THE COMPLETE AMERICA'S TEST KITCHEN TV SHOW COOKBOOK

2001 / 2019

AMERICA'S TEST KITCHEN

PHOTOGRAPHY **CARL TREMBLAY, KELLER + KELLER, STEVE KLISE, AND DANIEL J. VAN ACKERE**

AMERICA'S TEST KITCHEN
21 Drydock Avenue, Boston, MA 02210

THE COMPLETE AMERICA'S TEST KITCHEN TV SHOW COOKBOOK:
Every recipe from the hit TV show with product ratings and a look behind the scenes

Revised Edition

ISBN: 978-1-945256-54-7
ISSN: 2162-6944

Manufactured in the United States of America

10 9 8 7 6 5 4 3 2 1

Distributed by: Penguin Random House Publisher Services, tel: 800-733-3000

EDITORIAL DIRECTOR, BOOKS: **Elizabeth Carduff**

SENIOR MANAGING EDITOR: **Debra Hudak**

EDITORIAL ASSISTANTS: **Kelly Gauthier and Alyssa Langer**

ART DIRECTOR, BOOKS: **Lindsey Chandler**

ASSOCIATE ART DIRECTOR: **Katie Barranger**

PRODUCTION DESIGNER: **Reinaldo Cruz**

PHOTOGRAPHY DIRECTOR: **Julie Bozzo Cote**

SENIOR STAFF PHOTOGRAPHER: **Daniel J. van Ackere**

STAFF PHOTOGRAPHERS: **Steve Klise and Kevin White**

PHOTOGRAPHY PRODUCERS: **Mary Ball and Meredith Mulcahy**

FOOD STYLING: **Catrine Kelty, Marie Piraino, and Mary Jane Sawyer**

PRODUCTION MANAGER: **Christine Spanger**

IMAGING MANAGER: **Lauren Robbins**

PRODUCTION AND IMAGING SPECIALISTS: **Heather Dube, Dennis Noble, and Jessica Voas**

COPYEDITOR: **Cheryl Redmond**

PROOFREADERS: **Christine Corcoran Cox, Elizabeth Wray Emery, and Jeffrey Schier**

INDEXER: **Elizabeth Parson**

CHIEF CREATIVE OFFICER: **Jack Bishop**

EXECUTIVE EDITORIAL DIRECTORS: **Julia Collin Davison and Bridget Lancaster**

CONTENTS

WELCOME TO AMERICA'S TEST KITCHEN

This book has been tested, written, and edited by the folks at America's Test Kitchen. Located in Boston's Seaport District in the historic Innovation and Design Building, it features 15,000 square feet of kitchen space including multiple photography and video studios. It is the home of *Cook's Illustrated* magazine and *Cook's Country* magazine and is the workday destination for more than 60 test cooks, editors, and cookware specialists. Our mission is to test recipes over and over again until we understand how and why they work and until we arrive at the "best" version.

Our television show highlights the best recipes developed in the test kitchen during the past year—those recipes that our test kitchen staff makes at home time and time again. These recipes are accompanied by our most exhaustive equipment tests and our most interesting food tastings.

Julia Collin Davison and Bridget Lancaster co-host the show and ask the questions you might ask. It's the job of our chefs, Keith Dresser, Becky Hays, Lan Lam, Erin McMurrer, Elle Simone, and Dan Souza to demonstrate our recipes. The chefs show Julia and Bridget what works and what doesn't, and they explain why. In the process, they discuss (and show you) the best examples from our development process as well as the worst.

Adam Ried, our equipment expert, and Lisa McManus, our gadget expert, share the highlights from our detailed testing process in equipment corner and gadget critic segments. They bring with them our favorite (and least favorite) gadgets and tools. Jack Bishop is our ingredient expert. He has Julia and Bridget taste our favorite (and least favorite) brands of common food products. Julia and Bridget may not always enjoy these exercises (turmeric isn't exactly as fun to taste as fresh mozzarella or dark chocolate chips), but they usually learn something as Jack explains what makes one brand superior to another. And Dan Souza explains the science behind certain ingredients and recipes.

Although just 11 cooks and editors appear on the television show, another 50 people worked to make the show a reality. Executive Producer Mary Agnes conceived and developed each episode with help from Supervising Producer Kaitlin Keleher, Line Producer Diane Knox, and Producer Sara Joyner. The show is edited by Peter Hyzak, Sean Sandefur, and Herb Sevush, being overseen by Post-Production Supervisor Chen Margolis. Paul Adams, our science expert, researched the science behind the recipes along with science writer Eric Handler. Along with the on-air crew, executive chefs Erin McMurrer, Keith Dresser, and Andrea Geary

helped plan and organize the 26 television episodes shot in May 2018 and ran the "back kitchen," where all the food that appeared on camera originated. Kate Shannon, Miye Bromberg, and Carolyn Grillo organized the tasting and equipment segments.

During filming, chefs Tim Chin, Steve Dunn, Matthew Fairman, Hannah Fenton, Joseph Gitter, Andrew Janjigian, Lawman Johnson, Jane Katte, Nicole Konstantinakos, Lan Lam, Anne Petito, and Jessica Rudolph cooked all the food needed on set. Assistant Test Kitchen Director Alexxa Benson, Test Kitchen Manager Meridith Lippard, Test Kitchen Facilities Manager Kelly Ryan, and Senior Kitchen Assistant/Shopper Marissa Bunnewith were charged with making sure all the ingredients and kitchen equipment we needed were on hand. Kitchen assistants Ena Gudiel, Blanca Castanaza, Gladis Campos, Amarilys Merced, and Arlene Rosario also worked long hours. Chefs Allison Berkey, Dan Cellucci, Leah Colins, Sarah Ewald, Russell Selander, and Devon Shatkin helped coordinate the efforts of the kitchen with the television set by readying props, equipment, and food. Deva Djaafar led all tours of the test kitchen during filming.

Special thanks to director Herb Sevush and director of photography Dan Anderson.

We also appreciate the hard work of the production team, including Fletcher Burns, Phil Burns, Mikaela Bloomberg, Jason Bowen, Wilson Chao, Steve Damas, Jared Detsikas, Nick Dill, Clare Dingle, Eric Fisher, Shawn Gauvain, Eric Goddard, Alexandra Hadley, Harlem Logan, Jay Maurer, Stephen McCarthy, Claudia Moriel, Caroline Rickert, Jen Tawa, and Fred Young.

We also would like to thank Karen Fritz and Dani Cook at WETA Station Relations, and the team at American Public Television that presents the show: Cynthia Fenneman, Chris Funkhouser, Judy Barlow, and Tom Davison. Thanks also for production support from Zebra Productions, New York.

Bob's Red Mill, Holland America Line, Kohler, and Sub-Zero, Wolf, and Cove sponsored the show, and we thank them for their support. We also thank Sara Domville and Christine Anagnostis for serving our sponsors.

Meat was provided by Kinnealey Meats of Brockton, Mass. Fish was supplied by Wulf's Fish. Produce was supplied by Sid Wainer & Son. Bread was provided by Pain D'Avignon, Hyannis, Mass. Aprons were made by Crooked Brook.

JULIA AND BRIDGET TALK COOKING AND TV

What inspired your career in cooking?

Bridget: I've always been inspired by my mother, who is still a great cook, but I'd say that it goes back to watching Julia Child on PBS each Saturday morning.

Julia: I grew up cooking alongside my mother (she cooked full meals nearly every night), and I loved the hands-on work of preparing food. In my senior year of college, it dawned on me that culinary school should be my next step—it was the kind of work I naturally gravitated toward. So I enrolled in the Culinary Institute of America in Hyde Park, N.Y. I barely had enough kitchen experience to qualify for the admissions process, but as soon as I became a student there, I knew I had made the right decision. I loved it.

How did your long career at America's Test Kitchen prepare you to host the TV show?

Bridget: I started as a test cook in 1998, and back then, there were three of us working in the test kitchen, developing recipes, washing dishes, and shopping for all the ingredients ourselves. Over the years I've seen the evolution of the test kitchen: the physical space, the increase in the number of test cooks, the testing process. During this time I've worn many hats at ATK including running the kitchen for *Cook's Country* magazine in its early days, developing content for the online cooking school, and being our lead voice on the radio. Of course I've been on the TV show since its inception. I have a sense of pride for what we do, and after being on the show for all 19 seasons, it's easy for me to be a cheerleader.

Julia: I joined the *Cook's Illustrated* team in 1999 developing recipes for the magazine. When we shot our first half season of the TV show in 2000, I was one of the initial on-screen test cooks; in fact, pretty much everyone who worked in the kitchen was on the show. Nineteen seasons later, I've witnessed the incredible growth of the company, including the start of *Cook's Country* magazine and both TV shows, our cookbook department (where I spent more than a decade leading recipe development), the online cooking school . . . I could go on. In a sense, I grew up here at ATK. And at every turn, I've learned more about food and about what our viewers and readers really want from us: unbiased and well-vetted information about cooking and shopping that will help everyone cook better at home. Not only do I have all of the recipes ATK has developed over the past 15 to 20 years logged in my head, but I also have a clear vision for how we should continue to do this work in the years to come.

What are some of the most interesting recipes this season?

Bridget: I think what's interesting this season are our simplified takes on traditional recipes. Like Indoor Pulled Chicken (page 932). Traditional pulled chicken takes hours, but we developed a stovetop version that is so good and so quick. Its secret ingredients are powdered gelatin and liquid smoke. One-Hour Pizza (page 943) is another one. You can make really good pizza from scratch with a crisp and tender crust in just one hour, start to finish, with our foolproof method. Need I say more?

Julia: I think the balance this season between new exotic food and updates of well-loved classics is just right. We include recipes for Flat Hand-Pulled Noodles (Biang Biang Mian) with Chili Oil Vinaigrette (page 951) and an incredibly flavorful Brazilian Shrimp and Fish Stew called *moqueca* (page 931) as well as Hearty Beef and Vegetable Stew (page 930) that is loaded with vegetables and Roast Chicken with Warm Bread Salad (page 932).

The tastings and testings are a big part of the show. What's your favorite piece of equipment featured this season?

Julia: Our tastings have proven that you can elevate your cooking overall just by buying the right brand of an ingredient. My favorite tasting is of dry vermouth; our winner is good for cooking as well as drinking plain or in cocktails. My favorite piece of equipment we reviewed is the sous vide machine. I am a huge sous vide fan at home and the soft-poached egg recipe (page 961) is an absolute game changer.

Bridget: The tastings and testings are what set us apart from so many other cooking shows. They are there to provide the viewer with tangible information that they can use to better stock their kitchen. Take cocoa powder: Do you want to use one that's Dutched or not? We give you the facts. My favorite piece of equipment we reviewed is kitchen shears. A good pair is a must-have. This essential tool can make so many tasks faster, neater, and easier.

What do you hope the audience of the show will learn?

Julia: My number one hope is that viewers will simply think "I could do that. I could make that dish in my own kitchen and it will look and taste just like it does on TV."

Bridget: I always hope that folks will take away at least one piece of useful cooking info per show—something that they can use in a broader sense when they are cooking in their own kitchens.

There are more cast members now. How does that change the show?

Bridget: It's a brilliant move to feature more test cooks! We have so many talented people that work all year long to develop incredible content (recipes, tastings, and testings), and more of them will have a voice on the show, giving viewers a better glimpse into the test kitchen.

Julia: I think that it's great that we will have some fresh faces on camera to show more of the people who do the recipe development work in the kitchen all year round. I'm excited to pull back the curtain to show what our kitchen is really like and to show what it takes to develop one of our recipes start to finish.

What is your favorite ATK recipe?

Bridget: My favorite recipe of all time is still the coconut layer cake (page 765) that we made on the show many years ago. Coconut everywhere—in the cake, the frosting, the toasted crunchy coconut topping—so good.

Julia: I love Weeknight Roast Chicken (page 114) the best! A whole chicken is roasted in a preheated skillet and the oven is turned off during the second half of the cooking time, ensuring that both the white and dark meat are tender and juicy. The recipe is so easy (both my husband and I have it memorized by now) and turns out perfectly every time. It's the simple recipes, like roast chicken, that get me most excited because they are the hardest to get right; there are no bells and whistles to cover up any mistakes.

SOUP'S ON!

CLASSIC CHICKEN NOODLE SOUP

WHY THIS RECIPE WORKS: Classic chicken noodle soup is one of *the* all-time comfort foods. We eat it to nurse a cold or pair it with a simple sandwich for a satisfying meal. But making chicken noodle soup from scratch can take all day. We wanted a simple recipe but we wanted to make it the old-fashioned way—starting with a whole chicken—rather than cheating with store-bought broth.

We began by cutting the chicken into small pieces that could be browned in batches. To develop additional flavor, we sweated the browned pieces in a covered pot with an onion, then simmered them for less than half an hour. Now we had a stock that just needed some salt and bay leaves to round out its flavor. We reserved some of the skimmed fat from the stock to sauté aromatics and carrots for the soup, and we added in tender chicken breast pieces that had already been poached in our stock. For extra flavor, we cooked the egg noodles right in the soup pot so they could absorb rich, meaty flavor from the stock. With a final sprinkling of chopped parsley, our chicken noodle soup was complete—rich, home-made broth, moist pieces of chicken, tender vegetables, and perfectly cooked noodles.

Classic Chicken Noodle Soup
SERVES 6 TO 8

Make sure to reserve the chicken breast pieces until step 2; they should not be browned. If you use a cleaver, you will be able to cut up the chicken parts quickly. A chef's knife or kitchen shears will also work. Be sure to reserve 2 tablespoons of chicken fat for sautéing the aromatics in step 4; however, if you prefer not to use chicken fat, vegetable oil can be substituted.

STOCK
- 1 tablespoon vegetable oil
- 1 (4-pound) whole chicken, breast removed, split, and reserved; remaining chicken cut into 2-inch pieces (see note)
- 1 medium onion, chopped medium
- 2 quarts boiling water
- 2 teaspoons table salt
- 2 bay leaves

SOUP
- 2 tablespoons chicken fat, reserved from making stock, or vegetable oil (see note)
- 1 medium onion, chopped medium
- 1 large carrot, peeled and sliced ¼ inch thick
- 1 celery rib, sliced ¼ inch thick
- ½ teaspoon dried thyme
- 3 ounces egg noodles (about 2 cups)
- ¼ cup minced fresh parsley leaves
- Table salt and ground black pepper

1. FOR THE STOCK: Heat the oil in a large Dutch oven over medium-high heat until shimmering. Add half of the chicken pieces and cook until lightly browned, about 5 minutes per side. Transfer the cooked chicken to a bowl and repeat with the remaining chicken pieces; transfer to the bowl with the first batch. Add the onion and cook, stirring frequently, until the onion is translucent, 3 to 5 minutes. Return the chicken pieces to the pot. Reduce the heat to low, cover, and cook until the chicken releases its juices, about 20 minutes.

2. Increase the heat to high; add the boiling water, reserved chicken breast pieces, salt, and bay leaves. Reduce the heat to medium-low and simmer until the flavors have blended, about 20 minutes.

3. Remove the breast pieces from the pot. When cool, remove the skin and bones from the breast pieces and discard. Shred the meat with your fingers or two forks and set aside. Strain the stock through a fine-mesh strainer into a container, pressing on the solids to extract as much liquid as possible; discard the solids. Allow the liquid to settle about 5 minutes and skim off the fat; reserve 2 tablespoons, if desired (see note). (The shredded chicken, strained stock, and fat can be refrigerated in separate airtight containers for up to 2 days.)

4. FOR THE SOUP: Heat the reserved chicken fat in a large Dutch oven over medium-high heat. Add the onion, carrot, and celery and cook until softened, about 5 minutes. Add the thyme and reserved stock and simmer until the vegetables are tender, 10 to 15 minutes.

5. Add the noodles and reserved shredded chicken and cook until just tender, 5 to 8 minutes. Stir in the parsley, season with salt and pepper to taste, and serve.

HEARTY CHICKEN NOODLE SOUP

WHY THIS RECIPE WORKS: Sometimes we prefer a simple bowl of chicken soup—a brothy soup modestly enriched with chicken, noodles, and vegetables. Other times, a heartier version of chicken noodle soup is what we crave—one chock-full of chicken, noodles, and vegetables—a true meal in a bowl.

We began by jump-starting the flavor of our soup with a mixture of store-bought chicken broth and water, but the broth-and-water base had a distinctly flat flavor. A few pounds of chicken parts created a rich stock, but browning the parts and then simmering them was just too fussy for what we wanted. Instead, we turned to a somewhat unlikely but more convenient substitute—store-bought ground chicken. Ground chicken offers more surface area and exponentially more flavor, providing a great-tasting stock when sautéed with aromatics and then simmered with the broth and water. All the stock needed was some body and thickening, which we got from a little cornstarch. With our broth down, we were ready to add the chicken (breasts that had been poached in the stock until just cooked through and then shredded), vegetables, and noodles. Along with onion, celery, and carrots, we further enriched the soup with potato and Swiss chard. Our stream-lined hearty chicken noodle soup was now rich and satisfying.

Hearty Chicken Noodle Soup

SERVES 4 TO 6

When skimming the fat off the stock, we prefer to leave a little bit on the surface to enhance the soup's flavor.

STOCK

- 1 tablespoon vegetable oil
- 1 pound ground chicken
- 1 small onion, chopped medium
- 1 medium carrot, peeled and chopped medium
- 1 celery rib, chopped medium
- 2 quarts low-sodium chicken broth
- 4 cups water
- 2 bay leaves
- 2 teaspoons table salt
- 2 (12-ounce) bone-in, skin-on chicken breast halves, cut in half crosswise

SOUP

- ¼ cup cold water
- 3 tablespoons cornstarch
- 1 small onion, halved and sliced thin
- 2 medium carrots, peeled, halved lengthwise, and cut crosswise into ¾-inch pieces
- 1 medium celery rib, halved lengthwise and cut crosswise into ½-inch pieces
- 1 medium russet potato (about 8 ounces), peeled and cut into ¾-inch cubes
- 1½ ounces egg noodles (about 1 cup)
- 4-6 Swiss chard leaves, ribs removed, torn into 1-inch pieces (about 2 cups; optional)
- 1 tablespoon minced fresh parsley leaves
  Table salt and ground black pepper

1. FOR THE STOCK: Heat the oil in a large Dutch oven over medium-high heat until shimmering. Add the ground chicken, onion, carrot, and celery. Cook, stirring frequently, until the chicken is no longer pink, 5 to 10 minutes (do not brown the chicken).

2. Reduce the heat to medium-low. Add the broth, water, bay leaves, salt, and chicken breasts; cover and cook for 30 minutes. Remove the lid, increase the heat to high, and bring to a boil. (If the liquid is already boiling when the lid is removed, remove the chicken breasts immediately and continue with the recipe.) Transfer the chicken breasts to a large plate and set aside. Continue to cook the stock for 20 minutes, adjusting the heat to maintain a gentle boil. Strain the stock through a fine-mesh strainer into a container, pressing on the solids to extract as much liquid as possible; discard the solids. Allow the liquid to settle about 5 minutes and skim off the fat (see note). (The strained stock can be refrigerated in an airtight container for up to 2 days or frozen for up to 3 months. The chicken breasts can be stored in a zipper-lock bag with the air squeezed out.)

3. FOR THE SOUP: Return the stock to a Dutch oven set over medium-high heat. In a small bowl, combine the water and cornstarch until a smooth slurry forms; stir into the stock and bring to a gentle boil. Add the onion, carrots, celery, and potato and cook until the potato pieces are almost tender, 10 to 15 minutes, adjusting the heat as necessary to maintain a gentle boil. Add the egg noodles and continue to cook until all the vegetables and noodles are tender, about 5 minutes longer.

4. Meanwhile, remove the skin and bones from the reserved cooked chicken and discard. Shred the meat with your fingers or two forks. Add the shredded chicken, Swiss chard (if using), and parsley to the soup and cook until heated through, about 2 minutes. Season with salt and pepper to taste and serve.

OLD-FASHIONED SLOW-COOKER CHICKEN NOODLE SOUP

WHY THIS RECIPE WORKS: Making chicken noodle soup with a deep, satisfying flavor requires a few tricks when using a slow cooker. First, we used a combination of bone-in chicken thighs and breasts; cooked and shredded breast meat was the perfect choice for the final soup, but bone-in thighs were key for giving the broth its deep flavor during the long cooking time. We found browning the chicken thighs before adding them to the slow cooker really maximized the flavor. To prevent the breast meat from overcooking we wrapped the chicken breast inside a foil packet. Since we were already dirtying a skillet to brown the chicken thighs, it was no effort to brown and soften the vegetables and aromatics as well, and this step was well worth the depth of flavor it lent. An unlikely ingredient, tomato paste, gave the soup body and brought out the savory notes of our soup. We cooked the noodles separately to ensure perfect texture and added them in at the end, along with frozen peas that we simply let sit in the soup for 5 minutes to heat through.

Old-Fashioned Slow-Cooker Chicken Noodle Soup

SERVES 6 TO 8

Do not try to cook the noodles in the slow cooker or they will turn out mushy and taste raw.

1½   pounds bone-in, skin-on chicken thighs, trimmed
       Table salt and ground black pepper
  1   tablespoon vegetable oil
  3   medium carrots, peeled and chopped medium
  2   celery ribs, chopped medium
  1   medium onion, minced
  3   medium garlic cloves, minced or pressed through
       a garlic press (about 1 tablespoon)
  1   tablespoon tomato paste
  2   teaspoons minced fresh thyme
       or ½ teaspoon dried
 ⅛   teaspoon red pepper flakes
  8   cups low-sodium chicken broth
  2   bay leaves
  1   (12-ounce) bone-in, skin-on split chicken breast, trimmed
1½   ounces wide egg noodles (about 1 cup)
 ½   cup frozen peas
  2   tablespoons minced fresh parsley leaves

1. Dry the chicken thighs with paper towels and season with salt and pepper. Heat the oil in a 12-inch skillet over medium-high heat until just smoking. Brown the chicken thighs well on both sides, 6 to 8 minutes. Transfer to a plate, let cool slightly, and discard the skin.

2. Pour off all but 1 tablespoon fat left in the skillet. Add the carrots, celery, and onion and cook over medium heat until the vegetables are softened, 7 to 10 minutes. Stir in the garlic, tomato paste, thyme, and red pepper flakes and cook until fragrant, about 30 seconds. Stir in 1 cup of the chicken broth, scraping up any browned bits; transfer to the slow cooker.

3. Stir the remaining 7 cups broth and the bay leaves into the slow cooker. Nestle the browned chicken thighs with any accumulated juice into the slow cooker. Season the chicken breast with salt and pepper and place on one side of a large piece of aluminum foil. Fold the foil over the chicken and crimp to seal the edges. Place the foil packet on top of the soup, pressing gently as needed to fit. Cover and cook until the chicken is tender, 4 to 6 hours on low.

4. Remove the foil packet, open it carefully (watch for steam), and transfer the chicken breast to a cutting board. Transfer the chicken thighs to a cutting board. Let all of the chicken cool slightly, then shred it into bite-size pieces with two forks, discarding the skin and bones. Let the soup settle for 5 minutes, then skim the fat from the surface using a large spoon. Discard the bay leaves.

5. Bring 4 quarts water to a boil in a large pot. Add 1 tablespoon salt and the noodles to the boiling water and cook until tender, then drain. Stir the cooked noodles, shredded chicken, and peas into the soup and let sit until heated through, about 5 minutes. Stir in the parsley, season with salt and pepper to taste, and serve.

PRESSURE-COOKER CHICKEN NOODLE SOUP

WHY THIS RECIPE WORKS: With its velvety broth and deep flavor, old-fashioned chicken noodle soup is an ideal pressure-cooker candidate since the pressure cooker can extract flavor from the meat, skin, and bones of a whole chicken in just 20 minutes. We started by putting the chicken into the pot with some aromatics, carrots, celery, and water. Placing the chicken in the pot breast side up allowed the thighs and more delicate breast meat to cook through at the same time since the thighs were in contact with the pot's bottom. After 20 minutes, the meat practically fell off the bones, making it easy to shred and stir back in. Soy sauce gave the broth even deeper, richer meaty flavor. To keep things simple, we cooked the noodles in the broth while we shredded the chicken.

Pressure-Cooker Chicken Noodle Soup

SERVES 8

  1   tablespoon vegetable oil
  1   onion, chopped fine
  3   garlic cloves, minced (about 1 teaspoon)
  1   minced fresh thyme or ¼ teaspoon dried
  8   cups water
  4   carrots, peeled and sliced
  2   celery ribs, sliced ½ inch thick
  2   tablespoons soy sauce
  1   (4-pound) whole chicken, giblets discarded
       Salt and pepper
  4   ounces (2⅔ cups) wide egg noodles
 ¼   cup minced fresh parsley

1. Heat oil in pressure-cooker pot over medium heat until shimmering. Add onion and cook until softened, about 5 minutes. Stir in garlic and thyme and cook until fragrant, about 30 seconds. Stir in water, carrots, celery, and soy sauce, scraping up any browned bits. Season chicken with salt and pepper and place, breast side up, in pot.

2. Lock pressure-cooker lid in place and bring to high pressure over medium-high heat. As soon as pot reaches high pressure, reduce heat to medium-low and cook for 20 minutes, adjusting heat as needed to maintain high pressure.

3. Remove pot from heat. Quick release pressure, then carefully remove lid, allowing steam to escape away from you.

4. Transfer chicken to cutting board, let cool slightly, then shred meat into bite-size pieces, discarding skin and bones. Meanwhile, using large spoon, skim excess fat from surface of soup. Bring soup to boil, stir in noodles, and cook until tender, about 5 minutes. Stir in shredded chicken and parsley, season with salt and pepper to taste, and serve.

Pressure-Cooker Chicken and Rice Soup

Substitute 1 cup long-grain white rice for egg noodles and cook until tender, 15 to 18 minutes.

BEST BEEF STEW

WHY THIS RECIPE WORKS: The taste of beef stew is rarely as complex as its rich aroma would lead you to believe. We wanted a rich-tasting but approachable beef stew with tender meat, flavorful vegetables, and a rich brown gravy that justified the time it took to prepare. After browning the beef (chuck-eye is our preferred cut for stew), we caramelized the usual choices of onions and carrots, rather than just adding them raw to the broth. To mimic the luxurious, mouth-coating texture of beef stews made with homemade stock (provided by the collagen in bones that is transformed into gelatin when simmered), we included powdered gelatin and flour. We added frozen pearl onions toward the end of cooking along with some frozen peas.

Best Beef Stew

SERVES 6 TO 8

Use a good-quality medium-bodied wine, such as a Côtes du Rhône or Pinot Noir, for this stew. Try to find beef that is well marbled with white veins of fat. Meat that is too lean will come out slightly dry. Four pounds of blade steaks, trimmed of gristle and silver skin, can be substituted for the chuck-eye roast. While the blade steak will yield slightly thinner pieces after trimming, it should still be cut into 1½-inch pieces. Look for salt pork that looks meaty and is roughly 75 percent lean.

- 2 medium garlic cloves, minced or pressed through a garlic press (about 2 teaspoons)
- 4 anchovy fillets, minced fine (about 2 teaspoons)
- 1 tablespoon tomato paste
- 1 (4-pound) boneless chuck-eye roast, trimmed of excess fat and cut into 1½-inch pieces
- 2 tablespoons vegetable oil
- 1 large onion, halved and sliced ⅛ inch thick
- 4 carrots, peeled and cut into 1-inch pieces
- ¼ cup unbleached all-purpose flour
- 2 cups red wine (see note)
- 2 cups low-sodium chicken broth
- 4 ounces salt pork (see note), rinsed of excess salt
- 2 bay leaves
- 4 sprigs fresh thyme
- 1 pound Yukon Gold potatoes, scrubbed and cut into 1-inch pieces
- 1½ cups frozen pearl onions, thawed
- 2 teaspoons (about 1 packet) unflavored powdered gelatin
- ½ cup water
- 1 cup frozen peas, thawed
   Table salt and ground black pepper

1. Adjust an oven rack to the lower-middle position and heat the oven to 300 degrees. Combine the garlic and anchovies in a small bowl and press the mixture with the back of a fork to form a paste. Stir in the tomato paste and set the mixture aside.

2. Pat the meat dry with paper towels (do not season the meat). Heat 1 tablespoon of the vegetable oil in a large Dutch oven over high heat until just starting to smoke. Add half of the beef and cook until well browned on all sides, about 8 minutes total, reducing the heat if the oil begins to smoke or the fond begins to burn. Transfer the beef to a large plate. Repeat with the remaining 1 tablespoon vegetable oil and remaining beef, leaving the second batch of meat in the pot after browning.

3. Reduce the heat to medium and return the first batch of beef to the pot. Add the onion and carrots to the pot and stir to combine with the beef. Cook, scraping the bottom of the pan to loosen any browned bits, until the onion is softened, 1 to 2 minutes. Add the garlic mixture and cook, stirring constantly, until fragrant, about 30 seconds. Add the flour and cook, stirring constantly, until no dry flour remains, about 30 seconds.

4. Slowly add the wine, scraping the bottom of the pan to loosen any browned bits. Increase the heat to high and allow the wine to simmer until thickened and slightly reduced, about 2 minutes. Stir in the broth, salt pork, bay leaves, and thyme. Bring to a simmer, cover, transfer to the oven, and cook for 1½ hours.

5. Remove the pot from the oven. Remove and discard the bay leaves and salt pork. Stir in the potatoes, cover, return the pot to the oven, and cook until the potatoes are almost tender, about 45 minutes.

6. Using a large spoon, skim any excess fat from the surface of the stew. Stir in the pearl onions. Cook over medium heat until the potatoes and onions are cooked through and the meat offers little resistance when poked with a fork (the meat should not be falling apart), about 15 minutes. Meanwhile, sprinkle the gelatin over the water in a small bowl and allow to soften for 5 minutes.

7. Increase the heat to high and stir in the softened gelatin mixture and the peas. Simmer until the gelatin is fully dissolved and the stew is thickened, about 3 minutes. Season with salt and pepper to taste. Serve. (The stew can be cooled, covered tightly, and refrigerated for up to 2 days. Reheat it gently before serving.)

TUSCAN-STYLE BEEF STEW

WHY THIS RECIPE WORKS: Tuscany's rich beef stew, *peposo*, is meant to be a simple dish of slow-cooked beef shin, Chianti, garlic, and peppercorns, but following tradition to the letter yielded bland beef. To give our stew plenty of body, we salted chunks of short ribs and browned half of the meat to kickstart the sauce with flavorful fond. We deglazed the pot with red wine and stirred in the sauce's building blocks: water, shallots, carrots, garlic, rosemary, bay leaves, and peppercorns. Gelatin, tomato paste, and anchovy paste created a smooth texture and rich taste. We added in the uncooked beef chunks and brought the stew to a simmer before transferring it to the oven for a long, slow braise. Before serving, we removed the tender beef, strained and defatted the liquid, and returned the liquid to the pot. Adding more wine reinforced and freshened its impact before we reduced it to a thick, lush sauce. Just before spooning the sauce over the beef, we poured in one more hit of Chianti, this time mixed with a couple teaspoons of cornstarch for a final thickening boost.

Tuscan-Style Beef Stew

SERVES 6 TO 8

We prefer boneless short ribs in this recipe because they require very little trimming. If you cannot find them, substitute a 5-pound chuck roast. Trim the roast of large pieces of fat and sinew, and cut it into 2-inch pieces. If Chianti is unavailable, a medium-bodied wine such as Côtes du Rhône or Pinot Noir makes a nice substitute. Serve with polenta or crusty bread.

- 4 pounds boneless beef short ribs, trimmed and cut into 2-inch pieces
  Salt
- 1 tablespoon vegetable oil
- 1 (750-ml) bottle Chianti
- 1 cup water
- 4 shallots, halved lengthwise
- 2 carrots, peeled and halved lengthwise
- 1 garlic head, cloves separated, unpeeled, and crushed
- 4 sprigs fresh rosemary
- 2 bay leaves
- 1 tablespoon cracked black peppercorns, plus extra for serving
- 1 tablespoon unflavored gelatin
- 1 tablespoon tomato paste
- 1 teaspoon anchovy paste
- 2 teaspoons pepper
- 2 teaspoons cornstarch

1. Toss beef and 1½ teaspoons salt together in bowl and let stand at room temperature for 30 minutes. Adjust oven rack to lower-middle position and heat oven to 300 degrees.

2. Heat oil in large Dutch oven over medium-high heat until just smoking. Pat beef dry with paper towels. Add half of beef in single layer and cook until well browned on all sides, about 8 minutes total, reducing heat if fond begins to burn. Stir in 2 cups wine, water, shallots, carrots, garlic, rosemary, bay leaves, cracked peppercorns, gelatin, tomato paste, anchovy paste, and remaining beef. Bring to simmer and cover tightly with sheet of heavy-duty aluminum foil, then lid. Transfer to oven and cook until beef is tender, 2 to 2¼ hours, stirring halfway through cooking.

3. Using slotted spoon, transfer beef to bowl; cover tightly with foil and set aside. Strain sauce through fine-mesh strainer into fat separator. Wipe out pot with paper towels. Let liquid settle for 5 minutes, then return defatted liquid to pot.

4. Add 1 cup wine and pepper and bring mixture to boil over medium-high heat. Simmer briskly, stirring occasionally, until sauce is thickened to consistency of heavy cream, 12 to 15 minutes.

5. Combine remaining wine and cornstarch in small bowl. Reduce heat to medium-low, return beef to pot, and stir in cornstarch-wine mixture. Cover and simmer until just heated through, 5 to 8 minutes. Season with salt to taste. Serve, passing extra cracked peppercorns separately. (Stew can be refrigerated for up to 3 days.)

PORTUGUESE-STYLE BEEF STEW (ALCATRA)

WHY THIS RECIPE WORKS: *Alcatra*, a simple and meaty Portuguese beef stew, features tender chunks of beef braised with onions, garlic, spices, and wine. Unlike beef stews that require searing the beef to build savory flavor or adding flavor boosters like tomato paste and anchovies, this recipe skips those steps and ingredients, highlighting the warm and bright flavors of the spices and wine as much as the meatiness of the beef. We used beef shank because it is lean (which means the cooking liquid doesn't need to be skimmed) and full of collagen, which broke down into gelatin and gave the sauce full body. Submerging the sliced onions completely in the liquid under the meat caused them to form a meaty-tasting compound that amped up the savory flavor of the broth. Slices of smoky-sweet Spanish chorizo sausage matched up perfectly with the other flavors in the stew.

Portuguese-Style Beef Stew (Alcatra)

SERVES 6

Beef shank is sold both crosscut and long-cut (with and without bones). We prefer long-cut since it has more collagen. You can substitute 4 pounds of bone-in crosscut shank if that's all you can find. Remove the bones before cooking and save them for another use. Crosscut shank cooks more quickly, so check the stew for doneness in step 2 after 3 hours. A 3½- to 4-pound chuck roast, trimmed of fat and cut into 2½-inch pieces, can be substituted for the shank. Serve this dish with crusty bread or boiled potatoes.

3 pounds boneless long-cut beef shanks
  Salt and pepper
5 garlic cloves, peeled and smashed
5 allspice berries
4 bay leaves
1½ teaspoons peppercorns
2 large onions, halved and sliced thin
2¼ cups dry white wine
¼ teaspoon ground cinnamon
8 ounces Spanish-style chorizo sausage,
  cut into ¼-inch-thick rounds

1. Adjust oven rack to middle position and heat oven to 325 degrees. Trim away any fat or large pieces of connective tissue from exterior of shanks (silverskin can be left on meat). Cut each shank crosswise into 2½-inch pieces. Sprinkle meat with 1 teaspoon salt.

2. Cut 8-inch square of triple-thickness cheesecloth. Place garlic, allspice berries, bay leaves, and peppercorns in center of cheesecloth and tie into bundle with kitchen twine. Arrange onions and spice bundle in Dutch oven in even layer. Add wine and cinnamon. Arrange shank pieces in single layer on top of onions. Cover and cook until beef is tender, about 3½ hours.

3. Remove pot from oven and add chorizo. Using tongs, flip each piece of beef over, making sure that chorizo is submerged. Cover and let stand until chorizo is warmed through, about 20 minutes. Discard spice bundle. Season with salt and pepper to taste. Serve.

OUR FAVORITE CHILI

WHY THIS RECIPE WORKS: Our goal in creating an "ultimate" beef chili was to determine which of the "secret ingredients" recommended by chili experts around the world were spot-on—and which were expendable. We started with the beef. Most recipes call for ground beef, but we preferred meaty blade steaks, which don't require much trimming and stayed in big chunks in our finished chili. For complex chile flavor, we traded in the commercial chili powder in favor of ground dried ancho and de árbol chiles; for a grassy heat, we added fresh jalapeños. Dried beans, brined before cooking, stayed creamy for the duration of cooking. Beer and chicken broth outperformed red wine, coffee, and beef broth as the liquid components. For balancing sweetness, light molasses beat out other offbeat ingredients (including prunes and Coca-Cola). And finally, for the right level of thickness, flour and peanut butter didn't perform as promised; instead, a small amount of ordinary cornmeal sealed the deal, providing just the right consistency in our ultimate beef chili.

Our Favorite Chili

SERVES 6 TO 8

A 4-pound chuck-eye roast, well trimmed of fat, can be substituted for the steak. Because much of the chili flavor is held in the fat of this dish, refrain from skimming fat from the surface. Dried New Mexican or guajillo chiles make a good substitute for the anchos; each dried de árbol may be replaced with ⅛ teaspoon cayenne pepper. If you prefer not to work with any whole dried chiles, the anchos and de árbols can be replaced with ½ cup commercial chili powder and ¼ to ½ teaspoon cayenne pepper, though the texture of the chili will be slightly compromised. Good choices for condiments include diced avocado, finely chopped red onion, chopped cilantro leaves, lime wedges, sour cream, and shredded Monterey Jack or cheddar cheese.

  Table salt
8 ounces dried pinto beans (1¼ cups),
  picked over and rinsed
6 dried ancho chiles, stemmed, seeded,
  and torn into 1-inch pieces
2–4 dried de árbol chiles, stemmed, seeded,
  and split into 2 pieces
3 tablespoons cornmeal
2 teaspoons dried oregano
2 teaspoons ground cumin
2 teaspoons cocoa powder
2½ cups low-sodium chicken broth
2 medium onions, cut into ¾-inch pieces
3 small jalapeño chiles, stemmed, seeded,
  and cut into ½-inch pieces
3 tablespoons vegetable oil
4 medium garlic cloves, minced or pressed through
  a garlic press (about 4 teaspoons)
1 (14.5-ounce) can diced tomatoes
2 teaspoons light molasses
3½ pounds blade steak, ¾ inch thick, trimmed and
  cut into ¾-inch pieces
1 (12-ounce) bottle mild lager, such as Budweiser

1. Combine 3 tablespoons salt, 4 quarts water, and the beans in a Dutch oven and bring to a boil over high heat. Remove the pot from the heat, cover, and let sit for 1 hour. Drain and rinse well.

2. Adjust an oven rack to the lower-middle position and heat the oven to 300 degrees. Place the ancho chiles in a 12-inch skillet set over medium-high heat; toast, stirring frequently, until the flesh is fragrant, 4 to 6 minutes, reducing the heat if the chiles begin to smoke. Transfer to a food processor and cool. Do not wash out the skillet.

3. Add the de árbol chiles, cornmeal, oregano, cumin, cocoa, and ½ teaspoon salt to the food processor with the toasted ancho chiles; process until finely ground, about 2 minutes. With the processor running, slowly add ½ cup chicken broth until a smooth paste forms, about 45 seconds, scraping down the sides of the bowl as necessary. Transfer the paste to a small bowl. Place the onions in the now-empty processor and pulse until roughly chopped, about 4 pulses. Add the jalapeños and pulse until the consistency of chunky salsa, about 4 pulses, scraping down the bowl as necessary.

4. Heat 1 tablespoon oil in the Dutch oven over medium-high heat. Add the onion mixture and cook, stirring occasionally, until the moisture has evaporated and the vegetables are softened, 7 to 9 minutes. Add the garlic and cook until fragrant, about 1 minute. Add the chile paste, tomatoes, and molasses; stir until the chile paste is thoroughly combined. Add the remaining 2 cups chicken broth and the drained beans; bring to a boil, then reduce the heat to a simmer.

5. Meanwhile, heat 1 tablespoon more oil in the 12-inch skillet over medium-high heat until shimmering. Pat the beef dry with paper towels and sprinkle with 1 teaspoon salt. Add half of the beef and cook until browned on all sides, about 10 minutes. Transfer the meat to the Dutch oven. Add half of the beer to the skillet, scraping up any browned bits from the bottom of the skillet, and bring to a simmer. Transfer the beer to the Dutch oven. Repeat with the remaining 1 tablespoon oil, the remaining steak, and the remaining beer. Stir to combine and return the mixture to a simmer.

6. Cover the pot and transfer to the oven. Cook until the meat and beans are fully tender, 1½ to 2 hours. Let the chili stand, uncovered, for 10 minutes. Stir well, season with salt to taste, and serve. (The chili can be refrigerated for up to 3 days.)

BEST GROUND BEEF CHILI

WHY THIS RECIPE WORKS: Our ground beef chili can hold its own against the traditional chunky beef kind. We started by using 85 percent lean ground beef for flavor and tenderness. To protect the meat, we treated it with salt and baking soda. Both ingredients helped the meat hold on to moisture; since it didn't shed liquid during cooking the whole 2 pounds of beef could conveniently be browned in one batch. Simmering the meat for 90 minutes gave its collagen enough time to break down. We made a homemade chili powder for potent spicy flavor and used some tortilla chips to bulk it up and to add some corn flavor. Lastly we stirred any orange fat collected on the top back into the chili before serving since it contains much of the flavor from the fat-soluble spices.

Best Ground Beef Chili
SERVES 8 TO 10

Diced avocado, sour cream, and shredded Monterey Jack or cheddar cheese are also good options for garnishing. This chili is intensely flavored and should be served with tortilla chips and/or plenty of steamed white rice.

- 2 pounds 85 percent lean ground beef
- 2 tablespoons plus 2 cups water
- Salt and pepper
- ¾ teaspoon baking soda
- 6 dried ancho chiles, stemmed, seeded, and torn into 1-inch pieces
- 1 ounce tortilla chips, crushed (¼ cup)
- 2 tablespoons ground cumin
- 1 tablespoon paprika
- 1 tablespoon garlic powder
- 1 tablespoon ground coriander
- 2 teaspoons dried oregano
- ½ teaspoon dried thyme
- 1 (14.5-ounce) can whole peeled tomatoes
- 1 tablespoon vegetable oil
- 1 onion, chopped fine
- 3 garlic cloves, minced
- 1–2 teaspoons minced canned chipotle chile in adobo sauce
- 1 (15-ounce) can pinto beans
- 2 teaspoons sugar
- 2 tablespoons cider vinegar
- Lime wedges
- Coarsely chopped cilantro
- Chopped red onion

1. Adjust oven rack to lower-middle position and heat oven to 275 degrees. Toss beef with 2 tablespoons water, 1½ teaspoons salt, and baking soda in bowl until thoroughly combined. Set aside for 20 minutes.

2. Meanwhile, place anchos in Dutch oven set over medium-high heat; toast, stirring frequently, until fragrant, 4 to 6 minutes, reducing heat if anchos begin to smoke. Transfer to food processor and let cool.

3. Add tortilla chips, cumin, paprika, garlic powder, coriander, oregano, thyme, and 2 teaspoons pepper to food processor with anchos and process until finely ground, about 2 minutes. Transfer mixture to bowl. Process tomatoes and their juice in now-empty workbowl until smooth, about 30 seconds.

4. Heat oil in now-empty pot over medium-high heat until shimmering. Add onion and cook, stirring occasionally, until softened, 4 to 6 minutes. Add garlic and cook until fragrant, about 1 minute. Add beef and cook, stirring with wooden spoon to break meat up into ¼-inch pieces, until beef is browned and fond begins to form on pot bottom, 12 to 14 minutes. Add ancho mixture and chipotle; cook, stirring frequently, until fragrant, 1 to 2 minutes.

5. Add remaining 2 cups water, beans and their liquid, sugar, and tomato puree. Bring to boil, scraping bottom of pot to loosen any browned bits. Cover, transfer to oven, and cook until meat is tender and chili is slightly thickened, 1½ to 2 hours, stirring occasionally to prevent sticking.

6. Remove chili from oven and let stand, uncovered, for 10 minutes. Stir in any fat that has risen to top of chili, then add vinegar and season with salt to taste. Serve, passing lime wedges, cilantro, and chopped onion separately. (Chili can be refrigerated for up to 3 days.)

QUICK BEEF AND VEGETABLE SOUP

WHY THIS RECIPE WORKS: Rich and hearty beef and vegetable soup with old-fashioned flavor is a snap to make—if you have a few hours free and several pounds of beef and bones hanging around. We wanted to find another way to develop the same flavors and textures in under an hour.

We knew the key to this recipe would be finding the right cut of meat, one that had great beefy flavor and that would cook up tender in a reasonable amount of time. Tender cuts, like strip steak and rib eye, became tough, livery, and chalky when simmered in soup. Sirloin tip steak was the best choice—when cut into small pieces, the meat was tender and offered the illusion of being cooked for hours, plus its meaty flavor imparted richness to the soup.

In place of labor-intensive homemade beef broth, we doctored store-bought beef broth with aromatics and lightened its flavor profile with chicken broth. To further boost the flavor of the beef, we added cremini mushrooms, tomato paste, soy sauce, and red wine, ingredients that are rich in glutamates, naturally occurring compounds that accentuate the meat's hearty flavor. To mimic the rich body of a homemade meat stock (made rich through the gelatin released by the meat bones' collagen during the long simmering process), we relied on powdered gelatin. Our beef and vegetable soup now had the same richness and flavor as cooked-all-day versions in a whole lot less time.

Quick Beef and Vegetable Soup
SERVES 4 TO 6

Choose whole sirloin tip steaks over ones that have been cut into small pieces for stir-fries. If sirloin tip steaks are unavailable, substitute blade or flank steak, removing any hard gristle or excess fat. Button mushrooms can be used in place of the cremini mushrooms, with some trade-off in flavor. If you like, add 1 cup frozen peas, frozen corn, or frozen cut green beans during the last 5 minutes of cooking. For a heartier soup, add 10 ounces red potatoes, cut into ½-inch pieces (2 cups), during the last 15 minutes of cooking.

- 1 pound sirloin tip steaks, trimmed of excess fat and cut into ½-inch pieces (see note)
- 2 tablespoons soy sauce
- 1 teaspoon vegetable oil
- 1 pound cremini mushrooms, stems trimmed, caps wiped clean, and quartered (see note)
- 1 large onion, chopped medium
- 2 tablespoons tomato paste
- 1 medium garlic clove, minced or pressed through a garlic press (about 1 teaspoon)
- ½ cup red wine
- 4 cups beef broth
- 1¾ cups low-sodium chicken broth
- 4 medium carrots, peeled and cut into ½-inch pieces
- 2 medium celery ribs, cut into ½-inch pieces
- 1 bay leaf
- 1 tablespoon unflavored powdered gelatin
- ½ cup cold water
- 2 tablespoons minced fresh parsley leaves
  Table salt and ground black pepper

1. Combine the beef and soy sauce in a medium bowl; set aside for 15 minutes.

2. Heat the oil in a large Dutch oven over medium-high heat until just smoking. Add the mushrooms and onion; cook, stirring frequently, until the onion is browned and dark bits form on the pan bottom, 8 to 12 minutes. Transfer the vegetables to a bowl.

3. Add the beef and cook, stirring occasionally, until the liquid evaporates and the meat starts to brown, 6 to 10 minutes. Add the tomato paste and garlic; cook, stirring constantly, until fragrant, about 30 seconds. Add the red wine, scraping the bottom of the pot with a wooden spoon to loosen any browned bits, and cook until syrupy, 1 to 2 minutes.

4. Add the beef broth, chicken broth, carrots, celery, bay leaf, and browned mushrooms and onion; bring to a boil. Reduce the heat to low, cover, and simmer until the vegetables and meat are tender, 25 to 30 minutes. While the soup is simmering, sprinkle the gelatin over the cold water and let stand.

5. When the soup is finished, turn off the heat. Remove and discard the bay leaf. Add the gelatin mixture and stir until completely dissolved. Stir in the parsley, season with salt and pepper to taste, and serve.

VIETNAMESE BEEF PHO

WHY THIS RECIPE WORKS: Traditional versions of this Vietnamese beef and noodle soup call for simmering beef bones for hours to make a deeply flavorful broth. We wanted to make this soup suitable for the home cook, which meant that beef bones were out of the question. Instead, we simmered ground beef in spiced store-bought broth, which gave us the complexity and depth we were after in a fraction of the time. To serve the soup, we poured our broth over thinly sliced strip steak and gathered a variety of essential garnishes, such as lime wedges, hoisin and chile sauces, and bean sprouts.

Vietnamese Beef Pho

SERVES 4 TO 6

Our favorite store-bought beef broth is Rachael Ray Stock-in-a-Box All-Natural Beef Flavored Stock. Use a Dutch oven that holds 6 quarts or more. An equal weight of tri-tip steak or blade steak can be substituted for the strip steak; make sure to trim all connective tissue and excess fat. One 14- or 16-ounce package of rice noodles will serve four to six. Look for noodles that are about ⅛ inch wide; these are often labeled "small." Don't use Thai Kitchen Stir-Fry Rice Noodles since they are too thick and don't adequately soak up the broth.

1	pound 85 percent lean ground beef
2	onions, quartered through root end
12	cups beef broth
¼	cup fish sauce, plus extra for seasoning
1	(4-inch) piece ginger, sliced into thin rounds
1	cinnamon stick
2	tablespoons sugar, plus extra for seasoning
6	star anise pods
6	whole cloves
	Salt
1	teaspoon black peppercorns
1	(1-pound) boneless strip steak, trimmed and halved
14–16	ounces (⅛-inch-wide) rice noodles
⅓	cup chopped fresh cilantro
3	scallions, sliced thin (optional)
	Bean sprouts
	Sprigs fresh Thai or Italian basil
	Lime wedges
	Hoisin sauce
	Sriracha sauce

1. Break ground beef into rough 1-inch chunks and drop in Dutch oven. Add water to cover by 1 inch. Bring mixture to boil over high heat. Boil for 2 minutes, stirring once or twice. Drain ground beef in colander and rinse well under running water. Wash out pot and return ground beef to pot.

2. Place 6 onion quarters in pot with ground beef. Slice remaining 2 onion quarters as thin as possible and set aside for garnish. Add broth, 2 cups water, fish sauce, ginger, cinnamon, sugar, star anise, cloves, 2 teaspoons salt, and peppercorns to pot and bring to boil over high heat. Reduce heat to medium-low and simmer, partially covered, for 45 minutes.

3. Pour broth through colander set in large bowl. Discard solids. Strain broth through fine-mesh strainer lined with triple thickness of cheesecloth; add water as needed to equal 11 cups. Return broth to pot and season with extra sugar and salt (broth should taste overseasoned). Cover and keep warm over low heat.

4. While broth simmers, place steak on large plate and freeze until very firm, 35 to 45 minutes. Once firm, cut against grain into ⅛-inch-thick slices. Return steak to plate and refrigerate until needed.

5. Place noodles in large container and cover with hot tap water. Soak until noodles are pliable, 10 to 15 minutes; drain noodles. Meanwhile, bring 4 quarts water to boil in large pot. Add drained noodles and cook until almost tender, 30 to 60 seconds. Drain immediately and divide noodles among individual bowls.

6. Bring broth to rolling boil over high heat. Divide steak among individual bowls, shingling slices on top of noodles. Pile reserved onion slices on top of steak slices and sprinkle with cilantro and scallions, if using. Ladle hot broth into each bowl. Serve immediately, passing bean sprouts, basil sprigs, lime wedges, hoisin, Sriracha, and extra fish sauce separately.

QUINOA AND VEGETABLE STEW

WHY THIS RECIPE WORKS: Quinoa stews are common in many South American regions. But authentic recipes call for obscure ingredients, such as annatto powder or Peruvian varieties of potatoes and corn. We set out to make a traditional quinoa stew with an easy-to-navigate ingredient list. We found that paprika has a similar flavor profile to annatto powder; we rounded it out with cumin and coriander. Red bell pepper, tomatoes, red potatoes, sweet corn, and frozen peas were a nice mix of vegetables. We added the quinoa after the potatoes had softened and cooked it until it released starch to help give body to the stew. Finally, we added the traditional garnishes: *queso fresco*, avocado, and cilantro.

Quinoa And Vegetable Stew

SERVES 6 TO 8

We like the convenience of prewashed quinoa. If you buy unwashed quinoa (or are unsure whether it's washed), be sure to rinse it before cooking to remove its bitter protective coating (called saponin). This stew tends to thicken as it sits; add additional warm vegetable broth to loosen. Do not omit the garnishes; they are important to the flavor of the stew.

- 2 tablespoons vegetable oil
- 1 onion, chopped
- 1 red bell pepper, stemmed, seeded, and cut into ½-inch pieces
- 5 garlic cloves, minced
- 1 tablespoon paprika
- 2 teaspoons ground coriander
- 1½ teaspoons ground cumin
- 6 cups vegetable broth
- 1 pound red potatoes, unpeeled, cut into ½-inch pieces
- 1 cup prewashed white quinoa
- 1 cup fresh or frozen corn
- 2 tomatoes, cored and chopped coarse
- 1 cup frozen peas
  Salt and pepper
- 8 ounces queso fresco or feta cheese, crumbled (2 cups)
- 1 avocado, halved, pitted, and diced
- ½ cup minced fresh cilantro

1. Heat oil in Dutch oven over medium heat until shimmering. Add onion and bell pepper and cook until softened, 5 to 7 minutes. Stir in garlic, paprika, coriander, and cumin and cook until fragrant, about 30 seconds. Stir in broth and potatoes and bring to boil over high heat. Reduce heat to medium-low and simmer gently for 10 minutes.

2. Stir in quinoa and simmer for 8 minutes. Stir in corn and simmer until potatoes and quinoa are just tender, 5 to 7 minutes. Stir in tomatoes and peas and let heat through, about 2 minutes.

3. Off heat, season with salt and pepper to taste. Sprinkle individual portions with queso fresco, avocado, and cilantro before serving.

Quinoa and Vegetable Stew with Eggs

Serving this stew with a cooked egg on top is a common practice in Peru.

Crack 6 large eggs evenly over top of stew after removing from heat and seasoning with salt and pepper in step 3; cover and let eggs poach off heat until whites have set but yolks are still soft, about 4 minutes. To serve, carefully scoop cooked eggs and stew from pot with large spoon.

CLASSIC CREAM OF TOMATO SOUP

WHY THIS RECIPE WORKS: Canned cream of tomato soup is a childhood favorite. But grown-up tastes deserve something better—and let's face it, the canned soup's overly sweet flavors are just not all that appealing today. We wanted a well-balanced cream of tomato soup, one with rich color, great tomato flavor, and a silky texture.

Right away, we turned to canned tomatoes; fresh tomatoes are at their best just a few months out of the year and we didn't want to restrict our soup-making to just one season. To coax the most flavor from our canned whole tomatoes, it was essential to roast them in the oven. The intense dry heat worked to evaporate surface liquids and concentrate the flavor, and a sprinkling of brown sugar encouraged caramelization. We cooked our roasted tomatoes with shallots, chicken broth, and reserved tomato juice to develop robust flavor, then pureed the tomatoes (with broth) to keep the deep flavor of the tomato broth intact. Finished with heavy cream and a splash of brandy, this cream of tomato soup will satisfy everyone at the table.

Classic Cream of Tomato Soup

SERVES 6

Make sure to use canned whole tomatoes packed in juice. To obtain 3 cups of juice, use the packing juice as well as the liquid that falls from the tomatoes when they are seeded.

- 2 (28-ounce) cans whole tomatoes packed in juice, drained, 3 cups juice reserved (see note)
- 1½ tablespoons dark brown sugar
- 4 tablespoons (½ stick) unsalted butter
- 2 large shallots, minced (about ½ cup)
- 1 tablespoon tomato paste
  Pinch ground allspice
- 2 tablespoons unbleached all-purpose flour
- 1¾ cups low-sodium chicken broth
- ½ cup heavy cream
- 2 tablespoons brandy or dry sherry
  Table salt and cayenne pepper

1. Adjust an oven rack to the upper-middle position and heat the oven to 450 degrees. Line a large rimmed baking sheet with foil. With your fingers, carefully open the whole tomatoes over a fine-mesh strainer set in a bowl and push out the seeds, allowing the juices to fall through the strainer into the bowl; discard the seeds. Spread the seeded tomatoes in a single layer on the foil and sprinkle evenly with the brown sugar. Bake until all the liquid has evaporated and the tomatoes begin to color, about 30 minutes. Cool the tomatoes slightly, then peel them off the foil; transfer to a small bowl and set aside.

2. Melt the butter in a large saucepan over medium heat. Add the shallots, tomato paste, and allspice. Reduce the heat to low, cover, and cook, stirring occasionally, until the shallots are softened, 7 to 10 minutes. Add the flour and cook, stirring constantly, until thoroughly combined, about 30 seconds. Gradually add the chicken broth, whisking constantly to combine; stir in the reserved tomato juice and roasted tomatoes. Cover, increase the heat to medium, and bring to a boil. Reduce the heat to low and simmer, stirring occasionally, for 10 minutes.

3. Pour the mixture through a fine-mesh strainer into a medium bowl; rinse and dry the saucepan. Transfer the tomatoes and solids in the strainer to a blender; add 1 cup of the strained liquid and puree until smooth. Add the pureed mixture and the remaining strained liquid to the saucepan. Add the cream and warm over low heat until hot, about 3 minutes. Off the heat, stir in the brandy, season with salt and cayenne to taste, and serve. (The soup can be refrigerated in an airtight container for up to 2 days. Warm over low heat until hot; do not boil.)

BEHIND THE SCENES

WHY OUR EQUIPMENT RATINGS ARE DIFFERENT

For many viewers, the equipment corner is the most valuable part of the TV show. Why? Besides the fact that we save you big bucks (more often than not the expensive model is beaten by a much cheaper option), viewers know they can trust our ratings. That's because we're independent (we don't accept advertising) and because we put equipment through real-world tests.

On the television show, Adam has Bridget and Julia re-create some of the tests that were used when rating kitchen equipment. For example, to test the heat consistency of six different gas grills, Adam preheated the grills on high for 15 minutes and then mapped the heat distribution by covering the entire grill surface with white sandwich bread. As he and Julia saw, the top grills provided evenly browned toast, while other grills left the bread different shades of black, brown, and white.

Off camera, Adam and his team used thermocouples to check the accuracy of the grills' lid thermometers while grilling and tasting hamburgers and thick strip steaks and smoking 5-pound pork butts. They also tried grilling 12-pound turkeys to find out if they would fit under each grill lid with room to spare. The bottom line: You can rest assured that our winning grill is well-designed, responsive, and durable.

That's just a sample of the work involved in our equipment tests. The testing team often spends hundreds of kitchen hours on each one of our equipment ratings.

CREAMLESS CREAMY TOMATO SOUP

WHY THIS RECIPE WORKS: Creamy tomato soup boasts a bright, sweet tomato flavor when done right, but not everyone is a fan of rich cream soups. We wanted to keep the sharp tomatoey flavor in this classic soup, but ditch the dairy and tame the tartness in other ways.

Our first step was to choose canned tomatoes over fresh tomatoes—canned are simply more consistent in flavor than your average supermarket tomato. We mashed whole tomatoes (preferred over diced or crushed for their concentrated flavor) with a potato masher, then combined them with aromatics sautéed in extra-virgin olive oil, not butter, which guaranteed bright, clean flavor. Stirring in some olive oil before pureeing our soup added back vital flavor that was lost when we cooked the oil. To combat the acid in the tomatoes, we added full-flavored brown sugar. And for an ultra-creamy texture without the cream, we pureed sandwich bread into the soup. For a final touch, we stirred chicken broth into the pot and simmered the soup briefly to give our creamless creamy tomato soup a rich and velvety feel.

Creamless Creamy Tomato Soup
SERVES 6

If half of the soup fills your blender more than halfway, process the soup in three batches, but do not add more olive oil for the third batch. You can also use a hand-held blender to process the soup directly in the pot. Serve this soup topped with Classic Croutons (recipe follows), if desired. For an even smoother soup, strain the pureed mixture through a fine-mesh strainer before stirring in the chicken broth in step 2.

- ¼ cup extra-virgin olive oil, plus extra for drizzling (see note)
- 1 medium onion, chopped medium
- 3 medium garlic cloves, minced or pressed through a garlic press (about 1 tablespoon)
  Pinch red pepper flakes (optional)
- 1 bay leaf
- 2 (28-ounce) cans whole tomatoes
- 3 slices high-quality white sandwich bread, crusts removed, torn into 1-inch pieces
- 1 tablespoon brown sugar
- 2 cups low-sodium chicken broth
- 2 tablespoons brandy (optional)
  Table salt and ground black pepper
- ¼ cup chopped fresh chives

1. Heat 2 tablespoons of the oil in a large Dutch oven over medium-high heat until shimmering. Add the onion, garlic, red pepper flakes (if using), and bay leaf. Cook, stirring frequently, until the onion is translucent, 3 to 5 minutes. Stir in the tomatoes with their juice. Using a potato masher, mash until no pieces bigger than 2 inches remain. Stir in the bread and sugar and bring the soup to a boil. Reduce the heat to medium and cook, stirring occasionally, until the bread is completely saturated and starts to break down, about 5 minutes. Remove and discard the bay leaf.

2. Transfer half of the soup to a blender. Add 1 tablespoon more oil and process until the soup is smooth and creamy, 2 to 3 minutes. Transfer to a large bowl and repeat with the remaining soup and the remaining 1 tablespoon oil. Rinse and dry the Dutch oven and return the soup to the pot. Stir in the chicken broth and brandy (if using). Return the soup to a boil and season with salt and pepper to taste. Ladle the soup into bowls, sprinkle with the chopped chives, drizzle with olive oil, and serve. (The soup, minus the garnish, can be refrigerated in an airtight container for up to 2 days. Warm over low heat until hot; do not boil.)

Classic Croutons
MAKES ABOUT 1½ CUPS

3 slices high-quality white sandwich bread, crusts removed, cut into ½-inch cubes (about 1½ cups)
1½ tablespoons olive oil
Table salt and ground black pepper

1. Adjust an oven rack to the upper-middle position and heat the oven to 400 degrees. Combine the bread cubes and oil in a medium bowl and toss to coat. Season with salt and pepper to taste.

2. Spread the bread cubes in an even layer on a rimmed baking sheet and bake, stirring occasionally, until golden, 8 to 10 minutes. Cool on the baking sheet to room temperature. (The croutons can be stored in an airtight container or a plastic bag for up to 3 days.)

CARROT-GINGER SOUP

WHY THIS RECIPE WORKS: The coupling of sweet carrots and pungent ginger has the potential to produce an elegant, flavorful soup. But in most versions, the hapless addition of other vegetables, fruits, or dairy makes it difficult to truly taste the starring flavors. Another common problem is a grainy consistency. We wanted to bring this soup to its full potential and produce a version with a smooth, silken texture and pure, clean flavors.

For unadulterated carrot flavor, we used water in place of vegetable broth, eliminating the blurred vegetable background. Swapping ¾ cup of carrot juice for some of the water and stirring in another ¾ cup right before serving gave us intense carrot flavor. We also used peeled and sliced carrots; the earthy, sweet cooked carrots and the bright, raw carrot juice provided a well-balanced depth of flavor. To amp up ginger flavor, we used a combination of fresh and crystallized ginger, with the former supplying spiciness and the latter delivering the almost citrusy freshness that ginger is prized for. For the silkiest possible consistency, we turned to one of the test kitchen's secret weapons: baking soda. Just ½ teaspoon of baking soda helped to break down the cell walls of the carrots for

a soup that was downright velvety—without the need for lengthy cooking or fussy straining. As finishing touches, a sprinkle of fresh chives and a swirl of sour cream provided subtle onion flavor and mild tang. A few crispy, buttery croutons provided textural contrast.

Carrot-Ginger Soup
SERVES 6

In addition to sour cream and chives, serve the soup with Buttery Croutons (recipe follows).

2 tablespoons unsalted butter
2 onions, chopped fine
¼ cup minced crystallized ginger
1 tablespoon grated fresh ginger
2 garlic cloves, peeled and smashed
Salt and pepper
1 teaspoon sugar
2 pounds carrots, peeled and sliced ¼ inch thick
4 cups water
1½ cups carrot juice
2 sprigs fresh thyme
½ teaspoon baking soda
1 tablespoon cider vinegar
Chopped chives
Sour cream

1. Melt butter in large saucepan over medium heat. Add onions, crystallized ginger, fresh ginger, garlic, 2 teaspoons salt, and sugar; cook, stirring frequently, until onions are softened but not browned, 5 to 7 minutes.

2. Increase heat to high; add carrots, water, ¾ cup carrot juice, thyme sprigs, and baking soda and bring to simmer. Reduce heat to medium-low and simmer, covered, until carrots are very tender, 20 to 25 minutes.

3. Discard thyme sprigs. Working in batches, process soup in blender until smooth, 1 to 2 minutes. Return soup to clean pot and stir in vinegar and remaining ¾ cup carrot juice. (Soup can be refrigerated for up to 4 days.) Return to simmer over medium heat and season with salt and pepper to taste. Serve with sprinkle of chives and dollop of sour cream.

Buttery Croutons
MAKES ABOUT 2 CUPS

3 tablespoons unsalted butter
1 tablespoon olive oil
3 large slices high-quality sandwich bread, cut into ½-inch cubes (about 2 cups)
Table salt

Heat the butter and oil in a 12-inch skillet over medium heat. When the foaming subsides, add the bread cubes and cook, stirring frequently, until golden brown, about 10 minutes. Transfer the croutons to a paper towel–lined plate and season with salt to taste.

CREAMY PEA SOUP

WHY THIS RECIPE WORKS: Sweet pea soup is a labor of love—fresh peas are shelled, blanched, cooked with other vegetables, then passed through a sieve. We were after a fuss-free but still elegant version of this special soup. Our goal was a streamlined approach that would produce a soup with silky texture and real pea flavor.

Both garden and grocery store peas can be disappointing; fresh pods often reveal tough, starchy pellets that require a significant amount of time spent shelling. Instead, we decided to use frozen peas. For maximum pea flavor, we ground the frozen peas in a food processor before adding them to our simple soup base of chicken broth and shallots. Adding some Boston lettuce leaves gave the soup a wonderfully frothy texture. And a small dose of heavy cream added richness.

Creamy Pea Soup
SERVES 4 TO 6
A few Classic Croutons (page 13) are the perfect embellishment to this smooth soup.

- 4 tablespoons (½ stick) unsalted butter
- 4 large shallots, minced (about 1 cup), or 2 medium leeks, white and light green parts chopped fine and rinsed thoroughly (about 1⅓ cups)
- 2 tablespoons unbleached all-purpose flour
- 3½ cups low-sodium chicken broth
- 1½ pounds frozen peas (about 4½ cups), partially thawed at room temperature for 10 minutes
- 12 small leaves Boston lettuce (about 3 ounces), washed and dried
- ½ cup heavy cream
  Table salt and ground black pepper

1. Melt the butter in a large saucepan over low heat. Add the shallots and cook, covered, until softened, 8 to 10 minutes, stirring occasionally. Add the flour and cook, stirring constantly, until thoroughly combined, about 30 seconds. Whisking constantly, gradually add the chicken broth. Increase the heat to high and bring to a boil. Reduce the heat to medium-low and simmer for 3 to 5 minutes.

2. Meanwhile, process the peas in a food processor until coarsely chopped, about 20 seconds. Add the peas and lettuce to the saucepan. Increase the heat to medium-high, cover, and return to a simmer; cook for 3 minutes. Uncover, reduce the heat to medium-low, and continue to simmer 2 minutes longer.

3. Working in batches, puree the soup in a blender until smooth, filling the blender jar only halfway for each batch. Strain the soup through a fine-mesh strainer into a large bowl; discard the solids in the strainer. Rinse and dry the saucepan; return the pureed mixture to the saucepan and stir in the cream. Warm the soup over low heat until hot, about 3 minutes. Season with salt and pepper to taste and serve. (The soup can be refrigerated in an airtight container for up to 2 days. Warm over low heat until hot; do not boil.)

CREAMY CAULIFLOWER SOUP

WHY THIS RECIPE WORKS: For a creamy cauliflower soup that tasted first and foremost of cauliflower, we did away with the distractions—no cream, flour, or overpowering seasonings. Cauliflower, simmered until tender, produced a creamy, velvety smooth puree, without the aid of any cream, due to its low insoluble fiber content. For the purest flavor, we cooked it in salted water (instead of broth), skipped the spice rack entirely, and bolstered it with sautéed onion and leek. We added the cauliflower to the simmering water in two stages so our soup offered the grassy flavor of just-cooked cauliflower and the sweeter, nuttier flavor of long-cooked cauliflower. Finally, we fried a portion of the florets in butter until both the cauliflower and butter were golden brown and used each as a separate, richly flavored garnish.

Creamy Cauliflower Soup
SERVES 4 TO 6
White wine vinegar may be substituted for the sherry vinegar. For best flavor and texture, trim core thoroughly of green leaves and leaf stems, which can be fibrous and contribute to a grainy texture in the soup.

- 1 head cauliflower (2 pounds)
- 8 tablespoons unsalted butter, cut into 8 pieces
- 1 leek, white and light green parts only, halved lengthwise, sliced thin, and washed thoroughly
- 1 small onion, halved and sliced thin
  Salt and pepper
- 4½ cups water
- ½ teaspoon sherry vinegar
- 3 tablespoons minced fresh chives

1. Pull off outer leaves of cauliflower and trim stem. Using paring knife, cut around core to remove; thinly slice core and reserve. Cut heaping 1 cup of ½-inch florets from head of cauliflower; set aside. Cut remaining cauliflower crosswise into ½-inch-thick slices.

2. Melt 3 tablespoons butter in large saucepan over medium-low heat. Add leek, onion, and 1½ teaspoons salt; cook, stirring frequently, until onion is softened but not browned, about 7 minutes.

3. Increase heat to medium-high; add water, sliced core, and half of sliced cauliflower; and bring to simmer. Reduce heat to medium-low and simmer gently for 15 minutes. Add remaining sliced cauliflower, return to simmer, and continue to cook until cauliflower is tender and crumbles easily, 15 to 20 minutes longer.

4. While soup simmers, melt remaining 5 tablespoons butter in 8-inch skillet over medium heat. Add reserved florets and cook, stirring frequently, until florets are golden brown and butter is browned, 6 to 8 minutes. Remove skillet from heat and use slotted spoon to transfer florets to small bowl. Toss florets with vinegar and season with salt to taste. Pour browned butter in skillet into small bowl and reserve for garnishing.

5. Process soup in blender until smooth, about 45 seconds. Rinse out pan. Return pureed soup to pan and return to simmer over medium heat, adjusting consistency with up to ½ cup water as needed (soup should have thick, velvety texture, but should be thin enough to settle with a flat surface after being stirred) and seasoning with salt to taste. Serve, garnishing individual bowls with browned florets, drizzles of browned butter, and chives and seasoning with pepper to taste.

CREAMY MUSHROOM SOUP

WHY THIS RECIPE WORKS: Mushroom soups have great potential, but they often disappoint with their lackluster taste and less-than-stellar texture. We knew this pureed soup could be richly textured, neither too thick nor too thin, and showcase the deep, earthy flavor of mushrooms.

We chose to use readily available white mushrooms, which are often underestimated. To bring out the most flavor from the mushrooms, we had to slice them by hand (processing made for uneven and bruised pieces) and then sweat them in a covered pot with butter and shallots; roasted mushrooms were nixed because the juices released during roasting had browned on the pan and were lost, making for flavorless soup. Chicken broth proved a better addition than water for the liquid base, and dried porcini mushrooms amplified the mushroom flavor. After pureeing the soup, we added cream and a splash of Madeira for body. Our creamy mushroom soup was now texturally light and full of deep, rich flavor.

Creamy Mushroom Soup
SERVES 6 TO 8

The garnish of sautéed mushrooms (recipe follows) adds visual and textural appeal to this creamy soup.

- 6 tablespoons (¾ stick) unsalted butter
- 3 large shallots, minced (about ¾ cup)
- 1 medium garlic clove, minced or pressed through a garlic press (about 1 teaspoon)
- ½ teaspoon freshly grated nutmeg
- 2 pounds white mushrooms, wiped clean and sliced ¼ inch thick
- 4 cups hot water
- 3½ cups low-sodium chicken broth
- ½ ounce dried porcini mushrooms, rinsed well
- ⅓ cup Madeira or dry sherry
- 1 cup heavy cream
- 2 teaspoons juice from 1 lemon
  Table salt and ground black pepper
- 1 recipe Sautéed Wild Mushrooms, for garnish (recipe follows; see note)

1. Melt the butter in a large Dutch oven over medium-low heat. Add the shallots and sauté, stirring frequently, until softened, about 4 minutes. Stir in the garlic and nutmeg and cook until fragrant, about 30 seconds. Increase the heat to medium, add the white mushrooms, and stir to coat with the butter.

Cook, stirring occasionally, until the mushrooms release some liquid, about 7 minutes. Reduce the heat to medium-low, cover the pot, and cook, stirring occasionally, until the mushrooms have released all their liquid, about 20 minutes.

2. Add the water, chicken broth, and porcini mushrooms. Cover, bring to a simmer, then reduce the heat to low and simmer until the mushrooms are fully tender, about 20 minutes.

3. Working in batches, puree the soup in a blender until smooth, filling the blender jar only halfway for each batch. Rinse and dry the pot; return the soup to the pot. Stir in the Madeira and cream and bring to a simmer over low heat. Add the lemon juice and season with salt and pepper to taste. Ladle the soup into bowls, garnish with sautéed wild mushrooms, and serve. (The soup, minus the garnish, can be refrigerated in an airtight container for up to 2 days. Warm over low heat until hot; do not boil.)

Sautéed Wild Mushrooms
MAKES ENOUGH TO GARNISH 6 TO 8 BOWLS OF SOUP

- 2 tablespoons unsalted butter
- 8 ounces shiitake, chanterelle, oyster, or cremini mushrooms, stems trimmed and discarded, mushrooms wiped clean and sliced thin
  Table salt and ground black pepper

1. Melt the butter in a medium skillet over low heat. Add the mushrooms and season with salt and pepper to taste. Cover and cook, stirring occasionally, until the mushrooms release their liquid, about 10 minutes for shiitakes and chanterelles, about 5 minutes for oysters, and about 9 minutes for cremini.

2. Uncover and continue to cook, stirring occasionally, until the liquid released by the mushrooms has evaporated and the mushrooms are browned, about 2 minutes for shiitakes, oysters, and cremini and about 3 minutes for chanterelles. Serve immediately as garnish for the soup.

MUSHROOM BISQUE

WHY THIS RECIPE WORKS: Mushroom bisque should be luxuriously creamy but packed with distinct earthy flavor, so we started with the mushrooms. A combination of white, cremini, and shiitake mushrooms promised the perfect balance of buttery and earthy notes, and microwaving them concentrated their intensity by expelling the excess moisture. We saved the flavorful liquid for later and browned the mushrooms in oil in a Dutch oven. Adding a chopped onion, fresh thyme, and pepper boosted the base's flavors and a splash of sherry elevated the mushrooms' meaty profile. Stirring in the reserved mushroom juices at this point reinforced the fungi's impact. After adding water and broth, we brought the pot to a simmer, removed the thyme sprig, and blended the mushroom mixture into a creamy bisque with a blender. Taking a tip from Julia Child's recipe, we whisked together cream and egg yolks to form a classic French thickener called a *liaison*. The yolks contributed the same silkening effect of heavy cream but without dulling or diluting the bisque. A touch of lemon juice at the very end sharpened the flavor to perfection.

Mushroom Bisque

SERVES 6 TO 10

Tying the thyme sprig with twine makes it easier to remove from the pot. For the smoothest result, use a conventional blender rather than an immersion blender. Our Fried Shallots (recipe follows) can replace the garnish of cream and chopped chives.

1	pound white mushrooms, trimmed
8	ounces cremini mushrooms, trimmed
8	ounces shiitake mushrooms, stemmed
	Kosher salt and pepper
2	tablespoons vegetable oil
1	small onion, chopped fine
1	sprig fresh thyme, tied with kitchen twine
2	tablespoons dry sherry
4	cups water
3½	cups chicken broth
⅔	cup heavy cream, plus extra for serving
2	large egg yolks
1	teaspoon lemon juice
	Chopped fresh chives

1. Toss white mushrooms, cremini mushrooms, shiitake mushrooms, and 1 tablespoon salt together in large bowl. Cover with large plate and microwave, stirring every 4 minutes, until mushrooms have released their liquid and reduced to about one-third their original volume, about 12 minutes. Transfer mushrooms to colander set in second large bowl and drain well. Reserve liquid.

2. Heat oil in Dutch oven over medium heat until shimmering. Add mushrooms and cook, stirring occasionally, until mushrooms are browned and fond has formed on bottom of pot,

about 8 minutes. Add onion, thyme sprig, and ¼ teaspoon pepper and cook, stirring occasionally, until onion is just softened, about 2 minutes. Add sherry and cook until evaporated. Stir in reserved mushroom liquid and cook, scraping up any browned bits. Stir in water and broth and bring to simmer. Reduce heat to low and simmer for 20 minutes.

3. Discard thyme sprig. Working in batches, process soup in blender until very smooth, 1½ to 2 minutes per batch. Return soup to now-empty pot and bring to simmer over low heat. (Soup can be refrigerated for up to 2 days. Warm to 150 degrees before proceeding with recipe.)

4. Whisk cream and egg yolks together in medium bowl. Stirring slowly and constantly, add 2 cups soup to cream mixture. Stirring constantly, slowly pour cream mixture into simmering soup. Heat gently, stirring constantly, until soup registers 165 degrees (do not overheat). Stir in lemon juice and season with salt and pepper to taste. Serve immediately, garnishing each serving with 1 teaspoon extra cream and sprinkle of chives.

Fried Shallots

MAKES 1 CUP

Once cooled, you can store the shallots in an airtight container at room temperature for up to 3 days. You can strain the oil after cooking the shallots and reserve it for another use.

½	cup vegetable oil
3	shallots, sliced thin
	Salt

Cook oil and shallots in medium saucepan over high heat, stirring constantly, until shallots are deep golden, 11 to 13 minutes (they will still be soft; do not overcook). Using slotted spoon, transfer shallots to paper towel–lined plate, season with salt, and let drain and turn crisp, about 5 minutes, before serving.

WILD RICE AND MUSHROOM SOUP

WHY THIS RECIPE WORKS: For a rich, earthy, nutty-tasting soup, we had to figure out how to make the wild rice and mushrooms do more than just add bulk. Fresh cremini mushrooms provided a meaty texture, and dried shiitakes, ground into a powder and added to the broth, ensured full-bodied mushroom flavor. Simmering the wild rice with baking soda decreased the cooking time and brought out its complex flavor. Cooking the rice in the oven, instead of on the stovetop, made it tender with a pleasant chew. To infuse the entire soup with wild rice flavor, we replaced some of the water in the soup with the rice's leftover cooking liquid. Including tomato paste and soy sauce amplified the nutty, earthy flavor profile. A final addition of cornstarch helped suspend the rice in the broth to give our soup a velvety texture.

Wild Rice and Mushroom Soup

SERVES 6 TO 8

White mushrooms can be substituted for the cremini mushrooms. We use a spice grinder to process the dried shiitake mushrooms, but a blender also works.

¼ ounce dried shiitake mushrooms, rinsed
4¼ cups water
1 sprig fresh thyme
1 bay leaf
5 garlic cloves, peeled (1 whole, 4 minced)
  Salt and pepper
¼ teaspoon baking soda
1 cup wild rice
4 tablespoons unsalted butter
1 pound cremini mushrooms, trimmed and sliced ¼ inch thick
1 onion, chopped fine
1 teaspoon tomato paste
⅔ cup dry sherry
4 cups chicken broth
1 tablespoon soy sauce
¼ cup cornstarch
½ cup heavy cream
¼ cup minced fresh chives
¼ teaspoon finely grated lemon zest

1. Adjust oven rack to middle position and heat oven to 375 degrees. Grind shiitake mushrooms in spice grinder until finely ground (you should have about 3 tablespoons).

2. Bring 4 cups water, thyme sprig, bay leaf, garlic clove, ¾ teaspoon salt, and baking soda to boil in medium saucepan over high heat. Add rice and return to boil. Cover saucepan, transfer to oven, and bake until rice is tender, 35 to 50 minutes. Strain rice through fine-mesh strainer set in 4-cup liquid measuring cup; discard thyme sprig, bay leaf, and garlic clove. Add enough water to reserved cooking liquid to measure 3 cups.

3. Melt butter in Dutch oven over high heat. Add cremini mushrooms, onion, minced garlic, tomato paste, ¾ teaspoon salt, and 1 teaspoon pepper. Cook, stirring occasionally, until vegetables are browned and dark fond develops on bottom of pot, 15 minutes. Add sherry, scraping up any browned bits, and cook until reduced and pot is almost dry, about 2 minutes. Add ground shiitake mushrooms, reserved rice cooking liquid, broth, and soy sauce and bring to boil. Reduce heat to low and simmer, covered, until onion and mushrooms are tender, about 20 minutes.

4. Whisk cornstarch and remaining ¼ cup water in small bowl. Stir cornstarch slurry into soup, return to simmer, and cook until thickened, about 2 minutes. Remove pot from heat and stir in cooked rice, cream, chives, and lemon zest. Cover and let stand for 20 minutes. Season with salt and pepper to taste and serve.

BUTTERNUT SQUASH SOUP

WHY THIS RECIPE WORKS: Butternut squash soup strikes a perfect balance between nuttiness and sweetness. But getting that balance right depends on selecting just a few key ingredients so the sweet squash flavor can take center stage.

We found our answer to intense squash flavor in the squash's seeds and fibers. We sautéed shallots and butter with the seeds and fibers, simmered them in water, then used the liquid to steam the unpeeled quartered squash (thereby eliminating the pesky task of peeling raw squash). Once cooled, we scooped the flesh from the skin and pureed the squash with the steaming liquid (strained of seeds and fibers) for a soup with a perfectly smooth texture. A little dark brown sugar added to the soup also intensified the sweetness of the squash. Finally, we enriched the soup with a splash of heavy cream and a pinch of nutmeg to round out this velvety soup's rich flavors.

Butternut Squash Soup

SERVES 4 TO 6

Lightly toasted pumpkin seeds, drizzles of balsamic vinegar, or sprinklings of paprika or cracked black pepper make appealing accompaniments to this soup.

4 tablespoons (½ stick) unsalted butter
1 large shallot, minced (about ¼ cup)
3 pounds butternut squash (about 1 large squash), cut in half lengthwise, each half cut in half widthwise; seeds and fibers scraped out and reserved
6 cups water
  Table salt
½ cup heavy cream
1 teaspoon dark brown sugar
  Pinch grated nutmeg

1. Melt the butter in a large Dutch oven over medium-low heat. Add the shallot and cook, stirring frequently, until translucent, about 3 minutes. Add the seeds and fibers from the squash and cook, stirring occasionally, until the butter turns a saffron color, about 4 minutes.

2. Add the water and 1 teaspoon salt to the pot and bring to a boil over high heat. Reduce the heat to medium-low, place the squash, cut side down, in a steamer basket, and lower the basket into the pot. Cover and steam until the squash is completely tender, about 30 minutes. Take the pot off the heat and use tongs to transfer the squash to a rimmed baking sheet. When cool enough to handle, use a large spoon to scrape the flesh from the skin. Reserve the squash flesh in a bowl and discard the skin.

3. Strain the steaming liquid through a fine-mesh strainer into a second bowl; discard the solids in the strainer. (You should have 2½ to 3 cups liquid.) Rinse and dry the pot.

4. Working in batches and filling the blender jar only halfway for each batch, puree the squash, adding enough reserved steaming liquid to obtain a smooth consistency. Transfer the puree to the clean pot and stir in the remaining steaming liquid, the cream, and brown sugar. Warm the soup over medium-low heat until hot, about 3 minutes. Stir in the nutmeg, season with salt to taste, and serve. (The soup can be refrigerated in an airtight container for up to 2 days. Warm over low heat until hot; do not boil.)

SWEET POTATO SOUP

WHY THIS RECIPE WORKS: The secrets to a creamy sweet potato soup are to use the peels and turn off the heat. Most recipes call for so many other ingredients that the sweet potato flavor ends up muted and overpowered. By cutting back to shallot, thyme, and butter and using water instead of broth, we put the focus on the main ingredient. For extra earthiness, we also pureed some of the potato skins into the soup. However, the real key to intensifying the sweet potato flavor was to use only a minimal amount of flavor-diluting water. To do so, we let the sweet potatoes sit in hot water off heat to make use of an enzyme that converts their starch content to sugar. Less starch meant we could create a soup with less water, keeping the sweet potato flavor in the forefront.

Sweet Potato Soup
SERVES 4 TO 6 AS A MAIN DISH OR 8 AS A STARTER
To highlight the earthiness of the sweet potatoes, we incorporate a quarter of the skins into the soup. In addition to the chives, serve the soup with one of our suggested garnishes (recipes follow). The garnish can be prepared during step 1 while the sweet potatoes stand in the water.

- 4 tablespoons unsalted butter
- 1 shallot, sliced thin
- 4 sprigs fresh thyme
- 4¼ cups water, plus extra as needed

PUTTING PEELS TO WORK
Instead of discarding the sweet potato peels, we blend some of them into our soup to take advantage of an earthy-tasting compound they contain called methoxypyrazine.

Because the compound in the peels is potent—it's detectable in water in levels as low as one part per trillion—we use only one-quarter of the peels in order to avoid overwhelming the soup.

- 2 pounds sweet potatoes, peeled, halved lengthwise, and sliced ¼ inch thick, ¼ of peels reserved
- 1 tablespoon packed brown sugar
- ½ teaspoon cider vinegar
  Salt and pepper
  Minced fresh chives

1. Melt butter in large saucepan over medium-low heat. Add shallot and thyme sprigs and cook until shallot is softened but not browned, about 5 minutes. Add water, increase heat to high, and bring to simmer. Remove pot from heat, add sweet potatoes and reserved peels, and let stand uncovered for 20 minutes.

2. Add sugar, vinegar, 1½ teaspoons salt, and ¼ teaspoon pepper. Bring to simmer over high heat. Reduce heat to medium-low, cover, and cook until potatoes are very soft, about 10 minutes.

3. Discard thyme sprigs. Working in batches, process soup in blender until smooth, 45 to 60 seconds. Return soup to clean pot. Bring to simmer over medium heat, adjusting consistency with extra water if desired. Season with salt and pepper to taste. Serve, topping each portion with sprinkle of chives.

Buttery Rye Croutons
MAKES 1½ CUPS
The croutons can be made ahead and stored in an airtight container for up to 1 week.

- 3 tablespoons unsalted butter
- 1 tablespoon olive oil
- 2 slices light rye bread, cut into ½-inch cubes (about 1½ cups)
  Salt

Heat butter and oil in 10-inch skillet over medium heat. When foaming subsides, add bread cubes and cook, stirring frequently, until golden brown, about 10 minutes. Transfer croutons to paper towel–lined plate and season with salt to taste.

Candied Bacon Bits

MAKES ABOUT ¼ CUP

Break up any large chunks before serving.

- 4 slices bacon, cut into ½-inch pieces
- 2 teaspoons packed dark brown sugar
- ½ teaspoon cider vinegar

Cook bacon in 10-inch nonstick skillet over medium heat until crisp and well rendered, 6 to 8 minutes. Using slotted spoon, remove bacon from skillet and discard fat. Return bacon to skillet and add brown sugar and vinegar. Cook over low heat, stirring constantly, until bacon is evenly coated. Transfer to plate in single layer. Let bacon cool completely.

Maple Sour Cream

MAKES ⅓ CUP

Maple balances the sweet potatoes' earthiness.

- ⅓ cup sour cream
- 1 tablespoon maple syrup

Combine ingredients in bowl.

SUPER GREENS SOUP WITH LEMON-TARRAGON CREAM

WHY THIS RECIPE WORKS: We wanted a deceptively delicious, silky-smooth soup that delivered a big dose of healthy greens. It should be packed with all the essential nutrients of hearty greens and boast a deep, complex flavor brightened with a garnish of lemon and herb cream. First, we built a flavorful foundation of sweet caramelized onions and earthy sautéed mushrooms. We added broth, water, and lots of leafy greens (we liked a mix of chard, kale, arugula, and parsley), and simmered until the greens became tender before blending them smooth. We were happy with the soup's depth of flavor, but it was watery and too thin. Many recipes we found used potatoes as a thickener, but they lent an overwhelmingly earthy flavor. Instead, we tried using Arborio rice. The rice's high starch content thickened the soup to a velvety, lush consistency without clouding its bright, vegetal flavors. For a vibrant finish, we whisked together heavy cream, sour cream, lemon zest, lemon juice, and tarragon and drizzled it over the top.

Super Greens Soup with Lemon-Tarragon Cream

SERVES 4 TO 6

Our favorite brand of Arborio rice is RiceSelect.

- ¼ cup heavy cream
- 3 tablespoons sour cream
- 2 tablespoons plus ½ teaspoon extra-virgin olive oil
- ¼ teaspoon finely grated lemon zest plus ½ teaspoon juice
- ½ teaspoon minced fresh tarragon
-   Salt and pepper
- 1 onion, halved through root end and sliced thin
- ¾ teaspoon light brown sugar
- 3 ounces white mushrooms, trimmed and sliced thin
- 2 garlic cloves, minced
-   Pinch cayenne pepper
- 3 cups water
- 3 cups vegetable broth
- ⅓ cup Arborio rice
- 12 ounces Swiss chard, stemmed and chopped coarse
- 9 ounces kale, stemmed and chopped coarse
- ¼ cup fresh parsley leaves
- 2 ounces (2 cups) baby arugula

1. Combine cream, sour cream, ½ teaspoon oil, lemon zest and juice, tarragon, and ¼ teaspoon salt in bowl. Cover and refrigerate until ready to serve.

2. Heat remaining 2 tablespoons oil in Dutch oven over medium-high heat until shimmering. Stir in onion, sugar, and 1 teaspoon salt and cook, stirring occasionally, until onion releases some moisture, about 5 minutes. Reduce heat to low and cook, stirring often and scraping up any browned bits, until onion is deeply browned and slightly sticky, about 30 minutes. (If onion is sizzling or scorching, reduce heat. If onion is not browning after 15 to 20 minutes, increase heat.)

3. Stir in mushrooms and cook until they have released their moisture, about 5 minutes. Stir in garlic and cayenne and cook until fragrant, about 30 seconds. Stir in water, broth, and rice, scraping up any browned bits, and bring to boil. Reduce heat to low, cover, and simmer for 15 minutes.

4. Stir in chard, kale, and parsley, 1 handful at a time, until wilted and submerged in liquid. Return to simmer, cover, and cook until greens are tender, about 10 minutes.

5. Off heat, stir in arugula until wilted. Working in batches, process soup in blender until smooth, about 1 minute per batch. Return pureed soup to clean pot and season with salt and pepper to taste. Drizzle individual portions with lemon-tarragon cream and serve.

RUSTIC POTATO-LEEK SOUP

WHY THIS RECIPE WORKS: Rustic potato-leek soup often disappoints with soft, mealy potatoes and dingy, overcooked leeks. We wanted to perfect this soup so both ingredients would be at their best and the dish would retain its textural integrity and bright flavor.

We quickly eliminated potatoes with high or medium starch levels because they broke down too quickly in the chicken broth. Waxy, low-starch red potatoes were perfect—they kept their shape and didn't become waterlogged during cooking. To pump up the flavor of the soup, we used a substantial amount of leeks and sautéed both the white and light green parts in butter. Leeks and potatoes require different cooking times, so we staggered the cooking—leeks first, then potatoes, and then we removed the pot from the stove so the potatoes could gently cook through in the hot broth without becoming overcooked and mushy. We also added a bit of flour with the sautéed leeks to give our broth some body. At last, we had a flavorful, oniony soup, full of perfectly cooked potatoes and sweet, tender leeks.

Rustic Potato-Leek Soup

SERVES 6

Leeks can vary in size; if your leeks have large white and light green parts, use the smaller amount of leeks.

- 6 tablespoons (¾ stick) unsalted butter
- 4-5 pounds leeks, white and light green parts only, halved lengthwise, sliced crosswise 1 inch thick, and rinsed thoroughly (about 11 cups; see note)
- 1 tablespoon unbleached all-purpose flour
- 5¼ cups low-sodium chicken broth
- 1¾ pounds red potatoes (about 5 medium), peeled and cut into ¾-inch chunks
- 1 bay leaf
- Table salt and ground black pepper

1. Melt the butter in a large Dutch oven over medium-low heat. Add the leeks, increase the heat to medium, cover, and cook, stirring occasionally, until the leeks are tender but not mushy, 15 to 20 minutes; do not brown them. Add the flour and cook, stirring constantly, until thoroughly combined, about 2 minutes.

2. Increase the heat to high; whisking constantly, gradually add the broth. Add the potatoes and bay leaf, cover, and bring to a boil. Reduce the heat to medium-low and simmer, covered, until the potatoes are almost tender, 5 to 7 minutes. Remove the pot from the heat and let stand, covered, until the potatoes are tender, 10 to 15 minutes. Discard the bay leaf, season with salt and pepper to taste, and serve. (The soup can be refrigerated in an airtight container for up to 2 days. Warm over low heat until hot; do not boil.)

BROCCOLI-CHEESE SOUP

WHY THIS RECIPE WORKS: We were after a soup with pure broccoli flavor that wasn't hiding behind the cream or the cheese. Overcooked broccoli has a sulfurous flavor, but we discovered when we cooked our broccoli beyond the point of just overcooked—for a full hour—those sulfur-containing compounds broke down, leaving behind intense, nutty broccoli. Its texture was fairly soft, but that was perfect for use in a soup. Adding baking soda to the pot sped up the process, shortening the broccoli's cooking time to a mere 20 minutes. A little spinach lent bright green color to the soup without taking over the flavor. After adding cheddar and Parmesan, we had a soup so full of flavor and richness that it didn't even need the typical cream.

Broccoli-Cheese Soup

SERVES 6 TO 8

To make a vegetarian version of this soup, substitute vegetable broth for the chicken broth.

- 2 tablespoons unsalted butter
- 2 pounds broccoli, florets chopped into 1-inch pieces, stems peeled and sliced ¼ inch thick
- 1 medium onion, chopped coarse
- 2 medium garlic cloves, minced or pressed through a garlic press (about 2 teaspoons)
- 1½ teaspoons dry mustard
- Pinch cayenne pepper
- Table salt and ground black pepper
- 3-4 cups water
- ¼ teaspoon baking soda
- 2 cups low-sodium chicken broth
- 2 ounces baby spinach (about 2 cups)

3 ounces sharp cheddar cheese,
   shredded (about ¾ cup)
1½ ounces Parmesan cheese, grated fine
   (about ¾ cup), plus extra for serving
1 recipe Buttery Croutons (page 13)

1. Melt the butter in a Dutch oven over medium-high heat. Add the broccoli, onion, garlic, mustard, cayenne, and 1 teaspoon salt and cook, stirring frequently, until fragrant, about 6 minutes. Add 1 cup water and the baking soda. Bring to a simmer, cover, and cook until the broccoli is very soft, about 20 minutes, stirring once during cooking.

2. Add the broth and 2 cups more water and increase the heat to medium-high. When the mixture begins to simmer, stir in the spinach and cook until wilted, about 1 minute. Transfer half of the soup to a blender, add the cheddar and Parmesan, and process until smooth, about 1 minute. Transfer the soup to a medium bowl and repeat with the remaining soup. Return the soup to the Dutch oven, place over medium heat and bring to a simmer. Adjust the consistency of the soup with up to 1 cup water. Season with salt and pepper to taste. Serve, passing extra Parmesan.

MODERN HAM AND SPLIT PEA SOUP

WHY THIS RECIPE WORKS: We wanted a spoon-coating, richly flavorful broth studded with tender shreds of sweet-smoky meat. To avoid having to bake a ham beforehand, we needed a substitute for the traditional ham bone. Ham hock made the soup greasy and was skimpy on the meat. Ham steak, however, was plenty meaty and infused the soup with a fuller pork flavor—and we could get away with using just 1 pound. Our soup still needed richness and smokiness, and adding a few strips of raw bacon to the pot did the job. Unsoaked peas broke down just as well as soaked and were better at absorbing the flavor of the soup, so we skipped the traditional soaking step. To dress up our recipe, we garnished it with a handful of fresh peas; their sweetness popped against the hearty, smoky broth. Fresh chopped mint leaves and a drizzle of good balsamic vinegar added visual appeal and punched up the flavors even more. Floating gently fried croutons on the surface rounded off our updated version of this classic soup.

Modern Ham and Split Pea Soup
SERVES 6 TO 8

Four ounces of regular sliced bacon can be used, but the thinner slices are a little harder to remove from the soup. Depending on the age and brand of split peas, the consistency of the soup may vary slightly. If the soup is too thin at the end of step 3, increase the heat and simmer, uncovered, until the desired consistency is reached. If it is too thick, thin it with a little water. In addition to sprinkling the soup with Buttery Croutons (page 13), we also like to garnish it with fresh peas, chopped mint, and a drizzle of aged balsamic vinegar.

2 tablespoons unsalted butter
1 large onion, chopped fine
   Table salt and ground black pepper
2 medium garlic cloves, minced or pressed through
   a garlic press (about 2 teaspoons)
7 cups water
1 ham steak (about 1 pound), skin removed,
   cut into quarters
3 slices thick-cut bacon
1 pound (2 cups) green split peas, picked over and rinsed
2 sprigs fresh thyme
2 bay leaves
2 medium carrots, peeled and cut into ½-inch pieces
1 medium celery rib, cut into ½-inch pieces

1. Heat the butter in a Dutch oven over medium-high heat. Add the onion and ½ teaspoon salt and cook, stirring frequently, until the onion is softened, about 3 to 4 minutes. Add the garlic and cook until fragrant, about 30 seconds. Add the water, ham steak, bacon, peas, thyme, and bay leaves. Increase the heat to high and bring to a simmer, stirring frequently to keep the peas from sticking to the bottom. Reduce the heat to low, cover, and simmer until the peas are tender but not falling apart, about 45 minutes.

2. Remove the ham steak, cover with aluminum foil or plastic wrap to prevent drying out, and set aside. Stir in the carrots and celery and continue to simmer, covered, until the vegetables are tender and the peas have almost completely broken down, about 30 minutes longer.

3. When cool enough to handle, shred the ham into small bite-size pieces. Remove and discard the thyme, bay leaves, and bacon slices. Stir the ham back into the soup and return to a simmer. Season with salt and pepper to taste and serve. (The soup can be refrigerated for up to 3 days. If necessary, thin it with water when reheating.)

HEARTY HAM AND SPLIT PEA SOUP WITH POTATOES

WHY THIS RECIPE WORKS: Split pea soup tends to show up on the home cook's menu only when the previous meal (usually a holiday celebration) featured a big ham—and the leftovers are begging to be made into soup. We wanted a recipe for an old-fashioned ham and split pea soup that could be made anytime, with a readily available cut of ham that would also provide enough meat for really hearty soup. We found that we could get good, meaty ham stock with a picnic shoulder, a small, inexpensive cut that adds great flavor and provides plenty of meat for the soup (and some leftovers too). While it was easy enough to cook the peas in the ham stock, our vegetables benefited from a sauté in a separate pan. We found that caramelized vegetables gave this straightforward soup a richness and depth of flavor that had been missing—it was well worth the time spent washing an extra pan. Adding in a few red potatoes with the carrots, celery, and onions turned our soup into a truly satisfying meal.

vegetables are cooking, shred the meat with your fingers or two forks and set aside. Discard the rind and bone.

3. Meanwhile, heat the oil in a large skillet over medium-high heat until shimmering. Add the onions, carrots, and celery and sauté, stirring frequently, until most of the liquid evaporates and the vegetables begin to brown, 5 to 6 minutes. Reduce the heat to medium-low and add the butter, garlic, and sugar. Cook the vegetables, stirring frequently, until deeply browned, 30 to 35 minutes; set aside.

4. Add the sautéed vegetables, potatoes, and shredded ham to the pot with the split peas. Simmer until the potatoes are tender, the peas dissolve, and the soup thickens to the consistency of light cream, about 20 minutes. Season with pepper to taste. Discard the bay leaves and ladle the soup into bowls. Sprinkle with red onion (if using) and serve, passing balsamic vinegar separately. (The soup, minus the garnishes, can be refrigerated in an airtight container for up to 2 days. Warm over low heat until hot; do not boil.)

Hearty Ham and Split Pea Soup with Potatoes
SERVES 6

Use an entire small 2½-pound smoked picnic portion ham if you can find one. Otherwise, buy a half-picnic ham and remove some meat, which you can roast and use in sandwiches, salads, or omelets. To remove the meat, loosen the large comma-shaped muscles on top of the ham with your fingers, then use a knife to cut the membrane separating the comma-shaped muscles from the rest of the ham.

- 1 (2½-pound) smoked bone-in picnic ham (see note)
- 4 bay leaves
- 3 quarts water
- 1 pound (2 cups) green split peas, picked over and rinsed
- 1 teaspoon dried thyme
- 2 tablespoons extra-virgin olive oil
- 2 medium onions, chopped medium
- 2 medium carrots, peeled and chopped medium
- 2 celery ribs, chopped medium
- 1 tablespoon unsalted butter
- 2 medium garlic cloves, minced or pressed through a garlic press (about 2 teaspoons)
  Pinch sugar
- 3 small red potatoes (about ½ pound), scrubbed and cut into ½-inch chunks
  Ground black pepper
  Minced red onion (optional)
  Balsamic vinegar

1. Place the ham in a large Dutch oven, add the bay leaves and water, cover, and bring to a boil over medium-high heat. Reduce the heat to low and simmer until the meat is tender and pulls away from the bone, 2 to 2½ hours. Remove the ham meat and bone from the pot and set aside.

2. Add the split peas and thyme to the stock. Bring to a boil, reduce the heat, and simmer, uncovered, until the peas are tender but not dissolved, about 45 minutes. While the

HEARTY LENTIL SOUP

WHY THIS RECIPE WORKS: A hot bowl of lentil soup provides warm comfort on a cold day and, when properly prepared, tastes great—maybe even better—the next day. We wanted a hearty lentil soup worthy of a second bowl, not the tasteless variety we have so often encountered.

While *lentilles du Puy* are our top choice for lentil soup, we found that almost any lentil (other than red lentils) can be used. To keep the lentils from losing their shape as they cooked, we sweated them with sautéed aromatic vegetables before adding chicken broth to the soup pot. These lentils stayed intact in our final soup, but their flavor was weak. Revisiting this step, we added canned tomatoes and crisp bacon, which gave our lentils a huge flavor boost. And because we cooked the bacon first, we could then use the rendered fat to sauté our vegetables and aromatics, which brought a nice smoky flavor to the soup. For a texture that was neither too smooth nor too thick, we pureed a few cups of the soup and added it back to the pot to warm through. Lentil soup needs plenty of acidity, so we used white wine as part of the broth and finished the soup with balsamic vinegar.

Hearty Lentil Soup
SERVES 4 TO 6

Lentilles du Puy, sometimes called French green lentils, are our first choice for this recipe, but brown, black, or regular green lentils are fine, too. Note that cooking times will vary depending on the type of lentils used. Be sure to rinse and then carefully sort through the lentils to remove any small stones.

- 3 ounces (3 slices) bacon, cut into ¼-inch pieces
- 1 large onion, minced
- 2 medium carrots, peeled and chopped medium

3 medium garlic cloves, minced or pressed through
   a garlic press (about 1 tablespoon)
1 (14.5-ounce) can diced tomatoes, drained
1 bay leaf
1 teaspoon minced fresh thyme leaves
1 cup (7 ounces) lentils, rinsed and picked over (see note)
1 teaspoon table salt
   Ground black pepper
½ cup dry white wine
4½ cups low-sodium chicken broth
1½ cups water
1½ teaspoons balsamic vinegar
3 tablespoons minced fresh parsley leaves

1. Fry the bacon in a large Dutch oven over medium-high heat, stirring occasionally, until the fat is rendered and the bacon is crisp, 3 to 4 minutes. Add the onion and carrots; cook, stirring occasionally, until the vegetables begin to soften, about 2 minutes. Add the garlic and cook until fragrant, about 30 seconds. Stir in the tomatoes, bay leaf, and thyme; cook until fragrant, about 30 seconds. Stir in the lentils, salt, and pepper to taste; cover, reduce the heat to medium-low, and cook until the vegetables are softened and the lentils have darkened, 8 to 10 minutes.

2. Uncover, increase the heat to high, add the wine, and bring to a simmer. Add the chicken broth and water; bring to a boil, cover partially, and reduce the heat to low. Simmer until the lentils are tender but still hold their shape, 30 to 35 minutes; discard the bay leaf.

3. Puree 3 cups of the soup in a blender until smooth, then return to the pot. Stir in the vinegar and heat the soup over medium-low heat until hot, about 5 minutes. Stir in 2 tablespoons of the parsley. Ladle the soup into bowls, garnish with the remaining parsley, and serve. (The soup, minus the garnish, can be refrigerated in an airtight container for up to 2 days. Warm over low heat until hot; do not boil.)

HEARTY SPANISH-STYLE LENTIL AND CHORIZO SOUP

WHY THIS RECIPE WORKS: For our own version of Spain's thick and smoky lentil soup, we started with the lentils. Soaking them in a warm brine for 30 minutes before cooking prevented blowouts and ensured they were well seasoned. Browning links of Spanish chorizo and then simmering them in the soup ensured a juicy texture. Slowly sweating finely chopped aromatics in the chorizo's fat gave our soup incredible depth of flavor. For more intensity, we finished the soup with an Indian preparation called a *tarka*, which is a mixture of spices (smoked paprika ramped up the smoky notes) and finely minced aromatics (we used onion and garlic) bloomed in oil. Adding a little flour helped thicken the soup and some sherry vinegar brightened its flavors.

Hearty Spanish-Style Lentil and Chorizo Soup
SERVES 6 TO 8

We prefer French green lentils, or *lentilles du Puy*, for this recipe, but it will work with any type of lentil except red or yellow. Grate the onion on the large holes of a box grater. If Spanish-style chorizo is not available, kielbasa sausage can be substituted. Red wine vinegar can be substituted for the sherry vinegar. Smoked paprika comes in three varieties: sweet (dulce), bittersweet or medium hot (agridulce), and hot (picante). For this recipe, we prefer the sweet kind.

1 pound (2¼ cups) lentils, picked over and rinsed
   Salt and pepper
1 large onion
5 tablespoons extra-virgin olive oil
1½ pounds Spanish-style chorizo sausage,
   pricked with fork several times
3 carrots, peeled and cut into ¼-inch pieces
3 tablespoons minced fresh parsley
3 tablespoons sherry vinegar, plus extra for seasoning
7 cups water, plus extra as needed
2 bay leaves
⅛ teaspoon ground cloves
2 tablespoons sweet smoked paprika
3 garlic cloves, minced
1 tablespoon all-purpose flour

1. Place lentils and 2 teaspoons salt in heatproof container. Cover with 4 cups boiling water and let soak for 30 minutes. Drain well.

2. Meanwhile, finely chop three-quarters of onion (you should have about 1 cup) and grate remaining quarter (you should have about 3 tablespoons). Heat 2 tablespoons oil in Dutch oven over medium heat until shimmering. Add chorizo and cook until browned on all sides, 6 to 8 minutes. Transfer chorizo to large

plate. Reduce heat to low and add chopped onion, carrots, 1 tablespoon parsley, and 1 teaspoon salt. Cover and cook, stirring occasionally, until vegetables are very soft but not brown, 25 to 30 minutes. If vegetables begin to brown, add 1 tablespoon water to pot.

3. Add lentils and sherry vinegar to vegetables; increase heat to medium-high; and cook, stirring frequently, until vinegar starts to evaporate, 3 to 4 minutes. Add 7 cups water, chorizo, bay leaves, and cloves; bring to simmer. Reduce heat to low, cover, and cook until lentils are tender, about 30 minutes.

4. Heat remaining 3 tablespoons oil in small saucepan over medium heat until shimmering. Add paprika, grated onion, garlic, and ½ teaspoon pepper; cook, stirring constantly, until fragrant, 2 minutes. Add flour and cook, stirring constantly, 1 minute longer. Remove chorizo and bay leaves from lentils. Stir paprika mixture into lentils and continue to cook until flavors have blended and soup has thickened, 10 to 15 minutes. When chorizo is cool enough to handle, cut in half lengthwise, then cut each half into ¼-inch-thick slices. Return chorizo to soup along with remaining 2 tablespoons parsley and heat through, about 1 minute. Season with salt, pepper, and up to 2 teaspoons sherry vinegar to taste, and serve. (Soup can be made up to 3 days in advance.)

Hearty Spanish-Style Lentil and Chorizo Soup with Kale

Add 12 ounces kale, stemmed and cut into ½-inch pieces, to simmering soup after 15 minutes in step 3. Continue to simmer until lentils and kale are tender, about 15 minutes.

RED LENTIL SOUP WITH NORTH AFRICAN SPICES

WHY THIS RECIPE WORKS: Red lentils are one of our favorite legumes. They cook quickly and don't require any presoaking or brining like other beans. One of their best qualities, however, is that they disintegrate when cooked, forming a creamy, thick puree—perfect for a satisfying soup. Their mild flavor does require a bit of embellishment, so we started by sautéing onions in butter and used the warm mixture to bloom some fragrant North African spices. Tomato paste and garlic completed the base before the addition of the lentils, and a mix of chicken broth and water gave the soup a full, rounded character. After only 15 minutes of cooking, the lentils were soft enough to be pureed with a whisk. A generous dose of lemon juice brought the flavors into focus, and a drizzle of spice-infused butter and a sprinkle of fresh cilantro completed the transformation of commonplace ingredients into an exotic yet comforting soup.

Red Lentil Soup With North African Spices
SERVES 4 TO 6

Pair this soup with a salad and bread for lunch or a light supper.

4 tablespoons unsalted butter
1 large onion, chopped fine
   Salt and pepper
¾ teaspoon ground coriander
½ teaspoon ground cumin
¼ teaspoon ground ginger
⅛ teaspoon ground cinnamon
   Pinch cayenne pepper
1 tablespoon tomato paste
1 garlic clove, minced
4 cups chicken broth
2 cups water
10½ ounces (1½ cups) red lentils, picked over and rinsed
2 tablespoons lemon juice, plus extra for seasoning
1½ teaspoons dried mint, crumbled
1 teaspoon paprika
¼ cup chopped fresh cilantro

1. Melt 2 tablespoons butter in large saucepan over medium heat. Add onion and 1 teaspoon salt and cook, stirring occasionally, until softened but not browned, about 5 minutes. Add coriander, cumin, ginger, cinnamon, cayenne, and ¼ teaspoon pepper and cook until fragrant, about 2 minutes. Stir in tomato paste and garlic and cook for 1 minute. Stir in broth, water, and lentils and bring to simmer. Simmer vigorously, stirring occasionally, until lentils are soft and about half are broken down, about 15 minutes.

2. Whisk soup vigorously until it is coarsely pureed, about 30 seconds. Stir in lemon juice and season with salt and extra lemon juice to taste. Cover and keep warm. (Soup can be refrigerated for up to 3 days. Thin soup with water, if desired, when reheating.)

3. Melt remaining 2 tablespoons butter in small skillet over medium-low heat. Remove from heat and stir in mint and paprika. Ladle soup into individual bowls, drizzle each portion with 1 teaspoon spiced butter, sprinkle with cilantro, and serve.

MULLIGATAWNY SOUP

WHY THIS RECIPE WORKS: As with many other dishes of Indian origin, mulligatawny soup is mildly spicy and richly flavored, with a number of spices in its lineup. We wanted an elegant, but potent, rendition of this classic soup, not the thin, raw-tasting version found in many restaurants.

Chicken broth proved to be the best base for this pureed vegetable-laden soup; beef broth was too strong and vegetable broth gave us an overly vegetal soup. For the spices, good-quality curry powder is a must, and a little cumin and cayenne pepper made for the perfect spice mix. Garlic, ginger, and coconut were a given—essentials in mulligatawny—but the best way to incorporate them wasn't immediately clear. We ended up adopting a technique common in Indian cooking—we pureed the raw garlic and ginger with water so they could

be mixed into the soup for fresh bites of garlic and ginger. The best source for true coconut flavor turned out to be shredded unsweetened coconut.

Finally, to give the finished soup the right amount of body, we made a roux with our aromatics and pureed the soup with a banana, which imparted a rich, sweet flavor to the dish (a potato worked fine, too). A swirl of yogurt and sprinkling of cilantro were the crowning touches on our richly spiced, velvety mulligatawny.

Mulligatawny Soup

SERVES 6 TO 8

Leave the garlic and ginger puree from step 1 in the blender while making the soup; when the finished soup is pureed in the same blender, it will pick up a hit of spicy raw garlic and ginger. For a heartier soup, stir in cooked white rice.

- 4 medium garlic cloves, 2 peeled and 2 minced or pressed through a garlic press (see note)
- 1½ tablespoons minced or grated fresh ginger (see note)
- ¼ cup water
- 3 tablespoons unsalted butter
- 2 medium onions, chopped medium
- 1 teaspoon tomato paste
- ½ cup shredded unsweetened coconut
- ¼ cup unbleached all-purpose flour
- 1½ tablespoons curry powder
- 1 teaspoon ground cumin
- ¼ teaspoon cayenne pepper
- 7 cups low-sodium chicken broth
- 2 medium carrots, peeled and chopped medium
- 1 celery rib, chopped medium
- 1 medium very ripe banana (about 5 ounces), peeled, or 1 medium red potato (about 5 ounces), peeled and cut into 1-inch chunks

Table salt and ground black pepper
Plain yogurt
- 2 tablespoons minced fresh cilantro leaves

1. Puree the 2 peeled whole garlic cloves, 2 teaspoons of the ginger, and the water in a blender until smooth; leave the mixture in the blender and set aside.

2. Melt the butter in a large Dutch oven over medium heat. Add the onions and tomato paste and cook, stirring frequently, until the onions are softened and beginning to brown, about 3 minutes. Stir in the coconut and cook until fragrant, about 1 minute. Add the minced garlic, the remaining 2½ teaspoons ginger, the flour, curry powder, cumin, and cayenne; stir until evenly combined, about 1 minute. Whisking constantly, gradually add the chicken broth.

3. Add the carrots, celery, and banana to the pot. Increase the heat to medium-high and bring to a boil. Cover, reduce the heat to low, and simmer until the vegetables are tender, about 20 minutes.

4. Working in batches, puree the soup in the blender with the garlic and ginger until smooth, filling the blender jar only halfway for each batch. Wash and dry the pot. Return the pureed soup to the pot and season with salt and pepper to taste. Warm the soup over medium heat until hot, about 1 minute. Ladle the soup into bowls, spoon a dollop of yogurt into each bowl, sprinkle with the cilantro, and serve. (The soup, minus the garnishes, can be refrigerated in an airtight container for up to 3 days. Warm over low heat until hot; do not boil.)

CHICKEN AND SAUSAGE GUMBO

WHY THIS RECIPE WORKS: Most recipes for the beloved Louisiana soup, gumbo, start with a wet roux, a cooked paste of flour and fat that can take an hour or more to make. We streamlined this process by using a dry roux of oven-toasted flour, which gave the same effect as a wet roux but without the oil. To flavor our gumbo we used easy-to-work-with boneless, skinless chicken thighs and andouille sausage, rounding out the dish with garlic, thyme, bay leaves, and spices. We stirred in white vinegar rather than hot sauce at the end for acidity without adding heat to an already well-seasoned dish.

Chicken and Sausage Gumbo

SERVES 6

This recipe is engineered for efficiency: Get the flour toasting in the oven and then prep the remaining ingredients before you begin cooking. We strongly recommend using andouille, but in a pinch, kielbasa can be substituted. The salt level of the final dish may vary depending on the brand of sausage, so liberal seasoning with additional salt at the end may be necessary. Serve over white rice.

1 cup (5 ounces) all-purpose flour
1 tablespoon vegetable oil
1 onion, chopped fine
1 green bell pepper, chopped fine
2 celery ribs, chopped fine
3 garlic cloves, minced
2 bay leaves
1 tablespoon minced fresh thyme
1 teaspoon paprika
½ teaspoon cayenne pepper
  Salt and pepper
4 cups chicken broth, room temperature
2 pounds boneless, skinless chicken thighs, trimmed
8 ounces andouille sausage, sliced into ¼-inch thick half-moons
6 scallions, sliced thin
1 teaspoon distilled white vinegar
  Hot sauce

1. Adjust oven rack to middle position and heat oven to 425 degrees. Place flour in 12-inch skillet and bake, stirring occasionally, until color of ground cinnamon or dark brown sugar, 40 to 55 minutes. (As flour approaches desired color it will take on very nutty aroma that will smell faintly of burnt popcorn and it will need to be stirred more frequently.) Transfer flour to medium bowl and cool. (Toasted flour can be stored in airtight container for up to 1 week.)

2. Heat oil in Dutch oven over medium heat until shimmering. Add onion, pepper, and celery and cook, stirring frequently, until softened, 5 to 7 minutes. Stir in garlic, bay leaves, thyme, paprika, cayenne, ¼ teaspoon salt, and ¼ teaspoon pepper and cook until fragrant, about 1 minute. Stir in 2 cups broth. Add chicken thighs in single layer (they will not be completely submerged by liquid) and bring to simmer. Reduce heat to medium-low, cover, and simmer until chicken is fork tender, 15 to 17 minutes. Transfer chicken to plate.

3. Slowly whisk remaining 2 cups broth into toasted flour until thick, batter-like paste forms. (Add broth in small increments to prevent clumps from forming.) Return pot to medium heat and slowly whisk flour paste into gumbo, making sure each addition is incorporated before adding next. Stir sausage into gumbo. Simmer, uncovered, until gumbo thickens slightly, 20 to 25 minutes.

4. Once cool enough to handle, shred chicken into bite-size pieces. Stir chicken and scallions into gumbo. Remove pot from heat and stir in vinegar and season with salt to taste. Discard bay leaves. Serve, passing hot sauce at table. (Gumbo can be refrigerated in airtight container for up to 24 hours).

HEARTY MINESTRONE

WHY THIS RECIPE WORKS: Excellent minestrone soup relies on perfectly ripe vegetables. But we're often stuck with lackluster supermarket offerings. We wanted a soup that squeezed every ounce of flavor out of supermarket vegetables and was as satisfying as minestrone served in Italy.

To start, we limited our vegetables to a manageable six: onions, celery, carrots, cabbage, zucchini, and tomato. We began our soup by sautéing some finely diced pancetta in a Dutch oven, then browned the vegetables in the rendered fat, which helped develop sweetness and lent a rich flavor. We decided to use cannellini beans (a favorite for their creamy texture and buttery flavor), which we soaked overnight in salted water to ensure they cooked evenly and turned out well seasoned. We added the soaked beans along with the cooking liquid (and a Parmesan rind) and simmered them together vigorously—this helped the beans release their starch to thicken the soup. Once the beans were tender, we returned the vegetables to the pot and simmered everything together. Rather than using all water, we replaced a portion with chicken broth. But it wasn't until we landed on an unusual addition—V8 juice, rather than canned tomatoes—that our soup boasted consistent tomato flavor in every spoonful.

Hearty Minestrone
SERVES 6 TO 8
If you are pressed for time you can "quick-brine" your beans. In step 1, combine the salt, water, and beans in a large Dutch oven and bring to a boil over high heat. Remove the pot from the heat, cover, and let stand 1 hour. Drain and rinse the beans and proceed with the recipe. We prefer cannellini beans, but navy or great Northern beans can be used. We prefer pancetta, but bacon can be used in its place. A Parmesan rind is added for flavor, but can be replaced with a 2-inch chunk of the cheese. In order for the starch from the beans to thicken the soup, it is important to maintain a vigorous simmer in step 3.

  Table salt
½ pound dried cannellini beans (about 1 cup), rinsed and picked over (see note)
1 tablespoon extra-virgin olive oil, plus extra for serving
3 ounces pancetta, cut into ¼-inch pieces (see note)
2 medium celery ribs, cut into ½-inch pieces (about ¾ cup)

1 medium carrot, peeled and cut into
   ½-inch pieces (about ¾ cup)

2 small onions, peeled and cut into
   ½-inch pieces (about 1½ cups)

1 medium zucchini, trimmed and cut
   into ½-inch pieces (about 1 cup)

½ small head green cabbage, halved, cored,
   and cut into ½-inch pieces (about 2 cups)

2 medium garlic cloves, minced or pressed through
   a garlic press (about 2 teaspoons)

⅛–¼ teaspoon red pepper flakes

8 cups water

2 cups low-sodium chicken broth

1 piece Parmesan cheese rind, about 5 by 2 inches
   (see note)

1 bay leaf

1½ cups V8 juice

½ cup chopped fresh basil leaves

   Ground black pepper

   Grated Parmesan cheese, for serving

1. Dissolve 1½ tablespoons salt in 2 quarts cold water in a large bowl or container. Add the beans and soak at room temperature for at least 8 hours and up to 24 hours. Drain the beans and rinse well.

2. Heat the oil and pancetta in a large Dutch oven over medium-high heat. Cook, stirring occasionally, until the pancetta is lightly browned and the fat has rendered, 3 to 5 minutes. Add the celery, carrot, onions, and zucchini; cook, stirring frequently, until the vegetables are softened and lightly browned, 5 to 9 minutes. Stir in the cabbage, garlic, ½ teaspoon salt, and red pepper flakes; continue to cook until the cabbage starts to wilt, 1 to 2 minutes longer. Transfer the vegetables to a rimmed baking sheet and set aside.

3. Add the soaked beans, water, broth, Parmesan rind, and bay leaf to the now-empty Dutch oven and bring to a boil over high heat. Reduce the heat and vigorously simmer, stirring occasionally, until the beans are fully tender and the liquid begins to thicken, 45 to 60 minutes.

4. Add the reserved vegetables and V8 juice to the pot; cook until the vegetables are soft, about 15 minutes. Discard the bay leaf and Parmesan rind, stir in the basil, and season with salt and pepper to taste. Serve with olive oil and grated Parmesan.

FARMHOUSE VEGETABLE AND BARLEY SOUP

WHY THIS RECIPE WORKS: Most recipes for hearty winter vegetable soups, it turns out, are neither quick nor easy. For a satisfying soup that doesn't take the better part of a day to make, we started with canned chicken broth. To this we added soy sauce and ground dried porcini mushrooms. These ingredients added a savory, almost meaty flavor to the soup base. To make the soup more filling, we added barley to the hearty combination of carrots, potatoes, leeks, cabbage, and turnips.

Farmhouse Vegetable and Barley Soup

SERVES 6 TO 8

We prefer an acidic, unoaked white wine such as Sauvignon Blanc for this recipe. We love the richness added by the Lemon-Thyme Butter and the crunch of Herbed Croutons (recipes follow) but the soup can also be garnished with crisp bacon or crumbled cheddar cheese. You will need at least a 6-quart Dutch oven for this recipe.

⅛ ounce dried porcini mushrooms, rinsed

8 sprigs fresh parsley plus 3 tablespoons minced

4 sprigs fresh thyme

1 bay leaf

2 tablespoons unsalted butter

1½ pounds leeks, white and light green parts sliced
   ½ inch thick and washed thoroughly

2 carrots, peeled and cut into ½-inch pieces

2 celery ribs, cut into ¼-inch pieces

⅓ cup dry white wine

2 teaspoons soy sauce

   Salt and pepper

6 cups water

4 cups low-sodium chicken broth or vegetable broth

½ cup pearl barley

1 garlic clove, peeled and smashed

1½ pounds Yukon Gold potatoes, peeled and cut
   into ½-inch pieces

1 turnip, peeled and cut into ¾-inch pieces

1½ cups chopped green cabbage

1 cup frozen peas

1 teaspoon lemon juice

1. Grind mushrooms with spice grinder until they resemble fine meal, 10 to 30 seconds. Measure out 2 teaspoons porcini powder; reserve remainder for another use. Using kitchen twine, tie together parsley sprigs, thyme sprigs, and bay leaf.

2. Melt butter in large Dutch oven over medium heat. Add leeks, carrots, celery, wine, soy sauce, and 2 teaspoons salt.

Cook, stirring occasionally, until liquid has evaporated and celery is softened, about 10 minutes.

3. Add water, chicken broth, barley, porcini powder, herb bundle, and garlic; increase heat to high and bring to boil. Reduce heat to medium-low and simmer, partially covered, for 25 minutes.

4. Add potatoes, turnip, and cabbage; return to simmer and cook until barley, potatoes, turnip, and cabbage are tender, 18 to 20 minutes.

5. Remove pot from heat and remove herb bundle. Stir in peas, lemon juice, and minced parsley; season with salt and pepper to taste. Serve, passing Lemon-Thyme Butter and Herbed Croutons separately.

Lemon-Thyme Butter
MAKES 6 TABLESPOONS

- 6 tablespoons unsalted butter, softened
- 1 tablespoon minced fresh thyme
- ¾ teaspoon finely grated lemon zest plus ¼ teaspoon juice
  Pinch salt

Combine all ingredients in bowl.

Herbed Croutons
MAKES ABOUT 2½ CUPS

Our favorite brand of sandwich bread is Arnold Country Classic White Bread.

- 1 tablespoon unsalted butter
- 1 teaspoon minced fresh parsley
- ½ teaspoon minced fresh thyme
- 4 slices hearty white sandwich bread, cut into ½-inch pieces
  Salt and pepper

Melt butter in 10-inch skillet over medium heat. Add parsley and thyme; cook, stirring constantly, for 20 seconds. Add bread and cook, stirring frequently, until light golden brown, 5 to 10 minutes. Season with salt and pepper to taste.

CLASSIC GAZPACHO

WHY THIS RECIPE WORKS: Spain's famous chilled soup, gazpacho, boasts bright flavors, distinct pieces of vegetables, and a bracing tomato broth. But all too often, gazpacho is either grainy with the addition of too much bread (a common thickener) or watery from an abundance of macerated vegetables. We were after a chunky gazpacho that was well seasoned with vibrant tomato flavor.

We had to figure out the best method for preparing the vegetables. Although it was a breeze to use, the blender broke down our vegetables beyond recognition. Next, we tried the food processor, but even this machine pulverized some of our tomatoes, and the resulting soup was closer to a slushie than a good gazpacho. For the best texture, we had to chop the vegetables by hand.

Tomatoes are the star player in this dish, and early on we decided that full, ripe beefsteaks were the best option. As for peppers, we preferred red over green for their sweeter flavor. Onion and garlic are usually too overpowering in gazpacho, so we kept to modest levels. A combination of tomato juice and ice cubes—to help chill the soup—provided the right amount of liquid for our broth. And instead of using bread as a thickener, we saved it to make croutons. Now our gazpacho was nice and chunky, and brightly flavored.

Classic Gazpacho
SERVES 8 TO 10

This recipe makes a large quantity, but it can be easily halved if you prefer. Traditionally, the same vegetables used in the soup are also used as garnish. If that appeals to you, cut additional vegetables while you prepare those called for in the recipe. Other garnish possibilities include Garlic Croutons (recipe follows), chopped pitted black olives, chopped Foolproof Hard-Cooked Eggs (page 38), and finely diced avocado.

- 3 medium ripe beefsteak tomatoes (about 1½ pounds), cored and cut into ¼-inch cubes (about 4 cups)
- 2 medium red bell peppers (about 1 pound), stemmed, seeded, and cut into ¼-inch cubes (about 2 cups)
- 2 small cucumbers (about 1 pound), one peeled and the other with skin on, both seeded and cut into ¼-inch cubes (about 2 cups)
- ½ small sweet onion (such as Vidalia, Maui, or Walla Walla) or 2 large shallots, minced (about ½ cup)
- 2 medium garlic cloves, minced or pressed through a garlic press (about 2 teaspoons)
- ⅓ cup sherry vinegar
  Table salt and ground black pepper
- 5 cups tomato juice
- 8 ice cubes
- 1 teaspoon hot pepper sauce (optional)
  Extra-virgin olive oil, for serving

1. Combine the tomatoes, peppers, cucumbers, onion, garlic, vinegar, 2 teaspoons salt, and pepper to taste in a large (at least 4-quart) nonreactive bowl. Let stand until the vegetables just begin to release their juices, about 5 minutes. Stir in the tomato juice, ice cubes, and hot pepper sauce (if using). Cover tightly and refrigerate to blend flavors, at least 4 hours and up to 2 days.

2. Season with salt and pepper to taste and remove and discard any unmelted ice cubes. Serve cold, drizzling each portion with about 1 teaspoon olive oil and topping with the desired garnishes (see note).

Garlic Croutons
MAKES ABOUT 3 CUPS

- 3 tablespoons extra-virgin olive oil
- 3 medium garlic cloves, minced or pressed through a garlic press (about 1 tablespoon)
- ¼ teaspoon table salt
- 6 slices high-quality white sandwich bread, cut into ½-inch cubes (about 3 cups)

1. Adjust an oven rack to the middle position and heat the oven to 350 degrees. Combine the oil, garlic, and salt in a small bowl; let stand 20 minutes, then pour through a fine-mesh strainer into a medium bowl. Discard the garlic. Add the bread cubes to the bowl with the oil and toss to coat.

2. Spread the bread cubes in an even layer on a rimmed baking sheet and bake, stirring occasionally, until golden, about 15 minutes. Cool on the baking sheet to room temperature. (The croutons can be stored in an airtight container or a plastic bag for up to 1 day.)

GAZPACHO ANDALUZ

WHY THIS RECIPE WORKS: In the States, the classic "liquid salsa" style of gazpacho reigns supreme. But in Spain, the birthplace of gazpacho, a variety of styles abound. The most popular type by far comes from Andalusia, the southernmost region of the country. It starts with the same vegetables as its chunky cousin, but is blended with bread to give it some body. The result is a creamy, complex soup. But unless you have fresh, flavorful vegetables, in particular fresh, ripe tomatoes, this soup can be unremarkable and bland.

So how could we ensure a flavorful gazpacho if we had to rely on supermarket tomatoes? In a word, salt. Salting gave our tomatoes—even mid-winter specimens—a deep, full flavor. Figuring the same process could only improve the cucumbers, onions, and bell peppers, we salted them as well. To maximize the flavor of our soup even more, we soaked the bread in a portion of the vegetables' exuded liquid, rather than water. With a garnish of chopped vegetables, fresh herbs, and drizzles of extra-virgin olive oil and sherry vinegar, this Spanish classic can be enjoyed any time of the year.

Creamy Gazpacho Andaluz
SERVES 4 TO 6

For ideal flavor, allow the gazpacho to sit in the refrigerator overnight. Serve the soup with additional extra-virgin olive oil, sherry vinegar, ground black pepper, and the reserved diced vegetables. Red wine vinegar can be substituted for the sherry vinegar. Although we prefer kosher salt in this soup, half the amount of table salt can be used.

- 3 pounds (about 6 medium) ripe tomatoes, cored
- 1 small cucumber, peeled, halved, and seeded
- 1 medium green bell pepper, halved, cored, and seeded
- 1 small red onion, peeled and halved
- 2 medium garlic cloves, peeled and quartered
- 1 small serrano chile, stemmed and halved lengthwise
  Kosher salt (see note)
- 1 slice high-quality white sandwich bread, crust removed, torn into 1-inch pieces
- ½ cup extra-virgin olive oil, plus extra for serving
- 2 tablespoons sherry vinegar, plus extra for serving (see note)
- 2 tablespoons finely minced parsley, chives, or basil leaves
  Ground black pepper

1. Roughly chop 2 pounds of the tomatoes, half of the cucumber, half of the bell pepper, and half of the onion and place in a large bowl. Add the garlic, chile, and 1½ teaspoons salt; toss until well combined. Set aside.

2. Cut the remaining tomatoes, cucumber, and pepper into ¼-inch dice; place the vegetables in a medium bowl. Mince the remaining onion and add to the diced vegetables. Toss with ½ teaspoon salt and transfer to a fine-mesh strainer set over a medium bowl. Set aside for 1 hour.

3. Transfer the drained diced vegetables to a medium bowl and set aside. Add the bread pieces to the exuded liquid (there should be about ¼ cup) and soak for 1 minute. Add the soaked bread and any remaining liquid to the roughly chopped vegetables and toss thoroughly to combine.

4. Transfer half of the vegetable-bread mixture to a blender and process for 30 seconds. With the blender running, slowly drizzle in ¼ cup of the oil and continue to blend until completely smooth, about 2 minutes. Strain the soup through a fine-mesh strainer into a large bowl, using the back of a ladle or rubber spatula to press the soup through the strainer. Repeat with the remaining vegetable-bread mixture and ¼ cup more olive oil.

5. Stir the vinegar, parsley, and half of the diced vegetables into the soup and season with salt and pepper to taste. Cover and refrigerate overnight or for at least 2 hours to chill completely and develop the flavors. Serve, passing the remaining diced vegetables, olive oil, vinegar, and pepper separately.

WHITE GAZPACHO

WHY THIS RECIPE WORKS: Spanish white gazpacho, or *ajo blanco*, predates the familiar red version. It is a silky soup that requires only a handful of ingredients: almonds, garlic, bread, vinegar, and water. It's served ice-cold and garnished with almonds, sliced grapes, or even peppery olive oil. At its best, it is a study in contrasts: Some bites offer a nutty crunch, while others are sharply fruity and floral. But the first batches we whipped up were far from impressive. Some were watery and bland; others were grainy and salad dressing-esque. We wanted to nail down a foolproof way to make this chilled soup.

When it came to technique, we found that the order in which we added ingredients to the blender made all the difference. First, we buzzed the almonds until they were powdery, then added bread (which had been soaked in water), a clove of garlic, a splash of sherry vinegar, and salt and pepper. Once these ingredients were pureed, we drizzled in the olive oil and finally thinned the soup with more water. We liked the fruity, peppery pop that we got from premium olive oil. The sherry vinegar and a pinch of cayenne added brightness and bite. For just a hint of flowery bitter almond flavor, we mixed a tablespoon of the pureed soup with 1/8 teaspoon almond extract, then stirred a teaspoon of the mixture back into the soup. For garnishes, we thinly sliced green grapes and toasted a few almonds in oil to add crunch. An extra drizzle of olive oil made for a rich finish and a beautiful presentation.

Spanish Chilled Almond and Garlic Soup
SERVES 6 TO 8

This rich soup is best when served in small portions (about 6 ounces). Use a good-quality extra-virgin olive oil. Our favorite supermarket brand is California Olive Ranch Everyday Extra Virgin Olive Oil. Too much almond extract can ruin the soup. Hence, the unusual mixing technique in step 4.

- 6 slices hearty white sandwich bread, crusts removed
- 4 cups water
- 2½ cups (8¾ ounces) plus ⅓ cup sliced blanched almonds
- 1 garlic clove, peeled
- 3 tablespoons sherry vinegar
- Kosher salt and pepper
- Pinch cayenne pepper
- ½ cup extra-virgin olive oil, plus extra for drizzling
- ⅛ teaspoon almond extract
- 2 teaspoons vegetable oil
- 6 ounces seedless green grapes, sliced thin (1 cup)

1. Combine bread and water in bowl and let soak for 5 minutes. Process 2½ cups almonds in blender until finely ground, about 30 seconds, scraping down sides of blender jar as needed.

2. Using your hands, remove bread from water, squeeze it lightly, and transfer to blender with almonds. Measure 3 cups soaking water and set aside; transfer remaining soaking water to blender.

3. Add garlic, vinegar, 1¼ teaspoons salt, and cayenne to blender and process until mixture has consistency of cake batter, 30 to 45 seconds. With blender running, add olive oil in thin, steady stream, about 30 seconds. Add reserved soaking water and process for 1 minute. Season with salt and pepper to taste. Strain soup through fine-mesh strainer set in bowl, pressing on solids to extract liquid.

4. Measure 1 tablespoon of soup into second bowl and stir in almond extract. Return 1 teaspoon of extract mixture to soup; discard remainder. Chill for at least 3 hours or up to 24 hours.

5. Heat vegetable oil in 8-inch skillet over medium-high heat until oil begins to shimmer. Add remaining ⅓ cup almonds and cook, stirring constantly, until golden brown, 3 to 4 minutes. Immediately transfer to bowl and stir in ¼ teaspoon salt.

6. Ladle soup into shallow bowls. Mound an equal amount of grapes in center of each bowl. Sprinkle cooled almonds over soup and drizzle with extra-virgin olive oil. Serve immediately.

CALDO VERDE

WHY THIS RECIPE WORKS: This soup of sausage, potatoes, and hearty greens is a staple in many Portuguese households. While the flavors are rich, it's not a heavy soup. Without changing the soup's essentially light character, we wanted to create a slightly heartier result—something that could function as a main course.

To start, we replaced the hard-to-find Portuguese linguiça sausage with widely available Spanish-style chorizo, which boasts a similar garlicky profile. We sautéed the sausage right in the Dutch oven in just 1 tablespoon of olive oil, eliminating the need to dirty an extra skillet. For deeper flavor, we split the water with an equal amount of chicken broth. Collard greens offered a more delicate sweetness and a meatier bite than kale, and chopping the leaves into bite-size pieces made them more spoon-friendly. Finally, we swapped out starchy russet potatoes for sturdy Yukon Golds, which held their shape during cooking. Pureeing some of the potatoes and a few tablespoons of olive oil into our soup base made a creamier, heartier dish. A bit of white wine vinegar brightened the pot.

Caldo Verde

SERVES 6 TO 8

We prefer collard greens, but kale can be substituted. Serve this soup with hearty bread and, for added richness, a final drizzle of extra-virgin olive oil.

- ¼ cup extra-virgin olive oil
- 12 ounces Spanish-style chorizo sausage, cut into ½-inch pieces
- 1 onion, chopped fine
- 4 garlic cloves, minced
  Salt and pepper
- ¼ teaspoon red pepper flakes
- 2 pounds Yukon Gold potatoes, peeled and cut into ¾-inch pieces
- 4 cups chicken broth
- 4 cups water
- 1 pound collard greens, stemmed and cut into 1-inch pieces
- 2 teaspoons white wine vinegar

1. Heat 1 tablespoon oil in Dutch oven over medium-high heat until shimmering. Add chorizo and cook, stirring occasionally, until lightly browned, 4 to 5 minutes. Transfer chorizo to bowl and set aside. Reduce heat to medium and add onion, garlic, 1¼ teaspoons salt, and pepper flakes and season with pepper to taste. Cook, stirring frequently, until onion is translucent, 2 to 3 minutes. Add potatoes, broth, and water; increase heat to high and bring to boil. Reduce heat to medium-low and simmer, uncovered, until potatoes are just tender, 8 to 10 minutes.

2. Transfer ¾ cup solids and ¾ cup broth to blender jar. Add collard greens to pot and simmer for 10 minutes. Stir in chorizo and continue to simmer until greens are tender, 8 to 10 minutes longer.

3. Add remaining 3 tablespoons oil to soup in blender and process until very smooth and homogeneous, about 1 minute. Remove pot from heat and stir pureed soup mixture and vinegar into soup. Season with salt and pepper to taste, and serve. (Soup can be refrigerated for up to 2 days.)

CORN CHOWDER

WHY THIS RECIPE WORKS: We were looking for a corn chowder recipe that would pack lots of corn flavor in every spoonful while still maintaining a satisfying, yet not too thick, chowder texture. Inspired by a recipe we found that juiced corn kernels, a trick that delivered pronounced corn flavor, we strained the scrapings and pulp from several cobs through a kitchen towel to get unadulterated corn juice (when we added the unstrained pulp to the pot, the soup curdled). This delivered the intense corn flavor we were after. We lightened things up by using water as our primary liquid, which allowed the pure corn flavor to shine through, then added just 1 cup of half-and-half to give our chowder the right richness. A sprinkling of basil before serving lent a fresh finish.

Lighter Corn Chowder

SERVES 6

When removing the kernels from the cob make sure to remove only the part of the kernel sticking out of the cob. Cutting deeper will result in too much fibrous material coming off the corn. Yukon Gold potatoes can be substituted for the red potatoes. Minced chives can be used in place of the basil.

- 8 ears corn, husks and silk removed
- 3 tablespoons unsalted butter
- 1 medium onion, chopped fine
- 4 ounces (about 4 slices) bacon, halved lengthwise, then cut crosswise into ¼-inch pieces
- 2 teaspoons minced fresh thyme leaves
  Table salt and ground black pepper
- ¼ cup unbleached all-purpose flour
- 5 cups water
- 12 ounces red potatoes, cut into ½-inch cubes
- 1 cup half-and-half
  Sugar
- 3 tablespoons chopped fresh basil leaves

1. Using a chef's knife, cut the kernels from the ears of corn; transfer to a bowl and set aside (you should have 5 to 6 cups). Holding the cobs over a second bowl, use the back of a butter knife to firmly scrape any pulp remaining on the cobs into the bowl (you should have 2 to 2½ cups of pulp).

open completely meant they would overcook quickly when returned to the soup to heat through. We found waxy red potatoes to be the best choice for our creamy chowder; high-starch potatoes, like russets, broke down too much. Bacon made a nice substitute for the traditional salt pork and gave our chowder great smoky flavor. As for the creaminess factor, using a modest amount of heavy cream instead of milk meant that we could use less dairy for a rich, creamy chowder that tasted distinctly of clams.

New England Clam Chowder

SERVES 6

Don't skip the step of scrubbing the clams; many clams have bits of sand embedded in their shells that can ruin a pot of chowder. To remove the sand, simply scrub them under cold, running water using a soft brush.

7	pounds medium-size hard-shell clams, such as cherrystones, washed and scrubbed clean (see note)
5	ounces (about 3 slices) thick-cut bacon, cut into ¼-inch pieces
1	large onion, chopped medium
2	tablespoons unbleached all-purpose flour
1½	pounds red potatoes (about 4 medium), cut into ½-inch chunks
1	bay leaf
1	teaspoon fresh thyme leaves or ¼ teaspoon dried thyme
1	cup heavy cream
2	tablespoons minced fresh parsley leaves
	Table salt and ground black pepper

1. Bring 3 cups water to a boil in a large Dutch oven. Add the clams and cover with a tight-fitting lid. Cook for 5 minutes, uncover, and stir with a wooden spoon. Quickly cover the pot and steam until the clams just open, 2 to 4 minutes. (Don't let the clams open completely.) Transfer the clams to a large bowl and cool slightly; reserve the broth. Open the clams with a paring knife, holding the clams over a bowl to catch any juices. With the knife, sever the muscle that attaches the clam to the bottom shell and transfer the meat to a cutting board; discard the shells. Mince the clams and set aside. Pour the clam broth into a large bowl, holding back the last few tablespoons of broth in case of sediment; set the clam broth aside. (You should have about 5 cups. If not, add bottled clam juice or water to make this amount.) Rinse and dry the pot, then return the pot to the burner.

2. Fry the bacon in the pot over medium-low heat until the fat renders and the bacon crisps, 5 to 7 minutes. Add the onion and cook, stirring occasionally, until softened, about 5 minutes. Add the flour and stir until lightly colored, about 1 minute. Gradually whisk in the reserved clam broth. Add the potatoes, bay leaf, and thyme and simmer until the potatoes are tender, about 10 minutes. Add the clams, cream, parsley, and salt and pepper to taste; bring to a simmer. Remove from the heat, discard the bay leaf, and serve.

Transfer the pulp to the center of a clean kitchen towel set in a medium bowl. Wrap the towel tightly around the pulp and squeeze until dry. Discard the pulp in the towel and set the corn juice aside (you should have about ⅔ cup of juice).

2. Melt the butter in a Dutch oven over medium heat. Add the onion, bacon, thyme, 2 teaspoons salt, and 1 teaspoon pepper and cook, stirring frequently, until the onion is softened and beginning to brown, 8 to 10 minutes. Stir in the flour and cook, stirring constantly, for 2 minutes. Whisking constantly, gradually add the water and then bring to a boil. Add the corn kernels and the potatoes. Return to a simmer, reduce the heat to medium-low, and cook until the potatoes have softened, 15 to 18 minutes.

3. Transfer 2 cups of the chowder to a blender and process until smooth, 1 to 2 minutes. Return the puree to the pot, stir in the half-and-half, and return to a simmer. Remove the pot from the heat and stir in the reserved corn juice. Season with salt, pepper, and up to 1 tablespoon sugar to taste. Sprinkle with the basil and serve.

NEW ENGLAND CLAM CHOWDER

WHY THIS RECIPE WORKS: Good traditional chowder isn't that hard to make, but it can be daunting for the home cook. The biggest hurdle is a finicky ingredient that most people don't know how to work with—clams. We wanted to come up with a clam chowder that was economical, could be prepared quickly, and provided a simple method for working with the star ingredient.

We tested a variety of clams and ultimately found that medium-size hard-shell clams guaranteed the most clam flavor. Rather than shucking the raw clams (which can be tedious and time-consuming) and adding them to the pot, we steamed the clams to open them, then used the steaming liquid as our broth. The steamed clams had to be pulled from the pot when they had just opened; allowing them to

2 tablespoons kosher salt
1½ tablespoons tomato paste
3 tablespoons soy sauce

Process leeks, carrots, celery root, parsley, minced onions, and salt in food processor, scraping down sides of bowl frequently, until paste is as fine as possible, 3 to 4 minutes. Add tomato paste and process for 1 minute, scraping down sides of bowl every 20 seconds. Add soy sauce and continue to process 1 minute longer. Transfer mixture to airtight container and tap firmly on counter to remove air bubbles. Press small piece of parchment paper flush against surface of mixture and cover. Freeze for up to 6 months.

VEGETABLE BROTH BASE

WHY THIS RECIPE WORKS: Homemade broth enlivens any dish, but for vegetarian cooking, an overpowering broth can be ruinous. For our base, we focused on mild but impactful vegetables. Mirepoix, a mix of chopped onions, celery, and carrots, is a classic combination; we started there, swapping in leeks for their mild onion flavor and minimal moisture content. Celery root had a creamier, more complex celery taste. Dried minced onions reinforced the leeks and carrots contributed pleasant sweetness. Tomato paste and soy sauce bolstered the savory qualities and parsley added brightness. Kosher salt seasoned the broth while keeping it convenient: Salt lowers water's freezing point, so the concentrate would remain easy to scoop. Even better, our base had less salt than most store-bought broths. Creating the base was easy: We pulsed the ingredients in a food processor and froze the paste.

Vegetable Broth Base

MAKES ABOUT 1¾ CUPS BASE; ENOUGH FOR 7 QUARTS BROTH
For the best balance of flavors, measure the prepped vegetables by weight. Kosher salt aids in grinding the vegetables. The broth base contains enough salt to keep it from freezing solid, making it easy to remove 1 tablespoon at a time. To make 1 cup of broth, stir 1 tablespoon of fresh or frozen broth base into 1 cup of boiling water. If particle-free broth is desired, let the broth steep for 5 minutes and then strain it through a fine-mesh strainer.

2 leeks, white and light green parts only, chopped and washed thoroughly (2½ cups or 5 ounces)
2 carrots, peeled and cut into ½-inch pieces (⅔ cup or 3 ounces)
½ small celery root, peeled and cut into ½-inch pieces (¾ cup or 3 ounces)
½ cup (½ ounce) parsley leaves and thin stems
3 tablespoons dried minced onions

MAKING GOOD TV IN THE TEST KITCHEN

The process of creating our show begins several months before filming starts, in all-day script meetings. A group of six editors argues the merits of each recipe developed in the test kitchen for *Cook's Illustrated* magazine during the past year, choosing only the very best recipes to present on television. We're looking for recipes that not only taste great (obviously) but are also visually and editorially interesting. Passions run high, and coming to an agreement isn't always so easy or smooth. One year, for a show on drive-in specials, some editors rooted for pairing frothy chocolate milkshakes with hamburgers. Sounds good, but in the end, the process of making the milkshakes—dump ingredients into a blender and press a button—turned out to be as interesting as watching paint dry. The result? Goodbye milkshakes, hello oven-fried onion rings.

Once the recipe lineup is settled, we then spend several months hammering out scripts. Instead of mapping out dialogue, these scripts detail what the camera is going to see—for example: "Julia chops onions and then sautés them in a 12-inch skillet with pinch of salt until golden, about 5 minutes." So why do we write our scripts this way? Cooking is the heart of the show and it's why, we hope, you tune in. And frankly, Julia and Bridget and the chefs don't need scripts to banter (or argue) with each other. They've had plenty of practice at script meetings.

SALAD DAYS

FOOLPROOF VINAIGRETTES

WHY THIS RECIPE WORKS: Vinaigrettes often seem a little slipshod—harsh and bristling in one bite, dull and oily in the next. We were determined to nail down a formula for the perfect vinaigrette, one that would consistently yield a homogeneous, harmonious blend of bright vinegar and rich oil in every forkful.

For starters, top-notch ingredients are crucial. Balsamic vinegar works best with more assertive greens. Fruity extra-virgin olive oil is preferred as an all-purpose oil option, while walnut oil is best for nuttier vinaigrettes. As for mixing methods, whisking together the ingredients only gets you so far. A key ingredient—mayonnaise—is necessary to emulsify (bind together) the oil and vinegar for a stabilized, smooth dressing.

Foolproof Vinaigrette

MAKES ABOUT ¼ CUP, ENOUGH TO DRESS 8 TO 10 CUPS LIGHTLY PACKED GREENS

Red wine, white wine, or champagne vinegar will work in this recipe; however, it is important to use high-quality ingredients (see pages 926–927 for our top-rated brands of white wine vinegar and red wine vinegar and page 916 for our top-rated brand of extra-virgin olive oil). This vinaigrette works with nearly any type of green (as do the walnut and herb variations). For a hint of garlic flavor, rub the inside of the salad bowl with a cut clove of garlic before adding the lettuce.

- 1 tablespoon wine vinegar (see note)
- 1½ teaspoons very finely minced shallot
- ½ teaspoon regular or light mayonnaise
- ½ teaspoon Dijon mustard
- ⅛ teaspoon table salt
  Ground black pepper
- 3 tablespoons extra-virgin olive oil (see note)

1. Combine the vinegar, shallot, mayonnaise, mustard, salt, and pepper to taste in a small nonreactive bowl. Whisk until the mixture is milky in appearance and no lumps of mayonnaise remain.

2. Place the oil in a small measuring cup so that it is easy to pour. Whisking constantly, very slowly drizzle the oil into the vinegar mixture. If pools of oil are gathering on the surface as you whisk, stop adding the oil and whisk the mixture well to combine, then resume whisking in the oil in a slow stream. The vinaigrette should be glossy and lightly thickened, with no pools of oil on its surface.

Foolproof Lemon Vinaigrette

This vinaigrette is best for dressing mild greens.

Follow the recipe for Foolproof Vinaigrette, substituting lemon juice for the vinegar, omitting the shallot, and adding ¼ teaspoon finely grated lemon zest and a pinch of sugar along with the salt and pepper.

Foolproof Balsamic-Mustard Vinaigrette

This vinaigrette is best for dressing assertive greens. See page 926 for our top-rated brand of balsamic vinegar.

Follow the recipe for Foolproof Vinaigrette, substituting balsamic vinegar for the wine vinegar, increasing the mustard to 2 teaspoons, and adding ½ teaspoon chopped fresh thyme along with the salt and pepper.

Foolproof Walnut Vinaigrette

Follow the recipe for Foolproof Vinaigrette, substituting 1½ tablespoons roasted walnut oil and 1½ tablespoons regular olive oil for the extra-virgin olive oil.

Foolproof Herb Vinaigrette

Follow the recipe for Foolproof Vinaigrette, adding 1 tablespoon minced fresh parsley leaves or chives and ½ teaspoon minced fresh thyme, tarragon, marjoram, or oregano leaves to the vinaigrette just before use.

LEAFY GREEN SALAD WITH RED WINE VINAIGRETTE

WHY THIS RECIPE WORKS: A leafy green salad with red wine vinaigrette is a vital recipe to have in your arsenal. We wanted to develop a recipe for this basic salad—a mix of well-chosen greens tossed with a light vinaigrette that was neither harsh nor oily. We went back to the basics and revisited standard vinaigrette proportions. In most cases, 4 parts oil to 1 part vinegar produces the best balance of flavors in a vinaigrette, so that's where we started. Red wine vinegar was the foundation of our vinaigrette. Before whisking the vinaigrette ingredients together, we added salt and pepper to the vinegar. This step mutes these seasonings a bit and prevents them from becoming too overpowering. With the right mix of salad greens—we like a combination of mild, delicate greens and peppery greens—this leafy salad makes the perfect complement to any main dish.

Leafy Green Salad with Red Wine Vinaigrette

SERVES 4 TO 6

For the best results, use at least two kinds of greens. A blend of mild, delicate greens, such as Boston and leaf lettuces, and peppery greens, such as arugula and watercress, is ideal. Romaine adds crunch and texture. If you like, add mild fresh herbs, such as chives, tarragon, or basil, in small amounts.

2¼ teaspoons red wine vinegar
⅛ teaspoon table salt
    Pinch ground black pepper
3 tablespoons extra-virgin olive oil
8 cups mixed salad greens, washed, dried,
    and torn into bite-sized pieces (see note)

Combine the vinegar, salt, and pepper in a bowl; add the oil and whisk until combined. Place the greens in a large bowl, drizzle the vinaigrette over the greens, and toss to coat evenly. Serve.

LEAFY GREEN SALAD WITH RICH AND CREAMY BLUE CHEESE DRESSING

WHY THIS RECIPE WORKS: Cool and crunchy salad greens coated with creamy blue cheese dressing are simply irresistible. But getting the right proportion of dressing to greens can be tricky. We wanted lettuce lightly napped with a creamy, tangy dressing.

Starting with the dressing, we found that the secret to proper flavor and texture was in using the right creamy components. We determined that three creamy ingredients were essential: mayonnaise to give the dressing body, sour cream to supply tang, and buttermilk to thin out and further reinforce the dressing's bold flavors. A bit of sugar brought some much-needed sweetness, and white wine vinegar gave our dressing some zing. As for the main ingredient, we ruled out really pungent blue cheeses as too overpowering; a mild blue cheese works best. For the right chunky consistency, we mixed the crumbled blue cheese with the buttermilk before adding any other ingredients.

Leafy Green Salad with Rich and Creamy Blue Cheese Dressing

SERVES 4 TO 6

Sturdy romaine and curly leaf lettuce hold up well to this thick dressing. In a pinch, whole milk can be used in place of the buttermilk; the dressing will be a bit lighter and milder in flavor, but will still taste good.

2½ ounces blue cheese, crumbled (about ½ cup)
3 tablespoons buttermilk (see note)
3 tablespoons sour cream
2 tablespoons mayonnaise
2 teaspoons white wine vinegar
¼ teaspoon sugar
⅛ teaspoon garlic powder
    Table salt and ground black pepper
10 cups loosely packed sturdy salad greens,
    such as romaine or curly leaf lettuce, washed,
    dried, and torn into bite size pieces (see note)

1. Mash the blue cheese and buttermilk in a small bowl with a fork until the mixture resembles cottage cheese with small curds. Stir in the sour cream, mayonnaise, vinegar, sugar, and garlic powder and season with salt and pepper to taste. (The dressing can be refrigerated in an airtight container for up to 2 weeks.)

2. Place the greens in a large bowl. Pour the dressing over the greens and toss to coat evenly. Serve.

SPICY SALAD WITH MUSTARD AND BALSAMIC VINAIGRETTE

WHY THIS RECIPE WORKS: Some salads act as humble introductions to the main course, while other salads demand attention and pack a flavor punch all their own. We had a craving for a bold salad, one using spicy and bitter greens dressed in a pungent, mustardy vinaigrette.

We started by focusing on the greens, and chose peppery greens like arugula and watercress. We envisioned this salad as standing up to rich main dishes, like fettuccine Alfredo or a hearty meat stew, so we used both balsamic vinegar and Dijon mustard as the acidic components. Minced shallot provided another strong flavor and added a bit of texture to our vinaigrette. We mixed the greens and vinaigrette together a little at a time to ensure that all the greens were well covered. Boldly flavored, this spicy salad with mustard and balsamic vinaigrette will wake up any dulled palate.

Spicy Salad with Mustard and Balsamic Vinaigrette

SERVES 8 TO 10

This salad makes a perfect partner to rich main dishes, like lasagna, because its bitter greens and zesty vinaigrette help to cut the richness.

6 tablespoons extra-virgin olive oil
4 teaspoons balsamic vinegar
1 tablespoon Dijon mustard
1 teaspoon finely minced shallot
¼ teaspoon table salt
⅛ teaspoon ground black pepper
16 cups spicy greens, such as arugula, watercress, mizuna,
    and baby mustard greens, washed and dried

Whisk the oil, vinegar, mustard, shallot, salt, and pepper together in a bowl until combined. Place the greens in a large bowl, drizzle the dressing over the greens a little at a time, and toss to coat evenly, adding more vinaigrette if the greens seem dry. Serve.

WILTED SPINACH SALAD

WHY THIS RECIPE WORKS: Traditional wilted spinach salad, tossed with warm bacon dressing, makes for an appealing and elegant salad. But too often, this salad is a soggy mess of slimy spinach, bogged down from too much oil and too much heat. We wanted perfectly wilted spinach, a rich, balanced dressing, and crisp pieces of meaty bacon throughout.

Baby spinach was preferred over the mature variety for its tender, sweet qualities. Fried thick-cut bacon provided more textural interest than regular sliced bacon. And using the bacon fat left in the skillet to cook our onion and garlic gave the finished salad a smoky flavor. For the vinaigrette, a generous amount of cider vinegar, enhanced with sugar, cut the richness of the bacon fat. We found that pouring the hot vinaigrette right over the baby spinach provided enough heat to wilt the spinach without saturating it. With wedges of hard-cooked egg for some heartiness, this wilted spinach salad delivers on all fronts.

Wilted Spinach Salad with Warm Bacon Dressing
SERVES 4 TO 6

This salad comes together quickly, so have the ingredients ready before you begin cooking. When adding the vinegar mixture to the skillet, step back from the stovetop—the aroma is quite potent.

  6 ounces baby spinach (about 6 cups), washed and dried
  3 tablespoons cider vinegar
  ½ teaspoon sugar
  ¼ teaspoon ground black pepper
     Pinch table salt
10 ounces (about 8 slices) thick-cut bacon, cut into
     ½-inch pieces
  ½ medium red onion, chopped medium

  1 small garlic clove, minced or pressed through
     a garlic press (about ½ teaspoon)
  3 hard-cooked eggs (recipe follows),
     peeled and quartered

1. Place the spinach in a large bowl. Whisk the vinegar, sugar, pepper, and salt in a small bowl until the sugar dissolves; set aside.

2. Fry the bacon in a medium skillet over medium-high heat, stirring occasionally, until crisp, about 10 minutes. Using a slotted spoon, transfer the bacon to a paper towel–lined plate. Pour off all but 3 tablespoons of the bacon fat left in the pan. Add the onion to the skillet and cook over medium heat, stirring frequently, until softened, about 3 minutes. Stir in the garlic and cook until fragrant, about 15 seconds. Add the vinegar mixture, then remove the skillet from the heat. Working quickly, scrape the bottom of the skillet with a wooden spoon to loosen the browned bits. Pour the hot dressing over the spinach, add the bacon, and toss gently until the spinach is slightly wilted. Divide the salad among individual plates, arrange the egg quarters over each, and serve.

Foolproof Hard-Cooked Eggs
MAKES 3

You can double or triple this recipe as long as you use a pot large enough to hold the eggs in a single layer, covered by an inch of water.

  3 large eggs

1. Place the eggs in a medium saucepan, cover with 1 inch of water, and bring to a boil over high heat. Remove the pan from the heat, cover, and let sit for 10 minutes. Meanwhile, fill a medium bowl with 1 quart water and one tray of ice cubes.

2. Transfer the eggs to the ice bath with a slotted spoon and let sit for 5 minutes. Peel the eggs.

ARUGULA SALAD

WHY THIS RECIPE WORKS: Unlike everyday iceberg lettuce, spicy arugula is more than just a leafy backdrop for salad garnishes. But arugula's complex, peppery flavor also makes it something of a challenge to pair with other ingredients. We wanted a truly outstanding arugula-based salad with co-starring ingredients that would stand up to these spicy greens.

Salad combinations with harsh, one-dimensional flavor profiles (adding radishes and lemon-buttermilk dressing to arugula, for example) struck out, with too much abrasive flavor. What we did like were the salads containing fruit and cheese, so we decided to pair our arugula with sweet and salty ingredients. Fried prosciutto strips and shaved Parmesan fit the bill when it came to upping the saltiness of our salad. A spoonful of jam added to the vinaigrette helped to emulsify the dressing and provided a sweet contrast to arugula's peppery bite. For additional sweetness, dried figs worked well and toasted walnuts delivered just the right amount of crunch.

BEHIND THE SCENES

STAYING GREEN IN THE TEST KITCHEN

It's not unusual for the test kitchen fridge to be packed with salad greens. And although we try to work with the greens the day they arrive, it's not always a possibility. As a result, we've come up with a couple of storage tips for greens. First, remove any rubber band or tie from the greens. Constriction only encourages rotting. Gently wash the greens and spin them dry in a salad spinner. Then depending on the type of greens, store them one of two ways:

For delicate greens, line an empty salad spinner with paper towels. Layer the dried greens in the bowl, covering each layer with additional towels, and refrigerate. Greens stored in this manner should keep for at least two days.

For sturdier greens, loosely roll the leaves in paper towels, then seal in a zipper-lock bag and refrigerate. Greens stored this way should keep for up to one week.

We applied our storage techniques to basil too, especially because recipes often call for just a few leaves. First, we found that it's essential not to wash the basil before storage. In our tests, washing basil before storage decreased its storage life by half. Instead, gently wrap basil in a damp paper towel. It should keep for up to one week.

Arugula Salad with Figs, Prosciutto, Walnuts, and Parmesan

SERVES 6

Although frying the prosciutto adds crisp texture to the salad, if you prefer, you can simply cut it into ribbons and use it as a garnish. Honey can be substituted for the jam in either of these salads.

    4 tablespoons extra-virgin olive oil
    2 ounces thinly sliced prosciutto, cut into ¼-inch strips
    3 tablespoons balsamic vinegar
    1 tablespoon raspberry jam
    ½ cup dried figs, stems removed, fruit chopped
       into ¼-inch pieces
    1 small shallot, minced (about 1 tablespoon)
       Table salt and ground black pepper
    5 ounces loosely packed baby arugula (about 5 cups),
       washed and dried
    ½ cup walnuts, toasted and chopped
    2 ounces Parmesan cheese, shaved into thin
       strips with a vegetable peeler

1. Heat 1 tablespoon of the oil in a 10-inch nonstick skillet over medium heat; add the prosciutto and fry until crisp, stirring frequently, about 7 minutes. Using a slotted spoon, transfer to a paper towel–lined plate and set aside to cool.

2. Whisk the vinegar and jam together in a medium microwave-safe bowl until combined; stir in the figs. Cover with plastic wrap, cut several steam vents in the plastic, and microwave on high until the figs are plump, 30 seconds to 1 minute. Whisk in the remaining 3 tablespoons oil, the shallot, ¼ teaspoon salt, and ⅛ teaspoon pepper until combined. Cool to room temperature.

3. Toss the arugula with the vinaigrette in a large bowl; season with salt and pepper to taste. Divide the salad among individual plates; top each with a portion of the prosciutto, walnuts, and Parmesan. Serve.

BAKED GOAT CHEESE SALAD

WHY THIS RECIPE WORKS: Warm goat cheese salad has been a fixture on restaurant menus for years, featuring artisanal cheeses, organic greens, barrel-aged vinegars, and imported oils. But too often what arrives is an unremarkable salad at a price that defies reason. We wanted to bring this restaurant favorite home with creamy cheese rounds infused with the flavor of fresh herbs and surrounded by crisp, golden breading, all cradled by lightly dressed greens.

Ground Melba toasts (those ultra-dry and crispy crackers) made the crispiest crust for the goat cheese. After dipping the cheese rounds in beaten egg and herbs, we coated them with the crumbs, shaped them into attractive disks, and froze them to set the cheese and the crust. With the oven super hot and the cheese very cold, the cheese developed a crispy crust (with no oozing) and kept its shape, and a quick brush of olive oil on the outside of the disks lent flavor to the crumbs without turning them oily. A mix of greens paired well with the tangy flavor of the goat cheese, and a simple, light vinaigrette was all that was needed to finish this elegant salad.

Salad with Herbed Baked Goat Cheese and Vinaigrette

SERVES 6

The baked goat cheese should be served warm. Prepare the salad components while the cheese is in the freezer, then toss the greens and vinaigrette while the cheese cools a bit after baking.

GOAT CHEESE

    3 ounces white Melba toasts (about 2 cups)
    1 teaspoon ground black pepper
    3 large eggs
    2 tablespoons Dijon mustard
    1 tablespoon chopped fresh thyme leaves
    1 tablespoon chopped fresh chives
   12 ounces goat cheese
       Extra-virgin olive oil

SALAD

- 6 tablespoons extra-virgin olive oil
- 2 tablespoons red wine vinegar
- 1 tablespoon Dijon mustard
- 1 teaspoon minced shallot
- ¼ teaspoon table salt
  Ground black pepper
- 14 cups mixed delicate and spicy salad greens, such as arugula, baby spinach, and frisée, washed and dried

1. FOR THE CHEESE: In a food processor, process the Melba toasts to fine, even crumbs, about 1½ minutes; transfer the crumbs to a medium bowl and stir in the pepper. Whisk the eggs and mustard in a second medium bowl until combined. Combine the thyme and chives in a small bowl.

2. Using dental floss or kitchen twine, divide the cheese into 12 equal pieces by slicing the log lengthwise through the middle and each half into six even pieces. Roll each piece of cheese into a ball; roll each ball in the combined fresh herbs to coat lightly. Transfer 6 pieces to the egg mixture and turn each piece to coat; transfer to the Melba crumbs and turn each piece to coat, pressing the crumbs into the cheese. Flatten each ball gently with your fingertips into a disk about 1½ inches wide and 1 inch thick and set on a baking sheet. Repeat with the remaining 6 pieces of cheese. Transfer the baking sheet to the freezer and freeze the disks until firm, about 30 minutes. Adjust an oven rack to the top position and heat the oven to 475 degrees.

3. FOR THE SALAD: Meanwhile, whisk the oil, vinegar, mustard, shallot, and salt in a small bowl until combined; season with pepper to taste. Set aside.

4. Remove the cheese from the freezer and brush the tops and sides evenly with olive oil. Bake until the crumbs are golden brown and the cheese is slightly soft, 7 to 9 minutes (or 9 to 12 minutes if the cheese is completely frozen). Using a thin metal spatula, transfer the cheese to a paper towel–lined plate and cool for 3 minutes.

5. Place the greens in a large bowl, drizzle the vinaigrette over them, and toss to coat. Divide the greens among individual plates; place two rounds of goat cheese on each salad and serve.

NUT-CRUSTED CHICKEN WITH SPINACH SALAD

WHY THIS RECIPE WORKS: When leafy greens are paired with sautéed chicken, a simple salad becomes a satisfying, one-dish meal. We wanted to create an easy recipe for such a dish, and thought incorporating nuts in the coating of the chicken would make for a heartier, more elegant meal.

We started by pounding store-bought chicken breasts to the same thickness to ensure that they would cook evenly. Ground almonds paired with panko (Japanese-style bread crumbs) created a rich-tasting crust that was both light and crisp. After dipping the chicken breasts in eggs and the nut and panko mixture, we let them sit for a few minutes so the coating could set. Much like regular breaded chicken, the breasts had

to be pan-fried in a fair amount of oil. Pan-frying can make a mess in a traditional skillet, so we used a nonstick pan. To make a quick salad with bright flavors, we heated orange slices to create a dressing in the skillet, then used the hot dressing to wilt the spinach.

Almond-Crusted Chicken with Wilted Spinach Salad

SERVES 4

Don't process the nuts longer than directed or they will turn pasty and oily.

CHICKEN

- 4 (5 to 6-ounce) boneless, skinless chicken breasts, trimmed
  Table salt and ground black pepper
- 1 cup sliced almonds
- ½ cup panko (Japanese-style bread crumbs)
- 2 large eggs
- 1 teaspoon Dijon mustard
- 1¼ teaspoons grated zest from 1 orange
- ¾ cup plus 2 tablespoons vegetable oil

SALAD

- 5 ounces baby spinach (about 5 cups)
- 2 medium oranges, peel and pith removed (see page 250), quartered and sliced ¼ inch thick
- 1 small shallot, minced (about 1 tablespoon)

1. FOR THE CHICKEN: Adjust an oven rack to the middle position and heat the oven to 200 degrees. Pound each breast between two sheets of plastic wrap to a uniform ½-inch thickness. Pat the chicken dry with paper towels and season with salt and pepper.

2. Process the almonds in a food processor to fine crumbs, about 10 seconds (do not over process; see note). Toss the nuts with the panko in a shallow dish. Whisk the eggs, mustard, 1 teaspoon of the orange zest, ½ teaspoon salt, and ¼ teaspoon pepper together in another shallow dish. Working with 1 chicken breast at a time, dip the chicken into the egg mixture, turning to coat well and allowing the excess to drip off, then coat with the nut mixture, pressing gently so that the nuts adhere. Place the breaded chicken in a single layer on a wire rack set over a rimmed baking sheet and let sit for 5 minutes.

3. Heat 6 tablespoons of the oil in a 12-inch nonstick skillet over medium heat until shimmering. Add 2 of the chicken breasts and cook until browned on both sides, 4 to 6 minutes total. Drain the chicken briefly on a paper towel–lined plate, then transfer to a clean wire rack set over a rimmed baking sheet and keep warm in the oven. Discard the oil and wipe out the skillet with paper towels. Repeat with 6 tablespoons more oil and the remaining chicken. Discard the oil and wipe out the skillet with paper towels.

4. FOR THE SALAD: Place the spinach in a large bowl. Heat 1 tablespoon more oil in the skillet over high heat until just smoking. Add the orange slices and cook until lightly browned around the edges, 1½ to 2 minutes. Remove the pan from the heat and add the remaining 1 tablespoon oil, the shallot, remaining ¼ teaspoon zest, ¼ teaspoon salt, and ⅛ teaspoon pepper and allow residual heat to soften the shallot, about 30 seconds. Pour the warm dressing with the oranges over the spinach and toss gently. Divide the greens among individual plates. Remove the chicken from the oven, set a cutlet over each portion, and serve.

WARM SPINACH SALAD WITH PAN-SEARED SCALLOPS

WHY THIS RECIPE WORKS: Attempts to make perfectly seared, caramelized sea scallops usually result in overcooking these tender mollusks, rendering them rubbery and tough. We wanted a concentrated, nutty, rich-colored crust encasing an interior of sweet, creamy, perfectly cooked scallop meat. And for a complete meal, we wanted to incorporate our scallops into a main course salad that would be both elegant and satisfying.

We tackled the scallops first: To get scallops with a crusty exterior, using the unprocessed variety is a must. We found it was essential to dry the scallops thoroughly before adding them to the pan, to further guard against the scallops steaming rather than searing. Equally important is to avoid crowding the pan. We cooked the scallops in batches, browning each batch on just one side, then returned them all to the skillet at once to cook through on the other side, so that each salad would have hot, not tepid, scallops.

For the salad, we liked baby spinach and watercress for easy prep and moist, tender greens. A bright dressing with sherry vinegar and fresh orange complemented the rich scallops. For a finishing touch, toasted sliced almonds lent our salad nutty flavor and welcome crunch.

Pan-Seared Scallops with Wilted Spinach, Watercress, and Orange Salad

SERVES 4

Sea scallops can vary dramatically in size from 1 to 1½ ounces each. A dinner portion, therefore, can range from four to six scallops per person. To ensure that the scallops cook at the same rate, be sure to buy scallops of similar size. Note that scallops have a small, rough-textured, crescent-shaped muscle that toughens once cooked. It's easy to remove—simply peel it from the side of each scallop before cooking.

SALAD

 5 ounces baby spinach (about 5 cups)
 4 ounces watercress or arugula (about 4 cups)
 ¾ cup sliced almonds, toasted

SCALLOPS

 1½ pounds large sea scallops (16 to 24 scallops), tendons removed (see note)
   Table salt and ground black pepper
 ¼ cup vegetable oil

DRESSING

 3 tablespoons extra-virgin olive oil
 ½ medium red onion, sliced thin
 1 teaspoon minced fresh thyme leaves
 2 large oranges, peel and pith removed (see page 250), quartered and sliced ¼ inch thick
 2 tablespoons sherry vinegar

1. FOR THE SALAD: Toss the spinach, watercress, and almonds together in a large bowl; set aside.

2. FOR THE SCALLOPS: Place the scallops on a dish towel–lined plate or baking sheet and season with salt and pepper. Lay a single layer of paper towels over the scallops; set aside.

3. Add 2 tablespoons of the vegetable oil to a 12-inch skillet and heat over high heat until just smoking. Meanwhile, press the paper towel flush to the scallops to dry. Add half of the scallops to the skillet, dry side facing down, and cook until evenly golden, 1 to 2 minutes. Using tongs, transfer the scallops, browned side facing up, to a large plate; set aside. Wipe out the skillet using a wad of paper towels. Repeat with the remaining 2 tablespoons oil and the remaining scallops. Once the first side is golden, turn the heat to medium, turn the scallops over with tongs, and return the first batch of scallops to the pan, golden side facing up. Cook until the sides on all the scallops have firmed up and all but the middle third of each scallop is opaque, 30 to 60 seconds longer. Transfer all the scallops to a clean, large plate; set aside.

4. FOR THE DRESSING: Wipe the skillet clean with a wad of paper towels. Add the olive oil, onion, thyme, and ½ teaspoon salt to the skillet and return to medium-high heat; cook until the onion is slightly softened, about 1 minute. Add the oranges and vinegar to the pan and swirl to incorporate. Remove from the heat.

5. TO FINISH THE SALAD: Pour the warm dressing over the salad mixture and gently toss to wilt. Divide the spinach salad among four plates and arrange the scallops on top. Serve immediately.

KALE CAESAR SALAD

WHY THIS RECIPE WORKS: We weren't willing to sacrifice flavor in order to make a healthier version of classic Caesar salad. It had to include a rich, creamy dressing, but we did want to eliminate some of the usual fat. We tried both mayonnaise-based and egg-based dressings, but found that the heartier kale really needed a thicker mayonnaise base to stand up to it. Using that as a starting point, we cut out half the mayonnaise, replacing it with low-fat yogurt. We found we only needed a half cup of Parmesan to get the satisfying, nutty flavor so essential to Caesar dressing. The addition of anchovy fillets provided rich umami notes. A 10-minute soak in warm water tenderized the kale. We swapped the usual white bread croutons for croutons made from whole-grain bread, as the hearty greens paired well with the more rustic croutons.

Kale Caesar Salad
SERVES 4

- 12 ounces curly kale, stemmed and cut into 1-inch pieces (16 cups)
- 3 ounces rustic whole-grain bread, cut into ½-inch cubes (1½ cups)
- 2 tablespoons extra-virgin olive oil
  Salt and pepper
- 3 tablespoons mayonnaise
- 3 tablespoons plain low-fat yogurt
- 1 ounce Parmesan cheese, grated (½ cup)
- 1 tablespoon lemon juice
- 2 teaspoons white wine vinegar
- 2 teaspoons Worcestershire sauce
- 2 teaspoons Dijon mustard
- 3 anchovy fillets, rinsed and minced
- 1 garlic clove, minced

1. Adjust oven rack to middle position and heat oven to 350 degrees. Place kale in large bowl and cover with warm tap water (110 to 115 degrees). Swish kale around to remove grit. Let kale sit in warm water bath for 10 minutes. Remove kale from water and spin dry in salad spinner in multiple batches. Pat leaves dry with paper towels if still wet.

2. Toss bread, 1 tablespoon oil, ⅛ teaspoon salt, and ⅛ teaspoon pepper together in bowl. Spread on rimmed baking sheet and bake until golden and crisp, about 15 minutes. Let croutons cool completely on sheet. (Cooled croutons can be stored in airtight container at room temperature for up to 24 hours.)

3. In large bowl whisk mayonnaise, yogurt, ¼ cup Parmesan, lemon juice, vinegar, Worcestershire sauce, mustard, anchovies, garlic, ½ teaspoon salt, and ½ teaspoon pepper together until well combined. Whisking constantly, drizzle in remaining 1 tablespoon oil until combined.

4. Toss kale with dressing and refrigerate for at least 20 minutes or up to 6 hours. Toss dressed kale with croutons and remaining ¼ cup Parmesan. Serve.

BETTER CHOPPED SALADS

WHY THIS RECIPE WORKS: Chopped salads are often little better than a random collection of cut-up produce from the crisper drawer exuding moisture that turns the salad watery and bland. We wanted lively, thoughtfully chosen compositions of lettuce, vegetables, and perhaps fruit—cut into bite-size pieces—with supporting players like nuts and cheese contributing hearty flavors and textures. Salting some of the vegetables—cucumbers and tomatoes—to remove excess moisture was an important first step. As for the dressing, most recipes we tried called for a ratio of 3 parts oil to 1 part vinegar, but we found that a more assertive blend of equal parts oil and vinegar was far better at delivering the bright, acidic kick needed in salads boasting hearty flavors and chunky textures. We also found that marinating ingredients such as bell peppers, onions, and fruit in the dressing for 5 minutes before adding cheese and other tender components brought a welcome flavor boost.

Pear and Cranberry Chopped Salad
SERVES 4 TO 6

Chopped dried cherries can be substituted for the cranberries.

- 1 cucumber, peeled, halved lengthwise, seeded, and cut into ½-inch dice (about 1¼ cups; see page 47)
  Table salt
- 3 tablespoons extra-virgin olive oil
- 3 tablespoons sherry vinegar
- 1 red bell pepper, stemmed, seeded, and cut into ¼-inch pieces (about 1 cup)
- 1 ripe but firm pear, cut into ¼-inch pieces (about 1 cup)
- ½ small red onion, minced (about ¼ cup)
- ½ cup dried cranberries
- 1 romaine heart, cut into ½-inch pieces (about 3 cups)
- 4 ounces blue cheese, crumbled (about 1 cup)
- ½ cup pistachios, toasted and chopped coarse
  Ground black pepper

1. Combine the cucumber and ½ teaspoon salt in a colander set over a bowl and drain for 15 minutes.

2. Whisk the oil and vinegar together in a large bowl. Add the drained cucumber, bell pepper, pear, onion, and cranberries. Toss and let stand at room temperature to blend the flavors, 5 minutes.

3. Add the romaine, blue cheese, and pistachios and toss to combine. Season with salt and pepper to taste and serve.

Mediterranean Chopped Salad

SERVES 4 TO 6

For information on our top-rated brand of feta cheese, see page 907.

- 1 cucumber, peeled, halved lengthwise, seeded, and cut into ½-inch dice (about 1¼ cups; see page 47)
- 1 pint grape tomatoes, quartered (about 1½ cups)
  Table salt
- 3 tablespoons extra-virgin olive oil
- 3 tablespoons red wine vinegar
- 1 medium garlic clove, minced or pressed through a garlic press (about 1 teaspoon)
- 1 (15-ounce) can chickpeas, drained and rinsed
- ½ cup pitted kalamata olives, chopped
- ½ small red onion, minced (about ¼ cup)
- ½ cup chopped fresh parsley leaves
- 1 romaine heart, cut into ½-inch pieces (about 3 cups)
- 4 ounces feta cheese, crumbled (about 1 cup)
  Ground black pepper

1. Combine the cucumber, tomatoes, and 1 teaspoon salt in a colander set over a bowl and drain for 15 minutes.

2. Whisk the oil, vinegar, and garlic together in a large bowl. Add the drained cucumber and tomatoes, chickpeas, olives, onion, and parsley. Toss and let stand at room temperature to blend the flavors, 5 minutes.

3. Add the romaine and feta and toss to combine. Season with salt and pepper to taste and serve.

Fennel and Apple Chopped Salad

SERVES 4 TO 6

Braeburn, Jonagold, or Red Delicious apples all work well here. The cheese is sprinkled on the salads after plating because goat cheese tends to clump when tossed.

- 1 cucumber, peeled, halved lengthwise, seeded, and cut into ½-inch dice (about 1¼ cups; see page 47)
  Table salt
- 3 tablespoons extra-virgin olive oil
- 3 tablespoons white wine vinegar
- 1 fennel bulb, halved lengthwise, cored, and cut into ¼-inch dice (about 1½ cups; see photos)
- 2 apples, cored and cut into ¼-inch dice (about 2 cups; see note)
- ½ small red onion, minced (about ¼ cup)
- ¼ cup chopped fresh tarragon leaves
- 1 romaine heart, cut into ½-inch pieces (about 3 cups)

TRIMMING AND CORING FENNEL

1. Cut off the stems and feathery fronds.

2. Trim a very thin slice from the base of the bulb and remove any tough or blemished outer layers.

3. After cutting the bulb in half through the base, use a small, sharp knife to remove the pyramid-shaped core. Slice or chop the fennel as directed.

- ½ cup chopped walnuts, toasted
  Ground back pepper
- 4 ounces crumbled goat cheese (about 1 cup)

1. Combine the cucumber and ½ teaspoon salt in a colander set over a bowl and drain for 15 minutes.

2. Whisk the oil and vinegar together in a large bowl. Add the drained cucumber, fennel, apples, onion, and tarragon. Toss and let stand at room temperature to blend the flavors, 5 minutes.

3. Add the romaine and walnuts and toss to combine. Season with salt and pepper to taste. Divide the salad among individual plates; top each with some goat cheese and serve.

MANGO, ORANGE, AND JÍCAMA SALAD

WHY THIS RECIPE WORKS: When the summer fruit crops are at the peak of ripeness, it doesn't require much forethought to put together a stunning fruit salad. Come winter, however, and the task requires a little more creativity. Working with the abundant citrus and tropical fruits available in colder months, we set our sights on a nuanced salad. A pairing of 1 part citrus fruit to 4 parts tropical fruit produced a juicy—not waterlogged—salad. We started with oranges and mangoes and then we created a simple bright dressing by heating sugar, lime juice, lime zest, red pepper flakes, and a pinch of salt to form a tangy-sweet syrup infused with just a touch of spicy heat. The mild sweetness and supercrisp texture of jícama, softened slightly in the hot syrup, contributed just enough crunch to finish off the salad.

Mango, Orange, and Jícama Salad

SERVES 4 TO 6

Make sure that the syrup has cooled before pouring it over the fruit.

 3 tablespoons sugar
 ¼ teaspoon grated lime zest plus 3 tablespoons juice (2 limes)
 ¼ teaspoon red pepper flakes
   Pinch salt
 12 ounces jícama, peeled and cut into ¼-inch dice (1½ cups)
 2 oranges
 2 mangos, peeled, pitted, and cut into ½-inch dice

1. Bring sugar, lime zest and juice, pepper flakes, and salt to simmer in small saucepan over medium heat, stirring constantly, until sugar is dissolved, 1 to 2 minutes. Remove pan from heat, stir in jícama, and let syrup cool for 20 minutes.

2. Meanwhile, cut away peel and pith from oranges. Slice into ½-inch-thick rounds, then cut rounds into ½-inch pieces. Place oranges and mangos in large bowl.

3. When syrup is cool, pour over oranges and mangos and toss to combine. Refrigerate for 15 minutes before serving.

Papaya, Clementine, and Chayote Salad

Chayote, also called mirliton, is often sold with other tropical fruits and vegetables. If you can't find chayote, substitute an equal amount of jícama.

Substitute 2 teaspoons grated fresh ginger for red pepper flakes; 1 chayote, peeled, halved, pitted, and cut into ¼-inch dice, for jícama; 3 clementines, peeled and each segment cut into 3 pieces, for oranges; and 2 large papayas, peeled, seeded, and cut into ½-inch dice, for mangos.

Pineapple, Grapefruit, and Cucumber Salad

Substitute ground cardamom for red pepper flakes; 1 cucumber, peeled, halved lengthwise, seeded, and cut into ¼-inch dice, for jícama; 1 grapefruit for oranges; and 1 pineapple, peeled, cored, and cut into ½-inch dice, for mangos.

CHERRY TOMATO SALAD

WHY THIS RECIPE WORKS: Cherry tomatoes are sweet, juicy, and available year-round—and especially tempting during those cold winter months when summer seems eons away. We wanted an easy recipe that would make the most of their sweetness so we could enjoy fresh tomatoes anytime we wanted. Simply slicing cherry tomatoes in half and sprucing them up with vinaigrette resulted in a waterlogged salad

with no flavor at all. To prevent this soggy, watery outcome, we quartered and salted them, and then took them for a spin in a salad spinner to remove as much of the jelly and seeds as possible. Reducing the jelly with red wine vinegar concentrated its flavor, and adding olive oil made for a dressing that brought the tomato flavor to the forefront. Cucumber contributed welcome crunch, while chopped olives and crumbled feta added a briny touch that brought the whole dish together.

Cherry Tomato Salad with Feta and Olives

SERVES 4 TO 6

If in-season cherry tomatoes are unavailable, substitute vine-ripened cherry tomatoes or grape tomatoes from the supermarket. Cut grape tomatoes in half along the equator (rather than quartering them). If you don't have a salad spinner, after the salted tomatoes have stood for 30 minutes, wrap the bowl tightly with plastic wrap and gently shake to remove seeds and excess liquid. Strain the liquid and proceed with the recipe as directed. The amount of liquid given off by the tomatoes will depend on their ripeness. If you have less than ½ cup juice after spinning, proceed with the recipe using the entire amount of juice and reduce it to 3 tablespoons as directed (the cooking time will be shorter).

 2 pints ripe cherry tomatoes, quartered (about 4 cups; see note)
 ½ teaspoon sugar
   Table salt
 1 medium shallot, minced (about 3 tablespoons)
 1 tablespoon red wine vinegar
 2 medium garlic cloves, minced or pressed through a garlic press (about 2 teaspoons)
 ½ teaspoon dried oregano
 2 tablespoons extra-virgin olive oil
   Ground black pepper
 1 small cucumber, peeled, halved lengthwise, seeded, and cut into ½-inch pieces (see page 47)

½ cup chopped pitted kalamata olives

4 ounces feta cheese, crumbled (about 1 cup)

3 tablespoons chopped fresh parsley leaves

1. Toss the tomatoes, sugar, and ¼ teaspoon salt in a medium bowl; let stand for 30 minutes. Transfer the tomatoes to a salad spinner and spin until the seeds and excess liquid have been removed, 45 to 60 seconds, stirring to redistribute the tomatoes several times during spinning. Return the tomatoes to the bowl and set aside. Strain the tomato liquid through a fine-mesh strainer into a liquid measuring cup, pressing on the solids to extract as much liquid as possible.

2. Bring ½ cup of the tomato liquid (discard any extra), the shallot, vinegar, garlic, and oregano to a simmer in a small saucepan over medium heat. Simmer until reduced to 3 tablespoons, 6 to 8 minutes. Transfer the mixture to a small bowl and cool to room temperature, about 5 minutes. Whisk in the oil until combined and season with salt and pepper to taste.

3. Add the cucumber, olives, feta, parsley, and dressing to the bowl with the tomatoes; toss gently and serve.

ITALIAN BREAD SALAD

WHY THIS RECIPE WORKS: When the rustic Italian bread salad panzanella is done well, the sweet juice of the tomatoes mixes with a bright-tasting vinaigrette, moistening chunks of thick-crusted bread until they're soft and just a little chewy—but the line between lightly moistened and unpleasantly soggy is very thin. Toasting fresh bread in the oven, rather than using the traditional day-old bread, was a good start. With this method, the bread lost enough moisture in the oven to absorb the dressing without getting waterlogged. A 10-minute soak in the flavorful dressing yielded perfectly moistened, nutty-tasting bread ready to be tossed with the tomatoes, which we salted to intensify their flavor. A thinly sliced cucumber and shallot for crunch and bite plus a handful of chopped fresh basil perfected our salad.

Italian Bread Salad (Panzanella)

SERVES 4

The success of this recipe depends on high-quality ingredients, including ripe, in-season tomatoes and fruity olive oil. Fresh basil is also a must. Your bread may vary in density, so you may not need the entire loaf for this recipe.

1 (1-pound) loaf rustic Italian or French bread, cut or torn into 1-inch pieces (about 6 cups)

½ cup extra-virgin olive oil

Table salt and ground black pepper

1½ pounds tomatoes, cored, seeded, and cut into 1-inch pieces

3 tablespoons red wine vinegar

1 medium cucumber, peeled, halved lengthwise, seeded, and sliced thin (see page 47)

1 medium shallot, sliced thin

¼ cup chopped fresh basil leaves

1. Adjust an oven rack to the middle position and heat the oven to 400 degrees. Toss the bread pieces with 2 tablespoons of the oil and ¼ teaspoon salt; arrange the bread in a single layer on a rimmed baking sheet. Toast the bread pieces until just starting to turn light golden, 15 to 20 minutes, stirring halfway through baking. Set aside and let cool to room temperature.

2. Gently toss the tomatoes and ½ teaspoon salt in a large bowl. Transfer to a colander set over a bowl; set aside to drain for 15 minutes, tossing occasionally.

3. Whisk the remaining 6 tablespoons oil, the vinegar, and ¼ teaspoon pepper into the tomato juices. Add the bread pieces, toss to coat, and let stand for 10 minutes, tossing occasionally.

4. Add the tomatoes, cucumber, shallot, and basil to the bowl with the bread pieces and toss to coat. Season with salt and pepper to taste and serve immediately.

PITA BREAD SALAD WITH TOMATOES AND CUCUMBER

WHY THIS RECIPE WORKS: This Middle Eastern salad is at its best when it combines fresh, flavorful produce with crisp pita and bright herbs. Many recipes eliminate excess moisture from the salad by taking the time-consuming step of seeding and salting the cucumbers and tomatoes. We skipped that process, favoring the crisp texture of the cucumber (the English variety, which has fewer seeds) and the flavorful seeds and jelly of the tomato. We fended off soggy bread by making the pita moisture-repellent, brushing its craggy sides with plenty of olive oil before baking. The oil soaked into the bread and prevented the pita chips from absorbing the salad's moisture while still allowing them to take on some of its flavor. A fresh, summery blend of mint, cilantro, and peppery arugula comprised the salad's greenery and a vinaigrette of lemon juice, garlic, salt, and olive oil lent it an uncomplicated, bright finish.

Pita Bread Salad with Tomatoes and Cucumber (Fattoush)

SERVES 4

The success of this recipe depends on ripe, in-season tomatoes. A rasp-style grater makes quick work of turning the garlic into a paste.

    2   (8-inch) pita breads
    3   tablespoons plus ¼ cup extra-virgin olive oil
        Salt and pepper
    3   tablespoons lemon juice
    ¼   teaspoon garlic, minced to paste
    1   pound tomatoes, cored and cut into ¾-inch pieces
    1   English cucumber, peeled and sliced ⅛-inch thick
    1   cup arugula, chopped coarse
    ½   cup chopped fresh cilantro
    ½   cup chopped fresh mint
    4   scallions, sliced thin

1. Adjust oven rack to middle position and heat oven to 375 degrees. Using kitchen shears, cut around perimeter of each pita and separate into 2 thin rounds. Cut each round in half. Place pita bread, smooth side down, on wire rack set in rimmed baking sheet. Brush 3 tablespoons oil over surface of pita. (Pita does not need to be uniformly coated. Oil will absorb and spread as it bakes.) Season with salt and pepper. Bake until pita is crisp and pale golden brown, 10 to 14 minutes.

2. While pita toasts, whisk lemon juice, garlic, and ¼ teaspoon salt together in small bowl. Let stand 10 minutes

3. Place tomatoes, cucumber, arugula, cilantro, mint, and scallions in large bowl. Break pita into ½-inch pieces and place in bowl with vegetables. Add lemon-garlic mixture and remaining ¼ cup oil and toss to coat. Season with salt and pepper to taste. Serve immediately.

GREEK SALAD

WHY THIS RECIPE WORKS: Most versions of Greek salad consist of iceberg lettuce, chunks of green pepper, and a few pale wedges of tomato, sparsely dotted with cubes of feta and garnished with one or two olives. We wanted a salad with crisp ingredients and bold flavors. A combination of lemon juice, red wine vinegar, garlic, and olive oil made a zesty vinaigrette. We marinated onion and cucumber slices in the vinaigrette which helped mute the sting of raw onion in the salad. We swapped in crisp, flavorful romaine for the iceberg. And along with sliced tomatoes, we added jarred roasted red peppers for a bit of sweetness. A handful of kalamata olives and tangy feta cheese lent the traditional touches, and torn mint and parsley leaves gave our salad a fresh finish.

Classic Greek Salad

SERVES 6 TO 8

Marinating the onion and cucumber in the vinaigrette tones down the onion's harshness and flavors the cucumber. For efficiency, prepare the other salad ingredients while the onion and cucumber marinate.

VINAIGRETTE

    6   tablespoons extra-virgin olive oil
    3   tablespoons red wine vinegar
    2   teaspoons minced fresh oregano leaves
    1½ teaspoons juice from 1 lemon
    1   medium garlic clove, minced or pressed through a garlic press (about 1 teaspoon)
    ½   teaspoon table salt
    ⅛   teaspoon ground black pepper

SALAD

    ½   medium red onion, sliced thin (about ¾ cup)
    1   medium cucumber, peeled, halved lengthwise, seeded, and sliced ⅛ inch thick (see page 47)
    2   romaine hearts, washed, dried, and torn into 1½-inch pieces (about 8 cups)
    2   medium, firm, ripe tomatoes (6 ounces each), cored, seeded, and each tomato cut into 12 wedges
    6   ounces jarred roasted red bell peppers, cut into 2 by ½-inch strips (about 1 cup)
    ¼   cup loosely packed fresh parsley leaves, torn
    ¼   cup loosely packed fresh mint leaves, torn
    20 large pitted kalamata olives, quartered
    5   ounces feta cheese, crumbled (about 1¼ cups)

1. FOR THE VINAIGRETTE: Whisk the oil, vinegar, oregano, lemon juice, garlic, salt, and pepper in a large bowl until combined.

2. Add the onion and cucumber to the vinaigrette and toss; let stand to blend the flavors, about 20 minutes.

3. FOR THE SALAD: Add the romaine, tomatoes, peppers, parsley, and mint to the bowl with the onions and cucumbers; toss to coat with the vinaigrette.

4. Transfer the salad to a serving bowl or platter; sprinkle the olives and feta over the salad and serve.

CUCUMBER SALAD

WHY THIS RECIPE WORKS: More often than not, cucumbers in cucumber salad turn soft and watery, having lost their crunchy texture and released enough liquid to dilute the dressing. This phenomenon made the primary goal of our cucumber salad easy to identify: Maximize the crunch.

Because water makes cucumbers lose their texture, we had to salt and weight the cucumbers to draw off excess moisture. We also rinsed them and patted them dry before tossing the cucumbers with a rice vinegar, lemon juice, and sesame oil vinaigrette, a flavorful combination. Toasted sesame seeds added even more textural interest.

SEEDING CUCUMBERS

Peel the cucumber, cut it in half lengthwise, and scoop out the seeds with a spoon.

CHOPPING CUCUMBERS

1. Cut each half crosswise into 2 to 3-inch pieces.

2. Place the pieces cut side up on a cutting board, then slice them lengthwise into even batons.

3. Cut the batons crosswise into an even dice.

Sesame-Lemon Cucumber Salad

SERVES 4

Mild rice vinegar works well in this Asian-inspired dressing.

3   medium cucumbers (about 2 pounds), peeled, halved lengthwise, seeded, and sliced ¼ inch thick (see page 47)
1   tablespoon table salt
¼   cup rice vinegar (see note)
2   tablespoons toasted sesame oil
1   tablespoon juice from 1 lemon
1   tablespoon sesame seeds, toasted
2   teaspoons sugar
⅛   teaspoon red pepper flakes

1. Toss the cucumbers with the salt in a colander set over a large bowl. Weight the cucumbers with a gallon-sized zipper-lock bag filled with water; drain for 1 to 3 hours. Rinse and pat dry.

2. Whisk the remaining ingredients together in a medium bowl. Add the cucumbers; toss to coat. Serve chilled or at room temperature.

CREAMY COLESLAW

WHY THIS RECIPE WORKS: No other food embodies an outdoor grillfest quite like coleslaw. This summery salad offers a crunch and creaminess that contrasts well with sweet and savory barbecued meats and vegetables. But, despite its simplicity, coleslaw can be tough to get just right. Usually, the coleslaw ends up limp and sitting in a pool of water. We wanted a crisp salad and a creamy dressing that wouldn't be waterlogged. To prevent the salad from getting watery, we salted the cabbage until it wilted, then rinsed and dried it. Removing the excess water helped to keep our dressing thick and creamy, and ensured the cabbage stayed crunchy. For the dressing, we used mayonnaise and rice vinegar; these made a creamy dressing that was flavorful but not too harsh. All our coleslaw needed now was black pepper and some shredded carrot for color, further crunch, and a little sweetness.

Creamy Coleslaw

SERVES 4

If you like caraway or celery seeds, add ¼ teaspoon of either with the mayonnaise and vinegar. If you like a tangier slaw, replace some or all of the mayonnaise with an equal amount of sour cream. To serve the coleslaw immediately, rinse the salted cabbage and carrot in a large bowl of ice water, drain them in a colander, pick out any ice cubes, then pat the vegetables dry before dressing.

1   pound red or green cabbage (about ½ medium head), shredded (about 6 cups; see page 49)
1   large carrot, peeled and shredded
1   teaspoon table salt
½   small onion, minced
½   cup mayonnaise (see note)
2   tablespoons rice vinegar
    Ground black pepper

1. Toss the cabbage and carrot with the salt in a colander set over a medium bowl. Let stand until the cabbage wilts, at least 1 hour or up to 4 hours. Rinse the cabbage and carrot under cold running water (or in a large bowl of ice water if serving immediately). Press, but do not squeeze, to drain; pat dry with paper towels.

2. Combine the cabbage, carrot, onion, mayonnaise, and vinegar in a medium bowl; toss to coat and season with pepper to taste. Serve chilled or at room temperature. (The coleslaw can be refrigerated in an airtight container for up to 2 days.)

1. Toss the cabbage with 1 teaspoon salt in a colander set over a medium bowl. Let stand until the cabbage wilts, at least 1 hour or up to 4 hours. Rinse the cabbage under cold running water (or in a large bowl of ice water if serving immediately). Press, but do not squeeze, to drain; pat dry with paper towels. Transfer the cabbage to a large bowl; add the carrot.

2. Combine the remaining ingredients with ¼ teaspoon salt in a small bowl. Pour the buttermilk dressing over the cabbage and carrot and toss to coat. Serve chilled or at room temperature. (The coleslaw can be refrigerated in an airtight container for up to 2 days.)

CABBAGE SALAD

WHY THIS RECIPE WORKS: Cabbage makes a great salad—not just as coleslaw but as a crunchy, flavorful, dress-up kind of salad. We aimed to develop an Asian-inspired cabbage salad that incorporated spicy, sweet flavors for a salad side dish that was a refreshing change from the same old slaw.

Salting the cabbage and setting it over a colander helped to extract excess liquid, which otherwise would dilute the potent flavors of the dressing. Shredded carrot gave the salad some sweetness, and radishes brought a peppery crunch. For the dressing, we started with smooth peanut butter for its rich flavor and velvety texture. Rice vinegar and soy sauce provided bright, tangy notes. White sugar would have contributed too much sweetness, but a small amount of honey was just right. Last touches to the dressing came in the form of a spicy jalapeño chile and fresh ginger. Processed to a smooth consistency, our spicy peanut dressing provided the perfect lush coating to the crisp vegetables.

Confetti Cabbage Salad with Spicy Peanut Dressing
SERVES 6

Serve this Asian-inspired cabbage salad with simple pork or chicken dishes. To serve the salad immediately, rinse the salted cabbage and carrot in a large bowl of ice water, drain them in a colander, pick out any ice cubes, then pat the vegetables dry before dressing.

 1 pound red or green cabbage (about ½ medium head), shredded (about 6 cups)
 1 large carrot, peeled and shredded
    Table salt
 2 tablespoons smooth peanut butter
 2 tablespoons peanut oil
 2 tablespoons rice vinegar
 1 tablespoon soy sauce
 1 teaspoon honey
 2 medium garlic cloves, minced or pressed through a garlic press (about 2 teaspoons)
 1½ tablespoons minced or grated fresh ginger
 ½ jalapeño chile, seeds and ribs removed
 4 medium radishes, halved lengthwise and sliced thin
 4 scallions, sliced thin

BUTTERMILK COLESLAW

WHY THIS RECIPE WORKS: Order barbecue down South, and you won't just get coleslaw on the side, you'll get buttermilk coleslaw. Unlike all-mayonnaise coleslaw, buttermilk coleslaw is coated in a light, creamy, and refreshingly tart dressing. We wanted a recipe that showcased its best attributes: a pickle-crisp texture and a tangy dressing.

To prevent watery coleslaw, we salted, rinsed, and dried our shredded cabbage. This also gave us the texture we wanted—as the salted cabbage sat, moisture was pulled out of it, wilting it to the right crispy texture. For a tangy dressing that clung to the cabbage and didn't pool at the bottom of the bowl, we supplemented the buttermilk with mayonnaise and sour cream. For finishing touches, we added shredded carrot, which contributed both color and sweetness. The mild flavor of shallot was a welcome addition, and sugar, mustard, and cider vinegar amped up the slaw's tanginess.

Creamy Buttermilk Coleslaw
SERVES 4

To serve the coleslaw immediately, rinse the salted cabbage in a large bowl of ice water, drain it in a colander, pick out any ice cubes, then pat the cabbage dry before dressing.

 1 pound red or green cabbage (about ½ medium head), shredded (about 6 cups; see page 49)
    Table salt
 1 large carrot, peeled and shredded
 ½ cup buttermilk
 2 tablespoons mayonnaise
 2 tablespoons sour cream
 1 small shallot, minced (about 1 tablespoon)
 2 tablespoons minced fresh parsley leaves
 ½ teaspoon cider vinegar
 ¼ teaspoon Dijon mustard
 ½ teaspoon sugar
 ⅛ teaspoon ground black pepper

SHREDDING CABBAGE

1. Cut the cabbage into quarters, then trim and discard the hard core.

2. Separate the cabbage into small stacks of leaves that flatten when pressed.

3. Use a chef's knife to cut each stack of cabbage leaves into thin shreds.

1. Toss the cabbage and carrot with 1 teaspoon salt in a colander set over a medium bowl. Let stand until the cabbage wilts, at least 1 hour or up to 4 hours. Rinse the cabbage and carrot under cold running water (or in a large bowl of ice water if serving immediately). Press, but do not squeeze, to drain; pat dry with paper towels.

2. Process the peanut butter, oil, vinegar, soy sauce, honey, garlic, ginger, and jalapeño in a food processor until smooth. Combine the cabbage, carrot, radishes, scallions, and dressing in a medium bowl; toss to coat. Season with salt to taste. Cover and refrigerate; serve chilled. (The salad can be refrigerated in an airtight container for up to 2 days.)

MACARONI SALAD

WHY THIS RECIPE WORKS: Macaroni salad seems simple enough—toss elbow macaroni and a few seasonings with a mayo-based dressing. So why does this picnic salad often fall short, with mushy pasta and a bland, ho-hum dressing? We set out to make a picnic-worthy macaroni salad with tender pasta and a creamy, well-seasoned dressing.

First we had to get the pasta texture just right. To do this, we didn't drain the macaroni as thoroughly as we could have; the excess water is absorbed by the pasta as it sits and this prevents the finished salad from drying out. Also, cooking the macaroni to a point where it still has some bite left means the pasta won't get too soft when mixed with the mayonnaise. For the most flavor, we seasoned the pasta first—before adding the mayonnaise—so that the seasonings could penetrate and flavor the macaroni. Garlic powder added flavor to the salad (fresh garlic was too harsh), and lemon juice and Dijon mustard enlivened the creamy dressing.

Cool and Creamy Macaroni Salad
SERVES 8 TO 10
Don't drain the macaroni too well before adding the other ingredients—a little extra moisture will keep the salad from drying out. If you've made the salad ahead of time, simply stir in a little warm water to loosen the texture before serving.

Table salt
1 pound elbow macaroni
½ small red onion, minced
1 celery rib, chopped fine
¼ cup minced fresh parsley leaves
2 tablespoons juice from 1 lemon
1 tablespoon Dijon mustard
⅛ teaspoon garlic powder
Pinch cayenne pepper
1½ cups mayonnaise
Ground black pepper

1. Bring 4 quarts water to a boil in a large pot. Stir 1 tablespoon salt and the pasta into the boiling water and cook, stirring often, until nearly tender, about 5 minutes. Drain the pasta and rinse with cold water until cool, then drain briefly so that the macaroni remains moist. Transfer to a large bowl.

2. Stir in the onion, celery, parsley, lemon juice, mustard, garlic powder, and cayenne and let sit until the flavors are absorbed, about 2 minutes. Add the mayonnaise and let sit until the salad is no longer watery, 5 to 10 minutes. Season with salt and pepper to taste and serve. (The salad can be refrigerated in an airtight container for up to 2 days.)

PASTA SALAD WITH PESTO

WHY THIS RECIPE WORKS: Pasta salad with pesto should be light and refreshing, not dry and dull. We decided to perfect pesto pasta salad—and keep it fresh, green, garlicky, and full of herbal flavor. Using a pasta shape with a textured surface, like farfalle, guaranteed that the pesto wouldn't slide off. To ensure that the pesto coated the pasta, we didn't rinse it after cooking. Instead, we spread the pasta to cool in a single layer on a baking sheet; a splash of oil helped prevent it from sticking. For the pesto, we blanched the garlic to tame its harsh bite. Lots of basil made for vibrant herb flavor, and to keep the green color from fading, we added mild-tasting baby spinach, which lent the salad a vivid green color. For a creamy, not greasy, pesto, we enriched it with mayonnaise. Lemon juice brightened the pesto's flavor, and extra pine nuts, folded into the salad, provided an additional hit of nutty flavor and a pleasant crunchy texture.

Pasta Salad with Pesto

SERVES 8 TO 10

This salad is best served the day it is made; if it's been refrigerated, bring it to room temperature before serving. The pesto can be made a day ahead—just cook the garlic in a small saucepan of boiling water for 1 minute.

- 2 medium garlic cloves, unpeeled
  Table salt
- 1 pound farfalle (bow-tie pasta)
- ¼ cup plus 1 tablespoon extra-virgin olive oil
- 3 cups packed fresh basil leaves (about 4 ounces)
- 1 cup packed baby spinach (about 1 ounce)
- ¾ cup pine nuts (3¾ ounces), toasted
- 2 tablespoons juice from 1 lemon
- ½ teaspoon ground black pepper
- 1½ ounces Parmesan cheese, finely grated (about ¾ cup), plus extra for serving
- 6 tablespoons mayonnaise
- 1 pint cherry tomatoes, quartered, or grape tomatoes, halved (optional)

1. Bring 4 quarts water to a boil in a large pot. Add the garlic to the boiling water and let cook for 1 minute. Remove the garlic with a slotted spoon and rinse under cold water; set aside to cool. Stir 1 tablespoon salt and the pasta into the boiling water and cook, stirring often, until the pasta is just past al dente. Reserve ¼ cup of the pasta cooking water, drain the pasta, toss with 1 tablespoon of the oil, spread in a single layer on a rimmed baking sheet, and cool to room temperature, about 30 minutes.

2. Peel and mince the garlic or press it through a garlic press. Process the garlic, basil, spinach, ¼ cup of the nuts, lemon juice, pepper, remaining ¼ cup oil, and 1 teaspoon salt

in a food processor until smooth, scraping down the sides of the work bowl as necessary. Add the Parmesan and mayonnaise and process until thoroughly combined. Transfer the mixture to a large serving bowl. Cover and refrigerate until ready to assemble the salad.

3. Toss the pasta with the pesto, adding the reserved pasta water, 1 tablespoon at a time, until the pesto evenly coats the pasta. Fold in the remaining ½ cup nuts and the tomatoes (if using). Serve, passing extra Parmesan separately.

ANTIPASTO PASTA SALAD

WHY THIS RECIPE WORKS: We love the traditional antipasto platter served at Italian restaurants, chock-full of cured meats, cheese, and pickled vegetables. It's a full-flavored and satisfying dish—and something that we thought would translate well to a hearty pasta salad.

We quickly decided that short, curly pasta was the best shape to use, as its curves held on to the salad's other components, making for a more cohesive dish. Quickly rendering the meats in the microwave helped to keep this salad from becoming greasy. We used an increased ratio of vinegar to oil in the dressing—the sharp, acidic flavor cut the richness of the meats and cheese for a brighter-tasting salad. For well-seasoned pasta, we tossed the hot pasta with the dressing—hot pasta absorbs dressing better than cold pasta. Slicing the meat into thick strips meant that its hearty flavor wasn't lost among the other ingredients. And grating the cheese, rather than cubing it, made for evenly distributed sharp flavor throughout the salad.

Antipasto Pasta Salad

SERVES 6 TO 8

We also liked the addition of 1 cup chopped pitted kalamata olives or 1 cup jarred artichokes, drained and quartered, to this salad.

- 8 ounces sliced pepperoni, cut into ¼-inch strips
- 8 ounces thick-sliced sopresatta or salami, halved and cut into ¼-inch strips
- 10 tablespoons red wine vinegar
- 6 tablespoons extra-virgin olive oil
- 3 tablespoons mayonnaise
- 1 (12-ounce) jar pepperoncini, drained (2 tablespoons liquid reserved), stemmed, and chopped coarse
- 4 garlic cloves, minced or pressed through a garlic press (about 4 teaspoons)
- ¼ teaspoon red pepper flakes
  Table salt and ground black pepper
- 1 pound short, curly pasta, such as fusilli or campanelle
- 1 pound white mushrooms, wiped clean and quartered
- 4 ounces aged provolone cheese, grated (about 1 cup)
- 1 (12-ounce) jar roasted red peppers, drained, patted dry, and chopped coarse
- 1 cup minced fresh basil leaves

1. Bring 4 quarts water to a boil in a large pot. Place the pepperoni on a large paper towel–lined plate. Cover with another paper towel and place the sopresatta on top. Cover with another paper towel and microwave on high power for 1 minute. Discard the paper towels and set the pepperoni and sopresatta aside.

2. Whisk 5 tablespoons of the vinegar, the oil, mayonnaise, pepperoncini liquid, garlic, red pepper flakes, ½ teaspoon salt, and ½ teaspoon pepper together in a medium bowl.

3. Stir 1 tablespoon salt and the pasta into the boiling water and cook, stirring often, until the pasta is just past al dente. Drain the pasta and return it to the pot. Pour ½ cup of the dressing and the remaining 5 tablespoons vinegar over the pasta and toss to combine; season with salt and pepper to taste. Spread the pasta in a single layer on a rimmed baking sheet and cool to room temperature, about 30 minutes.

4. Meanwhile, bring the remaining dressing to a simmer in a large skillet over medium-high heat. Add the mushrooms and cook until lightly browned, about 8 minutes. Transfer to a large bowl and cool to room temperature.

5. Add the meat, provolone, peppers, basil, and pasta to the mushrooms and toss to combine. Season with salt and pepper to taste and serve.

RICE SALAD

WHY THIS RECIPE WORKS: Rice makes a light, refreshing salad when dressed properly and studded with vegetables—and it makes a nice change from pasta salad. But unlike pasta, rice can't stand up to assertive flavors or be bogged down by a heavy vinaigrette. To get rice salad just right, we would have to include a few bright, tangy ingredients and use a light hand when making the dressing.

To start out with as much flavor as possible, we toasted the rice to intensify its flavor and then boiled it in a large amount of water, as we would pasta. This method kept the rice tender when cool. To dry the rice, we spread it out on a large baking sheet—this guaranteed that the rice didn't clump or become waterlogged. As for the vinaigrette, restraint was key. We used small amounts of oil, vinegar, and seasonings to complement, but not overshadow, the grains of rice. Orange segments, slivered almonds, and chopped olives gave the salad character and textural interest. And a brief rest to blend the flavors yielded a rice salad that was bright and balanced.

Rice Salad with Oranges, Olives, and Almonds
SERVES 6 TO 8
Taste the rice as it nears the end of its cooking time; it should be cooked through and firm, but not crunchy. Be careful not to overcook the rice or the grains will be blown out.

1½ cups long-grain or basmati rice
   Table salt
2 tablespoons extra-virgin olive oil

¼ teaspoon grated zest plus 1 tablespoon juice from 1 orange
2 teaspoons sherry vinegar
1 small garlic clove, minced or pressed through a garlic press (about ½ teaspoon)
½ teaspoon ground black pepper
2 medium oranges, peel and pith removed, and cut into segments
⅓ cup chopped pitted green olives
⅓ cup slivered almonds, toasted
2 tablespoons fresh oregano leaves, minced

1. Bring 4 quarts water to a boil in a large pot. Heat a medium skillet over medium heat until hot, about 3 minutes; add the rice and toast, stirring frequently, until faintly fragrant and some grains turn opaque, about 5 minutes.

2. Stir 1½ teaspoons salt and the rice into the boiling water. Cook, uncovered, until the rice is tender but not soft, 8 to 10 minutes for long-grain rice or about 15 minutes for basmati (see note). Line a rimmed baking sheet with foil or parchment paper. Drain the rice in a colander and spread on the prepared baking sheet. Cool while preparing the salad ingredients.

3. Whisk the oil, orange zest and juice, vinegar, garlic, 1 teaspoon salt, and pepper together in a small bowl. Combine the rice, oranges, olives, almonds, and oregano in a large bowl; drizzle the dressing over the salad and toss to combine. Let stand for 20 minutes to blend the flavors, and serve.

AMERICAN POTATO SALAD

WHY THIS RECIPE WORKS: Few salads make a splash at potlucks or picnics the way potato salad does—this classic, all-American side always seems to disappear first. We wanted a recipe for a traditional, creamy (read: mayonnaise-based) potato salad that looked good—no mushy, sloppy spuds—and tasted even better.

2. Drain the potatoes and cool slightly; peel if desired. Cut the potatoes into ¾-inch pieces, using a serrated knife, while still warm, rinsing the knife occasionally in warm water to remove starch.

3. Combine the potatoes, vinegar, ½ teaspoon salt, and ¼ teaspoon pepper in a large bowl and toss gently. Cover and refrigerate until cool, about 20 minutes.

4. Meanwhile, combine the remaining ingredients and salt and pepper to taste. Add the potatoes, stir gently to combine, and serve. (The salad can be refrigerated in an airtight container for up to 1 day.)

AUSTRIAN POTATO SALAD

WHY THIS RECIPE WORKS: Austrian-style potato salad, seasoned with vinegar and mustard for a tart-and-tangy flavor, can be a welcome change of pace from traditional creamy potato salad. This style of potato salad calls on the starch from the potatoes along with an unexpected ingredient, chicken broth, to create the dressing. After cooking the sliced potatoes in broth, which we cut with an equal amount of water, we reduced the cooking liquid and mixed it with vinegar, mustard, chives, and cornichons for flavor. To give the dressing more body, and impart a rustic texture, we mashed in a small amount of our cooked potatoes. After mixing the rest of the sliced potatoes (which retained their shape but were soft and tender) with the thick vinaigrette, we had a luxurious, rich, and very different kind of potato salad.

Austrian-Style Potato Salad

SERVES 4 TO 6

If you can't find cornichons, chopped kosher dill pickles can be used in their place. To maintain its consistency, don't refrigerate the salad; it should be served within a few hours of preparation.

> 2 pounds Yukon Gold potatoes (about 4 medium),
>   peeled, quartered, and sliced ½ inch thick
> 1 cup low-sodium chicken broth
> 2 tablespoons white wine vinegar
> 1 tablespoon sugar
>   Table salt
> ¼ cup vegetable oil
> 1 small red onion, minced
> 6 cornichons, minced (about 2 tablespoons; see note)
> 2 tablespoons minced fresh chives
> 1 tablespoon Dijon mustard
>   Ground black pepper

1. Bring 1 cup water, the potatoes, broth, 1 tablespoon of the vinegar, the sugar, and 1 teaspoon salt to a boil in a 12-inch skillet over high heat. Reduce the heat to medium-low, cover, and cook until the potatoes are tender (a paring knife can be slipped in and out of the potatoes with little resistance), 15 to 17 minutes. Remove the cover, increase the heat to high, and cook until the liquid has reduced, about 2 minutes.

We began by choosing red potatoes. The skin adds color to a typically monochromatic salad. We boiled them whole for best flavor and then used a serrated knife to cut the potatoes into fork-friendly chunks—the serrated edge helps prevent the skins from tearing for a nicer presentation. While the potatoes were still warm, we drizzled them with vinegar and added a sprinkle of salt and pepper; this preseasoning gave the finished salad more flavor. When the potatoes were cool, we folded in the final traditional touches—mayonnaise, pickles, and red onion—for a perfect potluck potato salad, with a creamy dressing and firm bites of potato.

American Potato Salad with Hard-Cooked Eggs and Sweet Pickles

SERVES 4 TO 6

Use sweet pickles, not relish, for the best results. For potatoes that cook through at the same rate, buy potatoes that are roughly the same size.

> 2 pounds red potatoes (about 6 medium),
>   scrubbed (see note)
> ¼ cup red wine vinegar
>   Table salt and ground black pepper
> ½ cup mayonnaise
> ¼ cup sweet pickles, chopped fine (see note)
> 3 hard-cooked eggs (see page 38), peeled and
>   cut into ½-inch pieces
> 1 celery rib, chopped fine
> 2 tablespoons minced red onion
> 2 tablespoons minced fresh parsley leaves
> 2 teaspoons Dijon mustard

1. Place the potatoes in a large saucepan, cover with 1 inch of water, and bring to a boil over medium-high heat. Reduce the heat to medium and simmer, stirring occasionally, until the potatoes are tender (a paring knife can be slipped in and out of the potatoes with little resistance), 25 to 30 minutes.

2. Drain the potatoes in a colander set over a large bowl, reserving the cooking liquid. Set the potatoes aside. Pour off all but ½ cup cooking liquid (if ½ cup liquid does not remain, add water to make this amount). Whisk the cooking liquid, the remaining 1 tablespoon vinegar, the oil, onion, cornichons, chives, and mustard together in a large bowl.

3. Add ½ cup of the cooked potatoes to the bowl with the cooking liquid mixture and mash with a potato masher until a thick vinaigrette forms (the mixture will be slightly chunky). Add the remaining potatoes, stirring gently to combine. Season with salt and pepper to taste. Serve warm or at room temperature.

LENTIL SALADS

WHY THIS RECIPE WORKS: The most important step in making a lentil salad is perfecting the cooking of the lentils so they maintain their shape and firm-tender bite. It turns out there are two key steps. The first is to brine the lentils in warm salt water. With brining, the lentils' skins soften, which leads to fewer blowouts. The second step is to cook the lentils in the oven, which heats them gently and uniformly. Once we had perfectly cooked lentils, all we had left to do was to pair the earthy beans with a tart vinaigrette and boldly flavored mix-ins.

Lentil Salad with Olives, Mint, and Feta

SERVES 4 TO 6

French green lentils, or *lentilles du Puy*, are our preferred choice for this recipe, but it works with any type of lentil except red or yellow. Brining helps keep the lentils intact, but if you don't have time, they'll still taste good without it. The salad can be served warm or at room temperature.

- 1 cup lentils, picked over and rinsed
  Salt and pepper
- 6 cups water
- 2 cups low-sodium chicken broth
- 5 garlic cloves, lightly crushed and peeled
- 1 bay leaf
- 5 tablespoons extra-virgin olive oil
- 3 tablespoons white wine vinegar
- ½ cup pitted kalamata olives, chopped coarse
- ½ cup minced fresh mint
- 1 large shallot, minced
- 1 ounce feta cheese, crumbled (¼ cup)

1. Place lentils and 1 teaspoon salt in bowl. Cover with 4 cups warm water (about 110 degrees) and soak for 1 hour. Drain well. (Drained lentils can be refrigerated for up to 2 days before cooking.)

2. Adjust oven rack to middle position and heat oven to 325 degrees. Combine drained lentils, remaining 2 cups water, broth, garlic, bay leaf, and ½ teaspoon salt in ovensafe medium saucepan. Cover and bake until lentils are tender but remain intact, 40 minutes to 1 hour. Meanwhile, whisk oil and vinegar together in large bowl.

3. Drain lentils well; remove and discard garlic and bay leaf. Add drained lentils, olives, mint, and shallot to dressing and toss to combine. Season with salt and pepper to taste. Transfer to serving dish, sprinkle with feta, and serve.

Lentil Salad with Spinach, Walnuts, and Parmesan Cheese

Substitute sherry vinegar for white wine vinegar. Place 4 ounces baby spinach and 2 tablespoons water in bowl. Cover and microwave until spinach is wilted and volume is halved, 3 to 4 minutes. Remove bowl from microwave and keep covered for 1 minute. Transfer spinach to colander; gently press to release liquid. Transfer spinach to cutting board and chop coarse. Return to colander and press again. Substitute chopped spinach for olives and mint and ¾ cup coarsely grated Parmesan cheese for feta. Sprinkle with ⅓ cup coarsely chopped toasted walnuts before serving.

Lentil Salad with Hazelnuts and Goat Cheese

Substitute red wine vinegar for white wine vinegar and add 2 teaspoons Dijon mustard to dressing in step 2. Omit olives and substitute ¼ cup chopped parsley for mint. Substitute ½ cup crumbled goat cheese for feta and sprinkle with ⅓ cup coarsely chopped toasted hazelnuts before serving.

Lentil Salad with Carrots and Cilantro

Substitute lemon juice for white wine vinegar. Toss 2 carrots, peeled and cut into 2-inch-long matchsticks, with 1 teaspoon ground cumin, ½ teaspoon ground cinnamon, and ⅛ teaspoon cayenne pepper in bowl. Cover and microwave until carrots are tender but still crisp, 2 to 4 minutes. Substitute carrots for olives and ¼ cup minced fresh cilantro for mint. Omit shallot and feta.

CHAPTER 3

EASY SKILLET SUPPERS

PASTA FRITTATA

WHY THIS RECIPE WORKS: The classic Neapolitan pasta frittata starts with leftover cooked and sauced pasta (most often a long noodle shape) and half a dozen or so eggs beaten with salt, pepper, melted lard or butter, and grated Parmigiano-Reggiano cheese. The modest ingredients are transformed into a thick, creamy, golden-brown omelet laced with noodles. The best versions also feature small bites of meat or vegetables that contribute flavor without overly disrupting the creamy texture of the dish.

We rarely find ourselves with leftover pasta here in the test kitchen, but this dish sounded too good to pass up. Could we find a way to make a streamlined recipe that used dried pasta?

After a few tests, it was clear that angel hair was the best pasta for the job. These delicate strands brought a satisfying web of pasta to every bite without marring the tender egg texture. We found that we could cook the pasta in the same skillet we used to cook the frittata, saving time and dishes. By cooking off the water, we even skipped dirtying a strainer, and letting the pasta lightly "fry" after the water evaporated made for a lightly crispy, crunchy crust. Beating together 8 eggs provided the right balance and structure for 6 ounces of dried pasta. Gently cooking the eggs ensured that the exterior portions didn't overcook and turn rubbery while the interior came up to temperature. Three tablespoons of oil provided good richness and plenty of protection against toughness. Lastly, we added some bold flavorings, which provided richness and a bit of heat.

Pasta Frittata with Sausage and Hot Peppers
SERVES 6 TO 8

To ensure the proper texture, it's important to use angel hair pasta. We like to serve the frittata warm or at room temperature, with a green salad.

8 large eggs
1 ounce Parmesan cheese, grated (½ cup)
3 tablespoons extra-virgin olive oil
3 tablespoons coarsely chopped jarred hot cherry peppers
2 tablespoons chopped fresh parsley
  Salt and pepper
8 ounces sweet Italian sausage, casings removed, crumbled
2 garlic cloves, sliced thin
3 cups water
6 ounces angel hair pasta, broken in half
3 tablespoons vegetable oil

1. Whisk eggs, Parmesan, olive oil, cherry peppers, parsley, ½ teaspoon salt, and ½ teaspoon pepper together in large bowl until egg is even yellow color; set aside.

2. Cook sausage in 10-inch nonstick skillet over medium heat, breaking up sausage with wooden spoon, until fat renders and sausage is about half cooked, 3 to 5 minutes. Stir in garlic and cook for 30 seconds. Remove skillet from heat. Transfer sausage mixture (some sausage will still be raw) to bowl with egg mixture and wipe out skillet.

3. Bring water, pasta, vegetable oil, and ¾ teaspoon salt to boil in now-empty skillet over high heat, stirring occasionally. Cook, stirring occasionally, until pasta is tender, water has evaporated, and pasta starts to sizzle in oil, 8 to 12 minutes. Reduce heat to medium and continue to cook pasta, swirling pan and scraping under edge of pasta with rubber spatula frequently to prevent sticking (do not stir), until bottom turns golden and starts to crisp, 5 to 7 minutes (lift up edge of pasta to check progress).

4. Using spatula, push some pasta up sides of skillet so entire pan surface is covered with pasta. Pour egg mixture over pasta. Using tongs, lift up loose strands of pasta to allow egg to flow toward pan, being careful not to pull up crispy bottom crust. Cover skillet and continue to cook over medium heat until bottom crust turns golden brown and top of frittata is just set (egg below very top will still be raw), 5 to 8 minutes. Slide frittata onto large plate. Invert frittata onto second large plate and slide it browned side up back into skillet. Tuck edges of frittata into skillet with rubber spatula. Continue to cook second side of frittata until light brown, 2 to 4 minutes longer.

5. Remove skillet from heat and let stand for 5 minutes. Using your hand or pan lid, invert frittata onto cutting board. Cut into wedges and serve.

Pasta Frittata with Broccoli Rabe

Omit cherry peppers, parsley, and sausage. Heat 2 teaspoons vegetable oil in 10-inch nonstick skillet over medium heat until shimmering. Add garlic and ⅛ teaspoon red pepper flakes and cook for 1 minute. Stir in 8 ounces broccoli rabe, trimmed and cut into ½-inch pieces, 1 tablespoon water, and ¼ teaspoon salt; cover skillet and cook until broccoli rabe is crisp-tender, 2 to 3 minutes. Remove skillet from heat and add 1 tablespoon white wine vinegar. Transfer broccoli rabe to bowl with egg mixture. Proceed with recipe from step 3, cooking pasta with remaining 7 teaspoons vegetable oil.

PASTA FRITTATA MADE WITHOUT LEFTOVERS

1. Add water, broken angel hair, and oil to skillet.

2. Once pasta is tender, keep cooking until water evaporates and pasta starts sizzling in oil.

3. After about 5 minutes, pasta will start to crisp (check progress by lifting up the edge).

4. Pour eggs over pasta, then gently pull up top strands to allow eggs to flow into center.

5. To brown second side, slide frittata onto plate, invert onto second plate, and return to skillet.

SKILLET BAKED ZITI

WHY THIS RECIPE WORKS: Baked ziti, a hearty combination of pasta, tomato sauce, and gooey cheese, can be time-consuming and fussy, between making the sauce, boiling the pasta, and then assembling and baking the dish. We were looking for a method that would give us the same delicious results but in less time and without watching over, or dirtying, a multitude of pots.

Instead of preparing the components of the dish separately, we found we could get all our cooking done in a skillet—including the pasta. How did we do it? We thinned the sauce with water so that the pasta cooked through in the sauce without drying out. (And the thin sauce reduced to a nicely thick consistency.) To start building the sauce, we sautéed lots of garlic with red pepper flakes, then added crushed tomatoes, water, and the ziti. When the pasta was almost tender (it would finish cooking in the oven), we added some heavy cream, for richness and body, and shredded mozzarella cheese. A little grated Parmesan boosted the cheesy flavor, and minced fresh basil and pepper were all the seasonings we needed to finish our skillet version of this family favorite.

Skillet Baked Ziti

SERVES 4

To complete this recipe in 30 minutes, preheat your oven before assembling the ingredients. If your skillet is not oven-safe, transfer the pasta mixture to a shallow 2-quart casserole dish before sprinkling with the cheese and baking. Packaged preshredded mozzarella is a real time-saver here. Penne can be used in place of the ziti.

- 1 tablespoon olive oil
- 6 medium garlic cloves, minced or pressed through a garlic press (about 2 tablespoons)
- ¼ teaspoon red pepper flakes
  Table salt
- 1 (28-ounce) can crushed tomatoes
- 3 cups water
- 12 ounces ziti (3¾ cups; see note)
- ½ cup heavy cream
- 1 ounce Parmesan cheese, grated (about ½ cup)
- ¼ cup minced fresh basil leaves
  Ground black pepper
- 4 ounces whole milk mozzarella cheese, shredded (about 1 cup; see note)

1. Adjust an oven rack to the middle position and heat the oven to 475 degrees.

2. Heat the oil in a 12-inch ovensafe nonstick skillet over medium-high heat until hot. Add the garlic, red pepper flakes, and ½ teaspoon salt and sauté until fragrant, about 1 minute. Add the crushed tomatoes, water, ziti, and ½ teaspoon salt. Cover and cook, stirring often and adjusting the heat as needed to maintain a vigorous simmer, until the ziti is almost tender, 15 to 18 minutes.

3. Stir in the cream, Parmesan, and basil. Season with salt and pepper to taste. Sprinkle the mozzarella evenly over the ziti. Transfer the skillet to the oven and bake until the cheese has melted and browned, about 10 minutes. Using potholders (the skillet handle will be hot), remove the skillet from the oven. Serve.

SKILLET CHICKEN, BROCCOLI, AND ZITI

WHY THIS RECIPE WORKS: This classic restaurant dish rarely lives up to its promise. Our challenge would lie in getting the flavors and textures just right: tender chicken, crisp broccoli, and a light, fresh sauce. We also wanted to streamline preparation for an easy weeknight dinner. First we browned pieces of skinless, boneless chicken breasts in the skillet, then we removed the chicken to build our sauce. We started with a base of sautéed onion, garlic, oregano, and red pepper flakes. And to keep all our work limited to the skillet, we cooked the pasta right in the sauce. The broccoli went in next, along with chopped sun-dried tomatoes. We then covered the skillet and simmered everything just until the broccoli turned bright green. At this point, we returned the chicken to the pan to finish cooking. A little heavy cream made the sauce silky without obscuring the flavor of the broccoli and chicken. Grated Asiago cheese enriched the sauce and gave it a pleasantly tangy flavor. And a little lemon juice added a bright note.

Skillet Chicken, Broccoli, and Ziti
SERVES 4

This recipe also works well with 8 ounces of penne. Parmesan cheese can be substituted for the Asiago.

1	pound boneless, skinless chicken breasts, cut into 1-inch pieces
	Table salt and ground black pepper
2	tablespoons vegetable or olive oil
1	medium onion, minced
3	medium garlic cloves, minced or pressed through a garlic press (about 1 tablespoon)
¼	teaspoon dried oregano
⅛	teaspoon red pepper flakes
8	ounces ziti (2½ cups; see note)
2¾	cups water
1⅔	cups low-sodium chicken broth
12	ounces broccoli florets (4 cups)
¼	cup oil-packed sun-dried tomatoes, rinsed and chopped coarse
½	cup heavy cream
1	ounce Asiago cheese, grated (about ½ cup), plus extra for serving (see note)
1	tablespoon juice from 1 lemon

1. Season the chicken with salt and pepper. Heat 1 tablespoon of the oil in a 12-inch nonstick skillet over medium-high heat until just smoking. Add the chicken in a single layer and cook for 1 minute without stirring. Stir the chicken and continue to cook until most, but not all, of the pink color has disappeared and the chicken is lightly browned around the edges, 1 to 2 minutes longer. Transfer the chicken to a clean bowl and set aside.

2. Add the remaining 1 tablespoon oil, the onion, and ½ teaspoon salt to the skillet. Return the skillet to medium-high heat and cook, stirring often, until the onion is softened, 2 to 5 minutes. Stir in the garlic, oregano, and red pepper flakes and cook until fragrant, about 30 seconds.

3. Add the ziti, 2 cups of the water, and the broth. Bring to a boil over high heat and cook until the liquid is very thick and syrupy and almost completely absorbed, 12 to 15 minutes.

4. Add the broccoli, sun-dried tomatoes, and the remaining ¾ cup water. Cover, reduce the heat to medium, and cook until the broccoli turns bright green and is almost tender, 3 to 5 minutes.

5. Uncover and return the heat to high. Stir in the cream, Asiago, and reserved chicken with any accumulated juices and continue to simmer, uncovered, until the sauce is thickened and the chicken is cooked and heated through, 1 to 2 minutes. Off the heat, stir in the lemon juice and season with salt and pepper to taste. Serve, passing more grated Asiago at the table, if desired.

SKILLET LASAGNA

WHY THIS RECIPE WORKS: Lasagna isn't usually a dish you can throw together at the last minute. Even with no-boil noodles, it takes a good amount of time to get the components just right. Our goal was to transform traditional baked lasagna into a stovetop skillet dish without losing any of its flavor or appeal.

We built a hearty, flavorful meat sauce with onions, garlic, red pepper flakes, and meatloaf mix (a more flavorful alternative to plain ground beef). A large can of diced tomatoes along with tomato sauce provided juicy tomato flavor and a nicely chunky texture. We scattered regular curly-edged lasagna noodles, broken into pieces, over the top of the sauce (smaller pieces are easier to eat and serve). We then diluted the sauce with a little water so that the noodles would cook through. After a 20-minute simmer with the lid on, the pasta was tender, the sauce was properly thickened, and it was time for the cheese. Stirring Parmesan into the dish worked well, but we discovered that the sweet creaminess of ricotta was lost unless we placed it in heaping tablespoonfuls on top of the lasagna. Replacing the lid and letting the cheese warm through for several minutes was the final step for this super-easy one-pan dish.

Skillet Lasagna
SERVES 4 TO 6

Meatloaf mix is a combination of ground beef, pork, and veal, sold prepackaged in many supermarkets. If it's unavailable, use ground beef. A skillet with a tight-fitting lid works best for this recipe. To make this dish a bit richer, sprinkle lasagna with additional shredded cheese, such as mozzarella or provolone, along with the Parmesan in step 4.

1 (28-ounce) can diced tomatoes
   Water
1 tablespoon olive oil
1 medium onion, minced
   Table salt
3 medium garlic cloves, minced or pressed through
   a garlic press (about 1 tablespoon)
⅛ teaspoon red pepper flakes
1 pound meatloaf mix (see note)
10 curly-edged lasagna noodles, broken into 2-inch lengths
1 (8-ounce) can tomato sauce
1 ounce Parmesan cheese, grated (½ cup),
   plus extra for serving
   Ground black pepper
1 cup ricotta cheese
3 tablespoons chopped fresh basil leaves

1. Pour the tomatoes with their juice into a 4-cup liquid measuring cup. Add water until the mixture measures 4 cups.

2. Heat the oil in a 12-inch nonstick skillet over medium heat until shimmering. Add the onion and ½ teaspoon salt and cook until the onion begins to brown, 6 to 8 minutes. Stir in the garlic and red pepper flakes and cook until fragrant, about 30 seconds. Add the ground meat and cook, breaking apart the meat, until no longer pink, about 4 minutes.

3. Scatter the pasta over the meat but do not stir. Pour the diced tomatoes with their juice and the tomato sauce over the pasta. Cover and bring to a simmer. Reduce the heat to medium-low and simmer, stirring occasionally, until the pasta is tender, about 20 minutes.

4. Remove the skillet from the heat and stir in all but 2 tablespoons of the Parmesan. Season with salt and pepper to taste. Dot with heaping tablespoons of the ricotta, cover, and let stand off the heat for 5 minutes. Sprinkle with the basil and the remaining 2 tablespoons Parmesan. Serve.

SKILLET CHICKEN FAJITAS

WHY THIS RECIPE WORKS: To create indoor chicken fajitas that didn't require a slew of compensatory garnishes to be tasty, we took a fresh look at the key ingredients. For well-charred, juicy chicken we marinated boneless, skinless breasts in a potent mix of smoked paprika, garlic, cumin, cayenne, and sugar before searing them on one side and finishing them gently in a low oven. We revamped the usual bland mix of bell pepper and onion by charring poblano chiles and thinly sliced onion, and then cooking them down with cream and lime. Finally, we finished the dish with moderate amounts of complementary garnishes: pickled radish, queso fresco, and minced cilantro.

Skillet Chicken Fajitas
SERVES 4

We like to serve these fajitas with crumbled queso fresco or feta in addition to the other garnishes listed.

CHICKEN
¼ cup vegetable oil
2 tablespoons lime juice
4 garlic cloves, peeled and smashed
1½ teaspoons smoked paprika
1 teaspoon sugar
1 teaspoon salt
½ teaspoon ground cumin
½ teaspoon pepper
¼ teaspoon cayenne pepper
1½ pounds boneless, skinless chicken breasts,
   trimmed and pounded to ½-inch thickness

RAJAS CON CREMA
1 pound (3 to 4) poblano chiles, stemmed,
   halved, and seeded
1 tablespoon vegetable oil
1 onion, halved and sliced ¼ inch thick
2 garlic cloves, minced
¼ teaspoon dried thyme
¼ teaspoon dried oregano
½ cup heavy cream
1 tablespoon lime juice
½ teaspoon salt
¼ teaspoon pepper

8–12 (6-inch) flour tortillas, warmed
¼ cup minced fresh cilantro
   Spicy Pickled Radishes (recipe follows)
   Lime wedges

1. FOR THE CHICKEN: Whisk 3 tablespoons oil, lime juice, garlic, paprika, sugar, salt, cumin, pepper, and cayenne together in bowl. Add chicken and toss to coat. Cover and let stand at room temperature for at least 30 minutes or up to 1 hour.

2. FOR THE RAJAS CON CREMA: Meanwhile, adjust oven rack to highest position and heat broiler. Line rimmed baking sheet with aluminum foil, then arrange poblanos skin side up on baking sheet and press to flatten. Broil until skin is charred and puffed, 4 to 10 minutes, rotating baking sheet halfway through cooking. Transfer poblanos to bowl, cover, and let steam for 10 minutes. Rub most of skin from poblanos (leaving a little attached for flavor); slice into ¼-inch-thick strips. Adjust oven racks to middle and lowest positions and heat oven to 200 degrees.

3. Heat oil in 12-inch nonstick skillet over high heat until just smoking. Add onion and cook until charred and just softened, about 3 minutes. Add garlic, thyme, and oregano and cook until fragrant, about 15 seconds. Add cream and cook, stirring frequently, until reduced and cream lightly coats onion, 1 to 2 minutes. Add poblano strips, lime juice, salt, and pepper and toss to coat. Transfer vegetables to bowl, cover with foil, and place on middle oven rack. Wipe out skillet with paper towels.

4. Remove chicken from marinade and wipe off excess. Heat remaining 1 tablespoon oil in now-empty skillet over high heat until just smoking. Add chicken and cook without moving it until bottom side is well charred, about 4 minutes. Flip chicken; transfer skillet to lower oven rack. Bake until chicken registers 160 degrees, 7 to 10 minutes. Transfer to cutting board and let rest for 5 minutes; do not wash out skillet.

5. Slice chicken crosswise into ¼-inch-thick strips. Return chicken strips to skillet and toss to coat with pan juices. To serve, spoon a few pieces of chicken into center of warmed tortilla and top with spoonful of vegetable mixture, cilantro, and pickled radishes. Serve with lime wedges.

Spicy Pickled Radishes

MAKES ABOUT 1¾ CUPS

If you'd like a less spicy version of these pickled radishes, omit the seeds from the jalapeño.

10	radishes, trimmed and sliced thin
½	cup lime juice (4 limes)
½	jalapeño chile, stemmed and sliced thin
1	teaspoon sugar
¼	teaspoon salt

Combine all ingredients in bowl. Cover and let stand at room temperature for 30 minutes (or refrigerate for up to 24 hours).

SKILLET CHICKEN POT PIE

WHY THIS RECIPE WORKS: Quick versions of chicken pot pie are often plagued by dried-out leftover chicken, bland sauce made with canned soup, and biscuits popped out of a tube. We saw no reason why pot pie couldn't be a whole lot better. We wanted moist chicken, a richly flavored sauce, and a homemade biscuit crust.

Instead of the refrigerated biscuit dough used in most recipes, we turned to homemade biscuits, and it was easy enough to put together a simple dough for baking powder biscuits. We just whisked the dry ingredients together and stirred in heavy cream, kneaded the dough briefly, and cut it into rounds (wedges would also work fine). We then popped the biscuits into the oven to bake, while we turned to the filling.

Next, we decided to contain all our cooking to a skillet for ease of preparation. We first sautéed skinless, boneless breasts in butter, keeping the heat at medium so the exterior wouldn't toughen. We set the chicken aside after it was browned and started the sauce in the skillet with onion, celery, thyme, vermouth, and chicken broth—ingredients that contributed lots of flavor. Flour thickened the liquid, and heavy cream gave it richness and a lush texture. Gently simmering the browned chicken in this sauce not only enhanced the flavor of the sauce but also kept the chicken juicy. Using frozen peas and carrots made quick work of the vegetables. All that was left to do was to assemble our pie by placing the hot biscuits over the filling in the skillet. Our flavorful, meaty stew with tender biscuits on top was not only delicious but also fast and easy.

Skillet Chicken Pot Pie with Biscuit Topping

SERVES 4

If you don't have time to make your own biscuits for the topping, use packaged refrigerated biscuits and bake them according to the package instructions. We prefer the flavor of Pillsbury Golden Homestyle Biscuits but you can use your favorite brand (you will need anywhere from four to eight biscuits depending on their size). This pot pie can be served in a large pie plate with the biscuits arranged on top, or served directly from the skillet.

BISCUITS

2	cups (10 ounces) unbleached all-purpose flour, plus extra for the work surface
2	teaspoons sugar
2	teaspoons baking powder
½	teaspoon table salt
1½	cups heavy cream

FILLING

1½	pounds boneless, skinless chicken breasts
	Table salt and ground black pepper
4	tablespoons (½ stick) unsalted butter
1	medium onion, minced
1	celery rib, sliced thin
¼	cup unbleached all-purpose flour
¼	cup dry vermouth or dry white wine
2	cups low-sodium chicken broth
½	cup heavy cream
1½	teaspoons minced fresh thyme leaves
2	cups frozen pea-carrot medley, thawed

1. FOR THE BISCUITS: Adjust an oven rack to the upper-middle position and heat the oven to 450 degrees. Line a baking sheet with parchment paper and set aside.

2. Whisk the flour, sugar, baking powder, and salt together in a large bowl. Stir in the cream with a wooden spoon until a dough forms, about 30 seconds. Turn the dough out onto a lightly floured work surface and gather into a ball. Knead the dough briefly until smooth, about 30 seconds.

3. Pat the dough into a ¾-inch-thick circle. Cut the biscuits into rounds using a 2½-inch biscuit cutter or cut into eight wedges using a knife.

4. Place the biscuits on the prepared baking sheet. Bake until golden brown, about 15 minutes. Set aside on a wire rack.

5. FOR THE FILLING: While the biscuits bake, pat the chicken dry with paper towels and season with salt and pepper. Melt 2 tablespoons of the butter in a 12-inch skillet over medium heat until the foam subsides. Brown the chicken lightly on both sides, about 5 minutes total. Transfer the chicken to a clean plate.

6. Add the remaining 2 tablespoons butter to the skillet and return to medium heat until melted. Add the onion, celery, and ½ teaspoon salt and cook until the onion is softened, about 5 minutes. Stir in the flour and cook, stirring constantly, until incorporated, about 1 minute.

7. Stir in the vermouth and cook until evaporated, about 30 seconds. Slowly whisk in the broth, cream, and thyme, and bring to a simmer. Nestle the chicken into the sauce, cover, and cook over medium-low heat until the thickest part of the breasts registers 160 to 165 degrees on an instant-read thermometer, 8 to 10 minutes.

8. Transfer the chicken to a plate. Stir the peas and carrots into the sauce and simmer until heated through, about 2 minutes. When the chicken is cool enough to handle, cut or shred it into bite-size pieces and return it to the skillet. Season the filling with salt and pepper to taste.

9. FOR SERVING: Transfer the filling to a large pie plate and arrange the biscuits over the top, or serve directly from the skillet, topping individual portions with the biscuits.

SKILLET TAMALE PIE

WHY THIS RECIPE WORKS: Tamale pie—lightly seasoned, tomatoey ground beef with cornbread topping—is easy to prepare and makes a satisfying supper. But in many recipes, the filling either tastes bland and one-dimensional or turns heavy. As for the cornbread topping, it's usually from a mix and tastes like it. We wanted a skillet tamale pie with a rich, well-seasoned filling and a cornbread topping with real corn flavor.

For the beef, we found 90 percent lean ground sirloin gave us a good balance of richness and flavor. We started by sautéing minced onion and garlic. For seasoning, we used a generous amount of chili powder, which we added to the aromatics in the skillet to "bloom," or intensify, its flavor. The addition of canned black beans made our pie heartier, and canned diced tomatoes contributed additional flavor and texture. Cheddar cheese stirred into the mixture enriched the filling and also helped thicken it, and some minced fresh cilantro contributed a bright, fresh note. And to finish our pie, we skipped the

cornbread mix and instead devised an easy homemade version. We spread the cornbread batter over the filling in the skillet, put the skillet in the oven to bake through, and the result was crunchy, corny topping that perfectly complemented the spicy tamale filling.

Skillet Tamale Pie
SERVES 4
Parsley can be substituted for the cilantro, if desired.

TAMALE FILLING
- 2 tablespoons vegetable oil
- 1 medium onion, minced
- 2 tablespoons chili powder
- Table salt
- 2 medium garlic cloves, minced or pressed through a garlic press (about 2 teaspoons)
- 1 pound 90 percent lean ground sirloin
- 1 (15-ounce) can black beans, drained and rinsed
- 1 (14.5-ounce) can diced tomatoes, drained
- 4 ounces cheddar cheese, shredded (about 1 cup)
- 2 tablespoons minced fresh cilantro leaves (see note)
- Ground black pepper

CORNBREAD TOPPING
- ¾ cup (3¾ ounces) unbleached all-purpose flour
- ¾ cup (3¾ ounces) yellow cornmeal
- 3 tablespoons sugar
- ¾ teaspoon table salt
- ¾ teaspoon baking powder
- ¼ teaspoon baking soda
- ¾ cup buttermilk
- 1 large egg
- 3 tablespoons unsalted butter, melted and cooled

1. Adjust an oven rack to the middle position and heat the oven to 450 degrees.

2. FOR THE TAMALE FILLING: Heat the oil in a 12-inch ovensafe skillet over medium heat until shimmering. Add the onion, chili powder, and ½ teaspoon salt and cook until the onion is softened, about 5 minutes. Stir in the garlic and cook until fragrant, about 30 seconds.

3. Stir in the ground sirloin, beans, and tomatoes and bring to a simmer, breaking up the meat with a wooden spoon, about 5 minutes. Stir the cheddar and cilantro into the filling and season with salt and pepper to taste.

4. FOR THE CORNBREAD TOPPING: Whisk the flour, cornmeal, sugar, salt, baking powder, and baking soda together in a large bowl. In a separate bowl, whisk the buttermilk and egg together. Stir the buttermilk mixture into the flour mixture until uniform. Stir in the butter until just combined.

5. Dollop the cornbread batter evenly over the filling and spread into an even layer. Bake until the cornbread is cooked through in the center, 10 to 15 minutes. Using potholders (the skillet handle will be hot), remove the skillet from the oven. Serve.

SKILLET BEEF STROGANOFF

WHY THIS RECIPE WORKS: Beef stroganoff is more often associated with bad banquet fare than with a hearty, satisfying dinner. But originally, this dish was quite elegant and was even made with filet mignon. Our goal was twofold: find a less expensive option for the beef to turn it into a within-reach weeknight supper, and bring the too-rich, often gloppy sauce back to its refined roots.

We started with the beef. Blade steaks shrank too much during cooking; sirloin tips became tender and held their shape well, but the pieces of meat crinkled up oddly. We solved that problem by pounding the meat before cutting it into strips. We first seared the meat and removed it from the pan, then sautéed mushrooms and onion in the same pan. To finish cooking the beef, we built a braising liquid with equal amounts of chicken and beef broth (beef broth alone tasted flat) and a little flour to thicken the sauce. We didn't want to overload the dish with seasonings—they would mask the flavor of the beef and mushrooms—but we found that some brandy was essential. We then returned the meat to the sauce to cook through.

To avoid cooking the noodles separately, we borrowed our method of cooking pasta directly in sauce and added the egg noodles to the braising liquid. When the noodles were tender and the beef was cooked through, we added the final touches, sour cream and lemon juice—but off the heat so that it wouldn't curdle.

Skillet Beef Stroganoff
SERVES 4

To prepare the beef, pound it with a meat pounder to an even ½-inch thickness. Slice the meat, with the grain, into 2-inch strips, then slice each piece against the grain into ½-inch strips. Brandy can ignite if added to a hot, empty skillet. Be sure to add the brandy to the skillet after stirring in the broth.

1½	pounds sirloin tips, pounded and cut into ½-inch strips (see note)
	Table salt and ground black pepper
4	tablespoons vegetable oil
10	ounces white mushrooms, wiped clean and sliced thin
1	medium onion, minced
2	tablespoons unbleached all-purpose flour
1½	cups low-sodium chicken broth
1½	cups beef broth
⅓	cup brandy (see note)
6	ounces wide egg noodles (4 cups)
⅔	cup sour cream
2	teaspoons juice from 1 lemon

1. Pat the beef dry with paper towels and season with salt and pepper. Heat 1 tablespoon of the oil in a 12-inch skillet over medium-high heat until just smoking. Cook half of the beef

until well browned, 3 to 4 minutes per side. Transfer to a medium bowl and repeat with 1 tablespoon more oil and the remaining beef.

2. Heat the remaining 2 tablespoons oil in the now-empty skillet until shimmering. Cook the mushrooms, onion, and ½ teaspoon salt until the liquid from the mushrooms has evaporated, about 8 minutes. (If the pan becomes too brown, pour the accumulated beef juices into the skillet.) Stir in the flour and cook for 30 seconds. Gradually stir in the broths, then the brandy, and return the beef and accumulated juices to the skillet. Bring to a simmer, cover, and cook over low heat until the beef is tender, 30 to 35 minutes.

3. Stir the noodles into the beef mixture, cover, and cook, stirring occasionally, until the noodles are tender, 10 to 12 minutes. Off the heat, stir in the sour cream and lemon juice. Season with salt and pepper to taste and serve.

SKILLET-ROASTED CHICKEN DINNER

WHY THIS RECIPE WORKS: Roasted chicken and potatoes are a favorite combination for Sunday dinner. But on a busy weeknight, who has time to prepare a meal that requires at least an hour in the oven? We wanted to come up with a skillet preparation that would give us juicy, tender chicken and crispy potatoes in about half an hour.

To start, we borrowed the restaurant method of browning meat on the stovetop and finishing it in the oven. We swapped in bone-in split breasts for the whole chicken and seared the chicken in a skillet, then transferred it to a baking dish in the oven to finish cooking through.

Meanwhile, we turned to the potatoes. We chose red potatoes because their skins are tender and don't require peeling. This saved some prep time, but we couldn't get them to cook in the same amount of time as the chicken. The microwave turned out to be the solution; while the chicken was browning, we tossed the potatoes with a little olive oil, salt, and pepper and microwaved them for a few minutes to jump-start the cooking process. Placing the potatoes in a single layer in the skillet—the same one in which we'd browned the chicken—helped them cook up creamy and moist inside while their exteriors became crispy and caramelized, just when it was time to take the chicken out of the oven. Before serving, we drizzled a mixture of olive oil, lemon juice, garlic, red pepper flakes, and thyme over our chicken and potatoes for an extra hit of moisture and flavor.

Skillet-Roasted Chicken Breasts with Potatoes
SERVES 4

To complete this recipe in 30 minutes, preheat your oven before assembling the ingredients. If the split breasts are different sizes, check the smaller ones a few minutes early and remove them from the oven if they are done.

4 (10 to 12-ounce) bone-in, split chicken breasts
  Table salt and ground black pepper
6 tablespoons olive oil
1½ pounds red potatoes (4 to 5 medium), cut into
  1-inch wedges
2 tablespoons juice from 1 lemon
1 medium garlic clove, minced or pressed through
  a garlic press (about 1 teaspoon)
1 teaspoon minced fresh thyme leaves
  Pinch red pepper flakes

1. Adjust an oven rack to the lowest position and heat the oven to 450 degrees.

2. Pat the chicken dry with paper towels and season with salt and pepper. Heat 1 tablespoon of the oil in a 12-inch nonstick skillet over medium-high heat until just smoking. Add the chicken, skin side down, and cook until deep golden, about 5 minutes.

3. Meanwhile, toss the potatoes with 1 more tablespoon of the oil, ½ teaspoon salt, and ¼ teaspoon pepper in a microwave-safe bowl. Cover tightly with plastic wrap. Microwave on high power until the potatoes begin to soften, 5 to 10 minutes, shaking the bowl (without removing the plastic) to toss the potatoes halfway through.

4. Transfer the chicken, skin side up, to a baking dish and bake until the thickest part of the breasts registers 160 to 165 degrees on an instant-read thermometer, 15 to 20 minutes.

5. While the chicken bakes, pour off any fat in the skillet, add 1 tablespoon more oil, and return to medium heat until shimmering. Drain the microwaved potatoes, then add to the skillet and cook, stirring occasionally, until golden brown and tender, about 10 minutes.

6. Whisk the remaining 3 tablespoons oil, the lemon juice, garlic, thyme, and red pepper flakes together. Drizzle the oil mixture over the chicken and potatoes before serving.

SKILLET CHICKEN AND RICE

WHY THIS RECIPE WORKS: There are lots of bad recipes out there for quick chicken and rice. Most contain leftover chicken, instant rice, and canned cream-of-something soup. We aimed to improve this dish and still deliver it quickly.

Boneless, skinless chicken breasts are definitely convenient, but we needed to prevent them from drying out. Dredging them in flour not only gave the chicken a nice brown crust but also kept the meat juicy inside. After browning the breasts on one side in a nonstick skillet, we removed them to deal with the rice. We first sautéed minced onion, garlic, and red pepper flakes in butter, then added the rice and stirred to coat the grains. Coating and toasting the rice this way before adding liquid is a technique that imparts deeper flavor and keeps the rice grains distinct and firm. We added a little white wine to the skillet for brightness. We then added chicken broth and returned the chicken to the skillet to cook through. When the chicken was done, we removed it from the skillet and finished cooking the rice. Off the heat, we added frozen peas, which cooked in a just couple of minutes, and stirred in lemon juice and sliced scallions for a fresh, bright flavor. In about 30 minutes, this dish was perfectly cooked, flavorful, and ready to serve. In addition, we developed two variations: one with cheddar and broccoli and the other with the spicy flavors of curry.

Skillet Chicken and Rice with Peas and Scallions
SERVES 4

Be sure to use chicken breasts that are roughly the same size to ensure even cooking.

4 (6- to 8-ounce) boneless, skinless chicken breasts,
  trimmed (see note)
  Table salt and ground black pepper
½ cup unbleached all-purpose flour
2 tablespoons vegetable oil
2 tablespoons unsalted butter
1 medium onion, minced
3 medium garlic cloves, minced or pressed through
  a garlic press (about 1 tablespoon)
  Pinch red pepper flakes
1½ cups long-grain white rice
½ cup dry white wine
4½ cups low-sodium chicken broth
1 cup frozen peas
5 scallions, sliced thin
2 tablespoons juice from 1 lemon
  Lemon wedges, for serving

1. Pat the chicken dry with paper towels and season with salt and pepper. Dredge the chicken in the flour to coat and shake off any excess. Heat the oil in a 12-inch nonstick skillet over medium-high heat just until smoking. Brown the chicken well on one side, about 5 minutes. Transfer the chicken to a plate and set aside.

2. Off the heat, add the butter to the skillet, and swirl to melt. Add the onion and ½ teaspoon salt and return to medium-high heat until softened, 2 to 5 minutes. Stir in the garlic and red pepper flakes and cook until fragrant, about 30 seconds. Stir in the rice thoroughly and let toast for about 30 seconds.

3. Stir in the wine and let the rice absorb it completely, about 1 minute. Stir in the broth, scraping up any browned bits. Nestle the chicken into the rice, browned side up, and add any accumulated juices. Cover and cook over medium heat until the thickest part of the chicken registers 160 to 165 degrees on an instant-read thermometer, about 10 minutes.

4. Transfer the chicken to a clean plate. Gently brush off and discard any rice clinging to the chicken, then tent the chicken with foil and set aside. Return the skillet of rice to medium-low heat, cover, and continue to cook, stirring occasionally, until the liquid is absorbed and the rice is tender, 8 to 12 minutes longer.

5. Off the heat, sprinkle the peas over the rice, cover, and let warm through, about 2 minutes. Add the scallions and lemon juice to the rice. Season with salt and pepper to taste and serve with the chicken and lemon wedges.

Skillet Chicken and Rice with Broccoli and Cheddar

SERVES 4

Be sure to use chicken breasts that are roughly the same size to ensure even cooking.

    4 (6- to 8-ounce) boneless, skinless chicken breasts,
       trimmed (see note)
       Table salt and ground black pepper
    ½ cup unbleached all-purpose flour
    3 tablespoons vegetable oil
    1 onion, minced
 1½ cups long-grain white rice
    3 garlic cloves, minced or pressed through
       a garlic press (about 1 tablespoon)
 4½ cups low-sodium chicken broth
    1 (10-ounce) package frozen broccoli florets, thawed
    4 ounces cheddar cheese, shredded (about 1 cup)
    1 teaspoon hot sauce

1. Pat the chicken dry with paper towels and season with salt and pepper. Dredge the chicken in the flour to coat and shake off any excess. Heat 2 tablespoons of the oil in a 12-inch nonstick skillet over medium-high heat until just smoking. Brown the chicken well on one side, about 5 minutes. Transfer the chicken to a plate and set aside.

2. Add the remaining 1 tablespoon oil to the skillet and return to medium-high heat until shimmering. Add the onion and ½ teaspoon salt and cook until softened, about 5 minutes. Stir in the rice and garlic and cook until fragrant, about 30 seconds.

3. Stir in the broth, scraping up any browned bits. Nestle the chicken and any accumulated juices into the rice, browned side up. Cover and cook over medium heat until the liquid is

absorbed and the thickest part of the chicken registers 160 to 165 degrees on an instant-read thermometer, about 10 minutes.

4. Transfer the chicken to a clean plate. Gently brush off and discard any rice clinging to the chicken, then tent the chicken with foil and set aside. Return the skillet of rice to medium-low heat, cover, and continue to cook, stirring occasionally, until the liquid is absorbed and the rice is tender, 8 to 12 minutes longer.

5. Off the heat, gently fold the broccoli, ½ cup of the cheddar, and the hot sauce into the rice and season with salt and pepper to taste. Sprinkle the remaining ½ cup cheddar over the top, cover, and let sit until the cheese melts, about 2 minutes. Serve with the chicken.

Skillet Curried Chicken and Rice

SERVES 4

Be sure to use chicken breasts that are roughly the same size to ensure even cooking. The heat level of curry varies from brand to brand. If your curry powder is very spicy, you may need to reduce the amount.

    4 (6- to 8-ounce) boneless, skinless chicken breasts,
       trimmed (see note)
       Table salt and ground black pepper
    ½ cup unbleached all-purpose flour
    3 tablespoons vegetable oil
    1 onion, minced
    1 tablespoon curry powder (see note)
 1½ cups long-grain white rice
    3 garlic cloves, minced or pressed through
       a garlic press (about 1 tablespoon)
 4½ cups low-sodium chicken broth
    1 cup frozen peas, thawed
    ¼ cup raisins
    ¼ cup minced fresh cilantro leaves

1. Pat the chicken dry with paper towels and season with salt and pepper. Dredge the chicken in the flour to coat and shake off any excess. Heat 2 tablespoons of the oil in a 12-inch non-stick skillet over medium-high heat until just smoking. Brown the chicken well on one side, about 5 minutes. Transfer the chicken to a plate and set aside.

2. Add the remaining 1 tablespoon oil to the skillet and return to medium-high heat until shimmering. Add the onion, curry powder, and ½ teaspoon salt and cook until softened, about 5 minutes. Stir in the rice and garlic and cook until fragrant, about 30 seconds.

3. Stir in the broth, scraping up any browned bits. Nestle the chicken and any accumulated juices into the rice, browned side up. Cover and cook over medium heat until the liquid is absorbed and the thickest part of the chicken registers 160 to 165 degrees on an instant-read thermometer, about 10 minutes.

4. Transfer the chicken to a clean plate. Gently brush off and discard any rice clinging to the chicken, then tent the chicken with foil and set aside. Return the skillet of rice to medium-low heat, cover, and continue to cook, stirring occasionally, until the liquid is absorbed and the rice is tender, 8 to 12 minutes longer.

5. Off the heat, sprinkle the peas and raisins over the rice, cover, and let warm through, about 2 minutes. Add the cilantro and gently fold into the rice. Season with salt and pepper to taste and serve with the chicken.

SKILLET JAMBALAYA

WHY THIS RECIPE WORKS: Jambalaya, a hearty mix of chicken, andouille sausage, shrimp, and rice, is typically made in a Dutch oven and can take at least an hour to prepare. We wanted a quicker, easier version without sacrificing any of the complex flavors of this Creole classic.

Bone-in, skin-on chicken thighs rather than the typical whole cut-up chicken called for in many recipes saved us time and fuss. To mimic long-simmered flavor, we browned the sausage in the skillet, added the chicken, then cooked the vegetables in some of the rendered fat. We then stirred the rice in to coat it with the fat for deep flavor. For our cooking liquid, we relied on chicken broth and clam juice (to complement the shrimp). To prevent the shrimp from overcooking, we cooked it for only a few minutes, then allowed it to finish cooking through off the heat (the residual heat is hot enough to cook it through). Entirely made in a skillet, this jambalaya makes a fast and satisfying supper.

Skillet Jambalaya
SERVES 4 TO 6

If you cannot find andouille sausage, either chorizo or linguiça can be substituted. For a spicier jambalaya, you can add ¼ teaspoon of cayenne pepper along with the vegetables, and/or serve it with hot sauce.

- 4 bone-in, skin-on chicken thighs (about 1½ pounds), trimmed
  Table salt and ground black pepper
- 5 teaspoons vegetable oil
- ½ pound andouille sausage, halved lengthwise and sliced into ¼-inch pieces (see note)
- 1 medium onion, chopped medium
- 1 medium red bell pepper, stemmed, seeded, and chopped medium
- 5 medium garlic cloves, minced or pressed through a garlic press (about 1½ tablespoons)
- 1½ cups long-grain white rice
- 1 (14.5-ounce) can diced tomatoes, drained
- 1 (8-ounce) bottle clam juice
- 2½ cups low-sodium chicken broth
- 1 pound large shrimp (31 to 40 per pound), peeled and deveined (see page 240)
- 2 tablespoons chopped fresh parsley leaves

1. Dry the chicken thoroughly with paper towels, then season generously with salt and pepper. Heat 2 teaspoons of the oil in a 12-inch nonstick skillet over medium-high heat until just smoking. Carefully lay the chicken thighs in the skillet, skin-side down, and cook until golden, 4 to 6 minutes. Flip the chicken over and continue to cook until the second side is golden, about 3 minutes. Remove the pan from the heat and transfer the chicken to a plate. Using paper towels, remove and discard the browned chicken skin.

2. Pour off all but 2 teaspoons of the fat left in the skillet and return to medium-high heat until shimmering. Add the andouille and cook until lightly browned, about 3 minutes; transfer the sausage to a small bowl and set aside.

3. Add the remaining 3 teaspoons oil to the skillet and return to medium heat until shimmering. Add the onion, bell pepper, garlic, and ½ teaspoon salt; cook, scraping the browned bits off the bottom of the skillet, until the onion is softened, about 5 minutes. Add the rice and cook until the edges turn translucent, about 3 minutes. Stir in the tomatoes, clam juice, and chicken broth; bring to a simmer. Gently nestle the chicken and any accumulated juices into the rice. Cover, reduce the heat to low, and cook until the chicken is tender and cooked through, 30 to 35 minutes.

4. Transfer the chicken to a plate and cover with foil to keep warm. Stir the shrimp and sausage into the rice and continue to cook, covered, over low heat for 2 more minutes. Remove the skillet from the heat and let stand, covered, until the shrimp are fully cooked and the rice is tender, about 5 minutes. Meanwhile, shred the chicken into bite-size pieces. Stir the parsley and shredded chicken into the rice, season with salt and pepper to taste, and serve.

ONE-DISH SUPPERS

POT ROAST

WHY THIS RECIPE WORKS: The long braise that a pot roast needs can result in either a succulent roast or a dry, bland disappointment. We wanted our pot roast to be fall-apart tender with a savory sauce—a meal that would be worth the wait.

We first determined that chuck-eye is the best choice for pot roast; its fat and connective tissue break down and keep the meat moist during the long oven stay. Browning the meat first was important for flavor as well as color. Caramelizing the vegetables with a little sugar added another layer of flavor. For the braising liquid, equal amounts of beef and chicken broth tasted best; and we added just enough water for the liquid to come about halfway up the sides of the roast and prevent it from drying out. Before we moved the roast into the oven, we covered the pot with foil and then covered with the lid for a tight seal, so no steam (or flavor) escaped. The secret to tenderness is in the cooking time. Cook the meat in the oven until it reaches 210 degrees internally, then cook it for an hour longer. The reward is moist, flavorful meat that is also remarkably tender.

Simple Pot Roast

SERVES 6 TO 8

Our favorite cut for pot roast is a chuck-eye roast. Most markets sell this roast with twine tied around the center; if necessary, do this yourself. Seven-bone and top-blade roasts are also good choices for this recipe. Remember to add only enough water to come halfway up the sides of these thinner roasts, and begin checking for doneness after 2 hours. If using a top-blade roast, tie it before cooking to keep it from falling apart. Mashed or boiled potatoes are a good accompaniment to pot roast.

    1   (3½-pound) boneless chuck-eye roast (see note)
        Table salt and ground black pepper
    2   tablespoons vegetable oil
    1   medium onion, chopped medium
    1   small carrot, chopped medium
    1   small celery rib, chopped medium
    2   medium garlic cloves, minced or pressed through
        a garlic press (about 2 teaspoons)
    2   teaspoons sugar
    1   cup low-sodium chicken broth
    1   cup beef broth
    1   sprig fresh thyme
1–1½   cups water
    ¼   cup dry red wine

1. Adjust an oven rack to the middle position and heat the oven to 300 degrees. Thoroughly pat the roast dry with paper towels; sprinkle generously with salt and pepper.

2. Heat the oil in a large Dutch oven over medium-high heat until shimmering but not smoking. Brown the roast thoroughly on all sides, reducing the heat if the fat begins to smoke, 8 to 10 minutes. Transfer the roast to a large plate; set aside. Reduce the heat to medium; add the onion, carrot, and celery to the pot and cook, stirring occasionally, until beginning to brown, 6 to 8 minutes. Add the garlic and sugar; cook until fragrant, about 30 seconds. Add the chicken and beef broths and thyme, scraping the bottom of the pan with a wooden spoon to loosen the browned bits. Return the roast and any accumulated juices to the pot; add enough water to come halfway up the sides of the roast. Place a large piece of foil over the pot and cover tightly with the lid; bring the liquid to a simmer over medium heat, then transfer the pot to the oven. Cook, turning the roast every 30 minutes, until fully tender and a meat fork or sharp knife easily slips in and out of the meat, 3½ to 4 hours.

3. Transfer the roast to a carving board; tent with foil to keep warm. Allow the liquid in the pot to settle for about 5 minutes, then use a wide spoon to skim the fat off the surface; discard the thyme sprig. Boil over high heat until reduced to about 1½ cups, about 8 minutes. Add the red wine and reduce again to 1½ cups, about 2 minutes. Season with salt and pepper to taste.

4. Using a chef's or carving knife, cut the meat into ½-inch-thick slices, or pull apart into large pieces; transfer the meat to a warmed serving platter and pour about ½ cup sauce over the meat. Serve, passing the remaining sauce separately.

Simple Pot Roast with Root Vegetables

Add 1½ pounds carrots, sliced ½ inch thick; 1½ pounds small red potatoes, halved if larger than 1½ inches in diameter; and 1 pound parsnips, sliced ½ inch thick, to Dutch oven after cooking beef for about 3 hours, submerging them in liquid. Continue to cook until vegetables are almost tender, 30 minutes to 1 hour longer. Transfer roast to carving board; tent with foil to keep warm. Allow liquid in pot to settle for about 5 minutes, then use wide spoon to skim fat off surface; remove thyme sprig. Add wine and salt and pepper to taste; boil over high heat until vegetables are tender, 5 to 10 minutes. Using slotted spoon, transfer vegetables to warmed serving platter. Using carving knife, cut meat into ½-inch-thick slices or pull apart into large pieces; transfer meat to bowl or platter with vegetables and pour about ½ cup sauce over meat and vegetables. Serve, passing remaining sauce separately.

OLD-FASHIONED BEEF POT ROAST

WHY THIS RECIPE WORKS: Pot roast can be boring and bland, full of dry, stringy meat, stubborn bits of fat, and wan gravy. We wanted a meltingly tender roast sauced in savory, full-bodied gravy. To start, we separated the roast into two lobes, which allowed us to remove the knobs of fat that stubbornly refused to render and also shortened the cooking time. Salting the roast prior to cooking improved its flavor and allowed us to skip browning later. Sautéing the onion, celery, carrot, and garlic before we added them to the pot gave them more depth of flavor. Some recipes use water as a pot roast cooking liquid but when we tried this, the gravy turned out as you'd expect—watery. We had better luck with beef broth.

Garlic, tomato paste, red wine, thyme, and bay leaves boosted the flavor even further. The resulting gravy boasted a complex character. Finally, sealing the pot with aluminum foil before securing the lid concentrated the steam for an even simmer and fork-tender meat.

Old-Fashioned Pot Roast

SERVES 6 TO 8

To separate the roast into two pieces, simply pull apart at the natural seam and then trim away any large knobs of fat. The roast can be made up to 2 days ahead: Follow the recipe through step 4, transferring the cooked roasts to a large bowl and straining the liquid as directed in step 5. Transfer the vegetables to the bowl with the roasts, cover with plastic wrap, cut vents in the plastic, and refrigerate overnight or up to 48 hours. One hour before serving, adjust the oven rack to the middle position and heat the oven to 325 degrees. Transfer the cold roasts to a carving board, slice them against the grain into ½-inch-thick slices, place them in a 13 by 9-inch baking dish, cover tightly with foil, and bake until heated through, about 45 minutes. While the roasts heat, puree the sauce and vegetables as directed in step 5. Bring the sauce to a simmer and finish as directed in step 6 before serving with the meat.

- 1 (3½ to 4-pound) boneless chuck-eye roast, pulled into 2 pieces at the natural seam and fat trimmed (see note)
  Table salt and ground black pepper
- 2 tablespoons unsalted butter
- 2 medium onions, halved and sliced thin (about 2 cups)
- 1 large carrot, peeled and chopped medium (about 1 cup)
- 1 celery rib, chopped medium (about ¾ cup)
- 2 medium garlic cloves, minced or pressed through a garlic press (about 2 teaspoons)

- 1 cup beef broth, plus 1 to 2 cups for the sauce
- ½ cup dry red wine, plus ¼ cup for the sauce
- 1 tablespoon tomato paste
- 1 bay leaf
- 1 sprig fresh thyme plus ¼ teaspoon chopped fresh thyme leaves
- 1 tablespoon balsamic vinegar

1. Sprinkle the pieces of meat with 1½ teaspoons salt, place on a wire rack set over a rimmed baking sheet and let stand at room temperature for 1 hour.

2. Adjust an oven rack to the lower-middle position and heat the oven to 300 degrees. Heat the butter in a heavy-bottomed Dutch oven over medium heat. When the foaming subsides, add the onions and cook, stirring occasionally, until softened and beginning to brown, 8 to 10 minutes. Add the carrot and celery and continue to cook, stirring occasionally, for 5 minutes longer. Add the garlic and cook until fragrant, about 30 seconds. Stir in 1 cup of the broth, ½ cup of the wine, the tomato paste, bay leaf, and thyme sprig; bring to a simmer.

3. Season the beef generously with pepper. Using three pieces of kitchen twine, tie each piece of meat into a loaf shape for even cooking.

4. Nestle the roasts on top of the vegetables. Place a large piece of foil over the pot and cover tightly with the lid; transfer the pot to the oven. Cook the roasts until fully tender and a sharp knife easily slips in and out of the meat, 3½ to 4 hours, turning the roasts halfway through cooking.

5. Transfer the roasts to a carving board and tent loosely with foil. Strain the liquid through a fine-mesh strainer into a 4-cup liquid measuring cup. Discard the thyme sprig and bay leaf. Transfer the vegetables to a blender. Allow the liquid to settle for 5 minutes, then skim any fat off the surface. Add the remaining beef broth as necessary to bring the total amount of liquid to 3 cups. Place the liquid in the blender with the vegetables and blend until smooth, about 2 minutes. Transfer the sauce to a medium saucepan and bring to a simmer over medium heat.

6. While the sauce heats, remove the twine from the roasts and slice them against the grain into ½-inch-thick slices. Transfer the meat to a large serving platter. Stir the chopped thyme, remaining ¼ cup wine, and the balsamic vinegar into the sauce and season with salt and pepper to taste. Serve immediately, passing the sauce separately.

Old-Fashioned Pot Roast with Root Vegetables

Follow the recipe for Old-Fashioned Pot Roast, adding 1 pound carrots, peeled and cut crosswise into 2-inch pieces; 1 pound parsnips, peeled and cut crosswise into 2-inch pieces; and 1½ pounds russet potatoes, peeled, halved lengthwise, and each half quartered, to the pot in step 4 after the roasts have cooked for 3 hours. Once the pot roast and vegetables are fully cooked, transfer any large pieces of carrot, parsnip, and potato to a serving platter using a slotted spoon, cover tightly with foil, and proceed with the recipe as directed.

PRESSURE-COOKER POT ROAST

WHY THIS RECIPE WORKS: Most pressure-cooker pot roast recipes sell themselves on speed alone, often producing over-cooked vegetables, fatty meat, and bland, watery gravy. In order to put the pressure cooker to work for us, we made a few key adjustments. First we split the roast into two smaller pieces to speed cooking and allow for better trimming of fat. We decreased the liquid in the pot to account for very little evaporation. And we also chose to purposefully overcook the vegetables and then puree them into the gravy for better flavor and consistency. Finally, we added some baking soda to encourage the flavorful Maillard reaction in the pressurized pot.

Pressure-Cooker Pot Roast
SERVES 6 TO 8

If using an electric pressure cooker, turn off the cooker immediately after the pressurized cooking time and let the pressure release naturally for 10 minutes; do not let the cooker switch to the warm setting. To adjust for differences among pressure cookers, cook the roasts for the recommended time, check for doneness, and, if needed, repressurize and cook up to 10 minutes longer. A half teaspoon of red wine vinegar can be substituted for the wine.

- 1 (3 ½- to 4-pound) boneless beef chuck-eye roast, pulled into 2 pieces at natural seam and trimmed of large pieces of fat
  Kosher salt and pepper
- 4 tablespoons unsalted butter, cut into 4 pieces
- 1 onion, sliced thick
- 1 celery rib, sliced thick
- 1 carrot, peeled and sliced thick
- ¼ teaspoon baking soda
- 1 cup beef broth
- 2 teaspoons soy sauce
- 2 bay leaves
- 1 tablespoon red wine
- 1 sprig fresh thyme

1. Using 3 pieces of kitchen twine per roast, tie each roast crosswise at equal intervals into loaf shape. Season roasts with salt and pepper and set aside.

2. Melt 2 tablespoons butter in pressure cooker over medium heat; refrigerate remaining 2 tablespoons butter. Add onion, celery, carrot, and baking soda to pot and cook until onion breaks down and liquid turns golden brown, about 5 minutes. Stir in broth, soy sauce, and bay leaves, scraping up any browned bits. Nestle roasts side by side on top of vegetables in cooker.

3. Lock lid in place and bring pot to high pressure over high heat, 3 to 8 minutes. As soon as indicator signals that pot has reached high pressure, reduce heat to medium-low and cook for 55 minutes, adjusting heat as needed to maintain high pressure.

4. Remove pot from heat and let pressure release naturally for 10 minutes. Quick-release any remaining pressure, then remove lid, allowing steam to escape away from you. Transfer roasts to carving board, tent with aluminum foil, and let rest for 20 minutes.

5. Meanwhile, strain liquid through fine-mesh strainer into fat separator; discard bay leaves. Transfer vegetables in strainer to blender. Let liquid settle for 5 minutes, then pour defatted liquid into blender with vegetables. Blend until smooth, about 1 minute. Transfer sauce to medium saucepan. Add wine, thyme sprig, and 2 tablespoons chilled butter and bring to boil over high heat. Cook until sauce is thickened and measures 2 cups, 5 to 8 minutes.

6. Remove twine from roasts and slice against grain into ½-inch-thick slices. Transfer meat to serving platter and season with salt to taste. Remove thyme sprig from sauce and season sauce with salt and pepper to taste. Spoon half of sauce over meat. Serve, passing remaining sauce separately.

CATALAN-STYLE BEEF STEW WITH MUSHROOMS

WHY THIS RECIPE WORKS: Supremely meaty and complexly flavored, Spanish beef stew is a little different than its American counterpart. It starts with a *sofrito*, a slow-cooked jamlike mixture of onions, spices, and herbs that builds a flavor-packed base. We normally use chuck-eye for stew, but swapped it out for boneless beef short ribs, determining that they gave us a beefier-tasting stew. We finished the stew with a mixture of toasted bread, toasted almonds, garlic, and parsley. This mixture, called a *picada*, brightened the stew's flavor and thickened the broth.

Catalan-Style Beef Stew with Mushrooms
SERVES 4 TO 6

While we developed this recipe with Albariño, a dry Spanish white wine, you can also use a Sauvignon Blanc. Remove the woody base of the oyster mushroom stems before cooking. An equal amount of quartered button mushrooms may be substituted for the oyster mushrooms. Serve the stew with boiled or mashed potatoes or rice.

STEW

- 2 tablespoons olive oil
- 2 large onions, chopped fine
- ½ teaspoon sugar
  Kosher salt and pepper
- 2 plum tomatoes, halved lengthwise, pulp grated on large holes of box grater, and skins discarded
- 1 teaspoon smoked paprika
- 1 bay leaf
- 1½ cups dry white wine
- 1½ cups water
- 1 large sprig fresh thyme
- ¼ teaspoon ground cinnamon
- 2½ pounds boneless beef short ribs, trimmed and cut into 2-inch cubes

PICADA

¼ cup whole blanched almonds

2 tablespoons olive oil

1 slice hearty white sandwich bread,
   crusts removed, torn into 1-inch pieces

2 garlic cloves, peeled

3 tablespoons minced fresh parsley

8 ounces oyster mushrooms, trimmed

1 teaspoon sherry vinegar

1. FOR THE STEW: Adjust oven rack to middle position and heat oven to 300 degrees. Heat oil in Dutch oven over medium-low heat until shimmering. Add onions, sugar, and ½ teaspoon salt; cook, stirring often, until onions are deeply caramelized, 30 to 40 minutes. Add tomatoes, smoked paprika, and bay leaf; cook, stirring often, until darkened and thick, 5 to 10 minutes.

2. Add wine, water, thyme sprig, and cinnamon to pot, scraping up any browned bits. Season beef with 1½ teaspoons salt and ½ teaspoon pepper and add to pot. Increase heat to high and bring to simmer. Transfer to oven and cook, uncovered. After 1 hour stir stew to redistribute meat, return to oven, and continue to cook, uncovered, until meat is tender, 1½ to 2 hours longer.

3. FOR THE PICADA: While stew is in oven, heat almonds and 1 tablespoon oil in 10-inch skillet over medium heat; cook, stirring often, until almonds are golden brown, 3 to 6 minutes. Using slotted spoon, transfer almonds to food processor. Return now-empty skillet to medium heat, add bread, and cook, stirring often, until toasted, 2 to 4 minutes; transfer to food processor with almonds. Add garlic and process until mixture is finely ground, about 20 seconds, scraping down bowl as needed. Transfer mixture to bowl, stir in parsley, and set aside.

4. Return again-empty skillet to medium heat. Heat remaining 1 tablespoon oil until shimmering. Add mushrooms and ½ teaspoon salt; cook, stirring often, until tender, 5 to 7 minutes. Transfer to bowl and set aside.

5. Remove bay leaf and thyme sprig. Stir picada, mushrooms, and vinegar into stew. Season with salt and pepper to taste and serve.

BEEF CARBONNADE

WHY THIS RECIPE WORKS: Most recipes for this Belgian beef, onion, and beer stew go in one of two directions: In one version, the recipe masks its genuine flavors and, in others, the recipes rigidly adhere to the "three ingredients only" rule, so the stew is pale and tasteless. We wanted hearty chunks of beef and sliced sweet onion in a thickened broth, laced with the malty flavor of beer. We found that top blade steak, which has a fair amount of marbling, provided the best texture and a "buttery" flavor that worked well alongside the onions and beer. White and red onions were too sweet in our stew; yellow onions worked better. The onions should be browned only lightly; overcaramelization caused them to disintegrate. Tomato paste gave the stew depth, as did garlic. Fresh thyme and bay leaves provided seasoning, and a splash of cider vinegar added the right level of acidity. Beer is a staple of Belgian cooking, and we found that it's less forgiving than wine when used in a stew. The light lagers we tried resulted in pale, watery stews; better were dark ales and stouts. But beer alone often made for bitter-tasting stew, so we included some broth; a combination of chicken and beef broth gave us more solid and complex flavor.

Belgian Beef, Beer, and Onion Stew (Carbonnade à la Flamande)

SERVES 6

Top blade steaks (also called blade or flatiron steaks) are our first choice, but any boneless roast from the chuck will work. If you end up using a chuck roast, look for the chuck-eye roast, an especially flavorful cut that can easily be trimmed and cut into 1-inch pieces. Buttered egg noodles or mashed potatoes make excellent accompaniments to carbonnade.

3½ pounds top blade steaks, 1 inch thick, trimmed
    of gristle and fat and cut into 1-inch pieces
    (see note and page 72)
    Table salt and ground black pepper

3 tablespoons vegetable oil

2 pounds yellow onions (about 4 medium),
   halved and sliced ¼ inch thick

1 tablespoon tomato paste

2 medium garlic cloves, minced or pressed through
   a garlic press (about 2 teaspoons)

3 tablespoons unbleached all-purpose flour

¾ cup low-sodium chicken broth

¾ cup beef broth

1½ cups (12-ounce bottle or can) dark beer or stout

4 sprigs fresh thyme, tied with kitchen twine

2 bay leaves

1 tablespoon cider vinegar

1. Adjust an oven rack to the lower-middle position and heat the oven to 300 degrees. Dry the beef thoroughly with paper towels, then season generously with salt and pepper. Heat 2 teaspoons of the oil in a large Dutch oven over medium-high heat until beginning to smoke; add about one third of the beef to the pot. Cook without moving the pieces until well browned, 2 to 3 minutes; using tongs, turn each piece and continue cooking until the second side is well browned, about 5 minutes longer. Transfer the browned beef to a medium bowl. Repeat with 2 teaspoons more oil and half of the remaining beef. (If the drippings in the bottom of the pot are very dark, add ½ cup of the chicken or beef broth and scrape the pan bottom with a wooden spoon to loosen the browned bits; pour the liquid into the bowl with the browned beef, then proceed.) Repeat once more with 2 teaspoons more oil and the remaining beef.

2. Add the remaining 1 tablespoon oil to the now-empty Dutch oven; reduce the heat to medium-low. Add the onions, ½ teaspoon salt, and the tomato paste; cook, scraping the bottom of the pot with a wooden spoon to loosen the browned bits, until the onions have released some moisture, about 5 minutes. Increase the heat to medium and continue to cook, stirring occasionally, until the onions are lightly browned, 12 to 14 minutes. Stir in the garlic and cook until fragrant, about 30 seconds. Add the flour and stir until the onions are evenly coated and the flour is lightly browned, about 2 minutes. Stir in the broths, scraping the pan bottom to loosen any browned bits; stir in the beer, thyme, bay leaves, vinegar, browned beef with any accumulated juices, and salt and pepper to taste. Increase the heat to medium-high and bring to a full simmer, stirring occasionally; cover partially, then place the pot in the oven. Cook until a fork inserted into the beef meets little resistance, 2 to 2½ hours.

3. Discard the thyme and bay leaves. Season with salt and pepper to taste and serve. (The stew can be cooled and refrigerated in an airtight container for up to 4 days; reheat over medium-low heat.)

NOTES FROM THE TEST KITCHEN

TRIMMING BLADE STEAKS

To trim blade steaks, halve each steak lengthwise, leaving the gristle on one half. Then simply cut the gristle away.

HUNGARIAN BEEF STEW

WHY THIS RECIPE WORKS: The Americanized versions of Hungarian goulash served in the United States bear little resemblance to the authentic dish. Sour cream has no place in the pot, nor do mushrooms, green peppers, or most herbs. We wanted the real deal—a simple dish of tender braised beef packed with paprika flavor.

To achieve the desired spicy intensity, some recipes call for as much as half a cup of paprika per three pounds of meat, but that much fine spice gave the dish a gritty, dusty texture. The chefs at a few Hungarian restaurants introduced us to paprika cream, a condiment as common in Hungarian cooking as the dried spice—but hard to find in the U.S. Instead, we created our own quick version by pureeing dried paprika with roasted red peppers and a little tomato paste and vinegar. This mixture imparted vibrant paprika flavor without any offensive grittiness.

As for the meat, after settling on chuck-eye roast, we bought a whole roast and cut it ourselves into uniform, large pieces to ensure even cooking. Since searing the meat first—normally standard stew protocol—competed with the paprika's brightness, we referred back to a trend we noticed in the goulash recipes gathered during research: skipping the sear. We tried this, softening the onions in the pot first, adding paprika paste, carrots, and then meat before placing the covered pot in the oven. Sure enough, the onions and meat provided enough liquid to stew the meat, and the bits of beef that cooked above the liquid line browned in the hot air. A bit of broth added near the end of cooking thinned out the stewing liquid to just the right consistency.

Hungarian Beef Stew
SERVES 6

Do not substitute hot, half-sharp, or smoked Spanish paprika for the sweet paprika in the stew, as they will compromise the flavor of the dish. Since paprika is vital to this recipe, it is best to use a fresh container. We prefer chuck-eye roast, but any boneless roast from the chuck will work. Cook the stew in a Dutch oven with a tight-fitting lid. (Alternatively, to ensure a tight seal, place a sheet of foil over the pot before adding the lid.) Serve the stew over boiled potatoes or egg noodles.

1   boneless chuck-eye roast (about 3½ pounds), trimmed
    of excess fat and cut into 1½-inch cubes (see note)
    Table salt
1   (12-ounce) jar roasted red peppers, drained and rinsed
    (about 1 cup)
⅓   cup sweet paprika (see note)
2   tablespoons tomato paste
1   tablespoon white vinegar

2 tablespoons vegetable oil

6 medium onions, minced (about 6 cups)

4 large carrots, peeled and cut into 1-inch-thick rounds (about 2 cups)

1 bay leaf

1 cup beef broth, warmed

¼ cup sour cream (optional)

Ground black pepper

1. Adjust an oven rack to the lower-middle position and heat the oven to 325 degrees. Sprinkle the meat evenly with 1 teaspoon salt and let stand for 15 minutes. Process the roasted peppers, paprika, tomato paste, and 2 teaspoons of the vinegar in a food processor until smooth, 1 to 2 minutes, scraping down the sides as needed.

2. Combine the oil, onions, and 1 teaspoon salt in a large Dutch oven; cover and set over medium heat. Cook, stirring occasionally, until the onions have softened but have not yet begun to brown, 8 to 10 minutes. (If the onions begin to brown, reduce the heat to medium-low and stir in 1 tablespoon water.)

3. Stir in the paprika mixture; cook, stirring occasionally, until the onions stick to the bottom of the pan, about 2 minutes. Add the beef, carrots, and bay leaf; stir until the beef is well coated. Using a rubber spatula, scrape down the sides of the pot. Cover the pot and transfer to the oven. Cook until the meat is almost tender and the surface of the liquid is ½ inch below the top of the meat, 2 to 2½ hours, stirring every 30 minutes. Remove the pot from the oven and add enough beef broth that the surface of the liquid is ¼ inch from the top of the meat (the beef should not be fully submerged). Return the covered pot to the oven and continue to cook until a fork slips easily in and out of the beef, about 30 minutes longer.

4. Skim the fat off the surface using a wide spoon; stir in the remaining 1 teaspoon vinegar and the sour cream (if using). Remove the bay leaf, season with salt and pepper to taste, and serve. (The stew can be cooled, covered tightly, and refrigerated in an airtight container for up to 2 days; wait to add the optional sour cream until after reheating. Before reheating, skim the hardened fat from the surface and add enough water to the stew to thin it slightly.)

BRAISED SHORT RIBS

WHY THIS RECIPE WORKS: Short ribs have great flavor and luscious texture, but their excess fat can be a problem since so much fat is rendered during the ribs' stint in the oven. Most recipes call for resting them in the braising liquid overnight, so that the fat solidifies into an easy-to-remove layer. However, most people don't plan their dinners days in advance and skimming such a large amount of fat off with a spoon doesn't work well enough. The meat and sauce come out greasy, no matter how diligent one's spoon-wielding. We wanted a silky, grease-free sauce and fork-tender short rib meat, all in a few hours.

The first task was to choose the right rib. Instead of traditional bone-in short ribs, we used boneless short ribs, which rendered significantly less fat than bone-in. While we didn't miss much flavor from the bones, we did want the body that the bones' connective tissue added. To solve this, we sprinkled a bit of gelatin into the sauce to restore suppleness. We also wanted to ramp up the richness of the sauce. We jump-started flavor by reducing wine with browned aromatics (onions, garlic, and carrots) before using the liquid to cook the meat. This added the right intensity, but we needed another cup of liquid to keep the meat half-submerged—the right level for braises. More wine yielded too much wine flavor; we used beef broth instead. As for the excess fat, the level was low enough that we could strain and defat the liquid in a fat separator. Reducing the liquid concentrated the flavors and made for a rich, luxurious sauce for our fork-tender boneless short ribs.

Braised Beef Short Ribs

SERVES 6

Make sure that the ribs are at least 4 inches long and 1 inch thick. If boneless ribs are unavailable, substitute 7 pounds of bone-in beef short ribs at least 4 inches long with 1 inch of meat above the bone and bone them yourself (see page 74).

3½ pounds boneless beef short ribs, trimmed of excess fat (see note)

   Table salt and ground black pepper

2 tablespoons vegetable oil

2 large onions, sliced thin from pole to pole (about 4 cups)

1 tablespoon tomato paste

6 medium garlic cloves, peeled

2 cups red wine, such as Cabernet Sauvignon or Côtes du Rhône

1 cup beef broth

4 large carrots, peeled and cut crosswise into 2-inch pieces

4 sprigs fresh thyme

1 bay leaf

¼ cup cold water

½ teaspoon powdered gelatin

1. Adjust an oven rack to the lower-middle position and heat the oven to 300 degrees. Pat the beef dry with paper towels and season with 2 teaspoons salt and 1 teaspoon pepper. Heat 1 tablespoon of the oil in a large Dutch oven over medium-high heat until smoking. Add half of the beef and cook, without stirring, until well browned, 4 to 6 minutes. Turn the beef and continue to cook on the second side until well browned, 4 to 6 minutes longer, reducing the heat if the fat begins to smoke. Transfer the beef to a medium bowl. Repeat with the remaining 1 tablespoon oil and the remaining meat.

2. Reduce the heat to medium, add the onions, and cook, stirring occasionally, until softened and beginning to brown, 12 to 15 minutes. (If the onions begin to darken too quickly, add 1 to 2 tablespoons water to the pan.) Add the tomato paste and cook, stirring constantly, until it browns on the sides and bottom of the pan, about 2 minutes. Add the garlic and cook until aromatic, about 30 seconds. Increase the heat to medium-high, add the wine, and simmer, scraping the bottom of the pan with a wooden spoon to loosen the browned bits, until reduced by half, 8 to 10 minutes. Add the broth, carrots, thyme, and bay leaf. Add the beef and any accumulated juices to the pot; cover and bring to a simmer. Transfer the pot to the oven and cook, using tongs to turn the meat twice during cooking, until a fork slips easily in and out of the meat, 2 to 2½ hours.

3. Place the water in a small bowl and sprinkle the gelatin on top; let stand for at least 5 minutes. Using tongs, transfer the meat and carrots to a serving platter and tent with foil. Strain the cooking liquid through a fine-mesh strainer into a fat separator or bowl, pressing on the solids to extract as much liquid as possible; discard the solids. Allow the liquid to settle for about 5 minutes and strain off the fat. Return the cooking liquid to the Dutch oven and cook over medium heat until reduced to 1 cup, 5 to 10 minutes. Remove from the heat and stir in the gelatin mixture; season with salt and pepper to taste. Pour the sauce over the meat and carrots and serve.

NOTES FROM THE TEST KITCHEN

BONING SHORT RIBS

1. With a chef's knife as close as possible to the bone, carefully remove the meat.

2. Trim the excess hard fat and silverskin from both sides of the meat.

SLOW-COOKER BRAISED SHORT RIBS

WHY THIS RECIPE WORKS: Beef short ribs, which contain lots of fat and connective tissue, are ideal for long, slow cooking. We wanted to develop a recipe for the slow cooker that would produce meaty ribs in a rich, oniony sauce.

Thoroughly browning the ribs first gave us a good start. Next we browned lots of onions. Instead of stock or broth, we chose beer as the braising liquid, and dark beer worked best. Since flavors tend to become muted after hours in a slow cooker, we intensified the taste and color of the sauce with tomato paste and soy sauce. But we thought the dish lacked balance. We found our solution in an unusual source: prunes. They melted into the sauce and were unidentifiable, but their sweetness balanced the other flavors nicely. Livened up just before serving with some Dijon mustard and fresh thyme, these slow-cooker short ribs had the rich, complex flavor we were looking for.

Slow-Cooker Beer-Braised Short Ribs

SERVES 4 TO 6

The only way to remove fat from the braising liquid is to prepare this recipe a day or two before you want to serve it. Luckily, the short ribs actually taste better if cooked in advance and then reheated in the defatted braising liquid.

5 pounds English-style beef short ribs (6 to 8 ribs), trimmed of excess fat Table salt and ground black pepper
2 tablespoons vegetable oil
2 tablespoons unsalted butter
3 pounds yellow onions (about 6 medium), halved and sliced thin
2 tablespoons tomato paste
2 (12-ounce) bottles dark beer

12 pitted prunes

2 tablespoons soy sauce

2 tablespoons Minute tapioca

2 bay leaves

2 teaspoons minced fresh thyme leaves

3 tablespoons Dijon mustard

2 tablespoons minced fresh parsley leaves

1. Season the ribs with salt and pepper. Heat the oil in a 12-inch skillet over medium-high heat until just smoking. Add half of the ribs, meaty side down, and cook until well browned, about 5 minutes. Turn each rib on one side and cook until well browned, about 1 minute. Repeat with the remaining sides. Transfer the ribs to a slow-cooker insert, arranging them meaty side down. Repeat with the remaining ribs.

2. Pour off all but 1 teaspoon fat from the skillet. Add the butter and reduce the heat to medium. When the butter has melted, add the onions and cook, stirring occasionally, until well browned, 25 to 30 minutes. Stir in the tomato paste and cook, coating the onions with the tomato paste, until the paste begins to brown, about 5 minutes. Stir in the beer, bring to a simmer, and cook, scraping the browned bits from the pan bottom with a wooden spoon, until the foaming subsides, about 5 minutes. Remove the skillet from the heat and stir in the prunes, soy sauce, tapioca, bay leaves, and 1 teaspoon of the thyme. Transfer to the slow-cooker insert.

3. Set the slow cooker on low, cover, and cook until the ribs are fork-tender, 10 to 11 hours. (Alternatively, cook on high for 4 to 5 hours.) Transfer the ribs to a baking dish and strain the liquid through a fine-mesh strainer into a bowl. Cover and refrigerate for at least 8 hours or up to 2 days.

4. When ready to serve, use a spoon to skim off the hardened fat from the liquid. Place the short ribs, meaty side down, and the liquid in a Dutch oven and reheat over medium heat until warmed through, about 20 minutes. Transfer the ribs to a serving platter. Whisk the mustard and remaining 1 teaspoon thyme into the sauce and season with salt and pepper to taste. Pour 1 cup of the sauce over the ribs. Sprinkle with the parsley and serve, passing the remaining sauce separately.

NEW ENGLAND–STYLE HOME-CORNED BEEF AND CABBAGE

WHY THIS RECIPE WORKS: Corned beef and cabbage is a hearty winter favorite, but too many recipes result in overly salty beef and washed-out, mushy vegetables. To control the salt level in our beef, we eschewed commercially corned beef and set out to cure our own with an easy dry rub. We cooked our corned beef in the oven so it would benefit from the oven's slow, steady, and gentle heat. Cooking the vegetables separately in the meat's broth (while the meat rested) allowed the vegetables to be enriched by the meat's juices, but still retain their own flavor.

New England–Style Home-Corned Beef and Cabbage

SERVES 8

Leave a bit of fat attached to the brisket for better texture and flavor. A similar size point-cut brisket can be used in this recipe. The meat is cooked fully when it is tender, the muscle fibers have loosened visibly, and a skewer slides in with minimal resistance. Serve this dish with horseradish, either plain or mixed with whipped cream or sour cream, or with grainy mustard.

CORNED BEEF

½ cup kosher salt

1 tablespoon cracked black peppercorns

1 tablespoon dried thyme

2¼ teaspoons ground allspice

1½ teaspoons paprika

2 bay leaves, crumbled

1 (4- to 5-pound) beef brisket, flat cut, trimmed

VEGETABLES

1½ pounds carrots, peeled and halved crosswise, thick end halved lengthwise

1½ pounds small red potatoes

1 small rutabaga (1 pound), peeled and halved crosswise; each half cut into 6 chunks

1 small head green cabbage (2 pounds), uncored, cut into 8 wedges

1. FOR THE CORNED BEEF: Combine salt, peppercorns, thyme, allspice, paprika, and bay leaves in bowl.

2. Using metal skewer, poke about 30 holes on each side of brisket. Rub each side evenly with salt mixture. Place brisket in 2-gallon zipper-lock bag, forcing out as much air as possible. Place in 13 by 9-inch baking dish, cover with second, similar-size pan, and weight with 2 bricks or heavy cans of similar weight. Refrigerate for 5 to 7 days, turning once a day.

3. Rinse brisket and pat it dry. Place brisket in Dutch oven and cover brisket with water by 1 inch. Bring to boil over high heat, skimming any scum that rises to surface. Reduce heat to medium-low, cover, and simmer until skewer inserted in thickest part of brisket slides in and out with ease, 2 to 3 hours.

4. Adjust oven rack to middle position and heat oven to 200 degrees. Transfer meat to large platter, ladle 1 cup cooking liquid over meat, cover with aluminum foil, and place in oven to keep warm.

5. FOR THE VEGETABLES: Add carrots, potatoes, and rutabaga to Dutch oven and bring to a boil over high heat. Reduce heat to medium-low, cover, and simmer until vegetables begin to soften, about 7 minutes.

6. Add cabbage, increase heat to high and return to boil. Reduce heat to medium-low, cover, and simmer until all vegetables are tender, 13 to 18 minutes.

7. Meanwhile, remove meat from oven, transfer to carving board, and slice against grain into ¼-inch slices. Return meat to platter. Transfer vegetables to meat platter, moisten with additional broth, and serve.

HOME-CORNED BEEF WITH VEGETABLES

WHY THIS RECIPE WORKS: Making corned beef at home is actually quite simple. And though the process takes several days, it's almost entirely hands-off. After comparing wet-curing and dry-curing methods, we chose to go with the wet cure, which was considerably faster and easier, with no need for daily flipping. We soaked a flat-cut brisket for six days in a brine made with table and pink curing salts, which improved both the flavor and color of the meat. The remainder of the seasonings included brown sugar, garlic cloves, allspice berries, bay leaves, and coriander seeds—all of which put the meat a notch above commercial corned beef. After the soak, the seasoning had penetrated to the core of the meat. To break down the brisket's abundant collagen, we gently simmered the meat in a low oven after first bringing it to a simmer on the stovetop, which helped cut cooking time. As for the classic corned beef accompaniments, we added carrots, potatoes, and cabbage to the pot while the meat rested so that they simmered briefly in the seasoned cooking liquid. To add some last-minute subtle but clear depth to the dish, we filled a cheesecloth bundle with more garlic and curing spices and steeped it in the cooking liquid before serving.

Home-Corned Beef With Vegetables

SERVES 8 TO 10

Pink curing salt #1, which can be purchased online or in stores specializing in meat curing, is a mixture of table salt and nitrites; it is also called Prague Powder #1, Insta Cure #1, or DQ Curing Salt #1. In addition to the pink salt, we use table salt here. If using Diamond Crystal kosher salt, increase the salt to 1½ cups; if using Morton kosher salt, increase to 1⅛ cups.

This recipe requires six days to corn the beef, and you will need cheesecloth. Look for a uniformly thick brisket to ensure that the beef cures evenly. The brisket will look gray after curing but will turn pink once cooked.

CORNED BEEF
- 1 (4½- to 5-pound) beef brisket, flat cut
- ¾ cup salt
- ½ cup packed brown sugar
- 2 teaspoons pink curing salt #1
- 6 garlic cloves, peeled
- 6 bay leaves
- 5 allspice berries
- 2 tablespoons peppercorns
- 1 tablespoon coriander seeds

VEGETABLES
- 6 carrots, peeled, halved crosswise, thick ends halved lengthwise
- 1½ pounds small red potatoes, unpeeled
- 1 head green cabbage (2 pounds), uncored, cut into 8 wedges

1. FOR THE CORNED BEEF: Trim fat on surface of brisket to ⅛ inch. Dissolve salt, sugar, and curing salt in 4 quarts water in large container. Add brisket, 3 garlic cloves, 4 bay leaves, allspice berries, 1 tablespoon peppercorns, and coriander seeds to brine. Weigh brisket down with plate, cover, and refrigerate for 6 days.

2. Adjust oven rack to middle position and heat oven to 275 degrees. Remove brisket from brine, rinse, and pat dry with paper towels. Cut 8-inch square triple thickness of cheesecloth. Place remaining 3 garlic cloves, remaining 2 bay leaves, and remaining 1 tablespoon peppercorns in center of cheesecloth and tie into bundle with kitchen twine. Place brisket, spice bundle, and 2 quarts water in Dutch oven. (Brisket may not lie flat but will shrink slightly as it cooks.)

3. Bring to simmer over high heat, cover, and transfer to oven. Cook until fork inserted into thickest part of brisket slides in and out with ease, 2½ to 3 hours.

4. Remove pot from oven and turn off oven. Transfer brisket to large ovensafe platter, ladle 1 cup of cooking liquid over meat, cover, and return to oven to keep warm.

5. FOR THE VEGETABLES: Add carrots and potatoes to pot and bring to simmer over high heat. Reduce heat to medium-low, cover, and simmer until vegetables begin to soften, 7 to 10 minutes.

6. Add cabbage to pot, increase heat to high, and return to simmer. Reduce heat to low, cover, and simmer until all vegetables are tender, 12 to 15 minutes.

7. While vegetables cook, transfer beef to carving board and slice ¼ inch thick against grain. Return beef to platter. Using slotted spoon, transfer vegetables to platter with beef. Moisten with additional broth and serve.

SIMPLE POT-AU-FEU

WHY THIS RECIPE WORKS: For a pot-au-feu brimming with tradition but suited to today's modern kitchen, we needed a pared-down shopping list. Boneless chuck roast beat out harder-to-find cuts of meat for its relative tenderness and big meaty flavor. Marrow bones gave the broth a buttery, beefy quality when cooked together with the meat, onion, and celery. Gently simmering the broth kept it perfectly clear. We transferred the pot to the oven partially covered to cook low and slow and, in the meantime, stirred together a sauce reminiscent of traditional pot-au-feu accompaniments. The zesty, bright combination of parsley, Dijon, chives, white wine vinegar, minced cornichon pickles, and pepper was deepened with the addition of the soft, beefy marrow extracted from the bones after cooking.

Simple Pot-au-Feu

SERVES 6 TO 8

Marrow bones (also called soup bones) can be found in the freezer section or the meat counter at most supermarkets. Use small red potatoes measuring 1 to 2 inches in diameter.

MEAT

- 1 (3½- to 4-pound) boneless beef chuck-eye roast, pulled into two pieces at natural seam and trimmed
  Kosher salt
- 1½ pounds marrow bones
- 1 onion, quartered
- 1 celery rib, sliced thin
- 3 bay leaves
- 1 teaspoon black peppercorns

PARSLEY SAUCE

- ⅔ cup minced fresh parsley
- ¼ cup Dijon mustard
- ¼ cup minced fresh chives

- 3 tablespoons white wine vinegar
- 10 cornichons, minced
- 1½ teaspoons pepper

VEGETABLES

- 1 pound small red potatoes, unpeeled, halved
- 6 carrots, peeled and halved crosswise, thick halves quartered lengthwise, thin halves halved lengthwise
- 1 pound asparagus, trimmed
  Kosher salt and pepper

  Flake sea salt

1. FOR THE MEAT: Adjust oven rack to lower-middle position and heat oven to 300 degrees. Season beef with 1 tablespoon salt. Using 3 pieces of kitchen twine per piece, tie each into loaf shape for even cooking. Place beef, bones, onion, celery, bay leaves, and peppercorns in Dutch oven. Add 4 cups cold water (water should come halfway up roasts). Bring to simmer over high heat. Partially cover pot and transfer to oven. Cook until beef is fully tender and sharp knife easily slips in and out of meat (meat will not be shreddable), 3¼ to 3¾ hours, flipping beef over halfway through cooking.

2. FOR THE PARSLEY SAUCE: While beef cooks, combine all ingredients in bowl. Cover and set aside.

3. Remove pot from oven and turn off oven. Transfer beef to large platter, cover tightly with aluminum foil, and return to oven to keep warm. Transfer bones to cutting board and use end of spoon to extract marrow. Mince marrow into paste and add 2 tablespoons to parsley sauce (reserve any remaining marrow for other applications). Using ladle or large spoon, skim fat from surface of broth and discard fat. Strain broth through fine-mesh strainer into large liquid measuring cup; add water to make 6 cups. Return broth to pot. (Meat can be returned to broth, cooled, and refrigerated for up to 2 days. Skim fat from cold broth, then gently reheat and proceed with recipe.)

NOTES FROM THE TEST KITCHEN

ONE CUT IS PLENTY

Most pot-au-feu recipes call for a slew of different meats. To streamline, we settled on just one cut: chuck-eye roast, which delivers tender, beefy-tasting meat with a fraction of the effort and expense required by many classic renditions. This roast also needs very little prep.

Pull roast apart at seam to make two smaller roasts and then trim any large knobs of fat.

4. FOR THE VEGETABLES: Add potatoes to broth and bring to simmer over high heat. Reduce heat to medium and simmer for 6 minutes. Add carrots and cook 10 minutes longer. Add asparagus and continue to cook until all vegetables are tender, 3 to 5 minutes longer.

5. Using slotted spoon, transfer vegetables to large bowl. Toss with 3 tablespoons parsley sauce and season with salt and pepper to taste. Season broth with salt to taste.

6. Transfer beef to cutting board, remove twine, and slice against grain ½ inch thick. Arrange servings of beef and vegetables in large, shallow bowls. Dollop beef with parsley sauce, drizzle with ⅓ cup broth, and sprinkle with flake sea salt. Serve, passing remaining parsley sauce and flake sea salt separately.

CUBAN-STYLE PICADILLO

WHY THIS RECIPE WORKS: Authentic recipes for this Cuban dish of spiced ground meat, sweet raisins, and briny olives call for hand-chopping or grinding the beef, but we wanted our version to be a quick weeknight option. Store-bought ground beef provided a convenient substitute, and supplementing it with ground pork added a subtle sweetness and complexity. Browning the meat made it tough, so we skipped the extra step and soaked the meat in a mixture of baking soda and water to ensure it remained tender. Pinching it off into sizable 2-inch chunks before adding it to the pot to simmer also kept it moist. For the spices, we settled on just oregano, cumin, and cinnamon, then bloomed them to heighten their flavor. Beef broth added a savory boost, while drained canned whole tomatoes and white wine provided brightness. Raisins and green olives were a given, but we also liked briny capers and a splash of red wine vinegar.

Cuban-Style Picadillo
SERVES 6

We prefer this dish prepared with raisins, but they can be replaced with 2 tablespoons of brown sugar added with the broth in step 2. Picadillo is traditionally served with rice and black beans. It can also be topped with chopped parsley, toasted almonds, and/or chopped hard-cooked egg.

1 pound 85 percent lean ground beef
1 pound ground pork
2 tablespoons water
½ teaspoon baking soda
  Salt and pepper
1 green bell pepper, stemmed, seeded, and cut into 2-inch pieces
1 onion, halved and cut into 2-inch pieces
2 tablespoons vegetable oil
1 tablespoon dried oregano
1 tablespoon ground cumin
½ teaspoon ground cinnamon
6 garlic cloves, minced
1 (14.5-ounce) can whole tomatoes, drained and chopped coarse
¾ cup dry white wine
½ cup beef broth
½ cup raisins
3 bay leaves
½ cup pimento-stuffed green olives, chopped coarse
2 tablespoons capers, rinsed
1 tablespoon red wine vinegar, plus extra for seasoning

1. Toss beef and pork with water, baking soda, ½ teaspoon salt, and ¼ teaspoon pepper in bowl until thoroughly combined. Set aside for 20 minutes. Meanwhile, pulse bell pepper and onion in food processor until chopped into ¼-inch pieces, about 12 pulses.

2. Heat oil in large Dutch oven over medium-high heat until shimmering. Add chopped vegetables, oregano, cumin, cinnamon, and ¼ teaspoon salt; cook, stirring frequently, until vegetables are softened and beginning to brown, 6 to 8 minutes. Add garlic and cook, stirring constantly, until fragrant, about 30 seconds. Add tomatoes and wine and cook, scraping up any browned bits, until pot is almost dry, 3 to 5 minutes. Stir in broth, raisins, and bay leaves and bring to simmer.

3. Reduce heat to medium-low, add meat mixture in 2-inch chunks to pot, and bring to gentle simmer. Cover and cook, stirring occasionally with 2 forks to break meat chunks into ¼- to ½-inch pieces, until meat is cooked through, about 10 minutes.

4. Discard bay leaves. Stir in olives and capers. Increase heat to medium-high and cook, stirring occasionally, until sauce is thickened and coats meat, about 5 minutes. Stir in vinegar and season with salt, pepper, and extra vinegar to taste. Serve.

Cuban-Style Picadillo with Fried Potatoes

After pulsing vegetables in food processor, toss 1 pound russet potatoes, peeled and cut into ½-inch pieces, with 1 tablespoon vegetable oil in medium bowl. Cover and microwave until potatoes are just tender, 4 to 7 minutes, tossing halfway through microwaving. Line surface of large plate with double layer of coffee filters and lightly spray with vegetable oil spray. Drain potatoes well, transfer to coffee filters, and spread in even layer. Let cool for 10 minutes; proceed with recipe from step 2. After step 3, heat 1 cup vegetable oil in large saucepan over medium-high heat until shimmering. Add cooled potatoes and cook, stirring constantly until deep golden brown, 3 to 5 minutes. Using slotted spoon, transfer potatoes to paper towel–lined plate and set aside. Add potatoes to pot with vinegar in step 4.

SHEPHERD'S PIE

WHY THIS RECIPE WORKS: Shepherd's pie, a hearty mix of meat, gravy, and mashed potatoes, can take the better part of a day to prepare. And while the dish is indeed satisfying, traditional versions are simply too rich. We wanted to scale back its preparation and lighten the dish to fit in better with modern sensibilities. Per other modern recipes, we chose ground beef as our filling over ground lamb. To prevent the beef from turning dry and crumbly, we tossed it with a little baking soda (diluted in water) before browning it. This step raises the pH level of the beef, resulting in more tender meat. An onion and mushroom gravy, spiked with Worcestershire sauce, complemented the beef filling. For the mashed potatoes, we took our cue from an Irish dish called champ and cut way back on the dairy in favor of fresh scallions, which made for a lighter, more flavorful topping that was a good match for the meat filling underneath.

Shepherd's Pie
SERVES 4 TO 6

This recipe was developed with 93 percent lean ground beef. Using ground beef with a higher percentage of fat will make the dish too greasy.

- 1½ pounds 93 percent lean ground beef
- 2 tablespoons plus 2 teaspoons water
  Salt and pepper
- ½ teaspoon baking soda
- 2½ pounds russet potatoes, peeled and cut into 1-inch chunks
- 4 tablespoons unsalted butter, melted
- ½ cup milk
- 1 large egg yolk
- 8 scallions, green parts only, sliced thin
- 2 teaspoons vegetable oil
- 1 onion, chopped
- 4 ounces white mushrooms, trimmed and chopped
- 1 tablespoon tomato paste
- 2 garlic cloves, minced
- 2 tablespoons Madeira or ruby port
- 2 tablespoons all-purpose flour
- 1¼ cups beef broth
- 2 teaspoons Worcestershire sauce
- 2 sprigs fresh thyme
- 1 bay leaf
- 2 carrots, peeled and chopped
- 2 teaspoons cornstarch

1. Toss beef with 2 tablespoons water, 1 teaspoon salt, ¼ teaspoon pepper, and baking soda in bowl until thoroughly combined. Let sit for 20 minutes.

2. Meanwhile, place potatoes in medium saucepan; add water to just cover and 1 tablespoon salt. Bring to boil over high heat. Reduce heat to medium-low and simmer until potatoes are soft and tip of paring knife inserted into potato meets no resistance, 8 to 10 minutes. Drain potatoes and return to saucepan. Return saucepan to low heat and cook, shaking pot occasionally, until any surface moisture on potatoes has evaporated, about 1 minute. Remove pan from heat and mash potatoes well with potato masher. Stir in butter. Whisk together milk and egg yolk in small bowl, then stir into potatoes. Stir in scallions and season with salt and pepper to taste. Cover and set aside.

3. Heat oil in broiler-safe 10-inch skillet over medium heat until shimmering. Add onion, mushrooms, ½ teaspoon salt, and ¼ teaspoon pepper; cook, stirring occasionally, until vegetables are just starting to soften and dark bits form on bottom of skillet, 4 to 6 minutes. Stir in tomato paste and garlic; cook until bottom of skillet is dark brown, about 2 minutes. Add Madeira and cook, scraping up any browned bits, until evaporated, about 1 minute. Stir in flour and cook for 1 minute. Add broth, Worcestershire, thyme sprigs, bay leaf, and carrots; bring to boil, scraping up any browned bits. Reduce heat to medium-low, add beef in 2-inch pieces to broth and bring to gentle simmer. Cover and cook until beef is cooked through, 10 to 12 minutes, stirring and breaking up meat chunks with 2 forks

halfway through cooking. Stir cornstarch and remaining 2 teaspoons water together in bowl. Stir cornstarch mixture into filling and continue to simmer for 30 seconds. Remove thyme sprigs and bay leaf. Season with salt and pepper to taste.

4. Adjust oven rack 5 inches from broiler element and heat broiler. Place mashed potatoes in large zipper-lock bag and snip off 1 corner to create 1-inch opening. Pipe potatoes in even layer over filling, making sure to cover entire surface. Smooth potatoes with back of spoon, then use tines of fork to make ridges over surface. Place skillet on rimmed baking sheet and broil until potatoes are golden brown and crusty and filling is bubbly, 10 to 15 minutes. Let cool for 10 minutes before serving.

CHICKEN AND DUMPLINGS

WHY THIS RECIPE WORKS: Chicken and dumplings make chicken pot pie look easy: There's no disguising a leaden dumpling. Our goals were to develop a dumpling that was light yet substantial, and tender yet durable; and to develop a well-rounded recipe that, like chicken pot pie, included vegetables, therein providing the cook with a complete meal in one dish.

Dumplings can contain myriad ingredients, and there are just as many different ways to mix them. We tried them all—with disastrous results. But when we stumbled on a unique method of adding warm liquid rather than cold to the flour and fat, our dumplings were great—firm but light and fluffy. The reason? The heat expands and sets the flour so that the dumplings don't absorb liquid in the stew. The best-tasting dumplings were made with all-purpose flour, whole milk, and the chicken fat left from browning the chicken.

For the filling, we chose bone-in, skin-on chicken thighs for their deep flavor and added enough vegetables to make this dish into a meal. After browning the chicken and vegetables separately, we simmered them in the sauce until the chicken was done and the sauce thickened. We added some peas and parsley, then steamed the dumplings on top of everything until the dumplings turned light and tender.

Chicken and Dumplings

SERVES 6 TO 8

Don't use low-fat or fat-free milk in this recipe. Be sure to reserve 3 tablespoons of chicken fat for the dumplings in step 4; however, if you prefer not to use chicken fat, unsalted butter can be substituted. Start the dumpling dough only when you're ready to top the stew with the dumplings.

STEW

- 5 pounds bone-in, skin-on chicken thighs (about 12 thighs)
  Table salt and ground black pepper
- 4 teaspoons vegetable oil
- 4 tablespoons (½ stick) unsalted butter
- 4 carrots, peeled and sliced ¼ inch thick
- 2 celery ribs, sliced ¼ inch thick
- 1 medium onion, minced
- 6 tablespoons unbleached all-purpose flour
- ¼ cup dry sherry
- 4½ cups low-sodium chicken broth
- ¼ cup whole milk (see note)
- 1 teaspoon minced fresh thyme leaves
- 2 bay leaves
- 1 cup frozen green peas
- 3 tablespoons minced fresh parsley leaves

DUMPLINGS

- 2 cups unbleached all-purpose flour
- 1 tablespoon baking powder
- 1 teaspoon table salt
- 1 cup whole milk (see note)
- 3 tablespoons reserved chicken fat (see note)

1. FOR THE STEW: Pat the chicken dry with paper towels, then season with salt and pepper. Heat 2 teaspoons of the oil in a large Dutch oven over medium-high heat until just smoking. Add half of the chicken and cook until golden on both sides, about 10 minutes. Transfer the chicken to a plate and remove the browned skin. Pour off the chicken fat and reserve. Return the pot to medium-high heat and repeat with the remaining 2 teaspoons oil and the remaining chicken. Pour off and reserve any chicken fat.

2. Add the butter to the Dutch oven and melt over medium-high heat. Add the carrots, celery, onion, and ¼ teaspoon salt and cook until softened, about 7 minutes. Stir in the flour. Whisk in the sherry, scraping up any browned bits. Stir in the broth, milk, thyme, and bay leaves. Nestle the chicken, with any accumulated juices, into the pot. Cover and simmer until the chicken is fully cooked and tender, about 1 hour.

3. Transfer the chicken to a carving board. Discard the bay leaves. Allow the sauce to settle for a few minutes, then skim the fat from the surface using a wide spoon. Shred the chicken, discarding the bones, then return it to the stew.

4. FOR THE DUMPLINGS: Stir the flour, baking powder, and salt together. Microwave the milk and chicken fat in a microwave-safe bowl on high power until just warm (do not overheat), about 1 minute. Stir the warmed milk mixture into the flour mixture with a wooden spoon until incorporated and smooth.

5. Return the stew to a simmer, stir in the peas and parsley, and season with salt and pepper to taste. Following the photos, drop golf ball–sized dumplings over the top of the stew, about ¼ inch apart (you should have about 18 dumplings). Reduce the heat to low, cover, and cook until the dumplings have doubled in size, 15 to 18 minutes. Serve.

NOTES FROM THE TEST KITCHEN

ADDING THE DUMPLINGS

1. Gather a golf ball–sized portion of the dumpling batter onto a soup spoon, then push the dumpling onto the stew using a second spoon.

2. Cover the stew with the dumplings, leaving about ¼ inch between each.

3. When fully cooked, the dumplings will have doubled in size.

LIGHTER CHICKEN AND DUMPLINGS

WHY THIS RECIPE WORKS: A thick stew topped with sturdy dumplings makes a good cold-weather comfort food, but we wanted a version with dumplings as airy as drop biscuits in a light broth full of clean, concentrated chicken flavor.

For a streamlined rich and chickeny broth and tender meat, we poached browned chicken thighs in store-bought broth. To give our broth body, we added chicken wings to the pot. Boiling the wings converts the connective tissue in chicken wings to gelatin and thickens the broth. Dry sherry gave the broth complexity.

For light, airy dumplings sturdy enough to hold together in broth, we made some changes to our drop biscuit recipe—cutting back the buttermilk and eliminating the baking powder (which had led to overrising) were two steps in the right direction. Adding an egg white kept our dumplings from turning mushy. To help keep the dumplings intact, we waited until the broth was simmering to add them, which reduced their time in the broth and helped keep them whole. Finally, wrapping a kitchen towel around the lid of the Dutch oven trapped the moisture before it had a chance to drip down and saturate our light-as-air dumplings.

Lighter Chicken and Dumplings
SERVES 6

We strongly recommend buttermilk for the dumplings, but you can substitute ½ cup plain yogurt thinned with ¼ cup milk. If you want to include white meat (and don't mind losing a bit of flavor in the process), replace 2 chicken thighs with 2 boneless, skinless chicken breast halves (about 8 ounces each). Brown the chicken breasts along with the thighs and remove them from the stew once they reach an internal temperature of 160 to 165 degrees, 20 to 30 minutes. The collagen in the wings helps thicken the stew; do not omit or substitute. Since the wings yield only about 1 cup of meat, using their meat is optional.

STEW

- 2½ pounds bone-in, skin-on chicken thighs, trimmed
  Table salt and ground black pepper
- 2 teaspoons vegetable oil
- 2 small onions, minced
- 2 carrots, peeled and cut into ¾-inch pieces
- 1 celery rib, chopped fine
- ¼ cup dry sherry
- 6 cups low-sodium chicken broth
- 1 teaspoon minced fresh thyme leaves
- 1 pound chicken wings
- ¼ cup chopped fresh parsley leaves

DUMPLINGS

- 2 cups (10 ounces) unbleached all-purpose flour
- 1 teaspoon sugar
- 1 teaspoon table salt
- ½ teaspoon baking soda
- ¾ cup cold buttermilk (see note)
- 4 tablespoons (½ stick) unsalted butter, melted and cooled
- 1 large egg white

1. FOR THE STEW: Pat the chicken thighs dry with paper towels and season with 1 teaspoon salt and ¼ teaspoon pepper. Heat the oil in a large Dutch oven over medium-high heat until shimmering. Add the chicken thighs, skin side down, and cook until the skin is crisp and well browned, 5 to 7 minutes. Using tongs, turn the chicken pieces and brown the second side, 5 to 7 minutes longer; transfer to a large plate. Discard all but 1 teaspoon fat from the pot.

2. Add the onions, carrots, and celery to the pot. Cook, stirring occasionally, until caramelized, 7 to 9 minutes. Stir in the sherry, scraping up any browned bits. Stir in the broth and thyme. Return the chicken thighs, along with any accumulated juices, to the pot and add the chicken wings. Bring to a simmer, cover, and cook until the thigh meat offers no resistance when poked with the tip of a paring knife but still clings to the bones, 45 to 55 minutes.

3. Remove the pot from the heat and transfer the chicken to a cutting board. Allow the broth to settle for 5 minutes, then skim the fat from the surface using a wide spoon or ladle. When cool enough to handle, remove and discard the skin from the chicken. Using your fingers or a fork, pull the meat from the chicken thighs (and wings, if desired) and cut into 1-inch pieces. Return the meat to the pot.

4. FOR THE DUMPLINGS: Whisk the flour, sugar, salt, and baking soda in a large bowl. Combine the buttermilk and melted butter in a medium bowl, stirring until the butter forms small clumps. Whisk in the egg white. Add the buttermilk mixture to the dry ingredients and stir with a rubber spatula until just incorporated and the batter pulls away from the sides of the bowl.

5. Return the stew to a simmer, stir in the parsley, and season with salt and pepper to taste. Using a greased tablespoon measure (or #60 portion scoop), scoop level amounts of batter and drop them into the stew, spacing the dumplings about ¼ inch apart (you should have about 24 dumplings). Wrap the lid of the Dutch oven with a clean kitchen towel (keeping the towel away from the heat source) and cover the pot. Simmer gently until the dumplings have doubled in size and a toothpick inserted into the center comes out clean, 13 to 16 minutes. Serve immediately. (The stew can be prepared through step 3 up to 2 days in advance; bring the stew back to a simmer before proceeding with the recipe.)

BEST CHICKEN STEW

WHY THIS RECIPE WORKS: While recipes for chicken stew are few and far between, the ones we've come across are either too fussy or too fancy, or seem more soup than stew, with none of the complexity and depth we expect from the latter. We wanted to develop a chicken stew recipe that would satisfy like the beef kind—one with succulent bites of chicken, tender vegetables, and a truly robust gravy.

To start, we created an ultraflavorful gravy using chicken wings, which we later discarded. Browning the wings lent deep chicken flavor to the stew, and since wings are more about skin and bones than about meat, discarding them after they'd enriched the gravy didn't seem wasteful. A few strips of bacon, crisped in the pot before we browned the wings in the rendered fat, lent porky depth and just a hint of smoke. Soy sauce and anchovy paste, though unusual ingredients for chicken stew, lent more savory depth (without making the stew taste salty or fishy). Reducing the liquid with the aromatics at the beginning of cooking and then cooking the stew

uncovered further concentrated the flavor. To finish our hearty, savory stew, we added a splash of fresh white wine for a touch of brightness and a sprinkle of parsley for freshness.

Best Chicken Stew
SERVES 6 TO 8

Mashed anchovy fillets (rinsed and dried before mashing) can be used instead of anchovy paste. Use small red potatoes measuring 1½ inches in diameter.

2 pounds boneless, skinless chicken thighs, halved crosswise and trimmed
  Kosher salt and pepper
3 slices bacon, chopped
1 pound chicken wings, halved at joint
1 onion, chopped fine
1 celery rib, minced
2 garlic cloves, minced
2 teaspoons anchovy paste
1 teaspoon minced fresh thyme
5 cups chicken broth
1 cup dry white wine, plus extra for seasoning
1 tablespoon soy sauce
3 tablespoons unsalted butter, cut into 3 pieces
⅓ cup all-purpose flour
1 pound small red potatoes, unpeeled, quartered
4 carrots, peeled and cut into ½-inch pieces
2 tablespoons chopped fresh parsley

1. Adjust oven rack to lower-middle position and heat oven to 325 degrees. Arrange chicken thighs on baking sheet and lightly season both sides with salt and pepper; cover with plastic wrap and set aside.

2. Cook bacon in large Dutch oven over medium-low heat, stirring occasionally, until fat renders and bacon browns, 6 to 8 minutes. Using slotted spoon, transfer bacon to medium bowl. Add chicken wings to pot, increase heat to medium, and cook until well browned on both sides, 10 to 12 minutes; transfer wings to bowl with bacon.

3. Add onion, celery, garlic, anchovy paste, and thyme to fat in pot; cook, stirring occasionally, until dark fond forms on pan bottom, 2 to 4 minutes. Increase heat to high; stir in 1 cup broth, wine, and soy sauce, scraping up any browned bits; and bring to boil. Cook, stirring occasionally, until liquid evaporates and vegetables begin to sizzle again, 12 to 15 minutes. Add butter and stir to melt; sprinkle flour over vegetables and stir to combine. Gradually whisk in remaining 4 cups broth until smooth. Stir in wings and bacon, potatoes, and carrots; bring to simmer. Transfer to oven and cook, uncovered, for 30 minutes, stirring once halfway through cooking.

4. Remove pot from oven. Use wooden spoon to draw gravy up sides of pot and scrape browned fond into stew. Place over high heat, add thighs, and bring to simmer. Return pot to oven, uncovered, and continue to cook, stirring occasionally, until chicken offers no resistance when poked with fork and vegetables are tender, about 45 minutes longer. (Stew can be refrigerated for up to 2 days.)

5. Discard wings and season stew with up to 2 tablespoons extra wine. Season with salt and pepper to taste, sprinkle with parsley, and serve.

NOTES FROM THE TEST KITCHEN

BUILDING A RICH, FLAVORFUL GRAVY

1. Brown chopped bacon, then sear halved wings in rendered fat to develop meaty depth. Set bacon and wings aside.

2. Sauté aromatics, thyme, and anchovy paste in fat to create rich fond. Add chicken broth, wine, and soy sauce, then boil until liquid evaporates.

3. Cook reserved bacon and wings (with potatoes and carrots) in more broth. This extracts flavor from meats and body-enhancing collagen from wings (later discarded).

CHICKEN POT PIE

WHY THIS RECIPE WORKS: As homey as chicken pot pie sounds, this dish is a production. You've got to cook and cut up a chicken, make a sauce, parcook vegetables, and also prepare, chill, and roll out pie crust. We wanted to streamline the dish and get it on the table in 90 minutes, tops. And, we wanted a completely homemade pie (no prefab crust) full of tender, juicy chicken and bright vegetables.

To start, we swapped out a whole chicken for easy-to-poach chicken breasts—and we used the poaching liquid as the base of our sauce. But to boost the sauce's flavor, we turned to a few ingredients rich in glutamates, naturally occurring flavor compounds that accentuate savory qualities. Sautéed mushrooms, soy sauce, and tomato paste did the trick, turning into caramelized fond that gave our sauce deep flavor. Sautéing the vegetables—a medley of onions, carrots, and celery—while the chicken rested, also boosted the filling's flavor. (Later we'd add quick-cooking frozen peas straight to the filling to warm through.)

For the pot pie topping, we replaced traditional pastry with a savory crumble topping, enriched with grated cheese and pepper. To increase the crunch factor, we baked the crumble separately from the filling, then scattered it over the pot pie and slid it into the oven to warm through. Minutes later, our homemade pot pie emerged bubbling, fragrant, and topped with a crunchy, flavorful crust.

Chicken Pot Pie with Savory Crumble Topping
SERVES 6

This recipe relies on two unusual ingredients: soy sauce and tomato paste. Do not omit them. They don't convey their distinct tastes but greatly deepen the savory flavor of the filling. When making the topping, do not substitute milk or half-and-half for the heavy cream.

CHICKEN AND FILLING

- 1½ pounds boneless, skinless chicken breasts and/or thighs
- 3 cups low-sodium chicken broth
- 2 tablespoons vegetable oil
- 1 medium onion, minced
- 3 medium carrots, peeled and cut crosswise into ¼-inch-thick slices (about 1 cup)
- 2 small celery ribs, chopped fine
  Table salt and ground black pepper
- 10 ounces cremini mushrooms, stems trimmed, caps wiped clean and sliced thin
- 1 teaspoon soy sauce (see note)
- 1 teaspoon tomato paste (see note)
- 4 tablespoons (½ stick) unsalted butter
- ½ cup unbleached all-purpose flour
- 1 cup whole milk
- 2 teaspoons juice from 1 lemon
- 3 tablespoons minced fresh parsley leaves
- ¾ cup frozen baby peas

CRUMBLE TOPPING

- 2 cups (10 ounces) unbleached all-purpose flour
- 2 teaspoons baking powder
- ¾ teaspoon table salt
- ½ teaspoon ground black pepper
- ⅛ teaspoon cayenne pepper
- 6 tablespoons (¾ stick) unsalted butter, cut into ½-inch cubes and chilled
- 1 ounce Parmesan cheese, finely grated (about ½ cup)
- ¾ cup plus 2 tablespoons heavy cream (see note)

1. FOR THE CHICKEN: Bring the chicken and broth to a simmer in a covered Dutch oven over medium heat. Cook until the chicken is just done, 8 to 12 minutes. Transfer the cooked chicken to a large bowl. Pour the broth through a fine-mesh strainer into a liquid measuring cup and reserve. Do not wash the Dutch oven. Meanwhile, adjust an oven rack to the upper-middle position and heat the oven to 450 degrees.

2. FOR THE TOPPING: Combine the flour, baking powder, salt, black pepper, and cayenne in a large bowl. Sprinkle the butter pieces over the top of the flour. Using your fingers, rub the butter into the flour mixture until it resembles coarse cornmeal. Stir in the Parmesan. Add the cream and stir until just combined. Crumble the mixture into irregularly shaped pieces ranging from ½ to ¾ inch onto a parchment-lined rimmed baking sheet. Bake until fragrant and starting to brown, 10 to 13 minutes. Set aside.

3. FOR THE FILLING: Heat 1 tablespoon of the oil in the now-empty Dutch oven over medium heat until shimmering. Add the onion, carrots, celery, ¼ teaspoon salt, and ¼ teaspoon pepper; cover and cook, stirring occasionally, until just tender, 5 to 7 minutes. While the vegetables are cooking, shred the chicken into small bite-size pieces. Transfer the cooked vegetables to the bowl with the chicken; set aside.

4. Heat the remaining 1 tablespoon oil in the again-empty Dutch oven over medium heat until shimmering. Add the mushrooms; cover and cook, stirring occasionally, until the mushrooms have released their juices, about 5 minutes. Remove the cover, stir in the soy sauce and tomato paste. Increase the heat to medium-high and cook, stirring frequently, until the liquid has evaporated, the mushrooms are well browned, and a dark fond begins to form on the surface of the pan, about 5 minutes. Transfer the mushrooms to the bowl with the chicken and vegetables. Set aside.

5. Heat the butter in the again-empty Dutch oven over medium heat. When the foaming subsides, stir in the flour and cook for 1 minute. Slowly whisk in the reserved chicken broth and the milk. Bring to a simmer, scraping the pan bottom with a wooden spoon to loosen the browned bits, then continue to simmer until the sauce fully thickens, about 1 minute. Season with salt and pepper to taste. Remove from the heat and stir in the lemon juice and 2 tablespoons of the parsley.

6. Stir the chicken-vegetable mixture and peas into the sauce. Pour the mixture into a 13 by 9-inch baking dish or casserole dish of similar size. Scatter the crumble topping evenly over the filling. Bake on a rimmed baking sheet until the filling is bubbling and the topping is well browned, 12 to 15 minutes. Sprinkle with the remaining 1 tablespoon parsley and serve.

GREEK SPINACH AND FETA PIE

WHY THIS RECIPE WORKS: The roots of this savory dish run deep in Greek culture, yet most stateside versions are nothing more than soggy layers of phyllo with a sparse, bland filling. We wanted a casserole-style pie with a perfect balance of zesty spinach filling and shatteringly crisp, flaky phyllo crust—and we didn't want it to take all day. Using store-bought phyllo was an easy timesaver. Among the various spinach options (baby, frozen, mature curly-leaf), tasters favored the bold flavor of fresh curly-leaf spinach that had been microwaved, coarsely chopped, and squeezed of excess moisture. Crumbling the feta into fine pieces ensured a salty tang in every bite, while the addition of Greek yogurt buffered the assertiveness of the feta. We found that Pecorino Romano (a good stand-in for the traditional Greek hard sheep's milk cheese) added complexity to the filling and, when sprinkled between the sheets of phyllo, helped the flaky layers hold together. Using a baking sheet rather than a baking dish allowed excess moisture to easily evaporate, ensuring a crisp crust.

Greek Spinach and Feta Pie (Spanakopita)

SERVES 6 TO 8 AS A MAIN COURSE OR 10 TO 12 AS AN APPETIZER

It is important to rinse the feta; this step removes some of its salty brine, which would overwhelm the spinach. Full-fat sour cream can be substituted for whole-milk Greek yogurt.

Phyllo dough is also available in larger 14 by 18-inch sheets; if using, cut them in half to make 14 by 9-inch sheets. Don't thaw the phyllo in the microwave; let it sit in the refrigerator overnight or on the countertop for 4 to 5 hours. The filling can be made up to 24 hours in advance and refrigerated. The assembled, unbaked spanakopita can be frozen on a baking sheet, wrapped well in plastic wrap, or cut in half crosswise and frozen in smaller sections on a plate. To bake, unwrap and increase the baking time by 5 to 10 minutes.

FILLING

- 1¼ pounds curly-leaf spinach, stemmed
- ¼ cup water
- 12 ounces feta cheese, rinsed, patted dry, and crumbled into fine pieces (about 3 cups)
- ¾ cup whole-milk Greek yogurt
- 4 scallions, sliced thin
- 2 large eggs, beaten
- ¼ cup minced fresh mint leaves
- 2 tablespoons minced fresh dill leaves
- 3 medium garlic cloves, minced or pressed through a garlic press (about 1 tablespoon)
- 1 teaspoon grated zest plus 1 tablespoon juice from 1 lemon
- 1 teaspoon ground nutmeg
- ½ teaspoon ground black pepper
- ¼ teaspoon table salt
- ⅛ teaspoon cayenne pepper

PHYLLO LAYERS

- 7 tablespoons unsalted butter, melted
- 8 ounces (14 by 9-inch) phyllo, thawed
- 1½ ounces Pecorino Romano cheese, grated (¾ cup)
- 2 teaspoons sesame seeds (optional)

1. FOR THE FILLING: Place the spinach and water in a large bowl and cover with a large dinner plate. Microwave until the spinach is wilted and decreased in volume by half, about 5 minutes. Using potholders, remove the bowl from the microwave and keep covered for 1 minute. Carefully remove the plate and transfer the spinach to a colander. Using the back of a rubber spatula, gently press the spinach against the colander to release the excess liquid. Transfer the spinach to a cutting board and chop coarse. Transfer the spinach to a clean kitchen towel and squeeze to remove excess water. Place the drained spinach in a large bowl. Add the remaining filling ingredients and mix until thoroughly combined.

2. FOR THE PHYLLO LAYERS: Adjust an oven rack to the lower-middle position and heat the oven to 425 degrees. Line a rimmed baking sheet with parchment paper. Using a pastry brush, lightly brush a 14 by 9-inch rectangle in the center of the parchment with melted butter to cover an area the same size as the phyllo. Lay 1 phyllo sheet on the buttered parchment and brush thoroughly with melted butter. Repeat with 9 more phyllo sheets, brushing each with butter (you should have a total of 10 layers of phyllo).

3. Spread the spinach mixture evenly over the phyllo, leaving a ¼-inch border on all sides. Cover the spinach with 6 more phyllo sheets, brushing each with butter and sprinkling each with about 2 tablespoons Pecorino cheese. Lay 2 more phyllo sheets on top, brushing each with butter (do not sprinkle these layers with Pecorino).

4. Working from the center outward, use the palms of your hands to compress the layers and press out any air pockets. Using a sharp knife, score the spanakopita through the top 3 layers of phyllo into 24 equal pieces. Sprinkle with the sesame seeds (if using). Bake until the phyllo is golden and crisp, 20 to 25 minutes. Cool on a baking sheet for 10 minutes or up to 2 hours. Slide the spanakopita, still on the parchment, onto a cutting board. Cut into squares and serve.

MOROCCAN CHICKEN

WHY THIS RECIPE WORKS: Time-consuming techniques and esoteric ingredients make cooking authentic Moroccan chicken a daunting proposition. We wanted a recipe that was ready in an hour and relied on supermarket staples. For depth and flavor, we used a mix of white and dark meat chicken and browned the meat first. After removing the chicken from the pot, we sautéed onion, strips of lemon zest, garlic, and a spice blend in some oil and the browned bits left in the pot; this ensured that no flavor went to waste. A number of everyday spices were necessary to re-create the authentic notes in Moroccan chicken, including paprika, cumin, cayenne, ginger, coriander, and cinnamon; honey filled the bill for the missing sweetness. Greek green olives provided the meatiness and piquant flavor of hard-to-find Moroccan olives. Chopped cilantro, stirred in right before serving, was the perfect finishing touch to our exotic dinner.

Moroccan Chicken with Olives and Lemon

SERVES 4

Bone-in chicken parts can be substituted for the whole chicken. For best results, use four chicken thighs and two chicken breasts, each breast split in half; the dark meat contributes valuable flavor to the broth and should not be omitted. Use a vegetable peeler to remove wide strips of zest from the lemon before juicing it. Make sure to trim any white pith from the zest, as it can impart bitter flavor. If the olives are particularly salty, rinse them first. Serve with Simple Couscous (page 622).

1¼   teaspoons paprika
½   teaspoon ground cumin
½   teaspoon ground ginger
¼   teaspoon cayenne pepper
¼   teaspoon ground coriander
¼   teaspoon ground cinnamon
3   (2-inch) strips zest plus 3 tablespoons
       juice from 1 lemon
5   medium garlic cloves, minced or pressed through
       a garlic press (about 5 teaspoons)
1   (3½ to 4-pound) whole chicken, cut into 8 pieces
       (4 breast pieces, 2 thighs, 2 drumsticks), wings
       discarded, and trimmed
       Table salt and ground black pepper
1   tablespoon olive oil
1   large onion, halved and sliced ¼ inch thick
1¾   cups low-sodium chicken broth
1   tablespoon honey
2   medium carrots, peeled and cut crosswise
       into ½-inch-thick rounds, very large pieces
       cut into half-moons
1   cup cracked green olives, pitted and halved
2   tablespoons chopped fresh cilantro leaves

1. Combine the paprika, cumin, ginger, cayenne, coriander, and cinnamon in a small bowl and set aside. Mince 1 of the lemon zest strips, combine with 1 teaspoon of the minced garlic, and mince together until reduced to a fine paste; set aside.

2. Season both sides of the chicken pieces with salt and pepper. Heat the oil in a Dutch oven over medium-high heat until beginning to smoke. Brown the chicken pieces, skin side down, until deep golden, about 5 minutes; using tongs, flip the chicken pieces and brown on the second side, about 4 minutes longer. Transfer the chicken to a large plate; when cool enough to handle, remove and discard the skin. Pour off and discard all but 1 tablespoon fat from the pot.

3. Add the onion and the 2 remaining lemon zest strips to the pot and cook, stirring occasionally, until the onion slices have browned at the edges but still retain their shape, 5 to 7 minutes (add 1 tablespoon water if the pan gets too dark). Add the remaining 4 teaspoons garlic and cook, stirring, until fragrant, about 30 seconds. Add the spices and cook, stirring constantly, until darkened and very fragrant, 45 seconds to 1 minute. Stir in the broth and honey, scraping up the browned bits from the bottom of the pot. Add the thighs and drumsticks, reduce the heat to medium, and simmer for 5 minutes.

4. Add the carrots and breast pieces with any accumulated juices to the pot, arranging the breast pieces in a single layer on top of the carrots. Cover, reduce the heat to medium-low, and simmer until the breast pieces register 160 to 165 degrees, 10 to 15 minutes.

5. Transfer the chicken to a plate and tent with aluminum foil. Add the olives to the pot; increase the heat to medium-high and simmer until the liquid has thickened slightly and the carrots are tender, 4 to 6 minutes. Return the chicken to the pot and stir in the garlic mixture, lemon juice, and cilantro; season with salt and pepper to taste. Serve immediately.

Moroccan Chicken with Chickpeas and Apricots

Follow the recipe for Moroccan Chicken with Olives and Lemon, replacing 1 carrot with 1 cup dried apricots, halved, and replacing the olives with one 15-ounce can chickpeas, rinsed.

LATINO-STYLE CHICKEN AND RICE

WHY THIS RECIPE WORKS: The traditional way of cooking this bold-flavored cousin of American chicken and rice is time-consuming, requiring an overnight marinade of the chicken and then a long, slow stewing with rice and vegetables. Could we find a way to achieve the same results in a lot less time?

We began by choosing chicken thighs, not only for shopping convenience but also to ensure that all of the pieces would cook at the same rate—a problem when using a combination of white and dark meat. We poached the thighs in a broth preseasoned with a *sofrito*, a classic Latin American mixture of chopped onions and bell peppers. About half an hour before the chicken finished cooking, we added medium-grain rice (which we preferred over long-grain for

its creamy texture), stirring it a few times to ensure even cooking. And for maximum flavor, we devised two marinades. Before cooking, we marinated the chicken quickly in garlic, oregano, and distilled white vinegar; after cooking we tossed the cooked chicken with olive oil, vinegar, and cilantro.

We had one final dilemma: how to give the dish its traditional orange hue that comes from infusing oil with achiote, a tropical seed not readily available in local grocery stores. Adding canned tomato sauce solved the problem.

Latino-Style Chicken and Rice (Arroz con Pollo)
SERVES 4 TO 6

To keep the dish from becoming greasy, remove any visible pockets of waxy yellow fat from the chicken and most of the skin, leaving just enough to protect the meat. To use long-grain rice instead of medium-grain, increase the amount of water added in step 2 from ¼ to ¾ cup and add the additional ¼ cup water in step 3 as needed. When removing the chicken from the bone in step 4, we found it better to use two spoons rather than two forks; forks tend to shred the meat, while spoons pull it apart in chunks.

- 6 medium garlic cloves, minced or pressed through a garlic press (about 2 tablespoons)
  Table salt and ground black pepper
- 1 tablespoon plus 2 teaspoons distilled white vinegar
- ½ teaspoon dried oregano
- 4 pounds bone-in, skin-on chicken thighs (about 10 thighs), trimmed (see note)
- 2 tablespoons olive oil
- 1 medium onion, minced
- 1 small green pepper, stemmed, seeded, and chopped fine
- ¼ teaspoon red pepper flakes
- ¼ cup minced fresh cilantro leaves
- 1¾ cups low-sodium chicken broth
- 1 (8-ounce) can tomato sauce
- ¼ cup water, plus more if needed (see note)
- 3 cups medium-grain rice (see note)

- ½ cup green manzanilla olives, pitted and halved
- 1 tablespoon capers
- ½ cup jarred pimentos, cut into 2 by ¼-inch strips
  Lemon wedges, for serving

1. Adjust an oven rack to the middle position and heat the oven to 350 degrees. Place the garlic and 1 teaspoon salt in a large bowl; using a rubber spatula, mix to make a smooth paste. Add 1 tablespoon of the vinegar, the oregano, and ½ teaspoon black pepper to the garlic-salt mixture; stir to combine. Place the chicken in the bowl with the marinade. Coat the chicken pieces evenly with the marinade; set aside for 15 minutes.

2. Heat 1 tablespoon of the oil in a Dutch oven over medium heat until shimmering. Add the onion, green pepper, and red pepper flakes; cook, stirring occasionally, until the vegetables begin to soften, 4 to 8 minutes. Add 2 tablespoons of the cilantro; stir to combine. Push the vegetables to the sides of the pot and increase the heat to medium-high. Add the chicken to the clearing in the center of the pot, skin side down, in an even layer. Cook, without moving the chicken, until the outer layer of the meat becomes opaque, 2 to 4 minutes. (If the chicken begins to brown, reduce the heat to medium.) Using tongs, flip the chicken and cook on the second side until opaque, 2 to 4 minutes more. Add the broth, tomato sauce, and water; stir to combine. Bring to a simmer; cover, reduce the heat to medium-low, and simmer for 20 minutes.

3. Add the rice, olives, capers, and ¾ teaspoon salt; stir well. Bring to a simmer, cover, and place the pot in the oven. After 10 minutes, remove the pot from the oven and stir the chicken and rice once from the bottom up. Cover and return the pot to the oven. After another 10 minutes, stir once more, adding another ¼ cup water if the rice appears dry and the bottom of the pot is beginning to burn. Cover and return the pot to the oven; cook until the rice has absorbed all the liquid and is tender but still holds its shape and the thickest part of the thighs registers 175 degrees on an instant-read thermometer, about 10 minutes longer.

4. Using tongs, remove the chicken from the pot; replace the lid and set the pot aside. Remove and discard the chicken skin; using two spoons, pull the meat off the bones in large chunks. Using your fingers, remove the remaining fat and any dark veins from the chicken pieces. Place the chicken in a large bowl and toss with the remaining 1 tablespoon oil, remaining 2 teaspoons vinegar, remaining 2 tablespoons cilantro, and the pimentos; season with salt and pepper to taste. Place the chicken on top of the rice, cover, and let stand until warmed through, about 5 minutes. Serve, passing the lemon wedges separately.

Latino-Style Chicken and Rice with Bacon and Roasted Red Peppers

Bacon adds a welcome layer of richness, and red peppers bring subtle sweet flavor and color to this variation. To use long-grain rice, increase the amount of water to ¾ cup in step 2 and the salt added in step 3 to 1 teaspoon.

1. Follow the recipe for Latino-Style Chicken and Rice through step 1, substituting 2 teaspoons sweet paprika for the oregano and sherry vinegar for the white vinegar.

2. Fry 4 ounces (about 4 strips) bacon, cut into ½-inch pieces, in a Dutch oven over medium heat until crisp, 6 to 8 minutes. Using a slotted spoon, transfer the bacon to a paper towel–lined plate; pour off all but 1 tablespoon bacon fat. Continue with step 2, substituting 1 small red pepper, chopped fine, and 1 medium carrot, chopped fine, for the green pepper and sautéing the vegetables in the bacon fat.

3. Continue with the recipe, substituting ¼ cup minced fresh parsley leaves for the cilantro, omitting the olives and capers, and substituting ½ cup roasted red peppers, cut into 2 by ¼-inch strips, for the pimentos. Garnish the chicken and rice with the reserved bacon before serving.

Latino-Style Chicken and Rice with Ham, Peas, and Orange

Ham gives this variation further richness, and orange zest and juice provide a bright accent. To use long-grain rice, increase the amount of water to ¾ cup in step 2 and the salt added in step 3 to 1 teaspoon.

1. Follow the recipe for Latino-Style Chicken and Rice through step 1, substituting 1 tablespoon ground cumin for the oregano.

2. Continue with step 2, adding 8 ounces ham steak or Canadian bacon, cut into ½-inch pieces (about 1½ cups), with the onion, green pepper, and red pepper flakes.

3. With a vegetable peeler, remove three 3-inch strips of zest from 1 orange. Continue with step 3, adding the orange zest with the rice, olives, capers, and salt. Add 1 cup frozen peas to the pot with ¼ cup water, if necessary, after stirring the contents of the pot the second time.

4. In step 4, add 3 tablespoons juice from 1 orange to the bowl with the olive oil, vinegar, cilantro, and pimentos and proceed with the recipe.

CUBAN-STYLE BLACK BEANS AND RICE

WHY THIS RECIPE WORKS: Beans and rice is a familiar combination the world over, but Cuban black beans and rice is unique in that the rice is cooked in the inky concentrated liquid left over from cooking the beans, which renders the grains just as flavorful. For our own version, we expanded on this method, simmering a portion of the *sofrito* (the traditional combination of garlic, bell pepper, and onion) with our beans to infuse them with flavor and then using the liquid to cook our rice and beans together. Lightly browning the remaining sofrito vegetables and spices with rendered salt pork added complex, meaty flavor, and finishing the dish in the oven eliminated the crusty bottom that can form when the dish is cooked on the stove.

Cuban-Style Black Beans and Rice
SERVES 6 TO 8

It is important to use lean—not fatty—salt pork. If you can't find it, substitute 6 slices of bacon. If using bacon, decrease the cooking time in step 4 to 8 minutes. You will need a Dutch oven with a tight-fitting lid for this recipe. For a vegetarian version of this recipe, use water instead of chicken broth, omit the salt pork, add 1 tablespoon tomato paste with the vegetables in step 4, and increase the amount of salt in step 5 to 1½ teaspoons.

	Table salt
6½	ounces dried black beans (1 cup), picked over and rinsed
2	cups low-sodium chicken broth
2	cups water
2	large green bell peppers, stemmed, seeded, and halved
1	large onion, halved at equator and peeled, root end left intact
1	head garlic, 5 medium cloves minced or pressed through a garlic press (about 5 teaspoons), remaining head halved at equator with skin left intact
2	bay leaves
1½	cups long-grain white rice
2	tablespoons olive oil
6	ounces lean salt pork, cut into ¼-inch dice (see note)
4	teaspoons ground cumin
1	tablespoon minced fresh oregano leaves
2	tablespoons red wine vinegar
2	scallions, sliced thin, for serving
	Lime wedges, for serving

1. Dissolve 1½ tablespoons salt in 2 quarts cold water in a large bowl or container. Add the beans and soak at room temperature for at least 8 hours or up to 24 hours. Drain and rinse well.

2. In a Dutch oven, stir together the drained beans, broth, water, 1 bell pepper half, 1 onion half (with root end), the halved garlic head, bay leaves, and 1 teaspoon salt. Bring to a simmer over medium-high heat, cover, and reduce the heat to low. Cook until the beans are just soft, 30 to 35 minutes. Using tongs, remove and discard the pepper, onion, garlic, and bay leaves. Drain the beans in a colander set over a large bowl, reserving 2½ cups bean cooking liquid. (If you don't have enough bean cooking liquid, add water to equal 2½ cups.) Do not wash out the Dutch oven.

3. Adjust an oven rack to the middle position and heat the oven to 350 degrees. Place the rice in a large fine-mesh strainer and rinse under cold running water until the water runs clear, about 1½ minutes. Shake the strainer vigorously to remove all excess water; set the rice aside. Cut the remaining peppers and onion into 2-inch pieces and process in a food processor until broken into rough ¼-inch pieces, about 8 pulses, scraping down the bowl as necessary; set the vegetables aside.

4. In the now-empty Dutch oven, heat 1 tablespoon oil and the salt pork over medium-low heat and cook, stirring frequently, until lightly browned and rendered, 15 to 20 minutes. Add the remaining 1 tablespoon oil, the chopped bell peppers and onion, cumin, and oregano. Increase the heat to medium and continue to cook, stirring frequently, until the vegetables are softened and beginning to brown, 10 to 15 minutes longer. Add the minced garlic and cook, stirring constantly, until fragrant, about 1 minute. Add the rice and stir to coat, about 30 seconds.

5. Stir in the beans, reserved bean cooking liquid, vinegar, and ½ teaspoon salt. Increase the heat to medium-high and bring to a simmer. Cover and transfer to the oven. Cook until the liquid is absorbed and the rice is tender, about 30 minutes. Fluff with a fork and let rest, uncovered, for 5 minutes. Serve, passing the scallions and lime wedges separately.

PAELLA

WHY THIS RECIPE WORKS: Paella can be a big hit at restaurants but an unwieldy production at home. Could we re-create this Spanish classic in two hours without using any fancy equipment? The key to our paella was finding equipment and ingredients that stayed true to the dish's heritage. First, we substituted a Dutch oven for a single-purpose paella pan. Then we pared down our ingredients, dismissing lobster, diced pork, fish, rabbit, and snails. We were left with chorizo, chicken, shrimp, and mussels. We next simplified our sofrito—in this Spanish version, a combination of onions, garlic, and tomatoes—by mincing a can of drained diced tomatoes rather than seeding and grating a fresh tomato. For the rice, we found we preferred short-grain varieties. Valencia was our favorite, with Italian Arborio a close second. Sautéing the rice in the same pot used to brown the meat and make the sofrito boosted its flavor. For the cooking liquid and seasonings, we chose chicken broth, white wine, saffron, and a bay leaf. Once the rice had absorbed almost all the liquid, we added the mussels, shrimp, and peas to the mix. The result? A colorful, streamlined, yet flavorful rendition of the Spanish classic.

Paella
SERVES 6

Use a Dutch oven that is 11 to 12 inches in diameter with at least a 6-quart capacity. Dry-cured Spanish chorizo is the sausage of choice for paella, but fresh chorizo or linguiça is an acceptable substitute. *Soccarat,* a layer of crusty browned rice that forms on the bottom of the pan, is a traditional part of paella. In our version, soccarat does not develop because most of the cooking is done in the oven. We have provided instructions to develop soccarat in step 5; if you prefer, skip this step and go directly from step 4 to step 6.

1 pound extra-large shrimp (21 to 25 per pound), peeled and deveined (see page 240)
    Table salt and ground black pepper
2 tablespoons olive oil, plus extra as needed
8–9 medium garlic cloves, minced or pressed through a garlic press (2 generous tablespoons)
1 pound boneless, skinless chicken thighs (about 4 thighs), trimmed and halved crosswise
1 red bell pepper, stemmed, seeded, and cut pole to pole into ½-inch-wide strips
8 ounces Spanish chorizo, sliced ½ inch thick on the bias (see note)
1 medium onion, minced
1 (14.5-ounce) can diced tomatoes, drained, minced, and drained again
2 cups Valencia or Arborio rice
3 cups low-sodium chicken broth
⅓ cup dry white wine
½ teaspoon saffron threads, crumbled
1 bay leaf
1 dozen mussels, scrubbed and debearded
½ cup frozen peas, thawed
2 tablespoons chopped fresh parsley leaves
1 lemon, cut into wedges, for serving

1. Adjust an oven rack to the lower-middle position and heat the oven to 350 degrees. Toss the shrimp, ¼ teaspoon salt, ¼ teaspoon pepper, 1 tablespoon of the oil, and 1 teaspoon of the garlic in a medium bowl; cover with plastic wrap and refrigerate until needed. Season the chicken thighs with salt and pepper; set aside.

2. Heat 2 teaspoons more oil in a large Dutch oven over medium-high heat until shimmering but not smoking. Add the pepper strips and cook, stirring occasionally, until the skin begins to blister and turn spotty black, 3 to 4 minutes. Transfer the pepper to a small plate and set aside.

3. Add the remaining 1 teaspoon oil to the now-empty Dutch oven; heat the oil until shimmering but not smoking. Add the chicken pieces in a single layer; cook, without moving the pieces, until browned, about 3 minutes. Turn the pieces and brown on the second side, about 3 minutes longer; transfer the chicken to a medium bowl. Reduce the heat to medium and add the chorizo to the pot; cook, stirring frequently, until deeply browned and the fat begins to render, 4 to 5 minutes. Transfer the chorizo to the bowl with the chicken and set aside.

4. Add enough oil to the fat in the Dutch oven to equal 2 tablespoons; heat over medium heat until shimmering but not smoking. Add the onion and cook, stirring frequently, until softened, about 3 minutes; stir in the remaining garlic and cook until fragrant, about 1 minute. Stir in the tomatoes; cook until the mixture begins to darken and thicken slightly, about 3 minutes. Stir in the rice and cook until the grains are well coated with the tomato mixture, 1 to 2 minutes. Stir in the chicken broth, wine, saffron, bay leaf, and ½ teaspoon salt. Return the chicken and chorizo to the pot, increase the heat to medium-high, and bring to a boil, uncovered, stirring occasionally. Cover the pot and transfer it to the oven; cook until the rice absorbs almost all of the liquid, about 15 minutes. Remove the pot from the oven (close the oven door to retain heat). Uncover the pot; scatter the shrimp over the rice, insert the mussels, hinged side down, into the rice (so they stand upright), arrange the bell pepper strips in a pinwheel pattern, and scatter the peas over the top. Cover and return to the oven; cook until the shrimp are opaque and the mussels have opened, 10 to 12 minutes.

5. OPTIONAL: If soccarat is desired (see note), set the Dutch oven, uncovered, over medium-high heat for about 5 minutes, rotating the pot 180 degrees after about 2 minutes for even browning.

6. Let the paella stand, covered, for about 5 minutes. Discard any mussels that have not opened and the bay leaf, if it can be easily removed. Sprinkle with the parsley and serve, passing the lemon wedges separately.

GRILLED PAELLA

WHY THIS RECIPE WORKS: Grilling paella lends the dish subtle smoke flavor and a particularly rich crust and makes it a great dish for summer entertaining. In place of a traditional paella pan, we cooked ours in a large, sturdy roasting pan that maximized the amount of *socarrat*, the prized caramelized rice crust that forms on the bottom of the pan. Building a large (7-quart) fire and fueling it with fresh coals (which ignited during cooking) ensured that the heat output would last throughout cooking, but we also shortened the outdoor cooking time by using roasted red peppers and tomato paste (instead of fresh peppers and tomatoes), making an infused broth with the seasonings, and grilling (rather than searing) the chicken thighs. To ensure that the various components finished cooking at the same time, we staggered the addition of the proteins—first, the chicken thighs, followed by the shrimp, clams, and chorizo. We also deliberately placed the chicken on the perimeter of the pan, where it would finish cooking gently after grilling, and the sausage and seafood in the center, where they were partially submerged in the liquid so that they cooked through; once the liquid reduced, the steam kept them warm.

Paella on the Grill

SERVES 8

This recipe was developed with a light-colored 16 by 13.5-inch tri-ply roasting pan; however, it can be made in any heavy roasting pan that measures at least 14 by 11 inches. If your roasting pan is dark in color, the cooking times will be on the lower end of the ranges given. The recipe can also be made in a 15- to 17-inch paella pan. If littlenecks are unavailable, use 1½ pounds shrimp in step 1 and season it with ½ teaspoon salt.

1½ pounds boneless, skinless chicken thighs, trimmed and halved crosswise

   Salt and pepper

12 ounces jumbo shrimp (16 to 20 per pound), peeled and deveined (see page 240)

 6 tablespoons extra-virgin olive oil

 6 garlic cloves, minced

1¾ teaspoons smoked hot paprika

 3 tablespoons tomato paste

 4 cups chicken broth

⅔ cup dry sherry

 1 (8-ounce) bottle clam juice

   Pinch saffron threads (optional)

 1 onion, chopped fine

½ cup roasted red peppers, chopped fine

 3 cups Arborio rice

 1 pound littleneck clams, scrubbed

 1 pound Spanish-style chorizo, cut into ½-inch pieces

 1 cup frozen peas, thawed

   Lemon wedges

1. Place chicken on large plate and sprinkle both sides with 1 teaspoon salt and 1 teaspoon pepper. Toss shrimp with 1 tablespoon oil, ½ teaspoon garlic, ¼ teaspoon paprika, and ¼ teaspoon salt in bowl until evenly coated. Set aside.

2. Heat 1 tablespoon oil in medium saucepan over medium heat until shimmering. Add remaining garlic and cook, stirring constantly, until garlic sticks to bottom of saucepan and begins to brown, about 1 minute. Add tomato paste and remaining 1½ teaspoons paprika and continue to cook, stirring constantly, until dark brown bits form on bottom of saucepan, about 1 minute. Add broth, sherry, clam juice, and saffron, if using. Increase heat to high and bring to boil. Remove pan from heat and set aside.

3A. FOR A CHARCOAL GRILL: Open bottom vent completely. Light large chimney starter mounded with charcoal briquettes (7 quarts). When top coals are partially covered with ash, pour evenly over grill. Using tongs, arrange 20 unlit briquettes evenly over coals. Set cooking grate in place, cover, and open lid vent completely. Heat grill until hot, about 5 minutes.

3B. FOR A GAS GRILL: Turn all burners to high, cover, and heat grill until hot, about 15 minutes. Leave all burners on high.

4. Clean and oil cooking grate. Place chicken on grill and cook until both sides are lightly browned, 5 to 7 minutes total. Return chicken to plate. Clean cooking grate.

5. Place roasting pan on grill (turning burners to medium-high if using gas) and add remaining ¼ cup oil. When oil begins to shimmer, add onion, red peppers, and ½ teaspoon salt. Cook, stirring frequently, until onion begins to brown, 4 to 7 minutes. Add rice (turning burners to medium if using gas) and stir until grains are well coated with oil.

6. Arrange chicken around perimeter of pan. Pour broth mixture and any accumulated juices from chicken over rice. Smooth rice into even layer, making sure nothing sticks to sides of pan and no rice rests atop chicken. When liquid reaches gentle simmer, place shrimp in center of pan in single layer. Arrange clams in center of pan, evenly distributing with shrimp and pushing hinge sides of clams into rice slightly so they stand up. Distribute chorizo evenly over surface of rice. Cook, moving and rotating pan to maintain gentle simmer across entire surface of pan, until rice is almost cooked through, 12 to 18 minutes. (If using gas, heat can also be adjusted to maintain simmer.)

7. Sprinkle peas evenly over paella, cover grill, and cook until liquid is fully absorbed and rice on bottom of pan sizzles, 5 to 8 minutes. Continue to cook, uncovered, checking frequently, until uniform golden-brown crust forms on bottom of pan, 8 to 15 minutes longer. (Rotate and slide pan around grill as necessary to ensure even crust formation.) Remove from grill, cover with foil, and let stand for 10 minutes. Serve with lemon wedges.

CREOLE-STYLE GUMBO

WHY THIS RECIPE WORKS: With shrimp, sausage, and vegetables in a deeply flavored, rich brown sauce with a touch of heat, gumbo is a unique one-pot meal. We wanted a foolproof, streamlined technique for gumbo that featured a thick, smooth sauce with lots of well-seasoned vegetables, meat, and fish.

The basis of gumbo is the roux, which is flour cooked in fat. For a deep, dark roux in half the time, we heated the oil before adding the flour. We also added the roux to room-temperature shrimp stock (supplemented with clam juice) to prevent separating. Although tomatoes are traditional in gumbo, our tasters didn't think they were necessary—but garlic was, and lots of it. Some cayenne pepper added the requisite heat. We added spicy andouille sausage and simmered everything for half an hour, tossing in the shrimp only during the last few minutes of cooking. You can add filé powder if you like, but our gumbo is delicious even without it.

Creole-Style Shrimp and Sausage Gumbo

SERVES 6 TO 8

Making a dark roux can be dangerous, as the mixture reaches temperatures in excess of 400 degrees. Therefore, use a deep pot for cooking the roux and long-handled utensils for stirring it, and be careful not to splash it on yourself. One secret to smooth gumbo is adding shrimp stock that is neither too hot nor too cold to the roux. For a stock that is at the right temperature when the roux is done, start preparing it before you tend to the vegetables and other ingredients, strain it, and then give it a head start on cooling by immediately adding the ice water and clam juice. So that your constant stirring of the roux will not be interrupted, start the roux only after you've made the stock. Alternatively, you can make the stock well ahead of time and bring it back to room temperature before using it. Spicy andouille sausage is a Louisiana specialty that may not be available everywhere; kielbasa or any fully cooked smoked sausage makes a fine substitute. Gumbo is traditionally served over white rice.

- 1½ pounds small shrimp (51 to 60 per pound), shells removed and reserved
- 3½ cups ice water
- 1 (8-ounce) bottle clam juice
- ½ cup vegetable oil
- ½ cup all-purpose flour, preferably bleached
- 2 medium onions, minced
- 1 medium red bell pepper, stemmed, seeded, and chopped fine
- 1 medium celery rib, chopped fine
- 6 medium garlic cloves, minced or pressed through a garlic press (about 2 tablespoons)
- 1 teaspoon dried thyme
  Table salt
  Cayenne pepper
- 2 bay leaves
- 1 pound smoked sausage, such as andouille or kielbasa (see note), sliced ¼ inch thick
- ½ cup minced fresh parsley leaves
- 4 medium scallions, white and green parts, sliced thin
  Ground black pepper

1. Bring the reserved shrimp shells and 4½ cups water to a boil in a stockpot or large saucepan over medium-high heat. Reduce the heat to medium-low and simmer for 20 minutes. Strain the stock and add the ice water and clam juice (you should have about 2 quarts of tepid stock, 100 to 110 degrees); discard the shells. Set the stock aside.

2. Heat the oil in a Dutch oven or large, heavy-bottomed saucepan over medium-high heat until it registers 200 degrees on an instant-read thermometer, 1½ to 2 minutes. Reduce the heat to medium and gradually stir in the flour with a wooden spatula or spoon, making sure to work out any lumps that may form. Continue stirring constantly, reaching into the corners of the pan, until the mixture has a toasty aroma and is deep reddish brown, about 20 minutes. (The roux will thin as it cooks; if it begins to smoke, remove the pan from the heat and stir the roux constantly to cool slightly.)

3. Add the onions, bell pepper, celery, garlic, thyme, 1 teaspoon salt, and ¼ teaspoon cayenne to the roux and cook, stirring frequently, until the vegetables soften, 8 to 10 minutes. Add 4 cups of the reserved stock in a slow, steady stream while stirring vigorously. Stir in the remaining 4 cups of stock. Increase the heat to high and bring to a boil. Reduce the heat to medium-low, skim the foam from the surface with a wide spoon, add the bay leaves, and simmer, uncovered, skimming the foam as it rises to the surface, about 30 minutes. (The mixture can be covered and set aside for several hours. Reheat when ready to proceed.)

4. Stir in the sausage and continue simmering to blend the flavors, about 30 minutes. Stir in the shrimp and simmer until cooked through, about 5 minutes. Off the heat, stir in the parsley and scallions and season with salt, black pepper, and cayenne to taste.

CIOPPINO

WHY THIS RECIPE WORKS: Brought to San Francisco by Italian immigrants, the earliest versions of cioppino were uncomplicated affairs made by fishermen with the day's catch. Today's restaurant versions showcase a variety of fish and shellfish piled high in a bright, complex broth. Cioppino is an indulgence for a seafood lover—but many recipes are intimidating for home cooks. We wanted a restaurant-worthy cioppino in which every component was perfectly cooked but which could be on the table quickly and with minimal fuss. First, we scaled down the seafood. For the fish, halibut fillets worked perfectly—they were tender and had just enough heft. As for the shellfish, a combination of briny littleneck clams and

savory-sweet mussels had the flavors we were looking for. The only way to perfectly cook three varieties of seafood was to cook each one separately and bring them all together in the hot broth to serve. We poached the halibut in the broth while the clams and mussels steamed in a separate pan. Removing them as they opened ensured ideal doneness for each one, and using a shallow skillet made the task easy. We used white wine to steam the mussels and clams, and then added the briny cooking liquid to the stew for a boost of intense seafood flavor. Replacing the water in the broth with bottled clam juice improved the broth even further.

Cioppino

SERVES 4 TO 6

Any firm-fleshed, ¾- to 1-inch-thick whitefish (such as cod or sea bass) can be substituted for halibut. Discard clams or mussels with unpleasant odors, cracked shells, or shells that won't close. If littlenecks are not available, substitute Manila or mahogany clams, or use 2 pounds of mussels. If using only mussels, skip step 3 and cook them all at once with the butter and wine for 3 to 5 minutes.

- ¼ cup vegetable oil
- 2 large onions, chopped fine
  Salt and pepper
- ¼ cup water
- 4 garlic cloves, minced
- 2 bay leaves
- 1 teaspoon dried oregano
- ⅛–¼ teaspoon red pepper flakes
- 1 (28-ounce) can whole peeled tomatoes, drained with juice reserved, chopped coarse
- 1 (8-ounce) bottle clam juice
- 1 (1½-pound) skinless halibut fillet, ¾ to 1 inch thick, cut into 6 pieces
- 1 pound littleneck clams, scrubbed
- 1¼ cups dry white wine
- 4 tablespoons unsalted butter
- 1 pound mussels, scrubbed and debearded
- ¼ cup chopped fresh parsley
  Extra-virgin olive oil

1. Heat vegetable oil in Dutch oven over medium-high heat until shimmering. Add onions, ½ teaspoon salt, and ½ teaspoon pepper; cook, stirring frequently, until onions begin to brown, 7 to 9 minutes. Add water and cook, stirring frequently, until onions are soft, 2 to 4 minutes. Stir in garlic, bay leaves, oregano, and pepper flakes and cook for 1 minute. Stir in tomatoes and reserved juice and clam juice and bring to simmer. Reduce heat to low, cover, and simmer for 5 minutes.

2. Submerge halibut in broth, cover, and gently simmer until fish is cooked through, 12 to 15 minutes. Remove pot from heat and, using slotted spoon, transfer halibut to plate, cover with aluminum foil, and set aside.

3. Bring clams, wine, and butter to boil in covered 12-inch skillet over high heat. Steam until clams just open, 5 to 8 minutes, transferring them to pot with tomato broth as they open.

4. Once all clams have been transferred to pot, add mussels to skillet, cover, and cook over high heat until mussels have opened, 2 to 4 minutes, transferring them to pot with tomato broth as they open. Pour cooking liquid from skillet into pot, being careful not to pour any grit from skillet into pot. Return broth to simmer.

5. Stir parsley into broth and season with salt and pepper to taste. Divide halibut among serving bowls. Ladle broth over halibut, making sure each portion contains both clams and mussels. Drizzle with olive oil and serve immediately.

BEHIND THE SCENES

A PEEK INSIDE THE TEST KITCHEN FREEZER

Curious as to what we keep in our freezer? A whole lot more than you might think. In fact, we've found that some pantry staples are better preserved in the freezer. Here's a list of the more unusual items the test kitchen keeps on ice.

RIPE OR OVERRIPE BANANAS: Great to have for making banana bread or muffins, or drop them into a blender while still frozen for fruit smoothies. Peel bananas before freezing.

NUTS: Sealed in a zipper-lock freezer bag, nuts stay fresh tasting for months. And there's no need to defrost; frozen nuts chop just as easily as fresh.

HERBS: Dried bay leaves retain their potency much longer when stored in the freezer. Chopped fresh herbs such as parsley, sage, rosemary, and thyme can be covered with water in an ice cube tray and then frozen indefinitely. Keep the frozen cubes in a zipper-lock freezer bag until needed for sauces, soups, or stews. Homemade pesto can also be frozen in ice cube trays, and there's no need to add water.

BUTTER: When stored in the refrigerator, butter picks up off-odors and eventually turns rancid. You can prolong its life by storing it in the freezer. Transfer it to the refrigerator one stick at a time, as you need it.

DRY GOODS: Stored in the freezer, flour, bread crumbs, cornmeal, oats, and other grains are protected from humidity, bugs, and rancidity.

CHAPTER 5

SIMPLY CHICKEN

PERFECT POACHED CHICKEN BREASTS

WHY THIS RECIPE WORKS: Poaching can be a perfect way to gently cook delicate chicken breasts, but the standard approach can be fussy and it offers little in the way of flavor. To up the flavor ante, we added salt, soy sauce, garlic, and a bit of sugar to the poaching liquid for rich-tasting chicken. We found that our salty poaching liquid could double as a quick brine, simplifying the recipe and infusing the chicken with flavor. To ensure that the chicken cooked evenly, we used plenty of water and raised the chicken off the bottom of the pot in a steamer basket. Taking the pot off the heat partway through cooking allowed the delicate meat to cook through using residual heat and prevented overcooking. A couple of simple sauces made the perfect accompaniment.

Perfect Poached Chicken Breasts

SERVES 4

To ensure that the chicken cooks through, don't use breasts that weigh more than 8 ounces each. If desired, serve the chicken with one of our sauces (recipes follow) or in a salad or sandwiches.

- 4 (6- to 8-ounce) boneless, skinless chicken breasts, trimmed
- ½ cup soy sauce
- ¼ cup salt
- 2 tablespoons sugar
- 6 garlic cloves, smashed and peeled

1. Cover chicken breasts with plastic wrap and pound thick ends gently with meat pounder until ¾ inch thick. Whisk 4 quarts water, soy sauce, salt, sugar, and garlic in Dutch oven until salt and sugar are dissolved. Arrange breasts, skinned side up, in steamer basket, making sure not to overlap them. Submerge steamer basket in brine and let sit at room temperature for 30 minutes.

2. Heat pot over medium heat, stirring liquid occasionally to even out hot spots, until water registers 175 degrees, 15 to 20 minutes. Turn off heat, cover pot, remove from burner, and let stand until meat registers 160 degrees, 17 to 22 minutes.

3. Transfer breasts to cutting board, cover tightly with aluminum foil, and let rest for 5 minutes. Slice each breast on bias into ¼-inch-thick slices, transfer to serving platter or individual plates, and serve.

Cumin-Cilantro Yogurt Sauce

MAKES ABOUT 1 CUP

Mint may be substituted for the cilantro. This sauce is prone to curdle and thus does not reheat well; prepare it just before serving.

- 2 tablespoons extra-virgin olive oil
- 1 shallot, minced
- 1 garlic clove, minced
- 1 teaspoon ground cumin
- ⅛ teaspoon red pepper flakes
- ½ cup plain whole-milk yogurt
- ⅓ cup water
- 1 teaspoon lime juice
  Salt and pepper
- 2 tablespoons chopped fresh cilantro

Heat 1 tablespoon oil in small skillet over medium heat until shimmering. Add shallot and cook until softened, about 2 minutes. Stir in garlic, cumin, and pepper flakes and cook until fragrant, about 30 seconds. Remove from heat and whisk in yogurt, water, lime juice, and remaining 1 tablespoon oil. Season with salt and pepper to taste and cover to keep warm. Stir in cilantro just before serving.

Warm Tomato-Ginger Vinaigrette

MAKES ABOUT 2 CUPS

Parsley may be substituted for the cilantro.

- ¼ cup extra-virgin olive oil
- 1 shallot, minced
- 1½ teaspoons grated fresh ginger
- ⅛ teaspoon ground cumin
- ⅛ teaspoon ground fennel
- 12 ounces cherry tomatoes, halved
  Salt and pepper
- 1 tablespoon red wine vinegar
- 1 teaspoon packed light brown sugar
- 2 tablespoons chopped fresh cilantro

Heat 2 tablespoons oil in 10-inch nonstick skillet over medium heat until shimmering. Add shallot, ginger, cumin, and fennel and cook until fragrant, about 15 seconds. Stir in tomatoes and ¼ teaspoon salt and cook, stirring frequently, until tomatoes have softened, 3 to 5 minutes. Off heat, stir in vinegar and sugar and season with salt and pepper to taste; cover to keep warm. Stir in cilantro and remaining 2 tablespoons oil just before serving.

SAUTÉED CHICKEN WITH MUSTARD-CIDER SAUCE

WHY THIS RECIPE WORKS: Sautéed super-thin cutlets are satisfying midweek fare, except when they are tough and dry. We wanted juicy, ultra thin sautéed chicken cutlets, paired with a sauce that complements, rather than overpowers, the meat.

For evenly sized cutlets, we took a two-step approach. We halved the chicken breasts horizontally before pounding them to an even thickness under plastic wrap. Halving and pounding the breasts ensured that they cooked at the same rate, and turned out moist, tender, and juicy. To further ensure the cutlets were juicy, we browned them on only one side. And for the sauce, we kept the flavors simple, relying on the sweet, tangy combination of apple cider and cider vinegar complemented with the kick of whole grain mustard.

Sautéed Chicken Cutlets with Mustard-Cider Sauce
SERVES 4

To make slicing the chicken easier, freeze it for 15 minutes.

CHICKEN
- 4 (6- to 8-ounce) boneless, skinless chicken breasts, tenderloins removed and breasts trimmed
  Table salt and ground black pepper
- 2 tablespoons vegetable oil

MUSTARD-CIDER SAUCE
- 2 teaspoons vegetable oil
- 1 medium shallot, minced (about 3 tablespoons)
- 1¼ cups apple cider
- 2 tablespoons cider vinegar
- 2 teaspoons whole grain mustard
- 2 teaspoons minced fresh parsley leaves
- 2 tablespoons unsalted butter
  Table salt and ground black pepper

1. FOR THE CHICKEN: Adjust an oven rack to the middle position and heat the oven to 200 degrees. Halve the chicken horizontally, then cover the chicken halves with plastic wrap and use a meat pounder to pound the cutlets to an even ¼-inch thickness. Season both sides of each cutlet with salt and pepper. Heat 1 tablespoon of the oil in a 12-inch skillet over medium-high heat until just smoking. Place four cutlets in the skillet and cook without moving them until browned, about 2 minutes. Using a spatula, flip the cutlets and continue to cook until the second sides are opaque, 15 to 20 seconds. Transfer to a large heatproof plate. Add the remaining 1 tablespoon oil to the now-empty skillet and repeat to cook the remaining cutlets. Cover the plate loosely with foil and transfer it to the oven to keep warm while making the sauce.

2. FOR THE SAUCE: Off the heat, add the oil and shallot to the hot skillet. Using residual heat, cook, stirring constantly, until softened, about 30 seconds. Set the skillet over medium-high heat and add the cider and vinegar. Bring to a simmer, scraping the pan bottom with a wooden spoon to loosen any browned bits. Simmer until reduced to ½ cup, 6 to 7 minutes. Off the heat, stir in the mustard and parsley; whisk in the butter 1 tablespoon at a time. Season with salt and pepper to taste and serve immediately with the cutlets.

SAUTÉED CHICKEN CUTLETS

WHY THIS RECIPE WORKS: Sautéed chicken cutlets are a breeze to prepare, but their brief cooking time and lack of skin leaves very little fond behind with which to build a pan sauce. With this dilemma in mind, we sought out a sauce that packed big flavor and could be made before the chicken even hit the skillet. Romesco sauce—a thick, coarse Spanish concoction of roasted red peppers, toasted hazelnuts, bread, sherry vinegar, olive oil, smoked paprika, and garlic—was simple to whizz together in a food processor and boasted a bold flavor profile. Starting with those key elements, we added a touch of honey to focus the ingredients' impact and a pinch of cayenne for pleasant heat. With the pepper sauce under our belt, we used the same blueprint to create equally easy sun-dried tomato and tomatillo sauces. For the chicken, partially freezing the breasts before halving firmed them up for easy slicing. We browned the cutlets in a hot oiled pan and, in just under 3 minutes, they were ready to be served with our simple, bold red pepper sauce.

MAKING CHICKEN CUTLETS

Packaged chicken cutlets from the supermarket can be ragged or uneven in thickness. You can easily make your own using boneless, skinless chicken breasts.

1. Remove tenderloin from underside of breast if necessary. Lay chicken smooth side up on cutting board. To make cutlets, place your hand on top of chicken and carefully slice it in half horizontally.

2. Separate breast to yield 2 cutlets between ⅜ and ½ inch thick. If necessary, pound to even thickness.

Sautéed Chicken Cutlets

SERVES 4

The cutlets will be easier to slice in half if you freeze them for about 15 minutes.

- 4 (6- to 8-ounce) boneless, skinless chicken breasts, trimmed, halved horizontally, and pounded ¼ inch thick
  Kosher salt and pepper
- 4 teaspoons vegetable oil

Pat cutlets dry with paper towels; sprinkle each side of each cutlet with ⅛ teaspoon salt and season with pepper. Heat 2 teaspoons oil in 12-inch skillet over medium-high heat until just smoking. Place 4 cutlets in skillet and cook, without moving, until browned, about 2 minutes. Flip cutlets and continue to cook until second sides are opaque, about 30 seconds. Transfer to platter and tent loosely with aluminum foil. Repeat with remaining 4 cutlets and remaining 2 teaspoons oil. Serve.

Quick Roasted Red Pepper Sauce

MAKES ABOUT 1 CUP

You will need at least a 12-ounce jar of roasted red peppers for this recipe.

- ½ slice hearty white sandwich bread, cut into ½-inch pieces
- ¼ cup hazelnuts, toasted and skinned
- 2 tablespoons extra-virgin olive oil
- 2 garlic cloves, sliced thin

- 1 cup jarred roasted red peppers, rinsed and patted dry
- 1½ tablespoons sherry vinegar
- 1 teaspoon honey
- ½ teaspoon smoked paprika
- ½ teaspoon salt
  Pinch cayenne pepper

Heat bread, hazelnuts, and 1 tablespoon oil in 12-inch skillet over medium heat; cook, stirring constantly, until bread and hazelnuts are lightly toasted, 2½ to 3 minutes. Add garlic and cook, stirring constantly, until fragrant, about 30 seconds. Transfer bread mixture to food processor and pulse until coarsely chopped, about 5 pulses. Add red peppers, vinegar, honey, paprika, salt, cayenne, and remaining 1 tablespoon oil to processor. Pulse until finely chopped, 5 to 8 pulses. Transfer to bowl and let stand for at least 10 minutes. (Sauce can be refrigerated for up to 2 days.)

Quick Sun-Dried Tomato Sauce

MAKES ABOUT 1 CUP

For the best taste and texture, make sure to rinse all the dried herbs off the sun-dried tomatoes.

- ½ slice hearty white sandwich bread, cut into ½-inch pieces
- ¼ cup pine nuts
- 2 tablespoons extra-virgin olive oil
- 2 garlic cloves, sliced thin
- 1 small tomato, cored and cut into ½-inch pieces
- ½ cup oil-packed sun-dried tomatoes, rinsed
- 2 tablespoons coarsely chopped fresh basil
- 2 tablespoons balsamic vinegar
- ½ teaspoon salt

Heat bread, pine nuts, and 1 tablespoon oil in 12-inch skillet over medium heat; cook, stirring constantly, until bread and pine nuts are lightly toasted, 2½ to 3 minutes. Add garlic and cook, stirring constantly, until fragrant, about 30 seconds. Transfer bread mixture to food processor and pulse until coarsely chopped, about 5 pulses. Add tomato, sun-dried tomatoes, basil, vinegar, salt, and remaining 1 tablespoon oil to processor. Pulse until finely chopped, 5 to 8 pulses. Transfer to bowl and let stand for at least 10 minutes. (Sauce can be refrigerated for up to 2 days.)

Quick Tomatillo Sauce

MAKES ABOUT 1 CUP

You will need at least a 15-ounce can of tomatillos for this recipe.

- ½ slice hearty white sandwich bread, cut into ½-inch pieces
- ¼ cup pepitas
- 2 tablespoons extra-virgin olive oil
- 2 garlic cloves, sliced thin
- 1 cup canned tomatillos, rinsed

2 tablespoons jarred sliced jalapeños plus
   2 teaspoons brine
2 tablespoons fresh cilantro leaves
1 teaspoon honey
½ teaspoon salt

Heat bread, pepitas, and 1 tablespoon oil in 12-inch skillet over medium heat; cook, stirring constantly, until pepitas and bread are lightly toasted, 2½ to 3 minutes. Add garlic and cook, stirring constantly, until fragrant, about 30 seconds. Transfer bread mixture to food processor and pulse until coarsely chopped, about 5 pulses. Add tomatillos, jalapeños and brine, cilantro, honey, salt, and remaining 1 tablespoon oil to processor. Pulse until finely chopped, 5 to 8 pulses. Transfer to bowl and let stand for at least 10 minutes. (Sauce can be refrigerated for up to 2 days.)

BREADED CHICKEN CUTLETS

WHY THIS RECIPE WORKS: Breaded chicken cutlets, for all their apparent simplicity, can be problematic. Too often, they end up with either an underdone or burnt coating, which falls off the tasteless, rubbery chicken underneath. We wanted chicken cutlets with flavorful meat and a crunchy crust that would adhere nicely to the meat.

To ensure even cooking, we flattened the chicken breasts to ½ inch; thin enough to cook evenly, but thick enough to make a hearty, crisp cutlet. To prevent crust separation, we coated the chicken with flour, an egg and oil mixture, and flavorful, fresh bread crumbs. We then let them sit for five minutes to help set the crust. For the crispiest coating, we fried the cutlets in batches in vegetable oil. And for a tasty variation, we added Parmesan for a version of the classic Italian dish Chicken Milanese.

Breaded Chicken Cutlets
SERVES 4

If you'd rather not prepare fresh bread crumbs, use panko, the extra-crisp Japanese bread crumbs. The chicken is cooked in batches of two because the crust is noticeably more crisp if the pan is not overcrowded. Note that these cutlets are a bit thicker than others in the chapter and should not be halved horizontally.

4 (5- to 6-ounce) boneless, skinless chicken breasts, tenderloins removed and breasts trimmed
   Table salt and ground black pepper
3 slices high-quality white sandwich bread, torn into quarters
¾ cup unbleached all-purpose flour
2 large eggs
1 tablespoon plus ¾ cup vegetable oil
   Lemon wedges, for serving

1. Use a meat pounder to pound the chicken breasts to an even ½-inch thickness. Sprinkle the cutlets with salt and pepper and set aside. Set a large wire rack over a large baking sheet and set aside.

2. Adjust an oven rack to the lower-middle position, set a heatproof plate on the rack, and heat the oven to 200 degrees. Process the bread in a food processor until evenly fine-textured, 20 to 30 seconds. Transfer the crumbs to a pie plate or shallow dish. Spread the flour in a second plate. Beat the eggs with 1 tablespoon of the oil in a third plate.

3. Working with one cutlet at a time, dredge each cutlet in the flour, shaking off the excess. Using tongs, dip both sides of the cutlets in the egg mixture, allowing the excess to drip off. Dip both sides of the cutlets in the bread crumbs, pressing the crumbs with your fingers to form an even, cohesive coat. Place the breaded cutlets on the wire rack and allow the coating to dry for about 5 minutes.

4. Meanwhile, heat 6 tablespoons more oil in a 12-inch nonstick skillet over medium-high heat until shimmering but not smoking, about 2 minutes. Lay 2 cutlets gently in the skillet; cook until deep golden brown and crisp on the first side, gently pressing down on the cutlets with a metal spatula, about 2½ minutes. Using tongs, flip the cutlets, reduce the heat to medium, and continue to cook until the meat feels firm when pressed gently and the second side is deep golden brown and crisp, 2½ to 3 minutes longer. Line the warmed plate with a double layer of paper towels and set the cutlets on top; return the plate to the oven.

5. Discard the oil in the skillet and wipe the skillet clean with paper towels. Repeat step 4 using the remaining 6 tablespoons oil and remaining cutlets; serve with lemon wedges.

Chicken Milanese

Though Parmesan is classic in this dish, use Pecorino Romano if you prefer a more tangy flavor. Keep a close eye on the cutlets as they brown to make sure the cheese does not burn.

Follow the recipe for Breaded Chicken Cutlets, substituting ¼ cup finely grated Parmesan cheese for an equal amount of bread crumbs.

NUT-CRUSTED CHICKEN BREASTS

WHY THIS RECIPE WORKS: Adding chopped nuts to a coating is a great way to add robust flavor to otherwise lean and mild boneless, skinless chicken breasts. But nut coatings are often dense and leaden, and the rich flavor of the nuts rarely comes through. Using a combination of chopped almonds and panko bread crumbs—rather than all nuts—kept the coating light and crunchy, and the bread crumbs helped the coating adhere. Instead of frying the breaded breasts, we found that baking them in the oven was not only easier but also helped the meat stay juicy and ensured an even golden crust. But it wasn't until we cooked the coating in browned butter prior to breading the chicken that we finally achieved the deep nutty flavor we sought.

Nut-Crusted Chicken Breasts with Lemon and Thyme

SERVES 4

This recipe is best with almonds but works well with any type of nut. We prefer kosher salt in this recipe. If using table salt, reduce salt amounts by half.

- 4   (6- to 8-ounce) boneless, skinless chicken breasts, tenderloins removed and breasts trimmed
  Kosher salt
- 1   cup almonds, chopped coarse
- 4   tablespoons (½ stick) unsalted butter
- 1   medium shallot, minced (about 3 tablespoons)
- 1   cup panko bread crumbs
- 2   teaspoons finely grated zest from 1 lemon, zested lemon cut into wedges
- 1   teaspoon minced fresh thyme leaves
- ⅛   teaspoon cayenne pepper

- 1   cup unbleached all-purpose flour
- 3   large eggs
- 2   teaspoons Dijon mustard
- ¼   teaspoon ground black pepper

1. Adjust the oven rack to the lower-middle position and heat the oven to 350 degrees. Set a wire rack in a rimmed baking sheet. Pat the chicken dry with paper towels. Using a fork, poke the thickest half of the breasts 5 to 6 times and sprinkle with ½ teaspoon salt. Transfer the breasts to the prepared wire rack and refrigerate, uncovered, while preparing the coating.

2. Pulse the almonds in a food processor until they resemble coarse meal, about 20 pulses. Melt the butter in a 12-inch skillet over medium heat, swirling occasionally, until the butter is browned and releases a nutty aroma, 4 to 5 minutes. Add the shallot and ½ teaspoon salt and cook, stirring constantly, until just beginning to brown, about 3 minutes. Reduce the heat to medium-low, add the bread crumbs and ground almonds and cook, stirring often, until golden brown, 10 to 12 minutes. Transfer the panko mixture to a shallow dish or pie plate and stir in the lemon zest, thyme, and cayenne. Place the flour in a second dish. Lightly beat the eggs, mustard, and black pepper together in a third dish.

3. Pat the chicken dry with paper towels. Working with one breast at a time, dredge the chicken in the flour, shaking off the excess, then coat with the egg mixture, allowing the excess to drip off. Coat all sides of the breast with the panko mixture, pressing gently so that the crumbs adhere. Return the breaded breasts to the wire rack.

4. Bake until the chicken registers 160 degrees on an instant-read thermometer, 20 to 25 minutes. Let the chicken rest for 5 minutes before serving with the lemon wedges.

Nut-Crusted Chicken Breasts with Orange and Oregano

This version works particularly well with pistachios or hazelnuts.

Follow the recipe for Nut-Crusted Chicken Breasts with Lemon and Thyme, substituting 1 teaspoon orange zest for the lemon zest (reserving the orange wedges for the garnish) and 1 teaspoon oregano for the thyme.

STUFFED CHICKEN CUTLETS

WHY THIS RECIPE WORKS: Cutlets that are stuffed and breaded are special-occasion food. The filling moistens the chicken from the inside with a creamy, tasty sauce, while the crust makes a crunchy counterpoint. The problem is that these bundles can leak and getting the right proportion of filling to cutlet can be tricky. We wanted stuffed chicken cutlets with a creamy filling that wouldn't turn runny and flavors that would complement, not overpower, the chicken. And we wanted the crust to be crisp all over and completely seal in the filling so that none leaked out.

We pounded the chicken breasts thin so they rolled easily and cooked evenly. A combination of cream cheese and cheddar mixed with onion, garlic, and fresh thyme gave us a creamy, well-flavored filling. Thin-sliced ham added another layer of flavor to our cutlets. Before we breaded the cutlets, we chilled them in the refrigerator to help the filling set—this step prevented leaks during cooking. For perfectly cooked stuffed cutlets, we sautéed them just until brown, then moved them into the oven to finish cooking through.

Stuffed Chicken Cutlets with Ham and Cheddar

SERVES 4

To make slicing the chicken easier, freeze it for 15 minutes. The cutlets can be filled and rolled in advance, then refrigerated for up to 24 hours. To dry fresh bread crumbs, spread them out on a baking sheet and bake in a 200-degree oven, stirring occasionally, for 30 minutes. Removing some moisture from the crumbs cuts down on splattering when the breaded cutlets are pan-fried.

FILLING

- 1 tablespoon unsalted butter
- 1 small onion, minced
- 1 small garlic clove, minced or pressed through a garlic press (about ½ teaspoon)
- 4 ounces cream cheese, softened
- 1 teaspoon minced fresh thyme leaves
- 2 ounces cheddar cheese, shredded (about ½ cup)
  Table salt and ground black pepper
- 4 slices (about 4 ounces) thin-sliced cooked deli ham

CHICKEN

- 4 (5- to 6-ounce) boneless, skinless chicken breasts, tenderloins removed and breasts trimmed
  Table salt and ground black pepper
- ¾ cup unbleached all-purpose flour
- 2 large eggs
- 1 tablespoon plus ¾ cup vegetable oil
- 4 slices high-quality white sandwich bread, pulsed in a food processor to coarse crumbs and dried (see note)

1. FOR THE FILLING: Melt the butter in a medium skillet over low heat; add the onion and cook, stirring occasionally, until deep golden brown, 15 to 20 minutes. Stir in the garlic and cook until fragrant, about 30 seconds longer; set aside.

2. In a medium bowl and using an electric mixer, beat the cream cheese on medium speed until light and fluffy, about 1 minute. Stir in the onion mixture, thyme, and cheddar; season with salt and pepper to taste and set aside.

3. Following the photos, butterfly each chicken breast and pound between two sheets of plastic wrap to a uniform ¼-inch thickness. Pound the outer perimeter to ⅛ inch. Place the chicken cutlets, smooth side down, on a work surface and

BUTTERFLYING CHICKEN BREASTS

1. Starting on the thinnest side, butterfly the breast by slicing it lengthwise almost in half. Open the breast up to create a single flat breast. (To make cutlets, continue to cut through the meat until you have two cutlets.)

2. With the breast or cutlet in a zipper-lock bag or between sheets of plastic wrap, pound (starting at the center) to ¼-inch thickness. Pound the outer perimeter to ⅛ inch.

season with salt and pepper. Spread each cutlet with one-quarter of the cheese mixture, then place 1 slice of ham on top of the cheese, folding the ham as necessary to fit onto the surface of the cutlet. Roll up each cutlet from the tapered end, folding in the edges to form a neat cylinder. Refrigerate until the filling is firm, at least 1 hour.

4. FOR THE CHICKEN: Adjust an oven rack to the lower-middle position and heat the oven to 450 degrees. Set a large wire rack over a large baking sheet and set aside. Place the flour in a pie plate or shallow dish. Beat the eggs with 1 tablespoon of the oil in a second plate. Spread the bread crumbs in a third plate. Dredge 1 chicken roll in the flour, shaking off the excess, then coat with the egg mixture, allowing the excess to drip off. Coat all sides of the chicken roll with the bread crumbs, pressing gently so that the crumbs adhere. Place on the wire rack and repeat the flouring and breading with the remaining chicken. Allow the coating to dry for about 5 minutes. Transfer the chicken to a plate. Wipe the wire rack and baking sheet clean and set aside.

5. Heat the remaining ¾ cup oil in a 10-inch nonstick skillet over medium-high heat until shimmering, but not smoking. Using tongs, carefully add the chicken, seam side down, to the pan, and cook until medium golden brown, about 2 minutes. Turn each roll and cook until medium golden brown on all sides, 2 to 3 minutes longer. Transfer the chicken rolls, seam side down, to the now-clean wire rack on the baking sheet; bake until deep golden brown and an instant-read thermometer inserted into the center of a roll registers 160 to 165 degrees, about 15 minutes. Let stand for 5 minutes before slicing each roll crosswise on the diagonal with a serrated knife into five pieces; arrange on individual dinner plates and serve.

PAN-SEARED CHICKEN BREASTS

WHY THIS RECIPE WORKS: A boneless, skinless chicken breast doesn't have the bone and skin to protect it from the intensity of a hot pan. Inevitably, it emerges moist in the middle and dry at the edges, with an exterior that's leathery and tough. We wanted a boneless, skinless chicken breast that was every bit as flavorful, moist, and tender as its skin-on counterpart.

We decided to utilize a technique that we've used successfully in the test kitchen with thick-cut steaks, where we gently parcook the meat in the oven and then sear it on the stovetop. First, we salted the chicken to help it retain more moisture as it cooked. To expedite the process we poked holes in the breasts, creating channels for the salt to reach the interior of the chicken as it parcooked. We then placed the breasts in a baking dish and covered it tightly with foil. In this enclosed environment, any moisture released by the chicken stayed trapped under the foil, keeping the exterior from drying out without becoming so overly wet that it couldn't brown quickly.

The next step was figuring out how to achieve a crisp, even crust on our parcooked breasts. We turned to a Chinese cooking technique called velveting, in which meat is dipped in a mixture of oil and cornstarch to create a thin protective layer that keeps the protein moist and tender, even when exposed to ultra-high heat. We replaced the oil with butter (for flavor) and mixed flour in with the cornstarch to avoid any pasty flavor. The coating helped the chicken make better contact with the hot skillet, creating a thin, browned, crisp veneer that kept the breast's exterior as moist as the interior.

Pan-Seared Chicken Breasts

SERVES 4

For the best results, buy similarly sized chicken breasts. If your breasts have the tenderloin attached, leave it in place and follow the upper range of baking time in step 1. For optimal texture, sear the chicken immediately after removing it from the oven.

4 (6- to 8-ounce) boneless, skinless chicken breasts, trimmed (see note)
1 teaspoon table salt
1 tablespoon vegetable oil
2 tablespoons unsalted butter, melted
1 tablespoon unbleached all-purpose flour
1 teaspoon cornstarch
½ teaspoon ground black pepper
1 recipe Lemon and Chive Pan Sauce (optional; recipe follows)

1. Adjust an oven rack to the lower-middle position and heat the oven to 275 degrees. Use a fork to poke the thickest half of each breast five to six times, then sprinkle each breast with ¼ teaspoon salt. Place the chicken, skinned side down, in a 13 by 9-inch baking dish and cover tightly with foil. Bake until the chicken registers 145 to 150 degrees on an instant-read thermometer, 30 to 40 minutes.

2. Remove the chicken from the oven and transfer, skinned side up, to a paper towel–lined plate and pat dry with paper towels. Heat the oil in a 12-inch skillet over medium-high heat until smoking. While the pan is heating, whisk the butter, flour, cornstarch, and pepper together in a small bowl. Lightly brush the tops of the chicken with half of the butter mixture. Place the chicken in the skillet, coated side down, and cook until browned, 3 to 4 minutes. While the chicken browns, brush the second side with the remaining butter mixture. Using tongs, flip the chicken, reduce the heat to medium, and cook until the second side is browned and the chicken registers 160 to 165 degrees, 3 to 4 minutes. Transfer the chicken to a platter and let rest while preparing the pan sauce (if not making the pan sauce, let the chicken rest for 5 minutes before serving).

Lemon and Chive Pan Sauce

MAKES ABOUT ¾ CUP

1 medium shallot, minced (about 3 tablespoons)
1 teaspoon unbleached all-purpose flour
1 cup low-sodium chicken broth
1 tablespoon juice from 1 lemon
1 tablespoon minced fresh chives
1 tablespoon unsalted butter, chilled
Table salt and ground black pepper

Add the shallot to the empty skillet and cook over medium heat until softened, about 2 minutes. Add the flour and cook, stirring constantly, for 30 seconds. Add the broth, increase the heat to medium-high, and bring to a simmer, scraping the pan bottom to loosen the browned bits. Simmer rapidly until reduced to ¾ cup, 3 to 5 minutes. Stir in any accumulated chicken juices, return to a simmer, and cook for 30 seconds. Off the heat, whisk in the lemon juice, chives, and butter; season with salt and pepper to taste. Spoon the sauce over the chicken and serve immediately.

ROASTED BONE-IN CHICKEN BREASTS

WHY THIS RECIPE WORKS: People often view the chicken bones and skin as a complication rather than an asset, so we resolved to devise an easy method that would deliver juicy, well-seasoned meat and crispy, brown skin. We ran into some expected problems though: The bone-in chicken breasts roasted at a high temperature achieved a crispy, brown skin, but the resulting meat was dry and bland. Cooking the chicken at a lower temperature kept the meat juicy but left the skin pale and flabby. For the best of both worlds, we adapted a cooking technique that we more commonly use for steaks: reverse searing. We started by applying salt under the skin to season the meat and help it retain moisture. Then we poked small holes in the skin to help drain excess fat. Gently baking the breasts at 325 degrees minimized moisture loss and resulted in even cooking from the breasts' thick ends to their thin ends. It also allowed the surface of the skin to dry out so that a quick sear in a hot skillet was all that was required for a crackly finish.

Roasted Bone-In Chicken Breasts
SERVES 4

Be sure to remove excess fatty skin from the thick ends of the breasts when trimming. You may serve these chicken breasts on their own or prepare a sauce (recipe follows) while the chicken roasts.

    4 (10- to 12-ounce) bone-in chicken breasts, trimmed
 1½ teaspoons kosher salt
    1 tablespoon vegetable oil

1. Adjust oven rack to lower-middle position and heat oven to 325 degrees. Line rimmed baking sheet with aluminum foil. Working with 1 breast at a time, use your fingers to carefully separate chicken skin from meat. Peel skin back, leaving it attached at top and bottom of breast and at ribs. Sprinkle salt evenly over all chicken, then lay skin back in place. Using metal skewer or tip of paring knife, poke 6 to 8 holes in fat deposits in skin. Arrange breasts skin side up on prepared sheet. Roast until chicken registers 160 degrees, 35 to 45 minutes.

2. Heat 12-inch skillet over low heat for 5 minutes. Add oil and swirl to coat surface. Add chicken, skin side down, and increase heat to medium-high. Cook chicken without moving it until skin is well browned and crispy, 3 to 5 minutes. Using tongs, flip chicken and prop against side of skillet so thick side of breast is facing down; continue to cook until browned, 1 to 2 minutes longer. Transfer to platter and let rest for 5 minutes before serving.

Jalapeño and Cilantro Sauce
MAKES 1 CUP

For a spicier sauce, reserve and add some of the chile seeds to the blender.

    1 cup fresh cilantro leaves and stems,
       trimmed and chopped coarse
    3 jalapeño chiles, stemmed, seeded, and minced
  ½ cup mayonnaise
    1 tablespoon lime juice
    2 garlic cloves, minced
  ½ teaspoon kosher salt
    2 tablespoons extra-virgin olive oil

Process cilantro, jalapeños, mayonnaise, lime juice, garlic, and salt in blender for 1 minute. Scrape down sides of blender jar and continue to process until smooth, about 1 minute longer. With blender running, slowly add oil until incorporated. Transfer to bowl.

CRISPY-SKINNED CHICKEN BREASTS

WHY THIS RECIPE WORKS: Perfectly cooked chicken with shatteringly crispy, flavorful skin is a rare find, so we set out to develop a foolproof recipe that would work every time. Boning and pounding the chicken breasts was essential to creating a flat, even surface to maximize the skin's contact with the hot pan. We salted the chicken to both season the meat and dry out the skin; poking holes in the skin and the meat allowed the salt to penetrate deeply. Starting the chicken in a cold pan allowed time for the skin to crisp without overcooking the meat. Weighting the chicken for part of the cooking time with a heavy Dutch oven encouraged even contact with the hot pan for all-over crunchy skin. Finally, we created silky, flavorful sauces with a bright, acidic finish, which provided the perfect foil to the skin's richness.

Crispy-Skinned Chicken Breasts with Vinegar-Pepper Pan Sauce

SERVES 2

This recipe requires refrigerating the salted meat for at least 1 hour before cooking. Two 10- to 12-ounce chicken breasts are ideal, but three smaller ones can fit in the same pan; the skin will be slightly less crispy. A boning knife or sharp paring knife works best to remove the bones from the breasts. To maintain the crispy skin, spoon the sauce around, not over, the breasts when serving.

CHICKEN

- 2 (10- to 12-ounce) bone-in split chicken breasts
  Kosher salt and pepper
- 2 tablespoons vegetable oil

PAN SAUCE

- 1 shallot, minced
- 1 teaspoon all-purpose flour
- ½ cup chicken broth
- ¼ cup chopped pickled hot cherry peppers, plus ¼ cup brine
- 1 tablespoon unsalted butter, chilled
- 1 teaspoon minced fresh thyme
  Salt and pepper

1. FOR THE CHICKEN: Place 1 chicken breast, skin side down, on cutting board, with ribs facing away from knife hand. Run tip of knife between breastbone and meat, working from thick end of breast toward thin end. Angling blade slightly and following rib cage, repeat cutting motion several times to remove ribs and breastbone from breast. Find short remnant of wishbone along top edge of breast and run tip of knife along both sides of bone to separate it from meat. Remove tenderloin (reserve for another use) and trim excess fat, taking care not to cut into skin. Repeat with second breast.

2. Using tip of paring knife, poke skin on each breast evenly 30 to 40 times. Turn breasts over and poke thickest half of each breast 5 to 6 times. Cover breasts with plastic wrap and pound thick ends gently with meat pounder until ½ inch thick. Evenly sprinkle each breast with ½ teaspoon kosher salt. Place breasts, skin side up, on wire rack set in rimmed baking sheet, cover loosely with plastic, and refrigerate for 1 hour or up to 8 hours.

3. Pat breasts dry with paper towels and sprinkle each breast with ¼ teaspoon pepper. Pour oil in 12-inch skillet and swirl to coat. Place breasts, skin side down, in oil and place skillet over medium heat. Place heavy skillet or Dutch oven on top of breasts. Cook breasts until skin is beginning to brown and meat is beginning to turn opaque along edges, 7 to 9 minutes.

4. Remove weight and continue to cook until skin is well browned and very crispy, 6 to 8 minutes. Flip breasts, reduce heat to medium-low, and cook until second side is lightly browned and meat registers 160 to 165 degrees, 2 to 3 minutes. Transfer breasts to individual plates and let rest while preparing pan sauce.

5. FOR THE PAN SAUCE: Pour off all but 2 teaspoons oil from skillet. Return skillet to medium heat and add shallot; cook, stirring occasionally, until shallot is softened, about 2 minutes. Add flour and cook, stirring constantly, for 30 seconds. Increase heat to medium-high, add broth and brine, and bring to simmer, scraping up any browned bits. Simmer until thickened, 2 to 3 minutes. Stir in any accumulated chicken juices; return to simmer and cook for 30 seconds. Remove skillet from heat and whisk in peppers, butter, and thyme; season with salt and pepper to taste. Spoon sauce around breasts and serve.

Crispy-Skinned Chicken Breasts with Lemon-Rosemary Pan Sauce

In step 5, increase broth to ¾ cup and substitute 2 tablespoons lemon juice for brine. Omit peppers and substitute rosemary for thyme.

Crispy-Skinned Chicken Breasts with Maple–Sherry Vinegar Pan Sauce

In step 5, substitute 2 tablespoons sherry vinegar for brine, 1 tablespoon maple syrup for peppers, and sage for thyme.

NOTES FROM THE TEST KITCHEN

BONING A SPLIT CHICKEN BREAST

If you want to cook boneless breasts with skin, you'll have to do a little knife work. Removing the bones allows the entire surface of the meat to lie flat and even against the pan—a must for perfectly crispy skin.

1. With chicken breast skin side down, run tip of boning or sharp paring knife between breastbone and meat, working from thick end of breast toward thin end.

2. Angling blade slightly and following rib cage, repeat cutting motion several times to remove ribs and breastbone from breast.

3. Find short remnant of wishbone along top edge of breast and run tip of knife along both sides of bone to separate it from meat.

CRISPY PAN-FRIED CHICKEN CUTLETS

WHY THIS RECIPE WORKS: Chicken cutlets coated in bread crumbs and pan fried are a staple weeknight meal: They're quick cooking and a crowd pleaser. But the three-step breading process of flour, egg, and crumbs is fussy, so we set out to make a streamlined version. We ditched the flour step, which made for a more delicate coating. Instead of the usual homemade bread crumbs, we swapped Japanese-style panko that we poured into a zipper-lock bag and crushed with a rolling pin, creating a perfectly even coating. To avoid any spotty browning or burned bits of panko with our second batch of cutlets, we discarded the cooking oil from the first batch and started over with fresh oil. Once done cooking, we transferred the cutlets to a paper towel–lined rack, which helped to wick away excess oil while preventing the underside from turning soggy. To punch up the flavor, we turned east for inspiration and made a Japanese barbecue-style sauce with ketchup, Worcestershire sauce, Dijon mustard, and soy sauce.

Crispy Pan-Fried Chicken Cutlets (Chicken Katsu)
SERVES 4 TO 6

Be sure to remove any tenderloins from the breasts before halving. The cutlets will be easier to slice in half if you freeze them for about 15 minutes. If you are working with 8-ounce cutlets, the skillet will initially be crowded; the cutlets will shrink slightly as they cook. The first batch of cutlets can be kept warm in a 200-degree oven while the second batch cooks. These cutlets can be sliced into ½-inch-wide strips Japanese style and served over rice with sauce (recipes follow). They can also be served in a sandwich or over a green salad.

2 cups panko bread crumbs
2 large eggs
 Salt
4 (6- to 8-ounce) boneless, skinless chicken breasts, trimmed, halved horizontally, and pounded ¼ inch thick
½ cup vegetable oil

1. Place panko in large zipper-lock bag and finely crush with rolling pin. Transfer crushed panko to shallow dish. Whisk eggs and 1 teaspoon salt in second shallow dish until well-combined.

2. Working with 1 cutlet at a time, dredge cutlet in egg mixture, allowing excess egg to drip off, then coat all sides with panko, pressing gently so crumbs adhere. Transfer cutlet to rimmed baking sheet and repeat with remaining cutlets.

3. Place wire rack in second rimmed baking sheet. Line rack with layer of paper towels. Heat ¼ cup oil and small pinch of panko in 12-inch skillet over medium-high heat. When panko has turned golden brown, place 4 cutlets in skillet. Cook without moving them until bottoms are crispy and deep golden brown, 2 to 3 minutes. Using tongs, carefully flip cutlets and cook on second side until deep golden brown, 2 to 3 minutes. Transfer cutlets to towel-lined rack and season with salt to taste. Wipe out skillet with paper towels. Repeat with remaining ¼ cup oil and 4 cutlets. Serve immediately.

Tonkatsu Sauce
MAKES ABOUT ⅓ CUP
You can substitute yellow mustard for the Dijon, but do not use a grainy mustard.

¼ cup ketchup
2 tablespoons Worcestershire sauce
2 teaspoons soy sauce
1 teaspoon Dijon mustard

Whisk all ingredients together in bowl.

Garlic-Curry Sauce
MAKES ABOUT ½ CUP
Full-fat and nonfat yogurt will both work in this recipe.

⅓ cup mayonnaise
¼ cup plain yogurt
2 tablespoons ketchup
2 teaspoons curry powder
1 teaspoon lemon juice
¼ teaspoon minced garlic

Whisk all ingredients together in bowl.

CHICKEN KIEV

WHY THIS RECIPE WORKS: Chicken Kiev is a recipe that elevates the humdrum boneless, skinless chicken breast to star status. Traditionally, the dish is a crisp fried chicken breast encasing a buttery herb sauce that dramatically oozes out when cut. But today, the dish has sunk to the level of bad banquet food—a greasy, bread crumb–coated chicken breast whose meat is dry and chalky despite the butter filling. This dish needed its greatness restored. We found that butterflying the chicken breasts, then pounding them thin—and even thinner at the edges—helped create chicken bundles that wouldn't leak the butter filling. Instead of deep-frying the chicken as is traditionally done, we chose to oven-fry the chicken. Toasting the bread crumbs prior to breading the chicken helped mimic the flavorful, golden brown crust of the original. Traditional recipes stuff the Kievs with butter spiked with nothing more than parsley and chives, but we found that minced shallots were more flavorful than chives and a small amount of tarragon added a pleasant hint of sweetness. Lemon juice tamed the rich butter with a bit of acidity and Dijon mustard provided another layer of flavor for a chicken Kiev that was anything but bland.

Chicken Kiev

SERVES 4

To make slicing the chicken easier, freeze it for 15 minutes. Unbaked, breaded chicken Kievs can be refrigerated overnight and baked the next day or frozen for up to one month. To cook frozen chicken Kievs, increase the baking time to 50 to 55 minutes (do not thaw the chicken).

HERB BUTTER

- 8 tablespoons (1 stick) unsalted butter, softened
- 1 tablespoon juice from 1 lemon
- 1 small shallot, minced (about 1 tablespoon)
- 1 tablespoon minced fresh parsley leaves
- ½ teaspoon minced fresh tarragon leaves
- ⅜ teaspoon table salt
- ⅛ teaspoon ground black pepper

CHICKEN

- 4 slices high-quality white sandwich bread, torn into quarters
  Table salt and ground black pepper
- 2 tablespoons vegetable oil
- 4 (7- to 8-ounce) boneless, skinless chicken breasts, tenderloins removed and breasts trimmed
- 1 cup unbleached all-purpose flour
- 3 large eggs, beaten
- 1 teaspoon Dijon mustard

1. FOR THE HERB BUTTER: Mix the ingredients in a medium bowl with a rubber spatula until thoroughly combined. Following the photo, form into a 2 by 3-inch rectangle on a sheet of plastic wrap; wrap tightly and refrigerate until firm, about 1 hour.

NOTES FROM THE TEST KITCHEN

SHAPING THE BUTTER FOR CHICKEN KIEV

Shape the butter mixture into a 2 by 3-inch rectangle on plastic wrap, then wrap tightly and refrigerate until firm, about 1 hour.

ASSEMBLING CHICKEN KIEV

1. Cut the butter into four rectangular pieces. Place one butter piece near the tapered end of the cutlet.

2. Roll up the tapered end of the chicken over the butter, then fold in the sides and continue rolling, pressing on the seam to seal. Repeat with the remaining butter pieces and cutlets. The chicken is now ready to be breaded.

2. FOR THE CHICKEN: Adjust an oven rack to the lower-middle position and heat the oven to 300 degrees. Add half of the bread to a food processor and pulse until the bread is coarsely ground, about 16 pulses. Transfer the crumbs to a large bowl and repeat with the remaining bread. Add ⅛ teaspoon salt and ⅛ teaspoon pepper to the bread crumbs. Add the oil and toss until the crumbs are evenly coated. Spread the crumbs on a rimmed baking sheet and bake until golden brown and dry, about 25 minutes, stirring twice during the baking time. Cool to room temperature.

3. Following the photos on page 101, butterfly each chicken breast and pound between two sheets of plastic wrap to a uniform ¼-inch thickness. Pound the outer perimeter to ⅛ inch. Unwrap the herb butter and cut it into four rectangular pieces. Following the photos, place a chicken breast, cut side up, on a work surface; season both sides with salt and pepper. Place one piece of butter in the center of the bottom half of the breast. Roll the bottom edge of the chicken over the butter, then fold in the sides and continue rolling to form a neat, tight package, pressing on the seam to seal. Repeat with the remaining butter and chicken. Refrigerate the chicken, uncovered, to allow the edges to seal, about 1 hour.

4. Adjust an oven rack to the middle position and heat the oven to 350 degrees. Set a large wire rack over a large baking sheet and set aside. Place the flour, eggs, and bread crumbs in separate pie plates or shallow dishes. Season the flour with ¼ teaspoon salt and ⅛ teaspoon pepper; season the bread crumbs with ½ teaspoon salt and ¼ teaspoon pepper. Add the mustard to the eggs and whisk to combine. Dredge 1 chicken roll in the flour, shaking off the excess, then coat with the egg mixture, allowing the excess to drip off. Coat all sides of the chicken roll with the bread crumbs, pressing gently so that the crumbs adhere. Place on the wire rack set over a rimmed baking sheet. Repeat the flouring and breading with the remaining chicken rolls.

5. Bake until the center of the chicken registers 160 to 165 degrees on an instant-read thermometer, 40 to 45 minutes. Let rest for 5 minutes on the wire rack before serving.

CHICKEN MARBELLA

WHY THIS RECIPE WORKS: More than 25 years ago, this dinner-party mainstay put *The Silver Palate Cookbook* on the map. We wanted to retool the recipe for today's tastes. To save time and boost flavor, we ditched the original marinade and made a paste of the prunes, olives, capers, garlic, and oregano, which we spread on the chicken and caramelized into the sauce. Instead of using whole birds, which require butchering, we chose easy-prep chicken parts. To intensify the dish's meaty flavor and to create complexity, we added anchovies and red pepper flakes and browned the chicken skin in a skillet before baking it through.

Chicken Marbella

SERVES 4 TO 6

Any combination of split breasts and leg quarters can be used in this recipe.

PASTE

- ⅓ cup pitted green olives, rinsed
- ⅓ cup pitted prunes
- 3 tablespoons extra-virgin olive oil
- 2 tablespoons capers, rinsed
- 4 garlic cloves, peeled
- 3 anchovy fillets, rinsed
- ½ teaspoon dried oregano
- ½ teaspoon pepper
- ¼ teaspoon kosher salt
  Pinch red pepper flakes

CHICKEN

- 2½–3 pounds bone-in split chicken breasts and/or leg quarters, trimmed
  Kosher salt and pepper
- 2 teaspoons olive oil
- ¾ cup low-sodium chicken broth
- ⅓ cup white wine
- ⅓ cup pitted green olives, rinsed and halved

- 1 tablespoon capers, rinsed
- 2 bay leaves
- ⅓ cup pitted prunes, chopped coarse
- 1 tablespoon unsalted butter
- 1 teaspoon red wine vinegar
- 2 tablespoons minced fresh parsley

1. FOR THE PASTE: Adjust oven rack to middle position and heat oven to 400 degrees. Pulse all ingredients together in food processor until finely chopped, about 10 pulses. Scrape down bowl and continue to process until mostly smooth, 1 to 2 minutes. Transfer to bowl. (Paste can be refrigerated for up to 24 hours.)

2. FOR THE CHICKEN: Pat chicken dry with paper towels. Sprinkle chicken pieces with 1½ teaspoons salt and season with pepper.

3. Heat oil in 12-inch skillet over medium-high heat until just smoking. Add chicken, skin side down, and cook without moving until well browned, 5 to 8 minutes. Transfer chicken to large plate. Drain off all but 1 teaspoon fat from skillet and return to medium-low heat.

4. Add ⅓ cup paste to skillet and cook, stirring constantly, until fragrant and fond forms on bottom of pan, 1 to 2 minutes. Stir in broth, wine, olives, capers, and bay leaves, scraping up any browned bits. Return chicken, skin side up, to pan (skin should be above surface of liquid) and transfer to oven. Cook, uncovered, for 15 minutes.

5. Remove skillet from oven and use back of spoon to spread remaining paste over chicken pieces; sprinkle prunes around chicken. Continue to roast until paste begins to brown, breasts register 160 degrees, and leg quarters register 175 degrees, 7 to 12 minutes longer.

6. Transfer chicken to serving platter and tent loosely with aluminum foil. Remove bay leaves from sauce and whisk in butter, vinegar, and 1 tablespoon parsley; season with salt and pepper to taste. Pour sauce around chicken, sprinkle with remaining 1 tablespoon parsley, and serve.

SPANISH BRAISED CHICKEN WITH SHERRY AND SAFFRON

WHY THIS RECIPE WORKS: Nailing the classic Spanish dish called *pollo en pepitoria* hinges on achieving a balance between the richness and brightness of its creamy, nutty sherry sauce. We began with chicken thighs because their high collagen content breaks down into gelatin the longer they cook, making our slow-braised chicken tender. Onions, softened in rendered fat, created the base into which we added garlic, a bay leaf, and cinnamon. Dry, light-bodied sherries shine in savory applications, so we poured some in along with chicken broth. We also chopped canned peeled tomatoes, adding them for some bright acidity. We braised the chicken in the sauce at a gentle 300 degrees and removed the skin once the thighs were fully cooked. To finish, we poured a portion of the cooking liquid into a blender to create a *picada*, a flavorful thickener, adding chopped hard-boiled egg yolks, saffron threads, garlic, and almonds. We whirred the mixture into a thick, smooth paste. With a finishing touch of fresh lemon juice for brightness, we thickened the sauce before pouring it over the chicken. Fresh parsley and hard-boiled egg whites made for an authentic presentation.

Spanish Braised Chicken with Sherry and Saffron (Pollo en Pepitoria)

SERVES 4

Any dry sherry, such as fino or Manzanilla, will work in this dish. Serve with crusty bread.

- 8 (5- to 7-ounce) bone-in chicken thighs, trimmed
   Salt and pepper
- 1 tablespoon extra-virgin olive oil
- 1 onion, chopped fine
- 3 garlic cloves, minced
- 1 bay leaf
- ¼ teaspoon ground cinnamon
- ⅔ cup dry sherry
- 1 cup chicken broth
- 1 (14.5-ounce) can whole peeled tomatoes, drained and chopped fine
- 2 hard-cooked large eggs, peeled and yolks and whites separated
- ½ cup slivered blanched almonds, toasted
   Pinch saffron threads, crumbled
- 2 tablespoons chopped fresh parsley
- 1½ teaspoons lemon juice

1. Adjust oven rack to middle position and heat oven to 300 degrees.

2. Pat thighs dry with paper towels and season both sides of each with 1 teaspoon salt and ½ teaspoon pepper. Heat oil in 12-inch skillet over high heat until just smoking. Add thighs and brown on both sides, 10 to 12 minutes. Transfer thighs to large plate and pour off all but 2 teaspoons fat from skillet.

3. Return skillet to medium heat, add onion and ¼ teaspoon salt, and cook, stirring frequently, until just softened, about 3 minutes. Add 2 teaspoons garlic, bay leaf, and cinnamon and cook until fragrant, about 1 minute. Add sherry and cook, scraping up any browned bits, until sauce starts to thicken, about 2 minutes. Stir in broth and tomatoes and bring to simmer. Return thighs to skillet, cover, transfer to oven, and cook until chicken registers 195 degrees, 45 to 50 minutes. Transfer thighs to serving platter, remove and discard skin, and cover loosely with aluminum foil to keep warm. While thighs cook, finely chop egg whites.

4. Discard bay leaf. Transfer ¾ cup chicken cooking liquid, egg yolks, almonds, saffron, and remaining garlic to blender. Process until smooth, about 2 minutes, scraping down jar as needed. Return almond mixture to skillet. Add 1 tablespoon parsley and lemon juice; bring to simmer over medium heat. Simmer, whisking frequently, until thickened, 3 to 5 minutes. Season with salt and pepper to taste.

5. Pour sauce over chicken, sprinkle with remaining 1 tablespoon parsley and egg whites, and serve.

COQ AU RIESLING

WHY THIS RECIPE WORKS: This richer, subtler take on coq au vin swaps dry white wine for red, but creating this classic required more than just a change in wine. Sticking to tradition, we began by cutting a whole chicken into parts. To establish a meaty base, we cooked chopped bacon pieces and used the rendered fat to brown the chicken wings and back as well as the flavorful skins removed from the breasts, drumsticks, and thighs. These elements, though not part of the finished dish, contributed a rich base of flavor. A generous mirepoix of shallots, carrots, celery, and garlic, added with flour, solidified the complex flavor profile. Stirring in just 2½ cups of dry Riesling created a crisp, balanced finish. With the flavors in place, we added water, herbs, and the chicken pieces, cooking over low heat. Once cooked, we removed the chicken, discarded the back and wings, and strained the liquid to finish off the sauce. While the liquid settled, we used the empty pot to sauté white mushrooms with some of the reserved fat. We returned the liquid back to the pot, brought it to a simmer to thicken, and added tangy crème fraîche for an elegantly creamy finish.

Coq au Riesling

SERVES 4 TO 6

A dry Riesling is the best wine for this recipe, but a Sauvignon Blanc or Chablis will also work. Avoid a heavily oaked wine such as Chardonnay. Serve the stew with egg noodles or mashed potatoes.

- 1 (4- to 5-pound) whole chicken, cut into 8 pieces (4 breast pieces, 2 drumsticks, 2 thighs), wings and back reserved
   Salt and pepper
- 2 slices bacon, chopped

3 shallots, chopped

2 carrots, peeled and chopped coarse

2 celery ribs, chopped coarse

4 garlic cloves, lightly crushed and peeled

3 tablespoons all-purpose flour

2½ cups dry Riesling

1 cup water

2 bay leaves

6 sprigs fresh parsley, plus 2 teaspoons minced

6 sprigs fresh thyme

1 pound white mushrooms, trimmed and halved if small or quartered if large

¼ cup crème fraîche

1. Remove skin from chicken breast pieces, drumsticks, and thighs and set aside. Sprinkle both sides of chicken pieces with 1¼ teaspoons salt and ½ teaspoon pepper; set aside. Cook bacon in large Dutch oven over medium-low heat, stirring occasionally, until beginning to render, 2 to 4 minutes. Add chicken skin, back, and wings to pot; increase heat to medium; and cook, stirring frequently, until bacon is browned, skin is rendered, and chicken back and wings are browned on all sides, 10 to 12 minutes. Remove pot from heat and carefully transfer 2 tablespoons fat to small bowl and set aside.

2. Return pot to medium heat. Add shallots, carrots, celery, and garlic and cook, stirring occasionally, until vegetables are softened, 4 to 6 minutes. Add flour and cook, stirring constantly, until no dry flour remains, about 30 seconds. Slowly add wine, scraping up any browned bits. Increase heat to high and simmer until mixture is slightly thickened, about 2 minutes. Stir in water, bay leaves, parsley sprigs, and thyme and bring to simmer. Place chicken pieces in even layer in pot, reduce heat to low, cover, and cook until breasts register 160 degrees and thighs and legs register 175 degrees, 25 to 30 minutes, stirring halfway through cooking. Transfer chicken pieces to plate as they come up to temperature.

3. Discard back and wings. Strain cooking liquid through fine-mesh strainer set over large bowl, pressing on solids to extract as much liquid as possible; discard solids. Let cooking liquid settle for 10 minutes. Using wide shallow spoon, skim fat from surface and discard.

4. While liquid settles, return pot to medium heat and add reserved fat, mushrooms, and ¼ teaspoon salt; cook, stirring occasionally, until lightly browned, 8 to 10 minutes.

5. Return liquid to pot and bring to boil. Simmer briskly, stirring occasionally, until sauce is thickened to consistency of heavy cream, 4 to 6 minutes. Reduce heat to medium-low and stir in crème fraîche and minced parsley. Return chicken to pot along with any accumulated juices, cover, and cook until just heated through, 5 to 8 minutes. Season with salt and pepper to taste, and serve.

FILIPINO CHICKEN ADOBO

WHY THIS RECIPE WORKS: Adobo is the national dish of the Philippines, and chicken adobo is among the most popular versions. The dish consists of chicken simmered in a mixture of vinegar, soy sauce, garlic, bay leaves, and black pepper. The problem with most recipes we found was that they were aggressively tart and salty. Our secret to taming both of these elements was coconut milk. The coconut milk's richness tempered the bracing acidity of the vinegar and masked the briny soy sauce, bringing the sauce into balance. But the fat from the coconut milk and the chicken skin made the sauce somewhat greasy. To combat this, we borrowed a technique used in French bistros. We placed the meat skin side down in a cold pan and then turned up the heat. As the pan gradually got hotter, the fat under the chicken's skin melted away while the exterior browned.

Filipino Chicken Adobo

SERVES 4

Light coconut milk can be substituted for regular coconut milk. Serve this dish over rice.

8 (5- to 7-ounce) bone-in chicken thighs, trimmed

⅓ cup soy sauce

1 (13.5-ounce) can coconut milk

¾ cup cider vinegar

8 garlic cloves, peeled

4 bay leaves

2 teaspoons pepper

1 scallion, sliced thin

1. Toss chicken with soy sauce in large bowl. Refrigerate for at least 30 minutes or up to 1 hour.

2. Remove chicken from soy sauce, allowing excess to drip back into bowl. Transfer chicken, skin side down, to 12-inch nonstick skillet; set aside soy sauce.

3. Place skillet over medium-high heat and cook until chicken skin is browned, 7 to 10 minutes. While chicken is browning, whisk coconut milk, vinegar, garlic, bay leaves, and pepper into soy sauce.

4. Transfer chicken to plate and discard fat in skillet. Return chicken to skillet skin side down, add coconut milk mixture, and bring to boil. Reduce heat to medium-low and simmer, uncovered, for 20 minutes. Flip chicken skin side up and continue to cook, uncovered, until chicken registers 175 degrees, about 15 minutes. Transfer chicken to platter and tent loosely with aluminum foil.

5. Remove bay leaves and skim any fat off surface of sauce. Return skillet to medium-high heat and cook until sauce is thickened, 5 to 7 minutes. Pour sauce over chicken, sprinkle with scallion, and serve.

MAHOGANY CHICKEN THIGHS

WHY THIS RECIPE WORKS: Braising chicken thighs does an excellent job of rendering sneaky pockets of fat and producing luxurious, flavorful meat, but there is one drawback: we miss the crispy skin of roasted chicken. We wanted the best of both worlds.

We took a hybrid approach: braise for tenderness, then broil for crispy skin. We oven-braised the thighs in a flavor-infusing combination of soy sauce, sherry, white vinegar, a big piece of smashed ginger, smashed garlic, and sugar and molasses for sweetness (both would also caramelize and boost the mahogany hue). After braising for an hour, the fat was fully rendered, and although the meat was overcooked according to our usual standards, the melted connective tissue had converted to gelatin, which resulted in meat that was supple and juicy. Turning the chicken skin side up halfway through braising allowed the rendered skin to dry before broiling, which helped it crisp a little more. For a simple, streamlined finish, we used a portion of the braising liquid to make a quick sauce (thickened with a little cornstarch for body).

Mahogany Chicken Thighs
SERVES 4 TO 6

For best results, trim all visible fat and skin from the underside of the thighs. Serve with steamed rice and vegetables.

1½ cups water
1 cup soy sauce
¼ cup dry sherry
2 tablespoons sugar
2 tablespoons molasses
1 tablespoon distilled white vinegar
8 (5- to 7-ounce) bone-in chicken thighs, trimmed
1 (2-inch) piece ginger, peeled, halved, and smashed
6 garlic cloves, peeled and smashed
1 tablespoon cornstarch

1. Adjust oven rack to lower-middle position and heat oven to 300 degrees. Whisk 1 cup water, soy sauce, sherry, sugar, molasses, and vinegar together in ovensafe 12-inch skillet until sugar is dissolved. Arrange chicken, skin side down, in soy mixture and nestle ginger and garlic between pieces of chicken.

2. Bring soy mixture to simmer over medium heat and simmer for 5 minutes. Transfer skillet to oven and cook, uncovered, for 30 minutes.

3. Flip chicken skin side up and continue to cook, uncovered, until chicken registers 195 degrees, 20 to 30 minutes longer. Transfer chicken to platter, taking care not to tear skin. Pour cooking liquid through fine-mesh strainer into fat separator and let settle for 5 minutes. Heat broiler.

4. Whisk cornstarch and remaining ½ cup water together in bowl. Pour 1 cup defatted cooking liquid into now-empty skillet and bring to simmer over medium heat. Whisk cornstarch mixture into cooking liquid and simmer until thickened, about 1 minute. Pour sauce into bowl and set aside for serving.

5. Return chicken skin side up to now-empty skillet and broil until well browned, about 4 minutes. Return chicken to platter, and let rest for 5 minutes. Serve, passing reserved sauce separately.

OVEN-BARBECUED CHICKEN

WHY THIS RECIPE WORKS: Smoky, tender, and tangy, barbecued chicken is a real crowd pleaser. What do you do when a craving for this summertime favorite strikes in midwinter? Oven-barbecued chicken is the obvious solution. But while recipes for this dish abound, so do the disappointments: tough, rubbery, or unevenly cooked chicken in sauces ranging from pasty and candy-sweet to greasy, stale, thin, or commercial-tasting.

We started with boneless, skinless chicken breasts; the mild white meat is a perfect backdrop for the sauce. (Skinless breasts also meant that we wouldn't have to deal with the problem of flabby skin.) We lightly seared the chicken breasts in a skillet, then removed them from the pan to make a simple but flavorful barbecue sauce with pantry ingredients like grated onion, ketchup, Worcestershire sauce, mustard, molasses, and maple syrup. When we returned the chicken to the pan, the sauce clung nicely to the meat, thanks to the light searing we had given the chicken. We slid the chicken and sauce, still in the skillet, into the oven to cook through. Finally, for a nicely caramelized coating on the sauce, we finished the chicken under the high heat of the broiler. The result? Juicy chicken, thickly coated with a pleasantly tangy barbecue sauce.

Sweet and Tangy Oven-Barbecued Chicken
SERVES 4

Real maple syrup is preferable to imitation syrup, and "mild" or "original" molasses is preferable to darker, more bitter types. Use a rasp-style grater or the fine holes of a box grater to grate the onion. Make this recipe only in an in-oven broiler; do not use a drawer-type broiler. Broiling times may differ from one oven to another, so we urge you to check the chicken for doneness after only 3 minutes of broiling. You may also have to lower the oven rack if your broiler runs very hot. It is important to remove the chicken from the oven before switching to the broiler setting to allow the broiler element to come up to temperature.

- 1 cup ketchup
- 3 tablespoons molasses (see note)
- 3 tablespoons cider vinegar
- 2 tablespoons finely grated onion (see note)
- 2 tablespoons Worcestershire sauce
- 2 tablespoons Dijon mustard
- 2 tablespoons maple syrup (see note)
- 1 teaspoon chili powder
- ¼ teaspoon cayenne pepper
- 4 (5- to 6-ounce) boneless, skinless chicken breasts, tenderloins removed and breasts trimmed
  Table salt and ground black pepper
- 1 tablespoon vegetable oil

1. Adjust an oven rack to the upper-middle position, about 5 inches from the heating element, and heat the oven to 325 degrees. Whisk the ketchup, molasses, vinegar, onion, Worcestershire sauce, mustard, maple syrup, chili powder, and cayenne together in a small bowl; set aside. Pat the chicken dry with paper towels and season with salt and pepper.

2. Heat the oil in a 12-inch ovensafe skillet over high heat until just smoking. Add the chicken, smooth side down, and cook until very light golden, 1 to 2 minutes; using tongs, turn the chicken and cook until very light golden on the second side, 1 to 2 minutes longer. Transfer the chicken to a plate and set aside.

3. Discard the fat in the skillet; off the heat, add the sauce mixture and, using a wooden spoon, scrape up the browned bits on the bottom of the skillet. Simmer the sauce over medium heat, stirring frequently with a heatproof spatula, until the sauce is thick and glossy and a spatula leaves a clear trail in the sauce, about 4 minutes. Off the heat, return the chicken to the skillet and turn to coat thickly with the sauce; set the chicken pieces smooth side up and spoon extra sauce over each piece to create a thick coating.

4. Place the skillet in the oven and cook until the thickest part of the breasts registers 130 degrees on an instant-read thermometer, 8 to 12 minutes. Remove the skillet from the oven, turn the oven to broil, and heat for 5 minutes. Once the broiler is heated, place the skillet back in the oven and broil the chicken until the thickest part of the breasts registers 160 to 165 degrees, 3 to 8 minutes longer. Transfer the chicken to a platter and let rest for 5 minutes. Meanwhile, whisk the sauce in the skillet to recombine and transfer to a small bowl. Serve the chicken, passing the extra sauce separately.

PICNIC CHICKEN

WHY THIS RECIPE WORKS: Cold barbecued picnic chicken presents numerous challenges: the meat may be dry, the skin flabby, and the chicken covered with a sticky, messy sauce. We wanted a recipe for chicken that would be easy to pack (and eat) for a picnic; chicken with moist, tender meat flavored with robust spicy and slightly sweet barbecue flavors.

We first threw out the idea of a sticky sauce, substituting a robust dry rub (brown sugar, chili powder, paprika, and pepper) that reproduced the flavors of a good barbecue sauce. We partly solved the flabby skin problem by diligently trimming the chicken pieces as well as by slitting the skin before cooking (which allowed the excess fat to render). But the skin was still flabby from the moisture contributed by our traditional brine (we brine most poultry for better flavor and moister meat). We tried eliminating the brine, adding salt to the rub, and applying it the night before. Sure enough, when we oven-roasted the chicken the next day, we found the meat well seasoned throughout and very moist. Best of all, the skin was flavorful, delicate, and definitely not flabby.

Spice-Rubbed Picnic Chicken
SERVES 8

If you plan to serve the chicken later on the same day that you cook it, refrigerate it immediately after it has cooled, then let it come back to room temperature before serving. On the breast pieces, we use toothpicks to secure the skin, which otherwise shrinks considerably in the oven, leaving the meat exposed and prone to drying out. We think the extra effort is justified, but you can omit this step. This recipe halves easily.

5 pounds bone-in, skin-on chicken parts (split breasts, thighs, drumsticks, or a mix, with breasts cut into 3 pieces or halved if small), trimmed of excess fat and skin
3 tablespoons brown sugar
2 tablespoons chili powder
2 tablespoons sweet paprika
2 tablespoons kosher salt
2 teaspoons ground black pepper
¼–½ teaspoon cayenne pepper

1. Use a sharp knife to make two or three short slashes in the skin of each piece of chicken, taking care not to cut into the meat. Combine the sugar, chili powder, paprika, salt, and pepper in a small bowl and mix thoroughly. Coat the chicken pieces with the spices, gently lifting the skin to distribute the spice rub underneath but leaving it attached to the chicken. Transfer the chicken, skin side up, to a wire rack set over a large, rimmed baking sheet, lightly tent it with foil, and refrigerate for at least 6 hours or up to 24 hours.

2. If desired, secure the skin of each breast piece with two or three toothpicks placed near the edges of the skin (see note).

3. Adjust an oven rack to the middle position and heat the oven to 425 degrees. Roast the chicken until the thickest part of the smallest piece registers 140 degrees on an instant-read thermometer, 15 to 20 minutes. Increase the oven temperature to 500 degrees and continue roasting until the chicken is browned and crisp and the thickest part of the breasts registers 160 to 165 degrees, 5 to 8 minutes longer, removing the pieces from the oven and transferring them to a clean wire rack as they finish cooking. Continue to roast the thighs and/or drumsticks, if using, until the thickest part of the meat registers 175 degrees, about 5 minutes longer. Remove from the oven, transfer the chicken to a rack, and cool completely before refrigerating or serving.

PAN-ROASTED CHICKEN BREASTS

WHY THIS RECIPE WORKS: Cooking bone-in, skin-on chicken breasts can be a challenge. They are difficult to sauté or cook through on the stovetop because of their uneven shape. We wanted to find a method that would produce crisp skin, moist meat, and a quick, flavorful pan sauce.

We chose whole breasts, then split them ourselves to control their size. We brined the breasts for maximum moistness and then seared them on the stovetop before letting them cook through in a 450-degree oven. For the pan sauce, we sautéed minced shallot in the same skillet used to cook the chicken, so we could take advantage of the flavorful browned bits left in the pan. We deglazed the pan with chicken broth and vermouth, then added fresh sage for a sauce with deep herbal flavor. Butter whisked into the sauce after it had reduced lent the sauce body and richness—a perfect partner to our moist, juicy chicken.

TRIMMING SPLIT CHICKEN BREASTS

Using kitchen shears, trim off the rib sections from each breast, following the vertical line of fat from the tapered end of the breast up to the socket where the wing was attached.

Pan-Roasted Chicken Breasts with Sage-Vermouth Sauce

SERVES 4

We prefer to split whole chicken breasts ourselves because store-bought split chicken breasts are often sloppily butchered. However, if you prefer to purchase split chicken breasts, try to choose 10- to 12-ounce pieces with skin intact. If split breasts are of different sizes, check the smaller ones a few minutes early to see if they are cooking more quickly, and remove them from the skillet when they are done.

CHICKEN

½ cup table salt
2 (1½-pound) whole bone-in, skin-on chicken breasts, split in half along breast bone and trimmed of rib sections
Ground black pepper
1 teaspoon vegetable oil

SAGE-VERMOUTH SAUCE

1 large shallot, minced (about 4 tablespoons)
¾ cup low-sodium chicken broth
½ cup dry vermouth
4 medium fresh sage leaves, each leaf torn in half
3 tablespoons unsalted butter, cut into 3 pieces
Table salt and ground black pepper

1. FOR THE CHICKEN: Dissolve the salt in 2 quarts cold water in a large container; submerge the chicken in the brine, cover, and refrigerate for about 30 minutes. Rinse the chicken well and pat dry with paper towels. Season the chicken with pepper.

2. Adjust an oven rack to the lowest position and heat the oven to 450 degrees.

3. Heat the oil in a 12-inch ovensafe skillet over medium-high heat until beginning to smoke. Brown the chicken, skin side down, until deep golden, about 5 minutes; turn the chicken and brown until golden on the second side, about 3 minutes longer. Turn the chicken skin side down and place the skillet in the oven. Roast until the thickest part of the breasts registers 160 to 165 degrees on an instant-read thermometer, 15 to 18 minutes. Transfer the chicken to a platter, and let it rest while making the sauce. (If you're not making the sauce, let the chicken rest for 5 minutes before serving.)

4. FOR THE SAUCE: Using a potholder to protect your hands from the hot skillet handle, pour off all but 1 teaspoon of the fat from the skillet; add the shallot, then set the skillet over medium-high heat and cook, stirring frequently, until the shallot is softened, about 1½ minutes. Add the chicken broth, vermouth, and sage; increase the heat to high and simmer rapidly, scraping the skillet bottom with a wooden spoon to loosen the browned bits, until slightly thickened and reduced to about ¾ cup, about 5 minutes. Pour the accumulated chicken juices into the skillet, reduce the heat to medium, and whisk in the butter 1 piece at a time; season with salt and pepper to taste and discard the sage. Spoon the sauce around the chicken breasts and serve immediately.

SLOW-ROASTED CHICKEN PARTS

WHY THIS RECIPE WORKS: Slow roasting keeps chicken nice and juicy, but at a cost: The skin is often a bit flabby, padded with unrendered fat. For ultramoist roast chicken that boasted the shatteringly crisp skin we loved, we bypassed a whole chicken and turned to parts. We seared leg quarters and then split breasts in oil, rendering some of the fat and giving the crisping a head start. We moved the parts to a 250-degree oven, keeping the slower-cooking thighs on the back portion of the wire rack–lined sheet, facing the hotter side of the oven. While the chicken rested, we whisked together a simple pan sauce with butter, shallots, garlic, and coriander, adding a little powdered gelatin and cornstarch to give it the rich body of a jus. Before serving, we gave the skin a final crisping under the broiler.

Slow-Roasted Chicken Parts with Shallot-Garlic Pan Sauce

SERVES 8

To serve four people, halve the ingredient amounts.

5	pounds bone-in chicken pieces (4 split breasts and 4 leg quarters), trimmed
	Kosher salt and pepper
¼	teaspoon vegetable oil
1	tablespoon unflavored gelatin
2¼	cups chicken broth
2	tablespoons water
2	teaspoons cornstarch
4	tablespoons unsalted butter, cut into 4 pieces
4	shallots, sliced thin
6	garlic cloves, sliced thin
1	teaspoon ground coriander
1	tablespoon minced fresh parsley
1½	teaspoons lemon juice

1. Adjust 1 oven rack to lowest position and second rack 8 inches from broiler element. Heat oven to 250 degrees. Line rimmed baking sheet with aluminum foil and place wire rack on top. Sprinkle chicken pieces with 2 teaspoons salt and season with pepper (do not pat chicken dry).

2. Heat oil in 12-inch skillet over medium-high heat until shimmering. Place leg quarters skin side down in skillet; cook, turning once, until golden brown on both sides, 5 to 7 minutes total. Transfer to prepared sheet, arranging legs along 1 long side of sheet. Pour off fat from skillet. Place breasts skin side down in skillet; cook, turning once, until golden brown on both sides, 4 to 6 minutes total. Transfer to sheet with legs. Discard fat; do not clean skillet. Place sheet on lower rack, orienting so legs are at back of oven. Roast until breasts register 160 degrees and legs register 175 degrees, 1 hour 25 minutes to 1 hour 45 minutes. Let chicken rest on sheet for 10 minutes.

3. While chicken roasts, sprinkle gelatin over broth in bowl and let sit until gelatin softens, about 5 minutes. Whisk water and cornstarch together in small bowl; set aside.

4. Melt butter in now-empty skillet over medium-low heat. Add shallots and garlic; cook until golden brown and crispy, 6 to 9 minutes. Stir in coriander and cook for 30 seconds. Stir in gelatin mixture, scraping up any browned bits. Bring to simmer over high heat and cook until reduced to 1½ cups, 5 to 7 minutes. Whisk cornstarch mixture to recombine. Whisk into sauce and simmer until thickened, about 1 minute. Off heat, stir in parsley and lemon juice; season with salt and pepper to taste. Cover to keep warm.

5. Heat broiler. Transfer sheet to upper rack and broil chicken until skin is well browned and crisp, 3 to 6 minutes. Serve, passing sauce separately.

PERFECT ROAST CHICKEN

WHY THIS RECIPE WORKS: Most home-cooked chickens are either grossly overcooked or so underdone that they resemble an avian version of steak tartare. We wanted a method for producing perfectly roasted chicken, where the white meat cooks up juicy and tender, but with a hint of chew, and the dark meat is fully cooked, all the way to the bone.

For maximum juiciness and well-seasoned meat, we brined the chicken. And for further flavor and a moisture boost to the delicate breast, we rubbed butter under the skin and over the breast. Trussing and continuous basting both proved unnecessary for this ideal chicken. In fact, basting turned its skin greasy and chewy. We had hoped that the bird wouldn't have to be turned while cooking, but we found it was a must for even cooking. In the end, we found that roasting the bird for 15 minutes on each side and then putting it on its back rendered perfectly cooked white and dark meat as well as golden, crunchy skin.

Perfect Roast Chicken
SERVES 2 TO 3

If using a kosher chicken, skip the brining process and begin with step 2. We recommend using a V-rack to roast the chicken. If you don't have a V-rack, set the bird on a regular roasting rack and use balls of aluminum foil to keep the roasting chicken propped up on its side.

- ½ cup table salt
- ½ cup sugar
- 1 (3½- to 4-pound) whole chicken, giblets discarded (see note)
- 2 tablespoons unsalted butter, softened
- 1 tablespoon olive oil
- Ground black pepper

1. Dissolve the salt and sugar in 2 quarts cold water in a large container. Submerge the chicken in the brine, cover, and refrigerate for 1 hour.

2. Adjust an oven rack to the lower-middle position, place a roasting pan on the rack, and heat the oven to 400 degrees. Coat a V-rack with vegetable oil spray and set aside (see note). Remove the chicken from the brine, rinse well, and pat dry with paper towels.

3. Following the photo, use your fingers to gently loosen the center portion of the skin covering each breast; place the butter under the skin, directly on the meat in the center of each breast. Gently press on the skin to distribute the butter over the meat. Tuck the wings behind the back. Rub the skin with the oil, season with pepper, and place the chicken, wing side up, on the prepared V-rack. Place the V-rack in the pre-heated roasting pan and roast for 15 minutes.

4. Remove the roasting pan from the oven and, using two large wads of paper towels, rotate the chicken so that the opposite wing side is facing up. Return the roasting pan to the oven and roast for another 15 minutes.

5. Using two large wads of paper towels, rotate the chicken again so that the breast side is facing up and continue to roast until the thickest part of the breasts registers 160 to 165 degrees and the thickest part of the thighs registers 175 degrees on an instant-read thermometer, 20 to 25 minutes longer. Transfer the chicken to a carving board and let rest for 10 minutes. Carve the chicken and serve.

NOTES FROM THE TEST KITCHEN

APPLYING BUTTER UNDER THE SKIN

Loosen the skin on the breasts and thighs of the chicken by sliding your fingers between the skin and meat.

WEEKNIGHT ROAST CHICKEN

WHY THIS RECIPE WORKS: Roast chicken is often described as a simple dish, and it is, at least in terms of flavor—when done properly, the rich flavor and juicy meat of the chicken need little adornment. But the actual process of preparing and roasting chicken can be surprisingly complicated and time-consuming. And the most time-consuming part is salting or brining the bird, a step that ensures juiciness and well-seasoned meat. We wanted to find a way to get roast chicken on the table in just an hour without sacrificing flavor. After systematically testing the various components and steps of a typical recipe, we found we could skip complicated trussing and just tie the legs together and tuck the wings underneath. We also discovered we could skip both the V-rack and flipping the chicken by using a preheated skillet and placing the chicken breast side up; this gave the thighs a jump-start on cooking. Starting the chicken in a 450-degree oven and then turning the oven off while the chicken finished cooking slowed the evaporation of juices, ensuring moist, tender meat.

Weeknight Roast Chicken
SERVES 4

We prefer to use a 3½- to 4-pound chicken for this recipe; however this method can be used to cook a larger chicken. If roasting a larger bird, increase the cooking time in step 2 to 35 to 40 minutes. If you choose to serve the chicken with one of the pan sauces that follow, don't wash the skillet after removing the chicken. Prepare the pan sauce while resting the chicken.

1 tablespoon kosher salt

½ teaspoon ground black pepper

1 (3½- to 4-pound) whole chicken,
  giblets removed and discarded

1 tablespoon olive oil

1 recipe pan sauce (optional; recipes follow)

1. Adjust an oven rack to the middle position, place a 12-inch ovensafe skillet on the rack, and heat the oven to 450 degrees. Combine the salt and pepper in a bowl. Pat the chicken dry with paper towels and rub the entire surface with the oil. Sprinkle evenly all over with the salt mixture and rub in the mixture with your hands to coat evenly. Tie the legs together with twine and tuck the wing tips behind the back.

2. Transfer the chicken, breast side up, to the preheated skillet in the oven. Roast the chicken until the thickest part of the breasts registers 120 degrees and the thickest part of the thighs registers 135 degrees on an instant-read thermometer, 25 to 35 minutes. Turn off the oven and leave the chicken in the oven until the breasts register 160 degrees and the thighs register 175 degrees, 25 to 35 minutes.

3. Transfer the chicken to a carving board and rest, uncovered, for 20 minutes. Carve and serve with pan sauce.

Tarragon-Lemon Pan Sauce
MAKES ABOUT ¾ CUP

1 medium shallot, minced (about 3 tablespoons)

1 cup low-sodium chicken broth

2 teaspoons Dijon mustard

2 tablespoons unsalted butter

2 teaspoons chopped fresh tarragon leaves

2 teaspoons juice from 1 lemon
  Ground black pepper

While the chicken rests, remove all but 1 tablespoon of fat from the now-empty skillet using a large kitchen spoon, leaving any browned bits and juices in the skillet. Place the skillet over medium-high heat, add the shallot, and cook until softened, about 2 minutes. Stir in the chicken broth and mustard, scraping the skillet bottom with a wooden spoon to loosen the browned bits. Cook until reduced to ¾ cup, about 3 minutes. Off the heat, whisk in the butter, tarragon and lemon juice. Season with pepper to taste; cover and keep warm.

Thyme-Sherry Vinegar Pan Sauce
MAKES ABOUT ¾ CUP

1 medium shallot, minced (about 3 tablespoons)

2 medium garlic cloves, minced or pressed through
  a garlic press (about 2 teaspoons)

2 teaspoons chopped fresh thyme leaves

1 cup low-sodium chicken broth

2 teaspoons Dijon mustard

2 tablespoons unsalted butter

2 teaspoons sherry vinegar
  Ground black pepper

While the chicken rests, remove all but 1 tablespoon of fat from the now-empty skillet, leaving any browned bits and juices in the skillet. Place the skillet over medium-high heat, add the shallot, garlic, and thyme, and cook until softened, about 2 minutes. Stir in the chicken broth and mustard, scraping the skillet bottom with a wooden spoon to loosen the browned bits. Cook until reduced to ¾ cup, about 3 minutes. Off the heat, whisk in the butter and vinegar. Season with pepper to taste; cover and keep warm.

NOTES FROM THE TEST KITCHEN

CARVING A WHOLE CHICKEN

1. Cut the chicken where the leg meets the breast, then pull the leg quarter away. Push up on the joint, then carefully cut through it to remove the leg quarter.

2. Cut through the joint that connects the drumstick to the thigh. Repeat on the second side to remove the other leg.

3. Cut down along one side of the breastbone, pulling the breast meat away from the bone.

4. Remove the wing from the breast by cutting through the wing joint. Slice the breast into attractive slices.

CRISP-SKINNED ROAST CHICKEN

WHY THIS RECIPE WORKS: During roasting, juices and rendered fat can accumulate beneath the chicken skin and turn it wet and flabby. We wanted a juicy roasted chicken with skin that would crackle against your teeth with every bite.

A five-step process was the solution. We first cut an incision down the chicken's back to allow fat to escape and then loosened the skin from the thighs and breasts, poking holes in the fat deposits to allow multiple channels for excess fat and juices to escape. And since skin can't brown until all the surface moisture evaporates, we added baking powder to our salt rub. This helped dehydrate the skin and enhanced the effects of our fourth step: overnight air-drying. Finally, we roasted the bird at high heat to speed the browning. To prevent our kitchen from filling with smoke from the pan drippings, we placed a sheet of foil with holes punched into it under the chicken to shield the rendered fat from direct oven heat. The final result? Roast chicken with tender, juicy meat and the crispest skin ever.

Crisp-Skinned Roast Chicken

SERVES 2 TO 3

Do not brine the bird; it will prevent the skin from becoming crisp. The sheet of foil between the roasting pan and V-rack will keep the drippings from burning and smoking.

- 1 (3½- to 4-pound) whole chicken, giblets discarded (see note)
- 1 tablespoon kosher salt or 1½ teaspoons table salt
- 1 teaspoon baking powder
- ½ teaspoon ground black pepper

1. Place the chicken, breast side down, on a work surface. Following the photos, use the tip of a sharp knife to make four 1-inch incisions along the back of the chicken. Using your fingers or the handle of a wooden spoon, separate the skin from the thighs and breast, being careful not to break the skin. Using a metal skewer, poke 15 to 20 holes in the fat deposits on top of the breast halves and thighs. Tuck the wings behind the back.

2. Combine the salt, baking powder, and pepper in a small bowl. Pat the chicken dry with paper towels and sprinkle all over with the salt mixture. Rub in the mixture with your hands, coating the entire surface evenly. Set the chicken, breast side up, in a V-rack set on a rimmed baking sheet and refrigerate, uncovered, for at least 12 hours or up to 24 hours.

3. Adjust an oven rack to the lowest position and heat the oven to 450 degrees. Using a paring knife, poke 20 holes about 1½ inches apart in a 16 by 12-inch piece of foil. Place the foil loosely in a large roasting pan. Flip the chicken so the breast side faces down, and set the V-rack in the roasting pan on top of the foil. Roast the chicken for 25 minutes.

4. Remove the roasting pan from the oven. Using two large wads of paper towels, rotate the chicken breast side up. Continue to roast until the thickest part of the breasts registers 135 degrees on an instant-read thermometer, 15 to 25 minutes.

5. Increase the oven temperature to 500 degrees. Continue to roast until the skin is golden brown and crisp and the thickest part of the breasts registers 160 to 165 degrees and the thickest part of the thighs registers 175 degrees, 10 to 20 minutes.

6. Transfer the chicken to a carving board and let rest, uncovered, for 20 minutes. Following the photos on page 115, carve the chicken and serve immediately.

NOTES FROM THE TEST KITCHEN

PREPARING CRISP ROAST CHICKEN

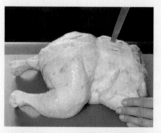

1. Cut incisions in the skin along the chicken's back for the fat to escape.

2. Loosen the skin from the thighs and breast to allow rendering fat to trickle out the openings.

3. Poke holes in the skin of the breast and thighs to create additional channels for fat and juices to escape.

4. Rub a mixture of baking powder and salt into the skin and air-dry the chicken in the refrigerator to help the skin crisp and brown.

BROILED CHICKEN

WHY THIS RECIPE WORKS: We found that one key to getting a whole chicken on the table in about an hour was broiling. Butterflying the chicken kept it flat so that it cooked evenly under the intense direct heat, and it also helped speed up cooking. Piercing the skin at ¾-inch intervals helped the fat render and created an escape route for steam. To get the delicate white meat to finish cooking at the same time as the dark meat, we used a two-pronged approach: A preheated skillet jump-started the cooking of the leg quarters, and starting that skillet under a cold broiler slowed down the cooking of the breasts. To account for carryover cooking, we pulled the chicken from the oven when the breast meat reached 155 degrees instead of 160 degrees (the temperature we'd normally target when roasting a chicken). Finally, the simple addition of garlic and thyme sprigs to the hot pan drippings created a flavorful sauce with almost no effort.

One-Hour Broiled Chicken and Pan Sauce
SERVES 4

If your broiler has multiple settings, choose the highest one. This recipe requires a broiler-safe skillet. In step 3, if the skin is dark golden brown but the breast has not yet reached 155 degrees, cover the chicken with aluminum foil and continue to broil. Monitor the temperature of the chicken carefully during the final 10 minutes of cooking, because it can quickly overcook. Do not attempt this recipe with a drawer broiler.

- 1 (4-pound) whole chicken, giblets discarded
- 1½ teaspoons vegetable oil
  Kosher salt and pepper
- 4 sprigs fresh thyme
- 1 garlic clove, peeled and crushed
  Lemon wedges

1. Adjust oven rack 12 to 13 inches from broiler element (do not preheat broiler). Place chicken breast side down on cutting board. Using kitchen shears, cut through bones on either side of backbone. Trim off any excess fat and skin and discard backbone. Flip chicken over and press on breastbone to flatten. Using tip of paring knife, poke holes through skin over entire surface of chicken, spacing them approximately ¾ inch apart.

2. Rub ½ teaspoon oil over skin and sprinkle with 1 teaspoon salt and ½ teaspoon pepper. Flip chicken over, sprinkle bone side with ½ teaspoon salt, and season with pepper. Tie legs together with kitchen twine and tuck wings under breasts.

3. Heat remaining 1 teaspoon oil in broiler-safe 12-inch skillet over high heat until just smoking. Place chicken in skillet, skin side up, and transfer to oven, positioning skillet as close to center of oven as handle allows (turn handle so it points toward one of oven's front corners.) Turn on broiler and broil chicken for 25 minutes. Rotate skillet by moving handle to opposite front corner of oven and continue to broil until skin is dark golden brown and thickest part of breast registers 155 degrees, 20 to 30 minutes longer.

4. Transfer chicken to carving board and let rest, uncovered, for 15 minutes. While chicken rests, stir thyme sprigs and garlic into juices in pan and let stand for 10 minutes.

5. Using spoon, skim fat from surface of pan juices. Carve chicken and transfer any accumulated juices to pan. Strain sauce through fine-mesh strainer and season with salt and pepper to taste. Serve chicken, passing pan sauce and lemon wedges separately.

CLASSIC ROAST LEMON CHICKEN

WHY THIS RECIPE WORKS: Simple as it sounds, roast lemon chicken can disappoint if the chicken is dry and uninteresting, tastes nothing like lemon, or, even worse, is bursting with citric acidity. The accompanying pan sauce usually suffers a similar fate: bland and lacking lemon or overly harsh. We wanted a way to bring out the full potential of this dish. The chicken should be evenly roasted and moist, with crispy skin, and the lemon flavor should be bright and pure, with no trace of bitterness.

We brined the chicken for extra juiciness. Then we filled the chicken cavity with a cut-up lemon and garlic cloves. To further ensure a juicy bird, we found that the roasting technique was key. We started the chicken breast side down in a moderately hot oven, then flipped it breast side up, added some broth to prevent the drippings from burning, and raised the oven temperature for the remainder of the cooking time. Once the chicken was cooked, we cut it into four pieces and broiled the pieces to get an evenly crisped skin. For the truest lemon flavor, we added a squirt of fresh lemon juice to a simple pan sauce of chicken broth, butter, and fresh herbs.

Classic Roast Lemon Chicken

SERVES 3 TO 4

If using a kosher chicken, skip the brining process and begin with step 2. Broiling the fully roasted and quartered chicken skin side up as it sits in a shallow pool of sauce crisps and browns the skin while keeping the meat succulent. If you decide to skip the broiling step, go directly from quartering the chicken to finishing the sauce with lemon juice, butter, and herbs.

½ cup table salt
1 (3½- to 4-pound) whole chicken, giblets discarded
2 lemons
6 medium garlic cloves, crushed and peeled
4 tablespoons (½ stick) unsalted butter, 2 tablespoons melted and 2 tablespoons chilled and cut into 2 pieces
   Ground black pepper
1¾ cups low-sodium chicken broth
1 tablespoon minced fresh parsley leaves
1 teaspoon minced fresh thyme leaves

1. Dissolve the salt in 2 quarts cold water in a large container. Submerge the chicken in the brine, cover, and refrigerate for 1 hour. Remove the chicken from the brine, rinse well, and pat dry with paper towels.

2. Adjust an oven rack to the lower-middle position; heat the oven to 375 degrees. Spray a V-rack with vegetable oil spray and set in a roasting pan.

3. Cut 1 of the lemons lengthwise into quarters. Place the lemon quarters and garlic in the cavity of the chicken. Brush the breast side of the chicken with 1 tablespoon of the melted butter and season generously with pepper. Place the chicken, breast side down, in the V-rack, then brush the back with the remaining 1 tablespoon melted butter and season generously with pepper.

4. Roast the chicken for 40 minutes. Remove the roasting pan from the oven; increase the oven temperature to 450 degrees. Using two large wads of paper towels, rotate the chicken breast

side up; add 1 cup of the chicken broth to the roasting pan. Return the roasting pan to the oven and continue roasting until the thickest part of the breasts registers 160 to 165 degrees and the thickest part of the thighs registers 175 degrees on an instant-read thermometer, 35 to 40 minutes longer. Remove the roasting pan from the oven; tip the V-rack to let the juices from the chicken cavity run into the roasting pan. Transfer the chicken to a carving board and let rest, uncovered, while making the sauce. Remove the V-rack from the roasting pan.

5. Adjust the oven rack to the upper-middle position and heat the broiler. Skim the fat from the drippings in the roasting pan, add the remaining ¾ cup chicken broth, and set the roasting pan on a burner over high heat. Simmer the liquid, scraping the pan bottom with a wooden spoon to loosen the browned bits, until reduced to ½ cup, about 4 minutes; set aside off the heat.

6. Discard the lemons and garlic from the chicken cavity. Following photos 1 and 3 on page 115, cut the chicken into quarters. Pour the accumulated chicken juices into the roasting pan, then place the chicken quarters, skin side up, into the sauce in the roasting pan; broil the chicken until the skin is crisp and deep golden brown, 3 to 5 minutes. Transfer the chicken to a serving platter.

7. Halve the remaining lemon lengthwise; squeeze the juice of one half into the roasting pan; cut the remaining half into four wedges and set aside. Whisk the remaining 2 tablespoons butter into the sauce until combined; stir in the parsley and thyme. Season with salt and pepper to taste. Serve the chicken with the pan sauce and lemon wedges.

GLAZED ROAST CHICKEN

WHY THIS RECIPE WORKS: Glazed chicken might sound simple but actually turns up a host of troubles, as the problems inherent in roasting chicken (dry breast meat, flabby skin) are compounded by the glaze (won't stick to the meat, burns in patches, introduces moisture). We wanted evenly glazed roast chicken with crisp skin and tender meat. We started with a large roaster chicken. We separated the skin from the meat and pricked holes in the fat deposits to allow rendered fat to escape, then rubbed it with salt and baking powder—to dehydrate the skin and help it to crisp—and we roasted the chicken straddled on top of a beer can set in a roasting pan (a popular grilling technique). The technique seemed like a winner—no awkward flipping, glazing every nook and cranny was easy, and fat dripped freely out of the bird. But cutting into the chicken revealed that the breast, now exposed to the high oven heat for the entire cooking time, was dry and tough. To solve these problems, we rested the chicken before putting it in the oven for blast of heat—the skin came out crisper than before and the breast meat was perfectly cooked. Second, we thickened our glaze with cornstarch and reduced it to a syrupy consistency, then applied it before the final five minutes of roasting. The result? Moist, tender chicken with crisp, glazed skin.

Glazed Roast Chicken

SERVES 4 TO 6

For best results, use a 16-ounce can of beer. A larger can will work, but avoid using a 12-ounce can, as it will not support the weight of the chicken. A vertical roaster can be used in place of the beer can, but we recommend only using a model that can be placed in a roasting pan. Taste your marmalade before using it; if it is overly sweet, reduce the amount of maple syrup in the glaze by 2 tablespoons. Trappist Seville Orange Marmalade is the test kitchen's preferred brand.

CHICKEN

- 1 (6- to 7-pound) whole chicken, giblets discarded
- 2½ teaspoons table salt
- 1 teaspoon baking powder
- 1 teaspoon ground black pepper
- 1 (16-ounce) can beer (see note)

GLAZE

- 1 tablespoon water
- 1 teaspoon cornstarch
- ½ cup maple syrup
- ½ cup orange marmalade (see note)
- ¼ cup cider vinegar
- 2 tablespoons unsalted butter
- 2 tablespoons Dijon mustard
- 1 teaspoon ground black pepper

1. FOR THE CHICKEN: Place the chicken, breast side down, on a work surface. Following the photos on page 116, use the tip of a sharp knife to make four 1-inch incisions along the back of the chicken. Using your fingers or the handle of a wooden spoon, separate the skin from the thighs and breast, being careful not to break the skin. Using a metal skewer, poke 15 to 20 holes in the fat deposits on top of the breast halves and thighs. Tuck the wings behind the back.

2. Combine the salt, baking powder, and pepper in a small bowl. Pat the chicken dry with paper towels and sprinkle evenly all over with the salt mixture. Rub in the mixture with your hands, coating the entire surface evenly. Set the chicken, breast side up, on a rimmed baking sheet and refrigerate, uncovered, for 30 to 60 minutes. Meanwhile, adjust an oven rack to the lowest position and heat the oven to 325 degrees.

3. Open the beer can and pour out (or drink) about half of the liquid. Spray the can lightly with vegetable oil spray and place in the middle of a roasting pan. Slide the chicken over the can so the drumsticks reach down to the bottom of the can, the chicken stands upright, and the breast is perpendicular to the bottom of the pan. Roast until the skin starts to turn golden and the thickest part of the breasts registers 140 degrees on an instant-read thermometer, 75 to 90 minutes. Carefully remove the chicken and pan from the oven and increase the oven temperature to 500 degrees.

4. FOR THE GLAZE: While the chicken cooks, stir the water and cornstarch together in a small bowl until no lumps remain; set aside. Bring the remaining glaze ingredients to a simmer in a medium saucepan over medium-high heat. Cook, stirring occasionally, until reduced to ¾ cup, 6 to 8 minutes. Slowly whisk the cornstarch mixture into the glaze. Return to a simmer and cook for 1 minute. Remove the pan from the heat.

5. When the oven is heated to 500 degrees, place 1½ cups water in the bottom of the roasting pan and return to the oven. Roast until the entire chicken skin is browned and crisp, the thickest part of the breasts registers 160 to 165 degrees, and the thickest part of the thighs registers 175 degrees on an instant-read thermometer, 24 to 30 minutes. Check the chicken halfway through roasting; if the top is becoming too dark, place a 7-inch square piece of foil over the neck and wingtips of the chicken and continue to roast (if the pan begins to smoke and sizzle, add ½ cup water to the roasting pan).

6. Brush the chicken with ¼ cup of the glaze and continue to roast until browned and sticky, about 5 minutes. (If the glaze has become stiff, return to low heat to soften.) Carefully remove the chicken from the oven, transfer the chicken, still on the can, to a carving board, and brush with ¼ cup more glaze. Let rest for 20 minutes.

7. While the chicken rests, strain the juices from the pan through a fine-mesh strainer into a fat separator; allow the liquid to settle for 5 minutes. Whisk ½ cup juices into the remaining ¼ cup glaze in a saucepan and set over low heat. Using a kitchen towel, carefully lift the chicken off the can and onto a platter or carving board. Following the photos on page 115, carve the chicken, adding any accumulated juices to the sauce. Serve, passing the sauce separately.

PERUVIAN ROAST CHICKEN

WHY THIS RECIPE WORKS: Authentic versions of Peruvian garlic-lime chicken require a wood-fired oven and hard-to-find ingredients. We wanted to replicate this robustly flavored dish using an oven and supermarket staples. A paste of salt, garlic, oil, lime zest, and cumin rubbed underneath and on top of the skin produced well-seasoned meat and a heady flavor. To this basic paste we added fresh mint (replacing the black mint paste called for in authentic recipes), oregano, pepper, and minced habanero chile for tangy spice, while a little smoked paprika subtly mimicked the smokiness we were missing from the rotisserie. Roasting the chicken vertically allowed it to cook evenly, while using two different oven temperatures helped us achieve both moist meat and well-browned skin.

Peruvian Roast Chicken with Garlic and Lime

SERVES 3 TO 4

If habanero chiles are unavailable, 1 tablespoon of minced serrano chile can be substituted. Wear gloves when working with hot chiles. This recipe calls for a vertical poultry roaster. If you don't have one, substitute a 12-ounce can of beer. Open the beer and pour out (or drink) about half of the liquid. Spray the can lightly with vegetable oil spray and proceed with the recipe. Serve with Spicy Mayonnaise (recipe follows) and lime wedges.

¼ cup fresh mint leaves

6 medium garlic cloves, chopped coarse

3 tablespoons extra-virgin olive oil

1 tablespoon table salt

1 tablespoon ground black pepper

1 tablespoon ground cumin

1 tablespoon sugar

2 teaspoons smoked paprika

2 teaspoons dried oregano

2 teaspoons finely grated zest plus ¼ cup juice from 2 limes

1 teaspoon minced habanero chile

1 (3½- to 4-pound) whole chicken, giblets discarded

1 cup Spicy Mayonnaise (recipe follows)

1. Process all the ingredients except the chicken and mayonnaise in a blender until a smooth paste forms, 10 to 20 seconds. Following the photos, use your fingers to gently loosen the skin covering the breast and thighs; place half of the paste under the skin, directly on the meat of the breast and thighs. Gently press on the skin to distribute the paste over the meat. Spread the entire exterior surface of the chicken with the remaining paste. Tuck the wings behind the back. Place the chicken in a 1-gallon zipper-lock bag and refrigerate for at least 6 hours or up to 24 hours.

NOTES FROM THE TEST KITCHEN

FLAVORING PERUVIAN ROAST CHICKEN

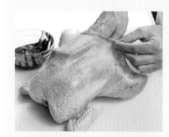

1. Use your fingers to gently loosen the chicken skin from over the thighs and breast and rub half of the paste directly over the meat.

2. Spread the remaining paste over the skin of the entire chicken.

3. Place the chicken in a gallon-size zipper-lock bag; refrigerate for at least 6 or up to 24 hours.

2. Adjust an oven rack to the lowest position and heat the oven to 325 degrees. Place a vertical roaster on a rimmed baking sheet. Slide the chicken onto the vertical roaster so the drumsticks reach down to the bottom of the roaster, the chicken stands upright, and the breast is perpendicular to the bottom of the pan. Roast the chicken until the skin just begins to turn golden and the thickest part of the breast registers 140 degrees, 45 to 55 minutes. Carefully remove the chicken and the pan from the oven and increase the oven temperature to 500 degrees.

3. Once the oven has reached 500 degrees, place 1 cup water in the bottom of the baking sheet and continue to roast until the entire chicken skin is browned and crisp, the breast registers 160 degrees, and the thighs register 175 degrees, about 20 minutes, rotating the pan halfway through roasting. Check the chicken halfway through roasting; if the top is becoming too dark, place a 7-inch square piece of aluminum foil over the neck and wingtips of the chicken and continue to roast (if the pan begins to smoke and sizzle, add additional water to the pan).

4. Carefully remove the chicken from the oven and let rest, still on the vertical roaster, for 20 minutes. Using 2 large wads of paper towels, carefully lift the chicken off the vertical roaster and onto a carving board. Carve the chicken and serve, passing the Spicy Mayonnaise separately.

Spicy Mayonnaise

MAKES ABOUT 1 CUP

If you have concerns about consuming raw eggs, ¼ cup of an egg substitute can be used in place of the egg.

1 large egg

2 tablespoons water

1 tablespoon minced onion

1 tablespoon juice from 1 lime

1 tablespoon minced fresh cilantro leaves

1 tablespoon minced jarred jalapeños

1 medium garlic clove, minced or pressed through
    a garlic press (about 1 teaspoon)
1 teaspoon yellow mustard
¼ teaspoon table salt
1 cup vegetable oil

Process all the ingredients except the oil in a food processor until combined, about 5 seconds. With the machine running, slowly drizzle in the oil in a steady stream until a mayonnaise-like consistency is reached, scraping down the bowl as necessary.

CHICKEN MOLE POBLANO

WHY THIS RECIPE WORKS: The most famous of Mexico's *moles*, mole poblano often relies on as many as six types of chiles for its deep richness. For simplicity's sake, we pared our recipe down to two: ancho, for a robust chile base, and chipotle, for smoky, intense chile flavor. Using almond butter instead of ground almonds was a simple shortcut that lent a luxurious, velvety texture to the sauce. Just 1 ounce of chocolate added richness and depth but didn't make the sauce taste chocolaty. We added warmth and a touch of sweetness with cinnamon, cloves, and raisins. Sautéing the chiles, chocolate, and spices along with the onion and garlic deepened the flavor of the final sauce. Simmering the mole for just 10 minutes thickened the sauce to the perfect consistency. Bone-in chicken pieces worked perfectly with our mole, and removing the skin kept it from turning soggy in the sauce.

Chicken Mole Poblano
SERVES 4 TO 6
Feel free to substitute ½ teaspoon ground chipotle chile powder or ½ teaspoon minced canned chipotles in adobo sauce for the chipotle chile (we noted little difference in flavor) and add with the cinnamon in step 2. Serve with rice.

2 dried ancho chiles, stemmed, seeded,
    and torn into ½-inch pieces (½ cup)
½ dried chipotle chile, stemmed, seeded, and
    torn into ½-inch pieces (scant tablespoon)
3 tablespoons vegetable oil
1 onion, chopped fine
1 ounce bittersweet, semisweet, or
    Mexican chocolate, chopped coarse
½ teaspoon ground cinnamon
⅛ teaspoon ground cloves
2 garlic cloves, minced
2 cups chicken broth
1 (14.5-ounce) can diced tomatoes, drained
¼ cup raisins
¼ cup almond butter
2 tablespoons sesame seeds,
    plus extra for garnish, toasted

MAKING MOLE POBLANO SAUCE
Mole poblano is a quintessential Mexican sauce, but traditional recipes can be very time-consuming. We streamlined the process by sautéing all of our aromatics together (rather than separately) and replacing ground almonds with almond butter for a mole with all the richness and depth of traditional versions.

1. Stem, seed, and tear chiles into ½-inch pieces. Toast chiles in 12-inch skillet over medium heat until fragrant, 2 to 6 minutes. Transfer chiles to plate.

2. Cook onion, then add chiles, spices, and chocolate. Stir in garlic, then broth, tomatoes, sesame seeds, raisins, and almond butter. Simmer until slightly thickened.

3. Transfer sauce to blender. Puree until smooth, about 20 seconds, then season with salt, pepper, and sugar to taste.

Salt and pepper
Sugar
3½ pounds bone-in chicken pieces (split breasts,
    legs, and/or thighs), skin removed, trimmed

1. Toast anchos and chipotle in 12-inch skillet over medium heat, stirring frequently, until fragrant, 2 to 6 minutes; transfer to plate. Add oil and onion to now-empty skillet and cook over medium-high heat until softened, 5 to 7 minutes.

2. Stir in chocolate, cinnamon, cloves, and toasted chiles and cook until chocolate is melted and bubbly, about 2 minutes. Stir in garlic and cook until fragrant, about 30 seconds. Stir in broth, tomatoes, raisins, almond butter, and sesame seeds and bring to simmer. Reduce heat to medium and simmer gently, stirring occasionally, until slightly thickened and measures about 3½ cups, about 7 minutes.

3. Transfer mixture to blender and process until smooth, about 20 seconds. Season with salt, pepper, and sugar to taste. (Sauce can be refrigerated for up to 3 days; loosen with water as needed before continuing.)

4. Adjust oven rack to middle position and heat oven to 400 degrees. Pat chicken dry with paper towels and season with salt and pepper. Arrange chicken in single layer in shallow baking dish and cover with mole sauce, turning to coat chicken evenly. Bake, uncovered, until breasts register 160 degrees, and thighs or drumsticks register 175 degrees, 35 to 45 minutes.

5. Remove chicken from oven, tent with aluminum foil, and let rest for 5 to 10 minutes. Sprinkle with extra sesame seeds and serve.

STOVETOP ROAST CHICKEN

WHY THIS RECIPE WORKS: Roasting chicken in the oven is the usual route to crisp skin and moist meat, but sometimes you want your oven for something else. Cooking chicken pieces in a skillet easily yields a flavorful pan sauce, but the skin on the chicken is often flabby and the meat unevenly cooked. We wanted to combine the best aspects of both roasted and skillet-cooked chicken. We started with four breast halves, two drumsticks, and two thighs. We tested a variety of approaches to achieve moist meat and crisp skin, but ran into numerous problems. Steaming the raw chicken in broth and then searing it in a hot pan, skin side down crisped the skin but caused it to shrink dramatically. To avoid this, we found that searing the chicken first and then steaming was the answer. After steaming, we poured off all the liquid from the pan (reserving it to use for the pan sauce) and returned the chicken to sear again skin side down. This second searing produced the deep, russet-hued crisp skin we had hoped for. After removing the finished chicken, we made our pan sauce with shallot, lemon, and herbs. This quick pan sauce was the perfect complement to our roast chicken.

Stovetop Roast Chicken with Lemon-Herb Sauce
SERVES 4

Use a splatter screen when browning the chicken.

CHICKEN

3½	pounds bone-in, skin-on chicken pieces (split breasts cut in half, drumsticks, and/or thighs), trimmed
	Table salt and ground black pepper
1	tablespoon vegetable oil
¾–1¼	cups low-sodium chicken broth

LEMON-HERB SAUCE

1	teaspoon vegetable oil
1	medium shallot, minced (about 3 tablespoons)
1	teaspoon unbleached all-purpose flour
1½	tablespoons minced fresh parsley leaves
1½	tablespoons minced fresh chives
1	tablespoon juice from 1 lemon
1	tablespoon unsalted butter, chilled
	Table salt and ground black pepper

1. FOR THE CHICKEN: Pat the chicken dry with paper towels and season with salt and pepper. Heat 2 teaspoons of the oil in a 12-inch nonstick skillet over medium-high heat until just smoking. Add the chicken pieces skin side down and cook without moving until golden brown, 5 to 8 minutes.

2. Using tongs, flip the chicken pieces skin side up. Reduce the heat to medium-low, add ¾ cup of the broth to the skillet, cover, and cook until the thickest part of the breasts registers 155 degrees and the thickest part of the thighs/drumsticks registers 170 degrees on an instant-read thermometer, 10 to 16 minutes. Transfer the chicken to a plate, skin side up.

3. Pour off the liquid from the skillet into a 2-cup measuring cup and reserve. Wipe out the skillet with paper towels. Add the remaining 1 teaspoon oil to the skillet and heat over medium-high heat until shimmering. Return the chicken pieces skin side down and cook undisturbed until the skin is deep golden brown and crisp, the thickest part of the breasts registers 160 to 165 degrees, and the thickest part of the thighs/drumsticks registers 175 degrees, 4 to 7 minutes. Transfer to a serving platter and tent loosely with foil. Using a spoon, skim any fat from the reserved cooking liquid and add enough broth to measure ¾ cup.

4. FOR THE SAUCE: Heat the oil in the now-empty skillet over low heat. Add the shallot and cook, stirring frequently, until softened, about 2 minutes. Add the flour and cook, stirring constantly, for 30 seconds. Increase the heat to medium-high, add the reserved cooking liquid, and bring to a simmer, scraping the skillet bottom with a wooden spoon to loosen any browned bits. Simmer rapidly until reduced to ½ cup, 2 to 3 minutes. Stir in any accumulated juices from the resting chicken; return to a simmer and cook for 30 seconds. Off the heat, whisk in the parsley, chives, lemon juice, and butter; season with salt and pepper to taste. Pour the sauce around the chicken and serve immediately.

RAO'S FAMOUS LEMON CHICKEN

WHY THIS RECIPE WORKS: Inspired by Rao's famous roast lemon chicken in New York City, we aspired to re-create this popular dish, while making it more accessible to home cooks. We used a mixture of white and dark meat bone-in chicken parts, instead of the small birds Rao's uses which can be difficult to find. Searing the chicken before transferring it to the oven provided flavorful fond for a pan sauce. Browning the dark meat on both sides ensured the white and dark meats cooked evenly. To get the right amount of lemony flavor, we introduced zest to the sauce right before the chicken was added. The most successful way to thicken the sauce was with flour, added to the aromatics in the beginning of cooking, which provided a full-bodied gravy. A last-minute sprinkle of oregano, parsley, and more lemon zest finished the dish, adding a fruity brightness that complemented the crisp skin, moist meat, and silky sauce.

Skillet-Roasted Chicken in Lemon Sauce
SERVES 4

We serve our version of Rao's chicken with crusty bread, but it can also be served with rice, potatoes, or egg noodles. To ensure crisp skin, dry the chicken well after brining and pour the sauce around, not on, the chicken right before serving.

- ½ cup salt
- 3 pounds bone-in chicken pieces (2 split breasts cut in half crosswise, 2 drumsticks, and 2 thighs), trimmed
- 1 teaspoon vegetable oil
- 2 tablespoons unsalted butter
- 1 large shallot, minced
- 1 garlic clove, minced
- 4 teaspoons all-purpose flour
- 1 cup chicken broth
- 4 teaspoons grated lemon zest plus ¼ cup juice (2 lemons)
- 1 tablespoon fresh parsley leaves
- 1 teaspoon fresh oregano leaves

1. Dissolve salt in 2 quarts cold water in large container. Submerge chicken in brine, cover, and refrigerate for 30 minutes to 1 hour. Remove chicken from brine and pat dry with paper towels.

2. Adjust oven rack to lower-middle position and heat oven to 475 degrees. Heat oil in ovensafe 12-inch skillet over medium-high heat until just smoking. Place chicken skin side down in skillet and cook until skin is well browned and crisp, 8 to 10 minutes. Transfer breasts to large plate. Flip thighs and legs and continue to cook until browned on second side, 3 to 5 minutes longer. Transfer thighs and legs to plate with breasts.

3. Pour off and discard fat in skillet. Return skillet to medium heat; add butter, shallot, and garlic and cook until fragrant, about 30 seconds. Sprinkle flour evenly over shallot-garlic mixture and cook, stirring constantly, until flour is lightly browned, about 1 minute. Slowly stir in broth and lemon juice, scraping up any browned bits, and bring to simmer. Cook until sauce is slightly reduced and thickened, 2 to 3 minutes.

Stir in 1 tablespoon zest and remove skillet from heat. Return chicken, skin side up (skin should be above surface of liquid), and any accumulated juices to skillet and transfer to oven. Cook, uncovered, until breasts register 160 degrees and thighs and legs register 175 degrees, 10 to 12 minutes.

4. While chicken cooks, chop parsley, oregano, and remaining 1 teaspoon zest together until finely minced and well combined. Remove skillet from oven and let chicken stand for 5 minutes.

5. Transfer chicken to serving platter. Whisk sauce, incorporating any browned bits from sides of pan, until smooth and homogeneous, about 30 seconds. Whisk half of herb-zest mixture into sauce and sprinkle remaining half over chicken. Pour some sauce around chicken. Serve, passing remaining sauce separately.

BEST ROAST CHICKEN WITH ROOT VEGETABLES

WHY THIS RECIPE WORKS: Our roast chicken and root vegetables recipe ensures perfect versions of both components by calling for cooking them separately. We brined the chicken to ensure that it stayed juicy and then placed it in a preheated skillet in a hot oven. The dark meat, which needed to be cooked to a higher temperature than the white meat, stayed in contact with the pan, ensuring that it finished cooking at the same time as the more delicate breast meat. We cooked the vegetables below the chicken on a baking sheet until they were tender. Once the chicken was done, we turned the oven up to 500 degrees and finished roasting the vegetables, using the drippings left behind in the skillet to infuse them with chicken flavor. We found that a variety of vegetables worked well as long as we cut them to the same size so they cooked evenly.

Best Roast Chicken With Root Vegetables
SERVES 4 TO 6

Cooking the chicken in a preheated skillet will ensure that the breast and thigh meat finish cooking at the same time. This recipe requires brining the chicken for 1 hour before cooking. If using a kosher chicken, do not brine in step 1, but season with ½ teaspoon salt in step 3.

- 1 (3½- to 4-pound) whole chicken, giblets discarded
  Salt and pepper
- ½ cup sugar
- 1½ pounds Yukon Gold potatoes, peeled and cut into 2-inch pieces
- 12 ounces carrots, peeled, halved crosswise, thick ends halved lengthwise
- 12 ounces parsnips, peeled, halved crosswise, thick ends halved lengthwise
- 4 teaspoons extra-virgin olive oil
- ¼ cup water
- 1 teaspoon minced fresh thyme
- 1 tablespoon chopped fresh parsley

1. With chicken breast side down, use tip of sharp knife to make four 1-inch incisions along back. Using your fingers, gently loosen skin covering breast and thighs. Use metal skewer to poke 15 to 20 holes in fat deposits on top of breast halves and thighs. Dissolve ½ cup salt and sugar in 2 quarts cold water in large container. Submerge chicken in brine, cover, and refrigerate for 1 hour.

2. Adjust oven racks to upper-middle and lower-middle positions and heat oven to 450 degrees. Place 12-inch ovensafe skillet on upper rack and heat for 15 minutes. Spray rimmed baking sheet with vegetable oil spray. Arrange potatoes, carrots, and parsnips with cut surfaces down in single layer on baking sheet and cover sheet tightly with aluminum foil.

3. Remove chicken from brine and pat dry with paper towels. Combine 1 tablespoon oil and ½ teaspoon pepper in small bowl. Rub entire surface of chicken with oil-pepper mixture. Tie legs together with twine and tuck wingtips behind back.

4. Carefully remove skillet from oven (handle will be hot). Add remaining 1 teaspoon oil to skillet and swirl to coat. Place chicken breast side up in skillet. Return skillet to upper rack and place sheet of vegetables on lower rack. Cook for 30 minutes.

5. Remove vegetables from oven, remove foil, and set aside. Rotate skillet and continue to cook chicken until breast registers 160 degrees and thighs register 175 degrees, 15 to 25 minutes longer.

6. Transfer chicken to carving board and let rest, uncovered, for 20 minutes. Increase oven temperature to 500 degrees. Add water to skillet. Using whisk, stir until brown bits have dissolved. Strain sauce through fine-mesh strainer into fat separator, pressing on solids to remove any remaining liquid. Let liquid settle for 5 minutes. Pour off liquid from fat separator and reserve. Reserve 3 tablespoons fat, discarding remaining fat.

7. Drizzle vegetables with reserved fat. Sprinkle vegetables with thyme, 1 teaspoon salt, and ½ teaspoon pepper and toss to coat. Place sheet on upper rack and roast for 5 minutes. Remove sheet from oven. Using thin, sharp metal spatula, turn vegetables. Continue to roast until browned at edges, 8 to 10 minutes longer.

8. Pour reserved liquid over vegetables. Continue to roast until liquid is thick and syrupy and vegetables are tender, 3 to 5 minutes. Toss vegetables to coat, then transfer to serving platter and sprinkle with parsley. Carve chicken and transfer to platter with vegetables. Serve.

CRISP ROAST BUTTERFLIED CHICKEN

WHY THIS RECIPE WORKS: One of the major perks of a butterflied chicken is that it takes considerably less time to cook than a traditional whole bird. Additionally, flattening the chicken encourages crisp skin, since most of the skin is in contact with the hot pan. However, during our testing we found that after initially crisping up, the skin turned soggy as the chicken continued to cook skin side down in its own juices. We set out to produce perfectly cooked chicken with crisp skin that could be on the table in less than an hour. We

started by heating a cast-iron skillet in a very hot oven. We then put the chicken into the preheated skillet skin side down and cooked it until the skin was golden brown. Flipping the chicken over for the remainder of the cooking time allowed us to take advantage of the hot, dry air of the oven to ensure that the skin remained crisp and intact. A simple mixture of extra-virgin olive oil, rosemary, and garlic brushed on the chicken during roasting elevated the flavor and crisped the skin further. We had four-star, perfectly browned roast chicken with spectacular skin on the table in under an hour. And as a bonus, the butterflied bird was a cinch to carve.

Crisp Roast Butterflied Chicken with Rosemary and Garlic

SERVES 4

Be aware that the chicken may slightly overhang the skillet at first, but once browned it will shrink to fit; do not use a chicken larger than 4 pounds. Serve with lemon wedges.

2 tablespoons extra-virgin olive oil
1 teaspoon minced fresh rosemary
1 garlic clove, minced
1 (3½- to 4-pound) whole chicken, giblets discarded
   Salt and pepper

1. Adjust oven rack to lowest position, place 12-inch cast-iron skillet on rack, and heat oven to 500 degrees. Meanwhile, combine 1 tablespoon oil, rosemary, and garlic in bowl; set aside.

2. With chicken breast side down, use kitchen shears to cut through bones on either side of backbone; discard backbone. Flip chicken over, tuck wingtips behind back, and press firmly on breastbone to flatten. Pat chicken dry with paper towels, then rub with remaining 1 tablespoon oil and season with salt and pepper.

3. When oven reaches 500 degrees, place chicken breast side down in hot skillet. Reduce oven temperature to 450 degrees and roast chicken until well browned, about 30 minutes.

4. Using potholders, remove skillet from oven. Being careful of hot skillet handle, gently flip chicken breast side up. Brush chicken with oil mixture, return skillet to oven, and continue to roast chicken until breast registers 160 degrees and thighs register 175 degrees, about 10 minutes. Transfer chicken to carving board, tent loosely with aluminum foil, and let rest for 15 minutes. Carve chicken and serve.

NOTES FROM THE TEST KITCHEN

BUTTERFLYING A CHICKEN

1. With the breast side down, cut along each side of the backbone and remove it.

2. Turn the chicken breast side up. Open the chicken on the work surface. Use the heel of your hand to flatten the breastbone.

3. Cover the chicken with plastic wrap, then pound it with a meat pounder to a fairly even thickness.

HIGH-ROAST CHICKEN

WHY THIS RECIPE WORKS: "High roasting"—cooking a bird at temperatures in excess of 450 degrees—is supposed to produce tastier chicken with crisper skin in record time. But recipes we've tried overcook the bird while producing enough smoke to be mistaken for a five-alarm fire. We wanted to improve upon this method for a quick roasted chicken with skin that is crisp and tanned to a deep golden hue and meat that is irresistibly tender and moist. And while we were at it, we wanted roasted potatoes too.

We began by brining the chicken for moist, well-seasoned meat. Then we butterflied the chicken, which allowed for more even and faster roasting. We found that we were able to add moisture and flavor to the chicken by rubbing flavored herb butter under the skin. (Some recipes instruct rubbing the butter over the skin, but the herbs burn and the butter doesn't season the meat.) We cooked the chicken on top of a broiler pan with a bottom attached. In the bottom of the pan under the chicken, we placed a layer of potatoes. To ensure that the potatoes cooked through, we sliced them thin—1⁄8 to 1⁄4 inch thick. As the chicken cooked, the potatoes absorbed the juices from the chicken and became well seasoned. In just one hour we had roast chicken with spectacularly crisp skin and moist meat—and potatoes too.

High-Roast Butterflied Chicken with Potatoes
SERVES 2 TO 3

If using a kosher bird, skip the brining process and begin with step 2. Because you'll be cooking the chicken under high heat, it's important that you rinse it thoroughly before proceeding—otherwise, the sugar remaining on the skin from the brine will caramelize and ultimately burn. For this cooking technique, russet potatoes offer the best potato flavor, but Yukon Golds develop a beautiful color and retain their shape better after cooking. Either works well in this recipe. A food processor makes quick and easy work of slicing the potatoes.

CHICKEN AND BRINE
- 1⁄2 cup table salt
- 1⁄2 cup sugar
- 1 (3½- to 4-pound) whole chicken, giblets discarded (see note)
- 1 recipe Mustard-Garlic Butter with Thyme (recipe follows)
- 1 tablespoon olive oil
  Ground black pepper

POTATOES
- 2½ pounds russet or Yukon Gold potatoes (4 to 5 medium), peeled and sliced 1⁄8 to 1⁄4 inch thick (see note)
- 1 tablespoon olive oil
- 1⁄2 teaspoon table salt
- 1⁄8 teaspoon ground black pepper

1. FOR THE CHICKEN AND BRINE: Dissolve the salt and sugar in 2 quarts cold water in a large container. Submerge the chicken in the brine, cover, and refrigerate for 1 hour.

2. Adjust an oven rack to the lower-middle position and heat the oven to 500 degrees. Line a broiler-pan bottom with foil. Remove the chicken from the brine, rinse well, and pat dry with paper towels. Following the photos, remove the backbone from the chicken, pound the chicken to a fairly even thickness, and tuck the wings behind the back.

3. Use your fingers to gently loosen the center portion of skin covering each side of the breast. Place the butter mixture under the skin, directly on the meat in the center of each side. Gently press on the skin to distribute the butter over the meat. Rub the skin with the oil and season with pepper. Place the chicken on the broiler-pan top and push each leg up to rest between the thigh and breast.

4. FOR THE POTATOES: Toss the potatoes with the oil, salt, and pepper. Spread the potatoes in an even layer in the prepared broiler-pan bottom. Place the broiler-pan top with the chicken on top.

5. Roast the chicken until just beginning to brown, about 20 minutes. Rotate the pan and continue to roast until the skin is crisped and deep brown and the thickest part of the breasts registers 160 to 165 degrees and the thickest part of the thighs registers 175 degrees on an instant-read thermometer, 20 to 25 minutes longer. Transfer the chicken to a carving board and let rest for 10 minutes.

6. While the chicken rests, remove the broiler-pan top and, using paper towels, soak up any excess grease from the potatoes. Transfer the potatoes to a serving platter. Carve the chicken, transfer to the platter with the potatoes, and serve.

Mustard-Garlic Butter with Thyme
MAKES ABOUT 3 TABLESPOONS

- 2 tablespoons unsalted butter, softened
- 1 tablespoon Dijon mustard
- 1 medium garlic clove, minced or pressed through a garlic press (about 1 teaspoon)
- 1 teaspoon minced fresh thyme leaves
  Pinch ground black pepper

Mash all the ingredients together in a small bowl.

"STUFFED" ROAST CHICKEN

WHY THIS RECIPE WORKS: Stuffed roast chicken can be a conundrum—it's either a perfectly cooked bird filled with lukewarm stuffing (risking salmonella) or safe-to-eat stuffing packed in parched poultry. And given the small cavity of a roasting chicken, there's often no more than a few tablespoons of stuffing per person. We wanted our stuffed roast chicken to produce both flavorful white and dark chicken meat along with an ample amount of intensely flavored stuffing. And we wanted to solve the problem of cooking the stuffing to a safe temperature without drying out the delicate breast meat of the chicken.

We ensured moist, savory meat by brining the bird before we stuffed and roasted it. While the chicken was brining, we jazzed up the stuffing mix by replacing the customary onion with a thinly sliced leek, adding it along with celery, mushrooms, minced garlic, fresh sage, thyme, and parsley, and chicken broth. Our most creative solution, however, was to make an aluminum foil bowl, mound the stuffing into it, and place the chicken—after butterflying it—on top. This improvised cooking vessel allowed the stuffing to become moist and flavorful throughout from the chicken juices, while also becoming brown and chewy on the bottom. And cleanup was a snap.

"Stuffed" Roast Butterflied Chicken
SERVES 4 TO 6

If using a kosher bird, skip the brining process and begin with step 2. Use a traditional (not nonstick) roasting pan to prepare this recipe. When arranging the chicken over the stuffing, it should extend past the edges of the bowl so that most of the fat renders into the roasting pan.

- ½ cup table salt
- ½ cup sugar
- 1 (5- to 6-pound) whole chicken, giblets discarded (see note)
- 1 tablespoon olive oil
  Ground black pepper
- 1 recipe Mushroom-Leek Bread Stuffing with Herbs (recipe follows)

1. Dissolve the salt and sugar in 2 quarts cold water in a large container. Submerge the chicken in the brine, cover, and refrigerate for 1½ hours.

2. Adjust an oven rack to the lower-middle position and heat the oven to 450 degrees. Remove the chicken from the brine, rinse well, and pat dry with paper towels. Following the photos on page 125, remove the backbone from the chicken, pound the chicken to a fairly even thickness, and tuck the wings behind the back. Rub the skin with the oil and season with pepper.

3. To make the foil bowl, place two 12-inch squares of foil on top of each other. Fold the edges to construct an 8 by 6-inch bowl. Coat the inside of the bowl with vegetable oil spray, and place the bowl in a roasting pan. Gently mound and pack the stuffing into the foil bowl and position the chicken over the stuffing. Roast the chicken until just beginning to brown, about

30 minutes. Rotate the pan and continue to roast until the skin is crisped and deep golden brown, the thickest part of the breasts registers 160 to 165 degrees, and the thickest part of the thighs registers 175 degrees on an instant-read thermometer, 25 to 35 minutes longer. Transfer the chicken to a carving board and let rest for 10 minutes.

4. While the chicken rests, transfer the stuffing to a serving bowl and fluff. Cover the stuffing with foil to keep warm. Carve the chicken and serve with the stuffing.

Mushroom-Leek Bread Stuffing with Herbs
MAKES ABOUT 6 CUPS

The dried bread cubes for this stuffing can be stored in an airtight container for up to 1 week.

- 6 slices high-quality white sandwich bread, cut into ¼-inch cubes
- 2 tablespoons unsalted butter
- 1 leek, white and light green parts only, halved lengthwise, sliced ⅛ inch thick, and rinsed thoroughly
- 1 celery rib, chopped fine
- 8 ounces white mushrooms, wiped clean and chopped medium
- ¼ cup minced fresh parsley leaves
- 2 medium garlic cloves, minced or pressed through a garlic press (about 2 teaspoons)
- ½ teaspoon minced fresh sage leaves or ¼ teaspoon dried sage
- ½ teaspoon minced fresh thyme leaves or ¼ teaspoon dried thyme
- ½ cup plus 2 tablespoons low-sodium chicken broth
- 1 large egg
- ½ teaspoon table salt
- ½ teaspoon ground black pepper

1. Adjust an oven rack to the middle position and heat the oven to 250 degrees. Spread the bread cubes in a single layer on a rimmed baking sheet. Bake until thoroughly dried but not browned, about 30 minutes, stirring halfway through the baking time.

2. Meanwhile, melt the butter in a 12-inch skillet over medium-high heat. Add the leek, celery, and mushrooms and cook, stirring occasionally, until the vegetables begin to brown, 6 to 8 minutes. Stir in the parsley, garlic, sage, and thyme and cook until fragrant, about 30 seconds.

3. Whisk the broth, egg, salt, and pepper together in a large bowl. Add the bread cubes and leek-mushroom mixture and toss gently until evenly moistened and combined. Use as directed.

ROASTED CORNISH GAME HENS

WHY THIS RECIPE WORKS: Quick-cooking roasted Cornish game hens are an easy, elegant dinner option, but achieving crispy skin and tender meat in the short cooking time can be a challenge. Poking holes in the skin helped the fat to render quickly. To help the skin crisp up and brown, we used a baking powder rub and let the hens air-dry in the refrigerator overnight. To guarantee evenly golden skin, we butterflied the hens and started cooking them skin side down on a preheated baking sheet. Finally, we flipped them over for a final stint under the broiler. To season the meat inside and out, we added a light coating of kosher salt and fragrant spices on the undersides of the birds.

Roasted Cornish Game Hens
SERVES 4

This recipe requires refrigerating the salted meat for at least 4 hours or up to 24 hours before cooking (a longer salting time is preferable). If your hens weigh 1½ to 2 pounds, cook three instead of four, and extend the initial cooking time in step 5 to 15 minutes. We prefer Bell and Evans Cornish Game Hens.

- 4 (1¼- to 1½-pound) Cornish game hens, giblets discarded
  Kosher salt and pepper
- ¼ teaspoon vegetable oil
- 1 teaspoon baking powder
  Vegetable oil spray

1. Using kitchen shears and working with 1 hen at a time, with hen breast side down, cut through bones on either side of backbone; discard backbone. Lay hens breast side up on counter. Using sharp chef's knife, cut through center of breast to make 2 halves.

2. Using your fingers, carefully separate skin from breasts and thighs. Using metal skewer or tip of paring knife, poke 10 to 15 holes in fat deposits on top of breasts and thighs. Tuck wingtips underneath hens. Pat hens dry with paper towels.

3. Sprinkle 1 tablespoon salt on underside (bone side) of hens. Combine 1 tablespoon salt and oil in small bowl and stir until salt is evenly coated with oil. Add baking powder and stir until well combined. Turn hens skin side up and rub salt–baking powder mixture evenly over surface. Arrange hens skin side up and in single layer on large platter or plates and refrigerate, uncovered, for at least 4 hours or up to 24 hours.

4. Adjust oven racks to upper-middle and lower positions, place rimmed baking sheet on lower rack, and heat oven to 500 degrees.

5. Once oven is fully heated, spray skin side of hens with oil spray and season with pepper. Carefully transfer hens, skin side down, to preheated sheet and cook for 10 minutes.

6. Remove hens from oven and heat broiler. Flip hens skin side up. Transfer sheet to upper rack and broil until well browned and breasts register 160 degrees and drumsticks/thighs register 175 degrees, about 5 minutes, rotating sheet as needed to promote even browning. Transfer to platter or individual plates and serve.

Herb-Roasted Cornish Game Hens

In step 3, combine 2 tablespoons salt with 1 teaspoon dried thyme, 1 teaspoon dried marjoram, and 1 teaspoon dried crushed rosemary. Sprinkle half of salt mixture on underside of hens; add oil to remaining salt-herb mixture until mixture is evenly coated with oil. Add baking powder to oil-salt mixture and proceed with recipe.

Cumin-Coriander Roasted Cornish Game Hens

In step 3, combine 2 tablespoons salt with 2 teaspoons ground cumin, 2 teaspoons ground coriander, 1 teaspoon paprika, and ¼ teaspoon cayenne pepper. Sprinkle half of salt mixture on underside of hens; add oil to remaining salt mixture until mixture is evenly coated with oil. Add baking powder to oil-salt mixture and proceed with recipe.

Oregano-Anise Roasted Cornish Game Hens

In step 3, combine salt with 1 teaspoon dried oregano, ½ teaspoon anise seeds, and ½ teaspoon hot smoked paprika. Sprinkle half of salt mixture on underside of hens; add oil to remaining salt mixture until mixture is evenly coated with oil. Add baking powder to oil-salt mixture and proceed with recipe.

NOTES FROM THE TEST KITCHEN

GETTING CORNISH GAME HENS TO CRISP QUICKLY AND EVENLY

Because the meat on Cornish game hens finishes cooking long before their skin crisps, we devised a few tricks to accelerate the skin's progress.

1. Cutting out the backbones and flattening the birds promotes uniform browning.

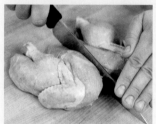

2. Halving the flattened hens (simple knife work with small birds) makes them easier to serve.

3. Loosening and poking holes in the skin allows the fat to drain during cooking, aiding crisping.

4. Rubbing the birds with salt and baking powder and then chilling them wicks away moisture.

5. Starting the birds skin side down on a preheated baking sheet effectively (and efficiently) crisps their skin.

FRIED CHICKEN

WHY THIS RECIPE WORKS: Frying chicken at home is a daunting task, with its messy preparation and spattering hot fat. In the end, the chicken often ends up disappointingly greasy, with a peeling crust and dry, tasteless meat. We wanted fried chicken worthy of the mess and splatter: moist, seasoned meat coated with a delicious, crispy mahogany crust.

We soaked chicken parts in a seasoned buttermilk brine for ultimate flavor and juiciness. Then we air-dried the brined chicken parts to help ensure a crisp skin. Flour made the crispest coating. We found that peanut oil can withstand the demands of frying and has the most neutral flavor of all the oils tested. Vegetable oil was a close runner-up. As for frying the chicken, we found that a Dutch oven worked best. With its high sides and lid, the Dutch oven minimized splatters and retained heat which helped the chicken cook through.

Crispy Fried Chicken
SERVES 4 TO 6

Avoid using kosher chicken in this recipe or it will be too salty. Maintaining an even oil temperature is key. After the chicken is added to the pot, the temperature will drop dramatically, and most of the frying will be done at about 325 degrees. Use an instant-read thermometer with a high upper range; a clip-on candy/deep-fry thermometer is fine, too, though it can be clipped to the pot only for the uncovered portion of frying.

CHICKEN
- ½ cup table salt
- ¼ cup sugar
- 2 tablespoons paprika
- 7 cups buttermilk
- 3 medium garlic heads, cloves separated and smashed
- 3 bay leaves, crumbled
- 4 pounds bone-in, skin-on chicken pieces (split breasts cut in half, drumsticks, and/or thighs), trimmed (see note)
- 3-4 quarts peanut oil or vegetable oil, for frying

COATING
- 4 cups (20 ounces) unbleached all-purpose flour
- 1 large egg
- 1 teaspoon baking powder
- ½ teaspoon baking soda
- 1 cup buttermilk

1. FOR THE CHICKEN: Dissolve the salt, sugar, and paprika in the buttermilk in a large container. Add the garlic and bay leaves, submerge the chicken in the brine, cover, and refrigerate for 2 to 3 hours.

2. Rinse the chicken well and place in a single layer on a wire rack set over a rimmed baking sheet. Refrigerate uncovered for 2 hours. (At this point, the chicken can be covered with plastic wrap and refrigerated for up to 6 more hours.)

3. Adjust an oven rack to the middle position and heat the oven to 200 degrees. In a large Dutch oven, heat 2 inches of oil over medium-high heat to 375 degrees (see note).

4. FOR THE COATING: Place the flour in a shallow dish. Whisk the egg, baking powder, and baking soda together in a medium bowl, then whisk in the buttermilk (the mixture will bubble and foam). Working with 3 chicken pieces at a time, dredge in the flour, shaking off the excess, then coat with the egg mixture, allowing the excess to drip off. Finally, coat with flour again, shake off the excess, and return to the wire rack.

5. When the oil is hot, add half of the chicken pieces to the pot, skin side down, cover, and fry until deep golden brown, 7 to 11 minutes, adjusting the heat as necessary to maintain an oil temperature of about 325 degrees. (After 4 minutes, check the chicken pieces for even browning and rearrange if some pieces are browning faster than others.) Turn the chicken pieces over and continue to cook until the thickest part of the breasts registers 160 to 165 degrees and the thickest part of the thighs or drumsticks registers 175 degrees on an instant-read thermometer, 6 to 8 minutes. Drain the chicken briefly on a paper towel–lined plate, then transfer to a clean wire rack set over a rimmed baking sheet and keep warm in the oven.

6. Return the oil to 375 degrees (if necessary) over medium-high heat and repeat with the remaining chicken pieces. Serve.

EASIER FRIED CHICKEN

WHY THIS RECIPE WORKS: Crackling-crisp, golden-brown, and juicy—what's not to love about fried chicken? In a word, frying. Heating more than a quart of fat on the stovetop can be daunting for home cooks. We wanted to find a way to prepare fried chicken without having to heat up a pot full of oil. To season the meat and ensure it turned out juicy, we soaked chicken parts in a buttermilk brine. We also incorporated baking powder, an unconventional ingredient in fried chicken, into our dredging mixture. As the chicken fried, the baking powder released carbon dioxide gas, leavening the crust and increasing its surface area, keeping it light and crisp. And while most dredging mixtures contain purely dry ingredients, we added a little buttermilk to our mixture because the small clumps of batter it formed turn ultra-crisp once fried. To streamline frying the chicken, we turned to a hybrid method where we fried the chicken until just lightly browned on both sides in less than half the amount of oil we'd typically use. Then we transferred the chicken to the oven to finish cooking through. Setting the chicken on a rack promoted air circulation all around the meat for an evenly crisp crust.

Easier Fried Chicken
SERVES 4

A whole 4-pound chicken, cut into eight pieces, can be used instead of the chicken parts. Skinless chicken pieces are also an acceptable substitute, but the meat will come out slightly drier. A Dutch oven with an 11-inch diameter can be used in place of the straight-sided sauté pan.

1¼ cups buttermilk

Table salt

Dash of hot sauce

3 teaspoons ground black pepper

1 teaspoon garlic powder

1 teaspoon paprika

¼ teaspoon cayenne pepper

3½ pounds bone-in, skin-on chicken parts (breasts, thighs, and drumsticks, or a mix, with breasts cut in half), trimmed of excess fat (see note)

2 cups unbleached all-purpose flour

2 teaspoons baking powder

1¾ cups vegetable oil

1. Whisk 1 cup of the buttermilk, 1 tablespoon salt, the hot sauce, 1 teaspoon of the black pepper, ¼ teaspoon of the garlic powder, ¼ teaspoon of the paprika, and a pinch of cayenne together in a large bowl. Add the chicken pieces and turn to coat. Refrigerate, covered, for at least 1 hour or up to overnight.

2. Adjust an oven rack to the middle position and heat the oven to 400 degrees. Whisk the flour, baking powder, 1 teaspoon salt, and the remaining 2 teaspoons black pepper, the remaining ¾ teaspoon garlic powder, the remaining ¾ teaspoon paprika, and the remaining cayenne together in a large bowl. Add the remaining ¼ cup buttermilk to the flour mixture and mix with your fingers until combined and small clumps form. Working with one piece at a time, dredge the chicken pieces in the flour mixture, pressing the mixture onto the pieces to form a thick, even coating. Place the dredged chicken on a large plate, skin side up.

3. Heat the oil in an 11-inch straight-sided sauté pan over medium-high heat to 375 degrees, about 5 minutes. Carefully place the chicken pieces in the pan, skin side down, and cook until golden brown, 3 to 5 minutes. Carefully flip the chicken pieces and continue to cook until golden brown on the second side, 2 to 4 minutes longer. Transfer the chicken to a wire rack set over a rimmed baking sheet. Bake the chicken until an instant-read thermometer inserted into the thickest part of the chicken registers 160 degrees for the breasts and 175 for the legs and thighs, 15 to 20 minutes. (Smaller pieces may cook faster than larger pieces. Remove the chicken pieces from the oven as they reach the correct temperature.) Let the chicken rest for 5 minutes before serving.

OVEN-FRIED CHICKEN

WHY THIS RECIPE WORKS: Oven-fried chicken never seems to taste as good as the real thing. The coating, often plain bread crumbs or cornflakes, never gets as crunchy or as flavorful as a deep-fried coating does. We wanted a good alternative to regular fried chicken that would have real crunch and good flavor. We soaked bone-in chicken legs and thighs in a buttermilk brine to achieve maximum juiciness. And we removed the skin from the chicken before brining because it didn't render in the oven. A mixture of eggs and mustard helped the crumbs stick to the chicken. Melba toast crumbs

made the crispest coating. We baked the chicken on a wire rack set over a baking sheet that we had lined with foil. This method allowed heat to circulate around the chicken during baking, resulting in crisp chicken all over without turning.

Oven-Fried Chicken

SERVES 4

Avoid using kosher chicken in this recipe or it will be too salty. If you don't want to buy whole chicken legs and cut them into drumsticks and thighs, simply buy four drumsticks and four thighs. To make Melba toast crumbs, place the toasts in a heavy-duty zipper-lock freezer bag, seal, and pound with a meat pounder or other heavy blunt object. Leave some crumbs in the mixture the size of pebbles, but most should resemble coarse sand.

CHICKEN

½ cup plus 2 tablespoons table salt

¼ cup sugar

2 tablespoons paprika

3 medium heads garlic, cloves separated

3 bay leaves, crumbled

7 cups buttermilk

4 whole chicken legs, separated into drumsticks and thighs and skin removed (see note)

COATING

¼ cup vegetable oil

1 box (about 5 ounces) plain Melba toast, crushed (see note)

2 large eggs

1 tablespoon Dijon mustard

1 teaspoon dried thyme

¾ teaspoon table salt

½ teaspoon ground black pepper

½ teaspoon dried oregano

¼ teaspoon garlic powder

¼ teaspoon cayenne pepper (optional)

1. FOR THE CHICKEN: In a large zipper-lock bag, combine the salt, sugar, paprika, garlic cloves, and bay leaves. With a flat meat pounder, smash the garlic into the salt and spice mixture thoroughly. Pour the mixture into a large container. Add the buttermilk and stir until the salt and sugar are completely dissolved. Submerge the chicken in the brine and refrigerate for 2 to 3 hours. Rinse the chicken well and place on a large wire rack set over a rimmed baking sheet. Refrigerate uncovered for 2 hours. (After 2 hours, the chicken can be covered with plastic wrap and refrigerated up to 6 hours longer.)

2. Adjust an oven rack to the upper-middle position and heat the oven to 400 degrees. Line a large, rimmed baking sheet with foil and set a large wire rack over the pan.

3. FOR THE COATING: Drizzle the oil over the Melba toast crumbs in a pie plate or shallow dish; toss well to coat. Mix the eggs, mustard, thyme, salt, pepper, oregano, garlic powder, and cayenne (if using) with a fork in a second plate.

4. Working with one piece at a time, coat the chicken on both sides with the egg mixture. Set the chicken in the Melba crumbs, sprinkle the crumbs over the chicken, and press to coat. Turn the chicken over and repeat on the other side. Gently shake off the excess and place on the rack. Bake until the chicken is deep nutty brown and the thickest part of a piece registers 175 degrees on an instant-read thermometer, about 40 minutes. Serve.

BUFFALO WINGS

WHY THIS RECIPE WORKS: Buffalo wings are the ultimate bar snack. Great wings boast juicy meat, a crisp coating, and a spicy, sweet, and vinegary sauce. But dry, flabby wings are often the norm and the sauce can be scorchingly hot. We wanted perfectly cooked wings, coated in a well-seasoned sauce—good enough to serve with our creamy blue cheese dressing. We coated the wings with cornstarch for a super crisp exterior and deep-fried the wings for the best texture. Then we deepened the flavor of the traditional hot sauce by adding brown sugar and cider vinegar. For heat, we chose Frank's RedHot Original Sauce, which is traditional, but not very spicy, so we added a little Tabasco for even more kick.

Buffalo Wings
SERVES 6 TO 8

Frank's RedHot Original Sauce is not terribly spicy. We like to combine it with a more potent hot sauce, such as Tabasco, to bring up the heat.

SAUCE
- 4 tablespoons (½ stick) unsalted butter
- ½ cup Frank's RedHot Original Sauce (see note)
- 2 tablespoons Tabasco or other hot sauce, plus more to taste (see note)
- 1 tablespoon packed dark brown sugar
- 2 teaspoons cider vinegar

WINGS
- 1–2 quarts peanut oil, for frying
- 3 tablespoons cornstarch
- 1 teaspoon table salt
- 1 teaspoon ground black pepper
- 1 teaspoon cayenne pepper
- 18 chicken wings (about 3 pounds), wings separated into 2 parts at joint and wingtips removed (see photos)

VEGETABLES AND DRESSING
- 2 medium carrots, peeled and cut into thin sticks
- 4 medium celery ribs, cut into thin sticks
- 1 recipe Rich and Creamy Blue Cheese Dressing (see page 37)

1. FOR THE SAUCE: Melt the butter in a small saucepan over low heat. Whisk in the hot sauces, brown sugar, and vinegar until combined. Remove from the heat and set aside.

CUTTING UP CHICKEN WINGS

1. Cut into the skin between the larger sections of the wing until you hit the joint.

2. Bend back the two sections to pop and break the joint.

3. Cut through the skin and flesh to completely separate the two meaty portions.

4. Hack off the wingtip and discard.

2. FOR THE WINGS: Heat the oven to 200 degrees. Line a baking sheet with paper towels. In a large Dutch oven fitted with a clip-on candy thermometer, heat 2½ inches of oil over medium-high heat to 360 degrees. While the oil heats, combine the cornstarch, salt, black pepper, and cayenne in a small bowl. Dry the chicken with paper towels and place the pieces in a large mixing bowl. Sprinkle the spice mixture over the wings and toss with a rubber spatula until evenly coated. Fry half of the chicken wings until golden and crisp, 10 to 12 minutes. With a slotted spoon, transfer the fried chicken wings to the prepared baking sheet. Keep the first batch of chicken warm in the oven while frying the remaining wings.

3. TO SERVE: Pour the sauce mixture into a large bowl, add the chicken wings, and toss until the wings are uniformly coated. Serve immediately with the carrot and celery sticks and blue cheese dressing on the side.

TALKING TURKEY
AND ALL THE TRIMMINGS

CLASSIC ROAST TURKEY

WHY THIS RECIPE WORKS: Few of us want to take chances when cooking the holiday bird. We wanted to find a way that guaranteed moist, flavorful meat and bronzed skin—a true holiday table centerpiece.

First we brined our turkey, which helped prevent the meat from drying out and also seasoned it right to the bone. After brining, we rinsed the bird of excess salt and let it rest on a wire rack in the refrigerator so that the skin dried out. This step helped ensure the skin would cook up crisp, not flabby. Placing the turkey on a V-rack allowed for air circulation all around so that the bird cooked evenly. And turning the turkey three times also helped to ensure even cooking. Finally, once the turkey was cooked, we waited 30 minutes before carving it. That might seem like a long time, but it allowed the juices in the turkey to redistribute so that, once carved, each slice was moist and full of flavor.

Classic Roast Turkey
SERVES 10 TO 12

Resist the temptation to tent the roasted turkey with foil while it rests on the carving board. Covering the bird will make the skin soggy.

- 2 cups table salt
- 1 (12- to 14-pound) turkey; giblets, neck, and tailpiece removed and reserved for gravy
- 2 medium onions, chopped coarse
- 2 medium carrots, chopped coarse
- 2 celery ribs, chopped coarse
- 6 sprigs fresh thyme
- 3 tablespoons unsalted butter, melted
- 1 cup water, plus more as needed
- 1 recipe Giblet Pan Gravy (recipe follows)

1. Dissolve the salt in 2 gallons cold water in a large container. Submerge the turkey in the brine, cover, and refrigerate or store in a very cool spot (40 degrees or less) for 4 to 6 hours.

2. Set a wire rack over a large rimmed baking sheet. Remove the turkey from the brine and rinse it well. Pat the turkey dry, inside and out, with paper towels. Place the turkey on the prepared baking sheet. Refrigerate, uncovered, for at least 8 hours or overnight.

3. Adjust an oven rack to the lowest position and heat the oven to 400 degrees. Line a V-rack with heavy duty foil and poke several holes in the foil. Set the V-rack in a roasting pan and spray the foil with vegetable oil spray.

4. Toss half of the onions, carrots, celery, and thyme with 1 tablespoon of the melted butter in a medium bowl and place inside the turkey. Tie the legs together with kitchen twine and tuck the wings under the bird. Scatter the remaining vegetables into the roasting pan.

5. Pour 1 cup water over the vegetable mixture. Brush the turkey breast with 1 tablespoon more melted butter, then place the turkey, breast side down, on the V-rack. Brush with the remaining 1 tablespoon melted butter.

6. Roast the turkey for 45 minutes. Remove the pan from the oven; baste with juices from the pan. With a dish towel in each hand, turn the turkey leg/thigh side up. If the liquid in the pan has totally evaporated, add another ½ cup water. Return the turkey to the oven and roast for 15 minutes. Remove the turkey from the oven again, baste, and turn the other leg/thigh side up; roast for another 15 minutes. Remove the turkey from the oven for a final time, baste, and turn it breast side up; roast until the thickest part of the breast registers 160 to 165 degrees and the thickest part of the thigh registers 175 degrees on an instant-read thermometer, 30 to 45 minutes.

7. Remove the turkey from the oven. Gently tip the turkey so that any accumulated juices in the cavity run into the roasting pan. Transfer the turkey to a carving board and let rest, uncovered, for 30 minutes. Carve the turkey and serve with the gravy.

Giblet Pan Gravy
MAKES ABOUT 6 CUPS

Complete step 1 up to a day ahead, if desired. Begin step 3 once the bird has been removed from the oven and is resting on a carving board.

- 1 tablespoon vegetable oil
  Reserved turkey giblets, neck, and tailpiece
- 1 medium onion, chopped
- 4 cups low-sodium chicken broth
- 2 cups water
- 2 sprigs fresh thyme
- 8 sprigs fresh parsley
- 3 tablespoons unsalted butter
- ¼ cup unbleached all-purpose flour
- 1 cup dry white wine
  Table salt and ground black pepper

1. Heat the oil in a large Dutch oven over medium heat until shimmering; add the giblets, neck, and tailpiece, and cook until golden and fragrant, about 5 minutes. Add the onion and continue to cook until softened, 3 to 4 minutes longer. Reduce the heat to low, cover, and cook until the turkey parts and onion release their juices, about 15 minutes. Add the broth, water, and herbs, bring to a boil, and adjust the heat to low. Simmer, uncovered, skimming any impurities that may rise to the surface, until the broth is rich and flavorful, about 30 minutes longer. Strain the broth into a large container and reserve the giblets. When cool enough to handle, chop the giblets. Refrigerate the giblets and broth until ready to use. (The broth can be stored in the refrigerator in an airtight container for up to 1 day.)

2. While the turkey is roasting, return the reserved turkey broth to a simmer. Heat the butter in a large saucepan over medium-low heat. Vigorously whisk in the flour (the mixture will froth and then thin out again). Cook slowly, stirring constantly, until nutty brown and fragrant, 10 to 15 minutes. Vigorously whisk all but 1 cup of the hot broth into the flour mixture. Bring to a boil, then continue to simmer, stirring occasionally, until the gravy is lightly thickened and very flavorful, about 30 minutes longer. Set aside until the turkey is done.

3. When the turkey has been transferred to a carving board to rest, spoon out and discard as much fat as possible from the roasting pan, leaving the caramelized herbs and vegetables. Place the roasting pan over two burners set on medium-high heat. Return the gravy to a simmer. Add the wine to the roasting pan of caramelized vegetables, scraping up any browned bits with a wooden spoon, and boil until reduced by half, about 5 minutes. Add the remaining 1 cup turkey broth and continue to simmer for 15 minutes; strain the pan juices into the gravy, pressing as much juice as possible out of the vegetables. Stir the reserved giblets into the gravy and return to a boil. Season with salt and pepper to taste and serve.

ROAST TURKEY FOR A CROWD

WHY THIS RECIPE WORKS: Unless you have access to multiple ovens, only a very large turkey will do when you've got a crowd coming to dinner. But finding a container large enough to brine a gargantuan bird can be tricky. And turning the bird in the oven, our usual method for evenly cooked meat, can be hot, heavy, and dangerous. We wanted the Norman Rockwell picture of perfection: a crisp, mahogany skin wrapped around tender, moist meat. And it had to be easy to prepare in a real home kitchen.

We chose a Butterball turkey, which has already been brined for juicy flavor (a kosher bird, which has been salted, works well too). A combination of high and low heat resulted in a tender, juicy bird with deeply browned skin. We made the meat and pan drippings more flavorful with the addition of onion, carrot, and celery. A quartered lemon added bright,

Once upon a time, the only thing the Thanksgiving turkey had going for it was tradition—and even that was tenuous, as many of us sometimes dreamed of cheating with a big buttery beef tenderloin. The problem was a familiar one. Sometimes the bird turned out juicy and flavorful, but most often, it was a dry disappointment. Passing the gravy didn't help much either. Then, 15 years ago, the test kitchen came upon an obscure technique called brining. Brining turkey involves soaking the turkey in a saltwater solution (which sometimes includes sugar) before cooking—this protects it from the ravages of heat and guarantees tender, flavorful meat from the surface all the way to the bone. (Brining does the same for other delicate white meat like chicken and pork.) How does brining work?

Simply put, the brining solution flows into the meat, distributing moisture and seasoning. In our testing, we found that while a turkey roasted straight out of its package will retain about 82 percent of its total weight after cooking, a brined turkey will retain about 93 percent of its total weight after cooking—and thus be moister and more flavorful. Once a little-known technique, brining has now become mainstream—and Thanksgiving dinners everywhere are all the better for it.

clean flavor. After roasting, we allowed the turkey to rest so the juices would redistribute, but didn't tent it with foil so the skin wouldn't become soggy. Serve with Giblet Pan Gravy for a Crowd (recipe follows).

Roast Turkey for a Crowd
SERVES ABOUT 20
Rotating the bird helps produce moist, evenly cooked meat, but for the sake of ease, you may opt not to rotate it. In that case, skip the step of lining the V-rack with foil and roast the bird breast side up for the entire cooking time. Because we do not brine the bird, we had the best results with a frozen Butterball (injected with salt and water) or a kosher bird (soaked in salt water during processing).

registers 160 to 165 degrees and the thickest part of the thigh registers 175 degrees on an instant-read thermometer, about 2 hours longer.

5. Remove the turkey from the oven. Gently tip the turkey up so that any accumulated juices in the cavity run into the roasting pan. Transfer the turkey to a carving board. Let rest, uncovered, for 35 to 40 minutes. Carve the turkey and serve with the gravy.

Giblet Pan Gravy for a Crowd
MAKES ABOUT 8 CUPS

Complete step 1 up to a day ahead, if desired. Begin step 3 once the bird has been removed from the oven and is resting on a carving board.

- 1 tablespoon vegetable oil
-     Reserved turkey giblets, neck, and tailpiece
- 1 medium onion, unpeeled and chopped
- 6 cups low-sodium chicken broth
- 3 cups water
- 2 sprigs fresh thyme
- 8 sprigs fresh parsley
- 5 tablespoons unsalted butter
- ¼ cup plus 2 tablespoons unbleached all-purpose flour
- 1½ cups dry white wine
-     Table salt and ground black pepper

1. Heat the oil in a large Dutch oven over medium heat until shimmering; add the giblets, neck, and tailpiece, and cook until golden and fragrant, about 5 minutes. Add the onion and continue to cook until softened, 3 to 4 minutes longer. Reduce the heat to low, cover, and cook until the turkey parts and onion release their juices, about 15 minutes. Add the broth, water, and herbs, bring to a boil, and adjust the heat to low. Simmer, uncovered, skimming any impurities that may rise to the surface, until the broth is rich and flavorful, about 30 minutes longer. Strain the broth into a large container and reserve the giblets. When cool enough to handle, chop the giblets. Refrigerate the giblets and broth until ready to use. (The broth can be stored in the refrigerator in an airtight container for up to 1 day.)

2. While the turkey is roasting, return the reserved turkey broth to a simmer. Heat the butter in a large saucepan over medium-low heat. Vigorously whisk in the flour (the mixture will froth and then thin out again). Cook slowly, stirring constantly, until nutty brown and fragrant, 10 to 15 minutes. Vigorously whisk all but 2 cups of the hot broth into the flour mixture. Bring to a boil, then continue to simmer, stirring occasionally, until the gravy is lightly thickened and very flavorful, about 35 minutes longer. Set aside until the turkey is done.

3. When the turkey has been transferred to a carving board to rest, spoon out and discard as much fat as possible from the roasting pan, leaving the caramelized herbs and vegetables.

- 3 medium onions, chopped coarse
- 3 medium carrots, chopped coarse
- 3 celery ribs, chopped coarse
- 1 lemon, quartered
- 2 sprigs fresh thyme
- 5 tablespoons unsalted butter, melted
- 1 (18- to 22-pound) frozen Butterball or kosher turkey, fully thawed (see note); giblets, neck, and tailpiece removed and reserved for gravy
- 1 cup water, plus more as needed
- 1 teaspoon table salt
- 1 teaspoon ground black pepper
- 1 recipe Giblet Pan Gravy for a Crowd (recipe follows)

1. Adjust an oven rack to the lowest position. Heat the oven to 425 degrees. Line a large V-rack with heavy-duty foil and poke several holes in the foil. Set the V-rack in a large roasting pan and spray the foil with vegetable oil spray.

2. Toss half of the onions, carrots, celery, lemon, and thyme with 1 tablespoon of the melted butter in a medium bowl and place inside the turkey. Tie the legs together with kitchen twine and tuck the wings under the bird. Scatter the remaining vegetables into the roasting pan.

3. Pour 1 cup water over the vegetable mixture. Brush the turkey breast with 2 tablespoons more of the melted butter, then sprinkle with half of the salt and half of the pepper. Place the turkey, breast side down, on the V-rack. Brush with the remaining 2 tablespoons melted butter and sprinkle with the remaining salt and pepper.

4. Roast the turkey for 1 hour. Remove the pan from the oven; baste with juices from the pan. With a dish towel in each hand, turn the turkey breast side up. If the liquid in the pan has totally evaporated, add another ½ cup water. Lower the oven temperature to 325 degrees. Return the turkey to the oven and continue to roast until the thickest part of the breast

Place the roasting pan over two burners set on medium-high heat. Return the gravy to a simmer. Add the wine to the roasting pan of caramelized vegetables, scraping up any browned bits with a wooden spoon, and boil until reduced by half, about 7 minutes. Add the remaining 2 cups turkey broth and continue to simmer for 15 minutes; strain the pan juices into the gravy, pressing as much juice as possible out of the vegetables. Stir the reserved giblets into the gravy and return to a boil. Season with salt and pepper to taste and serve.

OLD-FASHIONED STUFFED TURKEY

WHY THIS RECIPE WORKS: Perfecting one aspect of a roast turkey often comes at the cost of another. Crisp skin means dry white meat. Brining adds moisture, but can turn the skin soggy. And stuffing the cavity compounds the headache, slowing the roasting time and upping the chance for uneven cooking. We wanted a turkey with everything: juicy meat, crisply burnished skin, and rich-flavored stuffing that cooked inside the bird.

For the crispiest possible skin, we opted for salting over brining. Salting initially draws moisture out of the meat, but after a long rest in the refrigerator, all the moisture gets slowly drawn back in, seasoning the meat and helping it retain moisture. Next we turned to slow roasting and started the bird in a relatively low oven, then cranked the temperature to give it a final blast of skin-crisping heat and to bring the center up to temperature. It worked beautifully, yielding breast meat that was moist and tender. For even crispier skin, we massaged it with a baking powder and salt rub. The baking powder dehydrates the skin and raises its pH, making it more conducive to browning. We also poked holes in the skin to help rendering fat escape.

And for extra flavor, we draped the bird with meaty salt pork, which we removed and drained before cranking up the heat so the bird didn't taste too smoky. To make sure the stuffing was cooked through, we started half of it in the bird (in a cheesecloth bag for easy removal) to give it meaty flavor, then combined it with the uncooked batch to finish baking it while the turkey rested.

Old-Fashioned Stuffed Turkey

SERVES 10 TO 12

Table salt is not recommended for this recipe because it is too fine. To roast a kosher or self-basting turkey (such as a frozen Butterball), do not salt it in step 1. Look for salt pork that is roughly equal parts fat and lean meat. The bread can be toasted up to 1 day in advance. Serve with Make-Ahead Turkey Gravy (recipe follows).

TURKEY

- 1 (12- to 14-pound) turkey, giblets and neck reserved for gravy, if making (see note)
- 3 tablespoons plus 2 teaspoons kosher salt (see note)
- 2 teaspoons baking powder
- 12 ounces salt pork, cut into ¼-inch-thick slices and rinsed (see note)

STUFFING

- 1½ pounds (about 15 slices) high-quality white sandwich bread, cut into ½-inch cubes (about 12 cups)
- 4 tablespoons (½ stick) unsalted butter, plus extra for the baking dish
- 1 medium onion, minced
- 2 celery ribs, chopped fine
  Kosher salt and ground black pepper
- 2 tablespoons minced fresh thyme leaves
- 1 tablespoon minced fresh marjoram leaves
- 1 tablespoon minced fresh sage leaves
- 1½ cups low-sodium chicken broth
- 1 36-inch square cheesecloth, folded in quarters
- 2 large eggs

1. FOR THE TURKEY: Following the photos on page 147, use your fingers or the handle of a wooden spoon to separate the turkey skin from the meat on the breast, legs, thighs, and back; avoid breaking the skin. Rub 1 tablespoon of the salt evenly inside the cavity of the turkey, 1½ teaspoons salt under the skin of each breast half, and 1½ teaspoons salt under the skin of each leg. Wrap the turkey tightly with plastic wrap; refrigerate for 24 to 48 hours.

2. FOR THE STUFFING: Adjust an oven rack to the lowest position and heat the oven to 250 degrees. Spread the bread cubes in a single layer on a rimmed baking sheet; bake until the edges have dried but the centers are slightly moist (the cubes should yield to pressure), about 45 minutes, stirring several times during baking. Transfer to a large bowl and increase the oven temperature to 325 degrees.

STUFFING A TURKEY

1. After placing 4 to 5 cups of the preheated stuffing into the turkey, use metal skewers (or cut bamboo skewers) and thread them through the skin on both sides of the cavity to seal the cavity shut.

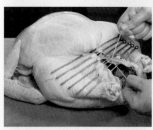

2. Center a 2-foot piece of kitchen twine on the top skewer and then cross the twine as you wrap each end of it around and under the skewers. Loosely tie the legs together with another short piece of twine.

3. Flip the turkey over onto its breast. Stuff the neck cavity loosely with approximately 1 cup of stuffing. Pull the skin flap over and use a skewer to pin the flap to the turkey.

3. While the bread dries, heat the butter in a 12-inch skillet over medium-high heat; when the foaming subsides, add the onion, celery, 2 teaspoons salt, and 1 teaspoon pepper; cook, stirring occasionally, until the vegetables begin to soften and brown slightly, 7 to 10 minutes. Stir in the herbs; cook until fragrant, about 1 minute. Add the vegetables to the bowl with the dried bread; add 1 cup of the broth and toss until evenly moistened.

4. TO ROAST THE TURKEY: Combine the remaining 2 teaspoons salt and the baking powder in a small bowl. Remove the turkey from the refrigerator and unwrap. Thoroughly dry the turkey inside and out with paper towels. Using a skewer, poke 15 to 20 holes in the fat deposits on top of the breast halves and thighs, 4 to 5 holes in each deposit. Sprinkle the surface of the turkey with the salt–baking powder mixture and rub in the mixture with your hands, coating the skin evenly. Tuck the wings underneath the turkey. Line the turkey cavity with the cheesecloth, pack with 4 to 5 cups stuffing, and tie the ends of the cheesecloth together. Cover the remaining stuffing with plastic wrap and refrigerate. Using kitchen twine, loosely tie the turkey legs together. Place the turkey breast side down in a V-rack set in a roasting pan and drape the salt pork slices over the back.

5. Roast the turkey breast side down until the thickest part of the breast registers 130 degrees on an instant-read thermometer, 2 to 2½ hours. Remove the roasting pan from the oven and increase the oven temperature to 450 degrees. Transfer the

turkey in the V-rack to a rimmed baking sheet. Remove and discard the salt pork. Using clean potholders or kitchen towels, rotate the turkey breast side up. Cut the twine binding the legs and remove the stuffing bag; empty into the reserved stuffing in the bowl. Pour the drippings from the roasting pan into a fat separator and reserve for gravy, if making.

6. Once the oven has come to temperature, return the turkey in the V-rack to the roasting pan and roast until the skin is golden brown and crisp, the thickest part of the breast registers 160 degrees, and the thickest part of the thigh registers 175 degrees, about 45 minutes, rotating the pan halfway through. Transfer the turkey to a carving board and let rest, uncovered, for 30 minutes.

7. While the turkey rests, reduce the oven temperature to 400 degrees. Whisk the eggs and remaining ½ cup broth together in a small bowl. Pour the egg mixture over the stuffing and toss to combine, breaking up any large chunks; spread in a buttered 13 by 9-inch baking dish. Bake until the stuffing registers 165 degrees and the top is golden brown, about 15 minutes. Carve the turkey and serve with the stuffing.

Make-Ahead Turkey Gravy
MAKES ABOUT 2 QUARTS

Note that the optional roast turkey drippings may be quite salty—add them carefully to the gravy in step 4 so the gravy does not become too salty.

  6 turkey thighs, trimmed, or 9 wings, separated at the joints
  2 medium carrots, chopped coarse
  2 medium celery ribs, chopped coarse
  2 medium onions, chopped coarse
  1 head garlic, halved
     Vegetable oil spray
10 cups low-sodium chicken broth, plus extra as needed
  2 cups dry white wine
12 sprigs fresh thyme
     Unsalted butter, as needed
  1 cup unbleached all-purpose flour
     Table salt and ground black pepper
     Defatted drippings from Old-Fashioned Stuffed Turkey (page 137; optional)

1. Adjust an oven rack to the middle position and heat the oven to 450 degrees. Toss the thighs, carrots, celery, onions, and garlic together in a roasting pan and spray with vegetable oil spray. Roast, stirring occasionally, until well browned, 1½ to 1¾ hours.

2. Transfer the contents of the roasting pan to a large Dutch oven. Add the broth, wine, and thyme and bring to a boil, skimming as needed. Reduce to a gentle simmer and cook until the broth is brown and flavorful and measures about 8 cups when strained, about 1½ hours. Strain the broth through a fine-mesh strainer into a large container, pressing on the solids to extract as much liquid as possible; discard the solids. (The turkey broth can be cooled and refrigerated in an airtight container for up to 2 days or frozen for up to 1 month.)

3. Let the strained turkey broth settle (if necessary) then spoon off and reserve ½ cup of the fat that has risen to the top (add butter as needed if short on turkey fat). Heat the fat in a Dutch oven over medium-high heat until bubbling. Whisk in the flour and cook, whisking constantly, until well browned, 3 to 7 minutes.

4. Slowly whisk in the turkey broth and bring to a boil. Reduce to a simmer and cook until the gravy is very thick, 10 to 15 minutes. Add the defatted drippings (if using) to taste, then season with salt and pepper to taste and serve. (The gravy can be refrigerated in an airtight container for up to 2 days; reheat gently, adding additional chicken broth as needed to adjust the consistency).

CLASSIC ROAST STUFFED TURKEY

WHY THIS RECIPE WORKS: There is something undeniably festive about a stuffed roasted turkey, but more and more people nowadays roast turkeys unstuffed out of concern for health and safety. We wanted to find a way to safely and success-fully roast a stuffed turkey, making sure that the breast meat would be succulent and the stuffing fully cooked.

At the outset, we decided to limit our turkey to a maximum of 14 pounds, because it is just too difficult to safely stuff and roast a larger bird. Often, the breast meat is a bone-dry 180 degrees by the time the stuffing reaches a safe 165 degrees. We got around this by heating the stuffing in the microwave before placing half of it in the bird to give it a head start on cooking. We baked the remaining stuffing separately in a casserole dish; this ensured that there would be enough stuffing to go around. We also brined the bird to add flavor and moisture (brining did not, as we feared, make the stuffing soggy or overly salty).

Classic Roast Stuffed Turkey

SERVES 10 TO 12

A 12- to 14-pound turkey will accommodate approximately half of the stuffing. Bake the remainder in a casserole dish while the bird rests before carving. If serving with Giblet Pan Gravy (page 134), note that you can complete step 1 up to a day ahead, if desired. Begin step 3 once the bird has been removed from the oven and is resting on a carving board.

- 2 cups table salt
- 1 (12- to 14-pound) turkey; giblets, neck, and tailpiece removed and reserved for gravy (see page 134)
- 2 medium onions, chopped coarse
- 1 medium carrot, chopped coarse
- 1 celery rib, chopped coarse
- 4 sprigs fresh thyme
- 1 cup water, plus more as needed
- 12 cups prepared stuffing (recipe follows)
- 3 tablespoons unsalted butter, plus extra for the casserole dish and foil
- ¼ cup low-sodium chicken broth
- 1 recipe Giblet Pan Gravy (page 134)

1. Dissolve the salt in 2 gallons cold water in a large container. Submerge the turkey in the brine, cover, and refrigerate or store in a very cool spot (40 degrees or less) for 4 to 6 hours.

2. Set a wire rack over a large rimmed baking sheet. Remove the turkey from the brine and rinse it well. Pat the turkey dry inside and out with paper towels. Place the turkey on the prepared baking sheet. Refrigerate, uncovered, and air-dry for at least 8 hours or overnight.

3. Adjust an oven rack to the lowest position and heat the oven to 400 degrees. Line a V-rack with heavy-duty foil and poke several holes in the foil. Set the V-rack inside a roasting pan and spray the foil with vegetable oil spray. Scatter the onions, carrot, celery, and thyme in the roasting pan. Pour 1 cup water over the vegetable mixture.

4. Place half of the stuffing in a buttered medium casserole dish, dot the surface with 1 tablespoon of the butter, cover with foil, and refrigerate until ready to use. Microwave the remaining stuffing on high power, stirring two or three times, until very hot (120 to 130 degrees on an instant-read thermometer), 6 to 8 minutes. Spoon 4 to 5 cups of stuffing into the turkey cavity until very loosely packed. Following the photos on page 138, secure the skin flap over the cavity opening with skewers. Melt the remaining 2 tablespoons butter. Tuck the wings under the bird, brush the turkey breast with half of the melted butter, then turn the turkey breast side down. Fill the neck cavity with the remaining heated stuffing and secure the skin flap over the opening. Place the turkey, breast side down, on the V-rack. Brush with the remaining butter.

5. Roast the turkey for 1 hour, then reduce the temperature to 250 degrees and roast for 2 hours longer, adding water if the pan becomes dry. Remove the pan from the oven (close the oven door) and, with a dish towel in each hand, turn the bird breast side up, and baste (the temperature of the thickest part of the breast should be 145 to 150 degrees). Increase the oven temperature to 400 degrees; continue to roast until the thick-est part of the breast registers 160 to 165 degrees, the thickest part of the thigh registers 175 degrees, and the center of the stuffing registers 165 degrees on an instant-read thermometer, 1 to 1½ hours longer. Remove the turkey from the oven, trans-fer to a carving board, and let rest for 30 minutes.

6. Add the broth to the dish of reserved stuffing, replace the foil, and bake until hot throughout, about 20 minutes. Remove the foil; continue to bake until the stuffing forms a golden brown crust, about 15 minutes longer.

7. Carve the turkey and serve with the stuffing and the gravy.

Bread Stuffing with Bacon, Apples, Sage, and Caramelized Onions

MAKES ABOUT 12 CUPS

To dry the bread, spread the cubes out onto 2 large baking sheets and dry in a 300-degree oven for 30 to 60 minutes. Let the bread cool before using in the stuffing.

1 pound bacon, cut crosswise into ¼-inch strips
6 medium onions, sliced thin (about 7 cups)
1 teaspoon table salt
2 Granny Smith apples, peeled, cored, and
   cut into ½-inch cubes (about 2 cups)
½ cup fresh parsley leaves, chopped fine
3 tablespoons minced fresh sage leaves
½ teaspoon ground black pepper
3 pounds high-quality white sandwich bread,
   cut into ¾-inch cubes (about 12 cups)
1 cup low-sodium chicken broth
3 large eggs, lightly beaten

1. Cook the bacon in a large skillet or Dutch oven over medium heat until crisp and browned, about 12 minutes. Remove the bacon from the pan with a slotted spoon and drain on paper towels. Discard all but 3 tablespoons of the rendered bacon fat.

2. Increase the heat to medium-high and add the onions and ¼ teaspoon of the salt. Cook the onions until golden in color, making sure to stir occasionally and scrape the sides and bottom of the pan, about 20 minutes. Reduce the heat to medium and continue to cook, stirring more often to prevent burning, until the onions are deep golden brown, another 5 minutes. Add the apples and continue to cook for another 5 minutes. Transfer the contents of the pan to a large bowl.

3. Add the parsley, sage, remaining ¾ teaspoon salt, and the pepper to the bowl and mix to combine. Add the bread cubes.

4. Whisk the broth and eggs together in a small bowl. Pour the mixture over the bread cubes. Gently toss to evenly distribute the ingredients.

JULIA CHILD'S STUFFED TURKEY, UPDATED

WHY THIS RECIPE WORKS: In her 1989 cookbook, *The Way to Cook*, Julia Child separates a raw turkey into legs and breast to ensure that both white and dark meat are roasted to perfection. Other benefits include a quicker cook time and a small mound of rich sausage stuffing that tastes as though it has been roasted inside the bird. We loved this idea, but saw a couple of opportunities for improvement. In our version, we brined the breast to keep it juicy and flavorful. Jump-starting the cooking of the breast at 425 degrees decreased the overall cooking time, which also helped the meat to retain moisture. To make even more stuffing, we increased the amount of bread, and we swapped the sausage for the brighter flavor of dried cranberries.

Julia Child's Stuffed Turkey, Updated
SERVES 10 TO 12

This recipe calls for a natural, unenhanced turkey and requires brining the turkey breast in the refrigerator for 6 to 12 hours before cooking. If using a self-basting turkey (such as a frozen Butterball) or a kosher turkey, do not brine

in step 3 and omit the salt in step 2. Trim any excess fat from the bird before cooking to ensure that the stuffing doesn't become greasy. The bottom of your roasting pan should be 7 to 8 inches from the top of the oven. In this recipe, we leave the stuffing in a warm oven while the turkey rests. If you need your oven during this time, you may opt to leave the stirred stuffing in the uncovered roasting pan at room temperature while the turkey rests and then reheat it in a 400-degree oven for 10 minutes before reassembling your turkey.

1   (12- to 15-pound) turkey, neck and giblets
    removed and reserved for gravy
1   teaspoon plus 2 tablespoons minced fresh sage
    Salt and pepper
    Wooden skewers
1½ pounds hearty white sandwich bread,
    cut into ½-inch cubes
1   tablespoon vegetable oil
3   tablespoons unsalted butter
3   onions, chopped fine
6   celery ribs, minced
1   cup dried cranberries
4   large eggs, beaten

1. With turkey breast side up, using boning or paring knife, cut through skin around leg quarter where it attaches to breast. Bend leg back to pop leg bone out of socket. Cut through joint to separate leg quarter. Repeat to remove second leg quarter. Working with 1 leg quarter at a time and with skin side down, use tip of knife to cut along sides of thighbone to expose bone, then slide knife under bone to free meat. Cut joint between thigh and leg and remove thighbone. Reserve thighbones for gravy.

2. Rub interior of each thigh with ½ teaspoon sage, ½ teaspoon salt, and ¼ teaspoon pepper. Truss each thigh closed using wooden skewers and kitchen twine. Place leg quarters on large plate, cover, and refrigerate for 6 to 12 hours.

DECONSTRUCTED TURKEY

Removing the leg quarters from a turkey and deboning the thighs may sound intimidating, but it really is a snap. Julia used a meat cleaver and rubber mallet to remove the backbone. But we found it easier to use only kitchen shears and a boning or paring knife, concentrating on severing the easy-to-cut ligaments, tendons, and cartilage between the bones instead of trying to hack through the bones themselves. Added bonus? Removing bones now makes it easier to carve later.

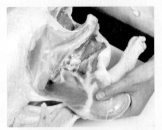

1. Using boning or paring knife, cut through skin around leg where it attaches to breast. Bend leg back to pop leg bone out of socket. Cut through joint to separate leg quarter.

2. With tip of knife, cut along sides of thighbone to expose bone, then slide knife under bone to free meat. Without severing skin, cut joint between thigh and leg and remove thighbone.

3. Rub interior of each thigh with sage, salt, and pepper. Truss thighs closed with wooden skewers and kitchen twine.

4. Using kitchen shears, cut through ribs, following line of fat running from tapered end of breast to wing joint.

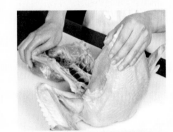

5. Using your hands, bend backbone away from breast to pop shoulder joint out of socket.

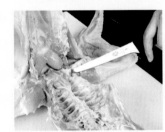

6. Cut through shoulder joint to separate back from breast.

3. Using kitchen shears, cut through ribs following vertical line of fat where breast meets back from tapered end of breast to wing joint. Using your hands, bend back away from breast to pop shoulder joint out of socket. Cut through joint between bones to separate back from breast. Reserve back for gravy. Trim excess fat from breast. Dissolve ¾ cup salt in 6 quarts cold water in large container. Submerge breast in brine, cover, and refrigerate for 6 to 12 hours.

4. Adjust oven racks to upper-middle and lower-middle positions and heat oven to 300 degrees. Spread bread cubes in even layer on 2 rimmed baking sheets and bake until mostly dry and very lightly browned, 25 to 30 minutes, stirring occasionally during baking. Transfer dried bread to large bowl. Increase oven temperature to 425 degrees.

5. While bread dries, remove breast from brine and pat dry with paper towels (leave leg quarters in refrigerator). Tuck wings behind back. Brush surface with 2 teaspoons oil. Melt butter in 12-inch nonstick ovensafe skillet over medium heat. Add onions and cook, stirring occasionally, until softened, 10 to 12 minutes. Add celery, remaining 2 tablespoons sage, and 1½ teaspoons pepper; continue to cook until celery is slightly softened, 3 to 5 minutes longer. Transfer vegetables

to bowl with bread and wipe out skillet with paper towels. Place turkey breast skin side down in skillet, and roast in oven for 30 minutes.

6. While breast roasts, add cranberries and eggs to bread mixture and toss to combine (mixture will be dry). Transfer stuffing to 16 by 13-inch roasting pan and, using rubber spatula, pat stuffing into level 12 by 10-inch rectangle.

7. Remove breast from oven, and using 2 wads of paper towels, flip breast and place over two-thirds of stuffing. Arrange leg quarters over remaining stuffing and brush with remaining 1 teaspoon oil. Lightly season breast and leg quarters with salt. Tuck any large sections of exposed stuffing under bird so most of stuffing is covered by turkey. Transfer pan to oven and cook for 30 minutes.

8. Reduce oven temperature to 350 degrees. Continue to roast until thickest part of breast registers 160 to 165 degrees and thickest part of thigh registers 175 to 180 degrees, 40 minutes to 1 hour 20 minutes longer. Transfer breast and leg quarters to cutting board and let rest for 30 minutes. While turkey rests, using metal spatula, stir stuffing well, scraping up any browned bits. Redistribute stuffing over bottom of roasting pan, return to oven, and turn off oven.

9. Before serving, season stuffing with salt and pepper to taste. Mound stuffing in center of platter. Place breast on top of stuffing with point of breast resting on highest part of mound. Remove skewers and twine from leg quarters and place on each side of breast. Carve and serve.

Turkey Gravy for Julia Child's Stuffed Turkey, Updated

MAKES ABOUT 4 CUPS

If you do not have ¼ cup of reserved turkey fat in step 4, supplement with unsalted butter.

> Reserved turkey giblets, neck, backbone, and thighbones, hacked into 2-inch pieces
> 2 onions, chopped coarse
> 1 carrot, peeled and cut into 1-inch pieces
> 1 celery rib, cut into 1-inch pieces
> 6 garlic cloves, unpeeled
> 1 tablespoon vegetable oil
> 3½ cups chicken broth
> 3 cups water
> 2 cups dry white wine
> 6 sprigs fresh thyme
> ¼ cup all-purpose flour
> Salt and pepper

1. Adjust oven rack to middle position and heat oven to 450 degrees. Place turkey parts, onions, carrot, celery, and garlic in large roasting pan. Drizzle with oil and toss to combine. Roast, stirring occasionally, until well browned, 40 to 50 minutes.

2. Remove pan from oven, and place over high heat. Add broth and bring to boil, scraping up any browned bits. Transfer contents of pan to Dutch oven. Add water, wine, and thyme sprigs; bring to boil over high heat. Reduce heat to low and simmer until reduced by half, about 1½ hours.

3. Strain contents of pot through fine-mesh strainer set in large bowl. Press solids with back of spatula to extract as much liquid as possible. Discard solids. Transfer liquid to fat separator and let settle, 5 minutes.

4. Transfer ¼ cup fat to medium saucepan and heat over medium-high heat until bubbling. Whisk in flour and cook, whisking constantly, until combined and honey-colored, about 2 minutes. Gradually whisk in hot liquid and bring to boil. Reduce heat to medium-low and simmer, stirring occasionally, until thickened, about 5 minutes. Season with salt and pepper to taste. (Gravy can be refrigerated for up to 2 days.)

SLOW-ROASTED TURKEY WITH GRAVY

WHY THIS RECIPE WORKS: Roasting a whole turkey is a race to keep the white meat from drying out while the dark meat cooks through. We wanted an approach that would get our fowl from supermarket to table in just a few hours. We

required meat as moist as prime rib and with crisp, crackling skin, and it all needed to be accompanied by rich gravy. For a greater challenge, we wanted to do it without salting the turkey or brining it, both of which take the better part of a day.

First, we roasted two nonbrined turkeys, one using our standard high-heat method and the other at 275 degrees the entire time. The outer layers of the high-heat breast dried out, but the slow-roasted breast cooked through moist, even without a brine. Coordinating the cooking between the breast and legs and thighs, however, was a problem. Instead we discovered that swapping in turkey parts for a whole turkey would help ensure the breast and thighs cooked through at about the same time. We roasted a breast and two leg quarters (thighs and drumsticks) on a rack over a baking sheet to promote air circulation. The results? Tender, juicy meat.

We next had to tackle crisping the skin. Most recipes achieve crisp skin by starting the bird in a hot oven to brown it, then lowering the heat. But that meant a higher oven temperature, which meant dried-out meat. Instead, we let the turkey cool before popping it back in the oven to crisp the skin. This turned out a perfect turkey from center to edge surrounded by flawless, crisp skin.

Slow-Roasted Turkey with Gravy

SERVES 10 TO 12

Instead of drumsticks and thighs, you may use 2 whole leg quarters, 1½ to 2 pounds each. The recipe will also work with turkey breast alone; in step 2, reduce the butter to 1½ tablespoons, the salt to 1½ teaspoons, and the pepper to 1 teaspoon. If you are roasting kosher or self-basting turkey parts, season the turkey with only 1½ teaspoons salt.

TURKEY

> 3 medium onions, chopped medium
> 3 medium celery ribs, chopped medium
> 2 medium carrots, peeled and chopped medium
> 5 sprigs fresh thyme

5 medium garlic cloves, peeled and halved
1 cup low-sodium chicken broth
1 (5- to 7-pound) whole bone-in, skin-on
turkey breast, trimmed (see note)
4 pounds turkey drumsticks and thighs,
trimmed (see note)
3 tablespoons unsalted butter, melted
1 tablespoon table salt
2 teaspoons ground black pepper

GRAVY

2 cups low-sodium chicken broth
3 tablespoons unsalted butter
3 tablespoons unbleached all-purpose flour
2 bay leaves
Table salt and ground black pepper

1. FOR THE TURKEY: Adjust an oven rack to the lower-middle position and heat the oven to 275 degrees. Arrange the onions, celery, carrots, thyme, and garlic in an even layer on a large rimmed baking sheet. Pour the broth into the baking sheet. Place a wire rack on top of the vegetables.

2. Pat the turkey pieces dry with paper towels. Brush the turkey pieces on all sides with the melted butter. Sprinkle the salt and pepper evenly over the turkey. Place the breast, skin side down, and the drumsticks and thighs, skin side up, on the rack on the vegetable-filled baking sheet, leaving at least ¼ inch between the pieces.

3. Roast the turkey pieces for 1 hour. With a dish towel in each hand, turn the turkey breast skin side up. Continue roasting until the thickest part of the breast registers 160 to 165 degrees the thickest part of the thigh registers 175 degrees on an instant-read thermometer, 1 to 2 hours longer. Remove the baking sheet from the oven and transfer the rack with the turkey to a second baking sheet. Allow the pieces to rest for at least 30 minutes or up to 1½ hours.

4. FOR THE GRAVY: Strain the vegetables and liquid from the baking sheet through a colander set in a large bowl. Press the solids with the back of a spatula to extract as much liquid as possible. Discard the vegetables. Transfer the liquid in the bowl to a 4-cup liquid measuring cup. Add the chicken broth to the measuring cup (you should have about 3 cups liquid).

5. In a medium saucepan, heat the butter over medium-high heat; add the flour and cook, stirring constantly, until the flour is dark golden brown and fragrant, about 5 minutes. Whisk in the broth mixture and bay leaves and gradually bring to a boil. Reduce the heat to medium-low and simmer, stirring occasionally, until the gravy is thick and reduced to 2 cups, 15 to 20 minutes. Discard the bay leaves. Remove the gravy from the heat and season with salt and pepper to taste. Keep the gravy warm.

6. TO SERVE: Heat the oven to 500 degrees. Place the baking sheet with the turkey in the oven. Roast until the skin is golden brown and crisp, about 15 minutes. Transfer the turkey to a carving board and let rest, uncovered, for 20 minutes. Carve and serve with the gravy.

CRISP-SKIN HIGH-ROAST TURKEY

WHY THIS RECIPE WORKS: High-roasting (oven-roasting at very high temperatures for the sake of speed and flavor) a turkey presents the home cook with two potential problems: billowing smoke from incinerated pan drippings and torched breast meat. We wanted to find a way to prepare a high-roast turkey with crisp, picture-perfect skin and moist, evenly cooked meat in less than two hours—without setting off the smoke alarm.

We butterflied the turkey for crisp skin and evenly cooked meat, and then roasted it on a broiler pan set over the stuffing—which absorbed the drippings. This step helped season the stuffing and kept the kitchen from filling with smoke. These techniques let us crank up the heat to get the bird done in record time. To complement our moist, crisp-skinned turkey, we made a corn bread and sausage stuffing that was both rich and easy to prepare.

Crisp-Skin High-Roast Butterflied Turkey with Sausage Dressing

SERVES 10 TO 12

The dressing can be made with corn bread or white bread, but note that they are not used in equal amounts. The turkey is roasted in a broiler pan top, or a sturdy wire rack, set in a 16 by 12-inch disposable aluminum roasting pan. If using a wire rack, choose one that measures about 17 by 11 inches so that it will span the roasting pan and sit above the dressing in the pan.

TURKEY

1 cup table salt
1 cup sugar
1 (12- to 14-pound) turkey; giblets, neck, and
tailpiece removed and reserved for gravy;
turkey butterflied (see photos on page 144)
and backbone and rib bones reserved for gravy
1 tablespoon unsalted butter, melted

SAUSAGE DRESSING

12 cups corn bread (recipe follows) broken into 1-inch
pieces (include crumbs), or 18 cups 1-inch challah
or Italian bread cubes (from about 1½ loaves)
1¾ cups low-sodium chicken broth
1 cup half-and-half
2 large eggs, beaten lightly
12 ounces bulk pork sausage, broken into 1-inch pieces
3 medium onions, minced (about 3 cups)
3 celery ribs, chopped fine (about 1½ cups)
2 tablespoons unsalted butter
2 tablespoons minced fresh thyme leaves
2 tablespoons minced fresh sage leaves
3 medium garlic cloves, minced or pressed through
a garlic press (about 1 tablespoon)
1½ teaspoons table salt
2 teaspoons ground black pepper
1 recipe Turkey Gravy (page 145)

1. TO BRINE THE TURKEY: Dissolve the salt and sugar in 2 gallons cold water in a large container. Submerge the turkey in the brine and refrigerate or store in a very cool spot (40 degrees or less) for 4 to 6 hours.

2. TO PREPARE THE DRESSING: While the turkey brines, adjust the oven racks to the upper-middle and lower-middle positions and heat the oven to 250 degrees. Spread the bread in an even layer on two rimmed baking sheets and dry in the oven for 50 to 60 minutes for corn bread or 40 to 50 minutes for challah or Italian bread.

3. Place the bread in a large bowl. Whisk the broth, half-and-half, and eggs together in a medium bowl; pour over the bread and toss very gently to coat so that the bread does not break into smaller pieces. Set aside.

4. Heat a 12-inch skillet over medium-high heat until hot, about 1½ minutes. Add the sausage and cook, stirring occasionally, until the sausage loses its raw color, 5 to 7 minutes. With a slotted spoon, transfer the sausage to a medium bowl. Add half the onions and celery to the fat in the skillet; sauté, stirring occasionally, over medium-high heat until softened, about 5 minutes. Transfer the onion mixture to the bowl with the sausage. Return the skillet to the heat and add the butter; when melted add the remaining onions and celery and sauté, stirring occasionally, until softened, about 5 minutes. Stir in the thyme, sage, and garlic; cook until fragrant, about 30 seconds; add the salt and pepper. Add this mixture along with the sausage and onion mixture to the bread and stir gently to combine (try not to break the bread into smaller pieces).

5. Spray a 16 by 12-inch disposable aluminum roasting pan with vegetable oil spray. Transfer the dressing to the roasting pan and spread in an even layer. Cover the pan with foil and refrigerate while preparing the turkey.

6. TO PREPARE THE TURKEY FOR ROASTING: Remove the turkey from the brine and rinse it well. Position the turkey on a broiler pan top or wire rack (see note); thoroughly pat the surface of the turkey dry with paper towels. Place the broiler pan top with the turkey on top of the roasting pan with the dressing; refrigerate, uncovered, for 8 to 24 hours.

7. TO ROAST THE TURKEY WITH THE DRESSING: Adjust an oven rack to the lower-middle position and heat the oven to 450 degrees. Remove the broiler pan top with the turkey and remove the foil from the dressing; place the broiler pan top with the turkey on the dressing in the roasting pan. Brush the turkey with the melted butter. Roast the turkey until the turkey skin is crisp and deep brown and the thickest part of the breast registers 160 to 165 degrees and the thickest part of the thigh registers 175 degrees on an instant-read thermometer, 1 hour 20 minutes to 1 hour 40 minutes, rotating the pan from front to back after 40 minutes.

8. Transfer the broiler pan top with the turkey to a carving board, tent loosely with foil, and let rest for 20 minutes. Meanwhile, adjust an oven rack to the upper-middle position, place the roasting pan with the dressing back in the oven, and bake until golden brown, about 10 minutes. Carve the turkey and serve with the dressing and gravy.

NOTES FROM THE TEST KITCHEN

PREPARING THE BUTTERFLIED TURKEY

1. Holding the turkey upright with the backbone facing front, use a hacking motion to cut through the turkey directly to one side of the backbone with a chef's knife.

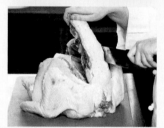

2. Holding the backbone with one hand, hack through the turkey directly to the other side of the backbone; the backbone will fall away.

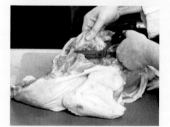

3. Using kitchen scissors, cut out the rib plate and remove any small pieces of bone.

4. Place the turkey, breast side up, on a cutting board and cover with plastic wrap. With a large rolling pin, whack the breastbone until it cracks and the turkey flattens.

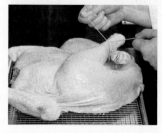

5. After brining and rinsing, place the turkey, breast side up, on a wire rack set over a rimmed baking sheet. Tuck the wings under the turkey. Push the legs up to rest between the thigh and breast. Tie the legs together.

Golden Corn Bread

MAKES ABOUT 16 CUPS CRUMBLED CORN BREAD

You need about three-quarters of this recipe for the dressing; the rest is for nibbling.

- 4 tablespoons (½ stick) unsalted butter, melted, plus extra for the baking dish
- 4 large eggs
- 1⅓ cups buttermilk
- 1⅓ cups milk
- 2 cups yellow cornmeal
- 2 cups (10 ounces) unbleached all-purpose flour
- 2 tablespoons sugar
- 4 teaspoons baking powder
- 1 teaspoon baking soda
- 1 teaspoon table salt

1. Adjust an oven rack to the middle position and heat the oven to 375 degrees. Grease a 13 by 9-inch baking dish with butter.

2. Beat the eggs in medium bowl; whisk in the buttermilk and milk.

3. Whisk the cornmeal, flour, sugar, baking powder, baking soda, and salt together in a large bowl. Push the dry ingredients up the sides of the bowl to make a well, then pour the egg and milk mixture into the well and stir with a whisk until just combined; stir in the melted butter.

4. Pour the batter into the prepared baking dish. Bake until the top is golden brown and the edges have pulled away from the sides of the pan, 30 to 40 minutes.

5. Transfer the baking dish to a wire rack and cool to room temperature before using, about 1 hour.

Turkey Gravy

MAKES ABOUT 4 CUPS

Because this gravy doesn't use drippings from the roasted turkey but instead uses the trimmings from butterflying the bird, the gravy can conveniently be made a day in advance (while the turkey brines and air-dries in the refrigerator) and then reheated before serving.

- Reserved giblets, neck, tailpiece, and backbone and rib bones from the turkey (see note)
- 2 small onions, chopped coarse
- 1 medium carrot, cut into 1-inch pieces
- 1 celery rib, cut into 1-inch pieces
- 6 garlic cloves, unpeeled
- 3½ cups low-sodium chicken broth
- 3 cups water
- 2 cups dry white wine
- 6 sprigs fresh thyme
- ¼ cup unbleached all-purpose flour
- Table salt and ground black pepper

1. Heat the oven to 450 degrees. Adjust an oven rack to the middle position. Place the turkey trimmings, onions, carrot, celery, and garlic in a large roasting pan or broiler pan bottom. Spray lightly with vegetable oil spray and toss to combine. Roast, stirring every 10 minutes, until well browned, 40 to 50 minutes.

2. Remove the pan from the oven and place over two burners set at high heat; add the chicken broth and bring to a boil, scraping up the browned bits on the bottom of the pan with a wooden spoon.

3. Transfer the contents of the pan to a large saucepan. Add the water, wine, and thyme; bring to a boil over high heat. Reduce the heat to low and simmer until reduced by half, about 1½ hours. Strain the stock into a large measuring cup or container. Cool to room temperature; cover with plastic wrap, and refrigerate until the fat congeals on the surface, about 2 hours.

4. Skim the fat from the stock using a soup spoon; reserve the fat. Pour the stock through a fine-mesh strainer to remove remaining bits of fat. Bring the stock to a simmer in a medium saucepan over medium-high heat. 5. In a second medium saucepan, heat ¼ cup reserved turkey fat over medium-high heat until bubbling; whisk in the flour and cook, whisking constantly, until combined and honey-colored, about 2 minutes. Continuing to whisk constantly, gradually add the hot stock; bring to a boil, then reduce the heat to medium-low and simmer, stirring occasionally, until slightly thickened, about 5 minutes. Season with salt and pepper to taste. (The gravy can be stored in an airtight container in the refrigerator for up to 1 day. While the turkey is resting, heat the gravy in a medium saucepan over medium heat until hot, about 8 minutes.)

EASIER ROAST TURKEY AND GRAVY

WHY THIS RECIPE WORKS: To season the meat and help it retain more juices as it cooked, we loosened the skin of the turkey and applied a mixture of salt and sugar onto the flesh. We preheated both a baking stone and roasting pan in the oven before placing the turkey in the pan. The stone absorbs heat and delivers it through the pan to the turkey's legs and thighs, which need to cook to a higher temperature than the delicate breast meat (which we protected with a foil shield). After the leg quarters had gotten a jump start on cooking, we reduced the oven temperature from 425 to 325 degrees and removed the shield to allow the breast to brown while the bird finished cooking. The boost of heat provided by the stone also helped the juices brown and reduce into concentrated drippings that can be turned into a flavorful gravy in the time that the turkey rests.

Easier Roast Turkey and Gravy

SERVES 10 TO 12

Note that this recipe requires salting the bird in the refrigerator for 24 to 48 hours. This recipe was developed and tested using Diamond Crystal Kosher Salt. If you have Morton's Kosher Salt, which is denser than Diamond Crystal, reduce the salt in step 1 to 3 tablespoons. Rub 1 tablespoon salt mixture into each breast, 1½ teaspoons into each leg, and remainder into cavity. Table salt is too fine and not recommended for this recipe. If you are roasting a kosher or self-basting turkey (such as a frozen Butterball), do not salt it; it already contains a good amount of sodium. The success of this recipe is dependent on saturating the pizza stone and roasting pan with heat. We recommend preheating the stone, pan, and oven for at least 30 minutes.

4	teaspoons sugar
	Kosher salt and pepper
1	(12- to 14-pound) turkey, neck and giblets removed and reserved for gravy
2½	tablespoons vegetable oil
1	teaspoon baking powder
1	small onion, chopped fine
1	carrot, peeled and sliced thin
5	sprigs fresh parsley
2	bay leaves
5	tablespoons all-purpose flour
3¼	cups water
¼	cup dry white wine

1. Combine sugar and 4 tablespoons salt in bowl. With turkey breast side up, use fingers or handle of wooden spoon to carefully separate skin from thighs and breast. Rub 4 teaspoons salt mixture under skin of each breast half, 2 teaspoons salt under skin of each leg, and remaining salt mixture into cavity. Tie legs together with kitchen twine. Place turkey on rack set in rimmed baking sheet and refrigerate uncovered for 24 to 48 hours.

2. At least 30 minutes before roasting turkey, adjust oven rack to lowest position and set pizza stone on oven rack. Place roasting pan on pizza stone and heat oven to 500 degrees. Combine 1½ teaspoons oil and baking powder in small bowl. Pat turkey dry with paper towels. Rub oil mixture evenly over turkey. Cover turkey breast with double layer of aluminum foil.

3. Remove roasting pan from oven. Place remaining 2 tablespoons oil in roasting pan. Place turkey into pan breast side up and return pan to oven. Reduce oven temperature to 425 degrees and cook for 45 minutes.

4. Remove foil shield, reduce temperature to 325 degrees, and continue to cook until breast registers 160 degrees and thighs register 175 degrees, 1 to 1½ hours longer.

5. Using spatula loosen turkey from roasting pan, transfer to carving board, and let rest uncovered for 45 minutes. While turkey rests, use wooden spoon to scrape any browned bits from bottom of roasting pan. Pour mixture through fine-mesh strainer set in bowl. Transfer drippings to fat separator and let rest 10 minutes. Reserve 3 tablespoons fat and defatted liquid (about 1 cup). Discard remaining fat.

6. Heat reserved fat in large saucepan over medium-high heat until shimmering. Add reserved neck and giblets and cook until well browned, 10 to 12 minutes. Transfer neck and giblets to large plate. Reduce heat to medium; add onion, carrot, parsley, and bay leaves; and cook, stirring frequently, until vegetables are softened, 5 to 7 minutes. Add flour and cook, stirring constantly, until flour is well coated with fat, about 1 minute. Slowly whisk in reserved defatted liquid and cook until thickened, about 1 minute. Whisk in water and wine, return neck and giblets, and bring to simmer. Simmer for 10 minutes. Season with salt and pepper to taste. Discard neck. Strain mixture through fine-mesh strainer and transfer to serving bowl. Carve turkey and arrange on serving platter. Serve with gravy.

ROAST SALTED TURKEY

WHY THIS RECIPE WORKS: Brining is the best way to guarantee a moist turkey, but it isn't always the most practical way, especially if you have limited refrigerator space. We wanted to develop an alternative method to brining that would season the meat and keep it moist. Instead of brining, we turned to salting. We wanted to make sure the salt penetrated the meat, but we didn't want to tear the skin. We found that either chopsticks or the handle of a wooden spoon worked well to help us gently separate the skin from the meat. To ensure moist breast meat, we chilled the breast by placing a small bag of ice inside the cavity against the breast and setting the turkey, breast side down, on ice. This trick brought down the temperature of the breast, thus allowing it to cook through over a longer period in the oven (more in line with the cooking time of the dark meat) without drying out.

Roast Salted Turkey

SERVES 10 TO 12

This recipe was developed and tested using Diamond Crystal Kosher Salt. If you have Morton's Kosher Salt, which is denser than Diamond Crystal, use only 4½ teaspoons of salt in the cavity, 2¼ teaspoons of salt per each half of the breast, and 1 teaspoon of salt per leg. Table salt is too fine and is not recommended for this recipe. If you are roasting a kosher or self-basting turkey (such as a frozen Butterball), do not salt it; it already contains a good amount of sodium. If serving with Giblet Pan Gravy (page 134), note that you can complete step 1 of the gravy recipe up to a day ahead, if desired. Begin step 3 once the bird has been removed from the oven and is resting on a carving board.

1	(12- to 14-pound) turkey; giblets, neck, and tailpiece removed and reserved for gravy (see page 134)
5	tablespoons kosher salt (see note)
1	(5-pound) bag ice cubes
4	tablespoons (½ stick) unsalted butter, melted
3	medium onions, chopped coarse
2	medium carrots, chopped coarse

2 celery ribs, chopped coarse

6 sprigs fresh thyme

1 cup water, plus more as needed

1. Following the photos, carefully separate the turkey skin from the meat on the breast, legs, thighs, and back; avoid breaking the skin. Then rub 2 tablespoons of the salt evenly inside the cavity of the turkey, 1 tablespoon more salt under the skin of each breast half, and 1½ teaspoons more salt under the skin of each leg. Wrap the turkey tightly with plastic wrap; refrigerate for 24 to 48 hours.

2. Remove the turkey from the refrigerator. Rinse off any excess salt between the meat and skin and in the cavity, then pat dry inside and out with paper towels. Add ice to two 1-gallon zipper-lock bags until each is half full. Place the bags in a large roasting pan and lay the turkey, breast side down, on top of the ice. Add ice to two 1-quart zipper-lock bags until each is one-third full; place one bag of ice in the large cavity of the turkey and the other bag in the neck cavity. (Make sure that the ice touches the breast only, not the thighs or legs; see the photo.) Keep the turkey on ice for 1 hour (the roasting pan should remain on the counter).

3. Meanwhile, adjust an oven rack to the lowest position and heat the oven to 425 degrees. Line a large V-rack with heavy-duty foil and poke several holes in the foil. Set the V-rack in a roasting pan and spray the foil with vegetable oil spray.

4. Remove the turkey from the ice and pat dry with paper towels (discard the ice). Tuck the tips of the drumsticks into the skin at the tail to secure and tuck the wings under the bird. Brush the turkey breast with 2 tablespoons of the melted butter. Scatter the vegetables and thyme in the roasting pan and pour 1 cup water over the vegetable mixture. Place the turkey, breast side down, on the V-rack. Brush the turkey with the remaining 2 tablespoons melted butter.

5. Roast the turkey for 45 minutes. Remove the pan from the oven (close the oven door to retain the oven heat) and reduce the oven temperature to 325 degrees. With a dish towel in each

HOW TO SALT A TURKEY

1. Use a chopstick or a thin wooden spoon handle to separate the skin from the meat over the breast, legs, thighs, and back.

2. Rub 2 tablespoons kosher salt inside the main cavity.

3. Lift the skin and apply 1 tablespoon kosher salt over each breast half, placing half of the salt on each end of each breast, then massaging the salt evenly over the meat.

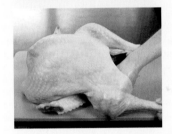

4. Apply 1½ teaspoons kosher salt over the top and bottom of each leg.

ICING THE TURKEY BREAST

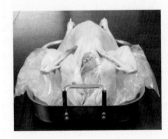

Cooling the breast down with ice ensures that it will cook more slowly than the legs and thighs, preventing the breast meat from drying out. Place bags of ice underneath the breast and inside both the large cavity and the neck area.

hand, rotate the turkey breast side up; continue to roast until the thickest part of the breast registers 160 to 165 degrees and the thickest part of the thigh registers 175 degrees on an instant-read thermometer, 1 to 1½ hours longer. Transfer the turkey to a carving board and let rest, uncovered, for 30 minutes. Carve the turkey and serve with the gravy (see note).

ROASTED BRINED TURKEY

WHY THIS RECIPE WORKS: Brining brings out the best in roasted turkey: It helps the bird retain moisture, seasons the meat, and helps the meat withstand hot oven temperatures, making for crisp skin. After brining, we let the turkey dry in the refrigerator for optimal crisping. Brushing the skin with melted butter before placing it breast-side down in a V-rack boosted its browning and added rich, buttery flavor to the finished turkey. To avoid overcooking the breast, we rotated the turkey after 45 minutes to an hour of roasting (depending on its size). This step kept the meat evenly moist and juicy. Before carving, we let the turkey rest for at least 30 minutes to give the juices time to redistribute through the meat.

Roasted Brined Turkey

SERVES 10 TO 22, DEPENDING ON TURKEY SIZE

We offer two brine formulas: one for a 4- to 6-hour brine and another for a 12- to 14-hour brine. The amount of salt used does not change with turkey size. If you're roasting a kosher or self-basting turkey, do not brine it; it already contains a good amount of sodium. Rotating the bird from a breast-side down position to a breast-side up position midway through cooking helps produce evenly cooked meat. If you're roasting a large (18- to 22-pound) bird and are reluctant to rotate it, skip the step of lining the V-rack with foil and roast the bird breast-side up for the full time.

Salt
1 turkey (12–22 pounds gross weight), rinsed thoroughly, giblets and neck reserved for gravy, if making
4 tablespoons unsalted butter, melted

1. Dissolve 1 cup salt per gallon cold water for 4- to 6-hour brine or ½ cup salt per gallon cold water for 12- to 14-hour brine in large stockpot or clean bucket. Two gallons of water will be sufficient for most birds; larger birds may require three gallons. Add turkey and refrigerate for predetermined amount of time.

2. Set wire rack in large rimmed baking sheet. Remove turkey from brine and pat dry, inside and out, with paper towels. Place turkey on prepared baking sheet. Refrigerate, uncovered, for at least 8 hours or overnight.

3. Before removing turkey from refrigerator, adjust oven rack to lowest position; heat oven to 400 degrees for 12- to 18-pound bird or 425 degrees for 18- to 22-pound bird. Line large V-rack with heavy-duty aluminum foil and use paring knife or skewer to poke 20 to 30 holes in foil; set V-rack in large roasting pan. Tuck tips of drumsticks into skin at tail to secure; tuck wing tips behind back. Brush breast with 2 tablespoons butter. Set turkey breast side down on prepared V-rack; brush back with remaining 2 tablespoons butter. Roast 45 minutes for 12- to 18-pound bird or 1 hour for 18- to 22-pound bird.

4. Remove roasting pan with turkey from oven (close oven door to retain oven heat); reduce oven temperature to 325 degrees if roasting 18- to 22-pound bird. Using clean potholders or dish towels, rotate turkey breast side up; continue to roast until thickest part of breast registers 160 degrees and thickest part of thigh registers 175 degrees, 50 to 60 minutes longer for 12- to 15-pound bird, about 1¼ hours for 15- to 18-pound bird, or about 2 hours for 18- to 22-pound bird. Transfer turkey to carving board; let rest for 30 minutes (or up to 40 minutes for 18- to 22-pound bird). Carve and serve.

HERBED ROAST TURKEY

WHY THIS RECIPE WORKS: Throwing a bunch of herbs into the cavity of a turkey or rubbing the outside of the bird with a savory paste only flirts with great herb flavor—it doesn't infuse that flavor into each and every bite. We wanted an intensely herby turkey, one with a powerful, aromatic flavor that permeated well beyond the meat's surface.

First we tried an intense brine, but it made the bird taste more pickled than infused with herbs. Next, we pumped the paste into the bird with a syringe, which created nothing but ugly blobs of overwhelmingly strong, raw-tasting herbs. Then we tried a technique we had developed for stuffing a thick-cut pork chop. We made a vertical slit in the breast meat and, using a paring knife, created an expansive pocket by sweeping the blade back and forth. This created a void into which we could rub a small amount of herb paste. This along with three other herbal applications—underneath the skin, inside the cavity, and over the skin—made for a successful four-pronged approach that gave every bite of turkey herb flavor. The herb paste itself, balanced with small amounts of pungent herbs (sage and rosemary) and greater amounts of softer flavors (thyme and parsley), also included lemon zest for a fresh, bright note and olive oil and Dijon mustard to make it spreadable. This was a moist roast turkey packed with bright herb flavor—a fresh alternative to the usual holiday bird.

APPLYING HERB PASTE TO THE TURKEY

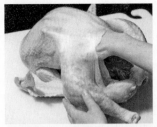

1. Carefully separate the skin from the meat on the breast, thigh, and drumstick areas.

2. Rub the herb paste under the skin and directly onto the flesh, distributing it evenly.

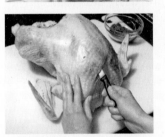

3. Make a 1½-inch slit in each breast. Swing a knife tip through the breast to create a large pocket.

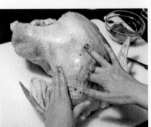

4. Place a thin layer of paste inside each pocket.

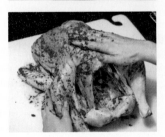

5. Rub the remaining paste inside the turkey cavity and on the skin.

Herbed Roast Turkey

SERVES 10 TO 12

If you have the time and the refrigerator space, air-drying produces extremely crisp skin and is worth the effort. After brining, rinsing, and patting the turkey dry, place the turkey, breast side up, on a wire rack set over a rimmed baking sheet and refrigerate, uncovered, for 8 to 24 hours. Proceed with the recipe. Serve with All-Purpose Turkey Gravy (recipe follows).

TURKEY AND BRINE

2 cups table salt

1 (12- to 14-pound) turkey; giblets, neck, and tailpiece removed and discarded

HERB PASTE

1¼ cups roughly chopped fresh parsley leaves

4 teaspoons minced fresh thyme leaves

2 teaspoons roughly chopped fresh sage leaves

1½ teaspoons minced fresh rosemary leaves

1 medium shallot, minced (about 3 tablespoons)

2 medium garlic cloves, minced or pressed through a garlic press (about 2 teaspoons)

¾ teaspoon grated zest from 1 lemon

¾ teaspoon table salt

1 teaspoon ground black pepper

¼ cup olive oil

1 teaspoon Dijon mustard

1 recipe All-Purpose Turkey Gravy (page 150)

1. FOR THE TURKEY AND BRINE: Dissolve the salt in 2 gallons cold water in a large container. Submerge the turkey in the brine, cover, and refrigerate or store in a very cool spot (40 degrees or less) for 4 to 6 hours.

2. Remove the turkey from the brine and rinse it well. Pat dry inside and out with paper towels. Place the turkey, breast side up, on a wire rack set over a rimmed baking sheet or roasting pan and refrigerate, uncovered, for 30 minutes. (Alternatively, air-dry the turkey; see note.)

3. FOR THE HERB PASTE: Pulse the parsley, thyme, sage, rosemary, shallot, garlic, lemon zest, salt, and pepper together in a food processor until a coarse paste is formed, 10 pulses. Add the olive oil and mustard; continue to pulse until the mixture forms a smooth paste, 10 to twelve 2-second pulses; scrape the sides of the processor bowl with a rubber spatula after 5 pulses. Transfer the mixture to a small bowl.

4. TO PREPARE THE TURKEY: Adjust an oven rack to the lowest position and heat the oven to 400 degrees. Line a large V-rack with heavy-duty foil and poke several holes in the foil. Set the V-rack in a large roasting pan and spray the foil with vegetable oil spray. Remove the turkey from the refrigerator and wipe away any water collected in the baking sheet; set the turkey, breast side up, on the baking sheet.

5. Following the photos on page 145, use your hands to carefully loosen the skin from the meat of the breast, thighs, and drumsticks. Using your fingers or a spoon, slip 1½ tablespoons of the paste under the breast skin on each side of the turkey. Using your fingers, distribute the paste under the skin over the breast, thigh, and drumstick meat.

6. Using a sharp paring knife, cut a 1½-inch vertical slit into the thickest part of each side of the breast. Starting from the top of the incision, swing the knife tip down to create a 4 to 5-inch pocket within the flesh. Place 1 tablespoon more paste in the pocket of each side of the breast; using your fingers, rub the paste in a thin, even layer.

7. Rub 1 tablespoon more paste inside the turkey cavity. Rotate the turkey breast side down; apply half the remaining herb paste to the turkey skin; flip the turkey breast side up and apply the remaining herb paste to the skin, pressing and patting to make the paste adhere; reapply the herb paste that falls onto the baking sheet. Tuck the tips of the drumsticks into the skin at the tail to secure, and tuck the wings under the bird.

8. TO ROAST THE TURKEY: Place the turkey, breast side down, on the V-rack. Roast the turkey for 45 minutes.

9. Remove the pan from the oven (close the oven door to retain the oven heat). With a dish towel in each hand, rotate the turkey breast side up. Continue to roast until the thickest part of the breast registers 160 to 165 degrees and the thickest part of the thigh registers 175 degrees on an instant-read thermometer, 50 to 60 minutes longer. Transfer the turkey to a carving board and let rest, uncovered, for 30 minutes. Following the photos, carve the turkey and serve with the gravy.

All-Purpose Turkey Gravy

MAKES ABOUT 2 CUPS

Adding drippings from the roasted turkey will enhance the flavor of the gravy.

- 1   small carrot, peeled and chopped coarse
- 1   small celery rib, chopped coarse
- 1   small onion, chopped coarse
- 3   tablespoons unsalted butter
- ¼   cup unbleached all-purpose flour
- 2   cups low-sodium chicken broth
- 2   cups beef broth
- 1   bay leaf
- 2   sprigs fresh thyme
- 5   whole black peppercorns
    Defatted pan drippings from Herbed Roast Turkey (optional; see note)
    Table salt and ground black pepper

1. Pulse the carrot into ¼-inch pieces in a food processor, about 5 pulses. Add the celery and onion and continue to pulse until all of the vegetables are chopped fine, 5 pulses.

2. Melt the butter in a large saucepan over medium-high heat. Add the vegetables and cook, stirring often, until softened and well browned, about 7 minutes. Reduce the heat to medium, stir in the flour, and cook, stirring constantly, until well browned, about 5 minutes.

3. Gradually whisk in the broths until smooth. Bring to a boil, skimming any foam that rises to the surface. Add the bay leaf, thyme, and peppercorns. Reduce the heat to medium-low and simmer, stirring occasionally, until the gravy is thickened and measures about 3 cups, 20 to 25 minutes. Stir in any juices from the roasted meat (if using) and continue to simmer the gravy as needed to re-thicken.

4. Strain the gravy through a fine-mesh strainer into a serving pitcher, pressing on the solids to extract as much liquid as possible; discard the solids. Season the gravy with salt and pepper to taste and cover to keep warm until needed.

CARVING THE BREAST

The wings and legs on our Herbed Roast Turkey can be carved just as they would be on any other turkey, but the breast, which is stuffed with herb paste, needs some special attention. Here's how to ensure that every slice has a nice swirl of herbs.

1. With the wings facing toward you, cut along both sides of the breast-bone, slicing from the tip of the breastbone to the cutting board.

2. Gently pull each breast half away to expose the wishbone. Then pull and remove the wishbone.

3. Using the knife tip, cut along the rib cage to remove the breast completely.

4. Place the entire breast half on a carving board and cut on the bias into thin slices. Repeat steps 3 and 4 on the other side.

BRAISED TURKEY

WHY THIS RECIPE WORKS: Separating turkey into parts and braising it for the holiday meal? It may sound heretical if you've never presented anything but a whole roasted bird at the table, but this break from tradition has a lot going for it. Roasting a large turkey is always a race to get the denser, fattier thighs and legs to come up to the ideal temperature of around 175 degrees before the leaner, more delicate breast dries out, once its temperature climbs past 160 degrees. An intact, upright bird compounds this problem because the slower-cooking thighs are shielded from the heat. So we wondered if there was an easier way to get perfectly cooked turkey on

the table without sacrificing flavor. Turkey parts provided a neat solution to the problem by giving both types of meat more even exposure to the heat—and without any cumbersome turning. Better yet, braising the pieces in a flavorful liquid created rich, ready-made gravy and infused the meat with all of its complex flavors. When we tasted this deeply flavored, moist and tender turkey, we found we didn't miss the traditional whole bird at all.

Braised Turkey
SERVES 10 TO 12

Instead of drumsticks and thighs, you may use 2 whole leg quarters, 1½ to 2 pounds each. The recipe will also work with turkey breast alone; in step 1, reduce the amount of salt and sugar to ½ cup each, and the amount of water to 4 quarts. If you are braising kosher or self-basting turkey parts, skip the brining step, and instead season the turkey parts with 1½ teaspoons salt.

BRAISED TURKEY

    Table salt and ground black pepper
1 cup sugar
1 (5- to 7-pound) whole bone-in, skin-on turkey breast, trimmed
4 pounds turkey drumsticks and thighs, trimmed
3 medium onions, chopped medium
3 medium celery ribs, chopped medium
2 medium carrots, peeled and chopped medium
6 medium garlic cloves, peeled and crushed
2 bay leaves
6 sprigs fresh thyme
6 sprigs fresh parsley
½ ounce dried porcini mushrooms, rinsed
4 tablespoons (½ stick) unsalted butter, melted
4 cups low-sodium chicken broth
1 cup dry white wine

GRAVY

3 tablespoons unbleached all-purpose flour
    Table salt and ground black pepper

1. FOR THE TURKEY: Dissolve 1 cup salt and the sugar in 2 gallons cold water in a large container. Submerge the turkey pieces in the brine, cover, and refrigerate for 3 to 6 hours.

2. Adjust an oven rack to the lower-middle position and heat the oven to 500 degrees. Remove the turkey from the brine and pat dry with paper towels. Toss the onions, celery, carrots, garlic, bay leaves, thyme, parsley, porcini, and 2 tablespoons of the melted butter in a large roasting pan; arrange in an even layer. Brush the turkey pieces with the remaining 2 tablespoons melted butter and season with pepper. Place the turkey pieces, skin side up, over the vegetables, leaving at least ¼ inch between the pieces. Roast until the skin is lightly browned, about 20 minutes.

3. While the turkey is roasting, bring the broth and wine to a simmer in a medium saucepan over medium heat. Cover and keep warm.

4. Remove the turkey from the oven and reduce the oven temperature to 325 degrees. Pour the broth mixture around the turkey pieces (it should come about three-quarters of the way up the legs and thighs.) Place a 12 by 16-inch piece of parchment paper over the turkey pieces. Cover the roasting pan tightly with aluminum foil. Return the covered roasting pan to the oven and cook until the breast registers 160 degrees and the thighs register 175 degrees on an instant-read thermometer, 1½ to 2 hours. Transfer the turkey to a carving board, tent loosely with foil, and let rest for 20 minutes.

5. FOR THE GRAVY: Strain the vegetables and liquid from the roasting pan through a fine-mesh strainer set in a large bowl. Press the solids with the back of a spatula to extract as much liquid as possible. Discard the vegetables. Transfer the liquid to a fat separator and allow to settle for 5 minutes. Reserve 3 tablespoons fat and measure off 3 cups broth (use any remaining broth for another use.)

6. Heat 3 tablespoons reserved turkey fat in a medium saucepan over medium-high heat; add the flour and cook, stirring constantly, until the flour is dark golden brown and fragrant, about 5 minutes. Whisk in 3 cups braising liquid and bring to a boil. Reduce the heat to medium-low and simmer, stirring occasionally, until the gravy is thick and reduced to 2 cups, 15 to 20 minutes. Remove the gravy from the heat and season with salt and pepper to taste.

7. Carve the turkey and serve, passing the gravy separately.

TURKEY BREAST EN COCOTTE WITH PAN GRAVY

WHY THIS RECIPE WORKS: Cooking turkey breast is a great alternative to tackling the whole bird; it's much easier to handle, yet still provides a substantial amount of meat. Having successfully developed a recipe for chicken en cocotte, we wondered if we could use this same method (cooking the poultry in a covered pot over low heat for an extended period of time) to get the same great results with a turkey breast—perfectly cooked, incredibly moist and tender meat. We found that bone-in breasts were more flavorful, and we decided that a 6- to 7-pound turkey breast was ideal—it's large enough to feed a small crowd (up to eight people), but small enough to fit in our 7-quart Dutch oven.To further ensure that a breast of this size easily fit into the pot, we found it helpful to trim the rib bones. Browning the turkey breast was an essential step in developing deep flavor. Adding some aromatics to the pot further rounded out the flavor, and we settled on a combination of onion, carrot, celery, garlic, thyme, and bay leaf. After 1 hour and 45 minutes, our turkey breast was done—we had an extremely tender, juicy, and moist piece of meat. After removing the turkey from the pot, we reduced the jus until it had all but evaporated, concentrating the turkey flavor, producing a mahogany fond on the bottom of the pot, and separating the fat from the jus. It was into this rendered fat that we stirred flour to make a roux. And by leaving the aromatics in the pot during the whole reduction process, we were sure to extract as much flavor from them as possible. We then added a full quart of chicken broth to the pot, brought it to a simmer, and reduced it to a proper gravy consistency. The result was a deeply flavored gravy reminiscent of Thanksgiving dinner.

Turkey Breast en Cocotte with Pan Gravy

SERVES 6 TO 8

Many supermarkets are now selling "hotel-style" turkey breasts. Try to avoid these if you can, as they still have the wings attached. If this is the only type of breast you can find, you will simply need to remove the wings before proceeding with the recipe. Be sure to use a 7- to 8-quart Dutch oven here. Don't buy a turkey breast larger than 7 pounds; it won't fit in the pot. For a smaller turkey breast, reduce the cooking time as necessary.

1 (6- to 7-pound) whole bone-in turkey breast
  Salt and ground black pepper
2 tablespoons olive oil
1 medium onion, chopped medium
1 medium carrot, chopped medium
1 celery rib, chopped medium
6 medium garlic cloves, peeled and crushed
2 sprigs fresh thyme
1 bay leaf
¼ cup unbleached all-purpose flour
4 cups low-sodium chicken broth

1. Adjust an oven rack to the lowest position and heat the oven to 250 degrees. Using kitchen shears or a chef's knife, trim the rib bones and any excess fat on both sides of the breast following the vertical line of fat. Pat the turkey dry with paper towels and season with salt and pepper.

2. Heat the oil in a large Dutch oven over medium-high heat until just smoking. Add the turkey, breast side down, and scatter the onion, carrot, celery, garlic, thyme, and bay leaf around the turkey. Cook, turning the breast on its sides and stirring the

vegetables as needed, until the turkey and vegetables are well browned, 12 to 16 minutes, reducing the heat if the pot begins to scorch. Turn turkey so breast side is facing up.

3. Off the heat, place a large sheet of foil over the pot and press to seal, then cover tightly with the lid. Transfer the pot to the oven and cook until the thickest part of the breast registers 160 to 165 degrees on an instant-read thermometer, 1½ to 1¾ hours.

4. Remove the pot from the oven. Transfer the turkey to a cutting board, tent loosely with foil, and let rest while making the gravy.

5. Place the pot with the juices and vegetables over medium-high heat and simmer until almost all of the liquid has evaporated, 15 to 20 minutes. Stir in the flour and cook, stirring constantly, until browned, 2 to 5 minutes. Slowly whisk in the chicken broth, bring to a simmer, and cook, stirring often, until the gravy is thickened and measures about 2½ cups, 10 to 15 minutes.

6. Strain the gravy through a fine-mesh strainer and season with salt and pepper to taste. Carve the turkey and serve, passing the gravy separately.

GRILL-ROASTED TURKEY

WHY THIS RECIPE WORKS: Grill-roasting a turkey can be hard to manage. Cooking times can vary depending on the weather, and it's much easier to burn the bird's skin on a grill. There also remain the usual problems inherent to roasting a turkey: dry, overcooked breast meat and undercooked thighs.

But grill-roasting can produce the best-tasting, best-looking turkey ever, with crispy skin and moist meat wonderfully perfumed with smoke. We wanted to take the guesswork out of preparing the holiday bird on the grill.

Because the skin on larger birds will burn before the meat is done, we chose a small turkey (less than 14 pounds). We ditched stuffing the turkey or trussing it—both can lead to burnt skin and undercooked meat. To season the meat and help prevent it from drying out on the grill, we brined the turkey. To protect the skin and promote slow cooking, we placed the turkey on the opposite side of the glowing coals or lit gas burner. Using a V-rack also helped, as it improved air circulation. And we turned the turkey three times instead of twice; this way, all four sides received equal exposure to the hot side of the grill for evenly bronzed skin.

Grill-Roasted Turkey

SERVES 10 TO 12

If using a self-basting turkey or kosher turkey, do not brine in step 1, and season with salt after brushing with melted butter in step 2. When using a charcoal grill, we prefer wood chunks to wood chips whenever possible; substitute 6 medium wood chunks, soaked in water for 1 hour, for the wood chip packets. The total cooking time is 2 to 2½ hours, depending on the size of the bird, the ambient conditions (the bird will require more time on a cool, windy day), and the intensity of the fire.

- 1   cup salt
- 1   (12- to 14-pound) turkey, trimmed, neck, giblets, and tailpiece removed, and wings tucked behind back
- 2   tablespoons unsalted butter, melted
- 6   cups wood chips, soaked in water for 15 minutes and drained (see note)

1. Dissolve salt in 2 gallons cold water in large container. Submerge turkey in brine, cover, and refrigerate or store in very cool spot (40 degrees or less) for 6 to 12 hours.

2. Lightly spray V-rack with vegetable oil spray. Remove turkey from brine and pat dry, inside and out, with paper towels. Brush both sides of turkey with melted butter and place breast side down in prepared V-rack.

3. Using 3 large pieces of heavy-duty aluminum foil, wrap soaked chips in 3 foil packets and cut several vent holes in top.

4A. FOR A CHARCOAL GRILL: Open bottom vent halfway. Light large chimney mounded with charcoal briquettes (7 quarts). When top coals are partially covered with ash, pour into steeply banked pile against side of grill. Place 1 wood chip packet on pile of coals. Set cooking grate in place, cover, and open lid vent halfway. Heat grill until hot and wood chips are smoking, about 5 minutes.

4B. FOR A GAS GRILL: Place 1 wood chip packet directly on primary burner. Turn all burners to high, cover, and heat grill until hot and wood chips are smoking, about 15 minutes. Turn primary burner to medium-high and turn off other burner(s). (Adjust primary burner as needed during cooking to maintain grill temperature around 325 degrees.)

Anyone who watches our show knows that we love to brine. Brining not only helps prevent delicate meat like chicken, turkey, and pork from drying out, it also seasons the meat for better flavor. What equipment do you need for brining? A clean container that's large enough to accommodate the meat and brine. For large containers (such as a washtub or cooler) that won't fit in a refrigerator, you need ice packs to keep the temperature at 40 degrees F. For a whole chicken, the test kitchen likes to use a Cambro storage container, which is a large, clear bucket marked with level graduations—Cambros make handy containers for rising bread dough, too. (Look for these containers at restaurant supply stores or online.)

As for brining tips, we've got a few after 15 plus years. After pulling your turkey out of the brine, make sure to thoroughly pat it dry to prevent soggy skin. You can also place the turkey on a wire rack set on a baking sheet and allow it to dry overnight in the refrigerator—this will further encourage crispy skin during roasting. And as for the salt, the test kitchen prefers table salt. Kosher salt works fine, but the size of the grains varies between the two major brands, which can make recipe testing (and writing) difficult. The ratio of salt to water varies a bit from recipe to recipe, but generally the test kitchen uses 1 cup table salt to 2 gallons of water (this is enough brine for a 12- to 14-pound turkey).

5. Clean and oil cooking grate. Place V-rack with turkey on cool side of grill with leg and wing facing coal, cover (position lid vent over turkey if using charcoal), and cook for 1 hour.

6. Using potholders, transfer V-rack with turkey to rimmed baking sheet or roasting pan. If using charcoal, remove cooking grate and add 12 new briquettes and second wood chip packet to pile of coals; set cooking grate in place. If using gas, place remaining wood chip packets directly on primary burner. With wad of paper towels in each hand, flip turkey breast side up in rack and return V-rack with turkey to cool side of grill, with other leg and wing facing heat. Cover (position lid vent over turkey if using charcoal) and cook for 45 minutes.

7. Using potholders, carefully rotate V-rack with turkey (breast remains up) 180 degrees. Cover and continue to cook until breast registers 160 degrees and thighs register 175 degrees, 15 to 45 minutes longer. Transfer turkey to carving board, tent loosely with foil, and let rest for 20 to 30 minutes. Carve and serve.

SIMPLE GRILL-ROASTED TURKEY

WHY THIS RECIPE WORKS: Besides freeing up your oven for other dishes, roasting your turkey out on the grill also means that you don't have to worry about constantly monitoring the bird to ensure a perfectly juicy, tender turkey. To make grilling turkey foolproof, we divided our coals into two piles on either side of the grill so that the turkey thighs would receive the highest heat. A combination of lit coals and unlit briquettes yielded a longer-burning fire, making replenishing coals unnecessary. The addition of a pan of water stabilized the temperature inside the grill for even cooking, and a quick salt rub before grilling yielded seasoned meat and crispy skin.

Simple Grill-Roasted Turkey
SERVES 10 TO 12

Table salt is not recommended for this recipe because it is too fine. If using a kosher or self-basting turkey (such as a frozen Butterball), do not salt it in step 1. Check the wings halfway through roasting; if they are getting too dark, fold a 12 by 8-inch piece of foil in half lengthwise and then again crosswise and slide the foil between the wing and the cooking grate to shield the wings from the flame. As an accompaniment, try our Gravy for Simple Grill-Roasted Turkey (recipe follows).

1   (12- to 14-pound) turkey, neck and giblets
    removed and reserved for gravy
    Kosher salt and pepper
1   teaspoon baking powder
1   tablespoon vegetable oil
    Large disposable aluminum roasting pan
    (if using charcoal) or 2 disposable aluminum
    pie plates (if using gas)

1. Place turkey breast side down on work surface. Make two 2-inch incisions below each thigh and breast along back of turkey (4 incisions total). Using fingers or handle of wooden spoon, carefully separate skin from thighs and breast. Rub 4 teaspoons salt evenly inside cavity of turkey, 1 tablespoon salt under skin of each side of breast, and 1 teaspoon salt under skin of each leg.

2. Combine 1 teaspoon salt, 1 teaspoon pepper, and baking powder in small bowl. Pat turkey dry with paper towels and evenly sprinkle baking powder mixture all over. Rub in mixture with hands, coating entire surface evenly. Wrap turkey tightly with plastic wrap; refrigerate for 24 to 48 hours.

3. Remove turkey from refrigerator and discard plastic. Tuck wings underneath turkey. Using hands, rub oil evenly over entire surface of turkey.

4A. FOR A CHARCOAL GRILL: Open bottom vent halfway and place disposable pan filled with 3 cups water in center of grill. Arrange 1½ quarts unlit charcoal briquettes on either side of pan in even layer. Light large chimney starter two-thirds filled with charcoal briquettes (4 quarts). When top coals are partially covered with ash, pour 2 quarts of lit coals on top of each pile of unlit coals. Set cooking grate in place, cover, and open lid vent halfway. Heat grill until hot, about 5 minutes.

4B. FOR A GAS GRILL: Place 2 disposable pie plates with 2 cups water in each directly on 1 burner over which turkey will be cooked. Turn all burners to high, cover, and heat grill until hot, about 15 minutes. Turn primary burner (burner opposite pie plates) to medium and turn other burner(s) off. Adjust primary burner as needed to maintain grill temperature of 325 degrees.

5. Clean and oil cooking grate. Place turkey, breast side up, in center of charcoal grill or on cooler side of gas grill, making sure bird is over disposable pans and not over flame. Cover (placing vents over turkey on charcoal grill) and cook until breasts register 160 degrees and thighs/drumsticks register 175 degrees, 2½ to 3 hours, rotating turkey after 1¼ hours if using gas grill.

6. Transfer turkey to carving board and let rest, uncovered, for 45 minutes. Carve turkey and serve.

Gravy for Simple Grill-Roasted Turkey
MAKES 6 CUPS

1   tablespoon vegetable oil
      Reserved turkey neck, cut into 1-inch pieces,
      and giblets
1   pound onions, chopped coarse
4   cups low-sodium chicken broth
4   cups beef broth
2   small carrots, peeled and chopped coarse
2   small celery ribs, chopped coarse
6   tablespoons unsalted butter
½   cup all-purpose flour
2   bay leaves
½   teaspoon dried thyme
10   whole black peppercorns
      Salt and pepper

1. Heat oil in Dutch oven over medium-high heat until shimmering. Add turkey neck and giblets; cook, stirring occasionally, until browned, about 5 minutes. Add half of onions and cook, stirring occasionally, until softened, about 3 minutes. Reduce heat to low; cover and cook, stirring occasionally, until turkey parts and onions release their juices, about 20 minutes.

2. Add chicken broth and beef broth; increase heat to high and bring to boil. Reduce heat to low and simmer, uncovered, skimming any scum that rises to surface, until broth is rich and flavorful, about 30 minutes. Strain broth into large bowl (you should have about 8 cups), reserving giblets, if desired; discard neck. Reserve broth. If using, when cool enough to handle, remove gristle from giblets, dice, and set aside. (Broth can be refrigerated for up to 2 days.)

3. Pulse carrots in food processor until broken into rough ¼-inch pieces, about 5 pulses. Add celery and remaining onions; pulse until all vegetables are broken into ⅛-inch pieces, about 5 pulses.

4. Melt butter in now-empty Dutch oven over medium-high heat. Add vegetables and cook, stirring frequently, until softened and well browned, about 10 minutes. Reduce heat to medium; stir in flour and cook, stirring constantly, until thoroughly browned and fragrant, 5 to 7 minutes. Whisking constantly, gradually add reserved broth; bring to boil, skimming off any foam that forms on surface. Reduce heat to medium-low and add bay leaves, thyme, and peppercorns; simmer, stirring occasionally, until thickened and reduced to 6 cups, 30 to 35 minutes.

5. Strain gravy through fine-mesh strainer into clean saucepan, pressing on solids to extract as much liquid as possible; discard solids. Stir in diced giblets, if using. Season with salt and pepper to taste.

GRILL-ROASTED TURKEY BREAST

WHY THIS RECIPE WORKS: Grill-roasting a turkey breast makes a nice change from the same old oven-roasted holiday bird. And unleashing the smoky fire of the grill on mild-mannered turkey breast is bound to add great flavor. The problem is that unlike fatty pork butt or brisket, which turns moist and tender after a stint on the grill, ultra-lean turkey breast easily dries out. Plus its irregular shape can lead to uneven cooking. We wanted to develop a recipe that would deliver a grill-roasted breast with all the richness and juiciness we associate with the thighs and legs, along with crisp, well-rendered skin, and meat that was moist all the way through.

We began by salting our turkey breast. Salting, much like brining, imparts flavor and moisture to the meat. When meat is salted, its juices are initially drawn out of the flesh and beads of liquid pool on its surface. Eventually, the salty liquid slowly migrates back into the meat, keeping it moist as it cooks. We grill-roasted the turkey breast over a modified two-level fire, starting the meat over the cool side of the grill and later moving it to the hot side to finish cooking. Although most of the meat turned out moist and flavorful, there were still desiccated spots on the tapered ends of the breast and in places where the skin didn't completely cover the meat. Inspired by a restaurant technique, we reshaped our turkey breast like a roulade so that it would cook through evenly. After carefully removing the skin, we rolled the boneless turkey breast into a tight cylinder. Then we rewrapped the skin around the roulade of meat to completely cover and protect it. Our roast held its shape beautifully on the grill and, once carved, the roulade revealed moist, evenly cooked meat and crisp skin.

Grill-Roasted Boneless Turkey Breast

SERVES 6 TO 8

We prefer either a natural (unbrined) or kosher turkey breast for this recipe. Using a kosher turkey breast (rubbed with salt and rinsed during processing) or self-basting turkey breast (injected with salt and water) eliminates the need for salting in step 2. If the breast has a pop-up timer, remove it before cooking.

When using a charcoal grill, we prefer wood chunks to wood chips whenever possible; substitute 1 small wood chunk, soaked in water for 1 hour, for the wood chip packet.

½ cup wood chips, soaked in water for 15 minutes and drained (optional)
1 (5- to 7-pound) whole bone-in turkey breast, trimmed
2 teaspoons salt
1 teaspoon vegetable oil
Pepper

1. Using large piece of heavy-duty aluminum foil, wrap soaked chips, if using, in foil packet and cut several vent holes in top.

2. Remove skin from breast meat and then cut along rib cage to remove breast halves (discard bones or save for stock). Pat turkey breast halves dry with paper towels and season with salt. Stack breast halves on top of one another with cut sides facing, and alternating thick and tapered ends. Stretch skin over exposed meat and tuck in ends. Tie kitchen twine lengthwise around roast. Then tie 5 to 7 pieces of twine at 1-inch intervals crosswise along roast. Transfer roast to wire rack set in rimmed baking sheet and refrigerate for 1 hour.

3A. FOR A CHARCOAL GRILL: Open bottom vent halfway. Light large chimney starter filled with charcoal briquettes (6 quarts). When top coals are partially covered with ash, pour evenly over half of grill. Place wood chip packet, if using, on coals. Set cooking grate in place, cover, and open lid vent halfway. Heat grill until hot and wood chips are smoking, about 5 minutes.

3B. FOR A GAS GRILL: Place wood chip packet, if using, directly on primary burner. Turn all burners to high, cover, and heat grill until hot and wood chips are smoking, about 15 minutes. Turn all burners to medium-low. (Adjust burner(s) as needed during cooking to maintain grill temperature around 300 degrees.)

4. Clean and oil cooking grate. Rub surface of roast with oil and season with pepper. Place roast on grill (cool side if using charcoal). Cover (position lid vents over meat if using charcoal) and cook until roast registers 150 degrees, 40 minutes to 1 hour, turning 180 degrees halfway through cooking.

5. Slide roast to hot side of grill (if using charcoal) or turn all burners to medium-high (if using gas). Cook until roast is browned and skin is crisp on all sides, 8 to 10 minutes, rotating every 2 minutes.

6. Transfer roast to carving board, tent loosely with foil, and let rest for 15 minutes. Cut into ½-inch-thick slices, removing twine as you cut. Serve.

NOTES FROM THE TEST KITCHEN

TURNING A BONE-IN TURKEY BREAST INTO A BONELESS TURKEY ROAST

1. Starting at one side of the breast and using your fingers to separate the skin from the meat, peel the skin off the breast meat and reserve.

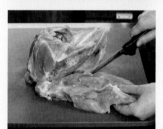

2. Using the tip of a knife, cut along the rib cage to remove each breast half completely.

3. Arrange one breast, cut side up; top with the second breast, cut side down, the thick end over the tapered end. Drape the skin over the breasts and tuck the ends under.

4. Tie a 3-foot piece of kitchen twine lengthwise around the roast. Then, tie five to seven pieces of twine at 1-inch intervals crosswise along the roast, starting at its center, then at either end, and then filling in the rest.

CRANBERRY SAUCE

WHY THIS RECIPE WORKS: The best cranberry sauce has a clean, pure cranberry flavor, with enough sweetness to temper the assertively tart fruit but not so much that the sauce is cloying or candylike. The texture should be that of a soft gel, neither too liquidy nor too stiff, cushioning some softened but still intact berries.

For the most part, it turned out that simpler was better. We used white table sugar, which, unlike brown sugar, honey, or syrup, balanced the tartness of the cranberries without adding a flavor profile of its own. Simpler was also better when it came to liquid: water proved the best choice. We also discovered that adding just a pinch of salt brought out an unexpected sweetness in the berries, heightening the flavor of the sauce overall.

Classic Cranberry Sauce

MAKES 2¼ CUPS

If you've got frozen cranberries, do not defrost them before use; just pick through them and add about 2 minutes to the simmering time.

  1 cup (7 ounces) sugar
  ¾ cup water
  ¼ teaspoon table salt
  1 (12-ounce) bag cranberries, picked through (see note)

Bring the sugar, water, and salt to a boil in a medium sauce-pan over high heat, stirring occasionally to dissolve the sugar. Stir in the cranberries; return to a boil. Reduce the heat to medium; simmer until saucy and slightly thickened, and about two-thirds of the berries have popped open, about 5 minutes. Transfer to a medium bowl, cool to room temperature, and serve. (The cranberry sauce can be covered and refrigerated for up to 7 days; let stand at room temperature for 30 minutes before serving.)

HOLIDAY CRANBERRY CHUTNEY

WHY THIS RECIPE WORKS: There's something to be said for the simplicity of a plain old sweet-tart cranberry sauce, but sometimes we want more. To create a more complexly flavored sauce, we looked to Indian chutneys. Adding vinegar, aromatics, and spices to slow-cooked cranberries and fruit yielded a jammy relish with kick and savor.

Cranberry Chutney with Apples and Crystallized Ginger

MAKES ABOUT 3 CUPS

If using frozen cranberries, thaw them before cooking.

1	teaspoon vegetable oil
1	shallot, minced
2	teaspoons finely grated fresh ginger
½	teaspoon salt
⅔	cup water
¼	cup cider vinegar
1	cup packed brown sugar
12	ounces (3 cups) fresh or frozen cranberries
2	Granny Smith apples, peeled, cored, and cut into ¼-inch pieces
⅓	cup minced crystallized ginger

1. Heat oil in medium saucepan over medium heat until shimmering. Add shallot, fresh ginger, and salt; cook, stirring occasionally, until shallot has softened, 1 to 2 minutes.

2. Add water, vinegar, and sugar. Increase heat to high and bring to simmer, stirring to dissolve sugar. Add 1½ cups cranberries and apples; return to simmer. Reduce heat to medium-low and simmer, stirring occasionally, until cranberries have almost completely broken down and mixture has thickened, about 15 minutes.

3. Add remaining 1½ cups cranberries and crystallized ginger; continue to simmer, stirring occasionally, until cranberries just begin to burst, 5 to 7 minutes. Transfer to serving bowl and cool for at least 1 hour before serving. (Sauce can be refrigerated for up to 3 days.)

Spicy Cranberry Chutney

Increase oil to 2 teaspoons and substitute 1 stemmed and seeded red bell pepper cut into ¼-inch pieces and 2 seeded and minced jalapeño chiles for fresh ginger in step 1. Increase cooking time in step 1 to 5 minutes. Increase water to ¾ cup and omit apples and crystallized ginger.

Cranberry Chutney with Fennel and Golden Raisins

Increase oil to 2 teaspoons and substitute 1 cored fennel bulb cut into ¼-inch pieces and ½ teaspoon fennel seeds for fresh ginger in step 1. Increase cooking time in step 1 to 5 minutes. Increase water to 1 cup, omit apples, and substitute ⅓ cup golden raisins for crystallized ginger.

Cranberry-Orange Chutney

Starting with 2 oranges, remove four 2-inch-wide strips zest from 1 orange, then peel both oranges and remove segments. Set aside zest and segments. Increase fresh ginger to 4 teaspoons and add 1 teaspoon yellow mustard seeds to oil together with fresh ginger in step 1. Increase water to ¾ cup and add orange zest and segments to pot with cranberries in step 2. Omit apples and crystallized ginger.

Cranberry Chutney with Pear, Lemon, and Rosemary

Remove two 2-inch-wide strips zest from 1 lemon, then peel and remove segments. Set aside zest and segments. Substitute 2 teaspoons chopped fresh rosemary for fresh ginger. Substitute 2 peeled Bosc pears cut into ¼-inch pieces for apples; omit crystallized ginger. Add lemon zest and segments to pot with cranberries in step 2.

BAKED BREAD STUFFING

WHY THIS RECIPE WORKS: Stuffing baked in a dish definitely has appeal—you can make as much as you want and you don't have to time its doneness to coincide with the doneness of the meat—but it lacks the rich flavor from the bird's juices. As the base for our stuffing we chose ordinary sandwich bread, which we "staled" in a low oven; this would allow it to soak up plenty of liquid. To infuse the stuffing with meaty turkey flavor, we browned turkey wings on the stovetop, then we used the same pan to sauté the aromatics. When we placed the stuffing in a baking dish, we arranged the seared wings on top—as they cooked, their rendered fat infused the stuffing with rich flavor. Covering the baking dish with foil prevented the top of the stuffing from drying out, while placing a baking sheet underneath the dish protected the bottom layer from the oven's heat.

Baked Bread Stuffing with Sausage, Dried Cherries, and Pecans

SERVES 10 TO 12

Two pounds of chicken wings can be substituted for the turkey wings. If using chicken wings, separate them into 2 sections (it's not necessary to separate the tips) and poke each segment 4 to 5 times. Also, increase the amount of broth to 3 cups, reduce the amount of butter to 2 tablespoons, and cook the stuffing for only 60 minutes (the wings should register over 175 degrees at the end of cooking). Use the meat from the cooked wings to make salad or soup. The bread can be toasted up to 1 day in advance.

2	pounds hearty white sandwich bread, cut into ½-inch cubes (16 cups)
3	pounds turkey wings, divided at joints
2	teaspoons vegetable oil
1	pound bulk pork sausage
4	tablespoons (½ stick) unsalted butter
1	large onion, chopped fine
3	medium celery ribs, minced
	Table salt
2	tablespoons minced fresh thyme
2	tablespoons minced fresh sage
1	teaspoon ground black pepper
2½	cups low-sodium chicken broth
3	large eggs
1	cup dried cherries
1	cup pecan halves, toasted and chopped fine

1. Adjust the oven racks to the upper-middle and lower-middle positions and heat the oven to 250 degrees. Spread the bread cubes in an even layer on 2 rimmed baking sheets. Bake until the edges have dried but the centers are slightly moist (the cubes should yield to pressure), 45 to 60 minutes, stirring several times during baking. Transfer the dried bread to a large bowl and increase the oven temperature to 375 degrees.

2. While the bread dries, use a paring knife to poke 10 to 15 holes in each wing segment. Heat the oil in a 12-inch skillet over medium-high heat until shimmering. Add the wings in a single layer and cook until golden brown on both sides, 8 to 12 minutes. Transfer the wings to a separate bowl and set aside.

3. Return the now-empty skillet to medium-high heat, add the sausage, and cook, breaking it up into ½-inch pieces with a wooden spoon, until browned, 5 to 7 minutes. Remove the sausage with a slotted spoon and transfer to a paper towel–lined plate.

4. Melt the butter in the fat left in the skillet over medium heat. Add the onion, celery, and ½ teaspoon salt and cook, stirring occasionally, until the vegetables are softened, 7 to 9 minutes. Stir in the thyme, sage, and pepper and cook until fragrant, about 30 seconds. Stir in 1 cup of the broth, scraping up any browned bits, and bring to a simmer. Add the vegetable mixture to the bowl with the dried bread and toss to combine.

5. Grease a 13 by 9-inch baking dish. Whisk the eggs, remaining 1½ cups broth, 1½ teaspoons salt, and any accumulated juices from the wings together in a bowl. Add the egg mixture, cherries, pecans, and sausage to the bread mixture and toss to combine; transfer to the prepared baking dish. Arrange the wings on top of the stuffing, cover tightly with aluminum foil, and place the baking dish on a rimmed baking sheet.

6. Bake on the lower rack until the wings register 175 degrees, 60 to 75 minutes. (The stuffing can be held at room temperature for up to 4 hours. To finish, remove the wings from the stuffing and re-cover the stuffing tightly with foil. Heat on a rimmed baking sheet in a 375-degree oven until hot, 20 to 25 minutes. Remove the foil, fluff with a fork, and serve immediately.)

7. Remove the foil and transfer the wings to a dinner plate to reserve for another use. Gently fluff the stuffing with a fork. Let rest for 5 minutes before serving.

Baked Bread Stuffing with Leeks, Bacon, and Apple

Follow the recipe for Baked Bread Stuffing with Sausage, Dried Cherries, and Pecans, substituting 12 ounces bacon, cut into ½-inch pieces, for the sausage. In step 3, cook the bacon in a skillet until crisp, about 5 minutes. Remove the bacon with a slotted spoon and transfer to a paper towel–lined plate; pour off all but 2 tablespoons fat from the skillet. Proceed with the recipe from step 4, substituting 2 leeks, white and light green parts, sliced thin, for the onion, and 3 Granny Smith apples, cut into 1/4-inch pieces, for the dried cherries. Omit the pecans.

Baked Bread Stuffing with Fresh Herbs

Follow the recipe for Baked Bread Stuffing with Sausage, Dried Cherries, and Pecans, omitting the sausage. After the browned turkey wings have been removed in step 2, increase the butter to 6 tablespoons and melt it in the skillet over medium heat. Proceed with the recipe from step 4, substituting 3 tablespoons chopped fresh parsley for the dried cherries and pecans.

GREEN BEAN CASSEROLE

WHY THIS RECIPE WORKS: The classic combination of green beans, condensed soup, and canned onions isn't bad. But for a holiday centered on homemade food, shouldn't every dish be great? We wanted to upgrade green bean casserole to give it fresh, homemade flavor.

Our first tasting determined that we definitely needed to use fresh green beans rather than frozen or canned beans. A preliminary blanching and shocking prepared the beans to finish cooking perfectly in the casserole, enabling them to keep a consistent texture and retain their beautiful green color. For our sauce, we made a mushroom variation of the classic French velouté sauce (chicken broth thickened with a roux made from butter and flour, then finished with heavy cream). Our biggest challenge was the onion topping. Ultimately we found that the canned onions couldn't be entirely replaced without sacrificing the level of convenience we thought appropriate to the dish, but we masked their "commercial" flavor with freshly made buttered bread crumbs.

Classic Green Bean Casserole

SERVES 8 TO 10

All the components of this dish can be cooked ahead of time. The assembled casserole needs only 15 minutes in a 375-degree oven to warm through and brown.

TOPPING

- 4 slices high-quality white sandwich bread, torn into quarters
- 2 tablespoons unsalted butter, softened
- ¼ teaspoon table salt
- ⅛ teaspoon ground black pepper
- 3 cups canned fried onions (about 6 ounces)

BEANS

- Table salt
- 2 pounds green beans, ends trimmed, cut on the diagonal into 2-inch pieces
- ½ ounce dried porcini mushrooms
- 6 tablespoons (¾ stick) unsalted butter
- 1 medium onion, minced
- 3 medium garlic cloves, minced or pressed through a garlic press (about 1 tablespoon)
- 12 ounces white button mushrooms, wiped clean and sliced ¼ inch thick
- 12 ounces cremini mushrooms, wiped clean and sliced ¼ inch thick
- 2 tablespoons minced fresh thyme leaves
- ¼ teaspoon ground black pepper
- 2 tablespoons unbleached all-purpose flour
- 1 cup low-sodium chicken broth
- 2 cups heavy cream

1. FOR THE TOPPING: Pulse the bread, butter, salt, and pepper in a food processor until the mixture resembles coarse crumbs, 10 to 15 pulses. Transfer to a large bowl and toss with the onions; set aside.

2. FOR THE BEANS: Heat the oven to 375 degrees. Bring 4 quarts water to a boil in a large pot. Add 2 tablespoons salt and the beans. Cook until bright green and slightly crunchy, 4 to 5 minutes. Drain the beans and plunge immediately into a large bowl filled with ice water to stop cooking. Spread the beans out onto a paper towel–lined baking sheet to drain.

3. Meanwhile, cover the dried porcini with ½ cup hot tap water in a small microwave-safe bowl; cover with plastic wrap, cut several steam vents with a paring knife, and microwave on high power for 30 seconds. Let stand until the mushrooms soften, about 5 minutes. Lift the mushrooms from the liquid with a fork and mince using a chef's knife (you should have about 2 tablespoons). Pour the liquid through a paper towel–lined sieve and reserve.

4. Melt the butter in a large nonstick skillet over medium-high heat. Add the onion, garlic, button mushrooms, and cremini mushrooms and cook until the mushrooms release their moisture, about 2 minutes. Add the porcini mushrooms along with their strained soaking liquid, the thyme, 1 teaspoon salt, and the pepper and cook until all the mushrooms are tender and the liquid has reduced to 2 tablespoons, about 5 minutes. Add the flour and cook for 1 minute. Stir in the chicken broth and reduce the heat to medium. Stir in the cream and simmer gently until the sauce has the consistency of dense soup, about 15 minutes.

5. Arrange the beans in a 3-quart gratin dish. Pour the mushroom mixture over the beans and mix to coat the beans evenly. Sprinkle with the bread-crumb mixture and bake until the top is golden brown and the sauce is bubbling around the edges, about 15 minutes. Serve immediately.

BEHIND THE SCENES

PRESS, DON'T MINCE, YOUR GARLIC

Newly hired test cooks (many of whom are fresh out of cooking school) often do a double take when they discover a test kitchen secret. When it comes to mincing garlic, we'd rather use a garlic press to do the job. Purists may insist on mincing their garlic the old-fashioned way (a chef's knife and cutting board), but let's face it—mincing garlic is quite a chore. First, its texture is defiantly sticky, so that little bits cling tenaciously to your cutting board, knife blade, and fingers. Second, despite the diminutive size of garlic cloves, mincing a couple of them finely and evenly is a time- and labor-intensive proposition. Enter the garlic press.

Most garlic presses share a common design, comprising two handles connected by a hinge. At the end of one handle is a small perforated hopper; at the end of the other is a plunger that fits snugly inside the hopper. The garlic cloves in the hopper get crushed by the descending plunger when you squeeze the handles together and the puree is extruded through the perforations in the bottom of the hopper. In thousands of hours of use in our test kitchen, we have found that this little tool delivers speed, ease, and a comfortable separation of garlic from fingers. (See page 879 for our recommended brand of garlic press.) And there are other advantages: A good garlic press breaks down the cloves more than an average cook would with a knife, resulting in a fuller, more pungent garlic flavor. A good garlic press also ensures a consistently fine texture, which in turns means better distribution throughout the dish. Lesson learned? They don't teach you everything in cooking school.

QUICK GREEN BEAN CASSEROLE

WHY THIS RECIPE WORKS: We love traditional green bean casserole, but we wanted a streamlined technique for preparing the dish—one with tender beans in a tasty sauce worthy of a holiday spread and yet speedy enough for a last-minute supper.

Rather than using two pots—one for the beans and one for the sauce—we cooked both in just one pot, a skillet. First, we built a sauce in the skillet with onion, garlic, chicken broth, cream, and a little flour; then we added the beans along with thyme and bay leaves, covered them, and allowed them to steam until the beans were almost done. We then stirred in meaty browned cremini mushrooms and thickened the sauce by uncovering the skillet during the final phase of cooking. And instead of canned fried onions, we sprinkled crunchy fried sliced shallots over our easy, tasty skillet casserole.

Quick Green Bean "Casserole"
SERVES 8

3	large shallots, sliced thin (about 1 cup)
	Table salt and ground black pepper
3	tablespoons unbleached all-purpose flour
5	tablespoons vegetable oil
10	ounces cremini mushrooms, wiped clean and sliced ¼ inch thick
2	tablespoons unsalted butter
1	medium onion, minced
2	medium garlic cloves, minced or pressed through a garlic press (about 2 teaspoons)
1½	pounds green beans, trimmed
3	sprigs fresh thyme
2	bay leaves
¾	cup heavy cream
¾	cup low-sodium chicken broth

1. Toss the shallots with ¼ teaspoon salt, ⅛ teaspoon pepper, and 2 tablespoons of the flour in a bowl. Heat 3 tablespoons of the oil in a 12-inch nonstick skillet over medium-high heat until smoking; add the shallots and cook, stirring frequently, until golden and crisp, about 5 minutes. Transfer the shallots with the oil to a baking sheet lined with paper towels.

2. Wipe out the skillet and return to medium-high heat. Add the remaining 2 tablespoons oil, the mushrooms, and ¼ teaspoon salt; cook, stirring occasionally, until the mushrooms are well browned, about 8 minutes. Transfer to a plate and set aside.

3. Wipe out the skillet. Melt the butter in the skillet over medium heat, then add the onion and cook, stirring occasionally, until the edges begin to brown, about 2 minutes. Stir in the garlic and remaining 1 tablespoon flour; toss in the green beans, thyme, and bay leaves. Add the cream and chicken broth, increase the heat to medium-high, cover, and cook until the beans are partly tender but still crisp at the center, about 4 minutes. Add the mushrooms and continue to cook, uncovered, until the green beans are tender, about 4 minutes. Off the heat, discard the bay leaves and thyme; season with salt and pepper to taste. Transfer to a serving dish, sprinkle evenly with the shallots, and serve.

CANDIED SWEET POTATO CASSEROLE

WHY THIS RECIPE WORKS: Sweet potato casserole is often claimed as a must-have at the Thanksgiving table. Kids love this sweet, sticky dish, but adults long for a side dish with more restrained sweetness, rather than one that could double as dessert. We set out to develop a sweet potato casserole with a bit of a savory accent to please everyone.

For the best texture and flavor, we steamed the sweet potatoes on the stovetop with a little water, butter, and brown sugar. We kept the other flavorings simple—just salt and pepper. In the topping, we used whole pecans instead of chopped; this gave the casserole a better texture and appearance. And a little cayenne and cumin lent a hit of spice to the topping that offset the sweetness of the potato.

Candied Sweet Potato Casserole

SERVES 10 TO 12

For a more intense molasses flavor, use dark brown sugar in place of light brown sugar.

SWEET POTATOES

- 8 tablespoons (1 stick) unsalted butter, cut into 1-inch chunks
- 5 pounds sweet potatoes (about 8 medium), peeled and cut into 1-inch cubes
- 1 cup (7 ounces) packed light brown sugar (see note)
- ½ cup water
- 1½ teaspoons table salt
- ½ teaspoon ground black pepper

PECAN TOPPING

- 2 cups pecan halves
- ½ cup packed (3½ ounces) light brown sugar (see note)
- 1 egg white, lightly beaten
- ⅛ teaspoon table salt
   Pinch cayenne pepper
   Pinch ground cumin

1. FOR THE SWEET POTATOES: Melt the butter in a large Dutch oven over medium-high heat. Add the sweet potatoes, brown sugar, water, salt, and black pepper; bring to a simmer. Reduce the heat to medium-low, cover, and cook, stirring often, until the sweet potatoes are tender (a paring knife can be slipped into and out of the center of the potatoes with very little resistance), 45 to 60 minutes.

2. When the sweet potatoes are tender, remove the lid and bring the sauce to a rapid simmer over medium-high heat. Continue to simmer until the sauce has reduced to a glaze, 7 to 10 minutes.

3. FOR THE TOPPING: Meanwhile, mix all the ingredients for the topping together in a medium bowl; set aside.

4. Adjust an oven rack to the middle position and heat the oven to 450 degrees. Pour the potato mixture into a 13 by 9-inch baking dish (or a shallow casserole dish of similar size). Spread the topping over the potatoes. Bake until the pecans are toasted and crisp, 10 to 15 minutes. Serve immediately.

CHAPTER 7

WE'LL HAVE THE STEAK

PAN-SEARED STEAKS

WHY THIS RECIPE WORKS: The flavor of a juicy, grilled steak is hard to beat. We wanted to produce outstanding steaks—indoors—that were every bit as good as those cooked on the grill. We found that heating a heavy-bottomed skillet until very hot is essential for a good sear and, thus, a good crust. Thoroughly drying the steaks is also key—soggy steaks will steam, not sear. For best flavor, we seasoned the steaks with salt and pepper prior to cooking. And we reduced the heat before adding the steaks—the skillet was still hot, but not so hot that it burned the fond, which we used to make a pan sauce. After removing the steaks from the pan, we let them rest for five minutes, enough time to prepare the pan sauce and allow the juices in the meat to redistribute.

Pan-Seared Steaks
SERVES 4

Serve these steaks with either Red Wine Pan Sauce or Shallot Butter Sauce (recipes follow). Prepare all the sauce ingredients before starting the steaks and don't wash the skillet after cooking the steaks; the fat left in the pan will be used for the sauce. Note that the wine reduction used in the red wine sauce should be started before the steaks are cooked.

- 1 tablespoon vegetable oil
- 4 (8-ounce) boneless strip or rib-eye steaks, each 1 to 1¼ inches thick, thoroughly dried with paper towels
  Table salt and ground black pepper

1. Heat the oil in a 12-inch skillet over high heat until just smoking. Meanwhile, season both sides of the steaks with salt and pepper.

2. Lay the steaks in the pan, leaving ¼ inch of space between them; reduce the heat to medium-high and cook, not moving the steaks until well browned, about 4 minutes. Using tongs, flip the steaks; cook until the center of the steaks registers 120 degrees on an instant-read thermometer for rare (4 minutes), 125 degrees for medium-rare (5 minutes), or 130 degrees for medium (6 minutes). Transfer the steaks to a large plate, tent with foil, and let rest for 5 minutes while preparing one of the pan sauces.

Red Wine Pan Sauce
MAKES ABOUT ½ CUP

Start cooking the steaks when the wine has almost finished reducing. Use a smooth, medium-bodied, fruity wine, such as a Côtes du Rhône.

WINE REDUCTION
- 1 cup red wine (see note)
- 1 medium shallot, minced (about 3 tablespoons)
- 2 white mushrooms, wiped clean and chopped fine (about 3 tablespoons)
- 1 small carrot, chopped fine (about 2 tablespoons)
- 1 bay leaf
- 3 sprigs fresh parsley

SAUCE
- 1 medium shallot, minced (about 3 tablespoons)
- ½ cup low-sodium chicken broth
- ½ cup low-sodium beef broth
- 3 tablespoons cold unsalted butter, cut into 6 pieces
- ½ teaspoon fresh thyme leaves
  Table salt and ground black pepper

1. FOR THE WINE REDUCTION: Heat the wine, shallot, mushrooms, carrot, bay leaf, and parsley in a 12-inch skillet over low heat; cook, without simmering (the liquid should be steaming but not bubbling), until the entire mixture reduces to 1 cup, 15 to 20 minutes. Strain through a fine-mesh strainer and return the liquid (about ½ cup) to the clean skillet. Continue to cook over low heat, without simmering, until the liquid is reduced to 2 tablespoons, 15 to 20 minutes. Transfer the reduction to a bowl.

2. FOR THE SAUCE: Follow the recipe for Pan-Seared Steaks. After removing the steaks from the skillet, add the shallot and cook over low heat until softened, about 1 minute. Turn the heat to high; add the chicken and beef broths. Bring to a boil, scraping up the browned bits on the pan bottom with a wooden spoon, until the liquid is reduced to 2 tablespoons, about 6 minutes. Turn the heat to medium-low, gently whisk in the reserved wine reduction and any accumulated juices from the plate with the steaks. Whisk in the butter, one piece at a time, until melted and the sauce is thickened and glossy; add the thyme and season with salt and pepper to taste. Spoon the sauce over the steaks and serve immediately.

Shallot Butter Sauce
MAKES ABOUT ½ CUP

- 2 medium shallots, minced (about ⅓ cup)
- 4 tablespoons (½ stick) cold unsalted butter, cut into 4 pieces
- 1 teaspoon juice from 1 lemon
- 1 teaspoon minced fresh parsley leaves
  Table salt and ground black pepper

Follow the recipe for Pan-Seared Steaks. After removing the steaks from the skillet, add the shallots and cook over low heat until softened, about 1 minute. Turn the heat to medium-low; stir in the butter, scraping up the browned bits on the pan bottom with a wooden spoon. When the butter is just melted, stir in the lemon juice and parsley; season with salt and pepper to taste. Spoon the sauce over the steaks and serve immediately.

RESTAURANT-STYLE STEAK SAUCE

WHY THIS RECIPE WORKS: We love the ultra-rich flavor and glossy consistency that a classic French demi-glace (a savory, full-bodied reduction traditionally made from veal bones and stock) adds to a sauce, but making it is a time-consuming process usually left to the expertise of professional cooks. We wanted to find a shortcut for making demi-glace at home, so that we could use it as the base of a variety of great sauces for crusty, pan-seared steaks. Chopping up vegetables (to increase their surface area, thus providing more opportunity for flavorful browning) as well as adding mushrooms, tomato paste, and seasonings to red wine and beef broth was a good start, but it wasn't enough. To replicate the meaty flavor and unctuous gelatin given up by roasted bones, we sautéed ground beef with the tomato paste and stirred powdered gelatin into the final reduction. Since it was easy to freeze and use again, making a big batch of our Sauce Base was worth our while; we made enough for two recipes of steak sauce and came up with variations that would make us want to eat steak every night.

Restaurant-Style Herb Sauce for Pan-Seared Steaks

SERVES 4

We like this sauce with strip or rib-eye steaks, but it will work with any type of pan-seared steak.

- 1 recipe Pan-Seared Steaks (page 164)
- 1 small shallot, minced (about 1 tablespoon)
- ½ cup white wine
- ¼ cup Sauce Base (½ recipe; page 165)
- ¼ teaspoon white wine vinegar
- 1½ teaspoons minced fresh chives
- 1½ teaspoons minced fresh parsley leaves
- 1 teaspoon minced fresh tarragon leaves
- 1 tablespoon unsalted butter
  Table salt and ground black pepper

After transferring the steaks to a plate to rest, return the now-empty skillet to medium-low heat; add the shallot and cook, stirring constantly, until lightly browned, about 2 minutes. Add the wine and bring to a simmer, scraping the bottom of the skillet with a wooden spoon to loosen any browned bits. Add the Sauce Base, vinegar, and any accumulated juices from the steaks; return to a simmer and cook until slightly reduced, about 1 minute. Off the heat, whisk in the chives, parsley, tarragon, and butter; season with salt and pepper to taste. Spoon the sauce over the steaks and serve.

Restaurant-Style Brandy and Green-Peppercorn Sauce for Pan-Seared Steaks

SERVES 4

- 1 recipe Pan-Seared Steaks (page 164)
- 1 small shallot, minced (about 1 tablespoon)
- ½ cup brandy
- ¼ cup Sauce Base (½ recipe; page 165)
- ¼ teaspoon red wine vinegar
- ¼ cup heavy cream
- 2 tablespoons green peppercorns, rinsed
- ¼ teaspoon chopped fresh thyme leaves
  Table salt and ground black pepper

After transferring the steaks to a plate to rest, return the now-empty skillet to medium-low heat; add the shallot and cook, stirring constantly, until lightly browned, about 2 minutes. Add the brandy and bring to a simmer, scraping the bottom of the skillet with a wooden spoon to loosen any browned bits. Add the Sauce Base, vinegar, heavy cream, peppercorns, thyme, and any accumulated juices from the steaks; return to a simmer and cook until slightly reduced, about 1 minute. Off the heat, season with salt and pepper to taste. Spoon the sauce over the steaks and serve.

Restaurant-Style Port Wine Sauce for Pan-Seared Steaks

SERVES 4

- 1 recipe Pan-Seared Steaks (page 164)
- 1 small shallot, minced (about 1 tablespoon)
- ½ cup ruby port
- ¼ cup Sauce Base (½ recipe; recipe follows)
- ¼ teaspoon balsamic vinegar
- ¼ teaspoon chopped fresh thyme leaves
- 1 tablespoon unsalted butter
  Table salt and ground black pepper

After transferring the steaks to a plate to rest, return the now-empty skillet to medium-low heat; add the shallot and cook, stirring constantly, until lightly browned, about 2 minutes. Add the port and bring to a simmer, scraping the bottom of the skillet with a wooden spoon to loosen any browned bits. Add the Sauce Base, vinegar, and any accumulated juices from the steaks; return to a simmer and cook until slightly reduced, about 1 minute. Off the heat, whisk in the thyme and butter; season with salt and pepper to taste. Spoon the sauce over the steaks and serve.

Sauce Base

MAKES ½ CUP

The sauce base recipe yields more than called for in the sauce recipes; leftovers can be refrigerated in an airtight container for up to 3 days or frozen for up to 1 month.

- 1 small onion, peeled and cut into rough ½-inch pieces
- 1 small carrot, peeled and cut into rough ½-inch pieces
- 8 ounces cremini mushrooms, trimmed and halved
- 2 medium garlic cloves, peeled
- 1 tablespoon vegetable oil
- 8 ounces 85 percent lean ground beef
- 1 tablespoon tomato paste
- 2 cups dry red wine
- 4 cups beef broth
- 4 sprigs fresh thyme
- 2 bay leaves
- 2 teaspoons whole black peppercorns
- 5 teaspoons unflavored gelatin

1. Pulse the onion, carrot, mushrooms, and garlic in a food processor into ⅛-inch pieces, 10 to 12 pulses, scraping down the sides as needed.

2. Heat the oil in a Dutch oven over medium-high heat until shimmering; add the beef and tomato paste and cook, stirring frequently, until the beef is well browned, 8 to 10 minutes. Add the vegetable mixture and cook, stirring occasionally, until any exuded moisture has evaporated, about 8 minutes. Add the wine and bring to a simmer, scraping the bottom of the pot with a wooden spoon to loosen any browned bits. Add the broth, thyme, bay leaves, and peppercorns; bring to a boil. Reduce the heat and gently boil, occasionally scraping the bottom and sides of the pot and skimming fat from the surface, until reduced to 2 cups, 20 to 25 minutes.

3. Strain the mixture through a fine-mesh strainer set over a small saucepan, pressing on the solids with a rubber spatula to extract as much liquid as possible (you should have about 1 cup stock). Sprinkle the gelatin over the stock and stir to dissolve. Place the saucepan over medium-high heat and bring the stock to a boil. Gently boil, stirring occasionally, until reduced to ½ cup, 5 to 7 minutes. Remove from the heat and cover to keep warm.

CAST-IRON THICK-CUT STEAKS

WHY THIS RECIPE WORKS: We were looking for a way to make a steak with the ultimate crust entirely on the stovetop— so we turned to a cast-iron skillet, since its heat-retention properties are ideal for a perfect sear. We chose the moderately expensive boneless strip steak for its big, beefy flavor. The first step to a great sear was an evenly heated cooking surface, which we accomplished by preheating the cast-iron skillet in the oven. This also gave us time to prepare a zesty compound butter with shallot, garlic, parsley, and chives—and to let the steaks warm up to room temperature, which helped them cook more quickly and evenly. Salting the outside of the steaks while they rested pulled moisture from the steaks while also seasoning the meat, helping us get a better sear. After testing different flipping techniques and heat levels, we found that flipping the steaks every 2 minutes and transitioning from medium-high to medium-low heat partway through cooking resulted in a perfectly browned, crisp crust and a juicy, evenly cooked interior every time.

Cast-Iron Thick-Cut Steaks with Herb Butter
SERVES 4

- 2 (1-pound) boneless strip steaks, 1½ inches thick, trimmed
  Salt and pepper
- 4 tablespoons unsalted butter, softened
- 2 tablespoons minced shallot
- 1 tablespoon minced fresh parsley
- 1 tablespoon minced fresh chives
- 1 garlic clove, minced
- 2 tablespoons vegetable oil

1. Adjust oven rack to middle position, place 12-inch cast-iron skillet on rack, and heat oven to 500 degrees. Meanwhile, season steaks with salt and let sit at room temperature. Mix butter, shallot, parsley, chives, garlic, ¼ teaspoon pepper, and pinch of salt together in bowl; set aside until needed.

2. When oven reaches 500 degrees, pat steaks dry with paper towels and season with pepper. Using potholders, remove skillet from oven and place over medium-high heat; turn off oven. Being careful of hot skillet handle, add oil and heat until just smoking. Cook steaks, without moving, until lightly browned on first side, about 2 minutes. Flip steaks and continue to cook until lightly browned on second side, about 2 minutes.

3. Flip steaks, reduce heat to medium-low, and cook, flipping every 2 minutes, until steaks are well browned and meat registers 120 to 125 degrees (for medium-rare), 7 to 9 minutes. Transfer steaks to carving board, dollop 2 tablespoons herb butter on each steak, tent loosely with aluminum foil, and let rest for 5 to 10 minutes. Slice steaks into ½-inch-thick slices and serve.

Cast-Iron Thick-Cut Steaks with Blue Cheese–Chive Butter

Omit shallot and parsley. Increase chives to 2 tablespoons and add ⅓ cup crumbled mild blue cheese to butter with chives.

PAN-SEARED THICK-CUT STEAKS

WHY THIS RECIPE WORKS: A nicely charred thick-cut steak certainly looks appealing. But cutting into the steak to find that the rosy meat is confined to a measly spot in the center—with the rest a thick band of overcooked gray—is a great disappointment. We wanted to find a surefire method for pan-searing thick-cut steaks that could deliver both a flavorful crust and juicy, perfectly pink meat throughout.

We found it was essential to sear the steaks quickly to keep the meat directly under the crust from turning gray. But we'd need to take an untraditional approach for these thick-cut steaks and sear them at the end of cooking, rather than at the beginning. We began by moving the steaks straight from the fridge into a 275-degree oven, which not only warmed them to 95 degrees but also dried the meat thoroughly—dry meat is essential for a well-browned crust. At this temperature, when the steak met the hot skillet, it developed a beautiful brown crust in less than four minutes, while the rest of the meat stayed pink, juicy, and tender.

Pan-Seared Thick-Cut Steaks

SERVES 4

Rib-eye or filet mignon of similar thickness can be substituted for strip steaks. If using filet mignon, buying a 2-pound center-cut tenderloin roast and portioning it into four 8-ounce steaks yourself will produce more consistent results. If using filet mignon, increase the oven time by about 5 minutes. When cooking lean strip steaks (without an external fat cap) or filet mignon, add an extra tablespoon of oil to the pan. To serve the steaks with the Red Wine–Mushroom Pan Sauce (recipe follows), prepare all the sauce ingredients while the steaks are in the oven, and don't wash the skillet after cooking the steaks.

> 2 (1-pound) boneless strip steaks, each
>   1½ to 1¾ inches thick (see note)
>   Table salt and ground black pepper
> 1 tablespoon vegetable oil

1. Adjust an oven rack to the middle position and heat the oven to 275 degrees. Pat the steaks dry with paper towels. Cut each steak in half vertically to create four 8-ounce steaks. Season the steaks liberally with salt and pepper; using your hands, gently shape into a uniform thickness. Place the steaks on a wire rack set over a rimmed baking sheet; transfer the baking sheet to the oven. Cook until an instant-read thermometer inserted horizontally into the center of the steaks registers 90 to 95 degrees for rare to medium-rare (20 to 25 minutes), or 100 to 105 degrees for medium (25 to 30 minutes).

2. Heat the oil in a 12-inch skillet over high heat until smoking. Place the steaks in the skillet and sear until well browned and crusty, 1½ to 2 minutes, lifting once halfway through to redistribute the fat underneath each steak. (Reduce the heat if the fond begins to burn.) Using tongs, turn the steaks and cook until well browned on the second side, 2 to 2½ minutes. Transfer the steaks to a clean rack and reduce the heat under the pan to medium. Use tongs to stand 2 steaks on their sides. Holding the steaks together, return to the skillet and sear on all edges until browned, about 1½ minutes (see photo on page 164). Repeat with the remaining 2 steaks.

3. Return the steaks to the wire rack and let rest, loosely tented with foil, for about 10 minutes. If desired, cook the sauce in the now-empty skillet. Serve immediately.

SEARING TWO STEAKS AT ONCE

Use tongs to sear the sides of two steaks at the same time.

Red Wine–Mushroom Pan Sauce

MAKES ABOUT 1 CUP

Prepare all the ingredients for the pan sauce while the steaks are in the oven.

> 1 tablespoon vegetable oil
> 8 ounces white mushrooms, wiped clean and
>   sliced thin (about 3 cups)
> 1 small shallot, minced (about 1 tablespoon)
> 1 cup dry red wine
> ½ cup low-sodium chicken broth
> 1 tablespoon balsamic vinegar
> 1 teaspoon Dijon mustard
> 2 tablespoons cold unsalted butter, cut into 4 pieces
> 1 teaspoon minced fresh thyme leaves
>   Table salt and ground black pepper

Follow the recipe for Pan-Seared Thick-Cut Steaks. After removing the steaks from the skillet, pour off the fat from the skillet. Heat the oil over medium-high heat until just smoking. Add the mushrooms and cook, stirring occasionally, until beginning to brown and the liquid has evaporated, about 5 minutes. Add the shallot and cook, stirring frequently, until beginning to soften, about 1 minute. Increase the heat to high; add the red wine and broth, scraping the bottom of the skillet with a wooden spoon to loosen any browned bits. Simmer rapidly until the liquid and mushrooms are reduced to 1 cup, about 6 minutes. Add the vinegar, mustard, and any juices from the resting steaks; cook until thickened, about 1 minute. Off the heat, whisk in the butter and thyme; season with salt and pepper to taste. Spoon the sauce over the steaks and serve immediately.

Thai Chili Butter

MAKES ABOUT ⅓ CUP

Prepare all the ingredients for the butter while the steaks are in the oven. If red curry paste isn't available, increase the chili-garlic sauce to 2½ teaspoons.

4 tablespoons (½ stick) unsalted butter, softened
1 tablespoon chopped fresh cilantro leaves
2 teaspoons Asian chili-garlic sauce (preferably Thai)
1½ teaspoons thinly sliced scallion, green part
   only (from 1 scallion)
1 small garlic clove, minced or pressed through
   a garlic press (about ½ teaspoon)
½ teaspoon red curry paste (preferably Thai; see note)
2 teaspoons juice from 1 lime
   Table salt

Beat the butter vigorously with a spoon until soft and fluffy. Add the cilantro, chili-garlic sauce, scallion, garlic, and red curry paste; beat to incorporate. Add the lime juice a little at a time, beating vigorously between each addition until fully incorporated. Add salt to taste. Spoon a dollop over each steak, giving it time to melt before serving.

PAN-SEARED INEXPENSIVE STEAKS

WHY THIS RECIPE WORKS: Buying cheap steak can be a gamble and a lesson in confusion. Names differ from region to region, some cuts are wonderfully tender while others are hopelessly tough, and some recipes recommend cuts that are almost impossible to find, leaving the consumer to make a blind substitution. We wanted inexpensive steak with the flavor and texture to rival its pricey counterparts.

We first visited meat purveyors to learn what makes some steaks more expensive than others as well as to decipher all the different names. After sorting through the confusion, we were left with a list of 12 candidates. We cooked them as we would any steak, creating a nice sear on both sides without overcooking or allowing the browned bits in the pan to burn. Tasters judged most to be too tough and/or lacking beefy flavor, while others were livery or gamy. We tried a variety of preparation methods—salting, aging, tenderizing, marinating—but none really improved flavor and texture. In the end, two cuts earned favored status: boneless shell sirloin steak (aka top butt) and flap meat steak (aka sirloin tips). To prepare the steak, season the steaks simply with salt and pepper and start with a very hot skillet. Allow the meat to rest before slicing. Slice the steak thin, against the grain and on the bias, to ensure the tenderest meat.

Pan-Seared Inexpensive Steaks
SERVES 4

Serve these steaks with Tomato-Caper Pan Sauce or Mustard-Cream Pan Sauce (recipes follow). Prepare all of the sauce ingredients before cooking the steaks, and don't wash the skillet after removing the steaks; the sauce will use some of the fat left in the pan. To serve two instead of four, use a 10-inch skillet to cook a 1-pound steak and halve the sauce ingredients. Bear in mind that even those tasters who usually prefer rare beef preferred these steaks cooked medium-rare or medium because the texture is firmer and not quite so chewy. The times in the recipe are for 1¼-inch-thick steaks.

2 tablespoons vegetable oil
2 1-pound whole boneless shell sirloin steaks
   (top butt) or whole flap meat steaks, each
   about 1¼ inches thick
   Table salt and ground black pepper

1. Heat the oil in a heavy-bottomed 12-inch skillet over medium-high heat until smoking. Meanwhile, season both sides of the steaks with salt and pepper. Place the steaks in the skillet; cook, without moving the steaks, until well browned, about 2 minutes. Using tongs, flip the steaks; reduce the heat to medium. Cook until well browned on the second side and the center of the steaks registers 125 degrees on an instant-read thermometer for medium-rare (about 5 minutes) or 130 degrees for medium (about 6 minutes).

2. Transfer the steaks to a large plate and tent loosely with foil; let rest for about 10 minutes. Meanwhile, prepare the pan sauce, if making.

3. Using a sharp chef's knife or carving knife, slice the steak about ¼ inch thick against the grain on the bias, arrange on a platter or on individual plates, and spoon some sauce (if using) over each steak; serve immediately.

Tomato-Caper Pan Sauce
MAKES ABOUT ¾ CUP

If ripe fresh tomatoes are not available, substitute 2 to 3 canned whole tomatoes, seeded and cut into ¼-inch pieces.

1 medium shallot, minced (about 3 tablespoons)
1 teaspoon unbleached all-purpose flour
2 tablespoons dry white wine
1 cup low-sodium chicken broth
2 tablespoons capers, drained
1 medium ripe tomato, seeded and cut into
   ¼-inch dice (about ¼ cup; see note)
¼ cup minced fresh parsley leaves
   Table salt and ground black pepper

Follow the recipe for Pan-Seared Inexpensive Steaks. After removing the steaks from the skillet, pour off all but 1 tablespoon of the fat. Return the skillet to low heat and add the shallot; cook, stirring frequently, until beginning to brown, 2 to 3 minutes. Sprinkle the flour over the shallot; cook, stirring constantly, until combined, about 1 minute. Add the wine and increase the heat to medium-high; simmer rapidly, scraping up the browned bits on the pan bottom with a wooden spoon. Simmer until the liquid is reduced to a glaze, about 30 seconds; add the broth and simmer until reduced to ⅔ cup, about 4 minutes. Reduce the heat to medium; add the capers, tomato, and any meat juices that have accumulated on the plate and cook until the flavors are blended, about 1 minute. Stir in the parsley and season with salt and pepper to taste; spoon the sauce over the sliced steak and serve immediately.

Mustard-Cream Pan Sauce
MAKES ABOUT ¾ CUP

- 1   medium shallot, minced (about 3 tablespoons)
- 2   tablespoons dry white wine
- ½   cup low-sodium chicken broth
- 6   tablespoons heavy cream
- 3   tablespoons grainy Dijon mustard
-      Table salt and ground black pepper

Follow the recipe for Pan-Seared Inexpensive Steaks. After removing the steaks from the skillet, pour off all but 1 tablespoon of the fat. Return the skillet to low heat and add the shallot; cook, stirring frequently, until beginning to brown, 2 to 3 minutes. Add the wine and increase the heat to medium-high; simmer rapidly, scraping up the browned bits on the pan bottom with a wooden spoon. Simmer until the liquid is reduced to a glaze, about 30 seconds; add the broth and simmer until reduced to ¼ cup, about 3 minutes. Add the cream and any meat juices that have accumulated on the plate; cook until heated through, about 1 minute. Stir in the mustard; season with salt and pepper to taste. Spoon over the sliced steak and serve immediately.

PAN-SEARED FILET MIGNON

WHY THIS RECIPE WORKS: Many cooks feel that filet mignon should be reserved for a celebratory restaurant meal. But we knew we could replicate the best restaurant filet at home, with a rich, brown crust and a tender interior, topped with a quick but luscious pan sauce.

For a great crust, we patted the steaks dry before searing them in a very hot skillet. Then we transferred the meat to a hot oven to cook through. Finishing the steak in the oven prevented the richly flavored browned bits in the bottom of the pan from burning and allowed us time to start the sauce, which can be made in minutes while the steaks rest.

Pan-Seared Filet Mignon
SERVES 4

If you are making one of the sauces, have all the sauce ingredients ready before searing the steaks, and don't wash the skillet after removing the steaks. Begin the sauce while the steaks are in the oven. To cook six steaks instead of four, use a 12-inch pan and use 6 teaspoons of olive oil.

- 4   (7- to 8-ounce) center-cut filets mignons, 1½ inches thick, each dried thoroughly with paper towels
- 4   teaspoons olive oil
-      Table salt and ground black pepper

1. Adjust an oven rack to the lower-middle position, place a large rimmed baking sheet on the oven rack, and heat the oven to 450 degrees. When the oven reaches 450 degrees, heat a large skillet over high heat on the stovetop until very hot.

2. Meanwhile, rub each side of the steaks with ½ teaspoon oil and sprinkle generously with salt and pepper. Place the steaks in the hot skillet and cook, without moving the steaks, until well browned and a nice crust has formed, about 3 minutes. Turn the steaks with tongs and cook until well browned and a nice crust has formed on the second side, about 3 minutes longer. Remove the pan from the heat and use tongs to transfer the steaks to the hot baking sheet in the oven.

3. Roast until the center of the steaks registers 120 degrees on an instant-read thermometer for rare (4 to 5 minutes), 125 degrees for medium-rare (6 to 8 minutes), or 130 degrees for medium (8 to 10 minutes). Transfer the steaks to a large plate; loosely tent with foil and let rest for about 10 minutes before serving.

Madeira Pan Sauce with Mustard and Anchovies

MAKES ABOUT ⅔ CUP

If you do not have Madeira on hand, sherry makes a fine substitute. The accumulated pan juices from the steaks in the oven are incorporated into the reduction. If the steaks haven't finished cooking once the sauce has reduced, simply set the sauce aside until the steaks (and accumulated juices) are ready.

- 1 medium shallot, minced (about 3 tablespoons)
- 1 cup Madeira (see note)
- 2 anchovy fillets, minced to a paste (about 1 teaspoon)
- 1 tablespoon minced fresh parsley leaves
- 1 tablespoon minced fresh thyme leaves
- 1 tablespoon Dijon mustard
- 1 tablespoon juice from 1 lemon
- 3 tablespoons unsalted butter, softened
  Table salt and ground black pepper

Follow the recipe for Pan-Seared Filet Mignon. While the steaks are in the oven, set the skillet over medium-low heat; add the shallot and cook, stirring constantly, until softened, about 1 minute. Add the Madeira, increase the heat to high, and scrape the pan bottom with a wooden spoon to loosen the browned bits. Simmer until the liquid is reduced to about ⅓ cup, 6 to 8 minutes. Add the accumulated juices from the baking sheet and reduce the liquid 1 minute longer. Off the heat, whisk in the anchovies, parsley, thyme, mustard, lemon juice, and butter until the butter has melted and the sauce is slightly thickened. Season with salt and pepper to taste, spoon the sauce over the steaks, and serve immediately.

Argentinian-Style Fresh Parsley and Garlic Sauce (Chimichurri)

MAKES ABOUT 1 CUP

For best results use flat-leaf parsley.

- 1 cup packed fresh parsley leaves from one large bunch, washed and dried (see note)
- 5 medium garlic cloves, peeled
- ½ cup extra-virgin olive oil
- ¼ cup red wine vinegar
- 2 tablespoons water
- 1 small red onion, finely minced
- 1 teaspoon table salt
- ¼ teaspoon red pepper flakes

Pulse the parsley and garlic in a food processor, stopping as necessary to scrape down the sides of the bowl with a rubber spatula, until the garlic and parsley are chopped fine, about 20 pulses; transfer to a medium bowl. Whisk in the oil, vinegar, water, onion, salt, and red pepper flakes until thoroughly blended. Spoon about 2 tablespoons over each steak and serve. (This sauce tastes best when used fresh but can be refrigerated, with plastic wrap pressed directly on the surface, for up to 3 days.)

PEPPER-CRUSTED FILET MIGNON

WHY THIS RECIPE WORKS: Filet mignon is ultra-tender, but it has only mild beefy flavor. Chefs often compensate by wrapping the delicate meat in bacon or puff pastry, serving it with rich wine sauces or flavored butter, or giving it a crust of cracked black peppercorns. We decided to pursue the peppercorn approach and found several problems to solve: The peppercorns tend to fall off in the pan, interfere with the meat's browning, and—when used in sufficient quantity to create a real crust—deliver punishing pungency.

Our first step was to mellow the peppercorns' heat by gently simmering them in olive oil. We then created a well-browned and attractive pepper crust using a two-step process: First, we rubbed the raw steaks with a paste of the cooked cracked peppercorns, salt, and oil, then we pressed the paste into each steak through a sheet of plastic wrap. We let the steaks sit, covered, for an hour before cooking. The paste not only added flavor to the meat but drew out the meat's own beefy flavor. While the steaks sat wrapped and covered in paste, we had plenty of time to simmer a rich reduction sauce—though a flavored butter also made an excellent accompaniment.

Pepper-Crusted Filet Mignon

SERVES 4

If you prefer a very mild pepper flavor, drain the cooled peppercorns in a fine-mesh strainer in step 1, toss them with 5 tablespoons of fresh oil, add the salt, and proceed. Serve with Port-Cherry Reduction or Blue Cheese–Chive Butter (recipes follow).

- 5 tablespoons black peppercorns, cracked
- 5 tablespoons plus 2 teaspoons olive oil
- 1½ teaspoons table salt
- 4 (7- to 8-ounce) center-cut filets mignons, 1½ to 2 inches thick, each dried thoroughly with paper towels

1. Heat the peppercorns and 5 tablespoons of the oil in a small saucepan over low heat until faint bubbles appear. Continue to cook at a bare simmer, swirling the pan occasionally, until the pepper is fragrant, 7 to 10 minutes. Remove from the heat and set aside to cool. When the mixture is at room temperature, add the salt and stir to combine. Rub the steaks with the pepper mixture, thoroughly coating the top and bottom of each steak with the peppercorns. Cover the steaks with plastic wrap and press gently to make sure the peppercorns adhere; let stand at room temperature for 1 hour.

2. Meanwhile, adjust an oven rack to the middle position, place a rimmed baking sheet on the oven rack, and heat the oven to 450 degrees. Heat the remaining 2 teaspoons oil in a 12-inch heavy-bottomed skillet over medium-high heat until faint smoke appears. Place the steaks in the skillet and cook, without moving the steaks, until a dark brown crust has formed, 3 to 4 minutes. Using tongs, turn the steaks and cook until well browned on the second side, about 3 minutes. Remove the pan from the heat and transfer the steaks to the hot baking sheet. Roast until the center of the steaks registers 120 degrees on an instant-read thermometer for rare (3 to 5 minutes), 125 degrees for medium-rare (5 to 7 minutes), and 130 degrees for medium (7 to 9 minutes). Transfer the steaks to a wire rack and let rest, loosely tented with foil, for about 10 minutes before serving.

Port-Cherry Reduction
MAKES ABOUT 1 CUP

- 1½ cups port
- ½ cup balsamic vinegar
- ½ cup dried tart cherries
- 1 large shallot, minced (about 4 tablespoons)
- 2 sprigs fresh thyme
- 1 tablespoon unsalted butter
- Table salt

1. Combine the port, balsamic vinegar, cherries, shallot, and thyme in a medium saucepan; simmer over medium-low heat until the liquid is reduced to ⅓ cup, about 30 minutes. Set aside, covered.

2. While the steaks are resting, reheat the sauce. Off the heat, remove the thyme, then whisk in the butter until melted. Season with salt to taste. Serve, passing the sauce at the table with the steak.

Blue Cheese–Chive Butter
MAKES ABOUT ½ CUP

- 3 tablespoons unsalted butter, softened
- ⅓ cup crumbled mild blue cheese, at room temperature
- ⅛ teaspoon table salt
- 2 tablespoons minced fresh chives

Combine the butter, cheese, and salt in a medium bowl and mix with a stiff rubber spatula until smooth. Fold in the chives. While the steaks are resting, spoon 1 to 2 tablespoons of the butter on each one.

We've all seen recipe instructions such as "Reduce sauce to ½ cup" or "Simmer until broth is reduced to 2 cups." Those directions are clear, but when you look into a pan of sauce, can you really discern volume? Unless you have wizard-like abilities, the answer is probably "No."

Here in the test kitchen, we know that getting the right amount of sauce can make or break a dish, and to be sure of success we keep a heatproof liquid measuring cup next to the stove. As the sauce appears to be getting near the targeted amount, we pour it into the cup to get an exact measure. If it needs more time on the stove, back into the pan it goes until just the right amount is obtained. No guessing, no problem.

PAN-SEARED FLANK STEAK

WHY THIS RECIPE WORKS: Cooking flank steak indoors often poses challenges—the cut of meat is too long to fit in most skillets, and it's quite thin, so it often overcooks before the exterior is well browned. We wanted a year-round, indoor cooking method that would produce a juicy, well-browned flank steak that was cooked to medium throughout. To start, we cut the flank into four steaks that would fit neatly in the skillet, but we didn't put them there right away. Instead, we sprinkled them with salt for seasoning and sugar for browning and baked them in a very low oven until they reached 120 degrees. Then we seared them in a hot skillet to develop the crust, flipping the steaks three times instead of just once. After enriching the lean steaks with a flavorful compound butter, we sliced them thinly against the grain for maximum tenderness.

Pan-Seared Flank Steak with Mustard-Chive Butter
SERVES 4 TO 6

Open the oven as infrequently as possible in step 1. If the meat is not yet up to temperature, wait at least 5 minutes before taking its temperature again. Slice the steak as thin as possible against the grain.

1 (1½- to 1¾-pound) flank steak, trimmed
2 teaspoons kosher salt
1 teaspoon sugar
½ teaspoon pepper
3 tablespoons unsalted butter, softened
3 tablespoons chopped fresh chives
2 teaspoons Dijon mustard
½ teaspoon grated lemon zest plus 1 teaspoon juice
2 tablespoons vegetable oil

1. Adjust oven rack to middle position and heat oven to 225 degrees. Pat steak dry with paper towels. Cut steak in half lengthwise. Cut each piece in half crosswise to create 4 steaks. Combine salt, sugar, and pepper in small bowl. Sprinkle half of salt mixture on 1 side of steaks and press gently to adhere. Flip steaks and repeat with remaining salt mixture. Place steaks on wire rack set in rimmed baking sheet; transfer sheet to oven. Cook until thermometer inserted through side into center of thickest steak registers 120 degrees, 30 to 40 minutes.

2. Meanwhile, combine butter, 1 tablespoon chives, mustard, and lemon zest and juice in small bowl.

3. Heat oil in 12-inch skillet over medium-high heat until just smoking. Sear steaks, flipping every 1 minute, until brown crust forms on both sides, 4 minutes total. (Do not move steaks between flips.) Return steaks to wire rack and let rest for 10 minutes.

4. Transfer steaks to cutting board with grain running from left to right. Spread 1½ teaspoons butter mixture on top of each steak. Slice steak as thin as possible against grain. Transfer sliced steak to warm platter, dot with remaining butter mixture, sprinkle with remaining 2 tablespoons chives, and serve.

STEAK SANDWICHES

WHY THIS RECIPE WORKS: Steak sandwiches run the gamut from oversized "bombs" with greasy, gristly meat (break out the napkins) to precious restaurant concoctions (hold the truffle butter, please) with a price tag to match. We wanted to find a satisfying steak sandwich with some middle ground—easy to eat and gussied up with flavorful, but not costly, ingredients.

We started with the choice of steak, and flank steak won out over all other cuts. It's relatively inexpensive, lean, and tender, as long as the meat is cooked correctly. For a flavorful browned crust, we generously seasoned the steak with salt and pepper and then pan-seared it in a very hot skillet on both sides until browned. To keep the steak tender and juicy, we allowed the meat to rest and then sliced it thin across the grain. Soft, squishy bread needn't apply here—only a crusty French baguette or similar artisan-style bread would do. We slathered the bread with mayonnaise doctored with soy sauce, honey, garlic, and ginger. And to finish, thinly sliced onion and arugula scattered on top of the steak provided a little spicy bite.

SLICING FLANK STEAK

Once the steak has rested, slice the meat across the grain into thin pieces.

Flank Steak and Arugula Sandwiches with Red Onion

SERVES 4

For juicy, tender meat, be sure to let the steak rest for 10 minutes after cooking and slice the steak thin across the grain.

1½ pounds flank steak, trimmed of excess fat and
     patted dry with paper towels
     Table salt and ground black pepper
1 tablespoon vegetable oil
1 baguette, cut into four 5-inch lengths, each
     piece split into top and bottom pieces
1 recipe Garlic-Soy Mayonnaise (recipe follows)
½ small red onion, sliced thin
3 ounces arugula, stemmed, washed, and dried
     (about 3 cups)

1. Heat a 12-inch skillet over high heat until very hot, about 4 minutes. While the skillet is heating, season the steak generously with salt and pepper. Add the oil to the pan and swirl to coat the bottom. Lay the steak in the pan and cook without moving it until well browned, about 5 minutes. Using tongs, flip the steak; cook until well browned on the second side, about 5 minutes longer. Transfer the steak to a carving board, tent with foil, and let rest for 10 minutes. Cut the steak into ¼-inch slices on the bias against the grain.

2. Spread each baguette piece with 1 tablespoon mayonnaise; portion the steak over the bottom pieces of the bread and sprinkle with salt and pepper to taste. Evenly divide the onion and arugula over the steak; top each with a baguette piece and serve.

Garlic-Soy Mayonnaise

MAKES ABOUT ½ CUP

Blue Plate is the test kitchen's favorite brand of mayonnaise—read why on page 915.

½ cup mayonnaise
1 tablespoon soy sauce
1 teaspoon minced or grated fresh ginger

½ teaspoon honey

1 small garlic clove, minced or pressed through a garlic press (about ½ teaspoon)

½ teaspoon toasted sesame oil

Mix all the ingredients together in a small bowl. (The mayonnaise can be covered and refrigerated for up to 1 day.)

PUB-STYLE STEAK AND ALE PIE

WHY THIS RECIPE WORKS: Intensely savory steak pie is a classic British comfort food, but making it can be a tedious multistep procedure. Our streamlined version has all the flavor and texture of the authentic dish with less work. We skipped the traditional browning of the meat, which requires working in batches, and browned the mushrooms and onion instead, building a flavorful fond. Adding flour early in the process and limiting the amount of beef broth we added to the pot meant that the gravy formed as the meat cooked so we could bypass the usual sauce-building steps. To make sure the limited moisture didn't mean limited flavor, we added bacon, garlic, and thyme. We substituted beer for some of the broth and boosted browning with the addition of a small amount of baking soda. Our sturdy dough included an egg for added structure, which together with sour cream also contributed fat, allowing us to decrease the amount of butter. The resulting dough could go over the filling while it was hot, but it baked up flaky and substantial, the perfect complement to the rich filling.

Pub-Style Steak and Ale Pie

SERVES 6

Don't substitute bone-in short ribs; their yield is too variable. Instead, use a 4-pound chuck-eye roast, well trimmed of fat. Use a good-quality beef broth for this recipe; the test kitchen's favorite is Better Than Bouillon Roasted Beef Base. If you don't have a deep-dish pie plate, use an 8 by 8-inch baking dish and roll the pie dough into a 10-inch square. We prefer pale and brown ales for this recipe.

FILLING

3 tablespoons water

½ teaspoon baking soda

3 pounds boneless beef short ribs, trimmed and cut into ¾-inch chunks

½ teaspoon salt

½ teaspoon pepper

2 slices bacon, chopped

1 pound cremini mushrooms, trimmed and halved if medium or quartered if large

1½ cups beef broth

1 large onion, chopped

1 garlic clove, minced

½ teaspoon dried thyme

¼ cup all-purpose flour

¾ cup beer

CRUST

1 large egg, lightly beaten

¼ cup sour cream, chilled

1¼ cups (6¼ ounces) all-purpose flour

½ teaspoon salt

6 tablespoons unsalted butter, cut into ½-inch pieces and chilled

1. FOR THE FILLING: Combine water and baking soda in large bowl. Add beef, salt, and pepper and toss to combine. Adjust oven rack to lower-middle position and heat oven to 350 degrees.

2. Cook bacon in large Dutch oven over high heat, stirring occasionally, until partially rendered but not browned, about 3 minutes. Add mushrooms and ¼ cup broth and stir to coat. Cover and cook, stirring occasionally, until mushrooms are reduced to about half their original volume, about 5 minutes. Add onion, garlic, and thyme and cook, uncovered, stirring occasionally, until onion is softened and fond begins to form on bottom of pot, 3 to 5 minutes. Sprinkle flour over mushroom mixture and stir until all flour is moistened. Cook, stirring occasionally, until fond is deep brown, 2 to 4 minutes. Stir in beer and remaining 1¼ cups broth, scraping up any browned bits. Stir in beef and bring to simmer, pressing as much beef as possible below surface of liquid. Cover pot tightly with aluminum foil, then lid; transfer to oven. Cook for 1 hour.

3. Remove lid and discard foil. Stir filling, cover, return to oven, and continue to cook until beef is tender and liquid is thick enough to coat beef, 15 to 30 minutes longer. Transfer filling to deep-dish pie plate. (Once cool, filling can be covered with plastic wrap and refrigerated for up to 2 days.) Increase oven temperature to 400 degrees.

4. FOR THE CRUST: While filling is cooking, measure out 2 tablespoons beaten egg and set aside. Whisk remaining egg and sour cream together in bowl. Process flour and salt in food processor until combined, about 3 seconds. Add butter and pulse until only pea-size pieces remain, about 10 pulses. Add half of sour cream mixture and pulse until combined, about 5 pulses. Add remaining sour cream mixture and pulse until dough begins to form, about 10 pulses. Transfer mixture to lightly floured counter and knead briefly until dough comes together. Form into 4-inch disk, wrap in plastic, and refrigerate for at least 1 hour or up to 2 days.

5. Roll dough into 11-inch round on lightly floured counter. Using knife or 1-inch round biscuit cutter, cut round from center of dough. Drape dough over filling (it's OK if filling is hot). Trim overhang to ½ inch beyond lip of plate. Tuck overhang under itself; folded edge should be flush with edge of plate. Crimp dough evenly around edge of plate using your fingers or press with tines of fork to seal. Brush crust with reserved egg. Place pie on rimmed baking sheet. Bake until filling is bubbling and crust is deep golden brown and crisp, 25 to 30 minutes. (If filling has been refrigerated, increase baking time by 15 minutes and cover with foil for last 15 minutes to prevent overbrowning.) Let cool for 10 minutes before serving.

CHAPTER 8

PORK CHOPS EVERY DAY

SAUTÉED PORK CUTLETS

WHY THIS RECIPE WORKS: Lean pork cutlets are flavorless without proper browning, but by the time the cutlets take on any color, they're dry and lacking any tenderness. We wanted tender, browned cutlets with meaty flavor and a rich pan sauce to accompany them.

Instead of supermarket pork cutlets, we opted for a meatier-tasting cut: boneless country-style spare ribs. These ribs combine a large portion of the flavorful shoulder meat with minimal connective tissue and only a bit of bland tenderloin. Even better, because the ribs are sold portioned into relatively small pieces, they require little work to be fashioned into cutlets. To guard against dry meat, we brined our cutlets to help them retain moisture. A quick brine worked well, but the retained moisture kept the meat so wet that it steamed, cooking the cutlets all the way through before they had a chance to brown. To trigger faster browning, we added sugar to the brine. The sugar in the brine helped the cutlets develop a golden-brown exterior without sweetening them too much. And for an even darker crust, we cooked the cutlets in a combination of olive oil and butter. The sugars and milk proteins in the butter promoted browning and boost flavor.

Sautéed Pork Cutlets with Mustard-Cider Sauce

SERVES 4

We prefer natural to enhanced pork (pork that has been injected with a salt solution to increase moistness and flavor). If the pork is enhanced, do not brine. Look for ribs that are 3 to 5 inches long. Cut ribs over 5 inches in half crosswise before slicing them lengthwise to make pounding more manageable.

Table salt and ground black pepper
1½ teaspoons sugar
1½ pounds boneless country-style pork spareribs, trimmed (see note)
1½ tablespoons unsalted butter, cut into 6 equal pieces
1 small shallot, minced (about 1 tablespoon)
1 teaspoon unbleached all-purpose flour
1 teaspoon dry mustard
½ cup low-sodium beef or chicken broth
¼ cup apple cider
½ teaspoon minced fresh sage
1 tablespoon olive oil
2 teaspoons whole-grain mustard

1. Dissolve 1 tablespoon salt and the sugar in 2 cups water in a medium bowl. Cut each pork rib lengthwise into 2 or 3 cutlets about ⅜ inch wide. Gently pound the cutlets to ¼-inch thickness between two layers of plastic wrap. Submerge the cutlets in the brine, cover with plastic wrap, and refrigerate for 30 minutes. (Do not overbrine.)

2. Meanwhile, melt 2 pieces of the butter in a small saucepan over medium heat. Add the shallot and cook until softened, about 1½ minutes. Stir in the flour and dry mustard and cook for 30 seconds. Gradually whisk in the broth, smoothing out

CUTTING COUNTRY-STYLE RIBS INTO CUTLETS

1. Slice each rib lengthwise to create 2 or 3 cutlets, each about ⅜ inch wide.

2. Lay each piece between 2 sheets of plastic wrap and pound until roughly ¼ inch thick.

any lumps. Stir in the cider and sage, bring to a boil, then reduce to a gentle simmer and cook for 5 minutes. Remove the pan from the heat, cover, and set aside.

3. Adjust an oven rack to the middle position and heat the oven to 200 degrees. Remove the cutlets from the brine, dry thoroughly with paper towels, and season with pepper. Heat the oil in a 12-inch skillet over medium-high heat until just smoking. Add 1 piece more butter, let it melt, then quickly lay half of the cutlets in the skillet. Cook until browned on the first side, 1 to 2 minutes.

4. Using tongs, flip the cutlets and continue to cook until browned on the second side, 1 to 2 minutes. Transfer the cutlets to a large plate and keep warm in the oven. Repeat with the remaining cutlets and 1 piece more butter.

5. Return the empty skillet to medium heat, add the reserved broth mixture, and bring to a simmer. Cook, scraping up the browned bits, until the sauce is slightly thickened and has reduced to about ½ cup, about 2 minutes. Stir in any accumulated pork juices and simmer for 30 seconds longer.

6. Off the heat, whisk in the whole-grain mustard and remaining 2 pieces butter. Season the sauce with salt and pepper to taste, spoon it over the cutlets, and serve immediately.

CRISPY PAN-FRIED PORK CHOPS

WHY THIS RECIPE WORKS: A breaded coating can be just the thing to give lean, bland pork chops a flavor boost—but not when it turns gummy and flakes off the meat. Using boneless chops was fast and easy. Dipping the chops in cornstarch was our first step toward creating an ultra-crisp sheath. Buttermilk brought a lighter texture and tangy flavor to the breading, and minced garlic and a bit of mustard perked up the breading's flavor. Crushed cornflakes added a craggy texture to the pork chops, especially once we combined them with more cornstarch. Finally, to ensure that our breading adhered to the chops, we gave the meat a short rest and we lightly scored the pork chops before adding them to the pan.

Crispy Pan-Fried Pork Chops
SERVES 4

We prefer natural to enhanced pork (pork that has been injected with a salt solution to increase moistness and flavor) for this recipe. Don't let the chops drain on the paper towels for longer than 30 seconds, or the heat will steam the crust and make it soggy. You can substitute ¾ cup store-bought cornflake crumbs for the whole cornflakes. If using crumbs, omit the processing step and mix the crumbs with the cornstarch, salt, and pepper.

- ⅔ cup cornstarch
- 1 cup buttermilk
- 2 tablespoons Dijon mustard
- 1 medium garlic clove, minced or pressed through a garlic press (about 1 teaspoon)
- 3 cups cornflakes
  Table salt and ground black pepper
- 8 (3- to 4-ounce) boneless pork chops, ½ to ¾ inch thick, trimmed
- ⅔ cup vegetable oil
  Lemon wedges, for serving

1. Place ⅓ cup of the cornstarch in a shallow dish or pie plate. In a second shallow dish, whisk the buttermilk, mustard, and garlic until combined. Process the cornflakes, ½ teaspoon salt, ½ teaspoon pepper, and the remaining ⅓ cup cornstarch in a food processor until the cornflakes are finely ground, about 10 seconds. Transfer the cornflake mixture to a third shallow dish.

NOTES FROM THE TEST KITCHEN

HELPING THE COATING STICK

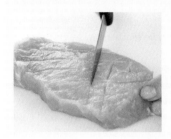

Making shallow slits on both sides of chops, spaced ½ inch apart, in a crosshatch pattern releases juices and sticky meat proteins that dampen the cornflake coating adhere.

2. Adjust the oven rack to the middle position and heat the oven to 200 degrees. With a sharp knife, cut ¹⁄₁₆-inch-deep slits on both sides of the chops, spaced ½ inch apart, in a crosshatch pattern. Season the chops with salt and pepper. Dredge 1 chop in cornstarch; shake off the excess. Using tongs, coat with the buttermilk mixture; let excess drip off. Coat with the cornflake mixture; gently pat off excess. Transfer the coated chop to a wire rack set in a rimmed baking sheet and repeat with the remaining 7 chops. Let the coated chops stand for 10 minutes.

3. Heat ⅓ cup of the oil in a 12-inch nonstick skillet over medium-high heat until shimmering. Place 4 chops in the skillet and cook until golden brown and crisp, 2 to 5 minutes. Carefully flip the chops and continue to cook until the second side is golden brown, crispy, and the chops register 145 degrees on an instant-read thermometer, 2 to 5 minutes longer. Transfer the chops to a paper towel–lined plate and let drain for 30 seconds on each side. Transfer to a clean wire rack set in a rimmed baking sheet, then transfer to the oven to keep warm. Discard the oil in the skillet and wipe clean with paper towels. Repeat the process with the remaining ⅓ cup oil and 4 pork chops. Serve with the lemon wedges.

PAN-SEARED THICK-CUT PORK CHOPS

WHY THIS RECIPE WORKS: Pan-seared thick-cut pork chops boast a juicy interior and crisp, browned exterior. Usually, though, they aren't prepared well and fall flat on both fronts. We wanted a simple skillet-roasting recipe that would give us plump, juicy meat and a well-formed crust every time.

Instead of brining our chops, we salted the meat and let it rest for almost an hour. This helped to draw out additional moisture, which would be pulled back in later to produce juicy, well-seasoned meat. Instead of cooking our chops on the stovetop, we turned to the oven. Slow-roasting the chops at a gentle temperature broke down connective tissue and tenderized the meat. This step also dried the exterior of the chops, creating a thin outer layer that, when seared, caramelized and turned into the crisp crust that we were after. For a completely browned crust, we seared the sides of the chops as well, using tongs to hold them up on their edges. While the cooked chops rested, we created a simple wine and garlic sauce using the browned bits left behind in the pan; now, we had the perfect rich, tangy accompaniment to our chops' tender meat and crisp surface.

Pan-Seared Thick-Cut Pork Chops
SERVES 4

We prefer natural to enhanced pork (pork that has been injected with a salt solution to increase moistness and flavor) for this recipe. If using enhanced pork, skip the salting in step 1. To serve the pork chops with the Garlic and Thyme Sauce (recipe follows), have all the sauce ingredients ready to go and don't wash the skillet after browning the chops; begin the sauce, using the fat left behind from browning the chops, when you set them aside to rest.

> 4 (12-ounce) bone-in rib loin pork chops, about 1½ inches thick, trimmed of excess fat (see note)
> Table salt and ground black pepper (see note)
> 1–2 tablespoons vegetable oil

1. Adjust an oven rack to the middle position and heat the oven to 275 degrees. Pat the chops dry with paper towels. Following the photo on page 179, use a sharp knife to cut two slits, about 2 inches apart, through the outer layer of fat and silver skin of each chop (do not cut into the meat of the chops). Sprinkle each chop with ½ teaspoon salt. Place the chops on a wire rack set over a rimmed baking sheet and let stand at room temperature for 45 minutes.

2. Season the chops with pepper; transfer the baking sheet to the oven. Cook until the center of the chops registers 120 to 125 degrees on an instant-read thermometer, 30 to 45 minutes.

3. Heat 1 tablespoon oil in a 12-inch skillet over high heat until smoking. Place 2 chops in the skillet and sear until well browned, 2 to 3 minutes, lifting once halfway through to redistribute the fat underneath each chop. (Reduce the heat if the browned bits on the pan bottom start to burn.) Flip the chops and cook until the second side is well browned, 2 to 3 minutes longer. Transfer the chops to a plate and repeat with the remaining 2 chops, adding 1 tablespoon more oil if the pan is dry.

4. Reduce the heat to medium. Using tongs, stand 2 pork chops on their sides. Hold them together with the tongs, return them to the skillet, and sear the sides (do not sear the bone side) until browned and the center of the chops registers 140 to 145 degrees on an instant-read thermometer, about 1½ minutes. Repeat with the remaining 2 chops. Transfer the chops to a platter, cover loosely with foil, and let rest until the internal temperature reaches 150 degrees, about 5 minutes, or while preparing the pan sauce.

Garlic and Thyme Sauce
MAKES ABOUT ½ CUP

> 1 large shallot, minced (about 4 tablespoons)
> 2 medium garlic cloves, minced or pressed through a garlic press (about 2 teaspoons)
> ¾ cup low-sodium chicken broth
> ½ cup dry white wine
> 1 teaspoon minced fresh thyme leaves
> ¼ teaspoon white wine vinegar
> 3 tablespoons unsalted butter, chilled and cut into 3 pieces
> Table salt and ground black pepper

Follow the recipe for Pan-Seared Thick-Cut Pork Chops. Pour off all but 1 teaspoon oil from the pan used to cook the chops and return the pan to medium heat. Add the shallot and garlic and cook, stirring constantly, until softened, about 1 minute. Add the broth and wine, scraping up any browned bits. Bring to a simmer and cook until the sauce measures ½ cup, 6 to 7 minutes. Off the heat, stir in the thyme and vinegar; whisk in the butter, 1 tablespoon at a time. Season with salt and pepper to taste and serve with the pork chops.

OVEN-ROASTED PORK CHOPS

WHY THIS RECIPE WORKS: Tender, juicy pork chops make for a satisfying dinner, but most home cooks pass up thick chops at the market because they assume the cooking time will be long. However, roasting these chops in a blazing hot oven (their thickness prevents them from drying out) cuts down on cooking time and frees up the stovetop so you can make an easy pan sauce at the same time.

We chose extra-thick rib loin pork chops and flavored them with a brown sugar and salt brine. We found that our thick chops couldn't go straight into the oven—they had to be cooked in three stages. First, we seared them in a hot pan to give them a nicely browned crust, then we transferred them to a preheated pan in the oven to cook most of the way through, and finally we moved them to a platter and covered them with foil to gently come up to serving temperature (while the meat stayed moist and tender). This last step also gave us time to make a speedy lemon-caper sauce right in the pan using the fond (browned bits) left behind from searing the chops.

Oven-Roasted Pork Chops

SERVES 4

We prefer natural to enhanced pork (pork that has been injected with a salt solution to increase moistness and flavor) for this recipe. If using enhanced pork, skip the brining in step 1. To serve the pork chops with the Lemon-Caper Sauce (recipe follows), have all the sauce ingredients ready to go and don't wash the skillet after browning the chops; begin the sauce, using the fat left behind from browning the chops, after the pork chops come out of the oven and are resting.

- ¾ cup (5¼ ounces) dark brown sugar
- ¼ cup table salt
- 10 medium garlic cloves, crushed
- 4 bay leaves, crumbled
- 8 whole cloves
- 3 tablespoons whole black peppercorns, crushed
- 4 (12-ounce) bone-in rib loin pork chops, about 1½ inches thick, trimmed of excess fat (see note)
- 2 tablespoons vegetable oil

1. Dissolve the sugar and salt in 6 cups cold water in a large bowl or container. Add the garlic, bay leaves, cloves, and peppercorns. Submerge the chops in the brine, cover with plastic wrap, and refrigerate for 1 hour. Remove the chops from the brine, rinse, and pat dry with paper towels. Following the photo on page 181, use a sharp knife to cut two slits, about 2 inches apart, through the outer layer of fat and silver skin of each chop (do not cut into the meat of the chops).

2. Adjust an oven rack to the lower-middle position, place a rimmed baking sheet on the rack, and heat the oven to 450 degrees. When the oven reaches 450 degrees, heat the oil in a 12-inch skillet over high heat until shimmering. Place the chops in the skillet and cook until well browned, about 2 minutes. Flip the chops and continue to cook until the second side is well browned, about 2 minutes longer.

3. Transfer the chops to the baking sheet in the oven. Roast until the center of the chops registers 140 to 145 degrees on an instant-read thermometer, about 15 minutes, turning the chops over once halfway through the cooking time. Transfer the chops to a platter, cover loosely with foil, and let rest until the internal temperature registers 150 degrees on an instant-read thermometer, 5 to 10 minutes or while preparing the pan sauce.

Lemon-Caper Sauce

MAKES ABOUT ½ CUP

- 1 medium shallot, minced (about 3 tablespoons)
- 1 cup low-sodium chicken broth
- ¼ cup juice from 2 lemons
- 2 tablespoons capers, drained
- 3 tablespoons unsalted butter, softened

Follow the recipe for Oven-Roasted Pork Chops. After removing the chops from the pan, add the shallot and cook over medium heat until softened, about 30 seconds. Increase the heat to high and stir in the broth, scraping up any browned bits. Add the lemon juice and capers, bring to a simmer, and cook until the sauce measures ⅓ cup, 3 to 4 minutes. Off the heat, whisk in the butter; serve with the pork chops.

SKILLET-BARBECUED PORK CHOPS

WHY THIS RECIPE WORKS: One of our favorite summer flavors is that of charred, salty-sweet grilled pork chops coated with spicy barbecue sauce. But because winter sometimes seems endless, we wanted to come up with an indoor method for replicating the tangy, sweet burnished crust and juicy meat of grilled chops.

Brining the chops first ensured that our meat would be juicy and well seasoned. We quickly learned that searing the chops in a blazing hot skillet and then turning the heat down once they had developed a nice crust only made the test kitchen smoky. Instead, we coated the chops with a dry spice rub—the rub charred rather than the pork chops and gave the meat the flavor and appearance of real barbecue. To prevent the rub from blackening, we cooked the chops over medium heat and used a nonstick skillet. Homemade barbecue sauce, made with ketchup, molasses, onion, and just a few other ingredients, provided a tangy flavor that contrasted nicely with the tender meat, and some reserved spice rub gave the sauce a spicy kick. A touch of liquid smoke gave our barbecue sauce more grill flavor. Finally, we brushed our chops with a small amount of sauce for a second sear so the sauce would caramelize and intensify in flavor—just as it would on the grill.

Skillet-Barbecued Pork Chops

SERVES 4

We prefer natural to enhanced pork (pork that has been injected with a salt solution to increase moistness and flavor) for this recipe. If using enhanced pork, skip the brining in step 1 and add ½ teaspoon salt to the spice rub. Grate the onion on the large holes of a box grater. In step 5, check your chops after 3 minutes. If you don't hear a definite sizzle and the chops have not started to brown on the underside, increase the heat to medium-high and continue cooking as directed (follow the indicated temperatures for the remainder of the recipe).

PORK CHOPS

½ cup table salt (see note)

4 (8- to 10-ounce) bone-in rib loin pork chops, ¾ to 1 inch thick, trimmed of excess fat (see note)

4 teaspoons vegetable oil

SPICE RUB

1 tablespoon paprika

1 tablespoon brown sugar

2 teaspoons ground coriander

1 teaspoon ground cumin

1 teaspoon ground black pepper

SAUCE

½ cup ketchup

3 tablespoons light or mild molasses

2 tablespoons grated onion (see note)

2 tablespoons Worcestershire sauce

2 tablespoons Dijon mustard

1 tablespoon cider vinegar

1 tablespoon brown sugar

1 teaspoon liquid smoke

1. FOR THE PORK CHOPS: Dissolve the salt in 2 quarts cold water in a large bowl or container. Submerge the chops in the brine, cover with plastic wrap, and refrigerate for 30 minutes.

2. FOR THE SPICE RUB: Combine the rub ingredients in a small bowl. Measure 2 teaspoons of the mixture into a medium bowl and set aside for the sauce. Transfer the remaining spice rub to a large plate.

3. FOR THE SAUCE: Whisk the sauce ingredients in the bowl with the reserved spice mixture until thoroughly combined; set aside.

4. Remove the chops from the brine, rinse, and pat dry with paper towels. Following the photo on page 181, use a sharp knife to cut two slits, about 2 inches apart, through the outer layer of fat and silver skin of each chop (do not cut into the meat of the chops). Coat both sides of the chops with the spice rub, pressing gently so the rub adheres. Shake off the excess rub.

5. Heat 1 tablespoon of the oil in a 12-inch nonstick skillet over medium heat until just smoking. Place the chops in the skillet in a pinwheel pattern, with the ribs pointing toward the center, and cook until browned and charred in spots, 5 to 8 minutes. Flip the chops and continue to cook until the second side is browned and the center of the chops registers 130 degrees on an instant-read thermometer, 4 to 8 minutes. Remove the skillet from the heat and transfer the chops to a plate. Lightly brush the top of each chop with 2 teaspoons of the sauce.

6. Wipe out the pan with paper towels and return to medium heat. Add the remaining 1 teaspoon oil and heat until just smoking. Add the chops to the pan, sauce side down, and cook without moving them until the sauce has caramelized and charred in spots, about 1 minute. While cooking, lightly brush the top of each chop with 2 more teaspoons sauce. Flip the chops and cook until the second side is charred and caramelized and the center of the chops registers 140 to 145 degrees on an instant-read thermometer, 1 to 2 minutes.

7. Transfer the chops back to the plate, cover loosely with foil, and let rest until the center of the chops registers 150 degrees on an instant-read thermometer, about 5 minutes.

8. Meanwhile, add the remaining sauce to the pan and cook over medium heat, scraping up any browned bits, until thickened and it measures ⅔ cup, about 3 minutes. Brush each chop with 1 tablespoon of the sauce and serve, passing the remaining sauce separately.

GLAZED PORK CHOPS

WHY THIS RECIPE WORKS: Thin boneless pork chops are readily available straight from the meat case—no butcher required. Plus they cook fast and are a bargain compared to other meats. But because they do cook quickly, they're prone to overcooking. We wanted to combine the convenience and speed of thin boneless pork chops with the flavor and moist, juicy interior of their thicker, bone-in counterparts.

To cook pork chops on the stove, it's best to stick with thin chops. Before searing the chops, it's important to cut through the fat and silver skin, which create a bowing effect (especially pronounced with thin chops) as it contracts. We found the chops needed an initial quick sear—we didn't want them to cook all the way through just yet but we still wanted a nicely browned side. A sweet and sticky glaze of cider, brown sugar, soy sauce, vinegar, and mustard went into the pan to finish cooking the chops. Not only did the sauce give the chops rich flavor, but it also reduced down to a nice, thick glaze, which perfectly coated the juicy, tender chops.

Cider-Glazed Pork Chops

SERVES 4

We prefer natural to enhanced pork (pork that has been injected with a salt solution to increase moistness and flavor) for this recipe, though either will work here. If your chops are on the thinner side, check their internal temperature after the initial sear. If they are already at the 140-degree mark, remove them from the skillet and allow them to rest, covered loosely with foil, for 5 minutes, then add the accumulated juices and glaze ingredients to the skillet and proceed with step 4. If your chops are a little thicker than we specify, you may need to increase the simmering time in step 3.

GLAZE

- ½ cup distilled white vinegar or cider vinegar
- ⅓ cup (2⅓ ounces) light brown sugar
- ⅓ cup apple cider or apple juice
- 2 tablespoons Dijon mustard
- 1 tablespoon soy sauce
- Pinch cayenne pepper

PORK CHOPS

- 4 (5- to 7-ounce) boneless center-cut or loin pork chops, ½ to ¾ inch thick, trimmed of excess fat (see note)
- Table salt and ground black pepper
- 1 tablespoon vegetable oil

1. FOR THE GLAZE: Combine the glaze ingredients in a medium bowl and set aside.

2. FOR THE PORK CHOPS: Following the photo, use a sharp knife to cut two slits, about 2 inches apart, through the outer layer of fat and silver skin of each chop (do not cut into the meat of the chops). Pat the chops dry with paper towels and season with salt and pepper. Heat the oil in a 12-inch skillet over medium-high heat until smoking. Add the chops to the skillet and cook until well browned, 4 to 6 minutes. Flip the chops and cook 1 minute longer; transfer the chops to a platter and pour off any oil in the skillet. (Check the internal temperature of the thinner chops; see note.)

3. Return the chops to the skillet, browned side up, and add the glaze mixture; cook over medium heat until the center of the chops registers 140 to 145 degrees on an instant-read thermometer, 5 to 8 minutes. Remove the skillet from the heat; transfer the chops to a clean platter, cover loosely with foil, and let rest until the center of the chops registers 150 degrees on an instant-read thermometer, about 5 minutes.

4. Stir any accumulated meat juices from the plate into the glaze in the skillet and simmer, whisking constantly, until the glaze has thickened, 2 to 6 minutes. Return the chops to the skillet and turn to coat both sides with the glaze. Transfer the chops back to the plate, browned side up, spread the remaining glaze over the top, and serve.

KOSHER? YES. ENHANCED? NO.

In the test kitchen we often brine chicken and pork to ensure moist, well-seasoned meat. But there are options at the store that allow you to skip this step. For chicken, that means buying a kosher bird. Koshering is a process similar to brining; it involves coating the chicken with salt to draw out any impurities. Kosher birds are also all-natural and contain no hormones or antibiotics.

Some people are surprised that pork is lean and prone to drying out. In fact, today's pork is 50 percent leaner than its 1950s counterpart, and less fat means less flavor and moisture. The industry has addressed this issue by introducing enhanced pork, which is meat injected with a solution of water, salt, and sodium phosphate. The idea is to both season the pork and prevent it from drying out. We've conducted countless tests comparing "enhanced" pork to natural pork and unequivocally prefer the latter. Natural pork has a better flavor and, if it's cooked correctly, moisture isn't an issue. We also strongly recommend brining most cuts of pork, which lends both moisture and seasoning to the meat. Manufacturers don't use the terms "enhanced" or "natural" on package labels, but if the pork has been enhanced it will have an ingredient list. Natural pork contains just pork and won't have an ingredient list. While natural pork benefits from brining, enhanced pork should not be brined because it's already pretty salty.

NOTES FROM THE TEST KITCHEN

HOW TO PREVENT CURLED PORK CHOPS

Whether your pork chops are boneless or bone-in, you can use the same technique to prevent them from buckling in a hot pan or oven. Simply cut two slits, about 2 inches apart, through one side of each chop.

SMOTHERED PORK CHOPS

WHY THIS RECIPE WORKS: Tender, flavorful chops stand up very well to rich, hearty gravy. But most of the time, the gravy misses the mark—it's either so thick you can't find the pork chop, or so thin and watery that the meat seems to be floating on the plate. We wanted a foolproof recipe for juicy chops smothered in rich gravy with a satiny, thick texture.

For a nice balance with the gravy and to allow for the best absorption of the gravy's flavors, we used thin, not thick, rib chops. Browning them well left meaty browned bits in the pan, essential for making a flavorful gravy. To build further flavor, we made a nut-brown, bacony roux. Thinly sliced yellow onions contributed a significant amount of moisture to the gravy. Garlic, thyme, and bay leaves rounded out the flavorful gravy; we skipped the salt because we had already salted the onions to encourage their browning and so they would give up liquid. For the tenderest chops, we combined the sauce and browned chops in the pan and braised them for half an hour. Not only did the lengthy braise result in moist, tender chops, it also allowed the gravy to thicken and its flavors to meld, so the chops had a rich, velvety coating when served.

Smothered Pork Chops
SERVES 4

We prefer natural to enhanced pork (pork that has been injected with a salt solution to increase moistness and flavor) for this recipe, though either will work here. Serve smothered chops with egg noodles or mashed potatoes to soak up the rich gravy.

- 3 ounces bacon (about 3 slices), cut into ¼-inch pieces
- 2 tablespoons unbleached all-purpose flour
- 1¾ cups low-sodium chicken broth
- 2 tablespoons vegetable oil, plus more as needed
- 4 (7-ounce) bone-in rib loin pork chops, ½ to ¾ inch thick, trimmed of excess fat (see note)
  Ground black pepper

- 2 medium yellow onions, halved and sliced thin (about 3½ cups)
  Table salt
- 2 tablespoons water
- 2 medium garlic cloves, minced or pressed through a garlic press (about 2 teaspoons)
- 1 teaspoon minced fresh thyme leaves
- 2 bay leaves
- 1 tablespoon minced fresh parsley leaves

1. Fry the bacon in a small saucepan over medium heat, stirring occasionally, until crisp, 8 to 10 minutes. Using a slotted spoon, transfer the bacon to a paper towel–lined plate, leaving the fat in the saucepan (you should have 2 tablespoons bacon fat; if not, add oil to make this amount). Whisk in the flour and cook over medium-low heat until golden, about 5 minutes. Whisk in the broth and bring to a boil, stirring occasionally, over medium-high heat; cover and set aside off the heat.

2. Heat 1 tablespoon of the oil in a 12-inch skillet over high heat until smoking. Pat the chops dry with paper towels. Following the photo on page 181, use a sharp knife to cut two slits, about 2 inches apart, through the outer layer of fat and silver skin of each chop (do not cut into the meat of the chops). Sprinkle each chop with ½ teaspoon pepper. Brown the chops in a single layer until browned on the first side, about 3 minutes. Flip the chops and cook until the second side is browned, about 3 minutes longer. Transfer the chops to a plate and set aside.

3. Add the remaining 1 tablespoon oil to the skillet and return to medium heat until shimmering. Add the onions, ¼ teaspoon salt, and the water, scraping up any browned bits, and cook until lightly browned, about 5 minutes. Stir in the garlic and thyme and cook until fragrant, about 30 seconds longer. Return the chops to the skillet and cover with the onions. Add the reserved sauce, the bay leaves, and any accumulated meat juices from the plate to the skillet. Cover and simmer over low heat until the chops are tender and a paring knife inserted into the chops meets little resistance, about 30 minutes.

4. Transfer the chops to a platter and cover loosely with foil. Simmer the sauce over medium-high heat, stirring frequently, until thickened, about 5 minutes. Discard the bay leaves, stir in the parsley, and season with salt and pepper to taste. Cover the chops with the sauce, sprinkle with the reserved bacon, and serve.

CRUNCHY BAKED PORK CHOPS

WHY THIS RECIPE WORKS: When done right, baked, breaded pork chops are the ultimate comfort food—juicy, tender chops covered with a well-seasoned, crunchy crust. We were on a mission to perfect these chops and avoid the common missteps of a soggy, flavorless crust, flabby meat, and a coating that just won't stay on.

We used center-cut boneless loin chops—which are easy to find and affordable—and brined them so the meat would stay moist and juicy. For the coating, only fresh bread crumbs would do; we toasted them first for crispness, then doctored them with garlic, shallots, Parmesan cheese, and minced herbs for flavor. To form a strong adhering agent for the crumbs, and prevent the chops from ending up bald in patches, we made a quick batterlike mixture by whisking flour and mustard into egg whites; whole eggs were a no-go because their higher amount of fat made for a soft, puffy layer under the bread crumbs. Baking the breaded chops on a wire rack set over a baking sheet allowed air to circulate completely around the chops, keeping the bottom crumbs crisp. Out of the oven, these chops were tender and moist, with a crisp coating that stayed put, even through some heavy knife-and-fork action.

Crunchy Baked Pork Chops
SERVES 4

We prefer natural to enhanced pork (pork that has been injected with a salt solution to increase moistness and flavor) for this recipe. If using enhanced pork, skip the brining in step 1. The breaded chops can be frozen for up to 1 week. They don't need to be thawed before baking; simply increase the cooking time in step 5 to 35 to 40 minutes.

    Table salt
 4 (6- to 8-ounce) boneless center-cut or loin pork chops,
    ¾ to 1 inch thick, trimmed of excess fat (see note)
 4 slices high-quality white sandwich bread, torn
    into 1-inch pieces
 2 tablespoons vegetable oil
 1 small shallot, minced (about 1 tablespoon)
 3 medium garlic cloves, minced or pressed through
    a garlic press (about 1 tablespoon)
    Ground black pepper
 2 tablespoons grated Parmesan cheese
 2 tablespoons minced fresh parsley leaves
 ½ teaspoon minced fresh thyme leaves
 ¼ cup plus 6 tablespoons unbleached all-purpose flour
 3 large egg whites
 3 tablespoons Dijon mustard
    Lemon wedges, for serving

1. Adjust an oven rack to the middle position and heat the oven to 350 degrees. Dissolve ¼ cup salt in 4 cups cold water in a medium bowl or gallon-sized zipper-lock bag. Submerge the chops in the brine, cover the container with plastic wrap or seal the bag, and refrigerate for 30 minutes. Remove the chops from the brine, rinse, and pat dry with paper towels.

2. Meanwhile, pulse the bread in a food processor to coarse crumbs, about 8 pulses (you should have about 3½ cups crumbs). Transfer the crumbs to a rimmed baking sheet, add the oil, shallot, garlic, ¼ teaspoon salt, and ¼ teaspoon pepper, and toss until the crumbs are evenly coated with the oil. Bake until golden brown and dry, about 15 minutes, stirring twice during the baking time. (Do not turn off the oven.) Cool to room temperature. Toss the crumbs with the Parmesan, parsley, and thyme. (The bread-crumb mixture can be stored in an airtight container for up to 3 days.)

3. Place ¼ cup of the flour in a pie plate. In a second pie plate, whisk the egg whites and mustard together; add the remaining 6 tablespoons flour and whisk until almost smooth, with pea-sized lumps remaining.

4. Increase the oven temperature to 425 degrees. Spray a wire rack with vegetable oil spray and place over a rimmed baking sheet. Season the chops with pepper. Dredge 1 pork chop in the flour; shake off the excess. Using tongs, coat with the egg mixture; let the excess drip off. Coat all sides of the chop with the bread-crumb mixture, pressing gently so that a thick layer of crumbs adheres to the chop. Transfer the breaded chop to the wire rack. Repeat with the remaining 3 chops.

5. Bake until the center of the chops registers 140 to 145 degrees on an instant-read thermometer, about 20 minutes. Let rest on the rack for 5 minutes; serve with the lemon wedges.

STUFFED PORK CHOPS

WHY THIS RECIPE WORKS: Thick-cut pork chops make the perfect home for a simple stuffing. Unfortunately, most stuffed pork chops are extremely dry and bland, with a filling that looks like it's trying to escape. We wanted the stuffing to be especially flavorful and rich to offset the mildness of the pork, and we wanted the chops to be moist and juicy.

Our stuffing was easy enough to make—we used a simple combination of aromatic vegetables, herbs, and fresh bread. But the stuffing was so loose, it crumbled and spilled out over the plate when the chops were served. Clearly, we needed a binder. Instead of eggs, we chose cream, which added richness and enough moisture to bring the stuffing together. Because the stuffing didn't contain eggs, the chops could be cooked to a lower (and more palatable) internal temperature, making for tender and juicy meat. After brining the chops and creating a small "pocket" to hold the stuffing, we started them in

a skillet to develop a nice brown crust but finished cooking them through on a baking sheet in a hot oven. A sweet chutney of ginger, apples, and apple cider provided a nice contrast to the savory filling.

For an alternative to chutney, flavorful gravy (sans big roast) is ideal for draping over the stuffed chops. Thoroughly browning both the aromatic vegetables and the flour added significant flavor, as did the inclusion of two kinds of broth: beef and chicken.

Stuffed Pork Chops

SERVES 4

We prefer natural to enhanced pork (pork that has been injected with a salt solution to increase moistness and flavor) for this recipe, though either will work here. Serve these pork chops with Quick All-Purpose Gravy or Ginger-Apple Chutney (recipes follow). The gravy is best made before you start the chops and reheated as needed. If you choose to serve the chops with the chutney, prepare it in the skillet used to cook the chops while the chops are in the oven.

PORK CHOPS

4 (12-ounce) bone-in rib loin pork chops, about 1½ inches
   thick, trimmed of excess fat (see note)
¾ cup packed light brown sugar
¼ cup table salt
   Ground black pepper
1 tablespoon vegetable oil

STUFFING

3 tablespoons unsalted butter
1 small onion, minced
1 celery rib, chopped fine
½ teaspoon table salt
1 tablespoon minced fresh parsley leaves
2 medium garlic cloves, minced or pressed through
   a garlic press (about 2 teaspoons)
2 teaspoons minced fresh thyme leaves
2 slices high-quality white sandwich bread,
   cut into ¼-inch cubes (about 2 cups)
2 tablespoons heavy cream
   Ground black pepper

1. FOR THE PORK CHOPS: Following the photos on page 185, cut a small pocket through the side of each chop. Dissolve the sugar and salt in 6 cups cold water in a large bowl or container. Submerge the chops in the brine, cover with plastic wrap, and refrigerate for 1 hour.

2. FOR THE STUFFING: Melt the butter in a 12-inch skillet over medium heat. Add the onion, celery, and salt and cook until the vegetables are softened, 6 to 8 minutes. Add the parsley, garlic, and thyme and cook until fragrant, about 30 seconds. Transfer to a medium bowl and toss with the bread cubes, cream, and ⅛ teaspoon pepper. Mix, lightly pressing the mixture against the sides of the bowl, until it comes together.

3. Adjust an oven rack to the lower-middle position, place a rimmed baking sheet on the rack, and heat the oven to 450 degrees. Remove the chops from the brine, rinse, and pat dry with paper towels. Place one-quarter of the stuffing (about ⅓ cup) in the pocket of each pork chop. Season the chops with pepper.

4. Heat the oil in a 12-inch skillet over high heat until shimmering. Place the chops in the skillet and cook until well browned, about 3 minutes. Flip the chops and cook until the second side is well browned, about 2 minutes longer.

5. Transfer the chops to the baking sheet in the oven. Roast until the center of the chops registers 140 degrees on an instant-read thermometer, about 15 minutes, turning the chops over halfway through the cooking time. Transfer the chops to a plate, cover loosely with foil, and let rest for 5 to 10 minutes. Serve.

Quick All-Purpose Gravy

MAKES 2 CUPS

This gravy can be served with almost any type of meat and with mashed potatoes as well. The recipe can be doubled. If doubling it, use a Dutch oven so that the vegetables brown properly and increase the cooking times by roughly half. The finished gravy can be frozen. To thaw it, place the gravy and 1 tablespoon of water in a saucepan over low heat and slowly bring it to a simmer. It may appear broken or curdled as it thaws, but a vigorous whisking will recombine it.

3 tablespoons unsalted butter
1 onion, minced
1 small carrot, peeled and chopped fine
1 celery rib, chopped fine
¼ cup unbleached all-purpose flour
2 cups low-sodium chicken broth
2 cups beef broth
1 bay leaf
¼ teaspoon dried thyme
5 whole black peppercorns
   Table salt and ground black pepper

1. Melt the butter in a large saucepan over medium-high heat. Add the onion, carrot, and celery and cook, stirring frequently, until softened, about 7 minutes. Reduce the heat to medium, add the flour, and cook, stirring constantly, until thoroughly browned, about 5 minutes. Gradually whisk in the broths and bring to a boil, skimming off any foam that forms on the surface. Add the bay leaf, thyme, and peppercorns and simmer, stirring occasionally, until thickened and reduced to 3 cups, 20 to 25 minutes.

2. Strain the gravy through a fine-mesh strainer into a clean saucepan, pressing on the solids to extract as much liquid as possible; discard the solids. Season with salt and pepper to taste and serve with the pork chops.

STUFFING PORK CHOPS

1. Using a paring knife, trim away the excess fat and connective tissue around the edge of the meat.

2. With the knife positioned as shown, insert the blade through the center of the side of the chop until the tip touches the bone.

3. Swing the tip of the blade through the middle of the chop to create a pocket (the opening should be about 1 inch wide).

4. With your fingers, gently press the stuffing mixture into the pocket, without enlarging the opening.

Ginger-Apple Chutney

MAKES ABOUT 3½ CUPS

If you want more heat, add a little more cayenne pepper.

- 1 tablespoon vegetable oil
- 1 small onion, chopped medium
- 2 Granny Smith apples, peeled, cored, and cut into ½-inch pieces
- 1 tablespoon minced ginger
- ¼ teaspoon ground allspice
- ⅛ teaspoon cayenne pepper (see note)
- 1 cup apple cider
- ¼ cup (1¾ ounces) packed light brown sugar
  Table salt and ground black pepper

Follow the recipe for Stuffed Pork Chops. After removing the chops from the pan, pour off any fat left in the skillet. Heat the oil over medium-high heat until shimmering. Add the onion and apples and cook, stirring occasionally, until softened, about 10 minutes. Add the ginger, allspice, and cayenne and cook until fragrant, about 30 seconds. Add the cider and sugar and bring to a boil, scraping up any browned bits, until the cider is slightly thickened, about 4 minutes. Season with salt and pepper to taste and serve with the pork chops.

RED WINE–BRAISED PORK CHOPS

WHY THIS RECIPE WORKS: When braising pork chops, we found it was important to avoid lean loin chops that have a tendency to dry out when even slightly overcooked. For moist, tender chops, we began with blade chops, which, like other braising cuts, have a larger amount of fat and connective tissue. We trimmed the chops of excess fat and connective tissue to prevent buckling when cooked, and used those trimmings to build a rich and flavorful braising liquid. When the chops were done braising, we used the same liquid as the foundation for a quick and tasty sauce.

Red Wine–Braised Pork Chops

SERVES 4

Look for chops with a small eye and a large amount of marbling, as these are the best suited to braising. The pork scraps can be removed when straining the sauce in step 4 and served alongside the chops. (They taste great.)

Salt and pepper
- 4 (10- to 12-ounce) bone-in pork blade chops, 1 inch thick
- 2 teaspoons vegetable oil
- 2 onions, halved and sliced thin
- 5 sprigs fresh thyme plus ¼ teaspoon minced
- 2 garlic cloves, peeled
- 2 bay leaves
- 1 (½-inch) piece ginger, peeled and crushed
- ⅛ teaspoon ground allspice
- ½ cup red wine
- ¼ cup ruby port
- 2 tablespoons plus ½ teaspoon red wine vinegar
- 1 cup low-sodium chicken broth
- 2 tablespoons unsalted butter
- 1 tablespoon minced fresh parsley

1. Dissolve 3 tablespoons salt in 1½ quarts cold water in large container. Submerge chops in brine, cover, and refrigerate for 30 minutes or up to 1 hour.

2. Adjust oven rack to lower-middle position and heat oven to 275 degrees. Remove chops from brine and pat dry with paper towels. Trim off meat cap and any fat and cartilage opposite rib bones. Cut trimmings into 1-inch pieces. Heat oil in Dutch oven over medium-high heat until shimmering. Add trimmings and brown on all sides, 6 to 9 minutes.

3. Reduce heat to medium and add onions, thyme sprigs, garlic, bay leaves, ginger, and allspice. Cook, stirring occasionally, until onions are golden brown, 5 to 10 minutes. Stir in wine, port, and 2 tablespoons vinegar and cook until reduced to thin syrup, 5 to 7 minutes. Add chicken broth, spread onions and pork scraps into even layer, and bring to simmer. Arrange pork chops on top of pork scraps and onions.

4. Cover, transfer to oven, and cook until meat is tender, 1¼ to 1½ hours. Remove from oven and let chops rest in pot, covered, for 30 minutes. Transfer chops to serving platter and tent with aluminum foil. Strain braising liquid through fine-mesh strainer; discard solids. Transfer braising liquid to fat separator and let stand for 5 minutes.

NOTES FROM THE TEST KITCHEN

MAKING RED WINE–BRAISED PORK CHOPS

1. The trimmed scraps from blade chops contain lots of fat and (in some cases) cartilage. Searing them builds so much flavorful browning that searing the chops themselves isn't necessary.

2. To build complex flavor, sauté the onions in the rendered pork fat until golden brown with garlic, thyme, bay leaves, ginger, and allspice.

3. To add acidity, sweetness, and complexity to the braising liquid, deglaze the pot with a combination of red wine, ruby port, and red wine vinegar.

4. Laying the chops on top of the trimmings raises them well above the liquid, where they will cook more gently and retain their flavorful juices.

---

5. Wipe out now-empty pot with wad of paper towels. Return defatted braising liquid to pot and cook over medium-high heat until reduced to 1 cup, 3 to 7 minutes. Off heat, whisk in butter, minced thyme, and remaining ½ teaspoon vinegar. Season with salt and pepper to taste. Pour sauce over chops, sprinkle with parsley, and serve.

FRENCH-STYLE PORK CHOPS WITH APPLES AND CALVADOS

WHY THIS RECIPE WORKS: For pork chops with big apple flavor, we took cues from the French. While our salted pork chops rested in the refrigerator, we created a base by frying up 2 slices of bacon, adding shallots and nutmeg to bloom and cook in the rendered fat. After adding a hit of Calvados, the woodsy apple brandy, we carefully ignited the sauce with a match to eliminate the alcohol's bite. We repeated this step, pouring in and flambéing a total of ½ cup of Calvados, and then rounded out the sauce's herbal, fruity flavors with apple cider, chicken broth, thyme, butter, and chopped apples. Vigorously simmering the liquid emulsified the butter. Once the sauce reduced and the apples softened, we turned our attention to the chops. After quickly browning them, we removed them from the skillet and then browned the apple rings. The apples cooked in chicken broth before we arranged the chops atop the rings, elevating the meat to finish cooking in the oven. Before serving, we strained the sauce, adding some minced thyme and cider vinegar to reinforce its apple flavor.

French-Style Pork Chops with Apples and Calvados

SERVES 4

We prefer natural pork, but if the pork is enhanced (injected with a salt solution; see page 181), decrease the salt in step 1 to ½ teaspoon per chop. To ensure that they fit in the skillet, choose apples that are approximately 3 inches in diameter. Applejack or regular brandy can be used in place of the Calvados. Before flambéing, be sure to roll up long shirtsleeves, tie back long hair, and turn off the exhaust fan and any lit burners. Use a long match or wooden skewer to flambé the Calvados. The amount of vinegar to add in step 4 will vary depending on the sweetness of your cider.

> 4 (12- to 14-ounce) bone-in pork rib chops,
>   1 inch thick, trimmed
>   Kosher salt and pepper
> 4 Gala or Golden Delicious apples, peeled and cored
> 2 slices bacon, cut into ½-inch pieces
> 3 shallots, sliced
>   Pinch ground nutmeg
> ½ cup Calvados
> 1¾ cups apple cider
> 1¼ cups chicken broth
> 4 sprigs fresh thyme, plus ¼ teaspoon minced

2 tablespoons unsalted butter
2 teaspoons vegetable oil
½–1 teaspoon apple cider vinegar

1. Evenly sprinkle each chop with ¾ teaspoon salt. Place chops on large plate, cover loosely with plastic wrap, and refrigerate for 1 hour.

2. While chops rest, cut 2 apples into ½-inch pieces. Cook bacon in medium saucepan over medium heat until crisp, 5 to 7 minutes. Add shallots, nutmeg, and ¼ teaspoon salt; cook, stirring frequently, until shallots are softened and beginning to brown, 3 to 4 minutes. Off heat, add ¼ cup Calvados and let warm through, about 5 seconds. Wave lit match over pan until Calvados ignites, then shake pan gently to distribute flames. When flames subside, 30 to 60 seconds, cover pan to ensure flame is extinguished, 15 seconds. Add remaining ¼ cup Calvados and repeat flambéing (flames will subside after 1½ to 2 minutes). (If you have trouble igniting second addition, return pan to medium heat, bring to bare simmer, and remove from heat and try again.) Once flames have extinguished, increase heat to medium-high; add cider, 1 cup broth, thyme sprigs, butter, and chopped apples; and bring to rapid simmer. Cook, stirring occasionally, until apples are very tender and mixture has reduced to 2⅓ cups, 25 to 35 minutes. Cover and set aside.

3. Adjust oven rack to middle position and heat oven to 300 degrees. Slice remaining 2 apples into ½-inch-thick rings. Pat chops dry with paper towels and evenly sprinkle each chop with pepper. Heat oil in 12-inch skillet over medium heat until just beginning to smoke. Increase heat to high and brown chops on both sides, 6 to 8 minutes total. Transfer chops to large plate and reduce heat to medium. Add apple rings and cook until lightly browned, 1 to 2 minutes. Add remaining ¼ cup broth and cook, scraping up any browned bits with rubber spatula, until liquid has evaporated, about 30 seconds. Remove pan from heat, flip apple rings, and place chops on top of apple rings. Place skillet in oven and cook until chops register 135 to 140 degrees, 11 to 15 minutes.

 WHY IS THAT PORK STILL PINK?

In the test kitchen, we steer clear of dishes like Parchingly Dry Pork Chops and No-Pink Pork Loin. But there's a reason that older recipes recommend cooking pork to startlingly high internal temperatures. Years ago, when pork quality was inconsistent and trichinosis concerns ran high, pink pork was considered a safety risk, thus most recipes recommended cooking pork to 190 degrees. Today, however, the risk of trichinosis is nearly nonexistent in the United States. What's more, even when the trichinosis parasite is present, it is killed when the temperature of the meat rises to 137 degrees.

Both the U.S. Department of Agriculture and the National Pork Board recommend cooking pork to a final internal temperature of 160 degrees. If you are concerned about contamination with salmonella (which is possible in any type of meat), you must cook the pork to 160 degrees to be certain that all potential pathogens are eliminated. Unfortunately, given the leanness of today's pork, these recommendations result in dry, tough meat. (In fact, today's pork has 50 percent less fat than it did 50 years ago, which explains why older recipes that called for cooking pork to 190 degrees weren't a total disaster—all that fat kept even overcooked pork moist.)

In the test kitchen, we have found cooking modern pork beyond 150 degrees to be a waste of time and money. We cook pork to an internal temperature of 140 to 145 degrees—the meat will still be slightly rosy in the center and juicy. As the meat rests and juices are redistributed throughout the meat, the internal temperature will continue to climb to the final serving temperature of 150. Of course, if safety is your top concern, cook all meat (including pork) until it is well-done; that is, when the internal temperature reaches 160 degrees.

4. Transfer chops and apple rings to serving platter, tent loosely with aluminum foil, and let rest for 10 minutes. While chops rest, strain apple-brandy mixture through fine-mesh strainer set in large bowl, pressing on solids with ladle or rubber spatula to extract liquid; discard solids. (Make sure to use rubber spatula to scrape any apple solids on bottom of strainer into sauce.) Stir in minced thyme and season sauce with vinegar, salt, and pepper to taste. Transfer sauce to serving bowl. Serve chops and apple rings, passing sauce separately.

ROASTS AND MORE

1 (3½- to 4½-pound) boneless eye-round roast (see note)
2 teaspoons table salt
1 tablespoon plus 2 teaspoons vegetable oil
2 teaspoons ground black pepper (see note)

1. Sprinkle all sides of the roast evenly with the salt. Wrap with plastic wrap and refrigerate for 18 to 24 hours.

2. Adjust an oven rack to the middle position and heat the oven to 225 degrees. Pat the roast dry with paper towels; rub with 2 teaspoons of the oil and sprinkle all sides evenly with the pepper. Heat the remaining 1 tablespoon oil in a 12-inch skillet over medium-high heat until starting to smoke. Sear the roast until browned on all sides, 3 to 4 minutes per side. Transfer the roast to a wire rack set over a rimmed baking sheet. Roast until the center of the roast registers 115 degrees on an instant-read thermometer for medium-rare (1¼ to 1¾ hours), or 125 degrees for medium (1¾ to 2¼ hours).

3. Turn the oven off; leave the roast in the oven, without opening the door, until the center of the roast registers 130 degrees for medium-rare or 140 degrees for medium, 30 to 50 minutes longer. Transfer the roast to a carving board and let rest for 15 minutes. Slice the meat crosswise as thin as possible and serve with the sauce, if using.

Horseradish Cream Sauce

MAKES ABOUT 1 CUP

See page 913 for information on our recommended brand of prepared horseradish.

½ cup heavy cream, chilled
½ cup prepared horseradish
1 teaspoon table salt
⅛ teaspoon ground black pepper

Whisk the cream in a medium bowl until thickened but not yet holding soft peaks, 1 to 2 minutes. Gently fold in the horseradish, salt, and pepper. Transfer to a serving bowl and refrigerate for at least 30 minutes or up to 1 hour before serving.

ROAST BEEF TENDERLOIN

WHY THIS RECIPE WORKS: There's nothing like the buttery texture of a roasted beef tenderloin. Ideally, it has rosy meat all the way through and a deep brown crust; too often, though, this roast has only one or the other. We wanted a technique that produced perfectly cooked and deeply flavored meat. We opted for a center-cut piece; it's already trimmed and lacks the narrow "tail" of the whole cut. We first tried searing the meat in the oven, but it never browned evenly. Stovetop browning was better for producing a crust, but the roast still came out of the oven with a gray band. The trick was to reverse the process, first roasting the meat in the oven, then searing at the end. Lowering the oven temperature eliminated the ring of overcooked meat altogether. To add flavor to this mild cut of beef, a simple technique of salting it before roasting worked wonders; rubbing the roast with a little softened butter added richness.

SLOW-ROASTED BEEF

WHY THIS RECIPE WORKS: Roasting inexpensive beef usually yields tough meat best suited for sandwiches. We wanted to take an inexpensive cut and turn it into a tender, rosy, beefy-tasting roast worthy of Sunday dinner. Our favorite cut, the eye round, has good flavor and tenderness and a uniform shape that guarantees even cooking. Next, we chose between the two classic methods for roasting meat—high and fast or low and slow. Low temperature was the way to go. Keeping the meat's internal temperature below 122 degrees as long as possible allowed the meat's enzymes to act as natural tenderizers, breaking down its tough connective tissue (this action stops at 122 degrees). Since most ovens don't heat below 200 degrees, we needed to devise a special method to lengthen this tenderizing period. We roasted the meat at 225 degrees (after searing it to give the meat a crusty exterior) and shut off the oven when the roast reached 115 degrees. The meat stayed below 122 degrees an extra 30 minutes, allowing the enzymes to continue their work before the temperature reached 130 degrees for medium-rare. As for seasoning, we found that salting the meat a full 24 hours before roasting made it even more tender and seasoned the roast throughout.

Slow-Roasted Beef

SERVES 6 TO 8

We don't recommend cooking this roast past medium. Open the oven door as little as possible and remove the roast from the oven while taking its temperature. If the roast has not reached the desired temperature in the time specified in step 3, heat the oven to 225 degrees for 5 minutes, shut it off, and continue to cook the roast to the desired temperature. For a smaller (2½- to 3½-pound) roast, reduce the amount of pepper to 1½ teaspoons. For a 4½- to 6-pound roast, cut in half crosswise before cooking to create two smaller roasts. Slice the roast as thin as possible and serve with Horseradish Cream Sauce (recipe follows), if desired.

A flavored butter served alongside was the final touch. With its uniformly rosy meat, deep brown crust, and beefy flavor, this beef tenderloin was worthy of its price tag.

Roast Beef Tenderloin

SERVES 4 TO 6

Ask your butcher to prepare a trimmed, center-cut Châteaubriand from the whole tenderloin, as this cut is not usually available without special ordering. If you are cooking for a crowd, this recipe can be doubled to make two roasts. Sear the roasts one after the other, wiping out the pan and adding new oil after searing the first roast. Both pieces of meat can be roasted on the same rack.

- 1 (2-pound) beef tenderloin center-cut Châteaubriand, trimmed (see note)
- 1 teaspoon table salt
- 1 teaspoon coarsely ground black pepper
- 2 tablespoons unsalted butter, softened
- 1 tablespoon vegetable oil
- 1 recipe flavored butter (recipes follow)

1. Using 12-inch lengths of kitchen twine, tie the roast crosswise at 1½-inch intervals. Sprinkle the roast evenly with the salt, cover loosely with plastic wrap, and let stand at room temperature for 1 hour. Meanwhile, adjust an oven rack to the middle position and heat the oven to 300 degrees.

2. Pat the roast dry with paper towels. Sprinkle the roast evenly with the pepper and spread the butter evenly over the surface. Transfer the roast to a wire rack set over a rimmed baking sheet. Roast until the center of the roast registers 125 degrees on an instant-read thermometer for medium-rare (40 to 55 minutes), or 135 degrees for medium (55 to 70 minutes), flipping the roast halfway through cooking.

3. Heat the oil in a 12-inch heavy-bottomed skillet over medium-high heat until just smoking. Place the roast in the skillet and sear until well browned on four sides, 1 to 2 minutes per side (a total of 4 to 8 minutes). Transfer the roast to a carving board and spread 2 tablespoons of the flavored butter evenly over the top of the roast; let rest for 15 minutes. Remove the twine and cut the meat crosswise into ½-inch-thick slices. Serve, passing the remaining flavored butter separately.

Shallot and Parsley Butter

MAKES ABOUT ½ CUP

- 4 tablespoons (½ stick) unsalted butter, softened
- 1 small shallot, minced (about 1 tablespoon)
- 1 medium garlic clove, minced or pressed through a garlic press (about 1 teaspoon)
- 1 tablespoon finely chopped fresh parsley leaves
- ¼ teaspoon table salt
- ¼ teaspoon ground black pepper

Combine all the ingredients in a medium bowl.

We're big advocates of brining in the test kitchen (see "How Brining Saved Thanksgiving" on page 135). But brining works best for lean types of meat like poultry and pork. Is there an alternative to brining for fattier meats like beef? There is—salting. Salting is a kind of "dry brine" in which meat is rubbed with salt and then refrigerated for several hours. How does salting do its work? Initially, the salt draws out moisture from the meat, and this moisture mixes with the salt to form a shallow brine. Over time, the salt migrates from the shallow brine into the meat, just as it does in our usual brining technique. Once inside the meat, the salt changes the structure of the muscle fibers, allowing the meat to hold on to more water, so that it turns out juicy and well-seasoned.

We tried salting in developing our Slow-Roasted Beef (page 190) and found that salting for 24 hours worked best—the results were remarkable. In addition to the slow-cooking technique we use in this recipe, salting helped transform our bargain eye round into a tender, juicy roast that rivals beef tenderloin. (Note that smaller cuts of meat, like steak, do not need to be salted nearly as long—about 40 minutes is sufficient.)

Chipotle and Garlic Butter with Lime and Cilantro

MAKES ABOUT ½ CUP

- 5 tablespoons unsalted butter, softened
- 1 medium chipotle chile in adobo sauce, seeded and minced, with 1 teaspoon adobo sauce
- 1 medium garlic clove, minced or pressed through a garlic press (about 1 teaspoon)
- 1 teaspoon honey
- 1 teaspoon grated zest from 1 lime
- 1 tablespoon minced fresh cilantro leaves
- ½ teaspoon table salt

Combine all the ingredients in a medium bowl.

HORSERADISH-CRUSTED BEEF TENDERLOIN

WHY THIS RECIPE WORKS: A crisp horseradish crust contrasts nicely with the mild flavor of beef tenderloin, but most horseradish-crusted recipes are uninspired, and when carving time comes around, the crust falls off the meat in patches. We wanted to combine the bracing flavor of horseradish with a crisp, golden crust that would add textural contrast to rosy, medium-rare meat—and we wanted it to stick.

We chose to use a center-cut roast—also called a Châteaubriand—because its uniform shape cooks evenly. After lightly flouring the meat and applying a thin wash of egg white, we rolled the roast in crushed potato chips and panko bread crumbs mixed with horseradish, mayonnaise, shallot, garlic, and herbs. Potato chips may seem unusual, but they kept their crunch and contributed lots of flavor, particularly when we made our own by frying shredded potato in oil until browned and crisp. To make the crust adhere to the meat after being sliced, we replaced the egg white with gelatin. Because both meat and gelatin are made up of linear proteins that form tight bonds with each other, the gelatin mixture bound the bread crumbs firmly to the meat, yet yielded slightly as we cut it.

And to prevent the crust from turning soggy from meat juices released during cooking, we seared the meat in a hot skillet and let it rest so that its juices could drain off before applying the paste and the crumbs. Then we coated only the top and sides of the tenderloin, leaving an "opening" on the bottom for meat juices to escape as it roasted.

Horseradish-Crusted Beef Tenderloin
SERVES 6

If using table salt, reduce the amount in step 1 to 1½ teaspoons. Add the gelatin to the horseradish paste at the last moment or the mixture will become unspreadable. If desired, serve the roast with Horseradish Cream Sauce (page 190; you will need 2 jars of prepared horseradish for both the roast and sauce). If you choose to salt the tenderloin in advance, remove it from the refrigerator 1 hour before cooking. To make this recipe 1 day in advance, prepare it through step 3, but in step 2 do not toss the bread crumbs with the other ingredients until you are ready to sear the meat.

1 (2-pound) beef tenderloin center-cut Châteaubriand, trimmed of fat and silver skin
Kosher salt (see note)
3 tablespoons panko (Japanese-style bread crumbs)
1 cup plus 2 teaspoons vegetable oil
1¼ teaspoons ground black pepper
1 small shallot, minced (about 1 tablespoon)
2 medium garlic cloves, minced or pressed through a garlic press (about 2 teaspoons)
¼ cup well-drained prepared horseradish (see note)
2 tablespoons minced fresh parsley leaves
½ teaspoon minced fresh thyme leaves
1 small russet potato (about 6 ounces), peeled and grated on the large holes of a box grater
1½ teaspoons mayonnaise
1½ teaspoons Dijon mustard
½ teaspoon powdered gelatin (see note)

1. Sprinkle the roast with 1 tablespoon salt, cover with plastic wrap, and let stand at room temperature for 1 hour or refrigerate for up to 24 hours. Adjust an oven rack to the middle position and heat the oven to 400 degrees.

2. Toss the bread crumbs with 2 teaspoons of the oil, ¼ teaspoon salt, and ¼ teaspoon of the pepper in a 10-inch nonstick skillet. Cook over medium heat, stirring frequently, until deep golden brown, 3 to 5 minutes. Transfer to a rimmed baking sheet and cool to room temperature (wipe out the skillet). Once cool, toss the bread crumbs with the shallot, garlic, 2 tablespoons of the horseradish, the parsley, and thyme.

3. Rinse the grated potato under cold water, then squeeze dry in a kitchen towel. Transfer the potatoes and remaining 1 cup oil to the skillet. Cook over high heat, stirring frequently, until the potatoes are golden brown and crisp, 6 to 8 minutes. Using a slotted spoon, transfer the potatoes to a paper towel–lined plate and season lightly with salt; let cool for 5 minutes. Reserve 1 tablespoon oil from the skillet and discard the remainder. Once the potatoes are cool, transfer to a quart-size zipper-lock bag and crush until coarsely ground. Transfer the potatoes to the baking sheet with the bread-crumb mixture and toss to combine.

4. Pat the exterior of the tenderloin dry with paper towels and sprinkle evenly with the remaining 1 teaspoon pepper. Heat the reserved 1 tablespoon oil in a 12-inch nonstick skillet over medium-high heat until just smoking. Sear the tenderloin until well browned on all sides, 5 to 7 minutes. Transfer to a wire rack set over a rimmed baking sheet and let rest for 10 minutes.

5. Combine the remaining 2 tablespoons horseradish, mayonnaise, and mustard in a small bowl. Just before coating the tenderloin, add the gelatin and stir to combine. Spread the horseradish paste on the top and sides of the meat, leaving the bottom and ends bare. Roll the coated sides of the tenderloin in the bread-crumb mixture, pressing gently so the crumbs adhere in an even layer that just covers the horseradish paste; pat off any excess.

6. Return the tenderloin to the wire rack. Roast until an instant-read thermometer inserted into the center of the roast registers 120 to 125 degrees for medium-rare, 25 to 30 minutes.

7. Transfer the roast to a carving board and let rest for 20 minutes. Carefully cut the meat crosswise into ½-inch-thick slices and serve.

ULTIMATE BEEF TENDERLOIN

WHY THIS RECIPE WORKS: Beef tenderloin is perfect holiday fare. Add a rich stuffing and you've got the ultimate main course—at least in theory. We found three problems with stuffed tenderloin. The tenderloin's thin, tapered shape made for uneven cooking; in the time it took to develop a nice crust, the meat overcooked; and "deluxe" fillings such as lobster and chanterelles were so chunky they fell out of the meat when sliced. We wanted a stuffed beef tenderloin with a deeply charred crust, a tender, rosy-pink interior, and an intensely flavored stuffing that stayed neatly rolled in the meat.

We had determined for our Roast Beef Tenderloin recipe (page 191) that a center-cut tenderloin cooks more evenly than a whole one, and its cylindrical shape had an added advantage here as it made the roast easier to stuff. But making a slit in

the roast didn't give us much room for stuffing; double-butterflying the meat, to open it up like a book, gave us more space. After we stuffed, rolled, and tied it, we rubbed the roast with salt, pepper, and olive oil, which added flavor and helped develop a good crust when we seared the meat. We could fit just a cupful of stuffing in the meat, so we knew the flavors had to be intense. Chunky stuffings fell out when the roast was sliced, and anything with bread in it became a sponge that soaked up the meat juice. We finally decided on woodsy cremini mushrooms and caramelized onions, seasoned with Madeira and garlic; this combination made a savory-sweet jam-like filling that spread easily on the meat and held together well. Baby spinach added color and freshness. This roast was juicy and flavorful, and the filling was the ultimate touch of luxury.

Roast Beef Tenderloin with Caramelized Onion and Mushroom Stuffing

SERVES 4 TO 6

The roast can be stuffed, rolled, and tied a day ahead, but don't season the exterior until you are ready to cook it. This recipe can be doubled to make two roasts. Sear the roasts one after the other, cleaning the pan and adding new oil after searing the first roast. Both pieces of meat can be roasted on the same rack.

STUFFING

- 8 ounces cremini mushrooms, cleaned, stems trimmed, and broken into rough pieces
- 1½ teaspoons unsalted butter
- 1½ teaspoons olive oil
- 1 medium onion, halved and sliced ¼ inch thick
- ¼ teaspoon table salt
- ⅛ teaspoon ground black pepper
- 1 medium garlic clove, minced or pressed through a garlic press (about 1 teaspoon)
- ½ cup Madeira or sweet Marsala wine

BEEF ROAST

- 1 (2- to 3-pound) beef tenderloin center-cut Châteaubriand, trimmed and butterflied (see page 194)
  Table salt and ground black pepper
- ½ cup lightly packed baby spinach
- 3 tablespoons olive oil

HERB BUTTER

- 4 tablespoons (½ stick) unsalted butter, softened
- 1 tablespoon chopped fresh parsley leaves
- ¾ teaspoon chopped fresh thyme leaves
- 1 medium garlic clove, minced or pressed through a garlic press (about 1 teaspoon)
- 1 tablespoon whole grain mustard
- ⅛ teaspoon table salt
- ⅛ teaspoon ground black pepper

1. FOR THE STUFFING: Pulse the mushrooms in a food processor until coarsely chopped, about 6 pulses. Heat the butter and oil in a 12-inch nonstick skillet over medium-high heat. Add the onion, salt, and pepper; cook, stirring occasionally, until the onion begins to soften, about 5 minutes. Add the mushrooms and cook, stirring occasionally, until all the moisture has evaporated, 5 to 7 minutes. Reduce the heat to medium and continue to cook, stirring frequently, until the vegetables are deeply browned and sticky, about 10 minutes. Stir in the garlic and cook until fragrant, about 30 seconds. Slowly stir in the Madeira and cook, scraping the bottom of the skillet to loosen any browned bits, until the liquid has evaporated, 2 to 3 minutes. Transfer the onion-mushroom mixture to a plate and cool to room temperature.

2. FOR THE ROAST: Pat the tenderloin dry and season the cut side of the tenderloin liberally with salt and pepper. Following the photos, spread the cooled stuffing mixture over the interior of the beef, leaving a ½-inch border on all sides; press the spinach leaves on top of the stuffing. Roll the roast lengthwise, making it as compact as possible without squeezing out any filling. Evenly space eight pieces of kitchen twine (each about 14 inches) beneath the roast. Tie each strand tightly around the roast, starting with the ends.

3. In a small bowl, stir together 1 tablespoon of the olive oil, 1½ teaspoons salt, and 1½ teaspoons pepper. Rub the roast with the oil mixture and let stand at room temperature for 1 hour.

4. Adjust an oven rack to the middle position and heat the oven to 450 degrees. Heat the remaining 2 tablespoons olive oil in a 12-inch skillet over medium-high heat until smoking. Add the beef to the pan and cook until well browned on all sides, 8 to 10 minutes total. Transfer the beef to a wire rack set over a rimmed baking sheet and place in the oven. Roast until the thickest part of the roast registers 120 degrees on an instant-read thermometer for rare (16 to 18 minutes), or 125 degrees for medium-rare (20 to 22 minutes).

5. FOR THE BUTTER: While the meat roasts, combine all the ingredients in a small bowl. Transfer the tenderloin to a carving board; spread half of the butter evenly over the top of the roast. Loosely tent the roast with foil; let rest for 15 minutes. Cut the roast between the pieces of twine into thick slices. Remove the twine and serve, passing the remaining butter separately.

NOTES FROM THE TEST KITCHEN

STUFFING AND TYING A TENDERLOIN

1. Insert a chef's knife about 1 inch from the bottom of the roast and cut horizontally, stopping just before the edge. Open the meat like a book.

2. Make another cut diagonally into the thicker portion of the roast. Open up this flap, smoothing out the butterflied rectangle of meat.

3. Spread the filling evenly over the entire surface, leaving a ½-inch border on all sides. Press the spinach leaves evenly on top of the filling.

4. Using both hands, gently but firmly roll up the stuffed tenderloin, making it as compact as possible without squeezing out the filling.

5. Evenly space eight pieces of kitchen twine (each about 14 inches) beneath the roast. Tie each strand tightly around the roast, starting with the ends.

PEPPER-CRUSTED BEEF TENDERLOIN ROAST

WHY THIS RECIPE WORKS: For a tender, rosy roast with a spicy, yet not harsh-tasting, peppercorn crust that didn't fall off, we relied on a few tricks. Rubbing the raw tenderloin with an abrasive mixture of kosher salt, sugar, and baking soda transformed its surface into a magnet for the pepper crust. To tame the heat of the pepper crust, we simmered cracked peppercorns in oil, then strained them from the oil. To replace some of the subtle flavors we had simmered away, we added some orange zest and nutmeg. With the crust in place, we gently roasted the tenderloin in the oven until it was perfectly rosy, then served it with a tangy, fruity sauce to complement the rich beef.

about 125 degrees for medium-rare (thinner parts of tenderloin will be slightly more done), 60 to 70 minutes. Transfer to carving board and let rest for 30 minutes.

4. Remove twine and slice meat into ½-inch-thick slices. Serve.

Pepper-Crusted Beef Tenderloin Roast

SERVES 10 TO 12

Not all pepper mills produce a coarse enough grind for this recipe. Coarsely cracked peppercorns are each about the size of a halved whole one.

4½ teaspoons kosher salt
1½ teaspoons sugar
¼ teaspoon baking soda
9 tablespoons olive oil
½ cup coarsely cracked black peppercorns
1 tablespoon finely grated orange zest
½ teaspoon ground nutmeg
1 (6-pound) whole beef tenderloin, trimmed

1. Adjust oven rack to middle position and heat oven to 300 degrees. Combine salt, sugar, and baking soda in bowl; set aside. Heat 6 tablespoons oil and peppercorns in small saucepan over low heat until faint bubbles appear. Continue to cook at bare simmer, swirling pan occasionally, until pepper is fragrant, 7 to 10 minutes. Using fine-mesh strainer, drain cooking oil from peppercorns. Discard cooking oil and mix peppercorns with remaining 3 tablespoons oil, orange zest, and nutmeg.

2. Set tenderloin on sheet of plastic wrap. Sprinkle salt mixture evenly over surface of tenderloin and rub into tenderloin until surface is tacky. Tuck tail end of tenderloin under about 6 inches to create more even shape. Rub top and side of tenderloin with peppercorn mixture, pressing to make sure peppercorns adhere. Spray three 12-inch lengths kitchen twine with vegetable oil spray; tie head of tenderloin to maintain even shape, spacing twine at 2-inch intervals.

3. Transfer prepared tenderloin to wire rack set in rimmed baking sheet, keeping tail end tucked under. Roast until thickest part of meat registers about 120 degrees for rare and

Red Wine–Orange Sauce
MAKES 1 CUP

2 tablespoons unsalted butter, plus 4 tablespoons cut into 4 pieces and chilled
2 shallots, minced
1 tablespoon tomato paste
2 teaspoons sugar
3 garlic cloves, minced
2 cups beef broth
1 cup red wine
¼ cup orange juice
2 tablespoons balsamic vinegar
1 tablespoon Worcestershire sauce
1 sprig fresh thyme
   Salt and pepper

1. Melt 2 tablespoons butter in medium saucepan over medium-high heat. Add shallots, tomato paste, and sugar; cook, stirring frequently, until deep brown, about 5 minutes. Add garlic and cook until fragrant, about 1 minute. Add broth, wine, orange juice, vinegar, Worcestershire, and thyme sprig, scraping up any browned bits. Bring to simmer and cook until reduced to 1 cup, 35 to 40 minutes.

2. Strain sauce through fine-mesh strainer and return to saucepan. Return saucepan to medium heat and whisk in remaining 4 tablespoons butter, 1 piece at a time. Season with salt and pepper to taste.

Pomegranate-Port Sauce
MAKES 1 CUP

2 cups pomegranate juice
1½ cups ruby port
1 shallot, minced
1 tablespoon sugar
1 teaspoon balsamic vinegar
1 sprig fresh thyme
   Salt and pepper
4 tablespoons cold unsalted butter, cut into 4 pieces

Bring juice, port, shallot, sugar, vinegar, thyme sprig, and 1 teaspoon salt to simmer over medium-high heat. Cook until reduced to 1 cup, 30 to 35 minutes. Strain sauce through fine-mesh strainer and return to saucepan. Return saucepan to medium heat and whisk in butter, 1 piece at a time. Season with salt and pepper to taste.

BEEF TENDERLOIN WITH SMOKY POTATOES AND PERSILLADE RELISH

WHY THIS RECIPE WORKS: For special occasions, few cuts top a beef tenderloin. This elegant roast cooks quickly and serves a crowd, and its rich, buttery slices are fork-tender. We found that a hot oven delivered rich, roasted flavor and perfectly rosy meat without overcooking this lean cut. Tying the roast helped to ensure even cooking. The roast needed company, and small whole red potatoes were a perfect pairing. To punch up the flavor, we tossed the potatoes with smoked paprika, which added a pleasant smokiness to complement our meat, along with garlic and scallions for a deep, flavorful backbone. The tender meat needed a sauce, so we made a simple yet bold persillade relish, which featured parsley, capers, and cornichons.

Beef Tenderloin with Smoky Potatoes and Persillade Relish

SERVES 6 TO 8

We prefer to use extra-small red potatoes measuring less than 1 inch in diameter. Larger potatoes can be used, but it may be necessary to return the potatoes to the oven to finish cooking, while the roast is resting in step 5. Center-cut beef tenderloin roasts are sometimes sold as Châteaubriand.

BEEF AND POTATOES

- 1 (3-pound) center-cut beef tenderloin roast, trimmed
  Kosher salt and pepper
- 1 teaspoon baking soda
- 3 tablespoons extra-virgin olive oil
- 3 pounds extra-small red potatoes, unpeeled
- 5 scallions, minced
- 4 garlic cloves, minced
- 1 tablespoon smoked paprika
- ½ cup water

PERSILLADE RELISH

- ¾ cup minced fresh parsley
- ½ cup extra-virgin olive oil
- 6 tablespoons minced cornichons plus 1 teaspoon brine
- ¼ cup capers, rinsed and chopped coarse
- 3 garlic cloves, minced
- 1 scallion, minced
- 1 teaspoon sugar
- ¼ teaspoon salt
- ¼ teaspoon pepper

1. FOR THE BEEF AND POTATOES: Pat roast dry with paper towels. Combine 2¼ teaspoons salt, 1 teaspoon pepper, and baking soda in small bowl. Rub salt mixture evenly over roast and let stand for 1 hour. After 1 hour, tie roast with kitchen twine at 1½ inch intervals. Adjust oven rack to middle position and heat oven to 425 degrees.

2. Heat 2 tablespoons oil in 16 by 12-inch roasting pan over medium-high heat (over 2 burners, if possible) until shimmering.

Add potatoes, scallions, garlic, paprika, 1 teaspoon salt, and ¼ teaspoon pepper and cook until scallions are softened, about 1 minute. Off heat, stir in water, scraping up any browned bits. Transfer roasting pan to oven and roast potatoes for 15 minutes.

3. Brush remaining 1 tablespoon oil over surface of roast. Remove roasting pan from oven, stir potato mixture, and lay beef on top. Reduce oven temperature to 300 degrees. Return pan to oven and roast until beef registers 120 to 125 degrees (for medium-rare), 45 to 55 minutes, rotating roasting pan halfway through cooking.

4. FOR THE PERSILLADE RELISH: While beef roasts, combine all ingredients in bowl.

5. Remove pan from oven. Transfer roast to carving board, tent with aluminum foil, and let rest 15 minutes. Cover potatoes left in pan with foil to keep warm. Remove twine from roast, slice into ½-inch-thick slices, and serve with potatoes and persillade relish.

FENNEL-CORIANDER TOP SIRLOIN ROAST

WHY THIS RECIPE WORKS: We wanted a holiday-caliber roast without the hefty price tag, so we set out to bring big flavor to a more affordable cut: top sirloin. We began by splitting the roast in half, creating two manageable roasts, salting the halves, and air-drying them in the refrigerator. This seasoned the meat, maximized its juiciness, and dried the surfaces for optimal browning. After 24 hours, we kickstarted the browning by quickly searing all sides of the two roasts in a skillet. Tying the roasts with kitchen twine turned the irregularly shaped roasts into two uniform cylinders. To compensate for the meat's leaner makeup, we created a rich, heavily seasoned paste that would further boost browning. We processed garlic, fennel, olive oil, and umami-boosting anchovy fillets to create a spreadable consistency, then added coriander, paprika, and oregano for extra flavor. After applying the spice paste, we roasted the meat in a 225-degree oven for 2 hours. This initial roast cooked the meat to our liking. To give it an attractive browned crust, we removed the roasts from the oven, ramped up the temperature to 500 degrees, and returned them (with twine removed) for a final crisping.

Fennel-Coriander Top Sirloin Roast

SERVES 8 TO 10

This recipe requires refrigerating the salted meat for at least 24 hours before cooking. The roast, also called a top sirloin roast, top butt roast, center-cut roast, spoon roast, shell roast, or shell sirloin roast, should not be confused with a whole top sirloin butt roast or top loin roast. Do not omit the anchovies; they provide great depth of flavor with no overt fishiness. Monitoring the roast with a meat-probe thermometer is best. If you use an instant-read thermometer, open the oven door as little as possible and remove the roast from the oven to take its temperature.

1   (5- to 6-pound) boneless top sirloin
    center-cut roast, trimmed
2   tablespoons kosher salt
4   teaspoons plus ¼ cup extra-virgin olive oil
4   garlic cloves, minced
6   anchovy fillets, rinsed and patted dry
2   teaspoons ground fennel
2   teaspoons ground coriander
2   teaspoons paprika
1   teaspoon dried oregano
1   teaspoon pepper
    Coarse sea salt

1. Cut roast lengthwise along grain into 2 equal pieces. Rub 1 tablespoon kosher salt over each piece. Transfer to large plate and refrigerate, uncovered, for at least 24 hours or up to 4 days.

2. Adjust oven rack to middle position and heat oven to 225 degrees. Heat 2 teaspoons oil in 12-inch skillet over high heat until just smoking. Brown 1 roast on all sides, 6 to 8 minutes. Return browned roast to plate. Repeat with 2 teaspoons oil and remaining roast. Let cool for 10 minutes.

3. While roasts cool, process garlic, anchovies, fennel, coriander, paprika, oregano, and remaining ¼ cup oil in food processor until smooth paste forms, about 30 seconds, scraping down sides of bowl as needed. Add pepper and pulse to combine, 2 to 3 pulses.

4. Using 5 pieces of kitchen twine per roast, tie each roast crosswise at equal intervals into loaf shape. Transfer roasts to wire rack set in rimmed baking sheet and rub roasts evenly with paste.

5. Roast until meat registers 125 degrees for medium-rare or 130 degrees for medium, 2 to 2¼ hours. Remove roasts from oven, leaving on wire rack, and tent loosely with aluminum foil; let rest for at least 30 minutes or up to 40 minutes.

6. Heat oven to 500 degrees. Remove foil from roasts and cut and discard twine. Return roasts to oven and cook until exteriors of roasts are well browned, 6 to 8 minutes.

7. Transfer roasts to carving board. Slice meat ¼ inch thick. Season with sea salt to taste, and serve.

GIVE THAT MEAT A REST

You'll never see anyone in the test kitchen cut into a roast, or any meat, straight from the oven. They always let it rest before slicing. Exposed to heat during cooking, proteins, which resemble coiled springs, undergo a radical transformation in which they uncoil and then reconnect to each other in haphazard structures. This process, called coagulation, is the reason that proteins become firm and lose moisture during the cooking process. The longer that proteins are exposed to heat, the tighter they coagulate and the more liquid they drive toward both the surface and the center of the meat, much like wringing a wet kitchen towel.

If you were to cut the meat immediately after removing it from the heat source, the liquid suspended between the interior proteins is driven toward the surface and would simply pool (or what many chefs call bleed) on the cutting board or plate because the proteins have not had time to relax. The best way to prevent this pooling of juices and a dry hunk of meat is to rest the roast. Although the process of coagulation is not reversible, allowing the protein molecules to relax after cooking slows the rate at which they continue to squeeze the liquid between their tight coils and increases their capacity to retain moisture. A short rest on the cutting board will decrease the amount of liquid lost during carving by about 40 percent. There's another good reason to have some patience and let your meat rest—it allows you some time to finish the other components of dinner, which is especially useful around the holidays when there are typically loads of sides to get to the table too.

Rosemary-Garlic Top Sirloin Roast

Omit fennel, coriander, paprika, and oregano. Add 3 tablespoons chopped fresh rosemary to food processor with oil in step 3. Add ¼ teaspoon red pepper flakes with pepper in step 3.

CLASSIC PRIME RIB

WHY THIS RECIPE WORKS: Most of us cook prime rib only once a year, if that, and don't want to risk experimenting with the cooking method—especially when the results are no better than mediocre. We thought that a special-occasion roast deserved better and wanted to find the best way to get the juicy, tender, rosy meat that prime rib should have.

The principal question for roasting prime rib was oven temperature, and our research turned up a wide range of recommendations. Most delivered meat that was well-done on the outside but increasingly rare toward the center—not too bad, but not exactly great. Surprisingly, the roast we cooked at a temperature of only 250 degrees was rosy from the center all the way out. Additionally, it retained more juice than a roast cooked at a higher temperature, and the internal temperature rose less during resting, so we had more control over the final degree of doneness. Searing before roasting gave us a crusty brown exterior. For seasoning, prime rib needs nothing more than salt and pepper. Now that we'd found a dependable cooking method, we could serve this once-a-year roast with confidence.

Classic Prime Rib

SERVES 6 TO 8

With two pieces of kitchen twine running parallel to the bone, tie the roast at both ends to prevent the outer layer of meat from pulling away from the rib-eye muscle and overcooking.

    1 (7-pound; 3-rib) standing rib roast,
       trimmed and tied (see note)
       Table salt and ground black pepper

1. Pat the roast dry with paper towels and season with salt and pepper. Cover the roast loosely with plastic wrap and let sit at room temperature for 1 to 2 hours.

2. Adjust an oven rack to the lowest position and heat the oven to 250 degrees. Heat a large roasting pan over two burners set at medium-high heat until hot, about 4 minutes. Place the roast in the hot pan and cook on all sides until nicely browned and about ½ cup fat has rendered, 6 to 8 minutes.

NOTES FROM THE TEST KITCHEN

CARVING CLASSIC PRIME RIB

1. Using a carving fork to hold the roast in place, cut along the rib bones to sever the meat from the bones.

2. Set the roast cut side down; carve the meat across the grain into thick slices.

---

3. Remove the roast from the pan. Set a wire rack in the pan, then set the roast on the rack.

4. Place the roast in the oven and roast until the meat registers 125 degrees on an instant-read thermometer for rare, 130 degrees for medium-rare, and 140 degrees for medium, 3 to 3½ hours. Remove the roast from the oven and tent with foil. Let stand for 20 to 30 minutes to allow the juices to redistribute evenly throughout the roast.

5. Remove the twine and set the roast on a carving board, with the rib bones at a 90-degree angle to the board. Following the photos, carve and serve immediately.

THE BEST PRIME RIB

WHY THIS RECIPE WORKS: The perfect prime rib should have a deep-colored, substantial crust encasing a tender, juicy rosy-pink center. To achieve superior results, we cut slits in the layer of fat to help it render efficiently, then salted the roast overnight. The long salting time enhanced the beefy flavor while dissolving some of the proteins, yielding a buttery-tender roast. To further enhance tenderness, we cooked the roast at a very low temperature, which allowed the meat's enzymes to act as natural tenderizers, breaking down its tough connective tissue. A brief stint under the broiler before serving ensured a crisp, flavorful crust.

Best Prime Rib

SERVES 6 TO 8

Look for a roast with an untrimmed fat cap (ideally ½ inch thick). We prefer the flavor and texture of Prime beef, but Choice grade will work as well. Monitoring the roast with a meat-probe thermometer is best. If you use an instant-read thermometer, open the oven door as little as possible and remove the roast from the oven while taking its temperature. If the roast has not reached the correct temperature in the time range specified in step 3, heat the oven to 200 degrees, wait for five minutes, then shut it off, and continue to cook the roast until it reaches the desired temperature.

    1 (7-pound) first-cut beef standing rib roast (3 bones),
       meat removed from bones, bones reserved
       Kosher salt and pepper
    2 teaspoons vegetable oil

1. Using sharp knife, cut slits in surface layer of fat, spaced 1 inch apart, in crosshatch pattern, being careful to cut down to, but not into, meat. Rub 2 tablespoons salt over entire roast and into slits. Place meat back on bones (to save space in refrigerator), transfer to large plate, and refrigerate, uncovered, for at least 24 hours or up to 4 days.

2. Adjust oven rack to middle position and heat oven to 200 degrees. Set wire rack in rimmed baking sheet. Heat oil in 12-inch skillet over high heat until just smoking. Sear sides and top of roast (reserving bones) until browned, 6 to 8 minutes total (do not sear side where roast was cut from

bones). Place meat back on ribs so bones fit where they were cut and let cool for 10 minutes; tie meat to bones with 2 lengths of kitchen twine between ribs. Transfer roast, fat side up, to prepared wire rack and season with pepper. Roast until meat registers 110 degrees, 3 to 4 hours.

3. Turn off oven; leave roast in oven, opening door as little as possible, until meat registers about 120 degrees (for rare) or about 125 degrees (for medium-rare), 30 minutes to 1¼ hours longer.

4. Remove roast from oven (leave roast on baking sheet), tent loosely with aluminum foil, and let rest for at least 30 minutes or up to 1¼ hours.

5. Adjust oven rack to about 8 inches from broiler element and heat broiler. Remove foil from roast, form into 3-inch ball, and place under ribs to elevate fat cap. Broil until top of roast is well browned and crisp, 2 to 8 minutes.

6. Transfer roast to carving board; cut twine and remove ribs from roast. Slice meat into ¾-inch-thick slices. Season with salt to taste, and serve.

NOTES FROM THE TEST KITCHEN

PREPARING BEST PRIME RIB

1. Removing ribs makes it easier to sear prime rib in skillet. Run sharp knife down length of bones, following contours as closely as possible to remove ribs.

2. Score fat cap in 1-inch crosshatch pattern to allow salt to contact meat directly and to improve fat rendering and crisping.

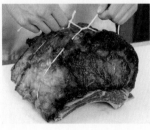

3. After searing meat, place meat back on ribs so bones fit where they were cut and let cool for 10 minutes; tie meat to bones with 2 lengths of kitchen twine between ribs. The bones provide insulation to the meat so it cooks evenly.

BRAISED BRISKET

WHY THIS RECIPE WORKS: Brisket is naturally flavorful, but because it is so lean, it requires long, slow braising to become tender—and the result is almost always stringy, dry meat. We wanted a better way to cook brisket so that it would remain moist, and we wanted to serve it with a flavorful sauce that would complement the beef. The fat in a piece of brisket is all on the surface; there's no marbling to keep the interior moist. We needed to find a way to get the moisture inside. We tried many different types and amounts of liquids and a variety of cooking vessels and techniques, but no matter what we did, the meat was still dry. Could the answer lie in adding moisture after the long braise? We left the meat in the sauce after cooking it, and after about an hour there was a noticeable difference. Taking this discovery further, we refrigerated the cooked meat and sauce overnight. The meat reabsorbed some of the liquid, becoming more moist and easier to carve without shredding. The sauce—based on red wine, chicken broth, and lots of onions—had improved as well; the fat had risen to the surface and congealed, making it easier to remove. All we had to do was reheat the sliced meat in the sauce, and this hearty dish was ready.

Onion-Braised Beef Brisket
SERVES 6

This recipe requires a few hours of unattended cooking. It also requires advance preparation. After cooking, the brisket must stand overnight in the braising liquid that later becomes the sauce. Defatting the sauce is essential. If the fat has congealed into a layer on top of the sauce, it can be easily removed while cold. Sometimes, however, fragments of solid fat are dispersed throughout the sauce; in this case, the sauce should be skimmed of fat after reheating. If you prefer a spicy sauce, increase the amount of cayenne to ¼ teaspoon. You will need 18-inch-wide heavy-duty foil for this recipe. If you own an electric knife, it will make easy work of slicing the cold brisket.

If you would like to make and serve the brisket on the same day, after removing the brisket from the oven in step 4, reseal the foil and let the brisket stand at room temperature for an hour. Then transfer the brisket to a carving board and continue with the recipe to strain, defat, and reheat the sauce and slice the meat; because the brisket will still be hot, there will be no need to put it back into the oven once the reheated sauce is poured over it.

1 (4- to 5-pound) beef brisket, preferably flat cut
  Table salt and ground black pepper
1 teaspoon vegetable oil, plus more as needed
3 large onions (about 2½ pounds), halved and sliced ½ inch thick
1 tablespoon brown sugar
3 medium garlic cloves, minced or pressed through a garlic press (about 1 tablespoon)
1 tablespoon tomato paste
1 tablespoon paprika
⅛ teaspoon cayenne pepper (see note)
2 tablespoons unbleached all-purpose flour
1 cup low-sodium chicken broth
1 cup dry red wine
3 bay leaves
3 sprigs fresh thyme
2 teaspoons cider vinegar (to season the sauce before serving)

1. Adjust an oven rack to the lower-middle position and heat the oven to 300 degrees. Line a 13 by 9-inch baking dish with two 24-inch-long sheets of 18-inch-wide heavy-duty foil, positioning the sheets perpendicular to each other and allowing the excess foil to extend beyond the edges of the pan. Pat the brisket dry with paper towels. Place the brisket, fat side up, on a cutting board; using a dinner fork, poke holes in the meat through the fat layer about 1 inch apart. Season both sides of the brisket liberally with salt and pepper.

2. Heat 1 teaspoon oil in a 12-inch skillet over medium-high heat until the oil just begins to smoke. Place the brisket, fat side up, in the skillet (the brisket may climb up the sides of the skillet); weight the brisket with a heavy Dutch oven or cast-iron skillet and cook until well browned, about 7 minutes. Remove the Dutch oven; using tongs, flip the brisket and cook on the second side without the weight until well browned, about 7 minutes longer. Transfer the brisket to a platter.

3. Pour off all but 1 tablespoon fat from the pan (or, if the brisket is lean, add enough oil to the fat in the skillet to equal 1 tablespoon); stir in the onions, brown sugar, and ¼ teaspoon salt and cook over medium-high heat, stirring occasionally, until the onions are softened and golden, 10 to 12 minutes. Add the garlic and cook, stirring frequently, until fragrant, about 1 minute; add the tomato paste and cook, stirring to combine, until the paste darkens, about 2 minutes. Add the paprika and cayenne and cook, stirring constantly, until fragrant, about 1 minute. Sprinkle the flour over the onions and

cook, stirring constantly, until well combined, about 2 minutes. Add the broth, wine, bay leaves, and thyme, stirring to scrape up the browned bits from the pan; bring to a simmer and simmer for about 5 minutes to fully thicken.

4. Pour the sauce and onions into the foil-lined baking dish. Nestle the brisket, fat side up, in the sauce and onions. Fold the foil extensions over and seal (do not tightly crimp the foil because it must later be opened to test for doneness). Place in the oven and cook until a fork can be inserted into and removed from the center of the brisket with no resistance, 3½ to 4 hours (when testing for doneness, open the foil with caution as the contents will be steaming). Carefully open the foil and let the brisket cool at room temperature for 20 to 30 minutes.

5. Transfer the brisket to a large bowl; set a mesh strainer over the bowl and strain the sauce over the brisket. Discard the bay leaves and thyme from the onions and transfer the onions to a small bowl. Cover both bowls with plastic wrap, cut vents in the plastic with a paring knife, and refrigerate overnight.

6. About 45 minutes before serving, adjust an oven rack to the lower-middle position and heat the oven to 350 degrees. While the oven heats, transfer the cold brisket to a carving board. Scrape off and discard any congealed fat from the sauce, then transfer the sauce to a medium saucepan and heat over medium heat until warm, skimming any fat on the surface with a wide shallow spoon (you should have about 2 cups of sauce without onions; if necessary, simmer the sauce over medium-high heat until reduced to 2 cups). While the sauce heats, use an electric knife, chef's knife, or carving knife to slice the brisket against the grain into ¼-inch-thick slices, trimming and discarding any excess fat, if desired; place the slices in a 13 by 9-inch baking dish. Stir the reserved onions and the vinegar into the warmed sauce and season with salt and pepper to taste. Pour the sauce over the brisket slices, cover the baking dish with foil, and bake until heated through, 25 to 30 minutes. Serve immediately.

CUBAN BRAISED AND SHREDDED BEEF

WHY THIS RECIPE WORKS: Tender yet hearty strands of beef napped in a bright and deeply savory sauce define *ropa vieja*. For braised and shredded beef dishes, we usually turn to chuck roast and short ribs, but this Cuban specialty calls for thicker, more fibrous shreds, so we used brisket. Slicing the beef into strips made for faster cooking and easy shredding, and a quick sear before braising gave the meat some ultrasavory browning. The accompanying vegetables would get overly soft if braised, so we cooked them ahead of time, browning sliced onions and red bell peppers then using their fond (as well as the beef's) to build the sauce. A fragrant combination of minced anchovies, minced garlic, ground cumin, and dried oregano created the meaty, aromatic base to which we added dry white wine for brightness. After letting the mixture reduce, we added chicken broth, tomato sauce, and bay leaves. We cooked the brisket in this seasoned sauce for 2 hours and it emerged juicy and richly flavored. Green olives are a traditional finishing touch, so we chopped and added them to the sauce while the beef cooled, stirring them in with the cooked onions and peppers. A splash of white wine vinegar made the flavors in our perfectly chewy Cuban shredded beef pop.

Cuban Braised and Shredded Beef

SERVES 6 TO 8

Look for a brisket that is 1½ to 2½ inches thick. Serve with steamed white rice and beans. Another good accompaniment is Fried Sweet Plantains (page 615).

1	(2-pound) beef brisket, fat trimmed to ¼ inch
	Salt and pepper
5	tablespoons vegetable oil
2	onions, halved and sliced thin
2	red bell peppers, stemmed, seeded, and sliced into ¼-inch-wide strips
2	anchovy fillets, rinsed, patted dry, and minced
4	garlic cloves, minced
2	teaspoons ground cumin
1½	teaspoons dried oregano
½	cup dry white wine
2	cups chicken broth
1	(8-ounce) can tomato sauce
2	bay leaves
¾	cup pitted green olives, chopped coarse
¾	teaspoon white wine vinegar, plus extra for seasoning

1. Adjust oven rack to middle position and heat oven to 300 degrees. Cut brisket against grain into 2-inch-wide strips. Cut any strips longer than 5 inches in half crosswise. Season beef on all sides with salt and pepper. Heat 4 tablespoons oil in Dutch oven over medium-high heat until just smoking. Brown beef on all sides, 7 to 10 minutes; transfer to large plate and set aside. Add onions and bell peppers and cook until softened and pan bottom develops fond, 10 to 15 minutes. Transfer vegetables to bowl and set aside. Add remaining 1 tablespoon oil to now-empty pot, then add anchovies, garlic, cumin, and oregano and cook until fragrant, about 30 seconds. Stir in wine, scraping up any browned bits, and cook until mostly evaporated, about 1 minute. Stir in broth, tomato sauce, and bay leaves. Return beef and any accumulated juices to pot and bring to simmer over high heat. Transfer to oven and cook, covered, until beef is just tender, 2 to 2¼ hours, flipping beef halfway through cooking.

2. Transfer beef to cutting board; when cool enough to handle, shred into ¼-inch-thick pieces. Meanwhile, add olives and reserved vegetables to pot and bring to boil over medium-high heat; simmer until thickened and measures 4 cups, 5 to 7 minutes. Stir in beef. Add vinegar. Season with salt, pepper, and extra vinegar to taste; serve.

CUBAN SHREDDED BEEF

WHY THIS RECIPE WORKS: *Vaca frita* is a Cuban classic that features beef (usually flank steak) that's been boiled, shredded, and fried so that the exterior develops a deep crust; a bit of lime juice and garlic contribute the bright, tart, and robust flavors typical of Caribbean cuisine. For our recipe, we were after meat with some textural contrast—we wanted a good exterior crust, plus a moister, more tender interior. We started with a collagen-rich chuck-eye roast and cut it into 1½-inch cubes to reduce the cooking time. Gently simmering it helped keep it moist. Pounding the meat flat was much more efficient than shredding it by hand. To reinforce the beefy flavor, we fried it, along with some thin-sliced onion, in its own fat before finishing everything with a mixture of garlic, cumin, oil, and citrus juices (lime as well as orange, to mellow the lime's acidity but maintain brightness).

Cuban Shredded Beef

SERVES 4 TO 6

Use a well-marbled chuck-eye roast in this recipe. When trimming the beef, don't remove all visible fat—some of it will be used in lieu of oil later in the recipe. If you don't have enough reserved fat in step 3, use vegetable oil. This dish pairs well with rice and beans, or it can be used as a filling for tacos, empanadas, or sandwiches.

2	pounds boneless beef chuck-eye roast, pulled apart at seams, trimmed, and cut into 1½-inch cubes
	Kosher salt and pepper
3	garlic cloves, minced
1	teaspoon vegetable oil
¼	teaspoon ground cumin
2	tablespoons orange juice
1½	teaspoons grated lime zest plus 1 tablespoon juice
1	onion, halved and sliced thin
2	tablespoons dry sherry
	Lime wedges

1. Bring beef, 2 cups water, and 1¼ teaspoons salt to boil in 12-inch nonstick skillet over medium-high heat. Reduce heat to low, cover, and gently simmer until beef is very tender, about 1 hour 45 minutes. (Check beef every 30 minutes, adding water so that bottom third of beef is submerged.) While beef simmers, combine garlic, oil, and cumin in bowl. Combine orange juice and lime zest and juice in second bowl.

2. Remove lid from skillet, increase heat to medium, and simmer until water evaporates and beef starts to sizzle, 3 to 8 minutes. Using slotted spoon, transfer beef to rimmed baking sheet. Pour off and reserve fat from skillet. Rinse skillet clean and dry with paper towels. Place sheet of aluminum foil over beef and, using meat pounder or heavy sauté pan, pound to flatten beef into ⅛-inch-thick pieces, discarding any large pieces of fat or connective tissue. (Some of beef should separate into shreds. Larger pieces that do not separate can be torn in half.)

3. Heat 1½ teaspoons reserved fat in now-empty skillet over high heat. When fat begins to sizzle, add onion and ¼ teaspoon salt. Cook, stirring occasionally, until onion is golden brown and charred in spots, 5 to 8 minutes. Add sherry and ¼ cup water and cook until liquid is absorbed, about 2 minutes. Transfer onion to bowl. Return skillet to high heat, add 1½ teaspoons reserved fat, and heat until it begins to sizzle. Add beef and cook, stirring frequently, until dark golden brown and crusty, 2 to 4 minutes.

4. Reduce heat to low and push beef to sides of skillet. Add garlic mixture to center and cook, stirring frequently, until fragrant and golden brown, about 30 seconds. Remove pan from heat, add orange juice mixture and onion, and toss to combine. Season with pepper to taste. Serve immediately with lime wedges.

ROAST BUTTERFLIED LEG OF LAMB

WHY THIS RECIPE WORKS: Roast leg of lamb is both delicious and daunting. The usual bone-in or boned, rolled, and tied leg options cook unevenly and are tricky to carve. Choosing a butterflied leg of lamb did away with these problems; we simply pounded it to an even thickness and salted it for an hour to encourage juicy, evenly cooked meat. We first roasted it gently in the oven until it was just medium-rare, then we passed it under the broiler to give it a crisp crust. A standard spice rub scorched under the broiler, so we opted for a spice-infused oil which seasoned the lamb during cooking and then became a quick sauce for serving.

Roast Butterflied Leg of Lamb with Coriander, Cumin, and Mustard Seeds

SERVES 8 TO 10

We prefer the subtler flavor and larger size of lamb labeled "domestic" or "American" for this recipe. The amount of salt (2 tablespoons) in step 1 is for a 6-pound leg. If using a larger leg (7 to 8 pounds), add an additional teaspoon of salt for every pound.

LAMB

- 1 (6- to 8-pound) butterflied leg of lamb
  Kosher salt
- ⅓ cup vegetable oil
- 3 shallots, sliced thin
- 4 garlic cloves, peeled and smashed
- 1 (1-inch) piece ginger, sliced into ½-inch-thick rounds and smashed
- 1 tablespoon coriander seeds
- 1 tablespoon cumin seeds
- 1 tablespoon mustard seeds
- 3 bay leaves
- 2 (2-inch) strips lemon zest

SAUCE

- ⅓ cup chopped fresh mint
- ⅓ cup chopped fresh cilantro
- 1 shallot, minced
- 2 tablespoons lemon juice
  Salt and pepper

1. FOR THE LAMB: Place lamb on cutting board with fat cap facing down. Using sharp knife, trim any pockets of fat and connective tissue from underside of lamb. Flip lamb over, trim fat cap so it's between ⅛ and ¼ inch thick, and pound roast to even 1-inch thickness. Cut slits, spaced ½ inch apart, in fat cap in crosshatch pattern, being careful to cut down to but not into meat. Rub 2 tablespoons salt over entire roast and into slits. Let stand, uncovered, at room temperature for 1 hour.

2. Meanwhile, adjust oven racks 4 to 5 inches from broiler element and to lower-middle position and heat oven to 250 degrees. Stir together oil, shallots, garlic, ginger, coriander seeds, cumin seeds, mustard seeds, bay leaves, and lemon zest on rimmed baking sheet and bake on lower-middle rack until spices are softened and fragrant and shallots and

garlic turn golden, about 1 hour. Remove sheet from oven and discard bay leaves.

3. Thoroughly pat lamb dry with paper towels and transfer, fat side up, to sheet (directly on top of spices). Roast on lower-middle rack until lamb registers 120 degrees, 30 to 40 minutes. Remove sheet from oven and heat broiler. Broil lamb on upper rack until surface is well browned and charred in spots and lamb registers 125 degrees, 3 to 8 minutes for medium-rare.

4. Remove sheet from oven and, using 2 pairs of tongs, transfer lamb to carving board (some spices will cling to bottom of roast); tent loosely with aluminum foil and let rest for 20 minutes.

5. FOR THE SAUCE: Meanwhile, carefully pour pan juices through fine-mesh strainer into medium bowl, pressing on solids to extract as much liquid as possible; discard solids. Stir in mint, cilantro, shallot, and lemon juice. Add any accumulated lamb juices to sauce and season with salt and pepper to taste.

6. With long side facing you, slice lamb with grain into 3 equal pieces. Turn each piece and slice across grain into ¼-inch-thick slices. Serve with sauce. (Briefly warm sauce in microwave if it has cooled and thickened.)

Roast Butterflied Leg of Lamb with Coriander, Rosemary, and Red Pepper

Omit cumin and mustard seeds. Toss 6 sprigs fresh rosemary and ½ teaspoon red pepper flakes with oil mixture in step 2. Substitute parsley for cilantro in sauce.

Roast Butterflied Leg of Lamb with Coriander, Fennel, and Black Pepper

Substitute 1 tablespoon fennel seeds for cumin seeds and 1 tablespoon black peppercorns for mustard seeds in step 2. Substitute parsley for mint in sauce.

ROAST RACK OF LAMB WITH ROASTED RED PEPPER RELISH

WHY THIS RECIPE WORKS: When you really think about it, roasting a rack of lamb is a simple process, but there's a fine line between a showstopper and a dried-out disappointment. For a rack that would make us proud at our next fête, the seasoning needed to be spot-on, the meat had to be juicy, and we'd need a bold relish to serve alongside it. Starting with the lamb, carving a shallow cross-hatch into the fat cap and rubbing the racks' surfaces with a blend of kosher salt and ground cumin ensured that our lamb would be loaded with flavor. We heated the oven to 250 degrees and arranged the lamb on a wire rack–lined baking sheet. In just over an hour, our racks emerged at a rosy medium-rare with big flavor to boot. While the racks roasted in the oven, we whipped up a relish to dress up the lamb, combining chopped roasted red pepper, minced parsley, olive oil, fresh lemon juice, and minced garlic. This simple sauce steeped while the lamb cooked. Because meat always tastes best with a bit of char, we browned the racks in a skillet before slicing and serving.

Roast Rack of Lamb with Roasted Red Pepper Relish

SERVES 4 TO 6

We prefer the milder taste and bigger size of domestic lamb, but you may substitute imported lamb from New Zealand and Australia. Since imported racks are generally smaller, in step 1 season each rack with ½ teaspoon of salt and reduce the cooking time to 50 to 70 minutes. A rasp-style grater makes quick work of turning the garlic into a paste.

LAMB
- 2 racks of lamb (1¾ to 2 pounds each), fat trimmed to ⅛ to ¼ inch, rib bones frenched
  Kosher salt and pepper
- 1 teaspoon ground cumin
- 1 teaspoon vegetable oil

RELISH
- ½ cup jarred roasted red peppers, rinsed, patted dry, and chopped fine
- ½ cup minced fresh parsley
- ¼ cup extra-virgin olive oil
- ¼ teaspoon lemon juice
- ⅛ teaspoon garlic, minced to paste
  Kosher salt and pepper

1. FOR THE LAMB: Adjust oven rack to middle position and heat oven to 250 degrees. Using sharp knife, cut slits in surface layer of fat, spaced ½-inch apart, in crosshatch pattern, being careful to cut down to, but not into, meat. Combine 2 tablespoons salt and cumin in bowl. Rub ¾ teaspoon salt mixture over entire surface of each rack and into slits. Reserve remaining salt mixture for serving. Place racks, bone-side down, on wire rack set in rimmed baking sheet. Roast until meat registers 125 degrees for medium-rare or 130 degrees for medium, 1 hour 5 minutes to 1 hour 25 minutes.

2. FOR THE RELISH: While lamb roasts, combine red peppers, parsley, olive oil, lemon juice, and garlic in bowl.

Season with salt and pepper to taste. Let stand at room temperature at least 1 hour before serving.

3. Heat vegetable oil in 12-inch skillet over high heat until just smoking. Place one rack, bone-side up, in skillet and cook until well-browned, 1 to 2 minutes. Transfer to carving board. Pour off all but 1 teaspoon fat from skillet and repeat with second rack. Tent racks loosely with aluminum foil and let rest for 20 minutes. Cut between ribs to separate chops and sprinkle cut side of chops with ½ teaspoon salt mixture. Serve, passing relish and remaining salt mixture separately.

Roast Rack of Lamb with Sweet Mint-Almond Relish

Substitute ground anise for cumin in salt mixture. Omit red pepper relish. While lamb roasts, combine ½ cup minced fresh mint; ¼ cup sliced almonds, toasted and chopped fine; ¼ cup extra-virgin olive oil; 2 tablespoons red currant jelly; 4 teaspoons red wine vinegar; and 2 teaspoons Dijon mustard in bowl. Season with salt and pepper to taste. Let stand at room temperature for at least 1 hour before serving with lamb.

SAUTÉED PORK TENDERLOIN

WHY THIS RECIPE WORKS: When cooked properly, pork tenderloin has a tenderness rivaling that of beef tenderloin; unfortunately it also has ultra-mild flavor. Long marinades and hybrid searing and roasting techniques help remedy the flavor deficiency, but they take the home cook a long way from the realm of the no-fuss meal. We wanted a recipe for a fast weeknight dinner that still offered maximum flavor. We needed to deal with the tenderloin's oblong, tapered shape as well as the fact that the tenderloins (which are usually sold in a pair in a vacuum pack) were almost guaranteed to be substantially different in weight and length. The solution was to cut them into 1½-inch-thick medallions (the end pieces were scored, creating a small flap of meat that folded underneath the larger half to yield the right-sized medallion). To preserve their tidy cylindrical shape, we developed two approaches: tying the medallions or wrapping blanched bacon around them, fastened with toothpicks. We found we could create a beautiful sear on all sides of these neat packages in the time it took to reach an internal temperature of 140 to 145 degrees, and the searing process had the extra benefit of producing enough fond (flavorful browned bits) to create a few easy, flavorful pan sauces.

Thick-Cut Pork Tenderloin Medallions
SERVES 4 TO 6

We prefer natural to enhanced pork (pork that has been injected with a salt solution to increase moistness and flavor), though both will work in this recipe. Begin checking the doneness of smaller medallions 1 or 2 minutes early; they may need to be taken out of the pan a little sooner. Be sure not to rinse out the skillet if serving with a pan sauce (recipes follow).

TURNING THE TAILPIECE INTO A MEDALLION

1. Score the tenderloin's tapered tail end.

2. Fold in half at the incision.

3. Tie the medallion with kitchen twine, making sure the outer surfaces are flat.

TYING THICK MEDALLIONS

Thick medallions allow for more browning, but they can flop over in the pan. To prevent this, tie each piece with kitchen twine.

2 (1- to 1¼-pound) pork tenderloins, trimmed, cut crosswise into 1½-inch pieces, and tied; thinner end pieces removed and tied together (see photos)
  Table salt and ground black pepper
2 tablespoons vegetable oil

1. Pat the pork medallions dry and season with salt and pepper.

2. Heat the oil in a 12-inch skillet over medium-high heat until shimmering. Add the pork and cook, without moving the pieces, until well browned, 3 to 5 minutes. Turn the pork and brown on the second side, 3 to 5 minutes more. Reduce the heat to medium. Using tongs, stand each piece on its side and cook, turning the pieces as necessary, until the sides are well browned and the internal temperature registers 140 to

145 degrees on an instant-read thermometer, 8 to 12 minutes. Transfer the pork to a platter, tent loosely with foil, and let rest until the temperature registers 150 degrees on an instant-read thermometer, while making a pan sauce (recipes follow). Serve with the sauce.

Maple-Mustard Sauce
MAKES ABOUT 1 CUP

  2 teaspoons vegetable oil
  1 medium onion, halved and sliced thin
  1 cup low-sodium chicken broth
  ⅓ cup maple syrup
  3 tablespoons balsamic vinegar
  3 tablespoons whole grain mustard
     Table salt and ground black pepper

Pour off any fat from the skillet in which the pork was cooked. Add the oil and heat the skillet over medium heat until shimmering. Add the onion and cook, stirring occasionally, until softened and beginning to brown, 3 to 4 minutes. Increase the heat to medium-high and add the broth; bring to a simmer, scraping the bottom of the skillet with a wooden spoon to loosen any browned bits. Simmer until the liquid is reduced to ½ cup, 3 to 4 minutes. Add the maple syrup, vinegar, mustard, and any juices from the resting meat and cook until thickened and reduced to 1 cup, 3 to 4 minutes longer. Season with salt and pepper to taste, pour the sauce over the pork, and serve immediately.

Apple Cider Sauce
MAKES ABOUT 1¼ CUPS
Complete step 1 of this recipe either before or during the cooking of the pork, then finish the sauce while the pork rests.

  1½ cups apple cider
   1 cup low-sodium chicken broth
   2 teaspoons cider vinegar
   1 cinnamon stick
   4 tablespoons (½ stick) unsalted butter,
      cut into 4 pieces
   2 large shallots, minced (about ½ cup)
   1 tart apple, such as Granny Smith, peeled,
      cored, and diced small
   ¼ cup Calvados or apple-flavored brandy
   1 teaspoon minced fresh thyme leaves
      Table salt and ground black pepper

1. Combine the cider, broth, vinegar, and cinnamon stick in a medium saucepan; simmer over medium-high heat until the liquid is reduced to 1 cup, 10 to 12 minutes. Remove the cinnamon stick and discard. Set the sauce aside until the pork is cooked.

2. Pour off any fat from the skillet in which the pork was cooked. Add 1 tablespoon of the butter and heat over medium heat until melted. Add the shallots and apple and cook, stirring occasionally, until softened and beginning to brown,

1 to 2 minutes. Remove the skillet from the heat and add the Calvados. Return the skillet to the heat and cook for about 1 minute, scraping the bottom of the skillet with a wooden spoon to loosen any browned bits. Add the reduced cider mixture, any juices from the resting meat, and the thyme; increase the heat to medium-high and simmer until thickened and reduced to 1¼ cups, 3 to 4 minutes. Off the heat, whisk in the remaining 3 tablespoons butter and season with salt and pepper to taste. Pour the sauce over the pork and serve immediately.

BREADED PORK CUTLETS

WHY THIS RECIPE WORKS: While classic *Wiener schnitzel* features a thin, tender veal cutlet coated in ultrafine bread crumbs and then fried until puffy and golden brown, many recipes—to avoid the toughness and high price of veal—substitute pork. But too often these recipes yield dry, tough pork cutlets with greasy coatings. We wanted tender pork cutlets with the crisp, wrinkled, puffy coating that is Wiener schnitzel's signature.

Dismissing pork chops and prepackaged cutlets, we chose tenderloin, which has a mild flavor similar to veal and isn't tough. We cut the tenderloin crosswise on an angle into four pieces, which when pounded thin gave us long, narrow cutlets that would fit two at a time in the pan. Schnitzel is breaded with a flour, egg, and bread-crumb sequence of coatings, but we had to figure out how to get the characteristic puffiness and "rumpled" appearance of the finished cutlets; with good schnitzel you should be able to slide a knife between the meat and the coating. Drying bread in the microwave produced extra-dry crumbs that helped with the crispness, and a little vegetable oil whisked into the egg helped separate the coating from the meat.

But the real breakthrough was in the frying method: Instead of sautéing the cutlets, we cooked them in a Dutch oven in an inch of oil, shaking the pot to get some of the oil over the top of the meat. The extra heat quickly solidified the egg in the coating, so that the steam from the meat couldn't escape and puffed the coating instead. With the traditional schnitzel garnishes of lemon, parsley, capers, and a sieved hard-cooked egg, these cutlets, with their tender meat and crisp coating, delivered on all fronts.

Breaded Pork Cutlets (Pork Schnitzel)

SERVES 4

To make cutlets, cut the tenderloin in half on a 20-degree angle, then cut each piece in half again at the same angle. Cut the tapered tail pieces slightly thicker than the middle ones. Using 2 cups of oil for cooking may seem like a lot, but it is necessary to get an authentic, wrinkled texture on the finished cutlets. When properly cooked, the cutlets absorb very little oil. To ensure ample room for the cutlets as they fry, it is essential to use a Dutch oven with a large surface area. Although spaetzle is the traditional side dish, boiled potatoes or egg noodles also make terrific accompaniments.

- 7 slices high-quality white sandwich bread, crusts removed, cut into ¾-inch cubes (about 4 cups)
- ½ cup unbleached all-purpose flour
- 2 large eggs
- 2 cups plus 1 tablespoon vegetable oil (see note)
- 1 (1¼-pound) pork tenderloin, trimmed of fat and silver skin and tenderloin cut on an angle into 4 equal pieces (see note)
  Table salt and ground black pepper

GARNISHES
- 1 lemon, cut into wedges
- 2 tablespoons chopped fresh parsley leaves
- 2 tablespoons capers, rinsed
- 1 large hard-cooked egg (page 38), yolk and white separated and passed separately through a fine-mesh strainer (optional)

1. Place the bread cubes on a large microwave-safe plate. Microwave on high power for 4 minutes, stirring well halfway through the cooking time. Microwave on medium power until the bread is dry and a few pieces start to lightly brown, 3 to 5 minutes longer, stirring every minute. Process the dry bread in a food processor to very fine crumbs, about 45 seconds. Transfer the bread crumbs to a shallow dish (you should have about 1¼ cups crumbs). Spread the flour in a second shallow dish. Beat the eggs with 1 tablespoon of the oil in a third shallow dish.

2. Place the pork, with one cut side down, between two sheets of plastic wrap and pound to an even thickness of between ⅛ and ¼ inch. Season the cutlets with salt and pepper. Working with one cutlet at a time, dredge the cutlets thoroughly in flour, shaking off the excess, then coat with the egg, allowing the excess to drip back into the dish to ensure a very thin coating, and coat evenly with the bread crumbs, pressing on the crumbs to adhere. Place the breaded cutlets in a single layer on a wire rack set over a baking sheet; let the coating dry for 5 minutes.

3. Heat the remaining 2 cups oil in a large Dutch oven over medium-high heat until it registers 375 degrees on an instant-read thermometer. Lay two cutlets, without overlapping, in the pan and cook, shaking the pan continuously and gently, until wrinkled and light golden brown on both sides, 1 to 2 minutes per side. Transfer the cutlets to a paper towel–lined plate and flip the cutlets several times to blot the excess oil. Repeat with the remaining cutlets. Serve immediately with the garnishes.

PAN-SEARED PORK TENDERLOIN

WHY THIS RECIPE WORKS: Because pork tenderloins are so lean, they cook relatively quickly and are therefore a good choice for an easy-to-prepare meal. But that same leanness means that the pork tends to overcook, and there's also less flavor. Although cutting the pork into medallions can alleviate some of these issues, we wanted a preparation for whole pork tenderloins that would deliver a flavor boost to this quick-cooking roast.

Simply roasted in the oven, the pork tended to dry out and never achieved the dark brown crust we wanted. We got that crust when we seared the tenderloins on the stovetop—but then the pork wasn't cooked through. A combination of searing the meat in a skillet, then transferring the pork to the oven to finish cooking, produced a flavorful crust and well-cooked meat. The browned crust added some flavor, but we wanted more. A dry rub of just salt and pepper, left on for half an hour before searing, provided enough seasoning and further encouraged a browned crust, and a pan sauce made with the browned bits left from sautéing was an additional flavor boost. Not only were these pork tenderloins delicious; they were also on the dinner table in about half an hour.

Pan-Seared Oven-Roasted Pork Tenderloin

SERVES 4

We prefer natural to enhanced pork (pork that has been injected with a salt solution to increase moisture and flavor) for this recipe. Enhanced pork can be used, but the meat won't brown as well. Because two are cooked at once, tenderloins larger than 1 pound apiece will not fit comfortably in a 12-inch skillet. If time permits, season the tenderloins up to 30 minutes before cooking; the seasonings will better penetrate the meat. The recipe will work in a nonstick or a traditional skillet. A pan sauce can be made while the tenderloins are in the oven (recipes follow); if you intend to make a sauce, make sure to prepare all of the sauce ingredients before cooking the pork.

2 (12- to 16-ounce) pork tenderloins, trimmed of
   fat and silver skin (see note)
1¼ teaspoons table salt
¾ teaspoon ground black pepper
2 teaspoons vegetable oil
1 recipe pan sauce (optional; recipes follow)

1. Adjust an oven rack to the middle position and heat the oven to 400 degrees. Sprinkle the tenderloins evenly with the salt and pepper; rub the seasoning into the meat. Heat the oil in a 12-inch skillet over medium-high heat until smoking. Place both tenderloins in the skillet; cook until well browned, about 3 minutes. Using tongs, rotate the tenderloins a quarter-turn; cook until well browned, 45 to 60 seconds. Repeat until all sides are browned, about 1 minute longer. Transfer the tenderloins to a rimmed baking sheet and place in the oven (reserve the skillet if making a pan sauce); roast until the internal temperature registers 140 to 145 degrees on an instant-read thermometer, 10 to 16 minutes. (Begin the pan sauce, if making, while the meat roasts.)

2. Transfer the tenderloins to a carving board and tent loosely with foil (continue with the pan sauce, if making); let rest until the internal temperature registers 150 degrees, 8 to 10 minutes. Cut the tenderloins crosswise into ½-inch-thick slices, arrange on a platter or individual plates, and spoon the sauce (if using) over; serve immediately.

Dried Cherry–Port Sauce with Onions and Marmalade

MAKES ABOUT ½ CUP

The flavors in this sauce are especially suited to the winter holiday season.

1 teaspoon vegetable oil
1 large onion, halved and sliced ½ inch thick
   (about 1½ cups)
¾ cup port
¾ cup dried cherries
2 tablespoons orange marmalade
3 tablespoons unsalted butter, cut into 3 pieces
   Table salt and ground black pepper

1. Immediately after placing the pork in the oven, add the oil to the still-hot skillet, swirl to coat, and set the skillet over medium-high heat; add the onion and cook, stirring frequently, until softened and browned around the edges, 5 to 7 minutes. (If the drippings are browning too quickly, add 2 tablespoons water and scrape up the browned bits with a wooden spoon.) Set the skillet aside off the heat.

2. While the pork is resting, set the skillet over medium-high heat and add the port and cherries; simmer, scraping up the browned bits with a wooden spoon, until the mixture is slightly thickened, 4 to 6 minutes. Add any accumulated pork juices and continue to simmer until thickened and reduced to about ⅓ cup, 2 to 4 minutes longer. Off the heat, whisk in the orange marmalade and butter, one piece at a time. Season with salt and pepper to taste.

Garlicky Lime Sauce with Cilantro

MAKES ABOUT ½ CUP

This assertive sauce is based on a Mexican sauce called *mojo de ajo*. A rasp grater is the best way to break down the garlic to a fine paste. Another option is to put the garlic through a press and then finish mincing it to a paste with a knife. If your garlic cloves contain green sprouts or shoots, remove the sprouts before grating—their flavor is bitter and hot. The initial cooking of the garlic off the heat will prevent scorching.

10 garlic cloves, peeled and grated to a fine paste on
    a rasp grater (about 2 tablespoons; see note)
2 tablespoons water
1 tablespoon vegetable oil
¼ teaspoon red pepper flakes
2 teaspoons light brown sugar
¼ cup chopped fresh cilantro leaves
3 tablespoons juice from 2 limes
1 tablespoon chopped fresh chives
4 tablespoons (½ stick) unsalted butter, cut into 4 pieces
   Table salt and ground black pepper

1. Immediately after placing the pork in the oven, mix the garlic paste with the water in a small bowl. Add the oil to the still-hot skillet and swirl to coat; off the heat, add the garlic paste and cook with the skillet's residual heat, scraping up the browned bits with a wooden spoon, until the sizzling subsides, about 2 minutes. Set the skillet over low heat and continue cooking, stirring frequently, until the garlic is sticky, 8 to 10 minutes; set the skillet aside off the heat.

2. While the pork is resting, set the skillet over medium heat; add the red pepper flakes and brown sugar to the skillet and cook until sticky and the sugar is dissolved, about 1 minute. Add the cilantro, lime juice, and chives; simmer to blend the flavors, 1 to 2 minutes. Add any accumulated pork juices and simmer for 1 minute longer. Off the heat, whisk in the butter, one piece at a time. Season with salt and pepper to taste.

MAPLE-GLAZED PORK TENDERLOIN

WHY THIS RECIPE WORKS: When done right, nothing can quite match pork tenderloin's fine-grained, buttery-smooth texture, but on its own, it can lack flavor. We thought a thick, sweet, fragrant glaze would be just the solution and decided it should feature New England's signature ingredient, maple syrup.

Getting the glaze right was comparatively easy: To temper the sweetness of the maple syrup, we added molasses, mustard, and a shot of bourbon; with a little cinnamon, cloves, and cayenne, the glaze was ready. To give the glaze something to hold on to, we rolled the tenderloins in a mixture of cornstarch and sugar before searing them. When we'd built a good crust in the skillet, we painted on some glaze and transferred the pork to the oven. It occurred to us that the painting analogy was a good one—why not put multiple coats on the tenderloins to get the best coverage? When the meat was nearly done, we put on more glaze, and we added yet another coat when the tenderloins were completely done. Finally, after letting the tenderloins rest, we glazed them one last time. Slicing into this roast revealed success: A thick maple glaze coated the meat.

Maple-Glazed Pork Tenderloin

SERVES 6

We prefer natural to enhanced pork (pork that has been injected with a salt solution to increase moistness and flavor) for this recipe. If your tenderloins are smaller than 1¼ pounds, reduce the cooking time in step 3 (and use an instant-read thermometer for best results). If the tenderloins don't fit in the skillet initially, let their ends curve toward each other; the meat will eventually shrink as it cooks. Make sure to cook the tenderloins until they turn deep golden brown in step 2 or they will appear pale after glazing. Be sure to pat off the cornstarch mixture thoroughly in step 1, as any excess will leave gummy spots on the tenderloins.

- ¾ cup maple syrup, preferably grade B
- ¼ cup light or mild molasses
- 2 tablespoons bourbon or brandy
- ⅛ teaspoon ground cinnamon
  Pinch ground cloves
  Pinch cayenne pepper
- ¼ cup cornstarch
- 2 tablespoons sugar
- 1 tablespoon table salt
- 2 teaspoons ground black pepper
- 2 (1¼- to 1½-pound) pork tenderloins (see note), trimmed of fat and silver skin
- 2 tablespoons vegetable oil
- 1 tablespoon whole grain mustard

1. Adjust an oven rack to the middle position and heat the oven to 375 degrees. Stir ½ cup of the maple syrup, the molasses, bourbon, cinnamon, cloves, and cayenne together in a 2-cup liquid measure; set aside. Whisk the cornstarch, sugar, salt, and black pepper in a small bowl until combined. Transfer the cornstarch mixture to a rimmed baking sheet. Pat the tenderloins dry with paper towels, then roll them in the cornstarch mixture until evenly coated on all sides. Thoroughly pat off the excess cornstarch mixture.

2. Heat the oil in a 12-inch heavy-bottomed nonstick skillet over medium-high heat until just beginning to smoke. Reduce the heat to medium and place both tenderloins in the skillet, leaving at least 1 inch between them. Cook until well browned on all sides, 8 to 12 minutes. Transfer the tenderloins to a wire rack set over a rimmed baking sheet.

3. Pour off the fat from the skillet and return to medium heat. Add the syrup mixture to the skillet, scraping up the browned bits with a wooden spoon, and cook until reduced to ½ cup, about 2 minutes. Transfer 2 tablespoons of the glaze

to a small bowl and set aside. Using the remaining glaze, brush each tenderloin with approximately 1 tablespoon glaze. Roast the pork until the thickest part of the tenderloins registers 130 degrees on an instant-read thermometer, 12 to 20 minutes. Brush each tenderloin with another tablespoon of the glaze and continue to roast until the thickest part of the tenderloins registers 140 degrees, 2 to 4 minutes longer. Remove the tenderloins from the oven and brush each with the remaining glaze; let rest, uncovered, until the temperature reaches 150 degrees, about 10 minutes.

4. While the tenderloins rest, stir the remaining ¼ cup maple syrup and the mustard into the reserved 2 tablespoons glaze. Brush each tenderloin with 1 tablespoon mustard glaze. Transfer the meat to a carving board and slice into ¼-inch-thick pieces. Serve, passing the extra mustard glaze at the table.

BROILED PORK TENDERLOIN

WHY THIS RECIPE WORKS: An easy way to prepare quick-cooking cuts like pork tenderloin is to simply put them under the broiler. The intense heat of the broiler promises to deeply brown the exterior and cook the roast through in one fell swoop. But the problem is that recipes calling for the broiler rely on a one-size-fits-all approach, when in reality no two broilers behave exactly the same way. We wanted to figure out a way to minimize differences among broilers so every oven would produce the same richly browned, juicy pork tenderloins.

To ensure that the tip of the tenderloin cooked at the same rate as the middle, we folded the thinner tail end underneath and tied the meat at 2-inch intervals to give it a rounded shape that would cook evenly. The best browning came from cooking the roasts 4 to 5 inches from the broiler element in a disposable roasting pan, which effectively reflected the heat of the broiler. A baking soda rub further enhanced browning. To correct for differences in broilers, we started by preheating the oven to 325 degrees, then turned on the broiler at the same time that we put the pork in the oven. We pulled the roasts from the oven when they reached a slightly lower-than-normal internal temperature to account for the increased carryover cooking effect of the broiler's intense heat.

Broiled Pork Tenderloin

SERVES 4 TO 6

We prefer natural pork, but enhanced pork (injected with a salt solution) can be used. If you're using enhanced pork, reduce the amount of salt in step 2 to 1½ teaspoons. A 13 by 9-inch aluminum roasting pan that is at least 3 inches deep is critical to the success of this recipe. We do not recommend broiling the pork in a pan that is a different size or material. This lean cut can be served by itself, but it's best accompanied by a richly flavored sauce (recipes follow). We developed this recipe with an in-oven broiler; do not attempt this with a drawer broiler (the type of broiler that is below the oven compartment).

- 2 (1-pound) pork tenderloins, trimmed
- 2 teaspoons kosher salt
- 1¼ teaspoons vegetable oil
- ½ teaspoon pepper
- ¼ teaspoon baking soda
- 1 (13 by 9-inch) disposable aluminum roasting pan

1. Adjust oven rack 4 to 5 inches from broiler element and heat oven to 325 degrees. Fold thin tip of each tenderloin under about 2 inches to create uniformly shaped roast. Tie tenderloins crosswise with kitchen twine at 2-inch intervals, making sure folded tip is secured underneath. Trim any excess twine close to meat to prevent it from scorching under broiler.

2. Mix salt, oil, and pepper in small bowl until salt is evenly coated with oil. Add baking soda and stir until well combined. Rub salt mixture evenly over pork. Place tenderloins in disposable pan, evenly spaced between sides of pan and each other.

3. Turn oven to broil. Broil tenderloins for 5 minutes. Flip tenderloins and continue to broil until golden brown and meat registers 125 to 130 degrees, 8 to 14 minutes. Remove disposable pan from oven, tent loosely with aluminum foil, and let rest for 10 minutes. Remove twine, slice tenderloins into ½-inch-thick slices, and serve.

Mustard–Crème Fraîche Sauce

MAKES ABOUT 1 CUP

- ½ cup crème fraîche
- 3 tablespoons Dijon mustard
- 3 tablespoons chopped fresh parsley
  Salt and pepper

Whisk crème fraîche, mustard, and parsley together in bowl. Season with salt and pepper to taste.

Sun-Dried Tomato and Basil Salsa

MAKES ABOUT 1 CUP

- ¼ cup oil-packed sun-dried tomatoes, rinsed and chopped fine
- ¼ cup chopped fresh basil
- ¼ cup chopped fresh parsley
- ¼ cup extra-virgin olive oil
- 2 tablespoons balsamic vinegar
- 1 small shallot, minced
  Salt and pepper

Combine all ingredients in bowl and season with salt and pepper to taste.

MILK-BRAISED PORK LOIN

WHY THIS RECIPE WORKS: Braising pork in milk is an Italian technique that produces moist pork paired with a rich, savory sauce. To maximize the pork loin roast's seasoning and moisture, we brined it in salt and sugar for 90 minutes. We wanted the sauce to be loaded with porky flavor, so we rendered salt pork (simmered in water to prevent burning) before introducing the roast to the pot. We browned the roast on all sides, removed it, and then began to build the sauce, stirring together milk, garlic cloves, and sage. Adding baking soda to the pot deepened the sauce's color and enriched its savory flavors. Once the sauce had thickened, we added the roast back to the pot and transferred it to a 275-degree oven. Adding white wine brightened the sauce, and we finished it with Dijon mustard for heat and parsley for a burst of freshness.

Milk-Braised Pork Loin

SERVES 4 TO 6

The milk will bubble up when added to the pot. If necessary, remove the pot from the heat and stir to break up the foam before returning it to the heat. We prefer natural pork, but if your pork is enhanced (injected with a salt solution; see page 181), do not brine. Instead, skip to step 2.

- Salt and pepper
- ¼ cup sugar
- 1 (2- to 2½-pound) boneless pork loin roast, trimmed
- 2 ounces salt pork, chopped coarse
- 3 cups whole milk
- 5 garlic cloves, peeled
- 1 teaspoon minced fresh sage
- ¼ teaspoon baking soda
- ½ cup dry white wine
- 3 tablespoons chopped fresh parsley
- 1 teaspoon Dijon mustard

1. Dissolve ¼ cup salt and sugar in 2 quarts cold water in large container. Submerge roast in brine, cover, and refrigerate for at least 1½ hours or up to 2 hours. Remove roast from brine and pat dry with paper towels.

2. Adjust oven rack to middle position and heat oven to 275 degrees. Bring salt pork and ½ cup water to simmer in Dutch oven over medium heat. Simmer until water evaporates and salt pork begins to sizzle, 5 to 6 minutes. Continue to cook, stirring frequently, until salt pork is lightly browned and fat has rendered, 2 to 3 minutes. Using slotted spoon, discard salt pork, leaving fat in pot.

3. Increase heat to medium-high, add roast to pot, and brown on all sides, 8 to 10 minutes. Transfer roast to large plate. Add milk, garlic, sage, and baking soda to pot and bring to simmer, scraping up any browned bits. Cook, stirring frequently, until milk is lightly browned and has consistency of heavy cream, 14 to 16 minutes. Reduce heat to medium-low and continue to cook, stirring and scraping bottom of pot constantly, until milk thickens to consistency of thin batter, 1 to 3 minutes longer. Remove pot from heat.

4. Return roast to pot, cover, and transfer to oven. Cook until meat registers 140 degrees, 40 to 50 minutes, flipping roast once halfway through cooking. Transfer roast to carving board, tent with aluminum foil, and let rest for 20 to 25 minutes.

5. Once roast has rested, pour any accumulated juices into pot. Add wine and return sauce to simmer over medium-high heat, whisking vigorously to smooth out sauce. Simmer until sauce has consistency of thin gravy, 2 to 3 minutes. Off heat, stir in 2 tablespoons parsley and mustard and season with salt and pepper to taste. Slice roast into ¼-inch-thick slices. Transfer slices to serving platter. Spoon sauce over slices, sprinkle with remaining 1 tablespoon parsley, and serve.

FRENCH-STYLE POT-ROASTED PORK LOIN

WHY THIS RECIPE WORKS: *Enchaud Perigordine* is a fancy name for what's actually a relatively simple French dish: slow-cooked pork loin. Cooked in the oven in a covered casserole dish, the roast turns out incredibly moist and flavorful, with a rich jus to accompany it. At least it does when it's prepared in France. But while pigs in France are bred to have plenty of fat, their American counterparts are lean, which translates to a bland and stringy roast. To improve the flavor and texture of our center-cut loin, we lowered the oven temperature (to 225 degrees) and removed the roast from the oven when it was medium-rare. Searing just three sides of the roast, rather than all four, prevented the bottom of the roast from overcooking from direct contact with the pot. Butterflying the pork allowed us to salt a maximum amount of surface area for a roast that was thoroughly seasoned throughout. And while we eliminated the hard-to-find trotter (or pig's foot), we added butter for richness while a sprinkling of gelatin lent body to the sauce.

French-Style Pot-Roasted Pork Loin

SERVES 4 TO 6

We strongly prefer the flavor of natural pork in this recipe, but enhanced pork (injected with a salt solution) can be used. If using enhanced pork, reduce the salt to 2 teaspoons (1 teaspoon per side) in step 2. The pork can be prepared through step 2, wrapped in plastic wrap, and refrigerated for up to 2 days.

- 2 tablespoons unsalted butter, cut into 2 pieces
- 6 medium garlic cloves, sliced thin
- 1 (2½-pound) boneless center-cut pork loin roast, trimmed
  Kosher salt and ground black pepper
- 1 teaspoon sugar
- 2 teaspoons herbes de Provence
- 2 tablespoons vegetable oil
- 1 Granny Smith apple, peeled, cored, and cut into ¼-inch pieces
- 1 medium onion, chopped fine
- ⅓ cup dry white wine
- 2 sprigs fresh thyme
- 1 bay leaf
- 1 tablespoon unflavored gelatin
- ¼–¾ cup low-sodium chicken broth
- 1 tablespoon chopped fresh parsley leaves

1. Adjust an oven rack to the lower-middle position and heat the oven to 225 degrees. Melt 1 tablespoon of the butter in an 8-inch skillet over medium-low heat. Add half of the garlic and cook, stirring frequently, until golden, 5 to 7 minutes. Transfer the mixture to a bowl and refrigerate while preparing the pork.

2. Following the photos, butterfly the pork loin. Sprinkle 1 tablespoon salt evenly over both sides of the loin (½ tablespoon per side) and thoroughly rub into the pork until the surface is slightly tacky. Sprinkle the sugar evenly over the inside of the loin and then spread with the cooled toasted garlic mixture. Fold the roast back together and tie tightly with kitchen twine at 1-inch intervals. Sprinkle the tied roast evenly with the herbes de Provence and season with pepper.

3. Heat 1 tablespoon of the oil in a large Dutch oven over medium heat until just smoking. Add the roast, fat side down, and brown on the top and sides (do not brown the bottom of the roast), 5 to 8 minutes. Transfer to a large plate. Add the remaining 1 tablespoon oil, the apple, and onion; cook, stirring frequently, until the onion is softened and browned, 5 to 7 minutes. Stir in the remaining sliced garlic and cook until fragrant, about 30 seconds. Stir in the wine, thyme, and bay leaf, and cook for 30 seconds. Return the roast, fat side up, to the pot; place a large sheet of foil over the pot and cover tightly with the lid. Transfer the pot to the oven and cook until the pork registers 140 degrees on an instant-read thermometer, 50 to 90 minutes

4. Transfer the roast to a carving board, tent loosely with foil, and let rest for 20 minutes. While the pork rests, sprinkle the gelatin over ¼ cup chicken broth and let sit until the gelatin softens, about 5 minutes. Remove and discard the thyme sprigs and bay leaf from the jus. Pour the jus into a 2-cup measuring cup and, if necessary, add chicken broth to measure 1¼ cups. Return the jus to the pot and bring to a simmer over medium heat. Whisk the softened gelatin mixture, the remaining 1 tablespoon butter, and the parsley into the jus and season with salt and pepper to taste; remove from the heat and cover to keep warm. Slice the pork into ½-inch-thick slices, adding any accumulated juices to the sauce. Serve the pork, passing the sauce separately.

NOTES FROM THE TEST KITCHEN

DOUBLE-BUTTERFLYING A ROAST

1. Holding a chef's knife parallel to the cutting board, insert the knife one-third of the way up from the bottom of the roast and cut horizontally, stopping ½ inch before the edge. Open up the flap.

2. Make another horizontal cut into the thicker portion of the roast. Open up this flap, smoothing out the butterflied rectangle of meat.

MAPLE-GLAZED PORK ROAST

WHY THIS RECIPE WORKS: Maple-glazed pork roast often falls short of its savory-sweet promise. Many roasts turn out dry, but the glazes often present even bigger problems. Most are too thin to coat the pork properly, some are too sweet, and few have a pronounced maple flavor. We wanted a glistening roast, which, when sliced, would combine the juices from tender, well-seasoned pork with a rich maple glaze to create complex flavor in every bite. For this dish we chose a blade-end loin roast, which has a deposit of fat that helps keep the meat moist. We tied it at intervals to make a neat bundle. Searing the roast first on the stovetop was a must for a flavorful exterior. We then removed the pork so that we could use the browned bits in the skillet to build the glaze. Maple syrup, with complementary spices and cayenne pepper for heat, made a thick, clingy glaze. Instead of brushing the glaze onto the pork, however, we decided to keep things simple and returned the pork to the skillet, rolled it in the glaze to coat it, and put the whole thing into the oven. The smaller area of the skillet kept the glaze from spreading out and burning, and the glaze reduced nicely while the roast cooked. Rolling the roast in the glaze periodically ensured even coverage and resulted in a tender, juicy roast.

Maple-Glazed Pork Roast

SERVES 4 TO 6

We prefer natural to enhanced pork (pork that has been injected with a salt solution to increase moisture and flavor) for this recipe. We prefer a nonstick ovensafe skillet because it is much easier to clean than a traditional one. Whichever you use, remember that the handle will be blistering hot when you take it out of the oven, so be sure to use a potholder or oven mitt. Note that you should not trim the pork of its thin layer of fat. This dish is unapologetically sweet, so we recommend side dishes that take well to the sweetness. Garlicky sautéed greens, braised cabbage, and soft polenta are good choices.

⅓ cup maple syrup, preferably grade B

⅛ teaspoon ground cinnamon

Pinch ground cloves

Pinch cayenne pepper

1 (2½-pound) boneless blade-end pork loin roast, tied at 1½-inch intervals (see note)

¾ teaspoon table salt

½ teaspoon ground black pepper

2 teaspoons vegetable oil

1. Adjust an oven rack to the middle position and heat the oven to 325 degrees. Stir the maple syrup, cinnamon, cloves, and cayenne together in a measuring cup or small bowl and set aside. Pat the roast dry with paper towels, then sprinkle evenly with the salt and pepper.

2. Heat the oil in a heavy-bottomed ovensafe 10-inch nonstick skillet over medium-high heat until just beginning to smoke, about 3 minutes. Place the roast, fat side down, in the skillet and cook until well browned, about 3 minutes. Using tongs, rotate the roast a quarter-turn and cook until well browned, about 2½ minutes; repeat until the roast is well browned on all sides. Transfer the roast to a large plate. Reduce the heat to medium and pour off the fat from the skillet; add the maple syrup mixture and cook until fragrant, about 30 seconds (the syrup will bubble immediately). Turn off the heat and return the roast to the skillet; using tongs, roll the roast to coat with the glaze on all sides.

3. Place the skillet in the oven and roast until the center of the pork registers 140 to 145 degrees on an instant-read thermometer, 35 to 45 minutes, using tongs to roll and spin the roast to coat with the glaze twice during the roasting time. Transfer the roast to a carving board; set the skillet aside to cool slightly to thicken the glaze, about 5 minutes. Pour the glaze over the roast and let rest for 15 minutes longer (the center of the loin should register 150 degrees on an instant-read thermometer). Remove the twine, cut the meat into ¼-inch slices, and serve immediately.

Maple-Glazed Pork Roast with Rosemary

Follow the recipe for Maple-Glazed Pork Roast, substituting 2 teaspoons minced fresh rosemary for the cinnamon, cloves, and cayenne.

Maple-Glazed Pork Roast with Orange Essence

Follow the recipe for Maple-Glazed Pork Roast, adding 1 tablespoon fresh grated orange zest to the maple syrup along with the spices.

Maple-Glazed Pork Roast with Star Anise

Follow the recipe for Maple-Glazed Pork Roast, adding 4 star anise pods to the maple syrup along with the spices.

Maple-Glazed Pork Roast with Smoked Paprika

Follow the recipe for Maple-Glazed Pork Roast, adding 2 teaspoons smoked hot paprika to the maple syrup along with the spices.

GARLIC-STUDDED ROAST PORK LOIN

WHY THIS RECIPE WORKS: Although it has a little more fat than pork tenderloin, a center loin pork roast is still quite lean and requires special handling to roast without drying out. We sought the best way to roast this cut so that the juices would remain inside the meat, not wind up on the carving board.

It turned out that a two-step roasting process was the key to juicy pork loin. After poking slivers of garlic into the meat and rubbing the surface with a mixture of thyme, cloves, salt, and pepper for extra flavor, we refrigerated the roast overnight. The next day we cranked up the oven to 475 degrees and added the pork directly from the fridge, leaving it in the oven for just half an hour before removing it. After we rested the roast, we returned it to the oven, this time at a lower temperature, to finish cooking. The texture of the meat was remarkably tender, and it had lost very little juice. The reason this method worked was that during the rest, the middle of the roast heated by conduction from the heat absorbed by the outside of the roast. When the meat went back into the oven, the center cooked through but the outside didn't overcook. A mustard-shallot sauce provides additional moisture and flavor.

Garlic-Studded Roast Pork Loin

SERVES 4 TO 6

We prefer natural to enhanced pork (pork that has been injected with a salt solution to increase moisture and flavor) for this recipe. For extra flavor and moisture, serve the sliced roast with the mustard-shallot sauce.

2 teaspoons dried thyme

2 teaspoons table salt

1 teaspoon ground black pepper

¼ teaspoon ground cloves or allspice

2 large garlic cloves, peeled and cut into slivers

1 (2¼-pound) boneless center loin pork roast, fat trimmed to about ⅛ inch thick and roast tied at 1½-inch intervals (see note)

1 recipe Mustard–Shallot Sauce with Thyme (optional; recipe follows)

1. Mix together the thyme, salt, pepper, and cloves. Coat the garlic slivers in the spice mixture. Poke slits in the roast with the point of a paring knife; insert the garlic slivers. Rub the remaining spice mixture onto the meat. Tie the roast with kitchen twine into a tight cylinder. Wrap the roast in plastic wrap and refrigerate for at least 2 hours or up to 24 hours.

2. Adjust an oven rack to the middle position and heat the oven to 475 degrees. Take the meat directly from the refrigerator, remove the plastic wrap, and place it on a wire rack set in a shallow roasting pan. Roast for exactly 30 minutes.

3. Remove the meat from the oven; immediately reduce the oven temperature to 325 degrees. Insert an instant-read thermometer at one end of the roast, going into the thickest part at the center (the temperature will range from 80 to 110 degrees); let the roast rest at room temperature, uncovered, for exactly

30 minutes. (At this point the roast's internal temperature will range from 115 to 140 degrees.) After this 30-minute rest, remove the thermometer, return the meat to the oven, and roast until the thickest part of the roast reaches an internal temperature of 140 to 145 degrees, 15 to 30 minutes longer, depending on the roast's internal temperature at the end of the resting period. Since the roast may cook unevenly, take temperature readings from a couple of locations, each time plunging the thermometer into the center of the meat and waiting 15 seconds.

4. Let the roast stand at room temperature, uncovered, for 15 to 20 minutes to finish cooking. (The temperature should register 150 degrees.) Remove the twine, slice the meat thin, and serve with the sauce (if using).

Mustard–Shallot Sauce with Thyme

MAKES ABOUT 1 CUP

Start making the sauce as soon as the roast comes out of the oven for the second time. Use a grainy, or country-style, mustard in this recipe. For extra body and richness, swirl another tablespoon or two of softened butter into the finished sauce.

- 2 tablespoons unsalted butter (see note)
- 4 medium shallots, minced (about ¾ cup)
- ¾ cup dry white wine or dry vermouth
- 1 cup low-sodium chicken broth
- ¾ teaspoon minced fresh thyme leaves or ¼ teaspoon dried thyme, crumbled
- ¼ cup whole grain mustard (see note)

Melt the butter in a medium skillet over medium-high heat. Add the shallots and sauté until softened, 3 to 4 minutes. Add the wine and boil until nearly evaporated, 8 to 10 minutes. Add the broth and thyme; boil until reduced by one third, about 5 minutes. Remove the pan from the heat and stir in the mustard. Serve immediately.

PORCHETTA

WHY THIS RECIPE WORKS: As a substitute for the traditional whole pig, we opted for easy-to-find pork butt (over pork belly or a pork belly–wrapped pork loin) since it cooked up evenly and offered the right balance of meat and fatty richness. To season and flavor the porchetta thoroughly and evenly, we cut slits in the meat every few inches; coated it with salt and an intensely flavored paste of garlic, rosemary, thyme, and fennel seeds; and let it sit overnight in the refrigerator. For quicker cooking and more presentable slices, we cut the roast into two pieces and tied each into a compact cylinder. We used a two-stage cooking method: First, we covered the roasting pan with foil, which trapped steam to cook the meat evenly and more quickly and also helped keep the meat moist. We then uncovered the pan and returned it to a 500-degree oven to brown and crisp the outer layer of the roasts. For the best layer of crisp "skin" on the tops of the roasts, we cut a crosshatch in the fat cap and rubbed it with a mixture of salt, pepper, and baking soda at the same time we applied the paste to help dry it out.

Porchetta

SERVES 8 TO 10

Pork butt roast is often labeled Boston butt in the supermarket. Look for a roast with a substantial fat cap. If fennel seeds are unavailable, substitute ¼ cup of ground fennel. The porchetta needs to be refrigerated for 6 to 24 hours once it is rubbed with the paste, but it is best when it sits for a full 24 hours.

- 3 tablespoons fennel seeds
- ½ cup fresh rosemary leaves (2 bunches)
- ¼ cup fresh thyme leaves (2 bunches)
- 12 garlic cloves, peeled
   Kosher salt and pepper
- ½ cup extra-virgin olive oil
- 1 (5- to 6-pound) boneless pork butt roast, trimmed
- ¼ teaspoon baking soda

1. Grind fennel seeds in spice grinder or mortar and pestle until finely ground. Transfer ground fennel to food processor and add rosemary, thyme, garlic, 1 tablespoon pepper, and 2 teaspoons salt. Pulse mixture until finely chopped, 10 to 15 pulses. Add oil and process until smooth paste forms, 20 to 30 seconds.

2. Using sharp knife, cut slits in surface fat of roast, spaced 1 inch apart, in crosshatch pattern, being careful not to cut into meat. Cut roast in half with grain into 2 equal pieces.

3. Turn each roast on its side so fat cap is facing away from you, bottom of roast is facing toward you, and newly cut side is facing up. Starting 1 inch from short end of each roast, use boning or paring knife to make slit that starts 1 inch from top of roast and ends 1 inch from bottom, pushing knife completely through roast. Repeat making slits, spaced 1 to 1½ inches apart, along length of each roast, stopping 1 inch from opposite end (you should have 6 to 8 slits, depending on size of roast).

4. Turn each roast so fat cap is facing down. Rub sides and bottom of each roast with 2 teaspoons salt, taking care to work salt into slits from both sides. Rub herb paste onto sides and bottom of each roast, taking care to work paste into slits from both sides. Flip each roast so that fat cap is facing up. Using 3 pieces of kitchen twine per roast, tie each roast into compact cylinder.

5. Combine 1 tablespoon salt, 1 teaspoon pepper, and baking soda in small bowl. Rub fat cap of each roast with salt–baking soda mixture, taking care to work mixture into crosshatches. Transfer roasts to wire rack set in rimmed baking sheet and refrigerate, uncovered, for at least 6 hours or up to 24 hours.

6. Adjust oven rack to middle position and heat oven to 325 degrees. Transfer roasts, fat side up, to large roasting pan, leaving at least 2 inches between roasts. Cover tightly with aluminum foil. Cook until pork registers 180 degrees, 2 to 2½ hours.

7. Remove pan from oven and increase oven temperature to 500 degrees. Carefully remove and discard foil and transfer roasts to large plate. Discard liquid in pan. Line pan with foil. Remove twine from roasts; return roasts to pan, directly on foil; and return pan to oven. Cook until exteriors of roasts are well browned and interiors register 190 degrees, 20 to 30 minutes.

8. Transfer roasts to carving board and let rest for 20 minutes. Slice roasts ½ inch thick, transfer to serving platter, and serve.

TUSCAN-STYLE ROAST PORK WITH GARLIC AND ROSEMARY

WHY THIS RECIPE WORKS: The Tuscan roast pork dish known as *arista* promises to turn lean, mild pork loin into a juicy roast flavored with plenty of garlic and rosemary and featuring a deeply browned crust. Yet most versions turn out dry and bland. To boost both flavor and juiciness, we salted the meat for 1 hour before cooking, using a double-butterfly technique to expose plenty of surface area and then salting both sides and rolling it back up. This technique also allowed us to maximize the distribution of the garlic and rosemary. Briefly simmering the herb-garlic mixture before spreading it over the pork tempered any raw flavors, and using plenty of oil (which we then strained off) and a nonstick skillet kept the garlic from browning, for a fresher garlic flavor. To boost richness and enhance the overall porky flavor, we processed pancetta with the garlic and rosemary (plus red pepper flakes and lemon zest for brightness) to make a paste. Using a low oven ensured that the meat was evenly cooked from edge to center. And instead of roasting, browning, and then resting the roast under foil, we let it rest after it came out of the oven and then browned it and served it immediately; this approach helped keep the crust crispy. For a finishing touch, we made a simple, bright, rich sauce by combining the reserved strained oil with the juice from a halved lemon that we quickly caramelized in the skillet for more complex flavor.

Tuscan-Style Roast Pork with Garlic and Rosemary (Arista)

SERVES 4 TO 6

We strongly prefer natural pork in this recipe, but if enhanced pork (injected with a salt solution; see page 181) is used, reduce the salt to 2 teaspoons (1 teaspoon per side) in step 3. After applying the seasonings, the pork needs to rest, refrigerated, for 1 hour before cooking.

    1   lemon
    ⅓   cup extra-virgin olive oil
    8   garlic cloves, minced
    ¼   teaspoon red pepper flakes
    1   tablespoon chopped fresh rosemary
    2   ounces pancetta, cut into ½-inch pieces
    1   (2½-pound) center-cut boneless pork
        loin roast, trimmed
        Kosher salt

1. Finely grate 1 teaspoon zest from lemon. Cut lemon in half and reserve. Combine lemon zest, oil, garlic, and pepper flakes in 10-inch nonstick skillet. Cook over medium-low heat, stirring frequently, until garlic is sizzling, about 3 minutes. Add rosemary and cook, about 30 seconds. Strain mixture through fine-mesh strainer set over bowl, pushing on garlic-rosemary mixture to extract oil. Set oil aside and let garlic-rosemary mixture cool. Using paper towels, wipe out skillet.

2. Process pancetta in food processor until smooth paste forms, 20 to 30 seconds, scraping down sides of bowl as needed. Add garlic-rosemary mixture and continue to process until mixture is homogeneous, 20 to 30 seconds longer, scraping down sides of bowl as needed.

3. Position roast fat side up. Insert knife one-third of way up from bottom of roast along 1 long side and cut horizontally, stopping ½ inch before edge. Open up flap. Keeping knife parallel to cutting board, cut through thicker portion of roast about ½ inch from bottom of roast, keeping knife level with first cut and stopping about ½ inch before edge. Open up this flap. If uneven, cover with plastic wrap and use meat pounder to even out. Sprinkle 1 tablespoon salt over both sides of roast (½ tablespoon per side) and rub into meat to adhere. Spread inside of roast evenly with pancetta-garlic paste, leaving about ¼-inch border on all sides. Starting from short side, roll roast (keeping fat on outside) and tie with twine at 1-inch intervals. Set wire rack in rimmed baking sheet and spray with vegetable oil spray. Set roast fat side up on prepared rack and refrigerate for 1 hour.

4. Adjust oven rack to middle position and heat oven to 275 degrees. Transfer roast to oven and cook until meat registers 135 degrees, 1½ to 2 hours. Remove roast from oven, tent with aluminum foil, and let rest for 20 minutes.

5. Heat 1 teaspoon reserved oil in now-empty skillet over high heat until just smoking. Add reserved lemon halves, cut side down, and cook until softened and cut surfaces are browned, 3 to 4 minutes. Transfer lemon halves to small plate.

6. Pat roast dry with paper towels. Heat 2 tablespoons reserved oil in now-empty skillet over high heat until just smoking. Brown roast on fat side and sides (do not brown bottom of roast), 4 to 6 minutes. Transfer roast to carving board and remove twine.

7. Once lemon halves are cool enough to handle, squeeze into fine-mesh strainer set over bowl. Press on solids to extract all pulp; discard solids. Whisk 2 tablespoons strained lemon juice into bowl with remaining reserved oil. Slice roast into ¼-inch-thick slices and serve, passing vinaigrette separately.

SLOW-ROASTED BONE-IN PORK RIB ROAST

WHY THIS RECIPE WORKS: A center-cut pork rib roast has a lot of potential: Some butchers call it the "pork equivalent of prime rib." Treated right, it can be truly impressive: moist, tender, and full of rich, meaty taste—and for far less money than a prime rib costs. We set out to make this cut worthy of an elegant holiday table.

To start, we pretreated the pork with a salt–brown sugar rub. The salt seasoned the meat and drew moisture into the flesh, helping to keep it juicy. The brown sugar contributed deep molasses notes and a gorgeous mahogany color, which allowed us to skip tedious searing. We also removed the bones from the meat so we could season it from all sides, then tied it back onto the bones to roast. Since heat travels more slowly through bone than through flesh, the bones helped keep the center of the roast moist. Another plus was that the finished roast, free of bones, was easier to carve. Scoring deep crosshatch marks into the fat with a sharp knife helped it melt and baste the meat during roasting. Cooking the roast in a gentle 250-degree oven ensured that the pork was evenly cooked all the way through. We crisped up the fat by blasting the roast

under the broiler for a couple of minutes just prior to serving. As a finishing touch, a classic beurre rouge sauce, made with tawny port and balsamic vinegar and studded with plump dried cherries, balanced the meaty roast with echoes of fruit and herbs.

Slow-Roasted Bone-In Pork Rib Roast
SERVES 6 TO 8
This recipe requires refrigerating the salted meat for at least 6 hours before cooking. For easier carving, ask the butcher to remove the chine bone. Monitoring the roast with an oven probe thermometer is best. If you use an instant-read thermometer, open the oven door as infrequently as possible and remove the roast from the oven while taking its temperature. The sauce may be prepared in advance or while the roast rests in step 3.

- 1 (4- to 5-pound) center-cut bone-in pork rib roast, chine bone removed
- 2 tablespoons packed dark brown sugar
- 1 tablespoon kosher salt
- 1½ teaspoons pepper
- 1 recipe Port Wine–Cherry Sauce (recipe follows)

1. Using sharp knife, remove roast from bones, running knife down length of bones and following contours as closely as possible. Reserve bones. Combine sugar and salt in small bowl. Pat roast dry with paper towels. If necessary, trim thick spots of surface fat layer to about ¼-inch thickness. Using sharp knife, cut slits, spaced 1 inch apart and in crosshatch pattern, in surface fat layer, being careful not to cut into meat. Rub roast evenly with sugar mixture. Wrap roast and ribs in plastic wrap and refrigerate for at least 6 hours or up to 24 hours.

2. Adjust oven rack to lower-middle position and heat oven to 250 degrees. Sprinkle roast evenly with pepper. Place roast back on ribs so bones fit where they were cut; tie roast to bones with lengths of kitchen twine between ribs. Transfer roast, fat side up, to wire rack set in rimmed baking sheet. Roast until meat registers 145 degrees, 3 to 4 hours.

3. Remove roast from oven (leave roast on sheet), tent loosely with aluminum foil, and let rest for 30 minutes.

4. Adjust oven rack 8 inches from broiler element and heat broiler. Return roast to oven and broil until top of roast is well browned and crispy, 2 to 6 minutes.

5. Transfer roast to carving board; cut twine and remove meat from ribs. Slice meat into ¾-inch-thick slices and serve, passing sauce separately.

Port Wine–Cherry Sauce

MAKES ABOUT 1¾ CUPS

- 2 cups tawny port
- 1 cup dried cherries
- ½ cup balsamic vinegar
- 4 sprigs fresh thyme, plus 2 teaspoons minced
- 2 shallots, minced
- ¼ cup heavy cream
- 16 tablespoons unsalted butter, cut into ½-inch pieces and chilled
- 1 teaspoon salt
- ½ teaspoon pepper

1. Combine port and cherries in bowl and microwave until steaming, 1 to 2 minutes. Cover and let stand until plump, about 10 minutes. Strain port through fine-mesh strainer into medium saucepan, reserving cherries.

2. Add vinegar, thyme sprigs, and shallots to port and bring to boil over high heat. Reduce heat to medium-high and reduce mixture until it measures ¾ cup, 14 to 16 minutes. Add cream and reduce again to ¾ cup, about 5 minutes. Discard thyme sprigs. Off heat, whisk in butter, a few pieces at a time, until fully incorporated. Stir in cherries, minced thyme, salt, and pepper. Cover pan and hold, off heat, until serving. Alternatively, let sauce cool completely and refrigerate for up to 2 days. Reheat in small saucepan over medium-low heat, stirring frequently, until warm.

SLOW-COOKER PORK LOIN

WHY THIS RECIPE WORKS: Cooking a lean roast like a pork loin in a slow cooker is tricky because it can quickly turn overcooked and dry. The key to this recipe was to monitor the temperature of the roast after a few hours and take it out of the slow cooker as soon as it reached 145 degrees. Whether you're cooking a pork loin in the oven or the slow cooker, pairing the lean meat with a sauce gives it a lot more appeal. We paired our loin with both dried cranberries and whole canned cranberries. Cinnamon, orange juice, and orange zest livened up our easy-to-make sauce, which goes directly into the slow cooker. After cooking the loin, we reduced the braising liquid until it became a sweet sauce that paired perfectly with our juicy pork loin.

Slow-Cooker Pork Loin with Cranberries and Orange

SERVES 6

When choosing a pork loin, we prefer the blade-end—be sure to choose a fatter, shorter loin over a longer, skinnier one. Use a vegetable peeler to remove wide strips of zest from the orange. Make sure to trim any white pith from the zest, as it can impart a bitter flavor.

- 1 (4½- to 5-pound) boneless pork loin roast, trimmed and tied at 1-inch intervals
  Table salt and ground black pepper
- 1 tablespoon vegetable oil
- 1 (14-ounce) can whole berry cranberry sauce
- ½ cup dried cranberries
- ½ cup juice and 3 (3-inch-long) strips zest from 1 orange
- ⅛ teaspoon ground cinnamon

1. Dry the pork with paper towels and season with salt and pepper. Heat the oil in a 12-inch skillet over medium-high heat until just smoking. Brown the pork well on all sides, 7 to 10 minutes.

2. Stir the cranberry sauce, cranberries, orange juice, orange zest, and cinnamon into the slow cooker. Nestle the browned pork into the slow cooker. Cover and cook until the pork is tender and registers 140 to 145 degrees on an instant-read thermometer, about 4 hours on low.

3. Transfer the pork to a cutting board, tent loosely with aluminum foil, and let rest for 10 minutes. Let the braising liquid settle for 5 minutes, then remove the fat from the surface using a large spoon. Discard the orange zest. Transfer the braising liquid to a saucepan and simmer until reduced to 2 cups, about 12 minutes. Season with salt and pepper to taste.

4. Remove the twine from the pork, slice into ½-inch-thick slices, and arrange on a serving platter. Spoon 1 cup sauce over the meat and serve with the remaining sauce.

SLOW-ROASTED PORK SHOULDER

WHY THIS RECIPE WORKS: Although most modern pork is leaner than it used to be, this is not true of every cut. We wanted to celebrate the glories of rich old-fashioned pork with the shoulder roast (also called Boston butt or pork butt). This tough cut is loaded with intramuscular fat that builds flavor and bastes the meat during roasting; outside, its thick fat cap renders to a bronze, bacon-like crust. Plus, at around $2 per pound, the shoulder offers value.

First, we salted the meat overnight—a technique we frequently use with large, tough roasts for improved texture and flavor. This helped, but to improve the roast's flavor even more, we turned to an idea taken from Chinese barbecued pork, where the meat is rubbed with a salt and sugar rub (we preferred brown sugar over white for its subtle molasses flavor and hints of caramel). As we hoped, the sugar caramelized and helped crisp the fat cap, giving it a bronze hue. For an accompanying sauce, peaches, white wine, sugar, vinegar, and a couple of sprigs of fresh thyme added to the drippings and then reduced delivered on all fronts. To round out the sweetness, we finished it with a spoonful of whole grain mustard.

Slow-Roasted Pork Shoulder with Peach Sauce
SERVES 8 TO 12

We prefer natural pork to enhanced pork (pork that has been injected with a salt solution to increase moistness and flavor), though both will work in this recipe. Add more water to the roasting pan as necessary during the last hours of cooking to prevent the fond from burning.

PORK ROAST
- 1 (6- to 8-pound) bone-in pork butt (see note)
- ⅓ cup kosher salt
- ⅓ cup packed light brown sugar
- Ground black pepper

PEACH SAUCE
- 10 ounces frozen peaches, cut into 1-inch chunks (about 2 cups) or 2 fresh peaches cut into ½-inch wedges
- 2 cups dry white wine
- ½ cup granulated sugar

- ¼ cup plus 1 tablespoon unseasoned rice vinegar
- 2 sprigs fresh thyme
- 1 tablespoon whole grain mustard

1. FOR THE ROAST: Using a sharp knife, cut slits 1 inch apart in the fat cap of the roast in a crosshatch pattern, being careful not to cut into the meat. Combine the salt and brown sugar in a medium bowl. Rub the salt mixture over the entire pork shoulder and into the slits. Wrap the roast tightly in a double layer of plastic wrap, place on a rimmed baking sheet, and refrigerate for at least 12 hours or up to 24 hours.

2. Adjust an oven rack to the lowest position and heat the oven to 325 degrees. Unwrap the roast and brush off any excess salt mixture from the surface. Season the roast with pepper. Transfer the roast to a V-rack coated with vegetable oil spray set in a large roasting pan. Add 1 quart water to the roasting pan.

3. Cook the roast, basting twice during cooking, until the meat is extremely tender and an instant-read thermometer inserted into the roast near, but not touching, the bone registers 190 degrees, 5 to 6 hours. Transfer the roast to a carving board and let rest, loosely tented with foil, for 1 hour. Transfer the liquid in the roasting pan to a fat separator and let stand for 5 minutes. Pour off ¼ cup jus and reserve, then discard any remaining jus and fat.

4. FOR THE SAUCE: Bring the peaches, wine, granulated sugar, ¼ cup of the vinegar, the reserved defatted jus, and the thyme to a simmer in a small saucepan; cook, stirring occasionally, until reduced to 2 cups, about 30 minutes. Stir in the remaining 1 tablespoon vinegar and the mustard. Remove the thyme sprigs, cover the pan, and keep warm.

5. Using a sharp paring knife, cut around the inverted T-shaped bone, until it can be pulled free from the roast (use a clean kitchen towel to grasp the bone). Using a serrated knife, slice the roast. Serve, passing the sauce separately.

INDOOR PULLED PORK

WHY THIS RECIPE WORKS: In recipes, the phrase "indoor barbecue" is usually code for "braised in a Dutch oven with bottled barbecue sauce." Unfortunately, this results in mushy, waterlogged meat and candy-sweet sauce. We wanted moist, tender, shreddable meat with deep smoke flavor all the way through, plus a dark, richly seasoned crust, often referred to as bark.

Be it indoor or outdoor, with barbecue a good amount of fat is necessary for moisture and flavor, so we chose to use boneless Boston butt because of its high level of marbling. To mimic the moist heat of a covered grill, we came up with a dual cooking method: covering the pork for part of the oven time to speed up cooking and keep it moist, then uncovering it for the remainder of the time to help the meat develop a crust.

To achieve smoky flavor without an actual barbecue pit, we turned to liquid smoke, a natural product derived from condensing the moist smoke of smoldering wood chips. We found that adding it to our brine infused it with smoky flavor without tasting unnatural. For even more smokiness, we employed a dry rub and a wet rub, which we also fortified with smoky flavorings. To serve alongside our pork, we developed three sauces inspired by the variety of barbecue regions and styles: a classic sweet and tangy sauce, a vinegar sauce, and a mustard sauce, all of which we flavored with some of the pork's defatted cooking liquid.

Indoor Pulled Pork with Sweet and Tangy Barbecue Sauce

SERVES 6 TO 8

Sweet paprika may be substituted for smoked paprika. Covering the pork with parchment and then foil prevents the acidic mustard from eating holes in the foil. Serve the pork on hamburger rolls with pickle chips and thinly sliced onion. In place of the Sweet and Tangy Barbecue Sauce or the variations that follow, you can use 2 cups of your favorite barbecue sauce thinned with ½ cup of the defatted pork cooking liquid in step 5. The shredded and sauced pork can be cooled, tightly covered, and refrigerated for up to 2 days. Reheat it gently before serving.

PORK

- 1 cup plus 2 teaspoons table salt
- ½ cup plus 2 tablespoons sugar
- 3 tablespoons plus 2 teaspoons liquid smoke
- 1 5-pound boneless pork butt roast, cut in half horizontally
- ¼ cup yellow mustard
- 2 tablespoons ground black pepper
- 2 tablespoons smoked paprika (see note)
- 1 teaspoon cayenne pepper

SWEET AND TANGY BARBECUE SAUCE

- 1½ cups ketchup
- ¼ cup light or mild molasses
- 2 tablespoons Worcestershire sauce
- 1 tablespoon hot sauce
- ½ teaspoon table salt
- ½ teaspoon ground black pepper

1. FOR THE PORK: Dissolve 1 cup of the salt, ½ cup of the sugar, and 3 tablespoons of the liquid smoke in 1 gallon cold water in a large container. Submerge the pork in the brine, cover with plastic wrap, and refrigerate for 2 hours.

2. While the pork brines, combine the mustard and remaining 2 teaspoons liquid smoke in a small bowl; set aside. Combine the black pepper, paprika, remaining 2 tablespoons sugar, remaining 2 teaspoons salt, and cayenne in a second small bowl; set aside. Adjust an oven rack to the lower-middle position and heat the oven to 325 degrees.

3. Remove the pork from the brine and dry thoroughly with paper towels. Rub the mustard mixture over the entire surface of each piece of pork. Sprinkle the entire surface of each piece with the spice mixture. Place the pork on a wire rack set over a foil-lined rimmed baking sheet. Place a piece of parchment paper over the pork, then cover with a sheet of aluminum foil, sealing the edges to prevent moisture from escaping. Roast the pork for 3 hours.

NOTES FROM THE TEST KITCHEN

CUTTING A PORK BUTT IN HALF

Halving the pork increases its surface area, which creates more flavorful bark. Holding your knife parallel to the cutting board, press one hand flat against the top of the pork while cutting horizontally.

4. Remove the pork from the oven; remove and discard the foil and parchment. Carefully pour off the liquid in the bottom of the baking sheet into a fat separator and reserve for the sauce. Return the pork to the oven and cook, uncovered, until well browned, tender, and the center of the roast registers 200 degrees on an instant-read thermometer, about 1½ hours. Transfer the pork to a serving dish, tent loosely with foil, and let rest for 20 minutes.

5. FOR THE SAUCE: While the pork rests, pour ½ cup of the defatted cooking liquid from the fat separator into a medium bowl; whisk in the sauce ingredients.

6. Using two forks, shred the pork into bite-size pieces. Toss with 1 cup sauce and season with salt and pepper to taste. Serve, passing the remaining sauce separately.

Lexington Vinegar Barbecue Sauce
MAKES ABOUT 2½ CUPS

- 1 cup cider vinegar
- ½ cup ketchup
- ½ cup water
- 1 tablespoon sugar
- ¾ teaspoon table salt
- ¾ teaspoon red pepper flakes
- ½ teaspoon ground black pepper

Combine all the ingredients in a medium bowl with ½ cup of the defatted cooking liquid in step 5 and whisk to combine.

South Carolina Mustard Barbecue Sauce
MAKES ABOUT 2½ CUPS

- 1 cup yellow mustard
- ½ cup white vinegar
- ¼ cup packed light brown sugar
- ¼ cup Worcestershire sauce
- 2 tablespoons hot sauce
- 1 teaspoon table salt
- 1 teaspoon ground black pepper

Combine all the ingredients in a medium bowl with ½ cup of the defatted cooking liquid in step 5 and whisk to combine.

ROAST FRESH HAM

WHY THIS RECIPE WORKS: Fresh ham is not cured like a Smithfield ham or salted and air-dried like prosciutto. It's not pressed or molded like a canned ham, and it's not smoked like a country ham. In fact, some people think there's no such thing as "fresh" ham. There is—and we wanted to find the best way to cook it for a roasted ham that boasted rich, moist meat and crackling crisp skin.

Fresh hams are large, so they're usually cut in half and sold as either the sirloin or the shank end; we chose the latter for its ease of carving. But even cut into these smaller roasts, fresh ham needs a long time in the oven, so the danger is drying out the meat. To prevent this, we brined our ham overnight. A garlic and herb rub added further flavor. We positioned the ham face down on a rack in a roasting pan; the rack allowed the heat to circulate all around the ham for more even cooking. A brief roasting at a high temperature followed by longer cooking at a lower temperature produced crunchy skin and succulent meat. The crowning touch was a sweet glaze, which we brushed on periodically while the meat roasted.

Roast Fresh Ham
SERVES 8 TO 10

Fresh ham comes from the pig's hind leg. Because a whole leg is quite large, it is usually cut into two sections. The sirloin, or butt, end is harder to carve than our favorite, the shank end. If you don't have room in your refrigerator, brine the ham in an insulated cooler or a small plastic garbage can; add five or six freezer packs to the brine to keep it well cooled.

ROAST
- 1 (6- to 8-pound) bone-in fresh half ham with skin, preferably shank end, rinsed (see note)

BRINE
- 3 cups packed brown sugar
- 2 cups table salt
- 2 heads garlic, cloves separated, lightly crushed and peeled
- 10 bay leaves
- ½ cup black peppercorns, crushed

GARLIC AND HERB RUB

- 1 cup lightly packed fresh sage leaves
- ½ cup parsley leaves
- ¼ cup olive oil
- 8 medium garlic cloves, peeled
- ½ tablespoon ground black pepper
- 1½ teaspoons table salt

GLAZE

- 1 recipe glaze (recipes follow)

1. FOR THE ROAST: Carefully slice through the skin and fat with a serrated knife, making a 1-inch diamond pattern. Be careful not to cut into the meat.

2. FOR THE BRINE: In a large container, dissolve the brown sugar and salt in 2 gallons cold water. Add the garlic, bay leaves, and crushed peppercorns. Submerge the ham in the brine and refrigerate for 8 to 24 hours.

3. Set a large disposable aluminum roasting pan on a baking sheet for extra support; place a flat wire rack in the roasting pan. Remove the ham from the brine; rinse under cold water and dry thoroughly with paper towels. Place the ham, wide cut side down, on the rack. (If using the sirloin end, place the ham skin side up.) Let the ham stand, uncovered, at room temperature for 1 hour.

4. FOR THE RUB: Meanwhile, adjust an oven rack to the lowest position and heat the oven to 500 degrees. Process the sage, parsley, oil, garlic, pepper, and salt in a food processor until the mixture forms a smooth paste, about 30 seconds. Rub all sides of the ham with the paste.

5. Roast the ham at 500 degrees for 20 minutes. Reduce the oven temperature to 350 degrees and continue to roast, brushing the ham with the glaze every 45 minutes, until the center of the ham registers 145 to 150 degrees on an instant-read thermometer, about 2½ hours longer. Remove from the oven and tent the ham loosely with foil and let stand until the center of the ham registers 155 to 160 degrees, 30 to 40 minutes. Carve and serve.

Cider and Brown Sugar Glaze
MAKES ABOUT 1⅓ CUPS

- 1 cup apple cider
- 2 cups packed brown sugar
- 5 whole cloves

Bring the cider, brown sugar, and cloves to a boil in a small saucepan over high heat; reduce the heat to medium-low and simmer until syrupy and reduced to about 1⅓ cups, 5 to 7 minutes. (The glaze will thicken as it cools between bastings; cook over medium heat for about 1 minute, stirring once or twice, before using.)

Spicy Pineapple-Ginger Glaze
MAKES ABOUT 1⅓ CUPS

- 1 cup pineapple juice
- 2 cups packed brown sugar
- 1 (1-inch) piece fresh ginger, grated (about 1 tablespoon)
- 1 tablespoon red pepper flakes

Bring the pineapple juice, brown sugar, ginger, and red pepper flakes to a boil in a small saucepan over high heat; reduce the heat to medium-low and simmer until syrupy and reduced to about 1⅓ cups, 5 to 7 minutes. (The glaze will thicken as it cools between bastings; cook over medium heat about for 1 minute, stirring once or twice, before using.)

Coca-Cola Glaze with Lime and Jalapeño
MAKES ABOUT 1⅓ CUPS

- 1 cup Coca-Cola
- ¼ cup juice from 2 limes
- 2 cups packed brown sugar
- 2 medium jalapeño chiles, cut crosswise into ¼-inch-thick slices

Bring the Coca-Cola, lime juice, brown sugar, and jalapeños to a boil in a small nonreactive saucepan over high heat; reduce the heat to medium-low and simmer until syrupy and reduced to about 1⅓ cups, 5 to 7 minutes. (The glaze will thicken as it cools between bastings; heat over medium heat for about 1 minute, stirring once or twice, before using.)

Orange, Cinnamon, and Star Anise Glaze
MAKES ABOUT 1⅓ CUPS

- 1 cup juice plus 1 tablespoon grated zest from 2 large oranges
- 2 cups packed brown sugar
- 4 pods star anise
- 1 (3-inch) cinnamon stick

Bring the orange juice, zest, brown sugar, star anise, and cinnamon stick to a boil in a small nonreactive saucepan over high heat; reduce the heat to medium-low and simmer until syrupy and reduced to about 1⅓ cups, 5 to 7 minutes. (The glaze will thicken as it cools between bastings; cook over medium heat for about 1 minute, stirring once or twice, before using.)

GLAZED HOLIDAY HAM

WHY THIS RECIPE WORKS: Nothing could be easier than heating up a cured ham, right? Well, we've made enough of them to know that as easy as it may be, the results are often leathery meat with an overly sweet glaze. We wanted to revisit the way to cook this roast to get moist meat accompanied by a glaze that didn't overwhelm it.

We have found that bone-in hams, labeled "with natural juices," have the best flavor, and spiral-sliced ones make carving a cinch. We knew that the longer the ham spent in the oven, the greater the chances we'd end up with dried-out meat, so we focused on reducing the cooking time. First we soaked the ham in hot water so that it wouldn't be ice-cold when it went into the oven; this step saved a full hour. Roasting the ham in an oven bag further reduced the cooking time, and using the bag had the added advantage of holding in moisture. For the glaze, we threw out the packet that came with our ham and made a fruit-based glaze with just a touch of sweetness to complement the moist, tender meat. This foolproof method will make the perfect holiday ham every time.

Glazed Spiral-Sliced Ham

SERVES 12 TO 14

You can bypass the 90-minute soaking time, but the heating time will increase to 18 to 20 minutes per pound for a cold ham. If there is a tear or hole in the ham's inner covering, wrap the ham in several layers of plastic wrap before soaking it in hot water. Instead of using the plastic oven bag, the ham may be placed cut side down in the roasting pan and covered tightly with foil, but you will need to add 3 to 4 minutes per pound to the heating time. If using an oven bag, be sure to cut slits in the bag so it does not burst.

1 (7- to 10-pound) spiral-sliced bone-in half ham
1 large plastic oven bag (see note)
1 recipe glaze (recipes follow)

1. Leaving the ham's inner plastic or foil covering intact, place the ham in a large container and cover with hot tap water; set aside for 45 minutes. Drain and cover again with hot tap water; set aside for another 45 minutes.

2. Adjust an oven rack to the lowest position and heat the oven to 250 degrees. Unwrap the ham; remove and discard the plastic disk covering the bone. Place the ham in the oven bag. Gather the top of the bag tightly so the bag fits snugly around the ham, tie the bag, and trim the excess plastic. Set the ham, cut side down, in a large roasting pan and cut four slits in the top of the bag with a paring knife.

3. Bake the ham until the center registers 100 degrees on an instant-read thermometer, 1 to 1½ hours (about 10 minutes per pound).

4. Remove the ham from the oven and increase the oven temperature to 350 degrees. Cut open the oven bag and roll back the sides to expose the ham. Brush the ham with one-third of the glaze and return to the oven until the glaze becomes sticky, about 10 minutes (if the glaze is too thick to brush, return it to the heat to loosen).

5. Remove the ham from the oven, transfer it to a carving board, and brush the entire ham with another third of the glaze. Let the ham rest, loosely tented with foil, for 15 minutes. While the ham rests, heat the remaining third of the glaze with 4 to 6 tablespoons of the ham juices until it forms a thick but fluid sauce. Carve and serve the ham, passing the sauce at the table.

Maple-Orange Glaze

MAKES 1 CUP

¾ cup maple syrup
½ cup orange marmalade
2 tablespoons unsalted butter
1 tablespoon Dijon mustard
1 teaspoon ground black pepper
¼ teaspoon ground cinnamon

Combine all the ingredients in a small saucepan. Cook over medium heat, stirring occasionally, until the mixture is thick, syrupy, and reduced to 1 cup, 5 to 10 minutes; set aside.

Cherry-Port Glaze

MAKES 1 CUP

½ cup ruby port
½ cup cherry preserves
1 cup packed dark brown sugar
1 teaspoon ground black pepper

Simmer the port in a small saucepan over medium heat until reduced to 2 tablespoons, about 5 minutes. Add the remaining ingredients and cook, stirring occasionally, until the sugar dissolves and the mixture is thick, syrupy, and reduced to 1 cup, 5 to 10 minutes; set aside.

CHAPTER 10

FAVORITE WAYS WITH FISH

SUPER-CRISPY OVEN-FRIED FISH

WHY THIS RECIPE WORKS: The golden brown coating and moist, flaky flesh of batter-fried fish come at a price: the oil. Cooks have turned to the oven to avoid the bother of deep-fat frying, but oven-frying often falls short. The coating never gets very crisp and the fish usually ends up overcooked. We aimed to put the crunch back into oven-frying.

We used thick fillets so that the fish and coating would finish cooking at the same time. Flaky cod and haddock provided the best contrast to the crunchy exterior we envisioned. A conventional bound breading—flour, egg, and fresh bread crumbs—wasn't as crisp as we wanted, so we toasted the bread crumbs with a little butter. (Precooking the crumbs also ensured we wouldn't have to overcook the fish to get really crunchy crumbs.) Placing the coated fish on a wire rack while baking allowed air to circulate all around the fish, crisping all sides. We boosted flavor in two ways, adding shallots and parsley to the breading and horseradish, cayenne, and paprika to the egg wash. As a final touch, we whipped up a creamy tartar sauce with mayonnaise, capers, and sweet relish.

Crunchy Oven-Fried Fish
SERVES 4

To prevent overcooking, buy fish fillets that are at least 1 inch thick. The bread crumbs can be made up to 3 days in advance and stored at room temperature in a tightly sealed container (allow to cool fully before storing). Serve the dish with Sweet and Tangy Tartar Sauce (recipe follows).

- 4 slices high-quality white sandwich bread, torn into quarters
- 2 tablespoons unsalted butter, melted
  Table salt and ground black pepper
- 2 tablespoons minced fresh parsley leaves
- 1 small shallot, minced (about 1 tablespoon)
- ¼ cup plus 5 tablespoons unbleached all-purpose flour
- 2 large eggs
- 3 tablespoons mayonnaise
- 2 teaspoons prepared horseradish (optional)
- ½ teaspoon paprika
- ¼ teaspoon cayenne pepper (optional)
- 1¼ pounds cod, haddock, or other thick whitefish fillets (1 to 1½ inches thick), cut into 4 pieces (see note)
  Lemon wedges, for serving

1. Adjust an oven rack to the middle position and heat the oven to 350 degrees. Pulse the bread, butter, ¼ teaspoon salt, and ¼ teaspoon black pepper in a food processor until the bread is coarsely ground, about 8 pulses. Transfer to a rimmed baking sheet and bake until deep golden brown and dry, about 15 minutes, stirring twice during the baking time. Cool the crumbs to room temperature, about 10 minutes. Transfer the crumbs to a pie plate and toss with the parsley and shallot. Increase the oven temperature to 425 degrees.

2. Place ¼ cup of the flour in a second pie plate. In a third pie plate, whisk together the eggs, mayonnaise, horseradish (if using), paprika, cayenne (if using), and ¼ teaspoon black pepper until combined; whisk in the remaining 5 tablespoons flour until smooth.

3. Spray a wire rack with vegetable oil spray and place over a rimmed baking sheet. Dry the fish thoroughly with paper towels and season with salt and black pepper. Dredge 1 fillet in the flour; shake off the excess. Using tongs, coat the fillet with the egg mixture. Coat all sides of the fillet with the bread-crumb mixture, pressing gently so that a thick layer of crumbs adheres to the fish. Transfer the breaded fish to the wire rack. Repeat with the remaining 3 fillets.

4. Bake the fish until the center of the fillets registers 140 degrees on an instant-read thermometer, 18 to 25 minutes. Using a thin spatula, transfer the fillets to individual plates and serve immediately with the lemon wedges.

Sweet and Tangy Tartar Sauce
MAKES ABOUT 1 CUP

This sauce can be refrigerated, tightly covered, for up to 1 week.

- ¾ cup mayonnaise
- 2 tablespoons drained capers, minced
- 2 tablespoons sweet pickle relish
- 1 small shallot, minced (about 1 tablespoon)
- 1½ teaspoons distilled white vinegar
- ½ teaspoon Worcestershire sauce
- ½ teaspoon ground black pepper

Mix all the ingredients together in a small bowl. Cover the bowl with plastic wrap and let sit until the flavors meld, about 15 minutes. Stir again before serving.

FISH AND CHIPS

WHY THIS RECIPE WORKS: The fish and chips served at most American pubs are mediocre at best. But the alternative—deep-frying fish at home—can be a hassle and a mess. Plus, by the time the fries finish frying, the fish is cold. We wanted fish with a light, crisp crust and moist interior, and we wanted to serve both the fish and the fries at their prime.

Our first challenge was to come up with a batter that not only would protect the fish as it cooked (allowing it to steam gently) but would also provide the fish with a nicely crisp contrast. We discovered that a wet batter was the most effective way to coat and protect the fish. We liked beer—the traditional choice—as the liquid component. What was the best way to keep the coating crisp? The answer was a 3–1 ratio of flour to cornstarch, along with a teaspoon of baking powder. Still, the coating was so tender it puffed away from the fish as it cooked. A final coating of flour on top of the battered fish solved the problem.

To solve the second challenge—delivering the fish and fries while both are still hot—we cooked them alternately. First, we precooked the fries in the microwave, which not only lessened cooking time but removed excess moisture that could dilute the oil and diminish crisping. Then we gave the fries their first, quick fry in hot oil. While the potatoes were draining, we battered and fried the fish. Then, as the fish drained, we gave the fries a quick final fry.

Fish and Chips
SERVES 4

For safety, use a Dutch oven with at least a 7-quart capacity. Serve with traditional malt vinegar or with Sweet and Tangy Tartar Sauce (page 224).

- 3 pounds russet potatoes (about 4 large potatoes), peeled, ends and sides squared off, and cut lengthwise into ½-inch by ½-inch fries (see page 407)
- 3 quarts plus ¼ cup peanut oil or canola oil
- 1½ cups unbleached all-purpose flour
- ½ cup cornstarch
- ½ teaspoon cayenne pepper
- ½ teaspoon paprika
- ⅛ teaspoon ground black pepper
- Table salt
- 1 teaspoon baking powder
- 1½ pounds cod or other thick whitefish fillets, such as hake or haddock, cut into eight 3-ounce pieces about 1 inch thick
- 1½ cups (12 ounces) cold beer

1. Place the cut fries in a large microwave-safe bowl, toss with ¼ cup of the oil, and cover with plastic wrap. Microwave on high power until the potatoes are partially translucent and pliable but still offer some resistance when pierced with the tip of a paring knife, 6 to 8 minutes, tossing them with a rubber spatula halfway through the cooking time. Carefully pull back the plastic wrap from the side farthest from you and drain the potatoes into a large mesh strainer set over a sink. Rinse well under cold running water. Spread the potatoes on a few clean kitchen towels and pat dry. Let rest until the fries have reached room temperature, at least 10 minutes or up to 1 hour.

2. While the fries cool, whisk the flour, cornstarch, cayenne, paprika, black pepper, and 2 teaspoons salt in a large mixing bowl; transfer ¾ cup of the mixture to a rimmed baking sheet. Add the baking powder to the bowl and whisk to combine.

3. In a large Dutch oven fitted with a clip-on candy thermometer, heat 2 quarts more oil over medium heat to 350 degrees. Add the fries to the hot oil and increase the heat to high. Fry, stirring with a mesh spider or slotted metal spoon, until the potatoes turn light golden and just begin to brown at the corners, 6 to 8 minutes. Transfer the fries to a thick paper bag or paper towels to drain.

4. Reduce the heat to medium-high, add the remaining 1 quart oil, and heat the oil to 375 degrees. Meanwhile, thoroughly dry the fish with paper towels and dredge each piece in the flour mixture on the baking sheet; transfer the pieces to a wire rack, shaking off any excess flour. Add 1¼ cups of the beer to the flour mixture in the mixing bowl and stir until the mixture is just combined (the batter will be lumpy). Add the remaining ¼ cup beer as needed, 1 tablespoon at a time, whisking after each addition, until the batter falls from the whisk in a thin, steady stream and leaves a faint trail across the surface of the batter. Using tongs, dip 1 piece of fish in the batter and let the excess run off, shaking gently. Place the battered fish back on the baking sheet with the flour mixture and turn to coat both sides. Repeat with the remaining fish, keeping the pieces in a single layer on the baking sheet.

5. When the oil reaches 375 degrees, increase the heat to high and add the battered fish to the oil with the tongs, gently shaking off any excess flour. Fry, stirring occasionally, until golden brown, 7 to 8 minutes. Transfer the fish to a thick paper bag or paper towels to drain. Allow the oil to return to 375 degrees.

6. Add all of the fries back to the oil and fry until golden brown and crisp, 3 to 5 minutes. Transfer to a fresh paper bag or paper towels to drain. Season the fries with salt to taste and serve immediately with the fish.

PAN-SEARED SALMON

WHY THIS RECIPE WORKS: We love salmon cooked on the grill, but when the weather makes grilling unpleasant or impossible, we don't want to forgo serving this flavorful fish. We wanted a great recipe for pan-seared salmon with a crisp, golden crust. Preheating the skillet over high heat and using just a teaspoon of neutral oil (butter tended to burn and was too rich) produced the brown crust we wanted—no flour or other coating was necessary. To prevent burning, we turned the heat down just after adding the fillets. Allowing plenty of space around the fillets kept them from merely steaming. We flipped the fillets when they turned opaque from the bottom to about halfway up; there was no need to shake the pan or move the fish until then. We found that removing the salmon just before it was done prevented overcooking; residual heat brought it up to serving temperature. Simply seasoned and perfectly cooked, these salmon fillets were easy to make and just as good as any cooked on the grill.

Pan-Seared Salmon
SERVES 4

To ensure uniform pieces of fish that cook at the same rate, buy a whole center-cut fillet and cut it into four pieces. With the addition of the fish fillets, the pan temperature drops; compensate for the heat loss by keeping the heat on high for 30 seconds after adding them. If cooking two or three fillets instead of the full recipe of four, use a 10-inch skillet and medium-high heat for both preheating the pan and cooking the salmon. A splatter screen helps reduce the mess of pan-searing.

    1 (1¾- to 2-pound) skinless salmon fillet, about
       1½ inches at the thickest part (see note)
    1 teaspoon canola or vegetable oil
       Table salt and ground black pepper
       Sweet-and-Sour Chutney (recipe follows) or lemon
       wedges, for serving

1. Use a sharp knife to trim any whitish fat from the belly of the fillet and cut it into four equal pieces. Heat the oil in a 12-inch skillet over high heat until shimmering but not smoking. Sprinkle the salmon with salt and pepper.

2. Add the fillets, skin-side down, and cook, without moving the fillets, until the skillet regains lost heat, about 30 seconds. Reduce the heat to medium-high; continue to cook until the skin side is well browned and the bottom half of the fillets turns opaque, 4½ minutes. Turn the fillets and cook, without moving them, until they are no longer translucent on the exterior and are firm, but not hard, when gently squeezed, 3 minutes for medium-rare and 3½ minutes for medium. Remove the fillets from the skillet; let stand for 1 minute. Pat the fillets with a paper towel to absorb excess fat on the surface, if desired. Serve immediately with the chutney or the lemon wedges.

Sweet-and-Sour Chutney
MAKES ABOUT ⅓ CUP

A little of this intensely flavored condiment goes a long way.

    1   teaspoon fennel seeds
    ½   teaspoon ground cumin
    ½   teaspoon ground coriander
    ¼   teaspoon ground cardamom
    ¼   teaspoon paprika
    ¼   teaspoon table salt
    2   teaspoons olive oil
    ½   medium onion, minced (about ½ cup)
    ¼   cup red wine vinegar
    1   tablespoon sugar
    1   tablespoon minced fresh parsley leaves

Mix the fennel, cumin, coriander, cardamom, paprika, and salt in a small bowl; set aside. Heat the oil in a medium skillet over medium heat; sauté the onion until soft, 3 to 4 minutes. Add the reserved spice mixture; sauté until fragrant, about 1 minute more. Increase the heat to medium-high and add the vinegar, sugar, and 2 tablespoons water; cook until the mixture reduces by about one third and reaches a syrupy consistency, about 1½ minutes. Stir in the parsley. Serve with the salmon.

PAN-SEARED BRINED SALMON

WHY THIS RECIPE WORKS: To achieve perfectly cooked salmon, we wanted to take advantage of the intense heat of the skillet and produce a golden-brown, ultracrisp crust on the fillets while keeping their interiors moist. We first brined the fish to season it and to keep it moist. Instead of adding the fish to an already-hot skillet, we placed it in a cold, dry nonstick skillet skin side down and then turned on the heat. The skin protected the fish from drying out while cooking and later was easy to peel off and discard. Also, because the skin released fat into the pan as it cooked, no extra oil was needed to sear the second side of the fish.

Pan-Seared Brined Salmon
SERVES 4

To ensure uniform cooking, buy a 1½- to 2-pound center-cut salmon fillet and cut it into four pieces. Using skin-on salmon is important here, as we rely on the fat underneath the skin as the cooking medium (as opposed to adding extra oil). If using wild salmon, cook it until it registers 120 degrees. If you don't want to serve the fish with the skin, we recommend peeling it off the fish after it is cooked. Serve with lemon wedges or Mango-Mint Salsa or Cilantro-Mint Chutney (recipes follow).

        Kosher salt and pepper
    4   (6- to 8-ounce) skin-on salmon fillets
        Lemon wedges

1. Dissolve ½ cup salt in 2 quarts cold water in large container. Submerge salmon in brine and let stand at room temperature for 15 minutes. Remove salmon from brine and pat dry with paper towels.

2. Sprinkle bottom of 12-inch nonstick skillet evenly with ½ teaspoon salt and ½ teaspoon pepper. Place fillets, skin side down, in skillet and sprinkle tops of fillets with ¼ teaspoon salt and ¼ teaspoon pepper. Heat skillet over medium-high heat and cook fillets without moving them until fat begins to render, skin begins to brown, and bottom ¼ inch of fillets turns opaque, 6 to 8 minutes.

3. Using tongs, flip fillets and continue to cook without moving them until centers are still translucent when checked with tip of paring knife and register 125 degrees, 6 to 8 minutes longer. Transfer fillets skin side down to serving platter and let rest for 5 minutes before serving with lemon wedges.

Mango-Mint Salsa

MAKES ABOUT 1 CUP

Adjust the salsa's heat level by reserving and adding the jalapeño seeds, if desired.

- 1 mango, peeled, pitted, and cut into ¼-inch pieces
- 1 shallot, minced
- 3 tablespoons lime juice (2 limes)
- 2 tablespoons chopped fresh mint
- 1 jalapeño chile, stemmed, seeded, and minced
- 1 tablespoon extra-virgin olive oil
- 1 garlic clove, minced
- ½ teaspoon salt

Combine all ingredients in bowl.

Cilantro-Mint Chutney

MAKES ABOUT 1 CUP

Adjust the chutney's heat level by reserving and adding the jalapeño seeds, if desired.

- 2 cups fresh cilantro leaves
- 1 cup fresh mint leaves
- ½ cup water
- ¼ cup sesame seeds, lightly toasted
- 1 (2-inch) piece ginger, peeled and sliced into ⅛-inch-thick rounds
- 1 jalapeño chile, stemmed, seeded, and sliced into 1-inch pieces
- 2 tablespoons vegetable oil
- 2 tablespoons lime juice
- 1½ teaspoons sugar
- ½ teaspoon salt

Process all ingredients in blender until smooth, about 30 seconds, scraping down sides of jar with spatula after 10 seconds.

BROILED SALMON

WHY THIS RECIPE WORKS: Cooking an entire side of salmon in the oven often results in fish that is either soggy or chalky. We wanted to pull off a crowd-pleasing side of salmon that is moist and firm, with a golden crumb crust that contrasts with the flavorful fish.

Most of the time, we achieve a crisp crust on salmon through pan-searing in a skillet on the stovetop. With a crumb crust, it made sense to use the broiler. A plain bread crumb-topping seemed bland, but when we toasted the crumbs and mixed in crushed potato chips and chopped dill, the result was a crisp and flavorful coating. To get the crumb mixture to adhere to the fish, we relied on a thin layer of mustard. One problem: The crust burned by the time the fish was cooked through. We switched gears and broiled the fish almost unadorned (save for salt, pepper, and a bit of olive oil) until it was nearly done, then spread on the mustard and crumbs for a second run under the broiler to crisp the crust. To get the fish onto a platter in one piece, we lined a baking sheet with heavy-duty foil before adding the fish, creating a sling with which we could move it. Our two-step broiling method resulted in firm, moist fish and a flavorful crunchy topping.

Broiled Salmon with Mustard and Crisp Dilled Crust

SERVES 8 TO 10

If you prefer to cook a smaller 2-pound fillet, ask to have it cut from the thick center of the fillet, not the thin tail end, and begin checking doneness a minute earlier.

- 3 slices high-quality white sandwich bread, torn into quarters
- 4 ounces plain high-quality potato chips, crushed into rough ⅛-inch pieces (about 1 cup)
- 6 tablespoons chopped fresh dill
- 1 whole side salmon fillet, about 3½ pounds, white belly fat trimmed
- 1 teaspoon olive oil
  Table salt and ground black pepper
- 3 tablespoons Dijon mustard

1. Adjust one oven rack to the top position (about 3 inches from the heat source) and the second rack to the upper-middle position; heat the oven to 400 degrees.

2. Pulse the bread in a food processor to fairly even ¼-inch pieces about the size of Grape-Nuts cereal (you should have about 1 cup), about 10 pulses. Spread the crumbs evenly on a rimmed baking sheet; toast on the lower oven rack, shaking the pan once or twice, until golden brown and crisp, 4 to 5 minutes. Toss the bread crumbs, crushed potato chips, and dill together in a small bowl; set aside.

3. Change the oven setting to broil. Cut a piece of heavy-duty foil 6 inches longer than the fillet. Fold the foil lengthwise in thirds and place lengthwise on a rimmed baking sheet; position the salmon lengthwise on the foil, allowing the excess foil to overhang the baking sheet. Rub the fillet evenly with the oil;

sprinkle with salt and pepper. Broil the salmon on the upper rack until the surface is spotty brown and the outer ½ inch of the thick end is opaque when gently flaked with a paring knife, 9 to 11 minutes. Remove the baking sheet from the oven, spread the fish evenly with the mustard, and press the bread-crumb mixture onto the fish. Return the baking sheet to the lower oven rack and continue broiling until the crust is deep golden brown, about 1 minute longer.

4. Grasping the ends of the foil sling, lift the salmon, sling and all, onto a platter. Slide an offset spatula under the thick end. Grasp the foil, press the spatula against the foil, and slide it under the fish down to the thin end, loosening the entire side of fish. Grasp the foil again, hold the spatula perpendicular to the fish to stabilize it, and pull the foil out from under the fish. Wipe the platter clean with a damp paper towel. Serve the salmon immediately.

MARINATED SALMON

WHY THIS RECIPE WORKS: Miso-marinated salmon promises firm, flavorful fish with a savory-sweet, lacquer-like exterior, but it takes 3 days to prepare. We wanted to make a dish that pulled back on the traditional approach (and shortened the process) but still achieved the depth of flavor that this dish is known for. And instead of a dense interior, we wanted fish that was silky and moist, contrasting with the texture of the crust. By reducing the marinating to between 6 and 24 hours, we found a window that allowed us to achieve such a goal. A marinade composed of miso, sugar, mirin, and sake allowed for flavor penetration, moisture retention, and better browning by firming up the fish's surface. Broiling the fish at a distance from the heating element allowed the fish to caramelize and cook to tender at the same time.

Miso-Marinated Salmon
SERVES 4

Note that the fish needs to marinate for at least 6 or up to 24 hours before cooking. Use center-cut salmon fillets of similar thickness. Yellow, red, or brown miso paste can be used instead of white.

- ½ cup white miso paste
- ¼ cup sugar
- 3 tablespoons sake
- 3 tablespoons mirin
- 4 (6- to 8-ounce) skin-on salmon fillets
  Lemon wedges

1. Whisk miso, sugar, sake, and mirin together in medium bowl until sugar and miso are dissolved (mixture will be thick). Dip each fillet into miso mixture to evenly coat all flesh sides. Place fish skin side down in baking dish and pour any remaining miso mixture over fillets. Cover with plastic wrap and refrigerate for at least 6 hours or up to 24 hours.

2. Adjust oven rack 8 inches from broiler element and heat broiler. Place wire rack in rimmed baking sheet and cover

with aluminum foil. Using your fingers, scrape miso mixture from fillets (do not rinse) and place fish skin side down on foil, leaving 1 inch between fillets.

3. Broil salmon until deeply browned and centers of fillets register 125 degrees, 8 to 12 minutes, rotating sheet halfway through cooking and shielding edges of fillets with foil if necessary. Transfer to platter and serve with lemon wedges.

FLAVORFUL POACHED SALMON

WHY THIS RECIPE WORKS: When salmon is poached incorrectly, not only is it dry, but the flavor is so washed out that not even the richest sauce can redeem it. We wanted irresistibly supple salmon accented by the delicate flavor of the poaching liquid, accompanied by a simple pan sauce—all in under half an hour.

We started our tests with a classic court-bouillon, which is made by boiling water, wine, herbs, vegetables, and aromatics and then straining out the solids. But discarding all those vegetables seemed wasteful for a simple weeknight supper. Using less liquid—poaching the salmon in just enough liquid to come half an inch up the side of the fillets—allowed us to cut back on the quantity of vegetables and aromatics; in fact, a couple of shallots, a few herbs, and some wine were all we needed to solve the flavor issue. However, the part of the salmon that wasn't submerged in liquid needed to be steamed for thorough cooking, and the low cooking temperature required to poach the salmon evenly didn't create enough steam. The solution was to increase the ratio of wine to water. The additional alcohol lowered the liquid's boiling point, producing more vapor even at the lower temperature. Meanwhile, the bottom of the fillets had the opposite problem, overcooking due to direct contact with the pan. Resting the salmon fillets on top of lemon slices provided sufficient insulation. For a finishing touch, after removing the salmon, we reduced the liquid and added a few tablespoons of olive oil to create an easy vinaigrette-style sauce.

Poached Salmon with Herb and Caper Vinaigrette
SERVES 4

To ensure uniform pieces of fish that cook at the same rate, buy a whole center-cut fillet and cut it into four pieces. If a skinless whole fillet is unavailable, remove the skin yourself (see photos on page 229) or follow the recipe as directed with a skin-on fillet, adding 3 to 4 minutes to the cooking time in step 2.

- 2 lemons
- 1 large shallot, minced (about 4 tablespoons)
- 2 tablespoons minced fresh parsley leaves, stems reserved
- 2 tablespoons minced fresh tarragon leaves, stems reserved
- ½ cup dry white wine
- ½ cup water
- 1 (1¾- to 2-pound) skinless salmon fillet, about 1½ inches at the thickest part (see note)

2 tablespoons capers, rinsed and roughly chopped

2 tablespoons extra-virgin olive oil

1 tablespoon honey

Table salt and ground black pepper

1. Cut the top and bottom off 1 lemon; cut the lemon into eight to ten ¼-inch-thick slices. Cut the remaining lemon into eight wedges and set aside. Arrange the lemon slices in a single layer across the bottom of a 12-inch skillet. Scatter 2 tablespoons of the shallot and the herb stems evenly over the lemon slices. Add the wine and water.

2. Use a sharp knife to trim any whitish fat from the belly of the fillet and cut it into four equal pieces. Place the salmon fillets in the skillet, skinned side down, on top of the lemon slices. Set the pan over high heat and bring the liquid to a simmer. Reduce the heat to low, cover, and cook until the sides of the fillets are opaque but the center of the thickest part of the fillets is still translucent (or until the thickest part of the fillets registers 125 degrees on an instant-read thermometer), 11 to 16 minutes. Remove the pan from the heat and, using a spatula, carefully transfer the salmon and lemon slices to a paper towel–lined plate. Tent loosely with foil.

3. Return the pan to high heat and simmer the cooking liquid until slightly thickened and reduced to 2 tablespoons, 4 to 5 minutes. Meanwhile, combine the remaining 2 tablespoons shallot, the minced herbs, capers, olive oil, and honey in a medium bowl. Strain the reduced cooking liquid through a fine-mesh strainer into the bowl with the herb-caper mixture, pressing on the solids to extract as much liquid as possible. Whisk to combine and season with salt and pepper to taste.

4. Season the salmon lightly with salt and pepper. Using a spatula, carefully lift and tilt the salmon fillets to remove the lemon slices. Place the salmon on a serving platter or individual plates and spoon the vinaigrette over the top. Serve, passing the reserved lemon wedges separately.

HERB-CRUSTED SALMON

WHY THIS RECIPE WORKS: Herb-crusted salmon rarely lives up to its name; it most often sports a dusty, bland sprinkling of bread crumbs and hardly any herb flavor. To make this dish the best it could be, we first brined the salmon to keep it moist (brining also inhibits the formation of the white protein albumin that appears on the fish when heated). For the herb, we thought the sweet, woodsy notes of tarragon paired especially well with our salmon. To protect its delicate flavor in the oven, we mixed the herb with mustard and mayonnaise, layered it on the fish, then sprinkled bread crumbs, which we'd seasoned with thyme, over the top. Toasting the bread crumbs in butter gave them some color and flavor. A little beaten egg helped them adhere, and a low oven kept the crust from scorching while the salmon cooked through.

Herb-Crusted Salmon
SERVES 4

For the fillets to cook at the same rate, they must be the same size and shape. To ensure uniformity, we prefer to purchase a 1½- to 2-pound center-cut salmon fillet and cut it into four pieces. Dill or basil can be substituted for the tarragon.

Salt and pepper

4 (6- to 8-ounce) skin-on salmon fillets

2 tablespoons unsalted butter

½ cup panko bread crumbs

2 tablespoons beaten egg

2 teaspoons minced fresh thyme

¼ cup chopped fresh tarragon

1 tablespoon whole-grain mustard

1½ teaspoons mayonnaise

Lemon wedges

1. Adjust oven rack to middle position and heat oven to 325 degrees. Dissolve 5 tablespoons salt in 2 quarts water in large container. Submerge salmon in brine and let stand at room temperature for 15 minutes. Remove salmon from brine, pat dry, and set aside.

2. Meanwhile, melt butter in 10-inch skillet over medium heat. Add panko and ⅛ teaspoon salt and season with pepper; cook, stirring frequently, until panko is golden brown, 4 to 5 minutes. Transfer to bowl and let cool completely. Stir in egg and thyme until thoroughly combined. Stir tarragon, mustard, and mayonnaise together in second bowl.

3. Set wire rack in rimmed baking sheet. Place 12 by 8-inch piece of aluminum foil on wire rack and lightly coat with vegetable oil spray. Evenly space fillets, skin side down, on foil. Using spoon, spread tarragon mixture evenly over top of each fillet. Sprinkle panko mixture evenly over top of each fillet, pressing with your fingers to adhere. Bake until center is still translucent when checked with tip of paring knife and registers 125 degrees (for medium-rare), 18 to 25 minutes. Transfer salmon to serving platter and let rest for 5 minutes before serving with lemon wedges.

SESAME-CRUSTED SALMON

WHY THIS RECIPE WORKS: The combination of fish and sesame shows up in cuisines from Asia to California to the Middle East. The simplest approach is to coat fillets with the seeds and then pan-sear the fish. But the duo of salmon and sesame often suffers from a common problem: Both salmon and sesame have a monotonous richness, so finishing a whole serving is a chore. We wanted a lively dish in which the salmon and sesame would be offset with bolder, brighter flavors. Brining the fish for just 15 minutes took care of any dryness. We dunked the seeds in the fish brine, which woke up the nutty flavor by infusing each with salt. Toasting the seeds gave them nice crunch. For extra sesame flavor, we "thickened" tahini with some lemon juice and used the thick paste to adhere the seeds. We also added scallion whites, lemon zest, fresh ginger, and a dash of cayenne for more layers of flavor.

Sesame-Crusted Salmon with Lemon and Ginger
SERVES 4

For even cooking, purchase fillets that are about the same size and shape. If any of your fillets have a thin belly flap, fold it over to create a more even thickness.

- Salt
- ¾ cup sesame seeds
- 4 (6- to 8-ounce) skinless salmon fillets
- 2 scallions, white parts minced, green parts sliced thin
- 1 tablespoon grated lemon zest plus 2 teaspoons juice
- 4 teaspoons tahini
- 2 teaspoons grated fresh ginger
- ⅛ teaspoon cayenne pepper
- 1 teaspoon vegetable oil

1. Adjust oven rack to middle position and heat oven to 325 degrees. Dissolve 5 tablespoons salt in 2 quarts water. Transfer 1 cup brine to bowl, stir in sesame seeds, and let stand at room temperature for 5 minutes. Submerge fillets in remaining brine and let stand at room temperature for 15 minutes.

2. Drain seeds and place in 12-inch nonstick skillet. Cook seeds over medium heat, stirring constantly, until golden brown, 2 to 4 minutes. Transfer seeds to pie plate and wipe out skillet with paper towels. Remove fillets from brine and pat dry.

3. Place scallion whites and lemon zest on cutting board and chop until whites and zest are finely minced and well combined. Transfer scallion-zest mixture to bowl and stir in lemon juice, tahini, ginger, cayenne, and ⅛ teaspoon salt.

4. Evenly distribute half of paste over bottoms (skinned sides) of fillets. Press coated sides of fillets in seeds and transfer, seed side down, to plate. Evenly distribute remaining paste over tops of fillets and coat with remaining seeds.

5. Heat oil in now-empty skillet over medium heat until shimmering. Place fillets in skillet, skinned side up, and reduce heat to medium-low. Cook until seeds begin to brown, 1 to 2 minutes. Remove skillet from heat and, using 2 spatulas, carefully flip fillets over. Transfer skillet to oven. Bake until center of fish is translucent when checked with tip of paring knife and registers 125 degrees, 10 to 15 minutes. Transfer to serving platter and let rest for 5 minutes. Sprinkle with scallion greens and serve.

Sesame-Crusted Salmon with Lime and Coriander

Substitute 4 teaspoons lime zest for lemon zest, lime juice for lemon juice, and ¼ teaspoon ground coriander for cayenne.

Sesame-Crusted Salmon with Orange and Chili Powder

Substitute orange zest for lemon zest, orange juice for lemon juice, and ¼ teaspoon chili powder for cayenne.

GLAZED SALMON

WHY THIS RECIPE WORKS: The traditional method for glazed salmon calls for broiling, but reaching into a broiling-hot oven every minute to baste the fish is a hassle and, even worse, the fillets often burn if your timing isn't spot-on. We wanted a foolproof method for glazed salmon that was succulent and pink throughout while keeping the slightly crusty, flavorful browned exterior typically achieved with broiling. First we found that reducing the temperature and gently baking the fish, instead of broiling, cooked the salmon perfectly. To rapidly caramelize the exterior of the fillets before they had a chance to toughen, we sprinkled the fillets with sugar and quickly pan-seared each side before transferring them to the oven. To ensure the glaze stayed put, we rubbed the fish with a mixture of cornstarch, brown sugar, and salt before searing.

Glazed Salmon

SERVES 4

To ensure uniform pieces of fish that cook at the same rate, buy a whole center-cut fillet and cut it into 4 pieces. Prepare the glaze before you cook the salmon. If your nonstick skillet isn't ovensafe, sear the salmon as directed in step 2, then transfer it to a rimmed baking sheet, glaze it, and bake as directed in step 3. You will need a 12-inch ovensafe nonstick skillet for this recipe.

- 1 teaspoon light brown sugar
- ½ teaspoon kosher salt
- ¼ teaspoon cornstarch
- 1 (1½- to 2-pound) skin-on salmon fillet, about 1½ inches thick
  Ground black pepper
- 1 teaspoon vegetable oil
- 1 recipe glaze (recipes follow)

1. Adjust an oven rack to the middle position and heat the oven to 300 degrees. Combine the brown sugar, salt, and cornstarch in a small bowl. Use a sharp knife to remove any whitish fat from the belly of the salmon and cut the fillet into 4 equal pieces. Pat the fillets dry with paper towels and season with pepper. Sprinkle the brown sugar mixture evenly over the top of the flesh side of the salmon, rubbing to distribute.

2. Heat the oil in a 12-inch ovensafe nonstick skillet over medium-high heat until just smoking. Place the salmon, flesh side down, in the skillet and cook until well browned, about 1 minute. Using tongs, carefully flip the salmon and cook on the skin side for 1 minute.

3. Remove the skillet from the heat and spoon the glaze evenly over the salmon fillets. Transfer the skillet to the oven and cook until the fillets register 125 degrees on an instant-read thermometer (for medium-rare) and are still translucent when cut into with a paring knife, 7 to 10 minutes. Transfer the fillets to a platter or individual plates and serve.

Pomegranate-Balsamic Glaze

MAKES ABOUT ½ CUP

This fruity, tangy glaze is a perfect match for rich salmon.

- 3 tablespoons light brown sugar
- 3 tablespoons pomegranate juice
- 2 tablespoons balsamic vinegar
- 1 tablespoon whole grain mustard
- 1 teaspoon cornstarch
  Pinch cayenne pepper

Whisk the ingredients together in a small saucepan. Bring to a boil over medium-high heat; simmer until thickened, about 1 minute. Remove from the heat and cover to keep warm.

Asian Barbecue Glaze

MAKES ABOUT ½ CUP

Toasted sesame oil gives this teriyaki-like glaze rich flavor.

- 2 tablespoons ketchup
- 2 tablespoons hoisin sauce
- 2 tablespoons rice vinegar
- 2 tablespoons packed light brown sugar
- 1 tablespoon soy sauce
- 1 tablespoon toasted sesame oil
- 2 teaspoons Asian chili-garlic sauce
- 1 teaspoon minced or grated fresh ginger

Whisk the ingredients together in a small saucepan. Bring to a boil over medium-high heat; simmer until thickened, about 3 minutes. Remove from the heat and cover to keep warm.

Orange-Miso Glaze

MAKES ABOUT ½ CUP

Miso is a fermented soybean paste that adds deep flavor to foods. We prefer milder, white miso here, rather than the strong-flavored red miso.

1   teaspoon grated zest plus ¼ cup juice from 1 orange
2   tablespoons white miso
1   tablespoon light brown sugar
1   tablespoon rice vinegar
1   tablespoon whole grain mustard
¾   teaspoon cornstarch
     Pinch cayenne pepper

Whisk the ingredients together in a small saucepan. Bring to a boil over medium-high heat; simmer until thickened, about 1 minute. Remove from the heat and cover to keep warm.

Soy-Mustard Glaze

MAKES ABOUT ½ CUP

Mirin, a sweet Japanese rice wine, can be found in Asian markets and the international section of most supermarkets.

3   tablespoons light brown sugar
2   tablespoons soy sauce
2   tablespoons mirin (see note)
1   tablespoon sherry vinegar
1   tablespoon whole grain mustard
1   tablespoon water
1   teaspoon cornstarch
⅛   teaspoon red pepper flakes

Whisk the ingredients together in a small saucepan. Bring to a boil over medium-high heat; simmer until thickened, about 1 minute. Remove from the heat and cover to keep warm.

OVEN-ROASTED SALMON

WHY THIS RECIPE WORKS: Roasting a salmon fillet can create a brown exterior, but often at the risk of a dry, overcooked interior. The best roasted salmon should have moist, flavorful flesh inside, with a contrasting crisp texture on the outside.

To ensure that the salmon fillets would cook evenly, we cut a whole center-cut fillet into four pieces. We roasted the fish at a low temperature and achieved the buttery flesh we were after, but no browning—and the fillets were a little mushy from the rendered fat. Taking the opposite approach, we put the fish on a preheated baking sheet and started the oven at a high temperature to firm up and brown the exterior. This gave us a crust, but we still needed to get rid of the fat; cutting slits in the skin released the fat rendered by the high heat. Lowering the temperature as soon as we put the fish in the oven enabled it to cook through gradually after the initial blast of heat, so it didn't dry out. Now we had the contrast between moist interior and crisp brown exterior that we wanted. Salmon is rich and flavorful all on its own, but we devised a couple of easy no-cook relishes that can be served alongside for even more flavor and contrast.

Oven-Roasted Salmon

SERVES 4

To ensure uniform pieces of fish that cook at the same rate, buy a whole center-cut fillet and cut it into four pieces. If your knife is not sharp enough to easily cut through the skin, try a serrated knife. It is important to keep the skin on during cooking; remove it afterward if you choose not to serve it.

1   (1¾- to 2-pound) skin-on salmon fillet, about
     1½ inches at the thickest part (see note)
2   teaspoons olive oil
     Table salt and ground black pepper
1   recipe relish (recipes follow)

1. Adjust an oven rack to the lowest position, place a rimmed baking sheet on the rack, and heat the oven to 500 degrees. Remove any whitish fat from the belly of the fillet and cut it into four equal pieces. Make four or five shallow slashes about an inch apart along the skin side of each piece, being careful not to cut into the flesh.

2. Pat the salmon dry with paper towels. Rub the fillets evenly with the oil and season liberally with salt and pepper. Reduce the oven temperature to 275 degrees and remove the baking sheet. Carefully place the salmon, skin-side down, on the baking sheet. Roast until the thickest part of the fillets is still translucent when cut into with a paring knife (or the thickest part of the fillets registers 125 degrees on an instant-read thermometer), 9 to 13 minutes. Transfer the fillets to individual plates or a platter. Top with relish and serve.

Tangerine and Ginger Relish

MAKES ABOUT 1¼ CUPS

4   tangerines, rind and pith removed and segments
     cut into ½-inch pieces (about 1 cup)
1   scallion, sliced thin (about ¼ cup)
1½   teaspoons minced or grated fresh ginger
2   teaspoons juice from 1 lemon
2   teaspoons extra-virgin olive oil
     Table salt and ground black pepper

1. Place the tangerines in a fine-mesh strainer set over a medium bowl and drain for 15 minutes.

2. Pour off all but 1 tablespoon tangerine juice from the bowl; whisk in the scallion, ginger, lemon juice, and oil. Stir in the tangerines and season with salt and pepper to taste.

Fresh Tomato Relish

MAKES ABOUT 1½ CUPS

¾   pound ripe tomatoes, cored, seeded, and cut
     into ¼-inch dice (about 1½ cups)
2   tablespoons chopped fresh basil leaves
1   small shallot, minced (about 1 tablespoon)
1   tablespoon extra-virgin olive oil

1 teaspoon red wine vinegar

1 small garlic clove, minced or pressed through
a garlic press (about ½ teaspoon)
Table salt and ground black pepper

Combine the tomatoes, basil, shallot, oil, vinegar, and garlic in a medium bowl. Season with salt and pepper to taste.

Spicy Cucumber Relish

MAKES ABOUT 2 CUPS

1 medium cucumber, peeled, seeded, and cut into ¼-inch
dice (about 2 cups)

2 tablespoons minced fresh mint leaves

1 small shallot, minced (about 1 tablespoon)

1 serrano chile, seeds and ribs removed, chile minced
(about 1 tablespoon)

1–2 tablespoons juice from 1 lime
Table salt

Combine the cucumber, mint, shallot, chile, 1 tablespoon of the lime juice, and ¼ teaspoon salt in a medium bowl. Let sit at room temperature until the flavors meld, about 15 minutes. Season with additional lime juice and salt to taste.

POACHED FISH FILLETS

WHY THIS RECIPE WORKS: Restaurant-style poached fish requires a potful of pricey olive oil and promises super-moist, delicately cooked fish. Using a small skillet and flipping the fish halfway through cooking allowed us to cut back to ¾ cup of oil, which we employed to crisp flavorful garnishes and finally blended into a vinaigrette.

Poached Fish Fillets with Crispy Artichokes and Sherry-Tomato Vinaigrette

SERVES 4

Fillets of meaty white fish like cod, halibut, sea bass, or snapper work best in this recipe. Just make sure the fillets are at least 1 inch thick. A neutral oil such as canola can be substituted for the olive oil. The onion half in step 3 is used to displace the oil; a 4-ounce porcelain ramekin may be used instead. Serve with couscous or steamed white rice.

FISH

4 (6-ounce) skinless white fish fillets, 1 inch thick
Kosher salt

4 ounces frozen artichoke hearts, thawed,
patted dry, and sliced in half lengthwise

1 tablespoon cornstarch

¾ cup olive oil

3 garlic cloves, minced

½ onion, peeled

VINAIGRETTE

4 ounces cherry tomatoes

½ small shallot, peeled

4 teaspoons sherry vinegar
Kosher salt and pepper

2 ounces cherry tomatoes, cut into ⅛-inch-thick rounds

1 tablespoon minced fresh parsley

1. FOR THE FISH: Adjust oven racks to middle and lower-middle positions and heat oven to 250 degrees. Pat fish dry with paper towels and season each fillet with ¼ teaspoon salt. Let sit at room temperature for 20 minutes.

2. Meanwhile, toss artichokes with cornstarch in bowl to coat. Heat ½ cup oil in 10-inch nonstick ovensafe skillet over medium heat until shimmering. Shake excess cornstarch from artichokes and add to skillet; cook, stirring occasionally, until crisp and golden, 2 to 4 minutes. Add garlic and continue to cook until garlic is golden, 30 to 60 seconds. Strain oil through fine-mesh strainer into bowl. Transfer artichokes and garlic to ovensafe paper towel–lined plate and season with salt. Do not wash strainer.

3. Return strained oil to skillet and add remaining ¼ cup oil. Place onion half in center of pan. Let oil cool until it registers about 180 degrees, 5 to 8 minutes. Arrange fish fillets, skinned side up, around onion (oil should come roughly halfway up fillets). Spoon a little oil over each fillet, cover skillet, transfer to middle oven rack, and cook for 15 minutes.

4. Remove skillet from oven (skillet handle will be hot). Using 2 spatulas, carefully flip fillets. Cover skillet, return to middle rack, and place plate with artichokes and garlic on lower-middle rack. Continue to cook fish until it registers 130 to 135 degrees, 9 to 14 minutes longer. Gently transfer fish to serving platter, reserving ½ cup oil, and tent fish loosely with aluminum foil. Turn off oven, leaving plate of artichokes in oven.

5. FOR THE VINAIGRETTE: Process cherry tomatoes, shallot, vinegar, ¾ teaspoon salt, and ½ teaspoon pepper with reserved ½ cup fish cooking oil in blender until smooth, 1 to 2 minutes. Add any accumulated fish juices from platter, season with salt to taste, and blend for 10 seconds. Strain sauce through fine-mesh strainer; discard solids.

6. To serve, pour vinaigrette around fish. Garnish each fillet with warmed crisped artichokes and garlic, tomato rounds, and parsley. Serve immediately.

Poached Fish Fillets with Jalapeño Vinaigrette

To make this dish spicier, add some of the reserved chile seeds to the vinaigrette in step 5. Serve with steamed white rice.

For fish, substitute 2 jalapeño chiles, stemmed, seeded, and cut into ⅛-inch-thick rings, for artichoke hearts and reduce cornstarch to 2 teaspoons. For vinaigrette, process 4 jalapeños, stemmed, halved, and seeded (seeds reserved); ½ small shallot, peeled; 6 sprigs fresh cilantro; 8 teaspoons lime juice; and ½ teaspoon kosher salt with ½ cup reserved fish cooking oil as directed in step 5. Garnish fish with 2 tablespoons fresh cilantro leaves and ½ avocado, cut into ¼-inch pieces.

Poached Fish Fillets with Crispy Scallions and Miso-Ginger Vinaigrette

For fish, substitute 8 scallion whites, sliced ¼ inch thick, for artichoke hearts; omit garlic; and reduce cornstarch to 2 teaspoons. For vinaigrette, process 6 scallion greens, 8 teaspoons lime juice, 2 tablespoons mirin, 4 teaspoons white miso paste, 2 teaspoons minced ginger, and ½ teaspoon sugar with ½ cup reserved fish cooking oil as directed in step 5. Garnish fish with 2 thinly sliced scallion greens and 2 halved and thinly sliced radishes.

PAN-SEARED TUNA STEAKS

WHY THIS RECIPE WORKS: Moist and rare in the middle with a seared crust, pan-seared tuna is a popular entrée in restaurants. This dish is so simple that we thought it would be easy to make at home, and set out to determine the best method. Starting with high-quality tuna—sushi grade if possible—is paramount; we prefer the flavor of yellowfin. A thickness of at least an inch is necessary for the center of the tuna to be rare while the exterior browns. Before searing the tuna in a nonstick skillet, we rubbed the steaks with oil, then coated them with sesame seeds; the oil helped the seeds stick to the fish. The sesame seeds browned in the skillet and formed a beautiful, nutty-tasting crust. We learned that tuna, like beef, will continue to cook from residual heat when removed from the stove, so when the interior of the tuna was near the desired degree of doneness (about 110 degrees on an instant-read thermometer), we transferred it to a platter.

Pan-Seared Sesame-Crusted Tuna Steaks
SERVES 4

If you plan to serve the fish with the sauce or salsa (recipes follow), prepare it before cooking the fish. Most members of the test kitchen staff prefer their tuna steaks rare to medium-rare; the cooking times given in this recipe are for tuna steaks cooked to these two degrees of doneness. For tuna steaks cooked medium, observe the timing for medium-rare, then tent the steaks loosely with foil for 5 minutes before slicing. If you prefer tuna steaks cooked so rare that they are still cold in the center, try to purchase steaks that are 1½ inches thick and cook them according to the timing below for rare steaks. Bear in mind, though, that the cooking times below are estimates; check for doneness by nicking the fish with a paring knife. To cook only two steaks, use half as many sesame seeds, reduce the amount of oil to 2 teaspoons both on the fish and in the pan, use a 10-inch nonstick skillet, and follow the same cooking times.

¾ cup sesame seeds
4 (8-ounce) tuna steaks, preferably yellowfin, about 1 inch thick (see note)
2 tablespoons vegetable oil
Table salt and ground black pepper
1 recipe sauce or salsa (recipes follow)

1. Spread the sesame seeds in a shallow baking dish or pie plate. Pat the tuna steaks dry with a paper towel; use 1 tablespoon of the oil to rub both sides of the steaks, then sprinkle them with salt and pepper. Press both sides of each steak in the sesame seeds to coat.

2. Heat the remaining 1 tablespoon oil in a 12-inch nonstick skillet over high heat until just beginning to smoke and swirl to coat the pan. Add the tuna steaks and cook 30 seconds without moving the steaks. Reduce the heat to medium-high and continue to cook until the seeds are golden brown, about 1½ minutes. Using tongs, flip the tuna steaks carefully and cook, without moving them, until golden brown on the second side and the centers register 110 degrees on an instant-read thermometer for rare (about 1½ minutes), or 120 degrees for medium-rare (about 3 minutes). Serve with Ginger-Soy Sauce with Scallions or Avocado-Orange Salsa.

Ginger-Soy Sauce with Scallions

MAKES ABOUT 1 CUP

If available, serve pickled ginger and wasabi, passed separately, with the tuna and this sauce.

- ¼ cup soy sauce
- ¼ cup rice vinegar
- ¼ cup water
- 1 medium scallion, sliced thin
- 2½ teaspoons sugar
- 2 teaspoons minced or grated fresh ginger
- 1½ teaspoons toasted sesame oil
- ½ teaspoon red pepper flakes

Combine all the ingredients in a small bowl, stirring to dissolve the sugar.

Avocado-Orange Salsa

MAKES ABOUT 1 CUP

To keep the avocado from discoloring, prepare this salsa just before you cook the tuna steaks.

- 1 large orange, cut into segments (see page 248)
- 1 ripe avocado, pitted, peeled, and diced medium (see page 414)
- 2 tablespoons minced red onion
- 2 tablespoons minced fresh cilantro leaves
- 4 teaspoons juice from 1 to 2 limes
- 1 small jalapeño chile, stemmed, seeded, and minced
  Table salt

Combine all the ingredients, including salt to taste, in a small nonreactive bowl.

PAN-ROASTED HALIBUT

WHY THIS RECIPE WORKS: Chefs often choose to braise halibut instead of pan-roasting or sautéing because this moist-heat cooking technique keeps the fish from drying out. The problem is that braising doesn't allow for browning, therefore producing a fish that the test kitchen considers bland-tasting. We didn't want to make any compromises on either texture or flavor, so we set out to develop a technique for pan-roasting halibut that would produce perfectly cooked, moist, and tender fish.

Halibut is most frequently sold as steaks, but there is quite a bit of range in size; to ensure that they cooked at the same rate, we chose steaks that were as close in size to each other as possible. We knew we could get a crust on the fish by pan-searing or oven-roasting, but neither technique proved satisfactory. A combination of the two proved best: browning on the stovetop and roasting in the oven. To be sure the steaks wouldn't overcook, we seared them on one side in a piping-hot skillet, then turned them over before placing them into the oven to finish cooking through. When they were done, the steaks were browned but still moist inside. To complement the lean fish, we paired the halibut with a rich flavored butter.

Pan-Roasted Halibut Steaks

SERVES 4 TO 6

If you plan to serve the fish with the flavored butter or vinaigrette (recipes follow), prepare it before cooking the fish. Even well-dried fish can cause the hot oil in the pan to splatter. You can minimize splattering by laying the halibut steaks in the pan gently and putting the edge closest to you in the pan first so that the far edge falls away from you.

NOTES FROM THE TEST KITCHEN

TRIMMING AND SERVING FULL HALIBUT STEAKS

BEFORE COOKING: Cut off the cartilage at each end of the steaks to ensure that they will fit neatly in the pan and diminish the likelihood that the small bones located there will wind up on your dinner plate.

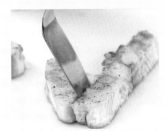

BEFORE SERVING: Remove the skin from the cooked steaks and separate the quadrants of meat from the bone by slipping a spatula gently between them.

2 tablespoons olive oil
2 (full) halibut steaks, about 1¼ inches thick and 10 to 12 inches long (about 2½ pounds total), gently rinsed, dried well with paper towels, and trimmed of cartilage at both ends (see photo on page 235)
Table salt and ground black pepper
1 recipe flavored butter or vinaigrette (recipes follow)

1. Adjust an oven rack to the middle position and heat the oven to 425 degrees. When the oven reaches 425 degrees, heat the oil in a 12-inch ovensafe skillet over high heat until the oil just begins to smoke.

2. Meanwhile, sprinkle both sides of the halibut steaks generously with salt and pepper. Reduce the heat to medium-high and swirl the oil in the pan to distribute; carefully lay the steaks in the pan and sear, without moving them, until spotty brown, about 4 minutes. (If the steaks are thinner than 1¼ inches, check browning at 3½ minutes; thicker steaks of 1½ inches may require extra time, so check at 4½ minutes.) Off the heat, flip the steaks over in the pan using two thin-bladed metal spatulas.

3. Transfer the skillet to the oven and roast until an instant-read thermometer inserted into the steaks reads 140 degrees and the fish flakes loosen and the flesh is opaque when checked with the tip of a paring knife, about 9 minutes (thicker steaks may take up to 10 minutes). Remove the skillet from the oven. Remove the skin from the cooked steaks and separate each quadrant of meat from the bones by slipping a spatula or knife gently between them (see photo). Transfer the fish to a warm platter and serve with the flavored butter or vinaigrette.

Chipotle-Garlic Butter with Lime and Cilantro
MAKES ABOUT ¼ CUP

4 tablespoons (½ stick) unsalted butter, softened
1 medium chipotle chile in adobo sauce, seeded and minced, plus 1 teaspoon adobo sauce
2 teaspoons minced fresh cilantro leaves
1 medium garlic clove, minced or pressed through a garlic press (about 1 teaspoon)
1 teaspoon honey
1 teaspoon grated zest from 1 lime
½ teaspoon table salt

Beat the butter with a fork until light and fluffy. Stir in the remaining ingredients until thoroughly combined. Dollop a portion of the butter over the pieces of hot cooked fish and allow the butter to melt. Serve immediately.

Chunky Cherry Tomato–Basil Vinaigrette
MAKES ABOUT 1½ CUPS

½ pint cherry or grape tomatoes, each tomato quartered (about 1 cup)
¼ teaspoon table salt
¼ teaspoon ground black pepper
2 medium shallots, minced (about 6 tablespoons)

6 tablespoons extra-virgin olive oil
3 tablespoons juice from 1 lemon
2 tablespoons minced fresh basil leaves

Mix the tomatoes with the salt and pepper in a medium bowl; let stand until juicy and seasoned, about 10 minutes. Whisk the shallots, oil, lemon juice, and basil together in a small mixing bowl, pour the vinaigrette over the tomatoes, and toss to combine. Pour over the pieces of hot cooked fish and serve immediately.

BRAISED HALIBUT WITH LEEKS AND MUSTARD

WHY THIS RECIPE WORKS: Braising is a technique usually reserved for tough cuts of meat, but the gentle, moist-heat cooking method also works wonders on fish. Halibut's dense flesh made it an easy fillet to manipulate and its clean, sweet flavor would pair well with a simple wine sauce. We began by gently cooking just one side of the fillets in butter in a skillet, then removing the fish to establish the braising liquid. We cooked sliced leeks in Dijon and their exuded moisture added to the thin sauce. Once the leeks had softened, we added some dry white wine, brought it to a simmer, and placed the halibut atop the vegetables with the uncooked side facing down. This arrangement allowed the parcooked side to steam while the rest of the fillet cooked through to perfection. To finish the sauce, we transferred the cooked fish and vegetables to a serving platter and let the wine sauce reduce, adding lemon juice for a burst of bright acidity.

Braised Halibut with Leeks and Mustard
SERVES 4

We prefer to prepare this recipe with halibut, but a similar firm-fleshed white fish such as striped bass or sea bass that is between ¾ and 1 inch thick can be substituted. To ensure that your fish cooks evenly, purchase fillets that are similarly shaped and uniformly thick.

4 (6- to 8-ounce) skinless halibut fillets, ¾ to 1 inch thick
Salt and pepper
6 tablespoons unsalted butter
1 pound leeks, white and light green parts only, halved lengthwise, sliced thin, and washed thoroughly
1 teaspoon Dijon mustard
¾ cup dry white wine
1 teaspoon lemon juice, plus lemon wedges for serving
1 tablespoon minced fresh parsley

1. Sprinkle fish with ½ teaspoon salt. Melt butter in 12-inch skillet over low heat. Place fish in skillet, skinned side up, increase heat to medium, and cook, shaking pan occasionally, until butter begins to brown (fish should not brown), 3 to 4 minutes. Using spatula, carefully transfer fish to large plate, raw side down.

juices from the fish, accelerating browning and giving the fish a rich color and deep flavor that's anything but sweet. We dusted a few fillets with a touch of granulated sugar and placed them in a hot skillet. A well-browned crust formed almost immediately, leaving no time for the interior to dry out. And after a short stay in the oven to finish cooking through, the fish emerged well-browned, tender and moist, and best of all, not one taster detected any out-of-place sweetness.

Pan-Roasted Thick-Cut Fish Fillets

SERVES 4

Thick white fish fillets with a meaty texture, like halibut, cod, sea bass, or red snapper, work best in this recipe. Because most fish fillets differ in thickness, some pieces may finish cooking before others—be sure to immediately remove any fillet that reaches 135 degrees. You will need an ovensafe nonstick skillet for this recipe. If you can't find skinless fillets, see page 229 for information on skinning fillets. Serve with lemon wedges or one of the relishes on page 232–233.

4   (6 to 8-ounce) skinless white fish fillets,
    1 to 1½ inches thick (see note)
    Table salt and ground black pepper
½   teaspoon sugar
1   tablespoon vegetable oil
    Lemon wedges or relish (see note), for serving

Adjust an oven rack to the middle position and heat the oven to 425 degrees. Dry the fish thoroughly with paper towels and season with salt and pepper. Sprinkle ⅛ teaspoon sugar evenly over one side of each fillet. Heat the oil in a 12-inch ovensafe nonstick skillet over high heat until smoking. Place the fillets in the skillet, sugared side down, and press down lightly to ensure even contact with the pan. Cook until browned, 1 to 1½ minutes. Using two spatulas, flip the fillets and transfer the skillet to the oven. Roast the fillets until the centers are just opaque and the fish registers 135 degrees on an instant-read thermometer, 7 to 10 minutes. Immediately transfer the fish to individual plates and serve with lemon wedges or relish.

2. Add leeks, mustard, and ½ teaspoon salt to skillet and cook, stirring frequently, until leeks begin to soften, 2 to 4 minutes. Add wine and bring to gentle simmer. Place fish, raw side down, on top of leeks. Cover skillet and cook, adjusting heat to maintain gentle simmer, until fish registers 135 to 140 degrees, 10 to 14 minutes. Remove skillet from heat and, using 2 spatulas, transfer fish and leeks to serving platter or individual plates. Tent loosely with aluminum foil.

3. Return skillet to high heat and simmer briskly until sauce is thickened, 2 to 3 minutes. Remove pan from heat, stir in lemon juice, and season with salt and pepper to taste. Spoon sauce over fish and sprinkle with parsley. Serve immediately with lemon wedges.

Braised Halibut with Carrots and Coriander

Substitute 1 pound carrots, peeled and shaved with vegetable peeler lengthwise into ribbons, and 4 shallots, halved and sliced thin, for leeks. Substitute ½ teaspoon ground coriander seed for Dijon mustard. Increase lemon juice to 1½ teaspoons and substitute cilantro for parsley.

PAN-ROASTED FISH FILLETS

WHY THIS RECIPE WORKS: Pan-roasted fish seems like a simple dish, but in reality it is usually only well executed by practiced chefs. At home, the dish often results in dry, over-baked fillets. We set out to develop a foolproof recipe for producing succulent, well-browned fillets.

From an initial round of testing, we knew we needed thick fillets; skinnier pieces end up overcooked by the time they achieved a serious sear. We then turned to a common restaurant method to cook the fish: Sear the fillet in a hot pan, flip, then transfer it to a hot oven to finish cooking. The technique was sound, but to brown the fish quickly before the hot pan had a chance to dry out the fish's exterior we turned to a sprinkling of sugar. The idea is that sugar commingles with exuded

BAKED SOLE FILLETS

WHY THIS RECIPE WORKS: We wanted a fuss-free, foolproof sole preparation that was suitable for a weeknight dinner yet impressive and elegant enough to serve to company. We found that rolling the fillets into compact bundles eased the transport from baking dish to plate and covering the baking dish with foil protected the delicate fish from the drying heat of the oven. To ramp up the fillets' mild flavor, we brushed them with Dijon mustard; seasoned them with salt, pepper, fresh herbs, and lemon zest; and drizzled them with melted butter and garlic. Then we rolled them up, drizzled them with more butter, and baked them. For texture, we added a mixture of herbs, butter, and panko bread crumbs to the sole at two intervals. We removed the foil before the fish was done cooking, basted the fillets with pan juices, topped them with most of the bread-crumb mixture, and then returned them to the oven uncovered. Just before serving, we sprinkled the remaining crumbs over the fillets.

Baked Sole Fillets with Herbs and Bread Crumbs

SERVES 6

Try to purchase fillets of similar size. If using smaller fillets (about 3 ounces each), serve 2 fillets per person and reduce the baking time in step 3 to 20 minutes. We strongly advise against using frozen fish in this recipe. Freezing can undermine the texture of the fish, making it hard to roll. Fresh basil or dill can be used in place of the tarragon.

- 3 tablespoons minced fresh parsley leaves
- 3 tablespoons minced fresh chives
- 1 tablespoon minced fresh tarragon leaves
- 1 teaspoon grated zest from 1 lemon
- 5 tablespoons unsalted butter, cut into 5 pieces
- 2 medium garlic cloves, minced or pressed through a garlic press (about 2 teaspoons)
- 6 (6-ounce) boneless, skinless sole or flounder fillets
  Table salt and ground black pepper
- 1 tablespoon Dijon mustard
- ⅔ cup panko bread crumbs
  Lemon wedges, for serving

1. Adjust an oven rack to the middle position and heat the oven to 325 degrees. Combine the parsley, chives, and tarragon in a small bowl. Reserve 1 tablespoon herb mixture; stir the lemon zest into the remaining herb mixture.

2. Heat 4 tablespoons of the butter in an 8-inch skillet over medium heat until just melted. Add half of the garlic and cook, stirring frequently, until fragrant, 1 to 2 minutes. Remove from the heat and set aside.

3. Pat the fillets dry with paper towels and season both sides with salt and pepper. Arrange the fillets, skinned side up, with the tail end pointing away from you. Spread ½ teaspoon mustard on each fillet, sprinkle each evenly with about 1 tablespoon of the herb–lemon zest mixture, and drizzle each with about 1½ teaspoons of the garlic butter. Tightly roll the fillets from the thick end to form cylinders. Set the fillets, seam side down, in a 13 by 9-inch baking dish. Drizzle the remaining garlic butter over the fillets, cover the baking dish with aluminum foil, and bake for 25 minutes. Wipe out the skillet but do not wash.

4. While the fillets are baking, melt the remaining 1 tablespoon butter in the now-empty skillet over medium heat. Add the panko and cook, stirring frequently, until the crumbs are deep golden brown, 5 to 8 minutes. Reduce the heat to low, add the remaining garlic, and cook, stirring constantly, until the garlic is fragrant and evenly distributed in the crumbs, about 1 minute. Transfer to a small bowl, stir in ¼ teaspoon salt, and season with pepper to taste. Let cool, then stir in the reserved 1 tablespoon herb mixture.

5. After the fillets have baked for 25 minutes, remove the baking dish from oven. Baste the fillets with melted garlic butter from the baking dish, sprinkle with all but 3 tablespoons of the bread crumbs, and continue to bake, uncovered, until the fillets register 135 degrees on an instant-read thermometer, 6 to 10 minutes longer. Using a thin metal spatula, transfer the fillets to plates, sprinkle with the remaining bread crumbs, and serve with the lemon wedges.

PAN-SEARED SCALLOPS

WHY THIS RECIPE WORKS: Producing, crisp-crusted restaurant-style scallops means overcoming two obstacles: chemically treated scallops and weak stovetops. We wanted to achieve superior pan-seared scallops that had a perfectly brown crust and no hint of off-flavors. We decided to work with wet scallops (those that are chemically treated with STP, a solution of water and sodium tripolyphosphate, to increase shelf life and retain moisture) first. If we could develop a good recipe for finicky wet scallops, it would surely work with premium dry (untreated) scallops. We found that waiting to add the scallops to the skillet until the oil was beginning to smoke, cooking the scallops in two batches instead of one, and switching to a nonstick skillet (so that the browned bits formed a crust on the meat instead of sticking to the skillet) were all steps in the right direction. But it wasn't until we tried a common restaurant technique—butter basting—that our scallops really improved. We seared the scallops in oil on one side and added butter to the skillet after flipping them. (Butter contains milk proteins and sugars that brown rapidly when heated.) We then used a large spoon to ladle the foaming butter over the scallops. Waiting to add the butter ensured that it had just enough time to work its browning magic on the scallops, but not enough time to burn.

Next we addressed the lingering flavor of STP. Unable to rinse it away, we decided to mask it by soaking the scallops in a saltwater brine containing lemon juice. For dry scallops, we simply skipped the soaking step and proceeded with the recipe. It produced scallops that rivaled those made on a powerful restaurant range, with golden brown exteriors and juicy and tender interiors.

Pan-Seared Scallops

SERVES 4

We strongly recommend purchasing dry scallops (those without chemical additives). If you can only find wet scallops, soak them in a solution of 1 quart cold water, ¼ cup lemon juice, and 2 tablespoons table salt for 30 minutes before proceeding with step 1, and season the scallops with pepper only in step 2. Prepare the sauce (if serving) while the scallops dry (between steps 1 and 2) and keep it warm while cooking them.

1½ pounds dry sea scallops (about 16 scallops),
   tendons removed (see note)
   Table salt and ground black pepper
2 tablespoons vegetable oil
2 tablespoons unsalted butter
   Lemon wedges or Lemon Browned Butter
   Sauce (recipe follows)

1. Place the scallops on a rimmed baking sheet lined with a clean kitchen towel. Place a second clean kitchen towel on top of the scallops and press gently on the towel to blot the liquid. Let the scallops sit at room temperature for 10 minutes while the towels absorb the moisture.

2. Remove the second towel and sprinkle the scallops on both sides with salt and pepper. Heat 1 tablespoon of the oil in a 12-inch nonstick skillet over high heat until just smoking. Add half of the scallops in a single layer, flat side down, and cook, without moving, until well browned, 1½ to 2 minutes.

3. Add 1 tablespoon of the butter to the skillet. Using tongs, flip the scallops and continue to cook, using a large spoon to baste the scallops with the melted butter, tilting the skillet so the butter runs to one side, until the sides of the scallops are firm and the centers are opaque, 30 to 90 seconds longer (remove the smaller scallops from the pan as they finish cooking). Transfer the scallops to a large plate and tent loosely with foil. Wipe out the skillet with a wad of paper towels and repeat with the remaining 1 tablespoon oil, remaining scallops, and remaining 1 tablespoon butter. Serve immediately with lemon wedges or sauce.

NOTES FROM THE TEST KITCHEN

ARE YOUR SCALLOPS WET OR DRY?

If you are unsure whether your scallops are wet (treated with chemicals) or dry (untreated), conduct this quick test: Place 1 scallop on a paper towel–lined, microwave-safe plate and microwave on high power for 15 seconds. If the scallop is dry, it will exude very little water. If it is wet, there will be a sizable ring of moisture on the paper towel. (The microwaved scallop can be cooked as is.)

PREPPING SCALLOPS

The small, crescent-shaped muscle that is sometimes attached to the scallop will be incredibly tough when cooked. Use your fingers to peel this muscle away from the sides of each scallop before cooking.

Lemon Browned Butter Sauce
MAKES ABOUT ¼ CUP

4 tablespoons (½ stick) unsalted butter,
   cut into 4 pieces
1 small shallot, minced (about 1½ tablespoons)
1 tablespoon minced fresh parsley leaves
½ teaspoon minced fresh thyme leaves
2 teaspoons juice from 1 lemon
   Table salt and ground black pepper

Heat the butter in a small heavy-bottomed saucepan over medium heat and cook, swirling the pan constantly, until the butter turns dark golden brown and has a nutty aroma, 4 to 5 minutes. Add the shallot and cook until fragrant, about 30 seconds. Remove the pan from the heat and stir in the parsley, thyme, and lemon juice. Season with salt and pepper to taste. Cover to keep warm.

PAN-SEARED SHRIMP

WHY THIS RECIPE WORKS: A good recipe for pan-seared shrimp is hard to find. Of the handful of recipes we uncovered, the majority resulted in shrimp that were either dry and flavorless or pale, tough, and gummy. We wanted shrimp that were well caramelized but still moist, briny, and tender.

We peeled the shrimp first and tried using a brine to add moisture, but found that it inhibited browning. Instead, we seasoned the shrimp with salt, pepper, and sugar, which brought out their natural sweetness and aided in browning. We cooked the shrimp in batches in a large, piping-hot skillet and then paired them with thick, glaze-like sauces with assertive ingredients and plenty of acidity as a foil for the shrimp's richness.

Pan-Seared Shrimp
SERVES 4

This recipe can also be prepared with large shrimp (31 to 40 per pound); the cooking time will be slightly shorter. Either a nonstick or a traditional skillet will work for this recipe, but a nonstick simplifies cleanup.

2 tablespoons vegetable oil
1½ pounds extra-large shrimp (21 to 25 per pound),
   peeled and deveined (see page 240; see note)
¼ teaspoon table salt
¼ teaspoon ground black pepper
⅛ teaspoon sugar

Heat 1 tablespoon of the oil in a 12-inch skillet over high heat until smoking. Meanwhile, toss the shrimp, salt, pepper, and sugar in a medium bowl. Add half of the shrimp to the pan in a single layer and cook until spotty brown and the edges turn

pink, about 1 minute. Remove the pan from the heat. Using tongs, flip each shrimp and let stand until all but the very center is opaque, about 30 seconds. Transfer the shrimp to a large plate. Repeat with the remaining 1 tablespoon oil and the remaining shrimp. After the second batch has stood off the heat, return the first batch to the skillet and toss to combine. Cover the skillet and let stand until the shrimp are cooked through, 1 to 2 minutes. Serve immediately.

Pan-Seared Shrimp with Garlic-Lemon Butter

Beat 3 tablespoons softened unsalted butter with a fork in a small bowl until light and fluffy. Stir in 1 medium garlic clove, minced or pressed through a garlic press, 1 tablespoon juice from 1 lemon, 2 tablespoons chopped fresh parsley leaves, and ⅛ teaspoon salt until combined. Follow the recipe for Pan-Seared Shrimp, adding the flavored butter when returning the first batch of shrimp to the skillet. Serve with lemon wedges, if desired.

Pan-Seared Shrimp with Ginger-Hoisin Glaze

Stir 2 tablespoons hoisin sauce, 1 tablespoon rice vinegar, 1½ teaspoons soy sauce, 2 teaspoons minced or grated fresh ginger, 2 teaspoons water, and 2 scallions, sliced thin, together in a small bowl. Follow the recipe for Pan-Seared Shrimp, substituting an equal amount of red pepper flakes for the black pepper and adding the hoisin mixture when returning the first batch of shrimp to the skillet.

Pan-Seared Shrimp with Chipotle-Lime Glaze

Stir 1 chipotle chile in adobo, minced, 2 teaspoons adobo sauce, 4 teaspoons brown sugar, 2 tablespoons juice from 1 lime, and 2 tablespoons chopped fresh cilantro leaves together in a small bowl. Follow the recipe for Pan-Seared Shrimp, adding the chipotle mixture when returning the first batch of shrimp to the skillet.

NOTES FROM THE TEST KITCHEN

DEVEINING SHRIMP

1. After removing the shell, use a paring knife to make a shallow cut along the back of the shrimp so that the vein is exposed.

2. Use the tip of the knife to lift the vein out of the shrimp. Discard the vein by wiping the blade against a paper towel.

CRISPY SALT AND PEPPER SHRIMP

WHY THIS RECIPE WORKS: The shrimp in this Chinese restaurant specialty are noted for their spicy heat and shells so crisp they're good enough to eat. Smaller shrimp are younger and have thinner shells, so we brought home a pound of 31- to 40-count shrimp and tossed them in rice wine and salt to infuse them with well-seasoned, savory flavor. A blend of black peppercorns and lively Sichuan peppercorns, ground together, combined with sugar and cayenne established the dish's flavor profile. Coating the shrimp with this blend and some cornstarch fused the flavors to the meat while also drawing out excess moisture for maximum crisping. We fried the shrimp in batches to prevent the oil's heat from flagging. Fried jalapeño slices would add extra heat at serving, and we reinforced the dish's big flavors by reserving some of the spicy frying oil and combining it with the spice blend, minced garlic, and grated fresh ginger. We heated this seasoned oil until it browned and tossed the cooked shrimp in it, scattering in sliced scallions for a dose of freshness.

Crispy Salt and Pepper Shrimp
SERVES 4 TO 6

In this recipe the shrimp are meant to be eaten shell and all. To ensure that the shells fry up crisp, avoid using shrimp that are overly large or jumbo. We prefer 31- to 40-count shrimp, but 26- to 30-count may be substituted. Serve with steamed rice.

- 1½ pounds shell-on shrimp (31 to 40 per pound)
- 2 tablespoons Chinese rice wine or dry sherry
  Kosher salt
- 2½ teaspoons black peppercorns
- 2 teaspoons Sichuan peppercorns
- 2 teaspoons sugar
- ¼ teaspoon cayenne pepper

4 cups vegetable oil

5 tablespoons cornstarch

2 jalapeño chiles, stemmed, seeded, and
   sliced into ⅛-inch-thick rings

3 garlic cloves, minced

1 tablespoon grated fresh ginger

2 scallions, sliced thin on bias

¼ head iceberg lettuce, shredded (1½ cups)

1. Adjust oven rack to upper-middle position and heat oven to 225 degrees. Toss shrimp, rice wine, and 1 teaspoon salt together in large bowl and set aside for 10 to 15 minutes.

2. Grind black peppercorns and Sichuan peppercorns in spice grinder or mortar and pestle until coarsely ground. Transfer peppercorns to small bowl and stir in sugar and cayenne.

3. Heat oil in large Dutch oven over medium heat until oil registers 385 degrees. While oil is heating, drain shrimp and pat dry with paper towels. Transfer shrimp to bowl, add 3 tablespoons cornstarch and 1 tablespoon peppercorn mixture, and toss until well combined.

4. Carefully add one-third of shrimp to oil and fry, stirring occasionally to keep shrimp from sticking together, until light brown, 2 to 3 minutes. Using wire skimmer or slotted spoon, transfer shrimp to paper towel–lined plate. Once paper towels absorb any excess oil, transfer shrimp to wire rack set in rimmed baking sheet and place in oven. Return oil to 385 degrees and repeat in 2 more batches, tossing each batch thoroughly with coating mixture before frying.

5. Toss jalapeño rings and remaining 2 tablespoons cornstarch in medium bowl. Shaking off excess cornstarch, carefully add jalapeño rings to oil and fry until crispy, 1 to 2 minutes. Using wire skimmer or slotted spoon, transfer jalapeño rings to paper towel–lined plate. After frying, reserve 2 tablespoons frying oil.

6. Heat reserved oil in 12-inch skillet over medium-high heat until shimmering. Add garlic, ginger, and remaining peppercorn mixture and cook, stirring occasionally, until mixture is fragrant and just beginning to brown, about 45 seconds. Add shrimp, scallions, and ½ teaspoon salt and toss to coat. Line platter with lettuce. Transfer shrimp to platter, sprinkle with jalapeño rings, and serve immediately.

GARLICKY SHRIMP WITH BREAD CRUMBS

WHY THIS RECIPE WORKS: Just about every all-purpose cookbook includes a recipe for a casserole of shrimp in a sherry-garlic sauce topped with bread crumbs, but the ones we tried produced rubbery shrimp and gluey toppings. We wanted all the potent flavors and contrasting textures that the name of this dish promises—tender, moist shrimp infused with garlic and blanketed with crisp, buttery bread crumbs.

Most recipes call for cooking the shrimp twice, first poaching them on the stovetop and then baking them in the casserole dish. No wonder they're usually overdone! Our experiments with skipping the poaching weren't very successful—the shrimp were just plain bland—so we abandoned the oven altogether and decided to make the entire dish in a skillet on top of the stove. After searing the shrimp on one side, sprinkled with a pinch of sugar to promote browning, we removed them to build the sauce; we would add the shrimp back at the end to heat through and finish cooking. For the sauce, we started with garlic. Sherry alone tasted too boozy, so we cut it with clam juice, which underscored the briny flavor of the shrimp. A pinch of flour and some butter thickened the sauce, and lemon juice brightened everything up. A chewy supermarket baguette made the perfect buttery bread crumbs; sprinkled on at the last minute, they were sturdy enough to stay crisp on the saucy shrimp. Our modernized skillet "casserole" was definitely an improvement on the tired old version.

Garlicky Shrimp with Buttered Bread Crumbs
SERVES 4

Vermouth can be substituted for the sherry. If using vermouth, increase the amount to ½ cup and reduce the amount of clam juice to ½ cup. To prepare this recipe in a 10-inch skillet, brown the shrimp in three batches for about 2 minutes each, using 2 teaspoons oil per batch. Serve the shrimp with rice and either broccoli or asparagus.

1 (3-inch) piece baguette, cut into small pieces

5 tablespoons unsalted butter, cut into 5 pieces

1 small shallot, minced (about 1 tablespoon)
   Table salt and ground black pepper

2 tablespoons minced fresh parsley leaves

2 pounds extra-large shrimp (21 to 25 per pound),
   peeled and deveined (see page 240)

¼ teaspoon sugar

4 teaspoons vegetable oil

4 medium garlic cloves, minced or pressed through
   a garlic press (about 4 teaspoons)

⅛ teaspoon red pepper flakes

2 teaspoons unbleached all-purpose flour

⅔ cup bottled clam juice

⅓ cup dry sherry (see note)

2 teaspoons juice from 1 lemon, plus lemon wedges
   for serving

1. Pulse the bread in a food processor until coarsely ground, about 8 pulses; you should have about 1 cup crumbs. Melt 1 tablespoon of the butter in a 12-inch nonstick skillet over medium heat. Add the crumbs, shallot, ⅛ teaspoon salt, and ⅛ teaspoon pepper. Cook, stirring occasionally, until the bread crumbs are golden brown, 7 to 10 minutes. Stir in 1 tablespoon of the parsley and transfer to a plate to cool. Wipe out the skillet with paper towels.

2. Pat the shrimp dry with paper towels and toss with the sugar, ¼ teaspoon salt, and ¼ teaspoon pepper in a bowl. Return the skillet to high heat, add 2 teaspoons of the oil, and heat until shimmering. Add half of the shrimp in a single layer and cook until spotty brown and the edges turn pink, about 3 minutes (do not flip the shrimp). Remove the pan from heat and transfer the shrimp to a large plate. Wipe out the skillet with paper towels. Repeat with the remaining 2 teaspoons oil and remaining shrimp; transfer the shrimp to the plate.

3. Return the skillet to medium heat and add 1 tablespoon more butter. When melted, add the garlic and red pepper flakes; cook, stirring frequently, until the garlic just begins to color, about 1 minute. Add the flour and cook, stirring frequently, for 1 minute. Increase the heat to medium-high and slowly whisk in the clam juice and sherry. Bring to a simmer and cook until the mixture reduces to ¾ cup, 3 to 4 minutes. Whisk in the remaining 3 tablespoons butter, 1 tablespoon at a time. Stir in the lemon juice and remaining 1 tablespoon parsley.

4. Reduce the heat to medium-low, return the shrimp to the pan, and toss to combine. Cook, covered, until the shrimp are pink and cooked through, 2 to 3 minutes. Uncover and sprinkle with the toasted bread crumbs. Serve with the lemon wedges.

GARLICKY ROASTED SHRIMP

WHY THIS RECIPE WORKS: We loved the idea of an easy weeknight meal of juicy roasted shrimp, but getting the lean, quick-cooking shrimp to develop color and roasted flavor before they turned rubbery required a few tricks. First we chose jumbo-size shrimp, which were the least likely to dry out and overcook. Butterflying the shrimp increased their surface area, giving us more room to add flavor. After brining the shrimp briefly to help them hold on to more moisture, we tossed them in a potent mixture of aromatic spices, garlic, herbs, butter, and oil. Then we roasted them under the broiler to get lots of color as quickly as possible, elevating them on a wire rack so they'd brown all over. To further protect them as they cooked and to produce a more deeply roasted flavor, we left their shells on; the sugar- and protein-rich shells browned quickly in the heat of the oven and transferred flavor to the shrimp itself.

Garlicky Roasted Shrimp with Parsley and Anise
SERVES 4 TO 6

Don't be tempted to use smaller shrimp with this cooking technique; they will be over seasoned and prone to overcook.

- ¼ cup salt
- 2 pounds shell-on jumbo shrimp (16 to 20 per pound)
- 4 tablespoons unsalted butter, melted
- ¼ cup vegetable oil
- 6 garlic cloves, minced
- 1 teaspoon anise seeds
- ½ teaspoon red pepper flakes
- ¼ teaspoon pepper
- 2 tablespoons minced fresh parsley
  Lemon wedges

1. Dissolve salt in 1 quart cold water in large container. Using kitchen shears or sharp paring knife, cut through shell of shrimp and devein but do not remove shell. Using paring knife, continue to cut shrimp ½ inch deep, taking care not to cut in half completely. Submerge shrimp in brine, cover, and refrigerate for 15 minutes.

2. Adjust oven rack 4 inches from broiler element and heat broiler. Combine melted butter, oil, garlic, anise seeds, pepper flakes, and pepper in large bowl. Remove shrimp from brine and pat dry with paper towels. Add shrimp and parsley to butter mixture; toss well, making sure butter mixture gets into interior of shrimp. Arrange shrimp in single layer on wire rack set in rimmed baking sheet.

3. Broil shrimp until opaque and shells are beginning to brown, 2 to 4 minutes, rotating sheet halfway through broiling. Flip shrimp and continue to broil until second side is opaque and shells are beginning to brown, 2 to 4 minutes longer, rotating sheet halfway through broiling. Transfer shrimp to serving platter and serve immediately, passing lemon wedges separately.

Garlicky Roasted Shrimp with Cilantro and Lime

Annatto powder, also called achiote, can be found with the Latin American foods at your supermarket. An equal amount of paprika can be substituted.

Omit butter and increase vegetable oil to ½ cup. Omit anise seeds and pepper. Add 2 teaspoons lightly crushed coriander seeds, 2 teaspoons grated lime zest, and 1 teaspoon annatto powder to oil mixture in step 2. Substitute ¼ cup minced fresh cilantro for parsley and lime wedges for lemon wedges.

Garlicky Roasted Shrimp with Cumin, Ginger, and Sesame

Omit butter and increase vegetable oil to ½ cup. Decrease garlic to 2 cloves and omit anise seeds and pepper. Add 2 teaspoons toasted sesame oil, 1½ teaspoons grated fresh ginger, and 1 teaspoon cumin seeds to oil mixture in step 2. Substitute 2 thinly sliced scallion greens for parsley and omit lemon wedges.

SPANISH-STYLE SIZZLING GARLIC SHRIMP

WHY THIS RECIPE WORKS: Sizzling *gambas al ajillo* is a tempting dish served in tapas bars. We knew we would have to make some adjustments to re-create this dish as an appetizer to serve at home, but our work would pay off when we could savor the juicy shrimp in spicy, garlic-infused oil.

The shrimp in the Spanish original are completely submerged in oil and cooked slowly. We didn't want to use that much oil, so we added just enough to a skillet to come halfway up the sides of the shrimp. We cooked them over very low heat and turned them halfway through; these shrimp cooked as evenly as they would have if completely covered with oil. We built heady garlic flavor in three ways: We added raw minced garlic to a marinade, we browned smashed cloves in the oil in which the shrimp would be cooked, and we cooked slices of garlic along with the shrimp. We included the traditional bay leaf and red chile, and added sherry vinegar (rather than sherry) and parsley, all of which brightened the richness of the oil. Served with plenty of bread to soak up the extra juices and flavorful oil, these garlicky shrimp rival the best restaurant versions.

Spanish-Style Garlic Shrimp
SERVES 6
Serve the shrimp with crusty bread for dipping in the richly flavored olive oil. This dish can be served directly from the skillet (make sure to use a trivet) or, for a sizzling effect, transferred to an 8-inch cast-iron skillet that's been heated for 2 minutes over medium-high heat. We prefer the slightly sweet flavor of dried chiles in this recipe, but ¼ teaspoon sweet paprika can be substituted. If sherry vinegar is unavailable, use 2 teaspoons dry sherry and 1 teaspoon white vinegar.

- 14 medium garlic cloves, peeled
- 1 pound large shrimp (31 to 40 per pound), peeled, deveined (see page 240), and tails removed
- 8 tablespoons olive oil
- ½ teaspoon table salt
- 1 bay leaf
- 1 (2-inch) piece mild dried chile, such as New Mexico, roughly broken, seeds included (see note)
- 1½ teaspoons sherry vinegar (see note)
- 1 tablespoon minced fresh parsley leaves

1. Mince 2 of the garlic cloves with a chef's knife or garlic press. Toss the minced garlic with the shrimp, 2 tablespoons of the olive oil, and salt in a medium bowl. Let the shrimp marinate at room temperature for 30 minutes.

2. Meanwhile, using the flat side of a chef's knife, smash 4 more garlic cloves. Heat the smashed garlic with the remaining 6 tablespoons olive oil in a 12-inch skillet over medium-low heat, stirring occasionally, until the garlic is light golden brown, 4 to 7 minutes. Remove the pan from the heat and allow the oil to cool to room temperature. Using a slotted spoon, remove the smashed garlic from the skillet and discard.

3. Slice the remaining 8 garlic cloves thin. Return the skillet to low heat and add the sliced garlic, bay leaf, and chile. Cook, stirring occasionally, until the garlic is tender but not browned, 4 to 7 minutes. (If the garlic has not begun to sizzle after 3 minutes, increase the heat to medium-low.) Increase the heat to medium-low and add the shrimp with the marinade to the pan in a single layer. Cook the shrimp, undisturbed, until the oil starts to gently bubble, about 2 minutes. Using tongs, flip the shrimp and continue to cook until almost cooked through, about 2 minutes longer. Increase the heat to high and add the sherry vinegar and parsley. Cook, stirring constantly, until the shrimp are cooked through and the oil is bubbling vigorously, 15 to 20 seconds. Serve immediately, discarding the bay leaf.

SPANISH-STYLE TOASTED PASTA WITH SHRIMP

WHY THIS RECIPE WORKS: Traditional recipes for *fideuà* can take several hours to prepare. We wanted to speed up the process but keep the deep flavors of the classic recipes. To replace the slow-cooked fish stock of the classics, we made a quick shrimp stock using the shrimp's shells, a combination of chicken broth and water, and a bay leaf. We also streamlined the *sofrito*, the aromatic base common in Spanish cooking, by finely mincing the onion and using canned tomatoes (instead of fresh), which helped the recipe components soften and brown more quickly. The final tweak to our recipe was boosting the flavor of the shrimp by quickly marinating them in olive oil, garlic, salt, and pepper.

Spanish-Style Toasted Pasta with Shrimp
SERVES 4
In step 5, if your skillet is not broiler-safe, once the pasta is tender transfer the mixture to a broiler-safe 13 by 9-inch baking dish lightly coated with olive oil; scatter the shrimp over the pasta and stir them in to partially submerge. Broil and serve as directed. Serve this dish with lemon wedges and Aïoli (recipe follows), stirring it into individual portions at the table.

3 tablespoons plus 2 teaspoons extra-virgin olive oil

3 garlic cloves, minced

Salt and pepper

1½ pounds extra-large shrimp (21 to 25 per pound), peeled and deveined (see page 240), shells reserved

2¾ cups water

1 cup low-sodium chicken broth

1 bay leaf

8 ounces spaghettini or thin spaghetti, broken into 1- to 2-inch lengths

1 onion, chopped fine

1 (14.5-ounce) can diced tomatoes, drained and chopped fine

1 teaspoon paprika

1 teaspoon smoked paprika

½ teaspoon anchovy paste

¼ cup dry white wine

1 tablespoon chopped fresh parsley

Lemon wedges

1 recipe Aïoli (optional) (recipe follows)

1. Combine 1 tablespoon oil, 1 teaspoon garlic, ¼ teaspoon salt, and ⅛ teaspoon pepper in medium bowl. Add shrimp, toss to coat, and refrigerate until ready to use.

2. Place reserved shrimp shells, water, broth, and bay leaf in medium bowl. Cover and microwave until liquid is hot and shells have turned pink, about 6 minutes. Set aside until ready to use.

3. Toss spaghettini and 2 teaspoons oil in broiler-safe 12-inch skillet until spaghettini is evenly coated. Toast spaghettini over medium-high heat, stirring frequently, until browned and nutty in aroma (spaghettini should be color of peanut butter), 6 to 10 minutes. Transfer spaghettini to bowl. Wipe out skillet with paper towel.

4. Heat remaining 2 tablespoons oil in now-empty skillet over medium-high heat until shimmering. Add onion and ¼ teaspoon salt; cook, stirring frequently, until onion is softened and beginning to brown around edges, 4 to 6 minutes. Add tomatoes and cook, stirring occasionally, until mixture is thick, dry, and slightly darkened in color, 4 to 6 minutes. Reduce heat to medium and add remaining garlic, paprika, smoked paprika, and anchovy paste. Cook until fragrant, about 1½ minutes. Add spaghettini and stir to combine. Adjust oven rack 5 to 6 inches from broiler element and heat broiler.

5. Pour shrimp broth through fine-mesh strainer into skillet. Add wine, ¼ teaspoon salt, and ½ teaspoon pepper and stir well. Increase heat to medium-high and bring to simmer. Cook uncovered, stirring occasionally, until liquid is slightly thickened and spaghettini is just tender, 8 to 10 minutes. Scatter shrimp over spaghettini and stir shrimp into spaghettini to partially submerge. Transfer skillet to oven and broil until shrimp are opaque and surface of spaghettini is dry with crisped, browned spots, 5 to 7 minutes. Remove from oven and let stand, uncovered, for 5 minutes. Sprinkle with parsley and serve immediately, passing lemon wedges and aïoli, if using, separately.

Spanish-Style Toasted Pasta with Shrimp and Clams

Reduce amount of shrimp to 1 pound and water to 2½ cups. In step 5, cook pasta until almost tender, about 6 minutes. Scatter 1½ pounds scrubbed littleneck or cherrystone clams over pasta, cover skillet, and cook until clams begin to open, about 3 minutes. Scatter shrimp over pasta, stir to partially submerge shrimp and clams, and proceed with recipe as directed.

Aïoli

MAKES ¾ CUP

1 garlic clove, grated fine

2 large egg yolks

4 teaspoons lemon juice

¼ teaspoon salt

⅛ teaspoon sugar

Ground white pepper

¾ cup olive oil

In large bowl, combine garlic, egg yolks, lemon juice, salt, sugar, and pepper to taste until combined. Whisking constantly, very slowly drizzle oil into egg mixture until thick and creamy. Season with salt and pepper to taste.

NOTES FROM THE TEST KITCHEN

IT'S A SNAP

Since traditional short *fideos* noodles are hard to find, we came up with an easy way to break long strands into even lengths.

1. Loosely fold 4 ounces of spaghettini in clean dish towel, keeping pasta flat, not bunched. Position so that 1 to 2 inches of pasta rests on counter and remainder of pasta hangs off edge.

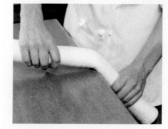

2. Pressing bundle against counter, press down on long end of towel to break strands into pieces, sliding bundle back over edge after each break.

GREEK SHRIMP

WHY THIS RECIPE WORKS: We can think of few examples where the unlikely combination of seafood and cheese marry as well as in Greece's shrimp *saganaki*. In this dish, sweet, briny shrimp are covered with a garlic-and-herb accented tomato sauce and topped with crumbles of creamy, salty feta cheese. Ordering this dish at a restaurant, however, can be a gamble. The shrimp can be tough and rubbery, the tomato sauce can turn out dull or overwhelming, and the feta can be lackluster. We set out to develop a foolproof version of this dish—one that is perfectly cooked and captures the bold and exuberant essence of Greek cuisine.

We started with the tomato sauce. Canned diced tomatoes along with sautéed onion and garlic provided our base. Dry white wine added acidity. Ouzo, the slightly sweet anise-flavored Greek liqueur, added welcome complexity when we simmered it in the sauce.

While the shrimp are typically layered with the tomato sauce and feta and baked, we found this method lacking. Since this should be a quick and easy dish, we opted to cook the shrimp right in the sauce; adding the shrimp raw to the sauce helped infuse them with the sauce's bright flavor. And for even more flavor, we marinated the shrimp with olive oil, ouzo, garlic, and lemon zest first while we made the sauce. Final touches included a generous sprinkling of feta over the sauced shrimp as well as a scattering of chopped fresh dill.

Greek-Style Shrimp with Tomatoes and Feta
SERVES 4 TO 6

This recipe works equally well with either jumbo shrimp (16 to 20 per pound) or extra-large shrimp (21 to 25 per pound); the cooking times in step 3 will vary slightly. Serve with crusty bread for soaking up the sauce.

1½   pounds shrimp, peeled and deveined (see page 240),
        tails left on, if desired (see note)
4   tablespoons extra-virgin olive oil
3   tablespoons ouzo
5   medium garlic cloves, minced or pressed through
        a garlic press (about 5 teaspoons)
1   teaspoon grated zest from 1 lemon
        Table salt and ground black pepper
1   small onion, diced medium
½   medium red bell pepper, stemmed, seeded,
        and diced medium
½   medium green bell pepper, stemmed, seeded,
        and diced medium
½   teaspoon red pepper flakes
1   (28-ounce) can diced tomatoes, drained,
        ⅓ cup juice reserved
¼   cup dry white wine
2   tablespoons coarsely chopped fresh parsley leaves
6   ounces feta cheese, preferably sheep's and/or
        goat's milk, crumbled (about 1½ cups)
2   tablespoons chopped fresh dill

1. Toss the shrimp, 1 tablespoon of the oil, 1 tablespoon of the ouzo, 1 teaspoon of the garlic, the lemon zest, ¼ teaspoon salt, and ⅛ teaspoon black pepper in a small bowl until well combined. Set aside while preparing the sauce.

2. Heat 2 tablespoons more oil in a 12-inch skillet over medium heat until shimmering. Add the onion, red and green bell peppers, and ¼ teaspoon salt and stir to combine. Cover the skillet and cook, stirring occasionally, until the vegetables release their moisture, 3 to 5 minutes. Uncover and continue to cook, stirring occasionally, until the moisture cooks off and the vegetables have softened, about 5 minutes longer. Add the remaining 4 teaspoons garlic and the red pepper flakes and cook until fragrant, about 1 minute. Add the tomatoes and reserved juice, the wine, and the remaining 2 tablespoons ouzo; increase the heat to medium-high and bring to a simmer. Reduce the heat to medium and simmer, stirring occasionally, until the flavors have melded and the sauce is slightly thickened (the sauce should not be completely dry), 5 to 8 minutes. Stir in the parsley and season with salt and pepper to taste.

3. Reduce the heat to medium-low and add the shrimp along with any accumulated liquid to the pan; stir to coat and distribute evenly. Cover and cook, stirring occasionally, until the shrimp are opaque throughout, 6 to 9 minutes for extra-large shrimp or 7 to 11 minutes for jumbo shrimp, adjusting the heat as needed to maintain a bare simmer. Remove the pan from the heat and sprinkle evenly with the feta. Drizzle the remaining 1 tablespoon oil evenly over the top and sprinkle with the dill. Serve immediately.

SHRIMP COCKTAIL

WHY THIS RECIPE WORKS: Nothing is more basic than shrimp cocktail and, given its simplicity, few dishes are more difficult to improve. Yet we set out to do just that; we wanted to work on the shrimp's flavor, the cooking method, and the cocktail sauce. Shrimp cook quickly, so there's little time to add flavor in the pan. We based our cooking liquid on shrimp stock, and added wine, lemon juice, herbs, and spices. To keep the shrimp in contact with this flavorful liquid as long as possible, we brought the mixture to a boil, turned off the heat, and then added the shrimp; the hot liquid cooked the shrimp slowly while they absorbed the stock's flavor. We determined that the classic sauce base, ketchup, was best. We added horseradish, which is the usual ingredient for spicing up the sauce, but we also included chili powder, cayenne, and lemon juice for extra spiciness.

Shrimp Cocktail
SERVES 4

When using larger or smaller shrimp, increase or decrease, respectively, the cooking times for the shrimp by one to two minutes. When using such large shrimp, we find it wise to remove the large black vein. Use horseradish from a freshly opened bottle and mild chili powder for the best flavor in the sauce.

SHRIMP
- 1 pound jumbo shrimp (16 to 20 per pound; see note), peeled, deveined (see page 240), and shells reserved
- 1 teaspoon table salt
- 1 cup dry white wine
- 4 peppercorns
- 5 coriander seeds
- ½ bay leaf
- 5 sprigs fresh parsley
- 1 sprig fresh tarragon
- 1 teaspoon juice from 1 lemon

COCKTAIL SAUCE
- 1 cup ketchup
- 1 tablespoon juice from 1 small lemon
- 2½ teaspoons prepared horseradish (see note)
- 1 teaspoon ancho or other mild chili powder (see note)
- Pinch cayenne pepper
- Table salt and ground black pepper

1. FOR THE SHRIMP: Bring the reserved shells, 3 cups water, and salt to a boil in a medium saucepan over medium-high heat; reduce the heat to low, cover, and simmer until fragrant, about 20 minutes. Strain the stock through a fine-mesh strainer, pressing on the shells to extract all the liquid.

2. Bring the stock and remaining ingredients except the shrimp to a boil in a 3- or 4-quart saucepan over high heat; boil for 2 minutes. Turn off the heat and stir in the shrimp; cover and let stand until the shrimp are firm and pink, 8 to 10 minutes. Meanwhile, fill a large bowl with ice water. Drain the shrimp, reserving the stock for another use. Immediately transfer the shrimp to the ice water to stop cooking and chill thoroughly, about 3 minutes. Remove the shrimp from the ice water and pat dry with paper towels.

3. FOR THE SAUCE: Stir all the ingredients together in a small bowl; season with salt and pepper to taste. Serve the chilled shrimp with the cocktail sauce.

BETTER SHRIMP SALAD

WHY THIS RECIPE WORKS: Most shrimp salads drown in a sea of mayonnaise, in part to hide the rubbery, flavorless boiled shrimp. We wanted perfectly cooked shrimp without the extra work of grilling, roasting, or sautéing. And we needed to coat them with the perfect deli-style dressing—something creamy but not overwhelming.

Overcooking is the culprit when shrimp turn out rubbery. We found that starting the shrimp in cold water (with lemon, parsley, tarragon, pepper, sugar, and salt), then cooking them over very gentle heat, resulted in tender shrimp. The longer cooking time infused the shrimp with the flavors of the poaching liquid. We didn't want to mask these tender, flavorful shrimp with too much dressing, so we scaled back the mayonnaise to a modest amount. Celery added a nice crunch, and shallot, herbs, and lemon juice perked up and rounded out the flavors.

Shrimp Salad
SERVES 4

This recipe can also be prepared with large shrimp (31 to 40 per pound); the cooking time will be 1 to 2 minutes shorter. The shrimp can be cooked up to 24 hours in advance, but hold off on dressing the salad until ready to serve. The recipe can be easily doubled; cook the shrimp in a 7-quart Dutch oven and increase the cooking time to 12 to 14 minutes. Serve the salad spooned over salad greens or on buttered and grilled buns.

1 pound extra-large shrimp (21 to 25 per pound; see note), peeled and deveined (see page 240)
¼ cup plus 1 tablespoon juice from 2 to 3 lemons, spent halves reserved
5 sprigs fresh parsley plus 1 teaspoon minced fresh parsley leaves
3 sprigs fresh tarragon plus 1 teaspoon minced fresh tarragon leaves
1 teaspoon whole black peppercorns plus ground black pepper
1 tablespoon sugar
Table salt
¼ cup mayonnaise
1 small celery rib, minced (about ⅓ cup)
1 small shallot, minced (about 1 tablespoon)

1. Combine the shrimp, ¼ cup of the lemon juice, the reserved lemon halves, parsley sprigs, tarragon sprigs, whole peppercorns, sugar, and 1 teaspoon salt with 2 cups cold water in a medium saucepan. Place the saucepan over medium heat and cook the shrimp, stirring several times, until pink, firm to the touch, and the centers are no longer translucent, 8 to 10 minutes (the water should be just bubbling around the edge of the pan and register 165 degrees on an instant-read thermometer). Remove the pan from the heat, cover, and let the shrimp sit in the broth for 2 minutes.

2. Meanwhile, fill a medium bowl with ice water. Drain the shrimp into a colander and discard the lemon halves, herbs, and spices. Immediately transfer the shrimp to the ice water to stop the cooking and chill thoroughly, about 3 minutes. Remove the shrimp from the ice water and pat dry with paper towels.

3. Whisk together the mayonnaise, celery, shallot, remaining 1 tablespoon lemon juice, the minced parsley, and minced tarragon in a medium bowl. Cut the shrimp in half lengthwise and then each half into thirds; add the shrimp to the mayonnaise mixture and toss to combine. Season with salt and pepper to taste and serve.

Shrimp Salad with Roasted Red Pepper and Basil

This Italian-style variation is especially good served over bitter greens.

Follow the recipe for Shrimp Salad, omitting the tarragon sprigs from the cooking liquid. Replace the celery, minced parsley, and minced tarragon with ⅓ cup thinly sliced jarred roasted red peppers, 2 teaspoons rinsed capers, and 3 tablespoons chopped fresh basil leaves.

Shrimp Salad with Avocado and Orange

Avocado and orange are a refreshing addition to this salad.

Follow the recipe for Shrimp Salad, omitting the tarragon sprigs from the cooking liquid. Replace the celery, minced parsley, and minced tarragon with 4 halved and thinly sliced radishes; 1 large orange, peeled and cut into ½-inch pieces; ½ ripe avocado, cut into ½-inch pieces; and 2 teaspoons minced fresh mint leaves.

MARYLAND CRAB CAKES

WHY THIS RECIPE WORKS: Making crab cakes at home is the only way to avoid the pricey crab-flecked dough balls that pass for crab cakes in many restaurants. We wanted traditional Maryland-style crab cakes with a crisp brown exterior and well-seasoned filling that tasted of sweet crab, not filler. Fresh crabmeat provided superior taste and texture, and jumbo lump crabmeat was worth the high price tag. Pasteurized crabmeat is not quite as good, but it is less expensive. After experimenting with different binders, we settled on fine dry bread crumbs; their flavor is mild, they held the cakes together well, and they mixed easily with the crab. We used just a few tablespoons of crumbs so that the crab's flavor and texture would shine. An egg and some mayonnaise bound the cakes together. Old Bay is the traditional seasoning for crab; some herbs and white pepper were the only additions we found necessary. Carefully folding the ingredients together rather than stirring them kept the texture chunky, and a short chill in the refrigerator ensured that the cakes wouldn't fall apart. Pan-frying in vegetable oil gave our crab cakes the crisp exterior we wanted.

Maryland Crab Cakes

SERVES 4

The amount of bread crumbs you add will depend on the crabmeat's juiciness. Start with the smallest amount, adjust the seasonings, then add the egg. If the cakes won't bind at this point, add more bread crumbs, 1 tablespoon at a time. If you can't find fresh jumbo lump crabmeat, pasteurized crabmeat, though not as good, is a decent substitute. At all costs, avoid the canned crabmeat sold near canned tuna. Either a nonstick or a traditional skillet will work for this recipe, but a nonstick simplifies cleanup.

1 pound fresh jumbo lump crabmeat, carefully picked over to remove cartilage and shell fragments (see note)
4 scallions, green parts only, minced (about ½ cup)
1 tablespoon chopped fresh herb, such as cilantro, dill, basil, or parsley
1½ teaspoons Old Bay seasoning
2-4 tablespoons plain dry bread crumbs (see note)
¼ cup mayonnaise
Table salt and ground white pepper
1 large egg
¼ cup unbleached all-purpose flour
¼ cup vegetable oil
Sweet and Tangy Tartar Sauce (page 224), Creamy Chipotle Chile Sauce (recipe follows), or lemon wedges

1. Gently mix the crabmeat, scallions, herb, Old Bay, 2 tablespoons of the bread crumbs, and the mayonnaise in a medium bowl, being careful not to break up the lumps of crab. Season with salt and white pepper to taste. Carefully fold in the egg with a rubber spatula until the mixture just clings together. Add more bread crumbs if necessary.

2. Divide the crab mixture into four portions and shape each into a fat, round cake, about 3 inches across and 1½ inches high. Arrange the cakes on a baking sheet lined with waxed or parchment paper; cover with plastic wrap and chill for at least 30 minutes. (The crab cakes can be refrigerated for up to 24 hours.)

3. Place the flour in a pie plate. Lightly dredge the crab cakes in the flour. Heat the oil in a large skillet over medium-high heat until hot but not smoking. Gently place the chilled crab cakes in the skillet; pan-fry until the outsides are crisp and browned, 4 to 5 minutes per side. Serve immediately with a sauce or lemon wedges.

Creamy Chipotle Chile Sauce
MAKES ABOUT ½ CUP

The addition of sour cream makes this sauce richer than traditional tartar sauce. The chipotles add smoky and spicy flavors.

- ¼ cup mayonnaise
- ¼ cup sour cream
- 2 teaspoons canned minced chipotle chiles in adobo sauce
- 1 small garlic clove, minced or pressed through a garlic press (about ½ teaspoon)
- 2 teaspoons minced fresh cilantro leaves
- 1 teaspoon juice from 1 lime

Mix all of the ingredients in a small bowl. Cover and refrigerate until the flavors blend, about 30 minutes. (The sauce can be refrigerated for up to 2 days.)

THE BEST CRAB CAKES

WHY THIS RECIPE WORKS: We wanted to come up with a recipe for crab cakes that were chock full of sweet, plump meat delicately seasoned and seamlessly held together with a binder that didn't mask the seafood flavor. And we didn't want shopping to be an issue—we wanted our crab cakes to work with either fresh crabmeat or the pasteurized variety found at the supermarket. To highlight and enhance the crabmeat's sweetness, we bound our cakes with a delicate shrimp mousse. Classic components like Old Bay seasoning and lemon juice bolstered the crab's flavor, and panko bread crumbs helped ensure a crisp crust.

Best Crab Cakes
SERVES 4

Either fresh or pasteurized crabmeat can be used in this recipe. With packaged crab, if the meat smells clean and fresh when you first open the package, skip steps 1 and 4 and simply blot away any excess liquid. Serve the crab cakes with lemon wedges.

- 1 pound lump crabmeat, picked over for shells
- 1 cup milk
- 1½ cups panko bread crumbs
   Salt and pepper

- 2 celery ribs, chopped
- ½ cup chopped onion
- 1 garlic clove, peeled and smashed
- 1 tablespoon unsalted butter
- 4 ounces shrimp, peeled, deveined (see page 240), and tails removed
- ¼ cup heavy cream
- 2 teaspoons Dijon mustard
- 1 teaspoon lemon juice
- ½ teaspoon hot sauce
- ½ teaspoon Old Bay seasoning
- ¼ cup vegetable oil

1. Place crabmeat and milk in bowl, making sure crab is totally submerged. Cover and refrigerate for 20 minutes.

2. Meanwhile, place ¾ cup panko in small zipper-lock bag and finely crush with rolling pin. Transfer crushed panko to 10-inch nonstick skillet and add remaining ¾ cup panko. Toast over medium-high heat, stirring constantly, until golden brown, about 5 minutes. Transfer panko to shallow dish and stir in ¼ teaspoon salt and pepper to taste. Wipe out skillet.

3. Pulse celery, onion, and garlic together in food processor until finely chopped, 5 to 8 pulses, scraping down bowl as needed. Transfer vegetables to large bowl. Rinse processor bowl and blade. Melt butter in now-empty skillet over medium heat. Add chopped vegetables, ½ teaspoon salt, and ⅛ teaspoon pepper; cook, stirring frequently, until vegetables are softened and all moisture has evaporated, 4 to 6 minutes. Return vegetables to large bowl and let cool to room temperature. Rinse out pan and wipe clean.

4. Strain crabmeat through fine-mesh strainer, pressing firmly to remove milk but being careful not to break up lumps of crabmeat.

5. Pulse shrimp in now-empty food processor until finely ground, 12 to 15 pulses, scraping down bowl as needed. Add cream and pulse to combine, 2 to 4 pulses, scraping down bowl as needed. Transfer shrimp puree to bowl with cooled vegetables. Add mustard, lemon juice, hot sauce, and Old Bay; stir until well combined. Add crabmeat and fold gently with rubber spatula, being careful not to overmix, and break up lumps of crabmeat. Divide mixture into 8 balls and firmly press into ½-inch-thick patties. Place cakes in rimmed baking sheet lined with parchment paper, cover tightly with plastic wrap, and refrigerate for 30 minutes.

6. Coat each cake with panko, firmly pressing to adhere crumbs to exterior. Heat 1 tablespoon oil in now-empty skillet over medium heat until shimmering. Place 4 cakes in skillet and cook without moving them until golden brown, 3 to 4 minutes. Using 2 spatulas, carefully flip cakes. Add 1 tablespoon oil, reduce heat to medium-low, and continue to cook until second side is golden brown, 4 to 6 minutes. Transfer cakes to platter. Wipe out skillet and repeat with remaining 4 cakes and remaining 2 tablespoons oil. Serve immediately.

EASY SALMON CAKES

WHY THIS RECIPE WORKS: Most salmon cakes are mushy and overly fishy, camouflaged by gluey binders and heavy-handed seasoning. Our goal was a quick and simple recipe for salmon cakes that first and foremost tasted like salmon, with a moist, delicate texture. To simplify preparation, we broke out our food processor. Pulsing small pieces of salmon (raw was preferred over cooked, which turned fishy) allowed for more even chopping and resulted in small, discrete pieces of fish. We also found a way to ditch the egg and flour steps of the breading process. Instead, we coated the salmon cakes with panko, which we had also used as a binder.

Easy Salmon Cakes
SERVES 4

If buying a skin-on salmon fillet, purchase 1⅓ pounds fish. This will yield 1¼ pounds fish after skinning. When processing the salmon, it is OK to have some pieces that are larger than ¼ inch. It is important to avoid overprocessing the fish. Serve the salmon cakes with lemon wedges and/or tartar sauce.

- 3 tablespoons plus ¾ cup panko bread crumbs
- 2 tablespoons minced fresh parsley
- 2 tablespoons mayonnaise
- 4 teaspoons lemon juice
- 1 scallion, sliced thin
- 1 small shallot, minced
- 1 teaspoon Dijon mustard
- ¾ teaspoon salt
- ¼ teaspoon pepper
  Pinch cayenne pepper
- 1 (1¼-pound) skinless salmon fillet, cut into 1-inch pieces
- ½ cup vegetable oil

1. Combine 3 tablespoons panko, parsley, mayonnaise, lemon juice, scallion, shallot, mustard, salt, pepper, and cayenne in bowl. Working in 3 batches, pulse salmon in food processor until coarsely chopped into ¼-inch pieces, about 2 pulses, transferring each batch to bowl with panko mixture. Gently mix until uniformly combined.

2. Place remaining ¾ cup panko in shallow dish. Using ⅓-cup measure, scoop level amount of salmon mixture and transfer to baking sheet; repeat to make 8 cakes. Carefully coat each cake with bread crumbs, gently patting into disk measuring 2¾ inches in diameter and 1 inch high. Return coated cakes to baking sheet.

3. Heat oil in 12-inch skillet over medium-high heat until shimmering. Place salmon cakes in skillet and cook without moving until bottoms are golden brown, about 2 minutes. Carefully flip cakes and cook until second side is golden brown, 2 to 3 minutes. Transfer cakes to paper towel–lined plate to drain for 1 minute. Serve.

Easy Salmon Cakes with Smoked Salmon, Capers, and Dill

Reduce fresh salmon to 1 pound and salt to ½ teaspoon. Substitute 1 tablespoon minced fresh dill for parsley. Add 4 ounces finely chopped smoked salmon and 1 tablespoon chopped capers to bowl with salmon mixture.

CRAB TOWERS WITH AVOCADO AND GAZPACHO SALSAS

WHY THIS RECIPE WORKS: Sometimes a dish served in a restaurant is so delicious and impressive-looking that we just have to try to make it ourselves. A crab salad molded into towers, from the Mayflower Park Hotel in Seattle, is one such dish, but a hotel restaurant can easily handle the recipe's 35 ingredients. Was there a way to re-create the flavors and presentation at home, with fewer ingredients and a lot less effort? By breaking down the recipe for this appetizer into

SEGMENTING ORANGES

1. Start by slicing a ½-inch piece from the top and bottom of the orange. With the fruit resting flat against a work surface, use a very sharp paring knife to slice off the rind, including the white pith.

2. Slip the knife blade between a membrane and one section of the fruit and slice to the center. Turn the blade so that it is facing out and slide the blade from the center out along the membrane to completely free the section.

ASSEMBLING CRAB TOWERS

1. Place the biscuit cutter in the center of the plate and, using the back of a soup spoon, press ⅓ cup of the Avocado Salsa evenly into the cutter. Lift the cutter off the plate slightly to reveal some but not all of the avocado.

2. Holding the cutter aloft, press ⅓ cup of the Crabmeat Salad evenly into the cutter, on top of the avocado. Lift the cutter farther off the plate and press ⅓ cup of the Gazpacho Salsa evenly into the cutter, on top of the crab.

3. Gently lift the cutter up and away from the plate to reveal the crab tower. Repeat with the remaining salsas and crabmeat salad.

its components—crab salad, avocado–hearts of palm salsa, and gazpacho salsa—we were able to address each one separately. For the crab salad, we used lump crabmeat mixed with a little mayonnaise and champagne vinaigrette. We eliminated the hearts of palm from the salsa; tasters felt the avocado alone worked quite well. For the gazpacho salsa, we used only one kind of bell pepper rather than two and omitted the diced lime and orange segments that were in the original recipe; we also cut back on some of the seasonings, limiting ourselves to sherry vinegar and olive oil. Now that we'd streamlined the components, we had to assemble the dish. The restaurant uses timbale rings, but we found our workaday biscuit cutter did the job just fine.

Crab Towers with Avocado and Gazpacho Salsas
SERVES 6

You can prepare the crabmeat salad and gazpacho salsa several hours ahead of serving, but the avocado salsa should be prepared just before assembly.

CRABMEAT SALAD
    3 tablespoons extra-virgin olive oil
    1 tablespoon champagne vinegar
    1 teaspoon minced or grated lemon zest
    ½ teaspoon Dijon mustard
    ½ teaspoon table salt
    ⅛ teaspoon ground black pepper
    2 tablespoons mayonnaise
   12 ounces lump or backfin Atlantic blue crabmeat,
       carefully picked over to remove cartilage and
       shell fragments

GAZPACHO SALSA
    1 small yellow bell pepper, cored, seeded,
       and cut into ⅛-inch pieces (about ½ cup)
    ½ small cucumber, peeled if desired, seeded,
       and cut into ⅛-inch pieces (about ½ cup)
    1 medium plum tomato, cored, seeded,
       and cut into ⅛-inch pieces (about ½ cup)
    1 small celery rib, cut into ⅛-inch pieces (about ½ cup)
    ½ small red onion, minced (about ¼ cup)
    ½ small jalapeño chile, stemmed, seeded, and minced
    1 tablespoon minced fresh cilantro leaves
    2 tablespoons extra-virgin olive oil
    1 tablespoon sherry vinegar
    ¾ teaspoon table salt
    ¼ teaspoon ground black pepper

AVOCADO SALSA
    3 ripe avocados, pitted, peed, and cut into ¼-inch
       dice (page 414)
    2 tablespoons juice from 1 lime
    ¼ teaspoon ground coriander
    ½ teaspoon table salt
    ⅛ teaspoon ground black pepper

GARNISH

1 cup frisée

2 oranges, peeled using a paring knife and segmented (optional)

1. FOR THE CRABMEAT SALAD: Whisk the olive oil, champagne vinegar, lemon zest, mustard, salt, and pepper together in a small bowl. Measure 3 tablespoons of the vinaigrette into a medium bowl and mix with the mayonnaise. Add the crabmeat to the mayonnaise mixture and toss to coat. Cover with plastic wrap and refrigerate until needed. Set the remaining vinaigrette aside.

2. FOR THE GAZPACHO SALSA: Toss the bell pepper, cucumber, tomato, celery, red onion, jalapeño, cilantro, olive oil, sherry vinegar, salt, and pepper in a medium bowl and set aside.

3. FOR THE AVOCADO SALSA: Toss the avocados, lime juice, coriander, salt, and pepper in a medium bowl and set aside.

4. TO ASSEMBLE: Place a 3-inch-wide round biscuit cutter in the center of an individual plate. Following the photos, press ⅓ cup of the Avocado Salsa into the bottom of the cutter using the back of a soup spoon. Lift the cutter off the plate slightly to reveal some but not all of the avocado. Holding the cutter aloft, press ⅓ cup of the Crabmeat Salad evenly into the cutter on top of the avocado. Lift the cutter further to reveal some but not all of the crab salad. Holding the cutter aloft, use a soup spoon to press ⅓ cup of the Gazpacho Salsa evenly into the cutter on top of the crab. Gently lift the cutter up and away from the plate to reveal the crab tower. Repeat the procedure five more times with the remaining ingredients.

5. Dress the frisée with the remaining champagne vinaigrette. Place a few sprigs of the dressed frisée on top of each crab tower and arrange the orange segments (if using) around the towers. Serve immediately.

FLAMBÉED PAN-ROASTED LOBSTER

WHY THIS RECIPE WORKS: Boiling and steaming are the usual ways of preparing lobster, and they're just fine. But we wanted an alternative cooking method that would be even tastier, and we didn't want to spend a whole lot more time in the kitchen. Our solution was a restaurant dish adapted for home cooking.

The New England restaurant chef Jasper White created a pan-roasted lobster dish that we took as our starting point. We quartered the lobsters and tossed them into a very hot skillet—shells down, so the meat wouldn't overcook—to pan-roast. The heat roasted the shells and permeated the lobster meat with intense flavor. To cook the exposed meat, we put the skillet under the broiler, returning it to the stovetop when the meat was cooked through. Now came the fun part: We flambéed the lobster with bourbon (carefully, of course!). A quick pan sauce, made in the skillet after we removed the lobsters, was the final touch; we used shallots, white wine, herbs, and, for unusual and intense flavor, the lobster tomalley.

PREPARING LOBSTER FOR PAN-ROASTING

1. Freeze the lobster for 5 to 10 minutes to sedate it. Plunge a chef's knife into the body at the point where the shell forms a "T" to kill the lobster. Move the blade straight down through the head.

2. Turn the lobster around and, while holding the upper body with one hand, cut through the body toward the tail.

3. Remove and discard the stomach and intestinal tract. Reserve the green tomalley for the sauce, if desired.

4. Cut the tail from the body.

5. Twist off the claws from the body. Remove the rubber bands from the claws. (Don't be put off if the lobster continues to twitch a little; it's a reflexive movement.)

This way of cooking lobsters is a little more trouble than dunking them in a pot of boiling water, but we think the results are well worth it.

Flambéed Pan-Roasted Lobster
SERVES 2

If you want to prepare more than two lobsters, we suggest that you engage some help. This dish requires close attention, and managing multiple extremely hot pans can be tricky. Before flambéing, make sure to roll up long shirtsleeves, tie back long hair, turn off the exhaust fan (otherwise the fan may pull up the flames), and turn off any lit burners (this is critical if you have a gas stove). For equipment, you will need a large ovensafe skillet, oven mitts, a pair of tongs, and long fireplace or grill matches.

2 (1½- to 2-pound) live lobsters
2 tablespoons peanut or canola oil
¼ cup bourbon or cognac
6 tablespoons (¾ stick) unsalted butter, cut into 6 pieces
2 medium shallots, minced (about 6 tablespoons)
3 tablespoons dry white wine
1 teaspoon minced fresh tarragon leaves
1 tablespoon minced fresh chives
   Table salt and ground black pepper
   Lemon wedges, for serving (optional)

1. Use a large heavy-duty chef's knife to quarter the lobsters (see page 251). (Don't be put off if the lobsters continue to twitch a little after quartering; it's a reflexive movement.)

2. Adjust an oven rack so it is 6 inches from the broiler element and heat the broiler. Heat the peanut oil in a large ovensafe skillet over high heat until smoking. Add the lobster pieces, shell-side down, in a single layer and cook, without disturbing, until the shells are bright red and lightly browned, 2 to 3 minutes. Transfer the skillet to the broiler and cook until the tail meat is just opaque, about 2 minutes.

3. Carefully remove the pan from the oven and return it to the stovetop. Off the heat, pour the bourbon over the lobsters. Wait for 10 seconds, then light a long match and wave it over the skillet until the bourbon ignites. Return the pan to medium-high heat and shake it until the flames subside. Transfer the lobster pieces to a warmed serving bowl and tent with foil to keep warm.

4. Using tongs, remove any congealed albumin (white substance) from the skillet and add 2 tablespoons of the butter and the shallots. Cook, stirring constantly, until the shallots are softened and lightly browned, 1 to 2 minutes. Add the tomalley (if using) and white wine and stir until completely combined. Remove the skillet from the heat and add the tarragon and chives. Stirring constantly, add the remaining 4 tablespoons butter, 1 piece at a time, until fully emulsified. Season with salt and pepper to taste. Pour the sauce over the lobster pieces. Serve immediately, accompanied by the lemon wedges, if desired.

NOTES FROM THE TEST KITCHEN

REMOVING LOBSTER MEAT FROM THE SHELL

There's a lot more meat in a lobster than just the tail and claws—if you know how to get it. Here's our tried-and-true approach to extracting every last bit, no special tools needed. The method works for both hard- and soft-shell lobsters.

1. SEPARATE TAIL: Once cooked lobster is cool enough to handle, set it on cutting board. Grasp tail with your hand and grab body with your other hand and twist to separate.

2. FLATTEN TAIL: Lay tail on its side on counter and use both hands to press down on tail until shell cracks.

3. TAKE OUT TAIL MEAT: Hold tail, flippers facing you and shell facing down. Pull back on sides to crack open shell and remove meat. Rinse meat under water to remove green tomalley if you wish; pat meat dry with paper towels and remove dark vein.

4. MOVE TO KNUCKLES: Twist "arms" to remove both claws and attached "knuckles". Twist knuckles to remove them from claw. Break knuckles at joint using back of chef's knife or lobster-cracking tool. Use handle of teaspoon to push out meat.

5. REMOVE CLAW MEAT: Wiggle hinged portion of each claw to separate. If meat is stuck inside small part, remove it with skewer. Break open claws, cracking 1 side and then flipping them to crack other side, and remove meat.

6. FINISH WITH LEGS: Twist legs to remove them. Lay legs flat on counter. Using rolling pin, start from claw end and roll toward open end, pushing out meat. Stop rolling before reaching end of legs; otherwise leg can crack and release pieces of shell.

NEW ENGLAND LOBSTER ROLL

WHY THIS RECIPE WORKS: We wanted to bring home a true New England–style lobster roll, complete with tender meat coated in a light dressing and tucked into a buttery toasted bun, but first we had to deal with the lobster. To make things easier, we sedated the lobster by placing it in the freezer for 30 minutes. Boiling was the easiest way to cook it, and removing it from the water when the tail registered 175 degrees ensured it was perfectly tender. For the lobster roll, we adhered mostly to tradition, tossing our lobster with just a bit of mayonnaise and adding a hint of crunch with lettuce leaves and a small amount of minced celery. Onion and shallot were overpowering, but minced chives offered bright herb flavor. Lemon juice and a pinch of cayenne provided a nice counterpoint to the rich lobster and mayo.

New England Lobster Roll

SERVES 6

This recipe is best when made with lobster you've cooked yourself. Use a very small pinch of cayenne pepper, as it should not make the dressing spicy. We prefer New England–style top-loading hot dog buns, as they provide maximum surface on the sides for toasting. If using other buns, butter, salt, and toast the interior of each bun instead of the exterior.

- 2 tablespoons mayonnaise
- 2 tablespoons minced celery
- 1½ teaspoons lemon juice
- 1 teaspoon minced fresh chives
  Salt
  Pinch cayenne pepper
- 1 pound lobster meat, tail meat cut into ½-inch pieces and claw meat cut into 1-inch pieces
- 2 tablespoons unsalted butter, softened
- 6 New England–style hot dog buns
- 6 leaves Boston lettuce

1. Whisk mayonnaise, celery, lemon juice, chives, ⅛ teaspoon salt, and cayenne together in large bowl. Add lobster and gently toss to combine.

2. Place 12-inch nonstick skillet over low heat. Butter both sides of hot dog buns and sprinkle lightly with salt. Place buns in skillet, with 1 buttered side down; increase heat to medium-low; and cook until crisp and brown, 2 to 3 minutes. Flip and cook second side until crisp and brown, 2 to 3 minutes longer. Transfer buns to large platter. Line each bun with lettuce leaf. Spoon lobster salad into buns and serve immediately.

Boiled Lobster

SERVES 4; YIELDS 1 POUND MEAT

To cook four lobsters at once, you will need a pot with a capacity of at least 3 gallons. If your pot is smaller, boil the lobsters in batches. Start timing the lobsters from the moment they go into the pot.

- 4 (1¼-pound) live lobsters
- ⅓ cup salt

1. Place lobsters in large bowl and freeze for 30 minutes. Meanwhile, bring 2 gallons water to boil in large pot over high heat.

2. Add lobsters and salt to pot, arranging with tongs so that all lobsters are submerged. Cover pot, leaving lid slightly ajar, and adjust heat to maintain gentle boil. Cook for 12 minutes, until thickest part of tail registers 175 degrees (insert thermometer into underside of tail to take temperature). If temperature registers lower than 175 degrees, return lobster to pot for 2 minutes longer, until tail registers 175 degrees, using tongs to transfer lobster in and out of pot.

3. Serve immediately or transfer lobsters to rimmed baking sheet and set aside until cool enough to remove meat, about 10 minutes. (Lobster meat can be refrigerated in airtight container for up to 24 hours.)

OVEN-STEAMED MUSSELS

WHY THIS RECIPE WORKS: We wanted to figure out a foolproof way to guarantee that our mussels cooked through at the same rate, so that they were all wide open and perfectly tender, even if they were different sizes. First, we moved them from the stovetop to the oven, where the even heat ensured they cooked through more gently, and we traded the Dutch oven for a large roasting pan so they weren't crowded. Covering the pan with aluminum foil trapped the moisture so the mussels didn't dry out. For a flavorful cooking liquid, we reduced white wine to concentrate its flavor and added thyme, garlic, and red pepper flakes for aromatic complexity. To avoid dirtying another pan, we simply cooked the aromatics and wine on the stovetop in the roasting pan before tossing in our mussels and transferring the pan to the oven. A few pats of butter, stirred in at the end, gave the sauce richness and body.

Oven-Steamed Mussels

SERVES 2 TO 4

Occasionally, mussels will have a harmless fibrous piece (known as the beard) protruding from between the shells. To remove it easily, trap the beard between the side of a small paring knife and your thumb and pull to remove it. The flat surface of the knife gives you some leverage to remove the beard. Unopened cooked mussels just need more cooking time. To open them, microwave briefly for 30 seconds or so. Serve mussels with crusty bread to sop up the flavorful broth.

- 1 tablespoon extra-virgin olive oil
- 3 garlic cloves, minced
  Pinch red pepper flakes
- 1 cup dry white wine
- 3 sprigs fresh thyme
- 2 bay leaves
- 4 pounds mussels, scrubbed and debearded
- ¼ teaspoon salt
- 2 tablespoons unsalted butter, cut into 4 pieces
- 2 tablespoons minced fresh parsley

1. Adjust oven rack to lowest position and heat oven to 500 degrees. Heat oil, garlic, and pepper flakes in large roasting pan over medium heat; cook, stirring constantly, until fragrant, about 30 seconds. Add wine, thyme sprigs, and bay leaves and bring to boil. Cook until wine is slightly reduced, about 1 minute. Add mussels and salt. Cover pan tightly with aluminum foil and transfer to oven. Cook until most mussels have opened (a few may remain closed), 15 to 18 minutes.

2. Remove pan from oven. Push mussels to sides of pan. Add butter to center and whisk until melted. Discard thyme sprigs and bay leaves, sprinkle parsley over mussels, and toss to combine. Serve immediately.

Oven-Steamed Mussels with Tomato and Chorizo

Omit red pepper flakes and increase oil to 3 tablespoons. Heat oil and 12 ounces Spanish-style chorizo sausage, cut into ½-inch pieces, in roasting pan until chorizo starts to brown, about 5 minutes. Add garlic and cook until fragrant, about 30 seconds. Proceed with recipe as directed, adding 1 (28-ounce) can crushed tomatoes to roasting pan before adding mussels and increasing butter to 3 tablespoons.

Oven-Steamed Mussels with Leeks and Pernod

Omit red pepper flakes and increase oil to 3 tablespoons. Heat oil; 1 pound leeks, white and light green parts only, halved lengthwise, sliced thin, and washed thoroughly; and garlic in roasting pan until leeks are wilted, about 3 minutes. Proceed with recipe as directed, omitting thyme sprigs and substituting ½ cup Pernod and ¼ cup water for wine, ¼ cup crème fraîche for butter, and chives for parsley.

Oven-Steamed Mussels with Hard Cider and Bacon

Omit garlic and red pepper flakes. Heat oil and 4 slices thick-cut bacon, cut into ½-inch pieces, in roasting pan until bacon has rendered and is starting to crisp, about 5 minutes. Proceed with recipe as directed, substituting dry hard cider for wine and ¼ cup heavy cream for butter.

NOTES FROM THE TEST KITCHEN

DEBEARDING MUSSELS

Because of the way they're cultivated, most mussels are free of the fibrous strands, or "beards," that wild mussels use to adhere to surfaces. If your mussel has a beard, hold it and use the back of a paring knife to remove it with a stern yank.

INDOOR CLAMBAKE

WHY THIS RECIPE WORKS: A clambake is perhaps the ultimate seafood meal: clams, mussels, and lobster, nestled with sausage, corn, and potatoes, all steamed together with hot stones in a sand pit by the sea. A genuine clambake is an all-day affair and, of course, requires a beach. But we wanted to re-create the great flavors of the clambake indoors, so we could enjoy this flavorful feast anywhere, without hours of preparation.

A large stockpot was the cooking vessel of choice. Many recipes suggest cooking the ingredients separately before adding them to the pot, but we found that with careful layering, we could cook everything in the same pot and have it all finish at the same time. And we didn't need to add water, because the shellfish released enough liquid to steam everything else. Sliced sausage went into the pot first (we liked kielbasa), so that it could sear before the steam was generated. Clams and mussels were next, wrapped in cheesecloth for easy removal. Then in went the potatoes, which would take the longest to cook; they were best placed near the heat source, and we cut them into 1-inch pieces to cook more quickly. Corn, with the husks left on to protect it from seafood flavors and lobster foam, was next, followed by the lobsters. It took less than half an hour for everything to cook—and we had all the elements of a clambake (minus the sand and surf) without having spent all day preparing them.

Indoor Clambake
SERVES 4 TO 6

Choose a large, narrow stockpot in which you can easily layer the ingredients. The recipe can be cut in half and layered in an 8-quart Dutch oven, but it should cook for the same amount of time. We prefer small littlenecks for this recipe. If your market carries larger clams, use 4 pounds. Mussels sometimes contain a weedy beard protruding from the crack between the two shells. It's fairly small and can be difficult to tug out of place. To remove it easily, trap the beard between the side of a small paring knife and your thumb and pull to remove it. The flat surface of the knife gives you some leverage to remove the beard.

- 2 pounds small littleneck or cherrystone clams, scrubbed (see note)
- 2 pounds mussels, scrubbed and debearded (see note)
- 1 pound kielbasa, sliced into ⅓-inch-thick rounds
- 1 pound small new or red potatoes, scrubbed and cut into 1-inch pieces
- 6 medium ears corn, silk and all but the last layer of husk removed
- 2 (1½-pound) live lobsters
- 8 tablespoons (1 stick) salted butter, melted

1. Place the clams and mussels on a large piece of cheesecloth and tie the ends together to secure; set aside. In a heavy-bottomed 12-quart stockpot, layer the sliced kielbasa, the sack of clams and mussels, the potatoes, the corn, and the lobsters on top of one another. Cover with the lid and place over high heat. Cook until the potatoes are tender (a paring knife can be slipped into and out of the center of a potato with little resistance), and the lobsters are bright red, 17 to 20 minutes.

2. Remove the pot from the heat and remove the lid (watch out for scalding steam). Remove the lobsters and set aside until cool enough to handle. Remove the corn from the pot and peel off the husks; arrange the ears on a large platter. Using a slotted spoon, remove the potatoes and arrange them on the platter with the corn. Transfer the clams and mussels to a large bowl and cut open the cheesecloth with scissors. Using a slotted spoon, remove the kielbasa from the pot and arrange it on the platter with the potatoes and corn. Pour the remaining steaming liquid in the pot over the clams and mussels. Using a kitchen towel to protect your hand, twist and remove the lobster tails, claws, and legs (if desired). Arrange the lobster parts on the platter. Serve immediately with the melted butter and napkins.

CHAPTER 11

DINNER AT THE DINER

TUNA SALAD

WHY THIS RECIPE WORKS: Tuna salads have been given a bad name by their typically mushy, watery, and bland condition. We wanted a tuna salad that was evenly textured, moist, and well seasoned. We learned that there are three keys to a great tuna salad. The first is to drain the tuna thoroughly in a colander; don't just tip the water out of the can. Next, instead of using a fork, break up the tuna with your fingers for a finer, more even texture. Finally, season the tuna before adding the mayonnaise for maximum flavor. Some additions to tuna salad are a matter of taste, but we thought that small amounts of garlic and mustard added another dimension, and minced pickle was a piquant touch. In addition to classic tuna salad, we developed a few variations that include tuna with balsamic vinegar and grapes, another with curry and apples, and a third with lime and horseradish.

Classic Tuna Salad

MAKES ABOUT 2 CUPS, ENOUGH FOR 4 SANDWICHES

Our favorite canned tuna is Wild Planet Wild Albacore. For more information on why we like this brand, see page 925.

- 2 (6-ounce) cans solid white tuna in water (see note)
- 1 small celery rib, minced (about ¼ cup)
- 2 tablespoons juice from 1 lemon
- 2 tablespoons minced red onion
- 2 tablespoons minced dill or sweet pickles
- 2 tablespoons minced fresh parsley leaves
- ½ small garlic clove, minced or pressed through a garlic press (about ½ teaspoon)
- ½ teaspoon table salt
- ¼ teaspoon ground black pepper
- ½ cup mayonnaise
- ¼ teaspoon Dijon mustard

Drain the tuna in a colander and shred with your fingers until no clumps remain and the texture is fine and even. Transfer the tuna to a medium bowl and mix in the celery, lemon juice, onion, pickles, parsley, garlic, salt, and pepper until evenly blended. Fold in the mayonnaise and mustard until the tuna is evenly moistened. (The tuna salad can be refrigerated in an airtight container for up to 3 days.)

Tuna Salad with Balsamic Vinegar and Grapes

Follow the recipe for Classic Tuna Salad, omitting the lemon juice, pickles, garlic, and parsley and adding 2 tablespoons balsamic vinegar, 6 ounces halved red seedless grapes (about 1 cup), ¼ cup lightly toasted slivered almonds, and 2 teaspoons minced thyme leaves to the tuna along with the salt and pepper.

Curried Tuna Salad with Apples and Currants

Follow the recipe for Classic Tuna Salad, omitting the pickles, garlic, and parsley and adding 1 medium firm, juicy apple, cut into ¼-inch dice (about 1 cup), ¼ cup currants, and 2 tablespoons minced fresh basil leaves to the tuna along with the lemon juice, salt, and pepper; mix 1 tablespoon curry powder into the mayonnaise before folding into the tuna.

Tuna Salad with Lime and Horseradish

Follow the recipe for Classic Tuna Salad, omitting the lemon juice, pickles, and garlic and adding 2 tablespoons juice and ½ teaspoon grated zest from 1 lime and 3 tablespoons prepared horseradish to the tuna along with the salt and pepper.

CLASSIC CHICKEN SALAD

WHY THIS RECIPE WORKS: Recipes for chicken salad are only as good as the chicken itself. If the chicken is dry or flavorless, no amount of dressing or add-ins will camouflage it. To ensure silky, juicy, and flavorful chicken, we used a method based on *sous vide* cooking (submerging vacuum-sealed foods in a temperature-controlled water bath). Our ideal formula was four chicken breasts and 6 cups of cold water heated to 170 degrees and then removed from the heat, covered, and left to stand for about 15 minutes. This yielded incomparably moist chicken that was perfect for chicken salad.

Classic Chicken Salad

SERVES 4 TO 6

To ensure that the chicken cooks through, don't use breasts that weigh more than 8 ounces or are thicker than 1 inch. Make sure to start with cold water in step 1. We like the combination of parsley and tarragon, but 2 tablespoons of one or the other is fine. This salad can be served in a sandwich or spooned over leafy greens.

- Salt and pepper
- 4 (6- to 8-ounce) boneless, skinless chicken breasts, no more than 1 inch thick, trimmed
- ½ cup mayonnaise

2 tablespoons lemon juice

1 teaspoon Dijon mustard

2 celery ribs, minced

1 shallot, minced

1 tablespoon minced fresh parsley

1 tablespoon minced fresh tarragon

1. Dissolve 2 tablespoons salt in 6 cups cold water in Dutch oven. Submerge chicken in water. Heat pot over medium heat until water registers 170 degrees. Turn off heat, cover pot, and let stand until chicken registers 165 degrees, 15 to 17 minutes.

2. Transfer chicken to paper towel–lined baking sheet. Refrigerate until chicken is cool, about 30 minutes. While chicken cools, whisk mayonnaise, lemon juice, mustard, and ¼ teaspoon pepper together in large bowl.

3. Pat chicken dry with paper towels and cut into ½-inch pieces. Transfer chicken to bowl with mayonnaise mixture. Add celery, shallot, parsley, and tarragon; toss to combine. Season with salt and pepper to taste. Serve. (Salad can be refrigerated for up to 2 days.)

Curried Chicken Salad with Cashews

Microwave 1 teaspoon vegetable oil, 1 teaspoon curry powder, and ⅛ teaspoon cayenne pepper together, uncovered, until oil is hot, about 30 seconds. Add curry oil to mayonnaise and substitute lime juice for lemon juice and 1 teaspoon grated fresh ginger for mustard in step 2. Substitute 2 tablespoons minced fresh cilantro for parsley and tarragon, and add ½ cup coarsely chopped toasted cashews and ⅓ cup golden raisins to salad with celery.

Waldorf Chicken Salad

Add ½ teaspoon ground fennel seeds to mayonnaise mixture in step 2. Substitute 1 teaspoon minced fresh thyme for parsley and add 1 peeled Granny Smith apple, cut into ¼-inch pieces, and ½ cup coarsely chopped toasted walnuts to salad with celery.

Chicken Salad with Red Grapes and Smoked Almonds

Add ¼ teaspoon grated lemon zest to mayonnaise mixture in step 2. Substitute 1 teaspoon minced fresh rosemary for tarragon, and add 1 cup quartered red grapes and ½ cup coarsely chopped smoked almonds to salad with celery.

GRILLED CHEESE SANDWICHES

WHY THIS RECIPE WORKS: The perfect grilled cheese consists of evenly melted cheese between crisp bread, but most don't turn out that way. We set out to find the keys to the ideal sandwich. We found that grating the cheese on a box grater enabled us to get an even layer of cheese onto the bread. Butter melted in the pan sometimes burned and didn't always coat the bread evenly, so we opted to butter the bread rather than the pan. And to coat the bread evenly and prevent it from tearing, we melted the butter first. Finally, we learned that the secret of a crisp exterior is low heat; the longer it takes for the bread to become golden, the crispier the bread will become—these are grilled cheese sandwiches worth the wait.

Classic Grilled Cheese Sandwiches
SERVES 2

The traditional grilled cheese sandwich usually uses a mild cheddar cheese, but our technique for this sandwich works with most any cheese. Grilled cheese sandwiches are best served hot out of the pan, though in a pinch they can be held, unsliced, for up to 20 minutes in a warm oven. If you want to make more than two sandwiches at once, get two skillets going or use an electric griddle set at medium-low (about 250 degrees), grilling 10 minutes per side. The possible variations on the basic grilled cheese sandwich are endless, but the extras are best sandwiched between the cheese. Try a few very thin slices of baked ham, prosciutto, turkey breast, or ripe, in-season tomato. Condiments such as Dijon mustard, pickle relish, or chutney can be spread on the bread instead of sandwiched in the cheese.

3 ounces cheese (preferably mild cheddar) or a combination of cheeses, shredded on the large holes of a box grater (about ¾ cup; see note)

4 slices high-quality white sandwich bread

2 tablespoons unsalted butter, melted

1. Heat a heavy 12-inch skillet over low to medium-low heat. Meanwhile, sprinkle the cheese evenly over two bread slices. Top each with a remaining bread slice, pressing down gently to set.

2. Brush the sandwich tops completely with half of the melted butter; place each sandwich, buttered side down, in the skillet. Brush the remaining side of each sandwich completely with the remaining butter. Cook until crisp and deep golden brown, 5 to 10 minutes per side, flipping the sandwiches back to the first side to reheat and crisp, about 15 seconds. Serve immediately.

GROWN-UP GRILLED CHEESE SANDWICHES

WHY THIS RECIPE WORKS: Melty American cheese on fluffy white bread is a childhood classic, but we wanted a grilled cheese for adults that offered more robust flavor. Aged cheddar gave us the complexity we were after, but it made for a greasy sandwich with a grainy filling. Adding a splash of wine and some Brie helped the aged cheddar melt evenly without separating or becoming greasy. Using a food processor to combine the ingredients ensured our cheese-and-wine mixture was easy to spread. A little bit of shallot ramped up the flavor without detracting from the cheese, and a smear of mustard butter livened up the bread.

Grown-Up Grilled Cheese Sandwiches with Cheddar and Shallot

SERVES 4

For the best flavor, look for a cheddar aged for about one year (avoid cheddar aged for longer; it won't melt well in this recipe). To quickly bring the cheese to room temperature, microwave the pieces until warm, about 30 seconds. The first two sandwiches can be held in a 200-degree oven on a wire rack set in a baking sheet while the second batch cooks.

- 7 ounces aged cheddar cheese, cut into 24 equal pieces, room temperature
- 2 ounces Brie cheese, rind removed
- 2 tablespoons dry white wine or dry vermouth
- 4 teaspoons minced shallot
- 3 tablespoons unsalted butter, softened
- 1 teaspoon Dijon mustard
- 8 slices hearty white sandwich bread

1. Process cheddar, Brie, and wine in food processor until smooth paste is formed, 20 to 30 seconds. Add shallot and pulse to combine, 3 to 5 pulses. Combine butter and mustard in small bowl.

2. Working on parchment paper–lined counter, divide mustard butter evenly among slices of bread. Spread butter evenly over surface of bread. Flip 4 slices of bread over and spread cheese mixture evenly over slices. Top with remaining 4 slices of bread, buttered sides up.

3. Preheat 12-inch nonstick skillet over medium heat for 2 minutes. (Droplets of water should just sizzle when flicked onto pan.) Place 2 sandwiches in skillet, reduce heat to medium-low, and cook until both sides are crisp and golden brown, 6 to 9 minutes per side, moving sandwiches to ensure even browning. Remove sandwiches from skillet and let stand for 2 minutes before serving. Repeat with remaining 2 sandwiches.

Grown-Up Grilled Cheese Sandwiches with Gruyère and Chives

Substitute Gruyère cheese for cheddar, chives for shallot, and rye sandwich bread for white sandwich bread.

Grown-Up Grilled Cheese Sandwiches with Asiago and Dates

Substitute Asiago cheese for cheddar, finely chopped pitted dates for shallot, and oatmeal sandwich bread for white sandwich bread.

Grown-Up Grilled Cheese Sandwiches with Comté and Cornichon

Substitute Comté cheese for cheddar, minced cornichon for shallot, and rye sandwich bread for white sandwich bread.

Grown-Up Grilled Cheese Sandwiches with Robiola and Chipotle

Substitute Robiola cheese, rind removed, for cheddar; ¼ teaspoon minced canned chipotle chile in adobo sauce for shallot; and oatmeal sandwich bread for white sandwich bread.

CLASSIC MACARONI AND CHEESE

WHY THIS RECIPE WORKS: Old-fashioned macaroni and cheese takes no shortcuts. This family favorite should boast tender pasta in a smooth, creamy sauce with great cheese flavor. Too often, the dish, which is baked in the oven, dries out or curdles. We aimed to create a foolproof version.

We cooked the pasta until just past al dente and then combined it with a béchamel-based cheese sauce. For the best flavor and a creamy texture, we used a combination of sharp cheddar and Monterey Jack. We combined the cooked pasta with the sauce and heated it through on the stovetop, rather than in the oven. This step helped ensure the dish didn't dry out, but remained smooth and creamy. And to give the dish a browned topping, we sprinkled it with bread crumbs and ran it briefly under the broiler.

Classic Macaroni and Cheese

SERVES 6 TO 8

It's crucial to cook the pasta until tender—that is, just past the al dente stage. Whole, low-fat, and skim milk all work well in this recipe. The recipe may be halved and baked in an 8-inch square, broiler-safe baking dish. If desired, offer celery salt or hot sauce for sprinkling at the table.

BREAD-CRUMB TOPPING

- 6 slices high-quality white sandwich bread, torn into quarters
- 3 tablespoons cold unsalted butter, cut into 6 pieces

MACARONI AND CHEESE

- 1 tablespoon plus 1 teaspoon table salt
- 1 pound elbow macaroni
- 5 tablespoons unsalted butter
- 6 tablespoons unbleached all-purpose flour
- 1½ teaspoons dry mustard
- ¼ teaspoon cayenne pepper (optional)
- 5 cups milk (see note)
- 8 ounces Monterey Jack cheese, shredded (about 2 cups)
- 8 ounces sharp cheddar cheese, shredded (about 2 cups)

1. FOR THE BREAD-CRUMB TOPPING: Pulse the bread and butter in a food processor until coarsely ground, 10 to 15 pulses. Set aside.

2. FOR THE MACARONI AND CHEESE: Adjust an oven rack to the lower-middle position and heat the broiler. Bring 4 quarts water to a rolling boil in a large pot. Add 1 tablespoon of the salt and the macaroni and stir to separate the noodles. Cook until tender, drain, and set aside.

3. In the now-empty pot, melt the butter over medium-high heat. Add the flour, mustard, cayenne (if using), and remaining 1 teaspoon salt and whisk well to combine. Continue whisking until the mixture becomes fragrant and deepens in color, about 1 minute. Whisking constantly, gradually add the milk; bring the mixture to a boil, whisking constantly (the mixture must reach a full boil to fully thicken), then reduce the heat to medium and simmer, whisking occasionally, until thickened to the consistency of heavy cream, about 5 minutes. Off the heat, whisk in the cheeses until fully melted. Add the pasta and cook over medium-low heat, stirring constantly, until the mixture is steaming and heated through, about 6 minutes.

4. Transfer the mixture to a broiler-safe 13 by 9-inch baking dish and sprinkle with the bread crumbs. Broil until deep golden brown, 3 to 5 minutes. Cool for 5 minutes, then serve.

STOVETOP MACARONI AND CHEESE

WHY THIS RECIPE WORKS: Just about the only thing boxed macaroni and cheese has going for it is its fast prep—and the fact that kids will almost always gobble it up. We wanted a quick stovetop macaroni and cheese with an ultra-creamy texture and authentic cheese flavor—so good that it would satisfy everyone at the table.

We cooked the macaroni to just shy of al dente, then drained and combined it with butter and an egg custard mixture that included evaporated milk, eggs, hot sauce, and dry mustard. For the cheese we chose cheddar, American, or Monterey Jack—and plenty of it. We stirred the cheese into the macaroni mixture until thick and creamy and then topped the mixture with toasted homemade bread crumbs–the final touch to this easy-to-prepare family favorite.

Stovetop Macaroni and Cheese

SERVES 4

If you're in a hurry or prefer to sprinkle the dish with crumbled crackers (saltines aren't bad), you can skip the bread-crumb step.

BREAD-CRUMB TOPPING

- 3 slices high-quality white sandwich bread, torn into quarters
- 2 tablespoons unsalted butter
  Table salt

MACARONI AND CHEESE

- 2 large eggs
- 1 (12-ounce) can evaporated milk
- 2 teaspoons table salt
- ¼ teaspoon ground black pepper
- 1 teaspoon dry mustard, dissolved in 1 teaspoon water
- ¼ teaspoon hot sauce
- 8 ounces elbow macaroni (about 2 cups)
- 4 tablespoons (½ stick) unsalted butter
- 12 ounces sharp cheddar, American, or Monterey Jack cheese, shredded (about 3 cups)

1. FOR THE BREAD CRUMBS: Pulse the bread in a food processor until coarsely ground, 10 to 15 pulses. Melt the butter in a large skillet over medium heat. Add the bread crumbs and cook, tossing to coat with the butter, until the crumbs just begin to color, about 10 minutes. Season with salt to taste; set aside.

2. FOR THE MACARONI AND CHEESE: Mix the eggs, 1 cup of the evaporated milk, ½ teaspoon of the salt, the pepper, mustard mixture, and hot sauce in a small bowl; set aside.

3. Meanwhile, bring 2 quarts water to a boil in a large heavy-bottomed saucepan or Dutch oven. Add the remaining 1½ teaspoons salt and the macaroni; cook until almost tender but still a little firm to the bite. Drain and return to the pan over low heat. Add the butter; toss to melt.

4. Pour the egg mixture over the buttered noodles along with three-quarters of the cheese; stir until thoroughly combined and the cheese starts to melt. Gradually add the remaining ½ cup milk and the remaining cheese, stirring constantly, until the mixture is hot and creamy, about 5 minutes. Serve immediately, topped with the toasted bread crumbs.

ADULT MACARONI AND CHEESE

WHY THIS RECIPE WORKS: We turned to science to help make our mac and cheese creamy and smooth. We were inspired by an innovative recipe calling for adding sodium citrate, an emulsifier, to cheese to keep it smooth when heated (instead of adding flour to make a béchamel). American cheese, which contains a similar stabilizing ingredient, was the solution. But because it tastes so plain, we combined it with Gruyère and blue cheese, as well as mustard and cayenne for more sophisticated flavor. We cooked the macaroni in a smaller-than-usual amount of water, so we didn't have to drain it; the liquid that was left after the elbows were hydrated was just enough to form the base of the sauce. Rather than bake the mac and cheese, we sprinkled toasted panko bread crumbs on top to keep things simple.

Grown-Up Stovetop Macaroni and Cheese
SERVES 4

Barilla makes our favorite elbow macaroni. Because the macaroni is cooked in a measured amount of liquid, we don't recommend using different shapes or sizes of pasta. Use a 4-ounce block of American cheese from the deli counter rather than presliced cheese.

1¾ cups water
1 cup milk
8 ounces elbow macaroni
4 ounces American cheese, shredded (1 cup)
½ teaspoon Dijon mustard
Small pinch cayenne pepper
3½ ounces Gruyère cheese, shredded (¾ cup)
2 tablespoons crumbled blue cheese
⅓ cup panko bread crumbs
1 tablespoon extra-virgin olive oil
Salt and pepper
2 tablespoons grated Parmesan cheese

1. Bring water and milk to boil in medium saucepan over high heat. Stir in macaroni and reduce heat to medium-low. Cook, stirring frequently, until macaroni is soft (slightly past al dente), 6 to 8 minutes. Add American cheese, mustard, and cayenne and cook, stirring constantly, until cheese is completely melted, about 1 minute. Off heat, stir in Gruyère and blue cheese until evenly distributed but not melted. Cover saucepan and let stand for 5 minutes.

2. Meanwhile, combine panko, oil, ⅛ teaspoon salt, and ⅛ teaspoon pepper in 8-inch nonstick skillet until panko is evenly moistened. Cook over medium heat, stirring frequently, until evenly browned, 3 to 4 minutes. Off heat, sprinkle Parmesan over panko mixture and stir to combine. Transfer panko mixture to small bowl.

3. Stir macaroni until sauce is smooth (sauce may look loose but will thicken as it cools). Season with salt and pepper to taste. Transfer to warm serving dish and sprinkle panko mixture over top. Serve immediately.

BEHIND THE SCENES

PASS THE PEPTO, PLEASE

During the tasting lab segments, Jack asks Bridget and Julia to pick out the test kitchen's winning brands from the losers. It doesn't look hard on television, but what viewers don't know is that we film as many as 11 tasting segments in a single day. That's because it takes the production team a few hours to light the tasting lab and position the cameras. Once the crew is in place, it makes sense to keep shooting one segment after another for two days straight. That means Bridget or Julia has to do at least one—often two—tasting segments every hour, starting as early as 8 a.m. and ending around 6 p.m. So what's on the menu? Here's a sample lineup from just one day in the tasting lab: jarred anchovies, olive oil, smoked paprika, whole-milk Greek yogurt, sherry vinegar, Parmesan cheese, and almond butter.

LIGHT MACARONI AND CHEESE

WHY THIS RECIPE WORKS: Weighing in at about 650 calories and 40 grams of fat per serving, a bowl of homemade mac and cheese should really be a treat every once in a while, like a slice of cake. But the truth is, most of us like to enjoy this family favorite a little more often. We aimed to develop a lighter version of mac and cheese—macaroni in a creamy (not rubbery or grainy), cheesy sauce—with a fraction of the calories.

We slashed both fat and calories by replacing full-fat cheddar with low-fat—its flavor and texture are vastly superior to nonfat cheddar. We also swapped in 2 percent milk for the whole milk and added 2 percent evaporated milk to ensure a creamy consistency. And we found that we could eliminate butter entirely by thickening the sauce with cornstarch instead of a classic roux. In the end, we cut the calories by almost half and the fat grams by 75 percent, turning full-fat macaroni and cheese into a dish you could eat every day.

Light Macaroni and Cheese
SERVES 4 TO 6

Don't be tempted to use either preshredded or nonfat cheddar cheese in this dish—the texture and flavor of the macaroni and cheese will suffer substantially. For best results, choose a low-fat cheddar cheese that is sold in block form and has roughly 50 percent of the fat and calories of regular cheese (we like Cracker Barrel brand).

> Table salt
> 8 ounces elbow macaroni (about 2 cups)
> 1 (12-ounce) can 2 percent reduced-fat evaporated milk
> ¾ cup 2 percent milk
> ¼ teaspoon dry mustard
> ⅛ teaspoon garlic powder or celery salt (optional)
> Pinch cayenne pepper
> 2 teaspoons cornstarch
> 8 ounces 50 percent light cheddar cheese, shredded (about 2 cups; see note)

1. Bring 2½ quarts water to a boil in a large saucepan. Stir in 2 teaspoons salt and the macaroni; cook until the pasta is completely cooked and tender, about 5 minutes. Drain the pasta and leave it in the colander; set aside.

2. Add the evaporated milk, ½ cup of the 2 percent milk, the mustard, garlic powder (if using), cayenne, and ½ teaspoon salt to the now-empty saucepan. Bring the mixture to a boil, then reduce to a simmer. Whisk the cornstarch and remaining ¼ cup milk together, then whisk it into the simmering mixture. Continue to simmer, whisking constantly, until the sauce has thickened and is smooth, about 2 minutes.

3. Off the heat, gradually whisk in the cheddar until melted and smooth. Stir in the macaroni and let the macaroni and cheese sit off the heat until the sauce has thickened slightly, 2 to 5 minutes, before serving.

TURKEY TETRAZZINI

WHY THIS RECIPE WORKS: Overcooking is the inevitable fate of many casseroles, as the contents are usually cooked twice: once on their own and once again when joined with the other casserole ingredients. We wanted a casserole with a silky sauce, a generous portion of turkey meat, and noodles cooked just until done.

We found we could cut the second cooking down to just 15 minutes by baking the recipe in a shallow dish that would allow it to heat through quickly. Most recipes for turkey Tetrazzini call for a béchamel sauce, in which milk is added to a roux (a paste made from fat and flour that is then cooked on the stovetop). In switching to a velouté, which is based on chicken stock rather than milk, we brightened up the texture and the flavor. We also used less sauce than most recipes call for, giving the other ingredients a chance to express themselves. Still looking for brighter flavor, we spruced things up with a shot of sherry and a little lemon juice and nutmeg. Parmesan cheese provided tang and bite, and a full 2 teaspoons of fresh thyme helped to freshen the overall impression of the dish.

Turkey Tetrazzini
SERVES 8

Don't skimp on the salt and pepper; this dish needs aggressive seasoning.

BREAD-CRUMB TOPPING
> 6 slices high-quality white sandwich bread, torn into quarters
> 4 tablespoons (½ stick) unsalted butter, melted
> Pinch table salt
> ½ ounce Parmesan cheese, grated (about ¼ cup)

COOKS WHO CAN MAKE THE CUT

Our recipes are created by a team of test cooks—more than three dozen cooks in total—who spend their day mincing, roasting, tasting, and talking about food. So what does it take to join our army of test cooks? It goes without saying that you must love to cook. Everyone in the test kitchen has professional cooking experience (this usually includes work in a restaurant kitchen as well as a degree from one of the top cooking schools in the country). But in-depth food knowledge and cooking skills are just a start.

To get hired, you must have a passion for understanding how things work in the kitchen. A curious mind is essential, as are attention to detail and a scientific approach to problem solving. Our test cooks are continually developing hypotheses to explain how a recipe works and then devising a testing protocol to prove (or disprove) their theory. Finally, we look for cooks who understand the realities of cooking at home—with imperfect equipment, the usual distractions (kids, pets, and phone calls), and no one to wash the dishes.

So how do we find test cooks? Our test kitchen director, Erin McMurrer, has developed a bench test for potential hires—it's like an audition, with knives. Erin gives potential hires two of our published recipes and watches them as they set to work preparing them. Chop those onions when the recipe says to mince them, and you're in trouble. Use a dry measuring cup to measure milk, and you're in serious trouble. Shape cookie dough into ½-inch balls when the recipe says 1-inch balls, and you're in very serious trouble. But job candidates can save the day when the cooking is done and Erin asks them to analyze their success and failures during the bench test. A candidate who can thoughtfully examine his or her work (and figure out how to remedy problems) might just make the cut.

FILLING

- 8 tablespoons (1 stick) unsalted butter, plus extra for the baking dish
- 8 ounces white mushrooms, wiped cleaned and sliced thin (about 3 cups)
- 2 medium onions, minced
  Table salt and ground black pepper (see note)
- 12 ounces spaghetti or other long-strand pasta, strands snapped in half
- 6 tablespoons unbleached all-purpose flour
- 3 cups low-sodium chicken broth
- 1½ ounces Parmesan cheese, grated (about ¾ cup)
- ¼ cup dry sherry
- 1 tablespoon juice from 1 lemon
- 2 teaspoons minced fresh thyme leaves
- ¼ teaspoon grated nutmeg
- 2 cups frozen peas
- 4 cups leftover cooked boneless turkey or chicken meat, cut into ¼-inch pieces

1. FOR THE TOPPING: Adjust an oven rack to the middle position and heat the oven to 350 degrees. Pulse the bread in a food processor until coarsely ground, 10 to 15 pulses. Mix the bread crumbs, butter, and salt in a small baking dish; bake until golden brown and crisp, 15 to 20 minutes. Cool to room temperature and mix with the Parmesan in a small bowl. Set aside.

2. FOR THE FILLING: Increase the oven temperature to 450 degrees. Melt 2 tablespoons of the butter in a large skillet over medium heat; add the mushrooms and onions and sauté, stirring frequently, until the liquid from the mushrooms evaporates, 12 to 15 minutes. Season with salt and pepper to taste; transfer the vegetables to a medium bowl and set aside. Clean the skillet.

3. Meanwhile, bring 4 quarts water to a boil in a large pot. Add 1 tablespoon salt and the pasta and cook until al dente. Reserve ¼ cup cooking water, drain the pasta, and return to the pot with the reserved liquid.

4. Melt the remaining 6 tablespoons butter in the clean skillet over medium heat. Whisk in the flour and cook, whisking constantly, until the flour turns golden, 1 to 2 minutes. Whisking constantly, gradually add the chicken broth. Increase the heat to medium-high and simmer until the mixture thickens, 3 to 4 minutes. Off the heat, whisk in the Parmesan, sherry, lemon juice, thyme, nutmeg, and ½ teaspoon salt. Add the sauce, sautéed vegetables, peas, and turkey to the pasta and mix well; season with salt and pepper to taste.

5. Turn the mixture into a buttered 13 by 9-inch gratin dish (or other shallow ovensafe baking dish of similar size), sprinkle evenly with the reserved bread crumbs, and bake until the bread crumbs brown and the mixture is bubbly, 13 to 15 minutes. Serve immediately.

½ teaspoon ground allspice

¼ teaspoon ground black pepper

2 cups tomato sauce

2 cups low-sodium chicken broth

2 cups water

2 tablespoons cider vinegar

2 teaspoons dark brown sugar

Hot sauce

ACCOMPANIMENTS

1 pound spaghetti, cooked, drained, and tossed with 2 tablespoons unsalted butter

12 ounces sharp cheddar cheese, shredded (about 3 cups)

1 (15-ounce) can red kidney beans, drained, rinsed, and warmed

1 medium onion, chopped

CINCINNATI CHILI

WHY THIS RECIPE WORKS: This Midwestern diner specialty is an unusual marriage of American chili and Middle Eastern spices. For an easy weeknight meal, we wanted to pare the list of ingredients down to the essentials without compromising the distinctive character of the dish.

The beef in Cincinnati Chili isn't sautéed like the beef in other chilis, so there is no way to remove the fat. To avoid greasiness, we blanched ground chuck for half a minute, which got rid of most of the fat but still left plenty of flavor. The spices used in this chili vary from recipe to recipe. We settled on a limited palette starring chili powder, oregano, cinnamon, and cocoa powder, which we bloomed in hot oil for more depth of flavor. Water and tomato sauce are the traditional base for the sauce; we added chicken broth for balance. Vinegar and brown sugar livened things up. After a long simmer, the chili was ready to be served, and we couldn't think of a better way to do it than "five-way"—over spaghetti, topped with cheddar cheese, chopped onions, and kidney beans.

Cincinnati Chili

SERVES 6 TO 8

Use canned tomato sauce for this recipe—do not use jarred spaghetti sauce.

CHILI

2 teaspoons table salt, plus more to taste

1½ pounds 80 percent lean ground chuck

2 tablespoons vegetable oil

2 medium onions, minced

2 medium garlic cloves, minced or pressed through a garlic press (about 2 teaspoons)

2 tablespoons chili powder

2 teaspoons dried oregano

2 teaspoons cocoa powder

1½ teaspoons ground cinnamon

½ teaspoon cayenne pepper

1. FOR THE CHILI: Bring 2 quarts water and 1 teaspoon of the salt to a boil in a large saucepan. Add the ground chuck, stirring vigorously to separate the meat into individual strands. As soon as the foam from the meat rises to the top (this takes about 30 seconds) and before the water returns to a boil, drain the meat into a strainer and set it aside.

2. Rinse and dry the empty saucepan. Set the pan over medium heat and add the oil. When the oil is warm, add the onions and cook, stirring frequently, until the onions are soft and browned around the edges, about 8 minutes. Add the garlic and cook until fragrant, about 1 minute. Stir in the chili powder, oregano, cocoa, cinnamon, cayenne, allspice, black pepper, and the remaining 1 teaspoon salt. Cook, stirring constantly, until the spices are fragrant, about 30 seconds. Stir in the tomato sauce, broth, water, vinegar, and sugar, scraping the pan bottom to remove any browned bits.

3. Add the blanched ground beef and increase the heat to high. As soon as the liquid boils, reduce the heat to medium-low and simmer, stirring occasionally, until the chili is deep red and has thickened slightly, about 1 hour. Season with salt and hot sauce to taste. (The chili can be refrigerated in an airtight container for up to 3 days. Bring to a simmer over medium-low heat before serving.)

4. TO SERVE: Divide the buttered spaghetti among individual bowls. Spoon the chili over the spaghetti and top with the cheese, beans, and onion. Serve immediately.

CHICKEN-FRIED STEAK

WHY THIS RECIPE WORKS: Although this truck-stop favorite often gets a bad rap, chicken-fried steak can be delicious when cooked just right. Poorly prepared versions feature dry, rubbery steaks that snap back with each bite, coated in damp, pale breading and topped with a bland, pasty white sauce. When cooked well, thin cutlets of beef are breaded and fried until a crisp, golden brown. The creamy gravy that accompanies the steak is well seasoned and not too thick. This was our goal.

A thin steak works best here, so we turned to cube steak and pounded the meat to an even thickness. What makes this steak special is the crisp coating. After trying a variety of coatings—Melba toast, corn flakes, panko, and the like—we determined simple was best. We dredged the steaks in heavily seasoned flour, dipped them in a thick buttermilk and egg mixture aerated with baking power and baking soda, and then returned them to the seasoned flour for a second coat. This coating fried up to an impressive dark mahogany color with a resilient texture to stand up to the gravy. For the gravy, we built in flavor by using the fried bits left in the pan after cooking the steaks and by making a roux. Onions and cayenne are traditional for the gravy, but we found that small additions of thyme and garlic also improved its flavor.

Chicken-Fried Steaks

SERVES 6

Getting the initial oil temperature to 375 degrees is key to the success of this recipe. Use an instant-read thermometer with a high upper range to check the temperature; a clip-on candy/deep-fry thermometer is also fine. If your Dutch oven measures 11 inches across (as ours does), you will need to fry the steaks in two batches.

STEAKS

- 3 cups unbleached all-purpose flour
  Table salt and ground black pepper
- ⅛ teaspoon cayenne pepper
- 1 large egg
- 1 teaspoon baking powder
- ½ teaspoon baking soda

- 1 cup buttermilk
- 6 (5-ounce) cube steaks, pounded ⅓ inch thick
- 4-5 cups peanut oil

CREAM GRAVY

- 1 medium onion, minced
- ⅛ teaspoon dried thyme
- 2 medium garlic cloves, minced or pressed through a garlic press (about 2 teaspoons)
- 3 tablespoons unbleached all-purpose flour
- ½ cup low-sodium chicken broth
- 2 cups whole milk
- ¾ teaspoon table salt
- ¼ teaspoon ground black pepper
  Pinch cayenne pepper

1. FOR THE STEAKS: Mix the flour, 5 teaspoons salt, 1 teaspoon black pepper, and the cayenne together in a large shallow dish. In a second large shallow dish, beat the egg, baking powder, and baking soda; stir in the buttermilk.

2. Set a wire rack over a large rimmed baking sheet. Pat the steaks dry with paper towels and sprinkle each side with salt and pepper. One at a time, drop the steaks into the flour and shake the dish to coat. Shake excess flour from each steak, then, using tongs, dip each steak into the egg mixture, turning to coat well and allowing the excess to drip off. Coat the steaks with flour again, shake off the excess, and place them on the wire rack.

3. Adjust an oven rack to the middle position, set a second wire rack over a second rimmed baking sheet, and place the sheet on the oven rack; heat the oven to 200 degrees. Line a large plate with a double layer of paper towels. Meanwhile, heat 1 inch of oil in a large (11-inch diameter) Dutch oven over medium-high heat to 375 degrees. Place 3 steaks in the oil and fry, turning once, until deep golden brown on each side, about 5 minutes (the oil temperature will drop to around 335 degrees). Transfer the steaks to the paper towel–lined plate to drain, then transfer them to the wire rack in the oven. Bring the oil back to 375 degrees and repeat the cooking and draining process (use fresh paper towels) with the 3 remaining steaks.

4. FOR THE GRAVY: Carefully pour the hot oil through a fine-mesh strainer into a clean pot. Return the browned bits from the strainer along with 2 tablespoons of the frying oil to the Dutch oven. Turn the heat to medium, add the onion and thyme, and cook until the onion has softened and is beginning to brown, 4 to 5 minutes. Add the garlic and cook until aromatic, about 30 seconds. Add the flour to the pan and stir until well combined and starting to dissolve, about 1 minute. Whisk in the broth, scraping any browned bits off the bottom of the pan. Whisk in the milk, salt, black pepper, and cayenne; bring to a simmer over medium-high heat. Cook until thickened (the gravy should have a loose consistency—it will thicken as it cools), about 5 minutes.

5. Transfer the chicken-fried steaks to individual plates. Spoon a generous amount of gravy over each steak. Serve immediately, passing any remaining gravy separately.

ALL-BEEF MEATLOAF

WHY THIS RECIPE WORKS: Every all-beef meatloaf we've tasted has had the same problems—chewy texture and uninteresting flavor, making it more of a hamburger in the shape of a log than bona fide meatloaf. In the past, when we wanted a great meatloaf, we turned to a traditional meatloaf mix consisting of beef, pork, and veal. Could we create an all-beef meatloaf to compete with this classic?

Supermarkets offer a wide selection of "ground beef," and after testing them alone and in combination we determined that equal parts of chuck (for moisture) and sirloin (for beefy flavor) were best. Beef has a livery taste that we wanted to subdue, and the usual dairy additions to meatloaf didn't work. Chicken broth, oddly enough, neutralized this off-flavor and provided moisture. For additional moisture and richness, we included mild-tasting Monterey Jack cheese, which also helped bind the mixture. To avoid pockets of oozing hot cheese in the meatloaf, we shredded the cheese and froze it briefly. Crushed saltines, our choice for the starchy filler, provided texture, but we felt our meatloaf needed more "sliceability." Surprisingly, gelatin gave us just the smooth, luxurious texture we sought. We seasoned the mixture with onions, celery, garlic (all sautéed), thyme, paprika, soy sauce, and mustard. A traditional ketchup glaze crowned our flavorful all-beef meatloaf.

Glazed All-Beef Meatloaf

SERVES 6 TO 8

If you can't find chuck and/or sirloin, substitute 85 percent lean ground beef.

MEATLOAF

- 3 ounces Monterey Jack cheese, shredded on the small holes of a box grater (about 1 cup)
- 1 tablespoon unsalted butter
- 1 medium onion, minced
- 1 medium celery rib, minced
- 2 teaspoons minced fresh thyme leaves
- 1 teaspoon paprika
- 1 medium garlic clove, minced or pressed through a garlic press (about 1 teaspoon)
- ¼ cup tomato juice
- ½ cup low-sodium chicken broth
- 2 large eggs
- ½ teaspoon unflavored powdered gelatin
- ⅔ cup crushed saltines
- 2 tablespoons minced fresh parsley leaves
- 1 tablespoon soy sauce
- 1 teaspoon Dijon mustard
- ¾ teaspoon table salt
- ½ teaspoon ground black pepper
- 1 pound 90 percent lean ground sirloin (see note)
- 1 pound 80 percent lean ground chuck (see note)

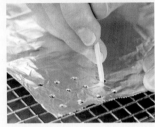
GLAZE

- ½ cup ketchup
- ¼ cup cider vinegar
- 3 tablespoons light brown sugar
- 1 teaspoon hot sauce
- ½ teaspoon ground coriander

1. FOR THE MEATLOAF: Adjust an oven rack to the middle position and heat the oven to 375 degrees. Spread the cheese on a plate and place in the freezer until ready to use. To prepare the baking sheet, set a wire rack over a rimmed baking sheet. Fold a sheet of heavy-duty aluminum foil to form a 10 by 6-inch rectangle. Center the foil on the rack and poke holes in the foil with a skewer (about half an inch apart). Spray the foil with vegetable oil spray or use nonstick foil.

2. Melt the butter in a 10-inch skillet over medium-high heat; add the onion and celery and cook, stirring occasionally, until beginning to brown, 6 to 8 minutes. Add the thyme, paprika, and garlic and cook, stirring, until fragrant, about 1 minute. Reduce the heat to low and add the tomato juice. Cook, stirring to scrape up the browned bits from the pan, until thickened, about 1 minute. Transfer the mixture to a small bowl and set aside to cool.

3. Whisk the broth and eggs together in a large bowl until combined. Sprinkle the gelatin over the liquid and let stand for 5 minutes. Stir in the saltines, parsley, soy sauce, mustard, salt, pepper, and onion mixture. Crumble the frozen cheese into a coarse powder and sprinkle over the mixture. Add the sirloin and chuck; mix gently with your hands until thoroughly combined, about 1 minute. Transfer the meat to the foil rectangle and shape into a 10 by 6-inch oval about 2 inches high. Smooth the top and edges of the meatloaf with a moistened spatula. Bake until the center of the loaf registers 135 to 140 degrees on an instant-read thermometer, 55 to 65 minutes. Remove the meatloaf from the oven and turn on the broiler.

4. FOR THE GLAZE: While the meatloaf cooks, combine the glaze ingredients in a small saucepan; bring to a simmer over medium heat and cook, stirring, until thick and syrupy, about 5 minutes. Spread half of the glaze evenly over the cooked meatloaf with a rubber spatula; place under the broiler and cook until the glaze bubbles and begins to brown at the edges, about 5 minutes. Remove the meatloaf from the oven and spread evenly with the remaining glaze; place back under the broiler and cook until the glaze is again bubbling and beginning to brown, about 5 minutes more. Let the meatloaf cool for about 20 minutes before slicing.

CLASSIC MEATLOAF

WHY THIS RECIPE WORKS: Not all meatloaves resemble Mom's. Some recipes go the canned soup route and, frankly, taste like it. Others become gussied up with ingredients that have no place in this humble family dish—canned pineapple, sun-dried tomatoes, and the like. Our goal was not to develop the ultimate meatloaf but to bring it back to its classic roots— a tender, well-seasoned loaf smothered with tangy sweet glaze.

We started, of course, with the meat. We determined that supermarkets haven't been selling "meatloaf mix" for no reason—a mixture of ground beef chuck, ground pork, and ground veal produced the best balance of flavors and textures. A starch turned out to be a necessity for binding the meat and giving it that classic meatloaf texture; cracker crumbs, quick-cooking oatmeal, and fresh bread crumbs all worked well. To prevent the filler from drying out the meatloaf, we knew we needed to add some moisture. After trying a host of options,

we determined that whole milk and plain yogurt are equally acceptable. Finally, we realized that the pan in which the meatloaf baked made a big difference. A standard loaf pan traps the fat and stews the meat, and the juice bubbles up and destroys the glaze. Baking the meatloaf free-form in a shallow baking pan gave the loaf a good crust, preserved our sweet-tart glaze, and helped the bacon topping crisp nicely.

Meatloaf with Brown Sugar–Ketchup Glaze
SERVES 6 TO 8

If you like, you can omit the bacon topping from the loaf. In this case, brush on half of the glaze before baking and the other half during the last 15 minutes of baking. If you choose not to special-order the mix of meat below, we recommend the standard meatloaf mix of equal parts beef, pork, and veal, available at most grocery stores. Lining the baking pan with foil makes for easier cleanup.

BROWN SUGAR–KETCHUP GLAZE
- ½   cup ketchup or chili sauce
- ¼   cup brown sugar
- 4   teaspoons cider vinegar or white vinegar

MEATLOAF
- 2   teaspoons vegetable oil
- 1   medium onion, chopped
- 2   medium garlic cloves, minced or pressed through a garlic press (about 2 teaspoons)
- 2   large eggs
- ½   cup whole milk or plain yogurt, plus more as needed
- 2   teaspoons Dijon mustard
- 2   teaspoons Worcestershire sauce
- 1   teaspoon table salt
- ½   teaspoon ground black pepper
- ½   teaspoon dried thyme
- ¼   teaspoon hot sauce
- 2   pounds meatloaf mix (50 percent ground chuck, 25 percent ground pork, 25 percent ground veal; see note)
- ⅔   cup crushed saltines (about 16) or quick oatmeal or 1⅓ cups fresh bread crumbs
- ⅓   cup minced fresh parsley leaves
- 6–8 ounces bacon (8 to 12 slices, depending on loaf shape) (see note)

1. FOR THE GLAZE: Mix all the ingredients together in a small saucepan; set aside.

2. FOR THE MEATLOAF: Line a 13 by 9-inch baking pan with foil; set aside. Heat the oven to 350 degrees. Heat the oil in a medium skillet over medium heat until shimmering. Add the onion and garlic; sauté until softened, about 5 minutes. Set aside to cool while preparing the remaining ingredients.

3. Mix the eggs with the milk, mustard, Worcestershire sauce, salt, pepper, thyme, and hot sauce. Combine the egg mixture with the meat in a large bowl and add the crackers, parsley, and cooked onion and garlic; mix with a fork until evenly blended and the meat mixture does not stick to the bowl. (If necessary, add more milk, a couple of tablespoons at a time, until the mixture no longer sticks.)

4. Turn the meat mixture onto a work surface. With wet hands, pat the mixture into an approximately 9 by 5-inch loaf shape. Place on the prepared baking pan. Brush with half the glaze, then arrange the bacon slices, crosswise, over the loaf, overlapping them slightly and tucking only the bacon tip ends under the loaf.

5. Bake the loaf until the bacon is crisp and the center of the loaf registers 160 degrees on an instant-read thermometer, about 1 hour. Cool for at least 20 minutes. Simmer the remaining glaze over medium heat until thickened slightly. Slice the meatloaf and serve with the extra glaze passed separately.

TURKEY MEATLOAF

WHY THIS RECIPE WORKS: Store-bought ground turkey is fine and pasty, and it produced a dense, mushy meatloaf when we simply swapped it into a traditional meatloaf recipe. We found a panade only exacerbated the mushiness. Instead, we stirred in quick oats, which added just the right amount of chew and helped open up the texture of the dense turkey. To help give the turkey's thin juices fuller body, we added cornstarch to the mix, boosted flavor with grated Parmesan cheese and butter, and used egg yolks instead of whole eggs. To avoid overwhelming the mild flavor of the meat with too many add-ins, we stirred in a modest amount of onion, as well as garlic, Worcestershire sauce, thyme, and Dijon mustard. To finish it off, we made a flavor-packed glaze and ensured that it stuck by applying a first coat to the meatloaf and letting it cook until the glaze was tacky. We then added a second coat of glaze, which stuck to this base coat in an even layer. To ensure the loaf cooked evenly, we baked it on an aluminum foil–lined wire rack set in a rimmed baking sheet.

Turkey Meatloaf with Ketchup–Brown Sugar Glaze

SERVES 4 TO 6

Do not use 99 percent lean ground turkey in this recipe; it will make a dry meatloaf. Three tablespoons of rolled oats, chopped fine, can be substituted for the quick oats; do not use steel-cut oats.

MEATLOAF

- 3 tablespoons unsalted butter
  Pinch baking soda
- ½ onion, chopped fine
  Salt and pepper
- 1 garlic clove, minced
- 1 teaspoon minced fresh thyme
- 2 tablespoons Worcestershire sauce
- 3 tablespoons quick oats
- 2 teaspoons cornstarch
- 2 large egg yolks
- 2 tablespoons Dijon mustard
- 2 pounds 85 or 93 percent lean ground turkey
- 1 ounce Parmesan, grated (½ cup)
- ⅓ cup chopped fresh parsley

GLAZE

- 1 cup ketchup
- ¼ cup packed brown sugar
- 2½ teaspoons cider vinegar
- ½ teaspoon hot sauce

1. FOR THE MEATLOAF: Adjust oven rack to upper-middle position and heat oven to 350 degrees. Line wire rack with aluminum foil and set in rimmed baking sheet. Melt butter in 10-inch skillet over low heat. Stir baking soda into melted butter. Add onion and ¼ teaspoon salt, increase heat to medium, and cook, stirring frequently, until onion is softened and beginning to brown, 3 to 4 minutes. Add garlic and thyme and cook until fragrant, about 1 minute. Stir in Worcestershire and continue to cook until slightly reduced, about 1 minute longer. Transfer onion mixture to large bowl and set aside. Combine oats, cornstarch, ¾ teaspoon salt, and ½ teaspoon pepper in second bowl.

2. FOR THE GLAZE: Whisk all ingredients in saucepan until sugar dissolves. Bring mixture to simmer over medium heat and cook until slightly thickened, about 5 minutes; set aside.

3. Stir egg yolks and mustard into cooled onion mixture until well combined. Add turkey, Parmesan, parsley, and oat mixture; using your hands, mix until well combined. Transfer turkey mixture to center of prepared rack. Using your wet hands, shape into 9 by 5-inch loaf. Using pastry brush, spread half of glaze evenly over top and sides of meatloaf. Bake meatloaf for 40 minutes.

4. Brush remaining glaze onto top and sides of meatloaf and continue to cook until meatloaf registers 160 degrees, 35 to 40 minutes longer. Let meatloaf cool for 20 minutes before slicing and serving.

Turkey Meatloaf with Apricot-Mustard Glaze

Microwave ¼ cup apricot preserves until hot and fluid, about 30 seconds. Strain preserves through fine-mesh strainer into bowl; discard solids. Stir in 2 tablespoons Dijon mustard, 2 tablespoons ketchup, and pinch salt. Proceed with recipe, substituting apricot mixture for glaze.

STUFFED PEPPERS

WHY THIS RECIPE WORKS: A vegetable can be more than just a side dish, and stuffed peppers are a perfect case in point. But slimy or too-crunchy peppers and tasteless fillings can ruin the show. We wanted to revamp this dish to be a flavorful option for a weeknight dinner. Cooking the peppers correctly is critical; they need to be sturdy enough to hold the filling but not crunchy and bitter. We found that blanching them before adding the filling gave us peppers that held their shape, had good color, and tasted sweeter. Rice is the classic stuffing for peppers, but alone it didn't have much flavor; a mixture of rice and ground beef did the trick. We cooked the rice in the water we'd used to blanch the peppers and for additional flavor, we included sautéed onion and garlic, tomatoes, cheddar cheese, and ketchup.

Classic Stuffed Bell Peppers

SERVES 4

When shopping for bell peppers to stuff, it's best to choose those with broad bases that will allow the peppers to stand up on their own. It's easier to fill the peppers after they have been placed in the baking dish because the sides of the dish will hold the peppers steady.

      Table salt
  4   medium red, yellow, or orange bell peppers
      (about 6 ounces each), ½ inch trimmed off
      tops, cores and seeds discarded (see note)
  ½   cup long-grain white rice
  1½ tablespoons olive oil
  1   medium onion, minced
  12 ounces ground beef, preferably 80 percent
      lean ground chuck
  3   medium garlic cloves, minced or pressed
      through a garlic press (about 1 tablespoon)
  1   (14.5-ounce) can diced tomatoes, drained,
      ¼ cup juice reserved
  5   ounces Monterey Jack cheese, shredded
      (about 1¼ cups)
  2   tablespoons chopped fresh parsley leaves
      Ground black pepper
  ¼   cup ketchup

1. Bring 4 quarts water to a boil in a large stockpot or Dutch oven over high heat. Add 1 tablespoon salt and the bell peppers. Cook until the peppers just begin to soften, about 3 minutes. Using a slotted spoon, remove the peppers from the pot, drain off the excess water, and place the peppers, cut side up, on paper towels. Return the water to a boil; add the rice and boil until tender, about 13 minutes. Drain the rice and transfer it to a large bowl; set aside.

2. Adjust an oven rack to the middle position and heat the oven to 350 degrees.

3. Meanwhile, heat the oil in a heavy-bottomed 12-inch skillet over medium-high heat until shimmering. Add the onion and cook, stirring occasionally, until softened and beginning to brown, about 5 minutes. Add the ground beef and cook, breaking the beef into small pieces with a spoon, until no longer pink, about 4 minutes. Stir in the garlic and cook until fragrant, about 30 seconds. Transfer the mixture to the bowl with the rice; stir in the tomatoes, 1 cup of the cheese, the parsley, and salt and pepper to taste.

4. Stir together the ketchup and the reserved tomato juice in a small bowl.

5. Place the peppers, cut side up, in a 9-inch square baking dish. Using a soup spoon, divide the filling evenly among the peppers. Spoon 2 tablespoons of the ketchup mixture over each filled pepper and sprinkle each with 1 tablespoon of the remaining ¼ cup cheese. Bake until the cheese is browned and the filling is heated through, 25 to 30 minutes. Serve immediately.

PHILLY CHEESESTEAKS

WHY THIS RECIPE WORKS: Authentic Philly cheesesteak recipes start with a rib eye and require a meat slicer and flat-top griddle to achieve ultrathin slices with crisp edges. To make this sandwich at home, we needed a stand-in for the meat and a way to slice it thin to get it super-crisp, without any fancy equipment. We started by looking for a more economical cut of meat and landed on skirt steak. When partially frozen, skirt steak's thin profile and open-grained texture made for easy slicing, and its flavor was nearest to rib eye. To best approximate the wide griddle typically used in Philadelphia, we cooked the meat in two batches, letting any excess moisture drain off before giving it a final sear. Finally, to bind it all together, we let slices of American cheese melt into the meat; a bit of grated Parmesan boosted the flavor.

Philly Cheesesteaks

SERVES 4

If skirt steak is unavailable, substitute sirloin steak tips (also called flap meat). Top these sandwiches with chopped pickled hot peppers, sautéed onions or bell peppers, sweet relish, or hot sauce.

- 2 pounds skirt steak, trimmed and sliced with grain into 3-inch-wide strips
- 4 (8-inch) Italian sub rolls, split lengthwise
- 2 tablespoons vegetable oil
- ½ teaspoon salt
- ⅛ teaspoon pepper
- ¼ cup grated Parmesan cheese
- 8 slices white American cheese (8 ounces)

1. Place steak pieces on large plate or baking sheet and freeze until very firm, about 1 hour.

2. Meanwhile, adjust oven rack to middle position and heat oven to 400 degrees. Spread split rolls on baking sheet and toast until lightly browned, 5 to 10 minutes.

3. Using sharp knife, shave steak pieces as thinly as possible against grain. Mound meat on cutting board and chop coarsely with knife 10 to 20 times.

4. Heat 1 tablespoon oil in 12-inch nonstick skillet over high heat until smoking. Add half of meat in even layer and cook without stirring until well browned on 1 side, 4 to 5 minutes. Stir and continue to cook until meat is no longer pink, 1 to 2 minutes. Transfer meat to colander set in large bowl. Wipe out skillet with paper towel. Repeat with remaining 1 tablespoon oil and sliced meat.

5. Return now-empty skillet to medium heat. Drain excess moisture from meat. Return meat to skillet (discard any liquid in bowl) and add salt and pepper. Heat, stirring constantly, until meat is warmed through, 1 to 2 minutes. Reduce heat to low, sprinkle with Parmesan, and shingle slices of American cheese over meat. Allow cheeses to melt, about 2 minutes. Using heatproof spatula or wooden spoon, fold melted cheese into meat thoroughly. Divide mixture evenly among toasted rolls. Serve immediately.

JUICY GRILLED TURKEY BURGERS

WHY THIS RECIPE WORKS: To create juicy, well-textured turkey burgers, we ditched store-bought ground turkey in favor of home-ground turkey thighs, which boast more fat and flavor. To ensure that our turkey burger recipe delivered maximum juiciness, we incorporated a paste with a portion of the ground turkey, gelatin, soy sauce, and baking soda, which trapped juice within the burgers. Finally, we added coarsely chopped raw white mushrooms to keep the meat from binding together too firmly.

Juicy Grilled Turkey Burgers

SERVES 6

If you are able to purchase boneless, skinless turkey thighs, substitute 1½ pounds for the bone-in thigh. To ensure the best texture, don't let the burgers stand for more than an hour before cooking. Serve the burgers with Malt Vinegar–Molasses Burger Sauce, Chile-Lime Burger Sauce, or Apricot-Mustard Burger Sauce (recipes follow).

- 1 (2-pound) bone-in turkey thigh, skinned, boned, trimmed, and cut into ½-inch pieces
- 1 tablespoon unflavored gelatin
- 3 tablespoons low-sodium chicken broth
- 6 ounces white mushrooms, trimmed
- 1 tablespoon soy sauce
  Pinch baking soda
- 2 tablespoons vegetable oil, plus extra for brushing
  Kosher salt and pepper
- 6 large hamburger buns

1. Place turkey pieces on large plate in single layer. Freeze meat until very firm and hardened around edges, 35 to 45 minutes. Meanwhile, sprinkle gelatin over chicken broth in small bowl and let sit until gelatin softens, about 5 minutes. Pulse mushrooms in food processor until coarsely chopped, about 7 pulses, stopping and redistributing mushrooms around bowl as needed to ensure even grinding. Set mushrooms aside; do not wash food processor.

2. Pulse one-third of turkey in food processor until coarsely chopped into ⅛-inch pieces, 18 to 22 pulses, stopping and redistributing turkey around bowl as needed to ensure even grinding. Transfer meat to large bowl and repeat two more times with remaining turkey.

3. Return ½ cup (about 3 ounces) ground turkey to bowl of food processor along with softened gelatin, soy sauce, and baking soda. Process until smooth, about 2 minutes, scraping down bowl as needed. With processor running, slowly drizzle in oil, about 10 seconds; leave paste in food processor. Return mushrooms to food processor with paste and pulse to combine, 3 to 5 pulses, stopping and redistributing mixture as needed to ensure even mixing. Transfer mushroom mixture to bowl with ground turkey and use hands to evenly combine.

4. With lightly greased hands, divide meat mixture into 6 balls. Flatten into ¾-inch-thick patties about 4 inches in diameter; press shallow indentation into center of each burger to ensure even cooking. (Shaped patties can be frozen for up to 1 month. Frozen patties can be cooked straight from freezer.)

5A. FOR A CHARCOAL GRILL: Open bottom vent completely. Light large chimney starter filled with charcoal briquettes (6 quarts). When top coals are partially covered with ash, pour evenly over half of grill. Set cooking grate in place, cover, and open lid vent completely. Heat grill until hot, about 5 minutes.

5B. FOR A GAS GRILL: Turn all burners to high, cover, and heat grill until hot, about 15 minutes. Leave primary burner on high and turn off other burner(s).

6. Clean and oil cooking grate. Brush 1 side of patties with oil and season with salt and pepper. Using spatula, flip patties, brush with oil, and season second side. Place burgers over hot part of grill and cook until burgers are well browned on both sides and register 160 degrees, 4 to 7 minutes per side. (If cooking frozen burgers: After burgers are browned on both sides, transfer to cool side of grill, cover, and continue to cook until burgers register 160 degrees.)

7. Transfer burgers to plate and let rest for 5 minutes. While burgers rest, grill buns over hot side of grill. Transfer burgers to buns, add desired toppings, and serve.

Malt Vinegar–Molasses Burger Sauce
MAKES ABOUT 1 CUP

- ¾ cup mayonnaise
- 4 teaspoons malt vinegar
- ½ teaspoon molasses
- ¼ teaspoon Worcestershire sauce
- ¼ teaspoon salt
- ¼ teaspoon pepper

Whisk all ingredients together in bowl.

Chile-Lime Burger Sauce
MAKES ABOUT 1 CUP

- ¾ cup mayonnaise
- 2 teaspoons chile-garlic paste
- 2 teaspoons lime juice
- 1 scallion, sliced thin
- ¼ teaspoon fish sauce
- ⅛ teaspoon sugar

Whisk all ingredients together in bowl.

Apricot-Mustard Burger Sauce
MAKES ABOUT 1 CUP

- ¾ cup mayonnaise
- 5 teaspoons apricot preserves
- 1 tablespoon lemon juice
- 1 tablespoon Dijon mustard
- 1 tablespoon whole-grain mustard
- ¼ teaspoon salt

Whisk all ingredients together in bowl.

OLD-FASHIONED BURGERS

WHY THIS RECIPE WORKS: The burger you find at most drive-ins is a rubbery, thin, gray patty with little beef flavor. We wanted to create, at home, the classic drive-in burger. Made from freshly ground beef, cooked on a flat griddle, this style of burger is ultracrisp, ultrabrowned, and ultrabeefy. Topped with melted cheese and tangy sauce, it's the burger fast food restaurants wish they could produce.

We learned right off the bat that the thin patty typical of this burger style requires freshly ground meat. Prepackaged hamburger is ground very fine and packaged tightly, which produced dense, rubbery, and dry patties. For the meat, we settled on short ribs ground up with sirloin steak tips. Numerous grinding tests revealed that while beefiness depended on cut, juiciness corresponded to fat. Well-marbled short ribs added the perfect amount of fat to complement the beefy flavor from the sirloin tips. And if you don't have a meat grinder? The food processor worked just fine as long as the meat was first chilled in the freezer until firm but still pliable. We still had to deal with a rubbery texture caused by meat collagen proteins shrinking and tightening when exposed to heat. To fight this, the meat needed to be as loosely packed as possible—not pressed but rather gently shaped into loose patties. To top our burgers, we went back to the tried-and-true flavors of a tangy and sweet Thousand Island–style dressing, American cheese, and thinly sliced onion.

Best Old-Fashioned Burgers

MAKES 4 BURGERS

Sirloin steak tips are also labeled "flap meat" by some butchers. Flank steak can be used in its place. This recipe yields juicy medium to medium-well burgers. If doubling the recipe, process the meat in three batches in step 2. Because the cooked burgers do not hold well, fry four burgers and serve them immediately before frying more. Or cook them in two pans. Extra patties can be frozen for up to 2 weeks. Stack the patties, separated by parchment paper, and wrap them in three layers of plastic wrap. Thaw burgers in a single layer on a baking sheet at room temperature for 30 minutes before cooking.

    10   ounces sirloin steak tips, cut into 1-inch chunks
         (see note)
     6   ounces boneless beef short ribs, cut into 1-inch chunks
         Table salt and ground black pepper
     1   tablespoon unsalted butter
     4   soft hamburger buns
     ½   teaspoon vegetable oil
     4   slices American cheese
         Thinly sliced onion
     1   recipe Classic Burger Sauce (recipe follows)

1. Place the beef chunks on a baking sheet in a single layer, leaving ½ inch of space around each chunk. Freeze the meat until very firm and starting to harden around the edges but still pliable, 15 to 25 minutes.

2. Place half of the meat in a food processor and pulse until the meat is coarsely ground, 10 to 15 pulses, stopping and redistributing the meat around the bowl as necessary to ensure the beef is evenly ground. Transfer the meat to a baking sheet by overturning the bowl, without touching the meat. Repeat the grinding with the remaining meat. Spread the meat over the sheet and inspect carefully, discarding any long strands of gristle or large chunks of hard meat or fat.

NOTES FROM THE TEST KITCHEN

MAKING LOOSELY PACKED PATTIES

1. Chill meat in freezer, separating cubes by at least ½ inch, until firm but still pliable, 15 to 25 minutes. Pulse meat in food processor.

2. Spread chopped meat over baking sheet and remove any large chunks or stringy connective tissue. Gently separate meat into 4 piles.

3. Without lifting or compressing, gently form meat into thin patties with rough edges and textured surface.

3. Gently separate the ground meat into four equal mounds. Without picking the meat up, with your fingers gently shape each mound into a loose patty ½ inch thick and 4 inches in diameter, leaving the edges and surface ragged. Season the top of each patty with salt and pepper. Using a spatula, flip the patties and season the other side. Refrigerate while toasting the buns.

4. Melt ½ tablespoon of the butter in a heavy-bottomed 12-inch skillet over medium heat. Add the bun tops, cut side down, and toast until light golden brown, about 2 minutes. Repeat with the remaining ½ tablespoon butter and the bun bottoms. Set the buns aside and wipe out the skillet with paper towels.

5. Return the skillet to high heat; add the oil and heat until just smoking. Using a spatula, transfer the burgers to the skillet and cook without moving them for 3 minutes. Using the spatula, flip the burgers over and cook for 1 minute. Top each patty with a slice of the cheese and continue to cook until the cheese is melted, about 1 minute longer.

6. Transfer the patties to the bun bottoms and top with the onion. Spread 2 teaspoons of the burger sauce on each bun top. Cover the burgers with the bun tops and serve immediately.

Classic Burger Sauce

MAKES ABOUT ¼ CUP

- 2 tablespoons mayonnaise
- 1 tablespoon ketchup
- ½ teaspoon sweet pickle relish
- ½ teaspoon sugar
- ½ teaspoon white vinegar
- ¼ teaspoon ground black pepper

Whisk all the ingredients together in a small bowl.

JUICY PUB-STYLE BURGERS

WHY THIS RECIPE WORKS: Few things are as satisfying as a thick, juicy pub-style burger. But by the time the center of these hefty burgers cooks through, there is often an overcooked band of meat. We wanted a patty that was evenly rosy from center to edge. Grinding our own meat in the food processor was a must (freezing the meat until just firm helped the processor chop it cleanly), and we found that sirloin steak tips were ideal. To give the burgers just enough structure, we cut the meat into small ½-inch chunks before grinding and lightly packed the meat into patties. Melted butter improved their flavor and juiciness. Transferring the burgers from the stovetop to the oven to finish cooking eliminated the overcooked gray zone. For extra pub-style appeal, we came up with flavorful topping combinations to finish off our burgers.

Juicy Pub-Style Burgers

SERVES 4

Sirloin steak tips are also labeled as "flap meat." When stirring the butter and pepper into the ground meat and shaping the patties, take care not to overwork the meat or the burgers will become dense. For the best flavor, season the burgers aggressively just before cooking. The burgers can be topped as desired, or try one of our variations that follow. The uncooked patties can be refrigerated for up to 1 day.

- 2 pounds sirloin steak tips or boneless beef short ribs, trimmed and cut into ½-inch chunks
- 4 tablespoons unsalted butter (½ stick), melted and cooled slightly
  Table salt and ground black pepper
- 1 teaspoon vegetable oil
- 4 large hamburger buns, toasted and buttered
- 1 recipe Pub-Style Burger Sauce (optional; recipe follows)

1. Place the beef chunks on a baking sheet in a single layer. Freeze the meat until very firm and starting to harden around the edges but still pliable, 15 to 25 minutes.

2. Place one-quarter of the meat in a food processor and pulse until finely ground into 1/16-inch pieces, about 35 pulses, stopping and redistributing the meat around the bowl as necessary to ensure the beef is evenly ground. Transfer the meat to the

baking sheet by overturning the processor bowl and without directly touching the meat. Repeat grinding with the remaining 3 batches of meat. Spread the meat over the sheet and inspect carefully, discarding any long strands of gristle or large chunks of hard meat or fat.

3. Adjust an oven rack to the middle position and heat the oven to 300 degrees. Drizzle the melted butter over the ground meat and add 1 teaspoon pepper. Gently toss with a fork to combine. Divide the meat into 4 lightly packed balls. Gently flatten into patties ¾ inch thick and about 4½ inches in diameter. Refrigerate the patties until ready to cook.

4. Season 1 side of the patties with salt and pepper. Using a spatula, flip the patties and season the other side. Heat the oil in a 12-inch skillet over high heat until just smoking. Using the spatula, transfer the burgers to the skillet and cook without moving for 2 minutes. Using the spatula, flip the burgers over and cook for 2 minutes longer. Transfer the patties to a rimmed baking sheet and bake until the burgers register 125 degrees (for medium-rare) on an instant-read thermometer, 3 to 5 minutes.

5. Transfer the burgers to a plate and let rest for 5 minutes. Transfer to the buns, top with Pub-Style Burger Sauce (if using), and serve.

Pub-Style Burger Sauce

MAKES ABOUT 1 CUP, ENOUGH TO TOP 4 BURGERS

- ¾ cup mayonnaise
- 2 tablespoons soy sauce
- 1 tablespoon dark brown sugar
- 1 tablespoon Worcestershire sauce
- 1 tablespoon minced chives
- 1 medium garlic clove, minced or pressed through a garlic press (about 1 teaspoon)
- ¾ teaspoon ground black pepper

Whisk all ingredients together in bowl.

Juicy Pub-Style Burgers with Crispy Shallots and Blue Cheese

Heat ½ cup vegetable oil and 3 thinly sliced shallots in a medium saucepan over high heat; cook, stirring frequently, until the shallots are golden, about 8 minutes. Using a slotted spoon, transfer the shallots to a paper towel–lined plate, season with table salt, and let drain until crisp, about 5 minutes. (The cooled shallots can be stored at room temperature in an airtight container for up to 3 days.) Follow the recipe for Juicy Pub-Style Burgers, topping each burger with 1 ounce crumbled blue cheese before transferring to the oven. Top with Pub-Style Burger Sauce and the crispy shallots just before serving.

Juicy Pub-Style Burgers with Peppered Bacon and Aged Cheddar

Adjust an oven rack to the middle position and heat the oven to 375 degrees. Arrange 6 bacon slices on a rimmed baking sheet and sprinkle with 2 teaspoons coarsely ground pepper. Place a second rimmed baking sheet on top of the bacon and bake until the bacon is crisp, 15 to 20 minutes. Transfer the bacon to a paper towel–lined plate and cool. Cut the bacon in half crosswise. Follow the recipe for Juicy Pub-Style Burgers, topping each burger with 1 ounce grated aged cheddar cheese before transferring to the oven. Top with Pub-Style Burger Sauce and the bacon just before serving.

Juicy Pub-Style Burgers with Sautéed Onions and Smoked Cheddar

Heat 2 tablespoons vegetable oil in a 12-inch skillet over medium-high heat until just smoking. Add 1 thinly sliced onion and ¼ teaspoon table salt; cook, stirring frequently, until softened and lightly browned, 5 to 7 minutes. Follow the recipe for Juicy Pub-Style Burgers, topping each burger with 1 ounce grated smoked cheddar cheese before transferring to the oven. Top with Pub-Style Burger Sauce and the onion just before serving.

Juicy Pub-Style Burgers with Pan-Roasted Mushrooms and Gruyère

Heat 2 tablespoons vegetable oil in a 12-inch skillet over medium-high heat until just smoking. Add 10 ounces thinly sliced cremini mushrooms, ¼ teaspoon table salt, and ¼ teaspoon pepper; cook, stirring frequently, until browned, 5 to 7 minutes. Add 1 minced shallot and 2 teaspoons minced thyme and cook until fragrant. Remove the skillet from the heat and stir in 2 tablespoons dry sherry. Follow the recipe for Juicy Pub-Style Burgers, topping each burger with 1 ounce grated Gruyère cheese before transferring to the oven. Top with Pub-Style Burger Sauce and the mushrooms just before serving.

BLACK BEAN BURGERS

WHY THIS RECIPE WORKS: As with many meatless patties, black bean burgers often get their structure from fillers that rob them of any trace of black bean flavor. We wanted that key ingredient to shine in our burgers. For convenient and reliable

beans, we turned to canned, rinsing and drying them completely to eliminate cohesion-compromising moisture. Eggs and flour served as our binding agents, and adding minced scallions, cilantro, and garlic contributed some personality. We stirred in a couple of spices with major impact—cumin and coriander—plus a hit of hot sauce for zip. In keeping with our Latin American flavor profile, we turned to the bright corn flavor of tortilla chips to build up our burger mix. After blitzing crushed chips in the food processor, we added in the beans and pulsed them into coarsely chopped pieces. We combined the beans with the flour-egg binder and refrigerated the mixture, allowing the starches to absorb some of the eggs' moisture. After an hour, we formed patties and cooked the burgers in an oiled skillet. After a quick browning on each side, these burgers were ready to serve with all of our favorite fixings.

Black Bean Burgers
SERVES 6

When forming the patties it is important to pack them firmly together. Serve the burgers with your favorite toppings or with Chipotle Mayonnaise (recipe follows).

- 2 (15-ounce) cans black beans, rinsed
- 2 large eggs
- 2 tablespoons all-purpose flour
- 4 scallions, minced (¼ cup)
- 3 tablespoons minced fresh cilantro
- 2 garlic cloves, minced
- 1 teaspoon ground cumin
- ½ teaspoon ground coriander
- ¼ teaspoon salt
- ¼ teaspoon pepper
- 1 teaspoon hot sauce (optional)
- 1 ounce tortilla chips, crushed coarse (½ cup)
- 8 teaspoons vegetable oil
- 6 burger buns

1. Line rimmed baking sheet with triple layer of paper towels and spread black beans over towels. Let stand for 15 minutes.

2. Whisk eggs and flour together in large bowl until uniform paste forms. Stir in scallions, cilantro, garlic, cumin, coriander, salt, pepper, and hot sauce, if using, until well combined.

3. Process tortilla chips in food processor until finely ground, about 30 seconds. Add black beans and pulse until beans are roughly broken down, about 5 pulses. Transfer black bean mixture to bowl with egg mixture and mix until well combined. Cover and refrigerate for at least 1 hour or up to 24 hours.

4. Divide bean mixture into 6 equal portions. Firmly pack each portion into tight ball, then flatten to 3½-inch patty. (Patties can be wrapped individually in plastic wrap, placed in a zipper-lock bag, and frozen for up to 2 weeks. Thaw patties before cooking.)

5. Heat 2 teaspoons oil in 10-inch nonstick skillet over medium heat until shimmering. Carefully lay 3 patties in skillet and cook until bottoms are well-browned and crisp, about 5 minutes. Flip patties, add 2 teaspoons oil, and cook second sides until well-browned and crisp, 3 to 5 minutes. Transfer patties to buns and repeat with remaining 3 patties and 4 teaspoons oil. Serve.

Chipotle Mayonnaise
MAKES ABOUT ⅓ CUP

- 3 tablespoons mayonnaise
- 3 tablespoons sour cream
- 2 teaspoons minced canned chipotle chile in adobo sauce
- 1 garlic clove, minced
- ⅛ teaspoon salt

Combine all ingredients. Cover and refrigerate for at least 1 hour.

VEGAN PINTO BEAN–BEET BURGERS

WHY THIS RECIPE WORKS: Vegan burgers are often bean-based; starchy, protein-packed beans taste great, hold together well, and are satisfying. Looking for a modern twist on the typical bean burger, we combined pinto beans with vibrant shredded beets, and we also packed in a generous amount of basil leaves. The result was a substantial but fresh-tasting burger with some sweetness from the beets and the bright, complementary aroma of basil. We incorporated bulgur for heft and ground nuts for meaty richness. Garlic and mustard deepened the savory flavors. While the bulgur cooked, we pulsed the other ingredients in the food processor to just the right consistency. To bind the burgers, we turned to a surprising ingredient: carrot baby food. The carrot added tackiness, and its subtle sweetness heightened that of the shredded beets; plus, it was already conveniently pureed. Panko bread crumbs further bound the mixture and helped the patties sear up with a crisp crust.

Pinto Bean–Beet Burgers
SERVES 8

When shopping, don't confuse bulgur with cracked wheat, which has a much longer cooking time and will not work in this recipe. Use a coarse grater or the shredding disk of a food processor to shred the beets.

  Salt and pepper
- ⅔ cup medium-grind bulgur, rinsed
- 1 large beet (9 ounces), peeled and shredded
- ¾ cup walnuts
- ½ cup fresh basil leaves
- 2 garlic cloves, minced
- 1 (15-ounce) can pinto beans, rinsed
- 1 (4-ounce) jar carrot baby food
- 1 tablespoon whole-grain mustard
- 1½ cups panko bread crumbs
- 6 tablespoons vegetable oil, plus extra as needed
- 8 burger buns

1. Bring 1½ cups water and ½ teaspoon salt to boil in small saucepan. Off heat, stir in bulgur, cover, and let stand until tender, 15 to 20 minutes. Drain bulgur, spread onto rimmed baking sheet, and let cool slightly.

2. Meanwhile, pulse beet, walnuts, basil, and garlic in food processor until finely chopped, about 12 pulses, scraping down sides of bowl as needed. Add beans, carrot baby food, 2 tablespoons water, mustard, 1½ teaspoons salt, and ½ teaspoon pepper and pulse until well combined, about 8 pulses. Transfer mixture to large bowl and stir in panko and cooled bulgur.

3. Adjust oven rack to middle position and heat oven to 200 degrees. Divide mixture into 8 equal portions and pack into 3½-inch-wide patties.

4. Heat 3 tablespoons oil in 12-inch nonstick skillet over medium-high heat until shimmering. Gently lay 4 patties in skillet and cook until crisp and well browned on first side, about 4 minutes. Gently flip patties and cook until crisp and well browned on second side, about 4 minutes, adding extra oil if skillet looks dry.

5. Transfer burgers to wire rack set in rimmed baking sheet and place in oven to keep warm. Wipe out skillet with paper towels and repeat with remaining 3 tablespoons oil and remaining patties. Transfer to buns and serve.

OVEN-FRIED ONION RINGS

WHY THIS RECIPE WORKS: Fried onion rings are the perfect accompaniment to burgers, barbecue, and other casual fare. But who wants the mess and smell of deep-fried onions? We wanted an oven method that produced tender, sweet onions with a super-crunchy coating.

We made a batter with buttermilk, egg, and flour, but when we put the baking sheet in the oven the batter slid right off the onions. Coating the onion rings with flour first gave the batter something to cling to. But we wanted even more crunch. For an extra layer of coating, we turned to crushed saltines and crushed potato chips. We preheated the oil in the baking sheet before adding the coated onions so they'd start crisping right away. The result: crispy, crunchy oven-fried onion rings with deep-fried flavor.

Oven-Fried Onion Rings
SERVES 4 TO 6
Slice the onions into ½-inch-thick rounds, separate the rings, and discard any rings smaller than 2 inches in diameter.

- ½ cup unbleached all-purpose flour
- 1 large egg, at room temperature
- ½ cup buttermilk, at room temperature
- ½ teaspoon table salt
- ¼ teaspoon ground black pepper
- ¼ teaspoon cayenne pepper
- 30 saltine crackers
- 4 cups kettle-cooked potato chips
- 2 large yellow onions, cut into 24 large rings (see note)
- 6 tablespoons vegetable oil

1. Adjust the oven racks to the lower-middle and upper-middle positions and heat the oven to 450 degrees. Place ¼ cup of the flour in a shallow baking dish. Beat the egg and buttermilk in a medium bowl. Whisk the remaining ¼ cup flour, the salt, black pepper, and cayenne into the buttermilk mixture. Pulse the saltines and chips together in a food processor until finely ground; place in a separate shallow baking dish.

2. Working one at a time, dredge each onion ring in the flour, shaking off the excess. Dip in the buttermilk mixture, allowing the excess to drip back into the bowl, then drop into the crumb coating, turning the ring over to coat evenly. Transfer to a large plate. (At this point, the onion rings can be refrigerated for up to 1 hour. Let them sit at room temperature for 30 minutes before baking.)

3. Pour 3 tablespoons of the oil onto each of two rimmed baking sheets. Place in the oven and heat until just smoking, about 8 minutes. Carefully tilt the heated sheets to coat evenly with the oil, then arrange the onion rings on the sheets. Bake, flipping the onion rings over and switching and rotating the baking sheets halfway through baking, until golden brown on both sides, about 15 minutes. Briefly drain the onion rings on paper towels. Serve immediately.

STEAK FRIES

WHY THIS RECIPE WORKS: Thick spears of skin-on potato, steak fries are the heartier, more rustic cousins of the crisp, skinny french fry. But getting steak fries crisp on the outside and tender inside can be tricky—soggy steak fries are too often the norm. We wanted to find a way to achieve a steak fry with hearty potato flavor and great crunch.

We found that the dense starchiness of russet potatoes makes them the best variety for frying. We got the proper ratio of crisp exterior to tender interior when we cut them into ¾-inch wedges. As for the frying oil, peanut oil was our top choice. Chilling the potatoes in cold water before frying proved to be an essential step. Prepared this way, they cooked more slowly and evenly, without burning. Even after chilling, though, our fries were overcooked when we simply fried them in oil. A two-step process worked wonders. After chilling and drying the potatoes, we par-fried them at a lower temperature to cook the interiors without browning them. Following a brief rest, we fried them again at a higher temperature to brown and crisp the exteriors. Neither greasy nor soggy, these fries boasted great flavor and crunch.

Steak Fries
SERVES 4
The potatoes must be soaked in cold water, fried once, cooled, and then fried a second time—so start this recipe at least one hour before dinner.

- 2½ pounds russet potatoes (about 4 large), scrubbed and cut lengthwise into ¾-inch-thick wedges (about 12 wedges per potato)
- 2 quarts peanut oil
  Table salt and ground black pepper

1. Place the cut potatoes in a large bowl, cover with cold water by at least 1 inch, and then cover with ice cubes. Refrigerate for at least 30 minutes or up to 3 days.

2. In a large Dutch oven fitted with a clip-on candy thermometer, heat the oil over medium-low heat to 325 degrees. (The oil will bubble up when you add the potatoes, so be sure you have at least 3 inches of room at the top of the pot.)

3. Pour off the ice and water, quickly wrap the potatoes in a clean kitchen towel, and thoroughly pat them dry. Increase the heat to medium-high and add the potatoes, one handful at a time, to the hot oil. Fry, stirring with a Chinese skimmer or large-holed slotted spoon, until the potatoes are limp and soft and have turned from white to gold, about 10 minutes. (The oil temperature will drop 50 to 60 degrees during this frying.) Use the skimmer or slotted spoon to transfer the fries to a triple thickness of paper towels to drain; let rest for at least 10 minutes. (The fries can stand at room temperature for up to 2 hours.)

4. When ready to serve the fries, reheat the oil to 350 degrees. Using the paper towels as a funnel, pour the potatoes into the hot oil. Discard the paper towels and line a wire rack with another triple thickness of paper towels. Fry the potatoes, stirring fairly constantly, until medium brown and puffed, 8 to 10 minutes. Transfer to the paper towel–lined rack to drain. Season with salt and pepper to taste. Serve immediately.

CLASSIC FRENCH FRIES

WHY THIS RECIPE WORKS: Efforts to re-create restaurant-style fries at home have always disappointed, with fries that were greasy, droopy, or burnt on the outside and raw on the inside. We wanted to find a recipe and method for the home cook that would rival those cooked by professionals—crunchy fries with deep potato flavor.

As we found in developing our recipe for Steak Fries (page 277), russet potatoes were preferred for their dense texture and hearty flavor. Because these are starchy potatoes, it was important to rinse the starch off the surface after cutting the potatoes into fries. To achieve evenly cooked fries, we first refrigerated the cut potatoes in a bowl of ice water for at least 30 minutes and then took a double-fry approach. During the first fry, because the potatoes are nearly frozen, the potatoes can cook long and slow, which ensures a soft, rich-tasting interior. A quick second fry at a higher temperature crisped and colored the exterior. We used peanut oil for frying but felt our fries lacked the flavor imparted by lard. A little strained bacon grease gave our fries a touch of meaty flavor just like those found in our favorite restaurant fries.

Classic French Fries
SERVES 4

We prefer to peel the potatoes. Leaving the skin on keeps the potato from forming those little airy blisters that we like. Peeling the potato also allows the removal of any imperfections and greenish coloring. Once the potatoes are peeled and cut, plan on at least an hour before the fries are ready to eat.

2½ pounds russet potatoes (about 4 large), peeled and cut into ¼-inch by ¼-inch lengths
2 quarts peanut oil
¼ cup bacon fat, strained (optional)
   Table salt and ground black pepper

1. Place the cut potatoes in a large bowl, cover with at least 1 inch of water, then cover with ice cubes. Refrigerate for at least 30 minutes or up to 3 days.

2. In a large Dutch oven fitted with a clip-on candy thermometer, heat the oil over medium-low heat to 325 degrees. (The oil will bubble up when you add the potatoes, so be sure you have at least 3 inches of room at the top of the pot.) Add the bacon grease (if using).

3. Pour off the ice and water, quickly wrap the potatoes in a clean kitchen towel, and thoroughly pat them dry. Increase the heat to medium-high and add the potatoes, one handful at a time, to the hot oil. Fry, stirring with a Chinese skimmer or large-holed slotted spoon, until the potatoes are limp and soft and have turned from white to gold, about 10 minutes. (The oil temperature will drop 50 to 60 degrees during this frying.) Use the skimmer or slotted spoon to transfer the fries to a triple thickness of paper towels to drain; let rest for at least 10 minutes. (The fries can stand at room temperature for up to 2 hours.)

4. When ready to serve the fries, reheat the oil to 350 degrees. Using the paper towels as a funnel, pour the potatoes into the hot oil. Discard the paper towels and line a wire rack with another triple thickness of paper towels. Fry the potatoes, stirring fairly constantly, until medium brown and puffed, about 1 minute. Transfer to the paper towel–lined rack to drain. Season with salt and pepper to taste. Serve immediately.

EASIER FRENCH FRIES

WHY THIS RECIPE WORKS: Our recipe for Classic French Fries works beautifully, but we'll admit that it sometimes seems like a lot of trouble. We challenged ourselves to devise a shortcut that would give us crisp, golden fries with less work. Oven-frying is the usual "quick" method, but we wanted real french fries. We started with an unorthodox procedure of starting the cut potatoes in a few cups of cold oil. To our surprise, the fries were pretty good, if a little dry. Because russets

Chive and Black Pepper Dipping Sauce
MAKES ABOUT ½ CUP

- 5 tablespoons mayonnaise
- 3 tablespoons sour cream
- 2 tablespoons chopped fresh chives
- 1½ teaspoons juice from 1 lemon
- ¼ teaspoon table salt
- ¼ teaspoon ground black pepper

Whisk all the ingredients together in a small bowl.

Belgian-Style Dipping Sauce
MAKES ABOUT ½ CUP

- 5 tablespoons mayonnaise
- 3 tablespoons ketchup
- 1 medium garlic clove, minced or pressed through a garlic press (about 1 teaspoon)
- ½ teaspoon hot sauce or more to taste
- ¼ teaspoon table salt

Whisk all the ingredients together in a small bowl.

are fairly dry, we wondered if a different type of potato would work better. Sure enough, Yukon Golds, which have more water and less starch, came out creamy and smooth inside and crisp outside. We found that leaving the fries undisturbed for 15 minutes, then stirring them, kept them from sticking and from breaking apart. Thinner batons were also less likely to stick. These fries had all the qualities of classic french fries, without all the bother.

Easier French Fries
SERVES 4

For those who like it, flavoring the oil with bacon fat gives the fries a mild meaty flavor. We prefer peanut oil for frying, but vegetable oil can be substituted. This recipe will not work with sweet potatoes or russets. Serve with dipping sauces (recipes follow), if desired.

- 2½ pounds Yukon Gold potatoes (about 6 medium), scrubbed, dried, sides squared off, and cut lengthwise into ¼-inch by ¼-inch batons (see note)
- 6 cups peanut oil (see note)
- ¼ cup bacon fat, strained (optional; see note)
  Table salt

1. Combine the potatoes, oil, and bacon fat (if using) in a large Dutch oven. Cook over high heat until the oil has reached a rolling boil, about 5 minutes. Continue to cook, without stirring, until the potatoes are pale golden and the exteriors are beginning to crisp, about 15 minutes.

2. Using tongs, stir the potatoes, gently scraping up any that stick, and continue to cook, stirring occasionally, until golden and crisp, 5 to 10 minutes longer. Using a skimmer or slotted spoon, transfer the fries to a thick paper bag or paper towels. Season with salt to taste and serve immediately.

NOTES FROM THE TEST KITCHEN

CUTTING POTATOES FOR FRENCH FRIES

1. Square off potato by cutting ¼-inch-thick slice from each of its 4 long sides.

2. Cut potato lengthwise into ¼-inch-thick planks.

3. Stack 3 or 4 planks and cut into ¼-inch-thick batons. Repeat with remaining planks.

CHAPTER 12

WHO WANTS PASTA?

PASTA WITH GARLIC AND OIL

WHY THIS RECIPE WORKS: Nothing sounds easier than pasta with olive oil and garlic, but too often this dish turns out oily or rife with burnt garlic. We were after a flawless version of this quick classic, with bright, deep garlic flavor and no trace of bitterness or harshness.

For a mellow flavor, we cooked most of the garlic over low heat until sticky and straw-colored; a modest amount of raw garlic added at the end brought in some potent fresh garlic flavor. Extra-virgin olive oil and reserved pasta cooking water helped to keep our garlic and pasta saucy. A splash of lemon juice and sprinkling of red pepper flakes added some spice and brightness to this simple, yet complex-flavored recipe.

Pasta with Garlic and Oil

SERVES 4 TO 6

For a twist on pasta with garlic and oil, try sprinkling toasted fresh bread crumbs over individual bowls, but prepare them in advance. Simply pulse two slices of high-quality white sandwich bread, torn into quarters, in a food processor to coarse crumbs. Combine with 2 tablespoons extra-virgin olive oil, season with salt and pepper, and bake on a rimmed baking sheet at 375 degrees until golden brown, 8 to 10 minutes.

　　Table salt
1　pound spaghetti
6　tablespoons extra-virgin olive oil
12　medium garlic cloves, minced or pressed through a garlic press (about 4 tablespoons)
¾　teaspoon red pepper flakes
3　tablespoons chopped fresh parsley leaves
2　teaspoons juice from 1 lemon
½　cup grated Parmesan cheese (optional)

1. Bring 4 quarts water to a boil in a large pot. Add 1 tablespoon salt and the pasta to the boiling water and cook, stirring often, until al dente; reserve ⅓ cup of the cooking water then drain the pasta and return it to the pot.

2. Meanwhile, heat 3 tablespoons of the oil, 3 tablespoons of the garlic, and ½ teaspoon salt over low heat in a 10-inch nonstick skillet. Cook, stirring constantly, until the garlic is sticky and straw-colored, 10 to 12 minutes. Off the heat, stir in the remaining 1 tablespoon garlic, the red pepper flakes, parsley, lemon juice, and 2 tablespoons of the reserved pasta cooking water.

3. Transfer the drained pasta to a warm serving bowl; add the remaining 3 tablespoons oil and remaining reserved pasta cooking water and toss to combine. Add the garlic mixture and ¾ teaspoon salt; toss to combine. Serve, sprinkling individual bowls with Parmesan cheese, if desired.

SPAGHETTI AL LIMONE

WHY THIS RECIPE WORKS: Unaccustomed to the spotlight, lemon can turn temperamental in this quick Italian classic—unless you provide it with the perfect costars. We wanted a dish bursting with bright, bracing lemon flavor and moistened with just enough fruity olive oil to coat each delicate strand. Starting with lemon flavor, we found the window for the right amount of juice per pound of pasta was extremely small, and if we leaned more to either side, the lemon flavor became either too tart or barely noticeable. To boost the lemon's power without extra acidity, we added some grated zest to the sauce. As for the base of the sauce, we relied on an olive oil–cream sauce. The cream neutralized some of the acids in the juice while augmenting the oils responsible for the fruity, floral notes.

Spaghetti with Lemon and Olive Oil (al Limone)

SERVES 4

Letting this dish rest briefly before serving allows the flavors to develop and the sauce to thicken.

　　Table salt and ground black pepper
1　pound spaghetti
¼　cup extra-virgin olive oil, plus extra for drizzling
1　medium shallot, minced (about 3 tablespoons)
¼　cup heavy cream
1　ounce Parmesan cheese, grated (about ½ cup), plus extra for serving
2　teaspoons grated zest plus ¼ cup juice from 2 lemons
2　tablespoons chopped fresh basil leaves

1. Bring 4 quarts water to a boil in a large pot. Add 1 tablespoon salt and the pasta to the boiling water and cook until al dente. Reserve 1¾ cups of the cooking water, then drain the pasta.

2. Heat 1 tablespoon of the oil in the now-empty pot over medium heat until shimmering. Add the shallot and ½ teaspoon salt and cook until softened, about 2 minutes. Stir in 1½ cups of the reserved cooking water and the cream, bring to a simmer, and cook for 2 minutes. Off the heat, add the drained pasta, remaining 3 tablespoons oil, Parmesan, lemon zest, lemon juice, and ½ teaspoon pepper, and toss to combine.

3. Cover and let the pasta rest for 2 minutes, tossing frequently and adding the remaining cooking water as needed to adjust the consistency. Stir in the basil and season with salt and pepper to taste. Drizzle individual portions with oil and serve, passing the additional Parmesan separately.

SPAGHETTI WITH PECORINO ROMANO AND BLACK PEPPER

WHY THIS RECIPE WORKS: With just three main ingredients (cheese, pepper, and pasta), this Roman dish makes a delicious and quick pantry supper. But in versions we tried, the creamy sauce quickly turns into clumps of solidified cheese. We wanted a sauce that was intensely cheesy but also creamy and smooth.

Our science editor explained why the cheese clumps in this dish. Cheese consists mainly of three basic substances: fat, protein, and water. When a hard cheese like Pecorino, our cheese of choice, is heated, its fat begins to melt and its proteins soften. The fat acts as a sort of glue, fusing the proteins together. In order to coat the cheese and prevent the proteins from sticking together, we needed to introduce a starch into the mix.

It occurred to us that as pasta cooks, it releases starch into the water. We reduced the amount of water to concentrate the starch and whisked some of the cooking liquid into the cheese. This helped to a point, but we found we also needed an emulsifier—something to bind together the sauce. We turned to cream. By switching the butter for cream, we created a light, perfectly smooth sauce that had all the cheese flavor we wanted. Even after sitting on the table for a full five minutes, there wasn't a clump in sight.

Spaghetti with Pecorino Romano and Black Pepper

SERVES 4 TO 6

High-quality ingredients are essential in this dish, most importantly, imported Pecorino Romano. For a slightly less rich dish, substitute half-and-half for the heavy cream. Do not adjust the amount of water for cooking the pasta; the amount used is critical to the success of the recipe. Make sure to stir the pasta frequently while cooking so that it

doesn't stick to the pot. Draining the pasta water into the serving bowl warms the bowl and helps keeps the dish hot until it is served. Letting the dish rest briefly before serving allows the flavors to develop and the sauce to thicken.

- 4 ounces Pecorino Romano, grated fine (about 2 cups), plus 2 ounces grated coarse (about 1 cup), for serving
- 1 pound spaghetti
  Table salt
- 2 tablespoons heavy cream
- 2 teaspoons extra-virgin olive oil
- 1½ teaspoons ground black pepper

1. Place the finely grated Pecorino in a medium bowl. Set a colander in a large bowl.

2. Bring 2 quarts water to a boil in a large Dutch oven. Add the pasta and 1½ teaspoons salt and cook, stirring frequently, until the pasta is al dente. Drain the pasta into the colander set in the bowl, reserving the cooking water. Pour 1½ cups of the cooking water into a liquid measuring cup and discard the remainder and then place the pasta in the empty bowl.

3. Slowly whisk 1 cup of the reserved pasta water into the finely grated Pecorino until smooth. Whisk in the cream, oil, and pepper. Gradually pour the cheese mixture over the pasta, tossing to coat. Let the pasta rest for 1 to 2 minutes, tossing frequently, adjusting the consistency with the remaining ½ cup reserved pasta cooking water as needed. Serve, passing the coarsely grated Pecorino separately.

FRESH PASTA WITHOUT A MACHINE

WHY THIS RECIPE WORKS: Not everyone has a pasta machine, and rolling out pasta dough by hand is no easy task. For an easy-to-roll pasta dough (that would still cook up into delicate, springy noodles), we added six extra egg yolks and a couple of tablespoons of olive oil to our dough. In addition, we incorporated an extended resting period to allow the gluten network to relax. To roll and cut the pasta, we first divided the pasta into smaller manageable pieces, then used a rolling pin to roll the dough and a sharp knife to cut the dough into noodles.

Fresh Pasta without a Machine

MAKES 1 POUND; SERVES 4 TO 6

If using a high-protein all-purpose flour like King Arthur brand, increase the number of egg yolks to 7. The longer the dough rests in step 2, the easier it will be to roll out. When rolling out the dough, avoid adding too much flour, which may result in excessive snapback.

- 2 cups (10 ounces) all-purpose flour
- 2 large eggs plus 6 large yolks
- 2 tablespoons olive oil
- 1 tablespoon salt
- 1 recipe sauce (recipes follow)

1. Process flour, eggs and yolks, and oil together in food processor until mixture forms cohesive dough that feels soft and is barely tacky to touch, about 45 seconds. (If dough sticks to fingers, add up to ¼ cup flour, 1 tablespoon at a time, until barely tacky. If dough doesn't become cohesive, add up to 1 tablespoon water, 1 teaspoon at a time, until it just comes together; process 30 seconds longer.)

2. Turn dough ball out onto dry counter and knead until smooth, 1 to 2 minutes. Shape dough into 6-inch-long cylinder. Wrap with plastic wrap and set aside at room temperature to rest for at least 1 hour or up to 4 hours.

3. Cut cylinder crosswise into 6 equal pieces. Working with 1 piece of dough (rewrap remaining dough), dust both sides with flour, place cut side down on clean counter, and press into 3-inch square. Using heavy rolling pin, roll into 6-inch square. Dust both sides of dough lightly with flour. Starting at center of square, roll dough away from you in 1 motion. Return rolling pin to center of dough and roll toward you in 1 motion. Repeat steps of rolling until dough sticks to counter and measures roughly 12 inches long. Lightly dust both sides of dough with flour and continue rolling dough until it measures roughly 20 inches long and 6 inches wide, frequently lifting dough to release it from counter. (You should be able to easily see outline of your fingers through dough.) If dough firmly sticks to counter and wrinkles when rolled out, dust dough lightly with flour.

4. Transfer pasta sheet to clean dish towel and let stand, uncovered, until firm around edges, about 15 minutes; meanwhile, roll out remaining dough. Starting with 1 short end, gently fold pasta sheet at 2-inch intervals until sheet has been folded into flat, rectangular roll. With sharp chef's knife, slice crosswise into 3/16-inch-wide noodles. Use fingers to unfurl pasta and transfer to baking sheet. Repeat folding and cutting remaining sheets of dough. Cook noodles within 1 hour.

5. Bring 4 quarts water to boil in large pot. Add pasta and salt and cook, stirring often, until al dente, about 3 minutes. Reserve 1 cup cooking water, then drain pasta. Toss with sauce; serve immediately.

TO MAKE AHEAD: Follow recipe through step 4, transfer baking sheet of pasta to freezer, and freeze until pasta is firm. Transfer to zipper-lock bag and store for up to 2 weeks. Cook frozen pasta straight from freezer as directed in step 5.

Tomato and Browned Butter Sauce
MAKES 3 CUPS; ENOUGH FOR 1 POUND PASTA

- 1 (28-ounce) can whole peeled tomatoes
- 4 tablespoons unsalted butter, cut into 4 pieces
- 2 garlic cloves, minced
- ½ teaspoon sugar
  Salt and pepper
- 2 teaspoons sherry vinegar
- 3 tablespoons chopped fresh basil
  Grated Parmesan cheese

1. Process tomatoes and their juice in food processor until smooth, about 30 seconds. Melt 3 tablespoons butter in 12-inch skillet over medium-high heat, swirling occasionally, until butter is dark brown and releases nutty aroma, about 1½ minutes. Stir in garlic and cook for 10 seconds. Stir in processed tomatoes, sugar, and ½ teaspoon salt and simmer until sauce is slightly reduced, about 8 minutes. Remove pan from heat; whisk in remaining 1 tablespoon butter and vinegar. Season with salt and pepper to taste; cover to keep warm.

2. To serve, return pan to medium heat. Add pasta, ¼ cup reserved cooking water, and basil; toss to combine. Season with salt and pepper to taste and add remaining cooking water as needed to adjust consistency. Serve immediately, passing Parmesan separately.

Walnut Cream Sauce
MAKES 2 CUPS; ENOUGH FOR 1 POUND PASTA

- 1½ cups (6 ounces) walnuts, toasted
- ¾ cup dry white wine
- ½ cup heavy cream
- 1 ounce Parmesan cheese, grated (½ cup)
  Salt and pepper
- ¼ cup minced fresh chives

1. Process 1 cup walnuts in food processor until finely ground, about 10 seconds. Transfer to small bowl. Pulse remaining ½ cup walnuts in food processor until coarsely chopped, 3 to 5 pulses. Bring wine to simmer in 12-inch skillet over medium-high heat; cook until reduced to ¼ cup, about 3 minutes. Whisk in cream, ground and chopped walnuts, Parmesan, ¼ teaspoon salt, and ½ teaspoon pepper. Remove pan from heat and cover to keep warm.

2. To serve, return pan to medium heat. Add pasta, ½ cup reserved cooking water, and chives; toss to combine. Season with salt and pepper to taste and add remaining cooking water as needed to adjust consistency. Serve immediately.

ROLLING AND CUTTING PASTA DOUGH BY HAND

What's the trick to turning a lump of pasta into long, silky, strands—without a pasta roller? Starting with a soft, malleable dough is half the battle. The other half: dividing the dough into small, manageable pieces and working with them one at a time.

1. Shape dough into 6-inch cylinder; wrap in plastic wrap and let rest for at least 1 hour. Divide into 6 equal pieces. Reserve 1 piece; rewrap remaining 5.

2. Working with reserved piece, dust both sides with flour, then press cut side down into 3-inch square. With rolling pin, roll into 6-inch square, then dust both sides again with flour.

3. Roll dough to 12 by 6 inches, rolling from center of dough 1 way at a time, then dust with flour. Continue rolling to 20 by 6 inches, lifting frequently to release from counter. Transfer dough to clean dish towel and air-dry for about 15 minutes.

4. Starting with short end, gently fold dried sheet at 2-inch intervals to create flat, rectangular roll.

5. With sharp knife, cut into 3/16-inch-wide noodles.

6. Use fingers to unfurl pasta; transfer to baking sheet.

PASTA WITH FRESH TOMATOES

WHY THIS RECIPE WORKS: Fully ripe tomatoes need little else besides high-quality olive oil and a smattering of fresh herbs to become a bright, summery dressing for pasta. We set out to create the perfect raw tomato sauce—ideal for a quick yet flavorful dinner.

Selecting the ripest tomatoes guaranteed fresh flavor in the sauce, but to prevent their sweetness and acidity from taking over, we mixed in a generous amount of extra-virgin olive oil and a hefty amount of fresh herbs—you can use basil, parsley, cilantro, mint, oregano, or tarragon. We let the flavors of the tomatoes, olive oil, herbs, and some minced garlic blend while we cooked the pasta. Short pasta shapes held on to the chunky sauce nicely

Pasta with Fresh Tomatoes and Herbs
SERVES 4 TO 6

This chunky sauce works best with tubular pasta shapes, such as penne or fusilli. The success of this dish depends on using ripe, flavorful tomatoes.

1½   pounds ripe tomatoes (about 3 large), cored and cut into ½-inch pieces (see note)
¼   cup minced fresh herbs, such as basil, parsley, cilantro, mint, oregano, or tarragon
1   medium garlic clove, minced or pressed through a garlic press (about 1 teaspoon)
¼   cup extra-virgin olive oil
  Table salt and ground black pepper
1   pound penne, fusilli, or other short tubular pasta (see note)

1. Combine the tomatoes, herbs, garlic, oil, and salt and pepper to taste in a medium bowl. Set aside.

2. Bring 4 quarts water to a boil in a large pot. Add 1 tablespoon salt and the pasta to the boiling water and cook, stirring often, until al dente. Reserve ½ cup of the cooking water then drain the pasta and return it to the pot. Add the tomatoes and toss to combine; adjust the consistency of the sauce with the reserved pasta cooking water as needed. Serve.

PASTA AND FRESH TOMATO SAUCE

WHY THIS RECIPE WORKS: The best fresh tomato sauces capture the contrasting sweet and tart flavors of ripe tomatoes. But often, these sauces get waterlogged from the tomato juice. We wanted a cooked sauce that allowed the flavors of the traditional players—tomatoes, basil, garlic, and oil—to meld, but not become watered down. Quick cooking was the key to preserving fresh tomato flavor and creating a sauce that was both hearty and brightly flavored. To prevent unattractive pieces of curled-up tomato skin floating in our finished sauce, we simply peeled the tomatoes by boiling them and pulling off their skins. Seeded tomatoes made for a less watery start to the sauce, and cooking them down for a brief period facilitated the evaporation of any remaining liquid. Chopped fresh basil rounded out the flavors of the sauce, and a last-minute drizzle of olive oil brought a richness that complemented the sweetness of the tomatoes.

Pasta and Fresh Tomato Sauce with Garlic and Basil

SERVES 4 TO 6

To peel the tomatoes, dunk the cored tomatoes in a pot of boiling water until the skins split and begin to curl around the cored area, 15 to 30 seconds; transfer the tomatoes to a bowl of ice water, then peel off the skins with your fingers. This chunky sauce works best with tubular pasta shapes, such as penne or fusilli. If you'd like to serve it with spaghetti or linguine, puree the sauce in a blender or food processor before adding the basil. This recipe can be doubled and prepared in a 12-inch skillet.

- 3 tablespoons extra-virgin olive oil
- 2 medium garlic cloves, minced or pressed through a garlic press (about 2 teaspoons)
- 2 pounds ripe tomatoes (about 4 large), cored, peeled, seeded, and cut into ½-inch pieces (see note)
- 2 tablespoons chopped fresh basil leaves
  Table salt
- 1 pound penne, fusilli, or other short tubular pasta (see note)

1. Cook 2 tablespoons of the oil and the garlic in a 10-inch skillet over medium heat until fragrant, about 30 seconds. Stir in the tomatoes and cook over medium-high heat until the liquid released by the tomatoes evaporates and the tomato pieces form a chunky sauce, about 10 minutes. Stir in the basil and salt to taste; cover.

2. Meanwhile, bring 4 quarts water to a boil in a large pot. Add 1 tablespoon salt and the pasta to the boiling water and cook, stirring often, until al dente. Reserve ½ cup of the cooking water then drain the pasta and return it to the pot. Add ¼ cup of the reserved cooking water, the sauce, and the remaining 1 tablespoon oil and toss to combine. Adjust the consistency of the sauce with the remaining reserved pasta cooking water as needed. Serve.

PASTA WITH CREAMY TOMATO SAUCE

WHY THIS RECIPE WORKS: In the best examples of creamy tomato sauce, the acidity of fruity tomatoes is balanced with the richness of dairy; the worst deliver instant heartburn. We wanted a smooth, full-flavored tomato sauce enriched with cream, and we wanted to use canned tomatoes for convenience. Readily available, canned crushed tomatoes trumped canned whole and diced tomatoes. Before adding the tomatoes, we cooked a few tablespoons of tomato paste with some onion, garlic, and sun-dried tomatoes. A pinch of red pepper flakes, a splash of wine, and a little minced prosciutto added depth and tamed some of the sauce's sweetness; a bit of reserved uncooked crushed tomatoes and another splash of wine stirred in before serving brought the sauce's ingredients together. We added cream to the just-finished sauce to enrich it without subduing the bright tomato flavor.

Pasta with Creamy Tomato Sauce

SERVES 4 TO 6

Use high-quality crushed tomatoes; our favorite brand is SMT.

- 3 tablespoons unsalted butter
- 1 small onion, minced
- 1 ounce prosciutto, minced (about 2 tablespoons)

1 bay leaf
  Pinch red pepper flakes
  Table salt
3 medium garlic cloves, minced or pressed through
  a garlic press (about 1 tablespoon)
2 ounces oil-packed sun-dried tomatoes, drained, rinsed,
  patted dry, and chopped coarse (about 3 tablespoons)
2 tablespoons tomato paste
¼ cup plus 2 tablespoons dry white wine
2 cups plus 2 tablespoons crushed tomatoes
  (from one 28-ounce can; see note)
1 pound ziti, penne, or other short tubular pasta
½ cup heavy cream
  Ground black pepper
¼ cup chopped fresh basil leaves
  Grated Parmesan cheese, for serving

1. Melt the butter in a medium saucepan over medium heat. Add the onion, prosciutto, bay leaf, red pepper flakes, and ¼ teaspoon salt; cook, stirring occasionally, until the onion is very soft and beginning to turn light gold, 8 to 12 minutes. Increase the heat to medium-high, add the garlic, and cook until fragrant, about 30 seconds. Stir in the sun-dried tomatoes and tomato paste and cook, stirring constantly, until slightly darkened, 1 to 2 minutes. Add ¼ cup of the wine and cook, stirring frequently, until the liquid has evaporated, 1 to 2 minutes.

2. Add 2 cups of the crushed tomatoes and bring to a simmer. Reduce the heat to low, partially cover, and cook, stirring occasionally, until the sauce is thickened, 25 to 30 minutes.

3. Meanwhile, bring 4 quarts water to a boil in a large pot. Add 1 tablespoon salt and the pasta to the boiling water and cook, stirring often, until al dente. Reserve ½ cup of the cooking water then drain the pasta and return it to the pot.

4. Remove the bay leaf from the sauce and discard. Stir the cream, remaining 2 tablespoons crushed tomatoes, and remaining 2 tablespoons wine into the sauce; season with salt and pepper to taste. Add the sauce to the pasta and adjust the consistency of the sauce with the reserved pasta cooking water as needed. Stir in the basil and serve, passing the Parmesan separately.

PASTA CAPRESE

WHY THIS RECIPE WORKS: The summer salad composed of creamy mozzarella, fresh basil, and sweet tomatoes has become so popular that we wanted to translate it to a simple-yet-elegant pasta dish, one in which the primary ingredients work in harmony with the pasta. Specifically, we wanted creamy pockets of milky mozzarella throughout the dish, rather than the chewy wads that can occur when cheese hits hot pasta. And we wanted to find a way to guarantee sweet tomato flavor, even when we were working with substandard tomatoes.

Supermarket mozzarella worked well in this dish; the trick was to dice and freeze it for just 10 minutes before tossing it with the hot pasta to keep the cheese soft and creamy (instead of dry and clumpy). Otherwise, handmade mozzarella (minus the freezing step) worked well. To boost the flavor of less-than-stellar tomatoes, we added a little sugar for sweetness and fresh lemon juice for brightness. Marinating the tomatoes and mozzarella with olive oil, minced shallot, salt, and a pinch of black pepper while the pasta was cooking added even more flavor. We decided not to cut corners with a substandard olive oil; because there are few flavors in this dish, the fruity nuances of a good extra-virgin olive oil really made a difference.

Pasta Caprese
SERVES 4 TO 6

This dish will be very warm, not hot. The success of this recipe depends on high-quality ingredients, including ripe, in-season tomatoes and a fruity olive oil (the test kitchen prefers Columela extra-virgin). Don't skip the step of freezing the mozzarella, as freezing prevents it from turning chewy when it comes in contact with the hot pasta. If handmade buffalo- or cow's-milk mozzarella is available (it's commonly found, packed in water, in gourmet and cheese shops), we highly recommend using it, but do not freeze it. Additional lemon juice or up to 1 teaspoon sugar can be added at the end to taste, depending on the ripeness of the tomatoes.

¼ cup extra-virgin olive oil (see note)

2–4 teaspoons juice from 1 lemon (see note)

1 small garlic clove, minced or pressed through a garlic press (about ½ teaspoon)

1 small shallot, minced (about 1 tablespoon)

Table salt and ground black pepper

1½ pounds ripe tomatoes (about 3 large), cored, seeded, and cut into ½-inch dice (see note)

12 ounces fresh mozzarella cheese, cut into ½-inch cubes (see note)

1 pound penne, fusilli, or campanelle

¼ cup chopped fresh basil leaves

1 teaspoon sugar (optional; see note)

1. Whisk the oil, 2 teaspoons of the lemon juice, the garlic, shallot, ½ teaspoon salt, and ¼ teaspoon pepper together in a large bowl. Add the tomatoes and gently toss to combine; set aside. Do not marinate the tomatoes for longer than 45 minutes.

2. While the tomatoes are marinating, place the mozzarella on a plate and freeze until slightly firm, about 10 minutes. Bring 4 quarts water to a boil in a large pot. Add 1 tablespoon salt and the pasta to the boiling water and cook, stirring often, until al dente. Drain well.

3. Add the pasta and mozzarella to the tomato mixture and gently toss to combine. Let stand for 5 minutes. Stir in the basil, season with salt and pepper to taste, and add additional lemon juice or sugar, if desired. Serve immediately.

PASTA WITH RICOTTA AND SPINACH

WHY THIS RECIPE WORKS: There are many recipes that pair simple boiled pasta with spinach and ricotta as a simplified, "deconstructed" version of stuffed shells, manicotti, or ravioli. But the versions we tried lacked complexity and suffered from a gritty texture. We wanted to punch up the flavor and make this simple pasta dish an easy weeknight option. To boost the flavor of the ricotta, we mixed in some extra-virgin olive oil, salt, and pepper. Then we set out to tackle the sauce's gritty, chalky texture. Heat caused the ricotta curds to release water and coagulate, rendering the sauce grainy. To minimize this effect, we dolloped most of the ricotta on top of the pasta so that tasters got concentrated hits of cheese here and there, much as they would when eating filled pasta. We mixed the rest of the ricotta with cream (to stabilize the milk proteins), along with sautéed garlic, cayenne, and nutmeg for warmth, and used this mixture to dress the warm pasta. As for the spinach, simply tossing the coarsely chopped leaves into the pot with the pasta at the end of cooking gave us slightly wilted but still brilliant green spinach. A generous dusting of grated Parmesan cheese over the finished dish provided additional depth, and a sprinkle of lemon zest and lemon juice introduced welcome brightness. Letting the pasta sit dressed for a few minutes before serving drew out some of the pasta's starches for a creamy, velvety texture.

Fusilli with Ricotta and Spinach
SERVES 4 TO 6

We like fusilli for this recipe since its corkscrew shape does a nice job of trapping the sauce, but penne and campanelle also work well.

11 ounces (1⅓ cups) whole-milk ricotta cheese

3 tablespoons extra-virgin olive oil

Salt and pepper

1 pound fusilli

1 pound (16 cups) baby spinach, chopped coarse

4 garlic cloves, minced

¼ teaspoon ground nutmeg

⅛ teaspoon cayenne pepper

¼ cup heavy cream

1 teaspoon grated lemon zest plus 2 teaspoons juice

1 ounce Parmesan cheese, grated (½ cup), plus extra for serving

1. Whisk 1 cup ricotta, 1 tablespoon oil, ¼ teaspoon pepper, and ⅛ teaspoon salt in medium bowl until smooth; set aside.

2. Bring 4 quarts water to boil in large pot. Add pasta and 1 tablespoon salt and cook, stirring often, until al dente. Reserve 1 cup cooking water. Stir spinach into pot with pasta and cook until wilted, about 30 seconds. Drain pasta and spinach and return them to pot.

3. While pasta cooks, heat remaining 2 tablespoons oil, garlic, nutmeg, and cayenne in saucepan over medium heat until fragrant, about 1 minute. Remove pan from heat and whisk in remaining ⅓ cup ricotta, cream, lemon zest and juice, and ¾ teaspoon salt until smooth.

4. Add ricotta-cream mixture and Parmesan to pasta and toss to combine. Let pasta rest, tossing frequently, until sauce has thickened slightly and coats pasta, 2 to 4 minutes, adjusting consistency with reserved cooking water as needed. Transfer pasta to serving platter, dot evenly with reserved ricotta mixture, and serve, passing extra Parmesan separately.

PASTA WITH TOMATOES AND OLIVES

WHY THIS RECIPE WORKS: When tomatoes are in season, there's no better time to make a simple, fresh tomato sauce. We like the classic pairing of tomatoes and olives, so we set out to make an easy, not too watery, sauce with Mediterranean flavors.

Seeding the tomatoes rid them of excess moisture and prevented a watery sauce. Instead of peeling the tomato skins, we decided to leave them on so the chopped tomatoes would have some structural integrity and not disintegrate. By making a no-cook sauce—the other components were fresh mint, chopped kalamata olives, and feta—we were able to prepare it quickly while the drained pasta waited on the sidelines. The potent olives and feta added a bright zestiness to our pasta, and the mint amplified the sauce's freshness.

Farfalle with Tomatoes, Olives, and Feta
SERVES 4 TO 6

To prevent the feta from melting into the pasta, add it only after the tomatoes have been tossed with the pasta, which gives the mixture the opportunity to cool slightly.

    Table salt
1   pound farfalle
1½ pounds ripe tomatoes (about 3 large), cored,
    seeded, and cut into ½-inch pieces
½   cup pitted kalamata olives, chopped coarse
¼   cup extra-virgin olive oil
1   tablespoon chopped fresh mint leaves
    Ground black pepper
6   ounces feta cheese, crumbled (about
    1½ cups; see note)

1. Bring 4 quarts water to a boil in a large pot. Add 1 tablespoon salt and the pasta to the boiling water and cook, stirring often, until al dente. Reserve ½ cup of the cooking water then drain the pasta and return it to the pot.

2. Meanwhile, combine the tomatoes, olives, oil, mint, ½ teaspoon salt, and ¼ teaspoon pepper in a medium bowl. Add the sauce to the pasta and adjust the consistency of the sauce with the reserved pasta cooking water as needed. Add the feta and toss to combine. Season with salt and pepper to taste and serve.

QUICK TOMATO SAUCE

WHY THIS RECIPE WORKS: In a perfect world, garden-ripe tomatoes make the best quick tomato sauce. But that isn't realistic for most of the year. We wanted to create a complex, brightly flavored sauce with the next best alternative—canned tomatoes—that tasted of full, fruity tomatoes, in the time it took to boil pasta. Choosing the right can of tomatoes was a critical first step. Crushed tomatoes were the best choice because they would save us the step of pureeing. We also shredded a small amount of onion on a box grater before sautéing; the shredded pieces cooked faster and became sweeter more quickly. We sautéed the onion in butter, which caramelized when heated, and added garlic, sugar, and the crushed tomatoes, then simmered the sauce briefly. To make up for the lost fragrance of fresh tomatoes, we added chopped fresh basil and extra-virgin olive oil.

Quick Tomato Sauce
MAKES ABOUT 3 CUPS

This recipe makes enough to sauce a pound of pasta. High-quality canned tomatoes will make a big difference in this sauce; our preferred brand of crushed tomatoes is SMT. Grate the onion on the large holes of a box grater.

2   tablespoons unsalted butter
¼   cup grated onion (see note)
¼   teaspoon dried oregano
    Table salt
2   medium garlic cloves, minced or pressed through
    a garlic press (about 2 teaspoons)
1   (28-ounce) can crushed tomatoes (see note)
¼   teaspoon sugar
2   tablespoons chopped fresh basil leaves
1   tablespoon extra-virgin olive oil
    Ground black pepper

Melt the butter in a medium saucepan over medium heat. Add the onion, oregano, and ½ teaspoon salt; cook, stirring occasionally, until the liquid has evaporated and the onion is golden brown, about 5 minutes. Add the garlic and cook until fragrant, about 30 seconds. Stir in the tomatoes and sugar; bring to a simmer over high heat. Lower the heat to medium-low and simmer until slightly thickened, about 10 minutes. Off the heat, stir in the basil and oil; season with salt and pepper to taste.

USE YOUR NOODLE—PERFECT PASTA TIPS

We love pasta in the test kitchen. As a result, we're pretty opinionated about how we cook it. Here's what you need to know.

COOKING PASTA:
Make sure you have all the necessary and utensils assembled before you begin. You'll need 4 quarts of water to cook 1 pound of dried pasta. Any less and the noodles may stick. Use a pot large enough to accommodate the water and pasta without boil-overs—we like an 8-quart pot. It's crucial to properly season the cooking water—we recommend 1 tablespoon table salt per 4 quarts water. Bring the water to a rolling boil before adding the salt and pasta and give it an immediate stir to prevent sticking. And don't add oil to the pot—oil will prevent sauce from sticking to the pasta.

DRAINING AND SERVING PASTA: If a sauce is too thick, we thin it with a little reserved pasta water. The trouble is, it's easy to forget to save some water. As a reminder, we place a measuring cup in the colander. As for draining pasta, just give it a shake or two. You don't want the pasta bone dry. The little bit of hot cooking water clinging to the pasta will help the sauce coat it. And if you're using a large serving bowl for the pasta, place it underneath the colander while draining the pasta. The hot water heats up the bowl, which keeps the pasta warmer longer.

MARINARA SAUCE

WHY THIS RECIPE WORKS: Making a tomato sauce with deep, complex flavor usually requires hours of simmering. We wanted to produce a multidimensional marinara sauce in under an hour, perfect for any night of the week.

Our first challenge was picking the right tomatoes. We found canned whole tomatoes, which we hand-crushed to remove the hard core, to be the best choice in terms of both flavor and texture. We boosted tomato flavor by sautéing the tomato pieces until they glazed the bottom of the pan, after which we added their liquid. We shortened the simmering time by using a skillet instead of a saucepan (the greater surface area of a skillet encourages faster evaporation and flavor concentration). Finally, we added just the right amount of sugar, red wine (we especially liked Chianti and Merlot), and, just before serving, a few uncooked canned tomatoes for texture, fresh basil for fresh herbal flavor, and olive oil for richness.

Marinara Sauce
MAKES 4 CUPS

You can figure on about 3 cups of sauce per pound of pasta. Chianti or Merlot work well for the dry red wine. Because canned tomatoes vary in acidity and saltiness, it's best to add salt, pepper, and sugar to taste just before serving. If you prefer a chunkier sauce, give it just three or four pulses in the food processor in step 4.

  2 (28-ounce) cans whole tomatoes packed in juice
  3 tablespoons extra-virgin olive oil
  1 medium onion, minced
  2 medium garlic cloves, minced or pressed through a garlic press (about 2 teaspoons)
  ½ teaspoon dried oregano
  ⅓ cup dry red wine (see note)
  3 tablespoons chopped fresh basil leaves
     Table salt and ground black pepper
1-2 teaspoons sugar, as needed (see note)

1. Pour the tomatoes into a strainer set over a large bowl. Open the tomatoes with your hands and remove and discard the fibrous cores; let the tomatoes drain excess liquid, about 5 minutes. Remove ¾ cup tomatoes from the strainer and set aside. Reserve 2½ cups tomato juice and discard the remainder.

2. Heat 2 tablespoons of the olive oil in a 12-inch skillet over medium heat until shimmering. Add the onion and cook, stirring occasionally, until softened and golden around the edges, 6 to 8 minutes. Add the garlic and oregano and cook, stirring constantly, until the garlic is fragrant, about 30 seconds.

3. Add the tomatoes from the strainer and increase the heat to medium-high. Cook, stirring every minute, until the liquid has evaporated and the tomatoes begin to stick to the bottom of the pan and browned bits form around the pan edges, 10 to 12 minutes. Add the wine and cook until thick and syrupy, about 1 minute. Add the reserved tomato juice and bring to a simmer; reduce the heat to medium and cook, stirring occasionally and loosening any browned bits, until the sauce is thickened, 8 to 10 minutes.

4. Transfer the sauce to a food processor and add the reserved tomatoes; process until slightly chunky, about 8 pulses. Return the sauce to the skillet, add the basil and remaining 1 tablespoon olive oil, and season with salt, pepper, and sugar to taste. (The sauce can be refrigerated in an airtight container for up to 3 days or frozen for up to 1 month.)

MEATLESS "MEAT" SAUCE

WHY THIS RECIPE WORKS: To create a vegetarian version of an unctuous tomato-meat sauce, we started with cremini mushrooms and tomato paste—both rich sources of savory flavor. We let the food processor do the work for us, using it to chop up our mushrooms, onions, and chickpeas, which added hearty texture. Extra-virgin olive oil did double duty, cooking the mushrooms and the classic Italian aromatics of garlic, dried oregano, and red pepper flakes and enriching the sauce. To loosen the sauce without diluting its flavor, we added vegetable broth. Chopped fresh basil added an authentic finish.

Meatless "Meat" Sauce with Chickpeas and Mushrooms

MAKES 6 CUPS; ENOUGH FOR 2 POUNDS PASTA

Make sure to rinse the chickpeas after pulsing them in the food processor or the sauce will be too thick. Our favorite canned chickpeas are from Pastene, our favorite crushed tomatoes are from SMT, and our favorite tomato paste is from Goya.

10	ounces cremini mushrooms, trimmed
6	tablespoons extra-virgin olive oil
	Salt and pepper
1	onion, chopped
5	garlic cloves, minced
1¼	teaspoons dried oregano
¼	teaspoon red pepper flakes
¼	cup tomato paste
1	(28-ounce) can crushed tomatoes
2	cups vegetable broth
1	(15-ounce) can chickpeas, rinsed
2	tablespoons chopped fresh basil

1. Pulse mushrooms in two batches in food processor until chopped into ⅛- to ¼-inch pieces, 7 to 10 pulses, scraping down sides of bowl as needed. (Do not clean workbowl.)

2. Heat 5 tablespoons oil in Dutch oven over medium-high heat until shimmering. Add mushrooms and 1 teaspoon salt and cook, stirring occasionally, until mushrooms are browned and fond has formed on bottom of pot, about 8 minutes.

3. While mushrooms cook, pulse onion in food processor until finely chopped, 7 to 10 pulses, scraping down sides of bowl as needed. (Do not clean workbowl.) Transfer onion to pot with mushrooms and cook, stirring occasionally, until onion is soft and translucent, about 5 minutes. Combine remaining 1 tablespoon oil, garlic, oregano, and pepper flakes in bowl.

4. Add tomato paste to pot and cook, stirring constantly, until mixture is rust-colored, 1 to 2 minutes. Reduce heat to medium and push vegetables to sides of pot. Add garlic mixture to center and cook, stirring constantly, until fragrant, about 30 seconds. Stir in tomatoes and broth; bring to simmer over high heat. Reduce heat to low and simmer sauce for 5 minutes, stirring occasionally.

5. While sauce simmers, pulse chickpeas in food processor until chopped into ¼-inch pieces, 7 to 10 pulses. Transfer chickpeas to fine-mesh strainer and rinse under cold running water until water runs clear; drain well. Add chickpeas to pot and simmer until sauce is slightly thickened, about 15 minutes. Stir in basil and season with salt and pepper to taste. (Sauce can be refrigerated for up to 2 days or frozen for up to 1 month.)

PASTA PUTTANESCA

WHY THIS RECIPE WORKS: Puttanesca is a gutsy tomato sauce punctuated by the brash, zesty flavors of garlic, anchovies, olives, and capers. But too often, the sauce comes off as too fishy, too garlicky, too briny, or just plain too salty. We wanted to harmonize the bold flavors in this Neapolitan dish and not let any one preside over the others.

For a sauce with the best tomato flavor and a slightly clingy consistency, we used canned diced tomatoes and kept the cooking time to a minimum to retain their fresh flavor and their meaty texture. To tame the garlic and prevent it from burning, we soaked minced garlic in a bit of water before sautéing it. Cooking the garlic and anchovies with red pepper flakes (before adding the tomatoes) helped their flavors bloom and added a subtle heat. We chose to add the olives and capers when the sauce was finished—this prevented them from disintegrating in the sauce. Reserved tomato juice from the canned tomatoes moistened the pasta, and a last-minute addition of minced parsley preserved the fresh flavors of the sauce.

Spaghetti Puttanesca

SERVES 4 TO 6

The pasta and sauce cook in about the same amount of time, so begin the sauce just after you add the pasta to the boiling water in step 1.

3 medium garlic cloves, minced or pressed through
a garlic press (about 1 tablespoon)
Table salt
1 pound spaghetti
1 (28-ounce) can diced tomatoes, drained and
½ cup juice reserved
2 tablespoons extra-virgin olive oil, plus extra for drizzling
4 teaspoons minced anchovy fillets (about 8 fillets)
1 teaspoon red pepper flakes
½ cup pitted kalamata olives, chopped coarse
¼ cup minced fresh parsley leaves
3 tablespoons capers, rinsed

1. Combine the garlic with 1 tablespoon water in a small bowl; set aside. Bring 4 quarts water to a boil in a large pot. Add 1 tablespoon salt and the pasta to the boiling water and cook, stirring often, until al dente. Reserve ½ cup of the cooking water then drain the pasta and return it to the pot. Add ¼ cup of the reserved tomato juice and toss to combine.

2. Meanwhile, heat the oil, anchovies, garlic mixture, and red pepper flakes in a 12-inch skillet over medium heat. Cook, stirring frequently, until the garlic is fragrant, 2 to 3 minutes. Add the tomatoes and simmer until slightly thickened, about 8 minutes.

3. Stir the olives, parsley, and capers into the sauce. Pour the sauce over the pasta and toss to combine; adjust the consistency of the sauce with the remaining reserved tomato juice or reserved pasta cooking water as needed. Season with salt to taste, drizzle with 1 tablespoon oil, if desired, and serve immediately.

PASTA WITH TOMATO, BACON, AND ONION

WHY THIS RECIPE WORKS: There are two versions of the classic Italian pasta dish *pasta all'amatriciana*: one from Amatrice, and one from Rome. The Roman version boasts a rich sauce containing tomatoes, bacon, onion, and Pecorino Romano cheese, and generally calls for a long, tubular pasta. (The version from Amatrice adds wine, leaves out the onions, and often calls for spaghetti.) We decided to re-create the rich, hearty Roman version for the American kitchen. In Rome, the dish traditionally uses a type of bacon called *guanciale* (made from pork jowls), which is easy to find in central Italy but not so easy to locate in the States. We wanted a recipe using ingredients found locally. Thickly sliced pancetta proved a good substitute for guanciale (if you can't find pancetta, bacon works). We cut the pancetta into strips and cooked them in a skillet until crisp, then removed the pancetta to ensure it stayed crisp while we built the sauce in the remaining fat. Canned diced tomatoes, minced onion, and red pepper flakes made a flavorful, aromatic backbone to our sauce. Finally, we tossed the crisp pancetta in with the tomato sauce and pasta (traditional long-strand pasta, like bucatini or linguine, worked best) and sprinkled grated Pecorino Romano cheese on top.

Pasta with Tomato, Bacon, and Onion
SERVES 4 TO 6

This dish is traditionally made with bucatini, also called perciatelli, which appear to be thick, round strands but are actually thin, extralong tubes. Linguine works fine, too. When buying pancetta, ask the butcher to slice it ¼ inch thick; if using bacon, buy slab bacon and cut it into ¼-inch-thick slices yourself. If the pancetta that you're using is very lean, it's unlikely that you will need to drain off any fat before adding the onion.

2 tablespoons extra-virgin olive oil
6 ounces pancetta or bacon, sliced ¼ inch thick and cut into strips 1 inch long and ¼ inch wide (see note)
1 medium onion, minced
½ teaspoon red pepper flakes, or to taste
1 (28-ounce) can diced tomatoes, drained and juice reserved
Table salt
1 pound bucatini, perciatelli, or linguine (see note)
⅓ cup grated Pecorino Romano cheese

1. Bring 4 quarts water to a boil in a large pot.

2. Meanwhile, heat the oil in a 12-inch skillet over medium heat until shimmering. Add the pancetta and cook, stirring occasionally, until lightly browned and crisp, about 8 minutes. Using a slotted spoon, transfer the pancetta to a paper towel–lined plate; set aside. Pour off all but 2 tablespoons of fat from the skillet. Add the onion and cook over medium heat until softened, about 5 minutes. Add the pepper flakes and cook, about 30 seconds. Stir in the tomatoes and reserved juice and simmer until slightly thickened, about 10 minutes.

3. While the sauce is simmering, add 1 tablespoon salt and the pasta to the boiling water and cook, stirring often, until al dente. Reserve ½ cup of the cooking water then drain the pasta and return it to the pot.

4. Add the pancetta to the sauce and season with salt to taste. Add the sauce to the pasta and toss over low heat to combine, about 30 seconds. Add the Pecorino and toss again. Adjust the consistency of the sauce with the reserved pasta cooking water as needed and serve immediately.

PASTA ALL'AMATRICIANA

WHY THIS RECIPE WORKS: Although the Roman version of this Italian pasta dish is understandably popular, there is another, slightly different version that hails from Amatrice, a town northeast of Rome. Rather than minced onions, the Amatrician version calls for wine in the sauce. We loved the simple concept, and knew we wanted to come up with a version that we could make at home. To create an authentic flavor profile, we first needed an alternative to hard-to-find *guanciale*, or cured pork jowl. Humble salt pork, though an unlikely solution, provided the rich, clean meatiness we were after, and proved to be a perfect foil for the bright acidity

2. Return skillet to medium heat and add tomato paste and pepper flakes; cook, stirring constantly, for 20 seconds. Stir in wine and cook for 30 seconds. Stir in tomatoes and their juice and rendered pork and bring to simmer. Cook, stirring frequently, until thickened, 12 to 16 minutes. While sauce simmers, stir 2 tablespoons reserved fat and ½ cup Pecorino together in bowl to form paste.

3. Meanwhile, bring 4 quarts water to boil in large Dutch oven. Add pasta and salt and cook, stirring often, until al dente. Reserve 1 cup cooking water, then drain pasta and return it to pot.

4. Add sauce, ⅓ cup cooking water, and Pecorino mixture to pasta and toss well to coat, adding cooking water as needed to adjust consistency. Serve, passing remaining ½ cup Pecorino separately.

PENNE ARRABBIATA

WHY THIS RECIPE WORKS: *Arrabbiata* means "angry" in Italian, and one bite of this peasant-style pasta sauce will confirm that it was aptly named. To deliver an arrabbiata with complex flavor and not just searing heat, we looked beyond the tradition of using only red pepper flakes and crafted a recipe that included three different types of pepper. By supplementing pepper flakes with paprika and pickled pepperoncini, we built deep flavor while keeping the spiciness in check. Pecorino Romano, tomato paste, and anchovies, while difficult to detect in the sauce, added umami notes and richness to this traditionally simple sauce. Finally, using canned tomatoes helped bring the sauce to the table quickly and means the dish can be enjoyed year-round.

Penne Arrabbiata
SERVES 6

This recipe will work with other short tubular pastas like ziti or rigatoni.

    1   (28-ounce) can whole peeled tomatoes
    ¼   cup extra-virgin olive oil
    ¼   cup stemmed, patted dry, and minced pepperoncini
    2   tablespoons tomato paste
    1   garlic clove, minced
    1   teaspoon red pepper flakes
    4   anchovy fillets, rinsed, patted dry, and minced to paste
    ½   teaspoon paprika
        Salt and pepper
    ¼   cup grated Pecorino Romano, plus extra for serving
    1   pound penne

1. Pulse tomatoes and their juice in food processor until finely chopped, about 10 pulses.

2. Heat oil, pepperoncini, tomato paste, garlic, pepper flakes, anchovies, paprika, ½ teaspoon salt, and ½ teaspoon pepper in medium saucepan over medium-low heat, stirring occasionally, until deep red in color, 7 to 8 minutes.

of the wine and tomatoes. To ensure tender bites of pork throughout, we first simmered it in water to gently cook it and render fat, a step that allowed the meat to quickly turn golden once the water evaporated. Finally, to ensure the grated Pecorino Romano didn't clump in the hot sauce, we first mixed it with a little cooled rendered pork fat. Now the flavor of pork, tomato, chili flakes, and Pecorino shone through in each bite.

Pasta all'Amatriciana
SERVES 4 TO 6

Look for salt pork that is roughly 70 percent fat and 30 percent lean meat; leaner salt pork may not render enough fat. If difficult to slice, the salt pork can be put in the freezer for 15 minutes to firm up. In this dish, it is essential to use high-quality imported Pecorino Romano—not the bland domestic cheese labeled "Romano."

    8   ounces salt pork, rind removed, rinsed thoroughly, and patted dry
    ½   cup water
    ½   teaspoon red pepper flakes
    2   tablespoons tomato paste
    ¼   cup red wine
    1   (28-ounce) can diced tomatoes
    2   ounces Pecorino Romano, grated fine (1 cup)
    1   pound spaghetti
    1   tablespoon salt

1. Slice salt pork into ¼-inch-thick strips, then cut each strip crosswise into ¼-inch pieces. Bring pork and water to simmer in 10-inch nonstick skillet over medium heat; cook until water evaporates and pork begins to sizzle, 5 to 8 minutes. Reduce heat to medium-low and continue to cook, stirring frequently, until fat renders and pork turns golden, 5 to 8 minutes longer. Using slotted spoon, transfer salt pork to bowl. Pour off all but 1 tablespoon fat from skillet. Reserve remaining fat.

3. Add tomatoes and Pecorino and bring to simmer. Cook, stirring occasionally, until thickened, about 20 minutes.

4. Bring 4 quarts water to boil in large pot. Add pasta and 1 tablespoon salt and cook, stirring often, until al dente. Reserve ½ cup cooking water, then drain pasta and return it to pot. Add sauce and toss to combine, adjusting consistency with reserved cooking water as needed. Season with salt and pepper to taste. Serve, passing extra Pecorino separately.

PASTA WITH CAULIFLOWER, BACON, AND BREAD CRUMBS

WHY THIS RECIPE WORKS: For an at-home version of pasta with cauliflower, a restaurant favorite, without the mountain of dirty pots and pans, we set out to streamline this recipe. We piled cauliflower florets into an oiled skillet and cooked them just enough to ensure a crisp-tender texture to contrast with the al dente pasta. Cooking the campanelle as we would a risotto—allowing the liquid to slowly absorb into the pasta—meant any of the starches we would otherwise lose after draining would stay in the pot, creating a creamy sauce. Chopped onion and minced fresh thyme established the flavorful base to which we added the uncooked campanelle and just enough chicken broth and white wine to cook the pasta, contributing complex flavor and lush texture. Once the liquid had absorbed, we stirred in the nutty cauliflower florets, plus parsley and lemon for liveliness. A sprinkling of crunchy panko crumbs cooked with salty bacon pieces offered a perfect crispy finish.

Pasta with Cauliflower, Bacon, and Bread Crumbs

SERVES 4 TO 6

Farfalle, orecchiette, or gemelli can be substituted for the campanelle. If the pasta seems too dry, stir in up to ¼ cup of hot water.

- 3 slices bacon, cut into ¼-inch pieces
- ½ cup panko bread crumbs
  Salt and pepper
- 2 tablespoons vegetable oil
- 1 large head cauliflower (3 pounds), cored and cut into 1-inch florets
- 1 onion, chopped fine
- ½ teaspoon minced fresh thyme
- 1 pound campanelle
- 5½ cups chicken broth
- ½ cup dry white wine
- 3 tablespoons minced fresh parsley
- 1 teaspoon lemon juice, plus lemon wedges for serving

1. Cook bacon in 12-inch skillet over medium-high heat until crispy, 5 to 7 minutes. Add panko and ¼ teaspoon pepper and cook, stirring frequently, until panko is well browned, 2 to 4 minutes. Transfer panko mixture to bowl and wipe out skillet.

2. Heat 5 teaspoons oil in now-empty skillet over medium-high heat until shimmering. Add cauliflower and 1 teaspoon salt; cook, stirring occasionally, until cauliflower is crisp-tender and browned in spots, 10 to 12 minutes. Remove pan from heat and cover to keep warm.

3. Heat remaining 1 teaspoon oil in Dutch oven over medium heat until shimmering. Add onion, thyme, and ½ teaspoon salt; cook, stirring frequently, until onion has softened, 4 to 7 minutes. Increase heat to high, add pasta, broth, and wine, and bring to simmer. Cook pasta, stirring frequently, until most of liquid is absorbed and pasta is al dente, 8 to 10 minutes.

4. Remove pot from heat; stir in parsley, lemon juice, and cauliflower; and season with salt and pepper to taste. Serve, passing panko mixture and lemon wedges separately.

PASTA WITH PESTO

WHY THIS RECIPE WORKS: Pasta with pesto makes for a satisfying, summery meal. But getting pesto right isn't always so easy; the sauce can be anywhere from too thin and watery to too thick and overpoweringly garlicky. Our goal was to heighten the basil and subdue the garlic flavors in pesto so that each major element balanced the next.

We started by briefly blanching whole unpeeled garlic cloves to tame their flavor and prevent them from taking over the sauce. Then we bruised the basil in a plastic bag with a meat pounder (you could also use a rolling pin) to unlock its flavor; we found that this method released the most herbal flavors from the basil. With the basil flavor boosted and the garlic toned down, it was time to process the ingredients with toasted nuts and stir in the Parmesan. Finally, we reserved some of the pasta cooking water, which was essential to thin out the pesto once it had been added to the pasta. The water also softened and blended the flavors a bit, and highlighted the creaminess of the cheese and nuts.

Farfalle with Pesto

SERVES 4 TO 6

Basil usually darkens in homemade pesto, but you can preserve the green color by adding the optional parsley. For sharper flavor, substitute 1 tablespoon finely grated Pecorino Romano cheese for 1 tablespoon of the Parmesan. For a change from farfalle, try curly shapes, such as fusilli, which can trap bits of the pesto.

- 3 medium garlic cloves, threaded on a skewer
- 2 cups packed fresh basil leaves
- 2 tablespoons fresh flat-leaf parsley leaves (optional; see note)
- ¼ cup pine nuts, walnuts, or almonds, toasted
- 7 tablespoons extra-virgin olive oil
  Table salt
- ¼ cup grated Parmesan (see note)
- 1 pound farfalle (see note)

1. Bring 4 quarts water to a boil in a large pot. Lower the skewered garlic into the water and boil for 45 seconds. Immediately run the garlic under cold water. Remove the garlic from the skewer, peel, and mince.

2. Place the basil and parsley (if using) in a zipper-lock bag and pound with the flat side of a meat pounder or a rolling pin until all the leaves are bruised.

3. Process the nuts, garlic, basil, oil, and ½ teaspoon salt in a food processor until smooth, scraping down the sides of the workbowl as necessary. Transfer the mixture to a small bowl, stir in the cheese, and season with salt to taste. (The pesto can be covered with a sheet of plastic wrap pressed against the surface and refrigerated for up to 5 days.)

4. Add 1 tablespoon salt and the pasta to the boiling water and cook, stirring often, until al dente. Reserve ½ cup of the cooking water then drain the pasta and return it to the pot. Stir in ¼ cup reserved cooking water and the pesto; adjust the consistency of the sauce with the remaining reserved pasta cooking water as needed. Serve immediately.

PASTA WITH PESTO, POTATOES, AND GREEN BEANS

WHY THIS RECIPE WORKS: The notion of putting pasta and potatoes in the same dish initially struck us as strange, but it's the preferred way to serve pesto in Liguria, Italy—the birthplace of the basil sauce. But the recipes we found needed work. The sauce was slightly grainy and the sharp, raw garlic dominated. Timing was another issue: When everything was cooked together, the green beans could be jarringly crisp and the pasta way too soft—or vice versa. How could we get all the elements of this dish to cook perfectly?

The traditional method called for cutting the potatoes into chunks and then, once cooked, vigorously mixing them with the pesto, pasta, and green beans. The agitation sloughed off

their corners, which dissolved into the dish, pulling the pesto and cooking water together to form a simple sauce. Simply trading out starchy russets for creamy, waxy red potatoes eliminated graininess and made our sauce smooth. We cooked the potatoes fully, then used the starchy water to cook the pasta. As for the pesto, we toasted the garlic and pine nuts for warm, mellow flavor (then used the same skillet to quickly steam the green beans). We used plenty of pasta water to bring the sauce together. Two tablespoons of butter made it even silkier, and a splash of lemon juice brought all the flavors into focus.

Pasta with Pesto, Potatoes, and Green Beans

SERVES 6

If gemelli is unavailable, penne or rigatoni make good substitutes. Use large red potatoes measuring 3 inches or more in diameter.

- ¼ cup pine nuts
- 3 garlic cloves, unpeeled
- 1 pound large red potatoes, peeled and cut into ½-inch pieces
  Salt and pepper
- 12 ounces green beans, trimmed and cut into 1½-inch lengths
- 2 cups fresh basil leaves
- 1 ounce Parmesan cheese, grated (½ cup)
- 7 tablespoons extra-virgin olive oil
- 1 pound gemelli
- 2 tablespoons unsalted butter, cut into ½-inch pieces and chilled
- 1 tablespoon lemon juice

1. Toast pine nuts and garlic in 10-inch skillet over medium heat, stirring frequently, until pine nuts are golden and fragrant and garlic darkens slightly, 3 to 5 minutes. Transfer to bowl and let cool. Peel garlic and chop coarsely.

2. Bring 3 quarts water to boil in large pot. Add potatoes and 1 tablespoon salt and cook until potatoes are tender but still hold their shape, 9 to 12 minutes. Using slotted spoon, transfer potatoes to rimmed baking sheet. (Do not discard water.)

3. Meanwhile, bring ½ cup water and ¼ teaspoon salt to boil in now-empty skillet over medium heat. Add green beans, cover, and cook until tender, 5 to 8 minutes. Drain green beans and transfer to sheet with potatoes.

4. Process basil, Parmesan, oil, pine nuts, garlic, and ½ teaspoon salt in food processor until smooth, about 1 minute.

5. Add gemelli to water in large pot and cook, stirring often, until al dente. Set colander in large bowl. Drain gemelli in colander, reserving cooking water in bowl. Return gemelli to pot. Add butter, lemon juice, potatoes and green beans, pesto, 1¼ cups reserved cooking water, and ½ teaspoon pepper and stir vigorously with rubber spatula until sauce takes on creamy appearance. Add additional cooking water as needed to adjust consistency and season with salt and pepper to taste. Serve immediately.

PASTA PARAPHERNALIA

What's our opinion on pasta gadgets? For the most part, *fuggedaboutit*. Pasta pots with perforated inserts tend to boil over if filled with the necessary amount of water. A pot with a strainer lid might look promising, but we found that if your grip isn't secure, the lid pops off and pasta can end up all over your sink. Ditto for crescent-shaped strainer plates that fit to the edge of the pot. The only pasta tool we've come across through the years that we've actually liked is a pasta fork, which is a long-handled spoon with ridged teeth. But no need to rush out and buy one; basic tongs work just fine.

PASTA WITH TOMATO AND ALMOND PESTO

WHY THIS RECIPE WORKS: In the Sicilian village of Trapani, there's a very different kind of pesto—it's basically pesto crossed with tomato sauce. Almonds replace pine nuts, but the big difference is the appearance of fresh tomatoes—not as the main ingredient, but as a fruity, sweet accent. We wanted a recipe for a clean, bright version of this sauce, not a chunky tomato salsa or thin, watery slush.

For this uncooked sauce, fresh tomatoes were best. Cherry and grape tomatoes proved equal contenders, sharing a similar brightness and juiciness that was far more reliable than that of their larger cousins. We processed the tomatoes with a handful of basil, garlic, and toasted almonds. The almonds contributed body and thickened the sauce while retaining just enough crunch to offset the tomatoes' pulpiness; using blanched, slivered almonds avoided the muddy flavor often contributed by papery skins. We added a scant amount of hot vinegar peppers for zing, then drizzled in olive oil in a slow, steady stream to emulsify the pesto. Parmesan was stirred in for the finishing touch to this light, bright, and texturally satisfying pesto.

Pasta with Tomato and Almond Pesto (Pesto alla Trapanese)

SERVES 4 TO 6

While we prefer linguine or spaghetti, any pasta shape will work here. You may substitute ½ teaspoon of red wine vinegar and ¼ teaspoon of red pepper flakes for the pepperoncini.

Table salt
1 pound linguine or spaghetti (see note)
¼ cup slivered almonds, toasted
12 ounces cherry or grape tomatoes (about 2½ cups)
½ cup packed fresh basil leaves
1 medium garlic clove, minced or pressed through a garlic press (about 1 teaspoon)
1 small pepperoncini (hot peppers in vinegar), stemmed, seeded, and minced (about ½ teaspoon; see note)
Pinch red pepper flakes (optional)
⅓ cup extra-virgin olive oil
1 ounce Parmesan cheese, grated (about ½ cup), plus extra for serving

1. Bring 4 quarts water to a boil in a large pot. Add 1 tablespoon salt and the pasta to the boiling water and cook, stirring often, until al dente. Reserve ½ cup of the cooking water then drain the pasta and return it to the pot.

2. Meanwhile, process the almonds, tomatoes, basil, garlic, pepperoncini, 1 teaspoon salt, and red pepper flakes (if using) in a food processor until smooth, about 1 minute. Scrape down the sides of the workbowl with a rubber spatula. With the machine running, slowly drizzle in the oil, about 30 seconds.

3. Add the pesto and ½ cup of the Parmesan to the cooked pasta and adjust the consistency of the sauce with the reserved pasta cooking water as needed. Serve immediately, passing extra Parmesan separately.

NONTRADITIONAL PESTOS

WHY THIS RECIPE WORKS: Pesto doesn't always mean basil, pine nuts, and Parmesan. We wanted to make quick pestos with a variety of other potent ingredients, like sun-dried tomatoes, goat cheese, and kalamata olives.

For pestos that were flavorful but not harsh, we tamed the garlic by toasting unpeeled cloves in a hot skillet or replaced most of it with sun-dried tomatoes. Then we processed the garlic or sun-dried tomatoes with olive oil, nuts, cheese, and olives, among other ingredients, to create smooth sauces that cling well to pasta. And to keep the pasta moist, we made sure to reserve some of the pasta cooking water to thin the pesto.

Campanelle with Arugula, Goat Cheese, and Sun-Dried Tomato Pesto

SERVES 4 TO 6

Make sure to rinse the herbs and seasonings from the sun-dried tomatoes. Farfalle can be substituted for the campanelle.

1 cup oil-packed sun-dried tomatoes (one 8½-ounce jar), drained, rinsed, patted dry, and chopped coarse (see note)
1 ounce Parmesan cheese, grated (about ½ cup)
6 tablespoons extra-virgin olive oil

¼ cup walnuts, toasted

1 small garlic clove, minced or pressed through a garlic press (about ½ teaspoon)

Table salt and ground black pepper

1 pound campanelle (see note)

1 medium bunch arugula, washed, dried, stemmed, and torn into bite-size pieces (about 6 cups)

3 ounces goat cheese, crumbled (about ¾ cup)

1. Process the sun-dried tomatoes, Parmesan, oil, walnuts, garlic, ½ teaspoon salt, and ⅛ teaspoon pepper in a food processor until smooth, scraping down the sides of the workbowl as necessary. Transfer the mixture to a small bowl and set aside.

2. Bring 4 quarts water to a boil in a large pot. Add 1 tablespoon salt and the pasta to the boiling water and cook, stirring often, until al dente. Reserve ¾ cup of the cooking water then drain the pasta and return it to the pot. Immediately stir in the arugula until wilted. Stir ½ cup of the reserved pasta cooking water into the pesto and add the pesto to the pasta. Toss to combine, adjusting the consistency of the sauce with the remaining reserved pasta cooking water as needed. Serve immediately, sprinkling the cheese over individual bowls.

Penne with Toasted Nut and Parsley Pesto

SERVES 4 TO 6

Toasting the unpeeled garlic in a skillet reduces its harshness and gives it a mellow flavor that works well in pesto.

3 medium garlic cloves, unpeeled

1 cup pecans, walnuts, whole blanched almonds, skinned hazelnuts, unsalted pistachios, or pine nuts, or any combination thereof, toasted

½ cup packed fresh parsley leaves

7 tablespoons extra-virgin olive oil

1 ounce Parmesan cheese, grated (about ½ cup)

Table salt and ground black pepper

1 pound penne

1. Toast the garlic in a small skillet over medium heat, shaking the pan occasionally, until softened and spotty brown, about 8 minutes; when cool, remove and discard the skins.

2. Process the garlic, nuts, parsley, and oil in a food processor until smooth, scraping down the sides of the workbowl as necessary. Transfer the mixture to a small bowl and stir in the Parmesan; season with salt and pepper to taste.

3. Bring 4 quarts water to a boil in a large pot. Add 1 tablespoon salt and the pasta to the boiling water and cook, stirring often, until al dente. Reserve ½ cup of the cooking water then drain the pasta and return it to the pot. Stir ¼ cup of the reserved pasta cooking water into the pesto and add the pesto to the pasta. Toss to combine, adjusting the consistency of the sauce with the remaining reserved pasta cooking water as needed. Serve immediately.

Spaghetti with Olive Pesto

SERVES 4 TO 6

This black pesto is called *olivada* in Italy. Make sure to use high-quality olives in this recipe. The anchovy adds flavor but not fishiness to the pesto and we recommend its inclusion.

3 medium garlic cloves, unpeeled

1½ cups pitted kalamata olives (see note)

1 ounce Parmesan cheese, grated (about ½ cup), plus extra for serving

6 tablespoons extra-virgin olive oil

¼ cup packed fresh parsley leaves

1 medium shallot, chopped coarse (about 3 tablespoons)

8 large basil leaves

1 tablespoon juice from 1 lemon

1 anchovy fillet, rinsed (optional; see note)

Table salt and ground black pepper

1 pound spaghetti

Lemon wedges, for serving

1. Toast the garlic in a small skillet over medium heat, shaking the pan occasionally, until the garlic is softened and spotty brown, about 8 minutes; when cool, remove and discard the skins.

2. Process the garlic, olives, ½ cup of the Parmesan, oil, parsley, shallot, basil, lemon juice, and anchovy (if using) in a food processor, scraping down the sides of the workbowl as necessary. Transfer the mixture to a small bowl and season with salt and pepper to taste.

3. Bring 4 quarts water to a boil in a large pot. Add 1 tablespoon salt and the pasta to the boiling water and cook, stirring often, until al dente. Reserve ½ cup of the cooking water then drain the pasta and return it to the pot. Stir ¼ cup of the reserved pasta cooking water into the pesto and add the pesto to the pasta. Toss to combine, adjusting the consistency of the sauce with the remaining reserved pasta cooking water as needed. Serve immediately, passing the lemon wedges and extra Parmesan separately.

SPRING VEGETABLE PASTA

WHY THIS RECIPE WORKS: In pasta primavera, the vegetables and pasta are tossed together in a sauce made with broth and heavy cream. We love this classic, but sometimes we want a lighter, brighter version. As for the vegetables, we wanted true spring vegetables. To start, we chose asparagus and green peas, adding chives for bite and garlic and leeks for depth and sweetness. For a deeply flavored sauce that would unify the pasta and vegetables, we borrowed a technique from risotto, lightly toasting the pasta in olive oil before cooking it in broth and white wine. The sauce flavored the pasta as it cooked while the pasta added starch to the sauce, thickening it without the need for heavy cream. This nontraditional approach gave us a light but creamy sauce with sweet, grassy flavors that paired perfectly with the vegetables. This was a dish that truly tasted like spring.

Spring Vegetable Pasta

SERVES 4 TO 6

Campanelle is our pasta of choice in this dish, but farfalle and penne are good substitutes.

- 1½ pounds leeks, white and light green parts halved lengthwise, sliced ½ inch thick, and washed; 3 cups coarsely chopped dark green parts, washed
- 1 pound asparagus, tough ends trimmed, chopped coarse, and reserved, spears cut on bias into ½-inch lengths
- 2 cups frozen peas, thawed
- 4 medium garlic cloves, minced or pressed through a garlic press (about 4 teaspoons)
- 4 cups vegetable broth
- 1 cup water
- 2 tablespoons minced fresh mint leaves
- 2 tablespoons minced fresh chives
- ½ teaspoon grated zest plus 2 tablespoons juice from 1 lemon
- 6 tablespoons extra-virgin olive oil
  Table salt and ground black pepper
- ¼ teaspoon red pepper flakes
- 1 pound campanelle (see note)
- 1 cup dry white wine
- 1 ounce grated Parmesan cheese (about ½ cup), plus extra for serving

1. Bring the leek greens, asparagus trimmings, 1 cup of the peas, half of the garlic, the broth, and water to simmer in a large saucepan. Reduce the heat to medium-low and simmer gently for 10 minutes. While the broth simmers, combine the mint, chives, and lemon zest in a bowl; set aside.

2. Strain the broth through a fine-mesh strainer into a large liquid measuring cup, pressing on the solids to extract as much liquid as possible (you should have 5 cups broth; add water as needed to measure 5 cups). Discard the solids and return the broth to the saucepan. Cover and keep warm.

3. Heat 2 tablespoons of the oil in a Dutch oven over medium heat until shimmering. Add the leeks and a pinch salt and cook, covered, stirring occasionally, until the leeks begin to brown, about 5 minutes. Add the asparagus spears and cook until the asparagus is crisp-tender, 4 to 6 minutes. Add the remaining garlic and the red pepper flakes and cook until fragrant, about 30 seconds. Add the remaining 1 cup peas and continue to cook for 1 minute longer. Transfer the vegetables to a plate and set aside. Wipe out the pot.

4. Heat the remaining ¼ cup oil in the now-empty pot over medium heat until shimmering. Add the pasta and cook, stirring often, until just beginning to brown, about 5 minutes. Add the wine and cook, stirring constantly, until absorbed, about 2 minutes.

5. When the wine is fully absorbed, add the warm broth and bring to a boil. Cook, stirring frequently, until most of the liquid is absorbed and the pasta is al dente, 8 to 10 minutes. Off the heat, stir in half of the herb mixture, the vegetables, lemon juice, and ½ cup of the Parmesan. Season with salt and pepper to taste and serve immediately, passing the additional Parmesan and the remaining herb mixture separately.

SUMMER PASTA PUTTANESCA

WHY THIS RECIPE WORKS: When we make pasta puttanesca with fresh tomatoes, we want the tomatoes to share equal billing with the pungently flavorful olives and anchovies typical of this robust sauce. For a puttanesca that would make the most of a bumper crop of fresh tomatoes, we opted to use grape or cherry tomatoes, which are both excellent in summer and among the best varieties of tomatoes available year-round. To retain the fresh tomato flavor, we pureed the tomatoes and strained the juices, which we cooked down briefly to thicken the sauce. We added the tomato pulp back in at the end of cooking so we wouldn't lose the fresh tomato flavor. We traded the traditional long pasta for frilly campanelle, which held on to the coarse sauce and gave our dish a summery flair.

Summer Pasta Puttanesca

SERVES 4

We prefer to make this dish with campanelle, but fusilli and orecchiette also work. Very finely mashed anchovy fillets (rinsed and dried before mashing) can be used instead of anchovy paste. Buy a good-quality black olive, such as kalamata, Gaeta, or Alfonso.

- 3 tablespoons extra-virgin olive oil
- 4 garlic cloves, minced
- 1 tablespoon anchovy paste
- ¼ teaspoon red pepper flakes
- ¼ teaspoon dried oregano
- 1½ pounds grape or cherry tomatoes

with their starchy liquid—to add even more body and flavor to the dish. Cooking the chickpeas and ditalini in the same pot blended the dish, and the additional starch released by the pasta created a silky, stick-to-your-ribs texture. We gave the chickpeas a brief head start, simmering them before adding the pasta, in order to achieve the perfect creamy softness. Using a food processor allowed us to get a finely minced *soffritto* of onions, garlic, carrot, celery, and pancetta, an addition that gave the dish a meaty backbone. And we achieved depth of flavor by adding anchovy, tomatoes, and Parmesan cheese. A last-minute addition of parsley and lemon juice provided a bright contrast just before serving.

Pasta e Ceci (Pasta with Chickpeas)
SERVES 4 TO 6

Another short pasta, such as orzo, can be substituted for the ditalini, but make sure to substitute by weight and not by volume.

- 2 ounces pancetta, cut into ½-inch pieces
- 1 small carrot, peeled and cut into ½-inch pieces
- 1 small celery rib, cut into ½-inch pieces
- 4 garlic cloves, peeled
- 1 onion, halved and cut into 1-inch pieces
- 1 (14-ounce) can whole peeled tomatoes, drained
- ¼ cup extra-virgin olive oil, plus extra for serving
- 1 anchovy fillet, rinsed, patted dry, and minced
- ¼ teaspoon red pepper flakes
- 2 teaspoons minced fresh rosemary
- 2 (15-ounce) cans chickpeas (do not drain)
- 2 cups water
    Salt and pepper
- 8 ounces (1½ cups) ditalini
- 1 tablespoon lemon juice
- 1 tablespoon minced fresh parsley
- 1 ounce Parmesan cheese, grated (½ cup)

1. Process pancetta in food processor until ground to paste, about 30 seconds, scraping down sides of bowl as needed. Add carrot, celery, and garlic and pulse until finely chopped, 8 to 10 pulses. Add onion and pulse until onion is cut into ⅛- to ¼-inch pieces, 8 to 10 pulses. Transfer pancetta mixture to large Dutch oven. Pulse tomatoes in now-empty food processor until coarsely chopped, 8 to 10 pulses. Set aside.

2. Add oil to pancetta mixture in Dutch oven and cook over medium heat, stirring frequently, until fond begins to form on bottom of pot, about 5 minutes. Add anchovy, pepper flakes, and rosemary and cook until fragrant, about 1 minute. Stir in tomatoes, chickpeas and their liquid, water, and 1 teaspoon salt and bring to boil, scraping up any browned bits. Reduce heat to medium-low and simmer for 10 minutes. Add pasta and cook, stirring frequently, until tender, 10 to 12 minutes. Stir in lemon juice and parsley and season with salt and pepper to taste. Serve, passing Parmesan and extra oil separately.

- 1 pound campanelle
    Salt
- ½ cup pitted kalamata olives, chopped coarse
- 3 tablespoons capers, rinsed and minced
- ½ cup minced fresh parsley

1. Combine oil, garlic, anchovy paste, pepper flakes, and oregano in bowl. Process tomatoes in blender until finely chopped but not pureed, 15 to 45 seconds. Transfer to fine-mesh strainer set in large bowl and let drain for 5 minutes, occasionally pressing gently on solids with rubber spatula to extract liquid (this should yield about ¾ cup). Reserve tomato liquid in bowl and tomato pulp in strainer.

2. Bring 4 quarts water to boil in large pot. Add campanelle and 1 tablespoon salt and cook, stirring often, until al dente. Reserve 1 cup cooking water, then drain campanelle and return it to pot.

3. While campanelle is cooking, cook garlic-anchovy mixture in 12-inch skillet over medium heat, stirring frequently, until garlic is fragrant but not brown, 2 to 3 minutes. Add tomato liquid and simmer until reduced to ⅓ cup, 2 to 3 minutes. Add tomato pulp, olives, and capers; cook until just heated through, 2 to 3 minutes. Stir in parsley.

4. Pour sauce over campanelle and toss to combine, adding reserved cooking water as needed to adjust consistency. Season with salt to taste. Serve immediately.

PASTA E CECI (PASTA WITH CHICKPEAS)

WHY THIS RECIPE WORKS: *Pasta e ceci*, a sibling of *pasta e fagioli*, is a hearty and fast one-pot meal that's simple to prepare, yet packed full of satisfying flavor. To keep the cooking time to under an hour, we used canned chickpeas—along

PASTA WITH ASPARAGUS

WHY THIS RECIPE WORKS: Asparagus is a natural starting point when trying to make a tomato-free vegetarian pasta sauce. Its sweet, vegetable flavor and quick-cooking nature is a terrific match to pasta. But more often than not, asparagus sauces are bland and boring. We wanted to keep it simple but make this dish livelier.

First, we focused on how to cook the asparagus. Boiling and steaming diluted the vegetable's grassy flavor, so they were out. Instead, we browned the asparagus in a hot skillet, after cutting it into bite-size pieces, for a sauce that was both quick and flavorful. The asparagus caramelized just a bit, and the heat brought out the flavors of the other ingredients, such as onions, walnuts, and garlic. To finish off the dish, we paired the asparagus with a balance of salty, sweet, and sour ingredients. In one dish, we teamed asparagus with balsamic vinegar, basil, and pecorino and in another, arugula, blue cheese, and apple worked well.

Campanelle with Asparagus, Basil, and Balsamic Glaze

SERVES 4 TO 6

Campanelle is a frilly trumpet-shaped pasta that pairs nicely with this sauce. If you cannot find it, fusilli works well, too. Use a vegetable peeler to shave the cheese.

>   Table salt
> 1   pound campanelle (see note)
> ¾   cup balsamic vinegar
> 5   tablespoons extra-virgin olive oil
> 1   pound asparagus, tough ends trimmed
>   (see photos), thick spears halved
>   lengthwise and cut into 1-inch lengths
> 1   medium red onion, halved and sliced thin
>   (about 1½ cups)
> ½   teaspoon ground black pepper
> ¼   teaspoon red pepper flakes
> 1   cup chopped fresh basil leaves
> 2   ounces Pecorino Romano cheese, shaved
>   (about 1 cup; see note)
> 1   tablespoon juice from 1 lemon

1. Bring 4 quarts water to a boil in a large pot. Add 1 tablespoon salt and the pasta to the boiling water and cook, stirring often, until al dente. Reserve ½ cup of the cooking water then drain the pasta and return it to the pot.

2. While the pasta is cooking, bring the balsamic vinegar to a boil in an 8-inch skillet over medium-high heat; reduce the heat to medium and simmer gently until reduced to ¼ cup, 15 to 20 minutes.

3. Meanwhile, heat 2 tablespoons of the oil in a 12-inch nonstick skillet over high heat until smoking. Add the asparagus, onion, black pepper, red pepper flakes, and ½ teaspoon salt

TRIMMING ASPARAGUS SPEARS

1. Before cooking asparagus, it's important to remove the tough ends. Remove one asparagus spear from the bunch and snap off the end.

2. Using the broken asparagus as a guide, trim off the ends of the remaining spears using a chef's knife.

and stir to combine. Cook, without stirring, until the asparagus begins to brown, about 1 minute, then stir and continue to cook, stirring occasionally, until the asparagus is crisp-tender, about 4 minutes longer.

4. Add the asparagus mixture, basil, ½ cup of the Pecorino, the lemon juice, and the remaining 3 tablespoons oil to the pasta and toss to combine. Adjust the consistency of the sauce with the reserved pasta cooking water as needed. Serve immediately, drizzling 1 to 2 teaspoons balsamic glaze over individual servings and passing the remaining ½ cup Pecorino separately.

Cavatappi with Asparagus, Arugula, Walnuts, and Blue Cheese

SERVES 4 TO 6

Cavatappi is a short, tubular corkscrew-shaped pasta; penne is a fine substitute. The grated apple balances the other flavors in this dish.

>   Table salt
> 1   pound cavatappi (see note)
> 5   tablespoons extra-virgin olive oil
> 1   pound asparagus, tough ends trimmed
>   (see photos), thick spears halved
>   lengthwise and cut into 1-inch lengths
> ½   teaspoon ground black pepper
> 1   cup walnuts, chopped
> 4   cups lightly packed arugula leaves from
>   1 large bunch, washed and dried
> 6   ounces strong blue cheese, such as Roquefort,
>   crumbled (about 1½ cups)
> 2   tablespoons cider vinegar
> 1   Granny Smith apple, peeled, for garnish

1. Bring 4 quarts water to a boil in a large pot. Add 1 tablespoon salt and the pasta to the boiling water and cook, stirring often, until al dente. Reserve ½ cup of the cooking water then drain the pasta and return it to the pot.

2. While the pasta is cooking, heat 2 tablespoons of the oil in a 12-inch nonstick skillet over high heat until smoking. Add the asparagus, pepper, and ½ teaspoon salt and cook, without stirring, until the asparagus begins to brown, about 1 minute. Add the walnuts and continue to cook, stirring frequently, until the asparagus is crisp-tender and the nuts are toasted, about 4 minutes longer. Add the arugula and toss to wilt.

3. Add the asparagus mixture, blue cheese, vinegar, and the remaining 3 tablespoons oil to the pasta and toss to combine. Adjust the consistency of the sauce with the reserved pasta cooking water as needed. Serve immediately, grating the apple over individual servings.

PASTA WITH MUSHROOMS

WHY THIS RECIPE WORKS: Pasta with mushrooms can be watery and tasteless. But when done right, this dish transforms an ordinary box of pasta and a package of mushrooms into something special. We wanted to combine the intense flavor of sautéed mushrooms with a light cream sauce to create a woodsy, full-flavored pasta dish.

For optimum flavor and texture, we used a combination of shiitake and cremini mushrooms; cremini mushrooms provided richness and meatiness, and the shiitakes contributed hearty flavor and a pleasant, chewy texture. Cooking the mushrooms in a skillet (not in the sauce) improved their flavor; adding salt to the pan helped the mushrooms release their juices and enhanced browning. We then added chicken broth and cream to the browned bits left in the skillet after the mushrooms were removed. Garlic, shallots, and thyme rounded out the flavors of our simple sauce, and lemon juice added brightness. We added the browned mushrooms back in for a chunky sauce that paired nicely with short pasta with lots of crevices—we liked either campanelle or farfalle.

Pasta with Sautéed Mushrooms and Thyme
SERVES 4 TO 6

Vegetable broth can be substituted for the chicken broth to make this dish vegetarian. If you add the pasta to the boiling water at the same time the cremini go into the skillet, the pasta and sauce will finish at the same time.

    Table salt
1   pound campanelle or farfalle
2   tablespoons unsalted butter
2   tablespoons extra-virgin olive oil
4   large shallots, minced (about 1 cup)
3   medium garlic cloves, minced or pressed through
    a garlic press (about 1 tablespoon)
10 ounces shiitake mushrooms, stems discarded,
    caps wiped clean and sliced ¼ inch thick

10 ounces cremini mushrooms, wiped clean and
    sliced ¼ inch thick
1   tablespoon plus 1 teaspoon minced fresh thyme leaves
1¼ cups low-sodium chicken broth (see note)
½   cup heavy cream
1   tablespoon juice from 1 lemon
    Ground black pepper
2   ounces Parmesan cheese, grated (about 1 cup)
2   tablespoons minced fresh parsley leaves

1. Bring 4 quarts water to a boil in a large pot. Add 1 tablespoon salt and the pasta to the boiling water and cook, stirring often, until al dente. Reserve ½ cup of the cooking water then drain the pasta and return it to the pot.

2. Meanwhile, melt the butter with the oil over medium heat in a 12-inch skillet. Add the shallots and cook, stirring occasionally, until softened and translucent, about 4 minutes. Add the garlic and cook until fragrant, about 30 seconds. Increase the heat to medium-high; add the shiitakes and cook, stirring occasionally, for 2 minutes. Add the cremini and ½ teaspoon salt; cook, stirring occasionally, until the moisture released by the mushrooms has evaporated and the mushrooms are golden brown, about 8 minutes. Add the thyme and cook until fragrant, about 30 seconds. Transfer the mushrooms to a bowl and set aside.

3. Add the chicken broth to the skillet and bring to a boil, scraping up the browned bits. Off the heat, stir in the cream and lemon juice and season with salt and pepper to taste.

4. Add the mushrooms, chicken broth mixture, cheese, and parsley to the pasta. Toss over medium-low heat until the cheese melts and the pasta absorbs most of the liquid, about 2 minutes. Adjust the consistency of the sauce with the reserved pasta cooking water as needed and serve immediately.

QUICK MUSHROOM RAGU

WHY THIS RECIPE WORKS: We wanted a mushroom ragu that combined the naturally hearty texture of fresh mushrooms with the concentrated flavor of dried ones—and that could be on the table in about 30 minutes. Using pancetta and its fat compensated for the lean nature of the mushrooms and made our mushroom ragu meatier. Portobello mushrooms gave our dish bulk, while smoky porcini gave it concentrated flavor. Adding tomato paste and fresh crushed tomatoes to our mushrooms after they'd browned sweetened our sauce but also let the mushrooms shine through. Finally, fresh rosemary finished our dish with brightness.

Spaghetti with Quick Mushroom Ragu
SERVES 4

Use a spoon to scrape the dark brown gills from the portobellos.

- 1 cup low-sodium chicken broth
- 1 ounce dried porcini mushrooms, rinsed
- 4 ounces pancetta, cut into ½-inch pieces
- 8 ounces portobello mushroom caps, gills removed, caps cut into ½-inch pieces (about 1½ cups)
- 3 tablespoons extra-virgin olive oil
- 4 medium garlic cloves, peeled and sliced thin
- 1 tablespoon tomato paste
- 2 teaspoons minced fresh rosemary leaves
- 1 (14.5-ounce) can whole peeled tomatoes, roughly crushed by hand
   Salt and pepper
- 1 pound spaghetti
   Grated Pecorino Romano cheese

1. Microwave broth and porcini in covered bowl until steaming, about 1 minute. Let sit until softened, about 10 minutes. Drain mushrooms through fine-mesh strainer lined with coffee filter into medium bowl, reserve broth, and chop mushrooms fine.

2. Heat pancetta in 12-inch skillet over medium heat; cook, stirring occasionally, until rendered and crisp, 7 to 10 minutes. Add portobellos, chopped porcini, oil, garlic, tomato paste, and rosemary; cook, stirring occasionally, until all liquid has evaporated and tomato paste starts to brown, 5 to 7 minutes. Add reserved broth and crushed tomatoes and their juice; increase heat to high and bring to simmer. Reduce heat to medium-low and simmer until thickened, 15 to 20 minutes. Season with salt and pepper to taste.

3. While sauce simmers, bring 4 quarts water to boil in large Dutch oven. Add pasta and 1 tablespoon salt; cook, stirring often, until al dente. Reserve ½ cup cooking water, then drain pasta and return it to pot. Add sauce to pasta and toss to combine. Add reserved cooking water as needed to adjust consistency and season with salt and pepper to taste. Serve, passing Pecorino separately.

TAGLIATELLE WITH PROSCIUTTO AND PEAS

WHY THIS RECIPE WORKS: Prosciutto and Parmesan are packed with complementary flavors, so when combining them in a pasta dish, we aimed to maximize their impact. Adding prosciutto in two stages created complex, porky flavor. Mincing an ounce of prosciutto and simmering it with softened shallots and cream created a meaty sauce. We opted for tagliatelle, its long ribbons of dried egg pasta a fitting substitute for fresh pasta. We stirred together the pasta, reserved water, and the prosciutto-cream mixture, adding in strips of raw prosciutto for the meat's fruity, nutty fragrance. Grated Parmesan plus Gruyère (another nutty, aromatic cheese) worked perfectly. We used frozen peas as a sweet, bright foil to the rich sauce.

Tagliatelle with Prosciutto and Peas
SERVES 4 TO 6

We prefer imported prosciutto di Parma sliced ¹⁄₁₆ inch thick or domestically made prepackaged Volpi Traditional Prosciutto. Look for a hard Gruyère that is aged for at least 10 months. Pappardelle can be substituted for the tagliatelle.

- 6 ounces thinly sliced prosciutto
- 1 tablespoon unsalted butter
- 1 shallot, minced
   Salt and pepper
- 1 cup heavy cream
- 1 pound tagliatelle
- 1½ cups frozen petite peas, thawed
- 1 ounce Parmesan cheese, grated (½ cup)
- 1 ounce Gruyère cheese, grated (½ cup)

1. Slice 5 ounces prosciutto crosswise into ¼-inch-wide strips; set aside. Mince remaining 1 ounce prosciutto. Melt butter in 10-inch skillet over medium-low heat. Add shallot and ¼ teaspoon salt and cook until softened, about 2 minutes. Stir in cream and minced prosciutto and bring to simmer. Cook, stirring occasionally, until cream mixture measures 1 cup, 5 to 7 minutes. Remove pan from heat and cover to keep warm.

2. Meanwhile, bring 4 quarts water to boil in large pot. Add pasta and 1 tablespoon salt and cook, stirring often, until al dente. Reserve 2 cups cooking water, then drain pasta and return it to pot.

3. Add 1 cup reserved cooking water, cream mixture, prosciutto strips, peas, Parmesan, Gruyère, and 1 teaspoon pepper to pasta. Gently toss until pasta is well coated. Transfer pasta to serving bowl and serve immediately, adjusting consistency with remaining reserved cooking water as needed.

PASTA WITH BROCCOLI RABE AND SAUSAGE

WHY THIS RECIPE WORKS: In southern Italy, broccoli rabe and *orecchiette* (loosely translated as "little ears") is a popular combination. The trick to this pasta dish is cooking the broccoli rabe just right and limiting the number of ingredients so that at the end, you have a moist and flavorful (but not oily) pasta dish.

For a hearty, filling dish, we decided to include some Italian sausage. Tasters preferred spicy Italian sausage to the sweet variety, but if you like less heat, the sweet sausage still makes for a satisfying dish. We started by browning the sausage in a skillet. We then added the broccoli rabe and chicken broth to absorb the rich, meaty flavors in the pan; covering the pan allowed us to steam the rabe with the other sauce ingredients. Besides eliminating the need for a separate pot to blanch the rabe, this cooking method didn't wash away the pleasantly bitter flavor of this Italian vegetable. Some red pepper flakes amplified the heat from the sausage, and a drizzle of olive oil and freshly grated Parmesan cheese brought the whole dish together.

Orecchiette with Broccoli Rabe and Sausage
SERVES 4 TO 6

If you prefer to use broccoli instead of broccoli rabe in this recipe, use 2 pounds broccoli cut into 1-inch florets and increase the cooking time by several minutes. If you prefer a less spicy dish, use sweet Italian sausage.

    Table salt
1   pound orecchiette
8   ounces hot Italian sausage, casings removed (see note)
6   medium garlic cloves, minced or pressed through
    a garlic press (about 2 tablespoons)
½   teaspoon red pepper flakes
1   bunch broccoli rabe (about 1 pound), washed,
    trimmed, and cut into 1½-inch pieces (see note)

REMOVING SAUSAGE FROM ITS CASING

Italian sausage is sold in links, bulk-style tubes, and patties. If using links, remove meat from its casing before cooking so that you can crumble it into bite-size pieces. Hold sausage firmly at 1 end and squeeze meat out of opposite end.

½   cup low-sodium chicken broth
1   tablespoon extra-virgin olive oil
1   ounce Parmesan cheese, grated (about ½ cup)

1. Bring 4 quarts water to a boil in a large pot. Add 1 tablespoon salt and the pasta to the boiling water and cook, stirring often, until al dente. Reserve ½ cup of the cooking water then drain the pasta and return it to the pot.

2. While the pasta is cooking, cook the sausage until browned in a 12-inch nonstick skillet over medium-high heat, breaking it into ½-inch pieces with a wooden spoon, about 3 minutes. Stir in the garlic, red pepper flakes, and ½ teaspoon salt. Cook, stirring constantly, until the garlic is fragrant, about 1½ minutes. Add the broccoli rabe and chicken broth, cover, and cook until the broccoli rabe turns bright green, about 2 minutes. Uncover and cook, stirring frequently, until most of the broth has evaporated and the broccoli rabe is tender, 2 to 3 minutes.

3. Add the sausage mixture, oil, and cheese to the pasta and toss to combine. Adjust the consistency of the sauce with the reserved pasta cooking water as needed and serve immediately.

PASTA ALLA NORCINA

WHY THIS RECIPE WORKS: *Pasta alla norcina*, from an Italian village in Umbria, features tender pasta and richly flavored pork sausage in a light cream sauce. To bring an authentic-tasting version of this dish to the American dinner table, we bypassed store-bought Italian sausage—the size of the grind and the fat levels varied too much, and the seasonings were out of place in this dish—and made our own. Brining ground pork and mixing it briefly with a spatula ensured it had a sausage-like snappy texture; rosemary, nutmeg, and garlic offered robust flavor. Adding baking soda and searing our sausage in patty form before chopping it into small pieces helped it stay juicy and tender when it finished cooking in the cream sauce. Finely chopped mushrooms provided earthy background notes, and a splash of wine balanced the richness of the dish. For the pasta, we preferred orecchiette, which cradled the chunky sauce nicely.

Pasta alla Norcina

SERVES 6

White mushrooms may be substituted for the cremini mushrooms. Short tubular or molded pastas such as mezze rigatoni or shells may be substituted for the orecchiette.

  Kosher salt and pepper
¼ teaspoon baking soda
4 teaspoons water
8 ounces ground pork
3 garlic cloves, minced
1¼ teaspoons minced fresh rosemary
⅛ teaspoon ground nutmeg
8 ounces cremini mushrooms, trimmed
7 teaspoons vegetable oil
¾ cup heavy cream
1 pound orecchiette
½ cup dry white wine
1½ ounces Pecorino Romano, grated (¾ cup)
3 tablespoons minced fresh parsley
1 tablespoon lemon juice

1. Spray large dinner plate with vegetable oil spray. Dissolve 1⅛ teaspoons salt and baking soda in water in medium bowl. Add pork and fold gently to combine; let stand for 10 minutes.

2. Add 1 teaspoon garlic, ¾ teaspoon rosemary, nutmeg, and ¾ teaspoon pepper to pork and stir and smear with rubber spatula until well combined and tacky, 10 to 15 seconds. Transfer pork mixture to greased plate and form into rough 6-inch patty. Pulse mushrooms in food processor until finely chopped, 10 to 12 pulses.

3. Heat 2 teaspoons oil in 12-inch skillet over medium-high heat until just smoking. Add patty and cook without moving it until bottom is well browned, 2 to 3 minutes. Flip patty and continue to cook until second side is well browned, 2 to

3 minutes longer (very center of patty will be raw). Remove pan from heat and transfer patty to cutting board. Using tongs to steady patty, roughly chop into ⅛- to ¼-inch pieces. Transfer meat to bowl and add cream; set aside.

4. Bring 4 quarts water to boil in large Dutch oven. Stir in orecchiette and 2 tablespoons salt and cook, stirring often, until al dente. Reserve 1½ cups cooking water, then drain orecchiette and return it to pot.

5. While orecchiette cooks, return now-empty skillet to medium heat. Add 1 tablespoon oil, mushrooms, and ⅛ teaspoon salt; cook, stirring frequently, until mushrooms are browned, 5 to 7 minutes. Stir in remaining 2 teaspoons oil, remaining 2 teaspoons garlic, remaining ½ teaspoon rosemary, and ½ teaspoon pepper; cook until fragrant, about 30 seconds. Stir in wine, scraping up any browned bits, and cook until completely evaporated, 1 to 2 minutes. Stir in meat-cream mixture and ¾ cup reserved cooking water and simmer until meat is no longer pink, 1 to 3 minutes. Remove pan from heat and stir in Pecorino until smooth.

6. Add sauce, parsley, and lemon juice to orecchiette and toss well to coat, adjusting consistency with remaining cooking water as needed. Season with salt and pepper to taste, and serve.

SHRIMP AND GARLIC WITH PASTA

WHY THIS RECIPE WORKS: In theory, garlic shrimp pasta has all the makings of an ideal weeknight meal—just toss a few quick-cooking ingredients with boiled pasta. In reality, delicate shrimp cooks fast, which translates to overcooked in a matter of seconds. Meanwhile, garlic can become bitter, depending on how it's treated. Add to that the challenge of getting a brothy sauce to coat the pasta, and this simple recipe turns into a precarious balancing act. We wanted al dente pasta and moist shrimp bound by a sauce infused with a deep garlic flavor. For the best flavor and texture, we used quick-frozen, extra-large shrimp and marinated them with minced garlic before a quick sauté in garlic oil. We also cut each shrimp into thirds before cooking to ensure that every bite of pasta had a tasty morsel of shrimp. With sweet low notes from the infused oil and brasher high notes from the garlic, we finally had a balanced garlic flavor. As for the sauce, to deglaze the pan, we preferred the clean taste of vermouth or white wine; bottled clam broth added complexity. Using a chunky tubular pasta instead of traditional linguine made it easy to find the shrimp. To get the sauce to cling to the pasta, we stirred flour into the oil just before adding the vermouth and clam juice and tossed in some cold butter to finish.

Garlicky Shrimp Pasta

SERVES 4 TO 6

Marinate the shrimp while you prepare the remaining ingredients. Any short tubular or curly pasta works well here. If you prefer more heat, use the greater amount of red pepper flakes given.

1 pound extra-large shrimp (21 to 25 per pound), peeled, deveined (see page 240), and each shrimp cut into 3 pieces

3 tablespoons olive oil

5 medium garlic cloves, minced or pressed through a garlic press (about 5 teaspoons), plus 4 medium garlic cloves, smashed

Table salt

1 pound mezze rigatoni, fusilli, or campanelle (see note)

¼–½ teaspoon red pepper flakes (see note)

2 teaspoons unbleached all-purpose flour

½ cup dry vermouth or white wine

¾ cup clam juice

½ cup chopped fresh parsley leaves

3 tablespoons unsalted butter, cut into 3 pieces

1 teaspoon lemon juice, plus lemon wedges for serving

Ground black pepper

1. Toss the shrimp, 1 tablespoon of the oil, 2 teaspoons of the minced garlic, and ¼ teaspoon salt in a medium bowl. Let the shrimp marinate at room temperature 20 minutes.

2. Heat the 4 smashed garlic cloves and the remaining 2 tablespoons oil in a 12-inch skillet over medium-low heat, stirring occasionally, until the garlic is light golden brown, 4 to 7 minutes. Remove the skillet from the heat and use a slotted spoon to remove the garlic from the skillet; discard the garlic. Set the skillet aside.

3. Bring 4 quarts water to a boil in a large pot. Add 1 tablespoon salt and the pasta to the boiling water and cook, stirring often, until al dente. Reserve ½ cup of the cooking water then drain the pasta and return it to the pot.

4. While the pasta cooks, return the skillet with the oil to medium heat; add the shrimp with the marinade to the skillet in a single layer. Cook the shrimp, undisturbed, until the oil starts to bubble gently, 1 to 2 minutes. Stir the shrimp and continue to cook until almost cooked through, about 1 minute longer. Using a slotted spoon, transfer the shrimp to a medium bowl. Add the remaining 3 teaspoons minced garlic and the red pepper flakes to the skillet and cook until fragrant, about 1 minute. Add the flour and cook, stirring constantly, for 1 minute; stir in the vermouth and cook for 1 minute. Add the clam juice and parsley; cook until the mixture starts to thicken, 1 to 2 minutes. Off the heat, whisk in the butter and lemon juice. Add the shrimp and sauce to the pasta and adjust the consistency of the sauce with the reserved pasta cooking water as needed. Season with black pepper to taste. Serve immediately, passing the lemon wedges separately.

CLASSIC SHRIMP FRA DIAVOLO

WHY THIS RECIPE WORKS: Most recipes for shrimp *fra diavolo* ("brother devil" in Italian) lack depth of flavor, with the star ingredients, shrimp and garlic, contributing little to an acidic, unbalanced tomato sauce. We wanted a classic shrimp fra diavolo with a seriously garlicky, spicy tomato sauce studded with sweet, firm shrimp.

For a streamlined procedure that would produce deep flavor, we seared the shrimp first to help them caramelize and enrich their sweetness. Following a brief sear with olive oil, salt, and red pepper flakes—the pepper flakes also benefited from the sear, as they took on toasty, earthy notes—we flambéed the shrimp with cognac. The combined forces of cognac and flame brought out the shrimp's sweet, tender notes and imbued our fra diavolo with the cognac's richness and complexity. We then sautéed the garlic slowly for a mellow nutty flavor, and reserved some raw garlic for a last-minute punch of heat and spice. Simmered diced tomatoes and a splash of white wine (balanced by a bit of sugar) completed our perfect fra diavolo in less than 30 minutes.

Classic Shrimp fra Diavolo

SERVES 4 TO 6

One teaspoon of red pepper flakes will give the sauce a little kick, but you may want to add more depending on your taste. For safety notes on flambéing, see page 408.

Table salt

1 pound linguine or spaghetti

1 pound large shrimp (31 to 40 per pound), peeled and deveined (see page 240)

6 tablespoons extra-virgin olive oil

1 teaspoon red pepper flakes, plus more to taste (see note)

¼ cup cognac or brandy

12 medium garlic cloves, minced or pressed through a garlic press (about ¼ cup)

1 (28-ounce) can diced tomatoes, drained

1 cup dry white wine

½ teaspoon sugar

¼ cup minced fresh parsley leaves

1. Bring 4 quarts water to a boil in a large pot. Add 1 tablespoon salt and the pasta to the boiling water and cook, stirring often, until al dente. Reserve ½ cup of the cooking water then drain the pasta and return it to the pot.

2. Meanwhile, toss the shrimp with 2 tablespoons of the oil, ½ teaspoon of the red pepper flakes, and ¾ teaspoon salt. Heat a 12-inch skillet over high heat. Add the shrimp to the skillet in a single layer and cook, without stirring, until the bottoms of the shrimp turn spotty brown, about 30 seconds. Remove the skillet from the heat, flip the shrimp, and add the cognac; wait until the cognac has warmed slightly, about 5 seconds, and return the skillet to high heat. Wave a lit match over the skillet until the cognac ignites, shaking the pan to distribute the flame over the entire pan. When the flames subside (this will take 15 to 30 seconds), transfer the shrimp to a medium bowl and set aside. Let the skillet cool, off the heat, about 2 minutes.

3. Add 3 tablespoons more oil and 3 tablespoons of the garlic to the cooled skillet and cook over low heat, stirring constantly, until the garlic becomes sticky and straw colored, 7 to 10 minutes. Add the remaining red pepper flakes, ¾ teaspoon salt, the tomatoes, wine, and sugar, increase the heat to medium-high, and simmer until thickened, about 8 minutes.

4. Stir the shrimp with accumulated juices, the remaining 1 tablespoon garlic, and the parsley into the tomato sauce. Simmer until the shrimp have heated through, about 1 minute. Off the heat, stir in the remaining 1 tablespoon oil. Add ½ cup of the tomato sauce (no shrimp) to the pasta; toss to coat and adjust the consistency of the sauce with the reserved pasta cooking water as needed. Serve immediately, topping individual bowls with the sauce and shrimp.

MODERN SHRIMP FRA DIAVOLO

WHY THIS RECIPE WORKS: Shrimp *fra diavolo* is a classic 20th-century Italian American combo of shrimp, tomatoes, garlic, and hot pepper, often served over spaghetti or with crusty bread. At its best, it's lively and piquant, the tangy tomatoes countering the sweet and briny shrimp, and the pepper and garlic providing a spirited kick. Unfortunately, the spice is often so heavy-handed that it completely overwhelms the other flavors, and the fragile shrimp are often overcooked and flavorless, identifiable only by their shape. We wanted to preserve the fiery character of fra diavolo but also heighten the other flavors—particularly the brininess of the shrimp—so that they could stand up to the heat.

To build a rich, briny seafood base, we borrowed a technique from shrimp bisque: sautéing the shrimp shells in a little oil until they and the surface of the pan were spotty brown, then deglazing the pan with wine to pick up the flavorful fond. Some canned tomato liquid rounded out our shrimp "stock." To bloom the flavors of our aromatics, we sautéed

some garlic, red pepper flakes, oregano, and a couple of anchovy fillets for extra savory (but not fishy) seafood flavor. We added our stock back to the aromatics and used this flavorful sauce to gently poach the shrimp. At the end of cooking, we stirred in some minced pepperoncini and their brine for a boost of tangy heat. Handfuls of chopped basil and parsley lent freshness, and a drizzle of fruity extra-virgin olive oil made for a rich finish.

Shrimp Fra Diavolo
SERVES 4

If the shrimp you are using have been treated with salt (check the bag's ingredient list), skip the salting in step 1 and add ¼ teaspoon of salt to the sauce in step 3. Adjust the amount of pepper flakes depending on how spicy you want the dish. Serve the shrimp with a salad and crusty bread or over spaghetti. If serving with spaghetti, adjust the consistency of the sauce with some reserved pasta cooking water.

1½	pounds large shrimp (26 to 30 per pound), peeled and deveined (see page 240), shells reserved
	Salt
1	(28-ounce) can whole peeled tomatoes
3	tablespoons vegetable oil
1	cup dry white wine
4	garlic cloves, minced
½–1	teaspoon red pepper flakes
½	teaspoon dried oregano
2	anchovy fillets, rinsed, patted dry, and minced
¼	cup chopped fresh basil
¼	cup chopped fresh parsley
1½	teaspoons minced pepperoncini, plus 1 teaspoon brine
2	tablespoons extra-virgin olive oil

1. Toss shrimp with ½ teaspoon salt and set aside. Pour tomatoes into colander set over large bowl. Pierce tomatoes with edge of rubber spatula and stir briefly to release juice. Transfer drained tomatoes to small bowl and reserve juice. Do not wash colander.

2. Heat 1 tablespoon vegetable oil in 12-inch skillet over high heat until shimmering. Add shrimp shells and cook, stirring frequently, until they begin to turn spotty brown and skillet starts to brown, 2 to 4 minutes. Remove skillet from heat and carefully add wine. When bubbling subsides, return skillet to heat and simmer until wine is reduced to about 2 tablespoons, 2 to 4 minutes. Add reserved tomato juice and simmer to meld flavors, 5 minutes. Pour contents of skillet into colander set over bowl. Discard shells and reserve liquid. Wipe out skillet with paper towels.

3. Heat remaining 2 tablespoons vegetable oil, garlic, pepper flakes, and oregano in now-empty skillet over medium heat, stirring occasionally, until garlic is straw-colored and fragrant, 1 to 2 minutes. Add anchovies and stir until fragrant, about

30 seconds. Remove from heat. Add drained tomatoes and mash with potato masher until coarsely pureed. Return to heat and stir in reserved tomato juice mixture. Increase heat to medium-high and simmer until mixture has thickened, about 5 minutes.

4. Add shrimp to skillet and simmer gently, stirring and turning shrimp frequently, until they are just cooked through, 4 to 5 minutes. Remove pan from heat. Stir in basil, parsley, and pepperoncini and brine and season with salt to taste. Drizzle with olive oil and serve.

LINGUINE WITH SEAFOOD

WHY THIS RECIPE WORKS: To create a seafood pasta dish with rich, savory seafood flavor in every bite (not just in the pieces of shellfish), we made a sauce with clam juice and four minced anchovies, which fortified the juices shed by the shellfish. Cooking the shellfish in a careful sequence—precooking hardier clams and mussels first and then adding the shrimp and squid during the final few minutes of cooking—ensured that every piece was plump and tender. We parboiled the linguine and then finished cooking it directly in the sauce; the noodles soaked up flavor while shedding starches that thickened the sauce so that it clung well to the pasta. Fresh cherry tomatoes, lots of garlic, fresh herbs, and lemon made for a bright, clean, complex-tasting sauce.

Linguine with Seafood (Linguine allo Scoglio)
SERVES 6

For a simpler version of this dish, you can omit the clams and squid and increase the amounts of mussels and shrimp to 1½ pounds each; you'll also need to increase the amount of salt in step 2 to ¾ teaspoon. If you can't find fresh squid, it's available frozen at many supermarkets and typically has the benefit of being precleaned. Bar Harbor makes our favorite clam juice.

- 6 tablespoons extra-virgin olive oil
- 12 garlic cloves, minced
- ¼ teaspoon red pepper flakes
- 1 pound littleneck clams, scrubbed
- 1 pound mussels, scrubbed and debearded
- 1¼ pounds cherry tomatoes (half of tomatoes halved, remaining left whole)
- 1 (8-ounce) bottle clam juice
- 1 cup dry white wine
- 1 cup minced fresh parsley
- 1 tablespoon tomato paste
- 4 anchovy fillets, rinsed, patted dry, and minced
- 1 teaspoon minced fresh thyme
   Salt and pepper
- 1 pound linguine
- 1 pound extra-large shrimp (21 to 25 per pound), peeled and deveined (see page 240)
- ½ pound squid, sliced crosswise into ½-inch-thick rings
- 2 teaspoons grated lemon zest, plus lemon wedges for serving

1. Heat ¼ cup oil in large Dutch oven over medium-high heat until shimmering. Add garlic and pepper flakes and cook until fragrant, 1 minute. Add clams, cover, and cook, shaking pan occasionally, for 4 minutes. Add mussels, cover, and continue to cook, shaking pan occasionally, until clams and mussels have opened, 3 to 4 minutes longer. Transfer clams and mussels to bowl, discarding any that haven't opened, and cover to keep warm; leave any broth in pot.

2. Add whole tomatoes, clam juice, wine, ½ cup parsley, tomato paste, anchovies, thyme, and ½ teaspoon salt to pot and bring to simmer over medium-high heat. Reduce heat to medium and cook, stirring occasionally, until tomatoes have started to break down and sauce is reduced by one-third, about 10 minutes.

3. Meanwhile, bring 4 quarts water to boil in large pot. Add pasta and 1 tablespoon salt and cook, stirring often, for 7 minutes. Reserve ½ cup cooking water, then drain pasta.

4. Add pasta to sauce in Dutch oven and cook over medium heat, stirring gently, for 2 minutes. Reduce heat to medium-low, stir in shrimp, cover, and cook for 4 minutes. Stir in squid, lemon zest, halved tomatoes, and remaining ½ cup parsley; cover and continue to cook until shrimp and squid are just cooked through, about 2 minutes longer. Gently stir in clams and mussels. Remove pot from heat, cover, and let stand until clams and mussels are warmed through, about 2 minutes. Season with salt and pepper to taste and adjust consistency with reserved cooking water as needed. Transfer to large serving dish, drizzle with remaining 2 tablespoons oil, and serve, passing lemon wedges separately.

THE TEST KITCHEN'S TOP FIVE ESSENTIAL KITCHEN TOOLS

Face it: Americans are crazy about gadgets. Since the time of Benjamin Franklin, we have valued the ingenuity of the inventor who designs a simple tool that makes the execution of an everyday task easier. But as anyone who watches late-night television knows, America's love of the gadget can—and does—go too far at times. No one needs a syringe to inject marinades into meat.

So how do you know which gadgets work and which ones don't? That's where we can help. Here's our list of five gadgets you might not own, but really should. (See pages 872–903 for recommended brands.)

1. DIGITAL INSTANT-READ THERMOMETER: How else do you know when food is done? And, because it's digital, it works in seconds so your hands don't tarry in hot spots like the oven or grill.

2. LOCKING TONGS: Don't use a fork. Sturdy, long-handled tongs (with scalloped edges that won't pierce food) can turn, flip, rotate, stir, and more.

3. GARLIC PRESS: Stop kidding yourself. You're never going to mince garlic finely and evenly enough. A garlic press ensures consistent (and perfect) results every time.

4. OVEN THERMOMETER: News flash—your oven probably isn't properly calibrated. How do we know? We tested 20 home ovens and only a handful came close. You could pay big bucks to get your oven serviced by a professional or spend a few dollars on an oven thermometer so cookies don't burn and roasts are perfectly cooked.

5. KNIFE SHARPENER: Using dull knives is slow and unsafe. You wouldn't drive a car with nearly flat tires, would you? A fancy electric sharpener is nice, but even a good (and cheap) manual sharpener is far better than nothing.

RIGATONI WITH BEEF AND ONION RAGU

WHY THIS RECIPE WORKS: This rich, supple meat sauce was born out of thrift in 16th-century Naples. *La Genovese* began as a combination of beef and aromatic vegetables that were cooked down to make two meals: a savory sauce for pasta and another, separate meal of cooked beef. Later, most of the vegetables took a backseat to the onions, which became the foundation of this deeply flavorful sauce. To make the ultra-savory recipe work in a modern context, we decided to turn all the elements into one substantial sauce by shredding the meat into the sauce. To eliminate the need for intermittent stirring and monitoring during cooking, we moved the process from the stovetop to the even heat of the oven. A surprising ingredient—water—proved essential to extracting maximum flavor from the onions. We also added tomato paste for an extra boost of flavor and color. To encourage the sauce to cling to the pasta, we vigorously stirred them together so that the starch from the pasta added body to the sauce. A bit of grated Pecorino Romano brought the flavors together and added a mild tang.

Rigatoni with Beef and Onion Ragu
SERVES 6 TO 8

If marjoram is unavailable, substitute an equal amount of oregano. Pair this dish with a lightly dressed salad of assertively flavored greens.

1	(1- to 1¼-pound) boneless beef chuck-eye roast, cut into 4 pieces and trimmed of large pieces of fat Kosher salt and pepper
2	ounces pancetta, cut into ½-inch pieces
2	ounces salami, cut into ½-inch pieces
1	small carrot, peeled and cut into ½-inch pieces
1	small celery rib, cut into ½-inch pieces
2½	pounds onions, halved and cut into 1-inch pieces
2	tablespoons tomato paste
1	cup dry white wine
2	tablespoons minced fresh marjoram
1	pound rigatoni
1	ounce Pecorino Romano cheese, grated (½ cup), plus extra for serving

1. Sprinkle beef with 1 teaspoon salt and ½ teaspoon pepper and set aside. Adjust oven rack to lower-middle position and heat oven to 300 degrees.

2. Process pancetta and salami in food processor until ground to paste, about 30 seconds, scraping down sides of bowl as needed. Add carrot and celery and process 30 seconds longer, scraping down sides of bowl as needed. Transfer paste to Dutch oven and set aside; do not clean out processor bowl. Pulse onions in processor in 2 batches, until ⅛- to ¼-inch pieces form, 8 to 10 pulses per batch.

3. Cook pancetta mixture over medium heat, stirring frequently, until fat is rendered and fond begins to form on bottom of pot, about 5 minutes. Add tomato paste and cook, stirring constantly, until browned, about 90 seconds. Stir in 2 cups water, scraping up any browned bits. Stir in onions and bring to boil. Stir in ½ cup wine and 1 tablespoon marjoram. Add beef and push into onions to ensure that it is submerged. Transfer to oven and cook, uncovered, until beef is fully tender, 2 to 2½ hours.

4. Transfer beef to carving board. Place pot over medium heat and cook, stirring frequently, until mixture is almost completely dry. Stir in remaining ½ cup wine and cook for

2 minutes, stirring occasionally. Using 2 forks, shred beef into bite-size pieces. Stir beef and remaining 1 tablespoon marjoram into sauce and season with salt and pepper to taste. Remove from heat, cover, and keep warm.

5. Bring 4 quarts water to boil in large pot. Add rigatoni and 2 tablespoons salt and cook, stirring often, until just al dente. Drain rigatoni and add to warm sauce. Add Pecorino and stir vigorously over low heat until sauce is slightly thickened and rigatoni is fully tender, 1 to 2 minutes. Serve, passing extra Pecorino separately.

PASTA WITH HEARTY ITALIAN MEAT SAUCE

WHY THIS RECIPE WORKS: Traditional "Sunday gravy" is more than just meat sauce—it's a labor of love, an all-day kitchen affair, involving several types of meat, a bunch of tomatoes, and at least one Italian grandmother. We wanted to honor this meaty extravaganza but shortcut the cooking so we could get this traditional dish on the table in a reasonable amount of time. When you're using six or seven types of meat, the browning alone can take up to 40 minutes. Our first step was to limit the dish to just one kind of sausage and one pork cut—plus meatballs. Hot Italian links gave the sauce a mild kick; baby back ribs were our favorite cut of pork because they weren't too fatty and turned moist and tender in just a few hours. Meatloaf mix, a combination of ground beef, pork, and veal, produced juicy, tender meatballs, especially when mixed with a panade of bread and buttermilk. To further bump up flavor, we mixed in minced garlic, parsley, and red pepper flakes, plus an egg yolk for richness. To help the meatballs retain their shape we browned them first in a skillet before adding them to the sauce. For the tomato sauce, canned crushed tomatoes were a winner, leading to a sauce with nice thickness and bright tomato flavor. Instead of merely browning the tomato paste for 30 seconds, we cooked it until it nearly blackened, which concentrated its sweetness. The sauce was still lacking some beefy undercurrents; the best booster turned out to be the simple, straightforward addition of an ingredient rarely found in tomato sauce: beef broth.

Pasta with Hearty Italian Meat Sauce (Sunday Gravy)

SERVES 8 TO 10

We prefer meatloaf mix (a combination of ground beef, pork, and veal) for the meatballs in this recipe. Ground beef may be substituted, but the meatballs won't be as flavorful. Six tablespoons of plain yogurt thinned with 2 tablespoons of milk can be substituted for the buttermilk. Our preferred brand of crushed tomatoes is SMT. This recipe can be prepared through step 4 and then cooled and refrigerated in the Dutch oven for up to 2 days. To reheat, drizzle ½ cup water over the sauce (do not stir in) and warm on the lower-middle rack of a preheated 325-degree oven for 1 hour before proceeding with the recipe.

SAUCE

- 2 tablespoons olive oil
- 1 (2¼-pound) rack baby back ribs, cut into 2-rib sections
  Table salt and ground black pepper
- 1 pound hot Italian sausage links
- 2 medium onions, minced
- 1¼ teaspoons dried oregano
- 3 tablespoons tomato paste
- 4 medium garlic cloves, minced or pressed through a garlic press (about 4 teaspoons)
- 2 (28-ounce) cans crushed tomatoes (see note)
- ⅔ cup low-sodium beef broth

MEATBALLS AND PASTA

- 2 slices high-quality white sandwich bread, crusts removed and bread cut into ½-inch cubes
- ½ cup buttermilk (see note)
- ¼ cup chopped fresh parsley leaves
- 2 medium garlic cloves, minced or pressed through a garlic press (about 2 teaspoons)
- 1 large egg yolk
  Table salt
- ¼ teaspoon red pepper flakes
- 1 pound meatloaf mix (see note)
- 2 ounces thinly sliced prosciutto, minced
- 1 ounce Pecorino Romano cheese, grated (about ½ cup)
- ½ cup olive oil
- 1½ pounds spaghetti or linguine
- ¼ cup chopped fresh basil leaves
  Grated Parmesan cheese, for serving

1. FOR THE SAUCE: Adjust an oven rack to the lower-middle position and heat the oven to 325 degrees. Heat the oil in a large Dutch oven over medium-high heat until just smoking. Pat the ribs dry with paper towels and season with salt and pepper. Add half of the ribs to the pot and brown on both sides, 5 to 7 minutes total. Transfer the ribs to a large plate and repeat with the remaining ribs. After transferring the second batch of ribs to the plate, brown the sausages on all four sides, 5 to 7 minutes total. Transfer the sausages to the plate with the ribs.

2. Reduce the heat to medium, add the onions and oregano; cook, stirring occasionally, until beginning to brown, about 5 minutes. Add the tomato paste and cook, stirring constantly, until very dark, about 3 minutes. Stir in the garlic and cook until fragrant, about 30 seconds. Add the crushed tomatoes and broth, scraping up any browned bits. Return the ribs and sausage to the pot; bring to a simmer, cover, and transfer to the oven. Cook until the ribs are tender, about 2½ hours.

3. FOR THE MEATBALLS: Meanwhile, combine the bread cubes, buttermilk, parsley, garlic, egg yolk, ½ teaspoon salt, and the red pepper flakes in a medium bowl and mash with a fork until no bread chunks remain. Add the meatloaf mix, prosciutto, and Pecorino Romano to the bread mixture; mix with your hands until thoroughly combined. Divide the mixture into 12 pieces; roll into balls, transfer to a plate, cover with plastic wrap, and refrigerate until ready to use.

4. When the sauce is 30 minutes from being done, heat the oil in a large nonstick skillet over medium-high heat until shimmering. Add the meatballs and cook until well browned all over, 5 to 7 minutes. Transfer the meatballs to a paper towel–lined plate to drain briefly. Remove the sauce from the oven and skim the fat from the top with a large spoon. Transfer the browned meatballs to the sauce and gently submerge. Return the pot to the oven and continue cooking until the meatballs are just cooked through, about 15 minutes.

5. Meanwhile, bring 6 quarts water to a boil in a large pot. Add 2 tablespoons salt and the pasta to the boiling water and cook, stirring often, until al dente. Reserve ½ cup of the cooking water then drain the pasta and return it to the pot.

6. Using tongs, transfer the meatballs, ribs, and sausage to a serving platter and cut the sausages in half. Stir the basil into the sauce and season with salt and pepper to taste. Add 1 cup of the sauce and the reserved pasta cooking water to the pasta; toss to coat. Serve, passing the remaining sauce, meat platter, and Parmesan separately.

PASTA AND SLOW-SIMMERED TOMATO SAUCE WITH MEAT

WHY THIS RECIPE WORKS: Slow-simmered Italian meat sauce—the kind without meatballs—relies on pork for rich flavor. But the pork found in supermarkets is so lean, we weren't convinced that any of the options could provide enough fat and flavor. So we set out to create a flavorful meat sauce with fall-off-the-bone-tender meat that was made from readily available supermarket products. We used fattier country-style pork ribs which turned meltingly tender when cooked for a long time and added meaty flavor. Beef short ribs can also be used, but since they tend to be thicker, it's important to remember to let them cook a little longer. Red wine accentuated the meatiness of the sauce, which was built on a simple combination of sautéed onion and canned diced tomatoes.

Pasta and Slow-Simmered Tomato Sauce with Meat

SERVES 4 TO 6

This sauce can be made with either beef or pork ribs. Depending on their size, you will need 4 or 5 ribs.

    1   tablespoon olive oil
    1½ pounds pork spareribs or country-style ribs or
        beef short ribs, trimmed of fat (see note)
        Table salt and ground black pepper
    1   medium onion, minced
    ½   cup red wine
    1   (28-ounce) can diced tomatoes
    1   pound ziti, rigatoni, or other short tubular pasta
        Grated Parmesan cheese, for serving

1. Heat the oil in a 12-inch skillet over medium-high heat until shimmering. Season the ribs with salt and pepper and brown on all sides, turning occasionally, 8 to 10 minutes. Transfer the ribs to a plate; pour off all but 1 teaspoon fat from the skillet. Add the onion and cook until softened, 2 to 3 minutes. Add the wine and simmer, scraping up any browned bits, until the wine reduces to a glaze, about 2 minutes.

2. Return the ribs and accumulated juices to the skillet; add the tomatoes with their juice. Bring to a boil, then reduce the heat to low, cover, and simmer gently, turning the ribs several times, until the meat is very tender and falling off the bones, 1½ hours (for pork spareribs or country-style ribs) to 2 hours (for beef short ribs).

3. Transfer the ribs to a clean plate. When cool enough to handle, remove the meat from the bones and shred, discarding the fat and bones. Return the shredded meat to the sauce. Bring the sauce to a simmer over medium heat and cook, uncovered, until heated through and slightly thickened, about 5 minutes. Season with salt and pepper to taste. (The sauce can be refrigerated in an airtight container for up to 4 days or frozen for up to 2 months.)

4. Meanwhile, bring 4 quarts water to a boil in a large pot. Add 1 tablespoon salt and the pasta to the boiling water and cook, stirring often, until al dente. Reserve ½ cup of the cooking water then drain the pasta and return it to the pot. Add the sauce to the pasta and toss to combine. Adjust the consistency of the sauce with the reserved pasta cooking water as needed. Serve immediately, passing the Parmesan separately.

SIMPLE ITALIAN-STYLE MEAT SAUCE

WHY THIS RECIPE WORKS: Old-fashioned Italian-style meat sauces are on an old-fashioned time line—they require hours of simmering. But just giving browned ground beef, onions, garlic, and canned tomatoes a quick simmer produced lackluster flavor and meat with the texture of a rubber band. We wanted a quick, weeknight meat sauce with long-simmered flavor.

Our goal required concentrated flavor and tender meat. Browned chopped onions and mushrooms gave the sauce a rich base of flavor, and browning the mushrooms made them so soft and supple they practically disappeared into the finished sauce. Deglazing the pan with tomato paste and tomato juice further boosted flavor. To tenderize the meat, we incorporated a panade—a paste of bread and milk—into the meat before cooking; we combined the panade and the meat in a food processor to avoid chili-like chunks. We cooked the meat mixture just until it lost its raw color; any longer, and the meat would have turned dry and mealy. Finishing the meat in a combination of canned diced and crushed tomatoes gave us the best mix of textures. A handful of grated Parmesan, added just before serving, lent the sauce a tangy, complex character.

Simple Italian-Style Meat Sauce

MAKES ABOUT 6 CUPS

You can figure on about 3 cups of sauce per pound of pasta. Except for ground round (which tasters found spongy and bland), this recipe will work with most types of ground beef, as long as it is 85 percent lean. Use high-quality crushed tomatoes; our favorite brand is SMT. If using dried oregano, add the entire amount with the canned tomato liquid in step 2.

- 4 ounces white mushrooms, wiped clean and broken into rough pieces
- 1 large slice high-quality white sandwich bread, torn into quarters
- 2 tablespoons whole milk
  Table salt and ground black pepper
- 1 pound 85 percent lean ground beef (see note)

- 1 tablespoon olive oil
- 1 medium onion, minced
- 6 medium garlic cloves, minced or pressed through a garlic press (about 2 tablespoons)
- 1 tablespoon tomato paste
- ¼ teaspoon red pepper flakes
- 1 (14.5-ounce) can diced tomatoes, drained, ¼ cup juice reserved
- 1 tablespoon minced fresh oregano leaves or 1 teaspoon dried oregano (see note)
- 1 (28-ounce) can crushed tomatoes (see note)
- ¼ cup grated Parmesan cheese

1. Pulse the mushrooms in a food processor until finely chopped, about 8 pulses, scraping down the sides of the work-bowl as needed; transfer to a medium bowl. Add the bread, milk, ½ teaspoon salt, and ½ teaspoon black pepper to the food processor and pulse until a paste forms, about 8 pulses. Add the beef and pulse until the mixture is well combined, about 6 pulses.

2. Heat the oil in a large saucepan over medium-high heat until just smoking. Add the onion and mushrooms; cook, stirring frequently, until the vegetables are browned and dark bits form on the pan bottom, 6 to 12 minutes. Stir in the garlic, tomato paste, and red pepper flakes; cook until fragrant and the tomato paste starts to brown, about 1 minute. Add the ¼ cup reserved tomato juice and 2 teaspoons of the fresh oregano (if using dried, add the full amount), scraping the bottom of the pan with a wooden spoon to loosen the browned bits. Add the meat mixture and cook, breaking the meat into small pieces with a wooden spoon, until no longer pink, 2 to 4 minutes, making sure that the meat does not brown.

3. Stir in the diced and crushed tomatoes and bring to a simmer; reduce the heat to low and gently simmer until the sauce has thickened and the flavors have blended, about 30 minutes. Stir in the cheese and the remaining 1 teaspoon fresh oregano; season with salt and pepper to taste. (The sauce can be refrigerated in an airtight container for up to 3 days or frozen for up to 1 month.)

RAGU ALLA BOLOGNESE

WHY THIS RECIPE WORKS: Unlike meat sauces in which tomatoes dominate, Bolognese sauce is about the meat, with the tomatoes in a supporting role. We wanted a traditional recipe for this complexly flavored sauce, with rich meatiness up front and a good balance of sweet, salty, and acidic flavors. We also wanted a velvety texture that would lightly cling to the noodles. For an ultrameaty version, we used six different types of meat: ground beef, pork, and veal; pancetta; mortadella (bologna-like Italian deli meat); and chicken livers. These meats and the combination of red wine and tomato paste gave us a rich, complex sauce with balanced acidity. The addition of gelatin lent the sauce an ultra-silky texture.

Ragu alla Bolognese

MAKES ABOUT 6 CUPS

This recipe makes enough sauce for 2 pounds of pasta. Eight teaspoons of gelatin is equivalent to one (1-ounce) box of gelatin. If you can't find ground veal, use an additional ¾ pound of ground beef.

1	cup low-sodium chicken broth
1	cup beef broth
8	teaspoons unflavored gelatin
1	onion, chopped coarse
1	large carrot, peeled and chopped coarse
1	celery rib, chopped coarse
4	ounces pancetta, chopped
4	ounces mortadella, chopped
6	ounces chicken livers, trimmed
3	tablespoons extra-virgin olive oil
¾	pound 85 percent lean ground beef
¾	pound ground veal
¾	pound ground pork
3	tablespoons minced fresh sage
1	(6-ounce) can tomato paste
2	cups dry red wine
	Salt and pepper
1	pound pappardelle or tagliatelle
	Grated Parmesan cheese

1. Combine chicken broth and beef broth in bowl; sprinkle gelatin over top and set aside. Pulse onion, carrot, and celery together in food processor until finely chopped, about 10 pulses, scraping down bowl as needed; transfer to separate bowl. Pulse pancetta and mortadella together in now-empty food processor until finely chopped, about 25 pulses, scraping down bowl as needed; transfer to second bowl. Process chicken livers in now-empty food processor until pureed, about 5 seconds; transfer to third bowl.

2. Heat oil in Dutch oven over medium-high heat until shimmering. Add beef, veal, and pork; cook, breaking up pieces with wooden spoon, until all liquid has evaporated and meat begins to sizzle, 10 to 15 minutes. Add pancetta mixture and sage; cook, stirring frequently, until pancetta is translucent, 5 to 7 minutes, adjusting heat as needed to keep fond from burning. Add chopped vegetables and cook, stirring frequently, until softened, 5 to 7 minutes. Add tomato paste and cook, stirring constantly, until rust-colored and fragrant, about 3 minutes.

3. Stir in wine, scraping up any browned bits. Simmer until sauce has thickened, about 5 minutes. Stir in broth mixture and return to simmer. Reduce heat to low and cook at bare simmer until thickened (wooden spoon should leave trail when dragged through sauce), about 1½ hours.

4. Stir in pureed chicken livers, bring to boil, and remove from heat. Season with salt and pepper to taste; cover and keep warm.

5. Bring 4 quarts water to boil in large pot. Add pasta and 1 tablespoon salt and cook, stirring often, until al dente. Reserve ¾ cup cooking water, then drain pasta and return it to pot. Add half of sauce and cooking water to pasta and toss to combine. Transfer to serving bowl and serve, passing Parmesan separately. (Leftover sauce may be refrigerated for up to 3 days or frozen for up to 1 month.)

PASTA WITH SLOW-SIMMERED BOLOGNESE SAUCE

WHY THIS RECIPE WORKS: There are many different ways to interpret what "real" bolognese sauce is. But no matter what the ingredients are, the sauce should be hearty and rich, with plenty of meaty character.

We started simple—with just onions, carrots, and celery, sautéed in butter. Meatloaf mix provided the right amount of meatiness and kept our shopping list short. For the most tender texture, we cooked the meat just until it lost its pink color and didn't let it brown. For dairy, which is used to tenderize the meat and give the sauce a rich, appealing flavor, we used milk. Once the milk had reduced, we added white wine, which gave the sauce a delicate brightness. For the tomato element, diced canned tomatoes imparted sweet, acidic notes. Finally, we simmered the sauce at the lowest possible heat for about three hours and served it with rich, eggy fettuccine.

Fettuccine with Slow-Simmered Bolognese Sauce

SERVES 4

Don't drain the pasta of its cooking water too meticulously when using this sauce; a little water left clinging to the noodles will help distribute the very thick sauce evenly over the noodles, as will the addition of 2 tablespoons of butter along with the sauce. If doubling this recipe, increase the simmering times for the milk and the wine to 30 minutes each, and increase the simmering time once the tomatoes are added to 4 hours. You can substitute equal amounts of 80 percent lean ground beef, ground veal, and ground pork for the meatloaf mix (the total amount of meat should be ¾ pound).

- 5 tablespoons unsalted butter
- 2 tablespoons minced onion
- 2 tablespoons minced carrot
- 2 tablespoons minced celery
- ¾ pound meatloaf mix (see note)
  Table salt
- 1 cup whole milk
- 1 cup dry white wine
- 1 (28-ounce) can diced tomatoes
- 1 pound fresh or dried fettuccine
  Grated Parmesan cheese, for serving

1. Melt 3 tablespoons of the butter in a large Dutch oven over medium heat. Add the onion, carrot, and celery and cook until softened but not browned, about 6 minutes. Add the meat and ½ teaspoon salt; crumble the meat into tiny pieces with a wooden spoon. Cook, continuing to crumble the meat, just until it loses its raw color but has not yet browned, about 3 minutes.

2. Add the milk and simmer until the milk evaporates and only rendered fat remains, 10 to 15 minutes. Add the wine and simmer until the wine evaporates, 10 to 15 minutes longer. Add the tomatoes with their juice and bring to a simmer. Reduce the heat to low so that the sauce continues to simmer just barely, with an occasional bubble or two at the surface, until the liquid has evaporated, about 3 hours. Season with salt to taste. (The sauce can be refrigerated in an airtight container for up to 3 days or frozen for up to 1 month.)

3. Bring 4 quarts water to a boil in a large pot. Add 1 tablespoon salt and the pasta to the boiling water and cook, stirring often, until al dente. Reserve ½ cup of the cooking water then drain the pasta and return it to the pot. Add the sauce and remaining 2 tablespoons butter; toss to combine. Adjust the consistency of the sauce with the reserved pasta cooking water as needed. Serve, passing the Parmesan separately.

NOTES FROM THE TEST KITCHEN

IMPROVING A FLAME TAMER

A flame tamer fits over the burner to reduce the heat to a bare simmer. To make one, take a long sheet of heavy-duty aluminum foil and shape it into a 1-inch-thick ring. Make sure the ring is of an even thickness so that the pot will rest flat on it.

PASTA WITH STREAMLINED BOLOGNESE SAUCE

WHY THIS RECIPE WORKS: Bolognese often gets its big flavor from braising ground meat and softened vegetables in slowly reducing milk, wine, and tomatoes. The process typically takes about three hours. But on a busy weeknight, we rarely have that much time to spend making dinner. We wanted to streamline Bolognese into a weeknight-friendly dinner. Using a food processor to chop the vegetables, including a big can of whole tomatoes with their juice, cut down on preparation time. To develop sweetness in the sauce without the day-long simmering, we reduced white wine in a separate pan and added it to the sauce at the end; a little bit of sugar, stirred in with the garlic to help it caramelize, amplified the sweetness. Instead of browning the ground meat, we cooked it with milk, which helped to break down and soften the meat in a short amount of time. To beef up the meaty flavor of the sauce, we added chopped pancetta, dried porcini mushrooms, and the flavorful liquid left behind from rehydrating the mushrooms. In about an hour, our sauce was ready, with all the rich meatiness of a long-simmered Bolognese.

Pasta with Streamlined Bolognese Sauce
SERVES 4 TO 6
Sweet white wines such as Gewürztraminer, Riesling, and even white Zinfandel work especially well in this sauce. To obtain the best texture, be careful not to break up the meat too much when cooking it with the milk in step 4; with additional cooking and stirring, it will continue to break up. Just about any pasta shape complements this meaty sauce, but spaghetti and linguine are the test kitchen favorites. If using pancetta that has been sliced thin rather than cut into 1-inch chunks, reduce the processing time in step 3 from 30 seconds to about 5 seconds. You can substitute equal amounts of 80 percent lean ground beef, ground veal, and ground pork for the meatloaf mix (the total amount of meat should be 1¼ pounds).

- ½ ounce dried porcini mushrooms
- 1¼ cups sweet white wine (see note)
- ½ small carrot, peeled and chopped coarse (about ½ cup)
- ½ small onion, chopped coarse (about ¼ cup)
- 3 ounces pancetta, cut into 1-inch chunks (see note)
- 1 (28-ounce) can whole tomatoes
- 1½ tablespoons unsalted butter
- 1 teaspoon sugar
- 1 small garlic clove, minced or pressed through a garlic press (about ½ teaspoon)
- 1¼ pounds meatloaf mix (see note)
- 1½ cups whole milk
- 2 tablespoons tomato paste
  Table salt
- ⅛ teaspoon ground black pepper
- 1 pound pasta (see note)
  Grated Parmesan cheese, for serving

1. Combine the porcini and ½ cup water in a small microwave-safe bowl; cover the bowl with plastic wrap, cut three vents for steam with a knife, and microwave on high power for 30 seconds. Let stand until the mushrooms have softened, about 5 minutes. Transfer the mushrooms to a second small bowl and reserve the liquid; pour the liquid through a paper towel–lined mesh strainer. Set the mushrooms and the strained liquid aside.

2. Bring the wine to a simmer in a 10-inch nonstick skillet over medium heat; reduce the heat to low and continue to simmer until the wine is reduced to 2 tablespoons, about 20 minutes. Set aside.

3. Meanwhile, pulse the carrot in a food processor until broken down into ¼-inch pieces, about 10 pulses. Add the onion and pulse until the vegetables are broken down into ⅛-inch pieces, about 10 pulses. Transfer the vegetables to a small bowl. Process the reserved mushrooms until well ground, about 15 seconds, scraping down the sides of the workbowl as needed. Transfer the mushrooms to the bowl with the vegetables. Process the pancetta until the pieces are no larger than ¼ inch, 30 to 35 seconds, scraping down the sides of the workbowl as needed; transfer to a small bowl. Pulse the tomatoes with their juice until chopped fine, about 8 pulses.

4. Melt the butter in a 12-inch skillet over medium-high heat. Cook the pancetta, stirring frequently, until well browned, about 2 minutes. Add the carrot, onion, and mushrooms and cook, stirring frequently, until the vegetables are softened but not browned, about 4 minutes. Add the sugar and garlic and cook until fragrant, about 30 seconds. Add the meat, breaking it into 1-inch pieces with a wooden spoon, and cook for about 1 minute. Add the milk and stir to break the meat into ½-inch pieces; bring to a simmer, reduce the heat to medium, and cook, stirring to break the meat into smaller pieces, until most of the liquid has evaporated and the meat begins to sizzle, 18 to 20 minutes. Stir in the tomato paste and cook until combined, about 1 minute. Add the tomatoes, reserved mushroom soaking liquid, ¼ teaspoon salt, and the pepper; bring to a simmer over medium-high heat, then reduce the heat to medium and simmer until the liquid is reduced and the sauce is thickened, 12 to 15 minutes. Stir in the reduced wine and simmer to blend the flavors, about 5 minutes.

5. Meanwhile, bring 4 quarts water to a boil in a large pot. Add 1 tablespoon salt and the pasta to the boiling water and cook, stirring often, until al dente. Reserve ½ cup of the cooking water then drain the pasta and return it to the pot. Add 2 cups of the sauce and 2 tablespoons of the reserved pasta cooking water to the pasta; toss to combine and adjust the consistency of the sauce with the remaining reserved pasta cooking water as needed. Serve immediately, topping individual bowls with ¼ cup sauce and passing the Parmesan separately.

WEEKNIGHT BOLOGNESE

WHY THIS RECIPE WORKS: To create a Bolognese sauce that could come together quickly on a busy weeknight but rival the depth and richness of a long-cooked version, we started by browning the aromatic vegetables (but not the ground beef, which would dry out and toughen if seared) to develop a flavorful fond; we also treated the ground beef with a baking soda solution to ensure that it stayed tender. Adding pancetta, which we ground and browned deeply with the aromatic vegetables, boosted the sauce's meaty flavor, and a healthy dose of tomato paste added depth and brightness. We also added Parmesan cheese, usually reserved for serving, directly to the sauce as it cooked for its umami richness. To develop concentrated flavor and a consistency that nicely coated the pasta, we boiled beef broth until it was reduced by half (mixing up a concentrated beef broth using our recommended product, Better Than Bouillon Roasted Beef Base, also works) and added it to the sauce, which then needed to simmer only 30 minutes longer. Finally, we intentionally made the sauce thin because the eggy noodles (traditionally tagliatelle or pappardelle) absorb a lot of liquid; once they have soaked up some of the sauce, it will coat the noodles beautifully.

Weeknight Tagliatelle with Bolognese Sauce
SERVES 4 TO 6

If you use our recommended beef broth, Better Than Bouillon Roasted Beef Base, you can skip step 2 and make a concentrated broth by adding 4 teaspoons paste to 2 cups water. To ensure the best flavor, be sure to brown the pancetta-vegetable mixture in step 4 until the fond on the bottom of the pot is quite dark. The cooked sauce will look thin but will thicken once tossed with the pasta. Tagliatelle is a long, flat, dry egg pasta that is about ¼ inch wide; if you can't find it, you can substitute pappardelle. Substituting other pasta may result in a too-wet sauce.

1 pound 93 percent lean ground beef

2 tablespoons water

¼ teaspoon baking soda

  Salt and pepper

4 cups beef broth

6 ounces pancetta, chopped coarse

1 onion, chopped coarse

1 large carrot, peeled and chopped coarse

1 celery rib, chopped coarse

1 tablespoon unsalted butter

1 tablespoon extra-virgin olive oil

3 tablespoons tomato paste

1 cup dry red wine

1 ounce Parmesan cheese, grated (½ cup),
  plus extra for serving

1 pound tagliatelle

1. Toss beef with water, baking soda, and ¼ teaspoon pepper in bowl until thoroughly combined. Set aside.

2. While beef sits, bring broth to boil over high heat in large pot (this pot will be used to cook pasta in step 6) and cook until reduced to 2 cups, about 15 minutes; set aside.

3. Pulse pancetta in food processor until finely chopped, 15 to 20 pulses. Add onion, carrot, and celery and pulse until vegetables are finely chopped and mixture has paste-like consistency, 12 to 15 pulses, scraping down sides of bowl as needed.

4. Heat butter and oil in large Dutch oven over medium-high heat until shimmering. When foaming subsides, add pancetta-vegetable mixture and ¼ teaspoon pepper and cook, stirring occasionally, until liquid has evaporated, about 8 minutes. Spread mixture in even layer in bottom of pot and continue to cook, stirring every couple of minutes, until very dark browned bits form on bottom of pot, 7 to 12 minutes longer. Stir in tomato paste and cook until paste is rust-colored and bottom of pot is dark brown, 1 to 2 minutes.

5. Reduce heat to medium, add beef, and cook, using wooden spoon to break meat into pieces no larger than ¼ inch, until beef has just lost its raw pink color, 4 to 7 minutes. Stir in wine, scraping up any browned bits, and bring to simmer. Cook until wine has evaporated and sauce has thickened, about 5 minutes. Stir in broth and Parmesan. Return sauce to simmer; cover, reduce heat to low, and simmer for 30 minutes (sauce will look thin). Remove from heat and season with salt and pepper to taste.

6. Rinse pot that held broth. While sauce simmers, bring 4 quarts water to boil in now-empty pot. Add pasta and 1 tablespoon salt and cook, stirring occasionally, until al dente. Reserve ¼ cup cooking water, then drain pasta. Add pasta to pot with sauce and toss to combine. Adjust sauce consistency with reserved cooking water as needed. Transfer to platter or individual bowls and serve, passing extra Parmesan separately.

SPAGHETTI AND MEATBALLS

WHY THIS RECIPE WORKS: One of the problems with meatballs is that they're thought of as smaller, rounder versions of hamburgers. This would be fine if meatballs were cooked to rare or medium-rare, as most hamburgers are, but meatballs are usually cooked to well-done. This can leave them flavorless, dry, and dense, so they need some help to lighten their texture. What we were after was nothing short of great meatballs: crusty and dark brown on the outside and soft and moist on the inside.

White bread soaked in buttermilk added as a binder gave the meatballs a creamy texture and an appealing tang. Eggs were also important for texture and flavor; their fats and emulsifiers added moistness and richness. Egg yolks alone worked best and kept the meatballs moist and light; the whites just made the mixture sticky and hard to handle, with no other added benefits. Adding some ground pork to the usual ground beef enhanced the flavor. Broiling dried out the meatballs; pan-frying was the best way to brown the meatballs and kept the interior moist. Finally, building the tomato sauce on top of the browned bits left in the pan after frying the meatballs made for a hearty, robust-tasting sauce.

Spaghetti and Meatballs

SERVES 4 TO 6

The shaped meatballs can be covered with plastic wrap and refrigerated for several hours ahead of serving time; fry the meatballs and make the sauce at the last minute. If you don't have buttermilk, you can substitute 6 tablespoons of plain yogurt thinned with 2 tablespoons of milk.

MEATBALLS

2 slices high-quality white sandwich bread, crusts
   removed and bread torn into small pieces
½ cup buttermilk (see note)
¾ pound 85 percent lean ground beef
¼ pound ground pork
¼ cup grated Parmesan cheese
2 tablespoons minced fresh parsley leaves
1 large egg yolk
1 medium garlic clove, minced or pressed through
   a garlic press (about 1 teaspoon)
¾ teaspoon table salt
⅛ teaspoon ground black pepper
   Vegetable oil, for pan-frying

TOMATO SAUCE AND PASTA

2 tablespoons extra-virgin olive oil
1 medium garlic clove, minced or pressed through
   a garlic press (about 1 teaspoon)
1 (28-ounce) can crushed tomatoes
1 tablespoon minced fresh basil leaves
   Table salt and ground black pepper
1 pound spaghetti
   Grated Parmesan cheese, for serving

1. FOR THE MEATBALLS: Mash the bread and buttermilk to a smooth paste in a large bowl. Let stand for 10 minutes.

2. Add the beef, pork, cheese, parsley, egg yolk, garlic, salt, and pepper to the mashed bread; stir gently until uniform. Gently form into 1½-inch round meatballs (about 14 meatballs). (When forming the meatballs use a light touch; if you compact the meatballs too much, they can become dense and hard.)

3. Pour the vegetable oil into a 12-inch skillet until it measures a depth of ¼ inch. Heat over medium-high heat until shimmering. Add the meatballs in a single layer and cook until nicely browned on all sides, about 10 minutes. Transfer the meatballs to a paper towel–lined plate and discard the oil left in the skillet.

4. FOR THE SAUCE: Add the olive oil and garlic to the skillet and cook over medium heat, scraping up any browned bits, until fragrant, about 30 seconds. Add the tomatoes with their juice, bring to a simmer, and cook until the sauce thickens, about 10 minutes. Stir in the basil and season with salt and pepper to taste. Add the meatballs and simmer, turning them occasionally, until heated through, about 5 minutes.

5. Meanwhile, bring 4 quarts water to a boil in a large pot. Add 1 tablespoon salt and the pasta to the boiling water and cook, stirring often, until al dente. Reserve ½ cup of the cooking water then drain the pasta and return it to the pot. Stir in several large spoonfuls of the tomato sauce (without meatballs) over the pasta and toss to coat. Adjust the consistency of the sauce with the reserved pasta cooking water as needed. Serve immediately, topping individual bowls with more tomato sauce and several meatballs and passing the Parmesan separately.

MAKING MEATBALLS

1. Use a fork to mash the bread and buttermilk into a smooth paste.

2. Working with 3 tablespoons of the meatball mixture at a time, form the mixture into a 1½-inch ball by gently rolling it between your palms.

3. Fry the meatballs, turning every so often, until they are a crusty golden brown all over.

SPAGHETTI AND MEATBALLS FOR A CROWD

WHY THIS RECIPE WORKS: Making spaghetti and meatballs for a crowd can try the patience of even the toughest Italian grandmother. We sought an easier way. Roasting them on a wire rack made our recipe faster. Adding powdered gelatin to a mix of ground chuck and pork served to plump the meatballs and lent them a soft richness. Prosciutto gave the meatballs extra meatiness, and a panade, which we made with panko, kept the meat moist and prevented it from getting tough. To create a rich sauce, we braised the meatballs in marinara sauce for about an hour. To make sure the sauce didn't overreduce, we swapped half the crushed tomatoes in our marinara recipe for an equal portion of tomato juice.

Classic Spaghetti and Meatballs for a Crowd
SERVES 12

If you don't have buttermilk, you can substitute 1 cup whole-milk plain yogurt thinned with ½ cup whole milk. Grate the onion on the large holes of a box grater. You can cook the pasta in two separate pots if you do not have a large enough pot to cook all of the pasta together. Once cooked, the sauce and the meatballs can be cooled and refrigerated for up to 2 days. To reheat, drizzle ½ cup of water over the sauce, without stirring, and reheat on the lower-middle rack of a 325-degree oven for 1 hour.

MEATBALLS

- 2¼ cups panko bread crumbs
- 1½ cups buttermilk (see note)
- 1½ teaspoons unflavored gelatin
- 3 tablespoons water
- 2 pounds 85 percent lean ground beef
- 1 pound ground pork
- 6 ounces thinly sliced prosciutto, chopped fine
- 3 large eggs
- 3 ounces Parmesan cheese, grated (about 1½ cups)
- 6 tablespoons minced fresh parsley leaves
- 3 medium garlic cloves, minced or pressed through a garlic press (about 1 tablespoon)
- 1½ teaspoons table salt
- ½ teaspoon ground black pepper

SAUCE

- 3 tablespoons extra-virgin olive oil
- 1 large onion, grated
- 6 medium garlic cloves, minced or pressed through a garlic press (about 2 tablespoons)
- 1 teaspoon dried oregano
- ½ teaspoon red pepper flakes
- 3 (28-ounce) cans crushed tomatoes
- 6 cups tomato juice
- 6 tablespoons dry white wine
  Table salt and ground black pepper
- ½ cup minced fresh basil leaves
- 3 tablespoons minced fresh parsley leaves
  Sugar

- 3 pounds spaghetti
- 2 tablespoons table salt
  Grated Parmesan cheese, for serving

1. FOR THE MEATBALLS: Adjust the oven racks to the lower-middle and upper-middle positions and heat the oven to 450 degrees. Set 2 wire racks in 2 aluminum foil–lined rimmed baking sheets and spray the racks with vegetable oil spray.

2. Combine the bread crumbs and buttermilk in a large bowl and let sit, mashing occasionally with a fork, until a smooth paste forms, about 10 minutes. Meanwhile, sprinkle the gelatin over the water in a small bowl and allow to soften for 5 minutes.

3. Mix the ground beef, ground pork, prosciutto, eggs, Parmesan, parsley, garlic, salt, pepper, and gelatin mixture into the bread-crumb mixture using your hands. Pinch off and roll the mixture into 2-inch meatballs (about 40 meatballs total) and arrange on the prepared sheets. Bake until well browned, about 30 minutes, switching and rotating the sheets halfway through baking.

4. FOR THE SAUCE: While the meatballs bake, heat the oil in a Dutch oven over medium heat until shimmering. Add the onion and cook until softened and lightly browned, 5 to 7 minutes. Stir in the garlic, oregano, and red pepper flakes and cook until fragrant, about 30 seconds. Stir in the crushed tomatoes, tomato juice, wine, 1½ teaspoons salt, and ¼ teaspoon pepper, bring to a simmer, and cook until thickened slightly, about 15 minutes.

5. Remove the meatballs from the oven and reduce the oven temperature to 300 degrees. Gently nestle the meatballs into the sauce. Cover, transfer to the oven, and cook until the meatballs are firm and the sauce has thickened, about 1 hour.

6. Meanwhile, bring 10 quarts water to boil in a 12-quart pot. Add the pasta and salt and cook, stirring often, until al dente. Reserve ½ cup of the cooking water, then drain the pasta and return it to the pot.

7. Gently stir the basil and parsley into the sauce and season with sugar, salt, and pepper to taste. Add 2 cups of the sauce (without meatballs) to the pasta and toss to combine, adding the reserved cooking water to adjust the consistency as needed. Serve, topping individual portions with more tomato sauce and several meatballs and passing the Parmesan separately.

SAUSAGE MEATBALLS AND SPAGHETTI

WHY THIS RECIPE WORKS: For a change of pace, we wanted to use Italian sausage to create meatballs that were full of bold flavor but still tender. To temper sausage's springy texture, we added ground pork, brined with baking soda and salt to impart tenderness and help the meat retain juices. A panade made with heavy cream brought more fat into the mix, which would coat the meat's proteins and prevent them from sticking

together. Pulsing the meat mixture in a food processor cut the panade into the meat for even incorporation, and processing the meat in stages kept it from turning tough from overworking. To really highlight the bold, seasoned flavors of Italian sausage, we added a reinforcing dose of the classic spices already present in the meat: coarsely ground fennel seeds, oregano, black pepper, and red pepper flakes. We baked the meatballs in a hot oven to quickly brown them in a single batch. A simple tomato sauce was all we needed to complement the spiced-up sausage meatballs, so we sautéed garlic in oil and added both crushed tomatoes and tomato sauce for bright but smooth results. After a quick simmer, we stirred in fresh basil and added the meatballs to the pot to finish cooking.

Sausage Meatballs and Spaghetti

SERVES 4 TO 6

The fennel seeds can be coarsely ground in a spice grinder or using the bottom of a heavy skillet. Use a light touch when rolling the meatballs to prevent them from being dense. A #30 scoop, loosely filled, works well for portioning the meatballs.

MEATBALLS

- ½ teaspoon salt
- ¼ teaspoon baking soda
- 4 teaspoons water
- 12 ounces ground pork
- 2 slices hearty white sandwich bread, crusts removed, cut into ½-inch pieces
- ⅓ cup heavy cream
- ⅓ cup grated Parmesan cheese, plus extra for serving
- 2 large egg yolks
- 2 garlic cloves, minced
- 1 teaspoon fennel seeds, coarsely ground
- 1 teaspoon dried oregano
- 1 teaspoon pepper
- ½ teaspoon red pepper flakes
- 12 ounces sweet Italian sausage, casings removed and broken into 1-inch pieces

TOMATO SAUCE

- 2 tablespoons extra-virgin olive oil
- 1 garlic clove, minced
- 1 (28-ounce) can crushed tomatoes
- 1 (15-ounce) can tomato sauce
  Salt
- 1 tablespoon chopped fresh basil

- 1 pound spaghetti

1. FOR THE MEATBALLS: Adjust oven rack to upper middle position and heat oven to 500 degrees. Place wire rack in aluminum foil–lined rimmed baking sheet. Spray wire rack with vegetable oil spray.

2. Dissolve salt and baking soda in water in large bowl. Add pork and fold gently to combine; let stand for 10 minutes.

3. Pulse bread, cream, Parmesan, egg yolks, garlic, fennel seeds, oregano, pepper, and pepper flakes in food processor until smooth paste forms, about 10 pulses, scraping down sides of bowl as needed. Add pork mixture (do not wash out bowl) and pulse until mixture is well combined, about 5 pulses.

4. Transfer half of pork mixture to now-empty large bowl. Add sausage to food processor and pulse until just combined, 4 to 5 pulses. Transfer sausage-pork mixture to large bowl with pork mixture. Using your hands, gently fold together until mixture is just combined.

5. With your wet hands, lightly shape mixture into 1¾-inch round meatballs (about 1 ounce each); you should have about 24 meatballs. Arrange meatballs, evenly spaced, on prepared rack and bake until browned, about 15 minutes, rotating sheet halfway through baking.

6. FOR THE TOMATO SAUCE: While meatballs bake, heat oil in Dutch oven over medium heat until shimmering. Add garlic and cook, stirring frequently, until fragrant, about 30 seconds. Stir in crushed tomatoes, tomato sauce, and ¼ teaspoon salt and bring to boil. Reduce heat and simmer gently until slightly thickened, about 10 minutes. Stir in basil and season with salt to taste.

7. Add meatballs to sauce and gently simmer, turning them occasionally, until cooked through, 5 to 10 minutes. Cover and keep warm over low heat.

8. Bring 4 quarts water to boil in large pot. Add pasta and 1 tablespoon salt and cook, stirring often, until al dente. Reserve ½ cup cooking water, then drain pasta and return it to pot.

9. Add ½ cup sauce and ¼ cup reserved cooking water to pasta and toss to combine. Transfer pasta to large serving platter and top with meatballs and remaining sauce, adjusting consistency with remaining reserved cooking water as needed. Serve, passing extra Parmesan separately.

ITALIAN-STYLE TURKEY MEATBALLS

WHY THIS RECIPE WORKS: Our turkey meatballs rival those made from beef or pork, thanks to a few test kitchen tricks. We started with 85 or 93 percent lean turkey; these fattier options produced moister meatballs. Next, we added an egg and fresh bread crumbs to help bind the meatballs. And a stint in the fridge was key to firming up the gelatin and creating juicy texture. To boost meaty flavor, we added glutamate-rich ingredients such as Parmesan cheese, anchovies, tomato paste, and rehydrated dried shiitake mushrooms.

Italian-Style Turkey Meatballs

SERVES 4 TO 6

Serve with spaghetti.

1 cup chicken broth
½ ounce dried shiitake mushrooms
2 slices hearty white sandwich bread, torn into 1-inch pieces
1 ounce Parmesan cheese, grated (½ cup), plus extra for serving
1 tablespoon chopped fresh parsley
1½ teaspoons unflavored gelatin
Salt and pepper
4 anchovy fillets, rinsed, patted dry, and minced
1½ pounds 85 or 93 percent lean ground turkey
1 large egg, lightly beaten
4 garlic cloves, minced
1 (14.5-ounce) can whole peeled tomatoes
½ teaspoon dried oregano
⅛ teaspoon red pepper flakes
3 tablespoons extra-virgin olive oil
2 tablespoons tomato paste
¼ cup chopped fresh basil
Sugar

1. Microwave broth and mushrooms in covered bowl until steaming, about 1 minute. Let sit until softened, about 5 minutes. Drain mushrooms in fine-mesh strainer and reserve liquid.

2. Pulse bread in food processor until finely ground, 10 to 15 pulses; transfer bread crumbs to large bowl (do not wash processor bowl). Add Parmesan, parsley, gelatin, 1 teaspoon salt, and ¼ teaspoon pepper to bowl with bread crumbs and mix until thoroughly combined. Pulse mushrooms and half of anchovies in food processor until chopped fine, 10 to 15 pulses.

Add mushroom mixture, turkey, egg, and half of garlic to bowl with bread-crumb mixture and mix with your hands until thoroughly combined. Divide mixture into 16 portions (about ¼ cup each). Using your hands, roll each portion into ball; transfer meatballs to plate and refrigerate for 15 minutes.

3. Pulse tomatoes and their juice in food processor to coarse puree, 10 to 15 pulses. Combine oregano, pepper flakes, remaining anchovies, remaining garlic, and ¼ teaspoon pepper in small bowl; set aside.

4. Heat oil in 12-inch nonstick skillet over medium-high heat until shimmering. Add meatballs and cook until well browned all over, 5 to 7 minutes. Transfer meatballs to paper towel–lined plate, leaving fat in skillet.

5. Add reserved anchovy mixture to skillet and cook, stirring constantly, until fragrant, about 30 seconds. Increase heat to high; stir in tomato paste, reserved mushroom liquid, and pureed tomatoes; and bring to simmer. Return meatballs to skillet, reduce heat to medium-low, cover, and cook until meatballs register 160 degrees, 12 to 15 minutes, turning meatballs once. Transfer meatballs to platter, increase heat to high, and simmer sauce until slightly thickened, 3 to 5 minutes. Stir in basil and season with sugar, salt, and pepper to taste. Pour sauce over meatballs and serve, passing extra Parmesan separately.

PENNE WITH VODKA SAUCE

WHY THIS RECIPE WORKS: Splashes of vodka and cream can turn run-of-the-mill tomato sauce into luxurious restaurant fare—or a heavy, boozy mistake. Despite the simple ingredients, we found recipes for penne alla vodka gave us results that varied widely. Many were absurdly rich (with more cream than tomatoes) and others were too harsh from a heavy hand with the vodka. We wanted to fine-tune this modern classic to strike the right balance of sweet, tangy, spicy, and creamy.

To achieve a sauce with the right consistency, we pureed half the tomatoes (which helped the sauce cling nicely to the pasta) and cut the rest into chunks. For sweetness, we added sautéed minced onions; for depth of flavor, we used a bit of tomato paste. We found we needed a liberal amount of vodka to cut through the richness and add "zinginess" to the sauce, but we needed to add it to the tomatoes early on to allow the alcohol to mostly (but not completely) cook off and prevent a boozy flavor. Adding a little heavy cream to the sauce gave it a nice consistency, and we finished cooking the penne in the sauce to encourage cohesiveness.

Penne with Vodka Sauce (Penne alla Vodka)

SERVES 4 TO 6

So that the sauce and pasta finish cooking at the same time, drop the pasta into the boiling water just after adding the vodka to the sauce.

1 (28-ounce) can whole tomatoes, drained, juice reserved
2 tablespoons olive oil
½ small onion, minced
1 tablespoon tomato paste
2 medium garlic cloves, minced or pressed through a garlic press (about 2 teaspoons)
¼ teaspoon red pepper flakes
  Table salt
⅓ cup vodka
½ cup heavy cream
1 pound penne
2 tablespoons minced fresh basil leaves
  Grated Parmesan cheese, for serving

1. Puree half of the tomatoes in a food processor until smooth. Dice the remaining tomatoes into ½-inch pieces, discarding the cores. Combine the pureed and diced tomatoes in a liquid measuring cup (you should have about 1⅔ cups). Add the reserved juice to equal 2 cups.

2. Heat the oil in a large saucepan over medium heat until shimmering. Add the onion and tomato paste and cook, stirring occasionally, until the onion is light golden around the edges, about 3 minutes. Add the garlic and red pepper flakes; cook, stirring constantly, until fragrant, about 30 seconds.

3. Stir in the tomatoes and ½ teaspoon salt. Remove the pan from the heat and add the vodka. Return the pan to medium-high heat and simmer briskly until the alcohol flavor is cooked off, 8 to 10 minutes; stir frequently and lower the heat to medium if the simmering becomes too vigorous. Stir in the cream and cook until hot, about 1 minute.

4. Meanwhile, bring 4 quarts water to a boil in a large pot. Add 1 tablespoon salt and the pasta to the boiling water. Cook, stirring often, until just shy of al dente. Reserve ½ cup of the cooking water then drain the pasta and return it to the pot. Add the sauce to the pasta and toss over medium heat until the pasta absorbs some of the sauce, 1 to 2 minutes. Adjust the consistency of the sauce with the reserved pasta cooking water as needed. Stir in the basil and season with salt to taste. Serve immediately, passing the Parmesan separately.

FOOLPROOF SPAGHETTI CARBONARA

WHY THIS RECIPE WORKS: This quintessential Roman pasta dish is made with simple ingredients, but the results are often disappointing. The finicky egg-based sauce (made from either whole eggs or just yolks, plus finely grated cheese) relies on the heat of the warm pasta to become lush and glossy, but that rarely happens without the addition of tons of fat. We wanted to make a classic carbonara that was foolproof but not so rich that eating a full serving was impossible.

We started by replacing the hard-to-find *guanciale*, or cured pork jowl, with good old American bacon. To approximate the meaty chew of guanciale, we cooked the bacon with a little water, which produced tender-chewy pieces. We used just a

touch of the rendered fat in our sauce for consistent bacon flavor in every bite. To make a richly eggy sauce that wouldn't become dry and clumpy when mixed with the pasta, we used three eggs and an extra yolk for richness. But the real secret here was adding starch in the form of pasta water. Boiling the pasta in half the usual amount of water gave us extra starchy water to coat the proteins and fats in the cheese, preventing them from separating or clumping, making for a perfectly velvety sauce. Tossing the spaghetti with the sauce in a warm serving bowl allowed the warm pasta to gently "cook" the carbonara sauce without overcooking the eggs.

Foolproof Spaghetti Carbonara
SERVES 4

It's important to work quickly in steps 2 and 3. The heat from the cooking water and the hot spaghetti will "cook" the sauce only if used immediately. Warming the mixing and serving bowls helps the sauce stay creamy. Use a high-quality bacon for this dish; our favorites are Farmland Thick Sliced Bacon and Vande Rose Farms Artisan Dry Cured Bacon, Applewood Smoked.

8 slices bacon, cut into ½-inch pieces
½ cup water
3 garlic cloves, minced
2½ ounces Pecorino Romano, grated (1¼ cups)
3 large eggs plus 1 large yolk
1 teaspoon pepper
1 pound spaghetti
1 teaspoon salt

1. Bring bacon and water to simmer in 10-inch nonstick skillet over medium heat; cook until water evaporates and bacon begins to sizzle, about 8 minutes. Reduce heat to medium-low and continue to cook until fat renders and bacon browns, 5 to 8 minutes longer. Add garlic and cook, stirring constantly, until fragrant, about 30 seconds. Strain bacon mixture through fine-mesh strainer set in bowl. Set aside bacon mixture. Measure out 1 tablespoon fat and place in medium bowl. Whisk Pecorino, eggs and yolk, and pepper into fat until combined.

2. Meanwhile, bring 2 quarts water to boil in Dutch oven. Set colander in large bowl. Add spaghetti and salt to pot; cook, stirring frequently, until al dente. Drain spaghetti in colander set in bowl, reserving cooking water. Pour 1 cup cooking water into liquid measuring cup and discard remainder. Return spaghetti to now-empty bowl.

3. Slowly whisk ½ cup reserved cooking water into Pecorino mixture. Gradually pour Pecorino mixture over spaghetti, tossing to coat. Add bacon mixture and toss to combine. Let spaghetti rest, tossing frequently, until sauce has thickened slightly and coats spaghetti, 2 to 4 minutes, adjusting consistency with remaining reserved cooking water if needed. Serve immediately.

CLASSIC SPAGHETTI ALLA CARBONARA

WHY THIS RECIPE WORKS: Spaghetti carbonara is a mainstay on Italian restaurant menus, but the velvety, bacon-laced sauce can be elusive for the home cook. Three eggs, mixed with a combination of Pecorino-Romano and Parmesan cheeses, made a silky sauce that could cling to the spaghetti. Raw garlic gave the sauce a bit of zing without being overpowering, but we deemed heavy cream an unnecessary addition, since it weighed down the dish and dulled the cheese flavor. In place of the traditional *guanciale* (salt-cured pork jowl), we used American bacon, which we sautéed to give our dish the perfect crunch and a hint of sweetness and smoke. For added brightness, white wine was just the thing. The acidity of the wine cut through the richness of the bacon for a lighter, brighter sauce. We found that the mixing method was key to this dish; mixing the hot spaghetti with the egg and cheese mixture before gently tossing in the crispy pieces of bacon ensured that every bite was perfect.

Classic Spaghetti alla Carbonara
SERVES 4 TO 6

Although we call for spaghetti in this recipe, you can substitute linguine or fettuccine.

- ¼ cup extra-virgin olive oil
- 8 ounces (about 8 slices) bacon, halved lengthwise and cut into ¼-inch pieces
- ½ cup dry white wine
- 3 large eggs
- 1½ ounces Parmesan cheese, grated (about ¾ cup)
- ¼ cup grated Pecorino Romano cheese
- 1 large garlic clove, minced or pressed through a garlic press (about 1½ teaspoons)
- 1 pound spaghetti (see note)
  Table salt and ground black pepper

1. Adjust an oven rack to the lower-middle position, set an ovensafe serving bowl on the rack, and heat the oven to 200 degrees. Bring 4 quarts water to a boil in a large pot.

2. While the water is heating, heat the oil in a large skillet over medium heat until shimmering. Add the bacon and cook, stirring occasionally, until crisp, about 8 minutes. Add the wine and simmer until it is slightly reduced, 6 to 8 minutes. Remove from the heat and cover. Whisk the eggs, cheeses, and garlic together in a small bowl; set aside.

3. When the water comes to a boil, add 1 tablespoon salt and the pasta. Cook, stirring often, until al dente. Reserve ½ cup of the cooking water; drain the pasta. Remove the warm bowl from the oven and add the pasta. Immediately pour the egg and bacon mixtures over the pasta, season with salt and pepper to taste, and toss to coat; adjust the consistency of the sauce with the reserved pasta cooking water as needed. Serve immediately.

FETTUCCINE ALFREDO

WHY THIS RECIPE WORKS: Fettuccine Alfredo—tender pasta bathed in a silky, creamy cheese sauce—always sounds so tempting. But too often, restaurant-style fettuccine Alfredo means gargantuan portions, overcooked pasta, and a sauce that quickly congeals in the bowl (or your stomach). We were after a better Alfredo, with a luxurious sauce that remained supple and velvety from the first bite of pasta to the last. We first discovered that fresh pasta was essential as a base—dried noodles didn't hold on to the sauce, and the delicate nature of fresh pasta brought a more sophisticated tone to the dish. Turning our attention to the sauce, we found that a light hand was necessary when adding two of the richer ingredients: the cheese and the butter. Smaller amounts were sufficient to add distinctive flavor without being overwhelming. To manage the heavy cream, we reduced a portion of it, then added the remaining amount uncooked. This technique produced not only a luxurious texture but also a fresher flavor. A pinch of freshly grated nutmeg added a spicy, sweet undertone to this elegant dish.

Fettuccine Alfredo
SERVES 4 TO 6

Fresh pasta is the best choice for this dish; supermarkets sell 9-ounce containers of fresh pasta in the refrigerated section. When boiling the pasta, undercook it slightly (just shy of al dente) because the pasta cooks an additional minute or two in the sauce just before serving. Note that fettuccine Alfredo must be served immediately; it does not hold or reheat well.

- 1½ cups heavy cream
- 2 tablespoons unsalted butter
  Table salt
- ¼ teaspoon ground black pepper
- 9 ounces fresh fettuccine (see note)
- 1½ ounces Parmesan cheese, grated (about ¾ cup)
- ⅛ teaspoon grated nutmeg

1. Bring 1 cup of the heavy cream and the butter to a simmer in a medium saucepan over medium heat; reduce the heat to low and simmer gently until the mixture reduces to ⅔ cup, 12 to 15 minutes. Off the heat, stir in the remaining ½ cup cream, ½ teaspoon salt, and the pepper.

2. While the cream reduces, bring 4 quarts water to a boil in a large pot. Add 1 tablespoon salt and the pasta to the boiling water and cook, stirring often, until just shy of al dente. Reserve ¼ cup of the cooking water then drain the pasta and return it to the pot.

3. Meanwhile, return the cream mixture to a simmer over medium-high heat; reduce the heat to low and add the pasta, cheese, and nutmeg to the cream mixture. Cook over low heat, tossing the pasta to combine, until the cheese is melted, the sauce coats the pasta, and the pasta is just al dente, 1 to 2 minutes. Stir in the reserved pasta cooking water and toss to coat; the sauce may look thin but will gradually thicken as the pasta is served. Serve immediately.

SEMOLINA GNOCCHI

WHY THIS RECIPE WORKS: Unlike the pillowy dumplings we often associate with gnocchi, Roman-style semolina gnocchi bears a stronger resemblance to polenta. The dough is made from a hearty combination of semolina flour, butter, egg, and cheese. To begin, we whisked flour into hot milk with a touch of woodsy nutmeg. Butter and egg were added to boost the dough's richness. Gruyère added big flavor without watering down the mixture and minced rosemary contributed warm, savory notes. Baking powder promised great lift without compromising the texture. While some traditional recipes stamp out the gnocchi rounds like biscuits, we used a wet measuring cup to portion out the gnocchi onto a tray. Chilling the rounds before baking kept the dumplings from fusing together in the oven.

Semolina Gnocchi (Gnocchi alla Romana)
SERVES 4 TO 6

Serve as a side dish or as a light entrée topped with Quick Tomato Sauce (recipe follows).

- 2½ cups whole milk
- ¾ teaspoon salt
-   Pinch ground nutmeg
- 1 cup (6 ounces) fine semolina flour
- 4 tablespoons unsalted butter
- 1 large egg, lightly beaten
- 1½ ounces Gruyère cheese, shredded (⅓ cup)
- 1 teaspoon minced fresh rosemary
- ½ teaspoon baking powder
- 2 tablespoons grated Parmesan cheese

MAKING SEMOLINA GNOCCHI
By making a very stiff dough and then refrigerating the shaped dumplings before shingling them in the pan, we ensure that they don't fuse together in the oven.

1. Slowly whisk semolina into warm milk mixture. Cook over low heat until stiff dough forms. Add butter, egg, cheese, rosemary, and baking powder.

2. Use moistened ¼ cup measure to portion gnocchi, inverting onto tray.

3. Shingle gnocchi in greased 8-inch square dish, then sprinkle with Parmesan and bake.

1. Adjust oven rack to middle position and heat oven to 400 degrees. Heat milk, salt, and nutmeg in medium saucepan over medium-low heat until bubbles form around edges of saucepan. Whisking constantly, slowly add semolina to milk mixture. Reduce heat to low and cook, stirring often with rubber spatula, until mixture forms stiff mass that pulls away from sides when stirring, 3 to 5 minutes. Remove from heat and let cool for 5 minutes.

2. Stir 3 tablespoons butter and egg into semolina mixture until incorporated. (Mixture will appear separated at first but will become smooth and a bit shiny.) Stir in Gruyère, rosemary, and baking powder until incorporated.

3. Fill small bowl with water. Moisten ¼-cup dry measuring cup with water and scoop even portion of semolina mixture. Invert gnocchi onto tray or large plate. Repeat, moistening measuring cup between scoops to prevent sticking. Place tray of gnocchi, uncovered, in refrigerator for 30 minutes. (Gnocchi can be refrigerated, covered, for up to 24 hours.)

4. Rub interior of 8-inch square baking dish with remaining 1 tablespoon butter. Shingle gnocchi in pan, creating 3 rows of 4 gnocchi each. Sprinkle gnocchi with Parmesan. Bake until tops of gnocchi are golden brown, 35 to 40 minutes. Let cool for 15 minutes before serving.

Quick Tomato Sauce

MAKES ABOUT 3 CUPS

Our favorite brand of crushed tomatoes is SMT.

- 2 tablespoons unsalted butter
- ¼ cup grated onion
- 1 teaspoon minced fresh oregano or ¼ teaspoon dried
  Salt and pepper
- 2 garlic cloves, minced
- 1 (28-ounce) can crushed tomatoes
- ¼ teaspoon sugar
- 2 tablespoons chopped fresh basil
- 1 tablespoon extra-virgin olive oil

Melt butter in medium saucepan over medium heat. Add onion, oregano, and ½ teaspoon salt and cook, stirring occasionally, until onion is softened and lightly browned, 5 to 7 minutes. Stir in garlic and cook until fragrant, about 30 seconds. Stir in tomatoes and sugar, bring to simmer, and cook until slightly thickened, about 10 minutes. Off heat, stir in basil and oil and season with salt and pepper to taste.

POTATO GNOCCHI

WHY THIS RECIPE WORKS: Good potato gnocchi are something of a culinary paradox; light, airy pillows created from dense, starchy ingredients. The method is simple: knead mashed potatoes into a dough with a minimum of flour; shape; and boil for a minute. And yet the potential pitfalls are numerous (lumpy mashed potatoes, too much or too little flour, a heavy hand when kneading, and bland flavor). We wanted a foolproof recipe for impossibly light gnocchi with unmistakable potato flavor. Baking russets (parcooked in the microwave for speed and ease) produced intensely flavored potatoes—an excellent start to our gnocchi base. To avoid lumps, which can cause gnocchi to break apart during cooking, we turned to a ricer for a smooth, supple mash. While many recipes offer a range of flour to use, which ups the chances of overworking the dough (and producing leaden gnocchi), we used an exact amount based on the ratio of potato to flour so that our gnocchi dough was mixed as little as possible. And we found that an egg, while not traditional, tenderized our gnocchi further, delivering delicate pillow-like dumplings.

Potato Gnocchi with Browned Butter and Sage Sauce

SERVES 4

Gnocchi, like many baking recipes, require accurate measurement to achieve the proper texture; it's best to weigh the potatoes and flour. After processing, you may have slightly more than the 3 cups (16 ounces) of potatoes required for this recipe; do not be tempted to use more than 3 cups. If you prefer, replace the browned butter sauce with Gorgonzola-Cream Sauce or Parmesan Sauce with Pancetta and Walnuts (recipes follow).

MAKING RIDGES ON GNOCCHI

To make ridges on gnocchi, hold a fork with the tines facing down. Press each dough piece (cut side down) against the tines with your thumb to make an indentation. Roll the dumpling down the tines to create ridges on the sides.

POTATO GNOCCHI

- 2 pounds russet potatoes
- 1 large egg, lightly beaten
- ¾ cup plus 1 tablespoon (4 ounces) unbleached all-purpose flour, plus extra for the work surface
  Table salt

BROWNED BUTTER AND SAGE SAUCE

- 4 tablespoons (½ stick) unsalted butter, cut into 4 pieces
- 1 small shallot, minced (about 2 tablespoons)
- 1 teaspoon minced fresh sage leaves
- 1½ teaspoons juice from 1 lemon
- ¼ teaspoon table salt

1. FOR THE GNOCCHI: Adjust an oven rack to the middle position and heat the oven to 450 degrees. Poke each potato 8 times with a paring knife over the entire surface. Place the potatoes on a plate and microwave until slightly softened at the ends, about 10 minutes, flipping the potatoes halfway through cooking. Transfer the potatoes directly to the oven rack and bake until a skewer glides easily through the flesh and the potatoes yield to gentle pressure, 18 to 20 minutes.

2. Hold a potato with a pot holder or kitchen towel and peel with a paring knife. Process the potato through a ricer or food mill onto a rimmed baking sheet. Repeat with the remaining potatoes. Gently spread the riced potatoes into an even layer and cool for 5 minutes.

3. Transfer 3 cups (16 ounces) warm potatoes to a large bowl. Using a fork, gently stir in the egg until just combined. Sprinkle the flour and 1 teaspoon salt over the potato mixture. Using a fork, gently combine until no pockets of dry flour remain. Press the mixture into a rough dough, transfer to a lightly floured work surface and gently knead until smooth but slightly sticky, about 1 minute, lightly dusting the work surface with flour as needed to prevent sticking.

4. Line 2 rimmed baking sheets with parchment paper and dust liberally with flour. Cut the dough into 8 pieces. Lightly dust the work surface with flour. Gently roll one piece of dough into a ½-inch-thick rope, dusting with flour to prevent sticking. Cut the rope into ¾-inch lengths. Following the photo, hold a fork, with the tines facing down, in one hand and press the side of each piece of dough against the ridged surface with your thumb to make an indentation in the center; roll the dough down and off the tines to form ridges. Transfer the formed gnocchi to the prepared sheets and repeat with the remaining dough.

5. FOR THE SAUCE: Melt the butter in a 12-inch skillet over medium-high heat, swirling occasionally, until the butter is browned and releases a nutty aroma, about 1½ minutes. Off the heat, add the shallot and sage, stirring until the shallot is fragrant, about 1 minute. Stir in the lemon juice and the salt and cover to keep warm.

6. Bring 4 quarts water to a boil in a large pot. Add 1 tablespoon salt. Using the parchment paper as a sling, add half of the gnocchi and cook until firm and just cooked through, about 90 seconds (the gnocchi should float to the surface after about 1 minute). Remove the gnocchi with a slotted spoon, transfer to the skillet with the sauce, and cover to keep warm. Repeat with the remaining gnocchi and transfer to the skillet. Gently toss the gnocchi with the sauce to combine, and serve.

Gorgonzola-Cream Sauce

MAKES ABOUT 1 CUP

Adjust the consistency of the sauce with up to 2 tablespoons cooking water before adding the gnocchi to it.

- ¾ cup heavy cream
- ¼ cup dry white wine
- 4 ounces Gorgonzola cheese, crumbled (about 1 cup)
- 2 tablespoons minced fresh chives
  Table salt and ground black pepper

Bring the cream and wine to a simmer in a 12-inch skillet over medium-high heat. Gradually add the Gorgonzola while whisking constantly and cook until melted and the sauce is thickened, 2 to 3 minutes. Stir in the chives and season with salt and pepper to taste. Remove from the heat and cover to keep warm.

Parmesan Sauce with Pancetta and Walnuts

MAKES ABOUT 1 CUP

Serve gnocchi prepared with this sauce with extra grated Parmesan cheese on the side.

- ½ cup low-sodium chicken broth
- 1 ounce Parmesan cheese, grated (about ½ cup)
- ¼ cup heavy cream
- 2 large egg yolks
- ⅛ teaspoon ground black pepper
- 2 teaspoons olive oil
- 3 ounces pancetta, chopped fine
- ½ cup walnuts, chopped coarse
  Table salt

Whisk the broth, Parmesan, cream, yolks, and pepper together in a bowl until smooth. Heat the oil in a 12-inch skillet over medium heat until shimmering. Add the pancetta and cook until crisp, 5 to 7 minutes. Stir in the walnuts and

cook until golden and fragrant, about 1 minute. Off the heat, gradually add the broth mixture, whisking constantly. Return the skillet to medium heat and cook, stirring often, until the sauce is thickened slightly, 2 to 4 minutes. Season with salt to taste. Remove from the heat and cover to keep warm.

BAKED CHEESY PASTA CASSEROLE

WHY THIS RECIPE WORKS: We love macaroni and cheese (who doesn't?), but sometimes we want a more sophisticated version than the typical neon orange mac and cheese. Enter the classic Italian iteration of macaroni and cheese, *pasta ai quattro formaggi*, made with four cheeses and heavy cream. We set out to make a four-cheese creamy pasta casserole with great flavor, properly cooked pasta, and a crisp bread-crumb topping.

The cheese was first up for consideration; for the best flavor and texture, we used Italian fontina, Gorgonzola, Pecorino Romano, and Parmesan cheeses. Heating the cheese and cream together made a greasy, curdled mess, so instead we built a basic white sauce (a béchamel) by cooking butter with flour and then adding cream. Combining the hot sauce and pasta with the cheese—and not cooking the cheese in the sauce—preserved the fresh flavor of the different cheeses. Knowing the pasta would spend some time in the oven, we drained it before it was al dente so it wouldn't turn to mush when baked. Topped with bread crumbs and more Parmesan, and baked briefly in a very hot oven, our pasta dinner was silky smooth and rich but not heavy—a grown-up, sophisticated version of macaroni and cheese with Italian flavors.

Creamy Baked Four-Cheese Pasta

SERVES 4 TO 6

To streamline the process, prepare the bread-crumb topping and shred, crumble, and grate the cheeses while you wait for the pasta water to boil.

    2   slices high-quality white sandwich bread,
        torn into quarters
    1   ounce Parmesan cheese, grated (about ½ cup)
        Table salt and ground black pepper
    4   ounces Italian fontina cheese, rind removed,
        shredded (about 1 cup)
    3   ounces Gorgonzola cheese, crumbled (about ¾ cup)
    1   ounce Pecorino Romano cheese, grated (about ½ cup)
    1   pound penne
    2   teaspoons unsalted butter
    2   teaspoons unbleached all-purpose flour
 1½   cups heavy cream

1. Pulse the bread in a food processor to coarse crumbs, about 10 to 15 pulses. Transfer to a small bowl. Stir in ¼ cup of the Parmesan, ¼ teaspoon salt, and ⅛ teaspoon pepper; set aside.

2. Adjust an oven rack to the middle position and heat the oven to 500 degrees.

3. Bring 4 quarts water to a boil in a large pot. Combine the remaining ¼ cup Parmesan and the fontina, Gorgonzola, and Pecorino Romano cheeses in a large bowl; set aside. Add 1 tablespoon salt and the pasta to the boiling water and cook, stirring often.

4. While the pasta is cooking, melt the butter in a small saucepan over medium-low heat. Whisk in the flour until no lumps remain, about 30 seconds. Gradually whisk in the cream, increase the heat to medium, and bring to a boil, stirring occasionally; reduce the heat to medium-low and simmer for 1 minute longer. Stir in ¼ teaspoon salt and ¼ teaspoon pepper; cover and set aside.

5. When the pasta is just shy of al dente, drain it, leaving it slightly wet. Add the pasta to the bowl with the cheeses; immediately pour the cream mixture over, then cover the bowl and let stand for 3 minutes. Uncover the bowl and stir with a rubber spatula, scraping the bottom of the bowl, until the cheeses are melted and the mixture is thoroughly combined.

6. Transfer the pasta to a 13 by 9-inch baking dish, then sprinkle evenly with the reserved bread crumbs, pressing down lightly. Bake until the topping is golden brown, about 7 minutes. Serve immediately.

BAKED ZITI

WHY THIS RECIPE WORKS: Most versions of baked ziti seem like they went directly from the pantry into the oven, calling for little more than cooked pasta, jarred tomato sauce, a container of ricotta, and some preshredded cheese. The results: overcooked ziti in a dull, grainy sauce topped with a rubbery mass of mozzarella. We wanted to rescue baked ziti so we could have perfectly al dente pasta, a rich and flavorful sauce, and melted cheese in every bite.

For a sauce that's big on flavor and light on prep, we cooked sautéed garlic with two canned products—diced tomatoes and tomato sauce. Fresh basil and dried oregano added aromatic flavor. Just when the tomato sauce seemed perfect, we added ricotta, and a familiar problem reared its head: Rather than baking up creamy and rich, the ricotta was grainy and dulled the sauce. Cottage cheese was the best choice for a replacement—its curds have a texture similar to ricotta, but are creamier and tangier. For more flavor, we combined the cottage cheese with eggs, Parmesan, and heavy cream thickened with cornstarch. Adding this milky, tangy mixture to the tomato sauce produced a sauce that was bright, rich, and creamy.

When it came to the pasta, we undercooked it and then baked it with a generous amount of sauce for perfectly al dente pasta and plenty of sauce left to keep our baked ziti moist. As for the mozzarella, we cut it into small cubes instead of shredding it, which dotted the finished casserole with gooey bits of cheese.

Baked Ziti

SERVES 8 TO 10

We prefer baked ziti made with heavy cream, but whole milk can be substituted by increasing the amount of cornstarch to 2 teaspoons and increasing the cooking time in step 3 by 1 to 2 minutes. Our preferred brand of mozzarella is Polly-O. Part-skim mozzarella can also be used.

    1   pound whole-milk or 1 percent cottage cheese
    2   large eggs, lightly beaten
    3   ounces Parmesan cheese, grated (about 1½ cups)
        Table salt
    1   pound ziti or other short tubular pasta
    2   tablespoons extra-virgin olive oil
    5   medium garlic cloves, minced or pressed through
        a garlic press (about 5 teaspoons)
    1   (28-ounce) can tomato sauce
    1   (14.5-ounce) can diced tomatoes
    1   teaspoon dried oregano
  ½   cup plus 2 tablespoons chopped fresh basil leaves
    1   teaspoon sugar
        Ground black pepper
  ¾   teaspoon cornstarch
    1   cup heavy cream (see note)
    8   ounces whole-milk mozzarella cheese, cut into
        ¼-inch pieces (about 1½ cups; see note)

1. Adjust an oven rack to the middle position and heat the oven to 350 degrees. Whisk the cottage cheese, eggs, and 1 cup of the Parmesan together in a medium bowl; set aside. Bring 4 quarts water to a boil in a large pot. Add 1 tablespoon salt and the pasta; cook, stirring occasionally, until the pasta begins to soften but is not yet cooked through, 5 to 7 minutes. Drain the pasta and leave in the colander (do not wash the pot).

2. Meanwhile, heat the oil and garlic in a 12-inch skillet over medium heat until the garlic is fragrant but not brown, about 2 minutes. Stir in the tomato sauce, diced tomatoes, and oregano; simmer until thickened, about 10 minutes. Off the heat, stir in ½ cup of the basil and the sugar; season with salt and pepper to taste.

3. Stir the cornstarch and heavy cream together in a small bowl; transfer the mixture to the now-empty pasta pot set over medium heat. Bring to a simmer and cook until thickened, 3 to 4 minutes. Remove the pot from the heat and add the cottage cheese mixture, 1 cup of the tomato sauce, and ¾ cup of the mozzarella; stir to combine. Add the pasta and stir to coat thoroughly with the sauce.

4. Transfer the pasta to a 13 by 9-inch baking dish and spread the remaining tomato sauce evenly over the pasta. Sprinkle the remaining ¾ cup mozzarella and remaining ½ cup Parmesan over the top. Cover the baking dish tightly with foil and bake for 30 minutes.

5. Remove the foil and continue to cook until the cheese is bubbling and beginning to brown, about 30 minutes longer. Cool for 20 minutes. Sprinkle with the remaining 2 tablespoons basil and serve.

MANICOTTI

WHY THIS RECIPE WORKS: Despite being composed of a straightforward collection of ingredients (pasta, cheese, and tomato sauce), manicotti is surprisingly fussy to prepare. Blanching, shocking, draining, and stuffing slippery pasta requires a lot of patience and time. We wanted an easy-to-prepare recipe that still produced great-tasting manicotti.

Our biggest challenge was filling the slippery manicotti tubes. We solved the problem by discarding the tubes completely and spreading the filling onto a lasagna noodle, which we then rolled up. For the lasagna noodles, we found that the no-boil variety were ideal. We soaked the noodles in boiling water for 5 minutes until pliable, then used the tip of a knife to separate them and prevent sticking. For the cheese filling, we taste-tested several ricottas and found that part-skim had an ideal level of richness. Eggs, Parmesan, and an ample amount of mozzarella added richness, flavor, and structure to the ricotta filling. For a quick but brightly flavored tomato sauce, we pureed canned diced tomatoes and simmered them until slightly thickened with sautéed garlic and red pepper flakes, then finished the sauce with fresh basil.

Baked Manicotti

SERVES 6 TO 8

We prefer Barilla no-boil lasagna noodles for their delicate texture resembling fresh pasta. Note that Pasta Defino and Ronzoni brands contain only 12 no-boil noodles per package; the recipe requires 16 noodles. The manicotti can be prepared through step 5, covered with a sheet of parchment paper, wrapped in aluminum foil, and refrigerated for up to 3 days or frozen for up to 1 month. (If frozen, thaw the manicotti in the refrigerator for 1 to 2 days.) To bake, remove the parchment, replace the aluminum foil, and increase the baking time to 1 to 1¼ hours.

TOMATO SAUCE

- 2 (28-ounce) cans diced tomatoes
- 2 tablespoons extra-virgin olive oil
- 3 medium garlic cloves, minced or pressed through a garlic press (about 1 tablespoon)
- ½ teaspoon red pepper flakes (optional)
  Table salt
- 2 tablespoons chopped fresh basil leaves

CHEESE FILLING AND PASTA

- 3 cups part-skim ricotta cheese
- 4 ounces Parmesan cheese, grated (about 2 cups)
- 8 ounces whole-milk mozzarella cheese, shredded (about 2 cups)
- 2 large eggs, lightly beaten
- 2 tablespoons chopped fresh parsley leaves
- 2 tablespoons chopped fresh basil leaves
- ¾ teaspoon table salt
- ½ teaspoon ground black pepper
- 16 no-boil lasagna noodles (see note)

1. FOR THE SAUCE: Adjust an oven rack to the middle position and heat the oven to 375 degrees. Pulse 1 can of the tomatoes with their juice in a food processor until coarsely chopped, 3 to 4 pulses. Transfer to a bowl. Repeat with the remaining can of tomatoes.

2. Heat the oil, garlic, and red pepper flakes (if using) in a large saucepan over medium heat until fragrant but not brown, 1 to 2 minutes. Stir in the tomatoes and ½ teaspoon salt and simmer until thickened slightly, about 15 minutes. Stir in the basil; season with salt to taste.

3. FOR THE CHEESE FILLING: Combine the ricotta, 1 cup of the Parmesan, the mozzarella, eggs, parsley, basil, salt, and pepper in a medium bowl; set aside.

4. Pour 2 inches boiling water into a 13 by 9-inch broiler-safe baking dish. Slip the noodles into the water, one at a time, and let them soak until pliable, about 5 minutes, separating them with the tip of a knife to prevent sticking. Remove the noodles from the water and place in a single layer on clean kitchen towels. Discard the water and dry the baking dish.

5. Spread the bottom of the baking dish evenly with 1½ cups of the sauce. Using a spoon, spread ¼ cup of the cheese mixture evenly onto the bottom three-quarters of each noodle (with the short side facing you), leaving the top quarter of the noodle exposed. Roll into a tube shape and arrange in the baking dish, seam side down. Top evenly with the remaining sauce, making certain that the pasta is completely covered.

6. Cover the baking dish tightly with foil and bake until bubbling, about 40 minutes. Remove the baking dish from the oven and remove the foil. Adjust the oven rack to the uppermost position (about 6 inches from the heating element) and heat the broiler. Sprinkle the manicotti evenly with the remaining 1 cup Parmesan. Broil until the cheese is spotty brown, 4 to 6 minutes. Cool for 15 minutes; cut into pieces and serve.

NOTES FROM THE TEST KITCHEN

BAKED MANICOTTI

1. Using spoon, spread about ¼ cup of filling evenly over bottom three-quarters of each noodle, leaving top quarter of noodles exposed.

2. Starting at bottom, roll each noodle up around filling, and lay in prepared baking dish, seam side down.

SIMPLE CHEESE LASAGNA

WHY THIS RECIPE WORKS: While removing both meat and vegetables from lasagna makes it a much simpler affair, it can result in a dish lacking in texture, flavor, and stature. This recipe works by upgrading the basic components—tomato sauce, cheese, and noodles—to star players. Tomato paste, minced anchovies, grated Pecorino Romano, and a dash of sugar boosted the complexity and body of the sauce, while a small can of diced tomatoes added texture to the smoother crushed tomato base. We switched out the usual trio of cheeses for more-flavorful alternatives, replacing ricotta with cottage cheese (mixed into a no-cook sauce with heavy cream, more Pecorino Romano, and seasonings); mozzarella with fontina; and Parmesan with Pecorino Romano. To give the casserole more structure and bite, we used traditional wavy lasagna noodles but treated them like the no-boil variety by briefly soaking them in boiling water. Staggering the noodles in the dish instead of lining them up parallel to one another prevented the casserole from buckling as it baked.

Simple Cheese Lasagna

SERVES 8

Do not substitute no-boil noodles for regular noodles, as they are too thin. Alternating the noodle arrangement in step 4 keeps the lasagna from buckling. For a vegetarian version, omit the anchovies.

CHEESE SAUCE

- 4 ounces Pecorino Romano cheese, grated (2 cups)
- 8 ounces (1 cup) cottage cheese
- ½ cup heavy cream
- 2 garlic cloves, minced
- 1 teaspoon cornstarch
- ¼ teaspoon salt
- ¼ teaspoon pepper

TOMATO SAUCE

- ¼ cup extra-virgin olive oil
- 1 onion, chopped fine
- 1½ teaspoons sugar
- ½ teaspoon red pepper flakes
- ½ teaspoon dried oregano
- ½ teaspoon salt
- 4 garlic cloves, minced
- 8 anchovy fillets, rinsed, patted dry, and minced
- 1 (28-ounce) can crushed tomatoes
- 1 (14.5-ounce) can diced tomatoes, drained
- ¼ cup tomato paste
- 1 ounce Pecorino Romano cheese, grated (½ cup)

LASAGNA

- 14 curly-edged lasagna noodles
- 8 ounces fontina cheese, shredded (2 cups)
- ⅛ teaspoon cornstarch
- ¼ cup grated Pecorino Romano cheese
- 3 tablespoons chopped fresh basil

1. FOR THE CHEESE SAUCE: Whisk all ingredients in bowl until homogeneous. Set aside.

2. FOR THE TOMATO SAUCE: Heat oil in large saucepan over medium heat. Add onion, sugar, pepper flakes, oregano, and salt and cook, stirring frequently, until onions are softened, about 10 minutes. Add garlic and anchovies and cook until fragrant, about 2 minutes. Stir in crushed tomatoes, diced tomatoes, tomato paste, and Pecorino and bring to simmer. Reduce heat to medium-low and simmer until slightly thickened, about 20 minutes.

3. FOR THE LASAGNA: While sauce simmers, lay noodles in 13 by 9-inch baking dish and cover with boiling water. Let noodles soak until pliable, about 15 minutes, separating noodles with tip of paring knife to prevent sticking. Place dish in sink, pour off water, and run cold water over noodles. Pat noodles dry with clean dish towel; dry dish. Cut two noodles in half crosswise.

4. Adjust oven rack to middle position and heat oven to 375 degrees. Spread 1½ cups tomato sauce in bottom of dish. Lay 3 noodles lengthwise in dish with ends touching 1 short side, leaving space on opposite short side. Lay 1 half noodle crosswise in empty space to create even layer of noodles. Spread half of cheese sauce over noodles, followed by ½ cup fontina. Repeat layering of noodles, alternating which short side gets half noodle (alternating sides will prevent lasagna from buckling). Spread 1½ cups tomato sauce over second layer of noodles, followed by ½ cup fontina. Create third layer using 3½ noodles (reversing arrangement again), remaining cheese sauce, and ½ cup fontina.

5. Lay remaining 3½ noodles over cheese sauce. Spread remaining tomato sauce over noodles. Toss remaining ½ cup fontina with cornstarch, then sprinkle over tomato sauce, followed by Pecorino.

6. Spray sheet of aluminum foil with vegetable oil spray and cover lasagna. Bake for 35 minutes. Remove lasagna from oven and increase oven temperature to 500 degrees.

7. Remove foil from lasagna, return to oven, and continue to bake until top is lightly browned, 10 to 15 minutes longer. Let lasagna cool for 20 minutes. Sprinkle with basil, cut into pieces, and serve.

FOUR-CHEESE LASAGNA

WHY THIS RECIPE WORKS: Cheese lasagna offers an elegant alternative to meat-laden, red sauce lasagna. But some cheese lasagna is just heavy and bland, due to the use of plain-tasting cheeses. And even those with good cheese flavor can have soupy, dry, or greasy textures. We wanted a robust cheese lasagna with great structure, creamy texture, and maximum flavor. For the best cheese flavor, we settled on a combination of fontina, Parmesan, Gorgonzola, and Gruyère cheeses. We found that making the white sauce (a béchamel) with a high ratio of flour to butter created a thick binder that provided

enough heft to keep the lasagna layers together. And replacing some of the milk with chicken broth was the key to balancing the richness of the sauce and bringing the cheese flavor forward. But the real secret of a great four-cheese lasagna proved to be a fifth cheese. While ricotta didn't add much flavor, it gave the lasagna body without making the dish heavy and starchy. Our final challenge was to keep the baking time short enough to avoid harming this delicate pasta dish. Both presoaking the no-boil noodles and using a low-heat/high-heat baking method—baking at a moderate temperature and then briefly broiling to brown the top—kept the lasagna from overbaking.

Four-Cheese Lasagna
SERVES 10

It's important not to overbake the lasagna. Once the sauce starts bubbling around the edges, uncover the lasagna and turn the oven to broil. If your lasagna pan is not broiler-safe, brown the lasagna at 500 degrees for about 10 minutes. Whole milk is best in the sauce, but skim and low-fat milk also work. Supermarket-brand cheeses work fine in this recipe. The Gorgonzola may be omitted, but the flavor of the lasagna won't be as complex. We prefer Barilla no-boil lasagna noodles for their delicate texture resembling fresh pasta. Note that Pasta Defino and Ronzoni brands contain only 12 no-boil noodles per package; this recipe requires 15 noodles. This lasagna is very rich; serve small portions with a green salad.

  6 ounces Gruyère cheese, shredded (about 1½ cups)

  2 ounces Parmesan cheese, grated (about 1 cup)

1½ cups part-skim ricotta cheese

  1 large egg, lightly beaten

  2 tablespoons plus 2 teaspoons minced fresh parsley leaves

 ¼ teaspoon ground black pepper

  3 tablespoons unsalted butter

  1 medium shallot, minced (about 2 tablespoons)

  1 medium garlic clove, minced or pressed through a garlic press (about 1 teaspoon)

 ⅓ cup unbleached all-purpose flour

2½ cups whole milk (see note)

1½ cups low-sodium chicken broth

 ½ teaspoon table salt

  1 bay leaf

    Pinch cayenne pepper

 15 no-boil lasagna noodles (see note)

  8 ounces fontina cheese, rind removed, shredded (about 2 cups)

  3 ounces Gorgonzola cheese, crumbled fine (about ¾ cup; see note)

1. Place the Gruyère and ½ cup of the Parmesan in a large ovensafe bowl. Combine the ricotta, egg, 2 tablespoons of the parsley, and the black pepper in a medium bowl. Set both bowls aside.

2. Melt the butter in a medium saucepan over medium heat; add the shallot and garlic and cook, stirring frequently, until beginning to soften, about 2 minutes. Add the flour and cook, stirring constantly, until thoroughly combined, about 1½ minutes; the mixture should not brown. Gradually whisk in the milk and broth; increase the heat to medium-high and bring to a full boil, whisking frequently. Add the salt, bay leaf, and cayenne; reduce the heat to medium-low and simmer until the sauce thickens and coats the back of a spoon, about 10 minutes, stirring occasionally with a heatproof rubber spatula or wooden spoon and making sure to scrape the bottom and corners of the saucepan.

3. Remove the saucepan from the heat and discard the bay leaf. Gradually whisk ¼ cup of the sauce into the ricotta mixture. Pour the remaining sauce over the Gruyère mixture and stir until smooth; set aside.

4. Adjust an oven rack to the upper-middle position and heat the oven to 350 degrees. Pour 2 inches boiling water into a 13 by 9-inch broiler-safe baking dish. Slip the noodles into the water, one at a time, and let them soak until pliable, about 5 minutes, separating them with the tip of a knife to prevent sticking. Remove the noodles from the water and place in a single layer on clean kitchen towels. Discard the water, dry the baking dish, and spray lightly with vegetable oil spray.

5. Spread the bottom of the baking dish evenly with ½ cup of the sauce. Place 3 noodles in a single layer on top of the sauce. Spread ½ cup of the ricotta mixture evenly over the noodles and sprinkle evenly with ½ cup of the fontina and 3 tablespoons of the Gorgonzola. Drizzle ½ cup of the sauce evenly over the cheese. Repeat the layering of noodles, ricotta, fontina, Gorgonzola, and sauce three more times. Place the final 3 noodles on top and cover completely with the remaining sauce, spreading with a rubber spatula and allowing it to spill over the noodles. Sprinkle evenly with the remaining ½ cup Parmesan.

6. Spray a large sheet of foil with vegetable oil spray and cover the lasagna; bake until the edges are just bubbling, 25 to 30 minutes, rotating the pan halfway through the baking time. Remove the foil and turn the oven to broil. Broil until the surface is spotty brown, 3 to 5 minutes. Cool for 15 minutes. Sprinkle with the remaining 2 teaspoons parsley; cut into pieces and serve.

GREAT VEGETABLE LASAGNA

WHY THIS RECIPE WORKS: For a complex vegetable lasagna with bold flavor, we started with a summery mix of zucchini, yellow squash, and eggplant, salting and microwaving the eggplant and sautéing all of the vegetables to cut down on excess moisture and deepen their flavor. Garlic, spinach, and olives added textural contrast and flavor without much work. We dialed up the typical cheese filling by switching mild-mannered ricotta for tangy cottage cheese mixed with heavy cream for richness and Parmesan and garlic for added flavor.

Our creamy, quick no-cook tomato sauce brought enough moisture to our lasagna that we found that we could skip the usual step of soaking the no-boil noodles before assembling the dish.

Vegetable Lasagna
SERVES 8 TO 10

Part-skim mozzarella can also be used in this recipe, but avoid preshredded cheese, as it does not melt well. We prefer kosher salt because it clings best to the eggplant. If using table salt, reduce salt amounts by half. To make assembly easier, the roasted vegetable filling can be made ahead and stored in the refrigerator for up to one day.

TOMATO SAUCE
- 1 (28-ounce) can crushed tomatoes
- ¼ cup minced fresh basil leaves
- 2 tablespoons extra-virgin olive oil
- 2 medium garlic cloves, minced or pressed through a garlic press (about 2 teaspoons)
- 1 teaspoon kosher salt
- ¼ teaspoon red pepper flakes

CREAM SAUCE
- 8 ounces whole-milk cottage cheese (about 1 cup)
- 1 cup heavy cream
- 4 ounces Parmesan cheese, grated (about 2 cups)
- 2 medium garlic cloves, minced or pressed through a garlic press (about 2 teaspoons)
- 1 teaspoon cornstarch
- ½ teaspoon kosher salt
- ½ teaspoon ground black pepper

VEGETABLE FILLING

- 1½ pounds eggplant, peeled and cut into ½-inch pieces
  Kosher salt and ground black pepper
- 1 pound zucchini, cut into ½-inch pieces
- 1 pound yellow squash, cut into ½-inch pieces
- 5 tablespoons plus 1 teaspoon extra-virgin olive oil
- 4 medium garlic cloves, minced or pressed through a garlic press (about 4 teaspoons)
- 1 tablespoon minced fresh thyme leaves
- 12 ounces baby spinach (12 cups)
- ½ cup pitted kalamata olives, minced
- 12 ounces whole-milk mozzarella cheese, shredded (about 3 cups)

- 12 no-boil lasagna noodles
- 2 tablespoons chopped fresh basil leaves

1. FOR THE TOMATO SAUCE: Whisk all the ingredients together in a bowl; set aside.

2. FOR THE CREAM SAUCE: Whisk all the ingredients together in a separate bowl; set aside.

3. FOR THE FILLING: Adjust an oven rack to the middle position and heat the oven to 375 degrees. Toss the eggplant with 1 teaspoon kosher salt in a large bowl. Line the surface of a large plate with a double layer of coffee filters and lightly spray with vegetable oil spray. Spread the eggplant in an even layer over the coffee filters; wipe out and reserve the bowl. Microwave the eggplant, uncovered, until dry to the touch and slightly shriveled, about 10 minutes, tossing halfway through cooking. Cool slightly. Return the eggplant to the bowl and toss with the zucchini and summer squash.

4. Combine 1 tablespoon of the oil, the garlic, and thyme in a small bowl. Heat 2 tablespoons more oil in a 12-inch nonstick skillet over medium-high heat until shimmering. Add half of the eggplant mixture, ¼ teaspoon kosher salt, and ¼ teaspoon pepper and cook, stirring occasionally, until the vegetables are lightly browned, about 7 minutes. Clear the center of the skillet, add half of the garlic mixture, and cook, mashing with a spatula, until fragrant, about 30 seconds. Stir the garlic mixture into the vegetables and transfer to a medium bowl. Repeat with the remaining eggplant mixture, 2 tablespoons more oil, and the remaining garlic mixture; transfer to the bowl.

5. Heat the remaining 1 teaspoon oil in the now-empty skillet over medium-high heat until shimmering. Add the spinach and cook, stirring frequently, until wilted, about 3 minutes. Transfer the spinach to a paper towel–lined plate and drain for 2 minutes. Stir into the eggplant mixture.

6. Grease a 13 by 9-inch baking dish. Spread 1 cup of the tomato sauce evenly over the bottom of the dish. Arrange 4 noodles on top of the sauce (the noodles will overlap). Spread half of the vegetable mixture over the noodles, followed by half of the olives. Spoon half of the cream sauce over the top and sprinkle with 1 cup of the mozzarella. Repeat the layering with 4 more noodles, 1 cup more tomato sauce, the remaining

vegetables, remaining olives, remaining cream sauce and 1 cup more mozzarella. For the final layer, arrange the remaining 4 noodles on top and cover completely with the remaining tomato sauce. Sprinkle with the remaining 1 cup mozzarella.

7. Cover the dish tightly with aluminum foil that has been sprayed with vegetable oil spray and bake until the edges are just bubbling, about 35 minutes, rotating the dish halfway through baking. Cool the lasagna for 25 minutes, then sprinkle with the basil and serve.

LASAGNA WITH MEAT SAUCE

WHY THIS RECIPE WORKS: Traditional meaty lasagna is one of the best comfort foods out there. Unfortunately, this hearty dish takes the better part of a day to make (not very comforting, if you ask us). The noodles must be boiled and the sauce slow-cooked. Then, once the cheese filling is mixed, the ingredients must be carefully layered before the whole thing is baked. We wanted a really good meat lasagna, with all of the rich, hearty meatiness of an all-day lasagna, but ready in a lot less time.

We made a speedy meaty tomato sauce by simmering onion, garlic, and meatloaf mix (a combination of ground beef, pork, and veal) together for about 15 minutes. Adding some heavy cream created a richer, creamier, more cohesive sauce; we stirred in pureed and diced tomatoes for a luxurious, soft sauce with chunks of tomatoes. Using no-boil lasagna noodles eliminated the tedious process of boiling and draining the pasta. For a classic cheese layer, we combined ricotta cheese, Parmesan cheese, fresh basil, and an egg, which helped thicken and bind the mixture; a layer of shredded mozzarella upped the creaminess and cheesiness of the filling. Covering the lasagna with foil before baking helped to soften the noodles; removing it during the last half-hour of baking ensured that the cheeses were properly browned.

Lasagna with Hearty Tomato-Meat Sauce
SERVES 6 TO 8

You can substitute equal amounts of 80 percent lean ground beef, ground veal, and ground pork for the meatloaf mix (the total amount of meat should be 1 pound). The assembled, unbaked lasagna will keep in the freezer for up to 2 months; wrap it tightly with plastic wrap, then foil, before freezing. To bake, defrost it in the refrigerator for up to 2 days and bake as directed, extending the covered baking time by 5 to 10 minutes.

TOMATO-MEAT SAUCE
- 1 tablespoon olive oil
- 1 medium onion, minced
- 6 medium garlic cloves, minced or pressed through a garlic press (about 2 tablespoons)
- 1 pound meatloaf mix (see note)

½ teaspoon table salt

½ teaspoon ground black pepper

¼ cup heavy cream

1 (28-ounce) can tomato puree

1 (28-ounce) can diced tomatoes, drained

CHEESE FILLING AND PASTA

1¾ cups whole-milk or part-skim ricotta cheese

2½ ounces Parmesan cheese, grated (about 1¼ cups)

½ cup chopped fresh basil leaves

1 large egg, lightly beaten

½ teaspoon table salt

½ teaspoon ground black pepper

12 no-boil lasagna noodles

1 pound whole-milk mozzarella cheese, shredded (about 4 cups)

1. Adjust an oven rack to the middle position and heat the oven to 375 degrees.

2. FOR THE SAUCE: Heat the oil in a large Dutch oven over medium heat until shimmering. Add the onion and cook, stirring occasionally, until softened but not browned, about 2 minutes. Add the garlic and cook until fragrant, about 2 minutes. Increase the heat to medium-high and add the meatloaf mix, salt, and pepper; cook, breaking the meat into small pieces with a wooden spoon, until the meat loses its raw color but has not browned, about 4 minutes. Add the cream and simmer, stirring occasionally, until the liquid evaporates and only rendered fat remains, about 4 minutes. Add the tomato puree and diced tomatoes and bring to a simmer; reduce the heat to low and simmer until the flavors have blended, about 3 minutes. Set aside. (The cooled sauce can be refrigerated in an airtight container for up to 2 days; reheat before assembling the lasagna.)

3. FOR THE CHEESE FILLING: Combine the ricotta, 1 cup of the Parmesan, the basil, egg, salt, and pepper in a medium bowl; set aside.

4. Spread the bottom of a 13 by 9-inch baking dish evenly with ¼ cup of the meat sauce (avoiding large chunks of meat). Place 3 noodles in a single layer on top of the sauce. Spread each noodle evenly with 3 tablespoons of the ricotta mixture and sprinkle the entire layer evenly with 1 cup of the mozzarella cheese. Spread the cheese evenly with 1½ cups of the meat sauce. Repeat the layering of noodles, ricotta, mozzarella, and sauce two more times. Place the remaining 3 noodles on top of the sauce, spread evenly with the remaining sauce, sprinkle with the remaining 1 cup mozzarella, then sprinkle with the remaining ¼ cup Parmesan. Spray a large sheet of foil with vegetable oil spray and cover the lasagna.

5. Bake for 15 minutes, then remove the foil. Continue to bake until the cheese is spotty brown and the sauce is bubbling, about 25 minutes longer. Cool the lasagna for 10 minutes; cut into pieces and serve.

BEHIND THE SCENES

A FRESH CRUSH IS BEST

We're always looking for ways to make our kitchen work more efficient and will often prep recipes in advance if we know we've got a lot of recipes to get through on a given day. But noticing that garlic can develop a particularly strong odor if minced too far in advance, we decided to run a quick test. We used garlic in three different applications: lightly cooked in Pasta with Garlic and Oil (page 282); raw, when stirred into mayonnaise; and as a subtle flavoring in a vinaigrette. For each recipe, we used freshly minced garlic, garlic that had been minced six hours in advance, and garlic that had been minced the day before. Both the six-hour-old and one-day-old minced garlic were so powerful they overwhelmed the other flavors in the dish.

Turns out, garlic flavor comes from a compound called allicin, which is not formed until after the garlic's cells are ruptured. As soon as you cut into garlic, the allicin will start to build and build until its flavor becomes overwhelmingly strong. So if you're going to prep a recipe in advance, make sure to leave the garlic cloves whole until the last minute.

BRINGING HOME
ITALIAN FAVORITES

HOMEMADE RICOTTA CHEESE

WHY THIS RECIPE WORKS: Creamy, milky, and luxuriously rich, fresh ricotta bears little-to-no resemblance to the grainy, clumpy cheese sold in supermarkets. The best part of fresh ricotta, however, is how simple it is to make at home. Using fresh homogenized and pasteurized milk yielded the most reliable results because ultra-pasteurized or ultra-heat-treated (UHT or long-life) milk wouldn't curdle properly. After lining a colander with butter muslin, we set about curdling a gallon of whole milk, heating it in a Dutch oven with salt. Once the milk reached 185 degrees, we took it off the heat and gently added the curdling agents: lemon juice and distilled white vinegar. Stirring gently and then leaving the mixture alone once the curds appeared allowed the ricotta to fully separate from the whey; adding more vinegar drew out any remaining curds from milky whey, if necessary. To finish, we emptied the pot into the colander to drain and then transferred the ricotta to a bowl to break up the curds and incorporate the whey.

Homemade Ricotta Cheese
MAKES ABOUT 2 POUNDS (4 CUPS)

For best results, don't stir the milk too hard, and be very gentle with the curds once they form.

- ⅓ cup lemon juice (2 lemons)
- ¼ cup distilled white vinegar, plus extra as needed
- 1 gallon pasteurized (not ultrapasteurized or UHT) whole milk
- 2 teaspoons salt

1. Line colander with butter muslin or triple layer of cheesecloth and place in sink. Combine lemon juice and vinegar in liquid measuring cup; set aside. Heat milk and salt in Dutch oven over medium-high heat, stirring frequently with rubber spatula to prevent scorching, until milk registers 185 degrees.

2. Remove pot from heat and slowly stir in lemon juice mixture until fully incorporated and mixture curdles, about 15 seconds. Let sit undisturbed until mixture fully separates into solid curds and translucent whey, 5 to 10 minutes. If curds do not fully separate and there is still milky whey in pot, stir in extra vinegar, 1 tablespoon at a time, and let sit another 2 to 3 minutes, until curds separate.

3. Gently pour mixture into prepared colander. Let sit, undisturbed, until whey has drained from edges of cheese but center is still very moist, about 8 minutes. Working quickly, gently transfer cheese to large bowl, retaining as much whey in center of cheese as possible. Stir well to break up large curds and incorporate whey. Refrigerate ricotta until cold, about 2 hours. Stir cheese before using. (Ricotta can be refrigerated for up to 5 days.)

FOCACCIA

WHY THIS RECIPE WORKS: Most of the focaccia we see in the States is heavy, thick, and strewn with pizza-like toppings. We wanted a lighter loaf, airy on the inside and topped with just a smattering of herbs. To start, we focused on flavor. To get the benefits of a long fermentation with minimal effort, many bakers use a "preferment" (also known as a "sponge," "starter," or *biga* in Italian): a mixture of flour, water, and a small amount of yeast that rests (often overnight) before being incorporated into the dough. We followed suit, but the interiors of the loaves weren't as tender and airy as we wanted. We wondered if our stand mixer was developing too much gluten (the strong, elastic network of cross-linked proteins that give bread its crumb structure). Instead we turned to a more gentle approach. In this method, a high hydration level (the weight of the water in relation to the weight of the flour) and a long autolysis (the dough resting process) take advantage of the enzymes naturally present in the wheat to produce the same effect as kneading. This method worked to a point—our loaves were light and airy, but squat. To improve the structure, we turned the dough at regular intervals while it proofed. To cut back on the long proofing time (three hours) and hasten gluten development, we held back the salt when mixing our dough, adding it later. We were able to shave an hour off our proofing time. To give our loaves a crisp crust, we oiled the baking pans and added coarse salt for flavor and an extra crunchy texture. This focaccia was a revelation: crackly crisp on the bottom, deeply browned on top, with an interior that was open and airy.

Rosemary Focaccia
MAKES TWO 9-INCH ROUND LOAVES

If you don't have a baking stone, bake the bread on an overturned, preheated rimmed baking sheet set on the upper-middle oven rack. The bread can be kept for up to 2 days well-wrapped at room temperature or frozen for several months wrapped in foil and placed in a zipper-lock bag.

BIGA

½ cup (2½ ounces) unbleached all-purpose flour

⅓ cup (2⅔ ounces) warm water (100–110 degrees)

¼ teaspoon instant or rapid-rise yeast

DOUGH

2½ cups (12½ ounces) unbleached all-purpose flour, plus extra for shaping

1¼ cups (10 ounces) warm water (100–110 degrees)

1 teaspoon instant or rapid-rise yeast

Kosher salt

4 tablespoons extra-virgin olive oil

2 tablespoons chopped fresh rosemary leaves

1. FOR THE BIGA: Combine the flour, water, and yeast in a large bowl and stir with a wooden spoon until a uniform mass forms and no dry flour remains, about 1 minute. Cover the bowl tightly with plastic wrap and let stand at room temperature (about 70 degrees) overnight (at least 8 hours or up to 24 hours). Use immediately or store in the refrigerator for up to 3 days (allow to stand at room temperature for 30 minutes before proceeding with the recipe).

2. FOR THE DOUGH: Stir the flour, water, and yeast into the biga with a wooden spoon until a uniform mass forms and no dry flour remains, about 1 minute. Cover with plastic wrap and let rise at room temperature for 15 minutes.

3. Sprinkle 2 teaspoons salt over the dough; stir into the dough until thoroughly incorporated, about 1 minute. Cover with plastic wrap and let rise at room temperature for 30 minutes. Spray a rubber spatula or bowl scraper with vegetable oil spray; fold the partially risen dough over itself by gently lifting and folding the edge of the dough toward the middle. Turn the bowl 90 degrees; fold again. Turn the bowl and fold the dough six more times (for a total of eight turns). Cover with plastic wrap and let rise for 30 minutes. Repeat the folding, turning, and rising two more times, for a total of three 30-minute rises. Meanwhile, adjust an oven rack to the upper-middle position, place a baking stone on the rack, and heat the oven to 500 degrees, at least 30 minutes before baking.

4. Gently transfer the dough to a lightly floured work surface. Lightly dust the top of the dough with flour and divide it in half. Shape each piece of dough into a 5-inch round by gently tucking under the edges. Coat two 9-inch round cake pans with 2 tablespoons olive oil each. Sprinkle each pan with ½ teaspoon kosher salt. Place a round of dough in one pan, top side down; slide the dough around the pan to coat the bottom and sides, then flip the dough over. Repeat with the second piece of dough in the second pan. Cover the pans with plastic wrap and let rest for 5 minutes.

5. Using your fingertips, press the dough out toward the edges of the pan, taking care not to tear it. (If the dough resists stretching, let it relax for 5 to 10 minutes before trying to stretch it again.) Using a dinner fork, poke the entire surface of the dough 25 to 30 times, popping any large bubbles. Sprinkle the rosemary evenly over the top of the dough. Let the dough rest in the pan until slightly bubbly, 5 to 10 minutes.

KEY STEPS TO MAKING FOCACCIA

1. Fold the partially risen dough over itself by gently lifting and folding the edge of the dough toward the middle. Turn the bowl 90 degrees; fold again. Turn the bowl and fold dough six more times (for a total of eight turns).

2. Cover with plastic wrap and let rise for 30 minutes. Repeat turning, folding, and rising two more times, for a total of three 30-minute rises.

3. Dust the dough with flour and divide in half. Shape the halves into 5-inch rounds. Place the rounds in the oiled pans and slide around to coat the dough. Flip and repeat. Cover the pans with plastic wrap and let rest for 5 minutes.

4. Using your fingertips, press the dough out toward the edges of the pan, taking care not to tear it. (If the dough resists stretching let it relax for 5 to 10 minutes before trying to stretch it again.)

5. Using a dinner fork, poke the surface of the dough 25 to 30 times. Deflate any remaining bubbles of dough with a fork. Sprinkle the rosemary over the dough. Let rest until slightly bubbly, 5 to 10 minutes, before baking.

6. Place the pans on the baking stone and lower the oven temperature to 450 degrees. Bake until the tops are golden brown, 25 to 28 minutes, switching the placement of the pans halfway through the baking time. Transfer the pans to a wire rack and let cool for 5 minutes. Remove the loaves from the pans and place on the wire rack. Brush the tops with any oil remaining in the pans. Cool for 30 minutes before serving.

NEAPOLITAN-STYLE PIZZA

WHY THIS RECIPE WORKS: Few dishes say "Italian" better than a slice of pizza, especially crisp-crust Neapolitan-style pizza. This style of crust is thinner than traditional parlor-style crusts, shatteringly crisp with a deeply caramelized flavor that bears no trace of raw yeast or flour.

For a pizza dough that came together quickly and easily, we turned to the food processor. Letting the dough rise slowly in the refrigerator overnight made it easier to handle the next day, and it developed good flavor from the slow fermentation. For the thinnest crust possible, we used a rolling pin. A sheet of plastic wrap on top of the dough made rolling easier; we didn't need to add more flour to prevent sticking. A bit of honey in the dough encouraged browning. This slim crust can't handle heavy toppings, nor should it. A thin layer of tomato sauce and a sprinkling of mozzarella pack lots of flavor.

Crisp Thin-Crust Pizza

SERVES 6 TO 8

Note that the pizza dough needs to be started at least 1 day before serving. Keep in mind that it is more important for the rolled dough to be of even thinness than to be a perfect circle. For topping the pizzas, we recommend buying shrink-wrapped mozzarella from the supermarket; do not use fresh because it is too moist and will make the crust soggy. If you don't have a pizza stone, bake the pizza on a rimless or overturned baking sheet that has been preheated just like the pizza stone.

DOUGH

1¾–2   cups (8¾ to 10 ounces) unbleached all-purpose
        flour, plus extra for the work surface
½   teaspoon instant or rapid-rise yeast
½   teaspoon honey
½   teaspoon table salt
¼   cup olive oil
¾   cup warm water (110 degrees)

TOPPINGS

1   cup Quick Tomato Sauce for Pizza (recipe follows)
8   ounces whole-milk mozzarella cheese, shredded
    (about 2 cups; see note)

1. FOR THE DOUGH: Pulse 1¾ cups of the flour, the yeast, honey, and salt in a food processor (fitted with the dough blade, if possible) until combined, about 5 pulses. With the machine running, pour the oil and then the water through the feed tube and process until the dough forms a ball, about 30 seconds. If after 30 seconds the dough is sticky and clings to the blade, add the remaining ¼ cup flour 1 tablespoon at a time. Turn the dough out onto a work surface.

2. Divide the dough in half and place each piece in a gallon-size, heavy-duty zipper-lock bag and seal. Refrigerate overnight or up to 48 hours.

3. TO MAKE THE PIZZA: One hour before baking the pizza, adjust an oven rack to the lowest position, set a pizza stone on the rack, and heat the oven to 500 degrees.

4. Remove the dough from the plastic bags. Set each piece in the center of a lightly floured large sheet of parchment paper. Cover each with two 18-inch lengths of plastic wrap, overlapping them in the center; let the dough rest for 10 minutes.

5. Setting one piece of dough aside, roll the other into a 14-inch round with an even thickness, using the tackiness of the dough against the parchment to help roll it. If the parchment wrinkles, flip the dough sandwich over and smooth the wrinkles with a metal bench scraper.

6. Peel the plastic wrap off the top of the rolled dough. Spread ½ cup of the tomato sauce to the edges of the dough. Sprinkle with 1 cup of the cheese.

7. Slip the dough with the parchment onto a pizza peel or rimless baking sheet. Slide the pizza, parchment and all, onto the hot pizza stone. Bake until a deep golden brown, about 10 minutes. Remove the pizza from the oven with a pizza peel or pull the parchment with the pizza onto a baking sheet. Transfer the pizza to a cutting board, slide the parchment out from under the pizza, and slide it onto a wire rack. Cool for 2 minutes until crisp; slide to a cutting board, cut into wedges, and serve.

8. While the first pizza is baking, repeat steps 5 and 6 to roll and top the second pizza; allow the baking stone to reheat for 15 minutes after baking the first pizza, then repeat step 7 to bake the second pizza.

Quick Tomato Sauce for Pizza

MAKES ABOUT 1½ CUPS

For pizza, you want the smoothest possible sauce. Start with crushed tomatoes and puree them in a food processor before cooking them with the garlic and oil. This recipe makes a bit more sauce than needed to sauce two thin-crust pizzas.

1   (14.5-ounce) can crushed tomatoes
1   tablespoon olive oil
1   medium garlic clove, minced or pressed through
    a garlic press (about 1 teaspoon)
    Table salt and ground black pepper

1. Process the tomatoes in a food processor until smooth, about 5 pulses.

2. Heat the oil and garlic in a medium saucepan over medium heat until the garlic is fragrant, about 30 seconds. Stir in the tomatoes; bring to a simmer and cook, uncovered, until the sauce thickens, about 15 minutes. Season with salt and pepper to taste.

NEW YORK–STYLE THIN-CRUST PIZZA

WHY THIS RECIPE WORKS: With home ovens that reach only 500 degrees and dough that's difficult to stretch thin, even the savviest cooks can struggle to produce parlor-quality pizza. We were in pursuit of a simple-to-make pizza with a New York–style crust: thin, crisp, and spottily charred on the exterior; tender yet chewy within. High-protein bread flour gave us a chewy, nicely tanned pizza crust and the right ratio of flour to water to yeast gave us dough that was easy to stretch and retained moisture as it baked. We kneaded the dough quickly in a food processor then let it proof in the refrigerator for 24 hours to develop its flavors. After we shaped and topped the pizza, it went onto a blazing hot baking stone to cook. Placing the stone near the top of the oven was a surprising improvement, allowing the top of the pizza to brown as well as the bottom. In minutes we had a pizza with everything in sync: a thoroughly crisp, browned crust with a slightly chewy texture, just like a good parlor slice.

New York–Style Thin-Crust Pizza

SERVES 4 TO 6

If you don't own a baking stone, bake the pizzas on a rimless or overturned baking sheet that has been preheated just like the pizza stone. If you don't own a pizza peel, stretch the dough on a large sheet of lightly floured parchment paper, transfer to a rimless or overturned baking sheet, and slide the pizza with the parchment onto the hot pizza stone. You can shape the second dough round while the first pizza bakes, but don't add the toppings until just before baking. It's important to use ice water in the dough to prevent it from overheating in the food processor. Semolina flour is ideal for dusting the peel; use it in place of bread flour if you have it. The sauce will yield more than needed in the recipe; extra sauce can be refrigerated for up to 1 week or frozen for up to 1 month.

DOUGH

- 3 cups (16½ ounces) bread flour, plus extra for the work surface
- 2 teaspoons sugar
- ½ teaspoon instant or rapid-rise yeast
- 1⅓ cups ice water
- 1 tablespoon vegetable oil
- 1½ teaspoons table salt

SAUCE

- 1 (28-ounce) can whole tomatoes, drained
- 1 tablespoon extra-virgin olive oil
- 2 medium garlic cloves, minced or pressed through a garlic press (about 2 teaspoons)
- 1 teaspoon red wine vinegar
- 1 teaspoon table salt
- 1 teaspoon dried oregano
- ¼ teaspoon ground black pepper

- 1 ounce Parmesan cheese, grated fine (about ½ cup)
- 8 ounces whole-milk mozzarella, shredded (about 2 cups)

1. FOR THE DOUGH: Pulse the flour, sugar, and yeast in a food processor (fitted with the dough blade, if possible) until combined, about 5 pulses. With the food processor running, slowly add the water; process until the dough is just combined and no dry flour remains, about 10 seconds. Let the dough sit for 10 minutes.

NOTES FROM THE TEST KITCHEN

PIZZA TOPPING TIPS

Our New York–Style Thin-Crust Pizza is great with just tomato sauce, shredded mozzarella, and Parmesan, but additional toppings are always an option—provided they're prepared correctly and added judiciously. (An overloaded pie will bake up soggy.) Here are a few guidelines for how to handle different types of toppings:

HEARTY VEGETABLES

Aim for a maximum of 6 ounces per pie, spread out in a single layer. Vegetables such as onions, peppers, and mushrooms should be thinly sliced and lightly sautéed (or microwaved for a minute or two along with a little olive oil) before using.

DELICATE VEGETABLES AND HERBS

Leafy greens and herbs like spinach and basil are best placed beneath the cheese to protect them or added raw to the fully cooked pizza.

MEATS

Proteins (no more than 4 ounces per pie) should be precooked and drained to remove excess fat. We like to poach meats like sausage (broken up into ½-inch chunks), pepperoni, or ground beef for 4 to 5 minutes in a wide skillet along with ¼ cup of water, which helps to render the fat while keeping the meat moist.

2. Add the oil and salt to the dough and process until the dough forms a satiny, sticky ball that clears the sides of the bowl, 30 to 60 seconds. Transfer the dough to a lightly oiled work surface and knead briefly by hand until smooth, about 1 minute. Shape the dough into a tight ball and place in a large, lightly oiled bowl; cover the bowl tightly with plastic wrap and refrigerate for at least 24 hours or up to 3 days.

3. FOR THE SAUCE: Process all the ingredients in the clean bowl of the food processor until smooth, about 30 seconds. Transfer to a bowl and refrigerate until ready to use.

4. TO BAKE THE PIZZA: One hour before baking, adjust an oven rack to the upper-middle position (the rack should be 4 to 5 inches from the broiler), set a baking stone on the rack, and heat the oven to 500 degrees. Transfer the dough to a clean work surface and divide in half. With cupped palms, form each half into a smooth, tight ball. Place the balls of dough on a lightly greased baking sheet, spacing them at least 3 inches apart; cover loosely with greased plastic wrap and let sit for 1 hour.

5. Coat 1 ball of dough generously with flour and place on a well-floured work surface (keep the other ball covered). Use your fingertips to gently flatten the dough into an 8-inch disk, leaving 1 inch of the outer edge slightly thicker than the center. Using your hands, gently stretch the disk into a 12-inch round, working along the edges and giving the disk quarter turns. Transfer the dough to a well-floured pizza peel and stretch into a 13-inch round. Using the back of a spoon or ladle, spread ½ cup of the tomato sauce in a thin layer over the surface of the dough, leaving a ¼-inch border around the edge. Sprinkle ¼ cup of the Parmesan evenly over the sauce, followed by 1 cup of the mozzarella. Slide the pizza carefully onto the baking stone and bake until the crust is well browned and the cheese is bubbly and beginning to brown, 10 to 12 minutes, rotating the pizza halfway through baking. Transfer the pizza to a wire rack and let cool for 5 minutes before slicing and serving. Repeat step 5 to shape, top, and bake the second pizza.

THIN-CRUST WHOLE-WHEAT PIZZA

WHY THIS RECIPE WORKS: For a whole-wheat pizza that was as crisp and chewy as traditional pizza and that offered a good, but not overwhelming, wheat flavor, we used a combination of 60 percent whole-wheat flour and 40 percent bread flour. To ensure that this higher-than-normal ratio of whole-wheat to bread flour still produced a great crust, we increased the hydration, which resulted in better gluten development and chew. To compensate for the added moisture, we employed the broiler to speed the baking process and guarantee a crisp crust and a moist, tender interior. We threw out traditional toppings, which tended to clash with the whole-wheat flavor, and opted for oil- and cream-based sauces and bold ingredients like blue cheese, pesto, and wine-braised onion.

Thin-Crust Whole-Wheat Pizza with Garlic Oil, Three Cheeses, and Basil

MAKES TWO 13-INCH PIZZAS

We recommend King Arthur brand bread flour for this recipe. Some baking stones, especially thinner ones, can crack under the intense heat of the broiler. Our recommended stone, by Old Stone Oven, is fine if you're using this technique. If you use another stone, you might want to check the manufacturer's website for guidance.

DOUGH

- 1½ cups (8¼ ounces) whole-wheat flour
- 1 cup (5½ ounces) bread flour
- 2 teaspoons honey
- ¾ teaspoon instant or rapid-rise yeast
- 1¼ cups ice water
- 2 tablespoons extra-virgin olive oil
- 1¾ teaspoons salt

GARLIC OIL

- ¼ cup extra-virgin olive oil
- 2 garlic cloves, minced
- 2 anchovy fillets, rinsed, patted dry, and minced (optional)
- ½ teaspoon pepper
- ½ teaspoon dried oregano
- ⅛ teaspoon red pepper flakes
- ⅛ teaspoon salt

- 1 cup fresh basil leaves
- 1 ounce Pecorino Romano cheese, grated (½ cup)
- 8 ounces whole-milk mozzarella cheese, shredded (2 cups)
- 6 ounces (¾ cup) whole-milk ricotta cheese

1. FOR THE DOUGH: Process whole-wheat flour, bread flour, honey, and yeast in food processor until combined, about 2 seconds. With processor running, add water and process until dough is just combined and no dry flour remains, about 10 seconds. Let dough stand for 10 minutes.

2. Add oil and salt to dough and process until it forms satiny, sticky ball that clears sides of workbowl, 45 to 60 seconds. Remove from bowl and knead on oiled countertop until smooth, about 1 minute. Shape dough into tight ball and place in large, lightly oiled bowl. Cover tightly with plastic wrap and refrigerate for at least 18 hours or up to 2 days.

3. FOR THE GARLIC OIL: Heat oil in 8-inch skillet over medium-low heat until shimmering. Add garlic; anchovies, if using; pepper; oregano; pepper flakes; and salt. Cook, stirring constantly, until fragrant, about 30 seconds. Transfer to bowl and let cool completely before using.

4. One hour before baking pizza, adjust oven rack 4½ inches from broiler element, set pizza stone on rack, and heat oven to 500 degrees. Divide dough in half. Shape each half into smooth, tight ball. Place balls on lightly oiled baking sheet, spacing them at least 3 inches apart. Cover loosely with plastic coated with vegetable oil spray; let stand for 1 hour.

5. Heat broiler for 10 minutes. Meanwhile, coat 1 ball of dough generously with flour and place on well-floured countertop. Using your fingertips, gently flatten into 8-inch disk, leaving 1 inch of outer edge slightly thicker than center. Lift edge of dough and, using back of your hands and knuckles, gently stretch disk into 12-inch round, working along edges and giving disk quarter turns as you stretch. Transfer dough to well-floured peel and stretch into 13-inch round. Using back of spoon, spread half of garlic oil over surface of dough, leaving ¼-inch border. Layer ½ cup basil leaves over pizza. Sprinkle with ¼ cup Pecorino, followed by 1 cup mozzarella. Slide pizza carefully onto stone and return oven to 500 degrees. Bake until crust is well browned and cheese is bubbly and partially browned, 8 to 10 minutes, rotating pizza halfway through baking. Remove pizza and place on wire rack. Dollop half of ricotta over surface of pizza. Let pizza rest for 5 minutes, slice, and serve.

6. Heat broiler for 10 minutes. Repeat process of stretching, topping, and baking with remaining dough and toppings, returning oven to 500 degrees when pizza is placed on stone.

Thin-Crust Whole-Wheat Pizza with Pesto and Goat Cheese

Process 2 cups basil leaves, 7 tablespoons extra-virgin olive oil, ¼ cup pine nuts, 3 minced garlic cloves, and ½ teaspoon salt in food processor until smooth, about 1 minute. Stir in ¼ cup finely grated Parmesan or Pecorino Romano and season with salt and pepper to taste. Substitute pesto for garlic oil. In step 5, omit basil leaves, Pecorino Romano, mozzarella, and ricotta. Top pizza with ½ cup crumbled goat cheese before baking.

Thin-Crust Whole-Wheat Pizza with Wine-Braised Onion and Blue Cheese

Bring 1 onion, halved through root end and sliced ⅛ inch thick, 1½ cups water, ¾ cup dry red wine, 3 tablespoons sugar, and ¼ teaspoon salt to simmer over medium-high heat in 10-inch skillet. Reduce heat to medium and simmer, stirring often, until liquid evaporates and onion is crisp-tender, about 30 minutes. Stir in 2 teaspoons red wine vinegar, transfer to bowl, and let cool completely before using. In step 5, omit garlic oil, basil leaves, Pecorino Romano, mozzarella, and ricotta. Spread ⅓ cup crème fraîche over each dough round. Top each with half of onion mixture, ½ cup coarsely chopped walnuts, and ½ cup crumbled blue cheese before baking. After letting pizza rest, top each with 2 tablespoons shredded fresh basil.

DEEP-DISH PIZZA

WHY THIS RECIPE WORKS: Unlike its thin-crust cousin, deep-dish pizza has a soft, chewy, thick crust and can stand up to substantial toppings. We wanted to try our hand at making this restaurant-style pizza at home. We were after a recipe that didn't require a lot of fuss and tasted better than takeout. Most of the allure of deep-dish pizza is in the crust, so it was important to get it right. After trying numerous ingredients and techniques, we discovered that a boiled potato gave the crust exactly the right qualities: It was soft and moist, yet with a bit of chew and good structure. The potato even made the unbaked dough easier to handle. To keep the outside of the crust from toughening during baking, we added a generous amount of olive oil to the pan before putting in the dough. Topping the pizza before it went into the oven weighed down the crust so that it didn't rise much, so we baked the crust untopped for a few minutes first. Our deep-dish crust wasn't just a platform for the topping; it had great flavor and texture of its own.

Deep-Dish Pizza with Tomatoes, Mozzarella, and Basil

SERVES 4

Prepare the topping while the dough is rising so the two will be ready at the same time. Baking the pizza in a deep-dish pan on a hot pizza stone will help produce a crisp, well-browned bottom crust. If you don't have a pizza stone, use an overturned or heavy rimless baking sheet. The amount of oil used to grease the pan may seem excessive, but it helps brown the crust while also preventing sticking. If you don't have a 14-inch deep-dish pizza pan, use two 10-inch cake pans. Grease them with 2 tablespoons oil each; divide the pizza dough in half and pat each half into a 9-inch round. Use shrink-wrapped supermarket cheese rather than fresh mozzarella.

DOUGH

1	medium russet potato (about 9 ounces), peeled and quartered
3¼–3½	cups (16¼ to 17½ ounces) unbleached all-purpose flour
1¾	teaspoons table salt
1½	teaspoons instant or rapid-rise yeast
6	tablespoons olive oil, plus extra for oiling the bowl (see note)
1	cup warm water (110 degrees)

- 1½ pounds plum tomatoes (5 to 6 medium), cored, seeded, and cut into 1-inch pieces
- 2 medium garlic cloves, minced or pressed through a garlic press (about 2 teaspoons)
  Table salt and ground black pepper
- 6 ounces whole-milk mozzarella cheese, shredded (about 1½ cups; see note)
- 1¼ ounces Parmesan cheese, grated (about ⅔ cup)
- 3 tablespoons shredded fresh basil leaves

1. FOR THE DOUGH: Bring 4 cups water and the potato to a boil in a small saucepan over medium-high heat; cook until tender, 10 to 15 minutes. Drain and cool until the potato can be handled; press the potato through the fine disk of a potato ricer or grate it on the large holes of a box grater. Measure 1⅓ cups lightly packed potato; discard the remaining potato.

2. Process 3¼ cups of the flour, the potato, salt and yeast in a food processor (fitted with the dough blade, if possible) until combined, about 5 seconds. With the motor running, pour 2 tablespoons of the oil and then the water through the feed tube and process until the dough comes together in a ball, about 30 seconds. If after 30 seconds the dough is sticky and clings to the blade, add the remaining ¼ cup flour 1 tablespoon at a time. Lightly coat a medium bowl with oil. Transfer the dough to the bowl; cover tightly with plastic wrap and set in a warm spot until doubled in volume, 1½ to 2 hours.

3. FOR THE TOPPING: Meanwhile, mix the tomatoes and garlic together in a medium bowl; season with salt and pepper to taste and set aside.

4. Oil the bottom of a 14-inch deep-dish pizza pan with the remaining 4 tablespoons olive oil. Remove the dough from the oven and gently punch it down; turn the dough onto a clean, dry work surface and pat it into a 12-inch round. Transfer the round to the oiled pan, cover with plastic wrap, and let rest until the dough no longer resists shaping, about 10 minutes.

5. Adjust the oven racks to the lowest and top positions, set a pizza stone on the lower rack, and heat the oven to 500 degrees. Uncover the dough and pull it into the edges and up the sides of the pan to form a 1-inch-high lip. Cover with plastic wrap; let rise in a warm, draft-free spot until doubled in size, about 30 minutes. Uncover the dough and prick it generously with a fork. Reduce the oven temperature to 425 degrees, place the pan with the pizza on the hot pizza stone, and bake until dry and lightly browned, about 15 minutes. Add the tomato mixture, followed by the mozzarella, then the Parmesan. Bake the pizza on the stone or baking sheet until the cheese melts, 10 to 15 minutes (5 to 10 minutes for 10-inch pizzas). Move the pizza to the top rack and bake until the cheese is spotty golden brown, about 5 minutes longer. Cool for 5 minutes, then, holding the pizza pan at an angle with a potholder, use a wide spatula to slide the pizza from the pan to a cutting board, cut into wedges, and serve.

CHICAGO DEEP-DISH PIZZA

WHY THIS RECIPE WORKS: Recipes for Chicago-style deep-dish pizzas—the kind with crusts like buttery pastries you can only get in Chicago pizzerias—are staunchly protected by the people who make them. We would have to invent our own recipe for the best deep-dish pizza Chicago has to offer: one that boasts a thick, crisp crust with an airy, flaky interior, and a rich taste that can hold its own under any kind of topping.

The recipes we came across in our research sounded a lot like classic pizza dough, with cornmeal added for crunch and butter for tenderness and flavor. These crusts weren't bad, but they weren't as flaky as a Chicago-made crust. To increase the flakiness factor, we turned to laminating. This baking term refers to the layering of butter and dough to create ultra-flaky pastries through a sequence of rolling and folding. A combination of adding melted butter to the dough and spreading the rolled out dough with softened butter before folding it did the trick. This crust was a huge improvement. Our only additional tweak was adding oil to each pan to crisp the edges.

With our crust all set, we turned to the toppings. Following Chicago tradition, we covered the dough with freshly shredded mozzarella and then topped the cheese with our thick, quick-to-make tomato sauce. The cheese formed a consistent barrier between the crust and our sauce, which prevented our thick, flavorful crust from turning soggy.

Chicago-Style Deep-Dish Pizza
MAKES TWO 9-INCH PIZZAS

You will need a stand mixer with a dough hook for this recipe. Place a damp kitchen towel under the mixer and watch it at all times during kneading to prevent it from wobbling off the counter. Handle the dough with slightly oiled hands to prevent sticking. The test kitchen prefers Polly-O Mozzarella; part-skim mozzarella can also be used, but avoid preshredded cheese here. Our preferred brand of crushed tomatoes is SMT. Grate the onion on the large holes of a box grater.

DOUGH

- 3¼ cups (16¼ ounces) unbleached all-purpose flour
- ½ cup (2¾ ounces) yellow cornmeal
- 2¼ teaspoons (about 1 envelope) instant or rapid-rise yeast
- 2 teaspoons sugar
- 1½ teaspoons table salt
- 1¼ cups water, room temperature
- 3 tablespoons unsalted butter, melted, plus 4 tablespoons, softened
- 1 teaspoon plus 4 tablespoons olive oil

SAUCE

- 2 tablespoons unsalted butter
- ¼ cup grated onion (see note)
- ¼ teaspoon dried oregano
  Table salt and ground black pepper

2 medium garlic cloves, minced or pressed through a garlic press (about 2 teaspoons)

1 (28-ounce) can crushed tomatoes (see note)

¼ teaspoon sugar

2 tablespoons chopped fresh basil

1 tablespoon extra-virgin olive oil

TOPPINGS

1 pound mozzarella, shredded (about 4 cups; see note)

¼ cup grated Parmesan cheese

1. FOR THE DOUGH: Mix the flour, cornmeal, yeast, sugar, and salt in the bowl of a stand mixer fitted with the dough hook on low speed until incorporated, about 1 minute. Add the water and melted butter and mix on low speed until fully combined, 1 to 2 minutes, scraping the sides and bottom of the bowl as needed. Increase the speed to medium and knead until the dough is glossy and smooth and pulls away from sides of the bowl, 4 to 5 minutes. (The dough will only pull away from the sides while the mixer is on. When the mixer is off, the dough will fall back to the sides.)

2. Using your fingers, coat a large bowl with 1 teaspoon of the olive oil, rubbing excess oil from your fingers onto the blade of a rubber spatula. Using the oiled spatula, transfer the dough to the oiled bowl, turning once to oil the top. Cover the bowl tightly with plastic wrap. Let the dough rise at room temperature until nearly doubled in volume, 45 to 60 minutes.

3. FOR THE SAUCE: While the dough rises, heat the butter in a medium saucepan over medium heat until melted. Add the onion, oregano, and ½ teaspoon salt and cook, stirring occasionally, until the liquid has evaporated and the onion is golden brown, about 5 minutes. Add the garlic and cook until fragrant, about 30 seconds. Stir in the tomatoes and sugar, increase the heat to high, and bring to a simmer. Lower the heat to medium-low and simmer until the sauce has reduced to 2½ cups, 25 to 30 minutes. Off the heat, stir in the basil and oil, then season with salt and pepper to taste.

4. TO LAMINATE THE DOUGH: Adjust an oven rack to the lowest position and heat the oven to 425 degrees. Using a rubber spatula, turn the dough out onto a dry work surface and roll into a 15 by 12-inch rectangle. Following the photos, use an offset spatula to spread the softened butter over the surface of the dough, leaving a ½-inch border along the edges. Starting at the short end, roll the dough into a tight cylinder. With the seam side down, flatten the cylinder into an 18 by 4-inch rectangle. Cut the rectangle in half crosswise. Working with one half, fold the dough into thirds like a business letter, then pinch the seams together to form a ball. Repeat with the remaining half of the dough. Return the dough balls to the oiled bowl, cover tightly with plastic wrap, and let rise in the refrigerator until nearly doubled in volume, 40 to 50 minutes.

5. Coat two 9-inch round cake pans with 2 tablespoons olive oil each. Transfer one dough ball to a dry work surface and roll out into a 13-inch disk about ¼ inch thick. Transfer the dough round to a cake pan by rolling the dough loosely around the rolling pin, then unrolling the dough into the pan. Lightly press the dough into the pan, working it into the corners and

MAKING CHICAGO DEEP-DISH PIZZA CRUST

1. After rolling out the dough into a 15 by 12-inch rectangle, spread the softened butter over the dough, leaving a ½-inch border along the edges.

2. Roll the dough into a tight cylinder, starting at the short end closest to you.

3. Flatten the dough cylinder into an 18 by 4-inch rectangle, then halve the cylinder crosswise.

4. Fold each dough half into thirds to form a ball, pinch the seams shut, and let the dough balls rise in the refrigerator for 40 to 50 minutes.

5. After rolling each ball of dough into a 13-inch disk about ¼ inch thick, transfer the dough disks to the oiled pans and lightly press the dough into the pans, working it into the corners and up the sides.

1 inch up the sides. If the dough resists stretching, let it relax for 5 minutes before trying again. Repeat with the remaining dough ball.

6. For each pizza, sprinkle 2 cups of the mozzarella evenly over the surface of the dough. Spread 1¼ cups of the tomato sauce over the cheese and sprinkle 2 tablespoons of the Parmesan over the sauce for each pizza. Bake until the crust is golden brown, 20 to 30 minutes. Remove the pizza from the oven and let rest for 10 minutes before slicing and serving.

THICK-CRUST SICILIAN-STYLE PIZZA

WHY THIS RECIPE WORKS: Unlike the thin pies you can get at any pizza parlor in town, Sicilian-style pizza boasts a thick crust with a tight, even crumb and a delicately crisp underside. To replicate that golden crust in our own kitchen, we created a dough with all-purpose and semolina flours, the latter contributing the distinct yellow color and cake-like crumb. We took things slowly, adding ice water and 3 tablespoons of olive oil for a tender texture, then letting the dough rest before adding salt and kneading and shaping it into a ball. Letting the dough proof for 24 hours under plastic wrap in the refrigerator helped create flavor: The cold kept carbon dioxide from forming bubbles while the extended fermentation period allowed an array of flavor compounds to form. To ensure bubbles didn't form during the second proof, we rolled the dough out with a rolling pin, moved it onto a rimmed baking sheet, and covered it with plastic wrap and a second baking sheet. Before baking, we topped the compressed dough with a boldly seasoned, slow-cooked homemade tomato sauce and a blend of gooey mozzarella and salty, sharp Parmesan.

Thick-Crust Sicilian-Style Pizza

SERVES 6 TO 8

This recipe requires refrigerating the dough for at least 24 hours before shaping it. King Arthur all-purpose flour and Bob's Red Mill semolina flour work best in this recipe. It is important to use ice water in the dough to prevent overheating during mixing. Anchovies give the sauce depth without a discernible fishy taste; if you decide not to use them, add an additional ¼ teaspoon of salt.

DOUGH

- 2¼ cups (11¼ ounces) all-purpose flour
- 2 cups (12 ounces) semolina flour
- 1 teaspoon sugar
- 1 teaspoon instant or rapid-rise yeast
- 1⅔ cups (13⅓ ounces) ice water
- 3 tablespoons extra-virgin olive oil
- 2¼ teaspoons salt

SAUCE

- 1 (28-ounce) can whole peeled tomatoes, drained
- 2 teaspoons sugar
- ¼ teaspoon salt
- ¼ cup extra-virgin olive oil
- 3 garlic cloves, minced
- 1 tablespoon tomato paste
- 3 anchovy fillets, rinsed, patted dry, and minced
- 1 teaspoon dried oregano
- ¼ teaspoon red pepper flakes

PIZZA

- ¼ cup extra-virgin olive oil
- 2 ounces Parmesan cheese, grated (1 cup)
- 12 ounces whole-milk mozzarella, shredded (3 cups)

1. FOR THE DOUGH: Using stand mixer fitted with dough hook, mix all-purpose flour, semolina flour, sugar, and yeast on low speed until combined, about 10 seconds. With machine running, slowly add water and oil until dough forms and no dry flour remains, 1 to 2 minutes. Cover with plastic wrap and let dough stand for 10 minutes.

2. Add salt to dough and mix on medium speed until dough forms satiny, sticky ball that clears sides of bowl, 6 to 8 minutes. Remove dough from bowl and knead briefly on lightly floured counter until smooth, about 1 minute. Shape dough into tight ball and place in large, lightly oiled bowl. Cover tightly with plastic wrap and refrigerate for at least 24 hours or up to 2 days.

3. FOR THE SAUCE: Process tomatoes, sugar, and salt in food processor until smooth, about 30 seconds. Heat oil and garlic in medium saucepan over medium-low heat, stirring occasionally, until garlic is fragrant and just beginning to brown, about 2 minutes. Add tomato paste, anchovies, oregano, and pepper flakes and cook until fragrant, about 30 seconds. Add tomato mixture and cook, stirring occasionally, until sauce measures 2 cups, 25 to 30 minutes. Transfer to bowl, let cool, and refrigerate until needed.

4. FOR THE PIZZA: One hour before baking pizza, place baking stone on upper-middle rack and heat oven to 500 degrees. Spray rimmed baking sheet (including rim) with vegetable oil spray, then coat bottom of a second baking sheet with oil.

Remove dough from refrigerator and transfer to lightly floured counter. Lightly flour top of dough and gently press into 12 by 9-inch rectangle. Using rolling pin, roll dough into 18 by 13-inch rectangle. Transfer dough to prepared baking sheet, fitting dough into corners. Spray top of dough with oil spray and lay sheet of plastic wrap over dough. Place second baking sheet on dough and let stand for 1 hour.

5. Remove top baking sheet and plastic wrap. Gently stretch and lift dough to fill pan. Using back of spoon or ladle, spread sauce in even layer over surface of dough, leaving ½-inch border. Sprinkle Parmesan evenly over entire surface of dough to edges followed by mozzarella.

6. Place pizza on stone; reduce oven temperature to 450 degrees and bake until bottom crust is evenly browned and cheese is bubbly and browned, 20 to 25 minutes, rotating pizza halfway through baking. Remove pan from oven and let cool on wire rack for 5 minutes. Run knife around rim of pan to loosen pizza. Transfer pizza to cutting board, cut into squares, and serve.

THE BEST GLUTEN-FREE PIZZA

WHY THIS RECIPE WORKS: Gluten-free pizza crusts are often either dense and doughy or cracker-crunchy. We wanted a gluten-free pizza crust that could hold its own against any wheat-flour crust, with a crispy exterior, a tender interior, and just enough chew. First, we developed a gluten-free flour blend that mimicked many of the properties of wheat flour. To imitate the strength and structure that gluten provides in wheat flour, we used a small amount of ground psyllium husk. To create a tender, airy crumb, we significantly increased the water in the dough and added a generous amount of baking powder. We also added a small amount of ground almond flour to introduce richness and increase crispiness without leaving the crust greasy. Since the added water made our dough sticky, we treated it like a batter and spread it onto a baking sheet with the help of a greased spatula. To ensure that the exterior of the crust didn't dry out before the interior had cooked through, we gently parbaked the crust at low heat before adding the toppings.

The Best Gluten-Free Pizza
MAKES TWO 12-INCH PIZZAS

This recipe requires letting the dough rise for 1½ hours and prebaking the crusts for about 45 minutes before topping and baking. If you don't have almond flour, you can process 2½ ounces of blanched almonds in a food processor until finely ground, about 30 seconds. Psyllium husk is available at natural foods stores. You can substitute 16 ounces (2⅔ cups plus ¼ cup) King Arthur Gluten-Free Multi-Purpose Flour or 16 ounces (2⅔ cup plus ½ cup) Bob's Red Mill GF All-Purpose Baking Flour for the America's Test Kitchen Gluten-Free Flour Blend. Note that pizza crust made with King Arthur will be slightly denser and not as chewy, and pizza crust made with Bob's Red Mill will be thicker and more airy and will have a distinct bean flavor.

SHAPING GLUTEN-FREE PIZZA DOUGH

Most traditional pizza dough requires a 60 percent hydration level, but gluten-free dough prepared with this ratio will be too stiff. We more than double the hydration—to 133 percent—for a gluten-free dough that can stretch and rise. But because it is so wet, it can't be shaped like traditional dough.

1. Drop batter onto parchment-lined baking sheet, then spread it into rough circle with rubber spatula. Spritz dough with vegetable oil spray.

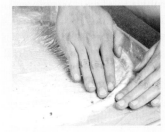

2. Cover with plastic wrap and press into even round with raised edge. To avoid gummy results, prebake crust, then top and bake to finish.

CRUST
- 16 ounces (3⅓ cups plus ¼ cup) The America's Test Kitchen Gluten-Free Flour Blend (recipe follows)
- 2½ ounces (½ cup plus 1 tablespoon) almond flour
- 1½ tablespoons powdered psyllium husk
- 2½ teaspoons baking powder
- 2 teaspoons salt
- 1 teaspoon instant or rapid-rise yeast
- 2½ cups warm water (100 degrees)
- ¼ cup vegetable oil
- Vegetable oil spray

SAUCE
- 1 (28-ounce) can whole peeled tomatoes, drained
- 1 tablespoon extra-virgin olive oil
- 1 teaspoon red wine vinegar
- 1 garlic clove, minced
- 1 teaspoon dried oregano
- ½ teaspoon salt
- ¼ teaspoon pepper

- 1 ounce Parmesan cheese, grated fine (½ cup)
- 8 ounces whole-milk mozzarella cheese, shredded (2 cups)

1. FOR THE CRUST: Using stand mixer fitted with paddle, mix flour blend, almond flour, psyllium, baking powder, salt, and yeast on low speed until combined. Slowly add warm water and oil in steady stream until incorporated. Increase speed to medium and beat until dough is sticky and uniform, about 6 minutes. (Dough will resemble thick batter.)

2. Remove bowl from mixer, cover with plastic wrap, and let stand until inside of dough is bubbly (use spoon to peer inside dough), about 1½ hours. (Dough will puff slightly but will not rise.)

3. Adjust oven racks to middle and lower positions. Line 2 rimmed baking sheets with parchment paper and spray liberally with oil spray. Transfer half of dough to center of 1 prepared sheet. Using oil-sprayed rubber spatula, spread dough into 8-inch circle. Spray top of dough with oil spray, cover with large sheet of plastic, and, using your hands, press out dough to 11½-inch round, about ¼ inch thick, leaving outer ¼ inch slightly thicker than center; discard plastic. Repeat with remaining dough and second prepared sheet.

4. Place prepared sheets in oven and heat oven to 325 degrees. Bake dough until firm to touch, golden brown on underside, and just beginning to brown on top, 45 to 50 minutes, switching and rotating sheets halfway through baking. Transfer crusts to wire rack and let cool.

5. FOR THE SAUCE: Process all ingredients in food processor until smooth, about 30 seconds. Transfer to bowl and refrigerate until ready to use.

6. One hour before baking pizza, adjust oven rack to upper-middle position, set baking stone on rack, and heat oven to 500 degrees.

7. Transfer 1 parbaked crust to pizza peel. Using back of spoon or ladle, spread ½ cup tomato sauce in thin layer over surface of crust, leaving ¼-inch border around edge. Sprinkle ¼ cup Parmesan evenly over sauce, followed by 1 cup mozzarella. Carefully slide crust onto stone and bake until crust is well browned and cheese is bubbly and beginning to brown, 10 to 12 minutes. Transfer pizza to wire rack and let cool for 5 minutes before slicing and serving. Repeat with second crust, ½ cup tomato sauce (you will have extra sauce), remaining ¼ cup Parmesan, and remaining 1 cup mozzarella.

TO MAKE AHEAD: Extra sauce can be refrigerated for up to 1 week or frozen for up to 1 month. Parbaked and cooled crusts can sit at room temperature for up to 4 hours. Completely cooled crusts can be wrapped with plastic wrap and then aluminum foil and frozen for up to 2 weeks. Frozen crusts can be topped and baked as directed without thawing.

The America's Test Kitchen Gluten-Free Flour Blend

MAKES 42 OUNCES (ABOUT 9⅓ CUPS)

Be sure to use potato starch, not potato flour, with this recipe. Tapioca starch is also sold as tapioca flour; they are interchangeable. We strongly recommend that you use Bob's Red Mill white and brown rice flours. We also recommend that you weigh your ingredients; if you measure by volume, spoon each ingredient into the measuring cup (do not pack or tap) and scrape off the excess.

24   ounces (4½ cups plus ⅓ cup) white rice flour
7½   ounces (1⅔ cups) brown rice flour
7   ounces (1⅓ cups) potato starch
3   ounces (¾ cup) tapioca starch
¾   ounce (¼ cup) nonfat dry milk powder

Whisk all ingredients in large bowl until well combined. Transfer to airtight container and refrigerate for up to 3 months.

PEPPERONI PAN PIZZA

WHY THIS RECIPE WORKS: Great pan pizza—named for the pan in which the dough rises and is cooked—has an irresistible crust that's crisp on the bottom and soft and chewy in the middle. A generous amount of oil poured into the pan creates the crisp bottom; getting the soft interior is harder to figure out. We found the secret in a novel ingredient: skim milk. Milk is often used in tender yeast breads, and when we tried it in our pan pizza dough, we got a tender crust with just the right chew. Whole milk worked fine as well, but dough made with skim milk rose better and baked up especially soft and light. Just a few teaspoons of sugar gave the yeast a jump start and improved the flavor of the dough. Rising the dough in a warmed oven sped up the process to just 30 minutes. We were determined to top our pizza with the quintessential pepperoni, but when just plopped on the pizza and baked, the pepperoni floated in pools of orange grease. We tried frying it, but this made it too crisp and turned it an ugly shade of brown. The solution was to use the microwave to render the excess fat before baking. Topped with chewy, spicy pepperoni, mozzarella, and a quick, fresh tomato sauce (and ready in just 90 minutes), this pizza beat delivery hands down.

Pepperoni Pan Pizza

MAKES TWO 9-INCH PIZZAS

DOUGH

½   cup olive oil
¾   cup skim milk plus 2 additional tablespoons, warmed to 110 degrees
2   teaspoons sugar
2⅓   cups (11⅝ ounces) unbleached all-purpose flour, plus extra for the work surface
1   envelope instant yeast
½   teaspoon table salt

TOPPING

1   (3.5-ounce) package sliced pepperoni
1½   cups Quick Tomato Sauce for Pizza (page 336)
12   ounces shredded part-skim mozzarella cheese (about 3 cups)

PAN PIZZA DOUGH WITHOUT A MIXER
In step 2 of Pepperoni Pan Pizza, mix the flour, yeast, and salt together in a large bowl. Make a well in the flour, then pour the milk mixture into the well. Using a wooden spoon, stir until the dough becomes shaggy and difficult to stir. Turn out onto a heavily floured work surface and knead, incorporating any shaggy scraps. Knead until the dough is smooth, about 10 minutes. Shape into a ball and proceed with recipe as directed.

1. TO MAKE THE DOUGH: Adjust an oven rack to the lowest position and heat the oven to 200 degrees. When the oven reaches 200 degrees, turn it off. Lightly coat a large bowl with vegetable oil spray. Coat each of two 9-inch cake pans with 3 tablespoons of the oil.

2. Mix the milk, sugar, and remaining 2 tablespoons oil in a measuring cup. Mix the flour, yeast, and salt in a stand mixer fitted with the dough hook. Turn the machine to low and slowly add the milk mixture. After the dough comes together, increase the speed to medium-low and mix until the dough is shiny and smooth, about 5 minutes. Turn the dough onto a lightly floured work surface, gently shape into a ball, and place in the greased bowl. Cover with plastic wrap and place in the warm oven until doubled in size, about 30 minutes.

3. TO SHAPE AND TOP THE DOUGH: Transfer the dough to a lightly floured work surface, divide it in half, and lightly roll each half into a ball. Working with 1 dough ball at a time, roll and shape the dough into a 9½-inch round and press into the oiled pans. Cover with plastic wrap and set in a warm spot (not in the oven) until puffy and slightly risen, about 20 minutes. Meanwhile, heat the oven to 400 degrees.

4. While the dough rises, put half of the pepperoni in a single layer on a microwave-safe plate lined with 2 paper towels. Cover with 2 more paper towels and microwave on high for 30 seconds. Discard the towels and set the pepperoni aside; repeat with new paper towels and the remaining pepperoni.

5. Remove the plastic wrap from the dough. Ladle ¾ cup of the sauce on each round, leaving a ½-inch border around the edges. Sprinkle each with 1½ cups of the cheese and top with the pepperoni. Bake until the cheese is melted and the pepperoni is browning around the edges, about 20 minutes. Remove from the oven; let the pizzas rest in the pans for 1 minute. Using a spatula, transfer the pizzas to a cutting board and cut each into 8 wedges. Serve.

PIZZA BIANCA

WHY THIS RECIPE WORKS: The Roman version of pizza has a crust like no other we've ever tasted: crisp but extraordinarily chewy. It's so good on its own that it is usually topped with just olive oil, rosemary, and kosher salt. We wanted to figure out how we could enjoy this marvel without taking a trip to Italy.

This pizza dough contains significantly more water than other styles, which is the secret to its chewy texture. But extra-wet doughs require more kneading, and we wanted to make this dish at home in a reasonable amount of time. Instead of a long knead, we let the dough rest for 20 minutes, which let us get away with just 10 minutes of kneading. After an initial rise, the dough was still sticky; we couldn't roll it out, but it was easy to pour out then press onto a baking sheet. After letting the dough rest briefly, we baked the crust, adding just kosher salt, oil, and rosemary to remain true to the authentic version.

Pizza Bianca
SERVES 6 TO 8
Serve the pizza by itself as a snack, or with soup or salad as a light entrée. Once the dough has been placed in the oiled bowl, it can be transferred to the refrigerator and kept for up to 24 hours. Bring the dough to room temperature, 2 to 2½ hours, before proceeding with step 4 of the recipe. While kneading the dough on high speed, the mixer tends to wobble and walk on the countertop. Place a towel or shelf liner under the mixer and watch it at all times while mixing. Handle the dough with lightly oiled hands. Resist flouring your fingers or the dough might stick further. This recipe was developed using an 18 by 13-inch baking sheet. Smaller baking sheets can be used, but because the pizza will be thicker, baking times will be longer. If you don't have a pizza stone, bake the pizza on a rimless or overturned baking sheet that has been preheated just like the pizza stone.

- 3 cups (15 ounces) unbleached all-purpose flour
- 1⅔ cups water, at room temperature
- 1¼ teaspoons table salt
- 1½ teaspoons instant or rapid-rise yeast
- 1¼ teaspoons sugar
- 5 tablespoons extra-virgin olive oil
- 1 teaspoon kosher salt
- 2 tablespoons whole fresh rosemary leaves

1. Mix the flour, water, and table salt in the bowl of a stand mixer fitted with the dough hook on low speed until no areas of dry flour remain, 3 to 4 minutes, occasionally scraping down the sides of the bowl. Turn off the mixer and let the dough rest for 20 minutes.

2. Sprinkle the yeast and sugar over the dough. Knead on low speed until fully combined, 1 to 2 minutes, occasionally scraping down the sides of the bowl. Increase the mixer speed to high and knead until the dough is glossy and smooth and pulls away from the sides of the bowl, 6 to 10 minutes. (The dough will pull away from the sides only while the mixer is on. When the mixer is off, the dough will fall back to the sides.)

3. Using your fingers, coat a large bowl with 1 tablespoon of the oil, rubbing the excess oil from your fingers onto the blade of a rubber spatula. Using the oiled spatula, transfer the dough to the bowl and pour 1 tablespoon more oil over the top. Flip the dough over once so that it is well coated with the oil; cover tightly with plastic wrap. Let the dough rise at room temperature until nearly tripled in volume and large bubbles have formed, 2 to 2½ hours.

4. One hour before baking the pizza, adjust an oven rack to the middle position, place a pizza stone on the rack, and heat the oven to 450 degrees.

5. Coat a rimmed baking sheet with 2 tablespoons more oil. Using a rubber spatula, turn the dough out onto the baking sheet along with any oil in the bowl. Using your fingertips, press the dough out toward the edges of the baking sheet, taking care not to tear it. (The dough will not fit snugly into corners. If the dough resists stretching, let it relax for 5 to 10 minutes before trying to stretch it again.) Let the dough rest until slightly bubbly, 5 to 10 minutes. Using a dinner fork, poke the surface of the dough 30 to 40 times and sprinkle with the kosher salt.

6. Bake until golden brown, 20 to 30 minutes, sprinkling the rosemary over the top and rotating the baking sheet halfway through baking. Using a metal spatula, transfer the pizza to a cutting board. Brush the dough lightly with the remaining 1 tablespoon oil. Slice and serve immediately.

SIMPLER GRILLED PIZZA

WHY THIS RECIPE WORKS: Most homemade versions of this restaurant classic disappoint with charred crusts and sauce and cheese that drip onto the coals. We set out to find the secret to great grilled pizza at home.

Regular pizza dough stuck to the cooking grate and burned easily. We found that the dough has to be both thinner and sturdier to work on the grill. We used high-protein bread flour to strengthen the dough, and adding water made it easier to stretch. The crust also needed more flavor to stand up to the heat of the fire, so we added extra salt, a little whole wheat flour, and some olive oil. The oil in the dough also kept the crust from sticking to the cooking grate. Salted chopped tomatoes rather than sauce and a mixture of soft fontina (which has more flavor than mozzarella) and nutty Parmesan

made a flavorful but light topping that didn't weigh down the crust or make it soggy. Spicy garlic oil and a scattering of fresh basil added complexity without heaviness. Full of flavor and with a cracker-crisp crust, these grilled pizzas are as good as any we've had in a restaurant.

Grilled Tomato and Cheese Pizza
MAKES FOUR 9-INCH PIZZAS, SERVING 4 TO 6

The pizzas cook very quickly on the grill, so before you begin, be sure to have all the equipment and ingredients you need at hand. Equipment includes a pizza peel (or baking sheet), a pair of tongs, a paring knife, a large cutting board, and a pastry brush. Ingredients includes all the toppings and a small bowl of flour for dusting. The pizzas are best served hot off the grill but can be kept warm for 20 to 30 minutes on a wire rack in a 200-degree oven.

DOUGH

- 1 cup water, room temperature
- 2 tablespoons olive oil
- 2 cups (11 ounces) bread flour
- 1 tablespoon whole-wheat flour (optional)
- 2 teaspoons sugar
- 1¼ teaspoons salt
- 1 teaspoon instant or rapid-rise yeast

TOPPING

- 1½ pounds plum tomatoes, cored, seeded, and cut into ½-inch pieces
- ¾ teaspoon salt
- 6 ounces fontina cheese, shredded (1½ cups)
- 1½ ounces Parmesan cheese, grated fine (¾ cup)
- 1 recipe Spicy Garlic Oil (recipe follows)
- ½ cup chopped fresh basil
  Kosher salt

1. FOR THE DOUGH: Combine water and 2 tablespoons oil in liquid measuring cup. Pulse 1¾ cup bread flour, whole wheat flour, if using, sugar, salt, and yeast in food processor (fitted with dough blade if possible) until combined, about 5 pulses. With food processor running, slowly add water mixture; process until dough forms ball, about 1½ minutes. (If after 1½ minutes dough is sticky and clings to blade, add remaining ¼ cup flour 1 tablespoon at a time.) Transfer dough to large, lightly greased bowl; cover tightly with plastic wrap and let rise at room temperature until doubled in size, 1½ to 2 hours.

2. Gently press down on center of dough to deflate. Transfer dough to clean counter and divide into 4 equal pieces. With cupped palms, form each piece into smooth, tight ball. Set dough balls on well-floured counter. Press dough rounds by hand to flatten; cover loosely with plastic and let rest for 15 minutes.

3. FOR THE TOPPING: Meanwhile, toss tomatoes and salt in bowl; transfer to colander and drain for 30 minutes (wipe out and reserve bowl). Shake colander to drain off excess liquid; transfer tomatoes to now-empty bowl and set aside. Combine fontina and Parmesan in second bowl and set aside.

4. Gently stretch 1 dough round (keep other rounds covered) into disk about ½ inch thick and 5 to 6 inches in diameter. Roll disk out to ⅛-inch thickness, 9 to 10 inches in diameter, on well-floured sheet of parchment paper, dusting with additional flour as needed to prevent sticking. (If dough shrinks when rolled out, cover with plastic and let rest until relaxed, 10 to 15 minutes.) Dust surface of rolled dough with flour and set aside. Repeat with remaining dough rounds, stacking sheets of rolled dough on top of each other (with parchment in between) and covering stack with plastic; set aside until grill is ready.

5A. FOR A CHARCOAL GRILL: Open bottom vent completely. Light large chimney starter filled with charcoal briquettes (6 quarts). When top coals are partially covered with ash, pour evenly over three-quarters of grill. Set cooking grate in place, cover, and open lid vent completely. Heat grill until hot, about 5 minutes.

5B. FOR A GAS GRILL: Turn all burners to high, cover, and heat grill until hot, about 15 minutes. Leave primary burner on high and turn off other burner(s).

6. Clean and oil cooking grate. Lightly flour pizza peel or baking sheet; invert 1 dough round onto peel, gently stretching it as needed to retain its shape (do not stretch dough too thin; thin spots will burn quickly). Peel off and discard parchment; carefully slide round onto hotter side of grill. Immediately repeat with another dough round. Cook (covered if using gas) until tops are covered with bubbles (pierce larger bubbles with paring knife) and bottoms are grill-marked and charred in spots, 1 to 4 minutes; while rounds cook, check undersides and slide to cooler area of grill if browning too quickly. Transfer crusts to cutting board, browned sides up. Repeat with 2 remaining dough rounds.

7. Brush 2 crusts generously with garlic oil; top each evenly with one-quarter of cheese mixture and one-quarter of tomatoes. Return pizzas to hotter side of grill and cover grill with lid; cook until bottoms are well browned and cheese is melted, 2 to 6 minutes, checking bottoms frequently to prevent burning. Transfer pizzas to cutting board; repeat with remaining 2 crusts. Sprinkle pizzas with basil and season with salt to taste; cut into wedges and serve.

Spicy Garlic Oil
MAKES ENOUGH FOR 4 PIZZAS

⅓ cup extra-virgin olive oil
4 medium garlic cloves, minced or pressed through a garlic press (about 4 teaspoons)
½–¾ teaspoon red pepper flakes

Cook all the ingredients in a small saucepan over medium heat, stirring occasionally, until the garlic begins to sizzle, 2 to 3 minutes. Transfer to a small bowl.

ULTIMATE GRILLED PIZZA

WHY THIS RECIPE WORKS: We let the food processor do the work making the dough for our grilled pizza, before letting it proof for at least 24 hours in the refrigerator to develop complex flavor. To ensure that the dough cooked up thin, we used a tiny amount of yeast to reduce air bubbles and a relatively high percentage of water that made a relatively slack dough that easily stretched. Stretching the dough on a generously oiled baking sheet prevented it from sticking to our hands and the grill and also helped the exterior fry and crisp. To ensure that the toppings cooked quickly on a grill, we preheated the sauce and used a combination of fast-melting fresh mozzarella and finely grated Parmesan; we also sprinkled the Parmesan evenly over the dough to create a flavorful barrier against moisture before dolloping (rather than slathering on) the sauce and scattering chunks of cheese, all of which helped maintain the dough's crisp texture. To prevent a hotspot at the center that would burn the crust, we placed the coals only around the perimeter of the grill rather than in an even layer.

Ultimate Grilled Pizza
SERVES 4 TO 6

The dough must sit for at least 24 hours before shaping. We prefer the high protein content of King Arthur bread flour for this recipe, though other bread flours are acceptable. For best results, weigh your ingredients. It's important to use ice water in the dough to prevent it from overheating in the food processor. Grilled pizza cooks quickly, so it's critical to have all of your ingredients and tools ready ahead of time. We recommend pargrilling, topping, and grilling in quick succession and serving the pizzas one at a time, rather than all at once.

DOUGH

- 3 cups (16½ ounces) King Arthur bread flour
- 1 tablespoon sugar
- ¼ teaspoon instant or rapid-rise yeast
- 1¼ cups plus 2 tablespoons ice water (11 ounces)
  Vegetable oil
- 1½ teaspoons salt

SAUCE

- 1 (14-ounce) can whole peeled plum tomatoes, drained, juice reserved
- 2 tablespoons extra-virgin olive oil
- 2 teaspoons minced fresh oregano
- ¼ teaspoon red pepper flakes
  Salt
  Sugar

PIZZA

  Extra-virgin olive oil
- 3 ounces Parmesan cheese, grated (1½ cups)
- 8 ounces fresh whole-milk mozzarella cheese, torn into grape-size pieces (about 2 cups)
- 3 tablespoons shredded fresh basil
  Coarse sea salt

1. FOR THE DOUGH: Process flour, sugar, and yeast in food processor until combined, about 2 seconds. With processor running, slowly add ice water; process until dough is just combined and no dry flour remains, about 10 seconds. Let dough stand for 10 minutes.

2. Add 1 tablespoon oil and salt to dough and process until dough forms satiny, sticky ball that clears sides of bowl, 30 to 60 seconds. Transfer dough to lightly oiled counter and knead until smooth, about 1 minute. Divide dough into 3 equal pieces (about 9⅓ ounces each). Shape each piece into tight ball and transfer to well-oiled baking sheet (alternatively, place dough balls in individual well-oiled bowls). Cover tightly with plastic wrap (taking care not to compress dough) and refrigerate for at least 24 hours or up to 3 days.

3. FOR THE SAUCE: Pulse tomatoes in food processor until finely chopped, 12 to 15 pulses. Transfer to medium bowl and stir in oil, oregano, pepper flakes, reserved juice, ½ teaspoon salt, and ½ teaspoon sugar. Season with additional salt and sugar to taste, cover, and refrigerate until ready to use.

4. One hour before cooking pizza, remove tray of dough from refrigerator and let stand at room temperature.

5A. FOR A CHARCOAL GRILL: Open bottom vent halfway. Light large chimney starter three-quarters filled with charcoal briquettes (4½ quarts). When top coals are partially covered with ash, pour into ring around perimeter of grill, leaving 8-inch clearing in center. Set cooking grate in place, cover, and open lid vent halfway. Heat grill until hot, about 5 minutes.

5B. FOR A GAS GRILL: Turn all burners to high, cover, and heat grill until hot, about 15 minutes. Leave all burners on high.

6. While grill is heating, place sauce in small saucepan and bring to simmer over medium heat. Cover and keep warm.

7. FOR THE PIZZA: Clean and oil cooking grate. Pour ¼ cup oil onto center of rimmed baking sheet. Transfer 1 dough round to sheet and coat both sides of dough with oil. Using your fingertips and palms, gently press and stretch dough toward edges of sheet to form rough 16 by 12-inch oval of even thickness. Using both of your hands, lift dough and carefully transfer to grill. (When transferring dough from sheet to grill, it will droop slightly to form half-moon or snowshoe shape.) Cook (over clearing if using charcoal and covered if using gas) until grill marks form, 2 to 3 minutes. Using tongs and spatula, carefully peel dough from grill grates, then rotate dough 90 degrees and continue to cook (covered if using gas) until second set of grill marks appears, 2 to 3 minutes longer. Flip dough and cook (covered if using gas) until second side of dough is lightly charred in spots, 2 to 3 minutes. Using tongs or pizza peel, transfer crust to cutting board, inverting so side that was grilled first is facing down. Repeat with remaining 2 dough rounds, adding 1 tablespoon oil to baking sheet for each round and keeping grill cover closed when not in use to retain heat.

8. Drizzle top of 1 crust with 1 tablespoon oil. Sprinkle one-third of Parmesan evenly over surface. Arrange one-third of mozzarella pieces, evenly spaced, on surface of pizza. Dollop one-third of sauce in evenly spaced 1-tablespoon mounds over surface of pizza. Using pizza peel or overturned rimmed baking sheet, transfer pizza to grill, cover, and cook until bottom is well browned and mozzarella is melted, 3 to 5 minutes, checking bottom and turning frequently to prevent burning. Transfer pizza to cutting board; repeat with remaining 2 crusts. Sprinkle pizzas with basil, drizzle lightly with oil, and season with salt to taste. Cut into wedges and serve.

NOTES FROM THE TEST KITCHEN

DON'T SKIMP ON THE OIL

Stretching the dough in a generous amount of olive oil not only prevents it from sticking to your hands and to the cooking grate but also crisps the exterior without rendering it greasy.

TOMATO TART

WHY THIS RECIPE WORKS: Falling somewhere in between pizza and quiche, tomato and mozzarella tart shares the flavors of both but features unique problems. For starters, this is not fast food, as some sort of pastry crust is required. Second, the moisture in the tomatoes almost guarantees a soggy crust. Third, despite their good looks, tomato tarts often fall short on flavor. We wanted a recipe that could easily be made at home with a solid bottom crust and great vine-ripened flavor.

Frozen puff pastry was the solution to an easy crust, and prebaking it was a start—but only a start—to solving the problem of sogginess. Sealing the puff pastry shell with an egg wash helped. Yet even with these preventive measures, the tomato juice still found its way into the crust. To extract more moisture from the tomatoes before baking the tart, we sliced and salted them, then pressed them lightly between paper towels. This removed much of the moisture. But even with a layer of grated mozzarella cheese (whole-milk worked best) between tomatoes and crust, the tart shell still came out a bit soggy. Our breakthrough came when we added a layer of grated Parmesan cheese, which sealed the crust fully and repelled moisture. After a short stay in the oven, our tart had a crisp and sturdy crust, nutty tang from the Parmesan, and rich flavors from the cheese and tomatoes.

Tomato and Mozzarella Tart

SERVES 4 TO 6

To keep the frozen dough from cracking, it's best to let it thaw slowly in the refrigerator overnight. For the best flavor, use authentic Parmesan cheese and very ripe, flavorful tomatoes. Fresh mozzarella will make the crust soggy, so be sure to use low-moisture, shrink-wrapped mozzarella.

PREPARING TOMATO TART

1. Fold the short edges of the pastry over by ½ inch and brush with egg. Then fold the long edges of the pastry over by ½ inch, making sure to keep the edges flush and square. Brush with egg.

2. Using a paring knife, cut through the folded edges and corners of the tart shell.

3. After sprinkling the bottom of the tart with the Parmesan, poke the dough repeatedly with a fork. Bake the pastry shell.

4. Sprinkle the mozzarella evenly over the crust and shingle the tomatoes attractively over the mozzarella.

1 (9 by 9½-inch) sheet frozen puff pastry, thawed (see note)

1 large egg, lightly beaten

1 ounce Parmesan cheese, grated (about ½ cup; see note)

½ pound plum tomatoes (2 medium), cored and sliced ¼ inch thick (see note)

½ teaspoon table salt

4 ounces whole-milk mozzarella cheese, shredded (about 1 cup; see note)

2 tablespoons extra-virgin olive oil

1 medium garlic clove, minced or pressed through a garlic press (about 1 teaspoon)

2 tablespoons minced fresh basil

1. Adjust an oven rack to the lowest position and heat the oven to 425 degrees. Line a large baking sheet with parchment paper. Lay the pastry in the center of the prepared baking sheet. Brush the pastry with the beaten egg. To form a rimmed crust, fold the long edges of the pastry over by ½ inch, then brush with the egg. Fold the short edges of the pastry over by ½ inch and brush with the egg. Use a paring knife to cut through the folded edges and corner of the pastry. Sprinkle the Parmesan evenly over the crust bottom. Poke the dough uniformly with a fork. Bake until golden brown and crisp, 15 to 20 minutes. Transfer to a wire rack to cool.

2. Meanwhile, spread the tomatoes over several layers of paper towels. Sprinkle with the salt and let drain for 30 minutes.

3. Sprinkle the mozzarella evenly over the crust bottom. Press excess moisture from the tomatoes, using additional paper towels. Following the photo (on page 349), shingle the tomatoes evenly over the mozzarella. Whisk the olive oil and garlic together and drizzle over the tomatoes. Bake until the shell is deep golden, 10 to 15 minutes.

4. Cool on a wire rack for 5 minutes and then sprinkle with the basil. Slide the tart onto a cutting board, slice into pieces, and serve.

GARLIC BREAD

WHY THIS RECIPE WORKS: Garlic bread is a classic accompaniment to spaghetti and meatballs, baked ziti, and countless other Italian favorites. It seems so simple, yet it often goes so wrong. We wanted to banish greasy, bland, and bitter-tasting garlic bread forever in favor of crisp toasted bread imbued with sweet, nutty garlic flavor.

Starting with the bread, we chose a substantial loaf of football-shaped Italian bread, the best quality we could find, to give us generous slices. We cut it in half horizontally, so that the surfaces would crisp up in the oven. We tamed the garlic's harshness by toasting whole cloves, which turned them rich and mellow. We cut out the step of melting butter and simply spread it, after softening and mixing in the garlic, on the bread—not too much, so the bread wouldn't be greasy or soggy. The addition of some grated Parmesan cheese was nearly undetectable, but it added a deep and complex flavor. For baking, we found that leaving the bread unwrapped on a baking sheet gave us the crispy crust we wanted, and exposure to the oven's heat further mellowed the garlic.

Classic Garlic Bread

SERVES 6 TO 8

Plan to pull the garlic bread from the oven when you are ready to serve the other dishes—it is best served piping hot.

- 9–10 medium garlic cloves, unpeeled
- 6 tablespoons (¾ stick) unsalted butter, softened
- 2 tablespoons grated Parmesan cheese
- ½ teaspoon table salt

- 1 (1-pound) loaf high-quality Italian bread (preferably football-shaped), halved horizontally
  Ground black pepper

1. Adjust an oven rack to the middle position and heat the oven to 500 degrees. Meanwhile, toast the garlic cloves in a small skillet over medium heat, shaking the pan occasionally, until fragrant and the color of the cloves deepens slightly, about 8 minutes. When cool enough to handle, peel and mince the cloves (you should have about 3 tablespoons). Using a dinner fork, mash the garlic, butter, cheese, and salt in a small bowl until thoroughly combined.

2. Spread the cut sides of the loaf evenly with the butter mixture; season with pepper to taste. Transfer the loaf halves, buttered side up, onto a rimmed baking sheet; bake, reversing the position of the baking sheet in the oven from front to back halfway through the baking time, until the surface of the bread is golden brown and toasted, 5 to 10 minutes. Cut each half into 2-inch slices; serve immediately.

REALLY GOOD GARLIC BREAD

WHY THIS RECIPE WORKS: Garlic bread is simple to make but is often a disappointment to eat, with either too much or too little garlic flavor and too crusty or too soft a texture. We briefly microwaved fresh garlic in butter and combined it with garlic powder, which provided sweet, roasty notes, some solid butter, and just a bit of cayenne and salt to make a smooth paste with just the right balance of full, complex garlic flavor. We then baked the garlic bread halves between two baking sheets to create a griddle-like set-up that crisped and browned the crust while keeping the interior soft and chewy.

Really Good Garlic Bread

SERVES 8

A 12 by 5-inch loaf of Italian bread from the bakery section of the supermarket, which has a soft, thin crust and fine crumb, works best in this recipe. We do not recommend using a rustic or crusty artisan-style loaf. A rasp-style grater makes quick work of turning the garlic into a paste. If you bake the bread on a dark baking sheet, start checking for doneness after 4 minutes after flipping the bread in step 3.

- 1 teaspoon garlic powder
- 1 teaspoon water
- 8 tablespoons unsalted butter
- ½ teaspoon salt
- ⅛ teaspoon cayenne pepper
- 4-5 garlic cloves, minced to paste (1 tablespoon)
- 1 (1-pound) loaf soft Italian bread, halved horizontally

1. Adjust oven rack to lower-middle position and heat oven 450 degrees. Combine garlic powder and water in medium bowl. Add 4 tablespoons butter, salt, and cayenne to bowl; set aside.

2. Place remaining 4 tablespoons butter in small bowl and microwave, covered, until melted, about 30 seconds. Stir in garlic and continue to microwave, covered, until mixture is bubbling around edges, about 1 minute, stirring halfway through. Transfer garlic-butter mixture to bowl with garlic powder mixture and whisk together until it forms homogenous loose paste. (If mixture melts, set aside until it solidifies before using.)

3. Spread cut sides of loaf evenly with butter mixture. Transfer bread, cut side up, to baking sheet. Bake until butter has melted into surface of bread and bread is hot, 3 to 4 minutes. Remove baking sheet from oven. Flip bread, cut side down, place second rimmed baking sheet on top and gently press. Return bread to oven, with second baking sheet on top of bread, and continue to bake until cut side of bread is golden brown and crisp, 5 to 10 minutes longer, rotating sheet halfway through baking. Transfer bread to cutting board. Using serrated knife, cut each half into 8 slices and serve immediately.

CHEESY GARLIC BREAD

WHY THIS RECIPE WORKS: Garlic bread is a balancing act between the butter, garlic, and bread. Add cheese to the mix and things get complicated. We wanted cheese-topped garlic bread that was crisp on the outside but chewy within, buttery all the way through, and with no bitter garlic aftertaste.

Supermarket baguettes already have a chewy interior and crisp crust, so we started there. Grating the garlic cloves made for a smoother butter, and to tone down the garlic's harshness we sautéed it in butter with a little water (to prevent burning). We mixed the garlic into more softened butter, spread it on our split baguette, and wrapped the bread in foil. Baking it this way "steamed" the bread and infused it with garlic-butter flavor. To crisp the crust, we took the bread out of the foil and baked it a little longer. The final adornment was the cheese; rather than shredding several different kinds ourselves, we took a shortcut and used a prepackaged mixture of shredded Italian cheeses. The last step was to run it under the broiler, which gave us both melted cheese and an extra-crisp crust.

Cheesy Garlic Bread

SERVES 6 TO 8

The serrated edges on a bread knife can pull off the cheesy crust. To prevent this, place the finished garlic bread cheese side down on a cutting board. Slicing through the crust first (rather than the cheese) will keep the cheese in place. Shredded Italian cheese blend is sold in bags in the supermarket case near other packaged cheeses.

- 5 medium garlic cloves, peeled and grated
- 8 tablespoons (1 stick) unsalted butter, softened
- ½ teaspoon water
- ¼ teaspoon table salt

- ¼ teaspoon ground black pepper
- 1 (18- to 20-inch) baguette, sliced in half horizontally
- 1½ cups shredded Italian cheese blend (see note)

1. Adjust an oven rack to the lower-middle position and heat the oven to 400 degrees. Cook the garlic, 1 tablespoon of the butter, and the water in a small nonstick skillet over low heat, stirring occasionally, until straw-colored, 7 to 10 minutes.

2. Mix the hot garlic, remaining 7 tablespoons butter, the salt, and pepper in a bowl and spread on the cut sides of the bread. Sandwich the bread back together and wrap the loaf in foil. Place on a baking sheet and bake for 15 minutes.

3. Carefully unwrap the bread and place the halves, buttered sides up, on a baking sheet. Bake until just beginning to color, about 10 minutes. Remove from the oven and set the oven to broil.

4. Sprinkle the bread with the cheese. Broil until the cheese has melted and the bread is crisp, 1 to 2 minutes. Transfer the bread to a cutting board with the cheese side facing down. Cut into pieces and serve.

FRICO

WHY THIS RECIPE WORKS: As an accompaniment to cocktails or eaten just as a snack, frico is a simple, crisp wafer of flavorful cheese, usually Montasio, that has been melted and browned. We wanted to find the secret behind great frico, and then determine the best substitute for Montasio cheese, which can be difficult to find.

Cheese simply grated into a hot pan could turn into a sticky mess, but we found that using a nonstick skillet allowed us to cook the frico without adding butter or oil. We discovered that it was easy to turn the frico to the other side once the first side was browned if we first took the skillet off the heat;

the slightly cooled cheese didn't stretch or tear when we flipped it. Turning the heat down to cook the second side gave the best results; a pan that was too hot turned the cheese bitter. Many recipes suggest Parmesan as a substitute for Montasio, but we found Asiago cheese to be a better stand-in—though the real thing is even better.

Frico

MAKES 8 LARGE WAFERS

Serve frico with drinks and a bowl of marinated olives or marinated sun-dried tomatoes. Frico is also good crumbled into a salad, crouton-style.

1 pound Montasio or aged Asiago cheese, grated fine (about 8 cups)

1. Sprinkle 2 ounces (about 1 cup) of the grated cheese over the bottom of a 10-inch nonstick skillet set over medium-high heat. Use a heat-resistant rubber spatula or a wooden spoon to tidy the lacy outer edges of the cheese. Cook, shaking the pan occasionally to ensure an even distribution of the cheese over the pan bottom, until the edges are lacy and toasted, about 4 minutes. Remove the pan from the heat and allow the cheese to set for about 30 seconds.

2. Using a fork on top and a heatproof spatula underneath, carefully flip the cheese wafer and return the pan to medium heat. Cook until the second side is golden brown, about 2 minutes. Slide the cheese wafer out of the pan and transfer to a plate. Repeat with the remaining cheese. Serve the frico within 1 hour.

PASTA E FAGIOLI

WHY THIS RECIPE WORKS: The American version of this hearty Italian bean-and-vegetable stew—sometimes called "pasta fazool"—often turns out bland, with mushy beans and pasta and too much tomato. And it can take hours to prepare. We wanted rich broth, perfectly cooked beans and pasta, and complex flavors—and we wanted to prepare it in a reasonable amount of time.

Substituting canned beans for dried would save the most preparation time, and we found cannellini beans to be the closest to the dried cranberry beans used in authentic recipes. We started to build deep flavor by sautéing pancetta (though bacon also works) and, for aromatics, onion, garlic, and celery. Tomatoes (diced worked better than crushed or sauce) went in next. A small amount of minced anchovies was unidentifiable but added complexity. Chicken broth diluted with water was our cooking liquid; chicken broth alone made the dish taste too much like chicken soup. A Parmesan rind added another layer of flavor. Last into the pot went the pasta. The flavors of our thick, hearty soup harmonized perfectly and, best of all, we had spent less than an hour at the stove.

Italian Pasta and Bean Soup (Pasta e Fagioli)

SERVES 8 TO 10

This soup does not hold well because the pasta absorbs the liquid, becomes mushy, and leaves the soup dry. You can, however, make the soup in two stages. Once the beans are simmered with the tomatoes, before the broth and water are added, the mixture can be cooled and refrigerated for up to 3 days. When ready to complete the soup, discard the Parmesan rind (otherwise it will become stringy), add the liquid, bring the soup to a boil, and proceed with the recipe.

1 tablespoon extra-virgin olive oil, plus extra for drizzling
3 ounces pancetta or bacon (about 3 slices), chopped fine
1 medium onion, minced
1 celery rib, chopped fine
4 medium garlic cloves, minced or pressed through a garlic press (about 4 teaspoons)
1 teaspoon dried oregano
¼ teaspoon red pepper flakes
3 anchovy fillets, minced to a paste (about 1½ teaspoons)
1 (28-ounce) can diced tomatoes
1 piece Parmesan cheese rind, about 5 inches by 2 inches
2 (15.5-ounce) cans cannellini beans, drained and rinsed
3½ cups low-sodium chicken broth
2½ cups water
    Table salt
8 ounces small pasta such as ditalini, tubetini, conchiglietti, or orzo
4 tablespoons chopped fresh parsley leaves
    Ground black pepper
    Grated Parmesan cheese, for serving

1. Heat the oil in a large Dutch oven over medium-high heat until shimmering. Add the pancetta and cook, stirring occasionally, until it begins to brown, 3 to 5 minutes. Add the onion and celery and cook, stirring occasionally, until the vegetables are softened, 5 to 7 minutes. Add the garlic, oregano, red pepper flakes, and anchovies and cook, stirring constantly, until fragrant, about 30 seconds. Add the tomatoes with their juice, scraping up any browned bits. Add the cheese rind and beans; bring to a boil, then reduce the heat to low and simmer to blend the flavors, 10 minutes. Add the chicken broth, water, and 1 teaspoon salt; increase the heat to high and bring to a boil. Add the pasta and cook until tender, about 10 minutes.

2. Discard the cheese rind. Off the heat, stir in 3 tablespoons of the parsley; season with salt and pepper to taste. Ladle the soup into individual bowls; drizzle each serving with olive oil and sprinkle with a portion of the remaining 1 tablespoon parsley. Serve immediately, passing the grated Parmesan separately.

ITALIAN VEGETABLE STEW (CIAMBOTTA)

WHY THIS RECIPE WORKS: Italy's ciambotta is a ratatouille-like stew chock-full of veggies that makes for a hearty one-bowl meal with nary a trace of meat. We wanted to avoid the sad fate of most recipes, which end in mushy vegetables drowning in a weak broth. To optimize the texture of the zucchini and peppers, we employed the dry heat of a skillet. To address the broth, we embraced eggplant's natural tendency to fall apart and cooked it until it completely assimilated into a thickened tomato-enriched sauce. Finally, we found that a traditional pestata of garlic and herbs provided the biggest flavor punch when added near the end of cooking.

Italian Vegetable Stew (Ciambotta)

SERVES 6 TO 8

Serve this hearty vegetable stew with crusty bread.

PESTATA

- ⅓ cup chopped fresh basil
- ⅓ cup fresh oregano leaves
- 6 garlic cloves, minced
- 2 tablespoons extra-virgin olive oil
- ¼ teaspoon red pepper flakes

STEW

- 12 ounces eggplant, peeled and cut into ½-inch pieces
  Salt
- ¼ cup extra-virgin olive oil
- 1 large onion, chopped
- 1 pound russet potatoes, peeled and cut into ½-inch pieces
- 2 tablespoons tomato paste
- 2¼ cups water
- 1 (28-ounce) can whole peeled tomatoes, drained with juice reserved, chopped coarse
- 2 zucchini (8 ounces each), halved lengthwise, seeded, and cut into ½-inch pieces
- 2 red or yellow bell peppers, stemmed, seeded, and cut into ½-inch pieces
- 1 cup shredded fresh basil

1. FOR THE PESTATA: Process all ingredients in food processor until finely ground, about 1 minute, scraping down sides as needed. Set aside.

2. FOR THE STEW: Toss eggplant with 1½ teaspoons salt in bowl. Line surface of large plate with double layer of coffee filters and lightly spray with vegetable oil spray. Spread eggplant in even layer over coffee filters. Microwave eggplant, uncovered, until dry to touch and slightly shriveled, 8 to 12 minutes, tossing once halfway through to ensure that eggplant cooks evenly.

3. Heat 2 tablespoons oil in Dutch oven over high heat until shimmering. Add eggplant, onion, and potatoes; cook, stirring frequently, until eggplant browns and surface of potatoes becomes translucent, about 2 minutes. Push vegetables to sides of pot; add 1 tablespoon oil and tomato paste to clearing. Cook paste, stirring frequently, until brown fond develops on bottom of pot, about 2 minutes. Add 2 cups water and chopped tomatoes and juice, scraping up any browned bits, and bring to boil. Reduce heat to medium, cover, and gently simmer until eggplant is completely broken down and potatoes are tender, 20 to 25 minutes.

4. Meanwhile, heat remaining 1 tablespoon oil in 12-inch skillet over high heat until smoking. Add zucchini, bell peppers, and ½ teaspoon salt; cook, stirring occasionally, until vegetables are browned and tender, 10 to 12 minutes. Push vegetables to sides of skillet; add pestata and cook until fragrant, about 1 minute. Stir pestata into vegetables and transfer vegetables to bowl. Add remaining ¼ cup water to skillet off heat, scraping up browned bits.

5. Remove Dutch oven from heat and stir reserved vegetables and water from skillet into vegetables in Dutch oven. Cover pot and let stand for 20 minutes to allow flavors to meld. Stir in basil and season with salt to taste; serve.

HEARTY TUSCAN BEAN STEW

WHY THIS RECIPE WORKS: Unlike *pasta e fagioli*, where beans and pasta share the spotlight, Tuscan bean soup boasts creamy, buttery cannellini beans in the starring role. Ideally, the beans should have a uniformly tender texture, but too often the skins are tough and the insides mealy—or the beans turn mushy. We wanted to fix the bean problem and convert this Italian classic into a hearty, rustic stew for a deeply flavorful one-pot meal.

Since the beans are the centerpiece of this stew, we concentrated on cooking them perfectly. After testing a variety of soaking times, we settled on soaking the beans overnight, a method that consistently produced the most tender and evenly cooked beans. But none of the methods we tested properly softened the skins. The answer was to soak the beans in salted water. Brining the beans, rather than the conventional approach of soaking them in plain water and then cooking them in salt water, allowed the salt to soften the skins but kept it from penetrating inside, where it could make the beans mealy. Tests showed that gently cooking the beans in a 250-degree oven produced perfectly cooked beans that stayed intact. The final trick was to add the tomatoes toward the end of cooking, since their acid interfered with the softening process. To complete our stew, we looked for other traditional Tuscan flavors, including pancetta, kale, lots of garlic, and a sprig of rosemary. And to make it even more substantial, we served the stew on a slab of toasted country bread, drizzled with fruity extra-virgin olive oil.

Hearty Tuscan Bean Stew
SERVES 8

We prefer the creamier texture of beans soaked overnight for this recipe. If you're short on time, quick-soak them: Place the rinsed beans in a large heat-resistant bowl. Bring 2 quarts water and 3 tablespoons salt to a boil. Pour the water over the beans and let them sit for 1 hour. Drain and rinse the beans well before proceeding with step 2. If pancetta is unavailable, substitute 4 ounces bacon (about 4 slices).

Table salt
1 pound (about 2 cups) dried cannellini beans, picked over and rinsed
1 tablespoon extra-virgin olive oil, plus extra for drizzling
6 ounces pancetta or bacon, cut into ¼-inch pieces (see note)
1 large onion, chopped medium (about 1½ cups)
2 medium celery ribs, cut into ½-inch pieces (about ¾ cup)
2 medium carrots, peeled and cut into ½-inch pieces (about 1 cup)
8 medium garlic cloves, peeled and crushed
4 cups low-sodium chicken broth
3 cups water
2 bay leaves

1 bunch kale or collard greens (about 1 pound), stems trimmed and leaves chopped into 1-inch pieces (about 8 cups loosely packed)
1 (14.5-ounce) can diced tomatoes, drained
1 sprig fresh rosemary
Ground black pepper
8 slices country white bread, each 1¼ inches thick, broiled until golden brown on both sides and rubbed with a garlic clove (optional)

1. Dissolve 3 tablespoons salt in 4 quarts cold water in a large bowl or container. Add the beans and soak at room temperature for at least 8 hours or up to 24 hours. Drain the beans and rinse well.

2. Adjust an oven rack to the lower-middle position and heat the oven to 250 degrees. Heat the oil and pancetta in a large Dutch oven over medium heat. Cook, stirring occasionally, until the pancetta is lightly browned and the fat has rendered, 6 to 10 minutes. Add the onion, celery, and carrots. Cook, stirring occasionally, until the vegetables are softened and lightly browned, 10 to 16 minutes. Stir in the garlic and cook until fragrant, about 1 minute. Stir in the broth, water, bay leaves, and soaked beans. Increase the heat to high and bring the mixture to a simmer. Cover the pot, transfer it to the oven, and cook until the beans are almost tender (the very center of the beans will still be firm), 45 minutes to 1 hour.

3. Remove the pot from the oven and stir in the kale and tomatoes. Return the pot to the oven and continue to cook until the beans and greens are fully tender, 30 to 40 minutes longer.

4. Remove the pot from the oven and submerge the rosemary sprig in the stew. Cover and let stand for 15 minutes. Discard the bay leaves and rosemary sprig and season the stew with salt and pepper to taste. If desired, use the back of a spoon to press some beans against the side of the pot to thicken the stew. Serve over the toasted bread (if using) and drizzle with olive oil.

ITALIAN WEDDING SOUP

WHY THIS RECIPE WORKS: Traditional recipes for this hearty soup featuring meatballs, tender greens, and pasta require an afternoon-long stint on the stovetop, which starts with building the *brodo*, a long-cooked broth made from the bones of meat and poultry. Wanting a quicker path to this richly flavored soup, we created a speedy yet ultrasavory broth by simmering ground beef and pork in a mixture of chicken and beef broth. Dried porcini mushrooms and Worcestershire sauce further boosted the meaty flavor. For the meatballs, we nixed the hard-to-find ground veal and stuck with ground beef and ground pork. To make up for the loss in texture from omitting the veal, we added baking powder and whipped the pork in a stand mixer to ensure the meatballs remained light, juicy, and supple. Chopped kale and ditalini, stirred in toward the end of the cooking time, became perfectly tender in a matter of minutes.

Italian Wedding Soup

SERVES 6 TO 8

Use a rasp-style grater to process the onion and garlic for the meatballs. Tubettini or orzo can be used in place of the ditalini.

BROTH

- 1 onion, chopped
- 1 fennel bulb, stalks discarded, bulb halved, cored, and chopped
- 4 garlic cloves, peeled and smashed
- ¼ ounce dried porcini mushrooms, rinsed
- 4 ounces ground pork
- 4 ounces 85 percent lean ground beef
- 1 bay leaf
- ½ cup dry white wine
- 1 tablespoon Worcestershire sauce
- 4 cups chicken broth
- 2 cups beef broth
- 2 cups water

MEATBALLS

- 1 slice hearty white sandwich bread, crusts removed, torn into 1-inch pieces
- 5 tablespoons heavy cream
- ¼ cup grated Parmesan cheese
- 4 teaspoons finely grated onion
- ½ teaspoon finely grated garlic
  Salt and pepper
- 6 ounces ground pork
- 1 teaspoon baking powder
- 6 ounces 85 percent lean ground beef
- 2 teaspoons minced fresh oregano
- 1 cup ditalini pasta
- 12 ounces kale, stemmed and cut into ½-inch pieces (6 cups)

1. FOR THE BROTH: Heat onion, fennel, garlic, porcini, pork, beef, and bay leaf in Dutch oven over medium-high heat; cook, stirring frequently, until meats are no longer pink, about 5 minutes. Add wine and Worcestershire; cook for 1 minute. Add chicken broth, beef broth, and water; bring to simmer. Reduce heat to low, cover, and simmer for 30 minutes.

2. FOR THE MEATBALLS: While broth simmers, combine bread, cream, Parmesan, onion, garlic, and pepper to taste in bowl; using fork, mash mixture to uniform paste. Using stand mixer fitted with paddle, beat pork, baking powder, and ½ teaspoon salt on high speed until smooth and pale, 1 to 2 minutes, scraping down bowl as needed. Add bread mixture, beef, and oregano; mix on medium-low speed until just incorporated, 1 to 2 minutes, scraping down bowl as needed. Using moistened hands, form heaping teaspoons of meat mixture into smooth, round meatballs; you should have 30 to 35 meatballs. Cover and refrigerate for up to 1 day.

3. Strain broth through fine-mesh strainer set over large bowl or container, pressing on solids to extract as much liquid as possible. Wipe out Dutch oven and return broth to pot. (Broth can be refrigerated for up to 3 days. Skim off fat before reheating.)

4. Return broth to simmer over medium-high heat. Add pasta and kale; cook, stirring occasionally, for 5 minutes. Add meatballs; return to simmer and cook, stirring occasionally, until meatballs are cooked through and pasta is tender, 3 to 5 minutes. Season with salt and pepper to taste and serve.

EGGPLANT PARMESAN

WHY THIS RECIPE WORKS: Frying the eggplant for this classic Italian dish not only is time-consuming but also can make the dish heavy and dull. In hopes of eliminating the grease as well as some of the prep time, we decided to cook the eggplant in the oven and see what other measures we could take to freshen up this Italian classic.

We salted and drained the eggplant slices to improve their texture. A traditional bound breading—flour, egg, and fresh bread crumbs—worked best for giving the eggplant a crisp coating. Baking the eggplant on preheated and oiled baking sheets resulted in crisp, golden brown slices. While the eggplant was in the oven, we made a quick tomato sauce using garlic, red pepper flakes, basil, and canned diced tomatoes. We layered the sauce, eggplant, and mozzarella in a baking dish and left the top layer of eggplant mostly unsauced, so that it would crisp up in the oven. Our re-engineered eggplant Parmesan was lighter and fresher tasting, and a lot less work.

Eggplant Parmesan

SERVES 6 TO 8

Use kosher salt when salting the eggplant. The coarse grains don't dissolve as readily as the fine grains of regular table salt, so any excess can be easily wiped away. It's necessary to divide the eggplant into two batches when tossing it with the salt. To be time-efficient, use the 30 to 45 minutes during which the salted eggplant sits to prepare the breading.

EGGPLANT

2 pounds globe eggplant (2 medium eggplants), cut crosswise into ¼-inch-thick rounds

1 tablespoon kosher salt (see note)

8 slices high-quality white sandwich bread, torn into quarters

2 ounces Parmesan cheese, grated (about 1 cup)

 Table salt and ground black pepper

1 cup unbleached all-purpose flour

4 large eggs

6 tablespoons vegetable oil

TOMATO SAUCE

3 (14.5-ounce) cans diced tomatoes

2 tablespoons extra-virgin olive oil

4 medium garlic cloves, minced or pressed through a garlic press (about 4 teaspoons)

¼ teaspoon red pepper flakes

½ cup coarsely chopped fresh basil leaves

 Table salt and ground black pepper

8 ounces whole-milk or part-skim mozzarella cheese, shredded (about 2 cups)

1 ounce Parmesan cheese, grated (about ½ cup)

10 fresh basil leaves, torn, for garnish

1. FOR THE EGGPLANT: Toss half of the eggplant slices and 1½ teaspoons of the kosher salt in a large bowl until combined; transfer the salted eggplant to a large colander set over a bowl. Repeat with the remaining eggplant and kosher salt, placing the second batch on top of the first. Let stand until the eggplant releases about 2 tablespoons liquid, 30 to 45 minutes. Spread the eggplant slices on a triple thickness of paper towels; cover with another triple thickness of paper towels. Press firmly on each slice to remove as much liquid as possible, then wipe off the excess salt.

2. While the eggplant is draining, adjust the oven racks to the upper-middle and lower-middle positions, place a rimmed baking sheet on each rack, and heat the oven to 425 degrees. Process the bread in a food processor to fine, even crumbs, about 20 to 30 seconds. Transfer the crumbs to a pie plate and stir in the Parmesan, ¼ teaspoon table salt, and ½ teaspoon pepper; set aside. Wipe out the workbowl (do not wash) and set aside.

3. Combine the flour and 1 teaspoon pepper in a large zipper-lock bag; shake to combine. Beat the eggs in a second pie plate. Place 8 to 10 eggplant slices in the bag with the flour; seal the bag and shake to coat the slices. Remove the slices, shaking off the excess flour, dip into the eggs, let the excess egg run off, then coat evenly with the bread-crumb mixture; set the breaded slices on a wire rack set over a baking sheet. Repeat with the remaining eggplant.

4. Remove the preheated baking sheets from the oven; add 3 tablespoons of the vegetable oil to each sheet, tilting to coat evenly with the oil. Place half of the breaded eggplant slices on each sheet in a single layer; bake until the eggplant is well browned and crisp, about 30 minutes, switching and rotating the baking sheets after 10 minutes, and flipping the eggplant slices with a wide spatula after 20 minutes. Do not turn off the oven.

5. FOR THE SAUCE: While the eggplant bakes, process 2 cans of the diced tomatoes in the food processor until almost smooth, about 5 seconds. Heat the olive oil, garlic, and red pepper flakes in a large heavy-bottomed saucepan over medium-high heat, stirring occasionally, until fragrant and the garlic is light golden, about 3 minutes; stir in the processed tomatoes and remaining can of diced tomatoes. Bring the sauce to a boil, then reduce the heat to medium-low and simmer, stirring occasionally, until slightly thickened and reduced, about 15 minutes (you should have about 4 cups). Stir in the basil and season with table salt and pepper to taste.

6. TO ASSEMBLE: Spread 1 cup of the tomato sauce in the bottom of a 13 by 9-inch baking dish. Layer in half of the eggplant slices, overlapping the slices to fit; distribute 1 cup more of the sauce over the eggplant; sprinkle with half of the mozzarella. Layer in the remaining eggplant and dot with 1 cup more of the sauce, leaving the majority of the eggplant exposed so it will remain crisp; sprinkle with the Parmesan and the remaining mozzarella. Bake until bubbling and the cheese is browned, 13 to 15 minutes. Cool for 10 minutes, scatter the basil over the top, and serve, passing the remaining tomato sauce separately.

EGGPLANT INVOLTINI

WHY THIS RECIPE WORKS: Eggplant *involtini* ("little bundles" in Italian) can be so complicated and messy that it makes the cook wonder whether these cheese-filled eggplant bundles are worth making. But the resulting dish—charmingly tidy involtini with homemade tomato sauce and a pleasantly cheesy filling—was too good to give up on. We wanted to come up with a version of involtini that would emphasize the eggplant and minimize the fuss.

First up for fixing: the eggplant. Generally this recipe calls for frying, but in order to fry eggplant, you must first get rid of the excess water or the eggplant will turn mushy and oily. Salting can fix this problem, but it's time-consuming. Instead, we opted for a lighter and more hands-off option: baking. We brushed the planks with oil, seasoned them with salt and pepper, and then baked them for about 30 minutes. They emerged light brown and tender, with a compact texture that was neither mushy nor sodden.

To lighten up our involtini filling, we decreased the amount of ricotta and replaced it with more flavorful Pecorino Romano, and brightened the filling with a squeeze of lemon juice. To ensure that our filling stayed creamy and didn't toughen up, we added bread crumbs to the mix. We made a bare-bones tomato sauce while the eggplant baked, then added the eggplant rolls directly to the sauce. Using a skillet meant that we could easily transfer the whole operation to the oven. We crowned the dish with an additional dusting of Pecorino and a sprinkling of basil before serving directly from the skillet.

Eggplant Involtini

SERVES 4 TO 6

Select shorter, wider eggplants for this recipe. Part-skim ricotta may be used, but do not use fat-free ricotta. Serve the eggplant with crusty bread and a salad.

    2   large eggplants (1½ pounds each), peeled
    6   tablespoons vegetable oil
        Kosher salt and pepper
    2   garlic cloves, minced
    ¼   teaspoon dried oregano
        Pinch red pepper flakes
    1   (28-ounce) can whole peeled tomatoes,
        drained with juice reserved, chopped coarse
    1   slice hearty white sandwich bread,
        torn into 1-inch pieces
    8   ounces (1 cup) whole-milk ricotta cheese
    1½ ounces grated Pecorino Romano (¾ cup)
    ¼   cup plus 1 tablespoon chopped fresh basil
    1   tablespoon lemon juice

1. Slice each eggplant lengthwise into ½-inch-thick planks (you should have 12 planks). Trim rounded surface from each end piece so it lies flat.

2. Adjust 1 oven rack to lower-middle position and second rack 8 inches from broiler element. Heat oven to 375 degrees. Line 2 rimmed baking sheets with parchment paper and spray generously with vegetable oil spray. Arrange eggplant slices in single layer on prepared sheets. Brush 1 side of eggplant slices with 2½ tablespoons oil and sprinkle with ½ teaspoon salt and ¼ teaspoon pepper. Flip eggplant slices and brush with 2½ tablespoons oil and sprinkle with ½ teaspoon salt and ¼ teaspoon pepper. Bake until tender and lightly browned, 30 to 35 minutes, switching and rotating sheets halfway through baking. Let cool for 5 minutes. Using thin spatula, flip each slice over. Heat broiler.

3. While eggplant cooks, heat remaining 1 tablespoon oil in 12-inch broiler-safe skillet over medium-low heat until just shimmering. Add garlic, oregano, pepper flakes, and ½ teaspoon salt and cook, stirring occasionally, until fragrant, about 30 seconds. Stir in tomatoes and their juice. Increase heat to high and bring to simmer. Reduce heat to medium-low and simmer until thickened, about 15 minutes. Cover and set aside.

4. Pulse bread in food processor until finely ground, 10 to 15 pulses. Combine bread crumbs, ricotta, ½ cup Pecorino, ¼ cup basil, lemon juice, and ½ teaspoon salt in medium bowl.

5. With widest short sides of eggplant slices facing you, evenly distribute ricotta mixture on bottom third of each slice. Gently roll up each eggplant slice and place seam side down in tomato sauce.

6. Bring sauce to simmer over medium heat. Simmer for 5 minutes. Transfer skillet to oven and broil until eggplant is well browned and cheese is heated through, 5 to 10 minutes. Sprinkle with remaining ¼ cup Pecorino and let stand for 5 minutes. Sprinkle with remaining 1 tablespoon basil and serve.

POLENTA

WHY THIS RECIPE WORKS: A creamy mound of hot polenta can be a comforting dish, especially when served with a stew or saucy braise. Composed of little more than cornmeal and water, it should be easy to prepare. But often it's lumpy or gummy, and getting it right requires constant stirring. We wanted the smooth, creamy texture and great corn flavor of real polenta, but without the hassle.

It turned out that the type of cornmeal made a difference in the end result, and we found that a medium-grind meal worked best. The traditional method of making polenta requires half an hour or more of constant stirring after the cornmeal is added to boiling salted water. Experimentation revealed that the way to avoid this continuous attention was very low heat. We added the cornmeal (very gradually, so it wouldn't seize up) to barely simmering water with the flame set as low as possible. With the cover on the pot to keep in moisture, the cornmeal had time to release its starches gradually and develop flavor, and we needed to stir it only every five minutes or so. Our polenta was smooth and creamy with lots of corn flavor, and we were able to serve it in half an hour without standing at the stove the whole time.

Basic Polenta

SERVES 4 TO 6

If you do not have a heavy-bottomed saucepan, you may want to use a flame tamer to manage the heat. A flame tamer can be purchased at most kitchen supply stores, or you can improvise one (see page 313). Use this polenta as the base for any stew or braise, especially Osso Buco (page 372), or serve with a chunk of Gorgonzola cheese. Cooked leafy greens also make an excellent topping for soft polenta.

6 cups water
Table salt
1½ cups medium-grind cornmeal, preferably stone-ground
3 tablespoons unsalted butter, cut into large chunks
Ground black pepper

1. Bring the water to a rolling boil in a 4-quart heavy-bottomed saucepan over medium-high heat. Reduce the heat to the lowest possible setting, add 1½ teaspoons salt, and pour the cornmeal into the water in a very slow stream from a measuring cup, all the while whisking in a circular motion to prevent lumps.

2. Cover and cook, vigorously stirring the polenta with a wooden spoon for about 10 seconds once every 5 minutes and making sure to scrape clean the bottom and corners of the pot, until the polenta has lost its raw cornmeal taste and becomes soft and smooth, about 30 minutes. Stir in the butter, season with salt and pepper to taste, and serve immediately.

MUSHROOM RISOTTO

WHY THIS RECIPE WORKS: Earthy wild mushrooms added to a basic Italian risotto make a great main course. But the difficulty, not to mention the expense, of finding exotic fungi prompted us to try our hand at reproducing these flavors with supermarket mushrooms.

Cultivated mushrooms just don't have enough flavor for a dish like this, so we turned to aromatic dried porcini, which pack quite a flavor punch. But they needed to be chopped, so for visual appeal and substantive texture we added fresh cremini. Because simmering the cremini in the rice-broth mixture would make them rubbery, we browned them in a separate skillet with some onion and garlic for added flavor, folding this mixture into the risotto only when the rice was done. We added extra wine to our basic risotto so that its acidity would balance the richness of the mushrooms, and used a decidedly un-Italian ingredient, soy sauce, to intensify the earthiness of the mushrooms and round out the flavors. Without relying on pricey fungi, we had created a risotto with the same exotic earthiness.

Mushroom Risotto
SERVES 4 TO 6

Cremini mushrooms are sometimes sold as baby bella mushrooms. If they're not available, button mushrooms make a fine, though somewhat less flavorful, substitute. Tie the thyme and parsley sprigs together with kitchen twine so they will be easy to retrieve from the pan.

2 bay leaves
6 sprigs fresh thyme (see note)
4 sprigs fresh parsley, plus 2 tablespoons minced parsley leaves (see note)
3½ cups low-sodium chicken broth
3½ cups water

1 ounce dried porcini mushrooms, rinsed in a mesh strainer under running water
2 teaspoons soy sauce
6 tablespoons (¾ stick) unsalted butter
1¼ pounds cremini mushrooms, wiped clean and cut into quarters if small or sixths if medium or large (see note)
2 medium onions, minced (about 2 cups)
Table salt
3 medium garlic cloves, minced or pressed through a garlic press (about 1 tablespoon)
2⅛ cups Arborio rice
1 cup dry white wine or dry vermouth
2 ounces Parmesan cheese, grated fine (about 1 cup)
Ground black pepper

1. Tie the bay leaves, thyme sprigs, and parsley sprigs together with kitchen twine. Bring the bundled herbs, chicken broth, water, porcini mushrooms, and soy sauce to a boil in a medium saucepan over medium-high heat; reduce the heat to medium-low and simmer until the dried mushrooms are softened and fully hydrated, about 15 minutes. Remove and discard the herb bundle and strain the broth through a fine-mesh strainer set over a medium bowl (you should have about 6½ cups strained liquid); return the liquid to the saucepan and keep warm over low heat. Finely mince the porcini and set aside.

2. Adjust an oven rack to the middle position and heat the oven to 200 degrees. Heat 2 tablespoons of the butter in a 12-inch nonstick skillet over medium-high heat. Add the cremini mushrooms, 1 cup of the onions, and ½ teaspoon salt; cook, stirring occasionally, until the moisture released by the mushrooms evaporates and the mushrooms are well browned, about 7 minutes. Stir in the garlic until fragrant, about 1 minute, then transfer the mushroom mixture to an ovensafe bowl and keep warm in the oven. Off the heat, add ¼ cup water to the now-empty skillet and scrape with a wooden spoon to loosen any browned bits on the pan bottom; pour the liquid from the skillet into the saucepan with the broth.

3. Melt 3 tablespoons more butter in a large saucepan over medium heat. Add the remaining 1 cup onions and ¼ teaspoon salt; cook, stirring occasionally, until the onions are softened and translucent, about 9 minutes. Add the rice and cook, stirring frequently, until the edges of the grains are transparent, about 4 minutes. Add the wine and cook, stirring frequently, until the rice absorbs the wine. Add the minced porcini and 3½ cups of the broth and cook, stirring every 2 to 3 minutes, until the liquid is absorbed, 9 to 11 minutes. Stir in ½ cup more broth every 2 to 3 minutes until the rice is cooked through but the grains are still somewhat firm at the center, 10 to 12 minutes (the rice may not require all of the broth). Stir in the remaining 1 tablespoon butter, then stir in the mushroom mixture (and any accumulated juice), cheese, and reserved chopped parsley. Season with salt and pepper to taste; serve immediately in warmed bowls.

BUTTERNUT SQUASH RISOTTO

WHY THIS RECIPE WORKS: Butternut squash and risotto should make a perfect culinary couple, but too often the squash and rice never become properly intertwined. The squash is reduced to overly sweet orange blobs or the whole dish becomes a gluey squash paste. We wanted to integrate the flavor of the squash with the risotto but still preserve their individual personalities—to create a creamy, orange-tinged rice fully infused with deep squash flavor. We started with our basic risotto recipe, then addressed the squash. We decided to brown the diced squash in a skillet and set it aside while we sautéed the aromatics and toasted the rice. We added only half of the squash with the first addition of liquid. This squash broke down somewhat during cooking and infused the rice with its flavor; the remaining squash, added when the rice was finished, retained its shape and texture. Chicken broth cut with water was the basis of the liquid, but we also simmered the squash seeds and fibers in it to intensify the squash flavor. A generous helping of white wine balanced the squash's sweetness. This creamy risotto had deep squash flavor and pleasing textures.

Butternut Squash Risotto

SERVES 4 TO 6

Infusing the chicken broth with the squash's seeds and fibers helps to reinforce the earthy squash flavor without adding more squash. We found that a 2-pound squash often yields more than the 3½ cups in step 1; this can be added to the skillet along with the squash scrapings in step 2. To make this dish vegetarian, vegetable broth can be used instead of chicken broth, but the resulting risotto will have more pronounced sweetness.

- 2 tablespoons olive oil
- 1 medium butternut squash (about 2 pounds), peeled, seeded (reserve fibers and seeds), and cut into ½-inch cubes (about 3½ cups; see note)
- ¾ teaspoon table salt
- ¾ teaspoon ground black pepper
- 4 cups low-sodium chicken broth (see note)
- 1 cup water
- 4 tablespoons (½ stick) unsalted butter
- 2 small onions, minced (about 1½ cups)
- 2 medium garlic cloves, minced or pressed through a garlic press (about 2 teaspoons)
- 2 cups Arborio rice
- 1½ cups dry white wine
- 1½ ounces Parmesan cheese, grated fine (about ¾ cup)
- 2 tablespoons minced fresh sage leaves
- ¼ teaspoon grated nutmeg

1. Heat the oil in a 12-inch nonstick skillet over medium-high heat until shimmering but not smoking. Add the squash in an even layer and cook without stirring until golden brown, 4 to 5 minutes; stir in ¼ teaspoon of the salt and ¼ teaspoon of the pepper. Continue to cook, stirring occasionally, until the squash is tender and browned, about 5 minutes longer. Transfer the squash to a bowl and set aside.

2. Return the skillet to medium heat; add the reserved squash fibers and seeds and any leftover diced squash. Cook, stirring frequently to break up the fibers, until lightly browned, about 4 minutes. Transfer to a large saucepan and add the chicken broth and water; cover the saucepan and bring the mixture to a simmer over high heat, then reduce the heat to medium-low to maintain a bare simmer.

3. Melt 3 tablespoons of the butter in the now-empty skillet over medium heat; add the onions, garlic, remaining ½ teaspoon salt, and remaining ½ teaspoon pepper. Cook, stirring occasionally, until the onions are softened, 4 to 5 minutes. Add the rice to the skillet and cook, stirring frequently, until the grains are translucent around the edges, about 3 minutes. (To prevent the rice from spilling out of the pan, stir inward, from the edges of the pan toward the center, not in a circular motion.) Add the wine and cook, stirring frequently, until the liquid is fully absorbed, 4 to 5 minutes. Meanwhile, strain the hot broth through a fine-mesh strainer into a medium bowl, pressing on the solids to extract as much liquid as possible. Return the strained broth to the saucepan and discard the solids in the strainer; cover the saucepan and set over low heat to keep the broth hot.

4. When the wine is fully absorbed, add 3 cups of the hot broth and half of the reserved squash to the rice. Simmer, stirring every 3 to 4 minutes, until the liquid is absorbed and the bottom of the pan is almost dry, about 12 minutes.

5. Stir in ½ cup more of the hot broth and cook, stirring constantly, until absorbed, about 3 minutes; repeat with additional broth until the rice is cooked through but the grains are still somewhat firm at the center. Off the heat, stir in the remaining 1 tablespoon butter, the Parmesan, sage, and nutmeg; gently fold in the remaining cooked squash. If desired, add up to ¼ cup more broth to loosen the texture of the risotto. Serve immediately in warmed bowls.

PARMESAN FARROTTO

WHY THIS RECIPE WORKS: The biggest challenge to making a satisfying *farrotto* is having it achieve the proper texture. We found that cracking about half the farro in a blender was the key to freeing enough starch from the grains to create a creamy, risotto-like consistency. Adding most of the liquid up front and cooking the farrotto in a lidded Dutch oven helped the grains cook evenly and meant we didn't have to stir constantly—just twice before stirring in the flavorings. We created variations with spring vegetables and mushrooms, which turned this simple side into a satisfying main course.

Parmesan Farrotto

SERVES 6

We prefer the flavor and texture of whole farro. Do not use quick-cooking or pearled farro. The consistency of farrotto is a matter of personal taste; if you prefer a looser texture, add more of the hot broth mixture in step 6.

1½ cups whole farro

3 cups chicken broth

3 cups water

4 tablespoons unsalted butter

½ onion, chopped fine

1 garlic clove, minced

2 teaspoons minced fresh thyme

Salt and pepper

2 ounces Parmesan, grated (1 cup)

2 tablespoons minced fresh parsley

2 teaspoons lemon juice

1. Pulse farro in blender until about half of grains are broken into smaller pieces, about 6 pulses.

2. Bring broth and water to boil in medium saucepan over high heat. Reduce heat to medium-low to maintain gentle simmer.

3. Melt 2 tablespoons butter in large Dutch oven over medium-low heat. Add onion and cook, stirring frequently, until softened, 3 to 4 minutes. Add garlic and stir until fragrant, about 30 seconds. Add farro and cook, stirring frequently, until grains are lightly toasted, about 3 minutes.

4. Stir 5 cups hot broth mixture into farro mixture, reduce heat to low, cover, and cook until almost all liquid has been absorbed and farro is just al dente, about 25 minutes, stirring twice during cooking.

5. Add thyme, 1 teaspoon salt, and ¾ teaspoon pepper and continue to cook, stirring constantly, until farro becomes creamy, about 5 minutes.

6. Remove pot from heat. Stir in Parmesan, parsley, lemon juice, and remaining 2 tablespoons butter. Season with salt and pepper to taste. Adjust consistency with remaining hot broth mixture as needed. Serve immediately.

Farrotto with Pancetta, Asparagus, and Peas

We prefer the flavor and texture of whole farro. Do not use quick-cooking or pearled farro. The consistency of farrotto is a matter of personal taste; if you prefer a looser texture, add more of the warm broth mixture in step 5.

1½ cups whole farro

3 cups chicken broth

3 cups water

4 ounces asparagus, trimmed and cut on bias into 1-inch lengths

4 ounces pancetta, cut into ¼-inch pieces

2 tablespoons extra-virgin olive oil

½ onion, chopped fine

1 garlic clove, minced

1 cup frozen peas, thawed

2 teaspoons minced fresh tarragon

Salt and pepper

1½ ounces Parmesan cheese, grated (¾ cup)

1 tablespoon minced fresh chives

1 teaspoon grated lemon zest plus 1 teaspoon juice

1. Pulse farro in blender until about half of grains are broken into smaller pieces, about 6 pulses.

2. Bring broth and water to boil in medium saucepan over high heat. Add asparagus and cook until crisp-tender, 2 to 3 minutes. Using slotted spoon, transfer asparagus to bowl and set aside. Reduce heat to low, cover broth mixture, and keep warm.

3. Cook pancetta in Dutch oven over medium heat until lightly browned and fat has rendered, about 5 minutes. Add 1 tablespoon oil and onion and cook until softened, about 5 minutes. Stir in garlic and cook until fragrant, about 30 seconds. Add farro and cook, stirring frequently, until grains are lightly toasted, about 3 minutes.

4. Stir 5 cups warm broth mixture into farro mixture, reduce heat to low, cover, and cook until almost all liquid has been absorbed and farro is just al dente, about 25 minutes, stirring twice during cooking.

5. Add peas, tarragon, ¾ teaspoon salt, and ½ teaspoon pepper and cook, stirring constantly, until farro becomes creamy, about 5 minutes. Off heat, stir in Parmesan, chives, lemon zest and juice, remaining 1 tablespoon oil, and reserved asparagus. Adjust consistency with remaining warm broth mixture as needed (you may have broth left over). Season with salt and pepper to taste. Serve.

Mushroom Farrotto

We prefer the flavor and texture of whole farro. Do not use quick-cooking or pearled farro. The consistency of farrotto is largely a matter of personal taste; if you prefer a looser texture, add more of the hot water in step 7.

1½ cups whole farro

¾ ounce dried porcini mushrooms, rinsed

6 cups water

4 tablespoons unsalted butter

12 ounces cremini mushrooms, trimmed and sliced thin

Salt and pepper

½ onion, chopped fine

1 garlic clove, minced

2 teaspoons minced fresh thyme

1½ ounces Parmesan, grated (¾ cup)

2 tablespoons minced fresh chives

2 teaspoons sherry vinegar

1. Pulse farro in blender until about half of grains are broken into smaller pieces, about 6 pulses.

2. Microwave porcini mushrooms and 1 cup water in covered bowl until steaming, about 1 minute. Let sit until softened, about 5 minutes. Drain mushrooms in fine-mesh strainer lined with coffee filter. Transfer liquid to medium saucepan and finely chop porcini mushrooms.

3. Add remaining 5 cups water to saucepan and bring to boil over high heat. Reduce heat to medium-low to maintain gentle simmer.

4. Melt 2 tablespoons butter in large Dutch oven over medium-low heat. Add cremini mushrooms and ½ teaspoon salt and cook, stirring frequently, until moisture released by mushrooms evaporates and pan is dry, 4 to 5 minutes. Add onion and chopped porcini mushrooms and continue to cook until onion has softened, 3 to 4 minutes. Add garlic and stir until fragrant, about 30 seconds. Add farro and cook, stirring frequently, until grains are lightly toasted, about 3 minutes.

5. Stir 5 cups hot water into farro, reduce heat to low, cover, and cook until almost all liquid has been absorbed and farro is just al dente, about 25 minutes, stirring twice during cooking.

6. Add thyme, 1 teaspoon salt, and ¾ teaspoon pepper and continue to cook, stirring constantly, until farro becomes creamy, about 5 minutes.

7. Remove pot from heat. Stir in Parmesan, chives, vinegar, and remaining 2 tablespoons butter. Season with salt and pepper to taste. Adjust consistency with remaining hot water as needed. Serve immediately.

CHICKEN MARSALA

WHY THIS RECIPE WORKS: Developed in Italy after a successful 19th-century marketing campaign to promote Marsala wine from Sicily, this combination of chicken and mushrooms in wine sauce has become an Italian restaurant staple. Too often, however, the chicken is dry, the mushrooms flabby, and the sauce nondescript. We felt a rescue was in order.

We browned chicken breasts in a skillet to start and kept them warm while we prepared the mushrooms and sauce. The mushrooms went into the skillet next, but the chicken drippings burned. Our solution was to sauté some pancetta before browning the mushrooms, which rendered additional fat as well as added meaty flavor. We preferred sweet (as opposed to dry) Marsala for its depth of flavor and smooth finish. Some lemon juice tempered the Marsala's sweetness, while a little garlic and tomato paste rounded out the flavors. Finally, butter, whisked into the sauce at the end, added a rich finish and beautiful sheen.

Chicken Marsala
SERVES 4

Our wine of choice for this dish is Sweet Marsala Fine, an imported wine that gives the sauce body, soft edges, and a smooth finish. To make slicing the chicken easier, freeze it for 15 minutes.

2 tablespoons vegetable oil

1 cup unbleached all-purpose flour

4 (5- to 6-ounce) boneless, skinless chicken breasts, tenderloins removed and breasts trimmed (see note)
  Table salt and ground black pepper

2½ ounces pancetta (about 3 slices), cut into pieces 1 inch long and ⅛ inch wide

8 ounces white mushrooms, wiped clean and sliced (about 2 cups)

1 medium garlic clove, minced or pressed through a garlic press (about 1 teaspoon)

1 teaspoon tomato paste

1½ cups sweet Marsala (see note)

1½ tablespoons juice from 1 lemon

4 tablespoons (½ stick) unsalted butter, cut into 4 pieces

2 tablespoons minced fresh parsley leaves

1. Adjust an oven rack to the lower-middle position, place a large ovensafe dinner plate on the oven rack, and heat the oven to 200 degrees. Heat the oil in a 12-inch skillet over medium-high heat until shimmering. Meanwhile, place the flour in a shallow baking dish or pie plate. Halve the chicken horizontally, then cover the chicken halves with plastic wrap and pound the cutlets to an even ¼-inch thickness. Pat the chicken breasts dry. Season both sides of the breasts with salt and pepper; working with one piece at a time, coat both sides with flour. Cooking the cutlets in two batches, place 4 floured cutlets in a single layer in the skillet and cook until golden brown, about 3 minutes. Using tongs, flip the cutlets and cook on the second side until golden brown and the meat feels firm when pressed with a finger, about 3 minutes longer. Transfer the chicken to the heated plate and return the plate to the oven while you cook the remaining cutlets.

2. Return the skillet to low heat and add the pancetta; sauté, stirring occasionally and scraping the pan bottom to loosen the browned bits, until the pancetta is brown and crisp, about 4 minutes. With a slotted spoon, transfer the pancetta to a paper towel–lined plate. Add the mushrooms and increase the heat to medium-high; sauté, stirring occasionally and scraping the pan bottom, until the liquid released by the mushrooms evaporates and the mushrooms begin to brown, about 8 minutes. Add the garlic, tomato paste, and cooked pancetta; sauté while stirring until the tomato paste begins to brown, about 1 minute. Off the heat, add the Marsala; return the pan to high heat and simmer vigorously, scraping the browned bits from the pan bottom, until the sauce is slightly syrupy and reduced to about 1¼ cups, about 5 minutes. Off the heat, add the lemon juice and any accumulated juices from the chicken; whisk in the butter 1 piece at a time. Season with salt and pepper to taste and stir in the parsley. Pour the sauce over the chicken and serve immediately.

BETTER CHICKEN MARSALA

WHY THIS RECIPE WORKS: In revisiting chicken Marsala, we took a new approach to fabricating and cooking chicken cutlets. First, we cut each chicken breast in half crosswise. Then, we cut the thicker half in half horizontally to make three identically sized pieces that could easily be pounded into cutlets. We salted the cutlets briefly to boost their ability to retain moisture and then dredged them in a light coating of flour, which accelerated browning and helped prevent the meat from overcooking. We seared the cutlets quickly on both sides and set them aside while we made the sauce. Our Marsala sauce used reduced dry Marsala and chicken broth, along with cremini and dried porcini mushrooms for rich flavor and gelatin for a silky texture. Once the Marsala and mushroom sauce was complete, we returned the cutlets to the pan to cook them through and wash any excess starch into the sauce, eliminating gumminess.

Better Chicken Marsala

SERVES 4 TO 6

It is worth spending a little extra for a moderately priced dry Marsala ($10 to $12 per bottle). Serve the chicken with potatoes, white rice, or buttered pasta.

- 2¼ cups dry Marsala
- 4 teaspoons unflavored gelatin
- 1 ounce dried porcini mushrooms, rinsed
- 4 (6- to 8-ounce) boneless, skinless chicken breasts, trimmed
  Kosher salt and pepper
- 2 cups chicken broth
- ¾ cup all-purpose flour
- ¼ cup plus 1 teaspoon vegetable oil
- 3 ounces pancetta, cut into ½-inch pieces
- 1 pound cremini mushrooms, trimmed and sliced thin
- 1 shallot, minced
- 1 tablespoon tomato paste
- 1 garlic clove, minced
- 2 teaspoons lemon juice
- 1 teaspoon minced fresh oregano
- 3 tablespoons unsalted butter, cut into 6 pieces
- 2 teaspoons minced fresh parsley

1. Bring 2 cups Marsala, gelatin, and porcini mushrooms to boil in medium saucepan over high heat. Reduce heat to medium-high and vigorously simmer until reduced by half, 6 to 8 minutes.

2. Meanwhile, cut each chicken breast in half crosswise, then cut thick half in half again horizontally, creating 3 cutlets of about same thickness. Place cutlets between sheets of plastic wrap and pound gently to even ½-inch thickness. Place cutlets in bowl and toss with 2 teaspoons salt and ½ teaspoon pepper. Set aside for 15 minutes.

3. Strain Marsala reduction through fine-mesh strainer, pressing on solids to extract as much liquid as possible; discard solids. Return Marsala reduction to saucepan, add broth, and return to boil over high heat. Lower heat to medium-high and simmer until reduced to 1½ cups, 10 to 12 minutes. Set aside.

4. Spread flour in shallow dish. Working with 1 cutlet at a time, dredge cutlets in flour, shaking gently to remove excess. Place on wire rack set in rimmed baking sheet. Heat 2 tablespoons oil in 12-inch skillet over medium-high heat until just smoking. Place 6 cutlets in skillet and lower heat to medium. Cook until golden brown on 1 side, 2 to 3 minutes. Flip and cook until golden brown on second side, 2 to 3 minutes. Return cutlets to wire rack. Repeat with 2 tablespoons oil and remaining 6 cutlets.

5. Return now-empty skillet to medium-low heat and add pancetta. Cook, stirring occasionally, scraping pan bottom to loosen any browned bits, until pancetta is brown and crisp, about 4 minutes. Add cremini mushrooms and increase heat to medium-high. Cook, stirring occasionally and scraping pan bottom, until liquid released by mushrooms evaporates and mushrooms begin to brown, about 8 minutes. Using slotted spoon, transfer cremini mushrooms and pancetta to bowl. Add remaining 1 teaspoon oil and shallot to pan and cook until softened, about 1 minute. Add tomato paste and garlic and cook until fragrant, about 30 seconds. Add reduced Marsala mixture, remaining ¼ cup Marsala, lemon juice, and oregano and bring to simmer.

6. Add cutlets to sauce and simmer for 3 minutes, flipping halfway through simmering. Transfer cutlets to platter. Off heat, whisk in butter. Stir in parsley and cremini mushroom mixture. Season with salt and pepper to taste. Spoon sauce over chicken and serve.

BEST CHICKEN PARMESAN

WHY THIS RECIPE WORKS: Classic chicken Parmesan should feature juicy chicken cutlets with a crisp pan-fried breaded coating, complemented by creamy mozzarella and a bright, zesty marinara sauce. But more often it ends up dry and overcooked, with a soggy crust and a chewy mass of cheese. To prevent the cutlets from overcooking, we halved them horizontally and pounded only the fatter halves thin. Then we salted them for 20 minutes to help them hold on to their moisture. To keep the crust crunchy, we replaced more than half of the sogginess-prone bread crumbs with flavorful grated Parmesan cheese. For a cheese topping that didn't turn chewy, we added some creamy fontina to the usual shredded mozzarella and ran it under the broiler for just 2 minutes to melt and brown. Melting the cheese directly on the fried cutlet formed a barrier between the crispy crust and the tomato sauce.

Best Chicken Parmesan
SERVES 4

Our preferred brand of crushed tomatoes is SMT. This recipe makes enough sauce to top the cutlets as well as four servings of pasta. Serve with pasta and a simple green salad.

SAUCE
- 2 tablespoons extra-virgin olive oil
- 2 garlic cloves, minced
  Kosher salt and pepper
- ¼ teaspoon dried oregano
  Pinch red pepper flakes
- 1 (28-ounce) can crushed tomatoes
- ¼ teaspoon sugar
- 2 tablespoons coarsely chopped fresh basil

CHICKEN
- 2 (6- to 8-ounce) boneless, skinless chicken breasts, trimmed, halved horizontally, and pounded ½ inch thick
- 1 teaspoon kosher salt
- 2 ounces whole-milk mozzarella cheese, shredded (½ cup)
- 2 ounces fontina cheese, shredded (½ cup)
- 1 large egg
- 1 tablespoon all-purpose flour
- 1½ ounces Parmesan cheese, grated (¾ cup)
- ½ cup panko bread crumbs
- ½ teaspoon garlic powder
- ¼ teaspoon dried oregano
- ¼ teaspoon pepper
- ⅓ cup vegetable oil
- ¼ cup torn fresh basil

1. FOR THE SAUCE: Heat 1 tablespoon oil in medium saucepan over medium heat until just shimmering. Add garlic, ¾ teaspoon salt, oregano, and pepper flakes; cook, stirring occasionally, until fragrant, about 30 seconds. Stir in tomatoes and sugar; increase heat to high and bring to simmer. Reduce heat to medium-low and simmer until thickened, about 20 minutes. Off heat, stir in basil and remaining 1 tablespoon oil; season with salt and pepper to taste. Cover and keep warm.

2. FOR THE CHICKEN: Sprinkle each side of each cutlet with ⅛ teaspoon salt and let stand at room temperature for 20 minutes. Combine mozzarella and fontina in bowl; set aside.

3. Adjust oven rack 4 inches from broiler element and heat broiler. Whisk egg and flour together in shallow dish or pie plate until smooth. Combine Parmesan, panko, garlic powder, oregano, and pepper in second shallow dish or pie plate. Pat chicken dry with paper towels. Working with 1 cutlet at a time, dredge cutlet in egg mixture, allowing excess to drip off. Coat all sides in Parmesan mixture, pressing gently so crumbs adhere. Transfer cutlet to large plate and repeat with remaining cutlets.

4. Heat oil in 10-inch nonstick skillet over medium-high heat until shimmering. Carefully place 2 cutlets in skillet and cook without moving them until bottoms are crispy and deep golden brown, 1½ to 2 minutes. Using tongs, carefully flip cutlets and cook on second side until deep golden brown, 1½ to 2 minutes. Transfer cutlets to paper towel–lined plate and repeat with remaining cutlets.

5. Place cutlets on rimmed baking sheet and sprinkle cheese mixture evenly over cutlets, covering as much surface area as possible. Broil until cheese is melted and beginning to brown, 2 to 4 minutes. Transfer chicken to serving platter and top each cutlet with 2 tablespoons sauce. Sprinkle with basil and serve immediately, passing remaining sauce separately.

LIGHTER CHICKEN PARMESAN

WHY THIS RECIPE WORKS: Crunchy fried chicken cutlets topped with cheese and tomato sauce, chicken Parmesan isn't exactly a dish for dieters. Not wanting to eliminate it as an option for healthy eating, we looked for a way to get the crispy coating without using all the oil.

Baking seemed to be the best alternative to frying. We toasted panko (ultracrisp Japanese-style bread crumbs) with a little oil for color and to give them "fried" flavor without the fat. Adopting the conventional breading technique of dipping the cutlets in flour (with garlic powder for flavor), then egg, then bread crumbs, we cut more calories by using only the egg whites. We baked the breasts on a wire rack until they were almost done, then topped them with tomato sauce and shredded low-fat mozzarella to finish. Leaving the breasts on the rack rather than putting them in a casserole dish ensured that they would stay crisp as they baked. Served with a little extra sauce and grated Parmesan on the side, these oven-baked chicken Parmesan cutlets were crisp and full of flavor. And with 310 calories and 8 grams of fat, they have one-third less calories and two-thirds less fat grams than traditional versions.

Lighter Chicken Parmesan

SERVES 6

If you are tight on time, you can substitute 2 cups of your favorite plain tomato sauce for the Simple Tomato Sauce. To make slicing the chicken easier, freeze it for 15 minutes.

- 1½ cups panko (Japanese-style bread crumbs)
- 1 tablespoon olive oil
- 1 ounce Parmesan cheese, grated (about ½ cup), plus extra for serving
- ½ cup unbleached all-purpose flour
- 1½ teaspoons garlic powder
  Table salt and ground black pepper
- 3 large egg whites
- 1 tablespoon water
- 3 (7- to 8-ounce) boneless, skinless chicken breasts, tenderloins removed and breasts trimmed (see note)
- 1 recipe Simple Tomato Sauce (recipe follows), warmed (see note)
- 3 ounces low-fat mozzarella cheese, shredded (about ¾ cup)
- 1 tablespoon minced fresh basil leaves

1. Adjust an oven rack to the middle position and heat the oven to 475 degrees. Combine the bread crumbs and oil in a 12-inch skillet and toast over medium heat, stirring often, until golden, about 10 minutes. Spread the bread crumbs in a shallow dish and cool slightly; when cool, stir in the Parmesan.

2. In a second shallow dish, combine the flour, garlic powder, 1 tablespoon salt, and ½ teaspoon pepper. In a third shallow dish, whisk the egg whites and water together.

3. Line a rimmed baking sheet with foil, place a wire rack over the sheet, and spray the rack with vegetable oil spray. Halve the chicken horizontally, then cover the chicken halves with plastic wrap and pound the cutlets to an even ¼-inch thickness. Pat the chicken dry with paper towels, then season with salt and pepper. Lightly dredge the cutlets in the flour, shaking off the excess. Using tongs, dip both sides of the cutlets into the egg whites and allow the excess egg to drip back into the dish. Finally, coat both sides of the chicken with the bread crumbs. Press on the bread crumbs to make sure they adhere. Lay the chicken on the wire rack.

4. Spray the tops of the chicken with vegetable oil spray. Bake until the meat is no longer pink in the center and feels firm when pressed with a finger, about 15 minutes.

5. Remove the chicken from the oven. Spoon 2 tablespoons of the sauce onto the center of each cutlet and top the sauce with 2 tablespoons of the mozzarella. Return the chicken to the oven and continue to bake until the cheese has melted, about 5 minutes. Sprinkle with the basil and serve, passing the remaining sauce and Parmesan separately.

Simple Tomato Sauce

MAKES ABOUT 2 CUPS

This easy sauce also works well with pasta.

- 1 (28-ounce) can diced tomatoes
- 4 medium garlic cloves, minced or pressed through a garlic press (about 4 teaspoons)
- 1 tablespoon tomato paste
- 1 teaspoon olive oil
- ⅛ teaspoon red pepper flakes
- 1 tablespoon minced fresh basil leaves
  Table salt and ground black pepper

Pulse the tomatoes in a food processor until mostly smooth, about 10 pulses; set aside. Cook the garlic, tomato paste, oil, and red pepper flakes in a medium saucepan over medium heat until the tomato paste begins to brown, about 2 minutes. Stir in the pureed tomatoes and cook until the sauce is thickened and measures 2 cups, about 20 minutes. Off the heat, stir in the basil and season with salt and pepper to taste. Cover and set aside until needed.

CHICKEN PICCATA

WHY THIS RECIPE WORKS: Many recipes for chicken piccata are either bland or overcomplicated, with extra ingredients that ruin the dish's simplicity. Many recipes contain just a tablespoon of lemon juice and a teaspoon of capers, neither of which provides much flavor. But chicken piccata is one of those appealing Italian recipes that taste complex but are actually easy to prepare. Our goal was properly cooked chicken with a streamlined sauce that really tasted of lemons and capers.

Many recipes suggest breading cutlets for chicken piccata, but we found that flour alone was sufficient; there was no point building a crisp crust that would end up drenched in sauce. After browning the chicken and sautéing aromatics, we deglazed the pan with chicken broth alone; although wine is sometimes suggested, we found it to be too acidic for this dish. We simmered slices from half a lemon in the broth for a few minutes; this was easier than grating the zest. For maximum lemon flavor in the sauce, we used a full quarter-cup of lemon juice, added when the sauce was nearly done so as not to blunt its impact. Butter gave the sauce body and was preferable to flour, which made it overly thick. Plenty of capers and a bit of parsley finished our ultra-lemony piccata.

Chicken Piccata

SERVES 4

To make slicing the chicken easier, freeze it for 15 minutes. If you like, use thinly sliced cutlets available at many supermarkets. These cutlets don't have any tenderloins and can be used as they are.

- 2 large lemons
- 4 boneless, skinless chicken breasts (about 1½ pounds), tenderloins removed and breasts trimmed
    Salt and ground black pepper
- ½ cup unbleached all-purpose flour
- 4 tablespoons vegetable oil
- 1 small shallot, minced (about 2 tablespoons), or 1 small garlic clove, minced (about 1 teaspoon)
- 1 cup chicken broth
- 2 tablespoons small capers, drained
- 3 tablespoons unsalted butter, softened
- 2 tablespoons minced fresh parsley leaves

1. Adjust oven rack to the lower-middle position, set large ovensafe plate on rack, and heat oven to 200 degrees.

2. Halve 1 lemon pole to pole. Trim ends from one half and cut it crosswise into slices ⅛ to ¼ inch thick; set aside. Juice remaining half and whole lemon to obtain ¼ cup juice; reserve.

3. Halve chicken horizontally, then cover chicken halves with plastic wrap and pound cutlets to even ¼-inch thickness. Sprinkle both sides of cutlets generously with salt and pepper. Place flour in shallow baking dish or pie plate. Working with 1 cutlet at a time, coat with flour and shake to remove excess.

4. Heat 2 tablespoons of oil in a heavy-bottomed 12-inch skillet over medium-high heat until shimmering. Lay half of chicken cutlets in skillet. Cook cutlets until lightly browned on first side, 2 to 3 minutes. Flip cutlets and cook until second side is lightly browned, 2 to 3 minutes longer. Remove pan from heat and transfer cutlets to plate in warm oven. Add remaining 2 tablespoons oil to now-empty skillet and heat until shimmering. Add remaining chicken cutlets and repeat.

5. Add shallot or garlic to now-empty skillet and return skillet to medium heat. Sauté until fragrant, about 30 seconds for shallot or 10 seconds for garlic. Add broth and lemon slices, increase heat to high, and scrape pan bottom with wooden spoon or spatula to loosen browned bits. Simmer until liquid reduces to about ⅓ cup, about 4 minutes. Add lemon juice and capers and simmer until sauce reduces again to ⅓ cup, about 1 minute. Remove pan from heat and swirl in butter until it melts and thickens sauce. Stir in parsley and season with salt and pepper to taste. Spoon sauce over chicken and serve immediately.

PARMESAN-CRUSTED CHICKEN BREASTS

WHY THIS RECIPE WORKS: With a short ingredient list of only chicken breasts and Parmesan cheese plus one or two binders such as eggs or flour, Parmesan-crusted chicken breasts should be straightforward. But we found pale, wet, and gummy baked versions as well as bitter and burnt pan-fried versions. We wanted moist and tender chicken coated with a thin, crispy-yet-chewy, wafer-like sheath of Parmesan cheese.

A standard breading in which we merely substituted cheese for the bread crumbs and flour was disappointing; the cheese didn't provide the dry base to which the rest of the coating would stick. So we went back to flour, with a bit of Parmesan for flavor, and we left out the egg yolks to eliminate the eggy taste. For the outermost layer, shredding the cheese on the large holes of a box grater made a sturdier, more even crust, and a little flour added to this cheese helped the coating turn crisp. Pan-frying in a nonstick skillet prevented sticking, and keeping the heat no higher than medium browned the cheese without making it bitter. These cutlets were pale golden rather than deep golden brown, but the nutty, crisp Parmesan crust was everything we hoped it would be.

Parmesan-Crusted Chicken Cutlets

SERVES 4

To make slicing the chicken easier, freeze it for 15 minutes. Note that part of the Parmesan is grated on the smallest holes of a box grater (or rasp grater) and the remaining Parmesan is shredded on the largest holes of the box grater. We like the flavor that authentic Parmigiano-Reggiano lends to this recipe. A less-expensive cheese, such as Boar's Head Parmesan cheese, can also be used, but the resulting cheese crust will be slightly saltier and chewier. Although the portion size (one cutlet per person) might seem small, these cutlets are rather rich due to the cheese content. To make eight cutlets, double the ingredients and cook the chicken in four batches, transferring the cooked cutlets to a warm oven and wiping out the skillet after each batch.

2 (7- to 8-ounce) boneless, skinless chicken breasts, tenderloins removed and breasts trimmed (see note)

Table salt and ground black pepper

5 tablespoons unbleached all-purpose flour

¼ cup grated Parmesan cheese plus 6 ounces, shredded (about 2 cups; see note)

3 large egg whites

2 tablespoons minced fresh chives (optional)

4 teaspoons olive oil

Lemon wedges, for serving

1. Adjust an oven rack to the middle position and heat the oven to 200 degrees. Halve the chicken horizontally, then cover the chicken halves with plastic wrap and pound the cutlets to an even ¼-inch thickness. Pat the chicken dry with paper towels and season with salt and pepper.

2. Whisk ¼ cup of the flour and the ¼ cup grated Parmesan together in a shallow dish. Whisk the egg whites and chives (if using) in a medium bowl until slightly foamy. Combine the 2 cups shredded Parmesan and remaining 1 tablespoon flour in a second shallow dish. Working with 1 chicken cutlet at a time, dredge in the flour mixture, shaking off the excess, then coat with the egg white mixture, allowing the excess to drip off. Finally, coat with the shredded Parmesan mixture, pressing gently so that the cheese adheres. Place the coated cutlets in a single layer on a wire rack set over a rimmed baking sheet.

3. Heat 2 teaspoons of the oil in a 12-inch nonstick skillet over medium heat until shimmering. Add 2 of the cutlets and cook until pale golden brown on both sides, 4 to 6 minutes in total. (While the chicken is cooking, use a thin nonstick spatula to gently separate any cheesy edges that have melted together.) Transfer to a clean wire rack set over a rimmed baking sheet and keep warm in the oven. Wipe out the skillet with paper towels. Repeat with the remaining 2 teaspoons oil and chicken. Serve with the lemon wedges.

CHICKEN FRANCESE

WHY THIS RECIPE WORKS: This fast-fading star of red-sauce Italian restaurants often features a rubbery coating and a puckery lemon sauce. Yet this quick dinner still holds promise for the home cook. We wanted our chicken to have a rich, eggy coating that would remain soft and tender yet be sturdy enough to stand up to a silky, well-balanced lemon sauce.

We found that a first coating of flour was essential for getting the egg to stick, and a little milk added to the egg prevented it from turning rubbery. A final dip into flour made a soft, delicate veneer. We sautéed the cutlets in butter for its flavor, adding a little oil to keep the butter from burning, and kept the cutlets warm in the oven while we made our sauce. Fresh lemon juice with some vermouth and chicken broth gave us the bright, fresh citrus flavor we wanted; a little sautéed shallot balanced the lemon but didn't overpower it. To get the sauce to cling to the chicken without making it soggy, we made a roux with butter and flour. Our sauce was just right,

but the chicken had dried out while waiting in the oven. Our solution was to make the sauce first, then cook the chicken and finish the sauce. We think this revitalized dish deserves a place in today's home kitchens.

Chicken Francese

SERVES 4

To make slicing the chicken easier, freeze it for 15 minutes. The sauce is very lemony—for less tartness, reduce the amount of lemon juice by about 1 tablespoon.

SAUCE

3 tablespoons unsalted butter

1 large shallot, minced (about 4 tablespoons)

1 tablespoon unbleached all-purpose flour

2¼ cups low-sodium chicken broth

½ cup dry vermouth or white wine

⅓ cup juice from 2 lemons (see note)

Table salt and ground black pepper

CHICKEN

4 (5- to 6-ounce) boneless, skinless chicken breasts, tenderloins removed and breasts trimmed (see note)

Table salt and ground black pepper

1 cup unbleached all-purpose flour

2 large eggs

2 tablespoons milk

2 tablespoons unsalted butter

2 tablespoons olive oil

2 tablespoons minced fresh parsley leaves

1. Adjust an oven rack to the middle position and heat the oven to 200 degrees.

2. FOR THE SAUCE: Melt 1 tablespoon of the butter in a medium saucepan over medium heat. Add the shallot and cook, stirring occasionally, until softened, about 2 minutes. Stir in the flour and cook until light golden brown, about 1 minute. Whisk in the broth, vermouth, and lemon juice and bring to a simmer. Cook, whisking occasionally, until the sauce measures 1½ cups, about 15 minutes. Strain the sauce through a fine-mesh strainer. Return the sauce to the saucepan and set aside, discarding the solids.

3. FOR THE CHICKEN: Halve the chicken horizontally, then cover the chicken halves with plastic wrap and pound the cutlets to an even ¼-inch thickness. Pat the chicken dry with paper towels and season with salt and pepper.

4. Combine the flour, 1 teaspoon salt, and ¼ teaspoon pepper in a shallow dish and whisk the eggs and milk together in a medium bowl. Working with 1 chicken cutlet at a time, dredge in the flour, shaking off the excess, then coat with the egg mixture, allowing the excess to drip off. Finally, coat with the flour again, shaking off the excess. Place the coated chicken in a single layer on a wire rack set over a rimmed baking sheet.

5. Heat 1 tablespoon each of the butter and oil in a 12-inch nonstick skillet over medium-high heat. Add 4 of the cutlets and cook until lightly browned on one side, 2 to 3 minutes. Flip the chicken over and continue to cook until no longer pink and lightly browned on the second side, about 1 minute. Transfer the chicken to a clean wire rack set over a rimmed baking sheet and keep warm in the oven. Wipe out the skillet with paper towels. Add the remaining 1 tablespoon each of the butter and oil to the skillet and repeat with the remaining cutlets, then transfer to the oven. Wipe out the skillet with paper towels.

6. TO FINISH THE SAUCE AND SERVE: Transfer the sauce to the now-empty skillet and cook over medium-low heat until warmed, about 2 minutes. Whisk in the remaining 2 tablespoons butter, 1 tablespoon at a time, and season with salt and pepper to taste. Transfer 4 of the chicken cutlets to the skillet, turn to coat with the sauce, then transfer each serving (2 cutlets) to individual plates. Repeat with the remaining cutlets. Spoon 2 tablespoons of the sauce over each serving and sprinkle with the parsley. Serve, passing the remaining sauce separately.

CHICKEN SALTIMBOCCA

WHY THIS RECIPE WORKS: In its classic Italian form, saltimbocca is made with veal, prosciutto, and sage, but chicken is frequently substituted for the veal. The combination of flavors is meant to "jump in the mouth," as the name suggests. Preparing this dish can be complicated, but we wanted to streamline it and ensure that the flavors were well balanced.

Flouring only the chicken, rather than the chicken-prosciutto package, avoided gummy spots. The prosciutto is usually secured to the chicken with a toothpick, but we found that searing the prosciutto side of the chicken first worked as well; once browned, the two stuck together just fine. Prosciutto can overwhelm the other flavors in this dish, so it's important to use thin slices, but not so thin that they disintegrate during cooking. A single sage leaf is the usual garnish, but we wanted more sage flavor, so we sprinkled some minced fresh sage over the floured chicken before adding the prosciutto. With a simple pan sauce of vermouth, lemon juice, butter, and parsley, our chicken saltimbocca was ready to serve and full of flavor.

Chicken Saltimbocca

SERVES 4

To make slicing the chicken easier, freeze it for 15 minutes. Although whole sage leaves make a beautiful presentation, they are optional and can be left out of step 3. A single fried sage leaf is another pretty but optional garnish. Make sure to buy prosciutto that is thinly sliced, not shaved; also avoid slices that are too thick, as they won't stick to the chicken. The prosciutto slices should be large enough to fully cover one side of each cutlet.

- 4 (5- to 6-ounce) boneless, skinless chicken breasts, tenderloins removed and breasts trimmed (see note)
- ½ cup unbleached all-purpose flour
  Ground black pepper
- 1 tablespoon minced fresh sage leaves, plus 8 large leaves (optional; see note)

MAKING CHICKEN SALTIMBOCCA

1. Flour just the chicken—not the prosciutto—before sautéing.

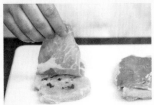

2. Sprinkle the cutlets evenly with the minced sage, then top each with a slice of prosciutto.

3. Cook the cutlets, prosciutto-side down, to help the ham adhere to the cutlets.

- 8 thin prosciutto slices (about 3 ounces; see note)
- 4 tablespoons olive oil
- 1¼ cups dry vermouth or white wine
- 2 teaspoons juice from 1 lemon
- 4 tablespoons (½ stick) unsalted butter, cut into 4 pieces and chilled
- 1 tablespoon minced fresh parsley leaves
  Table salt

1. Halve the chicken horizontally, then cover the chicken halves with plastic wrap and pound the cutlets to an even ¼-inch thickness.

2. Combine the flour and 1 teaspoon pepper in a shallow dish. Pat the chicken dry with paper towels. Dredge the chicken in the flour, shaking off any excess. Lay the cutlets flat and sprinkle evenly with the minced sage. Place 1 prosciutto slice on top of each cutlet, pressing lightly to adhere; set aside.

3. Heat 2 tablespoons of the oil in a 12-inch skillet over medium-high heat until shimmering. Add the sage leaves (if using) and cook until the leaves begin to change color and are fragrant, 15 to 20 seconds. Using a slotted spoon, transfer the sage to a paper towel–lined plate and set aside. Add 4 of the cutlets to the pan, prosciutto side down, and cook until lightly browned on one side, about 2 minutes. Flip the chicken over and continue to cook until no longer pink, 30 seconds to 1 minute. Transfer the chicken to a plate and tent loosely with foil. Add the remaining 2 tablespoons oil to the skillet and repeat with the remaining 4 cutlets. Transfer to the plate and tent loosely with foil while making the sauce.

4. Pour off the excess fat from the skillet. Stir in the vermouth, scraping up any browned bits, and simmer until reduced to about ⅓ cup, 5 to 7 minutes. Stir in the lemon juice. Turn the heat to low and whisk in the butter, 1 tablespoon at time. Off the heat, stir in the parsley and season with salt and pepper to taste. Spoon the sauce over the chicken, place a sage leaf (if using) on each cutlet, and serve.

ITALIAN BRAISED CHICKEN

WHY THIS RECIPE WORKS: Chicken *canzanese* is a regional Italian braised dish that transforms tough old birds into a moist and tender meal. Today's lean, mass-produced chickens, however, turn dried-out and bland when braised. We wanted old-fashioned results with a modern-day bird: tender, juicy chicken in an intensely flavored, well-developed sauce.

To start, we swapped out young, modern chickens for meaty chicken thighs that hold up especially well to braising. Next, we turned to the sauce. We browned diced prosciutto on the stovetop until it rendered enough fat to cook the garlic, which created a rich flavor base. Then we added white wine and chicken broth, and simmered them to concentrate flavors and burn off the raw alcohol flavor. We returned the chicken to the skillet and put it into the oven, uncovered to crisp the skin. To round out the flavors, we added a quick squeeze of lemon juice, a generous pat of butter, and a sprinkling of chopped rosemary.

Chicken Canzanese

SERVES 4 TO 6

When seasoning the dish at the end, be mindful that the prosciutto adds a fair amount of salt. It is important to use a piece of thickly sliced prosciutto in this recipe; thin strips will become tough and stringy. An equal amount of thickly sliced pancetta or bacon can be used in place of the prosciutto. Serve the chicken with boiled potatoes, noodles, or polenta.

> 1 tablespoon olive oil
> 2 ounces prosciutto (¼ inch thick), cut into ¼-inch cubes (see note)
> 4 medium garlic cloves, sliced thin lengthwise
> 3 pounds bone-in, skin-on chicken thighs (about 8 thighs), trimmed
>   Ground black pepper
> 2 teaspoons unbleached all-purpose flour
> 2 cups dry white wine
> 1 cup low-sodium chicken broth
> 4 whole cloves
> 1 (4-inch) sprig fresh rosemary, leaves removed and minced fine (about ½ teaspoon), stem reserved
> 12 whole fresh sage leaves
> 2 bay leaves
> ¼–½ teaspoon red pepper flakes
> 1 tablespoon juice from 1 lemon
> 2 tablespoons unsalted butter
>   Table salt

1. Adjust an oven rack to the lower-middle position and heat the oven to 325 degrees. Heat 1 teaspoon of the oil in a 12-inch heavy-bottomed ovensafe skillet over medium heat until shimmering. Add the prosciutto and cook, stirring frequently, until just starting to brown, about 3 minutes. Add the garlic slices and cook, stirring frequently, until the garlic is golden brown, about 1½ minutes. Using a slotted spoon, transfer the garlic and prosciutto to a small bowl and set aside. Do not rinse the pan.

2. Increase the heat to medium-high; add the remaining 2 teaspoons oil and heat until just smoking. Pat the chicken dry with paper towels and season with black pepper. Add the chicken, skin side down, and cook without moving until well browned, 5 to 8 minutes. Using tongs, turn the chicken and brown on the second side, about 5 minutes longer. Transfer the chicken to a large plate.

3. Remove all but 2 tablespoons fat from the pan. Sprinkle the flour over the fat and cook, stirring constantly, for 1 minute. Slowly add the wine and broth; bring to a simmer, scraping the bottom of the pan with a wooden spoon to loosen the browned bits. Cook until the liquid is slightly reduced, 3 minutes. Stir in the cloves, rosemary stem, sage leaves, bay leaves, red pepper flakes, and reserved prosciutto and garlic. Nestle the chicken into the liquid, skin side up (the skin should be above the surface of the liquid), and bake, uncovered, until the meat offers no resistance when poked with a fork but is not falling off the bones, about 1 hour 15 minutes. (Check the chicken after 15 minutes; the broth should be barely bubbling. If bubbling vigorously, reduce the oven temperature to 300 degrees.)

4. Using tongs, transfer the chicken to a serving platter and tent with foil. Remove and discard the sage leaves, rosemary stem, cloves, and bay leaves. Place the skillet over high heat and bring the sauce to a boil. Cook until the sauce is reduced to 1¼ cups, 2 to 5 minutes. Off the heat, stir in the minced rosemary, lemon juice, and butter. Season with salt and pepper to taste. Pour the sauce around the chicken and serve.

BEHIND THE SCENES

SHOPPING FOR CHICKEN—WHAT YOU NEED TO KNOW

Every good chicken dish starts with high-quality, fresh chicken. But there are an overwhelming number of choices at the supermarket—so how do you recognize superior poultry? Here are a few tips the test kitchen has learned over time. If you're buying boneless, skinless chicken breasts, you should be aware that breasts of different sizes are often packaged together, and it's usually impossible to tell what you've bought until you've opened the package. If possible, buy chicken breasts individually. If that isn't an option, pound the thicker ends of the larger pieces of chicken to match those of the smaller pieces. Some breasts will still be larger than others, but pounding will help make their thickness the same and ensure even cooking. As for chicken parts—say for making a dish such as fried chicken or stew—we prefer to butcher our own birds rather than buy packaged parts. Not only is this a less expensive option, but the parts will be consistently sized. (We also use this approach with stew meat—there's no guarantee that packaged stew meat is going to be cut into even-sized pieces or be from the same cut or even the same cow!) And what about ground chicken? Prepackaged ground chicken is made from either dark or white meat or a mix of the two. Higher-end markets often grind their chicken to order, so the choice is yours. In most of our testing, we found ground white meat chicken to be exceedingly dry and almost void of flavor. The dark meat was more flavorful and juicy due to its higher fat content. For our recommended brands of chicken, see page 909.

ITALIAN GRILLED CHICKEN

WHY THIS RECIPE WORKS: Anyone who has tried to grill a whole chicken knows that it's challenging at best, and the results are often inedible. Many cuisines have developed methods to overcome the problems of chicken cooked over a fire; the Italian way is to cook the chicken under bricks. This was one method we had to try.

One attempt to grill a butterflied chicken the Italian way was enough to let us know that we needed more than just bricks to make this recipe work. We thought of brining to keep the meat moist, but it produced burnt chicken when the liquid dripped into the fire. An alternative way to retain moisture in meat is salting; we rubbed the flesh under the skin with salt, mixed with garlic, red pepper flakes, and herbs for Italian flavor. With a modified two-level fire in the grill, we cooked the chicken under preheated bricks on the cooler side, skin side down, to firm up the flesh and release fat and liquid where the fire wouldn't cause flare-ups. We flipped the chicken and finished cooking it on the hot side; another flip and a few minutes without the bricks crisped up the skin. The combination of flipping and moving the chicken from the cool side to the hot side guaranteed even cooking, and the salting had kept the meat juicy. With a finishing embellishment of a quick vinaigrette, we had perfectly cooked chicken with zesty Italian flavor, and not a burnt piece in sight.

Italian-Style Grilled Chicken

SERVES 4

Use an oven mitt or kitchen towel to safely grip and maneuver the hot bricks. You will need two standard-size bricks for this recipe. Placing the bricks on the chicken while it cooks ensures that the skin will be evenly browned and well rendered. A cast-iron skillet or other heavy pan can be used in place of the bricks.

⅓   cup extra-virgin olive oil
8   garlic cloves, minced
1   teaspoon grated lemon zest plus 2 tablespoons juice
    Pinch red pepper flakes
4   teaspoons minced fresh thyme
1   tablespoon minced fresh rosemary
1   (3½- to 4-pound) whole chicken
    Salt and pepper

1. Heat oil, garlic, lemon zest, and pepper flakes in small saucepan over medium-low heat until sizzling, about 3 minutes. Stir in 1 tablespoon thyme and 2 teaspoons rosemary and continue to cook for 30 seconds longer. Strain mixture through fine-mesh strainer set over small bowl, pushing on solids to extract oil. Transfer solids to bowl and cool; set oil and solids aside.

2. **TO BUTTERFLY CHICKEN:** Use kitchen shears to cut along both sides of backbone to remove it. Flatten breastbone and tuck wings behind back. Use hands or handle of wooden spoon to loosen skin over breast and thighs and remove any excess fat.

3. Combine 1½ teaspoons salt and 1 teaspoon pepper in bowl. Mix 2 teaspoons salt mixture with cooled garlic solids. Spread salt-garlic mixture evenly under skin over chicken breast and thighs. Sprinkle remaining ½ teaspoon salt mixture on exposed meat of bone side. Place chicken skin side up on wire rack set in rimmed baking sheet and refrigerate for 1 to 2 hours.

4A. FOR A CHARCOAL GRILL: Open bottom vent halfway. Light large chimney starter three-quarters filled with charcoal briquettes (4½ quarts). When top coals are partially covered with ash, pour evenly over half of grill. Set cooking grate in place, wrap 2 bricks tightly in aluminum foil, and place on cooking grate. Cover and open lid vent halfway. Heat grill until hot, about 5 minutes.

4B. FOR A GAS GRILL: Wrap 2 bricks tightly in aluminum foil and place on cooking grate. Turn all burners to high, cover, and heat grill until hot, about 15 minutes. Leave primary burner on high and turn off other burner(s). (Adjust primary burner as needed during cooking to maintain grill temperature around 350 degrees.)

5. Clean and oil cooking grate. Place chicken on cooler side of grill, skin side down, with legs facing coals and flames. Place hot bricks lengthwise over each breast half, cover, and cook until skin is lightly browned and faint grill marks appear, 22 to 25 minutes. Remove bricks from chicken. Using tongs, grip legs and flip chicken (chicken should release freely from grill; use thin metal spatula to loosen if stuck), then transfer to hot side of grill, skin side up. Place bricks over breast, cover, and cook until chicken is well browned, 12 to 15 minutes.

6. Remove bricks, flip chicken skin side down, and continue to cook until skin is well browned and breast registers 160 degrees and thighs register 175 degrees, 5 to 10 minutes longer. Transfer chicken to carving board, tent loosely with foil, and let rest for 15 minutes.

7. Whisk lemon juice, remaining 1 teaspoon thyme, and remaining 1 teaspoon rosemary into reserved oil and season with salt and pepper to taste. Carve chicken and serve, passing sauce separately.

ITALIAN SAUSAGE WITH GRAPES AND BALSAMIC VINEGAR

WHY THIS RECIPE WORKS: Italian sausage with grapes is a great example of the affinity that pork and fruit flavors have for one another. We wanted to pay homage to this simple Italian dish and highlight the attributes that make it so appealing. We used a combination of sautéing and steaming to produce sausages that were nicely browned but moist and juicy. Building the sauce in the same skillet, we cooked down seedless red grapes and thinly sliced onion until caramelized to create a sweet but complex sauce. White wine, in addition to balsamic vinegar, gave the dish acidity and complemented the grapes. Oregano and pepper contributed earthiness and a touch of spice, while a finish of fresh mint added brightness.

Italian Sausage with Grapes and Balsamic Vinegar

SERVES 4 TO 6

Serve this dish with crusty bread and salad or over polenta for a heartier meal.

- 1 tablespoon vegetable oil
- 1½ pounds sweet Italian sausage
- 1 pound red seedless grapes, halved lengthwise (3 cups)
- 1 onion, halved and sliced thin (1½ cups)
- ¼ cup water
- ⅛ teaspoon salt
- ¼ teaspoon pepper
- ¼ cup dry white wine
- 1 tablespoon chopped fresh oregano
- 2 teaspoons balsamic vinegar
- 2 tablespoons chopped fresh mint

1. Heat oil in 12-inch skillet over medium heat until shimmering. Arrange sausage links in pan and cook, turning once, until browned on both sides, about 5 minutes. Tilt skillet and carefully remove excess fat with paper towel. Distribute grapes and onion over and around sausages. Add water and immediately cover. Cook, turning sausages once, until they register between 160 and 165 degrees and onions and grapes have softened, about 10 minutes.

2. Transfer sausages to paper towel–lined plate and tent with aluminum foil. Return skillet to medium-high heat and stir salt and pepper into grape-onion mixture. Spread grape-onion mixture in even layer in skillet and cook without stirring until browned, 3 to 5 minutes. Continue to cook, stirring frequently, until mixture is well browned and grapes are soft but still retain their shape, 3 to 5 minutes longer. Reduce heat to medium, stir in wine and oregano, and cook, scraping up any browned bits, until wine is reduced by half, 30 to 60 seconds. Remove pan from heat and stir in vinegar.

3. Arrange sausages on serving platter and spoon grape-onion mixture over top. Sprinkle with mint and serve.

PORK CHOPS WITH VINEGAR AND PEPPERS

WHY THIS RECIPE WORKS: This Italian-American dish was devised when pork chops had plenty of fat to keep them juicy; the leaner pork we have today tends to dry out and ruin the dish. But the thought of succulent pork with a tangy vinegar and pepper sauce spurred us to search for a way to make this dish taste the way it should. Bone-in rib chops of medium thickness had the best flavor, and the bone helped keep the meat juicy. Brining the chops in a solution of salt and sugar added moisture and flavor, and the sugar enhanced browning. We discovered that browning the chops, removing them from the pan to build the sauce, then finishing everything together in the oven worked best to get the flavors of the sauce into the meat. We also ditched the jarred vinegar peppers, which are traditional, and made our own; they were far superior to any we'd found at the supermarket.

Pork Chops with Vinegar and Sweet Peppers

SERVES 4

We prefer natural to enhanced pork (pork that has been injected with a salt solution to increase moistness and flavor) for this recipe, though enhanced pork can be used. If using enhanced pork, skip the brining in step 1. To keep the chops from overcooking and becoming tough and dry, remove them from the oven when they are just shy of fully cooked; as they sit in the hot skillet, they will continue to cook with residual heat.

- 1 cup sugar
  Table salt and ground black pepper
- 4 (8- to 10-ounce) bone-in rib loin pork chops, ¾ to 1 inch thick, trimmed of excess fat (see note)
- 2 tablespoons olive oil
- 1 medium onion, minced
- 1 medium red bell pepper, stemmed, seeded, and cut into ¼-inch-wide strips
- 1 medium yellow bell pepper, stemmed, seeded, and cut into ¼-inch-wide strips
- 2 anchovy fillets, minced (about 1 teaspoon)
- 1 medium sprig fresh rosemary
- 2 medium garlic cloves, minced or pressed through a garlic press (about 2 teaspoons)
- ¾ cup water
- ½ cup white wine vinegar, plus 2 tablespoons to finish the sauce (optional)
- 2 tablespoons cold unsalted butter
- 2 tablespoons chopped fresh parsley leaves

CUTTING BELL PEPPERS INTO MATCHSTICKS

1. Slice off the top and bottom of the pepper and remove the seeds and stem. Slice down through the side of the pepper.

2. Lay the pepper flat onto the cutting board and slice into ¼-inch-wide strips.

1. Dissolve the sugar and ½ cup salt in 2 quarts water in a large container; add the pork chops and refrigerate for 30 minutes. Remove the chops from the brine, rinse, and pat dry with paper towels. Using a sharp knife, cut two slits, about 2 inches apart, through the outer layer of fat and silver skin of each chop (do not cut into the meat of the chops). Season the chops with ¾ teaspoon pepper and set aside.

3. Set the skillet over medium-high heat. Add the onion and cook, stirring occasionally, until just beginning to soften, about 2 minutes. Add the peppers, anchovies, and rosemary; cook, stirring frequently, until the peppers just begin to soften, about 4 minutes. Add the garlic; cook, stirring constantly, until fragrant, about 30 seconds. Add the water and ½ cup of the vinegar and bring to a boil, scraping up the browned bits with a wooden spoon. Reduce the heat to medium; simmer until the liquid is reduced to about ⅓ cup, 6 to 8 minutes. Off the heat, discard the rosemary.

4. Return the pork chops, browner side up, to the skillet; nestle the chops in the peppers, but do not cover them. Add any accumulated juices to the skillet; set the skillet in the oven and cook until the center of the chops registers 140 to 145 degrees on an instant-read thermometer, 8 to 12 minutes (begin checking the temperature after 6 minutes). Using potholders, carefully remove the skillet from the oven (the handle will be very hot) and cover the skillet with a lid or foil; let stand until the center of the chops registers 150 degrees, 5 to 7 minutes. Transfer the chops to a platter or individual plates. Swirl the butter into the sauce and the peppers in the skillet; taste and stir in the remaining 2 tablespoons vinegar (if using) and the parsley. Season with salt and pepper to taste, then pour or spoon the sauce and peppers over the chops. Serve immediately.

OSSO BUCO

WHY THIS RECIPE WORKS: Osso buco, veal shanks braised in a rich sauce until tender, is incredibly rich and hearty. We felt that this time-honored recipe shouldn't be altered much, but we hoped to identify the keys to flavor so that we could perfect it.

To serve one shank per person, we searched for medium-sized shanks, and tied them around the equator to keep the meat attached to the bone for an attractive presentation. Most recipes suggest flouring the veal before browning it, but we got better flavor when we simply seared the meat, liberally seasoned with just salt and pepper. Browning in two batches enabled us to deglaze the pan twice, thus enriching the sauce. Celery, onion, and carrots formed the basis of the sauce; for the liquid we used a combination of chicken broth, white wine, and canned tomatoes. The traditional garnish of gremolata—minced garlic, lemon, and parsley—required no changes; we stirred half into the sauce and sprinkled the rest over individual servings for a fresh burst of citrus flavor.

Osso Buco
SERVES 6

To keep the meat attached to the bone during the long simmering process, tie a piece of kitchen twine around the thickest portion of each shank before it is browned. Just before serving, taste the liquid and, if it seems too thin, simmer it on the stovetop as you remove the strings from the osso buco and arrange them in individual bowls. Serve with rice or polenta.

OSSO BUCO
- 4 tablespoons vegetable oil
- 6 (8- to 10-ounce) veal shanks, 1½ inches thick, patted dry with paper towels and tied with kitchen twine at 1½-inch intervals
  Table salt and ground black pepper
- 2½ cups dry white wine

- 2 medium onions, cut into ½-inch pieces
- 2 medium carrots, cut into ½-inch pieces
- 2 medium celery ribs, cut into ½-inch pieces
- 6 medium garlic cloves, minced or pressed through a garlic press (about 2 tablespoons)
- 2 cups low-sodium chicken broth
- 2 small bay leaves
- 1 (14.5-ounce) can diced tomatoes, drained

GREMOLATA
- ¼ cup minced fresh parsley leaves
- 3 medium garlic cloves, minced or pressed through a garlic press (about 1 tablespoon)
- 2 teaspoons grated zest from 1 lemon

1. FOR THE OSSO BUCO: Adjust an oven rack to the lower-middle position and heat the oven to 325 degrees. Heat 1 tablespoon of the oil in a large Dutch oven over medium-high heat until shimmering. Meanwhile, sprinkle both sides of the shanks generously with salt and pepper. Place 3 shanks in the pan and cook until they are golden brown on one side, about 5 minutes. Using tongs, flip the shanks and cook on the second side until golden brown, about 5 minutes longer. Transfer the shanks to a bowl and set aside. Off the heat, add ½ cup of the wine to the Dutch oven, scraping the pan bottom with a wooden spoon to loosen any browned bits. Pour the liquid into the bowl with the browned shanks. Return the pot to medium-high heat, add 1 tablespoon more oil, and heat until shimmering. Brown the remaining shanks, about 5 minutes for each side. Transfer the shanks to the bowl. Off the heat, add 1 cup more wine to the pot, scraping the bottom to loosen the browned bits. Pour the liquid into the bowl with the shanks.

2. Set the pot over medium heat. Add the remaining 2 tablespoons oil and heat until shimmering. Add the onions, carrots, celery, ¼ teaspoon salt, and ⅛ teaspoon pepper and cook, stirring occasionally, until soft and lightly browned, about 9 minutes. Stir in the garlic and cook until fragrant, about 30 seconds. Increase the heat to high and stir in the broth, remaining 1 cup wine, and bay leaves. Add the tomatoes; return the veal shanks to the pot along with any accumulated juices (the liquid should just cover the shanks). Bring the liquid to a simmer. Cover the pot and transfer the pot to the oven. Cook the shanks until the meat is easily pierced with a fork but not falling off the bone, about 2 hours. (At this point the osso buco can be refrigerated for up to 2 days. Bring to a simmer over medium-low heat.)

3. FOR THE GREMOLATA: Combine the parsley, garlic, and lemon zest in a small bowl. Stir half of the gremolata into the pot, reserving the rest for garnish. Season with salt and pepper to taste. Let the osso buco stand, uncovered, for 5 minutes.

4. Using tongs, remove the shanks from the pot, cut off and discard the twine, and place 1 veal shank in each of six bowls. Ladle some of the braising liquid over each shank and sprinkle each serving with the remaining gremolata. Serve immediately.

BEEF IN BAROLO

WHY THIS RECIPE WORKS: Italian pot roast is an inexpensive cut of beef braised in wine. Full-bodied Barolo has been called the "wine of kings." It can be somewhat expensive, so this pot roast has to be special. We wanted tender meat in a rich, savory sauce that would do justice to the regal wine. A chuck-eye roast won't dry out after a long braise, but it has a line of fat in the middle that we felt was out of place in this refined dish. Separating one roast into two smaller ones enabled us to discard most of this fat before cooking. We then tied the roasts together and browned them in fat rendered from pancetta. We browned aromatics, then poured a whole bottle of wine into the pot. The Barolo's bold flavor needed something to temper it, and we liked a can of diced tomatoes. When the meat was done, we reduced the sauce and strained out the vegetables. Dark, full-flavored, and lustrous, this sauce bestowed nobility on our humble cut of meat.

Beef Braised in Barolo
SERVES 6

Don't skip tying the roasts—it keeps them intact during the long cooking time. Purchase pancetta that is cut to order, about ¼ inch thick. If pancetta is not available, substitute an equal amount of salt pork (find the meatiest piece possible), cut it into ¼-inch cubes, and boil it in 3 cups of water for about 2 minutes to remove excess salt. After draining, use it as you would pancetta.

- 1 (3½-pound) boneless chuck-eye roast
  Table salt and ground black pepper
- 4 ounces pancetta (about 4 slices), cut into ¼-inch cubes (see note)
- 2 medium onions, chopped medium
- 2 medium carrots, chopped medium
- 2 medium celery ribs, chopped medium
- 1 tablespoon tomato paste
- 3 medium garlic cloves, minced or pressed through a garlic press (about 1 tablespoon)
- 1 tablespoon unbleached all-purpose flour
- ½ teaspoon sugar
- 1 (750-milliliter) bottle Barolo wine
- 1 (14.5-ounce) can diced tomatoes, drained
- 1 sprig fresh thyme plus 1 teaspoon minced thyme leaves
- 1 sprig fresh rosemary
- 10 sprigs fresh parsley

1. Adjust an oven rack to the middle position and heat the oven to 300 degrees. Pull the roast apart at its major seams (delineated by lines of fat) into two halves. Use a knife as necessary. With the knife, remove the large knobs of fat from each piece, leaving a thin layer of fat on the meat. Tie three pieces of kitchen twine around each piece of meat. Thoroughly pat the beef dry with paper towels; sprinkle generously with salt and pepper. Place the pancetta in a large Dutch oven; cook over medium heat, stirring occasionally, until browned and crisp, about 8 minutes. Using a slotted spoon, transfer the pancetta to a paper towel–lined plate and reserve. Pour off all but 2 tablespoons of fat; set the Dutch oven over medium-high heat and heat the fat until beginning to smoke. Add the beef to the pot and cook until well browned on all sides, about 8 minutes total. Transfer the beef to a large plate; set aside.

2. Reduce the heat to medium; add the onions, carrots, celery, and tomato paste to the pot and cook, stirring occasionally, until the vegetables begin to soften and brown, about 6 minutes. Add the garlic, flour, sugar, and reserved pancetta; cook, stirring constantly, until combined and fragrant, about 30 seconds. Add the wine and tomatoes, scraping the bottom of the pan with a wooden spoon to loosen the browned bits; add the thyme sprig, rosemary, and parsley. Return the roast and any accumulated juice to the pot; increase the heat to high and bring the liquid to a boil, then place a large sheet of foil over the pot and cover tightly with the lid. Set the pot in the oven and cook, using tongs to turn the beef every 45 minutes, until a dinner fork easily slips in and out of the meat, about 3 hours.

3. Transfer the beef to a carving board and tent with foil to keep warm. Allow the braising liquid to settle for about 5 minutes, then, using a wide shallow spoon, skim the fat off the surface. Add the minced thyme, bring the liquid to a boil over high heat, and cook, whisking vigorously to help the vegetables break down, until the mixture is thickened and reduced to about 3½ cups, about 18 minutes. Strain the liquid through a large fine-mesh strainer, pressing on the solids with a spatula to extract as much liquid as possible; you should have 1½ cups strained sauce (if necessary, return the strained sauce to the Dutch oven and reduce to 1½ cups). Discard the solids in the strainer. Season the sauce with salt and pepper to taste.

4. Remove the kitchen twine from the meat and discard. Using a chef's knife or carving knife, cut the meat against the grain into ½-inch-thick slices. Divide the meat among warmed bowls or plates; pour about ¼ cup sauce over each portion and serve immediately.

SHRIMP SCAMPI

Restaurant versions of shrimp scampi often run the gamut from boiled shrimp and tomato sauce on a bed of pasta to rubbery shrimp overloaded in butter or olive oil. We wanted lightly cooked, moist shrimp in a light garlic and lemon sauce.

A quick sauté in batches was all the shrimp needed to cook fully without becoming rubbery; we then set them aside to build the sauce. We cooked minced garlic briefly in butter, so as not to scorch it, then added lemon juice and vermouth for depth of flavor; the liquids also protected the garlic from burning. Additional butter thickened the sauce, and parsley and cayenne provided the finishing touches to this light, flavorful Italian favorite.

Shrimp Scampi
SERVES 4 TO 6

Serve the scampi over long pasta like linguine or spaghetti or with chewy bread to soak up the extra juices.

- 2 tablespoons olive oil
- 2 pounds extra-large shrimp (21 to 25 per pound), peeled and deveined (see page 240)
- 3 tablespoons unsalted butter
- 4 medium garlic cloves, minced or pressed through a garlic press (about 4 teaspoons)
- 2 tablespoons juice from 1 lemon
- 1 tablespoon dry vermouth
- 2 tablespoons minced fresh parsley leaves
  Pinch cayenne pepper
  Table salt and ground black pepper

1. Heat 1 tablespoon of the oil in a 12-inch skillet over high heat until shimmering. Add 1 pound of the shrimp and cook, stirring occasionally, until just opaque, about 1 minute; transfer to a medium bowl. Return the pan to high heat and repeat with the remaining 1 tablespoon oil and remaining 1 pound shrimp.

2. Return the skillet to medium-low heat; melt 1 tablespoon of the butter. Add the garlic and cook, stirring constantly, until fragrant, about 30 seconds. Off the heat, add the lemon juice and vermouth. Whisk in the remaining 2 tablespoons butter; add the parsley and cayenne, and season with salt and black pepper to taste. Return the shrimp and any accumulated juices to the skillet. Toss to combine; serve immediately.

ULTIMATE SHRIMP SCAMPI

WHY THIS RECIPE WORKS: Our new shrimp scampi recipe uses a few test kitchen tricks to ensure flavorful and well-cooked shrimp, as well as a creamy and robust sauce to pair them with. First, we brined the shrimp in salt and sugar to season them throughout and to keep them moist and juicy. Then, because sautéing the shrimp led to uneven cooking, we instead poached them in wine, a gentler approach that was more consistent. To get more shrimp flavor into the sauce,

we didn't waste the shells; instead, we put them to use as the base of a stock and added wine and thyme. The key was to let it simmer for only 5 minutes, as a longer cooking time resulted in less flavor. For potent but clean garlic flavor, we used a generous amount of sliced, rather than minced, garlic. Just a teaspoon of cornstarch at the end of cooking kept the sauce emulsified and silky.

Ultimate Shrimp Scampi
SERVES 4

Extra-large shrimp (21 to 25 per pound) can be substituted for jumbo shrimp. If you use them, reduce the cooking time in step 3 by 1 to 2 minutes. We prefer untreated shrimp, but if your shrimp are treated with sodium or preservatives like sodium tripolyphosphate, skip the brining in step 1 and add ¼ teaspoon of salt to the sauce in step 4. Serve with crusty bread.

- 3 tablespoons salt
- 2 tablespoons sugar
- 1½ pounds jumbo shrimp (16 to 20 per pound), peeled, deveined (see page 240), and tails removed, shells reserved
- 2 tablespoons extra-virgin olive oil
- 1 cup dry white wine
- 4 sprigs fresh thyme
- 3 tablespoons lemon juice, plus lemon wedges for serving
- 1 teaspoon cornstarch
- 8 garlic cloves, sliced thin
- ½ teaspoon red pepper flakes
- ¼ teaspoon pepper
- 4 tablespoons unsalted butter, cut into ½-inch pieces
- 1 tablespoon chopped fresh parsley

1. Dissolve salt and sugar in 1 quart cold water in large container. Submerge shrimp in brine, cover, and refrigerate for 15 minutes. Remove shrimp from brine and pat dry with paper towels.

2. Heat 1 tablespoon oil in 12-inch skillet over high heat until shimmering. Add shrimp shells and cook, stirring frequently, until they begin to turn spotty brown and skillet starts to brown, 2 to 4 minutes. Remove skillet from heat and carefully add wine and thyme sprigs. When bubbling subsides, return skillet to medium heat and simmer gently, stirring occasionally, for 5 minutes. Strain mixture through colander set over large bowl. Discard shells and reserve liquid (you should have about ⅔ cup). Wipe out skillet with paper towels.

3. Combine lemon juice and cornstarch in small bowl. Heat remaining 1 tablespoon oil, garlic, pepper flakes, and pepper in now-empty skillet over medium-low heat, stirring occasionally, until garlic is fragrant and just beginning to brown at edges, 3 to 5 minutes. Add reserved wine mixture, increase heat to high, and bring to simmer. Reduce heat to medium, add shrimp, cover, and cook, stirring occasionally, until shrimp are just opaque, 5 to 7 minutes. Remove skillet from heat and, using slotted spoon, transfer shrimp to bowl.

4. Return skillet to medium heat, add lemon juice–cornstarch mixture, and cook until slightly thickened, about 1 minute. Remove from heat and whisk in butter and parsley until combined. Return shrimp and any accumulated juices to skillet and toss to combine. Serve, passing lemon wedges separately.

TUSCAN SHRIMP AND BEANS

WHY THIS RECIPE WORKS: To give this riff on Tuscan-style beans fuller seafood flavor, we made a quick concentrated stock with the shrimp shells and used it to simmer the beans. We also cooked the shrimp with the beans rather than separately and sautéed minced anchovies with the aromatics. To season the shrimp and keep them plump and juicy, we brined them briefly, added them late in the cooking process, and reduced the heat so they cooked gently. Canned beans and canned tomatoes made this dish fast and doable at any time of year; plus, the liquid from one of the cans of beans lent good body to the stew. Plenty of fresh basil and lemon juice and zest provide freshness and nice acidity.

Tuscan Shrimp and Beans
SERVES 4 TO 6

We prefer untreated shrimp, but if your shrimp are treated with added salt or preservatives like sodium tripolyphosphate, skip brining in step 1 and increase the salt to ½ teaspoon in step 3. Serve with crusty bread.

2 tablespoons sugar
  Salt and pepper
1 pound large shell-on shrimp (26 to 30 per pound), peeled, deveined (see page 240), and tails removed, shells reserved
¼ cup extra-virgin olive oil
1 onion, chopped fine
4 garlic cloves, peeled, halved lengthwise, and sliced thin
2 anchovy fillets, rinsed, patted dry, and minced
¼ teaspoon red pepper flakes
2 (15-ounce) cans cannellini beans (1 can drained and rinsed, 1 can left undrained)
1 (14.5-ounce) can diced tomatoes, drained
¼ cup shredded fresh basil
½ teaspoon grated lemon zest plus 1 tablespoon juice

1. Dissolve sugar and 1 tablespoon salt in 1 quart cold water in large container. Submerge shrimp in brine, cover, and refrigerate for 15 minutes. Remove shrimp from brine and pat dry with paper towels.

2. Heat 1 tablespoon oil in 12-inch skillet over medium heat until shimmering. Add shrimp shells and cook, stirring frequently, until they begin to turn spotty brown and skillet starts to brown, 5 to 6 minutes. Remove skillet from heat and carefully add 1 cup water. When bubbling subsides, return skillet to medium heat and simmer gently, stirring occasionally, for 5 minutes. Strain mixture through colander set over large bowl. Discard shells and reserve liquid (you should have about ¼ cup). Wipe skillet clean with paper towels.

3. Heat 2 tablespoons oil, onion, garlic, anchovies, pepper flakes, ¼ teaspoon salt, and ⅛ teaspoon pepper in now-empty skillet over medium-low heat. Cook, stirring occasionally, until onion is softened, about 5 minutes. Add 1 can drained beans, 1 can beans and their liquid, tomatoes, and shrimp stock and bring to simmer. Simmer, stirring occasionally, for 15 minutes.

4. Reduce heat to low, add shrimp, cover, and cook, stirring once during cooking, until shrimp are just opaque, 5 to 7 minutes. Remove skillet from heat and stir in basil and lemon zest and juice. Season with salt and pepper to taste. Transfer to serving dish, drizzle with remaining 1 tablespoon oil, and serve.

CHAPTER 14

THE FLAIR OF THE FRENCH

the cheese melts, then float them on top of the soup. For the best flavor, make the soup a day or two in advance. Alternatively, the onions can be prepared through step 1, cooled in the pot, and refrigerated for up to 3 days before proceeding with the recipe.

SOUP
- 3 tablespoons unsalted butter, cut into 3 pieces
- 4 pounds onions (about 6 large), halved pole to pole and sliced lengthwise ¼ inch thick (see note)
  Table salt
- 2 cups water, plus extra for deglazing
- ½ cup dry sherry
- 4 cups low-sodium chicken broth
- 2 cups beef broth
- 6 sprigs fresh thyme, tied together with kitchen twine
- 1 bay leaf
  Ground black pepper

CHEESE CROUTONS
- 1 small baguette, cut on the bias into ½-inch slices
- 8 ounces Gruyère cheese, shredded (about 2 cups)

CLASSIC FRENCH ONION SOUP

WHY THIS RECIPE WORKS: With too many onion soups, digging through a layer of congealed cheese unearths a disappointing broth that just doesn't taste like onions. The ideal French onion soup combines a satisfying broth redolent of sweet caramelized onions with a slice of toasted baguette and melted cheese. We wanted a foolproof method for achieving extraordinarily deep flavor from the humble onion—the star of this classic soup.

The secret to a rich broth was to caramelize the onions fully. The good news is that caramelizing the onions, deglazing the pot, and then repeating this process dozens of times will keep ratcheting up the flavor. The bad news is what a laborious, hands-on process this proved to be. Fortunately, we found that if we first cooked the onions, covered, in a hot oven for two and a half hours, we only needed to deglaze the onions on the stovetop three or four times. Just one type of onion (yellow) was sufficient, but a combination of three different liquids (water, chicken broth, and beef broth) added maximum flavor. For the topping, we toasted the bread before floating it on the soup to ward off sogginess and added only a modest sprinkling of nutty Gruyère so the broth wasn't overpowered.

Classic French Onion Soup

SERVES 6

Sweet onions, such as Vidalia or Walla Walla, will make this dish overly sweet. Be patient when caramelizing the onions in step 2; the entire process takes 45 to 60 minutes. Use broiler-safe crocks and keep the rims of the bowls 4 to 5 inches from the heating element to obtain a proper gratinée of melted, bubbly cheese. If using ordinary soup bowls, sprinkle the toasted bread slices with Gruyère and return them to the broiler until

1. FOR THE SOUP: Adjust an oven rack to the lower-middle position and heat the oven to 400 degrees. Generously spray the inside of a large (at least 7-quart) Dutch oven with vegetable oil spray. Add the butter, onions, and 1 teaspoon salt to the pot. Cook, covered, for 1 hour (the onions will be moist and slightly reduced in volume). Remove the pot from the oven and stir the onions, scraping the bottom and sides of the pot. Return the pot to the oven with the lid slightly ajar and continue to cook until the onions are very soft and golden brown, 1½ to 1¾ hours longer, stirring the onions and scraping the bottom and sides of the pot after 1 hour.

2. Carefully remove the pot from the oven and place over medium-high heat. Cook the onions, stirring frequently and scraping the bottom and sides of the pot, until the liquid evaporates and the onions brown, 15 to 20 minutes, reducing the heat to medium if the onions are browning too quickly. Continue to cook, stirring frequently, until the pot bottom is coated with a dark crust, 6 to 8 minutes, adjusting the heat as necessary. (Scrape any browned bits that collect on the spoon back into the onions.) Stir in ¼ cup water, scraping the pot bottom to loosen the crust, and cook until the water evaporates and the pot bottom has formed another dark crust, 6 to 8 minutes. Repeat the process of deglazing 2 to 3 more times, until the onions are very dark brown. Stir in the sherry and cook, stirring frequently, until the sherry evaporates, about 5 minutes.

3. Stir in 2 cups water, the chicken broth, beef broth, thyme, bay leaf, and ½ teaspoon salt, scraping up any final bits of browned crust on the bottom and sides of the pot. Increase the heat to high and bring to a simmer. Reduce the heat to low, cover, and simmer for 30 minutes. Remove and discard the thyme and bay leaf, then season with salt and pepper to taste.

4. FOR THE CROUTONS: While the soup simmers, heat the oven to 400 degrees. Arrange the baguette slices in a single layer on a rimmed baking sheet and bake until dry, crisp, and golden at the edges, about 10 minutes. Set aside.

5. Adjust an oven rack 6 inches from the broiler element and heat the broiler. Set individual broiler-safe crocks on the baking sheet and fill each with about 1¾ cups of the soup. Top each bowl with one or two baguette slices (do not overlap the slices) and sprinkle evenly with the Gruyère. Broil until the cheese is melted and bubbly around the edges, 3 to 5 minutes. Cool for 5 minutes; serve.

STREAMLINED FRENCH ONION SOUP

WHY THIS RECIPE WORKS: Streamlined versions of onion soup often amount to a sad crock of flavorless onions floating in super-salty beef bouillon topped with an oily blob of cheese. Or it might be just the opposite: a weak and watery affair. We wanted to make a better onion soup—a dark, rich broth, intensely flavored by an abundance of seriously cooked onions, covered by a broth-soaked crouton with a cheesy, crusty top—and we wanted to make it in record time.

We cheated from the get-go and created a simple broth with store-bought beef and chicken broths and wine. Red onions were chosen for their subtle complexity and nuance, and for the maximum flavor they offered when caramelized. Parsley, thyme, and a bay leaf rounded out the flavors and imparted freshness. To prevent the croutons from getting too soggy, we placed them atop the soup, so only the bottom was submerged. For the cheese, we liked a combination of pungent Swiss cheese topped with subdued Asiago; their flavors added some punch to our speedy but still irresistible soup.

Streamlined French Onion Soup

SERVES 6

Tie the parsley and thyme sprigs together with kitchen twine so they will be easy to retrieve from the soup pot. Use broiler-safe crocks and keep the rims of the bowls 4 to 5 inches from the heating element to obtain a proper gratinée of melted, bubbly cheese. If using ordinary soup bowls, top the toasted bread slices with the cheeses as directed in step 3 and return them to the broiler until the cheese melts, then float them on top of the soup.

SOUP

- 2 tablespoons unsalted butter
- 3 pounds red onions (about 6 medium), halved pole to pole and sliced crosswise ⅛ inch thick
  Table salt
- 6 cups low-sodium chicken broth

SHEDDING TEARS IN THE TEST KITCHEN

We can't tell you how many onions we've chopped over the years. Let's just say a lot. As a result, we've shed more than a few tears. What causes cut onions to be so pesky? When an onion is cut, the cells that are damaged in the process release sulfuric compounds as well as various enzymes, notably one called sulfoxide lyase. Those compounds and enzymes, which are separated when the onion's cell structure is intact, activate and mix to form the real culprit behind crying, a volatile new compound called thiopropanal sulfoxide. When thiopropanal sulfoxide evaporates in the air, it irritates the eyes, causing redness and tears.

Through the years we've collected dozens of ideas from readers, books, and conversations with colleagues, all aimed at reducing tears while cutting onions. We finally decided to put those ideas to the test. They ranged from common sense (work underneath an exhaust fan or freeze onions for 30 minutes before slicing) to the comical (wear ski goggles or hold a toothpick in your teeth). Overall, the methods that worked best were to protect our eyes by covering them with goggles or contact lenses or to introduce a flame near the cut onions. The flame, which can be produced by either a candle or a gas burner, changes the activity of the thiopropanal sulfoxide (the volatile compound that causes tearing) by completing its oxidization. Contact lenses and goggles form a physical barrier that the vapors cannot penetrate. So if you want to keep tears at bay when handling onions, light a candle or gas burner—or put on some ski goggles, even if it does look a bit silly.

- 1¾ cups beef broth
- ¼ cup dry red wine
- 2 sprigs fresh parsley (see note)
- 1 sprig fresh thyme (see note)
- 1 bay leaf
- 1 tablespoon balsamic vinegar
  Ground black pepper

CHEESE CROUTONS

- 1 small baguette, cut on the bias into ½-inch slices
- 4½ ounces thinly sliced Swiss cheese
- 1½ ounces Asiago cheese, grated (about ¾ cup)

1. FOR THE SOUP: Melt the butter in a large Dutch oven over medium-high heat. Add the onions and ½ teaspoon salt and cook, stirring frequently, until the onions are reduced and syrupy and the inside of the pot is coated with a deep brown crust, 30 to 35 minutes. Add the chicken and beef broths, red wine, parsley, thyme, and bay leaf, scraping the pot bottom with a wooden spoon to loosen the browned bits, and bring to a simmer. Simmer to blend the flavors, about 20 minutes; discard the herbs. Stir in the balsamic vinegar and season with salt and pepper to taste. (The cooled soup can be refrigerated in an airtight container for up to 2 days; return to a simmer before finishing the soup with the croutons and cheese.)

2. FOR THE CROUTONS: Adjust an oven rack to the upper-middle position and heat the oven to 350 degrees. Arrange the baguette slices on a rimmed baking sheet and bake, turning once, until lightly browned, about 15 minutes. Remove the bread from the oven, carefully adjust an oven rack 6 inches from the broiler element, and heat the broiler.

3. Set individual broiler-safe crocks on the baking sheet and fill each with about 1½ cups of the soup. Top each bowl with two baguette slices and divide the Swiss cheese slices, placing them in a single layer, if possible, on the bread; sprinkle with 2 tablespoons of the grated Asiago and broil until the cheese is browned and bubbly around the edges, 7 to 10 minutes. Cool for 5 minutes; serve.

FRENCH POTATO SALAD

WHY THIS RECIPE WORKS: French potato salad is served warm or at room temperature and is composed of sliced potatoes glistening with olive oil, white wine vinegar, and plenty of fresh herbs. We wanted a potato salad that was not only pleasing to the eye but to the palate as well. The potatoes should be tender but not mushy, and the flavor of the vinaigrette should penetrate the relatively bland potatoes but not be oily or dull. We learned the hard way that to prevent torn skins and broken slices, we had to slice the potatoes before boiling them. To tone down the flavor of harsh garlic, we blanched it before mixing the vinaigrette. A little extra vinegar—more than we would normally call for in a vinaigrette—added a pleasing sharpness, while some reserved potato water added just the right amount of moisture and saltiness to the salad. Dijon mustard combined with strong herbs also perked things up. Tossing the vinaigrette with the cooked potatoes led to mangled, shabby slices, but pouring the vinaigrette over the warm potatoes on a sheet pan, then folding in the other ingredients, kept the potato slices intact.

French Potato Salad

SERVES 4 TO 6

If fresh chervil isn't available, substitute an additional ½ tablespoon minced parsley and an additional ½ teaspoon minced tarragon. For best flavor, serve the salad warm, but to make ahead, follow the recipe through step 2, cover with plastic wrap, and refrigerate. Before serving, bring the salad to room temperature, then add the shallot and herbs.

2 pounds red potatoes (about 6 medium or 18 small), scrubbed and sliced ¼ inch thick

2 tablespoons table salt

1 medium garlic clove, peeled and threaded on a skewer

¼ cup olive oil

1½ tablespoons champagne vinegar or white wine vinegar

2 teaspoons Dijon mustard

½ teaspoon ground black pepper

1 small shallot, minced (about 1 tablespoon)

1 tablespoon minced fresh chervil leaves (see note)

1 tablespoon minced fresh parsley leaves

1 tablespoon minced fresh chives

1 teaspoon minced fresh tarragon leaves

1. Place the potatoes, 6 cups cold water, and the salt in a large saucepan. Bring to a boil over high heat, then reduce the heat to medium. Lower the skewered garlic into the simmering water and blanch, about 45 seconds. Immediately run the garlic under cold tap water to stop the cooking process; remove the garlic from the skewer and set aside. Simmer the potatoes, uncovered, until tender but still firm (a paring knife can be slipped into and out of the center of a potato slice with no resistance), about 5 minutes. Drain the potatoes, reserving ¼ cup cooking water. Arrange the hot potatoes close together in a single layer on a rimmed baking sheet.

2. Press the garlic through a garlic press or mince by hand. Whisk the garlic, reserved potato cooking water, oil, vinegar, mustard, and pepper together in a small bowl until combined. Drizzle the dressing evenly over the warm potato slices; let stand for 10 minutes.

3. Meanwhile, toss the shallot and herbs gently together in a small bowl. Transfer the potatoes to a large serving bowl. Add the shallot-herb mixture and mix lightly with a rubber spatula to combine. Serve immediately.

CHEESE SOUFFLÉ

WHY THIS RECIPE WORKS: Making a truly great cheese soufflé is like finding the Holy Grail for most cooks—unattainable. But this classic French dish doesn't have to be relegated to the realm of professional chefs. We wanted a cheese soufflé with bold cheese flavor, good stature, and a light but not-too-airy texture—all without the fussiness of most recipes.

To bump up the cheese flavor without weighing down the soufflé, we added lightweight-but-flavorful Parmesan cheese to the traditional Gruyère. Reducing the amount of butter and flour also amplified the cheese flavor. Filling the soufflé dish to an inch below the rim allowed ample room for the soufflé to rise high. To get the texture just right while keeping the preparation simple, we beat egg whites to stiff peaks, and then—rather than carefully folding them into the cheese sauce—added the sauce right to the stand mixer, and beat everything until uniform. When the center reached 170 degrees, our soufflé had a perfect luscious creamy center and lightly bronzed edges.

Cheese Soufflé

SERVES 4 TO 6

Serve this soufflé with a green salad for a light dinner. Comté, sharp cheddar, or gouda cheese can be substituted for the Gruyère. To prevent the soufflé from overflowing the soufflé dish, leave at least 1 inch of space between the top of the batter and the rim of the dish; any excess batter should be discarded. The most foolproof way to test for doneness is with an instant-read thermometer. To judge doneness without an instant-read thermometer, use two large spoons to pry open the soufflé so that you can peer inside it; the center should appear thick and creamy but not soupy.

- 1 ounce Parmesan cheese, grated (½ cup)
- ¼ cup (1¼ ounces) all-purpose flour
- ¼ teaspoon paprika
- ¼ teaspoon salt
- ⅛ teaspoon cayenne pepper
- ⅛ teaspoon white pepper
  Pinch ground nutmeg
- 4 tablespoons unsalted butter
- 1⅓ cups whole milk
- 6 ounces Gruyère cheese, shredded
  (1½ cups)
- 6 large eggs, separated
- 2 teaspoons minced fresh parsley
- ¼ teaspoon cream of tartar

1. Adjust oven rack to middle position and heat oven to 350 degrees. Spray 8-inch round (2-quart) soufflé dish with vegetable oil spray, then sprinkle with 2 tablespoons Parmesan.

2. Combine flour, paprika, salt, cayenne, white pepper, and nutmeg in bowl. Melt butter in small saucepan over medium heat. Stir in flour mixture and cook for 1 minute. Slowly whisk in milk and bring to simmer. Cook, whisking constantly, until mixture is thickened and smooth, about 1 minute. Remove pan from heat and whisk in Gruyère and 5 tablespoons Parmesan until melted and smooth. Let cool for 10 minutes, then whisk in egg yolks and 1½ teaspoons parsley.

3. Using stand mixer fitted with whisk, whip egg whites and cream of tartar on medium-low speed until foamy, about 1 minute. Increase speed to medium-high and whip until stiff peaks form, 3 to 4 minutes. Add cheese mixture and continue to whip until fully combined, about 15 seconds.

4. Pour mixture into prepared dish and sprinkle with remaining 1 tablespoon Parmesan. Bake until risen above rim, top is deep golden brown, and interior registers 170 degrees, 30 to 35 minutes. Sprinkle with remaining ½ teaspoon parsley and serve immediately.

FRENCH ONION TART

WHY THIS RECIPE WORKS: French onion tart is similar to quiche but delivers a more refined slice of pie, with more onions than custard. But re-creating this tart at home can produce a tough and crackery crust, which is doubly disappointing after spending long hours delicately cooking the onions, making the custard, and baking the whole thing together. We wanted to simplify the crust and shorten the overall preparation time.

We found that our onions would cook in half the usual time if we left the lid on the skillet throughout cooking. And covering the onions allowed them to cook entirely in their own juices, thereby becoming tender, retaining their pure onion flavor, and cooking more evenly. We liked bacon, which acted as a crisp foil to the creamy filling, but we found a traditional custard with the bacon to be simply too rich. To resolve the issue, we reduced the number of eggs and switched out the cream for half-and-half. And to ensure the bacon stayed crisp, we sprinkled it on top of the custard. We tried several classic crust recipes, looking for one that had the intense butteriness of traditional tart dough but could still be easily patted into a tart pan. We found that using a food processor to cut cold butter completely into the flour mixture required less ice water than a conventional crust, which kept the dough firm enough to press into the pan.

French Onion and Bacon Tart

SERVES 6 TO 8

Either yellow or white onions work well in this recipe, but stay away from sweet onions, such as Vidalias, which will make the tart watery. Use a 9-inch tinned-steel tart pan; see page 886 for our recommended brand. This tart can be served hot or at room temperature and pairs well with a green salad as a main course.

CRUST

1¼ cups (6¼ ounces) unbleached all-purpose flour
1 tablespoon sugar
½ teaspoon table salt
8 tablespoons (1 stick) unsalted butter, cut into ½-inch cubes and chilled
2–3 tablespoons ice water

FILLING

4 ounces bacon (about 4 slices), halved lengthwise and cut crosswise into ¼-inch pieces
  Vegetable oil, as needed
1½ pounds onions (about 3 medium), halved pole to pole and cut crosswise into ¼-inch slices (about 6 cups; see note)
¾ teaspoon table salt
1 sprig fresh thyme
2 large eggs
½ cup half-and-half
¼ teaspoon ground black pepper

1. FOR THE CRUST: Spray a 9-inch tart pan with a removable bottom with vegetable oil spray; set aside. Pulse the flour, sugar, and salt together in a food processor until combined, about 4 pulses. Scatter the butter pieces over the flour mixture and pulse until the mixture resembles coarse sand, about 15 pulses. Add 2 tablespoons of the ice water and continue to process until large clumps of dough form and no powdery bits remain, about 5 seconds. If the dough doesn't clump, add the remaining 1 tablespoon water and pulse to incorporate, about 4 pulses. Transfer the dough to the greased tart pan and, working outward from the center, pat the dough into an even layer, sealing any cracks. Working around the edge, press the dough firmly into the corners of the pan and up the sides, using your thumb to level off the top edge. Lay plastic wrap over the dough and smooth out any bumps or shallow areas. Place the tart shell on a plate and freeze for 30 minutes.

2. Adjust an oven rack to the middle position and heat the oven to 375 degrees. Place the frozen tart shell (still in the tart pan) on a rimmed baking sheet. Gently press a piece of extra-wide heavy-duty foil that has been sprayed with vegetable oil spray against the dough and over the edges of the tart pan. Fill the shell with pie weights and bake until the top edge of the dough just starts to color and the surface of dough under the foil no longer looks wet, about 30 minutes. Remove the tart shell from the oven and carefully remove the weights and foil. Return the baking sheet with the tart shell to the oven and continue to bake, uncovered, until golden brown, 5 to 10 minutes. Set the baking sheet with the tart shell on a wire rack to cool while making the filling. (Do not turn off the oven.)

3. FOR THE FILLING: While the crust is baking, cook the bacon in a 12-inch nonstick skillet over medium heat until browned and crisp, 8 to 10 minutes. Using a slotted spoon, transfer the bacon to a paper towel–lined plate; set aside. Pour off all but 2 tablespoons bacon fat from the skillet (or add vegetable oil if needed to make this amount).

4. Add the onions, salt, and thyme to the skillet. Cover and cook until the onions release their liquid and start to wilt, about 10 minutes. Reduce the heat to low and continue to cook, covered, until the onions are very soft, about 20 minutes, stirring once or twice (if after 15 minutes the onions look wet, remove the lid and continue to cook for another 5 minutes). Remove the pan from the heat and cool for 5 minutes.

5. Whisk the eggs, half-and-half, and pepper together in a large bowl. Remove the thyme from the onions; discard. Stir the onions into the egg mixture until just incorporated. Spread the onion mixture over the bottom of the baked crust and sprinkle the reserved bacon evenly on top.

6. Bake the tart on the baking sheet until the center of the tart feels firm to the touch, 20 to 25 minutes. Set the baking sheet with the tart on a wire rack and cool for at least 10 minutes. Remove the tart pan ring, gently slide a thin-bladed spatula between the pan bottom and crust to loosen, and slide the tart onto a serving plate. Cut into wedges and serve.

PISSALADIÈRE

WHY THIS RECIPE WORKS: *Pissaladière*, the classic olive, anchovy, and onion tart from Provence, is easy enough to prepare, but each ingredient must be handled carefully. We wanted to harmonize the onions, olives, and anchovies with a crisp crust to produce a tart worthy of the finest bakery in Nice.

We made the dough in a food processor and kneaded it as little as possible to create a pizza-like dough with a cracker-like exterior and a decently chewy crumb, a dough with the structure to stand up to the heavy toppings. Bread flour was our flour of choice as it has more protein than all-purpose flour, and that translates to a more substantial chew. Using a combination of high and low heat to cook the onions—starting the onions on high to release their juices and soften them, then turning the heat to medium-low to caramelize them—gave us perfectly browned and caramelized, but not burnt, onions. Adding a bit of water before spreading them on the crust kept them from clumping. We placed the onions on top of the chopped black olives, anchovies (also chopped; whole anchovies were too overpowering), and fresh thyme leaves to protect them from burning in the oven. Diehard fish lovers can add more anchovies as a garnish if desired.

Pissaladière

MAKES 2 TARTS, SERVING 6

For the best flavor, use high-quality oil-packed anchovies; in a tasting, King Oscar was our favorite brand (see page 904). If desired, you can slow down the dough's rising time by letting it rise in the refrigerator for 8 to 16 hours in step 1; let the refrigerated dough soften at room temperature for 30 minutes before using. The caramelized onions can also be made a day ahead and refrigerated.

DOUGH

- 2 cups (11 ounces) bread flour, plus extra for dusting the work surface
- 1 teaspoon instant or rapid-rise yeast
- 1 teaspoon table salt
- 1 tablespoon olive oil, plus extra for brushing the dough and greasing hands
- 1 cup warm water (110 degrees)

CARAMELIZED ONIONS

- 2 tablespoons olive oil
- 2 pounds onions (about 4 medium), halved and sliced ¼ inch thick
- 1 teaspoon brown sugar
- ½ teaspoon table salt
- 1 tablespoon water

   Olive oil
- ½ teaspoon ground black pepper
- ½ cup niçoise olives, pitted and chopped coarse
- 8 anchovy fillets, rinsed, patted dry, and chopped coarse (about 2 tablespoons), plus 12 fillets, rinsed and patted dry for garnish (optional; see note)
- 2 teaspoons minced fresh thyme leaves
- 1 teaspoon fennel seeds (optional)
- 1 tablespoon minced fresh parsley leaves (optional)

1. FOR THE DOUGH: Pulse the flour, yeast, and salt in a food processor (fitted with a dough blade, if possible) until combined, about 5 pulses. With the machine running, slowly add the oil, then the water, through the feed tube; continue to process until the dough forms a ball, about 15 seconds. Turn the dough out onto a lightly floured work surface and form it into a smooth, round ball. Place the dough in a large lightly oiled bowl and cover tightly with greased plastic wrap. Let rise in a warm place until doubled in volume, 1 to 1½ hours.

2. FOR THE CARAMELIZED ONIONS: While the dough is rising, heat the oil in a 12-inch nonstick skillet over medium-low heat until shimmering. Stir in the onions, sugar, and salt. Cover and cook, stirring occasionally, until the onions are softened and have released their juice, about 10 minutes. Remove the lid, increase the heat to medium-high, and continue to cook, stirring often, until the onions are deeply browned, 10 to 15 minutes. Off the heat, stir in the water, then transfer the onions to a bowl and set aside. Adjust the oven rack to the lowest position, set a baking stone on the rack, and heat the oven to 500 degrees. (Let the baking stone heat for at least 30 minutes but no longer than 1 hour.)

3. TO SHAPE, TOP, AND BAKE THE DOUGH: Turn the dough out onto a lightly floured work surface, divide it into two equal pieces, and cover with greased plastic wrap. Working with one piece at a time (keep the other piece covered), form each piece into a rough ball by gently pulling the edges of the dough together and pinching to seal. With floured hands, turn the dough ball seam side down. Cupping the dough with both hands, gently push the dough in a circular motion to form a taut ball. Repeat with the second piece. Brush each piece lightly with oil, cover with plastic wrap, and let rest for 10 minutes. Meanwhile, cut two 20-inch lengths of parchment paper and set aside.

4. Coat your fingers and palms generously with oil. Working with one piece of dough at a time, hold the dough up and gently stretch it to a 12-inch length. Place the dough on the parchment sheet and gently dimple the surface of the dough with your fingertips. Using your oiled palms, push and flatten the dough into a 14 by 8-inch oval. Brush the dough with oil and sprinkle with ¼ teaspoon of the pepper. Leaving a ½-inch border around the edge, sprinkle ¼ cup of the olives, 1 tablespoon of the chopped anchovies, and 1 teaspoon of the thyme evenly over the dough, then evenly scatter with half of the onions. Arrange 6 whole anchovy fillets (if using) on the tart and sprinkle with ½ teaspoon of the fennel seeds (if using). Slip the parchment with the tart onto a pizza peel (or inverted baking sheet), then slide it onto the hot baking stone. Bake until deep golden brown, 13 to 15 minutes. While the first tart bakes, shape and top the second tart.

5. Remove the first tart from the oven with a peel (or pull the parchment onto a baking sheet). Transfer the tart to a cutting board and slide the parchment out from under the tart; cool for 5 minutes. While the first tart cools, bake the second tart. Sprinkle with the parsley (if using) and cut each tart into 8 pieces before serving.

SUMMER VEGETABLE GRATIN

WHY THIS RECIPE WORKS: Layering summer's best vegetables into a gratin can lead to a memorable side dish—or a soggy mess. Juicy summer vegetables like zucchini and tomatoes can exude a torrent of liquid that washes away flavors. We wanted a simple, Provençal-style vegetable gratin, where a golden brown, cheesy topping provides a rich contrast to the fresh, bright flavor of the vegetables. The typical combination of tomatoes, zucchini, and summer squash won out. To eliminate excess moisture, we baked the casserole uncovered. Salting both seasoned and dried out the zucchini and summer squash, but proved insufficient to deal with all the tomato juice. While we could remove the watery jelly and seeds from the tomatoes, the jelly was crucial for full tomato flavor. We moved the tomatoes to the top gratin layer, which allowed them to roast and caramelize. The roasting added flavor, especially when drizzled with garlic-thyme oil. Finally, we added a layer of caramelized onions between the zucchini/squash and tomato layers and sprinkled the dish with Parmesan bread crumbs before baking.

Summer Vegetable Gratin
SERVES 6 TO 8

The success of this recipe depends on good-quality produce. Buy zucchini and summer squash of roughly the same diameter. We like the visual contrast zucchini and summer squash bring to the dish, but you can also use just one or the other. A similarly sized ovensafe gratin dish can be substituted for the 13 by 9-inch baking dish. Serve the gratin alongside grilled fish or meat, accompanied by bread to soak up any flavorful juices.

- 6 tablespoons extra-virgin olive oil
- 1 pound zucchini, ends trimmed and cut crosswise into ¼-inch-thick slices (see note)
- 1 pound yellow summer squash, ends trimmed and cut crosswise into ¼-inch-thick slices (see note)
- 2 teaspoons table salt
- 1½ pounds ripe tomatoes (3 to 4 large), cut into ¼-inch-thick slices
- 2 medium onions, halved pole to pole and sliced thin (about 3 cups)
- ¾ teaspoon ground black pepper
- 2 medium garlic cloves, minced or pressed through a garlic press (about 2 teaspoons)
- 1 tablespoon minced fresh thyme leaves
- 1 slice high-quality white sandwich bread, torn into quarters
- 2 ounces grated Parmesan cheese (about 1 cup)
- 2 medium shallots, minced (about 6 tablespoons)
- ¼ cup chopped fresh basil leaves

1. Adjust an oven rack to the upper-middle position and heat the oven to 400 degrees. Brush a 13 by 9-inch baking dish with 1 tablespoon of the oil; set aside.

2. Toss the zucchini and summer squash slices with 1 teaspoon of the salt in a large bowl; transfer to a colander set over a bowl. Let stand until the zucchini and squash release at least 3 tablespoons of liquid, about 45 minutes. Arrange the slices on a triple layer of paper towels; cover with another triple layer of paper towels. Firmly press each slice to remove as much liquid as possible.

3. Place the tomato slices in a single layer on a double layer of paper towels and sprinkle evenly with ½ teaspoon more salt; let stand for 30 minutes. Place a second double layer of paper towels on top of the tomatoes and press firmly to dry the tomatoes.

4. Meanwhile, heat 1 tablespoon more oil in a 12-inch nonstick skillet over medium heat until shimmering. Add the onions, the remaining ½ teaspoon salt, and ¼ teaspoon of the pepper; cook, stirring occasionally, until the onions are softened and dark golden brown, 20 to 25 minutes. Set the onions aside.

5. Combine the garlic, 3 tablespoons more oil, the remaining ½ teaspoon pepper, and the thyme in a small bowl. In a large bowl, toss the zucchini and summer squash in half of the oil mixture, then arrange in the greased baking dish. Arrange the caramelized onions in an even layer over the squash. Slightly overlap the tomato slices in a single layer on top of the onions. Spoon the remaining garlic-oil mixture evenly over the tomatoes. Bake until the vegetables are tender and the tomatoes are starting to brown on the edges, 40 to 45 minutes.

6. Meanwhile, process the bread in a food processor until finely ground, about 10 seconds. (You should have about 1 cup crumbs.) Combine the bread crumbs, remaining 1 tablespoon oil, the Parmesan, and shallots in a medium bowl. Remove the baking dish from the oven and increase the heat to 450 degrees. Sprinkle the bread-crumb mixture evenly on top of the tomatoes. Bake the gratin until bubbling and the cheese is lightly browned, 5 to 10 minutes. Sprinkle with the basil and cool for 10 minutes before serving.

WALKAWAY RATATOUILLE

WHY THIS RECIPE WORKS: Classic ratatouille recipes call for cutting vegetables into small pieces, labor- and time-intensive pretreatments like salting and/or pressing the vegetables to remove excess moisture, and cooking them in batches on the stovetop. Our secret to great yet easy ratatouille? Overcook some of the vegetables, barely cook the others—and let the oven do the work. Our streamlined recipe starts by sautéing onions and aromatics and then adding chunks of eggplant and tomatoes before moving the pot to the oven, where the dry, ambient heat thoroughly evaporated moisture, concentrated flavors, and caramelized some of the veggies. After 45 minutes, the tomatoes and eggplant became meltingly soft and could be mashed into a thick, silky sauce. Zucchini and bell peppers went into the pot last so that they retained some texture. Finishing the dish with fresh herbs, a splash of sherry vinegar, and a drizzle of extra-virgin olive oil tied everything together.

Walkaway Ratatouille

SERVES 6 TO 8

This dish is best prepared using ripe, in-season tomatoes. If good tomatoes are not available, substitute 1 (28-ounce) can of whole peeled tomatoes that have been drained, rinsed, and chopped coarse. Ratatouille can be served as an accompaniment to meat or fish. It can also be served on its own with crusty bread, topped with an egg, or over pasta or rice. This dish can be served warm, at room temperature, or chilled.

- ⅓ cup extra-virgin olive oil, plus extra for serving
- 2 large onions, cut into 1-inch pieces
- 8 large garlic cloves, peeled and smashed
  Salt and pepper
- 1½ teaspoons herbes de Provence
- ¼ teaspoon red pepper flakes
- 1 bay leaf
- 1½ pounds eggplant, peeled and cut into 1-inch pieces
- 2 pounds plum tomatoes, peeled and chopped coarse
- 2 small zucchini, halved lengthwise and cut into 1-inch pieces
- 1 red bell pepper, stemmed, seeded, and cut into 1-inch pieces
- 1 yellow bell pepper, stemmed, seeded, and cut into 1-inch pieces
- 2 tablespoons chopped fresh basil
- 1 tablespoon minced fresh parsley
- 1 tablespoon sherry vinegar

1. Adjust oven rack to middle position and heat oven to 400 degrees. Heat oil in Dutch oven over medium-high heat until shimmering. Add onions, garlic, 1 teaspoon salt, and ¼ teaspoon pepper and cook, stirring occasionally, until onions are starting to soften and have become translucent, about 10 minutes. Add herbes de Provence, pepper flakes, and bay leaf and cook, stirring frequently, for 1 minute. Stir in eggplant and tomatoes. Sprinkle with ½ teaspoon salt and ¼ teaspoon pepper and stir to combine. Transfer pot to oven and cook, uncovered, until vegetables are very tender and spotty brown, 40 to 45 minutes.

2. Remove pot from oven and, using potato masher or heavy wooden spoon, smash and stir eggplant mixture until broken down into sauce-like consistency. Stir in zucchini, bell peppers, ¼ teaspoon salt, and ¼ teaspoon pepper and return to oven. Cook, uncovered, until zucchini and peppers are just tender, 20 to 25 minutes.

3. Remove pot from oven, cover, and let stand until zucchini is translucent and easily pierced with tip of paring knife, 10 to 15 minutes. Using wooden spoon, scrape any browned bits from sides of pot and stir back into ratatouille. Stir in 1 tablespoon basil, parsley, and vinegar. Season with salt and pepper to taste. Transfer to large platter, drizzle with 1 tablespoon oil, sprinkle with remaining 1 tablespoon basil, and serve.

MUSHROOM AND LEEK GALETTE WITH GORGONZOLA

WHY THIS RECIPE WORKS: Most vegetable tarts rely on the same pastry dough used for fruit tarts. But vegetable tarts are more prone to leaking liquid into the crust or falling apart when the tart is sliced. We needed a crust that was extra sturdy and boasted a complex flavor of its own.

To increase the flavor of the crust and keep it tender, we swapped out part of the white flour for nutty whole wheat, and we used butter rather than shortening. To punch up its flaky texture and introduce more structure, we gave the crust a series of folds to create numerous interlocking layers. For a filling that was both flavorful and cohesive, we paired mushrooms and leeks with rich, potent binders like Gorgonzola cheese and crème fraîche.

Mushroom and Leek Galette with Gorgonzola

SERVES 6

Cutting a few small holes in the dough prevents it from lifting off the pan as it bakes. A pizza stone helps to crisp the crust but is not essential. An overturned baking sheet can be used in place of the pizza stone.

DOUGH

1¼ cups (6¼ ounces) all-purpose flour

½ cup (2¾ ounces) whole-wheat flour

1 tablespoon sugar

¾ teaspoon salt

10 tablespoons unsalted butter, cut into ½-inch pieces and chilled

7 tablespoons ice water

1 teaspoon distilled white vinegar

FILLING

1¼ pounds shiitake mushrooms, stemmed and sliced thin

5 teaspoons olive oil

1 pound leeks, white and light green parts only, sliced ½ inch thick and washed thoroughly (3 cups)

1 teaspoon minced fresh thyme

2 tablespoons crème fraîche

1 tablespoon Dijon mustard

Salt and pepper

3 ounces Gorgonzola cheese, crumbled (¾ cup)

1 large egg, lightly beaten

Kosher salt

2 tablespoons minced fresh parsley

1. FOR THE DOUGH: Pulse all-purpose flour, whole-wheat flour, sugar, and salt together in food processor until combined, 2 to 3 pulses. Add butter and pulse until it forms pea-size pieces, about 10 pulses. Transfer mixture to medium bowl.

2. Sprinkle water and vinegar over mixture. With rubber spatula, use folding motion to mix until loose, shaggy mass forms with some dry flour remaining (do not overwork). Transfer mixture to center of large sheet of plastic wrap, press gently into rough 4-inch square, and wrap tightly. Refrigerate for at least 45 minutes.

3. Transfer dough to lightly floured counter. Roll into 11 by 8-inch rectangle with short side of rectangle parallel to edge of counter. Using bench scraper, bring bottom third of dough up, then fold upper third over it, folding like business letter into 8 by 4-inch rectangle. Turn dough 90 degrees counterclockwise. Roll out dough again into 11 by 8-inch rectangle and fold into thirds again. Turn dough 90 degrees counterclockwise and repeat rolling and folding into thirds. After last fold, fold dough in half to create 4-inch square. Press top of dough gently to seal. Wrap in plastic and refrigerate for at least 45 minutes or up to 2 days.

4. FOR THE FILLING: Microwave mushrooms in covered bowl until just tender, 3 to 5 minutes. Transfer to colander to drain; return to bowl. Meanwhile, heat 1 tablespoon oil in 12-inch skillet over medium heat until shimmering. Add leeks and thyme, cover, and cook, stirring occasionally, until leeks are tender and beginning to brown, 5 to 7 minutes. Transfer to bowl with mushrooms. Stir in crème fraîche and mustard. Season with salt and pepper to taste. Set aside.

5. Adjust oven rack to lower-middle position, place pizza stone on rack, and heat oven to 400 degrees. Line rimmed baking sheet with parchment paper. Remove dough from refrigerator and let stand at room temperature for 15 to 20 minutes. Roll out on generously floured counter (use up to ¼ cup flour) to 14-inch circle about ⅛ inch thick. (Trim edges as needed to form rough circle.) Transfer dough to prepared baking sheet. With tip of paring knife, cut five ¼-inch circles in dough (one at center and four evenly spaced halfway from center to edge of dough). Brush top of dough with 1 teaspoon oil.

6. Spread half of filling evenly over dough, leaving 2-inch border around edge. Sprinkle with half of Gorgonzola, cover with remaining filling, and top with remaining Gorgonzola.

NOTES FROM THE TEST KITCHEN

PLEATING A FREE-FORM TART

It's surprisingly simple to create pleated edges around free-form tarts.

Gently grasp 1 edge of dough and make 2-inch-wide fold over filling. Lift and fold another segment of dough over first fold to form pleat. Repeat every 2 to 3 inches.

Drizzle remaining 1 teaspoon oil over filling. Gently grasp 1 edge of dough and fold up outer 2 inches over filling. Repeat around circumference of tart, overlapping dough every 2 to 3 inches; gently pinch pleated dough to secure but do not press dough into filling. Brush dough with egg and sprinkle evenly with kosher salt.

7. Lower oven temperature to 375 degrees. Bake until crust is deep golden brown and filling is beginning to brown, 35 to 45 minutes. Let tart cool on baking sheet on wire rack for 10 minutes. Using offset or wide metal spatula, loosen tart from parchment and carefully slide tart off parchment onto cutting board. Sprinkle with parsley, cut into wedges, and serve.

Potato and Shallot Galette with Goat Cheese

Substitute 1 pound Yukon Gold potatoes, sliced ¼ inch thick, for mushrooms and increase microwave cooking time to 4 to 8 minutes. Substitute 4 ounces thinly sliced shallots for leeks and rosemary for thyme. Increase amount of crème fraîche to ¼ cup and substitute ¼ cup chopped pitted kalamata olives and 1 teaspoon finely grated lemon zest for Dijon mustard. Substitute goat cheese for Gorgonzola.

Butternut Squash Galette with Gruyère

If desired, you can substitute rye flour for the whole-wheat flour in this recipe.

1. Microwave 6 ounces baby spinach and ¼ cup water in bowl until spinach is wilted and decreased in volume by half, 3 to 4 minutes. Using potholders, remove bowl from microwave and keep covered for 1 minute. Carefully remove plate and transfer spinach to colander. Gently press spinach with rubber spatula to release excess liquid. Transfer spinach to cutting board and chop coarse. Return spinach to colander and press again with rubber spatula; set aside.

2. Substitute 1¼ pounds butternut squash, peeled and cut into ½-inch cubes, for mushrooms and increase microwave cooking time to about 8 minutes. Substitute 1 thinly sliced red onion for leeks and ½ teaspoon minced fresh oregano for thyme. Substitute 1 teaspoon sherry vinegar for Dijon mustard and stir reserved spinach and 3 ounces shredded Gruyère cheese into filling along with crème fraîche and vinegar in step 4. Omit Gorgonzola.

SIMPLIFIED POTATO GALETTE

WHY THIS RECIPE WORKS: Pommes Anna, the classic French potato cake (or galette) in which thinly sliced potatoes are tossed with butter, tightly shingled in a skillet, and cooked slowly on the stovetop, delivers showstopping results, but it requires so much labor and time that we're willing to make it only once a year. We wanted a potato galette with a crisp, deeply bronzed crust encasing a creamy center that tastes of earthy potatoes and sweet butter—and we wanted one we could make on a weeknight.

We started by neatly arranging just the first layer of potatoes in the skillet, then casually packed the rest of the potatoes into the pan; once the galette was inverted onto the plate, only the tidy layer was visible. We swapped the traditional cast-iron skillet for a nonstick pan and achieved superior browning by starting the galette on the stovetop, then transferring it to the bottom rack of the oven. For a galette that held together but wasn't gluey, we rinsed the potatoes to rid them of excess starch, then incorporated a little cornstarch for just the right amount of adhesion. And in lieu of occasionally tamping down on the galette during cooking as in traditional recipes, we simply filled a cake pan with pie weights and set it on the galette for a portion of the baking time. A bit of fresh rosemary added another layer of earthy flavor.

Simplified Potato Galette
SERVES 6 TO 8

For the potato cake to hold together, it is important to slice the potatoes no more than ⅛ inch thick and to make sure the slices are thoroughly dried before assembling the cake. Use a mandoline slicer or the slicing attachment of a food processor to slice the potatoes uniformly thin. A pound of dried beans, rice, or coins can be substituted for the pie weights. You will need a 10-inch ovensafe nonstick skillet for this recipe.

1. Using a spatula, loosen the galette and slide it out of the skillet onto a large plate.

2. Gently place a cutting board over the galette. Do not use an overly heavy board, which may crush the cake.

3. Flip the plate over so the board is on the bottom. Remove the plate, and the galette is ready to be sliced and served.

2½ pounds Yukon Gold potatoes, sliced ⅛ inch thick
5 tablespoons unsalted butter, melted
1 tablespoon cornstarch
1½ teaspoons chopped fresh rosemary leaves (optional)
1 teaspoon table salt
½ teaspoon ground black pepper

1. Adjust an oven rack to the lowest position and heat the oven to 450 degrees. Place the potatoes in a large bowl and fill with cold water. Using your hands, swirl to remove excess starch, drain, then spread the potatoes onto kitchen towels and dry thoroughly.

2. Whisk 4 tablespoons of the butter, the cornstarch, rosemary (if using), salt, and pepper together in a large bowl. Add the dried potatoes and toss to thoroughly coat. Place the remaining 1 tablespoon butter in a 10-inch ovensafe nonstick skillet and swirl to coat. Place 1 potato slice in the center of the skillet, then overlap slices in a circle around the center slice, followed by an outer circle of overlapping slices. Gently place the remaining sliced potatoes on top of the first layer, arranging so they form an even thickness.

3. Place the skillet over medium-high heat and cook until sizzling and the potatoes around the edge of the skillet start to turn translucent, about 5 minutes. Spray a 12-inch square of aluminum foil with vegetable oil spray. Place the foil, sprayed side down, on top of the potatoes. Place a 9-inch cake pan on top of the foil and fill with 2 cups pie weights. Firmly press down on the cake pan to compress the potatoes. Transfer the skillet to the oven and bake for 20 minutes.

4. Remove the cake pan and the foil from the skillet. Continue to bake until the potatoes are tender when a paring knife is inserted in the center, 20 to 25 minutes. Return the skillet to the stovetop and cook over medium heat, gently shaking the pan, until the galette releases from the sides of the pan, 2 to 3 minutes.

5. Invert the galette onto a cutting board. Using a serrated knife, gently cut into wedges and serve immediately.

POMMES ANNA

WHY THIS RECIPE WORKS: Traditional *pommes Anna* is rarely seen on home or restaurant menus these days because it takes a long time to prepare, and it is hard to remove cleanly from the pan, resulting in an unsatisfactory time-consuming and messy dish. We wanted a traditionally elegant potato cake with a crisp, deep brown crust covering the soft, creamy potato layers within.

We used a nonstick skillet to ensure easy release of our potatoes. Most recipes for pommes Anna call for clarified butter, but we decided to cut down on time and waste (a good portion of the butter is lost with clarifying) and instead tossed the sliced potatoes with melted butter. To accelerate cooking, we arranged the potatoes in elegant, layered circles in the skillet as it was heating on the stovetop; when we were done layering the slices, we pressed the potatoes with the bottom

of a cake pan to compact them into a cohesive cake. To unmold, we simply inverted the potato cake onto a baking sheet and then slid it onto a serving dish.

Pommes Anna
SERVES 6 TO 8
Use a food processor fitted with a fine slicing disk or a mandoline to slice the potatoes, but do not slice them until you are ready to start assembling; see page 873 for our recommended mandoline. Remember to start timing when you begin arranging the potatoes in the skillet; they will need 30 minutes on the stovetop to brown properly no matter how quickly you arrange them.

3 pounds russet or Yukon Gold potatoes (about 6 medium), peeled and sliced ⅛ inch thick (see note)
5 tablespoons unsalted butter, melted
¼ cup vegetable oil or peanut oil
Table salt and ground black pepper

1. Adjust an oven rack to the lower-middle position and heat the oven to 450 degrees. Toss the potatoes with the butter to coat.

2. Heat the oil in an ovensafe 10-inch nonstick skillet over medium-low heat. Begin timing, and arrange the potato slices in the skillet, using the most attractive slices to form the bottom layer, by placing one slice in the center of the skillet and overlapping more slices in a circle around the center slice; form another circle of overlapping slices to cover the pan bottom. Season with ¼ teaspoon salt and pepper to taste. Arrange the second layer of potatoes, working in the opposite direction of the first layer; season with ¼ teaspoon salt and pepper to taste. Repeat, layering the potatoes in opposite directions and seasoning with ¼ teaspoon salt and pepper to taste, until no slices remain (broken or uneven slices can be pieced together to form a single slice; potatoes will mound in the center of the skillet). Continue to cook until 30 minutes elapse from when you began arranging the potatoes in the skillet.

3. Using the bottom of a 9-inch cake pan, press on the potatoes firmly to compact. Cover the skillet and place in the oven; bake until the potatoes begin to soften, about 15 minutes. Uncover and continue to bake until the potatoes are tender when pierced with the tip of a paring knife and the edge of the potatoes near the skillet is browned, about 10 minutes longer. Meanwhile, line a rimless baking sheet or an inverted rimmed baking sheet with foil and spray lightly with vegetable oil spray. Carefully drain off the excess fat from the potatoes by pressing the bottom of the cake pan against the potatoes while tilting the skillet. (Be sure to use heavy potholders.)

4. Set the baking sheet, foil side down, on top of the skillet. Using potholders, hold the baking sheet in place with one hand and carefully invert the skillet and baking sheet together. Lift the skillet off the potatoes; slide the potatoes from the baking sheet onto a platter. Cut into wedges and serve immediately.

FRENCH-STYLE MASHED POTATOES

WHY THIS RECIPE WORKS: *Aligot* is French cookery's intensely rich, cheesy take on mashed potatoes. These potatoes get their elastic, satiny texture through prolonged, vigorous stirring—which can easily go awry and lead to a gluey, sticky mess. We wanted to create cheesy, garlicky mashed potatoes with a smooth, elastic texture and the same signature stretch as the French original.

After making aligot with different potatoes, we found medium-starch Yukon Golds to be the clear winner, yielding a puree with a mild, buttery flavor and a light, creamy consistency. We boiled the potatoes, then used a food processor to "mash" them. Traditional aligot uses butter and crème fraîche to add flavor and creaminess and loosen the texture before mixing in the cheese. But crème fraîche isn't always easy to find, so we substituted whole milk, which provided depth without going overboard. For the cheese, a combination of mild mozzarella and nutty Gruyère proved just right. As for the stirring, we needed to monitor the consistency closely: too much stirring and the aligot turned rubbery, too little and the cheese didn't marry with the potatoes for that essential elasticity.

French Mashed Potatoes with Cheese and Garlic (Aligot)

SERVES 6

The finished potatoes should have a smooth and slightly elastic texture. White cheddar can be substituted for the Gruyère. For richer, stretchier aligot, double the mozzarella.

- 2 pounds Yukon Gold potatoes (about 4 medium), peeled, cut into ½-inch-thick slices, rinsed well, and drained
  Table salt
- 6 tablespoons (¾ stick) unsalted butter
- 2 medium garlic cloves, minced or pressed through a garlic press (about 2 teaspoons)
- 1–1½ cups whole milk
- 4 ounces mozzarella cheese, shredded (about 1 cup; see note)
- 4 ounces Gruyère cheese, shredded (about 1 cup; see note)
  Ground black pepper

1. Place the potatoes and 1 tablespoon salt in a large saucepan; add water to cover by 1 inch. Partially cover the saucepan with a lid and bring to a boil over high heat. Reduce the heat to medium-low and simmer until the potatoes are tender and just break apart when poked with a fork, 12 to 17 minutes. Drain the potatoes and dry the saucepan.

2. Add the potatoes, butter, garlic, and 1½ teaspoons salt to a food processor. Pulse until the butter is melted and incorporated, about 10 pulses. Add 1 cup of the milk and continue to process until the potatoes are smooth and creamy, about 20 seconds, scraping down the sides of the workbowl halfway through.

3. Return the potato mixture to the saucepan and set over medium heat. Stir in the cheeses, 1 cup at a time, until incorporated. Continue to cook the potatoes, stirring vigorously, until the cheese is fully melted and the mixture is smooth and elastic, 3 to 5 minutes. If the mixture is difficult to stir and seems thick, stir in 2 tablespoons milk at a time (up to ½ cup) until the potatoes are loose and creamy. Season with salt and pepper to taste. Serve immediately.

POTATO CASSEROLE WITH BACON

WHY THIS RECIPE WORKS: This casserole of potatoes and onions is traditionally baked beneath a roast, which allows the casserole to be seasoned by the savory fat and juices of the roast. To get the same luxurious results without the roast, we started by rendering a small amount of bacon, which lent the dish a meaty flavor with a hint of smokiness. We then browned the onions in the rendered bacon fat, which gave the dish remarkable complexity.

Potato Casserole with Bacon and Caramelized Onion

SERVES 6 TO 8

Do not rinse or soak the potatoes, as this will wash away their starch, which is essential to the dish. A mandoline makes slicing the potatoes much easier. For the proper texture, make sure to let the casserole stand for 20 minutes before serving.

3 slices thick-cut bacon, cut into ½-inch pieces
  1 large onion, halved and sliced thin
1¼ teaspoons salt
  2 teaspoons chopped fresh thyme
  ½ teaspoon pepper
1¼ cups low-sodium chicken broth
1¼ cups beef broth
  3 pounds Yukon Gold potatoes, peeled
  2 tablespoons unsalted butter, cut into 4 pieces

1. Adjust oven rack to lower-middle position and heat oven to 425 degrees. Grease 13 by 9-inch baking dish.

2. Cook bacon in medium saucepan over medium-low heat until crisp, 10 to 13 minutes. Using slotted spoon, transfer bacon to paper towel–lined plate. Remove and discard all but 1 tablespoon fat from pot. Return pot to medium heat and add onion and ¼ teaspoon salt; cook, stirring frequently, until onion is soft and golden brown, about 25 minutes, adjusting heat and adding water 1 tablespoon at a time if onion or bottom of pot becomes too dark. Transfer onion to large bowl; add bacon, thyme, remaining 1 teaspoon salt, and pepper. Add broths to now-empty saucepan and bring to simmer over medium-high heat, scraping bottom of pan to loosen any browned bits.

3. Slice potatoes ⅛ inch thick. Transfer to bowl with onion mixture and toss to combine. Transfer to prepared baking dish. Firmly press down on mixture to compress into even layer. Carefully pour hot broth over top of potatoes. Dot surface evenly with butter.

4. Bake, uncovered, until potatoes are tender and golden brown on edges and most of liquid has been absorbed, 45 to 55 minutes. Transfer to wire rack and let stand for 20 minutes to fully absorb broth before cutting and serving.

POTATOES LYONNAISE

WHY THIS RECIPE WORKS: Originally conceived as a way to use up leftover boiled potatoes, potatoes Lyonnaise came to represent the best of classic French bistro cuisine: buttery, browned potato slices with strands of sweet, caramelized onion and fresh parsley—a simple yet complex skillet potato dish. Sadly, many versions are greasy and heavy rather than rich and complex. We wanted a return to the original elegant, buttery potato and onion dish—but one that didn't require leftover potatoes to make.

First, we had to choose the right potato. Yukon Golds beat out high-starch russets and low-starch Red Bliss. We pre-cooked the potatoes in the microwave so that, once added to the skillet, they would cook through in the time they took to brown (without the microwave, the potatoes charred on the outside before cooking through). While the potatoes were

in the microwave, we cooked the onions just long enough to release moisture and cook in their own juices. To finish the dish, we united the onions and potatoes in a brief sauté for the perfect melding of flavors. A sprinkling of minced parsley gave the dish a fresh taste and bright color.

Potatoes Lyonnaise
SERVES 4

Toss the potatoes halfway through the microwave session to prevent uneven cooking. If using a lightweight skillet, you will need to stir the potatoes more frequently to prevent burning.

  3 tablespoons unsalted butter
  1 large onion, halved pole to pole and sliced
    ¼ inch thick (about 3 cups)
  ½ teaspoon table salt
  2 tablespoons water
1½ pounds Yukon Gold potatoes (about 3 medium),
    peeled and sliced crosswise into ¼-inch rounds
  ¼ teaspoon ground black pepper
  1 tablespoon minced fresh parsley leaves

1. Melt 1 tablespoon of the butter in a 12-inch heavy nonstick skillet over medium-high heat. Add the onion and ¼ teaspoon of the salt and stir to coat; cook, stirring occasionally, until the onion begins to soften, about 3 minutes. Reduce the heat to medium and cook, covered, stirring occasionally, until the onion is light brown and soft, about 12 minutes longer, deglazing with the water when the pan gets dry, about halfway through the cooking time. Transfer to a bowl and cover. Do not wash the skillet.

2. While the onion cooks, microwave 1 tablespoon more butter on high power in a large microwave-safe bowl until melted, about 15 seconds. Add the potatoes to the bowl and toss to coat with the melted butter. Microwave on high power until the potatoes just start to turn tender, about 6 minutes, tossing halfway through the cooking time. Toss the potatoes again and set aside.

3. Melt the remaining 1 tablespoon butter in the now-empty skillet over medium-high heat. Add the potatoes and shake the skillet to distribute evenly. Cook, without stirring, until browned on the bottom, about 3 minutes. Using a spatula, stir the potatoes carefully and continue to cook, stirring every 2 to 3 minutes, until the potatoes are well browned and tender when pierced with the tip of a paring knife, 8 to 10 minutes more. Season with the remaining salt and the pepper.

4. Add the onion back to the skillet and stir to combine. Cook until the onion is heated through and the flavors have melded, 1 to 2 minutes. Transfer to a large plate, sprinkle with the parsley, and serve.

CHICKEN FRICASSEE

WHY THIS RECIPE WORKS: In search of a streamlined technique that would give this classic French braise weeknight potential and a brighter sauce, we replaced the bone-in chicken parts with the busy cook's favorite timesaver: boneless, skinless breasts and thighs. Then we found two ways to add richness that we'd lost by omitting the skin and bones: We browned the meat in butter and oil, and we browned the vegetables until they developed fond to serve as the sauce base. Increasing the amount of mushrooms boosted the fricassee's meaty flavor, while finishing the sauce with sour cream added body and tang. Whisking an egg yolk into the sour cream thickened the sauce and made it silky.

Quick Chicken Fricassee

SERVES 4 TO 6

Two tablespoons of chopped fresh parsley leaves may be substituted for the tarragon in this recipe.

- 2 pounds boneless, skinless chicken breasts and/or thighs, trimmed
  Table salt and ground black pepper
- 1 tablespoon unsalted butter
- 1 tablespoon olive oil
- 1 pound cremini mushrooms, trimmed and sliced ¼ inch thick
- 1 medium onion, chopped fine
- ¼ cup dry white wine
- 1 tablespoon unbleached all-purpose flour
- 1 medium garlic clove, minced or pressed through a garlic press (about 1 teaspoon)
- 1½ cups low-sodium chicken broth
- ⅓ cup sour cream
- 1 large egg yolk
- 2 teaspoons juice from 1 lemon
- 2 teaspoons minced fresh tarragon leaves
- ½ teaspoon freshly grated nutmeg

1. Pat the chicken dry with paper towels and season with 1 teaspoon salt and ½ teaspoon pepper. Heat the butter and oil in a 12-inch skillet over medium-high heat until the butter is melted. Place the chicken in a skillet and cook until browned, about 4 minutes. Using tongs, flip the chicken and cook until browned on the second side, about 4 minutes longer. Transfer the chicken to a large plate.

2. Add the mushrooms, onion, and wine to the now-empty skillet and cook, stirring occasionally, until the liquid has evaporated and the mushrooms are browned, 8 to 10 minutes. Add the flour and garlic; cook, stirring constantly, for 1 minute. Add the broth and bring the mixture to a boil, scraping up the browned bits from the bottom of the pan. Add the chicken and any accumulated juices to the skillet. Reduce the heat to medium-low, cover, and simmer until the breasts register 160 to 165 degrees and the thighs register 175 degrees on an instant-read thermometer, 5 to 10 minutes.

3. Transfer the chicken to a clean platter and tent loosely with foil. Whisk the sour cream and the egg yolk together in a medium bowl. Whisking constantly, slowly stir ½ cup of the hot sauce from the skillet into the sour cream mixture to temper. Stirring constantly, slowly pour the sour cream mixture into the simmering sauce. Stir in the lemon juice, tarragon and nutmeg; return to a simmer. Season with salt and pepper to taste, pour the sauce over the chicken, and serve.

STUFFED CHICKEN BREASTS

WHY THIS RECIPE WORKS: Most American cooks stuff chicken breasts with cheesy, bready fillings. French chefs, on the other hand, use a forcemeat stuffing to transform ordinary chicken breasts into a four-star affair. The French technique requires some serious labor, and includes skinning and boning a whole chicken, stuffing the breasts with the leg meat, and wrapping them up in the skin. We wanted to achieve the same flavorful package of chicken and filling—using a much simpler procedure.

Starting with boneless, skinless chicken breasts eliminated the need to bone a whole chicken. We mimicked a forcemeat stuffing by trimming a bit of meat from each chicken breast, and combining the meat with mushrooms, herbs, and leeks. Pureeing the meat trimmings created a cohesive filling that stayed put inside the chicken breasts.

Turning to the mechanics, we needed to create easy-to-roll rectangles of chicken breast to encase the stuffing. After butterflying the chicken breasts, we pounded them thin and trimmed them into a rectangular shape. The stuffing was easy to spread on the breasts, which we simply rolled up and tied with twine. Finally, we browned the chicken in a hot skillet and then added chicken broth and wine to braise the meat in the pan. Not only did the chicken stay tender when simmered, but the liquid served as a base for a simple yet intensely flavored pan sauce.

French-Style Stuffed Chicken Breasts

SERVES 4

To make slicing the chicken easier, freeze it for 15 minutes. If your chicken breasts come with the tenderloins attached, pull them off and reserve them to make the puree (along with the breast meat you will trim in step 1). Because the stuffing contains raw chicken, it is important to check its temperature in step 5.

CHICKEN AND STUFFING

- 4 (7- to 8-ounce) boneless, skinless chicken breasts, tenderloins removed and breasts trimmed (see note)
- 3 tablespoons vegetable oil
- 10 ounces white mushrooms, wiped clean and sliced thin
- 1 small leek, white part only, chopped and rinsed thoroughly (about 1 cup)
- 2 medium garlic cloves, minced or pressed through a garlic press (about 2 teaspoons)
- ½ teaspoon minced fresh thyme leaves
- 1 tablespoon juice from 1 lemon
- ½ cup dry white wine
- 1 tablespoon minced fresh parsley leaves
  Table salt and ground black pepper
- 1 cup low-sodium chicken broth

SAUCE

- 1 teaspoon Dijon mustard
- 2 tablespoons unsalted butter
  Table salt and ground black pepper

1. FOR THE CHICKEN AND STUFFING: Butterfly the chicken horizontally, stopping ½ inch from the edges so the halves remain attached, then open up each breast, cover with plastic wrap, and pound the cutlets to an even ¼-inch thickness (each cutlet should measure about 8 by 6 inches). Trim about ½ inch from the long sides of the cutlets (1½ to 2 ounces of meat per cutlet, or a total of ½ cup from all 4 cutlets) to form rectangles that measure about 8 by 5 inches. Process all the trimmings in a food processor until smooth, about 20 seconds. Transfer the puree to a medium bowl and set aside. (Do not wash the food processor bowl.)

2. Heat 1 tablespoon of the oil in a 12-inch skillet over medium-high heat until shimmering. Add the mushrooms and cook, stirring occasionally, until all the moisture has evaporated and the mushrooms are golden brown, 8 to 11 minutes. Add 1 tablespoon more oil and the leek; continue to cook, stirring frequently, until softened, 2 to 4 minutes. Add the garlic and thyme and cook until fragrant, about 30 seconds. Add 1½ teaspoons of the lemon juice and cook until all the moisture has evaporated, about 30 seconds. Transfer the mixture to the bowl of the food processor. Return the pan to the heat, add the wine, and scrape the pan bottom to loosen any browned bits. Transfer the wine to a small bowl and set aside. Rinse and dry the skillet.

3. Pulse the mushroom mixture in the food processor until roughly chopped, about 5 pulses. Transfer the mushroom mixture to the bowl with the pureed chicken. Add 1½ teaspoons

STUFFING CHICKEN BREASTS

1. Slice each breast horizontally, stopping ½ inch from the edges so the halves remain attached.

2. Open up each breast, cover it with plastic wrap, and pound it to an even ¼-inch thickness.

3. Trim about ½ inch from the long side of each cutlet to form an 8 by 5-inch rectangle. Reserve the trimmings for the stuffing.

4. Spread the stuffing evenly over each cutlet, leaving a ¾-inch border along the short sides and a ¼-inch border along the long sides.

5. With the short side facing you, roll up each cutlet and secure it snugly with kitchen twine.

of the parsley, ¾ teaspoon salt, and ½ teaspoon pepper. Using a rubber spatula, fold together the stuffing ingredients until well combined (you should have about 1½ cups stuffing).

4. Spread one-quarter of the stuffing evenly over each cutlet with a rubber spatula, leaving a ¾-inch border along the short sides of the cutlet and a ¼-inch border along the long sides. Roll each breast up as tightly as possible without squeezing out the filling and place seam side down. Evenly space three pieces of kitchen twine (each about 12 inches long) beneath each breast and tie, trimming any excess.

5. Season the chicken with salt and pepper. Heat the remaining 1 tablespoon oil in the skillet over medium-high heat until just smoking. Add the chicken bundles and brown on all four sides, about 2 minutes per side. Add the broth and reserved wine to the pan and bring to a boil. Reduce the heat to low, cover the pan, and cook until the center of the chicken registers 160 to 165 degrees on an instant-read thermometer, 12 to 18 minutes. Transfer the chicken to a carving board and tent loosely with foil.

6. FOR THE SAUCE: While the chicken rests, whisk the mustard into the cooking liquid. Increase the heat to high and simmer, scraping the pan bottom to loosen the browned bits, until dark brown and reduced to ½ cup, 7 to 10 minutes. Off the heat, whisk in the butter and the remaining 1½ teaspoons parsley and 1½ teaspoons lemon juice; season with salt and pepper to taste. Remove the twine and cut each chicken bundle on the bias into six medallions. Spoon the sauce over the chicken and serve.

COQ AU VIN

WHY THIS RECIPE WORKS: Although conventional recipes for *coq au vin* take upwards of three hours to prepare, we felt that this rustic dish shouldn't be so time-consuming. After all, it's basically a chicken fricassee. We wanted to create a dish with tender, juicy chicken infused with the flavors of red wine, onions, mushrooms, and bacon in under two hours.

We decided to use chicken parts; this way, we could pick the parts we liked best. If using a mix of dark and white meat, we found it was essential to start the dark before the white, so that all the meat finished cooking at the same time and nothing was overcooked or undercooked. To thicken the stewing liquid, we sprinkled flour over the sautéed vegetables and whisked in butter toward the end of cooking; the butter also provided a nice richness in the sauce. Chicken broth added a savory note to the sauce and gave it some body; an entire bottle of red wine provided a great base of flavor. Tomato paste was a fuss-free way to add extra depth and body to the sauce, while a sprinkling of crisp, salty bacon rounded out the acidity of the wine.

Coq au Vin
SERVES 4

Use any $10 bottle of fruity, medium-bodied red wine, such as Pinot Noir, Côtes du Rhône, or Zinfandel. If using both chicken breasts and thighs/drumsticks, we recommend cutting the breast pieces in half so that each person can have some white meat and dark meat. The breasts and thighs/drumsticks do not cook at the same rate; if using both, note that the breast pieces are added partway through the cooking time. Serve with egg noodles.

6 ounces thick-cut bacon (about 5 slices), chopped medium
   Vegetable oil, as needed
4 pounds bone-in, skin-on chicken pieces (split breasts cut in half, drumsticks, and/or thighs; see note)
   Table salt and ground black pepper
8 ounces (about 2 cups) frozen pearl onions
10 ounces white mushrooms, wiped clean and quartered
2 medium garlic cloves, minced or pressed through a garlic press (about 2 teaspoons)
1 tablespoon tomato paste
3 tablespoons unbleached all-purpose flour
1 (750-milliliter) bottle medium-bodied red wine (see note)
2½ cups low-sodium chicken broth
1 teaspoon minced fresh thyme leaves or ¼ teaspoon dried
2 bay leaves
2 tablespoons unsalted butter, cut into 2 pieces, chilled
2 tablespoons minced fresh parsley leaves

1. Fry the bacon in a large Dutch oven over medium heat until crisp, 5 to 7 minutes. Transfer the bacon to a paper towel–lined plate, leaving the fat in the pot (you should have about 2 tablespoons; if necessary, add vegetable oil to make this amount). Set aside.

2. Pat the chicken dry with paper towels and season with salt and pepper. Return the pot with the bacon fat to medium-high heat until shimmering. Brown half of the chicken on both sides, 5 to 8 minutes per side, reducing the heat if the pan begins to scorch. Transfer the chicken to a plate, leaving the fat in the pot. Return the pot to medium-high heat and repeat with the remaining chicken; transfer the chicken to the plate.

3. Pour off all but 1 tablespoon of the fat in the pot (or add vegetable oil if needed to make this amount). Add the onions and mushrooms and cook over medium heat, stirring occasionally, until lightly browned, about 10 minutes. Stir in the garlic and tomato paste and cook until fragrant, about 30 seconds. Stir in the flour and cook for 1 minute. Stir in the wine, broth, thyme, and bay leaves, scraping up any browned bits.

4. Nestle the chicken, along with any accumulated juices, into the pot and bring to a simmer. Cover, turn the heat to medium-low, and simmer until the chicken is tender and the thickest part of the breasts registers 160 to 165 degrees on an instant-read thermometer, about 20 minutes, or the thickest part of the thighs and drumsticks registers 175 degrees on an instant-read thermometer, about 1 hour. (If using both types of chicken, simmer the thighs and drumsticks for 40 minutes before adding the breasts.)

5. Transfer the chicken to a serving dish, tent loosely with foil, and let rest while finishing the sauce. Skim as much fat as possible off the surface of the sauce and return to a simmer until the sauce is thickened and measures about 2 cups, about 20 minutes. Off the heat, remove the bay leaves, whisk in the butter, and season with salt and pepper to taste. Pour the sauce over the chicken, sprinkle with the reserved bacon and the parsley, and serve.

CHICKEN WITH 40 CLOVES OF GARLIC

WHY THIS RECIPE WORKS: In most versions of chicken with 40 cloves of garlic, the garlic is soft and spreadable, but its flavor is spiritless. The chicken is tender, but the breast meat takes on a dry, chalky quality, and its flavor is washed out. We wanted to revisit this classic French dish to make it faster and better, so it would boast well-browned, full-flavored chicken, sweet and nutty garlic, and a savory sauce.

Using a cut-up chicken rather than a whole bird ensured that the meat cooked quickly and evenly. We roasted the garlic cloves first to caramelize them and develop their flavor, then added them to the braising liquid with the chicken. Cooking it all with a two-part pan-roasting/braising technique kept the chicken moist, and finishing the chicken under the broiler made the chicken skin crispy. Some shallots and herbs added flavor to the sauce, and several roasted garlic cloves, smashed into a paste, thickened and flavored the sauce. A few tablespoons of butter, swirled in before serving, added richness.

Chicken with 40 Cloves of Garlic
SERVES 4

If using a kosher chicken, skip the brining process and begin with step 2. Avoid heads of garlic that have begun to sprout (the green shoots will make the sauce taste bitter). Tie the rosemary and thyme sprigs together with kitchen twine so they will be easy to retrieve from the pan. Serve the dish with slices of crusty baguette; you can spread them with the roasted garlic cloves.

Table salt and ground black pepper
1 (3½- to 4-pound) chicken, cut into 8 pieces (4 breast pieces, 2 thighs, 2 drumsticks; see page 395) and trimmed
3 medium heads garlic (about 8 ounces), outer papery skins removed, cloves separated and unpeeled (see note)
2 medium shallots, peeled and quartered
1 tablespoon olive oil
¾ cup dry vermouth or dry white wine
¾ cup low-sodium chicken broth
2 sprigs fresh thyme (see note)
1 sprig fresh rosemary (see note)
1 bay leaf
2 tablespoons unsalted butter

1. Adjust an oven rack to the middle position and heat the oven to 400 degrees. Dissolve ¼ cup salt in 2 quarts cold water in a large container; submerge the chicken in the brine, cover with plastic wrap, and refrigerate for 30 minutes. Remove the chicken from the brine, rinse, and pat dry with paper towels. Season both sides of the chicken pieces with pepper.

2. Meanwhile, combine the garlic, shallots, 2 teaspoons of the olive oil, ½ teaspoon salt, and ¼ teaspoon pepper in a 9-inch pie plate; cover tightly with foil and roast until softened and beginning to brown, about 30 minutes, shaking the pan once halfway through cooking. Uncover, stir, and continue to roast, uncovered, until browned and fully tender, about 10 minutes longer, stirring once or twice. Remove from the oven and increase the oven temperature to 450 degrees.

3. Heat the remaining 1 teaspoon oil in a 12-inch ovensafe skillet over medium-high heat until smoking. Brown the chicken, skin side down, until golden, about 5 minutes; flip the chicken pieces and brown until golden on the second side, about 4 minutes longer. Transfer the chicken to a large plate and pour off the fat from the skillet. Off the heat, add the vermouth, chicken broth, thyme, rosemary, and bay leaf to the pan, scraping up any browned bits. Set the skillet over medium heat, add the garlic mixture, and return the chicken, skin side up, to the pan, nestling the pieces on top of and between the garlic cloves. Place the skillet in the oven and roast until the thickest part of the breasts registers 160 to 165 degrees on an instant-read thermometer; remove the skillet from the oven.

4. Adjust an oven rack 6 inches from the broiler element and heat the broiler. Broil the chicken to crisp the skin, 3 to 5 minutes. Remove the skillet from the oven and transfer the chicken to a serving dish. Transfer 10 to 12 garlic cloves to a fine-mesh sieve and reserve. Using a slotted spoon, scatter the remaining garlic cloves and shallots around the chicken; discard the herbs. With a rubber spatula, push the reserved garlic cloves through the sieve and into a bowl; discard the skins. Add the garlic paste to the skillet and bring the liquid to a simmer over medium-high heat, whisking to incorporate the garlic. Whisk in the butter and season with salt and pepper to taste. Serve the chicken, passing the sauce separately.

CUTTING UP A WHOLE CHICKEN

Buying chicken parts is convenient, but packages often contain pieces of varying sizes. Cutting up a whole chicken yourself isn't difficult and it will guarantee evenly sized pieces of meat.

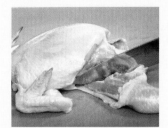

1. Using a chef's knife, cut off the legs, one at a time, by severing the joint between the leg and the body.

2. Cut each leg into two pieces—the drumstick and thigh—by slicing through the joint that connects them (marked by a thick white line of fat).

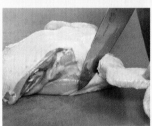

3. Flip the chicken over and remove the wings by slicing through each wing joint.

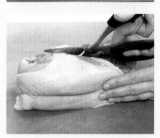

4. Turn the chicken (now without its legs and wings) on its side and, using scissors, remove the back from the chicken breast.

5. Flip the breast skin side down and, using a chef's knife, cut it in half through the breast plate (marked by a thin white line of cartilage), then cut each piece in half again.

FRENCH CHICKEN IN A POT

WHY THIS RECIPE WORKS: Poulet en cocotte (chicken in a pot) is a classic French specialty—at its best, it's a whole chicken baked with root vegetables in a covered pot that delivers incredibly tender and juicy meat. Sounds simple, but it's actually more challenging than throwing chicken in a pot with vegetables. One potential problem is too much moisture in the pot, which washes out the flavor; another pitfall is overcooking. We wanted chicken in a pot that delivered moist meat and satisfying flavor.

We removed the vegetables—the liquid they released made the pot too steamy—and cooked the chicken by itself (after browning it in a little oil to prevent it from sticking). We also tightly sealed the pot with foil before adding the lid. To keep the breast meat from drying out and becoming tough, we cooked the chicken very slowly. After developing the basic technique, we revisited the idea of vegetables, and found that a small amount of potently flavored aromatic vegetables could be added if they were lightly browned with the chicken to erase most of their moisture. Finally, defatting the liquid in the pot rewarded us with a richly flavored sauce.

French Chicken in a Pot

SERVES 4

The cooking times in the recipe are for a 4½- to 5-pound bird. A 3½- to 4½-pound chicken will take about an hour to cook, and a 5- to 6-pound bird will take close to 2 hours. We developed this recipe to work with a 5- to 8-quart Dutch oven with a tight-fitting lid. If using a 5-quart pot, do not cook a chicken larger than 5 pounds. If using a kosher chicken, reduce the amount of table salt to ½ teaspoon. If you choose not to serve the skin with the chicken, simply remove it before carving. The amount of sauce will vary depending on the size of the chicken; season it with about ¼ teaspoon lemon juice for every ¼ cup.

> 1 (4½- to 5-pound) whole chicken, giblets discarded, wings tucked under back (see note)
> 1 teaspoon table salt (see note)
> ¼ teaspoon ground black pepper
> 1 tablespoon olive oil
> 1 small onion, chopped medium
> 1 small celery rib, chopped medium
> 6 medium garlic cloves, peeled and trimmed
> 1 bay leaf
> 1 medium sprig fresh rosemary (optional)
> ½–1 teaspoon juice from 1 lemon (see note)

1. Adjust an oven rack to the lowest position and heat the oven to 250 degrees. Pat the chicken dry with paper towels and season with the salt and pepper.

2. Heat the oil in a large Dutch oven over medium heat until just smoking. Add the chicken, breast side down, and scatter the onion, celery, garlic cloves, bay leaf, and rosemary (if using) around the chicken. Cook until the breast is lightly browned, about 5 minutes. Flip the chicken breast side up and continue to cook until the chicken and vegetables are well browned, 6 to 8 minutes.

3. Off the heat, place a large sheet of foil over the pot and cover tightly with the lid. Transfer the pot to the oven and cook until the thickest part of the breast registers 160 to 165 degrees and the thickest part of the thighs registers 175 degrees on an instant-read thermometer, 1 hour and 20 minutes to 1 hour and 50 minutes.

4. Remove the pot from the oven. Transfer the chicken to a cutting board, tent loosely with foil, and let rest for 20 minutes. Strain the chicken juices from the pot into a fat separator, pressing on the solids to extract the liquid; discard the solids (you should have about ¾ cup juices). Let the liquid settle for 5 minutes, then pour into a saucepan and cook over low heat until hot. Carve the chicken, adding any accumulated juices to the saucepan. Season the sauce with lemon juice to taste (see note). Serve the chicken, passing the sauce separately.

FRENCH-STYLE CHICKEN AND STUFFING IN A POT

WHY THIS RECIPE WORKS: The French classic *poule au pot* is a rather unique take on stuffed chicken: Instead of being roasted, the stuffed bird is braised with vegetables in a Dutch oven to make a satisfying and hearty one-pot meal. Our first attempts gave us wan flavor and dry chicken. To ensure the pork and bread-crumb stuffing would cook through before the chicken was overdone, we skipped stuffing the bird and instead patted the stuffing into logs, wrapped them in parchment paper, and nestled them into the pot. To make room for the chicken and vegetables, we swapped out the whole bird for parts and browned them first to give the broth rich flavor. We layered them on top of the vegetables with just enough broth to cover the vegetables so the delicate breast meat could cook more gently raised above the simmering liquid. A simple herb sauce flavored with the traditional cornichons and mustard rounded out this rustic meal.

French-Style Chicken and Stuffing in a Pot
SERVES 4 TO 6

A neutral bulk sausage is best, but breakfast or sweet Italian sausage can be used. You'll need a Dutch oven with at least a 7¼-quart capacity. Use small red potatoes, measuring 1 to 2 inches in diameter. Serve this dish with crusty bread and cornichons and Dijon mustard or Herb Sauce (recipe follows).

SAUSAGE STUFFING
- 2 slices hearty white sandwich bread, crusts removed, torn into quarters
- 1 large egg
- 1 shallot, minced
- 2 garlic cloves, minced
- 2 tablespoons minced fresh parsley
- 2 tablespoons minced fennel fronds
- 2 teaspoons whole-grain mustard
- 1 teaspoon minced fresh marjoram
- ¼ teaspoon pepper
- 1 pound bulk pork sausage

CHICKEN
- 2 celery ribs, halved crosswise
- 8 sprigs plus 1 tablespoon minced fresh parsley
- 6 sprigs fresh marjoram
- 1 bay leaf
- 2 teaspoons vegetable oil
- 2 (12-ounce) bone-in split chicken breasts, trimmed
- 2 (12-ounce) bone-in chicken leg quarters, trimmed
  Salt and pepper
- 1½ pounds small red potatoes, unpeeled
- 2 carrots, peeled and cut into ½-inch lengths
- 1 fennel bulb, stalks trimmed, bulb quartered
- 8 whole peppercorns
- 2 garlic cloves, peeled
- 3–3½ cups low-sodium chicken broth

1. FOR THE SAUSAGE STUFFING: Adjust oven rack to middle position and heat oven to 300 degrees. Pulse bread in food processor until finely ground, 10 to 15 pulses. Add egg, shallot, garlic, parsley, fennel fronds, mustard, marjoram, and pepper to processor and pulse to combine, 6 to 8 pulses, scraping down sides of bowl as needed. Add sausage and pulse to combine, 3 to 5 pulses, scraping down sides of bowl as needed.

2. Place 18 by 12-inch piece of parchment paper on counter, with longer edge parallel to edge of counter. Place half of stuffing onto lower third of parchment, shaping it into rough 8 by 2-inch rectangle. Roll up sausage in parchment; gently but firmly twist both ends to compact mixture into 6- to 7-inch-long cylinder, approximately 2 inches in diameter. Repeat with second piece of parchment and remaining stuffing.

3. FOR THE CHICKEN: Using kitchen twine, tie together celery, parsley sprigs, marjoram, and bay leaf. Heat oil in large Dutch oven over medium-high heat until just smoking. Pat chicken breasts and leg quarters dry with paper towels, sprinkle with ½ teaspoon salt, and season with pepper. Add chicken, skin side down, and cook without moving it until browned, 4 to 7 minutes. Transfer chicken to large plate. Pour off and discard any fat in pot.

4. Remove Dutch oven from heat and carefully arrange celery bundle, potatoes, carrots, and fennel in even layer over bottom of pot. Sprinkle peppercorns, garlic, and ¼ teaspoon salt over vegetables. Add enough broth so that top ½ inch of vegetables is above surface of liquid. Place leg quarters on top of vegetables in center of pot. Place stuffing cylinders on either side of leg quarters. Arrange breasts on top of leg quarters. Place pot over high heat and bring to simmer. Cover, transfer to oven, and cook until breasts register 160 degrees, 60 to 75 minutes.

this dish, and create a chicken dish that was meltingly tender, moist, and flavorful, napped in an aromatic, garlicky tomato sauce that we could mop up with a good loaf of crusty bread.

For the best flavor and most tender texture, we used bone-in chicken thighs and browned them in a sheer film of olive oil. Skinless thighs stuck to the pan, and skin-on thighs developed a flabby texture when braised later on. So we settled on a compromise—browning the thighs with the skin on (to develop rich flavor and leave browned bits in the pan), then ditching the skins prior to the braising (to avoid flabby skin). To keep the sauce from becoming greasy, we spooned off the excess fat left behind from browning the chicken, but kept enough to sauté our garlic and onion. Diced tomatoes, white wine, and chicken broth also went into the sauce. We then braised the chicken until it was meltingly tender. As for flavor enhancers, a small amount of niçoise olives added an essential brininess to the dish, and some minced anchovy made the sauce taste richer and fuller.

5. Transfer chicken and stuffing cylinders to carving board. Using slotted spoon, transfer vegetables to serving platter, discarding celery bundle. Pour broth through fine-mesh strainer into fat separator; discard solids. Let stand for 5 minutes.

6. Unwrap stuffing cylinders and slice into ½-inch-thick disks; transfer slices to platter with vegetables. Remove skin from chicken pieces and discard. Carve breasts from bone and slice into ½-inch-thick pieces. Separate thigh from leg by cutting through joint. Transfer chicken to platter with stuffing and vegetables. Pour ½ cup defatted broth over chicken and stuffing to moisten. Sprinkle with minced parsley. Serve, ladling remaining broth over individual servings.

Herb Sauce
MAKES ABOUT ½ CUP

- ⅓ cup extra-virgin olive oil
- 6 cornichons, minced
- 2 tablespoons minced fresh parsley
- 1 tablespoon minced fennel fronds
- 2 teaspoons minced shallot
- 2 teaspoons whole-grain mustard
- 1 teaspoon minced fresh marjoram
- ½ teaspoon finely grated lemon zest plus 2 tablespoons juice
- ¼ teaspoon pepper

Whisk all ingredients together in bowl. Let stand for 15 minutes before serving.

CHICKEN PROVENÇAL

WHY THIS RECIPE WORKS: Chicken *Provençal* represents the best of rustic peasant food—bone-in chicken is simmered all day in a tomatoey, garlicky herb broth. But all too often, this formula results in dry, rubbery chicken, watery or overly thick sauce, and dulled or muddied flavors. We wanted to rejuvenate

Chicken Provençal
SERVES 4

This dish is often served with rice or slices of crusty bread, but soft polenta is also a good accompaniment. Niçoise olives are the preferred olives here; the flavor of kalamatas and other types of brined or oil-cured olives is too potent.

- 8 (5- to 6-ounce) bone-in, skin-on chicken thighs, trimmed
  - Table salt
- 1 tablespoon extra-virgin olive oil
- 1 small onion, minced
- 6 medium garlic cloves, minced or pressed through a garlic press (about 2 tablespoons)
- 1 anchovy fillet, minced (about ½ teaspoon)
- ⅛ teaspoon cayenne pepper
- 1 cup dry white wine
- 1 cup low-sodium chicken broth
- 1 (14.5-ounce) can diced tomatoes, drained
- 2½ tablespoons tomato paste
- 1½ tablespoons chopped fresh thyme leaves
- 1 teaspoon chopped fresh oregano leaves
- 1 teaspoon herbes de Provence (optional)
- 1 bay leaf
- 1½ teaspoons grated zest from 1 lemon
- ½ cup pitted niçoise olives (see note)
- 1 tablespoon chopped fresh parsley leaves

1. Adjust an oven rack to the lower-middle position and heat the oven to 300 degrees. Season both sides of the chicken thighs with salt. Heat 1 teaspoon of the oil in a large Dutch oven over medium-high heat until shimmering. Add 4 chicken thighs, skin side down, and cook, without moving, until the skin is crisp and well browned, about 5 minutes. Flip the chicken pieces and brown on the second side, about 5 minutes longer; transfer to a large plate. Repeat with the remaining 4 chicken thighs, then transfer them to the plate and set aside. Discard all but 1 tablespoon of fat from the pot.

2. Add the onion to the pot and cook, stirring occasionally, over medium heat until softened and browned, about 4 minutes. Add the garlic, anchovy, and cayenne; cook, stirring constantly, until fragrant, about 1 minute. Add the wine, scraping up any browned bits. Stir in the chicken broth, tomatoes, tomato paste, thyme, oregano, herbes de Provence (if using), and bay leaf. Remove and discard the skin from the chicken thighs, then submerge the chicken pieces in the liquid and add the accumulated chicken juices to the pot. Increase the heat to high, bring to a simmer, cover, and set the pot in the oven; cook until the chicken offers no resistance when poked with a knife but is still clinging to the bones, about 1¼ hours.

3. Using a slotted spoon, transfer the chicken to a serving platter and tent loosely with foil. Discard the bay leaf. Set the pot over high heat, stir in 1 teaspoon of the lemon zest, bring to a boil, and cook, stirring occasionally, until slightly thickened and reduced to 2 cups, about 5 minutes. Stir in the olives and cook until heated through, about 1 minute. Combine the remaining ½ teaspoon zest and the parsley. Spoon the sauce over the chicken, drizzle the chicken with the remaining 2 teaspoons oil, sprinkle with the parsley mixture, and serve.

DAUBE PROVENÇAL

WHY THIS RECIPE WORKS: *Daube Provençal*, also known as *daube niçoise*, has all the elements of the best French fare: tender beef, a luxurious sauce, and complex flavors. So why does it usually end up as beef stew with a few misplaced ingredients instead of being its own, coherent dish? We wanted to translate the flavors of Provence—olive oil, olives, garlic, wine, herbs, oranges, tomatoes, mushrooms, and anchovies—to an American home kitchen, and create a bold, brash, and full-flavored beef stew, with ingredients that married into a robust but unified dish. We started with the test kitchen's reliable set of techniques to turn tough but flavorful beef into a tender stew: Brown the beef; add the aromatics; sprinkle some flour in the pan to thicken the braising liquid; deglaze with more cooking liquid; add the meat back to the pot; and finally, cover and cook slowly in the oven until tender. Technique established, we concentrated on selecting and managing the complex blend of ingredients that defines this dish. We chose briny niçoise olives, bright tomatoes, floral orange peel, and the regional flavors of thyme and bay leaf. A few anchovies added complexity without a fishy taste, and salt pork contributed rich body. A whole bottle of wine added bold flavor and needed just a little cooking to tame its raw bite. Finally, to keep the meat from drying out during the long braising time required to create a complex-tasting sauce, we cut it into relatively large 2-inch pieces.

Daube Provençal

SERVES 4 TO 6

Serve this French beef stew with egg noodles or boiled potatoes. If niçoise olives are not available, kalamata olives, though not authentic, can be substituted. Cabernet Sauvignon is our favorite wine for this recipe, but Côtes du Rhône and Zinfandel also work. Our favorite cut of beef for this recipe is chuck-eye roast, but any boneless roast from the chuck will work. Because the tomatoes are added just before serving, it is preferable to use canned whole tomatoes and dice them yourself—uncooked, they are more tender than canned diced tomatoes. Once the salt pork, thyme, and bay leaves are removed in step 4, the daube can be cooled and refrigerated in an airtight container for up to 4 days. Before reheating, skim the hardened fat from the surface, then continue with the recipe.

- ¾ ounce dried porcini mushrooms, rinsed
- 1 (3½-pound) boneless beef chuck-eye roast, trimmed and cut into 2-inch chunks (see note)
- 1½ teaspoons table salt
- 1 teaspoon ground black pepper
- 4 tablespoons olive oil
- 5 ounces salt pork, rind removed
- 2 medium onions, halved pole to pole and cut into ⅛-inch-thick slices (about 4 cups)
- 4 large carrots, peeled and cut into 1-inch-thick rounds (about 2 cups)
- 2 tablespoons tomato paste
- 4 medium garlic cloves, peeled and sliced thin
- ⅓ cup unbleached all-purpose flour
- 1 (750-milliliter) bottle bold red wine (see note)
- 1 cup low-sodium chicken broth
- 1 cup water
- 1 cup pitted niçoise olives, drained well (see note)
- 4 strips zest from 1 orange, each strip about 3 inches long, removed with a vegetable peeler, cleaned of white pith, and cut lengthwise into thin strips
- 2 anchovy fillets, minced (about 1 teaspoon)
- 5 sprigs fresh thyme, tied together with kitchen twine
- 2 bay leaves
- 1 (14.5-ounce) can whole tomatoes, drained and cut into ½-inch cubes (see note)
- 2 tablespoons minced fresh parsley leaves

1. Combine the mushrooms and 1 cup water in a small microwave-safe bowl; cover with plastic wrap, cut three vents for steam with a knife, and microwave on high power for 30 seconds. Let stand until the mushrooms soften, about 5 minutes. Lift the mushrooms from the liquid with a fork and chop into ½-inch pieces (you should have about 4 tablespoons). Strain the liquid through a fine-mesh strainer lined with a paper towel into a medium bowl. Set the mushrooms and liquid aside.

2. Adjust an oven rack to the lower-middle position and heat the oven to 325 degrees. Dry the beef thoroughly with paper towels, then season with the salt and pepper. Heat 2 tablespoons of the oil in a large heavy-bottomed Dutch oven over medium-high heat until just smoking; add half of the beef. Cook without moving the pieces until well browned, about 2 minutes on each side, for a total of 8 to 10 minutes, reducing the heat if the fat begins to smoke. Transfer the meat to a medium bowl. Repeat with the remaining 2 tablespoons oil and the remaining beef.

3. Reduce the heat to medium and add the salt pork, onions, carrots, tomato paste, and garlic to the now-empty pot; cook, stirring occasionally, until light brown, about 2 minutes. Stir in the flour and cook, stirring constantly, about 1 minute. Slowly add the wine, gently scraping up any browned bits. Add the broth, water, and beef with any accumulated juices. Increase the heat to medium-high and bring to a simmer. Add the mushrooms and their liquid, ½ cup of the olives, the orange zest, anchovies, thyme, and bay leaves, distributing evenly and arranging the beef so it is completely covered by the liquid; partially cover the pot and place in the oven. Cook until a fork inserted in the beef meets little resistance (the meat should not be falling apart), 2½ to 3 hours.

4. Discard the salt pork, thyme, and bay leaves. Add the tomatoes and the remaining ½ cup olives; warm over medium-high heat until heated through, about 1 minute. Cover the pot and allow the stew to settle, about 5 minutes. Using a spoon, skim the excess fat from the surface of the stew. Stir in the parsley and serve.

BEEF BURGUNDY

WHY THIS RECIPE WORKS: Leave it to the French to make beef stew into an elegant affair. Unfortunately, when translated to the home kitchen, classic, intensely flavorful beef burgundy, also known as *boeuf bourguignon*, tends to lose its appeal. We've seen too many versions of this rustic French dish with tough meat or a dull sauce and no flavor complexity. We wanted to bring this dish to its earthy, robust, warm potential: satisfyingly large chunks of tender meat draped with a velvety sauce brimming with the flavor of good Burgundy wine and studded with caramelized mushrooms and pearl onions.

We started by rendering salt pork until crisp, then browned large chunks of beef chuck roast in the rendered fat. For the braising liquid, a combination of chicken broth and water, enhanced with a small amount of dried porcini mushrooms

and tomato paste, provided balanced, well-rounded flavor. Using anything less than a full bottle of red wine (preferably a Burgundy, but a good Pinot Noir will suffice) left the sauce lacking and unremarkable. We deglazed the pan twice, used a roux to thicken the sauce, and then added the wine. Wrapping the aromatic vegetables in cheesecloth made it easy to remove them from the braising liquid. While the liquid reduced to a velvety sauce, we simmered pearl onions then sautéed them briefly with mushrooms to create the perfect garnish for our rich, tender beef.

Beef Burgundy
SERVES 6

Thick-cut bacon can be substituted for the salt pork; cut the bacon crosswise into ¼-inch pieces and treat it just as you would the salt pork, but note that you will have no rind to include in the vegetable and herb pouch. Boiled potatoes are the traditional accompaniment, but mashed potatoes or buttered noodles are nice as well.

STEW

- 6 ounces salt pork, trimmed of rind and rind reserved, salt pork cut into ¼-inch pieces (see note)
- 2 medium onions, chopped coarse
- 2 medium carrots, chopped coarse
- 1 medium head garlic, cloves separated and crushed but unpeeled
- 10 sprigs fresh parsley, torn into pieces
- 6 sprigs fresh thyme
- 2 bay leaves, crumbled
- ½ teaspoon black peppercorns
- ½ ounce dried porcini mushrooms, rinsed (optional)
- 1 (4- to 4½-pound) boneless beef chuck-eye roast, trimmed and cut into 2-inch chunks
   Table salt and ground black pepper

2½   cups water
   4   tablespoons (½ stick) unsalted butter, cut into 4 pieces
   ⅓   cup unbleached all-purpose flour
1¾   cups low-sodium chicken broth
   1   (750-milliliter) bottle red Burgundy or Pinot Noir
   1   teaspoon tomato paste
   2   tablespoons brandy
   3   tablespoons minced fresh parsley leaves

ONION AND MUSHROOM GARNISH
   7   ounces (about 1¾ cups) frozen pearl onions
   ¾   cup water
   1   tablespoon unsalted butter
   1   tablespoon sugar
   ½   teaspoon table salt
  10   ounces medium white mushrooms, wiped clean
        and halved

1. FOR THE STEW: Bring the salt pork, reserved salt pork rind, and 3 cups water to a boil in a medium saucepan over high heat. Boil for 2 minutes, then drain well.

2. Lay a double layer of cheesecloth (each piece should measure 22 by 8 inches) in a medium bowl, placing the sheets perpendicular to each other. Place the onions, carrots, garlic, parsley pieces, thyme, bay leaves, peppercorns, porcini mushrooms (if using), and salt pork rind in the cheesecloth-lined bowl. Gather together the edges of the cheesecloth and fasten them securely with kitchen twine; trim the excess cheesecloth with scissors if necessary. Set the pouch in a large ovensafe Dutch oven. Adjust the oven rack to the lower-middle position and heat the oven to 300 degrees.

3. Cook the salt pork in a 12-inch skillet over medium heat until lightly browned and crisp, about 12 minutes. With a slotted spoon, transfer the salt pork to the pot. Pour off and reserve all but 2 teaspoons of the fat from the skillet. Pat the beef dry with paper towels and season with salt and pepper. Add half of the beef to the skillet, increase the heat to high, and brown in a single layer, turning once or twice, until deep brown, about 7 minutes; transfer the browned beef to the pot. Add ½ cup of the water to the skillet and scrape the pan with a wooden spoon to loosen the browned bits; add the liquid to the pot.

4. Heat 2 teaspoons of the reserved pork fat in the skillet over high heat until smoking. Add the remaining beef in a single layer, turning once or twice, until deep brown, about 7 minutes; transfer the browned beef to the pot. Add ½ cup more water to the skillet and scrape the pan with a wooden spoon to loosen the browned bits; add the liquid to the pot.

5. Melt the butter in the skillet over medium heat. Whisk in the flour and cook, stirring constantly, until light brown, about 5 minutes. Gradually whisk in the chicken broth and the remaining 1½ cups water. Increase the heat to medium-high and bring to a simmer, stirring frequently, until thickened; add the mixture to the pot. Add 3 cups of the wine and the tomato paste to the pot and season with salt and pepper

to taste; stir to combine. Set the pot over high heat and bring to a boil; cover and place in the oven. Cook until the meat is tender, 2½ to 3 hours.

6. Remove the pot from the oven and transfer the vegetable and herb pouch to a mesh strainer; set the strainer over the pot. Using the back of a spoon, press the liquid from the pouch into the pot; discard the pouch. With a slotted spoon, transfer the beef to a medium bowl; set aside. Let the pot contents settle for about 15 minutes, then skim off and discard the fat.

7. Bring the liquid in the pot to a boil over medium-high heat. Simmer, stirring occasionally, until thickened and reduced to about 3 cups, 15 to 25 minutes.

8. FOR THE ONION AND MUSHROOM GARNISH: Meanwhile, bring the pearl onions, ½ cup of the water, the butter, sugar, and ¼ teaspoon of the salt to a boil in a 10-inch skillet over high heat. Cover, reduce the heat to medium-low, and simmer, shaking the pan occasionally, until the onions are tender, about 5 minutes. Uncover, increase the heat to high, and simmer until all the liquid evaporates, about 3 minutes. Add the mushrooms and the remaining ¼ teaspoon salt. Cook, stirring occasionally, until the liquid released by the mushrooms evaporates and the vegetables are browned, about 5 minutes. Transfer the vegetables to a bowl and set aside. Add the remaining ¼ cup water to the skillet and scrape the pan with a wooden spoon to loosen the browned bits; add the liquid to the pot with the reducing sauce.

9. When the sauce has reduced, reduce the heat to medium-low and stir in the beef, the remaining 2 tablespoons wine, the brandy, and the mushrooms and onions (and any accumulated juices). Cover the pot and cook until heated through, 5 to 8 minutes. Season with salt and pepper to taste and serve, sprinkling individual servings with the parsley.

SLOW-COOKER BEEF BURGUNDY

WHY THIS RECIPE WORKS: Given the amount of simmering time required for classic Beef Burgundy (page 399), we thought this stew could be easily morphed into a slow-cooker version that would have the same tender beef chunks and rich, earthy sauce as the original.

For a long braise, chuck roast cut into pieces is the best choice. The usual first step in making a stew is to brown the meat, but we found that we could get the same meaty flavor base from browning only half the beef. We used rendered bacon fat instead of oil; the bacon would go back into the stew at the end, lending a smoky note. Sautéed carrots and onions went into the slow-cooker insert next, with plenty of garlic, thyme, and tomato paste. As our braising liquid, beef broth tasted tinny but chicken broth worked well. We mixed it with red wine and a surprising ingredient, soy sauce, which intensified the savory flavors in the stew as well as deepened its color. To enrich the sauce, we stirred in a small amount of tapioca, a common thickening agent, in place of flour. We prepared the traditional onion and mushroom garnish separately, when the stew was almost finished cooking, and folded it in. The final touch was more red wine, which we reduced first so that it wouldn't impart a sour alcoholic taste. This slow-cooker beef burgundy had everything we would expect from the refined French original.

Slow-Cooker Beef Burgundy

SERVES 6 TO 8

Make sure to use the low setting on your slow cooker; the stew will burn on the high setting. Don't spend a lot of money for the wine in this recipe—in our testing, we found that California Pinot Noir wines in the $6 to $20 price range worked just fine. Boiled potatoes are the traditional accompaniment, but mashed potatoes or buttered noodles are nice as well.

STEW

 8 ounces (about 8 slices) bacon, cut into ¼-inch pieces
 1 (4-pound) boneless beef chuck-eye roast, trimmed and cut into 1½-inch chunks
   Table salt and ground black pepper
 1 large onion, minced
 2 carrots, peeled and minced
 8 medium garlic cloves, minced or pressed through a garlic press (about 2 tablespoons plus 2 teaspoons)
 2 teaspoons chopped fresh thyme leaves
 4 tablespoons tomato paste
 2½ cups Pinot Noir (see note)
 1½ cups low-sodium chicken broth
 ⅓ cup soy sauce
 3 bay leaves
 3 tablespoons Minute tapioca
 3 tablespoons minced fresh parsley leaves

ONION AND MUSHROOM GARNISH

 8 ounces (about 2 cups) frozen pearl onions
 ½ cup water
 5 tablespoons unsalted butter
 1 tablespoon sugar
 10 ounces white mushrooms, wiped clean and quartered
   Table salt

1. FOR THE STEW: Cook the bacon in a 12-inch skillet over medium-high heat until crisp. Using a slotted spoon, transfer the bacon to a paper towel–lined plate and refrigerate. Pour half of the bacon fat into a small bowl; set the skillet with the remaining bacon fat aside.

2. Pat the beef dry with paper towels and season with salt and pepper; place half of the beef in a slow-cooker insert. Heat the skillet with the remaining bacon fat over medium-high heat until smoking. Cook the remaining beef in a single layer until deep brown on all sides, about 8 minutes. Transfer the browned beef to the slow-cooker insert.

3. Add the reserved bacon fat to the now-empty skillet and heat over medium-high heat until shimmering. Add the onion, carrots, and ¼ teaspoon salt and cook until the vegetables begin to brown, about 5 minutes. Add the garlic and thyme and cook until fragrant, about 30 seconds. Add the tomato paste and stir until beginning to brown, about 45 seconds. Transfer the mixture to the slow-cooker insert.

4. Return the now-empty skillet to high heat and add 1½ cups of the wine, the chicken broth, and soy sauce. Simmer, scraping up any browned bits, for about 1 minute. Transfer the wine mixture to the slow-cooker insert.

5. Stir the bay leaves and tapioca into the slow-cooker insert. Set the slow cooker on low, cover, and cook until the meat is fork-tender, about 9 hours.

6. FOR THE ONION AND MUSHROOM GARNISH: Bring the pearl onions, water, butter, and sugar to a boil in a 12-inch skillet over high heat. Cover and simmer over medium-low heat until the onions are tender, about 5 minutes. Uncover, increase the heat to high, and cook until the liquid evaporates, about 3 minutes. Add the mushrooms and ¼ teaspoon salt and cook until the vegetables are browned and glazed, about 5 minutes.

7. When ready to serve, discard the bay leaves and stir in the onion and mushroom garnish and the reserved bacon. Bring the remaining 1 cup wine to a boil in a 12-inch skillet over high heat and simmer until reduced by half, about 5 minutes. Stir the reduced wine and parsley into the stew and season with salt and pepper to taste. Serve.

MISE EN PLACE—A FRENCH PHRASE EVERY HOME COOK SHOULD KNOW

When Bridget, Julia, and Becky prepare recipes on TV they always have each ingredient prepared and measured into its own glass bowl. Yes, this looks nice on television, but our test cooks follow the same procedure when the cameras aren't rolling. This practice has a fancy French name—*mise en place*, which means "to put in place"—but the concept is really quite simple. Prepare your ingredients *before* you start cooking.

To stay organized from the get-go, the test cooks measure out the amounts required in their recipes and then individually label each ingredient with its corresponding quantity, such as 1 cup unbleached all-purpose flour, 2 large egg whites, 1 cup toasted chopped walnuts, and so on. (Note that some ingredients such as onions and garlic are best prepared just before cooking, rather than in advance.) The measured and labeled ingredients are then kept together, by recipe, on large baking sheets and stored. When the test cooks are ready to cook, they grab their prepped ingredients and are ready to go. Try mise en place at home—you'll find it useful not only in helping you keep on track when tackling an involved recipe (think labor-intensive holiday meals) but also for day-to-day cooking—prepping your ingredients the night before will allow you to walk in the door after work and get dinner on the table fast. And since you can focus on what's cooking (rather than preparing ingredients), you eliminate the risk that something will burn or overcook.

MODERN BEEF BURGUNDY

WHY THIS RECIPE WORKS: We wanted to update the French classic *boeuf bourguignon* to have tender braised beef napped with a silky sauce with bold red wine flavor—without all the work that traditional recipes require. To eliminate the time-consuming step of searing the beef, we cooked the stew uncovered in a roasting pan in the oven so that the exposed meat browned as it braised. This method worked so well that we also used the oven, rather than the stovetop, to render the salt pork and to caramelize the traditional mushroom and pearl onion garnish. Salting the beef before cooking and adding some anchovy paste and porcini mushrooms enhanced the meaty savoriness of the dish without making our recipe too fussy.

Modern Beef Burgundy
SERVES 6 TO 8

If the pearl onions have a papery outer coating, remove it by rinsing them in warm water and gently squeezing individual onions between your fingertips. Two minced anchovy fillets can be used in place of the anchovy paste. To save time, salt the meat and let it stand while you prep the remaining ingredients. Serve with mashed potatoes or buttered noodles.

- 1 (4-pound) boneless beef chuck-eye roast, trimmed and cut into 1½- to 2-inch pieces, scraps reserved
  Salt and pepper
- 6 ounces salt pork, cut into ¼-inch pieces
- 3 tablespoons unsalted butter
- 1 pound cremini mushrooms, trimmed, halved if medium or quartered if large
- 1½ cups frozen pearl onions, thawed
- 1 tablespoon sugar
- ⅓ cup all-purpose flour
- 4 cups beef broth
- 1 (750-ml) bottle red Burgundy or Pinot Noir
- 5 teaspoons unflavored gelatin
- 1 tablespoon tomato paste
- 1 teaspoon anchovy paste
- 2 onions, chopped coarse
- 2 carrots, peeled and cut into 2-inch lengths
- 1 garlic head, cloves separated, unpeeled, and crushed
- 2 bay leaves
- ½ teaspoon black peppercorns
- ½ ounce dried porcini mushrooms, rinsed
- 10 sprigs fresh parsley, plus 3 tablespoons minced
- 6 sprigs fresh thyme

1. Toss beef and 1½ teaspoons salt together in bowl and let stand at room temperature for 30 minutes.

2. Adjust oven racks to lower-middle and lowest positions and heat oven to 500 degrees. Place salt pork, beef scraps, and 2 tablespoons butter in large roasting pan. Roast on lower-middle rack until well browned and fat has rendered, 15 to 20 minutes.

3. While salt pork and beef scraps roast, toss cremini mushrooms, pearl onions, remaining 1 tablespoon butter, and sugar together on rimmed baking sheet. Roast on lowest rack, stirring occasionally, until moisture released by mushrooms evaporates and vegetables are lightly glazed, 15 to 20 minutes. Transfer vegetables to large bowl, cover, and refrigerate.

4. Remove roasting pan from oven and reduce temperature to 325 degrees. Sprinkle flour over rendered fat and whisk until no dry flour remains. Whisk in broth, 2 cups wine, gelatin, tomato paste, and anchovy paste until combined. Add onions, carrots, garlic, bay leaves, peppercorns, porcini mushrooms, parsley sprigs, and thyme sprigs to pan. Arrange beef in single layer on top of vegetables. Add water as needed to

come three-quarters up side of beef (beef should not be submerged). Return roasting pan to oven and cook until meat is tender, 3 to 3½ hours, stirring after 90 minutes and adding water to keep meat at least half-submerged.

5. Using slotted spoon, transfer beef to bowl with cremini mushrooms and pearl onions; cover and set aside. Strain braising liquid through fine-mesh strainer set over large bowl, pressing on solids to extract as much liquid as possible; discard solids. Stir in remaining wine and let cooking liquid settle, 10 minutes. Using wide shallow spoon, skim fat off surface and discard.

6. Transfer liquid to Dutch oven and bring mixture to boil over medium-high heat. Simmer briskly, stirring occasionally, until sauce is thickened to consistency of heavy cream, 15 to 20 minutes. Reduce heat to medium-low, stir in beef and mushroom-onion garnish, cover, and cook until just heated through, 5 to 8 minutes. Season with salt and pepper to taste. Stir in minced parsley and serve. (Stew can be made up to 3 days in advance.)

CASSOULET

WHY THIS RECIPE WORKS: Comforting and delectable as it is, cassoulet is just too much trouble for most cooks. It can take three days to make, and the ingredients can be both hard to find and difficult to prepare. We wanted to see if there was a way to streamline the preparation of this dish without compromising its essential character.

Instead of duck confit, which is difficult to find and time-consuming to prepare, we brined chicken thighs and cooked them in bacon fat to simulate the smoky flavor and moist texture of the confit. With our mock confit lined up, the other elements fell into place. We decided on the flavorful, fatty blade-end pork roast for stewing, dried beans instead of canned beans (canned beans were out because they fell apart

during cooking), and smoky kielbasa for the sausage component (the classically correct French sausage was too hard to find). We cooked the beans with onion and garlic to season them, then added some crisp bacon to infuse them with a salty smokiness. Cooking the dish entirely on the stove at a slow simmer, with a quick finish to brown our homemade croutons, gave us a quick and easy cassoulet that was worthy of the name.

Simplified Cassoulet with Pork and Kielbasa
SERVES 8

This dish can be made without brining the chicken, but we recommend that you do so. To ensure the most time-efficient preparation of the cassoulet, while the chicken is brining and the beans are simmering, prepare the remaining ingredients. Look for dried flageolet beans in specialty food stores. You can substitute a boneless Boston butt for the boneless blade-end pork loin roast. Additional salt is not necessary because the brined chicken adds a good deal of it, but if you skip the brining step, add salt to taste before serving.

CHICKEN
- 1   cup sugar
- ½   cup table salt
- 10 (5- to 6-ounce) bone-in, skin-on chicken thighs, trimmed and skin removed (see note)

BEANS
- 1   pound dried flageolet or great Northern beans, picked over and rinsed (see note)
- 1   medium onion, peeled, plus 1 small onion, minced
- 1   medium head garlic, outer papery skin removed and top ½ inch sliced off, plus 2 medium garlic cloves, minced or pressed through a garlic press (about 2 teaspoons)
- 1   teaspoon table salt
     Ground black pepper
- 6   ounces (about 6 slices) bacon, cut into ¼-inch pieces
- 1   (1-pound) boneless blade-end pork loin roast, trimmed and cut into 1-inch pieces (see note)
- 1   (14.5-ounce) can diced tomatoes, drained
- 1   tablespoon tomato paste
- 1   large sprig fresh thyme
- 1   bay leaf
- ¼   teaspoon ground cloves
- 3½ cups low-sodium chicken broth
- 1½ cups dry white wine
- ½   pound kielbasa, halved lengthwise and cut into ¼-inch slices

CROUTONS
- 6   slices high-quality white sandwich bread, cut into ½-inch cubes
- 3   tablespoons unsalted butter, melted

1. FOR THE CHICKEN: Dissolve the sugar and salt in 1 quart cold water in a gallon-size zipper-lock bag. Add the chicken, pressing out as much air as possible, seal the bag, and refrigerate for 1 hour. Remove the chicken from the brine, rinse, and pat dry with paper towels. Refrigerate until ready to use.

2. FOR THE BEANS: Bring the beans, the peeled onion, head of garlic, salt, ¼ teaspoon pepper, and 8 cups water to a boil in a large Dutch oven over high heat. Cover, reduce the heat to medium-low, and simmer until the beans are almost tender, 1¼ to 1½ hours. Drain the beans; discard the onion and garlic.

3. While the beans are cooking, fry the bacon in a large Dutch oven over medium heat until just beginning to crisp and most of the fat has rendered, 5 to 6 minutes. Using a slotted spoon, add half of the bacon to the pot with the beans; transfer the remaining bacon to a paper towel–lined plate and set aside. Increase the heat to medium-high and add half of the chicken, skinned side down; cook until lightly browned, 4 to 5 minutes. Flip the chicken thighs and cook until lightly browned on the second side, 3 to 4 minutes longer. Transfer the chicken to a large plate; repeat with the remaining thighs and set aside. Pour off all but 2 tablespoons fat from the pot. Return the pot to medium heat; add the pork pieces and cook, stirring occasionally, until lightly browned, about 5 minutes. Add the minced onion and cook, stirring occasionally, until softened, 3 to 4 minutes. Add the minced garlic, tomatoes, tomato paste, thyme, bay leaf, cloves, and pepper to taste and cook until fragrant, about 1 minute. Stir in the chicken broth and wine, scraping up any browned bits. Submerge the chicken in the pot, adding any accumulated juices, increase the heat to high, and bring to a boil. Reduce the heat to low, cover, and simmer for 40 minutes. Uncover and continue to simmer until the chicken and pork are fully tender, 20 to 30 minutes more.

4. FOR THE CROUTONS: While the chicken is simmering, adjust an oven rack to the lower-middle position and heat the oven to 400 degrees. Toss the bread cubes with the melted butter and spread out over a rimmed baking sheet. Bake until light golden brown and crisp, 8 to 12 minutes. Cool to room temperature; set aside (do not turn off the oven).

5. Gently stir the kielbasa, drained beans, and reserved bacon into the pot with the chicken and pork; remove and discard the thyme and bay leaf and season with pepper to taste (see note). Sprinkle the croutons evenly over the surface and bake, uncovered, until the croutons are deep golden brown, about 15 minutes. Let stand for 10 minutes; serve.

FRENCH-STYLE PORK STEW

WHY THIS RECIPE WORKS: In the French-style boiled dinner known as *potée*, multiple cuts of pork, sausages, and vegetables are simmered until tender, then served with their flavorful cooking liquid. We set out to turn this dish into a fork-friendly stew that was robust and satisfying, but not heavy. Pork butt, cut into chunks, became succulent and tender with the long cooking time. Supplementing it with a smoked ham shank

and kielbasa gave our stew the delicate smokiness and intense porky notes found in authentic versions, plus it provided such meaty flavor and complexity that we could skip the extra step of browning the pork. Chicken broth cut with water provided a subtle flavor base that kept the flavor clean; simmering it with aromatics and seasonings added depth. For ease, we limited the traditional roster of vegetables to just three—carrots, potatoes, and cabbage—which we added toward the end of cooking so they would retain their texture. Finally, moving our stew to the oven allowed it to cook through gently and evenly.

French-Style Pork Stew
SERVES 8 TO 10
Pork butt roast, often labeled Boston butt in the supermarket, is a very fatty cut, so don't be surprised if you lose a pound or even a little more in the trimming process (the weight called for in the recipe takes this loss into account). Serve with crusty bread.

- 6 sprigs fresh parsley
- 3 large sprigs fresh thyme
- 5 garlic cloves, unpeeled
- 2 bay leaves
- 1 tablespoon black peppercorns
- 2 whole cloves
- 5 cups water
- 4 cups chicken broth
- 3 pounds boneless pork butt roast, trimmed and cut into 1- to 1½-inch pieces
- 1 meaty smoked ham shank or 2–3 smoked ham hocks (1¼ pounds)
- 2 onions, halved through root end, root end left intact
- 4 carrots, peeled, narrow end cut crosswise into ½-inch pieces, wide end halved lengthwise and cut into ½-inch pieces
- 1 pound Yukon Gold potatoes, unpeeled, cut into ¾-inch pieces

12 ounces kielbasa sausage, halved lengthwise
   and sliced ½ inch thick
8 cups shredded savoy cabbage
   Salt and pepper
¼ cup chopped fresh parsley

1. Adjust oven rack to middle position and heat oven to 325 degrees. Cut 10-inch square of triple-thickness cheese-cloth. Place parsley sprigs (fold or break to fit), thyme sprigs, garlic, bay leaves, peppercorns, and cloves in center of cheese-cloth and tie into bundle with kitchen twine.

2. Bring water, chicken broth, pork butt, ham shank, onions, and herb bundle to simmer in large Dutch oven over medium-high heat, skimming off scum that rises to surface. Cover pot and place in oven. Cook until pork chunks are tender and skewer inserted into meat meets little resistance, 1¼ to 1½ hours.

3. Using slotted spoon, discard cheesecloth bundle and onion halves. Transfer shank to plate. Add carrots and potatoes to pot and stir to combine. Cover pot and return to oven. Cook until vegetables are almost tender, 20 to 25 minutes. When cool enough to handle, using two forks, remove meat from shank and shred into bite-size pieces; discard skin and bones.

4. Add shredded shank meat, kielbasa, and cabbage to pot. Stir to combine, cover, and return to oven. Cook until kielbasa is heated through and cabbage is wilted and tender, 15 to 20 minutes. Season with salt and pepper to taste, then stir in parsley. Ladle into bowls and serve.

STEAK AU POIVRE

WHY THIS RECIPE WORKS: Steak au poivre is often nothing more than uninspired skillet steak. We were after the real thing—a perfectly cooked steak with a well-seared crust of pungent, cracked peppercorns and a silky sauce.

The trick to successful steak au poivre is coating just one side of the steaks with peppercorns and cooking the steaks on the uncoated side as long as possible to promote browning and prevent scorching of the peppercorns. With the first side browned, we flipped the steaks and cooked them for less time on the peppered side. Pressing the steaks with a cake pan once they were placed in the hot skillet ensured that the pepper-corns stuck. After the steaks were done to our liking, we made a simple pan sauce with a mixture of beef broth and chicken broth that we first reduced, then flavored with brandy and lemon juice. Cream made the sauce luxurious and gave it some substance; butter whisked in at the end brought silkiness.

Steak au Poivre with Brandied Cream Sauce
SERVES 4

To save time, crush the peppercorns and trim the steaks while the broth mixture simmers. Many pepper mills do not have a sufficiently coarse setting. In that case, crush peppercorns with the back of a heavy pan. See page 879 for information on our top-rated pepper mill.

4 tablespoons (½ stick) unsalted butter
1 medium shallot, minced (about 3 tablespoons)
1 cup beef broth
¾ cup low-sodium chicken broth
4 (8- to 10-ounce) strip steaks, ¾ to 1 inch thick, trimmed
   Table salt
4 teaspoons black peppercorns, crushed (see note)
1 tablespoon vegetable oil
¼ cup plus 1 tablespoon brandy
¼ cup heavy cream
1 teaspoon juice from 1 lemon or 1 teaspoon
   champagne vinegar

1. Melt 1 tablespoon of the butter in a 12-inch skillet over medium heat. Add the shallot and cook, stirring occasionally, until softened, about 2 minutes. Add the beef and chicken broths and bring to a boil over high heat; cook until reduced to ½ cup, about 8 minutes. Transfer the broth mixture to a small bowl; wipe out the skillet with paper towels.

2. Meanwhile, pat the steaks dry with paper towels and season with salt. Sprinkle one side of each steak with 1 teaspoon of the crushed peppercorns and press them into the steaks with your fingers to adhere.

3. Heat the oil in the skillet over medium-high heat until just smoking. Carefully lay the steaks in the skillet, peppered side up. Press on the steaks with the bottom of a cake pan and cook until well-browned on the first side, 3 to 5 minutes. Flip the steaks over and continue to cook, pressing again with the cake pan, until the center of the steaks registers 120 degrees on an instant-read thermometer for rare (3 minutes), 125 degrees for medium-rare (4 minutes), or 130 degrees for medium (5 min-utes). Transfer the steaks to a plate, tent loosely with foil, and let rest while making the sauce.

4. Pour off any fat left in the pan and remove any stray pep-percorns. Add the broth mixture, ¼ cup of the brandy, and the cream to the skillet and bring to a boil over high heat, scraping up any browned bits. Simmer until golden brown and thick-ened, about 5 minutes. Off the heat, whisk in the remaining 3 tablespoons butter, the remaining 1 tablespoon brandy, the lemon juice, and any accumulated meat juices from the plate; season with salt to taste. Spoon the sauce over the steaks and serve immediately.

STEAK FRITES

WHY THIS RECIPE WORKS: Too often, steak frites in American restaurants misses the mark. The fries are usually too soggy and the steak just isn't as flavorful as it should be. We wanted to re-create the steak frites of our Parisian dreams, with perfectly cooked steak and fries that are fluffy on the inside and crisp on the outside, even when bathed in juices from the meat.

For our fries, we liked high-starch russet potatoes and found that double-cooking, or a low-temperature "blanch" in oil followed by a high-temperature "fry," yielded the crispiest exterior and fluffiest interior. Cooking multiple small batches of fries ensured that the oil's temperature wouldn't plunge too much. Soaking the potatoes in cold water before they were cooked further improved their crispiness, and a "rest" between the first and second frying allowed the fries to develop a thin coating of starch, which even further improved their crispiness. Tossing them with additional starch—in the form of cornstarch—made them perfect.

In France, steak frites is usually prepared with a cut called *entrecôte* (literally, "between the ribs"), which is a French cut you won't find in the States, but is actually quite similar to our rib-eye steak. Choosing the right size—or cutting them to fit—meant we could sear four steaks at once in a large skillet. Capped with a quick herb butter, the steaks tasted just like the bistro classic of our dreams.

Steak Frites

SERVES 4

Make sure to dry the potatoes well before tossing them with the cornstarch. For safety, use a Dutch oven with a capacity of at least 7 quarts. Use refined peanut oil (such as Planters) to fry the potatoes, not toasted peanut oil. A 12-inch skillet is essential for cooking four steaks at once. The recipe can be prepared through step 4 up to 2 hours in advance; shut off the heat under the oil, turning the heat back to medium

when you start step 6. The ingredients can be halved to serve two—keep the oil amount the same and forgo blanching and frying the potatoes in batches.

HERB BUTTER
- 4 tablespoons (½ stick) unsalted butter, softened
- ½ shallot, minced (about 1 tablespoon)
- 1 tablespoon minced fresh parsley leaves
- 1 tablespoon minced fresh chives
- 1 medium garlic clove, minced or pressed through a garlic press (about 1 teaspoon)
- ¼ teaspoon table salt
- ¼ teaspoon ground black pepper

STEAK AND POTATOES
- 2½ pounds russet potatoes (about 4 large), sides squared off, cut lengthwise into ¼ by ¼-inch fries (see note)
- 2 tablespoons cornstarch
- 3 quarts peanut oil (see note)
- 1 tablespoon vegetable oil
- 2 (1-pound) boneless rib-eye steaks, cut in half
  Table salt and ground black pepper

1. FOR THE BUTTER: Combine all the ingredients in a medium bowl; set aside.

2. FOR THE POTATOES: Rinse the cut potatoes in a large bowl under cold running water until the water turns clear. Cover with cold water and refrigerate for at least 30 minutes or up to 12 hours.

3. Pour off the water, spread the potatoes onto clean kitchen towels, and thoroughly dry. Transfer the potatoes to a large bowl and toss with the cornstarch until evenly coated. Transfer the potatoes to a wire rack set over a rimmed baking sheet and let rest until a fine white coating forms, about 20 minutes.

4. Meanwhile, heat the peanut oil over medium heat to 325 degrees in a large, heavy-bottomed Dutch oven fitted with a clip-on candy thermometer.

5. Add half of the potatoes, a handful at a time, to the hot oil and increase the heat to high. Fry, stirring with a mesh spider or slotted spoon, until the potatoes start to turn from white to blond, 4 to 5 minutes. (The oil temperature will drop about 75 degrees during this frying.) Transfer the fries to a thick paper bag or paper towels. Return the oil to 325 degrees and repeat with the remaining potatoes. Reduce the heat to medium and let the fries cool while cooking the steaks, at least 10 minutes.

6. FOR THE STEAK: Heat the vegetable oil in a 12-inch skillet over medium-high heat until smoking. Meanwhile, season the steaks with salt and pepper. Lay the steaks in the pan, leaving ¼ inch between them. Cook, without moving the steaks, until well browned, about 4 minutes. Flip the steaks and continue to cook until an instant-read thermometer inserted in the center registers 120 degrees for rare to medium-rare, 3 to 7 minutes. Transfer the steaks to a large plate, top with the herb butter, and tent loosely with foil; let rest while finishing the fries.

SQUARING THE SPUD

The best way to uniformly cut fries is to start by trimming a thin slice from each side of the potato. Once the potato is "squared," you can slice it into planks and then cut each plank into fries.

ONE STEAK BECOMES TWO

For steaks of the right thickness for Steak Frites (so they'll sear well without overcooking), it is necessary to buy two 1-pound steaks and cut them in half according to their thickness. If your steaks are 1¼ to 1¾ inches thick, cut them in half vertically into small, thick steaks. If your steaks are thicker than 1¾ inches, cut them in half horizontally into two thinner steaks.

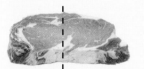

THIN STEAK
Cut in half vertically.

THICK STEAK
Cut in half horizontally.

7. Increase the heat under the Dutch oven to high and heat the oil to 375 degrees. Add half of the fries, a handful at a time, and fry until golden brown and puffed, 2 to 3 minutes. Transfer to a thick paper bag or paper towels. Return the oil to 375 degrees and repeat with the remaining fries. Season the fries with salt to taste and serve immediately with the steaks.

STEAK DIANE

WHY THIS RECIPE WORKS: For a different spin on the usual pan-seared steaks, we turn to the French classic, steak Diane. But the demanding rich sauce is based on an all-day veal stock reduction—and then the steaks still have to be cooked (if you have the energy, that is), and the sauce completed. We aimed to determine the right cut of steak, create a lighter, less labor-intensive sauce, and find a foolproof method for cooking the meat.

For a rich sauce base that mimicked the complexity of labor-intensive veal stock in a fraction of the time, we used a flavorful combination of sautéed tomato paste, aromatics such as garlic, onion, and carrots, both beef broth and chicken broth, red wine, peppercorns, and herbs. Omitting the traditional cream allowed the sauce to fully develop in intensity, and the inclusion of cognac gave the sauce a slightly sweet, complex flavor. For the meat, we selected strip steaks for great

beefy flavor and ease of preparation. To brown the steaks evenly and develop enough fond (the flavorful browned meaty bits that cling to the pan and give pan sauces their rich, meaty flavor), we weighted the steaks with a heavy-bottomed skillet when cooking the second side.

Steak Diane
SERVES 4

If you prefer not to make the sauce base (recipe follows), mix ½ cup glace de viande with ¾ cup water and ¼ cup red wine and use this mixture in place of the base in step 2. Glace de viande is meat stock, in this case veal stock, that's been reduced to a thick syrup; we recommend Provimi Glace de Veau and CulinArte' Bonewerks Glace de Veau. Before preparing the sauce, read "Tips for Fearless Flambé" on page 408, or, if you do not wish to flambé, simmer the cognac in step 2 for 10 to 15 seconds for a slightly less sweet flavor profile.

STEAKS
- 4 (12-ounce) strip steaks, 1 to 1¼ inches thick, trimmed
  Table salt and ground black pepper
- 2 tablespoons vegetable oil

SAUCE
- 1 tablespoon vegetable oil
- 1 small shallot, minced (about 1 tablespoon)
- ¼ cup cognac
- 1 recipe Sauce Base for Steak Diane (page 408; see note)
- 2 teaspoons Dijon mustard
- 2 tablespoons unsalted butter, chilled
- 1 teaspoon Worcestershire sauce
- 2 tablespoons minced fresh chives
  Table salt and ground black pepper

1. FOR THE STEAKS: Cover the steaks with plastic wrap and use a meat pounder to pound them to an even ½-inch thickness; season them with salt and pepper. Heat 1 tablespoon of the oil in a 12-inch skillet over medium-high heat until smoking. Place 2 steaks in the skillet and cook until well browned, about 1½ minutes. Flip the steaks and weight with a heavy-bottomed pan; continue to cook until well browned on the second side, about 1½ minutes longer. Transfer the steaks to a plate and tent with foil. Add the remaining 1 tablespoon oil to the skillet and repeat with the remaining 2 steaks; transfer the second batch of steaks to the plate.

2. FOR THE SAUCE: Off the heat, add the oil and shallot to the skillet. Using the skillet's residual heat, cook, stirring frequently, until the shallot is slightly softened and browned, about 45 seconds. Add the cognac and let stand until the cognac warms slightly, about 10 seconds, then set the skillet over high heat. Wave a lit match over the skillet until the cognac ignites, shaking the skillet until the flames subside, then simmer the cognac until reduced to about 1 tablespoon, about 10 seconds.

TIPS FOR FEARLESS FLAMBÉ

Flambéing is more than just tableside theatrics: As dramatic as it looks, igniting alcohol actually helps develop a deeper, more complex flavor in sauces—thanks to flavor-boosting chemical reactions that occur only at the high temperatures reached in flambéing. But accomplishing this feat at home can be daunting. Here are some tips for successful—and safe—flambéing at home.

BE PREPARED: Turn off the exhaust fan, tie back long hair, and have a lid at the ready to smother flare-ups.

USE THE PROPER EQUIPMENT: A pan with flared sides (such as a skillet) rather than straight sides will allow more oxygen to mingle with the alcohol vapors, increasing the chance that you'll spark the desired flame. If possible, use long chimney matches, and light the alcohol with your arm extended to full length.

IGNITE WARM ALCOHOL: If the alcohol becomes too hot, the vapors can rise to dangerous heights, causing large flare-ups once lit. Inversely, if the alcohol is too cold, there won't be enough vapors to light at all. We found that heating alcohol to 100 degrees Fahrenheit (best achieved by adding alcohol to a hot pan off heat and letting it sit for five to 10 seconds) produced the most moderate, yet long-burning, flames.

IF A FLARE-UP SHOULD OCCUR: Simply slide the lid over the top of the skillet (coming in from the side of, rather than over, the flames) to put out the fire quickly. Let the alcohol cool down and start again.

IF THE ALCOHOL WON'T LIGHT: If the pan is full of other ingredients (as is the case in Crêpes Suzette, page 832), the potency of the alcohol can be diminished as it becomes incorporated. For a more foolproof flame, ignite the alcohol in a separate small skillet or saucepan; once the flame has burned off, add the reduced alcohol to the remaining ingredients.

Add the sauce base and mustard and simmer until slightly thickened and reduced to 1 cup, 2 to 3 minutes. Whisk in the butter. Off the heat, add the Worcestershire sauce, any accumulated juices from the steaks, and 1 tablespoon of the chives. Season with salt and pepper to taste.

3. Serve immediately, spooning 2 tablespoons sauce and sprinkling a portion of the remaining 1 tablespoon chives over each steak, and passing the remaining sauce separately.

Sauce Base for Steak Diane
MAKES 1¼ CUPS

This recipe yields a sauce base that is an excellent facsimile of a demi-glace, a very labor-intensive and time-consuming classic French sauce base. Because the sauce base is very concentrated, make sure to use low-sodium chicken and beef broths; otherwise, the base may be unpalatably salty.

　2　tablespoons vegetable oil
　4　teaspoons tomato paste
　2　small onions, chopped medium
　1　medium carrot, chopped medium
　4　medium garlic cloves, peeled
　¼　cup water
　4　teaspoons unbleached all-purpose flour
1½　cups dry red wine
3½　cups low-sodium beef broth (see note)
1¾　cups low-sodium chicken broth (see note)
　2　teaspoons black peppercorns
　8　sprigs fresh thyme
　2　bay leaves

1. Heat the oil and tomato paste in a Dutch oven over medium-high heat and cook, stirring constantly, until the paste begins to brown, about 3 minutes. Add the onions, carrot, and garlic and cook, stirring frequently, until the mixture is reddish brown, about 2 minutes. Add 2 tablespoons of the water and continue to cook, stirring constantly, until the mixture is well browned, about 3 minutes, adding the remaining 2 tablespoons water as needed to prevent scorching. Add the flour and cook, stirring constantly, for about 1 minute. Add the wine, scraping up the browned bits on the bottom and sides of the pot; bring to a boil, stirring occasionally (the mixture will thicken slightly). Add the beef and chicken broths, peppercorns, thyme, and bay leaves; bring to a boil and cook, uncovered, occasionally scraping the bottom and sides of the pot with a spatula, until reduced to 2½ cups, 35 to 40 minutes.

2. Strain the mixture through a fine-mesh strainer, pressing on the solids to extract as much liquid as possible; you should have about 1¼ cups. (The sauce base can be refrigerated in an airtight container for up to 3 days.)

FISH MEUNIÈRE

WHY THIS RECIPE WORKS: Fish meunière typically features pale, soggy fillets in pools of greasy sauce—that is, if the fish doesn't stick to the pan or fall apart as it is plated. We wanted perfectly cooked fillets that were delicately crisp and golden brown on the outside and moist and flavorful on the inside, napped in a buttery yet light sauce.

Whole Dover sole is the most authentic choice, but it was also hard to come by and prohibitively expensive; either sole or flounder fillets were good stand-ins. To prevent the likelihood of overcooking the fish, the fillets needed to be no less than ⅜ inch thick. The fillets must be patted dry before being seasoned with salt and pepper and dredged in flour (no need for eggs and bread crumbs). Using a nonstick skillet for pan-frying meant there was less chance for our fillets to fall apart; lubricating the pan with a mixture of oil and butter added extra insurance. Removing the pan from the heat just before the fish was cooked prevented the fish from being dry (the fish will continue to cook off the heat). Butter browned in a traditional skillet (so the changing color was easy to monitor) and brightened with lemon juice made the ideal accompaniment to our crispy, golden fillets.

Fish Meunière with Browned Butter and Lemon
SERVES 4

Try to purchase fillets that are of similar size, and avoid those that weigh less than 5 ounces because they will cook too quickly. When placing the fillets in the skillet, be sure to place them skinned side up so that the opposite side, which had bones, will brown first. To flip the fillets while cooking, use two spatulas; gently lift one side of the fillet with one spatula, then support the fillet with the other spatula and gently

flip it so that the browned side faces up. A nonstick skillet ensures that the fillets will release from the pan, but for the sauce a traditional skillet is preferable because its light-colored surface will allow you to monitor the color of the butter as it browns.

FISH

½ cup unbleached all-purpose flour
4 (5- to 6-ounce) sole or flounder fillets, ⅜ inch thick (see note)
  Table salt and ground black pepper
2 tablespoons vegetable oil
2 tablespoons unsalted butter, cut into 2 pieces

BROWNED BUTTER

4 tablespoons (½ stick) unsalted butter, cut into 4 pieces
1 tablespoon chopped fresh parsley leaves
1½ tablespoons juice from 1 lemon
  Table salt
  Lemon wedges, for serving

1. FOR THE FISH: Adjust an oven rack to the lower-middle position, set four heatproof dinner plates on the rack, and heat the oven to 200 degrees. Place the flour in a large baking dish. Pat the fillets dry with paper towels and season with salt and pepper; let stand until the fillets are glistening with moisture, about 5 minutes. Coat both sides of the fillets with flour, shake off the excess, and place in a single layer on a rimmed baking sheet.

2. Heat 1 tablespoon of the oil in a 12-inch nonstick skillet over high heat until shimmering; add 1 tablespoon of the butter and swirl to coat the pan bottom. Carefully place 2 fillets, skinned side up, in the skillet. Immediately reduce the heat to medium-high and cook, without moving the fish, until the edges of the fillets are opaque and the bottoms are golden brown, about 3 minutes. Using two spatulas, gently flip the fillets and cook on the second side until the thickest part of the fillet easily separates into flakes when a toothpick is inserted, about 2 minutes longer. Transfer the fillets to two of the heated dinner plates, keeping them boned side up, and return the plates to the oven. Wipe out the skillet and repeat with the remaining 1 tablespoon oil, remaining 1 tablespoon butter, and the remaining fish fillets.

3. FOR THE BROWNED BUTTER: Melt the butter in a 10-inch traditional skillet over medium-high heat. Continue to cook, swirling the pan constantly, until the butter is golden brown and has a nutty aroma, 1 to 1½ minutes; remove the skillet from the heat. Remove the plates from the oven and sprinkle the fillets with the parsley. Add the lemon juice to the browned butter and season with salt to taste. Spoon the sauce over the fish and serve immediately, garnished with the lemon wedges.

CHAPTER 15

TEX-MEX TONIGHT

4 teaspoons grated zest plus ½ cup
juice from 4 limes (see note)
4 teaspoons grated zest plus ½ cup
juice from 3 lemons (see note)
¼ cup superfine sugar (see note)
Pinch table salt
2 cups crushed ice
1 cup 100 percent agave tequila, preferably reposado
1 cup triple sec

1. Combine the lime zest and juice, lemon zest and juice, sugar, and salt in a large liquid measuring cup; cover with plastic wrap and refrigerate until the flavors meld, 4 to 24 hours.

2. Divide 1 cup of the crushed ice among 4 or 6 margarita or double old-fashioned glasses. Strain the juice mixture into a 1-quart pitcher or cocktail shaker. Add the tequila, triple sec, and the remaining 1 cup crushed ice; stir or shake until thoroughly combined and chilled, 20 to 60 seconds. Strain into the ice-filled glasses and serve immediately.

MARGARITAS

WHY THIS RECIPE WORKS: The typical margarita tends to be a slushy, headache-inducing concoction made with little more than ice, tequila, and artificially flavored corn syrup. We wanted a margarita with a balanced blend of fresh citrus flavors and tequila.

We found that the key was using the right proportions of alcohol and citrus juice—equal parts of each one. For a mellow, delicate flavor, we preferred reposado tequila, made from 100 percent blue agave, which is aged about 12 months. Unaged tequilas gave our margaritas a raw, harsh flavor. And those made with superpremium tequilas, which are aged up to 6 years, tasted smooth, but their distinct tannic taste dominated the cocktail. As for orange-flavored liqueurs, a lower-alcohol liqueur, such as triple sec, worked best. Mixes and bottled citrus juice had no place in our cocktail—instead we steeped lemon and lime zest in their own juice for a deep, refreshing citrus flavor. And with a bit of easy-to-dissolve superfine sugar and crushed ice, our margaritas were complete.

Fresh Margaritas
SERVES 4 TO 6

The longer the zest and juice mixture is allowed to steep, the more developed the citrus flavors will be in the finished margaritas. We recommend steeping for the full 24 hours, although the margaritas will still be great if the mixture is steeped for only the minimum 4 hours. If you're in a rush and want to serve margaritas immediately, omit the zest and skip the steeping process altogether. If you can't find superfine sugar, process an equal amount of regular sugar in a food processor for 30 seconds.

SANGRIA

WHY THIS RECIPE WORKS: Many people mistake sangria for an unruly collection of fruit awash in a sea of overly sweetened red wine. We wanted a robust, sweet-tart wine punch.

After trying a variety of red wines, we found that inexpensive wine works best. (Experts told us that the sugar and fruit called for in sangria throw off the balance of any wine used, so why spend a lot on something that was carefully crafted?) We experimented with untold varieties of fruit to put in our sangria and finally concluded that simpler is better. We preferred the straightforward tang of citrus in the form of oranges and lemons. And we discovered that the zest and pith as well as the fruit itself make an important contribution to flavor. Orange liqueur is standard in recipes for sangria, and after experimenting we found that here, as with the wine, cheaper was just fine, this time in the form of triple sec. Fortification with any other alcoholic beverage, from gin to port to brandy, simply gave the punch too much punch. What we wanted, and what we now had, was a light, refreshing drink.

Sangria
SERVES 4

Although this punch hails from Spain, it has become a mainstay on Mexican restaurant menus and pairs well with the country's spicy dishes. The longer sangria sits before drinking, the more smooth and mellow it will taste. A full day is best, but if that's impossible, give it an absolute minimum of two hours to sit. Use large, heavy, juicy oranges and lemons for the best flavor. If you can't find superfine sugar, process an equal amount of regular sugar in a food processor for 30 seconds. Doubling or tripling the recipe is fine, but you'll have to switch to a large punch bowl in place of the pitcher. An inexpensive Merlot is the best choice for this recipe.

2   large juice oranges, washed; one orange sliced,
    remaining orange juiced (see note)
1   large lemon, washed and sliced (see note)
¼   cup superfine sugar (see note)
1   (750-milliliter) bottle inexpensive, fruity,
    medium-bodied red wine, chilled (see note)
¼   cup triple sec

1. Add the sliced orange and lemon and the sugar to a large pitcher. Mash the fruit gently with a wooden spoon until the fruit releases some juice, but is not totally crushed, and the sugar dissolves, about 1 minute. Stir in the orange juice, wine, and triple sec; refrigerate for at least 2 hours or up to 8 hours.

2. Before serving, add 6 to 8 ice cubes and stir briskly to distribute the settled fruit and pulp; serve immediately.

NACHOS

WHY THIS RECIPE WORKS: Prepackaged shredded cheese and jars of pre-made salsa and guacamole transform nachos from something delicious into bland fast food. We wanted nachos with hot, crisp tortilla chips, plentiful cheese and toppings, and the right amount of spicy heat.

To ensure that all of the chips would be cheesy and spicy, we layered tortilla chips with a full pound of shredded cheddar cheese and sliced jalapeños. Layering the jalapeños with the cheese also helped the chiles stick to the chips. We prepared a quick homemade salsa and chunky guacamole to spoon around the edges of the hot nachos after they came out of the oven. Spoonfuls of sour cream and a sprinkling of chopped fresh scallions provided final touches. Served with lime wedges, this fresh take on nachos is light-years beyond any fast-food version of the dish.

Cheesy Nachos with Guacamole and Salsa
SERVES 4 TO 6

8   ounces tortilla chips
1   pound cheddar cheese, shredded (about 4 cups)
2   large jalapeño chiles, sliced thin (about ¼ cup)
2   scallions, sliced thin
½   cup sour cream
1   recipe One-Minute Salsa (recipe follows)
1   recipe Chunky Guacamole (see right)
    Lime wedges, for serving

Adjust an oven rack to the middle position and heat the oven to 400 degrees. Spread half of the chips in an even layer in a 13 by 9-inch baking dish. Sprinkle the chips evenly with 2 cups of the cheese and half of the jalapeño slices. Repeat with the remaining chips, cheese, and jalapeños. Bake until the cheese is melted, 7 to 10 minutes. Remove the nachos from the oven and sprinkle with the scallions. Along the edge of the baking dish, drop scoops of the sour cream, salsa, and guacamole. Serve immediately, passing the lime wedges separately.

One-Minute Salsa
MAKES ABOUT 1 CUP

This quick salsa can be made with either fresh or canned tomatoes. If you like, replace the jalapeño with ½ chipotle chile in adobo sauce, minced.

2   tablespoons chopped red onion
2   tablespoons fresh cilantro leaves
2   teaspoons juice from 1 lime
½   small jalapeño chile, stemmed and seeded
    (about 1½ teaspoons; see note)
1   small garlic clove, minced or pressed through
    a garlic press (about ½ teaspoon)
¼   teaspoon table salt
    Pinch ground black pepper
2   small ripe tomatoes, each cored and cut into eighths,
    or one (14.5-ounce) can diced tomatoes, drained

Pulse all the ingredients except the tomatoes in a food processor until minced, about 5 pulses, scraping down the sides of the workbowl as necessary. Add the tomatoes and pulse until roughly chopped, about 2 pulses.

GUACAMOLE

WHY THIS RECIPE WORKS: Not only eaten as a party dip, guacamole is also the traditional accompaniment to several Mexican dishes. Unfortunately, it often has so many ingredients that the primary one—the avocado—becomes overshadowed by secondary ingredients. We wanted to get back to the basics of this dish, emphasizing the avocado.

Hass avocados, the dark, pebbly-skinned type, worked best, and they needed to be perfectly ripe; they should yield slightly to a gentle squeeze. We wanted a chunky texture in our guacamole, so instead of mashing or pureeing the avocados we diced two of them and mashed one lightly. Combining the avocados gave the guacamole a chunky, cohesive texture. As for flavorings, just a bit of finely minced onion provided some bite but not overwhelming onion flavor. Lime juice was essential for its bright citrus flavor. Cumin, a jalapeño, and fresh cilantro rounded out the dip's flavors. Cool and creamy, our guacamole makes a perfect partner to a bowl of tortilla chips or a garnish to a variety of Mexican dishes.

Chunky Guacamole
MAKES 2½ TO 3 CUPS

To minimize the risk of discoloration, prepare the minced ingredients first so they are ready to mix with the avocados as soon as they are cut. Ripe avocados are essential here. To test for ripeness, try to flick the small stem off the end of the avocado. If it comes off easily and you can see green underneath it, the avocado is ripe. If it does not come off or if you see brown underneath after prying it off, the avocado is not ripe. If you like, garnish the guacamole with diced tomatoes and chopped cilantro just before serving.

DICING AN AVOCADO

1. After halving and pitting the avocado, make ½-inch crosshatch incisions in the flesh of each half with a dinner knife, cutting down to but not through the skin.

2. Separate the diced flesh from the skin with a soup spoon, gently scooping out the avocado cubes.

3 medium, ripe avocados (see note)
¼ cup minced fresh cilantro leaves
2 tablespoons minced onion
1 small jalapeño chile, stemmed, seeded, and minced
1 medium garlic clove, minced or pressed through a garlic press (about 1 teaspoon)
½ teaspoon ground cumin (optional)
 Table salt
2 tablespoons juice from 1 lime

1. Halve 1 avocado, remove the pit, and scoop the flesh into a medium bowl. Mash the flesh lightly with the cilantro, onion, jalapeño, garlic, cumin (if using), and ¼ teaspoon salt with the tines of a fork until just combined.

2. Halve, pit, and cube the remaining 2 avocados. Add the cubes to the bowl with the mashed avocado mixture.

3. Sprinkle the lime juice over the diced avocado and mix the entire contents of the bowl lightly with a fork until combined but still chunky. Season with salt, if necessary, and serve. (The guacamole can be covered with plastic wrap, pressed directly onto the surface of the mixture, and refrigerated for up to 1 day. Return the guacamole to room temperature, removing the plastic wrap at the last moment, before serving.)

QUICK AND EASY QUESADILLAS

WHY THIS RECIPE WORKS: An authentic quesadilla is meant to be a quick snack, not an overstuffed tortilla with complicated fillings. We wanted a simple toasted tortilla, crisp and hot, filled with just the right amount of cheese.

We kept the tortillas crisp by lightly toasting them in a dry skillet. We then filled them with cheese and pickled jalapeños, lightly coated the tortillas with oil, and returned them to the skillet until they were well browned and the cheese was fully melted. Not yet satisfied that our recipe was speedy enough, we made the process even more convenient by switching to small 8-inch tortillas and folding them in half around the filling. This allowed us to cook two at one time in the same skillet, and the fold also kept our generous cheese filling from oozing out.

Quesadillas
MAKES 2 FOLDED 8-INCH QUESADILLAS
Cooling the quesadillas before cutting and serving them is important; straight from the skillet, the melted cheese will ooze out. Finished quesadillas can be held on a baking sheet in a 200-degree oven for up to 20 minutes.

2 (8-inch) flour tortillas
2 ounces Monterey Jack or cheddar cheese, shredded (about ½ cup)
1 tablespoon minced pickled jalapeños (optional)
 Vegetable oil for brushing the tortillas
 Kosher salt

1. Heat a 10-inch nonstick skillet over medium heat until hot, about 2 minutes. Place 1 tortilla in the skillet and toast until soft and puffed slightly at the edges, about 2 minutes. Flip the tortilla and toast until puffed and slightly browned, 1 to 2 minutes longer. Slip the tortilla onto a cutting board. Repeat to toast the second tortilla while assembling the first quesadilla. Sprinkle ¼ cup of the cheese and half of the jalapeños (if using) over half of the tortilla, leaving a ½-inch border around the edge. Fold the tortilla in half and press to flatten. Brush the top generously with oil, sprinkle lightly with salt, and set aside. Repeat to form the second quesadilla.

2. Place both quesadillas in the skillet, oiled sides down; cook over medium heat until crisp and well browned, 1 to 2 minutes. Brush the tops with oil and sprinkle lightly with salt. Flip the quesadillas and cook until the second sides are crisp, 1 to 2 minutes. Transfer the quesadillas to a cutting board; cool for 3 minutes, halve each quesadilla, and serve.

COOKING QUESADILLAS

To cook two quesadillas at the same time, arrange the folded edges at the center of a 10-inch nonstick skillet.

TORTILLA SOUP

WHY THIS RECIPE WORKS: The classic method of making this flavorful Mexican soup is not only arduous, but it relies on a long list of ingredients, many of which are difficult, if not impossible, to find outside of specialty markets. We wanted to make an intensely and authentically flavored tortilla soup in less than one hour, using supermarket ingredients.

By breaking the soup down to its three classic components—the flavor base (tomatoes, garlic, onion, and chiles), the chicken stock, and the garnishes (including fried tortilla chips)—we found we could devise techniques and substitute ingredients that together made a compelling version of tortilla soup. We began achieving maximum flavor by composing a puree made from chipotle chiles, tomatoes, onions, garlic, jalapeños, and a cilantro/oregano substitute for the Mexican ingredient *epazote*, and then frying the puree in oil over high heat. We then added the puree to low-sodium canned chicken broth that we strained after poaching chicken in it and infusing it with onions, garlic, cilantro, and oregano. Addressing the garnish issue, we oven-toasted our lightly oiled tortilla strips instead of frying them and substituted sour cream and Monterey Jack cheese for the harder-to-find Mexican crema and cotija.

Tortilla Soup

SERVES 6

Despite its somewhat lengthy ingredient list, this recipe is very easy to prepare. If desired, the soup can be completed short of adding the shredded chicken to the pot at the end of step 3. Return the soup to a simmer over medium-high heat before proceeding. The tortilla strips and the garnishes are best prepared the day of serving.

TORTILLA STRIPS

- 8 (6-inch) corn tortillas, cut into ½-inch-wide strips
- 1 tablespoon vegetable oil
  Table salt

SOUP

- 2 bone-in, skin-on split chicken breasts (about 1½ pounds) or 4 bone-in, skin-on chicken thighs (about 1¼ pounds), skin removed and trimmed
- 8 cups low-sodium chicken broth
- 1 very large white onion (about 1 pound), peeled and quartered
- 4 medium garlic cloves, peeled
- 2 sprigs fresh epazote or 8 to 10 sprigs fresh cilantro plus 1 sprig fresh oregano
  Table salt
- 2 medium tomatoes, cored and quartered
- ½ medium jalapeño chile
- 1 chipotle chile in adobo sauce, plus up to 1 tablespoon adobo sauce
- 1 tablespoon vegetable oil

GARNISHES

Lime wedges

Avocado, peeled, pitted, and diced fine (see page 414)

Cotija cheese, crumbled, or Monterey Jack cheese, diced fine

Fresh cilantro leaves

Jalapeño chile, minced

Crema Mexicana or sour cream

1. FOR THE TORTILLA STRIPS: Adjust an oven rack to the middle position and heat the oven to 425 degrees. Spread the tortilla strips on a rimmed baking sheet; drizzle with the oil and toss until evenly coated. Bake until the strips are deep golden brown and crisped, about 14 minutes, rotating the pan and shaking the strips (to redistribute) halfway through baking. Season the strips lightly with salt; transfer to a plate lined with several layers of paper towels.

2. FOR THE SOUP: While the tortilla strips bake, bring the chicken, broth, 2 of the onion quarters, 2 of the garlic cloves, the epazote, and ½ teaspoon salt to a boil over medium-high heat in a large saucepan; reduce the heat to low, cover, and simmer until the chicken is just cooked through, about 20 minutes. Using tongs, transfer the chicken to a large plate. Pour the broth through a fine-mesh strainer; discard the solids in the strainer. When cool enough to handle, shred the chicken into bite-size pieces; discard the bones.

3. Puree the tomatoes, remaining 2 onion quarters, remaining 2 garlic cloves, the jalapeño, chipotle chile, and 1 teaspoon of the adobo sauce in a food processor until smooth, about 20 seconds. Heat the oil in a Dutch oven over high heat until shimmering; add the tomato-onion puree and ⅛ teaspoon salt and cook, stirring frequently, until the mixture has darkened in color, about 10 minutes. Stir the strained broth into the tomato mixture, bring to a boil, then reduce the heat to low and simmer to blend the flavors, about 15 minutes. Taste the soup; if desired, add up to 2 teaspoons more adobo sauce. Add the shredded chicken and simmer until heated through, about 5 minutes. To serve, place portions of tortilla strips in the bottom of individual bowls and ladle the soup into the bowls; pass the garnishes separately.

BLACK BEAN SOUP

WHY THIS RECIPE WORKS: Making traditional black bean soup used to be an all-day affair. Generating full flavor required hours of simmering soaked beans with numerous ingredients, including parsnips, carrots, beef bones, and smoked ham hocks. But quicker versions developed for modern kitchens often produce watery, bland, and unattractive soups. We wanted a simplified procedure that would result in an attractive, dark-colored soup full of sweet, spicy, smoky flavors and brightened with fresh garnishes.

Though convenient, canned beans couldn't compare in flavor to dried, which imparted good flavor to the broth as they simmered, and we discovered that we didn't have to soak them. A touch of baking soda in the cooking water kept the beans from turning gray. Homemade stock would be time-consuming to prepare, so we focused on adding flavor to prepared broth. Ham steak provided the smoky pork flavor of the more conventional ham hock and more meat as well. We spiced up our aromatics—carrot, celery, onion, and garlic—with lots of cumin and some red pepper flakes. We wanted a chunky texture in our soup, so we pureed it only partially, thickening it further with a slurry of cornstarch and water. Some lime juice added brightness. The customary garnishes of sour cream, avocado, red onion, cilantro, and lime wedges topped our richly flavored but easy-to-make black bean soup.

Black Bean Soup

SERVES 6

Dried beans tend to cook unevenly, so be sure to taste several beans to determine their doneness in step 1. For efficiency, you can prepare the soup ingredients while the beans simmer and the garnishes while the soup simmers. Though you do not need to offer all of the garnishes listed below, do choose at least a couple; garnishes are essential for this soup, as they add not only flavor but texture and color as well. Leftover soup can

be refrigerated in an airtight container for up to 3 days; reheat it in a saucepan over medium heat until hot, stirring in additional chicken broth if it has thickened beyond your liking.

BEANS

- 1 pound (2 cups) dried black beans, rinsed and picked over
- 4 ounces ham steak, trimmed of rind
- 2 bay leaves
- 5 cups water
- ⅛ teaspoon baking soda
- 1 teaspoon table salt

SOUP

- 3 tablespoons olive oil
- 2 large onions, minced
- 3 celery ribs, chopped fine
- 1 large carrot, chopped
- ½ teaspoon table salt
- 5–6 medium garlic cloves, minced or pressed through a garlic press (about 2 tablespoons)
- 1½ tablespoons ground cumin
- ½ teaspoon red pepper flakes
- 6 cups low-sodium chicken broth
- 2 tablespoons cornstarch
- 2 tablespoons water
- 2 tablespoons juice from 1 lime

GARNISHES

Lime wedges

Minced fresh cilantro leaves

Red onion, diced fine

Avocado, peeled, pitted, and diced medium (see page 414)

Sour cream

1. FOR THE BEANS: Place the beans, ham, bay leaves, water, and baking soda in a large saucepan with a tight-fitting lid. Bring to a boil over medium-high heat; using a large spoon, skim the foam as it rises to the surface. Stir in the salt, reduce the heat to low, cover, and simmer briskly until the beans are tender, 1¼ to 1½ hours (if necessary, add 1 cup more water and continue to simmer until the beans are tender); do not drain the beans. Discard the bay leaves. Remove the ham steak (ham steak darkens to the color of the beans), cut it into ¼-inch cubes, and set aside.

2. FOR THE SOUP: Heat the oil in a large Dutch oven over medium-high heat until shimmering but not smoking; add the onions, celery, carrot, and salt and cook, stirring occasionally, until the vegetables are soft and lightly browned, 12 to 15 minutes. Reduce the heat to medium-low and add the garlic, cumin, and red pepper flakes; cook, stirring constantly, until fragrant, about 3 minutes. Stir in the beans, bean cooking liquid, and chicken broth. Increase the heat to medium-high and bring to a boil, then reduce the heat to low and simmer, uncovered, stirring occasionally, to blend the flavors, about 30 minutes.

3. TO FINISH THE SOUP: Ladle 1½ cups of the beans and 2 cups of the liquid into a food processor or blender, process until smooth, and return to the pot. Stir together the cornstarch and water in a small bowl until combined, then gradually stir half of the cornstarch mixture into the soup; bring to a boil over medium-high heat, stirring occasionally, to fully thicken. If the soup is still thinner than desired once boiling, stir the remaining cornstarch mixture to recombine and gradually stir the mixture into the soup; return to a boil to fully thicken. Off the heat, stir in the lime juice and reserved ham; ladle the soup into bowls and serve immediately, passing the garnishes separately.

TAMALES

WHY THIS RECIPE WORKS: Tamales are small, moist corn cakes that can be stuffed with a variety of fillings, wrapped in corn husks, and steamed. Often served during the holidays, tamales are time-consuming to prepare. We wanted to simplify the process while staying true to the tamales' subtle but hearty flavor and light texture. Although masa dough (made from corn kernels that have been cooked with slaked lime, ground to a flour, and mixed with water) is traditional, it can be difficult to find. Instead, we turned to widely available masa harina, but found that when used alone, it was too fine-textured and the corn flavor was bland. Grits, on the other hand, had a granular texture similar to authentic tamales and didn't sacrifice any of the flavor. To fold the tamales, most recipes require tying each one closed, a process we found we could do without by simply folding the tamales and placing them with the seam sides facing the edges of a steamer basket. For the filling, hearty chicken thighs worked best for the long cooking time. A combination of dried ancho and New Mexican chiles resulted in a sauce with subtle spice and sweetness. Once cooked, the tamales peeled easily away from the moist rich corn cakes.

Tamales

MAKES 18 TAMALES; SERVES 6 TO 8

We found it easiest to use large corn husks that measure about 8 inches long by 6 inches wide; if the husks are small, you may need to use two per tamale and shingle them as needed to hold all of the filling. You can substitute butter for the lard if desired, but the tamales will have a distinctive buttery flavor. Be sure to use quick, not instant, grits in this recipe. For an accurate measurement of boiling water, bring a full kettle of water to a boil and then measure out the desired amount.

1	cup plus 2 tablespoons quick grits
1½	cups boiling water
1	cup (4 ounces) plus 2 tablespoons masa harina
20	large dried corn husks
1½	cups frozen corn, thawed
6	tablespoons unsalted butter, cut into ½-inch cubes and softened
6	tablespoons lard, softened
1	tablespoon sugar
2¼	teaspoons baking powder
¾	teaspoon salt
1	recipe Red Chile Chicken Filling (recipe follows)

1. Place grits in medium bowl, whisk in boiling water, and let stand until water is mostly absorbed, about 10 minutes. Stir in masa harina, cover, and let cool to room temperature, about 20 minutes. Meanwhile, place husks in large bowl, cover with hot water, and let soak until pliable, about 30 minutes.

2. Process masa dough, corn, butter, lard, sugar, baking powder, and salt together in food processor until mixture is light, sticky, and very smooth, about 1 minute, scraping down sides as necessary. Remove husks from water and pat dry with dish towel.

3. Working with 1 husk at a time, lay on counter, cupped side up, with long side facing you and wide end on right side. Spread ¼ cup tamale dough into 4-inch square over bottom right-hand corner, pushing it flush to bottom edge but leaving ¼-inch border at wide edge. Mound 2 scant tablespoons filling in line across center of dough, parallel to bottom edge. Roll husk away from you and over filling, so that dough surrounds filling and forms cylinder. Fold up tapered end, leaving top open, and transfer seam side down to platter.

4. Fit large pot or Dutch oven with steamer basket, removing feet from steamer basket if pot is short. Fill pot with water until it just touches bottom of basket and bring to boil. Gently lay tamales in basket with open ends facing up and seam sides facing out. Cover and steam, checking water level often and adding additional water as needed, until tamales easily come free from husks, about 1 hour. Transfer tamales to large platter. Reheat remaining sauce from filling in covered bowl in microwave, about 30 seconds, and serve with tamales.

Red Chile Chicken Filling
MAKES ENOUGH FOR 18 TAMALES

4	dried ancho chiles, stemmed, seeded, and torn into ½-inch pieces (1 cup)
4	dried New Mexican chiles, stemmed, seeded, and torn into ½-inch pieces (1 cup)
3	tablespoons vegetable oil
1	large onion, chopped
6	garlic cloves, minced
¾	teaspoon ground cumin
¾	teaspoon dried oregano
	Salt and pepper
3	cups chicken broth
1¼	pounds boneless, skinless chicken thighs, trimmed
1½	tablespoons cider vinegar
	Sugar

1. Toast anchos and New Mexican chiles in 12-inch skillet over medium heat, stirring frequently, until fragrant, 2 to 6 minutes; transfer to bowl.

2. Heat oil in now-empty skillet over medium heat until shimmering. Add onion and cook until softened, 5 to 7 minutes. Stir in garlic, cumin, oregano, ½ teaspoon salt, and toasted chiles and cook for 30 seconds. Stir in broth and simmer until slightly reduced, about 10 minutes. Transfer mixture to blender and process until smooth, about 20 seconds; return to skillet.

3. Season chicken with salt and pepper, nestle into skillet, and bring to simmer over medium heat. Cover, reduce heat to low, and cook until chicken registers 160 degrees, 20 to 25 minutes.

4. Transfer chicken to carving board and let cool slightly. Using 2 forks, shred chicken into small pieces. Stir vinegar into sauce and season with salt, pepper, and sugar to taste. Toss shredded chicken with 1 cup sauce. Reheat remaining sauce and serve with tamales.

BEEF EMPANADAS

WHY THIS RECIPE WORKS: In Latin America, crisp pastry pockets stuffed with spiced beef make a savory, light lunch. We wanted to streamline the process but still get an empanada hearty enough to take center stage at dinner, with a moist, savory filling encased in a tender crust.

To streamline the filling, we first enhanced packaged ground chuck with a milk-and-bread mixture known as a panade. As the meat and panade cooked, the starches in the panade's bread absorbed moisture from the milk and formed a gel around the protein molecules, which lubricated the meat. But to intensify the meaty flavor, we replaced the milk with an equal amount of chicken broth. To round it out we added a hefty dose of aromatics. Finally, we threw in a handful of cilantro leaves and a splash of vinegar along with chopped hard-cooked eggs, raisins, and green olives.

For our crust, we made a few Latin-inspired changes to our Foolproof Double-Crust Pie Dough (page 844), a recipe that combines butter (for flavor) and shortening (for tenderness) with water and vodka for a dough that's both workable and tender (tequila can also be substituted for the vodka). We traded some of the flour for masa harina, the ground, dehydrated cornmeal used to make Mexican tortillas and tamales. This provided nutty richness and rough-hewn texture. Finally, a quick brush of oil on the top of the empanadas gave us a shiny, crunchy crust, and preheating the baking sheet and drizzling it with oil ensured the underside of the crust got as crispy as the top.

Beef Empanadas
SERVES 4 TO 6

The alcohol in the dough is essential to the texture of the crust and imparts no flavor—do not omit it or substitute water. Masa harina can be found in the international aisle of the supermarket with other Latin foods or in the baking aisle with the

ASSEMBLING EMPANADAS

1. Divide the dough in half, then divide each half into six equal pieces.

2. Roll each piece of dough into a 6-inch round about ⅛ inch thick.

3. Place about ⅓ cup of the filling on each round, then brush the edges with water.

4. Fold the dough over the filling, then crimp the edges using a fork to seal.

flour. If you cannot find masa harina, replace it with additional all-purpose flour (for a total of 4 cups). See page 38 for instructions on how to hard-cook eggs.

FILLING

1 slice high-quality white sandwich bread, torn into quarters
2 tablespoons plus ½ cup low-sodium chicken broth
1 pound 85 percent lean ground beef
   Table salt and ground black pepper
1 tablespoon olive oil
2 medium onions, minced
4 medium garlic cloves, minced or pressed through a garlic press (about 4 teaspoons)
1 teaspoon ground cumin
¼ teaspoon cayenne pepper
⅛ teaspoon ground cloves
½ cup fresh cilantro leaves, chopped coarse

2 hard-cooked eggs (see note), chopped coarse

⅓ cup raisins, chopped coarse

¼ cup pitted green olives, chopped coarse

4 teaspoons cider vinegar

DOUGH

3 cups (15 ounces) unbleached all-purpose flour

1 cup (5 ounces) masa harina (see note)

1 tablespoon sugar

2 teaspoons table salt

12 tablespoons (1½ sticks) unsalted butter,
    cut into ½-inch pieces and chilled

½ cup cold vodka or tequila

½ cup cold water

5 tablespoons olive oil

1. FOR THE FILLING: Process the bread and 2 tablespoons of the chicken broth in a food processor until a paste forms, about 5 seconds, scraping down the sides of the bowl as necessary. Add the beef, ¾ teaspoon salt, and ½ teaspoon pepper and pulse until the mixture is well combined, 6 to 8 pulses.

2. Heat the oil in a 12-inch nonstick skillet over medium-high heat until shimmering. Add the onions and cook, stirring frequently, until beginning to brown, about 5 minutes. Stir in the garlic, cumin, cayenne, and cloves and cook until fragrant, about 1 minute. Add the beef mixture and cook, breaking the meat into 1-inch pieces with a wooden spoon, until browned, about 7 minutes. Add the remaining ½ cup chicken broth and simmer until the mixture is moist but not wet, 3 to 5 minutes. Transfer the mixture to a bowl and cool for 10 minutes. Stir in the cilantro, eggs, raisins, olives, and vinegar. Season with salt and pepper to taste and refrigerate until cool, about 1 hour.

3. FOR THE DOUGH: Pulse 1 cup of the flour, the masa harina, sugar, and salt in a food processor until combined, about 2 pulses. Add the butter and process until the mixture is homogeneous and the dough resembles wet sand, about 10 seconds. Add the remaining 2 cups flour and pulse until the mixture is evenly distributed around the bowl, 4 to 6 quick pulses. Empty the mixture into a medium bowl.

4. Sprinkle the vodka and water over the mixture. Using your hands, mix the dough until it forms a tacky mass that sticks together. Following the photo, divide the dough in half, then divide each half into six equal pieces. Transfer the dough pieces to a plate, cover with plastic wrap, and refrigerate until firm, about 45 minutes.

5. TO ASSEMBLE: Adjust the oven racks to the upper-middle and lower-middle positions, place 1 baking sheet on each rack, and heat the oven to 425 degrees. While the baking sheets are preheating, remove the dough from the refrigerator. Following the photos on page 418, roll each dough piece out on a lightly floured work surface into a 6-inch circle about ⅛ inch thick, covering each rolled-out dough round with plastic wrap while rolling out the remaining dough. Place about ⅓ cup of the filling in the center of each dough round. Brush the edges of each round with water and fold the dough over the filling. Trim any ragged edges, then crimp the edges of the empanadas shut using a fork.

6. Drizzle 2 tablespoons of the oil over the surface of each hot baking sheet, then return the sheets to the oven for 2 minutes. Brush the empanadas with the remaining 1 tablespoon oil. Carefully place 6 empanadas on each baking sheet and cook until well browned and crisp, 25 to 30 minutes, switching and rotating the baking sheets halfway through baking. Cool the empanadas on a wire rack for 10 minutes before serving. (After step 5, the empanadas can be covered tightly with plastic wrap and refrigerated for up to 2 days.)

BEEF TACOS

WHY THIS RECIPE WORKS: Tacos made from supermarket kits are disappointing substitutes for the real thing. Easy as they may be to prepare, taco fillings made with store-bought spice mixes taste flat and stale, and the shells don't taste much different than the cardboard they're packaged in. We set out to develop a recipe for toasty, not greasy, taco shells filled with a boldly spiced beef mixture and fresh toppings.

Home-fried corn tortillas made superior homemade taco shells. For the filling, we seasoned lean ground beef with onions, garlic, and spices (chili powder, cumin, coriander, and oregano). To moisten and further flavor the beef filling, we added chicken broth, brown sugar, and vinegar. Spooned into our fresh, crisp taco shells and topped with tomatoes, lettuce, avocado, Monterey Jack, onion, and cilantro, these tacos have far better flavor than taco-kit versions.

Beef Tacos
SERVES 4

Taco toppings are highly individual. We consider the ones listed below essential, but you might also want to consider diced avocado, sour cream, and chopped onion.

BEEF FILLING

- 2 teaspoons vegetable oil
- 1 small onion, minced
- 3 medium garlic cloves, minced or pressed through a garlic press (about 1 tablespoon)
- 2 tablespoons chili powder
- 1 teaspoon ground cumin
- 1 teaspoon ground coriander
- ½ teaspoon dried oregano
- ¼ teaspoon cayenne pepper
  Table salt
- 1 pound 90 percent lean ground beef
- ½ cup canned tomato sauce
- ½ cup low-sodium chicken broth
- 2 teaspoons vinegar, preferably cider vinegar
- 1 teaspoon brown sugar
  Ground black pepper

SHELLS AND TOPPINGS

- 8 Home-Fried Taco Shells (recipe follows)
  Shredded Monterey Jack cheese
  Shredded iceberg lettuce
  Diced tomatoes
  Chopped fresh cilantro leaves

1. FOR THE FILLING: Heat the oil in a medium skillet over medium heat until shimmering. Add the onion and cook, stirring occasionally, until softened, about 4 minutes. Add the garlic, spices, and ½ teaspoon salt; cook, stirring constantly, until fragrant, about 30 seconds. Add the ground beef and cook, breaking up the meat with a wooden spoon and scraping the pan bottom to prevent scorching, until the beef is no longer pink, about 5 minutes. Add the tomato sauce, broth, vinegar, and brown sugar; bring to a simmer. Reduce the heat to medium-low and simmer uncovered, stirring frequently and breaking up the meat so that no chunks remain, until the liquid has reduced and thickened (the mixture should not be completely dry), about 10 minutes. Season with salt and pepper to taste.

2. Using a wide, shallow spoon, divide the mixture evenly among the taco shells; place two tacos on each plate. Serve immediately, passing the toppings separately.

Home-Fried Taco Shells

MAKES 8 SHELLS

Fry the taco shells before you make the filling, then rewarm them in a 200-degree oven for about 10 minutes before serving.

- ¾ cup corn oil, vegetable oil, or canola oil
- 8 (6-inch) corn tortillas

1. Line a rimmed baking sheet with a double thickness of paper towels and set aside. Heat the oil in an 8-inch skillet over medium heat to 350 degrees, about 5 minutes (the oil

MAKING YOUR OWN TACO SHELLS

1. Using tongs to hold the tortilla, slip half of it into the hot oil. With a metal spatula in the other hand, submerge the half in the oil. Fry until just set, but not brown, about 30 seconds.

2. Flip the tortilla and, using tongs, hold the tortilla open about 2 inches while keeping the bottom submerged in the oil. Fry until golden brown, about 1½ minutes. Flip again and fry the other side until golden brown, about 30 seconds.

3. Transfer the shell, upside down, to the paper towel-lined baking sheet to drain. Repeat with the remaining tortillas, adjusting the heat as necessary to keep the oil between 350 and 375 degrees.

should bubble when a small piece of tortilla is dropped in; the piece should rise to the surface in 2 seconds and be light golden brown in about 1 minute).

2. Following the photos, fry the tortillas. One at a time, place each fried taco shell on the prepared baking sheet (see note).

STEAK TACOS

WHY THIS RECIPE WORKS: Upscale steak tacos usually get their rich, beefy flavor from the grill, but cooking outdoors isn't always possible. We wanted an indoor cooking method that would always yield steak taco meat as tender, juicy, and rich-tasting as the grilled method.

We didn't want to wrap a pricey cut of beef in a taco, so we explored inexpensive cuts and chose flank steak for its good flavor and ready availability; when sliced against the grain, it can be just as tender as pricier cuts. To add flavor, we poked holes in the meat with a fork and rubbed it with a paste of oil, cilantro, jalapeño, garlic, and scallions; salt helped draw all the flavors into the steak and ensured juiciness. Pan-searing, with a sprinkling of sugar to enhance browning, gave us a crust that mimicked the char of the grill. To maximize this effect, we cut the steak into four long pieces, which gave us more sides to brown and turn crispy. For additional flavor, we tossed the cooked steak with some marinade that we had reserved and garnished the tacos simply with onion, cilantro, and lime wedges. In Mexico, steak tacos are often served with *curtido,* a relish of pickled vegetables; we devised a quick recipe for pickled onions to accompany our good-as-grilled steak tacos.

Steak Tacos

SERVES 4 TO 6

Our preferred method for warming tortillas is to place each one over the medium flame of a gas burner until slightly charred, about 30 seconds per side. We also like toasting them in a dry skillet over medium-high heat until softened and speckled with brown spots, 20 to 30 seconds per side. For a less spicy dish, remove some or all of the ribs and seeds from the jalapeños before chopping them for the marinade. In addition to the toppings suggested below, try serving the tacos with Sweet and Spicy Pickled Onions (recipe follows), thinly sliced radish or cucumber, or salsa.

MARINADE

- ½ cup packed fresh cilantro leaves
- 3 medium scallions, roughly chopped
- 1 medium jalapeño chile, stemmed and roughly chopped (see note)
- 3 medium garlic cloves, roughly chopped
- ½ teaspoon ground cumin
- ¼ cup vegetable oil
- 1 tablespoon juice from 1 lime

STEAK

- 1 (1½- to 1¾-pound) flank steak, trimmed and cut lengthwise (with the grain) into 4 equal pieces
- 1 tablespoon kosher salt or 1½ teaspoons table salt
- ½ teaspoon sugar
- ½ teaspoon ground black pepper
- 2 tablespoons vegetable oil

TACOS

- 12 (6-inch) corn tortillas, warmed (see note)
  Fresh cilantro leaves
  Minced white onion
  Lime wedges

1. FOR THE MARINADE: Pulse the cilantro, scallions, jalapeño, garlic, and cumin in a food processor until finely chopped, 10 to 12 pulses, scraping down the sides of the workbowl as necessary. Add the oil and process until the mixture is smooth and resembles pesto, about 15 seconds, scraping down the sides as necessary. Transfer 2 tablespoons of the herb paste to a medium bowl; whisk in the lime juice and set aside.

2. FOR THE STEAK: Using a dinner fork, poke each piece of steak 10 to 12 times on each side. Place in a large baking dish; rub all sides of the steak pieces evenly with the salt and then coat with the remaining herb paste. Cover with plastic wrap and refrigerate for at least 30 minutes or up to 1 hour.

3. Scrape the herb paste off the steak and sprinkle all sides of the pieces evenly with the sugar and black pepper. Heat the oil in a 12-inch nonstick skillet over medium-high heat until smoking. Place the steak in the skillet and cook until well browned, about 3 minutes. Flip the steak and sear until the second side is well browned, 2 to 3 minutes. Using tongs, stand each piece on a cut side and cook, turning as necessary, until all cut sides are well browned and the internal steak temperature registers 125 to 130 degrees on an instant-read thermometer, 2 to 7 minutes. Transfer the steak to a cutting board and let rest for 5 minutes.

4. FOR THE TACOS: Slice the steak against the grain into ⅛-inch-thick pieces. Transfer the sliced steak to the bowl with the herb paste–lime juice mixture and toss to coat. Season with salt to taste. Spoon a small amount of the sliced steak into the center of each warm tortilla and serve immediately, passing the toppings separately.

Sweet and Spicy Pickled Onions

MAKES ABOUT 2 CUPS

The onions can be refrigerated, tightly covered, for up to 1 week.

- 1 medium red onion, halved and sliced thin (about 1½ cups)
- 1 cup red wine vinegar
- ⅓ cup sugar
- 2 jalapeño chiles, stemmed, seeded, and cut into thin rings
- ¼ teaspoon table salt

Place the onions in a medium heat-resistant bowl. Bring the vinegar, sugar, jalapeños, and salt to a simmer in a small saucepan over medium-high heat, stirring occasionally, until the sugar dissolves. Pour the vinegar mixture over the onions, cover loosely, and let cool to room temperature, about 30 minutes. Once cool, drain and discard the liquid.

SHREDDED BEEF TACOS

WHY THIS RECIPE WORKS: The Mexican taco filling called *carne deshebrada* (shredded meat) is made by braising a large cut of beef (usually brisket, chuck roast, or even flank or skirt steak) until ultra tender and then shredding the meat and tossing it with a red or green sauce. We wanted an at-home version, made with a robust *rojo* (red) sauce.

Traditionally, the beef is cooked in water, which is then discarded—along with a lot of beefy flavor. Instead, we put the braising liquid to use in the sauce. Having it pull double duty not only ensured more flavor but also streamlined the recipe. We started by swapping out the water for a bright combination of beer and cider vinegar and swapping the large roast for meaty short ribs, cut into cubes to reduce the cooking time. To skip the extra step of browning the meat in batches, we propped up the cubes on slices of onion, which allowed the meat to brown in the ambient heat, contributing deep, meaty flavor

to the sauce. Tomato paste lent savory depth, and dried ancho chiles gave it a smoky, spicy kick. Ground cumin, cinnamon, and cloves provided a warm, earthy backbone. We pureed the sauce for a silky, unctuous texture that incorporated into the shredded meat seamlessly.

For a bright, fresh topping for our tacos, we made a quick *curtido*, a cabbage slaw from El Salvador. Marinating the shredded vegetables, onion, and jalapeño in a fruity cider vinegar–based pickling liquid gave them just the right amount of punch. A sprinkling of crumbled *queso fresco* introduced the right salty, creamy finish to the tacos.

Shredded Beef Tacos (Carne Deshebrada)

SERVES 6 TO 8

Use a full-bodied lager or ale such as Dos Equis or Sierra Nevada. If you can't find queso fresco, substitute feta. If your Dutch oven does not have a tight-fitting lid, cover the pot tightly with a sheet of heavy-duty aluminum foil and then replace the lid. To warm the tortillas, place them on a plate, cover them with a damp dish towel, and microwave them for 60 to 90 seconds. The shredded beef also makes a great filling for empanadas, tamales, and chiles rellenos.

BEEF

- 1½ cups beer
- ½ cup cider vinegar
- 2 ounces (4 to 6) dried ancho chiles, stemmed, seeded, and torn into 1-inch pieces
- 2 tablespoons tomato paste
- 6 garlic cloves, lightly crushed and peeled
- 3 bay leaves
- 2 teaspoons ground cumin
- 2 teaspoons dried oregano

Salt and pepper
- ½ teaspoon ground cloves
- ½ teaspoon ground cinnamon
- 1 large onion, sliced into ½-inch-thick rounds
- 3 pounds boneless beef short ribs, trimmed and cut into 2-inch cubes

CABBAGE-CARROT SLAW

- 1 cup cider vinegar
- ½ cup water
- 1 tablespoon sugar
- 1½ teaspoons salt
- ½ head green cabbage, cored and sliced thin (6 cups)
- 1 onion, sliced thin
- 1 large carrot, peeled and shredded
- 1 jalapeño chile, stemmed, seeded, and minced
- 1 teaspoon dried oregano
- 1 cup chopped fresh cilantro

- 18 (6-inch) corn tortillas, warmed
- 4 ounces queso fresco, crumbled (1 cup)
  Lime wedges

1. FOR THE BEEF: Adjust oven rack to lower-middle position and heat oven to 325 degrees. Combine beer, vinegar, anchos, tomato paste, garlic, bay leaves, cumin, oregano, 2 teaspoons salt, ½ teaspoon pepper, cloves, and cinnamon in Dutch oven. Arrange onion rounds in single layer on bottom of pot. Place beef on top of onion rounds in single layer. Cover and cook until meat is well browned and tender, 2½ to 3 hours.

2. FOR THE CABBAGE-CARROT SLAW: While beef cooks, whisk vinegar, water, sugar, and salt in large bowl until sugar is dissolved. Add cabbage, onion, carrot, jalapeño, and oregano and toss to combine. Cover and refrigerate for at least 1 hour or up to 24 hours. Drain slaw and stir in cilantro right before serving.

3. Using slotted spoon, transfer beef to large bowl, cover loosely with aluminum foil, and set aside. Strain liquid through fine-mesh strainer into 2-cup liquid measuring cup (do not wash pot). Discard onion rounds and bay leaves. Transfer remaining solids to blender. Let strained liquid settle for 5 minutes, then skim any fat off surface. Add water as needed to equal 1 cup. Pour liquid in blender with reserved solids and blend until smooth, about 2 minutes. Transfer sauce to now-empty pot.

4. Using two forks, shred beef into bite-size pieces. Bring sauce to simmer over medium heat. Add shredded beef and stir to coat. Season with salt to taste. (Beef can be refrigerated for up to 2 days; gently reheat before serving.)

5. Spoon small amount of beef into each warm tortilla and serve, passing slaw, queso fresco, and lime wedges separately.

SHREDDED CHICKEN TACOS

WHY THIS RECIPE WORKS: *Tinga de pollo* is typically made with cuts of meat that take several hours to turn tender—not exactly practical for a weeknight dish. We were determined to create a faster recipe that still brought authentic Mexican flavors to the table. At first, we poached chicken breast meat separately from the tomato-and-chipotle-based sauce and combined the two only briefly at the end. We realized, though, that we could achieve a deeper flavor by using boneless thighs and cooking them in the sauce. Fire-roasted tomatoes increased the sauce's smokiness, and a little brown sugar and lime juice and zest further boosted the dish's complexity. Simmering the cooked shredded chicken in the sauce for a full 10 minutes before serving gave the sauce a chance to thicken and loosened the chicken's muscle fibers so the sauce could really take hold and cling to the meat, making more cohesive tacos. Final toppings of fresh cilantro, scallions, avocado, crumbled Cotija cheese, and lime juice added the perfect amount of contrasting cool flavors.

Shredded Chicken Tacos (Tinga de Pollo)
SERVES 6

If you have a little extra time, homemade tortillas (recipe follows) will take these tacos to the next level. In addition to the Mexican-Style Pickled Vegetables (*Escabèche*) (recipe follows) and the toppings included here, Mexican *crema* (or sour cream) and minced onion are also good choices. If you can't find Cotija cheese, substitute feta. The shredded chicken mixture also makes a good topping for tostadas.

CHICKEN
- 2 pounds boneless, skinless chicken thighs, trimmed
  Salt and pepper
- 2 tablespoons vegetable oil
- 1 onion, halved and sliced thin
- 3 garlic cloves, minced
- 1 (14.5-ounce) can fire-roasted diced tomatoes
- ½ cup chicken broth
- 2 tablespoons minced canned chipotle chile in adobo sauce plus 2 teaspoons adobo sauce
- 1 teaspoon ground cumin
- ½ teaspoon brown sugar
- ¼ teaspoon cinnamon
- 1 teaspoon grated lime zest plus 2 tablespoons juice

TACOS
- 12 (6-inch) corn tortillas, warmed
- 1 avocado, halved, pitted, and cut into ½-inch pieces
  Fresh cilantro leaves
- 2 ounces Cotija cheese, crumbled (½ cup)
- 6 scallions, minced
  Lime wedges

1. FOR THE CHICKEN: Pat chicken dry with paper towels and season with salt and pepper. Heat 1 tablespoon oil in Dutch oven over medium-high heat until shimmering. Add half of chicken and brown on both sides, 3 to 4 minutes per side. Transfer to large plate. Repeat with remaining chicken.

2. Reduce heat to medium, add remaining 1 tablespoon oil to now-empty pot, and heat until shimmering. Add onion and cook, stirring frequently, until browned, about 7 minutes. Add garlic and cook until fragrant, about 1 minute. Add tomatoes and their juice, broth, chipotle and adobo sauce, cumin, sugar, and cinnamon and bring to boil, scraping bottom of pot to loosen any browned bits.

3. Return chicken to pot, reduce heat to medium-low, cover, and simmer until meat registers 195 degrees, about 15 minutes, flipping chicken after 5 minutes. Transfer chicken to cutting board.

4. Transfer cooking liquid to blender and process until smooth, 15 to 30 seconds. Return cooking liquid to pot. When cool enough to handle, use two forks to shred chicken into bite-size pieces. Return chicken to pot with cooking liquid. Cook over medium heat, stirring frequently, until sauce is thickened and clings to chicken, about 10 minutes. Stir in lime zest and juice. Season with salt and pepper to taste.

5. FOR THE TACOS: Spoon chicken into center of each warm tortilla and serve immediately, passing toppings separately.

Mexican-Style Pickled Vegetables (Escabèche)
MAKES ABOUT 2 CUPS

For a less spicy pickle, remove the seeds from the jalapeño.

- ½ teaspoon coriander seeds
- ¼ teaspoon cumin seeds
- 1 cup apple cider vinegar
- ½ cup water
- 1½ teaspoons sugar
- ¼ teaspoon salt
- 1 red onion, halved and sliced thin
- 2 carrots, peeled and sliced thin
- 1 jalapeño, stemmed and sliced thin into rings

Heat coriander seeds and cumin seeds in medium saucepan over medium heat, stirring frequently, until fragrant, about 2 minutes. Add vinegar, water, sugar, and salt and bring to boil, stirring to dissolve sugar and salt. Remove saucepan from heat and add onion, carrots, and jalapeno, pressing to submerge vegetables. Cover and let cool completely, 30 minutes. (Cooled vegetables can be refrigerated for up to 1 week.)

Corn Tortillas
MAKES ABOUT TWENTY-TWO 5-INCH TORTILLAS

Pressing the dough between a zipper-lock bag that has been cut open at the sides prevents it from sticking to the pie plate. Distribute your weight evenly over the dough when pressing. Using a clear pie plate makes it easy to see the tortilla. A tortilla press, of course, can also be used. You can find masa harina in the international aisle or near the flour.

2 cups (8 ounces) masa harina
2 teaspoons vegetable oil
¼ teaspoon salt
1¼ cups warm water, plus extra as needed

1. Cut sides of sandwich-size zipper-lock bag but leave bottom seam intact so that bag unfolds completely. Place open bag on counter and line large plate with 2 damp dish towels.

2. Mix masa, 1 teaspoon oil, and salt together in medium bowl. Using rubber spatula, stir in warm water to form soft dough. Using your hands, knead dough in bowl, adding extra warm water, 1 tablespoon at a time, until dough is soft and tacky but not sticky (texture is like Play-Doh). Cover dough and set aside for 5 minutes.

3. Meanwhile, heat remaining 1 teaspoon oil in 8-inch non-stick skillet over medium-high heat until shimmering. Using paper towel, wipe out skillet, leaving thin film of oil on bottom. Pinch off 1-ounce piece of dough (about 2 tablespoons) and roll into smooth 1¼-inch ball. Cover remaining dough with damp paper towel. Place ball in center of open bag and fold other side of bag over ball. Using clear pie plate, press down on plastic to flatten ball into 5-inch disk, rotating plastic during pressing to ensure even thickness. Working quickly, gently peel plastic away from tortilla.

4. Carefully place tortilla in skillet and cook, without moving it, until tortilla moves freely when pan is shaken, about 30 seconds. Flip tortilla and cook until edges curl and bottom surface is spotty brown, about 1 minute. Flip tortilla again and continue to cook until bottom surface is spotty brown and puffs up in center, 30 to 60 seconds. Place toasted tortilla between 2 damp dish towels; repeat shaping and cooking with remaining dough. (Cooled tortillas can be transferred to zipper-lock bag and refrigerated for up to 5 days. Reheat before serving.)

SAUSAGE AND POTATO TACOS

WHY THIS RECIPE WORKS: Juicy, seasoned Mexican chorizo is key to this classic taco, but it can be hard to find, so we devised a quick method for making our own. We started by toasting ancho chili powder, paprika, and spices in oil to intensify their flavors, and then we mixed the spiced oil into preground pork along with some cider vinegar. We cooked the mixture in a skillet and added parboiled diced potatoes to absorb the flavorful juices as they finished cooking. Mashing some of the potatoes and mixing them into the filling made it more cohesive and easier to eat. A creamy puree of tomatillos, avocado, cilantro, and jalapeños complemented the richness of the filling and was a cooling counterpoint to its spiciness.

Chorizo and Potato Tacos
SERVES 4

If you can purchase a good quality Mexican-style chorizo, skip step 2 and cook the chorizo as directed in step 3. The raw onions complement the soft, rich taco filling, so we do not recommend omitting them.

FILLING
1 pound Yukon Gold potatoes, peeled and cut into ½-inch chunks
Salt and pepper
1 tablespoon ancho chili powder
1 tablespoon paprika
1½ teaspoons ground coriander
1½ teaspoon dried oregano
¼ teaspoon ground cinnamon
Pinch cayenne pepper
Pinch ground allspice
3 tablespoons vegetable oil
3 tablespoons apple cider vinegar
1½ teaspoons sugar
1 garlic clove, minced
½ pound ground pork

SAUCE
8 ounces tomatillos, husks and stems removed, rinsed well and dried, and cut into 1-inch pieces
1 avocado, halved, pitted, and cut into 1-inch pieces
1–2 jalapeño chile(s), stemmed, seeded, and chopped
¼ cup chopped fresh cilantro leaves and stems
1 tablespoon lime juice
1 garlic clove, minced
¾ teaspoon salt

TACOS
12 (6-inch) corn tortillas, warmed
Finely chopped white onion
Fresh cilantro leaves
Lime wedges

1. FOR THE FILLING: Bring 4 cups water to boil in 12-inch non-stick skillet over high heat. Add potatoes and 1 teaspoon salt. Reduce heat to medium, cover, and cook until just tender, 3 to 5 minutes. Drain and set aside. Wipe out skillet.

2. Combine chili powder, paprika, coriander, oregano, cinnamon, cayenne, allspice, ¾ teaspoon salt, ½ teaspoon pepper, and oil in now-empty skillet. Cook over medium heat, stirring constantly, until mixture is bubbling and fragrant. Remove from heat and carefully stir in vinegar, sugar, and garlic (mixture will sputter). Let stand until steam subsides and skillet cools slightly, about 5 minutes. Add pork to skillet. Mash and mix with rubber spatula until spice mixture is evenly incorporated

3. Return skillet to medium-high heat and cook pork mixture over medium-high heat, mashing and stirring until pork has broken into fine crumbles and juices are bubbling over entire surface of skillet, about 3 minutes.

4. Stir in potatoes, cover, and reduce heat to low. Cook until potatoes are fully softened and have soaked up most of the pork juices, 6 to 8 minutes, stirring halfway through cooking time.

Remove skillet from heat and, using spatula, mash approximately one-eighth of potatoes. Stir mashed potatoes into mixture until lightly coated with juices. Cover and keep warm.

5. FOR THE SAUCE: Process all ingredients in food processor until smooth, about 1 minute, scraping down sides of bowl as needed. Transfer to serving bowl.

6. FOR THE TACOS: Spoon filling into center of each warm tortilla and serve with sauce, onion, cilantro, and lime wedges.

CHICKEN FAJITAS

WHY THIS RECIPE WORKS: Too often, chicken fajitas need to be slathered with guacamole, sour cream, and salsa to compensate for the bland flavor of the main ingredients. We wanted to go back to the basics, creating a simple combination of smoky grilled vegetables and strips of chicken wrapped up in warm flour tortillas. We wanted the chicken and vegetables to be flavorful enough to make condiments unnecessary.

To boost the flavor of the chicken, we used a marinade of lime juice and oil. We added jalapeño and cilantro for some bright spice and herbal flavor, and a surprising addition—Worcestershire sauce—lent a subtle but complex savory note. We marinated the chicken only briefly, so the acid wouldn't turn the delicate chicken to mush. Bell peppers and onions are the customary vegetables, and we found that their sweet-bitter flavors contrasted well with the chicken. To prepare the vegetables for grilling, we quartered the peppers, so they'd lie flat on the grill, and cut the onion into thick rounds that would hold together during cooking. A two-level fire enabled us to grill the chicken and vegetables at the same time, the latter on the cooler part so they wouldn't burn. We saved some of the marinade to toss with everything at the end for a bright flavor burst; nestled in a warm tortilla, the smoky vegetables and well-seasoned chicken were so good on their own that we forgot all about toppings.

Grilled Chicken Fajitas

SERVES 4 TO 6

You can use red, yellow, orange, or green bell peppers in this recipe. The chicken tenderloins can be reserved for another use or marinated and grilled along with the breasts. When you head outside to grill, bring a clean dish towel in which to wrap the tortillas and keep them warm. The chicken and vegetables have enough flavor on their own, but accompaniments (guacamole, salsa, sour cream, shredded cheddar or Monterey Jack cheese, and lime wedges) can be offered at the table.

    6   tablespoons vegetable oil
    ⅓   cup lime juice (3 limes)
    1   jalapeño chile, stemmed, seeded, and minced
    1½ tablespoons minced fresh cilantro
    3   garlic cloves, minced

    1   tablespoon Worcestershire sauce
    1½ teaspoons packed brown sugar
        Salt and pepper
    1½ pounds boneless, skinless chicken breasts, tenderloins
        removed, trimmed, pounded to ½-inch thickness
    1   large red onion, peeled and cut into ½-inch-thick rounds
        (do not separate rings)
    2   large bell peppers, quartered, stemmed, and seeded
 8–12 (6-inch) flour tortillas

1. Whisk ¼ cup oil, lime juice, jalapeño, cilantro, garlic, Worcestershire, sugar, 1 teaspoon salt, and ¾ teaspoon pepper together in bowl. Reserve ¼ cup marinade and set aside. Add 1 teaspoon salt to remaining marinade. Place marinade and chicken in 1-gallon zipper-lock bag and toss to coat; press out as much air as possible and seal bag. Refrigerate for at least 15 minutes, flipping bag halfway through marinating. Brush both sides of onion rounds and peppers with remaining 2 tablespoons oil and season with salt and pepper to taste.

2A. FOR A CHARCOAL GRILL: Open bottom vent completely. Light large chimney starter filled with charcoal briquettes (6 quarts). When top coals are partially covered with ash, pour coals over two-thirds of grill, leaving remaining one-third empty. Set cooking grate in place, cover, and open lid vent completely. Heat grill until hot, about 5 minutes.

2B. FOR A GAS GRILL: Turn all burners to high, cover, and heat grill until hot, about 15 minutes. Leave primary burner on high and turn other burner(s) to medium.

3. Clean and oil cooking grate. Remove chicken from bag, allowing excess marinade to drip off. Place chicken on hotter side of grill, smooth side down. Cook (covered if using gas) until well browned on first side, 4 to 6 minutes. Flip and continue to cook until chicken registers 160 degrees, 4 to 6 minutes longer. Transfer chicken to cutting board, tent loosely with aluminum foil, and let rest for 5 to 10 minutes.

4. While chicken cooks, place onion rounds and peppers (skin side down) on cooler side of grill and cook until tender and charred on both sides, 8 to 12 minutes, flipping every 3 minutes. Transfer onions and peppers to cutting board with chicken.

5. Working in 2 or 3 batches, place tortillas in single layer on cooler side of grill. Cook until warm and lightly browned, about 20 seconds per side (do not grill too long or tortillas will become brittle). As tortillas are done, wrap in dish towel or large sheet of foil.

6. Separate onions into rings and place in medium bowl. Slice peppers into ¼-inch-thick strips and place in bowl with onions. Add 2 tablespoons reserved marinade and toss to combine. Slice each breast on bias into ¼-inch-thick slices, place in second bowl, and toss with remaining 2 tablespoons reserved marinade.

7. Transfer chicken and vegetables to serving platter and serve with warmed tortillas.

STEAK FAJITAS

WHY THIS RECIPE WORKS: Steak fajitas were originally made with skirt steak, but the wider availability of flank steak has made it the cut of choice for this dish. Recipes for fajitas are fairly straightforward—grill the meat and vegetables and serve them in a warm tortilla. But too often, fajitas are lackluster or ruined by unnecessary complexity. We want fajitas that boasted flawless, flavorful meat with a rosy interior and browned crust.

Marinating is often recommended as a way to tenderize flank steak, but we learned that it's plenty tender without a marinade if sliced thin against the grain after being cooked. But we did want to add flavor. A long soak turned the meat mushy, but a squeeze of lime juice and a generous dose of salt and pepper just before grilling added all the extra flavor we wanted. The tried-and-true way of cooking flank steak—over high heat for a short period of time—required no changes. We found that the meat is juicier when allowed to rest after grilling, and that gave us time to grill the vegetables. Served in tortillas with freshly made guacamole, these fajitas delivered on all fronts.

Steak Fajitas
SERVES 8

The ingredients go on the grill in order as the fire dies down: steak over a medium-hot fire, vegetables over a medium fire, and tortillas around the edge of a medium to low fire just to warm them. Make sure to cover the grilled but unsliced flank steak with foil; it will take you at least 10 minutes to get the vegetables and tortillas ready. You can use red, yellow, orange, or green bell peppers in this recipe. When you head outside to grill, bring a clean kitchen towel in which to wrap the tortillas and keep them warm. Chunky Guacamole (page 413) and fresh salsa make good accompaniments.

1	(2- to 2½-pound) flank steak, trimmed
¼	cup lime juice
	Salt and pepper
1	large red onion, peeled and cut into ½-inch-thick rounds (do not separate rings)
2	large bell peppers, quartered, stemmed, and seeded
8-12	(6-inch) flour tortillas

1A. FOR A CHARCOAL GRILL: Open bottom vent completely. Light large chimney starter mounded with charcoal briquettes (7 quarts). When top coals are partially covered with ash, pour evenly over half of grill. Set cooking grate in place, cover, and open lid vent completely. Heat grill until hot, about 5 minutes.

1B. FOR A GAS GRILL: Turn all burners to high, cover, and heat grill until hot, about 15 minutes.

2. Clean and oil cooking grate. Pat steak dry with paper towels and sprinkle with lime juice, salt, and pepper. Place steak on grill (hot side if using charcoal) and cook (covered if using gas) until well browned on first side, 4 to 7 minutes. Flip steak and continue to cook until meat registers 120 to 125 degrees (for medium-rare) or 130 to 135 degrees (for medium), 3 to 8 minutes. Transfer steak to cutting board, tent loosely with aluminum foil, and let rest for 10 minutes.

NOTES FROM THE TEST KITCHEN

STEMMING AND SEEDING BELL PEPPERS

1. Slice ¼ inch from the top and bottom of each pepper and then gently remove the stem from the top lobe.

2. Pull the core out of the pepper. Make a slit down one side of the pepper and lay it flat, skin side down, in one long strip.

3. Slide a sharp knife along the inside of the pepper to remove all the ribs and seeds.

3. While steak rests, place onion rounds and peppers (skin side down) on hot side of grill (if using charcoal) or turn all burners to medium (if using gas). Cook until tender and charred on both sides, 8 to 12 minutes, flipping every 3 minutes. Transfer onions and peppers to carving board with beef.

4. Place tortillas in single layer on hot side of grill (if using charcoal) or turn all burners to low (if using gas). Cook until warm and lightly browned, about 20 seconds per side (do not grill too long or tortillas will become brittle). As tortillas are done, wrap in clean kitchen towel or large sheet of foil.

5. Separate onions into rings and slice peppers into ¼-inch strips. Slice steak, against grain, ¼-inch-thick. Transfer beef and vegetables to serving platter and serve with warmed tortillas.

CHICKEN ENCHILADAS

WHY THIS RECIPE WORKS: Chicken enchiladas are a complete meal that offers a rich and complex combination of flavors, textures, and ingredients. The problem with preparing enchiladas at home is that traditional cooking methods require a whole day of preparation. We wanted a recipe for an Americanized version of chicken enchiladas that could be made in 90 minutes from start to finish.

To save time preparing the tortillas, we sprayed them with vegetable oil spray and warmed them on a baking sheet in the oven. We created a quick chili sauce with onions, garlic, spices, and tomato sauce, and to further enhance the sauce's flavor, we poached the chicken right in the sauce. This step also made for moist, flavorful meat. And cheddar cheese spiked with canned jalapeños and fresh cilantro made a rich, flavorful filling.

Chicken Enchiladas with Red Chili Sauce

SERVES 4 TO 5

Monterey Jack can be used instead of cheddar, or for a mellower flavor and creamier texture, try farmer's cheese. Be sure to cool the chicken before filling the tortillas; otherwise the hot filling will make the enchiladas soggy.

SAUCE AND FILLING

- 1½ tablespoons vegetable oil
- 1 medium onion, chopped fine
- 3 medium garlic cloves, minced or pressed through a garlic press (about 1 tablespoon)
- 3 tablespoons chili powder
- 2 teaspoons ground coriander
- 2 teaspoons ground cumin
- 2 teaspoons sugar
- ½ teaspoon table salt
- 12 ounces boneless, skinless chicken thighs (about 4 thighs), trimmed and cut into ¼-inch-wide strips

- 2 (8-ounce) cans tomato sauce
- ¾ cup water
- 8 ounces sharp cheddar cheese (see note), shredded (about 2 cups)
- ½ cup coarsely chopped fresh cilantro leaves
- 1 (4-ounce) can pickled jalapeño chiles, drained and chopped (about ¼ cup)

TORTILLAS AND TOPPINGS

- 10 (6-inch) corn tortillas
  Vegetable oil spray
- 3 ounces sharp cheddar cheese (see note), shredded (about ¾ cup)
- ¾ cup sour cream
- 1 medium, ripe avocado, diced medium (see page 414)
- 5 romaine lettuce leaves, shredded
  Lime wedges

1. FOR THE SAUCE AND FILLING: Heat the oil in a medium saucepan over medium-high heat until shimmering. Add the onion and cook, stirring occasionally, until softened and beginning to brown, about 5 minutes. Add the garlic, chili powder, coriander, cumin, sugar, and salt and cook, stirring constantly, until fragrant, about 30 seconds. Add the chicken and cook, stirring constantly, until coated with the spices, about 30 seconds. Add the tomato sauce and water, stir to separate the chicken pieces, and bring to a simmer. Reduce the heat to medium-low and simmer, uncovered, stirring occasionally, until the chicken is cooked through and the flavors have melded, about 8 minutes. Pour the mixture through a medium-mesh strainer into a medium bowl, pressing on the chicken and onions to extract as much sauce as possible; set the sauce aside. Transfer the chicken mixture to a large plate; place in the freezer for 10 minutes to cool, then combine with the cheddar, cilantro, and jalapeños in a medium bowl.

2. Adjust the oven racks to the upper-middle and lower-middle positions and heat the oven to 300 degrees.

3. TO ASSEMBLE: Smear the bottom of a 13 by 9-inch baking dish with ¾ cup of the chili sauce. Place the tortillas in a single layer on two baking sheets. Spray both sides of the tortillas lightly with vegetable oil spray. Bake until the tortillas are soft and pliable, about 4 minutes. Transfer the warm tortillas to a work surface. Increase the oven temperature to 400 degrees. Spread ⅓ cup of the filling down the center of each tortilla. Roll each tortilla tightly by hand and place, seam side down, side by side on the sauce in the baking dish. Pour the remaining chili sauce over the top of the enchiladas. Use the back of a spoon to spread the sauce so it coats the top of each tortilla. Sprinkle the cheese down the center of the enchiladas.

4. Cover the baking dish with foil. Bake the enchiladas on the lower-middle rack until heated through and the cheese is melted, 20 to 25 minutes. Uncover and serve immediately, passing the sour cream, avocado, lettuce, and lime wedges separately.

ENCHILADAS VERDES

WHY THIS RECIPE WORKS: We love the bright taste of enchiladas verdes. But too often the green chili sauce is watery and lacks good green chile flavor. We wanted to re-create the memorable enchiladas verdes found in good Mexican restaurants: moist, tender chicken and fresh, citrusy flavors wrapped in soft corn tortillas and topped with just the right amount of melted cheese.

The chicken was easy; we poached it in chicken broth enhanced with sautéed onion, garlic, and cumin. The green sauce is based on tomatillos and chiles. Jalapeños and serranos are good for adding heat to a dish, but we wanted a more complex herbal flavor so we opted for poblanos. To get the characteristic char, which Mexican cooks achieve by roasting on a *comal*, we tossed the chiles and fresh tomatillos with a little oil and ran them under the broiler. Pulsed in a food processor and thinned with a bit of the broth left from poaching the chicken, the tomatillos and chiles formed a well-seasoned, chunky sauce. To enrich the filling, we liked pepper Jack cheese—and sprinkled more on top of the dish. To make the tortillas pliable and easy to roll, we picked up the same technique from our Chicken Enchiladas with Red Chili Sauce (page 427): We sprayed them with vegetable oil spray and baked them for a few minutes. The enchiladas required just a brief stint in the oven to heat through and melt the cheese. Garnished with sour cream, scallions, and radishes, these enchiladas may have the authentic restaurant version beat.

Enchiladas Verdes

SERVES 4 TO 6

You can substitute 3 (11-ounce) cans tomatillos, drained and rinsed, for the fresh ones in this recipe. Halve large tomatillos (more than 2 inches in diameter) and place them skin side up for broiling in step 2 to ensure even cooking and charring. If

you can't find poblanos, substitute 4 large jalapeño chiles (with seeds and ribs removed). To increase the spiciness of the sauce, reserve some of the chiles' ribs and seeds and add them to the food processor in step 3.

ENCHILADAS

- 4 teaspoons vegetable oil
- 1 medium onion, chopped medium
- 3 medium garlic cloves, minced or pressed through a garlic press (about 1 tablespoon)
- ½ teaspoon ground cumin
- 1½ cups low-sodium chicken broth
- 1 pound boneless, skinless chicken breasts (2 to 3 breasts), trimmed
- 1½ pounds tomatillos (16 to 20 medium), husks and stems removed, rinsed well and dried (see note)
- 3 medium poblano chiles, halved lengthwise, stemmed, and seeded (see note)
- 1-2 teaspoons sugar
  Table salt and ground black pepper
- ½ cup coarsely chopped fresh cilantro leaves
- 8 ounces pepper Jack or Monterey Jack cheese, grated (about 2 cups)
- 12 (6-inch) corn tortillas

GARNISHES

- 2 medium scallions, sliced thin
  Thinly sliced radishes
  Sour cream

1. Adjust the oven racks to the middle and highest positions and heat the broiler. Heat 2 teaspoons of the oil in a medium saucepan over medium heat until shimmering; add the onion and cook, stirring frequently, until golden, 6 to 8 minutes. Add 2 teaspoons of the garlic and the cumin; cook, stirring frequently, until fragrant, about 30 seconds. Decrease the heat to low and stir in the broth. Add the chicken, cover, and simmer until the thickest part of the chicken registers 160 to 165 degrees on an instant-read thermometer, 15 to 20 minutes, flipping the chicken halfway through cooking. Transfer the chicken to a large bowl; place in the refrigerator to cool, about 20 minutes. Remove ¼ cup liquid from the saucepan and set aside; discard the remaining liquid.

2. Meanwhile, toss the tomatillos and poblanos with the remaining 2 teaspoons oil; arrange on a rimmed baking sheet lined with foil, with the poblanos skin side up. Broil until the vegetables blacken and start to soften, 5 to 10 minutes, rotating the pan halfway through cooking. Cool for 10 minutes, then remove the skin from the poblanos (leave the tomatillo skins intact). Transfer the tomatillos and chiles to a food processor. Decrease the oven temperature to 350 degrees. Discard the foil from the baking sheet and set the baking sheet aside for warming the tortillas.

3. Add 1 teaspoon of the sugar, 1 teaspoon salt, the remaining 1 teaspoon garlic, and the reserved ¼ cup cooking liquid to the food processor; pulse until the sauce is somewhat chunky, about 8 pulses. Taste the sauce; season with salt and pepper to taste and adjust tartness by stirring in the remaining sugar, ½ teaspoon at a time. Set the sauce aside (you should have about 3 cups).

4. When the chicken is cool, pull into shreds using your hands or two forks, then chop into small bite-size pieces. Combine the chicken with the cilantro and 1½ cups of the cheese; season with salt to taste.

5. Smear the bottom of a 13 by 9-inch baking dish with ¾ cup of the tomatillo sauce. Place the tortillas in a single layer on two baking sheets. Spray both sides of the tortillas lightly with vegetable oil spray. Bake until the tortillas are soft and pliable, 2 to 4 minutes. Increase the oven temperature to 450 degrees. Place the warm tortillas on the work surface and spread ⅓ cup of the filling down the center of each tortilla. Roll each tortilla tightly by hand and place in the baking dish, seam side down. Pour the remaining tomatillo sauce over the top of the enchiladas. Use the back of a spoon to spread the sauce so that it coats the top of each tortilla. Sprinkle with the remaining ½ cup cheese and cover the baking dish with foil.

6. Bake the enchiladas on the middle oven rack until heated through and the cheese is melted, 15 to 20 minutes. Uncover, sprinkle with the scallions, and serve immediately, passing the radishes and sour cream separately.

SPICY PORK TACOS (AL PASTOR)

WHY THIS RECIPE WORKS: In Mexico, super-thin slices of pork butt and pork fat are marinated in chiles and tomato, stacked and roasted on a spit, and shaved, hot and crispy, into a corn tortilla. To mimic this popular taco filling, which is often garnished with sweet pineapple, without any special equipment, we had to get creative. We braised ½-inch-thick slabs of pork butt in a mix of guajillo chiles, tomatoes, and spices until tender, before basting them with sauce on the grill until crisped and charred. Chopped into bite-size strips and topped with grilled pineapple, our simple homemade spicy pork filling lives up to the original.

Spicy Pork Tacos (al Pastor)

SERVES 6 TO 8

Boneless pork butt is often labeled Boston butt in the supermarket. If you can't find guajillo chiles, New Mexican chiles may be substituted, although the dish may be spicier. To warm tortillas, place them on a plate, cover with a damp dish towel, and microwave for 60 to 90 seconds. Keep tortillas covered and serve immediately.

- 10 large dried guajillo chiles, wiped clean
- 1½ cups water
- 1¼ pounds plum tomatoes, cored and quartered
- 8 garlic cloves, peeled
- 4 bay leaves
  Salt and pepper
- ¾ teaspoon sugar
- ½ teaspoon ground cumin
- ⅛ teaspoon ground cloves
- 1 (3-pound) boneless pork butt roast
- 1 lime, cut into 8 wedges
- ½ pineapple, peeled, cored, and cut into ½-inch-thick rings
  Vegetable oil
- 18 (6-inch) corn tortillas, warmed
- 1 small onion, chopped fine
- ½ cup coarsely chopped fresh cilantro

1. Toast guajillos in large Dutch oven over medium-high heat until softened and fragrant, 2 to 4 minutes. Transfer to large plate and, when cool enough to handle, remove stems.

2. Return toasted guajillos to now-empty Dutch oven, add water, tomatoes, garlic, bay leaves, 2 teaspoons salt, ½ teaspoon pepper, sugar, cumin, and cloves, and bring to simmer over medium-high heat. Cover, reduce heat, and simmer, stirring occasionally, until guajillos are softened and tomatoes mash easily, about 20 minutes.

3. While sauce simmers, trim excess fat from exterior of pork, leaving ¼-inch-thick fat cap. Slice pork against grain into ½-inch-thick slabs.

4. Transfer guajillo-tomato mixture to blender and process until smooth, about 1 minute. Strain puree through fine-mesh strainer, pressing on solids to extract as much liquid as possible. Return puree to pot, submerge pork slices in liquid, and bring to simmer over medium heat. Partially cover, reduce heat, and gently simmer until pork is tender but still holds together, 1½ to 1¾ hours, flipping and rearranging pork halfway through cooking. (Pork can be left in sauce, cooled to room temperature, and refrigerated for up to 2 days.)

5. Transfer pork to large plate, season both sides with salt, and cover tightly with aluminum foil. Whisk sauce to combine. Transfer ½ cup sauce to bowl for grilling; pour off all but ½ cup remaining sauce from pot and reserve for another use. Squeeze 2 lime wedges into sauce in pot and add spent wedges; season with salt to taste.

6A. FOR A CHARCOAL GRILL: Open bottom vent halfway. Light large chimney starter filled with charcoal briquettes (6 quarts). When top coals are partially covered with ash, pour evenly over grill. Set cooking grate in place, cover, and open lid vent halfway. Heat grill until hot, about 5 minutes.

6B. FOR A GAS GRILL: Turn all burners to high, cover, and heat grill until hot, about 15 minutes. Turn all burners to medium.

7. Clean and oil cooking grate. Brush 1 side of pork with ¼ cup reserved sauce. Place pork on 1 side of grill, sauce side down, and cook until well browned and crisp, 5 to 7 minutes. Brush pork with remaining ¼ cup reserved sauce, flip, and continue to cook until second side is well browned and crisp, 5 to 7 minutes longer. Transfer to carving board. Meanwhile, brush both sides of pineapple rings with vegetable oil and season with salt to taste. Place on other half of grill and cook until pineapple is softened and caramelized, 10 to 14 minutes; transfer pineapple to carving board.

8. Coarsely chop grilled pineapple and transfer to serving bowl. Using tongs or carving fork to steady hot pork, slice each piece crosswise into ⅛-inch pieces. Bring remaining ½ cup sauce in pot to simmer, add sliced pork, remove pot from heat, and toss to coat pork well. Season with salt to taste.

9. Spoon small amount of pork into each warm tortilla and serve, passing chopped pineapple, remaining 6 lime wedges, onion, and cilantro separately.

SPICY MEXICAN SHREDDED PORK TOSTADAS

WHY THIS RECIPE WORKS: True Mexican shredded pork, or *tinga*, is a far cry from the bland burrito-joint version often found languishing on steam tables. We set out to perfect the methods that give tinga its characteristic crisp texture and smoky tomato flavor. We wanted tender, full-flavored Mexican shredded pork that we could serve atop crisp corn tortillas or spoon into taco shells.

We trimmed and cubed a Boston butt (chosen for its good marbling and little sinew), then simmered the pieces in water that we flavored with garlic, thyme, and onion. Once the pork was tender, we drained the meat (reserving some of the cooking liquid for the sauce) and returned it to the pot to shred. The meat was so tender, it fell apart with nothing more than the pressure of a potato masher. We then sautéed the meat in a hot frying pan along with the requisite additions of finely chopped onion and oregano. Minutes later, the pork had developed crackling edges crisp enough to survive the final step of simmering in tomato sauce. Unlike American barbecue with its sweet and tangy barbecue sauce, tinga relies on a complex smoke-flavored tomato sauce. For our version, we diluted canned tomato sauce with the reserved flavorful cooking liquid from the pork and added bay leaves for herbal complexity. And for tinga's all-important smokiness, we turned to ground chipotle powder, which was a little harder to find than the other option of canned chipotle chiles in adobo sauce, but had a deeper, more complex flavor.

Spicy Mexican Shredded Pork Tostadas
SERVES 4 TO 6

The trimmed pork should weigh about 1½ pounds. The shredded pork is traditionally served on tostadas (crisp fried corn tortillas), but you can also use the meat in tacos or burritos or simply served over rice. Make sure to buy tortillas made only with corn, lime, and salt—preservatives will compromise quality. We prefer the complex flavor of chipotle powder, but two minced canned chipotle chiles can be used in its place. The pork can be prepared through step 1 and refrigerated in an airtight container for up to 2 days. The tostadas can be made up to a day in advance and stored in an airtight container.

SHREDDED PORK
- 2 pounds boneless pork butt roast, trimmed of excess fat and cut into 1-inch pieces (see note)
- 2 medium onions, 1 quartered and 1 chopped fine
- 5 medium garlic cloves, 3 peeled and smashed and 2 minced or pressed through a garlic press (about 2 teaspoons)
- 4 sprigs fresh thyme
  Table salt
- 2 tablespoons olive oil
- ½ teaspoon dried oregano
- 1 (14.5-ounce) can tomato sauce
- 1 tablespoon ground chipotle powder (see note)
- 2 bay leaves

TOSTADAS
- ¾ cup vegetable oil
- 12 (6-inch) corn tortillas (see note)
  Table salt

GARNISHES

Queso fresco or feta cheese

Fresh cilantro leaves

Sour cream

Diced avocado

Lime wedges

1. FOR THE SHREDDED PORK: Bring the pork, quartered onion, smashed garlic cloves, thyme, 1 teaspoon salt, and 6 cups water to a simmer in a large saucepan over medium-high heat, skimming off any foam that rises to the surface. Reduce the heat to medium-low, partially cover, and cook until the pork is tender, 1¼ to 1½ hours. Drain the pork, reserving 1 cup cooking liquid. Discard the onion, garlic, and thyme. Return the pork to the saucepan and, using a potato masher, mash until shredded into rough ½-inch pieces; set aside.

2. Heat the olive oil in a 12-inch nonstick skillet over medium-high heat until shimmering. Add the shredded pork, chopped onion, and oregano; cook, stirring often, until the pork is well browned and crisp, 7 to 10 minutes. Add the minced garlic and cook until fragrant, about 30 seconds.

3. Stir in the tomato sauce, chipotle powder, reserved pork cooking liquid, and bay leaves; simmer until almost all the liquid has evaporated, 5 to 7 minutes. Remove and discard the bay leaves and season with salt to taste.

4. TO FRY THE TOSTADAS: Heat the vegetable oil in an 8-inch heavy-bottomed skillet over medium heat to 350 degrees. Using a fork, poke the center of each tortilla three or four times (to prevent puffing and allow for even cooking). Fry one at a time, holding a metal potato masher in the upright position on top of the tortilla to keep it submerged, until crisp and lightly browned, 45 to 60 seconds (no flipping is necessary). Drain on a paper towel–lined plate and season with salt to taste. Repeat with the remaining tortillas.

5. TO SERVE: Spoon a small amount of shredded pork onto the center of each tostada and serve, passing the garnishes separately.

MEXICAN PULLED PORK

WHY THIS RECIPE WORKS: Traditional *carnitas*, Mexico's version of pulled pork, is fried in gallons of lard or oil. The results are tasty, but who wants to deal with all that hot fat? We wanted restaurant-style carnitas—tender chunks of lightly crisped, caramelized pork, subtly accented with oregano and citrus—without the hassle of frying.

Our initial recipe for carnitas started by simmering the meat (taste tests proved boneless pork butt had the best flavor) in a seasoned broth in the oven and then sautéing it in some of the rendered fat. The flavor was OK, but too much of the pork flavor was lost when we discarded the cooking liquid. So we reduced the liquid on the stovetop (after the meat had been removed) to the consistency of a thick, syrupy glaze that was

perfect for coating the meat. Broiled on a rack set over a baking sheet, the glazed meat developed a wonderfully rich flavor, and the rack allowed the excess fat to drip off. We emulated the flavor of the Mexican sour oranges used in authentic carnitas with a mixture of fresh lime and orange juices. Bay leaves and oregano provided aromatic notes, and cumin brought an earthiness that complemented the other flavors.

Mexican Pulled Pork (Carnitas)
SERVES 6

We like serving carnitas spooned into tacos, but you can also use it as a filling for tamales, enchiladas, and burritos.

PORK

1 (3½- to 4-pound) boneless pork butt, fat cap trimmed to ⅛ inch thick, cut into 2-inch chunks

1 small onion, peeled and halved

2 bay leaves

1 teaspoon dried oregano

1 teaspoon ground cumin

   Table salt and ground black pepper

2 cups water

2 tablespoons juice from 1 lime

1 medium orange, halved

TORTILLAS AND GARNISHES

18 (6-inch) corn tortillas, warmed (see note on page 429)

   Lime wedges

   Minced white or red onion

   Fresh cilantro leaves

   Thinly sliced radishes

   Sour cream

1. Adjust an oven rack to the lower-middle position and heat the oven to 300 degrees. Combine the pork, onion, bay leaves, oregano, cumin, 1 teaspoon salt, ½ teaspoon pepper, water, and lime juice in a large Dutch oven (the liquid should just barely cover the meat). Juice the orange into a medium bowl and remove any seeds (you should have about ⅓ cup juice). Add the juice and spent orange halves to the pot. Bring the mixture to a simmer over medium-high heat, stirring occasionally. Cover the pot and transfer it to the oven; cook until the meat is soft and falls apart when prodded with a fork, about 2 hours, flipping the pieces of meat once during cooking.

2. Remove the pot from the oven and turn the oven to broil. Using a slotted spoon, transfer the pork to a bowl; remove the orange halves, onion, and bay leaves from the cooking liquid and discard (do not skim the fat from the liquid). Place the pot over high heat (use caution, as the handles will be very hot) and simmer the liquid, stirring frequently, until thick and syrupy (a heatproof spatula should leave a wide trail when dragged through the glaze), 8 to 12 minutes. You should have about 1 cup reduced liquid.

3. Using two forks, pull each piece of pork in half. Fold in the reduced liquid; season with salt and pepper to taste. Spread the pork in an even layer on a wire rack set over a rimmed baking sheet or on a broiler pan (the meat should cover almost the entire surface of the rack or broiler pan). Place the baking sheet on the lower-middle oven rack and broil until the top of the meat is well browned (but not charred) and the edges are slightly crisp, 5 to 8 minutes. Using a wide metal spatula, flip the pieces of meat and continue to broil until the top is well browned and the edges are slightly crisp, 5 to 8 minutes longer. Serve immediately with the warm tortillas and garnishes.

MEXICAN RICE

WHY THIS RECIPE WORKS: Rice cooked the Mexican way is a flavorful pilaf-style dish, but we've had our share of soupy, greasy, or just plain bland versions. We wanted tender rice infused with well-balanced fresh flavor.

Texture proved to be the backbone of this dish. To keep the rice grains distinct, we found it important to rinse the rice of excess starch before cooking it. And sautéing the rice in vegetable oil before adding the cooking liquid produced superior grains. The best texture for the rice was achieved by properly balancing the grain-to-liquid ratio. We found that equal portions of chicken broth and fresh tomatoes were ideal for a flavorful liquid base, which we combined in a 2:1 ratio with the rice. To further guarantee the right flavor, color, and texture, we added a little tomato paste and stirred the rice midway through cooking to reincorporate the tomato mixture. The garlic and jalapeños, meanwhile, fared best sautéed and then combined with a raw puree of tomato and onion. More than a garnish, fresh cilantro, minced jalapeño, and squirt of fresh lime juice complemented the richer tones of the cooked tomatoes, garlic, and onions. Our rice was neither greasy nor soggy, and the fresh flavors and easy preparation made it a unique side dish for a weeknight dinner.

Mexican Rice

SERVES 6 TO 8

Because the spiciness of jalapeños varies from chile to chile, we try to control the heat by removing the ribs and seeds (the source of most of the heat) from those chiles that are cooked into the rice. It is important to use an ovensafe pot about 12 inches in diameter so that the rice cooks evenly and in the time indicated. The pot's depth is less important than its diameter; we've successfully used both a straight-sided sauté pan and a Dutch oven. Whichever type of pot you use, it should have a tight-fitting, ovensafe lid. Vegetable broth can be substituted for the chicken broth.

- 2 medium ripe tomatoes (about 12 ounces), cored and quartered
- 1 medium onion, preferably white, peeled and quartered
- 3 medium jalapeño chiles (see note)
- 2 cups long-grain white rice
- ⅓ cup vegetable oil
- 4 medium garlic cloves, minced or pressed through a garlic press (about 4 teaspoons)
- 2 cups low-sodium chicken broth (see note)
- 1 tablespoon tomato paste
- 1½ teaspoons table salt
- ½ cup minced fresh cilantro leaves
  Lime wedges, for serving

1. Adjust an oven rack to the middle position and heat the oven to 350 degrees. Process the tomatoes and onion in a food processor until smooth and thoroughly pureed, about 15 seconds, scraping down the bowl if necessary. Transfer the mixture to a liquid measuring cup; you should have 2 cups (if necessary, spoon off the excess so that the volume equals 2 cups). Remove the ribs and seeds from 2 of the jalapeños and discard; mince the flesh and set aside. Mince the remaining jalapeño, including the ribs and seeds; set aside.

2. Place the rice in a large fine-mesh strainer and rinse under cold running water until the water runs clear, about 1½ minutes. Shake the rice vigorously in the strainer to remove all excess water.

3. Heat the oil in a heavy-bottomed straight-sided 12-inch ovenproof sauté pan or Dutch oven with a tight-fitting lid over medium-high heat for 1 to 2 minutes. Drop 3 or 4 grains of rice into the oil; if the grains sizzle, the oil is ready. Add the rice and fry, stirring frequently, until the rice is light golden and translucent, 6 to 8 minutes. Reduce the heat to medium, add the garlic and seeded minced jalapeños, and cook, stirring constantly, until fragrant, about 1½ minutes. Stir in the pureed tomato mixture, chicken broth, tomato paste, and salt. Increase the heat to medium-high and bring to a boil. Cover the pan and transfer to the oven. Bake until the liquid is absorbed and the rice is tender, 30 to 35 minutes, stirring well after 15 minutes.

4. Stir in the cilantro and reserved minced jalapeño with seeds to taste. Serve immediately, passing the lime wedges separately.

BEST VEGETARIAN CHILI

WHY THIS RECIPE WORKS: Vegetarian chilis are often little more than a mishmash of beans and vegetables. To create a robust, complex-flavored chili—not just a bean and vegetable stew—we found replacements for the different ways in which meat adds depth and savory flavor to chili. Walnuts, soy sauce, dried shiitake mushrooms, and tomatoes added hearty savoriness. Bulgur filled out the chili, giving it a substantial texture. The added oil and nuts lent a richness to the chili, for full, lingering flavor.

Best Vegetarian Chili

SERVES 6 TO 8

We prefer to use whole dried chiles, but the chili can be prepared with jarred chili powder. If using chili powder, grind the shiitakes and oregano and add them to the pot with ¼ cup of chili powder in step 4. Pinto, black, red kidney, small red, cannellini, or navy beans can be used in this recipe, either a single variety or a combination of beans. For a spicier chili use both jalapeños. Serve with diced avocado, chopped red onion, lime wedges, sour cream, and shredded Monterey Jack or cheddar cheese.

Salt
1 pound (2½ cups) dried beans, rinsed and picked over
2 dried ancho chiles
2 dried New Mexican chiles
½ ounce shiitake mushrooms, chopped coarse
4 teaspoons dried oregano
½ cup walnuts, toasted
1 (28-ounce) can diced tomatoes, drained with juice reserved
3 tablespoons tomato paste
1-2 jalapeño chiles, stemmed and chopped coarse
6 garlic cloves, minced
3 tablespoons soy sauce
¼ cup vegetable oil
2 pounds onions, chopped fine
1 tablespoon ground cumin
7 cups water
⅔ cup medium-grain bulgur
¼ cup chopped fresh cilantro

1. Bring 4 quarts water, 3 tablespoons salt, and beans to boil in Dutch oven over high heat. Remove pot from heat, cover, and let stand for 1 hour. Drain beans and rinse well.

2. Adjust oven rack to middle position and heat oven to 300 degrees. Arrange ancho and New Mexican chiles on rimmed baking sheet and toast until fragrant and puffed, about 8 minutes. Transfer to plate and let cool, about 5 minutes. Stem and seed toasted chiles. Working in batches, grind toasted chiles, shiitakes, and oregano in spice grinder or with mortar and pestle until finely ground.

3. Process walnuts in food processor until finely ground, about 30 seconds. Transfer to bowl. Process drained tomatoes, tomato paste, jalapeño(s), garlic, and soy sauce in food processor until tomatoes are finely chopped, about 45 seconds, scraping down bowl as needed.

4. Heat oil in Dutch oven over medium-high heat until shimmering. Add onions and 1¼ teaspoons salt; cook, stirring occasionally until onions begin to brown, 8 to 10 minutes. Lower heat to medium, add ground chile mixture and cumin, and cook, stirring constantly, until fragrant, about 1 minute. Add rinsed beans and water and bring to boil. Cover pot, transfer to oven, and cook for 45 minutes.

5. Remove pot from oven. Stir in bulgur, ground walnuts, tomato mixture, and reserved tomato juice. Return to oven and cook until beans are fully tender, about 2 hours.

6. Remove pot from oven, stir chili well, and let stand, uncovered, for 20 minutes. Stir in cilantro and serve. (Chili can be made up to 3 days in advance.)

BASIC CHILI

WHY THIS RECIPE WORKS: Many basic chili recipes yield a pot of under-spiced, under-flavored chili reminiscent of sloppy Joes. We wanted an easy recipe for a basic chili, made with supermarket staples, that would have some heat and great flavors—chili that would please almost everyone.

To start, we added the spices to the pan with the aromatics (bell peppers, onion, and lots of garlic) to get the most flavor, and used commercial chili powder with a boost from more cumin, oregano, cayenne, and coriander. For the meat, we found that 85 percent lean beef gave us full flavor. A combination of diced tomato and tomato puree gave our chili a well-balanced saucy backbone. We added quick-cooking canned red kidney beans with the tomatoes so that they heated through and absorbed flavor. For a rich, thick consistency, we cooked the chili with the lid on for half of the cooking time.

Beef Chili with Kidney Beans

SERVES 8 TO 10

Good choices for condiments include diced fresh tomatoes, diced avocado, sliced scallions, chopped red onion, chopped cilantro leaves, sour cream, and shredded Monterey Jack or cheddar cheese. If you are a fan of spicy food, consider using a little more of the red pepper flakes or cayenne—or both. The flavor of the chili improves with age; if possible, make it a day or up to 3 days in advance and reheat before serving. Leftovers can be frozen for up to 1 month.

2 tablespoons vegetable oil
2 medium onions, minced (about 2 cups)
1 medium red bell pepper, stemmed, seeded, and cut into ½-inch dice
6 medium garlic cloves, minced or pressed through a garlic press (about 2 tablespoons)
¼ cup chili powder
1 tablespoon ground cumin
2 teaspoons ground coriander
1 teaspoon red pepper flakes (see note)
1 teaspoon dried oregano
½ teaspoon cayenne pepper (see note)
2 pounds 85 percent lean ground beef
2 (15-ounce) cans dark red kidney beans, drained and rinsed
1 (28-ounce) can diced tomatoes
1 (28-ounce) can tomato puree
  Table salt
  Lime wedges, for serving

1. Heat the oil in a large heavy-bottomed nonreactive Dutch oven over medium heat until shimmering but not smoking. Add the onions, bell pepper, garlic, chili powder, cumin, coriander, red pepper flakes, oregano, and cayenne and cook, stirring occasionally, until the vegetables are softened and beginning to brown, about 10 minutes. Increase the heat to medium-high and add half of the beef. Cook, breaking up the pieces with a wooden spoon, until no longer pink and just beginning to brown, 3 to 4 minutes. Add the remaining beef and cook, breaking up the pieces with a wooden spoon, until no longer pink, 3 to 4 minutes.

2. Add the beans, tomatoes with juice, tomato puree, and ½ teaspoon salt. Bring to a boil, then reduce the heat to low and simmer, covered, stirring occasionally, for 1 hour. Remove the lid and continue to simmer for 1 hour longer, stirring occasionally (if the chili begins to stick to the bottom of the pot, stir in ½ cup water and continue to simmer), until the beef is tender and the chili is dark, rich, and slightly thickened. Season with salt to taste. Serve with the lime wedges and condiments (see note), if desired.

CHILI CON CARNE

WHY THIS RECIPE WORKS: Real Texas chili, made with dried chiles rather than chili powder, should have exceptional chile flavor but not overpowering heat, a smooth, rich sauce, and hearty chunks of meat. We wanted to develop the ultimate version. There are many types of dried chiles, and we chose a combination of ancho and New Mexican for a combination of earthy, fruity sweetness and crisp acidity. We got the best flavor by toasting and grinding chiles ourselves. Chuck-eye is our favored cut of beef for stews and it seemed right for our chili. We cut the meat into 1-inch chunks, which gave the chili a hearty texture. Then, we browned the meat in fat rendered from bacon, which added a smoky depth to the dish. From among the many recommended liquids to use in chili con carne, we chose plain old water—everything else diluted or competed with the flavor of the chiles. Although many "authentic" recipes include neither tomatoes nor onions, we found both to be valuable additions. To thicken the chili, we mixed in some masa harina, which also imparted a subtle corn flavor.

Chili con Carne

SERVES 6

To ensure the best chile flavor, we recommend toasting whole dried chiles and grinding them in a minichopper or spice-dedicated coffee grinder, all of which takes only 10 (very well-spent) minutes. Select dried chiles that are moist and pliant, like dried fruit. To toast and grind dried chiles: Place the chiles on a baking sheet in a 350-degree oven until fragrant and puffed, about 6 minutes. Cool, stem, and seed the pods, and tear them into pieces. Place pieces of the pods in a spice grinder and process until powdery, 30 to 45 seconds. For hotter chili, boost the heat with a pinch of cayenne pepper or a dash of hot sauce. Top with any of the following garnishes: chopped fresh cilantro leaves, minced white onion, diced avocado, shredded cheddar or Jack cheese, or sour cream.

3 medium ancho pods (about ½ ounce), toasted
   and ground (see note), or 3 tablespoons ancho
   chile powder

3 medium New Mexican pods (about ¾ ounce),
   toasted and ground (see note), or 3 tablespoons
   New Mexican chile powder

2 tablespoons cumin seeds, toasted in a dry skillet
   over medium heat until fragrant, about 4 minutes,
   and ground

2 teaspoons dried oregano, preferably Mexican

7½ cups water, plus extra for the masa
   harina or cornstarch

4 pounds beef chuck-eye roast, trimmed of
   excess fat and cut into 1-inch cubes
   Table salt

8 ounces bacon (about 8 slices), cut into ¼-inch pieces

1 medium onion, minced

5 medium garlic cloves, minced or pressed through
   a garlic press (about 5 teaspoons)

4–5 small jalapeño chiles, stemmed, seeded, and minced

1 cup canned crushed tomatoes or plain tomato sauce

2 tablespoons juice from 1 lime

5 tablespoons masa harina or 3 tablespoons cornstarch
   Ground black pepper

1. Mix the chili powders, cumin, and oregano in a small bowl and stir in ½ cup of the water to form a thick paste; set aside. Toss the beef cubes with 2 teaspoons salt in a large bowl; set aside.

2. Fry the bacon in a large Dutch oven over medium-low heat until the fat renders and the bacon crisps, about 10 minutes. Remove the bacon with a slotted spoon to a paper towel–lined plate; pour all but 2 teaspoons fat from the pot into a small bowl; set aside. Increase the heat to medium-high; sauté the meat in four batches until well browned on all sides, about 5 minutes per batch, adding 2 teaspoons more bacon fat to the pot each time as necessary. Set the browned meat aside in a large bowl.

3. Reduce the heat to medium and add 3 tablespoons more bacon fat to the now-empty pan. Add the onion and sauté until softened, 5 to 6 minutes. Add the garlic and jalapeños and sauté until fragrant, about 1 minute. Add the chili powder mixture and sauté until fragrant, 2 to 3 minutes. Add the reserved bacon and browned beef, the remaining 7 cups water, the crushed tomatoes, and lime juice. Bring to a simmer. Continue to cook at a steady simmer (lowering the heat as necessary) until the meat is tender and the juices are dark and rich and starting to thicken, about 2 hours.

4. Mix the masa harina with ⅔ cup water (or cornstarch with 3 tablespoons water) in a small bowl to form a smooth paste. Increase the heat to medium, stir in the paste, and simmer until thickened, 5 to 10 minutes. Season generously with salt and pepper to taste. Serve immediately or, for best flavor, cool slightly, cover, and refrigerate overnight or for up to 5 days. Reheat before serving.

WHITE CHICKEN CHILI

WHY THIS RECIPE WORKS: Chili made with chicken has become popular as a lighter, fresher alternative to the red kind. Though many recipes produce something more akin to chicken and bean soup, we thought there was potential to develop a rich stew-like chili with moist chicken, tender beans, and a complex flavor profile.

Ground chicken had a spongy texture and crumbly appearance, so we chose bone-in, skin-on breasts, later shredding the meat and discarding the skin and bones, and used the fat rendered from searing them to cook the aromatics. A single type of chile was one-dimensional; we used a combination of jalapeño, Anaheim, and poblano chiles, which have distinct characteristics that complemented one another. Simply sautéing the chiles with the other aromatics left them flat-tasting and too crisp, so we covered the pot and cooked them longer to soften them and deepen their flavors. Canned cannellini beans circumvented the hassle of dried beans and tasted just as good. We tried thickening the chili with masa harina, which we had used as a thickener in other chili recipes, but the texture and flavor didn't work well here. Instead, we pureed some of the chili mixture, beans, and broth, which made the chili thicker without compromising its flavor. To finish, a minced raw jalapeño stirred in before serving provided a shot of fresh chile flavor.

White Chicken Chili

SERVES 6 TO 8

Adjust the heat in this dish by adding the minced ribs and seeds from the jalapeño as directed in step 6. If Anaheim chiles cannot be found, add an additional poblano and jalapeño to the chili. This dish can also be successfully made by substituting chicken thighs for the chicken breasts. If using thighs, increase the cooking time in step 4 to about 40 minutes or

until the chicken registers 175 degrees on an instant-read thermometer. Serve the chili with sour cream, tortilla chips, and lime wedges.

3 pounds bone-in, skin-on chicken breast halves, trimmed
  Table salt and ground black pepper
1 tablespoon vegetable oil
3 medium jalapeño chiles (see note)
3 medium poblano chiles (see note), stemmed, seeded, and cut into large pieces
3 medium Anaheim chiles (see note), stemmed, seeded, and cut into large pieces
2 medium onions, cut into large pieces (about 2 cups)
6 medium garlic cloves, minced or pressed through a garlic press (about 2 tablespoons)
1 tablespoon ground cumin
1½ teaspoons ground coriander
2 (15-ounce) cans cannellini beans, drained and rinsed
3 cups low-sodium chicken broth
¼ cup minced fresh cilantro leaves
3 tablespoons juice from 2 limes
4 scallions, white and light green parts sliced thin

1. Season the chicken liberally with salt and pepper. Heat the oil in a large Dutch oven over medium-high heat until just smoking. Add the chicken, skin side down, and cook without moving until the skin is golden brown, about 4 minutes. Using tongs, turn the chicken and lightly brown the other side, about 2 minutes. Transfer the chicken to a plate; remove and discard the skin.

2. While the chicken is browning, remove and discard the ribs and seeds from 2 of the jalapeños; mince the flesh. In a food processor, pulse half of the poblanos, Anaheims, and onions until the consistency of chunky salsa, 10 to 12 pulses, scraping down the sides of the workbowl halfway through. Transfer the mixture to a medium bowl. Repeat with the remaining poblanos, Anaheims, and onions; combine with the first batch (do not wash the food processor blade or workbowl).

3. Pour off all but 1 tablespoon of the fat from the Dutch oven (adding more vegetable oil if necessary) and reduce the heat to medium. Add the minced jalapeños, chile-onion mixture, garlic, cumin, coriander, and ¼ teaspoon salt. Cover and cook, stirring occasionally, until the vegetables soften, about 10 minutes. Remove the pot from the heat.

4. Transfer 1 cup of the cooked vegetable mixture to the now-empty food processor workbowl. Add 1 cup of the beans and 1 cup of the broth and process until smooth, about 20 seconds. Add the vegetable-bean mixture, remaining 2 cups broth, and chicken breasts to the Dutch oven and bring to a boil over medium-high heat. Reduce the heat to medium-low and simmer, covered, stirring occasionally, until the chicken registers 160 degrees (175 degrees if using thighs) on an instant-read thermometer, 15 to 20 minutes (40 minutes if using thighs).

5. Using tongs, transfer the chicken to a large plate. Stir in the remaining beans and continue to simmer, uncovered, until the beans are heated through and the chili has thickened slightly, about 10 minutes.

6. Mince the remaining jalapeño, reserving and mincing the ribs and seeds (see note), and set aside. When cool enough to handle, shred the chicken into bite-size pieces, discarding the bones. Stir the shredded chicken, cilantro, lime juice, scallions, and minced jalapeño (with seeds if desired) into the chili and return to a simmer. Season with salt and pepper to taste and serve.

HUEVOS RANCHEROS

WHY THIS RECIPE WORKS: This Mexican egg dish was devised to use up leftover salsa and tortillas for a quick but filling "rancher-style" breakfast. What you get on this side of the border, however, is often spoiled with unnecessary ingredients and muddy flavors. We wanted to use readily available ingredients to produce as authentic a version of this dish as we could.

The salsa is a crucial element, and we know from experience that jarred salsa can't compare to freshly made, so we looked for ways to maximize the flavor of our supermarket tomatoes.

We found that roasting plum tomatoes turned them more flavorful, and we thought roasting the onion and jalapeños improved their flavor as well. It was difficult to get fried eggs from the skillet onto the tortillas neatly (and without breaking the yolks), so we turned to poaching the eggs for a tidier presentation. We made things even easier by poaching them right in the simmering salsa, saving ourselves a pot to clean in the bargain. To pep up the supermarket tortillas, we brushed them with a little oil, sprinkled them with salt, and toasted them in the oven. Crisp tortillas, creamy eggs, and fiery salsa combined for a great American version of this Mexican classic.

Huevos Rancheros

SERVES 2 TO 4

To save time, make the salsa the day before and store it in the refrigerator. If you like, serve with Refried Beans (recipe follows).

- 3 jalapeño chiles, halved, seeds and ribs removed
- 1½ pounds ripe plum tomatoes (about 6 medium), cored and halved
- ½ medium onion, cut into ½-inch wedges
- 3 tablespoons vegetable oil
- 1 tablespoon tomato paste
- 2 medium garlic cloves, peeled
  Table salt
- ½ teaspoon ground cumin
- ⅛ teaspoon cayenne pepper
- 3 tablespoons minced fresh cilantro leaves
  Ground black pepper
- 1-2 tablespoons juice from 1 lime, plus an additional lime cut into wedges, for serving
- 4 (6-inch) corn tortillas
- 4 large eggs

1. Adjust an oven rack to the middle position and heat the oven to 375 degrees. Mince 1 jalapeño and set aside. In a medium bowl, combine the tomatoes, remaining 2 jalapeños, onion, 2 tablespoons of the oil, the tomato paste, garlic, 1 teaspoon salt, cumin, and cayenne; toss to mix thoroughly. Place the vegetables, cut side down, on a rimmed baking sheet. Roast until the tomatoes are tender and the skins begin to shrivel and brown, 35 to 45 minutes; cool on the baking sheet for 10 minutes. Increase the oven temperature to 450 degrees. Using tongs, transfer the roasted onion, garlic, and jalapeños to a food processor. Process until almost completely broken down, about 10 seconds, pausing halfway through to scrape down the sides of the workbowl with a rubber spatula. Add the tomatoes and process until the salsa is slightly chunky, about 15 seconds more. Add 2 tablespoons of the cilantro, and the reserved minced jalapeño, salt, pepper, and lime juice to taste.

2. Brush both sides of each tortilla lightly with the remaining 1 tablespoon oil, sprinkle both sides with salt, and place on a clean baking sheet. Bake until the tops just begin to color, 5 to 7 minutes; flip the tortillas and continue to bake until golden brown, 2 to 3 minutes more.

3. Meanwhile, bring the salsa to a gentle simmer in a 12-inch nonstick skillet over medium heat. Remove from the heat and make four shallow wells in the salsa with the back of a large spoon. Break 1 egg into a cup, then carefully pour the egg into a well in the salsa; repeat with the remaining 3 eggs. Season each egg with salt and pepper, then cover the skillet and place over medium-low heat. Cook to the desired doneness: 4 to 5 minutes for runny yolks, 6 to 7 minutes for set yolks.

4. Place the tortillas on serving plates; gently scoop one egg onto each tortilla. Spoon the salsa around each egg, covering the tortillas but leaving a portion of the eggs exposed. Sprinkle with the remaining 1 tablespoon cilantro and serve with the lime wedges.

Refried Beans

MAKES ABOUT 3 CUPS

- 2 (15-ounce) cans pinto beans, drained and rinsed
- ¾ cup low-sodium chicken broth
- ½ teaspoon table salt
- 3 ounces (about 3 slices) bacon, minced
- 1 small onion, minced (about ¾ cup)
- 1 large jalapeño chile, stemmed, seeded, and minced (about 2 tablespoons)
- ½ teaspoon ground cumin
- 2 medium garlic cloves, minced or pressed through a garlic press (about 2 teaspoons)
- 2 tablespoons minced fresh cilantro leaves
- 2 teaspoons juice from 1 lime

1. Process all but 1 cup of the beans, the broth, and salt in a food processor until smooth, about 15 seconds, scraping down the sides of the workbowl with a rubber spatula if necessary. Add the remaining beans and pulse until slightly chunky, about 10 pulses.

2. Cook the bacon in a 12-inch nonstick skillet over medium heat until the bacon just begins to brown and most of the fat has rendered, about 4 minutes; transfer to a small bowl lined with a strainer; discard the bacon and add 1 tablespoon bacon fat back to the skillet. Increase the heat to medium-high, add the onion, jalapeño, and cumin, and cook until softened and just starting to brown, 3 to 5 minutes. Stir in the garlic and cook until fragrant, about 30 seconds. Reduce the heat to medium, stir in the pureed beans, and cook until thick and creamy, 4 to 6 minutes. Off the heat, stir in the cilantro and lime juice and serve.

LET'S DO TAKEOUT

CHINESE-STYLE CUCUMBER SALAD

WHY THIS RECIPE WORKS: Smashed cucumbers, or *pai huang gua*, is a Sichuan dish that is typically served with rich, spicy food. We started with English cucumbers, which are nearly seedless and have a thin, crisp skin. Placing them in a zipper-lock bag and smashing them into large, irregular pieces sped up a salting step that helped to expel excess water. The craggy pieces also did a better job of holding on to the dressing. Using black vinegar, an aged rice-based vinegar, added a mellow complexity to the soy and sesame dressing.

Smashed Cucumbers (Pai Huang Gua)
SERVES 4

We recommend using Chinese Chinkiang (or Zhenjiang) black vinegar in this dish because of its complex flavor. If you can't find it, you can substitute 2 teaspoons of rice vinegar and 1 teaspoon of balsamic vinegar. A rasp-style grater makes quick work of turning the garlic into a paste.

> 2 English cucumbers (about 14 ounces each)
> 1½ teaspoons kosher salt
> 4 teaspoons Chinese black vinegar
> 1 teaspoon garlic, minced to paste
> 1 tablespoon soy sauce
> 2 teaspoons toasted sesame oil
> 1 teaspoon sugar
> 1 teaspoon sesame seeds, toasted

1. Trim and discard ends from cucumbers. Cut cucumbers crosswise into three equal lengths. Place pieces in large zipper-lock bag and seal bag. Using small skillet or rolling pin, firmly but gently smash cucumbers until flattened and split lengthwise into 3 to 4 spears. Tear spears into rough 1- to 1½-inch pieces and transfer to colander set in large bowl. Toss pieces with salt and let stand for at least 15 minutes or up to 30 minutes.

2. While cucumber sits, whisk vinegar and garlic together in small bowl; let stand at least 5 minutes or up to 15 minutes.

3. Whisk soy sauce, sesame oil, and sugar into vinegar mixture until sugar has dissolved. Transfer cucumber pieces to medium bowl and discard any extracted liquid. Add dressing and sesame seeds to cucumbers and toss to combine. Serve immediately.

SCALLION PANCAKES

WHY THIS RECIPE WORKS: Scallion pancakes at Chinese restaurants tend to disappoint, so we wondered if we could end up with something better by making our own. The best scallion pancakes are crispy and browned on the outside and multilayered and delicately chewy inside. We opted for a boiling-water dough that stretched easily but did not spring back. To form alternating layers of dough and fat, we rolled the dough into a large, thin round; brushed it with a mixture of oil and flour; and sprinkled it with salt and scallions before rolling it into a cylinder. We coiled the cylinder into a spiral and then rolled it out into a round again. Making a small slit in the center of the pancake prevented steam from building up, so it laid flat and cooked evenly. A stir-together sauce complemented the richness of the pancakes.

Scallion Pancakes with Dipping Sauce
SERVES 4 TO 6

For this recipe we prefer the steady, even heat of a cast-iron skillet. A heavy stainless-steel skillet may be used, but you may have to increase the heat slightly. To make the pancakes ahead of time, stack the uncooked pancakes between layers of parchment paper, wrap them tightly in plastic wrap, and refrigerate for up to 24 hours or freeze for up to 1 month. If frozen, thaw the pancakes in a single layer for 15 minutes before cooking. These pancakes may be served as a side dish or appetizer.

DIPPING SAUCE

> 2 tablespoons soy sauce
> 1 scallion, sliced thin
> 1 tablespoon water
> 2 teaspoons rice vinegar
> 1 teaspoon honey
> 1 teaspoon toasted sesame oil
> Pinch red pepper flakes

PANCAKES

> 1½ cups (7½ ounces) plus 1 tablespoon all-purpose flour
> ¾ cup boiling water
> 7 tablespoons vegetable oil
> 1 tablespoon toasted sesame oil
> 1 teaspoon kosher salt
> 4 scallions, sliced thin

1. FOR THE DIPPING SAUCE: Whisk all ingredients together in small bowl; set aside.

2. FOR THE PANCAKES: Using wooden spoon, mix 1½ cups flour and boiling water in bowl to form rough dough. When cool enough to handle, transfer dough to lightly floured counter and knead until tacky (but not sticky) ball forms, about 4 minutes (dough will not be perfectly smooth). Cover loosely with plastic wrap and let rest for 30 minutes.

3. While dough is resting, stir together 1 tablespoon vegetable oil, sesame oil, and remaining 1 tablespoon flour. Set aside.

4. Place 10-inch cast-iron skillet over low heat to preheat. Divide dough in half. Cover one half of dough with plastic wrap and set aside. Roll remaining dough into 12-inch round on lightly floured counter. Drizzle with 1 tablespoon oil-flour mixture and use pastry brush to spread evenly over entire surface. Sprinkle with ½ teaspoon salt and half of scallions. Roll dough into cylinder. Coil cylinder into spiral, tuck end underneath, and flatten spiral with your palm. Cover with plastic and repeat with remaining dough, oil-flour mixture, salt, and scallions.

5. Roll first spiral into 9-inch round. Cut ½-inch slit in center of pancake. Place 2 tablespoons vegetable oil in skillet and increase heat to medium-low. Place one pancake in skillet (oil should sizzle). Cover and cook, shaking skillet occasionally, until pancake is slightly puffy and golden brown on underside, 1 to 1½ minutes. (If underside is not browned after 1 minute, turn heat up slightly. If it is browning too quickly, turn heat down slightly.) Drizzle 1 tablespoon vegetable oil over pancake. Use pastry brush to distribute over entire surface. Carefully flip pancake. Cover and cook, shaking skillet occasionally, until second side is golden brown, 1 to 1½ minutes. Uncover skillet and continue to cook until bottom is deep golden brown and crispy, 30 to 60 seconds longer. Flip and cook until deep golden brown and crispy, 30 to 60 seconds. Transfer to wire rack. Repeat with remaining 3 tablespoons vegetable oil and remaining pancake. Cut each pancake into 8 wedges and serve, passing dipping sauce separately.

NOTES FROM THE TEST KITCHEN

MAKING SCALLION PANCAKES

1. Roll dough into 12-inch round.

2. Brush round with oil and flour; sprinkle with salt and scallions.

3. Roll up round into cylinder.

4. Coil cylinder, tucking end underneath, then flatten.

5. Roll out flattened spiral into 9-inch round; cut slit.

PERFECT POTSTICKERS

WHY THIS RECIPE WORKS: Too often, potstickers are dense, flavorless meatballs wrapped in a doughy blanket. We wanted soft, savory pillows filled with tender ground meat and crunchy cabbage and spiked with a pleasing hit of garlic, ginger, and soy. And we weren't willing to make wrappers from scratch. To lighten up the filling a bit, we increased the amount of cabbage, after first salting and draining it to get rid of excess moisture, and then added lightly beaten egg whites. For the wrappers, we found that store-bought gyoza-style wrappers and wonton wrappers both made terrific potstickers, although tasters preferred the slightly chewy texture of the gyoza-style. To keep the filling in place and the wrapper from puffing up and away from the meat during cooking, we found it best to fold each meat-filled wrapper into a half-moon, pinch the middle closed, then carefully press out any air while sealing the edges. Our final challenge was the cooking method. A sequence of browning, steaming, then cranking up the heat produced potstickers with a perfect balance of soft and crispy textures.

Potstickers with Scallion Dipping Sauce

MAKES 24 DUMPLINGS

We prefer to use gyoza wrappers. You can substitute wonton wrappers, but the cooking time and recipe yield will vary. Potstickers are best served hot from the skillet; we recommend that you serve the first batch immediately, then cook the second batch.

SCALLION DIPPING SAUCE

- ¼ cup soy sauce
- 2 tablespoons rice vinegar
- 2 tablespoons mirin or sweet sherry
- 2 tablespoons water
- 1 teaspoon chili oil (optional)
- ½ teaspoon toasted sesame oil
- 1 scallion, minced

NOTES FROM THE TEST KITCHEN

WRAPPING POTSTICKERS

The instructions below are for round wrappers, our preferred shape. If using square wrappers, fold diagonally into a triangle (step 2) and proceed with the recipe. For rectangular wrappers, fold in half lengthwise.

1. Place a rounded tablespoon of the filling in the center of each gyoza wrapper.

2. After moistening the edge of the wrapper, fold it in half to make a half-moon shape.

3. With your forefinger and thumb, pinch the dumpling closed, pressing out any air pockets.

4. Place the dumpling on its side and press gently to flatten the bottom.

POTSTICKERS

- 12 ounces napa cabbage (½ medium head), cored and minced
- ¾ teaspoon table salt
- 12 ounces ground pork
- 4 scallions, minced
- 2 large egg whites, lightly beaten
- 4 teaspoons soy sauce
- 1½ teaspoons minced or grated fresh ginger
- 1 medium garlic clove, minced or pressed through a garlic press (about 1 teaspoon)
- ⅛ teaspoon ground black pepper
- 24 round gyoza wrappers (see note)
- 4 teaspoons peanut or vegetable oil

1. **FOR THE SAUCE:** Combine all the ingredients in a small bowl and set aside. (The sauce can be refrigerated in an airtight container for up to 24 hours.)

2. **FOR THE FILLING:** Toss the cabbage and salt together in a colander set over a bowl and let sit until the cabbage begins to wilt, about 20 minutes. Press the cabbage gently with a rubber spatula to squeeze out excess moisture, then transfer to a medium bowl. Stir the pork, scallions, egg whites, soy sauce, ginger, garlic, and pepper into the cabbage until combined. Cover and refrigerate until the mixture is cold, at least 30 minutes or up to 24 hours.

3. Working with 4 wrappers at a time (keep the remaining wrappers covered with plastic wrap), follow the photos on page 442 to fill, seal, and shape the dumplings using a generous 1 tablespoon of the chilled filling per dumpling. Transfer the dumplings to a baking sheet. (The filled dumplings can be refrigerated for up to 24 hours in a single layer on a baking sheet wrapped tightly with plastic wrap or frozen for up to 1 month. Once frozen, the dumplings can be transferred to a zipper-lock bag to save space in the freezer; do not thaw before cooking.)

4. Brush 2 teaspoons of the peanut oil over the bottom of a 12-inch nonstick skillet and arrange half of the dumplings in the skillet, with a flat side facing down (overlapping just slightly, if necessary). Place the skillet over medium-high heat and cook the dumplings, without moving, until golden brown on the bottom, about 5 minutes.

5. Reduce the heat to low, add ½ cup water, and cover immediately. Cook until most of the water is absorbed and the wrappers are slightly translucent, about 10 minutes. Uncover, increase the heat to medium-high, and cook, without stirring, until the dumpling bottoms are well browned and crisp, 3 to 4 minutes. Slide the dumplings from the skillet onto a paper towel–lined plate, browned side down, and let drain briefly.

6. Transfer the dumplings to a platter and serve with the sauce. Let the skillet cool until just warm, then wipe out the skillet with a wad of paper towels and repeat with the remaining peanut oil and dumplings.

SHU MAI

WHY THIS RECIPE WORKS: Every so often we'll land on an exemplary version of shu mai (steamed Chinese dumplings)—one that boasts a tender, thin skin and a moist, flavorful filling. Our goal was to replicate this version at home. Our favorite restaurant dumplings rely on coarse-ground pork and shrimp. To ensure proper flavor and texture, we chose to chop the pork (boneless country-style spareribs) in a food processor rather than relying on supermarket ground pork which is often inconsistent. To prevent the meat from drying out during steaming, we mixed in a little powdered gelatin dissolved in soy sauce. As for the shrimp, we added that to the food processor, too. Dried shiitake mushrooms, minced cilantro, fresh ginger, and water chestnuts were just a few of the ingredients we relied on to round out our flavorful filling. We chose widely available egg roll skins and cut them into rounds with a biscuit cutter.

Once we added the filling and gathered the edges of the wrappers up around each one, we steamed our dumplings in a steamer basket. Served with a hot chili sauce, our dumplings were full-flavored and virtually foolproof.

Steamed Chinese Dumplings (Shu Mai)

MAKES ABOUT 40 DUMPLINGS

Do not trim the excess fat from the spareribs, as the fat contributes flavor and moistness. Use any size shrimp except popcorn shrimp; there's no need to halve shrimp smaller than 26 to 30 per pound before processing. The dumplings may be frozen for up to 3 months; cook straight from the freezer for about an extra 5 minutes. Shu mai are traditionally served with a spicy chili oil (recipe follows), or use store-bought.

    2   tablespoons soy sauce
    ½   teaspoon unflavored powdered gelatin
    1   pound boneless country-style pork spareribs,
        cut into 1-inch pieces (see note)
    ½   pound shrimp, peeled, deveined (see page 240),
        tails removed, and halved lengthwise (see note)
    ¼   cup chopped water chestnuts
    4   dried shiitake mushroom caps (about ¾ ounce),
        soaked in hot water for 30 minutes, squeezed dry,
        and cut into ¼-inch dice
    2   tablespoons cornstarch
    2   tablespoons minced fresh cilantro leaves
    1   tablespoon toasted sesame oil
    1   tablespoon dry sherry or Chinese rice cooking wine
        (Shaoxing)
    1   tablespoon rice wine vinegar
    2   teaspoons sugar
    2   teaspoons grated fresh ginger
    ½   teaspoon table salt
    ½   teaspoon ground black pepper
    1   (1 pound) package 5½-inch square egg roll wrappers
    ¼   cup finely grated carrot (optional)

1. Combine the soy sauce and gelatin in a small bowl. Set aside to allow the gelatin to bloom, about 5 minutes.

2. Meanwhile, place half of the pork in a food processor and pulse until coarsely ground into pieces that are about ⅛ inch, about 10 pulses; transfer to a large bowl. Add the shrimp and remaining pork to the food processor and pulse until coarsely chopped into pieces that are about ¼ inch, about 5 pulses. Transfer to the bowl with the coarsely ground pork. Stir in the soy sauce mixture, water chestnuts, mushrooms, cornstarch, cilantro, sesame oil, cooking wine, vinegar, sugar, ginger, salt, and pepper until well combined.

3. Line a large baking sheet with parchment paper. Divide the egg roll wrappers into three stacks (six to seven per stack). Using a 3-inch biscuit cutter, cut two 3-inch rounds from each stack of egg roll wrappers (you should have 40 to 42 rounds). Cover the rounds with moist paper towels to prevent drying.

4. Working with six rounds at a time, brush the edges of each round lightly with water. Place a heaping tablespoon of filling in the center of each round. Following the photos, form the dumplings by crimping the wrapper around the sides of the filling and leaving the top exposed. Transfer to the prepared baking sheet, cover with a damp kitchen towel, and repeat with the remaining wrappers and filling. Top the center of each dumpling with a pinch of grated carrot (if using).

5. Cut a piece of parchment paper slightly smaller than the diameter of a steamer basket and place in the basket. Poke about 20 small holes in the parchment to allow steam to pass through and lightly coat with vegetable oil spray. Place batches of the dumplings on the parchment, making sure they are not touching. Set the steamer basket over simmering water and cook, covered, until no longer pink, 8 to 10 minutes. Serve immediately with chili oil.

Chili Oil
MAKES ABOUT ½ CUP

- 1 tablespoon soy sauce
- 2 teaspoons sugar
- ½ teaspoon table salt
- ½ cup peanut oil
- ¼ cup red pepper flakes
- 2 medium garlic cloves, peeled

Combine the soy sauce, sugar, and salt in a small bowl; set aside. Heat the oil in a small saucepan over medium heat until just shimmering and it registers 300 degrees on an instant-read thermometer. Remove the pan from the heat and stir in the red pepper flakes, garlic, and soy mixture. Let cool to room temperature, stirring occasionally, about 1 hour. Discard the garlic before storing.

NOTES FROM THE TEST KITCHEN

FILLING AND FORMING SHU MAI

1. Brush the edges of the dumpling wrapper lightly with water. Place a heaping tablespoon of filling in the center of each wrapper.

2. Pinch two opposing sides of the wrapper with your fingers. Rotate the dumpling 90 degrees, and, again, pinch the opposing sides of the wrapper with your fingers.

3. Continue to pinch the dumpling until you have eight equidistant pinches around the circumference of the dumpling.

4. Gather up the sides of the dumpling and squeeze gently at the top to create a "waist."

5. Hold the dumpling in your hand and gently but firmly pack the filling into the dumpling with a butter knife.

SHRIMP TEMPURA

WHY THIS RECIPE WORKS: A few preliminary attempts at making tempura made us see why some Japanese chefs devote their entire careers to this one technique. Success hinges almost entirely on the batter—which is maddeningly hard to get right. We wanted a recipe for perfectly cooked shrimp tempura—light, crisp, and so fresh-tasting that it barely seemed fried.

We settled on using the largest shrimp available, since it's easy to overcook small shrimp. Instead of a wok, we substituted a large Dutch oven, the test kitchen's preferred deep-frying vessel. Cooking the tempura in 400-degree oil also helped limit grease absorption. To prevent the batter from clumping on the inside curl of the shrimp, we made two shallow cuts on the underside of its flesh. For the batter, we replaced a bit of the flour with cornstarch to improve the structure and lightness. For a super tender coating, we used a combination of seltzer and vodka instead of the traditional tap water. Seltzer is a little more acidic than tap water and therefore slows down gluten development, while the vodka prevents the formation of gluten. Our tempura was now light and crisp with the essence of sweet, tender shrimp.

Shrimp Tempura

SERVES 8

Do not omit the vodka; it is critical for a crisp coating. For safety, use a Dutch oven with a capacity of at least 7 quarts. Be sure to begin mixing the batter when the oil reaches 385 degrees (the final temperature should reach 400 degrees). It is important to maintain a high oil temperature throughout cooking. If you are unable to find colossal shrimp (8 to 12 per pound), jumbo (16 to 20 per pound) or extra-large (21 to 25 per pound) may be substituted. Fry smaller shrimp in three batches, reducing the cooking time to 1½ to 2 minutes per batch.

3 quarts peanut or vegetable oil
1½ pounds colossal shrimp (8 to 12 per pound), peeled and deveined (see page 240), tails left on (see note)
1½ cups (7½ ounces) unbleached all-purpose flour
½ cup cornstarch
1 cup vodka (see note)
1 large egg
1 cup seltzer water
   Table salt
1 recipe Scallion Dipping Sauce (page 442)

1. Adjust an oven rack to the upper-middle position and heat the oven to 200 degrees. In a large, heavy Dutch oven fitted with a clip-on candy thermometer, heat the oil over high heat to 385 degrees, 18 to 22 minutes.

2. While the oil heats, make two shallow cuts about ¼ inch deep and 1 inch apart on the underside of each shrimp. Whisk the flour and cornstarch together in a large bowl. Whisk the vodka and egg together in a second large bowl, then whisk in the seltzer water.

3. When the oil reaches 385 degrees, whisk the vodka mixture into the bowl with the flour mixture until just combined (it is OK if small lumps remain). Submerge half of the shrimp in the batter. Using tongs, remove the shrimp from the batter one at a time, allowing the excess batter to drip off, and carefully place in the oil (the temperature should now be at 400 degrees). Fry, stirring with a chopstick or wooden skewer to prevent sticking, until light brown, 2 to 3 minutes. Using a slotted spoon, transfer the shrimp to a paper towel–lined plate and sprinkle with salt. Once the paper towels absorb the excess oil, transfer the shrimp to a wire rack set over a rimmed baking sheet and place in the oven to keep warm.

4. Return the oil to 400 degrees, about 4 minutes, then repeat with the remaining shrimp. Serve with the dipping sauce.

KOREAN RICE BOWL

WHY THIS RECIPE WORKS: The comforting combination of rice, vegetables, eggs, spicy sauce, and a crisp crust in Korean rice bowls, also known as *dolsot bibimbap*, is a restaurant favorite, and we wanted an efficient way to make it at home. Unfortunately, making bibimbap requires special stone bowls, a lot of sautéing, and a lot of knife work. To make a more approachable, family-style bibimbap, we substituted one enameled cast-iron Dutch oven for a set of stone bowls. To shorten the prep time and simplify the knife work involved, we decided to make three sautéed vegetable toppings instead of the usual six or more. We also turned the pickles, sauce, and vegetables into make-ahead options. Though it's traditional to rinse the rice before steaming it, after side-by-side tests we decided that skipping the rinsing saved time and ultimately made no discernible difference to the finished dish. A quickly pickled mixture of bean sprouts and cucumbers added crisp brightness in lieu of traditional kimchi.

VEGETABLES

- ½ cup water
- 3 scallions, minced
- 3 tablespoons soy sauce
- 3 garlic cloves, minced
- 1 tablespoon sugar
- 1 tablespoon vegetable oil
- 3 carrots, peeled and shredded (2 cups)
- 8 ounces shiitake mushrooms, stemmed, caps sliced thin
- 1 (10-ounce) bag curly-leaf spinach, stemmed and chopped coarse

BIBIMBAP

- 2 tablespoons plus 2 teaspoons vegetable oil
- 1 tablespoon toasted sesame oil
- 4 large eggs

1. FOR THE PICKLES: Whisk vinegar, sugar, and salt together in medium bowl. Add cucumber and bean sprouts and toss to combine. Gently press on vegetables to submerge. Cover and refrigerate for at least 30 minutes or up to 24 hours.

2. FOR THE CHILE SAUCE: Whisk gochujang, water, oil, and sugar together in small bowl. Cover and set aside.

3. FOR THE RICE: Bring rice, water, and salt to boil in medium saucepan over high heat. Cover, reduce heat to low, and cook for 7 minutes. Remove rice from heat and let sit, covered, until tender, about 15 minutes.

4. FOR THE VEGETABLES: While rice cooks, stir together water, scallions, soy sauce, garlic, and sugar. Heat 1 teaspoon oil in Dutch oven over high heat until shimmering. Add carrots and stir until coated. Add ⅓ cup scallion mixture and cook, stirring frequently, until carrots are slightly softened and moisture has evaporated, 1 to 2 minutes. Using slotted spoon, transfer carrots to small bowl.

5. Heat 1 teaspoon oil in now-empty pot until shimmering. Add mushrooms and stir until coated with oil. Add ⅓ cup scallion mixture and cook, stirring frequently, until mushrooms are tender and moisture has evaporated, 3 to 4 minutes. Using slotted spoon, transfer mushrooms to second small bowl.

6. Heat remaining 1 teaspoon oil in now-empty pot until shimmering. Add spinach and remaining ⅓ cup scallion mixture and stir to coat spinach. Cook, stirring frequently, until spinach is completely wilted but still bright green, 1 to 2 minutes. Using slotted spoon, transfer spinach to third small bowl. Discard any remaining liquid and wipe out pot with paper towel.

7. FOR THE BIBIMBAP: Heat 2 tablespoons vegetable oil and sesame oil in now-empty pot over high heat until shimmering. Carefully add cooked rice and gently press into even layer. Cook, without stirring, until rice begins to form crust on bottom of pot, about 2 minutes. Using slotted spoon, transfer carrots, spinach, and mushrooms to pot and arrange in piles that cover surface of rice. Reduce heat to low.

Korean Rice Bowl (Dolsot Bibimbap)

SERVES 6

For a quick dinner, prepare the pickles, chile sauce, and vegetables a day ahead (warm the vegetables to room temperature in the microwave before adding them to the rice). You can also substitute store-bought kimchi for the pickles to save time. The Korean chile paste *gochujang* is sold in Asian markets and some supermarkets. If you can't find it, an equal amount of Sriracha can be substituted. But because Sriracha is more watery than gochujang, omit the water from the chile sauce and stir just 1 tablespoon of sauce into the rice in step 9. For a true bibimbap experience, bring the pot to the table before stirring the vegetables into the rice in step 9.

PICKLES

- 1 cup cider vinegar
- 2 tablespoons sugar
- 1½ teaspoons salt
- 1 cucumber, peeled, quartered lengthwise, seeded, and sliced thin on bias
- 4 ounces (2 cups) bean sprouts

CHILE SAUCE

- ¼ cup gochujang
- 3 tablespoons water
- 2 tablespoons toasted sesame oil
- 1 teaspoon sugar

RICE

- 2½ cups short-grain white rice
- 2½ cups water
- ¾ teaspoon salt

8. While crust forms, heat remaining 2 teaspoons vegetable oil in 10-inch nonstick skillet over low heat for 5 minutes. Crack eggs into small bowl. Pour eggs into skillet; cover and cook (about 2 minutes for runny yolks, 2½ minutes for soft but set yolks, and 3 minutes for firmly set yolks). Slide eggs onto vegetables in pot.

9. Drizzle 2 tablespoons chile sauce over eggs. Without disturbing crust, use wooden spoon to stir rice, vegetables, and eggs until combined. Just before serving, scrape large pieces of crust from bottom of pot and stir into rice. Serve in individual bowls, passing pickles and extra chile sauce separately.

CHINESE CHICKEN LETTUCE WRAPS

WHY THIS RECIPE WORKS: This dish, popularized by chain restaurants, is based on a Cantonese dish called *sung choy bao*. Most recipes for this dish suffer from a similar fate—stringy, tasteless meat drowned in a bland sauce. To remedy this, we started with flavorful chicken thighs and marinated them in soy sauce and rice wine. To keep the meat from drying out when stir-fried, we coated it in a velvetizing cornstarch slurry, which helped it retain moisture as it cooked.

Chinese Chicken Lettuce Wraps
SERVES 4 AS A MAIN DISH OR 6 AS AN APPETIZER

To make it an entrée, serve this dish with Basic White Rice (page 453).

CHICKEN
- 1 pound boneless, skinless chicken thighs, trimmed and cut into 1-inch pieces
- 2 teaspoons Chinese rice wine or dry sherry
- 2 teaspoons soy sauce
- 2 teaspoons toasted sesame oil
- 2 teaspoons cornstarch

SAUCE
- 3 tablespoons oyster sauce
- 1 tablespoon Chinese rice wine or dry sherry
- 2 teaspoons soy sauce
- 2 teaspoons toasted sesame oil
- ½ teaspoon sugar
- ¼ teaspoon red pepper flakes

STIR-FRY
- 2 tablespoons vegetable oil
- 2 celery ribs, cut into ¼-inch pieces
- 6 ounces shiitake mushrooms, stemmed and sliced thin
- ½ cup water chestnuts, cut into ¼-inch pieces
- 2 scallions, white parts minced, green parts sliced thin
- 2 garlic cloves, minced
- 1 head Bibb lettuce (8 ounces), washed and dried, leaves separated and left whole
  Hoisin sauce

1. FOR THE CHICKEN: Place chicken pieces on large plate in single layer. Freeze meat until firm and starting to harden around edges, about 20 minutes.

2. Whisk rice wine, soy sauce, sesame oil, and cornstarch together in bowl. Pulse half of meat in food processor until coarsely chopped into ¼- to ⅛-inch pieces, about 10 pulses. Transfer meat to bowl with rice wine mixture and repeat with remaining chunks. Toss chicken to coat and refrigerate for 15 minutes.

3. FOR THE SAUCE: Whisk all ingredients together in bowl; set aside.

4. FOR THE STIR-FRY: Heat 1 tablespoon vegetable oil in 12-inch nonstick skillet over high heat until smoking. Add chicken and cook, stirring constantly, until opaque, 3 to 4 minutes. Transfer to bowl and wipe out skillet.

5. Heat remaining 1 tablespoon vegetable oil in now-empty skillet over high heat until smoking. Add celery and mushrooms; cook, stirring constantly, until mushrooms have reduced in size by half and celery is crisp-tender, 3 to 4 minutes. Add water chestnuts, scallion whites, and garlic; cook, stirring constantly, until fragrant, about 1 minute. Whisk sauce to recombine. Return chicken to skillet; add sauce and toss to combine. Spoon into lettuce leaves and sprinkle with scallion greens. Serve, passing hoisin sauce separately.

THAI PORK LETTUCE WRAPS

WHY THIS RECIPE WORKS: The classic Thai salad, *larb*, is made with finely chopped meat and nutty rice powder tossed with fresh herbs and a light dressing that embodies the cuisine's signature balance of sweet, sour, hot, and salty flavors. We aimed to develop a home-cook-friendly recipe.

Americanized recipes typically call for ground pork, but inconsistent results with supermarket ground pork inspired us to grind our own, using pork tenderloin and a food processor. To impart flavor and moisture to this lean cut, we marinated the meat in fish sauce. Toasted rice powder, which adds a nutty flavor and texture to the pork, can be found in Asian markets, but we found it was easier to just make our own by toasting rice until golden brown and grinding it in a mini food processor or with a mortar and pestle. As for the aromatic components, we found that the pungency of sliced shallots and the bright flavor of chopped mint and cilantro yielded a very flavorful salad without a trip to a specialty store. For serving, the pork is spooned into lettuce leaves and wrapped. We preferred the crisp spine, tender leaf, and mild taste of Bibb lettuce.

Thai Pork Lettuce Wraps
SERVES 6

We prefer natural pork in this recipe. If using enhanced pork (pork that has been injected with a salt solution to increase moistness and flavor), skip the marinating in step 1 and reduce the amount of fish sauce to 2 tablespoons, adding it all in step 4.

1 (1-pound) pork tenderloin, trimmed of silver skin and fat, cut into 1-inch chunks, and frozen for 20 minutes (see note)

2½ tablespoons fish sauce

1 tablespoon white rice

¼ cup low-sodium chicken broth

3 medium shallots, peeled and sliced into thin rings (about ½ cup)

3 tablespoons roughly chopped fresh mint leaves

3 tablespoons roughly chopped fresh cilantro leaves

3 tablespoons juice from 2 limes

2 teaspoons sugar

¼ teaspoon red pepper flakes

1 head Bibb lettuce, washed and dried, leaves separated and left whole

1. Pulse half of the pork in a food processor until coarsely chopped, about 6 pulses. Transfer the ground pork to a medium bowl and repeat with the remaining chunks. Stir 1 tablespoon of the fish sauce into the ground pork, cover, refrigerate, and let marinate for 15 minutes.

2. Toast the rice in a small skillet over medium-high heat, stirring constantly, until deep golden brown, about 5 minutes. Transfer to a small bowl and cool for 5 minutes. Grind the rice with a spice grinder, mini food processor, or mortar and pestle until it resembles fine meal, 10 to 30 seconds (you should have about 1 tablespoon rice powder).

3. Bring the broth to a simmer in a 12-inch nonstick skillet over medium-high heat. Add the pork and cook, stirring frequently, until about half of the pork is no longer pink, about 2 minutes. Sprinkle 1 teaspoon of the rice powder over the pork and continue to cook, stirring constantly, until the remaining pork is no longer pink, 1 to 1½ minutes longer. Transfer the pork to a large bowl and cool for 10 minutes.

4. Add the remaining 1½ tablespoons fish sauce, remaining 2 teaspoons rice powder, the shallots, mint, cilantro, lime juice, sugar, and red pepper flakes to the pork and toss to combine. Serve with the lettuce leaves, spooning the meat into the leaves at the table.

BEEF SATAY

WHY THIS RECIPE WORKS: This Southeast Asian street food should be simple enough, but more often than not it is tough, bland, and boring. We wanted tender meat that could easily be pulled apart into small bites right off the skewer, with great Southeast Asian flavors like garlic, chiles, and cilantro.

Choosing the right cut of meat proved to be more about texture than flavor. Flank steak was the winner. We used two techniques to slice it, first freezing the meat to firm it up enough to slice cleanly, then cutting the beef across the grain to keep it tender. Since the meat was so thin, cooking it was a breeze. Placing the skewered meat on a wire rack and cooking it 6 inches from the broiler's heating element proved just

right. We found our marinade ingredients in the supermarket (Asian chili sauce is now commonly available) and added generous amounts of cilantro and garlic.

Beef Satay
SERVES 8 TO 10

Asian chili sauce, also called Sriracha, is available in most supermarkets. Use 6-inch-long skewers for this recipe; you'll need about 24.

¼ cup soy sauce

¼ cup peanut or vegetable oil

¼ cup packed dark brown sugar

¼ cup minced fresh cilantro leaves

4 scallions, sliced thin

2 tablespoons Asian chili sauce, or more to taste (see note)

2 medium garlic cloves, minced or pressed through a garlic press (about 2 teaspoons)

1 (1½-pound) flank steak, trimmed, halved lengthwise, frozen for 30 minutes, and sliced across the grain into ¼-inch-thick strips

1 recipe Spicy Peanut Dipping Sauce (recipe follows)

1. Combine the soy sauce, oil, sugar, cilantro, scallions, chili sauce, and garlic in a large bowl. Stir in the beef, cover, and refrigerate for 1 hour.

2. Adjust an oven rack 6 inches from the heating element and heat the broiler.

3. Weave the meat onto 6-inch bamboo skewers (one piece per skewer). Lay the skewers on a wire rack set over a rimmed baking sheet and cover the skewer ends with foil. Broil the skewers until the meat is browned, 6 to 9 minutes, flipping the skewers over halfway through. Transfer the skewers to a serving platter and serve with the peanut sauce.

Spicy Peanut Dipping Sauce
MAKES ABOUT 1½ CUPS

This sauce can be refrigerated in an airtight container for up to 24 hours; bring to room temperature before serving.

½ cup creamy peanut butter

¼ cup hot water

2 tablespoons juice from 1 lime

2 tablespoons Asian chili sauce

1 tablespoon soy sauce

1 tablespoon dark brown sugar

1 tablespoon chopped fresh cilantro leaves

2 scallions, sliced thin

1 medium garlic clove, minced or pressed through a garlic press (about 1 teaspoon)

Whisk the peanut butter and hot water together in a small bowl until smooth. Stir in the remaining ingredients.

4 cups low-sodium chicken broth

2 (14-ounce) cans coconut milk (see note)

1 tablespoon sugar

8 ounces white mushrooms, wiped clean
and sliced ¼ inch thick

1 pound boneless, skinless chicken breasts, trimmed,
halved lengthwise, and cut on the bias into ⅛-inch
pieces (see note)

3 tablespoons juice from 2 limes

2 teaspoons Thai red curry paste (see note)

GARNISH

½ cup loosely packed fresh cilantro leaves

2 Thai, serrano, or jalapeño chiles, seeds and ribs
removed, chiles sliced thin

2 scallions, sliced thin on the bias
Lime wedges, for serving

THAI-STYLE CHICKEN SOUP

WHY THIS RECIPE WORKS: Replicating the complex flavors of Thai chicken soup at home can be difficult, since it relies on such exotica as galangal, kaffir lime leaves, lemon grass, and bird's eye chiles. We wanted a plausibly authentic version of Thai chicken soup that could be prepared with more readily available (i.e., supermarket) substitutions.

We started by making a classic version of the soup, then substituting one ingredient at a time. We developed an acceptably rich and definitely chicken-flavored broth by using equal parts chicken broth and coconut milk (adding the coconut milk in two stages: at the beginning and just before serving). We couldn't fake the flavor of lemon grass, but it proved to be easy enough to find. Our most exciting find was a "magic bullet" substitution: jarred red curry paste included all the other exotic ingredients we were missing. Just adding a dollop at the very end of cooking and whisking it with pungent fish sauce and tart lime juice allowed all the classic flavors to come through loud and clear.

Thai-Style Chicken Soup

SERVES 6 TO 8

To make slicing the chicken easier, freeze it for 15 minutes. Although we prefer the richer, more complex flavor of regular coconut milk, light coconut milk can be substituted for one or both cans. For a spicier soup, add additional red curry paste to taste.

SOUP

1 teaspoon peanut or vegetable oil

3 stalks lemon grass, bottom 5 inches only, trimmed
and sliced thin (see page 479)

3 large shallots, chopped coarse (about ¾ cup)

8 sprigs fresh cilantro, chopped coarse

3 tablespoons fish sauce

1. Heat the oil in a large saucepan over medium heat until just shimmering. Add the lemon grass, shallots, cilantro sprigs, and 1 tablespoon of the fish sauce and cook, stirring frequently, until just softened but not browned, 2 to 5 minutes.

2. Stir in the broth and 1 can of the coconut milk and bring to a simmer over high heat. Cover, reduce the heat to low, and simmer until the flavors have blended, about 10 minutes. Pour the broth through a fine-mesh strainer, discarding the solids in the strainer. (At this point, the soup can be refrigerated in an airtight container for up to 1 day.)

3. Return the strained soup to a clean saucepan and bring to a simmer over medium-high heat. Stir in the remaining can of coconut milk and the sugar and bring to a simmer. Reduce the heat to medium, add the mushrooms, and cook until just tender, 2 to 3 minutes. Add the chicken and cook, stirring constantly, until no longer pink, 1 to 3 minutes. Remove the soup from the heat.

4. Whisk the remaining 2 tablespoons fish sauce, the lime juice, and curry paste together, then stir into the soup. Ladle the soup into individual bowls and garnish with the cilantro, chiles, and scallions. Serve with the lime wedges.

HOT AND SOUR SOUP

WHY THIS RECIPE WORKS: Authentic versions of this soup have some hard-to-find ingredients such as mustard pickle, pig's-foot tendon, and dried sea cucumber—ingredients we couldn't find in the local grocery store. Using inventory only from our local supermarket, we wanted an authentic take on hot and sour soup, including spicy, bracing, pungent elements.

We created the "hot" side of the soup with two heat sources—distinctive, penetrating white pepper and a little chili oil. For the "sour" component, we preferred the traditional Chinese black vinegar, but found that a tablespoon each of balsamic and red wine vinegar made a suitable substitution. Cornstarch turned out to be a key ingredient: A cornstarch-based slurry thickened the soup; adding cornstarch to the pork marinade gave the pork a protective sheath that kept it tender; and beating the egg with cornstarch before drizzling it into the thickened soup kept the egg light, wispy, and cohesive. Pork and tofu are the usual, easy-to-find additions to the broth, but we had to come up with substitutes for a few other classic ingredients, settling on fresh shiitakes in lieu of wood ear mushrooms and canned bamboo shoots instead of lily buds. Spicy, bracing, rich, and complex, this soup has all the flavor of the classic version.

Hot and Sour Soup
SERVES 6 TO 8

To make slicing the pork chop easier, freeze it for 15 minutes. We prefer the distinctive flavor of Chinese black vinegar; look for it in Asian supermarkets. If you can't find it, use 1 tablespoon red wine vinegar and 1 tablespoon balsamic vinegar. This soup is very spicy. For a less spicy soup, omit the chili oil altogether or add only 1 teaspoon.

    7   ounces (½ block) extra-firm tofu
    ¼   cup soy sauce
    3   tablespoons plus 1½ teaspoons cornstarch
    1   teaspoon toasted sesame oil
    1   (6-ounce) boneless center-cut pork chop
        (about ½ inch thick), trimmed and cut into
        1-inch-long matchsticks (see note)
    3   tablespoons plus 1 teaspoon water
    1   large egg
    6   cups low-sodium chicken broth
    1   (5-ounce) can bamboo shoots, sliced into
        matchsticks (about 1 cup)
    4   ounces shiitake mushrooms, stemmed,
        wiped clean, caps sliced ¼ inch thick
    5   tablespoons Chinese black vinegar (see note)
    2   teaspoons chili oil (see note)
    1   teaspoon ground white pepper
    3   scallions, sliced thin

1. Place the tofu in a pie plate, top with a heavy plate, and weigh down with two heavy cans. Set the tofu aside until it has released about ½ cup liquid, about 15 minutes. When drained, cut the tofu into ½-inch cubes and set aside.

2. Meanwhile, whisk 1 tablespoon of the soy sauce, 1 teaspoon of the cornstarch, and the sesame oil together in a medium bowl. Stir in the pork, cover, and let marinate for at least 10 minutes or up to 30 minutes.

3. Combine 3 tablespoons more cornstarch with 3 tablespoons of the water in a small bowl. Mix the remaining ½ teaspoon cornstarch with the remaining 1 teaspoon water in a second small bowl, then add the egg and beat with a fork until combined.

4. Bring the broth to a simmer in a large saucepan over medium-low heat. Add the bamboo shoots and mushrooms and simmer until the mushrooms are just tender, 2 to 3 minutes.

Stir in the diced tofu and pork with its marinade and continue to simmer, stirring to separate any pieces of pork that stick together, until the pork is no longer pink, about 2 minutes.

5. Stir the cornstarch mixture to recombine, then add it to the soup, increase the heat to medium-high, and cook, stirring occasionally, until the soup thickens and turns translucent, about 1 minute. Stir in the remaining 3 tablespoons soy sauce, the vinegar, chili oil, and pepper and turn off the heat.

6. Without stirring the soup, use a soupspoon to slowly drizzle very thin streams of the egg mixture into the pot in a circular motion. Let the soup sit off the heat for 1 minute. Briefly return the soup to a simmer over medium-high heat, then remove from the heat immediately. Gently stir the soup once to evenly distribute the egg; ladle into individual bowls, sprinkle with the scallions, and serve.

COLD SESAME NOODLES

WHY THIS RECIPE WORKS: Cold noodles are underrated. Not as humble as they appear, these toothsome noodles tossed with shreds of tender chicken and fresh sesame sauce can be addicting if made properly. For this recipe, we set out to eliminate sticky noodles, gloppy sauce, and lackluster flavors.

We found that rinsing and tossing the noodles (either fresh Chinese noodles or dried spaghetti) with a little sesame oil after cooking prevents a rubbery texture and washes away much of their sticky starch. Boneless, skinless chicken breasts were the obvious choice for easy cooking and shredding, and broiling the meat helped retain the chicken's moisture and flavor. And for an authentic sauce, a combination of chunky peanut butter and freshly ground toasted sesame seeds was the best substitute for Asian sesame paste. After adding fresh garlic and ginger, as well as soy sauce, rice vinegar, hot sauce, and brown sugar, we achieved the perfect texture by thinning out the sauce with hot water.

Sesame Noodles with Shredded Chicken
SERVES 4 TO 6

Although our preference is for fresh Chinese noodles, we found that dried spaghetti works well, too. Because dried pasta swells so much more than fresh pasta during cooking, 12 ounces of dried spaghetti can replace 1 pound of fresh noodles.

    5   tablespoons soy sauce
    ¼   cup sesame seeds, toasted
    ¼   cup chunky peanut butter
    2   tablespoons rice vinegar
    2   tablespoons light brown sugar
    1   tablespoon minced or grated fresh ginger
    2   medium garlic cloves, minced or pressed through
        a garlic press (about 2 teaspoons)
    1   teaspoon hot sauce
        Hot water

1 pound fresh Chinese noodles or 12 ounces dried
   spaghetti (see note)
1 tablespoon table salt
2 tablespoons toasted sesame oil
1½ pounds boneless, skinless chicken breasts, trimmed
4 scallions, sliced thin on the bias
1 carrot, peeled and shredded

1. Process the soy sauce, 3 tablespoons of the sesame seeds, the peanut butter, vinegar, brown sugar, ginger, garlic, and hot sauce together in a blender or food processor until smooth, about 30 seconds. With the machine running, add hot water, 1 tablespoon at a time, until the sauce has the consistency of heavy cream (you should need about 5 tablespoons); set aside.

2. Position an oven rack 6 inches from the heating element and heat the broiler.

3. Bring 6 quarts water to a boil in a large pot. Add the noodles and salt and cook, stirring often, until tender, about 4 minutes for fresh and 10 minutes for dried. Drain the noodles, rinse them under cold running water until cold, then toss them with the sesame oil.

4. Set a wire rack over a foil-lined rimmed baking sheet and lightly coat the rack with vegetable oil spray. Lay the chicken on the rack and broil until lightly browned, 4 to 8 minutes. Flip the chicken over and continue to broil until the thickest part of the breast registers 160 to 165 degrees on an instant-read thermometer, 6 to 8 minutes longer. Transfer the chicken to a carving board and let rest for 5 minutes. Using two forks, shred the chicken into bite-size pieces and set aside.

5. Transfer the noodles to a large bowl, add the shredded chicken, sauce, scallions, and carrot and toss to combine. Divide the mixture among individual bowls, sprinkle with the remaining 1 tablespoon sesame seeds, and serve.

JAPANESE-STYLE STIR-FRIED NOODLES WITH BEEF

WHY THIS RECIPE WORKS: Japanese *yakisoba* stands out among noodle dishes for its sweet-savory-tangy sauce, tender meat, and hearty vegetables. For a flavor-packed noodle dish that rivaled our favorite takeout, we started with the beef. Coating bite-size strips of flank steak in baking soda and water tenderized the meat. To recreate the thick consistency and sweet, fruity flavor of yakisoba sauce, we whisked together ketchup, soy sauce, Worcestershire, brown sugar, minced garlic, minced anchovies, and rice vinegar. We cooked the remaining components in stages. Lo mein noodles (an easier supermarket find than traditional yakisoba noodles) turned tender after a few minutes in boiling water, and rinsing them under cold water after draining eliminated clingy starches. For the vegetable accompaniments to the noodles, sliced shiitakes and carrot cooked in chicken broth were an easy and traditional choice. Next, sliced napa cabbage and bright, grassy

scallions cooked up quickly, followed by the slices of beef. To tie everything together, we briefly cooked the sauce, chicken broth, and noodles before tossing them with the waiting vegetables and beef. A sprinkling of homemade Sesame-Orange Spice Blend brought the authentic flavors home.

Japanese-Style Stir-Fried Noodles with Beef
SERVES 4 TO 6

This recipe calls for lo mein noodles, but use yakisoba noodles if you can find them and follow the same cooking directions. Garnish the noodles with pickled ginger (often found in the refrigerated section of the grocery store near the tofu) and our Sesame-Orange Spice Blend (recipe follows) or, if you can find it, commercial shichimi togarashi.

⅛ teaspoon baking soda
12 ounces flank steak, trimmed, sliced lengthwise
   into 2- to 2½-inch strips, each strip sliced
   crosswise ¼ inch thick
¼ cup ketchup
¼ cup soy sauce
2 tablespoons Worcestershire sauce
1½ tablespoons packed brown sugar
3 garlic cloves, minced
3 anchovy fillets, rinsed, patted dry, and minced
1 teaspoon rice vinegar
1 pound fresh or 8 ounces dried lo mein noodles
1 tablespoon vegetable oil
6 ounces shiitake mushrooms, stemmed and
   sliced ¼ inch thick
1 carrot, peeled and sliced ⅛ inch thick on bias
¾ cup chicken broth
6 cups napa cabbage, sliced crosswise into ½-inch strips
7 scallions, cut on bias into 1-inch lengths
   Salt

1. Combine 1 tablespoon water and baking soda in medium bowl. Add beef and toss to coat. Let sit at room temperature for 5 minutes.

2. Whisk ketchup, soy sauce, Worcestershire, sugar, garlic, anchovies, and vinegar together in second bowl. Stir 2 tablespoons sauce into beef mixture and set aside remaining sauce.

3. Bring 4 quarts water to boil in large pot. Add noodles and cook, stirring often, until almost tender (center should still be firm with slightly opaque dot), 3 to 10 minutes (cooking time will vary depending on whether you are using fresh or dry noodles). Drain noodles and rinse under cold running water until water runs clear. Drain well and set aside.

4. Heat ½ teaspoon oil in 12-inch nonstick skillet over high heat until just smoking. Add mushrooms and carrot and cook, stirring occasionally, until vegetables are spotty brown, 2 to 3 minutes. Add ¼ cup broth and cook until all liquid has evaporated and vegetables are tender, about 30 seconds. Transfer vegetables to bowl.

5. Return skillet to high heat, add ½ teaspoon oil, and heat until just smoking. Add cabbage and scallions and cook, without stirring, for 30 seconds. Cook, stirring occasionally, until cabbage and scallions are spotty brown and crisp-tender, 2 to 3 minutes. Transfer to bowl with mushrooms and carrot.

6. Return skillet to high heat, add 1 teaspoon oil, and heat until just smoking. Add half of beef in single layer. Cook, without stirring, for 30 seconds. Continue to cook, stirring occasionally, until beef is spotty brown, 1 to 2 minutes. Transfer to bowl with vegetables. Repeat with remaining beef and remaining 1 teaspoon oil.

7. Return skillet to high heat; add reserved sauce, remaining ½ cup broth, and noodles. Cook, scraping up any browned bits, until noodles are warmed through, about 1 minute. Transfer noodles to bowl with vegetables and beef and toss to combine. Season with salt to taste, and serve immediately.

Sesame-Orange Spice Blend
MAKES ¼ CUP

In addition to garnishing our stir-fry, this blend makes a great seasoning for eggs, rice, and fish. Store for up to one week.

- ¾ teaspoon grated orange zest
- 2 teaspoons sesame seeds
- 1½ teaspoons paprika
- 1 teaspoon pepper
- ¼ teaspoon garlic powder
- ¼ teaspoon ground ginger
- ⅛ teaspoon cayenne pepper

Place orange zest in small bowl and microwave, stirring every 20 seconds, until zest is dry and no longer clumping together, 1 minute 30 seconds to 2 minutes 30 seconds. Stir in sesame seeds, paprika, pepper, garlic powder, ginger, and cayenne.

FRIED RICE

WHY THIS RECIPE WORKS: Fried rice is the perfect solution for leftover rice, but it often arrives in the bowl as a soggy mess of greasy rice doused in so much flavor-disguising soy sauce that you can hardly tell the vegetables from the chicken. We wanted fried rice with firm, separate grains, and we wanted a finished dish so clean and light that we could distinguish its many different flavors in every bite.

For fried rice that is light and flavorful rather than sodden and greasy, we found it essential to start with cold, dry rice (like leftover rice). Instead of gallons of soy sauce, we added a small amount in conjunction with complex oyster-flavored sauce to yield well-seasoned but not soggy rice. Cooking the vegetables and shrimp separately ensured that everything was cooked to perfection—no rubbery shrimp or mushy peas. And frying the rice in just a couple tablespoons of oil kept it from being greasy. Lastly, we finished the dish with tender vegetables including bean sprouts and a sprinkling of scallions.

Fried Rice with Shrimp, Pork, and Shiitakes
SERVES 4 TO 6

See the Basic White Rice recipe (page 453) for tips on preparing and cooling rice.

- ½ ounce (5 to 6 medium) dried shiitake mushrooms
- ¼ cup oyster-flavored sauce
- 1 tablespoon soy sauce
- 3 tablespoons plus 1½ teaspoons peanut or vegetable oil
- 2 large eggs, lightly beaten
- 8 ounces small shrimp (51 to 60 per pound), peeled and deveined (see page 240)
- 1 cup frozen peas, thawed
- 8 ounces sliced smoked ham, cut into ½-inch pieces
- 2 medium garlic cloves, minced or pressed through a garlic press (about 2 teaspoons)
- 5 cups cold cooked white rice, large clumps broken up with fingers (see note)
- 1 cup bean sprouts
- 5 scallions, sliced thin

1. Cover the dried shiitakes with 1 cup hot tap water in a small microwave-safe bowl. Cover the bowl with plastic wrap and microwave on high power for 30 seconds. Let sit until the mushrooms soften, about 5 minutes. Lift the mushrooms from the liquid with a fork. Trim the stems, slice into ¼-inch strips, and set aside.

2. Combine the oyster-flavored sauce and soy sauce in a small bowl and set aside.

3. Heat 1½ teaspoons of the oil in a 12-inch nonstick skillet over medium heat until shimmering. Add the eggs and cook, without stirring, until they just begin to set, about 20 seconds. Scramble and break into small pieces with a wooden spoon and continue to cook, stirring constantly, until the eggs are cooked through but not browned, about 1 minute longer. Transfer the eggs to a small bowl and set aside.

4. Add 1½ teaspoons more oil to the skillet and heat over medium heat until shimmering. Add the shrimp and cook, stirring constantly, until opaque and just cooked through, about 30 seconds. Transfer the shrimp to the bowl with the eggs and set aside.

5. Add the remaining 2½ tablespoons oil to the skillet and heat over medium heat until shimmering. Add the mushrooms, peas, and ham and cook, stirring constantly, for 1 minute. Stir in the garlic and cook until fragrant, about 30 seconds. Add the rice and oyster-flavored sauce mixture and cook, stirring constantly and breaking up any rice clumps, until the mixture is heated through, about 3 minutes. Stir in the eggs, shrimp, bean sprouts, and scallions and cook until heated through, about 1 minute. Serve.

Fried Rice with Peas and Bean Sprouts

SERVES 4 TO 6

See the Basic White Rice recipe for tips on preparing and cooling rice.

- ¼ cup oyster-flavored sauce
- 1 tablespoon soy sauce
- 3 tablespoons peanut or vegetable oil
- 2 large eggs, lightly beaten
- 1 cup frozen peas, thawed
- 2 medium garlic cloves, minced or pressed through a garlic press (about 2 teaspoons)
- 5 cups cold cooked white rice, large clumps broken up with fingers (see note)
- 1 cup bean sprouts
- 5 scallions, sliced thin

1. Combine the oyster-flavored sauce and soy sauce in a small bowl and set aside.

2. Heat 1½ teaspoons of the oil in a 12-inch nonstick skillet over medium heat until shimmering. Add the eggs and cook, without stirring, until they just begin to set, about 20 seconds. Scramble and break into small pieces with a wooden spoon and continue to cook, stirring constantly, until the eggs are cooked through but not browned, about 1 minute longer. Transfer the eggs to a small bowl and set aside.

3. Add the remaining 2½ tablespoons oil to the skillet and heat over medium heat until shimmering. Add the peas and cook, stirring constantly, for 1 minute. Stir in the garlic and cook until fragrant, about 30 seconds. Add the rice and oyster-flavored sauce mixture and cook, stirring constantly and breaking up any rice clumps, until the mixture is heated through, about 3 minutes. Stir in the eggs, bean sprouts, and scallions and cook until heated through, about 1 minute. Serve.

Basic White Rice

MAKES ABOUT 5 CUPS

To rinse the rice, you can either place it in a fine-mesh strainer and rinse it under cool water or place it in a medium bowl and repeatedly fill the bowl with water while swishing the rice around, then drain off the water. In either case, you must rinse the rice until the water runs clear.

- 3 cups water
- 2 cups long-grain white rice, rinsed (see note)

1. Bring the water and rice to a boil in a large saucepan over high heat. Reduce the heat to low, cover, and cook until all the water has been absorbed, about 10 minutes. Remove the pot from the heat and let sit, covered, until the rice is tender, about 15 minutes.

2. Serve, or to make fried rice, spread the cooked rice out over a baking sheet and let cool to room temperature, about 30 minutes. (The rice can be refrigerated in an airtight container for up to 24 hours.)

FRIED BROWN RICE WITH PORK AND SHRIMP

WHY THIS RECIPE WORKS: In this dish, using brown rice instead of the more conventional white rice offered several advantages. Because of its bran, brown rice holds up well if cooked aggressively in boiling water. The bran acted as a nonstick coating on each grain, so the dish required far less oil for frying. To balance the nuttier flavor of brown rice, we used plenty of ginger, garlic, and soy sauce. For a quick version of Chinese barbecued pork to turn our fried rice into a main course, we cut boneless country-style pork ribs across the grain into bite-size slices and tossed them in hoisin sauce, honey, and five-spice powder. We chopped scallions and shrimp, beat some eggs, grated some ginger, and minced some garlic, and we were ready to stir-fry. Preparing these components in batches, starting with the shrimp and eggs and then turning to the pork, yielded perfectly cooked ingredients ready to stir together with the fried brown rice.

Fried Brown Rice with Pork and Shrimp

SERVES 6

Boiling the rice gives it the proper texture for this dish. Do not use a rice cooker. The most efficient way to make this dish is to start the rice boiling and then to assemble the remaining ingredients while the rice cooks. The stir-fry portion of this recipe moves quickly, so make sure to have all your ingredients in place before starting. This recipe works best in a nonstick skillet with a slick surface. If your skillet is a bit worn, add an additional teaspoon of oil with the eggs in step 3. Serve with a simple steamed vegetable like broccoli, bok choy, or snow peas if desired.

2	cups short grain brown rice
	Salt
10	ounces boneless country-style pork ribs, trimmed
1	tablespoon hoisin sauce
2	teaspoons honey
⅛	teaspoon five-spice powder
	Small pinch cayenne pepper
4	teaspoons vegetable oil
8	ounces large shrimp (26 to 30 per pound), peeled, deveined (see page 240), tails removed, and cut into ½-inch pieces
3	large eggs, lightly beaten
1	tablespoon toasted sesame oil
6	scallions, whites and greens separated, sliced thin on bias
1½	teaspoons garlic, minced
1½	teaspoons grated fresh ginger
2	tablespoons soy sauce
1	cup frozen peas

1. Bring 3 quarts water to boil in large pot. Add rice and 2 teaspoons salt. Cook, stirring occasionally, until rice is tender, about 35 minutes. Drain well, and return to pot. Cover and set aside.

2. While rice cooks, cut pork into 1-inch pieces, and cut each piece into ¼-inch slices against grain. Combine pork with hoisin, honey, five-spice, cayenne, and ½ teaspoon salt, and toss to coat. Set aside.

3. Heat 1 teaspoon vegetable oil in 12-inch nonstick skillet over medium-high heat until shimmering. Add shrimp in even layer and cook without moving them until bottoms are browned, about 90 seconds. Stir and continue to cook until just cooked through, about 90 seconds longer. Push shrimp to 1 side of skillet. Add 1 teaspoon vegetable oil to cleared side of skillet. Add eggs to clearing and sprinkle with ¼ teaspoon salt. Using rubber spatula, stir eggs gently until set but still wet, about 30 seconds. Stir eggs into shrimp and continue to cook, breaking up large pieces of egg, until eggs are fully cooked, about 30 seconds longer. Transfer shrimp-egg mixture to clean bowl.

4. Heat remaining 2 teaspoons vegetable oil in now-empty skillet over medium-high heat until shimmering. Add pork in even layer. Cook without moving until pork is well browned on underside, 2 to 3 minutes. Flip pork and cook without moving until pork is cooked through and caramelized on second side, 2 to 3 minutes. Transfer to bowl with shrimp-egg mixture.

5. Heat sesame oil in now-empty skillet over medium-high heat until shimmering. Add scallion whites and cook, stirring frequently, until well-browned, about 1 minute. Add ginger and garlic and cook, stirring frequently, until fragrant and beginning to brown, 30 to 60 seconds. Add soy sauce and half of rice and stir until all ingredients are fully incorporated, making sure to break up clumps of ginger and garlic. Reduce heat to medium-low and add remaining rice, pork, shrimp, eggs, and peas. Stir until all ingredients are evenly incorporated and heated through, 2 to 4 minutes. Remove from heat and stir in scallion greens. Transfer to heated platter and serve.

INDONESIAN-STYLE FRIED RICE

WHY THIS RECIPE WORKS: Chinese takeout versions of fried rice are satisfying, to be sure, but frequently leave little to the imagination. We wanted to create a less heavy version of fried rice featuring the pungent, complex flavors of Indonesia—without heading to specialty markets for all of our ingredients. The primary source of this dish's flavor is chili paste, and we were happy to discover that the ingredients for this paste (staples like chiles, shallots, brown sugar, and soy sauce) are readily available at the average supermarket. To replicate the flavor of shrimp paste—another key but hard-to-find ingredient—we used a combination of fish sauce and chopped shrimp, which we added to the skillet with the chili paste. This dish requires chilled, firm rice, but most of us don't have leftover rice sitting in our fridge. For rice with the proper consistency, we cooked it in less water and then spread it out on a baking sheet to allow it to chill quickly in the fridge.

Indonesian-Style Fried Rice (Nasi Goreng)

SERVES 4 TO 6

If Thai chiles are unavailable, substitute two serranos or two medium jalapeños. Reduce the spiciness of this dish by removing the ribs and seeds from the chiles. This dish progresses very quickly at step 4; it's imperative that your ingredients are in place by then and ready to go. If desired, serve the rice with sliced cucumbers and tomato wedges.

5 green or red Thai chiles, stemmed (see note)

7 large shallots, peeled

4 large garlic cloves, peeled

2 tablespoons dark brown sugar

2 tablespoons light or mild molasses

2 tablespoons soy sauce

2 tablespoons fish sauce

Table salt

4 large eggs

½ cup vegetable oil

1 recipe Faux Leftover Rice (recipe follows)

12 ounces extra-large shrimp (21 to 25 per pound), peeled, deveined (see page 240), tails removed, and cut crosswise into thirds

4 large scallions, sliced thin

2 limes, cut into wedges

1. Pulse the chiles, 4 of the shallots, and the garlic in a food processor until a coarse paste is formed, about 15 pulses, scraping down the sides of the bowl as necessary. Transfer the mixture to a small bowl and set aside. In a second small bowl, stir together the brown sugar, molasses, soy sauce, fish sauce, and 1¼ teaspoons salt. Whisk the eggs and ¼ teaspoon salt together in a medium bowl.

2. Thinly slice the remaining 3 shallots and place in a 12-inch nonstick skillet with the oil. Cook over medium heat, stirring constantly, until the shallots are golden and crisp, 6 to 10 minutes. Using a slotted spoon, transfer the shallots to a paper towel–lined plate and season with salt to taste. Pour off the oil and reserve. Wipe out the skillet with paper towels.

3. Heat 1 teaspoon of the reserved oil in the now-empty skillet over medium heat until shimmering. Add half of the eggs to the skillet, gently tilting the pan to evenly coat the bottom. Cover and cook until the bottom of the omelet is spotty golden brown and the top is just set, about 1½ minutes. Slide the omelet onto a cutting board and gently roll up into a tight log. Using a sharp knife, cut the log crosswise into 1-inch segments (leaving the segments rolled). Repeat with 1 teaspoon more reserved oil and the remaining egg.

4. Remove the rice from the refrigerator and break up any large clumps with your fingers. Heat 3 tablespoons more reserved oil in the now-empty skillet over medium heat until just shimmering. Add the chile mixture and cook until the mixture turns golden, 3 to 5 minutes. Add the shrimp, increase the heat to medium-high, and cook, stirring constantly, until the exterior of the shrimp is just opaque, about 2 minutes. Push the shrimp to the sides of the skillet to clear the center; stir the molasses mixture to recombine and pour into the center of the skillet. When the molasses mixture bubbles, add the rice and cook, stirring and folding constantly, until the shrimp is cooked, the rice is heated through, and the mixture is evenly coated, about 3 minutes. Stir in the scallions, remove from the heat, and transfer to a serving platter. Garnish with the egg segments, fried shallots, and lime wedges; serve immediately.

Faux Leftover Rice

MAKES 6 CUPS

To rinse the rice, place it in a fine-mesh strainer and rinse under cool water until the water runs clear.

2 tablespoons vegetable oil

2 cups jasmine or long-grain white rice, rinsed (see note)

2⅔ cups water

Heat the oil in a large saucepan over medium heat until shimmering. Add the rice and stir to coat the grains with oil, about 30 seconds. Add the water, increase the heat to high, and bring to a boil. Reduce the heat to low, cover, and simmer until all the liquid is absorbed, about 18 minutes. Off the heat, remove the lid and place a clean kitchen towel, folded in half, over the saucepan; replace the lid. Let stand until the rice is just tender, about 8 minutes. Spread the cooked rice onto a rimmed baking sheet, set on a wire rack, and cool for 10 minutes. Transfer to the refrigerator and chill for 20 minutes.

CHICKEN TERIYAKI

WHY THIS RECIPE WORKS: Too many chicken teriyaki recipes are lackluster—they can include everything from skewered chicken chunks shellacked in a corn-syrupy sauce to over-marinated, preformed chicken breast patties. They're a long way away from the simple recipe promised in the name "teri-yaki"—meaning "to shine" (referring to the sauce) and meaning "to broil." We wanted a straightforward recipe that delivered the simple and authentic result of crisp and moist, sweet and salty, glazed chicken.

First, we decided against using breast meat. Bone-in, skin-on thighs stood up best to the salty profile of the teriyaki sauce. We set a weight on top of the chicken as it cooked (we used a heavy Dutch oven), which helped to brown a greater surface area of the chicken evenly, as well as to aid in pressing out most of the fat. We also found that a quick mixture of soy sauce, sugar, mirin, and a few other flavorings made an incredible teriyaki sauce that far surpassed any we could buy in a bottle.

Chicken Teriyaki

SERVES 4

A splatter screen (or an inverted large strainer or colander) is helpful for controlling the splatter that occurs when the second side of the chicken browns. There is a fair amount of soy sauce in this dish, so there is no need to salt it before serving. Serve with Basic White Rice (page 453).

- 8 (5- to 6-ounce) bone-in, skin-on chicken thighs, trimmed
  Ground black pepper
- 2 teaspoons peanut or vegetable oil
- ½ cup soy sauce
- ½ cup sugar
- 2 tablespoons mirin or sweet sherry
- 2 teaspoons minced or grated fresh ginger
- 1 medium garlic clove, minced or pressed through a garlic press (about 1 teaspoon)
- ½ teaspoon cornstarch
- ⅛ teaspoon red pepper flakes

1. Pat the chicken thighs dry with paper towels and season with pepper. Heat the oil in a 12-inch nonstick skillet over medium-high heat until just smoking. Carefully lay the chicken in the skillet, skin side down. Weigh down the chicken with a heavy pot and cook until the skin is a deep mahogany brown and very crisp, 15 to 20 minutes. (The chicken should be moderately brown after 10 minutes. If it is very brown, reduce the heat; if it is still pale, increase the heat.)

2. Remove the weight and flip the chicken over. Reduce the heat to medium and continue to cook, without the weight, until the second side is brown and the thickest part of the thighs registers 175 degrees on an instant-read thermometer, about 10 minutes longer.

3. Meanwhile, whisk the soy sauce, sugar, mirin, ginger, garlic, cornstarch, and red pepper flakes together in a small bowl; set aside.

4. Transfer the chicken to a plate. Pour off all of the fat from the skillet. Whisk the soy mixture to recombine, then add to the skillet and return to medium heat. Return the chicken to the skillet, skin side up, and spoon the sauce over the top. Continue to simmer until the sauce is thick and glossy, about 2 minutes longer. Serve.

ORANGE-FLAVORED CHICKEN

WHY THIS RECIPE WORKS: Chinese takeout orange-flavored chicken is never as good as its name promises—too often the dish delivers ultra-thick breading wrapped around scraps of greasy, gristly, tasteless chicken bathed in an "orange" sauce that tastes likes a mixture of corn syrup and orange food coloring. We wanted substantial, well-seasoned chicken chunks with a crisp, golden brown crust, and a sauce that offered a clear hit of fresh orange flavor with balanced sweet, sour, and spicy background notes.

We chose thigh meat over breast meat for its rich flavor and tendency to remain moist when deep-fried. We marinated the chicken in a mixture of soy sauce, garlic, ginger, sugar, vinegar, fresh orange juice, and chicken broth, reserving some marinade to become the base for the final sauce. Then, we created a tender/crisp coating by dunking the marinated chicken first in egg white, then cornstarch. The egg white created a thin sheath of protein beneath the cornstarch that kept it dry, helping it to brown more readily than a wet, gluey coating would. A touch of baking soda helped the chicken pieces develop golden color during frying.

Orange-Flavored Chicken

SERVES 4

We prefer the flavor and texture of thigh meat for this recipe, though an equal amount of boneless, skinless chicken breasts can be used. Unless you have a taste for the incendiary, do not eat the whole chiles in the finished dish. Serve with Basic White Rice (page 453).

MARINADE AND SAUCE

- ¾ cup low-sodium chicken broth
- ¾ cup juice, 1½ teaspoons grated zest, and 8 strips peel (each about 2 inches long by ½ inch wide) from 2 oranges
- ½ cup packed dark brown sugar
- 6 tablespoons distilled white vinegar
- ¼ cup soy sauce
- 3 medium garlic cloves, minced or pressed through a garlic press (about 1 tablespoon)
- 1 tablespoon minced or grated fresh ginger
- ¼ teaspoon cayenne pepper
- 1½ pounds boneless, skinless chicken thighs, trimmed and cut into 1½-inch pieces (see note)

2 tablespoons cold water

1 tablespoon plus 2 teaspoons cornstarch

8 small whole dried red chiles (optional; see note)

COATING AND FRYING OIL

3 large egg whites

1 cup cornstarch

½ teaspoon baking soda

¼ teaspoon cayenne pepper

3 cups peanut or vegetable oil

1. FOR THE MARINADE AND SAUCE: Whisk the broth, orange juice, grated zest, sugar, vinegar, soy sauce, garlic, ginger, and cayenne together in a large saucepan until the sugar is fully dissolved. Transfer ¾ cup of the mixture to a medium bowl and add the chicken. Let marinate for at least 10 minutes or up to 1 hour.

2. In a small bowl, stir the cold water and cornstarch together. Bring the remaining mixture in the saucepan to a simmer over high heat. Whisk the cornstarch mixture into the sauce, bring to a simmer, and cook, stirring occasionally, until thick and translucent, about 1 minute. Off the heat, stir in the orange peel and chiles (if using) and set aside. (The sauce should measure 1½ cups.)

3. FOR THE COATING: Using a fork, lightly beat the egg whites in a shallow dish until frothy. In a second shallow dish, whisk the cornstarch, baking soda, and cayenne together until combined. Drain the chicken and pat dry with paper towels. Place half of the chicken pieces in the egg whites and turn to coat. Transfer the chicken pieces to the cornstarch mixture and coat thoroughly. Place the dredged chicken pieces on a wire rack set over a baking sheet. Repeat with the remaining chicken pieces.

4. TO FRY THE CHICKEN: Heat the oil in a Dutch oven over high heat until the oil registers 350 degrees on an instant-read or deep-fry thermometer. Carefully place half of the chicken in the oil and fry until golden brown, about 5 minutes, turning each piece with tongs halfway through. Transfer the chicken pieces to a paper towel–lined plate. Return the oil to 350 degrees and repeat with the remaining chicken.

5. TO SERVE: Reheat the sauce over medium heat until simmering, about 2 minutes. Add the chicken and gently toss until evenly coated and heated through. Serve.

THREE-CUP CHICKEN

WHY THIS RECIPE WORKS: Originating in Dadu (modern Beijing), Three-Cup Chicken, or *San Bei Ji*, was named for its sparse ingredient list, with a sauce made up of just 1 cup each of soy sauce, sesame oil, and rice wine. Now adopted by neighboring Taiwan, it has evolved into a national dish of sorts. Its robust, aromatic flavors seemed ideal for adapting for the American kitchen. While traditional recipes involve butchering a whole bird into smaller pieces, we opted for boneless, skinless thighs, which didn't require using a cleaver. The rich

flavor of the thighs would stand up to the potent sauce better than that of milder breasts. Marinating the chicken in the sauce helped build deep flavor with minimal effort. We found that scallions, ginger, garlic, and red pepper flakes added even more flavor and complexity to this dish.

Three-Cup Chicken

SERVES 4

We prefer the flavor of Thai basil, but common sweet basil can be substituted. For a spicier dish, use the larger amount of red pepper flakes. Serve with Basic White Rice (page 453).

⅓ cup soy sauce

⅓ cup dry sherry

1 tablespoon packed brown sugar

1½ pounds boneless, skinless chicken thighs, trimmed and cut into 2-inch pieces

3 tablespoons vegetable oil

1 (2-inch) piece ginger, peeled, halved lengthwise, and sliced into thin half-rounds

12 garlic cloves, peeled and halved lengthwise

½–¾ teaspoon red pepper flakes

6 scallions, white and green parts separated and sliced thin on bias

1 tablespoon water

1 teaspoon cornstarch

1 cup Thai basil leaves, large leaves halved lengthwise

1 tablespoon toasted sesame oil

1. Whisk soy sauce, sherry, and sugar together in medium bowl. Add chicken and toss to coat; set aside.

2. Heat vegetable oil, ginger, garlic, and pepper flakes in 12-inch nonstick skillet over medium-low heat. Cook, stirring frequently, until garlic is golden brown and beginning to soften, 8 to 10 minutes.

3. Add chicken and marinade to skillet, increase heat to medium-high, and bring to simmer. Reduce heat to medium-low and simmer, stirring occasionally, for 10 minutes. Stir in scallion whites and continue to cook until chicken registers about 200 degrees, 8 to 10 minutes longer.

4. Whisk water and cornstarch together in small bowl, then whisk into sauce; simmer until sauce is slightly thickened, about 1 minute. Remove skillet from heat. Stir in basil, sesame oil, and scallion greens. Transfer to platter and serve.

KOREAN-STYLE FRIED CHICKEN

WHY THIS RECIPE WORKS: A thin, crispy exterior and a spicy-sweet-salty sauce are the hallmarks of Korean fried chicken. The biggest challenge, though, is preventing the sauce from destroying the crust. We dunked the wings (which offer a high exterior to interior ratio for maximum crunch and also cook quickly) in a loose batter of flour, cornstarch, and water, which clung nicely to the chicken and fried up brown and crispy. To help the coating withstand a wet sauce, we double-fried the

wings, which removed more water from the skin than a single fry did, making the coating extra-crispy. The Korean chili paste known as *gochujang* gives our sauce the proper spicy, fermented notes, while sugar tempered the heat and garlic and ginger—cooked briefly with sesame oil—provided depth.

Korean-Style Fried Chicken

SERVES 4 TO 6 AS A MAIN DISH

A rasp-style grater makes quick work of turning the garlic into a paste. *Gochujang*, Korean hot red chili paste, can be found in Asian markets and in some supermarkets. Tailor the heat level of your wings by adjusting its amount. If you can't find gochujang, substitute an equal amount of Sriracha sauce and add only 2 tablespoons of water to the sauce. For a complete meal, serve these wings with Basic White Rice (page 453) and a vegetable.

1	tablespoon toasted sesame oil
1	teaspoon garlic, minced to paste
1	teaspoon grated fresh ginger
1¾	cups water
3	tablespoons sugar
2–3	tablespoons gochujang
1	tablespoon soy sauce
2	quarts vegetable oil
1	cup all-purpose flour
3	tablespoons cornstarch
3	pounds chicken wings, cut at joints, wing tips discarded

1. Combine sesame oil, garlic, and ginger in large bowl and microwave until mixture is bubbly and fragrant but not browned, 40 to 60 seconds. Whisk in ¼ cup water, sugar, gochujang, and soy sauce until smooth and set aside.

2. Heat oil in large Dutch oven over medium-high heat to 350 degrees. While oil heats, whisk flour, cornstarch, and remaining 1½ cups water in second large bowl until smooth. Set wire rack in rimmed baking sheet and set aside.

3. Place half of wings in batter and stir to coat. Using tongs, remove wings from batter one at a time, allowing any excess batter to drip back into bowl, and add to hot oil. Increase heat to high and cook, stirring occasionally to prevent wings from sticking, until coating is light golden and beginning to crisp, about 7 minutes. (Oil temperature will drop sharply after adding chicken.) Transfer wings to prepared rack. Return oil to 350 degrees and repeat with remaining wings. Reduce heat to medium and let second batch of chicken rest for 5 minutes.

4. Return oil to 375 degrees. Carefully return all chicken to oil and cook, stirring occasionally, until exterior is deep golden brown and very crispy, about 7 minutes. Transfer to rack and let stand for 2 minutes. Add chicken to reserved sauce and toss until coated. Return chicken to rack and let stand for 2 minutes to allow surface to set. Transfer to platter and serve.

CHICKEN STIR-FRY WITH CRISPY NOODLE CAKE

WHY THIS RECIPE WORKS: Stir-fries are the quintessential weeknight dinner. And while a stir-fry served on top of rice is great, a pan-fried noodle cake—crispy and crunchy on the outside and tender and chewy in the middle—offers a welcome change of pace.

For the noodle cake, we had the most success with fresh Chinese egg noodles—they made for a cohesive cake with a crunchy exterior. A nonstick skillet was crucial—it kept the cake from sticking and falling apart and allowed us to use less oil so the cake wasn't greasy. We found the best way to flip the cake in the skillet was to slide it onto a plate, invert it onto another plate, and then slide it back in the pan to finish cooking. We kept the stir-fry simple; chicken and bok choy are a classic combination. A quick marinade gave our chicken welcome flavor, and a modified version of the Chinese technique called velveting prevented the chicken from drying out over high heat.

Stir-Fried Chicken with Bok Choy and Crispy Noodle Cake

SERVES 4

To make slicing the chicken easier, freeze it for 15 minutes. Fresh Chinese noodles are often kept in the produce section of the grocery store. If you can't find them, substitute an equal amount of fresh spaghetti.

SAUCE

¼	cup low-sodium chicken broth
2	tablespoons soy sauce
1	tablespoon dry sherry
1	tablespoon oyster-flavored sauce
1	teaspoon sugar
1	teaspoon cornstarch
¼	teaspoon red pepper flakes

NOODLE CAKE

- 1 (9-ounce) package fresh Chinese noodles (see note)
- 1 teaspoon table salt
- 2 scallions, sliced thin
- ¼ cup peanut or vegetable oil

CHICKEN AND VEGETABLES

- 1 pound boneless, skinless chicken breasts, trimmed and sliced thin (see note)
- 1 tablespoon soy sauce
- 1 tablespoon dry sherry
- 2 tablespoons toasted sesame oil
- 1 tablespoon cornstarch
- 1 tablespoon unbleached all-purpose flour
- 2 tablespoons plus 2 teaspoons peanut or vegetable oil
- 1 tablespoon minced or grated fresh ginger
- 1 medium garlic clove, minced or pressed through a garlic press (about 1 teaspoon)
- 1 small head bok choy, stalks cut on the bias into ¼-inch pieces and greens cut into ½-inch strips
- 1 small red bell pepper, stemmed, seeded, and cut into ¼-inch strips

1. FOR THE SAUCE: Combine all the ingredients in a small bowl and set aside.

2. FOR THE NOODLE CAKE: Bring 6 quarts water to a boil in a large pot. Add the noodles and salt and cook, stirring often, until almost tender, 2 to 3 minutes. Drain the noodles, then toss them with the scallions.

3. Heat 2 tablespoons of the peanut oil in a 12-inch nonstick skillet over medium heat until shimmering. Spread the noodles evenly across the bottom of the skillet and press with a spatula to flatten into a cake. Cook until crisp and golden brown, 5 to 8 minutes.

4. Slide the noodle cake onto a large plate. Add the remaining 2 tablespoons peanut oil to the skillet and swirl to coat. Invert the noodle cake onto a second plate and slide it, browned side up, back into the skillet. Cook until golden brown on the second side, 5 to 8 minutes.

5. Slide the noodle cake onto a cutting board and let sit for at least 5 minutes before slicing into wedges and serving. (The noodle cake can be transferred to a wire rack set over a baking sheet and kept warm in a 200-degree oven for up to 20 minutes.) Wipe out the skillet with a wad of paper towels.

6. FOR THE CHICKEN AND VEGETABLES: While the noodles boil, toss the chicken with the soy sauce and sherry in a medium bowl and let marinate for at least 10 minutes or up to 1 hour. In a large bowl, whisk the sesame oil, cornstarch, and flour together. In a small bowl, mix 1 teaspoon of the peanut oil, the ginger, and garlic together.

7. Stir the marinated chicken into the sesame oil–cornstarch mixture. Heat 2 teaspoons more peanut oil in the skillet over high heat until just smoking. Add half of the chicken, break up any clumps, then cook without stirring until the meat is browned at the edges, about 1 minute. Stir the chicken and continue to cook until cooked through, about 1 minute longer. Transfer the chicken to a clean bowl and cover with foil to

keep warm. Repeat with 2 teaspoons more peanut oil and the remaining chicken.

8. Add the remaining 1 tablespoon peanut oil to the skillet and return to high heat until just smoking. Add the bok choy stalks and bell pepper and cook until lightly browned, 2 to 3 minutes.

9. Clear the center of the skillet, add the ginger mixture, and cook, mashing the mixture into the pan, until fragrant, 15 to 20 seconds. Stir the ginger mixture into the vegetables, then stir in the bok choy greens and cook until beginning to wilt, about 30 seconds.

10. Stir in the chicken with any accumulated juices. Whisk the sauce to recombine, then add to the skillet and cook, tossing constantly, until the sauce is thickened, about 30 seconds. Transfer to a serving platter and serve with the noodle cake.

BEHIND THE SCENES

STIR-FRIES AT HOME? THROW OUT YOUR WOK!

We love the theatrics of the kitchen. And few pans seem as fun to use as a wok—watching a Chinese cook stir-fry with a wok can be as exciting as catching a great drum solo at a rock concert. So imagine our disappointment when we realized woks simply don't perform as well as we thought. A wok's shape is the culprit. A wok's conical bottom is designed for a pit-style stove; the flames lick and engulf the pan, making most of the surface area hot even when food is added. But when you set a wok over a conventional stovetop, the heat becomes concentrated in the pan's bottom, and the larger surface area—the sides—simply doesn't heat as well. And when food is added to the wok, the pan's temperature drops. The results? Meat that steams instead of sears and vegetables that turn soggy, rather than crisp-tender.

What does work on a conventional stovetop? A large nonstick skillet. Its flat-bottom design allows more surface area to come in direct contact with the flat burner, delivering more heat over more parts than a wok—and enabling it to remain hot even after food is added.

To quantify their differences, we heated oil in a wok and a heavy 12-inch skillet over high heat on gas burners. Once the oil was smoking (at around 415 degrees), we added stir-fry ingredients to each pan. The wok's temperature plummeted dramatically, to 220 degrees at its center, rising only another 50 degrees over the course of cooking. The skillet's temperature dipped to 345 degrees, then recovered quickly, continuing to rise to almost 500 degrees. This higher heat translated to better browning and more flavor. The bottom line? Don't invest in a wok—use what you probably already have: a skillet. And if you want theatrics, order some concert tickets.

STIR-FRIES MADE SIMPLE

WHY THIS RECIPE WORKS: A good stir-fry made with chicken, shrimp, or tofu is more difficult to prepare than a beef or pork stir-fry because these proteins, which have less fat, are often bland. Worse, they inevitably become dry and stringy or rubbery when cooked over high heat. We aimed to create stir-fry recipes that harmonized the flavors and textures of these lighter proteins with complementary vegetables and sauces. We paired the chicken with zucchini, red bell pepper, and a zesty ginger sauce. And asparagus, yellow bell pepper, and a brightly flavored lemon sauce were a natural fit for the shrimp. We selected a slightly more assertive hot and sour sauce, along with red onion and snow peas, to enhance the mild-flavored tofu. As with most of our stir-fries, we marinated the thinly sliced chicken and shrimp, and the tofu, in a combination of soy sauce and dry sherry to add flavor. After cooking the chicken, shrimp, or tofu and removing it from the pan, we stir-fried the vegetables in batches, quickly cooked the garlic and ginger, and returned the protein to the pan along with the sauce. This final mixture needed less than a minute over medium heat to finish.

Stir-Fried Chicken and Zucchini with Ginger Sauce

SERVES 4

To make slicing the chicken easier, freeze it for 15 minutes. Serve with Basic White Rice (page 453).

SAUCE

- ¼ cup soy sauce
- 3 tablespoons minced or grated fresh ginger
- 2 tablespoons low-sodium chicken broth
- 1 tablespoon dry sherry
- ½ teaspoon sugar

CHICKEN AND VEGETABLES

- 12 ounces boneless, skinless chicken breasts, trimmed and sliced thin (see note)
- 1 tablespoon soy sauce
- 1 tablespoon dry sherry
- 2 tablespoons toasted sesame oil
- 1 tablespoon cornstarch
- 1 tablespoon unbleached all-purpose flour
- 2 tablespoons peanut or vegetable oil
- 1 tablespoon minced or grated fresh ginger
- 3 medium garlic cloves, minced or pressed through a garlic press (about 1 tablespoon)
- 2 scallions, white parts only, minced
- 2 carrots, peeled and cut into 2-inch-long matchsticks
- 1 red bell pepper, stemmed, seeded, and cut into ½-inch strips
- 1 medium zucchini, halved lengthwise and sliced ½ inch thick

1. FOR THE SAUCE: Combine all the ingredients in a small bowl and set aside.

2. FOR THE CHICKEN AND VEGETABLES: Toss the chicken with the soy sauce and sherry in a medium bowl and let marinate for at least 10 minutes or up to 1 hour. In a large bowl, whisk the sesame oil, cornstarch, and flour together. In a small bowl, mix 1 teaspoon of the peanut oil, the ginger, garlic, and scallions together.

3. Stir the marinated chicken into the sesame oil–cornstarch mixture. Heat 2 teaspoons more peanut oil in a 12-inch non-stick skillet over high heat until just smoking. Add the chicken, break up any clumps, then cook without stirring until the meat is browned at the edges, about 1 minute. Stir the chicken and continue to cook until cooked through, about 1 minute longer. Transfer the chicken to a clean bowl and cover with foil to keep warm.

4. Add the remaining 1 tablespoon peanut oil to the skillet and return to high heat until just smoking. Add the carrots and cook until beginning to soften, about 1 minute. Add the bell pepper and cook until spotty brown, about 1 minute. Add the zucchini and cook for 15 to 30 seconds, until just tender.

5. Clear the center of the skillet, add the ginger mixture, and cook, mashing the mixture into the pan, until fragrant, 15 to 20 seconds. Stir the ginger mixture into the vegetables.

6. Stir in the chicken with any accumulated juices. Whisk the sauce to recombine, then add to the skillet and cook, tossing constantly, until the sauce is thickened, about 30 seconds. Transfer to a serving platter and serve.

Stir-Fried Shrimp, Asparagus, and Yellow Pepper with Lemon Sauce

SERVES 4

One large lemon yields enough juice and zest for this sauce. Serve with Basic White Rice (page 453).

SAUCE

- 3 tablespoons juice plus ½ teaspoon zest from 1 lemon
- 2 tablespoons low-sodium chicken broth
- 1 tablespoon soy sauce
- 2 teaspoons sugar

SHRIMP AND VEGETABLES

- 1 pound medium shrimp (41 to 50 per pound), peeled and deveined (see page 240)
- 1 tablespoon soy sauce
- 1 tablespoon dry sherry
- 2 tablespoons plus 2 teaspoons peanut or vegetable oil
- 1 tablespoon minced or grated fresh ginger
- 3 garlic cloves, minced or pressed through a garlic press (about 1 tablespoon)
- 2 scallions, white parts only, minced
- 1 pound asparagus (1 bunch), tough ends trimmed, cut on the bias into 1-inch lengths
- ¼ cup water
- 1 yellow bell pepper, stemmed, seeded, and cut into ½-inch strips
  Table salt and ground black pepper
- ¼ cup chopped fresh cilantro leaves

1. **FOR THE SAUCE:** Combine all the ingredients in a small bowl and set aside.

2. **FOR THE SHRIMP AND VEGETABLES:** Toss the shrimp with the soy sauce and sherry in a medium bowl and let marinate for at least 10 minutes or up to 1 hour. In a small bowl, mix 1 teaspoon of the oil, the ginger, garlic, and scallions together.

3. Heat 2 teaspoons more oil in a 12-inch nonstick skillet over high heat until just smoking. Add the shrimp and cook without stirring until bright pink, about 1 minute. Stir the shrimp and continue to cook until cooked through, 15 to 30 seconds longer. Transfer the shrimp to a clean bowl and cover with foil to keep warm.

4. Add 1 tablespoon more oil to the skillet and return to high heat until just smoking. Add the asparagus and cook, stirring frequently, until spotty brown, about 2 minutes. Add the water, cover the pan, and lower the heat to medium. Cook the asparagus until crisp-tender, about 2 minutes. Transfer the asparagus to the bowl with the shrimp. Add the remaining 2 teaspoons oil to the skillet and return to high heat until just smoking. Add the bell pepper and cook, stirring frequently, until spotty brown, about 1½ minutes.

5. Clear the center of the skillet, add the ginger mixture, and cook, mashing the mixture into the pan, until fragrant, 15 to 20 seconds. Stir the ginger mixture into the bell pepper.

6. Stir in the asparagus and shrimp with any accumulated juices. Whisk the sauce to recombine, then add to the skillet and cook, tossing constantly, until the sauce is thickened, about 30 seconds. Season with salt and pepper to taste. Transfer to a serving platter, sprinkle with the cilantro, and serve.

Stir-Fried Tofu, Snow Peas, and Red Onion with Hot and Sour Sauce

SERVES 4

Make sure to buy firm or extra-firm tofu; silken or soft tofu will crumble if stir-fried. To promote caramelization on the exterior of the tofu, turn the cubes as little as possible so that they have time to brown on several sides. For more heat, include the jalapeño seeds and ribs when mincing. Serve with Basic White Rice (page 453).

SAUCE

3 tablespoons cider vinegar
1 tablespoon low-sodium chicken broth
1 tablespoon soy sauce
2 teaspoons sugar

TOFU AND VEGETABLES

1 (14-ounce) block firm or extra-firm tofu, drained and cut into 1-inch cubes (see note)
1 tablespoon soy sauce
1 tablespoon dry sherry

2 tablespoons plus 1 teaspoon peanut or vegetable oil
1 tablespoon minced or grated fresh ginger
3 garlic cloves, minced or pressed through a garlic press (about 1 tablespoon)
2 scallions, white parts only, minced
1 jalapeño chile, seeds and ribs removed, chile minced (see note)
1 medium red onion, halved and sliced thin
1 pound snow peas, tips and strings removed
2 tablespoons water

1. **FOR THE SAUCE:** Combine all the ingredients in a small bowl and set aside.

2. **FOR THE TOFU AND VEGETABLES:** Toss the tofu with the soy sauce and sherry in a medium bowl and let marinate for at least 10 minutes or up to 1 hour. In a small bowl, mix 1 teaspoon of the oil, the ginger, garlic, scallions, and jalapeño together.

3. Heat 1 tablespoon more oil in a 12-inch nonstick skillet over high heat until just smoking. Add the tofu and cook until golden brown on several sides, 2 to 3 minutes, turning as needed. Transfer the tofu to a clean bowl and cover with foil to keep warm.

4. Add the remaining 1 tablespoon oil to the skillet and return to high heat until just smoking. Add the onion and cook, stirring frequently, until beginning to brown, about 2 minutes. Add the snow peas and cook until spotty brown, about 2 minutes. Add the water, cover the pan, and lower the heat to medium. Cook the snow peas until crisp-tender, about 1 minute.

5. Clear the center of the skillet, add the ginger mixture, and cook, mashing the mixture into the pan, until fragrant, 15 to 20 seconds. Stir the ginger mixture into the vegetables.

6. Stir in the tofu. Whisk the sauce to recombine, then add to the skillet and cook, tossing constantly, until the sauce is thickened, about 30 seconds. Transfer to a serving platter and serve.

CHINESE-STYLE MAPO TOFU

WHY THIS RECIPE WORKS: Our *mapo* tofu recipe is bold in flavor, but not too spicy, and balanced, as all Sichuan dishes should be. We used cubed soft tofu, poached gently in chicken broth to help the cubes stay intact in the braise. For the sauce base, we used plenty of ginger and garlic, along with four Sichuan pantry powerhouses: Asian broad bean chili paste (*doubanjiang* or *toban djan*), fermented black beans, Sichuan chili powder, and Sichuan peppercorns. In place of the chili oil often called for, we used a generous amount of vegetable oil, extra Sichuan chili powder, and added toasted sesame oil. Finally, just the right amount of cornstarch gave the dish a velvety thickness.

3. Process garlic, ginger, chili paste, and black beans in food processor until coarse paste forms, 1 to 2 minutes, scraping down sides of bowl as needed. Add ¼ cup vegetable oil, chili powder, and 1 teaspoon peppercorns and continue to process until smooth paste forms, 1 to 2 minutes longer. Transfer spice paste to bowl.

4. Heat 1 tablespoon vegetable oil and beef in large saucepan over medium heat; cook, breaking up meat with wooden spoon, until meat just begins to brown, 5 to 7 minutes. Transfer beef to bowl.

5. Add remaining 1 tablespoon vegetable oil and spice paste to now-empty saucepan and cook, stirring frequently, until paste darkens and oil begins to separate from paste, 2 to 3 minutes. Gently pour tofu with broth into saucepan, followed by hoisin, sesame oil, and beef. Cook, stirring gently and frequently, until dish comes to simmer, 2 to 3 minutes. Whisk water and cornstarch together in small bowl. Add cornstarch mixture to saucepan and continue to cook, stirring frequently, until thickened, 2 to 3 minutes longer. Transfer to serving dish, sprinkle with remaining peppercorns, and serve. (Mapo tofu can be refrigerated for up to 24 hours.)

STIR-FRIED BEEF AND BROCCOLI

WHY THIS RECIPE WORKS: Order beef and broccoli in most Chinese restaurants, and you are served a pile of tough meat and overcooked army-issue broccoli. Worst of all is the thick-as-pudding brown sauce, which, aside from being flavored with burnt garlic, is otherwise tasteless. We set out to rescue this dish from the tyranny of third-rate Chinese restaurants.

For the meat, we found that flank steak offered the biggest beefy taste and slicing it thin made it tender. We cooked the beef in two batches over high heat to make sure it browned and didn't steam. Then we cooked the broccoli until crisp-tender using a combination of methods—sautéing and steaming—and added some red bell pepper for sweetness and color. For the sauce, we made a simple mixture of oyster-flavored sauce, chicken broth, dry sherry, sugar, and sesame oil, which we lightly thickened with cornstarch so it clung beautifully to the beef and vegetables. Now we had it: Every component of the dish—the beef, the broccoli, and the sauce—was distinct and cooked to the best of its ability.

Stir-Fried Beef and Broccoli with Oyster Sauce
SERVES 4

To make slicing the flank steak easier, freeze it for 15 minutes. Serve with Basic White Rice (page 453).

SAUCE
- 5 tablespoons oyster-flavored sauce
- 2 tablespoons low-sodium chicken broth
- 1 tablespoon dry sherry
- 1 tablespoon light brown sugar
- 1 teaspoon toasted sesame oil
- 1 teaspoon cornstarch

Sichuan Braised Tofu with Beef (Mapo Tofu)
SERVES 4 TO 6

Ground pork can be used in place of beef, if desired. Asian broad bean chili paste (or sauce) is also known as *doubanjiang* or *toban djan*; our favorite, Pixian, is available online. Supermarket Lee Kum Kee Chili Bean Sauce is also a good option. If you can't find Sichuan chili powder, an equal amount of Korean red pepper flakes (*gochugaru*) is a good substitute. In a pinch, use 2½ teaspoons of ancho chile powder and ½ teaspoon of cayenne pepper. If you can't find fermented black beans, you can use an equal amount of fermented black bean paste or sauce or two additional teaspoons of Asian broad bean chili paste. Serve with Basic White Rice (page 453).

- 1 tablespoon Sichuan peppercorns
- 12 scallions
- 28 ounces soft tofu, cut into ½-inch cubes
- 2 cups chicken broth
- 9 garlic cloves, peeled
- 1 (3-inch) piece ginger, peeled and cut into ¼-inch rounds
- ⅓ cup Asian broad bean chili paste
- 1 tablespoon fermented black beans
- ¼ cup plus 2 tablespoons vegetable oil
- 1 tablespoon Sichuan chili powder
- 8 ounces 85 percent lean ground beef
- 2 tablespoons hoisin sauce
- 2 teaspoons toasted sesame oil
- 2 tablespoons water
- 1 tablespoon cornstarch

1. Place peppercorns in small bowl and microwave until fragrant, 15 to 30 seconds. Let cool completely. Once cool, grind in spice grinder or mortar and pestle (you should have 1½ teaspoons).

2. Using side of chef's knife, lightly crush white parts of scallions, then cut scallions into 1-inch pieces. Place tofu, broth, and scallions in large bowl and microwave, covered, until steaming, 5 to 7 minutes. Let stand while preparing remaining ingredients.

BEEF AND BROCCOLI

1 (1-pound) flank steak, trimmed and cut into 2-inch-wide strips with the grain, then sliced across the grain into ⅛-inch-thick slices (see note)

3 tablespoons soy sauce

3 tablespoons peanut or vegetable oil

6 medium garlic cloves, minced or pressed through a garlic press (about 2 tablespoons)

1 tablespoon minced or grated fresh ginger

1¼ pounds broccoli, florets cut into 1-inch pieces, stems trimmed and sliced thin

⅓ cup water

1 small red bell pepper, stemmed, seeded, and cut into ½-inch pieces

3 scallions, sliced ½ inch thick on the bias

1. FOR THE SAUCE: Combine all the ingredients in a small bowl and set aside.

2. FOR THE BEEF AND BROCCOLI: Toss the beef with the soy sauce in a medium bowl and let marinate for at least 10 minutes or up to 1 hour. In a small bowl, mix 1 teaspoon of the peanut oil, the garlic, and ginger together.

3. Heat 2 teaspoons more peanut oil in a 12-inch nonstick skillet over high heat until just smoking. Add half of the beef, break up any clumps, then cook without stirring until the meat is browned at the edges, about 1 minute. Stir the beef and continue to cook until cooked through, about 1 minute longer. Transfer the beef to a clean bowl and cover with foil to keep warm. Repeat with 2 teaspoons more peanut oil and the remaining beef.

4. Add 1 tablespoon more peanut oil to the skillet and return to high heat until just smoking. Add the broccoli and cook for 30 seconds. Add the water, cover the pan, and lower the heat to medium. Cook the broccoli until crisp-tender, about 2 minutes. Transfer the broccoli to a paper towel–lined plate.

5. Add the remaining 1 teaspoon peanut oil to the skillet and return to high heat until just smoking. Add the bell pepper and cook, stirring frequently, until spotty brown, about 1½ minutes. Clear the center of the skillet, add the garlic mixture, and cook, mashing the mixture into the pan, until fragrant, 15 to 20 seconds. Stir the garlic mixture into the bell pepper.

6. Stir in the broccoli and beef with any accumulated juices. Whisk the sauce to recombine, then add to the skillet and cook, tossing constantly, until the sauce is thickened, about 30 seconds. Transfer to a serving platter, sprinkle with the scallions, and serve.

CHINESE PEPPER STEAK

WHY THIS RECIPE WORKS: We discovered that in order to produce a stir-fry with velvety, tender beef normally only found in Chinese restaurants, we needed to choose the right cut of meat and treat it correctly. Flank steak, cut across the grain into bite-size pieces, delivered great beef flavor and a moderate chew. Then, our combination of meat tenderizing techniques—soaking the meat briefly in a mild baking soda solution and adding some cornstarch to the marinade before flash searing the steak in a very hot pan—finished the job of delivering a supertender, restaurant-quality beef stir-fry.

Beef Stir-Fry with Bell Peppers and Black Pepper Sauce

SERVES 4

Prepare the vegetables and aromatics while the beef is marinating. Serve with Basic White Rice (page 453).

1 tablespoon plus ¼ cup water

¼ teaspoon baking soda

1 pound flank steak, trimmed, cut into 2- to 2½-inch strips with grain, each strip cut crosswise against grain into ¼-inch-thick slices

3 tablespoons soy sauce

3 tablespoons dry sherry or Chinese rice wine

3 teaspoons cornstarch

2½ teaspoons packed light brown sugar

1 tablespoon oyster sauce

2 teaspoons rice vinegar

1½ teaspoons toasted sesame oil

2 teaspoons coarsely ground pepper

3 tablespoons plus 1 teaspoon vegetable oil

1 red bell pepper, stemmed, seeded, and cut into ¼-inch-wide strips

1 green bell pepper, stemmed, seeded, and cut into ¼-inch-wide strips

6 scallions, white parts sliced thin on bias, green parts cut into 2-inch pieces

3 garlic cloves, minced

1 tablespoon grated fresh ginger

1. Combine 1 tablespoon water and baking soda in medium bowl. Add beef and toss to coat. Let sit at room temperature for 5 minutes.

2. Whisk 1 tablespoon soy sauce, 1 tablespoon sherry, 1½ teaspoons cornstarch, and ½ teaspoon sugar together in small bowl. Add soy sauce mixture to beef, stir to coat, and let sit at room temperature for 15 to 30 minutes.

3. Whisk remaining ¼ cup water, remaining 2 tablespoons soy sauce, remaining 2 tablespoons sherry, remaining 1½ teaspoons cornstarch, remaining 2 teaspoons sugar, oyster sauce, vinegar, sesame oil, and pepper together in second bowl.

4. Heat 2 teaspoons vegetable oil in 12-inch nonstick skillet over high heat until just smoking. Add half of beef in single layer. Cook without stirring for 1 minute. Continue to cook, stirring occasionally, until spotty brown on both sides, about 1 minute longer. Transfer to bowl. Repeat with 2 teaspoons vegetable oil and remaining beef.

5. Return skillet to high heat, add 2 teaspoons vegetable oil, and heat until just beginning to smoke. Add bell peppers and scallion greens and cook, stirring occasionally, until vegetables are spotty brown and crisp-tender, about 4 minutes. Transfer vegetables to bowl with beef.

6. Return now-empty skillet to medium-high heat and add remaining 4 teaspoons vegetable oil, scallion whites, garlic, and ginger. Cook, stirring frequently, until lightly browned, about 2 minutes. Return beef and vegetables to skillet and stir to combine.

7. Whisk sauce to recombine. Add to skillet and cook, stirring constantly, until sauce has thickened, about 30 seconds. Serve immediately.

BEEF AND VEGETABLE STIR-FRIES

WHY THIS RECIPE WORKS: More often than not, beef and vegetable stir-fries consist of chewy, gray beef, surrounded by unevenly cooked vegetables, smothered in a gloppy sauce. We wanted browned, tender beef and crisp-tender vegetables coated in deep-flavored, silky sauces.

We chose flank steak for the best texture and flavor. We thinly sliced and marinated the steak in soy sauce and sugar and cooked it over high heat to achieve a good sear. We cooked the vegetables in batches for best texture. For one stir-fry, we paired the beef with green beans, shiitakes, and a teriyaki sauce. Next, we combined the beef with a tangerine sauce, snow peas, and onion. The sauces were lightly thickened with just 1 teaspoon of cornstarch, so they clung to the beef and vegetables but were not overly thick.

Teriyaki Stir-Fried Beef with Green Beans and Shiitakes

SERVES 4

To make slicing the flank steak easier, freeze it for 15 minutes. Serve with Basic White Rice (page 453).

SAUCE

½ cup low-sodium chicken broth
2 tablespoons soy sauce
2 tablespoons sugar

1 tablespoon mirin or sweet sherry
1 teaspoon cornstarch
¼ teaspoon red pepper flakes

BEEF AND VEGETABLES

12 ounces flank steak, trimmed and cut into 2-inch-wide strips with the grain, then sliced across the grain into ⅛-inch-thick slices (see note)
2 tablespoons soy sauce
1 teaspoon sugar
2 tablespoons peanut or vegetable oil
1 tablespoon minced or grated fresh ginger
3 medium garlic cloves, minced or pressed through a garlic press (about 1 tablespoon)
8 ounces shiitake mushrooms, stemmed, wiped clean, caps cut into 1-inch pieces
12 ounces green beans, ends trimmed, cut into 2-inch lengths (see photo on page 465)
¼ cup water
3 scallions, quartered lengthwise and cut into 1½-inch pieces

1. FOR THE SAUCE: Combine all the ingredients in a small bowl and set aside.

2. FOR THE BEEF AND VEGETABLES: Toss the beef with the soy sauce and sugar in a medium bowl and let marinate for at least 10 minutes or up to 1 hour. In a small bowl, mix 1 teaspoon of the oil, the ginger, and garlic together.

3. Heat 2 teaspoons more oil in a 12-inch nonstick skillet over high heat until just smoking. Add the beef, break up any clumps, then cook without stirring until the meat is browned at the edges, about 1 minute. Stir the beef and continue to cook until cooked through, about 1 minute longer. Transfer the beef to a clean bowl and cover with foil to keep warm.

4. Add the remaining 1 tablespoon oil to the skillet and return to high heat until just smoking. Add the mushrooms and cook until beginning to brown, about 2 minutes. Add the green beans and cook, stirring frequently, until spotty brown,

3 to 4 minutes. Add the water, cover the pan, and lower the heat to medium. Cook the green beans until crisp-tender, about 2 minutes.

5. Clear the center of the skillet, add the ginger mixture, and cook, mashing the mixture into the pan, until fragrant, 15 to 20 seconds. Stir the ginger mixture into the vegetables.

6. Stir in the beef with any accumulated juices. Whisk the sauce to recombine, then add to the skillet and cook, tossing constantly, until the sauce is thickened, about 30 seconds. Stir in the scallions. Transfer to a serving platter and serve.

NOTES FROM THE TEST KITCHEN

TRIMMING GREEN BEANS QUICKLY

Line up several green beans in a row on a cutting board. Trim about ½ inch from each end, then cut the beans as directed in the recipe.

Tangerine Stir-Fried Beef with Onion and Snow Peas

SERVES 4

To make slicing the flank steak easier, freeze it for 15 minutes. Two to three oranges can be substituted for the tangerines. Note that you should zest the tangerines before juicing them. Use the larger amount of red pepper flakes if you desire a spicier dish. If available, substitute 1 teaspoon toasted and ground Sichuan peppercorns for the red pepper flakes. Serve with Basic White Rice (page 453).

SAUCE
- ¾ cup juice from 3 to 4 tangerines (see note)
- 2 tablespoons soy sauce
- 1 tablespoon light brown sugar
- 1 teaspoon toasted sesame oil
- 1 teaspoon cornstarch

BEEF AND VEGETABLES
- 12 ounces flank steak, trimmed and cut into 2-inch-wide strips with the grain, then sliced across the grain into ⅛-inch-thick slices (see note)
- 2 tablespoons soy sauce
- 1 teaspoon light brown sugar
- 2 tablespoons peanut or vegetable oil
- 1 tablespoon minced or grated fresh ginger
- 3 medium garlic cloves, minced or pressed through a garlic press (about 1 tablespoon)
- 1 tablespoon Chinese black bean sauce
- 1 teaspoon grated zest from 1 tangerine (see note)
- ¼–½ teaspoon red pepper flakes (see note)
- 1 large onion, halved and cut into ½-inch wedges
- 10 ounces snow peas, tips and strings removed
- 2 tablespoons water

1. FOR THE SAUCE: Combine all the ingredients in a small bowl and set aside.

2. FOR THE BEEF AND VEGETABLES: Toss the beef with the soy sauce and sugar in a medium bowl and let marinate for at least 10 minutes or up to 1 hour. In a small bowl, mix 1 teaspoon of the peanut oil, the ginger, garlic, black bean sauce, tangerine zest, and red pepper flakes together.

3. Heat 2 teaspoons more peanut oil in a 12-inch nonstick skillet over high heat until just smoking. Add the beef, break up any clumps, then cook without stirring until the meat is browned at the edges, about 1 minute. Stir the beef and continue to cook until cooked through, about 1 minute longer. Transfer the beef to a clean bowl and cover with foil to keep warm.

4. Add the remaining 1 tablespoon peanut oil to the skillet and return to high heat until just smoking. Add the onion and cook, stirring frequently, until beginning to brown, about 2 minutes. Add the snow peas and cook until spotty brown, about 2 minutes. Add the water, cover the pan, and lower the heat to medium. Cook the snow peas until crisp-tender, about 1 minute.

5. Clear the center of the skillet, add the ginger mixture, and cook, mashing the mixture into the pan, until fragrant, 15 to 20 seconds. Stir the ginger mixture into the vegetables.

6. Stir in the beef with any accumulated juices. Whisk the sauce to recombine, then add to the skillet and cook, tossing constantly, until the sauce is thickened, about 30 seconds. Transfer to a serving platter and serve.

CHINESE BRAISED BEEF

WHY THIS RECIPE WORKS: Chinese braised beef (also called red-cooked beef) is a slow-braised dish in which a thick, ultra-flavorful, stew-like sauce envelops tender pieces of beef. We wanted to maintain the deeply complex flavors of the original but simplify the recipe for the home kitchen.

We decided to use readily available boneless beef short ribs in place of the traditional shank of beef. To streamline the classic cooking method, we opted to skip blanching the meat, and we moved the pot from the stovetop to the even heat of the oven. A pair of thickeners—gelatin and cornstarch—added body to the sauce. Five-spice powder provided characteristic flavor without the bother of whole spices, and a combination of hoisin sauce and molasses contributed an underlying sweetness that completed the dish.

3. Using slotted spoon, transfer beef to cutting board. Strain sauce through fine-mesh strainer into fat separator. Wipe out pot with paper towels. Let liquid settle for 5 minutes, then return defatted liquid to now-empty pot. Cook liquid over medium-high heat, stirring occasionally, until thickened and reduced to 1 cup, 20 to 25 minutes.

4. While sauce reduces, using 2 forks, break beef into 1½-inch pieces. Whisk cornstarch and remaining 1 tablespoon water together in small bowl.

5. Reduce heat to medium-low, whisk cornstarch mixture into reduced sauce, and cook until sauce is slightly thickened, about 1 minute. Return beef to sauce and stir to coat. Cover and cook, stirring occasionally, until beef is heated through, about 5 minutes. Sprinkle scallion greens over top. Serve.

Chinese Braised Beef

SERVES 6

With its generous amount of soy sauce, this dish is meant to taste salty, which is why we pair it with Basic White Rice (page 453). A simple steamed vegetable like bok choy or broccoli completes the meal. Boneless beef short ribs require little trimming, but you can also use a 4-pound chuck roast. Trim the roast of large pieces of fat and sinew, cut it across the grain into 1-inch-thick slabs, and cut the slabs into 4 by 2-inch pieces.

  1½ tablespoons unflavored gelatin
  2½ cups plus 1 tablespoon water
  ½ cup dry sherry
  ⅓ cup soy sauce
  2 tablespoons hoisin sauce
  2 tablespoons molasses
  3 scallions, white and green parts separated, green parts sliced thin on bias
  1 (2-inch) piece ginger, peeled, halved lengthwise, and crushed
  4 garlic cloves, peeled and smashed
  1½ teaspoons five-spice powder
  1 teaspoon red pepper flakes
  3 pounds boneless beef short ribs, trimmed and cut into 4-inch lengths
  1 teaspoon cornstarch

1. Sprinkle gelatin over 2½ cups water in Dutch oven and let sit until gelatin softens, about 5 minutes. Adjust oven rack to middle position and heat oven to 300 degrees.

2. Heat softened gelatin over medium-high heat, stirring occasionally, until melted, 2 to 3 minutes. Stir in sherry, soy sauce, hoisin, molasses, scallion whites, ginger, garlic, five-spice powder, and pepper flakes. Stir in beef and bring to simmer. Remove pot from heat. Cover tightly with sheet of heavy-duty aluminum foil, then lid. Transfer to oven and cook until beef is tender, 2 to 2½ hours, stirring halfway through cooking.

CRISPY ORANGE BEEF

WHY THIS RECIPE WORKS: Crispy orange beef has long remained a Chinese restaurant standard because its crunchy batter coating and tangy citrus sauce seem impossible in the home kitchen without a deep fryer. To make this recipe accessible without diminishing its big flavor and shatteringly crisp crust, we started with the beef. Tender flap meat cut into matchsticks maximized the surface area for extra crunch in each bite. Tossing the beef in soy sauce and cornstarch created a clingy, delicate coating and 45 minutes in the freezer dried the prepped beef's surface to boost crisping. We only needed 3 cups of oil to fry the beef to a beautiful golden brown, and thanks to the dry cornstarch coating, very little oil was absorbed, so the beef never turned greasy. For a sauce to complement the crispy beef, we recreated the bitter, citrusy tang of hard-to-find dried tangerine peels by using the juice and peels of two oranges. We whisked the fresh juice with soy sauce, molasses, dry sherry, rice vinegar, and sesame oil for a complex, complementary sauce and then, for some bite and heat, browned the peels with jalapeños in a skillet. Garlic, ginger, and red pepper flakes reinforced the spicy bite before the soy sauce mixture was added to the pan. We cooked the mixture until it thickened slightly, and then tossed in our beef along with sliced scallions for a finishing touch of brightness.

Crispy Orange Beef

SERVES 4

We prefer to buy flap meat and cut our own steak tips. Use a vegetable peeler on the oranges and make sure that your strips contain some pith. Do not use low-sodium soy sauce. Serve this dish with Basic White Rice (page 453).

  1½ pounds beef flap meat, trimmed
  3 tablespoons soy sauce
  6 tablespoons cornstarch
  10 (3-inch) strips orange peel, sliced thin lengthwise (¼ cup), plus ¼ cup juice (2 oranges)
  3 tablespoons molasses
  2 tablespoons dry sherry
  1 tablespoon rice vinegar

1½ teaspoons toasted sesame oil

3 cups vegetable oil

1 jalapeño chile, stemmed, seeded, and sliced thin lengthwise

3 garlic cloves, minced

2 tablespoons grated fresh ginger

½ teaspoon red pepper flakes

2 scallions, sliced thin on bias

1. Cut beef with grain into 2½- to 3-inch-wide lengths. Slice each piece against grain into ½-inch-thick slices. Cut each slice lengthwise into ½-inch-wide strips. Toss beef with 1 tablespoon soy sauce in bowl. Add cornstarch and toss until evenly coated. Spread beef in single layer on wire rack set in rimmed baking sheet. Transfer sheet to freezer until meat is very firm but not completely frozen, about 45 minutes.

2. Whisk remaining 2 tablespoons soy sauce, orange juice, molasses, sherry, vinegar, and sesame oil together in bowl.

3. Line second rimmed baking sheet with triple layer of paper towels. Heat vegetable oil in large Dutch oven over medium heat until oil registers 375 degrees. Carefully add one-third of beef and fry, stirring occasionally to keep beef from sticking together, until golden brown, about 1½ minutes. Using spider, transfer beef to paper towel–lined sheet. Return oil to 375 degrees and repeat twice more with remaining beef. After frying, reserve 2 tablespoons frying oil.

4. Heat reserved oil in 12-inch skillet over medium-high heat until shimmering. Add orange peel and jalapeño and cook, stirring occasionally, until about half of orange peel is golden brown, 1½ to 2 minutes. Add garlic, ginger, and pepper flakes; cook, stirring frequently, until garlic is beginning to brown, about 45 seconds. Add soy sauce mixture and cook, scraping up any browned bits, until slightly thickened, about 45 seconds. Add beef and scallions and toss. Transfer to platter and serve immediately.

CHINESE BARBECUED PORK

WHY THIS RECIPE WORKS: For a Chinese barbecued pork recipe suited to the home kitchen, we started by slicing a boneless pork butt into strips. Our marinade of soy sauce, sherry, hoisin sauce, five-spice powder, sesame oil, ginger, and garlic introduced traditional Asian flavors, especially after we pricked the meat with a fork to enhance penetration. For optimal browning and intense flavor, we needed a two-heat process—first cooking the meat, covered, at a low temperature to render fat and then cranking up the heat to develop a burnished crust. The classic lacquered appearance was achieved by applying a ketchup-honey glaze right before broiling, which also gave our pork its traditional red color.

Chinese Barbecued Pork

SERVES 6

To facilitate cleanup, spray the rack and pan with vegetable oil spray. The pork will release liquid and fat during the cooking process, so be careful when removing the pan from the oven. If you don't have a wire rack that fits in a rimmed baking sheet, substitute a broiler pan, although the meat may not darken as much. Pay close attention to the meat when broiling—you are looking for it to darken and caramelize, not blacken. Do not use a drawer broiler; the heat source will be too close to the meat. Instead, increase the oven temperature in step 5 to 500 degrees and cook for 8 to 12 minutes before glazing and 6 to 8 minutes once the glaze has been applied; flip meat and repeat on second side. This recipe can be made with boneless country-style ribs, but the meat will be slightly drier and less flavorful. To use ribs, reduce the uncovered cooking time in step 4 to 20 minutes and increase the broiling and glazing times in step 5 by 2 to 3 minutes per side.

4 pounds boneless pork butt (Boston butt), cut into 8 strips and excess fat removed

½ cup sugar

½ cup soy sauce

6 tablespoons hoisin sauce

¼ cup dry sherry

¼ teaspoon ground white pepper

1 teaspoon Chinese five-spice powder

1 tablespoon toasted sesame oil

2 tablespoons grated fresh ginger (from 4- to 6-inch piece)

2 medium cloves garlic, minced or pressed through a garlic press (about 2 teaspoons)

¼ cup ketchup

⅓ cup honey

1. Using fork, prick pork 10 to 12 times on each side. Place pork in large plastic zipper-lock bag. Combine sugar, soy, hoisin, sherry, pepper, five-spice powder, sesame oil, ginger, and garlic in medium bowl. Measure out ½ cup marinade and set aside. Pour remaining marinade into bag with pork. Press out as much air as possible; seal bag. Refrigerate for at least 30 minutes or up to 4 hours.

2. While meat marinates, combine ketchup and honey with reserved marinade in small saucepan. Cook glaze over medium heat until syrupy and reduced to 1 cup, 4 to 6 minutes.

3. Adjust oven rack to middle position and heat oven to 300 degrees. Line rimmed baking sheet with aluminum foil and set wire rack on sheet.

4. Remove pork from marinade, letting any excess drip off, and place on wire rack. Pour ¼ cup water into bottom of pan. Cover pan with heavy-duty aluminum foil, crimping edges tightly to seal. Cook pork for 20 minutes. Remove foil and continue to cook until edges of pork begin to brown, 40 to 45 minutes.

5. Turn on broiler. Broil pork until evenly caramelized, 7 to 9 minutes. Remove pan from oven and brush pork with half of glaze; broil until deep mahogany color, 3 to 5 minutes. Using tongs, flip meat and broil until other side caramelizes, 7 to 9 minutes. Brush meat with remaining glaze and continue to broil until second side is deep mahogany, 3 to 5 minutes. Cool for at least 10 minutes, then cut into thin strips and serve.

PORK AND VEGETABLE STIR-FRIES

WHY THIS RECIPE WORKS: Pork and vegetable stir-fries, homemade or ordered out, are usually nothing more than tough, tasteless pork and barely cooked vegetables in a thick sauce. We wanted to make pork and vegetable stir-fries that had tender, flavorful pork and perfectly cooked vegetables—dishes that would taste authentic but would not have unapproachable ingredient lists. We chose pork tenderloin for our stir-fry because it is so tender. Marinating improved the pork's flavor, and cooking quickly over high heat ensured browning. Because different vegetables cook at different rates, we batch-cooked the vegetables and added aromatics (like ginger and garlic) at the end so they would cook long enough to develop their flavors but not burn. For the sauce, we used chicken broth as the backbone and added an acid like lime juice or rice vinegar to brighten the flavors. As with our other stir-fries, cornstarch created a slightly thickened sauce that lightly cloaked the pork and vegetables.

Stir-Fried Pork, Eggplant, and Onion with Garlic and Black Pepper

SERVES 4

To make slicing the pork easier, freeze it for 15 minutes. This classic Thai stir-fry is not for those with timid palates. Serve with Basic White Rice (page 453).

SAUCE
- 2½ tablespoons soy sauce
- 2½ tablespoons fish sauce
- 2½ tablespoons light brown sugar
- 2 tablespoons low-sodium chicken broth
- 2 teaspoons juice from 1 lime
- 1 teaspoon cornstarch

PORK AND VEGETABLES
- 1 (12-ounce) pork tenderloin, trimmed of fat and silver skin and cut into ¼-inch strips (see note)
- 1 teaspoon soy sauce
- 1 teaspoon fish sauce
- 3 tablespoons peanut or vegetable oil
- 12 medium garlic cloves, minced or pressed through a garlic press (about ¼ cup)
- 2 teaspoons ground black pepper
- 1 medium eggplant (1 pound), cut into ¾-inch cubes
- 1 large onion, halved and cut into ¼-inch wedges
- ½ cup chopped fresh cilantro leaves

1. FOR THE SAUCE: Combine all the ingredients in a small bowl and set aside.

2. FOR THE PORK AND VEGETABLES: Toss the pork with the soy sauce and fish sauce in a medium bowl and let marinate for at least 10 minutes or up to 1 hour. In a small bowl, mix 2 teaspoons of the oil, the garlic, and pepper together.

3. Heat 2 teaspoons more oil in a 12-inch nonstick skillet over high heat until just smoking. Add the pork, break up any clumps, then cook without stirring until the meat is browned at the edges, about 1 minute. Stir the pork and continue to cook until cooked through, about 1 minute longer. Transfer the pork to a clean bowl and cover with foil to keep warm.

4. Add 1 tablespoon more oil to the skillet and return to high heat until just smoking. Add the eggplant and cook, stirring frequently, until browned and no longer spongy, about 5 minutes. Transfer the eggplant to the bowl with the pork. Add the remaining 2 teaspoons peanut oil to the skillet and return to high heat until just smoking. Add the onion and cook until beginning to brown and soften, about 2 minutes.

5. Clear the center of the skillet, add the garlic mixture, and cook, mashing the mixture into the pan, until fragrant, 15 to 20 seconds. Stir the garlic mixture into the onion.

6. Stir in the eggplant and pork with any accumulated juices. Whisk the sauce to recombine, then add to the skillet and cook, tossing constantly, until the sauce is thickened, about 30 seconds. Transfer to a serving platter, sprinkle with the cilantro, and serve.

Stir-Fried Pork, Green Beans, and Red Bell Pepper with Gingery Oyster Sauce

SERVES 4

To make slicing the pork easier, freeze it for 15 minutes. Serve with Basic White Rice (page 453).

SAUCE
- ⅓ cup low-sodium chicken broth
- 2½ tablespoons oyster-flavored sauce
- 1 tablespoon dry sherry
- 2 teaspoons toasted sesame oil
- 1 teaspoon rice vinegar
- 1 teaspoon cornstarch
- ¼ teaspoon ground white pepper

PORK AND VEGETABLES

- 1 (12-ounce) pork tenderloin, trimmed of fat and silver skin and cut into ¼-inch strips (see note)
- 2 teaspoons soy sauce
- 2 teaspoons dry sherry
- 3 tablespoons peanut or vegetable oil
- 2 tablespoons minced or grated fresh ginger
- 2 medium garlic cloves, minced or pressed through a garlic press (about 2 teaspoons)
- 12 ounces green beans, trimmed and cut on the bias into 2-inch lengths
- ¼ cup water
- 1 large red bell pepper, stemmed, seeded, and cut into ¾-inch squares
- 3 scallions, sliced thin on the bias

1. FOR THE SAUCE: Combine all the ingredients in a small bowl and set aside.

2. FOR THE PORK AND VEGETABLES: Toss the pork with the soy sauce and sherry in a medium bowl and let marinate for at least 10 minutes or up to 1 hour. In a small bowl, mix 2 teaspoons of the peanut oil, the ginger, and garlic together.

3. Heat 2 teaspoons more peanut oil in a 12-inch nonstick skillet over high heat until just smoking. Add the pork, break up any clumps, then cook without stirring until the meat is browned at the edges, about 1 minute. Stir the pork and continue to cook until cooked through, about 1 minute longer. Transfer the pork to a clean bowl and cover with foil to keep warm.

4. Add 1 tablespoon more peanut oil to the skillet and return to high heat until just smoking. Add the green beans and cook, stirring frequently, until spotty brown, 3 to 4 minutes. Add the water, cover the pan, and lower the heat to medium. Cook the green beans until crisp-tender, about 2 minutes. Transfer the green beans to the bowl with the pork. Add the remaining 2 teaspoons peanut oil to the skillet and return to high heat until just smoking. Add the bell pepper and cook until spotty brown, about 1½ minutes.

5. Clear the center of the skillet, add the ginger mixture, and cook, mashing the mixture into the pan, until fragrant, 15 to 20 seconds. Stir the ginger mixture into the bell pepper.

6. Stir in the green beans and pork with any accumulated juices. Whisk the sauce to recombine, then add to the skillet and cook, tossing constantly, until the sauce is thickened, about 30 seconds. Transfer to a serving platter, sprinkle with the scallions, and serve.

CHINESE-STYLE PORK IN GARLIC SAUCE

WHY THIS RECIPE WORKS: Recipes for this Sichuan staple are usually imbalanced. Some taste cloyingly sweet, while others overdo it on the vinegar. And the pork is usually dry, chewy, and stringy. We wanted a version as good as anything we'd order in a Sichuan restaurant. To re-create the succulent pork found in the best restaurant stir-fries (usually achieved by low-temperature deep frying), we soaked the pork in a baking

soda solution, which tenderized and moisturized the meat, and then coated it in a velvetizing cornstarch slurry, which helped it retain moisture as it cooked. Ketchup and fish sauce, both high in flavor-enhancing glutamates.

Sichuan Stir-Fried Pork in Garlic Sauce
SERVES 4 TO 6

If Chinese black vinegar is unavailable, substitute 2 teaspoons balsamic vinegar and 2 teaspoons rice vinegar. If Asian broad-bean chili paste is unavailable, substitute 2 teaspoons Asian chili-garlic paste or Sriracha sauce. Serve with Basic White Rice (page 453).

SAUCE

- ½ cup low-sodium chicken broth
- 2 tablespoons sugar
- 2 tablespoons soy sauce
- 4 teaspoons Chinese black vinegar (see note)
- 1 tablespoon toasted sesame oil
- 1 tablespoon Chinese rice wine or dry sherry
- 2 teaspoons ketchup
- 2 teaspoons fish sauce
- 2 teaspoons cornstarch

PORK

- 12 ounces boneless country-style pork ribs, trimmed
- 1 teaspoon baking soda
- 2 teaspoons Chinese rice wine or dry sherry
- 2 teaspoons cornstarch

STIR-FRY

- 2 scallions, white parts minced, green parts sliced thin
- 4 garlic cloves, minced
- 2 tablespoons Asian broad-bean chili paste (see note)
- ¼ cup vegetable oil
- 6 ounces shiitake mushrooms, stemmed and sliced thin
- 2 celery ribs, cut on bias into ¼-inch slices

1. FOR THE SAUCE: Whisk all ingredients together in bowl; set aside.

2. FOR THE PORK: Cut pork into 2-inch lengths, then cut each length into ¼-inch matchsticks. Combine pork with ½ cup cold water and baking soda in bowl. Let sit at room temperature for 15 minutes.

3. Rinse pork in cold water. Drain well and pat dry with paper towels. Whisk rice wine and cornstarch together in bowl. Add pork and toss to coat.

4. FOR THE STIR-FRY: Combine scallion whites, garlic, and chili paste in bowl.

5. Heat 1 tablespoon vegetable oil in 12-inch nonstick skillet over high heat until just smoking. Add mushrooms and cook, stirring frequently, until tender, 2 to 4 minutes. Add celery and continue to cook until celery is crisp-tender, 2 to 4 minutes. Transfer vegetables to separate bowl.

6. Add remaining 3 tablespoons vegetable oil to now-empty skillet and place over medium-low heat. Add scallion-garlic mixture and cook, stirring frequently, until fragrant, about 30 seconds. Transfer 1 tablespoon scallion-garlic oil to small bowl and set aside. Add pork to skillet and cook, stirring frequently, until no longer pink, 3 to 5 minutes. Whisk sauce mixture to recombine and add to skillet. Increase heat to high and cook, stirring constantly, until sauce is thickened and pork is cooked through, 1 to 2 minutes. Return vegetables to skillet and toss to combine. Transfer to serving platter, sprinkle with scallion greens and reserved scallion-garlic oil, and serve.

PORK LO MEIN

WHY THIS RECIPE WORKS: Ordinary takeout pork lo mein invariably disappoints, with greasy flavors and sodden vegetables. We wanted a dish representative of the best that a good Chinese home cook could turn out: chewy noodles tossed in a salty-sweet sauce and accented with bits of smoky, barbecued pork and still-crisp cabbage.

First we needed to tackle the *char siu*, preferably perfecting a stir-fried version since we were already stir-frying the vegetables. Country-style pork ribs won for best cut. Though fatty, these meaty ribs have the same rich flavor of pork shoulder—but don't need to be cooked for hours since they're naturally tender. To avoid an overly greasy dish, we trimmed the fat and cut the meat into thin strips that would allow our classic Chinese marinade to penetrate effectively. A few drops of liquid smoke mimicked char siu's characteristic smoky flavor. Turning to the noodles, ones labeled "lo mein" at the Asian market won raves. Fortunately, dried linguine, cooked al dente, also worked beautifully. For the vegetables, we opted for traditional choices—cabbage, scallions, and shiitake mushrooms—stir-frying them with garlic and fresh ginger. We used our meat marinade as a sauce base, with a little chicken broth and a teaspoon of cornstarch added for body. A splash of Asian chili-garlic sauce added a little kick.

Pork Lo Mein
SERVES 4

Use a cast-iron skillet for this recipe if you have one—it will help create the best sear on the pork. If boneless pork ribs are unavailable, substitute 1½ pounds bone-in country-style ribs, followed by the next-best option, pork tenderloin. Liquid smoke provides a flavor reminiscent of the Chinese barbecued pork traditional to this dish. It is important to cook the noodles at the last minute to avoid clumping.

- 3 tablespoons soy sauce
- 2 tablespoons oyster-flavored sauce
- 2 tablespoons hoisin sauce
- 1 tablespoon toasted sesame oil
- ¼ teaspoon Chinese five-spice powder
- 1 pound boneless country-style pork ribs, trimmed of fat and gristle, sliced crosswise into ⅛-inch pieces (see note)
- ¼ teaspoon liquid smoke (optional; see note)
- ½ cup low-sodium chicken broth
- 1 teaspoon cornstarch
- 2 tablespoons plus 1 teaspoon peanut or vegetable oil
- 2 teaspoons minced or grated fresh ginger
- 2 medium garlic cloves, minced or pressed through a garlic press (about 2 teaspoons)
- ¼ cup Chinese rice cooking wine (Shaoxing) or dry sherry
- 8 ounces shiitake mushrooms, stemmed, wiped clean, caps sliced ¼ inch thick
- 2 bunches scallions, whites sliced thin, greens cut into 1-inch pieces
- 1 pound napa cabbage (1 small head), cored and cut into ½-inch strips
- 12 ounces fresh Chinese noodles or 8 ounces dried linguine
- 1 tablespoon Asian chili-garlic sauce

1. Whisk the soy sauce, oyster-flavored sauce, hoisin sauce, sesame oil, and five-spice powder together in a small bowl. Transfer 3 tablespoons of the mixture to a medium bowl and add the pork and liquid smoke (if using). Let marinate for at least 10 minutes or up to 1 hour. Whisk the broth and cornstarch into the remaining soy sauce mixture and set aside. In a small bowl, mix 1 teaspoon of the peanut oil, the ginger, and garlic together and set aside.

2. Heat 2 teaspoons more peanut oil in a 12-inch nonstick or cast-iron skillet over high heat until just smoking. Add half of the pork, break up any clumps, then cook without stirring until the meat is browned at the edges, about 1 minute. Stir the pork and continue to cook until cooked through, about 1 minute longer. Add 2 tablespoons of the wine to the skillet and cook, stirring constantly, until the liquid is reduced and the pork is well coated, 30 to 60 seconds. Transfer the pork to a clean bowl and cover with foil to keep warm. Repeat with 2 teaspoons more peanut oil, the remaining pork, and the remaining 2 tablespoons wine. Wipe out the skillet with a wad of paper towels.

3. Add 1 teaspoon more peanut oil to the skillet and return to high heat until just smoking. Add the mushrooms and cook, stirring occasionally, until light golden brown, 4 to 6 minutes. Add the scallion whites and greens and cook, stirring occasionally, until wilted, 2 to 3 minutes. Transfer the vegetables to the bowl with the pork.

4. Add the remaining 1 teaspoon peanut oil to the skillet and heat over high heat until just smoking. Add the cabbage and cook, stirring occasionally, until spotty brown, 3 to 5 minutes. Clear the center of the skillet, add the ginger mixture, and cook, mashing the mixture into the pan, until fragrant, 15 to 20 seconds. Stir the ginger mixture into the cabbage.

5. Stir in the vegetables and pork with any accumulated juices. Whisk the sauce to recombine, then add to the skillet and cook, tossing constantly, until the sauce is thickened, about 30 seconds.

6. Bring 6 quarts water to a boil in a large pot. Add the noodles and cook, stirring often, until tender, about 4 minutes for fresh and 10 minutes for dried. Drain the noodles and return them to the pot. Add the cooked stir-fry mixture and the chili-garlic sauce to the noodles and toss to combine. Transfer to a serving platter and serve.

MU SHU PORK

WHY THIS RECIPE WORKS: Mu shu pork's thin, stretchy pancakes are the hallmark of the Chinese restaurant classic, so we started there. Stirring boiling water into flour kept the dough from turning sticky and made it easy to roll. After resting the dough, we rolled it into a log and cut it into 12 pieces, pressing them into rounds and brushing one side of 6 disks with sesame oil. After placing the unoiled disks on top of the

oiled ones, we rolled the doubled-up disks to a 7-inch diameter and cooked each in a warm skillet. These lightly browned, puffed pancakes were easily peeled into two thinner pancakes. We loaded up the filling with flavor-builders, first microwaving dried shiitakes in water to rehydrate them for an earthy component. We saved the shiitakes' soaking liquid to boost our sauce, whisking it with soy sauce, dry sherry, and cornstarch. To season the thinly sliced pork tenderloin, we tossed it in a blend of soy sauce, dry sherry, sugar, fresh ginger, and white pepper. Next, we scrambled 2 eggs, browned sliced scallion whites, and cooked the pork—a quick 1 to 2 minutes a side. With the pork and scrambled eggs in a bowl to the side, we finished up the vegetables. Simply heating the shiitakes and matchstick-cut bamboo shoots sufficed before adding in sliced green cabbage and scallion greens, cooking them in the mushroom liquid mixture for full umami-rich flavor. A smear of sweet and salty hoisin sauce on the pancakes tied the flavors together.

Mu Shu Pork

SERVES 4

We strongly recommend weighing the flour for the pancakes. For an accurate measurement of boiling water, bring a full kettle to a boil and then measure ¾ cup.

PANCAKES

1½ cups (7½ ounces) all-purpose flour
¾ cup boiling water
2 teaspoons toasted sesame oil
½ teaspoon vegetable oil

STIR-FRY

1 ounce dried shiitake mushrooms, rinsed
¼ cup soy sauce
2 tablespoons dry sherry
1 teaspoon sugar
1 teaspoon grated fresh ginger
¼ teaspoon white pepper
1 (12-ounce) pork tenderloin, trimmed, halved horizontally, and sliced thin against grain
2 teaspoons cornstarch
2 tablespoons plus 2 teaspoons vegetable oil
2 large eggs, beaten
6 scallions, white and green parts separated and sliced thin on bias
1 (8-ounce) can bamboo shoots, rinsed and sliced into matchsticks
3 cups thinly sliced green cabbage
¼ cup hoisin sauce

1. FOR THE PANCAKES: Using wooden spoon, mix flour and boiling water in bowl to form rough dough. When cool, transfer dough to lightly floured surface and knead until it forms ball that is tacky but no longer sticky, about 4 minutes (dough will not be perfectly smooth). Cover loosely with plastic wrap and let rest for 30 minutes.

2. Roll dough into 12-inch-long log on lightly floured surface and cut into 12 equal pieces. Turn each piece cut side up and pat into rough 3-inch disk. Brush 1 side of 6 disks with sesame oil; top each oiled side with unoiled disk and press lightly to form 6 pairs. Roll disks into 7-inch rounds, lightly flouring work surface as needed.

3. Heat vegetable oil in 12-inch nonstick skillet over medium heat until shimmering. Using paper towels, carefully wipe out oil. Place pancake in skillet and cook without moving it until air pockets begin to form between layers and underside is dry, 40 to 60 seconds. Flip pancake and cook until few light brown spots appear on second side, 40 to 60 seconds. Transfer to plate and, when cool enough to handle, peel apart into 2 pancakes. Stack pancakes moist side up and cover loosely with plastic. Repeat with remaining pancakes. Cover pancakes tightly and keep warm. Wipe out skillet with paper towel. (Pancakes can be wrapped tightly in plastic wrap, then aluminum foil, and refrigerated for up to 3 days or frozen for up to 2 months. Thaw wrapped pancakes at room temperature. Unwrap and place on plate. Invert second plate over pancakes and microwave until warm and soft, 60 to 90 seconds.)

4. FOR THE STIR-FRY: Microwave 1 cup water and mushrooms in covered bowl until steaming, about 1 minute. Let sit until softened, about 5 minutes. Drain mushrooms through fine-mesh strainer and reserve ⅓ cup liquid. Discard mushroom stems and slice caps thin.

5. Combine 2 tablespoons soy sauce, 1 tablespoon sherry, sugar, ginger, and pepper in large bowl. Add pork and toss to combine. Whisk together reserved mushroom liquid, remaining 2 tablespoons soy sauce, remaining 1 tablespoon sherry, and cornstarch; set aside.

6. Heat 2 teaspoons oil in now-empty skillet over medium-high heat until shimmering. Add eggs and scramble quickly until set but not dry, about 15 seconds. Transfer to bowl and break eggs into ¼- to ½-inch pieces with fork. Return now-empty skillet to medium-high heat and heat 1 tablespoon oil until shimmering. Add scallion whites and cook, stirring frequently, until well browned, 1 to 1½ minutes. Add pork mixture. Spread into even layer and cook without moving it until well browned on 1 side, 1 to 2 minutes. Stir and continue to cook, stirring frequently, until all pork is opaque, 1 to 2 minutes longer. Transfer to bowl with eggs.

7. Return now-empty skillet to medium-high heat and heat remaining 1 tablespoon oil until shimmering. Whisk mushroom liquid mixture to recombine. Add mushrooms and bamboo shoots to skillet and cook, stirring frequently, until heated through, about 1 minute. Add cabbage, all but 2 tablespoons scallion greens, and mushroom liquid mixture and cook, stirring constantly, until liquid has evaporated and cabbage is wilted but retains some crunch, 2 to 3 minutes. Add pork and eggs and stir to combine. Transfer to platter and top with remaining scallion greens.

8. Spread about ½ teaspoon hoisin in center of each warm pancake. Spoon stir-fry over hoisin and serve.

MAKING TWO PANCAKES AT A TIME
Cooking two rounds together produces pancakes twice as fast.

1. Brush 6 disks with sesame oil. Top with unoiled disks. Press pairs together, then roll into thin rounds.

2. Heat each round until air pockets form between layers and underside is dry. Flip and cook second side.

3. When pancakes are cool enough to handle, peel apart into 2 pieces.

SINGAPORE NOODLES

WHY THIS RECIPE WORKS: Singapore noodles have nothing to do with Singapore and are virtually unknown there. This light, almost fluffy stir-fry of thin, resilient rice noodles, vegetables, and shrimp is native to Hong Kong, and the name is something of a mystery. Along with the traditional Chinese flavorings of garlic, ginger, and soy, this dish prominently features curry powder. The heady spice mixture lends the dish a pervasive aroma and a pleasant chile burn. But because this dish is not saucy, the dry powder doesn't distribute evenly, leading to patchy curry flavor (and color), not to mention gritty texture. We set out to solve this problem, and also to revise the usual ratio of ingredients (mostly noodles with a smattering of veggies and protein) to make a satisfying one-dish meal.

We started with the curry powder. We knew that "blooming" the spice mix by cooking it in hot oil would release lots of complex flavor. This had the added benefit of providing a medium for the spice granules to disperse, which meant that the grittiness in the dish was gone. A spoonful of sugar dispelled lingering bitter notes. To make the noodles more manageable, we cut them after soaking to make them less tangle-prone. We also cut the shrimp into ½-inch pieces that

dispersed nicely throughout the noodles, and bulked up the protein and vegetables by adding 4 eggs (scrambled with a little salt), 4 scallions cut into ½-inch pieces, and a couple of cups of bean sprouts.

Singapore Noodles

SERVES 4 TO 6

For a spicier dish, add the optional cayenne pepper. Look for dried rice vermicelli in the Asian section of your supermarket. A rasp-style grater makes it easy to turn the garlic into a paste.

- 4 tablespoons plus 1 teaspoon vegetable oil
- 2 tablespoons curry powder
- ⅛ teaspoon cayenne pepper (optional)
- 6 ounces rice vermicelli
- 2 tablespoons soy sauce
- 1 teaspoon sugar
- 12 ounces large shrimp (26 to 30 per pound), peeled, deveined (see page 240), tails removed, and cut into ½-inch pieces
- 4 large eggs, lightly beaten
  Salt
- 1 teaspoon grated fresh ginger
- 3 garlic cloves, minced to paste
- 1 red bell pepper, stemmed, seeded, and cut into 2-inch-long matchsticks
- 2 large shallots, sliced thin
- ⅔ cup chicken broth
- 4 ounces (2 cups) bean sprouts
- 4 scallions, cut into ½-inch pieces
- 2 teaspoons lime juice, plus lime wedges for serving

1. Heat 3 tablespoons oil, curry powder, and cayenne (if using) in 12-inch nonstick skillet over medium-low heat, stirring occasionally, until fragrant, about 4 minutes. Remove skillet from heat and set aside.

2. Bring 6 cups water to boil. Place noodles in large bowl. Pour boiling water over noodles and stir briefly. Soak noodles until flexible, but not soft, about 2½ minutes, stirring once halfway through. Drain noodles briefly; do not wash bowl. Transfer noodles to cutting board. Using chef's knife, cut pile of noodles roughly into thirds. Return noodles to bowl, add curry mixture, soy sauce, and sugar; using tongs, toss until well combined. Set aside.

3. Wipe out skillet with paper towels. Heat 2 teaspoons oil in skillet over medium-high heat until shimmering. Add shrimp in even layer and cook without moving until bottom is browned, about 90 seconds. Stir and continue to cook until just cooked through, about 90 seconds longer. Push shrimp to one side of skillet. Add 1 teaspoon oil to cleared side of skillet. Add eggs to clearing, and sprinkle with ¼ teaspoon salt. Using rubber spatula, stir eggs gently until set but still wet, about 1 minute. Stir eggs into shrimp and continue to cook, breaking up large pieces of egg, until eggs are fully cooked, about 30 seconds longer. Transfer shrimp-egg mixture to second large bowl.

4. Lower heat to medium. Heat remaining 1 teaspoon oil in now-empty skillet until shimmering. Add ginger and garlic and cook, stirring constantly, until fragrant, about 15 seconds. Add bell pepper and shallots. Cook, stirring frequently, until vegetables are crisp-tender, about 2 minutes. Transfer to bowl with shrimp.

5. Return again-empty skillet to medium-high heat, add chicken broth to skillet, and bring to simmer. Add noodles and cook, stirring frequently, until liquid is absorbed, about 2 minutes. Add noodles to bowl with shrimp and vegetable mixture and toss to combine. Add bean sprouts, scallions, and lime juice, and toss to combine. Transfer to warmed platter and serve immediately, passing lime wedges separately.

NOTES FROM THE TEST KITCHEN

UNTANGLING SINGAPORE NOODLES

Two easy steps help avoid the usual "ball" of noodles that forms when you toss the rice vermicelli with the shrimp and vegetables.

1. Cutting the soaked and drained rice vermicelli into thirds makes the noodles less tangle-prone.

2. Coating the noodles with curry oil prevents them from sticking. "Blooming" the spice in oil also boosts its flavor, softens its gritty texture, and adds richness.

SHRIMP STIR-FRIES

WHY THIS RECIPE WORKS: Stir-fries are typically cooked over high heat to sear the food and develop flavor. This works well with chicken, beef, and pork, but delicate shrimp turns to rubber. We wanted a stir-fry with plump, juicy, well-seasoned shrimp in a balanced, flavorful sauce. We wondered if browning was really necessary. Abandoning the high-heat method, we turned down the burner to medium-low and gently parcooked a batch of shrimp, removed them from the skillet, then turned up the heat to sear the vegetables, sauté the aromatics, and finish cooking the shrimp with the sauce. This worked beautifully. Reversing the approach—cooking the veggies followed by the aromatics over high heat, then turning the heat down before adding the shrimp—made the process more efficient. We reduced our sweet and spicy sauce and reduced it so it tightly adhered to the shellfish.

Stir-Fried Shrimp with Snow Peas and Red Bell Pepper in Hot and Sour Sauce

SERVES 4

Serve with Basic White Rice (page 453).

- 1 pound extra-large shrimp (21 to 25 per pound), peeled, deveined (see page 240), and tails removed
- 3 tablespoons vegetable oil
- 1 tablespoon minced or grated fresh ginger
- 2 medium garlic cloves, 1 minced or pressed through a garlic press (about 1 teaspoon), 1 sliced thin
- ½ teaspoon table salt
- 3 tablespoons sugar
- 3 tablespoons white vinegar
- 1 tablespoon Asian chili-garlic sauce
- 1 tablespoon dry sherry or Chinese rice cooking wine (Shaoxing)
- 1 tablespoon ketchup
- 2 teaspoons toasted sesame oil
- 2 teaspoons cornstarch
- 1 teaspoon soy sauce
- 1 large shallot, sliced thin (about ⅓ cup)
- ½ pound snow peas or sugar snap peas, tips snapped off and strings removed
- 1 medium red bell pepper, stemmed, seeded, and cut into ¾-inch dice

1. Combine the shrimp with 1 tablespoon of the vegetable oil, the ginger, minced garlic, and salt in a medium bowl. Let the shrimp marinate at room temperature for 30 minutes.

2. Meanwhile, whisk the sugar, vinegar, chili-garlic sauce, sherry, ketchup, sesame oil, cornstarch, and soy sauce in a small bowl. Combine the sliced garlic with the shallot in a second small bowl.

3. Heat 1 tablespoon more vegetable oil in a 12-inch nonstick skillet over high heat until just smoking. Add the snow peas and bell pepper and cook, stirring frequently, until the vegetables begin to brown, 1½ to 2 minutes. Transfer the vegetables to a medium bowl.

4. Add the remaining 1 tablespoon vegetable oil to the now-empty skillet and heat until just smoking. Add the garlic-shallot mixture and cook, stirring frequently, until just beginning to brown, about 30 seconds. Reduce the heat to medium-low, add the shrimp, and cook, stirring frequently, until the shrimp are light pink on both sides, 1 to 1½ minutes. Whisk the soy sauce mixture to recombine and add to the skillet; return to high heat and cook, stirring constantly, until the sauce is thickened and the shrimp are cooked through, 1 to 2 minutes. Return the vegetables to the skillet, toss to combine, and serve.

Stir-Fried Shrimp with Garlicky Eggplant, Scallions, and Cashews

SERVES 4

To make quick work of cutting the scallions, use sharp kitchen shears. Serve with Basic White Rice (page 453).

- 1 pound extra-large shrimp (21 to 25 per pound), peeled, deveined (see page 240), and tails removed
- 3 tablespoons vegetable oil
- 6 medium garlic cloves, 1 minced or pressed through a garlic press (about 1 teaspoon), 5 sliced thin
- ½ teaspoon table salt
- 2 tablespoons soy sauce
- 2 tablespoons oyster-flavored sauce
- 2 tablespoons dry sherry or Chinese rice cooking wine (Shaoxing)
- 2 tablespoons sugar
- 1 tablespoon toasted sesame oil
- 1 tablespoon white vinegar
- 2 teaspoons cornstarch
- ⅛ teaspoon red pepper flakes
- 6 large scallions, greens cut into 1-inch pieces and whites sliced thin
- ½ cup unsalted cashews
- 1 medium eggplant (about ¾ pound), cut into ¾-inch dice

1. Combine the shrimp with 1 tablespoon of the vegetable oil, the minced garlic, and salt in a medium bowl. Let the shrimp marinate at room temperature for 30 minutes.

2. Meanwhile, whisk the soy sauce, oyster-flavored sauce, sherry, sugar, sesame oil, vinegar, cornstarch, and red pepper flakes in a small bowl. Combine the sliced garlic with the scallion whites and cashews in a small bowl.

3. Heat 1 tablespoon more vegetable oil in a 12-inch nonstick skillet over high heat until just smoking. Add the eggplant and cook, stirring frequently, until lightly browned, 3 to 6 minutes. Add the scallion greens and continue to cook until the scallion greens begin to brown and the eggplant is fully tender, 1 to 2 minutes longer. Transfer the vegetables to a medium bowl.

4. Continue with the recipe for Stir-Fried Shrimp with Snow Peas and Red Bell Pepper in Hot and Sour Sauce from step 4, replacing the garlic-shallot mixture with the garlic-scallion-cashew mixture.

KUNG PAO SHRIMP

WHY THIS RECIPE WORKS: Kung pao is meant to have a fiery personality, but many restaurant versions are dismal, featuring tiny, tough shrimp drenched in a quart of pale, greasy, bland sauce. We wanted to make this classic Sichuan stir-fry at home, with large, tender shrimp, crunchy peanuts, and an assertive, well-balanced brown sauce.

For tender, flavorful shrimp, we stir-fried marinated extra-large shrimp for just a few seconds, then added small whole red chiles and whole unsalted roasted peanuts. For vegetables, we kept things simple and added just one diced red bell pepper (tasters found other vegetables to be superfluous) and the usual aromatics, garlic and ginger. We made a potently flavored, syrupy sauce using a mixture of chicken broth, rice vinegar, toasted sesame oil, oyster-flavored sauce, hoisin sauce, and cornstarch. Stirring in sliced scallions just before serving put the final touch on our dish. We no longer need to rely on dull, gloppy restaurant renditions of this Sichuan classic.

Kung Pao Shrimp
SERVES 4

Roasted unsalted cashews can be substituted for the peanuts. Unless you have a taste for the incendiary, do not eat the whole chiles in the finished dish. Serve with Basic White Rice (page 453).

SAUCE
- ¾ cup low-sodium chicken broth
- 1 tablespoon oyster-flavored sauce
- 1 tablespoon hoisin sauce
- 2 teaspoons rice vinegar
- 2 teaspoons toasted sesame oil
- 1½ teaspoons cornstarch

SHRIMP AND VEGETABLES
- 1 pound extra-large shrimp (21 to 25 per pound), peeled and deveined (see page 240)
- 1 tablespoon Chinese rice cooking wine (Shaoxing) or dry sherry
- 2 teaspoons soy sauce
- 2 tablespoons plus 1 teaspoon peanut or vegetable oil
- 3 medium garlic cloves, minced or pressed through a garlic press (about 1 tablespoon)
- 2 teaspoons minced or grated fresh ginger
- ½ cup unsalted roasted peanuts (see note)
- 6 small whole dried red chiles (see note)
- 1 red bell pepper, stemmed, seeded, and cut into ½-inch pieces
- 3 scallions, sliced thin

1. FOR THE SAUCE: Combine all the ingredients in a small bowl and set aside.

2. FOR THE SHRIMP AND VEGETABLES: Toss the shrimp with the rice cooking wine and soy sauce in a medium bowl and let marinate for at least 10 minutes or up to 1 hour. In a small bowl, mix 1 teaspoon of the peanut oil, the garlic, and ginger together.

3. Heat 1 tablespoon more peanut oil in a 12-inch nonstick skillet over high heat until just smoking. Add the shrimp and cook until barely opaque, 30 to 40 seconds, stirring halfway through. Add the peanuts and chiles and continue to cook until the shrimp are bright pink and the peanuts have darkened slightly, 30 to 40 seconds longer. Transfer the shrimp, peanuts, and chiles to a clean bowl and cover with foil to keep warm.

4. Add the remaining 1 tablespoon peanut oil to the skillet and return to high heat until just smoking. Add the bell pepper and cook, stirring frequently, until spotty brown, about 1½ minutes. Clear the center of the skillet, add the garlic mixture, and cook, mashing the mixture into the pan, until fragrant, 15 to 20 seconds. Stir the garlic mixture into the bell pepper.

5. Stir in the peanuts, chiles, and shrimp with any accumulated juices. Whisk the sauce to recombine, then add to the skillet and cook, tossing constantly, until the sauce is thickened, about 30 seconds. Stir in the scallions, transfer to a serving platter, and serve.

VEGETABLE STIR-FRIES

WHY THIS RECIPE WORKS: Without meat, vegetable stir-fries can feel more like a side dish than a dinner. We wanted to make a satisfying, filling stir-fry—without meat.

We chose meaty portobello mushrooms as the main vegetable. We found that removing the gills kept them from tasting leathery and raw. We tried cutting them in a variety of sizes and settled on 2-inch wedges, which felt the most substantial. We cooked the mushrooms over medium-high heat until browned and tender, then added a mixture of broth, soy sauce, and sugar and reduced it to a glaze—this provided an intense flavor boost. For this stir-fry, we bulked up the amount of vegetables in our traditional stir-fries, mixing carrots, snow peas, and napa cabbage. Finally, the sauce—a mixture of broth, oyster-flavored sauce, soy sauce, cornstarch, and sesame oil—and a heavy dose of ginger tied the dish together, giving the vegetables great flavor—and nobody missed the meat!

Stir-Fried Portobellos with Ginger-Oyster Sauce

SERVES 4

Serve with Basic White Rice (see page 453).

GLAZE

¼ cup low-sodium chicken or vegetable broth

2 tablespoons soy sauce

2 tablespoons sugar

SAUCE

1 cup low-sodium chicken or vegetable broth

3 tablespoons oyster-flavored sauce

1 tablespoon soy sauce

1 tablespoon cornstarch

2 teaspoons toasted sesame oil

VEGETABLES

¼ cup peanut or vegetable oil

4 teaspoons minced or grated fresh ginger

2 medium garlic cloves, minced or pressed through a garlic press (about 2 teaspoons)

6–8 portobello mushrooms (each 4 to 6 inches), stemmed, wiped clean, gills removed, and cut into 2-inch wedges

4 carrots, peeled and sliced ¼ inch thick on the bias

½ cup low-sodium chicken or vegetable broth

3 ounces snow peas, tips and strings removed

1 pound napa cabbage (1 small head), cored and cut into ¾-inch strips

1 tablespoon sesame seeds, toasted (optional)

1. FOR THE GLAZE: Combine all the ingredients in a small bowl and set aside.

2. FOR THE SAUCE: Combine all the ingredients in a small bowl and set aside.

3. FOR THE VEGETABLES: In a small bowl, mix 1 teaspoon of the peanut oil, the ginger, and garlic together.

4. Heat 3 tablespoons more peanut oil in a 12-inch nonstick skillet over medium-high heat until shimmering. Add the mushrooms and cook without stirring until browned on one side, 2 to 3 minutes. Using tongs, flip the mushrooms, reduce the heat to medium, and cook until the second sides are browned and

the mushrooms are tender, about 5 minutes. Increase the heat to medium-high, add the glaze, and cook, stirring frequently, until the glaze is thick and the mushrooms are coated, 1 to 2 minutes. Transfer the mushrooms to a plate. Rinse the skillet clean and dry with a wad of paper towels.

5. Add 1 teaspoon more peanut oil to the skillet and return to high heat until just smoking. Add the carrots and cook, stirring frequently, until beginning to brown, 1 to 2 minutes. Add the broth, cover the pan, and lower the heat to medium. Cook the carrots until just tender, 2 to 3 minutes. Uncover and cook until the liquid evaporates, about 30 seconds. Transfer the carrots to the plate with the mushrooms.

6. Add the remaining 1 teaspoon peanut oil to the skillet and return to high heat until just smoking. Add the snow peas and cook until spotty brown, about 2 minutes. Add the cabbage and cook, stirring frequently, until wilted, about 2 minutes.

7. Clear the center of the skillet, add the ginger mixture, and cook, mashing the mixture into the pan, until fragrant, 15 to 20 seconds. Stir the ginger mixture into the vegetables.

8. Stir in the mushrooms and carrots. Whisk the sauce to recombine, then add to the skillet and cook, tossing constantly, until the sauce is thickened, 2 to 3 minutes. Transfer to a serving platter, sprinkle with the sesame seeds (if using), and serve.

Stir-Fried Portobellos with Sweet Chili-Garlic Sauce

Follow the recipe for Stir-Fried Portobellos with Ginger-Oyster Sauce, replacing the sugar in the glaze with 2 tablespoons honey. For the sauce, increase the soy sauce to 3 tablespoons, reduce the broth to ¾ cup, and replace the oyster-flavored sauce and toasted sesame oil with 2 tablespoons honey, 1 tablespoon rice vinegar, and 1 teaspoon Asian chili sauce. Increase the garlic to 4 cloves.

THAI CHICKEN WITH BASIL

WHY THIS RECIPE WORKS: In Thailand, street vendors have mastered an alternative to traditional Chinese high-heat stir-fry, using low flames to produce complex and flavorful dishes like chicken and basil—chopped pieces of moist chicken in a bright, basil-infused sauce. We set out to create our own version.

To start, we turned to the aromatics. Because Thai stir-fries are cooked over a lower temperature, the aromatics are added at the very beginning of cooking, where they infuse the oil with their flavors. To prevent scorching, we started our aromatics (garlic, chiles, and shallots) in a cold skillet.

It was too time-consuming to chop our chicken by hand, so we turned to the food processor. To ensure moist meat, we added fish sauce to the food processor when we ground the chicken, then rested the meat in the refrigerator—the fish sauce acted as a brine, seasoning the chicken and sealing in moisture. Next, we moved on to the sauce. For our sauce base, we liked Chinese-style oyster-flavored sauce brightened with a dash of white vinegar. We spiced up the flavor of the sauce by adding a reserved tablespoon of the raw garlic-chile mixture at the end of cooking. And for intense, bright basil flavor, we cooked a portion of chopped basil with the garlic, chile, and shallot mixture, and stirred in whole basil leaves just before serving.

Thai-Style Chicken with Basil

SERVES 4

Since tolerance for spiciness can vary, we've kept our recipe relatively mild. For a very mild version, remove the seeds and ribs from the chiles. If fresh Thai chiles are unavailable, substitute 2 serranos or 1 medium jalapeño. In Thailand, crushed red pepper and sugar are passed at the table, along with extra fish sauce and white vinegar. You do not need to wash the food processor bowl after step 1. Serve with Basic White Rice (page 453) and vegetables, if desired.

- 2 cups tightly packed fresh basil leaves
- 3 garlic cloves, peeled
- 6 green or red Thai chiles, stemmed (see note)
- 2 tablespoons fish sauce, plus extra for serving
- 1 tablespoon oyster-flavored sauce
- 1 tablespoon sugar, plus extra for serving
- 1 teaspoon white vinegar, plus extra for serving
- 1 pound boneless, skinless chicken breasts, trimmed and cut into 2-inch pieces
- 3 shallots, peeled and sliced thin (about ¾ cup)
- 2 tablespoons vegetable oil
  Red pepper flakes, for serving

1. Pulse 1 cup of the basil leaves, the garlic, and chiles in a food processor until chopped fine, 6 to 10 pulses, scraping down the sides of the bowl once during processing. Transfer 1 tablespoon of the basil mixture to a small bowl, stir in 1 tablespoon of the fish sauce, the oyster-flavored sauce, sugar, and vinegar and set aside. Transfer the remaining basil mixture to a 12-inch heavy-bottomed nonstick skillet.

2. Pulse the chicken and the remaining 1 tablespoon fish sauce in the food processor until the meat is chopped into ¼-inch pieces, 6 to 8 pulses. Transfer the chicken to a medium bowl and refrigerate for 15 minutes.

3. Stir the shallots and oil into the basil mixture in the skillet. Heat the mixture over medium-low heat (the mixture should start to sizzle after about 1½ minutes; if it doesn't, adjust the heat accordingly), stirring constantly, until the garlic and shallots are golden brown, 5 to 8 minutes.

4. Add the chicken, increase the heat to medium, and cook, stirring and breaking up the chicken with a potato masher or rubber spatula, until only traces of pink remain, 2 to 4 minutes. Add the reserved basil–fish sauce mixture and continue to cook, stirring constantly, until the chicken is no longer pink, about 1 minute. Stir in the remaining 1 cup basil leaves and cook, stirring constantly, until the basil is wilted, 30 to 60 seconds. Serve immediately, passing the extra fish sauce, sugar, vinegar, and red pepper flakes separately.

THAI CURRIES

WHY THIS RECIPE WORKS: Like most Thai food, Thai curries embrace a delicate balance of tastes, textures, temperatures, and colors that come together to create a harmonious whole. Unlike Indian curries, Thai curries almost always contain coconut milk. Also, they tilt the spice balance towards fresh aromatics, which are added in the form of a paste. We wanted an authentic Thai red curry and green curry, perfumed with lemon grass, hot chiles, and coconut milk, both of which could be made easily by the home cook.

A food processor made quick work of blending together the curry pastes. For the green curry, we favored Thai green chiles (although serrano or jalapeño chiles make great substitutes), while the red curry was best with small dried red chiles and a fresh red jalapeño. Shallots, lemon grass, cilantro stems, garlic, ginger, coriander, and cumin rounded out the flavors of the pastes. And to approximate the flavor of kaffir lime leaves, we added grated lime zest. To make the curries, we skimmed the coconut cream off the coconut milk and cooked it with the curry paste—this gave our curries silky body and intense, rich flavor. We paired the green curry with chicken, broccoli, mushrooms, and bell pepper, and the red curry with shrimp, pineapple, and peanuts. All that we needed now was rice to soak up the flavorful sauce.

Thai Green Curry with Chicken, Broccoli, and Mushrooms

SERVES 4

To make slicing the chicken easier, freeze it for 15 minutes. Serve with Basic White Rice (page 453).

2 (14-ounce) cans unsweetened coconut milk, not shaken

1 recipe Green Curry Paste (recipe follows)
or 2 tablespoons store-bought green curry paste

2 tablespoons fish sauce

2 tablespoons brown sugar

1½ pounds boneless, skinless chicken breasts,
trimmed and sliced thin (see note)
Table salt

8 ounces broccoli (½ small bunch), florets cut
into 1-inch pieces

4 ounces white mushrooms, wiped clean and quartered

1 red bell pepper, stemmed, seeded, and cut
into ¼-inch strips

1 Thai chile, stemmed, seeded, and quartered
lengthwise (optional)

½ cup loosely packed fresh basil leaves

½ cup loosely packed fresh mint leaves

1 tablespoon juice from 1 lime

1. Carefully spoon off about 1 cup of the top layer of cream from one can of the coconut milk. Whisk the coconut cream and curry paste together in a large Dutch oven, bring to a simmer over high heat, and cook until almost all of the liquid evaporates, 5 to 7 minutes. Reduce the heat to medium-high and continue to cook, whisking constantly, until the cream separates into a puddle of colored oil and coconut solids, 3 to 8 minutes. Continue cooking until the curry paste is very aromatic, 1 to 2 minutes.

2. Whisk in the remaining coconut milk, the fish sauce, and sugar, bring to a simmer, and cook until the flavors meld and the sauce thickens, about 5 minutes. Season the chicken with salt, stir into the sauce, and cook until evenly coated, about 1 minute. Stir in the broccoli and mushrooms and cook until the vegetables are almost tender, about 5 minutes. Stir in the bell pepper and chile (if using) and cook until the bell pepper is crisp-tender, about 2 minutes. Off the heat, stir in the basil, mint, and lime juice. Serve.

Green Curry Paste

MAKES ABOUT ½ CUP

We strongly prefer the flavor of Thai chiles here; however, serrano and jalapeño chiles are decent substitutes. For more heat, include the chile seeds and ribs when chopping.

⅓ cup water

12 fresh green Thai, serrano, or jalapeño chiles, seeds
and ribs removed, chiles chopped coarse (see note)

8 medium garlic cloves, peeled

3 medium shallots, peeled and quartered

2 stalks lemon grass, bottom 5 inches only, trimmed
and sliced thin

2 tablespoons grated zest from 2 limes

2 tablespoons vegetable oil

2 tablespoons minced fresh cilantro stems

1 tablespoon minced or grated fresh ginger

2 teaspoons ground coriander

1 teaspoon ground cumin

1 teaspoon table salt

Process all the ingredients in a food processor to a fine paste, about 3 minutes, scraping down the sides of the workbowl as needed.

Thai Red Curry with Shrimp, Pineapple, and Peanuts

SERVES 4

Roasted unsalted cashews can be substituted for the peanuts. For a more authentic appearance, leave the shells on the shrimp tails. Serve with Basic White Rice (page 453).

2 (14-ounce) cans unsweetened coconut milk, not shaken

1 recipe Red Curry Paste (recipe follows) or 2 tablespoons
store-bought red curry paste

2 tablespoons fish sauce

2 tablespoons brown sugar

1½ pounds medium shrimp (41 to 50 per pound),
peeled and deveined (see page 240; see note)
Table salt

1 pound peeled and cored pineapple,
cut into 1-inch pieces

4 ounces snow peas, tips and strings removed

1 red bell pepper, stemmed, seeded, and cut
into ¼-inch strips

1 Thai chile, stemmed, seeded, and quartered lengthwise
(optional)

½ cup loosely packed fresh basil leaves

½ cup loosely packed fresh mint leaves

1 tablespoon juice from 1 lime

½ cup unsalted roasted peanuts, chopped coarse
(see note)

1. Carefully spoon off about 1 cup of the top layer of cream from one can of the coconut milk. Whisk the coconut cream and curry paste together in a large Dutch oven, bring to a simmer over high heat, and cook until almost all of the liquid evaporates, 5 to 7 minutes. Reduce the heat to medium-high and continue to cook, whisking constantly, until the cream separates into a puddle of colored oil and coconut solids, 3 to 8 minutes. Continue cooking until the curry paste is very aromatic, 1 to 2 minutes.

2. Whisk in the remaining coconut milk, the fish sauce, and sugar, bring to a simmer, and cook until the flavors meld and the sauce thickens, about 5 minutes. Season the shrimp with salt, add them to the sauce with the pineapple, and cook, stirring occasionally, until the shrimp are almost opaque, about 4 minutes. Stir in the snow peas, bell pepper, and chile (if using) and cook until the vegetables are crisp-tender, about 2 minutes. Off the heat, stir in the basil, mint, and lime juice. Sprinkle with the peanuts and serve.

CUTTING LEMON GRASS

Because of its tough outer leaves, lemon grass can be difficult to slice or mince. We like this method, which relies on a sharp knife.

1. Trim all but the bottom 5 inches of the lemon grass stalk.

2. Remove the tough outer sheath from the trimmed lemon grass. If the lemon grass is particularly thick or tough, you may need to remove several layers to reveal the tender inner portion of the stalk.

3. TO SLICE: Thinly slice the trimmed and peeled lemon grass on a slight bias. **TO MINCE:** Cut the trimmed and peeled lemon grass in half lengthwise, then mince.

Red Curry Paste

MAKES ABOUT ½ CUP

If you can't find a red jalapeño chile, you can substitute a green jalapeño. For more heat, include the jalapeño seeds and ribs when chopping.

- 8 dried small red chiles, such as Thai, japonés, or de árbol
- ⅓ cup water
- 4 medium shallots, peeled and quartered
- 2 stalks lemon grass, bottom 5 inches only, trimmed and sliced thin
- 6 medium garlic cloves, peeled
- 1 medium fresh red jalapeño chile, seeds and ribs removed, chile chopped coarse (see note)
- 2 tablespoons minced fresh cilantro stems
- 2 tablespoons vegetable oil
- 1 tablespoon grated zest from 1 lime
- 2 teaspoons ground coriander
- 1 teaspoon ground cumin
- 1 teaspoon minced or grated fresh ginger
- 1 teaspoon tomato paste
- 1 teaspoon table salt

1. Adjust an oven rack to the middle position and heat the oven to 350 degrees. Place the dried red chiles on a baking sheet and toast in the oven until fragrant and puffed, about 5 minutes. Remove the chiles from the oven and set aside to cool. When cool enough to handle, seed and stem the chiles, then break them into small pieces.

2. Process the chile pieces with the remaining ingredients in a food processor to a fine paste, about 3 minutes, scraping down the sides of the workbowl as needed.

THAI CHICKEN CURRY WITH POTATOES AND PEANUTS

WHY THIS RECIPE WORKS: Warm-spiced, savory-sweet *massaman* curry is a Thai specialty, but it presents problems for the home cook with difficult-to-find ingredients and work-intensive processes. We set out to streamline the traditional recipe. To make a deeply flavorful curry paste, we broiled chiles, garlic, and shallots per tradition, but we replaced hard-to-find galangal with readily available ginger and traded out toasted, ground whole spices for preground five-spice powder. Coconut milk and lime juice rounded out the flavor of our curry. We stuck with the traditional potatoes, onion, chicken, and peanuts, simmered in the sauce until they were tender. A final garnish of lime zest and cilantro added a splash of color and brightness.

Thai Chicken Curry with Potatoes and Peanuts

SERVES 4 TO 6

Serve the curry with jasmine rice. The ingredients for the curry paste can be doubled to make extra for future use. Refrigerate the paste for up to one week or freeze it for up to two months.

CURRY PASTE

- 6 dried New Mexican chiles
- 4 shallots, unpeeled
- 7 garlic cloves, unpeeled
- ½ cup chopped fresh ginger
- ¼ cup water
- 4½ teaspoons lime juice
- 4½ teaspoons vegetable oil
- 1 tablespoon fish sauce
- 1 teaspoon five-spice powder
- ½ teaspoon ground cumin
- ½ teaspoon pepper

CURRY

- 1 teaspoon vegetable oil
- 1¼ cups chicken broth
- 1 (13.5-ounce) can coconut milk
- 1 pound Yukon Gold potatoes, unpeeled, cut into ¾-inch pieces
- 1 onion, cut into ¾-inch pieces
- ⅓ cup dry-roasted peanuts
- ¾ teaspoon salt
- 1 pound boneless, skinless chicken thighs, trimmed and cut into 1-inch pieces
- 2 teaspoons grated lime zest
- ¼ cup chopped fresh cilantro

1. FOR THE CURRY PASTE: Adjust oven rack to middle position and heat oven to 350 degrees. Line rimmed baking sheet with aluminum foil. Arrange chiles on prepared sheet and toast until puffed and fragrant, 4 to 6 minutes. Transfer chiles to large plate. Heat broiler.

2. Place shallots and garlic on foil-lined sheet and broil until softened and skin is charred, 6 to 9 minutes.

3. When cool enough to handle, stem and seed chiles and tear into 1½-inch pieces. Process chiles in blender until finely ground, about 1 minute. Peel shallots and garlic. Add shallots, garlic, ginger, water, lime juice, oil, fish sauce, five-spice powder, cumin, and pepper to blender. Process to smooth paste, scraping down sides of blender jar as needed, 2 to 3 minutes. You should have 1 cup paste.

4. FOR THE CURRY: Heat oil in large saucepan over medium heat until shimmering. Add curry paste and cook, stirring constantly, until paste begins to brown, 2½ to 3 minutes. Stir in broth, coconut milk, potatoes, onion, peanuts, and salt, scraping up any browned bits. Bring to simmer and cook until potatoes are just tender, 12 to 14 minutes.

5. Stir in chicken and continue to simmer until chicken is cooked through, 10 to 12 minutes. Remove pan from heat and stir in lime zest. Serve, passing cilantro separately.

CURRY BEEF

WHY THIS RECIPE WORKS: Made with an orange-red paste that usually includes ground peanuts, panang curry is a sweeter, more unctuous derivative of red curry. We wanted a panang curry just as rich and flavorful as traditional versions but quicker to make, so we turned to jarred red curry paste, which contains many of the same ingredients that go into panang paste. We doctored the paste with the distinct flavors of this dish: kaffir lime leaves, fish sauce, sugar, fresh chile, and peanuts. Following the typical method, we cooked the beef (we used thin-sliced boneless beef short ribs) separately in plain water until tender. Cooking the beef separately from the sauce ensured that its flavor didn't overpower the other flavors in the dish. Once the beef was cooked (which can be done well in advance), we added it to the coconut milk–based sauce and simmered it briefly.

Panang Beef Curry

SERVES 6

Red curry pastes from different brands vary in spiciness, so start by adding 2 tablespoons and then taste the sauce and add up to 2 tablespoons more. Kaffir lime leaves are well worth seeking out. If you can't find them, substitute three 3-inch strips each of lemon zest and lime zest, adding them to the sauce with the beef in step 2 (remove the zest strips before serving). Do not substitute light coconut milk. Serve this rich dish with rice and vegetables.

- 2 pounds boneless beef short ribs, trimmed
- 2 tablespoons vegetable oil
- 2–4 tablespoons Thai red curry paste
- 1 (14-ounce) can unsweetened coconut milk
- 4 teaspoons fish sauce
- 2 teaspoons sugar
- 1 Thai red chile, halved lengthwise (optional)
- 6 kaffir lime leaves, middle vein removed, sliced thin
- ⅓ cup unsalted dry-roasted peanuts, chopped fine

1. Cut each rib crosswise with grain into 3 equal pieces. Slice each piece against grain ¼ inch thick. Place beef in large saucepan and add water to cover. Bring to boil over high heat. Cover, reduce heat to low, and cook until beef is fork-tender, 1 to 1¼ hours. Using slotted spoon, transfer beef to bowl; discard water. (Beef can refrigerated for up to 24 hours; when ready to use, add it to curry as directed in step 2.)

2. Heat oil in 12-inch nonstick skillet over medium heat until shimmering. Add 2 tablespoons curry paste and cook, stirring frequently, until paste is fragrant and darkens in color to brick red, 5 to 8 minutes. Add coconut milk, fish sauce, sugar, and chile, if using; stir to combine and dissolve sugar. Taste sauce and add up to 2 tablespoons more curry paste to achieve desired spiciness. Add beef, stir to coat with sauce, and bring to simmer.

3. Rapidly simmer, stirring occasionally, until sauce is thickened and reduced by half and coats beef, 12 to 15 minutes. (Sauce should be quite thick, and streaks of oil will appear. Sauce will continue to thicken as it cools.) Add kaffir lime leaves and simmer until fragrant, 1 to 2 minutes. Transfer to serving platter, sprinkle with peanuts, and serve.

THAI CHILE BEEF

WHY THIS RECIPE WORKS: Most recipes for Thai chile beef require exotic ingredients and three hours of preparation—definitely not suitable for making midweek supper in an average American home kitchen. We wanted to create a sophisticated Thai chile beef recipe built around the traditional Thai flavors—spicy, sweet, sour, and salty—using readily available ingredients and requiring minimal cooking time.

A cheap and readily available cut—blade steak—won our taste test for its tenderness and very beefy flavor. We added the beef to our transformed stir-fry marinade—made with fish sauce for its briny flavor, white pepper for its spicy and almost gamy flavor, citrusy coriander, and a little light brown sugar for both sweetness and help in developing caramelization. With these elements, the beef only needed to marinate for 10 minutes to develop full flavor. We also wanted some heat and decided to use both a jalapeño and Asian chili-garlic paste (which added toasty garlicky flavors along with heat). More fish sauce, brown sugar, rice vinegar, fresh mint and cilantro, a few crunchy chopped peanuts, and a bright squirt of lime juice finished the dish.

Stir-Fried Thai-Style Beef with Chiles and Shallots

SERVES 4

To make slicing the blade steaks easier, freeze them for 15 minutes. If you cannot find blade steak, use flank steak; because flank steak requires less trimming, you will need only about 1¾ pounds. To cut a flank steak into the proper size slices for stir-frying, first cut the steak with the grain into 2-inch strips, then cut the strips against the grain into ⅛-inch-thick slices. Serve with Basic White Rice (page 453).

SAUCE

- 2 tablespoons fish sauce
- 2 tablespoons rice vinegar
- 2 tablespoons water
- 1 tablespoon light brown sugar
- 1 tablespoon Asian chili-garlic paste

BEEF AND VEGETABLES

- 2 pounds blade steaks, halved lengthwise, trimmed, and sliced into ⅛-inch-thick slices (see note)
- 1 tablespoon fish sauce
- 1 teaspoon light brown sugar
- ¾ teaspoon ground coriander
- ⅛ teaspoon ground white pepper
- 3 tablespoons peanut or vegetable oil
- 3 medium garlic cloves, minced or pressed through a garlic press (about 1 tablespoon)
- 3 serrano or jalapeño chiles, halved, seeds and ribs removed, chiles sliced thin
- 3 medium shallots, ends trimmed, peeled, quartered lengthwise, and layers separated
- ½ cup fresh mint leaves, large leaves torn into bite-size pieces
- ½ cup fresh cilantro leaves
- ⅓ cup unsalted roasted peanuts, chopped coarse
  Lime wedges, for serving

1. FOR THE SAUCE: Combine all the ingredients in a small bowl and set aside.

2. FOR THE BEEF AND VEGETABLES: Toss the beef with the fish sauce, sugar, coriander, and white pepper in a medium bowl and let marinate for at least 10 minutes or up to 1 hour. In a small bowl, mix 1 teaspoon of the oil and the garlic together.

3. Heat 2 teaspoons more oil in a 12-inch nonstick skillet over high heat until just smoking. Add one-third of the beef, break up any clumps, then cook without stirring until the meat is browned at the edges, about 1 minute. Stir the beef and continue to cook until cooked through, about 1 minute longer. Transfer the beef to a clean bowl and cover with foil to keep warm. Repeat with 4 teaspoons more oil and the remaining beef in two batches.

4. Add the remaining 2 teaspoons oil to the skillet and return to medium heat until shimmering. Add the chiles and shallots and cook until beginning to soften, 3 to 4 minutes. Clear the center of the skillet, add the garlic mixture, and cook, mashing the mixture into the pan, until fragrant, 15 to 20 seconds. Stir the garlic mixture into the shallots and chiles.

5. Stir in the beef with any accumulated juices. Whisk the sauce to recombine, then add to the skillet and cook, tossing constantly, until the sauce is thickened, about 30 seconds. Stir in the half of the mint and half of the cilantro. Transfer to a serving platter, sprinkle with the remaining mint, remaining cilantro, and peanuts, and serve with the lime wedges.

THAI-STYLE STIR-FRIED NOODLES WITH CHICKEN

WHY THIS RECIPE WORKS: We wanted to create a version of *pad see ew*—the traditional Thai dish of chewy, lightly charred rice noodles, with chicken, crisp broccoli, and moist egg, bound with a sweet and salty soy-based sauce—that would work in the American home kitchen. We substituted supermarket ingredients for hard-to-find fresh rice noodles, Chinese broccoli, and sweet Thai soy sauce, but it was simulating the high heat of a restaurant wok burner on a lower-output home stovetop that was the real challenge. Since we were already using maximum heat, we increased the surface area by using a 12-inch nonstick skillet, and we cooked the dish in batches, combining all of the components right before serving. Most important, we found that eliminating much of the stirring in our stir-fry helped us achieve the all-important char that characterizes pad see ew.

Thai-Style Stir-Fried Noodles with Chicken and Broccolini

SERVES 4

The flat pad thai–style rice noodles that are used in this recipe can be found in the Asian section of most supermarkets. If you can't find broccolini, you can substitute an equal amount of conventional broccoli, but be sure to trim and peel the stalks before cutting.

CHILE VINEGAR

⅓ cup white vinegar
1 serrano chile, stemmed and sliced into thin rings

STIR-FRY

2 (6-ounce) boneless, skinless chicken breasts, trimmed and cut against grain into ¼-inch-thick slices
1 teaspoon baking soda
8 ounces (¼-inch-wide) rice noodles
¼ cup vegetable oil
¼ cup oyster sauce
1 tablespoon plus 2 teaspoons soy sauce
2 tablespoons packed dark brown sugar
1 tablespoon white vinegar
1 teaspoon molasses
1 teaspoon fish sauce
3 garlic cloves, sliced thin
3 large eggs
10 ounces broccolini, florets cut into 1-inch pieces, stalks cut on bias into ½-inch pieces (5 cups)

1. FOR THE CHILE VINEGAR: Combine vinegar and serrano in bowl. Let stand at room temperature for at least 15 minutes.

2. FOR THE STIR-FRY: Combine chicken with 2 tablespoons water and baking soda in bowl. Let sit at room temperature for 15 minutes. Rinse chicken in cold water and drain well.

3. Bring 6 cups water to boil. Place noodles in large bowl. Pour boiling water over noodles. Stir, then soak until noodles are almost tender, about 8 minutes, stirring once halfway through soaking. Drain and rinse with cold water. Drain well and toss with 2 teaspoons oil.

4. Whisk oyster sauce, soy sauce, sugar, vinegar, molasses, and fish sauce together in bowl.

5. Heat 2 teaspoons oil and garlic in 12-inch nonstick skillet over high heat, stirring occasionally, until garlic is deep golden brown, 1 to 2 minutes. Add chicken and 2 tablespoons sauce mixture, toss to coat, and spread chicken into even layer. Cook, without stirring, until chicken begins to brown, 1 to 1½ minutes. Flip chicken and cook, without stirring, until second side begins to brown, 1 to 1½ minutes. Push chicken to 1 side of skillet. Add 2 teaspoons oil to cleared side of skillet. Add eggs to clearing. Using rubber spatula, stir eggs gently and cook until set but still wet. Stir eggs into chicken and continue to cook, breaking up large pieces of egg, until eggs are fully cooked, 30 to 60 seconds. Transfer chicken mixture to bowl.

6. Heat 2 teaspoons oil in now-empty skillet until smoking. Add broccolini and 2 tablespoons sauce and toss to coat. Cover skillet and cook for 2 minutes, stirring once halfway through cooking. Remove lid and continue to cook until broccolini is crisp and very brown in spots, 2 to 3 minutes, stirring once halfway through cooking. Transfer broccolini to bowl with chicken mixture.

7. Heat 2 teaspoons oil in again-empty skillet until smoking. Add half of noodles and 2 tablespoons sauce and toss to coat. Cook until noodles are starting to brown in spots, about 2 minutes, stirring halfway through cooking. Transfer noodles to bowl with chicken mixture. Repeat with remaining 2 teaspoons oil, noodles, and sauce. When second batch of noodles is cooked, add contents of bowl back to skillet and toss to combine. Cook, without stirring, until everything is warmed through, 1 to 1½ minutes. Transfer to platter and serve immediately, passing chile vinegar separately.

PAD THAI

WHY THIS RECIPE WORKS: Ordered out, pad thai suffers from indiscriminate amounts of sugar; slick, greasy noodles; or bloated, sticky, lifeless strands that clump together. We hoped to develop a pad thai with clean, fresh, not-too-sweet flavors, perfectly cooked noodles, and plenty of plump, juicy shrimp with tender bits of scrambled egg.

Soaking the rice sticks in boiling water for 10 minutes before stir-frying made for tender but not sticky noodles. We created the salty, sweet, sour, and spicy flavor profile of pad thai by combining fish sauce, sugar, ground chiles, and vinegar. For the fresh, bright, fruity taste that is essential to the dish, we used tamarind paste, which we soaked in hot water and passed through a fine-mesh strainer to make a smooth puree. Tossed with fresh and dried shrimp and eggs, and garnished with scallions, peanuts, and cilantro, this dish is an excellent rendition of the Thai classic.

Pad Thai

SERVES 4

Although pad thai cooks very quickly, the ingredient list is long, and everything must be prepared and within easy reach at the stovetop when you begin cooking. For maximum efficiency, use the time during which the tamarind and noodles soak to prepare the other ingredients. If tamarind paste is unavailable, substitute ⅓ cup lime juice and ⅓ cup water and use light brown sugar instead of granulated sugar.

SAUCE

- ¾ cup boiling water
- 2 tablespoons tamarind paste (see note)
- 3 tablespoons fish sauce
- 3 tablespoons sugar
- 2 tablespoons peanut or vegetable oil
- 1 tablespoon rice vinegar
- ¾ teaspoon cayenne pepper

NOODLES, SHRIMP, AND GARNISH

- 8 ounces dried rice stick noodles, ⅛ to ¼ inch wide
- 2 tablespoons peanut or vegetable oil
- 12 ounces medium shrimp (41 to 50 per pound), peeled and deveined (see page 240)
  Table salt
- 1 medium shallot, minced (about 2 tablespoons)
- 3 garlic cloves, minced or pressed through a garlic press (about 1 tablespoon)
- 2 large eggs, lightly beaten
- 2 tablespoons chopped Thai salted preserved radish (optional)
- 1 tablespoon dried shrimp, chopped fine (optional)
- 3 cups bean sprouts
- ½ cup unsalted roasted peanuts, chopped coarse
- 5 scallions, green parts only, sliced thin on the bias
- ¼ cup loosely packed fresh cilantro leaves (optional)
  Lime wedges, for serving

1. FOR THE SAUCE: Combine the water and tamarind paste in a small bowl and let sit until the tamarind is softened and mushy, 10 to 30 minutes. Mash the tamarind to break it up, then push it through a fine-mesh strainer into a medium bowl to remove the seeds and fibers and extract as much pulp as possible. Stir in the remaining sauce ingredients and set aside.

2. FOR THE NOODLES, SHRIMP, AND GARNISH: Bring 4 quarts water to a boil in a large pot. Remove the boiling water from the heat, add the rice noodles, and let sit, stirring occasionally, until almost tender, about 10 minutes. Drain the noodles and set aside.

3. Heat 1 tablespoon of the oil in a 12-inch nonstick skillet over high heat until just smoking. Add the shrimp, sprinkle with ⅛ teaspoon salt, and cook without stirring until bright pink, about 1 minute. Stir the shrimp and continue to cook until cooked through, 15 to 30 seconds longer. Transfer the shrimp to a clean bowl and cover with foil to keep warm.

4. Add the remaining 1 tablespoon oil to the skillet and return to medium heat until shimmering. Add the shallot and garlic and cook, stirring constantly, until light golden brown, about 1½ minutes. Stir in the eggs and cook, stirring constantly, until scrambled and barely moist, about 20 seconds.

5. Add the noodles and the salted radish and dried shrimp (if using) to the eggs and toss to combine. Add the sauce, increase the heat to high, and cook, tossing constantly, until the noodles are evenly coated, about 1 minute.

6. Add the cooked shrimp, bean sprouts, ¼ cup of the peanuts, and all but ¼ cup of the scallions and continue to cook, tossing constantly, until the noodles are tender, about 2½ minutes. (If not yet tender add 2 tablespoons water to the skillet and continue to cook until tender.) Transfer the noodles to a serving platter, sprinkle with the remaining ¼ cup peanuts, remaining ¼ cup scallions, and cilantro (if using) and serve with the lime wedges.

EVERYDAY PAD THAI

WHY THIS RECIPE WORKS: To create a truly authentic version of pad thai with distinct sweet, sour, and salty flavors and a mix of textures, it is necessary to source hard-to-find ingredients like preserved daikon, palm sugar, and dried shrimp. We wanted to develop a recipe that maintained the integrity of the dish while using accessible ingredients. Soaking rice noodles in boiling water softened them quickly, and a sauce of sugar, fish sauce, and tamarind concentrate (also increasingly found in supermarkets) resulted in balanced flavor. Shrimp and egg bulked up the dish while bean sprouts, scallion greens, and peanuts added crunch. Finally, we pickled regular red radishes to use in place of hard-to-find preserved daikon, and we created our own faux dried shrimp by microwaving and then frying small pieces of fresh shrimp.

Everyday Pad Thai

SERVES 4

Since pad thai cooks very quickly, prepare everything before you begin to cook. Use the time during which the radishes and noodles soak to prepare the other ingredients. We recommend using a tamarind juice concentrate made in Thailand in this recipe. If you cannot find tamarind, substitute 1½ tablespoons lime juice and 1½ tablespoons water and omit the lime wedges.

CHILE VINEGAR

⅓ cup distilled white vinegar
1 serrano chile, stemmed and sliced into thin rings

STIR-FRY

Salt
Sugar
2 radishes, trimmed and cut into 1½-inch by ¼-inch matchsticks
8 ounces (¼-inch-wide) rice noodles
3 tablespoons plus 2 teaspoons vegetable oil
¼ cup fish sauce
3 tablespoons tamarind juice concentrate
1 pound large shrimp (26 to 30 per pound), peeled and deveined (see page 240)
4 scallions, white and light green parts minced, dark green parts cut into 1-inch lengths
1 garlic clove, minced
4 large eggs, beaten
4 ounces (2 cups) bean sprouts
¼ cup roasted unsalted peanuts, chopped coarse
Lime wedges

1. FOR THE CHILE VINEGAR: Combine vinegar and chile in bowl and let stand at room temperature for at least 15 minutes.

2. FOR THE STIR-FRY: Combine ¼ cup water, ½ teaspoon salt, and ¼ teaspoon sugar in small bowl. Microwave until steaming, about 30 seconds. Add radishes and let stand for 15 minutes. Drain and pat dry with paper towels.

3. Bring 6 cups water to boil. Place noodles in large bowl. Pour boiling water over noodles. Stir, then let soak until noodles are almost tender, about 8 minutes, stirring once halfway through soaking. Drain noodles and rinse with cold water. Drain noodles well, then toss with 2 teaspoons oil.

4. Combine fish sauce, tamarind concentrate, and 3 tablespoons sugar in bowl and whisk until sugar is dissolved. Set sauce aside.

5. Remove tails from 4 shrimp. Cut shrimp in half lengthwise, then cut each half into ½-inch pieces. Toss shrimp pieces with ⅛ teaspoon salt and ⅛ teaspoon sugar. Arrange pieces in single layer on large plate and microwave at 50 percent power until shrimp are dried and have reduced in size by half, 4 to 5 minutes. (Check halfway through microwaving and separate any pieces that may have stuck together.)

6. Heat 2 teaspoons oil in 12-inch nonstick skillet over medium heat until shimmering. Add dried shrimp and cook,

stirring frequently, until golden brown and crispy, 3 to 5 minutes. Transfer to large bowl.

7. Heat 1 teaspoon oil in now-empty skillet over medium heat until shimmering. Add minced scallions and garlic and cook, stirring constantly, until garlic is golden brown, about 1 minute. Transfer to bowl with dried shrimp.

8. Heat 2 teaspoons oil in now-empty skillet over high heat until just smoking. Add remaining whole shrimp and spread into even layer. Cook, without stirring, until shrimp turn opaque and brown around edges, 2 to 3 minutes, flipping halfway through cooking. Push shrimp to sides of skillet. Add 2 teaspoons oil to center, then add eggs to center. Using rubber spatula, stir eggs gently and cook until set but still wet. Stir eggs into shrimp and continue to cook, breaking up large pieces of egg, until eggs are fully cooked, 30 to 60 seconds longer. Transfer shrimp-egg mixture to bowl with scallion-garlic mixture and dried shrimp.

9. Heat remaining 2 teaspoons oil in now-empty skillet over high heat until just smoking. Add noodles and sauce and toss with tongs to coat. Cook, stirring and tossing often, until noodles are tender and have absorbed sauce, 2 to 4 minutes. Transfer noodles to bowl with shrimp mixture. Add 2 teaspoons chile vinegar, drained radishes, scallion greens, and bean sprouts and toss to combine.

10. Transfer to platter and sprinkle with peanuts. Serve immediately, passing lime wedges and remaining chile vinegar separately.

THAI GRILLED CHICKEN

WHY THIS RECIPE WORKS: This herb- and spice-rubbed chicken is served in small pieces and eaten as finger food. We wanted to develop a recipe for Thai grilled chicken to offer a refreshing change of pace from typical barbecue fare. After testing numerous rub combinations, we liked cilantro, black pepper, lime juice, garlic, coriander, and ginger. We took some of the rub and placed it in a thick layer under the skin as well as on top of it. For perfectly cooked chicken, we made a modified two-level fire, first browning the chicken directly over the coals and then moving it to the cool side of the grill to finish cooking. The true Thai flavors of this dish come through in the sauce, a classic combination of sweet and spicy. We found balance in a blend of sugar, lime juice, white vinegar, red pepper flakes, fish sauce, and garlic.

Thai-Style Grilled Chicken with Spicy Sweet-and-Sour Dipping Sauce

SERVES 4

For even cooking, the chicken breasts should be of comparable size. Some of the rub is inevitably lost to the grill, but the chicken will still be flavorful.

CHICKEN AND BRINE

½ cup sugar
½ cup salt
4 (12-ounce) bone-in split chicken breasts, trimmed

DIPPING SAUCE

⅓ cup sugar

¼ cup distilled white vinegar

¼ cup lime juice (2 limes)

2 tablespoons fish sauce

3 small garlic cloves, minced

1 teaspoon red pepper flakes

RUB

⅔ cup chopped fresh cilantro

12 garlic cloves, minced

¼ cup lime juice (2 limes)

2 tablespoons grated fresh ginger

2 tablespoons pepper

2 tablespoons ground coriander

2 tablespoons vegetable oil

1 disposable aluminum roasting pan (if using charcoal)

1. **FOR THE CHICKEN AND BRINE:** Dissolve sugar and salt in 2 quarts cold water in large container. Submerge chicken in brine, cover, and refrigerate for at least 30 minutes or up to 1 hour. Remove chicken from brine and pat dry with paper towels.

2. **FOR THE DIPPING SAUCE:** Whisk all ingredients together in bowl until sugar dissolves. Let stand for 1 hour at room temperature to allow flavors to meld.

3. **FOR THE RUB:** Combine all ingredients in small bowl; work mixture with your fingers to thoroughly combine. Slide your fingers between chicken skin and meat to loosen skin, taking care not to detach skin. Rub about 2 tablespoons rub under skin of each breast. Thoroughly rub even layer of rub onto all exterior surfaces, including bottom and sides. Place chicken in bowl, cover with plastic wrap, and refrigerate while preparing grill.

4A. **FOR A CHARCOAL GRILL:** Open bottom vent completely. Light large chimney starter filled with charcoal briquettes (6 quarts). When top coals are partially covered with ash, pour evenly over half of grill. Set cooking grate in place, cover, and open lid vent completely. Heat grill until hot, about 5 minutes.

4B. **FOR A GAS GRILL:** Turn all burners to high, cover, and heat grill until hot, about 15 minutes. Leave primary burner on high and turn other burner(s) to low.

5. Clean and oil cooking grate. Place chicken, skin side down, on hotter side of grill; cook until browned, about 3 minutes (1 to 2 minutes longer for gas grill). Using tongs, flip chicken and cook until browned on second side, about 3 minutes longer. Move chicken, skin side up, to cooler side of grill and cover with disposable pan (or close lid if using gas grill). Continue to cook until thickest part of breast (not touching bone) registers 160 degrees, 10 to 15 minutes longer. Transfer chicken to platter; let rest for 10 minutes. Serve, passing dipping sauce separately.

GRILLED THAI BEEF SALAD

WHY THIS RECIPE WORKS: This traditional Thai salad features slices of charred steak tossed with shallots, mint, and cilantro in a bright dressing. We chose flank steak for its marbling and moderate price. Grilling the steak over a modified two-level fire and flipping it just when moisture beaded on the surface yielded perfectly charred, juicy meat. Adding a fresh Thai chile, toasted cayenne, and paprika gave the dressing a fruity, fiery heat. Toasted rice powder, a traditional Thai tableside condiment that gives the dressing fuller body and a subtle crunch, is not widely available here, but we made our own by toasting rice in a skillet on the stovetop, then grinding it in a food processor, spice grinder, or even with a mortar and pestle.

Grilled Thai Beef Salad

SERVES 4 TO 6

If fresh Thai chiles are unavailable, substitute ½ serrano chile. Don't skip the toasted rice; it's integral to the texture and flavor of the dish. Any variety of white rice can be used. Toasted rice powder (*kao kua*) can also be found in many Asian markets; substitute 1 tablespoon rice powder for the white rice. Serve with Basic White Rice (page 453), if desired.

1 teaspoon paprika

1 teaspoon cayenne pepper

1 tablespoon white rice

3 tablespoons lime juice (2 limes)

2 tablespoons fish sauce

2 tablespoons water

½ teaspoon sugar

1 (1½-pound) flank steak, trimmed
Salt and coarsely ground white pepper

1 seedless English cucumber, sliced ¼ inch thick on bias

4 shallots, sliced thin

1½ cups fresh mint leaves, torn

1½ cups fresh cilantro leaves

1 Thai chile, stemmed, seeded, and sliced thin into rounds

1. Heat paprika and cayenne in 8-inch skillet over medium heat; cook, shaking pan, until fragrant, about 1 minute. Transfer to small bowl. Return skillet to medium-high heat, add rice and toast, stirring constantly, until deep golden brown, about 5 minutes. Transfer to small bowl and let cool 5 minutes. Grind rice with spice grinder, mini food processor, or mortar and pestle until it resembles fine meal, 10 to 30 seconds (you should have about 1 tablespoon rice powder).

2. Whisk lime juice, fish sauce, water, sugar, and ¼ teaspoon toasted paprika mixture in large bowl and set aside.

3A. FOR A CHARCOAL GRILL: Open bottom vent completely. Light large chimney starter filled with charcoal briquettes (6 quarts). When top coals are partially covered with ash, pour in even layer over half of grill. Set cooking grate in place, cover, and open lid vent completely. Heat grill until hot, about 5 minutes.

3B. FOR A GAS GRILL: Turn all burners to high, cover, and heat grill until hot, about 15 minutes. Leave primary burner on high and turn off other burner(s).

4. Clean and oil grate. Season steak with salt and pepper. Place steak on grate over hot part of grill and cook until beginning to char and beads of moisture appear on outer edges of meat, 5 to 6 minutes. Flip steak, continue to cook on second side until meat registers 125 degrees, about 5 minutes longer. Transfer to carving board, tent loosely with aluminum foil, and rest for 10 minutes (or allow to cool to room temperature, about 1 hour).

5. Line large platter with cucumber slices. Slice meat, against grain, on bias, into ¼-inch-thick slices. Transfer sliced steak to bowl with fish sauce mixture, add shallots, mint, cilantro, chile, and half of rice powder, and toss to combine. Arrange steak over cucumber-lined platter. Serve, passing remaining rice powder and toasted paprika mixture separately.

VIETNAMESE-STYLE CARAMEL CHICKEN WITH BROCCOLI

WHY THIS RECIPE WORKS: In Vietnamese cooking, caramel sauce has a savory, bittersweet quality that gives a rich, molasses-like hue to meat, fish, and tofu alike. To prep our chicken for this flavorful sauce, we coated boneless, skinless thighs with a mixture of baking soda and water. Baking soda would help break down the muscle fibers, promising juicy, tender meat capable of taking on lots of flavor and moisture. For caramel that was savory, not sweet, we cooked sugar and water in a saucepan until the mixture took on a deep brown color and reached between 390 and 400 degrees. At that temperature, sugar molecules break down and the caramel takes on a pleasingly bitter, potent taste. We transferred the caramel to a 12-inch skillet and added fish sauce for a savory, salty punch and freshly grated ginger for spicy brightness. Simmering the boneless chicken in the sauce produced tender meat fully infused with bold Vietnamese flavor. Once the chicken was cooked, we prepared some steamed broccoli for textural and visual contrast and reduced the caramel, adding some cornstarch to further thicken and finish the sauce.

Vietnamese-Style Caramel Chicken with Broccoli

SERVES 4 TO 6

The saltiness of fish sauce can vary by brand; we recommend Red Boat. When taking the temperature of the caramel in step 2, tilt the pan and move the thermometer back and forth to equalize hot and cool spots; also make sure to have hot water at the ready. This dish is intensely seasoned, so serve it with Basic White Rice (page 453).

- 1 tablespoon baking soda
- 2 pounds boneless, skinless chicken thighs, trimmed and halved crosswise
- 7 tablespoons sugar
- ¼ cup fish sauce
- 2 tablespoons grated fresh ginger
- 1 pound broccoli, florets cut into 1-inch pieces, stalks peeled and sliced ¼ inch thick
- 2 teaspoons cornstarch
- ½ teaspoon pepper
- ½ cup chopped fresh cilantro leaves and stems

1. Combine baking soda and 1¼ cups cold water in large bowl. Add chicken and toss to coat. Let stand at room temperature for 15 minutes. Rinse chicken in cold water and drain well.

2. Meanwhile, combine sugar and 3 tablespoons water in small saucepan. Bring to boil over medium-high heat and cook, without stirring, until mixture begins to turn golden, 4 to 6 minutes. Reduce heat to medium-low and continue to cook, gently swirling saucepan, until sugar turns color of molasses and registers between 390 and 400 degrees, 4 to 6 minutes longer. (Caramel will produce some smoke during last 1 to 2 minutes of cooking.) Immediately remove saucepan

from heat and carefully pour in ¾ cup hot water (mixture will bubble and steam vigorously). When bubbling has subsided, return saucepan to medium heat and stir to dissolve caramel.

3. Transfer caramel to 12-inch skillet and stir in fish sauce and ginger. Add chicken and bring to simmer over medium-high heat. Reduce heat to medium-low, cover, and simmer until chicken is fork-tender and registers 205 degrees, 30 to 40 minutes, flipping chicken halfway through simmering. Transfer chicken to serving dish and cover to keep warm.

4. Bring 1 inch water to boil in Dutch oven. Lower insert or steamer basket with broccoli into pot so it rests above water; cover and simmer until broccoli is just tender, 4½ to 5 minutes. Transfer broccoli to serving dish with chicken.

5. While broccoli cooks, bring sauce to boil over medium-high heat and cook until reduced to 1¼ cups, 3 to 5 minutes. Whisk cornstarch and 1 tablespoon water together in small bowl, then whisk into sauce; simmer until slightly thickened, about 1 minute. Stir in pepper. Pour ¼ cup sauce over chicken and broccoli. Sprinkle with cilantro and serve, passing remaining sauce separately.

INDIAN FLATBREAD (NAAN)

WHY THIS RECIPE WORKS: Even in India, naan is considered "restaurant" bread. This may be because it calls for a traditional tandoor oven, which few home cooks own. We wanted an ideal version of this bread—light and airy, with a pliant, chewy crust—that we could easily make at home. We started with a moist dough with a fair amount of fat, which created a soft bread that was pleasantly chewy, but the real secret was the cooking method. While we thought a grill or preheated pizza stone would be the best cooking method, we discovered that they cooked the bread unevenly. A much better option was a covered skillet. The skillet delivered heat to the bottom and the top of the bread, producing loaves that were nicely charred but still moist.

Indian Flatbread (Naan)

MAKES 4 BREADS

This recipe works best with a high-protein all-purpose flour such as King Arthur brand. Do not use nonfat yogurt in this recipe. A 12-inch nonstick skillet may be used in place of the cast-iron skillet. For efficiency, stretch the next ball of dough while each naan is cooking.

½   cup ice water
⅓   cup plain whole-milk yogurt
3   tablespoons plus 1 teaspoon vegetable oil
1   large egg yolk
2   cups (10 ounces) all-purpose flour
1¼   teaspoons sugar
½   teaspoon instant or rapid-rise yeast
1¼   teaspoons salt
1½   tablespoons unsalted butter, melted

1. In measuring cup or small bowl, combine water, yogurt, 3 tablespoons oil, and egg yolk. Process flour, sugar, and yeast together in food processor until combined, about 2 seconds. With processor running, slowly add water mixture; process until dough is just combined and no dry flour remains, about 10 seconds. Let dough stand for 10 minutes.

2. Add salt to dough and process until dough forms satiny, sticky ball that clears sides of workbowl, 30 to 60 seconds. Transfer dough to lightly floured counter and knead until smooth, about 1 minute. Shape dough into tight ball and place in large, lightly oiled bowl. Cover tightly with plastic wrap and refrigerate for 16 to 24 hours.

3. Adjust oven rack to middle position and heat oven to 200 degrees. Place heatproof plate on rack. Transfer dough to lightly floured counter and divide into 4 equal pieces. Shape each piece into smooth, tight ball. Place dough balls on lightly oiled baking sheet, at least 2 inches apart; cover loosely with plastic coated with vegetable oil spray. Let stand for 15 to 20 minutes.

4. Transfer 1 ball to lightly floured counter and sprinkle with flour. Using hands and rolling pin, press and roll piece of dough into 9-inch round of even thickness, sprinkling dough and counter with flour as needed to prevent sticking. Using fork, poke entire surface of round 20 to 25 times. Heat remaining 1 teaspoon oil in 12-inch cast-iron skillet over medium heat until shimmering. Wipe oil out of skillet completely with paper towels. Mist top of dough lightly with water. Place dough in pan, moistened side down; mist top surface of dough with water; and cover. Cook until bottom is browned in spots across surface, 2 to 4 minutes. Flip naan, cover, and continue to cook on second side until lightly browned, 2 to 3 minutes longer. (If naan puffs up, gently poke with fork to deflate.) Flip naan, brush top with about 1 teaspoon melted butter, transfer to plate in oven, and cover plate tightly with aluminum foil. Repeat rolling and cooking remaining 3 dough balls. Once last naan is baked, serve immediately.

Quicker Indian Flatbread

This variation, which can be prepared in about 2 hours, forgoes the overnight rest, but the dough may be a little harder to roll out.

After shaping dough in step 2, let dough rise at room temperature for 30 minutes. After 30 minutes, fold partially risen dough over itself 8 times by gently lifting and folding edge of dough toward middle, turning bowl 90 degrees after each fold. Cover with plastic wrap and let rise for 30 minutes. Repeat folding, turning, and rising 1 more time, for total of three 30-minute rises. After last rise, proceed with recipe from step 3.

SAAG PANEER

WHY THIS RECIPE WORKS: *Saag paneer*, soft cubes of creamy cheese in a spicy pureed spinach sauce, is an Indian restaurant classic. We found that re-creating this dish at home wasn't so difficult. We made our own cheese by heating a combination of whole milk and buttermilk, squeezing the curds of moisture, then weighing the cheese down until it was firm enough to slice. We simply wilted the spinach in the microwave. Mustard greens gave our sauce additional complexity. Canned diced tomatoes brightened the dish. And buttery cashews gave our Indian classic a subtle nutty richness.

Indian-Style Spinach with Fresh Cheese (Saag Paneer)

SERVES 4 TO 6

To ensure that the cheese is firm, wring it tightly in step 2 and be sure to use two plates that nestle together snugly. Use commercially produced cultured buttermilk in this recipe. We found that some locally produced buttermilks didn't sufficiently coagulate the milk. Serve with basmati rice.

CHEESE

- 3 quarts whole milk
- 3 cups buttermilk
- 1 tablespoon salt

SPINACH SAUCE

- 1 (10-ounce) bag curly-leaf spinach, rinsed
- 12 ounces mustard greens, stemmed and rinsed
- 3 tablespoons unsalted butter
- 1 teaspoon cumin seeds
- 1 teaspoon ground coriander
- 1 teaspoon paprika
- ½ teaspoon ground cardamom
- ¼ teaspoon ground cinnamon
- 1 onion, chopped fine
  Salt and pepper
- 3 garlic cloves, minced
- 1 tablespoon grated fresh ginger
- 1 jalapeño chile, stemmed, seeded, and minced
- 1 (14.5-ounce) can diced tomatoes, drained and chopped coarse
- ½ cup roasted cashews, chopped coarse
- 1 cup water
- 1 cup buttermilk
- 3 tablespoons chopped fresh cilantro

1. FOR THE CHEESE: Line colander with triple layer of cheesecloth and set in sink. Bring milk to boil in Dutch oven over medium-high heat. Whisk in buttermilk and salt, turn off heat, and let stand for 1 minute. Pour milk mixture through cheesecloth and let curds drain for 15 minutes.

2. Pull edges of cheesecloth together to form pouch. Twist edges of cheesecloth together, firmly squeezing out as much liquid as possible from cheese curds. Place taut, twisted cheese pouch between 2 large plates and weigh down top plate with

heavy Dutch oven. Set aside at room temperature until cheese is firm and set, at least 45 minutes. Remove cheesecloth and cut cheese into ½-inch pieces. (Left uncut, cheese can be wrapped in plastic wrap and refrigerated for up to 3 days.)

3. FOR THE SPINACH SAUCE: Place spinach in large bowl, cover, and microwave until wilted, about 3 minutes. When cool enough to handle, chop enough spinach to measure ⅓ cup and set aside. Transfer remaining spinach to blender and wipe out bowl. Place mustard greens in now-empty bowl, cover, and microwave until wilted, about 4 minutes. When cool enough to handle, chop enough mustard greens to measure ⅓ cup and transfer to bowl with chopped spinach. Transfer remaining mustard greens to blender.

4. Meanwhile, melt butter in 12-inch skillet over medium-high heat. Add cumin seeds, coriander, paprika, cardamom, and cinnamon and cook until fragrant, about 30 seconds. Add onion and ¾ teaspoon salt; cook, stirring frequently, until softened, about 3 minutes. Add garlic, ginger, and jalapeño; cook, stirring frequently, until lightly browned and just beginning to stick to pan, 2 to 3 minutes. Stir in tomatoes and cook mixture until pan is dry and tomatoes are beginning to brown, 3 to 4 minutes. Remove skillet from heat.

5. Transfer half of onion mixture to blender with greens. Add ¼ cup cashews and water; process until smooth, about 1 minute. Return puree to skillet.

6. Return skillet to medium-high heat, stir in chopped greens and buttermilk, and bring to simmer. Reduce heat to low, cover, and cook until flavors have blended, 5 minutes. Season with salt and pepper to taste. Gently fold in cheese cubes and cook until just heated through, 1 to 2 minutes. Transfer to serving dish, sprinkle with remaining ¼ cup cashews and cilantro, and serve.

NOTES FROM THE TEST KITCHEN

MAKING PANEER

Even if you've never made cheese at home, our method for making paneer is very simple, and the flavor pay-off is well worth the effort.

1. Bring milk to boil, curdle it with buttermilk, and let rest for 1 minute off heat. Pour curdled milk through cheesecloth-lined colander; let drain. Twist cheesecloth to squeeze out liquid.

2. Press cheese between plates topped with Dutch oven; let drain until firm. Slice into ½-inch pieces.

CHICKEN TIKKA MASALA

WHY THIS RECIPE WORKS: Chicken tikka masala is arguably the single most popular Indian restaurant dish in the world. Turns out, it's not an authentic Indian dish—it was invented in a London curry house. Without historical roots, there is no definitive recipe. The variations we found had mushy or dry chicken and sauces that were unbearably rich and/or over-spiced. We wanted an approachable method for producing moist, tender chunks of chicken in a rich, lightly spiced tomato sauce. To season the chicken, we rubbed it with salt, coriander, cumin, and cayenne. Then we dipped it in yogurt mixed with oil, garlic, and ginger and broiled it. And since large pieces don't dry out as quickly as smaller ones under the broiler, we cooked the chicken breasts whole, cutting them into pieces only after cooking. While the chicken was cooking, we made the masala sauce. Masala means "hot spice," and the ingredients in a masala sauce depend on the whim of the cook, although tomatoes and cream are always present. We added onions, ginger, garlic, chile, and a readily available commercial garam masala spice mixture. A little tomato paste and sugar gave our sauce color and sweetness.

Chicken Tikka Masala

SERVES 4 TO 6

This dish is best when prepared with whole-milk yogurt, but low-fat yogurt can be substituted. For more heat, include the chile seeds and ribs when mincing. Serve with Rice Pilaf (see page 617).

CHICKEN

Table salt

½ teaspoon ground cumin
½ teaspoon ground coriander
¼ teaspoon cayenne pepper
2 pounds boneless, skinless chicken breasts, trimmed
1 cup plain whole-milk yogurt (see note)

2 tablespoons vegetable oil
1 tablespoon minced or grated fresh ginger
2 medium garlic cloves, minced or pressed through a garlic press (about 2 teaspoons)

SAUCE

3 tablespoons vegetable oil
1 medium onion, minced (about 1 cup)
1 tablespoon garam masala
1 tablespoon tomato paste
2 medium garlic cloves, minced or pressed through a garlic press (about 2 teaspoons)
2 teaspoons minced or grated fresh ginger
1 serrano chile, seeds and ribs removed, chile minced (see note)
1 (28-ounce) can crushed tomatoes
2 teaspoons sugar
½ teaspoon table salt
⅔ cup heavy cream
¼ cup chopped fresh cilantro leaves

1. FOR THE CHICKEN: Combine ½ teaspoon salt, cumin, coriander, and cayenne in a small bowl. Pat the chicken dry with paper towels and sprinkle with the spice mixture, pressing gently so the mixture adheres. Place the chicken on a plate, cover with plastic wrap, and refrigerate for 30 minutes or up to 1 hour. In a large bowl, whisk the yogurt, oil, ginger, and garlic together and set aside.

2. FOR THE SAUCE: Heat the oil in a large Dutch oven over medium heat until shimmering. Add the onion and cook, stirring frequently, until softened and light golden, 8 to 10 minutes. Stir in the garam masala, tomato paste, garlic, ginger, and serrano and cook, stirring frequently, until fragrant, about 3 minutes. Add the crushed tomatoes, sugar, and salt and bring to a boil. Reduce the heat to medium-low, cover, and simmer for 15 minutes, stirring occasionally. Stir in the cream and return to a simmer. Remove the pan from the heat and cover to keep warm. (The sauce can be refrigerated in an airtight container for up to 4 days and gently reheated before adding the hot chicken.)

3. TO COOK THE CHICKEN: While the sauce simmers, position an oven rack 6 inches from the heating element and heat the broiler. Line a rimmed baking sheet or broiler pan with foil and place a wire rack over the sheet.

4. Using tongs, dip the chicken into the yogurt mixture (the chicken should be coated with a thick layer of yogurt) and arrange on the wire rack. Discard the excess yogurt mixture. Broil the chicken until lightly charred and the thickest part of the breasts registers 160 to 165 degrees on an instant-read thermometer, 10 to 18 minutes, flipping the chicken halfway through.

5. Let the chicken rest for 5 minutes, then cut into 1-inch chunks and stir into the warm sauce (do not simmer the chicken in the sauce). Stir in the cilantro, season with salt to taste, and serve.

INDIAN-STYLE CHICKEN AND RICE

WHY THIS RECIPE WORKS: Chicken biryani is a complicated (and often greasy) "gourmet" Indian dish. Chicken and rice is a simple, but unremarkable, American one-pot meal. We wanted to find a happy medium between the two.

In biryani, long-grain basmati rice takes center stage, enriched with butter, saffron, and a variety of fresh herbs and pungent spices. Pieces of tender chicken and browned onions are layered with the rice and baked until the flavors have mingled. For our recipe, we browned bone-in, skin-on chicken thighs, then removed the skin and layered them with basmati rice, lots of caramelized onions, and just the right blend of spices. To get the most flavor out of the spices, we tied them into a cheesecloth bundle and simmered them in the rice cooking water—then we added some of that water to the biryani. For a finishing touch, we added saffron, currants, and plenty of ginger and chiles.

Chicken Biryani

SERVES 4

This recipe requires a 3½- to 4-quart saucepan about 8 inches in diameter. Do not use a large, wide Dutch oven, as it will adversely affect both the layering of the dish and the final cooking times. For more heat, add the jalapeño seeds and ribs when mincing.

YOGURT SAUCE

- 1 cup whole-milk or low-fat plain yogurt
- 2 tablespoons minced fresh cilantro leaves
- 2 tablespoons minced fresh mint leaves
- 1 medium garlic clove, minced or pressed through a garlic press (about 1 teaspoon)
  Table salt and ground black pepper

CHICKEN AND RICE

- 10 cardamom pods, preferably green, smashed with a chef's knife
- 1 cinnamon stick
- 1 (2-inch) piece fresh ginger, peeled, cut into ½-inch-thick coins, and smashed
- ½ teaspoon cumin seeds
- 3 quarts water
  Table salt and ground black pepper
- 4 (5- to 6-ounce) bone-in, skin-on chicken thighs, trimmed
- 3 tablespoons unsalted butter
- 2 medium onions, halved and sliced thin
- 2 jalapeño chiles, seeds and ribs removed, chiles minced (see note)
- 4 medium garlic cloves, minced or pressed through a garlic press (about 4 teaspoons)
- 1¼ cups basmati rice
- ½ teaspoon saffron threads, lightly crumbled
- ¼ cup dried currants or raisins
- 2 tablespoons chopped fresh cilantro leaves
- 2 tablespoons chopped fresh mint leaves

1. FOR THE YOGURT SAUCE: Combine all the ingredients in a small bowl, season with salt and pepper to taste, and set aside. (The sauce can be refrigerated in an airtight container for up to 2 days.)

2. FOR THE CHICKEN AND RICE: Wrap the cardamom pods, cinnamon stick, ginger, and cumin in a small piece of cheesecloth and secure with kitchen twine. In a 3½ to 4-quart heavy-bottomed saucepan about 8 inches in diameter, bring the spice bundle, water, and 1½ teaspoons salt to a boil over medium-high heat. Reduce the heat to medium and simmer, partially covered, until the spices have infused the water, at least 15 minutes (but no longer than 30 minutes).

3. Meanwhile, pat the chicken thighs dry with paper towels and season with salt and pepper. Melt the butter in a 12-inch nonstick skillet over medium-high heat. Add the onions and cook, stirring frequently, until soft and dark brown around the edges, 10 to 12 minutes. Stir in the jalapeños and garlic and cook, stirring frequently, until fragrant, about 2 minutes. Transfer the onion mixture to a bowl, season with salt, and set aside. Wipe out the skillet with a wad of paper towels.

4. Place the chicken, skin side down, in the skillet, return the skillet to medium-high heat, and cook until well browned on both sides, 8 to 10 minutes, flipping halfway through. Transfer the chicken to a plate and remove and discard the skin. Tent loosely with foil to keep warm.

5. If necessary, return the spice-infused water to a boil over high heat. Add the rice and cook, stirring occasionally, for 5 minutes. Drain the rice through a fine-mesh strainer, reserving ¾ cup of the cooking liquid; discard the spice bundle. Transfer the rice to a medium bowl and stir in the saffron and currants (the rice will turn splotchy yellow).

6. Spread half of the rice evenly in the bottom of the saucepan using a rubber spatula. Scatter half of the onion mixture over the rice, then place the chicken thighs, skinned side up, on top of the onions; add any accumulated chicken juices. Sprinkle evenly with the cilantro and mint, scatter the remaining onion mixture over the herbs, then cover with the remaining rice. Pour the reserved ¾ cup cooking liquid evenly over the rice.

7. Cover the saucepan and cook over medium-low heat until the rice is tender and the chicken registers 175 degrees on an instant-read thermometer, about 30 minutes (if a large amount of steam is escaping from the pot, reduce the heat to low).

8. Run a heatproof rubber spatula around the inside rim of the saucepan to loosen any affixed rice. Using a large serving spoon, spoon the biryani into individual bowls, scooping from the bottom of the pot. Serve, passing the yogurt sauce separately.

INDIAN CURRY

WHY THIS RECIPE WORKS: For many home cooks Indian cooking is a mystery, full of exotic spices and unfamiliar techniques. We hoped to bring Indian curry to the American home kitchen with a complex but not heavy-flavored curry that wouldn't take all day to prepare. Allowing the spices to cook completely provided the intense flavor we were after. We used a combination of whole spices—cinnamon sticks, cloves, green cardamom pods, black peppercorns, and a bay leaf—and toasted them in oil before adding aromatics, jalapeño, and ground spices. Instead of browning the meat), we stirred it into the pot along with crushed tomatoes and cooked the mixture until the liquid evaporated and the oil separated. This is a classic Indian technique that allows the spices to further develop their flavors in the oil, flavors which are then cooked into the meat. We then added water and simmered the mixture until the meat was tender, then stirred in the spinach and channa dal (yellow split peas) and cooked the dish until all the ingredients were melded and tender.

Indian Curry

SERVES 4 TO 6

If desired, 1½ pounds boneless, skinless chicken thighs, trimmed and cut into ¾-inch chunks, can be substituted for the lamb. For more heat, add the jalapeño seeds and ribs when mincing. For a creamier curry, choose yogurt over the crushed tomatoes. Serve with Yogurt Sauce (page 490), Onion Relish (page 492), Cilantro-Mint Chutney (page 492), and Rice Pilaf (page 617).

SPICE BLEND
1½ cinnamon sticks
4 whole cloves
4 green cardamom pods
8 whole black peppercorns
1 bay leaf

CURRY
¼ cup vegetable oil
1 medium onion, halved and sliced thin
5 medium garlic cloves, minced or pressed through a garlic press (about 5 teaspoons)
1 tablespoon minced or grated fresh ginger
1 jalapeño chile, stemmed and halved lengthwise, seeds and ribs removed (see note)
2 teaspoons ground cumin
2 teaspoons ground coriander
1 teaspoon ground turmeric
Table salt
1½ pounds boneless leg of lamb, trimmed and cut into ¾-inch cubes (see note)
⅔ cup crushed tomatoes or ½ cup plain low-fat yogurt (see note)
2 cups water
1½ pounds spinach, stemmed, washed, and chopped coarse (optional)
½ cup channa dal (yellow split peas)
¼ cup chopped fresh cilantro leaves

1. FOR THE SPICE BLEND: Combine all the ingredients in a small bowl and set aside.

2. FOR THE CURRY: Heat the oil in a Dutch oven over medium heat until shimmering. Add the spice blend and cook, stirring frequently, until the cinnamon stick unfurls and the cloves pop, about 5 seconds. Add the onion and cook, stirring occasionally, until softened, 5 to 7 minutes. Stir in the garlic, ginger, jalapeño, cumin, coriander, turmeric, and ½ teaspoon salt and cook until fragrant, about 30 seconds.

3. Stir in the lamb and the tomatoes. Bring to a simmer and cook, stirring frequently, until the liquid evaporates and the oil separates and turns orange, 5 to 7 minutes. Continue to cook until the spices are sizzling, about 30 seconds longer.

4. Stir in the water and bring to a simmer over medium heat. Reduce the heat to medium-low, cover, and cook until the lamb is almost tender, about 40 minutes.

5. Stir in the spinach (if using) and channa dal and cook until the channa dal are tender, about 15 minutes. Season with salt to taste, stir in the cilantro, and serve.

VEGETABLE CURRY

WHY THIS RECIPE WORKS: Vegetable curries can be complicated affairs, with lengthy ingredient lists and fussy techniques meant to compensate for the lack of meat. We wanted a curry we could make on a weeknight in less than an hour—without sacrificing flavor or overloading the dish with spices.

Although initially reluctant to use store-bought curry powder, we found that toasting the curry powder in a skillet turned it into a flavor powerhouse. Further experimentation proved that adding a few pinches of garam masala added even more spice flavor. To build the rest of our flavor base we started with a generous amount of sautéed onion, vegetable oil, garlic, ginger, fresh chile, and tomato paste for sweetness. When we chose our vegetables (chickpeas and potatoes for heartiness and cauliflower and peas for texture and color), we found that sautéing the spices and main ingredients together enhanced and melded the flavors. Finally, we rounded out our sauce with a combination of water, pureed canned tomatoes, and a splash of heavy cream or coconut milk.

Indian-Style Curry with Potatoes, Cauliflower, Peas, and Chickpeas

SERVES 4 TO 6

This curry is moderately spicy when made with one chile. For more heat, include the chile seeds and ribs when mincing. Serve with Yogurt Sauce (page 490), Onion Relish, Cilantro-Mint Chutney, and Rice Pilaf (page 617).

  2 tablespoons sweet or mild curry powder
1½ teaspoons garam masala
  4 tablespoons vegetable oil
  3 medium garlic cloves, minced or pressed through a garlic press (about 1 tablespoon)
  1 tablespoon minced or grated fresh ginger
  1 serrano chile, seeds and ribs removed, chile minced (see note)
  1 tablespoon tomato paste
  1 (14.5-ounce) can diced tomatoes
  2 medium onions, minced (about 2 cups)
 12 ounces red potatoes (about 2 medium), scrubbed and cut into ½-inch pieces
1¼ pounds cauliflower (½ medium head), trimmed, cored, and cut into 1-inch florets
1¼ cups water
  1 (15-ounce) can chickpeas, drained and rinsed
    Table salt
1½ cups frozen peas
  ¼ cup heavy cream or coconut milk

CONDIMENTS
    Onion Relish (recipe follows)
    Cilantro-Mint Chutney (recipe follows) or mango chutney

1. Toast the curry powder and garam masala in a small skillet over medium-high heat, stirring constantly, until the spices darken slightly and become fragrant, about 1 minute. Transfer the spices to a small bowl and set aside. In a separate small bowl, stir 1 tablespoon of the oil, the garlic, ginger, serrano, and tomato paste together. Pulse the tomatoes with their juice in a food processor until coarsely chopped, 3 to 4 pulses.

2. Heat the remaining 3 tablespoons oil in a large Dutch oven over medium-high heat until shimmering. Add the onions and potatoes and cook, stirring occasionally, until the onions are caramelized and the potatoes are golden brown around the edges, about 10 minutes. (Reduce the heat to medium if the onions darken too quickly.)

3. Reduce the heat to medium. Clear the center of the pot, add the garlic mixture, and cook, mashing the mixture into the pan, until fragrant, 15 to 20 seconds. Stir the garlic mixture into the vegetables. Add the toasted spices and cook, stirring constantly, for 1 minute longer. Add the cauliflower and cook, stirring constantly, until the spices coat the florets, about 2 minutes longer.

4. Add the tomatoes, water, chickpeas, and 1 teaspoon salt, scraping up any browned bits. Bring to a boil over medium-high heat. Cover, reduce the heat to medium, and cook, stirring occasionally, until the vegetables are tender, 10 to 15 minutes. Stir in the peas and cream and continue to cook until heated through, about 2 minutes longer. Season with salt to taste and serve, passing the condiments separately.

Indian-Style Curry with Sweet Potatoes, Eggplant, Green Beans, and Chickpeas

Follow the recipe for Indian-Style Curry with Potatoes, Cauliflower, Peas, and Chickpeas, substituting 12 ounces sweet potato (1 medium), peeled and cut into ½-inch pieces, for the red potatoes. Substitute 8 ounces green beans, trimmed and cut into 1-inch pieces, and 1 medium eggplant (1 pound), cut into ½-inch pieces, for the cauliflower. Omit the peas.

Onion Relish

MAKES ABOUT 1 CUP

If using a regular yellow onion, increase the sugar to 1 teaspoon. This relish can be refrigerated in an airtight container for up to 24 hours.

  1 medium Vidalia onion, minced (about 1 cup; see note)
  1 tablespoon juice from 1 lime
  ½ teaspoon sweet paprika
  ½ teaspoon sugar
  ⅛ teaspoon table salt
    Pinch cayenne pepper

Combine all the ingredients in a small bowl.

Cilantro-Mint Chutney

MAKES ABOUT 1 CUP

This chutney can be refrigerated in an airtight container for up to 24 hours.

  2 cups packed fresh cilantro leaves
  1 cup packed fresh mint leaves
  ⅓ cup plain yogurt
  ¼ cup minced onion
  1 tablespoon juice from 1 lime
1½ teaspoons sugar
  ½ teaspoon ground cumin
  ¼ teaspoon table salt

Process all the ingredients together in a food processor until smooth, about 20 seconds, scraping down the sides of the workbowl as needed.

TANDOORI CHICKEN

WHY THIS RECIPE WORKS: We weren't going to let a 24-hour marinade or the lack of a 900-degree oven keep us from turning this great Indian classic into an easy weeknight dinner. Traditional tandoors produce moist, smoky meat because the heat allows protein molecules on the meat's surface to contract, trapping moisture. Juices and fat fall on the coals, creating smoky flavor. Trying to mimic the tandoor by cooking chicken in a very hot oven gave us disappointing results. Instead, we baked the chicken in a low-temperature oven until almost done, then quickly broiled it to char the exterior. To get flavor into the meat, we turned to a salt-spice rub made with garam masala, cumin, and chili powder bloomed in oil. We massaged the rub into chicken pieces to lock in juices and infuse flavor. Following a dunk in yogurt flavored with the same spice mix, the chicken was ready for the oven.

Tandoori Chicken

SERVES 4

We prefer this dish with whole-milk yogurt, but low-fat yogurt can be substituted. It is important to remove the chicken from the oven before switching to the broiler setting to allow the heating element to come up to temperature. Serve with Yogurt Sauce (page 490), Onion Relish (page 492), Cilantro-Mint Chutney (page 492), and Rice Pilaf (page 617).

- 2 tablespoons vegetable oil
- 6 medium garlic cloves, minced or pressed through a garlic press (about 2 tablespoons)
- 2 tablespoons minced or grated fresh ginger
- 1 tablespoon garam masala
- 2 teaspoons ground cumin
- 2 teaspoons chili powder
- 1 cup plain whole-milk yogurt (see note)
- ¼ cup juice from 2 limes, plus 1 lime, cut into wedges (for serving)
- 2 teaspoons table salt
- 3 pounds bone-in, skin-on chicken pieces (split breasts cut in half, drumsticks, and/or thighs), trimmed and skin removed

1. Heat the oil in an 8-inch skillet over medium heat until shimmering. Add the garlic and ginger and cook until fragrant, about 1 minute. Stir in the garam masala, cumin, and chili powder and cook until fragrant, about 30 seconds. Transfer half of the garlic-spice mixture to a medium bowl, stir in the yogurt and 2 tablespoons of the lime juice, and set aside.

2. In a large bowl, combine the remaining garlic-spice mixture, remaining 2 tablespoons lime juice, and salt. Using a sharp knife, lightly score the skin side of each piece of chicken, making two or three shallow cuts about 1 inch apart and about ⅛ inch deep. Transfer the chicken to the bowl and gently rub with the salt-spice mixture until evenly coated. Let sit at room temperature for 30 minutes.

3. Adjust an oven rack to the upper-middle position (about 6 inches from the heating element) and heat the oven to 325 degrees. Set a wire rack over a foil-lined rimmed baking sheet or broiler pan bottom.

4. Pour the yogurt mixture over the chicken and toss until the chicken is evenly coated with a thick layer. Arrange the chicken pieces, scored side down, on the prepared wire rack. Discard the excess yogurt mixture. Bake the chicken until an instant-read thermometer inserted into the thickest part of the chicken registers 125 degrees for breasts and 130 degrees for legs and thighs, 15 to 25 minutes. (Smaller pieces may cook faster than larger pieces.) Transfer the chicken to a plate.

5. Turn the oven to broil and heat for 10 minutes. Flip the chicken pieces scored side up and broil until lightly charred in spots and the thickest part of the breasts registers 165 degrees and the thickest part of the legs and thighs registers 175 degrees, 8 to 15 minutes.

6. Transfer the chicken to a serving platter, tent loosely with foil, and let rest for 5 minutes. Serve with the lime wedges.

NOTES FROM THE TEST KITCHEN

TANDOORI CHICKEN WITHOUT THE TANDOOR

1. Massage chicken pieces with salt-spice rub to lock in juices and infuse flavor.

2. Toss chicken in spiced yogurt for another layer of flavor.

3. To ensure juicy meat, bake chicken slowly in 325-degree oven until not quite cooked through.

4. For smoky flavor, briefly broil chicken until lightly charred and fully cooked.

LET'S GET GRILLING: BEEF, PORK, AND LAMB

CLASSIC GRILLED HAMBURGERS

WHY THIS RECIPE WORKS: Burgers often come off the grill tough, dry, and bulging in the middle. We wanted a moist and juicy burger, with a texture that is tender and cohesive, not dense and heavy. Just as important, we wanted a flavorful, deeply caramelized reddish brown crust with an even surface capable of holding as many condiments as we could pile on.

Ground chuck gave us the most robustly flavored burgers when pitted head to head against burgers made from other cuts of ground beef. We selected meat with a ratio of 20 percent fat to 80 percent lean; more fat than that, and the burgers were too greasy. Burgers made with less fat lacked in juiciness and moisture. We formed the meat into 6-ounce patties that were fairly thick, with a depression in the middle. Rounds of testing taught us that indenting the center of each burger ensured that the patties would come off the grill with an even thickness instead of puffed up like a tennis ball. Cooking the burgers over the fire for just a few minutes kept them tender, and lightly oiling the cooking grate prevented them from sticking.

Grilled Hamburgers
SERVES 4

Weighing the meat on a kitchen scale is the most accurate way to portion it. If you don't own a scale, do your best to divide the meat evenly into quarters. Eighty percent lean ground chuck is our favorite for flavor, but 85 percent lean works, too.

- 1½ pounds 80 percent lean ground chuck
- 1 teaspoon salt
- ½ teaspoon pepper
- 4 hamburger rolls, toasted

1. Using hands, gently break up meat, season with salt and pepper, and toss lightly to incorporate. Divide meat into 4 portions and lightly toss 1 portion from hand to hand to form ball, then lightly flatten ball with fingertips into ¾-inch-thick patty. Press center of patty down with fingertips until it is about ½ inch thick, creating slight depression. Repeat with remaining portions.

2A. FOR A CHARCOAL GRILL: Open bottom vent completely. Light large chimney starter filled with charcoal briquettes (6 quarts). When top coals are partially covered with ash, pour evenly over grill. Set cooking grate in place, cover, and open lid vent completely. Heat grill until hot, about 5 minutes.

2B. FOR A GAS GRILL: Turn all burners to high, cover, and heat grill until hot, about 15 minutes.

3. Clean and oil cooking grate. Place burgers on grill and cook, without pressing on them, until well browned on first side, 2 to 3 minutes. Flip burgers and continue to grill, 2 to 3 minutes for rare, 2½ to 3½ minutes for medium-rare, and 3 to 4 minutes for medium.

4. Transfer burgers to serving platter, tent loosely with aluminum foil, and let rest for 5 to 10 minutes before serving on rolls.

Grilled Cheeseburgers

Since the cheese is evenly distributed in these burgers, just a little goes a long way.

Mix ¾ cup shredded cheddar, Swiss, or Monterey Jack cheese or ¾ cup crumbled blue cheese into meat with salt and pepper.

ULTIMATE GRILLED BURGERS

WHY THIS RECIPE WORKS: For us, the ideal burger has an ultra-craggy charred crust, a rich beefy taste, and an interior so juicy and tender that it practically falls apart at the slightest pressure—a particularly difficult achievement when grilling. The problem is, such a burger is pretty hard to come by. While the typical specimen may have a nicely browned crust, it's also heavy and dense with a pebbly texture that comes from using preground beef. We knew we wanted to grind our own meat to make the ultimate burger. In the test kitchen, we've found it easy to grind meat ourselves with a food processor. We trim gristle and excess fat from the meat, cut the meat into ½-inch pieces, freeze it for about 30 minutes to firm it up so that the blades cut it cleanly, and finally process it in small batches to ensure an even, precise grind. We chose to use beefy steak tips since they are decently tender, require virtually no trimming, and are relatively inexpensive. Adding a bit of butter to the food processor when grinding added richness but not buttery flavor.

To form the burgers so that they wouldn't fall apart on the grate but at the same time achieve that essential open texture, we froze them briefly before putting them on the grill. By the time they'd thawed at their centers, they had developed enough crust to ensure that they held together. A few minutes over a hot grill was all our burgers needed to achieve a

perfect medium-rare. Whether served with the classic fixings like lettuce and tomato or one of our creamy grilled-vegetable toppings, this was a grilled burger that lived up to our ideal.

Tender, Juicy Grilled Burgers

SERVES 4

This recipe requires freezing the meat twice, for a total of 65 to 80 minutes, before grilling. When stirring the salt and pepper into the ground meat and shaping the patties, take care not to overwork the meat or the burgers will become dense. Sirloin steak tips are also sold as flap meat. Serve the burgers with your favorite toppings or one of our grilled-vegetable toppings (recipes follow).

1½ pounds sirloin steak tips, trimmed and cut into ½-inch chunks
4 tablespoons unsalted butter, cut into ¼-inch pieces
Kosher salt and pepper
1 (13 by 9-inch) disposable aluminum pan (if using charcoal)
4 hamburger buns

1. Place beef chunks and butter on large plate in single layer. Freeze until meat is very firm and starting to harden around edges but still pliable, about 35 minutes.

2. Place one-quarter of meat and one-quarter of butter cubes in food processor and pulse until finely ground into pieces size of rice grains (about ¹/₃₂ inch), 15 to 20 pulses, stopping and redistributing meat around bowl as necessary to ensure beef is evenly ground. Transfer meat to baking sheet. Repeat grinding with remaining 3 batches of meat and butter. Spread mixture over sheet and inspect carefully, discarding any long strands of gristle or large chunks of hard meat, fat, or butter.

3. Sprinkle 1 teaspoon pepper and ¾ teaspoon salt over meat and gently toss with fork to combine. Divide meat into 4 balls. Toss each between hands until uniformly but lightly packed. Gently flatten into patties ¾ inch thick and about 4½ inches in diameter. Using thumb, make 1-inch-wide by ¼-inch-deep depression in center of each patty. Transfer patties to platter and freeze for 30 to 45 minutes.

4A. FOR A CHARCOAL GRILL: Using skewer, poke 12 holes in bottom of disposable pan. Open bottom vent completely and place disposable pan in center of grill. Light large chimney starter filled two-thirds with charcoal briquettes (4 quarts). When top coals are partially covered with ash, pour into disposable pan. Set cooking grate in place, cover, and open lid vent completely. Heat grill until hot, about 5 minutes.

4B. FOR A GAS GRILL: Turn all burners to high, cover, and heat grill until hot, about 15 minutes. Leave all burners on high.

5. Clean and oil cooking grate. Season 1 side of patties liberally with salt and pepper. Using spatula, flip patties and season other side. Grill patties (directly over coals if using charcoal), without moving them, until browned and meat easily releases from grill, 4 to 7 minutes. Flip burgers and continue to grill until browned on second side and meat registers 125 degrees for medium-rare or 130 degrees for medium, 4 to 7 minutes longer.

6. Transfer burgers to plate and let rest for 5 minutes. While burgers rest, lightly toast buns on grill, 1 to 2 minutes. Transfer burgers to buns and serve.

Grilled Scallion Topping

MAKES ABOUT ½ CUP

2 tablespoons sour cream
2 tablespoons mayonnaise
2 tablespoons buttermilk
1 tablespoon cider vinegar
1 tablespoon minced fresh chives
2 teaspoons Dijon mustard
¼ teaspoon sugar
Salt and pepper
20 scallions
2 tablespoons vegetable oil

1. Combine sour cream, mayonnaise, buttermilk, vinegar, chives, mustard, sugar, ½ teaspoon salt, and ⅛ teaspoon pepper in medium bowl. Set aside.

2. Toss scallions with oil in large bowl (do not wash out bowl). Grill scallions over hot fire until lightly charred and softened, 2 to 4 minutes per side. Return to bowl and let cool, 5 minutes. Slice scallions thinly, then transfer to bowl with reserved sour cream mixture. Toss to combine and season with salt and pepper to taste.

Grilled Shiitake Mushroom Topping

MAKES ABOUT ¾ CUP

2 tablespoons sour cream
2 tablespoons mayonnaise
2 tablespoons buttermilk
1 tablespoon cider vinegar
1 tablespoon minced fresh chives
2 teaspoons Dijon mustard
¼ teaspoon sugar
Salt and pepper
8½ ounces shiitake mushrooms, stems removed
2 tablespoons vegetable oil

1. Combine sour cream, mayonnaise, buttermilk, vinegar, chives, mustard, sugar, ½ teaspoon salt, and ⅛ teaspoon pepper in medium bowl. Set aside.

2. Toss mushrooms with oil in large bowl (do not wash out bowl). Grill mushrooms over hot fire until lightly charred and softened, 2 to 4 minutes per side. Return to bowl and let cool, 5 minutes. Slice mushrooms thinly, then transfer to bowl with reserved sour cream mixture. Toss to combine and season with salt and pepper to taste.

Grilled Napa Cabbage and Radicchio Topping

MAKES ABOUT ¾ CUP

    2   tablespoons sour cream
    2   tablespoons mayonnaise
    2   tablespoons buttermilk
    1   tablespoon cider vinegar
    1   tablespoon minced fresh parsley
    2   teaspoons Dijon mustard
    ¼   teaspoon sugar
        Salt and pepper
    ¼   small head napa cabbage
    ½   small head radicchio, cut into 2 wedges
    2   tablespoons vegetable oil

1. Combine sour cream, mayonnaise, buttermilk, vinegar, parsley, mustard, sugar, ½ teaspoon salt, and ⅛ teaspoon pepper in medium bowl. Set aside.

2. Place cabbage and radicchio wedges on rimmed baking sheet and brush with oil (do not wash sheet). Grill over hot fire until lightly charred and beginning to wilt, 2 to 4 minutes on each cut side. Return to baking sheet and let cool, 5 minutes. Slice cabbage and radicchio thinly, then transfer to bowl with reserved sour cream mixture. Toss to combine and season with salt and pepper to taste.

WELL-DONE BURGERS

WHY THIS RECIPE WORKS: We know that many backyard cooks grill their burgers to medium-well and beyond, but we aren't willing to accept the usual outcome of tough, desiccated hockey pucks with no beefy flavor. We wanted to work with supermarket ground beef to produce a tender and moist-as-can-be burger, with perfect grill marks and all, even when well-done.

Taste tests proved that well-done burgers made with 80 percent lean chuck were noticeably moister than burgers made from leaner beef, but they still weren't juicy enough. Because we couldn't force the meat to retain moisture, we opted to pack the patties with a panade, a paste made from bread and milk that's often used to keep meat loaf and meatballs moist. To punch up the flavor, we also added minced garlic and tangy steak sauce. To keep our burgers from puffing up the way most burgers do, we made use of a previous test kitchen discovery: If you make a slight depression in the center of the patty, it will puff slightly as it cooks and level out to form a flat top.

Grilled Well-Done Hamburgers

SERVES 4

Adding bread and milk to the beef creates burgers that are juicy and tender even when well-done. For cheeseburgers, follow the optional instructions below.

    1   slice hearty white sandwich bread, crust removed,
        bread cut into ¼-inch pieces
    2   tablespoons whole milk
    2   teaspoons steak sauce
    1   garlic clove, minced
    ¾   teaspoon salt
    ¾   teaspoon pepper
    1½ pounds 80 percent lean ground chuck
    6   ounces sliced cheese (optional)
    4   hamburger buns, toasted

1. Mash bread and milk in large bowl with fork until homogeneous. Stir in steak sauce, garlic, salt, and pepper. Using hands, gently break up meat over bread mixture and toss lightly to distribute. Divide meat into 4 portions and lightly toss 1 portion from hand to hand to form ball, then lightly flatten ball with fingertips into ¾-inch-thick patty. Press center of patty down with fingertips until it is about ½ inch thick, creating slight depression. Repeat with remaining portions.

2A. FOR A CHARCOAL GRILL: Open bottom vent completely. Light large chimney starter filled with charcoal briquettes (6 quarts). When top coals are partially covered with ash, pour evenly over grill. Set cooking grate in place, cover, and open lid vent completely. Heat grill until hot, about 5 minutes.

2B. FOR A GAS GRILL: Turn all burners to high, cover, and heat grill until hot, about 15 minutes.

3. Clean and oil cooking grate. Place burgers on grill (on hot side if using charcoal) and cook, without pressing on them, until well browned on first side, 2 to 4 minutes. Flip burgers and cook 3 to 4 minutes for medium-well or 4 to 5 minutes for well-done, adding cheese, if using, about 2 minutes before reaching desired doneness and covering grill to melt cheese.

4. Transfer burgers to serving platter, tent loosely with aluminum foil, and let rest for 5 to 10 minutes before serving on buns.

Well-Done Bacon-Cheeseburgers

Most bacon burgers simply top the burgers with bacon. We also add bacon fat to the ground beef, which adds juiciness and unmistakable bacon flavor throughout the burger.

Cook 8 slices bacon in skillet over medium heat until crisp, 7 to 9 minutes. Transfer bacon to paper towel–lined plate and set aside. Reserve 2 tablespoons fat and refrigerate until just warm. Follow recipe for Grilled Well-Done Hamburgers, including optional cheese and adding reserved bacon fat to beef mixture. Top each burger with 2 slices bacon before serving.

GRILLED LAMB-STUFFED PITA WITH YOGURT SAUCE

WHY THIS RECIPE WORKS: Seasoned with warm spices and herbs, pressed between pita, and grilled, these lamb sandwiches offer a flavorful, juicy, street food–style alternative to the everyday burger on a bun. Along with traditional cumin, coriander, and onion, we added lemon zest to our meat mixture as well as cayenne for heat and paprika for its complementary pepper flavor, and swapped out neutral, grassy parsley for brighter, more aromatic cilantro. The grill helped make the pita bread really crisp, providing contrasting texture to the filling within. We started cooking with the grill lid closed to jump-start the meat and keep the pita from getting dry and tough. The lamb's fat and juices helped turn the bread supercrisp as it cooked. To help balance the richness of the sandwich, we served it with a bright and cooling yogurt-tahini sauce.

Grilled Lamb-Stuffed Pitas with Yogurt Sauce

SERVES 4 TO 6

You can substitute 85 percent lean ground beef for the ground lamb, if desired. This recipe works best with ¼-inch-thick pitas that are fresh and pliable. To determine which side of the pita is thicker, look closely at the pattern of browning across its surface; the less-fragile side is usually covered with char marks in a dotted-line pattern. Serve with a dressed green salad or with Parsley-Cucumber Salad with Feta, Pomegranate, and Walnuts (recipe follows).

SAUCE

- 1 cup plain Greek yogurt
- ½ cup minced fresh mint
- 2 tablespoons lemon juice
- 2 tablespoons tahini
- 2 tablespoons extra-virgin olive oil
- ½ teaspoon salt

SANDWICHES

- 1 onion, cut into 1-inch pieces
- 1 cup fresh cilantro leaves
- ¼ cup extra-virgin olive oil
- 1 tablespoon grated lemon zest plus 3 tablespoons juice
- 1 tablespoon ground coriander
- 1 tablespoon ground cumin
- 1 tablespoon paprika
- 2 teaspoons salt
- 1½ teaspoons pepper
- ½ teaspoon cayenne pepper
- ¼ teaspoon ground cinnamon
- 2 pounds ground lamb
- 4 (8-inch) pita breads

1. FOR THE SAUCE: Whisk all ingredients together in bowl. Set aside.

2. FOR THE SANDWICHES: Pulse onion and cilantro in food processor until finely chopped, 10 to 12 pulses, scraping down sides of bowl as needed. Transfer mixture to large bowl. Stir in oil, lemon zest and juice, coriander, cumin, paprika, salt, pepper, cayenne, and cinnamon. Add lamb and knead gently with your hands until thoroughly combined.

3. Using kitchen shears, cut around perimeter of each pita and separate into 2 halves. Place 4 thicker halves on counter with interiors facing up. Divide lamb mixture into 4 equal portions and place 1 portion in center of each pita half. Using spatula, gently spread lamb mixture into even layer, leaving ½-inch border around edge. Top each with thinner pita half. Press each sandwich firmly until lamb mixture spreads to ¼ inch from edge of pita. Transfer assembled sandwiches to large plate, cover with plastic wrap, and set aside. (Sandwiches may be held for up to 1 hour before grilling.)

4A. FOR A CHARCOAL GRILL: Open bottom vent completely. Light large chimney starter two-thirds filled with charcoal briquettes (4 quarts). When top coals are partially covered with ash, spread coals in single layer over bottom of grill. Set cooking grate in place, cover, and open lid vent completely. Heat grill until hot, about 5 minutes.

4B. FOR A GAS GRILL: Turn all burners to high, cover, and heat grill until hot, about 15 minutes. Turn all burners to medium-high.

5. Clean and oil cooking grate. Place sandwiches on grill, cover, and cook until bottoms are evenly browned and edges are starting to crisp, 7 to 10 minutes, moving sandwiches as needed to ensure even cooking. Flip sandwiches, cover grill, and continue to cook until second sides are evenly browned and edges are crisp, 7 to 10 minutes longer. Transfer sandwiches to cutting board and cut each in half crosswise. Transfer sandwiches to platter and serve, passing sauce separately.

NAKED ROAST CHICKEN AND OTHER WACKY RECIPE TESTS

Our test cooks will do almost anything in pursuit of the perfect recipe. No idea is too silly or odd to try—not if it will make a recipe better. Here are some notable recipe tests performed over the years. Each one was deemed promising but ultimately never worked.

• Removing the skin from a chicken before it goes into the oven, pulling the skin taut with toothpicks, and then roasting the skin separately from the chicken pieces to maximize crispness. Too Hannibal Lecter.

• Cooking a roast beef in a 130-degree oven for 24 hours to maximize juiciness. Most ovens don't operate at such a low temperature, and it's probably just as well; this is a perfect recipe for food-borne illness.

• Rubbing the skin off every single chickpea to make extra-smooth hummus. Peeling chickpeas? What were we thinking?!

• Flipping a steak every 4 seconds—for a total of 176 flips over the course of the 11-minute cooking time—to ensure absolutely even heat distribution. Only cooks with Olympic aspirations need to try this.

• Attaching a still (yes, like you might devise to make moonshine) to a covered grill to make our own liquid smoke. The cost for 1 teaspoon of liquid smoke? Fifty bucks. And it didn't taste very good. Plus, this odd setup looked just a little suspicious (read: illegal) to our neighbors.

GRILLED FLANK STEAK

WHY THIS RECIPE WORKS: A common way to prepare flank steak is to marinate it in a bottle of Italian-style salad dressing. But while the resulting flavor can be interesting, the acid in the vinegar can ruin the texture, making the exterior mushy and gray. We wanted to develop a fresh, Mediterranean-style marinade without acid—a marinade that would really boost flavor without over-tenderizing the meat.

We turned to the optimal method for cooking a flank steak—use a two-level fire (which lets you move the thin part of the steak to the cooler side of the grill once it is done), cook the steak only to medium-rare to keep it from getting tough, and let the steak rest before slicing to reduce the loss of juices. Now we could concentrate on developing and applying an acid-free marinade.

Because fat carries flavor so well, we knew oil would be a key ingredient—the challenge was to infuse Mediterranean flavors (garlic, shallots, and rosemary) into the oil and then into the steak. We developed two key steps. First, we minced

the aromatics and combined them with the oil in a blender to create a marinade paste. Next, we invented a novel "marinating" technique—prick the steak all over with a fork, rub it first with salt and then with the marinade paste, then let it sit for up to 24 hours. After marinating, the paste is wiped off to prevent burning, and the steak is ready for the grill. Our technique was so successful, we were free to create two more marinades—one with Asian flavors, and the other with a smoky-spicy kick.

Grilled Marinated Flank Steak
SERVES 4 TO 6

Other thin steaks with a loose grain, such as skirt steak or steak tips, can be substituted for the flank steak.

- 1 (2- to 2½-pound) flank steak, trimmed
- 1 teaspoon salt
- 1 recipe wet paste marinade (recipes follow)
  Pepper

1. Pat steak dry with paper towels and place in large baking dish. Using dinner fork, prick steak about 20 times on each side. Rub both sides of steak evenly with salt, then with paste. Cover with plastic wrap and refrigerate for at least 1 hour or up to 24 hours.

2A. FOR A CHARCOAL GRILL: Open bottom vent completely. Light large chimney starter filled with charcoal briquettes (6 quarts). When top coals are partially covered with ash, pour two-thirds evenly over grill, then pour remaining coals over half of grill. Set cooking grate in place, cover, and open lid vent completely. Heat grill until hot, about 5 minutes.

2B. FOR A GAS GRILL: Turn all burners to high, cover, and heat grill until hot, about 15 minutes.

3. Clean and oil cooking grate. Using paper towels, wipe paste off steak and season with pepper. Place steak on grill (hot side if using charcoal) and cook (covered if using gas) until well browned on first side, 4 to 6 minutes. Flip steak and cook (covered if using gas) until meat registers 120 to 125 degrees (for medium-rare) or 130 to 135 degrees (for medium), 3 to 6 minutes. If exterior of meat is browned but steak is not yet cooked through, move to cooler side of grill (if using charcoal) or turn down burners (if using gas) and continue to cook to desired doneness.

4. Transfer steak to carving board, tent loosely with aluminum foil, and let rest for 10 minutes. Slice steak ¼ inch thick against grain on bias and serve.

Garlic-Shallot-Rosemary Wet Paste Marinade
MAKES ABOUT ⅔ CUP

- 6 tablespoons olive oil
- 1 shallot, minced
- 6 garlic cloves, minced
- 2 tablespoons minced fresh rosemary

Process all ingredients in blender until smooth, about 30 seconds, scraping down bowl as needed.

Garlic-Ginger-Sesame Wet Paste Marinade
MAKES ABOUT ⅔ CUP

- ¼ cup toasted sesame oil
- 3 tablespoons grated fresh ginger
- 2 tablespoons vegetable oil
- 2 scallions, minced
- 3 garlic cloves, minced

Process all ingredients in blender until smooth, about 30 seconds, scraping down bowl as needed.

Garlic-Chile Wet Paste Marinade
MAKES ABOUT ⅔ CUP

- 6 tablespoons vegetable oil
- 6 garlic cloves, minced
- 2 scallions, minced
- 1 tablespoon minced canned chipotle chile in adobo sauce
- 1 jalapeño chile, stemmed, seeded, and minced

Process all ingredients in blender until smooth, about 30 seconds, scraping down bowl as needed.

GRILLED STUFFED FLANK STEAK

WHY THIS RECIPE WORKS: Stuffed steak originated with Italian-American cooking as a way to transform an inexpensive steak into something more exciting and colorful. But when we tried a few of the premade stuffed "pinwheels" from our local grocery store, both the stuffing and the cheese tried to make a run for it, with the cheese oozing out all over the grill, and the stuffing—which can include prosciutto, nuts, or spinach, among other things—falling out onto the grill in big clumps. We were sure we could turn this dish into an easy dinner, with tender beef and a juicy, flavorful filling that stayed in place.

Thanks to its uniform shape and good beefy taste, flank steak was clearly the best bet. To guarantee the filling stayed in place, we butterflied and pounded the steak, so we were starting with the flattest and widest surface possible. As for the filling, we eliminated bread crumbs from consideration—after grilling, they contributed a taste of burnt toast. The classic Italian-American combo of prosciutto and provolone won raves for its salty savor and the way the dry cheese melted inside the pinwheel yet turned crisp where exposed to the grill. To prevent the meat from shrinking on the grill, and squeezing the centers of the pinwheels, we rolled up our flank steak, tied it with twine, and skewered it at 1-inch intervals before slicing and grilling. The twine kept the steak from unraveling, while the skewers prevented the meat from shrinking. Finally, we had stuffing that stayed stuffed and rich, smoky beef.

HOW TO BUTTERFLY AND STUFF FLANK STEAK

1. Lay the flank steak on the edge of a cutting board. Slice the steak horizontally, making sure to leave a ½-inch "hinge" along the top edge.

2. Open up the steak, cover with plastic wrap, and pound it to a 12 by 8-inch rectangle of even thickness.

3. Leaving the steak in place with the grain still running perpendicular to the edge of the cutting board, rub the steak evenly with the herb mixture, and layer it with the prosciutto and cheese, leaving a 2-inch border along the top edge.

4. Roll the steak away from you into a tight log, then tie it at even 1-inch intervals. Skewer the meat directly through each string, making sure to insert the skewer through the seam in the roll to prevent the beef from unraveling during cooking.

5. Slice the beef into 1-inch-thick pinwheels. Each spiral should be held together with a skewer and a piece of twine.

Grilled Stuffed Flank Steak
SERVES 4 TO 6

Look for a flank steak measuring approximately 8 by 6 inches, with the grain running the long way. Depending on the steak's size, you may have more or less than 8 slices of meat at the end of step 2. You will need both wooden skewers and kitchen twine for this recipe.

2 tablespoons olive oil

2 tablespoons minced fresh parsley

1 small shallot, minced

2 garlic cloves, minced

1 teaspoon minced fresh sage

1 (2- to 2½-pound) flank steak, trimmed

4 ounces thinly sliced prosciutto

4 ounces thinly sliced provolone cheese

   Salt and pepper

1. Combine oil, parsley, shallot, garlic, and sage in bowl.

2. Soak 8 to 12 wooden skewers in warm water to cover (you will need 1 skewer per inch of rolled steak length) for 30 minutes. Drain, dry, and set aside.

3. Lay steak on cutting board with grain running parallel to counter edge. Cut horizontally through meat, leaving ½-inch "hinge" along top edge. Open up steak and pound flat into rough rectangle, trimming any ragged edges. Rub herb mixture evenly over opened side of steak. Lay prosciutto evenly over steak, leaving 2-inch border along top edge. Cover prosciutto with even layer of cheese, leaving 2-inch border along top edge. Starting from short edge, roll beef into tight log and place on cutting board seam side down.

4. Starting ½ inch from end of rolled steak, evenly space eight to twelve 14-inch pieces of kitchen twine at 1-inch intervals underneath steak. Tie middle piece first, then, working from outer pieces toward center, tightly tie roll and turn tied steak 90 degrees so seam is facing you.

5. Skewer beef directly through outer flap of steak near seam through each piece of twine, allowing skewers to extend ½ inch on other side. Using chef's knife, slice roll between each piece of twine into 1-inch-thick pinwheels. Season pinwheels with salt and pepper.

6A. FOR A CHARCOAL GRILL: Open bottom vent completely. Light large chimney starter three-quarters filled with charcoal briquettes (4½ quarts). When top coals are partially covered with ash, pour evenly over half of grill. Set cooking grate in place, cover, and open lid vent completely. Heat grill until hot, about 5 minutes.

6B. FOR A GAS GRILL: Turn all burners to high, cover, and heat grill until hot, about 15 minutes.

7. Clean and oil cooking grate. Place pinwheels on grill (hot side if using charcoal) and cook (covered if using gas) until well browned on both sides, 6 to 12 minutes, flipping halfway through cooking. Move pinwheels to cool side of grill (if using charcoal) or turn all burners to medium (if using gas). Cover and cook until meat registers 125 to 130 degrees (for medium-rare) or 130 to 135 degrees (for medium), 1 to 5 minutes.

8. Transfer pinwheels to serving platter, tent loosely with aluminum foil, and let rest for 5 to 10 minutes. Remove and discard skewers and twine and serve.

Grilled Stuffed Flank Steak with Spinach and Pine Nuts

Microwave 4 ounces chopped spinach, 1 tablespoon water, ½ teaspoon pepper, and ½ teaspoon salt in bowl until spinach is wilted and decreased in volume by half, 3 to 4 minutes. Cool completely, then stir in ¼ cup toasted pine nuts. Replace prosciutto with spinach mixture.

GRILLED STEAK TIPS

WHY THIS RECIPE WORKS: Steak tips have long been the darling of all-you-can-eat restaurant chains where quantity takes precedence over quality. If they're not mushy, they land on the table tough and dry. We wanted to improve this classic bar food and instill it with deep flavor and a tender texture.

To stay true to the inexpensive nature of this dish, we set our sights on finding the best affordable (read: cheap) cut of meat that would stay tender and moist during a brief stint on the grill. The best cut, we found, is what butchers call flap meat. To tenderize and flavor the meat, we used a soy sauce–based marinade and let the meat marinate for at least an hour—just the right amount of time to allow the thicker parts of the meat to become tender while preventing the thinner sections from becoming too salty. Grilling the tips over a two-level fire, which has hotter and cooler areas, helps to cook this often unevenly shaped cut evenly. We let the meat rest for five minutes after grilling to ensure juicy meat, then sliced it thin so the meat would be tender and flavorful. Lime, orange, or lemon wedges provided a bright acidic counterpoint to the steak tips.

Grilled Steak Tips

SERVES 4 TO 6

Sirloin steak tips are sometimes labeled "flap meat." A two-level fire allows you to brown the steak over the hot side of the grill, then move it to the cooler side if it is not yet cooked through. If your steak is thin, however, you may not need to use the cooler side of the grill. Serve lime wedges with the Southwestern-marinated tips and orange wedges with the tips marinated in garlic, ginger, and soy sauce.

- 1 recipe marinade (recipes follow)
- 2 pounds sirloin steak tips, trimmed
  Lime, orange, or lemon wedges

1. Combine marinade and beef in 1-gallon zipper-lock bag and toss to coat; press out as much air as possible and seal bag. Refrigerate for 1 hour, flipping bag halfway through marinating.

2A. FOR A CHARCOAL GRILL: Open bottom vent completely. Light large chimney starter filled with charcoal briquettes (6 quarts). When top coals are partially covered with ash, pour two-thirds evenly over grill, then pour remaining coals over half of grill. Set cooking grate in place, cover, and open lid vent completely. Heat grill until hot, about 5 minutes.

2B. FOR A GAS GRILL: Turn all burners to high, cover, and heat grill until hot, about 15 minutes.

3. Clean and oil cooking grate. Remove beef from bag and pat dry with paper towels. Place steak tips on grill (on hotter side if using charcoal) and cook (covered if using gas) until well browned on first side, about 4 minutes. Flip steak tips and continue to cook (covered if using gas) until meat registers 120 to 125 degrees (for medium-rare) or 130 to 135 degrees (for medium), 6 to 10 minutes longer. If exterior of meat is browned but steak is not yet cooked through, move to cooler side of grill (if using charcoal) or turn down burners to medium (if using gas) and continue to cook to desired doneness.

4. Transfer steak tips to carving board, tent loosely with aluminum foil, and let rest for 5 to 10 minutes. Slice steak tips very thin on bias and serve with lime, orange, or lemon wedges.

Southwestern Marinade

MAKES ABOUT ¾ CUP

- ⅓ cup soy sauce
- ⅓ cup vegetable oil
- 3 garlic cloves, minced
- 1 tablespoon packed dark brown sugar
- 1 tablespoon tomato paste
- 1 tablespoon chili powder
- 2 teaspoons ground cumin
- ¼ teaspoon cayenne pepper

Combine all ingredients in bowl.

Garlic, Ginger, and Soy Marinade

MAKES ABOUT ⅔ CUP

- ⅓ cup soy sauce
- 3 tablespoons vegetable oil
- 3 tablespoons toasted sesame oil
- 2 tablespoons packed dark brown sugar
- 1 tablespoon grated fresh ginger
- 2 teaspoons grated orange zest
- 1 scallion, sliced thin
- 3 garlic cloves, minced
- ½ teaspoon red pepper flakes

Combine all ingredients in bowl.

GRILLED PREMIUM STEAKS

WHY THIS RECIPE WORKS: Grilled steaks have many tempting qualities—rich, beefy flavor, a thick, caramelized crust, and almost zero cleanup or prep for the cook. But the occasional small bonfire caused by the rendered fat can leave pricey cuts of meat charred and tasting like the inside of a smokestack. We wanted to develop a surefire technique for grilling the three most popular premium steaks—strip, rib eye, and filet mignon—so they would turn out juicy and tender every time.

To get the crust we wanted, a very hot fire was essential. But we quickly learned we couldn't cook a thick steak over consistently high heat without either burning the steak or causing the fat to drip down onto the charcoal and ignite. The solution was to cook these premium steaks over a two-level fire, searing them first over high heat and then moving them to the cooler part of the grill to cook through. For the strip and rib-eye steaks, lightly oiling the cooking grate was enough to get them going and keep them from sticking, but the lean filets mignons required a bit of olive oil to encourage browning. Otherwise, we didn't fuss with our steaks before cooking them—a light seasoning with salt and pepper was sufficient.

To add a little richness to the filets mignons, we made two compound butters, one with smoked paprika and roasted red peppers, the other with lemon, parsley, and garlic—perfect for melting down the sides of the still-warm steaks.

Grilled Strip or Rib-Eye Steaks

SERVES 6

Try to buy steaks of even thickness so they cook at the same rate.

- 4 (12- to 16-ounce) strip or rib-eye steaks, with or without bone, 1¼ to 1½ inches thick
  Salt and pepper

1A. FOR A CHARCOAL GRILL: Open lid vent completely. Light large chimney starter filled with charcoal briquettes (6 quarts). When top coals are partially covered with ash, pour two-thirds evenly over grill, then pour remaining coals over half of grill. Set cooking grate in place, cover, and heat grill until hot, about 5 minutes.

1B. FOR A GAS GRILL: Turn all burners to high, cover, and heat grill until hot, about 15 minutes. Leave one burner on high and turn other burner(s) to medium.

2. Clean and oil cooking grate. Pat steaks dry with paper towels and season with salt and pepper. Place steaks on grill (hotter side if using charcoal) and cook, uncovered, until well browned on both sides, 4 to 6 minutes, flipping steaks halfway through cooking. Move steaks to cooler side of grill (if using charcoal) or turn all burners to medium (if using gas) and continue to cook until meat registers 115 to 120 degrees (for rare) or 120 to 125 degrees (for medium-rare) 5 to 8 minutes longer.

3. Transfer steaks to serving platter, tent loosely with aluminum foil, and let rest for 10 minutes before serving.

Grilled Filets Mignons

SERVES 4

We suggest serving the steaks with one of our flavored butters (recipes follow).

- 4 (7- to 8-ounce) center-cut filets mignons, 1½ to 2 inches thick, trimmed
- 4 teaspoons olive oil
- Salt and pepper

1A. FOR A CHARCOAL GRILL: Open bottom vent completely. Light large chimney starter filled with charcoal briquettes (6 quarts). When top coals are partially covered with ash, pour two-thirds evenly over grill, then pour remaining coals over half of grill. Set cooking grate in place, cover, and open lid vent completely. Heat grill until hot, about 5 minutes.

1B. FOR A GAS GRILL: Turn all burners to high, cover, and heat grill until hot, about 15 minutes. Leave all burners on high.

2. Meanwhile, pat steaks dry with paper towels and lightly rub with oil. Season steaks with salt and pepper.

3. Clean and oil cooking grate. Place steaks on grill (hotter side if using charcoal) and cook (covered if using gas) until well browned on both sides, 4 to 6 minutes, flipping halfway through cooking. Move steaks to cooler side of grill (if using charcoal) or turn all burners to medium (if using gas) and continue to cook (covered if using gas), until meat registers 115 to 120 degrees (for rare) or 120 to 125 degrees (for medium-rare), 5 to 9 minutes longer.

4. Transfer steaks to serving platter, tent loosely with aluminum foil, and let rest for 10 minutes before serving.

Roasted Red Pepper and Smoked Paprika Butter

MAKES ¼ CUP

- 4 tablespoons unsalted butter, softened
- 2 tablespoons finely chopped jarred roasted red peppers
- 1 tablespoon minced fresh thyme
- ¾ teaspoon smoked paprika
- ½ teaspoon salt
- Pinch pepper

Combine all ingredients in bowl and mix until smooth. While steaks are resting, spoon 1 tablespoon of butter on each one.

Lemon, Garlic, and Parsley Butter

MAKES ¼ CUP

- 4 tablespoons unsalted butter, softened
- 1 tablespoon minced fresh parsley
- 1 garlic clove, minced
- ½ teaspoon grated lemon zest
- ½ teaspoon salt
- Pinch pepper

Combine all ingredients in bowl and mix until smooth. While steaks are resting, spoon 1 tablespoon of butter on each one.

GRILLED FROZEN STEAKS WITH ARUGULA AND PARMESAN

WHY THIS RECIPE WORKS: It may seem too good to be true, to have a steak go from freezer to grill to plate in just 30 minutes, but not only is it possible, it's delicious. We have cooked frozen steaks indoors in a skillet to great success, but we wanted to adapt this technique for the grill. The first big challenge was choosing the right type of steak. We tried thinner flank and skirt steaks but their interiors overcooked by the time we'd achieved an ideal char on the exterior. Thicker cuts like rib-eye and strip steaks turned out to be much more successful. Additionally, as those cuts tend to have more natural flavor, all they needed was a bit of salt and pepper—a spice-heavy rub was unnecessary. We took advantage of the steaks' ultrachilled state and started them over a hot fire to develop a well-browned crust on both sides, and then we slid them to the cooler side of the grill to cook until they reached the desired internal temperature.

Grilled Frozen Steaks with Arugula and Parmesan

SERVES 4 TO 6

Use the large holes of a box grater to shred the Parmesan. Do not substitute thinner steaks for the thick-cut steaks called for in this recipe. Thinner steaks cannot be grilled successfully when taken directly from the freezer.

ULTIMATE CHARCOAL-GRILLED STEAKS

WHY THIS RECIPE WORKS: For a thick steak that delivered a perfectly browned crust, even doneness, and only a minimal gray band—plus, great charred flavor from the grill—we ditched the actual grill in favor of a superhot charcoal chimney. After trimming the steaks' fat caps in order to eliminate flare-ups, we scored the steaks for better browning. We salted the steaks to ensure seasoning throughout and then baked them slowly in a low oven to cook them evenly and dehydrate their surfaces. Skewering them ahead of time made for easy handling and setup. Moving to the grill, we blasted the steaks over the chimney for about 60 seconds per side, and kept the seasoning simple with just a bit of black pepper to finish.

Ultimate Charcoal-Grilled Steaks

SERVES 4

Rib-eye steaks of a similar thickness can be substituted for strip steaks, although they may produce more flare-ups. You will need a charcoal chimney starter with a 7½-inch diameter and four 12-inch metal skewers for this recipe. If your chimney starter has a smaller diameter, skewer each steak individually and cook in four batches. It is important to remove the fat caps on the steaks to limit flare-ups during grilling.

> 2 (1-pound) boneless strip steaks, 1¾ inches thick,
>   fat caps removed
>   Kosher salt and pepper

1. Adjust oven rack to middle position and heat oven to 200 degrees. Cut each steak in half crosswise to create four 8-ounce steaks. Cut ¹⁄₁₆-inch-deep slits on both sides of steaks, spaced ¼ inch apart, in crosshatch pattern. Sprinkle both sides of each steak with ½ teaspoon salt (2 teaspoons total). Lay steak halves with tapered ends flat on counter and pass two 12-inch metal skewers, spaced 1½ inches apart, horizontally through steaks, making sure to keep ¼-inch space between steak halves. Repeat skewering with remaining steak halves.

2. Place skewered steaks on wire rack set in rimmed baking sheet, transfer to oven, and cook until centers of steaks register 120 degrees, flipping steaks over halfway through cooking and removing them as they come to temperature, 1½ hours to 1 hour 50 minutes. Tent skewered steaks (still on rack) with aluminum foil.

3. Light large chimney starter filled halfway with charcoal briquettes (3 quarts). When top coals are completely covered in ash, uncover steaks (reserving foil) and pat dry with paper towels. Using tongs, place 1 set of steaks directly over chimney so skewers rest on rim of chimney (meat will be suspended over coals). Cook until both sides are well browned and charred, about 1 minute per side. Using tongs, return first set of steaks to wire rack in sheet, season with pepper, and tent with reserved foil. Repeat with second set of skewered steaks. Remove skewers from steaks and serve.

> 2 (1-pound) frozen boneless strip or rib-eye steaks,
>   1½ inches thick, trimmed
>   Kosher salt and pepper
> 6 tablespoons extra-virgin olive oil
> 2 tablespoons lemon juice, plus lemon wedges for serving
> 8 ounces (8 cups) baby arugula
> 2 ounces Parmesan cheese, shredded (⅔ cup)

1A. FOR A CHARCOAL GRILL: Open bottom vent completely. Light large chimney starter mounded with charcoal briquettes (7 quarts). When top coals are partially covered with ash, pour evenly over half of grill. Set cooking grate in place, cover, and open lid vent completely. Heat grill until hot, about 5 minutes.

1B. FOR A GAS GRILL: Turn all burners to high, cover, and heat grill until hot, about 15 minutes. Leave primary burner on high and turn off other burner(s).

2. Clean and oil cooking grate. Place steaks on hotter side of grill and cook (covered if using gas) until browned and charred on first side, 5 to 7 minutes. Flip steaks, season with salt and pepper, and cook until browned and charred on second side, 5 to 7 minutes. Flip steaks, season with salt and pepper, and move to cooler side of grill, arranging so steaks are about 6 inches from heat source. Continue to cook until meat registers 115 to 120 degrees for rare or 120 to 125 degrees for medium-rare, 10 to 15 minutes longer. Transfer steaks to wire rack set in rimmed baking sheet and let rest for 5 minutes.

3. Slice steaks thin against grain. Fan slices on either side of large platter. Whisk oil, lemon juice, ¾ teaspoon salt, and ¼ teaspoon pepper together in large bowl. Add arugula and three-quarters of Parmesan and toss to combine. Arrange arugula down center of platter, allowing it to overlap steak. Sprinkle remaining Parmesan over steak and arugula. Serve with lemon wedges.

GRILLED INEXPENSIVE STEAKS

WHY THIS RECIPE WORKS: In this recipe, we used a two-stage rub to make the most of a comparatively inexpensive steak, the shell sirloin. We started with a savory rub of salt, onion powder, garlic powder, fish sauce, and tomato paste. This umami-rich rub made the steaks more savory and enhanced juiciness. For the second stage, we made our own coarsely ground rub based on toasted whole spices and dried chiles. By grinding our own spices, instead of using store-bought ground spices, we created a rub with much deeper flavor.

Grilled Steak with New Mexican Chile Rub
SERVES 6 TO 8

Shell sirloin steak is also known as top butt, butt steak, top sirloin butt, top sirloin steak, and center-cut roast. Spraying the rubbed steaks with oil helps the spices bloom, preventing a raw flavor.

STEAK
- 2 teaspoons tomato paste
- 2 teaspoons fish sauce
- 1½ teaspoons kosher salt
- ½ teaspoon onion powder
- ½ teaspoon garlic powder
- 2 (1½- to 1¾-pound) boneless shell sirloin steaks, 1 to 1¼ inches thick

SPICE RUB
- 2 dried New Mexican chiles, stemmed, seeded, and flesh torn into ½-inch pieces
- 4 teaspoons cumin seeds
- 4 teaspoons coriander seeds
- ½ teaspoon red pepper flakes
- ½ teaspoon black peppercorns
- 1 tablespoon sugar
- 1 tablespoon paprika
- ¼ teaspoon ground cloves
- Vegetable oil spray

1. FOR THE STEAK: Combine tomato paste, fish sauce, salt, onion powder, and garlic powder in bowl. Pat steaks dry with paper towels. With sharp knife, cut 1/16-inch-deep slits on both sides of steaks, spaced ½ inch apart, i n crosshatch pattern. Rub salt mixture evenly on both sides of steaks. Place steaks on wire rack set in rimmed baking sheet; let stand at room temperature for at least 1 hour. After 30 minutes, prepare grill.

2. FOR THE SPICE RUB: Toast chiles, cumin, coriander, pepper flakes, and peppercorns in 10-inch skillet over medium-low heat, stirring frequently, until just beginning to smoke, 3 to 4 minutes. Transfer to plate to cool, about 5 minutes. Grind spices in spice grinder or in mortar with pestle until coarsely ground. Transfer spices to bowl and stir in sugar, paprika, and cloves.

3A. FOR A CHARCOAL GRILL: Open bottom vent completely. Light large chimney starter mounded with charcoal briquettes (7 quarts). When top coals are partially covered with ash, pour two-thirds evenly over grill, then pour remaining coals over half of grill. Set cooking grate in place, cover, and open lid vent completely. Heat grill until hot, about 5 minutes.

3B. FOR A GAS GRILL: Turn all burners to high, cover, and heat grill until hot, about 15 minutes. Leave primary burner on high and turn other burner(s) to medium.

4. Clean and oil cooking grate. Sprinkle half of spice rub evenly over 1 side of steaks and press to adhere until spice rub is fully moistened. Lightly spray rubbed side of steak with vegetable oil spray, about 3 seconds. Flip steaks and repeat process of sprinkling with spice rub and coating with vegetable oil spray on second side.

5. Place steaks over hotter part of grill and cook until browned and charred on both sides and center registers 125 degrees for medium-rare or 130 degrees for medium, 3 to 4 minutes per side. If steaks have not reached desired temperature, move to cooler side of grill and continue to cook. Transfer steaks to clean wire rack set in rimmed baking sheet, tent loosely with aluminum foil, and let rest for 10 minutes. Slice meat thin against grain and serve.

Grilled Steak with Ancho Chile–Coffee Rub

Substitute 1 dried ancho chile for New Mexican chiles, 2 teaspoons ground coffee for paprika, and 1 teaspoon cocoa powder for ground cloves.

Grilled Steak with Spicy Chipotle Chile Rub

Substitute 2 dried chipotle chiles for New Mexican chiles, 1 teaspoon dried oregano for paprika, and ½ teaspoon ground cinnamon for ground cloves.

GRILLED ARGENTINE STEAKS

WHY THIS RECIPE WORKS: In Argentina, large 2-pound steaks are grilled low and slow over hardwood logs, not charcoal (and never over gas), which imbues them with a smokiness that is subtler and more complex that the typical "barbecue" flavor one comes to expect of grilled meat here in the States. With the piquant parsley, garlic, and olive oil sauce known as chimichurri served alongside, it's a world favorite. We wanted to duplicate the Argentinean method with American supermarket steaks and a kettle grill. For our choice of steak, we selected well-marbled New York strip steak for its big beefy flavor and meaty chew. To mimic a wood fire, we added unsoaked wood chunks to the perimeter of our grill fire. Setting the lid down on the grill for the first few minutes of cooking helped to quickly trap smoke flavor. To get a deep brown char on the meat without overcooking it, we used two strategies. First, we rubbed the meat with a mixture of salt and cornstarch. Salt seasons the meat and draws out moisture, as does cornstarch. Then we moved the steaks into the freezer for 30 minutes. The inside of a freezer is so dry that it often robs unprotected food of its moisture. In this instance, this was a good thing. Par-frozen steaks browned within moments of hitting the grill. Even better, these partially frozen steaks could stand about five more minutes of fire, adding up to more char and more flavor. To finish, garlicky chimichurri sauce cut through the rich, unctuous qualities of our great grilled steak.

Grilled Argentine Steaks with Chimichurri Sauce
SERVES 6 TO 8

Our preferred steak for this recipe is strip steak, also known as New York strip. A less expensive alternative is a boneless shell sirloin steak (or top sirloin steak).

SAUCE
- ¼ cup hot water
- 2 teaspoons dried oregano
- 1 teaspoon salt
- 1⅓ cups fresh parsley leaves
- ⅔ cup fresh cilantro leaves
- 6 garlic cloves, minced
- ½ teaspoon red pepper flakes
- ¼ cup red wine vinegar
- ½ cup extra-virgin olive oil

STEAKS
- 1 tablespoon cornstarch
  Salt and pepper
- 4 (1-pound) boneless strip steaks, 1½ inches thick, trimmed
- 4 (2-inch) wood chunks
- 1 (9-inch) disposable aluminum pie plate (if using gas)

1. FOR THE SAUCE: Combine water, oregano, and salt in small bowl and let sit until oregano is softened, about 15 minutes. Pulse parsley, cilantro, garlic, and pepper flakes in food processor until coarsely chopped, about 10 pulses. Add

water mixture and vinegar and pulse to combine. Transfer mixture to bowl and slowly whisk in oil until emulsified. Cover with plastic wrap and let sit at room temperature for 1 hour.

2. FOR THE STEAKS: Combine cornstarch and 1½ teaspoon salt in bowl. Pat steaks dry with paper towels and place on wire rack set in rimmed baking sheet. Rub entire surface of steaks with cornstarch mixture and place steaks, uncovered, in freezer until very firm, about 30 minutes.

3A. FOR A CHARCOAL GRILL: Open bottom vent halfway. Light large chimney starter filled with charcoal briquettes (6 quarts). When top coals are partially covered with ash, pour evenly over grill. Place wood chunks around perimeter of coals. Set cooking grate in place, cover, and open lid vent halfway. Heat grill until hot and wood chips are smoking, about 5 minutes.

3B. FOR A GAS GRILL: Using metal skewer, poke holes in bottom of disposable pie plate. Place wood chunks in pie plate and set on cooking grate. Turn all burners to high, cover, and heat grill until hot, about 15 minutes. Leave all burners on high.

4. Clean and oil cooking grate. Season steaks with pepper. Place steaks on grill (alongside pie plate if using gas), cover, and cook until beginning to brown on both sides, 4 to 6 minutes, flipping halfway through cooking.

5. Flip steaks again and cook, uncovered, until well browned on first side, 2 to 4 minutes. Flip steaks once more and continue to cook until meat registers 115 to 120 degrees (for rare) or 120 to 125 degrees (for medium-rare), 2 to 6 minutes longer.

6. Transfer steaks to carving board, tent loosely with aluminum foil, and let rest for 10 minutes. Cut each steak crosswise into ¼-inch-thick slices. Transfer to serving platter and serve, passing sauce separately.

NOTES FROM THE TEST KITCHEN

GETTING PERFECT CHAR ON ARGENTINE STEAKS
To get a deep brown char on the meat without overcooking it, the meat must be completely dry. To achieve this, we use a two-pronged approach.

1. Place steaks on wire rack set in rimmed baking sheet. Rub entire surface of steaks with cornstarch mixture.

2. Place steaks, uncovered, in freezer until very firm, about 30 minutes.

MEXICAN-STYLE GRILLED STEAK

WHY THIS RECIPE WORKS: These days *carne asada* usually refers to a super charred, thin steak, but traditionally the dish involves a platter of food. Created around 1940 at the Tampico Club in Mexico City, carne asada is traditionally served with a bevy of sides. We wanted to stick close to the original while keeping it approachable for the home cook. A juicy, thin, well-charred steak was a must, and we settled on just a few extras: a salsa that would complement the meat, some quick refried beans, and simple folded enchiladas.

We decided to use skirt steak, since it stayed tender when grilled to medium (the ideal doneness for both adequate charring and tender beef). A rub made with salt and cumin gave the steaks extra flavor, and the salt dried out the steaks' exteriors to promote browning. For our grill setup, we used a disposable aluminum roasting pan with the bottom removed to corral the coals and ensure high heat for fast browning and char. A smashed clove of garlic rubbed on the steaks after grilling brought a burst of fresh garlic flavor and aroma to the meat, and a squeeze of lime before serving provided fresh citrus flavor. The fruity, slightly smoky flavor of red chile salsa complemented the steak perfectly.

Mexican-Style Grilled Steak (Carne Asada)
SERVES 4 TO 6

Two pounds of sirloin steak tips, also sold as flap meat, may be substituted for the skirt steak. Serve with Red Chile Salsa, Simple Refried Beans, and Folded Enchiladas (recipes follow), if desired.

2 teaspoons kosher salt
¾ teaspoon ground cumin
1 (2-pound) skirt steak, trimmed, pounded ¼ inch thick, and cut with grain into 4 equal steaks
1 (13 by 9-inch) disposable aluminum roasting pan (if using charcoal)
1 garlic clove, peeled and smashed
Lime wedges

1. Combine salt and cumin in small bowl. Sprinkle salt mixture evenly over both sides of steaks. Transfer steaks to wire rack set in rimmed baking sheet and refrigerate, uncovered, for at least 45 minutes or up to 24 hours. Meanwhile, if using charcoal, use kitchen shears to remove bottom of disposable pan and discard, reserving pan collar.

2A. FOR A CHARCOAL GRILL: Open bottom vent completely. Light large chimney starter filled with charcoal briquettes (6 quarts). When top coals are partially covered with ash, place disposable pan collar in center of grill over bottom vent and pour coals into even layer in collar. Set cooking grate in place, cover, and open lid vent completely. Heat grill until hot, about 5 minutes.

2B. FOR A GAS GRILL: Turn all burners to high, cover, and heat grill until hot, about 15 minutes. Leave all burners on high.

3. Clean and oil cooking grate. Place steaks on grill (if using charcoal, arrange steaks over coals in collar) and cook, uncovered, until well browned on first side, 2 to 4 minutes. Flip steaks and continue to cook until well browned on second side and meat registers 130 degrees, 2 to 4 minutes longer. Transfer steaks to cutting board, tent loosely with aluminum foil, and let rest for 5 minutes.

4. Rub garlic thoroughly over 1 side of steaks. Slice steaks across grain into ¼-inch-thick slices and serve with lime wedges.

Red Chile Salsa
MAKES 2 CUPS

Guajillo chiles are tangy with just a bit of heat. Serve the salsa alongside the steak as a dipping sauce.

1¼ ounces dried guajillo chiles, wiped clean
1 (14.5-ounce) can fire-roasted diced tomatoes
¾ cup water
¾ teaspoon salt
1 garlic clove, peeled and smashed
½ teaspoon white vinegar
¼ teaspoon dried oregano
⅛ teaspoon pepper
Pinch ground clove
Pinch ground cumin

Toast guajillos in 10-inch nonstick skillet over medium-high heat until softened and fragrant, 1 to 2 minutes per side. Transfer to large plate and, when cool enough to handle, remove stems and seeds. Place guajillos in blender and process until finely ground, 60 to 90 seconds, scraping down sides of blender jar as needed. Add tomatoes and their juice, water, salt, garlic, vinegar, oregano, pepper, clove, and cumin to blender and process until very smooth, 60 to 90 seconds, scraping down sides of blender jar as needed. (Salsa can be stored in the refrigerator for up to 5 days or frozen for up to 1 month.)

Simple Refried Beans
MAKES ABOUT 1½ CUPS

Using the canning liquid from the beans helps develop a creamy texture.

- 2 slices bacon
- 1 small onion, chopped fine
- 2 garlic cloves, minced
- 1 (15-ounce) can pinto beans
- ¼ cup water
- Kosher salt

Heat bacon in 10-inch nonstick skillet over medium-low heat until fat renders and bacon crisps, 7 to 10 minutes, flipping bacon halfway through. Remove bacon and reserve for another use. Increase heat to medium, add onion to fat in skillet, and cook until lightly browned, 5 to 7 minutes. Add garlic and cook until fragrant, about 30 seconds. Add beans and their canning liquid and water and bring to simmer. Cook, mashing beans with potato masher, until mixture is mostly smooth, 5 to 7 minutes. Season with salt to taste, and serve.

Folded Enchiladas
SERVES 4 TO 6

Feta cheese can be substituted for the queso fresco. Guajillo chiles are tangy, with just a bit of heat.

- ⅔ ounce dried guajillo chiles, wiped clean
- 1 (8-ounce) can tomato sauce
- 1 cup chicken broth
- 1 tablespoon vegetable oil
- 1 garlic clove, peeled and smashed
- 1 teaspoon white vinegar
- ¼ teaspoon ground cumin
- Salt
- 12 (6-inch) soft corn tortillas
- Vegetable oil spray
- 1 small onion, chopped fine
- 2 ounces queso fresco, crumbled (½ cup)

1. Toast guajillos in 10-inch nonstick skillet over medium-high heat until softened and fragrant, 1 to 2 minutes per side. Transfer to large plate and, when cool enough to handle, remove stems and seeds. Place guajillos in blender and process until finely ground, 60 to 90 seconds, scraping down sides of blender jar as needed. Add tomato sauce, broth, oil, garlic, vinegar, and cumin to blender and process until very smooth, 60 to 90 seconds, scraping down sides of blender jar as needed. Season with salt to taste.

2. Place 1 cup enchilada sauce in large bowl. Spray both sides of tortillas with oil spray and stack on plate. Microwave, covered, until softened and warm, 60 to 90 seconds. Working with 1 tortilla at a time, dip into sauce in bowl to coat both sides, fold in quarters, and place in 8-inch square baking dish (enchiladas will overlap slightly in dish).

3. When ready to serve, pour remaining sauce evenly over enchiladas. Microwave enchiladas until hot throughout, 3 to 5 minutes. Sprinkle evenly with onion and queso fresco. Serve.

GRILL-ROASTED BEEF SHORT RIBS

WHY THIS RECIPE WORKS: Beef short ribs can require a lot of time and tending on the grill. We began our testing by coating our ribs with a simple spice rub. We jump-started the cooking process by giving the ribs a pit stop in the oven. In a foil-covered baking dish, the fat was rendered from the ribs, and the tough, chewy collagen began to transform into moisture-retaining gelatin. Then we headed out to the grill to complete the cooking while lacquering on one of our flavorful glazes.

Grill-Roasted Beef Short Ribs
SERVES 4 TO 6

Make sure to choose ribs that are 4 to 6 inches in length and have at least 1 inch of meat on top of the bone.

SPICE RUB
- 2 tablespoons kosher salt
- 1 tablespoon packed brown sugar
- 2 teaspoons pepper
- 2 teaspoons ground cumin
- 2 teaspoons garlic powder
- 1¼ teaspoons paprika
- ¾ teaspoon ground fennel
- ⅛ teaspoon cayenne pepper

SHORT RIBS
- 5 pounds bone-in English-style beef short ribs, trimmed
- 2 tablespoons red wine vinegar
- 1 recipe glaze (recipes follow)

1. FOR THE SPICE RUB: Combine all ingredients in bowl. Measure out 1 teaspoon rub and set aside for glaze.

2. FOR THE SHORT RIBS: Adjust oven rack to middle position and heat oven to 300 degrees. Sprinkle ribs with spice rub, pressing into all sides of ribs. Arrange ribs, bone side down, in 13 by 9-inch baking dish, placing thicker ribs around perimeter of baking dish and thinner ribs in center. Sprinkle vinegar evenly over ribs. Cover baking dish tightly with aluminum foil. Bake until thickest ribs register 165 to 170 degrees, 1½ to 2 hours.

3A. FOR A CHARCOAL GRILL: Open bottom vent halfway. Arrange 2 quarts unlit charcoal into steeply banked pile against 1 side of grill. Light large chimney starter half filled with charcoal (3 quarts). When top coals are partially covered with ash, pour on top of unlit charcoal to cover one-third of grill with coals steeply banked against side of grill. Set cooking grate in place, cover, and open lid vent halfway. Heat grill until hot, about 5 minutes.

3B. FOR A GAS GRILL: Turn all burners to high, cover, and heat grill until hot, about 15 minutes. Leave primary burner on medium and turn off other burner(s). Adjust primary burner as needed to maintain grill temperature of 275 to 300 degrees.

4. Clean and oil cooking grate. Place short ribs, bone side down, on cooler side of grill about 2 inches from flames. Brush with ¼ cup glaze. Cover and cook until ribs register 195 degrees, 1¾ to 2¼ hours, rotating and brushing ribs with ¼ cup glaze every 30 minutes. Transfer ribs to large platter, tent loosely with foil, and let rest for 5 to 10 minutes before serving.

Mustard Glaze
MAKES ABOUT 1 CUP

- ½ cup Dijon mustard
- ½ cup red wine vinegar
- ¼ cup packed brown sugar
- 1 teaspoon reserved spice rub
- ⅛ teaspoon cayenne pepper

Whisk all ingredients together in bowl.

Blackberry Glaze
MAKES ABOUT 1 CUP

- 10 ounces (2 cups) fresh or frozen blackberries
- ½ cup ketchup
- ¼ cup bourbon
- 2 tablespoons packed brown sugar
- 1½ tablespoons soy sauce
- 1 teaspoon reserved spice rub
- ⅛ teaspoon cayenne pepper

Bring all ingredients to simmer in small saucepan over medium-high heat. Simmer, stirring frequently to break up blackberries, until reduced to 1¼ cups, about 10 minutes. Strain through fine-mesh strainer, pressing on solids to extract as much liquid as possible. Discard solids.

Hoisin-Tamarind Glaze
MAKES ABOUT 1 CUP

- 1 cup water
- ⅓ cup hoisin sauce
- ¼ cup tamarind paste
- 1 (2-inch) piece ginger, peeled and sliced into ½-inch-thick rounds
- 1 teaspoon reserved spice rub
- ⅛ teaspoon cayenne pepper

Bring all ingredients to simmer in small saucepan over medium-high heat. Simmer, stirring frequently, until reduced to 1¼ cups, about 10 minutes. Strain through fine-mesh strainer, pressing on solids to extract as much liquid as possible. Discard solids.

INEXPENSIVE GRILLED ROAST BEEF

WHY THIS RECIPE WORKS: Trying to grill an uneven piece of meat usually results in a fibrous, chewy, and woefully dry roast. We wanted to turn an inexpensive cut of meat into a juicy, evenly cooked roast with a substantial, well-seasoned garlic-rosemary crust. After extensively testing five "cheap" roast beef options and subjecting each to a 24-hour salt rub, we settled on top sirloin, a beefy, relatively tender cut from the back half of the cow. To grill our roast, we set up a fire in which the coals cover one-third of the grill. In effect, this created hot zones for searing and cooler zones for gentler, indirect cooking. To prevent the meat from cooking too quickly, we placed the roast inside a disposable aluminum pan on the cooler side of the grill after searing it. Poking a few escape channels in the bottom of the aluminum allowed any liquid to drain away, preserving the meat's sear. We also found that cutting the roast into thin slices made the meat taste even more tender.

Inexpensive Grill-Roasted Beef with Garlic and Rosemary
SERVES 6 TO 8

A pair of kitchen shears works well for punching the holes in the aluminum pan. We prefer a top sirloin roast, but you can substitute a top round or bottom round roast. Start this recipe the day before you plan to grill so the salt rub has time to flavor and tenderize the meat.

- 6 garlic cloves, minced
- 2 tablespoons minced fresh rosemary
- 4 teaspoons kosher salt
- 1 tablespoon pepper
- 1 (3- to 4-pound) top sirloin roast
- 1 (13 by 9-inch) disposable aluminum roasting pan

GRILLING TOP SIRLOIN ROAST

1. Place roast over hot part of grill and cook until well browned on all sides, about 10 minutes.

2. Punch fifteen ¼-inch holes in center of 13 by 9-inch disposable aluminum roasting pan in area roughly same size as roast. Place browned beef in pan.

3. Set pan over cool side of grill and cover. After about 20 minutes, rotate pan 180 degrees and continue roasting until center of roast registers 120 to 125 degrees (for medium-rare) or 130 to 135 degrees (for medium), 20 to 40 minutes more.

4. Transfer meat to wire rack set in rimmed baking sheet. Tent loosely with aluminum foil and let rest for 20 minutes.

1. Combine garlic, rosemary, salt, and pepper in bowl. Sprinkle all sides of roast evenly with garlic mixture, wrap tightly in plastic wrap, and refrigerate for 18 to 24 hours.

2A. FOR A CHARCOAL GRILL: Open bottom vent halfway. Light large chimney starter half filled with charcoal briquettes (3 quarts). When top coals are partially covered with ash, pour evenly over one-third of grill. Set cooking grate in place, cover, and open lid vent halfway. Heat grill until hot, about 5 minutes.

2B. FOR A GAS GRILL: Turn all burners to high, cover, and heat grill until hot, about 15 minutes.

3. Clean and oil cooking grate. Place roast on grill (hotter side if using charcoal) and cook (covered if using gas) until well browned on all sides, 10 to 12 minutes, turning as needed. (If flare-ups occur, move roast to cooler side of grill until flames die down.)

4. Meanwhile, punch fifteen ¼-inch holes in center of disposable pan in area roughly same size as roast. Once browned, place beef in pan over holes and set pan over cooler side of grill (if using charcoal) or turn primary burner to medium and other burner(s) off (if using gas). (Adjust burners as needed to maintain grill temperature of 250 to 300 degrees.) Cover and cook until meat registers 120 to 125 degrees (for medium-rare) or 130 to 135 degrees (for medium), 40 minutes to 1 hour, rotating pan halfway through cooking.

5. Transfer roast to wire rack set in rimmed baking sheet, tent loosely with aluminum foil, and let rest for 20 minutes. Transfer roast to carving board, slice thin against grain, and serve.

GRILL-ROASTED BEEF TENDERLOIN

WHY THIS RECIPE WORKS: Grilling is a great way to add flavor that enhances but doesn't overwhelm beef tenderloin's delicate beefiness. Producing deep browning was the first step toward delivering flavor. To do this without overcooking the tenderloin's interior, we rubbed the exterior of the roast with baking soda. This raised the meat's pH, which sped up browning by allowing the Maillard reaction to occur more quickly. "Grilled" flavor also depends on drippings from the food, which hit the coals (charcoal) or heat diffusers (gas), transform into new compounds, vaporize, and then waft up and stick to the meat. Because lean tenderloin produces very little in the way of drippings, we looked to an outside source: bacon. Threading three strips onto a metal skewer and placing the skewer directly over the heat source while the tenderloin cooked, low-and-slow away from direct heat, allowed the bacon to slowly render and produce the "grilled" flavor the tenderloin needed.

Grill-Roasted Beef Tenderloin
SERVES 4 TO 6

Center-cut beef tenderloin roasts are sometimes sold as Châteaubriand. You will need one metal skewer for this recipe. The bacon will render slowly during cooking, creating a steady stream of smoke that flavors the beef. Serve the roast as is or with Chermoula Sauce (recipe follows).

2¼ teaspoons kosher salt
1 teaspoon pepper
2 teaspoons vegetable oil
1 teaspoon baking soda
1 (3-pound) center-cut beef tenderloin roast, trimmed and tied at 1½-inch intervals
3 slices bacon

1. Combine salt, pepper, oil, and baking soda in small bowl. Rub mixture evenly over roast and let stand while preparing grill.

2. Stack bacon slices. Keeping slices stacked, thread metal skewer through bacon 6 or 7 times to create accordion shape. Push stack together to compact into about 2-inch length.

¼ teaspoon salt

3 tablespoons lemon juice

½ cup extra-virgin olive oil

Pulse cilantro, garlic, cumin, paprika, cayenne, and salt in food processor until coarsely chopped, about 10 pulses. Add lemon juice and pulse briefly to combine. Transfer mixture to medium bowl and slowly whisk in oil until incorporated and mixture is emulsified. Cover with plastic wrap and let stand at room temperature for at least 1 hour. (Sauce can be refrigerated for up to 2 days; bring to room temperature and rewhisk before serving.)

GRILL-ROASTED BEEF TENDERLOIN FOR A CROWD

WHY THIS RECIPE WORKS: Grilled tenderloin sounds appealing, but with a whole tenderloin going for as much as $100, uneven cooking, bland flavor, and a tough outer crust just don't cut it. We wanted it cheaper and better. At its peak, tenderloin should be an even, rosy pink throughout, have a browned, crusty exterior, and boast a well-seasoned, grilled flavor.

In need of an affordable alternative to butcher prices, we found that beef at wholesale clubs was far more wallet-friendly. Though these tenderloins needed some home butchering, they were well worth the modest time and effort it took to trim them. Flavor-enhancement came next through just an hour of salting the meat, wrapping it in plastic wrap, and letting it rest on the counter before hitting the hot coals. Tucking the narrow tip end of the tenderloin under and tying it securely gave the tenderloin a more consistent thickness that allowed it to cook through more evenly on the grill. Direct fire was too hot for the roast to endure throughout the cooking stages, so after briefly searing the meat over the coals, we moved it away from the coals for grill-roasting via indirect heat. We removed it from the grill while still rare to account for carryover cooking, and we let the meat rest before slicing to ensure the meat stayed juicy.

Grill-Roasted Beef Tenderloin for a Crowd
SERVES 10 TO 12

Beef tenderloins purchased from wholesale clubs require a good amount of trimming before cooking. At the grocery store, however, you may have the option of having the butcher trim it for you. Once trimmed, and with the butt tenderloin still attached (the butt tenderloin is the lobe attached to the large end of the roast), the roast should weigh 4½ to 5 pounds. If you purchase an already-trimmed tenderloin without the butt tenderloin attached, begin checking for doneness about 5 minutes early. When using a charcoal grill, we prefer wood chunks to wood chips whenever possible; substitute 2 medium wood chunks, soaked in water for 1 hour, for the wood chip packet (if using). Serve with Salsa Verde (recipe follows), if desired.

3A. FOR A CHARCOAL GRILL: Open bottom vent halfway. Light large chimney starter two-thirds filled with charcoal briquettes (4 quarts). When top coals are partially covered with ash, pour evenly over half of grill. Set cooking grate in place, cover, and open lid vent halfway. Heat grill until hot, about 5 minutes.

3B. FOR A GAS GRILL: Turn all burners to high, cover, and heat grill until hot, about 15 minutes. Turn primary burner to medium and turn off other burner(s). (Adjust primary burner as necessary to maintain grill temperature of 300 degrees.)

4. Clean and oil cooking grate. Place roast on hotter side of grill and cook until lightly browned on all sides, about 12 minutes. Slide roast to cooler side of grill, arranging so roast is about 7 inches from heat source. Place skewered bacon on hotter side of grill. (For charcoal, place near center of grill, above edge of coals. For gas, place above heat diffuser of primary burner. Bacon should be 4 to 6 inches from roast and drippings should fall on coals or heat diffuser and produce steady stream of smoke and minimal flare-ups. If flare-ups are large or frequent, slide bacon skewer 1 inch toward roast.)

5. Cover and cook until beef registers 120 to 125 degrees (for medium-rare), 50 minutes to 1¼ hours. Transfer roast to carving board, tent with aluminum foil, and let rest for 20 minutes. Discard twine and slice roast ½ inch thick. Serve.

Chermoula Sauce
MAKES ABOUT 1 CUP

To keep the sauce from becoming bitter, whisk in the olive oil by hand.

¾ cup fresh cilantro leaves

4 garlic cloves, minced

1 teaspoon ground cumin

1 teaspoon paprika

¼ teaspoon cayenne pepper

1 (6-pound) beef tenderloin, trimmed of fat and
silver skin, tail end tucked and tied with kitchen
twine at 2-inch intervals
1½ tablespoons kosher salt
2 cups wood chips, soaked in water for 15 minutes
and drained (optional)
2 tablespoons olive oil
1 tablespoon pepper

1. Pat tenderloin dry with paper towels and rub with salt. Cover loosely with plastic wrap and let sit at room temperature for 1 hour.

2. Using large piece of heavy-duty aluminum foil, wrap soaked wood chips, if using, in foil packet and cut several vent holes in top.

3A. FOR A CHARCOAL GRILL: Open bottom vent halfway. Light large chimney starter filled with charcoal briquettes (6 quarts). When top coals are partially covered with ash, pour evenly over half of grill. Place wood chip packet, if using, on coals. Set cooking grate in place, cover, and open lid vent halfway. Heat grill until hot and wood chips are smoking, about 5 minutes.

3B. FOR A GAS GRILL: Place wood chip packet, if using, opposite primary burner. Turn all burners to high, cover, and heat grill until hot and wood chips are smoking, about 15 minutes.

4. Clean and oil cooking grate. Rub tenderloin with oil and season with pepper. Place roast on hot side of grill if using charcoal or opposite primary burner if using gas and cook (covered if using gas) until well browned on all sides, 8 to 10 minutes, turning as needed.

5. For gas grill, leave primary burner on, turning off other burner(s). (Adjust primary burner as needed during cooking to maintain grill temperature around 350 degrees.) Move roast to cool side of grill, cover (position lid vent over meat if using charcoal), and cook until meat registers 115 to 120 degrees (for rare) or 120 to 125 degrees (for medium-rare), 15 to 30 minutes.

6. Transfer roast to carving board, tent loosely with foil, and let rest for 10 to 15 minutes. Remove twine, cut into ½-inch-thick slices, and serve.

Salsa Verde
MAKES 1½ CUPS
Salsa verde is excellent with grilled or roasted meats, fish, or poultry; poached fish; boiled or steamed potatoes; or sliced tomatoes. It is also good on sandwiches.

2-3 slices hearty white sandwich bread, lightly toasted
and cut into ½-inch pieces (about 1½ cups)
1 cup extra-virgin olive oil
¼ cup lemon juice (2 lemons)
4 cups parsley leaves
¼ cup capers, rinsed

4 anchovy fillets, rinsed
1 garlic clove, minced
¼ teaspoon salt

Process bread, oil, and lemon juice in food processor until smooth, about 10 seconds. Add parsley, capers, anchovies, garlic, and salt and pulse until finely chopped (mixture should not be smooth), about 5 pulses. Transfer to serving bowl. (Salsa verde can be refrigerated for up to 2 days.)

FLAT-IRON STEAKS

WHY THIS RECIPE WORKS: Smoking steaks can lend them complexity, but treating them like larger, collagen-rich barbecue cuts like brisket can overwhelm the meat's delicate flavor with too much smoke. We found that the key was using a small amount of wood chips and cooking the steaks quickly over direct heat so that they were just kissed with smoke. To make sure we had a consistent amount of smoke, we weighed the wood chips for more control over the smoke quantity. Salting the steaks for an hour before cooking ensured that the seasoning penetrated below the meat's surface, and coating them with an herb-spice rub lent an extra layer of flavor that complemented the smoke. We also grilled lemons to serve with the steaks for a hit of brightness.

Grill-Smoked Herb-Rubbed Flat-Iron Steaks
SERVES 4 TO 6
This recipe requires rubbing the steaks with salt and letting them sit at room temperature for 1 hour before cooking. You can substitute blade steaks for the flat-iron steaks, if desired. We like both cuts cooked to medium (130 to 135 degrees). We like hickory chips in this recipe, but other kinds of wood chips will work. Gas grills are not as efficient at smoking meat as charcoal grills, so we recommend using 1½ cups of wood chips if using a gas grill.

2 teaspoons dried thyme
1 teaspoon dried rosemary
¾ teaspoon fennel seeds
½ teaspoon black peppercorns
¼ teaspoon red pepper flakes
4 (6- to 8-ounce) flat-iron steaks, ¾ to 1 inch thick, trimmed
1 tablespoon kosher salt
1-1½ cups (2½-3¾ ounces) wood chips
Vegetable oil spray
2 lemons, quartered lengthwise

1. Grind thyme, rosemary, fennel seeds, peppercorns, and pepper flakes in spice grinder or with mortar and pestle until coarsely ground. Transfer to small bowl. Pat steaks dry with paper towels. Rub steaks evenly on both sides with salt and place on wire rack set in rimmed baking sheet. Let stand at room temperature for 1 hour. (After 30 minutes, prepare grill.)

2. Using large piece of heavy-duty aluminum foil, wrap wood chips (1 cup if using charcoal; 1½ cups if using gas) in 8 by 4½-inch foil packet. (Make sure chips do not poke holes in sides or bottom of packet.) Cut 2 evenly spaced 2-inch slits in top of packet.

3A. FOR A CHARCOAL GRILL: Open bottom vent completely. Light large chimney starter filled with charcoal briquettes (6 quarts). When top coals are partially covered with ash, pour evenly over half of grill. Place wood chip packet on coals. Set cooking grate in place, cover, and open lid vent completely. Heat grill until hot and wood chips are smoking, about 5 minutes.

3B. FOR A GAS GRILL: Remove cooking grate and place wood chip packet directly on primary burner. Set grate in place, turn all burners to high, cover, and heat grill until hot and wood chips are smoking, about 15 minutes. Leave primary burner on high and turn other burner(s) to medium.

4. Clean and oil cooking grate. Sprinkle half of herb rub evenly over 1 side of steaks and press to adhere. Lightly spray herb-rubbed side of steaks with oil spray, about 3 seconds. Flip steaks and repeat process of sprinkling and pressing steaks with remaining herb rub and coating with oil spray on second side.

5. Place lemons and steaks on hotter side of grill, cover (position lid vent over steaks if using charcoal), and cook until lemons and steaks are well browned on both sides and meat registers 130 to 135 degrees (for medium), 4 to 6 minutes per side. (If steaks are fully charred before reaching desired temperature, move to cooler side of grill, cover, and continue to cook.) Transfer lemons and steaks to clean wire rack set in rimmed baking sheet, tent with foil, and let rest for 10 minutes. Slice steaks thin against grain and serve, passing lemons separately.

BARBECUED BRISKET

WHY THIS RECIPE WORKS: The main reason it's so hard to cook brisket is that it starts out as a very tough cut of meat. It's also big, sometimes weighing upward of 13 pounds, which is why most butchers separate it into two cuts: the "point" (the fattier of the two pieces) and the "flat" (which is leaner and also a little tougher). Slow cooking for as many as six to 12 hours at a low temperature tends to be the norm for cooking brisket, but we wanted to jump-start the cooking on the grill, to give us tender, smoky meat.

We didn't get the total cooking time below six hours, but we did make the job easier using the grill. First, we cooked the meat over the grill for two hours to let in those all-important smoky flavors; barbecuing the brisket fat side up allowed the fat to melt slowly over the meat. Then we moved it to the oven to cook for a few more hours unattended. For flavor, we turned to a dry rub; typical barbecuing methods like basting the meat or setting a pan of liquid on the cooking grate to create a moist environment just didn't work. Our grill-to-oven approach, although unconventional, gave us fork-tender meat with real barbecue flavor in about half the time it would take to cook the meat entirely on the grill.

Barbecued Whole Beef Brisket
SERVES 18 TO 24

Cooking a whole brisket, which weighs about 10 pounds, may seem like overkill. However, the process is easy, and the leftovers keep well in the refrigerator for up to 4 days. (Leave leftover brisket unsliced, and reheat the foil-wrapped meat in a 300-degree oven until warm.) Still, if you don't want to bother with a big piece of meat or if your grill has fewer than 400 square inches of cooking space, see the variation for Barbecued Half Beef Brisket (recipe follows). No matter how large or small a piece you cook, it's a good idea to save the juices the meat gives off while in the oven to enrich the barbecue sauce. If you'd like to use wood chunks instead of wood chips when using a charcoal grill, substitute 2 medium wood chunks, soaked in water for 1 hour, for the wood chip packet. You can either use store-bought barbecue sauce or our Quick Barbecue Sauce (page 533) in this recipe.

¼ cup paprika
2 tablespoons chili powder
2 tablespoons ground cumin
2 tablespoons salt
2 tablespoons dark brown sugar
1 tablespoon granulated sugar
1 tablespoon ground oregano
1 tablespoon ground black pepper
1 tablespoon ground white pepper
2 teaspoons cayenne pepper
1 (9- to 11-pound) whole beef brisket, fat trimmed to ¼ inch
2 cups wood chips
3 cups barbecue sauce, warmed

1. Combine paprika, chili powder, cumin, salt, brown sugar, granulated sugar, oregano, black pepper, white pepper, and cayenne in bowl. Rub brisket thoroughly with spice mixture. Wrap brisket in plastic wrap and refrigerate for at least 2 hours, or up to 2 days.

2. Just before grilling, soak wood chips in water for 15 minutes, then drain. Using large piece of heavy-duty aluminum foil, wrap soaked chips in foil packet and cut several vent holes in top.

3A. FOR A CHARCOAL GRILL: Open bottom vent halfway. Light large chimney starter half filled with charcoal briquettes (3 quarts). When top coals are partially covered with ash, pour into steeply banked pile against side of grill. Place wood chip packet on coals. Set cooking grate in place, cover, and open lid vent halfway. Heat grill until hot and wood chips are smoking, about 5 minutes.

3B. FOR A GAS GRILL: Remove cooking grate and place wood chip packet directly on primary burner. Set grate in place, turn all burners to high, cover, and heat grill until hot and wood chips are smoking, about 15 minutes. Turn primary burner to medium and turn off other burner(s). (Adjust primary burner as needed to maintain grill temperature around 275 degrees.)

4. Clean and oil cooking grate. Place brisket, fat side up, on cooler side of grill. Cover (position lid vent over meat if using charcoal) and cook for 2 hours without removing lid.

5. During final 20 minutes of grilling time, adjust oven rack to middle position and heat oven to 300 degrees. Assemble 4 by 3-foot rectangle of heavy-duty aluminum foil by piecing two, 4-foot-long pieces of foil together and folding over edges two or three times to seal.

6. Remove brisket from grill, place lengthwise in center of foil, then fold and crimp edges of foil together to completely seal brisket. Place brisket on rimmed baking sheet and cook in oven until meat is fork-tender, 3 to 3½ hours.

7. Remove brisket from oven, loosen foil at one end to release steam, and let rest for 30 minutes. Unwrap brisket and transfer to carving board, pouring any meat juices into fat separator. Separate meat into two sections and slice each thinly on bias against grain. Stir 1 cup of defatted juices into barbecue sauce, and serve with brisket.

Barbecued Half Beef Brisket

This smaller brisket will serve 8 to 10 people. Either a point cut or a flat cut brisket will work well here.

Substitute 4½- to 5½ pound brisket (either point cut or flat cut) for whole brisket and rub with only half of spice rub. Reduce cooking time on grill to 1½ hours and cooking time in oven to 2 hours. Reserve ½ cup of meat juices and reduce barbecue sauce to 1½ cups.

Spicy Chili Rub

MAKES ABOUT 1 CUP

If you cannot abide spicy food, reduce or eliminate the cayenne.

- 4 tablespoons paprika
- 2 tablespoons chili powder
- 2 tablespoons ground cumin
- 2 tablespoons dark brown sugar
- 2 tablespoons table salt
- 1 tablespoon ground oregano
- 1 tablespoon granulated sugar
- 1 tablespoon ground black pepper
- 1 tablespoon ground white pepper
- 2 teaspoons cayenne pepper (see note)

Combine all the ingredients in a small bowl. (The rub can be stored in an airtight container at room temperature for up to a month.)

GRILLED BONELESS PORK CHOPS

WHY THIS RECIPE WORKS: Pork chops are a prime candidate for the grill, which can imbue the lean chops with smoky, savory flavor, but too often, the results are disappointing. To produce juicy, well-charred boneless pork chops on the grill, we used a two-pronged approach. We brined the chops to improve their ability to hold on to juices during cooking, provide seasoning throughout, and increase their tenderness. To ensure we'd get a substantial browned crust before the interior overcooked, we looked to a unique coating of anchovy paste and honey. The anchovies' amino acids couple with the fructose from honey to rapidly begin the flavorful Maillard browning reaction. We developed some flavorful relishes using combinations of sweet and savory ingredients to complement the grilled chops.

Easy Grilled Boneless Pork Chops

SERVES 4 TO 6

If your pork is enhanced (see page 181), do not brine it in step 1. Very finely mashed anchovy fillets (rinsed and dried before mashing) can be used instead of anchovy paste.

- 6 (6- to 8-ounce) boneless pork chops, ¾ to 1 inch thick
- 3 tablespoons salt
- 1 tablespoon vegetable oil
- 1½ teaspoons honey
- 1 teaspoon anchovy paste
- ½ teaspoon pepper
- 1 recipe relish (optional) (recipes follow)

1. Cut 2 slits about 1 inch apart through outer layer of fat and connective tissue on each chop to prevent buckling. Dissolve salt in 1½ quarts cold water in large container. Submerge chops in brine and let stand at room temperature for 30 minutes.

2. Whisk together oil, honey, anchovy paste, and pepper to form smooth paste. Remove pork from brine and pat dry with paper towels. Using spoon, spread half of oil mixture evenly over 1 side of each chop (about ¼ teaspoon per side).

3A. FOR A CHARCOAL GRILL: Open bottom vent completely. Light chimney starter filled with charcoal briquettes (6 quarts). When top coals are partially covered with ash, pour evenly over half of grill. Set cooking grate in place, cover, and open lid vent completely. Heat grill until hot, about 5 minutes.

3B. FOR A GAS GRILL: Turn all burners to high, cover, and heat grill until hot, about 15 minutes. Leave primary burner on high and turn off other burner(s).

4. Clean and oil cooking grate. Place chops, oiled side down, over hot part of grill and cook, uncovered, until well browned on first side, 4 to 6 minutes. While chops are grilling, spread remaining oil mixture evenly over second side of chops. Flip chops and continue to cook until chops register 140 degrees, 4 to 6 minutes longer (if chops are well browned but register less than 140 degrees, move to cooler part of grill to finish cooking). Transfer chops to plate and let rest for 5 minutes. Serve with relish, if using.

Onion, Olive, and Caper Relish

MAKES ABOUT 2 CUPS

- ¼ cup olive oil
- 2 onions, cut into ¼-inch pieces
- 6 garlic cloves, sliced thin
- ½ cup pitted kalamata olives, chopped coarse
- ¼ cup capers, rinsed
- 3 tablespoons balsamic vinegar
- 2 tablespoons minced fresh parsley
- 1 teaspoon minced fresh marjoram
- 1 teaspoon sugar
- ½ teaspoon anchovy paste
- ½ teaspoon pepper
- ¼ teaspoon salt

Heat 2 tablespoons oil in 10-inch nonstick skillet over medium heat until shimmering. Add onions and cook until softened, about 5 minutes. Stir in garlic and cook until fragrant, about 30 seconds. Transfer onion mixture to medium bowl; stir in remaining 2 tablespoons oil, olives, capers, vinegar, parsley, marjoram, sugar, anchovy paste, pepper, and salt. Serve warm or at room temperature.

Tomato, Fennel, and Almond Relish

MAKES ABOUT 2 CUPS

- ¼ cup olive oil
- 1 fennel bulb, stalks discarded, bulb halved, cored, and cut into ¼-inch pieces
- 6 garlic cloves, sliced thin
- 2 tomatoes, cored and cut into ½-inch pieces
- ¼ cup green olives, pitted and chopped coarse
- 3 tablespoons sherry vinegar
- ¼ cup slivered almonds, toasted
- 3 tablespoons minced fresh parsley
- 1 teaspoon sugar
  Salt and pepper

Heat 2 tablespoons oil in 10-inch skillet over medium heat until shimmering. Add fennel and cook until slightly softened, about 5 minutes. Stir in garlic and cook until fragrant, about 30 seconds. Stir in tomatoes and continue to cook until tomatoes break down slightly, about 5 minutes. Transfer fennel mixture to medium bowl; stir in remaining 2 tablespoons oil, olives, vinegar, almonds, parsley, sugar, ¾ teaspoon salt, and ½ teaspoon pepper. Serve warm or at room temperature.

Orange, Jícama, and Pepita Relish
MAKES ABOUT 3 CUPS

    1   orange
    ¼   cup olive oil
    2   jalapeños, stemmed, seeded, and sliced into thin rings
    3   shallots, sliced thin
    6   garlic cloves, sliced thin
    2   cups jícama, peeled and cut into ¼-inch pieces
    ¼   cup pepitas, toasted
    3   tablespoons chopped fresh cilantro
    3   tablespoons lime juice (2 limes)
    1   teaspoon sugar
        Salt and pepper

Cut away peel and pith from orange. Quarter orange, then slice crosswise into ¼-inch-thick pieces. Heat 2 tablespoons oil in 10-inch skillet over medium heat until shimmering. Add jalapeños and shallots and cook until slightly softened, about 5 minutes. Stir in garlic and cook until fragrant, about 30 seconds. Transfer jalapeño-shallot mixture to medium bowl; stir in orange, jícama, pepitas, cilantro, lime juice, sugar, ¾ teaspoon salt, and ½ teaspoon pepper. Serve warm or at room temperature.

GRILLED BONE-IN PORK CHOPS

WHY THIS RECIPE WORKS: Too many grilled pork chops are burnt on the outside and raw on the inside. And even if they are cooked evenly, they can still be tough and bland. We wanted great-looking and great-tasting chops with a perfectly grilled, crisp crust and juicy, flavorful meat. What's more, we wanted our chops plump and meaty, not thin and tough.

We started with the right chops—tender and flavorful bone-in rib loin or center-cut loin chops worked best—and brined them to pump up their flavor and lock in moisture. To brown the pork chops, only a really hot fire would do. But keeping them over high heat long enough to cook through dried them out. So we grilled the chops over a two-level fire, with one side of the grill intensely hot to sear the chops, and the other only moderately hot to allow the chops to cook through without burning the exterior. So they wouldn't overcook, we pulled the chops from the grill when they were just underdone, and let the chops rest until the temperature rose to serving temperature and the juices were redistributed in the meat. A spice rub, made with potent spices and applied before grilling, added big flavor and gave our chops a nice crust.

Grilled Pork Chops
SERVES 4

Rib loin chops are our top choice for their big flavor and juiciness. The spice rub adds a lot of flavor for very little effort, but the chops can also be seasoned with pepper alone just before grilling. If the pork is enhanced (see page 181), do not brine and add 2 teaspoons salt along with spice rub or pepper.

    3   tablespoons salt
    3   tablespoons sugar
    4   (12-ounce) bone-in pork rib or center-cut chops, 1½ inches thick, trimmed
    1   recipe Basic Spice Rub for Pork Chops (recipe follows) or 2 teaspoons pepper

1. Dissolve salt and sugar in 1½ quarts cold water in large container. Submerge chops in brine, cover, and refrigerate for 30 minutes to 1 hour. Remove chops from brine and pat dry with paper towels. Rub chops with spice rub.

2A. FOR A CHARCOAL GRILL: Open bottom vent completely. Light large chimney starter filled with charcoal briquettes (6 quarts). When top coals are partially covered with ash, pour two-thirds evenly over grill, then pour remaining coals over half of grill. Set cooking grate in place, cover, and open lid vent completely. Heat grill until hot, about 5 minutes.

2B. FOR A GAS GRILL: Turn all burners to high, cover, and heat grill until hot, about 15 minutes. Leave primary burner on high and turn off other burner(s).

3. Clean and oil cooking grate. Place chops on hotter side of grill and cook (covered if using gas) until browned on both sides, 4 to 8 minutes. Move chops to cool side of grill, cover, and continue to cook, turning once, until meat registers 145 degrees, 7 to 9 minutes longer. Transfer chops to serving platter, tent loosely with aluminum foil, and let rest for 5 to 10 minutes. Serve.

Basic Spice Rub for Pork Chops
MAKES ¼ CUP

    1   tablespoon ground cumin
    1   tablespoon chili powder
    1   tablespoon curry powder
    2   teaspoons packed brown sugar
    1   teaspoon pepper

Combine all ingredients in bowl.

GRILL-SMOKED PORK CHOPS

WHY THIS RECIPE WORKS: Getting good smoke flavor and a charred crust is an elusive grilling goal. Smokiness generally requires a lengthy exposure to a slow fire, while a charred crust requires a blast of high heat to quickly sear the exterior of the meat before the interior turns dry. We wanted chops that had it all: charred crust, ultra-moist meat, and true smoke flavor. We decided to employ a technique we had used in previous pork chop recipes: reversing the cooking by starting low and finishing with a quick sear. To reap the benefits of both high and low heat on a charcoal grill, we used a double-banked fire (made by placing a disposable aluminum pan between two mounds of coals) and started our chops under cover on the cooler center of the grill, allowing the smoke to do its job for about 25 minutes. We then applied a few coats of sauce and finished by searing them, uncovered, over hot coals.

1. **FOR THE SAUCE:** Bring all ingredients to simmer in small saucepan over medium heat and cook, stirring occasionally, until reduced to about 1 cup, 5 to 7 minutes. Transfer ½ cup sauce to small bowl and set aside remaining sauce for serving.

2. **FOR THE CHOPS:** Using large piece of heavy-duty aluminum foil, wrap soaked chips in foil packet and cut several vent holes in top. Pat pork chops dry with paper towels. Use sharp knife to cut 2 slits about 1 inch apart through outer layer of fat and connective tissue. Season each chop with ½ teaspoon salt and ½ teaspoon pepper. Place chops side by side, facing in same direction, on cutting board with curved rib bone facing down. Pass 2 skewers through loin muscle of each chop, close to bone, about 1 inch from each end, then pull apart to create 1-inch space between each.

3A. **FOR A CHARCOAL GRILL:** Open bottom vent halfway and place roasting pan in center of grill. Light large chimney starter filled with charcoal briquettes (6 quarts). When top coals are partially covered with ash, pour into 2 even piles on either side of roasting pan. Place wood chip packet on 1 pile of coals. Set cooking grate in place, cover, and open lid vent halfway. Heat grill until hot and wood chips are smoking, about 5 minutes.

3B. **FOR A GAS GRILL:** Place wood chip packet over primary burner. Turn all burners to high, cover, and heat grill until hot and wood chips are smoking, about 15 minutes. Turn all burners to medium-high. (Adjust burners as needed during cooking to maintain grill temperature between 300 and 325 degrees.)

4. Clean and oil cooking grate. Place skewered chops bone side down on grill (over pan if using charcoal). Cover and cook until meat registers 120 degrees, 28 to 32 minutes.

As for arranging the chops on the grill, we found it best to rest each chop on its bone instead of laying it flat. To keep them from toppling over, we speared the chops together with skewers, making sure to leave a good inch between each one to allow smoke to circulate, then stood them upright in the center of the grill with bone, not meat, touching the grill. This allowed us to keep the chops over the fire for a full 30 minutes, after which we removed the skewers, applied the glaze, and finished the chops over hot coals for that crusty char.

Grill-Smoked Pork Chops

SERVES 4

Buy chops of the same thickness so they will cook uniformly. Use the large holes on a box grater to grate the onion for the sauce. Two medium wood chunks, soaked in water for 1 hour, can be substituted for the wood chip packet on a charcoal grill. You will need two 10-inch metal skewers for this recipe.

SAUCE

- ½ cup ketchup
- ¼ cup molasses
- 2 tablespoons grated onion
- 2 tablespoons Worcestershire sauce
- 2 tablespoons Dijon mustard
- 2 tablespoons cider vinegar
- 1 tablespoon packed light brown sugar

CHOPS

- 2 cups wood chips, soaked in water for 15 minutes and drained
- 4 (12-ounce) bone-in pork rib chops, 1½ inches thick, trimmed
- 2 teaspoons salt
- 2 teaspoons pepper
- 1 (13 by 9-inch) disposable aluminum roasting pan (if using charcoal)

NOTES FROM THE TEST KITCHEN

SKEWERING PORK CHOPS FOR THE GRILL

1. Pass two skewers through the loin muscle of each chop to provide stability when standing on the grill.

2. Stand the skewered chops, bone side down, on the cooking grate in the center of the grill so smoke can reach all sides.

5. Remove skewers from chops, tip chops onto flat side and brush surface of each with 1 tablespoon sauce. Transfer chops, sauce side down, to hotter parts of grill (if using charcoal) or turn all burners to high (if using gas) and cook until browned on first side, 2 to 6 minutes. Brush top of each chop with 1 tablespoon sauce, flip, and continue to cook until browned on second side and meat registers 140 degrees, 2 to 6 minutes longer.

6. Transfer chops to serving platter, tent loosely with aluminum foil, and let rest for 5 to 10 minutes. Serve, passing reserved sauce separately.

GRILLED PORK TENDERLOIN STEAKS

WHY THIS RECIPE WORKS: Although pork tenderloin medallions make for a nice presentation and offer lots of surface area to crisp and brown on the grill, they are inherently fussy: They require constant attention lest they overcook or, worse, slip through the grates. We wanted to take the spirit of the medallion approach but find a shape and a technique that, while it reliably delivered a maximum amount of flavorful, nicely browned crust, still kept this lean cut tender.

We started by cutting two tenderloin roasts in half and pounding them to an even thickness to make pork tenderloin "steaks." A two-level grill fire, with both hotter and cooler areas, allowed us to sear the steaks on the hotter side and then let them gently finish cooking on the cooler side. We added both bold seasoning and richness through a marinade. Plenty of salt ensured thorough seasoning and tender meat. Oil, lime juice and zest, garlic, fish sauce (which provided a savory boost without tasting fishy), and honey (the sugars in which would encourage browning) rounded out the marinade. We cut crosshatch marks in the steaks, which both made for extra crispy edges and allowed them to absorb even more marinade. A bit of reserved marinade, whisked with some mayo for body and cilantro for freshness, completed our tenderloin steaks.

Garlic-Lime Grilled Pork Tenderloin Steaks

SERVES 4 TO 6

Since marinating is a key step in this recipe, we don't recommend using enhanced pork (see page 181).

- 2 (1-pound) pork tenderloins, trimmed
- 1 tablespoon grated lime zest plus ¼ cup juice (2 limes)
- 4 garlic cloves, minced
- 4 teaspoons honey
- 2 teaspoons fish sauce
- ¾ teaspoon salt
- ½ teaspoon pepper
- ½ cup vegetable oil
- 4 teaspoons mayonnaise
- 1 tablespoon chopped fresh cilantro
  Flake sea salt (optional)

1. Slice each tenderloin in half crosswise to create 4 steaks total. Pound each half to ¾-inch thickness. Using sharp knife, cut ⅛-inch-deep slits spaced ½ inch apart in crosshatch pattern on both sides of steaks.

2. Whisk lime zest and juice, garlic, honey, fish sauce, salt, and pepper together in large bowl. Whisking constantly, slowly drizzle oil into lime mixture until smooth and slightly thickened. Transfer ½ cup lime mixture to small bowl and whisk in mayonnaise; set aside sauce. Add steaks to bowl with remaining marinade and toss thoroughly to coat; transfer steaks and marinade to large zipper-lock bag, press out as much air as possible, and seal bag. Let steaks sit at room temperature for 45 minutes.

3A. FOR A CHARCOAL GRILL: Open bottom vent completely. Light large chimney starter filled with charcoal briquettes (6 quarts). When top coals are partially covered with ash, pour evenly over half of grill. Set cooking grate in place, cover, and open lid vent completely. Heat grill until hot, about 5 minutes.

3B. FOR A GAS GRILL: Turn all burners to high, cover, and heat grill until hot, about 15 minutes. Leave primary burner on high and turn off other burner(s).

4. Clean and oil cooking grate. Remove steaks from marinade (do not pat dry) and place over hotter part of grill. Cook, uncovered, until well browned on first side, 3 to 4 minutes. Flip steaks and cook until well browned on second side, 3 to 4 minutes. Transfer steaks to cooler part of grill, with wider end of each steak facing hotter part of grill. Cover and cook until meat registers 140 degrees, 3 to 8 minutes longer (remove steaks as they come to temperature). Transfer steaks to cutting board and let rest for 5 minutes.

5. While steaks rest, microwave reserved sauce until warm, 15 to 30 seconds; stir in cilantro. Slice steaks against grain into ½-inch-thick slices. Drizzle with half of sauce; sprinkle with sea salt, if using; and serve, passing remaining sauce separately.

Lemon-Thyme Grilled Pork Tenderloin Steaks

Substitute grated lemon zest and juice (2 lemons) for lime zest and juice. Add 1 tablespoon minced fresh thyme to lemon mixture with garlic. Omit cilantro.

Spicy Orange-Ginger Grilled Pork Tenderloin Steaks

Reduce lime zest to 1½ teaspoons and juice to 2 tablespoons. Add 1½ teaspoons grated orange zest plus 2 tablespoons juice, 2 teaspoons grated fresh ginger, and ¼ teaspoon cayenne pepper to lime mixture with garlic.

GRILLED GLAZED PORK TENDERLOIN ROAST

WHY THIS RECIPE WORKS: Too often, delicate pork tenderloin turns out disappointing: The lean meat dries out easily, and it is plagued by uneven cooking because of its tapered shape. To make the pork cook more evenly and to create a more presentation-worthy roast, we tied two tenderloins together. Scraping the insides of the tenderloins with a fork created a sticky protein network that helped the tenderloins bind together. To ensure that our pork retained maximum juiciness, we brined the meat and cooked it mostly over indirect heat. Finally, we put together a few flavorful glazes. We made sure to use enough sugar (or ingredients containing sugar) to encourage browning, giving the pork a beautiful crust along with a flavor boost.

Grilled Glazed Pork Tenderloin Roast
SERVES 6

Since brining is a key step in having the two tenderloins stick together, we don't recommend using enhanced pork (see page 181) in this recipe.

- 2 (1-pound) pork tenderloins, trimmed
  Salt and pepper
  Vegetable oil
- 1 recipe glaze (recipes follow)

1. Lay tenderloins on cutting board, flat side (side opposite where silverskin was) up. Holding thick end of 1 tenderloin with paper towels and using dinner fork, scrape flat side

lengthwise from end to end 5 times, until surface is completely covered with shallow grooves. Repeat with second tenderloin. Dissolve 3 tablespoons salt in 1½ quarts cold water in large container. Submerge tenderloins in brine and let stand at room temperature for 1 hour.

2. Remove tenderloins from brine and pat completely dry with paper towels. Lay 1 tenderloin, scraped side up, on cutting board and lay second tenderloin, scraped side down, on top so that thick end of 1 tenderloin matches up with thin end of other. Spray five 14-inch lengths of kitchen twine thoroughly with vegetable oil spray; evenly space twine underneath tenderloins and tie. Brush roast with vegetable oil and season with pepper. Transfer ⅓ cup glaze to bowl for grilling; reserve remaining glaze for serving.

3A. FOR A CHARCOAL GRILL: Open bottom vent completely. Light large chimney starter filled with charcoal briquettes (6 quarts). When top coals are partially covered with ash, pour into steeply banked pile against side of grill. Set cooking grate in place, cover, and open lid vent completely. Heat grill until hot, about 5 minutes.

3B. FOR A GAS GRILL: Turn all burners to high, cover, and heat grill until hot, about 15 minutes. Leave primary burner on high and turn off other burner(s).

4. Clean and oil cooking grate. Place roast on cooler side of grill, cover, and cook until meat registers 115 degrees, 22 to 28 minutes, flipping and rotating halfway through cooking.

5. Slide roast to hotter side of grill and cook until lightly browned on all sides, 4 to 6 minutes. Brush top of roast with about 1 tablespoon glaze and grill, glaze side down, until glaze begins to char, 2 to 3 minutes; repeat glazing and grilling with remaining 3 sides of roast, until meat registers 140 degrees.

6. Transfer roast to carving board, tent loosely with aluminum foil, and let rest for 10 minutes. Carefully remove twine and slice roast into ½-inch-thick slices. Serve with remaining glaze.

Miso Glaze
MAKES ABOUT ¾ CUP

- 3 tablespoons sake
- 3 tablespoons mirin
- ⅓ cup white miso paste
- ¼ cup sugar
- 2 teaspoons Dijon mustard
- 1 teaspoon rice vinegar
- ¼ teaspoon grated fresh ginger
- ¼ teaspoon toasted sesame oil

Bring sake and mirin to boil in small saucepan over medium heat. Whisk in miso and sugar until smooth, about 30 seconds. Remove pan from heat and continue to whisk until sugar is dissolved, about 1 minute. Whisk in mustard, vinegar, ginger, and sesame oil until smooth.

Sweet and Spicy Hoisin Glaze

MAKES ABOUT ¾ CUP

- 1 teaspoon vegetable oil
- 3 garlic cloves, minced
- 1 teaspoon grated fresh ginger
- ½ teaspoon red pepper flakes
- ½ cup hoisin sauce
- 2 tablespoons soy sauce
- 1 tablespoon rice vinegar

Heat oil in small saucepan over medium heat until shimmering. Add garlic, ginger, and pepper flakes; cook until fragrant, about 30 seconds. Whisk in hoisin and soy sauce until smooth. Remove pan from heat and stir in vinegar.

Satay Glaze

MAKES ABOUT ¾ CUP

- 1 teaspoon vegetable oil
- 1 tablespoon red curry paste
- 2 garlic cloves, minced
- ½ teaspoon grated fresh ginger
- ½ cup canned coconut milk
- ¼ cup packed dark brown sugar
- 2 tablespoons peanut butter
- 1 tablespoon lime juice
- 2½ teaspoons fish sauce

Heat oil in small saucepan over medium heat until shimmering. Add curry paste, garlic, and ginger; cook, stirring constantly, until fragrant, about 1 minute. Whisk in coconut milk and sugar and bring to simmer. Whisk in peanut butter until smooth. Remove pan from heat and whisk in lime juice and fish sauce.

SIMPLE GRILLED PORK TENDERLOIN

WHY THIS RECIPE WORKS: To produce pork tenderloin with a rich crust and a tender, juicy interior, we used a half-grill fire and seared the roast on the hotter side of the grill. This allowed the exterior to develop flavorful browning before the interior was cooked through. Then we moved the meat to the cooler side of the grill to finish cooking gently. Seasoning the meat with a mixture of salt, cumin, and chipotle chile powder added smoky, savory flavor, and a touch of sugar encouraged browning. To add bright flavor and make the most of the fire, we grilled pineapple and red onion and, while the cooked pork rested, combined them with cilantro, a serrano chile, lime juice, and a bit of reserved spice mixture to make a quick salsa.

Grilled Pork Tenderloin with Grilled Pineapple–Red Onion Salsa

SERVES 4 TO 6

We prefer unenhanced pork in this recipe, but enhanced pork (injected with a salt solution; see page 181) can be used.

PORK
- 1½ teaspoons kosher salt
- 1½ teaspoons sugar
- ½ teaspoon ground cumin
- ½ teaspoon chipotle chile powder
- 2 (12- to 16-ounce) pork tenderloins, trimmed

SALSA
- ½ pineapple, peeled, cored, and cut lengthwise into 6 wedges
- 1 red onion, cut into 8 wedges through root end
- 4 teaspoons extra-virgin olive oil
- ½ cup minced fresh cilantro
- 1 serrano chile, stemmed, seeded, and minced
- 2 tablespoons lime juice, plus extra for seasoning
  Salt

1. FOR THE PORK: Combine salt, sugar, cumin, and chile powder in small bowl. Reserve ½ teaspoon spice mixture. Rub remaining spice mixture evenly over surface of both tenderloins. Transfer to large plate or rimmed baking sheet and refrigerate while preparing grill.

2A. FOR A CHARCOAL GRILL: Open bottom vent completely. Light large chimney starter filled with charcoal briquettes (6 quarts). When top coals are partially covered with ash, pour evenly over half of grill. Set cooking grate in place, cover, and open lid vent completely. Heat grill until hot, about 5 minutes.

2B. FOR A GAS GRILL: Turn all burners to high, cover, and heat grill until hot, about 15 minutes. Leave primary burner on high and turn off other burner(s).

3. Clean and oil cooking grate. Place tenderloins on hotter side of grill. Cover and cook, turning tenderloins every 2 minutes, until well browned on all sides, about 8 minutes.

4. FOR THE SALSA: Brush pineapple and onion with 1 teaspoon oil. Move tenderloins to cooler side of grill (6 to 8 inches from heat source) and place pineapple and onion on hotter side of grill. Cover and cook until pineapple and onion are charred on both sides and softened, 8 to 10 minutes, and until pork registers 140 degrees, 12 to 17 minutes, turning tenderloins every 5 minutes. As pineapple and onion and tenderloins reach desired level of doneness, transfer pineapple and onion to plate and transfer tenderloins to carving board. Tent tenderloins with aluminum foil and let rest for 10 minutes.

5. While tenderloins rest, roughly chop pineapple. Pulse pineapple, onion, cilantro, serrano, lime juice, reserved spice mixture, and remaining 1 tablespoon oil in food processor until mixture is roughly chopped, 4 to 6 pulses. Transfer to bowl and season with salt and extra lime juice to taste.

6. Slice tenderloins crosswise ½ inch thick. Serve with salsa.

GRILLED STUFFED PORK TENDERLOIN

WHY THIS RECIPE WORKS: Pork tenderloin has many advantages that make it an ideal candidate for the grill: It's quick cooking, is extremely tender, and has a uniform shape that allows for even cooking. But this cut is also mild and lean, making it prone to drying out. Stuffing this roast solves these problems by adding flavor and moisture. For more surface area for the filling and to help prevent leaks, we pounded, filled, then rolled the tenderloins. And for our flavor filling, we pulsed bold ingredients—such as olives, sun-dried tomatoes, and porcini mushrooms—in a food processor to produce an intense paste that didn't ooze out. When it came time to fire up the grill, we found that a two-level fire, with the coals spread over half the grill, allowed the pork to cook evenly without drying out. Our last touch was a brown sugar rub on the exterior of each tenderloin, which boosted browning significantly.

Grilled Stuffed Pork Tenderloin
SERVES 6 TO 8

We prefer natural to enhanced pork (pork that has been injected with a salt solution to increase moistness and flavor; see page 181) for this recipe.

    4   teaspoons packed dark brown sugar
        Salt and pepper
    2   (1¼- to 1½-pound) pork tenderloins, trimmed

    1   recipe stuffing (recipes follow)
    1   cup baby spinach
    2   tablespoons olive oil

1. Combine sugar, 1 teaspoon salt, and 1 teaspoon pepper in bowl. Cut each tenderloin in half horizontally, stopping ½ inch from edge so halves remain attached. Open up tenderloins, cover with plastic wrap, and pound to ¼-inch thickness. Trim any ragged edges to create rough rectangle about 10 inches by 6 inches. Season interior of pork with salt and pepper.

2. With long side of pork facing you, spread half of stuffing mixture over bottom half of pork followed by ½ cup of spinach. Roll away from you into tight cylinder, taking care not to squeeze stuffing out ends. Position tenderloin seam side down, evenly space 5 pieces kitchen twine underneath, and tie. Repeat with remaining tenderloin, stuffing, and spinach.

3A. FOR A CHARCOAL GRILL: Open bottom vent completely. Light large chimney starter filled with charcoal briquettes (6 quarts). When top coals are partially covered with ash, pour evenly over half of grill. Set cooking grate in place, cover, and open lid vent completely. Heat grill until hot, about 5 minutes.

3B. FOR A GAS GRILL: Turn all burners to high, cover, and heat grill until hot, about 15 minutes. Leave primary burner on high and turn off other burner(s). (Adjust primary burner as needed during cooking to maintain grill temperature between 325 and 350 degrees.)

4. Clean and oil cooking grate. Coat pork with oil, then rub entire surface with brown sugar mixture. Place pork on cool side of grill, cover, and cook until meat registers 140 degrees, 25 to 30 minutes, rotating pork halfway through cooking.

5. Transfer pork to carving board, tent loosely with aluminum foil, and let rest for 20 minutes. Remove twine, slice pork into ½-inch-thick slices, and serve.

Olive and Sun-Dried Tomato Stuffing

MAKES ABOUT 1 CUP

½ cup pitted kalamata olives
½ cup oil-packed sun-dried tomatoes, rinsed and chopped coarse
4 anchovy fillets, rinsed
2 garlic cloves, minced
1 teaspoon minced fresh thyme
1 teaspoon grated lemon zest
Salt and pepper

Pulse all ingredients except salt and pepper in food processor until coarsely chopped, 5 to 10 pulses; season with salt and pepper to taste.

Porcini and Artichoke Stuffing

MAKES ABOUT 1 CUP

Avoid jarred or canned artichokes; frozen artichokes have a much fresher flavor.

½ ounce dried porcini mushrooms, rinsed and minced
3 ounces frozen artichoke hearts, thawed and patted dry (¾ cup)
1 ounce Parmesan cheese, grated (½ cup)
¼ cup oil-packed sun-dried tomatoes, rinsed and chopped coarse
¼ cup fresh parsley leaves
2 tablespoons pine nuts, toasted
2 garlic cloves, minced
1 teaspoon grated lemon zest plus 2 teaspoons juice
Salt and pepper

Pulse all ingredients except salt and pepper in food processor until coarsely chopped, 5 to 10 pulses; season with salt and pepper to taste.

GRILLED STUFFED PORK LOIN ROAST

WHY THIS RECIPE WORKS: Center-cut pork loin is an especially lean cut, making it difficult to cook without drying out. We wanted to cook our pork loin on the grill but keep it moist using an approach other than traditional brines or sauces. We decided to use a moist, well-seasoned stuffing (and careful cooking) so our grilled pork loin would be juicy and flavorful.

We bought a short and wide roast, more square than cylindrical. This shape only required a few straight, short cuts to open to a long, flat sheet that was easy to fill and roll up. The best stuffing required both a deep flavor to counter the pork's rather bland taste and a texture thick enough to stay put. Poaching apples and cranberries in a blend of apple cider, apple cider vinegar, and spices developed a filling with the dense, chewy consistency we wanted. And this process had an added bonus—we had ample poaching liquid left, which could be reduced to a glaze. We had already decided not to give the loin a preliminary sear, which can create a tough exterior, but found we missed the brown color that searing produces. Rolling the loin in our glaze gave it a beautifully burnished finish.

Grilled Pork Loin with Apple-Cranberry Filling

SERVES 6

This recipe is best prepared with a loin that is 7 to 8 inches long and 4 to 5 inches wide and not enhanced (injected with a salt solution; see page 181). To make cutting the pork easier, freeze it for 30 minutes. If mustard seeds are unavailable, stir an equal amount of whole grain mustard into the filling after the apples have been processed. For a spicier stuffing, use the larger amount of cayenne. If you'd like to use wood chunks instead of wood chips when using a charcoal grill, substitute 2 medium wood chunks, soaked in water for 1 hour, for the wood chip packet. The pork loin can be stuffed and tied a day ahead of time, but don't season the exterior until you are ready to grill.

FILLING

1½ cups (4 ounces) dried apples
1 cup apple cider
¾ cup packed light brown sugar
½ cup cider vinegar
½ cup dried cranberries
1 large shallot, halved lengthwise and sliced thin crosswise
1 tablespoon grated fresh ginger
1 tablespoon yellow mustard seeds
½ teaspoon ground allspice
⅛–¼ teaspoon cayenne pepper

PORK

1 (2½-pound) boneless center-cut pork loin roast, trimmed
  Salt and pepper
2 cups wood chips, soaked in water for
  15 minutes and drained

1. FOR THE FILLING: Bring all ingredients to simmer in medium saucepan over medium-high heat. Cover, reduce heat to low, and cook until apples are very soft, about 20 minutes. Pour mixture through fine-mesh strainer set over bowl, pressing with back of spoon to extract as much liquid as possible. Return liquid to saucepan and simmer over medium-high heat until reduced to ⅓ cup, about 5 minutes; reserve for glazing. Pulse apple mixture in food processor until coarsely chopped, about 15 pulses. Transfer filling to bowl and refrigerate until needed.

2. FOR THE PORK: Position roast fat side up. Insert knife ½ inch from bottom of roast and cut horizontally, stopping ½ inch before edge. Open up this flap. Cut through thicker half of roast about ½ inch from bottom, stopping about ½ inch before edge. Open up this flap. Repeat until pork is even ½-inch thickness throughout. If uneven, cover with plastic wrap and use meat pounder to even out. Season interior with salt and pepper and spread filling in even layer, leaving ½-inch border. Roll tightly and tie with kitchen twine at 1-inch intervals. Season with salt and pepper.

3. Using large piece of heavy-duty aluminum foil, wrap soaked chips in foil packet and cut several vent holes in top.

4A. FOR A CHARCOAL GRILL: Open bottom vent halfway. Light large chimney starter three-quarters filled with charcoal briquettes (4½ quarts). When top coals are partially covered with ash, pour evenly over half of grill. Place wood chip packet on coals. Set cooking grate in place, cover, and open lid vent halfway. Heat grill until hot and wood chips are smoking, about 5 minutes.

4B. FOR A GAS GRILL: Place wood chip packet over primary burner. Turn all burners to high, cover, and heat grill until hot and wood chips are smoking, about 15 minutes. Leave primary burner on medium-high and turn off other burner(s). (Adjust primary burner as needed to maintain grill temperature of 300 to 325 degrees.)

5. Clean and oil cooking grate. Place pork, fat side up, on cooler side of grill, cover (position lid vent over roast if using charcoal), and cook until meat registers 130 to 135 degrees, 55 minutes to 1 hour 10 minutes, flipping halfway through cooking.

6. Brush roast evenly with reserved glaze. (Reheat glaze, if necessary, to make it spreadable.) Continue to cook until glaze is glossy and meat registers 145 degrees, 5 to 10 minutes longer. Transfer to carving board, tent loosely with foil, and let rest for 15 minutes. Remove twine, cut roast into ½-inch-thick slices, and serve.

HOW TO STUFF A PORK LOIN

1. Position the roast fat side up. Insert a knife ½ inch from the bottom of the roast and cut horizontally, stopping ½ inch before the edge. Open up this flap.

2. Cut through the thicker half of the roast about ½ inch from the bottom, stopping about ½ inch before the edge. Open up this flap.

3. Repeat until the pork loin is an even ½-inch thickness throughout. If uneven, cover with plastic wrap and use a meat pounder to even out.

4. With the long side of the meat facing you, season the meat and spread the filling, leaving a ½-inch border on all sides.

5. Starting from the short side, roll the pork loin tightly, then tie the roast with kitchen twine at 1-inch intervals.

GRILL-ROASTED PORK LOIN

WHY THIS RECIPE WORKS: When we're looking to dress up an outdoor dinner—and offer guests more than burgers or grilled chicken—we like to serve a juicy, crisp crusted pork loin. But because the roasts available at the supermarket nowadays are so incredibly lean, this cut of meat can dry out considerably when cooked with the dry heat of the grill. We planned to bring back the juiciness and produce a succulent roast with a deep brown crust and aromatic, smoke-flavored meat.

First, we chose the best cut. Our top choice—the blade-end roast—was moist and flavorful and was the hands-down winner over center-cut, sirloin, and tenderloin roasts. Brining ensured that our finished roast met with rave reviews from testers and stayed juicy and moist, and a generous coating of black pepper—or our own spicy rub—provided ample flavoring. We then used a two-step grilling process, searing the roast directly over hot coals for a nice crust and finishing it over indirect heat, so as not to overcook it. The final step was removing the roast from the grill when the internal temperature was just shy of done, then allowing it to rest until the temperature rose and the meat was juicy and tender.

Grill-Roasted Pork Loin

SERVES 4 TO 6

If the pork is enhanced (injected with a salt solution; see page 181), do not brine and add 1 tablespoon salt to the pepper or spice rub. Two medium wood chunks, soaked in water for 1 hour, can be substituted for the wood chip packet on a charcoal grill.

- ¼ cup salt
- 1 (2½- to 3-pound) boneless blade-end pork loin roast, trimmed and tied with kitchen twine at 1½-inch intervals
- 2 tablespoons olive oil
- 1 tablespoon pepper or 1 recipe spice rub (recipes follow)
- 2 cups wood chips, soaked in water for 15 minutes and drained

1. Dissolve salt in 2 quarts cold water in large container. Submerge pork loin in brine, cover, and refrigerate for 1 to 1½ hours. Remove pork from brine and pat dry with paper towels. Rub pork loin with oil and coat with pepper. Let sit at room temperature for 1 hour.

2. Using large piece of heavy-duty aluminum foil, wrap soaked chips in foil packet and cut several vent holes in top.

3A. FOR A CHARCOAL GRILL: Open bottom vent halfway. Light large chimney starter three-quarters filled with charcoal briquettes (4½ quarts). When top coals are partially covered with ash, pour evenly over half of grill. Place wood chip packet on coals. Set cooking grate in place, cover, and open lid vent halfway. Heat grill until hot and wood chips are smoking, about 5 minutes.

3B. FOR A GAS GRILL: Place wood chip packet directly on primary burner. Turn all burners to high, cover, and heat grill until hot and wood chips are smoking, about 15 minutes. Leave primary burner on high and turn off other burner(s). (Adjust primary burner as needed during cooking to maintain grill temperature between 300 and 325 degrees.)

4. Clean and oil cooking grate. Place pork loin on hot side of grill, fat side up, and cook (covered if using gas) until well browned on all sides, 10 to 12 minutes, turning as needed. Move to cool side of grill, positioning roast parallel with and as close as possible to heat. Cover (position lid vent over roast if using charcoal) and cook for 20 minutes.

5. Rotate roast 180 degrees, cover, and continue to cook until meat registers 145 degrees, 10 to 30 minutes longer, depending on thickness of roast.

6. Transfer roast to carving board, tent loosely with aluminum foil, and let rest for 15 minutes. Remove twine, cut roast into ½-inch-thick slices, and serve.

Chili-Mustard Spice Rub

MAKES ABOUT 2 TABLESPOONS

This rub packs some heat, so use the lesser amount of cayenne if you want a milder rub.

- 2 teaspoons chili powder
- 2 teaspoons dry mustard
- 1 teaspoon ground cumin
- ½–1 teaspoon cayenne pepper

Combine all ingredients in bowl.

SMOKED PORK LOIN

WHY THIS RECIPE WORKS: For a smoky, company-worthy pork roast that cooked in just a couple of hours, we looked to quick-cooking pork loin. Choosing a blade-end roast over a center-cut roast meant more fat and thus more flavor. An overnight rub of salt and brown sugar before grilling helped season the roast, kept it juicy, and delivered a nicely caramelized exterior. Low-and-slow indirect cooking was key for an evenly cooked, tender roast, so we poured lit coals over a layer of unlit coals to create a fire that wouldn't require refueling. Two cups of wood chips (in a single packet) provided just enough smoke to enhance the roast's meaty flavor without overwhelming it. A dried fruit chutney was the perfect complement to the smoky meat.

Smoked Pork Loin with Dried Fruit Chutney

SERVES 6

A blade roast is our preferred cut, but a center-cut boneless loin roast can also be used. If the pork is enhanced (injected with a salt solution; see page 181) skip step 1, but season with sugar-salt mixture in step 4. Any variety of wood chip except mesquite will work; we prefer hickory. If you'd like to use wood chunks instead of wood chips when using a charcoal grill, substitute 2 medium wood chunk(s), soaked in water for 1 hour, for the wood chip packet. To help maintain a constant charcoal grill temperature, do not remove the lid any more than necessary during cooking.

PORK

½ cup packed light brown sugar

¼ cup kosher salt

1 (3½- to 4-pound) blade-end boneless pork loin roast, trimmed

2 cups wood chips

1 (13 by 9-inch) disposable aluminum roasting pan (if using charcoal) or 1 (9-inch) disposable aluminum pie plate (if using gas)

CHUTNEY

¾ cup dry white wine

½ cup dried apricots, diced

½ cup dried cherries

¼ cup white wine vinegar

3 tablespoons water

3 tablespoons packed light brown sugar

1 shallot, minced

2 tablespoons grated fresh ginger

1 tablespoon unsalted butter

1 tablespoon Dijon mustard

1½ teaspoons dry mustard

Kosher salt

1. FOR THE PORK: Combine sugar and salt in small bowl. Tie roast with twine at 1-inch intervals. Rub sugar-salt mixture over entire surface of roast, making sure roast is evenly coated. Wrap roast tightly in plastic wrap, set in rimmed baking sheet, and refrigerate for at least 6 hours or up to 24 hours.

2. Just before grilling, soak wood chips in water for 15 minutes, then drain. Using large piece of heavy-duty aluminum foil, wrap soaked chips in 8 by 4½-inch foil packet. (Make sure chips do not poke holes in sides or bottom of packet.) Cut 2 evenly spaced 2-inch slits in top of packet.

3A. FOR A CHARCOAL GRILL: Open bottom vent halfway. Arrange 25 unlit charcoal briquettes over half of grill and place disposable pan filled with 3 cups water on other side of grill. Light large chimney starter two-thirds filled with charcoal briquettes (4 quarts). When top coals are partially covered with ash, pour evenly over unlit briquettes. Place wood chip packet on coals. Set cooking grate in place, cover, and open lid

vent halfway. Heat grill until hot and wood chips are smoking, about 5 minutes. (Adjust top and bottom vents as needed to maintain grill temperature of 300 degrees.)

3B. FOR A GAS GRILL: Remove cooking grate and place wood chip packet directly on primary burner. Place disposable pie plate filled with 1 inch water directly on other burner(s). Set grate in place, turn all burners to high, cover, and heat grill until hot and wood chips are smoking, about 15 minutes. Turn primary burner to medium and turn off other burner(s). (Adjust primary burner as needed to maintain grill temperature of 300 degrees.)

4. Clean and oil cooking grate. Unwrap roast and pat dry with paper towels. Place roast on grill (cooler side if using charcoal), directly over water pan. Cover (position lid vent over roast if using charcoal) and cook until meat registers 140 degrees, 1½ to 2 hours, rotating roast 180 degrees after 45 minutes.

5. FOR THE CHUTNEY: Combine wine, apricots, cherries, vinegar, water, sugar, shallot, and ginger in medium saucepan. Bring to simmer over medium heat. Cover and cook until fruit is softened, 10 minutes. Remove lid and reduce heat to medium-low. Add butter, Dijon, and dry mustard and continue to cook until slightly thickened, 4 to 6 minutes. Remove from heat and season with salt to taste. Transfer to bowl and let stand at room temperature.

6. Transfer roast to carving board, tent with foil, and let rest for 30 minutes. Remove and discard twine. Slice ¼ inch thick and serve, passing chutney separately.

GRILLED BONE-IN PORK ROAST

WHY THIS RECIPE WORKS: Grilling a bulky cut of meat like a pork roast may sound difficult, but we found that a tender, quick-cooking center-cut rib roast and a simple salt rub were all that we needed for a juicy grilled roast with a thick mahogany crust. We grilled it over indirect heat (on the cooler side of the grill) so it could cook through slowly, adding a single soaked wood chunk or a small amount of wood chips to the fire for a subtle tinge of smoke flavor. After a little more than an hour on the grill, our roast was tender and juicy, with plenty of rich, deep flavor. For the perfect counterpoint to the roast's richness, we whipped up a fresh orange salsa with bright citrus and fresh herbs, jalapeño, and a warm touch of cumin.

Grill-Roasted Bone-In Pork Rib Roast

SERVES 6 TO 8

If you buy a blade-end roast (sometimes called a "rib-end roast"), tie it into a uniform shape with kitchen twine at 1-inch intervals; this step is unnecessary with a center-cut roast. For easier carving, ask the butcher to remove the tip of the chine bone and to cut the remainder of the chine bone between each rib. One medium wood chunk, soaked in water for 1 hour, can be substituted for the wood chip packet on a charcoal grill.

Orange Salsa with Cuban Flavors

MAKES ABOUT 2½ CUPS

To make this salsa spicier, add the reserved chile seeds.

½ teaspoon grated orange zest plus 5 oranges peeled
   and segmented; each segment quartered crosswise
½ cup minced red onion
1 jalapeño chile, stemmed, seeds reserved, and minced
2 tablespoons lime juice
2 tablespoons minced fresh parsley
1 tablespoon extra-virgin olive oil
2 teaspoons packed brown sugar
1½ teaspoons distilled white vinegar
1½ teaspoons minced fresh oregano
1 garlic clove, minced
½ teaspoon ground cumin
½ teaspoon salt
½ teaspoon pepper

Combine all ingredients in medium bowl.

1 (4- to 5-pound) bone-in center-cut pork rib roast, tip of
   chine bone removed, fat trimmed to ¼-inch thickness
4 teaspoons kosher salt
1 cup wood chips, soaked in water
   for 15 minutes and drained
1½ teaspoons pepper
1 recipe Orange Salsa with Cuban Flavors
   (optional; recipe follows)

1. Pat roast dry with paper towels. Using sharp knife, cut slits in surface fat layer, spaced 1 inch apart, in crosshatch pattern, being careful not to cut into meat. Season roast with salt. Wrap with plastic wrap and refrigerate for at least 6 hours or up to 24 hours.

2. Using large piece of heavy-duty aluminum foil, wrap soaked chips in foil packet and cut several vent holes in top.

3A. FOR A CHARCOAL GRILL: Open bottom vent halfway. Light large chimney starter filled with charcoal briquettes (6 quarts). When top coals are partially covered with ash, pour into steeply banked pile against side of grill. Place wood chip packet on coals. Set cooking grate in place, cover, and open lid vent halfway. Heat grill until hot and wood chips are smoking, about 5 minutes.

3B. FOR A GAS GRILL: Place wood chip packet over primary burner. Turn all burners to high, cover, and heat grill until hot and wood chips are smoking, about 15 minutes. Turn primary burner to medium-high and turn off other burner(s). (Adjust primary burner as needed during cooking to maintain grill temperature around 325 degrees.)

4. Clean and oil cooking grate. Unwrap roast and season with pepper. Place roast on grate with meat near, but not over, coals and flames and bones facing away from coals and flames. Cover (position lid vent over meat if using charcoal) and cook until meat registers 140 degrees, 1¼ to 1½ hours.

5. Transfer roast to carving board, tent loosely with aluminum foil, and let rest for 30 minutes. Carve into thick slices by cutting between ribs. Serve, passing salsa, if using, separately.

GRILLED PORK KEBABS WITH HOISIN GLAZE

WHY THIS RECIPE WORKS: To bring out the best in mild pork tenderloins, we cut the meat into chunks and let them soak in salt. This simple mixture changed the structure of the raw meat's exterior proteins so that it wouldn't lose moisture on the grill. For a flavorful, sticky glaze that clung to the pork (and not to the grill), we combined five-spice powder, garlic powder, cornstarch, and hoisin sauce. Applying the glaze twice meant the pork developed great char from the sweet hoisin sauce during grilling and still had a thick, tasty coating when the kebabs were served.

Grilled Pork Kebabs with Hoisin Glaze

SERVES 4

You will need four 12-inch metal skewers for this recipe. We prefer natural pork, but if your pork is enhanced (injected with a salt solution; see page 181), do not salt it in step 1.

2 (12-ounce) pork tenderloins, trimmed and
   cut into 1-inch chunks
1 teaspoon kosher salt
1½ teaspoons five-spice powder
¾ teaspoon garlic powder
½ teaspoon cornstarch
4½ tablespoons hoisin sauce
   Vegetable oil spray
2 scallions, thinly sliced

1. Toss pork and salt together in large bowl and let sit for 20 minutes. Meanwhile, whisk five-spice powder, garlic powder, and cornstarch together in bowl. Add hoisin to five-spice mixture and stir to combine. Set aside 1½ tablespoons hoisin mixture.

2. Add remaining hoisin mixture to pork and toss to coat. Thread pork onto four 12-inch metal skewers, leaving ¼ inch between pieces. Spray both sides of meat generously with oil spray.

3A. FOR A CHARCOAL GRILL: Open bottom vent completely. Light large chimney starter filled with charcoal briquettes (6 quarts). When top coals are partially covered with ash, pour evenly over half of grill. Set cooking grate in place, cover, and open lid vent completely. Heat grill until hot, about 5 minutes.

3B. FOR A GAS GRILL: Turn all burners to high, cover, and heat grill until hot, about 15 minutes. Leave primary burner on high and turn off other burner(s).

4. Clean and oil cooking grate. Place skewers on hotter side of grill and grill until well charred, 3 to 4 minutes. Flip skewers, brush with reserved hoisin mixture, and continue to grill until second side is well charred and meat registers 140 degrees, 3 to 4 minutes longer. Transfer to serving platter, tent loosely with aluminum foil, and let rest for 5 minutes. Sprinkle with scallions and serve.

PULLED PORK

WHY THIS RECIPE WORKS: Pulled pork is classic summertime party food: slow-cooked pork roast, shredded and seasoned, served on the most basic of hamburger buns (or sliced white bread), with just enough of your favorite barbecue sauce, a couple of dill pickle chips, and a topping of coleslaw. However, many barbecue procedures demand the regular attention of the cook for eight hours or more. We wanted to find a way to make moist, fork-tender pulled pork without the marathon cooking time and constant attention to the grill.

After testing shoulder roasts (also called Boston butt), fresh ham, and picnic roasts, we determined that the shoulder roast, which has the most fat, retained the most moisture and flavor

during a long, slow cook. We massaged a spicy chili rub into the meat, then wrapped the roast in plastic wrap and refrigerated it for at least three hours to "marinate." The roast is first cooked on the grill to absorb smoky flavor (from wood chips—no smoker required), then finished in the oven. Finally, we let the pork rest in a paper bag so the meat would steam and any remaining collagen would break down, allowing the flavorful juices to be reabsorbed. We also developed a pair of sauce recipes to please barbecue fans with different tastes.

Barbecued Pulled Pork
SERVES 8

Pulled pork can be made with a fresh ham or picnic roast, although our preference is for Boston butt. If using a fresh ham or picnic roast, remove the skin by cutting through it with the tip of a chef's knife; slide the blade just under the skin and work around to loosen it while pulling it off with your other hand. Four medium wood chunks, soaked in water for 1 hour, can be substituted for the wood chip packets on a charcoal grill. Serve on plain white bread or warmed rolls with dill pickle chips and coleslaw.

1 (6- to 8-pound) bone-in Boston butt roast
¾ cup Dry Rub for Barbecue (recipe follows)
4 cups wood chips, soaked in water for 15 minutes and drained
1 (13 by 9-inch) disposable aluminum roasting pan
2 cups barbecue sauce (recipes follow)

1. Pat pork dry with paper towels, then massage dry rub into meat. Wrap meat in plastic wrap and refrigerate for at least 3 hours or up to 3 days.

2. At least 1 hour prior to cooking, remove roast from refrigerator, unwrap, and let sit at room temperature. Using 2 large pieces of heavy-duty aluminum foil, wrap soaked chips in 2 foil packets and cut several vent holes in tops.

3A. FOR A CHARCOAL GRILL: Open bottom vent halfway. Light large chimney starter three-quarters filled with charcoal briquettes (4½ quarts). When top coals are partially covered with ash, pour evenly over half of grill. Place wood chip packets on coals. Set cooking grate in place, cover, and open lid vent halfway. Heat grill until hot and wood chips are smoking, about 5 minutes.

3B. FOR A GAS GRILL: Place wood chip packets directly on primary burner. Turn all burners to high, cover, and heat grill until hot and wood chips are smoking, about 15 minutes. Turn primary burner to medium-high and turn off other burner(s). (Adjust primary burner as needed to maintain grill temperature around 325 degrees.)

4. Set roast in disposable pan, place on cool side of grill, and cook for 3 hours. During final 20 minutes of cooking, adjust oven rack to lower-middle position and heat oven to 325 degrees.

5. Wrap disposable pan with heavy-duty foil and cook in oven until meat is fork-tender, about 2 hours.

6. Carefully slide foil-wrapped pan with roast into brown paper bag. Crimp end shut and let rest for 1 hour.

7. Transfer roast to carving board and unwrap. Separate roast into muscle sections, removing fat, if desired, and tearing meat into shreds with your fingers. Place shredded meat in large bowl and toss with 1 cup barbecue sauce. Serve, passing remaining sauce separately.

Dry Rub for Barbecue
MAKES ABOUT 1 CUP

You can adjust the proportions of spices in this all-purpose rub or add or subtract a spice, as you wish.

¼ cup paprika
2 tablespoons chili powder
2 tablespoons ground cumin
2 tablespoons packed dark brown sugar
2 tablespoons salt
1 tablespoon dried oregano
1 tablespoon granulated sugar
1 tablespoon black pepper
1 tablespoon white pepper
1–2 teaspoons cayenne pepper

Combine all ingredients in small bowl.

Eastern North Carolina Barbecue Sauce
MAKES ABOUT 2 CUPS

This sauce can be refrigerated in an airtight container for up to 4 days.

1 cup distilled white vinegar
1 cup cider vinegar
1 tablespoon sugar
1 tablespoon red pepper flakes
1 tablespoon hot sauce
  Salt and pepper

Mix all ingredients except salt and pepper together in bowl and season with salt and pepper to taste.

Mid-South Carolina Mustard Sauce
MAKES ABOUT 2½ CUPS

This sauce can be refrigerated in an airtight container for up to 4 days.

1 cup cider vinegar
1 cup vegetable oil
6 tablespoons Dijon mustard
2 tablespoons maple syrup or honey
4 teaspoons Worcestershire sauce
1 teaspoon hot sauce
  Salt and pepper

Mix all ingredients except salt and pepper together in bowl and season with salt and pepper to taste.

SWEET AND TANGY GRILLED COUNTRY-STYLE PORK RIBS

WHY THIS RECIPE WORKS: In many ways, country-style ribs are actually more like pork chops—a point that can make them a little confusing for home cooks. Because they feature a combination of light, lean loin meat and richly flavored, fattier shoulder, the trick is figuring out how to grill them so that the white meat is juicy and the dark meat is tender. We applied a salty dry rub to boost the ribs' seasoning and help them stay moist, particularly the faster-drying light meat. We found that a doneness temperature of 150 degrees—a compromise between the usual 135 to 140 degrees required for light meat and 175 degrees for dark meat—delivered optimal results. Starting the ribs over high heat and then finishing on the cooler side of the grill ensured good browning and an evenly cooked interior. While the ribs were on the cooler side of the grill, we basted them with a sweet and tangy sauce of ketchup, molasses, Worcestershire sauce, cider vinegar, and Dijon mustard. Stirring in grated onion, minced garlic, chili powder, cayenne, and black pepper gave the sauce some depth.

Sweet and Tangy Grilled Country-Style Pork Ribs
SERVES 4 TO 6

Be sure to carefully trim the pork to reduce the number of flare-ups when the pork is grilled. This recipe requires refrigerating the spice-rubbed ribs for at least 1 hour or up to 24 hours before grilling.

PORK
4 teaspoons packed brown sugar
1 tablespoon kosher salt
1 tablespoon chili powder
⅛ teaspoon cayenne pepper
4 pounds bone-in country-style pork ribs, trimmed

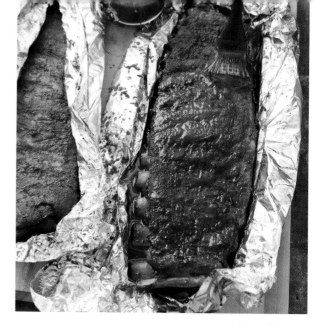

SAUCE

- 1 cup ketchup
- 5 tablespoons molasses
- 3 tablespoons cider vinegar
- 2 tablespoons Worcestershire sauce
- 2 tablespoons Dijon mustard
- ¼ teaspoon pepper
- 2 tablespoons vegetable oil
- ⅓ cup grated onion
- 1 garlic clove, minced
- 1 teaspoon chili powder
- ¼ teaspoon cayenne pepper

1. FOR THE PORK: Combine sugar, salt, chili powder and cayenne in bowl. Rub mixture all over ribs. Wrap tightly in plastic wrap and refrigerate for at least 1 hour or up to 24 hours.

2. FOR THE SAUCE: Whisk ketchup, molasses, vinegar, Worcestershire, mustard, and pepper together in bowl. Heat oil in medium saucepan over medium heat until shimmering. Add onion and garlic; cook until onion is softened, 2 to 4 minutes. Add chili powder and cayenne and cook until fragrant, about 30 seconds. Whisk in ketchup mixture and bring to boil. Reduce heat to medium-low and simmer gently for 5 minutes. Set aside ½ cup of sauce for basting pork and reserve remaining sauce for serving. (Sauce can be refrigerated for up to 1 week.)

3A. FOR A CHARCOAL GRILL: Open bottom vent halfway. Light large chimney starter filled with charcoal briquettes (6 quarts). When top coals are partially covered with ash, pour evenly over half of grill. Set cooking grate in place, cover, and open lid vent halfway. Heat grill until hot, about 5 minutes.

3B. FOR A GAS GRILL: Turn all burners to high, cover and heat grill until hot, about 15 minutes. Leave primary burner on high and turn other burner(s) off to maintain grill temperature around 350 degrees.

4. Clean and oil cooking grate. Place ribs over hotter part of grill and cook until well browned on both sides, 4 to 7 minutes. Move ribs to cooler part of grill and brush top sides with ¼ cup sauce. Cover and cook 6 minutes. Flip ribs and brush with remaining ¼ cup sauce. Cover and continue to cook until pork registers 150 degrees, 5 to 10 minutes longer. Transfer ribs to serving platter, tent loosely with aluminum foil and let rest for 10 minutes. Serve, passing sauce separately.

KANSAS CITY RIBS

WHY THIS RECIPE WORKS: Kansas City ribs are slow-smoked pork ribs slathered in a sauce so thick, sweet, and sticky that you need a case of wet naps to get your hands clean after eating them. But authentic ribs can take all day to prepare. We knew we could come up with a faster method for Kansas City ribs—one that would produce the same fall-off-the-bone, tender smoky meat of the long-cooked original recipe.

We quickly learned that spareribs, which are well marbled with fat, produce moist, tender ribs, but some racks are so big they barely fit on the grill. We turned to a more manageable cut, referred to as "St. Louis" ribs, which is a narrower, rectangular rack that offers all the taste of whole spareribs without any of the trouble. A spice rub added flavor and encouraged a savory crust on the meat.

We barbecued the ribs, covered with foil, over indirect heat for four hours—the foil traps some of the steam over the meat, so that it cooks up tender, not dry. Using wood chips on the grill imparted the meat with great smoky flavor. For sticky, saucy ribs, we brushed the ribs all over with barbecue sauce and finished them in the gentle, even heat of the oven until they were tender and falling off the bone.

Kansas City Sticky Ribs
SERVES 4 TO 6

We like St. Louis–style racks, but if you can't find them, baby back ribs will work fine; reduce the oven time in step 6 to 1 to 2 hours.

RIBS

- 3 tablespoons paprika
- 2 tablespoons brown sugar
- 1 tablespoon salt
- 1 tablespoon black pepper
- ¼ teaspoon cayenne pepper
- 2 (2½- to 3-pound) full racks pork spareribs (see note), trimmed of any large pieces of fat and membrane removed

SAUCE

- 1 tablespoon vegetable oil plus more for cooking grate
- 1 onion, minced
-   Salt
- 4 cups low-sodium chicken broth

1 cup root beer

1 cup cider vinegar

1 cup dark corn syrup

½ cup light or mild molasses

½ cup tomato paste

½ cup ketchup

2 tablespoons brown mustard

1 tablespoon hot sauce

½ teaspoon garlic powder

¼ teaspoon liquid smoke

 Pepper

2 cups wood chips, soaked, drained, and sealed in a foil packet

REMOVING THE MEMBRANE FOR KANSAS CITY RIBS

Ribs have a papery membrane on the underside that can make it hard to pull the meat off the bone. Before cooking, loosen this membrane with the tip of a paring knife and, with the aid of a paper towel, pull it off slowly, all in one piece.

1. FOR THE RIBS: Combine the paprika, sugar, salt, black pepper, and cayenne in a bowl. Pat the ribs dry with paper towels, and rub them evenly with the spice mixture. Wrap the meat in plastic wrap and let sit at room temperature for at least 1 hour, or refrigerate for up to 24 hours. (If refrigerated, let sit at room temperature for 1 hour before grilling.)

2. FOR THE SAUCE: Meanwhile, heat the oil in a large saucepan over medium heat until shimmering. Add the onion and a pinch of salt and cook until softened, 5 to 7 minutes. Whisk in the broth, root beer, vinegar, corn syrup, molasses, tomato paste, ketchup, mustard, hot sauce, and garlic powder. Bring the sauce to a simmer and cook, stirring occasionally, until reduced to 4 cups, about 1 hour. Stir in the liquid smoke. Cool to room temperature, and season with salt and pepper to taste. Measure out 1 cup of the barbecue sauce for cooking; set aside the remaining sauce for serving. (The sauce can be refrigerated in an airtight container for up to 4 days.)

3A. FOR A CHARCOAL GRILL: Open the bottom grill vents halfway. Light a large chimney starter three-quarters full with charcoal (4½ quarts, about 75 briquettes) and allow it to burn until the charcoal is partially covered with a layer of fine gray ash, about 20 minutes. Pour the coals into a steeply banked pile against 1 side of the grill and place the wood chip packet on top of the coals. Set the cooking grate in place, cover, and open the lid vents halfway. Heat the grill until hot and the wood chips begin to smoke heavily, about 5 minutes.

3B. FOR A GAS GRILL: Place the wood chip packet directly on the primary burner. Turn all the burners to high, cover, and heat the grill until hot and the wood chips begin to smoke heavily, about 15 minutes. Turn the primary burner to medium-high and turn off the other burner(s). (Adjust the primary burner as needed to maintain the grill temperature around 325 degrees.)

4. Use a grill brush to scrape the cooking grate clean. Lightly dip a wad of paper towels in oil; holding the wad with tongs, wipe the cooking grate. Place the ribs, meat side down, on the cooler side of the grill, away from the coals or flames; the ribs may overlap slightly. Place a sheet of foil on top of the ribs. Cover (positioning the lid vents over the meat if using charcoal) and cook until the ribs are deep red and smoky, about 2 hours, flipping and rotating the racks halfway through. During the final 20 minutes of grilling, adjust an oven rack to the middle position and heat the oven to 250 degrees.

5. Remove the ribs from the grill, brush them evenly with the 1 cup sauce reserved for cooking, and wrap tightly with foil. Lay the foil-wrapped ribs on a rimmed baking sheet and continue to cook in the oven until tender and a fork inserted into the ribs meets no resistance, 1½ to 2½ hours.

6. Remove the ribs from the oven and let rest, still wrapped, for 30 minutes. Unwrap the ribs and brush them thickly with 1 cup of the sauce set aside for serving. Slice the ribs between the bones and serve with the remaining sauce.

MEMPHIS DRY RUBBED PORK RIBS

WHY THIS RECIPE WORKS: Memphis pit masters pride themselves on their all-day barbecued pork ribs with a dark bark-like crust and distinctive chew. Up for a challenge, we decided to come up with our own version, but one that wouldn't involve tending a grill all day.

After failing to grill the ribs in a reasonable amount of time (less than seven hours), we opted for a grill-to-oven approach. We started first with the grill. For a fire that would maintain the key amount of indirect heat (roughly 250 to 275 degrees), we turned to a modified two-level fire where the hot coals are arranged over half the grill. In addition, we stowed a pan of water underneath the cooking grate on the cooler side of the grill, where it would absorb heat and work to keep the temperature stable, as well as help keep the meat moister. Then we transferred the ribs to a wire rack set over a rimmed baking sheet and cooked them in a moderate oven until tender and thick-crusted. We even mimicked our grill setup by pouring 1½ cups water into the rimmed baking sheet. In all, we'd shaved more than three hours off of our shortest recipe.

Memphis-Style Barbecued Spareribs

SERVES 4 TO 6

Don't remove the membrane that runs along the bone side of the ribs; it prevents some of the fat from rendering out and is authentic to this style of ribs.

- 1 recipe Spice Rub (recipe follows)
- 2 (2½- to 3-pound) racks St. Louis–style spareribs, trimmed
- ½ cup apple juice
- 3 tablespoons cider vinegar
- 1 (13 by 9-inch) disposable aluminum roasting pan (if using charcoal) or 2 (9-inch) disposable aluminum pie plates (if using gas)
- ¾ cup wood chips, soaked in water for 15 minutes and drained

1. Rub 2 tablespoons Spice Rub on each side of each rack of ribs. Let ribs sit at room temperature while preparing grill.

2. Combine apple juice and vinegar in small bowl and set aside.

3A. FOR A CHARCOAL GRILL: Open bottom vent halfway and evenly space 15 unlit charcoal briquettes on 1 side of grill. Place disposable pan filled with 2 cups water on other side of grill. Light large chimney starter one-third filled with charcoal briquettes (2 quarts). When top coals are partially covered with ash, pour evenly over unlit coals. Sprinkle soaked wood chips over lit coals. Set cooking grate in place, cover, and open lid vent halfway. Heat grill until hot and wood chips are smoking, about 5 minutes.

3B. FOR A GAS GRILL: Place soaked wood chips in pie plate with ¼ cup water and set over primary burner. Place second pie plate filled with 2 cups water on other burner(s).

Turn all burners to high, cover, and heat grill until hot and wood chips are smoking, about 15 minutes. Turn primary burner to medium-high and turn off other burner(s). (Adjust primary burner as needed to maintain grill temperature of 250 to 275 degrees.)

4. Clean and oil cooking grate. Place ribs meat side down on cooler side of grill over water-filled pan. Cover (position lid vent over meat if using charcoal) and cook until ribs are deep red and smoky, about 1½ hours, brushing with apple juice mixture and flipping and rotating racks halfway through cooking. About 20 minutes before removing ribs from grill, adjust oven rack to lower-middle position and heat oven to 300 degrees.

5. Set wire rack in rimmed baking sheet and transfer ribs to rack. Brush top of each rack with 2 tablespoons apple juice mixture. Pour 1½ cups water into bottom of sheet; roast for 1 hour. Brush ribs with remaining apple juice mixture and continue to cook until meat is tender and registers 195 degrees, 1 to 2 hours. Transfer ribs to cutting board and let rest for 15 minutes. Slice ribs between bones and serve.

Spice Rub

MAKES ABOUT ½ CUP

For less spiciness, reduce the amount of cayenne to ½ teaspoon.

- 2 tablespoons paprika
- 2 tablespoons packed light brown sugar
- 1 tablespoon salt
- 2 teaspoons chili powder
- 1½ teaspoons pepper
- 1½ teaspoons garlic powder
- 1½ teaspoons onion powder
- 1½ teaspoons cayenne pepper
- ½ teaspoon dried thyme

Combine all ingredients in bowl.

RAINY DAY BARBECUED RIBS

WHY THIS RECIPE WORKS: When the craving for barbecued ribs strikes in the dead of winter, you're out of luck unless you visit the local rib joint. There are recipes for oven barbecuing, but the smoke-flavored sauce they use is no substitute for actual smoke. We wanted the real thing, but prepared indoors.

St. Louis–style ribs, trimmed of skirt meat and excess cartilage, worked best here. We started with a spice rub as we would for grilling, and found that a thin coating of mustard, ketchup, and garlic helped the rub adhere. We tried wood chips in a stovetop smoker, but we had difficulty fitting the ribs in the pan, and it's hard to find wood chips in wintertime—however, the smoke-filled kitchen was the clincher.

We gave up on wood chips and instead borrowed a Chinese cooking method of smoking over tea leaves. Lapsang Souchong tea, which has a smoky flavor and worked perfectly when ground fine. Chilling the ribs first helped prevent toughening in the oven's initial high heat. Apple juice, a common ingredient in barbecue "mops," added moisture and more flavor. And running the ribs under the broiler at the end browned and crisped them. These tender, smoky, and spicy ribs taste amazingly like those barbecued on the grill, but can be made any time of the year.

Oven-Barbecued Spareribs

SERVES 4

To make this recipe, you will need a baking stone. It's fine if the ribs overlap slightly on the wire rack. Removing the surface fat keeps the ribs from being too greasy and removing the membrane from the ribs allows the smoke to penetrate both sides of the racks and also makes the ribs easier to eat. Note that the ribs must be coated with the rub and refrigerated at least 8 hours or up to 24 hours ahead of cooking. Be careful when opening the crimped foil to add the juice, as hot steam and smoke will billow out. Serve ribs with Quick Barbecue Sauce (recipe follows), if desired.

- 6 tablespoons yellow mustard
- 2 tablespoons ketchup
- 3 garlic cloves, minced
- 3 tablespoons packed brown sugar
- 1½ tablespoons kosher salt
- 1 tablespoon sweet paprika
- 1 tablespoon chili powder
- 2 teaspoons pepper
- ½ teaspoon cayenne pepper
- 2 (2½- to 3-pound) racks St. Louis–style spareribs, trimmed, membrane removed, and each rack cut in half
- ¼ cup finely ground Lapsang Souchong tea leaves (from about 10 tea bags, or ½ cup loose tea leaves ground to a powder in a spice grinder)
- ½ cup apple juice

1. Combine mustard, ketchup, and garlic in bowl; combine sugar, salt, paprika, chili powder, pepper, and cayenne in separate bowl. Spread mustard mixture in thin, even layer over both sides of ribs; coat both sides with spice mixture, then wrap ribs in plastic and refrigerate for 8 to 24 hours.

2. Transfer ribs from refrigerator to freezer for 45 minutes. Adjust oven racks to lowest and upper-middle positions (at least 5 inches below broiler). Place baking stone on lower rack; heat oven to 500 degrees. Sprinkle ground tea evenly over bottom of rimmed baking sheet; set wire rack in baking sheet. Place ribs meat side up on rack and cover with heavy-duty aluminum foil, crimping edges tightly to seal. Place baking

sheet on stone and roast ribs for 30 minutes, then reduce oven temperature to 250 degrees, leaving oven door open for 1 minute to cool. While oven is open, carefully open 1 corner of foil and pour apple juice into bottom of baking sheet; reseal foil. Continue to roast until meat is very tender and begins to pull away from bones, about 1½ hours. (Begin to check ribs after 1 hour; leave loosely covered with foil for remaining cooking time.)

3. Remove foil and carefully flip racks bone side up; place baking sheet on upper-middle rack. Turn on broiler; cook ribs until well browned and crispy in spots, 5 to 10 minutes. Flip ribs meat side up and cook until second side is well browned and crispy, 5 to 7 minutes more. Cool for at least 10 minutes before cutting into individual ribs. Serve with Quick Barbecue Sauce, if desired.

Quick Barbecue Sauce

MAKES ABOUT 1½ CUPS

Classic barbecue sauce must simmer for a long time for the whole tomatoes in it to break down. However, we found that starting with ketchup can shorten the process.

- 1 medium onion, peeled and quartered
- ¼ cup water
- 1 cup ketchup
- 5 tablespoons molasses
- 2 tablespoons cider vinegar
- 2 tablespoons Worcestershire sauce
- 2 tablespoons Dijon mustard
- 1½ teaspoons liquid smoke (optional)
- 1 teaspoon hot sauce
- ¼ teaspoon pepper
- 2 tablespoons vegetable oil
- 1 garlic clove, minced
- 1 teaspoon chili powder
- ¼ teaspoon cayenne pepper

1. Process onion and water in a food processor until pureed and mixture resembles slush, about 30 seconds. Strain mixture through fine mesh strainer into liquid measuring cup, pressing on solids with rubber spatula to obtain ½ cup juice. Discard solids.

2. Whisk onion juice, ketchup, molasses, vinegar, Worcestershire sauce, mustard, liquid smoke (if using), hot sauce, and pepper together in medium bowl.

3. Heat oil in large saucepan over medium heat until shimmering but not smoking. Add garlic, chili powder, and cayenne and cook until fragrant, about 30 seconds. Whisk in ketchup mixture and bring to a boil; reduce heat to medium-low and simmer gently, uncovered, until flavors meld and sauce is thickened, about 25 minutes. Cool sauce to room temperature before using. (Sauce can be refrigerated for up to 1 week.)

BARBECUED BABY BACK RIBS

WHY THIS RECIPE WORKS: Dry, flavorless ribs are a true culinary disaster. More often than not, baby back ribs cooked at home come out tasting like dry shoe leather on a bone. We wanted ribs that were juicy, tender, and fully seasoned, with an intense smokiness, ribs that would be well worth the time, money, and effort.

Meaty ribs—racks as close to 2 pounds as possible—provided substantial, satisfying portions. For ribs that were so good and moist they didn't even need barbecue sauce, they needed to be brined first—we used a salt, sugar, and water solution—then rubbed with a spice mix before barbecuing. Chili powder, cayenne pepper, cumin, and dark brown sugar formed a nice, crisp crust on the ribs and provided the best balance of sweet and spicy. For even more flavor, we placed wood chips or chunks on top of the coals before barbecuing and used the "low and slow" cooking method: Barbecue the ribs for a few hours on the cool side of the grill, then add fresh briquettes to the coals and continue to cook for another hour or two. This extended amount of time on the grill made for tender baby back ribs with an intensely smoky flavor.

Barbecued Baby Back Ribs

SERVES 4

For a more potent spice flavor, coat the ribs with the spice rub as directed and refrigerate them overnight, wrapped tightly in plastic wrap, If you'd like to use wood chinks rather than wood chips when using a charcoal grill, substitute 2 medium wood chunks, soaked in water for 1 hour, for the wood chip packet.

- Salt and pepper
- ½ cup granulated sugar
- 2 (2-pound) racks baby back or loin back ribs, trimmed, membrane removed
- 1 tablespoon plus ½ teaspoon paprika

- 1¾ teaspoons ground cumin
- 1½ teaspoons chili powder
- 1½ teaspoons packed dark brown sugar
- 1 teaspoon white pepper
- ¾ teaspoon dried oregano
- ½ teaspoon cayenne pepper
- 2 cups wood chips, soaked in water for 15 minutes and drained

1. Dissolve ½ cup salt and granulated sugar in 4 quarts cold water in a large bowl or container. Submerge ribs in brine, cover, and refrigerate for 1 hour. Remove ribs from brine and pat dry with paper towels.

2. Combine paprika, cumin, chili powder, brown sugar, white pepper, ¾ teaspoon salt, ¾ teaspoon pepper, oregano, and cayenne in a small bowl. Rub each rack with 1 tablespoon of spice rub and refrigerate for 30 minutes. Using large piece of heavy-duty aluminum foil, wrap soaked chips in foil packet and cut several vent holes in top.

3A. FOR A CHARCOAL GRILL: Open bottom vent halfway. Light large chimney starter three-quarters filled with charcoal briquettes (4½ quarts). When top coals are partially covered with ash, pour evenly over half of grill. Place wood chip packet on coals. Set cooking grate in place, cover, and open lid vent halfway. Heat grill until hot, about 5 minutes.

3B. FOR A GAS GRILL: Place wood chip packet over primary burner. Turn all burners to high, cover, and heat grill until hot and wood chips are smoking, about 15 minutes. Leave primary burner on high and turn off other burner(s).

4. Clean and oil cooking grate. Place ribs on cooler side of grill and cook for 2 hours, covered, until grill temperature drops to about 250 degrees, flipping, switching, and rotating ribs every 30 minutes so that rack that was nearest fire is on outside. Add 10 fresh briquettes to pile of coals (if using charcoal). Cover and continue to cook (grill temperature should register 275 to 300 degrees on grill thermometer), flipping, switching, and rotating ribs every 30 minutes, until meat easily pulls away from bone, 1½ to 2 hours longer. Transfer ribs to cutting board, cut between bones to separate ribs, and serve.

GRILLED GLAZED BABY BACK RIBS

WHY THIS RECIPE WORKS: Instead of spending hours tending a grill for flavorful, tender ribs, we started ours on the stovetop, then moved them outside. Boiling is an established rib-cooking shortcut, but we found this led to unevenly cooked ribs, so we turned down the heat and simmered them; the gentler heat kept the thinner ends from overcooking and becoming dry. Salting the water prevented them from losing too much of their pork flavor to the cooking liquid. Once they reached 195 degrees, we removed our ribs from the pot, applied a flavorful glaze, and tossed them on the grill, for tender-chewy ribs that were ready in a fraction of the time.

Grilled Glazed Baby Back Ribs

SERVES 4 TO 6

Try one of the glaze recipes that follow, or use 1 cup of your favorite glaze or barbecue sauce.

- 2 tablespoons salt
- 2 (2-pound) racks baby back or loin back ribs, trimmed, membrane removed, and each rack cut in half
- 1 recipe glaze (recipes follow)

1. Dissolve salt in 2½ quarts water in Dutch oven; place ribs in pot so they are fully submerged. Bring to simmer over high heat. Reduce heat to low, cover, and cook at bare simmer until thickest part of ribs registers 195 degrees, 15 to 25 minutes. While ribs are simmering, set up grill. (If ribs come to temperature before grill is ready, leave in pot, covered, until ready to use.)

2A. FOR A CHARCOAL GRILL: Open bottom vent halfway. Light large chimney starter filled with charcoal briquettes (6 quarts). When top coals are partially covered with ash, pour evenly over grill. Set cooking grate in place, cover, and open lid vent halfway. Heat grill until hot, about 5 minutes.

2B. FOR A GAS GRILL: Turn all burners to high, cover, and heat grill until hot, about 15 minutes. Turn all burners to medium-high.

3. Clean and oil cooking grate. Remove ribs from pot and pat dry with paper towels. Brush both sides of ribs with ⅓ cup glaze. Grill ribs, uncovered, flipping and rotating as needed, until glaze is caramelized and charred in spots, 15 to 20 minutes, brushing with another ⅓ cup glaze halfway through cooking. Transfer ribs to cutting board, brush both sides with remaining glaze, tent loosely with aluminum foil, and let rest for 10 minutes. Cut ribs between bones to separate, and serve.

Hoisin-Coconut Glaze

MAKES ABOUT 1 CUP

- ⅔ cup hoisin sauce
- ⅓ cup canned coconut milk
- 3 tablespoons rice vinegar
- ¾ teaspoon pepper

Whisk all ingredients together in bowl.

Lime Glaze

MAKES ABOUT 1 CUP

- ⅔ cup lime juice (6 limes)
- ⅓ cup ketchup
- ¼ cup packed brown sugar
- 1 teaspoon salt

Whisk all ingredients together in bowl.

Spicy Marmalade Glaze

MAKES ABOUT 1 CUP

- ⅔ cup orange marmalade
- ⅓ cup cider vinegar
- 2 tablespoons hot sauce
- ¾ teaspoon salt

Whisk all ingredients together in bowl.

TEXAS BEEF RIBS

WHY THIS RECIPE WORKS: In Texas, good beef ribs are all about intense meat flavor—not just smoke and spice. The barbecue chefs we've met get this flavor just right, thanks to the assistance of massive electric smokers with automated temperature controls. But can a backyard cook replicate this Lone Star classic without the help of special equipment? We were looking for a recipe that would yield potent meat flavor with a bit of honest Texas chew—on our conventional-size grill.

We began by debating whether to trim the fatty membrane that runs along the back side of the ribs. Surprisingly, the juiciest meat with the most flavor was accomplished by the path of least resistance: simply leaving the membrane in place. The fat not only basted the ribs as they cooked but also rendered to a crisp, bacon-like texture. A simple mixture of salt, pepper, cayenne, brown sugar, and chili powder rubbed into each rack was all that it took to bring out the flavor of the meat. To turn our grill into a backyard smoker, we made a slow, even fire with a single pile of coals on one side of the grill and kept the temperature in the range of 250 to 300 degrees. About an hour and a half of slow cooking was enough to render some of the fat and make the ribs juicy, tender, and slightly toothy. When cooked any longer, as is the case with pork ribs, the meat disintegrated into messy shreds, taking on a sticky, pot-roasted sort of texture that any real Texan would immediately reject.

For real Texas-style barbecue sauce to pair with our ribs, we pulled together the usual ingredients—vinegar, onion, and molasses, to name a few—with dry mustard and chili powder for bite. Savory Worcestershire sauce added depth while tomato juice (in place of ketchup) provided tangy flavor and helped thin the sauce out.

Texas-Style Barbecued Beef Ribs

SERVES 4

Beef ribs are sold in slabs with up to seven bones, but slabs with three to four bones are easier to manage on the grill. If you cannot find ribs with a substantial amount of meat on the bones, don't bother making this recipe. One medium wood chunk, soaked in water for one hour, can be substituted for the wood chips on a charcoal grill.

3. Adjust oven rack to middle position and heat oven to 300 degrees. Set wire rack set in rimmed baking sheet and add just enough water to cover pan bottom. Arrange ribs on rack and cover tightly with aluminum foil. Bake until fat has rendered and meat begins to pull away from bones, about 2 hours. Using large piece of heavy-duty foil, wrap soaked chips in foil packet and cut several vent holes in top.

4A. FOR A CHARCOAL GRILL: Open bottom vent halfway. Light large chimney starter filled with charcoal briquettes (6 quarts). When top coals are partially covered with ash, pour into steeply banked pile against 1 side of grill. Place wood chip packet on coals. Set cooking grate in place, cover, and open lid vent halfway. Heat grill until hot and wood chips are smoking, about 5 minutes.

4B. FOR A GAS GRILL: Place wood chip packet directly on primary burner. Turn all burners to high, cover, and heat grill until hot and wood chips are smoking, about 15 minutes. Leave primary burner on high and turn other burner(s) off. (Adjust primary burner as needed to maintain grill temperature between 250 and 300 degrees.)

5. Clean and oil cooking grate. Place ribs meat side down on cool side of grill; ribs may overlap slightly. Cover (positioning lid vent over meat if using charcoal) and cook until ribs are lightly charred and smoky, about 1½ hours, flipping and rotating racks halfway through grilling. Transfer to cutting board, tent with foil, and let rest for 10 minutes. Serve with barbecue sauce.

GRILLED BEEF KEBABS

WHY THIS RECIPE WORKS: Most beef kebabs are disappointing, with overcooked meat and vegetables that are raw or mushy. We wanted to develop a foolproof approach to creating meaty kebabs that looked and tasted like the real thing: chunks of beef with a caramelized char on the outside and a juicy interior, all thoroughly seasoned by a marinade and paired with tender-firm vegetables. For the meat, we chose well-marbled steak tips for their beefy flavor and tender texture. For the marinade, we included salt for moisture, oil for flavor, and sugar for browning. For even more depth, we used tomato paste, a host of seasonings and herbs, and beef broth. We settled on three grill favorites for the vegetables: peppers, onions, and zucchini. Grilling the beef kebabs and vegetables on separate skewers and building a fire that has hotter and cooler areas allowed us to cook the vegetables over a lower temperature while the beef seared over the hotter area.

Grilled Beef Kebabs with Lemon and Rosemary Marinade

SERVES 4 TO 6

If you can't find sirloin steak tips, sometimes labeled "flap meat," substitute 2½ pounds of blade steak; if you use blade steak, cut each steak in half to remove the gristle. You will need four 12-inch metal skewers for this recipe. If you have long, thin pieces of meat, roll or fold them into approximate 2-inch cubes before skewering.

TEXAS BARBECUE SAUCE
- 2 tablespoons unsalted butter
- ½ small onion, chopped fine
- 2 garlic cloves, minced
- 1½ teaspoons chili powder
- 1½ teaspoons pepper
- ½ teaspoon dry mustard
- 2 cups tomato juice
- 6 tablespoons distilled white vinegar
- 2 tablespoons Worcestershire sauce
- 2 tablespoons packed brown sugar
- 2 tablespoons molasses
  Salt

RIBS
- 3 tablespoons packed brown sugar
- 4 teaspoons chili powder
- 1 tablespoon salt
- 2 teaspoons pepper
- ½ teaspoon cayenne pepper
- 3-4 beef rib slabs (3 to 4 ribs per slab, about 5 pounds total), trimmed
- 1 cup wood chips, soaked in water for 15 minutes and drained

1. FOR THE SAUCE: Melt butter in medium saucepan over medium heat. Add onion and cook until softened, about 5 minutes. Stir in garlic, chili powder, pepper, and dry mustard and cook until fragrant, about 30 seconds. Stir in tomato juice, vinegar, Worcestershire, sugar, and molasses and simmer until sauce is reduced to 2 cups, about 20 minutes. Season with salt to taste. (Sauce can be refrigerated in airtight container for 1 week.)

2. FOR THE RIBS: Combine sugar, chili powder, salt, pepper, and cayenne in bowl. Pat ribs dry with paper towels and rub them evenly with spice mixture. Cover ribs with plastic wrap and let sit at room temperature for 1 hour.

MARINADE

- 1 onion, chopped
- ⅓ cup beef broth
- ⅓ cup vegetable oil
- 3 tablespoons tomato paste
- 6 garlic cloves, chopped
- 2 tablespoons chopped fresh rosemary
- 2 teaspoons grated lemon zest
- 2 teaspoons salt
- 1½ teaspoons sugar
- ¾ teaspoon pepper

BEEF AND VEGETABLES

- 2 pounds sirloin steak tips, trimmed and cut into 2-inch chunks
- 1 large zucchini or summer squash, halved lengthwise and sliced 1 inch thick
- 1 large red or green bell pepper, stemmed, seeded, and cut into 1½-inch pieces
- 1 large red or sweet onion, halved lengthwise, each half cut into 4 wedges and each wedge cut crosswise into thirds

1. FOR THE MARINADE: Process all ingredients in blender until smooth, about 45 seconds. Transfer ¾ cup marinade to large bowl and set aside.

2. FOR THE BEEF AND VEGETABLES: Place remaining marinade and beef in 1-gallon zipper-lock bag and toss to coat; press out as much air as possible and seal bag. Refrigerate for at least 1 to 2 hours, flipping bag every 30 minutes.

3. Add zucchini, bell pepper, and onion to bowl with reserved marinade and toss to coat. Cover and let sit at room temperature for at least 30 minutes.

4. Remove beef from bag and pat dry with paper towels. Thread beef tightly onto two 12-inch metal skewers. Alternating pattern of zucchini, bell pepper, and onion, thread vegetables onto two 12-inch metal skewers.

5A. FOR A CHARCOAL GRILL: Open bottom vent completely. Light large chimney starter mounded with charcoal briquettes (7 quarts). When top coals are partially covered with ash, pour evenly over center of grill, leaving 2-inch gap between grill wall and charcoal. Set cooking grate in place, cover, and open lid vent completely. Heat grill until hot, about 5 minutes.

5B. FOR A GAS GRILL: Turn all burners to high, cover, and heat grill until hot, about 15 minutes. Leave primary burner on high and turn other burner(s) to medium-low.

6. Clean and oil cooking grate. Place beef skewers on grill (directly over coals if using charcoal or over hotter side of grill if using gas). Place vegetable skewers on grill (near edge of coals but still over coals if using charcoal or over cooler side of grill if using gas). Cook (covered if using gas), turning skewers every 3 to 4 minutes, until beef is well browned and registers 120 to 125 degrees (for medium-rare) or 130 to 135 degrees (for medium), 12 to 16 minutes. Transfer beef skewers to platter and tent loosely with aluminum foil. Continue to cook vegetable skewers until tender and lightly charred, about 5 minutes; serve with beef skewers.

GRILLED SHISH KEBABS

WHY THIS RECIPE WORKS: Kebabs, for all their popularity and convenience, are usually over- or undercooked, with vegetables and meat that are either burnt or raw and falling off the skewer. But kebabs are so simple, they should be a go-to grilling recipe for most home cooks; they're easy to put together and take little time on the grill, thanks to the vegetables and meat already being in bite-size pieces. We decided to revisit the kebab. So we grabbed some metal skewers and headed to the grill in search of perfectly cooked lamb and crisp, slightly charred vegetables.

To avoid the raw lamb and burnt vegetables that cooking on skewers often delivers, we cut the meat (boneless leg of lamb, trimmed of fat and silver skin) into 1-inch cubes and narrowed the vegetable field. Onions and peppers were the vegetable combination most preferred by tasters; they aren't incredibly watery like tomatoes, which were out from the beginning, and they cooked at the same rate as the meat. Marinating the meat for 2 hours added extra flavor; for the marinades, we used fruity, sweet, and spicy ingredients that stood up well to the hearty lamb.

Grilled Lamb Kebabs

SERVES 6

You can use red, yellow, orange, or green bell peppers in this recipe. You will need four 12-inch metal skewers for this recipe. If you have long, thin pieces of meat, roll or fold them into approximate 1-inch cubes before skewering.

1 recipe marinade (recipes follow)
1 (2¼-pound) shank end boneless leg of lamb, trimmed and cut into 1-inch chunks
1 large bell pepper, stemmed, seeded, and cut into 1-inch pieces
1 large red or sweet onion, peeled, halved lengthwise, each half cut into 4 wedges and each wedge cut crosswise into thirds
Lemon or lime wedges (optional)

1. Place marinade and lamb in 1-gallon zipper-lock bag and toss to coat; press out as much air as possible and seal bag. Refrigerate for at least 2 hours or up to 24 hours, flipping bag every hour.

2. Remove lamb from bag and pat dry with paper towels. Starting and ending with meat, thread 4 pieces of meat, 3 pieces of onion (three 3-layer stacks), and 6 pieces of pepper in mixed order on four 12-inch metal skewers.

3A. FOR A CHARCOAL GRILL: Open bottom vent completely. Light large chimney starter mounded with charcoal briquettes (7 quarts). When top coals are partially covered with ash, pour evenly over grill. Set cooking grate in place, cover, and open lid vent completely. Heat grill until hot, about 5 minutes.

3B. FOR A GAS GRILL: Turn all burners to high, cover, and heat grill until hot, about 15 minutes.

4. Clean and oil cooking grate. Place skewers on grill and cook (covered if using gas), turning skewers every 3 to 4 minutes, until well browned and lamb registers 120 to 125 degrees (for medium-rare) or 130 to 135 degrees (for medium), 7 to 12 minutes.

5. Transfer skewers to serving platter, tent loosely with aluminum foil, and let rest for 5 to 10 minutes before serving with lemon wedges, if using.

Warm-Spiced Parsley Marinade with Ginger
MAKES ABOUT 1 CUP

½ cup olive oil
½ cup packed fresh parsley leaves
1 jalapeño chile, stemmed, seeded, and chopped coarse
2 tablespoons grated fresh ginger
3 garlic cloves, peeled
1 teaspoon ground cumin
1 teaspoon ground cardamom
1 teaspoon ground cinnamon
1 teaspoon salt
⅛ teaspoon pepper

Process all ingredients in food processor until smooth, about 1 minute.

Garlic and Cilantro Marinade with Garam Masala
MAKES ABOUT ¾ CUP

½ cup olive oil
½ cup fresh cilantro
¼ cup raisins
1½ tablespoons lemon juice
3 garlic cloves, peeled
1 teaspoon salt
½ teaspoon garam masala
⅛ teaspoon pepper

Process all ingredients in food processor until smooth, about 1 minute.

Sweet Curry Marinade with Buttermilk
MAKES ABOUT 1 CUP

¾ cup buttermilk
1 tablespoon lemon juice
3 garlic cloves, minced
1 tablespoon packed brown sugar
1 tablespoon curry powder
1 teaspoon red pepper flakes
1 teaspoon ground coriander
1 teaspoon chili powder
1 teaspoon salt
⅛ teaspoon pepper

Combine all ingredients in 1-gallon zipper-lock bag in which meat will marinate.

GRILLED BEEF SATAY

WHY THIS RECIPE WORKS: In the hands of American cooks, satay often comes out thick and chewy or overly marinated and mealy. To return this dish to its streetwise roots, we sliced beefy-flavored flank steak thin across the grain and threaded it onto skewers. To add flavor, we used an aromatic basting sauce consisting of authentic Thai ingredients, rather than the over tenderizing marinade used in many recipes. And to ensure that the quick-cooking beef achieved a burnished exterior, we corralled the coals in an aluminum pan in the center of the grill to bring them closer to the meat.

Grilled Beef Satay

SERVES 6

You will need ten to twelve 12-inch metal skewers for this recipe. Bamboo skewers soaked in water for 30 minutes can be substituted for metal skewers. The aluminum pan used for charcoal grilling should be at least 2¾ inches deep; you will not need the pan for a gas grill. Kitchen shears work well for punching the holes in the pan. Unless you have a very high-powered gas grill, these skewers will not be as well seared as they would be with charcoal. Serve with Peanut Sauce (recipe follows). To make it a meal, serve this dish with steamed white rice.

BASTING SAUCE

- ¾ cup regular or light coconut milk
- 3 tablespoons packed dark brown sugar
- 3 tablespoons fish sauce
- 2 tablespoons vegetable oil
- 3 shallots, minced
- 2 lemon grass stalks, trimmed to bottom 6 inches and minced
- 2 tablespoons grated fresh ginger
- 1½ teaspoons ground coriander
- ¾ teaspoon red pepper flakes
- ½ teaspoon ground cumin
- ½ teaspoon salt

BEEF

- 2 tablespoons vegetable oil
- 2 tablespoons packed dark brown sugar
- 1 tablespoon fish sauce
- 1 (1½- to 1¾-pound) flank steak, halved lengthwise and sliced on slight angle against grain into ¼-inch-thick slices
  Disposable aluminum deep roasting pan (if using charcoal)

1. FOR THE BASTING SAUCE: Whisk all ingredients together in bowl. Reserve one-third of sauce in separate bowl.

2. FOR THE BEEF: Whisk oil, sugar, and fish sauce together in medium bowl. Toss beef with marinade and let stand at room temperature for 30 minutes. Weave beef onto 12-inch metal skewers, 2 to 4 pieces per skewer, leaving 1½ inches at top and bottom of skewer exposed. You should have 10 to 12 skewers.

3A. FOR A CHARCOAL GRILL: Punch twelve ½-inch holes in bottom of disposable roasting pan. Open bottom vent completely and place roasting pan in center of grill. Light large chimney starter mounded with charcoal briquettes (7 quarts).

When top coals are partially covered with ash, pour into roasting pan. Set cooking grate over coals with grates parallel to long side of roasting pan, cover, and open lid vent completely. Heat grill until hot, about 5 minutes.

3B. FOR A GAS GRILL: Turn all burners to high, cover, and heat grill until hot, about 15 minutes. Leave all burners on high.

4. Clean and oil cooking grate. Place beef skewers on grill (directly over coals if using charcoal) perpendicular to grate. Brush meat with reserved one-third of basting sauce and cook (covered if using gas) until browned, about 3 minutes. Flip skewers, brush with half of remaining basting sauce, and cook until browned on second side, about 3 minutes. Brush meat with remaining basting sauce and cook 1 minute longer. Transfer to large platter and serve with Peanut Sauce.

Peanut Sauce

MAKES ABOUT 1½ CUPS

- 1 tablespoon vegetable oil
- 1 tablespoon Thai red curry paste
- 1 tablespoon packed dark brown sugar
- 2 garlic cloves, minced
- 1 cup regular or light coconut milk
- ⅓ cup chunky peanut butter
- ¼ cup dry-roasted unsalted peanuts, chopped
- 1 tablespoon lime juice
- 1 tablespoon fish sauce
- 1 teaspoon soy sauce

Heat oil in small saucepan over medium heat until shimmering. Add curry paste, sugar, and garlic; cook, stirring constantly, until fragrant, about 1 minute. Add coconut milk and bring to simmer. Whisk in peanut butter until smooth. Remove from heat and stir in peanuts, lime juice, fish sauce, and soy sauce. Cool to room temperature.

GRILLED LAMB KOFTE

WHY THIS RECIPE WORKS: In the Middle East, kebabs called *kofte* feature ground meat, not chunks, mixed with lots of spices and fresh herbs. For ours, we started with preground lamb for convenience. Kneading the meat ensured the kofte had a sausage-like spring. To help keep the meat firm, we added a small amount of gelatin and then refrigerated it. Ground pine nuts ensured a perfect texture and prevented toughness, plus they gave the kofte a noticeably richer flavor. Hot smoked paprika, cumin, and cloves contributed warm spice notes, while parsley and mint offered bright, grassy flavors. Adding a little tahini to the tangy garlic and yogurt serving sauce gave it more complexity.

Grilled Lamb Kofte

SERVES 4 TO 6

You will need 8 (12-inch) metal skewers for this recipe. Serve with rice pilaf or make sandwiches with warm pita bread, sliced red onion, and chopped fresh mint.

YOGURT-GARLIC SAUCE

- 1   cup plain whole-milk yogurt
- 2   tablespoons lemon juice
- 2   tablespoons tahini
- 1   garlic clove, minced
- ½   teaspoon salt

KOFTE

- ½   cup pine nuts
- 4   garlic cloves, peeled
- 1½ teaspoons hot smoked paprika
- 1   teaspoon salt
- 1   teaspoon ground cumin
- ½   teaspoon pepper
- ¼   teaspoon ground coriander
- ¼   teaspoon ground cloves
- ⅛   teaspoon ground nutmeg
- ⅛   teaspoon ground cinnamon
- 1½ pounds ground lamb
- ½   cup grated onion, drained
- ⅓   cup minced fresh parsley
- ⅓   cup minced fresh mint
- 1½ teaspoons unflavored gelatin
- 1   large disposable aluminum roasting pan (if using charcoal)

1. FOR THE YOGURT-GARLIC SAUCE: Whisk all ingredients together in bowl. Set aside.

2. FOR THE KOFTE: Process pine nuts, garlic, paprika, salt, cumin, pepper, coriander, cloves, nutmeg, and cinnamon in food processor until coarse paste forms, 30 to 45 seconds. Transfer mixture to large bowl. Add lamb, onion, parsley, mint, and gelatin; knead with your hands until thoroughly combined and mixture feels slightly sticky, about 2 minutes. Divide mixture into 8 equal portions. Shape each portion into 5-inch-long cylinder about 1 inch in diameter. Using 8 (12-inch) metal skewers, thread 1 cylinder onto each skewer, pressing gently to adhere. Transfer skewers to lightly greased baking sheet, cover with plastic wrap, and refrigerate for at least 1 hour or up to 24 hours.

3A. FOR A CHARCOAL GRILL: Using skewer, poke 12 holes in bottom of disposable pan. Open bottom vent completely and place pan in center of grill. Light large chimney starter filled two-thirds with charcoal briquettes (4 quarts). When top coals are partially covered with ash, pour into pan. Set cooking grate in place, cover, and open lid vent completely. Heat grill until hot, about 5 minutes.

3B. FOR A GAS GRILL: Turn all burners to high, cover, and heat grill until hot, about 15 minutes. Leave all burners on high.

4. Clean and oil cooking grate. Place skewers on grill (directly over coals if using charcoal) at 45-degree angle to grate. Cook (covered if using gas) until browned and meat easily releases from grill, 4 to 7 minutes. Flip skewers and continue to cook until browned on second side and meat registers 160 degrees, about 6 minutes longer. Transfer skewers to platter and serve, passing yogurt-garlic sauce separately.

Grilled Beef Kofte

Substitute 80 percent lean ground beef for lamb. Increase garlic to 5 cloves, paprika to 2 teaspoons, and cumin to 2 teaspoons.

GRILLED RACK OF LAMB

WHY THIS RECIPE WORKS: With its juicy, pink meat, rich crust, and classic stand-up-straight presentation, rack of lamb is a bona fide showstopper—and it has the price tag to prove it. But grill this piece of meat improperly and you've made a very costly mistake. That's why we wanted to come up with a foolproof technique for grilling rack of lamb—one that would deliver a great crust and flavorful, tender meat, every time.

1 (13 by 9-inch) disposable aluminum pan
   (if using charcoal)
4 teaspoons olive oil
4 teaspoons chopped fresh rosemary
2 teaspoons chopped fresh thyme
2 garlic cloves, minced
2 (1½- to 1¾-pound) racks of lamb (8 ribs each),
   frenched and trimmed
   Salt and pepper

1A. **FOR A CHARCOAL GRILL:** Open bottom vent completely and place pan in center of grill. Light large chimney starter filled with charcoal briquettes (6 quarts). When top coals are partially covered with ash, pour into two even piles on either side of pan. Set cooking grate in place, cover, and open lid vent completely. Heat grill until hot, about 5 minutes.

1B. **FOR A GAS GRILL:** Turn all burners to high, cover, and heat grill until hot, about 15 minutes. Leave primary burner on high, turning off other burners.

2. Combine 1 tablespoon oil, rosemary, thyme, and garlic in bowl. Pat lamb dry with paper towels, rub with remaining teaspoon oil, and season with salt and pepper. Place racks bone side up on cooler part of grill with meaty side of racks very close to, but not quite over, hot coals or lit burner. Cover and cook until meat is lightly browned, faint grill marks appear, and fat has begun to render, 8 to 10 minutes.

3. Flip racks over, bone side down, and move to hotter parts of grill. Cook until well browned, 3 to 4 minutes. Brush racks with herb mixture. Flip racks bone side up and continue to cook until well browned, 3 to 4 minutes longer. Stand racks up and lean them against each other; continue to cook (over hotter side of grill if using charcoal) until bottom is well browned and meat registers 120 to 125 degrees (for medium-rare) or 130 to 135 degrees (for medium), 3 to 8 minutes longer.

4. Transfer lamb to carving board, tent loosely with aluminum foil, and let rest for 15 minutes. Cut between ribs to separate chops and serve.

Our first challenge was choosing just the right cut. While the racks from butcher shops and high-end specialty stores cost more than those from the supermarket, they come already trimmed. And once we trimmed all the excess fat from our supermarket samples, we found this meat wasn't actually much cheaper. However, even the trimmed lamb needed additional butchering, both to remove the "cap" of fat that creates meat-scorching flare-ups and to trim away any excess meat and fat. (For perfect grilling results, we needed fairly lean racks of uniform thickness.)

To cook the lamb evenly as well as to effectively render its fat, we placed a disposable aluminum pan in the middle of the grill and heaped a small pile of coals on either side of the pan. Placing the lamb in the middle of the grill, over the pan, ensured the pan would catch the rendering fat, preventing flare-ups. A wet rub (garlic, rosemary, thyme, and olive oil) was the best way to flavor the meat—marinades turned the lamb mushy and dry rubs simply didn't work with our grilling method. For a rich crust that wasn't charred, we applied the wet rub during the last few minutes of grilling, keeping the surface crisp.

Grilled Rack of Lamb
SERVES 4 TO 6

We prefer the milder taste and bigger size of domestic lamb, but you may substitute lamb from New Zealand or Australia. Since imported racks are generally smaller, follow the shorter cooking times given in the recipe. While most lamb is sold frenched (meaning part of each rib bone is exposed), chances are there will still be some extra fat between the bones. Remove the majority of this fat, leaving an inch at the top of the small eye of meat. Also, make sure that the chine bone (along the bottom of the rack) has been removed to ensure that it will be easy to cut between the ribs after cooking. Ask the butcher to do it; it's very hard to cut off at home.

TRIMMING FAT FROM RACK OF LAMB

Use a boning or paring knife to cut away any thick portions of fat until a thin layer remains.

LET'S GET GRILLING: POULTRY, SEAFOOD, AND VEGETABLES

CHAPTER 18

GRILLED GLAZED CHICKEN BREASTS

WHY THIS RECIPE WORKS: Grilled glazed boneless chicken breasts are a quick and easy summer dinner, but too often the glaze burns or the chicken overcooks. To produce perfectly cooked chicken, we briefly brined the meat to keep it moist during cooking, and used a two-level grill fire to prevent the glaze from singeing. Lightly coating the chicken with milk powder hastened browning during the quick cooking time. We developed a variety of sweet-savory glazes that complemented but didn't overpower the chicken. A small amount of corn syrup provided a mild sweetness and just enough viscosity to help the glaze cling to the meat.

Grilled Glazed Boneless, Skinless Chicken Breasts

SERVES 4

- ¼ cup salt
- ¼ cup sugar
- 4 (6- to 8-ounce) boneless, skinless chicken breasts, trimmed
- 2 teaspoons nonfat dry milk powder
- ¼ teaspoon pepper
  Vegetable oil spray
- 1 recipe glaze (recipes follow)

1. Dissolve salt and sugar in 1½ quarts cold water. Submerge chicken in brine, cover, and refrigerate for at least 30 minutes or up to 1 hour. Remove chicken from brine and pat dry with paper towels. Combine milk powder and pepper in bowl.

2A. FOR A CHARCOAL GRILL: Open bottom vent completely. Light large chimney starter mounded with charcoal briquettes (7 quarts). When top coals are partially covered with ash, pour two-thirds evenly over half of grill, then pour remaining coals over other half of grill. Set cooking grate in place, cover, and open lid vent completely. Heat grill until hot, about 5 minutes.

2B. FOR A GAS GRILL: Turn all burners to high, cover, and heat grill until hot, about 15 minutes. Leave primary burner on high and turn other burner(s) to medium-high.

3. Clean and oil cooking grate. Sprinkle half of milk powder mixture over 1 side of chicken. Lightly spray coated side of chicken with oil spray until milk powder is moistened. Flip chicken and sprinkle remaining milk powder mixture over second side. Lightly spray with oil spray.

4. Place chicken, skinned side down, on hotter side of grill and cook until browned on first side, 2 to 2½ minutes. Flip chicken, brush with 2 tablespoons glaze, and cook until browned on second side, 2 to 2½ minutes. Flip chicken, move to cooler side of grill, brush with 2 tablespoons glaze, and cook for 2 minutes. Repeat flipping and brushing 2 more times, cooking for 2 minutes on each side. Flip chicken, brush with remaining glaze, and cook until chicken registers 160 degrees, 1 to 3 minutes. Transfer chicken to plate and let rest for 5 minutes before serving.

Spicy Hoisin Glaze

MAKES ABOUT ⅔ CUP

For a spicier glaze use the larger amount of Sriracha.

- 2 tablespoons rice vinegar
- 1 teaspoon cornstarch
- ⅓ cup hoisin sauce
- 2 tablespoons light corn syrup
- 1–2 tablespoons Sriracha sauce
- 1 teaspoon grated fresh ginger
- ¼ teaspoon five-spice powder

Whisk vinegar and cornstarch together in small saucepan until cornstarch has dissolved. Whisk in hoisin, corn syrup, Sriracha, ginger, and five-spice powder. Bring mixture to boil over high heat. Cook, stirring constantly, until thickened, about 1 minute. Transfer glaze to bowl.

Honey-Mustard Glaze

MAKES ABOUT ⅔ CUP

- 2 tablespoons cider vinegar
- 1 teaspoon cornstarch
- 3 tablespoons Dijon mustard
- 3 tablespoons honey
- 2 tablespoons corn syrup
- 1 garlic clove, minced
- ¼ teaspoon ground fennel seeds

Whisk vinegar and cornstarch together in small saucepan until cornstarch has dissolved. Whisk in mustard, honey, corn syrup, garlic, and fennel seeds. Bring mixture to boil over high heat. Cook, stirring constantly, until thickened, about 1 minute. Transfer glaze to bowl.

Coconut-Curry Glaze

MAKES ABOUT ⅔ CUP

2	tablespoons lime juice
1½	teaspoons cornstarch
⅓	cup canned coconut milk
3	tablespoons corn syrup
1	tablespoon fish sauce
1	tablespoon red curry paste
1	teaspoon grated fresh ginger
¼	teaspoon ground coriander

Whisk lime juice and cornstarch together in small saucepan until cornstarch has dissolved. Whisk in coconut milk, corn syrup, fish sauce, curry paste, ginger, and coriander. Bring mixture to boil over high heat. Cook, stirring constantly, until thickened, about 1 minute. Transfer glaze to bowl.

Miso-Sesame Glaze

MAKES ABOUT ⅔ CUP

3	tablespoons rice vinegar
1	teaspoon cornstarch
3	tablespoons white miso paste
2	tablespoons corn syrup
1	tablespoon sesame oil
2	teaspoons ginger
¼	teaspoon ground coriander

Whisk vinegar and cornstarch together in small saucepan until cornstarch has dissolved. Whisk in miso, corn syrup, sesame oil, ginger, and coriander. Bring mixture to boil over high heat. Cook, stirring constantly, until thickened, about 1 minute. Transfer glaze to bowl.

GRILLED BONE-IN CHICKEN BREASTS

WHY THIS RECIPE WORKS: We wanted glazed chicken breasts with tender meat and crisp, lacquered skin. Brining the bone-in chicken breasts before grilling helped ensure juicy, seasoned meat. For the glazes, we balanced sweet ingredients, like molasses and sugar, with bold flavors, like chipotle chiles, ginger, and curry powder. To keep the glazes from burning on the grill, we first seared the breasts over high heat, then moved them to the cool side of the grill, where we brushed them with the glaze in the last few minutes. For extra flavor, we reserved half of the glaze for serving.

Grilled Glazed Bone-In Chicken Breasts

SERVES 4

If using kosher chicken, do not brine in step 1, and season with salt as well as pepper. Remember to reserve half of the glaze for serving.

½	cup salt
4	(10- to 12-ounce) bone-in split chicken breasts, trimmed
	Pepper
1	recipe glaze (recipes follow)

1. Dissolve salt in 2 quarts cold water in large container. Submerge chicken breasts in brine, cover, and refrigerate for 30 minutes to 1 hour. Remove chicken from brine and pat dry with paper towels. Season chicken with pepper.

2A. FOR A CHARCOAL GRILL: Open bottom vent completely. Light large chimney starter filled with charcoal briquettes (6 quarts). When top coals are partially covered with ash, pour evenly over half of grill. Set cooking grate in place, cover, and open lid vent completely. Heat grill until hot, about 5 minutes.

2B. FOR A GAS GRILL: Turn all burners to high, cover, and heat grill until hot, about 15 minutes. Leave primary burner on high and turn off other burner(s). (Adjust primary burner as needed during cooking to maintain grill temperature around 350 degrees.)

3. Clean and oil cooking grate. Place chicken on hot side of grill, skin side up, and cook (covered if using gas) until lightly browned on both sides, 6 to 8 minutes, flipping halfway through cooking. Move chicken, skin side down, to cool side of grill, with thicker end of breasts facing coals and flames. Cover and continue to cook until chicken registers 150 degrees, 15 to 20 minutes longer.

4. Brush bone side of chicken generously with half of glaze, move to hot side of grill, and cook until browned, 5 to 10 minutes. Brush skin side of chicken with remaining glaze, flip chicken, and continue to cook until chicken registers 160 degrees, 2 to 3 minutes longer.

5. Transfer chicken to serving platter, tent loosely with aluminum foil, and let rest for 5 to 10 minutes before serving, passing reserved glaze separately.

Orange-Chipotle Glaze

MAKES ABOUT ¾ CUP

For a spicier glaze, use the greater amount of chipotle chiles.

- 1 teaspoon grated orange zest plus ⅔ cup juice (2 oranges)
- 1-2 tablespoons minced canned chipotle chile in adobo sauce
- 1 small shallot, minced
- 2 teaspoons minced fresh thyme
- 1 tablespoon molasses
- ¾ teaspoon cornstarch
- Salt

Combine orange zest and juice, chipotle, shallot, and thyme in small saucepan. Whisk in molasses and cornstarch, bring to simmer, and cook over medium heat until thickened, about 5 minutes. Season with salt to taste. Reserve half of glaze for serving and use remaining glaze to brush on chicken.

Soy-Ginger Glaze

MAKES ABOUT ¾ CUP

Reduce the amount of salt in the brine to ¼ cup when using this glaze.

- ⅓ cup water
- ¼ cup soy sauce
- 2 tablespoons mirin
- 1 tablespoon grated fresh ginger
- 2 garlic cloves, minced
- 3 tablespoons sugar
- ¾ teaspoon cornstarch
- 2 scallions, minced

Combine water, soy sauce, mirin, ginger, and garlic in small saucepan, then whisk in sugar and cornstarch. Bring to simmer over medium heat and cook until thickened, about 5 minutes; stir in scallions. Reserve half of glaze for serving and use remaining glaze to brush on chicken.

Curry-Yogurt Glaze

MAKES ABOUT ¾ CUP

- ¾ cup plain whole-milk yogurt
- 2 garlic cloves, minced
- 2 teaspoons grated fresh ginger
- 2 teaspoons minced fresh cilantro
- ½ teaspoon grated lemon zest
- 1½ teaspoons curry powder
- ½ teaspoon sugar
- Salt and pepper

Whisk all ingredients together in bowl and season with salt and pepper to taste. Reserve half of glaze for serving and use remaining glaze to brush on chicken.

GRILLED STUFFED CHICKEN BREASTS

WHY THIS RECIPE WORKS: Chicken cordon bleu solves the problem of dry, mild-flavored chicken breasts with a flavorful stuffing of sharp, nutty melted cheese and salty sliced ham. We wanted to bring this concept to the grill, but leaky cheese can cause flare-ups as it drips from the chicken and into the coals. We wanted great grilled chicken breasts with a flavorful stuffing that stayed put.

Off the bat, we knew we wanted a strongly flavored stuffing for our chicken to stand up to the grill's smoke. We settled on more flavorful prosciutto and fontina cheese rather than the usual deli ham and Swiss cheese. And we chose bone-in, skin-on breasts since the skin acts as a natural protector of the meat. We butterflied the breasts—cutting them horizontally nearly halfway through so the meat opened like a book. We placed prosciutto-wrapped fontina inside, folded over the breast to enclose it and tied each breast up with kitchen twine. Encasing the fontina in prosciutto rather than layering it on top, prevented the cheese from leaking. We also chose to add a simple compound butter enlivened by shallots and tarragon for additional moisture and flavor.

Cooking the stuffed breasts over a modified two-level fire (in which all the coals are banked on one side of the grill) allowed us to first sear the breasts over the hot coals for color and flavor, then finish cooking them over more moderate indirect heat. These boneless stuffed chicken breasts were so good, we could enjoy them straight through the grilling season.

Grilled Stuffed Chicken Breasts with Prosciutto and Fontina

SERVES 4

If using kosher chicken, do not brine in step 1. You can serve the chicken on the bone, but we prefer to carve it off and slice it before serving.

- 4 (10- to 12-ounce) bone-in split chicken breasts, trimmed
  Salt and pepper
- 4 tablespoons unsalted butter, softened
- 1 shallot, minced
- 4 teaspoons chopped fresh tarragon
- 2 ounces fontina cheese, rind removed, cut into four 3 by ½-inch sticks
- 4 thin slices prosciutto

1. Using sharp knife and starting on thick side of breast closest to breastbone, cut horizontal pocket in each breast, stopping ½ inch from edge so halves remain attached. Dissolve ¼ cup salt in 2 quarts cold water in large container. Submerge chicken breasts in brine, cover, and refrigerate for 30 minutes to 1 hour. Remove chicken from brine and pat dry with paper towels. Season chicken with pepper.

2A. FOR A CHARCOAL GRILL: Open bottom vent completely. Light large chimney starter filled with charcoal briquettes (6 quarts). When top coals are partially covered with ash, pour evenly over half of grill. Set cooking grate in place, cover, and open lid vent completely. Heat grill until hot, about 5 minutes.

2B. FOR A GAS GRILL: Turn all burners to high, cover, and heat grill until hot, about 15 minutes. Leave primary burner on high and turn off other burner(s). (Adjust primary burner as needed during cooking to maintain grill temperature around 350 degrees.)

3. Meanwhile, combine butter, shallot, and tarragon in bowl. Roll each piece of fontina in 1 slice prosciutto. Spread equal amount of butter mixture inside each breast. Place 1 prosciutto-wrapped piece of fontina inside each breast and fold breast over to enclose. Evenly space 3 pieces kitchen twine (each about 12 inches long) beneath each breast and tie, trimming any excess.

4. Clean and oil cooking grate. Place chicken on hot side of grill, skin side down. Cook (covered if using gas) until well browned on first side, 4 to 6 minutes. Flip chicken and cook until second side is just opaque, about 2 minutes. Move chicken to cool side of grill, skin side up with thicker side of breasts facing coals and flames. Cover and continue to cook until chicken registers 160 degrees, 25 to 35 minutes longer.

5. Transfer chicken to carving board, tent loosely with aluminum foil, and let rest for 5 to 10 minutes. Remove twine, cut meat from bone, slice ½ inch thick, and serve.

NOTES FROM THE TEST KITCHEN

ASSEMBLING STUFFED CHICKEN BREASTS FOR GRILLING

1. Starting on the thick side closest to the breastbone, cut a horizontal pocket in each breast, stopping ½ inch from the edge.

2. Spread an equal portion of compound butter inside each breast.

3. Place one prosciutto-wrapped piece of cheese inside each breast and fold the breast over to enclose.

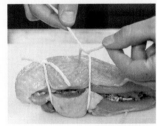

4. Tie each breast with three 12-inch pieces of kitchen twine at even intervals.

PERI PERI GRILLED CHICKEN

WHY THIS RECIPE WORKS: To bring this bold African chicken dish home, we started with a spice paste. We first blended garlic, shallot, bay leaves, lemon zest and juice, and pepper. Five-spice powder and tomato paste promised complexity, depth, and richness. Fruity-tasting arbol chiles, along with some cayenne pepper, replaced hard-to-find peri peri peppers. We tossed chicken pieces in the mixture along with chopped peanuts then let it sit overnight. The paste seasoned the meat and helped it stay juicy when cooked. We set up the grill with a cooler side and a hotter side, as well as a pan of water to help regulate the temperature. After rendering and charring the skin on the hotter side of the grill, we finished cooking the chicken on the cooler side.

Peri Peri Grilled Chicken
SERVES 6 TO 8

This recipe requires refrigerating the spice paste–coated chicken for at least 6 hours or up to 24 hours prior to cooking. When browning the chicken over the hotter side of the grill, move it away from the direct heat if any flare-ups occur. Serve with white rice.

4–10 arbol chiles, stemmed
3 tablespoons extra-virgin olive oil
2 tablespoons salt
8 garlic cloves, peeled
2 tablespoons tomato paste
1 shallot, chopped
1 tablespoon sugar
1 tablespoon paprika
1 tablespoon five-spice powder
2 teaspoons grated lemon zest plus ¼ cup juice (2 lemons)
1 teaspoon pepper
½ teaspoon cayenne pepper
3 bay leaves, crushed
6 pounds bone-in chicken pieces (breasts, thighs, and/or drumsticks), trimmed
½ cup dry-roasted peanuts, chopped fine
1 (13 by 9-inch) disposable aluminum pan (if using charcoal) or 2 (9-inch) disposable aluminum pie plates (if using gas)
Lemon wedges

1. Process 4 arbols, oil, salt, garlic, tomato paste, shallot, sugar, paprika, five-spice powder, lemon zest and juice, pepper, cayenne, and bay leaves in blender until smooth, 10 to 20 seconds. Taste paste and add up to 6 additional arbols, depending on desired level of heat (spice paste should be slightly hotter than desired heat level of cooked chicken), and

process until smooth. Using metal skewer, poke skin side of each chicken piece 8 to 10 times. Place chicken pieces, peanuts, and spice paste in large bowl or container and toss until chicken is evenly coated. Cover and refrigerate for at least 6 hours or up to 24 hours.

2A. FOR A CHARCOAL GRILL: Open bottom vent halfway and place disposable pan filled with 3 cups water on 1 side of grill. Light large chimney starter filled with charcoal briquettes (6 quarts). When top coals are partially covered with ash, pour evenly over other half of grill (opposite disposable pan). Set cooking grate in place, cover, and open lid vent halfway. Heat grill until hot, about 5 minutes.

2B. FOR A GAS GRILL: Place 2 disposable pie plates, each filled with 1½ cups water, directly on 1 burner of gas grill (opposite primary burner). Turn all burners to high, cover, and heat grill until hot, about 15 minutes. Turn primary burner to medium-high and turn off other burner(s). (Adjust primary burner as needed to maintain grill temperature between 325 and 350 degrees.)

3. Clean and oil cooking grate. Place chicken, skin side down, on hotter side of grill and cook until browned and blistered in spots, 2 to 5 minutes. Flip chicken and cook until second side is browned, 4 to 6 minutes. Move chicken to cooler side of grill and arrange, skin side up, with legs and thighs closest to fire and breasts farthest away. Cover (positioning lid vent over chicken if using charcoal) and cook until breasts register 160 degrees and legs and thighs register 175 degrees, 50 to 60 minutes.

4. Transfer chicken to serving platter, tent with aluminum foil, and let rest for 10 minutes before serving, passing lemon wedges separately.

GRILLED CHICKEN DRUMSTICKS

WHY THIS RECIPE WORKS: With the right treatment, economical chicken drumsticks can be a delicious choice for the grill. We started by soaking them in a saltwater brine to season them and help them retain their juices during cooking, then coated them with a flavorful rub. We cooked them to between 185 and 190 degrees over indirect heat, to ensure this collagen-rich cut turned tender. This also allowed the skin to render gently without the risk of flare-ups. We finished by cooking the drumsticks briefly over the coals to capture some char and crispiness.

Grilled Spice-Rubbed Chicken Drumsticks
SERVES 6

Before applying the spice rub, smooth the skin over the drumsticks so it is covering as much surface area as possible. This will help the skin render evenly and prevent the meat from drying out.

½ cup salt
5 pounds chicken drumsticks
1 recipe spice rub (recipes follow)

1. Dissolve salt in 2 quarts cold water in large container. Submerge drumsticks in brine, cover, and refrigerate for 30 minutes to 1 hour.

2. Place spice rub on plate. Remove drumsticks from brine and pat dry with paper towels. Holding 1 drumstick by bone end, press lightly into rub on all sides. Pat gently to remove excess rub. Repeat with remaining drumsticks.

3A. FOR A CHARCOAL GRILL: Open bottom vent halfway. Light large chimney starter filled with charcoal briquettes (6 quarts). When top coals are partially covered with ash, pour evenly over half of grill. Set cooking grate in place, cover, and open lid vent halfway. Heat grill until hot, about 5 minutes.

3B. FOR A GAS GRILL: Turn all burners to high, cover, and heat grill until hot, about 15 minutes. Leave primary burner on high and turn off other burner(s). (Adjust primary burner [or, if using three-burner grill, primary burner and second burner] as needed to maintain grill temperature between 325 and 350 degrees.)

4. Clean and oil cooking grate. Place drumsticks, skin side down, on cooler side of grill. Cover and cook for 25 minutes. Rearrange pieces so that drumsticks that were closest to edge are now closer to heat source and vice versa. Cover and cook until drumsticks register 185 to 190 degrees, 20 to 30 minutes.

5. Move all drumsticks to hotter side of grill and cook, turning occasionally, until skin is nicely charred, about 5 minutes. Transfer to platter, tent with aluminum foil, and let rest for 10 minutes. Serve.

Barbecue Spice Rub

MAKES ABOUT ⅓ CUP

You can substitute granulated garlic for the garlic powder, if desired.

- 3 tablespoons packed brown sugar
- 1 tablespoon paprika
- 1 tablespoon chili powder
- 2 teaspoons garlic powder
- ¾ teaspoon salt
- ¾ teaspoon pepper
- ¼ teaspoon cayenne pepper

Combine all ingredients in small bowl.

Jerk-Style Spice Rub

MAKES ABOUT ¼ CUP

If you can't find whole allspice berries, substitute 2 teaspoons of ground allspice.

- 1 tablespoon allspice berries
- 1 tablespoon black peppercorns
- 1½ teaspoons dried thyme
- 2 tablespoons packed brown sugar
- 2 teaspoons garlic powder
- 1½ teaspoons dry mustard
- ¾ teaspoon salt
- ¾ teaspoon cayenne pepper

Grind allspice, peppercorns, and thyme in spice grinder or mortar and pestle until coarsely ground. Transfer to bowl and stir in sugar, garlic powder, mustard, salt, and cayenne.

 BEHIND THE SCENES

LIGHT MY FIRE

Don't even think of using lighter fluid to light your charcoal. Sometimes we've found that we can taste the fluid residually on grilled food—and who wants that? Electric starters are fine, but most people don't have an electrical outlet near their grill. Where does that leave you? A chimney starter. A chimney starter is a metal cylinder with a heatproof handle. Simply dump in the charcoal, light, and wait until the coals are partially covered with a layer of ash. At this point the hot coals can be poured into the grill and arranged as necessary. One thing to keep in mind when buying a chimney starter is the charcoal capacity. We like a large chimney that holds about 6 quarts of charcoal briquettes—just the right amount for grilling most foods in a large kettle grill.

JERK CHICKEN

WHY THIS RECIPE WORKS: Traditional Jamaican jerk recipes rely on island ingredients for both marinade and cooking technique. Fortunately, we were able to achieve the characteristic spicy-sweet-fresh-smoky balance with the right combination of stateside staples. Keeping the marinade pastelike and cooking the meat first over indirect heat prevented the jerk flavors from dripping or peeling off during grilling. Enhancing our hickory chip packet with a few spice-cabinet ingredients allowed our jerk chicken recipe to mimic the unique smoke of authentic pimento wood.

Jerk Chicken

SERVES 4

For a milder dish, use one seeded chile. If you prefer your food very hot, use up to all three chiles including their seeds and ribs. Scotch bonnet chiles can be used in place of the habaneros. Wear gloves when working with the chiles.

JERK MARINADE

- 1½ tablespoons whole coriander seeds
- 1 tablespoon whole allspice berries
- 1 tablespoon whole peppercorns
- 1–3 habanero chiles, stemmed, quartered, and seeds and ribs reserved, if using
- 8 scallions, chopped
- 6 garlic cloves, peeled
- 3 tablespoons vegetable oil
- 2 tablespoons soy sauce
- 2 tablespoons finely grated lime zest (3 limes), plus lime wedges for serving
- 2 tablespoons yellow mustard
- 1 tablespoon dried thyme
- 1 tablespoon ground ginger
- 1 tablespoon packed brown sugar
- 2¼ teaspoons salt
- 2 teaspoons dried basil
- ½ teaspoon dried rosemary
- ½ teaspoon ground nutmeg

CHICKEN

- 3 pounds bone-in chicken pieces (split breasts cut in half, drumsticks, and/or thighs)
- 2 tablespoons whole allspice berries
- 2 tablespoons dried thyme
- 2 tablespoons dried rosemary
- 2 tablespoons water
- 1 cup wood chips, soaked in water for 15 minutes and drained

1. FOR THE JERK MARINADE: Grind coriander seeds, allspice berries, and peppercorns in spice grinder or mortar and pestle until coarsely ground. Transfer spices to blender jar. Add habanero(s), scallions, garlic, oil, soy sauce, lime zest, mustard, thyme, ginger, sugar, salt, basil, rosemary, and nutmeg and process until smooth paste forms, 1 to 3 minutes, scraping down sides as necessary. Transfer marinade to gallon-size zipper-lock bag.

2. FOR THE CHICKEN: Place chicken pieces in bag with marinade and toss to coat; press out as much air as possible and seal bag. Let stand at room temperature for 30 minutes while preparing grill, flipping bag after 15 minutes. (Marinated chicken can be refrigerated for up to 24 hours.)

3. Combine allspice berries, thyme, rosemary, and water in bowl and set aside to moisten for 15 minutes. Using large piece of heavy-duty aluminum foil, wrap soaked chips and moistened allspice mixture in foil packet and cut several vent holes in top.

4A. FOR A CHARCOAL GRILL: Open bottom vent halfway. Arrange 1 quart unlit charcoal briquettes in single layer over half of grill. Light large chimney starter one-third filled with charcoal briquettes (2 quarts). When top coals are partially covered with ash, pour evenly over unlit briquettes, keeping coals arranged over half of grill. Place wood chip packet on coals. Set cooking grate in place, cover, and open lid vent halfway. Heat grill until hot and wood chips are smoking, about 5 minutes.

4B. FOR A GAS GRILL: Place wood chip packet over primary burner. Turn all burners to high, cover, and heat grill until hot and wood chips begin to smoke, 15 to 25 minutes. Turn primary burner to medium and turn off other burner(s).

5. Clean and oil cooking grate. Place chicken, with marinade clinging and skin side up, as far away from fire as possible, with thighs closest to fire and breasts farthest away. Cover (positioning lid vent over chicken if using charcoal) and cook for 30 minutes.

6. Move chicken, skin side down, to hotter side of grill; cook until browned and skin renders, 3 to 6 minutes. Using tongs, flip chicken pieces and cook until browned on second side and breasts register 160 degrees and thighs/drumsticks register 175 degrees, 5 to 12 minutes longer.

7. Transfer chicken to serving platter, tent loosely with foil, and let rest for 5 to 10 minutes. Serve warm or at room temperature with lime wedges.

SMOKED CHICKEN

WHY THIS RECIPE WORKS: Smoked chicken needs to be cooked for a long time to be imbued with smoke flavor, but the meat dries out easily. We wanted perfectly cooked meat with a pervasive smoky flavor and crisp skin. A salt and sugar brine guaranteed moist, well-seasoned meat. Chicken parts were easier than whole chickens; the breasts could cook evenly on the coolest part of the grill and more of the bird was exposed to the smoke and heat, adding flavor and rendering more fat from the skin. To keep the skin moist, we brushed it with oil and added a pan of water to the grill. Two wood chip packets produced the ideal amount of smoke.

Smoked Chicken
SERVES 6 TO 8

If using kosher chicken, do not brine in step 1. Two medium wood chunks, soaked in water for 1 hour, can be substituted for the wood chip packet on a charcoal grill.

- 1 cup salt
- 1 cup sugar
- 6 pounds bone-in chicken parts (breasts, thighs, and/or drumsticks), trimmed
- 3 tablespoons vegetable oil
  Pepper
- 3 cups wood chips, 1½ cups soaked in water for 15 minutes and drained, plus 1½ cups unsoaked
- 1 (16 by 12-inch) disposable aluminum roasting pan (if using charcoal) or 1 disposable aluminum pie plate (if using gas)

1. Dissolve salt and sugar in 4 quarts cold water in large container. Submerge chicken pieces in brine, cover, and refrigerate for 30 minutes to 1 hour. Remove chicken from brine and pat dry with paper towels. Brush chicken evenly with oil and season with pepper.

2. Using large piece of heavy-duty aluminum foil, wrap soaked chips in foil packet and cut several vent holes in top. Repeat with another sheet of foil and unsoaked wood chips.

3A. FOR A CHARCOAL GRILL: Open bottom vent halfway. Arrange 2 quarts unlit charcoal banked against 1 side of grill and disposable pan filled with 2 cups water on empty side of grill. Light large chimney starter half filled with charcoal briquettes (3 quarts). When top coals are partially covered with ash, pour on top of unlit charcoal, to cover one-third of grill with coals steeply banked against side of grill. Place wood chip packets on top of coals. Set cooking grate in place, cover, and open lid vent halfway. Heat grill until hot and wood chips begin to smoke, about 5 minutes.

3B. FOR A GAS GRILL: Place wood chip packets directly on primary burner. Place disposable pie plate filled with 2 cups water on other burner(s). Turn all burners to high, cover, and heat grill until hot and wood chips begin to smoke, about 15 minutes. Turn primary burner to medium-high and turn off other burner(s). (Adjust primary burner as needed to maintain grill temperature around 325 degrees.)

4. Clean and oil cooking grate. Place chicken on cool side of grill, skin side up, as far away from heat as possible with thighs closest to heat and breasts farthest away. Cover (positioning lid vents over chicken if using charcoal) and cook until breasts register 160 degrees and thighs/drumsticks register 175 degrees, 1¼ to 1½ hours.

5. Transfer chicken to serving platter, tent loosely with foil, and let rest for 5 to 10 minutes before serving.

BARBECUED CHICKEN

WHY THIS RECIPE WORKS: To produce juicy, evenly cooked chicken parts on the grill, indirect cooking is key, as it provides a hotter side for briefly searing the parts and a cooler side for them to cook through gently. We lined up the fattier leg quarters closer to the coals and the leaner white meat farther from the heat, as well as adding a water pan underneath the cooler side, to help the dark and white pieces cook slowly and evenly. Applying a simple spice rub deeply seasoned the meat, and the salt in it helped retain moisture, while brushing on a homemade sauce in stages allowed it to cling nicely to the skin and also develop layers of tangy-sweet flavor.

Sweet and Tangy Barbecued Chicken
SERVES 6 TO 8

When browning the chicken over the hotter side of the grill, move it away from any flare-ups. Try to select similar-size chicken parts for even cooking.

CHICKEN
- 2 tablespoons packed dark brown sugar
- 4½ teaspoons kosher salt
- 1½ teaspoons onion powder
- 1½ teaspoons garlic powder
- 1½ teaspoons paprika
- ¼ teaspoon cayenne pepper
- 6 pounds bone-in chicken pieces (split breasts and/or leg quarters), trimmed

SAUCE
- 1 cup ketchup
- 5 tablespoons molasses
- 3 tablespoons cider vinegar
- 2 tablespoons Worcestershire sauce
- 2 tablespoons Dijon mustard
- ¼ teaspoon pepper
- 2 tablespoons vegetable oil
- ⅓ cup grated onion
- 1 garlic clove, minced
- 1 teaspoon chili powder
- ¼ teaspoon cayenne pepper

- 1 large disposable aluminum roasting pan (if using charcoal) or 2 disposable aluminum pie plates (if using gas)

5. Brush both sides of chicken with remaining ⅓ cup sauce and continue to cook, covered, until breasts register 160 degrees and leg quarters register 175 degrees, 25 to 35 minutes longer.

6. Transfer chicken to serving platter, tent loosely with aluminum foil, and let rest for 10 minutes. Serve, passing reserved sauce separately.

BARBECUED PULLED CHICKEN

WHY THIS RECIPE WORKS: Made-from-scratch barbecued pulled chicken sandwiches often rely on boneless chicken breasts and bottled barbecue sauce. The result is a sandwich with no smoke, tough meat, and artificial flavor. We wanted to take pulled chicken sandwiches seriously—using tender, smoky meat pulled off the bone in moist, soft shreds and then tossed with a tangy, sweet sauce—but we didn't want to take all day to make them.

We chose whole chicken legs for great flavor, low cost, and resistance to overcooking. The legs cooked gently but thoroughly over indirect heat, absorbing plenty of smoke flavor along the way. Cooking the chicken to a higher-than-usual temperature also dissolved connective tissue and rendered more fat, making the meat tender and less greasy. Once the chicken finished cooking, we hand-shredded half and machine-processed the other half to produce the perfect texture—one similar to pulled pork. The chicken then just had to be combined with a thin but tangy barbecue sauce to become truly bun-worthy.

Barbecued Pulled Chicken
SERVES 6 TO 8

Chicken leg quarters consist of drumsticks attached to thighs; often also attached are backbone sections that must be trimmed away. Two medium wood chunks, soaked in water for 1 hour, can be substituted for the wood chip packet on a charcoal grill. Serve the pulled chicken on hamburger rolls or sandwich bread, with pickles and coleslaw.

CHICKEN

- 2 cups wood chips, soaked in water for 15 minutes and drained
- 1 (16 by 12-inch) disposable aluminum roasting pan (if using charcoal)
- 1 tablespoon vegetable oil
- 8 (14-ounce) chicken leg quarters, trimmed
  Salt and pepper

SAUCE

- 1 large onion, peeled and quartered
- ¼ cup water
- 1½ cups ketchup
- 1½ cups apple cider
- ¼ cup molasses

1. FOR THE CHICKEN: Combine sugar, salt, onion powder, garlic powder, paprika, and cayenne in bowl. Arrange chicken on rimmed baking sheet and sprinkle both sides evenly with spice rub. Cover with plastic wrap and refrigerate for at least 6 hours or up to 24 hours.

2. FOR THE SAUCE: Whisk ketchup, molasses, vinegar, Worcestershire, mustard, and pepper together in bowl. Heat oil in medium saucepan over medium heat until shimmering. Add onion and garlic; cook until onion is softened, 2 to 4 minutes. Add chili powder and cayenne and cook until fragrant, about 30 seconds. Whisk in ketchup mixture and bring to boil. Reduce heat to medium-low and simmer gently for 5 minutes. Set aside ⅔ cup sauce to baste chicken and reserve remaining sauce for serving. (Sauce can be refrigerated for up to 1 week.)

3A. FOR A CHARCOAL GRILL: Open bottom vent halfway and place disposable pan filled with 3 cups water on 1 side of grill. Light large chimney starter filled with charcoal briquettes (6 quarts). When top coals are partially covered with ash, pour evenly over other half of grill (opposite disposable pan). Set cooking grate in place, cover, and open lid vent halfway. Heat grill until hot, about 5 minutes.

3B. FOR A GAS GRILL: Place 2 disposable pie plates, each filled with 1½ cups water, directly on 1 burner of gas grill (opposite primary burner). Turn all burners to high, cover, and heat grill until hot, about 15 minutes. Turn primary burner to medium-high and turn off other burner(s). (Adjust primary burner as needed to maintain grill temperature of 325 to 350 degrees.)

4. Clean and oil cooking grate. Place chicken, skin side down, over hotter part of grill and cook until browned and blistered in spots, 2 to 5 minutes. Flip chicken and cook until second side is browned, 4 to 6 minutes. Move chicken to cooler side of grill and brush both sides of chicken with ⅓ cup sauce. Arrange chicken, skin side up, with leg quarters closest to fire and breasts farthest away. Cover (positioning lid vent over chicken if using charcoal) and cook for 25 minutes.

¼ cup apple cider vinegar

3 tablespoons Worcestershire sauce

3 tablespoons Dijon mustard

½ teaspoon pepper

1 tablespoon vegetable oil

1½ tablespoons chili powder

2 garlic cloves, minced

½ teaspoon cayenne pepper

Hot sauce

1. FOR THE CHICKEN: Using large piece of heavy-duty aluminum foil, wrap soaked chips in foil packet and cut several vent holes in top.

2A. FOR A CHARCOAL GRILL: Open bottom vent halfway and place roasting pan in center of grill. Light large chimney starter three-quarters filled with charcoal briquettes (4½ quarts). When top coals are partially covered with ash, pour into 2 even piles on either side of roasting pan. Place wood chip packet on 1 pile of coals. Set cooking grate in place, cover, and open lid vent halfway. Heat grill until hot and wood chips are smoking, about 5 minutes.

2B. FOR A GAS GRILL: Place wood chip packet directly on primary burner. Turn all burners to high, cover, and heat grill until hot and wood chips are smoking, about 15 minutes. Turn all burners to medium. (Adjust burners as needed during cooking to maintain grill temperature between 250 and 300 degrees.)

3. Clean and oil cooking grate. Pat chicken dry with paper towels and season with salt and pepper. Place chicken in single layer on center of grill (over roasting pan if using charcoal), skin side up, or evenly over grill (if using gas). Cover (position lid vent over meat if using charcoal) and cook until chicken registers 185 degrees, 1 to 1½ hours, rotating the chicken pieces halfway through cooking. Transfer chicken to carving board, tent loosely with foil, and let rest until cool enough to handle.

4. FOR THE SAUCE: Meanwhile, process onion and water in food processor until mixture resembles slush, about 30 seconds. Pass through fine-mesh strainer into liquid measuring cup, pressing on solids with rubber spatula (you should have ¾ cup strained onion juice). Discard solids in strainer.

5. Whisk onion juice, ketchup, cider, molasses, 3 tablespoons vinegar, Worcestershire, mustard, and ½ teaspoon pepper together in bowl. Heat oil in large saucepan over medium heat until shimmering. Stir in chili powder, garlic, and cayenne and cook until fragrant, about 30 seconds. Stir in ketchup mixture, bring to simmer, and cook over medium-low heat until slightly thickened, about 15 minutes (you should have about 4 cups of sauce). Transfer 2 cups sauce to serving bowl; leave remaining sauce in saucepan.

6. TO SERVE: Remove and discard skin from chicken legs. Using your fingers, pull meat off bones, separating larger pieces (which should fall off bones easily) from smaller, drier pieces into 2 equal piles.

7. Pulse smaller chicken pieces in food processor until just coarsely chopped, 3 to 4 pulses, stirring chicken with rubber spatula after each pulse. Add chopped chicken to sauce in saucepan. Using your fingers or 2 forks, pull larger chicken pieces into long shreds and add to saucepan. Stir in remaining 1 tablespoon cider vinegar, cover, and heat chicken over medium-low heat, stirring occasionally, until heated through, about 10 minutes. Add hot sauce to taste and serve, passing remaining sauce separately.

Barbecued Pulled Chicken for a Crowd

SERVES 10 TO 12

This technique works well on a charcoal grill but not so well on a gas grill. If your gas grill is large and can accommodate more than 8 legs, follow the master recipe, adding as many legs as will comfortably fit in a single layer.

Increase amount of charcoal briquettes to 6 quarts. Use 12 chicken legs and slot them into V-shaped roasting rack set on top of cooking grate over disposable aluminum pan. Increase cooking time in step 3 to 1½ to 1¾ hours. In step 5, remove only 1 cup of sauce from saucepan. In step 7, pulse chicken in food processor in 2 batches.

NOTES FROM THE TEST KITCHEN

BARBECUED PULLED CHICKEN FOR A CROWD

To make barbecued pulled chicken for a crowd, we found that a roasting rack with six slots was the perfect tool for the job. By sliding two legs into each slot, a total of 12 legs fit (and finish cooking) at once—plenty to feed a hungry crowd.

GRILLED CHICKEN SOUVLAKI

WHY THIS RECIPE WORKS: *Souvlaki* is basically a Greek term for meat grilled on a stick. In modern Greece, souvlaki is usually made with pork, but at Greek restaurants here in the United States, boneless, skinless chicken breast is common. The chunks of white meat are marinated in a tangy mixture of lemon juice, olive oil, oregano, parsley, and garlic before being skewered and grilled until charred. The chicken is often placed on a lightly grilled pita, slathered with a yogurt-based *tzatziki* sauce, wrapped snugly, and eaten out of hand. At least as appealing as the dish itself is how easily it translates to a home grill. The ingredients are readily available, and small chunks of boneless chicken cook quickly, making souvlaki a prime candidate for weeknight fare. Instead of a long marinating time, which made the meat mushy and didn't add much flavor, we brined the chicken for a mere 30 minutes, then tossed it with olive oil, lemon juice, dried oregano, parsley, black pepper, and honey. The honey added complexity and encouraged browning. We also reserved a bit of the mixture to season the meat after cooking. We found that the meat on the outside of the skewers cooked faster than the chunks in the middle, so we made "shields" by threading bell peppers and onions onto the ends of the skewers. For soft pita, we wrapped a stack of four pitas tightly in foil after moistening the top and bottom surfaces of the stack with water. They steamed and softened while the chicken cooked. Topped with a cool, creamy tzatziki, our chicken souvlaki makes a perfect summer dinner.

Grilled Chicken Souvlaki

SERVES 4

This *tzatziki* is fairly mild; if you like a more assertive flavor, double the garlic. A rasp-style grater makes quick work of turning the garlic into a paste. We like the chicken as a wrap, but you may skip the pita and serve the chicken, vegetables, and tzatziki with rice. You will need four 12-inch metal skewers.

TZATZIKI SAUCE

- 1 tablespoon lemon juice
- 1 small garlic clove, minced to paste
- ¾ cup plain Greek yogurt
- ½ cucumber, peeled, halved lengthwise, seeded, and diced fine (½ cup)
- 3 tablespoons minced fresh mint
- 1 tablespoon minced fresh parsley
- ⅜ teaspoon salt

CHICKEN

- Salt and pepper
- 1½ pounds boneless, skinless chicken breasts, trimmed and cut into 1-inch pieces
- ⅓ cup extra-virgin olive oil
- 2 tablespoons minced fresh parsley
- 1 teaspoon finely grated lemon zest plus ¼ cup juice (2 lemons)
- 1 teaspoon honey
- 1 teaspoon dried oregano
- 1 green bell pepper, quartered, stemmed, and seeded, each quarter cut into 4 chunks
- 1 small red onion, ends trimmed, peeled, and halved lengthwise, each half cut into 4 chunks
- 4 (8-inch) pita breads

1. FOR THE TZATZIKI SAUCE: Whisk lemon juice and garlic together in small bowl. Let stand for 10 minutes. Stir in yogurt, cucumber, mint, parsley, and salt. Cover and set aside.

2. FOR THE CHICKEN: Dissolve 2 tablespoons salt in 1 quart cold water. Submerge chicken in brine, cover, and refrigerate for 30 minutes. While chicken is brining, combine oil, parsley, lemon zest and juice, honey, oregano, and ½ teaspoon pepper in medium bowl. Transfer ¼ cup oil mixture to large bowl and set aside to toss with cooked chicken.

3. Remove chicken from brine and pat dry with paper towels. Toss chicken with remaining oil mixture. Thread 4 pieces of bell pepper, concave side up, onto one 12-inch metal skewer. Thread one-quarter of chicken onto skewer. Thread 2 chunks of onion onto skewer, and place skewer on plate. Repeat skewering remaining chicken and vegetables on 3 more skewers. Lightly moisten 2 pita breads with water. Sandwich 2 unmoistened pita breads between moistened pita breads and wrap stack tightly in lightly greased heavy-duty aluminum foil.

4A. FOR A CHARCOAL GRILL: Open bottom vent completely. Light large chimney starter mounded with charcoal briquettes (7 quarts). When top coals are partially covered with ash, pour evenly over half of grill. Set cooking grate in place, cover, and open lid vent completely. Heat grill until hot, about 5 minutes.

4B. FOR A GAS GRILL: Turn all burners to high, cover, and heat grill until hot, about 15 minutes. Leave primary burner on high and turn off other burner(s).

5. Clean and oil cooking grate. Place skewers on hotter side of grill and cook, turning occasionally, until chicken and vegetables are well browned on all sides and chicken registers 160 degrees, 15 to 20 minutes. Using fork, push chicken and vegetables off skewers into bowl of reserved oil mixture. Stir gently, breaking up onion chunks; cover with foil and let sit for 5 minutes.

6. Meanwhile, place packet of pitas on cooler side of grill. Flip occasionally to heat, about 5 minutes.

7. Lay each warm pita on 12-inch square of foil. Spread each pita with 2 tablespoons tzatziki. Place one-quarter of chicken and vegetables in middle of each pita. Roll into cylindrical shape and serve.

GRILLED LEMON CHICKEN

WHY THIS RECIPE WORKS: Grilling a whole chicken can be a recipe for disaster thanks to flare-ups caused by the fatty skin. Usually recipes address this problem with a two-stage grilling process: low heat to gently render the fat and then high heat to char the meat and crisp the skin. We found a much faster way to solve the problem: We skipped the rendering step by removing the skin before grilling. To ensure that our chicken got plenty of color and char without overcooking, we butterflied it so it was an even thickness, then we brined it in a sugar and salt solution for juicy meat. For flavor that penetrated all the way to the bone, we cut deep channels in the meat and rubbed it with lemon and herb seasoning. Basting the chicken with a flavorful butter sauce and tenting it with aluminum foil partway through cooking kept the surface moist and tender as it cooked. We quickly charred lemon wedges to squeeze over each portion before serving for even more moisture and flavor.

Grilled Lemon Chicken with Rosemary

SERVES 4

For a better grip, use a paper towel to grasp the skin when removing it from the chicken.

NOTES FROM THE TEST KITCHEN

PREPPING A WHOLE CHICKEN FOR THE GRILL

For even, fast cooking, we remove the backbone, then flip the chicken and crack and flatten the breastbone. We peel off the skin, leaving it on the wings, and deeply slash the meat. Skewers inserted through the thighs and legs provide stability.

1   (3½- to 4-pound) whole chicken, giblets discarded
¾   cup sugar
     Salt and pepper
2   lemons
1   tablespoon vegetable oil
2   teaspoons minced fresh rosemary
1½   teaspoons Dijon mustard
2   tablespoons unsalted butter

1. With chicken breast side down, using kitchen shears, cut through bones on either side of backbone; discard backbone. Flip chicken over and press on breastbone to flatten. Using fingers and shears, peel skin off chicken, leaving skin on wings.

2. Tuck wings behind back. Turn legs so drumsticks face inward toward breasts. Using chef's knife, cut ½-inch-deep slits, spaced ½ inch apart, in breasts and legs. Insert skewer through thigh of 1 leg, into bottom of breast, and through thigh of second leg. Insert second skewer, about 1 inch lower, through thigh and drumstick of 1 leg and then through thigh and drumstick of second leg.

3. Dissolve sugar and ¾ cup salt in 3 quarts cold water in large, wide container. Submerge chicken in brine, cover, and refrigerate for at least 30 minutes or up to 1 hour.

4. Zest lemons (you should have 2 tablespoons grated zest). Juice 1 lemon (you should have 3 tablespoons juice) and quarter remaining lemon lengthwise. Combine zest, oil, 1½ teaspoons rosemary, 1 teaspoon mustard, and ½ teaspoon pepper in small bowl; set aside. Heat butter, remaining ½ teaspoon rosemary, remaining ½ teaspoon mustard, and ½ teaspoon pepper in small saucepan over low heat, stirring occasionally, until butter is melted and ingredients are combined. Remove pan from heat and stir in lemon juice; leave mixture in saucepan.

5. Remove chicken from brine and pat dry with paper towels. With chicken skinned side down, rub ½ teaspoon zest mixture over surface of legs. Flip chicken over and rub remaining zest mixture evenly over entire surface, making sure to work mixture into slits.

6A. FOR A CHARCOAL GRILL: Open bottom vent completely. Light large chimney starter mounded with charcoal briquettes (7 quarts). When top coals are partially covered with ash, pour evenly over half of grill. Set cooking grate in place, cover, and open lid vent completely. Heat grill until hot, about 5 minutes.

6B. FOR A GAS GRILL: Turn all burners to high, cover, and heat grill until hot, about 15 minutes. Leave primary burner on high and turn off other burner(s).

7. Clean and oil cooking grate. Place chicken, skinned side down, and lemon quarters over hotter side of grill. Cover and cook until chicken and lemon quarters are well browned, 8 to 10 minutes. Transfer lemon quarters to bowl and set aside. Flip chicken over and brush with one-third of butter mixture (place saucepan over cooler side of grill if mixture has solidified). Cover chicken loosely with aluminum foil. Continue to cook, covered, until chicken is well browned on second side, 8 to 10 minutes.

8. Remove foil and slide chicken to cooler side of grill. Brush with half of remaining butter mixture, and re-cover with foil. Continue to cook, covered, until breasts register 160 degrees and thighs/drumsticks register 175 degrees, 8 to 10 minutes longer.

9. Transfer chicken to carving board, brush with remaining butter mixture, tent loosely with foil, and let rest for 5 to 10 minutes. Carve into pieces and serve with reserved lemon quarters.

GRILL-ROASTED BEER CAN CHICKEN

WHY THIS RECIPE WORKS: We wanted to know if the curious cooking method of grill-roasting chicken over a can of beer really worked. To earn our approval, this technique would have to produce a tender, juicy, and deeply seasoned bird.

We found that beer can chicken is the real deal—why? The beer in the open can simmers and turns to steam as the chicken roasts, which makes the meat remarkably juicy and rich-textured, similar to braised chicken. As an added bonus, the dry heat of the grill crisps the skin and renders the fat away. To perfect the technique, we added a few hardwood chunks or chips to the fire for smoky flavor. The best grilling setup (for a charcoal grill) proved to be banking the lit coals on either side of the grill and propping the chicken up on an open can of beer on the grill in the center, using the bird's drumsticks to form a tripod. For the gas grill, a medium fire did the trick. Finally, we found we didn't have to spend money on an expensive beer—the beer flavor wasn't really detectable in the chicken, so a cheap brew worked just fine (so does lemonade, which proved an acceptable substitute for the beer).

Grill-Roasted Beer Can Chicken
SERVES 4

Two medium wood chunks, soaked in water for 1 hour, can be substituted for the wood chip packet on a charcoal grill. If you prefer, use lemonade instead of beer; fill an empty 12-ounce soda or beer can with 10 ounces (1¼ cups) of lemonade and proceed as directed.

1 (12-ounce) can beer
2 bay leaves
1 (3½- to 4-pound) whole chicken
3 tablespoons spice rub (recipe follows)
2 cups wood chips, soaked in water for 15 minutes and drained
1 (13 by 9-inch) disposable aluminum roasting pan (if using charcoal)

1. Open beer can and pour out (or drink) about ¼ cup. With church key can opener, punch 2 more large holes in the top of can (for total of 3 holes). Crumble bay leaves into beer.

2. Pat chicken dry with paper towels. Rub chicken evenly, inside and out, with spice rub, lifting up skin over breast and rubbing spice rub directly onto meat. Using skewer, poke skin all over. Slide chicken over beer can so that drumsticks reach down to bottom of can and chicken stands upright; set aside at room temperature.

3. Using large piece of heavy-duty aluminum foil, wrap soaked chips in foil packet and cut several vent holes in top.

4A. FOR A CHARCOAL GRILL: Open bottom vent halfway and place roasting pan in center of grill. Light large chimney starter two-thirds filled with charcoal briquettes (4 quarts). When top coals are partially covered with ash, pour into 2 even piles on either side of roasting pan. Place wood chip packet on 1 pile of coals. Set cooking grate in place, cover, and open lid vent halfway. Heat grill until hot and wood chips are smoking, about 5 minutes.

4B. FOR A GAS GRILL: Place wood chip packet directly on primary burner. Turn all burners to high, cover, and heat grill until hot and wood chips are smoking, about 15 minutes. Turn all burners to medium. (Adjust burners as needed to maintain grill temperature around 325 degrees.)

5. Clean and oil cooking grate. Place chicken (with can) in center of grill (over roasting pan if using charcoal), using drumsticks to help steady bird. Cover (position lid vent over chicken if using charcoal) and cook until breast registers 160 degrees and thighs register 175 degrees, 1 to 1½ hours.

6. Using large wad of paper towels, carefully transfer chicken (with can) to tray, making sure to keep can upright. Tent loosely with foil and let rest for 15 minutes. Carefully lift chicken off can and onto carving board. Discard remaining beer and can. Carve chicken and serve.

NOTES FROM THE TEST KITCHEN

SETTING UP BEER CAN CHICKEN

With legs pointing down, slide chicken over open beer can. Two legs and beer can form tripod that steadies chicken on grill.

Spice Rub

MAKES 1 CUP

Store leftover spice rub in an airtight container for up to 3 months.

- ½ cup paprika
- 2 tablespoons kosher salt
- 2 tablespoons garlic powder
- 1 tablespoon dried thyme
- 2 teaspoons ground celery seeds
- 2 teaspoons pepper
- 2 teaspoons cayenne pepper

Combine all ingredients in bowl.

GRILL-ROASTED CORNISH GAME HENS

WHY THIS RECIPE WORKS: Grilled Cornish game hens provide an attractive, elegant alternative to grilled chicken. We wanted to develop a foolproof technique that would deliver smoky notes, crisp skin, and juicy meat infused with great flavor. By butterflying the birds we could keep all of the skin on one side, which meant it crisped more quickly when placed facing the coals. Butterflying also produced a uniformly thick bird, which promoted even cooking. We needed to secure the legs to the body to keep the skin from tearing, so we developed a special skewering procedure that stabilized the legs, made it easier to fit the birds on the cooking grate, and created a restaurant-worthy presentation. A seven-ingredient rub gave the hens a sweet and savory complexity and helped crisp the skin even further, giving it a rich mahogany hue. A quick glaze provided the crowning touch.

Grill-Roasted Cornish Game Hens

SERVES 4

To add smoke flavor to the hens, use the optional wood chips; however, when using a charcoal grill, we prefer wood chunks to wood chips whenever possible; substitute 4 medium wood chunks, soaked in water for 1 hour, for the wood chip packets. You will need four 8- to 10-inch flat metal skewers for this recipe.

- ½ cup salt
- 4 (1¼- to 1½-pound) whole Cornish game hens
- 2 tablespoons packed brown sugar
- 1 tablespoon paprika
- 2 teaspoons garlic powder
- 2 teaspoons chili powder
- 1 teaspoon ground black pepper
- 1 teaspoon ground coriander
- ⅛ teaspoon cayenne pepper
- 4 cups wood chips, soaked in water for 15 minutes and drained (optional)
- 1 (16 by 12-inch) disposable aluminum roasting pan
- 1 recipe glaze (recipes follow)

1. TO BUTTERFLY GAME HENS: Use kitchen shears to cut along both sides of backbone to remove it. With skin side down, make ¼-inch cut into bone separating breast halves. Lightly press on ribs to flatten hen. Fold wing tips behind bird to secure them.

2. Dissolve salt in 4 quarts cold water in large container. Submerge hens in brine, cover, and refrigerate for 30 minutes to 1 hour.

3. Combine sugar, paprika, garlic powder, chili powder, pepper, coriander, and cayenne in bowl. Remove hens from brine and pat dry with paper towels.

4. TO SKEWER HENS: Insert flat metal skewer ½ inch from end of drumstick through skin and meat and out other side. Turn leg so that end of drumstick faces wing, then insert tip of skewer into meaty section of thigh under bone. Press skewer all the way through breast and second thigh. Fold end of drumstick toward wing and insert skewer ½ inch from end. Press skewer so that blunt end rests against bird and stretch skin tight over legs, thighs, and breast halves. Rub hens evenly with spice mixture and refrigerate while preparing grill.

5. Using 2 large pieces of heavy-duty aluminum foil, wrap soaked chips, if using, in 2 foil packets and cut several vent holes in tops.

6A. FOR A CHARCOAL GRILL: Open bottom vent completely and place roasting pan in center of grill. Light large chimney starter filled with charcoal briquettes (6 quarts). When top coals are partially covered with ash, pour into 2 even piles on either side of roasting pan. Place 1 wood chip packet, if using, on each pile of coals. Set cooking grate in place, cover, and open lid vent completely. Heat grill until hot and wood chips are smoking, about 5 minutes.

6B. FOR A GAS GRILL: Place wood chip packets, if using, directly on primary burner. Turn all burners to high, cover, and heat grill until hot and wood chips are smoking, about 15 minutes. Turn all burners to medium. (Adjust burners as needed during cooking to maintain grill temperature around 325 degrees.)

7. Clean and oil cooking grate. Place hens in center of grill (over roasting pan if using charcoal), skin side down. Cover (position lid vent over birds if using charcoal) and cook until thighs register 160 degrees, 20 to 30 minutes.

8. Using tongs, move the birds to the hot sides of the grill (if using charcoal; 2 hens per side), keeping them skin side down, or turn all burners to high (if using gas). Cover and continue to cook until browned, about 5 minutes. Brush the birds with half of glaze, flip, and cook for 2 minutes. Brush remaining glaze over hens, flip, and continue to cook until breasts register 160 degrees and thighs register 175 degrees, 1 to 3 minutes longer.

9. Transfer hens to carving board, tent loosely with foil, and let rest for 5 to 10 minutes. Cut hens in half through the breastbone and serve.

Barbecue Glaze
MAKES ABOUT ½ CUP

- ½ cup ketchup
- 2 tablespoons brown sugar
- 1 tablespoon soy sauce
- 1 tablespoon distilled white vinegar
- 1 tablespoon yellow mustard
- 1 garlic clove, minced

Combine all ingredients in small saucepan, bring to simmer, and cook, stirring occasionally, until thickened, about 5 minutes.

Asian Barbecue Glaze
MAKES ABOUT ½ CUP

- ¼ cup ketchup
- ¼ cup hoisin sauce
- 2 tablespoons rice vinegar
- 1 tablespoon soy sauce
- 1 tablespoon toasted sesame oil
- 1 tablespoon grated fresh ginger

Combine all ingredients in small saucepan, bring to simmer, and cook, stirring occasionally, until thickened, about 5 minutes.

THAI GRILLED CORNISH GAME HENS

WHY THIS RECIPE WORKS: For our take on Thai grilled chicken, we started with Cornish hens, which are similar in size to the hens traditionally used by street vendors in Thailand. Butterflying and flattening the hens helped them cook more quickly and evenly on the grill. We created a marinade consisting of cilantro leaves and stems (a substitute for hard-to-find cilantro root), lots of garlic, white pepper, ground coriander, brown sugar, and fish sauce; thanks to its pesto-like consistency, it clung to the hens instead of sliding off. We set up a half-grill fire and started cooking the hens skin side up over the cooler side of the grill so the fatty skin had time to slowly render while

NOTES FROM THE TEST KITCHEN

SKEWERING GAME HENS

1. Insert a flat metal skewer ½ inch from the end of a drumstick through the skin and meat and out the other side.

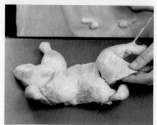

2. Turn the leg so that the end of the drumstick faces the wing, then insert the tip of the skewer into the meaty section of the thigh under the bone.

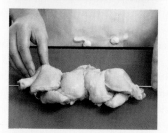

3. Press the skewer all the way through the breast and second thigh. Fold the end of the drumstick toward the wing and insert the skewer ½ inch from the end.

4. Press the skewer so that the blunt end rests against the bird and stretch the skin tight over the legs, thighs, and breast halves.

the meat cooked; then we finished them over the hotter side to crisp the skin. We whipped up a version of the traditional sweet-tangy-spicy dipping sauce by combining equal parts white vinegar and sugar and simmering the mixture until it was slightly thickened and would cling nicely to the chicken. Plenty of minced garlic and Thai chiles balanced the sauce with savory, fruity heat.

Thai Grilled Cornish Game Hens with Chili Dipping Sauce (Gai Yang)
SERVES 4

The hens need to marinate for at least 6 hours before cooking (a longer marinating time is preferable). If your hens weigh 1½ to 2 pounds, grill three hens instead of four and extend the initial cooking time in step 6 by 5 minutes. If you can't find Thai chiles, substitute Fresno or red jalapeño chiles. Serve with steamed white rice.

HENS

- 4 Cornish game hens (1¼ to 1½ pounds each), giblets discarded
- 1 cup fresh cilantro leaves and stems, chopped coarse
- 12 garlic cloves, peeled
- ¼ cup packed light brown sugar
- 2 teaspoons ground white pepper
- 2 teaspoons ground coriander
- 2 teaspoons salt
- ¼ cup fish sauce

DIPPING SAUCE

- ½ cup distilled white vinegar
- ½ cup granulated sugar
- 1 tablespoon minced Thai chiles
- 3 garlic cloves, minced
- ¼ teaspoon salt

1. FOR THE HENS: Working with 1 hen at a time, place hen breast side down on cutting board and use kitchen shears to cut through bones on either side of backbone; discard backbone. Flip hen and press on breastbone to flatten. Trim off any excess fat and skin.

2. Pulse cilantro leaves and stems, garlic, sugar, pepper, coriander, and salt in food processor until finely chopped, 10 to 15 pulses; transfer to small bowl. Add fish sauce and stir until marinade has consistency of loose paste.

3. Rub hens all over with marinade. Transfer hens and any excess marinade to large zipper-lock bag and refrigerate for at least 6 hours or up to 24 hours, turning bag halfway through marinating.

4. FOR THE DIPPING SAUCE: Bring vinegar to boil in small saucepan. Add sugar and stir to dissolve. Reduce heat to medium-low and simmer until vinegar mixture is slightly thickened, 5 minutes. Remove from heat and let vinegar mixture cool to room temperature. Add chiles, garlic, and salt

and stir until combined. Transfer sauce to airtight container and refrigerate until ready to use. (Sauce can be refrigerated for up to 2 weeks. Bring to room temperature before serving.)

5A. FOR A CHARCOAL GRILL: Open bottom vent completely. Light large chimney starter filled with charcoal briquettes (6 quarts). When top coals are partially covered with ash, pour evenly over half of grill. Set cooking grate in place, cover, and open lid vent completely. Heat grill until hot, about 5 minutes.

5B. FOR A GAS GRILL: Turn all burners to high, cover, and heat grill until hot, about 15 minutes. Leave primary burner and secondary burner (next to primary burner) on high and turn off other burner(s). Adjust secondary burner as needed to maintain grill temperature between 400 and 450 degrees.

6. Clean and oil cooking grate. Remove hens from bag, leaving any marinade that sticks to hens in place. Tuck wingtips behind backs and turn legs so drumsticks face inward toward breasts. Place hens, skin side up, on cooler side of grill (if using charcoal, arrange hens so that legs and thighs are facing coals). Cover and cook until skin has browned and breasts register 145 to 150 degrees, 30 to 35 minutes, rotating hens halfway through cooking.

7. Using tongs, carefully flip hens and place skin side down on hotter side of grill. Cover and cook until skin is crisp, deeply browned, and charred in spots and breasts register 160 degrees, 3 to 5 minutes, being careful to avoid burning.

8. Transfer hens, skin side up, to cutting board, tent with aluminum foil, and let rest for 10 minutes. Carve each hen in half or into 4 pieces and serve, passing dipping sauce separately.

GRILLED SALMON FILLETS

WHY THIS RECIPE WORKS: Cooking delicate salmon can be tricky. Even using a nonstick skillet, it's still easy to break the occasional fillet. Introduce that same fillet to a grill, and you've got a real challenge. We wanted grilled salmon with a tender interior and crisp skin, and with each fillet perfectly intact.

We chose thicker salmon fillets, which could stand the heat of the grill for a little while longer before the first turn. To prevent the fish from sticking, we dried the fish's exterior by wrapping it in kitchen towels and "seasoned" our cooking grate by brushing it over and over with multiple layers of oil until it developed a dark, shiny coating. After laying the fillets on the grate, we easily flipped each fillet without even the tiniest bit of sticking.

Grilled Salmon Fillets

SERVES 4

This recipe can be used with any thick, firm-fleshed white fish, including red snapper, grouper, halibut, and sea bass (cook white fish to 140 degrees, up to 2 minutes longer per side). If you are using skinless fillets, treat the skinned side of each as if it were the skin side. If desired, serve with Almond Vinaigrette or Olive Vinaigrette (recipes follow).

1 (1½- to 2-pound) skin-on salmon fillet, 1½ inches thick
  Vegetable oil
  Salt and pepper
  Lemon wedges

1. Use sharp knife to remove any whitish fat from belly of salmon and cut fillet into 4 equal pieces. Place fillets skin side up on large plate lined with clean kitchen towel. Place second clean kitchen towel on top of fillets and press down to blot liquid. Refrigerate fish, wrapped in towels, while preparing grill, at least 20 minutes.

2A. FOR A CHARCOAL GRILL: Open bottom vent completely. Light large chimney starter two-thirds filled with charcoal briquettes (4 quarts). When top coals are partially covered with ash, pour evenly over half of grill. Set cooking grate in place, cover, and open lid vent completely. Heat grill until hot, about 5 minutes.

2B. FOR A GAS GRILL: Turn all burners to high, cover, and heat grill until hot, about 15 minutes.

3. Clean cooking grate, then repeatedly brush grate with well-oiled paper towels until grate is black and glossy, 5 to 10 times. Lightly brush both sides of fish with oil and season with salt and pepper. Place fish skin side down on hot side of grill (if using charcoal) or turn all burners to medium (if using gas) with fillets diagonal to grate. Cover and cook until skin is well browned and crisp, 3 to 5 minutes. (Try lifting fish gently with spatula after 3 minutes; if it doesn't cleanly lift off grill, continue to cook, checking at 30-second intervals, until it releases.)

4. Flip fish and continue to cook, covered, until center is still translucent when checked with tip of paring knife and registers 125 degrees (for medium-rare) and is still translucent when cut into with paring knife, 2 to 6 minutes longer. Serve immediately with lemon wedges.

Almond Vinaigrette
MAKES ABOUT ½ CUP

⅓ cup whole almonds, toasted
1 small shallot, minced
4 teaspoons white wine vinegar
2 teaspoons honey
1 teaspoon Dijon mustard
⅓ cup extra-virgin olive oil
1 tablespoon cold water
1 tablespoon chopped fresh tarragon
  Salt and pepper

Place almonds in zipper-lock bag and, using rolling pin or bottom of skillet, pound until pieces no larger than ½ inch remain. Combine pounded almonds, shallot, vinegar, honey, and mustard in medium bowl. Whisking constantly, slowly drizzle in oil until smooth emulsion forms. Add water and tarragon and whisk to combine, then season with salt and pepper to taste. Whisk to recombine before serving.

Olive Vinaigrette
MAKES ABOUT ½ CUP

½ cup green or kalamata olives, pitted and chopped coarse
¼ cup extra-virgin olive oil
2 tablespoons chopped fresh parsley
1 small shallot, minced
2 teaspoons lemon juice
  Salt and pepper

Combine all ingredients except salt and pepper in bowl and season with salt and pepper to taste. Whisk to recombine before serving.

GLAZED SALMON

WHY THIS RECIPE WORKS: A burnt, stuck-to-the-grill crust and flavorless interior are too often the reality of glazed salmon. But truly great glazed salmon right off the grill is a thing of beauty—the sweet glaze not only forms a glossy, deeply caramelized crust, but it also permeates the flesh, making the last bite of fish every bit as good as the first. This was the salmon that we wanted to re-create—sweet, crisp, moist, and flavorful.

Our recipe coup came early on in development—we realized that the best way to prevent the glazed salmon from sticking to the cooking grate was by not letting it touch the grate at all. We grilled the salmon fillets in individual aluminum trays set over the grill. There was no need for special equipment—we simply folded heavy-duty foil into 7 by 5-inch trays. This way, the fish still picked up great smoky flavor, but didn't stick to the cooking grate. Jelly was the best base ingredient for a sweet and sticky glaze. For the deepest flavor, we brushed some glaze over

the fish toward the end of grilling, so it caramelized, and spooned the remaining glaze, enriched with butter, over the fish just before serving.

Sweet and Saucy Glazed Salmon

SERVES 4

Be sure to spray the foil trays with vegetable oil spray. You can also use Reynolds Wrap nonstick aluminum foil and skip the vegetable oil spray.

    ½ cup jalapeño jelly
    ½ cup packed fresh cilantro leaves and stems
    1 teaspoon grated fresh lime zest and
    2 tablespoons fresh lime juice
    2 scallions, chopped coarse
    2 garlic cloves, minced
    2 tablespoons unsalted butter
    4 (6- to 8-ounce) skinless salmon fillets,
       about 1¼ inches thick
       Salt and pepper

1. Process jelly, cilantro, lime zest, lime juice, scallions, and garlic in food processor or blender to a smooth glaze. Transfer glaze to small saucepan and cook over medium heat until just bubbling, 2 to 3 minutes. Measure out and reserve ¼ cup glaze. Stir butter into remaining glaze.

2. Use heavy-duty foil to make four 7 by 5-inch trays (see photo). Coat trays with vegetable oil spray. Season fillets with salt and pepper, and brush each thoroughly, on both sides, with 1 tablespoon of the reserved ¼ cup glaze. Place fillets, skinned side up, on trays.

3A. FOR A CHARCOAL GRILL: Open bottom grill vents completely. Light large chimney starter filled with charcoal briquettes (100 briquettes; 6 quarts). When coals are hot, pour evenly over grill. Set cooking grate in place, cover, and heat grill until hot, about 5 minutes.

3B. FOR A GAS GRILL: Turn all burners to high, cover, and heat grill until hot, about 15 minutes. (Adjust the burners as needed to maintain a hot fire.)

4. Clean and oil cooking grate. Place trays on grill. Cook (covered if using gas) until glaze forms a golden brown crust, 6 to 8 minutes. Flip fillets, keeping them in trays, and spoon half of buttered glaze over salmon. Continue to cook until fish is opaque and flakes apart when gently prodded with paring knife, about 2 to 4 minutes longer.

5. Transfer trays to wire rack, tent loosely with foil, and let rest for 5 minutes. Transfer salmon to platter, spoon remaining buttered glaze over the top, and serve.

Orange-Sesame Glazed Salmon

Follow the recipe for Sweet and Saucy Glazed Salmon, substituting orange marmalade for jalapeño jelly, and lemon zest and juice for lime zest and juice, in step 1. Add 2 tablespoons oyster-flavored sauce and 1 teaspoon toasted sesame oil to food processor or blender with other glaze ingredients. Stir 1 teaspoon toasted sesame seeds into glaze with butter.

NOTES FROM THE TEST KITCHEN

MAKING FOIL TRAYS

Cut four rectangles of heavy-duty aluminum foil, then crimp the edges of each piece to make a 7 by 5-inch tray.

REMOVING SKIN FROM SALMON

1. Using tip of boning knife (or sharp chef's knife), begin to cut skin away from fish at corner of fillet.

2. When enough skin is exposed, grasp it firmly with piece of paper towel, hold it taut, and carefully slice rest of skin off flesh.

Spicy Apple Glazed Salmon

Follow the recipe for Sweet and Saucy Glazed Salmon, substituting apple jelly for jalapeño jelly, and 2 tablespoons cider vinegar for lime zest and juice, in step 1. Add ½ teaspoon red pepper flakes to food processor or blender with other glaze ingredients.

BARBECUED SALMON

WHY THIS RECIPE WORKS: Store-bought smoked salmon is inconsistent in quality and also incredibly expensive—up to $8 for just 4 ounces. We wanted to create our own easy recipe for this dish that's often reserved for weekend brunch, and make moist (but not too moist), nicely crusted salmon with a hint of smoked flavor—in just two hours.

Surprisingly, impatience turned out to be the key to our success. Instead of the traditional cold-smoking technique, which keeps the salmon moist but lacks flavor, we developed a "hot-smoked" method, and kept the salmon moist by brining. We achieved full smoked salmon flavor on the grill using a whole side of salmon. To get a firm but not overly dry texture, complemented by a strong hit of smoke and wood, we slow-cooked the salmon with wood chips or chunks for more than an hour over a modified two-level fire, but kept the fish on the cooler part of the grill the whole time. Using two spatulas to transfer the cooked fish from the grill prevented it from falling apart, and cutting through the pink flesh, not the skin, to divide individual portions kept the meat intact while leaving the skin behind.

Barbecued Salmon
SERVES 4 TO 6

The cooking grate must be hot and thoroughly clean before you place the salmon on it; otherwise the fish might stick. Use foil or the back of a large rimmed baking sheet to get the fish onto the grill. If you'd like to use wood chunks instead of wood chips when using a charcoal grill, substitute 2 medium wood chunks, soaked in water for 1 hour, for the wood chip packet. If desired, serve the salmon with Horseradish Cream Sauce with Chives or Mustard-Dill Sauce (recipes follow).

    1   cup sugar
    ½   cup salt
    1   (2½-pound) skin-on salmon fillet
    2   cups wood chips, soaked in water for
        15 minutes and drained
    2   tablespoons vegetable oil
    1½ teaspoons sweet paprika
    1   teaspoon ground white pepper

1. Dissolve sugar and salt in 7 cups cold water in gallon-size zipper-lock bag. Add salmon, seal bag, and refrigerate for 3 hours. Remove salmon from brine, pat dry with paper towels, and rub thoroughly with oil. Lay salmon skin side down on 30-inch sheet of heavy-duty aluminum foil and season top and sides with paprika and pepper.

2A. FOR A CHARCOAL GRILL: Open bottom grill vent halfway. Light large chimney starter half filled with charcoal briquettes (3 quarts). When top coals are partially covered with ash, pour evenly over half of grill. Place wood chip packet on coals. Set cooking grate in place, cover, and open lid vent completely halfway. Heat grill until hot and wood chips are smoking, about 5 minutes.

2B. FOR A GAS GRILL: Remove grill grate and place wood chip packet directly on primary burner. Set cooking grate in place, turn all burners to high, cover, and heat grill until hot and wood chips are smoking, about 15 minutes. Leave primary burner on medium and turn off other burner(s). (Adjust primary burner as needed to maintain grill temperature around 275 degrees.)

3. Clean cooking grate, then repeatedly brush grate with well-oiled paper towels until black and glossy, 5 to 10 times. Gently slide salmon off foil onto cooler side of grill, skin-side down and perpendicular to grill grate. Cover (position lid vent over meat if using charcoal) and cook until heavily flavored with smoke, about 1½ hours.

4. Using two spatulas, gently remove salmon from grill. Serve hot or at room temperature.

Horseradish Cream Sauce with Chives
MAKES ABOUT 1 CUP

    1   cup crème fraîche or sour cream
    2   tablespoons prepared horseradish
    2   tablespoons minced fresh chives
        Pinch table salt

Combine the ingredients in a small bowl. (The sauce can be refrigerated in an airtight container for up to 1 day.)

Mustard-Dill Sauce
MAKES ABOUT 1 CUP

Use Dijon, honey, or grainy mustard, as desired. Depending on your choice of mustard, this sauce can be fairly hot.

    1   cup mustard (see note)
    ¼   cup minced fresh dill

Combine the ingredients in a small bowl. (The sauce can be refrigerated in an airtight container for up to 1 day.)

BEHIND THE SCENES

HOW TO AVOID A STICKY SITUATION: PREVENTING FISH (AND MORE) FROM STICKING TO THE GRILL

To prevent food from sticking, the cooking grate should be oiled once it is hot, after being scraped clean. Debris is more readily removed from a hot grate than a cool one, and once these stuck-on bits are gone, the grate can be more effectively slicked down with an oil-dipped wad of paper towels.

Oiling the cooking grate once it's hot also helps the oil to bond quickly to the metal and prevent proteins from sticking to the cooking grate. When oil is added to a cold cooking grate, the oil slowly vaporizes as the grill reaches the desired cooking temperature. The more the oil vaporizes, the less oil will be left on the cooking grate, making sticking more likely.

And for foods that are especially prone to sticking to the grill, like fish, multiple applications of oil work wonders. Simply apply the oil to the grate five to 10 times, re-dipping the towels in the oil between applications, until the grate is black and glossy.

One more point: Never try to take a shortcut by spraying a hot cooking grate with vegetable oil spray. You might save about 10 seconds, but you risk having a flare-up on your hands.

GRILL-SMOKED SALMON

WHY THIS RECIPE WORKS: We wanted to capture the intense, smoky flavor of hot-smoked fish and the firm but silky texture of the cold-smoked type, but we also wanted to skip specialized equipment and make this dish less of a project. We quick-cured the fish with a mixture of salt and sugar to draw moisture from the flesh, and we seasoned it inside and out. We then cooked it over a gentle fire with ample smoke to produce salmon that was sweet, smoky, and tender. We also cut our large fillet into individual serving-size portions. This ensured more thorough smoke exposure by creating more surface area. Plus, the smaller pieces of salmon were far easier to get off the grill intact than one large fillet.

Grill-Smoked Salmon

SERVES 6

Use center-cut salmon fillets of similar thickness so that they cook at the same rate. The best way to ensure uniformity is to buy a 2½- to 3-pound whole center-cut fillet and cut it into six pieces. Avoid mesquite wood chunks for this recipe. Serve the salmon with lemon wedges or with our "Smoked Salmon Platter" Sauce or Apple-Mustard Sauce (recipes follow).

- 2 tablespoons sugar
- 1 tablespoon kosher salt
- 6 (6- to 8-ounce) center-cut skin-on salmon fillets
- 2 wood chunks soaked in water for 30 minutes and drained (if using charcoal) or 2 cups wood chips, half of chips soaked in water for 15 minutes and drained (if using gas)

1. Combine sugar and salt in bowl. Set wire rack in rimmed baking sheet, set salmon on rack, and sprinkle flesh side evenly with sugar mixture. Refrigerate, uncovered, for 1 hour. With paper towels, brush any excess salt and sugar from salmon and blot dry. Return fish on wire rack to refrigerator, uncovered, while preparing grill.

2A. FOR A CHARCOAL GRILL: Open bottom vent halfway. Light large chimney starter one-third filled with charcoal briquettes (2 quarts). When top coals are partially covered with ash, pour into steeply banked pile against side of grill. Place wood chunks on top of coals. Set cooking grate in place, cover, and open lid vent halfway. Heat grill until hot and wood chunks begin to smoke, about 5 minutes.

2B. FOR A GAS GRILL: Combine soaked and unsoaked chips. Use large piece of heavy-duty aluminum foil to wrap chips into foil packet and cut several vent holes in top. Place wood chip packet directly on primary burner. Turn primary burner to high (leave other burners off), cover, and heat grill until hot and wood chips begin to smoke, 15 to 25 minutes. Turn primary burner to medium. (Adjust primary burner as needed to maintain grill temperature of 275 to 300 degrees.)

3. Clean and oil cooking grate. Fold piece of heavy-duty foil into 18 by 6-inch rectangle. Place foil rectangle over cool side of grill and place salmon pieces on foil, spaced at least ½ inch apart. Cover grill (positioning lid vent over fish if using charcoal) and cook until center of thickest part of fillet registers 125 degrees and is still translucent when checked with tip of paring knife, 30 to 40 minutes. Transfer to platter and serve, or allow to cool to room temperature.

"Smoked Salmon Platter" Sauce

MAKES 1½ CUPS

This sauce incorporates the three garnishes that are commonly served on a smoked salmon platter—hard-cooked egg, capers, and dill.

- 1 large egg yolk, plus 1 large hard-cooked egg, chopped fine
- 2 teaspoons Dijon mustard
- 2 teaspoons sherry vinegar
- ½ cup vegetable oil
- 2 tablespoons capers, rinsed, plus 1 teaspoon caper brine
- 2 tablespoons minced shallot
- 2 tablespoons minced fresh dill

Whisk egg yolk, mustard, and vinegar together in medium bowl. Whisking constantly, slowly drizzle in oil until emulsified, about 1 minute. Gently fold in capers and brine, hard-cooked egg, shallot, and dill.

Apple-Mustard Sauce

MAKES 1½ CUPS

- 2 Honeycrisp or Granny Smith apples, peeled, cored, and cut into ¼-inch dice
- ¼ cup whole-grain mustard
- 2 tablespoons Dijon mustard
- 2 tablespoons minced fresh chervil or parsley
- 1 tablespoon cider vinegar
- 1 tablespoon honey
- ¼ teaspoon salt

Combine all ingredients in bowl.

GRILLED TUNA STEAKS

WHY THIS RECIPE WORKS: Most grilled tuna steaks are either rare in the center with no char or have a great sear enveloping a dry, mealy interior. We wanted a thick layer of hot, grilled tuna with an intense smoky char wrapped around a cool, delicately flavored, tender, and moist center.

We began by selecting tuna steaks that were thick enough to stay on the grill long enough to achieve a decent crust without overcooking. Our initial test of cooking methods proved that using direct heat with a hot fire and getting the tuna on and off the grill as quickly as possible worked well. For the charred flavor we were after, we turned to an ingredient that can enhance browning—oil. Oil helped to distribute heat evenly over the surface of the fish, including those areas not actually touching the cooking grate, and it added a little fat to the lean tuna, which kept the exterior from getting too dry and stringy. But oil alone didn't infuse our fish with grill flavor. We discovered that to moisten the tuna's flesh, the oil needed to penetrate the meat's tiny muscle fibers. Instead, we turned to a vinaigrette. The dressing (and its oil) clung to the fish, moistening its exterior and solving the problem of dry flesh. To improve browning we added honey to our vinaigrette. The sugars caramelized quickly on the grill, helping deliver a perfectly browned crust on our tuna steaks.

Grilled Tuna Steaks with Vinaigrette
SERVES 6

We prefer our tuna served rare or medium-rare. If you like your fish cooked medium, observe the timing for medium-rare, then tent the steaks loosely with aluminum foil for 5 minutes before serving.

- 3 tablespoons plus 1 teaspoon red wine vinegar
- 2 tablespoons chopped fresh thyme or rosemary
- 2 tablespoons Dijon mustard
- 2 teaspoons honey
  Salt and pepper
- ¾ cup olive oil
- 6 (8-ounce) tuna steaks, 1 inch thick

1A. FOR A CHARCOAL GRILL: Open bottom vent completely. Light large chimney starter filled with charcoal briquettes (6 quarts). When top coals are partially covered with ash, pour evenly over half of grill. Set cooking grate in place, cover, and open lid vent completely. Heat grill until hot, about 5 minutes.

1B. FOR A GAS GRILL: Turn all burners to high, cover, and heat grill until hot, about 15 minutes. (Adjust burners as needed to maintain hot fire.)

2. Clean cooking grate, then repeatedly brush grate with well-oiled paper towels until grate is black and glossy, 5 to 10 times.

3. Meanwhile, whisk vinegar, thyme, mustard, honey, ½ teaspoon salt, and pinch pepper together in large bowl. Whisking constantly, slowly drizzle oil into vinegar mixture until lightly thickened and emulsified. Measure out ¾ cup vinaigrette and set aside for cooking fish. Reserve remaining vinaigrette for serving.

4. Pat fish dry with paper towels. Generously brush both sides of fish with vinaigrette and season with salt and pepper. Place fish on grill (hot side if using charcoal) and cook (covered if using gas) until grill marks form and bottom surface is opaque, 1 to 3 minutes.

5. Flip fish and cook until opaque at perimeter and translucent red at center when checked with tip of paring knife and registers 110 degrees (rare), about 1½ minutes, or until opaque at perimeter and reddish pink at center when checked with tip of paring knife and registers 125 degrees (medium-rare), about 3 minutes. Serve, passing reserved vinaigrette.

GRILLED BLACKENED RED SNAPPER

WHY THIS RECIPE WORKS: Blackened fish is usually prepared in a cast-iron skillet, but it can lead to one smoky kitchen. We thought we'd solve this issue by throwing our fish on the barbie (it works for more than just shrimp, right?). Unfortunately, this move created a host of other problems, including fish stuck to the grate, the outside of the fish being way overdone by the time the flesh had cooked through, and the skin-on fillets curling midway through cooking. We were done with the smoke—and were ready for our fillets to have a dark brown, crusty, sweet-smoky, toasted spice exterior, providing a rich contrast to the moist, mild-flavored fish inside.

The curling problem was easy to fix. We simply needed to score the skin. To prevent sticking, we made sure the grill was hot when we put the fish on and oiled the grate multiple times to ensure a clean surface. Finally, to give the fish its flavorful "blackened but not burned" coating, we bloomed our spice mixture in melted butter, allowed it to cool, and then applied the coating to the fish. Once on the grill, the spice crust acquired the proper depth and richness while the fish cooked through.

Grilled Blackened Red Snapper

SERVES 4

Striped bass, halibut, or grouper can be substituted for the snapper; if the fillets are thicker or thinner, they will have slightly different cooking times. Serve the fish with lemon wedges, Rémoulade, or Pineapple and Cucumber Salsa with Mint (recipes follow).

    2 tablespoons paprika
    2 teaspoons onion powder
    2 teaspoons garlic powder
    ¾ teaspoon ground coriander
    ¾ teaspoon salt
    ¼ teaspoon cayenne pepper
    ¼ teaspoon black pepper
    ¼ teaspoon white pepper
    3 tablespoons unsalted butter
    4 (6- to 8-ounce) skin-on red snapper fillets,
       ¾ inch thick

1. Combine paprika, onion powder, garlic powder, coriander, salt, cayenne, black pepper, and white pepper in bowl. Melt butter in 10-inch skillet over medium heat. Stir in spice mixture and cook, stirring frequently, until fragrant and spices turn dark rust color, 2 to 3 minutes. Transfer mixture to pie plate and let cool to room temperature. Use a fork to break up any large clumps.

2A. FOR A CHARCOAL GRILL: Open bottom vent completely. Light large chimney starter two-thirds filled with charcoal briquettes (4 quarts). When top coals are partially

covered with ash, pour evenly over half of grill. Set cooking grate in place, cover, and open lid vent completely. Heat grill until hot, about 5 minutes.

2B. FOR A GAS GRILL: Turn all burners to high, cover, and heat grill until hot, about 15 minutes.

3. Clean cooking grate, then repeatedly brush grate with well-oiled paper towels until black and glossy, 5 to 10 times.

4. Meanwhile, pat fillets dry with paper towels. Using sharp knife, make shallow diagonal slashes every inch along skin side of fish, being careful not to cut into flesh. Place fillets skin side up on large plate. Using your fingers, rub spice mixture in thin, even layer on top and sides of fish. Flip fillets over and repeat on other side (you should use all of spice mixture).

5. Place fish skin side down on grill (hot side if using charcoal) with fillets diagonal to grate. Cook until skin is very dark brown and crisp, 3 to 5 minutes. Carefully flip fish and continue to cook until dark brown and beginning to flake and center is opaque but still moist, about 5 minutes longer. Serve.

Rémoulade

MAKES ABOUT ½ CUP

The rémoulade can be refrigerated for up to 3 days.

    ½   cup mayonnaise
    1½ teaspoons sweet pickle relish
    1   teaspoon hot sauce
    1   teaspoon lemon juice
    1   teaspoon minced fresh parsley
    ½   teaspoon capers, rinsed
    ½   teaspoon Dijon mustard
    1   small garlic clove, minced
        Salt and pepper

Pulse all ingredients in food processor until well combined but not smooth, about 10 pulses. Season with salt and pepper to taste. Transfer to serving bowl.

Pineapple and Cucumber Salsa with Mint

MAKES ABOUT 3 CUPS

To make this dish spicier, add the reserved chile seeds.

    ½   large pineapple, peeled, cored, and cut
         into ¼-inch pieces
    ½   cucumber, peeled, halved lengthwise, seeded,
         and cut into ¼-inch pieces
    1   small shallot, minced
    1   serrano chile, stemmed, seeds reserved, and minced
    2   tablespoons chopped fresh mint
    1–2 tablespoons lime juice
    ½   teaspoon grated fresh ginger
         Salt
         Sugar

Combine pineapple, cucumber, shallot, serrano, mint, 1 tablespoon lime juice, ginger, and ½ teaspoon salt in bowl and let sit at room temperature for 15 to 30 minutes. Season with lime juice, salt, and sugar to taste. Transfer to serving bowl.

ABUSE TESTS: ADAM GETS TOUGH

Adam and our team of equipment experts spend weeks—often months—testing leading brands to see which are worth buying. We start by answering basic performance questions—such as "Does this skillet heat evenly?" or "Is this knife sharp?"—with controlled kitchen tests. We sauté onions in every skillet in the line-up or we slice tomatoes with each knife. Once we've evaluated each brand in terms of performance (and design), it's time to assess durability. Here's where Adam and our equipment testers can get pretty creative. They devise abuse tests—the kinds of things you might do at home, even though you shouldn't—to see how products will fare.

Some abuse tests are pretty straightforward. We cut and serve lasagna baked in nonstick baking dishes with a metal spatula to see how the nonstick coating will hold up. Other tests are downright wacky. Here are some favorites over the years:

• Trying to melt rubber spatulas by leaving them in a cast-iron skillet heated to 674 degrees, then simmering the spatulas in a pot of curry for an hour to see if they would stain and absorb odors.

• Dropping sealed food storage bags filled with spaghetti sauce from a height of 3 feet onto a plastic tarp to see which bags would survive without sending sauce all over the kitchen.

• Holding our mitt-covered hands in the gas flame on a cooktop for 5 seconds to see which mitts are truly flame-resistant.

Why are Adam and his team willing to abuse kitchen equipment (and their hands) to see how products will perform during worst-case scenarios? Simple. Because we want to know which items really work, and which ones don't.

GRILLED FISH TACOS

WHY THIS RECIPE WORKS: For a fish taco with fresh, bold flavors, we fired up the grill. For simplicity we opted for skinless fillets instead of the traditional whole butterflied fish. Meaty swordfish held up on the grill better than flaky options like hake and cod. A thick paste featuring ancho and chipotle chile powders, oregano, and just a touch of citrus juice developed deep, flavorful charring on the grill without promoting sticking. Refreshing grilled pineapple salsa, avocado, and crunchy iceberg lettuce completed our tacos with flavor and texture contrasts.

Grilled Fish Tacos
SERVES 6

Mahi-mahi, tuna, and halibut fillets are all suitable substitutes for the swordfish but to ensure the best results buy 1-inch-thick fillets and cut them in a similar fashion to the swordfish.

- 3 tablespoons vegetable oil
- 1 tablespoon ancho chile powder
- 2 teaspoons chipotle chile powder
- 1 teaspoon dried oregano
- 1 teaspoon ground coriander
- 2 garlic cloves, minced
- Salt
- 2 tablespoons tomato paste
- ½ cup orange juice
- 6 tablespoons lime juice (3 limes)
- 2 pounds skinless swordfish steaks, 1 inch thick, cut lengthwise into 1-inch-wide strips
- 1 pineapple, peeled, quartered lengthwise, cored, and each quarter halved lengthwise
- 1 jalapeño chile
- 18 (6-inch) corn tortillas
- 1 red bell pepper, stemmed, seeded, and cut into ¼-inch pieces
- 2 tablespoons minced fresh cilantro, plus extra for serving
- ½ head iceberg lettuce (4½ ounces), cored and thinly sliced
- 1 avocado, halved, pitted, and sliced thin
- Lime wedges

1. Heat 2 tablespoons oil, ancho chile powder, and chipotle chile powder in 8-inch skillet over medium heat, stirring constantly, until fragrant and some bubbles form, 2 to 3 minutes. Add oregano, coriander, garlic, and 1 teaspoon salt and continue to cook until fragrant, about 30 seconds longer. Add tomato paste and, using spatula, mash tomato paste with spice mixture until combined, about 20 seconds. Stir in orange juice and 2 tablespoons lime juice. Cook, stirring constantly, until thoroughly mixed and reduced slightly, about 2 minutes. Transfer chile mixture to large bowl and cool for 15 minutes.

2. Add swordfish to bowl with chile mixture, and stir gently with rubber spatula to coat fish. Cover and refrigerate for at least 30 minutes or up to 2 hours.

3A. FOR A CHARCOAL GRILL: Open bottom vent completely. Light large chimney starter mounded with charcoal briquettes (7 quarts). When top coals are partially covered with ash, pour evenly over grill. Set cooking grate in place, cover, and open lid vent completely. Heat grill until hot, about 5 minutes.

3B. FOR A GAS GRILL: Turn all burners to high, cover, and heat grill until hot, about 15 minutes. Turn all burners to medium-high.

4. Clean cooking grate, then repeatedly brush grate with well-oiled paper towels until grate is black and glossy, 5 to 10 times. Brush both sides of pineapple with remaining 1 tablespoon oil. Place fish on half of grill. Place pineapple and jalapeño on other half. Cover and cook until fish, pineapple, and jalapeño have begun to brown, 3 to 5 minutes. Using thin spatula, flip fish, pineapple, and jalapeño over. Cover and continue to cook until second sides of pineapple and jalapeño are browned and swordfish registers 140 degrees, 3 to 5 minutes. Transfer fish to large platter, flake into pieces, and tent with aluminum foil. Transfer pineapple and jalapeño to cutting board.

5. Clean cooking grate. Place half of tortillas on grill. Grill until softened and speckled with brown spots, 30 to 45 seconds per side. Wrap tortillas in dish towel or foil to keep warm until ready to use. Repeat with remaining tortillas.

6. When cool enough to handle, finely chop pineapple and jalapeño. Transfer to medium bowl and stir in bell pepper, cilantro, and remaining 4 tablespoons lime juice. Season with salt to taste. Top tortillas with flaked fish, salsa, lettuce, and avocado. Serve with lime wedges and extra cilantro.

GRILLED SEA SCALLOPS

WHY THIS RECIPE WORKS: In theory, the blazing-hot fire of a grill is perfect for cooking scallops with an extra-crisp crust and moist interior, but in practice they're usually rubbery and overcooked by the time they develop a good sear—and they inevitably stick to the grate. For great grilled scallops, we needed to figure out how to build the biggest fire possible. The solution for a charcoal grill was a disposable aluminum pan—it allowed us to corral the coals in just the center of the grill for a tall, even, super-hot fire that gave us scallops with impressive char and juicy centers. Drying the scallops with kitchen towels

before cooking helped ensure browning, and threading them onto two side-by-side skewers made them easy to flip all at once. To combat the problem of sticking, we lightly coated the scallops in a mixture of flour, cornstarch, oil, and sugar. With this simple coating, our scallops were crisp-crusted, moist and tender within, and they came off the grill without hesitation. To complement the scallops, a chile-lime vinaigrette contributed both brightness and heat, or a basil vinaigrette added a light, summery flavor.

Grilled Sea Scallops

SERVES 4

We recommend buying "dry" scallops, which don't have chemical additives and taste better than "wet." Dry scallops will look ivory or pinkish; wet scallops are bright white. If using wet scallops, soak them in a solution of 1 quart water, ¼ cup lemon juice, and 2 tablespoons salt for 30 minutes before step 1, and do not season with salt in step 3. You will need eight to twelve 12-inch metal skewers for this recipe. Double-skewering the scallops makes flipping easier. Serve with one recipe vinaigrette (recipes follow), if desired.

1½	pounds large dry sea scallops, tendons removed
1	(13 by 9-inch) disposable aluminum roasting pan
2	tablespoons vegetable oil
1	tablespoon all-purpose flour
1	teaspoon cornstarch
1	teaspoon sugar
	Salt and pepper
	Lemon wedges

1. Place scallops on rimmed baking sheet lined with clean dish towel. Place second clean dish towel on top of scallops and press gently on towel to blot liquid. Let scallops sit at room temperature, covered with towel, for 10 minutes. To double-skewer scallops, thread 4 to 6 scallops, 1 flat side down, onto 1 skewer and then place second skewer through scallops parallel to and about ¼ inch from first. Return skewered scallops to towel-lined baking sheet; refrigerate, covered with second towel, while preparing grill.

2A. FOR A CHARCOAL GRILL: Open bottom vent completely. Light large chimney starter mounded with charcoal briquettes (7 quarts). Meanwhile, poke twelve ½-inch holes in bottom of disposable pan and place in center of grill. When top coals are partially covered with ash, empty coals into pan. Set cooking grate in place, cover, and open lid vent completely. Heat grill until hot, about 5 minutes.

2B. FOR A GAS GRILL: Turn all burners to high, cover, and heat grill until hot, about 15 minutes.

3. While grill heats, whisk oil, flour, cornstarch, and sugar together in small bowl. Remove towels from scallops. Brush both sides of skewered scallops with oil mixture and season with salt and pepper.

4. Clean cooking grate, then repeatedly brush grate with well-oiled paper towels until grate is black and glossy, 5 to 10 times.

5. Place skewered scallops directly on grill (directly over hot coals if using charcoal). Cook (covered if using gas) without moving scallops until lightly browned, 2½ to 4 minutes. Carefully flip skewers and continue to cook until second side of scallops is browned, sides are firm, and centers are opaque, 2 to 4 minutes longer. Serve immediately with lemon wedges.

Chile-Lime Vinaigrette
MAKES ABOUT 1 CUP

- 1 teaspoon grated lime zest plus 3 tablespoons juice (2 limes)
- 2 tablespoons honey
- 1 tablespoon Sriracha sauce
- 2 teaspoons fish sauce
- ½ cup vegetable oil

Whisk lime zest and juice, honey, Sriracha, and fish sauce together in medium bowl until combined. Whisking constantly, slowly drizzle in oil until emulsified.

Basil Vinaigrette
MAKES ABOUT 1 CUP

- 1 cup packed fresh basil leaves
- 3 tablespoons minced fresh chives
- 2 tablespoons champagne vinegar
- 2 garlic cloves, minced
- 2 teaspoons sugar
- 1 teaspoon salt
- ½ teaspoon pepper
- ⅔ cup vegetable oil

Pulse basil, chives, vinegar, garlic, sugar, salt, and pepper in blender until roughly chopped, 5 to 7 pulses. With blender running, slowly drizzle in oil until emulsified, scraping down sides of blender jar as needed, about 1 minute.

GRILLED BACON-WRAPPED SCALLOPS

WHY THIS RECIPE WORKS: Smoky, salty bacon beautifully accents sweet, succulent scallops, and we thought taking it to the grill would make a great thing even better. We set out to make this classic appetizer into a grilled entrée.

We knew we needed to parcook the bacon to prevent the grease from dripping into the fire and incinerating our scallops. Microwaving proved a perfect solution: We layered strips of bacon between paper towels (to absorb grease) and weighed them down with a second plate to prevent curling. We wrapped each strip of bacon around two scallops for an ideal scallop to bacon ratio. Tossing the scallops in melted

butter added richness, and pressing the scallops firmly together on the skewers prevented them from spinning when flipped. A two-level fire cooked both scallops and bacon to perfection. A spritz of grilled lemon juice and a sprinkling of chopped chives gave the dish a bright finish.

Grilled Bacon-Wrapped Scallops
SERVES 4

Use ordinary bacon, as thick-cut bacon will take too long to crisp on the grill. When wrapping the scallops, the bacon slice should fit around both scallops, overlapping just enough to be skewered through both ends. We recommend buying "dry" scallops, which don't have chemical additives and taste better than "wet." Dry scallops will look ivory or pinkish; wet scallops are bright white. This recipe was developed with large sea scallops (sold 10 to 20 per pound).

- 12 slices bacon
- 24 large sea scallops, tendons removed
- 3 tablespoons unsalted butter, melted
- ½ teaspoon salt
- ⅛ teaspoon pepper
- 2 lemons, halved
- ¼ cup chopped fresh chives

1. Place 4 layers paper towels on large plate and arrange 6 slices bacon over towels in single layer. Top with 4 more paper towels and remaining 6 slices bacon. Cover with 2 layers of paper towels; place second large plate on top and press gently to flatten. Microwave until fat begins to render but bacon is still pliable, about 4 minutes. Toss scallops, butter, salt, and pepper together in bowl until scallops are thoroughly coated with butter.

2. Press 2 scallops together, side to side, and wrap with 1 slice bacon, trimming excess as necessary. Thread onto skewer through bacon. Repeat with remaining scallops and bacon, threading 3 bundles onto each of 4 skewers.

3A. FOR A CHARCOAL GRILL: Open bottom vent completely. Light large chimney starter filled with charcoal briquettes (6 quarts). When top coals are partially covered with ash, pour two-thirds evenly over half of grill, then pour remaining coals over other half of grill. Set cooking grate in place, cover, and open lid vent completely. Heat grill until hot, about 5 minutes.

3B. FOR A GAS GRILL: Turn all burners to high, cover, and heat grill until hot, about 15 minutes. Leave primary burner on high and turn other burner(s) to medium.

4. Clean and oil cooking grate. Place skewers, bacon side down, and lemon halves, cut side down, on cooler side of grill. Cook (covered, if using gas) until bacon is crispy on first side, about 4 minutes. Flip skewers onto other bacon side and cook until crispy, about 4 minutes longer. Flip skewers scallop side down and move to hot side of grill. Grill until sides of scallops are firm and centers are opaque, about 4 minutes on 1 side only. Transfer skewers to platter, squeeze lemon over, and sprinkle with chives. Serve.

GRILLED SHRIMP SKEWERS

WHY THIS RECIPE WORKS: Really great grilled shrimp—tender, moist, and flavorful—are hard to come by. Usually, they're overcooked and rubbery, giving the jaws a workout, thanks to their quick cooking time and the high temperature of the grill. Grilling shrimp in their shells can guarantee juiciness, but the seasoning tends to be lost when the shells are pulled off. We wanted tender, juicy, boldly seasoned grilled shrimp, with the flavor in the shrimp and not on our fingers.

Our decision to go with peeled shrimp for this recipe meant we had to revisit how we traditionally grilled shrimp. First we eliminated brining, which created waterlogged shrimp and hindered caramelization. Then we set the shrimp over a screaming-hot fire. This worked well with jumbo shrimp, but smaller shrimp overcooked before charring. With jumbo shrimp costing as much as $25 per pound, we decided against them. They did give us an idea, though. For our next step, we created faux jumbo shrimp by cramming a skewer with several normal-sized shrimp pressed tightly together. Our final revision was to take the shrimp off the fire before they were completely cooked (but after they had picked up attractive grill marks). We finished cooking them in a heated sauce waiting on the cool side of the grill; this final simmer gave them tons of flavor.

Grilled Shrimp Skewers
SERVES 4
The shrimp and sauce finish cooking together on the grill, so prepare the sauce ingredients while the grill is heating. To fit all of the shrimp on the cooking grate at once, you will need three 14-inch metal skewers. Serve with grilled bread.

1½   pounds extra-large shrimp (21 to 25 per pound), peeled and deveined (see page 240)
2–3 tablespoons olive oil
      Salt and pepper
¼   teaspoon sugar
1   recipe sauce (recipes follow)
      Lemon wedges

1. Pat shrimp dry with paper towels. Thread the shrimp onto 3 skewers, alternating direction of heads and tails. Brush both sides of shrimp with oil and season with salt and pepper. Sprinkle 1 side of each skewer evenly with sugar.

2A. FOR A CHARCOAL GRILL: Open bottom vent completely. Light large chimney starter filled with charcoal briquettes (6 quarts). When top coals are partially covered with ash, pour evenly over half of grill. Set cooking grate in place, cover, and open lid vent completely. Heat grill until hot, about 5 minutes.

2B. FOR A GAS GRILL: Turn all burners to high, cover, and heat grill until hot, about 15 minutes. Leave primary burner on high and turn other burner(s) to medium-low.

NOTES FROM THE TEST KITCHEN

ARRANGING SHRIMP ON A SKEWER

Pass the skewer through the center of each shrimp. As you add shrimp to the skewer, alternate the directions of the heads and tails for a compact arrangement of shrimp. The shrimp should fit snugly against one another.

3. Clean cooking grate, then repeatedly brush grate with well-oiled paper towels until grate is black and glossy, 5 to 10 times. Place disposable pan with sauce ingredients on hot side of grill and cook, stirring occasionally, until hot, 1 to 3 minutes. Move pan to cool side of grill.

4. Place shrimp skewers sugared side down on hot side of grill and use tongs to push shrimp together on skewers if they have separated. Cook shrimp until lightly charred, 4 to 5 minutes. Using tongs, flip and continue to cook until second side is pink and slightly translucent, 1 to 2 minutes longer.

5. Using potholder, carefully lift each skewer from grill and use tongs to slide shrimp off skewers into pan with sauce. Toss shrimp and sauce to combine. Place pan on hot side of grill and cook, stirring, until shrimp are opaque throughout, about 30 seconds. Remove from the grill, add remaining sauce ingredients, and toss to combine. Transfer to serving platter and serve with lemon wedges.

Spicy Lemon-Garlic Sauce
MAKES ABOUT ½ CUP

- 4 tablespoons unsalted butter, cut into 4 pieces
- ¼ cup lemon juice (2 lemons)
- 3 garlic cloves, minced
- ½ teaspoon red pepper flakes
- ⅛ teaspoon salt
- 1 (10-inch) disposable aluminum pie pan
- ⅓ cup minced fresh parsley

Combine butter, lemon juice, garlic, pepper flakes, and salt in aluminum pan. Cook over hot side of grill, stirring occasionally, until butter melts, about 1½ minutes. Move to cool side of grill and proceed to grill shrimp, adding parsley just before serving.

Fresh Tomato Sauce with Feta and Olives
MAKES ABOUT ½ CUP

- ¼ cup extra-virgin olive oil
- 1 large tomato, cored, seeded, and minced
- 1 tablespoon minced fresh oregano
- ⅛ teaspoon salt
- 1 (10-inch) disposable aluminum pie pan
- 4 ounces feta cheese, crumbled (1 cup)
- ⅓ cup kalamata olives, pitted and chopped fine
- 2 tablespoons lemon juice
- 3 scallions, sliced thin

Combine oil, tomato, oregano, and salt in aluminum pan. Cook over hot side of grill, stirring occasionally, until hot, about 1½ minutes. Move to cool side of grill and proceed to grill shrimp, adding feta, olives, lemon juice, and scallions just before serving.

GRILLED SHRIMP AND VEGETABLE KEBABS

WHY THIS RECIPE WORKS: Combined shrimp and vegetable kebabs are notoriously difficult to cook because the shrimp inevitably overcooks in the time it takes most vegetables to pass from raw to their crisp-tender ideal. As a result, you end up serving either overcooked shrimp or undercooked vegetables. This recipe works by pairing slower cooking jumbo shrimp with soft, quick-cooking vegetables. Mushrooms are nestled into the curve of the shrimp on the skewer to better insulate the shrimp and extend their cooking time, and the vegetables are cut to mimic the profile of the shrimp, so the entire skewer makes contact with the grill, promoting even cooking. Finally, some vegetables are precooked in the microwave before they are skewered to give them a head start. Simply seasoning with oil and pepper allows the kebabs to char beautifully on the grill, and dressing them with a fresh lemon-herb vinaigrette while they're hot from the fire finishes the dish in style.

Grilled Shrimp And Vegetable Kebabs
SERVES 4 TO 6

Small mushrooms about 1¼ to 1½ inches in diameter work best here. If using larger mushrooms, halve them before microwaving. You will need eight 12-inch metal skewers for this recipe.

SHRIMP

- Salt and pepper
- 2 tablespoons sugar
- 1½ pounds jumbo shrimp (16 to 20 per pound), peeled and deveined (see page 240)
- 3 large red or yellow bell peppers, stemmed, seeded, and cut into ¾-inch-wide by 3-inch-long strips

24 cremini mushrooms, trimmed

12 scallions, cut into 3-inch lengths

2 tablespoons vegetable oil

VINAIGRETTE

¼ cup lemon juice (2 lemons)

¼ cup extra-virgin olive oil

2 teaspoons minced fresh thyme

1 garlic clove, minced

½ teaspoon salt

¼ teaspoon Dijon mustard

⅛ teaspoon pepper

1. FOR THE SHRIMP: Dissolve 2 tablespoons salt and sugar in 1 quart cold water in large container. Submerge shrimp in brine, cover, and refrigerate for 15 minutes. Remove shrimp from brine and pat dry with paper towels.

2. Line large microwave-safe plate with double layer of paper towels. Spread half of bell peppers skin side down in even layer on plate and sprinkle with ⅛ teaspoon salt. Microwave for 2 minutes. Transfer peppers, still on towels, to cutting board and let cool. Repeat with fresh paper towels and remaining bell peppers.

3. Line second plate with double layer of paper towels. Spread mushrooms in even layer on plate and sprinkle with ⅛ teaspoon salt. Microwave for 3 minutes. Transfer mushrooms, still on towels, to cutting board and let cool.

4. Lay one shrimp on cutting board and run 12-inch metal skewer through center. Thread mushroom onto skewer through sides of cap, pushing so it nestles tightly into curve of shrimp. Follow mushroom with two pieces scallion and two pieces bell pepper, skewering so vegetables and shrimp form even layer. Repeat shrimp and vegetable sequence two more times. When skewer is full, gently press ingredients so they fit snugly together in center of each skewer. Skewer remaining shrimp and vegetables on seven more skewers for total of 8 kebabs. Brush each side of kebabs with vegetable oil and season with pepper.

5A. FOR A CHARCOAL GRILL: Open bottom vent completely. Light large chimney starter mounded with charcoal briquettes (7 quarts). When top coals are partially covered with ash, pour evenly over grill. Set cooking grate in place, cover, and open lid vent completely. Heat grill until hot, about 5 minutes.

5B. FOR A GAS GRILL: Turn all burners to high, cover, and heat grill until hot, about 15 minutes. Leave all burners on high.

6. FOR THE VINAIGRETTE: While grill heats, whisk all ingredients together in bowl.

7. Clean and oil cooking grate. Place kebabs on grill and grill (covered if using gas) until charred, about 2½ minutes. Flip skewers and grill until second side is charred and shrimp are cooked through, 2 to 3 minutes, moving skewers as needed to ensure even cooking. Transfer skewers to serving platter. Rewhisk vinaigrette and drizzle over kebabs. Serve.

GRILLED SWORDFISH SKEWERS WITH TOMATO-SCALLION CAPONATA

WHY THIS RECIPE WORKS: Swordfish is a favorite fish to grill along the Mediterranean and beyond. It has a robust taste and needs costarring ingredients with just as much oomph. We paired swordfish with a Sicilian-inspired grilled caponata relish. As a base, we grilled cherry tomatoes, lemons, and scallions alongside the swordfish and added an aromatic blend of warm spices for a potent sauce to complement the fish. Once grilled, the lemon transformed from tart and acidic to sweet. Rubbing the swordfish with ground coriander added complexity that popped with the tomato, scallions, and fresh basil.

Grilled Swordfish Skewers with Tomato-Scallion Caponata

SERVES 4 TO 6

If swordfish isn't available, you can substitute halibut. You will need six 12-inch metal skewers for this recipe.

1½ pounds skinless swordfish steaks, 1¼ to 1½ inches thick, cut into 1¼-inch pieces

5 teaspoons ground coriander

Salt and pepper

12 ounces cherry tomatoes

1 small eggplant (12 ounces), cut crosswise on bias into ½-inch-thick ovals

6 scallions, trimmed

¼ cup extra-virgin olive oil

1 tablespoon grated lemon zest, plus 2 lemons, halved

1½ tablespoons honey

2 garlic cloves, minced

1 teaspoon ground cumin

¼ teaspoon ground cinnamon

⅛ teaspoon ground nutmeg

¼ cup pitted kalamata olives, chopped

2 tablespoons minced fresh basil

1. Pat swordfish dry with paper towels, rub with 1 tablespoon coriander, and season with salt and pepper. Thread fish onto three 12-inch metal skewers. Thread tomatoes onto three 12-inch metal skewers. Brush swordfish, tomatoes, eggplant, and scallions with 2 tablespoons oil.

2A. FOR A CHARCOAL GRILL: Open bottom vent completely. Light large chimney starter filled with charcoal briquettes (6 quarts). When top coals are partially covered with ash, pour evenly over grill. Set cooking grate in place, cover, and open lid vent completely. Heat grill until hot, about 5 minutes.

2B. FOR A GAS GRILL: Turn all burners to high, cover, and heat grill until hot, about 15 minutes. Leave all burners on high.

3. Clean cooking grate, then repeatedly brush grate with well-oiled paper towels until black and glossy, 5 to 10 times. Place swordfish, tomatoes, eggplant, scallions, and lemon halves on grill. Cook (covered if using gas), turning as needed, until swordfish flakes apart when gently prodded with paring knife and registers 140 degrees and tomatoes, eggplant, scallions, and lemon halves are softened and lightly charred, 5 to 15 minutes. Transfer items to serving platter as they finish grilling and tent loosely with aluminum foil. Let swordfish rest while finishing caponata.

4. Whisk remaining 2 teaspoons coriander, remaining 2 tablespoons oil, lemon zest, honey, garlic, cumin, ¾ teaspoon salt, ¼ teaspoon pepper, cinnamon, and nutmeg together in large bowl. Microwave, stirring occasionally, until fragrant, about 1 minute. Once lemons are cool enough to handle, squeeze into fine-mesh strainer set over bowl with oil-honey mixture, extracting as much juice as possible; whisk to combine. Stir in olives.

5. Using tongs, slide tomatoes off skewers onto cutting board. Coarsely chop tomatoes, eggplant, and scallions, transfer to bowl with dressing, and gently toss to combine. Season with salt and pepper to taste. Remove swordfish from skewers, sprinkle with basil, and serve with caponata.

SHRIMP BURGERS

WHY THIS RECIPE WORKS: Shrimp burgers are a long-standing specialty in coastal towns in South Carolina and Georgia where seafood is abundant. Although the particulars may vary, a good shrimp burger should be first and foremost about the shrimp. Unfortunately, some of the shrimp burgers we've had were reminiscent of fish-flavored rubber patties; others were more bread ball than shrimp burger. We set out to develop a recipe for our ideal shrimp burger: moist, chunky yet still cohesive, and with seasoning that complements the sweet shrimp flavor but doesn't overpower it. Pan frying is the most common way to cook these burgers, but we thought they would be even better on the grill, where they could develop a nice crust.

The first issue was how to prepare the shrimp. After early testing we decided we needed a combination of textures—finely chopped shrimp to help bind the burgers, as well as some larger, bite-size chunks. We realized we could pulse the shrimp in the food processor, which resulted in an inconsistent, chunky texture. As for a binder, we wanted as little as possible. Most of the recipes we found used some combination of mayonnaise, egg, and bread crumbs, but these recipes yielded burgers with shrimp swathed in a soggy, unappealing mush. The mayonnaise was adding much-needed fat and moisture (unlike beef, shrimp have little fat of their own), but we found that we could eliminate the egg and decrease the bread crumbs. Since packing the patties makes them rubbery, we handled them as little as possible, instead allowing them to firm up in the refrigerator. Some minced scallion and parsley, lemon zest, and a touch of cayenne rounded out the flavor of our burgers. By themselves or on a bun with lettuce and tartar sauce, these burgers are sure to disappear as fast as they come off the grill.

Southern Shrimp Burgers
MAKES 4 BURGERS

Be sure to use raw, not cooked, shrimp here. Dry the shrimp thoroughly before processing, or the burgers will be mushy. Handle the burgers gently when shaping and grilling; if overhandled while being shaped, the burgers will be dense and rubbery, and if handled roughly during cooking, they will break apart. Serve with Tartar Sauce (recipe follows) or another flavored mayonnaise. If using shrimp with sodium added as a preservative, omit the salt in the recipe.

1 slice hearty white sandwich bread, torn into large pieces

1½ pounds extra-large shrimp (21 to 25 per pound), peeled, deveined (see page 240), and patted dry

¼ cup mayonnaise

2 scallions, minced

2 tablespoons minced fresh parsley

2 teaspoons grated fresh lemon zest

    Pinch cayenne pepper

¼ teaspoon salt

⅛ teaspoon pepper

1. Pulse bread in food processor to fine crumbs, 10 to 15 pulses; transfer to bowl. Pulse shrimp in now-empty food processor until some pieces are finely minced and others are coarsely chopped, about 7 pulses. Transfer shrimp to large bowl.

2. Combine mayonnaise, scallions, parsley, lemon zest, cayenne, salt, and pepper in large bowl until uniform, then gently fold into processed shrimp until just combined. Sprinkle bread crumbs over mixture and gently fold until thoroughly incorporated.

3. Divide shrimp mixture into 4 equal portions and shape each into 1-inch-thick patty. Cover and refrigerate patties for at least 30 minutes or up to 3 hours.

4A. FOR A CHARCOAL GRILL: Open bottom grill vents completely. Light large chimney starter three-quarters full with charcoal briquettes (75 briquettes; 4½ quarts). When coals are hot, pour evenly over grill. Set cooking grate in place, cover, and heat grill until hot, about 5 minutes.

4B. FOR A GAS GRILL: Turn all burners to high, cover, and heat grill until hot, about 15 minutes. Turn all burners to medium-high. (Adjust burners as needed to maintain medium-hot fire.)

5. Clean and oil cooking grate. Lightly brush tops of burgers with oil, lay them on grill, oiled side down, and lightly brush other side with oil. Cook burgers, without pressing on them, until lightly browned and register 140 to 145 degrees, 10 to 14 minutes, flipping halfway through. Transfer burgers to platter, tent loosely with foil, and let rest for 5 minutes before serving.

Tartar Sauce
MAKES ABOUT 1 CUP

¾ cup mayonnaise

1½ tablespoons minced cornichons

    (about 3 large)

1 teaspoon cornichon juice

1 tablespoon minced scallion

1 tablespoon minced red onion

1 tablespoon capers, minced

Whisk all ingredients together in bowl. Cover and refrigerate until flavors meld, at least 30 minutes. (Sauce can be refrigerated for up to 4 days.)

GRILLED CORN WITH FLAVORED BUTTER

WHY THIS RECIPE WORKS: Grilled corn is a go-to summer treat, but we wanted a way to spice it up—literally. To incorporate flavorful herbs and spices into the corn, we found that a two-step approach worked best. First, we brushed the ears with vegetable oil and seared them over a hot grill fire. When the corn had a nice char, we moved the ears to a disposable pan on the grill and added a dollop of butter seasoned with herbs and other aromatic ingredients. The butter infused every kernel with extra flavor, and the disposable pan made the process simple and prevented butter-induced flare-ups on the grill.

Grilled Corn with Flavored Butter
SERVES 4 TO 6

Use a disposable aluminum roasting pan that is at least 2¾ inches deep.

1 recipe flavored butter (recipes follow)

1 (13 by 9-inch) disposable aluminum roasting pan

8 ears corn, husks and silk removed

2 tablespoons vegetable oil

    Salt and pepper

1. Place flavored butter in disposable pan. Brush corn evenly with oil and season with salt and pepper to taste.

2. Grill corn over hot fire, turning occasionally, until lightly charred on all sides, 5 to 9 minutes. Transfer corn to pan and cover tightly with aluminum foil.

3. Place pan on grill and cook, shaking pan frequently, until butter is sizzling, about 3 minutes. Remove pan from grill and carefully remove foil, allowing steam to escape away from you. Serve corn, spooning any butter in pan over individual ears.

Basil and Lemon Butter

Serve with lemon wedges, if desired. We like to use a rasp grater for zesting citrus.

    6 tablespoons unsalted butter, softened
    2 tablespoons minced fresh basil
    1 tablespoon minced fresh parsley
    1 teaspoon finely grated lemon zest
    ½ teaspoon salt
    ¼ teaspoon pepper

Combine all ingredients in small bowl.

Honey Butter

This butter also works well with cornbread.

    6 tablespoons unsalted butter, softened
    2 tablespoons honey
    ½ teaspoon salt
    ¼ teaspoon red pepper flakes

Combine all ingredients in small bowl.

Latin-Spiced Butter

Serve with orange wedges, if desired. We like to use a rasp grater for zesting citrus.

    6 tablespoons unsalted butter, softened
    2 tablespoons minced fresh cilantro
    1 tablespoon minced fresh parsley
    1 teaspoon minced canned chipotle chile in
       adobo sauce
    ½ teaspoon finely grated orange zest
    ½ teaspoon salt

Combine all ingredients in small bowl.

New Orleans "Barbecue" Butter

    6 tablespoons unsalted butter, softened
    1 garlic clove, minced
    1 tablespoon Worcestershire sauce
    1 teaspoon tomato paste
    ½ teaspoon minced fresh rosemary
    ½ teaspoon minced fresh thyme
    ½ teaspoon cayenne pepper

Combine all ingredients in small bowl.

Spicy Old Bay Butter

Serve with lemon wedges, if desired.

    6   tablespoons unsalted butter, softened
    1   tablespoon hot sauce
    1   tablespoon minced fresh parsley
    1½ teaspoons Old Bay seasoning
    1   teaspoon finely grated lemon zest

Combine all ingredients in small bowl.

MEXICAN-STYLE GRILLED CORN

WHY THIS RECIPE WORKS: In Mexico, street vendors add kick to grilled corn by slathering it with a creamy, spicy sauce. The corn takes on a sweet, charred flavor, which is heightened by the lime juice and chili powder in the cheesy sauce. We wanted to develop our own rendition of this south-of-the-border street fare. We ditched the husks, coated the ears with oil to prevent sticking, and grilled them directly on the grate. Over a single-level fire, the corn emerged nicely smoky but insufficiently charred, so we pushed all the coals to one side to create a modified two-level fire, allowing the ears to cook closer to the coals. The traditional base for the sauce is crema, a thick, soured Mexican cream. But given its spotty availability, we replaced the crema with a combination of mayonnaise and sour cream. Most recipes call for queso fresco or Cotija, but these can be hard to find. Pecorino Romano made a good substitute. We included the usual seasonings of cilantro, lime juice, garlic, and chili powder. To provide more depth, we added chili powder to the oil used for coating the corn; once heated on the grill, the chili powder bloomed with a full flavor that penetrated the corn kernels.

Mexican-Style Grilled Corn

SERVES 6

If you can find queso fresco or Cotija, use either in place of the Pecorino Romano. If you prefer the corn spicy, add the optional cayenne pepper.

1½ ounces Pecorino Romano cheese, grated (¾ cup)
¼ cup mayonnaise
3 tablespoons sour cream
3 tablespoons minced fresh cilantro
4 teaspoons lime juice
1 garlic clove, minced
¾ teaspoon chili powder
¼ teaspoon pepper
¼ teaspoon cayenne pepper (optional)
4 teaspoons vegetable oil
¼ teaspoon salt
6 ears corn, husks and silk removed

1A. FOR A CHARCOAL GRILL: Open bottom vent completely. Light large chimney starter filled with charcoal briquettes (6 quarts). When top coals are partially covered with ash, pour evenly over half of grill. Set cooking grate in place, cover, and open lid vent completely. Heat grill until hot, about 5 minutes.

1B. FOR A GAS GRILL: Turn all burners to high, cover, and heat grill until hot, about 15 minutes.

2. Meanwhile, combine Pecorino, mayonnaise, sour cream, cilantro, lime juice, garlic, ¼ teaspoon chili powder, pepper, and cayenne, if using, in large bowl and set aside. In second large bowl, combine oil, salt, and remaining ½ teaspoon chili powder. Add corn to oil mixture and toss to coat evenly.

3. Clean and oil cooking grate. Place corn on grill (hot side if using charcoal) and cook (covered if using gas) until lightly charred on all sides, 7 to 12 minutes, turning as needed. Place corn in bowl with cheese mixture, toss to coat evenly, and serve.

GRILLED POTATOES

WHY THIS RECIPE WORKS: Grilled potatoes are a summer classic, but we wanted to put a new spin on them by adding rosemary and garlic for a heartier, more savory side. We found it harder than it sounded to add garlic and rosemary flavors to plain grilled potatoes. Coating the potatoes with oil, garlic, and rosemary produced burnt, bitter garlic and charred rosemary. We wanted potent garlic and rosemary flavors in our potatoes, without bitterness and charring. We learned that we needed to introduce the potatoes to the garlic-oil mixture not once, but three times. Before cooking, we pierced the potatoes, skewered them, seasoned them with salt, brushed on a garlic-rosemary oil, and precooked them in the microwave. Then, before grilling, we brushed them again with the infused oil. After grilling, we tossed them with the garlic and rosemary oil yet again. We finally had it—tender grilled potatoes infused with the smoky flavor of the grill and enlivened with the bold flavors of garlic and rosemary.

Grilled Potatoes with Garlic and Rosemary

SERVES 4

This recipe allows you to grill an entrée while the hot coals burn down in step 4. Once that item is done, start grilling the potatoes. This recipe works best with small potatoes that are about 1½ inches in diameter. If using medium potatoes, 2 to 3 inches in diameter, cut them into quarters. If the potatoes are larger than 3 inches in diameter, cut each potato into eighths. Since the potatoes are first cooked in the microwave, use wooden skewers.

¼ cup olive oil
9 garlic cloves, minced
1 teaspoon chopped fresh rosemary
Salt and pepper
2 pounds small red potatoes, halved and skewered
2 tablespoons chopped fresh chives

1. Heat oil, garlic, rosemary, and ½ teaspoon salt in small skillet over medium heat until sizzling, about 3 minutes. Reduce heat to medium-low and continue to cook until garlic is light blond, about 3 minutes. Pour mixture through fine-mesh strainer into small bowl; press on solids. Measure 1 tablespoon of solids and 1 tablespoon of oil into large bowl and set aside. Discard remaining solids but reserve remaining oil.

2. Place skewered potatoes in single layer on large plate and poke each potato several times with skewer. Brush with 1 tablespoon of strained oil and season with salt. Microwave until the potatoes offer slight resistance when pierced with paring knife, about 8 minutes, turning halfway through cooking. Transfer potatoes to baking sheet coated with 1 tablespoon of strained oil. Brush with remaining 1 tablespoon strained oil and season with salt and pepper to taste.

3A. FOR A CHARCOAL GRILL: Open bottom vent completely. Light large chimney starter filled with charcoal briquettes (6 quarts). When top coals are partially covered with ash, pour two-thirds evenly over grill, then pour remaining coals over half of grill. Set cooking grate in place, cover, and open lid vent completely. Heat grill until hot, about 5 minutes.

SKEWERING POTATOES FOR THE GRILL

Place a potato half, cut side down, on the work surface and pierce through the center with a skewer. Repeat, holding the already-skewered potatoes for better leverage.

3B. **FOR A GAS GRILL:** Turn all burners to high, cover, and heat grill until hot, about 15 minutes. Turn all burners down to medium-high.

4. Clean and oil cooking grate. Place potatoes on grill (hotter side if using charcoal) and cook (covered if using gas) until grill marks appear, 3 to 5 minutes, flipping halfway through cooking. Move potatoes to cooler side of grill (if using charcoal) or turn all burners to medium-low (if using gas). Cover and continue to cook until paring knife slips in and out of potatoes easily, 5 to 8 minutes longer.

5. Remove potatoes from skewers and transfer to bowl with reserved garlic-oil mixture. Add chives, season with salt and pepper to taste, and toss until thoroughly coated. Serve.

TUNISIAN-STYLE GRILLED VEGETABLES

WHY THIS RECIPE WORKS: Grilling brings out the best in summer vegetables, calling forth their sweetness and adding an accent of smoke. We took inspiration from the robustly flavored Tunisian dish called *mechouia*.

We opted to use bell peppers, eggplant, zucchini, and plum tomatoes. To avoid a waterlogged salad, we halved the zucchini and eggplant and cut deep crosshatch marks in their flesh to allow them to release their moisture. We also halved the tomatoes and opened the peppers into long planks so they would cook evenly all the way through. We sprinkled the vegetables with salt and oil flavored with traditional *tabil* seasonings. The spices bloomed on the grill and became full-flavored and aromatic. More tabil, plus lemon zest and a trio of fresh herbs, brought a tangy, lively taste to our finishing vinaigrette.

Tunisian-Style Grilled Vegetables (Mechouia)
SERVES 4 TO 6

Serve as a side dish to grilled meats and fish; with grilled pita as a salad course; or with hard-cooked eggs, olives, and premium canned tuna as a light lunch. Equal amounts of ground coriander and cumin can be substituted for the whole spices.

VINAIGRETTE

- 2 teaspoons coriander seeds
- 1½ teaspoons caraway seeds
- 1 teaspoon cumin seeds
- 5 tablespoons olive oil
- ½ teaspoon sweet paprika
- ⅛ teaspoon cayenne pepper
- 3 garlic cloves, minced
- ¼ cup chopped fresh parsley
- ¼ cup chopped fresh cilantro
- 2 tablespoons chopped fresh mint
- 1 teaspoon grated lemon zest plus 2 tablespoons juice
  Salt

VEGETABLES

- 2 bell peppers (1 red and 1 green)
- 1 small eggplant, halved lengthwise
- 1 zucchini (8 to 10 ounces), halved lengthwise
- 4 plum tomatoes, cored and halved lengthwise
  Salt and pepper
- 2 medium shallots, unpeeled

1. **FOR THE VINAIGRETTE:** Grind coriander seeds, caraway seeds, and cumin seeds in spice grinder until finely ground. Whisk ground spices, oil, paprika, and cayenne together in bowl. Reserve 3 tablespoons oil mixture. Heat remaining oil mixture and garlic in small skillet over low heat, stirring occasionally, until fragrant and small bubbles appear, 8 to 10 minutes. Transfer to large bowl and let cool, about 10 minutes. Whisk parsley, cilantro, mint, and lemon zest and juice into oil mixture; season with salt to taste.

2. **FOR THE VEGETABLES:** Slice ¼ inch off tops and bottoms of bell peppers and remove cores. Make slit down 1 side of each bell pepper and then press flat into 1 long strip, removing ribs and remaining seeds with knife as needed. Using sharp knife, cut slits in flesh of eggplant and zucchini, spaced ½ inch apart, in crosshatch pattern, being careful to cut into but not through skin. Brush cut sides of bell peppers, eggplant, zucchini, and tomatoes with reserved oil mixture and season with salt to taste.

3. Grill vegetables, starting with cut sides down, over medium-hot fire, until tender and well browned and skins of bell peppers, eggplant, tomatoes, and shallots are charred, 8 to 16 minutes, turning and moving vegetables as necessary. Transfer vegetables to baking sheet as they are done. Place bell peppers in bowl, cover with plastic wrap, and let steam to loosen skins.

4. When cool enough to handle, peel bell peppers, eggplant, tomatoes, and shallots. Chop all vegetables into ½-inch pieces and transfer to bowl with vinaigrette; toss to coat. Season with salt and pepper to taste, and serve warm or at room temperature.

BABA GHANOUSH

WHY THIS RECIPE WORKS: Baba ghanoush often appears on the appetizer table as a gray, bitter, watery mass of eggplant puree. We were after a dip that had realized its potential—full of smoky eggplant flavor and brightened with garlic and lemon juice. And one certain way to produce this creation was to start off by grilling our eggplant. For the best flavor, it's imperative to start out with firm, shiny, and unblemished eggplants. We grilled the eggplants directly over a hot fire until they were wrinkled and soft. To avoid a watery texture and any bitterness, we drained the pulp of excess fluid, but didn't bother spending time deseeding the eggplants. We processed the pulp with a modest amount of garlic, tahini paste, and lemon juice for the creaminess and bright flavor that baba ghanoush is known for.

Grilled Baba Ghanoush

MAKES 2 CUPS

When buying eggplants, select those with shiny, taut, and unbruised skins and an even shape (eggplants with a bulbous shape won't cook evenly). Grill until the eggplant walls have collapsed and the insides feel sloshy when pressed with tongs. We prefer to serve baba ghanoush only lightly chilled; if cold, let it stand at room temperature for about 20 minutes before serving. Baba ghanoush does not keep well, so plan to make it the day you want to serve it. Serve with pita bread, black olives, tomato wedges, or cucumber slices.

2 pounds eggplant (about 2 large globe eggplants, 5 medium Italian eggplants, or 12 medium Japanese eggplants), pricked all over with fork
2 tablespoons tahini
1 tablespoon lemon juice
1 tablespoon extra-virgin olive oil, plus extra for serving
1 small garlic clove, minced
Salt and pepper
2 teaspoons chopped fresh parsley

1A. FOR A CHARCOAL GRILL: Open bottom vent completely. Light large chimney starter filled with charcoal briquettes (6 quarts). When top coals are partially covered with ash, pour evenly over grill. Set cooking grate in place, cover, and open lid vent completely. Heat grill until hot, about 5 minutes.

1B. FOR A GAS GRILL: Turn all burners to high, cover, and heat grill until hot, about 15 minutes. Turn all burners to medium. (Adjust burners as needed to maintain grill temperature around 350 degrees.)

2. Clean and oil cooking grate. Set eggplants on cooking grate and cook until skins darken and wrinkle on all sides and eggplants are uniformly soft when pressed with tongs, about 25 minutes for large globe eggplants, 20 minutes for Italian eggplants, and 15 minutes for Japanese eggplants, turning every 5 minutes and reversing direction of eggplants on grill with each turn. Transfer eggplants to rimmed baking sheet and cool 5 minutes.

3. Set small colander over bowl. Trim top and bottom off each eggplant. Slit eggplants lengthwise and use spoon to scoop hot pulp from skins and place pulp in colander (you should have about 2 cups packed pulp); discard skins. Let pulp drain 3 minutes.

4. Transfer pulp to food processor. Add tahini, lemon juice, oil, garlic, ¼ teaspoon salt, and ¼ teaspoon pepper. Process until mixture has coarse, choppy texture, about 8 pulses. Season with salt and pepper to taste. Transfer to serving bowl, cover with plastic wrap flush with surface of dip, and refrigerate 45 to 60 minutes. Make trough in center of dip using large spoon and spoon olive oil into it. Sprinkle with parsley and serve.

SIDES OF PLENTY

SIMPLE APPLESAUCE

WHY THIS RECIPE WORKS: Applesauce should taste like apples, but all too often the tart, sweet, and fruity nuances of fresh apple flavor are overpowered by sweeteners and spices, and the sauce ends up tasting like bad pie filling. The texture, too, can vary from dry and chunky to loose and thin. We wanted a smooth, thick sauce that showcases fresh apple flavor without too much sweetness or spice—the perfect partner to pork chops or as a snack.

The first step was to find the right variety of apple. We began by gathering 18 varieties and making each into applesauce. We found that Jonagold, Jonathan, Pink Lady, and Macoun varieties all produce a sauce with a pleasing balance of tart and sweet. We tried blending varieties in combination with each other, but concluded that single-variety sauces had purer, stronger character. Cooking the apples with their skins on saved us the step of peeling and enhanced the flavor of the sauce. Processing the cooked apples through a food mill, not a food processor or blender, removed the skins and produced a sauce with the silky-smooth, thick texture we were after. Adding a little water, sugar, and a pinch of salt—and no spices—resulted in a perfectly sweetened sauce that tasted first and foremost of apples.

Simple Applesauce
MAKES ABOUT 3½ CUPS

If you do not own a food mill or prefer applesauce with a coarse texture, peel the apples before coring and cutting them and, after cooking, mash them against the side of the pot with a wooden spoon or against the bottom of the pot with a potato masher. Applesauce made with out-of-season apples may be somewhat drier than sauce made with peak-season apples, so it's likely that in step 2 of the recipe you will need to add more water to adjust the texture. If you double the recipe, the apples will need 10 to 15 minutes of extra cooking time.

- 4 pounds apples (about 10 medium), preferably Jonagold, Pink Lady, Jonathan, or Macoun, unpeeled, cored, and cut into rough 1½-inch pieces (see note)
- 1 cup water, plus more as needed
- ¼ cup sugar, plus more to taste
- Pinch table salt

1. Toss the apples, water, sugar, and salt in a large Dutch oven. Cover the pot and cook the apples over medium-high heat until they begin to break down, 15 to 20 minutes, checking and stirring occasionally with a wooden spoon to break up any large chunks.

2. Process the cooked apples through a food mill fitted with the medium disk. Season with extra sugar to taste or add water to adjust the consistency as desired. Serve hot, warm, at room temperature, or chilled.

BREAD-AND-BUTTER PICKLES

WHY THIS RECIPE WORKS: We wanted a bread-and-butter pickle with a crisp texture and a balance of sweet and sour. Most recipes combine cucumbers and onions in a spiced, syrupy brine; we cut back on the sugar and added red bell pepper. Cucumbers can lose their crunch when processed in a boiling-water bath; combining several crisping techniques gave us the best results. We tossed our sliced vegetables in salt to draw out excess water. Then we added a small amount of Ball Pickle Crisp to each jar, which helps keep the natural pectin from breaking down. Next, we employed low-temperature pasteurization, which involved maintaining our pickles in a hot-water bath at a temperature of 180 to 185 degrees Fahrenheit for 30 minutes—in this temperature range microorganisms are destroyed and pectin remains largely intact.

Bread-and-Butter Pickles
MAKES FOUR 1-PINT JARS

- 2 pounds pickling cucumbers, ends trimmed, sliced ¼ inch thick
- 1 onion, quartered and sliced thin
- 1 red bell pepper, stemmed, seeded, and cut into 1½-inch matchsticks
- 2 tablespoons canning and pickling salt
- 3 cups apple cider vinegar
- 2 cups sugar
- 1 cup water
- 1 tablespoon yellow mustard seeds
- ¾ teaspoon ground turmeric
- ½ teaspoon celery seeds
- ¼ teaspoon ground cloves
- ½ teaspoon Ball Pickle Crisp

1. Toss cucumbers, onion, and bell pepper with salt in large bowl and refrigerate for 3 hours. Drain vegetables in colander (do not rinse), then pat dry with paper towels.

2. Meanwhile, set canning rack in large pot, place four 1-pint jars in rack, and add water to cover by 1 inch. Bring to simmer over medium-high heat, then turn off heat and cover to keep hot.

3. Bring vinegar, sugar, water, mustard seeds, turmeric, celery seeds, and cloves to boil in large saucepan over medium-high heat; cover and remove from heat.

4. Place dish towel flat on counter. Using jar lifter, remove jars from pot, draining water back into pot. Place jars upside down on towel and let dry for 1 minute. Add ⅛ teaspoon Pickle Crisp to each hot jar, then pack tightly with vegetables.

5. Return brine to brief boil. Using funnel and ladle, pour hot brine over cucumbers to cover, distributing spices evenly and leaving ½ inch headspace. Slide wooden skewer along inside of jar, pressing slightly on vegetables to remove air bubbles, and add extra brine as needed.

6A. FOR SHORT-TERM STORAGE: Let jars cool to room temperature, cover with lids, and refrigerate for 1 day before serving. (Pickles can be refrigerated for up to 3 months; flavor will continue to mature over time.)

6B. FOR LONG-TERM STORAGE: While jars are warm, wipe rims clean, add lids, and screw on rings until fingertip-tight; do not overtighten. Before processing jars, heat water in canning pot to temperature between 120 and 140 degrees. Lower jars into water, bring water to 180 to 185 degrees, then cook for 30 minutes, adjusting heat as needed to maintain water between 180 and 185 degrees. Remove jars from pot and let cool for 24 hours. Remove rings, check seal, and clean rims. (Sealed jars can be stored for up to 1 year.)

NOTES FROM THE TEST KITCHEN

MAKING BREAD-AND-BUTTER PICKLES

1. We add ⅛ teaspoon of Ball Pickle Crisp to each jar before adding cucumbers and brine to help pickles retain their crispness. Pickle Crisp is simply a form of calcium chloride, which helps keep natural pectin in the cucumbers from softening.

2. It is key to have brine hot when pouring it over pickles. Be sure to distribute spices evenly between jars and leave ½ inch of headspace.

3. To remove any air bubbles trapped between layers of cucumbers, slide a wooden skewer along inside of jar and press it gently against vegetables. Once air bubbles have been dispersed, add extra brine as needed until headspace measures ½ inch.

4. Using low-temperature pasteurization processing means jars of pickles need to cook in 180- to 185-degree water. If water climbs above 185, pickles will turn mushy. If water falls below 180 degrees, harmful bacteria could grow inside jars.

BROILED ASPARAGUS

WHY THIS RECIPE WORKS: Broiling can intensify the flavor of asparagus, turning it sweet and nutty. But getting the asparagus to cook through evenly can be tricky. We wanted a foolproof broiling method for turning out browned, tender spears every time.

To start, we found that with thicker asparagus, the exterior began to char before the interior of the spears became fully tender. When we used thinner spears, however, the interior was tender by the time the exterior was browned. Keeping the spears about four inches away from the broiling element allowed them to caramelize properly without charring. To encourage browning, we tossed the asparagus with olive oil before broiling. Shaking the pan with the asparagus as it cooked ensured that the spears cooked evenly. The intense dry heat of the broiler concentrated the flavor of the asparagus, and the exterior caramelization made the spears especially sweet.

Broiled Asparagus
SERVES 6

Broilers vary significantly in intensity, thus the wide range of cooking times in this recipe. Choose asparagus no thicker than ½ inch near the base for this recipe.

    2 pounds thin asparagus (about 2 bunches), tough ends
       trimmed (see page 300; see note)
    1 tablespoon olive oil
       Table salt and ground black pepper

Adjust an oven rack to the highest position (about 4 inches from the heating element) and heat the broiler. Toss the asparagus with the oil and salt and pepper to taste, then lay the spears in a single layer on a rimmed baking sheet. Broil, shaking the pan halfway through cooking to turn the spears, until the asparagus is tender and lightly browned, 6 to 10 minutes. Serve hot or warm.

PAN-ROASTED ASPARAGUS

WHY THIS RECIPE WORKS: Recipes for pan-roasted asparagus promise ease and flavor, but the results are usually disappointing: limp, greasy, and shriveled spears. We wanted a simple stovetop method that would deliver crisp, nicely browned spears.

We quickly learned to choose thick spears because thinner spears overcooked too quickly. Taking a cue from restaurant chefs who blanch asparagus first, we developed a method to lightly steam and then brown the asparagus in the same skillet. For both flavor and browning, we used olive oil and butter. Positioning half the spears in one direction and the other half in the opposite direction ensured a better fit in the pan. Browning just one side of the asparagus provided a contrast in texture and guaranteed that the asparagus were firm and tender, never limp.

Pan-Roasted Asparagus

SERVES 3 TO 4

This recipe works best with asparagus that is at least ½ inch thick near the base. If using thinner spears, reduce the covered cooking time to 3 minutes and the uncovered cooking time to 5 minutes. Do not use pencil-thin asparagus; it cannot withstand the heat and overcooks too easily.

1 tablespoon olive oil
1 tablespoon unsalted butter
2 pounds thick asparagus (about 2 bunches), tough ends trimmed (see page 300; see note)
  Table salt and ground black pepper
½ lemon (optional)

1. Heat the oil and butter in a 12-inch skillet over medium-high heat. When the butter has melted, add half of the asparagus to the skillet with the tips pointed in one direction; add the remaining asparagus with the tips pointed in the opposite direction. Using tongs, distribute the spears in an even layer (the spears will not quite fit into a single layer); cover and cook until the asparagus is bright green and still crisp, about 5 minutes.

2. Uncover and increase the heat to high; season the asparagus with salt and pepper to taste. Cook until the spears are tender and well browned along one side, 5 to 7 minutes, using the tongs to occasionally move the spears from the center of the pan to the edge of the pan to ensure all are browned. Transfer the asparagus to a dish, season with salt and pepper to taste, and squeeze the lemon half (if using) over the spears. Serve.

STIR-FRIED ASPARAGUS WITH SHIITAKE MUSHROOMS

WHY THIS RECIPE WORKS: To achieve stir-fried asparagus with a flavorful browned exterior and a crisp-tender texture, we had to start with a hot pan and only stir the asparagus occasionally. This allowed the vegetables to char and caramelize. To ensure that the asparagus cooked evenly, we diluted the sauce with water. This diluted sauce created a small amount of steam, cooking the spears through, before evaporating and leaving behind a flavorful glaze.

Stir-Fried Asparagus with Shiitake Mushrooms

SERVES 4

To allow it to brown, stir the asparagus only occasionally. Look for spears that are no thicker than ½ inch.

2 tablespoons water
1 tablespoon soy sauce
1 tablespoon dry sherry
2 teaspoons packed brown sugar
2 teaspoons grated fresh ginger
1 teaspoon toasted sesame oil
1 tablespoon vegetable oil
1 pound asparagus, tough ends trimmed (see page 300) and cut on bias into 2-inch lengths
4 ounces shiitake mushrooms, stemmed and sliced thin
2 scallions, green parts only, sliced thin on bias

1. Combine water, soy sauce, sherry, sugar, ginger, and sesame oil in bowl.

2. Heat vegetable oil in 12-inch nonstick skillet over high heat until smoking. Add asparagus and mushrooms and cook, stirring occasionally, until asparagus is spotty brown, 3 to 4 minutes. Add soy sauce mixture and cook, stirring once or twice, until pan is almost dry and asparagus is crisp-tender, 1 to 2 minutes. Transfer to serving platter, sprinkle with scallion greens, and serve.

Stir-Fried Asparagus with Red Bell Pepper

Omit soy sauce, sherry, brown sugar, ginger, and sesame oil. Reduce water to 1 tablespoon. Whisk 1 tablespoon orange juice, 1 tablespoon rice vinegar, 1 tablespoon granulated sugar, 1 teaspoon ketchup, and ½ teaspoon salt into water. Substitute 1 stemmed and seeded red bell pepper cut into 2-inch-long matchsticks for shiitakes.

Stir-Fried Asparagus with Red Onion

Omit soy sauce, sherry, ginger, and sesame oil. Whisk 4 teaspoons fish sauce, 1 tablespoon lime juice, 2 teaspoons minced fresh lemon grass, and ⅛ teaspoon red pepper flakes into water, along with sugar. Substitute ½ red onion sliced through root end into ¼-inch-thick pieces for shiitakes and 2 tablespoons chopped fresh mint for scallion greens.

BRAISED BEETS

WHY THIS RECIPE WORKS: We sought a streamlined recipe for beets that maximized their sweet, earthy flavor. To achieve this goal in less than an hour, we braised the halved beets on the stovetop in minimal water, reduced the residual cooking liquid, and added light brown sugar and vinegar. This flavor-packed glaze was just thick enough to coat the wedges of peeled beets. For flavor and texture contrast, we added toasted nuts (or pepitas), fresh herbs, and aromatic citrus zest just before serving.

Beets with Lemon and Almonds

SERVES 4 TO 6

To ensure even cooking, we recommend using beets that are of similar size—roughly 2 to 3 inches in diameter. The beets can be served warm or at room temperature. If serving at room temperature, wait until right before serving to sprinkle on the almonds and herbs.

- 1½ pounds beets, trimmed and halved horizontally
- 1¼ cups water
  Salt and pepper
- 3 tablespoons white vinegar
- 1 tablespoon packed light brown sugar
- 1 shallot, sliced thin
- 1 teaspoon grated lemon zest
- ½ cup whole almonds, toasted and chopped
- 2 tablespoons chopped fresh mint
- 1 teaspoon chopped fresh thyme

1. Place beets, cut side down, in single layer in 11-inch straight-sided sauté pan or Dutch oven. Add water and ¼ teaspoon salt; bring to simmer over high heat. Reduce heat to low,

cover, and simmer until beets are tender and tip of paring knife inserted into beets meets no resistance, 45 to 50 minutes.

2. Transfer beets to cutting board. Increase heat to medium-high and reduce cooking liquid, stirring occasionally, until pan is almost dry, 5 to 6 minutes. Add vinegar and sugar, return to boil, and cook, stirring constantly with heat-resistant spatula, until spatula leaves wide trail when dragged through glaze, 1 to 2 minutes. Remove pan from heat.

3. When beets are cool enough to handle, rub off skins with paper towel or clean dish towel and cut into ½-inch wedges. Add beets, shallot, lemon zest, ½ teaspoon salt, and ¼ teaspoon pepper to glaze and toss to coat. Transfer beets to serving dish; sprinkle with almonds, mint, and thyme; and serve.

Beets with Lime and Pepitas

Omit thyme. Substitute lime zest for lemon zest, toasted pepitas for almonds, and cilantro for mint.

Beets with Orange and Walnuts

Substitute orange zest for lemon zest; walnuts, toasted and chopped, for almonds; and parsley for mint.

ROASTED BROCCOLI

WHY THIS RECIPE WORKS: Roasting can concentrate flavor to turn dull vegetables into something great, but roasting broccoli usually makes for spotty browning and charred, bitter florets. We wanted to figure out how to roast broccoli so that it turned out perfectly browned and deeply flavorful every time.

To ensure that the broccoli would brown evenly, we cut the crown into uniform wedges that lay flat on the baking sheet, increasing contact with the pan. To promote even cooking of the stem, we sliced away the exterior and cut the stalk into rectangular pieces slightly smaller than the more delicate wedges. After trial and error, we discovered that preheating the baking sheet helped the broccoli cook faster, crisping but not charring the florets, while a very hot oven delivered the best browning. Sprinkling a little sugar over the broccoli along with the salt and pepper helped it brown even more deeply. We finally had roasted broccoli with crispy-tipped florets and sweet, browned stems.

Roasted Broccoli

SERVES 4

It is important to trim away the outer peel from the broccoli stalks; otherwise they will turn tough when cooked.

- 1¾ pounds broccoli (about 1 large bunch)
- 3 tablespoons extra-virgin olive oil
- ½ teaspoon table salt
- ½ teaspoon sugar
  Ground black pepper
  Lemon wedges, for serving

1. Adjust an oven rack to the lowest position, place a large rimmed baking sheet on the rack, and heat the oven to 500 degrees. Cut the broccoli at the juncture of the florets and stems; remove the outer peel from the stalk. Cut the stalk into 2 to 3-inch lengths and each length into ½-inch-thick pieces. Cut the crowns into four wedges (if 3 to 4 inches in diameter) or six wedges (if 4 to 5 inches in diameter). Place the broccoli in a large bowl; drizzle with the oil and toss well until evenly coated. Season with the salt, sugar, and pepper to taste and toss to combine.

2. Carefully remove the baking sheet from the oven. Working quickly, transfer the broccoli to the baking sheet and spread into an even layer, placing the flat sides down. Return the baking sheet to the oven and roast until the stalks are well browned and tender and the florets are lightly browned, 9 to 11 minutes. Transfer to a dish and serve with the lemon wedges.

Roasted Broccoli with Garlic

Follow the recipe for Roasted Broccoli, adding 1 garlic clove, minced or pressed through a garlic press, to the oil before drizzling it over the broccoli in step 1.

ROASTED BRUSSELS SPROUTS

WHY THIS RECIPE WORKS: Roasting is a simple and quick way to produce Brussels sprouts that are well caramelized on the outside and tender on the inside. To ensure we achieved this balance, we started out roasting the "tiny cabbages," covered, with a little bit of water. This created a steamy environment, which cooked the vegetable through. We then removed the foil and allowed the exterior to dry out and caramelize.

Roasted Brussels Sprouts

SERVES 6 TO 8

If you are buying loose Brussels sprouts, select those that are about 1½ inches long. Quarter Brussels sprouts longer than 2½ inches; don't cut sprouts shorter than 1 inch.

2¼ pounds Brussels sprouts, trimmed and halved
3 tablespoons olive oil
1 tablespoon water
  Salt and pepper

1. Adjust oven rack to upper-middle position and heat oven to 500 degrees. Toss Brussels sprouts, oil, water, ¾ teaspoon salt, and ¼ teaspoon pepper together in large bowl until sprouts are coated. Transfer sprouts to rimmed baking sheet and arrange cut sides down.

2. Cover baking sheet tightly with aluminum foil and roast for 10 minutes. Remove foil and continue to cook until Brussels sprouts are well browned and tender, 10 to 12 minutes longer. Transfer to serving platter, season with salt and pepper to taste, and serve.

Roasted Brussels Sprouts with Garlic, Red Pepper Flakes, and Parmesan

While Brussels sprouts roast, heat 3 tablespoons olive oil in 8-inch skillet over medium heat until shimmering. Add 2 minced garlic cloves and ½ teaspoon red pepper flakes; cook until garlic is golden and fragrant, about 1 minute. Remove from heat. Toss roasted Brussels sprouts with garlic oil and season with salt and pepper to taste. Transfer to platter and sprinkle with ¼ cup grated Parmesan cheese before serving.

Roasted Brussels Sprouts with Bacon and Pecans

While Brussels sprouts roast, cook 4 slices bacon in 10-inch skillet over medium heat until crisp, 7 to 10 minutes. Using slotted spoon, transfer bacon to paper towel–lined plate and reserve 1 tablespoon bacon fat. Finely chop bacon. Toss roasted Brussels sprouts with 2 tablespoons olive oil, reserved bacon fat, chopped bacon, and ½ cup finely chopped toasted pecans. Season with salt and pepper to taste; transfer to platter and serve.

ROASTED CARROTS

WHY THIS RECIPE WORKS: Roasting carrots draws out their natural sugars and intensifies their flavor, but too often carrots shrivel up and turn jerky-like under the high heat of the oven. We wanted roasted carrots with a pleasingly al dente chew and earthy, sweet flavor.

To compensate for the oven's arid heat, we tried adding liquid to the roasting pan. While our carrots turned out moist, they weren't browned and lacked the intense roasted flavor we wanted. Our science editor then explained that no additional moisture was necessary. While a carrot's hard, woody structure doesn't suggest it, the average carrot is actually 87.5 percent water by weight. For our next test we tossed the carrots with melted butter, spread them onto a baking sheet, and covered the sheet tightly with foil. We roasted the carrots, covered, just until softened, then we removed the foil and continued to roast them to draw out their moisture and brown them. The result? Rich-tasting, tender carrots with a nutty flavor. Best of all, the technique worked just as well when we paired the carrots with other roasted root vegetables: parsnips, fennel, and shallots.

Roasted Carrots

SERVES 4 TO 6

Most bagged carrots come in a variety of sizes and must be cut lengthwise for evenly cooked results. After halving the carrots crosswise, leave small (less than ½ inch in diameter) pieces whole; halve medium pieces (½- to 1-inch diameter), and quarter large pieces (over 1 inch).

> 1½ pounds carrots, peeled, halved crosswise, and cut lengthwise if necessary (see note)
> 2 tablespoons unsalted butter, melted
> Table salt and ground black pepper

1. Adjust an oven rack to the middle position and heat the oven to 425 degrees. Line a large rimmed baking sheet with parchment or aluminum foil. In a large bowl, combine the carrots with the butter, ½ teaspoon salt, and ¼ teaspoon pepper; toss to coat. Transfer the carrots to the prepared baking sheet and spread in a single layer.

2. Cover the baking sheet tightly with foil and roast for 15 minutes. Remove the foil and continue to roast, stirring twice, until well-browned and tender, 30 to 35 minutes. Transfer to a serving platter, season with salt and pepper to taste, and serve.

Roasted Carrots and Fennel with Toasted Almonds and Lemon

Follow the recipe for Roasted Carrots, reducing the amount of carrots to 1 pound. Add ½ large fennel bulb, cored and sliced ½ inch thick, to the bowl with the carrots and roast as directed. Toss the roasted vegetables with ¼ cup toasted sliced almonds, 1 teaspoon juice from 1 lemon, and 2 teaspoons chopped fresh parsley leaves before serving in step 2.

Roasted Carrots and Parsnips with Rosemary

Follow the recipe for Roasted Carrots, reducing the amount of carrots to 1 pound. Add ½ pound peeled parsnips, cut like the carrots, and 1 teaspoon chopped fresh rosemary leaves to the bowl with the carrots and roast as directed. Toss the roasted vegetables with 2 teaspoons chopped fresh parsley leaves before serving in step 2.

QUICK ROASTED BABY CARROTS

WHY THIS RECIPE WORKS: Roasted carrots frequently end up either undercooked, with a bitter, hard center or, at the other end of the spectrum, are subjected to such intense heat that they become wan, limp, and utterly unpalatable. We wanted to release the sweetness from the carrots, yielding a caramelized exterior and a creamy, tender interior.

Roasting prepared baby carrots saved us time, because they require no cleaning or cutting. The flavor of the carrots needed a little help; plain olive oil with a little salt worked well—it neither masked the carrots' flavor nor changed their texture. Roasting the carrots uncovered at a high temperature created the caramelized exterior we were after, and using the bottom of a broiler pan prevented them from burning. We were now able to produce perfectly cooked, deeply flavorful roasted carrots in just 20 minutes.

Quick Roasted Baby Carrots

SERVES 8

When buying carrots, inspect the bag carefully for pockets of water. Bags taken from the top of the supermarket's pile are often waterlogged. This not only makes carrots mealy, it also prevents them from caramelizing properly.

> 2 pounds baby carrots (two 16-ounce bags; see note)
> 2 tablespoons olive oil
> ½ teaspoon table salt

Adjust an oven rack to the middle position and heat the oven to 475 degrees. Toss the carrots, oil, and salt in a broiler pan bottom. Spread into a single layer and roast for 12 minutes. Shake the pan to toss the carrots; continue roasting about 8 minutes longer, shaking the pan twice more, until the carrots are browned and tender. Serve.

GLAZED CARROTS

WHY THIS RECIPE WORKS: Glazing is probably the most popular way to prepare carrots, but they often turn out saccharine, with a limp and soggy or undercooked and fibrous texture. We wanted fully tender, well-seasoned carrots with a glossy and clingy—yet modest—glaze.

Peeling regular bagged carrots and cutting them on the bias yielded uniform ovals that cooked evenly. We cooked and glazed the carrots in one single operation, starting by cooking the sliced carrots in a covered skillet with chicken broth, salt, and sugar. After the carrots were cooked until almost tender, we removed the lid and turned up the heat to reduce the liquid. Finally, a little butter and a bit more sugar added to the skillet resulted in a pale amber glaze with light caramel flavor. A sprinkle of fresh lemon juice gave the dish sparkle, and a pinch of freshly ground black pepper provided depth.

Glazed Carrots

SERVES 4

We like to use a nonstick skillet here for easy cleanup, but any 12-inch skillet with a cover will work.

- 1 pound carrots (about 6 medium), peeled and sliced ¼ inch thick on the bias
- ½ cup low-sodium chicken broth
- 3 tablespoons sugar
- ½ teaspoon table salt
- 1 tablespoon unsalted butter, cut into 4 pieces
- 2 teaspoons juice from 1 lemon
  Ground black pepper

1. Bring the carrots, broth, 1 tablespoon of the sugar, and the salt to a boil in a 12-inch nonstick skillet, covered, over medium-high heat. Reduce the heat to medium and simmer, stirring occasionally, until the carrots are almost tender when poked with the tip of a paring knife, about 5 minutes. Uncover, increase the heat to high, and simmer rapidly, stirring occasionally, until the liquid is reduced to about 2 tablespoons, 1 to 2 minutes.

2. Add the remaining 2 tablespoons sugar and the butter to the skillet. Toss the carrots to coat and cook, stirring frequently, until the carrots are completely tender and the glaze is light gold, about 3 minutes. Off the heat, add the lemon juice and toss to coat. Transfer the carrots to a dish, scraping the glaze from the pan into the dish. Season with pepper to taste and serve.

SLOW-COOKED WHOLE CARROTS

WHY THIS RECIPE WORKS: We wanted a technique for cooking whole carrots that would yield a sweet and meltingly tender vegetable without the carrots becoming mushy. Cooking the tapered vegetable evenly from end to end was a challenge, so we looked to techniques that promised carrots with concentrated flavor and uniformly dense texture. Gently "steeping" the carrots in warm water, butter, and salt before cooking them firmed up the vegetable's cell walls so that they could be cooked for a long time without falling apart. We also took a tip from restaurant cooking and topped the carrots with a cartouche (a circle of parchment that sits directly on the food) during cooking to regulate the reduction of moisture. An easy relish finished the dish on a high note.

Slow-Cooked Whole Carrots

SERVES 4 TO 6

Use carrots that measure ¾ to 1¼ inches across at the thickest end. The carrots can be served plain, but we recommend topping them with Pine Nut Relish (recipe follows).

- 3 cups water
- 1 tablespoon unsalted butter
- ½ teaspoon salt
- 12 carrots (1½ to 1¾ pounds), peeled

1. Fold 12-inch square of parchment paper into quarters to create 6-inch square. Fold bottom right corner of square to top left corner to create triangle. Fold triangle again, right side over left, to create narrow triangle. Cut off ¼ inch of tip of triangle to create small hole. Cut base of triangle straight across where it measures 5 inches from hole. Open paper round.

2. Bring water, butter, and salt to simmer in 12-inch skillet over high heat. Remove pan from heat, add carrots in single layer, and place parchment round on top of carrots. Cover skillet and let stand for 20 minutes.

3. Remove lid from skillet, leaving parchment round in place, and bring to simmer over high heat. Reduce heat to medium-low and simmer until almost all water has evaporated and carrots are very tender, about 45 minutes.

4. Discard parchment round, increase heat to medium-high, and continue to cook carrots, shaking pan frequently, until they are lightly glazed and no water remains in skillet, 2 to 4 minutes longer. Transfer carrots to platter and serve.

Pine Nut Relish

MAKES ABOUT ¾ CUP

Pine nuts burn easily, so be sure to shake the pan frequently while toasting them.

- ⅓ cup pine nuts, toasted
- 1 shallot, minced
- 1 tablespoon sherry vinegar
- 1 tablespoon minced fresh parsley
- 1 teaspoon honey
- ½ teaspoon minced fresh rosemary
- ¼ teaspoon smoked paprika
- ¼ teaspoon salt
  Pinch cayenne pepper

Combine all ingredients in bowl.

BUFFALO CAULIFLOWER BITES

WHY THIS RECIPE WORKS: Deemed "better than wings" by our tasters, these crunchy, spicy vegan cauliflower bites will be the new star of your game day table. A mixture of cornstarch and cornmeal gave us an ultracrisp exterior. Because cauliflower is not naturally moist, the mixture didn't adhere; so we dunked the florets in canned coconut milk, which had the right viscosity. Frying helped achieve a crackly crust and tender interior.

Buffalo Cauliflower Bites

SERVES 4 TO 6

We used Frank's RedHot Original Cayenne Pepper Sauce, but other hot sauces can be used. Use a Dutch oven that holds 6 quarts or more for this recipe.

BUFFALO SAUCE
- ¼ cup coconut oil
- ½ cup hot sauce
- 1 tablespoon packed dark brown sugar
- 2 teaspoons cider vinegar

CAULIFLOWER
- 1–2 quarts peanut or vegetable oil
- ¾ cup cornstarch
- ¼ cup cornmeal
  Salt and pepper
- ⅔ cup canned coconut milk
- 1 tablespoon hot sauce
- 1 pound cauliflower florets, cut into 1½-inch pieces
- 1 recipe Ranch Dressing (recipe follows)

1. FOR THE BUFFALO SAUCE: Melt coconut oil in small saucepan over low heat. Whisk in hot sauce, brown sugar, and vinegar until combined. Remove from heat and cover to keep warm; set aside.

2. FOR THE CAULIFLOWER: Line platter with triple layer of paper towels. Add oil to large Dutch oven until it measures about 1½ inches deep and heat over medium-high heat to 400 degrees. While oil heats, combine cornstarch, cornmeal, ½ teaspoon salt, and ¼ teaspoon pepper in small bowl. Whisk coconut milk and hot sauce together in large bowl. Add cauliflower; toss to coat well. Sprinkle cornstarch mixture over cauliflower; fold with rubber spatula until thoroughly coated.

3. Fry half of cauliflower, adding 1 or 2 pieces to oil at a time, until golden and crisp, gently stirring as needed to prevent pieces from sticking together, about 3 minutes. Using slotted spoon, transfer fried cauliflower to prepared platter.

4. Return oil to 400 degrees and repeat with remaining cauliflower. Transfer ½ cup sauce to clean large bowl, add fried cauliflower and gently toss to coat. Serve immediately with dressing and remaining sauce.

Ranch Dressing

MAKES ABOUT ½ CUP

We strongly prefer our favorite vegan mayonnaise, Just Mayo, or our homemade Vegan Mayonnaise (recipe follows).

- ½ cup vegan mayonnaise
- 2 tablespoons unsweetened plain coconut milk yogurt
- 1 teaspoon white wine vinegar
- 1½ teaspoons minced fresh chives
- 1½ teaspoons minced fresh dill
- ¼ teaspoon garlic powder
- ⅛ teaspoon salt
- ⅛ teaspoon pepper

Whisk all ingredients in bowl until smooth. (Dressing can be refrigerated for up to 4 days.)

Vegan Mayonnaise

MAKES ABOUT 1 CUP

Aquafaba, the liquid found in a can of chickpeas, gives our mayo volume and emulsified body. It's devoid of off-flavors or off-textures, which was not the case when we tried creating mayo with soy milk, tofu, cashews, or miso.

- ⅓ cup aquafaba
- 1½ teaspoons lemon juice
- ½ teaspoon salt
- ½ teaspoon sugar
- ½ teaspoon Dijon mustard
- 1¼ cups vegetable oil
- 3 tablespoons extra-virgin olive oil

1. Process aquafaba, lemon juice, salt, sugar, and mustard in food processor for 10 seconds. With processor running, gradually add vegetable oil in slow, steady stream until mixture is thick and creamy, scraping down sides of bowl as needed, about 3 minutes.

2. Transfer mixture to bowl. Whisking constantly, slowly add olive oil until emulsified. If pools of oil form on surface, stop addition of oil and whisk mixture until well combined, then resume adding oil. Mayonnaise should be thick and glossy with no oil pools on surface. (Mayonnaise can be refrigerated for up to 1 week.)

CORN FRITTERS

WHY THIS RECIPE WORKS: Good corn fritters should be light—creamy in the middle and crisp on the outside. This is rarely the case, however; most corn fritters have little corn flavor and cook up dense and greasy. We wanted to make perfect corn fritters—light, crisp, and packed with fresh corn flavor.

We found that combining whole corn kernels and grated kernels worked best for visual appeal, textural contrast, and fullest corn flavor. Running the back of a knife over the cobs from which the corn had been grated helped us extract the flavorful pulp. Equal amounts of flour and cornmeal bound the mixture together without making the fritters heavy and kept the corn flavor strong. A bit of heavy cream added welcome richness. For pan-frying the cakes, vegetable oil was the cooking medium of choice for its high smoke point and neutral flavor, which didn't overpower the corn. Keeping the oil hot helped the fritters brown quickly.

Corn Fritters

MAKES TWELVE 2-INCH FRITTERS

Serve these fritters with hot sauce, salsa, or even maple syrup.

- 4 ears corn, husks and silk removed
- 1 large egg, lightly beaten
- 3 tablespoons unbleached all-purpose flour
- 3 tablespoons cornmeal
- 2 tablespoons heavy cream
- 1 small shallot, minced (about 1 tablespoon)
- ½ teaspoon salt
  Pinch cayenne pepper
- ¼ cup vegetable oil, plus more as needed

1. Stand the corn upright inside a large bowl and, using a paring knife, carefully cut the kernels from 2 ears of the corn; you should have about 1 cup. Transfer the kernels to a medium bowl. Use the back of a butter knife to scrape off any pulp remaining on the cobs and transfer it to the bowl. Grate the kernels from the remaining 2 ears of corn on the large holes of a box grater, then firmly scrape off any pulp remaining on the cobs with the back of a butter knife; you should have a generous cup of kernels and pulp. Transfer the grated kernels and pulp to the bowl with the cut kernels.

2. Mix the egg, flour, cornmeal, cream, shallot, salt, and cayenne into the corn mixture to form a thick batter.

3. Heat the oil in a 12-inch skillet over medium-high heat until almost smoking, about 2 minutes. Drop heaping tablespoons of batter into the oil (half the batter, or six fritters, should fit into the pan at once). Fry until golden brown, about 1 minute. Using a thin metal spatula, turn the fritters and fry until the second side is golden brown, about 1 minute longer. Transfer the fritters to a paper towel–lined plate. Repeat with the remaining batter, adding more oil to the skillet if necessary. Serve.

SOUTHERN CORN FRITTERS

WHY THIS RECIPE WORKS: For the lightest corn fritters, we minimized the number of fillers we added. We processed some of the kernels to act as a thickener rather than bulk up the batter with more flour or cornmeal. This step also let the fresh corn flavor shine through. Browning the corn puree in a skillet drove off excess moisture and deepened the flavor even more. Adding cayenne, nutty Parmesan cheese, and oniony chives balanced the natural sweetness of the corn, and a touch of cornstarch helped crisp the exterior and provide a textural contrast with the creamy interior.

Southern Corn Fritters

MAKES 12

Serve these fritters as a side dish with steaks, chops, or poultry or as an appetizer with a dollop of sour cream or with Red Pepper Mayonnaise, Maple-Chipotle Mayonnaise, Basil Mayonnaise, or Sriracha-Lime Yogurt Sauce (recipes follow).

- 4 ears corn, kernels cut from cobs (3 cups)
- 1 teaspoon plus ½ cup vegetable oil
  Salt and pepper
- ¼ cup all-purpose flour
- ¼ cup finely minced chives
- 2 tablespoons grated Parmesan cheese
- 1 tablespoon cornstarch
  Pinch cayenne pepper
- 1 large egg, lightly beaten

1. Process 1½ cups corn kernels in food processor to uniformly coarse puree, 15 to 20 seconds, scraping down bowl halfway through processing. Set aside.

2. Heat 1 teaspoon oil in 12-inch nonstick skillet over medium-high heat until shimmering. Add remaining 1½ cups corn kernels and ⅛ teaspoon salt, and cook, stirring frequently, until light golden, 3 to 4 minutes. Transfer to medium bowl.

3. Return skillet to medium heat, add corn puree, and cook, stirring frequently with heatproof spatula, until puree is consistency of thick oatmeal (puree clings to spatula rather than dripping off), about 5 minutes. Transfer puree to bowl with kernels and stir to combine. Rinse skillet and dry with paper towels.

4. Stir flour, 3 tablespoons chives, Parmesan, cornstarch, cayenne, ¼ teaspoon salt, and ⅛ teaspoon pepper into corn mixture until well combined. Gently stir in egg until incorporated.

5. Line rimmed baking sheet with paper towels. Heat remaining ½ cup oil in now-empty skillet over medium heat until shimmering. Drop six 2-tablespoon portions batter into skillet. Press with spatula to flatten into 2½- to 3-inch disks. Fry until deep golden brown on both sides, 2 to 3 minutes per side. Transfer fritters to prepared sheet. Repeat with remaining batter.

6. Transfer fritters to large plate or platter, sprinkle with remaining 1 tablespoon chives, and serve immediately.

Red Pepper Mayonnaise

MAKES ABOUT 1¼ CUPS

Letting the minced garlic sit in the lemon juice mellows its flavor.

- 1½ teaspoons lemon juice
- 1 clove garlic, minced
- ¾ cup jarred roasted red peppers, rinsed and patted dry
- ½ cup mayonnaise
- 2 teaspoons tomato paste
  Salt

Combine lemon juice and garlic in small bowl and let stand for 15 minutes. Process red peppers, mayonnaise, tomato paste, and lemon juice mixture in food processor until smooth, about 15 seconds, scraping down sides of bowl as needed. Season with salt to taste. Refrigerate until thickened, about 2 hours.

Maple-Chipotle Mayonnaise

MAKES ⅔ CUP

For the fullest maple flavor, use maple syrup labeled "Grade A, Dark Amber."

- ½ cup mayonnaise
- 1 tablespoon maple syrup
- 1 tablespoon minced canned chipotle in adobo sauce
- ½ teaspoon Dijon mustard

Combine all ingredients in small bowl.

Basil Mayonnaise

MAKES ¾ CUP

Blue Plate Real Mayonnaise is our favorite mayonnaise. It's one of the top-selling brands in the country, but you'll have to mail-order it unless you live in the South or Southeast. Hellmann's Real Mayonnaise, which is available nationwide (it's sold as Best Foods west of the Rockies), was our runner-up.

- ½ cup mayonnaise
- ½ cup fresh basil leaves
- 1 tablespoon water
- 1 teaspoon lemon juice
  Salt and pepper

Blend mayonnaise, basil, water, and lemon juice in blender until smooth, about 10 seconds, scraping down sides as needed. Transfer to bowl and season with salt and pepper to taste.

Sriracha-Lime Yogurt Sauce

MAKES ⅔ CUP

Our favorite Greek yogurt is Fage Total Classic Greek Yogurt.

- ½ cup plain Greek yogurt
- ½ teaspoon grated lime zest plus 1 teaspoon juice
- ½ teaspoon Sriracha sauce
- 1 tablespoon minced fresh cilantro
  Salt

Mix yogurt, lime zest and juice, Sriracha, and cilantro together in small bowl. Season with salt to taste.

BOILED CORN

WHY THIS RECIPE WORKS: For perfectly crisp, juicy corn, we figured out that the ideal doneness range is 150 to 170 degrees—when the starches have gelatinized but a minimum amount of the pectin has dissolved. Consistently cooking the corn to that temperature was easy once we realized we could use a *sous vide* method: bringing water to a boil, dropping in 6 ears of

corn, and shutting off the heat. The temperature of the water decreased quickly so the corn didn't overcook, while the temperature of the corn increased to the ideal zone. Even better, this method can accommodate between 6 and 8 ears of different sizes, and the corn can sit in the water for as long as 30 minutes without overcooking.

Boiled Corn
SERVES 4 TO 6

This recipe's success depends on using the proper ratio of hot water to corn. Use a Dutch oven with a capacity of at least 7 quarts, and bring the water to a rolling boil. Eight ears of corn can be prepared using this recipe, but let the corn sit for at least 15 minutes before serving. Serve with a flavored salt (recipes follow), if desired.

  6 ears corn, husks and silk removed
     Unsalted butter, softened
     Salt and pepper

1. Bring 4 quarts water to boil in large Dutch oven. Turn off heat, add corn to water, cover, and let stand for at least 10 minutes or up to 30 minutes.

2. Transfer corn to large platter and serve immediately, passing butter, salt, and pepper.

Chili-Lime Salt
MAKES 3 TABLESPOONS

  2 tablespoons kosher salt
  4 teaspoons chili powder
  ¾ teaspoon grated lime zest

Combine all ingredients in small bowl.

Pepper-Cinnamon Salt
MAKES 2 TABLESPOONS

  1 tablespoon kosher salt
  1 tablespoon coarsely ground pepper
  ¼ teaspoon ground cinnamon

Combine all ingredients in small bowl.

Cumin-Sesame Salt
MAKES 3 TABLESPOONS

  1 tablespoon cumin seeds
  1 tablespoon sesame seeds
  1 tablespoon kosher salt

Toast cumin seeds and sesame seeds in 8-inch skillet over medium heat, stirring occasionally, until fragrant and sesame seeds are golden brown, 3 to 4 minutes. Transfer mixture to cutting board and let cool for 2 minutes. Mince mixture fine until well combined. Transfer mixture to small bowl and stir in salt.

NEW ENGLAND BAKED BEANS

WHY THIS RECIPE WORKS: For a pot of classic New England baked beans, we made a few smart tweaks while keeping the traditional flavor. Brining the beans overnight helped jump-start hydration and also softened their skins so they cooked up tender in the oven, with few blowouts. Uncovering the pot for the last hour of cooking ensured that the liquid reduced sufficiently to coat the beans in a thick sauce. Flavorings such as molasses, brown sugar, dry mustard, bay leaf, and onion, plus one nontraditional ingredient (soy sauce), gave the beans rich flavor, while chunks of salt pork added meatiness.

New England Baked Beans
SERVES 4 TO 6

You'll get fewer blowouts if you soak the beans overnight, but if you're pressed for time, you can quick-salt-soak your beans. In step 1, combine the salt, water, and beans in a large Dutch oven and bring them to a boil over high heat. Remove the pot from the heat, cover it, and let it stand for 1 hour. Drain and rinse the beans and proceed with the recipe.

     Salt
  1 pound (2½ cups) dried navy beans,
     picked over and rinsed
  6 ounces salt pork, rinsed and cut into 3 pieces
  1 onion, halved
  ½ cup molasses
  2 tablespoons packed dark brown sugar
  1 tablespoon soy sauce
  2 teaspoons dry mustard
  ½ teaspoon pepper
  1 bay leaf

1. Dissolve 1½ tablespoons salt in 2 quarts cold water in large container. Add beans and let soak at room temperature for at least 8 hours or up to 24 hours. Drain and rinse well.

2. Adjust oven rack to lower-middle position and heat oven to 300 degrees. Combine beans, salt pork, onion, molasses, sugar, soy sauce, mustard, pepper, bay leaf, ¼ teaspoon salt, and 4 cups water in large Dutch oven. (Liquid should cover beans by about ½ inch. Add more water if necessary.) Bring to boil over high heat. Cover pot, transfer to oven, and cook until beans are softened and bean skins curl up and split when you blow on them, about 2 hours. (After 1 hour, stir beans and check amount of liquid. Liquid should just cover beans. Add water if necessary.)

3. Remove lid and continue to cook until beans are fully tender, browned, and slightly crusty on top, about 1 hour longer. (Liquid will reduce slightly below top layer of beans.)

4. Remove pot from oven, cover, and let stand for 5 minutes. Using wooden spoon or rubber spatula, scrape any browned bits from sides of pot and stir into beans. Discard onion and bay leaf. (Salt pork can be eaten, if desired.) Let beans stand, uncovered, until liquid has thickened slightly and clings to beans, 10 to 15 minutes, stirring once halfway through. Season with salt and pepper to taste, and serve. (Beans can be refrigerated for up to 4 days.)

BOSTON BAKED BEANS

WHY THIS RECIPE WORKS: Boston baked beans are both sweet and savory, a unique combination of the simplest ingredients, unified and refined during a long simmer. Unfortunately, recipes with lengthy lists of untraditional ingredients and mushy beans abound. We wanted tender beans in a thick, smoky, slightly sweet sauce.

For depth of flavor, we started by browning a combination of salt pork and bacon in a Dutch oven. Small white beans were preferred for their creamy texture and ability to remain intact during the long simmer. Mild molasses provided just the right amount of sweetness, while brown mustard and cider vinegar added welcome notes of spice and tanginess. We removed the lid for the last hour of cooking to reduce the sauce to a syrupy, intensified consistency that perfectly napped the beans.

Boston Baked Beans
SERVES 4 TO 6

The beans can be made ahead. After cooking, cool them to room temperature and refrigerate in an airtight container for up to 4 days.

- 4 ounces salt pork, trimmed of rind and cut into ½-inch cubes
- 2 ounces (about 2 slices) bacon, cut into ¼-inch pieces
- 1 medium onion, minced
- 9 cups water
- 1 pound (2 cups) dried small white beans, rinsed and picked over
- ½ cup plus 1 tablespoon mild molasses
- 1½ tablespoons prepared brown mustard, such as Gulden's

Table salt
- 1 teaspoon cider vinegar
Ground black pepper

1. Adjust an oven rack to the lower-middle position and heat the oven to 300 degrees. Place the salt pork and bacon in a large Dutch oven; cook over medium heat, stirring occasionally, until lightly browned and most of the fat is rendered, about 7 minutes. Add the onion and continue to cook, stirring occasionally, until the onion is softened, 5 to 7 minutes. Add the water, beans, ½ cup of the molasses, the mustard, and 1¼ teaspoons salt; increase the heat to medium-high and bring to a boil. Cover the pot and place in the oven.

2. Bake until the beans are tender, about 4 hours, stirring once after 2 hours. Remove the lid and continue to bake until the liquid has thickened to a syrupy consistency, 1 to 1½ hours longer. Remove the beans from the oven; stir in the remaining 1 tablespoon molasses, the vinegar, and salt and pepper to taste. Serve.

DRUNKEN BEANS

WHY THIS RECIPE WORKS: To give our drunken beans a rich, complex flavor without imparting booziness or bitterness, we turned to a mixture of beer and tequila. Canned beans were out of the question because this recipe required a full-flavored bean cooking liquid that only dried beans could impart. To preserve the bacon's flavor, we removed it from the pot after crisping it (to use as a garnish). Sautéing onion, garlic, and poblano chiles in the bacon fat created a flavorful base. Off heat, we poured in the tequila and let it evaporate, cooking off some of the alcohol and leaving behind its smoky sweetness. To ensure that our beans remained intact, we brined them overnight. Cilantro leaves are a classic garnish

for drunken beans, but the stems also have an aromatic quality to them, so we tied the stems into a bundle and added them to the pot. We cooked the beans gently in the oven, and held back the acidic beer and tomatoes until the beans were tender. A vigorous simmer to finish caused the beans to release starches that gave the cooking liquid pleasant body.

Drunken Beans

SERVES 6 AS A MAIN DISH

You'll get fewer blowouts if you soak the beans overnight, but if you are pressed for time, you can quick-brine your beans: In step 1, combine the salt, water, and beans in a large Dutch oven and bring to a boil over high heat. Remove the pot from the heat, cover, and let stand for 1 hour. Drain and rinse the beans and proceed with the recipe. Serve with rice.

      Salt
  1   pound (2½ cups) dried pinto beans,
      picked over and rinsed
 30   sprigs fresh cilantro (1 bunch)
  4   slices bacon, cut into ¼-inch pieces
  1   onion, chopped fine
  2   poblano chiles, stemmed, seeded, and chopped fine
  3   garlic cloves, minced
  ½   cup tequila
  2   bay leaves
  1   cup Mexican lager
  ¼   cup tomato paste
  2   limes, quartered
  2   ounces Cotija cheese, crumbled (½ cup)

1. Dissolve 3 tablespoons salt in 4 quarts cold water in large bowl or container. Add beans and soak at room temperature for at least 8 hours or up to 24 hours. Drain and rinse well.

2. Adjust oven rack to lower-middle position and heat oven to 275 degrees. Pick leaves from 20 cilantro sprigs (reserve stems), mince, and refrigerate until needed. Using kitchen twine, tie remaining 10 cilantro sprigs and reserved stems into bundle.

3. Cook bacon in Dutch oven over medium heat, stirring occasionally, until crisp, 5 to 8 minutes. Using slotted spoon, transfer bacon to paper towel–lined bowl and set aside. Add onion, poblanos, and garlic to fat in pot and cook, stirring frequently, until vegetables are softened, 6 to 7 minutes. Remove from heat. Add tequila and cook until evaporated, 3 to 4 minutes. Return to heat. Increase heat to high; stir in 3½ cups water, bay leaves, 1 teaspoon salt, beans, and cilantro bundle; and bring to boil. Cover, transfer to oven, and cook until beans are just soft, 45 to 60 minutes.

4. Remove pot from oven. Discard bay leaves and cilantro bundle. Stir in beer and tomato paste and bring to simmer over medium-low heat. Simmer vigorously, stirring frequently, until liquid is thick and beans are fully tender, about 30 minutes. Season with salt to taste. Serve, passing minced cilantro, lime wedges, Cotija, and reserved bacon separately.

TO MAKE AHEAD: The finished beans can be refrigerated for up to 2 days. Before reheating, thin beans slightly with water.

BLANCHED GREEN BEANS

WHY THIS RECIPE WORKS: Most vegetable side dishes require last-minute preparation, but green beans are an ideal side dish that can be prepared largely beforehand without sacrificing texture or flavor. We wanted a foolproof way of cooking beans ahead of time and then simply reheating and seasoning them just before serving.

The easiest way to do this was to blanch the beans in salted water, shock them in ice water to stop the cooking process, and then towel-dry and refrigerate them until needed—a process that could be completed up to three days before serving. To serve, we reheated the beans in a skillet with a little water and flavored them with a butter sauce. The small amount of water came to a boil quickly and evaporated almost completely, helping to heat the beans in just a minute or two for a quick and flavorful side dish.

Blanched Green Beans

SERVES 4

Blanched and cooled beans can be refrigerated in a zipper-lock bag for up to 3 days. To blanch, dress, and serve the beans without holding them first, increase the blanching time to 5 to 6 minutes and don't bother shocking them in ice water. Instead, quickly arrange the warm, drained beans on a serving platter and top them with the sauce you've prepared as the beans blanch (recipes follow).

  1   teaspoon table salt
  1   pound green beans, trimmed

Bring 2½ quarts water to a boil in a large saucepan over high heat; add the salt and green beans, return to a boil, and cook until the beans are bright green and crisp-tender, 3 to 4 minutes. Drain the beans and transfer them immediately to a large bowl filled with ice water. When the beans have cooled to room temperature, drain again and dry thoroughly with paper towels. Set aside (or refrigerate) until needed.

Green Beans with Sautéed Shallots and Vermouth

  4   tablespoons (½ stick) unsalted butter
  4   large shallots, sliced thin (about 1 cup)
  1   recipe Blanched Green Beans
      Table salt and ground black pepper
  2   tablespoons dry vermouth

1. Melt 2 tablespoons of the butter in a small skillet over medium heat. Add the shallots and cook, stirring frequently, until golden brown, fragrant, and just crisp around the edges, about 10 minutes. Set the skillet aside, off the heat.

2. Heat ¼ cup water and the beans in a 12-inch skillet over high heat; cook, tossing frequently, until warmed through, 1 to 2 minutes. Season with salt and pepper to taste and arrange on a warm platter.

3. Meanwhile, return the skillet with the shallots to high heat, stir in the vermouth, and bring to a simmer. Whisk in the remaining 2 tablespoons butter, 1 tablespoon at a time, and season with salt and pepper to taste. Top the beans with the shallots and sauce and serve.

Green Beans with Toasted Hazelnuts and Browned Butter

Use a light-colored traditional saucepan instead of a darker nonstick saucepan for this recipe to easily monitor the butter's browning.

- 4 tablespoons (½ stick) unsalted butter
- ½ cup hazelnuts, toasted and chopped fine
  Table salt and ground black pepper
- 1 recipe Blanched Green Beans

1. Melt the butter in a small saucepan over medium heat and cook, swirling frequently, until brown and fragrant, 4 to 5 minutes. Add the hazelnuts and cook, stirring constantly, until fragrant, about 1 minute. Season with salt and pepper to taste.

2. Meanwhile, heat ¼ cup water and the beans in a 12-inch skillet over high heat; cook, tossing frequently, until warmed through, 1 to 2 minutes. Season with salt and pepper to taste and arrange on a warm platter. Top the beans with the hazelnuts and butter and serve.

GREEN BEANS AMANDINE

WHY THIS RECIPE WORKS: A simple dish of green beans tossed with toasted almonds and a light lemon-butter sauce, green beans amandine is refined yet not intimidating. Unfortunately, recipes too often yield limp beans swimming in pools of overly acidic sauce, with soft, pale almonds thrown on as an afterthought. We wanted to revive this side dish with tender green beans, crisp almonds, and a balanced sauce.

For maximum flavor, we toasted the almonds then added some butter to the skillet and allowed it to brown for further nuttiness. Adding some lemon juice off the heat brightened our sauce considerably. After steaming the green beans in a little water in a covered skillet until they were crisp-tender, we tossed them with our sauce for a simple, flavorful take on this classic side.

Green Beans Amandine

SERVES 8

Use a light-colored traditional skillet instead of a darker nonstick skillet for this recipe to easily monitor the butter's browning.

- ⅓ cup sliced almonds
- 3 tablespoons unsalted butter, cut into pieces
- 2 teaspoons juice from 1 lemon
- 2 pounds green beans, trimmed
  Table salt

1. Toast the almonds in a large skillet over medium-low heat, stirring often, until just golden, about 6 minutes. Add the butter and cook, stirring constantly, until the butter is golden brown and has a nutty aroma, about 3 minutes. Transfer the almond mixture to a bowl and stir in the lemon juice.

2. Add the beans, ½ cup water, and ½ teaspoon salt to the now-empty skillet. Cover and cook over medium-low heat, stirring occasionally, until the beans are nearly tender, 8 to 10 minutes. Remove the lid and cook over medium-high heat until the liquid evaporates, 3 to 5 minutes. Off the heat, add the reserved almond mixture to the skillet and toss to combine. Season with salt to taste and serve.

ROASTED GREEN BEANS

WHY THIS RECIPE WORKS: Mature supermarket green beans are often tough and dull, needing special treatment to become tender and flavorful. Braising works, but the stovetop can get awfully crowded as dinnertime approaches. Roasting is a great option for many vegetables, and we wanted to find out if this technique could help transform older green beans, giving them a flavor comparable to sweet, fresh-picked beans.

A remarkably simple test produced outstanding results: Beans roasted in a 450-degree oven with only oil, salt, and pepper transformed aged specimens into deeply caramelized, full-flavored beans. Just 20 minutes of roasting reversed the aging process (converting starch back to sugar) and encouraged flavorful browning. Just 1 tablespoon of oil was enough to lend flavor and moisture without making the beans greasy. Lining the pan with foil prevented scorching and made for easy cleanup.

Roasted Green Beans

SERVES 4

Lining the baking sheet with foil makes for easy cleanup.

> 1 pound green beans, trimmed
> 1 tablespoon olive oil
> Table salt and ground black pepper

1. Adjust an oven rack to the middle position and heat the oven to 450 degrees. Line a large rimmed baking sheet with foil; spread the beans on the baking sheet. Drizzle with the oil; using your hands, toss to coat evenly. Sprinkle with ½ teaspoon salt, toss to coat, and distribute in an even layer. Roast for 10 minutes.

2. Remove the baking sheet from the oven. Using tongs, redistribute the beans. Continue roasting until the beans are dark golden brown in spots and have started to shrivel, 10 to 12 minutes longer. Season with salt and pepper to taste and serve.

SPINACH WITH GARLIC AND LEMON

WHY THIS RECIPE WORKS: Overcooked spinach, bitter burnt garlic, and pallid lemon flavor are all too often the hallmarks of this simple side dish. Instead, we sought tender sautéed spinach, seasoned with a perfect balance of garlic and lemon.

We preferred the hearty flavor and texture of curly-leaf spinach in this classic dish. We cooked the spinach in extra-virgin olive oil with slivered garlic (lightly browned in the pan before the spinach was added), which gave the spinach a sweet nuttiness. Once the spinach was cooked, we used tongs to squeeze the spinach in a colander over the sink to get rid of all the excess moisture. As for seasoning, a squeeze of lemon juice and some grated lemon zest, as well as a pinch of red pepper flakes gave the spinach some gentle heat. And finally, a drizzle of extra-virgin olive oil boosted the fruitiness of the dish.

Sautéed Garlic-Lemon Spinach

SERVES 4

The amount of spinach may seem excessive, but the spinach wilts considerably with cooking. We like to use a salad spinner to wash and dry the spinach.

> 2 tablespoons extra-virgin olive oil, plus 1 teaspoon for drizzling
> 4 medium garlic cloves, sliced thin crosswise (about 4 teaspoons)
> 3 (10-ounce) bags curly-leaf spinach, stems removed, leaves washed and dried (see note)
> Table salt
> Pinch red pepper flakes
> ½ teaspoon grated zest plus 2 teaspoons juice from 1 lemon

1. Heat 2 tablespoons of the oil and the garlic in a large Dutch oven over medium-high heat until shimmering; cook until the garlic is light golden brown, shaking the pan back and forth when the garlic begins to sizzle, about 3 minutes. Add the spinach by the handful, using tongs to stir and coat the spinach with the oil.

2. Once all the spinach is added, sprinkle ¼ teaspoon salt, the red pepper flakes, and lemon zest over the top and continue stirring with the tongs until the spinach is uniformly wilted and glossy, about 2 minutes. Using the tongs, transfer the spinach to a colander set in a sink and gently squeeze the spinach with the tongs to release the excess liquid. Return the spinach to the Dutch oven; sprinkle with the lemon juice and stir to coat. Drizzle with the remaining 1 teaspoon olive oil and season with salt to taste. Serve.

SAUTÉED BABY SPINACH

WHY THIS RECIPE WORKS: Baby spinach is convenient—no stems to remove or grit to rinse out—but cooking often turns this tender green into a watery, mushy mess. We were determined to find a method for cooking baby spinach that would give us a worthwhile side dish. Wilting, blanching, and steaming proved to be unsuccessful in removing excess water from baby spinach, but parcooking the spinach in the microwave with a little water added to the bowl worked great. After three minutes, the spinach had softened and shrunk to half its size, thanks to the release of a great deal of liquid. But there was still more water to remove. We found that pressing the spinach against the colander before roughly chopping it on a cutting board and then pressing it again removed any remaining excess liquid. The spinach was now tender, sweet, and ready to be combined with complementary ingredients. Pairing almonds and raisins introduced bold flavors and textures that enlivened this quick-cooking green.

Sautéed Baby Spinach with Almonds and Golden Raisins

SERVES 4

If you don't have a microwave-safe bowl large enough to accommodate the entire amount of spinach, cook it in a smaller bowl in two batches. Reduce the amount of water to 2 tablespoons per batch and cook each batch for about 1½ minutes.

> 3 (6-ounce) bags baby spinach (about 18 cups)
> ¼ cup water
> 2 tablespoons extra-virgin olive oil, plus 2 teaspoons for drizzling
> ½ cup golden raisins
> 4 medium garlic cloves, sliced thin crosswise (about 4 teaspoons)
> ¼ teaspoon red pepper flakes
> Table salt
> 2 teaspoons sherry vinegar
> ⅓ cup slivered almonds, toasted

1. Place the spinach and water in a large microwave-safe bowl. Cover the bowl with a large microwave-safe dinner plate (the plate should completely cover the bowl and not rest on the spinach). Microwave on high power until the spinach is wilted and decreased in volume by half, 3 to 4 minutes. Using potholders, remove the bowl from the microwave and keep covered for 1 minute. Carefully remove the plate and transfer the spinach to a colander set in the sink. Using the back of a rubber spatula, gently press the spinach against the colander to release excess liquid. Transfer the spinach to a cutting board and roughly chop. Return to the colander and press a second time.

2. Heat 2 tablespoons of the oil, the raisins, garlic, and red pepper flakes in a 10-inch skillet over medium-high heat. Cook, stirring constantly, until the garlic is light golden brown and beginning to sizzle, 3 to 6 minutes. Add the spinach to the skillet, using tongs to stir and coat with the oil. Sprinkle with ¼ teaspoon salt and continue stirring with the tongs until the spinach is uniformly wilted and glossy, about 2 minutes. Sprinkle with the vinegar and almonds; stir to combine. Drizzle with the remaining 2 teaspoons oil and season with salt to taste. Serve.

CREAMY HERBED SPINACH DIP

WHY THIS RECIPE WORKS: Spinach dip made with sour cream and soup mixes are flat, overly salty, and stale tasting. We wanted to ditch the mix and create a rich, thick, and creamy spinach dip brimming with big, bold flavors.

We were surprised to discover that frozen spinach actually made a better-tasting dip with a vibrant, more intense flavor than one made with fresh spinach. We used a food processor

to chop the spinach and then enriched it with sour cream, mayonnaise, and a mixture of fresh herbs and seasonings. The only problem was that our dip, which took just about 15 minutes to make, took almost two hours to chill. Fortunately the solution turned out to be a simple one. Instead of thawing the spinach completely, we only partially thawed it, allowing the chunks of icy spinach to thoroughly cool the dip as they broke down in the food processor. This dip is fresh-tasting, quick to make, and ready to serve immediately.

Creamy Herbed Spinach Dip
MAKES ABOUT 1½ CUPS

Partial thawing of the spinach produces a cold dip that can be served without further chilling. Instead of microwaving, the frozen spinach can also be thawed at room temperature for 1½ hours, then squeezed of excess liquid. The garlic must be minced or pressed before going into the food processor; otherwise, the dip will contain large chunks of garlic.

- 1 (10-ounce) box frozen chopped spinach
- ½ cup sour cream
- ½ cup mayonnaise
- 3 scallions, white parts only, sliced thin
- ½ cup packed fresh parsley leaves
- 1 tablespoon minced fresh dill
- 1 small garlic clove, minced or pressed through a garlic press (about ½ teaspoon; see note)
- ½ teaspoon table salt
- ¼ teaspoon ground black pepper
- ¼ teaspoon hot sauce
- ½ red bell pepper, chopped fine

1. Thaw the spinach in a microwave for 3 minutes at 40 percent power. (The edges should be thawed but not warm; the center should be soft enough to be broken into icy chunks.) Squeeze the partially frozen spinach to remove excess water.

2. Process the spinach, sour cream, mayonnaise, scallions, parsley, dill, garlic, salt, pepper, and hot sauce in a food processor until smooth and creamy, about 30 seconds. Transfer the mixture to a bowl and stir in the bell pepper; serve. (The dip can be covered with plastic wrap and refrigerated for up to 2 days.)

QUICK-COOKED TOUGH GREENS

WHY THIS RECIPE WORKS: Unlike tender greens, tougher greens such as kale, mustard, turnip, and collard greens don't have enough moisture to be wilted in a hot pan; they'll simply scorch before they wilt. Their flavor is much more assertive, even peppery in some cases, and can be overwhelming. We wanted a technique for cooking Southern-style greens that would mellow their assertive bite and render them tender—while still retaining just the right amount of chew.

Because they are relatively dry, these greens required the addition of some liquid as they cooked. Steaming the greens produced a texture tasters liked, but it didn't help tame their bitter flavor. Shallow blanching removed enough bitterness to make these assertive greens palatable, but didn't rob them of their character. After blanching the greens, we drained and then briefly cooked them with a little garlic and red pepper flakes for a spicy kick. To prevent them from becoming too dry, we added a little chicken broth to the pan for moistness and extra flavor.

Quick-Cooked Tough Greens

SERVES 4

Shallow-blanched greens should be shocked in cold water to stop the cooking process, drained, and then braised. Shocked and drained greens can be held for up to an hour before being braised.

> Table salt
> 2 pounds assertive greens, such as kale, collards, or mustard, stemmed, washed in several changes of cold water, and chopped coarse
> 3 tablespoons extra-virgin olive oil
> 3 medium garlic cloves, sliced thin crosswise (about 3 teaspoons)
> Red pepper flakes
> ⅓-½ cup low-sodium chicken broth
> Lemon wedges, for serving

1. Bring 2 quarts water to a boil in a large pot. Add 1½ teaspoons salt and the greens and stir until wilted, 1 to 2 minutes. Cover and cook until the greens are just tender, about 7 minutes. Drain the greens and pour them into a large bowl filled with ice water. Working with a handful of greens at a time, thoroughly squeeze them dry.

2. Heat the oil, garlic, and ¼ teaspoon red pepper flakes in a large skillet over medium heat until the garlic starts to sizzle, about 1 minute. Add the greens and toss to coat with the oil. Add ⅓ cup of the broth, cover, and cook over medium-high heat, adding more broth if necessary, until the greens are tender and juicy and most of the broth has been absorbed, about 5 minutes. Season with salt and additional red pepper flakes to taste. Serve with the lemon wedges.

SAUTÉED SWISS CHARD

WHY THIS RECIPE WORKS: Swiss chard, like spinach, is delicate and has an earthy flavor that mellows once cooked. A thick stalk runs through the center of each leaf, however, and can make cooking the greens a challenge. We set out to find a simple method for preparing Swiss chard—one that would yield tender, evenly cooked greens (both stalks and leaves) with deep flavor.

After testing blanching, steaming, microwaving, and wilting, the simplest, most straightforward method of cooking proved to be wilting our greens on the stovetop. First, however, we separated the leaves from the stalks and tossed the stalks, wet from washing, into the pan first. We added garlic for flavor, then added the leaves, covered the pan, and cooked, stirring occasionally, until the greens were wilted by the steam created by their own liquid. We then found that we got even better results when combining this technique with sautéing. To do this, we heated oil in the pan, then proceeded as before, adding the stalks before the leaves. Once the leaves wilted, we removed the lid, seasoned with salt and pepper, and sautéed the greens over high heat until all the liquid evaporated.

Simple Sautéed Swiss Chard

SERVES 4

A thick stalk runs through each Swiss chard leaf, so the leaf must be cut away from it.

> 3 tablespoons extra-virgin olive oil
> 2 pounds Swiss chard, stemmed, washed in several changes of cold water, stalks chopped medium and leaves chopped coarse
> 2 medium garlic cloves, minced or pressed through a garlic press (about 2 teaspoons)
> Table salt and ground black pepper
> Lemon wedges, for serving

1. Heat the oil in a large Dutch oven over medium heat until shimmering. Add the chard stalks and cook, stirring occasionally, until just tender, about 5 minutes. Add the garlic and cook until fragrant, about 30 seconds. Add the chard leaves, cover, increase the heat to medium-high, and cook, stirring occasionally, until the greens completely wilt, 2 to 3 minutes.

2. Uncover and season with salt and pepper to taste. Cook over high heat until the liquid evaporates, about 2 minutes. Serve with the lemon wedges.

ROASTED MUSHROOMS WITH PARMESAN AND PINE NUTS

WHY THIS RECIPE WORKS: Serving up a side of juicy, full-flavored roasted mushrooms started with an unusual step: brining. Soaking earthy cremini and meaty, smoky shiitakes in salty water for 10 minutes allowed the mushrooms' water-resistant proteins to break down, inviting in moisture and perfect seasoning. In order to cook the mushrooms evenly, we bypassed our stovetop in favor of oven-roasting. We spread the mushrooms on a baking sheet, drizzled them with olive oil, and roasted them for 35 minutes. After a quick stir and 10 more minutes in the oven, the mushrooms emerged deeply browned but still supremely juicy. As a final flourish before serving, we glossed them with butter and a touch of lemon juice and added Parmesan, pine nuts, and parsley to round out the side's hearty, herbal notes.

Roasted Mushrooms with Parmesan and Pine Nuts

SERVES 4

Quarter large (more than 2 inches) cremini mushrooms, halve medium (1 to 2 inches) ones, and leave small (under 1 inch) ones whole.

  Salt and pepper
1½ pounds cremini mushrooms, trimmed and left whole
  if small, halved if medium, or quartered if large
1 pound shiitake mushrooms, stemmed, caps larger
  than 3 inches halved
2 tablespoons extra-virgin olive oil
2 tablespoons unsalted butter, melted
1 teaspoon lemon juice
1 ounce Parmesan cheese, grated (½ cup)
2 tablespoons pine nuts, toasted
2 tablespoons chopped fresh parsley

1. Adjust oven rack to lowest position and heat oven to 450 degrees. Dissolve 5 teaspoons salt in 2 quarts room-temperature water in large container. Add cremini mushrooms and shiitake mushrooms to brine, cover with plate or bowl to submerge, and let stand for 10 minutes.

2. Drain mushrooms in colander and pat dry with paper towels. Spread mushrooms evenly on rimmed baking sheet, drizzle with oil, and toss to coat. Roast until liquid from mushrooms has completely evaporated, 35 to 45 minutes.

3. Remove sheet from oven (be careful of escaping steam when opening oven) and, using thin metal spatula, carefully stir mushrooms. Return to oven and continue to roast until mushrooms are deeply browned, 5 to 10 minutes longer.

4. Combine melted butter and lemon juice in large bowl. Add mushrooms and toss to coat. Add Parmesan, pine nuts, and parsley and toss. Season with salt and pepper to taste; serve immediately.

CRISPY POTATO LATKES

WHY THIS RECIPE WORKS: We wanted latkes that were light, not greasy, with buttery soft interiors and crisp outer crusts. We started with high-starch russets, shredded them, mixed them with some grated onion, then wrung the mixture out in a dish towel to rid it of excess moisture, which would prevent the latkes from crisping. To ensure that the latkes' centers were cooked before their crusts were too dark, we parcooked the potato-onion mixture in the microwave. This step also caused the starches in the potatoes to coalesce, further inhibiting the release of the potatoes' moisture when frying. We tossed the mixture with beaten egg to help bind the cakes and pan-fried them in just ¼ inch of oil. With the excess water taken care of, our latkes crisped up beautifully and absorbed minimal oil.

Crispy Potato Latkes

SERVES 4 TO 6

We prefer shredding the potatoes on the large holes of a box grater, but you can also use the large shredding disk of a food processor; cut the potatoes into 2-inch lengths first so you are left with short shreds. Serve with applesauce, sour cream, or gravlax.

2 pounds russet potatoes, unpeeled, scrubbed,
  and shredded
½ cup grated onion
  Salt and pepper
2 large eggs, lightly beaten
2 teaspoons minced fresh parsley
  Vegetable oil

1. Adjust oven rack to middle position, place rimmed baking sheet on rack, and heat oven to 200 degrees. Toss potatoes, onion, and 1 teaspoon salt in bowl. Place half of potato mixture in center of clean dish towel. Gather ends together and twist tightly to drain as much liquid as possible, reserving liquid in liquid measuring cup. Transfer drained potato mixture to second bowl and repeat process with remaining potato mixture. Set potato liquid aside and let stand so starch settles to bottom, at least 5 minutes.

2. Cover potato mixture and microwave until just warmed through but not hot, 1 to 2 minutes, stirring mixture with fork every 30 seconds. Spread potato mixture evenly over second rimmed baking sheet and let cool for 10 minutes. Don't wash out bowl.

3. Pour off water from reserved potato liquid, leaving potato starch in measuring cup. Add eggs and stir until smooth. Return cooled potato mixture to bowl. Add parsley, ¼ teaspoon pepper, and potato starch mixture and toss until evenly combined.

4. Set wire rack in clean rimmed baking sheet and line with triple layer of paper towels. Heat ¼-inch depth of oil in 12-inch skillet over medium-high heat until shimmering but not smoking (350 degrees). Place ¼-cup mound of potato mixture in oil and press with nonstick spatula into ⅓-inch-thick disk. Repeat until 5 latkes are in pan. Cook, adjusting heat so fat bubbles around latke edges, until golden brown on bottom, about 3 minutes. Turn and continue cooking until golden brown on second side, about 3 minutes longer. Drain on paper towels and transfer to baking sheet in oven. Repeat with remaining potato mixture, adding oil to maintain ¼-inch depth and returning oil to 350 degrees between batches. Season with salt and pepper to taste and serve immediately.

TO MAKE AHEAD: Cooled latkes can be covered loosely with plastic wrap and held at room temperature for up to 4 hours. Alternatively, they can be frozen on baking sheet until firm, transferred to zipper-lock bag, and frozen for up to 1 month. Reheat latkes in 375-degree oven until crisp and hot, 3 minutes per side for room-temperature latkes and 6 minutes per side for frozen latkes.

PATATAS BRAVAS

WHY THIS RECIPE WORKS: The best versions of *patatas bravas* showcase crispy, well-browned potatoes served with a smoky, spicy tomato-based sauce. To create an ultra-crispy crust without the need for double frying, we first parboiled russet potatoes with baking soda which helped develop into a thick crust. We also tossed the parcooked potatoes with kosher salt, which roughs up the surfaces of the potatoes, creating nooks and crannies through which steam can escape.

As the steam escaped, the nooks and crannies trapped oil, making an even more substantial crust. For our sauce, tomato paste, cayenne, smoked sweet paprika, garlic, and water made a smooth, smoky, and spicy mixture, which we finished with sherry vinegar for tang. Finally, adding mayonnaise allowed us to combine the bravas sauce and another common accompaniment, *aïoli*, into a single sauce.

Patatas Bravas

SERVES 4 TO 6

While this dish is traditionally served as part of a tapas spread, it can also be served as a side dish with grilled or roasted meat. Bittersweet or smoked hot paprika can be used in place of sweet, if desired. If you make this substitution, be sure to taste the sauce before deciding how much cayenne to add, if any. A rasp-style grater makes quick work of turning the garlic into a paste.

SAUCE

1	tablespoon vegetable oil
2	teaspoons garlic, minced to paste
1	teaspoon smoked sweet paprika
½	teaspoon kosher salt
½–¾	teaspoon cayenne pepper
¼	cup tomato paste
½	cup water
2	teaspoons sherry vinegar
¼	cup mayonnaise

POTATOES

2¼	pounds russet potatoes, peeled and cut into 1-inch pieces
½	teaspoon baking soda
	Kosher salt
3	cups vegetable oil

1. FOR THE SAUCE: Heat oil in small saucepan over medium-low heat until shimmering. Add garlic, paprika, salt, and cayenne and cook until fragrant, about 30 seconds. Add tomato paste and cook for 30 seconds. Whisk in water and bring to boil over high heat. Reduce heat to medium-low and simmer until slightly thickened, 4 to 5 minutes. Transfer sauce to bowl, stir in vinegar, and let cool completely. Once cool, whisk in mayonnaise. (Sauce can be refrigerated for up to 24 hours. Bring to room temperature before serving.)

2. FOR THE POTATOES: Bring 8 cups water to boil in large saucepan over high heat. Add potatoes and baking soda. Return to boil and cook for 1 minute. Drain potatoes.

3. Return potatoes to saucepan and place over low heat. Cook, shaking saucepan occasionally, until any surface moisture has evaporated, 30 seconds to 1 minute. Remove from heat. Add 1½ teaspoons salt and stir with rubber spatula until potatoes are coated with thick, starchy paste, about 30 seconds. Transfer potatoes to rimmed baking sheet in single layer to cool. (Potatoes can stand at room temperature for up to 2 hours.)

4. Heat oil in large Dutch oven over high heat to 375 degrees. Add all potatoes (they should just be submerged in oil) and cook, stirring occasionally with wire skimmer or slotted spoon, until deep golden brown and crispy, 20 to 25 minutes.

5. Transfer potatoes to paper towel–lined wire rack set in rimmed baking sheet. Season with salt to taste. Spoon ½ cup sauce onto bottom of large platter or 1½ tablespoons sauce onto individual plates. Arrange potatoes over sauce and serve immediately, passing remaining sauce separately.

BEST BAKED POTATOES

WHY THIS RECIPE WORKS: Baked potatoes are often bland, unevenly cooked, and dependent on toppings for flavor. To produce baked potatoes with an evenly fluffy interior, ideal doneness temperature of their center should reach 205 degrees. Baking them in a hot (450-degree) oven prevented a leathery "pellicle" or film from forming underneath the peel. To season the potato skin, we coated the potatoes in salty water before baking them. We also achieved a crisp skin by painting them with vegetable oil once the potatoes were cooked through and then baking the potatoes for an additional 10 minutes.

Best Baked Potatoes
SERVES 4

Open up the potatoes immediately after removal from the oven in step 3 so steam can escape. Top them as desired, or with one of our toppings.

Salt and pepper
4 (7- to 9-ounce) russet potatoes, unpeeled, each lightly pricked with fork in 6 places
1 tablespoon vegetable oil

1. Adjust oven rack to middle position and heat oven to 450 degrees. Dissolve 2 tablespoons salt in ½ cup water in large bowl. Place potatoes in bowl and toss so exteriors of potatoes are evenly moistened. Transfer potatoes to wire rack set in rimmed baking sheet and bake until center of largest potato registers 205 degrees, 45 minutes to 1 hour.

2. Remove potatoes from oven and brush tops and sides with oil. Return potatoes to oven and continue to bake for 10 minutes.

3. Remove potatoes from oven and, using paring knife, make 2 slits, forming X, in each potato. Using clean dish towel, hold ends and squeeze slightly to push flesh up and out. Season with salt and pepper to taste. Serve immediately.

Creamy Egg Topping
MAKES 1 CUP

3 hard-cooked large eggs, chopped
4 tablespoons sour cream
1½ tablespoons minced cornichons
1 tablespoon minced fresh parsley

1 tablespoon Dijon mustard
1 tablespoon capers, rinsed and minced
1 tablespoon minced shallot
Salt and pepper

Stir together eggs, sour cream, cornichons, parsley, mustard, capers, and shallot. Season with salt and pepper to taste.

Herbed Goat Cheese Topping
MAKES ¾ CUP

Our favorite goat cheese is Laura Chenel's Chèvre Fresh Chèvre Log.

4 ounces goat cheese, softened
2 tablespoons extra-virgin olive oil
2 tablespoons minced fresh parsley
1 tablespoon minced shallot
½ teaspoon grated lemon zest
Salt and pepper

Mash goat cheese with fork. Stir in oil, parsley, shallot, and lemon zest. Season with salt and pepper to taste.

Smoked Trout Topping
MAKES 1 CUP

We prefer trout for this recipe, but any hot-smoked fish, such as salmon or bluefish, may be substituted.

5 ounces smoked trout, chopped
⅓ cup crème fraîche
2 tablespoons minced fresh chives
4 teaspoons minced shallot
1¼ teaspoons grated lemon zest plus ¾ teaspoon lemon juice
Salt and pepper

Stir all ingredients together and season with salt and pepper to taste.

SMASHED POTATOES

WHY THIS RECIPE WORKS: Bold flavors and a rustic, chunky texture make smashed potatoes a satisfying side dish. But good smashed potatoes are hard to find. We were after a good contrast of textures, with the rich, creamy puree of mashed potatoes accented by chunks of potato and skins. Testing revealed that low-starch, high-moisture red potatoes were the best choice for this dish. Their compact structure held up well under pressure, maintaining its integrity. The thin skins were pleasantly tender and paired nicely with the chunky potatoes. Cooked whole in salted water, the potatoes became lightly seasoned while also retaining their naturally creamy texture, as the skins protected the potato flesh from the water. For the best chunky texture, we smashed the potatoes with a rubber spatula or the back of a wooden spoon. Cream cheese and butter lent tang and body to the dish, and stirring in a little of the potato cooking water added moisture to give it a creamy consistency. Seasoned with salt, freshly ground black pepper, and chopped chives, these potatoes are a quick, no-fuss side dish.

Smashed Potatoes
SERVES 4

Try to get potatoes of equal size; if that's not possible, test the larger potatoes for doneness (use a paring knife). If only large potatoes are available, increase the cooking time by about 10 minutes.

> 2 pounds red potatoes (about 12 small), scrubbed
> Table salt
> 1 bay leaf
> 4 tablespoons (½ stick) unsalted butter, melted
> 4 ounces cream cheese, at room temperature
> 3 tablespoons minced fresh chives (optional)
> Ground black pepper

1. Place the potatoes in a large saucepan and add cold water to cover by 1 inch; add 1 teaspoon salt and the bay leaf. Bring to a boil over high heat, then reduce the heat to medium-low and simmer gently until a paring knife can be inserted into the potatoes with no resistance, 35 to 45 minutes. Reserve ½ cup of the cooking water, then drain the potatoes. Return the potatoes to the pot, discard the bay leaf, and allow the potatoes to stand in the pot, uncovered, until the surfaces are dry, about 5 minutes.

2. While the potatoes dry, whisk the melted butter and softened cream cheese in a medium bowl until smooth and fully incorporated. Add ¼ cup of the reserved cooking water, the chives (if using), ½ teaspoon pepper, and ½ teaspoon salt. Using a rubber spatula or the back of a wooden spoon, smash the potatoes just enough to break the skins. Fold in the butter–cream cheese mixture until most of the liquid has been absorbed

and chunks of potatoes remain. Add more cooking water as needed, 1 tablespoon at a time, until the potatoes are slightly looser than desired (the potatoes will thicken slightly with standing). Season with salt and pepper to taste and serve.

CLASSIC MASHED POTATOES

WHY THIS RECIPE WORKS: Many people would never consider consulting a recipe when making mashed potatoes, instead adding chunks of butter and spurts of cream until their conscience tells them to stop. Little wonder then that mashed potatoes made this way are consistent only in their mediocrity. We wanted mashed potatoes that were perfectly smooth and creamy, with great potato flavor and plenty of buttery richness every time.

We began by selecting russet potatoes for their high starch content. Through trial and error, we learned to boil them whole and unpeeled—this method yielded mashed potatoes that were rich, earthy, and sweet. We used a food mill or ricer for the smoothest texture imaginable, but a potato masher can be used if you prefer your potatoes a little chunky. For smooth, velvety potatoes, we added melted butter first and then half-and-half. Melting, rather than merely softening, the butter enabled it to coat the starch molecules quickly and easily, so the potatoes turned out creamy and light.

Classic Mashed Potatoes
SERVES 4

Russet potatoes make fluffier mashed potatoes, but Yukon Golds have an appealing buttery flavor and can be used. This recipe yields smooth mashed potatoes. If you don't mind lumps, use a potato masher.

> 2 pounds russet potatoes (about 4 medium), scrubbed (see note)
> 8 tablespoons (1 stick) unsalted butter, melted
> 1 cup half-and-half, warmed
> 1½ teaspoons table salt
> Ground black pepper

1. Place the potatoes in a large saucepan and add cold water to cover by 1 inch. Bring to a boil over high heat, reduce the heat to medium-low, and simmer until the potatoes are just tender when pricked with a fork, 20 to 30 minutes. Drain the potatoes.

2. Set a ricer or food mill over the now-empty saucepan. Using a potholder (to hold the potatoes) and a paring knife, peel the skins from the potatoes. Working in batches, cut the peeled potatoes into large chunks and press or mill into the saucepan.

3. Stir in the butter until incorporated. Gently whisk in the half-and-half, and season with the salt and pepper to taste. Serve.

GARLIC AND OLIVE OIL MASHED POTATOES

WHY THIS RECIPE WORKS: The Mediterranean approach of flavoring mashed potatoes with olive oil and garlic is an appealing one, but it's not as simple as replacing the dairy with oil: olive oil can turn the texture pasty and garlic can be harsh and overpowering. We wanted to translate these bold flavors into a light and creamy mashed potato side dish that would partner well with simple grilled meats or fish.

We chose to use russets in this dish for their light, fluffy texture. We first simmered the potatoes and then put the drained, peeled, still-hot potatoes through a ricer or food mill for a smooth texture. We created a mild flavor base by slowly cooking minced garlic in oil, then heightened the garlic flavor a bit by adding just a little garlic, mashed to a paste. Fruity extra-virgin olive oil and a splash of fresh lemon juice brightened the final dish.

Garlic and Olive Oil Mashed Potatoes

SERVES 6

As this dish is denser and more intensely flavored than traditional mashed potatoes, our suggested serving size is smaller than you might expect.

- 2 pounds russet potatoes (about 4 medium), scrubbed
- 5 medium garlic cloves, minced or pressed through a garlic press (about 5 teaspoons)
- 2⅛ teaspoons table salt
- ½ cup plus 2 tablespoons extra-virgin olive oil
- ½ teaspoon ground black pepper
- 2 teaspoons juice from 1 lemon

1. Place the potatoes in a large saucepan and add cold water to cover by 1 inch. Bring to a boil over high heat; reduce the heat to medium-low and cook at a bare simmer until just tender (the potatoes will offer very little resistance when poked with a paring knife), 40 to 45 minutes.

2. Meanwhile, place 1 teaspoon of the garlic on a cutting board and sprinkle with ⅛ teaspoon of the salt. Using the flat side of a chef's knife, drag the garlic and salt back and forth across the cutting board in small circular motions until the garlic is ground into a smooth paste. Transfer to a medium bowl and set aside.

3. Place the remaining 4 teaspoons garlic in a small saucepan with ¼ cup of the oil and cook over low heat, stirring constantly, until the garlic begins to sizzle and is soft, fragrant, and golden, about 5 minutes. Transfer the oil and garlic to the bowl with the raw garlic paste.

4. Drain the cooked potatoes; set a ricer or food mill over the now-empty saucepan. Using a potholder (to hold the potatoes) and a paring knife, peel the skins from the potatoes. Working in batches, cut the peeled potatoes into large chunks and press or mill into the saucepan.

5. Add the remaining 2 teaspoons salt, the pepper, lemon juice, and remaining 6 tablespoons oil to the bowl with the cooked garlic and oil and whisk to combine. Fold the mixture into the potatoes and serve.

MASHED POTATOES WITH BLUE CHEESE AND PORT-CARAMELIZED ONIONS

WHY THIS RECIPE WORKS: When it comes to mashed potatoes, most cooks worry so much about getting the texture right that they forget about the flavor. Butter and half-and-half make for mashed potatoes that are rich tasting but not terribly exciting. Our goal was to jazz up the flavor of our classic mashed potatoes. Slowly cooking thinly sliced onions brought out their sweetness, which was further complemented by a reduced port glaze. The onions' sweetness paired well with the tanginess of blue cheese, which we stirred in just before serving.

Mashed Potatoes with Blue Cheese and Port-Caramelized Onions

SERVES 4

The port adds a sweet depth to the onions that perfectly complements the blue cheese.

ONIONS
- 1½ teaspoons unsalted butter
- 1½ teaspoons vegetable oil
- ½ teaspoon light brown sugar
- ¼ teaspoon salt
- 1 pound onions, halved and sliced ¼ inch thick
- 1 cup ruby port

POTATOES

¾ cup half-and-half
1 teaspoon chopped fresh thyme
2 pounds russet potatoes
6 tablespoons unsalted butter, melted
1¼ teaspoons salt
½ teaspoon pepper
4 ounces blue cheese, crumbled (1 cup)

1. FOR THE ONIONS: Heat butter and oil in 8-inch nonstick skillet over high heat until butter melts, then stir in sugar and salt. Add onions, stir to coat, and cook, stirring occasionally, until onions begin to soften and release some moisture, about 5 minutes. Reduce heat to medium and cook, stirring frequently, until onions are deeply browned and sticky, about 35 minutes longer (if onions are sizzling or scorching, reduce heat; if onions are not browning after 15 minutes, increase heat). Stir in port and continue to cook until port reduces to glaze, 4 to 6 minutes.

2. FOR THE POTATOES: While onions are cooking, bring half-and-half and thyme to boil in small saucepan; cover to keep warm.

3. Place potatoes in large saucepan and cover with 1 inch cold water. Bring to boil over high heat, reduce heat to medium-low, and simmer until potatoes are just tender (paring knife can be slipped in and out of potatoes with very little resistance), 20 to 30 minutes. Drain.

4. Set ricer or food mill over now-empty saucepan. Using potholder (to hold potatoes) and paring knife, peel skins from potatoes. Working in batches, cut peeled potatoes into large chunks and press or mill into saucepan.

5. Stir in butter until just incorporated. Add salt and pepper, then gently stir in half-and-half and blue cheese until just combined. Serve immediately topped with onions.

ULTIMATE CREAMY MASHED POTATOES

WHY THIS RECIPE WORKS: Sometimes we want a luxurious mash, one that is silky smooth and loaded with cream and butter. But there's a fine line between creamy and gluey. We wanted lush, creamy mashed potatoes, with so much richness and flavor they could stand on their own—no gravy necessary.

For a creamier, substantial mash, we found that Yukon Golds were perfect—creamier than russets but not as heavy as red potatoes. Slicing the peeled potatoes into rounds and then rinsing away the surface starch before boiling helped intensify their creamy texture without making them gluey. Setting the boiled and drained potatoes in their pot over a low flame helped further evaporate any excess moisture. Using 1½ sticks of butter and 1½ cups of heavy cream gives these potatoes luxurious flavor and richness without making the mash too thin. We found that melting the butter and warming the cream before adding them to the potatoes ensured that the finished dish arrived at the table piping hot.

Creamy Mashed Potatoes

SERVES 8 TO 10

This recipe can be cut in half, if desired.

4 pounds Yukon Gold potatoes (about 8 medium), scrubbed, peeled, and sliced ¾ inch thick
1½ cups heavy cream
12 tablespoons (1½ sticks) unsalted butter, cut into 6 pieces
2 teaspoons table salt

1. Place the potatoes in a colander and rinse under cool running water, tossing with your hands, for 30 seconds. Transfer the potatoes to a large Dutch oven, add cold water to cover by 1 inch, and bring to a boil over high heat. Reduce the heat to medium and boil until the potatoes are tender, 20 to 25 minutes.

2. Meanwhile, heat the heavy cream and butter in a small saucepan over medium heat until the butter is melted, about 5 minutes. Set aside and keep warm.

3. Drain the potatoes and return to the Dutch oven. Stir over low heat until the potatoes are thoroughly dried, 1 to 2 minutes. Set a ricer or food mill over a large bowl and press or mill the potatoes into the bowl. Gently fold in the warm cream mixture and salt with a rubber spatula until the cream is absorbed and the potatoes are thick and creamy. Serve.

FLUFFY MASHED POTATOES

WHY THIS RECIPE WORKS: In Classic Mashed Potatoes (page 600), we boil potatoes in their jackets for earthy potato flavor (and peel them while they're still hot). We don't mind this somewhat inconvenient method when we've got time to spare, but thought an easier alternative was in order.

Cooking potatoes in their skins preserves their earthy flavor and keeps the starch granules from absorbing too much water, thereby preventing gluey mashed potatoes. To give peeled potatoes the same protection, we made two alterations to our usual technique. Steaming rather than boiling the potatoes exposed the potato pieces to less water, reducing the chance of the granules swelling to the point of bursting. When they were cooked partway, we rinsed them under cold water to rid them of free amylose, the substance that results in gluey mashed potatoes, and returned them to the steamer to finish cooking. Because potatoes cooked this way are so full of rich potato flavor, we were able to use less butter and substitute whole milk for cream.

Fluffy Mashed Potatoes

SERVES 4

This recipe works best with either a metal colander that sits easily in a Dutch oven or a large pasta pot with a steamer insert. To prevent excess evaporation, it is important for the lid to fit as snugly as possible over the colander or steamer. For the lightest, fluffiest texture, use a ricer. A food mill is the next best alternative. Russets will also work in this recipe, but avoid red potatoes.

mashed potatoes from this fate. We then tackled the curdling problem. Buttermilk curdles at 160 degrees, a temperature reached almost instantly when the cold liquid hits steaming-hot potatoes. By adding the butter, melted, to room-temperature buttermilk, we coated the proteins in the buttermilk and protected them from the heat shock that causes curdling. We also simplified the recipe by choosing peeled and cut Yukon Gold potatoes rather than using unpeeled russets (which we have used in other mashed potato recipes). Because Yukon Golds have less starch and are less absorbent than russets, they didn't become soggy and thinned out when simmered without their jackets.

Buttermilk Mashed Potatoes

SERVES 4

To achieve the proper texture, it is important to cook the potatoes thoroughly; they are done if they break apart when a knife is inserted and gently wiggled. Buttermilk substitutes like clabbered milk do not produce sufficiently tangy potatoes. To reduce the likelihood of curdling, the buttermilk must be brought to room temperature and mixed with cooled melted butter.

- 2 pounds Yukon Gold potatoes (about 4 medium), peeled and cut into 1-inch chunks
  Table salt
- 6 tablespoons (¾ stick) unsalted butter, melted and cooled (see note)
- ⅔ cup buttermilk, room temperature (see note)
  Ground black pepper

1. Place the potatoes in a large saucepan and add cold water to cover by 1 inch; add 1 tablespoon salt. Bring to a boil over high heat, then reduce the heat to medium and simmer until the potatoes break apart very easily when a paring knife is inserted, about 18 minutes. Drain the potatoes briefly, then immediately return them to the saucepan set on the still-hot (but off) burner.

2. Using a potato masher, mash the potatoes until a few small lumps remain. Gently mix the melted butter and buttermilk in a small bowl until combined. Add the buttermilk mixture to the potatoes; using a rubber spatula, fold gently until just incorporated. Season with salt and pepper to taste and serve.

- 2 pounds Yukon Gold potatoes (about 4 medium), peeled, cut into 1-inch chunks, rinsed well, and drained (see note)
- 4 tablespoons (½ stick) unsalted butter, melted
  Table salt
- ⅔ cup whole milk, warmed
  Ground black pepper

1. Place a metal colander or steamer insert in a large pot or Dutch oven. Add enough water to barely reach the bottom of the colander. Bring the water to a boil over high heat. Add the potatoes, cover, and reduce the heat to medium-high. Cook the potatoes for 10 minutes. Transfer the colander to the sink and rinse the potatoes under cold water until no longer hot, 1 to 2 minutes. Return the colander and potatoes to the pot, cover, and continue to cook until the potatoes are soft and the tip of a paring knife inserted into the potatoes meets no resistance, 10 to 15 minutes longer. Drain the potatoes.

2. Set a ricer or food mill over the now-empty pot. Working in batches, transfer the potatoes to the hopper and process or mill, removing any potatoes stuck to the bottom. Using a rubber spatula, stir in the butter and ½ teaspoon salt until incorporated. Stir in the milk until incorporated. Season with salt and pepper to taste and serve.

BUTTERMILK MASHED POTATOES

WHY THIS RECIPE WORKS: Merely replacing butter and cream with buttermilk to create tangy, creamy buttermilk mashed potatoes doesn't work—the finished potatoes are curdled, crumbly, chalky, and dry. We wanted easy mashed potatoes with buttermilk's trademark distinctive tang, but we didn't want to sacrifice texture to get them.

Many recipes for buttermilk mashed potatoes remove so much butter that the potatoes taste lean and lack creaminess. We started by restoring just enough butter to save our

MASHED POTATOES AND ROOT VEGETABLES

WHY THIS RECIPE WORKS: Root vegetables like carrots, parsnips, turnips, and celery root can add an earthy, intriguing flavor to mashed potatoes, but because root vegetables and potatoes have different starch levels and water content, treating them the same way creates a bad mash. We wanted a potato and root vegetable mash with a creamy consistency and a balanced flavor that highlights the natural earthiness of these humble root cellar favorites.

1. Melt the butter in a large saucepan over medium heat. Add the root vegetables and cook, stirring occasionally, until the butter is browned and the vegetables are dark brown and caramelized, 10 to 12 minutes. (If after 4 minutes the vegetables have not started to brown, increase the heat to medium-high.)

2. Add the potatoes, broth, and ¾ teaspoon salt and stir to combine. Cook, covered, over low heat (the broth should simmer gently; do not boil), stirring occasionally, until the potatoes fall apart easily when poked with a fork and all the liquid has been absorbed, 25 to 30 minutes. (If the liquid does not gently simmer after a few minutes, increase the heat to medium-low.) Remove the pan from the heat; remove the lid and allow the steam to escape for 2 minutes.

3. Gently mash the potatoes and root vegetables in the saucepan with a potato masher (do not mash vigorously). Gently fold in the half-and-half and chives. Season with salt and pepper to taste and serve.

We found that a 1:3 ratio of root vegetables to potatoes provided an optimal consistency, although the root vegetable flavor was barely recognizable. Caramelizing the root vegetables first in a little butter helped bring out their natural earthy sweetness; this step also boosted the flavor of the overall dish. To use just one pot, we first sautéed the root vegetables in butter until caramelized and then added the potatoes with a little chicken broth. This gave us great flavor, but the mash had a gluey texture. The answer was to remove the starch from the potatoes by rinsing the peeled, sliced potatoes in several changes of water ahead of time.

Mashed Potatoes and Root Vegetables
SERVES 4

Russet potatoes will yield a slightly fluffier, less creamy mash, but they can be used in place of the Yukon Gold potatoes if desired. Rinsing the potatoes in several changes of water reduces the amount of starch and prevents the mashed potatoes from becoming gluey. It is important to cut the potatoes and root vegetables into even-sized pieces so they cook at the same rate. This recipe can be doubled and cooked in a large Dutch oven. If doubling, increase the cooking time in step 2 to 40 minutes.

    4   tablespoons (½ stick) unsalted butter
    8   ounces carrots, parsnips, turnips, or celery root,
        peeled; carrots or parsnips cut into ¼-inch-thick
        half-moons; turnips or celery root cut into ½-inch
        dice (about 1½ cups)
 1½   pounds Yukon Gold potatoes (about 3 medium),
        peeled, quartered lengthwise, and cut crosswise
        into ¼-inch-thick slices; rinsed well in 3 to 4 changes
        of cold water and drained well (see note)
    ⅓   cup low-sodium chicken broth
        Table salt
    ¾   cup half-and-half, warmed
    3   tablespoons minced fresh chives
        Ground black pepper

ROASTED ROOT VEGETABLES

WHY THIS RECIPE WORKS: Roasted root vegetables develop complex flavors with just a quick toss in oil, salt, and pepper and a stint in a hot oven—until you try to roast different vegetables at the same time. We wanted a medley of vegetables that would cook through evenly. The trick was to carefully prep each vegetable according to how long it took to cook through. With each vegetable cut into the right size and shape, we could roast them together in one batch for uniformly tender results. To speed up the roasting, we briefly microwaved the vegetables, then placed them on a preheated baking sheet to jump-start the browning. A fruity salsa garnish and a rich bacon topping gave us some flavorful seasoning options.

Roasted Root Vegetables
SERVES 6

Use turnips that are roughly 2 to 3 inches in diameter. Instead of sprinkling the roasted vegetables with chopped herbs, try garnishing them with one of the toppings that follow.

    1   celery root (14 ounces), peeled
    4   carrots, peeled and cut into 2½-inch lengths,
        halved or quartered lengthwise if necessary to
        create pieces ½ to 1 inch in diameter
   12   ounces parsnips, peeled and sliced 1 inch thick on bias
    5   ounces small shallots, peeled
        Kosher salt and pepper
   12   ounces turnips, peeled, halved horizontally,
        and each half quartered
    3   tablespoons vegetable oil
    2   tablespoons chopped fresh parsley, tarragon, or chives

1. Adjust oven rack to middle position, place rimmed baking sheet on rack, and heat oven to 425 degrees. Cut celery root into ¾-inch-thick rounds. Cut each round into ¾-inch-thick planks about 2½ inches in length.

2. Toss celery root, carrots, parsnips, and shallots with 1 teaspoon salt and pepper to taste in large microwave-safe bowl. Cover bowl and microwave until small pieces of carrot are just pliable enough to bend, 8 to 10 minutes, stirring once halfway through microwaving. Drain vegetables well. Return vegetables to bowl, add turnips and oil, and toss to coat.

3. Working quickly, remove baking sheet from oven and carefully transfer vegetables to baking sheet; spread into even layer. Roast for 25 minutes.

4. Using thin metal spatula, stir vegetables and spread into even layer. Rotate pan and continue to roast until vegetables are golden brown and celery root is tender when pierced with tip of paring knife, 15 to 25 minutes longer. Transfer to platter, sprinkle with parsley, and serve.

Bacon-Shallot Topping
MAKES ABOUT ⅓ CUP

- 4 slices bacon, cut into ¼-inch pieces
- ¼ cup water
- 2 tablespoons minced shallot
- 1 tablespoon sherry vinegar
- 2 tablespoons minced fresh chives

Bring bacon and water to boil in 8-inch skillet over high heat. Reduce heat to medium and cook until water has evaporated and bacon is crisp, about 10 minutes. Transfer bacon to paper towel–lined plate and pour off all but ½ teaspoon fat from skillet. Add shallot and cook, stirring frequently, until softened, 2 to 4 minutes. Remove pan from heat and add vinegar. Transfer shallot mixture to bowl and stir in bacon and chives. Sprinkle over vegetables before serving.

Orange-Parsley Salsa
MAKES ABOUT ½ CUP

- ¼ cup slivered almonds
- ¼ teaspoon ground cumin
- ¼ teaspoon ground coriander
- 1 orange
- ½ cup fresh parsley leaves, minced
- 2 garlic cloves, minced
- 2 teaspoons extra-virgin olive oil
- 1 teaspoon cider vinegar
- ¼ teaspoon kosher salt

1. Toast almonds in 10-inch skillet over medium-high heat until fragrant and golden brown, 5 to 6 minutes. Add cumin and coriander; continue to toast, stirring constantly, until fragrant, about 45 seconds. Immediately transfer to bowl.

2. Cut away peel and pith from orange. Use paring knife to slice between membranes to release segments. Cut segments into ¼-inch pieces. Stir orange pieces, parsley, garlic, oil, vinegar, and salt into almond mixture. Let stand for 30 minutes. Spoon over vegetables before serving.

BEHIND THE SCENES

ADAM'S EQUIPMENT HALL OF SHAME

Adam and the equipment testing team have spent thousands of hours over the past decade separating the good from the bad—and once in a while they come across gadgets and equipment that perform so poorly, they deserve special mention.

QUESADILLA MAKER: If we're going to shell out money for a gadget devoted to just one dish, it better be awfully good. This quesadilla maker, however, severely limits the amount of cheese that can be sandwiched between the tortillas. So, uh, what's the point? Unless you're on a diet, use a skillet instead.

SHRIMP BUTLER: Although this gadget is supposed to peel and devein shrimp, it only accomplishes the task partway by slitting the shell to reveal the vein. Even worse, we found that the shrimp sometimes became mangled in the machine. And since our testing, shrimp is now often sold deveined and slit for easy peeling, so a "butler" for shrimp is no longer necessary.

THERMOMETER FORK: Ouch! Put away your thermo fork and grab a pair of tongs and an instant-read thermometer instead (see our recommended brands on pages 877 and 884). Thermometer forks are designed to enable the user to move the food being cooked on the grill and take its temperature at the same time. We found this gadget awkward to use, especially when trying to flip or turn meat for even browning.

ALLIGATOR CHOPPER: This gadget claims to deliver perfectly cubed onions and elegant batons of carrots, bell peppers, or apples with one punch of the handheld chopper blades against its platform base. But too often, we found ourselves cautiously extracting suspended vegetables from the blade. We'll stick to chopping veggies the old-fashioned way—with a sharp knife and cutting board.

BANANA HANGER: Supermarkets often suspend unripe bananas from tall poles covered with small hooks. Banana hangers miniaturize this idea for the home kitchen. Sounds good, but we found no difference in the ripening time between hanging bananas . . . and simply setting them on the counter.

ROOT VEGETABLE GRATIN

WHY THIS RECIPE WORKS: For a lighter alternative to classic potato gratin, we wanted to supplement the starchy potatoes with more flavorful root vegetables—but first we needed to figure out how to cook them all evenly. To keep the potatoes from breaking down before the celery root and rutabaga slices were finished, we added dry white wine to the creamy cooking liquid. Incorporating flour into the liquid bound the layers of sliced vegetables. Dijon mustard offered a spicy, savory boost. A sprinkling of bold aromatics—chopped onion, fresh thyme, minced garlic, and black pepper—between the alternating layers infused the gratin with hearty flavors. Pressing the layers down after adding the liquid compacted the gratin, ensuring that the slices clung together nicely. A sprinkling of panko bread crumbs, Parmesan, and melted butter added with 15 minutes left in the oven created a golden crust.

Root Vegetable Gratin

SERVES 6 TO 8

Uniformly thin slices are necessary for a cohesive gratin. We recommend a mandoline for quick and even slicing, but a sharp chef's knife will also work. Because the vegetables in the gratin are tightly packed into the casserole dish, it will still be plenty hot after a 25-minute rest.

- 1 tablespoon plus 1½ cups water
- 1½ teaspoons Dijon mustard
- 2 teaspoons all-purpose flour
  Salt and pepper
- ⅔ cup dry white wine
- ½ cup heavy cream
- ½ onion, chopped fine
- 1¼ teaspoons minced fresh thyme
- 1 garlic clove, minced

- 2 pounds large Yukon Gold potatoes, peeled and sliced lengthwise ⅛ inch thick
- 1 large celery root (1 pound), peeled, quartered, and sliced ⅛ inch thick
- 1 pound rutabaga, peeled, quartered, and sliced ⅛ inch thick
- ¾ cup panko bread crumbs
- 1½ ounces Parmesan cheese, grated (¾ cup)
- 4 tablespoons unsalted butter, melted and cooled

1. Adjust oven rack to middle position and heat oven to 375 degrees. Grease 13 by 9-inch baking dish. Whisk 1 tablespoon water, mustard, flour, and 1½ teaspoons salt in medium bowl until smooth. Add wine, cream, and remaining 1½ cups water; whisk to combine. Combine onion, thyme, garlic, and ¼ teaspoon pepper in second bowl.

2. Layer half of potatoes in prepared dish, arranging so they form even thickness. Sprinkle half of onion mixture evenly over potatoes. Arrange celery root and rutabaga slices in even layer over onions. Sprinkle remaining onion mixture over celery root and rutabaga. Layer remaining potatoes over onions. Slowly pour water mixture over vegetables. Using rubber spatula, gently press down on vegetables to create even, compact layer. Cover tightly with aluminum foil and bake for 50 minutes. Remove foil and continue to bake until knife inserted into center of gratin meets no resistance, 20 to 25 minutes longer.

3. While gratin bakes, combine panko, Parmesan, and butter in bowl and season with salt and pepper to taste. Remove gratin from oven and sprinkle evenly with panko mixture. Continue to bake until panko is golden brown, 15 to 20 minutes longer. Remove gratin from oven and let stand for 25 minutes. Serve.

CAULIFLOWER GRATIN

WHY THIS RECIPE WORKS: We set out to create a cauliflower gratin that was flavorful and fresh, not rich and stodgy. We relied on cauliflower's ability to become an ultracreamy puree and used that as a sauce to bind florets together. To ensure that we had enough cauliflower to use in two ways, we used two heads. We removed the cores and stems and steamed them until soft; then blended them to make the sauce. We cut each cored head into slabs, which made for a more compact casserole and helped the florets cook more evenly. For an efficient cooking setup, we placed the cauliflower cores and stems in water in the bottom of a Dutch oven and set a steamer basket filled with the florets on top. Butter and Parmesan, plus a little cornstarch, gave the sauce a richer flavor and texture without making it too heavy, and a few pantry spices lent complexity. Tossing the florets in the sauce before placing them in the dish ensured that they were completely coated. A crisp topping of Parmesan and panko gave the gratin savory crunch, while a final garnish of minced chives added color.

Modern Cauliflower Gratin

SERVES 8 TO 10

When buying cauliflower, look for heads without many leaves. Alternatively, if your cauliflower does have a lot of leaves, buy slightly larger heads—about 2¼ pounds each. This recipe can be halved to serve 4 to 6; cook the cauliflower in a large saucepan and bake the gratin in an 8-inch square baking dish.

2	heads cauliflower (2 pounds each)
8	tablespoons unsalted butter
½	cup panko bread crumbs
2	ounces Parmesan cheese, grated (1 cup)
	Salt and pepper
½	teaspoon dry mustard
⅛	teaspoon ground nutmeg
	Pinch cayenne pepper
1	teaspoon cornstarch dissolved in 1 teaspoon water
1	tablespoon minced fresh chives

1. Adjust oven rack to middle position and heat oven to 400 degrees.

2. Pull off outer leaves of 1 head of cauliflower and trim stem. Using paring knife, cut around core to remove; halve core lengthwise and slice thin crosswise. Slice head into ½-inch-thick slabs. Cut stems from slabs to create florets that are about 1½ inches tall; slice stems thin and reserve along with sliced core. Transfer florets to bowl, including any small pieces that may have been created during trimming, and set aside. Repeat with remaining head of cauliflower. (After trimming you should have about 3 cups of sliced stems and cores and 12 cups of florets.)

3. Combine sliced stems and cores, 2 cups florets, 3 cups water, and 6 tablespoons butter in Dutch oven and bring to boil over high heat. Place remaining florets in steamer basket (do not rinse bowl). Once mixture is boiling, place steamer basket in pot, cover, and reduce heat to medium. Steam florets in basket until translucent and stem ends can be easily pierced with paring knife, 10 to 12 minutes. Remove steamer basket and drain florets. Re-cover pot, reduce heat to low, and continue to cook stem mixture until very soft, about 10 minutes longer. Transfer drained florets to now-empty bowl.

4. While cauliflower is cooking, melt remaining 2 tablespoons butter in 10-inch skillet over medium heat. Add panko and cook, stirring frequently, until golden brown, 3 to 5 minutes. Transfer to bowl and let cool. Once cool, add ½ cup Parmesan and toss to combine.

5. Transfer stem mixture and cooking liquid to blender and add 2 teaspoons salt, ½ teaspoon pepper, mustard, nutmeg, cayenne, and remaining ½ cup Parmesan. Process until smooth and velvety, about 1 minute (puree should be pourable; adjust consistency with additional water as needed). With blender running, add cornstarch slurry. Season with salt and pepper to taste. Pour puree over cauliflower florets and toss gently to evenly coat. Transfer mixture to 13 by 9-inch baking dish (it will be quite loose) and smooth top with spatula.

6. Scatter bread-crumb mixture evenly over top. Transfer dish to oven and bake until sauce bubbles around edges, 13 to 15 minutes. Let stand for 20 to 25 minutes. Sprinkle with chives and serve.

DUCK FAT–ROASTED POTATOES

WHY THIS RECIPE WORKS: For the ultimate side of roasted potatoes, we needed spuds that could take on meaty duck fat flavor and a crisp crust before drying out. Briefly boiling peeled, cut Yukon Golds in a solution of water, salt, and baking soda broke down the potatoes' pectin, causing them to release a wet starch that rapidly browns. After draining, we returned the pot to the stove to evaporate any moisture and then, off heat, stirred in enough duck fat to give the potatoes some distinct flavor. Stirring the potatoes released a thick paste that ensured a crunchy shell and roasting the pieces on a preheated baking sheet kick-started the crisping. To infuse the potatoes with richness and herbal flavors, we stirred in a mixture of rosemary and more duck fat toward the end of cooking.

Duck Fat–Roasted Potatoes

SERVES 6

Duck fat is available in the meat department in many supermarkets. Alternatively, substitute chicken fat, lard, or a mixture of 3 tablespoons of bacon fat and 3 tablespoons of extra-virgin olive oil.

We tested using different potatoes and found that we liked Yukon Golds best. Parcooking the potatoes before subjecting them to high oven temperatures helped them develop a somewhat crisper exterior, but the browning was uneven and they still weren't crispy enough. When we switched from cubing the potatoes to slicing them thick, we created more surface area for crisping but enough heft for a creamy interior. As an added bonus, with only two surfaces to cook, we now only had to flip the potatoes once halfway through roasting. We boiled the potatoes very briefly before roasting to prevent them from breaking up on the baking sheet, and we tossed the precooked potatoes with some olive oil to rough up the exteriors and increase crispiness.

Crispy Roasted Potatoes

SERVES 4 TO 6

Note that the potatoes should be just undercooked when removed from the boiling water—this helps ensure that they will roast up crispy.

2½ pounds Yukon Gold potatoes (about 5 medium), rinsed and cut into ½-inch-thick slices
    Table salt
5 tablespoons olive oil
    Ground black pepper

1. Adjust an oven rack to the lowest position, place a rimmed baking sheet on the rack, and heat the oven to 450 degrees. Place the potatoes and 1 tablespoon salt in a Dutch oven; add cold water to cover by 1 inch. Bring to a boil over high heat; reduce the heat and gently simmer until the exterior of a potato has softened, but the center offers resistance when pierced with a paring knife, about 5 minutes. Drain the potatoes well, and transfer to a large bowl. Drizzle with 2 tablespoons of the oil and sprinkle with ½ teaspoon salt; using a rubber spatula, toss to combine. Drizzle with 2 tablespoons more oil and ½ teaspoon more salt; continue to toss until the exteriors of the potato slices are coated with a starchy paste.

2. Working quickly, remove the baking sheet from the oven and drizzle the remaining 1 tablespoon oil over the surface. Carefully transfer the potatoes to the baking sheet and spread them into an even layer (skin side up for the end pieces). Bake until the bottoms of the potatoes are golden brown and crisp, 15 to 25 minutes, rotating the baking sheet after 10 minutes.

3. Remove the baking sheet from the oven and, using a metal spatula and tongs, loosen the potatoes from the pan and carefully flip each slice. Continue to roast until the second side is golden and crisp, 10 to 20 minutes longer, rotating the pan as needed to ensure the potatoes brown evenly. Season with salt and pepper to taste and serve.

3½ pounds Yukon Gold potatoes, peeled and cut into 1½-inch pieces
    Kosher salt and pepper
½ teaspoon baking soda
6 tablespoons duck fat
1 tablespoon chopped fresh rosemary

1. Adjust oven rack to top position, place rimmed baking sheet on rack, and heat oven to 475 degrees.

2. Bring 10 cups water to boil in Dutch oven over high heat. Add potatoes, ⅓ cup salt, and baking soda. Return to boil and cook for 1 minute. Drain potatoes. Return potatoes to pot and place over low heat. Cook, shaking pot occasionally, until surface moisture has evaporated, about 2 minutes. Remove from heat. Add 5 tablespoons fat and 1 teaspoon salt; mix with rubber spatula until potatoes are coated with thick paste, about 30 seconds.

3. Remove sheet from oven, transfer potatoes to sheet, and spread into even layer. Roast for 15 minutes.

4. Remove sheet from oven. Using thin, sharp, metal spatula, turn potatoes. Roast until golden brown, 12 to 15 minutes. While potatoes roast, combine rosemary and remaining 1 tablespoon fat in bowl.

5. Remove sheet from oven. Spoon rosemary-fat mixture over potatoes and turn again. Continue to roast until potatoes are well browned and rosemary is fragrant, 3 to 5 minutes. Season with salt and pepper to taste. Serve immediately.

ULTIMATE ROASTED POTATOES

WHY THIS RECIPE WORKS: The aroma of roasting potatoes draws everyone into the kitchen come meal time. Too often, though, the potatoes turn out brown and leathery with a mealy interior, or worse, soft with no crisp crust at all. We wanted oven-roasted potatoes that had a crisp crust with a silky interior.

SKILLET-ROASTED POTATOES

WHY THIS RECIPE WORKS: Skillet-roasted potatoes often cook up unevenly, with a mixture of scorched and pallid potatoes. We wanted to be able to make truly outstanding skillet-roasted potatoes, as good as oven-roasted—extra-crisp on the outside and moist and creamy on the inside, evenly browned, and never greasy. This would be the recipe we'd turn to when we craved roasted potatoes but there was no room in the oven for the conventional kind.

The solution turned out to be choosing the right potato and cutting it uniformly. Red Bliss potatoes, cut in half if small or quartered if medium, offered a great crust and a moist interior, thanks to their high moisture content. We rinsed the cut potatoes to remove surface starch, which otherwise caused the potatoes to stick to the pan and inhibited browning. Olive oil added flavor and richness to the dish. The winning cooking technique was to first brown the potatoes over high heat, then cover and finish cooking over low heat. This allowed the insides to cook through while the outsides stayed crisp.

Skillet-Roasted Potatoes

SERVES 3 TO 4

Small and medium potatoes can be used in this recipe, but they must be cut differently. Small potatoes (1½ to 2 inches in diameter) should be cut in half and medium potatoes (2 to 3 inches in diameter) should be cut into quarters to create ¾- to 1-inch chunks. Large potatoes should not be used because the cut pieces will be uneven and won't cook at the same rate. For even cooking and proper browning, the potatoes must be cooked in a single layer and should not be crowded in the pan.

- 1½ pounds small or medium red potatoes (about 9 small or 4 to 5 medium), scrubbed, halved if small, quartered if medium (see note)
- 2 tablespoons olive oil
- ¾ teaspoon table salt
- ¾ teaspoon ground black pepper

1. Rinse the potatoes in cold water and drain well; spread on a clean kitchen towel and thoroughly pat dry.

2. Heat the oil in a 12-inch skillet over medium-high heat until shimmering. Add the potatoes, cut side down, in a single layer. Cook, without stirring, until the potatoes are golden brown (the oil should sizzle but not smoke), 5 to 7 minutes. Using tongs, turn the potatoes skin side down if halved or second cut side down if quartered. Cook, without stirring, until the potatoes are deep golden brown, 5 to 6 minutes longer. Stir the potatoes, then redistribute in a single layer. Reduce the heat to medium-low, cover, and cook until the potatoes are tender (a paring knife can be inserted into the potatoes with no resistance), 6 to 9 minutes.

3. When the potatoes are tender, sprinkle with the salt and pepper and toss gently to combine; serve.

SALT-BAKED POTATOES

WHY THIS RECIPE WORKS: Let's be honest: Sometimes baked potatoes could use a flavor boost. And instead of light and fluffy, they are often dense and crumbly. Salt-baking potatoes promises to remedy these problems. We tried burying potatoes under a mound of salt, cooking them on a bed of salt, covering them with foil, and making a salt crust on the potatoes with an egg wash. All were good, but the bed of salt was best. Moisture that escaped during baking was trapped in the pan, then absorbed by the salt, and reabsorbed by the potatoes, making their skins tender and their flesh light. Uncovering the potatoes toward the end of cooking ensured dry, crisp skin. A 13 by 9-inch baking dish provided plenty of space so we didn't crowd the potatoes, and 2½ cups of salt allowed us to thoroughly cover the bottom of the pan. A little rosemary and garlic added helped flavor the spuds.

Salt-Baked Potatoes with Roasted Garlic and Rosemary Butter

SERVES 4

Kosher salt or table salt can be used in this recipe. The salt may be sifted through a strainer to remove any solid bits and reused for this recipe. These potatoes can be prepared without the roast garlic butter and topped with your favorite potato toppings such as sour cream, chives, crumbled bacon, or shredded cheese.

- 2½ cups plus ⅛ teaspoon salt
- 4 medium russet potatoes (about 8 ounces each), well scrubbed and dried
- 2 sprigs fresh rosemary plus ¼ teaspoon minced leaves
- 1 whole garlic head, outer papery skin removed and top quarter of head cut off and discarded
- 4 teaspoons olive oil
- 4 tablespoons (½ stick) unsalted butter, softened

1. Adjust an oven rack to the middle position and heat the oven to 450 degrees. Spread the salt into an even layer in a 13 by 9-inch baking dish. Gently nestle the potatoes in the salt, broad side down, leaving space between each potato. Add the rosemary sprigs and the garlic, cut side up, to the baking dish. Cover the baking dish with aluminum foil and crimp the edges to tightly seal. Bake for 1 hour and 15 minutes; remove the pan from the oven. Increase the oven temperature to 500 degrees.

2. Carefully remove the foil. Remove the garlic head from the baking dish and set aside to cool. Brush the exposed portion of each potato with 1 teaspoon oil. Return the uncovered baking dish to the oven and continue to bake until the potatoes are tender and the skins are glossy, 15 to 20 minutes.

3. Meanwhile, once the garlic is cool enough to handle, squeeze the root end until the cloves slip out of their skins.

Using a fork, mash the garlic, butter, minced rosemary, and remaining ⅛ teaspoon salt to a smooth paste. Remove any clumped salt from the potatoes (holding the potatoes with a kitchen mitt if necessary), split lengthwise, top with a portion of the butter and serve immediately.

Salt-Baked Potatoes with Roasted Shallot and Thyme Butter

Follow the recipe for Salt-Baked Potatoes with Roasted Garlic and Rosemary Butter, substituting 5 crumbled bay leaves for the rosemary sprigs and 1 teaspoon chopped fresh thyme leaves for the chopped rosemary. Substitute 2 medium shallots for the garlic head.

BRAISED RED POTATOES

WHY THIS RECIPE WORKS: What if you could get red potatoes with the creamy interiors created by steaming and the crispy browned exteriors produced by roasting—without doing either? That's the result promised by recipes for braised red potatoes, but they rarely deliver. To make good on the promise, we combined halved small red potatoes, butter, and salted water (plus thyme for flavoring) in a 12-inch skillet and simmered the spuds until their interiors were perfectly creamy and the water was fully evaporated. Then we let the potatoes continue to cook in the now-dry skillet until their cut sides browned in the butter, developing the rich flavor and crisp edges of roasted potatoes. These crispy, creamy potatoes were so good they needed only a minimum of seasoning: We simply tossed them with some minced garlic (softened in the simmering water along with the potatoes), lemon juice, chives, and pepper.

Braised Red Potatoes with Lemon and Chives
SERVES 4 TO 6

Use small red potatoes measuring about 1½ inches in diameter.

- 1½ pounds small red potatoes, unpeeled, halved
- 2 cups water
- 3 tablespoons unsalted butter
- 3 garlic cloves, peeled
- 3 sprigs fresh thyme
- ¾ teaspoon salt
- 1 teaspoon lemon juice
- ¼ teaspoon pepper
- 2 tablespoons minced fresh chives

1. Arrange potatoes in single layer, cut side down, in 12-inch nonstick skillet. Add water, butter, garlic, thyme, and salt and bring to simmer over medium-high heat. Reduce heat to medium, cover, and simmer until potatoes are just tender, about 15 minutes.

2. Remove lid and use slotted spoon to transfer garlic to cutting board; discard thyme. Increase heat to medium-high and vigorously simmer, swirling pan occasionally, until water

evaporates and butter starts to sizzle, 15 to 20 minutes. When cool enough to handle, mince garlic to paste. Transfer paste to bowl and stir in lemon juice and pepper.

3. Continue to cook potatoes, swirling pan frequently, until butter browns and cut sides of potatoes turn spotty brown, 4 to 6 minutes longer. Off heat, add garlic mixture and chives and toss to thoroughly coat. Serve immediately.

Braised Red Potatoes with Dijon and Tarragon

Substitute 2 teaspoons Dijon mustard for lemon juice and 1 tablespoon minced fresh tarragon for chives.

Braised Red Potatoes with Miso and Scallions

Reduce salt to ½ teaspoon. Substitute 1 tablespoon red miso paste for lemon juice and 3 thinly sliced scallions for chives.

BOILED POTATOES WITH BLACK OLIVE TAPENADE

WHY THIS RECIPE WORKS: Tapenade is an easy spread that shines as a quick go-to topping for bruschetta, pasta, or potatoes. A paste of processed pine nuts created a buttery base to keep the tapenade spreadable. Using brine-cured kalamata olives and salt-cured black olives created a perfect balance of tang. Rinsing the capers kept the salt under control. Anchovies bumped up the spread's subtle meatiness and some Dijon mustard and garlic contributed a sharp kick. We pulsed the ingredients into a finely chopped spread, stirring in olive oil by hand. Refrigerating the finished tapenade for at least 18 hours allowed the flavors to meld and develop. With our tapenade at the ready, we boiled halved red potatoes until just tender. Once drained, we folded in some of the spread. Chopped parsley and lemon juice livened the side.

Boiled Potatoes with Black Olive Tapenade

SERVES 4 TO 6

Use small red potatoes measuring about 1½ inches in diameter.

    2   pounds small red potatoes, unpeeled, halved
    1   tablespoon salt
    ⅓   cup Black Olive Tapenade
    1   tablespoon lemon juice
    1   tablespoon chopped fresh parsley
        Extra-virgin olive oil

1. Bring 6 cups water, potatoes, and salt to boil in large saucepan over medium-high heat. Reduce heat to medium-low and simmer until potatoes are just tender when pierced with knife, 10 to 15 minutes.

2. Reserve ¼ cup cooking water. Drain potatoes and return them to pan. Combine tapenade, lemon juice, and 2 tablespoons cooking water in bowl. Add tapenade mixture to potatoes and fold gently to incorporate. Add remaining 2 tablespoons cooking water as needed to adjust consistency. Transfer potatoes to serving bowl, sprinkle with parsley, drizzle with oil, and serve.

Black Olive Tapenade

MAKES ABOUT 1½ CUPS

The tapenade must be refrigerated for at least 18 hours before serving. It's important to use untoasted pine nuts in this recipe so that they provide creaminess but little flavor of their own. We prefer the rich flavor of kalamata olives, but any high-quality brine-cured black olive, such as niçoise, Sicilian, or Greek, can be substituted. Do not substitute brine-cured olives for the salt-cured olives. Serve extra tapenade as a spread with sliced crusty bread or as a dip with raw vegetables.

    ⅓   cup pine nuts
    1½   cups pitted kalamata olives
    ½   cup pitted salt-cured black olives
    3   tablespoons capers, rinsed
    2   anchovy fillets, rinsed and patted dry
    2   teaspoons Dijon mustard
    ½   garlic clove, minced
    ¼   cup extra-virgin olive oil

1. In food processor fitted with metal blade, process pine nuts until reduced to paste that clings to walls and avoids blade, about 20 seconds. Scrape down bowl to redistribute paste and process until paste again clings to walls and avoids blade, about 5 seconds. Repeat scraping and processing once more (pine nuts should form mostly smooth, tahini-like paste).

2. Scrape down bowl to redistribute paste and add olives, capers, anchovies, mustard, and garlic. Pulse until finely chopped, about 15 pulses, scraping down bowl halfway through pulsing. Transfer mixture to medium bowl and stir in oil until well combined.

3. Transfer to container, cover, and refrigerate for at least 18 hours or up to 2 weeks. Bring to room temperature and stir thoroughly before serving.

SCALLOPED POTATOES

WHY THIS RECIPE WORKS: Thinly sliced potatoes layered with cream and baked until they are bubbling and browned are a classic accompaniment to baked ham or roast beef. But scalloped potatoes can occupy the oven for over two hours and still produce unevenly cooked potatoes in a heavy, curdled sauce. We wanted to minimize the cooking time while turning out layers of thinly sliced, tender potatoes, a creamy sauce, and a nicely browned, cheesy crust.

We tried using flour to thicken the sauce, but this produced a thick, pasty sauce. Instead we relied on heavy cream lightened with whole milk. To cut the cooking time, we simmered the potatoes briefly in the cream in a covered pot, before transferring the mixture to a baking dish and finishing the potatoes in the oven. We found russet potatoes had the best texture and flavor, and we sliced them thin so they formed neat layers.

Scalloped Potatoes

SERVES 8 TO 10

For the fastest and most consistent results, slice the potatoes in a food processor or on a mandoline or V-slicer.

- 2 tablespoons unsalted butter
- 1 small onion, minced
- 2 medium garlic cloves, minced or pressed through a garlic press (about 2 teaspoons)
- 4 pounds russet potatoes (about 8 medium), peeled and cut into ⅛-inch-thick slices (see note)
- 3 cups heavy cream
- 1 cup whole milk
- 4 sprigs fresh thyme
- 2 bay leaves
- 2 teaspoons table salt
- ½ teaspoon ground black pepper
- 4 ounces cheddar cheese, shredded (about 1 cup)

1. Adjust an oven rack to the middle position and heat the oven to 350 degrees. Melt the butter in a large Dutch oven over medium-high heat. Add the onion and cook until softened and lightly browned, 5 to 7 minutes. Add the garlic and cook until fragrant, about 30 seconds. Add the potatoes, cream, milk, thyme, bay leaves, salt, and pepper, and bring to a simmer. Cover, adjusting the heat as necessary to maintain a light simmer, and cook until the potatoes are almost tender (a paring knife can be slipped into and out of the center of a potato slice with some resistance), about 15 minutes.

2. Remove and discard the thyme sprigs and bay leaves. Transfer the potato mixture to a 3-quart gratin dish and sprinkle with the cheese. Bake until the cream has thickened and is bubbling around the sides, and the top is golden brown, about 20 minutes. Cool for 5 minutes before serving.

TWICE-BAKED POTATOES

WHY THIS RECIPE WORKS: Twice-baked potatoes are not difficult to make, but the process can be time-consuming, and they're plagued by chewy skins and pasty, bland fillings. We wanted to perfect the process and have twice-baked potatoes with slightly crisp, chewy skins and a rich, creamy filling.

We had a head start, having already perfected a recipe for baked potatoes. Starting there, we oiled the potatoes before baking for a crisp skin, and we let the baked potatoes cool slightly before slicing them open and removing the flesh. We found that we could prevent the hollowed-out shells from turning soggy by keeping them in the oven while making the filling. And for the filling we found it best to combine the potato with tangy dairy ingredients—sour cream and buttermilk were ideal—a small amount of butter, and sharp cheddar cheese for its bold flavor. For a perfect finish, we placed the filled potatoes under the broiler, where they turned brown and crisp.

Twice-Baked Potatoes

SERVES 6 TO 8

Most potatoes have two relatively flat, blunt sides and two curved sides. Halve the baked potatoes lengthwise so the blunt sides are down once the shells are stuffed, making the potatoes much more stable in the pan during final baking. To vary the flavor a bit, try substituting other types of cheese, such as Gruyère, fontina, or feta, for the cheddar. Yukon Gold potatoes can be substituted for the russets.

- 4 medium russet potatoes (about 8 ounces each), scrubbed, dried, and rubbed lightly with vegetable oil (see note)
- 4 ounces sharp cheddar cheese, shredded (about 1 cup; see note)
- ½ cup sour cream
- ½ cup buttermilk
- 2 tablespoons unsalted butter, softened
- 3 scallions, sliced thin
- ½ teaspoon table salt
  Ground black pepper

1. Adjust an oven rack to the upper-middle position and heat the oven to 400 degrees. Bake the potatoes on a foil-lined baking sheet until the skin is crisp and deep brown and a skewer easily pierces the flesh, about 1 hour. Transfer the potatoes to a wire rack and cool slightly, about 10 minutes. (Leave the oven on.)

2. Using an oven mitt or folded kitchen towel to handle the hot potatoes, cut each potato in half so that the long, blunt sides rest on the work surface. Using a small spoon, scoop the flesh from each half into a medium bowl, leaving a ⅛ to ¼-inch thickness of the flesh in each shell. Arrange the shells on the foil-lined baking sheet and return to the oven until dry and slightly crisp, about 10 minutes. Meanwhile, mash the potato flesh with a fork until smooth. Stir in the remaining ingredients, including pepper to taste, until well combined.

3. Remove the shells from the oven and increase the oven setting to broil. Holding the shells steady on the pan with an oven mitt or towel-protected hand, spoon the mixture into the crisped shells, mounding it slightly at the center, and return the potatoes to the oven. Broil until spotty brown and crisp on top, 10 to 15 minutes. Cool for 10 minutes and serve warm.

CRISPY SMASHED POTATOES

WHY THIS RECIPE WORKS: Crispy smashed potatoes are the best of both worlds, delivering mashed potato creaminess with the crackling crisp crust of roasted potatoes. The technique looks straightforward: Skin-on spuds are parcooked in seasoned water, drained, and squashed just shy of an inch thick. Then the potatoes are oiled, and either pan-fried on the stovetop or spread out on a baking sheet in the oven to render the roughened edges browned and crispy and the interior flesh creamy and sweet. But parcooking the potatoes (waxy, thin-skinned Red Bliss) in water diluted their flavor, so they tasted flat, rather than rich and earthy.

2. Drizzle 3 tablespoons of the oil over the potatoes and roll to coat. Space the potatoes evenly on the baking sheet. Following the photos, place a second baking sheet on top; press down uniformly on the baking sheet until the potatoes are roughly ⅓ to ½ inch thick. Sprinkle with the thyme leaves and season generously with salt and pepper; drizzle evenly with the remaining 3 tablespoons oil. Roast the potatoes on the top rack for 15 minutes. Transfer the potatoes to the bottom rack and continue to roast until well browned, 20 to 30 minutes longer. Serve immediately.

MAKING CRISPY SMASHED POTATOES
You can smash each potato by hand with a potato masher, but we found that a baking sheet smashes the potatoes all at once.

1. After rolling the cooled, oven-steamed potatoes in olive oil, space the potatoes evenly on the baking sheet and place a second baking sheet on top; press down uniformly on the baking sheet until the potatoes are roughly ⅓ to ½ inch thick.

2. Sprinkle the smashed potatoes with the thyme leaves and season generously with salt and pepper; drizzle evenly with the remaining 3 tablespoons oil. Roast as directed.

To fix the flavor problem and streamline the cooking method, we turned to one pan to get the job done—a baking sheet. A baking sheet's roomy cooking surface allowed us to easily prepare potatoes for four at once rather than pan-frying them in fussy batches. To soften the potatoes, we spread them out on the baking sheet, added a little water, covered the pan with foil, and baked them until tender. To smash all the potatoes at once, we used a second baking sheet, which we simply pressed evenly and firmly on top of the pan of parcooked potatoes. To crisp the potatoes we opted for olive oil to coat the baking sheet and to drizzle over the broken spuds. The result? A welcome addition to the potato rotation: browned and crunchy potato patties, full of deep, earthy flavor.

Crispy Smashed Potatoes
SERVES 4 TO 6

This recipe is designed to work with potatoes that are 1½ to 2 inches in diameter. Do not attempt it with potatoes that are over 2 inches. Remove the potatoes from the baking sheet as soon as they are done browning—they will toughen if left on the baking sheet for too long. A potato masher can also be used to "smash" the potatoes.

2 pounds small Red Bliss potatoes (about 18),
   scrubbed (see note)
6 tablespoons extra-virgin olive oil
1 teaspoon chopped fresh thyme leaves
   Kosher salt and ground black pepper

1. Adjust the oven racks to the top and bottom positions and heat the oven to 500 degrees. Spread the potatoes on a rimmed baking sheet, pour ¾ cup water into the baking sheet, and wrap tightly with aluminum foil. Cook on the bottom rack until a skewer or paring knife slips in and out of the potatoes easily, 25 to 30 minutes (poke the skewer through the foil to test). Remove the foil and cool for 10 minutes. If any water remains on the pan, blot dry with a paper towel.

MASHED SWEET POTATOES

WHY THIS RECIPE WORKS: Mashed sweet potatoes often turn out overly thick and gluey or, at the other extreme, sloppy and loose. We wanted a recipe that would push sweet potatoes' deep, earthy sweetness to the fore and that would produce a silky puree with enough body to hold its shape on a fork.

We braised the sweet potatoes in a mixture of butter and heavy cream to impart a smooth richness. Adding a little salt brought out the sweet potatoes' delicate flavor, and just a teaspoon of sugar bolstered their sweetness. Once the potatoes were tender, we mashed them in the saucepan with a potato masher. We skipped the typical pumpkin pie seasoning and instead let the simple sweet potato flavor shine through.

Mashed Sweet Potatoes
SERVES 4

Cutting the sweet potatoes into slices of even thickness is important so that they cook at the same rate. The potatoes are best served immediately, but they can be covered tightly with plastic wrap and kept warm for 30 minutes. This recipe can be doubled and prepared in a Dutch oven; the cooking time will need to be doubled as well.

> 4 tablespoons (½ stick) unsalted butter, cut into 4 pieces
> 2 tablespoons heavy cream
> 1 teaspoon sugar
> ½ teaspoon table salt
> 2 pounds sweet potatoes (2 to 3 medium), peeled, quartered lengthwise, and cut crosswise into ¼-inch-thick slices (see note)
> Ground black pepper

1. Melt the butter in a large saucepan over low heat. Stir in the cream, sugar, and salt; add the sweet potatoes and cook, covered, stirring occasionally, until the potatoes fall apart when poked with a fork, 35 to 45 minutes.

2. Off the heat, mash the sweet potatoes in the saucepan with a potato masher or transfer the mixture to a food mill and process into a warmed serving bowl. Season with pepper to taste and serve.

SWEET POTATO FRIES

WHY THIS RECIPE WORKS: Too often, sweet potato fries simply don't do justice to their namesake. We wanted thick-cut fries with crispy exteriors and creamy interiors. Taking a cue from commercial frozen fries, we dunked the potato wedges in a slurry of water and cornstarch. Blanching the potatoes with salt and baking soda before dipping them in the slurry helped the coating stick to the potatoes, giving the fries a super-crunchy crust that stayed crispy. To keep the fries from sticking to the pan, we used a nonstick skillet, which

had the added benefit of allowing us to use less oil. For a finishing touch to complement the natural sweetness of the fries, we made a spicy Belgian-style dipping sauce.

Thick-Cut Sweet Potato Fries
SERVES 4 TO 6

If your sweet potatoes are shorter than 4 inches in length, do not cut the wedges crosswise. We prefer peanut oil for frying, but vegetable oil may be used instead. Leftover frying oil may be saved for further use; strain the cooled oil into an airtight container and store it in a cool, dark place for up to one month or in the freezer for up to two months. We like these fries with our Spicy Fry Sauce (recipe follows), but they are also good served plain.

> ½ cup cornstarch
> Kosher salt
> 1 teaspoon baking soda
> 3 pounds sweet potatoes, peeled and cut into ¾-inch-thick wedges, wedges cut in half crosswise
> 3 cups peanut oil

1. Adjust oven rack to middle position and heat oven to 200 degrees. Set wire rack in rimmed baking sheet. Whisk cornstarch and ½ cup cold water together in large bowl.

2. Bring 2 quarts water, ¼ cup salt, and baking soda to boil in Dutch oven. Add potatoes and return to boil. Reduce heat to simmer and cook until exteriors turn slightly mushy (centers will remain firm), 3 to 5 minutes. Whisk cornstarch slurry to recombine. Using wire skimmer or slotted spoon, transfer potatoes to bowl with slurry.

3. Using rubber spatula, fold potatoes with slurry until slurry turns light orange, thickens to paste, and clings to potatoes.

4. Heat oil in 12-inch nonstick skillet over high heat to 325 degrees. Using tongs, carefully add one third of potatoes to oil, making sure that potatoes aren't touching one another. Fry until crispy and lightly browned, 7 to 10 minutes, using tongs to flip potatoes halfway through frying (adjust heat as necessary to maintain oil temperature between 280 and 300 degrees). Using wire skimmer or slotted spoon, transfer fries to prepared wire rack (fries that stick together can be separated with tongs or forks). Season with salt to taste and transfer to oven to keep warm. Return oil to 325 degrees and repeat in 2 more batches with remaining potatoes. Serve immediately.

Spicy Fry Sauce
MAKES ABOUT ½ CUP

For a less spicy version, use only 2 teaspoons of Asian chili-garlic sauce. The sauce can be made up to four days in advance and stored, covered, in the refrigerator.

> 6 tablespoons mayonnaise
> 1 tablespoon Asian chili-garlic sauce
> 2 teaspoons white vinegar

Whisk all ingredients together in small bowl.

FRIED SWEET PLANTAINS

WHY THIS RECIPE WORKS: In Cuban restaurants, rich, meaty dishes are often accompanied by *plátanos maduros*, or fried sweet plantains. This savory-sweet side features thick, soft slices of very ripe plantains that are fried in oil to create a caramel-like browned crust encasing a soft, sweet interior; a sprinkling of salt balances the sweetness. We deep-fry our plantains and stir the slices occasionally so that they brown evenly.

Fried Sweet Plantains (Plátanos Maduros)
SERVES 6 TO 8

Make sure to use plantains that are very ripe and black.

- 3 cups vegetable oil
- 5 very ripe black plantains (8½ ounces each), peeled and sliced on bias into ½-inch pieces
  Kosher salt

Heat oil in medium saucepan over medium-high heat until it registers 350 degrees. Carefully add one-third of plantains and cook until dark brown on both sides, 3 to 5 minutes, stirring occasionally. Using wire skimmer or slotted spoon, transfer plantains to wire rack set in rimmed baking sheet. (Do not place plantains on paper towel or they will stick.) Season liberally with salt. Repeat with remaining plantains in two more batches. Serve immediately.

ROASTED BUTTERNUT SQUASH

WHY THIS RECIPE WORKS: Taking a cue from famed chef Yotam Ottolenghi, we sought to create a savory recipe for roasted butternut squash that was simple and presentation-worthy. We chose to peel the squash thoroughly to remove not only the tough outer skin but also the rugged fibrous layer of white flesh just beneath, ensuring supremely tender squash. To encourage the squash slices to caramelize, we used a hot 425-degree oven, placed the squash on the lowest oven rack, and increased the baking time to evaporate the water. We also swapped in melted butter for olive oil to promote the flavorful Maillard reaction. Finally, we selected a mix of toppings that added crunch, creaminess, brightness, and visual appeal.

Roasted Butternut Squash with Browned Butter and Hazelnuts
SERVES 4 TO 6

For plain roasted squash omit the topping. This dish can be served warm or at room temperature. For the best texture it's important to remove the fibrous flesh just below the squash's skin.

SQUASH
- 1 large (2½- to 3-pound) butternut squash
- 3 tablespoons unsalted butter, melted
- ½ teaspoon salt
- ½ teaspoon pepper

TOPPING
- 3 tablespoons unsalted butter, cut into 3 pieces
- ⅓ cup hazelnuts, toasted, skinned, and chopped coarse
- 1 tablespoon water
- 1 tablespoon lemon juice
  Pinch salt
- 1 tablespoon minced fresh chives

1. FOR THE SQUASH: Adjust oven rack to lowest position and heat oven to 425 degrees. Using sharp vegetable peeler or chef's knife, remove skin and fibrous threads from squash just below skin (peel until squash is completely orange with no white flesh remaining, roughly ⅛ inch deep). Halve squash lengthwise and scrape out seeds. Place squash, cut side down, on cutting board and slice crosswise ½ inch thick.

2. Toss squash with melted butter, salt, and pepper until evenly coated. Arrange squash on rimmed baking sheet in single layer. Roast squash until side touching sheet toward back of oven is well browned, 25 to 30 minutes. Rotate sheet and continue to bake until side touching sheet toward back of oven is well browned, 6 to 10 minutes. Remove squash from oven and use metal spatula to flip each piece. Continue to roast until squash is very tender and side touching sheet is browned, 10 to 15 minutes longer.

3. FOR THE TOPPING: While squash roasts, melt butter with hazelnuts in 8-inch skillet over medium-low heat. Cook, stirring frequently, until butter and hazelnuts are brown and fragrant, about 2 minutes. Immediately remove skillet from heat and stir in water (butter will foam and sizzle). Let cool for 1 minute; stir in lemon juice and salt.

4. Transfer squash to large serving platter. Drizzle butter mixture evenly over squash. Sprinkle with chives and serve.

Roasted Butternut Squash with Radicchio and Parmesan

Omit topping. Whisk 1 tablespoon sherry vinegar, ½ teaspoon mayonnaise, and pinch salt together in small bowl; gradually whisk in 2 tablespoons extra-virgin olive oil until smooth. Before serving, drizzle vinaigrette over squash and sprinkle with ½ cup coarsely shredded radicchio; ½ ounce Parmesan cheese, shaved into thin strips; and 3 tablespoons toasted pine nuts.

Roasted Butternut Squash with Goat Cheese, Pecans, and Maple

Omit topping. Stir 2 tablespoons maple syrup and pinch cayenne pepper together in small bowl. Before serving, drizzle maple mixture over squash and sprinkle with ⅓ cup crumbled goat cheese; ⅓ cup pecans, toasted and chopped coarse; and 2 teaspoons fresh thyme leaves.

Roasted Butternut Squash with Tahini and Feta

Omit topping. Whisk 1 tablespoon tahini, 1 tablespoon extra-virgin olive oil, 1½ teaspoons lemon juice, 1 teaspoon honey, and pinch salt together in small bowl. Before serving, drizzle tahini mixture over squash and sprinkle with ¼ cup finely crumbled feta cheese; ¼ cup shelled pistachios, toasted and chopped fine; and 2 tablespoons chopped fresh mint.

ACORN SQUASH

WHY THIS RECIPE WORKS: Cooked properly, acorn squash develops a sweet, almost nutty flavor and moist, smooth flesh—a result that should not take hours. But after what seems like eons in the oven, acorn squash often lands on the table with little flavor and a stringy texture. We wanted better, slow-roasted acorn squash in a fraction of the time. To our astonishment, microwaving was the ideal cooking method, presenting a squash that was tender and silky smooth, with nary a trace of dryness or stringiness. Microwaved on high power for 20 minutes, the squash was perfectly cooked. It was best to halve and seed the squash before cooking. Last, we learned that when added before cooking, salt seemed to better permeate the squash. Filling in the only remaining gap, equal portions of butter and dark brown sugar gave the squash ample, but not excessive, sweetness. And for a smooth, cohesive filling mixture, combining the butter and sugar with a pinch of salt and briefly broiling the final product eliminated the nagging sticky glaze problem. Finishing the squash under the broiler also gave it a welcome roasted texture and great caramelized flavor.

Quick Roasted Acorn Squash with Brown Sugar
SERVES 4

Squash smaller than 1½ pounds will likely cook a little faster than the recipe indicates, so begin checking for doneness a few minutes early. Likewise, larger squash will take slightly longer to cook. However, keep in mind that the cooking time is largely dependent on the microwave. If microwaving the squash in Pyrex, the manufacturer recommends adding water to the dish (or bowl) prior to cooking. To avoid a steam burn when uncovering the cooked squash, peel back the plastic wrap very carefully, starting from the side that is farthest away from you.

2 acorn squash (about 1½ pounds each), halved pole to pole and seeded (see note)
    Table salt
3 tablespoons unsalted butter
3 tablespoons dark brown sugar

1. Sprinkle the squash halves with salt and place the halves, cut side down, in a 13 by 9-inch microwave-safe baking dish or arrange the halves in a large (4-quart) microwave-safe bowl so that the cut sides face out. (If using Pyrex, add ¼ cup water to the dish or bowl.) Cover tightly with plastic wrap, using multiple sheets, if necessary; with a paring knife, poke four steam vents in the wrap. Microwave on high power until the squash is very tender and offers no resistance when pierced with a paring knife, 15 to 25 minutes. Using potholders, remove the baking dish or bowl from the microwave and set on a clean, dry surface (avoid damp or cold surfaces).

2. While the squash is cooking, adjust an oven rack to the highest position (about 6 inches from the broiler element) and heat the broiler. Melt the butter, brown sugar, and ⅛ teaspoon salt in a small saucepan over low heat, whisking occasionally, until combined.

3. When the squash is cooked, carefully pull back the plastic wrap from the side farthest from you. Using tongs, transfer the cooked squash halves, cut side up, to a rimmed baking sheet. Spoon a portion of the butter-sugar mixture onto each squash half. Broil until brown and caramelized, 5 to 8 minutes, rotating the baking sheet halfway through the cooking time and removing the squash halves as they are done. Set the squash halves on individual plates and serve immediately.

RICE PILAF

WHY THIS RECIPE WORKS: To make rice pilaf, rice is toasted or browned in fat to build flavor before being cooked through in liquid. The result should be rice that is fragrant, fluffy, and tender. Traditional recipes insist that for a truly great pilaf you must soak or at least repeatedly rinse the rice before cooking. We wondered if there was more to making perfect rice pilaf than this.

The variables included the kind of rice to use, the ratio of rice to cooking water, and whether or not to soak the rice before cooking. Testing revealed that using basmati rice was preferable, as was using a lower amount of water than is traditional for cooking rice. The step of rinsing the rice was also important for grains that were more tender, with a slightly shinier, smoother appearance. We also sautéed the rice in plenty of butter before adding the water. After the rice was cooked, we covered it with a kitchen towel and a lid and let it steam off the heat.

Rice Pilaf

SERVES 4

If you like, olive oil can be substituted for the butter depending on what you are serving with the pilaf. For the most evenly cooked rice, use a wide-bottomed saucepan with a tight-fitting lid.

- 1½ cups basmati or long-grain rice
- 2½ cups water
- 1½ teaspoons table salt
  Pinch ground black pepper
- 3 tablespoons unsalted butter (see note)
- 1 small onion, minced (about ½ cup)

1. Place the rice in a medium bowl and add enough water to cover by 2 inches; using your hands, gently swish the grains to release the excess starch. Carefully pour off the water, leaving the rice in the bowl. Repeat four to five times, until the water runs almost clear. Using a colander or fine-mesh strainer, drain the rice; place the colander over a bowl and set aside.

2. Bring the water to a boil, covered, in a small saucepan over medium-high heat. Add the salt and pepper; cover to keep hot. Meanwhile, melt the butter in a large saucepan over medium heat; add the onion and cook until softened but not browned, about 4 minutes. Stir in the rice until coated with the butter; cook until the edges of the rice grains begin to turn translucent, about 3 minutes. Stir the hot seasoned water into the rice; return to a boil, then reduce the heat to low, cover, and simmer until all the liquid is absorbed, 16 to 18 minutes. Off the heat, remove the lid and place a clean kitchen towel folded in half over the saucepan; replace the lid. Let stand for 10 minutes; fluff the rice with a fork and serve.

WILD RICE PILAF

WHY THIS RECIPE WORKS: Sometimes wild rice turns out undercooked and difficult to chew, other times the rice is overcooked and gluey. We wanted to figure out how to turn out properly cooked wild rice every time.

Through trial and error, we learned to simmer the rice slowly in plenty of liquid, making sure to stop the cooking process at just the right moment by checking it for doneness every couple of minutes past the 35-minute mark. For a simmering liquid, we used chicken broth—its mild yet rich profile tempered the rice's muddy flavor to a pleasant earthiness and affirmed its subdued nuttiness. To further tame the strong flavor of the wild rice, we added some white rice to the mixture, then added onions, carrots, dried cranberries, and toasted pecans for a winning pilaf.

Wild Rice Pilaf with Pecans and Dried Cranberries

SERVES 6 TO 8

Wild rice quickly goes from tough to pasty, so begin testing the rice at the 35-minute mark and drain the rice as soon as it is tender.

- 1¾ cups low-sodium chicken broth
- 2½ cups water
- 2 bay leaves
- 8 sprigs fresh thyme, divided into 2 bundles, each tied together with kitchen twine
- 1 cup wild rice, rinsed well in a strainer
- 1½ cups long-grain white rice
- 3 tablespoons unsalted butter
- 1 medium onion, minced
- 2 carrots, peeled and chopped fine
  Table salt
- ¾ cup sweetened or unsweetened dried cranberries
- ¾ cup pecans, toasted and chopped coarse
- 1½ tablespoons minced fresh parsley leaves
  Ground black pepper

1. Bring the chicken broth, ¼ cup of the water, the bay leaves, and 1 bundle of the thyme to a boil in a medium saucepan over medium-high heat. Add the wild rice, cover, and reduce the heat to low; simmer until the rice is plump and tender and has absorbed most of the liquid, 35 to 45 minutes. Drain the rice in a fine-mesh strainer. Return the rice to the saucepan; cover to keep warm and set aside.

2. While the wild rice is cooking, place the white rice in a medium bowl and add water to cover by 2 inches; gently swish the grains to release excess starch. Carefully pour off the water, leaving the rice in the bowl. Repeat four to five times, until the water runs almost clear. Drain the rice in a fine-mesh strainer.

3. Melt the butter in a medium saucepan over medium-high heat. Add the onion, carrots, and 1 teaspoon salt; cook, stirring frequently, until softened but not browned, about 4 minutes. Stir in the rinsed white rice until coated with the butter; cook, stirring frequently, until the grains begin to turn translucent, about 3 minutes. Meanwhile, bring the remaining 2¼ cups water to a boil in a small saucepan or a microwave. Add the boiling water and the second thyme bundle to the white rice; return to a boil, then reduce the heat to low, sprinkle the cranberries evenly over the rice, and cover. Simmer until all of the liquid is absorbed, 16 to 18 minutes. Off the heat, fluff the rice with a fork and discard the bay leaves and thyme bundles.

4. Combine the wild rice, white rice mixture, pecans, and parsley in a large bowl; toss with a rubber spatula until the ingredients are evenly mixed. Season with salt and pepper to taste and serve.

RICE AND PASTA PILAF

WHY THIS RECIPE WORKS: Typically, rice pilaf combines rice with pieces of vermicelli that have been toasted in butter to add richness and a nutty flavor. To produce rice that was as tender and fluffy as the pasta, we needed both elements to cook at the same rate. Jump-starting the rice by soaking it in hot water for a mere 10 minutes softened its outer coating and let it absorb water quickly. Once the pasta and rice were cooked perfectly, we let the pilaf stand for 10 minutes with a towel under the lid to absorb steam. A handful of fresh parsley lent brightness to the finished pilaf.

Rice and Pasta Pilaf
SERVES 4 TO 6
Use long, straight vermicelli or vermicelli nests.

- 1½ cups basmati or other long-grain white rice
- 3 tablespoons unsalted butter
- 2 ounces vermicelli, broken into 1-inch pieces
- 1 onion, grated
- 1 garlic clove, minced
- 2½ cups chicken broth
- 1¼ teaspoons salt
- 3 tablespoons minced fresh parsley

1. Place rice in medium bowl and cover with hot tap water by 2 inches; let stand for 15 minutes.

2. Using your hands, gently swish grains to release excess starch. Carefully pour off water, leaving rice in bowl. Add cold tap water to rice and pour off water. Repeat adding and pouring off cold water 4 to 5 times, until water runs almost clear. Drain rice in fine-mesh strainer.

3. Melt butter in saucepan over medium heat. Add pasta and cook, stirring occasionally, until browned, about 3 minutes. Add onion and garlic and cook, stirring occasionally, until onion is softened but not browned, about 4 minutes. Add rice and cook, stirring occasionally, until edges of rice begin to turn translucent, about 3 minutes. Add broth and salt and bring to boil. Reduce heat to low, cover, and cook until all liquid is absorbed, about 10 minutes. Off heat, remove lid, fold clean dish towel in half, and place over pan; replace lid. Let stand for 10 minutes. Fluff rice with fork, stir in parsley, and serve.

Herbed Rice and Pasta Pilaf
Stir ¼ cup plain whole-milk yogurt, ¼ cup minced fresh dill, and ¼ cup minced fresh chives into pilaf with parsley.

Rice and Pasta Pilaf with Golden Raisins and Almonds
Place ½ cup golden raisins in bowl and cover with boiling water. Let stand until plump, about 5 minutes. Drain and set aside. Stir 2 bay leaves and 1 teaspoon ground cardamom into rice with chicken broth. Discard bay leaves and stir raisins and ½ cup slivered almonds, toasted and chopped coarse, into rice with parsley.

Rice and Pasta Pilaf with Pomegranate and Walnuts
Omit onion and garlic. Add 2 tablespoons grated fresh ginger to pan with rice. Stir ½ teaspoon ground cumin into rice with chicken broth. Omit parsley and stir ½ cup walnuts, toasted and chopped coarse; ½ cup pomegranate seeds; ½ cup chopped fresh cilantro; and 1 tablespoon lemon juice into fluffed rice.

RICE AND LENTILS WITH CRISPY ONIONS

WHY THIS RECIPE WORKS: *Mujaddara*, the rice and beans of the Middle East, is a hearty, warm-spiced rice and lentil pilaf containing large brown or green lentils and crispy fried onion strings. We wanted a version of this dish in which all of the elements were cooked perfectly. We found that precooking the lentils and soaking the rice in hot water before combining them ensured that both components cooked evenly. For the crispiest possible onions, we removed some moisture by salting and microwaving them before frying. This allowed us to pare down the fussy process of batch-frying in several cups of oil to a single batch. And using some of the oil from the onions to dress our pilaf gave it ultrasavory depth.

Rice and Lentils with Crispy Onions (Mujaddara)

SERVES 4 TO 6

Large green or brown lentils will work interchangeably in this recipe; do not substitute smaller French lentils. When preparing the Crispy Onions, be sure to reserve 3 tablespoons of the onion cooking oil for cooking the rice and lentils.

YOGURT SAUCE

- 1 cup plain whole-milk yogurt
- 2 tablespoons lemon juice
- ½ teaspoon minced garlic
- ½ teaspoon salt

RICE AND LENTILS

- 8½ ounces (1¼ cups) green or brown lentils, picked over and rinsed
  Salt and pepper
- 1¼ cups basmati rice
- 1 recipe Crispy Onions, plus 3 tablespoons reserved oil (recipe follows)
- 3 garlic cloves, minced
- 1 teaspoon ground coriander
- 1 teaspoon ground cumin
- ½ teaspoon ground cinnamon
- ½ teaspoon ground allspice
- ⅛ teaspoon cayenne pepper
- 1 teaspoon sugar
- 3 tablespoons minced fresh cilantro

1. FOR THE YOGURT SAUCE: Whisk all ingredients together in bowl. Refrigerate while preparing rice and lentils.

2. FOR THE RICE AND LENTILS: Bring lentils, 4 cups water, and 1 teaspoon salt to boil in medium saucepan over high heat. Reduce heat to low and cook until lentils are tender, 15 to 17 minutes. Drain and set aside. While lentils cook, place rice in medium bowl and cover by 2 inches with hot tap water; let stand for 15 minutes.

3. Using your hands, gently swish rice grains to release excess starch. Carefully pour off water, leaving rice in bowl. Add cold tap water to rice and pour off water. Repeat adding and pouring off cold tap water 4 to 5 times, until water runs almost clear. Drain rice in fine-mesh strainer.

4. Heat reserved onion oil, garlic, coriander, cumin, cinnamon, allspice, ¼ teaspoon pepper, and cayenne in Dutch oven over medium heat until fragrant, about 2 minutes. Add rice and cook, stirring occasionally, until edges of rice begin to turn translucent, about 3 minutes. Add 2¼ cups water, sugar, and 1 teaspoon salt and bring to boil. Stir in lentils, reduce heat to low, cover, and cook until all liquid is absorbed, about 12 minutes.

5. Off heat, remove lid, fold clean dish towel in half, and place over pot; replace lid. Let stand for 10 minutes. Fluff rice and lentils with fork and stir in cilantro and half of crispy onions. Transfer to serving platter, top with remaining crispy onions, and serve, passing yogurt sauce separately.

Crispy Onions

MAKES 1½ CUPS

It is crucial to thoroughly dry the microwaved onions after rinsing. The best way to accomplish this is to use a salad spinner. Reserve 3 tablespoons of oil when draining the onions to use in Rice and Lentils with Crispy Onions. Remaining oil may be stored in an airtight container and refrigerated for up to 4 weeks.

- 2 pounds onions, halved and sliced crosswise into ¼-inch-thick pieces
- 2 teaspoons salt
- 1½ cups vegetable oil

1. Toss onions and salt together in large bowl. Microwave for 5 minutes. Rinse thoroughly, transfer to paper towel–lined baking sheet, and dry well.

2. Heat onions and oil in Dutch oven over high heat, stirring frequently, until onions are golden brown, 25 to 30 minutes. Drain onions in colander set in large bowl. Transfer onions to paper towel–lined baking sheet to drain. Serve.

PERSIAN-STYLE RICE

WHY THIS RECIPE WORKS: *Chelow* is a classic Iranian dish that marries a light and fluffy rice pilaf with a golden-brown, crispy crust (known as *tahdig*). Rinsing the rice and then soaking it for 15 minutes in hot salted water produced fluffy grains. Parboiling the rice and then steaming it was also essential to creating the best texture for the pilaf and the perfect crust. Steaming the grains for 45 minutes rather than the traditional hour was enough; we also wrapped the lid with a towel to absorb extra moisture. Combining a portion of the rice with thick Greek yogurt and oil created a flavorful crust, while chunks of butter enriched the pilaf portion. The yogurt also made the tahdig easier to remove from the pot, as did brushing the bottom of the pot with extra oil. Adding cumin seeds and parsley to the dish made for a more interesting and well-rounded flavor profile.

Persian-Style Rice with Golden Crust (Chelow)
SERVES 6

We prefer the nutty flavor and texture of basmati rice, but Texmati or another long-grain rice will work. For the best results, use a Dutch oven with a bottom diameter between 8½ and 10 inches. It is important not to overcook the rice during the parboiling step, as it will continue to cook during steaming. Begin checking the rice at the lower end of the given time range. Do not skip placing the pot on a damp towel in step 7—doing so will help free the crust from the pot. Serve this pilaf alongside stews or kebabs.

2	cups basmati rice
	Salt
1	tablespoon plus ¼ cup vegetable oil
¼	cup plain Greek yogurt
1½	teaspoons cumin seeds
2	tablespoons unsalted butter, cut into 8 cubes
¼	cup minced fresh parsley

1. Place rice in fine-mesh strainer and rinse under cold running water until water runs clear. Place rinsed rice and 1 tablespoon salt in medium bowl and cover with 4 cups hot tap water. Stir gently to dissolve salt; let stand for 15 minutes. Drain rice in fine-mesh strainer.

2. Meanwhile, bring 8 cups water to boil in Dutch oven over high heat. Add rice and 2 tablespoons salt. Boil briskly, stirring frequently, until rice is mostly tender with slight bite in center and grains are floating toward top of pot, 3 to 5 minutes (begin timing from when rice is added to pot).

3. Drain rice in large fine-mesh strainer and rinse with cold water to stop cooking, about 30 seconds. Rinse and dry pot well to remove any residual starch. Brush bottom and 1 inch up sides of pot with 1 tablespoon oil.

4. Whisk remaining ¼ cup oil, yogurt, 1 teaspoon cumin seeds, and ¼ teaspoon salt together in medium bowl. Add 2 cups parcooked rice and stir until combined. Spread yogurt-rice mixture evenly over bottom of prepared pot, packing it down well.

5. Stir remaining ½ teaspoon cumin seeds into remaining rice. Mound rice in center of pot on top of yogurt-rice base (it should look like small hill). Poke 8 equally spaced holes through rice mound but not into yogurt-rice base. Place 1 butter cube in each hole. Drizzle ⅓ cup water over rice mound.

6. Wrap pot lid with clean dish towel and cover pot tightly, making sure towel is secure on top of lid and away from heat. Cook over medium-high heat until rice on bottom is crackling and steam is coming from sides of pot, about 10 minutes, rotating pot halfway through for even cooking.

7. Reduce heat to medium-low and continue to cook until rice is tender and fluffy and crust is golden brown around edges, 30 to 35 minutes longer. Remove covered pot from heat and place on damp dish towel set in rimmed baking sheet; let stand for 5 minutes.

8. Stir 2 tablespoons parsley into rice, making sure not to disturb crust on bottom of pot, and season with salt to taste. Gently spoon rice onto serving platter.

9. Using thin metal spatula, loosen edges of crust from pot, then break crust into large pieces. Transfer pieces to serving platter, arranging evenly around rice. Sprinkle with remaining 2 tablespoons parsley and serve.

RED BEANS AND RICE

WHY THIS RECIPE WORKS: To replicate the traditional New Orleans red beans and rice recipe using ingredients easily found in supermarkets, we made some simple substitutions: small red beans for Camellia-brand dried red beans and bacon for hard-to-find tasso. Fine-tuning the proportions of sautéed green peppers, onions, and celery gave the recipe balance, and the right ratio of chicken broth to water added complexity to the dish.

Red Beans and Rice
SERVES 6 TO 8

If you are pressed for time you can "quick-brine" your beans. In step 1, combine the salt, water, and beans in a large Dutch oven and bring to a boil over high heat. Remove the pot from the heat, cover, and let stand 1 hour. Drain and rinse the beans and proceed with the recipe. If you can't find andouille sausage, substitute kielbasa. Tasso can be difficult to find, but if you use it, omit the bacon and paprika in step 2 and cook 4 ounces finely chopped tasso in 2 teaspoons vegetable oil until lightly browned, 4 to 6 minutes, then proceed. It is important to maintain a vigorous simmer in step 2. The beans can be cooled, covered tightly, and refrigerated for up to 2 days. To reheat, add enough water to the beans to thin them slightly.

Salt and pepper
1 pound (about 2 cups) dried small red beans, picked over and rinsed
4 slices bacon, chopped fine
1 onion, chopped fine
1 small green bell pepper, stemmed, seeded and chopped fine
1 celery rib, chopped fine
3 garlic cloves, minced
1 teaspoon minced fresh thyme
1 teaspoon sweet paprika
2 bay leaves
¼ teaspoon cayenne pepper
3 cups chicken broth
6 cups water
8 ounces andouille sausage, halved lengthwise and cut into ¼-inch slices
Basic White Rice (page 453)
1 teaspoon red wine vinegar, plus extra for seasoning
3 scallions, sliced thin
Hot sauce (optional)

1. Dissolve 3 tablespoons salt in 4 quarts cold water in large container. Add beans and soak at room temperature at least 8 hours or up to 24 hours. Drain and rinse well.

2. Heat bacon in Dutch oven over medium heat, stirring occasionally, until browned and almost fully rendered, 5 to 8 minutes. Add onion, bell pepper, and celery; cook, stirring frequently, until vegetables are softened, 6 to 7 minutes. Stir in garlic, thyme, paprika, bay leaves, cayenne pepper, and ¼ teaspoon black pepper; cook until fragrant, about 30 seconds. Stir in beans, broth, and water, and bring to boil over high heat. Reduce heat and vigorously simmer, stirring occasionally, until beans are just soft and liquid begins to thicken, 45 to 60 minutes.

3. Stir in sausage and 1 teaspoon vinegar and cook until liquid is thick and beans are fully tender and creamy, about 30 minutes. Season with salt, pepper, and additional vinegar to taste. Serve over rice, sprinkling with scallions and passing hot sauce separately, if using.

ALMOST HANDS-FREE RISOTTO

WHY THIS RECIPE WORKS: Classic risotto can demand half an hour of stovetop tedium for the best creamy results. Our goal was five minutes of stirring, tops.

First, we chose to cook our risotto in a Dutch oven, rather than a saucepan. A Dutch oven's thick, heavy bottom, deep sides, and tight-fitting lid are made to trap and distribute heat as evenly as possible. Typical recipes dictate adding the broth in small increments after the wine has been absorbed (and stirring constantly after each addition), but we added most of the broth at once. Then we covered the pan and simmered the rice until almost all the broth had been absorbed, stirring just twice during this time. After adding the second and final addition of broth, we stirred the pot for just a few minutes to ensure the bottom didn't cook more quickly than the top and turned off the heat. Without sitting over a direct flame, the sauce turned out perfectly creamy and the rice was thickened, velvety, and just barely chewy. To finish, we simply stirred in butter, herbs, and a squeeze of lemon juice to brighten the flavors.

Almost Hands-Free Risotto with Parmesan and Herbs

SERVES 6

This more hands-off method does require precise timing, so we strongly recommend using a timer. The consistency of risotto is largely a matter of personal taste; if you prefer a brothy risotto, add extra broth in step 4. This makes a great side dish for braised meats.

5 cups low-sodium chicken broth
1½ cups water
4 tablespoons (½ stick) unsalted butter
1 large onion, minced
Table salt
1 medium garlic clove, minced or pressed through a garlic press (about 1 teaspoon)
2 cups Arborio rice
1 cup dry white wine
2 ounces Parmesan cheese, grated (about 1 cup)
1 teaspoon juice from 1 lemon
2 tablespoons chopped fresh parsley leaves
2 tablespoons chopped fresh chives
Ground black pepper

1. Bring the broth and water to a boil in a large saucepan over high heat. Reduce the heat to medium-low to maintain a gentle simmer.

2. Heat 2 tablespoons of the butter in a large Dutch oven over medium heat. When the butter has melted, add the onion and ¾ teaspoon salt. Cook, stirring frequently, until the onion is softened but not browned, 5 to 7 minutes. Add the garlic and stir until fragrant, about 30 seconds. Add the rice and cook, stirring frequently, until the grains are translucent around the edges, about 3 minutes.

3. Add the wine and cook, stirring constantly, until fully absorbed, 2 to 3 minutes. Stir 5 cups of the warm broth mixture into the rice, reduce the heat to medium-low, cover, and simmer until almost all the liquid has been absorbed and the rice is just al dente, 16 to 19 minutes, stirring twice during cooking.

4. Add ¾ cup more broth mixture and stir gently and constantly until the risotto becomes creamy, about 3 minutes. Stir in the Parmesan. Remove the pot from the heat, cover, and let stand for 5 minutes. Stir in the remaining 2 tablespoons butter, the lemon juice, parsley, and chives. Season with salt and pepper to taste. If desired, add up to ½ cup remaining broth mixture to loosen the texture of the risotto. Serve immediately.

COUSCOUS

WHY THIS RECIPE WORKS: Although couscous traditionally serves as a sauce absorber under North African–style stews and braises, it can work equally well as a lighter, quicker alternative to everyday side dishes like rice pilaf. We wanted to develop a classic version as convenient as the box kind but much fresher tasting, as well as a handful of variations with a few flavorful add-ins. The box instructions—measure and boil water, stir in couscous, cover and let stand off heat for five minutes—gave us bland, clumpy grains. Toasting the couscous grains in butter deepened their flavor and helped them cook up fluffy and separate. And to bump up the flavor even further, we replaced half of the water with chicken broth. For our enriched variations, dried fruit, nuts, and citrus juice added textural interest and sweet, bright notes.

Simple Couscous
SERVES 4 TO 6

- 2 tablespoons unsalted butter
- 2 cups couscous
- 1 cup water
- 1 cup low-sodium chicken broth
- 1 teaspoon table salt
  Ground black pepper

Melt the butter in a medium saucepan over medium-high heat. Add the couscous and cook, stirring frequently, until the grains are just beginning to brown, about 5 minutes. Add the water, broth, and salt and stir briefly to combine. Cover and remove the pan from the heat. Let stand until the grains are tender, about 7 minutes. Uncover and fluff the grains with a fork. Season with pepper to taste and serve.

Couscous with Dates and Pistachios

Follow the recipe for Simple Couscous, increasing the butter to 3 tablespoons and adding ½ cup chopped dates, 1 tablespoon grated fresh ginger, and ½ teaspoon ground cardamom to the saucepan with the couscous. Increase the amount of water to 1¼ cups. Stir ¾ cup coarsely chopped toasted pistachios, 3 tablespoons minced fresh cilantro leaves, and 2 teaspoons juice from 1 lemon into the couscous before serving.

Couscous with Dried Cherries and Pecans

Follow the recipe for Simple Couscous, increasing the butter to 3 tablespoons and adding ½ cup coarsely chopped dried cherries, 2 minced garlic cloves, ¾ teaspoon garam masala, and ⅛ teaspoon cayenne pepper to the saucepan with the couscous. Increase the amount of water to 1¼ cups. Stir ¾ cup coarsely chopped toasted pecans, 2 thinly sliced scallions, and 2 teaspoons juice from 1 lemon into the couscous before serving.

Couscous with Carrots, Raisins, and Pine Nuts

Follow the recipe for Simple Couscous, increasing the butter to 3 tablespoons. Once the foaming subsides, add 2 grated carrots and ½ teaspoon ground cinnamon; cook, stirring frequently, until the carrot softens, about 2 minutes. Continue with the recipe, adding ½ cup raisins to the saucepan with the couscous and increasing the water to 1¼ cups. Stir ¾ cup toasted pine nuts, 3 tablespoons minced fresh cilantro leaves, ½ teaspoon grated orange zest, and 1 tablespoon orange juice into the couscous before serving.

Couscous with Shallots, Garlic, and Almonds

Follow the recipe for Simple Couscous, increasing the butter to 3 tablespoons. Once the foaming subsides, add 3 thinly sliced shallots and cook, stirring frequently, until softened and lightly browned, about 5 minutes. Add 1 minced garlic clove and cook until fragrant, about 30 seconds. Continue with recipe, stirring ¾ cup toasted sliced almonds, ¾ cup minced fresh parsley, and ½ teaspoon grated zest and 2 teaspoons juice from 1 lemon into the couscous before serving.

SIMPLE ISRAELI COUSCOUS

WHY THIS RECIPE WORKS: Israeli couscous is nuttier than its North African cousin, thanks to the practice of drying the pasta-like pearls over a flame. To prepare pasta salad using Israeli couscous, we toasted the spheres in oil to accentuate their earthy, nutty flavor. We then added water, brought it to a boil, and cooked the couscous covered and at a simmer, allowing it to slowly and evenly absorb the liquid. To turn the finished couscous into a salad, we spread the spheres on a baking sheet to cool (and to prevent it from cooking further in its own steam). Meanwhile, we quickly pickled shallot slices, dissolving sugar in red wine vinegar over medium-high heat before removing the pan from heat, stirring in the shallots, and letting them take on more flavor as the liquid cooled. We dressed the couscous in a bold vinaigrette, whisking together olive oil, lemon juice, Dijon, and red pepper flakes. Once the couscous was coated in the vinaigrette, we finished off the salad with mint, peas, toasted pistachios, and feta.

Simple Israeli Couscous

MAKES ABOUT 4 CUPS

Warm couscous can be tossed with butter or extra-virgin olive oil and salt and pepper for a simple side dish. If you're using it in a salad, transfer the couscous to a rimmed baking sheet and let it cool completely, about 15 minutes.

2 cups Israeli couscous
1 tablespoon extra-virgin olive oil
2½ cups water
½ teaspoon salt

Heat couscous and oil in medium saucepan over medium heat, stirring frequently, until about half of grains are golden brown, 5 to 6 minutes. Carefully add water and salt; stir briefly to combine. Increase heat to high and bring to boil. Reduce heat to medium-low, cover, and simmer, stirring occasionally, until water is absorbed, 9 to 12 minutes. Remove saucepan from heat and let stand, covered, for 3 minutes. Serve.

Israeli Couscous with Lemon, Mint, Peas, Feta, and Pickled Shallots

SERVES 6

For efficiency, let the shallots pickle while you prepare the remaining ingredients.

⅓ cup red wine vinegar
2 tablespoons sugar
Salt and pepper
2 shallots, sliced thin
3 tablespoons extra-virgin olive oil
3 tablespoons lemon juice
1 teaspoon Dijon mustard
⅛ teaspoon red pepper flakes
1 recipe Simple Israeli Couscous, cooled
4 ounces (4 cups) baby arugula, roughly chopped
1 cup fresh mint leaves, torn
½ cup frozen peas, thawed
½ cup shelled pistachios, toasted and chopped
3 ounces feta cheese, crumbled (¾ cup)

1. Bring vinegar, sugar, and pinch salt to simmer in small saucepan over medium-high heat, stirring occasionally, until sugar dissolves. Remove pan from heat, add shallots, and stir to combine. Cover and let cool completely, about 30 minutes. Drain and discard liquid.

2. Whisk oil, lemon juice, mustard, pepper flakes, and ⅛ teaspoon salt together in large bowl. Add cooled couscous, arugula, mint, peas, 6 tablespoons pistachios, ½ cup feta, and shallots and toss to combine. Season with salt and pepper to taste and transfer to serving bowl. Let stand for 5 minutes. Sprinkle with remaining ¼ cup feta and remaining 2 tablespoons pistachios and serve.

Israeli Couscous with Tomatoes, Olives, and Ricotta Salata

SERVES 6

Crumbled feta cheese can be substituted for the ricotta salata.

- 3 tablespoons extra-virgin olive oil
- 3 tablespoons red wine vinegar
- 1 teaspoon Dijon mustard
- Salt and pepper
- 1 recipe Simple Israeli Couscous (page 623), cooled
- 12 ounces grape tomatoes, quartered
- 3 ounces ricotta salata cheese, crumbled (¾ cup)
- 2 ounces (2 cups) baby spinach, sliced ¼ inch thick
- ⅔ cup pitted kalamata olives, sliced
- 1 bunch chives, cut into ¼-inch pieces (¼ cup)
- 1½ cups basil leaves, chopped coarse
- ½ cup pine nuts, toasted

Whisk oil, vinegar, mustard, and ⅛ teaspoon salt together in large bowl. Add couscous, tomatoes, ricotta salata, spinach, olives, chives, basil, and 6 tablespoons pine nuts and toss to combine. Season with salt and pepper to taste and transfer to serving bowl. Let stand for 5 minutes. Sprinkle with ricotta salata and remaining 2 tablespoons pine nuts and serve.

QUINOA PILAF

WHY THIS RECIPE WORKS: Most recipes for quinoa pilaf turn out woefully overcooked because they call for nearly twice as much liquid as they should. We cut the water back to ensure tender grains with a satisfying bite, and gave it a stir partway through cooking to ensure the grains cooked evenly. We let the quinoa rest for several minutes before fluffing to help further improve the texture. We also pre-toasted the quinoa in a dry skillet before simmering to develop its natural nutty flavor, and finished our pilaf with a judicious amount of boldly flavored ingredients.

Quinoa Pilaf with Herbs and Lemon

SERVES 4 TO 6

If you buy unwashed quinoa, rinse the grains in a fine-mesh strainer, drain them, and then spread them on a rimmed baking sheet lined with a clean dish towel and let them dry for 15 minutes before proceeding with the recipe. Any soft herbs, such as cilantro, parsley, chives, mint, and tarragon, can be used.

- 1½ cups prewashed quinoa
- 2 tablespoons unsalted butter, cut into 2 pieces
- 1 small onion, chopped fine
- ¾ teaspoon salt
- 1¾ cups water
- 3 tablespoons chopped fresh herbs
- 1 tablespoon lemon juice

1. Toast quinoa in medium saucepan over medium-high heat, stirring frequently, until quinoa is very fragrant and makes continuous popping sound, 5 to 7 minutes. Transfer quinoa to bowl and set aside.

2. Return now-empty pan to medium-low heat and melt butter. Add onion and salt; cook, stirring frequently, until onion is softened and light golden, 5 to 7 minutes.

3. Increase heat to medium-high, stir in water and quinoa, and bring to simmer. Cover, reduce heat to low, and simmer until grains are just tender and liquid is absorbed, 18 to 20 minutes, stirring once halfway through cooking. Remove pan from heat and let sit, covered, for 10 minutes. Fluff quinoa with fork, stir in herbs and lemon juice, and serve.

Quinoa Pilaf with Chipotle, Queso Fresco, and Peanuts

Add 1 teaspoon chipotle chile powder and ¼ teaspoon ground cumin with onion and salt. Substitute ½ cup crumbled queso fresco; ½ cup roasted unsalted peanuts, chopped coarse; and 2 thinly sliced scallions for herbs. Substitute 4 teaspoons lime juice for lemon juice.

Quinoa Pilaf with Apricots, Aged Gouda, and Pistachios

Add ½ teaspoon grated lemon zest, ½ teaspoon ground coriander, ¼ teaspoon ground cumin, and ⅛ teaspoon pepper with onion and salt. Stir in ½ cup dried apricots, chopped coarse, before letting quinoa sit for 10 minutes in step 3. Substitute ½ cup shredded aged gouda; ½ cup shelled pistachios, toasted and chopped coarse; and 2 tablespoons chopped fresh mint for herbs.

FARRO SALAD

WHY THIS RECIPE WORKS: Farro comes in a few different forms, but our favorite is minimally processed whole farro, in which the germ and bran have been retained. It has a nutty flavor and chewy texture and cooks in 20 minutes, making it one of the fastest-cooking whole grains. We found that the simplest cooking method was best: Boil in salted water for about 20 minutes until tender and drain well. Its versatility makes it ideal for salads, soups, and side dishes. Extra cooked farro can be stored in the refrigerator for up to five days.

Simple Farro

MAKES 2½ CUPS

We prefer the flavor and texture of whole-grain farro. Pearled farro can be used, but cooking times vary, so start checking for doneness after 10 minutes. Do not use quick-cooking farro in this recipe. Warm farro can be tossed with butter or olive oil and salt and pepper for a simple yet hearty side dish. It can also be added to soups or, when cooled, added to salads.

- 1½ cups whole farro, rinsed
- 1 tablespoon salt

Bring 2 quarts water to boil in large saucepan. Add farro and salt. Return to boil, reduce heat, and simmer until grains are tender with slight chew, 15 to 20 minutes. Drain well. (Farro can be refrigerated for up to 5 days.)

Farro Salad with Asparagus, Sugar Snap Peas, and Tomatoes

SERVES 6

- 6 ounces asparagus, trimmed and cut into 1-inch lengths
- 6 ounces sugar snap peas, strings removed, cut into 1-inch lengths
- Salt and pepper
- 3 tablespoons extra-virgin olive oil
- 2 tablespoons lemon juice
- 2 tablespoons minced shallot
- 1 teaspoon Dijon mustard
- 1 recipe Simple Farro, room temperature
- 6 ounces cherry tomatoes, halved
- 3 tablespoons chopped fresh dill
- 2 ounces feta cheese, crumbled (½ cup)

1. Bring 2 quarts water to boil in large saucepan. Add asparagus, snap peas, and 1 tablespoon salt. Cook until vegetables are crisp-tender, 2 to 3 minutes. Using slotted spoon, transfer vegetables to rimmed baking sheet and let cool for 15 minutes.

2. Whisk oil, lemon juice, shallot, mustard, ¼ teaspoon salt, and ¼ teaspoon pepper together in large bowl. Add cooled vegetables, farro, tomatoes, dill, and ¼ cup feta to dressing and toss to combine. Season with salt and pepper to taste and transfer to serving bowl. Sprinkle salad with remaining ¼ cup feta and serve.

Warm Farro with Lemon and Herbs

SERVES 6

- 3 tablespoons unsalted butter
- 1 onion, chopped
- Salt and pepper
- 1 garlic clove, minced
- 1 recipe Simple Farro
- ¼ cup chopped fresh parsley
- ¼ cup chopped fresh mint
- 2 teaspoons lemon juice

Melt butter in 12-inch skillet over medium heat. Add onion and ¼ teaspoon salt and cook, stirring frequently, until onion is softened but not browned, 6 to 8 minutes. Add garlic and cook until fragrant, about 1 minute. Add farro and cook until warmed through, 3 to 5 minutes. Remove from heat and stir in parsley, mint, and lemon juice. Season with salt and pepper to taste, and serve.

TABBOULEH

WHY THIS RECIPE WORKS: Tabbouleh has long been a *meze* staple in the Middle East, but these days it can be found in the refrigerated section of virtually every American supermarket. Its brief (and healthful) ingredient list explains its popularity: Chopped fresh parsley and mint, tomatoes, onion, and bits of nutty bulgur are tossed with lemon and olive oil for a refreshing appetizer or side dish. It all sounds easy enough, but following a recipe or picking up a pint at the market reveals that most versions are hopelessly soggy, with flavor that is either too bold or too bland. We wanted a flavorful dish that would feature a hefty amount of parsley as well as a decent amount of bulgur.

A high ratio of chopped parsley to chopped mint put the emphasis on the bright, peppery parsley but didn't overpower the other ingredients. Bulgur is made by boiling, drying, and grinding wheat kernels, so it only needs to be soaked, not cooked. We soaked it in lemon juice to infuse it with flavor. Extra-virgin olive oil tempered the tart lemon juice. To avoid soggy tabbouleh, we salted the tomatoes, and then, rather than throw out the exuded liquid, we added it to the bulgur-soaking liquid. Two sliced scallions (preferred over red or white onion) rounded out the mix.

Tabbouleh

SERVES 4

Serve the salad with the crisp inner leaves of romaine lettuce and wedges of pita bread.

3 medium round tomatoes, cored and cut
   into ½-inch pieces
   Salt and pepper
½ cup medium-grind bulgur
¼ cup lemon juice (2 lemons)
6 tablespoons extra-virgin olive oil
⅛ teaspoon cayenne pepper
1½ cups chopped fresh parsley
½ cup chopped fresh mint
2 scallions, sliced thin

1. Toss tomatoes and ¼ teaspoon salt in large bowl. Transfer to fine-mesh strainer, set strainer in bowl, and let stand for 30 minutes, tossing occasionally.

2. Rinse bulgur in fine-mesh strainer under cold running water. Drain well and transfer to second bowl. Stir in 2 tablespoons lemon juice and 2 tablespoons juice from draining tomatoes. Let stand until grains are beginning to soften, 30 to 40 minutes.

3. Whisk remaining 2 tablespoons lemon juice, oil, cayenne, and ¼ teaspoon salt together in large bowl. Add drained tomatoes, soaked bulgur, parsley, mint, and scallions; toss gently to combine. Cover and let stand at room temperature until flavors have blended and bulgur is tender, about 1 hour. Toss to recombine, season with salt and pepper to taste, and serve immediately.

EGYPTIAN BARLEY SALAD

WHY THIS RECIPE WORKS: We set out to develop a recipe for a vibrantly spiced pearl barley salad with the right balance of sweetness, tang, and nuttiness. Before we could focus on building these exciting flavors, we had to find a consistent cooking method for our barley. We wanted the grains to remain distinct, rather than cohesive as in a pilaf. We turned to what we call the "pasta method," in which we simply boil the grains until tender. With our perfectly cooked barley set aside, we turned our attention back to flavor. Inspired by the flavors of Egypt, we incorporated toasty pistachios, tangy pomegranate molasses, and bright, vegetal cilantro, all balanced by warm, earthy spices and sweet golden raisins. Salty feta cheese, pungent scallions, and pomegranate seeds adorned the top of the dish for a colorful composed salad with dynamic flavors and textures.

Egyptian Barley Salad
SERVES 6 TO 8
Do not substitute hulled barley or hull-less barley in this recipe. If using quick-cooking or presteamed barley (read the ingredient list on the package to determine this), you will need to decrease the barley cooking time in step 1.

1½ cups pearl barley
   Salt and pepper
3 tablespoons extra-virgin olive oil, plus extra for serving
2 tablespoons pomegranate molasses
½ teaspoon ground cinnamon
¼ teaspoon ground cumin
⅓ cup golden raisins
½ cup coarsely chopped cilantro
¼ cup shelled pistachios, toasted and chopped coarse
3 ounces feta cheese, cut into ½-inch cubes (¾ cup)
6 scallions, green parts only, sliced thin
½ cup pomegranate seeds

1. Bring 4 quarts water to boil in Dutch oven. Add barley and 1 tablespoon salt, return to boil, and cook until tender, 20 to 40 minutes. Drain barley, spread onto rimmed baking sheet, and let cool completely, about 15 minutes.

2. Whisk oil, molasses, cinnamon, cumin, and ½ teaspoon salt together in large bowl. Add barley, raisins, cilantro, and pistachios and gently toss to combine. Season with salt and pepper to taste. Spread barley salad evenly on serving platter and arrange feta, scallions, and pomegranate seeds in separate diagonal rows on top. Drizzle with extra oil and serve.

NO-FUSS CREAMY POLENTA

WHY THIS RECIPE WORKS: If you don't stir polenta almost constantly, it forms intractable lumps. We wanted creamy, smooth polenta with rich corn flavor, but we wanted to find a way around the fussy process.

The prospect of stirring continuously for an hour made our arms ache, so we set out to find a way to give the water a head start on penetrating the cornmeal (we prefer the soft texture and nutty flavor of degerminated cornmeal in polenta). Our research led us to consider the similarities between cooking dried beans and dried corn. With beans, water has to penetrate the hard outer skin to gelatinize the starch within. In a corn kernel, the water has to penetrate the endosperm. To soften bean skins and speed up cooking, baking soda is sometimes added to the cooking liquid. Sure enough, a pinch was all it took to cut the cooking time in half without affecting the texture or flavor. Baking soda also helped the granules break down and release their starch in a uniform way, so we could virtually eliminate the stirring if we covered the pot and adjusted the heat to low. Parmesan cheese and butter stirred in at the last minute finishes our polenta, which is satisfying and rich.

No-Fuss Creamy Parmesan Polenta

SERVES 6 TO 8

Coarse-ground degerminated cornmeal such as yellow grits (with grains the size of couscous) works best in this recipe. Avoid instant and quick-cooking products, as well as whole grain, stone-ground, and regular cornmeal. Do not omit the baking soda—it reduces the cooking time and makes for a creamier polenta. The polenta should do little more than release wisps of steam. If it bubbles or sputters even slightly after the first 10 minutes, the heat is too high and you may need a flame tamer. A flame tamer can be purchased at most kitchen supply stores, or you can improvise your own (see page 313). For a main course, serve the polenta with a wedge of rich cheese, meat sauce, or cooked leafy greens. Served plain, the polenta makes a great accompaniment to stews and braises.

7½ cups water

1½ teaspoons table salt
Pinch baking soda (see note)

1½ cups coarse-ground cornmeal (see note)

4 ounces Parmesan cheese, grated (about 2 cups), plus extra for serving

2 tablespoons unsalted butter
Ground black pepper

1. Bring the water to a boil in a heavy-bottomed 4-quart saucepan over medium-high heat. Stir in the salt and baking soda. Slowly pour the cornmeal into the water in a steady stream, while stirring back and forth with a wooden spoon or rubber spatula. Bring the mixture to a boil, stirring constantly, about 1 minute. Reduce the heat to the lowest possible setting and cover.

2. After 5 minutes, whisk the polenta to smooth out any lumps that may have formed, about 15 seconds. (Make sure to scrape the sides and bottom of the pan.) Cover and continue to cook, without stirring, until the grains of polenta are tender but slightly al dente, about 25 minutes longer. (The polenta should be loose and barely hold its shape; it will continue to thicken as it cools.)

3. Remove from the heat, stir in the Parmesan and butter, and season with pepper to taste. Let stand, covered, for 5 minutes. Serve, passing extra Parmesan separately.

SPICED PECANS WITH RUM GLAZE

WHY THIS RECIPE WORKS: Most spiced nuts are made with a heavily sugared syrup that causes the nuts to clump awkwardly and leaves your hands in a sticky mess. We wanted to get maximum flavor and balanced sweetness with minimum mess.

We tried two popular methods—boiling the nuts in syrup and tossing them in butter—and eliminated both straight off. The former made the nuts sticky, and the latter dulled their flavor. A third method, coating the nuts with an egg white mixture, pretty much overwhelmed them with a candy-like coating. What finally worked was a light glaze made from very small amounts of liquid (we like either rum or water), sugar, and butter, which left the nuts just tacky enough to pick up an even, light coating of dry spices.

Spiced Pecans with Rum Glaze

MAKES ABOUT 2 CUPS

The spiced nuts can be stored in an airtight container at room temperature for up to 5 days.

2 cups raw pecan halves

SPICE MIX

2 tablespoons sugar

¾ teaspoon table salt

½ teaspoon ground cinnamon

⅛ teaspoon ground cloves

⅛ teaspoon ground allspice

RUM GLAZE

1 tablespoon rum, preferably dark, or water

1 tablespoon unsalted butter

2 teaspoons vanilla extract

1 teaspoon light or dark brown sugar

1. Adjust an oven rack to the middle position and heat the oven to 350 degrees. Line a rimmed baking sheet with parchment paper and spread the pecans on it in an even layer; toast until fragrant and the color deepens slightly, about 8 minutes, rotating the sheet halfway through the baking time. Transfer the baking sheet with the nuts to a wire rack.

2. FOR THE SPICE MIX: While the nuts are toasting, combine all the spice mix ingredients in a medium bowl; set aside.

3. FOR THE RUM GLAZE: Bring the rum glaze ingredients to a boil in a medium saucepan over medium-high heat, whisking constantly. Stir in the pecans and cook, stirring constantly with a wooden spoon, until almost all the liquid has evaporated, about 1½ minutes.

4. Transfer the glazed pecans to the bowl with the spice mix; toss well to coat. Return the glazed spiced pecans to the parchment-lined baking sheet to cool before serving.

COME FOR BRUNCH

FLUFFY SCRAMBLED EGGS

WHY THIS RECIPE WORKS: Sometimes the simplest things can be the hardest to get right. Scrambled eggs are a good example. Seemingly easy to make, they can easily go wrong, and overcooking is probably the most common problem. We wanted scrambled eggs that turn out of the pan into a mound of large, soft curds—cooked enough to hold their shape but soft enough to eat with a spoon.

We learned that beating the eggs too much before cooking them can result in toughness, so we whisked our eggs just until they were combined. Milk was better than water as an addition to scrambled eggs; the sugar, proteins, and fat in milk helped create large curds, which trapped steam for that pillowy texture we were after. A nonstick skillet was a must to prevent sticking, and pan size mattered as well; if the skillet was too large, the eggs spread out in too thin a layer and overcooked. Getting the pan hot was crucial for moist, puffy curds, and constant gentle stirring—really more like pushing and folding—prevented overcooking. Cooked on the stove until they were almost done, which took only a couple of minutes, these eggs finished cooking on the way to the table, remaining moist and meltingly soft.

Fluffy Scrambled Eggs
SERVES 4

These eggs cook very quickly, so it's important to be ready to eat before you start to cook them.

- 8 large eggs
- ½ cup milk
- ½ teaspoon table salt
    Pinch ground black pepper
- 1 tablespoon unsalted butter

1. Whisk the eggs, milk, salt, and pepper together in a medium bowl until any streaks are gone and the color is pure yellow.

2. Melt the butter in a 10-inch nonstick skillet over high heat, swirling to coat the pan. Add the eggs and, using a heatproof rubber spatula, cook while gently pushing, lifting, and folding them from one side of the pan to the other as they form curds. Continue until the eggs are nicely clumped into a single mound but remain shiny and wet, 1½ to 2 minutes. Serve.

RICH AND CREAMY SCRAMBLED EGGS

WHY THIS RECIPE WORKS: Scrambled eggs often end up as either tough, dry slabs or pebbly, runny curds. We wanted foolproof rich scrambled eggs with fluffy, moist curds so creamy and light that they practically dissolved on the tongue.

The first step was to add salt to the uncooked eggs; salt dissolved some of the egg proteins so they were unable to bond when cooked, creating more tender curds. Beating the eggs until just combined, using the gentle action of a fork rather than a whisk, ensured our scramble didn't turn tough. For the intense creaminess we were after, we chose half-and-half over milk; it produced rich, clean-tasting curds that were both fluffy and stable. To replicate the richer flavor of farm-fresh eggs, we added extra yolks. Finally, when it came to the cooking process, we started the eggs on medium-high heat to create puffy curds, then finished them over low heat so they wouldn't overcook. Swapping out our 12-inch skillet for a 10-inch pan kept the eggs in a thicker layer, trapping more steam and producing heartier curds.

Rich and Creamy Scrambled Eggs
SERVES 4

It's important to follow the visual cues in this recipe, as pan thickness will affect cooking times. If using an electric stove, heat one burner on low heat and a second on medium-high heat; move the skillet between burners when it's time to adjust the heat. If you don't have half-and-half, substitute 8 teaspoons of whole milk and 4 teaspoons of heavy cream. To dress up the dish, add 2 tablespoons of chopped parsley, chives, basil, or cilantro or 1 tablespoon of dill or tarragon to the eggs after reducing the heat to low.

- 8 large whole eggs
- 2 large yolks
- ¼ cup half-and-half
    Table salt and ground black pepper
- 1 tablespoon unsalted butter, chilled

1. Beat the eggs, yolks, half-and-half, ⅜ teaspoon salt, and ¼ teaspoon pepper with a fork until the eggs are thoroughly combined and the color is pure yellow; do not over beat.

2. Heat the butter in a 10-inch nonstick skillet over medium-high heat until fully melted (the butter should not brown), swirling to coat the pan. Add the egg mixture and, using a heatproof rubber spatula, constantly and firmly scrape along the bottom and the sides of the skillet until the eggs begin to clump and the spatula just leaves a trail on the bottom of the

GETTING THE TIMING RIGHT FOR RICH AND CREAMY SCRAMBLED EGGS

When your spatula just leaves a trail through the eggs, that's your cue in our dual-heat method to turn the dial from medium-high to low.

pan, 1½ to 2½ minutes. Reduce the heat to low and gently but constantly fold the eggs until clumped and just slightly wet, 30 to 60 seconds. Immediately transfer the eggs to warmed plates and season with salt to taste. Serve immediately.

Rich and Creamy Scrambled Eggs for Two

Follow the recipe for Rich and Creamy Scrambled Eggs, reducing the whole eggs to 4, the yolks to 1, the half-and-half to 2 tablespoons, and the salt and pepper to ⅛ teaspoon each. In step 2, reduce the butter to ½ tablespoon. Cook the eggs in an 8-inch skillet for 45 to 75 seconds over medium-high heat, then for 30 to 60 seconds over low heat.

HEARTY SCRAMBLED EGGS

WHY THIS RECIPE WORKS: Having perfected the technique for cooking scrambled eggs, we figured that we could make a heartier dish by simply adding other ingredients. But even a sprinkling of some sausage or vegetables discolored the eggs and made them watery. We found that cooking in stages—sautéing our aromatics and removing them, cooking the eggs, then folding in all the other ingredients off the heat—prevented discoloration and helped with the wateriness. We were able to get rid of the last bit of wateriness when we substituted a smaller amount of half-and-half—with its higher-fat, lower-water content—for the milk. Breakfast meats, crunchy vegetables, and dry leafy greens were successful additions to these eggs, so long as we avoided any that were moisture-laden. These eggs were not as fluffy as eggs without adornment, but the difference was imperceptible once we added meats and vegetables—and there were no watery puddles on the plate.

Scrambled Eggs with Bacon, Onion, and Pepper Jack Cheese

SERVES 4 TO 6

Note that you'll need to reserve 2 teaspoons of bacon fat to sauté the onion. After removing the cooked bacon from the skillet, be sure to drain it well on paper towels; otherwise, the eggs will be greasy.

12 large eggs
6 tablespoons half-and-half
¾ teaspoon table salt
¼ teaspoon ground black pepper
4 ounces bacon (about 4 slices), halved lengthwise, then cut crosswise into ½-inch pieces
1 medium onion, chopped medium
1 tablespoon unsalted butter
1½ ounces pepper Jack or Monterey Jack cheese, shredded (about ⅓ cup)
1 teaspoon minced fresh parsley leaves (optional)

1. Whisk the eggs, half-and-half, salt, and pepper together in a medium bowl.

2. Cook the bacon in a 12-inch nonstick skillet over medium heat, stirring occasionally, until browned, 4 to 5 minutes. Using a slotted spoon, transfer the bacon to a paper towel–lined plate; discard all but 2 teaspoons bacon fat. Add the onion to the skillet and cook, stirring occasionally, until lightly browned, 2 to 4 minutes; transfer the onion to a second plate.

3. Thoroughly wipe out the skillet with paper towels, add the butter, and melt over medium heat, swirling to coat the pan. Add the eggs and, using a heatproof rubber spatula, cook while gently pushing, lifting, and folding them from one side of the pan to the other as they form curds. Cook until large curds form but the eggs are still very moist, 2 to 3 minutes. Off the heat, gently fold in the onion, pepper Jack, and half of the bacon until evenly distributed; if the eggs are still underdone, return the skillet to medium heat for no longer than 30 seconds. Divide the eggs among individual plates, sprinkle with the remaining bacon and parsley (if using), and serve.

Scrambled Eggs with Sausage, Sweet Pepper, and Cheddar Cheese

SERVES 4 TO 6

We prefer sweet Italian sausage here, especially for breakfast, but you can certainly use spicy sausage, if desired.

12 large eggs
6 tablespoons half-and-half
¾ teaspoon table salt
¼ teaspoon ground black pepper
1 teaspoon vegetable oil
8 ounces sweet Italian sausage, casings removed, sausage crumbled into ½-inch pieces (see note)
1 red bell pepper, stemmed, seeded, and cut into ½-inch cubes
3 scallions, white and green parts separated, both sliced thin on the bias
1 tablespoon unsalted butter
1½ ounces sharp cheddar cheese, shredded (about ⅓ cup)

1. Whisk the eggs, half-and-half, salt, and pepper together in a medium bowl.

2. Heat the oil in a 12-inch nonstick skillet over medium heat until shimmering. Add the sausage and cook until beginning to brown but still pink in the center, about 2 minutes.

Add the bell pepper and scallion whites; continue to cook, stirring occasionally, until the sausage is cooked through and the pepper is beginning to brown, about 3 minutes. Spread the mixture in a single layer on a medium plate; set aside.

3. Thoroughly wipe out the skillet with paper towels, add the butter, and melt over medium heat, swirling to coat the pan. Add the eggs and, using a heatproof rubber spatula, cook while gently pushing, lifting, and folding them from one side of the pan to the other as they form curds. Cook the eggs until large curds form but the eggs are still very moist, 2 to 3 minutes. Off the heat, gently fold in the sausage mixture and cheddar until evenly distributed; if the eggs are still underdone, return the skillet to medium heat for no longer than 30 seconds. Divide the eggs among individual plates, sprinkle with the scallion greens, and serve.

PERFECT FRIED EGGS

WHY THIS RECIPE WORKS: There are two common problems when it comes to fried eggs: undercooked whites and an overcooked yolk. A hot nonstick skillet, a touch of butter, and a lid combine to produce perfectly cooked fried eggs—with crisp edges, tender whites, and runny yolks—in just a few minutes.

Perfect Fried Eggs
SERVES 2

When checking the eggs for doneness, lift the lid just a crack to prevent loss of steam should they need further cooking. When cooked, the thin layer of white surrounding the yolk will turn opaque, but the yolk should remain runny. To cook two eggs, use an 8- or 9-inch nonstick skillet and halve the amounts of oil and butter. You can use this method with extra-large or jumbo eggs without altering the timing.

 2 teaspoons vegetable oil
 4 large eggs
    Salt and pepper
 2 teaspoons unsalted butter, cut into 4 pieces and chilled

1. Heat oil in 12- or 14-inch nonstick skillet over low heat for 5 minutes. Meanwhile, crack 2 eggs into small bowl and season with salt and pepper. Repeat with remaining 2 eggs and second small bowl.

2. Increase heat to medium-high and heat until oil is shimmering. Add butter to skillet and quickly swirl to coat pan. Working quickly, pour 1 bowl of eggs in 1 side of pan and second bowl of eggs in other side. Cover and cook for 1 minute. Remove skillet from burner and let stand, covered, 15 to 45 seconds for runny yolks (white around edge of yolk will be barely opaque), 45 to 60 seconds for soft but set yolks, and about 2 minutes for medium-set yolks. Slide eggs onto plates and serve.

MAKING PERFECT FRIED EGGS

1. HEAT SKILLET: Heat oil in nonstick skillet over low heat for 5 minutes.

2. CRACK EGGS INTO SMALL BOWLS: While skillet heats, crack 2 eggs into small bowl. Repeat with remaining eggs and second small bowl.

3. ADD EGGS ALL AT ONCE: Increase heat. Add butter and swirl to coat pan. Working quickly, position bowls on either side of skillet and add eggs simultaneously.

4. COVER PAN, THEN FINISH OFF HEAT: Cover and cook 1 minute. Remove skillet from burner and let stand, covered, until eggs achieve desired doneness.

POACHED EGGS

WHY THIS RECIPE WORKS: A poached egg should be a neat-looking pouch of tender egg, evenly cooked all the way through, with a yolk that is barely runny. But boiling water can agitate the eggs until they are a ragged mess; we needed to figure out how to cook these eggs gently.

Our first thought was to examine the type of pan used. Most recipes require a deep saucepan, but we found that a shallow pan—a skillet—was far better: The water boiled faster, and the egg hit bottom sooner, and thus more gently, so that it could solidify before becoming stringy. A touch of vinegar lowered the boiling point of the water so that we were able to cook the eggs over more gentle heat. Our most important discovery turned out to be the importance of cooking eggs in still, not bubbling, water—as long as it was hot enough. With this in mind, we covered the skillet and turned off the heat after adding the eggs to the boiling water, allowing the residual heat to cook the eggs through. Without bubbling water to tear them apart, our poached eggs came out of the pan perfectly shaped—and cooked—with no feathery whites in sight.

Poached Eggs

MAKES 4

To get four eggs into boiling water at the same time, crack each into a small cup with a handle. Holding two cups in each hand, lower the lip of each cup just into the water and then tip the eggs into the pan.

> Table salt
> 2 tablespoons distilled white vinegar
> 4 large eggs, each cracked into a small handled cup
>   (see note)
> Ground black pepper

1. Fill an 8- to 10-inch nonstick skillet nearly to the rim with water, add 1 teaspoon salt and the vinegar, and bring the mixture to a boil over high heat.

2. Lower the lip of each cup just into the water; tip the eggs into the boiling water, cover, and immediately remove the pan from the heat. Poach the eggs for 4 minutes for medium-firm yolks. (For firmer yolks, poach for 4½ minutes; for looser yolks, poach for 3 minutes.)

3. With a slotted spoon, carefully lift and drain each egg over the skillet. Season with salt and pepper to taste and serve.

EGGS BENEDICT

WHY THIS RECIPE WORKS: Overcoming one of the biggest challenges to poaching eggs—producing a tender, tidy white—started with draining the eggs in a colander. We also cracked the eggs into a liquid measuring cup and deposited them into the water one by one to prevent them from being jostled. Salted water with vinegar helped the whites set up quickly. Poaching the eggs in a Dutch oven filled with 6 cups of water left plenty of headspace so that steam fully cooked the notoriously gooey portion of the white. Our unconventional technique for hollandaise required whisking butter and egg yolks on the stovetop in a double boiler, creating a strong emulsion stable enough to be chilled and reheated. We served our poached eggs atop toasted English muffins and bacon, and topped them off with our velvety hollandaise.

Eggs Benedict with Perfect Poached Eggs and Foolproof Hollandaise

SERVES 4

For the best results, be sure to use the freshest eggs possible. Cracking the eggs into a colander will rid them of any watery, loose whites and result in perfectly shaped poached eggs. The hollandaise can be refrigerated in an airtight container for

3 days. Reheat in the microwave on 50 percent power, stirring every 10 seconds, until heated through, about 1 minute. You will need an instant-read thermometer to make this recipe.

HOLLANDAISE

> 8 tablespoons unsalted butter,
>   cut into 8 pieces and softened
> 4 large egg yolks
> ⅓ cup boiling water
> 2 teaspoons lemon juice
>   Pinch cayenne pepper
>   Salt

EGGS

> 1 tablespoon distilled white vinegar
>   Salt
> 8 large eggs

> 4 English muffins, split
> 8 slices Canadian bacon (see note)

1. FOR THE HOLLANDAISE: Whisk butter and egg yolks in large heat-resistant bowl set over medium saucepan filled with ½ inch of barely simmering water (don't let bowl touch water). Slowly add boiling water and cook, whisking constantly, until thickened and sauce registers 160 to 165 degrees, 7 to 10 minutes.

2. Off heat, stir in lemon juice and cayenne and season with salt. Cover and set aside in warm place until serving time.

3. FOR THE EGGS: Bring 6 cups water to boil in Dutch oven over high heat, and add vinegar and 1 teaspoon salt. Fill second Dutch oven halfway with water, heat over high heat until water registers 150 degrees; adjust heat as needed to maintain 150 degrees.

4. Crack 4 eggs, one at a time, into colander. Let stand until loose, watery whites drain away from eggs, 20 to 30 seconds. Gently transfer eggs to 2-cup liquid measuring cup. Remove first pot with added vinegar from heat. With lip of measuring cup just above surface of water, gently tip eggs into water, one at a time, leaving space between them. Cover pot and let stand until whites closest to yolks are just set and opaque, about 3 minutes. If after 3 minutes whites are not set, let stand in water, checking every 30 seconds, until eggs reach desired doneness. (For medium-cooked yolks, let eggs sit in pot, covered, for 4 minutes, then begin checking for doneness.)

5. Using slotted spoon, carefully lift and drain each egg over Dutch oven, then transfer to pot filled with 150-degree water and cover. Return Dutch oven used for cooking eggs to boil and repeat steps 4 and 5 with remaining 4 eggs.

6. Adjust oven rack 6 inches from broiler element and heat broiler. Arrange English muffins, split side up, on baking sheet and broil until golden brown, 2 to 4 minutes. Place 1 slice bacon on each English muffin and broil until beginning to brown, about 1 minute. Remove muffins from oven and transfer to serving plates. Using slotted spoon, carefully lift and drain each egg and lay on top of each English muffin. Spoon hollandaise over top and serve.

SOFT-COOKED EGGS

WHY THIS RECIPE WORKS: Traditional methods for making soft-cooked eggs are hit or miss. We wanted one that delivered a set white and a fluid yolk every time. Calling for fridge-cold eggs and boiling water has two advantages: It reduces temperature variables, which makes the recipe more foolproof, and it provides the steepest temperature gradient, which ensures that the yolk at the center stays fluid while the white cooks through. Using only ½ inch of boiling water instead of several cups to cook the eggs means that the recipe takes less time and energy from start to finish. Because of the curved shape of the eggs, they actually have very little contact with the water so they do not lower the water temperature when they go into the saucepan. This means that you can use the same timing for anywhere from one to six eggs without altering the consistency of the finished product.

Soft-Cooked Eggs
MAKES 4

Be sure to use large eggs that have no cracks and are cold from the refrigerator. Because precise timing is vital to the success of this recipe, we strongly recommend using a digital timer. You can use this method for one to six large, extra-large, or jumbo eggs without altering the timing. If you have one, a steamer basket makes lowering the eggs into the boiling water easier. We recommend serving these eggs in eggcups and with buttered toast for dipping, or you may simply use the dull side of a butter knife to crack the egg along the equator, break the egg in half, and scoop out the insides with a teaspoon.

4 large eggs
　 Salt and pepper

1. Bring ½ inch water to boil in medium saucepan over medium-high heat. Using tongs, gently place eggs in boiling water (eggs will not be submerged). Cover saucepan and cook eggs for 6½ minutes.

2. Remove cover, transfer saucepan to sink, and place under cold running water for 30 seconds. Remove eggs from pan and serve, seasoning with salt and pepper to taste.

Soft-Cooked Eggs with Salad
SERVES 2

Be sure to run the soft-cooked eggs under cold water for 30 seconds before peeling.

Combine 3 tablespoons olive oil, 1 tablespoon balsamic vinegar, 1 teaspoon Dijon mustard, and 1 teaspoon minced shallot in jar, seal lid, and shake vigorously until emulsified, 20 to 30 seconds. Toss with 5 cups assertively flavored salad greens (arugula, radicchio, watercress, or frisée). Season with salt and pepper to taste, and divide between 2 plates. Top each serving with 2 peeled soft-cooked eggs, split crosswise to release yolks, and season with salt and pepper to taste.

Soft-Cooked Eggs with Sautéed Mushrooms
SERVES 2

Be sure to run the soft-cooked eggs under cold water for 30 seconds before peeling.

Heat 2 tablespoons olive oil in large skillet over medium-high heat until shimmering. Add 12 ounces sliced white or cremini mushrooms and pinch salt and cook, stirring occasionally, until liquid has evaporated and mushrooms are lightly browned, 5 to 6 minutes. Stir in 2 teaspoons chopped fresh herbs (chives, tarragon, parsley, or combination). Season with salt and pepper to taste, and divide between 2 plates. Top each serving with 2 peeled soft-cooked eggs, split crosswise to release yolks, and season with salt and pepper to taste.

Soft-Cooked Eggs with Steamed Asparagus

SERVES 2

Be sure to run the soft-cooked eggs under cold water for 30 seconds before peeling.

Steam 12 ounces asparagus (spears about ½ inch in diameter, trimmed) over medium heat until crisp-tender, 4 to 5 minutes. Divide between 2 plates. Drizzle each serving with 1 tablespoon extra-virgin olive oil and sprinkle each serving with 1 tablespoon grated Parmesan. Season with salt and pepper to taste. Top each serving with 2 peeled soft-cooked eggs, split crosswise to release yolks, and season with salt and pepper to taste.

EGGS PIPERADE

WHY THIS RECIPE WORKS: When serving up eggs piperade for breakfast, one thing is for certain: All diners are in for a healthy serving of flavor-packed vegetables. This Basque dish serves up scrambled eggs in a vibrant sauté of tender bell peppers, onions, and tomatoes—the winning combination we love in ratatouille. We wanted our vegetables to soften but retain their structure, so we kept a close eye on our skillet. We started with the onions; as soon as the pieces began to brown in the hot oil, we brought in the aromatics: minced garlic, minced fresh thyme, paprika, and red pepper flakes. After allowing them to bloom, we introduced the peppers. Using both cubanelle and red bell peppers contributed great color and subtle sweetness. Once the peppers were just softened, coarsely chopped canned tomatoes brought in bright acidity and their juice helped meld the vegetables' flavors as the liquid reduced. Some minced fresh parsley and a touch of sherry vinegar tied the vegetables together before we turned our attention to the eggs. With the peppers and onions waiting on our serving platter, we prepared some lightly seasoned scrambled eggs, folding them in a hot oiled pan until cooked but still slightly wet. We served our sautéed vegetables and perfectly moist eggs with a final sprinkling of parsley.

Eggs Piperade

SERVES 4

We prefer to make this dish with cubanelle peppers, but green peppers can be substituted in a pinch. When serving, the eggs and pepper mixture can be served separately or the eggs can be gently folded into the pepper mixture, which is more traditional.

- 6 tablespoons extra-virgin olive oil
- 1 large onion, cut into ½-inch pieces
- 1 large bay leaf
  Salt and pepper
- 4 garlic cloves, minced
- 1 teaspoon minced fresh thyme
- 2 teaspoons paprika
- ¾ teaspoon red pepper flakes
- 3 red bell peppers (7 to 8 ounces each), stemmed, seeded, and cut into ⅜-inch strips
- 3 cubanelle peppers (3 to 4 ounces each), stemmed, seeded, and cut into ⅜-inch strips
- 1 (14-ounce) can whole peeled tomatoes, drained with ¼ cup juice reserved, chopped coarse
- 3 tablespoons minced fresh parsley
- 2 teaspoons sherry vinegar
- 8 large eggs

1. Heat 3 tablespoons oil in 12-inch nonstick skillet over medium heat until shimmering. Add onion, bay leaf, and ½ teaspoon salt and cook, stirring occasionally, until softened and just starting to brown, about 6 minutes. Add garlic, thyme, paprika, and pepper flakes and cook, stirring occasionally, until fragrant, about 1 minute. Add bell peppers, cubanelle peppers, and 1 teaspoon salt, cover, and cook, stirring occasionally, until peppers begin to soften, about 10 minutes.

2. Remove cover and stir in tomatoes and juice. Reduce heat to medium-low and cook, uncovered, stirring occasionally, until mixture appears dry and peppers are tender but not mushy, 10 to 12 minutes. Discard bay leaf; stir in 2 tablespoons parsley and vinegar. Season with salt and pepper to taste. Transfer pepper mixture to serving dish. Wipe out skillet with paper towels.

3. While pepper mixture cooks, beat eggs, 2 tablespoons oil, ½ teaspoon salt, and ¼ teaspoon pepper with fork until eggs are thoroughly combined and color is pure yellow.

4. Return now-empty skillet to medium-high heat, add remaining 1 tablespoon oil and heat until shimmering. Add egg mixture and, using rubber spatula, constantly and firmly scrape along bottom and sides of skillet until eggs begin to clump and spatula just leaves trail on bottom of pan, 30 to 60 seconds. Reduce heat to low and gently but constantly fold eggs until clumped and just slightly wet, 30 to 60 seconds. Immediately transfer eggs to serving dish with pepper mixture, sprinkle with remaining 1 tablespoon parsley, and serve.

HELP! MY RECIPE DOESN'T WORK!

It happens—even in America's Test Kitchen. Once in a while, we get a call from a viewer or reader that a recipe isn't working for them. And every time, our hearts sink. What did we do wrong? We not only test our recipes very carefully (as many as 100 times), but we also have our recipes vetted by a professional cook, and THEN we send them out to home cooks to test-drive our recipes. So why do recipes sometimes fail? The answers fall into three broad categories: substitutions, flawed equipment, or ingredient variables.

Substitutions are common (everyone does it), but if you decide to replace a key ingredient or piece of equipment, all bets are off. If you're on a diet, don't try making our crème brûlée with milk rather than cream. And don't sear four steaks in a 10-inch skillet when the recipe calls for a 12-inch pan—that is, unless you want them to taste steamed and bland. Our advice: Make the recipe once as it's written, then improvise.

Flawed equipment is harder to predict and control. Many home ovens are not properly calibrated and an oven that runs hot by 50 degrees (which is fairly common in home kitchens) will ruin many recipes. Always, always pay attention to the visual cues in our recipes, not the clock. And invest in an oven thermometer. It's cheap and will save you much frustration when cooking.

Ingredient variables are the hardest thing for us (or you) to control. Produce varies in sweetness and moisture content. The same cut of meat can have more or less fat. And brands of manufactured products are not all the same. In fact, we had trouble with a chocolate frosting recipe several years ago and realized that our recipe worked with the test kitchen's top-rated bittersweet chocolate (with 60 percent cacao) but failed when readers tried to use gourmet brands with a higher cacao content. We test all of our recipes with the ingredients that have won our blind taste tests (see pages 904 through 927). We suggest you do the same. Not only will your food taste better, but sometimes choosing the right brand can make the difference between a successful recipe and a failed one.

HOME FRIES

WHY THIS RECIPE WORKS: Whether made at home or eaten out, home fries frequently suffer from the same problems: greasy or undercooked potatoes, and bland or too-spicy flavors. We wanted a recipe that produced potatoes with a crisp crust and a tender interior. We determined that medium-starch Yukon Golds remained moist even when crisped on the outside. Attempts to cook raw diced potato in the skillet ended in failure; precooking was the way to go. We tried baking, boiling, and dicing the potatoes before frying them, but they overcooked. What finally worked was parcooking the potatoes—placing them in water and bringing them just to a boil, then immediately draining them before frying. This gave the interior of the potatoes a head start in the cooking process, but they weren't in the water long enough to absorb much liquid. The result: firm cubes of potato with crisp, browned exteriors. A combination of butter and oil worked best for frying. Onion was the perfect foil for these potatoes; we cooked it in the skillet before adding the potatoes.

Diner-Style Home Fries

SERVES 2 TO 3

If doubling this recipe, cook two batches of home fries separately. While making the second batch, keep the first batch hot and crisp by spreading the fries on a baking sheet placed in a 300-degree oven.

> 2½ tablespoons corn oil or peanut oil
> 1 medium onion, minced
> 1 pound (2 medium) Yukon Gold potatoes, scrubbed and cut into ½-inch cubes
> Table salt
> 1 tablespoon unsalted butter
> 1 teaspoon paprika (optional)
> 1 tablespoon minced fresh parsley leaves (optional)
> Ground black pepper

1. Heat 1 tablespoon of the oil in a 12-inch skillet over medium-high heat until shimmering. Add the onion and cook, stirring frequently, until browned, 8 to 10 minutes. Transfer the onion to a small bowl and set aside.

2. Meanwhile, place the potatoes in a large saucepan, cover with ½ inch of water, add 1 teaspoon salt, and bring to a boil over high heat. As soon as the water begins to boil, drain the potatoes thoroughly in a colander.

3. Heat the butter and the remaining 1½ tablespoons oil in the now-empty skillet over medium-high heat. Add the potatoes and shake the skillet to evenly distribute the potatoes in a single layer, making sure that one side of each piece is touching the surface of the skillet. Cook without stirring until one side of the potatoes is golden brown, 4 to 5 minutes, then carefully turn the potatoes, making sure the potatoes remain in a single layer. Repeat the process until the potatoes are tender and browned on most sides, turning three or four times, 10 to 15 minutes longer. Add the onions, paprika (if using), parsley (if using), ¼ teaspoon salt, and pepper to taste; serve.

surface moisture has evaporated, about 2 minutes. Remove from heat. Add butter, 1½ teaspoons salt, and cayenne; mix with rubber spatula until potatoes are coated with thick, starchy paste, about 30 seconds.

3. Remove baking sheet from oven and drizzle with 2 tablespoons oil. Transfer potatoes to baking sheet and spread into even layer. Roast for 15 minutes. While potatoes roast, combine onions, remaining 1 tablespoon oil, and ½ teaspoon salt in bowl.

4. Remove baking sheet from oven. Using thin, sharp metal spatula, scrape and turn potatoes. Clear about 8 by 5-inch space in center of baking sheet and add onion mixture. Roast for 15 minutes.

5. Scrape and turn again, mixing onions into potatoes. Continue to roast until potatoes are well browned and onions are softened and beginning to brown, 5 to 10 minutes. Stir in chives and season with salt and pepper to taste. Serve immediately.

HOME FRIES FOR A CROWD

WHY THIS RECIPE WORKS: Making home fries the traditional way requires constant monitoring while standing over a hot skillet, after which you get only three servings at most. We wanted a quicker, more hands-off method for making a larger amount. To speed things up, we developed a hybrid cooking technique: First, we parboiled diced russet potatoes, and then we coated them in oil and cooked them in a very hot oven. We discovered that boiling the potatoes with baking soda quickly broke down their exterior while leaving their insides nearly raw, ensuring home fries with a crisp, brown crust and a moist, fluffy interior. We added diced onions in the last 20 minutes of oven time and finished the home fries with chives to reinforce the onion flavor.

Home Fries for a Crowd
SERVES 6 TO 8

Don't skip the baking soda in this recipe. It's critical for home fries with just the right crisp texture.

- 3½ pounds russet potatoes, peeled and cut into ¾-inch dice
- ½ teaspoon baking soda
- 3 tablespoons unsalted butter, cut into 12 pieces
- Kosher salt and pepper
- Pinch cayenne pepper
- 3 tablespoons vegetable oil
- 2 onions, cut into ½-inch dice
- 3 tablespoons minced chives

1. Adjust oven rack to lowest position, place rimmed baking sheet on rack, and heat oven to 500 degrees.

2. Bring 10 cups water to boil in Dutch oven over high heat. Add potatoes and baking soda. Return to boil and cook for 1 minute. Drain potatoes. Return potatoes to Dutch oven and place over low heat. Cook, shaking pot occasionally, until any

BACON

WHY THIS RECIPE WORKS: A couple strips of crisp bacon are always a welcome accompaniment to a plate of eggs, but bacon requires frequent monitoring when cooked on the stovetop. The microwave produces unevenly cooked and flavorless strips, so we looked to the oven for an easier way. Bacon renders its fat while cooking, so it was important to choose a pan that would contain it; a rimmed baking sheet worked just fine, and it enabled us to cook more strips at the same time. We didn't have to turn the bacon because the heat of the oven cooked it evenly, though rotating the baking sheet front to back halfway through ensured even cooking. In comparison to the results from stovetop frying, bacon cooked in the oven wasn't quite as crisp, but it was certainly crisp enough, and it had the same great meaty flavor. Although preheating the oven and draining the bacon after cooking takes a little extra time, the payoff is that you don't have to stand at the stove while the bacon is in the oven.

Oven-Fried Bacon
SERVES 4 TO 6

A large rimmed baking sheet is important here to contain the rendered bacon fat. If cooking more than one tray of bacon, switch their oven positions once about halfway through cooking. You can use thin- or thick-cut bacon here, though the cooking times will vary.

- 12 slices bacon (see note)

Adjust an oven rack to the middle position and heat the oven to 400 degrees. Arrange the bacon slices on a rimmed baking sheet. Cook until the fat begins to render, 5 to 6 minutes; rotate the pan. Continue cooking until the bacon is crisp and browned, 5 to 6 minutes longer for thin-cut bacon, 8 to 10 minutes for thick-cut. Transfer the bacon to a paper towel–lined plate, drain, and serve.

BAKED EGGS FLORENTINE

WHY THIS RECIPE WORKS: Baked eggs can be hard to get right. We wanted a creamy, slightly runny yolk and a tender white—in the same ramekin. The answer turned out to be insulation—that is, adding a spinach cream sauce to provide a barrier between the egg and the very hot sides of the ramekin. We also found that pulling the eggs from the oven before they were done and allowing carryover cooking to finish the job, delivered first-rate baked eggs.

Baked Eggs Florentine
SERVES 6

For the eggs to cook properly, it is imperative to add them to the hot, filling-lined ramekins quickly. Prepare by cracking eggs into separate bowls or teacups while the filled ramekins are heating. Use 6-ounce ramekins with 3¼-inch diameters, measured from the inner lip. We developed this recipe using a glass baking dish; if using a metal baking pan, reduce the oven temperature to 425 degrees. This recipe can be doubled and baked in two 13 by 9-inch dishes. If doubling, increase the baking times in steps 3 and 4 by 1 minute.

- 2 tablespoons unsalted butter
- 1 large shallot, minced
- 1 tablespoon all-purpose flour
- ¾ cup half-and-half
- 10 ounces frozen spinach, thawed and squeezed dry
- 2 ounces Parmesan cheese, grated (1 cup)
  Salt and pepper
- ⅛ teaspoon dry mustard
- ⅛ teaspoon ground nutmeg
  Pinch cayenne pepper
  Vegetable oil spray
- 6 large eggs

1. Adjust oven rack to middle position and heat oven to 500 degrees.

2. Melt butter in medium saucepan over medium heat. Add shallot and cook, stirring occasionally, until softened, about 3 minutes. Stir in flour and cook, stirring constantly, for 1 minute. Gradually whisk in half-and-half; bring mixture to boil, whisking constantly. Simmer, whisking frequently, until thickened, 2 to 3 minutes. Remove pan from heat and stir in spinach, Parmesan, ¾ teaspoon salt, ½ teaspoon pepper, mustard, nutmeg, and cayenne.

3. Lightly spray six 6-ounce ramekins with oil spray. Evenly divide spinach filling among ramekins. Using back of spoon, push filling 1 inch up sides of ramekins, making shallow indentation in center of filling large enough to hold egg. Place filled ramekins in 13 by 9-inch glass baking dish. Bake ramekins until filling just starts to brown, about 7 minutes, rotating dish halfway through baking.

4. While filling is heating, crack eggs (taking care not to break yolks) into individual cups or bowls. Remove baking dish with ramekins from oven and place on wire rack. Gently pour eggs from cups into hot ramekins, centering yolk in filling. Lightly spray surface of each egg with oil spray and sprinkle each with pinch of salt. Return baking dish to oven and bake until whites are just opaque but still tremble, 6 to 8 minutes, rotating dish halfway through baking.

5. Remove dish from oven and, using tongs, transfer ramekins to wire rack. Let stand until whites are firm and set (yolks should still be runny), about 10 minutes. Serve immediately.

TO MAKE AHEAD: Follow recipe through step 3, skipping step of baking lined ramekins. Wrap ramekins with plastic wrap and refrigerate for up to 3 days. To serve, heat lined ramekins, directly from refrigerator, for additional 3 to 4 minutes (10 to 11 minutes total) before proceeding with recipe.

Baked Eggs Lorraine

Wash 1 pound leeks and slice white and light green parts thin. Cook 2 slices bacon cut into ½-inch pieces in medium saucepan over medium heat until crisp, about 10 minutes. Transfer bacon to paper towel–lined plate. Add leeks and cook until softened, about 10 minutes. Transfer leeks to plate with bacon. Proceed with recipe, omitting shallot and reducing butter to 1 tablespoon. Substitute bacon and leek mixture for spinach and ½ cup shredded Gruyère cheese for Parmesan.

FLUFFY OMELETS

WHY THIS RECIPE WORKS: A different breed than French-style rolled omelets or diner-style omelets folded into half-moons, fluffy omelets are made by baking whipped eggs in a skillet until they rise above the lip of the pan. We love their impressive height and delicate texture. But most recipes result in oozing soufflés or dry, bouncy rounds—or eggs that barely puff up at all. To give our omelet lofty height without making it tough, we folded butter-enriched yolks into stiffly whipped whites stabilized with cream of tartar. The whipped whites gave the omelet great lift while the yolks and butter kept it tender and rich-tasting. We chose light but flavorful fillings that satisfied without weighing down the omelet.

Fluffy Omelets

SERVES 2

A teaspoon of white vinegar or lemon juice can be used in place of the cream of tartar, and a hand-held mixer or a whisk can be used in place of a stand mixer. We recommend using the fillings that accompany this recipe; they are designed not to interfere with the cooking of the omelet.

    4 large eggs, separated
    1 tablespoon unsalted butter, melted, plus 1 tablespoon
       unsalted butter
    ¼ teaspoon salt
    ¼ teaspoon cream of tartar
    1 recipe filling (recipes follow)
    1 ounce Parmesan cheese, grated (½ cup)

1. Adjust oven rack to middle position and heat oven to 375 degrees. Whisk egg yolks, melted butter, and salt together in bowl. Place egg whites in bowl of stand mixer and sprinkle cream of tartar over surface. Fit stand mixer with whisk and whip egg whites on medium-low speed until foamy, 2 to 2½ minutes. Increase speed to medium-high and whip until stiff peaks just start to form, 2 to 3 minutes. Fold egg yolk mixture into egg whites until no white streaks remain.

2. Heat remaining 1 tablespoon butter in 12-inch ovensafe nonstick skillet over medium-high heat, swirling to coat bottom of pan. When butter foams, quickly add egg mixture, spreading into even layer with spatula. Remove pan from heat and gently sprinkle filling and Parmesan evenly over top of omelet. Transfer to oven and cook until center of omelet springs back when lightly pressed, 4½ minutes for slightly wet omelet and 5 minutes for dry omelet.

3. Run spatula around edges of omelet to loosen, shaking gently to release. Slide omelet onto cutting board and let stand for 30 seconds. Using spatula, fold omelet in half. Cut omelet in half crosswise and serve immediately.

Asparagus and Smoked Salmon Filling

MAKES ¾ CUP

    1 teaspoon olive oil
    1 shallot, sliced thin
    5 ounces asparagus, trimmed and cut on bias
       into ¼-inch lengths
       Salt and pepper
    1 ounce smoked salmon, chopped
    ½ teaspoon lemon juice

Heat oil in 12-inch nonstick skillet over medium-high heat until shimmering. Add shallot and cook until softened and starting to brown, about 2 minutes. Add asparagus, pinch salt, and pepper to taste, and cook, stirring frequently, until crisp-tender, 5 to 7 minutes. Transfer asparagus mixture to bowl and stir in salmon and lemon juice.

Mushroom Filling

MAKES ¾ CUP

    1 teaspoon olive oil
    1 shallot, sliced thin
    4 ounces white or cremini mushrooms, trimmed
       and chopped
       Salt and pepper
    1 teaspoon balsamic vinegar

Heat oil in 12-inch nonstick skillet over medium-high heat until shimmering. Add shallot and cook until softened and starting to brown, about 2 minutes. Add mushrooms, ⅛ teaspoon salt, and season with pepper to taste. Cook until liquid has evaporated and mushrooms begin to brown, 6 to 8 minutes. Transfer mixture to bowl and stir in vinegar.

Artichoke and Bacon Filling

MAKES ¾ CUP

    2 slices bacon, cut into ¼-inch pieces
    1 shallot, sliced thin
    5 ounces frozen artichoke hearts, thawed,
       patted dry, and chopped
       Salt and pepper
    ½ teaspoon lemon juice

Cook bacon in 12-inch nonstick skillet over medium-high heat until crisp, 3 to 6 minutes. Using slotted spoon, transfer bacon to paper towel–lined plate. Pour off all but 1 teaspoon fat from skillet. Add shallot and cook until softened and starting to brown, about 2 minutes. Add artichokes, ⅛ teaspoon salt, and pepper to taste. Cook, stirring frequently, until artichokes begin to brown, 6 to 8 minutes. Transfer artichoke mixture to bowl and stir in bacon and lemon juice.

FAMILY-SIZE OMELET

WHY THIS RECIPE WORKS: An omelet is a great breakfast or brunch dish, but cooking omelets one at a time for more than a couple of people is just not practical. We wanted to find a way to make an omelet that was big enough to serve four people. We wanted it to have tender, not rubbery, eggs and a rich, cheesy filling.

Flipping a huge eight-egg omelet was clearly not going to work, so we had to find a way to cook the top of the omelet as well as the bottom. Cooking the eggs longer over lower heat resulted in an unpleasant texture. Broiling to cook the top of the eggs worked, but it dried out the omelet, and we wanted it to be creamy. Then we had the idea of covering the pan after the bottom of the eggs was set but the top was still runny, which worked like a charm. The lid trapped the heat and moisture to steam the top of the omelet, and it partially melted the cheese as well. Now we had a perfectly cooked omelet for four, with tender eggs and bits of melted cheese in every bite.

Family-Size Cheese Omelet

SERVES 4

Monterey Jack, Colby, or any other good melting cheese can be substituted for the cheddar.

- 8 large eggs
- ½ teaspoon table salt
- ⅛ teaspoon ground black pepper
- 2 tablespoons unsalted butter
- 3 ounces cheddar cheese, shredded
  (about ¾ cup; see note)

1. Whisk the eggs, salt, and pepper together in a medium bowl. Melt the butter in a 12-inch nonstick skillet over medium heat, swirling to coat the pan.

2. Add the eggs and cook, stirring gently in a circular motion, until the mixture is slightly thickened, about 1 minute. Following the photos, use a heatproof rubber spatula to pull the cooked edges of the egg toward the center of the pan, tilting the pan so the uncooked egg runs to the cleared edge of the pan. Repeat until the bottom of the omelet is just set but the top is still runny, about 1 minute. Cover the skillet, reduce the heat to low, and cook until the top of the omelet begins to set but is still moist, about 5 minutes.

3. Remove the pan from the heat. Sprinkle the cheddar evenly over the eggs, cover, and let sit until the cheese partially melts, about 1 minute. Slide half of the omelet onto a warmed platter using the spatula, then tilt the skillet so the remaining omelet flips over onto itself, forming a half-moon shape. Cut into wedges and serve.

HOW TO MAKE AN OVERSIZED OMELET

1. Pull the cooked edges of the egg toward the center of the pan and allow the raw egg to run to the edges.

2. When the omelet is set on the bottom but still very runny on the top, cover the skillet and reduce the heat to low.

3. After the top of the omelet begins to set, sprinkle with the cheese and let the omelet rest off the heat, covered, until the cheese has partially melted.

4. After using a heatproof rubber spatula to slide half of the omelet out onto a platter, tilt the skillet so that the omelet folds over onto itself to make the traditional half-moon shape.

DENVER OMELETS

WHY THIS RECIPE WORKS: A substantial Denver omelet has become a breakfast feature in American restaurants and diners. Filled with ham and lots of vegetables in addition to cheese, it's a meal in itself. But it's hard to get the vegetables cooked without overcooking the eggs.

Cooking the filling separately, before the eggs, seemed to be the best way to avoid undercooked vegetables. In addition to the standard onion and green bell pepper, we also included red bell pepper, which made for a more colorful filling. Instead of julienning the vegetables, we finely chopped them; this made our filling easier to eat, and the peppers' skin was less intrusive. Ham steak was the easiest kind of ham to dice; it also imparted a welcome smoky flavor to the rest of the filling. For more complexity of flavor, we included garlic and parsley, which are unusual in a Denver omelet, and a dash of hot sauce livened things up without adding too much spiciness. We cooked the eggs according to our tried-and-true method, with some dairy (we used a little heavy cream, but milk worked as well) to keep the eggs from drying out, and added the warm filling just before folding the omelet onto a plate. Both components—eggs and filling—were perfectly cooked.

Denver Omelets

SERVES 2

You can make one omelet after another in the same pan, although you may need to reduce the heat. Refer to the photos for "How to Make an Oversized Omelet" on page 640—the steps are similar to the ones used here.

 6 large eggs
 2 tablespoons heavy cream or milk
 ½ teaspoon table salt
 ¼ teaspoon ground black pepper
 2 tablespoons unsalted butter
 4 ounces Monterey Jack cheese, shredded (about 1 cup)
 1 recipe Filling for Denver Omelets (recipe follows)

1. Whisk together 3 of the eggs, 1 tablespoon of the cream, ¼ teaspoon of the salt, and ⅛ teaspoon of the pepper in a small bowl until thoroughly combined.

2. Melt 1 tablespoon of the butter in a 10-inch nonstick skillet over medium-high heat until it just begins to brown, swirling to coat the pan. Add the eggs to the skillet and cook until the edges begin to set, 2 to 3 seconds, then, with a heat-

proof rubber spatula, stir in a circular motion until slightly thickened, about 10 seconds. Use the spatula to pull the cooked edges into the center, then tilt the pan to one side so that the uncooked egg runs to the edge of the pan. Repeat until the omelet is just set but still moist on the surface, 1 to 2 minutes.

3. Sprinkle ½ cup of the cheese evenly over the eggs and allow to partially melt, 15 to 20 seconds. With the handle of the pan facing you, spoon half the filling over the left side of the omelet. Following step 4 on page 640, slide the filling-topped half of the omelet onto a warmed plate using the spatula, then tilt the skillet so the remaining omelet folds over the filling in a half-moon shape; set aside. Repeat the instructions for the second omelet. Serve.

Filling for Denver Omelets

MAKES ENOUGH TO FILL 2 OMELETS

A ham steak is our top choice for this recipe, although canned ham and sliced deli ham will work. (If using sliced deli ham, add it with the garlic, parsley, and hot sauce.)

 1 tablespoon unsalted butter
 ½ red bell pepper, stemmed, seeded, and chopped fine
 ½ green bell pepper, stemmed, seeded, and chopped fine
 1 small onion, minced
 ¼ teaspoon table salt
 4 ounces ham steak, diced (about 1 cup; see note)
 1 tablespoon minced fresh parsley leaves
 1 garlic clove, minced or pressed through a garlic press (about 1 teaspoon)
 ½ teaspoon hot sauce

Melt the butter in a 10-inch nonstick skillet over medium-high heat. Add the peppers, onion, and salt and cook, stirring occasionally, until the onion begins to soften, 5 to 7 minutes. Add the ham and cook until the peppers begin to brown, about 2 minutes. Add the parsley, garlic, and hot sauce and cook for 30 seconds. Transfer to a small bowl and cover to keep warm.

FRENCH OMELETS

WHY THIS RECIPE WORKS: In contrast to half-moon diner-style omelets, the French omelet is a pristine rolled affair. The temperature of the pan must be just right, the eggs beaten just so, and hand movements must be swift. We decided to ditch the stuffy attitude and come up with a foolproof method for making the ideal French omelet—unblemished golden yellow with an ultra-creamy texture, rolled around minimal filling.

The classic method requires a black carbon steel omelet pan and a fork, but a nonstick skillet worked fine here. Instead of a fork, which scraped our nonstick pans, bamboo skewers and wooden chopsticks gave us small curds with a silky texture. Preheating the pan for 10 minutes over low heat eliminated any hot spots. For creaminess, we added very cold butter, which dispersed evenly and fused with the eggs for a moist, rich omelet. To keep the omelet light, we found the perfect number of strokes; excessive beating unravels egg proteins, leading to denseness. We tried different heat levels, but even at medium heat, the omelet cooked so quickly it was hard to judge when it was done, so we turned off the heat when it was still runny and covered it to finish cooking. Finally, for an easy rolling method, we slid the omelet onto a paper towel and used the towel to roll the omelet into the sought-after cylinder.

French Omelets

SERVES 2

Because making these omelets is such a quick process, make sure to have all your ingredients and equipment at the ready. If you don't have skewers or chopsticks to stir the eggs in step 3, use the handle of a wooden spoon. Warm the plates in a 200-degree oven.

> 2 tablespoons unsalted butter, cut into 2 pieces
> ½ teaspoon vegetable oil
> 6 large eggs, chilled
>   Table salt and ground black pepper
> 2 tablespoons shredded Gruyère cheese
> 4 teaspoons minced fresh chives

1. Cut 1 tablespoon of the butter in half. Cut the remaining 1 tablespoon butter into small pieces, transfer to a small bowl, and place in the freezer while preparing the eggs and the skillet, at least 10 minutes. Meanwhile, heat the oil in an 8-inch nonstick skillet over low heat for 10 minutes.

2. Crack 2 of the eggs into a medium bowl and separate a third egg; reserve the white for another use and add the yolk to the bowl. Add ⅛ teaspoon salt and a pinch of pepper. Break the yolks with a fork, then beat the eggs at a moderate pace, about 80 strokes, until the yolks and whites are well combined. Stir in half of the frozen butter cubes.

3. When the skillet is fully heated, use paper towels to wipe out the oil, leaving a thin film on the bottom and sides of the skillet. Add half of the reserved 1 tablespoon butter to the skillet and heat until melted. Swirl the butter to coat the skillet, add the egg mixture, and increase the heat to medium-high. Following the photos, use two chopsticks or wooden skewers to scramble the eggs using a quick circular motion to move around the skillet, scraping the cooked egg from the side of the skillet as you go, until the eggs are almost cooked but still slightly runny, 45 to 90 seconds. Turn off the heat (remove the skillet from the heat if using an electric burner) and smooth the eggs into an even layer using a heatproof rubber

spatula. Sprinkle the omelet with 1 tablespoon of the Gruyère and 2 teaspoons of the chives. Cover the skillet with a tight-fitting lid and let sit, 1 minute for a runnier omelet and 2 minutes for a firmer omelet.

4. Heat the skillet over low heat for 20 seconds, uncover, and, using a heatproof rubber spatula, loosen the edges of the omelet from the skillet. Place a folded square of paper towel onto a warmed plate and slide the omelet out of the skillet onto the paper towel so that the omelet lies flat on the plate and hangs about 1 inch off the paper towel. Roll the omelet into a neat cylinder and set aside. Return the skillet to low heat and heat for 2 minutes before repeating the instructions for the second omelet starting with step 2. Serve.

NOTES FROM THE TEST KITCHEN

MAKING A FRENCH OMELET

1. Add the beaten egg mixture to the skillet and stir with chopsticks to produce small curds, which result in a silkier texture.

2. Turn off the heat while the eggs are still runny; smooth with a spatula into an even layer.

3. After sprinkling with the cheese and chives, cover so the residual heat gently finishes cooking the omelet.

4. Slide the finished omelet onto a paper towel–lined plate. Use the paper towel to lift the omelet and roll it up.

6 tablespoons plus 1 teaspoon extra-virgin olive oil
   (see note)

1½ pounds (3 to 4 medium) Yukon Gold potatoes, peeled,
   quartered, and cut into ⅛-inch-thick slices

1 small onion, halved and sliced thin

1 teaspoon table salt

¼ teaspoon ground black pepper

8 large eggs

½ cup jarred roasted red peppers, rinsed, dried,
   and cut into ½-inch pieces

½ cup frozen peas, thawed
   Garlic Mayonnaise (optional; recipe follows)

SPANISH TORTILLA

WHY THIS RECIPE WORKS: This classic Spanish omelet is immensely appealing, but can be greasy, dense, and heavy if prepared incorrectly. Typical recipes call for up to 4 cups of extra-virgin olive oil to cook the potatoes, which can lead to an overly oily—and expensive—tortilla. We wanted an intensely rich, velvety, melt-in-your-mouth egg-and-potato omelet—that didn't require using a quart of oil.

We first stuck with the traditional volume of olive oil until we could determine the proper type and ratio of ingredients. We chose starchy russet potatoes, thinly sliced, and standard yellow onions, which had a sweet, mellow flavor. We also settled on the perfect ratio of eggs to potatoes that allowed the tortilla to set firm and tender, with the eggs and potatoes melding into one another. Next we set out to reduce the amount of oil. Unfortunately, with less oil in the pan, half the potatoes were frying, while the other half were steaming. We started over with slightly firmer, less starchy Yukon Golds. With a fraction of the oil in the skillet, they were a winner: starchy enough to become meltingly tender as they cooked, but sturdy enough to stir and flip halfway through cooking with few breaks. Finally, we had to determine the best way to flip the omelet. To do this, we simply slid the tortilla out of the pan and onto one plate. Then, placing another plate upside down over the tortilla, we easily flipped the whole thing and slid the tortilla back in the pan, making a once-messy task easy and foolproof.

Spanish Tortilla with Roasted Red Peppers and Peas

SERVES 4 TO 6

Spanish tortillas are often served warm or at room temperature with olives, pickles, and Garlic Mayonnaise (recipe follows) as an appetizer. They may also be served with a salad as a light entrée. For the most traditional tortilla, omit the roasted red peppers and peas. See page 916 for our top-rated extra-virgin olive oil.

1. Toss 4 tablespoons of the oil, the potatoes, onion, ½ teaspoon of the salt, and the pepper in a large bowl until the potato slices are thoroughly separated and coated in oil. Heat 2 tablespoons more oil in a 10-inch nonstick skillet over medium-high heat until shimmering. Reduce the heat to medium-low, add the potato mixture to the skillet, and set the bowl aside (do not rinse). Cover and cook, stirring occasionally with a heatproof rubber spatula, until the potatoes offer no resistance when poked with a paring knife, 22 to 28 minutes (some potato slices may break into smaller pieces).

2. Meanwhile, whisk the eggs and remaining ½ teaspoon salt in the reserved bowl until just combined. Using a heatproof rubber spatula, fold the hot potato mixture, red peppers, and peas into the eggs until combined, making sure to scrape all the potato mixture out of the skillet. Return the skillet to medium-high heat, add the remaining 1 teaspoon oil, and heat until just beginning to smoke. Add the egg-potato mixture and cook, shaking the pan and folding the mixture constantly for 15 seconds; smooth the top of the mixture with a heatproof rubber spatula. Reduce the heat to medium, cover, and cook, gently shaking the pan every 30 seconds, until the bottom is golden brown and the top is lightly set, about 2 minutes.

3. Using a heatproof rubber spatula, loosen the tortilla from the pan, shaking it back and forth until the tortilla slides around. Slide the tortilla onto a large plate. Invert the tortilla onto a second large plate and slide it, browned side up, back into the skillet. Tuck the edges of the tortilla into the skillet. Return the pan to medium heat and continue to cook, gently shaking the pan every 30 seconds, until the second side is golden brown, about 2 minutes longer. Slide the tortilla onto a cutting board; cool for at least 15 minutes. Cut the tortilla into cubes or wedges and serve with Garlic Mayonnaise (if using).

Spanish Tortilla with Chorizo and Scallions

Use a cured, Spanish-style chorizo for this recipe. Portuguese linguiça is a suitable substitute.

Follow the recipe for Spanish Tortilla with Roasted Red Peppers and Peas, omitting the roasted red peppers and peas. In step 1, heat 4 ounces Spanish-style chorizo, cut into ¼-inch pieces, with 1 tablespoon oil (reduced from 2 tablespoons) in a 10-inch nonstick skillet over medium-high heat, stirring occasionally, until the chorizo is browned and the fat has rendered, about 5 minutes. Proceed with the recipe as directed, adding the potato mixture to the skillet with the chorizo and rendered fat and folding 4 thinly sliced scallions into the eggs in step 2.

Garlic Mayonnaise
MAKES ABOUT 1¼ CUPS

- 2 large egg yolks
- 2 teaspoons Dijon mustard
- 2 teaspoons juice from 1 lemon
- 1 medium garlic clove, minced or pressed through a garlic press (about 1 teaspoon)
- ¾ cup vegetable oil
- 1 tablespoon water
- ¼ cup extra-virgin olive oil
- ½ teaspoon table salt
- ¼ teaspoon ground black pepper

Process the yolks, mustard, lemon juice, and garlic in a food processor until combined, about 10 seconds. With the machine running, slowly drizzle in the vegetable oil, about 1 minute. Transfer the mixture to a medium bowl and whisk in the water. Whisking constantly, slowly drizzle in the olive oil, about 30 seconds. Whisk in the salt and pepper. (The mayonnaise can be refrigerated in an airtight container for up to 4 days.)

THICK AND HEARTY FRITTATAS

WHY THIS RECIPE WORKS: A frittata loaded with meat and vegetables often ends up dry, overstuffed, and overcooked. We wanted a frittata big enough to make a substantial meal for 6 to 8 people—with a pleasing balance of egg to filling, firm yet moist eggs, and a lightly browned crust. We started with a dozen eggs, which we found required 3 cups of cooked vegetables and meat to create the best balance. When we chose our fillings, we needed to be a little selective about the cheese—Gruyère and goat cheese both had just the right amount of moisture. Most any vegetable or meat can be added to a frittata, with two caveats: The food must be cut into small pieces, and it must be precooked to drive off excess moisture and fat. A little half-and-half added a touch of creaminess. Given the large number of eggs, we had to shorten the time the frittata spent on the stovetop so the bottom wouldn't scorch. We started the eggs on medium heat and stirred them so they could cook quickly yet evenly. With the eggs still on the wet side, we slid the skillet under the broiler until the top had puffed and browned, but removed it while the eggs in the center were still slightly wet and runny, allowing the residual heat to finish the cooking.

Asparagus, Ham, and Gruyère Frittata
SERVES 6 TO 8
A 12-inch ovensafe nonstick skillet is necessary for this recipe. Because broilers vary so much in intensity, watch the frittata carefully as it cooks.

- 12 large eggs
- 3 tablespoons half-and-half
- ½ teaspoon table salt
- ¼ teaspoon ground black pepper
- 2 teaspoons olive oil
- 8 ounces asparagus, tough ends trimmed, spears cut on the bias into ¼-inch pieces
- 4 ounces ¼-inch-thick deli ham, cut into ½-inch cubes (about ¾ cup)
- 1 medium shallot, minced (about 3 tablespoons)
- 3 ounces Gruyère cheese, cut into ¼-inch cubes (about ¾ cup)

1. Adjust an oven rack about 5 inches from the broiler element and heat the broiler. Whisk the eggs, half-and-half, salt, and pepper together in a medium bowl. Set aside.

2. Heat the oil in a 12-inch ovensafe nonstick skillet over medium heat until shimmering; add the asparagus and cook, stirring occasionally, until lightly browned and almost tender, about 3 minutes. Add the ham and shallot and cook until the shallot softens, about 2 minutes.

3. Stir the Gruyère into the eggs; add the egg mixture to the skillet and cook, using a heatproof rubber spatula to stir and scrape the bottom of the skillet, until large curds form and the spatula begins to leave a wake but the eggs are still very wet, about 2 minutes. Shake the skillet to distribute the eggs evenly and cook without stirring to let the bottom set, about 30 seconds.

4. Slide the skillet under the broiler and cook until the surface is puffed and spotty brown, yet the center remains slightly wet and runny when cut into with a paring knife, 3 to 4 minutes. Using a potholder (the skillet handle will be hot), remove the skillet from the oven and let stand for 5 minutes to finish cooking; using the spatula, loosen the frittata from the skillet and slide it onto a platter or cutting board. Cut into wedges and serve.

Leek, Prosciutto, and Goat Cheese Frittata
SERVES 6 TO 8
A 12-inch ovensafe nonstick skillet is necessary for this recipe. The goat cheese will crumble more easily if it is chilled.

- 12 large eggs
- 3 tablespoons half-and-half
  Table salt and ground black pepper
- 2 tablespoons unsalted butter
- 2 small leeks, white and light green parts only, halved lengthwise, sliced thin, and rinsed thoroughly (about 3 cups)
- 3 ounces very thinly sliced prosciutto, cut into ½-inch-wide strips
- ¼ cup chopped fresh basil leaves
- 4 ounces goat cheese, crumbled (about 1 cup; see note)

1. Adjust an oven rack about 5 inches from the broiler element and heat the broiler. Whisk the eggs, half-and-half, ½ teaspoon salt, and ¼ teaspoon pepper together in a medium bowl. Set aside.

2. Melt the butter in a 12-inch ovensafe nonstick skillet over medium heat. Add the leeks and ¼ teaspoon salt; reduce the heat to low and cook, covered, stirring occasionally, until softened, 8 to 10 minutes.

3. Stir the prosciutto, basil, and ½ cup of the goat cheese into the eggs; add the egg mixture to the skillet and cook, using a heatproof rubber spatula to stir and scrape the bottom of the skillet, until large curds form and the spatula begins to leave a wake but the eggs are still very wet, about 2 minutes. Shake the skillet to distribute the eggs evenly and cook without stirring to let the bottom set, about 30 seconds.

4. Distribute the remaining ½ cup goat cheese evenly over the frittata. Slide the skillet under the broiler and cook until the surface is puffed and spotty brown, yet the center remains slightly wet and runny when cut into with a paring knife, 3 to 4 minutes. Using a potholder (the skillet handle will be hot), remove the skillet from the oven and let stand for 5 minutes to finish cooking; using the spatula, loosen the frittata from the skillet and slide it onto a platter or cutting board. Cut into wedges and serve.

QUICHE

WHY THIS RECIPE WORKS: A really good quiche should have a smooth, creamy custard in a tender pastry crust. The custard should be rich, but not overwhelmingly so, and moist, not dried out. We aimed to find a way to make this perfect pie.

We experimented with multiple combinations of egg and dairy to find the one that would provide just the right balance of richness and lightness. Eggs alone were not rich enough; whole eggs plus yolks provided the degree of richness we wanted. For the dairy component, we found that equal parts of milk and heavy cream worked best. This custard was creamy and smooth. After layering bacon and Gruyère over the bottom of the pie shell—for a classic quiche Lorraine—we poured the custard on top and baked the quiche until it was puffed and set around the edges but still jiggled in the center; the residual heat finished cooking the center without turning the top into a rubbery skin. Before serving the quiche, we let it cool on a wire rack, which is a small but important step; this allows air to circulate under the crust and prevents it from becoming soggy.

Quiche Lorraine
SERVES 8

The center of the quiche will be surprisingly soft when it comes out of the oven, but the filling will continue to set (and sink somewhat) as it cools. If the pie shell has been previously baked and cooled, place it in the heating oven for about five minutes to warm it, making sure that it does not burn.

- 1   recipe Basic Single-Crust Pie Dough (page 842), fitted into a 9-inch pie plate and chilled
- 8   ounces bacon (about 8 slices), cut into ½-inch pieces
- 2   large whole eggs plus 2 large egg yolks
- 1   cup whole milk

- 1   cup heavy cream
- ½   teaspoon table salt
- ½   teaspoon ground white pepper
      Pinch freshly grated nutmeg
- 4   ounces Gruyère cheese, shredded (about 1 cup)

1. Adjust an oven rack to the middle position and heat the oven to 375 degrees. Following the photos on page 856, line the chilled crust with a double layer of foil and fill with pie weights. Bake until the pie dough looks dry and is light in color, 25 to 30 minutes. Transfer the pie plate to a wire rack and remove the weights and foil.

2. Cook the bacon in a 12-inch nonstick skillet over medium heat until crisp, about 5 minutes. Using a slotted spoon, transfer the bacon to a paper towel–lined plate. Whisk the remaining ingredients except the Gruyère together in a medium bowl.

3. Spread the Gruyère and bacon evenly over the bottom of the warm pie shell and set the shell on the oven rack. Pour the custard mixture into the pie shell (it should come to about ½ inch below the crust's rim). Bake until light golden brown and a knife blade inserted about 1 inch from the edge comes out clean and the center feels set but still soft, 32 to 35 minutes. Transfer the quiche to a wire rack and cool. Serve warm or at room temperature.

BREAKFAST STRATA

WHY THIS RECIPE WORKS: A classic breakfast dish, strata is easy to prepare, presents a variety of flavors, can feed a crowd and, perhaps best of all, can and indeed should be made ahead of time. Too often, though, it is overloaded with fillings; we wanted a savory bread pudding with a balanced, well-seasoned filling.

Recipes recommend all kinds of bread to use; we liked supermarket French or Italian loaves, which were neutral in flavor but had a sturdy texture. Rather than cubing the bread, which is often recommended, we sliced it to retain the layered quality of the dish and let the slices dry slightly (stale bread held up better than fresh). We used whole eggs and half-and-half for the custard, with a tad more dairy than eggs, and increased the amount of custard to saturate the bread more fully. A surprisingly successful addition to the custard was white wine, which we reduced to evaporate the alcohol; it brightened all the flavors. A key to ensuring cohesiveness in the strata was weighting it while it rested for at least one hour; this way, every piece of bread absorbed some custard. We kept our fillings minimal so they wouldn't overwhelm the bread and custard, and we sautéed the filling ingredients before adding them to the casserole to keep moisture from turning the dish watery.

Breakfast Strata with Spinach and Gruyère

SERVES 6

To weigh down the assembled strata, use two 1-pound boxes of sugar, laid side by side over the plastic-covered surface. To double this recipe, use a 13 by 9-inch baking dish greased with 1½ tablespoons butter and increase the baking time in step 5 to 1 hour and 20 minutes.

8-10 (½-inch-thick) slices supermarket French
        or Italian bread
   5 tablespoons unsalted butter, softened
   4 medium shallots, minced (about ½ cup)
   1 (10-ounce) package frozen chopped spinach,
        thawed and squeezed dry
        Table salt and ground black pepper
   ½ cup dry white wine
   6 ounces Gruyère cheese, shredded (about 1½ cups)
   6 large eggs
  1¾ cups half-and-half

1. Adjust an oven rack to the middle position and heat the oven to 225 degrees. Arrange the bread in a single layer on a large baking sheet and bake until dry and crisp, about 40 minutes, turning the slices over halfway through the baking time. (Alternatively, leave the slices out overnight to dry.) Let the bread cool completely, then spread butter evenly over one side of each bread slice, using 2 tablespoons of the butter; set aside.

2. Heat 2 tablespoons more butter in a medium nonstick skillet over medium heat. Add the shallots and cook until softened, about 3 minutes; add the spinach and salt and pepper to taste and cook until the spinach is warm, about 2 minutes. Transfer to a medium bowl and set aside. Add the wine to the skillet, increase the heat to medium-high, and simmer until reduced to ¼ cup, 2 to 3 minutes; set aside.

3. Butter an 8-inch square baking dish with the remaining 1 tablespoon butter; arrange half of the bread slices, buttered-side up, in a single layer in the dish. Sprinkle half of the spinach mixture, then ½ cup of the shredded Gruyère, evenly over the bread slices. Arrange the remaining bread slices in a single layer over the cheese; sprinkle the remaining spinach mixture and ½ cup more Gruyère evenly over the bread. Whisk the eggs in a medium bowl until combined; whisk in the reduced wine, half-and-half, 1 teaspoon salt, and a pinch of pepper. Pour the egg mixture evenly over the bread layers.

4. Wrap the strata tightly with plastic wrap, pressing the wrap against the surface of the strata. Weigh the strata down (see note), and refrigerate for at least 1 hour or up to 24 hours.

5. Remove the dish from the refrigerator and let stand at room temperature for 20 minutes. Meanwhile, adjust an oven rack to the middle position and heat the oven to 325 degrees. Uncover the strata and sprinkle the remaining ½ cup Gruyère evenly over the surface; bake until both edges and center are puffed and the edges have pulled away slightly from the sides of the dish, 50 to 55 minutes. Cool on a wire rack for 5 minutes and serve.

Breakfast Strata with Sausage, Mushrooms, and Monterey Jack

To double this recipe, use a 13 by 9-inch baking dish greased with 1½ tablespoons butter and increase the baking time in step 5 to 1 hour and 20 minutes.

8-10 (½-inch-thick) slices supermarket French
        or Italian bread
   3 tablespoons unsalted butter, softened
   8 ounces bulk breakfast sausage, crumbled
   3 medium shallots, minced (about 6 tablespoons)
   8 ounces white mushrooms, wiped clean and quartered
        Table salt and ground black pepper
   ½ cup dry white wine
   6 ounces Monterey Jack cheese, shredded
        (about 1½ cups)
   6 large eggs
  1¾ cups half-and-half
   2 tablespoons minced fresh parsley leaves

Follow the recipe for Breakfast Strata with Spinach and Gruyère through step 1. Fry the sausage in a medium nonstick skillet over medium heat, breaking the sausage apart with a wooden spoon, until it loses its raw color and begins to brown, about 4 minutes; add the shallots and cook, stirring frequently, until softened, about 3 minutes. Add the mushrooms to the skillet and cook until the mushrooms no longer release liquid, about 6 minutes; transfer to a medium bowl and season with salt and pepper to taste. Reduce the wine as directed in step 2; continue with the recipe from step 3, adding the parsley to the egg mixture along with the salt and pepper and substituting the sausage mixture for the spinach and the Monterey Jack for the Gruyère.

BLUEBERRY PANCAKES

WHY THIS RECIPE WORKS: Blueberry pancakes sound appetizing, but they are often tough and rubbery or dense and soggy. And they inevitably take on an unappealing blue-gray hue. We wanted pancakes that cooked up light and fluffy and were studded with sweet, tangy bursts of summer's best berry.

Starting with the pancakes themselves, we determined that unbleached flour, sugar, a little salt, and both baking powder and baking soda were essential for the dry ingredients. One egg added just enough structure and richness without making the pancakes overly eggy. Buttermilk was the preferred dairy component, but since our ground rules were to use only what most home cooks would be likely to have on hand, we searched for a substitute. Lemon juice thickens milk almost to the consistency of buttermilk and adds a similar tang that tasters actually preferred. Some melted butter added to the mix prevented our pancakes from being dry and bland. Mixing the batter too strenuously leads to tough pancakes; it's time to stop mixing when there are still a few lumps and streaks of flour. Once we had great-tasting pancakes, we turned to the blueberries. Stirring them into the batter would obviously lead to smashing and those blue-gray streaks, so rather than incorporating the berries, we simply dropped some onto the batter after we'd ladled it into the skillet. Smaller wild berries are sweeter than the larger ones, but frozen berries work as well as fresh, which means we can have great blueberry pancakes any time of the year.

Blueberry Pancakes
MAKES ABOUT SIXTEEN 4-INCH PANCAKES, SERVING 4 TO 6
To make sure that frozen berries do not bleed, rinse them under cool water in a mesh strainer until the water runs clear, and then spread them on a paper towel–lined plate to dry. If you have buttermilk on hand, use 2 cups instead of the milk and lemon juice. To keep pancakes warm while cooking the remaining batter, hold them in a 200-degree oven on a greased rack set over a baking sheet.

2 cups milk (see note)
1 tablespoon juice from 1 lemon (see note)
2 cups (10 ounces) unbleached all-purpose flour
2 tablespoons sugar
2 teaspoons baking powder
½ teaspoon baking soda
½ teaspoon table salt
1 large egg
3 tablespoons unsalted butter, melted and cooled slightly
1-2 teaspoons vegetable oil
1 cup fresh or frozen blueberries, preferably wild, rinsed and dried (see note)

1. Whisk the milk and lemon juice together in a medium bowl or large measuring cup; set aside to thicken while preparing the other ingredients. Whisk the flour, sugar, baking powder, baking soda, and salt together in a medium bowl.

2. Whisk the egg and melted butter into the milk until combined. Make a well in the center of the dry ingredients in the bowl; pour in the milk mixture and whisk very gently until just combined (a few lumps should remain). Do not overmix.

3. Heat a 12-inch nonstick skillet over medium heat for 3 to 5 minutes; add 1 teaspoon of the oil and brush to coat the skillet bottom evenly. Pour ¼ cup batter onto three spots on the skillet; sprinkle 1 tablespoon of the blueberries over each pancake. Cook the pancakes until large bubbles begin to appear, 1½ to 2 minutes. Using a thin-bladed spatula, flip the pancakes and cook until golden brown on the second side, 1 to 1½ minutes longer. Serve and repeat with the remaining batter, using the remaining 1 teaspoon vegetable oil if necessary.

GERMAN PANCAKE

WHY THIS RECIPE WORKS: Our German pancake achieves its dramatic appearance and contrasting textures thanks to a few test kitchen tricks. First, we mixed up a simple batter containing just the right amounts of eggs, flour, and milk to produce a pancake with crispy yet tender edges and a custardy center. To produce a tall, puffy rim and an even, substantial center, we started the pancake in a cold oven and then turned the heat to 375 degrees. This allowed the center of the pancake to begin to set up before the rim got hot enough to puff up substantially. Finally, we put fruit and other ingredients on as a topping rather than baking them into the pancake. Without fruit to weigh things down, the pancake puffed dramatically and its texture remained delicate and uniform.

German Pancake

SERVES 4

A traditional 12-inch skillet may be used in place of the non-stick skillet; coat it lightly with vegetable oil spray before using. As an alternative to sugar and lemon juice, serve the pancake with maple syrup or our Brown Sugar–Apple Topping (recipe follows).

1¾	cups (8¾ ounces) all-purpose flour
¼	cup sugar
1	tablespoon grated lemon zest plus 1 tablespoon juice
½	teaspoon salt
⅛	teaspoon ground nutmeg
1½	cups milk
6	large eggs
1½	teaspoons vanilla extract
3	tablespoons unsalted butter

1. Whisk flour, 3 tablespoons sugar, lemon zest, salt, and nutmeg together in large bowl. Whisk milk, eggs, and vanilla together in second bowl. Whisk two-thirds of milk mixture

into flour mixture until no lumps remain, then slowly whisk in remaining milk mixture until smooth.

2. Adjust oven rack to lower-middle position. Melt butter in 12-inch ovensafe nonstick skillet over medium-low heat. Add batter to skillet, immediately transfer to oven, and set oven to 375 degrees. Bake until edges are deep golden brown and center is beginning to brown, 30 to 35 minutes.

3. Transfer skillet to wire rack and sprinkle pancake with lemon juice and remaining 1 tablespoon sugar. Gently transfer pancake to cutting board, cut into wedges, and serve.

Brown Sugar–Apple Topping

MAKES ABOUT 2 CUPS

You can substitute Honeycrisp or Fuji apples for the Braeburn apples, if desired.

2	tablespoons unsalted butter
⅓	cup water
¼	cup packed (1¾ ounces) brown sugar
¼	teaspoon ground cinnamon
⅛	teaspoon salt
1¼	pounds Braeburn apples (3 to 4 apples), peeled, cored, halved, and cut into ½-inch-thick wedges, wedges halved crosswise

Melt butter in 12-inch skillet over medium heat. Add water, sugar, cinnamon, and salt and whisk until sugar dissolves. Add apples, increase heat to medium-high, and bring to simmer. Cover and cook, stirring occasionally, for 5 minutes. Uncover and continue to cook until apples are translucent and just tender and sauce is thickened, 5 to 7 minutes longer. Transfer to bowl and serve. (Topping can be refrigerated for up to 2 days.)

GERMAN APPLE PANCAKE

WHY THIS RECIPE WORKS: More akin to popovers than American pancakes, German apple pancakes are golden and puffed outside, custardy inside, with sweet apples baked right in. The dish suffers from many of the same problems as popovers, too: not enough rise, dense texture, and a too-eggy flavor. We wanted to solve these problems and get this pancake just right.

Flour and eggs are the basis of the batter; half-and-half for the dairy component imparted richness and a light texture. Sugar, salt, and vanilla completed the batter. Steam, not leavening, is what puffs the pancake, so to get the maximum rise we needed to find the right oven temperature. A very hot oven burned the exterior of the pancake; preheating the oven to a high temperature as well as preheating the pan, then lowering the temperature when the pancake went in, proved the ideal method. Granny Smith apples were our top pick if you like a little tartness; otherwise Braeburns are a good choice for their sweetness. We cooked apples with brown sugar rather than granulated for a deeper flavor, along with butter, cinnamon, and a bright touch of lemon juice. To keep the apples from being pushed out of the pan when the pancake rose, we first poured the batter around the edge of the skillet, then over the apples. Our pancake puffed spectacularly, and when we served it, every bite contained warm, tender apples.

German Apple Pancake
SERVES 4

A 10-inch ovensafe skillet is necessary for this recipe; we highly recommend using a nonstick skillet for the sake of easy cleanup, but a regular skillet will work. If you prefer tart apples, use Granny Smiths; if you prefer sweet ones, use Braeburns.

- ½ cup (2½ ounces) unbleached all-purpose flour
- 1 tablespoon granulated sugar
- ½ teaspoon table salt
- 2 large eggs
- ⅔ cup half-and-half
- 1 teaspoon vanilla extract
- 2 tablespoons unsalted butter
- 1¼ pounds Granny Smith or Braeburn apples (3 to 4 large apples), peeled, quartered, cored, and cut into ½-inch-thick slices (see note)
- ¼ cup packed (1¾ ounces) light or dark brown sugar
- ¼ teaspoon ground cinnamon
- 1 teaspoon juice from 1 lemon
  Confectioners' sugar, for dusting
  Maple syrup or Caramel Sauce (recipe follows), for serving

1. Adjust an oven rack to the upper-middle position and heat the oven to 500 degrees.

2. Whisk the flour, granulated sugar, and salt together in a medium bowl. In a second medium bowl, whisk the eggs, half-and-half, and vanilla together until combined. Add the liquid ingredients to the dry ingredients and whisk until no lumps remain, about 20 seconds; set the batter aside.

3. Melt the butter in a 10-inch ovensafe nonstick skillet over medium-high heat. Add the apples, brown sugar, and cinnamon; cook, stirring frequently with a heatproof rubber spatula, until the apples are golden brown, about 10 minutes. Off the heat, stir in the lemon juice.

4. Working quickly, pour the batter around the edge of the pan and then over the apples. Place the skillet in the oven and immediately reduce the oven temperature to 425 degrees. Bake until the pancake edges are brown and puffy and have risen above the edges of the skillet, about 18 minutes.

5. Using a potholder (the skillet handle will be hot), remove the skillet from the oven and loosen the pancake edges with a heatproof rubber spatula; invert the pancake onto a platter. Dust with confectioners' sugar, cut into wedges, and serve with maple syrup or Caramel Sauce.

Caramel Sauce
MAKES ABOUT 1½ CUPS

Cooking the sugar with some water in a covered pot helps trap moisture and ensures that the sugar will dissolve. When the hot cream mixture is added in step 3, the hot sugar syrup will bubble vigorously (and dangerously), so don't use a smaller saucepan. If you make the caramel sauce ahead, reheat it in the microwave or a small saucepan over low heat until warm and fluid.

- ½ cup water
- 1 cup (7 ounces) sugar
- 1 cup heavy cream
- ⅛ teaspoon table salt
- ½ teaspoon vanilla extract
- ½ teaspoon juice from 1 lemon

1. Place the water in a 2-quart saucepan; pour the sugar into the center of the pan, taking care not to let the sugar crystals stick to the sides of the pan. Cover and bring the mixture to a boil over high heat; once the mixture is boiling, uncover the pan and continue to boil until the sugar syrup is thick and straw-colored and registers 300 degrees on an instant-read thermometer, about 7 minutes. Reduce the heat to medium and continue to cook until the syrup is deep amber and registers 350 degrees, 1 to 2 minutes.

2. Meanwhile, bring the cream and salt to a simmer in a small saucepan over high heat (if the cream boils before the sugar syrup reaches a deep amber color, remove the cream from the heat and cover to keep warm).

3. Remove the pan with the sugar syrup from the heat; very carefully pour about one-quarter of the hot cream into it (the mixture will bubble vigorously), and let the bubbling subside. Add the remaining cream, the vanilla, and lemon juice; whisk until the sauce is smooth. (The sauce can be cooled and refrigerated in an airtight container for up to 2 weeks.)

LEMON RICOTTA PANCAKES

WHY THIS RECIPE WORKS: Light, fluffy ricotta pancakes are sophisticated enough for special occasions, but getting the balance of ingredients just right is essential for pancakes that are puffy and tender, not dense and wet. To compensate for the extra weight of the ricotta, we decreased the amount of flour and stirred four whipped egg whites into the batter. Baking soda provided extra rise and aided with browning. Bright, tangy lemon juice complemented the rich, creamy ricotta, and lemon zest enhanced the citrus flavor without watering down the batter. A touch of vanilla extract brought depth and subtle sweetness. For a company-worthy finishing touch, we draped the pancakes with a warm fruit compote.

Lemon Ricotta Pancakes
MAKES 12 (4-INCH) PANCAKES; SERVES 3 TO 4

An electric griddle set at 325 degrees can also be used to cook the pancakes. We prefer the flavor of whole-milk ricotta, but part-skim will work, too; avoid nonfat ricotta. Serve with confectioners' sugar or Pear-Blackberry Topping.

- ⅔ cup (3⅓ ounces) all-purpose flour
- ½ teaspoon baking soda
- ½ teaspoon salt
- 8 ounces (1 cup) whole-milk ricotta cheese
- 2 large eggs, separated, plus 2 large whites
- ⅓ cup whole milk
- 1 teaspoon grated lemon zest plus 4 teaspoons juice
- ½ teaspoon vanilla extract
- 2 tablespoons unsalted butter, melted
- ¼ cup (1¾ ounces) sugar
- 1–2 teaspoons vegetable oil

1. Adjust oven rack to middle position and heat oven to 200 degrees. Spray wire rack set inside rimmed baking sheet with vegetable oil spray; place in oven. Whisk flour, baking soda, and salt together in medium bowl and make well in center. Add ricotta, egg yolks, milk, lemon zest and juice, and vanilla and whisk until just combined. Gently stir in butter.

2. Using stand mixer fitted with whisk, whip egg whites on medium-low speed until foamy, about 1 minute. Increase speed to medium-high and whip whites to soft, billowy mounds, about 1 minute. Gradually add sugar and whip until glossy, soft peaks form, 1 to 2 minutes. Transfer one-third of whipped egg whites to batter and whisk gently until mixture is lightened. Using rubber spatula, gently fold remaining egg whites into batter.

3. Heat 1 teaspoon oil in 12-inch nonstick skillet over medium heat until shimmering. Using paper towels, wipe out oil, leaving thin film on bottom and sides of pan. Using ¼-cup measure or 2-ounce ladle, portion batter into pan in 3 places, leaving 2 inches between portions. Gently spread each portion into a 4-inch round. Cook until edges are set and first side is deep golden brown, 2 to 3 minutes. Using thin, wide spatula, flip pancakes and continue to cook until second side is golden brown, 2 to 3 minutes longer. Serve pancakes immediately or transfer to wire rack in preheated oven. Repeat with remaining batter, using remaining oil as needed.

Pear-Blackberry Topping
MAKES 3 CUPS

- 3 ripe pears, peeled, halved, cored, and cut into ¼-inch pieces
- 1 tablespoon sugar
- 1 teaspoon cornstarch
  Pinch salt
  Pinch ground cardamom
- 5 ounces (1 cup) blackberries, berries more than 1 inch long cut in half crosswise

Combine pears, sugar, cornstarch, salt, and cardamom in bowl and microwave until pears are softened but not mushy and juices are slightly thickened, 4 to 6 minutes, stirring once halfway through microwaving. Stir in blackberries and serve.

100 PERCENT WHOLE-WHEAT PANCAKES

WHY THIS RECIPE WORKS: Most recipes for whole-wheat pancakes call for a mix of white and whole-wheat flours, and they also call for a host of extra flavorings like spices, vanilla, fruit juice, or fruit. Why not just whole-wheat flour? We discovered that using all whole-wheat flour actually delivers light, fluffy, and tender pancakes—not the dense cakes you'd imagine—because whole-wheat flour contains slightly less gluten-forming protein than white flour and because the bran in whole-wheat flour cuts through any gluten strands that do form. Recipes for pancakes made with white flour advise undermixing to avoid dense, tough pancakes, but with whole-wheat flour we were guaranteed light and tender cakes even as we whisked our batter to a smooth, thick consistency. We saw no need to cover up whole wheat's natural flavor with other add-ins; its earthy, nutty taste proved to be the perfect complement to maple syrup. As long as we used a bag of fresh or properly stored (in the freezer) whole-wheat flour, it had just the buttery, nutty flavor we wanted.

100 Percent Whole-Wheat Pancakes
MAKES 15 PANCAKES

An electric griddle set at 350 degrees can be used in place of a skillet. If substituting buttermilk powder and water for fresh buttermilk, use only 2 cups of water to prevent the pancakes from being too wet. To ensure the best flavor, use either recently purchased whole-wheat flour or flour that has been stored in the freezer for less than 12 months. Serve with maple syrup and butter.

- 2 cups (11 ounces) whole-wheat flour
- 2 tablespoons sugar
- 1½ teaspoons baking powder

½ teaspoon baking soda

¾ teaspoon salt

2¼ cups buttermilk

5 tablespoons plus 2 teaspoons vegetable oil

2 large eggs

1. Adjust oven rack to middle position and heat oven to 200 degrees. Spray wire rack set in rimmed baking sheet with vegetable oil spray; place in oven.

2. Whisk flour, sugar, baking powder, baking soda, and salt together in medium bowl. Whisk buttermilk, 5 tablespoons oil, and eggs together in second medium bowl. Make well in center of flour mixture and pour in buttermilk mixture; whisk until smooth. (Mixture will be thick; do not add more buttermilk.)

3. Heat 1 teaspoon oil in 12-inch nonstick skillet over medium heat until shimmering. Using paper towels, carefully wipe out oil, leaving thin film on bottom and sides of pan. Using ¼-cup dry measuring cup or 2-ounce ladle, portion batter into pan in 3 places. Gently spread each portion into 4½-inch round. Cook until edges are set, first side is golden brown, and bubbles on surface are just beginning to break, 2 to 3 minutes. Using thin, wide spatula, flip pancakes and continue to cook until second side is golden brown, 1 to 2 minutes longer. Serve pancakes immediately or transfer to wire rack in oven. Repeat with remaining batter, using remaining 1 teaspoon oil as necessary.

WAFFLES

WHY THIS RECIPE WORKS: You cannot simply put pancake batter in a waffle iron and make waffles; waffles should be moist and fluffy inside and crisp and brown outside—more like a soufflé with a crust than a pancake. We wanted to find the way to achieve this archetypal waffle.

Thick batter is the secret of the crisp exterior and custardy interior of a waffle, so we used a higher proportion of flour to liquid than that of standard recipes. With buttermilk (and buttermilk makes the best-tasting waffles) there's no need for baking powder, and we found that eliminating it also helped crisp up the waffles. A small amount of cornmeal added a pleasing crunch. Separating the egg and folding the whipped white into the batter was a definite improvement; we could see the pockets of air when we cut into a waffle made this way. Like pancakes, waffles turn tough when the batter is over mixed, so we used a light hand, adding the liquid gradually and using more of a folding motion to mix. Cooked to a medium toasty brown, these waffles were everything we wanted them to be.

Buttermilk Waffles
MAKES 3 TO 4 WAFFLES, DEPENDING ON THE SIZE OF THE IRON
The secret to great waffles is a thick batter, so don't expect a pourable batter. The optional dash of cornmeal adds a pleasant crunch to the finished waffle. This recipe can be doubled or tripled. Make toaster waffles out of leftover batter—undercook the waffles a bit, cool them on a wire rack, wrap them in plastic wrap, and freeze. Pop them in the toaster for a quick breakfast. The waffles are best served fresh from the iron but can be held in an oven until all of the batter is used. As you make the waffles, place them on a wire rack set in a rimmed baking sheet, cover them with a clean kitchen towel, and place the baking sheet in a 200-degree oven.

1 cup (5 ounces) unbleached all-purpose flour

1 tablespoon cornmeal (optional; see note)

½ teaspoon table salt

¼ teaspoon baking soda

⅞ cup buttermilk

1 large egg, separated

2 tablespoons unsalted butter, melted and cooled

1. Following the manufacturer's instructions, heat a waffle iron. Whisk the flour, cornmeal (if using), salt, and baking soda together in a medium bowl. In a separate medium bowl, whisk the buttermilk, egg yolk, and melted butter together.

2. Beat the egg white with an electric mixer on medium-low speed until foamy, about 1 minute. Increase the speed to medium-high and whip the whites to stiff peaks, 2 to 4 minutes.

3. Add the liquid ingredients to the dry ingredients in a thin, steady stream while mixing gently with a rubber spatula. (Do not add the liquid faster than you can incorporate it into the batter.) Toward the end of mixing, use a folding motion to incorporate the ingredients. Gently fold the egg white into the batter.

4. Spread an appropriate amount of batter onto the waffle iron. Following the manufacturer's instructions, cook the waffle until golden brown, 2 to 5 minutes. Serve.

EASY BUTTERMILK WAFFLES

WHY THIS RECIPE WORKS: Most waffle recipes are time-consuming affairs. We wanted waffles with a crisp, golden-brown, dimpled crust surrounding a moist, fluffy interior, but for rushed morning schedules, we wanted this recipe to require little more than measuring out some flour and cracking an egg.

To get crisp, the exterior of a waffle must first become dry, and the moist steam racing past the crisping waffle as it cooked was slowing down the process. We needed a drier batter with much more leavening oomph. To do this, we took a cue from a Japanese cooking technique, tempura. In tempura batters, seltzer or club soda is often used in place of still water. The tiny bubbles of carbon dioxide released from the water inflate the batter the same way as a chemical leavener—minus the metallic taste that baking soda and powder sometimes impart. We replaced the buttermilk in our pancake recipe with a mixture of seltzer and powdered buttermilk. The resulting waffles were incredibly light, but not as crisp as we wanted. For better texture, we replaced the melted butter in the recipe with oil—melted butter, which is partly water, had been imparting moisture to the waffles, preventing them from crisping. Best of all, tasters didn't notice the swap, just the excellent flavor and wonderfully crisp texture.

Easy Buttermilk Waffles

MAKES ABOUT EIGHT 7-INCH ROUND WAFFLES

While the waffles can be eaten directly from the waffle iron, they will have a crispier exterior if rested in a warm oven for 10 minutes. Buttermilk powder is available in most supermarkets and is generally located near the dried milk products or in the baking aisle (leftover powder can be kept in the refrigerator for up to a year). Seltzer or club soda gives these waffles their light texture; use a freshly opened container for maximum lift. Avoid Perrier, which is not bubbly enough. Serve with butter and warm maple syrup.

- 2 cups (10 ounces) unbleached all-purpose flour
- ½ cup dried buttermilk powder (see note)
- 1 tablespoon sugar
- ¾ teaspoon table salt
- ½ teaspoon baking soda
- ½ cup sour cream
- 2 large eggs
- ¼ cup vegetable oil
- ¼ teaspoon vanilla extract
- 1¼ cups unflavored seltzer water or club soda (see note)

1. Adjust an oven rack to the middle position and heat the oven to 250 degrees. Set a wire rack over a rimmed baking sheet and place the baking sheet in the oven. Whisk the flour, buttermilk powder, sugar, salt, and baking soda in a large bowl to combine. Whisk the sour cream, eggs, oil, and vanilla in a medium bowl to combine. Gently stir the seltzer into the wet ingredients. Make a well in the center of the dry ingredients and pour in the wet ingredients. Gently stir until just combined. The batter should remain slightly lumpy with streaks of flour.

2. Heat a waffle iron and bake the waffles according to the manufacturer's instructions (use about ⅓ cup for a 7-inch round iron). Transfer the waffles to the rack in the warm oven and hold for up to 10 minutes before serving.

FRENCH TOAST

WHY THIS RECIPE WORKS: When it comes to French toast, the results are rarely worth the trouble. The bread is soggy, too eggy, or just plain bland. We wanted to come up with French toast that's crisp on the outside and soft and puffy on the inside, with rich, custard-like flavor every time.

We first focused on determining which type of bread fared best in a typical batter made with milk and eggs. Tasters eliminated French and Italian breads for being chewy. We then turned to white sandwich bread, which comes in two kinds: regular and hearty. Regular bread was gloppy both inside and out. Hearty bread crisped up nicely on the outside, but still had mushiness. Drying out the bread in a low oven, however, produced French toast that was crisp on the outside and velvety on the inside. As for flavor, tasters thought the French toast tasted overly eggy. We recalled a recipe that required bread dipped in milk mixed with just yolks, versus whole eggs. The yolks-only soaking liquid made a huge difference, turning the taste rich and custardlike. Research revealed that most of the flavor in eggs comes not from the yolk but from the sulfur compounds in the whites, so problem solved. For flavorings, we settled on cinnamon, vanilla, and brown sugar. For nutty butter flavor, we incorporated melted butter into the soaking liquid, warming the milk first to prevent the butter from solidifying. A final bonus—the recipe worked just as well with challah.

French Toast

SERVES 4

For best results, choose a good challah or a firm sandwich bread, such as Arnold Country Classics White or Pepperidge Farm Farmhouse Hearty White. Thomas' English Muffin Toasting Bread also works well. To prevent the butter from clumping during mixing, warm the milk in a microwave or small saucepan until warm to the touch (about 80 degrees). The French toast can be cooked all at once on an electric griddle, but may take an extra 2 to 3 minutes per side. Set the griddle temperature to 350 degrees and use the entire amount of butter for cooking. Serve with warm maple syrup.

- 8 large slices high-quality hearty white sandwich bread or challah (see note)
- 1½ cups whole milk, warmed (see note)
- 3 large egg yolks
- 3 tablespoons light brown sugar
- ½ teaspoon ground cinnamon
- 2 tablespoons unsalted butter, melted, plus 2 tablespoons for cooking
- ¼ teaspoon table salt
- 1 tablespoon vanilla extract

1. Adjust an oven rack to the middle position and heat the oven to 300 degrees. Place the bread on a wire rack set over a rimmed baking sheet. Bake the bread until almost dry throughout (the center should remain slightly moist), about 16 minutes, flipping the slices halfway through cooking. Remove the bread from the rack and let cool for 5 minutes. Return the baking sheet with the wire rack to the oven and reduce the temperature to 200 degrees.

2. Whisk the milk, egg yolks, sugar, cinnamon, 2 tablespoons melted butter, salt, and vanilla in a large bowl until well blended. Transfer the mixture to a 13 by 9-inch baking pan.

3. Soak the bread in the milk mixture until saturated but not falling apart, 20 seconds per side. Using a firm slotted spatula, pick up a bread slice and allow the excess milk mixture to drip off; repeat with the remaining slices. Place the soaked bread on another baking sheet or platter.

4. Heat ½ tablespoon of the butter in a 12-inch skillet over medium-low heat. When the foaming subsides, use a slotted spatula to transfer 2 slices of the soaked bread to the skillet and cook until golden brown, 3 to 4 minutes. Flip and continue to cook until the second side is golden brown, 3 to 4 minutes longer. (If the toast is cooking too quickly, reduce the heat slightly.) Transfer to the baking sheet in the oven. Wipe out the skillet with paper towels. Repeat cooking with the remaining bread, 2 pieces at a time, adding ½ tablespoon more butter for each batch. Serve warm.

CLASSIC BANANA BREAD

WHY THIS RECIPE WORKS: Overripe bananas are a good excuse to make banana bread, but the loaf can be dry, heavy, and bland. We wanted a banana bread with deep banana flavor, plenty of moisture, and a nice, light texture.

Very ripe, darkly speckled bananas contributed moisture as well as flavor to this bread (they're sweeter, too); unripe ones did not work. Pureeing the bananas kept the bread from rising well, so instead we mashed them thoroughly by hand. For additional moisture we included yogurt, which contributed a nice tang without masking the flavor of the bananas. The quick-bread method of mixing—melting the butter and folding the wet ingredients into the dry ones—produced a golden brown loaf and delicate texture; when we tried creaming the butter and sugar first, the bread came out more like butter cake and wasn't as golden brown. However, we found it was important not to overmix the batter; overly vigorous stirring developed excess gluten that turned the loaf tough and dense.

Classic Banana Bread
MAKES ONE 9-INCH LOAF
For best flavor, use bananas that are very ripe.

- 2   cups (10 ounces) unbleached all-purpose flour
- ¾   cup (5¼ ounces) sugar
- ¾   teaspoon baking soda
- ½   teaspoon table salt
- 3   very ripe bananas, mashed well (about 1½ cups)
- ¼   cup plain yogurt
- 2   large eggs, lightly beaten
- 6   tablespoons (¾ stick) unsalted butter, melted and cooled
- 1   teaspoon vanilla extract
- 1¼ cup walnuts, toasted and chopped coarse

1. Adjust an oven rack to the lower-middle position and heat the oven to 350 degrees. Grease and flour a 9 by 5-inch loaf pan; set aside.

2. Whisk the flour, sugar, baking soda, and salt together in a large bowl; set aside.

3. Mix the mashed bananas, yogurt, eggs, butter, and vanilla together with a wooden spoon in a medium bowl. Lightly fold the banana mixture into the dry ingredients with a rubber spatula until just combined and the batter looks thick and chunky. Fold in the walnuts. Scrape the batter into the prepared loaf pan and smooth the surface with a rubber spatula.

4. Bake until the loaf is golden brown and a toothpick inserted in the center comes out clean, about 55 minutes. Cool in the pan for 5 minutes, then transfer to a wire rack. Serve warm or at room temperature.

ULTIMATE BANANA BREAD

WHY THIS RECIPE WORKS: Recipes for ultimate banana bread abound, but because they include an overload of bananas for flavor, the bread's texture is often soggy. We wanted a moist, not mushy, loaf that tasted of banana through and through.

To impart lots of banana flavor, we needed to use a generous amount of bananas, but we needed to rid them of excess moisture. We turned to the microwave to help us out. We piled as many bananas in a bowl as we dared and zapped them in the microwave. Then we drained the now-pulpy fruit and mixed the fruit into a batter. We didn't want to toss the flavorful liquid, so we reduced it and added it into the batter as well. Like a mock extract, our reduction infused the bread with ripe, intensely fruity banana flavor.

With the flavor problem solved, a few minor tweaks completed the recipe: We exchanged the granulated sugar for light brown sugar, finding that the latter's molasses notes better complemented the bananas. Swapping out the oil for the nutty richness of butter improved the loaf further. We also added toasted walnuts to the batter, finding that their crunch provided a pleasing contrast to the rich, moist crumb. Wondering if the crust might benefit from a little embellishment, we sliced a banana and shingled it on top of the batter. A final sprinkle of sugar helped the banana slices caramelize and gave this deeply flavored loaf an enticingly crisp, crunchy top.

Ultimate Banana Bread

MAKES ONE 9-INCH LOAF

Be sure to use very ripe, heavily speckled (or even black) bananas in this recipe. This recipe can be made using five thawed frozen bananas; since they release a lot of liquid naturally, they can bypass the microwaving in step 2 and go directly into the fine-mesh strainer. Do not use a thawed frozen banana in step 4; it will be too soft to slice. Instead, simply sprinkle the top of the loaf with sugar. The test kitchen's preferred loaf pan measures 8½ by 4½ inches; if you use a 9 by 5-inch loaf pan, start checking for doneness 5 minutes earlier than advised in the recipe. The texture is best when the loaf is eaten fresh, but it can be cooled completely and stored, covered tightly with plastic wrap, for up to 3 days.

- 1¾ cups (8¾ ounces) unbleached all-purpose flour
- 1 teaspoon baking soda
- ½ teaspoon table salt
- 6 large very ripe bananas (about 2¼ pounds), peeled (see note)
- 8 tablespoons (1 stick) unsalted butter, melted and cooled slightly
- 2 large eggs
- ¾ cup packed (5¼ ounces) light brown sugar
- 1 teaspoon vanilla extract
- ½ cup walnuts, toasted and chopped coarse (optional)
- 2 teaspoons granulated sugar

1. Adjust an oven rack to the middle position and heat the oven to 350 degrees. Spray an 8½ by 4½-inch loaf pan with vegetable oil spray. Whisk the flour, baking soda, and salt together in a large bowl.

2. Place 5 of the bananas in a microwave-safe bowl; cover with plastic wrap and cut several steam vents in the plastic with a paring knife. Microwave on high power until the bananas

SHINGLING THE LOAF

Layering thin bananas slices on either side of the loaf adds even more banana flavor to our bread (and brings the total number of bananas in the recipe to six). To ensure an even rise, leave a 1½-inch-wide space down the center.

are soft and have released their liquid, about 5 minutes. Transfer the bananas to a fine-mesh strainer placed over a medium bowl and allow to drain, stirring occasionally, for 15 minutes (you should have ½ to ¾ cup liquid).

3. Transfer the liquid to a medium saucepan and cook over medium-high heat until reduced to ¼ cup, about 5 minutes. Return drained bananas to bowl. Stir the reduced liquid into the bananas and mash them with a potato masher until fairly smooth. Whisk in the butter, eggs, brown sugar, and vanilla.

4. Pour the banana mixture into the flour mixture and stir until just combined with some streaks of flour remaining. Gently fold in the walnuts (if using). Scrape the batter into the prepared pan. Slice the remaining banana diagonally into ¼-inch-thick slices. Following the photo, shingle the banana slices on top of either side of the loaf, leaving a 1½-inch-wide space down the center to ensure even rise. Sprinkle the granulated sugar evenly over the loaf.

5. Bake until a toothpick inserted in the center of the loaf comes out clean, 55 to 75 minutes. Cool the bread in the pan on a wire rack for 15 minutes, then remove the loaf from the pan and continue to cool on a wire rack. Serve warm or at room temperature.

CREAM SCONES

WHY THIS RECIPE WORKS: Cream scones are a far cry from humongous coffeehouse creations. They are delicate and light, much like a biscuit. We set out to perfect a technique for making these tea-time (or breakfast) favorites.

Experimentation with different kinds of flour revealed that all-purpose was the best choice for these scones, and even better, for maximum tenderness, was a lower-protein brand of flour. Butter was important for flavor, but only a modest amount or the scones would practically melt in the oven. Cream won out over buttermilk and whole milk for the liquid; it made our scones rich and kept them tender. We increased the amount of sugar from that used in traditional recipes, but only slightly to keep them from being too sweet.

The discovery that the food processor did a great job of cutting the butter into the flour was a boon, making it even easier to make these treats. Our cream scones were just right served with a bit of jam.

Cream Scones

MAKES 8 SCONES

Use a low-protein all-purpose flour, such as Gold Medal or Pillsbury. The easiest and most reliable approach to mixing the butter into the dry ingredients is to use a food processor fitted with the metal blade. If you want a light glaze on the scones, brush the tops of the scones with 1 tablespoon heavy cream and then sprinkle them with 1 tablespoon sugar just before you put them in the oven. Resist the urge to eat the scones hot out of the oven. Letting them cool for at least 10 minutes firms them up and improves their texture.

- 2 cups (10 ounces) unbleached all-purpose flour (see note)
- 3 tablespoons sugar
- 1 tablespoon baking powder
- ½ teaspoon table salt
- 5 tablespoons unsalted butter, chilled and cut into ¼-inch cubes
- ½ cup currants
- 1 cup heavy cream

1. Adjust an oven rack to the middle position and heat the oven to 425 degrees.

2. Place the flour, sugar, baking powder, and salt in a food processor and pulse to combine, about 6 pulses.

3. Scatter the butter evenly over the top and continue to pulse until the mixture resembles coarse cornmeal with a few slightly larger butter lumps, about 12 more pulses. Transfer the mixture to a large bowl and stir in the currants. Stir in the heavy cream with a rubber spatula until a dough begins to form, about 30 seconds.

4. Transfer the dough and any dry, floury bits to a work surface and knead the dough by hand just until it comes together into a rough, slightly sticky ball, 5 to 10 seconds. Cut the dough into eight wedges. Place the wedges on an ungreased baking sheet. (The baking sheet can be covered in plastic wrap and refrigerated for up to 2 hours.)

5. Bake until the scone tops are light brown, 12 to 15 minutes. Cool on a wire rack for at least 10 minutes. Serve warm or at room temperature.

BLUEBERRY SCONES

WHY THIS RECIPE WORKS: Berry scones can be a treat—moist, sweet berries throughout a tender, light biscuit—but more often the berries weigh down the scone and impart little flavor. We wanted a rich, flaky scone studded with sweet, juicy blueberries.

Starting with traditional scone recipes, we increased the amounts of sugar and butter to add sweetness and richness to our scones. A combination of sour cream and milk lent both richness and tang. But now our scones were heavier than we wanted. We found two ways to lighten them. First, we borrowed a technique from puff pastry, where the dough is turned, rolled, and folded multiple times to create layers that are forced apart by steam when baked, and added a few quick folds to our scone dough. Then, to ensure that the butter would stay as cold and solid as possible while baking, we froze the butter and grated it into the dry ingredients using a box grater. Both tricks made for lighter, flakier scones. Adding the blueberries was a challenge. If we put them into the dry ingredients, they got mashed when we mixed the dough; when we added them to the already-mixed dough, we ruined our pockets of butter when we worked the berries in. The solution was pressing the berries into the dough, rolling the dough into a log, then pressing the log into a rectangle and cutting the scones. We had successfully transformed the scone into a fruit-filled, rich yet light treat.

Blueberry Scones

MAKES 8 SCONES

It is important to work the dough as little as possible—work quickly and knead and fold the dough only the number of times called for. The butter should be frozen solid before grating. If your kitchen is hot and humid, chill the flour mixture and bowls before use. The recipe calls for two whole sticks of butter, but only 10 tablespoons are actually used (see step 1). If fresh berries are unavailable, an equal amount of frozen berries, unthawed, can be substituted. An equal amount of raspberries, blackberries, or strawberries can also be used in place of the blueberries. Cut larger berries into ¼- to ½-inch pieces before incorporating. Refrigerate or freeze leftover scones, wrapped in foil, in an airtight container. To serve, remove the foil and place the scones on a baking sheet in a 375-degree oven. Heat until warmed through and recrisped, 8 to 10 minutes if refrigerated, 16 to 20 minutes if frozen.

16 tablespoons (2 sticks) unsalted butter, frozen whole (see note)

1½ cups (about 7½ ounces) fresh blueberries, picked over (see note)

½ cup whole milk

½ cup sour cream

2 cups (10 ounces) unbleached all-purpose flour, plus extra for the work surface

½ cup (3½ ounces) sugar, plus 1 tablespoon for sprinkling

2 teaspoons baking powder

½ teaspoon table salt

¼ teaspoon baking soda

1 teaspoon grated zest from 1 lemon

1. Adjust an oven rack to the middle position and heat the oven to 425 degrees. Score and remove half of the wrapper from each stick of frozen butter. Grate the unwrapped ends on the large holes of a box grater (you should grate a total of 8 tablespoons). Place the grated butter in the freezer until needed. Melt 2 tablespoons of the remaining ungrated butter and set aside. Save the remaining 6 tablespoons butter for another use. Place the blueberries in the freezer until needed.

2. Whisk the milk and sour cream together in a medium bowl; refrigerate until needed. Whisk the flour, ½ cup of the sugar, the baking powder, salt, baking soda, and lemon zest together in a medium bowl. Add the frozen butter to the flour mixture and toss with your fingers until the butter is thoroughly coated.

3. Add the milk mixture to the flour mixture; fold with a rubber spatula until just combined. Using the spatula, transfer the dough to a liberally floured work surface. Dust the surface of the dough with flour; with floured hands, knead the dough six to eight times, until it just holds together in a ragged ball, adding flour as needed to prevent sticking.

4. Roll the dough into an approximate 12-inch square. Following the photos, fold the dough into thirds like a business letter, using a bench scraper or metal spatula to release the dough if it sticks to the work surface. Lift the short ends of the dough and fold into thirds again to form an approximate 4-inch square. Transfer the dough to a plate lightly dusted with flour and chill in the freezer for 5 minutes.

5. Transfer the dough to a floured work surface and roll into an approximate 12-inch square again. Sprinkle the blueberries evenly over the surface of the dough, then press down so they are slightly embedded in the dough. Using a bench scraper or a thin metal spatula, loosen the dough from the work surface. Roll the dough, pressing to form a tight log. Lay the log seam side down and press it into a 12 by 4-inch rectangle. Using a sharp, floured knife, cut the rectangle crosswise into four equal rectangles. Cut each rectangle diagonally to form two triangles and transfer to a parchment-lined baking sheet.

6. Brush the tops of the scones with the melted butter and sprinkle with the remaining 1 tablespoon sugar. Bake until the tops and bottoms are golden brown, 18 to 25 minutes. Transfer to a wire rack and cool for 10 minutes before serving.

FOLDING AND SHAPING THE SCONES

1. Start by folding the dough into thirds (like a business letter). Then fold in the ends of the dough to form a 4-inch square. Chill the dough.

2. Reroll the dough into a 12-inch square. Press the berries into the dough.

3. Roll the dough into a jellyroll-like log to incorporate the blueberries.

4. Lay the log seam side down and press into an even 12 by 4-inch rectangle.

5. Cut the dough into eight triangular pieces.

OATMEAL SCONES

WHY THIS RECIPE WORKS: The oatmeal scones served in a typical coffeehouse are so dry and leaden that they seem like a ploy to get people to buy more coffee to wash them down. We wanted rich toasted oat flavor in a tender, flaky, not-too-sweet scone.

Whole rolled oats and quick oats performed better than instant and steel-cut oats. The rolled oats had a deeper oat flavor, but the quick-cooking oats made scones with a softer

CUTTING OATMEAL SCONES

After shaping scone dough into evenly thick round, use bench scraper to cut dough into 8 equal wedges.

texture; either type will work. Toasting the oats brought out their nutty flavor. We used a minimal amount of sugar and baking powder, but plenty of cold butter. A mixture of milk and heavy cream added richness without making the scones too heavy. An egg proved to be the ultimate touch of richness. Cutting the cold butter into the flour, instead of using melted butter, resulted in a lighter texture; we were careful not to overmix the dough, which toughened the scones. A very hot oven made the scones rise spectacularly and also gave them a craggy appearance; the high heat meant less time in the oven and therefore less time to dry out. You won't need a gallon of coffee to wash down these light, oaty scones.

Oatmeal Scones

MAKES 8 SCONES

Half-and-half is a suitable substitute for the milk-cream combination.

1½	cups (4½ ounces) old-fashioned oats or quick oats
¼	cup whole milk (see note)
¼	cup heavy cream (see note)
1	large egg
1½	cups (7½ ounces) unbleached all-purpose flour
⅓	cup (2⅓ ounces) sugar, plus 1 tablespoon for sprinkling
2	teaspoons baking powder
½	teaspoon table salt
10	tablespoons (1¼ sticks) unsalted butter, chilled and cut into ½-inch cubes

1. Adjust an oven rack to the middle position and heat the oven to 375 degrees. Spread the oats evenly on a rimmed baking sheet and toast in the oven until fragrant and lightly browned, 7 to 9 minutes; cool the oats on the baking sheet on a wire rack. Increase the oven temperature to 450 degrees. Line a second baking sheet with parchment paper. When the oats are cooled, measure out 2 tablespoons (for dusting the work surface and the dough) and set aside.

2. Whisk the milk, cream, and egg together in a large measuring cup; remove 1 tablespoon of the mixture and reserve for glazing.

3. Pulse the flour, ⅓ cup of the sugar, the baking powder, and salt in a food processor until combined, about 4 pulses. Scatter the cold butter evenly over the dry ingredients and pulse until the mixture resembles coarse cornmeal, about 12 pulses. Transfer the mixture to a medium bowl and stir in the cooled oats. Using a rubber spatula, fold in the liquid ingredients until large clumps form. Mix the dough by hand in the bowl until the dough forms a cohesive mass.

4. Dust a work surface with half of the reserved oats, turn the dough out onto the work surface, and dust the top with the remaining oats. Gently pat into a 7-inch circle about 1 inch thick. Using a bench scraper or chef's knife, cut the dough into eight wedges and set on the prepared baking sheet, spacing the scones about 2 inches apart. Brush the surfaces with the reserved egg mixture and sprinkle with the remaining 1 tablespoon sugar. Bake until golden brown, 12 to 14 minutes; cool the scones on the baking sheet on a wire rack for 5 minutes, then transfer the scones to the rack and cool to room temperature, about 30 minutes. Serve.

Glazed Maple-Pecan Oatmeal Scones

Follow the recipe for Oatmeal Scones, toasting ½ cup chopped pecans with the oats, whisking ¼ cup maple syrup into the milk mixture, and omitting the sugar. When the scones are cooled, whisk 3 tablespoons maple syrup and ½ cup confectioners' sugar together in a small bowl until combined; drizzle the glaze over the scones.

BRITISH-STYLE CURRANT SCONES

WHY THIS RECIPE WORKS: Compared to American scones, British scones are lighter, fluffier, and less sweet; perfect for serving with butter and jam. Rather than leaving pieces of cold butter in the dry ingredients as we would with American scones, we thoroughly worked in softened butter until it was fully integrated. This protected some of the flour granules from moisture, which in turn limited gluten development and kept the crumb tender and cakey. For a higher rise, we added more than the usual amount of leavening and started the scones in a 500-degree oven to boost their lift before turning the temperature down. We brushed some reserved milk and egg on top for enhanced browning, and added currants for tiny bursts of fruit flavor throughout.

British-Style Currant Scones

MAKES 12 SCONES

We prefer whole milk in this recipe, but low-fat milk can be used. The dough will be quite soft and wet; dust your work surface and your hands liberally with flour. For a tall, even rise, use a sharp-edged biscuit cutter and push straight down; do not twist the cutter. These scones are best served fresh, but leftover scones may be stored in the freezer and reheated in a 300-degree oven for 15 minutes before serving. Serve these scones with jam as well as salted butter or clotted cream.

 3 cups (15 ounces) all-purpose flour
 ⅓ cup (2⅓ ounces) sugar
 2 tablespoons baking powder
 ½ teaspoon salt
 8 tablespoons unsalted butter, cut into
   ½-inch pieces and softened
 ¾ cup dried currants
 1 cup whole milk
 2 large eggs

1. Adjust oven rack to upper-middle position and heat oven to 500 degrees. Line rimmed baking sheet with parchment paper. Pulse flour, sugar, baking powder, and salt in food processor until combined, about 5 pulses. Add butter and pulse until fully incorporated and mixture looks like very fine crumbs with no visible butter, about 20 pulses. Transfer mixture to large bowl and stir in currants.

2. Whisk milk and eggs together in second bowl. Set aside 2 tablespoons milk mixture. Add remaining milk mixture to flour mixture and, using rubber spatula, fold together until almost no dry bits of flour remain.

3. Transfer dough to well-floured counter and gather into ball. With floured hands, knead until surface is smooth and free of cracks, 25 to 30 times. Press gently to form disk. Using floured rolling pin, roll disk into 9-inch round, about 1 inch thick. Using floured 2½-inch round cutter, stamp out 8 rounds, recoating cutter with flour if it begins to stick. Arrange scones on prepared sheet. Gather dough scraps, form into ball, and knead gently until surface is smooth. Roll dough to 1-inch thickness and stamp out 4 rounds. Discard remaining dough.

4. Brush tops of scones with reserved milk mixture. Reduce oven temperature to 425 degrees and bake scones until risen and golden brown, 10 to 12 minutes, rotating sheet halfway through baking. Transfer scones to wire rack and let cool for at least 10 minutes. Serve scones warm or at room temperature.

CROISSANTS

WHY THIS RECIPE WORKS: We wanted to create an approachable croissant recipe for home bakers—one that would deliver authentic flavor. The layered structure that characterizes croissants is formed through a process called lamination. First, a basic dough of flour, water, yeast, sugar, salt, and a small amount of butter is made. Then a larger amount of butter is formed into a block and encased in the relatively lean dough. This dough and butter package is rolled out and folded multiple times (each is called a "turn") to form paperthin layers of dough separated by even thinner layers of butter. Once baked, it's these layers that make croissants so flaky and decadent. To start, we found that more turns didn't necessarily produce more layers; we stopped at three turns, as any more produced a homogeneous bready texture. As for the star ingredient, butter, we found that great croissants demanded higher-fat European-style butter. And one essential tip we discovered during our recipe development was to give the dough a 30-minute quick freeze to firm it to the consistency of the butter, thus ensuring perfectly distinct layers.

Croissants

MAKES 22 CROISSANTS

These croissants take at least 10 hours to make from start to finish, but the process can be spread over 2 days Europeanstyle cultured butters have a higher butterfat content, which makes it easier to fold them into the dough. (Our favorite is from Plugrá.) Any brand of all-purpose flour will produce acceptable croissants, but we recommend using King Arthur All-Purpose Flour, which has a slightly higher protein content. Do not attempt to make these croissants in a room that is warmer than 80 degrees. If at any time during rolling the dough retracts, dust it lightly with flour, fold it loosely, cover it, and return it to the freezer to rest for 10 to 15 minutes. This recipe makes 22 croissants, but only 12 are baked. Shaped croissants can be evenly spaced 1 inch apart on a parchmentlined baking sheet, wrapped with plastic wrap, and frozen until solid, about 2 hours. Once frozen, transfer the croissants from the baking sheet to a zipper-lock bag. Croissants can be kept frozen for up to 2 months. Bake frozen croissants as directed from step 8, increasing the rising time by 1 to 2 hours.

24 tablespoons European-style unsalted butter, very cold, plus 3 tablespoons unsalted butter at room temperature (see note)
1¾ cups whole milk
4 teaspoons instant or rapid-rise yeast
4¼ cups (21¼ ounces) unbleached all-purpose flour (see note)
¼ cup (1¾ ounces) sugar
Table salt
1 large egg
1 teaspoon cold water

1. Melt 3 tablespoons of the butter in a medium saucepan over low heat. Remove from the heat and immediately stir in the milk (the temperature should be lower than 90 degrees). Whisk in yeast; transfer the milk mixture to the bowl of a stand mixer. Add the flour, sugar, and 2 teaspoons salt. Using the mixer's dough hook, knead on low speed until a cohesive dough forms, 2 to 3 minutes. Increase the speed to medium-low and knead for 1 minute. Remove the bowl from the mixer,

remove the dough hook, and cover the bowl with plastic wrap. Let the dough rest at room temperature for 30 minutes.

2. Transfer the dough to a parchment paper–lined baking sheet and shape into a 10 by 7-inch rectangle about 1 inch thick. Wrap tightly with plastic and refrigerate for 2 hours.

3. TO MAKE THE BUTTER BLOCK: While the dough chills, fold a 24-inch length of parchment in half to create a 12-inch rectangle. Following the photos, fold over 3 open sides of the rectangle to form an 8-inch square with enclosed sides. Crease the folds firmly. Place the cold butter directly on the work surface and beat with a rolling pin for about 60 seconds until the butter is just pliable, but not warm, folding the butter in on itself using a bench scraper. Beat into a rough 6-inch square. Unfold the parchment envelope. Using the bench scraper, transfer the butter to the center of the parchment square, re-folding at the creases to enclose. Turn the packet over so that the flaps are underneath and gently roll the butter packet until the butter fills the parchment square, taking care to achieve an even thickness. Refrigerate for at least 45 minutes.

4. TO LAMINATE THE DOUGH: Transfer the dough to the freezer. After 30 minutes, transfer the dough to a lightly floured work surface and roll into a 17 by 8-inch rectangle with the long side of the rectangle parallel to the edge of the work surface. Following the photos, unwrap the butter and place it in the center of the dough so that the butter and dough

NOTES FROM THE TEST KITCHEN

MAKING THE BUTTER BLOCK FOR CROISSANTS

1. Fold a 24-inch length of parchment in half to create a 12-inch rectangle. Fold over 3 open sides of the rectangle to form an 8-inch enclosed square. Crease the folds firmly.

2. Using a rolling pin, beat the butter until it is just pliable, then fold the butter in on itself using a bench scraper. Beat the butter into a rough 6-inch square.

3. Unfold the envelope and, using a bench scraper, transfer the butter to the parchment, re-folding at the creases to enclose. Turn the packet over; gently roll the butter to fill the parchment square, taking care to achieve an even thickness.

LAMINATING THE CROISSANT DOUGH

1. Roll the dough into a 17 by 8-inch rectangle. Unwrap the butter and place in the center of the dough so that the edges of the butter and dough are flush at the top and bottom. Fold two sides of the dough over the butter so they meet in the center of the butter square.

2. Using your fingertips, press the seam together. Using a rolling pin, press firmly on each open end of the packet. Roll the dough out lengthwise until it is 24 inches long and 8 inches wide.

3. Starting at the bottom of the dough, fold it into thirds. Turn the dough 90 degrees; roll and fold again. Place it on a baking sheet, wrap with plastic wrap, and return to the freezer for 30 minutes. Roll and fold into thirds one more time.

are flush at the top and bottom. Fold 2 sides of the dough over the butter square so they meet in the center. Press the seam together. With the rolling pin, press firmly on each open end of the packet. Roll out the dough, perpendicular to the edge of the work surface, until it is 24 inches long and 8 inches wide. Bring the bottom third of the dough up, then fold the upper third over it, folding like a business letter into an 8-inch square. Turn the dough 90 degrees counterclockwise. Roll out the dough again, perpendicular to the edge of the work surface, into a 24 by 8-inch rectangle and fold into thirds. Place the dough on the baking sheet, wrap tightly with plastic wrap, and return to the freezer for 30 minutes.

5. Transfer the dough to a lightly floured work surface so that the top flap of the dough is facing right. Roll once more, perpendicular to the edge of the work surface, into a 24 by 8-inch rectangle and fold into thirds. Place the dough on the baking sheet, wrap tightly with plastic wrap, and refrigerate for 2 hours.

6. Transfer the dough to the freezer. After 30 minutes, transfer to a lightly floured work surface and roll into an 18 by 16-inch rectangle with the long side of the rectangle parallel

---

NOTES FROM THE TEST KITCHEN

SHAPING THE CROISSANTS

1. Transfer the dough from the freezer to a lightly floured work surface and roll it into an 18 by 12-inch rectangle. (If it begins to retract, fold it into thirds, wrap it, and return it to the freezer for 10 to 15 minutes.) Fold the upper half of the dough over the lower half.

2. Using a ruler, mark the dough at 3-inch intervals along the bottom edge. Move the ruler to the top of the dough, measure in 1½ inches from the left, then use this mark to measure out 3-inch intervals.

3. Using a sharp pizza wheel or knife, cut the dough into triangles from mark to mark; discard any scraps.

4. You should have 12 single triangles and 5 double triangles. Unfold the double triangles and cut in half to form 10 single triangles (making 22 triangles in all).

5. Cut a ½-inch slit in the center of the short end of a triangle. If the dough begins to soften, return it to the freezer for 10 minutes.

6. Grasp the triangle by the 2 corners on either side of the slit and stretch gently, then grasp the point and stretch.

7. Place the triangle on the work surface so the point is facing toward you. Fold both sides of the slit down.

8. Positioning your palms on the folds, roll partway toward the point.

9. Gently grasp the point with one hand and stretch again. Resume rolling, tucking the point underneath.

10. Curve the ends gently toward one another to form a crescent shape. Repeat with the remaining triangles.

to the edge of the work surface. Fold the upper half of the dough over the lower half. Using a ruler, mark the dough at 3-inch intervals along the bottom edge with a bench scraper (you should have 5 marks). Move the ruler to the top of the dough, measure in 1½ inches from the left, then use this mark to measure out 3-inch intervals (you should have 6 marks). Starting at the lower left corner, use a pizza wheel or knife to cut the dough into triangles from mark to mark. You will have 12 single triangles and 5 double triangles; discard any scraps. Unfold the double triangles and cut into 10 single triangles (making 22 equal-size triangles in total). If the dough begins to soften, return to the freezer for 10 minutes.

7. TO SHAPE THE CROISSANTS: Position 1 triangle on the work surface. (Keep the remaining triangles covered with plastic while shaping.) Following the photos on page 660, cut a ½-inch slit in the center of the short end of the triangle. Grasp the triangle by 2 corners on either side of the slit and stretch gently, then grasp the bottom point and stretch. Fold both sides of the slit down. Positioning your palms on the folds, roll partway toward the point. Gently stretch the point again; continue to roll, tucking the point underneath. Curve the ends gently toward one another to create a crescent shape. Repeat with the remaining triangles.

8. Place 12 croissants on 2 parchment-lined baking sheets, leaving at least 2½ inches between the croissants, 6 croissants per sheet. Lightly wrap the baking sheets with plastic, leaving room for the croissants to expand. Let stand at room temperature until nearly doubled in size, 2½ to 3 hours. (Shaped croissants can be refrigerated on trays for up to 18 hours. Remove from the refrigerator to rise and add at least 30 minutes to the rising time.)

9. After the croissants have been rising for 2 hours, adjust the oven racks to the upper-middle and lower-middle positions and heat the oven to 425 degrees. In a small bowl, whisk together the egg, water, and a pinch of salt. Brush the croissants with the egg wash using a pastry brush. Place the croissants in the oven and reduce the temperature to 400 degrees. Bake for 12 minutes then switch and rotate the baking sheets. Continue to bake until deep golden brown, 8 to 12 minutes longer. Transfer the croissants to a wire rack and allow to cool until just warm, about 15 minutes. Serve warm or at room temperature.

BLUEBERRY MUFFINS

WHY THIS RECIPE WORKS: Blueberry muffins should be packed with blueberry flavor and boast a moist crumb. But too often, the blueberry flavor is fleeting, thanks to the fact that the berries in the produce aisle have suffered from long-distance shipping. We wanted blueberry muffins that would taste great with blueberries of any origin, even the watery supermarket kind.

To intensify the blueberry in our muffins, we tried combining blueberry jam with fresh supermarket blueberries. The muffins baked up with a pretty blue filling, but tasters thought the jam made them too sweet. To solve this, we

made our own fresh, low-sugar berry jam by simmering fresh blueberries on the stovetop with a bit of sugar. Adding our cooled homemade jam to the batter along with fresh, uncooked berries gave us the best of both worlds: intense blueberry flavor and the liquid burst that only fresh berries could provide.

As for the muffin base, we found that the quick-bread method—whisking together eggs and sugar before adding milk and melted butter, and then gently folding in the dry ingredients—produced a hearty, substantial crumb that could support a generous amount of fruit. We found that an equal amount of butter and oil gave us just the right combination of buttery flavor and moist, tender texture. To make the muffins even richer, we swapped the whole milk for buttermilk. Finally, for a nice crunch, we sprinkled lemon-scented sugar on top of the batter just before baking.

Blueberry Muffins
MAKES 12 MUFFINS
For finely grated lemon zest, use a rasp grater.

LEMON-SUGAR TOPPING
- ⅓ cup (2⅓ ounces) sugar
- 1½ teaspoons finely grated zest from 1 lemon (see note)

MUFFINS
- 2 cups (about 10 ounces) fresh blueberries, picked over
- 1 teaspoon plus 1⅛ cups (8 ounces) sugar
- 2½ cups (12½ ounces) unbleached all-purpose flour
- 2½ teaspoons baking powder
- 1 teaspoon table salt
- 2 large eggs
- 4 tablespoons (½ stick) unsalted butter, melted and cooled slightly
- 4 tablespoons vegetable oil
- 1 cup buttermilk
- 1½ teaspoons vanilla extract

1. FOR THE TOPPING: Stir the sugar and lemon zest together in a small bowl until combined and set aside.

2. FOR THE MUFFINS: Adjust an oven rack to the upper-middle position and heat the oven to 425 degrees. Spray a standard-size muffin pan with vegetable oil spray. Bring 1 cup of the blueberries and 1 teaspoon of the sugar to a simmer in a small saucepan over medium heat. Cook, mashing the berries with a spoon several times and stirring frequently, until the berries have broken down and the mixture is thickened and reduced to ¼ cup, about 6 minutes. Transfer to a small bowl and cool to room temperature, 10 to 15 minutes.

3. Whisk the flour, baking powder, and salt together in a large bowl. Whisk the remaining 1⅛ cups sugar and the eggs together in a medium bowl until thick and homogeneous, about 45 seconds. Slowly whisk in the butter and oil until combined. Whisk in the buttermilk and vanilla until combined. Using a rubber spatula, fold the egg mixture and remaining 1 cup blueberries into the flour mixture until just moistened. (The batter will be very lumpy with a few spots of dry flour; do not overmix.)

4. Using a ⅓-cup measure or an ice cream scoop, divide the batter equally among the prepared muffin cups (the batter should completely fill the cups and mound slightly). Following the photos, spoon 1 teaspoon of the cooked berry mixture into the center of each mound of batter. Using a chopstick or skewer, gently swirl the berry filling into the batter using a figure-eight motion. Sprinkle the lemon sugar evenly over the muffins.

5. Bake until the muffin tops are golden and just firm, 17 to 19 minutes, rotating the pan halfway through baking. Cool the muffins in the pan for 5 minutes, then transfer them to a wire rack and cool for 5 minutes before serving.

NOTES FROM THE TEST KITCHEN

SWIRLING JAM INTO BLUEBERRY MUFFINS

1. Place 1 teaspoon of cooled berry jam in the center of each batter-filled cup, pushing it below the surface.

2. Using a chopstick, swirl the jam into the batter following a figure-eight pattern.

BRAN MUFFINS

WHY THIS RECIPE WORKS: We've made bran muffins with unprocessed wheat bran, so we know how they're supposed to look and taste. But there are so many bran cereals at the supermarket with a muffin recipe on the box that we wondered if we could achieve the same thing without a special trip to the natural foods store.

Twig-style cereal worked better than flakes, but soaking the twigs in milk, as most recipes recommend, left our muffins dense and heavy—they were soaking up all the moisture. Instead, we stirred together the wet ingredients first and then added the cereal; grinding half of the twigs in the food processor and leaving the rest whole gave us the rustic texture we wanted, and the cereal softened in just a few minutes. Whole-milk yogurt added needed moisture to the batter. Molasses and brown sugar reinforced the earthy bran flavor. To improve the texture, we swapped baking soda for baking powder and used one egg plus a yolk—two eggs made the muffins too springy. To ensure that they would soften fully, we plumped the raisins in water in the microwave. These muffins were tender and moist, rustic but not dense, with hearty bran flavor—and all the ingredients came from the supermarket.

Bran Muffins

MAKES 12 MUFFINS

The test kitchen prefers Kellogg's All-Bran Original cereal in this recipe. Dried cranberries or dried cherries may be substituted for the raisins. Low-fat or nonfat yogurt can be substituted for whole-milk yogurt, though the muffins will be slightly less flavorful.

- 1 cup raisins (see note)
- 1 teaspoon water
- 2¼ cups (5 ounces) All-Bran Original cereal (see note)
- 1¼ cups (6¼ ounces) unbleached all-purpose flour
- ½ cup (2½ ounces) whole wheat flour
- 2 teaspoons baking soda
- ½ teaspoon table salt
- 1 large whole egg plus 1 large egg yolk
- ⅔ cup packed (4⅔ ounces) light brown sugar
- 3 tablespoons mild or light molasses
- 1 teaspoon vanilla extract
- 6 tablespoons (¾ stick) unsalted butter, melted and cooled
- 1¾ cups plain whole-milk yogurt (see note)

1. Adjust an oven rack to the middle position and heat the oven to 400 degrees. Spray a standard-size muffin pan with vegetable oil spray. Combine the raisins and water in a small microwave-safe bowl, cover with plastic wrap, cut several steam vents in the plastic with a paring knife, and microwave on high power for 30 seconds. Let stand, covered, until the raisins are softened and plump, about 5 minutes. Transfer the raisins to a paper towel–lined plate to cool.

2. Process half of the bran cereal in a food processor until finely ground, about 1 minute. Whisk the flours, baking soda, and salt in a large bowl to combine; set aside. Whisk the egg and egg yolk together in a medium bowl until well combined and light-colored, about 20 seconds. Add the sugar, molasses, and vanilla; whisk until the mixture is thick, about 30 seconds. Add the melted butter and whisk to combine; add the yogurt and whisk to combine. Stir in the processed cereal and unprocessed cereal; let the mixture sit until the cereal is evenly moistened (there will still be some small lumps), about 5 minutes.

3. Add the wet ingredients to the dry ingredients and gently mix with a rubber spatula until the batter is combined and evenly moistened. Do not overmix. Gently fold the raisins into the batter. Using a ⅓-cup measure or an ice cream scoop, divide the batter evenly among the prepared muffin cups, dropping the batter to form mounds. Do not level or flatten the surfaces of the mounds.

4. Bake until the muffins are dark golden and a toothpick inserted into the center of a muffin comes out with a few crumbs attached, 16 to 20 minutes, rotating the pan halfway through the baking time. Cool the muffins in the pan for 5 minutes, then transfer to a wire rack and cool for 10 minutes before serving.

CORN MUFFINS

WHY THIS RECIPE WORKS: A corn muffin shouldn't be as sweet and fluffy as a cupcake, nor should it be dense and "corny" like corn bread. It should taste like corn, but not overpoweringly, and should be moist with a tender crumb and a crunchy top. Our mission was to come up with a recipe for these seemingly simple muffins that struck just the right balance in both texture and flavor.

The cornmeal itself proved to be an important factor, and degerminated meal just didn't have enough corn flavor. A fine-ground, whole grain meal provided better flavor and texture. Our first batches of muffins were too dry, so we experimented with various ways to add moisture; butter, sour cream, and milk provided the moisture, fat (for richness), and acidity (for its tenderizing effect) that we wanted. We tried mixing the ingredients with both the quick-bread and creaming methods; not only was the former the easier way to go, but it also resulted in less airy, cakey muffins. We got our crunchy top from a 400-degree oven. All in all, we'd resolved all of our issues with corn muffins; these were subtly sweet, rich but not dense, and with a texture that was neither cake nor corn bread.

Corn Muffins

MAKES 12 MUFFINS

Whole grain cornmeal has a fuller flavor than regular cornmeal milled from degerminated corn. To determine what kind of cornmeal a package contains, look closely at the label.

2 cups (10 ounces) unbleached all-purpose flour
1 cup (5 ounces) fine-ground, whole grain yellow cornmeal (see note)
1½ teaspoons baking powder
1 teaspoon baking soda
½ teaspoon table salt
2 large eggs
¾ cup (5¼ ounces) sugar
8 tablespoons (1 stick) unsalted butter, melted
¾ cup sour cream
½ cup milk

1. Adjust an oven rack to the middle position and heat the oven to 400 degrees. Spray a standard-size muffin pan with vegetable oil spray.

2. Whisk the flour, cornmeal, baking powder, baking soda, and salt together in a medium bowl; set aside. Whisk the eggs in a second medium bowl. Add the sugar to the eggs; whisk vigorously until thick and homogeneous, about 30 seconds; add the melted butter in three additions, whisking to combine after each addition. Add half of the sour cream and half of the milk and whisk to combine; whisk in the remaining sour cream and milk until combined. Add the wet ingredients to the dry ingredients; mix gently with a rubber spatula until the batter is just combined and evenly moistened. Do not overmix. Using a ⅓-cup measure or ice cream scoop, divide the batter evenly among the prepared muffin cups, dropping the batter to form mounds. Do not level or flatten the surface of the mounds.

3. Bake until the muffins are light golden brown and a skewer inserted into the center of the muffins comes out clean, about 18 minutes, rotating the pan halfway through the baking time. Cool the muffins in the pan for 5 minutes, then transfer to a wire rack and cool for 10 minutes before serving.

Corn and Apricot Muffins with Orange Essence
MAKES 12 MUFFINS

1. In a food processor, process ⅔ cup granulated sugar and 1½ teaspoons grated orange zest until pale orange, about 10 seconds. Transfer to a small bowl and set aside.

2. In a food processor, pulse 1½ cups (10 ounces) dried apricots for 10 pulses, until chopped fine. Transfer to a medium microwave-safe bowl; add ⅔ cup orange juice to the apricots, cover the bowl tightly with plastic wrap, and microwave on high power until simmering, about 1 minute. Let the apricots stand, covered, until softened and plump, about 5 minutes. Strain the apricots and discard the juice.

3. Follow the recipe for Corn Muffins, substituting ¼ cup packed dark brown sugar for an equal amount of the granulated sugar and stirring ½ teaspoon grated orange zest and the strained apricots into the wet ingredients before adding them to the dry ingredients. Before baking, sprinkle a portion of the orange sugar over each mound of batter. Cool the muffins in the pan for 5 minutes, then gently lift them out using the tip of a paring knife. Cool on a wire rack for 10 minutes before serving.

SAVORY CORN MUFFINS

WHY THIS RECIPE WORKS: For a corn muffin with great cornmeal flavor and proper muffin structure, we used a ratio of 2 parts cornmeal to 1 part flour for the former's big flavor and the latter's gluten-forming power. Cutting back on sugar promised a perfectly savory muffin, but we needed to keep a few tablespoons of the sweet stuff in order to boost the batter's moisture retention. To make up for the moisture that extra sugar normally provides, we used a mix of milk, butter, and sour cream for the right amount of water and fat. We incorporated extra liquid into the batter by precooking a portion of the cornmeal with additional milk to make a polenta-like porridge. With this technique, we were able to add nearly double the liquid in the batter, promising a supermoist crumb while still allowing the batter to rise into a pretty dome.

Savory Corn Muffins

MAKES 12 MUFFINS

Don't use coarse-ground or white cornmeal.

- 2 cups (10 ounces) cornmeal
- 1 cup (5 ounces) all-purpose flour
- 1½ teaspoons baking powder
- 1 teaspoon baking soda
- 1¼ teaspoons salt
- 1¼ cups whole milk
- 1 cup sour cream
- 8 tablespoons unsalted butter, melted and cooled slightly
- 3 tablespoons sugar
- 2 large eggs, beaten

1. Adjust oven rack to upper-middle position and heat oven to 425 degrees. Grease 12-cup muffin tin. Whisk 1½ cups cornmeal, flour, baking powder, baking soda, and salt together in medium bowl.

2. Combine milk and remaining ½ cup cornmeal in large bowl. Microwave milk-cornmeal mixture for 1½ minutes. Whisk thoroughly and continue to microwave, whisking every 30 seconds, until thickened to batter-like consistency (whisk will leave channel in bottom of bowl that slowly fills in), 1 to 3 minutes longer. Whisk in sour cream, melted butter, and sugar until combined. Whisk in eggs until combined. Fold in flour mixture until thoroughly combined. Using portion scoop or large spoon, divide batter evenly among prepared muffin cups (about ½ cup batter per cup; batter will mound slightly above rim).

3. Bake until tops are golden brown and toothpick inserted in center comes out clean, 13 to 17 minutes, rotating muffin tin halfway through baking. Let muffins cool in muffin tin on wire rack for 5 minutes. Remove muffins from muffin tin and let cool 5 minutes longer. Serve warm.

Savory Corn Muffins with Rosemary and Black Pepper

Whisk in 1 tablespoon minced fresh rosemary and 1½ teaspoons pepper with eggs.

CRANBERRY-NUT MUFFINS

WHY THIS RECIPE WORKS: Cranberry-nut muffins can make a quick and hearty breakfast, but all too often they are dense and leaden, with an overwhelming sour berry flavor and soggy nuts distributed haphazardly throughout. We wanted a moist, substantial muffin accented—but not overtaken—by tart cranberries and toasted, crunchy nuts. Hand mixing the batter was quick and gave our muffins enough structure to accommodate the fruit and nuts. Grinding some of the nuts and using them in place of some of the flour added complexity and nutty flavor throughout. Chopping the berries and tossing them with a little sugar toned down their tartness. Finally, adding a streusel topping added back the crunch lost from grinding up the nuts.

Cranberry-Pecan Muffins

MAKES 12 MUFFINS

If fresh cranberries aren't available, substitute frozen cranberries. Before using, place the cranberries in a microwave-safe bowl and microwave on high power until the cranberries are partially thawed, 30 to 45 seconds. Do not overthaw the cranberries.

STREUSEL TOPPING

- 3 tablespoons unbleached all-purpose flour
- 1 tablespoon packed light brown sugar
- 1 tablespoon plus 1 teaspoon granulated sugar
  Table salt
- 2 tablespoons unsalted butter, cut into ½-inch pieces, softened
- ½ cup pecan halves

MUFFINS

- 1⅓ cups (6⅔ ounces) unbleached all-purpose flour
- 1½ teaspoons baking powder
- 1 teaspoon table salt
- 1¼ cups pecan halves, toasted and cooled
- 1 cup plus 1 tablespoon (7½ ounces) granulated sugar
- 2 large eggs
- 6 tablespoons (¾ stick) unsalted butter, melted and cooled
- ½ cup whole milk
- 2 cups fresh cranberries
- 1 tablespoon confectioners' sugar

1. Adjust an oven rack to the upper-middle position and heat the oven to 425 degrees. Spray a 12-cup muffin tin with vegetable oil spray.

2. FOR THE STREUSEL: Pulse the flour, brown sugar, granulated sugar, a pinch of salt, and the butter in a food processor until the mixture resembles coarse sand, 4 to 5 pulses. Add the pecans and pulse until the pecans are chopped coarse, about 4 pulses. Transfer to a small bowl; set aside.

3. FOR THE MUFFINS: Whisk the flour, baking powder, and ¾ teaspoon of the salt together in a bowl; set aside.

4. Process the toasted pecans and granulated sugar until the mixture resembles coarse sand, 10 to 15 seconds. Transfer to a large bowl and whisk in the eggs, butter, and milk until combined. Whisk the flour mixture into the egg mixture until just moistened and no streaks of flour remain. Set the batter aside for 30 minutes to thicken.

5. Pulse the cranberries, remaining ¼ teaspoon salt, and confectioners' sugar in the food processor until very coarsely chopped, 4 to 5 pulses. Using a rubber spatula, fold the cranberries into the batter. Using an ice cream scoop or large spoon, divide the batter equally among the prepared muffin cups (the batter should completely fill the cups and mound slightly). Evenly sprinkle the streusel topping over the muffins, gently pressing into the batter to adhere. Bake until the muffin tops are golden and just firm, 17 to 18 minutes, rotating the muffin tin halfway through baking. Cool the muffins in the muffin tin on a wire rack for 10 minutes. Remove the muffins from the tin and cool for 10 minutes before serving.

OATMEAL MUFFINS

WHY THIS RECIPE WORKS: For an oatmeal muffin that is packed with oats but also has a fine, tender texture, we processed old-fashioned rolled oats into a flour in the food processor. To boost oat flavor, we first toasted the oats in a couple of tablespoons of butter and eliminated extraneous spices from the batter. To ensure a lump-free batter, we used a whisk to fold the wet and dry ingredients together and allowed the batter to sit and hydrate for 20 minutes before baking. Finally, we made an apple crisp–inspired topping of crunchy oats, nuts, and brown sugar.

Oatmeal Muffins

MAKES 12 MUFFINS

Do not use quick or instant oats in this recipe. Walnuts may be substituted for the pecans. The easiest way to grease and flour the muffin tin is with a baking spray with flour.

TOPPING

- ½ cup (1½ ounces) old-fashioned rolled oats
- ⅓ cup (1⅔ ounces) all-purpose flour
- ⅓ cup pecans, chopped fine
- ⅓ cup packed (2⅓ ounces) light brown sugar
- 1¼ teaspoons ground cinnamon
- ⅛ teaspoon salt
- 4 tablespoons unsalted butter, melted

MUFFINS

- 2 tablespoons unsalted butter, plus 6 tablespoons melted
- 2 cups (6 ounces) old-fashioned rolled oats
- 1¾ cups (8¾ ounces) all-purpose flour
- 1½ teaspoons salt
- ¾ teaspoon baking powder
- ¼ teaspoon baking soda
- 1⅓ cups packed (9⅓ ounces) light brown sugar
- 1¾ cups milk
- 2 large eggs, beaten

1. FOR THE TOPPING: Combine oats, flour, pecans, sugar, cinnamon, and salt in medium bowl. Drizzle melted butter over mixture and stir to thoroughly combine; set aside.

2. FOR THE MUFFINS: Grease and flour 12-cup muffin tin. Melt 2 tablespoons butter in 10-inch skillet over medium heat. Add oats and cook, stirring frequently, until oats turn golden brown and smell of cooking popcorn, 6 to 8 minutes. Transfer oats to food processor and process into fine meal, about 30 seconds. Add flour, salt, baking powder, and baking soda to oats and pulse until combined, about 3 pulses.

3. Stir 6 tablespoons melted butter and sugar together in large bowl until smooth. Add milk and eggs and whisk until smooth. Using whisk, gently fold half of oat mixture into wet ingredients, tapping whisk against side of bowl to release clumps. Add remaining oat mixture and continue to fold with whisk until no streaks of flour remain. Set aside batter for 20 minutes to thicken. Meanwhile, adjust oven rack to middle position and heat oven to 375 degrees.

4. Using ice cream scoop or large spoon, divide batter equally among prepared muffin cups (about ½ cup batter per cup; cups will be filled to rim). Evenly sprinkle topping over muffins (about 2 tablespoons per muffin). Bake until toothpick inserted in center comes out clean, 18 to 25 minutes, rotating muffin tin halfway through baking.

5. Let muffins cool in muffin tin on wire rack for 10 minutes. Remove muffins from muffin tin and serve or let cool completely before serving.

CRUMB CAKE

WHY THIS RECIPE WORKS: The original crumb cake was brought to New York by German immigrants; sadly, the bakery-fresh versions have all but disappeared, and most people know only the commercially baked (and preservative-laden) type. We wanted a recipe closer to the original version that could be made at home.

Most modern recipes use butter cake rather than the traditional yeast dough, which made our job that much easier. The essence of this cake is the balance between the tender, buttery cake and the thick, lightly spiced crumb topping. Starting with our favorite yellow cake recipe, we realized we needed to reduce the amount of butter or the richness would be overwhelming. We compensated for the resulting dryness by substituting buttermilk for milk, which also helped make the cake sturdy enough to support the crumbs, and we left out an egg white so the cake wouldn't be rubbery. We wanted our crumb topping to be soft and cookie-like, not a crunchy streusel, so we mixed granulated and brown sugars and melted the butter for a dough-like consistency, flavoring the mixture only with cinnamon. Broken into little pieces and sprinkled over the cake batter, our topping held together during baking and made a thick layer of moist crumbs with golden edges that didn't sink into the cake.

New York–Style Crumb Cake

SERVES 8 TO 10

Don't be tempted to substitute all-purpose flour for the cake flour; doing so will make a dry, tough cake. If you can't find buttermilk, you can use an equal amount of plain low-fat yogurt, but do not substitute powdered buttermilk because it will make a sunken cake. When topping the cake, take care to not push the crumbs into the batter. This recipe can be easily doubled and baked in a 13 by 9-inch baking dish. If doubling, increase the baking time to about 45 minutes.

CRUMB TOPPING

- ⅓ cup (2⅔ ounces) granulated sugar
- ⅓ cup packed (2⅓ ounces) dark brown sugar
- ¾ teaspoon ground cinnamon
- ⅛ teaspoon table salt
- 8 tablespoons (1 stick) unsalted butter, melted and still warm
- 1¾ cups (7 ounces) cake flour (see note)

CAKE

- 1¼ cups (5 ounces) cake flour (see note)
- ½ cup (3½ ounces) granulated sugar
- ¼ teaspoon baking soda
- ¼ teaspoon table salt
- 6 tablespoons (¾ stick) unsalted butter, cut into 6 pieces, softened but still cool
- 1 large whole egg plus 1 large egg yolk
- ⅓ cup buttermilk (see note)
- 1 teaspoon vanilla extract
  Confectioners' sugar, for dusting

1. FOR THE CRUMB TOPPING: Whisk the sugars, cinnamon, salt, and butter together in a medium bowl to combine. Add the flour and stir with a rubber spatula or wooden spoon until the mixture resembles a thick, cohesive dough; set aside to cool to room temperature, 10 to 15 minutes.

2. FOR THE CAKE: Adjust an oven rack to the upper-middle position and heat the oven to 325 degrees. Cut a 16-inch length of parchment paper or aluminum foil and fold lengthwise to a 7-inch width. Spray an 8-inch square baking dish with vegetable oil spray and fit the parchment into the dish, pushing it into the corners and up the sides; allow the excess to overhang the edges of the dish.

3. In the bowl of a stand mixer fitted with the paddle attachment, mix the flour, sugar, baking soda, and salt on low speed to combine. With the mixer running at low speed, add the butter one piece at a time; continue beating until the mixture resembles moist crumbs, with no visible butter chunks remaining, 1 to 2 minutes. Add the egg, egg yolk, buttermilk, and vanilla; beat on medium-high speed until light and fluffy, about 1 minute, scraping once if necessary.

4. Transfer the batter to the prepared baking pan; using a rubber spatula, spread the batter into an even layer. Break apart the crumb topping into large pea-size pieces, rolling them between your thumb and forefinger to form crumbs, and spread in an even layer over the batter, beginning with the edges and then working toward the center. Bake until the crumbs are golden and a wooden skewer inserted into the center of the cake comes out clean, 35 to 40 minutes. Cool on a wire rack for at least 30 minutes. Remove the cake from the pan by lifting the parchment overhang. Dust with confectioners' sugar before serving.

BLUEBERRY BOY BAIT

WHY THIS RECIPE WORKS: This coffee cake, a moist cake with blueberries and a light streusel topping, is so called because the girl who created it for the Pillsbury Grand National Baking Contest said that teenage boys found it irresistible. We tracked down a version of the contest-winning recipe and decided to see if we could improve it.

The original recipe called for shortening and granulated sugar. We swapped butter for the shortening and brown sugar for some of the granulated sugar. Both exchanges resulted in richer, deeper flavor in the cake. We doubled the amount of blueberries; half went into the cake batter and the other half on top. An extra egg in the cake batter firmed up the structure so that the extra fruit wouldn't make the cake mushy. The topping couldn't be simpler: in addition to the blueberries, just sugar and cinnamon instead of a streusel, which baked into a light, crisp, sweet coating. If the quick disappearance of this cake is any indication, it's not only teenage boys who can't refuse a second piece.

Blueberry Boy Bait
SERVES 12

If using frozen blueberries, do not let them thaw, as they will turn the batter a blue-green color.

CAKE
- 2 cups (10 ounces) plus 1 teaspoon unbleached all-purpose flour
- 1 tablespoon baking powder
- 1 teaspoon table salt
- 16 tablespoons (2 sticks) unsalted butter, softened
- ¾ cup packed (5¼ ounces) light brown sugar
- ½ cup (3½ ounces) granulated sugar

- 3 large eggs
- 1 cup whole milk
- ½ cup blueberries, fresh or frozen (see note)

TOPPING
- ½ cup blueberries, fresh or frozen (see note)
- ¼ cup (1¾ ounces) granulated sugar
- ½ teaspoon ground cinnamon

1. FOR THE CAKE: Adjust an oven rack to the middle position and heat the oven to 350 degrees. Grease and flour a 13 by 9-inch baking pan.

2. Whisk 2 cups of the flour, the baking powder, and salt together in a medium bowl. With an electric mixer, beat the butter and sugars on medium-high speed until fluffy, about 2 minutes. Add the eggs, one at a time, beating until just incorporated. Reduce the speed to medium and beat in one-third of the flour mixture until incorporated; beat in ½ cup of the milk. Beat in half of the remaining flour mixture, then the remaining ½ cup milk, and finally the remaining flour mixture. Toss the blueberries in a small bowl with the remaining 1 teaspoon flour. Using a rubber spatula, gently fold in the blueberries. Spread the batter into the prepared pan.

3. FOR THE TOPPING: Scatter the blueberries over the top of the batter. Stir the sugar and cinnamon together in a small bowl and sprinkle over the batter. Bake until a toothpick inserted in the center of the cake comes out clean, 45 to 50 minutes. Cool in the pan for 20 minutes, then turn out and place on a serving platter (topping side up). Serve warm or at room temperature. (The cake can be stored in an airtight container at room temperature for up to 3 days.)

CINNAMON BUNS

WHY THIS RECIPE WORKS: A tender, fluffy bun with a sweet filling and glaze is a brunch treat no one will turn down. Most recipes, though, require yeast, which makes them time-consuming. Eliminating the yeast would reduce the prep time substantially, so we started with the assumption that our leavener would be baking powder. A cream biscuit recipe, which could be mixed all in one bowl, was our starting point; buttermilk rather than cream (plus baking soda to balance the acidity of the buttermilk) made the interior of the buns light and airy. Melted butter restored some of the richness we had lost by eliminating the cream. A brief kneading ensured that the rolls would rise. We patted out the dough rather than rolling it out and covered it with the filling of brown and granulated sugars, cinnamon, cloves, and salt, with melted butter to help the mixture adhere. We rolled up the dough, cut the buns, and put them in a nonstick cake pan to bake. We topped the buns with a glaze of confectioners' sugar, buttermilk, and cream cheese. These cinnamon buns were on the table in less than a quarter of the time it would have taken for yeast buns—and they were just as tasty.

Quick Cinnamon Buns with Buttermilk Icing

MAKES 8 BUNS

Melted butter is used in both the filling and the dough and to grease the pan; melt the total amount (8 tablespoons) at once and measure it out as you need it. The buns are best eaten warm, but they will hold for up to 2 hours.

1 tablespoon unsalted butter, melted, for the pan (see note)

CINNAMON-SUGAR FILLING
¾ cup packed (5¼ ounces) dark brown sugar
¼ cup (1¾ ounces) granulated sugar
2 teaspoons ground cinnamon
⅛ teaspoon ground cloves
⅛ teaspoon table salt
1 tablespoon unsalted butter, melted (see note)

BISCUIT DOUGH
2½ cups (12½ ounces) unbleached all-purpose flour, plus extra for the work surface
2 tablespoons granulated sugar
1¼ teaspoons baking powder
½ teaspoon baking soda
½ teaspoon table salt
1¼ cups buttermilk
6 tablespoons (¾ stick) unsalted butter, melted (see note)

ICING
2 tablespoons cream cheese, softened
2 tablespoons buttermilk
1 cup (4 ounces) confectioners' sugar

1. Adjust an oven rack to the upper-middle position and heat the oven to 425 degrees. Pour 1 tablespoon of the melted butter into a 9-inch nonstick cake pan; brush to coat the pan. Spray a wire rack with vegetable oil spray and set aside.

2. FOR THE CINNAMON-SUGAR FILLING: Combine the sugars, spices, and salt in a small bowl. Add the melted butter and stir with a fork or your fingers until the mixture resembles wet sand; set the filling mixture aside.

3. FOR THE BISCUIT DOUGH: Whisk the flour, sugar, baking powder, baking soda, and salt together in a large bowl. Whisk the buttermilk and 2 tablespoons of the melted butter together in a measuring cup or small bowl. Add the liquid to the dry ingredients and stir with a wooden spoon until the liquid is absorbed (the dough will look very shaggy), about 30 seconds. Transfer the dough to a lightly floured work surface and knead until just smooth and no longer shaggy.

4. Pat the dough with your hands into a 12 by 9-inch rectangle. Brush the dough with 2 tablespoons more melted butter. Sprinkle evenly with the filling, leaving a ½-inch border of plain dough around the edges. Press the filling firmly into the dough. Using a bench scraper or metal spatula, loosen the dough from the work surface. Starting at a long side, roll the dough, pressing lightly, to form a tight log. Pinch the seam to seal. Roll the log seam side down and cut it evenly into eight pieces. With your hand, slightly flatten each piece of dough to seal the open edges and keep the filling in place. Place one roll in the center of the prepared pan, then place the remaining seven rolls around the perimeter of the pan. Brush with the remaining 2 tablespoons melted butter.

5. Bake until the edges are golden brown, 23 to 25 minutes. Use an offset metal spatula to loosen the buns from the pan. Wearing an oven mitt, place a large plate over the pan and invert the buns onto a plate. Place the greased wire rack over the plate and invert the buns onto the rack. Cool for 5 minutes.

6. FOR THE ICING: While the buns are cooling, line a rimmed baking sheet with parchment paper; set the rack with the buns over the baking sheet. Whisk the cream cheese and buttermilk together in a large nonreactive bowl until thick and smooth (the mixture will look like cottage cheese at first). Sift the confectioners' sugar over the mixture; whisk until a smooth glaze forms, about 30 seconds. Spoon the glaze evenly over the buns and serve.

STICKY BUNS

WHY THIS RECIPE WORKS: Sticky buns are often too sweet, too big, too rich—just too much. We wanted a bun that was neither dense nor bready, but tender and feathery. The sticky glaze should be gently chewy and gooey; the flavor should be warm and spicy, buttery and sweet—but just enough so that devouring one isn't a feat.

To keep the sticky bun glaze from hardening into a taffy-like shell, we hit on the idea of including cream, which kept the glaze supple. The yeast dough for these buns should be rich, so we added buttermilk, which gave the buns a complex

flavor and a little acidity that balanced the sweetness. Butter and eggs enriched the dough further. After the first rise, we spread the filling—dark brown sugar, cinnamon, cloves, and butter—over the dough, rolled it, cut the individual buns, and laid them in the pan with the caramel to rise once more before being baked. We found that setting the pan (a metal nonstick pan was preferable) on a baking stone in the oven ensured that the bottoms of the buns (which would end up on top) baked completely. We wanted pecans in our sticky buns, too, but they lost their crunch when we put them into the filling or the topping. To preserve their crispness, we topped the rolls with the toasted nuts in a lightly sweetened glaze before serving.

Sticky Buns with Pecans

MAKES 12 BUNS

This recipe has four components: the dough that is shaped into buns, the filling that creates the swirl in the shaped buns, the caramel glaze that bakes in the bottom of the baking dish along with the buns, and the pecan topping that garnishes the buns once they're baked. Although the ingredient list may look long, note that many ingredients are repeated. Leftover sticky buns can be wrapped in foil or plastic wrap and refrigerated for up to 3 days, but they should be warmed through before serving. They reheat quickly in a microwave oven (for two buns, about 2 minutes at 50 percent power works well).

DOUGH

- 3 large eggs, at room temperature
- ¾ cup buttermilk, at room temperature
- ¼ cup (1¾ ounces) granulated sugar
- 1¼ teaspoons table salt
- 2¼ teaspoons (1 envelope) instant or rapid-rise yeast
- 4¼ cups (21¼ ounces) unbleached all-purpose flour, plus extra for the work surface
- 6 tablespoons (¾ stick) unsalted butter, melted and still warm

CARAMEL GLAZE

- ¾ cup packed (5¼ ounces) light brown sugar
- 6 tablespoons (¾ stick) unsalted butter
- 3 tablespoons light or dark corn syrup
- 2 tablespoons heavy cream
  Pinch table salt

CINNAMON-SUGAR FILLING

- ¾ cup packed (5¼ ounces) light brown sugar
- 2 teaspoons ground cinnamon
- ¼ teaspoon ground cloves
  Pinch table salt
- 1 tablespoon unsalted butter, melted

PECAN TOPPING

- ¼ cup packed (1¾ ounces) light brown sugar
- 3 tablespoons light or dark corn syrup
- 3 tablespoons unsalted butter
  Pinch table salt
- ¾ cup (3 ounces) pecans, toasted in a small, dry skillet over medium heat until fragrant and browned, about 5 minutes, then cooled and chopped coarse
- 1 teaspoon vanilla extract

1. FOR THE DOUGH: In the bowl of a stand mixer, whisk the eggs to combine; add the buttermilk and whisk to combine. Whisk in the granulated sugar, salt, and yeast. Add about 2 cups of the flour and the butter; stir with a wooden spoon or rubber spatula until evenly moistened and combined. Add all but about ¼ cup of the remaining flour and knead with the dough hook at low speed for 5 minutes. Check the consistency of the dough (it should feel soft and moist but should not be wet and sticky; add more flour, if necessary); knead at low speed 5 minutes longer (the dough should clear the sides of the bowl but stick to the bottom). Turn the dough out onto a lightly floured work surface; knead by hand for about 1 minute to ensure that the dough is uniform (the dough should not stick to the work surface during hand kneading; if it does, knead in additional flour 1 tablespoon at a time).

2. Lightly spray a large bowl or plastic container with vegetable oil spray. Transfer the dough to the bowl, spray the dough lightly with vegetable oil spray, then cover the bowl tightly with plastic wrap and set in a warm, draft-free spot until doubled in volume, 2 to 2½ hours.

3. FOR THE CARAMEL GLAZE: Meanwhile, combine all the glaze ingredients in a small saucepan; cook over medium heat, whisking occasionally, until the butter is melted and the mixture is thoroughly combined. Pour the mixture into a nonstick metal 13 by 9-inch baking dish; using a rubber spatula, spread the mixture to cover the surface of the baking dish; set the baking dish aside.

4. FOR THE FILLING: Combine the brown sugar, cinnamon, cloves, and salt in a small bowl and mix until thoroughly combined, using your fingers to break up any sugar lumps; set aside.

5. TO ASSEMBLE AND BAKE THE BUNS: Turn the dough out onto a lightly floured work surface. Gently shape the dough into a rough rectangle with a long side nearest you. Lightly flour the dough and roll to a 16 by 12-inch rectangle. Brush the dough with the melted butter, leaving a ½-inch border along the top edge; brush the sides of the baking dish with the butter remaining on the brush. Sprinkle the filling mixture over the dough, leaving a ¾-inch border along the top edge; smooth the filling in an even layer with your hand, then gently press the mixture into the dough to adhere. Beginning with the long edge nearest you, roll the dough into a taut cylinder. Firmly pinch the seam to seal and roll the cylinder seam side down. Very gently stretch to form a cylinder of even diameter and 18-inch length; push the ends in to create an even thickness. Using a serrated knife and gentle sawing motion, slice the cylinder in half, then slice each half in half again to create evenly sized quarters. Slice each quarter evenly into thirds, yielding 12 buns (the end pieces may be slightly smaller).

6. Arrange the buns cut side down in the prepared baking dish; cover tightly with plastic wrap and set in a warm, draft-free spot until puffy and pressed against one another, about 1½ hours. Meanwhile, adjust an oven rack to the lowest position, place a baking stone on the rack, and heat the oven to 350 degrees.

7. Place the baking pan on the baking stone; bake until golden brown and the center of the dough registers 180 degrees on an instant-read thermometer, 25 to 30 minutes. Cool on a wire rack for 10 minutes; invert onto a rimmed baking sheet, large rectangular platter, or cutting board. With a rubber spatula, scrape any glaze remaining in the baking pan onto the buns; cool while making the pecan topping.

8. FOR THE PECAN TOPPING: Combine the brown sugar, corn syrup, butter, and salt in a small saucepan and bring to a simmer over medium heat, whisking occasionally to thoroughly combine. Off the heat, stir in the pecans and vanilla until the pecans are evenly coated. Using a soupspoon, spoon a heaping tablespoon of nuts and topping over the center of each sticky bun. Continue to cool until the sticky buns are warm, 15 to 20 minutes. Pull apart or use a serrated knife to cut apart the sticky buns; serve.

PERFECT STICKY BUNS

WHY THIS RECIPE WORKS: Sticky buns look inviting, but most are dry and overly sweet, with a topping that threatens your dental work. We wanted a version that fulfilled its promise. To make a softer, more tender, and moist sticky bun, we added a cooked flour-and-water paste to the dough. The paste traps water, so the dough isn't sticky or difficult to work with, and the increased hydration converts to steam during baking, which makes the bread fluffy and light. The added water also keeps the crumb moist and tender. To ensure that the soft bread wouldn't collapse under the weight of the topping, we strengthened the crumb by adding a resting period and withholding the sugar and salt until the gluten was firmly established. Dark corn syrup plus water was the key to a

gooey, sticky topping that was substantial enough to sit atop the buns without sinking in but not so firm that it presented a danger to our teeth.

Perfect Sticky Buns
MAKES 12 BUNS

These buns take about 4 hours to make from start to finish. For dough that is easy to work with and produces light, fluffy buns, we strongly recommend that you measure the flour for the dough by weight. The slight tackiness of the dough aids in flattening and stretching it in step 6, so resist the urge to use a lot of dusting flour. Rolling the dough cylinder tightly in step 7 will result in misshapen rolls; keep the cylinder a bit slack. Bake these buns in a metal, not glass or ceramic, baking pan. We like dark corn syrup and pecans here, but light corn syrup may be used, and the nuts may be omitted, if desired.

FLOUR PASTE
- ⅔ cup water
- ¼ cup (1⅓ ounces) bread flour

DOUGH
- ⅔ cup milk
- 1 large egg plus 1 large yolk
- 2¾ cups (15⅛ ounces) bread flour
- 2 teaspoons instant or rapid-rise yeast
- 3 tablespoons granulated sugar
- 1½ teaspoons salt
- 6 tablespoons unsalted butter, softened

TOPPING
- 6 tablespoons unsalted butter, melted
- ½ cup packed (3½ ounces) dark brown sugar
- ¼ cup (1¾ ounces) granulated sugar
- ¼ cup dark corn syrup
- ¼ teaspoon salt
- 2 tablespoons water
- 1 cup pecans, toasted and chopped (optional)

FILLING
- ¾ cup packed (5¼ ounces) dark brown sugar
- 1 teaspoon ground cinnamon

1. FOR THE FLOUR PASTE: Whisk water and flour together in small bowl until no lumps remain. Microwave, whisking every 25 seconds, until mixture thickens to stiff, smooth, pudding-like consistency that forms mound when dropped from end of whisk into bowl, 50 to 75 seconds.

2. FOR THE DOUGH: In bowl of stand mixer, whisk flour paste and milk together until smooth. Add egg and yolk and whisk until incorporated. Add flour and yeast. Fit stand mixer with dough hook and mix on low speed until all flour is moistened, 1 to 2 minutes. Let stand for 15 minutes. Add sugar and salt and mix on medium-low speed for 5 minutes. Stop mixer and add butter. Continue to mix on medium-low speed for 5 minutes longer, scraping down dough hook and sides of bowl halfway through (dough will stick to bottom of bowl).

3. Transfer dough to lightly floured counter. Knead briefly to form ball and transfer seam side down to lightly greased bowl; lightly coat surface of dough with vegetable oil spray and cover bowl with plastic wrap. Let dough rise until just doubled in volume, 40 minutes to 1 hour.

4. FOR THE TOPPING: While dough rises, grease 13 by 9-inch metal baking pan. Whisk melted butter, brown sugar, granulated sugar, corn syrup, and salt together in medium bowl until smooth. Add water and whisk until incorporated. Pour mixture into prepared pan and tilt pan to cover bottom. Sprinkle evenly with pecans, if using.

5. FOR THE FILLING: Combine sugar and cinnamon in small bowl and mix until thoroughly combined; set aside.

6. Turn out dough onto lightly floured counter. Press dough gently but firmly to expel air. Working from center toward edge, pat and stretch dough to form 18 by 15-inch rectangle with long edge nearest you. Sprinkle filling over dough, leaving 1-inch border along top edge; smooth filling into even layer with your hand, then gently press mixture into dough to adhere.

7. Beginning with long edge nearest you, roll dough into cylinder, taking care not to roll too tightly. Pinch seam to seal and roll cylinder seam side down. Mark gently with knife to create 12 equal portions. To slice, hold strand of dental floss taut and slide underneath cylinder, stopping at first mark. Cross ends of floss over each other and pull. Slice cylinder into 12 portions and transfer, cut sides down, to prepared baking pan. Cover tightly with plastic wrap and let rise until buns are puffy and touching one another, 40 minutes to 1 hour. (Buns may be refrigerated immediately after shaping for up to 14 hours. To bake, remove baking pan from refrigerator and let sit until buns are puffy and touching one another, 1 to 1½ hours.) Meanwhile, adjust oven racks to lowest and lower-middle positions. Place rimmed baking sheet on lower rack to catch any drips and heat oven to 375 degrees.

8. Bake buns on upper rack until golden brown, about 20 minutes. Tent with aluminum foil and bake until center of dough registers at least 200 degrees, 10 to 15 minutes longer. Let buns cool in pan on wire rack for 5 minutes. Place rimmed baking sheet over buns and carefully invert. Using spoon, scoop any glaze from baking pan onto buns. Let cool for at least 10 minutes longer before serving.

NOTES FROM THE TEST KITCHEN

ROLLING DOUGH FOR STICKY BUNS

Because these sticky buns bake up so soft and fluffy, it's important to roll the dough loosely when forming the cylinder in step 7. If rolled too tightly, the buns will expand upward.

SOUR CREAM COFFEE CAKE

WHY THIS RECIPE WORKS: Sour cream coffee cakes should be buttery and rich. But some recipes yield a heavy cake that borders on greasy. We wanted a pleasantly rich cake with lots of streusel. All-purpose flour gave us a better texture than the cake flour specified in many recipes. For richness, we used plenty of butter, sour cream, and eggs; the eggs also contributed a tight crumb. Baking powder and baking soda were necessary to make this hefty batter rise. Rather than creaming the butter and sugar, which made the cake too light and airy, we cut softened butter and some of the sour cream into the dry ingredients, then added the eggs and the rest of the sour cream. In addition to the streusel in the middle of the cake, we wanted more on top, so we started with a mixture of brown and granulated sugars and added a big hit of cinnamon and some flour (to keep the streusel from congealing). We then divided the mixture—some for the interior streusel layers, which we sweetened further with more brown sugar, and the rest for the topping. To the latter, we added pecans and butter; the nuts toasted as the cake baked, so we didn't have to toast them first. With two layers of streusel in our moist, rich cake and another layer on top with toasty, crunchy nuts, this was a coffee cake worth getting up for.

Sour Cream Coffee Cake with Brown Sugar–Pecan Streusel

SERVES 12 TO 16

A 10-inch tube pan is best for this recipe.

STREUSEL

- ¾ cup (3¾ ounces) unbleached all-purpose flour
- ¾ cup (5¼ ounces) granulated sugar
- ½ cup packed (3½ ounces) dark brown sugar
- 2 tablespoons ground cinnamon
- 1 cup pecans, chopped
- 2 tablespoons unsalted butter, chilled and cut into 2 pieces

CAKE

12 tablespoons (1½ sticks) unsalted butter, softened
but still cool, cut into ½-inch cubes, plus 2 tablespoons
softened butter, for greasing the pan

4 large eggs

1½ cups sour cream

1 tablespoon vanilla extract

2¼ cups (11½ ounces) unbleached all-purpose flour

1¼ cups (8¾ ounces) granulated sugar

1 tablespoon baking powder

¾ teaspoon baking soda

¾ teaspoon table salt

1. FOR THE STREUSEL: In a food processor, process the flour, granulated sugar, ¼ cup of the brown sugar, and the cinnamon until combined, about 15 seconds. Transfer 1¼ cups of the flour-sugar mixture to a small bowl; stir in the remaining ¼ cup brown sugar and set aside to use for the streusel filling. Add the pecans and butter to the flour-sugar mixture in the food processor; pulse until the nuts and butter resemble small pebbly pieces, about 10 pulses; set aside.

2. FOR THE CAKE: Adjust an oven rack to the lowest position and heat the oven to 350 degrees. Grease a 10-cup tube pan with 2 tablespoons of the softened butter. Whisk the eggs, 1 cup of the sour cream, and the vanilla together in a medium bowl until combined.

3. Mix the flour, granulated sugar, baking powder, baking soda, and salt in the bowl of a stand mixer on low speed until combined, about 30 seconds. Add the remaining 12 tablespoons butter and remaining ½ cup sour cream; mix on low speed until the dry ingredients are moistened and the mixture resembles wet sand, with a few large butter pieces remaining, about 1½ minutes. Increase the speed to medium and beat until the batter comes together, about 10 seconds, scraping down the sides of the bowl with a rubber spatula as necessary. Lower the speed to medium-low and gradually add the egg mixture in three additions, beating for 20 seconds after each addition and scraping down the sides of the bowl as necessary. Increase the speed to medium-high and beat until the batter is light and fluffy, about 1 minute.

4. Using a rubber spatula, spread 2 cups of the batter in the bottom of the prepared pan, smoothing the surface. Sprinkle evenly with ¾ cup of the streusel filling without butter or nuts. Repeat with 2 cups more batter and the remaining ¾ cup streusel filling without butter or nuts. Spread the remaining batter over, then sprinkle with the streusel topping with butter and nuts.

5. Bake until the cake feels firm to the touch and a long toothpick or skewer inserted into the center comes out clean (bits of sugar from the streusel may cling to the tester), 50 to 60 minutes. Cool the cake in the pan on a wire rack for 30 minutes. Invert the cake onto a rimmed baking sheet (the cake will be streusel side down); remove the tube pan, place a wire rack on top of the cake, and reinvert the cake streusel side up. Cool to room temperature, about 2 hours. Cut into wedges and serve. (The cake can be wrapped in foil and stored at room temperature for up to 5 days.)

CREAM CHEESE COFFEE CAKE

WHY THIS RECIPE WORKS: This brunch staple is fraught with pitfalls—from dry, bland cake to lackluster fillings that sink to the bottom as they cook. We wanted a rich, moist cake with a texture that could support a tangy swirl of cream cheese filling.

We assembled a batter of flour, granulated sugar, salt, butter, eggs, whole milk, and baking powder and settled on a straightforward creaming method: Beat softened butter with sugar, then add the eggs, milk, and dry ingredients. The resulting cake was full of flavor and capable of supporting our cheese filling—but it was also a bit dry. To add moisture, we replaced the milk with rich sour cream, added baking soda, and upped the amount of butter. Our cake now had a lush texture as well as subtle acidity—a perfect backdrop for the cheese filling. We settled on a base mixture of softened cream cheese and sugar and added lemon juice to cut the richness and a hint of vanilla extract for depth of flavor. To prevent graininess, we incorporated some of the cake batter into the cheese. The filling not only stayed creamy, but it fused to the cake during baking, eliminating gaps that had afflicted our earlier tests. For a topping, we decided upon a crisp yet delicate coating of sliced almonds, sugar, and lemon zest. As it baked, the topping formed a glistening, crackly crust on our now-perfect coffee cake.

Cream Cheese Coffee Cake
SERVES 12 TO 16

Leftovers should be stored in the refrigerator, covered tightly with plastic wrap. For optimal texture, allow the cake to return to room temperature before serving.

LEMON SUGAR-ALMOND TOPPING

¼ cup (1¾ ounces) sugar

1½ teaspoons finely grated zest from 1 lemon

½ cup sliced almonds

CAKE

2¼ cups (11¼ ounces) unbleached all-purpose flour

1⅛ teaspoons baking powder

1⅛ teaspoons baking soda

1 teaspoon table salt

10 tablespoons (1¼ sticks) unsalted butter, softened
but still cool

1 cup (7 ounces) plus 7 tablespoons sugar

1 tablespoon finely grated zest plus 4 teaspoons
juice from 1 to 2 lemons

4 large eggs

5 teaspoons vanilla extract

1¼ cups sour cream

8 ounces cream cheese, softened

1. FOR THE TOPPING: Adjust an oven rack to the middle position and heat the oven to 350 degrees. Stir together the sugar and lemon zest in a small bowl until combined and the sugar is moistened. Stir in the almonds; set aside.

MAKING CREAM CHEESE COFFEE CAKE

1. Reserve 1¼ cups of the batter, then fill the pan with the remaining batter; smooth the top.

2. Beat ¼ cup of the reserved batter with the filling ingredients; spoon the filling evenly over the batter.

3. Top the filling with the remaining 1 cup reserved batter; smooth the top.

4. Using a figure-8 motion, swirl the filling into the batter. Tap the pan on the counter.

5. Sprinkle the lemon sugar–almond topping onto the batter, then gently press to adhere.

2. FOR THE CAKE: Spray a 10-inch tube pan with vegetable oil spray. Whisk the flour, baking powder, baking soda, and salt together in a medium bowl; set aside. In a stand mixer fitted with the paddle attachment, beat the butter, 1 cup plus 2 tablespoons of the sugar, and the lemon zest at medium speed until light and fluffy, about 3 minutes, scraping down the sides and bottom of the bowl with a rubber spatula. Add the eggs one at a time, beating well after each addition, about 20 seconds, and scraping down the beater and sides of the bowl as necessary. Add 4 teaspoons of the vanilla and mix

to combine. Reduce the speed to low and add one-third of the flour mixture, followed by half of the sour cream, mixing until incorporated after each addition, 5 to 10 seconds. Repeat, using half of the remaining flour mixture and all of the remaining sour cream. Scrape the bowl and add the remaining flour mixture; mix at low speed until the batter is thoroughly combined, about 10 seconds. Remove the bowl from the mixer and fold the batter once or twice with a rubber spatula to incorporate any remaining flour.

3. Reserve 1¼ cups of the batter and set aside. Spoon the remaining batter into the prepared pan and smooth the top. Return the now-empty bowl to the mixer and beat the cream cheese, remaining 5 tablespoons sugar, lemon juice, and remaining 1 teaspoon vanilla on medium speed until smooth and slightly lightened, about 1 minute. Add ¼ cup of the reserved batter and mix until incorporated. Spoon the cheese filling mixture evenly over the batter, keeping the filling about 1 inch from the edges of the pan; smooth the top. Spread the remaining 1 cup reserved batter over the filling and smooth the top. With a butter knife or offset spatula, gently swirl the filling into the batter using a figure-eight motion, being careful not to drag the filling to the bottom or edges of the pan. Firmly tap the pan on the counter two or three times to dislodge any bubbles. Sprinkle the lemon sugar–almond topping evenly over the batter and gently press into the batter to adhere.

4. Bake until the top is golden and just firm and a long skewer inserted into the cake comes out clean (a skewer will be wet if inserted into the cheese filling), 45 to 50 minutes. Remove the pan from the oven and firmly tap on the counter two or three times (the top of the cake may sink slightly). Cool the cake in the pan on a wire rack for 1 hour. Gently invert the cake onto a rimmed baking sheet (the cake will be topping side down); remove the tube pan, place a wire rack on top of the cake, and invert the cake sugar side up. Cool to room temperature, about 1½ hours, before serving.

CHUNKY GRANOLA WITH DRIED FRUIT

WHY THIS RECIPE WORKS: Store-bought granola suffers from many shortcomings. It's often loose and gravelly and/or infuriatingly expensive. We wanted to make our own granola at home, with big, satisfying clusters and crisp texture. The secret was to firmly pack the granola mixture into a rimmed baking sheet before baking. Once it was baked, we had a granola "bark" that we could break into crunchy lumps of any size.

Almond Granola with Dried Fruit
MAKES ABOUT 9 CUPS
Chopping the almonds by hand is the first choice for superior texture and crunch. If you prefer not to hand chop, substitute an equal quantity of slivered or sliced almonds. (A food processor does a lousy job of chopping whole nuts evenly.) Use a single type of your favorite dried fruit or a combination. Do not use quick oats.

⅓ cup maple syrup

⅓ cup packed (2⅓ ounces) light brown sugar

4 teaspoons vanilla extract

½ teaspoon salt

½ cup vegetable oil

5 cups (15 ounces) old-fashioned rolled oats

2 cups (10 ounces) raw almonds, chopped coarse

2 cups raisins or other dried fruit, chopped

1. Adjust oven rack to upper-middle position and heat oven to 325 degrees. Line rimmed baking sheet with parchment paper.

2. Whisk maple syrup, brown sugar, vanilla, and salt in large bowl. Whisk in oil. Fold in oats and almonds until thoroughly coated.

3. Transfer oat mixture to prepared baking sheet and spread across sheet into thin, even layer (about ⅜ inch thick). Using stiff metal spatula, compress oat mixture until very compact. Bake until lightly browned, 40 to 45 minutes, rotating pan once halfway through baking. Remove granola from oven and cool on wire rack to room temperature, about 1 hour. Break cooled granola into pieces of desired size. Stir in dried fruit. (Granola can be stored in airtight container for up to 2 weeks.)

Pecan-Orange Granola with Dried Cranberries

Add 2 tablespoons finely grated orange zest and 2½ teaspoons ground cinnamon to maple syrup mixture in step 2. Substitute coarsely chopped pecans for almonds. After granola is broken into pieces, stir in 2 cups dried cranberries.

Spiced Walnut Granola with Dried Apple

Add 2 teaspoons ground cinnamon, 1½ teaspoons ground ginger, ¾ teaspoon ground allspice, ½ teaspoon freshly grated nutmeg, and ½ teaspoon pepper to maple syrup mixture in step 2. Substitute coarsely chopped walnuts for almonds. After granola is broken into pieces, stir in 2 cups chopped dried apples.

Tropical Granola with Dried Mango

Reduce vanilla extract to 2 teaspoons and add 1½ teaspoons ground ginger and ¾ teaspoon freshly grated nutmeg to maple syrup mixture in step 2. Substitute coarsely chopped macadamias for almonds and 1½ cups unsweetened shredded coconut for 1 cup oats. After granola is broken into pieces, stir in 2 cups chopped dried mango or pineapple.

Hazelnut Granola with Dried Pear

Substitute coarsely chopped, skinned hazelnuts for almonds. After granola is broken into pieces, stir in 2 cups chopped dried pears.

TEN-MINUTE STEEL-CUT OATMEAL

WHY THIS RECIPE WORKS: Most oatmeal fans agree that the steel-cut version of the grain offers the best flavor and texture, but many balk at the 40-minute cooking time. We decreased the cooking time to only 10 minutes by stirring steel-cut oats into boiling water the night before. This enabled the grains to hydrate and soften overnight. In the morning, more water (or fruit juice or milk) was added and the mixture was simmered for 4 to 6 minutes, until thick and creamy. A brief resting period off the heat ensured the perfect consistency.

Ten-Minute Steel-Cut Oatmeal

SERVES 4

The oatmeal will continue to thicken as it cools. If you prefer a looser consistency, thin the oatmeal with boiling water. Customize your oatmeal with toppings such as brown sugar, toasted nuts, maple syrup, or dried fruit.

4 cups water

1 cup steel-cut oats

¼ teaspoon salt

1. Bring 3 cups water to boil in large saucepan over high heat. Remove pan from heat; stir in oats and salt. Cover pan and let stand overnight.

2. Stir remaining 1 cup water into oats and bring to boil over medium-high heat. Reduce heat to medium and cook, stirring occasionally, until oats are softened but still retain some chew and mixture thickens and resembles warm pudding, 4 to 6 minutes. Remove pan from heat and let stand for 5 minutes. Stir and serve, passing desired toppings separately.

Apple-Cinnamon Steel-Cut Oatmeal

Increase salt to ½ teaspoon. Substitute ½ cup apple cider and ½ cup whole milk for water in step 2. Stir ½ cup peeled, grated sweet apple, 2 tablespoons packed dark brown sugar, and ½ teaspoon ground cinnamon into oatmeal with cider and milk. Sprinkle each serving with 2 tablespoons coarsely chopped toasted walnuts.

Carrot-Spice Steel-Cut Oatmeal

Increase salt to ¾ teaspoon. Substitute ½ cup carrot juice and ½ cup whole milk for water in step 2. Stir ½ cup finely grated carrot, ¼ cup packed dark brown sugar, ⅓ cup dried currants, and ½ teaspoon ground cinnamon into oatmeal with carrot juice and milk. Sprinkle each serving with 2 tablespoons coarsely chopped toasted pecans.

Cranberry-Orange Steel-Cut Oatmeal

Increase salt to ½ teaspoon. Substitute ½ cup orange juice and ½ cup whole milk for water in step 2. Stir ½ cup dried cranberries, 3 tablespoons packed dark brown sugar, and ⅛ teaspoon ground cardamom into oatmeal with orange juice and milk. Sprinkle each serving with 2 tablespoons toasted sliced almonds.

Banana-Coconut Steel-Cut Oatmeal

Increase salt to ½ teaspoon. Substitute 1 cup canned coconut milk for water in step 2. Stir ½ cup toasted shredded coconut, 2 diced bananas, and ½ teaspoon vanilla extract into oatmeal before serving.

Peanut, Honey, and Banana Steel-Cut Oatmeal

Increase salt to ½ teaspoon. Substitute ½ cup whole milk for ½ cup water in step 2. Stir 3 tablespoons honey into oatmeal with milk and water. Add ¼ cup of peanut butter and 1 tablespoon unsalted butter to oatmeal after removing from heat in step 2. Stir 2 diced bananas into oatmeal before serving. Sprinkle each serving with 2 tablespoons coarsely chopped toasted peanuts.

FRUIT SALAD

WHY THIS RECIPE WORKS: A bowl of cut-up fresh fruit is a nice complement to the sweets and heavier egg dishes at a brunch, but it can be a little boring without additional flavors. Yogurt-based sauces mask the fresh flavors of the fruit, and sweet syrups make the fruit too much like a dessert. We were looking for a lighter, more flavorful alternative. We adapted a French dressing called a *gastrique*, a reduction of an acidic liquid with sugar that usually accompanies savory dishes made with fruit. It's a simple technique, and our experiments with reducing different types of acid—wine, citrus juice, and balsamic vinegar—were an unqualified success. We were able to use additional flavorings in the dressing, such as spices, extracts, and citrus zests, that would complement the flavors of the fruit. Served at room temperature or chilled, fresh fruit bathed in a light but sweet-tart dressing is not only delicious but easy to make.

Strawberries and Grapes with Balsamic and Red Wine Reduction

MAKES ABOUT 6 CUPS

An inexpensive balsamic vinegar is fine for use in this recipe. Save high-quality vinegar for other preparations in which the vinegar is not cooked.

- ¾ cup balsamic vinegar (see note)
- ¼ cup dry red wine
- ¼ cup sugar
- Pinch table salt
- 1 tablespoon grated zest plus 1 tablespoon juice from 1 lemon
- ¼ teaspoon vanilla extract
- 3 whole cloves
- 1 quart strawberries, hulled and halved lengthwise (about 4 cups)
- 9 ounces large seedless red or black grapes, each grape halved pole to pole (about 2 cups)

1. Simmer the vinegar, wine, sugar, and salt in a small saucepan over high heat until syrupy and reduced to ¼ cup, about 15 minutes. Off the heat, stir in the lemon zest and juice, vanilla, and cloves; steep for 1 minute to blend the flavors and strain.

2. Combine the strawberries and grapes in a medium bowl; pour the warm dressing over the fruit and toss to coat. Serve at room temperature, or cover with plastic wrap, refrigerate for up to 4 hours, and serve chilled.

Nectarines, Blueberries, and Raspberries with Champagne-Cardamom Reduction

MAKES ABOUT 6 CUPS

Dry white wine can be substituted for the champagne.

- 1 cup champagne (see note)
- ¼ cup sugar
- Pinch table salt
- 1 tablespoon grated zest plus 1 tablespoon juice from 1 lemon
- 5 cardamom pods, crushed
- 3 medium nectarines (about 18 ounces), cut into ½-inch wedges (about 3 cups)
- 1 pint blueberries
- ½ pint raspberries

1. Simmer the champagne, sugar, and salt in a small saucepan over high heat until syrupy, honey-colored, and reduced to ¼ cup, about 15 minutes. Off the heat, stir in the lemon zest and juice and cardamom; steep for 1 minute to blend the flavors and strain.

2. Combine the nectarines, blueberries, and raspberries in a medium bowl; pour the warm dressing over the fruit and toss to coat. Serve at room temperature, or cover with plastic wrap, refrigerate for up to 4 hours, and serve chilled.

Honeydew, Mango, and Blueberries with Lime-Ginger Reduction

MAKES ABOUT 6 CUPS

Be sure to zest one of the limes before juicing. Cantaloupe can be used in place of honeydew, although the color contrast with the mango won't be as vivid.

1 cup juice plus 1 tablespoon grated zest from 8 limes (see note)
¼ cup sugar
Pinch table salt
1 (1-inch) piece fresh ginger, peeled and minced (about 1 tablespoon)
1 tablespoon juice from 1 lemon
½ small honeydew melon (see note), seeds and rind removed, cut into 1-inch pieces (about 2 cups)
1 mango (about 10 ounces), peeled and cut into ½-inch pieces (about 1½ cups)
1 pint blueberries

1. Simmer the lime juice, sugar, and salt in a small saucepan over high heat until syrupy, honey-colored, and reduced to ¼ cup, about 15 minutes. Off the heat, stir in the lime zest, ginger, and lemon juice; steep for 1 minute to blend the flavors and strain.

2. Combine the melon, mango, and blueberries in a medium bowl; pour the warm dressing over the fruit and toss to coat. Serve at room temperature, or cover with plastic wrap, refrigerate for up to 4 hours, and serve chilled.

CLASSIC STRAWBERRY JAM

WHY THIS RECIPE WORKS: Strawberry jam is a universal favorite. Naturally low in pectin, strawberries are often cooked too long, causing the fruit to lose its bright flavor. We shortened the cooking time by cutting the strawberries into smaller pieces and then mashing them to release their juices and jump-start the cooking process. Shredded apple added natural pectin and fresh flavor to the mix. Lemon juice added acidity to balance the sugar's sweetness and helped the natural pectin to gel. Small, fragrant berries produce the best jam.

Classic Strawberry Jam

MAKES FOUR 1-CUP JARS

For safety reasons, be sure to use bottled lemon juice, not fresh-squeezed juice, in this recipe.

3 pounds strawberries, hulled and cut into ½-inch pieces (10 cups)
3 cups sugar
1¼ cups peeled and shredded Granny Smith apple (1 large apple)
2 tablespoons bottled lemon juice

1. Place 2 small plates in freezer to chill. Set canning rack in large pot, place four 1-cup jars in rack, and add water to cover by 1 inch. Bring to simmer over medium heat, then turn off heat and cover to keep hot.

2. In Dutch oven, crush strawberries with potato masher until fruit is mostly broken down. Stir in sugar, apple, and lemon juice and bring to boil, stirring often, over medium-high heat. Once sugar is completely dissolved, boil mixture, stirring and adjusting heat as needed, until thickened and registers 217 to 220 degrees, 20 to 25 minutes. (Temperature will be lower at higher elevations.) Remove pot from heat.

3. To test consistency, place 1 teaspoon jam on chilled plate and freeze for 2 minutes. Drag your finger through jam on plate; jam has correct consistency when your finger leaves distinct trail. If runny, return pot to heat and simmer for 1 to 3 minutes longer before retesting. Skim any foam from surface of jam using spoon.

4. Place dish towel flat on counter. Using jar lifter, remove jars from pot, draining water back into pot. Place jars upside down on towel and let dry for 1 minute. Using funnel and ladle, portion hot jam into hot jars, leaving ¼ inch headspace. Slide wooden skewer along inside edge of jar and drag upward to remove air bubbles.

5A. FOR SHORT-TERM STORAGE: Let jam cool to room temperature, cover, and refrigerate until jam is set, 12 to 24 hours. (Jam can be refrigerated for up to 2 months.)

5B. FOR LONG-TERM STORAGE: While jars are hot, wipe rims clean, add lids, and screw on rings until fingertip-tight; do not overtighten. Return pot of water with canning rack to boil. Lower jars into water, cover, bring water back to boil, then start timer. Cooking time will depend on your altitude: Boil 10 minutes for up to 1,000 feet, 15 minutes for 1,001 to 3,000 feet, 20 minutes for 3,001 to 6,000 feet, or 25 minutes for 6,001 to 8,000 feet. Turn off heat and let jars sit in pot for 5 minutes. Remove jars from pot and let cool for 24 hours. Remove rings, check seal, and clean rims. (Sealed jars can be stored for up to 1 year.)

NOTES FROM THE TEST KITCHEN

KEYS TO STRAWBERRY JAM SUCCESS

Stir sugar, shredded apple, and lemon juice into mashed berries and bring mixure to a vigorous boil. Boil mixture vigorously until it has thickened and registers between 217 and 220 degrees (at sea level).

To test jam's consistency, place 1 teaspoon of hot jam on a chilled plate and freeze it for 2 minutes. Drag your finger through the chilled jam on the plate; jam has the correct consistency when your finger leaves a distinct trail.

CHOCOLATE HAZELNUT SPREAD

WHY THIS RECIPE WORKS: Much as we love Nutella, we couldn't resist making our own homemade version of the habit-forming chocolate-hazelnut spread. Without the additives and palm oil, we hoped for a spread with a texture closer to natural peanut butter with a deeply nutty, chocolaty punch. After blanching raw hazelnuts in water and baking soda, we immediately transferred them to ice water. Their skin was easily removed by rubbing with a dish towel. Roasting the hazelnuts on a baking sheet brought out their buttery fragrance and toasty, nutty flavor. The remaining steps were as easy as pulling out our food processor and whirling the nuts into a smooth paste before adding in sugar, cocoa, oil, vanilla, and salt.

Chocolate Hazelnut Spread

MAKES 1½ CUPS

Hazelnut oil work best to reinforce the spread's flavors, but walnut and vegetable oils are also passable.

- 2 cups hazelnuts
- 6 tablespoons baking soda
- 1 cup (4 ounces) confectioners' sugar
- ⅓ cup (1 ounce) unsweetened cocoa powder
- 2 tablespoons hazelnut oil
- 1 teaspoon vanilla extract
- ⅛ teaspoon salt

1. Fill large bowl halfway with ice and water. Bring 4 cups water to boil. Add hazelnuts and baking soda and boil for 3 minutes. Transfer nuts to ice bath with slotted spoon, drain, and slip skins off with dish towel.

2. Adjust oven rack to middle position and heat oven to 375 degrees. Place hazelnuts in single layer on rimmed baking sheet and roast until fragrant and golden brown, 12 to 15 minutes, rotating sheet halfway through roasting.

3. Process hazelnuts in food processor until oil is released and smooth, loose paste forms, about 5 minutes, scraping down sides of bowl often.

4. Add sugar, cocoa, oil, vanilla, and salt and process until fully incorporated and mixture begins to loosen slightly and becomes glossy, about 2 minutes, scraping down sides of bowl as needed.

5. Transfer spread to jar with tight-fitting lid. Chocolate hazelnut spread can be stored at room temperature or refrigerated for up to 1 month.

MEXICAN HOT CHOCOLATE

WHY THIS RECIPE WORKS: For an always-ready Mexican hot chocolate mix that delivered rich texture, indulgent taste, and a touch of heat, we needed our chocolate to come in two forms. Cocoa powder is loaded with chocolate flavor and made for a thick drink, and unsweetened chocolate promised a creamy, smooth texture. Nonfat dry milk powder introduced a creamy sweetness to the blend plus a bit of extra thickening, further boosted with some cornstarch. Vanilla extract and salt heightened the chocolate's flavor. To infuse the mix with some heat, we added ground cinnamon, ancho chile powder, and cayenne. Whizzing the ingredients in the food processor created a fine, even powder that would stay combined during storage.

Mexican Hot Chocolate

MAKES 3 CUPS OF MIX; ENOUGH FOR TWELVE 1-CUP SERVINGS

Our preferred unsweetened chocolate is Hershey's Unsweetened Baking Bar. Both natural and Dutch-processed cocoa will work in this recipe. Our favorite natural cocoa powder is Hershey's Natural Cocoa Unsweetened; our favorite Dutch-processed cocoa powder is Droste Cocoa. For one serving of hot chocolate, heat 1 cup of whole, 2 percent low-fat, or 1 percent low-fat milk in a small saucepan over medium heat until it starts to steam and bubbles appear around the edge of the saucepan. Add ¼ cup of hot chocolate mix and continue to heat, whisking constantly, until simmering, 2 to 3 minutes longer. Pour the hot chocolate into a mug and serve.

- 1 cup (7 ounces) sugar
- 6 ounces unsweetened chocolate, chopped fine
- 1 cup (3 ounces) unsweetened cocoa powder
- ½ cup (1½ ounces) nonfat dry milk powder
- 5 teaspoons cornstarch
- 1 teaspoon vanilla extract
- ¾ teaspoon kosher salt
- 1 teaspoon ground cinnamon
- ¾ teaspoon ancho chile powder
  Pinch cayenne pepper

Process all ingredients in food processor until ground to powder, 30 to 60 seconds. Transfer to airtight container and store at room temperature for up to 2 months.

CHAPTER 21

PLEASE PASS THE BREAD

CREAM BISCUITS

WHY THIS RECIPE WORKS: With a high rise, light texture, and rich flavor, fresh-from-the-oven biscuits tend to disappear quicker than cookies in the test kitchen. So it's a shame that many prospective bakers pass them up, just because the recipe calls for the strenuous step of cutting butter into flour, or the messy move of rolling out dough time and again to get every last piece into a round for the baking sheet. We wanted to make great biscuits that cut out these extra steps and used a basic combination of heavy cream, flour, baking powder, and salt.

Instead of cutting butter into flour, we included a generous amount of heavy cream in our biscuits, which gave them a lighter and more tender texture. Kneading for just 30 seconds was enough to get our dough smooth and uniform. We used an extra bit of cream to soak up all the last bits of flour in the bowl, ensuring that nothing was wasted. To enhance the light flavor of our biscuits, we added a small amount of sugar. All there was left to do was shape them, then pop them into the oven immediately to keep them from spreading. Although it is easy enough to pat out this dough and cut it into rounds with a biscuit cutter, we devised a second strategy of simply pressing the dough into an 8-inch cake pan, turning out the dough, and then slicing it into wedges.

Cream Biscuits
MAKES 8 BISCUITS

Bake the biscuits immediately after cutting them; letting them stand for any length of time can decrease the leavening power and thereby prevent the biscuits from rising properly in the oven.

> 2 cups (10 ounces) unbleached all-purpose flour, plus extra for the work surface
> 2 teaspoons sugar
> 1 teaspoon baking powder
> ½ teaspoon table salt
> 1½ cups heavy cream

1. Adjust an oven rack to the upper-middle position and heat the oven to 425 degrees. Line a large rimmed baking sheet with parchment paper. Whisk the flour, sugar, baking powder, and salt together in a medium bowl.

2. Add 1¼ cups of the cream to the flour mixture and stir with a wooden spoon until a dough forms, about 30 seconds. Transfer the dough to a lightly floured work surface, leaving all dry, floury bits behind in the bowl. Add the remaining ¼ cup cream, 1 tablespoon at a time, to the bowl, mixing with a wooden spoon after each addition, until all the loose flour is just moistened; add these moistened bits to the dough. Knead the dough briefly just until smooth, about 30 seconds.

3. Pat the dough into a ¾-inch-thick circle or press it into an 8-inch cake pan and turn it out onto a lightly floured surface. Cut the biscuits into rounds using a 2½-inch biscuit cutter or into eight wedges using a knife. Place the rounds or wedges onto the prepared baking sheet and bake until golden brown, about 15 minutes. Serve immediately.

Cream Biscuits with Fresh Herbs
Use the herb of your choice in this variation.

Follow the recipe for Cream Biscuits, adding 2 tablespoons minced fresh herbs to the flour mixture in step 1. Proceed as directed.

Cheddar Biscuits
Follow the recipe for Cream Biscuits, adding 2 ounces sharp cheddar cheese, shredded (about ½ cup), to the flour mixture in step 1. Proceed as directed, increasing the baking time to 18 minutes.

BEST DROP BISCUITS

WHY THIS RECIPE WORKS: Drop biscuits have many things going for them: a crisp outer crust, a tender, flaky interior, and a simple, no-nonsense method. There's only one problem—they're often not very good. Too many are dense, gummy, and doughy or, on the flip side, lean and dry. Drop biscuits should, by nature, be simple to make and tender. We wanted a biscuit that could be easily broken apart and eaten piece by buttery piece.

Identifying the best ingredients was the first task. While oil-based biscuits were easy to work with, they lacked flavor, so butter was a must. Replacing the usual milk with buttermilk helped heighten flavor; the biscuits now had a rich, buttery tang and were crisper on the exterior and fluffier on the interior. Choosing the right leavener was also important. We needed a substantial amount, but too much baking powder left a metallic taste. Since we'd added buttermilk, we could replace some of the baking powder with baking soda (buttermilk provides the acid that soda needs to act), which gave us the rise we needed without the metallic bitterness. Once the ingredients had been identified, we were left with only one problem. Properly combining the butter and buttermilk required that both ingredients be at just the right temperature; if they weren't, the melted butter clumped in the buttermilk. But when we had trouble avoiding this, we made a batch with lumpy buttermilk anyway. The result was a surprisingly better biscuit, slightly higher and with better texture. The water in the lumps of butter (butter is 20 percent water) had turned to steam in the oven, helping create additional height.

Best Drop Biscuits

MAKES 12 BISCUITS

A ¼-cup (#16) portion scoop can be used to portion the batter. To refresh day-old biscuits, heat them in a 300-degree oven for 10 minutes.

- 2 cups (10 ounces) unbleached all-purpose flour
- 2 teaspoons baking powder
- 1 teaspoon sugar
- ¾ teaspoon table salt
- ½ teaspoon baking soda
- 1 cup buttermilk, chilled
- 8 tablespoons (1 stick) unsalted butter, melted and cooled slightly, plus 2 tablespoons melted butter for brushing the biscuits

1. Adjust an oven rack to the middle position and heat the oven to 475 degrees. Line a large rimmed baking sheet with parchment paper. Whisk the flour, baking powder, sugar, salt, and baking soda together in a large bowl. Combine the buttermilk and 8 tablespoons of the melted butter in a medium bowl, stirring until the butter forms small clumps.

2. Add the buttermilk mixture to the dry ingredients and stir with a rubber spatula until just incorporated and the batter pulls away from the sides of the bowl. Using a greased ¼-cup measuring cup, scoop a level amount of batter and drop onto the prepared baking sheet. Repeat with the remaining batter, spacing the biscuits about 1½ inches apart. Bake until the tops are golden brown and crisp, 12 to 14 minutes.

3. Brush the biscuit tops with the remaining 2 tablespoons melted butter. Transfer to a wire rack and cool for 5 minutes before serving.

PUMPKIN BREAD

WHY THIS RECIPE WORKS: Although most recipes for pumpkin bread are pleasantly sweet and spicy, they're nothing to write home about. For a bread with rich pumpkin flavor and enough spices to enhance rather than overwhelm the flavor of our pumpkin, we used a few strategies. To rid canned pumpkin puree of its raw flavor and bring out its richness, we cooked it on top of the stove just until it began to caramelize. To replace some of the lost moisture from cooking the puree and offset some of the sweetness, we added softened cream cheese to the mix. A modest hand with spices and a sweet streusel sprinkled over the top of the loaf gave us perfect pumpkin bread.

Pumpkin Bread

MAKES 2 LOAVES

The test kitchen's preferred loaf pan measures 8½ by 4½ inches; if using a 9 by 5-inch loaf pan, start checking for doneness 5 minutes early.

TOPPING

- 5 tablespoons packed (2¼ ounces) light brown sugar
- 1 tablespoon all-purpose flour
- 1 tablespoon unsalted butter, softened
- 1 teaspoon ground cinnamon
- ⅛ teaspoon salt

BREAD

- 2 cups (10 ounces) all-purpose flour
- 1½ teaspoons baking powder
- ½ teaspoon baking soda
- 1 (15-ounce) can unsweetened pumpkin puree
- 1 teaspoon salt
- 1½ teaspoons ground cinnamon
- ¼ teaspoon ground nutmeg
- ⅛ teaspoon ground cloves
- 1 cup (7 ounces) granulated sugar
- 1 cup packed (7 ounces) light brown sugar
- ½ cup vegetable oil
- 4 ounces cream cheese, cut into 12 pieces
- 4 large eggs
- ¼ cup buttermilk
- 1 cup walnuts, toasted and chopped fine

1. FOR THE TOPPING: Using fingers, mix all ingredients together in bowl until well combined and topping resembles wet sand; set aside.

2. FOR THE BREAD: Adjust oven rack to middle position and heat oven to 350 degrees. Grease two 8½ by 4½-inch loaf pans. Whisk flour, baking powder, and baking soda together in bowl.

3. Combine pumpkin puree, salt, cinnamon, nutmeg, and cloves in large saucepan over medium heat. Cook mixture, stirring constantly, until reduced to 1½ cups, 6 to 8 minutes. Remove pot from heat; stir in granulated sugar, brown sugar, oil, and cream cheese until combined. Let mixture stand for 5 minutes. Whisk until no visible pieces of cream cheese remain and mixture is homogeneous.

4. Whisk together eggs and buttermilk. Add egg mixture to pumpkin mixture and whisk to combine. Fold flour mixture into pumpkin mixture until combined (some small lumps of flour are OK). Fold walnuts into batter. Scrape batter into prepared pans. Sprinkle topping evenly over top of each loaf. Bake until skewer inserted in center of loaf comes out clean, 45 to 50 minutes. Let loaves cool in pans on wire rack for 20 minutes. Remove loaves from pans and let cool for at least 1½ hours. Serve warm or at room temperature.

Pumpkin Bread with Candied Ginger

Substitute ½ teaspoon ground ginger for cinnamon in topping. Fold ⅓ cup minced crystallized ginger into batter after flour mixture has been added in step 4.

ZUCCHINI BREAD

WHY THIS RECIPE WORKS: In the health food–crazed 1960s and '70s, recipes for zucchini bread popped up everywhere. With bits of healthy green vegetable speckling the crumb, the bread was a sweet treat you could not only enjoy but also feel virtuous about eating. But zucchini can also be a liability, as too much leads to a soggy loaf. That's why, in spite of the oft-stated goal of using up surplus squash, most recipes top out at a mere 10 to 12 ounces. And despite being associated with a health-food movement, the recipes tend to call for copious amounts of oil that turn the loaf greasy and overly rich.

We found that coarsely grated, thoroughly squeezed squash produced a crumb that was super moist but not gummy. This had the added benefit of removing some of the key compounds in zucchini—called Amadori compounds—which are responsible for zucchini's vegetal flavor, giving our loaf a sweet, mildly earthy (but not vegetal) flavor. For deeper flavor, we switched from granulated sugar to molasses-y brown sugar, increased the cinnamon to 1 tablespoon, and added nutmeg and vanilla. Swapping some of the all-purpose flour for whole-wheat gave the loaf even better structure and ensured that it wasn't soggy.

Zucchini Bread

MAKES 1 LOAF

Use the large holes of a box grater to shred the zucchini. The test kitchen's preferred loaf pan measures 8½ by 4½ inches; if you use a 9 by 5-inch loaf pan, start checking for doneness 5 minutes early.

1½   pounds zucchini, shredded
1¼   cups (8¾ ounces) packed brown sugar
¼   cup vegetable oil
2   large eggs
1   teaspoon vanilla extract
1½   cups (7½ ounces) all-purpose flour
½   cup (2¾ ounces) whole-wheat flour
1   tablespoon ground cinnamon
1½   teaspoons salt
1   teaspoon baking powder
1   teaspoon baking soda
½   teaspoon ground nutmeg
¾   cup walnuts, toasted and chopped (optional)
1   tablespoon granulated sugar

1. Adjust oven rack to middle position and heat oven to 325 degrees. Grease 8½ by 4½-inch loaf pan.

2. Place zucchini in center of clean dish towel. Gather ends together and twist tightly to drain as much liquid as possible, discarding liquid (you should have ½ to ⅔ cup liquid). Whisk brown sugar, oil, eggs, and vanilla together in medium bowl. Fold in zucchini.

3. Whisk all-purpose flour, whole-wheat flour, cinnamon, salt, baking powder, baking soda, and nutmeg together in large bowl. Fold in zucchini mixture until just incorporated. Fold in walnuts, if using. Pour batter into prepared pan and sprinkle with granulated sugar.

4. Bake until top bounces back when gently pressed and toothpick inserted in center comes out with a few moist crumbs attached, 65 to 75 minutes. Let bread cool in pan on wire rack for 30 minutes. Remove bread from pan and cool completely on wire rack. Serve.

Zucchini Bread with Walnuts and Dried Cherries

Substitute cocoa powder for cinnamon and ground cloves for nutmeg. Add ¾ cup dried cherries, chopped, to batter with walnuts in step 3.

BOSTON BROWN BREAD

WHY THIS RECIPE WORKS: When colonists started making this unyeasted, one-bowl bread in the 18th century, most cooking was done over an open hearth—a tricky environment for bread baking. To get around this, brown bread was steamed in lidded tin pudding molds in a kettle of simmering water over an open fire, giving the loaves a distinctive shape and a smooth, crustless exterior—and keeping the whole-grain crumb remarkably moist. To get the right balance of flavor in our brown bread, we combined whole-wheat flour, rye flour, and finely ground cornmeal in equal amounts. Molasses, the traditional sweetener, added the right hint of bitterness. Baking soda and baking powder reacted with the acid in the batter to lighten the bread, and melted butter added some richness. We steamed the batter on the stovetop in two 28-ounce tomato cans, which produced moist loaves inside and out.

Boston Brown Bread
MAKES 2 SMALL LOAVES; SERVES 6 TO 8

BPA-free 28-ounce tomato cans are a good substitute for traditional (but increasingly uncommon) coffee cans. This recipe requires two empty 28-ounce cans. Use cans that are labeled "BPA-free." We prefer Quaker white cornmeal in this recipe, though other types will work; do not use coarse grits. Any style of molasses will work except for blackstrap. This recipe requires a 10-quart or larger stockpot that is at least 7 inches deep. Brown bread is traditionally served with baked beans but is also good toasted and buttered.

- ¾ cup (4⅛ ounces) rye flour
- ¾ cup (4⅛ ounces) whole-wheat flour
- ¾ cup (3¾ ounces) fine white cornmeal
- 1¾ teaspoons baking soda
- ½ teaspoon baking powder
- 1 teaspoon salt
- 1⅔ cups buttermilk

- ½ cup molasses
- 3 tablespoons butter, melted and cooled slightly
- ¾ cup raisins

1. Bring 3 quarts water to simmer in large stockpot over high heat. Fold two 16 by 12-inch pieces of aluminum foil in half to yield two rectangles that measure 8 by 12 inches. Spray 4-inch circle in center of each rectangle with vegetable oil spray. Spray insides of two clean 28-ounce cans with vegetable oil spray.

2. Whisk rye flour, whole-wheat flour, cornmeal, baking soda, baking powder, and salt together in large bowl. Whisk buttermilk, molasses, and melted butter together in second bowl. Stir raisins into buttermilk mixture. Add buttermilk mixture to flour mixture and stir until combined and no dry flour remains. Evenly divide batter between cans. Wrap tops of cans tightly with prepared foil, positioning sprayed side of foil over can openings.

3. Place cans in stockpot (water should come about halfway up sides of cans). Cover pot and cook, maintaining gentle simmer, until skewer inserted in center of loaves comes out clean, about 2 hours. Check pot occasionally and add hot water as needed to maintain water level.

4. Using jar lifter, carefully transfer cans to wire rack set in rimmed baking sheet and let cool for 20 minutes. Slide loaves from cans onto rack and let cool completely, about 1 hour. Slice and serve. (Bread can be wrapped tightly in plastic wrap and stored at room temperature for up to 3 days or frozen for up to 2 weeks.)

IRISH SODA BREAD

WHY THIS RECIPE WORKS: Authentic Irish soda bread has a tender, dense crumb and a rough-textured, thick crust—definitely a departure from the more common Americanized soda bread, which is closer to a supersized scone. We wanted to try our hand at the authentic version of this bread, which relies on a simple ingredient list of flour, baking soda, salt, and buttermilk. A loaf made with all-purpose flour produced a doughy, heavy bread with an overly thick crust. To soften the crumb, we added some cake flour. A version made with all cake flour, however, was heavy and compact. A ratio of 3 parts all-purpose flour to 1 part cake flour proved best. With only the flour, buttermilk, baking soda, and salt, our bread was lacking in flavor and still tough. Traditionally, very small amounts of butter and sugar are sometimes added, so we felt justified in using a minuscule amount of each. The sugar added flavor without making the bread sweet, and the butter softened the dough without making it overly rich.

Irish Soda Bread
MAKES 1 LOAF

If you do not have a cast-iron skillet, the bread can be baked on a baking sheet, although the crust won't be quite as crunchy. Soda bread is best eaten on the day it is baked but does keep well covered and stored at room temperature for a couple of days, after which time it will become dry.

3 cups (15 ounces) unbleached all-purpose flour
1 cup (4 ounces) cake flour
2 tablespoons sugar
1½ teaspoons baking soda
1½ teaspoons cream of tartar
1½ teaspoons table salt
2 tablespoons unsalted butter, softened, plus 1 tablespoon melted butter for brushing the loaf (optional)
1¾ cups buttermilk

1. Adjust an oven rack to the middle position and heat the oven to 400 degrees. Whisk the flours, sugar, baking soda, cream of tartar, and salt together in a large bowl. Add the softened butter and rub it into the flour using your fingers until it is completely incorporated. Make a well in the center of the flour mixture and add 1½ cups of the buttermilk. Work the buttermilk into the flour mixture using a fork until the dough comes together in large clumps and there is no dry flour in the bottom of the bowl, adding up to ¼ cup more buttermilk, 1 tablespoon at a time, until all the loose flour is just moistened. Turn the dough onto a lightly floured work surface and pat together to form a 6-inch round. The dough will be scrappy and uneven.

2. Place the dough in a 12-inch cast-iron skillet. Score a deep cross, about 5 inches long and ¾ inch deep, on the top of the loaf and place in the oven. Bake until nicely browned and a knife inserted in the center of the loaf comes out clean, 40 to 45 minutes. Remove from the oven and brush with the melted butter (if using). Cool for at least 30 minutes before slicing.

Whole-Wheat Soda Bread

This variation is known as brown bread in Ireland. The dough will be sticky and you may need to add a small amount of all-purpose flour as you mix it.

Follow the recipe for Irish Soda Bread, reducing the unbleached all-purpose flour to 1½ cups (7½ ounces) and the cake flour to ½ cup (2 ounces) and increasing the sugar to 3 tablespoons. Add 1½ cups (8¼ ounces) whole-wheat flour and ½ cup toasted wheat germ with the flours, sugar, baking soda, cream of tartar, and salt in step 1.

QUICK CHEESE BREAD

WHY THIS RECIPE WORKS: Run-of-the-mill cheese bread is both dry and greasy, with almost no cheese flavor. We wanted to create a rich loaf topped with a bold, crust. We started with all-purpose flour and added whole milk and sour cream for a creamy flavor and moist texture. Just a few tablespoons of butter added enough richness without greasiness, and using less fat made the texture heartier. A single egg gave rise and structure without an overly eggy flavor. As for cheese, small chunks of Asiago or cheddar mixed into the dough offered rich, cheesy pockets throughout the bread; a moderate amount added plenty of flavor without weighing it down. For added cheesy flavor and a crisp crust, we coated the pan and sprinkled the top of the loaf with shredded Parmesan.

Quick Cheese Bread
MAKES ONE 8-INCH LOAF

If using Asiago, choose a mild supermarket cheese that yields to pressure when pressed. Aged Asiago that is as firm as Parmesan is too sharp and piquant for this bread. If, when testing the bread for doneness, the toothpick comes out with what looks like uncooked batter clinging to it, try again in a different, but still central, spot; if the toothpick hits a pocket of cheese, it may give a false indication.

3 ounces Parmesan cheese, shredded on the large holes of a box grater (about 1 cup)
3 cups (15 ounces) unbleached all-purpose flour
1 tablespoon baking powder
1 teaspoon table salt
¼ teaspoon cayenne pepper
⅛ teaspoon ground black pepper
4 ounces extra-sharp cheddar cheese, cut into ½-inch cubes, or mild Asiago (see note), crumbled into ¼- to ½-inch pieces (about 1 cup)
1¼ cups whole milk
3 tablespoons unsalted butter, melted
1 large egg, lightly beaten
¾ cup sour cream

1. Adjust an oven rack to the middle position and heat the oven to 350 degrees. Spray an 8½ by 4½-inch loaf pan with vegetable oil spray; sprinkle ½ cup of the Parmesan evenly over the bottom of the pan.

2. Whisk the flour, baking powder, salt, cayenne, and black pepper together in a large bowl. Using a rubber spatula, mix in the cheddar, breaking up clumps. Whisk the milk, melted butter, egg, and sour cream together in a medium bowl. Using a rubber spatula, gently fold the wet ingredients into the dry ingredients until just combined (the batter will be heavy and thick); do not overmix. Scrape the batter into the prepared loaf pan; smooth the surface with a rubber spatula. Sprinkle the remaining ½ cup Parmesan evenly over the surface.

3. Bake until deep golden brown and a toothpick inserted in the center comes out clean, 45 to 50 minutes. Cool on a wire rack for 5 minutes; invert the loaf onto the wire rack, then turn right side up and continue to cool until warm, about 45 minutes. Cut into slices and serve.

Quick Cheese Bread with Bacon, Onion, and Gruyère

Cook 5 ounces (about 5 slices) bacon, cut into ½-inch pieces, in a 10-inch nonstick skillet over medium heat, stirring occasionally, until crisp, about 8 minutes. Using a slotted spoon, transfer the bacon to a paper towel–lined plate and pour off all but 3 tablespoons fat from the skillet. Add ½ cup minced onion to the skillet and cook, stirring frequently, until softened, about 3 minutes; set the skillet with the onion aside. Follow the recipe for Quick Cheese Bread, substituting Gruyère for the cheddar, adding the bacon and onion to the flour mixture with the cheese, and omitting the butter.

ALL-PURPOSE CORNBREAD

WHY THIS RECIPE WORKS: Cornbread can be sweet and cakey (the Northern version) or savory and light (the Southern version). We wanted a combination of the two. And most important, we wanted our cornbread to be bursting with corn flavor.

The secret to cornbread with real corn flavor was pretty simple: Use corn, not just cornmeal. While fresh corn was best, we wanted to be able to make this cornbread year round. We found that frozen kernels were nearly as good as fresh, and pureeing the kernels in a food processor made them easy to use while minimizing tough, chewy kernels. For flavoring, buttermilk provided a tangy flavor, while light brown sugar enhanced the naturally sweet flavor of the corn. Baking the bread at a higher than conventional temperature produced a crunchy crust full of toasted corn flavor.

All-Purpose Cornbread

MAKES ONE 8-INCH SQUARE

Before preparing the baking dish or any of the other ingredients, measure out the frozen corn kernels and let them stand at room temperature until thawed. When corn is in season, fresh cooked kernels can be substituted for the frozen corn. This recipe was developed with Quaker yellow cornmeal; a stone-ground whole-grain cornmeal will work but will yield a drier and less tender cornbread. We prefer a Pyrex glass baking dish because it yields a nice golden brown crust, but a metal baking dish (nonstick or traditional) will also work. The cornbread is best served warm; leftovers can be wrapped in foil and reheated in a 350-degree oven for 10 to 15 minutes.

1½ cups (7½ ounces) unbleached all-purpose flour
1 cup (about 5 ounces) yellow cornmeal (see note)
2 teaspoons baking powder
¾ teaspoon table salt
¼ teaspoon baking soda
1 cup buttermilk
¾ cup frozen corn kernels, thawed (see note)
¼ cup packed (1¾ ounces) light brown sugar
2 large eggs
8 tablespoons (1 stick) unsalted butter, melted and cooled slightly

1. Adjust an oven rack to the middle position and heat the oven to 400 degrees. Spray an 8-inch square baking dish with vegetable oil spray. Whisk the flour, cornmeal, baking powder, salt, and baking soda together in a medium bowl until combined; set aside.

2. Process the buttermilk, thawed corn kernels, and brown sugar in a food processor or blender until combined, about 5 seconds. Add the eggs and process until well combined (corn lumps will remain), about 5 seconds longer.

3. Using a rubber spatula, make a well in the center of the dry ingredients; pour the wet ingredients into the well. Begin folding the dry ingredients into the wet ingredients, giving the mixture only a few turns to barely combine; add the melted butter and continue folding until the dry ingredients are just moistened. Pour the batter into the prepared baking dish; smooth the surface with a rubber spatula. Bake until deep golden brown and a toothpick inserted in the center comes out clean, 25 to 35 minutes. Cool on a wire rack for 10 minutes; invert the cornbread onto the wire rack, then turn right side up and continue to cool until warm, about 10 minutes longer. Cut into pieces and serve.

Spicy Jalapeño-Cheddar Cornbread

Follow the recipe for All-Purpose Cornbread, reducing the table salt to ½ teaspoon; add ⅜ teaspoon cayenne pepper, 1 medium jalapeño chile, seeds and ribs removed, minced, and 2 ounces sharp cheddar cheese, shredded (about ½ cup), to the flour mixture in step 1 and toss well to combine. Reduce the brown sugar to 2 tablespoons and sprinkle 2 ounces more sharp cheddar, shredded (about ½ cup), over the batter in the baking dish just before baking.

FRESH CORN CORNBREAD

WHY THIS RECIPE WORKS: For cornbread packed with fresh, concentrated corn flavor, we pureed fresh corn kernels and cooked them down into a "corn butter" that we incorporated into the batter. Buttermilk added tang, while egg yolks and a little bit of extra butter ensured that the bread would be moist.

SOUTHERN CORNBREAD

WHY THIS RECIPE WORKS: Classic Southern cornbread is made in a ripping hot skillet greased with bacon fat, which causes it to develop a thin, crispy crust as the bread bakes. The resulting bread is moist and tender, with the aroma of toasted corn and the subtle flavor of dairy. Traditionally, Southern-style cornbread is made from white cornmeal and has only trace amounts of sugar and flour. We wanted to perfect the proportions of ingredients and come up with our own crusty, savory Southern-style cornbread baked in a cast-iron skillet.

Departing from tradition, we chose yellow cornmeal over white—cornbreads made with yellow cornmeal consistently had a more potent corn flavor than those made with white cornmeal. We chose a rustic method to incorporate the cornmeal—combining part of the cornmeal with boiling water to create a cornmeal "mush." Cornbread that started with some mush had the most corn flavor, and it also produced a fine, moist crumb. We then stirred the buttermilk and egg into the mush before adding the remaining cornmeal and other dry ingredients. As for sugar, a small amount enhanced the natural sweetness of the corn. Finally, we poured the batter into a hot, greased cast-iron skillet to bake until crusty and fragrant.

Fresh Corn Cornbread
SERVES 6 TO 8

We prefer to use a well-seasoned cast-iron skillet in this recipe, but an ovensafe 10-inch skillet can be used in its place. Alternatively, in step 4 you can add 1 tablespoon of butter to a 9-inch cake pan and place it in the oven until the butter melts, about 3 minutes.

- 1⅓ cups (6⅔ ounces) stone-ground cornmeal
- 1 cup (5 ounces) all-purpose flour
- 2 tablespoons sugar
- 1½ teaspoons baking powder
- ¼ teaspoon baking soda
- 1¼ teaspoons salt
- 3 ears corn, kernels cut from cobs (2¼ cups)
- 6 tablespoons unsalted butter, cut into 6 pieces
- 1 cup buttermilk
- 2 large eggs plus 1 large yolk

1. Adjust oven rack to middle position and heat oven to 400 degrees. Whisk cornmeal, flour, sugar, baking powder, baking soda, and salt together in large bowl.

2. Process corn kernels in blender until very smooth, about 2 minutes. Transfer puree to medium saucepan (you should have about 1½ cups). Cook puree over medium heat, stirring constantly, until very thick and deep yellow and it measures ¾ cup, 5 to 8 minutes.

3. Remove pan from heat. Add 5 tablespoons butter and whisk until melted and incorporated. Add buttermilk and whisk until incorporated. Add eggs and yolk and whisk until incorporated. Transfer corn mixture to bowl with cornmeal mixture and, using rubber spatula, fold together until just combined.

4. Melt remaining 1 tablespoon butter in 10-inch cast-iron skillet over medium heat. Scrape batter into skillet and spread into even layer. Bake until top is golden brown and toothpick inserted in center comes out clean, 23 to 28 minutes. Let cool on wire rack for 5 minutes. Remove cornbread from skillet and let cool for 20 minutes before cutting into wedges and serving.

Southern Cornbread
MAKES ONE 8-INCH LOAF

Cornmeal mush of just the right texture is essential to this bread. Make sure that the water is at a rapid boil when it is added to the cornmeal. And for an accurate measurement of boiling water, bring a kettle of water to a boil, then measure out the desired amount. Though we prefer to make cornbread in a preheated cast-iron skillet, a 9-inch round cake pan or 9-inch square baking pan, greased lightly with butter and not preheated, will also produce acceptable results if you double the recipe and bake the bread for 25 minutes. For our top-rated cast-iron skillet, see page 875.

- 4 teaspoons bacon drippings or vegetable oil
- 1 cup (about 5 ounces) yellow cornmeal, preferably stone-ground
- 2 teaspoons sugar
- 1 teaspoon baking powder
- ½ teaspoon table salt
- ¼ teaspoon baking soda
- ⅓ cup boiling water (see note)
- ¾ cup buttermilk
- 1 large egg, lightly beaten

1. Adjust an oven rack to the lower-middle position and heat the oven to 450 degrees. Add the bacon drippings to an 8-inch cast-iron skillet and place the skillet in the heating oven.

2. Place ⅓ cup of the cornmeal in a medium bowl. Whisk the remaining ⅔ cup cornmeal, the sugar, baking powder, salt, and baking soda together in a small bowl; set aside.

3. Add the boiling water to the ⅓ cup cornmeal and stir to make a stiff mush. Whisk in the buttermilk gradually, breaking up lumps until smooth, then whisk in the egg. When the oven is preheated and the skillet is very hot, add the dry ingredients to the cornmeal mush and stir until just moistened. Carefully remove the skillet from the oven (skillet handle will be hot). Pour the hot bacon fat from the pan into the batter and stir to incorporate, then quickly pour the batter into the heated skillet. Bake until golden brown, about 20 minutes. Remove from the oven and immediately turn the cornbread onto a wire rack. Cool for 5 minutes; serve.

BEHIND THE SCENES

WEIGHING IN ON WEIGHTS AND MEASURES

Variations in measurement can have a significant effect on baked goods. To prove this point, we asked 10 home cook volunteers to measure out 1 cup of flour and 3 tablespoons of water. The weights of the measured flour and water varied by as much as 20 percent! From these findings, we recommend three things to guarantee more consistent results from your baked goods:

WEIGH FLOUR: Don't rely on cup measurements alone. (One cup of all-purpose flour weighs 5 ounces; 1 cup of bread or whole-wheat flour weighs 5½ ounces; and 1 cup of cake flour weighs 4 ounces.)

USE THE RIGHT MEASURING CUP: Liquid measurements should be made in a liquid cup measure (not a dry cup measure). To measure accurately, place the cup on a level surface and bring your eyes down to the level of the measurement markings. Add liquid until the bottom of the curved top surface of the liquid (called the meniscus)—not the edges of the surface, which can cling and ride up the walls of the measuring cup—is level with the measurement marking.

BE PRECISE: When measuring tablespoon or teaspoon amounts of liquid, make sure that the teaspoon is completely filled and that there is no excess liquid clinging to the bottom of the spoon after pouring.

POTATO BURGER BUNS

WHY THIS RECIPE WORKS: Mashed potatoes are hefty and substantial, but in recipes for potato rolls, they give the crumb a light, tender, moist texture. That's because the starches in potatoes dilute the gluten-forming proteins in flour, which weakens the structural network of the dough and makes it softer, moister, and more tender. For the lightest potato rolls, we combined ½ pound of mashed russet potatoes with high-protein bread flour. This created a potato roll dough with a stable structure, producing rolls that were not only perfectly risen but also light and airy.

Potato Burger Buns

MAKES 9 ROLLS

Don't salt the cooking water for the potatoes. A pound of russet potatoes should yield just over 1 very firmly packed cup (½ pound) of mash. To ensure optimum rise, your dough should be warm; if your potatoes or potato water are too hot to touch, let cool before proceeding with the recipe. This dough looks very dry when mixing begins but will soften as mixing progresses. If you prefer, you may portion the rolls by weight in step 5 (2.75 ounces of dough per roll).

1	pound russet potatoes, peeled and cut into 1-inch pieces
2	tablespoons unsalted butter, cut into 4 pieces
2¼	cups (12⅓ ounces) bread flour
1	tablespoon sugar
2	teaspoons instant or rapid-rise yeast
1	teaspoon salt
2	large eggs, 1 lightly beaten with 1 teaspoon water and pinch salt
1	tablespoon sesame seeds (optional)

1. Place potatoes in medium saucepan and add water to just cover. Bring to boil over high heat; reduce heat to medium-low and simmer until potatoes are cooked through, 8 to 10 minutes.

2. Transfer 5 tablespoons cooking water to bowl to cool; drain potatoes. Return potatoes to saucepan and place over low heat. Cook, shaking pot occasionally, until any surface moisture has evaporated, about 1 minute. Remove from heat. Process potatoes through ricer or food mill or mash well with potato masher. Measure 1 very firmly packed cup potatoes and transfer to bowl. Reserve any remaining potatoes for another use. Stir in butter until melted.

3. Combine flour, sugar, yeast, and salt in bowl of stand mixer. Add warm potato mixture to flour mixture and mix with hands until combined (some large lumps are OK). Add 1 egg and reserved potato water; mix with dough hook on low speed until dough is soft and slightly sticky, 8 to 10 minutes.

4. Shape dough into ball and place in lightly greased container. Cover tightly with plastic wrap and allow to rise at room temperature until almost doubled in volume, 30 to 40 minutes.

5. Turn out dough onto counter, dusting with flour only if dough is too sticky to handle comfortably. Pat gently into 8-inch square of even thickness. Using bench scraper or chef's knife, cut dough into 9 pieces (3 rows by 3 rows). Separate pieces and cover loosely with plastic.

6. Working with 1 piece of dough at a time and keeping remaining pieces covered, form dough pieces into smooth, taut rounds. (To round, set piece of dough on unfloured work surface. Loosely cup hand around dough and, without applying pressure to dough, move hand in small circular motions. Tackiness of dough against work surface and circular motion should work dough into smooth, even ball, but if dough sticks to hands, lightly dust fingers with flour.) Cover rounds with plastic and allow to rest for 15 minutes.

7. Line 2 rimmed baking sheets with parchment paper. On lightly floured surface, firmly press each dough round into 3½-inch disk of even thickness, expelling large pockets of air. Arrange on prepared baking sheets. Cover loosely with plastic and let rise at room temperature until almost doubled in size, 30 to 40 minutes. While rolls rise, adjust oven racks to middle and upper-middle positions and heat oven to 425 degrees.

8. Brush rolls gently with egg wash and sprinkle with sesame seeds, if using. Bake rolls until deep golden brown, 15 to 18 minutes, rotating and switching baking sheets halfway through baking. Transfer baking sheets to wire racks and let cool for 5 minutes. Transfer rolls from baking sheets to wire racks. Serve warm or at room temperature.

Potato Dinner Rolls

MAKES 12 ROLLS

Line rimmed baking sheet with parchment paper. In step 5, divide dough square into 12 pieces (3 rows by 4 rows). Shape pieces into smooth, taut rounds as directed in step 6. Transfer rounds to prepared baking sheet and let rise at room temperature until almost doubled in size, 30 to 40 minutes. Bake on upper-middle rack until rolls are deep golden brown, 12 to 14 minutes, rotating baking sheet halfway through baking.

RUSTIC DINNER ROLLS

WHY THIS RECIPE WORKS: The remarkably crisp crust of European-style dinner rolls is what keeps these rolls in the domain of professionals, who typically rely on a steam-injected oven to expose the developing crust to moisture. We wanted to create a reliable recipe for rustic dinner rolls with a crisp crust and chewy crumb that looked—and tasted—like they came from an artisanal bakery.

We baked our first batch using bread flour, but when we broke the rolls open, we found a dense, bland crumb beneath a leathery crust. The flavor was easy to improve—we replaced a few tablespoons of bread flour with whole-wheat flour, which contributed earthiness, while honey added sweetness. A little extra yeast improved the crumb slightly, but not enough; making the dough wetter was the fix. Lots of water in the dough created more steam bubbles during baking, which produced an airier crumb. Giving the dough a couple of turns also encouraged the yeast to produce more carbon dioxide, creating more bubbles and a lighter crumb.

As for baking, we came up with a two-step baking process to mimic a steam-injected oven: First, we misted the rolls with water before baking them for an even crisper crust. We then partially baked them in a cake pan at a high temperature to help set their shape. Halfway through baking, we removed the cake pan from the oven, lowered the temperature, pulled the rolls apart, and returned them to the oven spaced out on a baking sheet for uniformly golden rolls with the crust and crumb we were looking for.

Rustic Dinner Rolls

MAKES 16 ROLLS

Because this dough is sticky, keep your hands well floured when handling it. Use a spray bottle to mist the rolls with water. The rolls will keep for up to 2 days at room temperature stored in a zipper-lock bag. To recrisp the crust, place the rolls in a 450-degree oven for 6 to 8 minutes. The rolls will keep frozen for several months wrapped in foil and placed in a large zipper-lock freezer bag. Thaw the rolls at room temperature and recrisp using the instructions above.

1½ cups plus 1 tablespoon water, at room temperature
2 teaspoons honey
1½ teaspoons instant or rapid-rise yeast
3 cups plus 1 tablespoon (16½ ounces) bread flour, plus extra for the dough and work surface
3 tablespoons whole-wheat flour
1½ teaspoons table salt

1. Whisk the water, honey, and yeast in the bowl of a stand mixer until well combined, making sure no honey sticks to the bottom of the bowl. Add the flours and mix on low speed with the dough hook until a cohesive dough is formed, about 3 minutes. Cover the bowl with plastic wrap and let sit at room temperature for 30 minutes.

2. Remove the plastic wrap and sprinkle the salt evenly over the dough. Knead on low speed for 5 minutes. (If the dough

creeps up on the attachment, stop the mixer and scrape it down.) Increase the speed to medium and continue to knead until the dough is smooth and slightly tacky, about 1 minute. If the dough is very sticky, add 1 to 2 tablespoons flour and continue mixing for 1 minute. Lightly oil a medium bowl; transfer the dough to the bowl and cover with plastic wrap. Let the dough rise in a warm, draft-free place until doubled in size, about 1 hour.

3. Fold the dough over itself; rotate the bowl a quarter turn and fold again. Rotate the bowl again and fold once more. Cover with plastic wrap and let rise for 30 minutes. Repeat the folding, replace the plastic wrap, and let the dough rise until doubled in size, about 30 minutes. Spray two 9-inch round cake pans with vegetable oil spray and set aside.

4. Transfer the dough to a floured work surface and sprinkle the top with more flour. Using a bench scraper, cut the dough in half and gently stretch each half into a 16-inch log. Divide each log into quarters, then each quarter into two pieces (you should have 16 pieces total), and dust the top of each piece with more flour. With floured hands, gently pick up each piece and roll it in your palms to coat with flour, shaking off the excess, and place in the prepared cake pan. Arrange eight dough pieces in each cake pan, placing one piece in the middle and the others around it, with the long side of each piece running from the center of the pan to the edge and making sure the cut side faces up. Loosely cover the cake pans with plastic wrap and let the rolls rise until doubled in size, about 30 minutes (the dough is ready when it springs back slowly when pressed lightly with a knuckle). Thirty minutes before baking, adjust an oven rack to the middle position and heat the oven to 500 degrees.

5. Remove the plastic wrap from the cake pans, spray the rolls lightly with water, and place in the oven. Bake until the tops of the rolls are brown, 10 minutes, then remove them from the oven. Reduce the oven temperature to 400 degrees; using kitchen towels or oven mitts, invert the rolls from both cake pans onto a rimmed baking sheet. When the rolls are cool enough to handle, turn them right side up, pull apart, and space evenly on the baking sheet. Continue to bake until the rolls develop a deep golden brown crust and sound hollow when tapped on the bottom, 10 to 15 minutes, rotating the baking sheet halfway through baking. Transfer the rolls to a wire rack and cool to room temperature, about 1 hour.

AUTHENTIC BAGUETTES

WHY THIS RECIPE WORKS: A great baguette is hard to come by, at least outside of France. The ideal: a moist, wheaty interior punctuated with irregular holes and a deeply browned crust so crisp it shatters into millions of tiny shards.

For the ideal structure and open crumb, we opted for a hybrid mixing approach: We mixed the dough in a stand mixer, then folded the dough several times during the initial proofing. As for fermentation, the best flavor (and most convenient method) was a slow rise in the fridge. At least 24 hours, or up to 72, produced the most flavorful loaves.

As a bonus, this dough could be portioned out to make baguettes as desired within that window. Some sifted wheat flour provided extra depth of flavor without any bitterness. The key to shaping was a three-stage process, starting with pressing the dough into a square and then rolling it like a log. Leaving the ends of the loaves unsealed until the very end allowed air bubbles to escape. For slashes with the right wide almond shape, we found that we needed to keep the blade at a shallow angle while making the cuts, about 30 degrees to the work surface. Using a *lame*, which has a slightly curved blade, made this job easy and also created a ridge, or "ear" along the edge of the slash that baked up deliciously crisp. For a shatteringly crisp crust, we covered the bread with a disposable roasting pan while it baked to allow it to begin cooking in its own steam, which promoted good color and flavor as well as crispiness.

Authentic Baguettes at Home
MAKES FOUR 15-INCH-LONG BAGUETTES

We recommend using a *couche, lame*, flipping board, and diastatic malt powder for this recipe (see right for more information). You will also need a baking stone and a baking peel (see page 887 for our recommended brands). If you can't find King Arthur all-purpose flour, substitute bread flour, not another all-purpose flour. For best results, weigh your ingredients. This recipe makes enough dough for four loaves, which can be baked anytime during the 24- to 72-hour window after placing the dough in the fridge.

¼ cup (1⅓ ounces) whole-wheat flour

3 cups (15 ounces) King Arthur all-purpose flour

1 teaspoon instant or rapid-rise yeast

1 teaspoon diastatic malt powder (optional; see page 690)

1½ teaspoons salt

1½ cups (12 ounces) water

2 (16 by 12-inch) disposable aluminum roasting pans

1. Sift whole-wheat flour through fine-mesh strainer into bowl of stand mixer; discard bran remaining in strainer. Add all-purpose flour; yeast; malt, if using; and salt to mixer bowl. Fit stand mixer with dough hook, add water, and knead on low speed until cohesive dough forms and no dry flour remains, 5 to 7 minutes. Transfer dough to lightly oiled large bowl, cover with plastic wrap, and let rest at room temperature for 30 minutes.

NOTES FROM THE TEST KITCHEN

BAGUETTE BAKER'S KIT

Baguettes require a few specialty items, though we did find some alternatives. For more information on these items, see pages 896 and 897.

COUCHE: To proof baguettes, bakers cradle them in the folds of a piece of heavy linen called a *couche*. It maintains their shape while wicking away moisture, and the fabric releases the dough without tugging it out of shape. Our favorite is the **San Francisco Baking Institute 18″ Linen Canvas (Couche)** ($8 for a 36 by 18-inch couche). Alternatively, use a double layer of 100 percent linen tea towels at least 16 inches long and 12 inches wide.

FLIPPING BOARD: To move baguettes from the couche to the oven, professional bakers use a flipping board or transfer peel. While these boards aren't expensive ($12 from breadtopia.com), a homemade substitute, made by taping two 16 by 4-inch pieces of cardboard together with packaging tape, works equally well.

LAME: For the proper almond-shaped slashes, with one edge that bakes up into a crispy ridge, you must cut the loaf at a low angle, something much more easily done with the curved blade of a *lame*. Our favorite, the **Breadtopia Bread Lame** ($9.50), scored baguettes perfectly (we did have to choke up a bit on the long handle), and its blades are easy to change (it came with five extras). Alternatively, an unused box cutter blade will work.

DIASTATIC MALT POWDER: Because of the long proofing time, nearly all the sugars in this dough will be consumed by the yeast. Since sugars are responsible for browning and caramelization, this will leave the crust pale and dull-tasting. Adding diastatic malt powder, a naturally occurring enzyme that converts the starches in flour into sugar, guarantees a supply of sugar at baking time and thus a crust that browns quickly and deeply. It's not critical, but it definitely makes a difference. Purchase diastatic malt powder (available from Amazon, $7.63 for 1 pound), not plain malt powder or malt syrup.

2. Holding edge of dough with your fingertips, fold dough over itself by gently lifting and folding edge of dough toward center. Turn bowl 45 degrees; fold again. Turn bowl and fold dough 6 more times (total of 8 folds). Cover with plastic and let rise for 30 minutes. Repeat folding and rising every 30 minutes, 3 more times. After fourth set of folds, cover bowl tightly with plastic and refrigerate for at least 24 hours or up to 72 hours.

3. Transfer dough to lightly floured counter, pat into 8-inch square (do not deflate), and divide in half. Return 1 piece of dough to container, wrap tightly with plastic, and refrigerate (dough can be shaped and baked anytime within 72-hour window). Divide remaining dough in half crosswise, transfer to lightly floured rimmed baking sheet, and cover loosely with plastic. Let rest for 45 minutes.

4. On lightly floured counter, roll each piece into loose 3- to 4-inch-long cylinder; return to floured baking sheet and cover with plastic. Let rest at room temperature for 30 minutes.

5. Lightly mist underside of couche with water, drape over inverted baking sheet and dust with flour. Gently press 1 piece of dough into 6 by 4-inch rectangle on lightly floured counter, with long edge facing you. Fold upper quarter of dough toward center and press gently to seal. Rotate dough 180 degrees and repeat folding step to form 8 by 2-inch rectangle.

6. Fold dough in half toward you, using thumb of your other hand to create crease along center of dough, sealing with heel of your hand as you work your way along the loaf. Without pressing down on loaf, use heel of your hand to reinforce seal (do not seal ends of loaf).

7. Cup your hand over center of dough and roll dough back and forth gently to tighten (it should form dog-bone shape).

8. Starting at center of dough and working toward ends, gently and evenly roll and stretch dough until it measures 15 inches long by 1¼ inches wide. Moving your hands in opposite directions, use back and forth motion to roll ends of loaf under your palms to form sharp points.

9. Transfer dough to floured couche, seam side up. Gather edges of couche into 2 pleats on either side of loaf, then cover loosely with large plastic garbage bag.

10. Repeat steps 4 through 9 with second piece of dough and place on opposite side of pleat. Fold edges of couche over loaves to cover completely, then carefully place sheet inside bag, and tie or fold under to enclose.

11. Let stand until loaves have nearly doubled in size and dough springs back minimally when poked gently with your fingertip, 45 to 60 minutes. While bread rises, adjust oven rack to middle position, place baking stone on rack, and heat oven to 500 degrees.

12. Line pizza peel with 16 by 12-inch piece parchment paper with long edge perpendicular to handle. Unfold couche, pulling from ends to remove pleats. Gently pushing with side of flipping board, roll 1 loaf over, away from other loaf, so it is seam side down. Using your hand, hold long edge of flipping board between loaf and couche at 45-degree angle, then lift couche with your other hand and flip loaf seam side up onto board.

SHAPING AND BAKING BAGUETTES

Once your dough has gone through the initial rising, folding, and resting stages, it's ready to be shaped. For more information on the *couche* and *lame*, see pages 896 and 897.

1. On lightly floured counter, roll each piece of refrigerated and rested dough into loose 3- to 4-inch-long cylinder. Move dough to floured baking sheet and cover with plastic. Let rest at room temperature for 30 minutes.

2. Gently press 1 piece of dough into 6 by 4-inch rectangle with long edge facing you. Fold upper quarter of dough toward center and press gently to seal. Rotate dough 180 degrees and repeat folding step to form 8 by 2-inch rectangle.

3. Fold dough in half toward you, using thumb of your other hand to create crease along center of dough, sealing with heel of your hand as you work your way along the loaf. Do not seal ends of loaf.

4. Cup your hand over center of dough and roll dough back and forth gently to form dog-bone shape. Working toward ends, gently roll and stretch dough until it measures 15 inches long by 1¼ inches wide.

5. Moving your hands in opposite directions, use back and forth motion to roll ends of loaf under your palms to form sharp points.

6. Transfer dough to floured couche, seam side up. On either side of loaf, pinch edges of couche into pleat. Cover loosely with large plastic garbage bag.

7. Place second loaf on opposite side of pleat. Fold edges of couche over loaves to cover, then carefully place sheet inside bag, and tie or fold under to enclose. Let rise for 45 to 60 minutes. While bread rises, preheat baking stone.

8. Unfold couche. For each loaf, use flipping board to roll loaf over so it is seam side down. Hold long edge of flipping board between loaf and couche at 45-degree angle. Lift couche and flip loaf seam side up onto board. Invert loaf onto parchment-lined peel.

9. Holding lame concave side up at 30-degree angle to loaf, make series of three 4-inch-long, ½-inch-deep slashes along length of each loaf, using swift, fluid motion, overlapping each slash slightly.

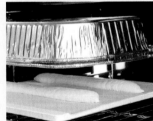

10. Transfer loaves, on parchment, to baking stone, cover with stacked inverted disposable pans, and bake for 5 minutes. Carefully remove pans and bake until loaves are evenly browned, 12 to 15 minutes longer, rotating parchment halfway through baking.

13. Invert loaf onto parchment-lined peel, seam side down, about 2 inches from long edge of parchment, then use flipping board to straighten loaf. Repeat with remaining loaf, leaving at least 3 inches between loaves.

14. Holding lame concave side up at 30-degree angle to loaf, make series of three 4-inch-long, ½-inch-deep slashes along length of loaf, using swift, fluid motion, overlapping each slash slightly. Repeat with second loaf.

15. Transfer loaves, on parchment, to baking stone, cover with stacked inverted disposable pans, and bake for 5 minutes. Carefully remove pans and bake until loaves are evenly browned, 12 to 15 minutes longer, rotating parchment halfway through baking. Transfer to cooling rack and let cool for at least 20 minutes before serving. Consume within 3 to 4 hours.

RUSTIC COUNTRY BREAD

WHY THIS RECIPE WORKS: Authentic rustic country bread should be made with little more than flour, water, yeast, and salt. We aimed to develop a reliable recipe for a big, crusty, pleasant loaf—made the old-fashioned way.

We decided to focus our tests around using a sponge starter—a mixture of flour, water, and yeast, left to ferment and then combined with additional flour, water, and other ingredients. A sponge starter gave our bread a complex flavor that yeast alone could not provide. We soon learned that bread with a high water content produces a chewier texture. So we ended up working with a wet dough, to which we could add more flour if necessary. This wet dough was tricky to work with but resulted in a bread with a texture so rough, chewy, and substantial that it was a meal all by itself. For a finishing touch, we added whole-wheat and rye flours to the ingredients to enhance this bread's full flavor.

Rustic Country Bread
MAKES 1 ROUND LOAF

Because of its high water content, the bread will be gummy if pulled from the oven too soon. To ensure the bread's doneness, make sure its internal temperature reads 210 degrees by inserting an instant-read thermometer into the loaf. The crust should be very dark brown, almost black. Leftover bread can be wrapped in a double layer of plastic wrap and stored at room temperature for up to 3 days; wrapped with an additional layer of aluminum foil, the bread can be frozen for up to one month. To recrisp the crust, place the unwrapped bread in a 450-degree oven for 10 minutes (frozen bread should be thawed at room temperature before recrisping).

SPONGE
- 1 cup water, at room temperature
- ½ teaspoon instant or rapid-rise yeast
- 1 cup (5½ ounces) bread flour
- 1 cup (5½ ounces) whole-wheat flour

DOUGH
- 3–3½ cups (16½ to 19¼ ounces) bread flour, plus extra for the dough and work surface
- ½ cup (2¾ ounces) rye flour
- 1⅓ cups water, at room temperature
- 2 tablespoons honey
- 2 teaspoons table salt

1. FOR THE SPONGE: Combine the water and yeast in a medium bowl and stir until the yeast is dissolved. Add the flours and stir with a rubber spatula to create a stiff, wet dough. Cover the bowl with plastic wrap and let sit at room temperature for at least 5 hours or up to 24 hours. (The sponge can be refrigerated for up to 24 hours; return to room temperature before continuing with the recipe.)

2. FOR THE DOUGH: Using a rubber spatula, combine 3 cups of the bread flour, the rye flour, water, honey, and sponge in the bowl of a stand mixer. Knead the dough on low speed with the dough hook until smooth, about 15 minutes, adding the salt during the final 3 minutes. If more flour is needed, add the remaining ½ cup bread flour, 1 tablespoon at a time, until the dough clears the sides of the bowl but sticks to the bottom. Lightly oil a large bowl; transfer the dough to the bowl and cover with plastic wrap. Let the dough rise until tripled in size, about 2 hours.

3. Transfer the dough to a lightly floured work surface. Flour the top of the dough. With floured hands, shape the dough into a round by pulling the edges into the middle and gathering it loosely together. Transfer the dough, seam side down, to an inverted baking sheet lined with parchment paper. Cover with plastic wrap and let rise until almost doubled in size, about 45 minutes. (The dough should barely spring back when poked with a knuckle.)

4. Meanwhile, adjust an oven rack to the lower-middle position, place a baking stone on the rack, and heat the oven to 450 degrees at least 30 minutes before baking.

5. Use a razor blade or sharp knife to cut three slashes on the top of the dough. With scissors, trim the excess parchment around the dough. Lightly spray the dough with water.

6. Carefully slide the parchment with the dough onto the baking stone using a jerking motion. Bake until the crust is very dark brown and the center registers 210 degrees on an instant-read thermometer, 35 to 40 minutes, rotating the bread halfway through baking (see note). Turn the oven off, open the oven door, and let the bread remain in the oven 10 minutes longer. Remove from the oven, transfer to a wire rack, and cool to room temperature, about 2 hours.

ALMOST NO-KNEAD BREAD

WHY THIS RECIPE WORKS: The no-knead method of bread making first came to our attention in an article on baker Jim Lahey in the *New York Times*. The article claimed that Lahey's method produces artisanal-style loaves with minimum effort. Lahey uses two approaches to replace kneading (the mechanical process that forms gluten, which gives bread structure): a very high hydration level (85 percent—meaning that for every 10 ounces of flour, there are 8.5 ounces of water) and a 12-hour autolysis period that allows the flour to hydrate and rest before the dough is kneaded. After the dough is briefly kneaded, it is baked in a covered Dutch oven; the lid trapped released steam, creating a springy loaf. By finishing the baking with the loaf uncovered, we created a beautifully browned crust.

However, as we baked loaf after loaf, we found two big problems: The dough didn't have enough structure, and it lacked flavor. To give the dough more strength (and make it easier to handle), we lowered the hydration and added the bare minimum of kneading time (under a minute) to compensate. To solve the lack of flavor, we needed to introduce two elements that a starter adds to artisan breads: an acidic tang with vinegar and a shot of yeasty flavor with beer.

MAKING ALMOST NO-KNEAD BREAD

1. Mix the dough by stirring the wet ingredients into the dry ingredients with a rubber spatula, then leave the dough to rest for 8 to 18 hours.

2. Turn the dough out onto a lightly floured surface and knead the dough 10 to 15 times.

3. After kneading the dough, shape it into a ball by pulling the edges into the middle.

4. Transfer the loaf, seam side down, to a large sheet of greased parchment and, using the paper, transfer it to a Dutch oven. Mist the bread with vegetable oil spray, cover it loosely with plastic, and let it rise until doubled in size, about 2 hours.

5. Sprinkle the dough with flour and cut a ½-inch-deep X into the loaf. Cover the pot, place it in the oven, and turn the oven to 425 degrees. Bake for 30 minutes, then remove the lid and bake until the loaf registers 210 degrees.

Almost No-Knead Bread

MAKES 1 ROUND LOAF

Use a mild-flavored lager, such as Budweiser (mild nonalcoholic lager also works). In step 3, start the 30-minute timer as soon as you put the bread in the cold oven. Do not wait until the oven has preheated to start your timer or the bread will burn. The bread is best eaten the day it is baked, but it can be wrapped in aluminum foil and stored in a cool, dry place for up to two days.

3 cups (15 ounces) all-purpose flour
1½ teaspoons salt
¼ teaspoon instant or rapid-rise yeast
¾ cup plus 2 tablespoons water, room temperature
6 tablespoons mild-flavored lager
1 tablespoon distilled white vinegar
Vegetable oil spray

1. Whisk flour, salt, and yeast together in large bowl. Add water, lager, and vinegar. Using rubber spatula, fold mixture, scraping up dry flour from bottom of bowl, until shaggy ball forms. Cover bowl with plastic wrap and let dough sit at room temperature for at least 8 hours or up to 18 hours.

2. Lay 18 by 12-inch sheet of parchment paper on counter and coat lightly with vegetable oil spray. Transfer dough to lightly floured counter and knead by hand to form smooth, round ball, 10 to 15 times. Shape dough into ball by pulling edges into middle. Transfer dough, seam side down, to center of parchment and spray surface of dough with oil spray. Pick up dough by lifting parchment overhang and lower into heavy-bottomed Dutch oven (let any excess parchment hang over pot edge). Cover loosely with plastic and let rise at room temperature until dough has doubled in size and does not readily spring back when poked with finger, about 2 hours.

3. Adjust oven rack to middle position. Remove plastic from pot. Lightly flour top of dough and, using razor blade or sharp knife, make one 6-inch-long, ½-inch-deep slit along top of dough. Cover pot and place in oven. Heat oven to 425 degrees. Bake bread for 30 minutes.

4. Remove lid and continue to bake until loaf is deep brown and registers 210 degrees, 20 to 30 minutes. Carefully remove bread from pot; transfer to wire rack and let cool completely, about 2 hours.

BEST SOURDOUGH BREAD

WHY THIS RECIPE WORKS: Making one's own sourdough culture (starter) is a commitment, but one that's rewarding—even addictive. For a simple, straightforward sourdough starter, we began by mixing all-purpose flour with whole-wheat flour, which provided extra nutrition for the developing bacteria and yeasts. We then added enough water to form a wet dough and let it sit at room temperature. After 3 days or so, when it started to show signs of life in the form of gas bubbles and a pungent aroma, we began a routine of daily feedings, mixing some of the culture with fresh flour and water. After 10 to 14 days, it smelled pleasantly yeasty and doubled in volume 8 to 12 hours after refreshing, a sure sign that it was mature enough to use. For a simple recipe in which to use the culture, we developed a sourdough version of our Almost No-Knead Bread, which rises overnight and is baked in a Dutch oven. We also came up with an easy way to maintain the culture between uses. We found we could refresh the food supply just once a week by letting the culture sit for 5 hours at room temperature after feeding it and then moving it to the refrigerator for storage.

Sourdough Starter

MAKES ABOUT 2 CUPS

It's okay to occasionally miss a daily feeding in step 2, but don't let it go for more than 48 hours. For the best results, weigh your ingredients and use organic flour and bottled or filtered water to create the starter. Once the starter is mature, all-purpose flour should be used to maintain it. Placing the starter in a glass bowl will allow for easier observation of activity beneath the surface. Discarding some starter before each feeding gets rid of waste and keeps the amount of starter manageable.

4½ cups (24¾ ounces) whole-wheat flour
5 cups (25 ounces) all-purpose flour, plus extra for maintaining starter
Water, room temperature

1. Combine whole-wheat flour and all-purpose flour in large container. Using wooden spoon, mix 1 cup (5 ounces) flour mixture and ⅔ cup (5⅓ ounces) room-temperature water in glass bowl until no dry flour remains (reserve remaining flour mixture). Cover with plastic wrap and let sit at room temperature until bubbly and fragrant, 48 to 72 hours.

2. FEED STARTER: Measure out ¼ cup (2 ounces) starter and transfer to clean bowl or jar; discard remaining starter. Stir ½ cup (2½ ounces) flour mixture and ¼ cup (2 ounces) water into starter until no dry flour remains. Cover with plastic wrap and let sit at room temperature for 24 hours.

3. Repeat step 2 every 24 hours until starter is pleasantly aromatic and doubles in size 8 to 12 hours after being refreshed, about 10 to 14 days. At this point starter is mature and ready to be baked with, or it can be moved to storage. (If baking, use starter once it has doubled in size during 8- to 12-hour window. Use starter within 1 hour after it starts to deflate once reaching its peak.)

4A. TO STORE AND MAINTAIN MATURE STARTER: Measure out ¼ cup (2 ounces) starter and transfer to clean bowl; discard remaining starter. Stir ½ cup (2½ ounces) all-purpose flour and ¼ cup (2 ounces) room-temperature water into starter until no dry flour remains. Transfer to clean container that can be loosely covered (plastic container or mason jar with its lid inverted) and let sit at room temperature for 5 hours. Cover and transfer to refrigerator. If not baking regularly, repeat process weekly.

4B. TO PREPARE FOR BAKING: Eighteen to 24 hours before baking, measure out ½ cup (4 ounces) starter and transfer to clean bowl; discard remaining starter. Stir 1 cup (5 ounces) all-purpose flour and ½ cup (4 ounces) room-temperature water into starter until no dry flour remains. Cover and let sit at room temperature for 5 hours. Measure out amount of starter called for in bread recipe and transfer to second bowl. Cover and transfer to refrigerator for at least 12 hours or up to 18 hours. Remaining starter should be refrigerated and maintained as directed.

Almost No-Knead Sourdough Bread

MAKES 1 LARGE ROUND LOAF

We prefer King Arthur all-purpose flour here; if you can't find it, you can substitute bread flour. For the best results, weigh your ingredients. The dough can rise at room temperature in step 3 (instead of in the oven), but it will take 3 to 4 hours. Do not wait until the oven has preheated in step 4 to start timing 30 minutes or the bread will burn.

3⅔ cups (18⅓ ounces) King Arthur all-purpose flour
1¾ teaspoons salt
1½ cups plus 4 teaspoons (12⅔ ounces) water, room temperature
⅓ cup (3 ounces) mature sourdough starter

1. Whisk flour and salt together in medium bowl. Whisk room-temperature water and starter in large bowl until smooth. Add flour mixture to water mixture and stir using wooden spoon, scraping up dry flour from bottom of bowl, until dough comes together, and then knead by hand in bowl until shaggy ball forms and no dry flour remains. Cover bowl with plastic wrap and let sit at room temperature for at least 12 hours or up to 18 hours.

2. Lay 12 by 12-inch sheet of parchment paper on counter and spray generously with vegetable oil spray. Transfer dough to lightly floured counter and knead 10 to 15 times. Shape dough into ball by pulling edges into middle. Transfer dough, seam side down, to center of parchment. Pick up dough by lifting parchment edges and lower into heavy-bottomed Dutch oven. Cover with plastic wrap.

3. Adjust oven rack to middle position and place loaf pan or cake pan in bottom of oven. Place Dutch oven on middle rack and pour 3 cups of boiling water into pan below. Close oven

door and let dough rise until doubled in size and does not readily spring back when poked with your floured finger, 2 to 3 hours.

4. Remove Dutch oven and water pan from oven; discard plastic from Dutch oven. Lightly flour top of dough and, using razor blade or sharp knife, make one 7-inch-long, ½-inch-deep slit along top of dough. Cover pot and place on middle rack in oven. Heat oven to 425 degrees. Bake bread for 30 minutes (starting timing as soon as you turn on oven).

5. Remove lid and continue to bake until bread is deep brown and registers 210 degrees, 20 to 30 minutes longer. Carefully remove bread from pot; transfer to wire rack and let cool completely before serving.

NO-KNEAD BRIOCHE

WHY THIS RECIPE WORKS: The average brioche recipe is 50 percent butter, and the high fat content can make the brioche incredibly tender—or it can cause the dough to separate into a greasy mess. For rich, tender brioche without the hassle of painstakingly adding softened butter to the dough little by little as it is kneaded, we melted the butter and added it directly to the eggs. Then we dispensed with the stand mixer and opted for an equally effective no-knead approach that lets time do most of the work: An overnight rest in the fridge developed both structure and flavor. We used two simple loaf pans and then, to build structure and ensure an even, fine crumb, we shaped the dough into four tight balls before placing two in each pan. The dough can also be divided to make brioche buns or traditionally shaped loaves using fluted brioche molds.

No-Knead Brioche
MAKES 2 LOAVES
High-protein King Arthur Bread Flour works best with this recipe, though other bread flours will suffice. The test kitchen's preferred loaf pan measures 8½ by 4½ inches; if you use a 9 by 5-inch pan, start checking for doneness 5 minutes earlier. If you don't have a baking stone, bake the bread on a preheated rimmed baking sheet.

- 3¼ cups (17¾ ounces) bread flour
- 2¼ teaspoons instant or rapid-rise yeast
- 1½ teaspoons salt
- 7 large eggs (1 lightly beaten with pinch salt)
- ½ cup water, room temperature
- ⅓ cup (2⅓ ounces) sugar
- 16 tablespoons unsalted butter, melted and cooled slightly

1. Whisk flour, yeast, and salt together in large bowl. Whisk 6 eggs, water, and sugar together in medium bowl until sugar has dissolved. Whisk in butter until smooth. Add egg mixture to flour mixture and stir with wooden spoon until uniform mass forms and no dry flour remains, about 1 minute. Cover bowl with plastic wrap and let stand for 10 minutes.

2. Holding edge of dough with your fingertips, fold dough over itself by gently lifting and folding edge of dough toward middle. Turn bowl 45 degrees; fold again. Turn bowl and fold dough 6 more times (total of 8 folds). Cover with plastic and let rise for 30 minutes. Repeat folding and rising every 30 minutes, 3 more times. After fourth set of folds, cover bowl tightly with plastic and refrigerate for at least 16 hours or up to 48 hours.

3. Transfer dough to well-floured counter and divide into 4 equal pieces. Working with 1 piece of dough at a time, pat dough into 4-inch disk. Working around circumference of dough, fold edges of dough toward center until ball forms. Flip dough over and, without applying pressure, move your hands in small circular motions to form dough into smooth, taut round. (If dough sticks to your hands, lightly dust top of dough with flour.) Repeat with remaining dough. Cover dough rounds loosely with plastic and let rest for 5 minutes.

4. Grease two 8½ by 4½-inch loaf pans. After 5 minutes, flip each dough ball so seam side is facing up, pat into 4-inch disk, and repeat rounding step. Place 2 rounds, seam side down, side by side into prepared pans and press gently into corners. Cover loaves loosely with plastic and let rise at room temperature until almost doubled in size (dough should rise to about ½ inch below top edge of pan), 1½ to 2 hours. Thirty minutes before baking, adjust oven rack to middle position, place baking stone on rack, and heat oven to 350 degrees.

5. Remove plastic and brush loaves gently with remaining 1 egg beaten with salt. Set loaf pans on stone and bake until golden brown and internal temperature registers 190 degrees, 35 to 45 minutes, rotating pans halfway through baking. Transfer pans to wire rack and let cool for 5 minutes. Remove loaves from pans, return to wire rack, and let cool completely before slicing and serving, about 2 hours.

No-Knead Brioche Buns
MAKES 10 BUNS

1. Line 2 rimmed baking sheets with parchment paper. Transfer dough to well-floured counter and divide into 10 equal pieces. Working with 1 piece of dough at a time, pat dough into disk. Working around circumference of dough, fold edges of dough toward center until ball forms. Flip dough over and, without applying pressure, move your hands in small circular motions to form dough into smooth, taut round. (Tackiness of dough against counter and circular motion should work dough into smooth, even ball, but if dough sticks to your hands, lightly dust top of dough with flour.) Repeat with remaining dough.

2. Arrange buns on prepared sheets, five per sheet. Cover loosely with plastic and let rise at room temperature until almost doubled in size, 1 to 1½ hours. Thirty minutes before baking, adjust oven racks to upper-middle and lower-middle positions and heat oven to 350 degrees.

3. Remove plastic and brush rolls gently with remaining 1 egg beaten with salt. Bake until golden brown and internal temperature registers 190 degrees, 15 to 20 minutes, rotating and switching sheets halfway through baking. Transfer sheets to wire rack and let cool for 5 minutes. Transfer buns to wire rack. Serve warm or at room temperature.

No-Knead Brioche à Tête

MAKES 2 LOAVES

Traditional loaves of *brioche à tête* achieve their fluted sides and conical shape from a brioche mold.

1. Transfer dough to well-floured counter and divide into 2 equal pieces. Remove golf ball–size piece of dough from each. Pat 2 large pieces of dough into 4-inch disks and 2 small pieces of dough into ½-inch disks. Working with 1 piece of dough at a time, work around circumference of dough; fold edges of dough toward center until ball forms. Flip dough over and, without applying pressure, move your hands in small circular motions to form dough into smooth, taut round. (Tackiness of dough against counter and circular motion should work dough into smooth, even ball, but if dough sticks to your hands, lightly dust top of dough with flour.) Repeat with remaining dough. Cover dough rounds loosely with plastic and let rest for 5 minutes.

2. Grease two 8- to 8½-inch fluted brioche pans. After 5 minutes, flip each dough ball so seam side is facing up, pat into 4-inch and ½-inch disks, and repeat rounding step. Place larger rounds, seam side down, into prepared pans and press gently into corners. Place smaller rounds, seam side down, in center of larger rounds, pushing down gently so only top halves of smaller rounds are showing. Cover loaves loosely with plastic and let rise at room temperature until almost doubled in size (dough should rise to about ½ inch below top edge of pan), 1½ to 2 hours. Thirty minutes before baking, adjust oven rack to middle position, place baking stone on rack, and heat oven to 350 degrees.

3. Remove plastic and brush loaves gently with remaining 1 egg beaten with salt. Set pans on stone and bake until golden brown and internal temperature registers 190 degrees, 35 to 45 minutes, rotating pans halfway through baking. Transfer pans to wire rack and let cool for 5 minutes. Remove loaves from pans, return to wire rack, and let cool completely before slicing and serving, about 2 hours.

CINNAMON SWIRL BREAD

WHY THIS RECIPE WORKS: This American classic frequently disappoints due to either precious little cinnamon flavor or, just as bad, a gloppy, oozing filling reminiscent of sticky buns. The bread itself is often an afterthought of pedestrian white bread, or else it's a cakey, dense affair. We swapped in an airy, cottony Japanese white bread called *shokupan* and created a filling with a balanced mixture of cinnamon, confectioners' sugar, and vanilla. To ensure that our filling stayed put and could be tasted with every bite, we traded the traditional swirl shape for a simple yet elegant Russian braid.

Cinnamon Swirl Bread

MAKES 2 LOAVES

To achieve the proper dough consistency, make sure to weigh your ingredients. The dough will appear very wet and sticky until the final few minutes of kneading; do not be tempted to add supplemental flour.

DOUGH

- 8 tablespoons unsalted butter
- 3¾ cups (20⅔ ounces) bread flour
- ¾ cup (2¾ ounces) nonfat dry milk powder
- ⅓ cup (2⅓ ounces) granulated sugar
- 1 tablespoon instant or rapid-rise yeast
- 1½ cups (12 ounces) water, heated to 110 degrees
- 1 large egg, lightly beaten
- 1½ teaspoons salt
- 1½ cups (7½ ounces) golden raisins

FILLING

- 1 cup (4 ounces) confectioners' sugar
- 3 tablespoons ground cinnamon
- 1 teaspoon vanilla extract
- ½ teaspoon salt
- 1 large egg, lightly beaten with pinch salt

1. FOR THE DOUGH: Cut butter into 32 pieces and toss with 1 tablespoon flour; set aside to soften while mixing dough. Whisk remaining flour, milk powder, sugar, and yeast together in bowl of stand mixer fitted with dough hook. Add water and egg and mix on medium-low speed until cohesive mass forms, about 2 minutes, scraping down bowl as needed. Cover mixing bowl with plastic wrap and let stand for 20 minutes.

2. Adjust oven rack to middle position and place loaf or cake pan on bottom of oven. Grease large bowl. Remove plastic from mixer bowl, add salt, and mix on medium-low speed until dough is smooth and elastic and clears sides of bowl, 7 to 15 minutes. With mixer running, add butter a few pieces at a time, and continue to knead until butter is fully incorporated and dough is smooth and elastic and clears sides of bowl, 3 to 5 minutes longer. Add raisins and mix until incorporated, 30 to 60 seconds. Transfer dough to prepared bowl and, using bowl scraper or rubber spatula, fold dough over itself by gently lifting and folding edge of dough toward middle.

WEAVING CINNAMON SWIRL BREAD, RUSSIAN-STYLE

The benefit of a Russian braid—other than good looks—is that it solves the gapping that plagues swirl breads. The twisted shape tightly seals the pieces of dough together while providing plenty of escape routes for the excess air that would otherwise compress the dough and create tunnels in the loaf.

1. Using bench scraper or sharp chef's knife, cut filled dough in half lengthwise. Turn halves so cut sides are facing up.

2. With cut sides up, stretch each half into 14-inch length.

3. Pinch 2 ends of strips together. To braid, take left strip of dough and lay it over right strip of dough. Repeat braiding, keeping cut sides face up, until pieces are tightly twisted. Pinch ends together.

Turn bowl 90 degrees; fold again. Turn bowl and fold dough 6 more times (total of 8 folds). Cover tightly with plastic and transfer to middle rack of oven. Pour 3 cups boiling water into loaf pan in oven, close oven door, and allow dough to rise for 45 minutes.

3. Remove bowl from oven and gently press down on center of dough to deflate. Repeat folding (making total of 8 folds), re-cover, and return to oven until doubled in volume, about 45 minutes.

4. FOR THE FILLING: Whisk all ingredients together in bowl until well combined; set aside.

5. Grease two 8½ by 4½-inch loaf pans. Transfer dough to lightly floured counter and divide into 2 pieces. Working with 1 piece of dough, pat into rough 6 by 11-inch rectangle. With short side facing you, fold long sides in like a business letter to form 3 by 11-inch rectangle. Roll dough away from you into ball. Dust ball with flour and flatten with rolling pin into 7 by 18-inch rectangle with even ¼-inch thickness. Using spray bottle, spray dough lightly with water. Sprinkle half of filling mixture evenly over dough, leaving ¼-inch border on sides and ¾-inch border on top and bottom; spray filling lightly with water.

(Filling should be speckled with water over entire surface.) With short side facing you, roll dough away from you into firm cylinder. Turn loaf seam side up and pinch closed; pinch ends closed. Dust loaf lightly on all sides with flour and let rest for 10 minutes. Repeat with second ball of dough and remaining filling.

6. Working with 1 loaf at a time, use bench scraper to cut loaf in half lengthwise; turn halves so cut sides are facing up. Gently stretch each half into 14-inch length. Line up pieces of dough and pinch 2 ends of strips together. Take piece on left and lay over piece on right. Repeat, keeping cut side up, until pieces of dough are tightly twisted. Pinch ends together. Transfer loaf, cut side up, to prepared loaf pan; push any exposed raisins into seams of braid. Repeat with second loaf. Cover loaves loosely with plastic, return to oven, and allow to rise for 45 minutes. Remove loaves and water pan from oven; heat oven to 350 degrees. Allow loaves to rise at room temperature until almost doubled in size, about 45 minutes (tops of loaves should rise about 1 inch over lip of pans).

7. Brush loaves with egg mixture. Bake until crust is well browned, about 25 minutes. Reduce oven temperature to 325 degrees, tent loaves with aluminum foil, and continue to bake until internal temperature registers 200 degrees, 15 to 25 minutes longer.

8. Transfer pans to wire rack and let cool for 5 minutes. Remove loaves from pans, return to rack, and cool to room temperature before slicing, about 2 hours.

CIABATTA

WHY THIS RECIPE WORKS: Unless your source is an artisanal bakery, most loaves of ciabatta available just aren't any good. Some lack flavor, others are too flat, and still others have holes so big there's hardly any bread. Ideally, this Italian loaf should boast a crisp, flavorful crust, a full and tangy flavor, and a chewy, open crumb. Uninterested in yet another lackluster loaf from the supermarket, we decided to make our own.

We started with the flour selection—whole-wheat, bread, or all-purpose? We preferred all-purpose, which is made from both hard and soft wheat and has less protein than bread flour, producing loaves with a more open, springy texture. The next step was to build flavor through the sponge (or *biga* in Italian), which we also used in our Rustic Country Bread (page 692). As it ferments, the yeast in the biga produces lactic and acetic acids as by-products, which give the bread its characteristic sourness. Kneading the sponge and remaining dough ingredients in a stand mixer for only a few minutes produced loaves that spread out instead of rising, so we turned to a combination of kneading and folding the dough over itself a few times before letting it rest. This two-step process gave the dough structure but also supported oversized holes. Adding a small amount of milk, which contains a protein that slightly weakens the gluten strands, remedied the problem and took down the size of those big bubbles.

To avoid extra handling of the dough, we formed the loaves,

then moved them to parchment paper and slid the parchment onto the baking surface after another rest. We opted to bake the loaves at a cooler temperature than 500 degrees (as most recipes recommend). A final enhancement was to spray the loaves with water in the first minutes of baking for a crisper crust and loaves that rose a bit higher.

Ciabatta

MAKES 2 LOAVES

As you make this bread, keep in mind that the dough is wet and very sticky. The key to manipulating it is working quickly and gently; rough handling will result in flat, tough loaves. When possible, use a large rubber spatula or bowl scraper to move the dough. If you have to use your hands, make sure they are well floured. Because the dough is so sticky, it must be prepared in a stand mixer. If you don't have a baking stone, bake the bread on an overturned and preheated rimmed baking sheet set on the lowest oven rack. Leftover bread can be wrapped in a double layer of plastic wrap and stored at room temperature for up to 3 days; wrapped with an additional layer of aluminum foil, the bread can be frozen for up to 1 month. To recrisp the crust, place the unwrapped bread in a 450-degree oven for 6 to 8 minutes (frozen bread should be thawed at room temperature before recrisping).

SPONGE

- 1 cup (5 ounces) unbleached all-purpose flour
- ⅛ teaspoon instant or rapid-rise yeast
- ½ cup water, at room temperature

DOUGH

- 2 cups (10 ounces) unbleached all-purpose flour, plus extra for the dough and work surface
- 1½ teaspoons table salt
- ½ teaspoon instant or rapid-rise yeast
- ¾ cup water, at room temperature
- ¼ cup milk, at room temperature

1. FOR THE SPONGE: Combine the flour, yeast, and water in a medium bowl and stir with a wooden spoon until a uniform mass forms, about 1 minute. Cover the bowl tightly with plastic wrap and let stand at room temperature (about 70 degrees) for at least 8 hours or up to 24 hours.

2. FOR THE DOUGH: Place the sponge and dough ingredients in the bowl of a stand mixer fitted with the paddle attachment. Mix on low speed until roughly combined and a shaggy dough forms, about 1 minute; scrape down the sides of the bowl as necessary. Increase the speed to medium-low and continue mixing until the dough becomes a uniform mass that collects on the paddle and pulls away from the sides of the bowl, 4 to 6 minutes. Change to the dough hook and knead the bread on medium speed until smooth and shiny (the dough will be very sticky), about 10 minutes. (If the dough creeps up on the attachment, stop the mixer and scrape it down.) Transfer the dough to a large bowl and cover tightly with plastic wrap. Let the dough rise at room temperature until doubled in size, about 1 hour. (The dough should barely spring back when poked with a knuckle.)

3. Spray a rubber spatula or bowl scraper with vegetable oil spray; fold the partially risen dough over itself by gently lifting and folding the edge of the dough toward the middle. Turn the bowl 90 degrees; fold again. Turn the bowl and fold the dough six more times (for a total of eight turns). Cover with plastic wrap and let rise for 30 minutes. Repeat folding, replace the plastic wrap, and let rise until doubled in size, about

---

NOTES FROM THE TEST KITCHEN

MAKING CIABATTA

1. After mixing the dough and allowing it to rest, turn the partially risen dough by folding it in on itself to gently encourage more gluten development. Let it rest again, then repeat this step.

2. Transfer the dough to a lightly floured surface and halve it with a bench scraper.

3. Press each half into a rough 12 by 6-inch rectangle.

4. Fold each dough half like a business letter into a 7 by 4-inch loaf. Transfer each loaf, seam side down, to sheets of parchment, dust with flour, and cover with plastic wrap. Let rest for 30 minutes.

5. Use floured fingertips to evenly poke the entire surface of each loaf to form a 10 by 6-inch rectangle; spray the loaves lightly with water. Transfer the loaves, parchment and all, onto the hot baking stone and bake.

30 minutes longer. Meanwhile, adjust an oven rack to the lower-middle position, place a baking stone on the rack, and heat the oven to 450 degrees at least 30 minutes before baking.

4. Cut two 12 by 6-inch pieces of parchment paper and liberally dust with flour. Transfer the dough to a floured work surface, being careful not to deflate it completely. Liberally flour the top of the dough and divide it in half with a bench scraper. Turn one piece of dough cut side up and dust with flour. Following the photos on page 698, with well-floured hands, press the dough into a rough 12 by 6-inch shape. Fold the shorter sides of the dough toward the center, overlapping them like a business letter to form a 7 by 4-inch loaf. Repeat with the second dough piece. Gently transfer each loaf, seam side down, to the parchment sheets, dust with flour, and cover with plastic wrap. Let the loaves sit at room temperature for 30 minutes (the surface of the loaves will develop small bubbles).

5. Slide the parchment with the loaves onto an inverted rimmed baking sheet or pizza peel. Using floured fingertips, evenly poke the entire surface of each loaf to form a 10 by 6-inch rectangle; spray the loaves lightly with water. Carefully slide the parchment with the loaves onto the baking stone using a jerking motion. Bake, spraying the loaves with water twice more during the first 5 minutes of baking time, until the crust is a deep golden brown and the center of the loaves registers 210 degrees on an instant-read thermometer, 22 to 27 minutes. Transfer to a wire rack, discard the parchment, and cool the loaves to room temperature, about 1 hour, before slicing and serving.

EASY SANDWICH BREAD

WHY THIS RECIPE WORKS: A freshly baked loaf of bread is one of life's great pleasures. But most people don't have 4 hours to devote to mixing dough, waiting for it to rise, kneading, shaping, and baking. Could we find a quicker way? We started with basic batter bread, which relies on a high hydration level and a single rise, but falls short on flavor. Adding melted butter was a good start toward a tastier loaf, and substituting some whole-wheat flour provided nutty depth. Swapping the rest of the all-purpose flour for bread flour lent better structure. We also traded 1 tablespoon of honey for sugar, which contributed complexity and encouraged browning. Two 20-minute proofs were enough for flavor development. Adding salt only after the initial rise allowed the bread to rise high. An egg wash before baking and a brush of melted butter provided a shiny, tender crust.

Easy Sandwich Bread
MAKES 1 LOAF

The test kitchen's preferred loaf pan measures 8½ by 4½ inches; if using a 9 by 5-inch pan, check for doneness 5 minutes early. To prevent the loaf from deflating as it rises, do not let the batter come in contact with the plastic wrap. This loaf is best eaten the day it is made, but leftovers may be wrapped in plastic wrap and stored for up to two days at room temperature or frozen for up to one month.

2	cups (11 ounces) bread flour
6	tablespoons (2 ounces) whole-wheat flour
2¼	teaspoons instant or rapid-rise yeast
1¼	cups plus 2 tablespoons warm water (120 degrees)
3	tablespoons unsalted butter, melted
1	tablespoon honey
¾	teaspoon salt
1	large egg, lightly beaten with 1 teaspoon water and pinch salt

1. In bowl of stand mixer, whisk bread flour, whole-wheat flour, and yeast together. Add 1¼ cups warm water, 2 tablespoons melted butter, and honey. Fit stand mixer with paddle and mix on low speed for 1 minute. Increase speed to medium and mix for 2 minutes. Scrape down bowl and paddle with greased rubber spatula. Continue to mix 2 minutes longer. Remove bowl and paddle from mixer. Scrape down bowl and paddle, leaving paddle in batter. Cover with plastic wrap and let batter rise in warm place until doubled in size, about 20 minutes.

2. Adjust oven rack to lower-middle position and heat oven to 375 degrees. Spray 8½ by 4½-inch loaf pan with vegetable oil spray. Dissolve salt in remaining 2 tablespoons warm water. When batter has doubled, attach bowl and paddle to mixer. Add salt-water mixture and mix on low speed until water is mostly incorporated, about 40 seconds. Increase speed to medium and mix until thoroughly combined, about 1 minute, scraping down paddle if necessary. Transfer batter to prepared pan and smooth surface with greased rubber spatula. Cover and leave in warm place until batter reaches ½ inch below edge of pan, 15 to 20 minutes. Uncover and let rise until center of batter is level with edge of pan, 5 to 10 minutes longer.

3. Gently brush top of risen loaf with egg mixture. Bake until deep golden brown and loaf registers 208 to 210 degrees, 40 to 45 minutes. Using clean dish towels, carefully invert bread onto wire rack. Reinvert loaf and brush top and sides with remaining 1 tablespoon melted butter. Let cool completely before slicing.

WHOLE-WHEAT SANDWICH BREAD

WHY THIS RECIPE WORKS: Most whole-wheat bread recipes turn out either squat bricks or white bread in disguise. We wanted a nutty, light-textured sandwich loaf. We started with a good white-flour recipe and worked our way backward to "unrefine" it. We made a series of white bread loaves, replacing different amounts of all-purpose flour with whole-wheat to find the highest percentage of whole-wheat flour we could use before the texture suffered, landing on 60 percent. We also substituted bread flour for the all-purpose flour. Next, we soaked the flour overnight in milk, with some wheat germ for added flavor. This softened the grain's fiber, kept the dough moist, and coaxed out some sweetness. Finally, we turned to a sponge, a mixture of flour, water, and yeast left to sit overnight to develop a full range of flavor. Adding honey lent complexity and swapping out some of the butter for vegetable oil cut the richness.

Best Whole-Wheat Sandwich Bread
MAKES TWO 8-INCH LOAVES

If you don't have a stand mixer, you can mix the dough by hand following the instructions on page 701. If you don't have a baking stone, bake the bread on an overturned and preheated rimmed baking sheet set on the lowest oven rack. The bread can be wrapped in a double layer of plastic wrap and stored at room temperature for up to 3 days. Wrapped with an additional layer of aluminum foil, the bread can be frozen for up to 1 month.

SPONGE
- 2 cups (11 ounces) bread flour
- 1 cup water, heated to 110 degrees
- ½ teaspoon instant or rapid-rise yeast

SOAKER
- 3 cups (16½ ounces) whole-wheat flour
- ½ cup wheat germ
- 2 cups whole milk

DOUGH
- 6 tablespoons unsalted butter, softened
- ¼ cup honey
- 2 tablespoons instant or rapid-rise yeast
- 2 tablespoons vegetable oil
- 4 teaspoons table salt

1. FOR THE SPONGE: Combine the flour, water, and yeast in a large bowl and stir with a wooden spoon until a uniform mass forms and no dry flour remains, about 1 minute. Cover the bowl tightly with plastic wrap and let sit at room temperature for at least 8 hours or up to 24 hours.

2. FOR THE SOAKER: Combine the flour, wheat germ, and milk in a separate large bowl and stir with a wooden spoon until a shaggy mass forms, about 1 minute. Transfer the dough to a lightly floured work surface and knead by hand until smooth, 2 to 3 minutes. Return the soaker to the bowl, cover tightly with plastic wrap, and refrigerate for at least 8 hours or up to 24 hours.

3. FOR THE DOUGH: Tear the soaker apart into 1-inch pieces and place in the bowl of a stand mixer fitted with the dough hook. Add the sponge, butter, honey, yeast, oil, and salt and mix on low speed until a cohesive mass starts to form, about 2 minutes. Increase the speed to medium and knead until the dough is smooth and elastic, 8 to 10 minutes. Transfer the dough to a lightly floured work surface and knead by hand to form a smooth, round ball, about 1 minute. Place the dough in a large, lightly greased bowl. Cover tightly with plastic wrap and let rise at room temperature for 45 minutes.

4. Gently press down on the center of the dough to deflate. Spray a rubber spatula or bowl scraper with vegetable oil spray; fold the partially risen dough over itself by gently lifting and folding the edge of the dough toward the middle. Turn the bowl 90 degrees; fold again. Turn the bowl and fold the dough 6 more times (for a total of 8 folds). Cover tightly with plastic wrap and allow to rise at room temperature until doubled in size, about 45 minutes.

5. Grease two 8½ by 4½-inch loaf pans. Transfer the dough to a well-floured work surface and divide in half. Press 1 piece of the dough into a 17 by 8-inch rectangle, with the short side facing you. Roll the dough toward you into a firm cylinder, keeping the roll taut by tucking it under itself as you go. Turn the loaf seam side up and pinch it closed. Place the loaf seam side down in a prepared pan, pressing gently into the corners. Repeat with the second piece of dough. Cover the loaves loosely with greased plastic wrap and let rise at room temperature until nearly doubled in size, 1 to 1½ hours (the top of the loaves should rise about 1 inch over the lip of the pan).

6. Thirty minutes before baking, adjust the oven racks to the middle and lowest positions, place a baking stone on the middle rack, place an empty loaf pan or other heatproof pan on the bottom rack, and heat the oven to 400 degrees. Bring 2 cups water to boil on the stovetop.

7. Using a sharp serrated knife or a single-edge razor blade, make one ¼-inch-deep slash lengthwise down the center of each loaf. Working quickly, pour the boiling water into the empty loaf pan in the oven and set the loaves on the baking stone. Reduce the oven temperature to 350 degrees. Bake until the crust is dark brown and the loaves register 200 degrees on an instant-read thermometer, 40 to 50 minutes, rotating the loaves front to back and side to side halfway through baking. Transfer the pans to a wire rack and let cool for 5 minutes. Remove the loaves from the pans, return to the rack, and let cool to room temperature, about 2 hours, before slicing and serving.

MIXING WHOLE-WHEAT SANDWICH DOUGH BY HAND

Stir the wet and dry ingredients together along with the sponge with a stiff rubber spatula until the dough comes together and looks shaggy. Transfer the dough to a clean work surface and knead by hand to form a smooth, round ball, 15 to 25 minutes, adding additional flour if necessary to prevent the dough from sticking to the work surface. Proceed with the recipe as directed.

FOLDING AND FORMING WHOLE-WHEAT SANDWICH BREAD

1. Deflate the center of the dough, then fold it in on itself. Turn the bowl 90 degrees; fold again. Repeat for a total of 8 folds. Let rise for 45 minutes.

2. Halve the dough and pat each portion into an 8 by 17-inch rectangle, with the short side facing you.

3. Roll each sheet toward you into a tight cylinder. Keep the roll taut by tucking it under itself as you go. Pinch the seams to seal.

4. Place each loaf seam side down in the prepared loaf pans. Let the dough rise until almost doubled in size, 60 to 90 minutes.

5. Using a knife, make a shallow slash down the center of each loaf to stop the bread from tearing when it rises. Bake for 40 to 50 minutes.

MULTIGRAIN BREAD

WHY THIS RECIPE WORKS: Although multigrain bread often has great flavor, the quantity of ingredients weighs it down so much that the loaf becomes dense and heavy. On the other end of the spectrum are loaves with a sandwich-style texture but so little grain that they're hard to distinguish from white bread. We wanted a multigrain bread with great flavor and balanced texture. Our first challenge was to develop more gluten in the dough. Because the protein content of any flour is an indicator of how much gluten it will produce, we thought first to switch out all-purpose flour for bread flour, but this move only made the bread chewier. The solution was twofold: long kneading preceded by an autolyse, a resting period just after the initial mixing of water and flour that gives flour time to hydrate. This combination also made the dough easier to work with. The result was a loaf that baked up light yet chewy, without being tough. To incorporate grains into the bread, we used a one-stop-shopping alternative: packaged seven-grain hot cereal. To soften the grains, we made a thick porridge with the cereal before adding it to the dough. A final step of rolling the shaped loaves in oats yielded a finished, professional look.

Multigrain Bread

MAKES TWO 8-INCH LOAVES

Don't confuse seven-grain hot cereal mix with boxed, cold breakfast cereals that may also be labeled "seven-grain." Our favorite brands of seven-grain mix are Bob's Red Mill and Arrowhead Mills. Leftover bread can be wrapped in a double layer of plastic wrap and stored at room temperature for up to 3 days; wrapped with an additional layer of aluminum foil, the bread can be frozen for up to 1 month. For an accurate measurement of boiling water, bring a kettle of water to a boil, then measure out the desired amount. See page 885 for information on our top-rated loaf pan.

- 1¼ cups (6¼ ounces) seven-grain hot cereal mix (see note)
- 2½ cups boiling water (see note)
- 3 cups (15 ounces) unbleached all-purpose flour, plus extra for the dough and work surface
- 1½ cups (8¼ ounces) whole-wheat flour
- ¼ cup honey
- 4 tablespoons (½ stick) unsalted butter, melted and cooled slightly
- 1 envelope (2¼ teaspoons) instant or rapid-rise yeast
- 1 tablespoon table salt
- ¾ cup unsalted pumpkin seeds or sunflower seeds
- ½ cup old-fashioned rolled oats or quick oats

1. Place the cereal mix in the bowl of a stand mixer and pour the boiling water over it; let stand, stirring occasionally, until the mixture cools to 100 degrees and resembles thick porridge, about 1 hour. Whisk the flours together in a medium bowl.

2. Once the grain mixture has cooled, add the honey, melted butter, and yeast and stir to combine. Attach the bowl to a stand mixer fitted with the dough hook. With the mixer running on low speed, add the flours, ½ cup at a time, and knead until the dough forms a ball, 1½ to 2 minutes; cover the bowl with plastic wrap and let the dough rest for 20 minutes. Add the salt and knead on medium-low speed until the dough clears the sides of the bowl, 3 to 4 minutes (if it does not clear the sides, add 2 to 3 tablespoons additional all-purpose flour and continue mixing); continue to knead the dough for 5 more minutes. Add the seeds and knead for another 15 seconds. Transfer the dough to a floured work surface and knead by hand until the seeds are dispersed evenly and the dough forms a smooth, taut ball. Place the dough in a greased container with a 4-quart capacity; cover with plastic wrap and allow to rise until doubled in size, 45 to 60 minutes.

3. Adjust an oven rack to the middle position and heat the oven to 375 degrees. Spray two 9 by 5-inch loaf pans with vegetable oil spray. Transfer the dough to a lightly floured work surface and pat into a 12 by 9-inch rectangle; cut the dough in half crosswise with a knife or bench scraper. With a short side facing you, starting at the farthest end, roll one dough piece into a log, keeping the roll taut by tucking it under itself as you go. Seal the loaf by pinching the seam together gently with your thumb and forefinger; repeat with the remaining dough. Spray the loaves lightly with water or vegetable oil spray. Roll each dough log in oats to coat evenly and place, seam side down, in the greased loaf pans, pressing gently into the corners; cover lightly with plastic wrap and let rise until almost doubled in size, 30 to 40 minutes. (The dough should barely spring back when poked with a knuckle.) Bake until the center of the loaves registers 200 degrees on an instant-read thermometer, 35 to 40 minutes. Remove the loaves from the pans and cool on a wire rack before slicing, about 3 hours.

NEW YORK BAGELS

WHY THIS RECIPE WORKS: For the chewy center and crackly-crisp shell of an authentic New York bagel, we needed to take the obvious steps—mixing flour, water, yeast and salt; shaping the dough into rings; letting the rings proof—and add some extra at-home finesse. For a fine, uniform crumb with plenty of chew, the dough's gluten network needed tightening. Mixing vital wheat gluten with bread flour elevated the gluten and ice water kept the dough cool during mixing. Dissolving malt syrup in the water ahead of time infused the dough with distinct malty flavor. Flattening, rolling, and twisting the dough into a compact spiral stressed it, eliminating air pockets and promising a bagel with substantial chew. After the bagels proofed in the refrigerator, we boiled them in an alkaline mixture of water, sugar, and baking soda to wake up the yeast and cook some of the surface starches for a glossy, crisp crust. Preheating a baking stone in the oven created a hearth-like cooking environment while the bagels boiled. We arranged them on a wire rack–lined rimmed baking sheet and placed the sheet directly on the baking stone. Before leaving the bagels to bake, we poured boiling water into the bottom of the sheet for plenty of steam. A flip halfway through baking ensured even browning.

New York Bagels
MAKES 8 BAGELS

This recipe requires refrigerating the shaped bagels for 16 to 24 hours before baking them. This recipe works best with King Arthur bread flour, although other bread flours will work. Vital wheat gluten and malt syrup are available in most supermarkets in the baking and syrup aisles, respectively. If you cannot find malt syrup, substitute 4 teaspoons of molasses. The bagels are best eaten within a day of baking; fully cooled bagels can be transferred to heavy-duty zipper-lock bags and frozen for up to one month.

 1   cup plus 2 tablespoons ice water (9 ounces)
 2   tablespoons malt syrup
2⅔   cups (14⅔ ounces) bread flour
 4   teaspoons vital wheat gluten
 2   teaspoons instant or rapid-rise yeast
 2   teaspoons salt
 ¼   cup (1¼ ounces) cornmeal
 ¼   cup (1¾ ounces) sugar
 1   tablespoon baking soda

1. Stir ice water and malt syrup together in 2-cup liquid measuring cup until malt syrup has fully dissolved. Process flour, wheat gluten, and yeast in food processor until combined, about 2 seconds. With processor running, slowly add ice water mixture; process until dough is just combined and no dry flour remains, about 20 seconds. Let dough stand for 10 minutes.

2. Add salt to dough and process, stopping processor and redistributing dough as needed, until dough forms shaggy mass that clears sides of workbowl (dough may not form one single mass), 45 to 90 seconds. Transfer dough to unfloured counter and knead until smooth, about 1 minute. Divide dough into 8 equal pieces (3½ ounces each) and cover loosely with plastic wrap.

3. Working with 1 piece of dough at a time and keeping remaining pieces covered, form dough pieces into smooth, taut rounds. (To round, set piece of dough on unfloured counter. Loosely cup your hand around dough and, without applying pressure to dough, move your hand in small circular motions. Tackiness of dough against counter and circular motion should work dough into smooth, even ball, but if dough sticks to your hands, lightly dust your fingers with flour.) Let dough balls rest on counter, covered, for 15 minutes.

4. Sprinkle rimmed baking sheet with cornmeal. Working with 1 dough ball at a time and keeping remaining pieces covered, coat dough balls lightly with flour and then, using your hands and rolling pin, pat and roll dough balls into 5-inch rounds. Starting with edge of dough farthest from you, roll into tight cylinder. Starting at center of cylinder and working toward ends, gently and evenly roll and stretch dough into 8- to 9-inch-long rope. Do not taper ends. Rolling ends of dough under your hands in opposite directions, twist rope to form tight spiral. Without unrolling spiral, wrap rope around your fingers, overlapping ends of dough by about 2 inches under your palm, to create ring shape. Pinch ends of dough gently together. With overlap under your palm, press and roll seam using circular motion on counter to fully seal. Transfer rings to prepared sheet and cover loosely with plastic, leaving at least 1 inch between bagels. Let bagels stand at room temperature for 1 hour. Cover sheet tightly with plastic and refrigerate for at least 16 hours or up to 24 hours.

5. One hour before baking, adjust oven rack to upper-middle position, place baking stone on rack, and heat oven to 450 degrees.

6. Bring 4 quarts water, sugar, and baking soda to boil in large Dutch oven. Set wire rack in rimmed baking sheet and spray rack with vegetable oil spray.

7. Transfer 4 bagels to boiling water and cook for 20 seconds. Using wire skimmer or slotted spoon, flip bagels over and cook 20 seconds longer. Using wire skimmer or slotted spoon, transfer bagels to prepared wire rack, with cornmeal side facing down. Repeat with remaining 4 bagels.

8. Place sheet with bagels on preheated baking stone and pour ½ cup boiling water into bottom of sheet. Bake until tops of bagels are beginning to brown, 10 to 12 minutes. Using metal spatula, flip bagels and continue to bake until golden brown, 10 to 12 minutes longer. Remove sheet from oven and let bagels cool on wire rack for at least 15 minutes. Serve warm or at room temperature.

Bagel Toppings

Place ½ cup poppy seeds, sesame seeds, caraway seeds, dehydrated onion flakes, dehydrated garlic flakes, or coarse/pretzel salt in small bowl. Press tops of just-boiled bagels (side without cornmeal) gently into topping and return to wire rack, topping side up.

NOTES FROM THE TEST KITCHEN

SHAPING BAGELS LIKE A PRO
Thoroughly working the dough during shaping helps a New York bagel develop its characteristic chew.

1. Pat and roll dough ball (lightly coated with flour) with rolling pin into 5-inch round. Roll into tight cylinder, starting with far side of dough.

2. Roll and stretch dough into 8- to 9-inch-long rope, starting at center of cylinder (don't taper ends). Twist rope to form tight spiral by rolling ends of dough under hands in opposite directions.

3. Wrap rope around fingers, overlapping ends by 2 inches, to create ring. Pinch ends together. Press and roll seam (positioned under your palm) using circular motion on counter to fully seal.

CHAPTER 22

COOKIE JAR FAVORITES

CHEWY SUGAR COOKIES

WHY THIS RECIPE WORKS: Traditional recipes for sugar cookies require obsessive attention to detail. The butter must be at precisely the right temperature and it must be creamed to the proper degree of airiness. Slight variations in measures can result in cookies that spread or cookies that become brittle and hard upon cooling. We didn't want a cookie that depended on such a finicky process, we wanted an approachable recipe for great sugar cookies that anyone could make anytime. We melted the butter so our sugar cookie dough could easily be mixed together with a spoon—no more fussy creaming. Replacing a portion of the melted butter with vegetable oil ensured a chewy cookie without affecting flavor. And incorporating an unusual addition, cream cheese, into the cookie dough kept our cookies tender, while the slight tang of the cream cheese made for a rich, not-too-sweet cookie.

Chewy Sugar Cookies

MAKES ABOUT 24 COOKIES

The final dough will be slightly softer than most cookie doughs. For best results, handle the dough as briefly and gently as possible when shaping the cookies. Overworking the dough will result in flatter cookies.

- 2¼ cups (11¼ ounces) unbleached all-purpose flour
- 1 teaspoon baking powder
- ½ teaspoon baking soda
- ½ teaspoon table salt
- 1½ cups (10½ ounces) sugar, plus ⅓ cup for rolling
- 2 ounces cream cheese, cut into 8 pieces
- 6 tablespoons (¾ stick) unsalted butter, melted and still warm
- ⅓ cup vegetable oil
- 1 large egg
- 1 tablespoon whole milk
- 2 teaspoons vanilla extract

1. Adjust an oven rack to the middle position and heat the oven to 350 degrees. Line 2 large rimmed baking sheets with parchment paper. Whisk the flour, baking powder, baking soda, and salt together in a medium bowl. Set aside.

2. Place 1½ cups of the sugar and the cream cheese in a large bowl. Place the remaining ⅓ cup sugar in a shallow baking dish or pie plate and set aside. Pour the warm butter over the sugar and cream cheese and whisk to combine (some small lumps of cream cheese will remain but will smooth out later). Whisk in the oil until incorporated. Add the egg, milk, and vanilla; continue to whisk until smooth. Add the flour mixture and mix with a rubber spatula until a soft homogeneous dough forms.

3. Divide the dough into 24 equal pieces, about 2 tablespoons each. Using your hands, roll each piece of dough into a ball (see note). Working in batches, roll the balls in sugar to coat and set on the prepared baking sheet, 12 dough balls per sheet. Using the bottom of a drinking glass, flatten the dough balls until 2 inches in diameter. Sprinkle the tops of the cookies evenly with the remaining sugar, using 2 teaspoons for each sheet. (Discard the remaining sugar.)

4. Bake the cookies, one sheet at a time, until the edges are set and beginning to brown, 11 to 13 minutes, rotating the sheet after 7 minutes. Cool the cookies on the baking sheet for 5 minutes; using a wide metal spatula, transfer the cookies to a wire rack and cool to room temperature.

BROWN SUGAR COOKIES

WHY THIS RECIPE WORKS: Simple sugar cookies, while classic, can seem too basic—even dull—at times. We wanted to turn up the volume on the sugar cookie by switching out the granulated sugar in favor of brown sugar. We had a clear vision of this cookie. It would be oversized, with a crackling crisp exterior and a chewy interior. And, like Mick Jagger, this cookie would scream "brown sugar."

We wanted butter for optimal flavor, but the traditional creaming method (creaming softened butter with sugar until fluffy, beating in an egg, and then adding the dry ingredients) gave us a cakey texture. Cutting the butter into the flour produced crumbly cookies. What worked was first melting the butter. We then tweaked the amount of eggs, dark brown sugar, flour, and leavener to give us a good cookie, but we wanted even more brown sugar flavor. We made progress by rolling the dough balls in a combination of brown and granulated sugar and adding a healthy amount of vanilla and table salt. But our biggest success came from an unlikely refinement. Browning the melted butter added a complex nuttiness that made a substantial difference.

Brown Sugar Cookies

MAKES ABOUT 24 COOKIES

Avoid using a nonstick skillet to brown the butter. The dark color of the nonstick coating makes it difficult to gauge when the butter is sufficiently browned. Use fresh brown sugar, as hardened brown sugar will make the cookies too dry. Achieving the proper texture—crisp at the edges and chewy in the middle—is critical to this recipe. Because the cookies are so dark, it's hard to judge doneness by color. Instead, gently press halfway between the edge and center of the cookie. When it's done, it will form an indentation with slight resistance. Check early and err on the side of underdone.

- 14 tablespoons (1¾ sticks) unsalted butter
- 2 cups packed (14 ounces) dark brown sugar (see note)
- ¼ cup (1¾ ounces) granulated sugar
- 2 cups plus 2 tablespoons (about 10⅔ ounces) unbleached all-purpose flour
- ½ teaspoon baking soda
- ¼ teaspoon baking powder
- ½ teaspoon table salt
- 1 large whole egg
- 1 large egg yolk
- 1 tablespoon vanilla extract

1. Melt 10 tablespoons of the butter in a 10-inch skillet over medium-high heat, about 2 minutes. Continue to cook, swirling the pan constantly until the butter is dark golden brown and has a nutty aroma, 1 to 3 minutes. Transfer the browned butter to a large heatproof bowl. Stir the remaining 4 tablespoons butter into the hot butter to melt; set aside for 15 minutes.

2. Meanwhile, adjust an oven rack to the middle position and heat the oven to 350 degrees. Line 2 large baking sheets with parchment paper. In a shallow baking dish or pie plate, mix ¼ cup of the brown sugar and the granulated sugar, rubbing the mixture between your fingers until well combined; set aside. Whisk the flour, baking soda, and baking powder together in a medium bowl; set aside.

3. Add the remaining 1¾ cups brown sugar and the salt to the bowl with the cooled butter; mix until no sugar lumps remain, about 30 seconds. Scrape down the bowl with a rubber spatula; add the whole egg, egg yolk, and vanilla and mix until fully incorporated, about 30 seconds. Scrape down the bowl. Add the flour mixture and mix until just combined, about 1 minute. Give the dough a final stir to ensure that no flour pockets remain and the ingredients are evenly distributed.

4. Divide the dough into 24 portions, each about 2 tablespoons, rolling them between your hands into balls about 1½ inches in diameter. Working in batches, drop 12 dough balls into the baking dish with the sugar mixture and toss to coat. Set the dough balls on the prepared baking sheet, spacing them about 2 inches apart; repeat with the second batch of 12.

5. Bake one sheet at a time until the cookies are browned and still puffy and the edges have begun to set but the centers are still soft (the cookies will look raw between the cracks and seem underdone), 12 to 14 minutes, rotating the baking sheet halfway through the baking time. Do not overbake.

6. Cool the cookies on the baking sheet for 5 minutes; using a wide metal spatula, transfer the cookies to a wire rack and cool to room temperature.

SNICKERDOODLES

WHY THIS RECIPE WORKS: With their crinkly tops and liberal dusting of cinnamon sugar, snickerdoodles are a New England favorite. Cream of tartar is essential to these cookies, as it provided their subtle tang, and, when combined with baking soda, it created a short-lived leavening effect that caused the cookies to rise and fall quickly while baking, leaving them with a distinctive crinkly appearance. We found that using equal amounts of shortening and butter gave us nicely shaped cookies that were chewy and buttery. Rolling the balls of dough in cinnamon sugar—a full tablespoon for warm spice flavor—imparted a spicy sweet crunch to the cookies. For the best results, we baked the cookies one sheet at a time and pulled them from the oven just as they were beginning to brown but were still soft and puffy in the middle. They continued to cook as they cooled on the baking sheet and were perfectly done and chewy once cooled.

Snickerdoodles

MAKES 24 COOKIES

Cream of tartar is essential to the flavor of these cookies, and it works in combination with the baking soda to give the cookies lift; do not substitute baking powder. For the best results, bake only one sheet of cookies at a time.

- 2½ cups (12½ ounces) all-purpose flour
- 2 teaspoons cream of tartar
- 1 teaspoon baking soda
- ½ teaspoon salt
- 8 tablespoons unsalted butter, softened
- 8 tablespoons vegetable shortening
- 1½ cups (10½ ounces) sugar, plus ¼ cup for rolling
- 2 large eggs
- 1 tablespoon ground cinnamon

1. Adjust oven rack to middle position and heat oven to 375 degrees. Line 3 baking sheets with parchment paper. Whisk flour, cream of tartar, baking soda, and salt together in bowl.

2. Using stand mixer fitted with paddle, beat butter, shortening, and 1½ cups sugar together on medium speed until light and fluffy, about 3 minutes. Beat in eggs, one at a time, until incorporated, about 30 seconds, scraping down bowl as needed.

3. Reduce speed to low and slowly add flour mixture until combined, about 30 seconds. Give dough final stir by hand to ensure no flour pockets remain.

4. Combine remaining ¼ cup sugar and cinnamon in shallow dish. Working with 2 tablespoons dough at a time, roll into balls, then roll in sugar to coat; measure and space 2 inches apart on prepared baking sheets. (Dough balls can be frozen for up to 1 month; bake frozen cookies in 300-degree oven for 18 to 20 minutes.)

5. Bake cookies, 1 sheet at a time, with 8 cookies per sheet, until edges are just set and beginning to brown but centers are still soft, puffy, and cracked (cookies will look raw between cracks and seem underdone), 8 to 12 minutes, rotating sheet halfway through baking. Let cookies cool on sheet for 10 minutes, then transfer to wire rack and let cool completely before serving.

MOLASSES SPICE COOKIES

WHY THIS RECIPE WORKS: Molasses spice cookies are often miserable specimens, no more than flat, tasteless cardboard rounds of gingerbread. They can be dry and cakey without the requisite chew; others are timidly flavored with molasses and scantily spiced. We wanted to create the ultimate molasses spice cookie—soft, chewy, and gently spiced with deep, dark molasses flavor. We also wanted it to have the traditional cracks and crinkles so characteristic of these charming cookies.

We started with all-purpose flour and butter for full, rich flavor. Using just the right amount of molasses and brown sugar and flavoring the cookies with a combination of vanilla, ginger, cinnamon, cloves, black pepper, and allspice gave these spiced cookies the warm tingle that we were after. We found that to keep the cookies mild, using a light or mild molasses was imperative; but if it's a stronger flavor you want, dark molasses is in order. We pulled the cookies from the oven when they still looked a bit underdone; residual heat finished the baking and kept the cookies chewy and moist.

Molasses Spice Cookies
MAKES ABOUT 22 COOKIES

For best flavor, make sure that your spices are fresh. Light or mild molasses gives the cookies a milder flavor; for a stronger flavor, use dark molasses. Either way, measure molasses in a liquid measure. If you find that the dough sticks to your palms as you shape the balls, moisten your hands occasionally in a bowl filled with cold tap water and shake off the excess. Bake the cookies one sheet at a time; if baked two sheets at a time, the cookies started on the bottom rack won't develop attractive crackly tops. Remove the cookies from the oven when they still look slightly raw and underbaked.

- ⅓ cup (2⅓ ounces) granulated sugar, plus ½ cup for coating
- 2¼ cups (11¼ ounces) unbleached all-purpose flour
- 1 teaspoon baking soda
- 1½ teaspoons ground cinnamon
- 1½ teaspoons ground ginger
- ½ teaspoon ground cloves
- ¼ teaspoon ground allspice
- ¼ teaspoon ground black pepper
- ¼ teaspoon table salt
- 12 tablespoons (1½ sticks) unsalted butter, softened
- ⅓ cup packed (2⅓ ounces) dark brown sugar
- 1 large egg yolk
- 1 teaspoon vanilla extract
- ½ cup light or dark molasses (see note)

1. Adjust an oven rack to the middle position and heat the oven to 375 degrees. Line 2 large baking sheets with parchment paper. Place ½ cup of the granulated sugar in a shallow baking dish or pie plate; set aside.

2. Whisk the flour, baking soda, spices, and salt together in a medium bowl; set aside.

3. In a stand mixer fitted with the paddle attachment, beat the butter, brown sugar, and remaining ⅓ cup granulated sugar on medium-high speed until light and fluffy, about 3 minutes. Decrease the speed to medium-low and add the egg yolk and vanilla; increase the speed to medium and beat until incorporated, about 20 seconds. Decrease the speed to medium-low and add the molasses; beat until fully incorporated, about 20 seconds, scraping down the bowl once with a rubber spatula. Decrease the speed to low and add the flour mixture; beat until just incorporated, about 30 seconds, scraping down the bowl once. Give the dough a final stir to ensure that no flour pockets remain. The dough will be soft.

4. Divide the dough into 22 portions, each about 1 tablespoon, and roll them between your hands into balls about 1¼ to 1½ inches in diameter. Working in batches, drop five dough balls into the baking dish with the sugar and toss to coat. Set the dough balls on the prepared baking sheets, spacing them about 2 inches apart. Repeat with the remaining dough.

5. Bake one sheet at a time, rotating the baking sheets halfway through the baking time, until the cookies are browned, still puffy, and the edges have begun to set but the centers are still soft (the cookies will look raw between the cracks and seem underdone), about 11 minutes. Do not overbake.

6. Cool the cookies on the baking sheets for 5 minutes; using a wide metal spatula, transfer the cookies to a wire rack and cool to room temperature.

Molasses Spice Cookies with Dark Rum Glaze

If the glaze is too thick to drizzle, whisk in up to an additional ½ tablespoon rum.

Follow the recipe for Molasses Spice Cookies. Whisk 1 cup (4 ounces) confectioners' sugar and 2½ tablespoons dark rum together in a medium bowl until smooth. Drizzle or spread the glaze using the back of a spoon on the cooled cookies. Allow the glazed cookies to dry for at least 15 minutes.

CLASSIC CHOCOLATE CHIP COOKIES

WHY THIS RECIPE WORKS: Rich and buttery, with their soft cores and crispy edges, chocolate chip cookies are the American cookie-jar standard. Since Nestlé first began printing the recipe for Toll House cookies on the back of chocolate chip bags in 1939, generations of bakers have packed them into lunches and taken them to potlucks. But we wondered if this was really the best that a chocolate chip cookie could be. We wanted something more than the standard bake sale offering; we wanted a moist and chewy cookie with crisp edges and deep notes of toffee and butterscotch to balance its sweetness.

Melting the butter before combining it with the other ingredients gave us the chewy texture we wanted, and browning a portion of it added nutty flavor. Upping the brown sugar enhanced chewiness, while a combination of one whole egg and one egg yolk gave us supremely moist cookies. For the crisp edges and deep toffee flavor, we allowed the sugar to dissolve and rest in the melted butter. We baked the cookies until golden brown and just set, but still soft in the center. The resulting cookies were crisp, chewy, and gooey with chocolate and boasted a complex medley of sweet, buttery, caramel, and toffee flavors.

Classic Chocolate Chip Cookies
MAKES ABOUT 16 LARGE COOKIES

Avoid using a nonstick skillet to brown the butter; the dark color of the nonstick coating makes it difficult to gauge when the butter is browned. Use fresh, moist brown sugar instead of hardened brown sugar, which will make the cookies dry. This recipe works with light brown sugar, but the cookies will be less full-flavored. For our winning brand of chocolate chips, see page 910. If you're using smaller baking sheets, put fewer cookies on each sheet and bake them in batches.

- 1¾ cups (8¾ ounces) unbleached all-purpose flour
- ½ teaspoon baking soda
- 14 tablespoons (1¾ sticks) unsalted butter
- ¾ cup packed (5¼ ounces) dark brown sugar (see note)
- ½ cup (3½ ounces) granulated sugar
- 1 teaspoon table salt
- 2 teaspoons vanilla extract
- 1 large whole egg
- 1 large egg yolk
- 1¼ cups (7½ ounces) semisweet chocolate chips or chunks (see note)
- ¾ cup chopped pecans or walnuts, toasted (optional)

1. Adjust an oven rack to the middle position and heat the oven to 375 degrees. Line 2 large baking sheets with parchment paper.

2. Whisk the flour and baking soda together in a medium bowl; set aside.

3. Heat 10 tablespoons of the butter in a 10-inch skillet over medium-high heat until melted, about 2 minutes. Continue cooking, swirling the pan constantly until the butter is dark golden brown and has a nutty aroma, 1 to 3 minutes. Transfer the browned butter to a large heatproof bowl. Add the remaining 4 tablespoons butter and stir until completely melted.

4. Add the sugars, salt, and vanilla to the melted butter; whisk until fully incorporated. Add the whole egg and egg yolk; whisk until the mixture is smooth with no sugar lumps remaining, about 30 seconds. Let the mixture stand for 3 minutes, then whisk for 30 seconds. Repeat the process of resting and whisking two more times until the mixture is thick, smooth, and shiny. Using a rubber spatula, stir in the flour mixture until just combined, about 1 minute. Stir in the chocolate chips and nuts (if using), giving the dough a final stir to ensure that no flour pockets remain.

5. Divide the dough into 16 portions, each about 3 tablespoons. Place the cookies on the prepared baking sheets, spacing them about 2 inches apart.

6. Bake one sheet at a time, rotating the sheet halfway through the baking time, until the cookies are golden brown and still puffy, and the edges have begun to set but the centers are still soft, 10 to 14 minutes. Transfer the baking sheet to a wire rack; cool to room temperature.

THICK AND CHEWY CHOCOLATE CHIP COOKIES

WHY THIS RECIPE WORKS: Nowadays, chocolate chip cookies sold in gourmet shops and cafés always come jumbo-sized (think saucer plate). These cookies are incredibly appealing and satisfying—thick and chewy rounds loaded with as many chocolate chips as they can hold. We wanted our own version that retained the soft and tender texture of these café cookies, even after a day or two (not that they'd be hanging around that long).

One key element in achieving this cookie was melting the butter, which created a product with a chewy texture. But to keep the cookie from becoming tough, we had to add a little extra fat, which we did in the form of an egg yolk; the added fat acts a tenderizer and prevents the cookies from hardening after several hours. The usual suspects of all-purpose flour, baking soda, an egg, brown sugar, and granulated sugar made an appearance in our cookie recipe, and vanilla provided a light flavor. A good amount of chocolate chips guaranteed that every bite was rich and chocolaty. Finally, we formed the dough into balls, then pulled each ball into two pieces and rejoined them with the uneven surface facing up; now our cookies had the rustic, craggy appearance we wanted.

Thick and Chewy Chocolate Chip Cookies
MAKES ABOUT 18 LARGE COOKIES

To ensure the proper texture, cool the cookies on the baking sheets. See page 876 for our top-rated baking sheet.

- 2 cups plus 2 tablespoons (about 10⅔ ounces) unbleached all-purpose flour
- ½ teaspoon baking soda
- ½ teaspoon table salt
- 12 tablespoons (1½ sticks) unsalted butter, melted and cooled
- 1 cup packed (7 ounces) light or dark brown sugar
- ½ cup (3½ ounces) granulated sugar
- 1 large whole egg
- 1 large egg yolk
- 2 teaspoons vanilla extract
- 1½ cups (9 ounces) semisweet chocolate chips

1. Adjust the oven racks to the upper-middle and lower-middle positions and heat the oven to 325 degrees. Line 2 large baking sheets with parchment paper.

2. Whisk the flour, baking soda, and salt together in a medium bowl; set aside.

3. In a stand mixer fitted with the paddle attachment, beat the butter and sugars at medium speed until smooth, about 1 minute. Add the whole egg, egg yolk, and vanilla and beat on medium-low speed until fully incorporated, about 30 seconds, scraping down the bowl and beater as needed with a rubber spatula. Add the dry ingredients and mix on low speed until combined, about 30 seconds. Mix in the chocolate chips until just incorporated.

4. Divide the dough into 18 portions, each about ¼ cup, and roll them between your hands into balls. Holding one dough ball with your fingers, pull the dough apart into two equal halves. Rotate the halves 90 degrees and, with the jagged surfaces facing up, join the halves together at their base, again forming a single ball, being careful not to smooth the dough's uneven surface. Place the cookies on the prepared baking sheets, spacing them about 2½ inches apart.

5. Bake until the cookies are light golden brown and the edges start to harden but the centers are still soft and puffy, 15 to 18 minutes, switching and rotating the baking sheets halfway through the baking time. Cool the cookies on the baking sheets.

THIN, CRISPY CHOCOLATE CHIP COOKIES

WHY THIS RECIPE WORKS: Too often, thin and crispy chocolate chip cookies are brittle and crumbly or tough and lacking flavor. We wanted cookies that were thin and packed a big crunch without breaking teeth or shattering into a million pieces when eaten. And they had to have the simple, gratifying flavors of deeply caramelized sugar and rich butter. For cookies with a notable butterscotch flavor and sufficient crunch, we turned to a combination of light brown sugar and white sugar. Next we focused on the thickness of our cookies. When butter is creamed with sugar, air cells are created in the batter; these cells expand during baking, leading to cookies that rise—and cookies with height were not what we wanted. So we used melted butter and milk to create a batter that would spread (not rise) in the oven, resulting in cookies with the perfect thin crispiness. A bit of baking soda and corn syrup promoted maximum browning and caramelization, and vanilla and salt gave our cookies the best flavor.

Thin and Crispy Chocolate Chip Cookies

MAKES ABOUT 40 COOKIES

The dough, en masse or shaped into balls and wrapped well, can be refrigerated for up to 2 days or frozen for up to 1 month; bring it to room temperature before baking.

- 1½ cups (7½ ounces) unbleached all-purpose flour
- ¾ teaspoon baking soda
- ¼ teaspoon table salt
- 8 tablespoons (1 stick) unsalted butter, melted and cooled
- ½ cup (3½ ounces) granulated sugar
- ⅓ cup packed (2⅓ ounces) light brown sugar
- 2 tablespoons light corn syrup
- 1 large egg yolk
- 2 tablespoons milk
- 1 tablespoon vanilla extract
- ¾ cup (4½ ounces) semisweet chocolate chips

1. Adjust an oven rack to the middle position and heat the oven to 375 degrees. Line 2 large baking sheets with parchment paper.

2. Whisk the flour, baking soda, and salt together in a medium bowl; set aside.

3. In a stand mixer fitted with the paddle attachment, beat the melted butter, granulated sugar, brown sugar, and corn syrup at low speed until thoroughly blended, about 1 minute. Add the egg yolk, milk, and vanilla; mix until fully incorporated and smooth, about 1 minute, scraping down the bowl and beater as needed. With the mixer still running on low, slowly add the dry ingredients and mix until just combined. Do not over beat. Add the chocolate chips and mix until evenly distributed throughout the batter, about 5 seconds.

4. Divide the dough into 40 portions, each about 1 tablespoon, and roll them between your hands into balls. Place the cookies on the prepared baking sheets, spacing them about 2 inches apart. Bake, one sheet at a time, until the cookies are deep golden brown and flat, about 12 minutes, switching and rotating the baking sheets halfway through the baking time.

5. Cool the cookies on the baking sheet for 3 minutes. Using a wide metal spatula, transfer the cookies to a wire rack and cool to room temperature.

GLUTEN-FREE CHOCOLATE CHIP COOKIES

WHY THIS RECIPE WORKS: Chocolate chip cookies are a classic favorite, but most gluten-free versions turn out crumbly, gritty, and greasy. Using the test kitchen's gluten-free flour blend, we set out to create a gluten-free cookie that would be as good as the original version. Cutting back on butter helped to minimize greasiness. Melting the butter, rather than creaming (as called for in traditional recipes), gave the cookies a chewier texture. Some xanthan gum helped give the cookies structure, allowing them to hold together. To alleviate grittiness, we added more liquid in the form of milk and let the

A RULE TO COOK BY

Contrary to what you may think, the test kitchen isn't packed with the latest high-tech kitchen gadgets. In fact, one of our favorite gadgets isn't even found in a kitchenware store. Wondering why that cake didn't rise properly? Or why those cookies ran together? Did your expensive steak overcook? Pull out a ruler. It can prove that the 8-inch cake pan you are using is actually 9 inches, that the cookies have been spaced together too closely, and that the supposedly 1-inch-thick steak the butcher sold you is only ½ inch thick. We prefer 18-inch stainless steel rulers, which can be thrown right into the dishwasher. They can be purchased at any office supply store for about $4.

batter rest for 30 minutes so that the starches had time to hydrate and soften. Upping the ratio of brown sugar to granulated sugar made our cookies crispy on the edges and chewy in the center, and also gave the cookies more complex, toffee-like flavor.

Gluten-Free Chocolate Chip Cookies

MAKES ABOUT 24 COOKIES

Not all brands of chocolate chips are processed in a gluten-free facility, so read labels carefully. We highly recommend you weigh the ingredients for this recipe, rather than rely on cup measurements. You can substitute 8 ounces (¾ cup plus ⅔ cup) King Arthur Gluten-Free Multi-Purpose Flour or 8 ounces (1½ cups plus 2 tablespoons) Bob's Red Mill GF All-Purpose Baking Flour for the ATK Blend. Note that cookies made with King Arthur will spread more and be more delicate, while cookies made with Bob's Red Mill will spread more and have a distinct bean flavor.

- 8 ounces (1¾ cups) The America's Test Kitchen Gluten-Free Flour Blend (page 344)
- 1 teaspoon baking soda
- ¾ teaspoon xanthan gum
- ½ teaspoon salt
- 8 tablespoons unsalted butter, melted
- 5¼ ounces (¾ cup packed) light brown sugar
- 2⅓ ounces (⅓ cup) granulated sugar
- 1 large egg
- 2 tablespoons milk
- 1 tablespoon vanilla extract
- 7½ ounces (1¼ cups) semisweet chocolate chips

1. Whisk flour blend, baking soda, xanthan gum, and salt together in medium bowl; set aside. Whisk melted butter, brown sugar, and granulated sugar together in large bowl until well combined and smooth. Whisk in egg, milk, and vanilla and continue to whisk until smooth. Stir in flour mixture with rubber spatula and mix until soft, homogeneous dough forms. Fold in chocolate chips. Cover bowl with plastic wrap and let dough rest for 30 minutes. (Dough will be sticky and soft.)

2. Adjust oven rack to middle position and heat oven to 350 degrees. Line 2 baking sheets with parchment paper. Using 2 soupspoons and working with about 1½ tablespoons of dough at a time, portion dough and space 2 inches apart on prepared sheets. Bake cookies, 1 sheet at a time, until golden brown and edges have begun to set but centers are still soft, 11 to 13 minutes, rotating sheet halfway through baking.

3. Let cookies cool on sheet for 5 minutes, then transfer to wire rack. Serve warm or at room temperature. (Cookies are best eaten on day they are baked, but they can be cooled and placed immediately in airtight container and stored at room temperature for up to 1 day.)

CHOCOLATE COOKIES

WHY THIS RECIPE WORKS: Cookie recipes that trumpet their extreme chocolate flavor always leave us a bit suspicious. While they provide plenty of intensity, these over-the-top confections also tend to be delicate and crumbly, more like cakey brownies than cookies. We set out to make an exceptionally rich chocolate cookie that we could sink our teeth into—without having it fall apart.

Our first batch, with modest amounts of cocoa powder and melted chocolate, baked up too cakey and tender—just what we didn't want. The chocolate was the culprit; its fat was softening the dough. Cutting out the chocolate made the cookies less cakey and tender, and more like cookies. To restore chocolate flavor without adding too much fat, we increased the cocoa powder and reduced the flour. Using an egg white rather than a whole egg gave us the structure we wanted, and adding dark corn syrup gave the cookies a nice chewiness and lent a hint of caramel flavor. For more richness, we folded in chopped bittersweet chocolate; the chunks stayed intact and added intense chocolate flavor. A dip in granulated sugar before baking gave the cookies a sweet crunch and an attractive crackled appearance once they were out of the oven.

Chocolate Cookies
MAKES ABOUT 16 COOKIES

We recommend using one of the test kitchen's favorite baking chocolates, Ghirardelli Bittersweet Chocolate or Callebaut Intense Dark Chocolate, but any high-quality dark, bittersweet, or semisweet chocolate will work. Light brown sugar can be substituted for the dark, as can light corn syrup for the dark, but with some sacrifice in flavor.

⅓ cup (2⅓ ounces) granulated sugar, plus ½ cup for coating

1½ cups (7½ ounces) unbleached all-purpose flour

¾ cup Dutch-processed cocoa powder

½ teaspoon baking soda

¼ teaspoon plus ⅛ teaspoon table salt

½ cup dark corn syrup (see note)

1 large egg white

1 teaspoon vanilla extract

12 tablespoons (1½ sticks) unsalted butter, softened

⅓ cup packed (2⅓ ounces) dark brown sugar (see note)

4 ounces bittersweet chocolate, chopped into ½-inch pieces (see note)

1. Adjust the oven racks to the upper-middle and lower-middle positions and heat the oven to 375 degrees. Line 2 large baking sheets with parchment paper. Place ½ cup of the granulated sugar in a shallow baking dish or pie plate. Whisk the flour, cocoa powder, baking soda, and salt together in a medium bowl. Whisk the corn syrup, egg white, and vanilla together in a small bowl.

2. In a stand mixer fitted with the paddle attachment, beat the butter, brown sugar, and remaining ⅓ cup granulated sugar at medium-high speed until light and fluffy, about 2 minutes. Decrease the speed to medium-low, add the corn syrup mixture, and beat until fully incorporated, about 20 seconds, scraping down the bowl and beater as needed with a rubber spatula. Decrease the speed to low, add the flour mixture and chopped chocolate, and mix until just incorporated, about 30 seconds, scraping down the bowl and beater as needed. Give the dough a final stir to ensure that no pockets of flour remain. Chill the dough for 30 minutes to firm slightly (do not chill longer than 30 minutes).

3. Divide the dough into 16 equal portions, each a generous 2 tablespoons, and roll them between your hands into balls about 1½ inches in diameter. Working in batches, drop eight dough balls into the baking dish with the sugar and toss to coat. Place the dough balls on the prepared baking sheet, spacing them about 2 inches apart; repeat with the second batch of eight. Bake, switching and rotating the sheets halfway through the baking time, until the cookies are puffed and cracked and the edges have begun to set but the centers are still soft (the cookies will look raw between the cracks and seem underdone), 10 to 11 minutes. Do not overbake.

4. Cool the cookies on the baking sheets for 5 minutes; using a wide metal spatula, transfer the cookies to a wire rack and cool to room temperature.

DOUBLE-CHOCOLATE COOKIES

WHY THIS RECIPE WORKS: Our goal in creating a traditional double-chocolate cookie recipe seemed more like a fantasy: The first bite of the cookie would reveal a center of hot fudge sauce, the texture would call to mind chocolate bread pudding, and the overall flavor would be of deep and complex chocolate. Was it possible?

In the end, the fulfillment of our fantasy relied on very basic ingredients: chocolate, sugar, eggs, butter, flour, baking powder, and salt. We used a modified creaming method with minimal beating to produce moist cookies that weren't cakey, and we let the batter rest for a half-hour to develop a certain fudginess. Ingredient proportions were all-important—for moist, rich cookies, we used more chocolate than flour. The more highly processed semisweet chocolate tasted smoother and richer than unsweetened, and Dutch-processed cocoa and instant coffee further enriched the chocolate flavor. At last, we had a cookie that was both rich and soft, with an intense chocolaty center.

Thick and Chewy Double-Chocolate Cookies
MAKES ABOUT 42 COOKIES

To melt the chocolate using a microwave, heat it at 50 percent power for 2 minutes; stir the chocolate and continue heating until melted, stirring once every additional minute. Resist the urge to bake the cookies longer than indicated; they may appear underbaked at first but will firm up as they cool.

- 2 cups (10 ounces) unbleached all-purpose flour
- ½ cup Dutch-processed cocoa powder
- 2 teaspoons baking powder
- ½ teaspoon table salt
- 16 ounces semisweet chocolate, chopped
- 4 large eggs
- 2 teaspoons vanilla extract
- 2 teaspoons instant coffee or espresso powder
- 10 tablespoons (1¼ sticks) unsalted butter, softened
- 1½ cups packed (10½ ounces) light brown sugar
- ½ cup (3½ ounces) granulated sugar

1. Whisk the flour, cocoa powder, baking powder, and salt together in a medium bowl; set aside.

2. Melt the chocolate in a medium heatproof bowl set over a saucepan of barely simmering water, stirring occasionally, until smooth; set aside to cool slightly. Whisk the eggs and vanilla together in a medium bowl, sprinkle the coffee powder over the top to dissolve, and set aside.

3. In a stand mixer fitted with the paddle attachment, beat the butter and sugars at medium speed until combined, about 45 seconds; the mixture will look granular. Decrease the speed to low, gradually add the egg mixture, and mix until incorporated, about 45 seconds. Add the melted chocolate in a steady stream and mix until combined, about 40 seconds, scraping down the bowl and beater as needed with a rubber spatula. With the mixer still running on low, add the dry ingredients and mix until just combined. Do not over beat. Cover the bowl of dough with plastic wrap and let stand at room temperature until the consistency is scoopable and fudge-like, about 30 minutes.

4. Meanwhile, adjust the oven racks to the upper-middle and lower-middle positions and heat the oven to 350 degrees. Line 2 baking sheets with parchment paper. Divide the dough into 42 equal portions, each about 2 tablespoons, and roll them between your hands into balls about 1¾ inches in diameter. Set the dough balls on the prepared baking sheets, spacing them about 1½ inches apart.

5. Bake two sheets at a time, switching and rotating the baking sheets halfway through the baking time, until the edges have just begun to set but the centers are still very soft, about 10 minutes. Cool the cookies on the baking sheets for 10 minutes; using a wide metal spatula, transfer the cookies to a wire rack and cool to room temperature.

Thick and Chewy Triple-Chocolate Cookies

The addition of chocolate chips will slightly increase the yield of the cookies.

Follow the recipe for Thick and Chewy Double-Chocolate Cookies, adding 2 cups (12 ounces) semisweet chocolate chips to the batter after the dry ingredients are incorporated in step 3.

CHOCOLATE CRINKLE COOKIES

WHY THIS RECIPE WORKS: The name says it all—these cookies are as much about looks as they are about flavor. Rolled in powdered sugar before going in the oven, chocolate crinkle cookies (aka earthquakes) form dark chocolaty fissures that break through the bright white surface during baking. They're eye-catching, with an irresistible deep chocolaty richness to back it up. Or at least, that's how they should be. Too often, these cookies turn out tooth-achingly sweet, with just a couple of wide gaping cracks instead of a crackly surface. We wanted a cookie with deep chocolate flavor and only enough sweetness to balance the chocolate's bitterness; a moist and tender—but not gooey—interior; and plenty of small irregular crinkly fissures breaking through a bright-white surface.

For the best chocolate flavor, we used a combination of unsweetened chocolate and cocoa powder, which got an additional flavor boost from espresso powder. Using brown sugar instead of granulated lent a more complex, tempered sweetness with a bitter molasses edge that complemented the chocolate. A combination of both baking powder and baking soda gave us cookies with the right amount of lift and spread and contributed to a crackly surface. But the real key was rolling the cookies in granulated sugar before the traditional powdered sugar. It not only helped produce the perfect crackly exterior by creating a "shell" that broke into numerous fine fissures as the cookie rose and spread, but it also helped the powdered sugar coating stay in place. We finally had chocolate crinkle cookies that lived up to their name.

Chocolate Crinkle Cookies

MAKES 22 COOKIES

Both natural and Dutch-processed cocoa will work in this recipe. Our favorite brand of natural cocoa is Hershey's Natural Cocoa Unsweetened; our favorite Dutch-processed cocoa is Droste Cocoa.

- 1 cup (5 ounces) all-purpose flour
- ½ cup (1½ ounces) unsweetened cocoa powder
- 1 teaspoon baking powder
- ¼ teaspoon baking soda
- ½ teaspoon salt
- 1½ cups packed (10½ ounces) brown sugar
- 3 large eggs
- 4 teaspoons instant espresso powder (optional)
- 1 teaspoon vanilla extract
- 4 ounces unsweetened chocolate, chopped
- 4 tablespoons unsalted butter
- ½ cup (3½ ounces) granulated sugar
- ½ cup (2 ounces) confectioners' sugar

1. Adjust oven rack to middle position and heat oven to 325 degrees. Line 2 baking sheets with parchment. Whisk flour, cocoa, baking powder, baking soda, and salt together in bowl.

2. Whisk brown sugar, eggs, espresso powder (if using), and vanilla together in large bowl. Microwave chocolate and butter in bowl at 50 percent power, stirring occasionally, until melted, 2 to 3 minutes.

3. Whisk chocolate mixture into egg mixture until combined. Fold in flour mixture until no dry streaks remain. Allow dough to sit at room temperature, 10 minutes.

4. Place granulated sugar and confectioners' sugar in two separate shallow baking dishes or pie plates. Divide dough into 2-tablespoon portions and roll into balls (or use #30 scoop). Drop balls of dough directly into granulated sugar and roll to coat. Transfer balls to confectioners' sugar and roll to coat. Evenly space dough balls on prepared baking sheets, 11 dough balls per sheet.

5. Bake cookies, 1 sheet at a time, until cookies are puffed and cracked and edges have begun to set but centers are still soft (cookies will look raw between cracks and will seem underdone), about 12 minutes, rotating sheet halfway through baking. Cool completely on baking sheet before serving.

PEANUT BUTTER COOKIES

WHY THIS RECIPE WORKS: Recipes for peanut butter cookies tend to fall into one of two categories: sweet and chewy with a mild peanut flavor, and sandy and crumbly with a strong peanut flavor. What we wanted, of course, was the best of both worlds—that is, cookies that were crisp on the edges and chewy in the center, with lots of peanut flavor.

First off, we had to determine the amount and type of sugar. Granulated sugar was necessary for crisp edges and chewy centers, while dark brown sugar enriched the peanut flavor. As for flour, too little resulted in an oily cookie, whereas too much made for dry cookies. Baking soda contributed to browning and amplified the peanut flavor and baking powder provided lift, making both leaveners necessary. Extra-crunchy peanut butter also helped the cookie rise and achieve a crisper edge and a softer center. But the best way to get the true peanut flavor we sought was to use peanuts and salt. Adding some roasted, salted peanuts, ground in a food processor, and then adding still more salt (directly to the batter as well in the form of salted rather than unsalted butter) produced a strong roasted nut flavor without sacrificing anything in terms of texture.

Peanut Butter Cookies

MAKES ABOUT 36 COOKIES

These cookies have a strong peanut flavor that comes from extra-crunchy peanut butter as well as from roasted salted peanuts that are ground in a food processor and worked into the dough. In our testing, we found that salted butter brings out the flavor of the nuts. If using unsalted butter, increase the salt to 1 teaspoon.

2½ cups (12½ ounces) unbleached all-purpose flour

½ teaspoon baking soda

½ teaspoon baking powder

½ teaspoon table salt

16 tablespoons (2 sticks) salted butter, softened (see note)

1 cup packed (7 ounces) dark brown sugar

1 cup (7 ounces) granulated sugar

1 cup extra-crunchy peanut butter, at room temperature

2 large eggs

2 teaspoons vanilla extract

1 cup (5 ounces) roasted salted peanuts, ground in a food processor to resemble bread crumbs, about 14 pulses

1. Adjust the oven racks to the upper-middle and lower-middle positions and heat oven to 350 degrees. Line 2 large baking sheets with parchment paper.

2. Whisk the flour, baking soda, baking powder, and salt together in a medium bowl; set aside.

3. In a stand mixer fitted with the paddle attachment, beat the butter and sugars at medium speed until light and fluffy, about 2 minutes, scraping down the bowl and beater as needed with a rubber spatula. Add the peanut butter and mix until fully incorporated, about 30 seconds; add the eggs, one at a time, and the vanilla and mix until combined, about 30 seconds. Decrease the speed to low and add the dry ingredients; mix until combined, about 30 seconds. Mix in the ground peanuts until just incorporated.

4. Divide the dough into 36 portions, each a generous 2 tablespoons, and roll them between your hands into balls about 2 inches in diameter. Place the dough balls on the prepared baking sheets, spacing them about 2½ inches apart. Press each dough ball twice, at perpendicular angles, with a dinner fork dipped in cold water to make a crisscross design.

5. Bake, switching and rotating the sheets halfway through the baking time, until the cookies are puffy and slightly brown around the edges but not on top, 10 to 12 minutes; the cookies will not look fully baked. Cool the cookies on the baking sheets for 5 minutes; using a wide metal spatula, transfer the cookies to a wire rack and cool to room temperature.

PEANUT BUTTER SANDWICH COOKIES

WHY THIS RECIPE WORKS: We wanted a cookie so packed with peanut flavor that it needed no crosshatch to identify it. In the research for our testing, we found that peanut butter flavor molecules can be trapped by flour in baked applications, so we ratcheted up the flavor's intensity by sandwiching an uncooked peanut butter filling between our cookies. Adding a full cup of confectioners' sugar to the filling made it firm enough to stay in place, and we balanced the sweetness with a relatively low-sugar cookie component. Extra liquid and extra baking soda gave our cookies the thin, flat dimensions and sturdy crunch that are vital to a sandwich cookie.

Peanut Butter Sandwich Cookies

MAKES 24 COOKIES

Do not use unsalted peanut butter for this recipe.

COOKIES

1¼ cups (6¼ ounces) raw peanuts, toasted and cooled

¾ cup (3¾ ounces) all-purpose flour

1 teaspoon baking soda

½ teaspoon salt

3 tablespoons unsalted butter, melted

½ cup creamy peanut butter

½ cup (3½ ounces) granulated sugar

½ cup packed (3½ ounces) light brown sugar

3 tablespoons whole milk

1 large egg

FILLING

¾ cup creamy peanut butter

3 tablespoons unsalted butter

1 cup (4 ounces) confectioners' sugar

1. FOR THE COOKIES: Adjust oven racks to upper-middle and lower-middle positions and heat oven to 350 degrees. Line 2 baking sheets with parchment paper. Pulse peanuts in food processor until finely chopped, about 8 pulses. Whisk flour, baking soda, and salt together in bowl. Whisk melted butter, peanut butter, granulated sugar, brown sugar, milk, and egg together in second bowl. Stir flour mixture into peanut butter mixture with rubber spatula until combined. Stir in peanuts until evenly distributed.

2. Using #60 scoop or tablespoon measure, place 12 mounds, evenly spaced, on each prepared baking sheet. Using damp hand, flatten mounds until 2 inches in diameter.

3. Bake until deep golden brown and firm to touch, 15 to 18 minutes, switching and rotating baking sheets halfway through baking. Let cookies cool on baking sheets for 5 minutes. Transfer cookies to wire rack and let cool completely, about 30 minutes. Repeat portioning and baking remaining dough.

FILLING COOKIES EVENLY

1. Using #60 scoop or tablespoon measure, portion warm filling onto bottom cookies (turned upside down).

2. Rather than spreading filling with knife or offset spatula, top bottom cookie with second cookie and press gently until filling spreads to edges.

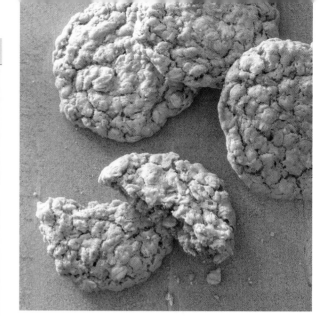

4. FOR THE FILLING: Microwave peanut butter and butter together until butter is melted and warm, about 40 seconds. Using rubber spatula, stir in confectioners' sugar until combined.

5. TO ASSEMBLE: Place 24 cookies upside down on counter. Place 1 level tablespoon (or #60 scoop) warm filling in center of each cookie. Place second cookie on top of filling, right side up, pressing gently until filling spreads to edges. Allow filling to set for 1 hour before serving. Assembled cookies can be stored at room temperature for up to 3 days.

Peanut Butter Sandwich Cookies with Honey-Cinnamon Filling

Omit butter from filling. Stir 5 tablespoons honey and ½ teaspoon ground cinnamon into warm peanut butter before adding confectioners' sugar.

Peanut Butter Sandwich Cookies with Milk Chocolate Filling

Reduce peanut butter to ½ cup and omit butter from filling. Stir 6 ounces finely chopped milk chocolate into warm peanut butter until melted, microwaving for 10 seconds at a time if necessary, before adding confectioners' sugar.

CLASSIC CHEWY OATMEAL COOKIES

WHY THIS RECIPE WORKS: Many oatmeal cookies are dry, cakey, and overly spiced. To make ours dense and chewy, we combined unsaturated fat (vegetable oil) and saturated fat (butter) in a ratio of nearly 3 to 1, and we decreased the proportion of flour. Adding an extra egg yolk boosted moistness and richness, while a touch more salt than most recipes call for tempered the sweetness and complemented the oaty

flavor. Most recipes call for using a stand mixer, but we found this counterproductive to our goal of chewy, dense cookies because the mixer beats air into the dough. Instead we made our dough by hand, melting the butter for easier mixing. Browning the butter delivered more complexity, and blooming a small amount of cinnamon in the butter rounded out its flavor. Raisins added pops of brightness and reinforced the chewy texture.

Classic Chewy Oatmeal Cookies
MAKES 20 COOKIES

Regular old-fashioned rolled oats worked best in this recipe. Do not use extra-thick rolled oats. For cookies with just the right amount of spread and chew, we strongly recommend that you weigh your ingredients. If you omit the raisins, the recipe will yield 18 cookies.

- 1 cup (5 ounces) all-purpose flour
- ¾ teaspoon salt
- ½ teaspoon baking soda
- 4 tablespoons unsalted butter
- ¼ teaspoon ground cinnamon
- ¾ cup packed (5¼ ounces) dark brown sugar
- ½ cup (3½ ounces) granulated sugar
- ½ cup vegetable oil
- 1 large egg plus 1 large yolk
- 1 teaspoon vanilla extract
- 3 cups (9 ounces) old-fashioned rolled oats
- ½ cup raisins (optional)

1. Adjust oven rack to middle position and heat oven to 375 degrees. Line 2 rimmed baking sheets with parchment paper. Whisk flour, salt, and baking soda together in medium bowl; set aside.

2. Melt butter in 8-inch skillet over medium-high heat, swirling pan occasionally, until foaming subsides. Continue to cook, stirring and scraping bottom of pan with heatproof spatula, until milk solids are dark golden brown and butter has nutty aroma, 1 to 2 minutes. Immediately transfer browned butter to large heatproof bowl, scraping skillet with spatula. Stir in cinnamon.

3. Add brown sugar, granulated sugar, and oil to bowl with butter and whisk until combined. Add egg and yolk and vanilla and whisk until mixture is smooth. Using wooden spoon, stir in flour mixture until fully combined, about 1 minute. Add oats and raisins, if using, and stir until evenly distributed (mixture will be stiff).

4. Divide dough into 20 portions, each about 3 tablespoons (or use #24 cookie scoop). Arrange dough balls 2 inches apart on prepared sheets, 10 dough balls per sheet. Using your damp hand, press each ball into 2½-inch disk.

5. Bake, 1 sheet at a time, until cookie edges are set and lightly browned and centers are still soft but not wet, 8 to 10 minutes, rotating sheet halfway through baking. Let cookies cool on sheet on wire rack for 5 minutes; using wide metal spatula, transfer cookies to wire rack and let cool completely.

CHEWY OATMEAL-RAISIN COOKIES

WHY THIS RECIPE WORKS: Big, moist, and craggy, oatmeal raisin cookies are so good and so comforting, but also so hard to get just right. Too often, they have textural issues and other times the flavor is off, with cookies that lack any sign of oatiness. We wanted an oversize, chewy cookie with buttery oat flavor. After numerous rounds of testing, we discovered three key changes that made a significant difference in the research recipes we uncovered. First, we substituted baking powder for baking soda, which gave the dough more lift and made the cookies less dense and a bit chewier. Second, we eliminated the cinnamon recommended in lots of recipes; by taking away the cinnamon, we revealed more oat flavor. We wanted some spice, however, and chose nutmeg, which has a cleaner, subtler flavor that we like with oats. Finally, we increased the sugar in our cookies, and this made a huge difference in terms of texture and moistness.

Big and Chewy Oatmeal-Raisin Cookies
MAKES ABOUT 18 LARGE COOKIES

If you prefer a less sweet cookie, you can reduce the granulated sugar to ¾ cup, but you will lose some crispness. Do not overbake these cookies. The edges should be brown, but the rest of the cookie should be very light in color.

1½	cups (7½ ounces) unbleached all-purpose flour
½	teaspoon table salt
½	teaspoon baking powder
¼	teaspoon freshly grated nutmeg
16	tablespoons (2 sticks) unsalted butter, softened
1	cup packed (7 ounces) light brown sugar
1	cup (7 ounces) granulated sugar (see note)
2	large eggs
3	cups (9 ounces) old-fashioned oats
1½	cups raisins (optional)

1. Adjust the oven racks to the upper-middle and lower-middle positions and heat the oven to 350 degrees. Line 2 large baking sheets with parchment paper. Whisk the flour, salt, baking powder, and nutmeg together in a medium bowl; set aside.

2. In a stand mixer fitted with the paddle attachment, beat the butter and sugars at medium speed until light and fluffy, about 2 minutes. Add the eggs, one at a time, and mix until combined, about 30 seconds.

3. Decrease the speed to low and slowly add the dry ingredients until combined, about 30 seconds. Mix in the oats and raisins (if using) until just incorporated.

4. Divide the dough into 18 portions, each a generous 2 tablespoons, and roll them between your hands into balls about 2 inches in diameter. Place the dough balls on the prepared baking sheets, spacing them about 2 inches apart.

5. Bake, switching and rotating the sheets halfway through the baking time, until the cookies turn golden brown around the edges, 22 to 25 minutes. Cool the cookies on the baking sheets for 2 minutes; using a wide metal spatula, transfer the cookies to a wire rack and cool to room temperature.

Big and Chewy Oatmeal-Date Cookies
Follow the recipe for Big and Chewy Oatmeal-Raisin Cookies, substituting 1½ cups chopped dates for the raisins.

THIN AND CRISPY OATMEAL COOKIES

WHY THIS RECIPE WORKS: Thin and crispy oatmeal cookies can be irresistible—crunchy and delicate, these cookies really let the flavor of the oats take center stage. But the usual ingredients that give thick, chewy oatmeal cookies great texture—generous amounts of sugar and butter, a high ratio of oats to flour, raisins, and nuts—won't all fit in a thin, crispy cookie. We wanted to adjust the ingredients to create a crispy, delicate cookie in which the simple flavor of buttery oats really stands out. Given this cookie's simplicity, creating a rich butter flavor was critical, so we kept almost the same amount of butter as in our standard big, chewy oatmeal cookie, but we scaled back the amount of sugar. During baking, large carbon dioxide bubbles created by the baking soda and baking powder caused the cookies to puff up, collapse, and spread out, producing the thin, flat cookies. Baking the cookies until they were fully set and evenly browned from center to edge made them crisp throughout but not tough.

Thin and Crispy Oatmeal Cookies

MAKES ABOUT 24 COOKIES

To ensure that the cookies bake evenly and are crisp throughout, bake them one sheet at a time. Place them on the baking sheet in three rows, with three cookies in the outer rows and two cookies in the center row. If you reuse a baking sheet, allow the cookies on it to cool for at least 15 minutes before transferring them to a wire rack, then reline the sheet with fresh parchment before baking more cookies. We developed this recipe using Quaker Old Fashioned Oats. Other brands of old-fashioned oats can be substituted but may cause the cookies to spread more. Do not use instant or quick oats.

- 1 cup (5 ounces) unbleached all-purpose flour
- ¾ teaspoon baking powder
- ½ teaspoon baking soda
- ½ teaspoon table salt
- 14 tablespoons (1¾ sticks) unsalted butter, softened but still cool
- 1 cup (7 ounces) granulated sugar
- ¼ cup packed (1¾ ounces) light brown sugar
- 1 large egg
- 1 teaspoon vanilla extract
- 2½ cups (7½ ounces) old-fashioned oats (see note)

1. Adjust an oven rack to the middle position and heat the oven to 350 degrees. Line 3 large baking sheets with parchment paper. Whisk the flour, baking powder, baking soda, and salt in a medium bowl; set aside.

2. In a stand mixer fitted with the paddle attachment, beat the butter and sugars at medium-low speed until just combined, about 20 seconds. Increase the speed to medium and continue to beat until light and fluffy, about 1 minute longer, scraping down the bowl and beater as needed with a rubber spatula. Add the egg and vanilla and beat on medium-low until fully incorporated, about 30 seconds, scraping down the bowl and beater as needed. Decrease the speed to low, add the flour mixture, and mix until just incorporated and smooth, about 10 seconds. With the mixer still running on low, gradually add the oats and mix until well incorporated, about 20 seconds. Give the dough a final stir to ensure that no flour pockets remain and the ingredients are evenly distributed.

3. Divide the dough into 24 portions, each about 2 tablespoons, and roll them between your hands into balls. Place the cookies on the prepared baking sheets, spacing them about 2½ inches apart, eight dough balls per sheet (see note). Using your fingertips, gently press each dough ball to a ¾-inch thickness.

4. Bake one sheet at a time until the cookies are deep golden brown, the edges are crisp, and the centers yield to slight pressure when pressed, 13 to 16 minutes, rotating the sheet halfway through the baking time. Cool the cookies completely on the sheet.

Salty Thin and Crispy Oatmeal Cookies

We prefer the texture and flavor of a coarse-grained sea salt, like Maldon or *fleur de sel*, but kosher salt can be used. If using kosher salt, reduce the amount sprinkled over the cookies to ¼ teaspoon.

Follow the recipe for Thin and Crispy Oatmeal Cookies, reducing the amount of salt in the dough to ¼ teaspoon. Lightly sprinkle ½ teaspoon coarse sea salt evenly over the flattened dough balls before baking.

ULTIMATE OATMEAL COOKIES

WHY THIS RECIPE WORKS: Oatmeal cookies can be great vehicles for additional flavors, but it's easy to get carried away and overload the dough with a crazy jumble of ingredients resulting in a poorly textured cookie monster. Our ultimate oatmeal cookie would have just the right amount of added ingredients and an ideal texture—crisp around the edges and chewy in the middle.

We wanted to add four flavor components—sweet, tangy, nutty, and chocolaty—to the underlying oat flavor. Bittersweet chocolate, dried sour cherries (or cranberries), and toasted pecans gave the right balance of flavors. We also analyzed the cookie dough ingredients and discovered that cookies made with brown sugar were moister and chewier than cookies made with granulated sugar. A combination of baking powder and baking soda (we doubled the usual amount) produced cookies that were light and crisp on the outside, but chewy, dense, and soft in the center. Finally, we focused on appearance to decide when to remove the cookies from the oven— they should be set but still look wet between the fissures; if they look matte rather than shiny, they've been overbaked.

Chocolate-Chunk Oatmeal Cookies with Pecans and Dried Cherries

MAKES ABOUT 16 LARGE COOKIES

We like these cookies made with pecans and dried sour cherries, but walnuts or skinned hazelnuts can be substituted for the pecans, and dried cranberries for the cherries. Quick oats used in place of the old-fashioned oats will yield a cookie with slightly less chewiness. These cookies keep for 4 to 5 days stored in an airtight container or zipper-lock bag, but they will lose their crisp exterior and become uniformly chewy after a day or so. To recrisp the cookies, place them on a baking sheet and in a 425-degree oven for 4 to 5 minutes. Make sure to let the cookies cool on the baking sheet for a few minutes before removing them, and eat them while they're warm.

1¼ cups (6¼ ounces) unbleached all-purpose flour

¾ teaspoon baking powder

½ teaspoon baking soda

½ teaspoon table salt

1¼ cups (3¾ ounces) old-fashioned oats (see note)

1 cup (4 ounces) pecans, toasted and chopped (see note)

1 cup dried sour cherries, chopped coarse (see note)

4 ounces bittersweet chocolate, chopped into chunks about the size of chocolate chips (about ¾ cup)

12 tablespoons (1½ sticks) unsalted butter, softened

1½ cups packed (10½ ounces) brown sugar, preferably dark

1 large egg

1 teaspoon vanilla extract

1. Adjust the oven racks to the upper-middle and lower-middle positions and heat the oven to 350 degrees. Line 2 large baking sheets with parchment paper.

2. Whisk the flour, baking powder, baking soda, and salt together in a medium bowl. In a second medium bowl, stir together the oats, pecans, cherries, and chocolate.

3. In a stand mixer fitted with the paddle attachment, beat the butter and sugar at medium speed until no sugar lumps remain, about 1 minute, scraping down the bowl and beater as needed with a rubber spatula. Add the egg and vanilla and beat on medium-low until fully incorporated, about 30 seconds, scraping down the bowl and beater as needed. Decrease the speed to low, add the flour mixture, and mix until just combined, about 30 seconds. With the mixer still running on low, gradually add the oat-nut mixture; mix until just incorporated. Give the dough a final stir to ensure that no flour pockets remain and the ingredients are evenly distributed.

4. Divide the dough into 16 portions, each about ¼ cup, and roll them between your hands into balls; stagger eight balls on each prepared baking sheet, spacing them about 2½ inches apart. Using your fingertips, gently press each dough ball to a 1-inch thickness. Bake the cookies for 20 to 22 minutes, switching and rotating the baking sheets halfway through the baking time, until the cookies are medium brown and the edges have begun to set but the centers are still soft (the cookies will seem underdone and will appear raw, wet, and shiny in the cracks).

5. Cool the cookies on the baking sheets for 5 minutes; using a wide metal spatula, transfer the cookies to a wire rack and cool to room temperature.

GINGERSNAPS

WHY THIS RECIPE WORKS: We wanted to put the "snap" back in gingersnap cookies. This meant creating a cookie that not only breaks cleanly in half and crunches satisfyingly with every bite but also has an assertive ginger flavor and heat. The key to texture was reducing the moisture in the final baked cookie. We achieved this by reducing the amount of sugar (which holds on to moisture), increasing the baking soda

(which created cracks in the dough where more moisture could escape), and lowering the oven temperature (which increased the baking time.) For flavor we doubled the normal amount of dried ginger but also added fresh ginger, black pepper, and cayenne to ensure our cookie had real "snap."

Gingersnaps
MAKES 80 1½-INCH COOKIES

For the best results, use fresh spices. For efficiency, form the second batch of cookies while the first batch bakes. The 2 teaspoons of baking soda are essential to getting the right texture.

2½ cups (12½ ounces) all-purpose flour

2 teaspoons baking soda

½ teaspoon salt

12 tablespoons unsalted butter

2 tablespoons ground ginger

1 teaspoon ground cinnamon

¼ teaspoon ground cloves

¼ teaspoon pepper

Pinch cayenne pepper

1¼ cups packed (8¾ ounces) dark brown sugar

¼ cup molasses

2 tablespoons finely grated fresh ginger

1 large egg plus 1 large yolk

½ cup (3½ ounces) granulated sugar

1. Whisk flour, baking soda, and salt together in bowl. Heat butter in 10-inch skillet over medium heat until melted. Lower heat to medium-low and continue to cook, swirling pan frequently, until foaming subsides and butter is just beginning to brown, 2 to 4 minutes. Transfer butter to large bowl and whisk in ground ginger, cinnamon, cloves, pepper, and cayenne. Let cool slightly, about 2 minutes. Add brown sugar, molasses, and fresh ginger to butter mixture and whisk to combine. Add egg and yolk and whisk to combine. Add flour mixture and stir until just combined. Cover dough tightly with plastic wrap and refrigerate until firm, about 1 hour.

2. Adjust oven racks to upper-middle and lower-middle positions and heat oven to 300 degrees. Line 2 baking sheets with parchment paper. Place granulated sugar in shallow dish. Divide dough into heaping teaspoon portions; roll dough into 1-inch balls. Working in batches of 10, roll balls in sugar to coat. Evenly space dough balls on prepared baking sheets, 20 dough balls per sheet.

3. Place 1 sheet on upper rack and bake for 15 minutes. Transfer partially baked top sheet to lower rack, rotating 180 degrees, and place second sheet of dough balls on upper rack. Continue to bake until cookies on lower tray just begin to darken around edges, 10 to 12 minutes longer. Remove lower sheet of cookies and transfer upper sheet to lower rack, rotating 180 degrees, and continue to bake until cookies begin to darken around edges, 15 to 17 minutes longer. Slide baked cookies, still on parchment, to wire rack and let cool completely before serving. Let baking sheets cool slightly and line with parchment again. Repeat step 2 with remaining dough balls. (Cooled cookies can be stored at room temperature for up to 2 weeks.)

TO MAKE AHEAD: Dough can be refrigerated for up to 2 days or frozen for up to 1 month. Let frozen dough thaw overnight in refrigerator before proceeding with recipe. Let dough stand at room temperature for 30 minutes before shaping.

FLORENTINE LACE COOKIES

WHY THIS RECIPE WORKS: Wafer-thin almond Florentines have a reputation for being fussy and unpredictable, but these elegant, confection-like cookies have undeniable appeal. To make our recipe foolproof, we ground the almonds and decreased the flour to allow the cookies to spread more. Instead of getting out a thermometer to make the caramel-like base of the dough, we removed the pan from the heat when the sugar mixture thickened and began to brown. Substituting orange marmalade for the usual candied orange peel and corn syrup produced a more concentrated, complex citrus flavor. A flourish of faux-tempered chocolate completed the professional pastry shop effect.

Florentine Lace Cookies
MAKES 24 COOKIES

It's important to cook the cream mixture in the saucepan until it is thick and starting to brown at the edges; undercooking will result in a dough that is too runny to portion. Do not be concerned if some butter separates from the dough while you're portioning the cookies. For the most uniform cookies, use the flattest baking sheets you have and make sure that your parchment paper lies flat. When

melting the chocolate, pause the microwave and stir the chocolate often to ensure that it doesn't get much warmer than body temperature.

2 cups slivered almonds
¾ cup heavy cream
4 tablespoons unsalted butter, cut into 4 pieces
½ cup (3½ ounces) sugar
¼ cup orange marmalade
3 tablespoons all-purpose flour
1 teaspoon vanilla extract
¼ teaspoon grated orange zest
¼ teaspoon salt
4 ounces bittersweet chocolate, chopped fine

1. Adjust oven racks to upper-middle and lower-middle positions and heat oven to 350 degrees. Line 2 baking sheets with parchment paper. Process almonds in food processor until they resemble coarse sand, about 30 seconds.

2. Bring cream, butter, and sugar to boil in medium saucepan over medium-high heat. Cook, stirring frequently, until mixture begins to thicken, 5 to 6 minutes. Continue to cook, stirring constantly, until mixture begins to brown at edges and is thick enough to leave trail that doesn't immediately fill in when spatula is scraped along pan bottom, 1 to 2 minutes longer (it's OK if some darker speckles appear in mixture). Remove pan from heat and stir in almonds, marmalade, flour, vanilla, orange zest, and salt until combined.

3. Drop 6 level tablespoons dough at least 3½ inches apart on prepared sheets. When cool enough to handle, use damp fingers to press each portion into 2½-inch circle.

4. Bake until deep brown from edge to edge, 15 to 17 minutes, switching and rotating sheets halfway through baking. Transfer cookies, still on parchment, to wire racks and let cool. Let baking sheets cool for 10 minutes, line with fresh parchment, and repeat portioning and baking with remaining dough.

5. Microwave 3 ounces chocolate in bowl at 50 percent power, stirring frequently, until about two-thirds melted, 1 to 2 minutes. Remove bowl from microwave, add remaining 1 ounce chocolate, and stir until melted, returning to microwave for no more than 5 seconds at a time to complete melting if necessary. Transfer chocolate to small zipper-lock bag and snip off corner, making hole no larger than ¹/₁₆ inch.

6. Transfer cooled cookies directly to wire racks. Pipe zigzag of chocolate over each cookie, distributing chocolate evenly among all cookies. Refrigerate until chocolate is set, about 30 minutes, before serving. (Cookies can be stored at cool room temperature for up to 4 days.)

COCONUT MACAROONS

WHY THIS RECIPE WORKS: Not that long ago, macaroons (cone-shaped cookies flavored with shredded coconut) were quite elegant and very popular. But today, they have deteriorated into lackluster mounds of beaten egg whites and

coconut shreds or, at their worst, nothing more than a baked mixture of condensed milk and sweetened coconut. We set out to create a great coconut macaroon, with a pleasing texture and real, honest coconut flavor.

When we began looking at recipes for modern coconut macaroons, we found that they varied widely, some calling for vanilla or almond extract in addition to different kinds of coconut and sweeteners. We knew that narrowing the field when it came to the coconut and other flavorings would make a big difference in both taste and texture. After rounds of testing, we determined that unsweetened shredded coconut resulted in a less sticky, more appealing texture. But sweetened shredded coconut packed more flavor than the unsweetened coconut, so we decided to use both; together they worked very well in the cookie. To add one more layer of coconut flavor, we tried cream of coconut and hit the jackpot. As for the structure of our cookie, a few egg whites and some corn syrup ensured that the macaroons held together well and were moist and pleasantly chewy.

Triple-Coconut Macaroons
MAKES ABOUT 48 COOKIES

Cream of coconut, available canned, is a very sweet product commonly used in piña colada cocktails. Be sure to mix the can's contents thoroughly before using, as the mixture separates upon standing. Unsweetened desiccated coconut is commonly sold in natural foods stores and Asian markets. If you are unable to find any, use all sweetened flaked or shredded coconut, but reduce the amount of cream of coconut to ½ cup, omit the corn syrup, and toss 2 tablespoons cake flour with the coconut before adding the liquid ingredients. For larger macaroons, shape haystacks from a generous ¼ cup of batter and increase the baking time to 20 minutes.

1　cup cream of coconut (see note)
2　tablespoons light corn syrup
4　large egg whites

2　teaspoons vanilla extract
½　teaspoon table salt
3　cups unsweetened, shredded, desiccated (dried) coconut (see note)
3　cups sweetened flaked or shredded coconut

1. Adjust the oven racks to the upper-middle and lower-middle positions and heat the oven to 375 degrees. Line 2 baking sheets with parchment paper and lightly spray the parchment with vegetable oil spray.

2. Whisk the cream of coconut, corn syrup, egg whites, vanilla, and salt together in a small bowl; set aside. Combine the unsweetened and sweetened coconuts in a large bowl; toss together, breaking up clumps with your fingertips. Pour the liquid ingredients over the coconut and mix with a rubber spatula until evenly moistened. Chill for 15 minutes.

3. Drop heaping tablespoons of batter onto the prepared baking sheets, spacing them about 1 inch apart. Using moistened fingertips, form the cookies into loose haystacks. Bake until light golden brown, about 15 minutes, switching and rotating the sheets halfway through the baking time.

4. Cool the cookies on the baking sheets until slightly set, about 2 minutes; using a wide metal spatula, transfer the cookies to a wire rack and cool to room temperature.

Chocolate-Dipped Triple-Coconut Macaroons

Using the two-stage melting process for the chocolate helps ensure that it will be at the proper consistency for dipping the cookies. To melt the 8 ounces of chocolate in a microwave, heat it at 50 percent power for 2 minutes; stir the chocolate and continue heating until melted, stirring once every additional minute.

Follow the recipe for Triple-Coconut Macaroons. Cool the baked macaroons to room temperature; line two large baking sheets with parchment paper. Chop 10 ounces semisweet chocolate; melt 8 ounces of the chocolate in a small heatproof bowl set over a saucepan of barely simmering water, stirring occasionally, until smooth. Off the heat, stir in the remaining 2 ounces of chocolate until smooth. Holding a macaroon by its pointed top, dip the bottom ½ inch up the sides in the chocolate, scrape off the excess, and place the macaroon on the prepared baking sheet. Repeat with the remaining macaroons. Refrigerate until the chocolate sets, about 15 minutes.

HOLIDAY SPRITZ COOKIES

WHY THIS RECIPE WORKS: Spritz cookies, those golden-swirled holiday cookies, often end up bland, gummy, and tasteless. How come they never taste as good as they look? Unfortunately, this Scandinavian treat has fallen victim to many recipe modifications, such as the use of vegetable shortening instead of butter, an overload of eggs, and an excess of starchy confectioners' sugar. We set out to spruce up spritz cookies and make them light, crisp, buttery treats—the life of any holiday party. The success of these confections rests primarily in the management of a finicky ingredient list. Carefully balancing the butter, sugar, flour, egg yolk, heavy cream (just a drop), vanilla, and salt is the only recipe for success—a few simple ingredients gathered in the proper proportions. Creaming the butter and sugar in the traditional fashion worked well and produced a dough light enough to easily press or pipe the cookies. As for shaping, either a cookie press or a pastry bag can be used—it's up to you.

Spritz Cookies

MAKES ABOUT 72 SMALL COOKIES

If using a pastry bag, use a star tip to create the various shapes. For stars, a ½ to ⅝-inch tip (measure the diameter of the tip at the smallest point) works best, but for rosettes and S shapes, use a ⅜-inch tip. To create stars, see the photo; stars should be about 1 inch in diameter. To create rosettes, pipe the dough while moving the bag in a circular motion, ending at the center of the rosette; rosettes should be about 1¼ inches in diameter. To create S shapes, pipe the dough into compact S's; they should be about 2 inches long and 1 inch wide. If you make an error while piping, the dough can be scraped off the baking sheet and re-piped.

We had the best results baking these cookies one sheet at a time. When reusing a baking sheet, make sure that it has completely cooled before forming more cookies on it. Unbaked dough can be refrigerated in an airtight container for up to 4 days; to use, let it stand at room temperature until softened, about 45 minutes. Baked cookies will keep for more than a week if stored in an airtight container or zipper-lock bag.

1	large egg yolk
1	tablespoon heavy cream
1	teaspoon vanilla extract
16	tablespoons (2 sticks) unsalted butter, softened but still cool
⅔	cup (4⅔ ounces) granulated sugar
¼	teaspoon table salt
2	cups (10 ounces) unbleached all-purpose flour

1. Adjust an oven rack to the middle position and heat the oven to 375 degrees. Line 2 large baking sheets with parchment paper. Whisk the egg yolk, cream, and vanilla in a small bowl until combined; set aside.

NOTES FROM THE TEST KITCHEN

PIPING SPRITZ COOKIES

Using a ½-inch star tip, hold the bag at a 90-degree angle to the baking sheet and pipe the dough straight down, about 1 inch in diameter. If you make an error while piping, the dough can be scraped off the baking sheet and re-piped.

---

2. In a stand mixer fitted with the paddle attachment, beat the butter, sugar, and salt at medium-high speed until light and fluffy, about 3 minutes, scraping down the bowl and beater as needed with a rubber spatula. With the mixer running at medium speed, add the yolk-cream mixture and beat until incorporated, about 30 seconds. With the mixer running at low speed, gradually beat in the flour until combined, scraping down the bowl and beater as needed. Give the dough a final stir to ensure that no flour pockets remain.

3. If using a cookie press to form the cookies, follow the manufacturer's instructions to fill the press. If using a pastry bag (see note), fit it with a star tip and fill the bag with half of the dough. Press or pipe cookies onto the prepared baking sheet, spacing them about 1½ inches apart, refilling the cookie press or pastry bag as needed. Bake one sheet at a time, until the cookies are light golden brown, 10 to 12 minutes, rotating the baking sheet halfway through the baking time. Cool the cookies on the baking sheet for 10 to 15 minutes; using a metal spatula, transfer them to a wire rack and cool to room temperature.

Spritz Cookies with Lemon Essence

Follow the recipe for Spritz Cookies, adding 1 teaspoon juice from 1 lemon to the yolk-cream mixture in step 1 and adding 1 teaspoon finely grated zest from 1 lemon to the butter along with the sugar and salt in step 2.

Almond Spritz Cookies

Grind ½ cup sliced almonds and 2 tablespoons of the flour in a food processor until powdery and evenly fine, about 12 pulses; combine the almond mixture with the remaining flour. Follow the recipe for Spritz Cookies, substituting ¾ teaspoon almond extract for the vanilla.

SABLÉ COOKIES

WHY THIS RECIPE WORKS: During the holidays, these French butter cookies offer sophistication and style. That is, if you can capture their elusive sandy texture (*sablé* is French for sandy), which separates them from sturdy American butter cookies. Most of the sablé recipes we came across had only slight differences in ingredient proportions—but they all baked up without the delicate crumbliness that defines this cookie. To create the hallmark sandy texture of sablés—light, with an inviting granular quality similar to shortbread—we would have to do some detective work. We started with a basic recipe using the typical method of creaming butter and sugar, then adding egg and flour. We found that we needed to decrease the liquid in the dough so there would be less moisture to dissolve the sugar particles. Cutting back on butter helped, as did the inclusion of a hard-cooked egg yolk, an addition we came across in our research. Adding the mashed yolk during creaming eliminated moisture and perfected the texture of the cookies. Brushing the cookies with a beaten egg white and sprinkling them with coarse sugar before baking added a delicate crunch and an attractive sparkle.

Sablés (French Butter Cookies)

MAKES ABOUT 40 COOKIES

Turbinado sugar is commonly sold as Sugar in the Raw. Demerara sugar, sanding sugar, or another coarse sugar can be substituted. Make sure the cookie dough is well chilled and firm so that it can be uniformly sliced. After the dough has been wrapped in parchment, it can be double-wrapped in plastic wrap and frozen for up to 2 weeks.

1	large egg
10	tablespoons (1¼ sticks) unsalted butter, softened
⅓	cup plus 1 tablespoon (2¾ ounces) granulated sugar
¼	teaspoon table salt
1	teaspoon vanilla extract
1½	cups (7½ ounces) unbleached all-purpose flour
1	large egg white, lightly beaten with 1 teaspoon water
4	teaspoons turbinado sugar (see note)

1. Place the egg in a small saucepan, cover with water by 1 inch, and bring to a boil over high heat. Remove the pan from the heat, cover, and let sit for 10 minutes. Meanwhile, fill a small bowl with ice water. Using a slotted spoon, transfer the egg to the ice water and let stand for 5 minutes. Crack the egg and peel the shell. Separate the yolk from the white; discard the white. Press the yolk through a fine-mesh strainer into a small bowl.

2. In a stand mixer fitted with the paddle attachment, beat the butter, granulated sugar, salt, and cooked egg yolk on medium speed until light and fluffy, about 4 minutes, scraping down the bowl and beater as needed with a rubber spatula. Decrease the speed to low, add the vanilla, and mix until incorporated. Stop the mixer; add the flour and mix on low speed until just combined, about 30 seconds. Using a rubber spatula, press the dough into a cohesive mass.

NOTES FROM THE TEST KITCHEN

FORMING SPIRAL COOKIES

1. Halve each batch of dough. Roll out each portion on parchment paper into an 8 by 6-inch rectangle, ¼ inch thick. Briefly chill the dough until firm enough to handle.

2. Using a bench scraper, place one plain cookie dough rectangle on top of one chocolate dough rectangle. Repeat to make two double rectangles.

3. Roll out each double rectangle on parchment into a 9 by 6-inch rectangle (if too firm, let rest until malleable). Then, starting at the long end, roll each into a tight log.

4. Twist the ends of the parchment to seal. Chill the logs for 1 hour. Slice the logs into ¼-inch-thick rounds.

FORMING PRETZEL COOKIES

1. Slice slightly chilled dough into ¼-inch-thick rounds and roll into balls.

2. Roll each ball into a 6-inch rope, tapering the ends.

3. Pick up one end of the rope and cross it over to form half of a pretzel shape.

4. Bring the second end over to complete the pretzel shape.

3. Divide the dough in half; roll each piece into a log about 6 inches long and 1¾ inches in diameter. Wrap each log in a 12-inch square of parchment paper and twist the ends to seal and firmly compact the dough into a tight cylinder. Chill until firm, about 1 hour.

4. Adjust the oven racks to the upper-middle and lower-middle positions and heat the oven to 350 degrees. Line 2 large baking sheets with parchment paper. Using a chef's knife, slice the dough into ¼-inch-thick rounds, rotating the dough so that it won't become misshapen from the weight of the knife. Place the cookies 1 inch apart on the baking sheets. Using a pastry brush, gently brush the cookies with the egg white mixture and sprinkle evenly with the turbinado sugar.

5. Bake until the centers of the cookies are pale golden brown with edges slightly darker than the centers, about 15 minutes, switching and rotating the baking sheets halfway through the baking time. Cool the cookies on the baking sheets for 5 minutes; using a thin metal spatula, transfer the cookies to a wire rack and cool to room temperature. (The cookies can be stored between sheets of parchment paper in an airtight container for up to 1 week.)

Chocolate Sablés

Follow the recipe for Sablés, reducing the flour to 1⅓ cups (6⅔ ounces) and adding ¼ cup Dutch-processed cocoa powder with the flour in step 2.

Black and White Spiral Cookies
MAKES ABOUT 80 COOKIES

Follow the recipes for Sablés and Chocolate Sablés through step 2. Following the "Forming Spiral Cookies" photos on page 723, form the dough into spiral logs. Proceed with the

Sablés recipe from step 4, slicing the logs into ¼-inch-thick rounds, omitting the egg white mixture and turbinado sugar in both recipes, and baking as directed.

Chocolate Sandwich Cookies
MAKES ABOUT 40 COOKIES

Follow the recipe for Sablés through step 3. In step 4, slice one dough log into ⅛-inch-thick rounds, omitting the egg white mixture and turbinado sugar. Bake the cookies as directed in step 5, reducing the baking time to 10 to 13 minutes. Repeat with the second dough log. When all the cookies are completely cool, melt 3½ ounces dark or milk chocolate and cool slightly. Spread the melted chocolate on the bottom of one cookie. Place a second cookie on top, slightly off-center, so some chocolate shows. Repeat with the remaining melted chocolate and cookies.

Vanilla Pretzel Cookies
MAKES ABOUT 40 COOKIES

Follow the recipe for Sablés through step 3, increasing the vanilla extract to 1 tablespoon and reducing the chilling time to 30 minutes (the dough will not be fully hardened). Slice the dough into ¼-inch-thick rounds and roll into balls. Roll each ball into a 6-inch rope, tapering the ends. Following the "Forming Pretzel Cookies" photos on page 723, form the ropes into pretzel shapes. Proceed with the recipe, brushing with the egg white mixture, sprinkling with the turbinado sugar, and baking as directed.

HOLIDAY ROLLED COOKIES

WHY THIS RECIPE WORKS: Baking holiday cookies should be a fun endeavor but so often it's an exercise in frustration. The dough clings to the rolling pin, it rips and tears as it is rolled out, and the tactic of moving the dough in and out of the fridge to make it easier to work with turns a simple one-hour process into a half-day project. We wanted a simple recipe that would yield a forgiving, workable dough, producing cookies that would be sturdy enough to decorate yet tender enough to be worth eating.

Our first realization was that we had to use enough butter to stay true to the nature of a butter cookie but not so much that the dough became greasy. All-purpose flour had enough gluten to provide structure, while superfine sugar provided a fine, even crumb and a compact, crisp cookie. Cream cheese—a surprise ingredient—gave the cookies flavor and richness without altering their texture.

Glazed Butter Cookies
MAKES ABOUT 38 COOKIES

If you cannot find superfine sugar, process granulated sugar in a food processor for 30 seconds. If desired, the cookies can be finished with sprinkles or other decorations immediately after glazing (see page 726).

BUTTER COOKIE DOUGH

2½ cups (12½ ounces) unbleached all-purpose flour
¾ cup (5⅔ ounces) superfine sugar (see note)
¼ teaspoon table salt
16 tablespoons (2 sticks) unsalted butter, cut into 16 pieces, softened
2 tablespoons cream cheese, at room temperature
2 teaspoons vanilla extract

GLAZE

1 tablespoon cream cheese, at room temperature
3 tablespoons milk
1½ cups (6 ounces) confectioners' sugar

1. FOR THE COOKIES: In a stand mixer fitted with the paddle attachment, mix the flour, sugar, and salt at low speed until combined, about 5 seconds. With the mixer running on low, add the butter 1 piece at a time; continue to mix until the mixture looks crumbly and slightly wet, 1 to 2 minutes longer. Beat in the cream cheese and vanilla until the dough just begins to form large clumps, about 30 seconds.

2. Knead the dough by hand in the bowl, about two to three turns, until it forms a large, cohesive mass. Transfer the dough to a clean work surface and divide it into two even pieces. Press each piece into a 4-inch disk, wrap the disks in plastic wrap, and refrigerate until the dough is firm but malleable, about 30 minutes. (The disks can be refrigerated for up to 3 days or frozen for up to 2 weeks; defrost in the refrigerator before using.)

3. Adjust an oven rack to the middle position and heat the oven to 375 degrees. Working with one piece of dough at a time, roll out the dough to an even ⅛-inch thickness between 2 large sheets of parchment paper; slide the rolled dough, still on the parchment, onto a baking sheet and refrigerate until firm, about 10 minutes.

4. Line 2 large baking sheets with parchment paper. Working with 1 sheet of dough at a time, cut into desired shapes using cookie cutters and place the cookies on the prepared sheet, spacing them about 1½ inches apart. Bake 1 sheet at a time, until the cookies are light golden brown, about 10 minutes, rotating the sheet halfway through the baking time. (The dough scraps can be patted together, chilled, and rerolled once.) Cool the cookies on the baking sheet for 3 minutes; using a wide metal spatula, transfer the cookies to a wire rack and cool to room temperature.

5. FOR THE GLAZE: Whisk the cream cheese and 2 tablespoons of the milk together in a medium bowl until combined and no lumps remain. Add the confectioners' sugar and whisk until smooth, adding the remaining 1 tablespoon milk as needed until the glaze is thin enough to spread easily. Using the back of a spoon, drizzle or spread a scant teaspoon of the glaze onto each cooled cookie. Allow the glazed cookies to dry for at least 30 minutes.

CUTTING AND FILLING JAM SANDWICHES

1. Using a 2-inch round fluted cookie cutter, cut out cookies from one piece of the dough.

2. Sprinkle the second piece of rolled dough evenly with turbinado sugar and cut out 2-inch rounds.

3. Using a ¾-inch round fluted cookie cutter, cut out the centers of the sugared rounds.

4. When the cookies have cooled, spread the reduced jam on the solid cookies, then place the cut-out cookies on top.

Jam Sandwiches

MAKES ABOUT 30 COOKIES

See the photos to prepare these cookies. Turbinado sugar is commonly sold as Sugar in the Raw. Demerara sugar, sanding sugar, or another coarse sugar can be substituted.

1 recipe Butter Cookie Dough, prepared through step 3
2 tablespoons turbinado sugar (see note)
1¼ cups (12 ounces) raspberry jam, strained, simmered until reduced to 1 cup, and cooled to room temperature

1. Line 2 large baking sheets with parchment paper. Using a 2-inch round fluted cookie cutter, cut rounds from 1 piece of rolled dough and bake on a prepared sheet in a 375-degree oven, rotating the baking sheet halfway through the baking time, until the cookies are light golden brown, 8 to 10 minutes.

2. Sprinkle the second piece of rolled dough evenly with the sugar.

3. Using a 2-inch round fluted cookie cutter, cut rounds of sugar-sprinkled dough. Using a ¾-inch round fluted cookie cutter, cut out the centers of the sugared rounds. Place the cookies on a prepared sheet and bake, rotating the baking sheet halfway through the baking time, until the cookies are light golden brown, about 8 minutes.

4. When the cookies have cooled, spread 1 teaspoon jam on the top of each solid cookie, then cover with a cut-out cookie. Let the filled cookies stand until set, about 30 minutes.

Lime-Glazed Coconut Snowballs
MAKES ABOUT 40 COOKIES

 1 recipe Butter Cookie Dough, with 1 teaspoon grated lime zest added with the dry ingredients, prepared through step 2
 1 recipe Glaze, with 3 tablespoons juice from 2 limes substituted for the milk
 1½ cups sweetened shredded coconut, pulsed in a food processor until finely chopped, about 15 pulses

1. Line 2 baking sheets with parchment paper. Roll the dough between your hands into 1-inch balls. Place the balls on the prepared sheets, spacing them about 1½ inches apart. Bake one sheet at a time in a 375-degree oven until lightly browned, about 12 minutes. Cool to room temperature.

2. Dip the tops of the cookies into the glaze and scrape off the excess, then dip them into the coconut. Place the cookies on a wire rack and let stand until the glaze sets, about 20 minutes.

Chocolate-Cherry Bar Cookies with Hazelnuts
MAKES ABOUT 50 COOKIES

 1 recipe Butter Cookie Dough, with 1 cup chopped dried cherries added with the dry ingredients, prepared through step 2
 1½ cups (9 ounces) semisweet chocolate chips
 1½ cups (6 ounces) hazelnuts, toasted, skinned, and chopped

1. Adjust an oven rack to the lower-middle position and heat the oven to 375 degrees. Line a 17 by 12-inch rimmed baking sheet with parchment paper. Press the dough evenly into the prepared sheet and bake until golden brown, about 20 minutes, rotating the sheet halfway through the baking time.

2. Immediately after removing the baking sheet from the oven, sprinkle evenly with the chocolate chips; let stand to melt, about 3 minutes.

3. Using an offset spatula, spread the chocolate into an even layer, then sprinkle the chopped hazelnuts evenly over the chocolate. Cool on a wire rack until just warm, 15 to 20 minutes.

4. Using a pizza wheel, cut on the diagonal into 1½-inch diamonds. Transfer the cookies to a wire rack to cool completely.

BEST SHORTBREAD

WHY THIS RECIPE WORKS: When made well, shortbread, with its moderately sweet, buttery flavor and distinctive sandy texture, is the perfect partner to a cup of tea or served alongside fruit for dessert, but often shortbread turns out bland and chalky. We wanted superlative shortbread with an alluring tawny brown crumb and pure, buttery richness.

In initial tests, we tinkered with various mixing methods and found that reverse creaming—mixing the flour and sugar before adding the butter, creating less aeration—yielded the most reliable results. To smooth out an objectionable granular texture, we swapped the white sugar for confectioners' sugar. Still, our shortbread was unpleasantly tough. The problems were gluten and moisture. Gluten, the protein matrix that lends baked goods structure and chew, forms naturally when liquid and all-purpose flour are combined, even without kneading. The liquid in our recipe was coming from butter, which contains 20 percent water. To curb gluten development, we replaced some of our flour with powdered old-fashioned oats. We ground some oats to a powder and supplemented it with a modest amount of cornstarch (using all oat powder muted the buttery flavor). The cookies were now perfectly crisp and flavorful, with an appealing hint of oat flavor.

As for the moisture problem, we took a hint from recipes from historic cookbooks: We cooked the dough briefly, then shut off the heat and let it sit in the still-warm oven. The batch was dry through and through, with an even golden brown exterior. Crisp and buttery, our shortbread was anything but bland.

Best Shortbread

MAKES 16 WEDGES

Use the collar of a springform pan to form the shortbread into an even round. Mold the shortbread with the collar in the closed position, then open the collar, but leave it in place. This allows the shortbread to expand slightly but keeps it from spreading too far. The extracted round of dough in step 2 is baked alongside the rest of the shortbread. Wrapped well and stored at room temperature, the shortbread will keep for up to 7 days.

- ½ cup (1½ ounces) old-fashioned oats
- 1½ cups (7½ ounces) unbleached all-purpose flour
- ¼ cup cornstarch
- ⅔ cup (2⅔ ounces) confectioners' sugar
- ½ teaspoon table salt
- 14 tablespoons (1¾ sticks) unsalted butter, chilled, cut into ⅛-inch-thick slices

1. Adjust an oven rack to the middle position and heat the oven to 450 degrees. Pulse the oats in a spice grinder or blender until reduced to a fine powder, about ten 5-second pulses (you should have ¼ to ⅓ cup oat flour). In a stand mixer fitted with the paddle attachment, mix the oat flour, all-purpose flour, cornstarch, sugar, and salt on low speed until combined, about 5 seconds. Add the butter to the dry ingredients and continue to mix on low speed until the dough just forms and pulls away from the sides of the bowl, 5 to 10 minutes.

2. Place an upside-down (the grooved edge should be at the top) collar of a 9- or 9½-inch springform pan on a parchment-lined rimmed baking sheet (do not use the springform pan bottom). Following the photos, press the dough into

FORMING AND BAKING THE SHORTBREAD

1. Press the dough into a closed springform pan collar; smooth with the back of a spoon.

2. Cut a hole in the center of the dough with a 2-inch biscuit cutter and remove the round of dough—place it on the baking sheet next to the collar; replace the cutter in the hole.

3. Open the collar, but leave it in place. Bake 5 minutes at 450 degrees, then 10 to 15 minutes at 250 degrees.

4. Score the partially baked shortbread into wedges, then poke 8 to 10 holes in each wedge.

5. Return the shortbread to the turned-off oven to dry; prop the door open with a wooden spoon or stick.

the collar in an even ½-inch-thick layer, smoothing the top of the dough with the back of a spoon. Place a 2-inch biscuit cutter in the center of the dough and cut out the center. Place the extracted round alongside the springform collar on the baking sheet and replace the cutter in the center of the dough. Open the springform collar, but leave it in place.

3. Bake the shortbread for 5 minutes, then reduce the oven temperature to 250 degrees. Continue to bake until the edges turn pale golden, 10 to 15 minutes longer. Remove the baking sheet from the oven; turn off the oven. Remove the springform pan collar; use a chef's knife to score the surface of the short-bread into 16 even wedges, cutting halfway through the shortbread. Using a wooden skewer, poke 8 to 10 holes in each wedge. Return the shortbread to the oven and prop the door open with the handle of a wooden spoon, leaving a 1-inch gap at the top. Allow the shortbread to dry in the turned-off oven until pale golden in the center (the shortbread should be firm but giving to the touch), about 1 hour.

4. Transfer the baking sheet to a wire rack; cool the short-bread to room temperature, at least 2 hours. Cut the shortbread at the scored marks to separate and serve.

NUT CRESCENT COOKIES

WHY THIS RECIPE WORKS: When nut crescent cookies are well made, they can be delicious: buttery, nutty, slightly crisp, slightly crumbly, with a melt-in-your mouth quality. Too often, however, they turn out bland and dry. We wanted to develop a recipe that would put them back in their proper place.

The ratio of 1 cup butter to 2 cups flour in almost all of the recipes we looked at is what worked for us. We tried three kinds of sugar in the batter: granulated, confectioners', and superfine. The last resulted in just what we wanted: cookies that melted in our mouths. In determining the amount, we had to remember that the cookies would be sweetened once more by their traditional coating of confectioners' sugar. Before rolling them, we let the cookies cool to room temperature; coating them with sugar while still warm results in the pasty outer layer we wanted to avoid.

Pecan or Walnut Crescent Cookies
MAKES ABOUT 48 SMALL COOKIES

If you cannot find superfine sugar, you can obtain a close approximation by processing regular granulated sugar in a food processor for about 30 seconds. If you don't have a food processor, you can finely grind the chopped nuts by rolling them between two large sheets of plastic wrap with a rolling pin, applying moderate pressure, until broken down to a coarse cornmeal-like texture.

- 2 cups (8 ounces) whole pecans or walnuts, chopped fine
- 2 cups (10 ounces) unbleached all-purpose flour
- ½ teaspoon table salt
- 16 tablespoons (2 sticks) unsalted butter, softened
- ⅓ cup (2½ ounces) superfine sugar (see note)
- 1½ teaspoons vanilla extract
- 1½ cups (6 ounces) confectioners' sugar

1. Adjust the oven racks to the upper-middle and lower-middle positions and heat the oven to 325 degrees. Line 2 large baking sheets with parchment paper.

2. Whisk 1 cup of the chopped nuts, the flour, and salt together in a medium bowl; set aside. Process the remaining 1 cup chopped nuts in a food processor (see note) until they are the texture of coarse cornmeal, 10 to 15 seconds (do not over process). Stir the nuts into the flour mixture and set aside.

3. In a stand mixer fitted with the paddle attachment, beat the butter and superfine sugar at medium-low speed until light and fluffy, about 2 minutes; add the vanilla, scraping down the bowl and beater with a rubber spatula. Add the flour mixture and beat on low speed until the dough just begins to come together but still looks scrappy, about 15 seconds. Scrape down the bowl and beater again with a rubber spatula; continue beating at low speed until the dough is cohesive, 6 to 9 seconds longer. Do not over beat.

4. Divide the dough into 48 portions, each about 1 table-spoon, and roll them between your hands into 1¼-inch balls. Roll each ball between your palms into a rope that measures 3 inches long. Place the ropes on the prepared baking sheets and turn up the ends to form a crescent shape. Bake until the tops are pale golden and the bottoms are just begin-ning to brown, 17 to 19 minutes, switching and rotating the baking sheets halfway through the baking time.

5. Cool the cookies on the baking sheets for 2 minutes; using a wide metal spatula, transfer the cookies to a wire rack and cool to room temperature, about 30 minutes. Place the confec-tioners' sugar in a shallow baking dish or pie plate. Working with three or four cookies at a time, roll the cookies in the sugar to coat them thoroughly; gently shake off the excess. (The cookies can be stored in an airtight container for up to 5 days.) Before serving, roll the cookies in the confectioners' sugar again and tap off the excess.

Almond or Hazelnut Crescent Cookies
Almonds can be used raw for cookies that are light in both color and flavor or toasted to enhance the almond flavor and darken the crescents.

Follow the recipe for Pecan or Walnut Crescent Cookies, substituting 1¾ cups (7¾ ounces) whole blanched almonds (toasted, if desired) or 2 cups (8 ounces) toasted, skinned hazelnuts for the pecans or walnuts. If using almonds, add ½ teaspoon almond extract along with the vanilla extract.

MERINGUE COOKIES

WHY THIS RECIPE WORKS: A classic meringue cookie may have only two ingredients—egg whites and sugar—but it requires precise timing. Otherwise, you'll end up with a meringue that's as dense as Styrofoam or weepy, gritty, and cloyingly sweet. A great meringue cookie should emerge from the oven glossy and white, with a shatteringly crisp texture that dissolves instantly in your mouth.

We chose a basic French meringue over a fussier Italian meringue. The French version, in which egg whites are whipped with sugar, is the simpler of the two; the Italian meringue, in which hot sugar syrup is poured into the whites, produces cookies that are dense and candy-like. The key to

scrape down the sides and bottom of the bowl with a rubber spatula. Increase the speed to high and beat until glossy and stiff peaks have formed, 30 to 45 seconds.

3. Working quickly, place the meringue in a pastry bag fitted with a ½-inch plain tip or a large zipper-lock bag with ½ inch of the corner cut off. Pipe meringues into 1¼-inch-wide mounds about 1 inch high on the baking sheets, six rows of four meringues on each sheet. Bake for 1 hour, switching and rotating the baking sheets halfway through the baking time. Turn off the oven and allow the meringues to cool in the oven for at least 1 hour. Remove the meringues from the oven and let cool to room temperature before serving, about 10 minutes.

Chocolate Meringue Cookies

Follow the recipe for Meringue Cookies, gently folding 2 ounces finely chopped bittersweet chocolate into the meringue mixture at the end of step 2.

Toasted Almond Meringue Cookies

Follow the recipe for Meringue Cookies, substituting ½ teaspoon almond extract for the vanilla extract. In step 3, sprinkle the meringues with ⅓ cup coarsely chopped toasted almonds and 1 teaspoon coarse sea salt, such as Maldon (optional), before baking.

BISCOTTI

WHY THIS RECIPE WORKS: We wanted biscotti that were hard and crunchy, but not hard to eat, and bold in flavor. To keep the crumb crisp, we used just a small amount of butter (4 tablespoons), and to keep the biscotti from being too hard, we ground some of the nuts to a fine meal, which helped minimize gluten development in the crumb. To ensure bold flavor in a biscuit that gets baked twice, we increased the quantities of almond extract and of the aromatic herbs and spices used in our variations, such as anise, rosemary, lavender, cardamom, and cloves.

Almond Biscotti

MAKES 30 COOKIES

The almonds will continue to toast while the biscotti bake, so toast the nuts only until they are just fragrant.

- 1¼ cups whole almonds, lightly toasted
- 1¾ cups (8¾ ounces) all-purpose flour
- 2 teaspoons baking powder
- ¼ teaspoon salt
- 2 large eggs, plus 1 large white beaten with pinch salt
- 1 cup (7 ounces) sugar
- 4 tablespoons unsalted butter, melted and cooled
- 1½ teaspoons almond extract
- ½ teaspoon vanilla extract
  Vegetable oil spray

glossy, evenly textured meringue was adding the sugar at just the right time—when the whites have been whipped enough to gain some volume, but still have enough free water left in them for the sugar to dissolve completely. Surprisingly, we found that cream of tartar wasn't necessary. Without it, the whites formed more slowly, giving a wider time frame in which to add the sugar. It was also important to form the cookies in a uniform shape, so we piped them from either a pastry bag or a zipper-lock bag with a corner cut off.

Meringue Cookies

MAKES ABOUT 48 SMALL COOKIES

Meringues may be a little soft immediately after being removed from the oven but will stiffen as they cool. To minimize stickiness on humid or rainy days, allow the meringues to cool in a turned-off oven for an additional hour (for a total of 2 hours) without opening the door, then transfer them immediately to airtight containers and seal. Cooled cookies can be kept in an airtight container for up to 2 weeks.

- ¾ cup (5¼ ounces) sugar
- 2 teaspoons cornstarch
- 4 large egg whites
- ¾ teaspoon vanilla extract
- ⅛ teaspoon table salt

1. Adjust the oven racks to the upper-middle and lower-middle positions and heat the oven to 225 degrees. Line 2 large baking sheets with parchment paper. Combine the sugar and cornstarch in a small bowl.

2. In a stand mixer fitted with the whisk attachment, beat the egg whites, vanilla, and salt together at high speed until very soft peaks start to form (the peaks should slowly lose their shape when the whip is removed), 30 to 45 seconds. Decrease the speed to medium and slowly add the sugar mixture in a steady stream down the side of the mixer bowl (the process should take about 30 seconds). Stop the mixer and

1. Adjust oven rack to middle position and heat oven to 325 degrees. Using ruler and pencil, draw two 8 by 3-inch rectangles, spaced 4 inches apart, on piece of parchment paper. Grease baking sheet and place parchment on it, marked side down.

2. Pulse 1 cup almonds in food processor until coarsely chopped, 8 to 10 pulses; transfer to bowl and set aside. Process remaining ¼ cup almonds in food processor until finely ground, about 45 seconds. Add flour, baking powder, and salt; process to combine, about 15 seconds. Transfer flour mixture to second bowl. Process 2 eggs in now-empty food processor until lightened in color and almost doubled in volume, about 3 minutes. With processor running, slowly add sugar until thoroughly combined, about 15 seconds. Add melted butter, almond extract, and vanilla and process until combined, about 10 seconds. Transfer egg mixture to medium bowl. Sprinkle half of flour mixture over egg mixture and, using spatula, gently fold until just combined. Add remaining flour mixture and chopped almonds and gently fold until just combined.

3. Divide batter in half. Using floured hands, form each half into 8 by 3-inch rectangle, using lines on parchment as guide. Spray each loaf lightly with oil spray. Using rubber spatula lightly coated with oil spray, smooth tops and sides of rectangles. Gently brush tops of loaves with egg white wash. Bake until loaves are golden and just beginning to crack on top, 25 to 30 minutes, rotating pan halfway through baking.

4. Let loaves cool on baking sheet for 30 minutes. Transfer loaves to cutting board. Using serrated knife, slice each loaf on slight bias into ½-inch-thick slices. Lay slices, cut side down, about ¼ inch apart on wire rack set in rimmed baking sheet. Bake until crisp and golden brown on both sides, about 35 minutes, flipping slices halfway through baking. Let cool completely before serving. Biscotti can be stored in airtight container for up to 1 month.

Anise Biscotti

Add 1½ teaspoons anise seeds to flour mixture in step 2. Substitute anise-flavored liqueur for almond extract.

Hazelnut-Orange Biscotti

Substitute lightly toasted and skinned hazelnuts for almonds. Add 2 tablespoons minced fresh rosemary to flour mixture in step 2. Substitute orange-flavored liqueur for almond extract and add 1 tablespoon grated orange zest to egg mixture with butter.

Hazelnut-Lavender Biscotti

Substitute lightly toasted and skinned hazelnuts for almonds. Add 2 teaspoons dried lavender flowers to flour mixture in step 2. Substitute 1½ teaspoons water for almond extract and add 2 tablespoons grated lemon zest to egg mixture with butter.

Pistachio-Spice Biscotti

Substitute shelled pistachios for almonds. Add 1 teaspoon ground cardamom, ½ teaspoon ground cloves, ½ teaspoon pepper, ¼ teaspoon ground cinnamon, and ¼ teaspoon ground ginger to flour mixture in step 2. Substitute 1 teaspoon water for almond extract and increase vanilla extract to 1 teaspoon.

BLONDIES

WHY THIS RECIPE WORKS: Blondies are first cousins to both brownies and chocolate chip cookies. Although blondies are baked in a pan like brownies, the flavorings are similar to those in chocolate chip cookies. They're sometimes laced with nuts and chocolate chips or butterscotch chips. But even with these extras, blondies can be pretty bland, floury, and dry. We set out to fix the blondie so it would be chewy but not dense, sweet but not cloying, and loaded with nuts and chocolate. We found that the key to chewy blondies was using melted, not creamed, butter because the creaming process incorporated too much air into the batter. Light brown sugar lent the right amount of molasses flavor. And combined with vanilla extract and salt, the light brown sugar developed a rich butterscotch flavor. To add both texture and flavor, we included chocolate chips and pecans. We also tried butterscotch chips, but we found that they did little for this recipe. On a whim, we included white chocolate chips with the semisweet chips, and we were surprised that they produced the best blondie yet.

Blondies

MAKES 36 BARS

If you have trouble finding white chocolate chips, chop a bar of white chocolate into small chunks.

- 1½ cups (7½ ounces) unbleached all-purpose flour
- 1 teaspoon baking powder
- ½ teaspoon table salt
- 1½ cups packed (10½ ounces) light brown sugar

CLASSIC BROWNIES

WHY THIS RECIPE WORKS: Chewy and chocolaty, brownies should be a simple and utterly satisfying affair. But too often, brownies are heavy, dense, and remarkably low on chocolate flavor. We wanted old-fashioned brownies that had serious chocolate flavor. They had to be the simple treats we enjoyed in our youth—Mom's brownies—but altered to cater to adult tastes.

To get that tender texture and delicate chew, we shelved the all-purpose flour in favor of cake flour; a bit of baking powder further lightened the crumb. Getting the number of eggs just right prevented our brownies from being cakey or dry. As for chocolatiness, plenty of unsweetened chocolate provided maximum chocolate flavor—not too sweet, with profound chocolate notes. Nailing the baking time was essential—too little time in the oven and the brownies were gummy and underbaked, too much time and they were dry. Finally, for nut-lovers, we toasted pecans and topped the brownies with them just before baking; baked inside the brownies, they steamed and got soft.

Classic Brownies

MAKES 24 BROWNIES

Be sure to test for doneness before removing the brownies from the oven. If underbaked (the toothpick has batter clinging to it), the texture of the brownies will be dense and gummy; if overbaked (the toothpick comes out completely clean), the brownies will be dry and cakey. To melt the chocolate using a microwave, heat it with the butter at 50 percent power for 2 minutes; stir the chocolate and continue heating until melted, stirring once every additional minute.

- 12 tablespoons (1½ sticks) unsalted butter, melted and cooled
- 2 large eggs
- 1½ teaspoons vanilla extract
- 1 cup (4 ounces) pecans, toasted and chopped coarse
- ½ cup (3 ounces) semisweet chocolate chips
- ½ cup (3 ounces) white chocolate chips (see note)

1. Adjust an oven rack to the middle position and heat the oven to 350 degrees. Line a 13 by 9-inch baking pan with 2 pieces of foil (see the photos on page 732) and spray with vegetable oil spray.

2. Whisk the flour, baking powder, and salt together in a medium bowl; set aside.

3. Whisk the brown sugar and melted butter together in a medium bowl until combined. Add the eggs and vanilla and mix well. Using a rubber spatula, fold the dry ingredients into the egg mixture until just combined. Do not overmix. Fold in the nuts and semisweet and white chocolate chips and turn the batter into the prepared pan, smoothing the top with a rubber spatula.

4. Bake until the top is shiny and cracked and feels firm to the touch, 22 to 25 minutes. Transfer the pan to a wire rack and cool completely. Loosen the edges with a paring knife and lift the bars from the pan using the foil sling. Cut into 2 by 1½-inch bars.

Congo Bars

If you have trouble locating unsweetened shredded coconut, try a natural foods store or an Asian market. Keep a close eye on the coconut when toasting, as it can burn quickly.

Toast 1½ cups unsweetened shredded coconut on a rimmed baking sheet on the middle oven rack at 350 degrees, stirring two to three times, until light golden, 4 to 5 minutes. Transfer to a small bowl to cool. Follow the recipe for Blondies, adding the toasted coconut with the chocolate chips and nuts in step 3.

- 1¼ cups (5 ounces) cake flour
- ¾ teaspoon baking powder
- ½ teaspoon table salt
- 6 ounces unsweetened chocolate, chopped fine
- 12 tablespoons (1½ sticks) unsalted butter, cut into 6 pieces
- 2¼ cups (15¾ ounces) sugar
- 4 large eggs
- 1 tablespoon vanilla extract
- 1 cup (4 ounces) pecans or walnuts, toasted and coarsely chopped (optional)

1. Adjust an oven rack to the middle position and heat the oven to 325 degrees. Line a 13 by 9-inch baking pan with 2 pieces of foil (see the photos on page 732) and spray with vegetable oil spray.

2. Whisk the flour, baking powder, and salt in a medium bowl until combined; set aside.

3. Melt the chocolate and butter in a medium heatproof bowl set over a saucepan of barely simmering water, stirring occasionally, until smooth. Off the heat, gradually whisk in the sugar. Add the eggs, one at a time, whisking after each

MAKING A FOIL SLING

1. Place two sheets of aluminum foil perpendicular to each other in the baking pan, with the extra foil hanging over the edges of the pan.

2. Push the foil into the corners and up the sides of the pan, smoothing out any wrinkles in the foil.

3. After the bars or brownies have baked and cooled, use the foil sling to lift and transfer them to a cutting board before cutting into squares.

addition, until thoroughly combined. Whisk in the vanilla. Add the flour mixture in three additions, folding with a rubber spatula until the batter is completely smooth and homogeneous.

4. Transfer the batter to the prepared pan; using a spatula, spread the batter into the corners of the pan and smooth the surface. Sprinkle the toasted nuts (if using) evenly over the batter. Bake until a toothpick or wooden skewer inserted into the center of the brownies comes out with a few moist crumbs attached, 30 to 35 minutes. Cool on a wire rack to room temperature, about 2 hours; loosen the edges with a paring knife and lift the brownies from the pan using the foil sling. Cut the brownies into 2-inch squares and serve. (The brownies can be stored in an airtight container at room temperature for up to 3 days.)

FUDGY BROWNIES

WHY THIS RECIPE WORKS: Classic Brownies (page 731) boast a balance of cakey and chewy. We wanted a brownie that was distinctly chewy and fudgy—a moist, dark brownie with a firm, smooth texture. To develop a rich, deep chocolate flavor, we ultimately found it necessary to use three types of chocolate. Unsweetened chocolate laid a solid, intense foundation; semisweet chocolate provided a mellow, even somewhat sweet, flavor; and cocoa powder smoothed out any rough edges introduced by the unsweetened chocolate and

added complexity to what can be the bland flavor of semisweet chocolate. We focused on flour, butter, and eggs to arrive at the chewy texture we wanted. Too little flour and the batter was goopy; too much made the brownies dry and muted the flavor. We melted the butter instead of creaming softened butter with the sugar and eggs; as with our Classic Brownies, the melted butter produced a more dense and fudgy texture.

Fudgy Triple-Chocolate Brownies
MAKES 64 SMALL BROWNIES

To melt the chocolates in a microwave, heat them with the butter at 50 percent power for 2 minutes; stir the chocolate and continue heating until melted, stirring once every additional minute. Either Dutch-processed or natural cocoa powder works well in this recipe. These brownies are very rich, so we prefer to cut them into very small squares for serving.

5	ounces semisweet or bittersweet chocolate, chopped
2	ounces unsweetened chocolate, chopped
8	tablespoons (1 stick) unsalted butter, cut into quarters
3	tablespoons cocoa powder (see note)
3	large eggs
1¼	cups (8¾ ounces) sugar
2	teaspoons vanilla extract
½	teaspoon table salt
1	cup (5 ounces) unbleached all-purpose flour

1. Adjust an oven rack to the lower-middle position and heat the oven to 350 degrees. Following the photos, line an 8-inch square baking pan with 2 pieces of foil and spray with vegetable oil spray.

2. Melt the chocolates and butter in a medium heatproof bowl set over a saucepan of barely simmering water, stirring occasionally, until smooth. Whisk in the cocoa powder until smooth. Set aside to cool slightly.

3. Whisk the eggs, sugar, vanilla, and salt together in a medium bowl until combined, about 15 seconds. Whisk the warm chocolate mixture into the egg mixture. Using a wooden spoon, stir in the flour until just combined. Transfer the batter to the prepared pan; using a spatula, spread the batter into the corners and smooth the surface. Bake until slightly puffed and a toothpick or wooden skewer inserted into the center of the brownies comes out with a few moist crumbs attached, 35 to 40 minutes. Cool the brownies on a wire rack to room temperature, about 2 hours; loosen the edges with a paring knife and lift the brownies from the pan using the foil sling. Cut the brownies into 1-inch squares and serve. (Do not cut the brownies until ready to serve; the brownies can be wrapped in plastic wrap and refrigerated for up to 5 days.)

Triple-Chocolate Espresso Brownies

Follow the recipe for Fudgy Triple-Chocolate Brownies, whisking in 1½ tablespoons instant espresso or coffee powder along with the cocoa powder in step 2.

CHEWY BROWNIES

WHY THIS RECIPE WORKS: Brownies are a tricky business: Homemade recipes have better flavor, while boxed mixes claim best texture. Our goal was clear: a homemade brownie with chewiness to rival the boxed-mix standard—but flush with a rich, deep chocolate flavor. Boxed brownie mixes derive their chewy texture from the right combination of saturated (solid) and unsaturated (liquid) fats. Unsaturated vegetable oil and powdered solid fat combine in a ratio designed to deliver maximum chew. To get the same chew at home, we tested and tested until we finally homed in on the ratio that produced the chewiest brownie. To combat greasiness, we replaced some of the oil with egg yolks, whose emulsifiers prevented fat from separating and leaking out during baking. We focused on flavor next. Because unsweetened chocolate contains a similar ratio of saturated and unsaturated fat to butter, we could replace some of the butter with unsweetened chocolate, thereby providing more chocolate flavor. Espresso powder improved the chocolate taste as well. And finally, folding in bittersweet chocolate chunks just before baking gave our chewy, fudgy brownies gooey pockets of melted chocolate and rounded out their complex chocolate flavor.

Chewy Brownies

MAKES 2 DOZEN 2-INCH BROWNIES

For an accurate measurement of boiling water, bring a full kettle of water to a boil, then measure out the desired amount. For the chewiest texture, it is important to let the brownies cool thoroughly before cutting. If your baking dish is glass, cool the brownies for 10 minutes, then remove them promptly from the pan (otherwise, the superior heat retention of glass can lead to overbaking). While any high-quality chocolate can be used, our preferred brands of bittersweet chocolate are Callebaut Intense Dark Chocolate and Ghirardelli Bittersweet Chocolate. Our preferred brand of unsweetened chocolate is Hershey's.

⅓ cup (1 ounce) Dutch-processed cocoa powder
1½ teaspoons instant espresso (optional)
½ cup plus 2 tablespoons boiling water (see note)
2 ounces unsweetened chocolate (see note), chopped fine
½ cup plus 2 tablespoons vegetable oil
4 tablespoons (½ stick) unsalted butter, melted
2 large whole eggs plus 2 large egg yolks
2 teaspoons vanilla extract
2½ cups (17½ ounces) sugar
1¾ cups (8¾ ounces) unbleached all-purpose flour
¾ teaspoon table salt
6 ounces bittersweet chocolate (see note),
  cut into ½-inch pieces

1. Adjust an oven rack to the lowest position and heat the oven to 350 degrees. Following the photos on page 732, line a 13 by 9-inch baking pan with a foil sling, lightly coat with vegetable oil spray, and set aside.

2. Whisk the cocoa, espresso powder (if using), and boiling water together in a large bowl until smooth. Add the unsweetened chocolate and whisk until the chocolate is melted. Whisk in the oil and melted butter. (The mixture may look curdled.) Add the whole eggs, egg yolks, and vanilla and continue to whisk until smooth and homogeneous. Whisk in the sugar until fully incorporated. Add the flour and salt and mix with a rubber spatula until combined. Fold in the bittersweet chocolate pieces.

3. Scrape the batter into the prepared pan and bake until a toothpick inserted halfway between the edge and the center comes out with just a few moist crumbs attached, 30 to 35 minutes. Transfer the pan to a wire rack and cool for 1½ hours.

4. Loosen the edges with a paring knife and lift the brownies from the pan using the foil sling. Return the brownies to the wire rack and let cool completely, about 1 hour. Cut into 2-inch squares and serve. (The brownies can be stored in an airtight container at room temperature for up to 4 days.)

CREAM CHEESE BROWNIES

WHY THIS RECIPE WORKS: Rich, decadent cream cheese brownies are hard to get just right: They are plagued by chalky cream cheese, dry brownie, and uneven distribution of each element. To fix these issues, we started with a cakey brownie, which would absorb some of the moisture from the cream cheese. Unsweetened chocolate gave us the most intense chocolate flavor, and a bit of extra sugar eliminated bitter notes. For the cream cheese swirl, we mixed in some sour cream for tang and richness. Dolloping the cream cheese into the brownie batter made for unevenly dispersed swirls; we fixed this problem by layering some of the brownie batter, then the cream cheese, then dolloping more brownie batter on top and giving the whole construction a few quick swirls with a knife.

4. Whisk sugar, eggs, and vanilla together in medium bowl. Add melted chocolate mixture (do not clean bowl) and whisk until incorporated. Add flour mixture and fold to combine.

5. Transfer ½ cup batter to bowl used to melt chocolate. Spread remaining batter in prepared pan. Spread cream cheese filling evenly over batter.

6. Microwave bowl of reserved batter until warm and pourable, 10 to 20 seconds. Using spoon, dollop softened batter over cream cheese filling, 6 to 8 dollops. Using knife, swirl batter through cream cheese filling, making marbled pattern, 10 to 12 strokes, leaving ½-inch border around edges.

7. Bake until toothpick inserted in center comes out with a few moist crumbs attached, 35 to 40 minutes, rotating pan halfway through baking. Let cool in pan on wire rack for 1 hour.

8. Using foil overhang, lift brownies out of pan. Return brownies to wire rack and let cool completely, about 1 hour. Cut into 2-inch squares and serve.

Cream Cheese Brownies
MAKES SIXTEEN 2-INCH BROWNIES

To accurately test the doneness of the brownies, be sure to stick the toothpick into the brownie portion, not the cream cheese. Leftover brownies should be stored in the refrigerator. Let leftovers stand at room temperature for 1 hour before serving.

CREAM CHEESE FILLING
  4 ounces cream cheese, cut into 8 pieces
  ½ cup sour cream
  2 tablespoons sugar
  1 tablespoon all-purpose flour

BROWNIE BATTER
  ⅔ cup (3⅓ ounces) all-purpose flour
  ½ teaspoon baking powder
  ½ teaspoon salt
  4 ounces unsweetened chocolate, chopped fine
  8 tablespoons unsalted butter
1¼ cups (8¾ ounces) sugar
  2 large eggs
  1 teaspoon vanilla extract

1. FOR THE CREAM CHEESE FILLING: Microwave cream cheese until soft, 20 to 30 seconds. Add sour cream, sugar, and flour and whisk to combine. Set aside.

2. Adjust oven rack to middle position and heat oven to 325 degrees. Make foil sling for 8-inch square baking pan by folding 2 long sheets of aluminum foil so each is 8 inches wide. Lay sheets of foil in pan perpendicular to each other, with extra foil hanging over edges of pan. Push foil into corners and up sides of pan, smoothing foil flush to pan. Grease foil.

3. FOR THE BROWNIE BATTER: Whisk flour, baking powder, and salt together in bowl and set aside. Microwave chocolate and butter in bowl at 50 percent power, stirring occasionally, until melted, 1 to 2 minutes.

FUDGY LOW-FAT BROWNIES

WHY THIS RECIPE WORKS: We have tried many recipes for "healthy" brownies, but it usually takes just one bite to regret the effort. Either the texture is incredibly dry or the chocolate flavor is anemic. We wanted a moist, fudgy, chocolaty brownie that had a lower fat and calorie count than a traditional brownie, which can weigh in at over 200 calories and 12 grams of fat.

We knew the richness and flavor would have to come from somewhere if we were cutting back on butter and unsweetened chocolate. We started our tests with "alternative" ingredients, such as prune puree, applesauce, and yogurt, but they resulted in everything from oddly flavored brownies to flavorless hockey pucks. We had more success replacing some of the butter with low-fat sour cream, which yielded moist, fudgy brownies. A blend of cocoa powder and bittersweet chocolate (which has less fat per ounce than unsweetened chocolate) added deep chocolate flavor. And to boost both the brownies' chocolate flavor and moisture without adding any fat, we used a shot of chocolate syrup. Our brownies were now rich and decadent, but with half the calories (just 110 per serving) and less than half the fat (only 4.5 grams) of traditional brownies.

Fudgy Low-Fat Brownies
MAKES 16 BROWNIES

For a truly fudgy consistency, don't overbake the brownies; as soon as a toothpick inserted into the center comes out with moist crumbs attached, the brownies are done. If the toothpick emerges with no crumbs, the brownies will be cakey. To melt the chocolate in a microwave, heat it with the butter at 50 percent power for 2 minutes; stir and continue heating until melted, stirring once every additional minute.

¾ cup (3¾ ounces) unbleached all-purpose flour

⅓ cup Dutch-processed cocoa powder

½ teaspoon baking powder

¼ teaspoon table salt

2 ounces bittersweet chocolate, chopped

2 tablespoons unsalted butter

1 cup (7 ounces) sugar

2 tablespoons low-fat sour cream

1 tablespoon chocolate syrup

2 teaspoons vanilla extract

1 large whole egg

1 large egg white

1. Adjust an oven rack to the middle position and heat the oven to 350 degrees. Line an 8-inch square baking pan with 2 pieces of foil (see photos on page 732) and spray with vegetable oil spray.

2. Whisk the flour, cocoa powder, baking powder, and salt together in a medium bowl. Melt the chocolate and butter in a large heatproof bowl set over a saucepan of barely simmering water, stirring occasionally, until smooth. Set aside to cool slightly, 2 to 3 minutes. Whisk in the sugar, sour cream, chocolate syrup, vanilla, whole egg, and egg white. Using a rubber spatula, fold the dry ingredients into the chocolate mixture until combined.

3. Transfer the batter to the prepared pan; using a spatula, spread the batter into the corners and smooth the surface. Bake until slightly puffed and a toothpick or wooden skewer inserted into the center of the brownies comes out with a few moist crumbs attached, 20 to 25 minutes. Cool the brownies on a wire rack to room temperature, about 1 hour. Loosen the edges with a paring knife and lift the brownies from the pan using the foil sling. Cut the brownies into 2-inch squares and serve. (Do not cut the brownies until ready to serve; the brownies can be wrapped in plastic wrap and refrigerated for up to 3 days.)

MILLIONAIRE'S SHORTBREAD

WHY THIS RECIPE WORKS: Millionaire's shortbread has a lot going for it: a crunchy shortbread base topped with a chewy, caramel-like layer, all covered in shiny, snappy chocolate. We wanted foolproof methods for producing all three layers. We started by making a quick pat-in-the-pan shortbread with melted butter. Sweetened condensed milk was important to the creaminess of the middle layer, but we needed to add a little heavy cream to keep it from separating. Gently heating the chocolate in the microwave and stirring in grated chocolate created a firm top layer, which made a suitably elegant finish for this rich yet refined cookie.

Millionaire's Shortbread

MAKES 40 COOKIES

For a caramel filling with the right texture, monitor the temperature with an instant-read thermometer. We prefer Ghirardelli 60% Cacao Bittersweet Chocolate Premium Baking Bar for this recipe. Grating a portion of the chocolate is important for getting the chocolate to set properly; the small holes on a box grater work well for this task. Stir often while melting the chocolate and don't overheat it.

CRUST

2½ cups (12½ ounces) all-purpose flour

½ cup (3½ ounces) granulated sugar

¾ teaspoon salt

16 tablespoons unsalted butter, melted

FILLING

1 (14-ounce) can sweetened condensed milk

1 cup packed (7 ounces) brown sugar

½ cup heavy cream

½ cup corn syrup

8 tablespoons unsalted butter

½ teaspoon salt

CHOCOLATE

8 ounces bittersweet chocolate (6 ounces chopped fine, 2 ounces grated)

1. FOR THE CRUST: Adjust oven rack to lower-middle position and heat oven to 350 degrees. Make foil sling for 13 by 9-inch baking pan by folding 2 long sheets of aluminum foil; first sheet should be 13 inches wide and second sheet should be 9 inches wide. Lay sheets of foil in pan perpendicular to each other, with extra foil hanging over edges of pan. Push foil

into corners and up sides of pan, smoothing foil flush to pan. Combine flour, sugar, and salt in medium bowl. Add melted butter and stir with rubber spatula until flour is evenly moistened. Crumble dough evenly over bottom of prepared pan. Using your fingertips and palm of your hand, press and smooth dough into even thickness. Using fork, pierce dough at 1-inch intervals. Bake until light golden brown and firm to touch, 25 to 30 minutes. Transfer pan to wire rack. Using sturdy metal spatula, press on entire surface of warm crust to compress (this will make finished bars easier to cut). Let crust cool until it is just warm, at least 20 minutes.

2. FOR THE FILLING: Stir all ingredients together in large, heavy-bottomed saucepan. Cook over medium heat, stirring frequently, until mixture registers between 236 and 239 degrees (temperature will fluctuate), 16 to 20 minutes. Pour over crust and spread to even thickness (mixture will be very hot). Let cool completely, about 1½ hours.

3. FOR THE CHOCOLATE: Microwave chopped chocolate in bowl at 50 percent power, stirring every 15 seconds, until melted but not much warmer than body temperature (check by holding in palm of your hand), 1 to 2 minutes. Add grated chocolate and stir until smooth, returning to microwave for no more than 5 seconds at a time to finish melting if necessary. Spread chocolate evenly over surface of filling. Refrigerate shortbread until chocolate is just set, about 10 minutes.

4. Using foil overhang, lift shortbread out of pan and transfer to cutting board; discard foil. Using serrated knife and gentle sawing motion, cut shortbread in half crosswise to create two 6½ by 9-inch rectangles. Cut each rectangle in half to make four 3½ by 9-inch strips. Cut each strip crosswise into 10 equal pieces. (Shortbread can be stored at room temperature, between layers of parchment, for up to 1 week.)

RASPBERRY SQUARES

WHY THIS RECIPE WORKS: Raspberry squares are one of the best, and easiest, bar cookies to prepare, especially since the filling is ready-made (a jar of raspberry preserves). But sometimes the proportions are uneven, leaving one parched from too much sandy crust, or with a puckered face from an overload of tart filling. We were after a buttery, tender, golden brown crust and crumb topping with just the right amount of sweet and tart raspberry preserves in the middle.

For the tender, almost (but not quite) sandy crumb, we had to get the right combination of ingredients, especially the butter and sugar. Too much butter made the raspberry squares greasy, but too little left them on the dry side. We found that equal amounts of white and light brown sugar made for a deeper flavor than white alone; oats and nuts made a subtle contribution to flavor while also adding some textural interest. For a golden brown bottom crust, we prebaked it before layering it with raspberry preserves and sprinkling on the top crust, which was a small amount of the reserved bottom crust mixture.

Raspberry Squares
MAKES 25 SQUARES

For a nice presentation, trim ¼ inch off the outer rim of the uncut baked block. The outside edges of all cut squares will then be neat.

- 1½ cups (7½ ounces) unbleached all-purpose flour
- 1¼ cups (3¾ ounces) quick oats
- ½ cup pecans or almonds, chopped fine
- ⅓ cup (2⅓ ounces) granulated sugar
- ⅓ cup packed (2⅓ ounces) light brown sugar
- ¼ teaspoon baking soda
- ¼ teaspoon table salt
- 12 tablespoons (1½ sticks) unsalted butter, cut into 12 pieces and softened
- 1 cup raspberry preserves

1. Adjust an oven rack to the lower-middle position and heat the oven to 350 degrees. Line a 9-inch square baking pan with 2 pieces of foil (see the photos on page 732) and spray with vegetable oil spray.

2. Whisk the flour, oats, nuts, sugars, baking soda, and salt together in a large bowl. In a stand mixer fitted with the paddle attachment, beat the flour mixture and butter at low speed until well blended and the mixture resembles wet sand, about 2 minutes.

3. Transfer two-thirds of the mixture to the prepared pan. Press the crumbs evenly and firmly into the bottom of the pan. Bake until just starting to brown, about 20 minutes. Using a rubber spatula, spread the preserves evenly over the hot crust; sprinkle the remaining flour mixture evenly over the preserves. Bake until bubbling around the edges and the top is golden brown, about 30 minutes, rotating the pan halfway through the baking time. Cool on a wire rack to room temperature, 1 to 1½ hours. Lift the bars from the baking pan using the foil sling; cut the bars into 25 squares and serve.

KEY LIME BARS

WHY THIS RECIPE WORKS: Key lime pie is a luscious, bright, summery dessert, but like all pies, it's not very portable. Thus, we decided to bring all the essence of Key lime pie to a Key lime bar, creating a cookie that balanced tart and creamy flavors as well as soft and crispy textures.

To support our handheld bars, we needed a thicker, sturdier crust, which required more crumbs and butter than used in traditional pie crust. Tasters found the traditional graham cracker flavor too assertive in such a crust and preferred the more neutral flavor of animal crackers. As for the filling, it also had to be firmer. By adding cream cheese and an egg yolk to the usual sweetened condensed milk, lime juice, and lime zest, we created a firm, rich filling that didn't fall apart when the bars were picked up. Two issues remained: Were Key limes really key? Did we need a topping? While tasters preferred Key lime juice to regular lime juice by a narrow margin, regular juice was judged acceptable, especially considering that we needed to squeeze far fewer regular limes (three) than Key limes (20) to get the same amount of juice. For a topping, a heavy streusel was rejected. The favorite was an optional toasted-coconut topping.

Key Lime Bars

MAKES 16 BARS

If you cannot find fresh Key limes, use regular (Persian) limes. Do not use bottled lime juice. Grate the zest from the limes before juicing them, avoiding the bitter white pith that lies just beneath the outermost skin. The optional coconut garnish adds textural interest and tames the lime flavor for those who find it too intense. The recipe can be doubled and baked in a 13 by 9-inch baking pan; you will need a double layer of extra-wide foil for the pan (each sheet about 20 inches in length) and should increase the baking times by a minute or two.

CRUST

- 5 ounces animal crackers
- 3 tablespoons brown sugar
  Pinch table salt
- 4 tablespoons (½ stick) unsalted butter, melted and cooled slightly

FILLING

- 2 ounces cream cheese, at room temperature
- 1 tablespoon grated zest from 1 lime
  Pinch table salt
- 1 (14-ounce) can sweetened condensed milk
- 1 large egg yolk
- ½ cup juice from about 20 Key limes or from about 3 Persian limes (see note)

GARNISH (OPTIONAL)

- ¾ cup sweetened shredded coconut, toasted until golden and crisp (see note)

1. Adjust an oven rack to the middle position and heat the oven to 325 degrees. Line an 8-inch square baking pan with 2 pieces of foil (see the photos on page 732) and spray with vegetable oil spray.

2. FOR THE CRUST: Pulse the animal crackers in a food processor until broken down, about 10 pulses; process the crumbs until evenly fine, about 10 seconds (you should have about 1¼ cups crumbs). Add the brown sugar and salt; process to combine, 10 to 12 pulses (if large sugar lumps remain, break them apart with your fingers). Drizzle the butter over the crumbs and pulse until the crumbs are evenly moistened with the butter, about 10 pulses. Press the crumbs evenly and firmly into the bottom of the prepared pan. Bake until deep golden brown, 18 to 20 minutes. Cool on a wire rack while making the filling. Do not turn off the oven.

3. FOR THE FILLING: While the crust cools, in a medium bowl, stir the cream cheese, zest, and salt with a rubber spatula until softened, creamy, and thoroughly combined. Add the sweetened condensed milk and whisk vigorously until incorporated and no lumps of cream cheese remain; whisk in the egg yolk. Add the lime juice and whisk gently until incorporated (the mixture will thicken slightly).

NOTES FROM THE TEST KITCHEN

ZESTING CITRUS

Hold a rasp-style grater upside down with the fruit on the bottom and the inverted grater on the top. This method is neater and makes it easy to see exactly how much zest you have.

4. Pour the filling into the crust; spread to the corners and smooth the surface with a rubber spatula. Bake until set and the edges begin to pull away slightly from the sides, 15 to 20 minutes. Cool on a wire rack to room temperature, 1 to 1½ hours. Cover with foil and refrigerate until thoroughly chilled, at least 2 hours.

5. Loosen the edges with a paring knife and lift the bars from the baking pan using the foil sling; cut the bars into 16 squares. Sprinkle with the toasted coconut (if using) and serve. (Leftovers can be refrigerated for up to 2 days; the crust will soften slightly. Let the bars stand at room temperature for about 15 minutes before serving.)

Triple Citrus Bars

Using three types of citrus (orange, lemon, and lime) gives these bars a slightly more complex, floral flavor.

Follow the recipe for Key Lime Bars, substituting 1½ teaspoons each grated lime zest, lemon zest, and orange zest for the lime zest, and using 6 tablespoons lime juice, 1 tablespoon lemon juice, and 1 tablespoon orange juice in place of all the lime juice.

PECAN BARS

WHY THIS RECIPE WORKS: Pecan bars usually take the lead from pecan pie and are more about a thick, custardy filling than the pecans. We wanted a bar cookie that emphasized the star ingredient. For the filling, we increased the amount of pecans to a full pound and tossed them in a thick mixture of brown sugar, corn syrup, and melted butter for an easy dump-and-stir filling that spread itself evenly in the heat of the oven. Using so many nuts gave these pecan bars

a variety of textures; depending on the bite, some parts were chewy and some crunchy—a quality we enjoyed. Instead of making a crust using cold butter in a food processor, we found that melted butter helped form an easy press-in crust with no special equipment necessary. And after we eliminated the wet custardy filling, we discovered the crust also didn't need parbaking. A final sprinkling of flaky sea salt as the bars came out of the oven elevated the flavor and appearance of this nutty treat.

Ultranutty Pecan Bars

MAKES 24 BARS

It is important to use pecan halves, not pieces. The edges of the bars will be slightly firmer than the center. If desired, trim ¼ inch from the edges before cutting into bars. Toast the pecans on a rimmed baking sheet in a 350-degree oven until fragrant, 8 to 12 minutes, shaking the sheet halfway through.

CRUST

  1¾ cups (8¾ ounces) all-purpose flour
   6 tablespoons (2⅔ ounces) granulated sugar
   ½ teaspoon salt
   8 tablespoons unsalted butter, melted

TOPPING

  ¾ cup packed (5¼ ounces) light brown sugar
   ½ cup light corn syrup
   7 tablespoons unsalted butter, melted and hot
   1 teaspoon vanilla extract
   ½ teaspoon salt
   4 cups (1 pound) pecan halves, toasted
   ½ teaspoon flake sea salt (optional)

1. FOR THE CRUST: Adjust oven rack to lowest position and heat oven to 350 degrees. Make foil sling for 13 by 9-inch baking pan by folding 2 long sheets of aluminum foil; first sheet should be 13 inches wide and second sheet should be 9 inches wide. Lay sheets of foil in pan perpendicular to each other, with extra foil hanging over edges of pan. Push foil into corners and up sides of pan, smoothing foil flush to pan. Lightly spray foil with vegetable oil spray.

2. Whisk flour, sugar, and salt together in medium bowl. Add melted butter and stir with wooden spoon until dough begins to form. Using your hands, continue to combine until no dry flour remains and small portion of dough holds together when squeezed in palm of your hand. Evenly scatter tablespoon-size pieces of dough over surface of pan. Using your fingertips and palm of your hand, press and smooth dough into even thickness in bottom of pan.

3. FOR THE TOPPING: Whisk sugar, corn syrup, melted butter, vanilla, and salt together in medium bowl until smooth (mixture will look separated at first but will become homogeneous), about 20 seconds. Fold pecans into sugar mixture until nuts are evenly coated.

HOW TO TOAST NUTS

Nuts (especially irregularly shaped ones) toast more evenly in the oven, but the stovetop is more convenient for amounts less than 1 cup. To avoid overbrowning, transfer toasted nuts to a plate to cool.

IN THE OVEN
Spread nuts in single layer on rimmed baking sheet and toast in 350-degree oven until fragrant and slightly darkened, 8 to 12 minutes, shaking sheet halfway through.

ON THE STOVETOP
Place nuts in single layer in dry skillet set over medium heat and toast, stirring frequently, until fragrant and slightly darkened, 3 to 5 minutes.

4. Pour topping over crust. Using spatula, spread topping over crust, pushing to edges and into corners (there will be bare patches). Bake until topping is evenly distributed and rapidly bubbling across entire surface, 23 to 25 minutes.

5. Transfer pan to wire rack and lightly sprinkle with flake sea salt, if using. Let bars cool completely in pan on rack, about 1½ hours. Using foil overhang, lift bars out of pan and transfer to cutting board. Cut into 24 bars. (Bars can be stored at room temperature for up to 5 days.)

BAKLAVA

WHY THIS RECIPE WORKS: Baklava is rich with butter, sugar, and nuts, but it can be too soggy and too sweet. We wanted our baklava to be crisp, flaky, and buttery, light yet decadent, filled with fragrant nuts and spices, and sweetened just assertively enough. To achieve this goal, we sprinkled store-bought phyllo dough with three separate layers of nuts (a combination of almonds and walnuts) flavored with cinnamon and cloves and clarified butter for even browning. Fully cutting the baklava rather than just scoring it before baking helped it to absorb the sugar syrup. A low oven and slow baking time proved best. Finally, allowing the baklava to stand overnight before serving improved both its flavor and texture.

Baklava

MAKES 32 TO 40 PIECES

A straight-sided traditional (not nonstick) metal baking pan works best for making baklava; the straight sides ensure that the pieces will have nicely shaped edges, and the surface of a traditional pan will not be marred by the knife during cutting, as would a nonstick surface. If you don't have this type of pan, a glass baking dish will work. Make sure that the phyllo is fully thawed before use; leave it in the refrigerator overnight or on the countertop for four to five hours. When assembling, use the nicest, most intact phyllo sheets for the bottom and top layers; use sheets with tears or ones that are smaller than the size of the pan in the middle layers, where their imperfections will go unnoticed.

SUGAR SYRUP

- 1¼ cups granulated sugar
- ¾ cup water
- ⅓ cup honey
- 1 tablespoon lemon juice from 1 lemon, plus 3 strips zest, removed in large strips with vegetable peeler
- 1 cinnamon stick
- 5 whole cloves
- ⅛ teaspoon salt

NUT FILLING

- 8 ounces blanched slivered almonds
- 4 ounces walnuts
- 1¼ teaspoons ground cinnamon
- ¼ teaspoon ground cloves
- 2 tablespoons granulated sugar
- ⅛ teaspoon salt

24 tablespoons (3 sticks) unsalted butter, cut into 1-inch pieces

1 pound frozen phyllo, thawed (see note)

1. FOR THE SUGAR SYRUP: Combine syrup ingredients in small saucepan and bring to full boil over medium-high heat, stirring occasionally to ensure that sugar dissolves. Transfer to 2-cup liquid measuring cup and set aside to cool while making and baking baklava; when syrup is cool, discard spices and lemon zest. (Cooled syrup can be refrigerated in airtight container for up to 4 days.)

2. FOR THE NUT FILLING: Pulse almonds in food processor until very finely chopped, about twenty 1-second pulses; transfer to medium bowl. Pulse walnuts in food processor until very finely chopped, about fifteen 1-second pulses; transfer to bowl with almonds and toss to combine. Measure out 1 tablespoon nuts and set aside for garnish. Add cinnamon, cloves, sugar, and salt; toss well to combine.

3. TO ASSEMBLE AND BAKE: Melt butter in small saucepan over medium-low heat. Remove pan from heat and let stand for 10 minutes. Using spoon, carefully skim off foam from surface. Spoon butterfat into bowl, leaving water and milk solids in saucepan and tipping saucepan gently and only when it becomes necessary. Brush 13 by 9-inch traditional (not non-stick) baking pan with some of melted butter. Adjust oven rack to lower-middle position and heat oven to 300 degrees. Unwrap and unfold phyllo on large cutting board; carefully smooth with hands to flatten. Using baking pan as guide, cut sheets cross-wise with chef's knife, yielding two roughly evenly sized stacks of phyllo (one may be narrower than other). Cover with plastic wrap, then damp dish towel to prevent drying.

4. Place one phyllo sheet (from wider stack) in bottom of baking pan and brush until completely coated with butter. Repeat with 7 more phyllo sheets (from wider stack), brushing each with butter.

5. Evenly distribute about 1 cup nuts over phyllo. Cover nuts with phyllo sheet (from narrower stack) and dab with butter (phyllo will slip if butter is brushed on). Repeat with 5 more phyllo sheets (from narrower stack), staggering sheets slightly if necessary to cover nuts, and brushing each with butter. Repeat layering with additional 1 cup nuts, 6 sheets phyllo, and remaining 1 cup nuts. Finish with 8 to 10 sheets phyllo (from wider stack), using nicest and most intact sheets for uppermost layers and brushing each except final sheet with butter. Use palms of hands to compress layers, working from center outward to press out any air pockets. Spoon 4 tablespoons butter on top layer and brush to cover all surfaces. Use bread knife or other serrated knife with pointed tip in gentle sawing motion to cut baklava into diamonds, rotating pan as necessary to complete cuts. (Cut on bias into eighths on both diagonals.)

6. Bake until golden and crisped, about 1½ hours, rotating baking pan halfway through baking. Immediately after removing baklava from oven, pour cooled syrup over cut lines until about 2 tablespoons remain (syrup will sizzle when it hits hot pan); drizzle remaining syrup over surface. Garnish center of each piece with pinch of reserved ground nuts. Cool to room temperature on wire rack, about 3 hours, then cover with foil and let stand at least 8 hours before serving. (Once cooled, baklava can be served, but flavor and texture improve if left to stand at least 8 hours. Baklava can be wrapped tightly in foil and kept at room temperature for up to 10 days.)

Pistachio Baklava with Cardamom and Rose Water

Omit honey, lemon zest, and cinnamon in sugar syrup and increase sugar to 1¾ cups. Substitute 10 whole peppercorns for cloves and stir in 1 tablespoon rose water after discarding peppercorns. Substitute 2¾ cups shelled pistachios for almonds and walnuts and 1 teaspoon ground cardamom for cinnamon and cloves in nut filling.

CHOCOLATE TRUFFLES

WHY THIS RECIPE WORKS: The problem with many homemade truffles is that they have a dry, grainy texture. There are three keys to creating creamy, silky-smooth truffles. First, start with melted chocolate. Melting the chocolate before adding the cream allowed us to stir—rather than whisk—the two together, reducing the incorporation of air that can cause grittiness. Second, add corn syrup and butter. Corn syrup smoothed over the gritty texture of the sugar, and butter introduced silkiness. Finally, cooling down the ganache gradually before chilling prevented the formation of grainy crystals.

Chocolate Truffles

MAKES 64 TRUFFLES

In step 5, running your knife under hot water and wiping it dry makes cutting the chocolate easier. We recommend using Callebaut Intense Dark L-60-40NV or Ghirardelli Bittersweet Chocolate Baking Bar. If giving the truffles as a gift, set them in 1½-inch candy cup liners in a gift box and keep them chilled.

GANACHE

- 2 cups (12 ounces) bittersweet chocolate, roughly chopped
- ½ cup heavy cream
- 2 tablespoons light corn syrup
- ½ teaspoon vanilla extract
- Pinch salt
- 1½ tablespoons unsalted butter, cut into 8 pieces and softened

COATING

- 1 cup (3 ounces) Dutch-processed cocoa
- ¼ cup (1 ounce) confectioners' sugar

1. FOR THE GANACHE: Lightly coat 8-inch baking dish with vegetable oil spray. Make parchment sling by folding 2 long sheets of parchment so that they are as wide as baking pan. Lay sheets of parchment in pan perpendicular to each other, with extra hanging over edges of pan. Push parchment into corners and up sides of pan, smoothing flush to pan.

2. Microwave chocolate in medium bowl at 50 percent power, stirring occasionally, until mostly melted and a few small chocolate pieces remain, 2 to 3 minutes; set aside. Microwave cream in measuring cup until warm to touch, about 30 seconds. Stir corn syrup, vanilla, and salt into cream and pour mixture over chocolate. Cover bowl with plastic wrap, set aside for 3 minutes, and then stir with wooden spoon to combine. Stir in butter, one piece at a time, until fully incorporated.

3. Using rubber spatula, transfer ganache to prepared pan and set aside at room temperature for 2 hours. Cover pan and transfer to refrigerator; chill for at least 2 hours. (Ganache can be stored, refrigerated, for up to 2 days.)

4. FOR THE COATING: Sift cocoa and sugar through fine-mesh strainer into large bowl. Sift again into large cake pan and set aside.

5. Gripping overhanging parchment, lift ganache from pan. Cut ganache into sixty-four 1-inch squares (8 rows by 8 rows). (If ganache cracks during slicing, let sit at room temperature for 5 to 10 minutes and then proceed.) Dust hands lightly with cocoa mixture to prevent ganache from sticking and roll each square into ball. Transfer balls to cake pan with cocoa mixture and roll to evenly coat. Lightly shake truffles in hand over pan to remove excess coating. Transfer coated truffles to airtight container and repeat until all ganache squares are rolled and coated. Cover container and refrigerate for at least 2 hours or up to 1 week. Let truffles sit at room temperature for 5 to 10 minutes before serving.

Hazelnut-Mocha Truffles

Substitute 2 tablespoons Frangelico (hazelnut-flavored liqueur) and 1 tablespoon espresso powder for vanilla. For coating, omit confectioners' sugar and use enough cocoa to coat hands while shaping truffles. Roll shaped truffles in 1½ cups finely chopped toasted hazelnuts.

BEHIND THE SCENES

ERIN KNOWS BEST

Erin McMurrer is our test kitchen director. She oversees all the recipe testing and development in the test kitchen, but one of her most important jobs is to keep an eye on new test cooks to make sure they're keeping up with test kitchen standards. And like the proverbial mother with eyes in the back of her head, Erin doesn't miss much. You'll often hear her issuing gentle admonitions to new test cooks throughout the day. Where do the test cooks sometimes fall short? Cutting vegetables into perfect dice? Filleting fish properly? Efficiently frenching racks of lamb? Not even close. They sometimes neglect to thoroughly scrape out the contents of their measuring cups. Other than the waste factor, there is a second important reason Erin wants to make sure all the ingredients make it into the mixing bowl—it can often make or break a recipe.

To prove this point, we baked two batches of molasses spice cookies. In one batch we used a rubber spatula to scrape every last bit of molasses (an especially viscous ingredient) from the measuring cup and in the other, we simply poured the molasses from the cup, which left some residue behind (nearly 2 tablespoons!). The results were remarkable. The cookies made with less molasses were less flavorful and they were also dry and cakey as opposed to the cookies using the full amount of molasses, which were richly flavored, moist, and chewy.

So whether you're a test cook or home cook, heed Erin's advice and take a few extra minutes to scrape out your measuring cups—it makes a difference.

CHAPTER 23

A PIECE OF CAKE

OLIVE OIL CAKE

WHY THIS RECIPE WORKS: We wanted our simple olive oil cake to have a light yet plush crumb, with a subtle but noticeable olive oil flavor. Whipping the sugar with whole eggs, rather than just the whites, produced a fine texture that was airy but sturdy enough to support the olive oil–rich batter. To emphasize the defining flavor, we opted for a good-quality extra-virgin olive oil and accentuated its fruitiness with a tiny bit of lemon zest. Sugar created a crackly topping that added a touch of sweetness and sophistication.

Olive Oil Cake
SERVES 8 TO 10

For the best flavor, use a fresh, high-quality extra-virgin olive oil. If your springform pan is prone to leaking, place a rimmed baking sheet on the oven floor to catch any drips. Leftover cake can be wrapped in plastic wrap and stored at room temperature for up to three days.

- 1¾ cups (8¾ ounces) all-purpose flour
- 1 teaspoon baking powder
- ¾ teaspoon salt
- 3 large eggs
- 1¼ cups (8¾ ounces) plus 2 tablespoons sugar
- ¼ teaspoon grated lemon zest
- ¾ cup extra-virgin olive oil
- ¾ cup milk

1. Adjust oven rack to middle position and heat oven to 350 degrees. Grease 9-inch springform pan. Whisk flour, baking powder, and salt together in bowl.

2. Using stand mixer fitted with whisk attachment, whip eggs on medium speed until foamy, about 1 minute. Add 1¼ cups sugar and lemon zest, increase speed to high, and whip until mixture is fluffy and pale yellow, about 3 minutes. Reduce speed to medium and, with mixer running, slowly pour in oil. Mix until oil is fully incorporated, about 1 min-

ute. Add half of flour mixture and mix on low speed until incorporated, about 1 minute, scraping down bowl as needed. Add milk and mix until combined, about 30 seconds. Add remaining flour mixture and mix until just incorporated, about 1 minute, scraping down bowl as needed.

3. Transfer batter to prepared pan; sprinkle remaining 2 tablespoons sugar over entire surface. Bake until cake is deep golden brown and toothpick inserted in center comes out with few crumbs attached, 40 to 45 minutes. Transfer pan to wire rack and let cool for 15 minutes. Remove side of pan and let cake cool completely, about 1½ hours. Cut into wedges and serve.

ANGEL FOOD CAKE

WHY THIS RECIPE WORKS: At its heavenly best, an angel food cake should be tall and perfectly shaped, have a snowy-white, tender crumb, and be encased in a thin, delicate golden crust. The difficulty with making a great angel food cake is that it requires a delicate balance of ingredients and proper cooking techniques. In particular, since this cake is leavened only with beaten egg whites, it is critical that you whip them correctly. Over beaten egg whites produce a flatter cake.

First, we found it key to create a stable egg-white base, starting the whites at medium-low speed just to break them up into a froth and increasing the speed to medium-high speed to form soft, billowy mounds. Next, the sugar should be added, a tablespoon at a time. Once all the sugar is added, the whites become shiny and form soft peaks when the beater is lifted. A delicate touch is required when incorporating the remaining ingredients, such as the flour, which should be sifted over the batter and gently folded in. Angel food cakes are baked in a tube pan. We like to use a tube pan with a removable bottom but a pan without one can be lined with parchment paper. We avoid greasing the sides of the pan so that the cake can climb up and cling to the sides as it bakes—a greased pan will produce a disappointingly short cake. Follow our instructions and you'll be rewarded with the perfect tall, light yet firm angel food cake.

Angel Food Cake
SERVES 10 TO 12

If your tube pan has a removable bottom, you do not need to line it with parchment. Angel food cake can be served plain or dusted with confectioners' sugar.

- 1½ cups (10½ ounces) sugar
- ¾ cup (3 ounces) cake flour
- 12 large egg whites, at room temperature
- 1 teaspoon cream of tartar
- ¼ teaspoon table salt
- 1½ teaspoons juice from 1 lemon
- 1½ teaspoons vanilla extract
- ½ teaspoon almond extract

1. Adjust an oven rack to the lower-middle position and heat the oven to 325 degrees. Line the bottom of a 16-cup tube pan with parchment paper but do not grease. Whisk ¾ cup of the sugar and the flour together in a medium bowl.

2. In a stand mixer fitted with the whisk attachment, whip the egg whites and cream of tartar together on medium-low speed until foamy, about 1 minute. Increase the mixer speed to medium-high and whip the whites to soft, billowy mounds, about 1 minute. Gradually whip in the salt and remaining ¾ cup sugar, 1 tablespoon at a time, about 1 minute. Continue to whip the whites until they are shiny and form soft peaks, 1 to 3 minutes.

3. Whisk the lemon juice and extracts into the whipped whites by hand. Sift ¼ cup of the flour mixture over the top of the whites, then gently fold to combine with a large rubber spatula until just a few streaks of flour remain. Repeat with the remaining flour mixture, ¼ cup at a time.

4. Scrape the batter into the prepared pan and smooth the top. Wipe any drops of batter off the sides of the pan and lightly tap the pan against the countertop two or three times to settle the batter. Bake the cake until golden brown and the top springs back when pressed firmly, 50 to 60 minutes.

5. Invert the tube pan over a large metal kitchen funnel or the neck of a sturdy bottle (or, if your pan has "feet" that rise above the top edge of the pan, simply let the cake rest upside down). Cool the cake completely, upside down, 2 to 3 hours.

6. Run a small knife around the edge of the cake to loosen. Gently tap the pan upside down on the countertop to release the cake. Peel off the parchment paper, turn the cake right side up onto a serving platter, and serve.

CHOCOLATE BUNDT CAKE

WHY THIS RECIPE WORKS: A Bundt cake is the pinnacle of cake-baking simplicity. With its decorative shape, this cake doesn't require frosting or fussy finishing techniques. We wanted a cake that would deliver that moment of pure chocolate ecstasy with the first bite—a chocolate Bundt cake that tastes every bit as good as it looks, with a fine crumb, moist texture, and rich chocolate flavor.

We intensified the chocolate flavor by using both bittersweet chocolate and natural cocoa and dissolving them in boiling water, which "bloomed" their flavor. We used sour cream and brown sugar instead of white to add moisture and flavor. Finally, we further enhanced flavor with a little espresso powder and a generous amount of vanilla extract, both of which complemented the floral nuances of the chocolate.

Rich Chocolate Bundt Cake
SERVES 12

We prefer natural cocoa here because Dutch-processed cocoa will result in a compromised rise. For an accurate measurement of boiling water, bring a kettle of water to a boil, then measure out the desired amount. The cake can be served with just a dusting of confectioners' sugar but is easily made more impressive with lightly sweetened whipped cream and raspberries.

12	tablespoons (1½ sticks) unsalted butter, softened, plus 1 tablespoon, melted, for the pan
¾	cup natural cocoa powder, plus 1 tablespoon for the pan (see note)
6	ounces bittersweet chocolate, chopped coarse
1	teaspoon instant espresso powder (optional)
¾	cup boiling water (see note)
1	cup sour cream, at room temperature
1¾	cups (8¾ ounces) unbleached all-purpose flour
1	teaspoon table salt
1	teaspoon baking soda
2	cups packed (14 ounces) light brown sugar
1	tablespoon vanilla extract
5	large eggs, at room temperature
	Confectioners' sugar, for dusting (see note)

1. Stir together the 1 tablespoon melted butter and 1 tablespoon of the cocoa in a small bowl until a paste forms. Using a pastry brush, coat all the interior surfaces of a standard 12-cup Bundt pan. (If the mixture becomes too thick to brush on, microwave it for 10 to 20 seconds, or until warm and softened.) Adjust an oven rack to the lower-middle position and heat the oven to 350 degrees.

2. Combine the remaining ¾ cup cocoa, the chocolate, and espresso powder (if using) in a medium heatproof bowl. Pour the boiling water over and whisk until smooth. Cool to room temperature; then whisk in the sour cream. Whisk the flour, salt, and baking soda in a second bowl to combine.

3. In a stand mixer fitted with the paddle attachment, beat the remaining 12 tablespoons butter, the brown sugar, and vanilla on medium-high speed until pale and fluffy, about 3 minutes. Reduce the speed to medium and add the eggs one at a time, mixing for about 30 seconds after each addition and scraping down the bowl with a rubber spatula after the first two additions. Reduce to medium-low speed (the batter may appear separated); add about one-third of the flour mixture and half of the chocolate mixture and mix until just incorporated, about 20 seconds. Scrape the bowl and repeat using half of the remaining flour mixture and all of the remaining chocolate mixture; add the remaining flour mixture and beat until just incorporated, about 10 seconds. Scrape the bowl and mix on medium-low speed until the batter is thoroughly combined, about 30 seconds.

4. Transfer the batter to the prepared pan, smoothing the top with a rubber spatula. Lightly tap the pan against the countertop two or three times to settle the batter. Bake until a toothpick inserted into the center comes out with a few crumbs attached, 45 to 50 minutes, rotating the pan halfway through the baking time. Cool the cake in the pan on a wire rack for 10 minutes, then invert the cake directly onto the wire rack; cool to room temperature, about 2 hours. Dust with confectioners' sugar, transfer to a serving platter, cut into slices, and serve.

CIDER-GLAZED APPLE BUNDT CAKE

WHY THIS RECIPE WORKS: We managed to pack the equivalent of 4½ pounds of fruit into our apple cake and its glaze. Baking the thick, dense batter in a Bundt pan rather than a round pan allowed heat to flow through the center of the cake, ensuring that it baked evenly edge to edge. Mixing reduced apple cider into the batter, brushing it onto the cake, and using it to flavor the icing drizzled on top provided layers of pervasive apple flavor. Minimizing the spices allowed true apple flavor to shine.

Cider-Glazed Apple Bundt Cake
SERVES 12 TO 16

For the sake of efficiency, we recommend that you begin boiling the cider before assembling the rest of the ingredients. Reducing the cider to exactly 1 cup is important to the success of this recipe. If you accidentally over-reduce the cider, make up the difference with water. Baking spray that contains flour can be used to grease and flour the pan. We like the tartness of Granny Smith apples in this recipe, but any variety of apple will work. You may shred the apples with the large shredding disc of a food processor or with the large holes of a box grater.

4	cups apple cider
3¾	cups (18¾ ounces) all-purpose flour
1½	teaspoons salt
1½	teaspoons baking powder
½	teaspoon baking soda
¾	teaspoon ground cinnamon
¼	teaspoon ground allspice
¾	cup (3 ounces) confectioners' sugar
16	tablespoons (2 sticks) unsalted butter, melted
1½	cups packed (10½ ounces) dark brown sugar
3	large eggs
2	teaspoons vanilla extract
1½	pounds Granny Smith apples, peeled, cored, and shredded (3 cups)

1. Boil cider in 12-inch skillet over high heat until reduced to 1 cup, 20 to 25 minutes. While cider is reducing, adjust oven rack to middle position and heat oven to 350 degrees. Grease and flour 12-cup nonstick Bundt pan. Whisk flour, salt, baking powder, baking soda, cinnamon, and allspice together in large bowl until combined. Place confectioners' sugar in small bowl.

2. Add 2 tablespoons reduced cider to confectioners' sugar, and whisk to form smooth icing. Cover icing with plastic wrap and set aside. Pour ½ cup reduced cider into large bowl. Set remaining 6 tablespoons reduced cider aside to brush over baked cake.

3. Add butter, brown sugar, eggs, and vanilla to ½ cup cider reduction and whisk until smooth. Pour cider mixture over flour mixture, and stir with rubber spatula until almost fully combined (some streaks of flour will remain). Stir in apples and any accumulated juices until evenly distributed. Transfer mixture to prepared Bundt pan and smooth top. Bake until skewer inserted in center of cake comes out clean, 55 to 65 minutes.

4. Transfer pan to wire rack set in rimmed baking sheet. Brush exposed surface of cake lightly with 1 tablespoon reserved cider reduction. Allow cake to cool for 10 minutes. Invert cake onto wire rack. Brush top and sides with remaining 5 tablespoons reserved cider reduction. Cool cake for 20 minutes. Stir icing to loosen, and drizzle over cake. Cool cake completely, at least 2 hours, before serving. (Leftover cake may be wrapped loosely and stored at room temperature for up to three days.)

MARBLED BLUEBERRY BUNDT CAKE

WHY THIS RECIPE WORKS: Oversize, bland cultivated blueberries wreak havoc in a cake. The berries refuse to stay suspended in the batter and burst into bland, soggy pockets in the heat of the oven. We solved these problems by pureeing the fruit, seasoning it with sugar and lemon, and bumping up its natural pectin content with low-sugar pectin for a thickened, fresh-tasting filling that can be swirled throughout the cake.

Marbled Blueberry Bundt Cake

SERVES 12

Spray the pan well in step 1 to prevent sticking. If you don't have baking spray with flour, mix 1 tablespoon melted butter and 1 tablespoon flour into a paste and brush inside the pan. For fruit pectin we recommend both Sure-Jell for Less or No Sugar Needed Recipes and Ball RealFruit Low or No-Sugar Needed Pectin. If using frozen berries, thaw them before blending in step 3. This cake can be served plain or with Lemon Glaze or Cinnamon Whipped Cream (recipes follow).

CAKE

- 3 cups (15 ounces) all-purpose flour
- 1½ teaspoons baking powder
- ¾ teaspoon baking soda
- 1 teaspoon salt
- ½ teaspoon ground cinnamon
- ¾ cup buttermilk
- 2 teaspoons grated lemon zest plus 3 tablespoons juice
- 2 teaspoons vanilla extract
- 3 large eggs plus 1 large yolk, room temperature
- 18 tablespoons (2¼ sticks) unsalted butter, softened
- 2 cups (14 ounces) sugar

FILLING

- ¾ cup (5¼ ounces) sugar
- 3 tablespoons low- or no-sugar-needed fruit pectin
  Pinch salt
- 10 ounces (2 cups) fresh or thawed frozen blueberries
- 1 teaspoon grated lemon zest plus 1 tablespoon juice

1. FOR THE CAKE: Adjust oven rack to lower-middle position and heat oven to 325 degrees. Heavily spray 12-cup nonstick Bundt pan with baking spray with flour. Whisk flour, baking powder, baking soda, salt, and cinnamon together in large bowl. Whisk buttermilk, lemon zest and juice, and vanilla together in medium bowl. Gently whisk eggs and yolk to combine in third bowl.

2. Using stand mixer fitted with paddle, beat butter and sugar on medium-high speed until pale and fluffy, about 3 minutes, scraping down bowl as needed. Reduce speed to medium and beat in half of eggs until incorporated, about 15 seconds. Repeat with remaining eggs, scraping down bowl after incorporating. Reduce speed to low and add one-third of flour mixture, followed by half of buttermilk mixture, mixing until just incorporated after each addition, about 5 seconds. Repeat using half of remaining flour mixture and all of remaining buttermilk mixture. Scrape down bowl, add remaining flour mixture, and mix at medium-low speed until batter is thoroughly combined, about 15 seconds. Remove bowl from mixer and fold batter once or twice with rubber spatula to incorporate any remaining flour. Cover bowl with plastic wrap and set aside while preparing filling (batter will inflate a bit).

3. FOR THE FILLING: Whisk sugar, pectin, and salt together in small saucepan. Process blueberries in blender until mostly smooth, about 1 minute. Transfer ¼ cup puree and lemon zest to saucepan with sugar mixture and stir to thoroughly combine. Heat sugar-blueberry mixture over medium heat until just simmering, about 3 minutes, stirring frequently to dissolve sugar and pectin. Transfer mixture to medium bowl and let cool for 5 minutes. Add remaining puree and lemon juice to cooled mixture and whisk to combine. Let sit until slightly set, about 8 minutes.

4. Spoon half of batter into prepared pan and smooth top. Using back of spoon, create ½-inch-deep channel in center of batter. Spoon half of filling into channel. Using butter knife or small offset spatula, thoroughly swirl filling into batter (there should be no large pockets of filling remaining). Repeat swirling step with remaining batter and filling.

5. Bake until top is golden brown and skewer inserted in center comes out with no crumbs attached, 60 to 70 minutes. Let cake cool in pan on wire rack for 10 minutes, then invert cake directly onto wire rack. Let cake cool for at least 3 hours before serving.

Lemon Glaze

MAKES ABOUT 2 CUPS

This glaze can be used with Marbled Blueberry Bundt Cake or another Bundt cake.

3–4 tablespoons lemon juice (2 lemons)
2 cups (8 ounces) confectioners' sugar

1. While cake is baking, whisk together 3 tablespoons lemon juice and sugar until smooth, gradually adding more lemon juice as needed until glaze is thick but still pourable (mixture should leave faint trail across bottom of mixing bowl when drizzled from whisk).

2. After cake has been removed from pan and inverted onto wire rack set in baking sheet, pour half of glaze over warm cake and let cool for 1 hour. Pour remaining glaze evenly over cake and continue to let cool to room temperature, at least 2 hours longer.

Cinnamon Whipped Cream

MAKES ABOUT 2 CUPS

For the best texture, whip the cream until soft peaks just form. Do not over whip.

1 cup heavy cream
2 tablespoons confectioners' sugar
¼ teaspoon ground cinnamon
  Pinch salt

Using stand mixer fitted with whisk, whip all ingredients on medium-low speed until foamy, about 1 minute. Increase speed to high and whip until soft peaks form, 1 to 3 minutes.

LEMON BUNDT CAKE

WHY THIS RECIPE WORKS: Lemons are tart, brash, and aromatic. Why, then, is it so hard to capture their assertive flavor in a straightforward Bundt cake? The flavor of lemon juice is drastically muted when exposed to the heat of an oven, and its acidity can wreak havoc on the delicate nature of baked goods. We wanted to develop a Bundt cake with potent lemon flavor without ruining its texture.

We developed a battery of tests challenging classic lemon Bundt cake ingredient proportions, finally deciding to increase the butter and to replace the milk with buttermilk. We also found that creaming was necessary to achieve a light and even crumb. But we still needed to maximize the lemon flavor; we couldn't get the flavor we needed from lemon juice alone without using so much that the cake fell apart when sliced. We turned to zest and found that three lemons' worth gave the cake a perfumed lemon flavor, though we needed to give the zest a brief soak in lemon juice to eliminate its fibrous texture. The final challenge was the glaze, and a simple mixture of lemon juice, buttermilk, and confectioners' sugar made the grade.

Lemon Bundt Cake

SERVES 12

The cake has a light, fluffy texture when eaten the day it is baked, but if well wrapped and held at room temperature overnight its texture becomes more dense—like that of pound cake—the following day.

CAKE

18 tablespoons (2¼ sticks) unsalted butter, at room temperature, plus 1 tablespoon, melted, for the pan
3 cups (15 ounces) unbleached all-purpose flour, plus 1 tablespoon for the pan
3 tablespoons grated zest plus 3 tablespoons juice from 3 lemons
1 teaspoon baking powder
½ teaspoon baking soda
1 teaspoon table salt
¾ cup buttermilk
1 teaspoon vanilla extract
3 large eggs plus 1 large egg yolk, at room temperature
2 cups (14 ounces) granulated sugar

GLAZE

2 cups (8 ounces) confectioners' sugar
2–3 tablespoons juice from 1 lemon
1 tablespoon buttermilk

1. FOR THE CAKE: Adjust an oven rack to the lower-middle position and heat the oven to 350 degrees. Stir together the 1 tablespoon melted butter and 1 tablespoon of the flour in a small bowl until a paste forms. Using a pastry brush, coat all the interior surfaces of a standard 12-cup Bundt pan. (If the mixture becomes too thick to brush on, microwave it for 10 to 20 seconds, or until warm and softened.) Mince the lemon zest to a fine paste (you should have about 2 tablespoons). Combine the zest and lemon juice in a small bowl; set aside to soften, 10 to 15 minutes.

2. Whisk the remaining 3 cups flour, the baking powder, baking soda, and salt in a large bowl. Combine the lemon juice mixture, buttermilk, and vanilla in a medium bowl. In a small bowl, gently whisk the whole eggs and yolk to combine.

In a stand mixer fitted with the paddle attachment, beat the remaining 18 tablespoons butter and the granulated sugar at medium-high speed until pale and fluffy, about 3 minutes. Reduce to medium speed and add half of the eggs, mixing until incorporated, about 15 seconds; scrape down the bowl with a rubber spatula. Repeat with the remaining eggs; scrape down the bowl again. Reduce to low speed; add about one-third of the flour mixture, followed by half of the buttermilk mixture, mixing until just incorporated after each addition (about 5 seconds). Repeat using half of the remaining flour mixture and all of the remaining buttermilk mixture. Scrape down the bowl and add the remaining flour mixture; mix at medium-low speed until the batter is thoroughly combined, about 15 seconds. Transfer the batter to the prepared pan, smoothing the top with a rubber spatula. Lightly tap the pan against the countertop two or three times to settle the batter.

3. Bake until the top is golden brown and a toothpick inserted into the center comes out with no crumbs attached, 45 to 50 minutes, rotating the pan halfway through the baking time.

4. FOR THE GLAZE: While the cake is baking, whisk the confectioners' sugar, 2 tablespoons of the lemon juice, and the buttermilk until smooth, adding more lemon juice gradually as needed until the glaze is thick but still pourable. Cool the cake in the pan on a wire rack set over a baking sheet for 10 minutes, then invert the cake directly onto the rack. Pour half of the glaze over the warm cake and cool for 1 hour; pour the remaining glaze evenly over the top of the cake and continue to cool to room temperature, at least 2 hours. Cut into slices and serve.

LEMON POUND CAKE

WHY THIS RECIPE WORKS: Pound cakes often turn out spongy, rubbery, heavy, and dry—and lemon pound cakes often lack true lemon flavor. We wanted to produce a superior pound cake (fine-crumbed, rich, moist, and buttery) while making the process as simple and foolproof as possible.

After less-than-successful results with a stand mixer and a hand mixer, we turned to the food processor to mix our cake. It ensured a perfect emulsification of the eggs, sugar, and melted butter (we found that a blender worked, too). Cake flour produced a tender crumb, but our cake was still a bit heavy. We fixed matters with the addition of baking powder, which increased lift and produced a consistent, fine crumb. Finally, in addition to mixing lemon zest into the cake batter, we glazed the finished cake with lemon sugar syrup—but first we poked holes all over the cake to ensure that the tangy, sweet glaze infused the cake with a blast of bright lemon flavor.

Lemon Pound Cake

MAKES ONE 8-INCH LOAF, SERVING 8

You can use a blender instead of a food processor to mix the batter. To add the butter, remove the center cap of the lid so it can be drizzled into the whirling blender with minimal splattering. This batter looks almost like a thick pancake batter and is very fluid.

CAKE

- 16 tablespoons (2 sticks) unsalted butter, plus 1 tablespoon, softened, for the pan
- 1½ cups (6 ounces) cake flour, plus 1 tablespoon for the pan
- 1 teaspoon baking powder
- ½ teaspoon table salt
- 1¼ cups (8¾ ounces) sugar
- 2 tablespoons grated zest plus 2 teaspoons juice from 1 lemon
- 4 large eggs, at room temperature
- 1½ teaspoons vanilla extract

GLAZE

- ½ cup (3½ ounces) sugar
- ¼ cup juice from 2 lemons

1. FOR THE CAKE: Adjust an oven rack to the middle position and heat the oven to 350 degrees. Grease an 8½ by 4½-inch loaf pan with 1 tablespoon of the softened butter; dust with 1 tablespoon of the flour, tapping out the excess. In a medium bowl, whisk together the remaining 1½ cups flour, the baking powder, and salt; set aside.

2. Melt the remaining 16 tablespoons butter in a small saucepan over medium heat. Whisk the melted butter thoroughly to reincorporate any separated milk solids.

3. In a food processor, pulse the sugar and zest until combined, about 5 pulses. Add the lemon juice, eggs, and vanilla; process until combined, about 5 seconds. With the machine running, add the melted butter through the feed tube in a steady stream (this should take about 20 seconds). Transfer the mixture to a large bowl. Sift the flour mixture over the egg mixture in three additions, whisking gently after each addition until just combined.

4. Pour the batter into the prepared pan and bake for 15 minutes. Reduce the oven temperature to 325 degrees and continue to bake until deep golden brown and a toothpick inserted in the center comes out clean, about 35 minutes, rotating the pan halfway through the baking time. Cool in the pan for 10 minutes, then turn onto a wire rack. Poke the top and sides of the cake throughout with a toothpick. Cool to room temperature, at least 1 hour. (The cooled cake can be wrapped tightly in plastic wrap and stored at room temperature for up to 5 days.)

5. FOR THE GLAZE: While the cake is cooling, bring the sugar and lemon juice to a boil in a small saucepan, stirring occasionally to dissolve the sugar. Reduce the heat to low and simmer until thickened slightly, about 2 minutes. Brush the top and sides of the cake with the glaze and cool to room temperature.

APPLESAUCE CAKE

WHY THIS RECIPE WORKS: Applesauce cakes run the gamut from dense, chunky fruitcakes to gummy "health" cakes without much flavor. We wanted a moist and tender cake that actually tasted like its namesake.

It was easy to achieve the looser, more casual crumb that is best suited to a rustic snack cake. Since this texture is similar to that of quick breads and muffins, we used the same technique, i.e., mixing the wet ingredients separately and then gently adding the dry ingredients by hand. The harder challenge was to develop more apple flavor—simply adding more applesauce made for a gummy cake and fresh apples added too much moisture. But two other sources worked well. Apple cider, reduced to a syrup, contributed a pleasing sweetness and a slight tang without excess moisture. And plumping dried apples in the cider while it was reducing added even more apple taste without making the cake chunky. With such great apple flavor, we didn't want the cake to be too sweet or rich, so we rejected the idea of topping the cake with a glaze or frosting. But we found we liked the modicum of textural contrast provided by a simple sprinkling of spiced granulated sugar.

Applesauce Snack Cake

SERVES 9

This recipe can be easily doubled and baked in a 13 by 9-inch baking dish. If doubling the recipe, give the cider and dried apple mixture about 20 minutes to reduce, and bake the cake for about 45 minutes. The cake is very moist, so it is best to err on the side of overdone when testing its doneness. The test kitchen prefers the rich flavor of cider, but apple juice can be substituted.

    1 cup apple cider (see note)
    ¾ cup (2 ounces) dried apples, cut into ½-inch pieces
    1½ cups (7½ ounces) unbleached all-purpose flour
    1 teaspoon baking soda
    ⅔ cup (4⅔ ounces) sugar
    ½ teaspoon ground cinnamon
    ¼ teaspoon ground nutmeg
    ⅛ teaspoon ground cloves
    1 cup unsweetened applesauce, at room temperature
    1 large egg, at room temperature, lightly beaten
    ½ teaspoon table salt
    8 tablespoons (1 stick) unsalted butter, melted and
       cooled slightly
    1 teaspoon vanilla extract

1. Adjust an oven rack to the middle position and heat the oven to 325 degrees. Cut a 16-inch length of parchment paper or foil and fold lengthwise to a 7-inch width. Grease an 8-inch square baking dish and fit the parchment into the dish, pushing it into the corners and up the sides; allow the excess to overhang the edges of the dish.

2. Bring the cider and dried apples to a simmer in a small saucepan over medium heat; cook until the liquid evaporates and the mixture appears dry, about 15 minutes. Cool to room temperature.

3. Whisk the flour and baking soda in a medium bowl to combine; set aside. In a second medium bowl, whisk the sugar, cinnamon, nutmeg, and cloves together. Measure

2 tablespoons of the sugar-spice mixture into a small bowl and set aside for the topping.

4. In a food processor, process the cooled dried-apple mixture and applesauce until smooth, 20 to 30 seconds, scraping down the sides of the bowl as needed; set aside. Whisk the egg and salt in a large bowl to combine. Add the sugar-spice mixture and whisk continuously until well combined and light colored, about 20 seconds. Add the butter in three additions, whisking after each addition. Add the applesauce mixture and vanilla and whisk to combine. Add the flour mixture to the wet ingredients; using a rubber spatula, fold gently until just combined and evenly moistened.

5. Transfer the batter to the prepared pan, smoothing the top with a rubber spatula. Lightly tap the pan against the countertop two or three times to settle the batter. Sprinkle the reserved 2 tablespoons sugar-spice mixture evenly over the batter. Bake until a toothpick inserted into the center comes out clean, 35 to 40 minutes, rotating the pan halfway through the baking time. Cool the cake to room temperature in the pan on a wire rack, about 2 hours. Remove the cake from the pan by lifting the parchment overhang and transfer to a cutting board. Cut the cake into squares and serve.

OATMEAL CAKE

WHY THIS RECIPE WORKS: While we love the broiled icing on this classic snack cake, we find that the cake itself is often dense, gummy, and bland. And the icing isn't always perfect, either; it can be saccharine sweet and tend toward greasiness. We wanted a moist, not dense, cake with buttery undertones topped by a broiled icing that features chewy coconut, crunchy nuts, and a butterscotch-like flavor.

We solved the problem of denseness by replacing some of the brown sugar with granulated sugar—less moist than brown sugar, granulated sugar lightened the cake's texture. We also reduced the proportion of flour to oats, using the minimum amount of flour needed to keep the cake from collapsing into crumbs. The cake was now sufficiently light, and its more moderate sweetness made it better suited to a sugary icing. We still had to tackle the gumminess, however, which was created partly by soaking the oats in water; the hydrated oats were a sticky mess when we stirred them into the batter. But simply folding in dried oats didn't work—they never fully hydrated during baking, and tasted raw and chewy in the finished cake. The answer proved to be soaking the oats in room-temperature rather than boiling water, minimizing the amount of released starch. As for the type of oats, quick-cooking worked best. Unlike the cake, the icing only required a few tweaks. Cutting back on the sugar brought the sweetness in line, using melted butter (rather than creaming the butter into the sugar) simplified the recipe, and adding a splash of milk made the icing more pliable. Keeping the cake about 9 inches from the heating element produced the "crun-chewy" texture we wanted.

Oatmeal Cake with Broiled Icing

SERVES 9

Do not use old-fashioned or instant oats for this recipe. Be sure to use a metal baking dish; glass pans are not recommended when broiling. If you have a drawer-style broiler (underneath the oven), position the rack as far as possible from the broiler element and monitor the icing carefully as it cooks in step 5. A vertical sawing motion with a serrated knife works best for cutting through the crunchy icing and tender crumb.

CAKE

- 1 cup (3 ounces) quick-cooking oats (see note)
- ¾ cup water, at room temperature
- ¾ cup (3¾ ounces) unbleached all-purpose flour
- ½ teaspoon baking soda
- ½ teaspoon baking powder
- ½ teaspoon table salt
- ¼ teaspoon ground cinnamon
- ⅛ teaspoon ground nutmeg
- 4 tablespoons (½ stick) unsalted butter, softened
- ½ cup (3½ ounces) granulated sugar
- ½ cup packed (3½ ounces) light brown sugar
- 1 large egg, at room temperature
- ½ teaspoon vanilla extract

BROILED ICING

- ¼ cup packed (1¾ ounces) light brown sugar
- 3 tablespoons unsalted butter, melted and cooled
- 3 tablespoons milk
- ¾ cup sweetened shredded coconut
- ½ cup (2½ ounces) pecans, chopped

1. FOR THE CAKE: Adjust an oven rack to the middle position and heat the oven to 350 degrees. Cut two 16-inch lengths of aluminum foil and fold both lengthwise to 5-inch widths. Grease an 8-inch square metal baking dish. Fit the foil pieces into the baking dish, one overlapping the other, pushing them into the corners and up the sides of the pan; allow the excess to overhang the pan edges. Spray the foil lightly with vegetable oil spray.

2. Combine the oats and water in a medium bowl and let sit until the water is absorbed, about 5 minutes. In a second medium bowl, whisk the flour, baking soda, baking powder, salt, cinnamon, and nutmeg together.

3. In the bowl of a stand mixer fitted with the paddle attachment, beat the butter and sugars on medium speed until combined and the mixture has the consistency of damp sand, 2 to 4 minutes, scraping down the bowl with a rubber spatula halfway through mixing. Add the egg and vanilla; beat until combined, about 30 seconds. Add the flour mixture in two additions and mix until just incorporated, about 30 seconds. Add the soaked oats and mix until combined, about 15 seconds.

4. Give the batter a final stir with a rubber spatula to make sure it is thoroughly combined. Transfer the batter to the prepared pan and lightly tap it against the countertop two or three times to settle the batter; smooth the surface with the spatula. Bake the cake until a toothpick inserted into the center comes out with a few crumbs attached, 30 to 35 minutes, rotating the pan halfway through the baking time. Cool the cake slightly in the pan, at least 10 minutes.

5. FOR THE BROILED ICING: While the cake cools, adjust an oven rack about 9 inches from the broiler element and heat the broiler. In a medium bowl, whisk the brown sugar, melted butter, and milk together; stir in the coconut and pecans. Spread the mixture evenly over the warm cake. Broil until the topping is bubbling and golden, 3 to 5 minutes.

6. Cool the cake in the pan for 1 hour. To remove the cake from the pan, pick up the overhanging edges of the foil and transfer the cake to a platter. Gently push the side of the cake with a knife and remove the foil, one piece at a time. Cut the cake into squares and serve.

PEAR-WALNUT UPSIDE-DOWN CAKE

WHY THIS RECIPE WORKS: Pears are sometimes referred to as the queen of fruit, but, despite their subtle floral flavor and graceful shape, their popularity in desserts has always been a distant second to apples. We were determined to create an elegant cake that really showcased the pears. We settled on Bosc pears; since they have dense flesh, they hold their shape after baking. Cutting the pears into wedges allowed them to be baked raw but still be manageable to eat with the cake. Instead of a sweet, somewhat dense yellow cake, we made a walnut-based cake, which was light but sturdy, earthy-tasting and less sweet, and visually attractive. Lining the cake pan (a light-colored pan helped the cake cook more evenly) with parchment and removing the cake from

the pan after 15 minutes—good practice for any upside-down cake—allowed the top to set while preventing the bottom of the cake from steaming and turning soggy.

Pear-Walnut Upside-Down Cake

SERVES 8 TO 10

We strongly recommend baking this cake in a light-colored cake pan with sides that are at least 2 inches tall. If using a dark-colored pan, start checking for doneness at 1 hour, and note that the cake may dome in the center and the topping may become too sticky. Serve with crème fraîche or lightly sweetened whipped cream.

TOPPING

- 4 tablespoons unsalted butter, melted
- ½ cup packed (3½ ounces) dark brown sugar
- 2 teaspoons cornstarch
- ⅛ teaspoon salt
- 3 ripe but firm Bosc pears (8 ounces each)

CAKE

- 1 cup walnuts, toasted
- ½ cup (2½ ounces) all-purpose flour
- ½ teaspoon salt
- ¼ teaspoon baking powder
- ⅛ teaspoon baking soda
- 3 large eggs
- 1 cup (7 ounces) granulated sugar
- 4 tablespoons unsalted butter, melted
- ¼ cup vegetable oil

1. FOR THE TOPPING: Adjust oven rack to middle position and heat oven to 300 degrees. Grease 9-inch round cake pan and line bottom with parchment paper. Pour melted butter over bottom of pan and swirl to evenly coat. Combine sugar, cornstarch, and salt in small bowl and sprinkle evenly over melted butter.

NOTES FROM THE TEST KITCHEN

UNMOLDING UPSIDE-DOWN CAKES

If an upside-down cake is turned out of the pan too quickly, the bottom of the cake steams and turns gummy; if the cake cools completely in the pan, the fruit will stick.

Our approach is to line the pan with parchment paper, which ensures that the fruit releases cleanly; let the cake rest in the pan for just 15 minutes before turning it out onto a rack.

2. Peel, halve, and core pears. Set aside 1 pear half and reserve for other use. Cut remaining 5 pear halves into 4 wedges each. Arrange pears in circular pattern around cake pan with tapered ends pointing inward. Arrange two smallest pear wedges in center.

3. FOR THE CAKE: Pulse walnuts, flour, salt, baking powder, and baking soda in food processor until walnuts are finely ground, 8 to 10 pulses. Transfer walnut mixture to bowl.

4. Process eggs and sugar in now-empty processor until very pale yellow, about 2 minutes. With processor running, add melted butter and oil in steady stream until incorporated. Add walnut mixture and pulse to combine, 4 to 5 pulses. Pour batter evenly over pears (some pear may show through; cake will bake up over fruit).

5. Bake until center of cake is set and bounces back when gently pressed and toothpick inserted in center comes out clean, 1 hour 10 minutes to 1¼ hours, rotating pan after 40 minutes. Let cake cool in pan on wire rack for 15 minutes. Carefully run paring knife or offset spatula around sides of pan. Invert cake onto wire rack set in rimmed baking sheet; discard parchment. Let cake cool for about 2 hours. Transfer to serving platter, cut into wedges, and serve.

APPLE UPSIDE-DOWN CAKE

WHY THIS RECIPE WORKS: Ever since canned pineapple was introduced into this country in the early 1900s, pineapple has been synonymous with upside-down cake. But at one time, upside-down cakes were made with seasonal fruit, such as apples. We loved the idea of resurrecting apple upside-down cake. We wanted a rich buttery cake topped with tightly packed, burnished, sweet apples.

We started our testing with choosing the type of apple. Most apples turned mushy and watery and were simply too sweet, but crisp, tart Granny Smiths made the cut. Following the lead of recipes found in our research, we shingled the apples in the pan and poured the cake batter over the top. But once baked and inverted, our apple layer was shrunken and dry. The solution turned out to be increasing the number of apples, for a hefty layer of fruit.

This effort yielded better results, but we found the apples to be overcooked, so we turned to a method uncovered in our recipe for Deep-Dish Apple Pie (page 847)—we pre-cooked half the apples by sautéing them on the stovetop, then we cut the remainder thin, so they baked through evenly. For the butter cake, we tested milk, buttermilk, yogurt, and sour cream. Sour cream won hands down—its subtle tang balanced the sweetness of the cake and complemented the caramelized apples. And another addition—cornmeal—gave the cake a hint of earthy flavor and a pleasantly coarse texture. Our final discovery came when we attempted to release the cake cleanly from the pan. Typical recipes instruct a 5 to 10-minute cooling period, but we found that a full 20 minutes was required to allow the apple filling to set. And turning the cake out onto a rack to finish cooling let the bottom of the cake breathe, preventing sogginess, which is typical of so many upside-down cakes.

Apple Upside-Down Cake

SERVES 8

We like the slight coarseness that cornmeal adds to the cake, but it's fine to omit it. Golden Delicious apples can be substituted for the Granny Smiths. You will need a 9-inch nonstick cake pan with sides that are at least 2 inches high; anything shallower and the cake will overflow. Alternatively, a 10-inch ovensafe stainless steel skillet (don't use cast iron) can be used to both cook the apples and bake the cake, with the following modifications: Cook the apples in the skillet and set them aside while mixing the batter (it's OK if the skillet is still warm when the batter is added) and increase the baking time by 7 to 9 minutes. If you don't have either a 2-inch-high cake pan or an ovensafe skillet, use an 8-inch square pan.

TOPPING

- 4 tablespoons (½ stick) unsalted butter, cut into 4 pieces, plus extra for the pan
- 4 Granny Smith apples (about 2 pounds), peeled and cored (see note)
- ⅔ cup packed (4⅔ ounces) light brown sugar
- 2 teaspoons juice from 1 lemon

CAKE

- 1 cup (5 ounces) unbleached all-purpose flour
- 1 tablespoon cornmeal (optional; see note)
- 1 teaspoon baking powder
- ½ teaspoon table salt
- ¾ cup (5¼ ounces) granulated sugar
- ¼ cup packed (1¾ ounces) light brown sugar
- 2 large eggs, at room temperature
- 6 tablespoons (¾ stick) unsalted butter, melted and cooled slightly
- ½ cup sour cream
- 1 teaspoon vanilla extract

1. FOR THE TOPPING: Butter the bottom and sides of a nonstick 9-inch-wide by 2-inch-high round cake pan; set aside. Adjust an oven rack to the lowest position and heat the oven to 350 degrees.

2. Halve the apples from pole to pole. Cut 2 apples into ¼-inch-thick slices; set aside. Cut the remaining 2 apples into ½-inch-thick slices. Melt the butter in a 12-inch skillet over medium-high heat. Add the ½-inch-thick apple slices and cook, stirring two or three times, until the apples begin to caramelize, 4 to 6 minutes. (Do not fully cook the apples.) Add the ¼-inch-thick apple slices, brown sugar, and lemon juice; continue cooking, stirring constantly, until the sugar dissolves and the apples are coated, about 1 minute longer.

Transfer the apple mixture to the prepared pan and lightly press into an even layer. Set aside while preparing the cake.

3. FOR THE CAKE: Whisk the flour, cornmeal (if using), baking powder, and salt together in a medium bowl; set aside. Whisk the sugars and eggs together in a large bowl until thick and homogeneous, about 45 seconds. Slowly whisk in the butter until combined. Add the sour cream and vanilla; whisk until combined. Add the flour mixture and whisk until just combined. Pour the batter into the pan and spread evenly over the fruit. Lightly tap the pan against the countertop two or three times to settle the batter. Bake until the cake is golden brown and a toothpick inserted into the center comes out clean, 35 to 40 minutes, rotating the pan halfway through the baking time.

4. Cool the pan on a wire rack for 20 minutes. Run a small knife around the sides of the cake to loosen. Place a wire rack over the cake pan. Holding the rack tightly, invert the cake pan and wire rack together; lift off the cake pan. Place the wire rack over a baking sheet or large plate to catch any drips. If any fruit sticks to the pan bottom, remove and position it on top of the cake. Cool the cake for 20 minutes (or longer to cool it completely), then transfer it to a serving platter, cut into pieces, and serve.

Apple Upside-Down Cake with Almond

Follow the recipe for Apple Upside-Down Cake, combining ⅓ cup finely ground toasted almonds with the flour and adding 1 teaspoon almond extract with the sour cream and vanilla in step 3.

Apple Upside-Down Cake with Lemon and Thyme

Follow the recipe for Apple Upside-Down Cake, adding 1 teaspoon finely grated lemon zest and 1 teaspoon finely chopped fresh thyme leaves with the sour cream and vanilla in step 3.

FRENCH APPLE CAKE

WHY THIS RECIPE WORKS: For our own version of this classic French dessert, we wanted the best of both worlds: a dessert with a custardy, apple-rich base beneath a light, cake-like topping. To ensure that the apple slices softened fully, we microwaved them briefly to break the enzyme responsible for firming up pectin. And to create two differently textured layers from one batter, we divided the batter and added egg yolks to one part to make the custardy base and added flour to the rest to form the cake layer above it.

French Apple Cake
SERVES 8 TO 10

The microwaved apples should be pliable but not completely soft when cooked. To test for doneness, take one apple slice and try to bend it. If it snaps in half, it's too firm; microwave it for an additional 30 seconds and test again. If Calvados is unavailable, 1 tablespoon of apple brandy or white rum can be substituted.

1½	pounds Granny Smith apples, peeled, cored, cut into 8 wedges, and sliced ⅛ inch thick crosswise
1	tablespoon Calvados
1	teaspoon lemon juice
1	cup (5 ounces) plus 2 tablespoons all-purpose flour
1	cup (7 ounces) plus 1 tablespoon granulated sugar
2	teaspoons baking powder
½	teaspoon salt
1	large egg plus 2 large yolks
1	cup vegetable oil
1	cup whole milk
1	teaspoon vanilla extract
	Confectioners' sugar

1. Adjust oven rack to lower-middle position and heat oven to 325 degrees. Spray 9-inch springform pan with vegetable oil spray. Place prepared pan on rimmed baking sheet lined with aluminum foil. Place apple slices in microwave-safe pie plate, cover, and microwave until apples are pliable and slightly translucent, about 3 minutes. Toss apple slices with Calvados and lemon juice and let cool for 15 minutes.

2. Whisk 1 cup flour, 1 cup granulated sugar, baking powder, and salt together in bowl. Whisk egg, oil, milk, and vanilla together in second bowl until smooth. Add dry ingredients to wet ingredients and whisk until just combined. Transfer 1 cup batter to separate bowl and set aside.

3. Add egg yolks to remaining batter and whisk to combine. Using spatula, gently fold in cooled apples. Transfer batter to prepared pan; using offset spatula, spread batter evenly to pan edges, gently pressing on apples to create even, compact layer, and smooth surface.

4. Whisk remaining 2 tablespoons flour into reserved batter. Pour over batter in pan and spread batter evenly to pan edges and smooth surface. Sprinkle remaining 1 tablespoon granulated sugar evenly over cake.

5. Bake until center of cake is set, toothpick inserted in center comes out clean, and top is golden brown, about 1¼ hours. Transfer pan to wire rack; let cool for 5 minutes. Run paring knife around sides of pan and let cool completely, 2 to 3 hours. Dust lightly with confectioners' sugar, cut into wedges, and serve.

CARROT CAKE

WHY THIS RECIPE WORKS: A relic of the health food craze, carrot cake was once heralded for its use of vegetable oil in place of butter and carrots as a natural sweetener. Sure, the carrots add some sweetness, but they also add a lot of moisture, which is why carrot cake is invariably soggy. And oil? It makes this cake dense and, well, oily. We didn't want a greasy cake. We wanted a moist, rich cake with a tight and tender crumb and balanced spice.

We started with all-purpose flour—cake flour proved too delicate to support the grated carrots that get mixed in. For lift, we liked a combination of baking soda and baking powder. Some carrot cakes use a heavy hand with the spices and taste too much like spice cake. We took a conservative approach and used modest amounts of cinnamon, nutmeg, and cloves. After trying varying amounts of grated carrots, we settled on 3 cups for a pleasantly moist texture. One and one-half cups of vegetable oil gave us a rich, but not greasy, cake. Cream cheese frosting is the perfect partner to carrot cake—we enriched our version with sour cream for extra tang and vanilla for depth of flavor.

Carrot Cake

SERVES 15 TO 18

You can serve the cake right out of the pan, in which case you'll only need 3 cups of frosting for the top of the cake.

- 2½ cups (12½ ounces) unbleached all-purpose flour
- 1¼ teaspoons ground cinnamon
- 1¼ teaspoons baking powder
- 1 teaspoon baking soda
- ½ teaspoon table salt
- ½ teaspoon ground nutmeg
- ⅛ teaspoon ground cloves
- 4 large eggs, at room temperature
- 1½ cups (10½ ounces) granulated sugar
- ½ cup packed (3½ ounces) light brown sugar
- 1½ cups vegetable oil
- 1 pound carrots (about 6 medium), peeled and grated (about 3 cups)
- 4 cups Cream Cheese Frosting (recipe follows; see note)

1. Adjust an oven rack to the middle position and heat the oven to 350 degrees. Grease a 13 by 9-inch baking pan, then line the bottom with parchment paper. Whisk the flour, cinnamon, baking powder, baking soda, salt, nutmeg, and cloves together in a medium bowl.

2. In a large bowl, whisk the eggs and sugars together until the sugars are mostly dissolved and the mixture is frothy. Continue to whisk, while slowly drizzling in the oil, until thoroughly combined and emulsified. Whisk in the flour mixture until just incorporated. Stir in the carrots.

3. Give the batter a final stir with a rubber spatula to make sure it is thoroughly combined. Scrape the batter into the prepared pan, smooth the top, and lightly tap the pan against the countertop two or three times to settle the batter. Bake the cake until a toothpick inserted in the center comes out with a few moist crumbs attached, 35 to 40 minutes, rotating the pan halfway through the baking time.

4. Cool the cake completely in the pan, set on a wire rack, about 2 hours. Run a small knife around the edge of the cake and flip the cake out onto a wire rack. Peel off the parchment paper, then flip the cake right side up onto a serving platter. Spread the frosting evenly over the top and sides of the cake and serve.

Cream Cheese Frosting

MAKES ABOUT 4 CUPS

If the frosting becomes too soft to work with, let it chill in the refrigerator until firm.

- 2 (8-ounce) packages cream cheese, softened
- 10 tablespoons (1¼ sticks) unsalted butter, cut into chunks and softened
- 2 tablespoons sour cream
- 1½ teaspoons vanilla extract
- ¼ teaspoon table salt
- 2 cups (8 ounces) confectioners' sugar

1. Beat the cream cheese, butter, sour cream, vanilla, and salt together in a large bowl with an electric mixer on medium-high speed until smooth, 2 to 4 minutes.

2. Reduce the mixer speed to medium-low, slowly add the confectioners' sugar, and beat until smooth, 4 to 6 minutes. Increase the mixer speed to medium-high and beat until the frosting is light and fluffy, 4 to 6 minutes.

LIGHT CARROT CAKE

WHY THIS RECIPE WORKS: Although carrot cake sounds healthy, most versions tip the scales at 500 calories and 31 grams of fat per slice. We wanted to create a moist and rich carrot cake and we wanted the cake to be lighter in both calories and fat.

We made four significant changes to satisfy our goal of a tasty dessert we could enjoy more than once in a while. We reduced the amount of oil from 1½ cups to ½ cup and also reduced the number of eggs from four to three. We whipped air into the eggs to keep the cake from being dense and leaden. And, finally, we replaced the cream cheese and butter in the frosting with Neufchâtel reduced-fat cream cheese and mixed it by hand to prevent it from being runny. In the end, we reduced the calories to 350 and the fat grams to 13 and still had a cake that was tender, moist, and flavorful.

Light Carrot Cake

SERVES 16

You can use either the large holes of a box grater or the large-holed shredding disk in a food processor for grating the carrots. Use a metal cake pan, not a glass or Pyrex pan, for best results. This cake is terrific with our Light Cream Cheese Frosting (recipe follows) or a simple dusting of confectioners' sugar.

2½ cups (12½ ounces) unbleached all-purpose flour
1¼ teaspoons baking powder
1 teaspoon baking soda
1¼ teaspoons ground cinnamon
½ teaspoon ground nutmeg
½ teaspoon table salt
⅛ teaspoon ground cloves
3 large eggs, at room temperature
1 cup packed (7 ounces) light brown sugar
1 cup (7 ounces) granulated sugar
½ cup vegetable oil
1 pound carrots (about 6 medium), peeled and grated (about 3 cups; see note)

1. Adjust an oven rack to the middle position and heat the oven to 350 degrees. Grease a 13 by 9-inch cake pan, then line the bottom with parchment paper. Whisk the flour, baking powder, baking soda, cinnamon, nutmeg, salt, and cloves together in a medium bowl.

2. Beat the eggs, brown sugar, and granulated sugar together in a large bowl with an electric mixer on medium speed until the mixture turns thick and creamy, 1 to 3 minutes. Reduce the mixer speed to low and slowly beat in the oil until thoroughly combined and emulsified, 30 to 60 seconds.

3. Sift half the flour mixture over the batter and gently whisk in by hand. Repeat with the remaining flour mixture and continue to whisk the batter gently until most of the lumps are gone (do not overmix). Using a rubber spatula, gently stir in the carrots.

4. Pour the batter into the prepared pan and smooth the top. Bake until a wooden skewer inserted into the center of the cake comes out with a few moist crumbs attached, 35 to 40 minutes, rotating the pan halfway through the baking time.

5. Cool the cake completely in the pan, about 2 hours. Run a paring knife around the edge of the cake and flip the cake out onto a wire rack. Peel off the parchment paper, then flip the cake right side up onto a serving platter. If desired, spread the frosting (see note) evenly over the top and sides of the cake and serve.

Light Cream Cheese Frosting

MAKES ABOUT 2 CUPS

12 ounces Neufchâtel (⅓ less fat) cream cheese, softened
1 teaspoon vanilla extract
1½ cups (6 ounces) confectioners' sugar

Mix the cream cheese and vanilla together in a large bowl with a rubber spatula. Add the confectioners' sugar and stir until thoroughly combined and smooth.

CARROT LAYER CAKE

WHY THIS RECIPE WORKS: This American classic has a lot going for it: moist cake, delicate spices, tangy cream cheese frosting. But its presentation could use some refinement. We wanted to reengineer humble carrot cake as a four-tier, nut-crusted confection that could claim its place among the most glamorous desserts. To start, we found that baking this cake in a half sheet pan meant that it baked and cooled in far less time than a conventional layer cake, and—cut into quarters—it produced four thin, level layers that did not require splitting or trimming. Extra baking soda raised the pH of the batter, ensuring that the coarsely shredded carrots softened during the shortened baking time. Buttermilk powder in the frosting reinforced the tangy flavor of the cream cheese.

Carrot Layer Cake

SERVES 10 TO 12

Shred the carrots on the large holes of a box grater or in a food processor fitted with the shredding disk. Do not substitute liquid buttermilk for the buttermilk powder. To ensure the proper spreading consistency for the frosting, use cold cream cheese. If your baked cake is of an uneven thickness, adjust the orientation of the layers as they are stacked to produce a level cake. Assembling this cake on a cardboard cake round trimmed to about a 6 by 8-inch rectangle makes it easy to press the pecans onto the sides of the frosted cake.

CAKE

1¾ cups (8¾ ounces) all-purpose flour
2 teaspoons baking powder
1 teaspoon baking soda
1½ teaspoons ground cinnamon
¾ teaspoon ground nutmeg
½ teaspoon salt
¼ teaspoon ground cloves
1¼ cups packed (8¾ ounces) light brown sugar
¾ cup vegetable oil
3 large eggs
1 teaspoon vanilla extract
2⅔ cups shredded carrots (4 carrots)
⅔ cup dried currants

and spread 1 cup frosting evenly over top. Spread remaining frosting evenly over sides of cake. (It's fine if some crumbs show through frosting on sides, but if you go back to smooth top of cake, be sure that spatula is free of crumbs.)

7. Hold cake with 1 hand and gently press chopped pecans onto sides with other hand. Chill for at least 1 hour before serving. (The frosted cake can be refrigerated for up to 24 hours before serving.)

SPICE CAKE

WHY THIS RECIPE WORKS: The problem with spice cakes? Spice. Some variations suffer from spice overload, which makes them gritty and dusty. Others are so lacking in spice flavor that it seems as if a cinnamon stick has only been waved in their general direction. We wanted an old-fashioned, moist, and substantial spice cake with spices that were warm and bold without being overpowering. We needed a less-than-tender cake, one with a substantial and open crumb that could stand up to the spices. We found that all-purpose flour, rather than cake flour, added volume and heft. Butter and eggs contributed richness. We bloomed the spices in butter, a process that intensified their aromas and gave the cake a heightened spice impact throughout. We used the classic mixture of cinnamon, cloves, cardamom, allspice, and nutmeg, but found that a tablespoon of grated fresh ginger and a couple of tablespoons of molasses gave the cake an extra zing. And reserving a little of the spice mixture to add to the cream cheese frosting united the frosting and the cake.

Spice Cake
SERVES 15 TO 18

Using fresh ginger instead of dried ground ginger gives this cake a brighter flavor. You can serve the cake right out of the pan, in which case you'll only need 3 cups of frosting for the top of the cake.

FROSTING

  3 cups (12 ounces) confectioners' sugar
 16 tablespoons unsalted butter, softened
 ⅓ cup buttermilk powder
  2 teaspoons vanilla extract
 ¼ teaspoon salt
 12 ounces cream cheese, chilled and cut into 12 equal pieces
  2 cups (8 ounces) pecans, toasted and chopped coarse

1. FOR THE CAKE: Adjust oven rack to middle position and heat oven to 350 degrees. Grease 18 by 13-inch rimmed baking sheet, line with parchment paper, and grease parchment. Whisk flour, baking powder, baking soda, cinnamon, nutmeg, salt, and cloves together in large bowl.

2. Whisk sugar, oil, eggs, and vanilla together in second bowl until mixture is smooth. Stir in carrots and currants. Add flour mixture and fold with rubber spatula until mixture is just combined.

3. Transfer batter to prepared sheet and smooth surface with offset spatula. Bake until center of cake is firm to touch, 15 to 18 minutes. Cool in pan on wire rack for 5 minutes. Invert cake onto wire rack (do not remove parchment), then reinvert onto second wire rack. Cool cake completely, about 30 minutes.

4. FOR THE FROSTING: Using stand mixer fitted with paddle, beat sugar, butter, buttermilk powder, vanilla, and salt together on low speed until smooth, about 2 minutes, scraping down bowl as needed. Increase speed to medium-low; add cream cheese, 1 piece at a time; and mix until smooth, about 2 minutes.

5. Transfer cooled cake to cutting board, parchment side down. Using sharp chef's knife, cut cake and parchment in half crosswise, then lengthwise into 4 even quarters.

6. Place 6 by 8-inch cardboard rectangle on cake platter. Place 1 cake layer, parchment side up, on cardboard and carefully remove parchment. Using offset spatula, spread ⅔ cup frosting evenly over top, right to edge of cake. Repeat with 2 more layers of cake, pressing lightly to adhere and frosting each layer with ⅔ cup frosting. Top with last cake layer

  1 tablespoon ground cinnamon
 ¾ teaspoon ground cardamom
 ½ teaspoon ground allspice
 ½ teaspoon ground cloves
 ¼ teaspoon ground nutmeg
 16 tablespoons (2 sticks) unsalted butter, cut into
    16 pieces and softened
 2¼ cups (11¼ ounces) all-purpose flour
 ½ teaspoon baking powder
 ½ teaspoon baking soda
 ½ teaspoon table salt
  2 large whole eggs plus 3 large egg yolks,
    at room temperature
  1 teaspoon vanilla extract
 1¾ cups (12¼ ounces) sugar
  2 tablespoons light or mild molasses
  1 tablespoon minced or grated fresh ginger (see note)
  1 cup buttermilk, room temperature
  4 cups Cream Cheese Frosting (page 755; see note)

1. Adjust an oven rack to the middle position and heat the oven to 350 degrees. Grease a 13 by 9-inch baking pan, then line the bottom with parchment paper.

2. Combine the cinnamon, cardamom, allspice, cloves, and nutmeg in a small bowl; reserve ½ teaspoon of the spice mixture for the frosting. Melt 4 tablespoons of the butter in a small skillet over medium heat and continue to cook, swirling the pan constantly, until the butter is light brown, 3 to 6 minutes. Stir in the spice mixture and cook until fragrant, about 15 seconds. Set the mixture aside to cool slightly.

3. In a medium bowl, whisk the flour, baking powder, baking soda, and salt together. In a small bowl, whisk the whole eggs, egg yolks, and vanilla together.

4. In a stand mixer fitted with the paddle attachment, beat the remaining 12 tablespoons butter, the sugar, and molasses on medium-high speed until light and fluffy, 3 to 6 minutes; scrape down the bowl with a rubber spatula. Beat in the ginger, cooled butter-spice mixture, and half of the egg mixture until combined, about 30 seconds. Beat in the remaining egg mixture until combined, about 30 seconds, and scrape down the bowl again.

5. Reduce the mixer speed to low and beat in one-third of the flour mixture, followed by half of the buttermilk. Repeat with half of the remaining flour mixture and the remaining buttermilk. Beat in the remaining flour mixture until just combined; scrape down the bowl.

6. Give the batter a final stir with a rubber spatula to make sure it is thoroughly combined. Scrape the batter into the prepared pan, smooth the top, and lightly tap the pan against the countertop two or three times to settle the batter. Bake the cake until a toothpick inserted in the center comes out with a few moist crumbs attached, 30 to 35 minutes, rotating the pan halfway through the baking time.

7. Cool the cake completely in the pan, set on a wire rack, about 2 hours. Run a small knife around the edge of the cake and flip the cake out onto a wire rack. Peel off the parchment paper, then flip the cake right side up onto a serving platter. Stir the reserved spice mixture into the frosting, spread the frosting evenly over the top and sides of the cake, and serve.

BEST ALMOND CAKE

WHY THIS RECIPE WORKS: Simple, rich almond cake makes a sophisticated dessert, but traditional European versions can be heavy and dense. For a slightly cakier version with plenty of nutty flavor, we swapped out traditional almond paste for toasted blanched sliced almonds and added a bit of almond extract for extra depth. Lemon zest in the batter provided citrusy brightness. For a lighter crumb, we increased the flour slightly and added baking powder. Making the batter in a food processor broke down some of the protein structure in the eggs, ensuring that the cake had a level, not domed, top. We swapped some butter for oil and lowered the oven temperature to produce an evenly baked, moist cake. For a crunchy finishing touch, we topped the cake with sliced almonds and a sprinkle of lemon zest–infused sugar.

Best Almond Cake
SERVES 8 TO 10

If you can't find blanched sliced almonds, grind slivered almonds for the batter and use unblanched sliced almonds for the topping. Serve plain or with Orange Crème Fraîche (recipe follows).

1½ cups plus ⅓ cup blanched sliced almonds, toasted
¾ cup (3¾ ounces) all-purpose flour
¾ teaspoon salt
¼ teaspoon baking powder
⅛ teaspoon baking soda
4 large eggs
1¼ cups (8¾ ounces) plus 2 tablespoons sugar
1 tablespoon plus ½ teaspoon grated lemon zest (2 lemons)
¾ teaspoon almond extract
5 tablespoons unsalted butter, melted
⅓ cup vegetable oil

1. Adjust oven rack to middle position and heat oven to 300 degrees. Grease 9-inch round cake pan and line with parchment paper. Pulse 1½ cups almonds, flour, salt, baking powder, and baking soda in food processor until almonds are finely ground, 5 to 10 pulses. Transfer almond mixture to bowl.

2. Process eggs, 1¼ cups sugar, 1 tablespoon lemon zest, and almond extract in now-empty processor until very pale yellow, about 2 minutes. With processor running, add melted butter and oil in steady stream, until incorporated. Add almond mixture and pulse to combine, 4 to 5 pulses. Transfer batter to prepared pan.

3. Using your fingers, combine remaining 2 tablespoons sugar and remaining ½ teaspoon lemon zest in small bowl until fragrant, 5 to 10 seconds. Sprinkle top of cake evenly with remaining ⅓ cup almonds followed by sugar-zest mixture.

4. Bake until center of cake is set and bounces back when gently pressed and toothpick inserted in center comes out clean, 55 to 65 minutes, rotating pan after 40 minutes. Let cake cool in pan on wire rack for 15 minutes. Run paring knife around sides of pan. Invert cake onto greased wire rack, discard parchment, and reinvert cake onto second wire rack. Let cake cool, about 2 hours. Cut into wedges and serve. (Store cake in plastic wrap at room temperature for up to 3 days.)

Orange Crème Fraîche
MAKES ABOUT 2 CUPS

2	oranges
1	cup crème fraîche
2	tablespoons sugar
⅛	teaspoon salt

Remove 1 teaspoon zest from 1 orange. Cut away peel and pith from oranges. Slice between membranes to release segments and cut segments into ¼-inch pieces. Combine orange pieces and zest, crème fraîche, sugar, and salt in bowl and mix well. Refrigerate for 1 hour.

GÂTEAU BRETON

WHY THIS RECIPE WORKS: The rich, dense texture of gâteau Breton lies somewhere between shortbread and pound cake. To avoid introducing too much air into the batter of our French butter cake, which would lead to a fluffy, airy texture, we creamed the butter and sugar for only 3 minutes before adding the egg yolks and flour. Briefly freezing a layer of the batter in the cake pan helped us spread a bright homemade apricot filling onto the batter. The pan then went back into the freezer to firm so that the top layer of batter could also easily be added. All that was left to do was pretty up the cake with an egg wash and diamond-patterned design.

Gâteau Breton with Apricot Filling
SERVES 8

We strongly prefer the flavor of California apricots in the filling. Mediterranean (or Turkish) apricots can be used, but increase the amount of lemon juice to 2 tablespoons. This cake is traditionally served plain with coffee or tea but can be dressed up with fresh berries, if desired.

FILLING

⅔	cup water
½	cup dried California apricots, chopped
⅓	cup (2⅓ ounces) sugar
1	tablespoon lemon juice

CAKE

16	tablespoons (2 sticks) unsalted butter, softened
¾	cup plus 2 tablespoons (6⅛ ounces) sugar
6	large egg yolks (1 lightly beaten with 1 teaspoon water)
2	tablespoons dark rum
1	teaspoon vanilla extract
2	cups (10 ounces) all-purpose flour
½	teaspoon salt

1. FOR THE FILLING: Process water and apricots in blender until uniformly pureed, about 2 minutes. Transfer puree to 10-inch nonstick skillet and stir in sugar. Set skillet over medium heat and cook, stirring frequently, until puree has darkened slightly and rubber spatula leaves distinct trail when dragged across bottom of pan, 10 to 12 minutes. Transfer filling to bowl and stir in lemon juice. Refrigerate filling until cool to touch, about 15 minutes.

2. FOR THE CAKE: Adjust oven rack to lower-middle position and heat oven to 350 degrees. Grease 9-inch round cake pan.

3. Using stand mixer fitted with paddle, beat butter on medium-high speed until smooth and lightened in color, 1 to 2 minutes. Add sugar and continue to beat until pale and fluffy, about 3 minutes longer. Add 5 egg yolks, one at a time, and beat until combined. Scrape down bowl, add rum and vanilla, and mix until incorporated, about 1 minute. Reduce speed to low, add flour and salt, and mix until flour is just incorporated, about 30 seconds. Give batter final stir by hand.

4. Spoon half of batter into bottom of prepared pan. Using small offset spatula, spread batter into even layer. Freeze for 10 minutes.

5. Spread ½ cup filling in even layer over chilled batter, leaving ¾-inch border around edge (reserve remaining filling for another use). Freeze for 10 minutes.

6. Gently spread remaining batter over filling. Using offset spatula, carefully smooth top of batter. Brush with egg yolk wash. Using tines of fork, make light scores in surface of cake, spaced about 1½ inches apart, in diamond pattern, being careful not to score all the way to sides of pan. Bake until top is golden brown and edges of cake start to pull away from sides of pan, 45 to 50 minutes. Let cake cool in pan on wire rack for 30 minutes. Run paring knife between cake and sides of pan, remove cake from pan, and let cool completely on rack, about 1 hour. Cut into wedges and serve.

Gâteau Breton with Prune Filling

Increase water to 1 cup, substitute 1 cup pitted prunes for apricots, and omit sugar. Bring water and prunes to simmer in small saucepan over medium heat. Reduce heat to medium-low and cook until all liquid is absorbed and prunes are very soft, 10 to 12 minutes. Remove saucepan from heat, add lemon juice, and stir with wooden spoon, pressing prunes against side of saucepan, until coarsely pureed. Transfer filling to bowl and refrigerate until cool to touch, about 15 minutes.

STRAWBERRY CREAM CAKE

WHY THIS RECIPE WORKS: What could possibly ruin the heavenly trio of cake, cream, and ripe strawberries? How about soggy cake, bland berries, and squishy cream? We wanted a sturdy cake, a firm filling, and strawberry flavor fit for a starring role—a cake that would serve a formal occasion better than a simple strawberry shortcake.

To start, we had to solve three crucial problems. First, we realized that tender butter cakes couldn't support a substantial strawberry filling, so we developed a chiffon-style cake that combined the rich flavor of a butter cake with the light-yet-sturdy texture of a sponge cake. Second, we made a flavorful berry "mash" with half of the berries and then reduced the macerated juice in a saucepan (with a little kirsch) to help concentrate and round out the flavor. We sliced the rest of the berries and placed them around the edges of the cake for visual appeal. Another problem arose when the cake was sliced: The filling squirted out and the layers fell apart. To correct the problem, we reduced the number of layers from four to three and fortified the whipped-cream filling with cream cheese. This filling stayed put and didn't mar the glorious layers of this spectacular summertime cake.

Strawberry Cream Cake
SERVES 8 TO 10

You will need a cake pan with straight sides that are at least 2 inches high.

CAKE
- 1¼ cups (5 ounces) cake flour, plus extra for the pan
- 1½ teaspoons baking powder
- ¼ teaspoon table salt
- 1 cup (7 ounces) sugar

- 5 large eggs (2 whole and 3 separated), at room temperature
- 6 tablespoons (¾ stick) unsalted butter, melted and cooled slightly
- 2 tablespoons water
- 2 teaspoons vanilla extract

STRAWBERRY FILLING
- 2 pounds fresh strawberries (medium or large, about 2 quarts), washed, dried, and stemmed
- 4–6 tablespoons sugar
- 2 tablespoons kirsch
- Pinch table salt

WHIPPED CREAM
- 8 ounces cream cheese, at room temperature
- ½ cup (3½ ounces) sugar
- 1 teaspoon vanilla extract
- ⅛ teaspoon table salt
- 2 cups heavy cream

1. FOR THE CAKE: Adjust an oven rack to the lower-middle position and heat the oven to 325 degrees. Grease and flour a 9-inch-wide by 2-inch-high round cake pan or 9-inch springform pan and line it with parchment paper. Whisk the flour, baking powder, salt, and all but 3 tablespoons of the sugar in a mixing bowl. Whisk in 2 whole eggs and 3 yolks (reserving the whites), the butter, water, and vanilla; whisk until smooth.

2. In the clean bowl of a stand mixer fitted with the whisk attachment, beat the remaining 3 egg whites at medium-low speed until frothy, 1 to 2 minutes. With the machine running, gradually add the remaining 3 tablespoons sugar, increase the speed to medium-high, and beat until soft peaks form, 60 to 90 seconds. Stir one-third of the whites into the batter to lighten; add the remaining whites and gently fold into the batter until no white streaks remain. Transfer the batter to the prepared pan, smoothing the top with a rubber spatula. Lightly tap the pan against the countertop two or three times to settle the batter. Bake until a toothpick inserted into the center comes out clean, 30 to 40 minutes, rotating the pan halfway through the baking time. Cool the cake in the pan on a wire rack for 10 minutes, then invert onto the wire rack and peel off the parchment. Invert the cake again and cool completely on the rack, about 2 hours.

3. FOR THE STRAWBERRY FILLING: Halve 24 of the best-looking berries and reserve. Quarter the remaining berries; toss with 4 to 6 tablespoons sugar (depending on the sweetness of the berries) in a medium bowl and let sit for 1 hour, stirring occasionally. Strain the juices from the berries and reserve (you should have about ½ cup). In a food processor, give the macerated berries 5 pulses (you should have about 1½ cups). In a small saucepan over medium-high heat, simmer the reserved juices and the kirsch until syrupy and reduced to about 3 tablespoons, 3 to 5 minutes. Pour the reduced syrup over the processed, macerated berries, add the salt, and toss to combine. Set aside until the cake has cooled.

BUILDING A STRAWBERRY CREAM CAKE

1. With a serrated knife, use a sawing motion to cut the cake into three layers, rotating the cake as you go.

2. Place sliced berries evenly around the edges (they will be visible once the layers are assembled).

3. Cover the center of the cake completely with half of the pureed strawberries.

4. Spread one-third of the whipped cream over the berries, leaving a ½-inch border. Repeat the layering.

5. Press the last layer into place, spread with the remaining cream, and decorate with the remaining berries.

4. FOR THE WHIPPED CREAM: When the cake has cooled, place the cream cheese, sugar, vanilla, and salt in the clean bowl of a stand mixer fitted with the whisk attachment. Whisk at medium-high speed until light and fluffy, 1 to 2 minutes, scraping down the bowl with a rubber spatula as needed. Reduce the speed to low and add the heavy cream in a slow, steady stream; when almost fully combined, increase the speed to medium-high and beat until the mixture holds stiff peaks, 2 to 2½ minutes more, scraping down the bowl as needed (you should have about 4½ cups).

5. TO ASSEMBLE THE CAKE: Line the edges of a cake platter with strips of parchment paper to keep the platter clean. Following the photos, use a serrated knife to cut the cake horizontally into three even layers. Place the bottom layer on the platter and arrange a ring of 20 strawberry halves, cut sides down and stem ends facing out, around the perimeter of the cake layer. Pour one-half of the pureed berry mixture (about ¾ cup) in the center, then spread to cover any exposed cake. Gently spread about one-third of the whipped cream (about 1½ cups) over the berry layer, leaving a ½-inch border from the edge. Place the middle cake layer on top and press down gently (the whipped cream layer should become flush with the cake edge). Repeat with 20 additional strawberry halves, the remaining berry mixture, and half of the remaining whipped cream; gently press the last cake layer on top. Spread the remaining whipped cream over the top; decorate with the remaining cut strawberries. Remove the parchment strips from the platter and serve.

RASPBERRY CHARLOTTE

WHY THIS RECIPE WORKS: Raspberry charlotte is a show-stopping dessert, but the traditional steps are so labor intensive that many home cooks shy away. We wanted to deliver a creamy filling and tender cake without the hassle, so we started from the inside out where a bright raspberry curd would serve as the filling's base. First, we sprinkled gelatin over water—just enough to eventually give the filling some spring without turning it to Jell-O. We mashed raspberries with sugar, butter, and salt in a saucepan and cooked the mixture to break down the berries. Whisking cornstarch into the egg yolks prevented curdling as the hot raspberry mixture was added in. The curd slowly formed once we brought the raspberry-yolk mixture back to the stove, whisking constantly. We poured the curd into the gelatin mixture through a sieve to remove the berries' seeds, stirring the filling together and letting it cool and thicken. The cake base and sides are traditionally made with ladyfingers, but we preferred the tender, rich texture (and superior structure) of chiffon cake. For easy assembly, we baked one round cake and one square cake, using the round as the bottom and slicing the square cake into strips to line the walls of a springform pan. Before assembling, we spread the cakes with a zesty, bright spread of raspberry jam boosted with lemon-soaked gelatin. We lightened the filling before pouring it into the cake ring by whipping heavy cream to soft peaks, whisking a third of it into the curd and folding the rest in to finish. After pouring in and smoothing the top of the filling, we created a dramatic marbled pattern with the remaining jam.

Raspberry Charlotte

SERVES 12 TO 16

It is fine to use frozen raspberries in the filling. Thaw frozen berries completely before using and use any collected juices, too. It is important to measure the berries for the filling by weight. If you wish to garnish the top of the charlotte with berries, arrange 1 to 1½ cups fresh berries (depending on size) around the edge of the assembled charlotte before refrigerating. For clean, neat slices, dip your knife in hot water and wipe it dry before each slice.

FILLING

- 1¼ teaspoons unflavored gelatin
- 2 tablespoons water
- 3 large egg yolks (reserve whites for cake)
- 2 teaspoons cornstarch
- 1 pound (3¼ cups) fresh or thawed frozen raspberries
- ⅔ cup (4⅔ ounces) sugar
- 2 tablespoons unsalted butter
  Pinch salt
- 1¾ cups heavy cream

JAM MIXTURE

- ½ teaspoon unflavored gelatin
- 1 tablespoon lemon juice
- ½ cup seedless raspberry jam

CAKE

- ⅔ cup (2⅔ ounces) cake flour
- 6 tablespoons (2⅔ ounces) sugar
- ¾ teaspoon baking powder
- ⅛ teaspoon salt
- ¼ cup vegetable oil
- 1 large egg plus 3 large egg whites (reserved from filling)
- 2 tablespoons water
- 1 teaspoon vanilla extract
- ¼ teaspoon cream of tartar

1. FOR THE FILLING: Sprinkle gelatin over water in large bowl and set aside. Whisk egg yolks and cornstarch together in medium bowl until combined. Combine raspberries, sugar,

butter, and salt in medium saucepan. Mash lightly with whisk and stir until no dry sugar remains. Cook over medium heat, whisking frequently, until mixture is simmering and raspberries are almost completely broken down, 4 to 6 minutes.

2. Remove raspberry mixture from heat and, whisking constantly, slowly add ½ cup raspberry mixture to yolk mixture to temper. Whisking constantly, return tempered yolk mixture to mixture in saucepan. Return saucepan to medium heat and cook, whisking constantly, until mixture thickens and bubbles, about 1 minute. Pour through fine-mesh strainer set over gelatin mixture and press on solids with back of ladle or rubber spatula until only seeds remain. Discard seeds and stir raspberry mixture until gelatin is dissolved. Set aside, stirring occasionally, until curd is slightly thickened and reaches room temperature, at least 30 minutes or up to 1 hour 15 minutes.

3. FOR THE JAM MIXTURE: Sprinkle gelatin over lemon juice in small bowl and let sit until gelatin softens, about 5 minutes. Heat jam in microwave, whisking occasionally, until hot and fluid, 30 to 60 seconds. Add softened gelatin to jam and whisk until dissolved. Set aside.

4. FOR THE CAKE: Adjust oven rack to upper-middle position and heat oven to 350 degrees. Lightly grease 8-inch round cake pan and 8-inch square baking pan, line with parchment paper, and lightly grease parchment. Whisk flour, sugar, baking powder, and salt together in medium bowl. Whisk oil, whole egg, water, and vanilla into flour mixture until smooth batter forms.

5. Using stand mixer fitted with whisk, whip egg whites and cream of tartar on medium-low speed until foamy, about 1 minute. Increase speed to medium-high and whip until soft peaks form, 2 to 3 minutes. Transfer one-third of egg whites to batter; whisk gently until mixture is lightened. Using rubber spatula, gently fold remaining egg whites into batter.

6. Pour 1 cup batter into round pan and spread evenly. Pour remaining batter into square pan and spread evenly. Place pans on rimmed baking sheet and bake until cakes spring back when pressed lightly in center and surface is no longer sticky, 8 to 11 minutes (round cake, which is shallower, will be done before square cake). Cakes should not brown.

7. Let cakes cool in pans on wire rack for 5 minutes. Invert round cake onto wire rack. Carefully remove parchment, then reinvert onto second wire rack. Repeat with square cake. Let cool completely, at least 15 minutes.

8. Place round cake in center of serving platter. Spread with 2 tablespoons jam mixture. Place ring from 9-inch springform pan around cake, leaving equal space on all sides. Leave clasp of ring slightly loose. Using sharp chef's knife, trim ⅛ inch off all edges of square cake. Spread square cake with 2 tablespoons jam mixture. Cut cake in half. Cut each half lengthwise into two pieces to make four equal-size long strips. Place cake strips vertically around round cake, jam side in, taking care to nestle ends together neatly. Fasten clasp of springform ring.

9. Using stand mixer fitted with whisk, whip cream on medium-low speed until foamy, about 1 minute. Increase speed to high and whip until soft peaks form, 1 to 2 minutes.

Transfer one-third of whipped cream to curd; whisk gently until mixture is lightened. Using rubber spatula, gently fold in remaining cream until mixture is homogenous.

10. Pour filling into cake ring and spread evenly to edge. (Surface of filling will be above edge of cake.) Drizzle remaining jam mixture over surface of filling. Using knife, swirl jam through surface of filling, making marbled pattern. Refrigerate for at least 5 hours or up to 24 hours.

11. To unmold, run thin knife around edge of ring (just ½ inch down). Release ring and lift to remove. Let stand at room temperature for 20 minutes before slicing and serving.

NOTES FROM THE TEST KITCHEN

ASSEMBLING RASPBERRY CHARLOTTE
Our charlotte requires 2 cakes—one round cake as the base and a square cake, cut into strips, to line the sides. We construct our charlotte inside the ring of a springform pan, right on the serving platter.

1. Spread round cake with jam mixture and place springform pan ring around cake. Spread square cake with jam mixture, cut into strips, and place strips vertically around round cake. Fasten clasp of ring.

2. Whip cream and fold into curd, then pour filling into cake-lined pan.

3. Drizzle remaining jam mixture over cake and swirl.

SUMMER PEACH CAKE

WHY THIS RECIPE WORKS: Marrying cake with fresh summer peaches, this dessert is a bakery favorite, yet most versions are plagued by soggy cake and barely noticeable peach flavor. We wanted a buttery cake that was moist and not at all soggy, with a golden-brown exterior and plenty of peach flavor. Roasting chunks of peaches tossed in sugar and a little lemon juice helped concentrate their flavor and expel excess moisture before we combined them with our cake batter. However, during roasting, the peach chunks became swathed in a flavorful but unpleasantly gooey film. Coating our roasted peaches in panko bread crumbs before combining them with the batter ensured the film was absorbed by the crumbs, which then dissolved into the cake during baking. To amplify the peach flavor, we tossed the fruit with peach schnapps before roasting, and a little almond extract added to the batter lent a subtle complementary note. Fanning peach slices (macerated with a little more of the schnapps) over the top, sprinkled with almond extract–flavored sugar for a light glaze, ensured our cake looked as good as it tasted.

Summer Peach Cake
SERVES 8

To crush the panko bread crumbs, place them in a zipper-lock bag and smash them with a rolling pin. If you can't find panko, ¼ cup of plain, unseasoned bread crumbs can be substituted. Orange liqueur can be substituted for the peach schnapps. If using peak-of-season, farm-fresh peaches, omit the peach schnapps.

2½	pounds peaches, halved, pitted, and cut into ½-inch wedges
5	tablespoons peach schnapps (see note)
4	teaspoons juice from 1 lemon
6	tablespoons plus ⅓ cup (5 ounces) granulated sugar
1	cup (5 ounces) unbleached all-purpose flour
1¼	teaspoons baking powder
¾	teaspoon table salt
½	cup packed (3½ ounces) light brown sugar
2	large eggs, at room temperature
8	tablespoons (1 stick) unsalted butter, melted and cooled
¼	cup sour cream
1½	teaspoons vanilla extract
¼	teaspoon plus ⅛ teaspoon almond extract
⅓	cup panko bread crumbs, crushed fine (see note)

1. Adjust an oven rack to the middle position and heat the oven to 425 degrees. Line a rimmed baking sheet with aluminum foil and spray with vegetable oil spray. Grease and flour a 9-inch springform pan. Gently toss 24 peach wedges with 2 tablespoons of the schnapps, 2 teaspoons of the lemon juice, and 1 tablespoon of the granulated sugar in a bowl; set aside.

2. Cut the remaining peach wedges crosswise into 3 chunks. In a large bowl, gently toss the chunks with the remaining 3 tablespoons schnapps, remaining 2 teaspoons lemon juice, and 2 tablespoons more granulated sugar. Spread the peach chunks in a single layer on the prepared baking sheet and bake until the exuded juices begin to thicken and caramelize at the edges of the pan, 20 to 25 minutes. Transfer the pan to a wire rack and let the peaches cool to room temperature, about 30 minutes. Reduce the oven temperature to 350 degrees.

3. Whisk the flour, baking powder, and salt together in a bowl. Whisk ⅓ cup more granulated sugar, the brown sugar, and eggs together in a bowl until thick and thoroughly combined, about 45 seconds. Slowly whisk in the butter until combined. Add the sour cream, vanilla, and ¼ teaspoon of the almond extract; whisk until combined. Add the flour mixture and whisk until just combined.

4. Pour half of the batter into the prepared pan. Using an offset spatula, spread the batter evenly to the pan edges and smooth the top. Sprinkle the crushed panko evenly over the cooled peach chunks and gently toss to coat. Arrange the peach chunks on the batter in the pan in an even layer, gently pressing the peaches into the batter. Gently spread the remaining batter over the peach chunks and smooth the top. Arrange the reserved peach wedges, slightly overlapped, in a ring over the surface of the batter, placing the smaller wedges in the center. Stir the remaining 3 tablespoons granulated sugar and the remaining ⅛ teaspoon almond extract together in a small bowl until the sugar is moistened. Sprinkle the sugar mixture evenly over the top of the cake.

5. Bake until the center of the cake is set and a toothpick inserted in the center comes out clean, 50 to 60 minutes. Transfer the pan to a wire rack and let cool for 5 minutes. Run a thin knife between the cake and the sides of the pan; remove the sides of the pan. Let the cake cool completely, 2 to 3 hours, before serving.

CLASSIC GINGERBREAD

WHY THIS RECIPE WORKS: Most recipes for gingerbread suffer from a dense, sunken center, and flavors range from barely gingery to spicier than a curry dinner. Our ideal gingerbread should be moist through and through and utterly simple. Focusing on flavor first, we bumped up the ginger with both a hefty dose of ground ginger and grated fresh ginger. Cinnamon and freshly ground pepper produced a complex, lingering heat. Dark stout, gently heated to minimize its booziness, had a bittersweet flavor that brought out the caramel undertones of the molasses. Finally, swapping out the butter for vegetable oil and replacing some of the brown sugar with granulated let the spice flavors come through.

To prevent a sunken center, we looked at our leaveners first. Baking powder isn't as effective at leavening if too many other acidic ingredients are present in the batter. Incorporating the baking soda with the wet ingredients instead of the other dry ones helped to neutralize those acidic ingredients before they got incorporated into the batter and allowed the baking powder to do a better job. While stirring is typically the enemy of tenderness since it develops the flour's gluten, our batter was so loose that vigorous stirring actually gave our gingerbread the structure necessary to further ensure the center didn't collapse. With that, we had a flawless cake with plenty of spice and warmth.

Classic Gingerbread Cake
SERVES 8
This cake packs potent yet well-balanced spice. If you prefer less spice, you can decrease the amount of ground ginger to 1 tablespoon. Avoid opening the oven door until the minimum baking time has elapsed. Serve the gingerbread plain or with lightly sweetened whipped cream.

- ¾ cup stout, such as Guinness
- ½ teaspoon baking soda
- ⅔ cup molasses
- ¾ cup (5¼ ounces) packed light brown sugar
- ¼ cup (1¾ ounces) granulated sugar
- 1½ cups (7½ ounces) unbleached all-purpose flour
- 2 tablespoons ground ginger
- ½ teaspoon baking powder
- ½ teaspoon table salt
- ¼ teaspoon ground cinnamon
- ¼ teaspoon ground black pepper
- 2 large eggs, at room temperature
- ⅓ cup vegetable oil
- 1 tablespoon grated fresh ginger

1. Adjust an oven rack to the middle position and heat the oven to 350 degrees. Grease an 8-inch square baking pan, line with parchment paper, grease the parchment, and flour the pan.

2. Bring the stout to a boil in a medium saucepan over medium heat, stirring occasionally. Remove from the heat and stir in the baking soda (the mixture will foam vigorously). When the foaming subsides, stir in the molasses, brown sugar, and granulated sugar until dissolved; set aside. Whisk the flour, ground ginger, baking powder, salt, cinnamon, and pepper together in a large bowl.

3. Transfer the stout mixture to a second large bowl. Whisk in the eggs, oil, and grated ginger until combined. Whisk the wet mixture into the flour mixture in thirds, stirring vigorously until completely smooth after each addition.

4. Scrape the batter into the prepared pan, smooth the top with a rubber spatula, and gently tap the pan on the counter to release any air bubbles. Bake until the top of the cake is just firm to the touch and a toothpick inserted into the center comes out clean, 35 to 45 minutes. Let the cake cool in the pan on a wire rack, about 1½ hours, before serving.

COCONUT LAYER CAKE

WHY THIS RECIPE WORKS: Too often, a coconut cake is just plain white cake with plain white frosting sprinkled with shredded coconut, lacking any real coconut flavor. Coconut cake should be perfumed inside and out with the cool, subtle, mysterious essence of coconut. Its layers of snowy white cake should be moist and tender, with a delicate, yielding crumb, and the icing a silky, gently sweetened coat covered with a deep drift of downy coconut.

For this type of cake, we found a traditional butter cake to be best. To infuse this cake with maximum coconut flavor, we relied on coconut extract and cream of coconut in the cake and the buttercream icing. We also coated the cake with a generous amount of shredded coconut for more flavor and textural interest.

Coconut Layer Cake

SERVES 10 TO 12

Be sure to use cream of coconut (such as Coco López), and not coconut milk here. If you like, before decorating, toast the shredded coconut in a 350-degree oven, stirring often, until golden, about 10 minutes. Toasting the coconut, which is optional, adds a golden halo to the finished cake, as well as a nutty flavor.

CAKE

2¼ cups (9 ounces) cake flour, plus extra for the pans
¾ cup cream of coconut (see note)
5 large egg whites plus 1 large egg, at room temperature
¼ cup water
1 teaspoon coconut extract
1 teaspoon vanilla extract
1 cup (7 ounces) granulated sugar
1 tablespoon baking powder
¾ teaspoon table salt
12 tablespoons (1½ sticks) unsalted butter, cut into 12 pieces and softened

FROSTING

2 tablespoons heavy cream
1 teaspoon coconut extract
1 teaspoon vanilla extract
Pinch table salt
16 tablespoons (2 sticks) unsalted butter, cut into chunks and softened
¼ cup cream of coconut (see note)
3 cups (12 ounces) confectioners' sugar
2 cups sweetened shredded coconut (see note)

1. FOR THE CAKE: Adjust an oven rack to the middle position and heat the oven to 325 degrees. Grease and flour two 9-inch round cake pans, then line the bottoms with parchment paper. Whisk the cream of coconut, egg whites, whole egg, water, and extracts together in a medium bowl.

2. In a stand mixer fitted with the paddle attachment, mix the flour, granulated sugar, baking powder, and salt on low speed until combined, about 30 seconds. Increase the speed to medium and beat the butter into the flour mixture, one piece at a time, about 30 seconds. Continue to beat the mixture until it resembles moist crumbs, about 1 minute.

3. Beat in all but ½ cup of the cream of coconut mixture, then increase the mixer speed to medium and beat the batter until smooth, light, and fluffy, about 1 minute. Reduce the mixer speed to low and slowly beat in the remaining cream of coconut mixture until the batter is combined, about 30 seconds.

4. Scrape the batter into the prepared pans, smooth the tops, and lightly tap the pans against the countertop two or three times to settle the batter. Bake the cakes until a toothpick inserted in the center comes out with a few crumbs attached, 30 to 35 minutes, rotating the pans halfway through the baking time.

5. Cool the cakes in the pans for 10 minutes. Run a small knife around the edge of the cakes, then flip them out onto a wire rack. Peel off the parchment paper, flip the cakes right side up, and cool completely before frosting, about 2 hours.

6. FOR THE FROSTING: In a small bowl, stir the cream, extracts, and salt together. In a stand mixer fitted with the paddle attachment, beat the butter and cream of coconut together on medium-high speed until smooth, about 20 seconds. Reduce the mixer speed to medium-low and gradually beat in the confectioners' sugar, then continue to beat until smooth, about 2 minutes. Beat in the cream mixture. Increase the mixer speed to medium-high and beat until the mixture is light and fluffy, about 4 minutes.

7. Line the edges of a cake platter with strips of parchment paper to keep the platter clean while you assemble the cake. Place one of the cake layers on the platter. Spread 1 cup of the frosting over the cake, right to the edges. Place the other cake layer on top and press lightly to adhere. Frost the cake with the remaining frosting. Press the coconut into the sides of the cake and sprinkle it over the top. Remove the parchment strips from the platter before serving.

EASY CARAMEL CAKE

WHY THIS RECIPE WORKS: A Southern favorite, caramel cake boasts a rich toffee-flavored caramel frosting spread over yellow cake layers. But the best part—the caramel frosting that develops a thin, crystalline crust on its exterior while remaining silky-smooth closer to the cake—is notoriously troublesome to make. We wanted an easier, even foolproof, caramel icing that would stay creamy long enough to frost a two-layer cake. First, we needed a cake sturdy enough to support the thick frosting. Using the reverse creaming method—beating the butter into the dry ingredients—and switching from cake flour to all-purpose flour gave us a tender, fine-crumbed cake with enough structure. For a truly easy frosting, we simmered brown sugar and butter before adding cream, and rather than use a candy thermometer we relied on simple visual cues to know when to add the cream and when to remove the mixture from the heat. To ensure that the frosting wouldn't stiffen before we frosted the cake, we beat in a little softened butter. The fat from the butter kept the frosting soft and spreadable for a few precious extra minutes. After about 30 minutes, it transformed into the classic coating of frosting that we were after.

Easy Caramel Cake

SERVES 8

In step 5, the cooled frosting stays soft and spreadable longer than with other recipes, but it will harden over time. If the frosting does begin to stiffen, you can microwave it for about 10 seconds (or until it returns to a spreadable consistency).

CAKE

- ½ cup buttermilk, at room temperature
- 4 large eggs, at room temperature
- 2 teaspoons vanilla extract
- 2¼ cups (11¼ ounces) unbleached all-purpose flour
- 1½ cups (10⅛ ounces) granulated sugar
- 1½ teaspoons baking powder
- ½ teaspoon baking soda
- ¾ teaspoon table salt
- 16 tablespoons (2 sticks) unsalted butter, cut into 16 pieces and softened

FROSTING

- 12 tablespoons (1½ sticks) unsalted butter, cut into 12 pieces and softened
- 2 cups packed (14 ounces) dark brown sugar
- ½ teaspoon table salt
- ½ cup heavy cream
- 1 teaspoon vanilla extract
- 2½ cups (10 ounces) confectioners' sugar, sifted

1. FOR THE CAKE: Adjust an oven rack to the middle position and heat the oven to 350 degrees. Grease and flour two 9-inch cake pans, then line the bottoms with parchment paper. Whisk the buttermilk, eggs, and vanilla in a large measuring cup. With an electric mixer on low speed, mix the flour, granulated sugar, baking powder, baking soda, and salt until combined. Beat in the butter, 1 piece at a time, until only pea-size pieces remain. Pour in half of the buttermilk mixture and beat over medium-high speed until light and fluffy, about 1 minute. Slowly add the remaining buttermilk mixture to the bowl and beat until incorporated, about 15 seconds.

2. Scrape equal amounts of the batter into the prepared pans and bake until golden and a toothpick inserted in the center comes out clean, 20 to 25 minutes. Cool the cakes in the pans for 10 minutes, then turn out onto wire racks. Cool completely, at least 1 hour.

3. FOR THE FROSTING: Following the photo, heat 8 tablespoons of the butter, the brown sugar, and salt in a large saucepan over medium heat until small bubbles appear around the perimeter of the pan, 4 to 8 minutes. Whisk in the cream and cook until the ring of bubbles reappears, about 1 minute. Off the heat, whisk in the vanilla.

4. Transfer the hot frosting mixture to a bowl and, with the electric mixer on low speed, gradually mix in the confectioners' sugar until incorporated. Increase the speed to medium and beat until the frosting is pale brown and just warm, about 5 minutes. Add the remaining butter, 1 piece at a time, and beat until light and fluffy, about 2 minutes.

5. Line the edges of a cake platter with strips of parchment paper to keep the platter clean. Place 1 cake round on a serving platter. Spread ¾ cup of the frosting over the cake, then top with the second cake round. Spread the remaining frosting evenly over the top and sides of the cake. Serve.

NOTES FROM THE TEST KITCHEN

GETTING THE TIMING RIGHT FOR CARAMEL

When a ring of bubbles appears around the perimeter of the pan, it's time to add the cream.

CHOCOLATE-CARAMEL LAYER CAKE

WHY THIS RECIPE WORKS: Many chocolate-caramel cakes barely contain enough caramel flavor to merit the name. To ensure a hit of caramel flavor in each and every bite, we sandwiched three layers of thick but spreadable caramel filling between layers of deep, dark, moist chocolate cake. We started with a simple chocolate cake recipe and added a little extra water and swapped melted butter for more neutral-tasting vegetable oil. Combining the dry ingredients and wet ingredients separately before whisking them together could not have been easier, and greasing and then lining two cake pans with parchment paper made for a clean release after baking. For a not-too-sweet caramel that was spreadable but thick enough to stand out between the layers, we cooked it until it turned dark (but not burnt) and added extra butter to ensure that it set up at room temperature without any unpleasant oozing. Because the cake and filling both had deep, rich flavors, we determined that the frosting could afford to be on the slightly sweeter side. Using a food processor, we combined softened butter, confectioners' sugar, cocoa powder, corn syrup (for a guaranteed smooth texture), vanilla, and melted bittersweet chocolate. For a dramatic layered look, we split our two cake rounds in half, creating four layers, and sandwiched our lush caramel filling between each before spreading the thick chocolate frosting over the sides and top of the cake.

Chocolate-Caramel Layer Cake

SERVES 12

Baking spray with flour can be used to grease and flour the pans. Both natural and Dutch-processed cocoa will work in this recipe. Our favorite natural cocoa is Hershey's Natural Cocoa Unsweetened; our favorite Dutch-processed cocoa is Droste Cocoa. When taking the temperature of the caramel in steps 3 and 4, remove the pot from heat and tilt the pan to one side. Use your thermometer to stir the caramel back and forth to equalize hot and cool spots and make sure you are getting an accurate reading. When cooking the caramel in step 4, be sure the caramel is between 240 and 245 degrees to ensure a filling with the correct consistency.

CAKE

- 1½ cups (7½ ounces) all-purpose flour
- ¾ cup (2¼ ounces) unsweetened cocoa powder
- 1½ cups (10½ ounces) granulated sugar

- 1¼ teaspoons baking soda
- ¾ teaspoon baking powder
- ¾ teaspoon salt
- ¾ cup buttermilk
- ½ cup water
- ¼ cup vegetable oil
- 2 large eggs
- 1 teaspoon vanilla extract

CARAMEL FILLING

- 1¼ cups (8¾ ounces) granulated sugar
- ¼ cup light corn syrup
- ¼ cup water
- 1 cup heavy cream
- 8 tablespoons unsalted butter, cut into 8 pieces
- 1 teaspoon vanilla extract
- ¾ teaspoon salt

FROSTING

- 16 tablespoons unsalted butter, softened
- ¾ cup (3 ounces) confectioners' sugar
- ½ cup (1½ ounces) unsweetened cocoa powder
  Pinch salt
- ½ cup light corn syrup
- ¾ teaspoon vanilla extract
- 6 ounces bittersweet chocolate, melted and cooled

¼–½ teaspoon coarse sea salt (optional)

1. FOR THE CAKE: Adjust oven rack to middle position and heat oven to 325 degrees. Grease two 9-inch round cake pans, line with parchment paper, grease parchment, and flour pans. Sift flour and cocoa into large bowl. Whisk in sugar, baking soda, baking powder, and salt. Whisk buttermilk, water, oil, eggs, and vanilla together in second bowl. Whisk buttermilk mixture into flour mixture until smooth batter forms. Divide batter evenly between prepared pans and smooth tops with rubber spatula.

2. Bake until toothpick inserted in center comes out clean, 22 to 28 minutes, rotating and switching pans halfway through baking. Let cakes cool in pans on wire rack for 15 minutes. Remove cakes from pans, discard parchment, and let cool completely on rack, at least 2 hours.

3. FOR THE CARAMEL FILLING: Lightly grease 8-inch square baking pan. Combine sugar, corn syrup, and water in medium saucepan. Bring to boil over medium-high heat and cook, without stirring, until mixture is amber colored, 8 to 10 minutes. Reduce heat to low and continue to cook, swirling saucepan occasionally, until dark amber, 2 to 5 minutes longer. (Caramel will register between 375 and 380 degrees.)

4. Off heat, carefully stir in cream, butter, vanilla, and salt (mixture will bubble and steam). Return saucepan to medium heat and cook, stirring frequently, until smooth and caramel reaches 240 to 245 degrees, 3 to 5 minutes. Carefully transfer caramel to prepared pan and let cool until just warm to touch (100 to 105 degrees), 20 to 30 minutes.

5. FOR THE FROSTING: Process butter, sugar, cocoa, and salt in food processor until smooth, about 30 seconds, scraping down sides of bowl as needed. Add corn syrup and vanilla and process until just combined, 5 to 10 seconds. Scrape down sides of bowl, then add chocolate and pulse until smooth and creamy, 10 to 15 seconds. (Frosting can be made 3 hours in advance. For longer storage, cover and refrigerate frosting. Let stand at room temperature for 1 hour before using.)

6. Using long serrated knife, score 1 horizontal line around sides of each cake layer; then, following scored lines, cut each layer into 2 even layers.

7. Using rubber spatula or large spoon, transfer ⅓ of caramel to center of 1 cake layer and use small offset spatula to spread over surface, leaving ½-inch border around edge. Repeat with remaining caramel and 2 of remaining cake layers. (Three of your cake layers should be topped with caramel.)

8. Line edges of cake platter with 4 strips of parchment to keep platter clean. Place 1 caramel-covered cake layer on platter. Top with second caramel-covered layer. Repeat with third caramel-covered layer and top with final layer. Spread frosting evenly over sides and top of cake. Carefully remove parchment strips. Let cake stand for at least 1 hour. (Cake can be made up to 2 days in advance and refrigerated. Let stand at room temperature for at least 5 hours before serving.) Sprinkle with coarse sea salt, if using. Cut and serve.

LEMON LAYER CAKE

WHY THIS RECIPE WORKS: Most versions of lemon layer cake are poorly executed concoctions of heavy cake stacked with filling and frosting that taste more like butter than lemon. We wanted an old-fashioned cake in which tangy, creamy lemon filling divides layers of tender, delicate cake draped in sweet frosting—an ideal contrast of sweet and tart.

Most layer cakes are substantial butter cakes, but we suspected that the light, fresh flavor of lemon would be better served by something more ethereal. After trying a sponge cake and a classic yellow cake, we found that a white butter cake was the perfect compromise: a cake nicely flavored by butter yet light enough for our flavors, with a fine crumb and tender texture.

Lemon layer cake is often filled with lemon-scented buttercream, but this filling can mute the lemon flavor and make the cake far too rich. We preferred the brightness of lemon curd. We also wanted something lighter than buttercream for our frosting, eventually landing on an old-fashioned classic: seven-minute icing. We needed to make some adjustments, as the traditional version was a little too sweet, slightly thick, and required holding a hand-held mixer for longer than was comfortable. We cut back on the sugar and added a squeeze of lemon juice to solve the first two problems. After some trial and error, we learned that if we heated the mixture to at least 160 degrees and then transferred it to the stand mixer for whipping (rather than holding a hand mixer for seven minutes), the end result was just as billowy and shiny as the old-fashioned version.

Lemon Layer Cake with Fluffy White Icing
SERVES 10 TO 12

You will need a cake pan with straight sides that are at least 2 inches high. For neater slices, dip a knife into hot water before cutting the cake.

LEMON CURD FILLING
- 1 cup juice from about 6 lemons
- 1 teaspoon powdered gelatin
- 1½ cups (10½ ounces) sugar
- ⅛ teaspoon table salt
- 4 large whole eggs plus 6 large egg yolks (reserve the egg whites for the cake)
- 8 tablespoons (1 stick) unsalted butter, cut into ½-inch cubes and frozen

CAKE
- 2¼ cups (9 ounces) cake flour, plus extra for the pans
- 1 cup whole milk, at room temperature
- 6 large egg whites, at room temperature
- 2 teaspoons vanilla extract
- 1¾ cups (12¼ ounces) sugar
- 4 teaspoons baking powder
- 1 teaspoon table salt
- 12 tablespoons (1½ sticks) unsalted butter, cut into 12 pieces, softened but still cool

FLUFFY WHITE ICING
- 1 cup (7 ounces) sugar
- 2 large egg whites, at room temperature
- ¼ cup water
- 1 tablespoon juice from 1 lemon
- 1 tablespoon corn syrup

1. FOR THE FILLING: Measure 1 tablespoon of the lemon juice into a small bowl; sprinkle the gelatin over the top. Heat the remaining lemon juice, the sugar, and salt in a medium saucepan over medium-high heat, stirring occasionally, until the sugar dissolves and the mixture is hot but not boiling. Whisk the eggs and yolks in a large bowl. Whisking constantly, slowly pour the hot lemon-sugar mixture into the eggs, then return the mixture to the saucepan. Cook over medium-low heat, stirring constantly with a heatproof spatula, until the mixture registers 170 degrees on an instant-read thermometer and is thick enough to leave a trail when the spatula is scraped along the pan bottom, 4 to 6 minutes. Immediately remove the pan from the heat and stir in the gelatin mixture until dissolved. Stir in the frozen butter until incorporated. Pour the filling through a fine-mesh strainer into a bowl (you should have 3 cups). Lay a sheet of plastic wrap directly on the surface and refrigerate until firm enough to spread, at least 4 hours.

2. FOR THE CAKE: Adjust an oven rack to the middle position and heat the oven to 350 degrees. Grease and flour two 9-inch-wide by 2-inch-high round cake pans and line with parchment paper. In a 2-cup liquid measure or medium bowl, whisk together the milk, egg whites, and vanilla.

3. In a stand mixer fitted with the paddle attachment, mix the flour, sugar, baking powder, and salt at low speed until combined, about 30 seconds. With the mixer running at low speed, add the butter one piece at a time; continue beating until the mixture resembles moist crumbs with no visible butter chunks. Add all but ½ cup of the milk mixture to the crumbs and beat at medium speed until the mixture is pale and fluffy, about 1½ minutes. With the mixer running at low speed, add the remaining ½ cup milk mixture; increase the speed to medium and beat for 30 seconds more. Stop the mixer and scrape the sides of the bowl. Return the mixer to medium speed and beat for 20 seconds longer. Divide the batter evenly between the pans, smoothing the tops with a rubber spatula. Lightly tap the pan against the countertop two or three times to settle the batter.

4. Bake until a toothpick inserted in the center of the cakes comes out clean, 23 to 25 minutes, rotating the pans halfway through the baking time. Cool the cakes in the pans on a wire rack for 10 minutes. Run a small knife around the edges of the cakes, then flip them out onto a wire rack. Peel off the parchment paper, flip the cakes right side up, and cool completely before frosting, about 2 hours.

5. TO ASSEMBLE: Line the edges of a cake platter with strips of parchment paper to keep the platter clean while you assemble the cake. Use a serrated knife to cut each cake horizontally into two even layers. Place the bottom layer of one cake on the platter. Using a spatula, spread 1 cup of the lemon filling evenly on the cake, leaving a ½-inch border around the edge. Carefully place the upper cake layer on top of the filling. Spread 1 cup of the filling on top; repeat using the remaining filling and cake layers. Smooth out any filling that has leaked from the sides of the cake; cover with plastic wrap and refrigerate while making the icing.

6. FOR THE ICING: Combine all the ingredients in the bowl of a stand mixer or a large heatproof bowl and set over a medium saucepan filled with 1 inch of barely simmering water (do not let the bowl touch the water). Cook, stirring constantly, until the mixture registers 160 degrees on an instant-read thermometer, 5 to 10 minutes. Remove the bowl

from the heat and transfer the mixture to a stand mixer fitted with the whisk attachment. Beat on medium speed until soft peaks form, about 5 minutes. Increase the speed to medium-high and continue to beat until the mixture has cooled to room temperature and stiff peaks form, 5 minutes longer. Using a spatula, spread the frosting evenly over the top and sides of the cake. Remove the parchment strips from the platter and serve.

OLD-FASHIONED BIRTHDAY CAKE

WHY THIS RECIPE WORKS: White layer cakes have been the classic birthday cake for more than 100 years. White cake is simply a basic butter cake made with egg whites instead of whole eggs. The whites produce the characteristic color, and they are also supposed to make the cake soft and fine-grained—that's what we wanted. Unfortunately, the white cakes that we have baked over the years, though good enough, always fell short of our high expectations. They came out a little dry and chewy—one might say cottony—and we noticed that they were riddled with tunnels and small holes. What were we doing wrong?

Every traditional recipe for white cake calls for stiffly beaten egg whites folded into the batter at the end. We began to suspect that it was the beaten egg whites that were forming the large air pockets and those unsightly holes in the baked cakes. We solved this problem by mixing the egg whites with the milk before beating them into the flour-and-butter mixture. The results were fantastic. The cake was not only fine-grained and free from holes but, to our surprise, it was also larger and lighter than the ones we'd prepared with beaten whites. And the method couldn't be simpler, quicker, or more foolproof. To make this cake birthday-special, we iced it with an easy butter frosting and added a layer of raspberry jam and chopped toasted almonds.

Classic White Layer Cake with Butter Frosting and Raspberry-Almond Filling

SERVES 10 TO 12

There will be enough frosting left to pipe a border around the base and top of the cake; to decorate the cake more elaborately, you should make 1½ times the frosting recipe. If desired, finish the sides of the cake with 1 cup of sliced almonds.

CAKE

2¼ cups (9 ounces) cake flour, plus extra for the pans
1 cup whole milk, at room temperature
6 large egg whites, at room temperature
1 teaspoon vanilla extract
1 teaspoon almond extract
1¾ cups (12¼ ounces) granulated sugar
4 teaspoons baking powder
1 teaspoon table salt
12 tablespoons (1½ sticks) unsalted butter, cut into 12 pieces and softened

FROSTING AND FILLING

- 16 tablespoons (2 sticks) unsalted butter, softened
- 4 cups (1 pound) confectioners' sugar
- 1 tablespoon vanilla extract
- 1 tablespoon milk
  Pinch table salt
- ½ cup (2¼ ounces) blanched slivered almonds, toasted and chopped coarse
- ⅓ cup seedless raspberry jam

1. FOR THE CAKE: Adjust an oven rack to the middle position and heat the oven to 350 degrees. Grease and flour two 8- or 9-inch round cake pans, then line the bottoms with parchment paper. Whisk the milk, egg whites, and both extracts together in a small bowl.

2. In a stand mixer fitted with the paddle attachment, mix the flour, sugar, baking powder, and salt together on low speed until combined, about 30 seconds. Increase the speed to medium-low and beat the butter into the flour mixture, one piece at a time, about 30 seconds. Continue to beat the mixture until it resembles moist crumbs, about 1 minute.

3. Beat in all but ½ cup of the milk mixture, then increase the mixer speed to medium and beat until smooth, light, and fluffy, about 1 minute. Reduce the mixer speed to low and slowly beat in the remaining ½ cup milk mixture until the batter looks slightly curdled, about 15 seconds.

4. Give the batter a final stir with a rubber spatula to make sure it is thoroughly combined. Scrape the batter into the prepared pans, smooth the tops, and lightly tap the pans against the countertop two or three times to settle the batter. Bake the cakes until a toothpick inserted in the center comes out with a few crumbs attached, 20 to 25 minutes, rotating the pans halfway through the baking time.

NOTES FROM THE TEST KITCHEN

LINING CAKE PANS

1. Trace the outline of the bottom of the pan onto a sheet of parchment paper. Cut out the outline, cutting on the inside of the line so that the round fits snugly inside the pan.

2. Fit the trimmed piece of parchment into the pan.

5. Cool the cakes in the pans for 10 minutes. Run a small knife around the edge of the cakes, then flip them out onto a wire rack. Peel off the parchment paper, flip the cakes right side up, and cool completely before frosting, about 2 hours.

6. FOR THE FROSTING AND FILLING: In the bowl of a stand mixer fitted with the paddle attachment, beat the butter, confectioners' sugar, vanilla, milk, and salt on low speed until the sugar is moistened, about 30 seconds. Increase the speed to medium-high; beat, stopping twice to scrape down the bowl, until creamy and fluffy, about 1½ minutes.

7. Line the edges of a cake platter with strips of parchment to keep the platter clean while you assemble the cake. Place one cake layer on the platter. Combine ½ cup of the frosting with the almonds in a small bowl. Spread the almond frosting over the first layer. Carefully spread the jam on top, then cover with the second cake layer. Spread the remaining frosting evenly over the top and sides of the cake. Remove the parchment strips from the platter before serving.

CLASSIC YELLOW LAYER CAKE

WHY THIS RECIPE WORKS: Traditional yellow layer cake should melt in the mouth and taste of butter and eggs. But many recipes we tried came out crumbly, sugary, and hard. And the flavor? It tasted merely sweet. We wanted a yellow cake that was tender and buttery and could stand up to a slathering of frosting, if desired.

Most versions of yellow layer cake rely on the classic 1–2–3–4 formula (1 cup butter, 2 cups sugar, 3 cups flour, and four eggs—plus milk, baking powder, vanilla, and salt) and follow the classic way of mixing together the ingredients—creaming the butter and sugar, adding the eggs one at a time, and finally adding the milk and dry ingredients alternately. This worked okay, but we wanted something easier for this cake. The two-stage method fit the bill. In this technique, the dry ingredients are combined and then two-thirds of the milk and eggs are added and beaten until thick and fluffy. Then in the second stage, the rest of the milk and eggs are poured in and the batter is beaten again. This technique is simpler and quicker, and produced a tender cake. The flavor still needed some improvement. We tackled the proportions of the ingredients, increasing the butter, eggs, and sugar. This cake turned out fine-grained, soft, and meltingly rich—just what we wanted. As for the frosting, we chose a traditional vanilla buttercream. Rich with egg yolks, butter, sugar, and corn syrup for sheen, this supple frosting is the perfect complement to our cake.

Classic Yellow Layer Cake with Vanilla Buttercream

SERVES 8 TO 10

Cake flour gives this buttery yellow cake its tender crumb; do not substitute all-purpose flour. When making the buttercream, make sure that the sugar mixture is poured into the egg yolks while still hot. For a decorative finish, press toasted sliced almonds on the sides of the cake.

CAKE

- 1¾ cups (7 ounces) cake flour (see note), plus extra for the pans
- ½ cup whole milk, at room temperature
- 4 large eggs, at room temperature
- 2 teaspoons vanilla extract
- 1½ cups (10½ ounces) sugar
- 2 teaspoons baking powder
- ¾ teaspoon table salt
- 16 tablespoons (2 sticks) unsalted butter, cut into 16 pieces and softened

VANILLA BUTTERCREAM

- 6 large egg yolks, at room temperature
- ¾ cup (5¼ ounces) sugar
- ½ cup light corn syrup
- 2½ teaspoons vanilla extract
- ¼ teaspoon table salt
- 4 sticks unsalted butter, cut into chunks and softened

1. FOR THE CAKE: Adjust an oven rack to the middle position and heat the oven to 350 degrees. Grease and flour two 8- or 9-inch round cake pans, then line the bottoms with parchment paper. Whisk the milk, eggs, and vanilla together in a small bowl.

2. In a stand mixer fitted with the paddle attachment, whisk the flour, sugar, baking powder, and salt together on low speed until combined, about 30 seconds. Increase the speed to medium-low and beat the butter into the flour mixture, one piece at a time, about 30 seconds. Continue to beat the mixture until it resembles moist crumbs, about 1 minute.

3. Beat in all but ½ cup of the milk mixture, then increase the mixer speed to medium and beat the batter until smooth, light, and fluffy, about 1 minute. Reduce the mixer speed to low and slowly beat in the remaining ½ cup milk mixture until the batter looks slightly curdled, about 15 seconds.

4. Give the batter a final stir with a rubber spatula to make sure it is thoroughly combined. Scrape the batter into the prepared pans and smooth the tops with a rubber spatula. Lightly tap the pans against the countertop two or three times to settle the batter. Bake the cakes until a toothpick inserted in the center comes out with a few crumbs attached, 20 to 25 minutes, rotating the pans halfway through the baking time.

5. Cool the cakes in the pans for 10 minutes. Run a small knife around the edge of the cakes, then flip them out onto a wire rack. Peel off the parchment paper, flip the cakes right side up, and cool completely before frosting, about 2 hours.

6. FOR THE FROSTING: Whip the egg yolks in a large bowl with an electric mixer on medium speed until slightly thickened and pale yellow, 4 to 6 minutes.

7. Meanwhile, bring the sugar and corn syrup to a boil in a small saucepan over medium heat, stirring occasionally to dissolve the sugar, about 3 minutes.

8. Without letting the hot sugar mixture cool off, turn the mixer to low and slowly pour the warm sugar syrup into the whipped egg yolks without hitting the side of the bowl or the beaters. Increase the mixer speed to medium-high and whip the mixture until it is light and fluffy and the bowl is no longer warm, 5 to 10 minutes.

9. Reduce the mixer speed to medium-low and add the vanilla and salt. Gradually add the butter, one piece at a time, until completely incorporated, about 2 minutes. Increase the mixer speed to medium-high and whip the buttercream until smooth and silky, about 2 minutes. (If the mixture looks curdled, wrap a hot wet towel around the bowl and continue to whip until smooth, 1 to 2 minutes.)

10. Line the edges of a cake platter with strips of parchment to keep the platter clean while you assemble the cake. Place one cake layer on the platter. Spread 1½ cups of the frosting evenly across the top of the cake with a spatula. Place the second cake layer on top, then spread the remaining frosting evenly over the top and sides of the cake. Remove the parchment strips from the platter before serving.

FLUFFY YELLOW CAKE

WHY THIS RECIPE WORKS: It's easy to create a supremely fluffy layer cake with additives, but most cakes made entirely from natural ingredients are either unpleasantly dense or too fragile to support layers of frosting. We wanted a frosted yellow layer cake with an ethereal texture and the great flavor of real butter and eggs.

Chiffon cakes are especially weightless, springy, and moist. But unlike butter cakes, they are too light to stand up to a serious slathering of frosting. We decided to blend the two types of cake. We adapted a chiffon technique (using a large quantity of whipped egg whites to get a high volume and light texture) to combine the ingredients from our butter cake recipe. This worked beautifully, creating a light, porous cake that was hefty

enough to hold the frosting's weight. But the cake lacked moistness and some tenderness. A combination of fats (butter plus vegetable oil), kept the butter flavor intact while improving the moistness of the cake. For extra tenderness, we increased the sugar and substituted buttermilk for milk. The buttermilk not only introduced a new flavor dimension, but also allowed us to replace some of the baking powder with a little baking soda to ensure an even rise.

As for the frosting, a fluffy chocolate frosting is the perfect partner to this cake. A hefty amount of cocoa powder combined with melted chocolate gave the frosting a deep chocolate flavor. A combination of confectioners' sugar and corn syrup made it smooth and glossy. To keep the frosting from separating and turning greasy, we moved it out of the stand mixer and into the food processor. The faster machine minimized any risk of over beating, as it blended the ingredients quickly without melting the butter or incorporating too much air. The result is a thick, fluffy chocolate frosting that spreads like a dream.

Fluffy Yellow Layer Cake with Milk Chocolate Frosting

SERVES 10 TO 12

Bring all the ingredients to room temperature before beginning. For the frosting, cool the chocolate to between 85 and 100 degrees before adding it to the butter mixture. The frosting can be made 3 hours in advance. For longer storage, refrigerate the frosting, covered, and let it stand at room temperature for 1 hour before using.

CAKE

2½ cups (10 ounces) cake flour, plus extra for the pans
1¾ cups (12¼ ounces) granulated sugar
1¼ teaspoons baking powder
¼ teaspoon baking soda
¾ teaspoon table salt
1 cup buttermilk, at room temperature
10 tablespoons (1¼ sticks) unsalted butter, melted and cooled slightly
3 tablespoons vegetable oil
2 teaspoons vanilla extract
6 large egg yolks plus 3 large egg whites, at room temperature

FROSTING

20 tablespoons (2½ sticks) unsalted butter, softened
1 cup (4 ounces) confectioners' sugar
¾ cup Dutch-processed cocoa powder
Pinch table salt
¾ cup light corn syrup
1 teaspoon vanilla extract
8 ounces milk chocolate, melted and cooled slightly (see note)

1. FOR THE CAKE: Adjust an oven rack to the middle position and heat the oven to 350 degrees. Grease and flour two 9-inch-wide by 2-inch-high round cake pans and line with parchment paper. Whisk the flour, 1½ cups of the granulated sugar, the baking powder, baking soda, and salt together in a large bowl. In a 4-cup liquid measuring cup or medium bowl, whisk together the buttermilk, melted butter, oil, vanilla, and egg yolks.

2. In a stand mixer fitted with the whisk attachment, beat the egg whites at medium-high speed until foamy, about 30 seconds. With the machine running, gradually add the remaining ¼ cup granulated sugar; continue to beat until stiff peaks just form, 30 to 60 seconds (the whites should hold a peak but the mixture should appear moist). Transfer to a bowl and set aside.

NOTES FROM THE TEST KITCHEN

FROSTING A LAYER CAKE

1. Dollop a portion of frosting in the center of the cake and spread into an even layer right to the edge.

2. Lay the second layer on top. Brush away any large crumbs, dollop more frosting in the center, and spread slightly over the edge.

3. Gather a few tablespoons of frosting onto the top of the spatula, then gently smear it onto the side of the cake. Repeat to frost the sides completely.

4. For smooth sides, gently run the edge of the spatula around the cake. Or, to create billows in the frosting, press the back of a soup spoon into the frosting, then twirl the spoon as you lift it away.

3. Add the flour mixture to the now-empty mixing bowl. With the mixer still fitted with the whisk attachment, and running at low speed, gradually pour in the butter mixture and mix until almost incorporated (a few streaks of dry flour will remain), about 15 seconds. Stop the mixer and scrape the whisk and the sides of the bowl. Return the mixer to medium-low speed and beat until smooth and fully incorporated, 10 to 15 seconds.

4. Using a rubber spatula, stir one-third of the whites into the batter to lighten, then add the remaining whites and gently fold into the batter until no white streaks remain. Divide the batter evenly between the prepared pans, smoothing the tops with a rubber spatula. Lightly tap the pans against the countertop two or three times to settle the batter.

5. Bake until the cake layers begin to pull away from the sides of the pans and a toothpick inserted into the centers comes out clean, 20 to 22 minutes, rotating the pans halfway through the baking time. Cool the cakes in the pans on a wire rack for 10 minutes. Run a small knife around the edge of the cakes, then flip them out onto a wire rack. Peel off the parchment paper, flip the cakes right side up, and cool completely before frosting, about 2 hours.

6. FOR THE FROSTING: In a food processor, process the butter, confectioners' sugar, cocoa, and salt until smooth, about 30 seconds, scraping down the sides of the bowl as needed. Add the corn syrup and vanilla and process until just combined, 5 to 10 seconds. Scrape down the sides of the bowl, then add the chocolate and process until smooth and creamy, 10 to 15 seconds. The frosting can be used immediately or held (see note).

7. Line the edges of a cake platter with strips of parchment to keep the platter clean while you assemble the cake. Place one cake layer on the platter. Spread 1½ cups of the frosting evenly across the top of the cake with a spatula. Place the second cake layer on top, then spread the remaining frosting evenly over the top and sides of the cake. Remove the parchment strips from the platter before serving.

OLD-FASHIONED CHOCOLATE LAYER CAKE

WHY THIS RECIPE WORKS: Over the years, chocolate cakes have become denser, richer, and squatter. Many contemporary cakes are so intense that just a few forkfuls satisfy. These cakes taste great—it's hard to imagine a bad chocolate cake—but sometimes we'd rather have a real piece of cake, not a fudge-like confection. We wanted an old-style, mile-high chocolate layer cake with a tender, airy, open crumb and a soft, billowy frosting.

The mixing method was the key to getting the right texture. After trying a variety of techniques, we turned to ribboning, a popular old-fashioned method used for cakes like genoise (a moist, light sponge cake). Ribboning involves whipping eggs with sugar until they double in volume, then adding the butter, dry ingredients, and milk. The egg foam aerated

the cake, giving it both structure and tenderness. To achieve a moist cake with rich chocolate flavor, we once again looked to historical sources, which suggested using buttermilk and making a "pudding" with a mixture of chocolate, water, and sugar. We simply melted unsweetened chocolate and cocoa powder in hot water over a double boiler, then stirred in sugar until it dissolved. Turning to the frosting, we wanted to combine the best elements of classic chocolate frostings: the intense chocolate flavor of a ganache (a mixture of chocolate and cream) and the volume of a meringue or buttercream. The solution turned out to be a simple reversal of the conventional ganache procedure: We poured cold (rather than heated) cream into warm (rather than room-temperature) chocolate, waited for it to cool to room temperature, then whipped until fluffy.

Old-Fashioned Chocolate Layer Cake with Chocolate Frosting

SERVES 10 TO 12

For a smooth, spreadable frosting, use chopped semisweet chocolate, not chocolate chips—chocolate chips contain less cocoa butter than bar chocolate and will not melt as readily. As for other bar chocolate, bittersweet chocolate that is 60 percent cacao can be substituted but it will produce a stiffer, but still spreadable, frosting. Bittersweet chocolate with 70 percent cacao, however, should be avoided—it will produce a frosting that is crumbly and it will not spread. For best results, don't make the frosting until the cakes are cooled, and use the frosting as soon as it is ready. If the frosting gets too cold and stiff to spread easily, wrap the mixer bowl with a towel soaked in hot water and mix on low speed until the frosting appears creamy and smooth.

CAKE

1¾ cups (8¾ ounces) unbleached all-purpose flour, plus extra for the pans

4 ounces unsweetened chocolate, chopped coarse

¼ cup Dutch-processed cocoa powder

½ cup hot water

1¾ cups (12¼ ounces) sugar

1½ teaspoons baking soda

1 teaspoon table salt

1 cup buttermilk

2 teaspoons vanilla extract

4 large whole eggs plus 2 large egg yolks, at room temperature

12 tablespoons (1½ sticks) unsalted butter, very soft

FROSTING

1 pound semisweet chocolate, chopped fine (see note)

8 tablespoons (1 stick) unsalted butter

⅓ cup (2⅓ ounces) sugar

2 tablespoons corn syrup

2 teaspoons vanilla extract

¼ teaspoon table salt

1¼ cups heavy cream, chilled

1. FOR THE CAKE: Adjust an oven rack to the middle position and heat the oven to 350 degrees. Grease and flour two 9-inch-wide by 2-inch-high round cake pans and line with parchment paper. Combine the chocolate, cocoa powder, and hot water in a medium heatproof bowl set over a saucepan filled with 1 inch of barely simmering water, stirring occasionally until smooth. Add ½ cup of the sugar to the chocolate mixture and stir until thick and glossy, 1 to 2 minutes. Remove the bowl from the heat and set aside to cool.

2. Whisk the flour, baking soda, and salt in a medium bowl. Combine the buttermilk and vanilla in a small bowl. In the bowl of a stand mixer fitted with the whisk attachment, whisk the whole eggs and egg yolks on medium-low speed until combined, about 10 seconds. Add the remaining 1¼ cups sugar, increase the speed to high, and whisk until fluffy and lightened in color, 2 to 3 minutes. Replace the whisk with the paddle attachment. Add the cooled chocolate mixture to the egg-sugar mixture and mix on medium speed until thoroughly incorporated, 30 to 45 seconds, pausing to scrape down the sides of the bowl with a rubber spatula as needed. Add the softened butter 1 tablespoon at a time, mixing for about 10 seconds after each addition. Add about one-third of the flour mixture followed by half of the buttermilk mixture, mixing until incorporated after each addition (about 15 seconds). Repeat, using half of the remaining flour mixture and all of the remaining buttermilk mixture (the batter may appear separated). Scrape down the sides of the bowl and add the remaining flour mixture; mix at medium-low speed until the batter is thoroughly combined, about 15 seconds. Remove the bowl from the mixer and fold the batter once or twice with a rubber spatula to incorporate any remaining flour. Divide the batter evenly between the prepared pans, smoothing the tops with a rubber spatula. Lightly tap the pans against the countertop two or three times to settle the batter.

3. Bake the cakes until a toothpick inserted into the center comes out with a few crumbs attached, 25 to 30 minutes, rotating the pans halfway through the baking time. Cool the cakes in the pans on a wire rack for 15 minutes. Run a small knife around the edge of the cakes, then flip them out onto a wire rack. Peel off the parchment paper, flip the cakes right side up, and cool completely before frosting, about 2 hours.

4. FOR THE FROSTING: Melt the chocolate in a heatproof bowl set over a saucepan containing 1 inch of barely simmering water, stirring occasionally until smooth. Remove from the heat and set aside. Meanwhile, heat the butter in a small saucepan over medium-low heat until melted. Increase the heat to medium; add the sugar, corn syrup, vanilla, and salt and stir with a heatproof spatula until the sugar is dissolved, 4 to 5 minutes. Add the melted chocolate, butter mixture, and cream to the clean bowl of a stand mixer and stir to thoroughly combine.

5. Place the mixer bowl over an ice bath and stir the mixture constantly with a rubber spatula until the frosting is thick and just beginning to harden against the sides of the bowl, 1 to 2 minutes (the frosting should be at 70 degrees). Place the bowl on a stand mixer fitted with the paddle attach-

ment and beat on medium-high speed until the frosting is light and fluffy, 1 to 2 minutes. Stir with a rubber spatula until completely smooth.

6. Line the edges of a cake platter with strips of parchment to keep the platter clean while you assemble the cake. Place one cake layer on the platter. Spread 1½ cups of the frosting evenly across the top of the cake with a spatula. Place the second cake layer on top, then spread the remaining frosting evenly over the top and sides of the cake. Remove the parchment strips from the platter before serving.

CHOCOLATE SHEET CAKE

WHY THIS RECIPE WORKS: Sheet cakes, for all their simplicity, can still turn out dry, sticky, or flavorless and, on occasion, can even sink in the middle. We wanted a simple, dependable recipe that delivered a moist yet tender cake. We started with the mixing method—testing everything from creaming butter to beating yolks, whipping whites, and gently folding together everything in the end. The best of the lot was the most complicated to make, so we took a step back. The simplest technique we tried was simply whisking all the ingredients together without beating, creaming, or whipping. The recipe needed work, but the approach was clearly a good match for the simple all-purpose nature of a sheet cake. First we added buttermilk and baking soda to lighten the batter. To increase the chocolate flavor, we reduced the sugar, flour, and butter. To further deepen the chocolate taste, we used semisweet chocolate in addition to the cocoa. We baked the cake at a low temperature for 40 minutes to produce a perfect cake with a flat top. Though this cake can be frosted with almost anything, we like a classic American milk chocolate frosting, which pairs well with the darker flavor of the cake.

Chocolate Sheet Cake with Easy Chocolate Frosting

SERVES 15 TO 18

We prefer Dutch-processed cocoa for the deeper chocolate flavor it gives the cake. The frosting needs about an hour to cool before it can be used, so begin making it when the cake comes out of the oven. You can also serve the cake lightly dusted with confectioners' sugar or with lightly sweetened whipped cream.

CAKE

- 12 tablespoons (1½ sticks) unsalted butter
- ¾ cup cocoa powder, preferably Dutch-processed (see note)
- 1¼ cups (6¼ ounces) unbleached all-purpose flour
- ½ teaspoon baking soda
- ¼ teaspoon table salt
- 8 ounces semisweet chocolate, chopped
- 4 large eggs, at room temperature
- 1½ cups (10½ ounces) granulated sugar
- 1 teaspoon vanilla extract
- 1 cup buttermilk

FROSTING

½ cup heavy cream
  Pinch table salt
1 tablespoon light or dark corn syrup
10 ounces milk chocolate, chopped
½ cup (2 ounces) confectioners' sugar
8 tablespoons (1 stick) cold unsalted butter,
  cut into 8 pieces

1. FOR THE CAKE: Adjust an oven rack to the middle position and heat the oven to 325 degrees. Grease a 13 by 9-inch baking pan, then line the bottom with parchment paper.

2. Sift together the cocoa, flour, baking soda, and salt in a medium bowl; set aside. Melt the chocolate and butter in a heatproof bowl set over a saucepan filled with 1 inch of barely simmering water, stirring occasionally until smooth. Whisk together the eggs, sugar, and vanilla in a medium bowl. Whisk in the buttermilk until smooth.

3. Whisk the chocolate into the egg mixture until combined. Whisk in the dry ingredients until the batter is smooth and glossy. Pour the batter into the prepared pan; bake until firm in the center when lightly pressed and a toothpick inserted in the center comes out clean, about 40 minutes, rotating the pan halfway through the baking time. Let the cake cool completely in the pan, set on a wire rack, about 2 hours. Run a small knife around the cake and flip the cake out onto a wire rack. Peel off the parchment paper, then flip the cake right side up onto a serving platter.

4. FOR THE FROSTING: Heat the cream, salt, and corn syrup in a microwave-safe measuring cup on high power until simmering, about 1 minute, or bring to a simmer in a small saucepan over medium heat.

5. Place the chocolate in a food processor. With the machine running, gradually add the hot cream mixture through the feed tube; process for 1 minute after the cream has been added. Stop the machine; add the confectioners' sugar and process to combine, about 30 seconds. With the machine running, add the butter through the feed tube one piece at a time; process until incorporated and smooth, about 20 seconds longer.

6. Transfer the frosting to a medium bowl and cool at room temperature, stirring frequently, until thick and spreadable, about 1 hour. Spread the frosting evenly over the top and sides of the cake and serve.

SIMPLE CHOCOLATE SHEET CAKE

WHY THIS RECIPE WORKS: For a simple cake that boasted deep chocolate flavor and color, we used a combination of Dutch-processed cocoa and melted bittersweet chocolate; the cocoa offered pure, assertive chocolate flavor while the chocolate contributed complexity as well as fat and sugar. Neutral-tasting oil allowed the chocolate flavor to shine. To minimize cleanup, we mixed the wet and dry ingredients directly into the saucepan where we'd melted the chocolate with cocoa and milk. A milk chocolate ganache frosting contrasted nicely with the deeper flavor of the cake. To make the ganache thick, rich, and creamy, we added plenty of softened butter to the warm chocolate-cream mixture, refrigerated the frosting to cool it quickly so that it would spread nicely, and gave it a quick whisk to smooth it out and lighten its texture.

Simple Chocolate Sheet Cake with Milk Chocolate Frosting

SERVES 12

While any high-quality chocolate can be used here, our preferred bittersweet chocolates are Ghirardelli 60% Cacao Bittersweet Chocolate Premium Baking Bar and Callebaut Intense Dark Chocolate, L-60-40NV, and our favorite milk chocolate is Dove Silky Smooth Milk Chocolate. We recommend making this cake with a Dutch-processed cocoa powder; our favorite is from Droste. Using a natural cocoa powder will result in a drier cake.

CAKE

1½ cups (10½ ounces) granulated sugar
1¼ cups (6¼ ounces) all-purpose flour
½ teaspoon baking soda
½ teaspoon salt
1 cup whole milk
8 ounces bittersweet chocolate, chopped fine
¾ cup (2¼ ounces) Dutch-processed cocoa powder
⅔ cup vegetable oil
4 large eggs
1 teaspoon vanilla extract

FROSTING

1 pound milk chocolate, chopped
⅔ cup heavy cream
16 tablespoons (2 sticks) unsalted butter,
   cut into 16 pieces and softened

1. **FOR THE CAKE:** Adjust oven rack to middle position and heat oven to 325 degrees. Lightly spray 13 by 9-inch baking pan with vegetable oil spray. Whisk sugar, flour, baking soda, and salt together in medium bowl; set aside.

2. Combine milk, chocolate, and cocoa in large saucepan. Place saucepan over low heat and cook, whisking frequently, until chocolate is melted and mixture is smooth. Remove from heat and let cool slightly, about 5 minutes. Whisk oil, eggs, and vanilla into chocolate mixture (mixture may initially look curdled) until smooth and homogeneous. Add sugar mixture and whisk until combined, making sure to scrape corners of saucepan.

3. Transfer batter to prepared pan; bake until firm in center when lightly pressed and toothpick inserted in center comes out with few crumbs attached, 30 to 35 minutes, rotating pan halfway through baking. Let cake cool completely in pan on wire rack before frosting, 1 to 2 hours.

4. **FOR THE FROSTING:** While cake is baking, combine chocolate and cream in large heatproof bowl set over saucepan filled with 1 inch barely simmering water, making sure that water does not touch bottom of bowl. Whisk mixture occasionally until chocolate is uniformly smooth and glossy, 10 to 15 minutes. Remove bowl from saucepan. Add butter, whisking once or twice to break up pieces. Let mixture stand for 5 minutes to finish melting butter, then whisk until completely smooth. Refrigerate frosting, without stirring, until cooled and thickened, 30 minutes to 1 hour.

5. Once cool, whisk frosting until smooth. (Whisked frosting will lighten in color slightly and should hold its shape on whisk.) Spread frosting evenly over top of cake. Cut cake into squares and serve out of pan. (Leftover cake can be refrigerated in airtight container for up to 2 days.)

GERMAN CHOCOLATE CAKE

WHY THIS RECIPE WORKS: Most German chocolate cake recipes are similar, if not identical, to the one on the German's Sweet Chocolate box. Our tasters found several shortcomings in this recipe. It produced a cake that was too sweet, with chocolate flavor that was too mild, and with a texture so listless that the filling and cake together formed a soggy, sweet mush. We wanted a cake that was less sweet and more chocolaty than the original, but we didn't want to sacrifice the overall blend of flavors and textures that makes German chocolate cake so appealing in the first place.

The first order of business was to scale back the recipe by one quarter, which allowed us to fit the batter into two cake pans, thereby producing a cake with four thinner layers rather than three thicker layers. After testing, we discovered that the texture of the cake actually improved when we used whole eggs instead of laboriously separating the eggs, beating the whites, and folding them into the batter. We increased chocolate flavor with a combination of cocoa powder and good-quality semisweet or bittersweet chocolate. By adjusting the level and proportions of the sugar (both

brown and white) and butter in the cake and filling, as well as toasting the pecans, we finished the necessary adjustments to create a definitely easier-to-make cake, with better texture and flavor than the original.

German Chocolate Cake

SERVES 12 TO 16

When you assemble the cake, the filling should be cool or cold. To be time-efficient, first make the filling, then use the refrigeration time to prepare, bake, and cool the cakes. For an accurate measurement of boiling water, bring a kettle of water to a boil, then measure out the desired amount. Note that the toasted pecans are stirred into the filling just before assembly to keep them from becoming soft and soggy.

FILLING

- 4 large egg yolks, at room temperature
- 1 (12-ounce) can evaporated milk
- 1 cup (7 ounces) granulated sugar
- ¼ cup packed (1¾ ounces) light brown sugar
- 6 tablespoons (¾ stick) unsalted butter, cut into 6 pieces
- ⅛ teaspoon table salt
- 2 teaspoons vanilla extract
- 2⅓ cups sweetened shredded coconut
- 1½ cups (6 ounces) finely chopped pecans, toasted (see note)

CAKE

- 4 ounces semisweet or bittersweet chocolate, chopped fine
- ¼ cup Dutch-processed cocoa powder
- ½ cup boiling water (see note)
- 2 cups (10 ounces) unbleached all-purpose flour, plus extra for the pans
- ¾ teaspoon baking soda
- 12 tablespoons (1½ sticks) unsalted butter, softened

1 cup (7 ounces) granulated sugar

⅔ cup packed (4⅔ ounces) light brown sugar

¾ teaspoon table salt

4 large whole eggs, at room temperature

1 teaspoon vanilla extract

¾ cup sour cream, at room temperature

1. FOR THE FILLING: Whisk the egg yolks in a medium saucepan; gradually whisk in the evaporated milk. Add the sugars, butter, and salt and cook over medium-high heat, whisking constantly, until the mixture is boiling, frothy, and slightly thickened, about 6 minutes. Transfer the mixture to a bowl, whisk in the vanilla, then stir in the coconut. Cool until just warm, cover with plastic wrap, and refrigerate until cool or cold, at least 2 hours or up to 3 days. (The pecans are stirred in just before cake assembly.)

2. FOR THE CAKE: Adjust an oven rack to the lower-middle position; heat the oven to 350 degrees. Combine the chocolate and cocoa in a small bowl; pour the boiling water over and let stand to melt the chocolate, about 2 minutes. Whisk until smooth; set aside until cooled to room temperature.

3. Meanwhile, grease and flour two 9-inch-wide by 2-inch-high round cake pans and line with parchment paper. Sift the flour and baking soda into a medium bowl or onto a sheet of parchment or waxed paper.

4. In a stand mixer fitted with the paddle attachment, beat the butter, sugars, and salt at medium-low speed until the sugar is moistened, about 30 seconds. Increase the speed to medium-high and beat until the mixture is light and fluffy, about 4 minutes, scraping down the bowl with a spatula halfway through. With the mixer running at medium speed, add the eggs one at a time, beating well after each addition and scraping down the bowl halfway through. Beat in the vanilla; increase the speed to medium-high and beat until light and fluffy, about 45 seconds. With the mixer running at low speed, add the chocolate mixture, then increase the speed to medium and beat until combined, about 30 seconds, scraping down the bowl once (the batter may appear curdled). Add about one-third of the flour mixture, followed by half of the sour cream, mixing until just incorporated after each addition (about 5 seconds). Repeat using half of the remaining flour mixture and all of the remaining sour cream. Scrape down the bowl and add the remaining flour mixture; mix at medium-low speed until the batter is thoroughly combined, about 15 seconds. Divide the batter evenly between the prepared cake pans, smoothing the tops with a rubber spatula. Lightly tap the pans against the countertop two or three times to settle the batter.

5. Bake the cakes until a toothpick inserted into the centers comes out clean, about 30 minutes, rotating the pans halfway through the baking time. Cool the cakes in the pans on a wire rack for 10 minutes. Run a small knife around the edges of the cakes, then flip them out onto a wire rack. Peel off the parchment, flip the cakes right side up, and cool completely before frosting, about 2 hours.

6. TO ASSEMBLE: Stir the toasted pecans into the chilled filling. Line the edges of a cake platter with strips of parchment paper to keep the platter clean while you assemble the cake. Use a serrated knife to cut each cake horizontally into two even layers. Place one bottom layer on the platter. Spread about 1 cup of the filling evenly across the top of the cake with a spatula. Carefully place the upper cake layer on top of the filling; repeat using the remaining filling and cake layers. Remove the parchment strips before serving.

CHOCOLATE CUPCAKES

WHY THIS RECIPE WORKS: Cupcakes shouldn't be complicated, but homemade versions can take a lot of time and store-bought mixes don't deliver good chocolate flavor. We wanted the consummate chocolate cupcake—one with a rich, buttery flavor, a light, moist, cakey texture, and just the right amount of sugar—but we wanted it to be almost as quick and easy to make as the cupcakes that come from a box.

For the mixing method, we found that the melted-butter method often used for mixing muffins, quick breads, and brownies—a method that requires no mixer and no time spent waiting for butter to soften—worked best. The same procedure won out over the more conventional creaming method for our cupcakes, delivering a light texture with a tender, fine crumb. Moving on to tackle our desire for deep chocolate flavor, we found that a combination of cocoa powder and bittersweet chocolate delivered deep chocolate flavor and that mixing the cocoa powder with the butter and chocolate as they melted (rather than adding the cocoa to the dry ingredients) made the chocolate flavor even stronger and richer. Sour cream gave our cupcakes moistness and a little tang, while just the right amounts of baking soda and baking powder helped them rise to a gently domed shape that was perfect for frosting.

Dark Chocolate Cupcakes

MAKES 12 CUPCAKES

Store leftover cupcakes (frosted or unfrosted) in the refrigerator, but let them come to room temperature before serving.

8 tablespoons (1 stick) unsalted butter, cut into 4 pieces

2 ounces bittersweet chocolate, chopped

½ cup cocoa powder, preferably Dutch-processed

¾ cup (3¾ ounces) unbleached all-purpose flour

¾ teaspoon baking powder

½ teaspoon baking soda

2 large eggs, at room temperature

¾ cup (5¼ ounces) sugar

1 teaspoon vanilla extract

½ teaspoon table salt

½ cup sour cream

1 recipe Easy Vanilla Bean Buttercream, Easy Chocolate Buttercream, or Easy Coffee Buttercream (recipes follow)

1. Adjust an oven rack to the lower-middle position and heat the oven to 350 degrees. Line a standard-size muffin pan with baking cup liners.

2. Melt the butter, chocolate, and cocoa in a medium heat-proof bowl set over a saucepan filled with 1 inch of barely simmering water, stirring occasionally. Set aside to cool until just warm to the touch.

3. Whisk the flour, baking powder, and baking soda in a small bowl to combine.

4. Whisk the eggs in a medium bowl to combine; add the sugar, vanilla, and salt and whisk until fully incorporated. Add the cooled chocolate mixture and whisk until combined. Sift about one-third of the flour mixture over the chocolate mixture and whisk until combined; whisk in the sour cream until combined, then sift the remaining flour mixture over the batter and whisk until homogeneous and thick.

5. Divide the batter evenly among the muffin cups. Bake until a toothpick or wooden skewer inserted into the center of the cupcakes comes out clean, 18 to 20 minutes, rotating the pan halfway through the baking time.

6. Cool the cupcakes in the pan on a wire rack until cool enough to handle, about 15 minutes. Carefully lift each cupcake from the muffin pan and set on a wire rack. Cool to room temperature before icing, about 30 minutes. To frost: Mound about 2 tablespoons of icing on the center of each cupcake. Using a small spatula or butter knife, spread the icing to the edge of the cupcake, leaving a slight mound in the center.

Easy Vanilla Bean Buttercream

MAKES ABOUT 1½ CUPS, ENOUGH TO FROST 12 CUPCAKES

If you prefer to skip the vanilla bean, increase the extract to 1½ teaspoons. Any of the buttercream frostings can be made ahead and refrigerated; if refrigerated, however, the frosting must stand at room temperature to soften before use. If using a hand-held mixer, increase mixing times significantly (by at least 50 percent).

- 10 tablespoons (1¼ sticks) unsalted butter, softened
- ½ vanilla bean, halved lengthwise (see note)
- 1¼ cups (5 ounces) confectioners' sugar
  Pinch table salt
- 1 tablespoon heavy cream
- ½ teaspoon vanilla extract

In a stand mixer fitted with the whisk attachment, beat the butter at medium-high speed until smooth, about 20 seconds. Using a paring knife, scrape the seeds from the vanilla bean into the butter and beat the mixture at medium-high speed to combine, about 15 seconds. Add the confectioners' sugar and salt and beat at medium-low speed until most of the sugar is moistened, about 45 seconds. Scrape down the bowl and beat at medium speed until the mixture is fully combined, about 15 seconds. Scrape down the bowl, add the heavy cream and vanilla extract, and beat at medium speed until incorporated, about 10 seconds, then increase the speed to medium-high and beat until light and fluffy, about 4 minutes, scraping down the bowl once or twice.

Easy Chocolate Buttercream

Follow the recipe for Easy Vanilla Bean Buttercream, omitting the vanilla bean and heavy cream and reducing the sugar to 1 cup. After beating in the vanilla extract, reduce the speed to low and gradually beat in 4 ounces melted and cooled semi-sweet or bittersweet chocolate.

Easy Coffee Buttercream

Follow the recipe for Easy Vanilla Bean Buttercream, omitting the vanilla bean and dissolving 1½ teaspoons instant espresso powder in the heavy cream and vanilla extract.

ULTIMATE CHOCOLATE CUPCAKES

WHY THIS RECIPE WORKS: A cupcake catch-22 befalls bakery and homemade confections alike: If the cupcakes are packed with decent chocolate flavor, their structure can be too crumbly for out-of-hand consumption. Conversely, if the cakes balance moisture and tenderness without crumbling, the core elements—cake and frosting—are barely palatable. We wanted a moist, tender (but not crumbly) crumb capped with just enough creamy, not-too-sweet frosting.

Figuring that a cupcake is just a pint-size cake, we made cupcakes using our favorite chocolate cake recipe. Tasters liked the real chocolate flavor, but their crumbly texture made them impossible to eat without a fork. Though we were loath to compromise the chocolate's intensity, we knew that to strengthen the batter we had to cut back on both kinds of chocolate. We tweaked the ingredients to achieve a perfectly portable batch of cupcakes before we turned our attention to working in more chocolate without disrupting the batter's structure. Mixing the cocoa with hot coffee eked out more chocolate flavor. To make the chocolate even more pronounced, we replaced the butter with more neutral-flavored vegetable oil.

Next, we tried enhancing the structure of the cupcake. That would give us a base for adding back extra chocolate without over tenderizing. To do this, we substituted bread flour for all-purpose flour. Specifically engineered for gluten development, bread flour turned out a cupcake that was markedly less crumble-prone, but not tough. For a final chocolate burst, we spooned ganache onto the cupcakes before baking, which gave them a truffle-like center. A velvety buttercream with just enough sweetness crowned the cake perfectly.

Ultimate Chocolate Cupcakes with Ganache Filling

MAKES 12 CUPCAKES

Use a high-quality bittersweet or semisweet chocolate for this recipe, such as one of the test kitchen's favorite baking chocolates, Callebaut Intense Dark Chocolate or Ghirardelli Bittersweet Chocolate. Though we highly recommend the ganache filling, you can omit it for a more traditional cupcake.

GANACHE FILLING

- 2 ounces bittersweet chocolate, chopped fine (see note)
- ¼ cup heavy cream
- 1 tablespoon confectioners' sugar

CHOCOLATE CUPCAKES

- 3 ounces bittersweet chocolate, chopped fine (see note)
- ⅓ cup (1 ounce) Dutch-processed cocoa powder
- ¾ cup hot coffee
- ¾ cup (4⅛ ounces) bread flour
- ¾ cup (5¼ ounces) granulated sugar
- ½ teaspoon table salt
- ½ teaspoon baking soda
- 6 tablespoons vegetable oil
- 2 large eggs
- 2 teaspoons white vinegar
- 1 teaspoon vanilla extract
- 1 recipe Creamy Chocolate Frosting (recipe follows)

1. FOR THE GANACHE FILLING: Place the chocolate, cream, and confectioners' sugar in a medium microwave-safe bowl. Microwave until the mixture is warm to the touch, 20 to 30 seconds. Whisk the mixture until smooth, then refrigerate until just chilled, no longer than 30 minutes.

2. FOR THE CUPCAKES: Adjust an oven rack to the middle position and heat the oven to 350 degrees. Line a standard-size muffin pan (cups have ½-cup capacity) with baking cup liners. Place the chocolate and cocoa in a medium bowl. Pour the hot coffee over the mixture and whisk until smooth. Refrigerate until completely cool, about 20 minutes. Whisk the flour, granulated sugar, salt, and baking soda together in a medium bowl and set aside.

3. Whisk the oil, eggs, vinegar, and vanilla into the cooled chocolate-cocoa mixture until smooth. Add the flour mixture and whisk until smooth.

4. Divide the batter evenly among the muffin pan cups. Place one slightly rounded teaspoon of the ganache filling on top of each cupcake. Bake until the cupcakes are set and just firm to the touch, 17 to 19 minutes. Cool the cupcakes in the muffin pan on a wire rack until cool enough to handle, about 10 minutes. Carefully lift each cupcake from the muffin pan and set on a wire rack. Cool to room temperature before frosting, about 1 hour.

5. TO FROST: Mound 2 to 3 tablespoons of the frosting on the center of each cupcake. Use a small icing spatula or butter knife to ice each cupcake. (The cupcakes can be made up to 24 hours in advance and stored unfrosted in an airtight container.)

Creamy Chocolate Frosting

MAKES ABOUT 2¼ CUPS

Cool the chocolate to between 85 and 100 degrees before adding it to the frosting. If the frosting seems too soft after adding the chocolate, chill it briefly in the refrigerator and then rewhip it until creamy.

- ⅓ cup (2⅓ ounces) sugar
- 2 large egg whites
  Pinch salt
- 12 tablespoons (1½ sticks) unsalted butter, cut into 12 pieces and softened
- 6 ounces bittersweet chocolate, melted and cooled (see note)
- ½ teaspoon vanilla extract

1. Combine the sugar, egg whites, and salt in the bowl of a stand mixer, then place the bowl over a pan of simmering water. Whisking gently but constantly, heat the mixture until slightly thickened and foamy and it registers 150 degrees on an instant-read thermometer, 2 to 3 minutes.

2. Using the whisk attachment, beat the mixture on medium speed in a stand mixer until it reaches the consistency of shaving cream and is slightly cooled, 1 to 2 minutes. Add the butter, one piece at a time, until smooth and creamy. (The frosting may look curdled after half of the butter has been added; it will smooth with additional butter.) Once all the butter is added, add the cooled melted chocolate and the vanilla and mix until combined. Increase the mixer speed to medium-high and beat until light, fluffy, and thoroughly combined, about 30 seconds, scraping the beater and sides of the bowl with a rubber spatula as necessary. (The frosting can be made up to 24 hours in advance and refrigerated in an airtight container. When ready to frost, place the frosting in a microwave-safe container and microwave briefly until just slightly softened, 5 to 10 seconds. Once warmed, stir until creamy.)

CHOCOLATE TORTE

WHY THIS RECIPE WORKS: Sachertorte, the classic Viennese dessert with layers of chocolate cake sandwiching apricot jam and enrobed in a creamy-rich chocolate glaze, always sounds more promising than it typically is in reality—dry, flavorless cake and sweet jam with little fruity complexity, all covered in a glaze that is nothing more than a thin, overly sugary coating. We set out to create a rich, deeply chocolaty dessert using Sachertorte as the inspiration, giving it our own spin by pairing the chocolate with raspberries.

For a rich, fudgy base, we started by baking our Flourless Chocolate Cake (page 781) in two 9-inch pans, so we could sandwich the two cakes together rather than deal with halving a single delicate cake. But when we tried to stack the layers, the dense cake tore and fell apart. Adding ground nuts gave it the structure it needed, plus a good boost of flavor. Since we were using the food processor to grind the nuts, we tweaked our cake recipe so that it could be prepared using the same appliance. The winning approach for our filling was to combine jam with lightly mashed fresh berries for a tangy-sweet mixture that clung to the cake. For the glaze, we kept things simple, melting bittersweet chocolate with heavy cream to create a rich-tasting, glossy ganache that poured smoothly over the cake. For simple but tasty decorating, we dotted fresh raspberries around the top of the torte and pressed sliced, toasted almonds along its sides.

Chocolate-Raspberry Torte

SERVES 12 TO 16

Be sure to use cake pans with at least 2-inch-tall sides.

CAKE

- 8 ounces bittersweet chocolate, chopped fine
- 12 tablespoons (1½ sticks) unsalted butter, cut into ½-inch pieces
- 2 teaspoons vanilla extract
- ¼ teaspoon instant espresso powder
- 1¾ cups (6⅛ ounces) sliced almonds, toasted
- ¼ cup (1¼ ounces) unbleached all-purpose flour
- ½ teaspoon table salt
- 5 large eggs, at room temperature
- ¾ cup (5¼ ounces) sugar

FILLING

- 2½ ounces (½ cup) raspberries, plus 16 individual raspberries
- ¼ cup seedless raspberry jam

GLAZE

- 5 ounces bittersweet chocolate, chopped fine
- ½ cup plus 1 tablespoon heavy cream

1. FOR THE CAKE: Adjust an oven rack to the middle position and heat the oven to 325 degrees. Grease and flour two 9-inch round cake pans, line the bottoms with parchment paper, then grease and flour the parchment. Melt the chocolate and butter in a large heatproof bowl set over a saucepan filled with 1 inch of simmering water, stirring occasionally until smooth. Remove from the heat and let cool to room temperature, about 30 minutes. Stir in the vanilla and espresso powder.

2. Pulse ¾ cup of the almonds in a food processor until coarsely chopped, 6 to 8 pulses, and set aside. Process the remaining 1 cup almonds until very finely ground, about 45 seconds. Add the flour and salt and continue to process until combined, about 15 seconds. Transfer the almond-flour mixture to a medium bowl. Process the eggs until lightened in color and almost doubled in volume, about 3 minutes. With the processor running, slowly add the sugar and process until thoroughly combined, about 15 seconds. Using a whisk, gently fold the egg mixture into the chocolate mixture until some streaks of egg remain. Sprinkle half of the almond-flour mixture over the chocolate mixture and gently whisk until just combined. Sprinkle with the remaining almond-flour mixture and gently whisk until just combined.

3. Divide the batter evenly between the prepared pans and smooth the tops with a rubber spatula. Bake until the center is firm and a toothpick inserted in the center comes out with a few moist crumbs attached, 14 to 16 minutes. Transfer the cakes to a wire rack and let cool completely in the pans, about 30 minutes.

4. Run a paring knife around the sides of the cakes to loosen and invert the cakes onto cardboard rounds cut the same size as the diameter of the cake; discard the parchment. Using a wire rack, turn 1 cake right side up, then slide from the rack back onto the cardboard round.

5. FOR THE FILLING: Place ½ cup of the raspberries in a medium bowl and coarsely mash with a fork. Stir in the raspberry jam until just combined.

NOTES FROM THE TEST KITCHEN

DECORATING CHOCOLATE-RASPBERRY TORTE

1. With the fully assembled cake placed on a cardboard round, hold the bottom of the cake in one hand and gently press the chopped nuts onto its side with the other hand.

2. Place one raspberry on the cake at 12 o'clock, then another at 6 o'clock. Place a third berry at 9 o'clock and a fourth at 3 o'clock. Continue to place raspberries directly opposite each other until all have been arranged in an evenly spaced circle.

6. TO ASSEMBLE THE TORTE: Spread the raspberry mixture onto the cake layer that is right side up. Top with the second cake layer, leaving it upside down. Transfer the assembled cake, still on the cardboard round, to a wire rack set in a rimmed baking sheet.

7. FOR THE GLAZE: Melt the chocolate and cream in a medium heatproof bowl set over a saucepan filled with 1 inch of simmering water, stirring occasionally until smooth. Remove from the heat and gently whisk until very smooth. Pour the glaze onto the center of the assembled cake. Using an offset spatula, spread the glaze evenly over the top of the cake, letting it drip down the sides. Spread the glaze along the sides of the cake to coat evenly.

8. Using a fine-mesh strainer, sift the reserved chopped almonds to remove any fine bits. Holding the bottom of the cake on the cardboard round with 1 hand, gently press the sifted almonds onto the cake sides with the other hand. Arrange the remaining 16 raspberries around the circumference. Refrigerate the cake on the rack until the glaze is set, at least 1 hour or up to 24 hours (if refrigerating the cake for more than 1 hour, let sit at room temperature for about 30 minutes before serving). Transfer the cake to a platter and serve.

FLOURLESS CHOCOLATE CAKE

WHY THIS RECIPE WORKS: While all flourless chocolate cake recipes share common ingredients (chocolate, butter, and eggs), the techniques used to make them vary, as do the results. You can end up with anything from a fudge brownie to a bittersweet chocolate soufflé. We wanted something dense, moist, and ultra-chocolaty.

We started with the type of chocolate. A cake made with unsweetened chocolate was neither smooth nor silky enough for this kind of cake. Bittersweet or semisweet chocolate was ideal, with deep chocolate flavor and a smooth texture. Next we turned to the eggs—we compared cakes made with room temperature eggs and eggs taken straight from the fridge. The batter made with chilled eggs produced a denser foam and the resulting cake boasted a smooth, velvety texture. And the gentle, moist heat of a water bath further preserved the cake's lush texture.

Flourless Chocolate Cake
SERVES 12 TO 16

This cake is best when baked a day ahead to mellow its flavor. Even though the cake may not look done, pull it from the oven when an instant-read thermometer registers 140 degrees. (Do not let the tip of the thermometer hit the bottom of the pan.) It will continue to firm up as it cools. If you use a 9-inch springform pan instead of the preferred 8-inch pan, reduce the baking time to 18 to 20 minutes. See page 910 for our top-rated brands of chocolate.

8   large eggs, chilled
1   pound bittersweet or semisweet chocolate,
    chopped (see note)
½   pound (2 sticks) unsalted butter, cut into ½-inch chunks
¼   cup strong coffee
    Confectioners' sugar or cocoa powder, for decoration

1. Adjust an oven rack to the lower-middle position and heat the oven to 325 degrees. Grease an 8-inch springform pan, then line the bottom with parchment paper. Wrap the outside of the pan with two 18-inch-square pieces of heavy-duty foil; set the springform pan in a roasting pan. Bring a kettle of water to a boil.

2. In a stand mixer fitted with the whisk attachment, beat the eggs at medium speed until doubled in volume, about 5 minutes.

3. Meanwhile, melt the chocolate and butter in a large heatproof bowl set over a saucepan filled with 1 inch of barely simmering water until smooth, stirring once or twice; stir in the coffee. Using a large rubber spatula, fold one-third of the egg mixture into the chocolate mixture until only a few streaks of egg are visible; fold the remaining egg mixture, in two additions, until the batter is totally homogeneous.

4. Scrape the batter into the prepared pan and smooth the surface with the spatula. Set the roasting pan on the oven rack and pour in enough boiling water to come about halfway up the sides of the pan. Bake until the cake has risen slightly, the edges are just beginning to set, a thin glazed crust (like a brownie) has formed on the surface, and an instant-read thermometer inserted halfway through the center of the cake registers 140 degrees, 22 to 25 minutes. Remove the pan from the water bath and set on a wire rack; cool to room temperature. Cover and refrigerate overnight to mellow the flavors. (The cake can be covered and refrigerated for up to 4 days.)

5. About 30 minutes before serving, remove the springform pan sides, then flip the cake out onto the wire rack. Peel off the parchment and flip the cake right side up onto a serving platter. Lightly dust the cake with confectioners' sugar or unsweetened cocoa powder, if desired, and serve.

HOT FUDGE PUDDING CAKE

WHY THIS RECIPE WORKS: Those who have eaten hot fudge pudding cake know its charms: moist, brownie-like chocolate cake sitting on a pool of thick, chocolate pudding–like sauce, baked together in one dish, as if by magic. Served warm with vanilla ice cream, this cake has a flavor that more than makes up for its homespun looks. We set out to master this humble dessert. Pudding cake is made by sprinkling brownie batter with a mixture of sugar and cocoa, then pouring hot water on top, and baking. To bump up the chocolate flavor, we used a combination of Dutch-processed cocoa and bittersweet chocolate. We also added instant coffee to the water that is poured over the batter to cut the sweetness of the cake. We baked the cake slow and low to promote a good top crust and a silky sauce. And we found that letting the cake rest for 20 to 30 minutes before eating allows the sauce to become pudding-like and the cake brownie-like.

Hot Fudge Pudding Cake
SERVES 8

If you have cold brewed coffee on hand, it can be used in place of the instant coffee and water, but to make sure it isn't too strong, use 1 cup of cold coffee mixed with ½ cup of water. Serve the cake warm with vanilla or coffee ice cream.

- 2 teaspoons instant coffee powder (see note)
- 1½ cups water
- 1 cup (7 ounces) granulated sugar
- ⅔ cup Dutch-processed cocoa powder
- ⅓ cup packed (2⅓ ounces) brown sugar
- 6 tablespoons (¾ stick) unsalted butter
- 2 ounces bittersweet or semisweet chocolate, chopped
- ¾ cup (3¾ ounces) unbleached all-purpose flour
- 2 teaspoons baking powder
- ⅓ cup whole milk
- 1 tablespoon vanilla extract
- ¼ teaspoon table salt
- 1 large egg yolk, at room temperature

1. Adjust an oven rack to the lower-middle position and heat the oven to 325 degrees. Lightly grease an 8-inch square glass or ceramic baking dish. Stir the instant coffee into the water; set aside to dissolve. Stir together ⅓ cup of the granulated sugar, ⅓ cup of the cocoa, and the brown sugar in a small bowl, breaking up large clumps with your fingers; set aside. Melt the butter, the remaining ⅓ cup cocoa, and the chocolate in a small bowl set over a saucepan filled with 1 inch of barely simmering water; whisk until smooth and set aside to cool slightly. Whisk the flour and baking powder in a small bowl to combine; set aside. Whisk the remaining ⅔ cup granulated sugar, the milk, vanilla, and salt in a medium bowl until combined; whisk in the egg yolk. Add the chocolate mixture and whisk to combine. Add the flour mixture and whisk until the batter is evenly moistened.

2. Pour the batter into the prepared baking dish and spread evenly to the sides and corners. Sprinkle the cocoa-sugar mixture evenly over the batter (the cocoa mixture should cover the entire surface of the batter); pour the coffee mixture gently over the cocoa mixture. Bake until the cake is puffed and bubbling and just beginning to pull away from the sides of the baking dish, about 45 minutes, rotating the pan halfway through the baking time. (Do not overbake.) Cool the cake in the dish on a wire rack for about 25 minutes and serve.

Individual Hot Fudge Pudding Cakes

Follow the recipe for Hot Fudge Pudding Cake, heating the oven to 400 degrees and lightly greasing eight 6- to 8-ounce ramekins; set the ramekins on a baking sheet. Divide the batter evenly among the ramekins (about ¼ cup per ramekin) and level with the back of a spoon; sprinkle about 2 tablespoons cocoa-sugar mixture over the batter in each ramekin. Pour 3 tablespoons coffee mixture over the cocoa-sugar mixture in each ramekin. Bake until puffed and bubbling, about 20 minutes. (Do not overbake.) Cool the pudding cakes for about 15 minutes before serving (the cakes will fall as they cool).

BITTERSWEET CHOCOLATE ROULADE

WHY THIS RECIPE WORKS: A chocolate roulade can be a baker's nightmare—a hard-to-roll cake with a dry texture and a filling that won't stay put. We wanted a recipe for a true showcase roulade, a cake with a velvety texture and deep chocolate flavor, a thick, rich filling, and a decadent icing that covers it all.

We used bitter- or semisweet chocolate for maximum chocolate flavor. Six eggs gave our cake great support. A combination of cocoa and flour provided further structure and extra chocolate flavor. Once the cake was baked, we cooled it briefly in the pan, then unmolded it onto a kitchen towel rubbed with cocoa to prevent sticking. While the cake was still warm, we rolled it up with the towel inside, cooled it briefly, and then unrolled the cake—this method gave the cake a "memory" so it could be filled and re-rolled. For the filling, we made a simple espresso-flavored cream with just four ingredients, including the lush Italian cream cheese, mascarpone. Mascarpone provided both structural support and rich flavor. For the icing, we chose dark chocolate ganache, made with bittersweet chocolate and cognac for complex flavor.

Bittersweet Chocolate Roulade
SERVES 8 TO 10

We suggest that you make the filling and ganache first, then make the cake while the ganache is setting up. Or, if you prefer, the cake can be baked, filled, and rolled—but not iced—then wrapped in plastic wrap and refrigerated for up to 24 hours. If serving this cake in the style of a holiday yule log, make wood-grain striations in the ganache with a fork. The roulade is best served at room temperature.

¼ cup (1¼ ounces) unbleached all-purpose flour, plus extra for the pan

6 ounces bittersweet or semisweet chocolate, chopped fine

2 tablespoons cold unsalted butter, cut into 2 pieces

2 tablespoons cold water

¼ cup Dutch-processed cocoa powder, sifted, plus 1 tablespoon for unmolding

⅛ teaspoon table salt

6 large eggs, at room temperature and separated

⅓ cup (2⅓ ounces) sugar

1 teaspoon vanilla extract

⅛ teaspoon cream of tartar

1 recipe Espresso-Mascarpone Cream (recipe follows)

1 recipe Dark Chocolate Ganache (recipe follows)

1. Adjust an oven rack to the upper-middle position and heat the oven to 400 degrees. Spray a 17½ by 12-inch rimmed baking sheet with vegetable oil spray, cover the pan bottom with parchment paper, and spray the parchment with vegetable oil spray; dust with flour and tap out the excess.

2. Heat the chocolate, butter, and water in a small heatproof bowl set over a saucepan filled with 1 inch of barely simmering water, stirring occasionally until smooth. Set aside to cool slightly. Sift ¼ cup of the cocoa, the flour, and salt together into a small bowl and set aside.

3. In a stand mixer fitted with the whisk attachment, beat the egg yolks at medium-high speed until just combined, about 15 seconds. With the mixer running, add half of the sugar. Continue to beat, scraping down the sides of the bowl as necessary, until the yolks are pale yellow and the mixture falls in a thick ribbon when the whisk is lifted, about 8 minutes. Add the vanilla and beat to combine, scraping down the bowl once, about 30 seconds. Turn the mixture into a medium bowl; wash and dry the mixer bowl and whisk attachment.

4. In the clean bowl with the clean whisk attachment, beat the egg whites and cream of tartar at medium speed until foamy, about 30 seconds. With the mixer running, add about 1 teaspoon more sugar; continue beating until soft peaks form, about 40 seconds. Gradually add the remaining sugar and beat until the egg whites are glossy and hold stiff peaks when the whisk is lifted, about 1 minute longer. Do not over beat.

5. Stir the chocolate mixture into the egg yolks. With a rubber spatula, stir one-quarter of the egg whites into the chocolate mixture to lighten it. Fold in the remaining egg whites until almost no streaks remain. Sprinkle the cocoa-flour mixture over the top and fold in quickly but gently.

6. Pour the batter into the prepared pan; using a spatula and working quickly, even the surface and smooth the batter into the pan corners. Lightly tap the pan against the countertop two or three times to settle the batter. Bake until the center of the cake springs back when touched with a finger, 8 to 10 minutes, rotating the pan halfway through the baking time. Cool the cake in the pan on a wire rack for 5 minutes.

7. While the cake is cooling, lay a clean kitchen towel over the work surface and sift the remaining 1 tablespoon cocoa over the towel; rub the cocoa into the towel. Run a small knife around the baking sheet to loosen the cake. Flip the cake onto the towel and peel off the parchment.

8. Roll the cake, towel and all, into a jellyroll shape. Cool for 15 minutes, then unroll the cake and towel. Using a spatula, immediately spread the filling evenly over the cake, almost to the edges. Roll up the cake gently but snugly around the filling. Set a large sheet of parchment paper on an overturned rimmed baking sheet and set the roulade, seam side down, on top. Trim both ends on the diagonal. Spread the ganache evenly over the roulade. Use a fork to make wood-grain striations, if desired, on the surface of the ganache before the icing has set. Refrigerate the cake, on the baking sheet, uncovered, to slightly set the icing, about 20 minutes.

9. Carefully slide two wide metal spatulas under the cake and transfer the cake to a serving platter. Cut into slices and serve.

Espresso-Mascarpone Cream

MAKES ABOUT 2½ CUPS

Mascarpone is a fresh Italian cheese. Its flavor is unique—mildly sweet and refreshing. It is sold in small containers in some supermarkets as well as most gourmet stores, cheese shops, and Italian markets.

½ cup heavy cream

2 teaspoons espresso powder or instant coffee

6 tablespoons confectioners' sugar

16½ ounces mascarpone cheese (generous 2 cups)

1. Bring the cream to a simmer in a small saucepan over high heat. Off the heat, stir in the espresso and confectioners' sugar; cool slightly.

2. With a spatula, beat the mascarpone in a medium bowl until softened. Gently whisk in the cooled cream mixture until combined. Cover with plastic wrap and refrigerate until ready to use.

Dark Chocolate Ganache

MAKES ABOUT 1½ CUPS

If your kitchen is cool and the ganache becomes too stiff to spread, set the bowl over a saucepan of simmering water, then stir briefly until it is smooth and icing-like.

- ¾ cup heavy cream
- 2 tablespoons unsalted butter
- 6 ounces high-quality bittersweet or semisweet chocolate, chopped
- 1 tablespoon cognac

Microwave the cream and butter in a microwave-safe measuring cup on high power until bubbling, about 1½ minutes. (Alternatively, bring to a simmer in a small saucepan over medium-high heat.) Place the chocolate in a food processor. With the machine running, gradually add the hot cream mixture and cognac through the feed tube and process until smooth and thickened, about 3 minutes. Transfer the ganache to a medium bowl and let stand at room temperature for 1 hour, until spreadable (the ganache should have the consistency of soft icing).

TRIPLE-CHOCOLATE MOUSSE CAKE

WHY THIS RECIPE WORKS: Triple chocolate mousse cake is a truly decadent dessert. Most times, though, the mousse texture is exactly the same from one layer to the next and the flavor is so rich it's hard to finish more than a few forkfuls. We set out to tweak this showy confection. By finessing one layer at a time, we aimed to create a triple-decker that was incrementally lighter in texture—and richness. For simplicity's sake, we decided to build the whole dessert, layer by layer, in the same springform pan. For a base layer that had the heft to support the upper two tiers, we chose flourless chocolate cake instead of the typical mousse. Folding egg whites into the batter helped lighten the cake without affecting its structural integrity. For the middle layer, we started with a traditional chocolate mousse, but the texture seemed too heavy when combined with the cake, so we removed the eggs and cut back on the chocolate a bit—this resulted in the lighter, creamier layer we desired. And for the crowning layer to our cake, we made an easy white chocolate mousse by folding whipped cream into melted white chocolate—and to prevent the soft mousse from oozing during slicing, we added a little gelatin to the mix.

Triple-Chocolate Mousse Cake

SERVES 12 TO 16

This recipe requires a springform pan at least 3 inches high for all three layers to fit. It is imperative that each layer is made in sequential order. Cool the base completely before topping with the middle layer. We recommend Ghirardelli

Bittersweet Chocolate for the base and middle layers; our other recommended brand of chocolate, Callebaut Intense Dark Chocolate, may be used but will produce drier, slightly less sweet results. Our preferred brand of white chocolate is Guittard Choc-Au-Lait White Chips. For best results, chill the mixer bowl before whipping the heavy cream. For neater slices, clean the knife thoroughly between slices.

BASE LAYER

- 6 tablespoons (¾ stick) unsalted butter, cut into 6 pieces
- 7 ounces bittersweet chocolate, chopped fine (see note)
- ¾ teaspoon instant espresso powder
- 4 large eggs, at room temperature and separated
- 1½ teaspoons vanilla extract
  Pinch table salt
- ⅓ cup packed (2⅓ ounces) light brown sugar, crumbled with fingers to remove lumps

MIDDLE LAYER

- 5 tablespoons hot water
- 2 tablespoons cocoa powder, preferably Dutch-processed
- 7 ounces bittersweet chocolate, chopped fine (see note)
- 1½ cups heavy cream, chilled
- 1 tablespoon granulated sugar
- ⅛ teaspoon table salt

TOP LAYER

- ¾ teaspoon powdered gelatin
- 1 tablespoon water
- 6 ounces white chocolate, chopped fine (see note)
- 1½ cups heavy cream, chilled
  Shaved chocolate or cocoa powder, for serving (optional)

1. FOR THE BASE LAYER: Adjust an oven rack to the middle position and heat the oven to 325 degrees. Grease the bottom and sides of a 9-inch-wide by 3-inch-high round springform pan. Melt the butter, chocolate, and espresso powder in a large heatproof bowl set over a saucepan filled with 1 inch of barely simmering water, stirring occasionally until smooth. Remove from the heat and cool the mixture slightly, about 5 minutes. Whisk in the egg yolks and vanilla; set aside.

2. In a stand mixer fitted with the whisk attachment, beat the egg whites and salt at medium speed until frothy, about 30 seconds. Add half of the brown sugar and beat until combined, about 15 seconds. Add the remaining brown sugar and beat at high speed until soft peaks form when the whisk is lifted, about 1 minute longer, scraping down the sides of the bowl halfway through. Using a whisk, fold one-third of the beaten egg whites into the chocolate mixture to lighten. Using a rubber spatula, fold in the remaining egg whites until no white streaks remain. Carefully transfer the batter to the prepared pan, gently smoothing the top with a spatula.

3. Bake until the cake has risen, is firm around the edges, and the center has just set but is still soft (the center of the cake will spring back after pressing gently with a finger), 13 to 18 minutes. Transfer the cake to a wire rack to cool completely, about 1 hour. (The cake will collapse as it cools.) Do not remove the cake from the pan.

4. FOR THE MIDDLE LAYER: Combine the hot water and cocoa powder in a small bowl; set aside. Melt the chocolate in a large heatproof bowl set over a saucepan filled with 1 inch of barely simmering water, stirring occasionally until smooth. Remove from the heat and cool slightly, 2 to 5 minutes.

5. In the clean bowl of a stand mixer fitted with the whisk attachment, whip the heavy cream, sugar, and salt at medium speed until it begins to thicken, about 30 seconds. Increase the speed to high and whip until soft peaks form when the whisk is lifted, 15 to 60 seconds. Whisk the cocoa powder mixture into the melted chocolate until smooth. Using a whisk, fold one-third of the whipped cream mixture into the chocolate mixture to lighten. Using a rubber spatula, fold in the remaining whipped cream mixture until no white streaks remain. Spoon the mousse into the springform pan over the cooled cake and lightly tap the pan against the countertop two or three times to settle the mousse; gently smooth the top with a spatula. Wipe the inside edge of the pan with a damp cloth to remove any drips. Refrigerate the cake for at least 15 minutes while preparing the top layer.

6. FOR THE TOP LAYER: In a small bowl, sprinkle the gelatin over the water; let stand for at least 5 minutes. Place the white chocolate in a medium bowl. Bring ½ cup of the cream to a simmer in a small saucepan over medium-high heat. Remove from the heat; add the gelatin mixture and stir until fully dissolved. Pour the cream mixture over the white chocolate and whisk until the chocolate is melted and the mixture is smooth, about 30 seconds. Cool to room temperature, stirring occasionally, 5 to 8 minutes (the mixture will thicken slightly).

7. In the bowl of a stand mixer fitted with the whisk attachment, whip the remaining 1 cup cream at medium speed until it begins to thicken, about 30 seconds. Increase the speed to high and whip until soft peaks form when the whisk is lifted, 15 to 60 seconds. Using a whisk, fold one-third of the whipped cream into the white chocolate mixture to lighten. Using a rubber spatula, fold the remaining whipped cream into the white chocolate mixture until no white streaks remain. Spoon the white chocolate mousse into the pan over the bittersweet chocolate mousse layer. Smooth the top with a spatula. Return the cake to the refrigerator and chill until set, at least 2½ hours.

8. TO SERVE: Garnish the top of the cake with chocolate curls or dust with cocoa (if using). Run a thin knife between the cake and sides of the springform pan; remove the sides of the pan. Run the cleaned knife along the outside of the cake to smooth the sides. Serve.

CHOCOLATE VOLCANO CAKES WITH ESPRESSO ICE CREAM

WHY THIS RECIPE WORKS: A common restaurant dessert, volcano cake, or molten chocolate cake, is an intensely chocolate cake that boasts a warm, liquid center. In addition to its great flavor and alluring contrasting textures, the cake can often be made ahead and baked just before serving. The make-ahead appeal of such a cake inspired us to master this dessert for the home cook.

The initial recipes we tried revealed a host of problems with this cake—unbalanced chocolate flavor and a soggy or dry texture were just a few issues we faced. After testing various chocolates, we settled on a combination of bittersweet chocolate and unsweetened chocolate—this gave us maximum chocolate flavor. Chocolate alone seemed a little flat, so we added Grand Marnier for another layer of flavor. Whole eggs and egg yolks contributed richness and cornstarch helped make the batter remarkably stable. To help the cakes fall right out of the ramekins without a struggle, we buttered and sugared the ramekins before pouring in the batter. The cakes alone were great, but we felt they were even better when accompanied by a cold, creamy scoop of doctored "espresso" ice cream.

Chocolate Volcano Cakes with Espresso Ice Cream

SERVES 8

Use a bittersweet bar chocolate in this recipe, not chips—the chips include emulsifiers that will alter the cakes' texture. The cake batter can be mixed and portioned into the ramekins, wrapped tightly with plastic wrap, and refrigerated up to 24 hours in advance. The cold cake batter should be baked straight from the refrigerator.

ESPRESSO ICE CREAM
2 pints coffee ice cream, softened
1½ tablespoons finely ground espresso beans

CAKES

- 10 tablespoons (1¼ sticks) unsalted butter, cut into ½-inch pieces, plus extra for the ramekins
- 1½ cups (10½ ounces) granulated sugar, plus extra for the ramekins
- 8 ounces bittersweet chocolate, chopped fine (see note)
- 2 ounces unsweetened chocolate, chopped fine
- 2 tablespoons cornstarch
- 3 large eggs plus 4 large egg yolks, at room temperature
- 2 teaspoons Grand Marnier (or other orange-flavored liqueur)
- Confectioners' sugar, for dusting the cakes

1. FOR THE ICE CREAM: Transfer the ice cream to a medium bowl and, using a rubber spatula, fold in the ground espresso until incorporated. Press a sheet of plastic wrap directly on the ice cream to prevent freezer burn and return it to the freezer. (The ice cream can be prepared up to 24 hours ahead.)

2. FOR THE CAKES: Lightly coat eight 4-ounce ramekins with butter. Dust with sugar, tapping out any excess, and set aside.

3. Melt the bittersweet and unsweetened chocolates and the 10 tablespoons butter in a large heatproof bowl set over a pan filled with 1 inch of barely simmering water, stirring occasionally until smooth. In a large bowl, whisk the 1½ cups sugar and cornstarch together. Add the chocolate mixture and stir to combine. Add the whole eggs, egg yolks, and Grand Marnier and whisk until fully combined. Using a ½-cup measure, scoop the batter into each of the prepared ramekins. (The ramekins can be covered tightly with plastic wrap and refrigerated for up to 24 hours.)

4. Adjust an oven rack to the upper-middle position and heat the oven to 375 degrees. Place the filled ramekins on a rimmed baking sheet and bake until the tops of the cakes are set, have formed shiny crusts, and are beginning to crack, 16 to 20 minutes.

5. Transfer the ramekins to a wire rack and cool slightly, about 2 minutes. Run a small knife around the edge of each cake. Using a towel to protect your hand from the hot ramekins, invert each cake onto a small plate, then immediately invert again right side up onto eight individual plates. Sift confectioners' sugar over each cake. Remove the ice cream from the freezer and scoop a portion next to each cake. Serve immediately.

CHOCOLATE-ESPRESSO DACQUOISE

WHY THIS RECIPE WORKS: We made this elaborate and impressive-looking dessert more approachable by reworking the meringue and buttercream, making them simpler and more foolproof. We swapped the traditional individually piped layers of meringue for a single sheet that was trimmed into layers after baking, and we shortened the usual 4-plus hours of oven time by increasing the oven temperature.

While many recipes call for a Swiss or French buttercream made with a hot sugar syrup, we opted for a German buttercream. With equal parts pastry cream and butter, this option required no hot syrup and it enabled us to use up the egg yolks left over from the meringue.

Chocolate-Espresso Dacquoise
SERVES 10 TO 12

The components in this recipe can easily be prepared in advance. Use a rimless baking sheet or an overturned rimmed baking sheet to bake the meringue. Instant coffee may be substituted for the espresso powder. To skin the hazelnuts, simply place the warm toasted nuts in a clean dish towel and rub gently. We recommend Ghirardelli Bittersweet Chocolate Baking Bar with 60 percent cacao for this recipe.

MERINGUE

- ¾ cup blanched sliced almonds, toasted
- ½ cup hazelnuts, toasted and skinned
- 1 tablespoon cornstarch
- ⅛ teaspoon salt
- 1 cup (7 ounces) sugar
- 4 large egg whites, room temperature
- ¼ teaspoon cream of tartar

BUTTERCREAM

- ¾ cup whole milk
- 4 large egg yolks
- ⅓ cup (2⅓ ounces) sugar
- 1½ teaspoons cornstarch
- ¼ teaspoon salt
- 2 tablespoons amaretto or water
- 1½ tablespoons instant espresso powder
- 16 tablespoons unsalted butter, softened

GANACHE

- 6 ounces bittersweet chocolate, chopped fine
- ¾ cup heavy cream
- 2 teaspoons corn syrup

- 12 whole hazelnuts, toasted and skinned
- 1 cup blanched sliced almonds, toasted

1. FOR THE MERINGUE: Adjust oven rack to middle position and heat oven to 250 degrees. Using ruler and pencil, draw 13 by 10½-inch rectangle on piece of parchment paper. Grease baking sheet and place parchment on it, marked side down.

2. Process almonds, hazelnuts, cornstarch, and salt in food processor until nuts are finely ground, 15 to 20 seconds. Add ½ cup sugar and pulse to combine, 1 to 2 pulses.

3. Using stand mixer fitted with whisk, whip egg whites and cream of tartar on medium-low speed until foamy, about 1 minute. Increase speed to medium-high and whip whites to soft, billowy mounds, about 1 minute. With mixer running at medium-high speed, slowly add remaining ½ cup sugar and continue to whip until glossy, stiff peaks form, 2 to 3 minutes. Fold nut mixture into egg whites in 2 batches. With offset spatula, spread meringue evenly into 13 by 10½-inch rectangle on parchment, using lines on parchment as guide. Using spray bottle, evenly mist surface of meringue with water until glistening. Bake for 1½ hours. Turn off oven and allow meringue to cool in oven for 1½ hours. (Do not open oven during baking and cooling.) Remove from oven and let cool to room temperature, about 10 minutes. (Cooled meringue can be kept at room temperature, tightly wrapped in plastic wrap, for up to 2 days.)

4. FOR THE BUTTERCREAM: Heat milk in small saucepan over medium heat until just simmering. Meanwhile, whisk yolks, sugar, cornstarch, and salt in bowl until smooth. Remove milk from heat and, whisking constantly, add half of milk to yolk mixture to temper. Whisking constantly, return tempered yolk mixture to remaining milk in saucepan. Return saucepan to medium heat and cook, whisking constantly, until mixture is bubbling and thickens to consistency of warm pudding, 3 to 5 minutes. Transfer pastry cream to bowl. Cover and refrigerate until set, at least 2 hours or up to 24 hours. Before using, warm gently to room temperature in microwave at 50 percent power, stirring every 10 seconds.

5. Stir together amaretto and espresso powder; set aside. Using stand mixer fitted with paddle, beat butter at medium speed until smooth and light, 3 to 4 minutes. Add pastry cream in 3 batches, beating for 30 seconds after each addition. Add amaretto mixture and continue to beat until light and fluffy, about 5 minutes longer, scraping down bowl thoroughly halfway through mixing.

NOTES FROM THE TEST KITCHEN

ASSEMBLING THE DACQUOISE

Here's how to assemble the three different components of dacquoise—cooled, baked meringue; buttercream; and ganache—into a dessert that looks like it was made in a professional bakery.

1. Using serrated knife and gentle, repeated scoring motion, trim edges of cooled meringue to form 12 by 10-inch rectangle.

2. With long side of meringue parallel to counter, mark top and bottom edges at 3-inch intervals.

3. Repeatedly score surface by gently drawing knife from top mark to corresponding bottom mark until cut through. Repeat to make four 10 by 3-inch strips.

4. Place 3 strips on wire rack and spread ¼ cup ganache evenly over each. Refrigerate for 15 minutes. Spread remaining strip with ½ cup buttercream.

5. Invert one ganache-coated strip on top of buttercream-coated strip and press gently. Spread top with buttercream. Repeat twice to form 4 layers.

6. Lightly coat sides of cake with half of remaining buttercream; coat top with remaining buttercream. Smooth edges and surfaces; refrigerate until firm.

7. Pour ganache over top of cake and spread in thin, even layer, letting excess flow down sides. Spread thinly across sides.

8. Place toasted whole hazelnuts in line on top of cake and gently press sliced almonds onto sides.

6. FOR THE GANACHE: Place chocolate in heatproof bowl. Bring cream and corn syrup to simmer in small saucepan over medium heat. Pour cream mixture over chocolate and let stand for 1 minute. Stir mixture until smooth. Set aside to cool until chocolate mounds slightly when dripped from spoon, about 5 minutes.

7. Carefully invert meringue and peel off parchment. Reinvert meringue and place on cutting board. Using serrated knife and gentle, repeated scoring motion, trim edges of meringue to form 12 by 10-inch rectangle. Discard trimmings. With long side of rectangle parallel to counter, use ruler to mark both long edges of meringue at 3-inch intervals. Using serrated knife, score surface of meringue by drawing knife toward you from mark on top edge to corresponding mark on bottom edge. Repeat scoring until meringue is fully cut through. Repeat until you have four 10 by 3-inch rectangles. (If any rectangles break during cutting, use them as middle layers.)

8. Place 3 rectangles on wire rack set in rimmed baking sheet. Using offset spatula, spread ¼ cup ganache evenly over surface of each meringue. Refrigerate until ganache is firm, about 15 minutes. Set aside remaining ganache.

9. Using offset spatula, spread top of remaining rectangle with ½ cup buttercream; place on wire rack with ganache-coated meringues. Invert 1 ganache-coated meringue, place on top of buttercream, and press gently to level. Repeat, spreading meringue with ½ cup buttercream and topping with inverted ganache-coated meringue. Spread top with buttercream. Invert final ganache-coated meringue on top of cake. Use 1 hand to steady top of cake and spread half of remaining buttercream to lightly coat sides of cake, then use remaining buttercream to coat top of cake. Smooth until cake resembles box. Refrigerate until buttercream is firm, about 2 hours. (Once buttercream is firm, assembled cake may be wrapped tightly in plastic and refrigerated for up to 2 days.)

10. Warm remaining ganache in heatproof bowl set over barely simmering water, stirring occasionally, until mixture is very fluid but not hot. Keeping assembled cake on wire rack, pour ganache over top of cake. Using offset spatula, spread ganache in thin, even layer over top of cake, letting excess flow down sides. Spread ganache over sides in thin layer (top must be completely covered, but some small gaps on sides are OK).

11. Garnish top of cake with hazelnuts. Holding bottom of cake with 1 hand, gently press almonds onto sides with other hand. Chill on wire rack, uncovered, for at least 3 hours or up to 12 hours. Transfer to platter. Cut into slices with sharp knife that has been dipped in hot water and wiped dry before each slice. Serve.

TIRAMISÙ

WHY THIS RECIPE WORKS: There's a reason restaurant menus (Italian or not) offer tiramisù. Delicate ladyfingers soaked in a spiked coffee mixture layered with a sweet, creamy filling make an irresistible combination. Preparing tiramisù, however, can be labor intensive. Some versions are overly rich with ladyfingers that turn soggy. We wanted to avoid these issues and find a streamlined approach—one that highlights the luxurious combination of flavors and textures that have made this dessert so popular. Instead of hauling out a double boiler to make the fussy custard-based filling (called *zabaglione*), we instead simply whipped egg yolks, sugar, salt, rum, and mascarpone together. Salt heightened the filling's subtle flavors. And to lighten the filling, we chose whipped cream instead of egg whites. For the coffee soaking mixture, we combined strong brewed coffee and espresso powder (along with more rum). To moisten the ladyfingers so that they were neither too dry nor too saturated, we dropped them one at a time into the spiked coffee mixture and rolled them over to moisten the other side for just a couple of seconds. For best flavor and texture, we discovered that it was important to allow the tiramisù to chill in the refrigerator for at least six hours.

Tiramisù

SERVES 10 TO 12

Brandy and even whiskey can stand in for the dark rum. The test kitchen prefers a tiramisù with a pronounced rum flavor; for a less potent rum flavor, halve the amount of rum added to the coffee mixture in step 1. Do not allow the mascarpone to warm to room temperature before using it; it has a tendency to break if allowed to do so.

2½ cups strong brewed coffee, at room temperature
9 tablespoons dark rum (see note)
1½ tablespoons instant espresso powder
6 large egg yolks, at room temperature
⅔ cup (4⅔ ounces) sugar
¼ teaspoon table salt
1½ pounds mascarpone (generous 3 cups; see note)

¾ cup heavy cream, chilled

14 ounces (42 to 60, depending on size) dried ladyfingers

3½ tablespoons cocoa powder, preferably Dutch-processed

¼ cup grated semisweet or bittersweet chocolate (optional)

1. Stir together the coffee, 5 tablespoons of the rum, and the espresso powder in a wide bowl or baking dish until the espresso dissolves; set aside.

2. In a stand mixer fitted with the whisk attachment, beat the egg yolks at low speed until just combined. Add the sugar and salt and beat at medium-high speed until pale yellow, 1½ to 2 minutes, scraping down the sides of the bowl with a rubber spatula once or twice. Add the remaining 4 tablespoons rum and beat at medium speed until just combined, 20 to 30 seconds; scrape the bowl. Add the mascarpone and beat at medium speed until no lumps remain, 30 to 45 seconds, scraping down the sides of the bowl once or twice. Transfer the mixture to a large bowl and set aside.

3. In the now-empty mixer bowl (no need to clean the bowl), beat the cream at medium speed until frothy, 1 to 1½ minutes. Increase the speed to high and continue to beat until the cream holds stiff peaks, 1 to 1½ minutes longer. Using a rubber spatula, fold one-third of the whipped cream into the mascarpone mixture to lighten, then gently fold in the remaining whipped cream until no white streaks remain. Set the mascarpone mixture aside.

4. Working one at a time, drop half of the ladyfingers into the coffee mixture, roll, remove, and transfer to a 13 by 9-inch glass or ceramic baking dish. (Do not submerge the ladyfingers in the coffee mixture; the entire process should take no longer than 2 to 3 seconds for each cookie.) Arrange the soaked cookies in a single layer in the baking dish, breaking or trimming the ladyfingers as needed to fit neatly into the dish.

5. Spread half of the mascarpone mixture over the ladyfingers; use a rubber spatula to spread the mixture to the sides and into the corners of the dish and smooth the surface. Place 2 tablespoons of the cocoa in a fine-mesh strainer and dust the cocoa over the mascarpone.

6. Repeat the dipping and arrangement of the ladyfingers; spread the remaining mascarpone mixture over the ladyfingers and dust with the remaining 1½ tablespoons cocoa. Wipe the edges of the dish with a dry paper towel. Cover with plastic wrap and refrigerate for 6 to 24 hours. Sprinkle with the grated chocolate (if using); cut into pieces and serve chilled.

Tiramisù with Cooked Eggs

This recipe involves cooking the yolks in a double boiler, which requires a little more effort and makes for a slightly thicker mascarpone filling, but the results are just as good as with our traditional method. You will need an additional ⅓ cup heavy cream.

Follow the recipe for Tiramisù through step 1. In step 2, add ⅓ cup cream to the egg yolks after the sugar and salt; do not whisk in the rum. Set the bowl with the yolks over a medium saucepan containing 1 inch gently simmering water; cook, constantly scraping along the bottom and sides of the bowl with a heatproof spatula, until the mixture coats the back of a spoon and registers 160 degrees on an instant-read thermometer, 4 to 7 minutes. Remove from the heat and stir vigorously to cool slightly, then set aside to cool to room temperature, about 15 minutes. Whisk in the remaining 4 tablespoons rum until combined. Transfer the bowl to a stand mixer fitted with the whisk attachment, add the mascarpone, and beat at medium speed until no lumps remain, 30 to 45 seconds. Transfer the mixture to a large bowl and set aside. Continue with the recipe from step 3, using the full amount of cream specified (¾ cup).

BOSTON CREAM PIE

WHY THIS RECIPE WORKS: This triple-component dessert deserved a revival—if only we could make the filling foolproof and keep the glaze from cracking off. A hot-milk sponge cake made a good base because it didn't require any finicky folding or separating of eggs. Baking the batter in two pans eliminated the need to slice a single cake horizontally before adding the filling. We used butter to firm up our pastry cream, and added corn syrup to heavy cream and melted chocolate to make a smooth glaze that clung to the top of our Boston Cream Pie and dripped artistically down its sides.

Wicked Good Boston Cream Pie

SERVES 8 TO 10

Chill the assembled cake for at least 3 hours to make it easy to cut and serve.

PASTRY CREAM

2 cups half-and-half

6 large egg yolks

½ cup (3½ ounces) sugar

Pinch salt

¼ cup all-purpose flour

4 tablespoons cold unsalted butter, cut into four pieces

1½ teaspoons vanilla extract

CAKE

1½ cups (7½ ounces) all-purpose flour

1½ teaspoons baking powder

¾ teaspoon salt

¾ cup whole milk

6 tablespoons unsalted butter

1½ teaspoons vanilla extract

3 large eggs

1½ cups (10½ ounces) sugar

GLAZE

½ cup heavy cream

2 tablespoons light corn syrup

4 ounces bittersweet chocolate, chopped fine

8. TO ASSEMBLE: Place one cake round on large plate. Whisk pastry cream briefly, then spoon onto center of cake. Using offset spatula, spread evenly to cake edge. Place second layer on pastry cream, bottom side up, making sure layers line up properly. Press lightly on top of cake to level. Refrigerate cake while preparing glaze.

9. FOR THE GLAZE: Bring cream and corn syrup to simmer in small saucepan over medium heat. Remove from heat and add chocolate. Whisk gently until smooth, 30 seconds. Let stand, whisking occasionally, until thickened slightly, about 5 minutes.

10. Pour glaze onto center of cake. Use offset spatula to spread glaze to edge of cake, letting excess drip decoratively down sides. Chill finished cake for 3 hours before slicing. Cake may be made up to 24 hours before serving.

NEW YORK–STYLE CHEESECAKE

WHY THIS RECIPE WORKS: The ideal New York cheesecake should be a tall, bronze-skinned, and dense affair. The flavor should be pure and minimalist, sweet and tangy, and rich. But many recipes fall short, with textures that range from fluffy to rubbery and leaden, and flavors that are starchy or overly citrusy. We wanted to perfect New York cheesecake. After trying a variety of crusts, we settled on the classic graham cracker crust—a simple combination of graham crackers, butter, and sugar. For the filling, cream cheese, boosted by the extra tang of a little sour cream, delivered the best flavor. A little lemon juice and vanilla added just the right sweet, bright accents without calling attention to themselves. A combination of eggs and egg yolks yielded a texture that was dense but not heavy. We found that the New York method worked better for this cheesecake than the typical water bath—baking the cake in a hot oven for 10 minutes then in a low oven for a full 90 minutes yielded the satiny texture we were after.

New York Cheesecake
SERVES 12

For neater slices, clean the knife thoroughly between slices. Serve as is or with Strawberry Topping (recipe follows). If you are concerned about the precision of your oven's temperature, try our Foolproof New York Cheesecake, page 791.

CRUST

- 8 whole graham crackers, broken into 1-inch pieces
- 7 tablespoons unsalted butter, melted and cooled
- 3 tablespoons sugar

FILLING

- 2½ pounds cream cheese, cut into chunks and softened
- 1½ cups (10½ ounces) sugar
- ⅛ teaspoon table salt
- ⅓ cup sour cream
- 2 teaspoons juice from 1 lemon
- 2 teaspoons vanilla extract
- 6 large eggs plus 2 large egg yolks, at room temperature

1. FOR THE PASTRY CREAM: Heat half-and-half in medium saucepan over medium heat until just simmering. Meanwhile, whisk yolks, sugar, and salt in medium bowl until smooth. Add flour to yolk mixture and whisk until incorporated. Remove half-and-half from heat and, whisking constantly, slowly add ½ cup to yolk mixture to temper. Whisking constantly, return tempered yolk mixture to half-and-half in saucepan.

2. Return saucepan to medium heat and cook, whisking constantly, until mixture thickens slightly, about 1 minute. Reduce heat to medium-low and continue to simmer, whisking constantly, 8 minutes.

3. Increase heat to medium and cook, whisking vigorously, until bubbles burst on surface, 1 to 2 minutes. Remove saucepan from heat; whisk in butter and vanilla until butter is melted and incorporated. Strain pastry cream through fine-mesh strainer set over medium bowl. Press lightly greased parchment paper directly on surface and refrigerate until set, at least 2 hours and up to 24 hours.

4. FOR THE CAKE: Adjust oven rack to middle position and heat oven to 325 degrees. Lightly grease two 9-inch round cake pans with vegetable oil spray and line with parchment. Whisk flour, baking powder, and salt together in medium bowl. Heat milk and butter in small saucepan over low heat until butter is melted. Remove from heat, add vanilla, and cover to keep warm.

5. In stand mixer fitted with whisk attachment, whip eggs and sugar at high speed until light and airy, about 5 minutes. Remove mixer bowl from stand. Add hot milk mixture and whisk by hand until incorporated. Add dry ingredients and whisk until incorporated.

6. Working quickly, divide batter evenly between prepared pans. Bake until tops are light brown and toothpick inserted in center of cakes comes out clean, 20 to 22 minutes.

7. Transfer cakes to wire rack and cool completely in pan, about 2 hours. Run small plastic knife around edge of pans, then invert cakes onto wire rack. Carefully remove parchment, then reinvert cakes.

1. FOR THE CRUST: Adjust an oven rack to the middle position and heat the oven to 325 degrees. Process the graham cracker pieces in a food processor to fine, even crumbs, about 30 seconds. Sprinkle 6 tablespoons of the melted butter and the sugar over the crumbs and pulse to incorporate. Sprinkle the mixture into a 9-inch springform pan. Press the crumbs firmly into an even layer using the bottom of a measuring cup. Bake the crust until fragrant and beginning to brown, 10 to 15 minutes. Cool the crust to room temperature, about 30 minutes.

2. FOR THE FILLING: Meanwhile, increase the oven temperature to 500 degrees. In the bowl of a stand mixer fitted with the paddle attachment, beat the cream cheese on medium-low speed until smooth, 1 to 3 minutes. Scrape down the bowl and beaters as needed.

3. Beat in ¾ cup of the sugar and the salt until incorporated, 1 to 3 minutes. Beat in the remaining ¾ cup sugar until incorporated, 1 to 3 minutes. Beat in the sour cream, lemon juice, and vanilla until incorporated, 1 to 3 minutes. Beat in the whole eggs and egg yolks, two at a time, until combined, 1 to 3 minutes.

4. Being careful not to disturb the baked crust, brush the inside of the prepared springform pan with the remaining 1 tablespoon melted butter. Set the pan on a rimmed baking sheet. Carefully pour the filling into the pan. Bake the cheesecake for 10 minutes.

5. Without opening the oven door, reduce the oven temperature to 200 degrees and continue to bake until the center of the cheesecake registers 150 degrees on an instant-read thermometer, about 1½ hours.

6. Transfer the cheesecake to a wire rack and run a knife around the edge of the cake. Cool the cheesecake until just barely warm, 2½ to 3 hours, running a knife around the edge of the cake every hour or so. Wrap the pan tightly in plastic wrap and refrigerate until cold, about 3 hours.

7. To unmold the cheesecake, wrap a wet, hot kitchen towel around the cake pan and let sit for 1 minute. Remove the sides of the pan and carefully slide the cake onto a cake platter. Let the cheesecake sit at room temperature for 30 minutes before serving.

Strawberry Topping
MAKES ABOUT 6 CUPS

This accompaniment to cheesecake is best served the same day it is made.

- 2 pounds fresh strawberries, cleaned, hulled, and cut lengthwise into ¼ to ⅛-inch slices
- ½ cup (3½ ounces) sugar
- Pinch table salt
- 1 cup strawberry jam
- 2 tablespoons juice from 1 lemon

1. Toss the berries, sugar, and salt in a medium bowl; let stand until the berries have released their juices and the sugar has dissolved, about 30 minutes, tossing occasionally to combine.

2. Process the jam in a food processor until smooth, about 8 seconds; transfer to a small saucepan. Bring the jam to a simmer over medium-high heat; simmer, stirring frequently, until dark and no longer frothy, about 3 minutes. Stir in the lemon juice; pour the warm liquid over the strawberries and stir to combine. Let cool, then cover with plastic wrap and refrigerate until cold, at least 2 hours or up to 12 hours. To serve, spoon a portion of topping over each slice of cheesecake.

FOOLPROOF NEW YORK CHEESECAKE

WHY THIS RECIPE WORKS: Our original New York Cheesecake (page 790) has a luxurious texture and brown surface, but some ovens yielded inconsistent cakes. To revise our recipe for everyone's ovens, we first created a pastry–graham cracker hybrid crust that wouldn't become soggy. Pulsing graham crackers, sugar, flour, and salt with melted butter coated the starches, making a crisp crust. Straining and resting the filling released bubble-producing air pockets. New York–style cheesecakes usually start in a hot oven before the temperature is dropped, but we found the time it took for the oven temperature to change varied. We flipped the order, baking at a low temperature to set the filling and then removing it before ramping up the oven's heat. Once the oven hit 500 degrees, we put the cheesecake on the upper rack to brown. This cheesecake would now have the same texture, flavor, and appearance no matter what oven was used.

Foolproof New York Cheesecake
SERVES 12 TO 16

This cheesecake takes at least 12 hours to make (including chilling), so we recommend making it the day before serving. An accurate oven thermometer and instant-read thermometer are essential. To ensure proper baking, check that the oven thermometer is holding steady at 200 degrees and refrain from frequently taking the temperature of the cheesecake (unless it is within a few degrees of 165, allow 20 minutes between checking). Keep a close eye on the cheesecake in step 5 to prevent overbrowning.

CRUST
- 6 whole graham crackers, broken into pieces
- ⅓ cup packed (2⅓ ounces) dark brown sugar
- ½ cup (2½ ounces) all-purpose flour
- ¼ teaspoon salt
- 7 tablespoons unsalted butter, melted

FILLING
- 2½ pounds cream cheese, softened
- 1½ cups (10½ ounces) granulated sugar
- ⅛ teaspoon salt
- ⅓ cup sour cream
- 2 teaspoons lemon juice
- 2 teaspoons vanilla extract
- 6 large eggs plus 2 large egg yolks

1. FOR THE CRUST: Adjust oven racks to upper-middle and lower-middle positions and heat oven to 325 degrees. Process cracker pieces and sugar in food processor until finely ground, about 30 seconds. Add flour and salt and pulse to combine, 2 pulses. Add 6 tablespoons melted butter and pulse until crumbs are evenly moistened, about 10 pulses. Brush bottom of 9-inch springform pan with ½ tablespoon melted butter. Using your hands, press crumb mixture evenly into pan bottom. Using flat bottom of measuring cup or ramekin, firmly pack crust into pan. Bake on lower-middle rack until fragrant and beginning to brown around edges, about 13 minutes. Transfer to rimmed baking sheet and set aside to cool completely. Reduce oven temperature to 200 degrees.

2. FOR THE FILLING: Using stand mixer fitted with paddle, beat cream cheese, ¾ cup sugar, and salt at medium-low speed until combined, about 1 minute. Beat in remaining ¾ cup sugar until combined, about 1 minute. Scrape beater and bowl well; add sour cream, lemon juice, and vanilla and beat at low speed until combined, about 1 minute. Add egg yolks and beat at medium-low speed until thoroughly combined, about 1 minute. Scrape bowl and beater. Add whole eggs two at a time, beating until thoroughly combined, about 30 seconds after each addition. Pour filling through fine-mesh strainer set in large bowl, pressing against strainer with rubber spatula or back of ladle to help filling pass through strainer.

3. Brush sides of springform pan with remaining ½ tablespoon melted butter. Pour filling into crust and set aside for 10 minutes to allow air bubbles to rise to top. Gently draw tines of fork across surface of cake to pop air bubbles that have risen to surface.

4. When oven thermometer reads 200 degrees, bake cheesecake on lower rack until center registers 165 degrees, 3 to 3½ hours. Remove cake from oven and increase oven temperature to 500 degrees.

5. When oven is at 500 degrees, bake cheesecake on upper rack until top is evenly browned, 4 to 12 minutes. Let cool for 5 minutes; run paring knife between cheesecake and side of springform pan. Let cheesecake cool until barely warm, 2½ to 3 hours. Wrap tightly in plastic wrap and refrigerate until cold and firmly set, at least 6 hours.

6. To unmold cheesecake, remove sides of pan. Slide thin metal spatula between crust and pan bottom to loosen, then slide cheesecake onto serving plate. Let cheesecake stand at room temperature for about 30 minutes. To slice, dip sharp knife in very hot water and wipe dry between cuts. Serve. (Leftovers can be refrigerated for up to 4 days.)

LIGHT CHEESECAKE

WHY THIS RECIPE WORKS: Of all the desserts that people long for in low-fat form, cheesecake is probably the most popular—but it's also the most difficult to lighten. Why? One modest slice of cheesecake boasts nearly 600 calories and about 40 grams of fat. Start removing the fat and sugar in the cake and flavor and texture can suffer terribly, as evidenced by the light recipes we tried. These cheesecakes were rubbery, gummy, and full of artificial flavors. We set out to develop a light cheesecake worth eating.

Three key steps produced our desired results. We replaced full-fat cream cheese and sour cream with a combination of light cream cheese, low-fat cottage cheese, and low-fat yogurt cheese. And to ensure a firm, not loose, filling, we drained the cottage cheese—this rid it of excess moisture. We cut the fat further by using a reduced number of whole eggs instead of whole eggs and yolks. And, finally, we pureed the filling in a food processor for an ultra smooth texture. The result? A rich, creamy cheesecake with about half the calories and three-quarters less fat than the original.

Light New York Cheesecake
SERVES 12

You can buy low-fat yogurt cheese (also called *labne*) or make your own with low-fat yogurt—allow at least 10 hours for the yogurt to drain. To make 1 cup yogurt cheese, line a fine-mesh strainer with 3 paper coffee filters or a double layer of cheesecloth. Spoon 2 cups of plain low-fat yogurt into the lined strainer, cover, and refrigerate for 10 to 12 hours (about 1 cup of liquid will have drained out of the yogurt to yield 1 cup yogurt cheese). Serve cake as is, or with Strawberry Topping (page 791).

CRUST

- 9 whole graham crackers, broken into 1-inch pieces
- 4 tablespoons (½ stick) unsalted butter, melted
- 1 tablespoon sugar

FILLING

- 1 pound 1 percent cottage cheese
- 1 pound light cream cheese, cut into chunks and softened
- 8 ounces (1 cup) low-fat yogurt cheese (see note)

1½   cups (10½ ounces) sugar
1   tablespoon vanilla extract
1   teaspoon grated zest from 1 lemon
¼   teaspoon table salt
3   large eggs, at room temperature

1. FOR THE CRUST: Adjust an oven rack to the middle position and heat the oven to 325 degrees. Process the graham cracker pieces in a food processor to fine, even crumbs, about 30 seconds. Mix the cracker crumbs, melted butter, and sugar together, then pour into a 9-inch springform pan. Press the crumbs firmly into an even layer using the bottom of a measuring cup. Bake the crust until fragrant, 10 to 15 minutes. Cool on a wire rack, about 30 minutes.

2. FOR THE FILLING: Meanwhile, increase the oven temperature to 500 degrees. Line a medium bowl with a clean dish towel or several layers of paper towels. Spoon the cottage cheese into the bowl and let drain for 30 minutes.

3. Process the drained cottage cheese in a food processor until smooth and no visible lumps remain, about 1 minute, scraping down the bowl as needed. Dollop the cream cheese and yogurt cheese into the food processor and continue to process until smooth, 1 to 2 minutes, scraping down the bowl as needed. Add the sugar, vanilla, lemon zest, and salt and continue to process until smooth, about 1 minute. With the processor running, add the eggs one at a time and continue to process until smooth.

4. Being careful not to disturb the baked crust, spray the insides of the springform pan with vegetable oil spray. Set the pan on a rimmed baking sheet. Pour the processed cheese mixture into the cooled crust and bake for 10 minutes.

5. Without opening the oven door, reduce the oven temperature to 200 degrees and continue to bake until the center of the cheesecake registers 150 degrees on an instant-read thermometer, about 1½ hours.

6. Transfer the cake to a wire rack and run a paring knife around the edge of the cake. Cool until barely warm, 2½ to 3 hours, running a paring knife around the edge of the cake every hour or so. Wrap the pan tightly in plastic wrap and refrigerate until cold, about 3 hours.

7. To unmold the cheesecake, wrap a wet, hot kitchen towel around the springform pan and let stand for 1 minute. Remove the sides of the pan. Blot any excess moisture from the top of the cheesecake with paper towels and slide onto a cake platter. Let the cheesecake stand at room temperature for about 30 minutes before slicing.

PUMPKIN CHEESECAKE

WHY THIS RECIPE WORKS: Those who suffer from pumpkin pie ennui embrace pumpkin cheesecake as "a nice change," but the expectations are low. Textures run the gamut from dry and dense to wet, soft, and mousse-like. Flavors veer from far too cheesy and tangy to pungently overspiced to totally bland. We wanted a creamy pumpkin cheesecake with a velvety smooth texture that tasted of sweet, earthy pumpkin as well as tangy cream cheese, that struck a harmonious spicy chord, and, of course, that had a crisp, buttery, cookie-crumb crust. For a cookie crust that complemented the earthy, warm flavors of pumpkin, we spiced up a graham cracker crust with ginger, cinnamon, and cloves. For a smooth and creamy texture, we blotted canned pumpkin puree with paper towels to remove excess moisture—this solved the sogginess issue. For dairy, we liked heavy cream, not sour cream, for added richness. We also preferred white sugar to brown, which tended to overpower the pumpkin flavor. Whole eggs, vanilla, salt, lemon juice, and a moderate blend of spices rounded out our cake. And for a smooth, velvety texture, we baked the cheesecake in a water bath in a moderate oven.

Spiced Pumpkin Cheesecake

SERVES 12

Be sure to buy unsweetened canned pumpkin, not pumpkin pie filling, which is preseasoned and sweetened. For neater slices, clean the knife thoroughly between slices.

CRUST

8   whole graham crackers, broken into 1-inch pieces
7   tablespoons unsalted butter, melted and cooled
3   tablespoons sugar
½   teaspoon ground ginger
½   teaspoon ground cinnamon
¼   teaspoon ground cloves

FILLING

1   (15-ounce) can pumpkin puree (see note)
1⅓   cups (9⅓ ounces) sugar
1   teaspoon ground cinnamon
½   teaspoon ground ginger
¼   teaspoon ground nutmeg
¼   teaspoon ground cloves
¼   teaspoon ground allspice
½   teaspoon table salt
1½   pounds cream cheese, cut into chunks and softened
1   tablespoon juice from 1 lemon
1   tablespoon vanilla extract
5   large eggs, at room temperature
1   cup heavy cream

1. FOR THE CRUST: Adjust an oven rack to the middle position and heat the oven to 325 degrees. Process the graham cracker pieces in a food processor to fine, even crumbs, about 30 seconds. Sprinkle 6 tablespoons of the melted butter, the sugar, and spices over the crumbs and pulse to incorporate. Sprinkle the mixture into a 9-inch springform pan. Press the crumbs firmly into an even layer using the bottom of a measuring cup. Bake the crust until fragrant and beginning to brown, 10 to 15 minutes. Let the crust cool to room temperature, about 30 minutes. Once cool, wrap the outside of the pan with two sheets of heavy-duty foil and set in a large roasting pan lined with a dish towel. Bring a kettle of water to a boil.

2. FOR THE FILLING: Pat the pumpkin puree dry with several layers of paper towels. Whisk the sugar, spices, and salt together in a small bowl.

3. In a stand mixer fitted with the paddle attachment, beat the cream cheese on medium-low speed until smooth, about 1 minute. Scrape down the bowl and beaters as needed.

4. Beat in half of the sugar mixture until incorporated, about 1 minute. Beat in the remaining sugar mixture until incorporated, about 1 minute. Beat in the dried pumpkin, lemon juice, and vanilla until incorporated, about 1 minute. Beat in the eggs, one at a time, until combined, about 1 minute. Beat in the heavy cream until incorporated, about 1 minute.

5. Being careful not to disturb the baked crust, brush the inside of the springform pan with the remaining 1 tablespoon melted butter. Carefully pour the filling into the pan. Set the roasting pan, with the cheesecake, on the oven rack and pour the boiling water into the roasting pan until it reaches about halfway up the sides of the pan. Bake the cheesecake until the center registers 150 degrees on an instant-read thermometer, about 1½ hours.

6. Cool the cheesecake in the roasting pan for 45 minutes, then transfer to a wire rack and cool until barely warm, 2½ to 3 hours, running a knife around the edge of the cake every hour or so. Wrap the pan tightly in plastic wrap and refrigerate until cold, about 3 hours.

7. To unmold the cheesecake, wrap a wet, hot kitchen towel around the cake pan and let sit for 1 minute. Remove the sides of the pan and carefully slide the cake onto a cake platter. Let the cheesecake sit at room temperature for 30 minutes before serving.

LEMON CHEESECAKE

WHY THIS RECIPE WORKS: Cheesecake is decadently rich. We love it in its unadulterated form, but sometimes the fresh flavor of citrus can take cheesecake to a refreshing new level. We aimed to develop a creamy cheesecake with a bracing but not overpowering lemon flavor.

Graham crackers, our usual cookie for cheesecakes, were too overpowering for the filling's lemon flavor. Instead, we turned to biscuit-type cookies, such as animal crackers, for a mild-tasting crust that allowed the lemon flavor of the cheesecake to shine. For maximum lemon flavor, we ground lemon zest with a portion of the sugar. This released its flavorful oils dramatically. Grinding the zest also improved the filling's texture (minced lemon zest baked up into fibrous bits in the cake). Heavy cream, in addition to cream cheese, provided richness, and vanilla rounded out the flavors. For ultimate creaminess, we baked the cake in a water bath. And finally, for an additional layer of bright lemon flavor, we topped off the cake with lemon curd.

Lemon Cheesecake
SERVES 12

Be sure to zest the lemons before juicing them. For neater slices, clean the knife thoroughly between slices.

CRUST

- 5 ounces Nabisco Barnum's Animal Crackers or Social Tea Biscuits
- 7 tablespoons unsalted butter, melted and cooled
- 3 tablespoons sugar

FILLING

- 1¼ cups (8¾ ounces) sugar
- 1 tablespoon grated zest from 1 lemon
- 1½ pounds cream cheese, cut into chunks and softened
- ¼ teaspoon table salt
- ¼ cup juice from 2 lemons
- 2 teaspoons vanilla extract
- 4 large eggs, at room temperature
- ½ cup heavy cream

CURD

- ⅓ cup juice from 2 lemons
- ½ cup (3½ ounces) sugar
  Pinch table salt
- 2 large whole eggs plus 1 large egg yolk
- 2 tablespoons unsalted butter, cut into ½-inch pieces and frozen
- 1 tablespoon heavy cream
- ¼ teaspoon vanilla extract

1. FOR THE CRUST: Adjust an oven rack to the middle position and heat the oven to 325 degrees. Process the cookies in a food processor to fine, even crumbs, about 30 seconds. Sprinkle 6 tablespoons of the melted butter and the sugar over the crumbs and pulse to incorporate. Sprinkle the mixture into a 9-inch springform pan. Press the crumbs firmly into an even layer using the bottom of a measuring cup. Bake the crust until fragrant and beginning to brown, 10 to 15 minutes. Let the crust cool to room temperature, about 30 minutes. Once cool, wrap the outside of the pan with two sheets of heavy-duty foil and set in a large roasting pan lined with a dish towel. Bring a kettle of water to a boil.

2. FOR THE FILLING: Process ¼ cup of the sugar and the lemon zest in a food processor until the sugar is yellow and the zest is very fine, about 15 seconds. Pulse in the remaining 1 cup sugar to combine.

3. In a stand mixer fitted with the paddle attachment, beat the cream cheese on medium speed until smooth, about 1 minute. Scrape down the bowl and beaters as needed.

4. Beat in half of the lemon sugar and the salt until incorporated. Beat in the remaining lemon sugar until incorporated, about 1 minute. Beat in the lemon juice and vanilla until incorporated, about 1 minute. Beat in the eggs, one at a time, until combined, about 1 minute. Beat in the heavy cream until incorporated, about 1 minute.

5. Being careful not to disturb the baked crust, brush the inside of the prepared springform pan with the remaining 1 tablespoon melted butter. Carefully pour the filling into the pan. Set the roasting pan, with the cheesecake, on the oven rack and pour the boiling water into the roasting pan until it reaches about halfway up the sides of the springform pan. Bake the cheesecake until the center registers 150 degrees on an instant-read thermometer, about 1½ hours.

6. Cool the cheesecake in the roasting pan for 45 minutes, then transfer to a wire rack and cool until barely warm, 2½ to 3 hours, running a knife around the edge of the cake every hour or so. Wrap the pan tightly in plastic wrap and refrigerate until cold, about 3 hours.

7. FOR THE CURD: Meanwhile, cook the lemon juice, sugar, and salt together in a small saucepan over medium-high heat until the sugar dissolves and the mixture is hot (do not boil). In a medium bowl, whisk the whole eggs and egg yolk together until combined, then slowly whisk in the hot lemon mixture to temper. Return the mixture to the saucepan and cook over medium-low heat, stirring constantly, until the mixture is thickened and a spatula scraped along the bottom of the pan leaves a trail (170 degrees on an instant-read thermometer), 2 to 4 minutes.

8. Off the heat, stir in the frozen butter until melted and incorporated, then stir in the cream and vanilla. Strain the curd through a fine-mesh strainer into a small bowl. Press plastic wrap directly on the surface of the curd and refrigerate until needed.

9. TO FINISH THE CAKE: When the cheesecake is cold, spoon the lemon curd over the top of the cake and spread into an even layer. Wrap the pan tightly in plastic wrap and refrigerate until the curd and cake have set, at least 5 hours.

10. To unmold the cheesecake, wrap a wet, hot kitchen towel around the cake pan and let sit for 1 minute. Remove the sides of the pan and carefully slide the cake onto a cake platter. Let the cheesecake sit at room temperature for 30 minutes before serving.

LEMON PUDDING CAKES

WHY THIS RECIPE WORKS: Despite the appeal of a single batter that produces two texturally distinct layers, lemon pudding cake can be unpredictable, sporting underbaked cake or grainy pudding. We wanted lots of lemon flavor, tender cake, and rich, creamy pudding. Whipping the egg whites to soft peaks and decreasing the amount of flour gave us the best ratio of pudding to cake. Baking powder gave the cake layer some lift, while also producing a golden top. Using a cold water bath in a large roasting pan prevented the pudding from curdling while still allowing the cake to cook through. By infusing the milk and cream with lemon zest, we achieved maximum lemon flavor without a disruption in the smooth texture of the dessert. We finished off the cakes with a sweet, fruity blueberry compote to complement the tart lemon flavor.

Lemon Pudding Cakes

SERVES 6

To take the temperature of the pudding layer, touch the probe tip to the bottom of the ramekin and pull it up ¼ inch. The batter can also be baked in an 8-inch square glass baking

dish. We like this dessert served at room temperature, but it can also be served chilled (the texture will be firmer). Spoon Blueberry Compote (recipe follows) over the top of each ramekin or simply dust with confectioners' sugar.

- 1 cup whole milk
- ½ cup heavy cream
- 3 tablespoons grated lemon zest plus ½ cup juice (3 lemons)
- 1 cup (7 ounces) sugar
- ¼ cup (1¼ ounces) all-purpose flour
- ½ teaspoon baking powder
- ⅛ teaspoon salt
- 2 large eggs, separated, plus 2 large whites
- ½ teaspoon vanilla extract

1. Adjust oven rack to middle position and heat oven to 325 degrees. Bring milk and cream to simmer in medium saucepan over medium-high heat. Remove pan from heat, whisk in lemon zest, cover pan, and let stand for 15 minutes. Meanwhile, fold dish towel in half and place in bottom of large roasting pan. Place six 6-ounce ramekins on top of towel and set aside pan.

2. Strain milk mixture through fine-mesh strainer into bowl, pressing on lemon zest to extract liquid; discard lemon zest. Whisk ¾ cup sugar, flour, baking powder, and salt in second bowl until combined. Add egg yolks, vanilla, lemon juice, and milk mixture and whisk until combined. (Batter will have consistency of milk.)

3. Using stand mixer fitted with whisk, whip egg whites on medium-low speed until foamy, about 1 minute. Increase speed to medium-high and whip whites to soft, billowy mounds, about 1 minute. Gradually add remaining ¼ cup sugar and whip until glossy, soft peaks form, 1 to 2 minutes.

4. Whisk one-quarter of whites into batter to lighten. With rubber spatula, gently fold in remaining whites until no clumps or streaks remain. Ladle batter into ramekins (ramekins should be nearly full). Pour enough cold water into roasting pan to come one-third of way up sides of ramekins. Bake until cake is set and pale golden brown and pudding layer registers 172 to 175 degrees at center, 50 to 55 minutes.

5. Remove pan from oven and let ramekins stand in water bath for 10 minutes. Transfer ramekins to wire rack and let cool completely. Serve.

Blueberry Compote

MAKES ABOUT 1 CUP

To use fresh blueberries, crush one-third of them against the side of the saucepan with a wooden spoon after adding them to the butter and then proceed as directed.

   1   tablespoon unsalted butter
  10 ounces (2 cups) frozen blueberries
   2   tablespoons sugar, plus extra for seasoning
        Pinch salt
  ½   teaspoon lemon juice

Melt butter in small saucepan over medium heat. Add blueberries, 2 tablespoons sugar, and salt; bring to boil. Lower heat and simmer, stirring occasionally, until thickened and about one-quarter of juice remains, 8 to 10 minutes. Remove pan from heat and stir in lemon juice. Season with extra sugar to taste.

BAKED ALASKA

WHY THIS RECIPE WORKS: Though making a baked Alaska can be intimidating to some, the dessert is essentially a dressed-up ice cream cake that's no more difficult to make than any other version. Plenty of insulation was the key to a baked Alaska that is toasty on the outside but still firm at the center. Most recipes use cake only as a base, but we used it to encase the ice cream entirely, thereby decreasing the amount of meringue by more than one-third without sacrificing heat resistance. To further improve the balance, we added cocoa to our cake, boosting flavor without adding sweetness. Rather than packing softened ice cream into a mold (refrozen ice cream can be icy, and it can be hard to match cake pans and bowls), we simply cut the cardboard off two pints of firm ice cream and stuck them together to form the core of our dessert. We opted for coffee ice cream, which complements the flavor of the cake and the sweetness of the meringue perfectly.

Baked Alaska

SERVES 8

Coffee ice cream provides the best contrast with sweet meringue in this recipe, but other flavors may be substituted, if desired. A high-quality ice cream such as Häagen-Dazs works best because it is slower to melt. To ensure the proper texture when serving, it is necessary to remove the cake from the freezer before making the meringue. This recipe leaves just enough leftover cake and ice cream to make an additional for-two version (recipe follows).

   2   (1-pint) containers coffee ice cream

CAKE
   1   cup (4 ounces) cake flour
  ⅓   cup (1 ounce) unsweetened cocoa powder
  ⅔   cup (4⅔ ounces) sugar
  1½ teaspoons baking powder
  ¼   teaspoon salt
  ½   cup vegetable oil
   6   tablespoons water
   4   large eggs, separated

MERINGUE
  ¾   cup (5¼ ounces) sugar
  ⅓   cup light corn syrup
   3   large egg whites
   2   tablespoons water
        Pinch salt
   1   teaspoon vanilla extract

1. Lay 12-inch square sheet of plastic wrap on counter and remove lids from ice cream. Use scissors to cut cardboard tubs from top to bottom. Peel away cardboard and discard. Place ice cream blocks on their sides in center of plastic with wider ends facing each other. Grasp each side of plastic and firmly press blocks together to form barrel shape. Wrap plastic tightly around ice cream and roll briefly on counter to form uniform cylinder. Place cylinder, standing on end, in freezer until completely solid, at least 1 hour.

2. FOR THE CAKE: Adjust oven rack to middle position and heat oven to 350 degrees. Lightly grease 18 by 13-inch rimmed baking sheet, line with parchment paper, and lightly grease parchment. Whisk flour, cocoa, ⅓ cup sugar, baking powder, and salt together in large bowl. Whisk oil, water, and egg yolks into flour mixture until smooth batter forms.

3. Using stand mixer fitted with whisk attachment, whip egg whites on medium-low speed until foamy, about 1 minute. Increase speed to medium-high and whip whites to soft, billowy mounds, about 1 minute. Gradually add remaining ⅓ cup sugar and whip until glossy, soft peaks form, 1 to 2 minutes. Transfer one-third of egg whites to batter; whisk gently until mixture is lightened. Using rubber spatula, gently fold remaining egg whites into batter.

4. Pour batter into prepared sheet; spread evenly. Bake until cake springs back when pressed lightly in center, 10 to 13 minutes. Transfer cake to wire rack and let cool for 5 minutes. Run knife around edge of sheet, then invert cake onto wire rack. Carefully remove parchment, then reinvert cake onto second wire rack. Let cool completely, at least 15 minutes.

5. Transfer cake to cutting board with long side of rectangle parallel to edge of counter. Using serrated knife, trim ¼ inch off left side of cake and discard. Using ruler, measure 4½ inches from cut edge and make mark with knife. Using mark as guide, cut 4½-inch rectangle from cake. Trim piece to create 4½ by 11-inch rectangle and set aside. (Depending on pan size and how much cake has shrunk during baking, it may not be necessary to trim piece to measure 11 inches.)

Measure 4 inches from new cut edge and make mark. Using mark as guide, cut 4-inch rectangle from cake. Trim piece to create 4 by 10-inch rectangle, wrap rectangle in plastic, and set aside. Cut 3½-inch round from remaining cake and set aside (biscuit cutter works well). Save scraps for Bonus Baked Alaska.

6. Unwrap ice cream. Trim cylinder to 4½ inches in length and return remainder to freezer for Bonus Baked Alaska. Place ice cream cylinder on 4½ by 11-inch cake rectangle and wrap cake around ice cream. (Cake may crack slightly.) Place cake circle on one end of cylinder. Wrap entire cylinder tightly in plastic. Place cylinder, standing on cake-covered end, in freezer until cake is firm, at least 30 minutes.

7. Unwrap cylinder and place on cutting board, standing on cake-covered end, and cut in half lengthwise. Unwrap reserved 4 by 10-inch cake rectangle and place halves on top, ice cream side down, with open ends meeting in middle. Wrap tightly with plastic and press ends gently to close gap between halves. Return to freezer for at least 2 hours and up to 2 weeks.

8. FOR THE MERINGUE: Adjust oven rack to upper-middle position and heat oven to 500 degrees. Spray wire rack set in rimmed baking sheet with vegetable oil spray. Unwrap cake and place on rack. Combine sugar, corn syrup, egg whites, water, and salt in bowl of stand mixer; place bowl over saucepan filled with 1 inch simmering water, making sure that water does not touch bottom of bowl. Whisking gently but constantly, heat until sugar is dissolved and mixture registers 160 degrees, 5 to 8 minutes.

9. Place bowl in stand mixer fitted with whisk attachment. Beat mixture on medium speed until bowl is only slightly warm to touch, about 5 minutes. Increase speed to high and beat until mixture begins to lose its gloss and forms stiff peaks, about 5 minutes. Add vanilla and beat until combined.

10. Using offset spatula, spread meringue over top and sides of cake, avoiding getting meringue on rack. Use back of spoon to create peaks all over meringue.

11. Bake until browned and crisp, about 5 minutes. Run offset spatula or thin knife under dessert to loosen from rack, then use two spatulas to transfer to serving platter. To slice, dip sharp knife in very hot water and wipe dry after each cut. Serve immediately.

Bonus Baked Alaska

SERVES 2

Our Baked Alaska recipe leaves just enough leftover cake and ice cream to make an additional for-two version.

From remaining cake, cut two 3⅓-inch rounds and one 11 by 2-inch strip. Place leftover ice cream disk on top of 1 cake round. Wrap strip of cake around sides of disk. Place remaining cake round on top, wrap tightly in plastic, and freeze. Following step 10, spread meringue over cake and bake as directed.

BUILDING A NEW BAKED ALASKA

1. Cut ice cream tubs from top to bottom and peel away cardboard. Place blocks on plastic wrap on their sides with wider ends facing each other.

2. Wrap plastic tightly around ice cream and roll on counter to form even cylinder. Place in freezer, standing on end, for 1 hour.

3. Trim ¼ inch off left side of cake. Cut 4½ by 11-inch rectangle, 4 by 10-inch rectangle, and 3½-inch round. Save scraps for Bonus Baked Alaska.

4. Unwrap ice cream and trim cylinder to 4½ inches in length. Return remainder to freezer.

5. Place ice cream on 11 by 4½-inch cake rectangle and wrap cake around ice cream. Place cake circle on 1 end of cylinder. Wrap in plastic. Freeze, standing on cake-covered end, for 30 minutes.

6. Unwrap cylinder, stand on cake-covered end, and cut in half lengthwise. Place halves on 10 by 4-inch rectangle, ice cream side down, with open ends meeting in middle.

PUDDINGS, SOUFFLÉS, AND MORE

BREAD PUDDING

WHY THIS RECIPE WORKS: Contemporary versions of this humble dish vary in texture, from mushy porridge to chewy, desiccated cousins of overcooked holiday stuffing. We wanted a dessert as refined as any French soufflé. We chose challah for its rich flavor, cut the bread into cubes, toasted them until lightly browned, and soaked them with basic custard. Once the cubes were saturated, we transferred them to a baking dish and slid our pudding into a low-temperature oven to prevent curdling. The custard turned out creamy and smooth, but not as set as we'd have liked. Adding another egg or two would help, but it already tasted somewhat eggy. It turns out that eggy flavor comes from the sulfur compounds in egg whites. We got rid of the whites and just used the yolks. We now had a luscious, silky custard with no trace of egginess. For a crackly crust, we dotted the top of the pudding with additional toasted bread cubes. Then we brushed it with melted butter and sprinkled it with a flavorful mixture of white and brown sugar before transferring it to the oven. The crunchy, buttery, sugary crust was the perfect partner to the satiny-smooth custard that lay below.

Classic Bread Pudding
SERVES 8 TO 10

Challah is an egg-enriched bread that can be found in most bakeries and supermarkets. If you cannot find challah, a firm high-quality sandwich bread such as Arnold Country Classics White or Pepperidge Farm Farmhouse Hearty White may be substituted. If desired, serve this pudding with softly whipped cream or with Bourbon–Brown Sugar Sauce (recipe follows). Store leftovers tightly wrapped in the refrigerator. To retain a crisp top crust when reheating leftovers, cut the bread pudding into squares and heat, uncovered, in a 450-degree oven until warmed through, 6 to 8 minutes.

2	tablespoons light brown sugar
¾	cup (5¼ ounces) plus 1 tablespoon granulated sugar
1	(14-ounce) loaf challah bread, cut into ¾-inch cubes (about 10 cups; see note)
9	large egg yolks
4	teaspoons vanilla extract
¾	teaspoon table salt
2½	cups heavy cream
2½	cups milk
2	tablespoons unsalted butter, melted

1. Adjust the oven racks to the middle and lower-middle positions and heat the oven to 325 degrees. Combine the brown sugar and 1 tablespoon of the granulated sugar in a small bowl; set aside.

2. Spread the bread cubes in a single layer on two rimmed baking sheets. Bake, tossing occasionally, until just dry, about 15 minutes, switching the baking sheets halfway through the baking time. Cool the bread cubes for about 15 minutes; set aside 2 cups.

3. Whisk the egg yolks, remaining ¾ cup sugar, the vanilla, and salt together in a large bowl. Whisk in the cream and milk until combined. Add the remaining 8 cups cooled bread cubes and toss to coat. Transfer the mixture to a 13 by 9-inch baking dish and let stand, occasionally pressing the bread cubes into the custard, until the cubes are thoroughly saturated, about 30 minutes.

4. Spread the reserved bread cubes evenly over the top of the soaked bread mixture and gently press into the custard. Using a pastry brush, dab the melted butter over the top of the unsoaked bread pieces. Sprinkle the brown sugar mixture evenly over the top. Place the bread pudding on a rimmed baking sheet and bake on the middle rack until the custard has just set and pressing the center of the pudding with your finger reveals no runny liquid, 45 to 50 minutes. (An instant-read thermometer inserted into the center of the pudding should read 170 degrees.) Transfer to a wire rack and cool until the pudding is set and just warm, about 45 minutes. Serve.

Bourbon–Brown Sugar Sauce
MAKES ABOUT 1 CUP

½	cup packed (3½ ounces) light brown sugar
7	tablespoons heavy cream
2½	tablespoons unsalted butter
1½	tablespoons bourbon

Whisk the brown sugar and heavy cream in a small saucepan over medium heat until combined. Continue to cook, whisking frequently, until the mixture comes to a boil, about 5 minutes. Whisk in the butter and bring the mixture back to a boil, about 1 minute. Remove from the heat and whisk in the bourbon. Cool to just warm; serve with the bread pudding.

SLOW-COOKER CHOCOLATE BREAD PUDDING

WHY THIS RECIPE WORKS: Making bread pudding in a slow cooker may seem like a stretch, but we were determined to make a company-worthy version in the slow cooker that boasted both decadence and hands-off (and oven-freeing) convenience. Getting the texture of this dessert just right was the real challenge; early tests yielded mushy or dry puddings, not the creamy and moist texture we were after. After testing various types of bread, we agreed challah, with its rich flavor, had the upper hand. We cut the bread into cubes and toasted it in the oven before adding it to the slow cooker. This extra step dried out the bread so it would be able to soak up as much custard as possible. Once toasted, we transferred the bread to the slow cooker and added the custard (a combination of egg yolks, milk, heavy cream, sugar, and vanilla). Pressing the bread into the custard ensured every cube soaked up its share. A chocolate bread pudding seemed like the right indulgent route to take, and opting for Nutella as our chief chocolaty component took our recipe to the next level. To give our recipe another chocolaty boost, we stirred in chocolate chips, which melted into the pudding and made this dessert that much more decadent.

Chocolate-Hazelnut Slow-Cooker Bread Pudding
SERVES 8 TO 10

- 1 (14-ounce) loaf challah bread, cut into 1-inch cubes (about 12 cups; see note on page 800)
- ½ cup chocolate chips
- 2 cups heavy cream
- 2 cups whole milk
- 9 large egg yolks
- 1 cup Nutella
- ¾ cup plus 1 tablespoon (5⅔ ounces) granulated sugar
- 4 teaspoons vanilla extract
- ¾ teaspoon table salt
- 2 tablespoons light brown sugar

1. Following the photos, line the slow cooker with an aluminum foil collar, then line with a foil sling, and spray with vegetable oil spray. Adjust the oven rack to the middle position and heat the oven to 225 degrees. Spread the bread over a rimmed baking sheet and bake, shaking the pan occasionally, until dry and crisp, about 40 minutes. Let the bread cool slightly, then transfer to a very large bowl.

2. Mix the chocolate chips into the dried bread; transfer to the prepared slow cooker. Whisk the cream, milk, egg yolks, Nutella, ¾ cup of the granulated sugar, the vanilla, and salt together in a bowl, then pour the mixture evenly over the bread. Press gently on the bread to submerge.

3. Mix the remaining 1 tablespoon granulated sugar with the brown sugar then sprinkle over the top of the casserole. Cover and cook until the center is set, about 4 hours on low. Let cool for 30 minutes before serving.

PREPARING THE SLOW COOKER

1. TO MAKE A FOIL COLLAR: Layer and fold sheets of heavy-duty foil until you have a six-layered foil rectangle that measures roughly 16 inches long by 4 inches wide. Press the collar into the back side of the slow-cooker insert.

2. TO MAKE A FOIL SLING: Fit two large sheets of heavy-duty foil into the slow cooker, perpendicular to one another and hanging over the edges of the slow cooker. Use the overhanging foil to lift the dish out of the slow cooker fully intact.

STOVETOP RICE PUDDING

WHY THIS RECIPE WORKS: At its best, rice pudding is lightly sweet and tastes of its primary component, rice. At its worst, the rice flavor is lost to cloying sweetness, overcooked milk, and a pasty, leaden consistency. We wanted a rice pudding with intact, tender grains bound loosely in a subtly sweet, creamy pudding.

For simple, straightforward rice flavor, we avoided aromatic rices like basmati and jasmine. Arborio rice, used for risotto, was stiff and gritty. Overall, medium-grain rice produced the best texture (with long-grain rice a close second). We found that cooking the rice in water rather than milk left its flavor intact. After the rice absorbed the water, we added sugar and equal amounts of milk and half-and-half, which delivered the proper degree of richness; the eggs and butter found in other recipes were just too overpowering. When we cooked the rice in water with the lid on the pan, then removed the lid while the rice simmered in the milk mixture, we got the results we wanted: distinct, tender grains of rice in a milky, subtly sweet sauce.

Stovetop Rice Pudding
SERVES 6 TO 8

We prefer pudding made with medium-grain rice, but long-grain rice works, too.

- 2 cups water
- 1 cup medium-grain rice (see note)
- ¼ teaspoon table salt
- 2½ cups whole milk
- 2½ cups half-and-half
- ⅔ cup (4⅔ ounces) sugar
- ½ cup raisins
- 1½ teaspoons vanilla extract
- 1 teaspoon ground cinnamon

1. Bring the water to a boil in a large saucepan. Stir in the rice and salt, cover, and simmer over low heat, stirring once or twice, until the water is almost fully absorbed, 15 to 20 minutes.

2. Stir in the milk, half-and-half, and sugar. Increase the heat to medium-high and bring to a simmer, then reduce the heat to maintain a simmer. Cook, uncovered and stirring frequently, until the mixture starts to thicken, about 30 minutes. Reduce the heat to low and continue to cook, stirring every couple of minutes to prevent sticking and scorching, until a spoon is just able to stand up in the pudding, about 15 minutes longer.

3. Remove from the heat and stir in the raisins, vanilla, and cinnamon. Serve warm, at room temperature, or chilled. (To store, press plastic wrap directly onto the surface of the pudding and refrigerate for up to 2 days. If serving at room temperature or chilled, stir in up to 1 cup warm milk, 2 tablespoons at a time, as needed to loosen before serving.)

Coconut Rice Pudding

To toast the coconut, spread it out on a rimmed baking sheet and toast it in a 325-degree oven, stirring often, until light golden, 10 to 15 minutes.

Follow the recipe for Stovetop Rice Pudding, substituting coconut milk for the whole milk and garnishing with 1 cup shredded sweetened coconut, toasted, before serving.

BEST BUTTERSCOTCH PUDDING

WHY THIS RECIPE WORKS: For butterscotch pudding with rich, bittersweet flavor, we made butterscotch sauce by cooking butter, brown and white sugar, corn syrup, lemon juice, and salt together into a dark caramel. Because making caramel can be finicky—it can go from caramelized to burnt in a matter of seconds—we used a two-step process that gave us a larger window in which to gauge the doneness of the caramel. We first brought the mixture to a rolling boil and then we reduced the heat to a low simmer where it slowly came up to temperature and we could stop the cooking at just the right moment. To turn our butterscotch into pudding, we ditched the classical (yet time-consuming) tempering method in favor of a revolutionary technique that calls for pouring the boiling caramel sauce directly over the thickening agents (egg yolks and cornstarch thinned with a little milk). The result is the sophisticated bittersweet flavor of traditional butterscotch with less mess and fuss.

Best Butterscotch Pudding

SERVES 8

When taking the temperature of the caramel in step 1, tilt the pan and move the thermometer back and forth to equalize hot and cool spots. Work quickly when pouring the caramel mixture over the egg mixture in step 4 to ensure proper thickening. Serve the pudding with lightly sweetened whipped cream.

12 tablespoons unsalted butter, cut into ½-inch pieces
½ cup (3½ ounces) granulated sugar
½ cup packed (3½ ounces) dark brown sugar
¼ cup water
2 tablespoons light corn syrup
1 teaspoon lemon juice
¾ teaspoon salt
1 cup heavy cream
2¼ cups whole milk
4 large egg yolks
¼ cup cornstarch
2 teaspoons vanilla extract
1 teaspoon dark rum

1. Bring butter, granulated sugar, brown sugar, water, corn syrup, lemon juice, and salt to boil in large saucepan over medium heat, stirring occasionally to dissolve sugar and melt butter. Once mixture is at full rolling boil, cook, stirring occasionally, for 5 minutes (caramel will register about 240 degrees). Immediately reduce heat to medium-low and gently simmer (caramel should maintain steady stream of lazy bubbles—if not, adjust heat accordingly), stirring frequently, until mixture is color of dark peanut butter, 12 to 16 minutes longer (caramel will register about 300 degrees and should have slight burnt smell).

2. Remove pan from heat; carefully pour ¼ cup cream into caramel mixture and swirl to incorporate (mixture will bubble and steam); let bubbling subside. Whisk vigorously and scrape corners of pan until mixture is completely smooth, at least 30 seconds. Return pan to medium heat and gradually whisk in remaining ¾ cup cream until smooth. Whisk in 2 cups milk until mixture is smooth, making sure to scrape corners and edges of pan to remove any remaining bits of caramel.

3. Meanwhile, microwave remaining ¼ cup milk until simmering, 30 to 45 seconds. Whisk egg yolks and cornstarch together in large bowl until smooth. Gradually whisk in hot milk until smooth; set aside (do not refrigerate).

4. Return saucepan to medium-high heat and bring mixture to full rolling boil, whisking frequently. Once mixture is boiling rapidly and beginning to climb toward top of pan, immediately pour into bowl with yolk mixture in 1 motion (do not add gradually). Whisk thoroughly for 10 to 15 seconds (mixture will thicken after a few seconds). Whisk in vanilla and rum. Spray piece of parchment paper with vegetable oil spray and press on surface of pudding. Refrigerate until cold and set, at least 3 hours. Whisk pudding until smooth before serving.

PANNA COTTA

WHY THIS RECIPE WORKS: Though its name is lyrical, the literal translation of panna cotta, "cooked cream," does nothing to suggest its ethereal qualities. In fact, panna cotta is not cooked at all. Neither is it complicated with eggs, as is a custard. Instead, sugar and gelatin are melted in cream and milk, and the whole mixture is then turned into individual ramekins and chilled. Panna cotta is more often found on restaurant menus, but we wanted a version for the home cook—one that would guarantee a pudding with the rich flavor of cream and vanilla and a delicate texture.

After trying several different recipes, we concluded that we needed a higher proportion of cream to milk to achieve the creamiest flavor and texture. The amount of gelatin proved critical—too much turned the panna cotta rubbery; it needs to be just firm enough to unmold, so we used a light hand. And because gelatin sets more quickly at cold temperatures, we minimized the amount of heat by softening the gelatin in cold milk, then heating it very briefly until it was melted. To avoid premature hardening, we gradually added cold vanilla-infused cream to the gelatin mixture and stirred everything over an ice bath to incorporate the gelatin. Chilled until set and served with a raspberry sauce, our panna cotta was creamy, smooth, and light.

Panna Cotta
SERVES 8

A vanilla bean gives the panna cotta the deepest flavor, but 2 teaspoons of vanilla extract can be used instead. If you like, you can omit the Raspberry Coulis and simply serve the panna cotta with lightly sweetened berries. Though traditionally unmolded, panna cotta may be chilled and served in wine glasses and sauced on top. If you would like to make the panna cotta a day ahead, decrease the amount of gelatin to 2½ teaspoons, and chill the filled wine glasses or ramekins for 18 to 24 hours.

- 1 cup whole milk
- 2¾ teaspoons gelatin (see note)
- 3 cups heavy cream
- 1 vanilla bean, halved lengthwise (see note)
- 6 tablespoons sugar
  Pinch table salt
  Raspberry Coulis (recipe follows)

1. Pour the milk into a medium saucepan; sprinkle the surface evenly with the gelatin and let stand for 10 minutes. Meanwhile, turn the contents of two ice cube trays (about 32 cubes) into a large bowl; add 4 cups cold water. Pour the cream into a large measuring cup or pitcher. With a paring knife, scrape the vanilla seeds into the cream; place the pod in the cream along with the seeds and set the mixture aside. Set eight 4-ounce ramekins on a rimmed baking sheet.

2. Heat the milk and gelatin mixture over high heat, stirring constantly, until the gelatin is dissolved and the mixture registers 135 degrees on an instant-read thermometer, about 1½ minutes. Off the heat, add the sugar and salt; stir until dissolved, about 1 minute.

3. Stirring constantly, slowly pour the cream with the vanilla into the saucepan containing the milk, then transfer the mixture to a medium bowl and set the bowl over the ice water bath. Stir frequently until thickened to the consistency of eggnog and the mixture registers 50 degrees on an instant-read thermometer, about 10 minutes. Strain the mixture into a large measuring cup or pitcher, then distribute evenly among the ramekins. Cover the baking sheet with plastic wrap, making sure that the plastic does not mar the surface of the cream; refrigerate until just set (the mixture should wobble when shaken gently), about 4 hours.

4. To serve, spoon a portion of the raspberry coulis onto eight individual serving plates. Pour 1 cup boiling water into a small wide-mouthed bowl, dip a ramekin filled with panna cotta into the water for 3 seconds and lift the ramekin out of the water. With a moistened finger, press lightly on the periphery of the panna cotta to loosen the edges. Dip the ramekin back into the hot water for another 3 seconds. Invert the ramekin over your palm and loosen the panna cotta by cupping your fingers between the panna cotta and the edges of the ramekin. Gently lower the panna cotta onto a serving plate with the coulis. Repeat the process with the remaining ramekins of panna cotta. Serve.

Raspberry Coulis
MAKES ABOUT 1½ CUPS

- 24 ounces (about 5 cups) frozen raspberries
- ⅓ cup (2⅓ ounces) sugar
- ¼ teaspoon juice from 1 lemon
  Pinch table salt

1. Place the frozen raspberries in a 4-quart saucepan. Cover and simmer over medium-high heat, stirring occasionally, for 10 to 12 minutes. Add the sugar and increase the heat to high. Boil for 2 minutes.

2. Strain the berries through a fine-mesh strainer into a bowl, using a rubber spatula to push the berries through the strainer; discard the seeds. Stir in the lemon juice and salt. Cover and refrigerate until chilled, at least 2 hours or up to 3 days.

crust, we recommend turbinado or Demerara sugar. Regular granulated sugar will work, too, but use only 1 scant teaspoon on each ramekin or 1 teaspoon on each shallow fluted dish. It's important to use 4- to 5-ounce ramekins.

4	cups heavy cream, chilled
⅔	cup (4⅔ ounces) granulated sugar
	Pinch table salt
1	vanilla bean, halved lengthwise (see note)
12	large egg yolks (see note)
8–12	teaspoons turbinado or Demerara sugar (see note)

1. Adjust an oven rack to the lower-middle position and heat the oven to 300 degrees.

2. Combine 2 cups of the cream, the sugar, and salt in a medium saucepan. With a paring knife, scrape the seeds from the vanilla bean into the pan, submerge the pod in the cream, and bring the mixture to a boil over medium heat, stirring occasionally to ensure that the sugar dissolves. Take the pan off the heat and let steep for 15 minutes.

3. Meanwhile, place a kitchen towel in the bottom of a large baking dish or roasting pan and arrange eight 4- or 5-ounce ramekins (or shallow fluted dishes) on the towel (making sure they do not touch). Bring a kettle or large sauce-pan of water to a boil.

4. After the vanilla bean has steeped, stir in the remaining 2 cups cream to cool down the mixture. Whisk the egg yolks in a large bowl until broken up and combined. Whisk about 1 cup of the cream mixture into the yolks until loosened and combined; repeat with 1 cup more cream. Add the remaining cream and whisk until evenly colored and thoroughly combined. Strain the mixture through a fine-mesh strainer into a large measuring cup or pitcher (or clean medium bowl); discard the solids in the strainer. Pour or ladle the mixture into the ramekins, dividing it evenly among them.

5. Carefully place the baking dish with the ramekins on the oven rack; pour the boiling water into the dish, taking care not to splash water into the ramekins, until the water reaches two-thirds of the way up the sides of the ramekins. Bake until the centers of the custards are just barely set and are no longer sloshy and register 170 to 175 degrees on an instant-read thermometer, 30 to 35 minutes (25 to 30 minutes for shallow fluted dishes). Begin checking the temperature about 5 minutes before the recommended time.

6. Transfer the ramekins to a wire rack and cool to room temperature, about 2 hours. Set the ramekins on a rimmed baking sheet, cover tightly with plastic wrap, and refrigerate until cold, at least 4 hours or up to 4 days.

7. Uncover the ramekins; if condensation has collected on the custards, blot the moisture with a paper towel. Sprinkle each with about 1 teaspoon turbinado sugar (1½ teaspoons for shallow fluted dishes); tilt and tap each ramekin for even coverage. Ignite a torch and caramelize the sugar. Refrigerate the ramekins, uncovered, to rechill, 30 to 45 minutes (but no longer); serve.

CRÈME BRÛLÉE

WHY THIS RECIPE WORKS: Crème brûlée is all about the contrast between the crisp sugar crust and the silky custard underneath. But too often the crust is either stingy or rock-hard and the custard is heavy and tasteless. Because crème brûlée requires so few ingredients, we knew that finding just the right technique would be key in creating the quintessential version of this elegant dessert.

The texture of the custard should not be firm but rather soft and supple. The secret, we found, is using egg yolks—and lots of them—rather than whole eggs. Heavy cream gave the custard a luxurious richness. Sugar, a vanilla bean, and a pinch of salt were the only other additions. Despite instructions in many recipes to use scalded cream, we found that this technique was more likely to result in overcooked custard, so we thought we would leave the ingredients cold. The downside, however, was that we needed heat to extract flavor from the vanilla bean and dissolve the sugar. Our compromise was to heat only half of the cream with the sugar and vanilla bean and add the remaining cream cold, which worked perfectly. For the crust, we used crunchy turbinado sugar, which was easy to spread on the baked and chilled custards. A propane or butane torch worked better than the broiler for caramelizing the sugar, and because the blast of heat inevitably warms the custard beneath the crust, we chilled our crèmes brûlées once more before serving.

Classic Crème Brûlée

SERVES 8

Separate the eggs and whisk the yolks after the cream has finished steeping; if left to sit, the surface of the yolks will dry and form a film. A vanilla bean gives the custard the deepest flavor, but 2 teaspoons of vanilla extract, whisked into the yolks in step 4, can be used instead. The best way to judge doneness is with an instant-read thermometer. For the caramelized sugar

Espresso Crème Brûlée

Place ¼ cup espresso beans in a zipper-lock bag and crush lightly with a rolling pin or meat pounder until coarsely cracked. Follow the recipe for Classic Crème Brûlée, substituting the cracked espresso beans for the vanilla bean and whisking 1 teaspoon vanilla extract into the egg yolks in step 4 before adding the cream.

CRÈME CARAMEL

WHY THIS RECIPE WORKS: This simple, classic French dessert is essentially a baked custard, but what makes it really stand out is the caramel sauce. We found that making the caramel is relatively simple; what we needed to address was the custard, which should be silky smooth, modestly sweet, and firm but not rubbery.

We discovered that the proportion of egg whites to yolks in the custard was critical for the texture. Too many whites caused the custard to solidify too much, and too few left it almost runny. We settled on a formula of three whole eggs and two yolks. Light cream and milk for the dairy component provided the proper amount of richness. For contrast with the sweet caramel, we kept the amount of sugar in the custard to a minimum. The caramel comes together quickly; sugar is dissolved in water and cooked until caramel-colored. Baking the ramekins in a water bath was essential for even cooking and ensured a delicate custard; a dish towel on the bottom of the pan stabilized the ramekins and prevented the bottoms of the custards from overcooking. When we unmolded our crème caramel on serving plates, the sweet caramel sauce bathed the rounds of perfectly cooked custard.

Classic Crème Caramel
SERVES 8

You can vary the amount of sugar in the custard to suit your taste. Most tasters preferred the full ⅔ cup, but you can reduce that amount to as little as ½ cup to create a greater contrast between the custard and the caramel. Cook the caramel in a pan with a light-colored interior, since a dark surface makes it difficult to judge the color of the syrup. Caramel can leave a real mess in a pan, but it is easy to clean. Simply boil water in the pan for 5 to 10 minutes to loosen the hardened caramel.

CARAMEL
- ⅓ cup water
- 2 tablespoons light corn syrup
- ¼ teaspoon juice from 1 lemon
- 1 cup (7 ounces) sugar

CUSTARD
- 1½ cups whole milk
- 1½ cups light cream
- 3 large eggs, plus 2 large yolks
- ⅔ cup (4⅔ ounces) sugar (see note)
- 1½ teaspoons vanilla extract
- Pinch table salt

1. FOR THE CARAMEL: Combine the water, corn syrup, and lemon juice in a 2 to 3-quart saucepan. Pour the sugar into the center of the saucepan, taking care not to let the sugar granules touch the sides of the pan. Gently stir with a clean spatula to moisten the sugar thoroughly. Bring to a boil over medium-high heat and cook, without stirring, until the sugar is completely dissolved and the liquid is clear, 6 to 10 minutes. Reduce the heat to medium-low and continue to cook (swirling occasionally) until the caramel darkens to a honey color, 4 to 5 minutes longer. Remove the pan immediately from the heat and, working quickly but carefully (the caramel is above 300 degrees and will burn if it touches your skin), pour a portion of the caramel into each of eight ungreased 6-ounce ramekins. Allow the caramel to cool and harden, about 15 minutes. (The caramel-coated ramekins can be covered with plastic wrap and refrigerated for up to 2 days; return to room temperature before adding the custard.)

2. FOR THE CUSTARD: Adjust an oven rack to the middle position and heat the oven to 350 degrees. Heat the milk and cream in a medium saucepan over medium heat, stirring occasionally, until steam appears and/or the mixture registers 160 degrees on an instant-read thermometer, 6 to 8 minutes; remove from the heat. Meanwhile, gently whisk the whole eggs, egg yolks, and sugar in a large bowl until just combined. Off the heat, gently whisk the warm milk mixture, vanilla, and salt into the eggs until just combined but not at all foamy. Strain the mixture through a fine-mesh strainer into a large measuring cup or pitcher (or clean medium bowl); set aside.

3. Bring a kettle or large saucepan of water to a boil. Meanwhile, place a kitchen towel in the bottom of a large baking dish or roasting pan. Arrange the ramekins on the towel (making sure they do not touch). Divide the reserved custard mixture among the ramekins and carefully place the baking dish on the oven rack. Pour the boiling water into the dish, taking care not to splash water into the ramekins, until the water reaches halfway up the sides of the ramekins; cover the entire pan loosely with aluminum foil. Bake until a paring knife inserted halfway between the center and the edge of the custards comes out clean, 35 to 40 minutes. Transfer the custards to a wire rack and cool to room temperature. (The custards can be covered with plastic wrap and refrigerated for up to 2 days.)

4. To unmold, slide a paring knife around the perimeter of each ramekin, pressing the knife against the side of the dish. Hold a serving plate over the top of the ramekin and invert; set the plate on a work surface and shake the ramekin gently to release the custard. Repeat with the remaining ramekins and serve.

LATIN AMERICAN–STYLE FLAN

WHY THIS RECIPE WORKS: The Latin style of this baked custard isn't light and quivering like its European counterparts. It is far richer and more densely creamy, with a texture somewhere between pudding and cheesecake. It also boasts a more deeply caramelized, toffee-like flavor. The custard gets its thick, luxurious texture from canned milk—evaporated as well as sweetened condensed. But in many recipes, much of the caramel sticks to the bottom of the pan, and the custard is stiff with an unpleasantly thick skin where the flan is exposed to the direct heat of the oven. We got to work on a version that was as dense and rich-tasting as it was creamy.

We realized that the high protein content of canned milk products was to blame for the stiff texture. Removing one egg from the mix helped, but not enough. To further improve creaminess, we added ½ cup of fresh milk. Wrapping the cake pan in foil before baking prevented the skin from forming on top, and reducing the oven temperature ensured that the custard baked evenly. We also switched from a shallow cake pan to a loaf pan, which produced a gorgeous, tall flan less prone to cracking. Adding a bit of water to the warm caramel and then letting the baked flan sit overnight helped more of the caramel to come out of the dish, creating a substantial layer of gooey caramel.

Perfect Latin Flan
SERVES 8 TO 10

This recipe should be made at least 1 day before serving. We recommend an 8½ by 4½-inch loaf pan for this recipe. If your pan is 9 by 5 inches, begin checking for doneness at 1 hour and 15 minutes. You may substitute 2 percent milk for the whole milk, but do not use skim milk. Serve the flan on a platter with a raised rim to contain the liquid caramel.

⅔ cup (4⅔ ounces) sugar
¼ cup water plus 2 tablespoons warm tap water
2 large eggs, plus 5 large yolks
1 (14-ounce) can sweetened condensed milk
1 (12-ounce) can evaporated milk
½ cup whole milk
1½ tablespoons vanilla extract
½ teaspoon salt

1. Stir together sugar and ¼ cup water in medium heavy saucepan until sugar is completely moistened. Bring to boil over medium-high heat, 3 to 5 minutes, and cook without stirring until mixture begins to turn golden, another 1 to 2 minutes. Gently swirling pan, continue to cook until sugar is the color of peanut butter, 1 to 2 minutes. Remove from heat and swirl pan until sugar is reddish-amber and fragrant, 15 to 20 seconds. Carefully swirl in 2 tablespoons warm tap water until incorporated; mixture will bubble and steam. Pour caramel into 8½ by 4½-inch loaf pan; do not scrape out saucepan. Set loaf pan aside.

2. Adjust oven rack to middle position and heat oven to 300 degrees. Line bottom of 13 by 9-inch baking pan with dish towel, folding towel to fit smoothly, and set aside. Bring 2 quarts water to boil.

3. Whisk eggs and yolks until combined. Add sweetened condensed milk, evaporated milk, whole milk, vanilla, and salt, and whisk until incorporated. Strain mixture through fine-mesh strainer into prepared loaf pan.

4. Cover loaf pan tightly with aluminum foil and place in prepared baking pan. Place baking pan in oven and carefully pour boiling water into pan. Bake until center of custard jiggles slightly when shaken and custard registers 180 degrees, 1¼ to 1½ hours. Remove foil and leave custard in water bath until loaf pan has cooled to room temperature. Wrap loaf pan tightly with plastic wrap and chill overnight or up to 4 days.

5. To unmold, slide paring knife around edges of pan. Invert serving platter on top of pan and turn pan and platter over. When flan is released, remove loaf pan. Use rubber spatula to scrape residual caramel onto flan. Slice and serve. Leftover flan may be covered loosely and refrigerated for up to 4 days.

Coffee Flan

Whisk 4 teaspoons of instant espresso powder into the egg-milk mixture until dissolved.

Orange-Cardamom Flan

Whisk 2 tablespoons orange zest and ¼ teaspoon ground cardamom into the egg-milk mixture before straining.

Almond Flan

Reduce vanilla to 1 tablespoon and whisk 1 teaspoon almond extract into the egg-milk mixture.

CHOCOLATE POTS DE CRÈME

WHY THIS RECIPE WORKS: Classic *pots de crème* can be finicky and laborious, requiring a hot water bath that threatens to splash the custards every time the pan is moved. In addition, the individual custards don't always cook at the same rate. We wanted a user-friendly recipe that delivered a decadent dessert with a satiny texture and intense chocolate flavor.

First we moved the dish out of the oven, concentrating on an unconventional approach in which the custard is cooked on the stovetop in a saucepan, then poured into ramekins. Our next challenge was developing the right amount of richness and body, which we did by choosing a combination of heavy cream and half-and-half, along with egg yolks only, for maximum richness. For intense chocolate flavor, we focused on bittersweet chocolate—and a lot of it. Our chocolate content was at least 50 percent more than in any other recipe we had encountered.

Chocolate Pots de Crème

SERVES 8

We prefer pots de crème made with 60 percent bittersweet chocolate (our favorite brands are Callebaut Intense Dark Chocolate and Ghirardelli Bittersweet Chocolate), but 70 percent bittersweet chocolate can also be used. If using a 70 percent bittersweet chocolate, reduce the amount of chocolate to 8 ounces. An instant-read thermometer is the most reliable way to judge when the custard has reached the proper temperature. However, you can also judge the progress of the custard by its thickness. Dip a wooden spoon into the custard and run your finger across the back. The custard is ready when it coats the spoon and a line drawn maintains neat edges. The pots de crème (minus the whipped cream garnish) can be covered tightly with plastic wrap and refrigerated for up to 3 days.

POTS DE CRÈME

- 10 ounces bittersweet chocolate, chopped fine (see note)
- 5 large egg yolks
- 5 tablespoons sugar
- ¼ teaspoon table salt
- 1½ cups heavy cream
- ¾ cup half-and-half
- 1 tablespoon vanilla extract
- ½ teaspoon instant espresso powder mixed with 1 tablespoon water

WHIPPED CREAM AND GARNISH

- ½ cup heavy cream, chilled
- 2 teaspoons sugar
- ½ teaspoon vanilla extract
  Cocoa, for dusting (optional)
  Chocolate shavings, for sprinkling (optional)

1. FOR THE POTS DE CRÈME: Place the chocolate in a medium heatproof bowl; set a fine-mesh strainer over the bowl and set aside.

2. Whisk the egg yolks, sugar, and salt together in a medium bowl until combined, then whisk in the heavy cream and half-and-half. Transfer the mixture to a medium saucepan. Cook the mixture over medium-low heat, stirring constantly and scraping the bottom of the pot with a wooden spoon, until it is thickened and silky and registers 175 to 180 degrees on an instant-read thermometer, 8 to 12 minutes. (Do not let the custard overcook or simmer.)

3. Immediately pour the custard through the strainer over the chocolate. Let the mixture stand to melt the chocolate, about 5 minutes. Whisk gently until smooth, then whisk in the vanilla and dissolved espresso. Divide the mixture evenly among eight 5-ounce ramekins. Gently tap the ramekins against the counter to remove any air bubbles.

4. Cool the pots de crème to room temperature, then cover with plastic wrap and refrigerate until chilled, at least 4 hours or up to 3 days. Before serving, let the pots de crème stand at room temperature for 20 to 30 minutes.

5. FOR THE WHIPPED CREAM AND GARNISH: Using an electric mixer, whip the cream, sugar, and vanilla on medium-low speed until small bubbles form, about 30 seconds. Increase the speed to medium-high and continue to whip the mixture until it thickens and forms stiff peaks, about 1 minute. Dollop each pot de crème with about 2 tablespoons of the whipped cream and garnish with cocoa and/or chocolate shavings (if using). Serve.

Milk Chocolate Pots de Crème

Milk chocolate behaves differently in this recipe than bittersweet chocolate, and more of it must be used to ensure that the custard sets. And because of the increased amount of chocolate, it's necessary to cut back on the amount of sugar so that the custard is not overly sweet.

Follow the recipe for Chocolate Pots de Crème, substituting 12 ounces milk chocolate for the 10 ounces bittersweet chocolate. Reduce the amount of sugar to 2 tablespoons and proceed as directed.

CHOCOLATE PUDDING

WHY THIS RECIPE WORKS: Homemade chocolate pudding often suffers either from lackluster chocolate flavor, caused by a dearth of chocolate, or a grainy texture, caused by too much cocoa butter. We were after chocolate pudding that tasted deeply of chocolate and was thickened to a perfectly silky, creamy texture.

We found that using a moderate amount of bittersweet chocolate in combination with unsweetened cocoa and espresso powder helped us achieve maximum chocolate flavor. Cornstarch proved the right thickener for our pudding; using mostly milk, and just half a cup of heavy cream, along with three egg yolks ensured that our pudding had a silky smooth texture. Salt and vanilla enhanced the chocolate flavor for the perfect classic chocolate pudding.

Creamy Chocolate Pudding
SERVES 6

We recommend using one of the test kitchen's favorite baking chocolates, Callebaut Intense Dark Chocolate or Ghirardelli Bittersweet Chocolate, for this recipe, but any high-quality dark, bittersweet, or semisweet chocolate will work. This recipe was developed using a 60 percent cacao chocolate. Using a chocolate with a higher cacao percentage will result in a thicker pudding. Low-fat milk (1 percent or 2 percent) may be substituted for the whole milk with a small sacrifice in richness. Do not use skim milk as a substitute. Serve the pudding with lightly sweetened whipped cream and chocolate shavings.

2 teaspoons vanilla extract
½ teaspoon instant espresso powder
½ cup (3½ ounces) sugar
3 tablespoons Dutch-processed cocoa powder
2 tablespoons cornstarch
¼ teaspoon table salt
3 large egg yolks
½ cup heavy cream
2½ cups whole milk (see note)
5 tablespoons unsalted butter, cut into 8 pieces
4 ounces bittersweet chocolate, finely chopped (see note)

1. Stir together the vanilla extract and espresso powder in a bowl; set aside. Whisk the sugar, cocoa, cornstarch, and salt together in a large saucepan. Whisk in the egg yolks and cream until fully incorporated, making sure to scrape the corners of the saucepan. Whisk in the milk until incorporated.

2. Place the saucepan over medium heat and cook, whisking constantly, until the mixture is thickened and bubbling over the entire surface, 5 to 8 minutes. Cook for 30 seconds longer, remove from the heat, add the butter and chocolate, and whisk until melted and fully incorporated. Whisk in the vanilla mixture.

3. Strain the pudding through a fine-mesh strainer into a bowl. Place lightly greased parchment paper against the surface of the pudding, and place in a refrigerator to cool, at least 4 hours. Serve. (The pudding can be refrigerated for up to 2 days.)

CHOCOLATE MOUSSE

WHY THIS RECIPE WORKS: Rich, creamy, and dense, chocolate mousse can be delicious but too filling after a few mouthfuls. On the other hand, light and airy mousse usually lacks deep chocolate flavor. We wanted chocolate mousse with both a light, meltingly smooth texture and a substantial chocolate flavor.

To start, we addressed the mousse's dense, heavy texture. Most recipes for chocolate mousse contain butter. Could we do without it? We eliminated the butter and found that our mousse tasted less heavy. We further lightened the mousse's texture by reducing the number of egg whites and yolks. To make up for the lost volume of the eggs, we whipped the cream to soft peaks before adding it to the chocolate.

Next we tackled the mousse's flavor. We maximized the chocolate flavor with a combination of bittersweet chocolate and cocoa powder. And to further deepen the chocolate flavor, we found that a small amount of instant espresso powder, salt, and brandy did the trick.

Dark Chocolate Mousse
SERVES 6 TO 8

When developing this recipe, we used our winning brands of dark chocolate, Callebaut Intense Dark Chocolate and Ghirardelli Bittersweet Chocolate, which each contain about

60 percent cacao. If you want to use a chocolate with a higher percentage of cacao, see our variation, Premium Dark Chocolate Mousse (recipe follows). If you choose to make the mousse a day in advance, let it sit at room temperature for 10 minutes before serving. Serve with very lightly sweetened whipped cream and chocolate shavings, if desired.

  8 ounces bittersweet chocolate, chopped
     fine (see note)
  5 tablespoons water
  2 tablespoons cocoa powder, preferably
     Dutch-processed
  1 tablespoon brandy
  1 teaspoon instant espresso powder
  2 large eggs, separated
  1 tablespoon sugar
  ⅛ teaspoon table salt
  1 cup plus 2 tablespoons heavy cream, chilled

1. Melt the chocolate with the water, cocoa powder, brandy, and espresso powder in a medium heatproof bowl set over a saucepan filled with 1 inch of barely simmering water, stirring frequently until smooth. Remove from the heat.

2. Whisk the egg yolks, 1½ teaspoons of the sugar, and the salt in a medium bowl until the mixture lightens in color and thickens slightly, about 30 seconds. Pour the melted chocolate into the egg mixture and whisk until combined. Cool until just warmer than room temperature, 3 to 5 minutes.

3. Using an electric mixer, whip the egg whites at medium-low speed until frothy, 1 to 2 minutes. Add the remaining 1½ teaspoons sugar, increase the mixer speed to medium-high, and whip until soft peaks form when the whisk is lifted, about 1 minute. Whisk the last few strokes by hand, making sure to scrape any unbeaten whites from the bottom of the bowl. Using the whisk, stir about one-quarter of the whipped egg whites into the chocolate mixture to lighten it; gently fold in the remaining egg whites with a rubber spatula until a few white streaks remain.

4. In the now-empty bowl, whip the heavy cream at medium speed until it begins to thicken, about 30 seconds. Increase the speed to high and whip until soft peaks form when the whisk is lifted, about 15 seconds more. Using a rubber spatula, fold the whipped cream into the mousse until no white streaks remain. Spoon the mousse into six to eight individual serving dishes or goblets. Cover with plastic wrap and refrigerate until set and firm, at least 2 hours or up to 24 hours. Serve.

Chocolate-Orange Mousse

For best flavor, the orange zest needs to steep in the heavy cream overnight, so plan accordingly. Garnish each serving of mousse with a thin strip of orange zest, if desired.

Follow the recipe for Dark Chocolate Mousse with the following changes: Start by bringing the heavy cream to a simmer in a medium saucepan. Remove from the heat and transfer to a liquid measuring cup; add 3 strips orange zest (each about 2 inches long and ½ inch wide). Cool until just warm, cover, and refrigerate overnight. Remove and discard the zest; add more heavy cream, if necessary, to equal 1 cup plus 2 tablespoons. Continue with step 1, reducing the amount of water to 4 tablespoons and omitting the brandy. Once the chocolate is melted, stir in 2 tablespoons Grand Marnier and proceed as directed in step 2.

Chocolate-Raspberry Mousse

Chambord is our preferred brand of raspberry-flavored liqueur for this recipe. Serve the mousse with fresh raspberries, if desired.

Follow the recipe for Dark Chocolate Mousse, reducing the amount of water to 4 tablespoons, omitting the brandy, and, once the chocolate is melted at the end of step 1, stirring in 2 tablespoons raspberry-flavored liqueur.

Premium Dark Chocolate Mousse

This recipe is designed to work with a boutique chocolate that contains a higher percentage of cacao than the Callebaut or Ghirardelli chocolate recommended for our Dark Chocolate Mousse.

Follow the recipe for Dark Chocolate Mousse, replacing the bittersweet chocolate (containing about 60 percent cacao) with an equal amount of bittersweet chocolate containing 62 to 70 percent cacao. Increase the amount of water to 7 tablespoons, add 1 egg (for a total of 3 eggs), and increase the amount of sugar to 3 tablespoons (adding the extra 2 tablespoons sugar to the chocolate mixture in step 1).

LOW-FAT CHOCOLATE MOUSSE

WHY THIS RECIPE WORKS: When presented with the challenge of developing a low-fat chocolate mousse, we admit we were daunted. After all, traditional chocolate mousse gets its lush, creamy texture and decadent richness chiefly from heavy cream—and lots of it. We wanted to ditch the cream but preserve the rich chocolate flavor and silky, fluffy texture.

We found the solution in an Italian meringue (egg whites beaten until fluffy, and then cooked in hot sugar syrup). It made a fat-free base that mimicked the volume and texture of a traditional mousse made with heavy cream. Semisweet chocolate and Dutch-processed cocoa added rich chocolate flavor, and a surprise ingredient—melted white chocolate chips—mellowed and rounded out the flavors of each.

Low-Fat Chocolate Mousse

SERVES 6

The meringue and chocolate mixture are combined in two stages so the meringue doesn't collapse. For the best texture, chill the mousse overnight. The mousse can be refrigerated for up to 4 days.

    4   ounces semisweet chocolate,
        broken into pieces
    ⅓   cup white chocolate chips
    2   tablespoons Dutch-processed cocoa powder
    6   tablespoons plus ½ cup water
    1   teaspoon vanilla extract
    ½   cup (3½ ounces) sugar
    3   large egg whites
    ¼   teaspoon cream of tartar

1. Melt the semisweet chocolate, white chocolate, cocoa powder, 6 tablespoons of the water, and the vanilla in a medium bowl set over a pot of barely simmering water, stirring until smooth. Set aside to cool slightly.

2. Bring the remaining ½ cup water and the sugar to a vigorous boil in a small saucepan over high heat. Boil until slightly thickened and large bubbles rise to the top, about 4 minutes. Remove from the heat.

3. With an electric mixer on medium-low speed, beat the egg whites in a large bowl until frothy, about 1 minute. Add the cream of tartar and beat, gradually increasing the speed to medium-high, until the whites hold soft peaks, about 2 minutes. With the mixer running, slowly pour the hot syrup into the whites (avoid pouring the syrup onto the beaters or it will splash). Increase the speed to high and beat until the meringue has cooled to just warm and becomes very thick and shiny, 2 to 3 minutes.

4. Whisk one-third of the meringue into the chocolate mixture until combined, then whisk in the remaining meringue. Spoon the mousse into six 6-ounce ramekins or pudding cups. Cover tightly with plastic wrap. Chill overnight.

FRESH STRAWBERRY MOUSSE

WHY THIS RECIPE WORKS: There's a good reason that strawberry mousse recipes aren't very prevalent: The berries contain lots of juice that can easily ruin the texture of a mousse that should be creamy and rich. Plus, the fruit flavor produced by most strawberry mousse recipes is too subtle. To achieve a creamy yet firm texture without losing the strawberry flavor,

we replaced some of the cream with cream cheese. We processed the berries into small pieces and macerated them with sugar and a little salt to draw out their juice. We then reduced the released liquid to a syrup before adding it to the mousse, which standardized the amount of moisture in the dessert and also concentrated the berry flavor. Fully pureeing the juiced berries contributed bright, fresh berry flavor. A dollop of lemon whipped cream made for a tangy finish, and extra diced strawberries made for a pretty presentation.

Fresh Strawberry Mousse

SERVES 4 TO 6

This recipe works well with supermarket strawberries and farmers' market strawberries. In step 1, be careful not to overprocess the berries. If you like, substitute 1½ pounds (5¼ cups) of thawed frozen strawberries for fresh strawberries. If using frozen strawberries skip step 1 (do not process berries). Proceed with the recipe, adding the ½ cup of sugar and the salt to the whipped cream in step 4. For more-complex berry flavor, replace the 3 tablespoons of raw strawberry juice in step 2 with strawberry or raspberry liqueur. In addition to the diced berries, or if you're using frozen strawberries, you can serve the mousse with Lemon Whipped Cream (recipe follows).

    2   pounds strawberries, hulled (6½ cups)
    ½   cup (3½ ounces) sugar
        Pinch salt
    1¾ teaspoons unflavored gelatin
    4   ounces cream cheese, cut into 8 pieces and softened
    ½   cup heavy cream, chilled

1. Cut enough strawberries into ¼-inch dice to measure 1 cup; refrigerate until ready to garnish. Pulse remaining strawberries in food processor in 2 batches until most pieces are ¼ to ½ inch thick (some larger pieces are fine), 6 to 10 pulses. Transfer strawberries to bowl and toss with ¼ cup sugar and salt. (Do not clean processor.) Cover bowl and let strawberries stand for 45 minutes, stirring occasionally.

2. Strain processed strawberries through fine-mesh strainer into bowl (you should have about ⅔ cup juice). Measure out 3 tablespoons juice into small bowl, sprinkle gelatin over juice, and let sit until gelatin softens, about 5 minutes. Place remaining juice in small saucepan and cook over medium-high heat until reduced to 3 tablespoons, about 10 minutes. Remove pan from heat, add softened gelatin mixture, and stir until gelatin has dissolved. Add cream cheese and whisk until smooth. Transfer mixture to large bowl.

3. While juice is reducing, return strawberries to now-empty processor and process until smooth, 15 to 20 seconds. Strain puree through fine-mesh strainer into medium bowl, pressing on solids to remove seeds and pulp (you should have about 1⅔ cups puree). Discard any solids in strainer. Add strawberry puree to juice-gelatin mixture and whisk until incorporated.

4. Using stand mixer fitted with whisk, whip cream on medium-low speed until foamy, about 1 minute. Increase speed to high and whip until soft peaks form, 1 to 3 minutes. Gradually add remaining ¼ cup sugar and whip until stiff peaks form, 1 to 2 minutes. Whisk whipped cream into strawberry mixture until no white streaks remain. Portion into dessert dishes and chill for at least 4 hours or up to 48 hours. (If chilled longer than 6 hours, let mousse sit at room temperature for 15 minutes before serving.) Serve, garnishing with reserved diced strawberries.

Lemon Whipped Cream
MAKES ABOUT 1 CUP
If preferred, you can replace the lemon with lime.

- ½ cup heavy cream
- 2 tablespoons sugar
- 1 teaspoon finely grated lemon zest plus 1 tablespoon juice

Using stand mixer fitted with whisk, whip cream on medium-low speed until foamy, about 1 minute. Add sugar and lemon zest and juice, increase speed to medium-high, and whip until soft peaks form, 1 to 3 minutes.

GRAND MARNIER SOUFFLÉ

WHY THIS RECIPE WORKS: Home cooks are wary of attempting soufflés, which have the reputation of being difficult and temperamental and so are relegated to being eaten only in restaurants. The reality, however, is that they are relatively easy to make. To prove the point, we set out to develop a reliable recipe for a classic Grand Marnier soufflé.

The best soufflés have a crusty top layer above the rim of the dish and a contrasting rich, creamy, almost-fluid center, so we needed to produce height without making the entire dish foamy. For the base we began with a *bouillie*—a paste of flour and milk. Butter kept the egginess at bay, and increasing the usual amount of flour prevented the frothiness we wanted to avoid. An equal number of egg whites and yolks was the right

proportion for rise versus richness. Adding a little sugar and some cream of tartar to the whites while we whipped them stabilized the whites so that they would hold their structure. We discovered that the sugar must be added gradually and partway through the beating process, not at the beginning, or the soufflé will not rise properly and will taste too sweet. We also found it important to remove the soufflé from the oven while the center was still loose and moist to prevent overcooking. With a luxuriously creamy interior and crusty top, our foolproof soufflé is an impressive dessert that can easily be made at home.

Grand Marnier Soufflé
SERVES 6 TO 8
Make the soufflé base and immediately begin beating the whites before the base cools too much. Once the whites have reached the proper consistency, they must be used at once. Do not open the oven door during the first 15 minutes of baking time; as the soufflé nears the end of its baking, you may check its progress by opening the oven door slightly. (Be careful here; if your oven runs hot, the top of the soufflé may burn.) A quick dusting of confectioners' sugar is a nice finishing touch, but a soufflé waits for no one, so be ready to serve it immediately.

SOUFFLÉ DISH PREPARATION
- 1 tablespoon unsalted butter, softened
- ¼ cup sugar
- 2 teaspoons sifted cocoa powder

SOUFFLÉ
- 5 tablespoons unbleached all-purpose flour
- ½ cup (3½ ounces) sugar
- ¼ teaspoon table salt
- 1 cup whole milk
- 2 tablespoons unsalted butter, at room temperature
- 5 large eggs, separated
- 1 tablespoon grated zest from 1 orange
- 3 tablespoons Grand Marnier
- ⅛ teaspoon cream of tartar

1. TO PREPARE THE SOUFFLÉ DISH: Adjust an oven rack to the upper-middle position and heat the oven to 400 degrees. Grease a 1½-quart porcelain soufflé dish with the butter, making sure to coat all of the interior surfaces. Stir the sugar and cocoa together in a small bowl; pour into the buttered soufflé dish and shake to coat the bottom and sides with a thick, even coating. Tap out the excess and set the dish aside.

2. FOR THE SOUFFLÉ: Whisk the flour, ¼ cup of the sugar, and the salt in a small saucepan. Gradually whisk in the milk, whisking until smooth and no lumps remain. Bring the mixture to a boil over high heat, whisking constantly, until thickened and the mixture pulls away from the sides of the pan, about 3 minutes. Scrape the mixture into a medium bowl; whisk in the butter until combined. Whisk in the yolks until incorporated; stir in the orange zest and Grand Marnier.

3. Using an electric mixer, whip the egg whites, cream of tartar, and 1 teaspoon more sugar at medium-low speed until combined, about 10 seconds. Increase the speed to medium-high and whip until frothy and no longer translucent, about 2 minutes. With the mixer running, sprinkle in half of the remaining sugar; continue whipping until the whites form soft, billowy peaks, about 30 seconds. With the mixer still running, sprinkle in the remaining sugar and whip until just combined, about 10 seconds. The whites should form soft peaks when the beater is lifted but should not appear Styrofoam-like or dry.

4. Using a rubber spatula, immediately stir one-quarter of the beaten whites into the soufflé base to lighten until almost no white streaks remain. Scrape the remaining whites into the base and fold in the whites with a balloon whisk until the mixture is just combined, gently flicking the whisk after scraping up the sides of the bowl to free any of the mixture caught in the whisk. Gently pour the mixture into the prepared dish and run your index finger through the mixture, tracing the circumference about ½ inch from the side of the dish, to help the soufflé rise properly. Bake until the surface of the soufflé is deep brown, the center jiggles slightly when shaken, and the soufflé has risen 2 to 2½ inches above the rim of the dish, 20 to 25 minutes. Serve immediately.

Grand Marnier Soufflé with Grated Chocolate

A rotary cheese grater is the perfect tool for grating the chocolate, though a box grater works well, too.

Finely grate ½ ounce bittersweet chocolate (you should have about ⅓ cup). Follow the recipe for Grand Marnier Soufflé, folding the grated chocolate into the soufflé base along with the beaten egg whites.

CHILLED LEMON SOUFFLÉ

WHY THIS RECIPE WORKS: "Chilled lemon soufflé" can be interpreted in many ways, from cooled baked pudding cake to lemony, eggy foam. But no matter what the desired outcome, what typically results is a dense, rubbery mass or a mouthful of tart egg white foam. The delicate balance of ingredients is hard for home cooks to get right. We wanted to perfect the unusual marriage of cream and foam, sweet and sour, high lemony notes and rich custard.

A starting point of egg whites, gelatin, sugar, and lemon juice had none of the creaminess we desired, so we cooked a custard base of milk, egg yolks, and sugar, adding a little cornstarch to prevent the yolks from curdling. To our custard we then added lemon juice and gelatin (to stabilize the mixture so it would set up while chilling). Because this was to be a soufflé, not a pudding, we lightened the custard with whipped cream and beaten egg whites. The egg yolks and dairy tended to mute the lemon flavor, so for more citrus punch we included grated lemon zest. Now we had the balance of flavor and texture that we sought: a satisfying but light custard with bright lemon flavor.

Chilled Lemon Soufflé
SERVES 4 TO 6

To make this lemon soufflé "soufflé" over the rim of the dish, use a 1-quart soufflé dish and, following the photo on page 814, make a foil collar for it before beginning the recipe. For those less concerned about appearance, this dessert can be served from any 1½-quart serving bowl. For the best texture, serve the soufflé after 1½ hours of chilling. It may be chilled for up to 6 hours; though the texture will stiffen slightly because of the gelatin, it will taste just as good.

½ cup juice plus 2½ teaspoons grated zest from 3 lemons
1 (¼-ounce) package gelatin
1 cup whole milk
¾ cup (5¼ ounces) sugar
5 large egg whites plus 2 large egg yolks, at room temperature
¼ teaspoon cornstarch
Pinch cream of tartar
¾ cup heavy cream
Mint, raspberries, confectioners' sugar, or finely chopped pistachios, for garnish (optional)

1. Place the lemon juice in a small bowl; sprinkle the gelatin over and set aside.

2. Heat the milk and ½ cup of the sugar in a medium saucepan over medium-low heat, stirring occasionally, until steaming and the sugar is dissolved, about 5 minutes. Meanwhile, whisk the egg yolks, 2 tablespoons more sugar, and the cornstarch in a medium bowl until pale yellow and thickened. Whisking constantly, gradually add the hot milk to the yolks. Return the milk-egg mixture to the saucepan and cook, stirring constantly, over medium-low heat until the foam has dissipated to a thin layer and the mixture thickens to the consistency of heavy cream and registers 185 degrees on an instant-read thermometer, about 4 minutes. Pour the mixture through a fine-mesh strainer into a medium bowl; stir in the lemon juice mixture and zest. Set the bowl with the custard in a large bowl of ice water; stir occasionally to cool.

3. While the custard mixture is chilling, use an electric mixer to whip the egg whites and cream of tartar on medium speed until foamy, about 1 minute. Increase the speed to medium-high; gradually add the remaining 2 tablespoons sugar and continue to whip until glossy and the whites hold soft peaks when the beater is lifted, about 2 minutes longer. Do not over whip. Remove the bowl containing the custard mixture from the ice water bath; gently whisk in about one-third of the egg whites, then fold in the remaining whites with a large rubber spatula until almost no white streaks remain.

4. In the same mixer bowl, whip the cream on medium-high speed until soft peaks form when the beater is lifted, 2 to 3 minutes. Fold the cream into the custard and egg-white mixture until no white streaks remain.

5. Pour into a 1½ quart soufflé dish or bowl (see note). Chill until set but not stiff, about 1½ hours; remove the foil collar, if using, and serve, garnishing if desired.

Chilled Lemon Soufflé with White Chocolate

The white chocolate in this variation subdues the lemony kick.

Follow the recipe for Chilled Lemon Soufflé, adding 2 ounces chopped white chocolate to the warm custard before adding the lemon juice mixture and the zest. Stir until melted and fully incorporated.

Individual Chilled Lemon Soufflés

Follow the recipe for Chilled Lemon Soufflé, dividing the batter equally among eight ¾-cup ramekins (filled to the rim) or six 6-ounce ramekins with foil collars (see photo).

LEMON POSSET

WHY THIS RECIPE WORKS: Lemon posset is a silky, rich British dessert with bright citrus flavor. We found that using just the right proportions of sugar and lemon juice was the key to custard with a smooth, luxurious consistency and a bright enough flavor to balance the richness of the cream. Lemon zest was essential to making the lemon flavor even more prominent. For a posset with an optimally dense, firm set, we reduced the cream-sugar mixture to 2 cups to evaporate some of the water before adding the lemon juice, which in turn caused the mixture to solidify. Letting the warm mixture rest for 20 minutes before straining and portioning allowed the flavors to meld even more and ensured a silky-smooth consistency. Pairing the dessert with fresh berries for textural contrast helps keep it from feeling overly rich.

Lemon Posset with Berries

SERVES 6

This dessert requires portioning into individual servings. Reducing the cream mixture to exactly 2 cups creates the best consistency. Transfer the liquid to a 2-cup heatproof liquid

measuring cup once or twice during boiling to monitor the amount. Do not leave the cream unattended, as it can boil over easily.

> 2   cups heavy cream
> ⅔   cup (4⅔ ounces) sugar
> 1   tablespoon grated lemon zest plus
> 6   tablespoons juice (2 lemons)
> 1½ cups (7½ ounces) blueberries or raspberries

1. Combine cream, sugar, and lemon zest in medium saucepan and bring to boil over medium heat. Continue to boil, stirring frequently to dissolve sugar. If mixture begins to boil over, briefly remove from heat. Cook until mixture is reduced to 2 cups, 8 to 12 minutes.

2. Remove saucepan from heat and stir in lemon juice. Let sit until mixture is cooled slightly and skin forms on top, about 20 minutes. Strain through fine-mesh strainer into bowl; discard zest. Divide mixture evenly among 6 individual ramekins or serving glasses.

3. Refrigerate, uncovered, until set, at least 3 hours. Once chilled, possets can be wrapped in plastic wrap and refrigerated for up to 2 days. Unwrap and let sit at room temperature for 10 minutes before serving. Garnish with berries and serve.

MAKE-AHEAD CHOCOLATE SOUFFLÉS

WHY THIS RECIPE WORKS: A chocolate soufflé is a grand dessert to serve dinner guests, but most cooks wouldn't risk the anxiety of all the last-minute preparation when entertaining. It seemed a shame to cross this dessert off the list of possibilities for a dinner party, so we challenged ourselves to find a way to make it in advance. We wanted the chocolate to be front and center, so we used a base of egg yolks beaten with sugar, with no flour or milk to mute the chocolate flavor. Instead of the equal number of egg yolks and whites that worked for our Grand Marnier Soufflé (page 811), two extra whites were necessary to lighten and lift our chocolaty base. Now that we had the flavor and texture we wanted, it was time to address the problem of making the soufflés ahead of time. To our amazement, the answer was simple: freezing. Adding a little confectioners' sugar to the egg whites helped stabilize them so they held up better in the freezer, and individual ramekins produced better results than a single large soufflé dish. Now we could make our dinner party dessert ahead of time, confident that we could pull perfectly risen, rich chocolate soufflés from the oven at the end of the meal.

Make-Ahead Chocolate Soufflés

SERVES 6 TO 8

The yolk whipping time in step 3 depends on the type of mixer you use; a stand mixer will take about 3 minutes, and a hand-held mixer will take about 8 minutes. If using 6-ounce ramekins, reduce the cooking time to 20 to 22 minutes. See the photo for making a collar for the ramekins.

RAMEKIN PREPARATION

2 tablespoons unsalted butter, softened
2 tablespoons granulated sugar

SOUFFLÉS

8 ounces bittersweet or semisweet chocolate,
    chopped coarse
4 tablespoons (½ stick) unsalted butter,
    cut into ½-inch pieces
1 tablespoon Grand Marnier
½ teaspoon vanilla extract
⅛ teaspoon table salt
6 large egg yolks plus 8 large egg whites
⅓ cup (2⅓ ounces) granulated sugar
¼ teaspoon cream of tartar
2 tablespoons confectioners' sugar

1. FOR THE RAMEKINS: Grease the inside of eight 8-ounce ramekins with the softened butter, then coat the inside of each dish evenly with the granulated sugar.

2. FOR THE SOUFFLÉS: Melt the chocolate and butter together in a medium heatproof bowl set over a saucepan filled with 1 inch of barely simmering water, stirring frequently until smooth. Remove from the heat and stir in the Grand Marnier, vanilla, and salt; set aside.

3. Using an electric mixer, whip the egg yolks and granulated sugar at medium speed until the mixture triples in volume and is thick and pale yellow, 3 to 8 minutes (see note). Fold the yolk mixture into the chocolate mixture. Thoroughly clean and dry the mixing bowl and the beaters.

4. Using the clean beaters, whip the egg whites at medium-low speed until frothy, 1 to 2 minutes. Add the cream of tartar, increase the mixer speed to medium-high, and whip until soft peaks form when the beaters are lifted, 1 to 2 minutes. Add the confectioners' sugar and continue to whip until stiff peaks form, 2 to 4 minutes (do not over whip). Whisk the last few strokes by hand, making sure to scrape any unwhipped whites from the bottom of the bowl.

5. Vigorously stir one-quarter of the whipped egg whites into the chocolate mixture. Gently fold the remaining whites into the chocolate mixture until just incorporated. Carefully spoon the mixture into the prepared ramekins almost to the rim, wiping the excess filling from the rims with a wet paper towel. If making a foil collar for the ramekins, see the photo. (To serve right away, bake as directed in step 7, reducing the baking time to 12 to 15 minutes.)

6. TO STORE: Cover each ramekin tightly with plastic wrap and then foil and freeze for at least 3 hours or up to 1 month. (Do not thaw before baking.)

7. TO BAKE AND SERVE: Adjust an oven rack to the lower-middle position and heat the oven to 400 degrees. Unwrap the frozen ramekins and spread them out on a baking sheet. Bake the soufflés until fragrant, fully risen, and the exterior is set but the interior is still a bit loose and creamy, about 25 minutes. (To check the interior, use two spoons to pull open the top of one and peek inside.) Serve immediately.

Make-Ahead Mocha Soufflés

Follow the recipe for Make-Ahead Chocolate Soufflés, adding 1 tablespoon instant coffee or espresso powder dissolved in 1 tablespoon hot water to the melted chocolate with the vanilla in step 2.

NOTES FROM THE TEST KITCHEN

MAKING A FOIL COLLAR

Baking our individual chocolate soufflés from the freezer gives them a high rise and a domed top, just as we like them. But placing a collar around the ramekins yields an even higher rise with an iconic, perfectly flat top.

Secure a strip of foil that has been sprayed with vegetable oil spray around each ramekin so that it extends 2 inches above the rim (do this after the ramekins have been filled). You can tape the foil collar to the dish to prevent it from slipping.

SKILLET SOUFFLÉ

WHY THIS RECIPE WORKS: Having taken the mystique out of soufflé making and even developing a recipe for making soufflés ahead of time, we wondered if we could take our expertise one step further. If we could make a soufflé in a skillet, we would guarantee that this great dessert was in the realm of everyday cooking.

We theorized that the heat on the stovetop would activate the batter and ensure an even rise from the egg whites. To determine what to use for the soufflé base, we pitted the bases used in our other soufflés—béchamel and *bouillie*—against a simpler base of whipped egg yolks. All tasted fine, but the whipped egg yolks were so much less complicated that we decided to start there. A little flour added to the yolks kept the soufflé creamy rather than foamy. We decided that lemon would be the best flavoring, since it would shine through the eggy base well; lemon juice and zest provided bright, natural citrus flavor. We beat the egg whites separately, adding sugar partway through, folded them into the egg-lemon base, and poured the mixture into a buttered ovensafe skillet. After a few minutes on the stovetop the soufflé was just set around the edges and on the bottom (and the crust that eventually formed on the bottom was a bonus our tasters applauded), so we moved the skillet to the oven to finish. A few minutes later our soufflé was puffed, golden on top, and creamy in the middle— a successful transformation from fussy to easy.

Skillet Lemon Soufflé

SERVES 6

Don't open the oven door during the first 7 minutes of baking, but do check the soufflé regularly for doneness during the final few minutes in the oven. Be ready to serve the soufflé immediately after removing it from the oven. Using a 10-inch traditional (not nonstick) skillet is essential to getting the right texture and height in the soufflé.

- 5 large eggs, separated
- ¼ teaspoon cream of tartar
- ⅔ cup (4⅔ ounces) granulated sugar
- ⅛ teaspoon table salt
- ⅓ cup juice plus 1 teaspoon grated zest from 2 lemons
- 2 tablespoons unbleached all-purpose flour
- 1 tablespoon unsalted butter
  Confectioners' sugar, for dusting

1. Adjust an oven rack to the middle position and heat the oven to 375 degrees. Using an electric mixer, whip the egg whites and cream of tartar together on medium-low speed until foamy, about 1 minute. Slowly add ⅓ cup of the granulated sugar and the salt, then increase the mixer speed to medium-high, and continue to whip until stiff peaks form, 3 to 5 minutes. Gently transfer the whites to a clean bowl and set aside.

2. Using an electric mixer (no need to wash the mixing bowl), whip the egg yolks and the remaining ⅓ cup granulated sugar together on medium-high speed until pale and thick, about 1 minute. Whip in the lemon juice, zest, and flour until incorporated, about 30 seconds.

3. Fold one-quarter of the whipped egg whites into the yolk mixture until almost no white streaks remain. Gently fold in the remaining egg whites until just incorporated.

4. Melt the butter in a 10-inch ovensafe skillet over medium-low heat. Swirl the pan to coat it evenly with the melted butter, then gently scrape the soufflé batter into the skillet and cook until the edges begin to set and bubble slightly, about 2 minutes.

5. Transfer the skillet to the oven and bake the soufflé until puffed, the center jiggles slightly when shaken, and the surface is golden, 7 to 11 minutes. Using a potholder (the skillet handle will be hot), remove the skillet from the oven. Dust the soufflé with the confectioners' sugar and serve immediately.

Skillet Chocolate-Orange Soufflé

Grating the chocolate fine is key here; we find it easiest to use either a rasp grater or the fine holes of a box grater.

Follow the recipe for Skillet Lemon Soufflé, substituting 1 tablespoon grated zest from 1 orange for the lemon zest and ⅓ cup orange juice for the lemon juice. Gently fold 1 ounce finely grated bittersweet chocolate (about ½ cup) into the soufflé batter after incorporating all of the whites in step 3.

VANILLA ICE CREAM

WHY THIS RECIPE WORKS: Homemade vanilla ice cream is never as creamy or dense as the impossibly smooth "super-premium" ice cream found at gourmet markets or high-end ice cream shops. Instead of thick, dense, and velvety, ice cream made at home invariably turns out crumbly, fluffy, and icy. We wanted an incredibly creamy custard-based vanilla ice cream that would rival any pricey artisanal batch.

Creating smooth ice cream means reducing the size of the ice crystals; the smaller they are, the less perceptible they are. Our first move was to replace some of the sugar in our custard base with corn syrup, which interferes with crystal formation, making for a super-smooth texture. To speed up the freezing process, further ensuring small ice crystals, we froze a portion of the custard prior to churning, then mixed it with the remaining refrigerated custard. Finally, instead of freezing the churned ice cream in a tall container, we spread it into a thin layer in a cold metal baking pan and chilled it, which allowed the ice cream to firm up more quickly and delivered the flawlessly smooth texture we were after.

Homemade Vanilla Ice Cream

MAKES ABOUT 1 QUART

Two teaspoons of vanilla extract can be substituted for the vanilla bean; stir the extract into the cold custard in step 3. An instant-read thermometer is critical for the best results. Using a prechilled metal baking pan and working quickly in step 4 will help prevent melting and refreezing of the ice cream and will speed the hardening process. If using a canister-style ice cream maker, be sure to freeze the empty canister at least 24 hours and preferably 48 hours before churning. For self-refrigerating ice cream makers, prechill the canister by running the machine for 5 to 10 minutes before pouring in the custard. The ice cream can be stored for up to 5 days.

1 vanilla bean
1¾ cups heavy cream
1¼ cups whole milk
½ cup plus 2 tablespoons (4⅖ ounces) sugar
⅓ cup light corn syrup
¼ teaspoon table salt
6 large egg yolks

1. Place an 8- or 9-inch-square metal baking pan in the freezer. Cut the vanilla bean in half lengthwise. Using the tip of a paring knife, scrape out the vanilla seeds. Combine the vanilla bean, seeds, cream, milk, ¼ cup plus 2 tablespoons of the sugar, the corn syrup, and salt in a medium saucepan. Heat over medium-high heat, stirring occasionally, until the mixture is steaming steadily and registers 175 degrees on an instant-read thermometer, 5 to 10 minutes. Remove the saucepan from the heat.

2. While the cream mixture heats, whisk the egg yolks and the remaining ¼ cup sugar in a bowl until smooth, about 30 seconds. Slowly whisk 1 cup of the heated cream mixture into the egg yolk mixture. Return the mixture to the saucepan and cook over medium-low heat, stirring constantly, until the mixture thickens and registers 180 degrees, 7 to 14 minutes. Immediately pour the custard into a large bowl and let cool until no longer steaming, 10 to 20 minutes. Transfer 1 cup of the custard to a small bowl. Cover both bowls with plastic wrap. Place the large bowl in the refrigerator and the small bowl in the freezer and cool completely, at least 4 hours or up to 24 hours. (The small bowl of custard will freeze solid.)

3. Remove the custards from the refrigerator and freezer. Scrape the frozen custard from the small bowl into the large bowl of custard. Stir occasionally until the frozen custard has fully dissolved. Strain the custard through a fine-mesh strainer and transfer to an ice cream maker. Churn until the mixture resembles thick soft-serve ice cream and registers

about 21 degrees, 15 to 25 minutes. Transfer the ice cream to the frozen baking pan and press plastic wrap on the surface. Return to the freezer until firm around the edges, about 1 hour.

4. Transfer the ice cream to an airtight container, pressing firmly to remove any air pockets, and freeze until firm, at least 2 hours, before serving.

FROZEN YOGURT

WHY THIS RECIPE WORKS: We wanted to make frozen yogurt that put the tart, fresh flavor of yogurt up front and had the texture of a dense, creamy premium ice cream. We found that Greek yogurt produced a chalky frozen yogurt, so instead we used regular plain yogurt that we had strained of excess liquid (the whey) to help minimize the number of ice crystals. Swapping in a few tablespoons of Lyle's Golden Syrup for some of the granulated sugar not only gave us a frozen yogurt with fewer ice crystals but also one that was more scoopable straight from the freezer. This is because about half of Lyle's sugar is invert sugar (the other half is glucose). Unlike granulated sugar, which is made up of large sucrose molecules, invert sugar is made up of the "small sugars" glucose and fructose, which are much better at depressing the freezing point, which kept more of the water in the frozen yogurt base in liquid form for a smoother, more scoopable final product. The final step in managing the water in our base was to trap some of it using unflavored gelatin. By dissolving and heating just 1 teaspoon of gelatin in a portion of the strained whey, we prevented water molecules from joining together and forming large ice crystals.

Frozen Yogurt

MAKES ABOUT 1 QUART

We prefer the flavor and texture that Lyle's Golden Syrup lends this frozen yogurt, but light corn syrup may be substituted. Any brand of whole-milk yogurt will work in this recipe. Low-fat yogurt can be used, but the results will be less creamy and less flavorful. If more than 1¼ cups of whey drains from the yogurt in step one, simply stir the extra back in.

1 quart plain whole-milk yogurt
1 teaspoon unflavored gelatin
¾ cup sugar
3 tablespoons Lyle's Golden Syrup
⅛ teaspoon salt

1. Line colander or fine-mesh strainer with triple layer of cheesecloth and place over large bowl or measuring cup. Place yogurt in colander, cover with plastic wrap (plastic should not touch yogurt), and refrigerate until 1¼ cups whey has drained from yogurt, at least 8 hours and up to 12 hours.

2. Discard ¾ cup of drained whey. Sprinkle gelatin over remaining ½ cup whey in bowl and let sit until gelatin softens, about 5 minutes. Microwave until mixture is bubbling around edges and gelatin dissolves, about 30 seconds. Let cool for 5 minutes. In large bowl, whisk sugar, Lyle's Golden Syrup, salt, drained yogurt, and cooled gelatin mixture together until sugar is completely dissolved. Cover and refrigerate (or place bowl over ice bath) until yogurt mixture registers 40 degrees or less.

3. Churn yogurt mixture in ice cream maker until mixture resembles thick soft-serve frozen yogurt and registers about 21 degrees, 25 to 35 minutes. Transfer frozen yogurt to airtight container and freeze until firm, at least 2 hours. Serve. (Frozen yogurt can be stored for up to 5 days.)

Ginger Frozen Yogurt

Stir 1 tablespoon grated fresh ginger and 1 teaspoon ground ginger into whey-gelatin mixture as soon as it is removed from microwave. After mixture has cooled for 5 minutes, strain through fine-mesh strainer, pressing on solids to extract all liquid. Proceed with recipe as directed.

Orange Frozen Yogurt

Substitute ½ cup fresh orange juice for ½ cup whey in step 2. Stir ½ teaspoon grated orange zest into whey-gelatin mixture as soon as it is removed from microwave.

Strawberry Frozen Yogurt

Substitute ¾ cup strawberry puree for ½ cup whey in step 2.

RASPBERRY SORBET

WHY THIS RECIPE WORKS: For our raspberry sorbet recipe, we super-chilled the base and used just the right ratio of sweeteners to water to ensure the finest-textured ice crystals possible. We also bumped up the berries' natural amount of pectin to give the sorbet stability both in the freezer and out.

Raspberry Sorbet

MAKES 1 QUART

Super-chilling part of the sorbet base before transferring it to the ice cream maker will keep ice crystals to a minimum. If using a canister-style ice cream maker, be sure to freeze the empty canister for at least 24 hours and preferably 48 hours before churning. For self-refrigerating ice cream makers, prechill the canister by running the machine for five to 10 minutes before pouring in the sorbet mixture. Allow the sorbet to sit at room temperature for five minutes to soften before serving. Fresh or frozen berries may be used. If using frozen berries, thaw them before proceeding. Make certain that you use Sure-Jell engineered for low- or no-sugar recipes (packaged in a pink box) and not regular Sure-Jell (in a yellow box).

    1   cup water
    1   teaspoon Sure-Jell for Less or
        No Sugar Needed Recipes
    ⅛   teaspoon salt
    1¼ pounds (4 cups) raspberries
    ½   cup (3½ ounces) plus 2 tablespoons sugar
    ¼   cup light corn syrup

1. Combine water, Sure-Jell, and salt in medium saucepan. Heat over medium-high heat, stirring occasionally, until Sure-Jell is fully dissolved, about 5 minutes. Remove saucepan from heat and allow mixture to cool slightly, about 10 minutes.

2. Process raspberries, sugar, corn syrup, and water mixture in blender or food processor until smooth, about 30 seconds. Strain mixture through fine-mesh strainer, pressing on solids to extract as much liquid as possible. Transfer 1 cup mixture to small bowl and place remaining mixture in large bowl. Cover both bowls with plastic wrap. Place large bowl in refrigerator and small bowl in freezer and cool completely, at least 4 hours or up to 24 hours. (Small bowl of base will freeze solid.)

3. Remove mixtures from refrigerator and freezer. Scrape frozen base from small bowl into large bowl of base. Stir occasionally until frozen base has fully dissolved. Transfer mixture to ice cream maker and churn until mixture has consistency of thick milkshake and color lightens, 15 to 25 minutes.

4. Transfer sorbet to airtight container, pressing firmly to remove any air pockets, and freeze until firm, at least 2 hours. Serve. (Sorbet can be frozen for up to 5 days.)

Raspberry–Lime Rickey Sorbet

Reduce water to ¾ cup. Add 2 teaspoons grated lime zest and ¼ cup lime juice to blender with raspberries.

Raspberry-Port Sorbet

Substitute ruby port for water in step 1.

Raspberry Sorbet with Ginger and Mint

Substitute ginger beer for water in step 1. Add 2-inch piece of peeled and thinly sliced ginger and ¼ cup mint leaves to blender with raspberries. Decrease amount of sugar to ½ cup.

CHAPTER 25

CLASSIC FRUIT DESSERTS

STRAWBERRY SHORTCAKES

WHY THIS RECIPE WORKS: While some cooks like to spoon strawberries over pound cake, sponge cake, and even angel food cake, our idea of strawberry shortcake definitely involves a biscuit. We wanted a juicy strawberry filling and mounds of freshly whipped cream sandwiched in between a lightly sweetened, tender biscuit.

While eggs are not traditional, we found that one whole egg gave our biscuits a light, tender texture. And we used just enough dairy (half-and-half or milk) to bind the dough together. A modest amount of sugar yielded a lightly sweetened biscuit. For the strawberries, we wanted to avoid both a mushy puree and dry chunks of fruit. We found our solution in a compromise—mashing a portion of the berries and slicing the rest for a chunky, juicy mixture that didn't slide off the biscuit. And lightly sweetened whipped cream, flavored with vanilla, provided a cool, creamy contrast to the berries and biscuits.

Strawberry Shortcakes

SERVES 6

Start the recipe by preparing the fruit, then set the fruit aside while preparing the biscuits to allow the juices to become syrupy.

FRUIT

- 8 cups (40 ounces) strawberries, hulled
- 6 tablespoons sugar

SHORTCAKE

- 2 cups (10 ounces) unbleached all-purpose flour, plus extra for the work surface and biscuit cutter
- 5 tablespoons sugar
- 1 tablespoon baking powder
- ½ teaspoon table salt
- 8 tablespoons (1 stick) unsalted butter, cut into ½-inch pieces and chilled

- ½ cup plus 1 tablespoon half-and-half or milk
- 1 large whole egg, lightly beaten
- 1 large egg white, lightly beaten

WHIPPED CREAM

- 1 cup heavy cream, chilled
- 1 tablespoon sugar
- 1 teaspoon vanilla extract

1. FOR THE FRUIT: Crush 3 cups of the strawberries in a large bowl with a potato masher. Slice the remaining 5 cups of berries and stir them into the crushed berries along with the sugar. Set aside until the sugar has dissolved and the berries are juicy, at least 30 minutes or up to 2 hours.

2. FOR THE SHORTCAKE: Adjust an oven rack to the lower-middle position and heat the oven to 425 degrees. Line a large baking sheet with parchment paper. Pulse the flour, 3 tablespoons of the sugar, the baking powder, and salt in a food processor until combined. Sprinkle the butter pieces over the top and pulse until the mixture resembles coarse meal, about 15 pulses. Transfer the mixture to a large bowl.

3. Whisk the half-and-half and lightly beaten whole egg together in a small bowl, then stir into the flour mixture with a rubber spatula until large clumps form. Turn the dough onto a lightly floured work surface and knead lightly until it comes together.

4. Pat the dough into a 9 by 6-inch rectangle, about ¾ inch thick. Do not overwork the dough. Using a floured 2¾-inch biscuit cutter, cut out six dough rounds. Arrange the short-cakes on the prepared baking sheet, spaced about 1½ inches apart. Brush the tops with the lightly beaten egg white and sprinkle evenly with the remaining 2 tablespoons sugar. (The unbaked shortcakes can be covered with plastic wrap and refrigerated for up to 2 hours.)

5. Bake until the shortcakes are golden brown, 12 to 14 minutes, rotating the sheet halfway through the baking time. Transfer the sheet to a wire rack and cool the shortcakes until warm, about 10 minutes.

6. FOR THE WHIPPED CREAM: In a medium bowl, whip the cream, sugar, and vanilla with an electric mixer on medium-low speed until frothy, about 1 minute. Increase the speed to high and continue to whip until the cream forms soft peaks, 1 to 3 minutes.

7. TO ASSEMBLE: When the shortcakes have cooled slightly, split them in half horizontally. Place each shortcake bottom on an individual plate, spoon a portion of the berries over each bottom, dollop with whipped cream, and cap with the shortcake tops. Serve immediately.

CHERRY COBBLER

WHY THIS RECIPE WORKS: Most cherry cobblers are no more than canned pie filling topped with dry, heavy biscuits. We wanted a filling that highlighted the unique, sweet-tart flavor of sour cherries and, on top, we wanted a tender, feather-light biscuit crust.

Because fresh sour cherries are so hard to find most of the year, we picked jarred Morello cherries—easy to find and available year-round. Embellishing the cherries with cherry juice, cinnamon, and vanilla was a step in the right direction but the filling still tasted a bit flat, so we switched out some of the juice for red wine and replaced the vanilla with almond extract. The resulting sauce was better, but a little thin. A small amount of cornstarch thickened the filling nicely. As for the biscuits, we favored buttermilk biscuits, which have a light and fluffy texture. To ensure nicely browned biscuits that didn't become soggy over the filling, we parbaked them on their own ahead of time, then slid the biscuits over the warm cherry filling and put it in the oven to finish cooking.

Sour Cherry Cobbler

SERVES 12

Use the smaller amount of sugar in the filling if you prefer your fruit desserts on the tart side and the larger amount if you like them sweet. Serve with vanilla ice cream or lightly sweetened whipped cream.

BISCUIT TOPPING

- 2 cups (10 ounces) unbleached all-purpose flour
- ½ cup (3½ ounces) sugar
- ½ teaspoon baking powder
- ½ teaspoon baking soda
- ½ teaspoon table salt
- 6 tablespoons (¾ stick) unsalted butter, cut into ½-inch pieces and chilled
- 1 cup buttermilk

FILLING

- 8 cups jarred Morello cherries from 4 (24-ounce) jars, drained, 2 cups juice reserved
- ¾–1 cup (5¼ to 7 ounces) sugar (see note)
- 3 tablespoons plus 1 teaspoon cornstarch
  Pinch table salt
- 1 cup dry red wine
- 1 (3-inch) cinnamon stick
- ¼ teaspoon almond extract

1. Adjust an oven rack to the middle position and heat the oven to 425 degrees. Line a large baking sheet with parchment paper.

2. FOR THE BISCUIT TOPPING: Pulse the flour, 6 tablespoons of the sugar, the baking powder, baking soda, and salt in a food processor until combined. Sprinkle the butter pieces over the top and pulse until the mixture resembles coarse meal, about 15 pulses. Transfer the mixture to a large bowl; add the buttermilk and stir with rubber spatula until combined. Using a greased ¼-cup measure ice cream scoop, scoop 12 biscuits onto the prepared baking sheet, spacing them 1½ inches apart.

Sprinkle the biscuits evenly with the remaining 2 tablespoons sugar and bake until lightly browned, about 15 minutes, rotating the sheet halfway through baking. (Do not turn the oven off.)

3. FOR THE FILLING: Meanwhile, arrange the drained cherries in an even layer in a 13 by 9-inch glass baking dish. Combine the sugar, cornstarch, and salt in a medium saucepan. Stir in the reserved cherry juice and wine and add the cinnamon stick; cook over medium-high heat, stirring frequently, until the mixture simmers and thickens, about 5 minutes. Discard the cinnamon stick, stir in the almond extract, and pour the hot liquid over the cherries in the baking dish.

4. TO BAKE: Arrange the hot biscuits in three rows of four biscuits over the warm filling. Bake the cobbler until the filling is bubbling and the biscuits are deep golden brown, about 10 minutes. Transfer the baking dish to a wire rack and cool for 10 minutes; serve.

Fresh Sour Cherry Cobbler

Morello or Montmorency cherries can be used in this cobbler made with fresh sour cherries. Do not use sweet Bing cherries. If the cherries do not release enough juice after 30 minutes in step 1, add cranberry juice to make up the difference.

- 1¼ cups (8¾ ounces) sugar
- 3 tablespoons plus 1 teaspoon cornstarch
  Pinch table salt
- 8 cups (4 pounds) fresh sour cherries, pitted, juice reserved (see note)
- 1 cup dry red wine
  Cranberry juice, as needed (see note)
- 1 recipe Biscuit Topping
- 1 (3-inch) cinnamon stick
- ¼ teaspoon almond extract

1. Whisk the sugar, cornstarch, and salt together in a large bowl; add the cherries and toss well to combine. Pour the wine over the cherries; let stand for 30 minutes. Drain the cherries in a colander set over a medium bowl. Combine the drained and reserved juices (from pitting the cherries); you should have 3 cups (if not, add cranberry juice to make this amount).

2. Meanwhile, prepare and bake the biscuit topping.

3. Arrange the drained cherries in an even layer in a 13 by 9-inch glass baking dish. Bring the juices, wine, and cinnamon stick to a simmer in a medium saucepan over medium-high heat, stirring frequently, until the mixture thickens, about 5 minutes. Discard the cinnamon stick, stir in the almond extract, and pour the hot juices over the cherries in the baking dish.

4. Arrange the hot biscuits in three rows of four biscuits over the warm filling. Bake the cobbler until the filling is bubbling and the biscuits are deep golden brown, about 10 minutes. Transfer the baking dish to a wire rack and cool for 10 minutes; serve.

BLUEBERRY COBBLER

WHY THIS RECIPE WORKS: Too often, blueberry cobbler means a filling that is too sweet, overspiced, and unappealingly thick. We wanted a not-too-thin, not-too-thick filling where the blueberry flavor would be front and center. And over the fruit, we wanted a light, tender biscuit topping that could hold its own against the fruit filling, with an ingredient list simple enough to allow the blueberries to play a starring role.

We prepared a not-too-sweet filling using 6 cups of fresh berries and less than a cup of sugar. Cornstarch worked well as a thickener—it thickened the fruit's juice without leaving a starchy texture behind. A little lemon and cinnamon were all that were needed to enhance the filling without masking the blueberry flavor. For the topping, ease of preparation was our guiding principle, so we made light, rustic drop biscuits enriched with a little cornmeal. Adding the biscuit topping to the cobbler after the filling had baked on its own allowed the biscuits to brown evenly and cook through. A sprinkling of cinnamon sugar on the dropped biscuit dough added a pleasing sweet crunch.

Blueberry Cobbler

SERVES 6 TO 8

While the blueberries are baking, prepare the ingredients for the topping, but do not stir the wet ingredients into the dry ingredients until just before the berries come out of the oven. A standard or deep-dish 9-inch pie plate works well; an 8-inch square baking dish can also be used. Vanilla ice cream or lightly sweetened whipped cream is the perfect accompaniment. To reheat leftovers, put the cobbler in a 350-degree oven for 10 to 15 minutes, until heated through.

FILLING

- ½ cup (3½ ounces) sugar
- 1 tablespoon cornstarch
- Pinch ground cinnamon
- Pinch table salt
- 6 cups (30 ounces) fresh blueberries, rinsed and picked over
- 1½ teaspoons grated zest plus 1 tablespoon juice from 1 lemon

BISCUIT TOPPING

- 1 cup (5 ounces) unbleached all-purpose flour
- ¼ cup (1¾ ounces) plus 2 teaspoons sugar
- 2 tablespoons stone-ground cornmeal
- 2 teaspoons baking powder
- ¼ teaspoon baking soda
- ¼ teaspoon table salt
- 4 tablespoons (½ stick) unsalted butter, melted
- ⅓ cup buttermilk
- ½ teaspoon vanilla extract
- ⅛ teaspoon ground cinnamon

1. Adjust an oven rack to the lower-middle position and heat the oven to 375 degrees.

2. **FOR THE FILLING:** Whisk the sugar, cornstarch, cinnamon, and salt together in a large bowl. Add the berries and mix gently with a rubber spatula until evenly coated; add the lemon zest and juice and mix to combine. Transfer the berry mixture to a 9-inch glass pie plate, place the pie plate on a rimmed baking sheet, and bake until the filling is hot and bubbling around the edges, about 25 minutes.

3. **FOR THE BISCUIT TOPPING:** Meanwhile, whisk the flour, ¼ cup of the sugar, the cornmeal, baking powder, baking soda, and salt together in a large bowl. Whisk the melted butter, buttermilk, and vanilla together in a small bowl. Mix the remaining 2 teaspoons sugar with the cinnamon in a second small bowl and set aside. One minute before the berries come out of the oven, add the wet ingredients to the dry ingredients; stir with a rubber spatula until just combined and no dry pockets remain.

4. **TO ASSEMBLE AND BAKE:** Remove the berries from the oven; increase the oven temperature to 425 degrees. Divide the biscuit dough into eight equal pieces and place them on the hot berry filling, spacing them at least ½ inch apart (they should not touch). Sprinkle each mound of dough evenly with the cinnamon sugar. Bake until the filling is bubbling and the biscuits are golden brown on top and cooked through, 15 to 18 minutes. Transfer the cobbler to a wire rack; cool for 20 minutes and serve.

PEACH CRISP

WHY THIS RECIPE WORKS: There is seldom anything crisp about most crisps. This simple fruit dessert usually comes out of the oven with a soggy, mushy topping—quite a letdown from the ideal of a warm, fruity filling covered in a crunchy, sweet topping. We set out to make peach crisp that wouldn't disappoint, one with the perfect balance of nicely thickened filling and a lightly sweetened, crisp topping.

We tried everything from Grape-Nuts to cookie crumbs and found the ideal topping mixture to be chopped nuts, butter, and flour. Cutting the butter into the flour was crucial for creating a crisp topping, and we found that a food processor was ideally suited to producing a mixture that resembled crumbly wet sand. Another issue to tackle was sugar: what kind and how much. White sugar alone was too bland, while brown sugar on its own was too strong tasting. A 50–50 mix of the two proved to be the perfect combination. We decided not to use too much sugar in the fruit filling so there would be some contrast with the topping. And we nixed the idea of a thickener—the filling without one had a nicely bright fresh fruit flavor and the topping remained crisp whether we used one or not.

Peach Crisp

SERVES 4 TO 6

Lightly sweetened whipped cream or vanilla ice cream is the perfect accompaniment, especially if serving the crisp warm. A standard or deep-dish 9-inch pie plate works well; an 8-inch square baking dish can also be used.

TOPPING

- 6 tablespoons unbleached all-purpose flour
- ¼ cup packed (1¾ ounces) light brown sugar
- ¼ cup (1¾ ounces) granulated sugar
- ¼ teaspoon ground cinnamon
- ¼ teaspoon ground nutmeg
- ¼ teaspoon table salt
- 5 tablespoons unsalted butter, cut into ½-inch pieces and chilled
- ¾ cup (about 4 ounces) coarsely chopped pecans, walnuts, or almonds

FILLING

- 3 pounds peaches (6 to 8 medium), peeled, pitted, and cut into ½-inch slices
- ¼ cup (1¾ ounces) granulated sugar
- ½ teaspoon grated zest plus 1½ tablespoons juice from 1 lemon

1. FOR THE TOPPING: Pulse the flour, sugars, cinnamon, nutmeg, and salt in a food processor until combined. Sprinkle the butter pieces over the top and pulse until the mixture resembles coarse meal, about 15 pulses. Add the nuts and pulse until the mixture clumps together and resembles wet sand, about 5 pulses; do not overmix. Transfer the mixture to a bowl and refrigerate while preparing the filling, at least 15 minutes.

2. FOR THE FILLING: Adjust an oven rack to the lower-middle position and heat the oven to 375 degrees. Combine the peaches, sugar, zest, and juice in a large bowl and toss gently to combine. Transfer the peach mixture to a 9-inch glass pie plate, place the pie plate on a rimmed baking sheet, and sprinkle the chilled topping evenly over the top.

3. Bake for 40 minutes. Increase the oven temperature to 400 degrees and continue to bake until the filling is bubbling and the topping is deep golden brown, about 5 minutes longer. Serve warm.

Peach Crisp for a Crowd

SERVES 10

Follow the recipe for Peach Crisp, doubling all the ingredients and using a 13 by 9-inch baking dish. Increase the baking time to 55 minutes and bake at 375 degrees without increasing the oven temperature.

CHERRY CLAFOUTI

WHY THIS RECIPE WORKS: For a clafouti that featured juicy cherries in every bite (and no pits to get in the way, as most traditional recipes have), we pitted and halved the cherries. To concentrate their flavor and prevent excess moisture from leaking into the custard, we roasted them in a hot oven for 15 minutes and then tossed them with a couple of teaspoons of absorbent flour. To recover the slightly spicy, floral flavor the pits contributed, we added ⅛ teaspoon of cinnamon to the flour. We found that too much flour made the custard too bready, whereas an excess of dairy made it too loose. Ultimately, we settled on a moderate amount of each for a tender yet slightly resilient custard void of pastiness. Switching from a casserole dish to a preheated 12-inch skillet gave us better browning and made the custard easy to slice and serve. A last-minute sprinkle of granulated sugar added a touch of sweetness and a delicate crunch.

Cherry Clafouti

SERVES 6 TO 8

We prefer whole milk in this recipe, but 1 or 2 percent low-fat milk may be substituted. Do not substitute frozen cherries for the fresh cherries.

1½ pounds fresh sweet cherries, pitted and halved
1 teaspoon lemon juice
2 teaspoons plus ½ cup (2½ ounces) all-purpose flour
⅛ teaspoon ground cinnamon
4 large eggs
⅔ cup (4⅔ ounces) plus 2 teaspoons sugar
2½ teaspoons vanilla extract
¼ teaspoon salt
1 cup heavy cream
⅔ cup whole milk
1 tablespoon unsalted butter

1. Adjust oven racks to upper-middle and lowest positions; place 12-inch ovensafe skillet on lower rack and heat oven to 425 degrees. Line rimmed baking sheet with aluminum foil and place cherries, cut side up, on sheet. Roast cherries on upper rack until just tender and cut sides look dry, about 15 minutes. Transfer cherries to medium bowl, toss with lemon juice, and let cool 5 for minutes. Combine 2 teaspoons flour and cinnamon in small bowl; dust flour mixture evenly over cherries and toss to coat thoroughly.

2. While cherries roast, whisk eggs, ⅔ cup sugar, vanilla, and salt in large bowl until smooth and pale, about 1 minute. Whisk in remaining ½ cup flour until smooth. Whisk in cream and milk until incorporated.

3. Remove skillet (skillet handle will be hot) from oven and set on wire rack. Add butter and swirl to coat bottom and sides of skillet (butter will melt and brown quickly). Pour batter into skillet and place cherries evenly over top (some will sink). Transfer skillet to lower rack and bake until clafouti puffs and surface is golden brown (edges will be dark brown), and center registers 195 degrees, 18 to 22 minutes, rotating skillet halfway through baking. Transfer skillet to wire rack, and let cool for 25 minutes. Sprinkle evenly with remaining 2 teaspoons sugar. Slice into wedges and serve.

RASPBERRY GRATIN

WHY THIS RECIPE WORKS: Quicker than a crisp and dressier than a shortcake, a gratin is a layer of fresh fruit piled into a shallow baking dish, dressed up with bread crumbs, and run under a broiler. The topping browns and the fruit is warmed just enough to release a bit of juice. We wanted to find the quickest, easiest route to this pleasing dessert.

We started with perfect raspberries: ripe, dry, unbruised, and clean. Tossing the sweet-tart berries with just a bit of sugar and kirsch (a clear cherry brandy; vanilla extract can be substituted) provided enough additional flavor and sweetness. For the topping, we combined soft white bread, brown

sugar, cinnamon, and butter in the food processor and topped the berries with the fluffy crumbs. Instead of broiling the gratin, which can produce a crust that's burnt in spots, we simply baked it. We found that a moderately hot oven gave the berries more time to soften and browned the crust more evenly.

Simple Raspberry Gratin

SERVES 4 TO 6

If you prefer, you can substitute blueberries, blackberries, or strawberries for part or all of the raspberries. If using strawberries, hull them and slice them in half lengthwise if small or into quarters if large. Later in the summer season, ripe, peeled peaches or nectarines, sliced, can be used in combination with the blueberries or raspberries.

4 cups (20 ounces) fresh or frozen (not thawed) raspberries (see note)
1 tablespoon granulated sugar
1 tablespoon kirsch or vanilla extract (optional)
Pinch table salt
3 slices high-quality white sandwich bread, torn into quarters
¼ cup packed (1¾ ounces) light or dark brown sugar
2 tablespoons unsalted butter, softened
Pinch ground cinnamon

1. Adjust an oven rack to the lower-middle position and heat the oven to 400 degrees. Gently toss the raspberries, granulated sugar, kirsch (if using), and salt in a medium bowl. Transfer the mixture to a 9-inch glass pie plate.

2. Pulse the bread, brown sugar, butter, and cinnamon in a food processor until the mixture resembles coarse crumbs, about 10 pulses. Sprinkle the crumbs evenly over the fruit and bake until the crumbs are deep golden brown, 15 to 20 minutes. Transfer to a wire rack; cool for 5 minutes and serve.

FRESH BERRY GRATIN

WHY THIS RECIPE WORKS: Gratins can be very humble, as in our Simple Raspberry Gratin, where the topping is little more than sweetened bread crumbs. Or they can be a bit more sophisticated, as when they are topped with the foamy Italian custard called zabaglione. Zabaglione is made with just three simple ingredients—egg yolks, sugar, and alcohol—but it requires constant watching so that the mixture doesn't overcook. It also needs to be whisked just long enough to transform the egg yolks to the ideal thick, creamy texture. We were after a foolproof method for this topping for a gratin that could serve as an elegant finale to a special summer meal.

We chose to make individual gratins—perfect for entertaining—and settled on raspberries, strawberries, blueberries, and blackberries. We tossed the berries with sugar and a pinch of salt to draw out their juices and let the mixture

sit while we worked on the custard. To prevent scrambled eggs, we kept the heat low; for the right texture, we didn't stop whisking when soft peaks formed—instead we waited until the custard became slightly thicker. As for flavor, tasters thought that zabaglione made with the traditional Marsala wine was a bit sweet and cloying on top of the berries. We switched to a crisp, dry Sauvignon Blanc and found that its clean flavor allowed the berries to shine. However, with that change, our zabaglione was almost runny. After trying to thicken it with cornstarch and gelatin (with disappointing results), we turned to whipped cream. After carefully folding a few tablespoons of whipped cream into the cooked and slightly cooled zabaglione base, we spooned it over the berries. Finally, we sprinkled the custard with a mixture of brown and white sugar before broiling for a crackly, caramelized crust.

Individual Fresh Berry Gratins with Zabaglione
SERVES 4

When making the zabaglione, make sure to cook the egg mixture in a glass bowl over water that is barely simmering; glass conducts heat more evenly and gently than metal. If the heat is too high, the yolks around the edges of the bowl will start to scramble. Constant whisking is required. Do not use frozen berries for this recipe. You will need four shallow 6-inch gratin dishes, but a broiler-safe pie plate or gratin dish can be used instead. To prevent scorching, pay close attention to the gratins when broiling.

BERRY MIXTURE

- 3 cups (about 15 ounces) mixed berries (raspberries, blueberries, blackberries, and strawberries; strawberries hulled and halved lengthwise if small, quartered if large), at room temperature (see note)
- 2 teaspoons granulated sugar
  Pinch table salt

ZABAGLIONE

- 3 large egg yolks
- 3 tablespoons granulated sugar
- 3 tablespoons dry white wine, such as Sauvignon Blanc
- 2 teaspoons light brown sugar
- 3 tablespoons heavy cream, chilled

1. FOR THE BERRY MIXTURE: Toss the berries, sugar, and salt together in a medium bowl. Divide the berry mixture evenly among four shallow 6-ounce gratin dishes set on a rimmed baking sheet; set aside.

2. FOR THE ZABAGLIONE: Whisk the egg yolks, 2 tablespoons plus 1 teaspoon of the granulated sugar, and the wine together in a medium glass bowl until the sugar is dissolved, about 1 minute. Set the bowl over a saucepan of barely simmering water and cook, whisking constantly, until the mixture is frothy. Continue to cook, whisking constantly, until the mixture is slightly thickened, creamy, and glossy, 5 to 10 minutes (the mixture will form loose mounds when dripped from the whisk). Remove the bowl from the saucepan and whisk constantly for 30 seconds to cool slightly. Transfer the bowl to the refrigerator and chill until the egg mixture is completely cool, about 10 minutes.

3. Meanwhile, adjust an oven rack 6 inches from the broiler element and heat the broiler. Combine the brown sugar and the remaining 2 teaspoons granulated sugar in a small bowl.

4. Whisk the heavy cream in a large bowl until it holds soft peaks, 30 to 90 seconds. Using a rubber spatula, gently fold the whipped cream into the cooled egg mixture. Spoon the zabaglione over the berries and sprinkle the sugar mixture evenly on top; let stand at room temperature for 10 minutes, until the sugar dissolves.

5. Broil the gratins until the sugar is bubbly and caramelized, 1 to 4 minutes. Serve immediately.

Individual Fresh Berry Gratins with Lemon Zabaglione

Follow the recipe for Individual Fresh Berry Gratins with Zabaglione, replacing 1 tablespoon of the wine with 1 tablespoon juice from 1 lemon and adding 1 teaspoon grated zest from 1 lemon to the yolk mixture in step 2.

BAKED APPLES

WHY THIS RECIPE WORKS: This homey dessert is often plagued with a mushy texture and one-dimensional, cloyingly sweet flavor. We wanted baked apples that were tender and firm with a filling that perfectly complemented their sweet, tart flavor. We knew picking the right variety of apple was paramount to our success and, after extensive testing, we arrived at a surprising winner: Granny Smith was the best apple for the job, with its firm flesh and tart, fruity flavor. To ensure that our fruit avoided even the occasional collapse, we peeled the apples after cutting off the top.

The skin traps steam from the extra moisture released by the breakdown of the apples' interior cells, and removing it allows the steam to escape and the apple to retain its tender-firm texture. Sautéing our apples cut side down intensified their flavor. Our filling base of dried cranberries, brown sugar, and pecans benefited from some finessing by way of cinnamon, orange zest, and a pat of butter. We intensified the nuttiness with chewy rolled oats, and diced apple was an obvious addition. A melon baller helped us to scoop out a spacious cavity that accommodated plenty of filling. We then capped off the filled apples with the tops we had previously lopped off. Once in the oven, the apples were basted with an apple cider and maple syrup sauce and emerged full of flavor.

Best Baked Apples

SERVES 6

If you don't have an ovensafe skillet, transfer the browned apples to a 13 by 9-inch baking dish and bake as directed. The recipe calls for seven apples; six are left whole and one is diced and added to the filling. Serve the apples with vanilla ice cream, if desired.

    7 large (about 6 ounces each) Granny Smith apples
       (see note)
    6 tablespoons (¾ stick) unsalted butter, softened
    ⅓ cup dried cranberries, chopped coarse
    ⅓ cup coarsely chopped pecans, toasted
    ¼ cup packed (1¾ ounces) brown sugar
    3 tablespoons old-fashioned oats
    1 teaspoon finely grated zest from 1 orange
    ½ teaspoon ground cinnamon
       Pinch table salt
    ⅓ cup maple syrup
    ⅓ cup plus 2 tablespoons apple cider

1. Adjust an oven rack to the middle position and heat the oven to 375 degrees. Peel, core, and cut 1 apple into ¼-inch dice. Combine 5 tablespoons of the butter, the cranberries, pecans, brown sugar, oats, orange zest, cinnamon, salt, and diced apple in a large bowl; set aside.

2. Shave a thin slice off the bottom (blossom end) of the remaining 6 apples to allow them to sit flat. Cut the top ½ inch off the stem end of the apples and reserve. Peel the apples and use a melon baller or small measuring spoon to remove a 1½-inch-diameter core, being careful not to cut through the bottom of the apple.

3. Melt the remaining 1 tablespoon butter in a 12-inch oven-safe nonstick skillet over medium heat. Once the foaming subsides, add the apples, stem side down, and cook until the cut surface is golden brown, about 3 minutes. Flip the apples, reduce the heat to low, and spoon the filling inside, mounding the excess filling over the cavities; top with the reserved apple caps. Add the maple syrup and ⅓ cup of the cider to the skillet. Transfer the skillet to the oven and bake until a skewer inserted into the apples meets little resistance, 35 to 40 minutes, basting every 10 minutes with the maple syrup mixture in the skillet.

4. Transfer the apples to a serving platter. Stir up to 2 tablespoons of the remaining cider into the sauce in the skillet to adjust the consistency. Pour the sauce over the apples and serve.

APPLE CRISP

WHY THIS RECIPE WORKS: Most apple crisp recipes are what you'd expect—unevenly cooked fruit and an unremarkable topping that rarely lives up to its crisp moniker. We wanted an exemplary apple crisp—a lush (but not mushy) sweet-tart apple filling covered with truly crisp morsels of buttery, sugary topping.

For apple crisp, we prefer crisp apples such as Golden Delicious, because they are hardier and turn tender but not mushy. But they posed two problems. One, their mellower, more honeyed flesh lacked fruity punch. And while complete apple blowouts had been averted, the apples were still cooking unevenly. Stirring the fruit helped solve the problem but donning oven mitts to reach into a hot oven and stir bubbling fruit was a hassle. Instead, we turned to softening our fruit on the stovetop—in a skillet. The shallow, flared shape of the skillet also encouraged evaporation, browning, and better flavor overall. But to improve the flavor further, we turned to apple cider, first reducing it in the skillet to a syrupy consistency. This super-potent reduction contributed an intense, almost *tarte Tatin*–like fruity depth.

As for the topping, we added brown sugar to white to play up the apples' caramel notes. Rolled oats gave the topping character and chew. Chopped pecans not only improved the crunch factor, but added rich flavor as well. We then slid the skillet into the oven for a quick browning and to finish cooking the apples.

Skillet Apple Crisp

SERVES 6 TO 8

If your skillet is not ovensafe, prepare the recipe through step 3 and then transfer the filling to a 13 by 9-inch baking dish. Top the filling as directed and bake for an additional 5 minutes. We like Golden Delicious apples for this recipe, but any sweet, crisp apple such as Honeycrisp or Braeburn can be substituted. Do not use Granny Smith apples in this recipe. While old-fashioned oats are preferable in this recipe, quick-cooking oats can be substituted. Serve the apple crisp warm or at room temperature with vanilla ice cream or whipped cream.

TOPPING

- ¾ cup (3¾ ounces) unbleached all-purpose flour
- ¾ cup (3 ounces) pecans, chopped fine
- ¾ cup (2¼ ounces) old-fashioned oats (see note)
- ½ cup packed (3½ ounces) light brown sugar
- ¼ cup (1¾ ounces) granulated sugar
- ½ teaspoon ground cinnamon
- ½ teaspoon table salt
- 8 tablespoons (1 stick) unsalted butter, melted

FILLING

- 3 pounds Golden Delicious apples (about 7 medium), peeled, cored, halved, and cut into ½-inch-thick wedges (see note)
- ¼ cup (1¾ ounces) granulated sugar
- ¼ teaspoon ground cinnamon (optional)
- 1 cup apple cider
- 2 teaspoons juice from 1 lemon
- 2 tablespoons unsalted butter

1. FOR THE TOPPING: Adjust an oven rack to the middle position and heat the oven to 450 degrees. Combine the flour, pecans, oats, brown sugar, granulated sugar, cinnamon, and salt in a medium bowl. Stir in the butter until the mixture is thoroughly moistened and crumbly. Set aside while preparing the fruit filling.

2. FOR THE FILLING: Toss the apples, sugar, and cinnamon (if using) together in a large bowl; set aside. Bring the cider to a simmer in a 12-inch ovensafe skillet over medium heat; cook until reduced to ½ cup, about 5 minutes. Transfer the reduced cider to a bowl or liquid measuring cup; stir in the lemon juice and set aside.

3. Heat the butter in the now-empty skillet over medium heat. When the foaming subsides, add the apple mixture and cook, stirring frequently, until the apples are beginning to soften and become translucent, 12 to 14 minutes. (Do not fully cook the apples.) Remove the pan from the heat and gently stir in the cider mixture until the apples are coated.

4. Sprinkle the topping evenly over the fruit, breaking up any large chunks. Place the skillet on a baking sheet and bake until the fruit is tender and the topping is deep golden brown, 15 to 20 minutes. Cool on a wire rack until warm, at least 15 minutes, and serve.

APPLE BROWN BETTY

WHY THIS RECIPE WORKS: In its most basic form, apple brown betty contains only four ingredients: apples, bread crumbs, sugar, and butter. Sadly, this simple combination inevitably results in a soggy, mushy mess—not the classic Colonial dish of tender, lightly spiced chunks of apple topped with toasted bread crumbs. We decided it was time to give "Betty" a serious makeover. For a lightly sweetened, crisp topping, we toasted white sandwich bread crumbs with butter and a bit of sugar. The sweet/tart combination of Granny Smith and Golden Delicious apples made a not-too-sweet apple filling. Instead of baking the dessert, we prepared it in a skillet on the stovetop and cooked the apples in two batches to ensure even cooking. After preparing the bread crumbs, we removed them from the pan and caramelized the apples. Adding brown sugar to the apples along with ginger and cinnamon gave the dessert a deepened, lightly spiced flavor. The addition of apple cider to the fruit brought moisture and a further dimension of apple flavor; a bit of lemon juice brightened the filling. For a thicker filling, we added a portion of the toasted bread crumbs to the apples and reserved the remainder for sprinkling over the top.

Skillet Apple Brown Betty

SERVES 6 TO 8

If your apples are especially tart, omit the lemon juice. If, on the other hand, your apples are exceptionally sweet, use the full amount. Leftovers can be refrigerated in an airtight container; topped with vanilla yogurt, they make an excellent breakfast.

BREAD CRUMBS

- 4 slices high-quality white sandwich bread, torn into quarters
- 3 tablespoons unsalted butter, cut into 4 pieces
- 2 tablespoons packed light brown sugar

FILLING

- ¼ cup packed (1¾ ounces) light brown sugar
- ¼ teaspoon ground ginger
- ¼ teaspoon ground cinnamon
  Pinch table salt
- 3 tablespoons unsalted butter
- 1½ pounds Granny Smith apples (about 3 large), peeled, cored, and cut into ½-inch cubes (about 4 cups)
- 1½ pounds Golden Delicious apples (about 3 large), peeled, cored, and cut into ½-inch cubes (about 4 cups)
- 1¼ cups apple cider
- 1–3 teaspoons juice from 1 lemon (see note)

1. FOR THE BREAD CRUMBS: Pulse the bread, butter, and sugar in a food processor until coarsely ground, 5 to 7 pulses. Transfer the bread crumbs to a 12-inch skillet and toast over medium heat, stirring constantly, until they are deep golden brown, 8 to 10 minutes. Transfer to a paper towel–lined plate; wipe out the skillet.

2. FOR THE FILLING: Combine the sugar, spices, and salt in a small bowl. Melt 1½ tablespoons of the butter in the now-empty skillet over high heat. Stir in the Granny Smith apples and half of the sugar mixture. Distribute the apples in an even layer and cook, stirring two or three times, until medium brown, about 5 minutes; transfer to a medium bowl. Repeat with the remaining butter, the Golden Delicious apples, and the remaining sugar mixture, returning the first batch of apples to the skillet when the second batch is done.

3. Add the apple cider to the skillet and scrape the bottom and sides of the pan with a wooden spoon to loosen the browned bits; cook until the apples are tender but not mushy and the liquid has reduced and is just beginning to thicken, 2 to 4 minutes.

4. Remove the skillet from the heat; stir in the lemon juice (if using) and ⅓ cup of the toasted bread crumbs. Using a wooden spoon, lightly flatten the apples into an even layer in the skillet and evenly sprinkle with the remaining toasted bread crumbs. Spoon the warm betty into individual bowls and serve with vanilla ice cream, if desired.

APPLE STRUDEL

WHY THIS RECIPE WORKS: Most modern phyllo-based versions of strudel have tough layers of phyllo on the underside, while the sheets on top shatter before you even cut a slice. Meanwhile, fillings collapse and leak everywhere, despite the bread crumbs supposedly added to soak up liquid and prevent leaking (instead, they just make the filling taste pasty). We parcooked the apples in the microwave to activate an enzyme that sets the pectin in the fruit and allows them to bake without collapsing. We stirred in ultradry panko bread crumbs instead of homemade toasted crumbs since we could use less of them to soak up a comparable amount of liquid (thus avoiding pastiness). To avoid a compressed, tough underside, we used fewer sheets of phyllo and changed the typical wrapping technique so the seam was on the top instead of on the bottom. We were able to minimize the flyaways on top by dusting a small amount of confectioners' sugar between the phyllo layers so that they fused in the oven, and by slicing our strudel while it was warm. Making two smaller strudels simplified assembly.

Apple Strudel

SERVES 6

Gala apples can be substituted for Golden Delicious. Phyllo dough is also available in larger 18 by 14-inch sheets; if using, cut them in half to make 14 by 9-inch sheets. Thaw phyllo in the refrigerator overnight or on the counter for 4 to 5 hours; don't thaw it in the microwave.

1¾	pounds Golden Delicious apples, peeled, cored, and cut into ½-inch pieces
3	tablespoons granulated sugar
½	teaspoon grated lemon zest plus 1½ teaspoons juice

¼	teaspoon ground cinnamon
¼	teaspoon ground ginger
	Salt
3	tablespoons golden raisins
1½	tablespoons panko bread crumbs
7	tablespoons unsalted butter, melted
14	(14 by 9-inch) phyllo sheets, thawed
1	tablespoon confectioners' sugar, plus extra for serving

1. Toss apples, granulated sugar, lemon zest and juice, cinnamon, ginger, and ⅛ teaspoon salt together in large bowl. Cover and microwave until apples are warm to touch, about 2 minutes, stirring once halfway through microwaving. Let apples stand, covered, for 5 minutes. Transfer apples to colander set in second large bowl and let drain, reserving liquid. Return apples to bowl; stir in raisins and panko.

2. Adjust oven rack to upper-middle position and heat oven to 375 degrees. Spray rimmed baking sheet with vegetable oil spray. Stir ⅛ teaspoon salt into melted butter.

3. Place 16½ by 12-inch sheet of parchment paper on counter with long side parallel to edge of counter. Place 1 phyllo sheet on parchment with long side parallel to edge of counter. Place 1½ teaspoons confectioners' sugar in fine-mesh strainer (rest strainer in bowl to prevent making mess). Lightly brush sheet with melted butter and dust sparingly with confectioners' sugar. Repeat with 6 more phyllo sheets, melted butter, and confectioners' sugar, stacking sheets one on top of the other as you go.

4. Arrange half of apple mixture in 2½ by 10-inch rectangle 2 inches from bottom of phyllo and about 2 inches from each side. Using parchment, fold sides of phyllo over filling, then fold bottom edge of phyllo over filling. Brush folded portions of phyllo with reserved apple liquid. Fold top edge over filling, making sure top and bottom edges overlap by about 1 inch. (If they do not overlap, unfold, rearrange filling into slightly narrower strip, and refold.) Press firmly to seal. Using thin metal spatula, transfer strudel to 1 side of prepared baking sheet, facing seam toward center of sheet. Lightly brush top and sides of strudel with half of remaining apple liquid. Repeat process with remaining phyllo, melted butter, confectioners' sugar, filling, and apple liquid. Place second strudel on other side of prepared sheet, with seam facing center of sheet.

5. Bake strudels until golden brown, 27 to 35 minutes, rotating sheet halfway through baking. Using thin metal spatula, immediately transfer strudels to cutting board. Let cool for 3 minutes. Slice each strudel into thirds and let cool for at least 20 minutes. Serve warm or at room temperature, dusting with extra confectioners' sugar before serving.

EASY APPLE STRUDEL

WHY THIS RECIPE WORKS: Apple strudel, lightly spiced apples in a thin, flaky pastry, is meant to be savored by the forkful, preferably with a strong cup of coffee. We wanted all the flavor and charm of this apple dessert, but we didn't want to bother with the hours of preparation the paper-thin dough requires. So we set out to simplify this classic dessert while keeping the rich apple filling and as much of the crisp, flaky texture as possible.

Replacing homemade strudel dough with purchased phyllo dough made for a crust with perfect flaky layers in a fraction of the time. We brushed the phyllo sheets with melted butter to keep them crisp and flaky. A combination of Golden Delicious and McIntosh apples, sliced thin, gave us a filling with layered apple flavor and just the right texture. A small amount of bread crumbs, browned in butter, thickened the filling without weighing it down. Golden raisins, plumped on the stove with Calvados (apple brandy), added a sophisticated, fruity dimension to the apple filling; for brightness and to lighten the filling, we added in some fresh lemon juice. We found that the phyllo on most strudels, including this one, curled and shattered as it cooled; sprinkling sugar between the layers of phyllo "glued" them together in the oven and prevented this problem.

Easy Apple Strudel

SERVES 6

The best ways to thaw the phyllo are in the refrigerator overnight or at room temperature for 3 to 4 hours; it doesn't defrost well in the microwave. Make sure that the phyllo sheets you use for the strudel are not badly torn. If they have small cuts or tears in the same location (sometimes an entire package sustains cuts in the same spot), when forming the strudel, flip alternating layers so that the cuts will not line up, thereby creating a weak spot that can cause the strudel to burst during baking. To make the fresh bread crumbs, process one slice of high-quality white sandwich bread in a food processor until fine, 20 to 30 seconds. Serve the strudel warm with Tangy Whipped Cream (recipe follows) or regular whipped cream.

ASSEMBLING EASY APPLE STRUDEL

1. Brush 1 sheet of phyllo with melted butter and sprinkle with sugar. Place another sheet of phyllo next to it, overlapping the sheets. Brush with more butter and sprinkle with sugar. Repeat this process four times.

2. Mound the filling along the bottom edge of the phyllo, leaving a 2½-inch border on the bottom and a 2-inch border on the sides.

3. Fold the dough on the sides over the apples. Fold the dough on the bottom over the apples and continue to roll the dough around the filling to form the strudel.

4. After the strudel has been assembled and rolled, gently lay it seam side down on the prepared baking sheet.

½ cup golden raisins

2 tablespoons Calvados or apple cider

8 tablespoons (1 stick) unsalted butter, melted and cooled

¼ cup fresh bread crumbs (see note)

1 pound Golden Delicious apples (about 2 large), peeled, cored, and sliced ¼ inch thick

1 medium McIntosh apple, peeled, cored, and sliced ¼ inch thick

¼ cup (1¾ ounces) plus 2 tablespoons granulated sugar

⅓ cup finely chopped walnuts (optional), toasted

¼ teaspoon ground cinnamon

⅛ teaspoon table salt

1 teaspoon juice from 1 lemon

10 (14 by 9-inch) sheets phyllo, thawed (see note)

1½ teaspoons confectioners' sugar

1. Adjust an oven rack to the lower-middle position and heat the oven to 475 degrees. Line a large baking sheet with parchment paper. Bring the raisins and Calvados to a simmer in a small saucepan over medium heat. Cover, remove from the heat, and let stand until needed.

2. Combine 1 tablespoon of the butter and the bread crumbs in a small skillet and cook over medium heat, stirring frequently, until golden brown, about 2 minutes. Transfer the bread crumbs to a small bowl and set aside.

3. Drain off and discard any remaining liquid from the raisins. Toss the apples, raisins, bread crumbs, ¼ cup of the granulated sugar, the walnuts (if using), cinnamon, salt, and lemon juice in a large bowl to combine.

4. Melt the remaining 7 tablespoons butter. Place a large sheet of parchment paper horizontally on a work surface. Following the photos on page 829, lay 1 sheet of phyllo on the left side of the sheet of parchment paper, then brush with melted butter and sprinkle with ½ teaspoon more of the granulated sugar. Place another sheet of phyllo on the right side of the parchment, overlapping the sheets by 1 inch, then brush with more butter and sprinkle with sugar. Repeat this process with the remaining 8 sheets of phyllo, more butter, and more sugar. Mound the filling along the bottom edge of the phyllo, leaving a 2½-inch border on the bottom and a 2-inch border on the sides. Fold the dough on the sides over the apples. Fold the dough on the bottom over the apples and continue to roll the dough around the filling to form the strudel.

5. Place the strudel, seam side down, on the prepared baking sheet; brush with the remaining butter and sprinkle with the remaining 1 teaspoon sugar. Cut four 1-inch crosswise vents into the top of the strudel and bake until golden brown, 15 minutes. Transfer the baking sheet to a wire rack and cool until warm, about 40 minutes.

6. Dust the strudel with the confectioners' sugar before serving; slice with a serrated knife and serve warm or at room temperature.

Tangy Whipped Cream
MAKES ABOUT 2 CUPS

Adding sour cream to whipped cream mimics the pleasantly tart flavor of the rich French-style whipped cream, crème fraîche.

 1 cup heavy cream
 ½ cup sour cream
 1 tablespoon sugar
 1 teaspoon vanilla extract

Whip the heavy cream and sour cream in a large bowl with an electric mixer on medium-low speed until frothy, about 1 minute. Add the sugar and vanilla. Increase the mixer speed to high and continue to whip until the cream forms soft peaks, 1 to 3 minutes.

APPLE PANDOWDY

WHY THIS RECIPE WORKS: Apple pandowdy harks back to Colonial-era New England—the dessert takes a more rustic approach to apple pie in that it features just one pastry crust, placed on top of a lightly sweetened apple filling. During or after baking, the pastry is broken and pushed into the filling—a technique known as "dowdying." We found the idea of an easier approach to apple pie very appealing—no fussy crimping and only one piece of pastry dough to roll out, so we set out to make our own version—one with a flaky crust and tender, juicy apples.

For a juicy apple filling with bright fruit flavor, we added cider to the apples and sweetened the filling with maple syrup—the tart intensity of the cider deepened the apple flavor and maple syrup's rich character added the right degree of sweetness. Both additions also made for a pleasantly saucy filling. Parcooking the apples in a skillet until caramelized before adding the other ingredients helped to deepen their flavor. For the crust, we cut a standard pie crust into squares after rolling it over the fruit right in the skillet—this encouraged a multitude of crispy edges that contrast nicely with the tender fruit and recall (in a less dowdy way) the broken-up crusts of a traditional pandowdy.

Skillet Apple Pie
SERVES 6 TO 8

If your skillet is not ovensafe, precook the apples and stir in the cider mixture as instructed, then transfer the apples to a 13 by 9-inch baking dish. Roll out the dough to a 13 by 9-inch rectangle and cut the crust and bake the pandowdy as instructed. If you do not have apple cider, reduced apple juice may be used as a substitute; simmer 1 cup apple juice in a small saucepan over medium heat until reduced to ½ cup (about 10 minutes). Serve the pandowdy warm or at room temperature with vanilla ice cream or whipped cream. Use a combination of sweet, crisp apples such as Golden Delicious and firm, tart apples such as Cortland or Empire.

CRUST

- 1 cup (5 ounces) unbleached all-purpose flour, plus extra for the work surface
- 1 tablespoon sugar
- ½ teaspoon table salt
- 2 tablespoons vegetable shortening, chilled
- 6 tablespoons (¾ stick) unsalted butter, cut into ¼-inch pieces and chilled
- 3–4 tablespoons ice water

FILLING

- ½ cup apple cider
- ⅓ cup maple syrup
- 2 tablespoons juice from 1 lemon
- 2 teaspoons cornstarch
- ⅛ teaspoon ground cinnamon (optional)
- 2 tablespoons unsalted butter
- 2½ pounds sweet and tart apples (about 4 large), peeled, cored, and cut into ½-inch-thick wedges (see note)
- 1 large egg white, lightly beaten
- 2 teaspoons sugar

1. FOR THE CRUST: Pulse the flour, sugar, and salt in a food processor until combined, about 4 pulses. Add the shortening and pulse until the mixture has the texture of coarse sand, about 10 pulses. Sprinkle the butter pieces over the flour mixture and pulse until the mixture is pale yellow and resembles coarse crumbs, with the butter bits no larger than small peas, about 10 pulses. Transfer the mixture to a medium bowl.

2. Sprinkle 3 tablespoons of the ice water over the mixture. With a rubber spatula, use a folding motion to mix, pressing down on the dough until the dough is slightly tacky and sticks together, adding up to 1 tablespoon more ice water if the dough does not come together. Flatten the dough into a 4-inch disk. Wrap the disk in plastic wrap and refrigerate for at least 1 hour or up to 2 days. Let the dough stand at room temperature for 15 minutes before rolling.

3. FOR THE FILLING: Adjust an oven rack to the upper-middle position (between 7 and 9 inches from the heating element) and heat the oven to 500 degrees. Whisk the cider, syrup, lemon juice, cornstarch, and cinnamon (if using) together in a medium bowl until smooth. Melt the butter in a 12-inch oven-safe skillet over medium-high heat. Add the apples and cook, stirring two or three times, until the apples begin to caramelize, about 5 minutes. (Do not fully cook the apples.) Remove the pan from the heat, add the cider mixture, and gently stir until the apples are well coated. Set aside to cool slightly.

4. TO ASSEMBLE AND BAKE: Roll the dough out on a lightly floured work surface to an 11-inch circle. Roll the dough loosely around the rolling pin and unroll over the apple filling. Brush the dough with the egg white and sprinkle with the sugar. With a sharp knife, gently cut the dough into six pieces by making one vertical cut followed by two evenly spaced horizontal cuts (perpendicular to the first cut). Bake until the apples are tender and the crust is a deep golden brown, about 20 minutes, rotating the skillet halfway through the baking time. Cool for 15 minutes and serve.

BANANAS FOSTER

WHY THIS RECIPE WORKS: Although the New Orleans dessert bananas Foster is quick and simple, with few ingredients (butter, brown sugar, rum, and bananas), things can go wrong. Sometimes the bananas are overcooked and mushy. Or the sauce can be too thin, overly sweet, or taste too strongly of alcohol. We wanted to fix these issues and come up with a quick, reliable dessert with tender bananas and a flavorful but not boozy sauce.

First we kept the amounts of butter and brown sugar in check—most recipes use a high ratio of butter to brown sugar, which makes for a thin, greasy sauce. For the rum, we found that a small amount was just enough to impart a definite rum flavor without turning the dessert into a cocktail. We decided to add some rum to the sauce and use the rest to flambé the bananas. We also enhanced the sauce with a little cinnamon and lemon zest, which added some complexity. As for the bananas, we cooked them in the sauce until soft, flipping them over halfway through cooking so they turned out tender, not mushy.

Bananas Foster
SERVES 4

While the bananas cook, scoop the ice cream into individual bowls so they are ready to go once the sauce has been flambéed. Before preparing this recipe, read "Tips for Fearless Flambé" on page 408.

- 4 tablespoons (½ stick) unsalted butter
- ½ cup packed (3½ ounces) dark brown sugar
- 1 (3-inch) cinnamon stick
- 1 (2-inch) strip zest from 1 lemon
- 4 tablespoons dark rum
- 2 large, firm, ripe bananas, peeled and quartered
- 1 pint vanilla ice cream, divided among four bowls

1. Combine the butter, sugar, cinnamon stick, zest, and 1 tablespoon of the rum in a 12-inch skillet. Cook over medium-high heat, stirring constantly, until the sugar dissolves and the mixture has thickened, about 2 minutes.

2. Reduce the heat to medium and add the bananas to the pan, spooning some sauce over each quarter. Cook until the bananas are glossy and golden on the bottom, about 1½ minutes. Flip the bananas; continue to cook until very soft but not mushy or falling apart, about 1½ minutes longer.

3. Off the heat, add the remaining 3 tablespoons rum and allow the rum to warm slightly, about 5 seconds. Wave a lit match over the pan until the rum ignites, shaking the pan to distribute the flame over the entire pan. When the flames subside (this will take 15 to 30 seconds), discard the cinnamon stick and zest and divide the bananas and sauce among the four bowls of ice cream. Serve.

CRÊPES SUZETTE

WHY THIS RECIPE WORKS: Classic French restaurants have mastered the fiery theatrics of this tableside treat—a sophisticated combination of crêpes, oranges, liqueur, and a showy flambé. We wanted to develop a recipe that would comfortably guide the home cook through the flambé process so this dessert could be prepared for an elegant dinner party. For a foolproof flambé that didn't create a frightening fireball or, conversely, didn't burn at all, we ignited the cognac alone in the skillet before building the sauce. We enriched a reduction of butter, sugar, and fresh orange juice with additional orange juice, fresh orange zest, and triple sec. For tender but sturdy crêpes that would stand up to the sauce without turning soggy, we skipped the usual resting of the batter, meant to relax the gluten, before cooking. Then, once the crêpes were cooked, we sprinkled them with sugar and ran them under the broiler for a sweet and crunchy coating.

Crêpes Suzette

SERVES 6

Note that it takes a few crêpes to get the heat of the pan right; your first two or three will almost inevitably be unusable. (To allow for practice, the recipe yields about 16 crêpes; only 12 are needed for the dish.) A dry measuring cup with a ¼-cup capacity is useful for portioning the batter. We prefer crêpes made with whole milk, but low-fat or skim milk can also be used. Before preparing this recipe, read "Tips for Fearless Flambé" on page 408.

CRÊPES

    3 large eggs
 1½ cups whole milk (see note)
 1½ cups (7½ ounces) unbleached all-purpose flour
   ½ cup water
    5 tablespoons unsalted butter, melted, plus extra
       for brushing the pan
    3 tablespoons sugar
    2 tablespoons cognac
   ½ teaspoon table salt

ORANGE SAUCE

    4 tablespoons cognac
 1¼ cups juice plus 1 tablespoon finely grated zest
       from 3 to 4 large oranges
    6 tablespoons (¾ stick) unsalted butter, cut into 6 pieces
   ¼ cup (1¾ ounces) sugar
    2 tablespoons orange-flavored liqueur, preferably
       triple sec

1. FOR THE CRÊPES: Combine the eggs, milk, flour, water, melted butter, sugar, cognac, and salt in a blender until a smooth batter forms, about 10 seconds. Transfer the batter to a medium bowl.

2. Using a pastry brush, brush the bottom and sides of a 10-inch nonstick skillet very lightly with melted butter and heat the skillet over medium heat. When the butter stops sizzling, tilt the pan slightly to the right and begin pouring in a scant ¼ cup batter. Continue to pour the batter in a slow, steady stream, rotating your wrist and twirling the pan slowly counterclockwise until the pan bottom is covered with an even layer of batter. Cook until the crêpe starts to lose its opaqueness and turns spotty light golden brown on the bottom, loosening the crêpe from the side of the pan with a heatproof rubber spatula, 30 seconds to 1 minute. To flip the crêpe, loosen the edge with the spatula and, with your fingertips on the top side, slide the spatula under the crêpe and flip. Cook until dry on the second side, about 20 seconds.

3. Place the cooked crêpe on a plate and repeat the cooking process with the remaining batter, brushing the pan very lightly with butter before making each crêpe. As they are done, stack the crêpes on a plate (you will need 12 crêpes). (The crêpes can be double-wrapped in plastic wrap and refrigerated for up to 3 days; bring them to room temperature before making the sauce.)

4. FOR THE ORANGE SAUCE: Adjust an oven rack to the lower-middle position and heat the broiler. Add 3 tablespoons of the cognac to a broiler-safe 12-inch skillet; heat the pan over medium heat just until the vapors begin to rise from the cognac, about 5 seconds. Remove the pan from the heat and wave a lit match over the pan until the cognac ignites, shaking the pan until the flames subside, about 15 seconds; reignite if the flame dies too soon.

5. Add 1 cup of the orange juice, the butter, and 3 tablespoons of the sugar and simmer briskly over high heat, stirring occasionally, until many large bubbles appear and the mixture reduces to a thick syrup, 6 to 8 minutes (you should have just over ½ cup sauce). Transfer the sauce to a small bowl; do not wash the skillet. Stir the remaining ¼ cup orange juice, zest, liqueur, and the remaining 1 tablespoon cognac into the sauce; cover.

6. TO ASSEMBLE: Fold each crêpe in half, then in half again to form a wedge shape. Arrange nine folded crêpes around the edge of the now-empty skillet, with the rounded edges facing inward, overlapping as necessary to fit. Arrange the remaining three crêpes in the center of the pan. Sprinkle the crêpes evenly with the remaining 1 tablespoon sugar. Broil until the sugar caramelizes and the crêpes turn spotty brown, about 5 minutes. (Watch the crêpes constantly to prevent scorching; turn the pan as necessary.) Carefully remove the pan from the oven and pour half of the sauce over the crêpes, leaving some areas uncovered. Transfer the crêpes to individual serving dishes and serve immediately, passing the extra sauce separately.

CLASSIC CRÊPES

WHY THIS RECIPE WORKS: A crêpe is nothing but a thin pancake cooked quickly on each side and wrapped around a sweet or savory filling, but it has a reputation for being difficult. We wanted an easy method for crêpes that were thin and delicate yet rich and flavorfully browned in spots.

Finding the perfect ratio of milk to flour and sugar gave us rich-tasting, lightly sweet pancakes. We were surprised to find that neither the type of flour nor the mixing method seemed to matter, and a plain old 12-inch nonstick skillet worked as well as a specialty crêpe pan. What does matter is heating the pan properly (over low heat for at least 10 minutes), using the right amount of batter (we settled on ¼ cup), and flipping the crêpe at precisely the right moment, when the edges appear dry, matte, and lacy. To transform our perfectly cooked crêpes into decadent desserts, we whipped up a few sweet fillings: the simple classic of sugar and lemon; a decadent chocolate and orange; and a banana and Nutella sure to please kids and adults alike.

Crêpes with Sugar and Lemon

SERVES 4

The crêpes will give off steam as they cook, but if at any point the skillet begins to smoke, remove it from the heat immediately and turn down the heat. Stacking the crêpes on a wire rack allows excess steam to escape so they won't stick together. To allow for practice, the recipe yields 10 crêpes; only eight are needed for the filling.

- ½ teaspoon vegetable oil
- 1 cup (5 ounces) unbleached all-purpose flour
- 1 teaspoon sugar, plus 8 teaspoons for sprinkling
- ¼ teaspoon table salt
- 1½ cups whole milk
- 3 large eggs
- 2 tablespoons unsalted butter, melted and cooled
  Lemon wedges, for serving

1. Heat the oil in a 12-inch nonstick skillet over low heat for at least 10 minutes.

MAKING A CRÊPE

1. Pour ¼ cup batter into far side of skillet.

2. Tilt and shake skillet gently until batter evenly covers bottom of skillet.

3. Gently slide spatula underneath edge of crêpe, grasp edge with your fingertips, and flip crêpe.

2. While the skillet is heating, whisk the flour, 1 teaspoon of the sugar, and the salt together in a medium bowl. In a separate bowl, whisk together the milk and eggs. Add half of the milk mixture to the dry ingredients and whisk until smooth. Add the butter and whisk until incorporated. Whisk in the remaining milk mixture until smooth.

3. Using a paper towel, wipe out the skillet, leaving a thin film of oil on the bottom and sides of the pan. Increase the heat to medium and let the skillet heat for 1 minute. After 1 minute, test the heat of the skillet by placing 1 teaspoon of the batter in the center; cook for 20 seconds. If the mini crêpe is golden brown on the bottom, the skillet is properly heated; if it is too light or too dark, adjust the heat accordingly and retest.

4. Pour ¼ cup batter into the far side of pan and tilt and shake gently until the batter evenly covers the bottom of the pan. Cook the crêpe without moving until the top surface is dry and the edges are starting to brown, loosening the crêpe from the side of the pan with a rubber spatula, about 25 seconds. Gently slide the spatula underneath the edge of the crêpe, grasp the edge with your fingertips, and flip the crêpe. Cook until the second side is lightly spotted, about 20 seconds. Transfer the cooked crêpe to a wire rack, inverting so the spotted side is facing up. Return the pan to the heat and heat for 10 seconds before repeating with the remaining batter. As the crêpes are done, stack on the wire rack.

5. Transfer the stack of crêpes to a large plate and invert a second plate over the crêpes. Microwave until the crêpes are warm, 30 to 45 seconds (45 to 60 seconds if the crêpes have cooled completely). Remove the top plate and wipe dry with a paper towel. Sprinkle half of the top crêpe with 1 teaspoon sugar. Fold the unsugared bottom half over the sugared half, then fold into quarters. Transfer the sugared crêpe to a second plate. Continue with the remaining crêpes. Serve immediately, passing the lemon wedges separately.

Crêpes with Chocolate and Orange

Follow the recipe for Crêpes with Sugar and Lemon, omitting the 8 teaspoons sugar for sprinkling and the lemon wedges. Using your fingertips, rub 1 teaspoon finely grated orange zest into ¼ cup sugar. Stir in 2 ounces finely grated bittersweet chocolate. In step 5, sprinkle 1½ tablespoons of the chocolate-orange mixture over half of each crêpe. Fold the crêpes into quarters. Serve immediately.

Crêpes with Bananas and Nutella

Follow the recipe for Crêpes with Sugar and Lemon, omitting the 8 teaspoons sugar for sprinkling and the lemon wedges. In step 5, spread 2 teaspoons Nutella over half of each crêpe, followed by eight to ten ¼-inch-thick banana slices. Fold the crêpes into quarters. Serve immediately.

SUMMER PUDDING

WHY THIS RECIPE WORKS: If any food speaks of summer, the English dessert called summer pudding does. Ripe, fragrant, lightly sweetened berries are gently cooked to coax out their juices and then packed into a bowl lined with slices of bread. The berry juices soak and soften the bread to make it meld with the fruit. We set out to master this summertime classic.

Instead of lining the mold with bread and then filling it with berries, we opted to layer bread (cut out with a biscuit cutter) and berries together in ramekins; this way, the layers of bread on the inside would almost melt into the fruit. Combining the berries—we used strawberries, raspberries, blueberries, and blackberries—with sugar and lemon juice, and gently cooking the mixture for just five minutes, released just the right amount of juice and offset the tartness of the berries. Fresh bread became too gummy in the pudding, but day-old bread had just the right consistency. We used potato bread; its even, tight-crumbed, tender texture and light sweetness was a perfect match for the berries (challah makes a good substitute). To ensure that the puddings would come together and hold their shape, we weighted and refrigerated them for at least eight hours.

Individual Summer Berry Puddings
SERVES 6

The bread should be dry to the touch but not brittle. If working with fresh bread, dry the slices by heating them on an oven rack in a single layer in a 200-degree oven for about 1 hour, flipping them once halfway through the time. For this recipe, you will need six 6-ounce ramekins and a round cookie cutter of a slightly smaller diameter than the ramekins. If you don't have the right size cutter, use a paring knife and the bottom of a ramekin (most ramekins taper toward the bottom) as a guide for trimming the rounds. Challah will need to be cut into slices about ½ inch thick; if both potato bread and challah are unavailable, use high-quality white sandwich bread. Summer pudding can be made up to 24 hours before serving; held any longer, the berries begin to lose their freshness. Lightly sweetened whipped cream is the perfect accompaniment.

- 4 cups (20 ounces) strawberries, hulled and sliced
- 2 cups (about 10 ounces) raspberries
- 1 cup (about 5 ounces) blueberries
- 1 cup (about 5 ounces) blackberries
- ¾ cup (5¼ ounces) sugar
- 2 tablespoons juice from 1 lemon
- 12 slices stale potato bread, challah, or high-quality white sandwich bread (see note)

1. Cook the strawberries, raspberries, blueberries, blackberries, and sugar in a large saucepan over medium heat, stirring occasionally, until the berries begin to release their juice and the sugar has dissolved, about 5 minutes. Off the heat, stir in the lemon juice; cool to room temperature.

2. While the berries are cooling, spray six 6-ounce ramekins with vegetable oil spray and place on a rimmed baking sheet. Use a cookie cutter to cut out 12 bread rounds that are slightly smaller in diameter than the ramekins.

3. Using a slotted spoon, place ¼ cup of the fruit mixture in each ramekin. Lightly soak one bread round in the fruit juice in the saucepan and place on top of the fruit in a ramekin; repeat with five more bread rounds and the remaining ramekins. Diving the remaining fruit among the ramekins. Lightly soak one bread round in the juice and place on top of the fruit in a ramekin (it should sit above the lip of the ramekin); repeat with the remaining five bread rounds and the remaining ramekins. Pour the remaining fruit juice over the bread and cover the ramekins loosely with plastic wrap. Place a second baking sheet on top of the ramekins and weight it with heavy cans. Refrigerate the puddings for at least 8 hours or up to 24 hours.

4. Remove the cans and baking sheet and uncover the puddings. Loosen the puddings by running a paring knife around the edge of each ramekin, unmold into individual bowls, and serve immediately.

Large Summer Berry Pudding

SERVES 6 TO 8

You will need a 9 by 5-inch loaf pan for this recipe. Because there is no need to cut out rounds for this version, you will need only about 8 slices bread, depending on their size.

Follow the recipe for Individual Summer Berry Puddings through step 1. While the berries are cooling, spray a 9 by 5-inch loaf pan with vegetable oil spray, line it with plastic wrap, and place it on a rimmed baking sheet. Trim the crusts from the bread and trim the slices to fit in a single layer in the loaf pan (you will need about 2½ slices per layer; there will be three layers). Using a slotted spoon, spread about 2 cups of the fruit mixture evenly over the bottom of the prepared pan. Lightly soak enough bread slices for one layer in the fruit juice in the saucepan and place on top of the fruit. Repeat with two more layers of fruit and bread. Pour the remaining fruit juice over the bread and cover loosely with plastic wrap. Place a second baking sheet on top of the loaf pan and weight it with heavy cans. Refrigerate the pudding for at least 8 hours or up to 24 hours. Remove the cans and baking sheet and uncover the pudding. Invert the pudding onto a serving platter, remove the loaf pan and plastic wrap, slice, and serve.

CARAMELIZED PEARS

WHY THIS RECIPE WORKS: Pears and blue cheese are a classic combination, but we wanted to up the flavor ante with another component—caramel. We had encountered this triple play in restaurants, where a caramel sauce is draped over seared pears, and a modest amount of pungent blue cheese provides a nice contrast to the dessert's sweetness. We decided to adapt this dish so it would be easy for the home cook to get it just right (meaning no mushy pears and no sticky, overcooked caramel).

To streamline the recipe, we cooked the pears right in the caramel sauce, instead of separately, saving time and eliminating some dirty dishes. We brought water and sugar (the basis for caramel sauce) to a boil in a skillet and slid the pears into the hot mixture to cook in the browning caramel. We added cream to the pan to transform the sticky sugar syrup into a smooth sauce that clung lightly to the pears. After removing the pears, we were able to season the sauce left in the skillet with just the right amount of black pepper and salt. For an attractive presentation, we stood the pears upright on a plate (we had already trimmed the bottom off each pear for a flat base) and drizzled the caramel sauce around them, then added wedges of strong blue cheese—the perfect foil to the sweet caramel.

Caramelized Pears with Blue Cheese and Black Pepper–Caramel Sauce

SERVES 6

Any type of pear can be used in this recipe, but the pears must be firm to withstand the heat. If desired, the pears can be served upright on a large platter instead of on individual plates, with the warm caramel sauce and the blue cheese passed separately. Many pepper mills do not have a sufficiently coarse setting; in that case, crush peppercorns with the back of a heavy pan or a rolling pin. See page 879 for information on our top-rated pepper mill.

- ⅓ cup water
- ⅔ cup (4⅔ ounces) sugar
- 3 ripe, firm pears, halved, cored, and ¼ inch trimmed off the bottom (see note)
- ⅔ cup heavy cream
    Table salt
- ¼ teaspoon black peppercorns, crushed (see note)
- 3 ounces strong blue cheese (such as Stilton), cut into 6 wedges

1. Pour the water into a 12-inch nonstick skillet, then pour the sugar into the center of the pan, being careful not to let it hit the sides of the pan. Bring to a boil over high heat, stirring occasionally, until the sugar is fully dissolved and the liquid is bubbling. Add the pears to the skillet, cut side down, cover, reduce the heat to medium-high, and cook until the pears are almost tender and a paring knife inserted into the center of the pears meets slight resistance, 13 to 15 minutes.

2. Uncover, reduce the heat to medium, and cook until the sauce is golden brown and the cut sides of the pears are beginning to brown, 3 to 5 minutes. Pour the heavy cream around the pears and cook, shaking the pan until the sauce is a smooth, deep caramel color and the cut sides of the pears are golden brown, 3 to 5 minutes.

3. Off the heat, transfer the pears, cut side up, to a wire rack set over a rimmed baking sheet and cool slightly. Season the sauce left in the pan with salt to taste and the crushed peppercorns, then transfer it to a small bowl.

4. Carefully (the pears will still be hot) stand each pear half upright on an individual plate and arrange a wedge of the blue cheese beside it. Drizzle the caramel sauce over the plate and the pear. Serve immediately.

ROASTED PEARS WITH DRIED APRICOTS AND PISTACHIOS

WHY THIS RECIPE WORKS: Tender, caramelized roasted pears are a delightfully simple dessert, but it took a two-step cooking process to perfect their texture. To eliminate any excess moisture that might weigh down the fruit, we cooked our peeled, halved pears in butter in a hot skillet. Once the pears began to brown, we transferred the skillet to the oven for 30 minutes. We plated the fork-tender fruit and started in on the sauce, deglazing the pan with white wine and adding sweet dried apricots, sugar, cardamom, and salt, plus a pat of butter for a creamy dimension. A touch of lemon juice stirred in once the liquid had thickened contributed citrusy brightness, and a sprinkling of pistachios, added right at serving, gave the dessert some toasty, textural contrast.

Roasted Pears with Dried Apricots and Pistachios

SERVES 4 TO 6

Select pears that yield slightly when pressed. We prefer Bosc pears in this recipe, but Comice and Bartlett pears also work. The fruit can be served as is or with vanilla ice cream or plain Greek yogurt.

- 2½ tablespoons unsalted butter
- 4 ripe but firm Bosc pears (6 to 7 ounces each), peeled, halved, and cored
- 1¼ cups dry white wine
- ½ cup dried apricots, quartered
- ⅓ cup (2⅓ ounces) sugar
- ¼ teaspoon ground cardamom
- ⅛ teaspoon salt
- 1 teaspoon lemon juice
- ⅓ cup pistachios, toasted and chopped

1. Adjust oven rack to middle position and heat oven to 450 degrees. Melt 1½ tablespoons butter in ovensafe 12-inch skillet over medium-high heat. Place pear halves, cut side down, in skillet. Cook, without moving them, until pears are just beginning to brown, 3 to 5 minutes.

2. Transfer skillet to oven and roast pears for 15 minutes. Using tongs, flip pears and continue to roast until fork easily pierces fruit, 10 to 15 minutes longer (skillet handle will be hot).

3. Using tongs, transfer pears to platter. Return skillet to medium-high heat and add wine, apricots, sugar, cardamom, salt, and remaining 1 tablespoon butter. Bring to vigorous simmer, whisking to scrape up any browned bits. Cook until sauce is reduced and has consistency of maple syrup, 7 to 10 minutes. Remove pan from heat and stir in lemon juice.

4. Pour sauce over pears, sprinkle with pistachios, and serve.

Roasted Apples with Dried Figs and Walnuts

Substitute Gala apples for pears, red wine for white wine, dried figs for apricots, ¾ teaspoon pepper for cardamom, and walnuts for pistachios.

STRAWBERRIES WITH BALSAMIC VINEGAR

WHY THIS RECIPE WORKS: Strawberries with balsamic vinegar may sound a bit trendy, but this combination actually goes back in time—hundreds of years at least—to northern Italy. We wanted to pay homage to this time-honored tradition and create our own dessert, with the vinegar enhancing but not overwhelming the flavor of bright, summer berries.

We didn't want to pay big bucks for a super-pricey balsamic vinegar, so we opted to use an inexpensive vinegar. To coax big flavor out of our bargain balsamic, we simmered it with some sugar to approximate the syrupy texture of an aged vinegar. Next we tried to enhance the flavor with honey or vanilla, but these flavors were too overpowering; a squirt of fresh lemon juice brought just the right amount of brightness. We tossed the berries with light brown sugar—rather than the traditional granulated sugar—for the most complex flavor. Once we mixed the sliced berries and sugar together, it took about 15 minutes for the sugar to dissolve and the berries to release their juice; if the strawberries sat any longer than this, they continued to soften and became quite mushy.

Strawberries with Balsamic Vinegar

SERVES 6

If you don't have light brown sugar on hand, sprinkle the berries with an equal amount of granulated sugar. Serve the berries and syrup as is or with a scoop of vanilla ice cream or a dollop of lightly sweetened whipped cream.

- ⅓ cup balsamic vinegar
- 2 teaspoons granulated sugar
- ½ teaspoon juice from 1 lemon
- 6 cups (30 ounces) strawberries, hulled, sliced lengthwise ¼ inch thick if large, halved or quartered if small
- ¼ cup packed (1¾ ounces) light brown sugar (see note)
  Ground black pepper

1. Bring the vinegar, granulated sugar, and lemon juice to a simmer in a small saucepan over medium heat. Simmer until the syrup is reduced by half (about 3 tablespoons), about 3 minutes. Transfer to a small bowl and cool completely.

2. Gently toss the berries and brown sugar in a large bowl. Let stand until the sugar dissolves and the berries exude some juice, 10 to 15 minutes. Pour the vinegar syrup over the berries, add pepper to taste, and toss to combine. Serve immediately.

BERRY FOOL

WHY THIS RECIPE WORKS: Traditionally, fruit fool is made by folding pureed stewed fruit (traditionally gooseberries) into sweet custard. Modern fool recipes skip the traditional custard and use whipped cream. But whipped cream blunts the fruit flavor and is too light and insubstantial—or, worse, it can turn the dessert soupy. We wanted a dessert with intense fruitiness and rich body—and we wanted to use raspberries or strawberries rather than the traditional gooseberries.

Gooseberries are naturally high in pectin—when exposed to heat, sugar, and acid, pectin breaks down and causes fruit to thicken, which made them ideal for fruit fool. We wanted to use raspberries and strawberries, which are low in pectin, so our first challenge was to thicken the fruit properly. We turned to gelatin to thicken our berries, but used a judicious hand (just 2 teaspoons), softening the gelatin in some uncooked berry puree, and then combined the softened mixture with some heated puree to help melt and distribute the gelatin. The result? A smooth, thickened puree with intense fruit flavor.

Now we just needed a richer, sturdier cream base to partner with the fruit puree. We liked the ease of using whipped cream rather than custard, so why not make whipped cream more custard-like? Combined with sour cream, the mixture was airy yet substantial, and the sour cream added just the right touch of richness, along with a tangy undertone. For even more fruit flavor, we layered the fruit puree and cream base with fresh berries that had been macerated in sugar to release excess juice. Finally, topping the dessert with crumbled sweet wheat crackers added a pleasant, nutty contrast.

Berry Fool

SERVES 6

Blueberries or blackberries can be substituted for raspberries in this recipe. You may also substitute frozen fruit for fresh, but there will be a slight compromise in texture. If using frozen fruit, reduce the amount of sugar in the puree by 1 tablespoon. The thickened fruit puree can be made up to 4 hours in advance; just make sure to whisk it well in step 4 to break up any clumps before combining it with the whipped cream. For the best results, chill your beater and bowl before whipping the cream. We like the granular texture and nutty flavor of Carr's Whole Wheat Crackers, but graham crackers or gingersnaps will also work.

- 2 quarts strawberries (about 2 pounds), washed, dried, and stemmed
- 1 pint raspberries (about 12 ounces), washed and dried (see note)
- ½ cup (3½ ounces) plus 4 tablespoons sugar
- 2 teaspoons unflavored powdered gelatin
- 1 cup heavy cream
- ¼ cup sour cream
- ½ teaspoon vanilla extract
- 4 Carr's Whole Wheat Crackers, crushed fine (about ¼ cup; see note)
- 6 sprigs fresh mint (optional)

1. Process 1 quart of the strawberries, ½ pint of the raspberries, and ½ cup of the sugar in a food processor until the mixture is completely smooth, about 1 minute. Strain the berry puree through a fine-mesh strainer into a 4-cup liquid measuring cup (you should have about 2½ cups puree; reserve any excess for another use). Transfer ½ cup of the puree to a small bowl and sprinkle the gelatin over the top; stir until the gelatin is incorporated and let stand for at least 5 minutes. Heat the remaining 2 cups puree in a small saucepan over medium heat until it begins to bubble, 4 to 6 minutes. Remove the pan from the heat and stir in the gelatin mixture until dissolved. Transfer the gelatin-puree mixture to a medium bowl, cover with plastic wrap, and refrigerate until cold, about 2 hours.

2. Meanwhile, chop the remaining 1 quart strawberries into rough ¼-inch pieces. Toss the strawberries, remaining ½ pint raspberries, and 2 tablespoons more sugar together in a medium bowl. Set aside for 1 hour.

3. Place the cream, sour cream, vanilla, and remaining 2 tablespoons sugar in the chilled bowl of a stand mixer. Beat on low speed until bubbles form, about 30 seconds. Increase the mixer speed to medium and continue beating until the beaters leave a trail, about 30 seconds. Increase the mixer speed to high; continue beating until the mixture has nearly doubled in volume and holds stiff peaks, about 30 seconds. Transfer ⅓ cup of the whipped cream mixture to a small bowl and set aside.

4. Remove the thickened berry puree from the refrigerator and whisk until smooth. With the mixer running at medium speed, slowly add two-thirds of the puree to the whipped cream mixture; mix until incorporated, about 15 seconds. Using a spatula, gently fold in the remaining thickened puree, leaving streaks of puree.

5. Transfer the uncooked berries to a fine-mesh strainer; shake gently to remove any excess juice. Divide two-thirds of the berries evenly among six tall parfait or sundae glasses. Divide the creamy berry mixture evenly among the glasses, followed by the remaining uncooked berries. Top each glass with the reserved plain whipped cream mixture. Sprinkle with the crushed crackers and garnish with mint sprigs (if using). Serve immediately.

RHUBARB FOOL

WHY THIS RECIPE WORKS: A fool is a quick, everyday dessert that just so happens to have a quaint and quirky British name. We decided to try our hand at this simple dessert—cooked fruit with whipped cream folded in—using rhubarb as the foundation. Although fool is in itself no culinary feat, the challenges lie in the rhubarb, with its sometimes overpowering sourness and tendency to cook into a thick, drab gray mess. We knew that before we could finalize a fool, we would have to tame the rhubarb. We wanted the perfect balance—pinkish-red, sweet/tart, toothsome fruit mixed with light cream. Baking, stewing, and sautéing the rhubarb all led to gray, mushy fruit. Eventually, we hit on soaking the rhubarb in cold water for 20 minutes—this removed some of the bitterness—and simmering it with orange juice. For the whipped cream, we decided that a soft-to-medium peak gave the fool just enough body. For the best presentation and flavor, we arranged the rhubarb and whipped cream in layers rather than folding the two elements together, making for a pleasing contrast of color and flavor.

Rhubarb Fool
SERVES 8

For a more elegant presentation, use a pastry bag to pipe the whipped cream into individual glasses. To make one large fool, double the recipe and layer the rhubarb and whipped cream in a 12-cup glass bowl.

- 2¼ pounds rhubarb, trimmed and cut into 6-inch lengths
- ⅓ cup juice from 1 large orange
- 1 cup (7 ounces) plus 2 tablespoons sugar
- Pinch table salt
- 2 cups heavy cream, chilled

1. Soak the rhubarb in cold water for 20 minutes. Drain, pat dry with paper towels, and cut crosswise into ½-inch-thick pieces.

2. Bring the orange juice, ¾ cup of the sugar, and the salt to a boil in a medium saucepan over medium-high heat. Add the rhubarb and return to a boil, then reduce the heat to medium-low and simmer, stirring two or three times, until the rhubarb begins to break down and is tender, 7 to 10 minutes. Transfer the rhubarb to a large bowl, cool to room temperature, cover with plastic wrap, and refrigerate until cold, at least 1 hour or up to 24 hours.

3. Whip the cream and remaining 6 tablespoons sugar in a large bowl with an electric mixer on medium-low speed until frothy, about 1 minute. Increase the speed to high and continue to whip until the cream forms soft peaks, 1 to 3 minutes.

4. To assemble, spoon about ¼ cup rhubarb into each of eight 8-ounce glasses, then layer about ¼ cup whipped cream on top. Repeat, ending with a dollop of cream; serve. (The fools can be refrigerated, covered with plastic wrap, for up to 6 hours.)

Strawberry-Rhubarb Fool
Follow the recipe for Rhubarb Fool, substituting 4 cups strawberries, hulled and quartered, for 1¼ pounds of the rhubarb and adding the strawberries to the saucepan with the rhubarb in step 2.

SUMMER BERRY TRIFLE

WHY THIS RECIPE WORKS: Trifles usually look a lot better than they taste because busy cooks simplify the complicated preparation by subbing in shortcut ingredients like storebought cake and pudding from a box. We wanted to streamline, but not shortchange, the components so that the entire trifle could be made from scratch in just a few hours. We added a little extra flour to a classic chiffon cake so we could bake it in an 18 by 13-inch sheet, which baked and cooled much more quickly than the traditional tall chiffon cake, and we prevented our pastry cream from turning runny during assembly by adding a little more cornstarch. We mashed one-third of the berries so their juices would provide moisture to the cake. A bit of cream sherry added a sophisticated layer of flavor.

Summer Berry Trifle
SERVES 12 TO 16

For the best texture, this trifle should be assembled at least 6 hours before serving. Use a glass bowl with at least a 3½-quart capacity; straight sides are preferable.

PASTRY CREAM
- 3½ cups whole milk
- 1 cup (7 ounces) sugar
- 6 tablespoons cornstarch
- Pinch salt
- 5 large egg yolks (reserve whites for cake)
- 4 tablespoons unsalted butter, cut into ½-inch pieces and chilled
- 4 teaspoons vanilla extract

CAKE

- 1⅓ cups (5⅓ ounces) cake flour
- ¾ cup (5¼ ounces) sugar
- 1½ teaspoons baking powder
- ¼ teaspoon salt
- ⅓ cup vegetable oil
- ¼ cup water
- 1 large egg
- 2 teaspoons vanilla extract
- 5 large egg whites (reserved from pastry cream)
- ¼ teaspoon cream of tartar

FRUIT FILLING

- 1½ pounds strawberries, hulled and cut into ½-inch pieces (4 cups), reserving 3 halved for garnish
- 12 ounces (2⅓ cups) blackberries, large berries halved crosswise, reserving 3 whole for garnish
- 12 ounces (2⅓ cups) raspberries, reserving 3 for garnish
- ¼ cup (1¾ ounces) sugar
- ½ teaspoon cornstarch
- Pinch salt

WHIPPED CREAM

- 1 cup heavy cream
- 1 tablespoon sugar
- 1 tablespoon plus ½ cup cream sherry

1. FOR THE PASTRY CREAM: Heat 3 cups milk in medium saucepan over medium heat until just simmering. Meanwhile, whisk sugar, cornstarch, and salt together in medium bowl. Whisk remaining ½ cup milk and egg yolks into sugar mixture until smooth. Remove milk from heat and, whisking constantly, slowly add 1 cup to sugar mixture to temper. Whisking constantly, return tempered sugar mixture to milk in saucepan.

2. Return saucepan to medium heat and cook, whisking constantly, until mixture is very thick and bubbles burst on surface, 4 to 7 minutes. Remove saucepan from heat; whisk in butter and vanilla until butter is melted and incorporated. Strain pastry cream through fine-mesh strainer set over medium bowl. Press lightly greased parchment paper directly on surface and refrigerate until set, at least 2 hours or up to 24 hours.

3. FOR THE CAKE: Adjust oven rack to middle position and heat oven to 350 degrees. Lightly grease 18 by 13-inch rimmed baking sheet, line with parchment, and lightly grease parchment. Whisk flour, sugar, baking powder, and salt together in medium bowl. Whisk oil, water, egg, and vanilla into flour mixture until smooth batter forms.

4. Using stand mixer fitted with whisk, whip reserved egg whites and cream of tartar on medium-low speed until foamy, about 1 minute. Increase speed to medium-high and whip until soft peaks form, 2 to 3 minutes. Transfer one-third of whipped egg whites to batter; whisk gently until mixture is lightened. Using rubber spatula, gently fold remaining egg whites into batter.

5. Pour batter into prepared sheet; spread evenly. Bake until top is golden brown and cake springs back when pressed lightly in center, 13 to 16 minutes.

6. Transfer cake to wire rack; let cool for 5 minutes. Run knife around edge of sheet, then invert cake onto wire rack. Carefully remove parchment, then reinvert cake onto second wire rack. Let cool completely, at least 30 minutes.

7. FOR THE FRUIT FILLING: Place 1½ cups strawberries, 1 cup blackberries, 1 cup raspberries, sugar, cornstarch, and salt in medium saucepan. Place remaining berries (except those reserved for garnish) in large bowl; set aside. Using potato masher, thoroughly mash berries in saucepan. Cook over medium heat until sugar is dissolved and mixture is thick and bubbling, 4 to 7 minutes. Pour over berries in bowl and stir to combine. Set aside.

8. FOR THE WHIPPED CREAM: Using stand mixer fitted with whisk, whip cream, sugar, and 1 tablespoon sherry on medium-low speed until foamy, about 1 minute. Increase speed to high and whip until soft peaks form, 1 to 2 minutes.

9. Trim ¼ inch off each side of cake; discard trimmings. Using serrated knife, cut cake into 24 equal pieces (each piece about 2½ inches square).

10. Briefly whisk pastry cream until smooth. Spoon ¾ cup pastry cream into trifle bowl; spread over bottom. Shingle 12 cake pieces, fallen domino–style, around bottom of trifle, placing 10 pieces against dish wall and 2 remaining pieces in center. Drizzle ¼ cup sherry evenly over cake. Spoon half of berry mixture evenly over cake, making sure to use half of liquid. Using back of spoon, spread half of remaining pastry cream over berries, then spread half of whipped cream over pastry cream (whipped cream layer will be thin). Repeat layering with remaining 12 cake pieces, sherry, berries, pastry cream, and whipped cream. Cover bowl with plastic wrap and refrigerate for at least 6 hours or up to 36 hours. Garnish top of trifle with reserved berries and serve.

KEEP YOUR FORK— THERE'S PIE!

BASIC PIE DOUGH

WHY THIS RECIPE WORKS: Basic pie dough often contains vegetable shortening, which makes the dough easier to handle and yields a crust that is remarkably flaky. The primary issue with vegetable shortening crusts, however, is that they lack flavor. We set out to master basic pie dough by determining the right fat, the right proportion of fat to flour, and the right method for combining them.

Flakiness is important to a crust, but so is flavor—and nothing beats butter. We experimented with a variety of combinations and ultimately settled on a proportion of 3 parts butter to 2 parts shortening as optimal for both flavor and texture. We also settled on a ratio of 2 parts flour to 1 part fat. This crust is relatively high in fat, but we found that the 2–1 proportion produces dough that is easier to work with and a baked crust that is more tender and flavorful than any other. You can make this pie dough by hand, but the food processor is faster and easier and does the best job of cutting the fat into the flour.

Basic Double-Crust Pie Dough

MAKES ENOUGH FOR ONE 9-INCH PIE

The dough, wrapped tightly in plastic wrap, can be refrigerated for up to 2 days or frozen for up to 1 month. If frozen, let the dough thaw completely on the counter before rolling it out.

- 2½ cups (12½ ounces) unbleached all-purpose flour, plus extra for the work surface
- 2 tablespoons sugar
- 1 teaspoon table salt
- ½ cup vegetable shortening, cut into ½-inch pieces and chilled
- 12 tablespoons (1½ sticks) unsalted butter, cut into ¼-inch pieces and chilled
- 6–8 tablespoons ice water

1. Process the flour, sugar, and salt together in a food processor until combined. Scatter the shortening over the top and process until the mixture resembles coarse cornmeal, about 10 seconds. Scatter the butter pieces over the top and pulse the mixture until it resembles coarse crumbs, about 10 pulses. Transfer the mixture to a large bowl.

2. Sprinkle 6 tablespoons of the ice water over the mixture. Stir and press the dough together, using a stiff rubber spatula, until the dough sticks together. If the dough does not come together, stir in the remaining water, 1 tablespoon at a time, until it does.

3. Divide the dough into two even pieces. Turn each piece of dough onto a sheet of plastic wrap and flatten each into a 4-inch disk. Wrap each piece tightly in plastic wrap and refrigerate for 1 hour. Before rolling the dough out, let it sit on the counter to soften slightly, about 10 minutes.

ROLLING AND FITTING PIE DOUGH

1. Lay the disk of dough on a lightly floured work surface and roll the dough outward from its center into a 12-inch circle. Between every few rolls, give the dough a quarter turn to help keep the circle nice and round.

2. Toss additional flour underneath the dough as needed to keep the dough from sticking to the work surface.

3. Loosely roll the dough around the rolling pin, then gently unroll it over the pie plate.

4. Lift the dough and gently press it into the pie plate, letting the excess hang over the plate. For a double-crust pie, cover the crust lightly with plastic wrap and refrigerate for at least 30 minutes. To crimp a single-crust pie, see page 825.

Hand Mixed Basic Double-Crust Pie Dough

Freeze the butter in its stick form until very firm. Whisk the flour, sugar, and salt together in a large bowl. Add the chilled shortening and press it into the flour using a fork. Grate the frozen butter on the large holes of a box grater into the flour mixture, then cut the mixture together using two butter or dinner knives, until the mixture resembles coarse crumbs. Follow the recipe for Basic Double-Crust Pie Dough, adding the water as directed.

Basic Single-Crust Pie Dough

MAKES ENOUGH FOR ONE 9-INCH PIE

The dough, wrapped tightly in plastic wrap, can be refrigerated for up to 2 days or frozen for up to 1 month. If frozen, let the dough thaw completely on the counter before rolling it out.

1¼ cups (6¼ ounces) unbleached all-purpose flour, plus extra for the work surface

1 tablespoon sugar

½ teaspoon table salt

3 tablespoons vegetable shortening, cut into ½-inch pieces and chilled

5 tablespoons unsalted butter, cut into ¼-inch pieces and chilled

4–6 tablespoons ice water

1. Process the flour, sugar, and salt together in a food processor until combined. Scatter the shortening over the top and process until the mixture resembles coarse cornmeal, about 10 seconds. Scatter the butter pieces over the top and pulse the mixture until it resembles coarse crumbs, about 10 pulses. Transfer the mixture to a medium bowl.

2. Sprinkle 4 tablespoons of the ice water over the mixture. Stir and press the dough together, using a stiff rubber spatula, until the dough sticks together. If the dough does not come together, stir in the remaining water, 1 tablespoon at a time, until it does.

3. Turn the dough onto a sheet of plastic wrap and flatten into a 4-inch disk. Wrap the dough tightly in plastic wrap and refrigerate for 1 hour. Before rolling the dough out, let it sit on the counter to soften slightly, about 10 minutes.

4. Following the photos on page 842, roll the dough into a 12-inch circle and fit it into a pie plate. Following the photos at right, trim, fold, and crimp the edge of the dough. Wrap the dough-lined pie plate loosely in plastic wrap and place in the freezer until the dough is fully chilled and firm, about 30 minutes, before using.

Hand Mixed Basic Single-Crust Pie Dough

Freeze the butter in its stick form until very firm. Whisk the flour, sugar, and salt together in a medium bowl. Add the chilled shortening and press it into the flour using a fork. Grate the frozen butter on the large holes of a box grater into the flour mixture, then cut the mixture together using two butter or dinner knives, until the mixture resembles coarse crumbs. Follow the recipe for Basic Single-Crust Pie Dough, adding the water as directed.

Single-Crust Pie Dough for Custard Pies

We like rolling our single-crust dough in fresh graham cracker crumbs because it adds flavor and crisp textural appeal to many of our custard pies.

Crush 3 whole graham crackers to fine crumbs. (You should have about ½ cup crumbs.) Follow the recipe for Basic Single-Crust Pie Dough, dusting the work surface with the graham cracker crumbs instead of flour. Continue sprinkling the dough with the crumbs, both underneath and on top, as it is being rolled out.

CRIMPING A SINGLE-CRUST PIE DOUGH

For a traditional single-crust pie, you need to make an evenly thick edge before crimping. Trim the pie dough so that it hangs over the pie plate by ½ inch, then tuck the dough underneath itself to form a tidy, even edge that sits on the lip of the pie plate.

FOR A FLUTED EDGE:
Use the index finger of one hand and the thumb and index finger of the other to create fluted ridges perpendicular to the edge of the pie plate.

FOR A RIDGED EDGE:
Press the tines of a fork into the dough to flatten it against the rim of the pie plate.

ALL-BUTTER PIE DOUGH

WHY THIS RECIPE WORKS: All-butter pie doughs possess great flavor, but they often fail to be flaky and are notoriously difficult to work with. We wanted an all-butter pie pastry that was easier to mix, handle, and roll, producing a pie crust with all the tenderness and flavor that the description "all-butter" promises.

We initially tried to make the dough easier to handle by reducing the amount of butter, but this resulted in bland flavor and dry texture. Rather than adding back the subtracted butter, we experimented with other forms of fat, including heavy cream, cream cheese, and sour cream. We found that sour cream not only added flavor but, because acid reduces gluten development, also helped keep the dough tender and flaky. And to mix the dough, we used a food processor, which brought the ingredients together quickly and evenly.

All-Butter Double-Crust Pie Dough

MAKES ENOUGH FOR ONE 9-INCH PIE

Freezing the butter for 10 to 15 minutes is crucial to the flaky texture of this crust. If preparing the dough in a very warm kitchen, refrigerate all of the ingredients before making the dough. The dough, wrapped tightly in plastic wrap, can be refrigerated for up to 2 days or frozen for up to 1 month. If frozen, let the dough thaw completely on the counter before rolling it out.

⅓ cup ice water, plus extra as needed

3 tablespoons sour cream

2½ cups (12½ ounces) unbleached all-purpose flour, plus extra for the work surface

1 tablespoon sugar

1 teaspoon table salt

16 tablespoons (2 sticks) unsalted butter, cut into ¼-inch pieces and frozen for 10 to 15 minutes (see note)

1. Mix ⅓ cup of the ice water and the sour cream in a small bowl until combined. Process the flour, sugar, and salt together in a food processor until combined. Following the photos, scatter the butter pieces over the top and pulse the mixture until the butter is the size of large peas, about 10 pulses.

2. Pour half of the sour cream mixture over the flour mixture and pulse until incorporated, about 3 pulses. Repeat with the remaining sour cream mixture. Pinch the dough with your fingers; if the dough feels dry and does not hold together, sprinkle 1 to 2 tablespoons more ice water over the mixture and pulse until the dough forms large clumps and no dry flour remains, 3 to 5 pulses.

3. Divide the dough into two even pieces. Turn each piece of dough onto a sheet of plastic wrap and flatten each into a 4-inch disk. Wrap each piece tightly in plastic wrap and refrigerate for 1 hour. Before rolling the dough out, let it sit on the counter to soften slightly, about 10 minutes.

NOTES FROM THE TEST KITCHEN

MAKING ALL-BUTTER DOUBLE-CRUST PIE DOUGH

1. Pulse the butter and flour mixture together in a food processor until the butter is the size of large peas, about 10 pulses.

2. After adding the sour cream and water mixture, pinch the dough with your fingers. If the dough is dry and does not hold together, sprinkle 1 to 2 tablespoons ice water over the mixture and pulse 3 to 5 times.

3. Divide the dough into two pieces and flatten each into a 4-inch disk. Wrap the disks tightly in plastic wrap and refrigerate for 1 hour. Before rolling the dough out, let it sit on the counter to soften slightly, about 10 minutes.

Hand Mixed All-Butter Double-Crust Pie Dough

Freeze the butter in its stick form until very firm. Whisk the flour, sugar, and salt together in a large bowl. Grate the frozen butter on the large holes of a box grater into the flour mixture, then cut the mixture together using two butter or dinner knives, until the mixture resembles coarse crumbs. Follow the recipe for All-Butter Double-Crust Pie Dough, adding the liquid as directed, stirring it with a rubber spatula.

FOOLPROOF PIE DOUGH

WHY THIS RECIPE WORKS: Unless you're a practiced pie baker, it's hard to get the same results every time. While we think our All-Butter Pie Dough (page 843) and Basic Pie Dough (page 842) are great, we wanted a recipe for pie dough that rolls out easily every time and produces a tender, flaky crust. The first step was to determine the right fat. As with our basic dough, a combination of butter and shortening provided the best balance of flavor and tenderness. Once again, the best tool to cut the fat into the flour was the food processor. To ensure the butter was incorporated evenly, we skipped cutting it into pieces and made a paste instead. Rather than starting with all the flour in the processor, we put aside 1 cup of flour and processed the remaining 1½ cups with all of the fat until it formed a unified paste. We added the reserved flour to the bowl and pulsed it until it was just evenly distributed. Finally, we tackled the tenderness issue, which is partially determined by the amount of water added. For the dough to roll easily, it needs a generous amount of water, but more water makes crusts tough. We found the answer in the liquor cabinet: vodka. While gluten (the protein that makes crust tough) forms readily in water, it doesn't form in ethanol, and vodka is 60 percent water and 40 percent ethanol. So adding ¼ cup of vodka produced a moist, easy-to-roll dough that stayed tender. (The alcohol vaporizes in the oven, so you won't taste it in the baked crust.)

Foolproof Double-Crust Pie Dough

MAKES ENOUGH FOR ONE 9-INCH PIE

Vodka is essential to the tender texture of this crust and imparts no flavor—do not substitute water. This dough is moister than most standard pie doughs and will require lots of flour to roll out (up to ¼ cup). The dough, wrapped tightly in plastic wrap, can be refrigerated for up to 2 days or frozen for up to 1 month. If frozen, let the dough thaw completely on the counter before rolling it out.

2½ cups (12½ ounces) unbleached all-purpose flour, plus extra for the work surface (see note)

2 tablespoons sugar

1 teaspoon table salt

12 tablespoons (1½ sticks) unsalted butter, cut into ¼-inch pieces and chilled

½ cup vegetable shortening, cut into 4 pieces and chilled

¼ cup vodka, chilled (see note)

¼ cup ice water

1. Process 1½ cups of the flour, the sugar, and salt together in a food processor until combined. Scatter the butter and shortening over the top and continue to process until incorporated and the mixture begins to form uneven clumps with no remaining floury bits, about 15 seconds.

2. Scrape down the workbowl and redistribute the dough evenly around the processor blade. Sprinkle the remaining 1 cup flour over the dough and pulse until the mixture has broken up into pieces and is evenly distributed around the bowl, 4 to 6 pulses.

3. Transfer the mixture to a medium bowl. Sprinkle the vodka and water over the mixture. Stir and press the dough together, using a stiff rubber spatula, until the dough sticks together.

4. Divide the dough into two even pieces. Turn each piece of dough onto a sheet of plastic wrap and flatten each into a 4-inch disk. Wrap each piece tightly in plastic wrap and refrigerate for 1 hour. Before rolling the dough out, let it sit on the counter to soften slightly, about 10 minutes.

Foolproof Single-Crust Pie Dough

MAKES ENOUGH FOR ONE 9-INCH PIE

Vodka is essential to the tender texture of this crust and imparts no flavor—do not substitute water. This dough is moister than most standard pie doughs and will require lots of flour to roll out (up to ¼ cup). The dough, wrapped tightly in plastic wrap, can be refrigerated for up to 2 days or frozen for up to 1 month. If frozen, let the dough thaw completely on the counter before rolling it out.

1¼   cups (6¼ ounces) all-purpose flour
 1   tablespoon sugar
 ½   teaspoon salt
 6   tablespoons unsalted butter, cut into ¼-inch
     pieces and chilled
 4   tablespoons vegetable shortening, cut into
     2 pieces and chilled
 2   tablespoons vodka, chilled
 2   tablespoons ice water

1. Process ¾ cups of the flour, the sugar, and salt together in a food processor until combined. Scatter the butter and shortening over the top and continue to process until incorporated and the mixture begins to form uneven clumps with no remaining floury bits, about 10 seconds.

2. Scrape down the workbowl and redistribute the dough evenly around the processor blade. Sprinkle the remaining ½ cup flour over the dough and pulse until the mixture has broken up into pieces and is evenly distributed around the bowl, 4 to 6 pulses.

3. Transfer the mixture to a medium bowl. Sprinkle the vodka and water over the mixture. Stir and press the dough together, using a stiff rubber spatula, until the dough sticks together.

4. Turn the dough onto a sheet of plastic wrap and flatten into a 4-inch disk. Wrap tightly in plastic wrap and refrigerate for 45 minutes or up to 2 days. Before rolling the dough out, let it sit on the counter to soften slightly, about 10 minutes.

BEHIND THE SCENES

YOU CAN NEVER HAVE ENOUGH RECIPES FOR PIE DOUGH

Viewers of our television show and readers of our recipes may wonder why we revisit the same recipes (roast chicken, mashed potatoes, and pie dough, to name a few) and develop alternate versions of them. Simply put, personal choice is a big factor. Take pie dough. There are few recipes that divide the test kitchen like the humble pie crust. Some in the test kitchen are purists when it comes to pie dough—they wouldn't dream of using anything but an all-butter dough. The flavor of our All-Butter Pie Dough (page 843) is undeniably buttery and delicious, but let's face it—this dough can be difficult to work with and isn't quite as flaky as a pie dough made with vegetable shortening. Next are the cooks who prefer the ease of working with a dough made with vegetable shortening as well as butter, like our Basic Pie Dough (page 842). Vegetable shortening, such as Crisco, is made from vegetable oil that has been hydrogenated, a process in which hydrogen gas is pumped into vegetable oil so it solidifies. Adding vegetable shortening makes the dough easier to work with and it does a good job of lightening and tenderizing the dough. That said, this pie dough still takes some patience to roll out.

The problem is that most pie dough recipes are stingy with the water (and thus really hard to roll out). Adding more water may seem to help matters, but once baked, the resulting crust is tougher. So to solve this problem, we developed a third pie dough, based on our Basic Pie Dough but with an unlikely ingredient—vodka.

While gluten (the protein that makes crust tough) forms readily in water, it doesn't form in ethanol, and vodka is 60 percent water and 40 percent ethanol. So adding ¼ cup of vodka and ¼ cup of water produces a moist, easy-to-roll dough that stays tender because the alcohol vaporizes in the oven, leaving the final crust with only about 6 tablespoons of water. This dough bakes into a crust that is tender and flavorful and that rolls out easily every time. For those in the test kitchen who demand an easy-to-roll pie dough, this is their dream recipe. (And for those who aren't practiced bakers and make a pie maybe once a year around the holidays, this dough makes a lot of sense.) Does that mean we're through developing pie doughs? Maybe, maybe not.

GRAHAM CRACKER CRUST

WHY THIS RECIPE WORKS: Saving time is always a good idea—just as long as you're not sacrificing quality. But while store-bought graham cracker pie crusts are tempting (all you have to do is fill, chill, then serve), they taste stale and bland. We wanted a fresh-tasting homemade crust that wasn't too sweet, with a crisp texture.

Turns out, a classic graham cracker crust couldn't be easier to make: Combine crushed crumbs with a little butter and sugar to bind them, then use a measuring cup or flat-bottomed glass to pack the crumbs into the pie plate. And producing a perfect graham cracker crust has a lot to do with the type of graham crackers used. After experimenting with the three leading brands, we discovered subtle but distinct differences among them and found that these differences carried over into crumb crusts made with each kind of cracker. Here in the test kitchen, we prefer Nabisco Original Graham Crackers for their hearty molasses flavor.

Graham Cracker Crust
MAKES ENOUGH FOR ONE 9-INCH PIE

We don't recommend using store-bought graham cracker crumbs here as they can often be stale. Be sure to note whether the crust needs to be warm or cool before filling (the pie recipes will specify) and plan accordingly.

    8   whole graham crackers, broken into 1-inch pieces
    5   tablespoons unsalted butter, melted and cooled
    3   tablespoons sugar

1. Adjust an oven rack to the middle position and heat the oven to 325 degrees. Process the graham cracker pieces in a food processor to fine, even crumbs, about 30 seconds. Sprinkle the butter and sugar over the crumbs and pulse to incorporate.

2. Sprinkle the mixture into a 9-inch pie plate. Following the photo, use the bottom of a measuring cup to press the crumbs into an even layer on the bottom and sides of the pie plate. Bake until the crust is fragrant and beginning to brown, 13 to 18 minutes. Following the particular pie recipe, use the crust while it is still warm or let it cool completely.

NOTES FROM THE TEST KITCHEN

MAKING A GRAHAM CRACKER OR COOKIE CRUST

Press the crumb mixture firmly and evenly across the bottom of the pie plate, using the bottom of a measuring cup. Then tightly pack the crumbs against the sides of the pie plate, using your thumb and the measuring cup simultaneously.

APPLE PIE

WHY THIS RECIPE WORKS: In the test kitchen, we have found that it's difficult to produce an apple pie with a filling that is tart as well as sweet and juicy. We wanted to develop a classic apple pie recipe—one with the clean, bright taste of apples that could be made year-round, based on apple types that are always available in the supermarket.

To arrive at the tartness and texture we were after, we had to use two kinds of apples in our pie, Granny Smith and McIntosh. The Grannies could be counted on for tartness and for keeping their shape during cooking; the Macs added flavor, and their otherwise frustrating tendency to become mushy was a virtue, providing a nice, juicy base for the harder Grannies. While many bakers add butter to their apple pie fillings, we found that it dulled the fresh taste of the apples and so did without it. Lemon juice, however, was essential, counterbalancing the sweetness of the apples. To give the apples the upper hand, we settled on quite modest amounts of cinnamon, nutmeg, and allspice.

Classic Apple Pie
SERVES 8

You can use All-Butter Double-Crust Pie Dough (page 843), Basic Double-Crust Pie Dough (page 842), or Foolproof Double-Crust Pie Dough (page 844) for this pie. The pie is best eaten when cooled to room temperature, or even the next day. Serve with vanilla ice cream or lightly sweetened whipped cream.

    1   recipe double-crust pie dough (see note)
    2   tablespoons unbleached all-purpose flour, plus extra
        for the work surface
    ¾   cup (5¼ ounces) plus 1 tablespoon sugar

1 teaspoon grated zest plus 1 tablespoon juice
from 1 lemon

¼ teaspoon table salt

¼ teaspoon ground nutmeg

¼ teaspoon ground cinnamon

⅛ teaspoon ground allspice

2 pounds firm McIntosh apples (about 4 large), peeled,
cored, and sliced ¼ inch thick

1½ pounds Granny Smith apples (about 3 large), peeled,
cored, and sliced ¼ inch thick

1 large egg white, lightly beaten

1. Following the photos on page 842, roll one disk of dough into a 12-inch circle on a lightly floured work surface, then fit it into a 9-inch pie plate, letting the excess dough hang over the edge; cover with plastic wrap and refrigerate for 30 minutes. Roll the other disk of dough into a 12-inch circle on a lightly floured work surface, then transfer to a parchment-lined baking sheet; cover with plastic wrap and refrigerate for 30 minutes.

2. Adjust an oven rack to the lowest position and heat the oven to 500 degrees.

3. Mix the flour, ¾ cup of the sugar, the zest, salt, nutmeg, cinnamon, and allspice together in a large bowl. Add the lemon juice and apples and toss until combined. Spread the apples with their juice into the dough-lined pie plate, mounding them slightly in the middle. Following the photos on page 848, loosely roll the second piece of dough around the rolling pin and gently unroll it over the pie. Trim, fold, and crimp the edges, and cut four vent holes in the top. Brush the dough with the egg white and sprinkle with the remaining 1 tablespoon sugar.

4. Place the pie on a rimmed baking sheet, reduce the oven temperature to 425 degrees, and bake until the crust is golden, about 25 minutes. Reduce the oven temperature to 375 degrees, rotate the baking sheet, and continue to bake until the juices are bubbling and the crust is deep golden brown, 35 to 45 minutes longer. Cool the pie on a wire rack to room temperature, about 4 hours. Serve.

Apple Pie with Crystallized Ginger

Follow the recipe for Classic Apple Pie, adding 3 tablespoons chopped crystallized ginger to the apple mixture.

Apple Pie with Dried Fruit

Toss 1 cup raisins, dried sweet cherries, or dried cranberries with the lemon juice plus 1 tablespoon applejack, brandy, or cognac. Follow the recipe for Classic Apple Pie, adding the dried fruit and liquid to the apple mixture.

Apple Pie with Fresh Cranberries

Follow the recipe for Classic Apple Pie, increasing the sugar to 1 cup (7 ounces) and adding 1 cup fresh or frozen cranberries to the apple mixture.

DEEP-DISH APPLE PIE

WHY THIS RECIPE WORKS: The problem with deep-dish apple pie is that the apples are often unevenly cooked and the exuded juice leaves the apples swimming in liquid, producing a bottom crust that is pale and soggy. Then there is the gaping hole left between the apples (which are shrunken from the loss of all that moisture) and the arching top crust, making it impossible to slice and serve a neat piece of pie. We wanted our piece of deep-dish pie to be a towering wedge of tender, juicy apples, fully framed by a buttery, flaky crust. Precooking the apples solved the shrinking problem, helped the apples hold their shape, and prevented juices from collecting in the bottom of the pie plate, giving us a nicely browned bottom crust. All that was left to do was to choose the right combination of apples and stir in a little brown sugar, salt, lemon, and cinnamon, for flavor and sweetness.

Deep-Dish Apple Pie

SERVES 8

You can use All-Butter Double-Crust Pie Dough (page 843), Basic Double-Crust Pie Dough (page 842), or Foolproof Double-Crust Pie Dough (page 844) for this pie. Use a combination of tart and sweet apples for this pie. Good choices for tart are Granny Smiths, Empires, or Cortlands; for sweet we recommend Golden Delicious, Jonagolds, or Braeburns. Serve with vanilla ice cream or lightly sweetened whipped cream.

1 recipe double-crust pie dough (see note)
Unbleached all-purpose flour, for the work surface

2½ pounds firm tart apples (about 5 large), peeled, cored, and sliced ¼ inch thick (see note)

2½ pounds firm sweet apples (about 5 large), peeled, cored, and sliced ¼ inch thick (see note)

½ cup (3½ ounces) plus 1 tablespoon granulated sugar

¼ cup packed (1¾ ounces) light brown sugar

½ teaspoon grated zest plus 1 tablespoon juice
from 1 lemon

¼ teaspoon table salt

⅛ teaspoon ground cinnamon

1 large egg white, lightly beaten

1. Following the photos on page 842, roll one disk of dough into a 12-inch circle on a lightly floured work surface, then fit it into a 9-inch pie plate, letting the excess dough hang over the edge; cover with plastic wrap and refrigerate for 30 minutes. Roll the other disk of dough into a 12-inch circle on a lightly floured work surface, then transfer to a parchment-lined baking sheet; cover with plastic wrap and refrigerate for 30 minutes.

2. Toss the apples, ½ cup of the granulated sugar, the brown sugar, zest, salt, and cinnamon together in a Dutch oven. Cover and cook over medium heat, stirring frequently, until the apples are tender when poked with a fork but still hold their shape, 15 to 20 minutes. Transfer the apples and their juice to a rimmed baking sheet and cool to room temperature, about 30 minutes.

3. Adjust an oven rack to the lowest position and heat the oven to 425 degrees. Drain the cooled apples thoroughly through a colander, reserving ¼ cup of the juice. Stir the lemon juice into the reserved ¼ cup apple juice.

4. Spread the apples into the dough-lined pie plate, mounding them slightly in the middle, and drizzle with the lemon juice mixture. Following the photos, loosely roll the second piece of dough around the rolling pin and gently unroll it over the pie. Trim, fold, and crimp the edges and cut four vent holes in the top. Brush the dough with the egg white and sprinkle with the remaining 1 tablespoon sugar.

5. Place the pie on a rimmed baking sheet and bake until the crust is golden, about 25 minutes. Reduce the oven temperature to 375 degrees, rotate the baking sheet, and continue to bake until the juices are bubbling and the crust is deep golden brown, 30 to 40 minutes longer. Cool the pie on a wire rack until the filling has set, about 2 hours; serve slightly warm or at room temperature.

NOTES FROM THE TEST KITCHEN

MAKING A DOUBLE-CRUST PIE

1. Loosely roll the chilled top crust around the rolling pin, then gently unroll it over the filled pie crust bottom.

2. Using scissors, trim all but ½ inch of the dough overhanging the edge of the pie plate.

3. Press the top and bottom crusts together, then tuck the edges underneath.

4. Crimp the dough evenly around the edge of the pie, using your fingers. Cut vent holes attractively in the center of the top crust with a paring knife (drier pies only require four vents, while very juicy pies require eight vents).

FRESH PEACH PIE

WHY THIS RECIPE WORKS: Juicy summer peaches often produce soupy peach pies, and the amount of moisture changes from pie to pie. To control the moisture, we macerated the peaches to draw out some of their juices and then added a measured amount back to the filling. Cornstarch and pectin helped hold the filling together without making it gluey or bouncy, and mashing some of the peaches helped make neat, attractive slices. A buttery, tender lattice-top crust allowed moisture to evaporate and made for an impressive presentation.

Fresh Peach Pie
SERVES 8

If your peaches are too soft to withstand the pressure of a peeler, cut a shallow X in the bottom of the fruit, blanch them in a pot of simmering water for 15 seconds, and then shock them in a bowl of ice water before peeling. For fruit pectin we recommend both Sure-Jell for Less or No Sugar Needed Recipes and Ball RealFruit Low or No-Sugar Needed Pectin. For illustrations of our no-weave lattice, see page 849.

3	pounds peaches, peeled, quartered, and pitted, each quarter cut into thirds
½	cup (3½ ounces) plus 3 tablespoons sugar
1	teaspoon grated lemon zest plus 1 tablespoon juice
⅛	teaspoon salt
2	tablespoons low- or no-sugar-needed fruit pectin
¼	teaspoon ground cinnamon
	Pinch ground nutmeg
1	recipe Pie Dough for Lattice-Top Pie (recipe follows)
1	tablespoon cornstarch

1. Toss peaches, ½ cup sugar, lemon zest and juice, and salt in medium bowl. Let stand at room temperature for at least 30 minutes or up to 1 hour. Combine pectin, cinnamon, nutmeg, and 2 tablespoons sugar in small bowl and set aside.

2. Remove dough from refrigerator. Before rolling out dough, let it sit on counter to soften slightly, about 10 minutes. Roll 1 disk of dough into 12-inch circle on lightly floured counter. Transfer to parchment paper–lined baking sheet. With pizza wheel, fluted pastry wheel, or paring knife, cut round into ten 1¼-inch-wide strips. Freeze strips on sheet until firm, about 30 minutes.

3. Adjust oven rack to lowest position, place rimmed baking sheet on rack, and heat oven to 425 degrees. Roll other disk of dough into 12-inch circle on lightly floured counter. Loosely roll dough around rolling pin and gently unroll it onto 9-inch pie plate, letting excess dough hang over edge. Ease dough into plate by gently lifting edge of dough with your hand while pressing into plate bottom with your other hand. Leave any dough that overhangs plate in place. Wrap dough-lined pie plate loosely in plastic wrap and refrigerate until dough is firm, about 30 minutes.

4. Meanwhile, transfer 1 cup peach mixture to small bowl and mash with fork until coarse paste forms. Drain remaining peach mixture through colander set in large bowl. Transfer

peach juice to liquid measuring cup (you should have about ½ cup liquid; if liquid measures more than ½ cup, discard remainder). Return peach pieces to bowl and toss with cornstarch. Transfer peach juice to 12-inch skillet, add pectin mixture, and whisk until combined. Cook over medium heat, stirring occasionally, until slightly thickened and pectin is dissolved (liquid should become less cloudy), 3 to 5 minutes. Remove skillet from heat, add peach pieces and peach paste, and toss to combine.

5. Transfer peach mixture to dough-lined pie plate. Remove dough strips from freezer; if too stiff to be workable, let stand at room temperature until malleable and softened slightly but still very cold. Lay 2 longest strips across center of pie perpendicular to each other. Using 4 shortest strips, lay 2 strips across pie parallel to 1 center strip and 2 strips parallel to other center strip, near edges of pie; you should have 6 strips in place. Using remaining 4 strips, lay each one across pie parallel and equidistant from center and edge strips. If dough becomes too soft to work with, refrigerate pie and dough strips until dough firms up.

6. Trim overhang to ½ inch beyond lip of pie plate. Press edges of bottom crust and lattice strips together and fold under. Folded edge should be flush with edge of pie plate. Crimp dough evenly around edge of pie using your fingers. Using spray bottle, evenly mist lattice with water and sprinkle with remaining 1 tablespoon sugar.

7. Place pie on rimmed baking sheet and bake until crust is set and begins to brown, about 25 minutes. Reduce oven temperature to 375 degrees, rotate sheet, and continue to bake until crust is deep golden brown and filling is bubbly at center, 30 to 40 minutes longer. Let pie cool on wire rack for 3 hours before serving.

Pie Dough for Lattice-Top Pie

MAKES ENOUGH FOR ONE 9-INCH PIE

- 3 cups (15 ounces) all-purpose flour
- 2 tablespoons sugar
- 1 teaspoon salt

- 7 tablespoons vegetable shortening, cut into ½-inch pieces and chilled
- 10 tablespoons unsalted butter, cut into ¼-inch pieces and frozen for 30 minutes
- 10–12 tablespoons ice water

1. Process flour, sugar, and salt in food processor until combined, about 5 seconds. Scatter shortening over top and process until mixture resembles coarse cornmeal, about 10 seconds. Scatter butter over top and pulse until mixture resembles coarse crumbs, about 10 pulses. Transfer to bowl.

2. Sprinkle 5 tablespoons ice water over flour mixture. With rubber spatula, use folding motion to evenly combine water and flour mixture. Sprinkle 5 tablespoons ice water over mixture and continue using folding motion to combine until small portion of dough holds together when squeezed in palm of your hand, adding up to 2 tablespoons remaining ice water if necessary. (Dough should feel quite moist.) Turn out dough onto clean, dry counter and gently press together into cohesive ball. Divide dough into 2 even pieces and flatten each into 4-inch disk. Wrap disks tightly in plastic wrap and refrigerate for 1 hour or up to 2 days.

NOTES FROM THE TEST KITCHEN

BUILDING A "NO-WEAVE" LATTICE TOP

Making a lattice top for our Fresh Peach Pie can be intimidating. But it need not be if you use our simple technique: Freeze strips of dough and then arrange them in a particular order over the filling. Done properly, our approach gives the illusion of a woven lattice with less effort.

1. Roll dough into 12-inch circle, transfer to parchment paper–lined baking sheet, and cut into ten 1¼-inch-wide strips with a fluted pastry wheel, pizza wheel, or paring knife. Freeze for 30 minutes.

2. Lay 2 longest strips perpendicular to each other across center of pie to form cross. Place 4 shorter strips along edges of pie, parallel to center strips.

3. Lay 4 remaining strips between each edge strip and center strip. Trim off excess lattice ends, press edges of bottom crust and lattice strips together, and fold under.

STRAWBERRY PIE

WHY THIS RECIPE WORKS: Because uncooked berries shed so much liquid, the filling for strawberry pie is usually firmed up with a thickener, which produces results that range from stiff and bouncy to runny and gloppy. We wanted a strawberry pie featuring fresh berries lightly held together by a sheer, glossy glaze in a buttery shell. We knew that the success of our strawberry pie hinged on getting the thickener just right. When none of the thickeners we tried worked on their own, we decided to use a combination of two: pectin (in the form of a homemade strawberry jam) and cornstarch. By themselves, pectin produced a filling that was too firm and cornstarch one that was too loose, but together they created just the right supple, lightly clingy glaze. Fresh, flavorful strawberries make this dessert a perfect summery treat.

Fresh Strawberry Pie

SERVES 8

To account for any imperfect strawberries, the ingredient list calls for several more ounces of berries than will be used in the pie. If possible, seek out ripe, farmers' market–quality berries. Make sure to thoroughly dry the strawberries after washing. Make certain that you use fruit pectin engineered for low- or no-sugar recipes (we recommend Sure-Jell Premium Fruit Pectin) and not regular pectin; otherwise, the glaze will not set properly. The pie is at its best after two or three hours of chilling; as it continues to chill, the glaze becomes softer and wetter, though the pie will taste just as good.

1 recipe Foolproof Single-Crust Pie Dough (page 845), fitted into a 9-inch pie plate and chilled

3 pounds strawberries, hulled (9 cups)

¾ cup (5¼ ounces) sugar

2 tablespoons cornstarch

1½ teaspoons Sure-Jell for low-sugar recipes (see note)
Pinch table salt

1 tablespoon juice from 1 lemon

1 cup heavy cream, cold

1 tablespoon sugar

1. Adjust an oven rack to the middle position and heat the oven to 375 degrees. Following the photos on page 856, line the chilled pie shell with a double layer of foil and fill with pie weights.

2. Bake until the pie dough looks dry and is light in color, 25 to 30 minutes. Remove the weights and foil and continue to bake the crust until deep golden brown, 10 to 12 minutes longer. Transfer the pie plate to a wire rack and let cool completely, about 1 hour.

3. Select 6 ounces misshapen, underripe, or otherwise unattractive berries, halving those that are large; you should have about 1½ cups. Process the berries in a food processor to a smooth puree, 20 to 30 seconds, scraping down the bowl as needed (you should have about ¾ cup puree).

4. Whisk the sugar, cornstarch, Sure-Jell, and salt together in a medium saucepan. Stir in the berry puree, making sure to scrape the corners of the pan. Cook over medium-high heat, stirring constantly, and bring to a boil. Boil, scraping the bottom and sides of the pan to prevent scorching, for 2 minutes to ensure that the cornstarch is fully cooked (the mixture will appear frothy when it first reaches a boil, then will darken and thicken with further cooking). Transfer the glaze to a large bowl and stir in the lemon juice; let cool to room temperature.

5. Meanwhile, pick over the remaining berries and measure out 2 pounds of the most attractive ones; halve only any extra-large berries. Add the berries to the bowl with the glaze and fold gently with a rubber spatula until the berries are evenly coated. Scoop the berries into the cooled prebaked pie shell, piling into a mound. If any cut sides face up on top, turn them face down. If necessary, rearrange the berries so that holes are filled and the mound looks attractive. Refrigerate the pie until the filling is chilled and has set, about 2 hours. Serve within 5 hours of chilling.

6. Just before serving, beat the cream and sugar with an electric mixer on low speed until small bubbles form, about 30 seconds. Increase the speed to medium; continue beating until the beaters leave a trail, about 30 additional seconds. Increase the speed to high; continue beating until the cream is smooth, thick, and nearly doubled in volume and forms soft peaks, 30 to 60 seconds.

7. Cut the pie into wedges and serve with whipped cream.

STRAWBERRY-RHUBARB PIE

WHY THIS RECIPE WORKS: The key to pairing sweet strawberries and tart rhubarb in a pie is to keep their high water content in check. Microwaving rhubarb pieces with sugar allowed them to shed some liquid. We tossed in some of our cut strawberries to macerate among the microwaved

rhubarb and used the juices to create a jammy filling. We cooked the rest of the cut strawberries in the liquid, softening them until they were easy to mash into a jam. Adding tapioca to the filling mixture gelatinized the juices, protecting the crust from turning soggy. A sugary crust offered a contrast to the tart rhubarb, and brushing the surface with water before sprinkling it with sugar ensured the granules stayed put during baking.

Strawberry-Rhubarb Pie

SERVES 8

This dough is unusually moist and requires a full ¼ cup of flour when rolling it out to prevent it from sticking. Rhubarb varies in the amount of trimming required. Buy 2 pounds to ensure that you end up with 7 cups of rhubarb pieces. For tips on crimping the dough, see page 843. If desired, serve the pie with whipped cream or ice cream.

CRUST

2½ cups (12½ ounces) all-purpose flour

2 tablespoons sugar, plus 3 tablespoons for sprinkling

1 teaspoon salt

12 tablespoons unsalted butter, cut into ¼-inch slices and chilled

½ cup vegetable shortening, cut into 4 pieces and chilled

¼ cup vodka, chilled

¼ cup cold water, plus extra for brushing

FILLING

2 pounds rhubarb, trimmed and cut into ½-inch pieces (7 cups)

1¼ cups (8¾ ounces) sugar

1 pound strawberries, hulled, halved if less than 1 inch, quartered if more than 1 inch (3 to 4 cups)

3 tablespoons instant tapioca

1. FOR THE CRUST: Process 1½ cups flour, 2 tablespoons sugar, and salt in food processor until combined, about 5 sec-

onds. Scatter butter and shortening over top and process until incorporated and mixture begins to form uneven clumps with no remaining floury bits, about 15 seconds.

2. Scrape down sides of bowl and redistribute dough evenly around processor blade. Sprinkle remaining 1 cup flour over dough and pulse until mixture has broken up into pieces and is evenly distributed around bowl, 4 to 6 pulses.

3. Transfer mixture to large bowl. Sprinkle vodka and cold water over mixture. Using rubber spatula, stir and press dough until it sticks together.

4. Divide dough in half. Turn each half onto sheet of plastic wrap and form into 4-inch disk. Wrap disks tightly in plastic and refrigerate for 1 hour. Let chilled dough sit on counter to soften slightly, about 10 minutes, before rolling. (Wrapped dough can be refrigerated for up to 2 days or frozen for up to 1 month. If frozen, let dough thaw completely on counter before rolling.)

5. FOR THE FILLING: While dough chills, combine rhubarb and sugar in bowl and microwave for 1½ minutes. Stir and continue to microwave until sugar is mostly dissolved, about 1 minute longer. Stir in 1 cup strawberries and set aside for 30 minutes, stirring once halfway through.

6. Drain rhubarb mixture through fine-mesh strainer set over large saucepan. Return drained rhubarb mixture to bowl and set aside. Add remaining strawberries to rhubarb liquid and cook over medium-high heat until strawberries are very soft and mixture is reduced to 1½ cups, about 10 to 15 minutes. Mash berries with fork (mixture does not have to be smooth). Add strawberry mixture and tapioca to drained rhubarb mixture and stir to combine. Set aside.

7. Roll 1 disk of dough into 12-inch circle on well-floured counter. Loosely roll dough around rolling pin and gently unroll onto 9-inch pie plate, letting excess dough hang over edge. Ease dough into plate by gently lifting edge of dough with your hand while pressing into plate bottom with your other hand. Wrap dough-lined plate loosely in plastic and refrigerate until dough is firm, about 30 minutes.

8. Roll other disk of dough into 12-inch circle on well-floured counter, then transfer to parchment paper–lined baking sheet; cover with plastic and refrigerate for 30 minutes. Adjust rack to middle position and heat oven to 425 degrees.

9. Transfer filling to chilled dough-lined plate and spread into even layer. Loosely roll remaining dough round around rolling pin and gently unroll it onto filling. Trim overhang to ½ inch beyond lip of plate. Pinch edges of top and bottom crusts firmly together. Tuck overhang under itself; folded edge should be flush with edge of plate. Crimp dough evenly around edge of plate using your fingers or butter knife. Brush surface thoroughly with extra water and sprinkle with 3 tablespoons sugar. Cut eight 2-inch slits in top crust.

10. Place pie on parchment-lined rimmed baking sheet and bake until crust is set and begins to brown, about 25 minutes. Rotate pie and reduce oven temperature to 375 degrees; continue to bake until crust is deep golden brown and filling is bubbling, 30 to 40 minutes longer. If edges of pie begin to get too brown before pie is done, cover loosely with aluminum foil. Let cool on wire rack for 2½ hours before serving.

BLUEBERRY PIE

WHY THIS RECIPE WORKS: If the filling in blueberry pie doesn't jell, a sliced wedge can collapse into a soupy puddle topped by a sodden crust. Too much thickener and the filling can be so dense that cutting into it is like slicing through gummi bears. We wanted a pie that had a firm, glistening filling full of fresh, bright flavor and still-plump berries.

To thicken the pie, we favored tapioca because it didn't mute the fresh yet subtle blueberry flavor as cornstarch and flour did. The back of the tapioca box recommended 6 tablespoons, but this produced a stiff, congealed mass. Cooking and reducing half of the berries helped us cut down on the tapioca required, but not enough. A second inspiration came from a peeled and grated Granny Smith apple. Apples are high in pectin, a type of carbohydrate that acts as a thickener when cooked. Combined with a modest 2 tablespoons of tapioca, the apple thickened the filling to a soft, even consistency that was neither gelatinous nor slippery. The crust posed a much simpler challenge. As with all of our fruit pies, baking on a rimmed baking sheet on the bottom oven rack produced a crisp, golden bottom crust. And we found a fast, easy alternative to a lattice top in a small biscuit cutter, which we used to cut out circles in the top crust before transferring the dough onto the pie. The attractive, unusual-looking top crust vented the steam from the berries as successfully as a classic lattice top.

Blueberry Pie

SERVES 8

You can use All-Butter Double-Crust Pie Dough (page 843), Basic Double-Crust Pie Dough (page 842), or Foolproof Double-Crust Pie Dough (page 844) for this pie. This recipe was developed using fresh blueberries, but unthawed frozen blueberries (our favorite brands are Wyman's and Cascadian Farm) will work as well. In step 3, cook half the frozen berries over medium-high heat, without mashing, until reduced to 1¼ cups, 12 to 15 minutes. Grind the tapioca to a powder in a spice grinder or mini food processor. If using pearl tapioca, reduce the amount to 5 teaspoons. Serve with vanilla ice cream or lightly sweetened whipped cream.

1 recipe double-crust pie dough (see note)
  Unbleached all-purpose flour, for the work surface
6 cups (30 ounces) fresh blueberries (see note)
1 Granny Smith apple, peeled, cored, and shredded on the large holes of a box grater
¾ cup (5¼ ounces) sugar
2 tablespoons instant tapioca, ground (see note)
2 teaspoons grated zest plus 2 teaspoons juice from 1 lemon
  Pinch table salt
2 tablespoons unsalted butter, cut into ¼-inch pieces
1 large egg white, lightly beaten

1. Following the photos on page 842, roll one disk of dough into a 12-inch circle on a lightly floured work surface, then fit it into a 9-inch pie plate, letting the excess dough hang over the edge; cover with plastic wrap and refrigerate for 30 minutes.

2. Roll the other disk of dough into a 12-inch circle on a lightly floured work surface. Following the photo, use a 1¼-inch round biscuit cutter to cut a round from the center of the dough. Cut 6 more rounds from the dough, 1½ inches from the edge of the center hole and equally spaced around the center hole. Transfer the dough to a parchment-lined baking sheet; cover with plastic wrap and refrigerate for 30 minutes.

3. Place 3 cups of the berries in a medium saucepan and set over medium heat. Using a potato masher, mash the berries several times to release the juices. Continue to cook, stirring

---

NOTES FROM THE TEST KITCHEN

MAKING A CUT-OUT CRUST

1. Use a 1¼-inch round biscuit cutter (or spice jar lid) to cut holes in the dough.

2. The cut-out crust vents the steam from the berry filling and is an easy alternative to a lattice-top pie.

frequently and mashing occasionally, until about half of the berries have broken down and the mixture is thickened and reduced to 1½ cups, about 8 minutes. Cool slightly.

4. Adjust an oven rack to the lowest position and heat the oven to 400 degrees.

5. Place the shredded apple in a clean kitchen towel and wring dry. Transfer the apple to a large bowl and stir in the cooked berries, remaining 3 cups uncooked berries, sugar, tapioca, lemon zest and juice, and salt until combined. Spread the mixture into the dough-lined pie plate and scatter the butter pieces over the top.

6. Following the photos on page 848, loosely roll the second piece of dough around the rolling pin and gently unroll it over the pie. Trim, fold, and crimp the edges. Brush the dough with the egg white.

7. Place the pie on a rimmed baking sheet and bake until the crust is golden, about 25 minutes. Reduce the oven temperature to 350 degrees, rotate the baking sheet, and continue to bake until the juices are bubbling and the crust is deep golden brown, 35 to 50 minutes longer. Cool the pie on a wire rack to room temperature, about 4 hours. Serve.

SUMMER BERRY PIE

WHY THIS RECIPE WORKS: A fresh berry pie might seem like an easy-to-pull-off summer dessert, but most of the recipes we tried buried the berries in gluey thickeners or embedded them in bouncy gelatin. We wanted a simple pie with great texture and flavor. We started with the test kitchen's quick and easy homemade graham cracker crust. For the filling, we used a combination of raspberries, blackberries, and blueberries. After trying a few different methods, we found a solution that both bound the berries in the graham cracker crust and intensified their bright flavor. We processed a portion of berries in the food processor until they made a smooth puree, then we thickened the puree with cornstarch. Next, we tossed the remaining berries with warm jelly for a glossy coat and a shot of sweetness. Pressed gently into the puree, the berries stayed put and tasted great.

Summer Berry Pie
SERVES 8

Feel free to vary the amount of each berry as desired as long as you have 6 cups of berries total; do not substitute frozen berries here. Serve with lightly sweetened whipped cream.

- 2 cups (10 ounces) raspberries (see note)
- 2 cups (10 ounces) blackberries (see note)
- 2 cups (10 ounces) blueberries (see note)
- ½ cup (3½ ounces) sugar
- 3 tablespoons cornstarch
- ⅛ teaspoon table salt
- 1 tablespoon juice from 1 lemon
- 1 recipe Graham Cracker Crust (page 846), baked and cooled
- 2 tablespoons red currant or apple jelly

1. Gently toss the berries together in a large bowl. Process 2½ cups of the berries in a food processor until very smooth, about 1 minute (do not under-process). Strain the puree through a fine-mesh strainer into a small saucepan, pressing on the solids to extract as much puree as possible (you should have about 1½ cups); discard the solids.

2. In a small bowl, whisk the sugar, cornstarch, and salt together, then whisk into the strained puree. Bring the puree to a boil over medium heat, stirring constantly, and cook until it is as thick as pudding, about 7 minutes. Off the heat, stir in the lemon juice and set aside to cool slightly.

3. Pour the warm berry puree into the baked and cooled pie crust. Melt the jelly in a small saucepan over low heat, then pour over the remaining 3½ cups berries and toss to coat. Spread the berries evenly over the puree and lightly press them into the puree. Cover the pie loosely with plastic wrap and refrigerate until the filling is chilled and set, about 3 hours. Serve chilled or at room temperature.

CHERRY PIE

WHY THIS RECIPE WORKS: Great cherry pie is typically made with sour cherries because their soft, juicy flesh and bright, punchy flavor isn't dulled by oven heat or sugar. But cherry season is cruelly short and chances are the cherries that are available are the sweet variety. Sweet cherries have mellower flavors and meaty, firm flesh—traits that make them ideal for eating straight off the stem but don't translate well to baking. Our challenge was obvious: Develop a recipe for sweet cherry pie with all the intense, jammy flavor and softened but still intact fruit texture of the best sour cherry pie.

To mimic the bright, tart flavor of a sour cherry pie filling, we supplemented sweet cherries with chopped plums, which are tart and helped tame the cherries' sweet flavor. To fix the texture problem, we cut the cherries in half to expose their sturdy flesh. This step encouraged the cherries to soften and give up their juices. A splash of bourbon and lemon juice also offset the sweetness and added flavorful depth. To keep the filling juicy, rather than dry, we switched out the typical lattice pie crust in favor of a traditional top crust, which prevented any moisture from evaporating.

Sweet Cherry Pie

SERVES 8

You can use All-Butter Double-Crust Pie Dough (page 843), Basic Double-Crust Pie Dough (page 842), or Foolproof Double-Crust Pie Dough (page 844) for this recipe. The tapioca should be measured first, then ground in a coffee grinder or food processor for 30 seconds. If you are using frozen fruit, measure it frozen, but let it thaw before filling the pie. If not, you run the risk of partially cooked fruit and undissolved tapioca.

- 1 recipe double-crust pie dough (see note)
  Unbleached all-purpose flour, for the work surface
- 2 red plums, halved and pitted
- 6 cups (about 2 pounds) pitted sweet cherries or 6 cups pitted frozen cherries, halved (see note)
- ½ cup (3½ ounces) sugar
- ⅛ teaspoon table salt
- 1 tablespoon juice from 1 lemon
- 2 teaspoons bourbon (optional)
- 2 tablespoons instant tapioca, ground (see note)
- ⅛ teaspoon ground cinnamon (optional)
- 2 tablespoons unsalted butter, cut into ¼-inch pieces
- 1 large egg, lightly beaten with 1 teaspoon water

1. Following the photos on page 842, roll one disk of the dough into a 12-inch circle on a lightly floured work surface, then fit it into a 9-inch pie plate, letting the excess dough hang over the edge; cover with plastic wrap and refrigerate for 30 minutes. Roll the other disk of dough into a 12-inch circle on a lightly floured work surface, then transfer to a parchment-lined baking sheet; cover with plastic wrap and refrigerate for 30 minutes.

2. Adjust an oven rack to the lowest position and heat the oven to 400 degrees. Process the plums and 1 cup of the halved cherries in a food processor until smooth, about 1 minute, scraping down the sides of the bowl as necessary. Strain the puree through a fine-mesh strainer into a large bowl, pressing on the solids to extract the liquid; discard the solids. Stir in the remaining 5 cups halved cherries, sugar, salt, lemon juice, bourbon (if using), tapioca, and cinnamon (if using) into the puree; let stand for 15 minutes.

3. Transfer the cherry mixture, including all the juices, to the dough-lined plate. Scatter the butter pieces over the fruit. Following the photos on page 848, loosely roll the second piece of dough around the rolling pin and gently unroll it over the pie. Trim, fold, and crimp the edges, and cut eight evenly spaced vent holes in the top. Brush the dough with the egg mixture. Freeze the pie for 20 minutes.

4. Place the pie on a rimmed baking sheet and bake for 30 minutes. Reduce the oven temperature to 350 degrees and continue to bake until the juices bubble and the crust is deep golden brown, 35 to 50 minutes longer.

5. Cool the pie on a wire rack to room temperature, about 4 hours, before serving.

PUMPKIN PIE

WHY THIS RECIPE WORKS: Too often, pumpkin pie appears at the end of a Thanksgiving meal as a grainy, overspiced, canned-pumpkin custard encased in a soggy crust. We wanted to create a pumpkin pie recipe destined to be a new classic: velvety smooth, packed with pumpkin flavor, and redolent of just enough fragrant spices.

Canned pumpkin contains moisture, which dilutes a pie's flavor. To maximize flavor, we concentrated this liquid by cooking the pumpkin with sugar and spices, then whisked in heavy cream, milk, and eggs. This improved the flavor and the hot filling let the custard firm up quickly in the oven, preventing it from soaking into the crust. For spices, we chose nutmeg, cinnamon, and, surprisingly, freshly grated ginger. Sugar and maple syrup sweetened things, but tasters still craved a more complex pie. On a whim, we added mashed roasted yams to the filling and tasters appreciated the deeper flavor. To streamline the recipe we switched to canned candied yams and cooked them with the pumpkin. To keep the custard from curdling, we started the pie at a high temperature for 10 minutes, followed by a reduced temperature for the remainder of the baking time. This cut the baking time to less than one hour and the dual temperatures produced a creamy pie fully and evenly cooked from edge to center.

Pumpkin Pie

SERVES 8

If candied yams are unavailable, regular canned yams can be substituted. When the pie is properly baked, the center 2 inches of the pie should look firm but jiggle slightly. The pie finishes cooking with residual heat; to ensure that the filling sets, cool it at room temperature and not in the refrigerator. The crust and filling must both be warm when the filling is added. Serve with lightly sweetened whipped cream.

- 1 recipe Basic Single-Crust Pie Dough (page 842), fitted into a 9-inch pie plate and chilled
- 1 cup heavy cream
- 1 cup whole milk
- 3 large whole eggs plus 2 large egg yolks
- 1 teaspoon vanilla extract
- 1 (15-ounce) can pumpkin puree
- 1 cup candied yams, drained (see note)
- ¾ cup (5¼ ounces) sugar
- ¼ cup maple syrup
- 2 teaspoons grated or minced fresh ginger
- 1 teaspoon table salt
- ½ teaspoon ground cinnamon
- ¼ teaspoon ground nutmeg

1. Adjust an oven rack to the middle position and heat the oven to 375 degrees. Following the photos on page 856, line the chilled pie shell with a double layer of foil and fill with pie weights.

2. Bake until the pie dough looks dry and is light in color, 25 to 30 minutes. Remove the weights and foil and continue to bake the crust until deep golden brown, 10 to 12 minutes longer. Transfer the pie plate to a wire rack. (The crust must still be warm when the filling is added.)

3. While the pie shell is baking, whisk the cream, milk, whole eggs, egg yolks, and vanilla together in a medium bowl. Bring the pumpkin puree, yams, sugar, maple syrup, ginger, salt, cinnamon, and nutmeg to a simmer in a large saucepan over medium heat and cook, stirring constantly and mashing the yams against the sides of the pot, until thick and shiny, 15 to 20 minutes.

4. Remove the pan from the heat and whisk in the cream mixture until fully incorporated. Strain the mixture through a fine-mesh strainer set over a medium bowl, using the back of a ladle or spatula to press the solids through the strainer. Whisk the mixture, then transfer to the warm prebaked pie crust.

5. Bake the pie on a rimmed baking sheet for 10 minutes. Reduce the oven temperature to 300 degrees and continue to bake until the edges of the pie are set and the center registers 175 degrees on an instant-read thermometer, 25 to 45 minutes longer. Cool the pie on a wire rack to room temperature, 2 to 3 hours, before serving.

PECAN PIE

WHY THIS RECIPE WORKS: Pecan pies can be overwhelmingly sweet, with no real pecan flavor. And they too often turn out curdled and separated. What's more, the weepy filling makes the bottom crust soggy and leathery. The fact that the crust usually seems underbaked to begin with doesn't help matters. We wanted to create a recipe for a not-too-sweet pie with a smooth-textured filling and a properly baked bottom crust.

We tackled this pie's problems by using brown sugar and reducing the amount, which helped bring out the pecan flavor. We also partially baked the crust, which kept it crisp. We found that it's important to add the hot filling to a warm pie crust as this helps keep the crust from getting soggy. In addition, we discovered that simulating a double boiler when you're melting the butter and making the filling is an easy way to maintain gentle heat, which helps ensure that the filling doesn't curdle.

Pecan Pie

SERVES 8

The crust must still be warm when the filling is added. To serve the pie warm, cool it thoroughly so that it sets completely, then warm it in a 250-degree oven for about 15 minutes and slice. Serve with vanilla ice cream or lightly sweetened whipped cream.

- 1 recipe Basic Single-Crust Pie Dough (page 842), fitted into a 9-inch pie plate and chilled
- 6 tablespoons (¾ stick) unsalted butter, cut into 1-inch pieces
- 1 cup packed (7 ounces) dark brown sugar
- ½ teaspoon table salt
- 3 large eggs
- ¾ cup light corn syrup
- 1 tablespoon vanilla extract
- 2 cups (8 ounces) pecans, toasted and chopped into small pieces

BLIND BAKING A PIE CRUST

1. Line the chilled pie shell with a double layer of aluminum foil, covering the edges to prevent burning.

2. Fill the shell with pie weights and bake until dry and light in color. After baking, carefully remove the weights and let the crust cool (for a partially baked crust) or continue to bake until deep golden brown (for a fully baked crust).

1. Adjust an oven rack to the middle position and heat the oven to 375 degrees. Following the photos, line the chilled pie shell with a double layer of foil and fill with pie weights. Bake until the pie dough looks dry and is light in color, 25 to 30 minutes. Transfer the pie plate to a wire rack and remove the weights and foil. Adjust the oven rack to the lower-middle position and reduce the oven temperature to 275 degrees. (The crust must still be warm when the filling is added.)

2. Melt the butter in a heatproof bowl set in a skillet of water maintained at just below a simmer. Remove the bowl from the skillet and stir in the sugar and salt until the butter is absorbed. Whisk in the eggs, then the corn syrup and vanilla until smooth. Return the bowl to the hot water and stir until the mixture is shiny and hot to the touch and registers 130 degrees on an instant-read thermometer. Off the heat, stir in the pecans.

3. Pour the pecan mixture into the warm pie crust. Bake the pie until the filling looks set but yields like Jell-O when gently pressed with the back of a spoon, 50 to 60 minutes. Cool the pie on a wire rack until the filling has firmed up, about 2 hours; serve slightly warm (see note) or at room temperature.

Triple Chocolate Chunk Pecan Pie

SERVES 8

Use either just one type of chocolate listed or a combination of two or three types. See page 910 for information on our top-rated brands of chocolate. The crust must still be warm when the filling is added.

- 1 recipe Basic Single-Crust Pie Dough (page 842), fitted into a 9-inch pie plate and chilled
- 3 tablespoons unsalted butter, cut into 3 pieces
- ¾ cup packed (5¼ ounces) dark brown sugar
- ½ teaspoon table salt

- 2 large eggs
- ½ cup light corn syrup
- 1 teaspoon vanilla extract
- 1 cup (4 ounces) pecans, toasted and chopped coarse
- 6 ounces semisweet, milk, and/or white chocolate, chopped coarse (see note)

1. Adjust an oven rack to the middle position and heat the oven to 375 degrees. Following the photos, line the chilled pie shell with a double layer of foil and fill with pie weights. Bake until the pie dough looks dry and is light in color, 25 to 30 minutes. Transfer the pie plate to a wire rack and remove the weights and foil. Adjust the oven rack to the lower-middle position and reduce the oven temperature to 275 degrees. (The crust must still be warm when the filling is added.)

2. Melt the butter in a heatproof bowl set in a skillet of water maintained at just below a simmer. Remove the bowl from the skillet and stir in the sugar and salt until the butter is absorbed. Whisk in the eggs, then the corn syrup and vanilla until smooth. Return the bowl to the hot water and stir until the mixture is shiny and hot to the touch and registers 130 degrees on an instant-read thermometer. Off the heat, stir in the pecans.

3. Pour the pecan mixture into the warm pie crust. Scatter the chocolate over the top and lightly press it into the filling with the back of a spoon. Bake the pie until the filling looks set but yields like Jell-O when gently pressed with the back of a spoon, 50 to 60 minutes. Cool the pie on a wire rack until the filling has firmed up, about 2 hours; serve slightly warm or at room temperature.

KEY LIME PIE

WHY THIS RECIPE WORKS: Some of us have been served Key lime pie in restaurants and found it disappointing, usually harsh and artificial tasting. We wanted a recipe for classic Key lime pie with a fresh flavor and silky filling. Traditional Key lime pie is usually not baked; instead, the combination of egg yolks, lime juice, and sweetened condensed milk firms up when chilled because the juice's acidity causes the proteins in the eggs and milk to bind.

Although we had suspected that the sweetened condensed milk was the party guilty of giving Key lime pies their "off" flavor, we found that the real culprit was the lime juice—bottled, reconstituted lime juice, that is. When we substituted the juice and zest from fresh limes, the pie became an entirely different experience: pungent and refreshing, cool and yet creamy, and very satisfying. We also discovered that while the pie filling will set without baking (most recipes call only for mixing and then chilling), it set much more nicely after being baked for only 15 minutes. We tried other, more dramatic, departures from the "classic" recipe—folding in egg whites, substituting heavy cream for condensed milk—but they didn't work. Just two seemingly minor adjustments to the recipe made all the difference in the world.

Key Lime Pie

SERVES 8

We found that tasters could not tell the difference between pies made with regular supermarket limes (called Persian limes) and true Key limes. Since Persian limes are easier to find and juice, we recommend them. You need to make the filling first, then prepare the crust.

PIE

- 4 large egg yolks
- 4 teaspoons grated zest plus ½ cup juice from 3 or 4 limes (see note)
- 1 (14-ounce) can sweetened condensed milk
- 1 recipe Graham Cracker Crust (page 846)

TOPPING (OPTIONAL)

- 1 cup heavy cream, chilled
- ¼ cup (1 ounce) confectioners' sugar

1. FOR THE PIE: Whisk the egg yolks and lime zest together in a medium bowl until the mixture has a light green tint, about 2 minutes. Whisk in the condensed milk until smooth, then whisk in the lime juice. Cover the mixture and set aside at room temperature until thickened, about 30 minutes.

2. Meanwhile, prepare and bake the crust. Transfer the pie plate to a wire rack and leave the oven at 325 degrees. (The crust must still be warm when the filling is added.)

3. Pour the thickened filling into the warm pie crust. Bake the pie until the center is firm but jiggles slightly when shaken, 15 to 20 minutes. Let the pie cool slightly on a wire rack, about 1 hour, then cover loosely with plastic wrap and refrigerate until the filling is chilled and set, about 3 hours.

4. FOR THE TOPPING (IF USING): Before serving, whip the cream and sugar together in a large bowl with an electric mixer on medium-low speed until frothy, about 1 minute. Increase the mixer speed to high and continue to whip until the cream forms soft peaks, 1 to 3 minutes. Spread the whipped cream attractively over the top of the pie and serve.

LEMON MERINGUE PIE

WHY THIS RECIPE WORKS: Most everybody loves lemon meringue pie—at least the bottom half of it. The most controversial part is the meringue. On any given day it can shrink, bead, puddle, deflate, burn, sweat, break down, or turn rubbery. We wanted a pie with a crisp, flaky crust and a rich filling that would balance the airy meringue, without blocking the clear lemon flavor. The filling should be soft but not runny; firm enough to cut but not stiff and gelatinous. Most important, we wanted a meringue that didn't break down and puddle on the bottom or "tear" on top.

We consulted a food scientist, who told us that the puddling underneath the meringue is from undercooking. The beading on top of the pie is from overcooking. We discovered that if the filling is piping hot when the meringue is applied, the underside of the meringue will not undercook; if the oven temperature is relatively low, the top of the meringue won't overcook. Baking the pie in a relatively cool (325-degree) oven also produces the best-looking, most evenly baked meringue. To further stabilize the meringue and keep it from weeping (even on hot, humid days), we beat in a small amount of cornstarch.

Lemon Meringue Pie

SERVES 8

Make the pie crust, let it cool, and then begin work on the filling. As soon as the filling is made, cover it with plastic wrap to keep it hot and then start working on the meringue topping. You want to add hot filling to the pie crust, apply the meringue topping, and then quickly get the pie into the oven.

- 1 recipe Single-Crust Pie Dough for Custard Pies (page 843), fitted into a 9-inch pie plate and chilled

FILLING

- 1½ cups water
- 1 cup (7 ounces) sugar
- ¼ cup (1 ounce) cornstarch
- ⅛ teaspoon table salt
- 6 large egg yolks
- 1 tablespoon grated zest plus ½ cup juice from 3 lemons
- 2 tablespoons unsalted butter, cut into 2 pieces

MERINGUE

- ⅓ cup water
- 1 tablespoon cornstarch
- ½ cup (3½ ounces) sugar
- ¼ teaspoon cream of tartar
- 4 large egg whites
- ½ teaspoon vanilla extract

1. Adjust an oven rack to the middle position and heat the oven to 375 degrees. Following the photos on page 856, line the chilled pie shell with a double layer of foil and fill with pie weights. Bake until the pie dough looks dry and is light in color, 25 to 30 minutes. Remove the weights and foil and continue to bake the crust until deep golden brown, 10 to 12 minutes longer. Cool the crust to room temperature. Reduce the oven temperature to 325 degrees.

2. FOR THE FILLING: Bring the water, sugar, cornstarch, and salt to a simmer in a large saucepan over medium heat, whisking constantly. When the mixture starts to turn translucent, whisk in the egg yolks, 2 at a time. Whisk in the lemon zest and juice and the butter. Return the mixture to a brief simmer, then remove the pan from the heat. Lay a sheet of plastic wrap directly on the surface of the filling to keep warm and prevent a skin from forming.

3. FOR THE MERINGUE: Bring the water and cornstarch to a simmer in a small saucepan and cook, whisking occasionally, until thickened and translucent, 1 to 2 minutes. Set aside off the heat to cool slightly.

4. Combine the sugar and cream of tartar in a small bowl. In a large bowl, whip the egg whites and vanilla together with an electric mixer on medium-low speed until foamy, about 1 minute. Increase the mixer speed to medium-high, add the sugar mixture, 1 tablespoon at a time, and whip the whites until shiny and soft peaks form, 1 to 3 minutes. Add the cornstarch mixture, 1 tablespoon at a time, and continue to whip the meringue to stiff peaks, 1 to 3 minutes longer.

5. Meanwhile, remove the plastic wrap from the filling and return to very low heat during the last minute or so of beating the meringue (to ensure the filling is hot).

6. Pour the warm filling into the pie crust. Using a rubber spatula, immediately distribute the meringue evenly around the edge and then the center of the pie, attaching the meringue to the pie crust to prevent shrinking. Use the back of a spoon to create attractive swirls and peaks in the meringue. Bake until the meringue is golden brown, about 20 minutes. Cool the pie on a wire rack until the filling has set, about 2 hours. Serve.

LEMON CHIFFON PIE

WHY THIS RECIPE WORKS: We love the elegant simplicity of lemon chiffon pie but found the gelatin used in most recipes difficult to work with. We use a combination of cornstarch and gelatin to get a creamy pie and add a burst of lemon flavor by tucking a layer of lemon curd beneath the chiffon. Our graham cracker crust adds just a hint of flavor and is a crisp contrast to the soft and fluffy filling.

Lemon Chiffon Pie
SERVES 8 TO 10

Before cooking the curd mixture, be sure to whisk thoroughly so that no clumps of cornstarch or streaks of egg white remain. Pasteurized egg whites can be substituted for the 3 raw egg whites. Serve with lightly sweetened whipped cream.

CRUST
- 9 whole graham crackers
- 3 tablespoons sugar
- ⅛ teaspoon salt
- 5 tablespoons unsalted butter, melted

FILLING
- 1 teaspoon unflavored gelatin
- 4 tablespoons water
- 5 large eggs (2 whole, 3 separated)
- 1¼ cups (8¾ ounces) sugar
- 1 tablespoon cornstarch
- ⅛ teaspoon salt
- 1 tablespoon grated lemon zest plus ¾ cup juice (4 lemons)
- ¼ cup heavy cream
- 4 ounces cream cheese, cut into ½-inch pieces, softened

1. FOR THE CRUST: Adjust oven rack to lower-middle position and heat oven to 325 degrees. Process graham crackers in food processor until finely ground, about 30 seconds (you should have about 1¼ cups crumbs). Add sugar and salt and pulse to combine. Add melted butter and pulse until mixture resembles wet sand.

2. Transfer crumbs to 9-inch pie plate. Press crumbs evenly into bottom and up sides of plate. Bake until crust is lightly browned, 15 to 18 minutes. Allow crust to cool completely.

3. FOR THE FILLING: Sprinkle ½ teaspoon gelatin over 2 tablespoons water in small bowl and let sit until gelatin softens, about 5 minutes. Repeat with second small bowl, remaining ½ teaspoon gelatin, and remaining 2 tablespoons water.

4. Whisk 2 eggs and 3 yolks together in medium saucepan until thoroughly combined. Whisk in 1 cup sugar, cornstarch, and salt until well combined. Whisk in lemon zest and juice and heavy cream. Cook over medium-low heat, stirring constantly, until thickened and slightly translucent, 4 to 5 minutes (mixture should register 170 degrees). Stir in 1 water-gelatin mixture until dissolved. Remove pan from heat and let stand for 2 minutes.

5. Remove 1¼ cups curd from pan and pour through fine-mesh strainer set in bowl. Transfer strained curd to prepared pie shell (do not wash out strainer or bowl). Place filled pie shell in freezer. Add remaining water-gelatin mixture and cream cheese to remaining curd in pan and whisk to combine. (If cream cheese does not melt, briefly return pan to low heat.) Pour through strainer into now-empty bowl.

6. Using stand mixer, whip 3 egg whites on medium-low speed until foamy, about 2 minutes. Increase speed to medium-high and slowly add remaining ¼ cup sugar. Continue whipping until whites are stiff and glossy, about 4 minutes. Add curd–cream cheese mixture and whip on medium speed until few streaks remain, about 30 seconds. Remove bowl from mixer and, using spatula, scrape sides of bowl and stir mixture until no streaks remain. Remove pie shell from freezer and carefully pour chiffon over curd, allowing chiffon to mound slightly in center. Refrigerate for at least 4 hours or up to 2 days before serving.

COCONUT CREAM PIE

WHY THIS RECIPE WORKS: Most recipes for this diner dessert are nothing more than a redecorated vanilla cream pie. A handful of coconut shreds stirred into the filling or sprinkled on the whipped cream might be enough to give it a new name, but certainly not enough to give it flavor. We wanted a coconut cream pie with the exotic and elusive flavor of tropical coconut rather than a thinly disguised vanilla custard.

We found that using not-too-sweet graham crackers made a crust with a delicate, cookie-like texture that didn't overshadow the coconut filling. For the filling, we started with a basic custard, using a combination of unsweetened coconut milk and whole milk. For more coconut flavor, we stirred in unsweetened shredded coconut and cooked it so the shreds softened slightly in the hot milk. Lastly, we topped the pie with simple sweetened whipped cream and dusted it with crunchy shreds of toasted coconut.

Coconut Cream Pie

SERVES 8

Do not use low-fat coconut milk here because it does not have enough flavor. Also, don't confuse coconut milk with cream of coconut. The filling should be warm—neither piping hot nor room temperature—when poured into the cooled pie crust. To toast the coconut, place it in a small skillet over medium heat and cook, stirring frequently, for 3 to 5 minutes. It burns quite easily, so keep a close eye on it.

FILLING

- 1 (14-ounce) can coconut milk (see note)
- 1 cup whole milk
- ½ cup (1¼ ounces) unsweetened shredded coconut
- ⅔ cup (4⅔ ounces) sugar
- ¼ teaspoon table salt
- 5 large egg yolks

- ¼ cup (1 ounce) cornstarch
- 2 tablespoons unsalted butter, cut into 2 pieces
- 1½ teaspoons vanilla extract

- 1 recipe Graham Cracker Crust (page 846), baked and cooled

TOPPING

- 1½ cups heavy cream, chilled
- 1½ tablespoons sugar
- 1½ teaspoons dark rum (optional)
- ½ teaspoon vanilla extract
- 1 tablespoon unsweetened shredded coconut, toasted (see note)

1. FOR THE FILLING: Bring the coconut milk, whole milk, shredded coconut, ⅓ cup of the sugar, and the salt to a simmer in a medium saucepan over medium-high heat, stirring occasionally.

2. As the milk mixture begins to simmer, whisk the remaining ⅓ cup sugar, the egg yolks, and cornstarch together in a separate bowl. Slowly whisk 1 cup of the simmering coconut milk mixture into the yolk mixture to temper, then slowly whisk the tempered yolks back into the simmering saucepan. Reduce the heat to medium and cook, whisking vigorously, until the mixture is thickened and a few bubbles burst on the surface, about 30 seconds.

3. Off the heat, whisk in the butter and vanilla. Cool the mixture until just warm, stirring often, about 5 minutes.

4. Pour the warm filling into the baked and cooled pie crust. Lay a sheet of plastic wrap directly on the surface of the filling and refrigerate the pie until the filling is chilled and set, about 4 hours.

5. FOR THE TOPPING: Before serving, whip the cream, sugar, rum (if using), and vanilla together with an electric mixer on medium-low speed until frothy, about 1 minute. Increase the mixer speed to high and continue to whip until the cream forms soft peaks, 1 to 3 minutes. Spread the whipped cream attractively over the top of the pie and sprinkle with the toasted coconut.

CHOCOLATE CREAM PIE

WHY THIS RECIPE WORKS: Chocolate cream pies can look superb but are often gummy, gluey, overly sweet, and impossible to slice. We wanted a voluptuously creamy pie, with a well-balanced chocolate flavor somewhere between milkshake and melted candy bar, and a delicious, easy-to-slice crust.

After testing every type of cookie on the market, we hit on pulverized Oreos and a bit of melted butter for the tastiest, most tender, sliceable crumb crust. We found that the secret to perfect chocolate cream pie filling was to combine two different types of chocolate for a deeper, more complex flavor. Bittersweet or semisweet chocolate provides the main thrust of flavor, and intensely flavored unsweetened chocolate lends depth. One ounce of unsweetened chocolate may not seem like much, but it gives this pie great flavor. We also discovered that the custard's texture depended upon carefully pouring the egg yolk mixture into simmering half-and-half, then whisking in butter.

Chocolate Cream Pie
SERVES 8

For the best chocolate flavor and texture, we recommend Callebaut semisweet chocolate or Hershey's Special Dark and Hershey's unsweetened chocolate. Other brands of chocolate sandwich cookies may be substituted for the Oreos, but avoid any "double-filled" cookies because the proportion of cookie to filling won't be correct. Do not combine the egg yolks and sugar in advance of making the filling—the sugar will begin to break down the yolks, and the finished cream will be pitted.

CRUST

16 Oreo cookies, broken into rough pieces (see note)
4 tablespoons (½ stick) unsalted butter, melted and cooled

FILLING

2½ cups half-and-half
⅓ cup (2⅓ ounces) sugar
Pinch table salt
6 large egg yolks
2 tablespoons cornstarch
6 tablespoons (¾ stick) unsalted butter, cut into 6 pieces
6 ounces semisweet or bittersweet chocolate, chopped fine (see note)
1 ounce unsweetened chocolate, chopped fine (see note)
1 teaspoon vanilla extract

TOPPING

1½ cups heavy cream, chilled
2 tablespoons sugar
½ teaspoon vanilla extract

1. FOR THE CRUST: Adjust an oven rack to the middle position and heat the oven to 350 degrees. Pulse the cookies in a food processor until coarsely ground, about 15 pulses, then continue to process to fine, even crumbs, about 15 seconds. Sprinkle the butter over the crumbs and pulse to incorporate.

2. Sprinkle the mixture into a 9-inch pie plate. Following the photo on page 846, use the bottom of a measuring cup to press the crumbs into an even layer on the bottom and sides of the pie plate. Bake until the crust is fragrant and looks set, 10 to 15 minutes. Transfer the crust to a wire rack and cool completely.

3. FOR THE FILLING: Bring the half-and-half, 3 tablespoons of the sugar, and the salt to a simmer in a medium saucepan over medium-high heat, stirring occasionally.

4. As the half-and-half mixture begins to simmer, whisk the egg yolks, cornstarch, and remaining sugar together in a medium bowl until smooth. Slowly whisk about 1 cup of the simmering half-and-half mixture into the yolk mixture to temper, then slowly whisk the tempered yolks back into the simmering saucepan. Reduce the heat to medium and cook, whisking vigorously, until the mixture is thickened and a few bubbles burst on the surface, about 30 seconds.

5. Off the heat, whisk in the butter and chocolates until completely smooth and melted. Stir in the vanilla. Pour the warm filling into the baked and cooled pie crust. Lay a sheet of plastic wrap directly on the surface of the filling and refrigerate the pie until the filling is chilled and set, about 4 hours.

6. FOR THE TOPPING: Before serving, whip the cream, sugar, and vanilla together with an electric mixer on medium-low speed until frothy, about 1 minute. Increase the mixer speed to high and continue to whip until the cream forms soft peaks, 1 to 3 minutes. Spread the whipped cream attractively over the top of the pie.

CLASSIC TART DOUGH

WHY THIS RECIPE WORKS: The problem with most tarts is the crust—it's usually either too tough or too brittle. While regular pie crust is tender and flaky, classic tart crust should be fine-textured, buttery-rich, crisp, and crumbly—it is often described as being shortbread-like. We set out in the test kitchen to achieve the perfect tart dough, one that we could use in several of our tart recipes.

We found that using a full stick of butter made tart dough that tasted great and was easy to handle, yet still had a delicate crumb. Instead of using the hard-to-find superfine sugar and pastry flour that many other recipes call for, we used confectioners' sugar and all-purpose flour to achieve a crisp texture. Rolling the dough and fitting it into the tart pan was easy, and we had ample dough to patch any holes.

Classic Tart Dough

MAKES ENOUGH FOR ONE 9-INCH TART

Tart crust is sweeter, crisper, and less flaky than pie crust—it is more similar in texture to a cookie. The dough, wrapped tightly in plastic wrap, can be refrigerated for up to 2 days or frozen for up to 1 month. If frozen, let the dough thaw completely on the counter before rolling out.

- 1 large egg yolk
- 1 tablespoon heavy cream
- ½ teaspoon vanilla extract
- 1¼ cups (6¼ ounces) unbleached all-purpose flour
- ⅔ cup (2⅔ ounces) confectioners' sugar
- ¼ teaspoon table salt
- 8 tablespoons (1 stick) unsalted butter, cut into ¼-inch pieces and chilled

NOTES FROM THE TEST KITCHEN

MAKING A TART SHELL

1. After rolling the dough out into an 11-inch circle on a lightly floured work surface, wrap it loosely around the rolling pin and unroll the dough over a 9-inch tart pan with a removable bottom.

2. Lifting the edge of the dough, gently ease the dough into the pan. Press the dough into the corners and fluted sides of the pan.

3. Run the rolling pin over the top of the tart pan to remove any excess dough and make a clean edge.

4. If parts of the edge are too thin, reinforce them by pressing in some of the excess dough. If the edge is too thick, press some of the dough up over the edge of the pan and trim it away.

1. Whisk the egg yolk, cream, and vanilla together in a small bowl. Process the flour, sugar, and salt together in a food processor until combined. Scatter the butter pieces over the top and pulse until the mixture resembles coarse cornmeal, about 15 pulses.

2. With the machine running, add the egg mixture through the feed tube and continue to process until the dough just comes together around the processor blade, about 12 seconds.

3. Turn the dough onto a sheet of plastic wrap and flatten into a 6-inch disk. Wrap the dough tightly in plastic wrap and refrigerate for 1 hour. Before rolling the dough out, let it sit on the counter to soften slightly, about 10 minutes.

LEMON TART

WHY THIS RECIPE WORKS: Despite its apparent simplicity, there is much that can go wrong with a lemon tart. It can slip over the edge of sweet into cloying; its tartness can grab at your throat; it can be gluey or eggy or, even worse, metallic-tasting. Its crust can be too hard, too soft, too thick, or too sweet. We wanted a proper tart, one in which the filling is baked with the shell. For us, that meant only one thing: lemon curd. For just enough sugar to offset the acid in the lemons, we used 3 parts sugar to 2 parts lemon juice, plus a ¼ cup of lemon zest. To achieve a curd that was creamy and dense with a vibrant lemony yellow color, we used a combination of whole eggs and egg yolks. We cooked the curd over direct heat, then whisked in cold butter. And for a smooth texture, we strained the curd and stirred in heavy cream just before baking.

Lemon Tart

SERVES 8 TO 10

Once the lemon curd ingredients have been combined, cook the curd immediately; otherwise it will have a grainy finished texture. Dust with confectioners' sugar before serving, or serve with lightly whipped cream.

- 1 recipe Classic Tart Dough
  Unbleached all-purpose flour, for the work surface
- 7 large egg yolks plus 2 large whole eggs
- 1 cup (7 ounces) sugar
- ¼ cup grated zest plus ⅔ cup juice from 4 to 5 lemons
  Pinch table salt
- 4 tablespoons (½ stick) unsalted butter, cut into 4 pieces
- 3 tablespoons heavy cream

1. Roll the dough out to an 11-inch circle on a lightly floured work surface and, following the photos, fit it into a 9-inch tart pan with a removable bottom. Set the tart pan on a large plate and freeze the tart shell for 30 minutes.

2. Adjust an oven rack to the middle position and heat the oven to 375 degrees. Set the tart pan on a large baking sheet. Press a double layer of foil into the frozen tart shell and over the edges of the pan and fill with pie weights. Bake until the tart shell is golden brown and set, about 30 minutes, rotating the baking sheet halfway through.

tangy and firm enough to slice cleanly. Arranging thin-sliced peaches in lines that radiated from the center of the tart to its outer edge created cutting guides between which we artfully arranged a mix of berries. These cutting guides ensured that we could slice the tart into neat portions without marring the arrangement of the fruit. An apricot preserves and lime juice glaze brightened the fruit, and gave the tart a polished, professional look.

The Best Summer Fruit Tart

SERVES 8

This recipe calls for extra berries to account for any bruising. Ripe, unpeeled nectarines can be substituted for the peaches, if desired. Use white baking chips here, not white chocolate bars, which contain cocoa butter and will result in a loose filling. Be sure to use a light hand when dabbing on the glaze as too much force will dislodge the fruit. If the glaze begins to solidify while dabbing, microwave it for 5 to 10 seconds.

CRUST

- 1 cup (6 ounces) all-purpose flour
- ¼ cup (1¾ ounces) sugar
- ⅛ teaspoon salt
- 10 tablespoons unsalted butter
- 2 tablespoons water

TART

- ⅓ cup (2 ounces) white baking chips
- ¼ cup heavy cream
- 1 teaspoon grated lime zest plus 7 teaspoons juice (2 limes)
  Pinch salt
- 6 ounces (¾ cup) mascarpone, room temperature
- 2 ripe peaches, peeled
- 20 ounces (4 cups) raspberries, blackberries, and blueberries
- ⅓ cup apricot preserves

1. FOR THE CRUST: Adjust oven rack to middle position and heat oven to 350 degrees. Whisk flour, sugar, and salt together in bowl. Melt butter in small saucepan over medium-high heat, swirling pan occasionally, until foaming subsides. Continue to cook, stirring and scraping bottom of pan with heatproof spatula, until milk solids are dark golden brown and butter has nutty aroma, 1 to 3 minutes. Remove pan from heat and add water. When bubbling subsides, transfer butter to bowl with flour mixture, scraping pan with spatula. Stir until mixture is well combined. Transfer dough to 9-inch tart pan with removable bottom and let dough rest until warm to the touch, about 10 minutes.

2. Use hands to evenly press and smooth dough over bottom and up side of pan (using two-thirds of dough for bottom crust and remaining third for side). Place tart pan on wire rack set in rimmed baking sheet. Bake until crust is golden brown, 25 to 30 minutes, rotating pan halfway through baking. Let

3. Carefully remove the weights and foil and continue to bake the tart shell until it is fully baked and golden, 5 to 10 minutes longer. Transfer the tart crust with the baking sheet to a wire rack and cool the tart shell slightly while making the filling.

4. Whisk the egg yolks and whole eggs together in a medium saucepan. Whisk in the sugar until combined, then whisk in the lemon zest and juice and salt. Add the butter and cook over medium-low heat, stirring constantly, until the mixture thickens slightly and registers 170 degrees on an instant-read thermometer, about 5 minutes. Immediately pour the mixture through a fine-mesh strainer into a bowl and stir in the cream.

5. Pour the lemon filling into the warm tart shell. Bake the tart on the baking sheet until the filling is shiny and opaque and the center jiggles slightly when shaken, 10 to 15 minutes. Let the tart cool completely on the baking sheet, about 1½ hours. To serve, remove the outer metal ring of the tart pan, slide a thin metal spatula between the tart and the tart pan bottom, and carefully slide the tart onto a serving platter or cutting board.

THE BEST SUMMER FRUIT TART

WHY THIS RECIPE WORKS: By trading the traditional rolled pastry and pastry cream filling for easier, faster alternatives, we produced a fresh fruit tart that is as appealing to make as it is to eat. Stirring melted butter into the dry ingredients yielded a malleable dough that could be pressed into the pan; for extra flavor, we browned the butter first and added back water that we lost so that there was enough moisture to help the flour form gluten (the protein network that would give the dough structure). A mix of mascarpone cheese, melted white baking chips, and lime juice and zest gave us a quick-to-make filling that was lush and creamy but also cool completely, about 1 hour. (Cooled crust can be wrapped loosely in plastic wrap and stored at room temperature for up to 24 hours before filling.)

3. FOR THE TART: Microwave baking chips, cream, lime zest, and salt in medium bowl, stirring every 10 seconds, until chips are melted, 30 to 60 seconds. Whisk in one-third of mascarpone to cool mixture, then whisk in 6 teaspoons lime juice and remaining mascarpone until smooth. Transfer filling to cooled tart shell and smooth into even layer.

4. Place peach stem side down on cutting board. Placing knife just to side of pit, cut down to remove one side of peach. Turn peach 180 degrees and cut off opposite side. Slice off remaining 2 sides. Arrange pieces cut side down on cutting board and slice into ¼-inch thick half-moon shapes. Repeat with second peach. Select the 24 best slices.

5. Arrange 8 berries, evenly spaced, around outer edge of tart. Using berries as guide, arrange 8 sets of 3 peach slices in filling, slightly overlapping them with rounded side up, starting at center and ending on right side of each berry at outer edge of tart. Arrange remaining berries in attractive pattern between peach slices, covering as much of filling as possible and keeping fruit in even layer.

6. Microwave preserves and remaining 1 teaspoon lime juice in small bowl until fluid, 20 to 30 seconds. Strain mixture through fine-mesh strainer. Using pastry brush, gently dab mixture over fruit, avoiding crust. Refrigerate tart for 30 minutes.

7. Remove outer metal ring of tart pan. Insert thin metal spatula between crust and pan bottom to loosen tart; carefully slide tart onto serving platter. Let tart sit at room temperature for 15 minutes. Using peaches as guide, cut into wedges and serve. (Tart can be refrigerated for up to 24 hours. If refrigerated for more than 1 hour, let tart sit at room temperature for 1 hour before serving.)

FRESH FRUIT TART WITH PASTRY CREAM

WHY THIS RECIPE WORKS: Fresh fruit tarts usually offer little substance beyond their dazzling beauty, with rubbery or institutionalized pudding fillings, soggy crusts, and underripe, flavorless fruit. We set out to create a buttery, crisp crust filled with rich, lightly sweetened pastry cream, topped with fresh, glistening fruit. We started with our classic tart dough as the crust and baked it until it was golden brown. We then filled the tart with pastry cream, made with half-and-half that was enriched with butter and thickened with just enough cornstarch to keep its shape without becoming gummy. For the fruit, we chose a combination of kiwi, which we peeled and sliced into half-moons, raspberries, and blueberries. We found that it was important not to wash the berries, as washing causes them to bruise and bleed and makes for a less than attractive tart. The finishing touch: a drizzle with a jelly glaze for a glistening presentation.

Fresh Fruit Tart with Pastry Cream

SERVES 8 TO 10

The pastry cream can be made a day or two in advance, but do not fill the prebaked tart shell until just before serving. Once filled, the tart should be topped with fruit, glazed, and served within half an hour or so. Don't wash the berries or they will lose their flavor and shape.

PASTRY CREAM

- 2 cups half-and-half
- ½ cup (3½ ounces) sugar
- Pinch table salt
- 5 large egg yolks
- 3 tablespoons cornstarch
- 4 tablespoons (½ stick) unsalted butter, cut into 4 pieces
- 1½ teaspoons vanilla extract

TART SHELL AND FRUIT

- 1 recipe Classic Tart Dough (page 861)
  Unbleached all-purpose flour, for the work surface
- 2 large kiwis, peeled, halved lengthwise, and sliced ⅜ inch thick
- 2 cups (10 ounces) raspberries (see note)
- 1 cup (5 ounces) blueberries (see note)
- ½ cup red currant or apple jelly

1. FOR THE PASTRY CREAM: Bring the half-and-half, 6 tablespoons of the sugar, and the salt to a simmer in a medium saucepan over medium-high heat, stirring occasionally.

2. As the half-and-half mixture begins to simmer, whisk the egg yolks, cornstarch, and remaining 2 tablespoons sugar together in a medium bowl until smooth. Slowly whisk about 1 cup of the simmering half-and-half mixture into the yolks to temper, then slowly whisk the tempered yolks back into the simmering saucepan. Reduce the heat to medium and cook, whisking vigorously, until the mixture is thickened and a few bubbles burst on the surface, about 30 seconds.

3. Off the heat, stir in the butter and vanilla. Transfer the mixture to a medium bowl, lay a sheet of plastic wrap directly on the surface, and refrigerate the pastry cream until chilled and firm, about 3 hours.

4. FOR THE TART SHELL AND FRUIT: Roll the dough out to an 11-inch circle on a lightly floured work surface and, following the photos on page 861, fit it into a 9-inch tart pan with a removable bottom. Set the tart pan on a large plate and freeze the tart shell for 30 minutes.

5. Adjust an oven rack to the middle position and heat the oven to 375 degrees. Set the tart pan on a large baking sheet. Press a double layer of foil into the frozen tart shell and over the edges of the pan and fill with pie weights. Bake until the tart shell is golden brown and set, about 30 minutes, rotating the baking sheet halfway through.

6. Carefully remove the weights and foil and continue to bake the tart shell until it is fully baked and golden, 5 to 10 minutes longer. Transfer the tart shell with the baking sheet to a wire rack and cool the tart shell completely, about 1 hour.

7. Spread the chilled pastry cream evenly over the bottom of the cooled tart shell. Shingle the kiwi slices around the edge of the tart, then arrange three rows of raspberries inside the kiwi. Finally, arrange a mound of blueberries in the center.

8. Melt the jelly in a small saucepan over medium-high heat, stirring occasionally to smooth out any lumps. Using a pastry brush, dab the melted jelly over the fruit. To serve, remove the outer metal ring of the tart pan, slide a thin metal spatula between the tart and the tart pan bottom, and carefully slide the tart onto a serving platter or cutting board.

Mixed Berry Tart with Pastry Cream

Follow the recipe for Fresh Fruit Tart with Pastry Cream, omitting the kiwi and adding 2 cups (10 ounces) extra berries (including blackberries or quartered strawberries). Combine the berries in a large plastic bag and toss them gently to mix. Carefully spread the berries in an even layer over the tart. Glaze and serve as directed.

FREE-FORM FRUIT TART

WHY THIS RECIPE WORKS: Few things are better than a summer fruit pie, but that takes time (and skill). What we wanted was simpler: a buttery, flaky crust paired with juicy summer fruit—with half the work of a regular pie. A free-form tart (a single layer of buttery pie dough folded up around fresh fruit) seemed the obvious solution.

Without the support of a pie plate, tender crusts are prone to leak juice, and this results in soggy bottoms. For our crust, we used a high proportion of butter to flour, which provided the most buttery flavor and tender texture without compromising the structure. We then turned to a French technique in pastry making called *fraisage*. To begin, butter is only partially cut into the dry ingredients. Then, with the heel of the hand, the cook presses the barely mixed dough firmly against the counter. As a result, the chunks of butter are pressed into long, thin sheets that create lots of flaky layers when the dough is baked. We rolled the dough into a 12-inch circle for a crust that was thick enough to contain a lot of fruit but thin enough to bake evenly and thoroughly. We placed the fruit in the middle, then lifted the dough up and back over the fruit and pleated it loosely to allow for shrinkage. The bright summer fruit needed only the simple addition of sugar.

Free-Form Summer Fruit Tart
SERVES 6

The dough, wrapped tightly in plastic wrap, can be refrigerated for up to 2 days or frozen for up to 1 month. If frozen, let the dough thaw completely on the counter before rolling it out. Though we prefer a tart made with a mix of stone fruits and berries, you can use only one type of fruit if you prefer. Taste the fruit before adding sugar to it; use the lesser amount if the fruit is very sweet, more if it is tart. However much sugar you use, do not add it to the fruit until you are ready to fill and form the tart. Serve with vanilla ice cream, lightly sweetened whipped cream, or crème fraîche.

RUSTIC TART DOUGH

1½ cups (7½ ounces) unbleached all-purpose flour, plus extra for the work surface

½ teaspoon table salt

10 tablespoons (1¼ sticks) unsalted butter, cut into ½-inch pieces and chilled

4–6 tablespoons ice water

FILLING

1 pound peaches, nectarines, apricots, or plums, pitted and sliced into ½-inch-thick wedges (see note)

1 cup (5 ounces) blueberries, raspberries, or blackberries (see note)

3–5 tablespoons plus 1 tablespoon sugar (see note)

1. FOR THE RUSTIC TART DOUGH: Process the flour and salt in a food processor until combined. Scatter the butter pieces over the top and pulse until the mixture resembles coarse bread crumbs and the butter pieces are about the size of small peas, about 10 pulses. Continue to pulse, adding the water through the feed tube 1 tablespoon at a time, until the dough begins to form small curds that hold together when pinched with your fingers (the dough will be crumbly), about 10 pulses.

2. Following the photos, turn the dough crumbs out onto a lightly floured work surface and gather into a rectangular-shaped pile. Starting at the farthest end, use the heel of your hand to smear a small amount of dough against the work surface. Continue to smear the dough until all the crumbs have been worked. Gather the smeared crumbs together in another rectangular-shaped pile and repeat the process. Flatten the dough into a 6-inch disk, wrap it tightly in plastic wrap, and refrigerate for 1 hour. Before rolling the dough out, let it sit on the counter to soften slightly, about 10 minutes.

3. Roll the dough into a 12-inch circle between two large sheets of floured parchment paper. Slide the dough, still between the parchment sheets, onto a large baking sheet and refrigerate until firm, about 20 minutes.

4. FOR THE FILLING: Adjust an oven rack to the middle position and heat the oven to 375 degrees. Gently toss the fruit and sugar together in a large bowl. Remove the top sheet of parchment paper from the dough. Mound the fruit in the center of the dough, leaving a 2½-inch border around the edge. Following photo 2 on page 868, and being careful to leave a ½-inch border of dough around the fruit, fold the outermost 2 inches of dough over the fruit, pleating it every 2 to 3 inches as needed; gently pinch the pleated dough to secure, but do not press the dough into the fruit. Working quickly, brush the dough with water and sprinkle evenly with the additional 1 tablespoon sugar.

5. Bake the tart until the crust is deep golden brown and the fruit is bubbling, about 1 hour, rotating the baking sheet halfway through.

MIXING A FLAKY DOUGH

1. Starting at one end of the rectangular pile of dough, smear a small amount of the dough against the work surface with the heel of your hand. Repeat this process (called fraisage) until the rest of the buttery crumbs have been worked.

2. Gather the smeared bits into another rectangular pile and repeat the smearing process until all of the crumbs have been worked again. This second time won't take as long and will result in large flakes of dough.

6. Cool the tart on the baking sheet on a wire rack for 10 minutes, then use the parchment paper to gently transfer the tart to a wire rack. Use a metal spatula to loosen the tart from the parchment and remove the parchment. Cool the tart on the rack until the juices have thickened, about 25 minutes. Serve warm or at room temperature.

APPLE GALETTE

WHY THIS RECIPE WORKS: The French tart known as an apple galette should have a flaky crust and a layer of shingled caramelized apples. But it's challenging to make a crust strong enough to hold the apples and still be eaten out of hand—most recipes create a tough, bland crust. Choosing the right flour put us on the right track. All-purpose flour contained too much gluten; it made the pastry tough. Lower-protein pastry flour created a flaky and sturdy pastry. As pastry flour is hard to find, we mixed regular all-purpose flour with instant flour. Technique also proved to be important. We used the French fraisage method of blending butter into dough (see page 864). We found that any thinly sliced apple would work, although we slightly preferred Granny Smith.

Apple Galette
SERVES 10 TO 12
The most common brands of instant flour are Wondra and Shake & Blend; they are sold in canisters in the baking aisle. The galette can be made without instant flour, using 2 cups unbleached all-purpose flour and 2 tablespoons cornstarch; however, you might have to increase the amount of ice water. The dough, wrapped tightly in plastic wrap, can be refrigerated for up to 2 days or frozen for up to 1 month. If frozen, let the dough thaw completely on the counter before rolling out. Serve with ice cream, whipped cream, or crème fraîche.

DOUGH

1½ cups (7½ ounces) unbleached all-purpose flour, plus extra for the work surface

½ cup (2½ ounces) instant flour (see note)

½ teaspoon table salt

½ teaspoon sugar

12 tablespoons (1½ sticks) unsalted butter, cut into ¼-inch pieces and chilled

7–9 tablespoons ice water

TOPPING

1½ pounds Granny Smith apples (about 3 large), peeled, cored, and sliced ⅛ inch thick

2 tablespoons unsalted butter, cut into ¼-inch pieces

¼ cup (1¾ ounces) sugar

3 tablespoons apple jelly

NOTES FROM THE TEST KITCHEN

PREPARING APPLE GALETTE

1. Cut a piece of parchment to measure exactly 16 by 12 inches, then roll the dough out on top of the parchment until it just overhangs the edge and is about ⅛ inch thick.

2. Trim the dough so that the edges are even with the parchment paper. We use the parchment as a guide to cut a perfectly even rectangle of dough from which we can make a large thin crust.

3. Roll up 1 inch of each edge to create a ½-inch-thick border. This border is decorative and helps keep the apple slices in place.

4. Slide the parchment and dough onto a rimmed baking sheet. Starting in one corner, shingle the apple slices in tidy rows on the diagonal over the dough, overlapping each row by a third.

---

1. FOR THE DOUGH: Process the flours, salt, and sugar together in a food processor until combined. Scatter the butter pieces over the top and pulse until the mixture resembles coarse cornmeal, about 15 pulses. Continue to pulse, adding the water through the feed tube 1 tablespoon at a time until the dough begins to form small curds that hold together when pinched with your fingers (the dough will be crumbly), about 10 pulses.

2. Following the photos on page 865, turn the dough crumbs onto a lightly floured work surface and gather into a rectangular-shaped pile. Starting at the farthest end, use the heel of your hand to smear a small amount of dough against the work surface. Continue to smear the dough until all the crumbs have been worked. Gather the smeared crumbs together in another rectangular-shaped pile and repeat the process. Press the dough into a 4-inch square, wrap it tightly in plastic wrap, and refrigerate for 1 hour. Before rolling the dough out, let it sit on the counter to soften slightly, about 10 minutes.

3. Adjust an oven rack to the middle position and heat the oven to 400 degrees. Cut a piece of parchment to measure exactly 16 by 12 inches. Following the photos, roll the dough out over the parchment, dusting with flour as needed, until it just overhangs the parchment. Trim the edges of the dough even with the parchment. Roll the outer 1 inch of the dough up to create a ½-inch-thick border. Slide the parchment paper with the dough onto a large rimmed baking sheet.

4. FOR THE TOPPING: Starting in one corner of the tart, shingle the apple slices onto the crust in tidy diagonal rows, overlapping them by a third. Dot with the butter and sprinkle evenly with the sugar. Bake the tart until the bottom is deep golden brown and the apples have caramelized, 45 to 60 minutes, rotating the baking sheet halfway through.

5. Melt the jelly in a small saucepan over medium-high heat, stirring occasionally to smooth out any lumps. Brush the glaze over the apples and let the tart cool slightly on the baking sheet for 10 minutes. Slide the tart onto a large platter or cutting board and slice the tart in half lengthwise, then crosswise into square pieces. Serve warm or at room temperature.

FRENCH APPLE TART

WHY THIS RECIPE WORKS: Classically elegant French apple tart is little more than apples and pastry, but such simplicity means that imperfections like tough or mushy apples, unbalanced flavor, and a sodden crust are hard to hide. We wanted a foolproof way to achieve tender apples and a flavorful, buttery crust. We parbaked our quick pat-in-pan dough for a cookie-like texture that gave the tart a sturdy base. For intense fruit flavor, we packed the tart with a whopping 5 pounds of Golden Delicious apples. We cooked half into a concentrated puree, which we made more luxurious with butter and apricot preserves. For textural contrast, we sliced and parcooked the remaining apples and used them to adorn the top. A thin coat of preserves and a final stint under the broiler provided an attractively caramelized finish.

French Apple Tart

SERVES 8

You may have extra apple slices after topping the tart in step 6. If you don't have a potato masher, you can puree the applesauce in a food processor. For the best flavor and texture, be sure to bake the crust thoroughly. The tart is best served the day it is assembled. To ensure that the outer ring of the pan releases easily from the tart, avoid getting apple puree and apricot glaze on the crust.

CRUST

- 1⅓ cups (6⅔ ounces) all-purpose flour
- 5 tablespoons (2¼ ounces) sugar
- ½ teaspoon salt
- 10 tablespoons unsalted butter, melted

FILLING

- 10 Golden Delicious apples (8 ounces each), peeled and cored
- 3 tablespoons unsalted butter
- 1 tablespoon water
- ½ cup apricot preserves
- ¼ teaspoon salt

1. FOR THE CRUST: Adjust 1 oven rack to lowest position and second rack 5 to 6 inches from broiler element. Heat oven to 350 degrees. Whisk flour, sugar, and salt together in bowl. Add melted butter and stir until dough forms. Using your hands, press two-thirds of dough into bottom of 9-inch tart pan with removable bottom. Press remaining dough into fluted sides of pan. Press and smooth dough with your hands to even thickness. Place pan on wire rack set in rimmed baking sheet and bake on lowest rack, until crust is deep golden brown and firm to touch, 30 to 35 minutes, rotating pan halfway through baking. Set aside until ready to fill.

2. FOR THE FILLING: Cut 5 apples lengthwise into quarters and cut each quarter lengthwise into 4 slices. Melt 1 tablespoon butter in 12-inch skillet over medium heat. Add apple slices and water and toss to combine. Cover and cook, stirring occasionally, until apples begin to turn translucent and are slightly pliable, 3 to 5 minutes. Transfer apples to large plate, spread into single layer, and set aside to cool.

3. While apples cook, microwave apricot preserves until fluid, about 30 seconds. Strain preserves through fine-mesh strainer into small bowl, reserving solids. Set aside 3 tablespoons strained preserves for brushing tart.

4. Cut remaining 5 apples into ½-inch-thick wedges. Melt remaining 2 tablespoons butter in now-empty skillet over medium heat. Add remaining strained apricot preserves, reserved apricot solids, apples, and salt. Cover and cook, stirring occasionally, until apples are very soft, about 10 minutes.

5. Mash apples to puree with potato masher. Continue to cook, stirring occasionally, until puree is reduced to 2 cups, about 5 minutes.

6. Transfer apple puree to baked tart shell and smooth surface. Select 5 thinnest slices of sautéed apple and set aside. Starting at outer edge of tart, arrange remaining slices, tightly overlapping in concentric circles. Bend reserved slices to fit in center. Bake tart, still on wire rack in sheet, on lowest rack, for 30 minutes. Remove tart from oven and heat broiler.

7. While broiler heats, warm reserved preserves in microwave until fluid, about 20 seconds. Brush evenly over surface of apples, avoiding tart crust. Broil tart, checking every 30 seconds and turning as necessary, until apples are attractively caramelized, 1 to 3 minutes. Let tart cool for at least 1½ hours. Remove outer metal ring of tart pan, slide thin metal spatula between tart and pan bottom, and carefully slide tart onto serving platter. Cut into wedges and serve.

TO MAKE AHEAD: Baked crust, apple slices, and apple puree can be made up to 24 hours in advance. Apple slices and puree should be refrigerated separately. Assemble tart with refrigerated apple slices and puree and bake as directed, adding 5 minutes to baking time.

NOTES FROM THE TEST KITCHEN

MAKING AN APPLE ROSETTE

1. Starting at edges and working toward center, arrange most of the cooled sautéed apple slices in tightly overlapping concentric circles.

2. Bend remaining slices to fit in center.

FREE-FORM APPLE TART

WHY THIS RECIPE WORKS: Apple tarts are easier to make than apple pie, but they have their problems: The filling can dry out owing to the lack of a top crust, and the dough can be limp and tacky. We wanted a simple free-form tart with moist, flavorful apples neatly contained by a flaky, easy-to-handle dough.

Off the bat, we decided to borrow the crust from our Free-Form Summer Fruit Tart recipe (see page 864)—it's sturdy yet flaky, with a great buttery flavor. As with our Classic Apple Pie (see page 846), we favored a combination of Granny Smith and McIntosh apples. To ensure that the apples cooked through in a short amount of time, we sliced them ¼ inch thick. All the apples needed in the way of flavor enhancement was lemon juice, sugar, and cinnamon.

Free-Form Apple Tart
SERVES 6

Serve with vanilla ice cream or lightly sweetened whipped cream.

- 1 pound Granny Smith apples (about 2 large), peeled, cored, and sliced ¼ inch thick
- 1 pound McIntosh apples (about 2 large), peeled, cored, and sliced ¼ inch thick
- ½ cup (3½ ounces) plus 1 tablespoon sugar
- 1 tablespoon juice from 1 lemon
- ⅛ teaspoon ground cinnamon
- 1 recipe Rustic Tart Dough (page 864), rolled into a 12-inch circle and chilled

1. Adjust an oven rack to the middle position and heat the oven to 375 degrees. Toss the apples, ½ cup of the sugar, the lemon juice, and cinnamon together in a large bowl.

NOTES FROM THE TEST KITCHEN

MAKING A FREE-FORM APPLE TART

1. Discard the top piece of parchment. Stack the apple slices into a circular wall, leaving a 2½-inch border of dough. Fill the center with the remaining apples.

2. Fold 2 inches of the dough up over the fruit, leaving a ½-inch border between the fruit and the edge of the tart shell. This ½-inch space helps prevent the tart juices from leaking through the folds in the shell.

2. Remove the top sheet of parchment paper from the dough. Following the photos, stack some of the apples into a circular wall, leaving a 2½-inch border around the edge. Fill in the middle of the tart with the remaining apples. Being careful to leave a ½-inch border of dough around the fruit, fold the outermost 2 inches of dough over the fruit, pleating it every 2 to 3 inches as needed; gently pinch the pleated dough to secure, but do not press the dough into the fruit. Working quickly, brush the dough with water and sprinkle evenly with the remaining 1 tablespoon sugar.

3. Bake the tart on a large rimmed baking sheet until the crust is deep golden brown and the apples are tender, about 1 hour, rotating the baking sheet halfway through.

4. Cool the tart on the baking sheet on a wire rack for 10 minutes, then use the parchment paper to gently transfer the tart to the wire rack. Use a metal spatula to loosen the tart from the parchment and remove the parchment. Cool the tart on the rack until the juices have thickened, about 25 minutes. Serve warm or at room temperature.

TARTE TATIN

WHY THIS RECIPE WORKS: Making a true *tarte Tatin* requires an investment of time and a certain amount of skill. Traditionally, the apples are cooked in a skillet until caramelized, then topped with homemade pastry and cooked in the oven. Before serving, the tart is masterfully flipped onto a serving platter. Yes, this version is great, but we wanted to simplify it enough for a weeknight dessert.

We first baked a sheet of store-bought puff pastry until it was beautifully golden brown. While the pastry baked, we caramelized the apples in a skillet until they were tender. We then spooned the apples over the pastry, arranging them in three even rows with a ½-inch border around the outside of the pastry. As a final touch, we created a simple sauce by adding heavy cream and Grand Marnier to the juices left behind after the apples were cooked.

30-Minute Tarte Tatin
SERVES 6 TO 8

To get this dessert on the table in 30 minutes, peel the apples while the oven preheats and the pastry thaws, and then bake the pastry while the apples are caramelizing. This dessert is especially good with Tangy Whipped Cream (page 830).

- 1 (9½ by 9-inch) sheet frozen puff pastry, thawed
- 8 tablespoons (1 stick) unsalted butter
- ¾ cup (5¼ ounces) sugar
- 2 pounds Granny Smith apples (about 4 large), peeled, quartered, and cored
- ¼ cup heavy cream
- 2 tablespoons Grand Marnier, spiced rum, or Calvados (optional)

1. Adjust an oven rack to the middle position and heat the oven to 400 degrees. Line a rimmed baking sheet with parchment paper. Unfold the puff pastry, lay it on the prepared baking sheet, and bake until golden brown and puffed, 15 to 20 minutes, rotating the baking sheet halfway through. Transfer the baked pastry sheet to a serving platter and press lightly to flatten if domed.

2. Meanwhile, melt the butter in a 12-inch nonstick skillet over high heat. Remove the pan from the heat and sprinkle evenly with the sugar. Lay the apples in the skillet, return the skillet to high heat, and cook until the juice in the pan turns a rich amber color and the apples are caramelized, about 15 minutes, turning the apples halfway through.

3. Remove the apples from the pan one at a time and arrange in three overlapping rows on the baked pastry sheet, leaving a ½-inch border. Spoon about half of the pan juice over the apples.

4. Whisk the cream and Grand Marnier (if using) into the remaining juice in the pan and bring to a simmer. Pour some sauce over the tart and serve, passing the remaining sauce separately.

Pear Tatin

We like to use Bosc or Bartlett pears here because they maintain their shape nicely when cooked. If you have it on hand, substitute Poire William (or other pear liqueur) for the Grand Marnier.

Follow the recipe for 30-Minute Tarte Tatin, substituting 2 pounds Bosc or Bartlett pears for the apples. Increase the cooking time by 5 to 10 minutes if necessary.

BEST CHOCOLATE TART

WHY THIS RECIPE WORKS: For us, a great chocolate tart should possess deep chocolate flavor, a rich, lush texture, and a sophisticated presentation. First we made a custardy filling by melting intense dark chocolate into hot cream, adding eggs, and baking. To enrich the filling's flavor, we added some butter and a little instant espresso to echo the bittersweetness of the chocolate. Because custards tend to curdle under high heat, we baked the tart in a very low 250-degree oven for a smooth and silky texture. To make our tart a showstopper, we topped it with a simple glossy glaze of chocolate, cream, and corn syrup. A classic sweet pastry dough flavored with ground almonds made the perfect complement to the chocolate filling.

Best Chocolate Tart

SERVES 12

Toasted and skinned hazelnuts can be substituted for the almonds. Use good-quality dark chocolate containing a cacao percentage between 60 and 65 percent; our favorites are Ghirardelli 60% Cacao Bittersweet Chocolate and Callebaut Intense Dark Chocolate, L-60-40NV. Let tart sit at room temperature for 30 minutes before glazing in step 6.

The tart can be garnished with chocolate curls or with a flaky coarse sea salt, such as Maldon. Serve with lightly sweetened whipped cream; if you like, flavor the whipped cream with cognac or vanilla extract.

CRUST
- 1 large egg yolk
- 2 tablespoons heavy cream
- ½ cup sliced almonds, toasted
- ¼ cup (1¾ ounces) sugar
- 1 cup (5 ounces) all-purpose flour
- ¼ teaspoon salt
- 6 tablespoons unsalted butter, cut into ½-inch pieces

FILLING
- 1¼ cups heavy cream
- ½ teaspoon instant espresso powder
- ¼ teaspoon salt
- 9 ounces bittersweet chocolate, chopped fine
- 4 tablespoons unsalted butter, cut into thin slices and softened
- 2 large eggs, lightly beaten, room temperature

GLAZE
- 3 tablespoons heavy cream
- 1 tablespoon light corn syrup
- 2 ounces bittersweet chocolate, chopped fine
- 1 tablespoon hot water

1. **FOR THE CRUST:** Beat egg yolk and cream together in small bowl. Process almonds and sugar in food processor until nuts are finely ground, 15 to 20 seconds. Add flour and salt; pulse to combine, about 10 pulses. Scatter butter over

flour mixture; pulse to cut butter into flour until mixture resembles coarse meal, about 15 pulses. With processor running, add egg yolk mixture and process until dough forms ball, about 10 seconds. Transfer dough to large sheet of plastic wrap and press into 6-inch disk; wrap dough in plastic and refrigerate until firm but malleable, about 30 minutes. (Dough can be refrigerated for up to 3 days; before using, let stand at room temperature until malleable but still cool.)

2. Roll out dough between 2 large sheets of plastic into 11-inch round about ⅜ inch thick. (If dough becomes too soft and sticky to work with, slip it onto baking sheet and refrigerate until workable.) Place dough round (still in plastic) on baking sheet and refrigerate until firm but pliable, about 15 minutes.

3. Adjust oven rack to middle position and heat oven to 375 degrees. Spray 9-inch tart pan with removable bottom with vegetable oil spray. Keeping dough on sheet, remove top layer of plastic. Invert tart pan (with bottom) on top of dough round. Press on tart pan to cut dough. Using both hands, pick up sheet and tart pan and carefully invert both, setting tart pan right side up. Remove sheet and peel off plastic; reserve plastic. Roll over edges of tart pan with rolling pin to cut dough. Gently ease and press dough into bottom of pan, reserving scraps. Roll dough scraps into ¾-inch rope (various lengths are OK). Line edge of tart pan with rope(s) and gently press into fluted sides. Line tart pan with reserved plastic and, using measuring cup, gently press and smooth dough to even thickness (sides should be about ¼ inch thick). Using paring knife, trim any excess dough above rim of tart; discard scraps. Freeze dough-lined pan until dough is firm, 20 to 30 minutes.

4. Set dough-lined pan on baking sheet. Spray 12-inch square of aluminum foil with oil spray and press foil, sprayed side down, into pan; fill with 2 cups pie weights. Bake until dough is dry and light golden brown, about 25 minutes, rotating sheet halfway through baking. Carefully remove foil and weights and continue to bake until pastry is rich golden brown and fragrant, 8 to 10 minutes longer. Let cool completely on baking sheet on wire rack.

5. FOR THE FILLING: Heat oven to 250 degrees. Bring cream, espresso powder, and salt to simmer in small saucepan over medium heat, stirring once or twice to dissolve espresso powder and salt. Meanwhile, place chocolate in large heatproof bowl. Pour simmering cream mixture over chocolate, cover, and let stand for 5 minutes to allow chocolate to soften. Using whisk, stir mixture slowly and gently (so as not to incorporate air) until homogeneous. Add butter and continue to whisk gently until fully incorporated. Pour beaten eggs through fine-mesh strainer into chocolate mixture; whisk slowly until mixture is homogeneous and glossy. Pour filling into tart crust and shake gently from side to side to distribute and smooth surface; pop any large bubbles with toothpick or skewer. Bake tart, on baking sheet, until outer edge of filling is just set and very faint cracks appear on

surface, 30 to 35 minutes; filling will still be very wobbly. Let cool completely on baking sheet on wire rack. Refrigerate, uncovered, until filling is chilled and set, at least 3 hours or up to 18 hours.

6. FOR THE GLAZE: Thirty minutes before glazing, remove tart from refrigerator. Bring cream and corn syrup to simmer in small saucepan over medium heat; stir once or twice to combine. Remove pan from heat, add chocolate, and cover. Let stand for 5 minutes to allow chocolate to soften. Whisk gently (so as not to incorporate air) until mixture is smooth, then whisk in hot water until glaze is homogeneous, shiny, and pourable. Working quickly, pour glaze onto center of tart. To distribute glaze, tilt tart and allow glaze to run to edge. (Spreading glaze with spatula will leave marks on surface.) Pop any large bubbles with toothpick or skewer. Let cool completely, about 1 hour.

7. Remove outer ring from tart pan. Insert thin-bladed metal spatula between crust and pan bottom to loosen tart; slide tart onto serving platter. Cut into wedges and serve.

NOTES FROM THE TEST KITCHEN

FITTING DELICATE PASTRY INTO A TART PAN

After your dough has been refrigerated, follow these easy steps to get it into the tart pan. This novel method works with any tart dough, but it is especially helpful when working with higher-fat, more fragile pastry.

1. Invert tart pan (with bottom) onto dough round. Press down on tart pan to perforate dough. Invert baking sheet, holding tart pan in place, then set down so that tart pan is right side up. Remove baking sheet and plastic wrap.

2. Roll over dough edges with rolling pin to cut off excess, reserving scraps. Gently press dough into bottom of pan in even layer.

3. Roll dough scraps into ¾-inch rope(s). Line fluted edges of pan with ropes and press evenly into sides.

THE AMERICA'S TEST KITCHEN SHOPPING GUIDE

SHOPPING FOR EQUIPMENT

With a well-stocked kitchen, you'll be able to take on any recipe. But with so much equipment out there on the market, how do you figure out what's what? Price often correlates with design, not performance. Over the years, our test kitchen has evaluated thousands of products. We've gone through copious rounds of testing and have identified the most important attributes in every piece of equipment, so when you go shopping you'll know what to look for. And because our test kitchen accepts no support from product manufacturers, you can trust our ratings. Prices in this chart are based on shopping at online retailers and will vary. See AmericasTestKitchen.com for updates to these testings.

KNIVES AND MORE	ITEM	WHAT TO LOOK FOR	TEST KITCHEN FAVORITES
MUST-HAVE ITEMS	CHEF'S KNIFE	• High-carbon stainless-steel knife • Thin, curved 8-inch blade • Lightweight • Comfortable grip and nonslip handle	**Victorinox Swiss Army Fibrox Pro 8" Chef's Knife** $39.95 For older kids: **Victorinox Swiss Army Fibrox Pro 6" Chef's Knife** $20.99 For younger kids: **Opinel Le Petit Chef + Finger Guard** $39.95
	SERRATED KNIFE	• 10-inch blade • Fewer broader, deeper, pointed serrations • Thinner blade angle • Comfortable, grippy handle • Medium weight	**Mercer Culinary Millennia 10" Wide Bread Knife** $22.10
	SLICING/ CARVING KNIFE	• Tapered 12-inch blade for slicing large cuts of meat • Oval scallops (called a granton edge) carved into blade • Fairly rigid blade with rounded tip	**Victorinox Swiss Army 12" Fibrox Pro Granton Edge Slicing/Carving Knife** $54.65
	PARING KNIFE	• Comfortable grip • Thin, flexible blade with pointed tip • 3- to 3½-inch blade	**Victorinox Swiss Army Fibrox Pro 3¼-Inch Spear Point Paring Knife** $9.47
	SERRATED PARING KNIFE	•Thin blade with razor-sharp serrations for safe, precise slicing • Hefty but nimble	**Wüsthof Classic 3.5-Inch Fully Serrated Paring Knife** $59.95 Best Buy: **Victorinox Serrated Paring Knife** $5.95
	STEAK KNIVES	• Super-sharp, straight-edged blade • Sturdy—not wobbly—blade	**Victorinox Swiss Army 6-Piece Rosewood Steak Set, Spear Point, Straight Edge** $170.74 for set of 6 Best Buy: **Chicago Cutlery Walnut Tradition 4-Piece Steak Knife Set** $17.95 for set of 4

KNIVES AND MORE	ITEM	WHAT TO LOOK FOR	TEST KITCHEN FAVORITES
	SANTOKU KNIFE	• Narrow, curved, and short blade • Comfortable grip	Misono UX10 Santoku 7.0" $179.50
	BONING KNIFE	• Sharp, moderately flexible, 5.5-inch blade that maintains its edge • Slender handle and slim profile for easy grasp	Zwilling Pro 5.5" Flexible Boning Knife $99.95
	MEAT CLEAVER	• Razor-sharp blade • Balanced weight between handle and blade • Comfortable grip	Shun Classic Meat Cleaver $149 Best Buy: Lamson Products 7.25" Walnut Handle Meat Cleaver $59.95
	VEGETABLE CLEAVER	• Slim blade for slicing through thick, hard vegetables • Lightweight	MAC Japanese Series 6½-Inch Japanese Vegetable Cleaver $75
	HYBRID CHEF'S KNIFE	• High-carbon stainless-steel knife • Lightweight • Thin blade that tapers from spine to cutting edge and from handle to tip	Masamoto VG-10 Gyutou, 8.2" $136.50
	CARBON-STEEL KNIFE	• 8-inch blade • Sloping ergonomic handle • Narrow, razor-sharp blade	Bob Kramer 8" Carbon Steel Chef's Knife by Zwilling J.A. Henckels $299.95 Best Buy: Togiharu Virgin Carbon Steel Gyutou, 8.2" $98.50
	MANDOLINE	• Razor-sharp blade(s) • Hand guard to shield fingers • Gripper tongs to grasp food • Measurement-marked dial for precision cuts • Storage for extra blades	Swissmar Börner Original V-Slicer Plus Mandoline $29.99
	CARVING BOARD	• Trenches can contain ½ cup of liquid • Large and stable enough to hold large roasts • Midweight for easy carrying, carving, and cleaning	J.K. Adams Maple Reversible Carving Board $69.95
MUST-HAVE ITEM	CUTTING BOARD	• Roomy work surface at least 20 by 15 inches • Teak board for minimal maintenance • Durable edge-grain construction (wood grain runs parallel to surface of board)	Large: Proteak Edge Grain Teak Cutting Board $84.99 Small: OXO Good Grips Utility Cutting Board $14.95 Best Buy: OXO Good Grips Carving & Cutting Board $21.99

KNIVES AND MORE	ITEM	WHAT TO LOOK FOR	TEST KITCHEN FAVORITES
	FLEXIBLE CUTTING MAT	• Thick and sturdy but still flexible • Textured sides keep mat in place and prevent food from sliding • Textured surface conceals nicks	**Dexas Heavy Duty Grippmats** $19.99 for set of 4 ($5 per mat)
	KNIFE SHARPENER	• Diamond abrasives and a spring-loaded chamber to precisely guide blade • Quickly removes nicks in blades • Can convert a 20-degree edge to a sharper 15 degrees	Electric: **Chef'sChoice Trizor XV Knife Sharpener, Model #15** $149.99 Electric, Best Buy: **Chef'sChoice Diamond Sharpener for Asian Knives** $79.99 Manual: **Chef'sChoice Pronto Manual Diamond Hone Asian Knife Sharpener** $49.99
	UNIVERSAL KNIFE BLOCK	• Heavy, ultrastable block with rotating base • Durable bamboo exterior for easy cleaning • Well-placed, medium-strength magnets for easy knife attachment	**Design Trifecta 360 Knife Block** $248.64
	MAGNETIC KNIFE STRIP	• Medium strength magnets to hold knives with just the right amount of pull • Easy to install and clean • Bamboo surface that is gentle on blades	**Messermeister 16.75-inch Bamboo Knife Magnet** $59.95
	CUT-RESISTANT GLOVE	• Tightly woven fabric for durability • Stretchy fabric for comfortable fit • Fits either right or left hand	**Microplane Specialty Series Cut Resistant Glove** $14.95
POTS AND PANS	ITEM	WHAT TO LOOK FOR	TEST KITCHEN FAVORITES
	TRADITIONAL SKILLET	• Stainless-steel interior and fully clad for even heat distribution • 12-inch diameter and flared sides • Comfortable, ovensafe handle • Tight-fitting lid included	**All-Clad d3 Stainless Steel 12″ Fry Pan with Lid** $96.85
	NONSTICK SKILLET	• Dark, nonstick surface • 12- or 12½-inch diameter, thick bottom • Comfortable, ovensafe handle • Cooking surface of at least 9 inches	**OXO Good Grips Non-Stick 12-inch Open Frypan** $39.99
	CARBON-STEEL SKILLET	• Affordable • Thick, solid construction; ergonomically angled handle • Sides flared up just right for easy access but high enough to contain splashes	**Matfer Bourgeat Black Steel Round Frying Pan, 11⅞″** $44.38

MUST-HAVE ITEM (Knife Sharpener)

MUST-HAVE ITEMS (Pots and Pans)

POTS AND PANS	ITEM	WHAT TO LOOK FOR	TEST KITCHEN FAVORITES
	CAST-IRON SKILLET Traditional	• Thick bottom and straight sides • Roomy interior (cooking surface of 9¼ inches or more) • Preseasoned	**Lodge Classic Cast Iron Skillet, 12"** $33.31
	Enameled	• Boasts flaring sides, an oversize helper handle, wide pour spouts, satiny interior, and balanced weight	**Le Creuset Signature 11¾" Iron Handle Skillet** $179.95
	GREEN SKILLET	• PFOA-free (perfluorooctanoic acid) surfaces are nonstick and more durable than silicone coatings • Roomy interior (cooking surface of 9 inches or more) NOTE: We prefer our favorite nonstick skillet for its superior performance.	**Scanpan Professional 12.50" Fry Pan** $129.95
MUST-HAVE ITEM	DUTCH OVEN	• Enameled cast iron or stainless steel • Capacity of at least 6 quarts • Diameter of at least 9 inches • Tight-fitting lid • Wide, sturdy handles	Heavier: **Le Creuset 7¼ Quart Round Dutch Oven** $367.99 Best Buy: **Cuisinart Chef's Classic Enameled Cast Iron Covered Casserole** $83.70
	DUTCH OVEN, INNOVATIVE	• Large capacity • Sturdy, thick base • Silicone oil chamber in base spreads heat slowly and evenly • Good heat retention	**Pauli Cookware Never Burn Sauce Pot, 10 Quart** $229.99
MUST-HAVE ITEMS	SAUCEPAN Large	• Steady heating and good visibility to monitor browning • Stay-cool, easy to grip handle • Helper handle for extra grabbing point	**All-Clad 4 Quart Stainless Steel Sauce Pan with Loop Helper Handle** $179.13 Best Buy: **Cuisinart MultiClad Unlimited 4-Quart Saucepan with Cover** $65.12
	Small	• Heavy, solid, well-priced • Easy to control • Shallow shape and generous diameter	**Calphalon Contemporary Nonstick 2½ Quart Shallow Saucepan with Cover** $39.95

POTS AND PANS	ITEM	WHAT TO LOOK FOR	TEST KITCHEN FAVORITES
MUST-HAVE ITEM	RIMMED BAKING SHEET	• Light-colored surface (heats and browns evenly) • Thick, sturdy pan • Dimensions of 18 by 13 inches • Good to have at least two	**Nordic Ware Bakers Half Sheet** $14.97
	SAUTÉ PAN	• Aluminum core surrounded by layers of stainless steel • Relatively lightweight • 9¾-inch diameter • Stay-cool helper handle	**All-Clad Stainless 3-Quart Tri-Ply Sauté Pan** $224.95 Best Buy: **Cuisinart MultiClad Pro Stainless 3½-Quart Sauté Pan with Helper and Cover** $78.13
	OMELET PAN	• Gently sloped sides for easy turning and rolling of omelets • Nonstick finish • Heavy construction for durability and even heat distribution • 8-inch size for French omelets	**Original French Chef Omelette Pan** $139.95
	PAELLA PAN	• Shallow, wide shape maximizes the surface area of the paella • Distributes heat evenly	**Matfer Bourgeat Black Steel Paella Pan** $49.98
	CANNING POT	• Comfortable, grippy handles • Clear lid that allows user to easily monitor contents	**Victorio Stainless Steel Multi-Use Canner** $75.19
MUST-HAVE ITEMS	STOCKPOT	• 12-quart capacity • Thick bottom to prevent scorching • Wide body for easy cleaning and storage • Flat or round handles that extend at least 1¾ inches	**All-Clad Stainless 12-Quart Stock Pot** $389.95 Best Buy: **Cuisinart Chef's Classic Stainless 12-Quart Stock Pot** $69.99
	ROASTING PAN	• At least 15 by 11 inches • Stainless-steel interior with aluminum core for even heat distribution • Upright handles for easy gripping • Light interior for better food monitoring	**Calphalon Contemporary Stainless Roasting Pan with Rack** $99.99 Best Buy: **Calphalon Commercial Hard-Anodized Roasting Pan with Nonstick Rack** $59.99

POTS AND PANS	ITEM	WHAT TO LOOK FOR	TEST KITCHEN FAVORITES
	ROASTING RACK	• Fixed, not adjustable, to provide sturdiness • Tall, vertical handles positioned on long side of rack	**All-Clad Nonstick Large Rack** $24.95
	GRILL PAN	• Cast-iron pan with enamel coating for heat retention and easy cleanup • Tall ridges (4- to 5.5-mm high) to keep food above rendered fat • Generous cooking area	**Staub 12-Inch American Square Grill Pan and Press** $219.95, including press Best Buy: **Lodge Square Grill Pan and Lodge Ribbed Panini Press** $18.97, grill pan $14.58, panini press
	COOKWARE SET	• Fully clad stainless steel with aluminum core for even heat distribution • Moderately heavy, durable construction • Lids included • Ideal mix of pans includes 12-inch skillet, 10-inch skillet, 2-quart saucepan, 4-quart saucepan, 8-quart stockpot	**All-Clad Stainless Steel Cookware Set, 10-piece** $799.95 Best Buy: **Tramontina 18/10 Stainless Steel TriPly-Clad Cookware Set, 8-piece** $144.97

HANDY TOOLS	ITEM	WHAT TO LOOK FOR	TEST KITCHEN FAVORITES
	KITCHEN SHEARS	• Take-apart scissors (for easy cleaning) • Super-sharp blades • Sturdy construction • Work for both right- and left-handed users	**Kershaw Taskmaster Shears/ Shun Multi-Purpose Shears** $26.30
	TONGS	• Scalloped edges • Slightly concave pincers • Length of 12 inches (to keep your hand far from the heat) • Open and close easily	12-Inch: **OXO Good Grips 12-Inch Tongs** $12.95 9-Inch: **OXO Good Grips 9-Inch Tongs** $11.99
	WOODEN SPOON	• Slim yet broad bowl • Stain-resistant bamboo • Comfortable handle	**SCI Bamboo Wood Cooking Spoon** $2.40
	SLOTTED SPOON	• Lightweight • Wide, shallow bowl • Thin-edged bowl • Long, comfortable handle	**Cuisinart Stainless Steel Slotted Spoon** $9.12
	SPOONULA	• Lightweight thanks to lightly textured silicone material and gently rounded handle • Odor-resistant • Vibrant color hides stains	**Starpack Premium Silicone Spoonula** $8.49

MUST-HAVE ITEMS

HANDY TOOLS	ITEM	WHAT TO LOOK FOR	TEST KITCHEN FAVORITES
MUST-HAVE ITEMS	ALL-AROUND SPATULA	• Head about 3 inches wide and 5 inches long • Long, vertical slots • Useful to have a metal spatula to use with traditional cookware and plastic for nonstick cookware • Comfortable, easy to control handle • Thin and flexible head	Metal: **Wüsthof Gourmet Turner/Fish Spatula** $49.95 Best Buy: **MIU France Flexible Fish Turner—Slotted** $16.57 Plastic: **Matfer Bourgeat Pelton Spatula** $8.23
	SILICONE SPATULA	• Firm enough for scraping and scooping • Fits neatly into tight corners • Straight sides and wide, flat blade to ensure no food is left unmixed	**Di Oro Living Seamless Silicone Spatula–Large** $10.97 Large: **Rubbermaid 13.5" High-Heat Scraper** $14.50
	OFFSET SPATULA	• Flexible blade offset to a roughly 30-degree angle • Enough usable surface area to frost the radius of a 9-inch cake • Comfortable handle	**OXO Good Grips Bent Icing Knife** $9.99
	COMPACT SPATULA	• High heat resistance • Comfortable grip with 2-inch-wide head	**KitchenAid Cookie/Pastry Lifter** $8
	JAR SPATULA	• Slim, flexible head maneuvers tight corners and edges • Strong enough to lift heavy food • Seamless silicone for easy cleaning and comfortable feel	**GIR Skinny Spatula** $12.95 Best Buy: **OXO Good Grips Silicone Jar Spatula** $5.95
MUST-HAVE ITEM	ALL-PURPOSE WHISK	• At least 10 wires • Wires of moderate thickness • Comfortable rubber handle • Balanced, lightweight feel	**OXO Good Grips 11" Balloon Whisk** $9.99
	FLAT WHISK	• Comfortable to use for longer periods • Grippy TPE handle • Tines with good rigidity and spacing	**OXO Good Grips Flat Whisk** $6.95

HANDY TOOLS	ITEM	WHAT TO LOOK FOR	TEST KITCHEN FAVORITES
PEPPER MILL	• Easy-to-adjust, clearly marked grind settings • Efficient, comfortable grinding mechanism • Generous capacity	**Cole & Mason Derwent Gourmet Precision Pepper Mill** $40
LADLE	• Stainless steel • Hook handle • Pouring rim to prevent dripping • Handle 9 to 10 inches in length	**Rösle Hook Ladle with Pouring Rim** $34 Best Buy: **OXO Good Grips Brushed Stainless Steel Ladle** $9.99
CAN OPENER	• Easy to attach • Smooth and comfortable turning motions • Pulls off removed lid for safe and easy disposal	**Fissler Magic Smooth-Edge Can Opener** $29
JAR OPENER	• Strong, sturdy clamp grip • Adjusts quickly to any size jar	**Amco Swing-A-Way Jar Opener** $5.99
GARLIC PRESS	• Large capacity that holds multiple garlic cloves • Long handle and short distance between pivot point and plunger	**Kuhn Rikon Stainless Steel Epicurean Garlic Press** $44.95
CHEESE PLANE	• Comfortable handle with relatively long blade • Thin, flexible head produces perfect, clean-edged, even cheese slices	**Wüsthof Gourmet 4¾-inch Cheese Plane** $19.95
SERRATED FRUIT PEELER	• Comfortable grip and nonslip handle • Sharp blade	**Messermeister Serrated Swivel Peeler** $5.50
VEGETABLE PEELER	• Sharp, carbon steel blade • 1-inch space between blade and peeler to prevent jamming • Lightweight and comfortable	For adults and older kids: **Kuhn Rikon Original Swiss Peeler** $3.50 For younger kids and beginners: **Le Petit Chef Peeler by Opinel** $17
AVOCADO SLICER	• Compact • Relatively comfortable to hold • Double-headed configuration with knife on one end and slicer on the other	**OXO Good Grips 3-in-1 Avocado Slicer** $9.95

MUST-HAVE ITEMS · MUST-HAVE ITEM · MUST-HAVE ITEM

HANDY TOOLS	ITEM	WHAT TO LOOK FOR	TEST KITCHEN FAVORITES
	RASP GRATER	• Sharp teeth (require little effort or pressure when grating) • Maneuverable over round shapes • Comfortable handle	**Microplane Premium Classic Zester/Grater** $14.95
	GRATER	• Four super-sharp grating planes framed by tough plastic, making it easy to handle • Large holes for quick, flawless mozzarella grating and fine holes for perfect shredded ginger or Parmesan	**Microplane Specialty Series 4-Sided Box Grater** $34.95
	GINGER GRATER	• Ample surface area and razor-sharp etched holes • Comfortable grip • Wide paddle shape makes it easy to collect ginger puree and clean	**Microplane Home Series Fine Grater** $14.95
	ROTARY GRATER	• Barrel at least 2 inches in diameter • Classic turn-crank design • Comfortable handle • Simple to disassemble for easy cleanup	**Zyliss All Cheese Grater** $19.95
	MANUAL CITRUS JUICER	• Handheld squeezer with comfortable handle • Durable, plastic exterior • Large, slat-like holes for efficient draining	**Chef'n FreshForce Citrus Juicer** $23.04
	ICE CREAM SCOOP	• Comfortable handle • Gently curved bowl for easy releasing • Scoop warms on contact with your hand to slightly melt ice cream	**Zeroll Original Ice Cream Scoop** $18.44
	MEAT POUNDER	• At least 1½ pounds in weight • Vertical handle for better leverage and control	**Norpro GRIP-EZ Meat Pounder** $17.50
	BENCH SCRAPER	• Sturdy blade • Comfortable handle with plastic, rubber, or nylon grip	**Dexter-Russell 6" Dough Cutter/Scraper— Sani-Safe Series** $7.01
	BOWL SCRAPER	• Curved shape with comfortable grip • Rigid enough to move dough but flexible enough to scrape up batter • Thin, straight edge doubles as dough cutter or bench scraper	**iSi Basics Silicone Scraper Spatula** $5.99

MUST-HAVE ITEMS

HANDY TOOLS	ITEM	WHAT TO LOOK FOR	TEST KITCHEN FAVORITES
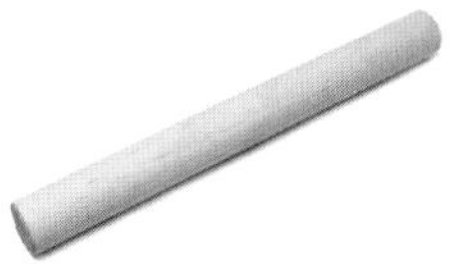	ROLLING PIN	• Moderate weight (1 to 1½ pounds) • 19-inch straight barrel • Slightly textured wooden surface to grip dough for easy rolling	**J.K. Adams Plain Maple Rolling Dowel** $13.95
	MIXING BOWLS Stainless Steel	• Lightweight and easy to handle • Durability • Conducts heat well for double boiler	**Vollrath Economy Stainless Steel Mixing Bowls** $2.90, 1.5 quart $4.50, 3 quart $6.90, 5 quart
	Glass	• Tempered to increase impact and thermal resistance • Can be used in microwave • Durability	**Pyrex Smart Essentials Mixing Bowl Set with Colored Lids** $27.98 for 4-bowl set
	MINI PREP BOWLS	• Wide, shallow bowls are easy to hold, fill, empty, and clean • Can be used in the microwave and oven	**Anchor Hocking 6-Piece Nesting Prep Bowl Set** $11
	BOWL STABILIZER	• Firmly attaches bowls to every work surface in the kitchen • Accommodates bowls from 6 to 21 inches in diameter • Forms a tight seal in double boilers	Staybowlizer $19.95
	OVEN MITT	• Form-fitting and not overly bulky for easy maneuvering • Machine washable • Flexible, heat-resistant material	**San Jamar Cool Touch Flame Oven Mitt** $44.95 each For kids: **Williams Sonoma Junior Chef Oven Mitt** $7.95 each
	JAR LIFTER	• Spring-loaded hinge that pops grabbers open when handles are released • Broad, molded handles comfortable and secure • Does not rust	**Ball Secure-Grip Jar Lifter** $10.99
	COOKIE PRESS	• Produces visually appealing, uniform cookies • Withstands prolonged use with no decline in performance • Consistently produces cookies with intact designs without dough jamming	MARCATO Biscuit Maker $42

MUST-HAVE ITEMS

MUST-HAVE ITEM

HANDY TOOLS	ITEM	WHAT TO LOOK FOR	TEST KITCHEN FAVORITES
	PASTRY BRUSH	• Bristles of moderate length and density • Grippy handle • Loses few bristles	**Winco Flat Pastry and Basting Brush, 1½ inch** $6.93
	SPLATTER SCREEN	• Diameter of at least 13 inches • Lollipop-shaped design • Tightly woven mesh face	**HIC Stainless Steel Splatter Screen** $9.99
	BOUILLON STRAINER/ CHINOIS	• Conical shape • Depth of 7 to 8 inches • At least one hook on rim for stability	**Winco Reinforced Extra Fine Mesh Bouillon Strainer** $33.78
	COLANDER	• 4- to 7-quart capacity • Metal ring attached to the bottom for stability • Many holes for quick draining • Small holes so pasta doesn't slip through	**RSVP International Endurance Precision Pierced 5 Qt. Colander** $25.99
	FINE-MESH STRAINER	• Roomy, medium-depth basket with fine, stiff mesh • Long wide hook and rounded steel handle	**Rösle Fine Mesh Strainer, Round Handle, 7.9 inches, 20 cm** $45
	SPIDER SKIMMER	• Long handle for protection from hot water and oil • Well-balanced and easy to maneuver	**Rösle Wire Skimmer** $41.68
	COLLAPSIBLE MINI COLANDER	• Large, comfortable, rubberized grip • Perfectly sized webbed basket	**Progressive International Collapsible Mini Colander** $13.70
	TEA INFUSER	• Large capacity (13.5 tablespoons) allows for good water circulation • Easy to fill and clean • Tightly woven mesh basket keeps even the finest leaves out of finished tea	**Finum Brewing Basket L** $9.95
	FOOD MILL	• Interchangeable disks for fine, medium, and coarse purees • Easy to turn	**RSVP Classic Rotary Food Mill** $24.95

MUST-HAVE ITEMS

HANDY TOOLS	ITEM	WHAT TO LOOK FOR	TEST KITCHEN FAVORITES
	FAT SEPARATOR	• Bottom-draining model • Detachable bowl for easy cleaning • Strainer for catching solids	**Cuisipro Fat Separator** $33.95
	POTATO MASHER	• Solid mashing disk with small holes • Comfortable grip	**Zyliss Stainless Steel Potato Masher** $12.99
	SALAD SPINNER	• Ergonomic and easy-to-operate hand pump • Wide base for stability • Flat lid for easy cleaning and storage	**OXO Good Grips Salad Spinner** $29.99
	STEAMER BASKET	• Stainless-steel basket with feet • Roomy and collapsible	**OXO Good Grips Stainless Steel Steamer with Extendable Handle** $17.95
	MORTAR AND PESTLE	• Heavy, stable base with tall, narrow walls • Rough interior to help grip and grind ingredients • Comfortable, heavy pestle	**Frieling "Goliath" Mortar and Pestle Set** $49.95

MEASURING EQUIPMENT	ITEM	WHAT TO LOOK FOR	TEST KITCHEN FAVORITES
	DRY MEASURING CUPS	• Accurate measurements • Easy-to-read measurement markings • Stack and store neatly • Durable measurement markings • Stable when empty and filled • Handles perfectly flush with cups	**OXO Good Grips Stainless Steel Measuring Cups** $19.99
	LIQUID MEASURING CUP	• Crisp, unambiguous markings that include ¼- and ⅓-cup measurements • Heatproof, sturdy cup with handle • Good to have in a variety of sizes (1, 2, and 4 cups)	**Pyrex 2-Cup Measuring Cup** $5.99

MUST-HAVE ITEMS

MEASURING EQUIPMENT	ITEM	WHAT TO LOOK FOR	TEST KITCHEN FAVORITES
	ADJUSTABLE MEASURING CUP	• Plunger-like bottom (with a tight seal between plunger and tube) that you can set to correct measurement, then push up to cleanly extract sticky ingredients (such as shortening or peanut butter) • 1- or 2-cup capacity • Dishwasher-safe	**KitchenArt Adjust-A-Cup Professional Series, 2-Cup** $12.95
	MEASURING SPOONS	• Long, comfortable handles • Rim of bowl flush with handle (makes it easy to "dip" into a dry ingredient and "sweep" across the top for accurate measuring) • Slim design	**Cuisipro Stainless Steel Measuring Spoons Set** $11.95
	KITCHEN RULER	• Stainless steel and easy to clean • 18 inches in length • Large, easy-to-read markings	**Empire 18-inch Stainless Steel Ruler** $8.49
	DIGITAL SCALE	• Easy-to-read display not blocked by weighing platform • At least 7-pound capacity • Accessible buttons • Gram-to-ounce conversion feature • Roomy platform	**OXO Good Grips 11 lb Food Scale with Pull Out Display** $49.95 Best Buy: **Ozeri Pronto Digital Multifunction Kitchen and Food Scale** $11.79

THERMOMETERS AND TIMERS	ITEM	WHAT TO LOOK FOR	TEST KITCHEN FAVORITES
	INSTANT-READ THERMOMETER	• Digital model with automatic shut-off • Quick-response readings in 10 seconds or fewer • Wide temperature range (-40 to 450 degrees) • Long stem that can reach interior of large cuts of meat • Water-resistant	**ThermoWorks Thermapen Mk4** $99 Best Buy: **ThermoWorks ThermoPop** $29 Best Mid-Price: **The Javelin Pro Duo** $49.95
	OVEN THERMOMETER	• Clearly marked numbers for easy readability • Large, sturdy base • Large temperature range (up to 600 degrees)	**CDN Pro Accurate Oven Thermometer** $8.70
	MEAT PROBE/ CANDY/ DEEP-FRY THERMOMETER	• Digital model • Easy-to-read console • Intuitive design and ovensafe probe	**ThermoWorks ChefAlarm** $59 Best Buy: **Polder Classic Digital Thermometer/Timer** $24.99

MUST-HAVE ITEMS

THERMOMETERS AND TIMERS	ITEM	WHAT TO LOOK FOR	TEST KITCHEN FAVORITES
	REFRIGERATOR/ FREEZER THERMOMETER	• Accurate and customizable • Alerts when temperatures remain outside safe zone for over 30 minutes	ThermoWorks Fridge/Freezer Alarm $22
MUST-HAVE ITEM	KITCHEN TIMER	• Lengthy time range (1 second to at least 10 hours) • Able to count up after alarm goes off • Easy to use and read • Able to track multiple events	OXO Good Grips Triple Timer $19.99

BAKEWARE	ITEM	WHAT TO LOOK FOR	TEST KITCHEN FAVORITES
	GLASS BAKING DISH	• Large handles • Lightweight • Easy to grip and maneuver	Pyrex Easy Grab 3-Quart Oblong Baking Dish $7.29
	METAL BAKING PAN	• Dimensions of 13 by 9 inches • Straight sides • Nonstick coating for even browning and easy release of cakes and bar cookies	Williams-Sonoma Goldtouch Nonstick Rectangular Cake Pan, 9" x 13" $32.95
	SQUARE BAKING PAN	• Straight sides • Light gold or dark nonstick surface for even browning and easy release of cakes • Good to have both 9-inch and 8-inch square pans	Williams-Sonoma Goldtouch Nonstick 8-Inch Square Cake Pan $21
MUST-HAVE ITEMS	ROUND CAKE PAN Best All Around	• Best for cake • Straight sides • Light finish for tall, evenly baked cakes • Nonstick surface for easy release	Nordic Ware Naturals Nonstick 9-inch Round Cake Pan $14.99
	Best for Browning	• Dark finish is ideal for pizza and cinnamon buns • Nonstick	Chicago Metallic Non-Stick 9" Round Cake Pan $10.97
	PIE PLATE	• Gold-hued metal for even browning and crisping • Nonfluted lip for maximum crust-crimping flexibility • Good to have two	Williams-Sonoma Goldtouch Nonstick Pie Dish $18.95
	LOAF PAN	• Light gold or dark nonstick surface for even browning and easy release • Good to have both 8½ by 4½-inch and 9 by 5-inch pans	Williams-Sonoma Goldtouch Nonstick Loaf Pan $21

BAKEWARE	ITEM	WHAT TO LOOK FOR	TEST KITCHEN FAVORITES
	SPRINGFORM PAN	• Tight seal between band and bottom of pan prevents leakage • Raised base makes cutting and removing slices easy • Light finish for controlled, even browning	**Williams-Sonoma Goldtouch Springform Pan, 9″** $49.95 Best Buy: **Nordic Ware 9″ Leakproof Springform Pan** $16.22
	MUFFIN TIN	• Easy to hold and turn • Oversize rim for secure grasping • Gold finish for perfectly browned baked goods	**OXO Good Grips Non-Stick Pro 12-Cup Muffin Pan** $24.99
	COOLING RACK	• Grid-style rack with tightly woven bars • Six feet on three bars for extra stability • Should fit inside standard 18 by 13-inch rimmed baking sheet • Dishwasher-safe	**Libertyware Half Size Sheet Pan Cooling Rack** $15.99 for set of two ($7.99 each)
	BAKER'S COOLING RACK	• Sturdy rack • Four collapsible shelves • Unit folds down for easy storage	**Linden Sweden Baker's Cooling Rack** $17.99
	BISCUIT CUTTERS	• Sharp edges • A set with a variety of sizes	**Ateco 5357 11-Piece Round Cutter Set** $14.95
	BUNDT PAN	• Thick, easy-to-grip handles • Deep, well-defined ridges that produce perfect cakes	**Nordic Ware Anniversary Bundt Pan** $30.99
	MINI BUNDT PAN	• Tray-style model with six ¾-cup molds • Silver platinum nonstick surface for even browning and easy release • Clearly defined ridges	**Nordic Ware Platinum Anniversary Bundtlette Pan** $40
	TART PAN	• Nonstick coating for easy transfer • Professional-looking edges • If you bake a lot, it's good to have multiple sizes, though 9 inches is standard	**Matfer Steel Non-stick Fluted Tart Mold with Removable Bottom 9½″** $27

MUST-HAVE ITEMS

BAKEWARE	ITEM	WHAT TO LOOK FOR	TEST KITCHEN FAVORITES
	TUBE PAN	• Heavy pan (at least 1 pound) • Heavy bottom for leak-free seal • Dark nonstick surface for even browning and easy release • 16-cup capacity • Feet on the rim	**Chicago Metallic Professional Nonstick Angel Food Cake Pan with Feet** $19.95
	PULLMAN LOAF PAN	• Squared-off pan (4 by 4 inches) • Nonstick aluminized steel for easy cleanup • Light surface for even browning	**USA Pan 13 by 4-Inch Pullman Loaf Pan and Cover** $33.95
	BAKER'S EDGE PAN	• Attached cutting grid • Dark nonstick surface for easy release	**Baker's Edge Brownie Pan** $34.95
	SOUFFLÉ DISH	• Round dish with straight sides • Not-too-thick side walls	**HIC 64-Ounce Soufflé** $15.12
	BAKING STONE	• Substantial but not too heavy to handle • Dimensions of 16 by 14 inches • Clay, not cement, for evenly browned crusts	**Old Stone Oven Pizza Baking Stone** $59.95
	BAKING PEEL	• Polymer coating guards against moisture • Innovative cloth conveyer belt	**EXO Polymer Sealed Super Peel** $54.95 Best Buy: **Pizzacraft 14″ Wood Pizza Peel** $27.31
	BAKING MAT	• Fits perfectly inside rimmed baking sheets • Heavy enough to stay put • Dishwasher-safe	**DeMarle Silpat U.S. Half-Size Non-Stick Silicone Baking Mat** $22.35

SMALL APPLIANCES	ITEM	WHAT TO LOOK FOR	TEST KITCHEN FAVORITES
	AIR FRYER	• Compact, slim machine that doesn't take up too much counterspace • Roomy cooking basket holds one pound of food and has nonstick coating • Easy, intuitive time and temperature controls • Safe and easy to clean	**Philips TurboStar Airfryer, Avance Digital** $249.95

SMALL APPLIANCES	ITEM	WHAT TO LOOK FOR	TEST KITCHEN FAVORITES
MUST-HAVE ITEM	FOOD PROCESSOR	• 14-cup capacity • Sharp and sturdy blades • Wide feed tube • Should come with basic blades and discs: steel blade, dough blade, shredding/slicing disc	**Cuisinart Custom 14-Cup Food Processor** $199.99
MUST-HAVE ITEMS	STAND MIXER	• Planetary action (stationary bowl and single mixing arm) • Powerful motor • Bowl size of at least 4½ quarts • Slightly squat bowl to keep ingredients in beater's range • Should come with basic attachments: paddle, dough hook, metal whisk	**KitchenAid Pro Line Series 7-Qt Bowl Lift Stand Mixer** $549.95 Best Buy: **KitchenAid Classic Plus Stand Mixer** $199.99
	HANDHELD MIXER	• Lightweight model • Slim wire beaters without central post • Variety of speeds	**KitchenAid 5-Speed Ultra Power Hand Mixer** $69.99 Best Buy: **Cuisinart PowerSelect 3-Speed Hand Mixer** $26.77
	BLENDER	• Mix of straight and serrated blades at different angles • Jar with curved base • At least 44-ounce capacity • Heavy base for stability	**Vitamix 5200** $449 Best Midpriced: **Breville The Hemisphere Control** $199.95
	PERSONAL BLENDER	• Quick and effective blending thanks to sharp, six-pronged blades angled both up and down • Travel lid well-designed with drinking spout and hinged arm that seals tight	**Ninja Nutri Ninja Pro** $89
	IMMERSION BLENDER	• Grippy rubber handle • Easy to change speeds	**Braun Multiquick 5 Hand Blender** $59.99

SMALL APPLIANCES	ITEM	WHAT TO LOOK FOR	TEST KITCHEN FAVORITES
	ELECTRIC GRIDDLE	• Large cooking area (about 21 by 12 inches) • Attached pull-out grease trap (won't tip over) • Nonstick surface for easy cleanup	**Broilking Professional Griddle** $99.99
	ELECTRIC JUICER	• Ideal for making a large amount of fruit or vegetable juice • Centrifugal, not masticating, model for fresher-tasting juice • 3-inch-wide feed tube • Easy to assemble and clean	**Breville Juice Fountain Plus** $149.99
	ADJUSTABLE ELECTRIC KETTLE	• Heats water to a range of different temperatures • Automatic shutoff • Separate base for cordless pouring • Visible water level	**Zojirushi Micom Water Boiler & Warmer** $114.95
	STOVETOP KETTLE	• Lightweight and easy to fill • Generous capacity • Easy to clean surface • Comfortable, grippy handle • Gently curved spout provides smooth pouring • Not induction-compatible	**OXO Good Grips Classic Tea Kettle in Brushed Stainless Steel** $39.95
	COFFEE MAKER	• Thermal carafe that keeps coffee hot and fresh with capacity of at least 10 cups • Short brewing time (6 minutes is ideal) • Copper, not aluminum, heating element • Easy-to-fill water tank • Clear, intuitive controls	**Technivorm Moccamaster 10-Cup Coffee Maker with Thermal Carafe** $299 Best Buy: **Bonavita 8-Cup Coffee Maker with Thermal Carafe** $189.99 "Smart" System: **Behmor Connected 8-Cup Brew System** $167
	ESPRESSO MACHINE	• Compact, well-made machine • Consistent, excellent espresso • Easy adjustment of flavor, temperature, and shot strength • Simple attached steam wand with silicone grip for easy cleaning • Clear display and well-designed controls	**Gaggia Anima Automatic Coffee Machine** $690.06 Best for DIY Types: **Breville BES870XL Barista Express Espresso Machine** $578

SMALL APPLIANCES	ITEM	WHAT TO LOOK FOR	TEST KITCHEN FAVORITES
	MANUAL PASTA MACHINE	• Laser-sharp noodle attachment for perfectly shaped pasta • Wide and narrow thickness settings • Easy-to-use dial	**Marcato Atlas 150 Wellness Pasta Machine** $69.25
	WARMING TRAY	• Features a range of heat settings to keep food at a safe serving temperature • Keeps food hot for 4 hours • Stay-cool handles for easy maneuvering • Easily wipes clean and is cool after use in 20 minutes' time	**BroilKing Professional Stainless Warming Tray** $126.06 Best Buy: **Oster Stainless Steel Warming Tray** $38.15
	SMART COOKING SYSTEM	• Easy, intuitive Bluetooth system • Sturdy, well-built skillet and pot • Smooth, stainless-steel cooking surface	**Hestan Cue Smart Cooking System: Pan, Burner & Chef's Pot** $799.90
	ICE CREAM MAKER	• Compact size for easy storage • Simple to use and clean • Produces dense, smooth ice cream	**Cuisinart Frozen Yogurt, Ice Cream, and Sorbet Maker** $53.99
	ICE CREAM CONE MAKER	• Easy to use • Solidly constructed • Channel around edge to catch excess batter for easy cleanup	**Chef's Choice 838 Waffle Cone Express** $49.95
	STOVETOP PRESSURE COOKER	• Solidly built • Stovetop model with low sides and wide base for easy access and better browning and heat retention • Easy-to-read pressure indicator	**Fissler Vitaquick 8½-Quart Pressure Cooker** $279.95 Best Buy: **Fagor Duo 8-Quart Stainless Steel Pressure Cooker** $109.95
	SLOW COOKER	• At least 6-quart capacity • Insert handles • Clear lid to see progress of food • Dishwasher-safe insert • Intuitive control panel with programmable timer and warming mode	**KitchenAid 6-Quart Slow Cooker with Solid Glass Lid** $99.99

SMALL APPLIANCES	ITEM	WHAT TO LOOK FOR	TEST KITCHEN FAVORITES
	RICE COOKER	• Produces tender-chewy white, brown, and sushi rice • Digital timer with clear audio alert and a delayed-start function • Removable lid for hassle-free cleanup • Small countertop footprint	**Aroma 8-Cup Digital Rice Cooker and Food Steamer** $29.92
	INTELLIGENT OVEN	• Easy to use with responsive control panel • Well-designed app that does not lose connectivity with oven • Compatible with Amazon Alexa • Sturdy nonstick sheet pan with rack requires hand-washing	**The June Intelligent Oven** $1,495
	TOASTER OVEN	• Quartz heating elements for steady, controlled heat • Roomy but compact interior • Simple to use	**The Smart Oven by Breville** $249.95
	WAFFLE IRON	• Indicator lights and audible alert • Makes two waffles at a time • Six-point dial for customizing waffle doneness	**Cuisinart Double Belgian Waffle Maker** $99.95

GRILLING EQUIPMENT	ITEM	WHAT TO LOOK FOR	TEST KITCHEN FAVORITES
	GAS GRILL	• Large main grate • Built-in thermometer • Two burners for varying heat levels (three is even better) • Made of thick, heat-retaining materials such as cast aluminum and enameled steel	**Weber Spirit E-310 Gas Grill** $499
	CHARCOAL GRILL	• Sturdy construction for maintaining heat • Well-designed cooking grate, handles, lid, and wheels • Generous cooking and charcoal capacity • Well-positioned vents to control air flow • Gas ignition instantly and easily lights coals • Ash catcher for easy cleanup	**Weber Performer Deluxe Charcoal Grill** $399 Best Buy: **Weber Original Kettle Premium Charcoal Grill, 22-Inch** $149

GRILLING EQUIPMENT	ITEM	WHAT TO LOOK FOR	TEST KITCHEN FAVORITES
	SMOKER	• Large cooking area • Water pan • Multiple vents for precise temperature control	**Weber Smokey Mountain Cooker Smoker 18"** $298.95
	CHIMNEY STARTER	• 6-quart capacity • Holes in the canister so air can circulate around the coals • Sturdy construction • Heat-resistant handle • Dual handle for easy control	**Weber Rapidfire Chimney Starter** $14.99
	GRILL TONGS	• 16 inches in length • Scalloped, not sharp and serrated, edges • Open and close easily • Lightweight • Moderate amount of springy tension	**OXO Good Grips 16" Locking Tongs** $14.93
	GRILL BRUSH	• Long handle (about 14 inches) • Large woven-mesh detachable stainless-steel scrubbing pads	**Grill Wizard 18-Inch China Grill Brush** $31.50
	GRILL GRATE CLEANING BLOCK	• Use for once-per-season grill reconditioning • Pumice scrubber to strip all accumulated gunk even from cold grates	**GrillStone Value Pack Cleaning Kit by Earthstone International** $9.99
	BASTING BRUSH	• Silicone bristles • Angled brush head • Handle 8 to 13 inches in length • Heat-resistant	**Elizabeth Karmel Super Silicone Angled BBQ Brush** $9.16
	SKEWERS	• Flat and metal • 3/16 inch thick	**Norpro 12-Inch Stainless Steel Skewers** $6.85 for set of 6
	GRILL GLOVES	• Excellent heat protection • Gloves, rather than mitts, for dexterity • Long sleeves to protect forearms	**Steven Raichlen Ultimate Suede Grilling Gloves** $29.99 per pair
	GRILL LIGHTER	• Flexible neck • Refillable chamber with large, easy-to-read fuel window • Comfortable grip	**Zippo Flexible Neck Utility Lighter** $18.35

GRILLING EQUIPMENT	ITEM	WHAT TO LOOK FOR	TEST KITCHEN FAVORITES
	OUTDOOR GRILL PAN	• Narrow slits and raised sides so food can't fall through or off • Sturdy construction with handles	**Weber Professional-Grade Grill Pan** $19.99
	GRILL GRATE SET	• Stainless-steel grate for 22½-inch charcoal grill • Removable inner circle of grate can be replaced with crosshatched sear grate (shown), griddle, or wok (sold separately)	**Weber 7420 Gourmet BBQ System Sear Grate Set** $54.99
	PIZZA GRILLING KIT	• Metal collar that elevates the grill's lid • Brings grill heat to over 900 degrees • Cutout that lets you insert pizzas without losing heat	**KettlePizza Pro 22 Kit** $299.95
	STOVETOP SMOKER	• Sliding snug, flat metal lid • Large drip tray • Rack with parallel wires • Stay-cool handle	**Camerons Stovetop Smoker** $54.95
	SMOKER BOX	• Cast iron for slow heating and steady smoke • Easy to fill, empty, and clean	**GrillPro Cast Iron Smoker Box Made by Onward Manufacturing Company** $12.79
	GRILLING BASKET FOR WHOLE FISH	• Two-piece metal cage with nonstick coating to keep fish from sticking • Wires less than 2 inches apart to secure both large and small fish • Removable handle for easy cleanup	**Charcoal Companion Ultimate Nonstick Fish-Grilling Basket** $24.99
	VERTICAL ROASTER	• Helps poultry cook evenly • 8-inch shaft keeps chicken above fat and drippings in pan • Attached basin catches drippings for pan sauce • Sturdy construction	**Vertical Roaster with Infuser by Norpro** $22.11 Best Buy: **Elizabeth Karmel's Grill Friends Porcelain Chicken Sitter** $11.99
	CHARCOAL STARTERS	• Relatively water-resistant • Ignite easily without impacting food flavor	**Weber Lighter Cubes** $3.29 for 24 cubes ($0.14 per cube)

SPECIALTY PIECES	ITEM	WHAT TO LOOK FOR	TEST KITCHEN FAVORITES
	APPLE CORER	• Sharp, serrated barrel edges • Blade diameter measuring ¾ to 1 inch	**Cuisipro Apple Corer** $9.95
	GRAPEFRUIT KNIFE	• Sturdy, lightweight handle • Gently angled blade for precise cutting	**Messermeister Pro-Touch 4-Inch Grapefruit Knife** $15.39
	STRAWBERRY HULLER	• Huller with four spring-loaded metal prongs that slice out leaves, stem, and core • Easy and safe to use • Compact for easy storage	**StemGem Strawberry Hull Remover by Chef'n** $7.95
	PINEAPPLE SLICER	• Corkscrew design • Easy to use • Narrow slicing base for easy storage	**OXO Good Grips Stainless Steel Ratcheting Pineapple Slicer** $19.99
	CORN STRIPPER	• Safer than using chef's knife • Attached cup to catch kernels • Comfortable grip and sharp blade	**OXO Good Grips Corn Stripper** $11.99
	MANUAL NUT CHOPPER	• Sharp, sturdy stainless-steel chopping tines • Dishwasher-safe	**Prepworks from Progressive Nut Chopper with Non-Skid Base** $11.70
	NUTCRACKER	• Lever-style model • Solidly built • Extra-long handle for good leverage and easy cracking	**Get Crackin' Heavy Duty Steel Lever Nutcracker** $35.99

SPECIALTY PIECES	ITEM	WHAT TO LOOK FOR	TEST KITCHEN FAVORITES
	SPIRAL SLICER (SPIRALIZER)	• Includes three blades that are stored in the base • Stabilizing suction cups make for safer slicing • Pronged to hold fruit and vegetables against blade for optimal spiralizing • Large rectangular chamber accommodates vegetables up to 10 inches long or 7 inches thick	Paderno World Cuisine Tri-Blade Plastic Spiral Vegetable Slicer $33.24
	TORTILLA PRESS	• Wood or heavy cast iron • Large pressing surface of 8 inches • Easy to use	La Mexicana Tortilladora de Madera Barnizada/Mesquite Tortilla Press $64.95 Best Buy: Norpro Cast Aluminum Tortilla Press $15.20
	STOVETOP GRIDDLE	• Anodized aluminum for even heating • Nonstick coating • Lightweight (about 4 pounds) • Heat-resistant loop handles • At least 17 by 9 inches (large enough to span two burners) • Pour spout for draining grease	Anolon Advanced Double Burner Griddle $68.99
	MILK FROTHER	• Easy to use and clean • Immersion blender–style wand • Battery operated	Aerolatte Milk Frother $19.99
	OYSTER KNIFE	• Sturdy, flat blade with slightly curved tip for easy penetration • Slim, nonstick handle for secure, comfortable grip	R. Murphy New Haven Oyster Knife with Stainless Steel Blade $16.65
	SEAFOOD SCISSORS	• Thin, curved blades to fit into shells • Strong and sturdy	RSVP International Endurance Seafood Scissors $14.99
	SILICONE MICROWAVE LID	• Thin, silicone round to cover splatter-prone food during microwave heating • Easy to clean • Doubles as jar opener	Piggy Steamer $18
	RECIPE HOLDER	• Holds pages at perfect angle for viewing • Compact yet sturdy • Strong magnet	Recipe Rock by Architec $9.99

SPECIALTY PIECES	ITEM	WHAT TO LOOK FOR	TEST KITCHEN FAVORITES
	OIL MISTER	• Clear plastic makes it easy to monitor oil level • Consistent, fine spray • Easy to refill • Dishwasher-safe (top shelf only)	Mastrad Oil and Flavor Mister $17.29
	MICROWAVE RICE COOKER	• Sturdy and compact • 6-cup capacity • Easy to clean	Progressive International Microwave Rice Cooker Set $8.99
	MICROWAVE CHIP MAKER	• Perforated 11-inch silicone disk that holds 15 to 20 chips • Slicer that produces wafer-thin chips	Topchips Chips Maker $19.99
	PIPING SET	• Large bag (about 18 inches in length) for easier gripping and twisting • Contains all of the essentials: twelve 16-inch pastry bags; four plastic couplers; and the following Wilton tips: #4 round, #12 round, #70 leaf, #103 petal, #2D large closed star, #1M open star	Test Kitchen Self-Assembled à La Carte Decorating Set $15.32
	CHEESE WIRE	• Comfortable plastic handles • Narrow wire	Fante's Handled Cheese Wire $2.99
	PIZZA CUTTER	• Comfortable, soft-grip handle • Thumb guard to protect fingers	OXO Good Grips 4" Pizza Wheel $12.99
	COUCHE	• Maintains baguettes' shape and wicks moisture effectively • Fabric easily releases dough	San Francisco Baking Institute 18" Linen Canvase (Couche) $8 for 36 x 18-inch couche
	LAME	• Scores baguettes cleanly and evenly • Easy to change blades	Breadtopia Bread Lame $9.50

SPECIALTY PIECES	ITEM	WHAT TO LOOK FOR	TEST KITCHEN FAVORITES
	POTATO RICER	• Hopper with many holes so more food can travel through • Comfortable handles • Easy to assemble and clean	**RSVP International Potato Ricer** $13.95
	PANCAKE BATTER DISPENSER	• Tall plastic cylinder • Easy to use • Heat-resistant silicone tip	**Tovolo Pancake Pen** $9.95
	MAPLE SYRUP DISPENSER	• Snug-closing spout cover that allows control of flow and precise pouring • Easy to fill and clean • Dishwasher-safe	**American Metalcraft Beehive Syrup Dispenser, 6 oz.** $7.80
	INSULATED ICE CREAM KEEPER	• Foam-core insulated base and gel pack-lined lid • Can hold 1 pint of ice cream • Keeps ice cream frozen for 90 minutes	**Zak! Designs Ice Cream Tubbie** $10.12
	ICE POP MOLDS	• Easy to fill, transport, and store • Easy to remove and clean pops • Long, grippy, reusable popsicle sticks	**Zoku Classic Pop Molds** $15.45
	CUPCAKE AND CAKE CARRIER	• Fits both round and square cakes and cupcakes • Snap locks • Nonskid base • Collapses for easy storage	**Progressive Collapsible Cupcake and Cake Carrier** $29.95
	PIE CARRIER	• Collapsible plastic tote expands to accommodate larger pies • Large, nonstick base	**Prepworks Collapsible Party Carrier** $23.81 Best Buy: **Pyrex Portables Pie Carrier with 9" Pie Plate** $11.88

SPECIALTY PIECES	ITEM	WHAT TO LOOK FOR	TEST KITCHEN FAVORITES
	REVOLVING CAKE STAND	• Tall stand with excellent visibility and comfort • Easy to carry • Rotates quickly and smoothly	**Winco Revolving Cake Decorating Stand** $29.98
	CREAM WHIPPER	• Rubber grip • Responsive lever for effortless control	**ISI Gourmet Whip** $99.27
	SPICE GRINDER	• Fine grind of all spices • Electric, not manual, grinders • Deep bowl to hold ample amount of spices • Easy-to-control texture of grind	**Krups Fast-Touch Coffee Mill** $19.99
	MOKA POT	• Classic design that uses steam pressure to force hot water from bottom chamber up through coffee grounds • Stovetop, not electric, model • Easy to use	**Bialetti Moka Express, 3 cups** $24.95
	FRENCH PRESS	• Fine-mesh filter to eliminate sediment • Insulated pot to keep coffee hot • Smooth, simple, dishwasher-safe parts for easy cleanup	**Bodum Columbia French Press Coffee Maker, Double Wall, 8 Cup** $79.95
	COLD BREW COFFEE MAKER	• Easy to use • Produces smooth, rich-tasting cold brew concentrate • Enough concentrate to make sixty-four 4-ounce cups of coffee	**Toddy Cold Brew System** $34.95
	MANUAL ESPRESSO MAKER	• Includes milk foamer, measuring scoop, and adapter for making two shots simultaneously • Easy and intuitive to use	**ROK Manual Espresso Maker** $150

SPECIALTY PIECES	ITEM	WHAT TO LOOK FOR	TEST KITCHEN FAVORITES
	INNOVATIVE TEAPOT	• Contained ultrafine-mesh strainer keeps tea leaf dregs separate • One-piece design for easy cleaning	ingenuiTEA by Adagio Teas $14.95
	TEA MACHINE	• Perforated tea basket for thorough infusion • Programmable temperature and steep times • Fully automated brewing • Dishwasher-safe accessories	Breville Tea Maker $249.99 Best Buy: Cuisinart PerfecTemp Programmable Tea Steeper & Kettle $99
	TWIST CORKSCREW	• 4.75-inch worm accommodates corks of any length • Nonstick coating ensures smooth, neat piercing • Slim and lightweight, making it easy to handle and store	Le Creuset Table Model Corkpull $19.95
	ELECTRIC WINE OPENER	• Sturdy, quiet corkscrew • Broad base that rests firmly on bottle	Cuisinart Cordless Wine Opener with Vacuum Sealer $39.95
	WINE AERATOR	• Long, tubelike design that exposes wine to air as it is being poured • Neat, hands-free aerating	Nuance Wine Finer $19.95
	WINE SAVER	• Minimizes amount of contact wine has with air • Easy, reliable mechanism • Keeps wine drinkable for at least one month	Air Cork The Wine Preserver $24.95
	CHAMPAGNE SAVER	• Inexpensive • Attaches with an easy one-handed motion • Fits easily in the fridge	Cilio Champagne Bottle Sealer $7.50

MUST-HAVE ITEM

SPECIALTY PIECES	ITEM	WHAT TO LOOK FOR	TEST KITCHEN FAVORITES
	COCKTAIL SHAKER	• Leakproof and easy to use • Domed top doubles as a 1- and 2-ounce jigger • Comfortable grip • Wide mouth for effortless filling, muddling, and cleaning • Includes reamer attachment	Best Cobbler Style Shaker: **Tovolo Stainless Steel 4-in-1 Cocktail Shaker** $8.99 Best Boston Style Shaker: **The Boston Shaker Professional Boston Shaker, Weighted** $14.50
	SILICONE ICE CUBE TRAY	• Sturdy silicone construction • Large cubes that keep drinks from tasting watered-down	**Tovolo King Cube Silicone Ice Cube Tray** $7.95
	COOLER	• Insulating layer of plastic lining • Lightweight, durable, sturdy, and easy to move, even when full • Easy to clean	**California Cooler Bags T-Rex Large Collapsible Rolling Cooler** $75
	INSULATED FOOD CARRIER	• Designed to carry two 13 by 9-inch baking dishes • Sturdy, expandable frame • Insulation keeps food above 140 degrees for more than 3 hours	**Rachael Ray Expandable Lasagna Lugger** $26.95
	WINE CARRIER	• Reusable and washable • Folds up for easy transport • Fits taller and wider bottles	**VinniBag** $28
	INSULATED SHOPPING TOTE	• Shoulder straps for easy toting • Insulation keeps groceries at a food-safe temperature for 2 hours in a 90-degree room	**Rachael Ray ChillOut Thermal Tote** $17.99
	SELTZER MAKER	• Easy to use and easy-to-control level of fizz • Cartridges carbonate up to 60 liter-size bottles	**SodaStream Source Starter Kit** $99.95
	SOUS VIDE MACHINE	• Slim, lightweight machine • Heats water quickly and accurately • Magnetic bottom allows it to stand stably in center of metal pots • Small enough to store in a drawer • Requires smartphone app	**Joule** $199

SPECIALTY PIECES	ITEM	WHAT TO LOOK FOR	TEST KITCHEN FAVORITES
	ROBOT VACUUM	• Easy to use and program • Recharging dock • Efficient, grid-pattern cleaning program • Unique shape fits into corners and along walls	Neato Botvac D80 $499.99
	NEW GENERATION KITCHEN TRASH CANS	• Sleek, spacious frame • Foot pedal flips lid open completely and allows it to close slowly when released • Fingerprint-proof stainless-steel exterior • Easy bag changes	Simplehuman 50L Rectangular Step Can $180 Best Buy: Sterilite Lift-Top Wastebasket $17.99
	COMPOST BUCKET	• Plastic pail to collect food scraps for composter • Carbon filter prevents odors from escaping and allows oxygen to enter so decomposition can occur • Easy-to-open lid that latches securely in place • 2.4-gallon capacity	Exaco Trading Kitchen Compost Waste Collector $19.98

KITCHEN SUPPLIES	ITEM	WHAT TO LOOK FOR	TEST KITCHEN FAVORITES
	FIRE EXTINGUISHER	• Fast, effective, and easy to figure out • Manageable size • Powerful spray that quickly puts out fires	First Alert Tundra Fire Extinguishing Spray $23.88 Amerex 2.5 lb ABC Dry Chemical Fire Extinguisher $41.13
	PARCHMENT PAPER	• Stores flat • Fits perfectly into a standard rimmed baking sheet • Precut sheets for superior convenience	King Arthur Flour Parchment Paper 100 Half-Sheets $19.95 per package ($0.20 per sheet), plus shipping
	PLASTIC WRAP	• Clings to vessels of different materials • Dispenses easily • Resilient and strong over long periods of time	Freeze-Tite Clear High Cling Freezer Wrap $13.21 for 315 sq. feet ($4.19 per 100 sq. feet)
	PLASTIC WRAP DISPENSERS	• Concealed metal teeth for easy, clean cuts • Slightly elevated for easier wrapping	Stretch-Tite Wrap'n Snap 7500 Dispenser $22

MUST-HAVE ITEMS

KITCHEN SUPPLIES	ITEM	WHAT TO LOOK FOR	TEST KITCHEN FAVORITES
	FOOD STORAGE BAGS	• Thick plastic and tight seal • Order online at webrestaurantstore.com	Elkay Plastics Ziplock Heavy Weight Freezer Bag $9.69 for 100 bags
	PARCHMENT COOKING BAGS	• Easy to fill and fold	PaperChef Culinary Parchment Cooking Bags $7.98 for 10 bags
	CHEESE STORAGE WRAPS	• Two-ply wax-coated paper • Easy to fill and fold	Formaticum Cheese Bags and Cheese Paper $9 for 15 bags $9 for 15 sheets with stickers
	FOOD STORAGE CONTAINERS Glass	• Large capacity of 8 cups • Airtight, leakproof seal • Plastic lid that attaches easily	OXO Good Grips 8 Cup Smart Seal Rectangle Container $14.99
	Plastic	• Lightweight material that remains stain-free like glass • Lid with vents for convenient microwaving • Extended rims that stay cool for easy handling • BPA-free	Rubbermaid Brilliance, Large, 9.6 Cup $12.99
	For dry foods	• Sturdy, spacious, and simple to use and clean • Available in a range of sizes • Note: lid sold separately	Cambro 6-Quart Square Storage Container $23.74 ($16.67 for container, $7.07 for lid)
	SOAP-FILLED DISH BRUSH	• Handle for easy gripping and to keep hands dry • Tight seal to prevent soap from leaking	OXO Steel Soap Squirting Dish Brush $11.99
	ALL-PURPOSE CLEANER	• Natural, green product • Cuts through grease and food splatters quickly and efficiently • Pleasant, not overpowering, scent	Method All-Purpose Natural Surface Cleaner (French Lavender) $3.79 for 28 oz

MUST-HAVE ITEM

KITCHEN SUPPLIES	ITEM	WHAT TO LOOK FOR	TEST KITCHEN FAVORITES
	CAST-IRON POT SCRUBBER	• 5-inch square of chain mail made of 316-grade stainless steel • Ideal for cleaning traditional cast-iron cookware	Knapp Made Small Ring CM Scrubber $19.98
	HEAVY-DUTY HANDLED SCRUB BRUSH	• Short, stiff bristles • Compact size • Thick nonslip handle	Caldrea Dishwashing Brush $5
	DISH TOWEL	• Thin cotton for absorbency and flexibility • Dries glassware without streaks • Washes clean without shrinking	Williams-Sonoma Striped Towels, Set of 4 $19.95 ($4.99 per towel)
	PAPER TOWEL HOLDER	• Sturdy, secure, and easy to carry • Angled arm uses spring-loaded tension and tilts to accommodate rolls of all sizes	Simplehuman Tension Arm Paper Towel Holder $24.99
	APRON	• Adjustable neck strap and long strings • Full coverage; chest area reinforced with extra layer of fabric • Stains wash out completely	Bragard Travail Bib Apron $27.95
	LIQUID DISH SOAP	• High concentration of surfactants to wash away oil • Clean scent	Mrs. Meyer's Clean Day Liquid Dish Soap, Lavender $3.99 for 16 ounces
	LAUNDRY STAIN REMOVER	• Clear instructions • Contains enzymes and surfactants to eliminate old and new stains from fabric • Stained fabrics emerged bright as new	OxiClean Versatile Stain Remover $8.59 for 3-lb tub
	UNDER APPLIANCE CLEANER	• Long, thin duster easily and efficiently picks up dust and flour • Fits under most standard home appliances and long enough to reach into far corners • Microfiber head can be washed in the washing machine	OXO Good Grips Under Appliance Duster $15.51

MUST-HAVE ITEM

MUST-HAVE ITEM

SHOPPING FOR INGREDIENTS

Using the best ingredients is one way to guarantee success in the kitchen. But how do you know what to buy? Shelves are filled with a dizzying array of choices—and price does not equal quality. Over the years, the test kitchen's blind-tasting panels have evaluated thousands of ingredients, brand by brand, side by side, plain and in prepared applications, to determine which brands you can trust and which brands to avoid. In the chart that follows, we share the results, revealing our top-rated choices and the attributes that made them stand out among the competition. And because our test kitchen accepts no support from product manufacturers, you can trust our ratings. See AmericasTestKitchen.com for updates to these tastings.

ITEM	TEST KITCHEN FAVORITES	WHY WE LIKE IT
ANCHOVIES	**King Oscar—Flat Fillets in Olive Oil**	• Right amount of salt • Savory without being fishy • Firm, meaty texture • Minimal bones • Aged 4 to 6 months
APPLESAUCE	**Musselman's Lite**	• An unusual ingredient, sucralose, sweetens this applesauce without overpowering its fresh, bright apple flavor • Pinch of salt boosts flavor above weak, bland, and too-sweet competitors • Coarse, almost chunky texture, not slimy like applesauces sweetened with corn syrup
BACON, SUPERMARKET	**Farmland Thick Sliced** and **Plumrose Premium Thick Sliced**	• Good balance of saltiness and sweetness • Smoky and full flavored • Very meaty, not too fatty or insubstantial • Crisp yet hearty texture, not tough or dry
BACON, TURKEY	**Wellshire All Natural Uncured**	• Smoky, salty, sweet flavor of bacon • Pleasantly chewy texture that crisped up more than its competitors
BARBECUE SAUCE, SUPERMARKET	**Bull's-Eye Original**	• Spicy, fresh tomato taste • Good balance of tanginess, smokiness, and sweetness • Robust flavor from molasses • Sweetened with sugar and molasses, not high-fructose corn syrup, which caramelizes and burns quickly
BARBECUE SAUCE, HIGH-END	**Pork Barrel Original**	• Generous amounts of vinegar, salt, chili paste, and liquid smoke for bold spicy flavor • Tangy kick • Good body
BEANS, CANNED BAKED	**B&M Vegetarian**	• Firm and pleasant texture with some bite • Sweetened with molasses for complexity and depth

	ITEM	TEST KITCHEN FAVORITES	WHY WE LIKE IT
	BEANS, CANNED BLACK	**Bush's Best**	• Clean, mild, and slightly earthy flavor • Firm, almost al dente texture, not mushy or pasty • Good amount of salt
	BEANS, CANNED CHICKPEAS	**Goya**	• Nutty flavor • Plump, buttery chickpeas • Enough salt to enhance but not overwhelm the flavor
	BEANS, CANNED WHITE	**Goya**	• Clean, earthy flavor • Smooth, creamy interior with tender skins • Not full of broken beans like some competitors
	BEANS, DRIED WHITE	**Rancho Gordo Classic Cassoulet**	• Creamy and smooth texture • Fresh taste • Nutty and sweet flavors
	BEANS, REFRIED	**Taco Bell Home Originals**	• Well-seasoned mixture • Super-smooth texture, not overly thick, pasty, or gluey
	BREAD, WHITE SANDWICH	**Arnold Country Classics**	• Subtle sweetness, not tasteless or sour • Perfect structure, not too dry or too soft
	BREAD, WHOLE-WHEAT SANDWICH	**Arnold Whole Grains 100%**	• Mild nuttiness with clean wheat flavor and a touch of sweetness • Tender and chewy with crunchy flecks of bulgur on the crust
	BREAD CRUMBS	**Ian's Original Style**	• Crisp, with a substantial crunch • Not too delicate, stale, sandy, or gritty • Oil-free and without seasonings or undesirable artificial flavors

	ITEM	TEST KITCHEN FAVORITES	WHY WE LIKE IT
	BROTH, BEEF	Better Than Bouillon	• Contains good amount of salt and multiple powerful flavor enhancers • Paste is economical, stores easily, and dissolves quickly in hot water
	BROTH, VEGETABLE	Orrington Farms Vegan Chicken Flavored Broth Base & Seasoning	• Savory depth without off-tasting vegetable undertones • Easy to store • Yeast extract adds depth and richness
	BROTH, VEGETABLE, LOW-SODIUM	Edward & Sons Low Sodium Not-Chick'n Natural Bouillon Cubes	• Mild, chicken-y flavor • Unctuous, meaty body • Lends a clean, fresh flavor to risottos and vegetable soups
	BROWNIE MIX	Ghirardelli Chocolate Supreme and Barefoot Contessa Outrageous	• Rich, balanced chocolate flavor from both natural and Dutch-processed cocoa powders • Moist, chewy, and fudgy with perfect texture
	BUTTER, ALMOND	Jif Creamy	• Homogeneous, creamy texture • Clean and distinct almond flavor • Well seasoned with salt and sugar • Made with almonds that are blanched and roasted
	BUTTER, UNSALTED	Plugrá European-Style	• Sweet and creamy • Complex tang and grassy flavor • Moderate amount of butterfat so that it's decadent and glossy but not so rich that baked goods are greasy
	CHEESE, AMERICAN	Boar's Head	• Strong cheesy flavor, unlike some competitors • Higher content of cheese culture contributes to better flavor
	CHEESE, BRIE	Fromager d'Affinois	• Buttery, earthy flavor with gooey, silky texture • Soft, pillowy rind
	CHEESE, BURRATA	Lioni	• Distinct shell with balanced amount of filling • Bright, fresh dairy flavor • Nicely salted • Thick, luscious cream

ITEM	TEST KITCHEN FAVORITES	WHY WE LIKE IT
CHEESE, CHEDDAR, ARTISANAL	Milton Creamery Prairie Breeze	• Earthy complexity with nutty, buttery, and fruity flavors • Dry and crumbly with crystalline crunch, not rubbery or overly moist • Aged no more than 12 months to prevent overly sharp flavor
CHEESE, CHEDDAR, EXTRA-SHARP	Cracker Barrel Extra Sharp White	• Perfect amount of tang • Moderate amounts of fat and moisture ensure toothsome, crumbly texture when eaten plain and melty, creamy texture when cooked
CHEESE, CHEDDAR, REDUCED-FAT	Cracker Barrel Reduced Fat Sharp	• Ample creaminess • Strong cheesy flavor • Good for cooking
CHEESE, CHEDDAR, SHARP	Cabot Vermont	• Nutty, smoky, caramel flavor • Firm, crumbly texture, not moist, rubbery, or springy • Aged a minimum of 9 months for complex flavor
CHEESE, COTTAGE	Daisy Regular	• Large, uniform curds • Thick, creamy consistency • Clean, tart, tangy flavor
CHEESE, CREAM, ARTISANAL	Zingerman's Creamery	• Supercreamy and smooth texture • Impressive depth of flavor
CHEESE, CREAM, SUPERMARKET	Philadelphia Brick Original	• Rich, tangy, and milky flavor • Thick, creamy texture, not pasty, waxy, or chalky
CHEESE, FETA	Real Greek	• Silky, luxurious texture • Savory, complex flavor
CHEESE, FONTINA For Cheese Plate	Fontina Val d'Aosta	• Strong, earthy aroma • Somewhat elastic texture with small irregular holes • Grassy, nutty flavor—but can be overpowering in cooked dishes
For Cooking	Italian Fontina	• Semisoft, super-creamy texture • Mildly tangy, nutty flavor • Melts well

ITEM	TEST KITCHEN FAVORITES	WHY WE LIKE IT
CHEESE, GOAT	**Laura Chenel's Fresh Chèvre Log**	• Rich-tasting, grassy, tangy flavor • Salt content enhances flavor and texture • Smooth and creamy both unheated and baked
CHEESE, GRUYÈRE	**1655 Le Gruyère AOP**	• Aged for 12 to 14 months • High fat and low moisture content provide dense, fudgy texture • Excellent crystalline structure • Deeply aged, caramelized, grassy flavors shine through even when cooked
CHEESE, MASCARPONE	**Polenghi**	• Made with all cream and no milk • Soft and creamy but able to hold shape in desserts • Perfect consistency
CHEESE, MOZZARELLA	**Polly-O Whole Milk**	• Creamy and milky with hint of salt • Elastic but not gooey when melted
CHEESE, MOZZARELLA FRESH	**Belgioioso**	• Plush, pillowy, tender texture • Well-seasoned with a balanced tang • Buttery, creamy, fresh flavor
CHEESE, PARMESAN, PRE-SHREDDED	**Sargento Artisan Blends**	• Mix of small and large shreds • Blends 10- and 18-month-aged Parmesan • Rich, nutty flavor
CHEESE, PARMESAN, SUPERMARKET	**Boar's Head Parmigiano-Reggiano**	• Rich and complex flavor balances tanginess and nuttiness • Dry, crumbly texture yet creamy with a crystalline crunch, not rubbery or dense • Aged a minimum of 12 months for better flavor and texture
CHEESE, PECORINO ROMANO	**Boar's Head**	• High sodium content provides super savory flavor • Pungent, sharp, and creamy in pasta
CHEESE, PEPPER JACK	**Boar's Head Monterey Jack with Jalapeño**	• Buttery, tangy cheese • Clean, balanced flavor with assertive spice

	ITEM	TEST KITCHEN FAVORITES	WHY WE LIKE IT
	CHEESE, PROVOLONE	Provolone Vernengo	• Bold, nutty, and tangy flavor, not plasticky or bland • Firm, dry texture
	CHEESE, RICOTTA	Belgioso Ricotta Con Latte Whole Milk	• Rich, dense consistency • Slight sweetness thanks to sweet whey and small amount of milk • Rich but not overwhelming in manicotti
	CHEESE, SWISS For Cheese Plate	Edelweiss Creamery Emmentaler	• Subtle flavor with sweet, buttery, nutty, and fruity notes • Firm yet gently giving texture, not rubbery • Aged longer for better flavor, resulting in larger eyes • Mildly pungent yet balanced
	For Cooking	Boar's Head Gold Label	• Mild, nutty flavor • Smooth texture when melted
	For Cheese Plate or Cooking	Emmi Emmentaler Cheese AOC	• Creamy texture • Salty mildness preferable for grilled cheese sandwiches
	CHICKEN, BREASTS, BONELESS, SKINLESS	Bell & Evans Air-Chilled	• Juicy and tender with clean chicken flavor • Not salted or brined • Air-chilled • Aged on bone for at least 12 hours after slaughter for significantly more tender meat
	CHICKEN, WHOLE	Mary's Free Range Air Chilled (also sold as Pitman's)	• Great, savory chicken flavor • Very tender • Air-chilled for minimum water retention and cleaner flavor
	CHILI POWDER	Morton & Bassett	• Blend of chile peppers with added seasonings, not assertively hot, overly smoky, or one-dimensional • Balance of sweet and smoky flavors • Potent but not overwhelming

ITEM	TEST KITCHEN FAVORITES	WHY WE LIKE IT
CHOCOLATE, DARK	Ghirardelli 60% Cacao Bittersweet Chocolate Premium Baking Bar	• Creamy texture, not grainy or chalky • Dark, bold flavor with notes of cherries, wine, and smoke • Balance of sweetness and bitterness
CHOCOLATE, DARK CHIPS	Ghirardelli 60% Premium Baking Chips	• Rich, chocolate flavor • Higher cacao and fat percentages • Dew drop shaped chips for even distribution
CHOCOLATE, MILK	Dove Silky Smooth	• Intense, full, rich chocolate flavor • Super-creamy texture from abundant milk fat and cocoa butter • Not overwhelmingly sweet
CHOCOLATE, MILK CHIPS	Hershey's Kitchens	• Bold chocolate flavor outshines too-sweet, weak chocolate flavor of other chips • Complex with caramel and nutty notes • Higher fat content makes texture creamier than grainy, artificial competitors
CHOCOLATE, UNSWEETENED	Hershey's Baking Bar	• Well-rounded, complex flavor • Assertive chocolate flavor and deep notes of cocoa
CHOCOLATE, WHITE CHIPS	Guittard Choc-Au-Lait	• Creamy texture, not waxy or crunchy • Silky smooth meltability from high fat content • Complex flavor like high-quality real chocolate, no artificial or off-flavors
CINNAMON	Morton & Bassett	• Perfect balance of sweet and spicy • Desirable, mellow flavor when baked into cinnamon rolls and on pita chips
COCOA POWDER	Droste	• Dark color with earthy flavor • High fat content and less starch • Ensures decadent chocolate desserts with perfectly moist textures and complex, sophisticated flavors
COCONUT MILK	Aroy-D	• Velvety, luxurious texture that's not too thick • Tastes strongly of coconut but doesn't overwhelm other ingredients

	ITEM	TEST KITCHEN FAVORITES	WHY WE LIKE IT
	COFFEE, DECAF	Maxwell House Original Roast	• Smooth, mellow flavor without being acidic or harsh • Complex, with a slightly nutty aftertaste • Made with only flavorful Arabica beans
	COFFEE, MEDIUM ROAST Bolder	Peet's Coffee Café Domingo	• Extremely smooth but bold-tasting with a strong finish • Rich chocolate and toast flavors • Few defective beans and low acidity
	Brighter	Millstone Breakfast Blend	• Good balance of acidity, earthiness, and complexity • Few defective beans and ideal moisture
	CORNMEAL	Arrowhead Mills Organic Yellow	• Clean, pure corn flavor comes from using whole-grain kernels • Ideal texture resembling slightly damp, fine sand, not too fine or too coarse
	COUSCOUS, ISRAELI	Roland	• Large pearls with a firm, springy texture • Sweet, toasty flavor • Sold in an airtight jar
	CRABMEAT	Phillips Premium Crab Jumbo	• Moist, plump, meaty chunks • Taste comparable to freshly picked crabmeat
	CURRY POWDER	Penzeys Sweet	• Balanced, neither too sweet nor too hot • Complex and vivid earthy flavor, not thin, bland, or one-dimensional NOTE: Available through Amazon.com or mail order (800-741-7787, Penzeys.com).
	DINNER ROLLS, FROZEN	Pepperidge Farm Stone Baked Artisan French	• Pleasantly wheaty and yeasty flavor • Chewy, tender insides and crispy crust • Tastes closest to fresh homemade

ITEM	TEST KITCHEN FAVORITES	WHY WE LIKE IT
FIVE-SPICE POWDER	**Frontier Natural Products Co-Op**	• Woodsy, sweet, and aromatic taste • Harmonious flavor with a nice spice kick
FLOUR, ALL-PURPOSE	**King Arthur Unbleached Enriched**	• Fresh, toasty flavor • No metallic taste or other off-flavors • Consistent results across recipes • Made tender, flaky pie crust, hearty biscuits, crisp cookies, and chewy, sturdy bread
	Pillsbury Unbleached Enriched	• Clean, toasty, and hearty flavor • No metallic or other off-flavors • Consistent results across recipes • Made flaky pie crust, chewy cookies, and tender biscuits, muffins, and cakes
FLOUR, WHOLE-WHEAT	**King Arthur Premium**	• Finely ground for hearty but not overly coarse texture in bread and pancakes • Sweet, nutty flavor
GIARDINIERA	**Pastene**	• Sharp, vinegary tang • Crunchy mix of vegetables • Mellow heat that's potent but not overpowering
HAM, BLACK FOREST DELI	**Dietz & Watson**	• Good texture • Nice ham flavor

	ITEM	TEST KITCHEN FAVORITES	WHY WE LIKE IT
	HAM, SPIRAL-SLICED	Johnston County	• Good balance of smokiness and sweetness • Moist, tender yet firm texture, not dry or too wet • Classic ham flavor
	HOISIN SAUCE	Kikkoman	• Balances sweet, salty, pungent, and spicy flavors • Initial burn mellows into harmonious and aromatic blend without bitterness
	HORSERADISH	Boar's Head	• No preservatives, just horseradish, vinegar, and salt (found in refrigerated section) • Natural flavor and hot without being overpowering
	HOT DOGS	Nathan's Famous	• Meaty, robust, and hearty flavor, not sweet, sour, or too salty • Juicy but not greasy • Firm, craggy texture, not rubbery, mushy, or chewy
	HOT FUDGE SAUCE	Hershey's	• True fudge flavor, not weak or overly sweet • Thick, smooth, and buttery texture
	HOT SAUCE	Frank's Original RedHot	• Complex flavor • Aged peppers as first ingredient • 190-200mg sodium
	HUMMUS	Sabra Classic	• Nutty, earthy flavor • Thick, creamy texture • Clean flavor of tahini

ITEM	TEST KITCHEN FAVORITES	WHY WE LIKE IT
ICE CREAM BARS	Dove Vanilla Ice Cream with Milk Chocolate	• Rich, prominent chocolate flavor • Thick, crunchy chocolate coating • Dense, creamy ice cream with pure vanilla flavor • Milk chocolate, not coconut oil, listed first in coating ingredients
ICE CREAM, CHOCOLATE	Turkey Hill Premium Dutch	• Smooth, creamy texture • Well-rounded chocolate flavor • Clean aftertaste with no bitterness
ICE CREAM, VANILLA	Ben & Jerry's	• Complex yet balanced vanilla flavor from real vanilla extract • Sweetness solely from sugar rather than corn syrup • Creamy richness from both egg yolks and small amount of stabilizers
ICED TEA, BLACK Loose Leaf	Tazo	• Distinctive flavor with herbal notes • Balanced level of strength and astringency
Bottled, with Lemon	Lipton PureLeaf with Lemon	• Bright, balanced, and natural tea and lemon flavors • Uses concentrated tea leaves to extract flavor
KETCHUP	Heinz Organic	• Clean, pure sweetness from sugar, not high-fructose corn syrup • Bold, harmonious punch of saltiness, sweetness, tang, and tomato flavor
LEMONADE	Natalie's Natural	• Natural-tasting lemon flavor without artificial flavors or off-notes • Perfect balance of tartness and sweetness, unlike many overly sweet competitors • Contains 20% lemon juice
MACARONI & CHEESE	Kraft Homestyle Dinner Classic Cheddar Cheese Sauce	• Reinforces flavor with blue and cheddar cheeses • Uses creamy, clingy liquid cheese sauce • Dry noodles, rather than frozen, for substantial texture and bite • Crunchy, buttery bread-crumb topping

ITEM	TEST KITCHEN FAVORITES	WHY WE LIKE IT
MAPLE SYRUP	**Uncle Luke's Grade A Dark Amber**	• Rich caramel flavor and deep molasses-like hue NOTE: We found that all Grade A Dark Amber maple syrups at supermarkets taste similar, so our advice is to buy the cheapest all-maple product available.
MAYONNAISE	**Blue Plate**	• Great balance of taste and texture • Richer, deeper flavor from using egg yolks alone (no egg whites) • Short ingredient list that's close to homemade
MAYONNAISE, LIGHT	**Hellmann's Light**	• Bright, balanced flavor close to full-fat counterpart, not overly sweet like other light mayos • Not as creamy as full-fat but passable texture NOTE: Hellmann's is known as Best Foods west of the Rocky Mountains.
MAYONNAISE, VEGAN	**Hampton Creek Just Mayo, Original**	• Tangy taste and smooth, supercreamy texture • Tasters liked it as much as Hellmann's Real Mayonnaise when tasted side by side
MEXICAN LAGER	**Tecate**	• Light bodied and straw colored • Crisp and clean with lingering bitterness • Refreshing citrusy flavor
MIRIN (JAPANESE RICE WINE)	**Mitoku Organic Mikawa Sweet Rice Seasoning** Best Buy: **Eden Mirin Rice Cooking Wine**	• Good straight up or in teriyaki sauce • Balanced flavors with woodsy overtones and smoky aftertaste
MISO PASTE	**Hikari Organic White**	• Intense umami flavor combined with tropical, sweet, and subtly tart flavors • Full-flavored but not overwhelmingly salty
MOLASSES	**Brer Rabbit All Natural Unsulphured Mild Flavor**	• Acidic yet balanced • Strong and straightforward raisin-y taste • Pleasantly bitter bite

ITEM	TEST KITCHEN FAVORITES	WHY WE LIKE IT
MUSTARD, COARSE-GRAIN	**Grey Poupon Harvest** and **Grey Poupon Country Dijon**	• Spicy, tangy burst of mustard flavor • High salt content amplifies flavor • Contains no superfluous ingredients that mask mustard flavor • Big, round seeds add pleasant crunch • Just enough vinegar, not too sour or thin
MUSTARD, DIJON	**Trois Petits Cochons Moutarde de Dijon**	• Potent, bold, and very hot, not weak or mild • Good balance of sweetness, tanginess, and sharpness • High ratio of mustard seeds for balanced but impactful heat
MUSTARD, YELLOW	**Annie's Naturals Organic**	• Lists mustard seeds second in the ingredients for rich mustard flavor • Good balance of heat and tang • Relatively low salt content
OATS, ROLLED	**Bob's Red Mill Old-Fashioned**	• Toasty, nutty flavor • Hearty, tender
OATS, STEEL-CUT	**Bob's Red Mill Organic**	• Rich and complex oat flavor with buttery, earthy, nutty, and whole-grain notes • Creamy yet toothsome texture • Moist but not sticky NOTE: Not recommended for baking.
OLIVE OIL, EXTRA-VIRGIN, CALIFORNIA	**California Olive Ranch Arbequina**	• Round and full, sweet olive flavor with little bitterness or pungency • Complex with fruity, nutty, and buttery notes and fresh, pure olive aftertaste
OLIVE OIL, EXTRA-VIRGIN, PREMIUM	**Gaea Fresh Extra Virgin**	• Buttery, smooth, lemony, sweet olive fruitiness • Nicely balanced • Aroma like tomato stems with a lightly peppery aftertaste
OLIVE OIL, EXTRA-VIRGIN, SUPERMARKET	**California Olive Ranch Everyday Extra Virgin**	• Complex finish with fresh flavors • Aromatic and fruity, not bland or bitter • Clean taste, comparable to a fresh-squeezed olive • Outshines bland, greasy competitors

ITEM	TEST KITCHEN FAVORITES	WHY WE LIKE IT
OLIVES, PIMENTO-STUFFED GREEN	**Mezzetta Super Colossal Spanish Queen**	• Meaty and juicy • Bright taste when cooked • Calcium chloride helps to firm flesh
ORANGE JUICE	**Natalie's 100% Florida, Gourmet Pasteurized**	• Squeezed within 24 hours of shipping • Superfresh taste with no flavor manipulation • Gentler pasteurization helps retain fresh-squeezed flavor • Pleasantly variable flavor with notes of guava and mango
OYSTER CRACKERS	**Sunshine Krispy**	• Wheaty, toasty flavor • Flaky, delicate crackers that retain their crispness in soup
PANCAKE MIX	**Hungry Jack Buttermilk**	• Flavorful balance of sweetness and tang well-seasoned with sugar and salt • Light, extra fluffy texture • Requires vegetable oil (along with milk and egg) to reconstitute the batter
PAPRIKA, SMOKED	**Simply Organic**	• Deep, rich smoky taste • Balanced flavor • Made in Spain according to traditional methods
PAPRIKA, SWEET	**The Spice House Hungarian Sweet**	• Complex flavor with earthy, fruity notes • Bright and bold, not bland and boring • Rich, toasty aroma NOTE: Available only through mail order, The Spice House (312-274-0378, TheSpiceHouse.com).
PASTA, CHEESE RAVIOLI, SUPERMARKET	**Rosetto**	• Creamy, plush, and rich blend of ricotta, Romano, and Parmesan cheeses • Pasta with nice, springy bite • Perfect dough-to-filling ratio
PASTA, CHEESE TORTELLINI, SUPERMARKET	**Barilla Three Cheese**	• Robustly flavored filling from combination of ricotta, Emmentaler, and Grana Padano cheeses • Tender pasta that's sturdy enough to withstand boiling but not so thick that it becomes doughy

ITEM	TEST KITCHEN FAVORITES	WHY WE LIKE IT
PASTA, EGG NOODLES	Pennsylvania Dutch Wide (also sold as Mueller's)	• Balanced, buttery taste with no off-flavors • Light and fluffy texture, not gummy or starchy
PASTA, ELBOW MACARONI	Barilla	• Rich, wheaty taste with no off-flavors • Pleasantly hearty texture, not mushy or chewy • Ridged surface and slight twist in shape hold sauce especially well
PASTA, LASAGNA NOODLES No-Boil	Barilla	• Taste and texture of fresh pasta • Delicate, flat noodles
Whole-Wheat	Bionaturae Organic	• Complex nutty, rich wheat flavor • Substantial chewy texture without any grittiness
PASTA, PENNE	Mueller's Penne Rigate	• Hearty texture, not insubstantial or gummy • Wheaty, slightly sweet flavor, not bland
PASTA, SPAGHETTI	De Cecco No. 12	• Rich, nutty, wheaty flavor • Firm, ropy strands with good chew, not mushy, gummy, or mealy • Semolina flour for resilient texture • Dried at moderately low temperature for 18 hours to preserve flavor
PASTA, SPAGHETTI, GLUTEN-FREE	Jovial Organic Brown Rice	• Springy texture • Clean-tasting flavor • No off-flavors or gumminess
PASTA, SPAGHETTI, WHOLE-WHEAT	Bionaturae Organic 100%	• Chewy, firm, and toothsome, not mushy or rubbery • Full and nutty wheat flavor

ITEM	TEST KITCHEN FAVORITES	WHY WE LIKE IT
PASTA SAUCE, JARRED	Rao's Homemade Marinara Sauce	• Vibrant tomato flavor reminiscent of homemade sauce • Bright acidity and gentle aromatic undertones of garlic and basil • Uses whole tomatoes
PEANUT BUTTER Creamy	Skippy	• Smooth, creamy, and spreadable • Good balance of sweet and salty flavors
Crunchy	Skippy Super Chunk	• Light, smooth, creamy butter with peanut chunks evenly dispersed • Toasty flavor with a hint of sweetness
PEPPERCORNS, BLACK Artisanal	Kalustyan's Indian Tellicherry	• Enticing and fragrant, not musty, aroma with flavor to back it up and moderate heat • Fresh, complex flavor at once sweet and spicy, earthy and smoky, fruity and floral NOTE: Available only by mail order, Kalustyan's (800-352-3451, Kalustyans.com).
Supermarket	Morton & Bassett Organic Whole	• Spicy but not too hot • Sharp, fresh, classic pepper flavor
PEPPERCORNS, SICHUAN	Dean & DeLuca Best Buy: Savory Spice Shop	• Fresh, potent aroma with floral, citrus, herbal, and black tea notes • Sharp, zippy tingling effect
PEPPERONI	Margherita Italian Style	• Nice balance of meatiness and spice • Tangy, fresh flavor with hints of fruity licorice and peppery fennel • Thin slices with the right amount of chew

ITEM	TEST KITCHEN FAVORITES	WHY WE LIKE IT
PEPPERS, ROASTED RED	Dunbars Sweet	• Balance of smokiness and sweetness • Mild, sweet, and earthy red pepper flavor • Firm texture, not slimy or mushy • Packed in simple yet strong brine of salt and water without distraction of other strongly flavored ingredients
PICKLES, BREAD-AND-BUTTER	Bubbies Chips	• Subtle, briny tang • All-natural solution that uses real sugar, not high-fructose corn syrup
PICKLES, WHOLE KOSHER DILL	Boar's Head	• Authentic, garlicky flavor and firm, snappy crunch • Balanced salty, sour, and garlic flavors • Fresh and refrigerated, not processed and shelf-stable
PORK, PREMIUM	Snake River Farms: American Kurobuta Berkshire	• Deep pink tint, which indicates higher pH level and more flavorful meat • Tender texture and juicy, intensely porky flavor
POTATO CHIPS Kettle Style	Utz's Kettle Classics, Original	• Perfectly salted, flavorful chips • Slightly thick chips that are crunchy • Not too greasy
Regular	Herr's Crisp 'N Tasty	• Thin and crispy without being flimsy
PRESERVES, APRICOT	Smucker's	• Deep, authentic apricot taste • Visible fruit suspended in spreadable jam • Sweetened with sugar and syrup rather than with flavor-muting fruits
PRESERVES, RASPBERRY	Smucker's	• Clean, strong raspberry flavor, not too tart or sweet • Not overly seedy • Ideal, spreadable texture, not too thick, artificial, or overprocessed
PRESERVES, STRAWBERRY	Welch's	• Big, distinct strawberry flavor • Natural-tasting and not overwhelmingly sweet • Thick and spreadable texture, not runny, slimy, or too smooth

ITEM	TEST KITCHEN FAVORITES	WHY WE LIKE IT
PROSCIUTTO, SUPERMARKET	Volpi Traditional Best Buy: Del Duca	• Tender and buttery flavor • Silky and supple texture • Very thin slices
RELISH, SWEET PICKLE	Cascadian Farm	• Piquant, sweet flavor, lacks out-of-place flavors such as cinnamon and clove present in competitors • Fresh and natural taste, free of yellow dye #5 and high-fructose corn syrup • Good texture, not mushy like competitors
RICE, ARBORIO	RiceSelect	• Creamier than competitors • Smooth grains • Characteristic good bite of Arborio rice in risotto where al dente is ideal
RICE, BASMATI	Daawat	• Pleasantly chewy, long, intact, fluffy grains • Fragrant, aromatic flavor • Aged 18–24 months • Imported from India
RICE, BROWN	Lundberg Organic Long Grain	• Firm yet tender grains • Bold, toasty, nutty flavor
RICE, JASMINE	Dynasty	• Floral fragrance • Separate, toothsome grains
RICE, LONG-GRAIN WHITE	Lundberg Organic	• Nutty, buttery, and toasty flavor • Distinct, smooth grains that offer some chew without being overly chewy
RICE, READY, WHITE	Minute Ready to Serve	• Parboiled long-grain white rice that is ready in less than 2 minutes • Toasted, buttery flavor • Firm grains with al dente bite
RICE, WILD	Goose Valley	• Plump grains • Firm texture • Woodsy flavor

ITEM	TEST KITCHEN FAVORITES	WHY WE LIKE IT
SALSA, HOT	Pace Hot Chunky	• Good balance of bright tomato, chile, and vegetal flavors • Chunky, almost crunchy texture, not mushy or thin • Spicy and fiery but not overpowering
SALT	Maldon	• Light and airy texture • Delicately crunchy flakes • Not so coarse as to be overly crunchy or gritty nor so fine as to disappear
SAUCE, FISH	Red Boat 40° N	• Intensely rich and flavorful thanks to an abundance of protein • High in sodium but not overly salty
SAUSAGE, BREAKFAST	Jimmy Dean Fully Cooked Original	• Nice and plump with crisp golden crust • Good balance of sweetness and spiciness with hints of maple • Tender, super-juicy meat, not rubbery, spongy, or greasy
SAUSAGE, KIELBASA	Wellshire Farms Smoked Polska	• Deeply smoked and distinctive garlicky flavor • Nice, coarse texture
SMOKED SALMON	Spence & Co. Traditional Scottish Style	• Subtle smoky flavor balanced with clean fresh salmon taste • Thinly sliced for easy eating • Firm and flaky, even when cooked • Uniformly silky and buttery thanks to manufacturer's trimming of pellicle
SOUP, CANNED CHICKEN NOODLE	Muir Glen Organic	• Organic chicken and vegetables and plenty of seasonings give it a fresh taste and spicy kick • Firm, not mushy, vegetables and noodles • No off-flavors
SOUP, CANNED TOMATO	Progresso Vegetable Classics Hearty	• Includes fresh, unprocessed tomatoes, not just tomato puree like some competitors • Tangy, slightly herbaceous flavor • Balanced seasoning and natural sweetness • Medium body and slightly chunky texture

	ITEM	TEST KITCHEN FAVORITES	WHY WE LIKE IT
	SOY SAUCE	Kikkoman	• Good salty-sweet balance • Long fermentation (6–8 months) • Simple ingredient list (wheat, soybeans, water, and salt) with no added sugar or flavor enhancers
	STOCK, CHICKEN	Swanson	• Rich, meaty flavor • More robust and savory than unsalted version
	STOCK, CHICKEN, UNSALTED	Swanson Unsalted	• Subtle and clean-tasting with mellow chicken flavor • High percentage of meat-based proteins
	SWEETENED CONDENSED MILK	Borden Eagle Brand and Nestlé Carnation	• Made with whole milk • Creamy in desserts and balances more assertive notes with other ingredients
	TAHINI	Ziyad	• Distinct, intense sesame flavor • Smooth, fluid consistency made creamy, buttery hummus
	TARTAR SAUCE	Legal Sea Foods	• Creamy, nicely balanced sweet-tart base • Lots of vegetable chunks
	TEA, BLACK For Plain Tea	Twinings English Breakfast	• Bright, bold, and flavorful yet not too strong • Fruity, floral, and fragrant • Smooth, slightly astringent profile preferred for tea without milk
	For Tea with Milk and Sugar	Tetley British Blend	• Clean, strong taste • Caramel notes and pleasant bitterness • Full, deep, smoky flavors • Good balance of flavor and intensity • More astringent profile stands up to milk

ITEM	TEST KITCHEN FAVORITES	WHY WE LIKE IT
TERIYAKI SAUCE	Annie Chun's All Natural	• Distinct teriyaki flavor without offensive or dominant flavors, unlike competitors • Smooth, rich texture, not too watery or gluey
TOFU, FIRM	Nasoya Organic Firm	• Delicate, clean soy flavor • Consistent, even texture that holds its shape and offers right amount of chew when cooked
TOMATOES, CANNED CRUSHED	SMT	• Bright and sweet, full tomato flavor • Added diced tomatoes contribute a firm, tender texture
TOMATOES, CANNED DICED	Hunt's	• Bright, fresh tomato flavor that balances sweet and tart • Firm yet tender texture
TOMATOES, CANNED FIRE-ROASTED	DeLallo Diced Tomatoes in Juice with Seasonings	• Intense smoky flavor • Natural tomato texture
TOMATOES, CANNED PUREED	Muir Glen Organic	• Full tomato flavor without any bitter, sour, or tinny notes • Pleasantly thick, even consistency, not watery or thin
TOMATOES, CANNED WHOLE	Muir Glen Organic Peeled	• Pleasing balance of bold acidity and fruity sweetness • Firm yet tender texture, even after hours of simmering
TOMATO PASTE	Goya	• Bright, robust tomato flavor • Balance of sweet and tart flavors

	ITEM	TEST KITCHEN FAVORITES	WHY WE LIKE IT
	TORTILLA CHIPS	**On the Border Café Style**	• Buttery, sweet corn flavor, not bland, artificial, or rancid • Sturdy yet crunchy and crisp texture, not brittle, stale, or cardboardlike
	TORTILLAS, FLOUR	**Old El Paso Soft Tacos & Fajitas**	• Thin, flaky tortilla with tender texture • Made with plenty of fat and salt
	TOSTADAS, CORN	**Mission Tostadas Estilo Casero**	• Crisp, crunchy texture • Good corn flavor • Flavor and texture that are substantial enough to stand up to hearty toppings
	TUNA, CANNED Premium	**Nardin Bonito Del Norte Ventresca Fillets**	• Creamy, delicate meat and tender yet firm fillets • Full, rich tuna flavor
	Regular	**Wild Planet Wild Albacore** Best Buy: **Tonnino Ventresca Yellowfin in Olive Oil**	• Rich, fresh-tasting, and flavorful, not fishy • Hearty, substantial chunks of tuna
	TURKEY Heritage	**Mary's Free-Range** Best Buy: **Heritage Turkey Farm**	• Distinct layer of fat below the skin for moist, flavorful meat • Long-legged with an angular breast and almost bluish-purple dark meat (the sign of a well-exercised bird)
	Supermarket	**Mary's Free-Range Non-GMO Verified** Best Buy: **Plainville Farms**	• Juicy, moist texture • Rich, colorful turkey taste

	ITEM	TEST KITCHEN FAVORITES	WHY WE LIKE IT
	TURMERIC	**Frontier Co-Op Ground**	• Warm, moderate heat • Aromatic and pleasantly earthy
	VANILLA BEANS	**McCormick Madagascar**	• Moist, seed-filled pods • Complex, robust flavor with caramel notes
	VANILLA EXTRACT	**McCormick Pure**	• Strong, rich vanilla flavor where others are weak and sharp • Complex flavor with spicy, caramel notes and a sweet undertone
	VEGETABLE OIL, ALL-PURPOSE	**Crisco Blends**	• Unobtrusive, mild flavor for stir-frying and sautéing and for use in baked goods and in uncooked applications such as mayonnaise and vinaigrette • Neutral taste and absence of fishy or metallic flavors when used for frying
	VERMOUTH	**Dolin Dry Vermouth de Chambéry**	• Versatile and crisp with notes of fresh fruit, citrus, and mint • Good for cooking and for drinking plain or in cocktails
	VINEGAR, APPLE CIDER	**Heinz Filtered**	• Good balance of sweet and tart • Distinct apple flavor with a floral aroma and assertive, tangy qualities
	VINEGAR, BALSAMIC, SUPERMARKET	**Bertolli of Modena**	• Syrupy texture when used in a vinaigrette • Notes of apple, molasses, and dried fruit when served plain

ITEM	TEST KITCHEN FAVORITES	WHY WE LIKE IT
VINEGAR, RED WINE	Laurent Du Clos	• Crisp red wine flavor balanced by stronger than average acidity and subtle sweetness • Complex yet pleasing taste from multiple varieties of grapes
VINEGAR, SHERRY	Napa Valley Naturals Reserve	• Slightly sweet with just the right amount of tang • Boasts flavors ranging from "lemony" to "smoky"
VINEGAR, WHITE WINE	Napa Valley Naturals Organic	• High levels of acidity and sweetness • Made from a wine based on crisp-tasting Trebbiano grapes
YOGURT, FROZEN, SUPERMARKET	TCBY Classic Vanilla Bean	• Balanced sweetness • Straightforward vanilla flavor • Smooth texture
YOGURT, GREEK NONFAT	Fage Total 0%	• Smooth, creamy consistency, not watery or puddinglike from added thickeners such as pectin or gelatin • Pleasantly tangy, well-balanced flavor, not sour or metallic
YOGURT, GREEK WHOLE-MILK	Fage Total Classic	• Rich taste and satiny texture, not thin, watery, or soupy • Buttery, tangy flavor
YOGURT, WHOLE-MILK	Brown Cow Cream Top Plain	• Rich, well-rounded flavor, not sour or bland • Especially creamy, smooth texture, not thin or watery • Higher fat content contributes to flavor and texture

2019 EPISODE DIRECTORY

MOROCCAN LENTIL AND CHICKPEA SOUP

WHY THIS RECIPE WORKS: If you only know lentil soup as a plain and rather homogeneous dish, prepare to be wowed by the Moroccan version known as *harira*. Like countless other regional dishes, harira's exact ingredients vary from region to region and even from family to family. We wanted our version to be doable on a weeknight and ideally call mainly for staples we already had on hand. We decided to omit any meat—it seemed unnecessary with all the other robust flavors and textures in the mix. To save time, we opted for convenient canned chickpeas rather than dried beans, plus quick-cooking lentils. We pared down the number of spices to a key five, which made it a dish most people can prepare without a special trip to the market. For more depth of flavor, we also replaced half the water with chicken broth. Using large amounts of just two herbs made for quicker prep and a more efficient use of fresh ingredients. Finishing the dish with fresh lemon juice helped focus all the flavors. This wonderfully complex-tasting, spice-filled soup, made almost entirely from pantry ingredients, brought humble lentils to a whole new level.

Moroccan Lentil and Chickpea Soup (Harira)
SERVES 6 TO 8

For a vegetarian version, substitute vegetable broth for the chicken broth and water. We like to garnish this soup with a small amount of harissa, a fiery North African chili paste, which is available at some supermarkets.

- ⅓ cup extra-virgin olive oil
- 1 large onion, chopped fine
- 2 celery ribs, chopped fine
- 5 garlic cloves, minced
- 1 tablespoon grated fresh ginger
- 2 teaspoons ground coriander
- 2 teaspoons smoked paprika
- 1 teaspoon ground cumin
- ½ teaspoon ground cinnamon
- ⅛ teaspoon red pepper flakes
- ¾ cup minced fresh cilantro
- ½ cup minced fresh parsley
- 4 cups chicken broth
- 4 cups water
- 1 (15-ounce) can chickpeas, rinsed
- 1 cup brown lentils, picked over and rinsed
- 1 (28-ounce) can crushed tomatoes
- ½ cup orzo
- 4 ounces Swiss chard, stemmed and cut into ½-inch pieces
- 2 tablespoons lemon juice
  Salt and pepper
  Lemon wedges

1. Heat oil in large Dutch oven over medium-high heat until shimmering. Add onion and celery and cook, stirring frequently, until translucent and starting to brown, 7 to 8 minutes. Reduce heat to medium, add garlic and ginger, and cook until fragrant, 1 minute. Stir in coriander, paprika, cumin, cinnamon, and pepper flakes and cook for 1 minute. Stir in ½ cup cilantro and ¼ cup parsley and cook for 1 minute.

2. Stir in broth, water, chickpeas, and lentils; increase heat to high and bring to simmer. Reduce heat to medium-low, partially cover, and gently simmer until lentils are just tender, about 20 minutes.

3. Stir in tomatoes and pasta and simmer, partially covered, for 7 minutes, stirring occasionally. Stir in chard and continue to cook, partially covered, until pasta is tender, about 5 minutes longer. Off heat, stir in lemon juice, remaining ¼ cup cilantro, and remaining ¼ cup parsley. Season with salt and pepper to taste. Serve, passing lemon wedges separately.

HEARTY BEEF AND VEGETABLE STEW

WHY THIS RECIPE WORKS: We wanted a satisfying yet healthy beef stew packed with hearty winter vegetables. Instead of using a 4-pound chuck roast, we used a much smaller roast to both lighten our stew and make way for all the vegetables. To start we browned the beef to get a good base on which to build layers of flavor. We then cooked portobello mushrooms in the fat left behind, infusing them with plenty of meaty flavor. Onions, garlic, and thyme gave the stew a savory profile, before adding flour and tomato paste to help thicken the stew. For more complex flavor, we used a mixture of wine, chicken broth, and beef broth. We then returned the browned meat back into the pot, along with the root vegetables. Kale, peas, and parsley came last, as they required less time to cook through.

Hearty Beef and Vegetable Stew
SERVES 4 TO 6

- 2 pounds boneless beef chuck-eye roast, trimmed and cut into 1½-inch pieces
  Salt and pepper
- 5 teaspoons canola oil
- 1 large portobello mushroom cap, cut into ½-inch pieces
- 2 onions, chopped fine
- 3 garlic cloves, minced
- 1 tablespoon minced fresh thyme or 1 teaspoon dried
- 3 tablespoons all-purpose flour
- 1 tablespoon tomato paste
- 1½ cups dry red wine
- 2 cups chicken broth
- 2 cups beef broth
- 2 bay leaves
- 12 ounces red potatoes, unpeeled, cut into 1-inch pieces
- 4 carrots, peeled, halved lengthwise, and sliced 1 inch thick
- 4 parsnips, peeled, halved lengthwise, and sliced 1 inch thick

8   ounces kale, stemmed and sliced into ½-inch-wide strips

½   cup frozen peas

¼   cup minced fresh parsley

1. Adjust oven rack to lower-middle position and heat oven to 300 degrees. Pat beef dry with paper towels and season with salt and pepper. Heat 1 teaspoon oil in Dutch oven over medium-high heat until just smoking. Brown half of meat on all sides, 5 to 10 minutes; transfer to bowl. Repeat with 1 teaspoon oil and remaining beef; transfer to bowl.

2. Add mushroom pieces to fat left in pot, cover, and cook over medium heat until softened and wet, about 5 minutes. Uncover and continue to cook until mushroom pieces are dry and browned, 5 to 10 minutes.

3. Stir in remaining 1 tablespoon oil and onions and cook until softened, 5 to 7 minutes. Stir in garlic and thyme and cook until fragrant, about 30 seconds. Stir in flour and tomato paste and cook until flour is lightly browned, about 1 minute.

4. Slowly whisk in wine, scraping up any browned bits. Slowly whisk in chicken broth and beef broth until smooth. Stir in bay leaves and browned meat and bring to simmer. Cover, transfer pot to oven, and cook for 1½ hours.

5. Stir in potatoes, carrots, and parsnips and continue to cook in oven until meat and vegetables are tender, about 1 hour. Stir in kale and continue to cook in oven until tender, about 10 minutes. Remove stew from oven and remove bay leaves. Stir in peas and parsley and let stew sit for 5 to 10 minutes. Season with salt and pepper to taste. Serve.

BRAZILIAN SHRIMP AND FISH STEW

WHY THIS RECIPE WORKS: For a bright, fresh, and filling version of this traditional Brazilian stew, we started with the seafood. Cod and shrimp made for a nice balance of flavor and texture, and both were easy to find. After tossing the seafood with garlic, salt, and pepper, we looked to the other components of the stew. To balance the richness and sweetness of the coconut milk with the bright, fresh flavor of the aromatics, we blended the onion, tomatoes, and a portion of the cilantro in the food processor until they had the texture of a slightly chunky salsa, which added body to the stew. We kept the bell peppers diced for contrasting texture and bite. To ensure that the seafood was properly cooked, we brought the broth to a boil to make sure the pot was super-hot, added the seafood and lime juice, covered the pot, and removed it from the heat, allowing the seafood to gently cook in the residual heat. To finish our *moqueca*, we added more cilantro and a couple of tablespoons of homemade pepper sauce, which elevated the stew with its bright, vinegary tang.

Brazilian Shrimp and Fish Stew (Moqueca)

SERVES 6

Pickled hot cherry peppers are usually sold jarred, next to the pickles or jarred roasted red peppers at the supermarket. Haddock or other firm-fleshed, flaky whitefish may be substituted for cod. We prefer untreated shrimp, but if your shrimp are treated with sodium, do not add salt to the shrimp in step 2. Our favorite coconut milk is made by Aroy-D. Serve with steamed white rice.

PEPPER SAUCE

4   pickled hot cherry peppers (3 ounces)

½   onion, chopped coarse

¼   cup extra-virgin olive oil

⅛   teaspoon sugar

   Salt

STEW

1   pound large shrimp (26 to 30 per pound), peeled, deveined, and tails removed

1   pound skinless cod fillets (¾ to 1 inch thick), cut into 1½-inch pieces

3   garlic cloves, minced

   Salt and pepper

1   onion, chopped coarse

1   (14.5-ounce) can whole peeled tomatoes

¾   cup chopped fresh cilantro

2   tablespoons extra-virgin olive oil

1   red bell pepper, stemmed, seeded, and cut into ½-inch pieces

1   green bell pepper, stemmed, seeded, and cut into ½-inch pieces

1   (14-ounce) can coconut milk

2   tablespoons lime juice

1. FOR THE PEPPER SAUCE: Process all ingredients in food processor until smooth, about 30 seconds, scraping down sides of bowl as needed. Season with salt to taste and transfer to separate bowl. Rinse out processor bowl.

2. FOR THE STEW: Toss shrimp and cod with garlic, ½ teaspoon salt, and ¼ teaspoon pepper in bowl. Set aside.

3. Process onion, tomatoes and their juice, and ¼ cup cilantro in food processor until finely chopped and mixture has texture of pureed salsa, about 30 seconds.

4. Heat oil in large Dutch oven over medium-high heat until shimmering. Add red and green bell peppers and ½ teaspoon salt and cook, stirring frequently, until softened, 5 to 7 minutes. Add onion-tomato mixture and ½ teaspoon salt. Reduce heat to medium and cook, stirring frequently, until puree has reduced and thickened slightly, 3 to 5 minutes (pot should not be dry).

5. Increase heat to high, stir in coconut milk, and bring to boil (mixture should be bubbling across entire surface). Add seafood mixture and lime juice and stir to evenly distribute seafood, making sure all pieces are submerged in liquid. Cover pot and remove from heat. Let stand until shrimp and cod are opaque and just cooked through, 15 minutes.

6. Gently stir in 2 tablespoons pepper sauce and remaining ½ cup cilantro, being careful not to break up cod too much. Season with salt and pepper to taste. Serve, passing remaining pepper sauce separately.

ROAST CHICKEN WITH WARM BREAD SALAD

WHY THIS RECIPE WORKS: Few dishes are as beloved and crowd-pleasing as roast chicken. Perhaps no one knew this better than the late, renowned chef Judy Rodgers of Zuni Café in San Francisco. When she put her roast chicken with warm bread salad on the menu in the late '80s, it was a real hit. Now, some 30 years later, it still is. We wanted our own take on Zuni Café's roast chicken with bread salad, so we started by butterflying a whole chicken and salting it overnight; this would allow it to cook quickly and evenly and be juicy and well seasoned. Before roasting the chicken in a 475-degree oven, we covered the bottom of a skillet with bread cubes that we had moistened with oil and broth and then draped the chicken on top. The bread cubes toasted and browned beneath the bird while absorbing its juices to create a mix of moistened, crispy-fried, and chewy pieces all packed with savory flavor. To finish the dish, we built a vinaigrette of champagne vinegar, oil, currants, thinly sliced scallions, Dijon mustard, and chicken drippings that we tossed with peppery arugula and the toasted bread. To ensure the greens didn't wilt, we served the salad alongside the carved chicken.

Roast Chicken with Warm Bread Salad

SERVES 4 TO 6

Note that this recipe requires refrigerating the seasoned chicken for 24 hours. This recipe was developed and tested using Diamond Crystal Kosher Salt. If you have Morton Kosher Salt, which is denser than Diamond Crystal, put only ½ teaspoon of salt onto the cavity. Red wine or white wine vinegar may be substituted for champagne vinegar, if desired. For the bread, we prefer a round rustic loaf with a chewy, open crumb and a sturdy outer crust.

- 1 (4-pound) whole chicken, giblets discarded
  Kosher salt and pepper
- 4 (1-inch-thick) slices country-style bread (8 ounces), bottom crust removed, cut into ¾- to 1-inch pieces (5 cups)
- ¼ cup chicken broth
- 6 tablespoons plus 2 teaspoons extra-virgin olive oil
- 2 tablespoons champagne vinegar
- 1 teaspoon Dijon mustard
- 3 scallions, sliced thin
- 2 tablespoons dried currants
- 5 ounces (5 cups) baby arugula

1. Place chicken, breast side down, on cutting board. Using kitchen shears, cut through bones on either side of backbone; discard backbone. Do not trim off any excess fat or skin. Flip chicken over and press on breastbone to flatten.

2. Using your fingers, carefully loosen skin covering breast and legs. Rub ½ teaspoon salt under skin of each breast, ½ teaspoon under skin of each leg, and 1 teaspoon salt onto bird's cavity. Tuck wings behind back and turn legs so drumsticks face inward toward breasts. Place chicken on wire rack set in rimmed baking sheet or on large plate and refrigerate, uncovered, for 24 hours.

3. Adjust oven rack to middle position and heat oven to 475 degrees. Spray 12-inch skillet with vegetable oil spray. Toss bread with broth and 2 tablespoons oil until pieces are evenly moistened. Arrange bread in skillet in single layer, with majority of crusted pieces near center, crust side up.

4. Pat chicken dry with paper towels and place, skin side up, on top of bread. Brush 2 teaspoons oil over chicken skin and sprinkle with ¼ teaspoon salt and ¼ teaspoon pepper. Roast chicken until skin is deep golden brown and thickest part of breast registers 160 degrees and thighs register 175 degrees, 45 to 50 minutes, rotating skillet halfway through roasting.

5. While chicken roasts, whisk vinegar, mustard, ¼ teaspoon salt, and ¼ teaspoon pepper together in small bowl. Slowly whisk in remaining ¼ cup oil. Stir in scallions and currants and set aside. Place arugula in large bowl.

6. Transfer chicken to carving board and let rest, uncovered, for 15 minutes. Run thin metal spatula under bread to loosen from bottom of skillet. (Bread should be mix of softened, golden-brown, and crunchy pieces.) Carve chicken and whisk any accumulated juices into vinaigrette. Add bread and vinaigrette to arugula and toss to evenly coat. Transfer salad to serving platter and serve with chicken.

INDOOR PULLED CHICKEN

WHY THIS RECIPE WORKS: Traditional pulled chicken is a true labor of love, so we wanted to find a stovetop version of really good pulled chicken that still had the texture and flavor of outdoor slow-smoked pulled chicken but in just a fraction of the time. We started by braising boneless, skinless chicken thighs in a mixture of chicken broth, salt, sugar, molasses, gelatin, and liquid smoke, which simulated the flavor of traditional smoked chicken. The gelatin and broth helped mimic the unctuous texture and intense chicken flavor of whole chicken parts. To mimic the richness of skin-on chicken, we skipped trimming the fat from the thighs and added the rendered fat back to the finished pulled chicken. Finally, we mixed the shredded meat with a homemade barbecue sauce and cooked it briefly to drive off excess moisture.

Indoor Pulled Chicken

SERVES 6 TO 8

Do not trim the fat from the chicken thighs; it contributes to the flavor and texture of the pulled chicken. If you don't have 3 tablespoons of fat to add back to the pot in step 3, add melted butter to make up the difference. We like mild molasses in this recipe; do not use blackstrap. Serve the pulled chicken on white bread or hamburger buns with pickles and coleslaw.

1 cup chicken broth

2 tablespoons molasses

1 tablespoon sugar

1 tablespoon liquid smoke

1 teaspoon unflavored gelatin

Salt and pepper

2 pounds boneless, skinless chicken thighs, halved crosswise

1 recipe barbecue sauce (recipes follow)

Hot sauce

1. Bring broth, molasses, sugar, 2 teaspoons liquid smoke, gelatin, and 1 teaspoon salt to boil in large Dutch oven over high heat, stirring to dissolve sugar. Add chicken and return to simmer. Reduce heat to medium-low, cover, and cook, stirring occasionally, until chicken is easily shredded with fork, about 25 minutes.

2. Transfer chicken to medium bowl and set aside. Strain cooking liquid through fine-mesh strainer set over bowl (do not wash pot). Let liquid settle for 5 minutes; skim fat from surface. Set aside fat and defatted liquid.

3. Using tongs, squeeze chicken until shredded into bite-size pieces. Transfer chicken, 1 cup barbecue sauce, ½ cup reserved defatted liquid, 3 tablespoons reserved fat, and remaining 1 teaspoon liquid smoke to now-empty pot. Cook mixture over medium heat, stirring frequently, until liquid has been absorbed and exterior of meat appears dry, about 5 minutes. Season with salt, pepper, and hot sauce to taste. Serve, passing remaining barbecue sauce separately.

Lexington Vinegar Barbecue Sauce
MAKES ABOUT 2 CUPS
For a spicier sauce, add hot sauce to taste.

1 cup cider vinegar

½ cup ketchup

½ cup water

1 tablespoon sugar

¾ teaspoon salt

¾ teaspoon red pepper flakes

½ teaspoon pepper

Whisk all ingredients together in bowl.

South Carolina Mustard Barbecue Sauce
MAKES ABOUT 2 CUPS
You can use either light or dark brown sugar in this recipe.

1 cup yellow mustard

½ cup distilled white vinegar

¼ cup packed brown sugar

¼ cup Worcestershire sauce

2 tablespoons hot sauce

1 teaspoon salt

1 teaspoon pepper

Whisk all ingredients together in bowl.

Sweet and Tangy Barbecue Sauce
MAKES ABOUT 2 CUPS
We like mild molasses in this recipe.

1½ cups ketchup

¼ cup molasses

2 tablespoons Worcestershire sauce

1 tablespoon hot sauce

½ teaspoon salt

½ teaspoon pepper

Whisk all ingredients together in bowl.

PERFECT SEARED STEAKS

WHY THIS RECIPE WORKS: Though we often think of the grill when it comes to steaks, sous vide cooking is a game changer. The water bath technique takes all of the risk, guesswork, and stress out of the dinner-preparation equation. With sous vide, steaks are cooked to the same temperature, and thus same doneness (of your choosing!), all the way through. This eliminates the gray band of overcooked meat around the exterior of the meat, which often occurs with traditional pan-roasted methods. Once the steaks are taken out of the water bath, all we had to do was give them a quick sear in a screaming hot pan to create a brown, flavorful crust. Then we created a luscious pan sauce from the drippings left behind in the pan.

Sous Vide Perfect Seared Steaks
SERVES 4
This recipe was developed for tender steaks such as strip, rib eye, shell sirloin, top sirloin, and tenderloin; avoid tougher cuts such as top round, bottom round, blade, and flank. Serve with Red Wine–Peppercorn Pan Sauce or Mustard-Fennel Pan Sauce (recipes follow), if desired.

2 pounds boneless beef steaks, 1 to 1½ inches thick, trimmed

Salt and pepper

7 tablespoons vegetable oil

1. Using sous vide circulator, bring water to 130 degrees in 7-quart container.

2. Season steaks with salt and pepper. Place steaks and ¼ cup (56 grams) oil in 1-gallon zipper-lock freezer bag and toss to coat. Arrange steaks in single layer and seal bag, pressing out as much air as possible. Gently lower bag into prepared water bath until steaks are fully submerged, and then clip top corner of bag to side of water bath container, allowing remaining air bubbles to rise to top of bag. Reopen 1 corner of zipper, release remaining air bubbles, and reseal bag. Cover and cook for at least 1½ hours or up to 3 hours.

3. Transfer steaks to paper towel–lined plate and let rest for 5 to 10 minutes. Pat steaks dry with paper towels. Heat remaining 3 tablespoons (42 grams) oil in 12-inch skillet over medium-high heat until just smoking. Sear steaks, about 1 minute per side, until well browned. Transfer to cutting board and slice into ½-inch-thick slices. Serve.

Red Wine–Peppercorn Pan Sauce
MAKES ABOUT ½ CUP

Note that this recipe is meant to be started after you have seared the steaks. Use a good quality medium-bodied wine, such as a Côtes du Rhône or Pinot Noir, for this sauce.

      Vegetable oil, if needed
  1   large shallot, minced
  ½   cup dry red wine
  ¾   cup chicken broth
  2   teaspoons packed brown sugar
  3   tablespoons unsalted butter, cut into 3 pieces and chilled
  1   teaspoon coarsely ground pepper
  ¼   teaspoon balsamic vinegar
      Salt

1. Pour off all but 1 tablespoon fat from skillet used to sear steak. (If necessary, add oil to equal 1 tablespoon.) Add shallot and cook over medium heat until softened, 1 to 2 minutes. Stir in wine, scraping up any browned bits. Bring to simmer and cook until wine is reduced to glaze, about 3 minutes.

2. Stir in broth and sugar and simmer until reduced to ⅓ cup, 4 to 6 minutes. Off heat, whisk in butter, 1 piece at a time, until melted and sauce is thickened and glossy. Whisk in pepper, vinegar, and any accumulated meat juices. Season with salt to taste. Serve immediately.

Mustard-Fennel Pan Sauce
MAKES ABOUT ½ CUP

Note that this recipe is meant to be started after you have seared the steaks. Sauvignon Blanc is our preferred white cooking wine.

      Vegetable oil, if needed
  1   shallot, minced
  ½   teaspoon fennel seeds, cracked
  ½   cup chicken broth
  ¼   cup dry white wine
  1½ tablespoons Dijon mustard
  2   tablespoons unsalted butter, cut into 2 pieces and chilled
  1   teaspoon chopped fresh tarragon
      Salt and pepper

1. Pour off all but 1 tablespoon fat from skillet used to sear steak. (If necessary, add oil to equal 1 tablespoon.) Add shallot and fennel seeds and cook over medium heat until shallot is softened, 1 to 2 minutes. Stir in broth, wine, and mustard, scraping up any browned bits. Bring to simmer and cook until liquid is reduced to ½ cup, about 6 minutes.

2. Off heat, whisk in butter, 1 piece at a time, until melted and sauce is thickened and glossy. Whisk in tarragon any accumulated meat juices and season with salt and pepper to taste. Serve immediately.

DEVILED PORK CHOPS

WHY THIS RECIPE WORKS: Most recipes call for pan-searing or broiling pork chops, but those techniques often yield dried out meat, so we wanted to slow-roast them in a low oven, which wouldn't require fussy flipping and would allow them to cook evenly and retain as much moisture as possible—a must for lean cuts to taste juicy. To punch up their mild flavor, we "deviled" them by painting the tops and sides of the chops with a bold, balanced, complex-tasting paste of spicy, sharp Dijon mustard mixed with dry mustard (for an extra jolt of heat), minced garlic, and cayenne and black peppers. A bit of brown sugar and salt balanced the paste's heat and acidity. For textural contrast and visual appeal, we coated the tops of the chops with crispy panko bread crumbs, which we toasted in butter to render them deep golden brown and make them water-resistant so that they didn't absorb too much moisture from the mustard coating and turn soggy.

Deviled Pork Chops
SERVES 4

For the best results, be sure to buy chops of similar size. This recipe was developed using natural pork; if using enhanced pork (injected with a salt solution), do not add salt to the mustard paste in step 2. Serve the pork chops with mashed potatoes, rice, or buttered egg noodles.

  2   tablespoons unsalted butter
  ½   cup panko bread crumbs
      Kosher salt and pepper
  ¼   cup Dijon mustard
  2   teaspoons packed brown sugar
  1½ teaspoons dry mustard
  ½   teaspoon garlic, minced to paste
  ¼   teaspoon cayenne pepper
  4   (6- to 8-ounce) boneless pork chops,
      ¾ to 1 inch thick

1. Adjust oven rack to middle position and heat oven to 275 degrees.

2. Melt butter in 10-inch skillet over medium heat. Add panko and cook, stirring frequently, until golden brown, 3 to 5 minutes. Transfer to bowl and sprinkle with ⅛ teaspoon salt. Stir Dijon, sugar, dry mustard, garlic, cayenne, 1 teaspoon salt, and 1 teaspoon pepper in second bowl until smooth.

3. Set wire rack in rimmed baking sheet and spray with vegetable oil spray. Pat chops dry with paper towels. Transfer chops to prepared wire rack, spacing them 1 inch apart. Brush 1 tablespoon mustard mixture over top and sides of each chop (leave bottoms uncoated). Spoon 2 tablespoons toasted panko evenly over top of each chop and press lightly to adhere.

4. Roast until meat registers 140 degrees, 40 to 50 minutes. Remove from oven and let rest on rack for 10 minutes before serving.

BRAISED BRISKET WITH POMEGRANATE, CUMIN, AND CILANTRO

WHY THIS RECIPE WORKS: We know well that braising brisket breaks down what can be a tough cut into something satisfyingly tender. For a foolproof modern take on a timeless cooking method, we wanted to spare no detail for the ultimate brisket dish—one that stood apart from the rest for the holidays or an elegant dinner party. For braised brisket that would be both tender and moist, we started by salting the meat (halved lengthwise for quicker cooking and easier slicing and poked all over to allow the salt to penetrate) and letting it sit for at least 16 hours, which helped it retain moisture as it cooked; the salt also seasoned it. From there, we brought the meat to 180 degrees—the sweet spot for the collagen breakdown that is necessary for the meat to turn tender—relatively quickly in a 325-degree oven and then lowered the oven temperature to 250 degrees so that the brisket finished cooking gently and retained as much moisture as possible. We reduced the braising liquid (chicken broth, pomegranate juice, lots of onions and garlic, anchovies, tomato paste, herbs, and spices) in the pan to achieve rich flavor. Reducing the sauce also built body, which we enhanced with flour and gelatin for a velvety consistency. This recipe requires salting the brisket for at least 16 hours; if you have time, you can salt it for up to 48 hours. If you have a probe thermometer, we recommend using it to monitor the temperature of the brisket.

Braised Brisket with Pomegranate, Cumin, and Cilantro

SERVES 6 TO 8

This recipe requires salting the brisket for at least 16 hours; if you have time, you can salt it for up to 48 hours. We recommend using a remote probe thermometer to monitor the temperature of the brisket. Serve with boiled or mashed potatoes or buttered noodles.

1	(4- to 5-pound) beef brisket, flat cut, fat trimmed to ¼ inch
	Kosher salt and pepper
2	tablespoons vegetable oil
2	large onions, chopped
¼	teaspoon baking soda
6	garlic cloves, minced
4	anchovy fillets, rinsed, patted dry, and minced to paste
1	tablespoon tomato paste
1	tablespoon ground cumin
1½	teaspoons ground cardamom
⅛	teaspoon cayenne pepper
¼	cup all-purpose flour
2	cups pomegranate juice
1½	cups chicken broth
3	bay leaves
2	tablespoons unflavored gelatin
1	cup pomegranate seeds
3	tablespoons chopped fresh cilantro

1. Place brisket, fat side down, on cutting board and cut in half lengthwise with grain. Using paring knife or metal skewer, poke each roast 20 times, pushing all the way through roast. Flip roasts and repeat on second side.

2. Sprinkle each roast evenly on all sides with 2½ teaspoons salt (5 teaspoons salt total). Wrap each roast in plastic wrap and refrigerate for at least 16 hours or up to 48 hours.

3. Adjust oven rack to middle position and heat oven to 325 degrees. Heat oil in large roasting pan over medium heat until shimmering. Add onions and baking soda and cook, stirring frequently, until onions have started to soften and break down, 4 to 5 minutes. Add garlic and cook until fragrant, about 30 seconds. Stir in anchovies, tomato paste, cumin, cardamom, cayenne, and ½ teaspoon pepper. Add flour and cook, stirring constantly, until onions are evenly coated and flour begins to stick to pan, about 2 minutes. Stir in pomegranate juice, broth, and bay leaves, scraping up any browned bits. Stir in gelatin. Increase heat to medium-high and bring to boil.

4. Unwrap roasts and place in pan. Cover pan tightly with aluminum foil, transfer to oven, and cook until meat registers 180 to 185 degrees at center, about 1½ hours. Reduce oven temperature to 250 degrees and continue to cook until fork slips easily in and out of meat, 2 to 2½ hours longer. Transfer roasts to baking sheet and wrap sheet tightly in foil.

5. Strain braising liquid through fine-mesh strainer set over large bowl, pressing on solids to extract as much liquid as possible; discard solids. Let liquid settle for 10 minutes. Using wide, shallow spoon, skim fat from surface and discard. Wipe roasting pan clean with paper towels and return defatted liquid to pan.

6. Increase oven temperature to 400 degrees. Return pan to oven and cook, stirring occasionally, until liquid is reduced by about one-third, 30 to 40 minutes. Remove pan from oven and use wooden spoon to draw liquid up sides of pan and scrape browned bits around edges of pan into liquid.

7. Transfer roasts to carving board and slice against grain ¼ inch thick; transfer to wide serving platter. Season sauce with salt and pepper to taste and pour over brisket. Tent platter with foil and let stand for 5 to 10 minutes to warm brisket through. Sprinkle with pomegranate seeds and cilantro and serve.

TO MAKE AHEAD: Follow recipe through step 6 and let sauce and brisket cool completely. Cover and refrigerate sauce and roasts separately for up to 2 days. To serve, slice each roast against grain ¼ inch thick and transfer to 13 by 9-inch baking dish. Heat sauce in small saucepan over medium heat until just simmering. Pour sauce over brisket, cover dish with aluminum foil, and cook in 325-degree oven until meat is heated through, about 20 minutes.

BRAISED OXTAILS WITH WHITE BEANS, TOMATOES, AND ALEPPO PEPPER

WHY THIS RECIPE WORKS: Oxtails are succulent, beefy, and hugely underutilized, so we gave them star status in our spin on a Turkish dish, *etli kuru fasulye*, which means "white beans with meat" that's often served with rice pilaf and pickled vegetables. In our version, the white beans offer a creamy, nutty counterpoint to hearty oxtails. To be sure our braise didn't turn out greasy, we started by roasting the oxtails in the oven for an hour, rather than browning them in a Dutch oven; this way we rendered and discarded a significant amount of fat (about a half-cup!). We then transferred the oxtails to the pot and deglazed the roasting pan with chicken broth to create a flavorful liquid for braising. We added a simple yet flavorful trio of eastern Mediterranean elements to give the braising liquid its character: sweet whole tomatoes, warm and earthy Aleppo pepper, and pungent oregano. After braising, we were careful to remove the fat (about another half-cup) from the cooking liquid using a fat separator. We added canned navy beans, sherry vinegar, and fresh oregano to create a hearty sauce in which we reheated the oxtails. Try to buy oxtails that are approximately 2 inches thick and 2 to 4 inches in diameter. Oxtails can often be found in the freezer section of the grocery store; if using frozen oxtails, thaw them completely before using. If you can't find Aleppo pepper, you can substitute 1½ teaspoons paprika and 1½ teaspoons finely chopped red pepper flakes.

Braised Oxtails with White Beans, Tomatoes, and Aleppo Pepper

SERVES 6 TO 8

Try to buy oxtails that are approximately 2 inches thick and 2 to 4 inches in diameter. Oxtails can often be found in the freezer section of the grocery store; if using frozen oxtails, be sure to thaw them completely before using. If you can't find Aleppo pepper, you can substitute 1½ teaspoons paprika and 1½ teaspoons finely chopped red pepper flakes.

    4 pounds oxtails, trimmed
       Salt and pepper
    4 cups chicken broth
    2 tablespoons extra-virgin olive oil
    1 onion, chopped fine
    1 carrot, peeled and chopped fine
    6 garlic cloves, minced
    2 tablespoons tomato paste
    2 tablespoons ground dried Aleppo pepper
    1 tablespoon minced fresh oregano
    1 (28-ounce) can whole peeled tomatoes
    1 (15-ounce) can navy beans, rinsed
    1 tablespoon sherry vinegar

1. Adjust oven rack to lower-middle position and heat oven to 450 degrees. Pat oxtails dry with paper towels and season with salt and pepper. Arrange oxtails cut side down in single layer in large roasting pan and roast until meat begins to brown, about 45 minutes.

2. Discard any accumulated fat and juices in pan and continue to roast until meat is well browned, 15 to 20 minutes. Transfer oxtails to bowl and tent loosely with aluminum foil; set aside. Stir chicken broth into pan, scraping up any browned bits; set aside.

3. Reduce oven temperature to 300 degrees. Heat oil in Dutch oven over medium heat until shimmering. Add onion and carrot and cook until softened, about 5 minutes. Stir in garlic, tomato paste, Aleppo, and 1 teaspoon oregano and cook until fragrant, about 30 seconds.

4. Stir in broth mixture from roasting pan and tomatoes and their juice and bring to simmer. Nestle oxtails into pot and bring to simmer. Cover, transfer pot to oven, and cook until oxtails are tender and fork slips easily in and out of meat, about 3 hours.

5. Transfer oxtails to bowl and tent loosely with aluminum foil. Strain braising liquid through fine-mesh strainer into fat separator; return solids to now-empty pot. Let braising liquid settle for 5 minutes, then pour defatted liquid into pot with solids.

6. Stir in beans, vinegar, and remaining 2 teaspoons oregano. Return oxtails and any accumulated juices to pot, bring to gentle simmer over medium heat, and cook until oxtails and beans are heated through, about 5 minutes. Season with salt and pepper to taste. Transfer oxtails to serving platter and spoon 1 cup sauce over top. Serve, passing remaining sauce separately.

PERFECT PAN-SEARED PORK TENDERLOIN STEAKS

WHY THIS RECIPE WORKS: We've all suffered through dry, chalky, or tough pork tenderloin. That's because traditional techniques usually use high heat in an attempt to give the mild meat a flavorful browned crust. But these methods typically overcook the lean pork. We were looking for a way to guarantee juicy, flavorful, and fork-tender meat. We began by lightly pounding the pork to create two flat sides that would be easy to sear. Halving the tenderloins crosswise created moderately sized steaks that were easy to maneuver. We placed the pork on a wire rack set in a rimmed baking sheet to raise it off the hot sheet and help it cook evenly. Slowly cooking the pork in a low oven ensured that the meat cooked evenly from edge to edge so that every bite was moist and tender. To achieve browning, we thoroughly patted the pork dry before searing it in a hot skillet. After letting the meat rest, we sliced into pork tenderloin perfection: juicy, tender, and evenly rosy meat encased in a flavorful mahogany crust.

Perfect Pan-Seared Pork Tenderloin Steaks

SERVES 4

Choose tenderloins that are equal in size to ensure that the pork cooks at the same rate. We prefer natural pork in this recipe. If using enhanced pork (injected with a salt solution), reduce the salt in step 2 to ¼ teaspoon per steak. Open the oven as infrequently as possible in step 2. If the meat is not yet up to temperature, wait at least 5 minutes before taking its temperature again. Serve the pork with Scallion-Ginger Relish (recipe follows), if desired.

> 2 (1-pound) pork tenderloins, trimmed
> Kosher salt and pepper
> 2 tablespoons vegetable oil

1. Adjust oven rack to middle position and heat oven to 275 degrees. Set wire rack in rimmed baking sheet and lightly spray rack with vegetable oil spray.

2. Pound each tenderloin to 1-inch thickness. Halve each tenderloin crosswise. Sprinkle each steak with ½ teaspoon salt and ⅛ teaspoon pepper. Place steaks on prepared wire rack and cook until meat registers between 137 and 140 degrees, 25 to 35 minutes.

3. Move steaks to 1 side of rack. Line cleared side with double layer of paper towels. Transfer steaks to paper towels, cover with another double layer of paper towels, and let stand for 10 minutes.

4. Pat steaks until surfaces are very dry. Heat oil in 12-inch skillet over medium-high heat until just smoking. Increase heat to high, place steaks in skillet, and sear until well browned on both sides, 1 to 2 minutes per side. Transfer to carving board and let stand for 5 minutes. Slice steaks against grain ¾ inch thick and transfer to serving platter. Season with salt to taste, and serve.

Scallion-Ginger Relish

MAKES ABOUT ⅔ CUP

We like the complexity of white pepper in this recipe.

> 6 scallions, white and green parts separated
> and sliced thin
> 2 teaspoons grated fresh ginger
> ½ teaspoon ground white pepper
> ½ teaspoon grated lime zest plus 2 teaspoons juice
> ¼ cup vegetable oil
> 2 teaspoons soy sauce

Combine scallion whites, ginger, pepper, and lime zest in heatproof bowl. Heat oil in small saucepan over medium heat until shimmering. Pour oil over scallion mixture. (Mixture will bubble.) Stir until well combined. Let cool completely, about 15 minutes. Stir in scallion greens, lime juice, and soy sauce. Let mixture sit for 15 minutes to allow flavors to meld.

CRISPY SLOW-ROASTED PORK BELLY

WHY THIS RECIPE WORKS: Pork belly is a boneless cut featuring alternating layers of deeply flavorful, well-marbled meat and buttery fat which, when properly cooked, turn silky and sumptuous, with a crisp crown of skin. To tackle this special cut, we started by scoring the skin and rubbing it with a mixture of salt and brown sugar. We then air-dried the belly overnight in the refrigerator to dehydrate the skin. Roasting the pork belly low and slow further dried the skin and broke down the tough collagen, making the meat juicy and supple. We finished by frying the belly skin side down, which caused it to dramatically puff up and crisp. A quick, bracing mustard sauce balanced the richness of the pork belly.

Crispy Slow-Roasted Pork Belly

SERVES 8 TO 10

This recipe requires refrigerating the seasoned pork belly for at least 12 hours or up to 24 hours before cooking (a longer time is preferable). Be sure to ask for a flat, rectangular center-cut section of skin-on pork belly that's 1½ inches thick with roughly equal amounts of meat and fat. Serve with white rice and steamed greens or boiled potatoes and salad.

PORK

> 1 (3-pound) skin-on center-cut fresh pork belly,
> about 1½ inches thick
> Kosher salt
> 2 tablespoons packed dark brown sugar
> Vegetable oil

MUSTARD SAUCE

> ⅔ cup Dijon mustard
> ⅓ cup cider vinegar
> ¼ cup packed dark brown sugar
> 1 tablespoon hot sauce
> 1 teaspoon Worcestershire sauce

1. FOR THE PORK: Using sharp chef's knife, slice pork belly lengthwise into 3 strips about 2 inches wide, then cut slits, spaced 1 inch apart in crosshatch pattern, in surface fat layer, being careful not to cut into meat. Combine 2 tablespoons salt and sugar in bowl. Rub salt mixture into bottom and sides of pork belly (do not rub into skin). Season skin of each strip evenly with ½ teaspoon salt. Place pork belly, skin side up, in 13 by 9-inch baking dish and refrigerate, uncovered, for at least 12 hours or up to 24 hours.

2. Adjust oven rack to middle position and heat oven to 250 degrees. Set wire rack in rimmed baking sheet and spray with vegetable oil spray. Transfer pork belly, skin side up, to wire rack and roast until pork registers 195 degrees and paring knife inserted in pork meets little resistance, 3 to 3½ hours, rotating sheet halfway through roasting.

3. FOR THE MUSTARD SAUCE: Whisk all ingredients together in bowl; set aside.

4. Transfer pork belly, skin side up, to large plate. (Pork belly can be held at room temperature for up to 1 hour.) Pour fat from sheet into 1-cup liquid measuring cup. Add vegetable oil as needed to equal 1 cup and transfer to 12-inch skillet. Arrange pork belly, skin side down, in skillet (strips can be sliced in half crosswise if skillet won't fit strips whole) and place over medium heat until bubbles form around pork belly. Continue to fry, tilting skillet occasionally to even out hot spots, until skin puffs, crisps, and turns golden, 6 to

10 minutes. Transfer pork belly, skin side up, to carving board and let rest for 5 minutes. Flip pork belly skin side down and slice ½ inch thick (being sure to slice through original score marks). Reinvert slices and serve with sauce.

Crispy Slow-Roasted Pork Belly with Tangy Hoisin Sauce

Omit mustard sauce. Whisk ½ cup hoisin, 4 teaspoons rice vinegar, 1 teaspoon grated fresh ginger, and 2 thinly sliced scallions together in bowl and serve with pork.

NOTES FROM THE TEST KITCHEN

COOKING PORK BELLY

Our mostly hands-off approach produces rich, tender meat capped with a layer of shatteringly crisp skin.

1. SPLIT IT LENGTHWISE: Cutting the pork belly into three strips provides more surface area for seasoning. The smaller pieces of meat and skin also cook more quickly and evenly.

2. GIVE IT A RUB: Seasoning the meat with salt and brown sugar adds flavor, encourages browning, and helps it retain moisture. Sprinkling salt on the skin (scored for deeper penetration) helps it dehydrate.

3. GIVE IT A REST: Letting the seasoned meat sit overnight in the refrigerator gives the rub time to penetrate. It also dries out the surface of the skin so that it can crisp.

4. ROAST IT SLOW: Slow roasting browns the meat and further dehydrates the skin while converting the rigid collagen in both to gelatin. Gelatin keeps the meat moist and helps the skin puff when crisped.

5. CRISP THE SKIN: Frying just the skin portion of the pork belly (start it in cold oil so that all the skin heats at the same pace) forces its remaining water to evaporate, leaving it puffed up and ultracrisp.

ROASTED WHOLE SIDE OF SALMON

WHY THIS RECIPE WORKS: When it comes to serving a crowd, most cooks turn to a large roast or bird. But salmon is ideal for entertaining, too. We wanted to come up with an approach for a whole roasted fillet that would be evenly moist inside and gorgeously browned on top. To start, we salted it for an hour, which helped the flesh retain moisture and protein. Placing it on a greased aluminum foil sling ensured that it was easy to transfer to a serving platter. We set the salmon on a wire rack set in a rimmed baking sheet to encourage air circulation. Evenly brushing the surface with honey encouraged rapid browning. We preheated the oven to 250 degrees to warm the entire oven, which ensured that cooking happened quickly and evenly. Then, we broiled the fillet until it just began to brown. Lastly, we again turned the oven heat to 250 degrees to allow the fillet to gently cook through. A squeeze of fresh lemon juice was all it took to temper the richness of the salmon, but a pair of vibrant, no-cook condiments—an arugula-based pesto and a crisp cucumber relish—offered even more dress-up potential.

Roasted Whole Side of Salmon

SERVES 8 TO 10

This recipe requires salting the fish for at least 1 hour. Look for a fillet that is uniformly thick from end to end. The surface will continue to brown after the oven temperature is reduced in step 4; if the surface starts to darken too much before the fillet's center registers 125 degrees, shield the dark portion with aluminum foil. If using wild salmon, which contains less fat than farmed salmon, remove it from the oven when the center of the fillet registers 120 degrees. Serve as is or with Arugula and Almond Pesto or Cucumber-Ginger Relish (recipes follow).

    1   (4-pound) skin-on side of salmon, pinbones removed
        and belly fat trimmed
        Kosher salt
    2   tablespoons honey
        Lemon wedges

1. Sprinkle flesh side of salmon evenly with 1 tablespoon salt and refrigerate, uncovered, for at least 1 hour or up to 4 hours.

2. Adjust oven rack 7 inches from broiler element and heat oven to 250 degrees. Line rimmed baking sheet with aluminum foil and place wire rack in sheet. Fold 18 by 12-inch piece of foil lengthwise to create 18 by 6-inch sling. Place sling on wire rack and spray with vegetable oil spray.

3. Heat broiler. Pat salmon dry with paper towels and place, skin side down, on foil sling. Brush salmon evenly with honey and broil until surface is lightly but evenly browned, 8 to 12 minutes, rotating sheet halfway through broiling.

4. Return oven temperature to 250 degrees and continue to cook until center of fillet registers 125 degrees, 10 to 15 minutes longer, rotating sheet halfway through cooking. Using foil sling, transfer salmon to serving platter, then carefully remove foil. Serve, passing lemon wedges separately.

Arugula and Almond Pesto
MAKES ABOUT 1½ CUPS

For a spicier pesto, reserve, mince, and add the ribs and seeds from the chile. The pesto can be refrigerated for up to 24 hours. If refrigerated, let the pesto sit at room temperature for 30 minutes before serving.

- ¼ cup almonds, lightly toasted
- 4 garlic cloves, peeled
- 4 anchovy fillets, rinsed and patted dry
- 1 serrano chile, stemmed, seeded, and halved lengthwise
- 6 ounces (6 cups) arugula
- ¼ cup lemon juice (2 lemons)
- ¼ cup extra-virgin olive oil
- 1½ teaspoons kosher salt

Process almonds, garlic, anchovies, and serrano in food processor until finely chopped, about 15 seconds, scraping down sides of bowl as needed. Add arugula, lemon juice, oil, and salt and process until smooth, about 30 seconds.

Cucumber-Ginger Relish
MAKES ABOUT 2 CUPS

For a spicier relish, reserve, mince, and add the ribs and seeds from the chile. To keep the cucumbers crisp, serve this relish within 30 minutes of assembling it.

- ½ cup rice vinegar
- 6 tablespoons extra-virgin olive oil
- ¼ cup lime juice (2 limes)
- 2 tablespoons whole-grain mustard
- 1 tablespoon grated fresh ginger
- ½ teaspoon kosher salt
- 1 English cucumber, seeded and cut into ¼-inch dice
- 1 cup minced fresh mint
- 1 cup minced fresh cilantro
- 1 serrano chile, stemmed, seeded, and minced

Whisk vinegar, oil, lime juice, mustard, ginger, and salt in bowl until smooth. Add cucumber, mint, cilantro, and serrano and stir to combine.

COD BAKED IN FOIL

WHY THIS RECIPE WORKS: Cooking mild fish like cod en papillote—in a tightly sealed, artfully folded parchment package so it can steam in its own juices—is an easy, mess-free way to enhance its delicate flavor. If you throw in vegetables, it should add up to a light but satisfying meal. However, without the right blend of flavorings, the fish can taste lean and bland, and not all vegetables pair well with cod. We found that foil was easier to work with than parchment. Placing the packets on the oven's lower-middle rack concentrated the exuded liquid and deepened the flavor. Leeks, carrots, fennel, and zucchini all worked well as the vegetable component and complemented the mild fish.

Cod Baked in Foil with Leeks and Carrots
SERVES 4

Haddock, red snapper, halibut, and sea bass also work well in this recipe and those that follow as long as the fillets are 1 to 1¼ inches thick. The packets may be assembled several hours ahead of time and refrigerated until ready to cook. If the packets have been refrigerated for more than 30 minutes, increase the cooking time by 2 minutes. Open each packet promptly after baking to prevent overcooking. Zest the lemon before cutting it into wedges.

- 4 tablespoons unsalted butter, softened
- 1¼ teaspoons finely grated zest from 1 lemon; lemon cut into wedges
- 2 medium garlic cloves, minced or pressed through garlic press (about 2 teaspoons)
- 1 teaspoon minced fresh thyme leaves
  Salt and pepper
- 2 tablespoons minced fresh parsley leaves
- 2 medium carrots, peeled and cut into matchsticks (about 1½ cups)
- 2 medium leeks, white and light green parts halved lengthwise, washed, and cut into matchsticks (about 2 cups)
- 4 tablespoons vermouth or dry white wine
- 4 skinless cod fillets, 1 to 1¼ inches thick (about 6 ounces each)

1. Combine butter, ¼ teaspoon zest, 1 teaspoon garlic, thyme, ¼ teaspoon salt, and ⅛ teaspoon pepper in small bowl. Combine parsley, remaining teaspoon zest, and remaining teaspoon garlic in another small bowl; set aside. Place carrots and leeks in medium bowl, season with salt and pepper, and toss together.

2. Adjust oven rack to lower-middle position and heat oven to 450 degrees. Cut eight 12-inch sheets of foil; arrange four flat on counter. Divide carrot and leek mixture among foil sheets, mounding in center of each. Pour 1 tablespoon vermouth over each mound of vegetables. Pat fish dry with paper towels; season with salt and pepper and place one fillet on top of each vegetable mound. Spread quarter of butter mixture on top of each fillet. Place second square of foil on top of fish; crimp edges together in ½-inch fold, then fold over three more times to create a packet about 7 inches square. Place packets on rimmed baking sheet (overlapping slightly if necessary).

3. Bake packets 15 minutes. Carefully open foil, allowing steam to escape away from you. Using thin metal spatula, gently slide fish and vegetables onto plate with any accumulated juices; sprinkle with parsley mixture. Serve immediately, passing lemon wedges separately.

Cod Baked in Foil with Zucchini and Tomatoes
SERVES 4

- 1 pound zucchini (2 medium), ends trimmed and sliced crosswise into ¼-inch-thick rounds
  Salt
- ½ pound plum tomatoes (2 medium), cored, seeded, and chopped into ½-inch pieces (about 1 cup)
- 2 tablespoons extra-virgin olive oil
- 2 medium garlic cloves, minced or pressed through garlic press (about 2 teaspoons)
- 1 teaspoon minced fresh oregano leaves
- ⅛ teaspoon red pepper flakes
  Pepper
- 4 tablespoons vermouth or dry white wine
- 4 skinless cod fillets, 1 to 1¼ inches thick (about 6 ounces each)
- ¼ cup minced fresh basil leaves
- 1 lemon, cut into wedges

1. Toss zucchini with ½ teaspoon salt in large bowl; transfer to colander set over bowl. Let stand until zucchini releases 1 to 2 tablespoons liquid, about 30 minutes. Arrange zucchini on triple layer paper towels; cover with another triple layer paper towels. Firmly press each slice to remove as much liquid as possible. Meanwhile, combine tomatoes, oil, garlic, oregano, pepper flakes, ¼ teaspoon salt, and ⅛ teaspoon pepper in medium bowl.

2. Follow recipe for Cod Baked in Foil with Leeks and Carrots from step 2, mounding salted zucchini in center of foil, drizzling with vermouth, placing fish on top, then spooning quarter of tomato mixture over each fillet. Bake and arrange on plates as directed in step 3, sprinkling basil over fish and passing lemon wedges separately.

Cod Baked in Foil with Fennel and Shallots
SERVES 4
Zest the orange before it is peeled and quartered.

- 1 large fennel bulb (about 1 pound), trimmed, halved, cored, and sliced into ¼-inch strips (about 4 cups)
- 2 medium shallots, sliced thin (about ½ cup)
- 4 tablespoons unsalted butter, softened

- 2 medium oranges, ¼ teaspoon finely grated zest removed from one; both peeled, quartered, and cut crosswise into ¼-inch-thick pieces
- 1 medium garlic clove, minced or pressed through garlic press (about 1 teaspoon)
- 2 teaspoons minced fresh tarragon leaves
  Salt and pepper
- 4 tablespoons vermouth or dry white wine
- 4 skinless cod fillets, 1 to 1¼ inches thick (about 6 ounces each)

1. Combine fennel and shallots in large microwave-safe bowl; cover tightly with plastic wrap. Microwave on high power until fennel has started to wilt, 3 to 4 minutes, stirring once halfway through cooking. Combine butter, zest, garlic, 1 teaspoon tarragon, ¼ teaspoon salt, and ⅛ teaspoon pepper in small bowl. Combine orange pieces and remaining 1 teaspoon tarragon in another small bowl; set aside.

2. Follow recipe for Cod Baked in Foil with Leeks and Carrots from step 2, mounding fennel mixture in center of foil, drizzling with vermouth, placing fish on top, then spreading quarter of butter mixture over each fillet. Bake and arrange on plates as directed in step 3, spooning orange and tarragon mixture over fish before serving.

PERUVIAN-STYLE SEAFOOD CEVICHE

WHY THIS RECIPE WORKS: Ceviche, the Latin American dish in which pieces of raw fish are "cooked" in an acidic marinade until the flesh firms and turns opaque, is a great summertime go-to dinner because it's easy and quick, it doesn't require turning on the stove or oven or even firing up the grill, and it's the only dish that truly allows the fresh, clean, delicate flavor of seafood to shine. To create a flavorful yet balanced "cooking" liquid for our Peruvian-style fish ceviche, we made what's known as a *leche de tigre* by blending lime juice, aji amarillo chile paste, garlic, extra-virgin olive oil, and a small amount of fish. Once strained, we were left with an intensely flavorful and silky-textured emulsion. We then soaked thinly sliced and briefly salted fish (red snapper, sea bass, halibut, and grouper were all good options) in the leche for 30 to 40 minutes until it was just opaque and slightly firm. To complete the dish, we added sweet oranges; crisp, peppery radishes; and chopped cilantro. We served the ceviche with corn nuts and popcorn, which provided salty crunch.

Peruvian-Style Fish Ceviche with Radishes and Orange
SERVES 4 TO 6 AS A MAIN DISH OR 6 TO 8 AS AN APPETIZER
It is imperative that you use the freshest fish possible in this recipe. Do not use frozen fish. Sea bass, halibut, or grouper can be substituted for the snapper, if desired. For more information about cutting citrus segments, see page 250. Aji

amarillo chile paste can be found in the Latin section of grocery stores; if you can't find it, you can substitute 1 stemmed and seeded habanero chile. Serving the popcorn and corn nuts separately allows diners to customize their ceviche to suit their taste.

- 1 pound skinless red snapper fillets, ½ inch thick
  Kosher salt
- ¾ cup lime juice (6 limes)
- 3 tablespoons extra-virgin olive oil
- 1 tablespoon aji amarillo chile paste
- 2 garlic cloves, peeled
- 3 oranges
- 8 ounces radishes, trimmed, halved, and sliced thin
- ¼ cup coarsely chopped fresh cilantro
- 1 cup corn nuts
- 1 cup lightly salted popcorn

1. Using sharp knife, cut fish lengthwise into ½-inch-wide strips. Slice each strip crosswise ⅛ inch thick. Set aside ⅓ cup (2½ ounces) fish pieces. Toss remaining fish with 1 teaspoon salt and refrigerate for at least 10 minutes or up to 30 minutes.

2. Meanwhile, process reserved fish pieces, 2½ teaspoons salt, lime juice, 2 tablespoons oil, chile paste, and garlic in blender until smooth, 30 to 60 seconds. Strain mixture through fine-mesh strainer set over large bowl, pressing on solids to extract as much liquid as possible. Discard solids. (Sauce can be refrigerated for up to 24 hours. It will separate slightly; whisk to recombine before proceeding with recipe.)

3. Cut away peel and pith from oranges. Holding fruit over bowl, use paring knife to slice between membranes to release segments. Cut orange segments into ¼-inch pieces. Add oranges, salted fish, and radishes to bowl with sauce and toss to combine. Refrigerate for 30 to 40 minutes (for more-opaque fish, refrigerate for 45 minutes to 1 hour).

4. Add cilantro to ceviche and toss to combine. Portion ceviche into individual bowls and drizzle with remaining 1 tablespoon oil. Serve, passing corn nuts and popcorn separately.

Peruvian Scallop Ceviche with Cucumber and Grapefruit

SERVES 4 TO 6 AS A MAIN DISH OR 6 TO 8 AS AN APPETIZER

It is imperative that you use the freshest scallops possible in this recipe. We recommend buying "dry" scallops, which don't have chemical additives and taste better than "wet." Dry scallops will look ivory or pinkish; wet scallops are bright white. Serving the plantain chips and corn nuts separately allows diners to customize their ceviche to suit their taste.

- 1 pound large sea scallops, tendons removed and reserved
  Kosher salt
- 2 red grapefruits
- 20 sprigs fresh cilantro, plus ¼ cup coarsely chopped
- ⅓ cup lime juice (3 limes)
- 1 jalapeño chile, stemmed and seeded
- 1 (1-inch) piece fresh ginger, peeled and sliced into ⅛-inch-thick rounds

- 3 tablespoons extra-virgin olive oil
- 1 small shallot, peeled
- 2 garlic cloves, peeled
- ½ English cucumber, quartered lengthwise, seeded, and cut into ⅛-inch pieces
- 2 cups plantain chips
- 1 cup corn nuts

1. Using sharp knife, cut scallops into ¼-inch pieces. Combine reserved tendons and enough scallop pieces to measure ⅓ cup (2½ ounces) and set aside. Toss remaining scallops with 1 teaspoon salt and refrigerate for at least 10 minutes or up to 30 minutes.

2. Juice 1 grapefruit and set aside ½ cup juice. Cut away peel and pith from remaining grapefruit. Holding fruit over bowl, use paring knife to slice between membranes to release segments. Cut grapefruit segments into ¼-inch pieces; set aside.

3. Process reserved ⅓ cup scallop pieces, 2½ teaspoons salt, reserved grapefruit juice, cilantro sprigs, lime juice, jalapeño, ginger, 2 tablespoons oil, shallot, and garlic in blender until smooth, 30 to 60 seconds. Strain mixture through fine-mesh strainer set over large bowl, pressing on solids to extract as much liquid as possible. Discard solids. (Sauce can be refrigerated for up to 24 hours. It will separate slightly; whisk to recombine before proceeding with recipe.)

4. Add salted scallops, reserved grapefruit segments, and cucumber to bowl with sauce and toss to combine. Refrigerate for at least 5 minutes or up to 15 minutes.

5. Add chopped cilantro to ceviche and toss to combine. Portion ceviche into individual bowls and drizzle with remaining 1 tablespoon oil. Serve, passing plantain chips and corn nuts separately.

Peruvian Shrimp Ceviche with Tomato, Jícama, and Avocado

SERVES 4 TO 6 AS A MAIN DISH OR 6 TO 8 AS AN APPETIZER

Shrimp of other sizes may be used in this recipe; be sure to adjust the cooking time accordingly. If Vidalia onions are unavailable, you can substitute another sweet onion or ¼ cup of chopped red onion. Serving the corn nuts and popcorn separately allows diners to customize their ceviche to suit their taste.

- 5 sprigs fresh cilantro, plus ¼ cup coarsely chopped
- 4 garlic cloves, lightly crushed and peeled
  Kosher salt
- 1¼ pounds large (26 to 30 per pound) shrimp, peeled, tails removed, and deveined
- 2 tomatoes, cored
- ¾ cup lime juice (6 limes)
- 1 jalapeño chile, stemmed and seeded
- 3 tablespoons extra-virgin olive oil
- 8 ounces jícama, peeled and cut into ¼-inch dice (1 cup)
- ½ cup chopped Vidalia onion
- 1 avocado, halved, pitted, and cut into ½-inch pieces
- 1 cup corn nuts
- 1 cup lightly salted popcorn

1. Bring 2 cups water, cilantro sprigs, 2 garlic cloves, and 1 teaspoon salt to boil in large saucepan over high heat. Add shrimp, cover, and remove saucepan from heat. Let stand, stirring occasionally, until shrimp are just opaque, 1 to 2 minutes. Transfer shrimp to bowl of ice and let cool. Once cool, cut shrimp in half lengthwise, then cut each half into ½-inch pieces. Transfer ⅓ cup (2½ ounces) cut shrimp to blender. Refrigerate remaining shrimp.

2. Cut 1 tomato into ¼-inch pieces and set aside. Cut remaining tomato into quarters and add to blender with shrimp. Add lime juice, jalapeño, 2 tablespoons oil, 2½ teaspoons salt, and remaining 2 garlic cloves to blender and process until mixture is smooth, 30 to 60 seconds. Strain mixture through fine-mesh strainer set over large bowl, pressing on solids to extract as much liquid as possible. Discard solids. (Sauce can be refrigerated for up to 24 hours. It will separate slightly; whisk to recombine before proceeding with recipe.)

3. Add refrigerated shrimp, reserved tomato, jícama, and onion to bowl with sauce and toss to combine. Refrigerate for 30 minutes.

4. Add chopped cilantro to ceviche and toss to combine. Portion ceviche into individual bowls; garnish each bowl with avocado and drizzle with remaining 1 tablespoon oil. Serve, passing corn nuts and popcorn separately.

BEEF SHORT RIB RAGU

WHY THIS RECIPE WORKS: A typical Sunday gravy is an all-day affair and calls for several different kinds of meats. We wanted a simplified version that could be on the table in about 2 hours and would only use one cut of beef. We chose a rich, beefy cut of meat—boneless short ribs—and paired it with umami-rich porcini mushrooms, tomato paste, and anchovies. To prevent scorching, we moved the braising operation to the oven, making the dish largely hands-off. Removing the lid partway through cooking helped to thicken the sauce and browned the meat, deepening its flavor and eliminating the messy step of browning it before braising. The addition of five-spice powder contributed subtle background notes that underscored the savory taste of the beef and mushrooms.

Beef Short Rib Ragu

MAKES 5 CUPS; ENOUGH FOR 1 POUND PASTA

If you can't find boneless short ribs, don't substitute bone-in short ribs. Instead, use a 2½-pound chuck-eye roast, trimmed and cut into 1-inch chunks. This recipe yields enough to sauce 1 pound of pasta or a batch of No-Fuss Creamy Parmesan Polenta (page 627) (our favorite way to serve it). This recipe can be doubled, and the sauce can be frozen. Better Than Bouillon Roasted Beef Base is our taste test winner.

1½ cups beef broth
½ ounce dried porcini mushrooms, rinsed
1 tablespoon extra-virgin olive oil

1 onion, chopped fine
2 garlic cloves, minced
1 tablespoon tomato paste
3 anchovy fillets, rinsed, patted dry, and minced
½ teaspoon five-spice powder
½ cup dry red wine
1 (14.5-ounce) can whole peeled tomatoes, drained with juice reserved, chopped fine
2 pounds boneless beef short ribs, trimmed
Salt and pepper

1. Adjust oven rack to middle position and heat oven to 350 degrees. Microwave ½ cup broth and mushrooms in covered bowl until steaming, about 1 minute. Let sit until softened, about 5 minutes. Drain mushrooms in fine-mesh strainer lined with coffee filter, pressing to extract all liquid; reserve liquid and chop mushrooms fine.

2. Heat oil in Dutch oven over medium heat until shimmering. Add onion and cook, stirring occasionally, until softened, about 5 minutes. Add garlic and cook until fragrant, about 1 minute. Add tomato paste, anchovies, and five-spice powder and cook, stirring frequently, until mixture has darkened and fond forms on pot bottom, 3 to 4 minutes. Add wine, increase heat to medium-high, and bring to simmer, scraping up any browned bits. Continue to cook, stirring frequently, until wine is reduced and pot is almost dry, 2 to 4 minutes. Add tomatoes and reserved juice, remaining 1 cup broth, reserved mushroom soaking liquid, and mushrooms and bring to simmer.

3. Toss beef with ¾ teaspoon salt and season with pepper. Add beef to pot, cover, and transfer to oven. Cook for 1 hour.

4. Uncover and continue to cook until beef is tender, 1 to 1¼ hours longer.

5. Remove pot from oven; using slotted spoon, transfer beef to cutting board and let cool for 5 minutes. Using 2 forks, shred beef into bite-size pieces, discarding any large pieces of fat or connective tissue. Using large spoon, skim off any excess fat that has risen to surface of sauce. Return beef to sauce and season with salt and pepper to taste. (Sauce can be refrigerated for up to 3 days or frozen for up to 2 months.)

ITALIAN PASTA SALAD

WHY THIS RECIPE WORKS: We wanted to give this summertime staple a makeover, which would involve improving the texture of the noodles, picking the perfect mix-ins, and creating a flavorful dressing that would cling well. First, we opted for corkscrew-shaped fusilli pasta, as the shape has plenty of nooks and crannies for capturing dressing and is easy to spear with a fork. We purposefully cooked the pasta until it was a little too soft so that as it cooled and firmed up, it would have just the right tender texture. Rather than toss raw vegetables into the mix, we took inspiration from Italian antipasto platters and used intensely flavored jarred ingredients like sun-dried tomatoes, kalamata olives, and pepperoncini—a mix of textures that didn't overshadow the pasta. For heartiness, we included salami, and to balance the salt and tang, we add chunks of creamy mozzarella, fresh basil, and peppery arugula. To ensure the pasta itself was just as flavorful as the rest of the dish, we made a thick, punchy dressing by processing some of the salad ingredients themselves—capers and pepperoncini plus their tangy liquid—with olive oil infused with garlic, red pepper flakes, and anchovies.

Italian Pasta Salad

SERVES 8 TO 10 AS A SIDE DISH

The pasta firms as it cools, so overcooking is key to ensuring the proper texture. We prefer a small, individually packaged, dry Italian-style salami such as Genoa or soppressata, but unsliced deli salami can be used. If the salad is not being eaten right away, don't add the arugula and basil until right before serving.

1	pound fusilli
	Salt and pepper
¼	cup extra-virgin olive oil
3	anchovy fillets, rinsed, patted dry, and minced
3	garlic cloves, minced
¼	teaspoon red pepper flakes
1	cup pepperoncini, stemmed, plus 2 tablespoons reserved liquid
2	tablespoons capers, rinsed
½	cup oil-packed sun-dried tomatoes, sliced thin
½	cup pitted Kalamata olives, quartered
8	ounces salami, cut into ⅜-inch dice
8	ounces fresh mozzarella cheese, cut into ⅜-inch dice and patted dry with paper towels
2	cups (2 ounces) baby arugula
1	cup chopped fresh basil

1. Bring 4 quarts water to boil in large pot. Add pasta and 1 tablespoon salt and cook, stirring often, until pasta is tender throughout, 2 to 3 minutes past al dente. Drain pasta and rinse under cold water until chilled. Drain well and transfer to large bowl.

2. Meanwhile, combine oil, anchovies, garlic, and pepper flakes in 1-cup liquid measuring cup. Cover and microwave until oil is bubbling and fragrant, 30 to 60 seconds. Set aside.

3. Slice half of pepperoncini into thin rings and set aside. Transfer remaining pepperoncini to food processor. Add capers and pulse until finely chopped, 8 to 10 pulses, scraping down sides of bowl as necessary. Add 2 tablespoons reserved pepperoncini liquid and warm oil mixture and process until combined, about 20 seconds.

4. Add dressing to pasta and toss to combine. Add sun-dried tomatoes, olives, salami, mozzarella, arugula, basil, and reserved pepperoncini rings and toss well. Season to taste with salt and pepper. Serve. (Salad can be refrigerated for up to 3 days. Bring to room temperature before serving.)

ONE-HOUR PIZZA

WHY THIS RECIPE WORKS: We were determined to make a really good pizza from scratch in just one hour. Doing so required a handful of tricks to get a crust that was crisp, tender, and light without prolonged proofing. First, we used a high percentage of yeast and warm water in the dough to make sure it proofed in 30 minutes. We also found that a combination of semolina and all-purpose flours worked best, providing crispness, stretch, and enough structure. Finally, we rolled the dough between sheets of oiled parchment paper immediately after mixing so that the air bubbles that developed during proofing wouldn't be knocked out by shaping. We made our quick no-cook pizza sauce in the food processor. The last step was the cheese: we first sprinkled grated Parmesan on top of the sauce, followed by creamy shredded mozzarella. Just a few minutes in the oven browned the crust to perfection, while the cheese melted and turned bubbly.

One-Hour Pizza

MAKES TWO 11½-INCH PIZZAS

For the best results, weigh your ingredients. We like the depth anchovies add to the sauce, but you can omit them, if desired. For the mild lager, we recommend Budweiser or Stella Artois. Extra sauce can be refrigerated for up to a week or frozen for up to a month. Some baking stones can crack under the intense heat of the broiler. Our recommended stone from Old Stone Oven won't, but if you're using another stone, check the manufacturer's website. If you don't have a pizza peel, use an overturned rimmed baking sheet instead.

DOUGH

1⅓	cups (7⅓ ounces) bread flour
½	cup (3 ounces) semolina flour
2	teaspoons instant or rapid-rise yeast
2	teaspoons sugar
½	cup plus 2 tablespoons (5 ounces) warm water (115 degrees)
¼	cup (2 ounces) mild lager
2	teaspoons distilled white vinegar
1½	teaspoons extra-virgin olive oil
1	teaspoon salt
	Vegetable oil spray
	All-purpose flour

SAUCE

1	(28-ounce) can whole peeled tomatoes, drained
1	tablespoon extra-virgin olive oil
3	anchovy fillets, rinsed and patted dry (optional)
1	teaspoon salt
1	teaspoon dried oregano
½	teaspoon sugar
¼	teaspoon pepper
⅛	teaspoon red pepper flakes

PIZZA

1	ounce Parmesan cheese, grated fine (½ cup)
6	ounces whole-milk mozzarella, shredded (1½ cups)

1. FOR THE DOUGH: Adjust oven rack 4 to 5 inches from broiler element, set pizza stone on rack, and heat oven to 500 degrees.

2. While oven heats, process bread flour, semolina flour, yeast, and sugar in food processor until combined, about 2 seconds. With processor running, slowly pour warm water, lager, vinegar, and oil through feed tube; process until dough is just combined and no dry flour remains, about 10 seconds. Let dough stand for 10 minutes.

3. Add salt to dough and process until dough forms satiny, sticky ball that clears sides of workbowl, 30 to 60 seconds. Transfer dough to lightly floured counter and gently knead until smooth, about 15 seconds. Divide dough into 2 equal pieces and shape each into smooth ball.

4. Spray 11-inch circle in center of large sheet of parchment paper with oil spray. Place 1 ball of dough in center of parchment. Spray top of dough with oil spray. Using rolling pin, roll dough into 10-inch circle. Cover with second sheet of parchment. Using rolling pin and your hands, continue to roll and press dough into 11½-inch circle. Set aside and repeat rolling with second ball of dough. Let dough stand at room temperature until slightly puffy, 30 minutes.

5. FOR THE SAUCE: Process all ingredients in food processor until smooth, about 30 seconds. Transfer to medium bowl.

6. FOR THE PIZZA: When dough has rested for 20 minutes, heat broiler for 10 minutes. Remove top piece of parchment from 1 disk of dough and dust top of dough lightly with all-purpose flour. Using your hands or pastry brush, spread flour evenly over dough, brushing off any excess. Liberally dust pizza peel with all-purpose flour. Flip dough onto peel, parchment side up. Carefully remove parchment and discard.

7. Using back of spoon or ladle, spread ½ cup sauce in thin layer over surface of dough, leaving ¾-inch border around edge. Sprinkle ¼ cup Parmesan evenly over sauce, followed by ¾ cup mozzarella. Slide pizza carefully onto stone and return oven to 500 degrees. Bake until crust is well browned and cheese is bubbly and beginning to brown, 8 to 12 minutes, rotating pizza halfway through baking.

8. Transfer pizza to wire rack and let cool for 5 minutes before slicing and serving. Repeat steps 6 and 7 to top and bake second pizza.

CHICKEN PICCATA

WHY THIS RECIPE WORKS: Chicken piccata needs little introduction, for better or for worse. A good version—chicken breasts pounded thin, lightly dusted with flour, pan-seared, and bathed in a lemon-butter pan sauce—deserves nothing but praise. Yet piccata can also be punishingly bad, featuring dry, tough chicken drowning in sauce that's either boring or brash. We wanted a recipe for tender chicken and a complex, lemony sauce that could rival the best of Italian restaurants. First, we used our easy approach to butchering and cooking chicken cutlets: we cut each chicken breast in half crosswise, and then halved the thicker portion horizontally to make three similar-size pieces that required only minimal pounding to become cutlets. We salted the cutlets briefly to boost their ability to retain moisture and then lightly coated them in flour, which helped with browning. We seared the cutlets quickly on both sides and set them aside while making the sauce. We chose to include both lemon juice and lemon slices in the sauce for complexity and textural appeal. We then returned the cutlets to the pan to cook through and to wash any excess starch into the sauce, eliminating a gummy coating. A hearty amount of briny capers and a few tablespoons of butter finished the sauce, while a sprinkling of parsley added freshness.

Next-Level Chicken Piccata
SERVES 4 TO 6

Serve with buttered pasta, white rice, potatoes, or crusty bread and a simple steamed vegetable.

- 4 (6- to 8-ounce) boneless, skinless chicken breasts, trimmed
  Kosher salt and pepper
- 2 large lemons
- ¾ cup all-purpose flour
- ¼ cup plus 1 teaspoon vegetable oil
- 1 shallot, minced
- 1 garlic clove, minced
- 1 cup chicken broth
- 3 tablespoons unsalted butter, cut into 6 pieces
- 2 tablespoons capers, drained
- 1 tablespoon minced fresh parsley

1. Cut each chicken breast in half crosswise, then cut thick half in half again horizontally, creating 3 cutlets of similar thickness. Place cutlets between sheets of plastic wrap and gently pound to even ½-inch thickness. Place cutlets in bowl and toss with 2 teaspoons salt and ½ teaspoon pepper. Set aside for 15 minutes.

2. Halve 1 lemon lengthwise. Trim ends from 1 half, halve lengthwise again, then cut crosswise ¼-inch-thick slices; set aside. Juice remaining half and whole lemon and set aside 3 tablespoons juice.

3. Spread flour in shallow dish. Working with 1 cutlet at a time, dredge cutlets in flour, shaking gently to remove excess. Place on wire rack set in rimmed baking sheet. Heat 2 tablespoons oil in 12-inch skillet over medium-high heat until smoking. Place 6 cutlets in skillet, reduce heat to medium, and cook until golden brown on 1 side, 2 to 3 minutes. Flip and cook until golden brown on second side, 2 to 3 minutes. Return cutlets to wire rack. Repeat with 2 tablespoons oil and remaining 6 cutlets.

4. Add remaining 1 teaspoon oil and shallot to skillet and cook until softened, 1 minute. Add garlic and cook until fragrant, 30 seconds. Add broth, reserved lemon juice, and reserved lemon slices and bring to simmer, scraping up any browned bits.

5. Add cutlets to sauce and simmer for 4 minutes, flipping halfway through simmering. Transfer cutlets to platter. Sauce should be thickened to consistency of heavy cream; if not, simmer 1 minute longer. Off heat, whisk in butter. Stir in capers and parsley. Season with salt and pepper to taste. Spoon sauce over chicken and serve.

CHICKEN VESUVIO

WHY THIS RECIPE WORKS: Chicken Vesuvio is a classic Chicago restaurant dish: crisp-skinned chicken and deeply browned potatoes in a potent garlic and white wine sauce. Line cooks make it one order at a time in a big skillet, which provides plenty of space for browning and for reduction of the sauce, and goes handily from stovetop to oven. We set out to transfer Vesuvio to the home kitchen. We traded the customary skillet for a large, heavy roasting pan, which gave us plenty of room for four servings, and we swapped the usual half chickens for just thighs. We heated oil in the roasting pan on the stovetop, browned the chicken thighs and halved Yukon Gold potatoes, and added traditional dried herbs and plenty of garlic cloves. We then poured wine into the pan and transferred it to the oven so the chicken, potatoes, and garlic could finish cooking. After placing the cooked chicken and potatoes on a platter, we returned the pan to the stovetop to further reduce the sauce. Mashing the cooked garlic cloves released polysaccharides, which brought the oil and wine together in a rich emulsion, and fresh minced garlic, tempered with lemon juice, delivered robust flavor.

Chicken Vesuvio
SERVES 4 TO 6

For this recipe you'll need a roasting pan that measures at least 16 by 12 inches. Trim all the skin from the underside of the chicken thighs, but leave the skin on top intact. To ensure that all of the potatoes fit in the pan, halve them crosswise to minimize their surface area. For the most efficient browning, heat the roasting pan over 2 burners. Mixing lemon juice into the garlic in step 1 makes the garlic taste less harsh, but only if the lemon juice is added immediately after the garlic is minced.

    8   (5- to 7-ounce) bone-in chicken thighs, trimmed
    2½ teaspoons kosher salt
    ½   teaspoon pepper
    2   tablespoons vegetable oil
    1½ pounds Yukon Gold potatoes, 2 to 3 inches, halved
    14 garlic cloves, peeled (2 whole, 12 halved lengthwise)
    1   tablespoon lemon juice
    1½ teaspoons dried oregano
    ½   teaspoon dried thyme
    1½ cups dry white wine
    2   tablespoons minced fresh parsley

1. Adjust oven rack to upper-middle position, and heat oven to 450 degrees. Pat chicken dry with paper towels and season both sides with 1½ teaspoons salt and ½ teaspoon pepper. Toss potatoes with 1 tablespoon oil and remaining 1 teaspoon salt. Mince 2 whole garlic cloves and immediately combine with lemon juice in small bowl and set aside.

2. Heat remaining 1 tablespoon oil in large roasting pan over medium-high heat until shimmering. Place chicken skin-side down in single layer in pan and cook without moving until chicken has rendered about 2 tablespoons of fat, 2 to 3 minutes. Place potatoes cut side down in chicken fat, arranging so that cut sides are in complete contact with surface of pan. Sprinkle chicken and potatoes with oregano and thyme. Continue to cook until chicken and potatoes are deeply browned and crisp, 8 to 12 minutes longer, moving chicken and potatoes to ensure even browning and turning pieces over when fully browned. When all pieces have been flipped, tuck halved garlic cloves in between chicken and potatoes. Remove roasting pan from heat and pour wine into pan (do not pour over chicken or potatoes). Transfer to oven. Roast until potatoes are tender when pierced with tip of paring knife and chicken registers 185 to 190 degrees, 15 to 20 minutes.

3. Transfer chicken and potatoes to deep platter, browned sides up. Place roasting pan over medium heat (handles will be hot) and stir to incorporate any browned bits. Using slotted spoon, transfer garlic cloves to cutting board. Chop coarse, and then mash to smooth paste with side of knife. Whisk garlic into sauce. Continue to cook until sauce coats back of spoon, 3 to 5 minutes. Remove from heat and whisk in reserved lemon juice mixture and 1 tablespoon parsley. Pour sauce around chicken and potatoes. Sprinkle with remaining 1 tablespoon parsley, and serve.

ROASTED POBLANO AND BLACK BEAN ENCHILADAS

WHY THIS RECIPE WORKS: For great vegetarian enchiladas, we wanted a bright yet rich green enchilada sauce featuring the sweet-tart flavor of tomatillos. We rounded out the flavor of the tomatillo sauce with onion, garlic, cilantro, and lime juice. A splash of heavy cream lent richness. For the filling, we started with roasted poblano chiles. We smashed canned black beans to create a quick "refried" bean base and stirred in a little of the tomatillo sauce, Monterey Jack cheese, and some heady seasonings, which we bloomed on the stovetop with basic aromatics. When choosing tomatillos, look for pale-green orbs with firm flesh that fills and splits open the fruit's outer papery husk, which must be removed before cooking. Serve with sour cream, diced avocado, sliced radishes, shredded romaine lettuce, and lime wedges.

Roasted Poblano and Black Bean Enchiladas

SERVES 4 TO 6

- 1 pound tomatillos, husks and stems removed, rinsed well, dried, and halved
- 4 poblano chiles, halved, stemmed, and seeded
- 1 teaspoon plus ¼ cup vegetable oil
- 2 onions, chopped fine
- 1 cup fresh cilantro leaves
- ⅓ cup vegetable broth
- ¼ cup heavy cream
- 4 garlic cloves, minced
- 1 tablespoon lime juice
- 1 teaspoon sugar
- Salt and pepper
- 1 teaspoon chili powder
- ½ teaspoon ground coriander
- ½ teaspoon ground cumin
- 1 (15-ounce) can black beans, rinsed, half of beans mashed smooth
- 8 ounces Monterey Jack cheese, shredded (2 cups)
- 12 (6-inch) corn tortillas

1. Adjust oven rack 6 inches from broiler element and heat broiler. Line rimmed baking sheet with aluminum foil. Toss tomatillos and poblanos with 1 teaspoon oil. Arrange tomatillos cut side down and poblanos skin side up on prepared sheet. Broil until vegetables are blackened and beginning to soften, 5 to 10 minutes. Let vegetables cool slightly. Remove skins and seeds from poblanos (leave tomatillo skins intact), then chop into ½-inch pieces.

2. Meanwhile, process broiled tomatillos, 1 cup onion, ½ cup cilantro, broth, cream, 1 tablespoon oil, half of garlic, lime juice, sugar, and 1 teaspoon salt in food processor until sauce is smooth, about 2 minutes. Season with salt and pepper to taste.

3. Heat 1 tablespoon oil in 12-inch skillet over medium heat until shimmering. Add remaining onion and ¼ teaspoon salt and cook until softened, 5 to 7 minutes. Stir in chili powder, coriander, cumin, and remaining garlic and cook until fragrant, about 30 seconds. Stir in mashed and whole beans and chopped poblanos and cook until warmed through, about 2 minutes. Transfer mixture to large bowl and let cool slightly. Stir in 1 cup Monterey Jack, ½ cup tomatillo sauce, and remaining ½ cup cilantro. Season with salt and pepper to taste.

4. Adjust oven rack to middle position and heat oven to 400 degrees. Spread ½ cup tomatillo sauce over bottom of 13 by 9-inch baking dish. Brush both sides of tortillas with remaining 2 tablespoons oil. Arrange tortillas, overlapping, on rimmed baking sheet in 2 rows (6 tortillas each). Bake until tortillas are warm and pliable, about 5 minutes.

5. Working with 1 warm tortilla at a time, spread ¼ cup bean-cheese filling across center of tortilla. Roll tortilla tightly around filling and place seam side down in baking dish; arrange enchiladas in 2 columns across width of dish.

6. Pour remaining sauce over top to cover completely and sprinkle remaining 1 cup cheese down center of enchiladas.

Cover dish tightly with greased aluminum foil. Bake until enchiladas are heated through and cheese is melted, about 25 minutes. Let cool for 5 minutes and serving.

CRISPY GROUND BEEF TACOS

WHY THIS RECIPE WORKS: Commercial taco kits are convenient, but the seasoning packets taste dusty and flat and the shells tend to be short on flavor and are prone to cracking. And while frying your own shells results in great taste and texture, the process is tedious and messy. Instead, we made *tacos dorados*, a Mexican preparation in which tortillas are stuffed with a beef filling before being folded in half and fried. The tacos are then opened like books and loaded with garnishes. We first tossed ground beef with a bit of baking soda to help it stay juicy before adding it to a savory base of sautéed onion, spices, and tomato paste. Next, we stirred in some shredded cheddar to make the filling more cohesive. To build the tacos, we brushed corn tortillas with oil, warmed them in the oven to make them pliable, and stuffed them with the filling. Instead of fussy deep frying, we pan-fried the tacos in just two batches until they were supercrispy and golden.

Crispy Tacos (Tacos Dorados)

SERVES 4

Arrange the tacos so they face the same direction in the skillet to make them easy to fit and flip. To ensure crispy tacos, cook the tortillas until they are deeply browned. To garnish, open each taco like a book and load it with your preferred toppings; close it to eat.

- 1 tablespoon water
- ¼ teaspoon baking soda
- 12 ounces 90 percent lean ground beef
- 7 tablespoons vegetable oil
- 1 onion, chopped fine
- 1½ tablespoons chili powder
- 1½ tablespoons paprika
- 1½ teaspoons ground cumin
- 1½ teaspoons garlic powder
- Salt
- 2 tablespoons tomato paste
- 2 ounces cheddar cheese, shredded (½ cup), plus extra for serving
- 12 (6-inch) corn tortillas

  Shredded iceberg lettuce
  Chopped tomato
  Sour cream
  Pickled jalapeño slices
  Hot sauce

1. Adjust oven rack to middle position and heat oven to 400 degrees. Combine water and baking soda in large bowl. Add beef and mix until thoroughly combined. Set aside.

2. Heat 1 tablespoon oil in 12-inch nonstick skillet over medium heat until shimmering. Add onion and cook, stirring occasionally, until softened, 4 to 6 minutes. Add chili powder, paprika, cumin, garlic powder, and 1 teaspoon salt and cook, stirring frequently, until fragrant, about 1 minute. Stir in tomato paste and cook until paste is rust-colored, 1 to 2 minutes. Add beef mixture and cook, using wooden spoon to break meat into pieces no larger than ¼ inch, until beef is no longer pink, 5 to 7 minutes. Transfer beef mixture to bowl; stir in cheddar until cheese has melted and mixture is homogeneous. Wipe skillet clean with paper towels.

3. Thoroughly brush both sides of tortillas with 2 tablespoons oil. Arrange tortillas, overlapping, on rimmed baking sheet in 2 rows (6 tortillas each). Bake until tortillas are warm and pliable, about 5 minutes. Remove tortillas from oven and reduce oven temperature to 200 degrees.

4. Place 2 tablespoons filling on 1 side of 1 tortilla. Fold and press to close tortilla (edges will be open, but tortilla will remain folded). Repeat with remaining tortillas and remaining filling. (At this point, filled tortillas can be covered and refrigerated for up to 12 hours.)

5. Set wire rack in second rimmed baking sheet and line rack with double layer of paper towels. Heat remaining ¼ cup oil in now-empty skillet over medium-high heat until shimmering. Arrange 6 tacos in skillet with open sides facing away from you. Cook, adjusting heat so oil actively sizzles and bubbles

appear around edges of tacos, until tacos are crispy and deeply browned on 1 side, 2 to 3 minutes. Using tongs and thin spatula, carefully flip tacos. Cook until deeply browned on second side, 2 to 3 minutes, adjusting heat as necessary.

6. Remove skillet from heat and transfer tacos to prepared wire rack. Blot tops of tacos with double layer of paper towels. Place sheet with fried tacos in oven to keep warm. Return skillet to medium-high heat and cook remaining tacos. Serve tacos immediately, passing extra cheddar, lettuce, tomato, sour cream, jalapeños, and hot sauce separately.

BRAISED PORK IN RED CHILE SAUCE

WHY THIS RECIPE WORKS: To make *carne adovada*, a classic, ultrasimple New Mexican pork braise, we started by cutting boneless pork shoulder into large chunks and salting them (so that they would be well-seasoned and retain moisture during cooking). We started with a generous 4 ounces of dried red New Mexican chiles, which are fruity and relatively mild. But rather than toast them, we simply steeped them in water to preserve their bright flavor. When they were pliable, we blended them with aromatics and spices, as well as honey, white vinegar, and just enough of the chile soaking liquid to form a thick paste; when the paste was smooth, we added the remaining water to form a puree, making sure to leave in small bits of chile skin that contributed rustic texture and vibrant flavor. We tossed the pork with the puree in a Dutch oven, then braised it in a low oven until the meat was very tender. A squeeze of lime added brightness and acidity.

Braised New Mexico–Style Pork in Red Chile Sauce (Carne Adovada)

SERVES 6

Pork butt roast is often labeled Boston butt. If you can't find New Mexican chiles, substitute dried California chiles. Dried chiles should be pliable and smell slightly fruity. Kitchen shears can be used to cut them. If you can't find Mexican oregano, substitute Mediterranean oregano. Serve with rice and beans, crispy potatoes, or flour tortillas with shredded lettuce and chopped tomato. Alternatively, shred the pork as a filling for tacos and burritos.

- 1 (3½- to 4-pound) boneless pork butt roast, trimmed and cut into 1½-inch pieces
  Kosher salt
- 4 ounces dried New Mexican chiles, wiped clean, stemmed, seeded, and torn into 1-inch pieces
- 2 tablespoons honey
- 2 tablespoons distilled white vinegar
- 5 garlic cloves, peeled
- 2 teaspoons dried Mexican oregano
- 2 teaspoons ground cumin
- ½ teaspoon cayenne pepper
- ⅛ teaspoon ground cloves
  Lime wedges

1. Toss pork and 1 tablespoon salt together in bowl; refrigerate for 1 hour.

2. Bring 4 cups water to boil. Place chile pieces in medium bowl. Pour boiling water over chiles, making sure they are completely submerged, and let stand until chiles are softened, 30 minutes. Adjust oven rack to lower-middle position and heat oven to 325 degrees.

3. Drain chiles and reserve 2 cups of soaking liquid (discard remaining soaking liquid). Process chiles, honey, vinegar, garlic, oregano, cumin, cayenne, cloves, and 1 teaspoon salt in blender until chiles are finely ground and thick paste forms, about 30 seconds. With blender running, add 1 cup soaking liquid and blend until puree is smooth, 1½ to 2 minutes, adding up to additional ¼ cup liquid to maintain vortex. Add remaining soaking liquid and continue to blend sauce at high speed, 1 minute longer.

4. Add pork and chile sauce to Dutch oven, stirring to make sure pork is evenly coated. Bring to boil over high heat. Cover pot, transfer to oven, and cook until pork is tender and fork inserted into pork meets little to no resistance, 2 to 2½ hours.

5. Using wooden spoon, scrape any browned bits from sides of pot and stir until pork and sauce are recombined, and sauce is smooth and homogeneous. Let stand, uncovered, for 10 minutes. Season to taste with salt. Serve, passing lime wedges separately.

MEXICAN-STYLE CORN SALAD

WHY THIS RECIPE WORKS: There's nothing like the sweet, nutty flavor of charred corn right off the grill, but we wanted a simpler route to enjoying Mexican street corn (*elote*) that didn't require firing up the grill, and we wanted it in salad form (*esquites*) so it wouldn't be messy to eat. First, we looked to the stovetop and cooked our kernels in a little oil in a covered skillet. The kernels that were in contact with the skillet's surface browned and charred, and the lid prevented the kernels from popping out of the hot skillet and trapped steam, which helped cook the corn. To maximize flavorful browning, we cooked the corn in two batches, which allowed more kernels to have contact with the skillet. Once the corn was perfectly toasted and cooked through, we used the already hot skillet to bloom chili powder and lightly cook minced garlic, which tempered its bite. To tie everything together, we made a simple crema with mayonnaise, sour cream, and lime juice, which we tossed with the charred corn and spices before adding crumbled cotija, chopped cilantro, and sliced scallions. Letting the corn cool before adding the cilantro, scallions, and cheese preserved their fresh flavors.

Mexican-Style Corn Salad (Esquites)
SERVES 6 TO 8

If desired, substitute plain Greek yogurt for the sour cream. We like serrano chiles here, but you can substitute a jalapeño chile that has been halved lengthwise and sliced into ⅛-inch-thick half-moons. Adjust the amount of chiles to suit your taste. If cotija cheese is unavailable, substitute feta cheese.

3 tablespoons lime juice, plus extra for seasoning (2 limes)
3 tablespoons sour cream
1 tablespoon mayonnaise
1–2 serrano chiles, stemmed and cut into ⅛-inch-thick rings
Salt
2 tablespoons plus 1 teaspoon vegetable oil
6 ears corn, kernels cut from cobs (6 cups)
2 garlic cloves, minced
½ teaspoon chili powder
4 ounces cotija cheese, crumbled (1 cup)
¾ cup coarsely chopped fresh cilantro
3 scallions, sliced thin

1. Combine lime juice, sour cream, mayonnaise, serrano(s), and ¼ teaspoon salt in large bowl. Set aside.

2. Heat 1 tablespoon oil in 12-inch nonstick skillet over high heat until shimmering. Add half of corn and spread into even layer. Sprinkle with ¼ teaspoon salt. Cover and cook, without stirring, until corn touching skillet is charred, about 3 minutes. Remove skillet from heat and let stand, covered, for 15 seconds, until any popping subsides. Transfer corn to bowl with sour cream mixture. Repeat with 1 tablespoon oil, ¼ teaspoon salt, and remaining corn.

3. Return now-empty skillet to medium heat and add remaining 1 teaspoon oil, garlic, and chili powder. Cook, stirring constantly, until fragrant, about 30 seconds. Transfer garlic mixture to bowl with corn mixture and toss to combine. Let cool for at least 15 minutes.

4. Add cotija, cilantro, and scallions and toss to combine. Season salad with salt and up to 1 tablespoon extra lime juice to taste. Serve.

CHINESE PORK DUMPLINGS

WHY THIS RECIPE WORKS: If you have the right recipe, Chinese dumplings can be as much fun to make as they are to eat. We started by making a dough with just two ingredients—boiling water and flour—that would be easy to roll out and remain moist but not sticky. For the filling, we started with ground pork, saving ourselves the traditional step of finely chopping a fatty cut like pork shoulder. We then mixed in vegetable oil and sesame oil to provide richness to the relatively lean meat. Soy sauce, ginger, Chinese rice wine, hoisin sauce, and white pepper added flavor to the meat, and cabbage and scallions contributed subtle crunch. Mixing the filling in the food processor was quick and tidy; it also developed myosin, a protein that helped the filling hold together when cooked. When it came time to shape the dumplings, we developed a simpler two-pleat approach that achieved the appearance and functionality of a traditional multipleat crescent. To ensure even browning, we brushed a cold nonstick skillet with oil and snugly arranged 20 dumplings before turning on the heat. The results were ideal—a flavorful, juicy, cohesive filling tucked inside a soft, slightly chewy wrapper—and the method was user-friendly and fun.

Chinese Pork Dumplings

MAKES 40 DUMPLINGS

For dough that has the right moisture level, we strongly recommend weighing the flour. For an accurate measurement of boiling water, bring a full kettle of water to a boil and then measure out the desired amount. To ensure that the dumplings seal completely, use minimal flour when kneading, rolling, and shaping so that the dough remains slightly tacky. Keep all the dough covered with a damp towel except when rolling and shaping. There is no need to cover the shaped dumplings. A shorter, smaller-diameter rolling pin works well here, but a conventional pin will also work.

DOUGH

2½ cups (12½ ounces) all-purpose flour
1 cup boiling water

FILLING

5 cups 1-inch napa cabbage pieces
   Salt
12 ounces ground pork
1½ tablespoons soy sauce, plus extra for dipping
1½ tablespoons toasted sesame oil
1 tablespoon vegetable oil, plus 2 tablespoons for pan-frying (optional)
1 tablespoon Chinese rice wine or dry sherry
1 tablespoon hoisin sauce
1 tablespoon grated fresh ginger
¼ teaspoon ground white pepper
4 scallions, chopped fine
   Black or rice vinegar
   Chili oil

1. FOR THE DOUGH: Place flour in food processor. With processor running, add boiling water. Continue to process until dough forms ball and clears sides of bowl, 30 to 45 seconds longer. Transfer dough to counter and knead until smooth, 2 to 3 minutes. Wrap dough in plastic wrap and let rest for 30 minutes.

2. FOR THE FILLING: While dough rests, scrape any excess dough from now-empty processor bowl and blade. Pulse cabbage in processor until finely chopped, 8 to 10 pulses. Transfer cabbage to medium bowl and stir in ½ teaspoon salt; let sit for 10 minutes. Using your hands, squeeze excess moisture from cabbage. Transfer cabbage to small bowl and set aside.

3. Pulse pork, soy sauce, sesame oil, 1 tablespoon vegetable oil, rice wine, hoisin, ginger, pepper, and ½ teaspoon salt in now-empty food processor until blended and slightly sticky, about 10 pulses. Scatter cabbage over pork mixture. Add scallions and pulse until vegetables are evenly distributed, about 8 pulses. Transfer pork mixture to small bowl and, using rubber spatula, smooth surface. Cover with plastic and refrigerate.

4. Line 2 rimmed baking sheets with parchment paper. Dust lightly with flour and set aside. Unwrap dough and transfer to counter. Roll dough into 12-inch cylinder and cut cylinder into 4 equal pieces. Set 3 pieces aside and cover with plastic. Roll remaining piece into 8-inch cylinder. Cut cylinder in half and cut each half into 5 equal pieces. Place dough pieces on 1 cut side on lightly floured counter and lightly dust with flour. Using palm of your hand, press each dough piece into 2-inch disk. Cover disks with damp towel.

5. Roll 1 disk into 3½-inch round (wrappers needn't be perfectly round) and re-cover disk with damp towel. Repeat with remaining disks. (Do not overlap disks.)

6. Using rubber spatula, mark filling with cross to divide into 4 equal portions. Transfer 1 portion to small bowl and refrigerate remaining filling. Working with 1 wrapper at a

---

NOTES FROM THE TEST KITCHEN

ASSEMBLING CHINESE DUMPLINGS

1. Place scant 1 tablespoon filling in center of wrapper.

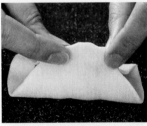

2. Seal top and bottom edges to form 1½-inch-wide seam.

3. Bring far left corner to center of seam and pinch together.

4. Pinch rest of left side to seal. Repeat process on right side.

5. Gently press dumpling into crescent shape.

time (keep remaining wrappers covered), place scant 1 tablespoon filling in center of wrapper. Brush away any flour clinging to surface of wrapper. Lift side of wrapper closest to you and side farthest away and pinch together to form 1½-inch-wide seam in center of dumpling. (When viewed from above, dumpling will have rectangular shape with rounded open ends.) Lift left corner farthest away from you and bring to center of seam. Pinch to seal. Pinch together remaining dough on left side to seal. Repeat pinching on right side. Gently press dumpling into crescent shape and transfer to prepared sheet. Repeat with remaining wrappers and filling in bowl. Repeat dumpling-making process with remaining 3 pieces dough and remaining 3 portions filling.

7A. TO PAN-FRY: Brush 12-inch nonstick skillet with 1 tablespoon vegetable oil. Evenly space 16 dumplings, flat sides down, around edge of skillet and place four in center. Cook over medium heat until bottoms begin to turn spotty brown, 3 to 4 minutes. Off heat, carefully add ½ cup water (water will sputter). Return skillet to heat and bring water to boil. Cover and reduce heat to medium-low. Cook for 6 minutes. Uncover, increase heat to medium-high, and cook until water has evaporated and bottoms of dumplings are crispy and browned, 1 to 3 minutes. Transfer dumplings to platter, crispy sides up. (To cook second batch of dumplings, let skillet cool for 10 minutes. Rinse skillet under cool water and wipe dry with paper towels. Repeat cooking process with 1 tablespoon vegetable oil and remaining dumplings.)

7B. TO BOIL: Bring 4 quarts water to boil in large Dutch oven over high heat. Add 20 dumplings, a few at a time, stirring gently to prevent them from sticking. Return to simmer, adjusting heat as necessary to maintain simmer. Cook dumplings for 7 minutes. Drain well.

8. Serve dumplings hot, passing vinegar, chili oil, and extra soy sauce separately for dipping.

TO MAKE AHEAD: Freeze uncooked dumplings on rimmed baking sheet until solid. Transfer to zipper-lock bag and freeze for up to 1 month. To pan-fry, increase water to ⅔ cup and covered cooking time to 8 minutes. To boil, increase cooking time to 8 minutes.

BEIJING-STYLE MEAT SAUCE AND NOODLES

WHY THIS RECIPE WORKS: *Zha jiang mian* is an easy-to-make and deeply satisfying Chinese noodle dish that comes together in just 30 minutes. Because two of the ingredients, sweet bean sauce and ground bean sauce, are difficult to find outside of specialty Asian markets, we wanted to find pantry-staple substitutes. We discovered that a combination of red miso paste, soy sauce, hoisin, and molasses did the trick. We mixed a baking soda solution into the ground pork to keep it moist and tender. Shiitake mushrooms added even more meaty depth to the dish. We spooned the sauce over chewy lo mein noodles and finished it off with bean sprouts, cucumber matchsticks, and scallion greens for a crisp, fresh contrast.

Beijing-Style Meat Sauce and Noodles (Zha Jiang Mian)

SERVES 6

We prefer red miso in this recipe. You can use white miso, but the color will be lighter and the flavor milder. You can substitute 8 ounces of dried linguine for the lo mein noodles, if desired, but be sure to follow the cooking time listed on the package. For an authentic presentation, bring the bowl to the table before tossing the noodles in step 5.

- 8   ounces ground pork
- ⅛   teaspoon baking soda
- 5   tablespoons red miso paste
- 5   tablespoons soy sauce
- 3   tablespoons hoisin sauce
- 1   tablespoon molasses
- 8   scallions, white and light green parts cut into ½-inch pieces, dark green parts sliced thin on bias
- 2   garlic cloves, peeled
- 1   (½-inch) piece ginger, peeled and sliced into ⅛-inch rounds
- 4   ounces shiitake mushrooms, stemmed and sliced ½ inch thick
- 1   tablespoon vegetable oil
- 1   pound fresh lo mein noodles
- ½   English cucumber, unpeeled, cut into 2½-inch-long matchsticks (2 cups)
- 6   ounces (3 cups) bean sprouts

1. Toss pork, 2 teaspoons water, and baking soda in bowl until thoroughly combined. Let stand for 5 minutes. Whisk ½ cup water, miso paste, soy sauce, hoisin, and molasses together in second bowl.

2. Pulse white and light green scallion parts, garlic, and ginger in food processor until coarsely chopped, 5 to 10 pulses, scraping down sides of bowl as needed. Add mushrooms and pulse until mixture is finely chopped, 5 to 10 pulses.

3. Heat oil and pork mixture in large saucepan over medium heat for 1 minute, breaking up meat with wooden spoon. Add mushroom mixture and cook, stirring frequently, until mixture is dry and just begins to stick to saucepan, 5 to 7 minutes. Add miso mixture to saucepan and bring to simmer. Cook, stirring occasionally, until mixture thickens, 8 to 10 minutes. Cover and keep warm while noodles cook.

4. Bring 4 quarts water to boil in large pot. Add noodles and cook, stirring often, until almost tender (center should still be firm with slightly opaque dot), 3 to 5 minutes. Drain noodles and transfer to wide, shallow serving bowl.

5. Ladle sauce over center of noodles and sprinkle with cucumber, sprouts, and dark green scallion parts. Toss well and serve.

FLAT HAND-PULLED NOODLES WITH CHILI OIL VINAIGRETTE

WHY THIS RECIPE WORKS: Biang Biang noodles are a popular dish from the Shaanxi province of China. They are handmade, flat, belt-like noodles often served with lots of hot peppers and chili oil in the cold winter months. The name describes the sound made when the noodles are slapped against a table to stretch them. To achieve the perfect chew and texture, we used high-protein bread flour and an extended resting time, which allowed the strong gluten network to relax and make the stretching process easier. We then dressed the noodles in a simple Sichuan-inspired chili oil vinaigrette. A sprinkle of fresh cilantro and scallions just before serving added a pop of freshness and burst of color.

Flat Hand-Pulled Noodles (Biang Biang Mian) with Chili Oil Vinaigrette

SERVES 4

Bird chiles are dried red chiles, and are pretty spicy; scale back accordingly. Black vinegar can be found at Asian markets or online. In step 1, you can mix the dough in a food processor instead of a stand mixer. Process flour and salt in food processor until combined, about 2 seconds. With processor running, add water and oil and process until dough forms satiny ball that clears sides of workbowl, about 90 seconds. It is critical to rest the dough for at least 12 hours (and up to 48 hours). During this long rest, the gluten network becomes more extensible, making it easier to pull long, flat noodles by hand. Note that after 24 hours the surface of the dough may develop small black speckles. This oxidation has no impact on flavor or safety.

DOUGH

- 2⅓ cups (12¾ ounces) bread flour
- ¾ teaspoon salt
- 1 cup (8 ounces) water
- 1 tablespoon vegetable oil

CHILI VINAIGRETTE

- 10–20 bird chiles, ground fine
- ½ cup vegetable oil
- 2 garlic cloves, sliced thin
- 1 (1-inch) piece fresh ginger, peeled and sliced thin
- 1 tablespoon Sichuan peppercorns
- ½ cinnamon stick
- 1 star anise pod
- 2 tablespoons soy sauce
- 2 tablespoons black vinegar
- 1 tablespoon toasted sesame oil
- 1 teaspoon sugar
- 4 quarts water
- 1 tablespoon salt
- 12 fresh cilantro sprigs, trimmed and cut into 2-inch pieces
- 6 scallions, sliced thin on bias

1. FOR THE DOUGH: Whisk flour and salt together in bowl of stand mixer. Add water and oil. Fit stand mixer with dough hook and mix on low speed until all flour is moistened, 1 to 2 minutes. Increase speed to medium and knead until dough is smooth and satiny, 10 to 12 minutes. (Alternatively, mix dough in food processor.) Transfer dough to counter, knead for 30 seconds, and shape into 9-inch log. Wrap log in plastic wrap and refrigerate for at least 12 hours or up to 48 hours.

2. FOR THE CHILI VINAIGRETTE: Place chiles in large heatproof bowl. Place fine-mesh strainer over bowl and set aside. Combine vegetable oil, garlic, ginger, peppercorns, cinnamon, and star anise pod in small saucepan and heat over medium-high heat until sizzling. Reduce heat to low and gently simmer until garlic and ginger are slightly browned, 10 to 12 minutes. Pour through strainer into bowl with chiles; discard solids in strainer. Stir chile oil to combine and let cool for 5 minutes. Stir in soy sauce, vinegar, sesame oil, and sugar until combined; set aside.

NOTES FROM THE TEST KITCHEN

PULLING FLAT NOODLES BY HAND

1. Divide dough log into 6 equal pieces; cover with plastic and let rest for 5 minutes.

2. Flatten 1 piece of oiled dough into 7 by 3-inch rectangle, with long side parallel to edge of counter.

3. Gently grasp short ends of dough. Using quick repetitive flapping motion, stretch and slap center of dough strand against counter until noodle is 32 to 36 inches long.

4. Pinch center of noodle with forefingers and thumbs of both hands and pull apart with even pressure in both directions to rip seam in middle of noodle and create 1 continuous loop. Cut loop to create 2 equal-length noodles.

3. Unwrap dough, transfer to lightly oiled counter, and, using bench scraper or knife, divide into 6 equal pieces (each 1½ inches wide). Cover with plastic wrap and let rest for 5 minutes. Meanwhile, bring water and salt to boil in large pot; reduce heat to low and cover to keep hot. Working with 1 piece at a time, oil both sides of dough and flatten into 7 by 3-inch rectangle, with long side parallel to edge of counter. With both hands, gently grasp short ends of dough. Stretch dough and slap against counter until noodle is 32 to 36 inches long (noodle will be between 1/16 and 1/8 inch thick). Place noodle on counter. Pinch center of noodle with forefingers and thumbs of both hands and pull apart with even pressure in both directions to rip seam in middle of noodle and create 1 continuous loop. Cut loop to create 2 equal-length noodles. Set noodles aside on lightly oiled counter (do not let noodles touch) and cover with plastic wrap. Repeat stretching and cutting with remaining pieces of dough.

4. Return water to boil over high heat. Add half of noodles to water and cook, stirring occasionally, until noodles float and turn chewy-tender, 45 to 60 seconds. Using wire skimmer, transfer noodles to bowl with chili vinaigrette; toss to combine. Return water to boil and repeat with remaining noodles. Divide noodles among individual bowls, top with cilantro and scallions, and serve.

CHINESE-STYLE BARBECUED SPARERIBS

WHY THIS RECIPE WORKS: Chinese barbecued spareribs are typically associated with Cantonese buffets and pupu platters, but unlike the questionable provenance of platter-mates such as crab rangoons and chicken fingers, spareribs have real roots in Chinese cuisine. These ribs are usually marinated for several hours and then slow-roasted and basted repeatedly to build up a thick crust. We skipped both of those time-consuming steps and instead braised the ribs, which we cut into individual pieces to speed up the cooking process and create more surface area. We also made a highly seasoned liquid, which helped the flavor penetrate the meat thoroughly and quickly. Then we strained, defatted, and reduced the braising liquid to make a full-bodied glaze in which we tossed the ribs before roasting them on a rack in a hot oven to color and crisp their exteriors.

Chinese-Style Barbecued Spareribs
SERVES 6 TO 8 AS AN APPETIZER OR 4 TO 6 AS A MAIN DISH
It's not necessary to remove the membrane on the bone side of the ribs. These ribs are chewier than American-style ribs; if you prefer them more tender, cook them for an additional 15 minutes in step 1. Adding water to the baking sheet during roasting helps prevent smoking. Serve the ribs alone as an appetizer or with vegetables and rice as a main course. You can serve the first batch immediately or tent them with foil to keep them warm.

1 (6-inch) piece fresh ginger, peeled and sliced thin
8 garlic cloves, peeled
1 cup honey
¾ cup hoisin sauce
¾ cup soy sauce
½ cup Chinese rice wine or dry sherry
2 teaspoons five-spice powder
1 teaspoon red food coloring (optional)
1 teaspoon ground white pepper
2 (2½- to 3-pound) racks St. Louis–style spareribs, cut into individual ribs
2 tablespoons toasted sesame oil

1. Pulse ginger and garlic in food processor until finely chopped, 10 to 12 pulses, scraping down sides of bowl as needed. Transfer ginger-garlic mixture to Dutch oven. Add honey; hoisin; soy sauce; ½ cup water; rice wine; five-spice powder; food coloring, if using; and pepper and whisk until combined. Add ribs and stir to coat (ribs will not be fully submerged). Bring to simmer over high heat, then reduce heat to low, cover, and cook for 1¼ hours, stirring occasionally.

2. Adjust oven rack to middle position and heat oven to 425 degrees. Using tongs, transfer ribs to large bowl. Strain braising liquid through fine-mesh strainer set over large container, pressing on solids to extract as much liquid as possible; discard solids. Let cooking liquid settle for 10 minutes. Using wide, shallow spoon, skim fat from surface and discard.

3. Return braising liquid to pot and add sesame oil. Bring to boil over high heat and cook until syrupy and reduced to 2½ cups, 16 to 20 minutes.

4. Set wire rack in aluminum foil–lined rimmed baking sheet and pour ½ cup water into sheet. Transfer half of ribs to pot with braising liquid and toss to coat. Arrange ribs, bone sides up, on prepared rack, letting excess glaze drip off. Roast until edges of ribs start to caramelize, 5 to 7 minutes. Flip ribs and continue to roast until second side starts to caramelize, 5 to 7 minutes longer. Transfer ribs to serving platter; repeat process with remaining ribs. Serve.

JAPANESE GRILLED STEAK AND SCALLION ROLLS

WHY THIS RECIPE WORKS: *Negimaki* pairs the flavor of grilled beef, grassy scallions, and a salty-sweet teriyaki glaze with the elegant presentation of sushi, making a summer dish that can be served as an appetizer or entrée. While many versions call for cuts like tenderloin or round, we opted for flank steak (briefly frozen first to firm it up for easy slicing), which was affordable, flavorful, and mostly uniform. We pounded the pieces until they were thin and arranged the slices in a slightly overlapping pattern to form rectangular meat "wrappers." Then we laid 4 scallion halves on each wrapper in alternating directions so that the green and white portions were evenly distributed, tightly rolled the meat around the scallions, and pinned the roll shut with 3 toothpicks. To char the meat quickly, we grilled the rolls over a hot fire, turning them every 5 minutes so all sides browned evenly, and glazed the meat partway through cooking with a salty-sweet teriyaki-like reduction of sake, mirin, soy sauce, and sugar. We found that the meat slices were too thin to probe for doneness, so instead we took the temperature of the scallion core; when it registered between 150 and 155 degrees, the meat was fully cooked. Finally, we sliced the rolls into bite-size pieces, drizzled them with extra glaze, and sprinkled them with toasted sesame seeds.

Japanese Grilled Steak and Scallion Rolls (Negimaki)

SERVES 8 TO 10 AS AN APPETIZER OR 4 TO 6 AS A MAIN DISH

Look for a flank steak that is as rectangular as possible as this will yield the most uniform slices. Depending on how you slice the steak you may end up with extra slices; you can grill these alongside the rolls or make several smaller rolls. Serve either as an appetizer or as an entrée with steamed white rice and a vegetable.

- 1 (2-pound) flank steak, trimmed
- ⅓ cup soy sauce
- 3 tablespoons sugar
- 2 tablespoons mirin
- 2 tablespoons sake
- 16 scallions, trimmed and halved crosswise
- 1 tablespoon sesame seeds, toasted

1. Place flank steak on large plate and freeze until firm, about 30 minutes.

2. Bring soy, sugar, mirin, and sake to simmer in small saucepan over high heat, stirring to dissolve sugar. Reduce heat to medium and cook until slightly syrupy and reduced to ½ cup, 3 to 5 minutes. Divide evenly between two bowls and let cool. Cover one bowl with plastic wrap and set aside for serving.

3. Place flank steak on cutting board. Starting at thinner end, slice steak ⅜ inch thick, against grain, on bias until width of steak is about 7 inches across (usually 2 to 3 slices). Cut steak in half lengthwise. Continue to slice each half, against grain, on bias. You should end up with at least 24 slices. Pound each slice into ³⁄₁₆-inch thickness between two sheets of plastic wrap.

4. Arrange 3 slices on cutting board, overlapping slices by ¼ inch and alternating tapered ends as needed, to form rough rectangle that measures 4 to 6 inches wide and at least 4 inches long. Place 4 scallion halves along edge of rectangle nearest to edge of work surface, with white tips slightly overhanging edges on either side. Starting from bottom edge and rolling away from you, roll into tight log. Insert three equally spaced toothpicks into end flaps and through center of roll. Transfer to platter and repeat with remaining steak and scallions. (Rolls can be assembled and refrigerated for up to 24 hours.)

5A. FOR A CHARCOAL GRILL: Open bottom vent completely. Light large chimney starter three-quarters filled with charcoal briquettes (5 quarts). When top coals are partially covered with ash, pour evenly over half of grill. Set cooking grate in place, cover, and open lid vent completely. Heat grill until hot, about 5 minutes.

NOTES FROM THE TEST KITCHEN

WRAPPING AND ROLLING NEGIMAKI
Slicing, pounding and arranging the meat strategically are the keys to producing a sturdy, tight log.

1. Slice chilled steak against grain on bias into 24 pieces.

2. Pound slices to ³⁄₁₆-inch thickness.

3. Arrange slices like jigsaw puzzle, overlapping them by ¼ inch to form rough 4- to 6-inch by 4-inch rectangle.

4. Lay scallion halves head to toe over beef, letting white tips overhang edge.

5. Roll steak away from you into tight log and fasten with three toothpicks.

5B. FOR A GAS GRILL: Turn all burners to high, cover, and heat grill until hot, about 15 minutes.

6. Clean and oil cooking grate. Place rolls over hot part of grill and cook until first side is beginning to char, 4 to 6 minutes. Flip rolls, brush cooked sides with glaze, and continue to cook until second side is beginning to char, 4 to 6 minutes. Cook remaining two sides, glazing after each turn, until all 4 sides of rolls are evenly charred and thermometer inserted from end of roll into scallions at core registers 150 to 155 degrees, 16 to 24 minutes total. Transfer rolls to cutting board, tent loosely with foil, and let rest for 5 minutes. Discard remaining glaze.

7. Remove toothpicks from rolls and cut rolls crosswise into 1-inch pieces. Arrange rolls cut-side down on clean platter, drizzle with 2 tablespoons reserved glaze, sprinkle with sesame seeds, and serve, passing remaining reserved glaze separately.

VIETNAMESE PORK PATTIES WITH RICE NOODLES AND SALAD

WHY THIS RECIPE WORKS: Vietnamese *bun cha* is an ideal one-dish meal, each bite containing an extraordinary balance of smoky, juicy meat; tangy, salty-sweet sauce; cool, tender greens; and delicately springy noodles. We started by boiling dried rice vermicelli, after which we rinsed the noodles well and spread them on a platter to dry. Then we mixed up the bold and zesty sauce known as *nuoc cham* from lime juice, sugar, and fish sauce. To ensure that every drop of the sauce was flavored with garlic and chile, we used a portion of the sugar to help grind the pungent ingredients into a fine paste. Mixing baking soda into ground pork helped the meat retain moisture and brown during the brief grilling time. Per tradition, we also seasoned the pork with shallot, fish sauce, sugar, and pepper. Briefly dunking the grilled patties in the sauce further flavored them and their meaty char flavors infused the sauce. We then arranged the components separately on platters to allow diners to combine them according to their taste.

Vietnamese Grilled Pork Patties with Rice Noodles and Salad (Bun Cha)

SERVES 4 TO 6

Look for dried rice vermicelli in the Asian section of your supermarket. We prefer the more delicate springiness of vermicelli made from 100 percent rice flour to those that include a secondary starch such as cornstarch. If you can find only the latter, just cook them longer—up to 12 minutes. For a less spicy sauce, use only half the Thai chile. For the cilantro, use the leaves and the thin, delicate stems, not the thicker ones close to the root. To serve, place platters of noodles, salad, sauce, and pork patties on the table and allow diners to combine components to their taste. The sauce is potent, so use it sparingly.

NOODLES AND SALAD

- 8 ounces rice vermicelli
- 1 head Boston lettuce (8 ounces), torn into bite-size pieces
- 1 English cucumber, peeled, quartered lengthwise, seeded, and sliced thin on bias
- 1 cup fresh cilantro leaves and stems
- 1 cup fresh mint leaves, torn if large

SAUCE

- 1 small Thai chile, stemmed and minced
- 3 tablespoons sugar
- 1 garlic clove, minced
- ⅔ cup hot water
- 5 tablespoons fish sauce
- ¼ cup lime juice (2 limes)

PORK PATTIES

- 1 large shallot, minced
- 1 tablespoon fish sauce
- 1½ teaspoons sugar
- ½ teaspoon baking soda
- ½ teaspoon pepper
- 1 pound ground pork

1. FOR THE NOODLES AND SALAD: Bring 4 quarts water to boil in large pot. Stir in noodles and cook until tender but not mushy, 4 to 12 minutes. Drain noodles and rinse under cold running water until cool. Drain noodles very well, spread on large plate, and let stand at room temperature to dry. Arrange lettuce, cucumber, cilantro, and mint separately on large platter and refrigerate until needed.

2. FOR THE SAUCE: Using mortar and pestle (or on cutting board using flat side of chef's knife), mash Thai chile, 1 tablespoon sugar, and garlic to fine paste. Transfer to medium bowl and add hot water and remaining 2 tablespoons sugar. Stir until sugar is dissolved. Stir in fish sauce and lime juice. Set aside.

3. FOR THE PORK PATTIES: Combine shallot, fish sauce, sugar, baking soda, and pepper in medium bowl. Add pork and mix until well combined. Shape pork mixture into 12 patties, each about 2½ inches wide and ½ inch thick.

4A. FOR A CHARCOAL GRILL: Open bottom vent completely. Light large chimney starter filled with charcoal briquettes (6 quarts). When top coals are partially covered with ash, pour over half of grill. Set cooking grate in place, cover, and open lid vent completely. Heat grill until hot, about 5 minutes.

4B. FOR A GAS GRILL: Turn all burners to high, cover, and heat grill until hot, about 15 minutes. Leave all burners on high.

5. Clean and oil cooking grate. Cook patties (directly over coals if using charcoal; covered if using gas) until well charred, 3 to 4 minutes per side. Transfer grilled patties to bowl with sauce and gently toss to coat. Let stand for 5 minutes.

6. Transfer patties to serving plate, reserving sauce. Serve noodles, salad, sauce, and pork patties separately.

FALAFEL

WHY THIS RECIPE WORKS: The best falafel are moist, tender, packed with vibrant fresh herbs and aromatics, and sturdy enough to form and fry. We started by soaking dried chickpeas overnight to soften them slightly, then grinding them into coarse bits along with onion, herbs, garlic, and spices. Though many recipes call for mixing starch into the dough (either flour, cornstarch, or chickpea flour), we found success using a technique associated with Asian bread baking called *tangzhong*, a cooked flour paste. This paste added moisture without making the batter too fragile to form and fry. Adding a bit of baking powder to the dough helped to lighten the fritters as they fried. Frying the fritters at 325 degrees allowed the moist interiors to fully cook through just as the exteriors turned brown and crisp.

Falafel
MAKES 24 PIECES, ENOUGH TO SERVE 4 TO 6

This recipe requires that the chickpeas be soaked for at least 8 hours. Use a Dutch oven that holds 6 quarts or more. An equal amount of chickpea flour can be substituted for the all-purpose flour; if using, increase the amount of water to ½ cup in step 4. Do not substitute canned beans or quick-soaked chickpeas. They will make stodgy falafel. Serve the falafel with the tahini sauce as an appetizer or in pita bread with lettuce, chopped tomatoes, chopped cucumbers, fresh cilantro, Quick Pickled Turnips and Carrots with Lemon and Coriander and Tomato-Chile Sauce (recipes follow). Serve the first batch of falafel immediately or hold them in a 200-degree oven while the second batch cooks.

FALAFEL

- 8 ounces dried chickpeas, picked over and rinsed
- ¾ cup fresh cilantro leaves and stems
- ¾ cup fresh parsley leaves
- ½ onion, chopped fine (½ cup)
- 2 garlic cloves, minced
- 1½ teaspoons ground coriander
- 1 teaspoon ground cumin
- 1 teaspoon salt
- ¼ teaspoon cayenne pepper
- ¼ cup all-purpose flour
- 2 teaspoons baking powder
- 2 quarts vegetable oil

TAHINI SAUCE

- ⅓ cup tahini
- ⅓ cup plain Greek yogurt
- ¼ cup lemon juice (2 lemons)
- ¼ cup water
- Salt

1. FOR THE FALAFEL: Place chickpeas in large container and cover with 2 to 3 inches of cold water. Let soak at room temperature for at least 8 hours or up to 24 hours. Drain well.

2. FOR THE TAHINI SAUCE: Whisk tahini, yogurt, and lemon juice together in medium bowl until smooth. Whisk in water to thin sauce as desired. Season with salt to taste; set aside. (Sauce can be refrigerated for up to 4 days. Let come to room temperature and stir to combine before serving.)

3. Process cilantro, parsley, onion, garlic, coriander, cumin, salt, and cayenne in food processor for 5 seconds. Scrape down sides of bowl. Continue to process until mixture resembles pesto, about 5 seconds longer. Add chickpeas and pulse 6 times. Scrape down sides of bowl. Continue to pulse until chickpeas are coarsely chopped and resemble sesame seeds, about 6 pulses more. Transfer mixture to large bowl and set aside.

4. Whisk flour and ⅓ cup water in bowl until no lumps remain. Microwave, whisking every 10 seconds, until mixture thickens to stiff, smooth, pudding-like consistency that forms mound when dropped from end of whisk into bowl, 40 to 80 seconds. Stir baking powder into flour paste.

5. Add flour paste to ground chickpea mixture and, using rubber spatula, mix until fully incorporated. Divide mixture into 24 pieces and gently roll into golf ball–size spheres, transferring spheres to parchment paper–lined rimmed baking sheet once they are formed. (Formed falafel can be refrigerated for up to 2 hours.)

6. Heat oil in large Dutch oven over medium-high heat to 325 degrees. Add half of falafel and fry, stirring occasionally, until deep brown, about 5 minutes. Adjust burner, if necessary, to maintain oil temperature of 325 degrees. Using slotted spoon or wire skimmer, transfer to paper towel–lined baking sheet. Return oil to 325 degrees and repeat with remaining falafel. Serve immediately with tahini sauce.

Quick Pickled Turnips and Carrots with Lemon and Coriander
MAKES ABOUT 4 CUPS

To ensure that the turnips are tender, peel them thoroughly to remove not only the tough outer skin but also the fibrous layer of flesh just beneath.

- 1 teaspoon coriander seeds
- 1 teaspoon mustard seeds
- 1½ cups cider vinegar
- ¾ cup water
- 1 tablespoon sugar
- ½ teaspoon red pepper flakes
- ½ teaspoon salt
- 1 pound turnips, peeled and cut into ½-inch by ½-inch by 2-inch batons
- 1 red onion, halved and sliced thin
- 2 carrots, peeled and sliced thin on bias
- 4 (3-inch) strips lemon zest

Toast coriander seeds and mustard seeds in medium saucepan over medium heat, stirring frequently, until fragrant, about 2 minutes. Add vinegar, water, sugar, pepper flakes, and salt, and bring to boil, stirring to dissolve sugar and salt. Remove saucepan from heat and add turnips, onion, carrots, and lemon zest, pressing to submerge vegetables. Cover and let cool completely, 30 minutes. (Cooled vegetables can be refrigerated for up to 1 week.)

Tomato-Chile Sauce

MAKES ABOUT 1½ CUPS

The test kitchen's favorite canned diced tomatoes are made by Hunt's.

1 (15 ounce) can diced tomatoes, drained
½ cup fresh cilantro leaves and stems
3 garlic cloves, minced
1 tablespoon red pepper flakes
1 tablespoon red wine vinegar, plus extra for seasoning
1 teaspoon ground cumin
1 teaspoon ground coriander
½ teaspoon smoked paprika
⅛ teaspoon sugar
   Salt
2 tablespoons extra-virgin olive oil

Process tomatoes, cilantro, garlic, pepper flakes, vinegar, cumin, coriander, paprika, sugar, and ¾ teaspoon salt in food processor until smooth paste is formed, 20 to 30 seconds. With food processor running, slowly add oil through feed tube until fully incorporated, about 5 seconds. Transfer to bowl and season with salt and vinegar to taste.

GRILLED MOJO-MARINATED SKIRT STEAK

WHY THIS RECIPE WORKS: If you're not grilling skirt steak, you should be: It's a great cut for marinating, it cooks in minutes, and it's especially beefy, tender, and juicy—as long as you buy the right kind. For this recipe, we chose the outside skirt steak, which is 3 to 4 inches wide, and avoided the wider, far less tender inside skirt steak. To make the most of this steak's ample surface area, we submerged it in a citrusy, garlicky Cuban-style mojo marinade. Adding soy sauce to the marinade, though untraditional, helped season the meat and added even more savory flavor; one hour of marinating did the trick. We also added baking soda to the oil we rubbed onto the steak before grilling, which created even more browning during cooking. We reused the marinade as a serving sauce, pouring it into a saucepan and boiling it so it would be safe to eat. To give the sauce some added richness and acidity, we added lime juice and olive oil, plus some orange and lime zest to achieve a bright, tropical flavor.

Grilled Mojo-Marinated Skirt Steak

SERVES 4 TO 6

Skirt steak is most tender when cooked to medium (130 to 135 degrees). Thin steaks cook very quickly, so we recommend using an instant-read thermometer for a quick and accurate measurement.

6 garlic cloves, minced
2 tablespoons soy sauce
1 teaspoon grated lime zest plus ¼ cup juice (2 limes)
1 teaspoon ground cumin
1 teaspoon dried oregano
   Salt
½ teaspoon grated orange zest plus ½ cup juice
¼ teaspoon red pepper flakes
2 pounds skirt steak, trimmed and cut with grain into 6- to 8-inch-long steaks
2 tablespoons extra-virgin olive oil
1 teaspoon baking soda

1. Combine garlic, soy sauce, 2 tablespoons lime juice, cumin, oregano, ¾ teaspoon salt, orange juice, and pepper flakes in 13 by 9-inch baking dish. Place steaks in dish. Flip steaks to coat both sides with marinade. Cover and refrigerate for 1 hour, flipping steaks halfway through refrigerating.

2. Remove steaks from marinade and transfer marinade to small saucepan. Pat steaks dry with paper towels. Combine 1 tablespoon oil and baking soda in small bowl. Rub oil mixture evenly onto both sides of each steak.

3. Bring marinade to boil over high heat and boil for 30 seconds. Transfer to bowl and stir in lime zest, orange zest, remaining 2 tablespoons lime juice, and remaining 1 tablespoon oil. Set aside sauce.

4A. FOR A CHARCOAL GRILL: About 25 minutes before grilling, open bottom vent completely. Light large chimney starter filled with charcoal briquettes (6 quarts). When top coals are partially covered with ash, pour evenly over half of grill. Set cooking grate in place, cover, and open lid vent completely. Heat grill until hot, about 5 minutes.

4B. FOR A GAS GRILL: Turn all burners to high, cover, and heat grill until hot, about 15 minutes. Turn off 1 burner (if using grill with more than 2 burners, turn off burner farthest from primary burner) and leave other burner(s) on high.

5. Clean and oil cooking grate. Cook steaks on hotter side of grill until well browned and meat registers 130 to 135 degrees (for medium), 2 to 4 minutes per side. (Move steaks to cooler side of grill before taking temperature to prevent them from overcooking.) Transfer steaks to cutting board, tent with aluminum foil, and let rest for 10 minutes. Cut steaks on bias against grain into ½-inch-thick slices. Arrange slices on serving platter, drizzle with 2 tablespoons sauce, and serve, passing extra sauce separately.

GRILLED CHICKEN THIGHS

WHY THIS RECIPE WORKS: We wanted a recipe that would produce juicy, flavorful grilled chicken thighs that had well-rendered, crispy skin—minus the all too frequent inferno. Cooking the chicken over indirect heat for a relatively long time (about 40 minutes), until it registered between 185 to 190 degrees, allowed collagen in the meat to break down into gelatin, which lubricated the meat so that it tasted moist and silky. We also grilled the thighs skin side down for all but the last few minutes of cooking, which allowed fat under the surface of the skin to thoroughly render and the collagen in the skin to break down, both of which led to thin, crispy, well-browned skin. For extra flavor, we wanted to coat the chicken with a bold paste and found that spreading two-thirds of the paste on the flesh side of each thigh worked best, as there were lots of nooks and crannies to capture it. We then rubbed the remaining third of the paste over the skin, which seasoned and flavored it without adding so much moisture that crisping was inhibited. The only hitch: If the chicken cooked skin side down the whole time, the paste on the flesh side looked and tasted a bit raw. So after the skin crisped over the hotter side of the grill, we flipped the pieces onto the flesh side for a minute or two to take the raw edge off the paste.

Best Grilled Chicken Thighs
SERVES 4 TO 6

In step 1, the chicken can be refrigerated for up to 2 hours before grilling.

  8 (5- to 7-ounce) bone-in chicken thighs, trimmed
  ½ teaspoon kosher salt
  1 recipe paste (recipes follow)

1. Place chicken, skin side up, on large plate. Sprinkle skin side with salt and spread evenly with one-third of spice paste. Flip chicken and spread remaining two-thirds of paste evenly over flesh side. Refrigerate while preparing grill.

2A. FOR A CHARCOAL GRILL: Open bottom vent halfway. Light large chimney starter mounded with charcoal briquettes (7 quarts). When top coals are partially covered with ash, pour evenly over half of grill. Set cooking grate in place, cover, and open lid vent halfway. Heat grill until hot, about 5 minutes.

2B. FOR A GAS GRILL: Turn all burners to high, cover, and heat grill until hot, about 15 minutes. Leave primary burner on high and turn off other burner(s). (Adjust primary burner [or, if using 3-burner grill, primary burner and second burner] as needed to maintain grill temperature around 350 degrees.)

3. Clean and oil cooking grate. Place chicken, skin side down, on cooler side of grill. Cover and cook for 20 minutes. Rearrange chicken, keeping skin side down, so that pieces that were positioned closest to edge of grill are now closer to heat source and vice versa. Cover and continue to cook until chicken registers 185 to 190 degrees, 15 to 20 minutes longer.

4. Move all chicken, skin side down, to hotter side of grill and cook until skin is lightly charred, about 5 minutes. Flip chicken and cook until flesh side is lightly browned, 1 to 2 minutes. Transfer to platter, tent with aluminum foil, and let rest for 10 minutes. Serve.

Gochujang Paste
MAKES ABOUT ⅓ CUP

Gochujang, or Korean red chili paste, can be found in Asian markets or in the Asian section of large supermarkets.

  3 tablespoons gochujang
  1 tablespoon soy sauce
  2 garlic cloves, minced
  2 teaspoons sugar
  1 teaspoon kosher salt

Combine all ingredients in bowl.

Mustard-Tarragon Paste
MAKES ABOUT ⅓ CUP

Rosemary or thyme can be substituted for the tarragon, if desired. When using this paste, we like to serve the chicken with lemon wedges.

  3 tablespoons Dijon mustard
  5 garlic cloves, minced
  1 tablespoon finely grated lemon zest
  2 teaspoons minced fresh tarragon
1½ teaspoons kosher salt
  1 teaspoon water
  ½ teaspoon pepper

Combine all ingredients in bowl.

Garam Masala Paste
MAKES ABOUT ⅓ CUP

Adjust the amount of cayenne to suit your taste. When using this paste, we like to serve the chicken with lime wedges.

  3 tablespoons vegetable oil
1½ tablespoons garam masala
  2 garlic cloves, minced
  2 teaspoons grated fresh ginger
  2 teaspoons finely grated lime zest
1¼ teaspoons kosher salt
⅛–¼ teaspoon cayenne pepper

Combine all ingredients in bowl.

SKILLET-ROASTED BRUSSELS SPROUTS

WHY THIS RECIPE WORKS: All too often, Brussels sprouts wind up either overcooked or undercooked and rarely receive the praise they deserve. We wanted a foolproof stovetop recipe that would produce Brussels sprouts that were deeply browned on the cut sides, while still bright green on the uncut sides and crisp-tender within. After several unsuccessful attempts in a hot skillet, we tried starting the sprouts in a cold skillet (which also made it easier to arrange them), adding plenty of oil and cooking them covered. This gently heated the sprouts and created a steamy environment that cooked them through without adding any extra moisture. We then removed the lid and continued to cook the sprouts cut sides down so they had time to develop a substantial, cara-melized crust. Using enough oil to completely coat the skillet ensured that all the sprouts made full contact with the fat to brown from edge to edge, resulting in gorgeously, evenly browned sprouts that weren't greasy. To balance their nutty sweetness, we stirred in some lemon juice and sprinkled Pecorino Romano as a finishing touch.

Skillet-Roasted Brussels Sprouts with Lemon and Pecorino Romano

SERVES 4

Look for Brussels sprouts that are similar in size, with small, tight heads that are no more than 1½ inches in diameter, as they're likely to be sweeter and more tender than larger sprouts. Parmesan cheese can be substituted for the Pecorino, if desired.

- 1 pound small (1 to 1½ inches in diameter) Brussels sprouts, trimmed and halved
- 5 tablespoons extra-virgin olive oil
- 1 tablespoon lemon juice
  Salt and pepper
- ¼ cup shredded Pecorino Romano cheese

1. Arrange Brussels sprouts in single layer, cut sides down, in 12-inch nonstick skillet. Drizzle oil evenly over sprouts. Cover skillet, place over medium-high heat, and cook until sprouts are bright green and cut sides have started to brown, about 5 minutes.

2. Uncover and continue to cook until cut sides of sprouts are deeply and evenly browned and paring knife slides in with little to no resistance, 2 to 3 minutes longer, adjusting heat and moving sprouts as necessary to prevent them from overbrowning. While sprouts cook, combine lemon juice and ¼ teaspoon salt in small bowl.

3. Off heat, add lemon juice mixture to skillet and stir to evenly coat sprouts. Season with salt and pepper to taste. Transfer sprouts to large plate, sprinkle with Pecorino, and serve.

Skillet-Roasted Brussels Sprouts with Cider Vinegar and Honey

Substitute 2 teaspoons cider vinegar, 2 teaspoons honey, and ¼ teaspoon red pepper flakes for lemon juice and omit pepper and Pecorino.

Skillet-Roasted Brussels Sprouts with Maple Syrup and Smoked Almonds

Omit pepper. Substitute 1 tablespoon maple syrup and 1 table-spoon sherry vinegar for lemon juice and ¼ cup smoked almonds, chopped fine, for Pecorino.

Skillet-Roasted Brussels Sprouts with Pomegranate and Pistachios

Substitute 1 tablespoon pomegranate molasses and ½ tea-spoon ground cumin for lemon juice. Omit pepper. Substi-tute ¼ cup shelled pistachios, toasted and chopped fine, and 2 tablespoons pomegranate seeds for Pecorino.

Skillet-Roasted Brussels Sprouts with Chile, Peanuts, and Mint

Substitute 1 Fresno chile, stemmed, seeded, and minced; 2 teaspoons lime juice; and 1 teaspoon fish sauce for lemon juice. Omit pepper. Substitute 2 tablespoons finely chopped dry-roasted peanuts and 2 tablespoons chopped fresh mint for Pecorino.

Skillet-Roasted Brussels Sprouts with Gochujang and Sesame Seeds

Omit pepper. Substitute 1 tablespoon gochujang and 1 table-spoon rice vinegar for lemon juice and 2 teaspoons toasted sesame seeds for Pecorino.

Skillet-Roasted Brussels Sprouts with Mustard and Brown Sugar

Substitute 1 tablespoon Dijon mustard, 1 tablespoon packed brown sugar, 2 teaspoons white wine vinegar, and ⅛ teaspoon cayenne pepper for lemon juice. Omit pepper and Pecorino.

BUTTERY SPRING VEGETABLES

WHY THIS RECIPE WORKS: Crisp-tender spring vegetables coated in a rich yet light butter sauce sounds ideal, but many of these recipes wind up dull, waterlogged, and ultimately lacking in buttery flavor. We wanted spring vegetables that retained their vibrant colors and crisp textures and a butter sauce that would cling to the vegetables, not the platter. To prevent our medley of vegetables from becoming water-logged, we cooked them in a steamer basket, staggering their additions so that each ended up perfectly crisp-tender. Spreading the vegetables on a platter immediately after cooking allowed excess heat to dissipate, so the vegetables didn't overcook while we made the sauce. Instead of plain melted butter, which had a tendency to slip off the vegetables and pool on the platter below, we made a version of the creamy, tangy French butter sauce beurre blanc by emulsify-ing chilled butter into a mixture of sautéed shallot, vinegar, salt, sugar, and water. The emulsified sauce clung to and coated each vegetable. A sprinkle of chives made this simple platter of vegetables worthy of a special occasion.

Buttery Spring Vegetables

SERVES 6

To ensure that the turnips are tender, peel them thoroughly to remove not only the tough outer skin but also the fibrous layer of flesh just beneath. This recipe works best with thick asparagus spears that are between ½ and ¾ inch in diameter.

- 1 pound turnips, peeled and cut into ½-inch by ½-inch by 2-inch batons
- 1 pound asparagus, trimmed and cut on bias into 2-inch lengths
- 8 ounces sugar snap peas, strings removed, trimmed
- 4 large radishes, halved and sliced thin
- 1 tablespoon minced shallot

1½ teaspoons white wine vinegar

¾ teaspoon salt

¼ teaspoon sugar

6 tablespoons unsalted butter, cut into 6 pieces and chilled

1 tablespoon minced fresh chives

1. Bring 1 cup water to boil in large saucepan over high heat. Place steamer basket over boiling water. Add turnips and asparagus to basket, cover saucepan, and reduce heat to medium. Cook until vegetables are slightly softened, about 2 minutes. Add snap peas, cover, and cook until snap peas are crisp-tender, about 2 minutes. Add radishes, cover, and cook for 1 minute. Lift basket out of saucepan and transfer vegetables to platter. Spread into even layer to allow steam to dissipate. Discard all but 3 tablespoons liquid from saucepan.

2. Return saucepan to medium heat. Add shallot, vinegar, salt, and sugar and cook until mixture is reduced to 1½ tablespoons (it will barely cover bottom of saucepan), about 2 minutes. Reduce heat to low. Add butter, 1 piece at a time, whisking vigorously after each addition, until butter is incorporated and sauce has consistency of heavy cream, 4 to 5 minutes. Remove saucepan from heat. Add vegetables and stir to coat. Dry platter and return vegetables to platter. Sprinkle with chives and serve.

FAVA BEANS WITH ARTICHOKES, ASPARAGUS, AND PEAS

WHY THIS RECIPE WORKS: Italian *vignole* is a vibrant braise that highlights the best of spring produce. Since fresh fava beans are traditional, we started there. The favas are usually eaten skin on, but tasters found their fibrous skins tough and unpleasant. We were happy to find that we could tenderize the skins by blanching the beans in a baking soda solution. However, the baking soda solution had one drawback: The high pH of the water caused the favas to slowly turn purple during cooking—and they continued to change color after draining. We found that the most effective way to counteract this was to simply rinse them thoroughly after cooking. With our skin-on favas perfected, we turned to the remaining vegetables. Sweet peas, savory baby artichokes, and grassy asparagus added layers of springtime flavor. A speedy stovetop braise was the ideal method for cooking each vegetable perfectly; we added the artichokes first to allow them time to cook almost all the way through before adding the more delicate asparagus and peas, and finally the favas to warm through. We finished the dish with fresh herbs and lemon zest to reinforce the lively flavor profile.

Fava Beans with Artichokes, Asparagus, and Peas

SERVES 6

This recipe works best with fresh, in-season vegetables; however, if you can't find fresh fava beans and peas, you can substitute 1 cup of frozen, thawed fava beans and 1¼ cups of frozen peas; add the peas to the skillet with the beans in step 4.

2 teaspoons grated lemon zest, plus 1 lemon

4 baby artichokes (3 ounces each)

1 teaspoon baking soda

1 pound fava beans, shelled (1 cup)

1 tablespoon extra-virgin olive oil, plus extra for serving

1 leek, white and light green parts only, halved lengthwise, sliced thin, and washed thoroughly

Salt and pepper

3 garlic cloves, minced

1 cup chicken or vegetable broth

1 pound asparagus, trimmed and cut on bias into 2-inch lengths

1 pound fresh peas, shelled (1¼ cups)

2 tablespoons shredded fresh basil

1 tablespoon chopped fresh mint

1. Cut lemon in half, squeeze halves into container filled with 2 quarts water, then add spent halves. Working with 1 artichoke at a time, trim stem to about ¾ inch and cut off top quarter of artichoke. Break off bottom 3 or 4 rows of tough outer leaves by pulling them downward. Using paring knife, trim outer layer of stem and base, removing any dark green parts. Cut artichoke into quarters and submerge in lemon water.

2. Bring 2 cups water and baking soda to boil in small saucepan. Add beans and cook until edges begin to darken, 1 to 2 minutes. Drain and rinse well with cold water.

3. Heat oil in 12-inch skillet over medium heat until shimmering. Add leek, 1 tablespoon water, and 1 teaspoon salt and cook until softened, about 3 minutes. Stir in garlic and cook until fragrant, about 30 seconds.

4. Remove artichokes from lemon water, shaking off excess water, and add to skillet. Stir in broth and bring to simmer. Reduce heat to medium-low, cover, and cook until artichokes are almost tender, 6 to 8 minutes. Stir in asparagus and peas, cover, and cook until crisp-tender, 5 to 7 minutes. Stir in beans and cook until heated through and artichokes are fully tender, about 2 minutes. Off heat, stir in basil, mint, and lemon zest. Season with salt and pepper to taste and drizzle with extra oil. Serve immediately.

DUCHESS POTATO CASSEROLE

WHY THIS RECIPE WORKS: *Pommes duchesse* is a classic French preparation of piped mounds of egg-enriched mashed potatoes. They can be made in advance, they look festive, and they taste great with a variety of entrées; however, they are rather fussy to prepare, require a pastry bag, and, since they're rather petite, they cool rapidly. To make this dish easier to pull off, we skipped the piping and baked the mashed potatoes in a larger casserole-style dish, which kept them hotter longer. We enhanced mashed Yukon Golds with butter, egg yolks, half-and-half, and nutmeg, being sure to add the butter first to coat the potatoes' starch granules and protect them from being overworked and turning gluey. To give the casserole an attractive finish, we coated the top with a mixture of butter and egg white (which produced a crisp, golden-brown crust) and then scored the surface before baking, creating plenty of sharp edges to brown.

Duchess Potato Casserole
SERVES 8 TO 10
Freshly ground nutmeg contributes heady flavor, so be sure to use it sparingly.

3½ pounds Yukon Gold potatoes, peeled and sliced ½ inch thick
⅔   cup half-and-half
1   large egg, separated, plus 2 large yolks
    Salt and pepper
    Pinch nutmeg
10 tablespoons unsalted butter, melted

1. Adjust oven rack to middle position and heat oven to 450 degrees. Grease 13 by 9-inch baking dish. Place potatoes in large saucepan and add cold water to cover by 1 inch. Bring to simmer over medium-high heat. Adjust heat to maintain gentle simmer and cook until paring knife can be slipped into and out of centers of potatoes with no resistance, 18 to 22 minutes. Drain potatoes.

2. While potatoes cook, combine half-and-half, 3 egg yolks, 1¾ teaspoons salt, ½ teaspoon pepper, and nutmeg in bowl. Set aside.

3. Place now-empty saucepan over low heat; set ricer or food mill over saucepan. Working in batches, transfer potatoes to hopper and process. Using rubber spatula, stir in 8 tablespoons melted butter until incorporated. Stir in reserved half-and-half mixture until combined. Transfer potatoes to prepared dish and smooth into even layer.

4. Combine egg white, remaining 2 tablespoons melted butter, and pinch salt in bowl and beat with fork until combined. Pour egg white mixture over potatoes, tilting dish so mixture evenly covers surface. Using flat side of paring knife, make series of ½-inch-deep, ¼-inch-wide parallel grooves across surface of casserole. Make second series of parallel grooves across surface, at angle to first series, to create crosshatch pattern. Bake casserole until golden brown, 25 to 30 minutes, rotating dish halfway through baking. Let cool for 20 minutes. Serve.

TO MAKE AHEAD: At end of step 3, wrap dish in plastic wrap and refrigerate for up to 24 hours. To serve, top and score casserole as directed in step 4 and bake in 375-degree oven for 45 to 50 minutes.

THICK-CUT OVEN FRIES

WHY THIS RECIPE WORKS: Most people's alternative to deep-fried fries is oven fries, which are usually less fussy to make, often less greasy—but usually a disappointment. We wanted the flavor and crispiness of deep-fried fries with no more work than roasting potatoes. Taking a closer look at how French fries cook, we discovered that when traditional fries are fried, water is rapidly driven out of the starch cells

at the surface of the potato, leaving behind tiny cavities; it's these cavities that create a delicate, crispy crust. Since oven fries don't heat fast enough for air pockets to form, we looked to alternatives and instead coated the potatoes in a cornstarch slurry that crisped up like a deep-fried fry would. We arranged the coated planks on a rimmed baking sheet that we coated with both vegetable oil spray and vegetable oil; the former contains a surfactant called lecithin, which prevented the oil from pooling and, in turn, prevented the potatoes from sticking. Using the oil spray also allowed us to use only 3 tablespoons of oil, just enough to evenly coat the fries. Covering the baking sheet with aluminum foil for the first half of cooking ensured that the potatoes were fully tender by the time they browned to perfection.

Thick-Cut Oven Fries
SERVES 4
Choose potatoes that are 4 to 6 inches in length to ensure well-proportioned fries. Trimming thin slices from the ends of the potatoes in step 2 ensures that each fry has two flat surfaces for even browning. This recipe's success is dependent on a heavy-duty rimmed baking sheet that will not warp in the heat of the oven. Spraying the sheet with vegetable oil spray will help the oil spread evenly and prevent sticking. The rate at which the potatoes brown is dependent on your baking sheet and oven. After removing the foil from the baking sheet in step 5, monitor the color of the potatoes carefully to prevent scorching.

3 tablespoons vegetable oil
2 pounds Yukon gold potatoes, unpeeled
3 tablespoons cornstarch
   Salt

1. Adjust oven rack to lowest position and heat oven to 425 degrees. Generously spray rimmed baking sheet with vegetable oil spray. Pour oil into prepared sheet and tilt sheet until surface is evenly coated with oil.

2. Halve potatoes lengthwise and turn halves cut sides down on cutting board. Trim thin slice from both long sides of each potato half; discard trimmings. Slice potatoes lengthwise into ⅓- to ½-inch-thick planks.

3. Combine ¾ cup water and cornstarch in large bowl, making sure no lumps of cornstarch remain on bottom of bowl. Microwave, stirring every 20 seconds, until mixture begins to thicken, 1 to 3 minutes. Remove from microwave and continue to stir until mixture thickens to pudding-like consistency. (If necessary, add up to 2 tablespoons water to achieve correct consistency.)

4. Transfer potatoes to bowl with cornstarch mixture and toss until each plank is evenly coated. Arrange planks on prepared sheet, leaving small gaps between planks. (Some cornstarch mixture will remain in bowl.) Cover sheet tightly with lightly greased aluminum foil and bake for 12 minutes.

5. Remove foil from sheet and bake until bottom of each fry is golden brown, 10 to 18 minutes. Remove sheet from oven and, using thin metal spatula, carefully flip each fry. Return sheet to oven and continue to bake until second sides are golden brown, 10 to 18 minutes longer. Sprinkle fries with ½ teaspoon salt. Using spatula, carefully toss fries to distribute salt. Transfer fries to paper towel–lined plate and season with salt to taste. Serve.

CREAMY FRENCH-STYLE SCRAMBLED EGGS

WHY THIS RECIPE WORKS: American-style scrambled eggs are the speediest of home-cooked breakfasts, but French cooks (and often British ones) employ a more leisurely approach, cooking their eggs slowly over low heat. This technique can take five times as long as the American version, but the reward is eggs that are extravagantly creamy and rich. The velvety texture of traditional French-style scrambled eggs is believed to be the combined result of slow cooking and the addition of plenty of cream and butter, but we found a way to make them without all the added fat. We used steaming water, rather than melted butter, to indicate when our nonstick skillet was hot enough to begin cooking the eggs. Stirring constantly controlled the coagulation of the proteins so that some formed delicate curds while the rest thickened into a saucy consistency. Adding a tablespoon of water at the end of cooking diluted the proteins, giving our eggs the perfect texture. Finally, a sprinkle of fresh minced herbs complemented their richness.

Creamy French-Style Scrambled Eggs
SERVES 4

For the creamiest, richest-tasting result, be sure to cook these eggs slowly, following the visual cues provided. It should take 12 to 14 minutes total. Though the eggs will be rather loose, their extended cooking time ensures that they reach a safe temperature. You can prepare two servings by halving the amounts of all the ingredients and using an 8-inch skillet. Chives or tarragon can be substituted for the parsley, if desired. Serve with buttered toast.

- 8 large eggs
- ½ teaspoon salt
- 3 tablespoons water
- 1 teaspoon minced fresh parsley

1. Using fork, beat eggs and salt until blended. Heat 2 tablespoons water in 10-inch nonstick skillet over low heat until steaming. Add egg mixture and immediately stir with rubber spatula. Cook, stirring slowly and constantly, scraping edges and bottom of skillet, for 4 minutes. (If egg mixture is not steaming after 4 minutes, increase heat slightly.)

2. Continue to stir slowly until eggs begin to thicken and small curds begin to form, about 4 minutes longer (if curds have not begun to form, increase heat slightly). If any large curds form, mash with spatula. As curds start to form, stir

vigorously, scraping edges and bottom of skillet, until eggs are thick enough to hold their shape when pushed to 1 side of skillet, 4 to 6 minutes. Remove skillet from heat. Add remaining 1 tablespoon water and parsley and stir vigorously until incorporated, about 30 seconds. Serve.

SOUS VIDE SOFT-POACHED EGGS

WHY THIS RECIPE WORKS: There's no getting around it: Eggs are tricky to cook. The white and the yolk behave differently when subjected to heat. Because they contain different proportions of proteins, fats, and water, they coagulate and set at different temperatures, and they have different final textures. However, eggs are perhaps the poster child for sous vide cooking: The technique can produce eggs with unique texture; the method is hands-off; and the recipe is easily scalable. Typically, sous vide eggs are cooked at a low temperature (around 145°F/63°C) for at least an hour. This will provide a yolk that is slightly thickened but still runny and a barely set white. We found the white to be too loose when cooked in this temperature range, most of it running off when we cracked into the eggs. Some recipes, though, call for cracking "63-degree eggs," such as these, into simmering water to better set the whites. We wanted to ditch that extra step and still produce a perfectly poached egg, so we opted to cook at a higher temperature for a shorter time to set more of the white. This method produced a traditional poached egg—right out of the shell. And with the ability to make these eggs ahead of time—just reheat them in a 140°F/60°C water bath for anywhere from 15 to 60 minutes—this recipe is perfect for the brunch crowd.

Be sure to use large eggs that have no cracks and are cold from the refrigerator. Fresher eggs have tighter egg whites and are better suited for this recipe. Serve with crusty bread or toast.

Sous Vide Soft-Poached Eggs
MAKES 1 TO 16 EGGS

- 1–16 large eggs, chilled
  Salt and pepper

1. Using sous vide circulator, bring water to 167 degrees in 7-quart container. Using slotted spoon, gently lower eggs into prepared water bath, cover, and cook for 12 minutes.

2. Meanwhile, fill large bowl halfway with ice and water. Using slotted spoon, transfer eggs to ice bath and let sit until cool enough to touch, about 1 minute. To serve, crack eggs into individual bowls and season with salt and pepper to taste.

TO MAKE AHEAD: Eggs can be rapidly chilled in ice bath for 10 minutes and then refrigerated for up to 5 days. To reheat, lower eggs into water bath set to 140 degrees and cook until heated through, at least 15 minutes or up to 60 minutes. Crack into bowls as directed.

BROCCOLI AND FETA FRITTATA

WHY THIS RECIPE WORKS: The frittata is sometimes called a lazy cook's omelet. After all, it contains the same ingredients but doesn't require folding the eggs around the filling, a skill that takes practice to master. But even the practical frittata requires a little know-how, lest the bottom turn rubbery or the center end up loose and wet. We wanted to uncover the keys to a tender, evenly cooked, cohesive frittata, and we wanted it to be big and hearty enough to serve at least four for dinner. We started with a well-seasoned filling made with bold ingredients and combined it with a dozen eggs to make a substantial dinner. To ensure that the frittata was cohesive, we chopped the filling ingredients small so that they could be surrounded and held in place by the eggs. To help the eggs stay tender even when cooked to a relatively high temperature, we added milk and salt. The liquid diluted the proteins, making it harder for them to coagulate and turn the eggs rubbery, and salt weakened the interactions between proteins, producing a softer curd. Finally, for eggs that were cooked fully and evenly, we started the frittata on the stovetop, stirring until a spatula left a trail in the curds, and then transferred the skillet to the oven to gently finish.

Broccoli and Feta Frittata
SERVES 4 TO 6
This frittata can also be served warm or at room temperature. When paired with a salad, it can serve as a meal.

- 12 large eggs
- ⅓ cup whole milk
- Salt
- 1 tablespoon extra-virgin olive oil
- 12 ounces broccoli florets, cut into ½-inch pieces (4 cups)
- Pinch red pepper flakes
- 3 tablespoons water
- ½ teaspoon grated lemon zest plus ½ teaspoon juice
- 4 ounces feta cheese, crumbled into ½-inch pieces (1 cup)

1. Adjust oven rack to middle position and heat oven to 350 degrees. Whisk eggs, milk, and ½ teaspoon salt in bowl until well combined.

2. Heat oil in 12-inch ovensafe nonstick skillet over medium-high heat until shimmering. Add broccoli, pepper flakes, and ¼ teaspoon salt; cook, stirring frequently, until broccoli is crisp-tender and spotty brown, 7 to 9 minutes. Add water and lemon zest and juice; continue to cook, stirring constantly, until broccoli is just tender and no water remains in skillet, about 1 minute longer.

3. Add feta and egg mixture and cook, using rubber spatula to stir and scrape bottom of skillet until large curds form and spatula leaves trail through eggs but eggs are still very wet, about 30 seconds. Smooth curds into even layer and cook,

without stirring, for 30 seconds. Transfer skillet to oven and bake until frittata is slightly puffy and surface bounces back when lightly pressed, 6 to 9 minutes. Using rubber spatula, loosen frittata from skillet and transfer to cutting board. Let stand for 5 minutes before slicing and serving.

Asparagus and Goat Cheese Frittata
This recipe works best with thin and medium-size asparagus.

Substitute 1 pound asparagus, trimmed and cut into ¼-inch lengths, for broccoli and ¼ teaspoon pepper for pepper flakes. Reduce cooking time in step 2 to 3 to 4 minutes. Omit water. Substitute goat cheese for feta and add 2 tablespoons chopped fresh mint to eggs with cheese.

Shiitake Mushroom Frittata with Pecorino Romano
While the shiitake mushrooms needn't be cut into exact ½-inch pieces, for a cohesive frittata, make sure that no pieces are much larger than ¾ inch.

Substitute 1 pound shiitake mushrooms, stemmed and cut into ½-inch pieces, for broccoli and ¼ teaspoon pepper for pepper flakes. Reduce water to 2 tablespoons and substitute 2 minced scallion whites, 1 tablespoon sherry vinegar, and 1½ teaspoons minced fresh thyme for lemon zest and juice. Substitute ¾ cup shredded Pecorino Romano for feta and add 2 thinly sliced scallion greens to eggs with cheese.

Chorizo and Potato Frittata
Be sure to use Spanish-style chorizo, which is dry-cured and needs only to be heated through.

Substitute 1 pound Yukon Gold potatoes, peeled and cut into ½-inch pieces, for broccoli and ¼ teaspoon ground cumin for pepper flakes. In step 2, cook potatoes until half are lightly browned, 8 to 10 minutes. Substitute 6 ounces Spanish-style chorizo sausage, cut into ¼-inch pieces, and 1 teaspoon sherry vinegar for lemon zest and juice. Substitute ½ cup chopped fresh cilantro for feta.

NOTES FROM THE TEST KITCHEN

THE TRAIL TO SUCCESS

Stirring the eggs with a rubber spatula helps them set up evenly. When the spatula leaves a trail, transfer the pan to the oven. Look for a trail that fills in slowly; if it fills in quickly, not enough egg has coagulated and some will be undercooked.

EASY PANCAKES

WHY THIS RECIPE WORKS: Everyone loves sitting down to a plate of fluffy, golden, flavorful pancakes, but making them is another matter. Nobody wants to run out for buttermilk before the first meal of the day, never mind haul out (and then clean) their stand mixer to whip egg whites. That's where box mixes come in, but their convenience is hardly worth the results they deliver: rubbery pancakes with a Styrofoam-like flavor. We wanted tender, fluffy, flavorful pancakes that were simple to make using pantry-friendly ingredients and basic kitchen tools. To make them tall and fluffy, we prepared a thick batter by using a relatively small amount of liquid and lots of baking powder. We also mixed the batter minimally to ensure that lumpy pockets of flour remained, and we let the batter rest briefly, allowing the flour pockets to hydrate slightly. Sugar, vanilla, and baking soda provided sweetness, depth, and saline tang, respectively.

Easy Pancakes

MAKES SIXTEEN 4-INCH PANCAKES; SERVES 4 TO 6

The pancakes can be cooked on an electric griddle set to 350 degrees. They can be held in a preheated 200-degree oven on a wire rack set in a rimmed baking sheet. Serve with salted butter and maple syrup or with one of our flavored butters (recipes follow).

- 2   cups (10 ounces) all-purpose flour
- 3   tablespoons sugar
- 4   teaspoons baking powder
- ½   teaspoon baking soda
- 1   teaspoon salt
- 2   large eggs
- ¼   cup plus 1 teaspoon vegetable oil
- 1½ cups milk
- ½   teaspoon vanilla extract

1. Whisk flour, sugar, baking powder, baking soda, and salt together in large bowl. Whisk eggs and ¼ cup oil in second medium bowl until well combined. Whisk milk and vanilla into egg mixture. Add egg mixture to flour mixture and stir gently until just combined (batter should remain lumpy with few streaks of flour). Let batter sit for 10 minutes before cooking.

2. Heat ½ teaspoon oil in 12-inch nonstick skillet over medium-low heat until shimmering. Using paper towels, carefully wipe out oil, leaving thin film on bottom and sides of skillet. Drop 1 tablespoon batter in center of skillet. If pancake is pale golden brown after 1 minute, skillet is ready. If it is too light or too dark, adjust heat accordingly.

3. Using ¼-cup dry measuring cup, portion batter into skillet in 3 places, leaving 2 inches between portions. If necessary, gently spread batter into 4-inch round. Cook until edges are set, first sides are golden brown, and bubbles on surface are just beginning to break, 2 to 3 minutes. Using thin, wide spatula, flip pancakes and continue to cook until

second sides are golden brown, 1 to 2 minutes longer. Serve. Repeat with remaining batter, using remaining ½ teaspoon oil as necessary.

Ginger-Molasses Butter

MAKES ½ CUP

Do not use blackstrap molasses; its intense flavor will overwhelm the other flavors. Our favorite is Brer Rabbit All Natural Unsulphured Molasses Mild Flavor.

- 8   tablespoons unsalted butter, cut into ¼-inch pieces
- 2   teaspoons molasses
- 1   teaspoon grated fresh ginger
- ⅛   teaspoon salt

Microwave 2 tablespoons butter in medium bowl until melted, about 1 minute. Stir in molasses, ginger, salt, and remaining 6 tablespoons butter. Let mixture stand for 2 minutes. Whisk until smooth. (Butter can be refrigerated for up to 3 days.)

Orange-Almond Butter

MAKES ½ CUP

Do not use buckwheat honey; its intense flavor will overwhelm the other flavors.

- 8   tablespoons unsalted butter, cut into ¼-inch pieces
- 2   teaspoons grated orange zest
- 2   teaspoons honey
- ¼   teaspoon almond extract
- ⅛   teaspoon salt

Microwave 2 tablespoons butter in medium bowl until melted, about 1 minute. Stir in orange zest, honey, almond extract, salt, and remaining 6 tablespoons butter. Let mixture stand for 2 minutes. Whisk until smooth. (Butter can be refrigerated for up to 3 days.)

Pumpkin Spice Butter

MAKES ½ CUP

Do not use buckwheat honey; its intense flavor will overwhelm the other flavors. You can substitute ¼ teaspoon of ground cinnamon, ⅛ teaspoon of ground ginger, a pinch of nutmeg, and a pinch of allspice for the pumpkin pie spice, if desired.

- 8   tablespoons unsalted butter, cut into ¼-inch pieces
- 2   teaspoons honey
- ½   teaspoon pumpkin pie spice
- ⅛   teaspoon salt

Microwave 2 tablespoons butter in medium bowl until melted, about 1 minute. Stir in honey, pumpkin pie spice, salt, and remaining 6 tablespoons butter. Let mixture stand for 2 minutes. Whisk until smooth. (Butter can be refrigerated for up to 3 days.)

STREUSEL COFFEE CAKE

WHY THIS RECIPE WORKS: We wanted to streamline the process for this breakfast treat and still produce a soft, tender crumb crowned with a crunchy, nutty streusel. We decided to use a food processor to mix both the cake and the topping. To make sure our cake was tender despite the aggressive action of the food processor's blades, we opted to use the reverse-creaming method (combining butter and flour before adding the wet ingredients). This mixing method coated the flour's proteins with fat and prevented them from linking up and forming gluten when water was added to the batter. Building a thick batter kept it from rising over and covering the streusel at the edges of the pan. And adding just a teaspoon of water to the streusel ingredients while pulsing them helped the mixture adhere to the cake. Finally, baking the cake in a springform pan instead of the typical round cake pan allowed for fuss-free unmolding that kept the streusel intact. Each bite of this coffee cake offered an appealing combination of crunchy cinnamon-pecan streusel and rich, tender cake. And, as an added bonus, it could be made quickly and using a single kitchen appliance.

Coffee Cake with Pecan-Cinnamon Streusel

SERVES 8 TO 10

For the best results, we recommend weighing the flour in this recipe. Do not insert a skewer into this cake to test for doneness until the center appears firm when the pan is shaken. If you do, the weight of the streusel may squeeze out air and the cake may sink. This cake can be stored at room temperature, wrapped in plastic wrap, for up to 24 hours.

STREUSEL

- 1 cup pecans, toasted
- ⅓ cup packed (2⅓ ounces) brown sugar
- ½ cup (2½ ounces) all-purpose flour
- ¾ teaspoon ground cinnamon
- ¼ teaspoon salt
- 4 tablespoons unsalted butter, melted and cooled
- 1 teaspoon water

CAKE

- 1⅔ cups (8⅓ ounces) all-purpose flour
- 1 cup (7 ounces) sugar
- 1 teaspoon ground cinnamon
- 1 teaspoon baking powder
- ½ teaspoon baking soda
- ¾ teaspoon salt
- 7 tablespoons unsalted butter, cut into 7 pieces and softened
- ¾ cup milk
- 1 large egg plus 1 large yolk
- 1 teaspoon vanilla extract

1. Adjust oven rack to lower-middle position and heat oven to 350 degrees. Grease and flour 9-inch springform pan and place on rimmed baking sheet.

2. FOR THE STREUSEL: Process pecans and sugar in food processor until finely ground, about 10 seconds. Add flour, cinnamon, and salt and pulse to combine, about 5 (1-second) pulses. Add melted butter and water and pulse until butter is fully incorporated and mixture begins to form clumps, 8 to 10 (1-second) pulses. Transfer streusel to bowl and set aside.

3. FOR THE CAKE: In now-empty processor, process flour, sugar, cinnamon, baking powder, baking soda, and salt until combined, about 10 seconds. Add butter and pulse until very small but visible pieces of butter remain, 5 to 8 (5-second) pulses. Add milk, egg and yolk, and vanilla; pulse until dry ingredients are moistened, 4 to 5 (1-second) pulses. Scrape down sides of bowl. Pulse until mixture is well combined, 4 to 5 (1-second) pulses (some small pieces of butter will remain). Transfer batter to prepared pan and smooth top with rubber spatula.

4. Starting at edges of pan, sprinkle streusel in even layer over batter. Bake cake on sheet until center is firm and skewer inserted into center of cake comes out clean, 45 to 55 minutes. Transfer pan to wire rack and let cake cool in pan for 15 minutes. Remove side of pan and let cake cool completely, about 2 hours. Using offset spatula, transfer cake to serving platter. Using serrated knife, cut cake into wedges and serve.

PANE FRANCESE

WHY THIS RECIPE WORKS: The Italian cousin to the baguette, *pane francese* (which means "French bread") is a long loaf with a moist and open crumb. Pane francese has a crisp yet forgiving exterior, and it's slightly fatter in shape than a baguette. It's nice for sandwiches or for dipping into olive oil. We started this bread with a sponge, which developed structure, depth of favor, and a hint of tang in the loaf. After preparing this mixture (made with water, yeast, and 20 percent of the bread's total weight of flour), we let it sit on the counter for 6 to 24 hours before mixing it into the dough. During this period the yeast consumed sugars in the flour. This fermentation process, visible by the rise and collapse of the mixture, created acid as a byproduct, which helps develop the strong gluten network that supports the loaf's open crumb. Also, extending the overall fermentation time for the dough is what provides great flavor. A repeated series of gentle folds helped develop the gluten structure even further while also incorporating air for an open interior crumb. We proofed the loaf on a couche—a heavy linen cloth—to help the wet dough keep its shape. We slash the top of rustic loaves like pane francese with a lame, a curved-blade tool that gives our scores a dramatic raised edge that bakes up crisp. The last step? We preheated pans filled with lava rocks and added water to them to create a steamy oven, which encouraged a crisp crust.

Pane Francese

MAKES 2 LOAVES

Lava rocks are available at many hardware stores for use in gas grills.

SPONGE

- ⅔ cup (3⅔ ounces) bread flour
- ½ cup (4 ounces) water, room temperature
- ⅛ teaspoon instant or rapid-rise yeast

DOUGH

- 2⅔–3 cups (14⅔ to 6½ ounces) bread flour
- 1½ teaspoons instant or rapid-rise yeast
- 1¼ cups (10 ounces) water, room temperature
- 1 tablespoon extra-virgin olive oil
- 2¼ teaspoons salt

1. FOR THE SPONGE: Stir all ingredients in 4-cup liquid measuring cup with wooden spoon until well combined. Cover tightly with plastic wrap and let sit at room temperature until sponge has risen and begins to collapse, about 6 hours (sponge can sit at room temperature for up to 24 hours).

2. FOR THE DOUGH: Whisk 2⅔ cups flour and yeast together in bowl of stand mixer. Stir water into sponge with wooden spoon until well combined. Using dough hook on low speed, slowly add sponge mixture to flour mixture and mix until cohesive dough starts to form and no dry flour remains, about 2 minutes, scraping down bowl as needed. Cover bowl tightly with plastic and let dough rest for 20 minutes.

3. Add oil and salt to dough and knead on medium-low speed until dough is smooth and elastic and clears sides of bowl, about 10 minutes. If more flour is needed, add remaining ⅓ cup flour, 1 tablespoon at a time, until dough clears sides of bowl but sticks to bottom. Transfer dough to lightly greased large bowl or container, cover tightly with plastic, and let rise for 30 minutes.

4. Using greased bowl scraper (or your fingertips), fold dough over itself by gently lifting and folding edge of dough toward middle. Turn bowl 45 degrees and fold dough again; repeat turning bowl and folding dough 6 more times (total of 8 folds). Cover tightly with plastic and let rise for 30 minutes. Repeat folding, then cover bowl tightly with plastic and let dough rise until nearly doubled in size, 1 to 1½ hours.

5. Mist underside of couche with water, drape over inverted rimmed baking sheet, and dust evenly with flour. Transfer dough to lightly floured counter. Using lightly floured hands press and stretch dough into 12 by 6-inch rectangle, deflating any gas pockets larger than 1 inch, and divide in half crosswise. Cover loosely with greased plastic.

6. Gently press and stretch 1 piece of dough (keep remaining piece covered) into 7-inch square. Fold top corners of dough diagonally into center of square and press gently to seal. Stretch and fold upper third of dough toward center and press seam gently to seal.

7. Stretch and fold dough in half toward you to form rough loaf with tapered ends and pinch seam closed. Roll loaf seam side down. Starting at center of loaf and working toward ends, gently and evenly roll and stretch dough until it measures 15 inches long by 2½ inches wide. Moving your hands in opposite directions, use back and forth motion to roll ends of loaf under your palms to form sharp points.

8. Gently slide your hands underneath each end of loaf and transfer seam side up to prepared couche. On either side of

loaf, pinch couche into pleat, then cover loosely with large plastic garbage bag. Repeat steps 6 through 7 with remaining piece of dough and place on opposite side of 1 pleat. Fold edges of couche over loaves to cover completely, then carefully place sheet inside garbage bag. Tie, or fold under, open end of bag to fully enclose. Let rise until loaves increase in size by about half and dough springs back minimally when poked gently with your knuckle, 30 minutes to 1 hour (remove loaf from bag to test).

9. One hour before baking, adjust oven racks to lower-middle and lowest positions. Place baking stone on upper rack, place 2 disposable aluminum pie plates filled with 1 quart lava rocks each on lower rack, and heat oven to 450 degrees. Line pizza peel with 16 by 12-inch piece of parchment paper, with long edge perpendicular to handle. Bring 1 cup water to boil.

10. Remove sheet with loaves from bag. Unfold couche, pulling from ends to remove pleats. Dust top of loaves with flour. (If any seams have reopened, pinch closed before dust-

---

NOTES FROM THE TEST KITCHEN

SHAPING CLASSIC ITALIAN BREAD

1. Gently press and stretch dough into 7-inch square. Fold top corners of dough diagonally into center of square; press gently to seal.

2. Stretch and fold upper third of dough toward center; press seam gently to seal.

3. Stretch and fold dough in half toward you to form rough loaf with tapered ends. Pinch seam closed, then roll loaf seam side down.

4. Roll and stretch loaf until it measures 15 inches long by 2½ inches wide. Moving your hands in opposite directions, use back and forth motion to roll ends of loaf under your palms to form sharp points.

ing with flour.) Gently pushing with side of flipping board, roll 1 loaf over, away from other loaf, so it is seam side down. Using your hand, hold long edge of flipping board between loaf and couche at 45-degree angle, then lift couche with your other hand and flip loaf seam side up onto board. Invert loaf seam side down onto prepared pizza peel, about 2 inches from long edge of parchment, then use flipping board to straighten loaf and reshape as needed. Repeat with second loaf, leaving at least 3 inches between loaves.

11. Carefully pour ½ cup boiling water into 1 disposable pie plate of preheated rocks and close oven door for 1 minute to create steam. Meanwhile, holding lame concave side up at 30-degree angle to loaf, make one ½-inch deep slash with swift, fluid motion lengthwise along top of loaf, starting and stopping about ½ inch from ends. Repeat with second loaf.

12. Working quickly, slide parchment with loaves onto baking stone and pour remaining ½ cup boiling water into second disposable pie plate of preheated rocks. Bake until crust is golden brown and loaves register 205 to 210 degrees, 20 to 25 minutes, rotating loaves halfway through baking. Transfer loaves to wire rack, discard parchment, and let cool completely, about 3 hours, before serving.

FLAKY BUTTERMILK BISCUITS

WHY THIS RECIPE WORKS: For the ultimate flaky biscuits, we grated the butter so that it would be evenly distributed in the flour mixture, which we learned was key to an ideal flakiness. Freezing the butter prior to grating ensured that it stayed in individual pieces throughout the mixing and shaping process. Using a higher-protein all-purpose flour (such as King Arthur) provided the right amount of structure for flakiness (rather than fluffiness, which you'd get with a lower-protein flour) without toughness, while buttermilk gave the biscuits tang and sugar lent complexity. To produce the maximum number of layers, we rolled out and folded the dough like a letter five times. Cutting the biscuits into squares was easy and avoided any wasted scraps (or tough rerolls). And finally, we learned that letting the dough rest for 30 minutes and trimming away the edges ensured that the biscuits rose up tall in the oven.

Ultimate Flaky Buttermilk Biscuits
MAKES 9 BISCUITS

We prefer King Arthur all-purpose flour for this recipe, but other brands will work. Use sticks of butter. In hot or humid environments, chill the flour mixture, grater, and work bowls before use. The dough will start out very crumbly and dry in pockets but will be smooth by the end of the folding process; do not be tempted to add extra buttermilk. Flour the counter and the top of the dough as needed to prevent sticking, but be careful not to incorporate large pockets of flour into the dough when folding.

3 cups (15 ounces) King Arthur all-purpose flour
2 tablespoons sugar
4 teaspoons baking powder
½ teaspoon baking soda
1½ teaspoons salt
16 tablespoons (2 sticks) unsalted butter, frozen for 30 minutes
1¼ cups buttermilk, chilled

1. Line rimmed baking sheet with parchment paper and set aside. Whisk flour, sugar, baking powder, baking soda, and salt together in large bowl. Coat sticks of butter in flour mixture, then grate 7 tablespoons from each stick on large holes of box grater directly into flour mixture. Toss gently to combine. Set aside remaining 2 tablespoons butter.

2. Add buttermilk to flour mixture and fold with spatula until just combined (dough will look dry). Transfer dough to liberally floured counter. Dust surface of dough with flour; using your floured hands, press dough into rough 7-inch square.

3. Roll dough into 12 by 9-inch rectangle with short side parallel to edge of counter. Starting at bottom of dough, fold into thirds like business letter, using bench scraper or metal spatula to release dough from counter. Press top of dough firmly to seal folds. Turn dough 90 degrees clockwise. Repeat rolling into 12 by 9-inch rectangle, folding into thirds, and turning clockwise 4 more times, for total of 5 sets of folds. After last set of folds, roll dough into 8½-inch square about 1 inch thick. Transfer dough to prepared sheet, cover with plastic wrap, and refrigerate for 30 minutes. Adjust oven rack to upper-middle position and heat oven to 400 degrees.

4. Transfer dough to lightly floured cutting board. Using sharp, floured chef's knife, trim ¼ inch of dough from each side of square and discard. Cut remaining dough into 9 squares, flouring knife after each cut. Arrange biscuits at least 1 inch apart on sheet. Melt reserved butter; brush tops of biscuits with melted butter.

5. Bake until tops are golden brown, 22 to 25 minutes, rotating sheet halfway through baking. Transfer biscuits to wire rack and let cool for 15 minutes before serving.

BRAZILIAN CHEESE BREAD

WHY THIS RECIPE WORKS: *Pão de queijo* are traditional Brazilian rolls made using a classic French pâte à choux dough. Comprised of butter, water, flour, and eggs, choux pastry relies on steam rather than chemical leavening agents to create rise; this type of dough is used for both sweet (éclairs, profiteroles) and savory (Parisian gnocchi, gougères) items. But, in developing our own recipe for this bread, many of the recipes we tried baked up with a too-gooey interior. So we played with the hydration level until we nailed our favorite version. At 91 percent hydration (most recipes have hydration levels well over 100 percent, which makes them more of a batter than a dough), our rolls baked up crackly on the outsides, bready just under the crusts, and gooey at the very centers. As an added bonus, these little rolls are gluten-free.

Brazilian Cheese Bread (Pão de Queijo)

MAKES 8 ROLLS

    3 cups tapioca starch
    2¼ teaspoons kosher salt
    ¼ teaspoon baking powder
    ⅔ cup plus 2 tablespoons whole milk
    ½ cup vegetable oil
    1½ tablespoons unsalted butter
    3 large eggs
    3½ ounces Parmesan cheese, finely grated (1¾ cups)
    3½ ounces Pecorino Romano, finely grated (1¾ cups)
    1 teaspoon water

1. Using stand mixer fitted with paddle, mix tapioca starch, 2 teaspoons salt, and baking powder on low speed until combined, about 30 seconds.

2. Combine milk, oil, and butter in medium saucepan and bring to boil over high heat. With mixer running on low speed, working quickly, pour milk mixture over tapioca mixture and continue to mix on low speed until all ingredients are incorporated, about 3 minutes longer.

3. Add 2 eggs and mix on low speed until dough comes together, turns shiny and sticky, and clings to sides of bowl, about 8 minutes, scraping down paddle and bowl halfway through mixing.

4. Add Parmesan and Pecorino and mix on low speed until cheeses are incorporated, 30 to 60 seconds. Mix with rubber spatula to ensure mixture is fully incorporated. Remove bowl from stand mixer and press plastic wrap directly onto surface of dough. Refrigerate for at least 2 hours or overnight.

5. Adjust oven rack to middle position and heat oven to 450 degrees. Stack 2 baking sheets and line top sheet with parchment paper. Divide dough into 8 balls (about 3½ ounces each). To form rolls, lightly dampen your hands with water and roll balls between your palms until smooth. Evenly space rolls on prepared sheet.

6. Whisk 1 egg, 1 teaspoon water, and ¼ teaspoon salt together in small bowl. Brush egg mixture over tops of rolls. Place rolls in oven and immediately reduce oven temperature to 375 degrees. Bake for 20 minutes. Rotate sheet and continue to bake until rolls are deep golden brown and outer crusts are dry and crunchy, about 20 minutes longer. Transfer rolls to serving platter and let cool for 5 minutes. Serve.

EASY HOLIDAY SUGAR COOKIES

WHY THIS RECIPE WORKS: Our holiday roll-and-cut sugar cookies taste as great as they are easy to make. For a crisp and sturdy texture with no hint of graininess, we made superfine sugar by grinding granulated sugar briefly in the food processor, and we added small amounts of baking powder and baking soda to the dough. A touch of almond extract, added along with the usual vanilla, made these cookies taste more interesting without giving them overt almond flavor. We skipped creaming softened butter and sugar in favor of whizzing cold butter with sugar in the food processor, which let the dough come together in just minutes. The just-made dough was cold enough to be rolled out immediately, and we chilled it after rolling. For an even, golden color; minimal browning; and a crisp, crunchy texture from edge to edge, we baked the cookies at a gentle 300 degrees on a rimless cookie sheet (to promote air circulation) on the oven's lower-middle rack.

Easy Holiday Sugar Cookies

MAKES ABOUT FORTY 2½-INCH COOKIES

For the dough to have the proper consistency when rolling, make sure to use cold butter directly from the refrigerator. In step 3, use a rolling pin and a combination of rolling and a pushing or smearing motion to form the soft dough into an oval. A rimless cookie sheet helps achieve evenly baked cookies; if you do not have one, use an overturned rimmed baking sheet. Dough scraps can be combined and rerolled once, though the cookies will be slightly less tender. If desired, stir 1 or 2 drops of food coloring into the icing. For a pourable icing, whisk in milk, 1 teaspoon at a time, until the desired consistency is reached. You can also decorate the shapes with sanding sugar or sprinkles before baking.

COOKIES

    1 large egg
    1 teaspoon vanilla extract
    ¾ teaspoon salt
    ¼ teaspoon almond extract
    2½ cups (12½ ounces) all-purpose flour
    ¼ teaspoon baking powder
    ¼ teaspoon baking soda
    1 cup (7 ounces) granulated sugar
    16 tablespoons unsalted butter, cut into ½-inch pieces
       and chilled

ROYAL ICING

    2⅔ cups (10⅔ ounces) confectioners' sugar
    2 large egg whites
    ½ teaspoon vanilla extract
    ⅛ teaspoon salt

1. FOR THE COOKIES: Whisk egg, vanilla, salt, and almond extract together in small bowl. Whisk flour, baking powder, and baking soda together in second bowl.

2. Process sugar in food processor until finely ground, about 30 seconds. Add butter and process until uniform mass forms and no large pieces of butter are visible, about 30 seconds, scraping down sides of bowl as needed. Add egg mixture and process until smooth and paste-like, about 10 seconds. Add flour mixture and process until no dry flour remains but mixture remains crumbly, about 30 seconds, scraping down sides of bowl as needed.

3. Turn out dough onto counter and knead gently by hand until smooth, about 10 seconds. Divide dough in half. Place 1 piece of dough in center of large sheet of parchment paper and press into 7 by 9-inch oval. Place second large sheet of parchment over dough and roll dough into 10 by 14-inch oval of even ⅛-inch thickness. Transfer dough with parchment to rimmed baking sheet. Repeat pressing and rolling with second piece of dough, then stack on top of first piece on sheet. Refrigerate until dough is firm, at least 1½ hours (or freeze for 30 minutes). (Rolled dough can be wrapped in plastic wrap and refrigerated for up to 5 days.)

4. Adjust oven rack to lower-middle position and heat oven to 300 degrees. Line rimless cookie sheet with parchment. Working with 1 piece of rolled dough, gently peel off top layer of parchment. Replace parchment, loosely covering dough. (Peeling off parchment and returning it will make cutting and removing cookies easier.) Turn over dough and parchment and gently peel off and discard second piece of parchment. Using cookie cutter, cut dough into shapes. Transfer shapes to prepared cookie sheet, spacing them about ½ inch apart. Bake until cookies are lightly and evenly browned around edges, 14 to 17 minutes, rotating sheet halfway through baking. Let cookies cool on sheet for 5 minutes. Using wide metal spatula, transfer cookies to wire rack and let cool completely. Repeat cutting and baking with remaining dough. (Dough scraps can be patted together, rerolled, and chilled once before cutting and baking.)

5. FOR THE ROYAL ICING: Using stand mixer fitted with whisk attachment, whip all ingredients on medium-low speed until combined, about 1 minute. Increase speed to medium-high and whip until glossy, soft peaks form, 3 to 4 minutes, scraping down bowl as needed.

6. Spread icing onto cooled cookies. Let icing dry completely, about 1½ hours, before serving.

Easy Holiday Cocoa Sugar Cookies

Reduce vanilla extract to ½ teaspoon and substitute 1½ teaspoons espresso powder for almond extract. Add ⅓ cup (1 ounce) Dutch-processed cocoa powder to flour mixture in step 1.

BEST LEMON BARS

WHY THIS RECIPE WORKS: For the lemoniest lemon bars with a sweet-tart flavor, a silky-smooth filling, and a crisp, well-browned crust, we started at the bottom. Our pat-in-the-pan crust is made with melted—not cold—butter and can therefore be stirred together instead of requiring a food processor. For a truly crisp texture, we used granulated sugar instead of the usual confectioners' sugar and baked the crust until it was dark golden brown to ensure that it retained its crispness even after we topped it with the lemon filling. We cooked our lemon filling on the stove to shorten the oven time and keep it from curdling or browning at the edges when it baked. A combination of lemon juice and lemon zest provided complex flavor and aroma, and a unique ingredient—cream of tartar (tartaric acid)—gave the bars a bold sharpness and bright, lingering finish.

Best Lemon Bars
MAKES 12 BARS

Do not substitute bottled lemon juice for fresh here.

CRUST

- 1 cup (5 ounces) all-purpose flour
- ¼ cup (1¾ ounces) granulated sugar
- ½ teaspoon salt
- 8 tablespoons unsalted butter, melted

FILLING

- 1 cup (7 ounces) granulated sugar
- 2 tablespoons all-purpose flour
- 2 teaspoons cream of tartar
- ¼ teaspoon salt
- 3 large eggs plus 3 large yolks
- 2 teaspoons grated lemon zest plus ⅔ cup juice (4 lemons)
- 4 tablespoons unsalted butter, cut into 8 pieces

Confectioners' sugar (optional)

1. FOR THE CRUST: Adjust oven rack to middle position and heat oven to 350 degrees. Make foil sling for 8-inch square baking pan by folding 2 long sheets of aluminum foil so each is 8 inches wide. Lay sheets of foil in pan perpendicular to each other, with extra foil hanging over edges of pan. Push foil into corners and up sides of pan, smoothing foil flush to pan.

2. Whisk flour, sugar, and salt together in bowl. Add melted butter and stir until combined. Transfer mixture to prepared pan and press into even layer over entire bottom of pan (do not wash bowl). Bake crust until dark golden brown, 19 to 24 minutes, rotating pan halfway through baking.

3. FOR THE FILLING: While crust bakes, whisk sugar, flour, cream of tartar, and salt together in now-empty bowl. Whisk in eggs and yolks until no streaks of egg remain. Whisk in lemon zest and juice. Transfer mixture to saucepan and cook over medium-low heat, stirring constantly, until mixture thickens and registers 160 degrees, 5 to 8 minutes. Off heat, stir in butter. Strain filling through fine-mesh strainer set over bowl.

4. Pour filling over hot crust and tilt pan to spread evenly. Bake until filling is set and barely jiggles when pan is shaken, 8 to 12 minutes. (Filling around perimeter of pan may be

---

NOTES FROM THE TEST KITCHEN

PAT-IN-THE-PAN CRUST

Most lemon bar crust recipes call for cutting cold butter into flour. Our recipe calls for simply stirring melted butter into a mixture of flour, sugar, and salt. The upshot: a no-fuss, pliable dough that's easy to press into an even layer.

slightly raised.) Let bars cool completely, at least 1½ hours. Using foil overhang, lift bars out of pan and transfer to cutting board. Cut into bars, wiping knife clean between cuts as necessary. Before serving, dust bars with confectioners' sugar, if using.

GINGERBREAD LAYER CAKE

WHY THIS RECIPE WORKS: We wanted the dark, moist crumb and spicy bite of gingerbread in a tender, sophisticated layer cake. For fiery flavor, we added 2 tablespoons each of ground ginger and freshly grated ginger, and we enhanced that heat with both white pepper and cayenne pepper. Molasses and coffee contributed moisture, rich color, and pleasantly bitter notes that worked well with the spices and sweetness. Cocoa powder, an unexpected ingredient in gingerbread, added depth to the color and the flavor and, as it is mostly gluten-free starch and fat, it increased the cake's tenderness. To avoid the challenge of slicing thicker layers in half horizontally, we baked four thin layers in two batches. Finally, a silky, fluffy, and not-too-sweet ermine frosting, made by beating softened butter into a cooked gel made with milk, sugar, and starch, showed off the spicy, tender cake to its best advantage.

Gingerbread Layer Cake

SERVES 12 TO 16

Transferring the milk mixture to a wide bowl will ensure that it cools within 2 hours. A rasp-style grater makes quick work of grating the ginger. Use a 2-cup liquid measuring cup to portion the cake batter. Baking four thin cake layers two at a time eliminates the need to halve thicker layers. Do not use blackstrap molasses here, as it is too bitter.

FROSTING

- 1½ cups (10½ ounces) sugar
- ¼ cup (1¼ ounces) all-purpose flour
- 3 tablespoons cornstarch
- ½ teaspoon salt
- 1½ cups milk
- 24 tablespoons (3 sticks) unsalted butter, softened
- 2 teaspoons vanilla extract

CAKE

- 1¾ cups (8¾ ounces) all-purpose flour
- ¼ cup (¾ ounce) unsweetened cocoa powder
- 2 tablespoons ground ginger
- 1½ teaspoons baking powder
- 1 teaspoon ground cinnamon
- ¾ teaspoon salt
- ½ teaspoon ground white pepper
- ⅛ teaspoon cayenne pepper
- 1 cup brewed coffee
- ¾ cup molasses
- ½ teaspoon baking soda
- 1½ cups (10½ ounces) sugar

- ¾ cup vegetable oil
- 3 large eggs, beaten
- 2 tablespoons finely grated fresh ginger
- ¼ cup chopped crystallized ginger (optional)

1. FOR THE FROSTING: Whisk sugar, flour, cornstarch, and salt together in medium saucepan. Slowly whisk in milk until smooth. Cook over medium heat, whisking constantly and scraping corners of saucepan, until mixture is boiling and is very thick, 5 to 7 minutes. Transfer milk mixture to wide bowl and let cool completely, about 2 hours.

2. FOR THE CAKE: Adjust oven rack to middle position and heat oven to 350 degrees. Grease and flour two 8-inch round cake pans and line pans with parchment paper. Whisk flour, cocoa, ground ginger, baking powder, cinnamon, salt, pepper, and cayenne together in large bowl. Whisk coffee, molasses, and baking soda in second large bowl until combined. Add sugar, oil, eggs, and fresh ginger to coffee mixture and whisk until smooth.

3. Whisk coffee mixture into flour mixture until smooth. Pour 1⅓ cups batter into each prepared pan. Bake until toothpick inserted in center of cake comes out clean, 12 to 14 minutes. Let cakes cool in pans on wire rack for 10 minutes. Invert cakes onto wire rack and peel off parchment; reinvert cakes. Wipe pans clean with paper towels. Grease and flour pans and line with fresh parchment. Repeat baking and cooling process with remaining batter.

4. Using stand mixer fitted with paddle, beat butter on medium-high speed until light and fluffy, about 5 minutes. Add cooled milk mixture and vanilla; mix on medium speed until combined, scraping down bowl if necessary. Increase speed to medium-high and beat until frosting is light and fluffy, 3 to 5 minutes.

5. Place 1 cake layer on platter or cardboard round. Using offset spatula, spread ¾ cup frosting evenly over top, right to edge of cake. Repeat stacking and frosting with 2 more cake layers and 1½ cups frosting. Place final cake layer on top and spread remaining frosting evenly over top and sides of cake. Garnish top of cake with crystallized ginger, if using. Refrigerate cake until frosting is set, about 30 minutes. (Cake can be refrigerated, covered, for up to 2 days. Let cake come to room temperature before serving.)

STICKY TOFFEE PUDDING CAKE

WHY THIS RECIPE WORKS: Sticky toffee pudding is a British dessert that's sticky in a good way: It features a moist date-studded cake soaked in toffee sauce. To bring this dessert stateside, we knew we'd have to find a substitute for treacle, a sweetener similar to molasses that's traditionally used in these cakes. We also wanted to perfect the texture of the cake and showcase the rich, fruity flavor of the dates. Cakes made using the creaming method disintegrated once soaked in sauce. Happily, the easier quick-bread technique (dry and wet ingredients are mixed separately and then combined) produced the desired dense-yet-springy crumb. Substituting brown sugar for treacle was a good option, but the dates needed a flavor boost. Typically, sliced dates are soaked in baking soda–laced water to soften their skins. Replacing the water that was already in our batter recipe with the date soaking liquid improved the flavor significantly, and pulverizing half the dates in the food processor before mixing them in guaranteed that every bite was laced with date flavor. Baking the cakes in a water bath ensured they remained moist.

Individual Sticky Toffee Pudding Cakes

SERVES 8

You will need eight 6-ounce ramekins to make these cakes. Be sure to form a tight seal with the foil before baking the cakes.

CAKES

- 8 ounces pitted dates, cut crosswise into ¼-inch-thick slices (1⅓ cups)
- ¾ cup warm water (110 degrees)
- ½ teaspoon baking soda
- 1¼ cups (6¼ ounces) all-purpose flour
- ½ teaspoon baking powder
- ½ teaspoon salt
- ¾ cup packed (5¼ ounces) brown sugar
- 2 large eggs
- 4 tablespoons unsalted butter, melted
- 1½ tablespoons vanilla extract

SAUCE

- 4 tablespoons unsalted butter
- 1 tablespoon water
- 1 cup packed (7 ounces) brown sugar
- ¼ teaspoon salt
- 1 cup heavy cream
- 1 tablespoon rum
- ¼ teaspoon lemon juice

1. FOR THE CAKES: Adjust oven rack to middle position and heat oven to 350 degrees. Grease and flour eight 6-ounce ramekins. Fold dish towel in half and place in bottom of large roasting pan. Place prepared ramekins on top of towel; set aside pan. Bring kettle of water to boil.

2. Combine half of dates, warm water, and baking soda in 2-cup liquid measuring cup (dates should be submerged beneath water); soak dates for 5 minutes. Meanwhile, whisk flour, baking powder, and salt together in large bowl.

3. Process sugar and remaining dates in food processor until no large chunks remain and mixture has texture of damp, coarse sand, about 45 seconds, scraping down sides of bowl as needed. Drain soaked dates and add soaking liquid to processor. Add eggs, melted butter, and vanilla and process until smooth, about 15 seconds. Transfer sugar mixture to bowl with flour mixture and sprinkle soaked dates on top. Using rubber spatula or wooden spoon, gently fold sugar mixture into flour mixture until just combined and date pieces are evenly dispersed.

4. Divide batter evenly among prepared ramekins (ramekins should be two-thirds full). Quickly pour enough boiling water into roasting pan to come ¼ inch up sides of ramekins. Cover pan tightly with aluminum foil, crimping edges to seal. Bake until cakes are puffed and surfaces are spongy, firm, and moist to touch, about 40 minutes. Immediately transfer ramekins from water bath to wire rack and let cool for 10 minutes.

5. FOR THE SAUCE: While cakes cool, melt butter with water in medium saucepan over medium-high heat. Whisk in sugar and salt until smooth. Continue to cook, stirring occasionally, until sugar is dissolved and slightly darkened, 3 to 4 minutes. Stir in ⅓ cup cream until smooth, about 30 seconds. Slowly pour in rum and remaining ⅔ cup cream, whisking constantly until smooth. Reduce heat to low; simmer until frothy, 3 to 5 minutes. Remove from heat and stir in lemon juice.

6. Using toothpick, poke 25 holes in top of each cake and spoon 1 tablespoon toffee sauce over each cake. Let cakes sit until sauce is absorbed, about 5 minutes. Invert each ramekin onto plate or shallow bowl; lift off ramekin. Divide remaining toffee sauce evenly among cakes and serve immediately.

Large Sticky Toffee Pudding Cake

Substitute 8-inch square baking dish, greased and floured, for ramekins. Bake cake until outer 2 inches develop small holes and center is puffed and firm to touch, about 40 minutes. Cool as directed. Using toothpick, poke about 100 holes in cake and glaze with ½ cup sauce. Let cake sit until sauce is absorbed, about 5 minutes. Cut cake into squares and pour remaining toffee sauce over each square before serving.

CHOCOLATE SEMIFREDDO

WHY THIS RECIPE WORKS: *Semifreddo*, a classic Italian dessert that's often described as a frozen mousse, typically starts with a custard base. For a chocolate semifreddo that was rich and creamy, we started by preparing a custard-style base of whole eggs, sugar, cream, and water directly on the stovetop (rather than over a fussy water bath). We conveniently melted the chocolate by straining the hot custard directly over it. To ensure a rich, creamy, and sliceable semifreddo that was also cold and refreshing, we had to balance fat and water: Using whole eggs instead of yolks and cutting the cream in the custard base with a bit of water were key. Garnishing the semifreddo with a sweet cherry sauce and crunchy candied nuts added contrast and made for an elegant presentation. Semifreddo can sit out of the freezer without melting, makng it ideal for serving to company.

Chocolate Semifreddo

SERVES 12

The semifreddo needs to be frozen for at least 6 hours before serving. We developed this recipe with our favorite dark chocolate, Ghirardelli 60% Cacao Bittersweet Chocolate Premium Baking Bar. Do not whip the heavy cream until the chocolate mixture has cooled. If the semifreddo is difficult to release from the pan, run a thin offset spatula around the edges of the pan or carefully run the sides of the pan under hot water for 5 to 10 seconds. If frozen overnight, the semifreddo should be tempered before serving for the best texture. To temper, place slices on individual plates or a large tray, and refrigerate for 30 minutes. Serve the semifreddo as is or with our Cherry Sauce (recipe follows). For some crunch, sprinkle each serving with Quick Candied Nuts (recipe follows).

    8 ounces bittersweet chocolate, chopped fine
    1 tablespoon vanilla extract
    ½ teaspoon instant espresso powder
    3 large eggs
    5 tablespoons sugar
    ¼ teaspoon salt
    2 cups heavy cream, chilled
    ¼ cup water

1. Lightly spray loaf pan with vegetable oil spray and line with plastic wrap, leaving 3-inch overhang on all sides. Place chocolate in large heatproof bowl; set fine-mesh strainer over bowl and set aside. Stir vanilla and espresso powder in small bowl until espresso powder is dissolved.

2. Whisk eggs, sugar, and salt in medium bowl until combined. Heat ½ cup cream (keep remaining 1½ cups chilled) and water in medium saucepan over medium heat until simmering. Slowly whisk hot cream mixture into egg mixture until combined. Return mixture to saucepan and cook over medium-low heat, stirring constantly and scraping bottom of saucepan with rubber spatula, until mixture is very slightly thickened and registers 160 to 165 degrees, about 5 minutes. Do not let mixture simmer.

3. Immediately pour mixture through strainer set over chocolate. Let mixture stand to melt chocolate, about 5 minutes. Whisk until chocolate is melted and smooth, then whisk in vanilla-espresso mixture. Let chocolate mixture cool completely, about 15 minutes.

4. Using stand mixer fitted with whisk attachment, beat remaining 1½ cups cream on low speed until bubbles form, about 30 seconds. Increase speed to medium and beat until whisk leaves trail, about 30 seconds. Increase speed to high and continue to beat until nearly doubled in volume and whipped cream forms soft peaks, 30 to 45 seconds longer.

5. Whisk one-third of whipped cream into chocolate mixture. Using rubber spatula, gently fold remaining whipped cream into chocolate mixture until incorporated and no streaks of whipped cream remain. Transfer mixture to prepared pan and spread evenly with rubber spatula. Fold overhanging plastic over surface. Freeze until firm, at least 6 hours.

6. When ready to serve, remove plastic from surface and invert pan onto serving plate. Remove plastic and smooth surface with spatula as necessary. Dip slicing knife in very hot water and wipe dry. Slice semifreddo ¾ inch thick, trans-ferring slices to individual plates and dipping and wiping knife after each slice. Serve immediately. (Semifreddo can be wrapped tightly in plastic wrap and frozen for up to 2 weeks.)

Cherry Sauce
MAKES ABOUT 2 CUPS
This recipe was developed with frozen cherries. Do not thaw the cherries before using. Water can be substituted for the kirsch, if desired.

    12 ounces frozen sweet cherries
    ¼ cup sugar
    2 tablespoons kirsch
    1½ teaspoons cornstarch
    1 tablespoon lemon juice

1. Combine cherries and sugar in bowl and microwave for 1½ minutes. Stir, then continue to microwave until sugar is mostly dissolved, about 1 minute longer. Combine kirsch and cornstarch in small bowl.

2. Drain cherries in fine-mesh strainer set over small saucepan. Return cherries to bowl and set aside.

3. Bring juice in saucepan to simmer over medium-high heat. Stir in kirsch mixture and bring to boil. Boil, stirring occasionally, until mixture has thickened and appears syrupy, 1 to 2 minutes. Remove saucepan from heat and stir in cherries and lemon juice. Let sauce cool completely before serving. (Sauce can be refrigerated for up to 1 week.)

Quick Candied Nuts
MAKES ½ CUP
We like this recipe prepared with shelled pistachios, walnut or pecan halves, roasted cashews, salted or unsalted peanuts, and sliced almonds. If you want to make a mixed batch, cook the nuts individually and then toss to combine once you've chopped them.

    ½ cup nuts
    1 tablespoon granulated sugar
    1 tablespoon hot water
    ⅛ teaspoon salt

1. Adjust oven rack to middle position and heat oven to 350 degrees. Spread nuts in single layer on rimmed baking sheet and toast until fragrant and slightly darkened, 8 to 12 minutes, shaking sheet halfway through toasting. Transfer nuts to plate and let cool for 10 to 15 minutes. Do not wash sheet.

2. Line now-empty sheet with parchment paper. Whisk sugar, hot water, and salt in large bowl until sugar is mostly dissolved. Add nuts and stir to coat. Spread nuts on prepared sheet in single layer and bake until nuts are crisp and dry, 10 to 12 minutes.

3. Transfer sheet to wire rack and let nuts cool completely, about 20 minutes. Transfer nuts to cutting board and chop as desired. (Nuts can be stored at room temperature for up to 1 week.)

DARK CHOCOLATE FUDGE SAUCE

WHY THIS RECIPE WORKS: Many chocolate fudge sauces are more sweet than chocolaty and are overly thick; we wanted a sauce that was less sugary, boasted a luxurious, pourable consistency, and could be refrigerated and reheated. So we got to work. Using both cocoa powder and unsweetened chocolate provided a foundation of complex flavor and richness, and choosing milk, rather than cream, allowed the deep chocolate flavor to shine. As far as sweeteners go, we stuck with granulated sugar because it was simplest and we didn't notice enough of a difference when trying other options. To thicken the sauce, we swirled in a few knobs of butter, which gave it body and a glossier appearance. A bit of vanilla extract and salt helped the chocolate flavor pop.

Dark Chocolate Fudge Sauce
MAKES 2 CUPS

We like to serve this sauce over ice cream, but it can also be drizzled over fresh fruit. We prefer to use Dutch-processed cocoa powder in this recipe (our favorite is from Droste), but other cocoa powders will work. Our favorite unsweetened chocolate is Hershey's Unsweetened Baking Bar.

- 1¼ cups sugar
- ⅔ cup whole or 2 percent low-fat milk
- ¼ teaspoon salt
- ⅓ cup unsweetened cocoa powder, sifted
- 3 ounces unsweetened chocolate, chopped fine
- 4 tablespoons unsalted butter, cut into 8 pieces and chilled
- 1 teaspoon vanilla extract

1. Heat sugar, milk, and salt in medium saucepan over medium-low heat, whisking gently, until sugar has dissolved and liquid starts to bubble around edges of saucepan, 5 to 6 minutes. Reduce heat to low, add cocoa, and whisk until smooth.

2. Remove saucepan from heat, stir in chocolate, and let stand for 3 minutes. Whisk sauce until smooth and chocolate is fully melted. Add butter and whisk until fully incorporated and sauce thickens slightly. Whisk in vanilla and serve. (Sauce can be refrigerated for up to 1 month. Gently reheat sauce in microwave [do not let it exceed 110 degrees], stirring every 10 seconds, until just warmed and pourable.)

Dark Chocolate–Orange Fudge Sauce
Bring milk and 8 (3-inch) strips orange zest to simmer in medium saucepan over medium heat. Remove saucepan from heat, cover, and let stand for 15 minutes. Strain milk mixture through fine-mesh strainer into bowl, pressing on zest to extract liquid; discard zest. Return milk to saucepan and proceed with recipe as directed.

Mexican Dark Chocolate Fudge Sauce
Add ¼ teaspoon ground cinnamon and ¼ teaspoon chipotle chili powder to saucepan with milk in step 1.

Dark Chocolate–Peanut Butter Fudge Sauce
Increase salt to ½ teaspoon. Whisk ¼ cup creamy peanut butter into sauce after butter in step 2.

CHOCOLATE CREAM PIE WITH FOOLPROOF ALL-BUTTER DOUGH

WHY THIS RECIPE WORKS: Our goal was to create a moist all-butter pie dough that rolled out easily and baked up tender and flaky. We first used the food processor to coat two-thirds of the flour with butter, creating a pliable mixture that was water resistant. Then we broke that dough into pieces, coated the pieces with the remaining flour, and tossed in some grated butter. When we folded in the water, it was absorbed only by the dry flour that coated the butter-flour chunks. Since gluten can develop only when flour is hydrated, this resulted in a supertender crust. Grating some of the butter and adding it to the dough left a little more flour available to form gluten, so the crust had enough structure to support a flaky texture. After a 2-hour chill, the dough had hydrated completely and was easy to roll out, and once baked, the crust held a perfect, crisp edge and was rich-tasting while being both tender and truly flaky.

There's no better match for our tender, flaky pie crust than a luxurious chocolate cream filling. For a deeply chocolaty mixture that wasn't too heavy, we made a milk-based cocoa pudding and then whisked in bittersweet chocolate, along with vanilla for extra depth. A few tablespoons of butter helped the filling set up with a silky consistency once it was poured into the prebaked pie shell and refrigerated. Finally, we finished off the pie with a complementary topping of lightly sweetened whipped cream.

Chocolate Cream Pie
SERVES 8 TO 10

We developed this recipe with whole milk, but you can use 2 percent low-fat milk, if desired. Avoid using 1 percent low-fat or skim milk, as the filling will be too thin. Ghirardelli 60% Cacao Bittersweet Chocolate Premium Baking Bar is our favorite dark chocolate.

- 1 recipe Foolproof All-Butter Dough for Single-Crust Pie

FILLING
- ⅓ cup (2⅓ ounces) sugar
- ¼ cup (1-ounce) cornstarch
- 2 tablespoons unsweetened cocoa powder
- ¼ teaspoon salt
- 3 cups whole or 2 percent low-fat milk
- 6 ounces bittersweet chocolate, chopped fine
- 3 tablespoons unsalted butter, cut into 3 pieces
- 2 teaspoons vanilla extract

TOPPING
- 1 cup heavy cream
- 1 tablespoon confectioners' sugar

1. Roll dough into 12-inch circle on well-floured counter. Roll dough loosely around rolling pin and unroll it onto 9-inch pie plate, leaving at least 1-inch overhang around edge. Ease dough into plate by gently lifting edge of dough with your hand while pressing into plate bottom with your other hand.

2. Trim overhang to ½ inch beyond lip of plate. Tuck overhang under itself; folded edge should be flush with edge of plate. Crimp dough evenly around edge of plate using your fingers. Refrigerate dough-lined plate until firm, about 30 minutes. Adjust oven rack to middle position and heat oven to 350 degrees.

3. Line chilled pie shell with aluminum foil, covering edges to prevent burning, and fill with pie weights. Bake until edges are set and just beginning to turn golden, 15 to 20 minutes. Remove foil and weights, rotate plate, and continue to bake until golden brown and crisp, 15 to 20 minutes longer. If crust begins to puff, pierce gently with tip of paring knife. Let crust cool completely in plate on wire rack, about 30 minutes.

4. FOR THE FILLING: Whisk sugar, cornstarch, cocoa, and salt together in large saucepan. Whisk in milk until incorporated, making sure to scrape corners of saucepan. Place saucepan over medium heat; cook, whisking constantly, until mixture is thickened and bubbling over entire surface, 8 to 10 minutes. Cook 30 seconds longer; remove from heat. Add chocolate and butter and whisk until melted and fully incorporated. Whisk in vanilla. Pour filling into cooled pie crust. Press lightly greased parchment paper against surface of filling and let cool completely, about 1 hour. Refrigerate until filling is firmly set, at least 2½ hours or up to 24 hours.

5. FOR THE TOPPING: Using stand mixer fitted with whisk attachment, whip cream and sugar on medium-low speed until foamy, about 1 minute. Increase speed to high and whip until stiff peaks form, 1 to 2 minutes. Spread whipped cream evenly over chilled pie and serve.

Foolproof All-Butter Dough for Single-Crust Pie
MAKES ONE 9-INCH SINGLE CRUST

Be sure to weigh the flour for this recipe. This dough will be more moist than most pie doughs, but as it chills it will absorb a lot of excess moisture. Roll the dough on a well-floured counter.

- 10 tablespoons unsalted butter, chilled
- 1¼ cups (6¼ ounces) all-purpose flour
- 1 tablespoon sugar
- ½ teaspoon salt
- ¼ cup ice water

1. Grate 2 tablespoons butter on large holes of box grater and place in freezer. Cut remaining 8 tablespoons butter into ½-inch cubes.

2. Pulse ¾ cup flour, sugar, and salt in food processor until combined, 2 pulses. Add cubed butter and process until homogeneous paste forms, about 30 seconds. Using your hands, carefully break paste into 2-inch chunks and redistribute evenly around processor blade. Add remaining ½ cup flour and pulse until mixture is broken into pieces no larger

than 1 inch (most pieces will be much smaller), 4 to 5 pulses. Transfer mixture to medium bowl. Add grated butter and toss until butter pieces are separated and coated with flour.

3. Sprinkle 2 tablespoons ice water over mixture. Toss with rubber spatula until mixture is evenly moistened. Sprinkle remaining 2 tablespoons ice water over mixture and toss to combine. Press dough with spatula until dough sticks together. Transfer dough to sheet of plastic wrap. Draw edges of plastic over dough and press firmly on sides and top to form compact, fissure-free mass. Wrap in plastic and form into 5-inch disk. Refrigerate dough for at least 2 hours or up to 2 days. Let chilled dough sit on counter to soften slightly, about 10 minutes, before rolling. (Wrapped dough can be frozen for up to 1 month. If frozen, let dough thaw completely on counter before rolling.)

NOTES FROM THE TEST KITCHEN

NOT YOUR TYPICAL PIE DOUGH
Both the flour and the butter in this pie dough are added in two stages. This dough will look wetter than others you may have made, but fear not: As it chills, it will absorb extra moisture and will eventually form a smooth, easy-to-roll dough.

1. MAKE FLOUR-AND-BUTTER PASTE: Process most of flour (and sugar and salt) and cubed butter until homogeneous paste forms, about 30 seconds.

2. BREAK IT UP; ADD MORE FLOUR: Separate paste into 2-inch chunks and distribute around processor blade, then pulse in remaining flour.

3. TOSS IN GRATED BUTTER: Transfer mixture to bowl, add frozen grated butter, and gently toss to coat butter shreds with flour.

4. ADD WATER: Using rubber spatula, mix in ice water in 2 additions to form wet, sticky dough. Transfer to plastic wrap, press into disk, and refrigerate.

CONVERSIONS AND EQUIVALENTS

Some say cooking is a science and an art. We would say that geography has a hand in it, too. Flour milled in the United Kingdom and elsewhere will feel and taste different from flour milled in the United States. So, while we cannot promise that the loaf of bread you bake in Canada or England will taste the same as a loaf baked in the States, we can offer guidelines for converting weights and measures. We also recommend that you rely on your instincts when making our recipes. Refer to the visual cues provided. If the bread dough hasn't "come together in a ball," as described, you may need to add more flour—even if the recipe doesn't tell you so. You be the judge.

The recipes in this book were developed using standard U.S. measures following U.S. government guidelines. The charts below offer equivalents for U.S. and metric (U.K.) measures. All conversions are approximate and have been rounded up or down to the nearest whole number.

EXAMPLES:

1 teaspoon = 4.929 milliliters, rounded up to 5 milliliters
1 ounce = 28.349 grams, rounded down to 28 grams

VOLUME CONVERSIONS

U.S.	METRIC
1 teaspoon	5 milliliters
2 teaspoons	10 milliliters
1 tablespoon	15 milliliters
2 tablespoons	30 milliliters
¼ cup	59 milliliters
⅓ cup	79 milliliters
½ cup	118 milliliters
¾ cup	177 milliliters
1 cup	237 milliliters
1¼ cups	296 milliliters
1½ cups	355 milliliters
2 cups	473 milliliters
2½ cups	591 milliliters
3 cups	710 milliliters
4 cups (1 quart)	0.946 liter
1.06 quarts	1 liter
4 quarts (1 gallon)	3.8 liters

WEIGHT CONVERSIONS

OUNCES	GRAMS
½	14
¾	21
1	28
1½	43
2	57
2½	71
3	85
3½	99
4	113
4½	128
5	142
6	170
7	198
8	227
9	255
10	283
12	340
16 (1 pound)	454

CONVERSIONS FOR INGREDIENTS COMMONLY USED IN BAKING

Baking is an exacting science. Because measuring by weight is far more accurate than measuring by volume, and thus more likely to achieve reliable results, in our recipes we provide ounce measures in addition to cup measures for many ingredients. Refer to the chart below to convert these measures into grams.

INGREDIENT	OUNCES	GRAMS
Flour		
1 cup all-purpose flour*	5	142
1 cup cake flour	4	113
1 cup whole-wheat flour	5½	156
Sugar		
1 cup granulated (white) sugar	7	198
1 cup packed brown sugar (light or dark)	7	198
1 cup confectioners' sugar	4	113
Cocoa Powder		
1 cup cocoa powder	3	85
Butter†		
4 tablespoons (½ stick, or ¼ cup)	2	57
8 tablespoons (1 stick, or ½ cup)	4	113
16 tablespoons (2 sticks, or 1 cup)	8	227

* U.S. all-purpose flour, the most frequently used flour in this book, does not contain leaveners, as some European flours do. These leavened flours are called self-rising or self-raising. If you are using self-rising flour, take this into consideration before adding leavening to a recipe.

† In the United States, butter is sold both salted and unsalted. We generally recommend unsalted butter. If you are using salted butter, take this into consideration before adding salt to a recipe.

OVEN TEMPERATURES

FAHRENHEIT	CELSIUS	GAS MARK
225	105	¼
250	120	½
275	135	1
300	150	2
325	165	3
350	180	4
375	190	5
400	200	6
425	220	7
450	230	8
475	245	9

CONVERTING TEMPERATURES FROM AN INSTANT-READ THERMOMETER

We include doneness temperatures in many of our recipes, such as those for poultry, meat, and bread. We recommend an instant-read thermometer for the job. Refer to the table above to convert Fahrenheit degrees to Celsius. Or, for temperatures not represented in the chart, use this simple formula:

Subtract 32 degrees from the Fahrenheit reading, then divide the result by 1.8 to find the Celsius reading.

EXAMPLE:
"Roast chicken until thighs register 175 degrees."
To convert:

175° F – 32 = 143°
143° ÷ 1.8 = 79.44°C, rounded down to 79°C

INDEX

Note: Page references in *italics* indicate photographs.

Asparagus

Artichokes, and Peas, Fava Beans with, 959

Arugula, Walnuts, and Blue Cheese, Cavatappi with, 300–301

Basil, and Balsamic Glaze, Campanelle with, 300

Broiled, 581

Buttery Spring Vegetables, 958–59

and Goat Cheese Frittata, 962

Ham, and Gruyère Frittata, 644

Pancetta, and Peas, Farrotto with, 360

Pan-Roasted, 581–82

Shrimp, and Yellow Pepper, Stir-Fried, with Lemon Sauce, 460–61

Simple Pot-au-Feu, 77, *77*

and Smoked Salmon Omelet Filling, 639

Spring Vegetable Pasta, 297–98, *298*

Steamed, Soft-Cooked Eggs with, 635

Stir-Fried, with Red Bell Pepper, 582

Stir-Fried, with Red Onion, 582

Stir-Fried, with Shiitake Mushrooms, 582, *582*

Sugar Snap Peas, and Tomatoes, Farro Salad with, 625, *625*

trimming tough ends, 300

Austrian-Style Potato Salad, 52–53

Authentic Baguettes at Home, *689*, 689–91

Avocado(s)

Chunky Guacamole, 413–14

dicing, 414

and Orange, Shrimp Salad with, 247

-Orange Salsa, 235

Salsa, 250–51

Tomato, and Jícama, Peruvian Shrimp Ceviche with, 941–42

B

Bacon

Apples, Sage, and Caramelized Onions, Bread Stuffing with, 139–40

and Artichoke Omelet Filling, 639

Bits, Candied, 19

and Caramelized Onion, Potato Casserole with, *389*, 389–90

Cauliflower, and Bread Crumbs, Pasta with, 294, *294*

-Cheeseburgers, Well-Done, 498

Classic Spaghetti alla Carbonara, 321

Foolproof Spaghetti alla Carbonara, *320*, 320–21

and Hard Cider, Oven-Steamed Mussels with, 254

Leeks, and Apple, Baked Bread Stuffing with, 158

Onion, and Gruyère, Quick Cheese Bread with, 684

Onion, and Pepper Jack Cheese, Scrambled Eggs with, 631

and Onion Tart, French, 381–82

Oven-Fried, 637

and Pecans, Roasted Brussels Sprouts with, 584

Peppered, and Aged Cheddar, Juicy Pub-Style Burgers with, 275

Quiche Lorraine, 645, *645*

and Roasted Red Peppers, Latino-Style Chicken and Rice with, *87*, 87–88

-Shallot Topping, 605

Bacon (*cont.*)

taste tests on, 904

Tomato, and Onion, Pasta with, 292

Warm, Dressing, Wilted Spinach Salad with, 38, *38*

-Wrapped Scallops, Grilled, *568*, 568–69

Bagels, New York, 702–3, *703*

Bakeware buying guide

baker's edge pan, 887

baking mat, 887

baking peel, 887

baking stone, 887

biscuit cutters, 886

Bundt pans, 886

cooling racks, 886

glass baking dish, 885

loaf pans, 885, 887

metal baking pan, 885

muffin tin, 886

pie plate, 885

round cake pans, 885

soufflé dish, 887

springform pan, 886

square baking pan, 885

tart pan, 886

tube pan, 887

Baklava, *739*, 739–40

Baklava, Pistachio, with Cardamom and Rose Water, 740

Balsamic-Mustard Vinaigrette, Foolproof, 36

Balsamic Vinegar, Strawberries with, *836*, 836–37

Balsamic vinegar, taste tests on, 926

Banana(s)

Bread, Classic, 653

Bread, Ultimate, 653–54, *654*

-Coconut Steel-Cut Oatmeal, 675

Foster, 831

frozen, uses for, 93

and Nutella, Crêpes with, 834

Peanut, and Honey Steel-Cut Oatmeal, 675

Barbecued Baby Back Ribs, 534, *534*

Barbecued Half Beef Brisket, 515

Barbecued Pulled Chicken, 552–53, *553*

Barbecued Pulled Chicken for a Crowd, 553

Barbecued Pulled Pork, 528–29

Barbecued Salmon, 561–62

Barbecued Whole Beef Brisket, 514–15, *515*

Barbecue Glaze, 558

Barbecue Spice Rub, 549

Barley

Salad, Egyptian, 626, *626*

and Vegetable Soup, Farmhouse, 27, 27–28

Bars

Baklava, *739*, 739–40

Blondies, 730–31, *731*

Chocolate-Cherry, with Hazelnuts, 726

Congo, 731

F

K

L

M

Macaroni

and Cheese, Classic, 260–61

and Cheese, Grown-Up Stovetop, 262, *262*

and Cheese, Light, 263

and Cheese, Stovetop, 261

and cheese, taste tests on, 914

Salad, Cool and Creamy, 49

taste tests on, 918

Macaroons, Triple-Coconut, 720–21

Macaroons, Triple-Coconut, Chocolate-Dipped, 721, *721*

Madeira Pan Sauce with Mustard and Anchovies, 170

Mahogany Chicken Thighs, 110, *110*

Make-Ahead Chocolate Soufflés, 813–14, *814*

Make-Ahead Mocha Soufflés, 814

Make-Ahead Turkey Gravy, 138–39

Malt Vinegar–Molasses Burger Sauce, 272

Mango

Dried, Tropical Granola with, 674

Honeydew, and Blueberries with Lime-Ginger Reduction, 675–76

-Mint Salsa, 227, *227*

Orange, and Jícama Salad, 43–44

Maple (syrup)

Best Baked Apples, 825–26, *826*

-Chipotle Mayonnaise, 589

-Glazed Pork Roast, *211*, 211–12

with Orange Essence, 212

with Rosemary, 212

with Smoked Paprika, 212

with Star Anise, 212

-Glazed Pork Tenderloin, 207–8, *208*

-Mustard Sauce, 205

-Orange Glaze, 223

-Pecan Oatmeal Scones, Glazed, 657

–Sherry Vinegar Pan Sauce, Crispy-Skinned Chicken Breasts with, 104

Skillet Apple Pie, *830*, 830–31

and Smoked Almonds, Skillet-Roasted Brussels Sprouts with, 958

Sour Cream, 19

taste tests on, 915

Marbled Blueberry Bundt Cake, *747*, 747–48

Margaritas, Fresh, 412, *412*

Marinades

Garlic, Ginger, and Soy, 503

Garlic and Cilantro, with Garam Masala, 538

Garlic-Chile Wet Paste, 501

Garlic-Ginger-Sesame Wet Paste, 501

Garlic-Shallot-Rosemary Wet Paste, 500

Parsley, Warm-Spiced, with Ginger, 538

Southwestern, 503

Sweet Curry, with Buttermilk, 538

Marinara Sauce, 290

Marmalade

Glaze, Spicy, 535

Maple-Orange Glaze, 223

and Onions, Dried Cherry–Port Sauce with, 207

Maryland Crab Cakes, 247–48

Masa harina

Corn Tortillas, 423–24

Tamales, 417–18

Mayonnaise

Aïoli, 244

Basil, 589

Chipotle, 276

Garlic, 644

Garlic-Soy, 172–73

Maple-Chipotle, 589

Red Bell Pepper, 589

Spicy, 120–21

taste tests on, 915

Vegan, 587, *587*

Measuring equipment buying guide

adjustable measuring cup, 884

digital scale, 884

dry measuring cups, 883

kitchen ruler, 884

liquid measuring cup, 883

measuring spoons, 884

Meat

resting, before carving, 197

roasts, "double-butterflying," 211

salting, effect of, 191

see also Beef; Lamb; Pork; Veal

Meatballs

Pasta with Hearty Italian Meat Sauce (Sunday Gravy), *309*, 309–10

Sausage, and Spaghetti, *317*, 317–18

Spaghetti and, *315*, 315–16

Spaghetti and, Classic, for a Crowd, 316–17

Turkey

Asian-Style, 319

Italian-Style, 318–19, *319*

Moroccan-Style, 319

Meatless "Meat" Sauce with Chickpeas and Mushrooms, 290–91, *291*

Meatloaf

All-Beef, Glazed, 267–68

with Brown Sugar–Ketchup Glaze, *268*, 268–69

Turkey, with Apricot-Mustard Glaze, 270

Turkey, with Ketchup–Brown Sugar Glaze, *269*, 269–70

Mediterranean Chopped Salad, 43

Memphis-Style Barbecued Spareribs, 531–32, *532*

Meringue Cookies, 728–29, *729*

Chocolate, 729

Toasted Almond, 729

Mexican Chocolate Fudge Sauce, 972

Mexican Hot Chocolate, 677

Mexican Pulled Pork (Carnitas), 431–32

Mexican Rice, 432, *432*

Mexican-Style Corn Salad (Esquites), 948

Mexican-Style Grilled Corn, *574*, 574–75

Mexican-Style Grilled Steak (Carne Asada), 508, *508*

Mexican-Style Pickled Vegetables (Escabeche), 423

Mid–South Carolina Mustard Sauce, 529